THE ZONDERVAN
ENCYCLOPEDIA
OF THE BIBLE

THE ZONDERVAN ENCYCLOPEDIA OF THE BIBLE

Volume 2
D–G

Merrill C. Tenney, General Editor / Moisés Silva, Revision Editor

Revised, Full-Color Edition

ZONDERVAN.com/
AUTHORTRACKER
follow your favorite authors

ZONDERVAN

The Zondervan Encyclopedia of the Bible
Copyright © 2009 by The Zondervan Corporation
First edition copyright © 1975, 1976 by The Zondervan Corporation

Requests for information should be addressed to:
Zondervan, Grand Rapids, Michigan 49530

Library of Congress Cataloging-in-Publication Data

The Zondervan encyclopedia of the Bible / Moisés Silva, revision editor ; Merrill C. Tenney, general editor. — Rev. full-color ed.
    p. cm.
  Rev. ed. of: The Zondervan pictorial encyclopedia of the Bible.
  Includes bibliographical references.
  ISBN 978-0-310-24132-4 (hardcover, printed)
  ISBN 978-0-310-24136-2 (set)
  1. Bible — Encyclopedias. I. Silva, Moisés. II. Tenney, Merrill Chapin, 1904-1985. III. Zondervan pictorial encyclopedia of the Bible. IV. Title: Encyclopedia of the Bible.
BS440.Z63 2009
220.3—dc22   2009004956

All Scripture quotations, unless otherwise indicated, are taken from the *Holy Bible, New International Version*®. NIV®. Copyright © 1973, 1978, 1984 by International Bible Society. Used by permission of Zondervan. All rights reserved.

Any Internet addresses (websites, blogs, etc.) and telephone numbers printed in this book are offered as a resource. They are not intended in any way to be or imply an endorsement by Zondervan, nor does Zondervan vouch for the content of these sites and numbers for the life of this book.

All rights reserved. No part of this publication may be reproduced, stored in a retrieval system, or transmitted in any form or by any means — electronic, mechanical, photocopy, recording, or any other — except for brief quotations in printed reviews, without the prior permission of the publisher.

Interior design by Tracey Walker

Printed in China

09 10 11 12 13 14 15 • 23 22 21 20 19 18 17 16 15 14 13 12 11 10 9 8 7 6 5 4 3 2 1

IMAGE SOURCES

The Amman Archaeological Museum. Amman, Jordan.
Todd Bolen/www.BiblePlaces.com
The British Museum. London, England.
The Cairo Museum. Cairo, Egypt.
The Church of Annunciation Museum. Nazareth, Israel.
Direct Design. Amarillo, Texas.
The Egyptian Ministry of Antiquities.
The Ephesus Archaeological Museum. Selchok, Turkey.
The Eretz Israel Museum. Tel Aviv, Israel.
The House of Anchors. Kibbutz Ein Gev. Sea of Galilee, Israel.
International Mapping.
The Isma-iliya Museum. Isma-iliya, Egypt.
The Israel Museum, Jerusalem, courtesy of the Israel Antiquities Authority.
The Istanbul Archaeological Museum. Istanbul, Turkey.
Dr. James C. Martin.
The Jordanian Ministry of Antiquities. Amman, Jordan.
Ministero per I Beni e le Attivita Culturali—Soprintendenza Archaeologica di Roma. Rome, Italy.
Mosaic Graphics.
Musée du Louvre. Paris, France.
Phoenix Data Systems
Reproduction of the City of Jerusalem at the time of the Second Temple—located on the grounds of the Holy Land Hotel, Jerusalem.
Sola Scriptura. The Van Kampen Collection on display at the Holy Land Experience. Orlando, Florida.
The Turkish Ministry of Antiquities. Ankara, Turkey.
The Yigal Allon Center. Kibbutz Ginosar, on the western shore of the Sea of Galilee, Israel.

ABBREVIATIONS

I. General

א	(Aleph) Codex Sinaiticus
A	Codex Alexandrinus
AASOR	Annual of the American Schools of Oriental Research
AB	Anchor Bible
ABD	*Anchor Bible Dictionary*
ABR	*Australian Biblical Review*
ad loc.	*ad locum*, at the place
AHR	*American Historical Review*
AJA	*American Journal of Archaeology*
AJP	*American Journal of Philology*
AJSL	*American Journal of Semitic Languages and Literature*
AJT	*American Journal of Theology*
Akk.	Akkadian
ANE	Ancient Near East(ern)
ANEP	*The Ancient Near East in Pictures Relating to the Old Testament*, ed. J. B. Pritchard (1954)
ANET	*Ancient Near East Texts Relating to the Old Testament*, ed. J. B. Pritchard, 3rd ed. (1969)
ANF	*Ante-Nicene Fathers*
ANRW	*Aufstieg und Niedergang der römischen Welt* (1972–)
aor.	aorist
APOT	*Apocrypha and Pseudepigrapha of the Old Testament*, ed. R. H. Charles, 2 vols. (1913)
Apoc.	Apocrypha
approx.	approximate(ly)
Aq.	Aquila
ARAB	*Ancient Records of Assyria and Babylonia*, ed. D. D. Luckenbill, 2 vols. (1926–27)
Arab.	Arabic
Aram.	Aramaic
Arch	Archaeology
ARM	*Archives royales de Mari*
Assyr.	Assyrian
ASV	American Standard Version
AThR	*Anglican Theological Review*
AUSS	*Andrews University Seminary Studies*
B	Codex Vaticanus
b.	born
BA	*Biblical Archaeologist*
BAR	*Biblical Archaeology Review*
BASOR	*Bulletin of the American Schools of Oriental Research*
BASORSup	*Bulletin of the American Schools of Oriental Research Supplemental Studies*
BBR	*Bulletin for Biblical Research*
BC	F. J. Foakes-Jackson and K. Lake, eds., *The Beginnings of Christianity*, 5 vols. (1920–33)
BDAG	W. Bauer, *A Greek-English Lexicon of the New Testament and Other Early Christian Literature*, 3rd ed., rev. F. W. Danker (2000)
BDB	F. Brown, S. R. Driver, and C. A. Briggs, *A Hebrew and English Lexicon of the Old Testament* (1907)
BDF	F. Blass, A. Debrunner, and R. W. Funk, *A Greek Grammar of the New Testament and Other Early Christian Literature* (1961)
BDT	*Baker's Dictionary of Theology*, ed. E. F. Harrison (1960)
BECNT	Baker Exegetical Commentary on the New Testament
BETS	*Bulletin of the Evangelical Theological Society*
BHK	*Biblia Hebraica*, ed. R. Kittel, 3rd ed. (1937)
BHS	*Biblia Hebraica Stuttgartensia*, ed. K. Elliger and W. Rudolph (1983)
Bib.	*Biblica*
BJRL	*Bulletin of the John Rylands Library*
BKAT	Biblischer Kommentar, Altes Testament
BNTC	Black's New Testament Commentaries
BRev	*Bible Review*
BSac	*Bibliotheca Sacra*
BWL	*Babylonian Wisdom Literature*, ed. W. G. Lambert (1960)
BZ	*Biblische Zeitschrift*
C	Codex Ephraemi Syri
c.	*circa*, about

CAH	*Cambridge Ancient History*	*DOTT*	*Documents from Old Testament Times*, ed. D. W. Thomas (1958)
CANE	*Civilizations of the Ancient Near East*, ed. J. M. Sasson, 4 vols. (1995)	*DPL*	*Dictionary of Paul and his Letters*, ed. G. F. Hawthorne et al. (1993)
CBQ	*Catholic Biblical Quarterly*	DSS	Dead Sea Scrolls
CBSC	Cambridge Bible for Schools and Colleges	E	east
CD	Cairo: Damascus (i.e., *Damascus Document*)	EA	El-Amarna Tablets. See *Die el-Amarna-Tafeln, mit Einleitung und Erläuterung*, ed. J. A. Knudtzon, 2 vols. (1908–15; suppl. by A. F. Rainey, 2nd ed., 1978)
cent.	century		
CEV	Contemporary English Version		
cf.	*confer*, compare	*EBC*	*The Expositor's Bible Commentary*, ed. F. E. Gaebelein et al., 12 vols. (1979–92)
CGTC	Cambridge Greek Testament Commentary		
		EBr	*Encyclopedia Britannica*
ch(s).	chapter(s)	ed(s).	editor(s), edited, edition
CT	*Christianity Today*	e.g.	*exempli gratia*, for example
CIG	*Corpus inscriptionum graecarum*	*EGT*	*Expositor's Greek Testament*, ed. W. R. Nicoll, 5 vols. (1897–1910)
CIL	*Corpus inscriptionum latinarum*		
CIS	*Corpus inscriptionum semiticarum*	Egyp.	Egyptian
col(s).	column(s)	EKKNT	Evangelisch-katholischer Kommentar zum Neuen Testament
COS	*The Context of Scripture*, ed. W. W. Hallo, 3 vols. (1997–2002)		
		EncBib	*Encyclopaedia Biblica*, ed. T. K. Cheyne and J. S. Black, 4 vols. (1899–1903)
CRINT	Compendia rerum iudaicarum ad Novum Testamentum		
		EncJud	*Encyclopedia Judaica*, 16 vols. (1972)
D	Codex Bezae	Eng.	English
d.	died, date of death	*ERE*	*Encyclopedia of Religion and Ethics*, ed. J. Hastings, 13 vols. (1908–27)
DAC	*Dictionary of the Apostolic Church*, ed. J. Hastings, 2 vols. (1915–18)		
		ERV	English Revised Version
DBI	*Dictionary of Biblical Interpretation*, ed. J. H. Hayes, 2 vols. (1999)	esp.	especially
		ESV	English Standard Version
DBSup	*Dictionnaire de la Bible: Supplément*, ed. L. Pirot and A. Robert (1928–)	et al.	*et alii*, and others
		ETR	*Etudes théologiques et religieuses*
DCG	*Dictionary of Christ and the Gospels*, ed. J. Hastings, 2 vols. (1906–08)	*ETSB*	*Evangelical Theological Society Bulletin*
		Euseb.	Eusebius
DDD	*Dictionary of Deities and Demons in the Bible*, ed. K. van der Toorn et al., 2nd ed. (1999)	*EvQ*	*Evangelical Quarterly*
		EvT	*Evangelische Theologie*
		Exp	*The Expositor*
DJD	Discoveries in the Judaean Desert	*ExpTim*	*Expository Times*
DJG	*Dictionary of Jesus and the Gospels*, ed. J. B. Green et al. (1992)	ff.	following (verses, pages, etc.)
		FCI	*Foundations of Contemporary Interpretation*, ed. M. Silva, 6 vols. in 1 (1996)
DLNT	*Dictionary of the Later New Testament and Its Developments*, ed. R. P. Martin and P. H. Davids (1997)		
		fem.	feminine
DNTB	*Dictionary of New Testament Background*, ed. C. A. Evans and S. E. Porter (2000)	*FFB*	*Fauna and Flora of the Bible*, UBS Handbook Series, 2nd ed. (1980)
		fig.	figure, figurative(ly)
DOTHB	*Dictionary of the Old Testament: Historical Books*, ed. B. T. Arnold and H. G. M. Williamson (2005)	fl.	*floruit*, flourished
		FOTL	Forms of the Old Testament Literature
		ft.	foot, feet
DOTP	*Dictionary of the Old Testament: Pentateuch*, ed. T. D. Alexander and D. W. Baker (2003)	GCS	Die griechische christliche Schriftsteller

Ger.	German		impv.	imperative
GKC	Gesenius-Kautzsch-Cowley, *Gesenius' Hebrew Grammar*, 2nd ed. (1910)		inscr.	inscription
			Int	*Interpretation*
Gk.	Greek		*IPN*	*Die israelitischen Personennamen*, by M. Noth (1928)
GNB	Good News Bible			
HAL	*Hebräisches und aramäisches Lexikon zum Alten Testament*, by L. Koehler et al., 5 fascicles (1967–95)		Iren.	Irenaeus
			ISBE	*International Standard Bible Encyclopedia*, ed. M. G. Kyle, 4 vols. (1929); rev. ed., G. W. Bromiley, 4 vols. (1979–88)
HALOT	*Hebrew and Aramaic Lexicon of the Old Testament*, by L. Koehler et al., 5 vols. (1994–2000)			
			JANESCU	*Journal of the Ancient Near Eastern Society of Columbia University*
HAT	Handbuch zum Alten Testament			
HDB	Hastings' *Dictionary of the Bible*, 5 vols. (1898–1904); rev. ed. in 1 vol. by F. C. Grant and H. H. Rowley (1963)		*JAOS*	*Journal of American Oriental Society*
			JASA	*Journal of the American Scientific Affiliation*
Heb.	Hebrew		*JB*	Jerusalem Bible
HGHL	*Historical Geography of the Holy Land*, by G. A. Smith, 25th ed. (1931)		*JBL*	*Journal of Biblical Literature*
			JBR	*Journal of Bible and Religion*
Hitt.	Hittite		*JCS*	*Journal of Cuneiform Studies*
HibJ	*Hibbert Journal*		*JE*	*The Jewish Encyclopedia*, ed. I. Singer, 12 vols. (1925)
HJP	*A History of the Jewish People in the Time of Jesus Christ*, by E. Schürer, 5 vols., 2nd ed. (1885–90); rev. ed., *The History of the Jewish People in the Age of Jesus Christ (175 B.C.–A.D. 135)*, by G. Vermès and F. Millar, 4 vols. (1973–87)			
			JEA	*Journal of Egyptian Archaeology*
			JETS	*Journal of the Evangelical Theological Society*
			JJS	*Journal of Jewish Studies*
			JNES	*Journal of Near Eastern Studies*
			JNSL	*Journal of North Semitic Languages*
HNT	Handbuch zum Neuen Testament		Jos.	Josephus
HNTC	Harper's New Testament Commentaries		*JPOS*	*Journal of the Palestine Oriental Society*
			JPS	Jewish Publication Society, *The Holy Scriptures according to the Masoretic Text: A New Translation…* (1945)
HTKAT	Herders theologischer Kommentar zum Alten Testament			
HTKNT	Herders theologischer Kommentar zum Neuen Testament		*JQR*	*Jewish Quarterly Review*
			JR	*Journal of Religion*
HTR	*Harvard Theological Review*		*JRS*	*Journal of Roman Studies*
HUCA	*Hebrew Union College Annual*		*JSJ*	*Journal for the Study of Judaism in the Persian, Hellenistic, and Roman Periods*
IB	*Interpreter's Bible*, ed. G. A. Buttrick et al., 12 vols. (1951–57)			
			JSNT	*Journal for the Study of the New Testament*
ibid.	*ibidem*, in the same place			
ICC	International Critical Commentary		*JSOT*	*Journal for the Study of the Old Testament*
id.	*idem*, the same (as previously mentioned)		*JSP*	*Journal for the Study of the Pseudepigrapha*
IDB	*Interpreter's Dictionary of the Bible*, ed. G. A. Buttrick, 4 vols. (1962); supplementary vol., ed K. Crim (1976)		*JSS*	*Journal of Semitic Studies*
			JTS	*Journal of Theological Studies*
			KAI	*Kanaanäishce und aramäische Inschriften*, by H. Donner and W. Röllig, 2nd ed., 3 vols. (1966–69)
i.e.	*id est*, that is			
IEJ	*Israel Exploration Journal*		KAT	Kommentar zum Alten Testament
Ign.	Ignatius		KB	L. Koehler and W. Baumgartner, *Lexicon in Veteris Testamenti libros*, 2nd ed. (1958; for 3rd ed., see *HAL*)
illus.	illustration			
impf.	imperfect			

KD	C. F. Keil and F. Delitzsch, *Biblical Commentary on the Old Testament*, 25 vols. (1857–78)
KEK	Kritisch-exegetischer Kommentar über das Neue Testament (= Meyer-Kommentar)
KJV	King James Version
Lat.	Latin
LCL	Loeb Classical Library
lit.	literal(ly), literature
LN	J. P. Louw and E. A. Nida, *Greek-English Lexicon of the New Testament Based on Semantic Domains*, 2 vols., 2nd ed. (1989)
LSJ	H. G. Liddell, R. Scott, and H. S. Jones, *A Greek-English Lexicon*, 9th ed., with rev. supplement (1996)
LXX	The Seventy = Septuagint
Maj. Text	Majority Text
masc.	masculine
mg.	margin
mi.	mile(s)
MM	J. H. Mouton and G. Milligan, *The Vocabulary of the Greek Testament* (1930)
MNTC	Moffatt New Testament Commentary
MS(S)	manuscript(s)
McClintock and Strong	J. McClintock and J. Strong, *Cyclopedia of Biblical, Theological, and Ecclesiastical Literature*, 12 vols. (1867–87)
MT	Masoretic text
N	north
n.	note
NA	Nestle-Aland, *Novum Testamentum Graecum*
NAB	New American Bible
NAC	New American Commentary
NASB	New American Standard Bible
NBD	*New Bible Dictionary*, ed. J. D. Douglas et al.; unless otherwise noted, references are to the 3rd ed. (1996)
NCB	New Century Bible
NCBC	New Century Bible Commentary
NCE	*New Catholic Encyclopedia*, ed. W. J. McDonald et al., 15 vols. (1967)
NCV	New Century Version
n.d.	no date
NE	northeast
NEAEHL	*The New Encyclopedia of Archaeological Excavations in the Holy Land*, ed. E. Stern et al., 4 vols. (1993)
NEB	New English Bible
neut.	neuter
NewDocs	*New Documents Illustrating Early Christianity*, ed. G. H. R. Horsley and S. Llewelyn (1981–)
NHC	Nag Hammadi Codex
NHL	*Nag Hammadi Library in English*, ed. J. M. Robinson, 4th ed. (1996)
NIBCNT	New International Bible Commentary on the New Testament
NIBCOT	New International Bible Commentary on the Old Testament
NICNT	New International Commentary on the New Testament
NICOT	New International Commentary on the Old Testament
NIDNTT	*New International Dictionary of New Testament Theology*
NIDOTTE	*New International Dictionary of Old Testament Theology and Exegesis*
NIGTC	New International Greek Testament Commentary
NIV	New International Version
NIVAC	New International Version Application Commentary
NJB	New Jerusalem Bible
NJPS	*Tanakh: The Holy Scriptures. The New JPS translation according to the Traditional Hebrew Text*
NKJV	New King James Version
NLT	New Living Translation
NovT	*Novum Testamentum*
NPNF	Nicene and Post-Nicene Fathers
NRSV	New Revised Standard Version
NT	New Testament
NTAp	*New Testament Apocrypha*, ed. E. Hennecke, 2 vols., trans. R. McL. Wilson (1963–65); unless otherwise indicated, references are to the rev. ed. by W. Schneemelcher, trans. R. McL. Wilson (1991–92)
NTD	Das Neue Testament Deutsch
NTS	*New Testament Studies*
NW	northwest
OCD	*Oxford Classical Dictionary* (1949)
ODCC	*Oxford Dictionary of the Christian Church*, ed. F. L. Cross and E. A. Livingstone, 3rd ed. (1997)
Onom.	Eusebius's *Onomasticon*, according to E. Klostermann, ed., *Das Onomastikon der biblischen Ortsnamen* (1904)

op. cit.	*opere citato*, in the work previously cited	SHERK	*The New Schaff-Herzog Encyclopedia of Religious Knowledge*, 13 vols. (1908–14)
orig.	original(ly)		
OT	Old Testament	SIG	*Sylloge inscriptionum graecarum*, ed. W. Dittenberger, 4 vols., 3rd ed. (1915–24)
OTL	Old Testament Library		
OTP	*Old Testament Pseudepigrapha*, ed. J. H. Charlesworth, 2 vols. (1983–85)	sing.	singular
		SJT	*Scottish Journal of Theology*
p., pp.	page, pages	SP	Sacra Pagina
pass.	passive	*ST*	*Studia theologica*
PEQ	*Palestine Exploration Quarterly*	Str-B	H. L. Strack and P. Billerbeck, *Kommentar zum Neuen Testament aus Talmud und Midrash*, 6 vols. (1922–61)
Pers.	Persian		
pf.	perfect		
PG	*Patrologia graeca*, ed. J.-P. Migne, 162 vols. (1857–96)	Sumer.	Sumerian
		s.v.	*sub verbo*, under the word
PJ	*Palästina-Jahrbuch*	SW	southwest
pl.	plural	Syr.	Syriac
PL	*Patrologia latina*, ed. J.-P. Migne, 217 vols. (1844–64)	Symm.	Symmachus
		Tac.	Tacitus
POxy	Oxyrhynchus Papyri	*TDNT*	*Theological Dictionary of the New Testament*, ed. G. Kittel and G. Friedrich, 10 vols. (1964–76)
prob.	probably		
Pseudep.	Pseudepigrapha		
ptc.	participle	*TDOT*	*Theological Dictionary of the Old Testament*, ed. G. J. Botterweck and H. Ringgren (1974–)
PTR	*Princeton Theological Review*		
RA	*Revue d'assyriologie et d'archéologie orientale*		
		TEV	Today's English Version
Rahlfs	A. Rahlfs, *Septuaginta, id est, Vetus Testamentum graece iuxta LXX interpretes*, 3rd ed. (1949)	Tg.	Targum
		Theod.	Theodotion
		THKNT	*Theologischer Handkommentar zum Neuen Testament*
RB	*Revue biblique*		
RE	*Realencyclopädie für protestantische Theologie und Kirche*, ed. J. J. Herzog and A. Hauck, 24 vols. (1896–1913)	*ThTo*	*Theology Today*
		TNIV	Today's New International Version
		TNTC	Tyndale New Testament Commentaries
REB	Revised English Bible	TOTC	Tyndale Old Testament Commentaries
repr.	reprint(ed)	TR	Textus Receptus
rev.	revised	trans.	translation, translator, translated
RevExp	*Review and Expositor*	*TWNT*	*Theologisches Wörterbuch zum Neuen Testament*, ed. ed. G. Kittel and G. Friedrich, 10 vols. (1932–79)
RevQ	*Revue de Qumran*		
RGG	*Die Religion in Geschichte und Gegenwart*, ed. K. Galling, 7 vols., 3rd ed. (1857–65)		
		TynBul	*Tyndale Bulletin*
		TZ	*Theologische Zeitschrift*
Rom.	Roman	UBS	United Bible Society, *The Greek New Testament*
RSPT	*Révue des sciences philosophiques et théologiques*		
		UF	*Ugarit-Forschungen*
RSV	Revised Standard Version	Ugar.	Ugaritic
RV	Revised Version	*UM*	*Ugaritic Manual*, by C. H. Gordon, 3 parts (1955)
S	south		
SacBr	A. F. Rainey and R. S. Notley, *The Sacred Bridge: Carta's Atlas of the Biblical World* (2005)	*UT*	*Ugaritic Textbook*, by C. H. Gordon, 3 parts (1965)
		v., vv.	verse, verses
Sansk.	Sanskrit	*VT*	*Vetus Testamentum*
SE	southeast	viz.	*videlicet*, namely
sec.	section	v.l.	*varia lectio*, variant reading

vol(s).	volume(s)
vs.	versus
Vulg.	Vulgate
W	west
WBC	Word Biblical Commentary
WEB	World English Bible
WH	B. F. Westcott and F. J. A. Hort, *The New Testament in the Original Greek*, 2 vols. (1881)
WTJ	*Westminster Theological Journal*
ZAW	*Zeitschrift für die alttestamentliche Wissenschaft*
ZDMG	*Zeitschrift der deutschen morgenländischen Gesellschaft*
ZDPV	*Zeitschrift der deutschen Palästina-Vereins*
ZNW	*Zeitschrift für die neutestamentliche Wissenschaft*
ZRGG	*Zeitschrift für Religions und Geistesgeschichte*

II. Books of the Bible

Old Testament

Gen.	Genesis
Exod.	Exodus
Lev.	Leviticus
Num.	Numbers
Deut.	Deuteronomy
Josh.	Joshua
Jdg.	Judges
Ruth	Ruth
1 Sam.	1 Samuel
2 Sam.	2 Samuel
1 Ki.	1 Kings
2 Ki.	2 Kings
1 Chr.	1 Chronicles
2 Chr.	2 Chronicles
Ezra	Ezra
Neh.	Nehemiah
Esth.	Esther
Job	Job
Ps.	Psalm(s)
Prov.	Proverbs
Eccl.	Ecclesiastes
Cant.	Canticles (Song of Songs)
Isa.	Isaiah
Jer.	Jeremiah
Lam.	Lamentations
Ezek.	Ezekiel
Dan.	Daniel
Hos.	Hosea
Joel	Joel
Amos	Amos
Obad.	Obadiah
Jon.	Jonah
Mic.	Micah
Nah.	Nahum
Hab.	Habakkuk
Zeph.	Zephaniah
Hag.	Haggai
Zech.	Zechariah
Mal.	Malachi

New Testament

Matt.	Matthew
Mk.	Mark
Lk.	Luke
Jn.	John
Acts	Acts
Rom.	Romans
1 Cor.	1 Corinthians
2 Cor.	2 Corinthians
Gal.	Galatians
Eph.	Ephesians
Phil.	Philippians
Col.	Colossians
1 Thess.	1 Thessalonians
2 Thess.	2 Thessalonians
1 Tim.	1 Timothy
2 Tim.	2 Timothy
Tit.	Titus
Phlm.	Philemon
Heb.	Hebrews
Jas.	James
1 Pet.	1 Peter
2 Pet.	2 Peter
1 Jn.	1 John
2 Jn.	2 John
3 Jn.	3 John
Jude	Jude
Rev.	Revelation

Apocrypha

1 Esd.	1 Esdras
2 Esd.	2 Esdras (= *4 Ezra*)
Tob.	Tobit
Jdt.	Judith
Add. Esth.	Additions to Esther
Wisd.	Wisdom of Solomon

Sir.	Ecclesiasticus (Wisdom of Jesus the Son of Sirach)	2 En.	2 Enoch
Bar.	Baruch	4 Ezra	4 Ezra (= 2 Esdras)
Ep. Jer.	Epistle of Jeremy	Jub.	Book of Jubilees
Pr. Azar.	Prayer of Azariah	Let. Aris.	Letter of Aristeas
Sg. Three	Song of the Three Children (or Young Men)	Life Adam	Life of Adam and Eve
		3 Macc.	3 Maccabees
		4 Macc.	4 Maccabees
Sus.	Susanna	Mart. Isa.	Martyrdom of Isaiah
Bel	Bel and the Dragon	Pss. Sol.	Psalms of Solomon
Pr. Man.	Prayer of Manasseh	Sib. Or.	Sibylline Oracles
1 Macc.	1 Maccabees	T. Benj.	Testament of Benjamin (etc.)
2 Macc.	2 Maccabees	T. 12 Patr.	Testaments of the Twelve Patriarchs
		Zad. Frag.	Zadokite Fragments

III. Pseudepigrapha

As. Moses	*Assumption of Moses*
2 Bar.	*2 Baruch*
3 Bar.	*3 Baruch*
1 En.	*1 Enoch*

Other Christian, Jewish, and Greco-Roman texts are referred to by their standard abbreviations. See, e.g., *The SBL Handbook of Style* (1999), ch. 8, appendix F, and appendix H.

THE ZONDERVAN
ENCYCLOPEDIA
OF THE BIBLE

Dor was an important harbor along the Mediterranean Sea used by Phoenicians and Israelites during the period of the Israelite monarchy. (View to the S.)

D

D. The symbol used to designate two different NT MSS, CODEX BEZAE (for the Gospels and Acts) and CODEX CLAROMONTANUS (Pauline Epistles). See also SEPTUAGINT; TEXTS AND MANUSCRIPTS (NT).

D (Deuteronomist). An abbreviation used (along with E, J, and P) to designate one of the supposed sources of the PENTATEUCH, according to the Documentary Hypothesis. It refers primarily to the author or editor of the book of DEUTERONOMY, but also to the material or outlook peculiar to it. Characteristic are the centralization of worship (Deut. 12:5–7), the Holy War demanding the massacre of the inhabitants of the land (chs. 7 and 20), and the concept of earthly reward for doing right (11:13–17).

Dabareh dab´uh-ruh. KJV alternate form of DABERATH (only in Josh. 21:28).

Dabbasheth. See DABBESHETH.

Dabbesheth dab´uh-sheth (דַּבֶּשֶׁת H1833, "hump"). KJV Dabbasheth. A town on the S border of the tribe of ZEBULUN between SARID and JOKNEAM (Josh. 19:11), perhaps a little E of the Brook KISHON. Dabbesheth should possibly be identified with Tell esh-Shammam, 6 mi. NW of MEGIDDO.

Daberath dab´uh-rath (דָּבְרָת H1829, "pasture"). A town at the NW foot of Mount TABOR, in the territory of the tribe of ISSACHAR, allotted to the Levites descended from GERSHON (Josh. 21:28 [KJV, "Dabareh"]; 1 Chr. 6:72 [MT, 6:57]); it was apparently on the border with ZEBULUN (Josh. 19:12). Daberath lay by an international route that provided passage between DAMASCUS and the Mediterranean. JOSEPHUS refers to it as *Dabaritta* (e.g., *Life* 318). The site is identified with the village of Daburiyeh (more precisely, Khirbet Dabbura), 5 mi. E of NAZARETH. Some think Daberath is the same place as RABBITH (Josh. 19:20).   R. F. GRIBBLE

Dabria dab´ree-uh. One of five scribes trained to "write rapidly" and commissioned to record the apocalyptic vision of EZRA on "many writing tablets" (2 Esd. 14:24).

Dacobi day´kuh-b*i*. KJV Apoc. form of AKKUB (1 Esd. 5:28).

Dagan. See DAGON.

dagger. See ARMOR, ARMS IV.A.

Dagon day´gon (דָּגוֹן H1837, derivation disputed). A popular Semitic deity and the chief god of the PHILISTINES. Two locations mentioned in the Bible use the name of this god (Josh. 15:41; 19:27; see BETH DAGON); moreover, the name *ʾr ʿdgwn* was applied to the area of Joppa and Dor c. 300 B.C. These uses indicate the widespread worship of Dagon by the inhabitants. Dagon was most prominent in the days of SAMUEL and SAUL, because by this time Philistine power was reaching down into the JORDAN Valley and moving southward toward the DEAD SEA. For a brief period the ARK OF THE COVENANT was captured by the Philistines and deposited in Dagon's temple in ASHDOD (1 Sam. 5:1–7). The presence of the ark of Yahweh in the same sanctuary with the idol of Dagon gave rise to a series of judgments on the idol, including the severing of its hands and head. In a remarkably similar manner the Philistine capture of SAMSON,

D

the man of God, had earlier brought disaster to the temple of Dagon in GAZA (Jdg. 16:23–30). The present article shows the development in the cultus of Dagon and the principal centers of worship in the Syro-Palestinian area.

    I. The problem of the origin of the name
    II. The meaning of the name
    III. Philistine Dagon
    IV. The temples of Dagon
        A. Ugarit
        B. Ashdod
        C. Gaza
        D. Beth Shan
    V. Conclusions

I. The problem of the origin of the name. Etymologically the name has been thought by some to have come from *dāg* H1834 and *ʾôn* (= *ʾāwen* H224), meaning, according to JEROME, "fish of sorrow" (i.e., sorrow to the devotees because of the burdens of idolatry; see R. A. S. Macalister, *The Philistines: Their History and Civilization* [1913], 100 n. 1). Others have argued it comes from *dāgān* H1841, "grain" (cf. already PHILO OF BYBLOS). In the Middle Ages, the name was thought by the rabbis to have been derived simply from *dāg*, "fish," but to early writers like Jerome and JOSEPHUS, Dagon was not known as a fish god, so this popular derivation probably resulted from similarity of sound (but see K. Holter in *Scandinavian Journal of the Old Testament* no vol. [1989]: 142–47). The meaning must be sought in its association with earlier eras and in other areas. Some have considered -*ôn* as indicative of a diminutive, whereas others see the name as derived from a root represented in Arabic by *dagga*, with the meaning "cloudy."

II. The meaning of the name. King Sargon of AKKAD (c. 2360 B.C.), in his account of the campaign to the upper EUPHRATES country and CILICIA, relates his stop at Tuttul (modern Tell Biʾa) to worship Dagan (*ANET*, 268). His son Naram-Sin conquered the same territory and claimed it was a gift to him by the same god (ibid.), which implies that the worship of Dagan/Dagon had spread westward beyond the W Syrian mountains. We now know that about the same time the cult to Dagan was established in EBLA, where he was the principal deity (see G. Pettinato and H. Waetzoldt in *Orientalia* 54 [1985]: 234–56). The name occurs also in the Ur III period, the Isin-Larsa period, and well beyond the HAMMURABI epoch (from 1530 B.C.; cf. F. J. Montalbano in *CBQ* 13 [1951]: 381–97).

It is possible on the basis of certain specific uses of the name to derive its meaning. Naram-Sin's texts of the conquest of SYRIA (I. J. Gelb, *Inscriptions from Alishar and Vicinity* [1935], 6) cannot be used to describe Dagon as the war god, for this function was served by Ninurta. Dagon could not have achieved widespread popularity in a role secondary to the chief Ninurta. It is first in the Ur III period that a suggestion as to meaning is given. His "wife's" name is written as *ša-la-aš*, probably equivalent to *ša-la*, the wife of Adad the weather God (Montalbano in *CBQ* 13 [1951]: 386). See HADAD (DEITY). Final confirmation is found in the HAMMURABI period, for in a letter to Zimrilim (c. 1730 B.C.) of MARI, Dagon is equated with Enlil the Babylonian storm god (ibid., 388). The victory cited in the letter was promised from Dagon for suggested reverence on achievement of victory, which reverence was made in offerings in the temple of Dagon, most likely at Tirqa, c. 60 mi. N of Mari, which could be called the locus of the cult of Dagon. The letter strongly suggests a palace revolt of some kind. By this equation is shown the nature of Dagon as the weather god of the Upper Euphrates River country between the Ḫabur River and Tuttul.

Dagon is mentioned in the TELL EL-AMARNA tablets, c. 1375 B.C., by the name *Dagan-takala* (see *The Tell El Amarna Tablets in the British Museum* [1892], 74:3; 129:2), and c. 1400 B.C. at UGARIT on commemorative sacrificial stelae (R. Dussaud in *Syria* 16 [1935]: 179–80). In other Ras Shamra texts, Dagon is presented as the father of BAAL, the Canaanite storm god, who had a temple erected to him in Ugarit, probably from the Middle Bronze period. Thus down to the 2nd millennium B.C. and later, as Assyro-Babylonian records show, Dagon was widely popular for a time span of some 1,500 years. It is in the Amarna era that his worship appears to have reached widespread permanence in Syro-Palestinian areas. It is necessary to find the causes of his adoption by Palestinians and the significance of his name. The temples dedicated to him show distinctly the influence of the occupying power.

In Syria, as in the upper Euphrates, Dagon was associated with the weather gods (C. H. Gordon, *Ugaritic Literature* [1949], lists Dagon with his son twelve times). Adad, another Babylonian-Assyrian weather god, was associated with Dagon. Later Adad was assimilated into Syria as HADAD and then became the son of Dagon (Montalbano in *CBQ* 13 [1951]: 396; cf. N. Wyatt in *Ugarit-Forschung*en 12 [1980]: 375–79). Hadad became the Baal of Ugarit. Thus the transference of a fixed association tending toward Dagon's identity as a weather god is established. In Palestine and Syria weather is important from the standpoint of rain for the crops. It is not too difficult to transfer the power of Dagon from a weather god to the status of a grain god, particularly since good harvests generally coincided with the appeals to him for rain so the grainfields would flourish. In Ugarit was found a word for grain that is synonymous with the name of Dagon (Gordon, *Ugaritic Handbook*, 3 vols. [1947], 3:223 n. 519). Baal, his "son," by virtue of the process of amalgamation begun with Dagon, was known as the god of both weather and productivity (Montalbano in *CBQ* 13 [1951]: 397).

Therefore Dagon as a storm god of the upper Euphrates country was brought into Syro-Palestine by conquerors from Mesopotamia, was adopted there, and by a process of accretion became also the storm god. Along with the usage of the upper Euphrates area, one must look for a word that would provide a root for the name, perhaps best supplied in the root *dg*, cognate to Arabic *dagga*, *dagā*, ("cloudy, rainy"). The final long syllable *-ôn* (but not the Aramaic long *-ân*) derives from the Akkadian *-an*; the vowel was accented in Hebrew and then became long (*ā/ô*).

III. Philistine Dagon.

The references to Dagon in the Bible are Jdg. 16:23; 1 Sam. 5:1–7; 1 Chr. 10:10 (cf. also the coupling of his name with *bayit* H1074 in Josh. 15:41 and 19:27; see BETH DAGON). In ABRAHAM's time, the Philistines were not the warriors depicted later in the days of Samson and Samuel. They were distinctly aggressive to acquire territory first in Egypt, where they were repulsed by RAMSES III. They later settled in Palestine, but some were subsequently hired by the Egyptians as mercenaries (G. E. Wright in *BA* 22 [1959]: 65), and as such were quartered at BETH SHAN. This town was controlled by the pharaoh of Egypt, as indicated by a door lintel inscription left there by one of his officers. This was also the era of Egyptian hegemony over the land, particularly along the trade routes (see W. F. Albright in *AJA* 54 [1950]: 162–76). But the evidence of Philistine pottery, which shows AEGEAN affinities, does not appear in Palestine before the 13th cent. B.C.; thus the period of the judges must be moved down in time, since the first and earliest reference to the warrior Philistines

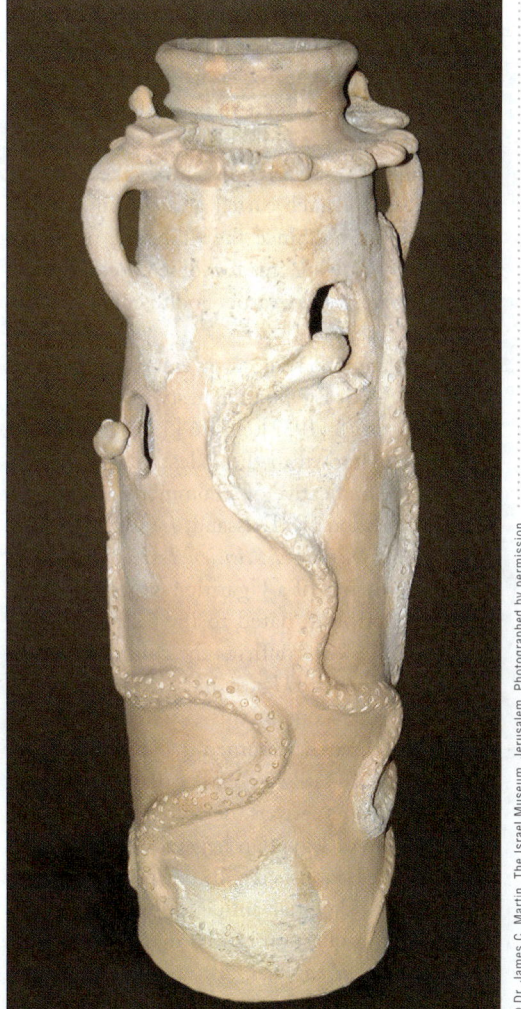

Snake imagery is used in this Philistine cult stand of Dagon (from Beth Shan, 11th cent. B.C.).

as established in Philistia (Josh. 13:2, 13) occurs in the era of the conquest (cf. *BA* 22 [1959]: 61–62, esp. n. 11). Since also Ramses II (1290–1224) and Merneptah (1224–1216) beat off the Sea Peoples, among whom were the *Peleste* (or the Philistines), it appears that the 13th cent. is established for the advent of these people in Palestine.

How did the Philistines take up the worship of Dagon? The answer is found first in a tablet found at Ugarit dated to the 18th dynasty of Egypt (c. 1580–1314 B.C.), which includes the name of Ashdod with those of Ashkelon and Acco as Palestinian cities (Y. Yadin in *BA* 26 [1963]: 135–36), indicating commercial relations with the area. It mentions linen as an article of that commerce and also names the governor of Ashdod. It would seem that since Dagon appeared earlier in Syria and later in Palestine, and since there is provable commercial traffic, Dagon migrated with those traders and their families from Ugarit. It is probable that trade was established much earlier and continued for a considerable time. Since the Philistine plain had been a grain-growing area for some time, this was a most likely area for a weather god to come to active acknowledgment.

Now a temple to Dagon was erected at Ugarit as early as the 12th Egyptian dynasty (c. 1963–1759 B.C.; cf. *Syria* 13 [1932]: 20; 16 [1935]: 177ff.), so this city was known to the Palestinians from the Amarna age, indicative of a commerce wider than just with Ashdod (R. Dussaud, *Les découvertes du Ras Shamra (Ugarit) et l'Ancien Testament* [1941], 28). The presence of a Ugaritic invoice or receipt tablet in Taanach, dated to the 12th cent. (*BA* 30 [1967]: 21–22), confirms the commerce of the area of Palestine with Ugarit and widens the understanding of the scope of this city's cultural influence. Thus it may be assumed that the worship of Dagon traveled southward earlier than the Amarna period, perhaps as early as the 16th cent. when, still within the era of Egyptian hegemony, commercial relations were established and continued thereafter. Indications of Egyptian influence in Ugarit in the area and era in question is seen in the Mani Stela (Dussaud, *Les découvertes*, 28) in its dedication to Seth Zapouna, an Egyptian god equivalent to Baal Zaphon, thus using a form of localized paraphrase that pinpoints the locale.

It would seem evident that the Dagon of the Philistines was the same as the Syrian type and perhaps the aspect emphasized would be that of fertility, since Philistia was a grain-producing area.

IV. The temples of Dagon. Temples to this god existed in Ugarit (Dussaud, *Les découvertes*), in Beth Shan (1 Chr. 10:10; cf. 1 Sam. 31:7–10), in Gaza (Jdg. 16:23), and in Ashdod (1 Sam. 5:1–7).

A. Ugarit. The peculiarity about the temple of Dagon in Ugarit is that it is of the same size and arrangements and orientation as the temple of Baal (*Syria* 16 [1935]: 177). It is situated c. 170 ft. E-SE of the temple of Baal and was discovered after that of Baal. Dussaud remarked that the honors the father had received were accorded likewise to the son (*Les découvertes*, 29). The temple was situated within an open court where the religious ceremonies were performed and in which was situated the altar. That of the Baal temple had two steps; probably that of Dagon had steps also. Beyond the altar was the holy place and back of that the holy of holies itself.

One is at once impressed with the similarity of these temples to the later Ishtar temple of Asshur (13th cent. B.C.; *Syria* 16 [1935]: 406–47; W. Andrae, *Das wiedererstandene Assur* [1938], 109 for plan, and 110 for perspective). The striking and common element is the arrangement of the altar; one entered the holy of holies and then turned to the right to view the altar and the idol, which was on a platform served by a series of steps. Since the Baal temple was built after that to Dagon, and since inscriptional evidence points to the founding of the latter c. 1910 (*Syria* 13 [1932]: 20), the temple of Dagon began its history late in the 20th cent. B.C.

That the identification of the temple with Dagon is certain is seen by the finding of two dedicatory stelae on the site. One stela (A), complete, is that of a woman, reading: "The stela that Tryl erected to Dagan. A monument (commemorating) [a head of small] and a head of large cattle as food." The other (B), incomplete, reads in part: "The monument that -zn erected to Dagan, his master, (commemorating) [a head of small and a head of large] cattle in the *mhrt* (temple refectory?)" (Gordon, *Ugaritic Literature*, 108). The stelae had the usual rounded heads

Close-up of a cult stand depicting a snake (from Beth Shan, 11th cent. B.C.).

and a tennon at the bottom to fit into a stone socket (*Syria* 6 [1925], plate XXXI).

B. Ashdod. Excavations were conducted at Ashdod in May-June of 1962 and in June-July of 1963 (*IEJ* 12 [1962]: 147–50; 13 [1963]: 340–42). In the first campaign, the only Philistine pottery finds occurred in a large pit. In the second season two levels of Philistine occupation dating to the 12th and 11th centuries B.C. were exposed, the principal structure being a fortress. So far no temple has appeared (cf. Jdg. 16:23), but such may be unearthed in the future (see *BA* 26 [1963]: 134ff.). The fortress testifies to the prowess of the Philistines.

C. Gaza. Excavations of Gaza by W. J. Phythian-Adams (*PEQ* no vol. [1923]: 11–36) give no data since the soundings were limited by present occupation. As this was a Philistine city, one would expect a temple there, and perhaps future excavations will disclose it.

D. Beth Shan. Of the four temples found by the Museum of the University of Pennsylvania excavations in 1925–1926, the two temples of Ramses III (1175–1144 B.C.) are from the era of Philistine occupation (A. Rowe, *The Four Canaanite Temples of Beth-shan*, 2 vols. [1940], 1:22). The southern temple is of minor hypo-style construction on an irregular plan. The outer walls are of mud brick on basalt stone bases; the central hall is divided into side aisles and a central one by three columns in each of two rows that support the clerestory above the center aisle. Between the columns in each row are dwarf walls separating the clerestory aisle from the side aisles (ibid., 24, fig. 5 and plate X). This central hall measures 71 ft. E to W and 25 ft. N to S. It is flanked by two small store rooms and one long one on the N and by two small ones on the S, plus a third room to their E, which opens off the E end of the central hall. At this end of the hall is a transept, longer toward the S than to the N. At its E wall is a type of pedestal on a raised floor level at the E end of the hall and extends around both to the N and S sides of the transept. From the center aisle, steps ascend to this level with a small, low pedestal immediately in front of them. In a general way this is similar to the pedestal feature at Ugarit and at Asshur. The low pedestal on the upper level may have carried an idol, but there is no evidence of any curtain at the near columns. The clerestory wall was of brick construction supported by wood beams bearing on the wood columns below. The clay roof was supported on a framework of beams and branches.

Since the southern temple is the larger of the two, and since Dagon was the chief god of the Philistines, it may be assumed that this was the temple of Dagon. It was here that the head of Saul was fastened (1 Chr. 10:10). The reconstruction of the northern temple may be seen in Rowe (*Four Canaanite Temples*, 33, figure; plate XII). This is similar to the southern temple but having one less column in each row, a slightly higher platform for the idol, and no store rooms. Its identity as the house of Ashtoreth (1 Sam. 31:10) seems assured by the finding of the figures of Antit, the warrior goddess, dressed as an Ashtoreth. Here was placed the armor of Saul by the Philistines (1 Chr. 10:10).

V. Conclusions. The similarities among the separate temples vary somewhat, but one may note that those of Ugarit and Assyria are closest, whereas those of Ashdod and Beth Shan are most alike. This conclusion is based on the fact that, although no temple of Dagon at Gaza has been found yet, Jdg. 16:25–30 indicates that there were pillars in it, perhaps somewhat like those at Beth Shan in arrangement. There was most likely a large forecourt framed by a colonnade, indicated by the large number of observers (3,000) on the roofs, with the court side being supported by a series of columns according to the Egyptian style. The temple itself under this arrangement would have been fitted into one side. It was there that Samson was placed; pushing down the columns, he initiated a domino-like action of destruction that brought down the temple and court colonnade.

A comparison of the Ugaritic and Assyrian temples shows preference for the Mesopotamian model, whereas those of the Philistines reveal a preference for the Egyptian type. This latter conclusion is based on the usage in Egypt of the clerestory and a more open sanctuary. Therefore, the temple plans followed the typical arrangement of the political area exerting greatest influence over the respective areas. Ugarit derived her religion and temple from Mesopotamia; the Philistines owed their allegiance to Egypt and took inspiration from her ARCHITECTURE.

The use in Solomon's temple of a plan akin to the temple of Dagon in Ugarit is dictated by the requirements of the worship of Yahweh, and this arrangement was not available in the examples from Egypt. A "wall of separation" between the worshiper and Yahweh was required, but even in this arrangement, it is not the heavy masonry dividing wall characteristic of the examples from the north. (See further J. F. Healey in *DDD*, 216–19.)

H. G. STIGERS

daily bread. See LORD'S PRAYER, THE.

dainty. This English term (either in the pl. "dainties" or in the phrase "dainty meats") is used a few times by the KJV and other versions to render several words or expressions, such as Hebrew *maṭ'ām* H4761 (Prov. 23:3, 6; NIV, "delicacies" [this Heb. word occurs also several times in Gen. 27:4–31]) and Greek *liparos* G3353, lit. "fat," fig. "luxurious" (Rev. 18:14; NIV, "riches"). Note also that when JACOB blessed his children, he predicted that ASHER would "provide delicacies [*ma'ădannim* H5052] fit for a king" (Gen. 49:20; cf. the same word in Prov. 29:17 ["delight"] and Lam. 4:5).

Daisan day'suhn (Δαισαν). Ancestor of a family of temple servants (NETHINIM) that returned from Babylon (1 Esd. 5:31; the RSV renders "Rezin" because that is the corresponding name found in the parallels, Ezra 2:48; Neh. 7:50).

Dalaiah duh-lay'yuh. KJV alternate form of DELAIAH (only in 1 Chr. 3:24).

Dale, King's. See KING'S VALLEY.

daleth dah'leth (from דָּלֶת H1946, "door"). The fourth letter of the Hebrew ALPHABET (ד), with a numerical value of four. It was originally shaped like a triangle, but later on, when "square Hebrew" characters developed (apparently in Aramaic circles during the 6th cent. B.C.), it assumed the shape of an upside-down "L." The letter *resh* assumed a similar shape (ר), except that the angle corner was somewhat rounded, and it never developed a tittle (or projection to the right of the vertical stroke) as *daleth* did. This letter was pronounced *d* as in English, although in later times it became spirantized (cf. the *th* sound in English *this*) when it was preceded by a vowel sound.   G. L. ARCHER

Dalmanutha dal-muh-noo'thuh (Δαλμανουθά G1236). A village near the W shore of the Sea of Galilee (only in Mk. 8:10, with several textual variants). See GALILEE, SEA OF. Jesus and his disciples came to this region (*ta merē Dalmanoutha*) following the feeding of the 4,000, an area seemingly contingent or identical with MAGADAN in the parallel passage (Matt. 15:39, *ta horia Magadan* [variant *Magdala*]). The ruins on the W shore of the lake, 3 mi. NW of TIBERIAS near modern Majdel (Magdala), may be the location. The name Dalmanutha is not attested elsewhere, and various theories, none of them persuasive, have been proposed regarding its derivation (cf. G. Dalman, *Die*

Worte Jesu [1930], 52–53; B. Hjerl-Hansen in *RB* 53 [1946]: 372–84).   W. H. Mare

Dalmatia dal-may′shee-uh (Δαλματία *G1237*). A district in the southern part of Illyricum to which Titus went during Paul's final imprisonment (2 Tim. 4:10). Dalmatia was a somewhat vaguely defined area of coast and mountain hinterland that lay E of the Adriatic Sea confronting Italy. Rome first compelled the warlike tribes of this area to acknowledge her sovereignty in the middle years of the 2nd cent. B.C. Subjugation was precarious and far from complete, and the Dalmatians remained a military problem until Octavian, the future emperor Augustus, brought the area more firmly under Roman control. The Pax Romana was finally established by his successor, Tiberius. It was a vital area in the prosecution of Rome's project of a Rhine-Danube frontier. Paul's brief and unexplained reference to Illyricum in writing to Rome (Rom. 15:19) may mean that the apostle himself had founded Christian churches in the southern and more hellenized parts of the region. He possibly visited the area from Macedonia after his Ephesian ministry (Acts 20:1).   E. M. Blaiklock

Dalphon dal′fon (דַּלְפוֹן *H1943*, possibly from Akk. *dullupu*, "sleepless"). The second of the ten sons of Haman who were put to death by the Jews (Esth. 9:7).

Damaris dam′uh-ris (Δάμαρις *G1240*, meaning uncertain, though some derive the name from δάμαρ, "wife," and others believe it is a variant of δάμαλις, "heifer"; cf. C. J. Hemer, *The Book of Acts in the Setting of Hellenistic History* [1989], 232). One of Paul's converts at Mars Hill in Athens (Acts 17:34; see Areopagus). Beyond this we know nothing of her. Since Luke singled her out as one of several converts, and since she was named with Dionysius the Areopagite, one of the judges of the Athenian court, she may have been a woman of high social rank (some have proposed, without evidence, that she was the wife of Dionysius). However, because a respectable woman of Athens likely would not have attended such a public gathering, others have suggested that she was one of the *hetairai*, an educated courtesan and thus a woman of low moral character (cf. W. M. Ramsay, *St. Paul the Traveller and the Roman Citizen*, 14th ed. [1920], 252; B. Witherington III, *Women in the Earliest Churches* [1988], 6–9).   H. J. Miles

Damascus duh-mas′kuhs (דַּמֶּשֶׂק *H1966* [in Chronicles, usually דַּרְמֶשֶׂק *H2008*; cf. also דּוּמֶשֶׂק *H1877* in 2 Ki. 16:10a and מֶשֶׂק in Gen. 15:2]; Δαμασκός *G1242*, gentilic Δαμασκηνός *G1241*, "Damascene"). This name can be applied to (1) the well-known city NE of Mount Hermon, (2) the general geographic region in S Syria (see Aram) where the city was located, and (3) at times, the state of which the city was the capital. Today Damascus is the capital of the modern state of Syria.

I. Locale. Damascus is located in a plain of about 2,200 ft. elevation surrounded on three sides by mountains: Mount Hermon and the Antilebanon range on the W; a ridge jutting from the range on the N; and Jebel Aswad (Mt. Aswad), which separates

City of Damascus.

it from the fertile HAURAN (biblical BASHAN) on the S. Toward the E marshy lakes and low hills separate the region from the desert. Rainfall is a sparse ten inches per year so that agriculture must depend upon irrigation waters from the streams flowing off the Antilebanon (El-Barada ["The Cool"], biblical Abana) and from Mount Hermon (El-Awaj ["The Crooked"], biblical Pharpar). By careful usage these transform the plain into a green garden surrounded by barren, brown hills and desert sands. Agricultural products include olives, various fruits, almonds, walnuts, pistachios, grains, tobacco, cotton, flax, and hemp.

II. History

A. Prior to 1200 B.C. The earliest history of Damascus is known only from occasional references in documents of surrounding peoples and by inferences from the general state of affairs. The general region (called Abina, Apina, Aba, Abu, Api, Upe, etc.) is referred to in the Egyptian EXECRATION TEXTS (18th and 19th cent. B.C.) and in the MARI Letters (c. 18th cent.). Biblical "Mesheq" may be a name for Damascus from the time of Abraham (Gen. 15:2, Heb. text). The name Damascus first appears among the conquests of THUTMOSE III (1484–1450). It remained a part of the Egyptian empire until AKHENATEN (c. 1372–1354). With the collapse of Egyptian power under Akhenaten, the HITTITES penetrated as far S as Damascus, but the city does not seem to have been incorporated into the Hittite empire as were regions farther north. Seti I (1312–1298) returned Damascus to the Egyptian sphere of influence, but in the latter part of the reign of RAMSES II (1301–1225), Egyptian power in Asia again faltered.

B. From 1200 B.C. to the Assyrian conquest (732 B.C.). The extensive migrations of people of the late 13th cent. B.C. jolted Egypt and destroyed the Hittite empire. They left the Hebrews, the Arameans, the Philistines, and numerous other peoples settled in new homelands. They set the stage for the biblical conflicts between the Hebrews and the Arameans, especially those of Damascus. The Hebrew tribes lay directly across the trade routes extending SW from Damascus, thus assuring enmity between the two. Likewise Damascus was a threat to Assyrian trade routes to the Mediterranean.

SAUL fought against Aramean kingdoms such as ZOBAH (1 Sam. 14:47). DAVID incorporated a number of Aramean kingdoms, including Damascus, into his empire (2 Sam. 8:5–6). Shortly afterward, however, Damascus regained her independence under REZON and took the lead in Syrian resistance to Hebrew domination (1 Ki. 11:23–25; c. 940 B.C.). The death of SOLOMON and the subsequent division of his kingdom ended all Hebrew pretensions of an empire in Syria (Aram). Under Rezon, Hezion, and Tabrimmon (the latter two known from 1 Ki. 15:18 and the Ben-Hadad Stela; some identify Rezon and Hezion), Damascus became the leader of the Aramean states of Syria.

History of Damascus now turns on three kings, BEN-HADAD I (i.e., HADADEZER or Adadidri; 883–843 B.C.), HAZAEL (843–c. 801), and Ben-Hadad II. Their policies were (1) suppression of the Hebrews in order to keep the southeastern trade routes open, and (2) maintenance of an anti-Assyrian coalition of Syrian states—including the Hebrews whenever possible.

Under Ben-Hadad I, Damascus dominated Syria and was easily able to intervene in Hebrew affairs (cf. 1 Ki. 15:16–22; c. 879). The dynasty of OMRI offered more effective resistance: AHAB defeated Ben-Hadad I twice in battle (c. 855 and 854; 1 Ki. 20:1–21, 23–34). The following year, however, Ahab and Ben-Hadad were allies against Assyria at the Battle of Qarqar (853). Ben-Hadad remained the soul of resistance to Assyria through three more hard-fought campaigns (849, 848, 845) and seems to have been generally successful in checking Assyrian expansion. He also saw his great enemy, Ahab, die in the battle of RAMOTH GILEAD (c. 851; 22:34–36). Ben-Hadad was killed by the usurper, Hazael.

The role of the prophet ELISHA in Hazael's rise to power (2 Ki. 8:10–15) is significant. This incident also gives a graphic view of Hebrew fear of Hazael (v. 12). Hazael decisively defeated the Hebrews; he suppressed JEHU and reduced JEHOAHAZ to vassalage (13:1–9). Against the Assyrians, he was less successful. SHALMANESER III boasted of slaying some 16,000 of Hazael's men, besieging

Damascus, despoiling gardens outside the wall, and plundering the region as far S as the Hauran.

Ben-Hadad II was defeated both by the Hebrews and the Assyrians. Adad-Nirari III of Assyria boasts of besieging Damascus and receiving tribute. Then a revitalized Israel, under JOASH and JEROBOAM II, not only gained independence but even succeeded in making Damascus the vassal state (2 Ki. 14:28). The end for Damascus came when AHAZ of Judah called for Assyrian help against Israel under PEKAH and Damascus under Rezon (biblical Rezin; 2 Ki. 16:5–9). In response, TIGLATH-PILESER III (i.e., Pul, 745–727 B.C.) defeated Israel, annexing part of her territory, and then sacked Damascus, putting an end to her history as an independent Aramean state.

C. Under foreign rule (732 B.C. to A.D. 636).

Damascus's economic importance endured through Assyrian, Babylonian, and Persian rule until ANTIOCH became the commercial leader of Syria in the Hellenistic Age. Warfare between the Ptolemies of Egypt and the Seleucids left Damascus under Seleucid control. However, after Roman intervention Damascus was at various times controlled by the NABATEANS (e.g., c. 85 B.C. and then again during the time of Paul), by HEROD, and even by CLEOPATRA. Other times Damascus was a "free" member of the DECAPOLIS, but finally became a part of the Roman empire under NERO after being temporarily controlled by Augustus and Tiberius. With the division of the Roman empire, Damascus became one of the major frontier cities of the Byzantine empire.

D. Arab rule (A.D. 636 to the present).

Arab rule began with the Battle of Yarmuk in 636. Since then Damascus has generally retained her economic importance and at times has added a significant political and cultural role. Her period as capital of the Umayyad Empire (639–744), and also in the 14th cent. under the control of the Egyptian Mamelukes, was brilliant. Her most serious disaster was the sacking at the hands of Timur's Mongols in 1401. In modern times, Damascus has regained her role as leading city and capital of Syria, though her former economic importance is shared with ALEPPO. Modern Damascus combines clean, wide thoroughfares with the narrow, crowded lanes of the older quarters of the city. Traditional handicraft industries can be seen within walking distance of the site of the annual Damascus trade fair.

III. Remains.

Historic remains and sacred sites abound in the region. Muslim pilgrims can visit Adam's Cave at Jebel Qasiyun, the Cave of Blood where Abel is said to have been murdered, the Cavern of Gabriel, and Moses' Tomb. The Umayyad Mosque built on the site of the basilica of St. John the Baptist—which in turn occupied the site of a classical temple of Jupiter—still shows some elements of the old pagan temple. Muslim tradition asserts that the Prophet Jesus (i.e., Jesus of Nazareth) will return to the Minaret of Jesus of this mosque to fight the Antichrist.

For the Christian there is the street called STRAIGHT, the place in the wall—including the very window—from which PAUL was lowered in a basket, the site of Paul's vision, and the house of ANANIAS. All of these are of dubious authenticity.

For the historian there are the Citadel (chiefly from the 13th cent. but built on the site of a Roman fortress), portions of the city wall, and the National Museum. For the student of biblical backgrounds,

The wall of this church in Damascus is built into the traditional location of Paul's escape from the city (Acts 9:25).

the Museum features the Mari Room with an outstanding collection of statues and objects, and the Ras Shamra Room containing the major finds from UGARIT. Also of interest is the reconstruction of the DURA-EUROPOS synagogue and the objects from Palmyra (TADMOR). (See M. F. Unger, *Israel and the Aramaeans of Damascus* [1957]; C. Thubron, *Mirror to Damascus* [1967]; W. T. Pitard, *Ancient Damascus* [1987]).   A. BOWLING

Damascus Document (CD). See ZADOKITE FRAGMENTS.   F. B. HUEY, JR.

damnation. This English term and its cognates *damned, damnable* (from Latin *damnare*, "to condemn") are used in the KJV (only the NT) but seldom in modern versions. See CONDEMN; JUDGMENT.

damsel. This term, seldom used in contemporary English, occurs over thirty times in the KJV OT, almost always as the rendering of Hebrew *naʿărâ* H5855, "girl" (Gen. 24:14 et al.). In the KJV NT, where it occurs over a dozen times, it renders several Greek terms (e.g., *korasion* G3166, Matt. 14:11). See GIRL; MAID; YOUTH.

Dan (person and tribe) dan (דָּן H1968, "judge"; gentilic דָּנִי H1974, "Danites"). Son of JACOB through BILHAH, and ancestor of the tribe that bore his name. RACHEL, unable to bear children (and thus jealous of her sister LEAH, who had already given birth to four sons), gave to Jacob her maid Bilhah as a wife. When the latter bore a son, Rachel said, "God has vindicated [or judged, *dîn* H1906] me," and so named him Dan (Gen. 30:6; Bilhah also bore NAPHTALI). Rachel saw in the birth of this child God's acceptance of her claim to motherhood and the evidence that he had heard her prayer. Nothing more is said about Dan except that he had a son named HUSHIM (46:23; apparently the same as SHUHAM in Num. 26:42).

When Jacob blessed his sons, Dan was placed after the last two sons of Leah, although he was born before them (the relative position of the tribe differs in various lists, such as Num. 1:38–39; 34:22; 1 Chr. 27:22). The blessing again played on the meaning of the name: "Dan will provide justice [*dîn*] for his people / as one of the tribes of Israel. / Dan will be a serpent by the roadside, / a viper along the path, / that bites the horse's heels / so that its rider tumbles backward" (Gen. 49:16–17). The prophecy clearly suggests that Dan would show the subtlety and venom of a snake in dealing with his enemies.

Surprisingly (if indeed Dan had only one son), the Danites constituted the second largest Hebrew tribe (64,400, according to the census recorded in Num. 26:43; the descendants of JUDAH numbered 76,500, v. 22). One of its members was OHOLIAB, a skilled craftsman who assisted BEZALEL in the construction of the TABERNACLE. Tribe leaders included Ahiezer, Ammiel, and Bukki (7:66; 13:12; 34:22). In the encampments Dan's standard, which included Asher and Naphtali, was on the N side of the tabernacle. In the line of march Dan headed the last of the four standards (10:25–26). Likewise when the offerings for the dedication of the altar were presented, Dan offered on the tenth day (7:66–71), being followed by Asher and Naphtali. At the great ceremony at EBAL, Dan was among the tribes that were to pronounce the curses (Deut. 27:13).

Dan was mentioned briefly in MOSES' blessing of the tribes (Deut. 33:22). The comparison with "a lion's cub" suggests vigor and ferocity; and the words "springing out of Bashan" suggest events that took place after the conquest of Laish (see below). At the distribution of the land by JOSHUA, Dan's lot was the last (Josh. 19:40–48). Their portion was between Judah on the S and Ephraim on the N, with Benjamin to the E and the sea to the W. See TRIBES, LOCATION OF II.C. Seventeen cities assigned to Dan are listed. These were cramped quarters, because of the resistance of the AMORITES (Jdg. 1:34), and because the PHILISTINES were in possession of much of their seacoast (3:3). Only a brief reference is made to the way in which they remedied the situation (Josh. 19:47).

The most spectacular event (or series of events) in their history was their trek to the N. Instead of endeavoring to gain possession of all their allotted portion in the land of Canaan, they secured for themselves by violent means lands in the far N that had not been occupied by an Israelite tribe. They sent out five spies to search out for them an inheritance in which to dwell (Jdg. 18:1–2). The spies came first to the house of MICAH in Mount Ephraim. Instead of being shocked that Micah had installed a Levite as his priest and had household idols (v. 14), they sought counsel concerning their journey and its possible results. Having received encouragement attributed to the Lord (v. 6), they went to Leshem/Laish, which apparently was under the nominal protection of Sidon; and discovering that it was likely to fall an easy prey to an invader, they brought back a most favorable report and declared that God would bless them.

Thereupon 600 armed men of ZORAH and ESHTAOL, apparently with families and livestock (Jdg. 18:21), departed for Laish. En route they came to the house of Micah, guided there by the spies, and possessing themselves of Micah's priest and objects of idol worship, they went to Laish, surprised and destroyed it, and then named it Dan. See DAN (PLACE). The story of this successful foray ends with the statement that they set up a graven image as the evidence and guarantee of their conquest. Finally the name of the priest whom they had taken away from Micah is given, Jonathan, the son of Gershom, the son of Moses (if "Moses" is the correct reading rather than the Masoretic emendation, "Manasseh"), and it is stated that he and his sons were priests to the tribe of Dan "until the time of the captivity of the land" (Jdg. 18:30–31). See JONATHAN #2. The parallel statement, "all the time the house of God was in Shiloh," may be defined as ending with the disastrous battle in the days of ELI (1 Sam. 4:10), when the ARK OF THE COVENANT was taken by the Philistines and SHILOH apparently destroyed (many scholars find here a reference to the invasion of Tiglath-Pileser in 734 B.C., which would indicate a late date of composition for this narrative). The well-known IDOLATRY of the Danites may have been mainly responsible for Jeroboam's placing one of his golden calves at Dan (2 Ki. 10:29), although the location probably figured to some extent, Dan and Bethel being on the northern and southern boundaries of the northern kingdom.

The conquest of Laish in the time of the judges apparently was followed by the gradual removal from there of many or most of the tribe, although the Bible says nothing concerning this development.

SAMSON was a Danite, and in his day there were many Danites still living in the portion assigned to them by Joshua. ZORAH, ESHTAOL, TIMNAH, ELTEKEH, and EKRON were "Danite" cities (Josh. 19:41–46; cf. 21:23), although the last one was, in the days of Samson, one of the five cities of the lords of the Philistines (Jdg. 13:2, 25), and others were more or less under their control. If MAHANEH DAN (v. 25) is the same as the place mentioned in 18:12, the inference is justified that the conquest of Laish took place before the time of Samson. The meaning of Jdg. 5:17 is too uncertain to be referred to in this connection.

Dan is not listed in the genealogies of 1 Chronicles (1 Chr. 1–8), but 28,600 Danites came to DAVID in HEBRON to make him king over all Israel (1 Chr. 12:35). The listing of the Danites after Issachar, Zebulun, and Naphtali, and before

The tribal territory of Dan and, farther north, the city of Dan.

Asher, indicates that during the reign of David the Danites were regarded as a northern tribe, which means that by this time or long before, the Danites had completed the trek, the beginning of which is described in the book of Judges. Note that HIRAM king of Tyre stated in his letter to SOLOMON that he was sending a skillful workman whose father was a Tyrian but his mother a Danite (2 Chr. 2:14); such a mixed marriage was more likely to have taken place after the Danite migration to the N. (Cf. A. Malamat in *Bib* 51 [1971]: 1–16; F. Spina in *JSOT* issue 4 [1977]: 60–71; H. M. Nieman, *Die Daniten: Studien zur Geschichte eines altisraelitischen Stammes* [1985].)

In Ezekiel's vision of the Holy Land and the Holy City, Dan is named as occupying the northernmost portion (Ezek. 48:1). Dan was one of the so-called "lost tribes" that were carried away by the Assyrians and disappeared. But it is to be remembered that, when EZRA came to Jerusalem, the Israelites offered in sacrifice "twelve bulls for all Israel" (Ezra 8:35), and that the aged ANNA, who was present when the infant Jesus was presented to the Lord, was of another "lost tribe," Asher (Lk. 2:36). PAUL also, speaking before Agrippa (see HEROD VIII), referred to "the promise our twelve tribes are hoping to see fulfilled as they earnestly serve God day and night" (Acts 26:7). This statement would seem to indicate that after the carrying away there was a remnant of grace in the northern kingdom, including Danites, even as there had been 7,000 in the days of ELIJAH who had not bowed the knee to Baal (1 Ki. 19:18). Yet it is remarkable that in Rev. 7 the name of Dan does not appear, a fact that is probably responsible for the ancient tradition that the antichrist was to come from the tribe of Dan. (See further M. Bartusch, *Understanding Dan: An Exegetical Study of a Biblical City, Tribe and Ancestor* [2003].)

O. T. ALLIS

Dan (place) (דן *H1969*, "judge"). A city of the northern extremity of ancient Israel, situated on the S base of Mount HERMON close to one of the tributaries of the JORDAN River, the Nahr Leddan. It was commonly used as a symbol of the extent of Israelite territory in the phrase, "from Dan to Beersheba" (Jdg. 20:1 et al.). The mound where the ancient city stood is known in Arabic as Tell el-Qadi (in Hebrew as Tel Dan) and rises about 75 ft. above the grass land roundabout. In ancient Canaanite times it was known as LAISH (*layiš H4332*, Jdg. 18:7; variant LESHEM *lešem H4386*, Josh. 19:47), a name probably derived from an old Semitic word for "lion" (e.g., Isa. 30:6, NIV "lionesses"). It is known that the site was occupied as early as the Bronze Age and probably was inhabited by 3500 B.C. The town was on

Aerial view of the ancient city of Dan (looking SSW).

the trade route to the Syrian coast; specifically, it was about midway between ancient ARAM, TYRE, and SIDON. The city lay above the great valley of BETH REHOB, which stretches from N to S between Mount Lebanon and Mount Hermon. It was in this region that ABRAHAM and his retinue pursued the Elamite king KEDORLAOMER (Gen. 14:14).

The Danite conquest of the city is reviewed in Jdg. 18, which also states that its inhabitants "were living in safety, like the Sidonians, unsuspecting and secure. And since their land lacked nothing, they were prosperous" (v. 7). After the revolt of JEROBOAM, Dan along with BETHEL became the locations of the two shrines that he set up with golden calves, probably as symbols of BAAL worship (1 Ki. 12:29; see CALF, GOLDEN). So ingrained did this worship at the shrines become that even the massacre of Baal worshipers by JEHU did not stamp out the worship at Dan (2 Ki. 10:28–31). Subsequently it was one of the towns taken by the Aramean king BEN-HADAD, in fulfillment of the warning in 2 Ki. 10:32: "the LORD began to trim off parts of Israel" (NRSV). Dan was recaptured by Israel under Jeroboam II (14:25), but was again taken by the Assyrian TIGLATH-PILESER III (745–727 B.C.). In accord with his usual policy often depicted on Assyrian reliefs of the period, he deported the inhabitants of captured towns, thus the Israelites were carried off to resettle the cities of the Medes (17:6). On Ezek. 27:19, see VEDAN.

Dan is mentioned in extrabiblical sources as early as the conquest annals of THUTMOSE III (1490–1436), in which it appears as *rwś* (representing La-wish or Ra-wish). It is also mentioned by JOSEPHUS as the area in which TITUS, at his father VESPASIAN's orders, stamped out a revolt in the fall of A.D. 67 (*War* 4.4). See also DAN (PERSON AND TRIBE).

(A. Biran has produced a synthesis, *Biblical Dan* [1994], and edited a detailed chronicle of excavations entitled *Dan I* and *Dan II* [1996, 2002]; for a summary, see *NEAEHL*, 1:323–32. On the Danite migration, see A. Malamat in *Bib* 51 [1971]: 1–16. On the Gate of Laish at Tel Dan, see A. Biran in *IEJ* 34 [1984]: 1–19. On a recently discovered Old Aramaic inscription from Tel Dan that appears to refer to the "house of David," see A. Biran and J. Naveh in *IEJ* 43 [1993]: 81–98 and 45 [1995]: 1–18; cf. also V. Sasson in *JSS* 40 [1995]: 11–30, and G. Athas, *The Tel Dan Inscription: A Reappraisal and a New Interpretation* [2003].)

W. WHITE, JR.

dancing. Several Hebrew words describe the joyous, rhythmic movements of the dance, which evidently played a significant part in Israelite life and religion. The verb *rāqad* H8376 ("to skip about") means "to dance" in the piel stem (cf. Ugaritic *mrqdm*, "dancers," who appear with drums, cymbals, and lyre). It is used of children's merriment (Job 21:11) and is the opposite of mourning (Eccl. 3:4). Another verb, *ḥûl* H2565, can mean "to whirl" or "to dance" (Jdg. 21:23), while its cognate nouns, *mĕḥōlâ* H4703 (v. 21; 1 Sam. 18:6) and *māḥôl* H4688 (in praise of Yahweh, Pss. 149:3; 150:4) seem to indicate "circle-dancing." DAVID's lengthy dance before the ARK OF THE COVENANT is described with the unique root *kārar* H4159 (2 Sam. 6:14, 16, pilpel stem; cf. Ugar. *krkr* "to twist, twiddle fingers"). David's movements included leaping (v. 16), so the dancing of the whirling dervishes of Islam seems to afford some parallel to this type. (For other possible ways to refer to dancing, cf. 1 Sam. 18:7; 30:16; 2 Sam. 6:5, 21.)

The religious involvements of dancing are clear from several passages already cited. Added to these could be the dance led by MIRIAM's timbrel playing celebrating Israel's preservation at the RED SEA (Exod. 15:20). The narrative in Jdg. 21:16–24 records the dancing of girls connected with the annual feast at SHILOH. There is likewise evidence based on post-OT practice that dancing may have taken place during other religious celebrations, such as the Feast of Tabernacles (see FEASTS I.B.3). The Psalms scarcely mention dancing, but do frequently describe religious processions. It is possible that dancing was included on these occasions, inasmuch as singers and instrumentalists are mentioned (Ps. 68:25). If Ps. 132 commemorates the transference of the ark, the procession in vv. 8–10 could include a repetition of the dance of David in 2 Sam. 6:14–16.

Pagan societies utilized the dance for various purposes, including religious ritual. The prophets of BAAL employed a kind of limping dance while imploring their god on Mount Carmel (1 Ki. 18:26).

In Babylon, dancing was so closely tied to the religious cult that it could not be properly called an independent activity (H. W. F. Saggs, *The Greatness that Was Babylon* [1962], 190). Egyptian paintings and reliefs portray the dancing of girls to the beating of drums and other instruments. C. H. Gordon (in *Yehezkel Kaufmann Jubilee*, ed. M. Haran [1960], 46–49) has related the dancing of David to the war dances used by the Spartans of Tyrtaeus. These dances were performed in time to the elegiac poems composed by the Spartan leader. Just as David used poetry to inspire and teach his troops (2 Sam. 1:18), so he may have utilized the dance. He could have learned this technique from his tenure among the PHILISTINES, whose AEGEAN connections are well-known.

In the NT *orcheomai G4004* can be used of the playful dancing of children (Matt. 11:17; Lk. 7:32) or of the performance of the daughter of HERODIAS (Matt. 14:6; Mk. 6:22). The latter dance was undoubtedly a sensuous display before the immoral king. The noun *choros G5962* is used to describe the joyous dancing celebrating the return of the prodigal son (Lk. 15:25). While the mode of dancing is not known in detail, it is clear that men and women did not generally dance together, since social amusement was hardly a major purpose of dancing. (See W. O. E. Oesterley, *The Sacred Dance* [1923]; W. Sorell in *The Hebrew Impact on Western Civilization*, ed. D. D. Runes [1951], 505–11; M.-G. Wosien, *Sacred Dance: Encounter with the Gods* [1974]; S. Lonsdale, *Dance and Ritual Play in Greek Religion* [1993].) H. M. WOLF

dandle. This English term, meaning "to move [a small child] up and down playfully," is used once by several versions, including the NIV, to render the Hebrew verb *šāʿaʿ H9130* (pulpal stem, Isa. 66:12). In addition, the ASV and RSV use it to translate *ṭāpaḥ H3254* (piel, occurring only in Lam. 2:22; NIV, "cared for"; NRSV, "bore"). Both contexts illustrate God's love for his children by alluding to the care of a parent.

Daniel dan'yuhl (דָּנִיֵּאל *H1975* [*Ketib* דנאל in Ezek.], "God is my judge"; Δανιήλ *G1248*). **(1)** The second son of DAVID born to him in HEBRON (1 Chr. 3:1). See KILEAB (2 Sam. 3:3).

(2) A descendant of AARON through ITHAMAR and priest of the postexilic period; he was among those who affixed their seals to Nehemiah's covenant (Ezra 8:2; Neh. 10:6; named "Gamael" in 1 Esd. 8:29).

(3) The exilic seer traditionally credited with authorship of the book of Daniel (see DANIEL, BOOK OF). He is commonly accorded the status of a prophet, but this is technically incorrect. His life experiences show that he was more of a statesman in a foreign court than a mediator of divine revelation to a theocratic community. Yet it is also true that his outlook contains elements that are in full accord with the highest spiritual traditions of Hebrew prophecy generally.

Daniel seems to have been born into an unidentified family of Judean nobility somewhat prior to JOSIAH's reformation in 621 B.C. While nothing is known about the life and career of Daniel aside from what is narrated in the canonical book of that name, the fact that he was among the first selection of Jewish captives taken to BABYLON in 605 by NEBUCHADNEZZAR indicates that he claimed considerable social standing. The advance of the Babylonians against the Egyptians, who had marched to HARAN to assist the beleaguered remnants of the Assyrian armies, has been well documented by cuneiform texts. The discovery in 1956 by D. J. Wiseman of four additional tablets of the *Babylonian Chronicle* in the British Museum archives furnished an account of the shattering defeat the Babylonians inflicted upon the Egyptians at

The cuneiform inscription on this terra-cotta cylinder describes various building projects by Nebuchadnezzar II. It informs us that a year after Daniel was taken to Babylon, the king repaired his father's palace that had been damaged by flooding.

Carchemish in 605. One result of this victory was that the Babylonians seem to have demanded hostages of Judah as evidence of good faith toward Babylonia, and it was this group that went into captivity in the third year of JEHOIAKIM (Dan. 1:1, 3), including the young man Daniel.

For a three-year period Daniel was instructed in all the lore of the Chaldeans (Dan. 1:4–5) in preparation for the royal service. He was also given the Babylonian name of BELTESHAZZAR, probably a transliteration of *balāṭsu-uṣur*, "protect his life," the name of the protective deity having been omitted in the Hebrew. However, despite his superficial conformity to the court customs of Babylonia, Daniel remained true to his Jewish heritage. Thus, when he and his three friends (SHADRACH, MESHACH, ABEDNEGO) were invited to accept the royal food and drink, they declined courteously rather than violate the ancient dietary laws of Leviticus, since the food in question (1:8) had been tainted through contact with idols. God honored the witness of this group by giving them outstanding learning abilities (1:20), which enabled them to qualify as official "wise men" after three years (1:20; cf. 2:13). In addition, Daniel received the ability to experience visions and interpret dreams.

In 602 B.C. Nebuchadnezzar was troubled by a dream that he had forgotten on waking (Dan. 2:5, 8). The priestly diviners were ordered to disclose the nature of the dream and interpret its meaning, and when they proved unequal to this challenge they were promptly sentenced to death. This unfortunate fate included Daniel also, but after prayer God revealed the dream and its meaning to him (2:11, 18–19). It depicted a fourfold image representing the four world empires of Babylon, Persia, Greece, and Rome, which would precede the introduction of the messianic kingdom. Nebuchadnezzar was so impressed with this performance that he made Daniel "ruler over the entire province of Babylon and placed him in charge of all its wise men" (2:48). Toward the end of Nebuchadnezzar's reign (604–562 B.C.), Daniel was called upon to interpret the dream of the fallen tree (4:8–27). It required both courage and tact for Daniel to tell the king that for a specified period he would be afflicted with a mental condition, a prediction fulfilled within a year (4:28–33).

When NABONIDUS, the last ruler of imperial Babylon, retired to Teimaʿ (TEMA) in Arabia c. 556 B.C., his son BELSHAZZAR acted as coregent. About 555 Daniel saw a vision of four great beasts (Dan. 7:1–14) that paralleled Nebuchadnezzar's earlier dream of the composite image. In the meantime Babylonian political power was diminishing and being overshadowed by the rising influence of CYRUS (559–530 B.C.). About 552 Daniel had a vision of a ram and a he-goat that related to the fortunes of Persia and Greece (8:20–21) down to the Maccabean period (8:25). Late in 539 Gubaru and Ugbaru led the armies of Cyrus to victory over the Chaldeans, and during the drunken revelries that immediately preceded the fall of Babylon, Daniel was summoned to the court and asked to explain the "handwriting on the wall." He predicted a Medo-Persian victory, condemned the dissolute Belshazzar, and witnessed the collapse of the regime that very night (5:23–31).

This basalt stela represents Nabonidus (555–539 B.C.), the last ruler of the Neo-Babylonian empire, wearing the traditional official dress of a king of Babylon. In front of him are shown the crescent of the moon-god Sin, the star of Ishtar or Venus, and the winged disc of the sun-god Shamash. The larger size of the moon symbol reflects the prominence that Nabonidus gave to this deity.

On assuming his office as king of Babylon, DARIUS THE MEDE (prob. Gubaru) invited Daniel to become one of his three "presidents" (Dan. 6:2). Jealous colleagues tried to cause the downfall of Daniel through charges of corruption (6:4), and when this failed they instituted a royal edict prohibiting all prayers or petitions except those addressed to King Darius himself. The intractable laws of the Medes and Persians left Darius no course but to throw Daniel into a den of lions for breaking them. God intervened to save his servant but allowed the fate intended for Daniel to overtake his accusers. As the Israelite exile in Babylon drew to a close in 538 B.C., the angel GABRIEL answered Daniel's prayers by revealing the time span of SEVENTY WEEKS or 490 years (9:24–27) intervening between the decree enabling Jerusalem to be rebuilt and the time when the Messiah's work would begin.

Daniel continued to function as a wise man during the early years of Cyrus (Dan. 6:28), and having seniority in this position he would doubtless have been accorded great veneration by the superstitious Persians. What appears to be the last recorded event in the life of the seer occurred in the third year of Cyrus (536 B.C.), when Daniel saw a vision of the conflict between the archangel MICHAEL and the demonic powers of society. This unfolded in terms of the history of ANE nations, dealing at some length with the persecutions of ANTIOCHUS Epiphanes (175 B.C.) and the rise of the eschatological antichrist. It culminated in a revelation concerning resurrection and the final judgment of God (10:10—12:4), during which Daniel was assured that, although he would die before all this was fulfilled, he would nevertheless receive his reward at the consummation (12:13).

It seems probable that Daniel was well over eighty when he died. He left behind an impressive reputation for inspiring faith through the exercise of courage when confronted by mortal danger. He also manifested complete dedication to the ideals of God in a pagan society, and set an example of persistence in prayer. His popularity in later times among the Jews is indicated by the numerous legendary accretions, as well as by MSS and fragments of the book discovered at Qumran.

The Ugaritic *Legend of Aqht* referred to an ancient Phoenician king named *Dnʾil* (prob. vocalized as *Danʾilu*) who was reputedly wise and upright (see UGARIT). The reference to "Daniel" in Ezek. 14:14 and 20 may point to some such antediluvian person, and not a contemporary of EZEKIEL. So also in Ezek. 28:3, where the prophet mocks Tyre sarcastically for pretending to be "wiser than Daniel." (See further A. Lacocque, *Daniel in His Time* [1987].)   R. K. HARRISON

Daniel, Additions to. See AZARIAH, PRAYER OF; BEL AND THE DRAGON; SUSANNAH, HISTORY OF.

Daniel, Apocalypse of. A pseudepigraphic document dated to the beginning of the 9th cent. A.D.; one MS attributes it to "Daniel the Prophet," but another one to "Bishop Methodius" (Methodius of Olympus, bishop in Lycia, died early in the 4th cent.). The work is based largely on the book of Revelation and clearly alludes to medieval conflicts between Byzantium and the invading Arabs. According to some scholars, however, it incorporates much earlier apocalyptic material. (English trans. in *OTP*, 1:755–70.)

Daniel, Book of. The fourth book among the Major Prophets of the OT (following the order of the SEPTUAGINT), but included among the KETUBIM (third section) in the Hebrew Bible.

    I. Historical background
   II. Unity
  III. Authorship and special problems
  IV. Date
   V. Place of origin
  VI. Destination
 VII. Occasion
VIII. Purpose
  IX. Canonicity
   X. Text
  XI. Content
 XII. Theology and Interpretation

I. Historical background. The period of time covered by the historical and visionary sections of the book is slightly in excess of the full period of Hebrew EXILE in Babylonia. Daniel was apparently taken by NEBUCHADNEZZAR to BABYLON along with other Judean hostages in 605 B.C., following a Babylonian attempt to subjugate Judah (see

Daniel #3). This would indicate that Daniel was descended from a noble family, since normally only prominent persons were taken captive in this manner. According to the book, the attributive author was trained for service in the royal court, and it was not long before he gained an outstanding reputation as a seer and wise man. With divine help he was able to recall and interpret visions that other men had had, and subsequently he experienced several visions himself by which he was able to predict the future triumph of the messianic kingdom. The book covers the activities of Daniel under successive rulers including BELSHAZZAR and DARIUS THE MEDE. His last recorded vision occurred on the banks of the river TIGRIS in the third year of CYRUS, 536 B.C. Thus the historical period involved corresponds to slightly more than the full extent of the Hebrew exile, after the decree of Cyrus had been promulgated in 538.

The background of both the historical and visionary sections is clearly Babylonian, and there is no question as to whether the author was ever in any other place than Babylonia during his mature years. Babylonian traditions and imagery are clearly in evidence, and the book reflects precisely the same historical background as that found in Ezekiel. Quite possibly the book of Daniel covers a greater length of time than that of his contemporary EZEKIEL, since the latter has no specific references to the Persian regime as master of the contemporary political scene.

II. Unity. The book falls quite readily into two distinct sections: Dan. 1–6, which consists of narratives set against a historical background, and chs. 7–12, which contain the visions experienced by Daniel. There seems little doubt that similarity of subject matter was the primary reason for such an arrangement. Although a general chronological order was followed in the first six chapters, it was modified in the remainder of the book in favor of relating the various visions to one another in terms of theme and content rather than the actual time when they occurred. This division indicates that the book was compiled as a literary bifid, furnishing in effect a two-volume work whose parts could circulate independently if necessary and still provide an adequate understanding of the prophet's activities and outlook. The compilation of works in bifid form was by no means uncommon in antiquity, and in the case of large books like ISAIAH it served to reduce the composition to more manageable proportions without at the same time losing any of the essential teachings of the author concerned.

Elementary though this bifid division is, a great many scholars have failed to recognize it as a genuine literary structure. Consequently a number of

Excavated mud-brick remains of Belshazzar's palace, where this king saw the writing on the wall.

Daniel in exile.

contributing authors have been suggested for the book in some circles, ranging up to nine different hands. Yet, concurrent with theories of multiple authorship have been staunch avowals of the unity of Daniel from both liberal and conservative sources. The wide diversity of opinion regarding the unity of the book is unfortunately self-defeating, and reflects unfavorably upon the critical methods employed. It is now no longer possible to maintain the diversity of authorship of the work on the ground that it contains two languages, an ARAMAIC section (Dan. 2:4b—7:28) enclosed by a Hebrew prologue and epilogue (1:1—2:4a; 8:1—12:13). As a result of archaeological discoveries, it is now known that the ancient Mesopotamian writers not infrequently enclosed the main body of a unified literary work within a linguistic form of a contrasting nature in order to heighten the general effect. This is true of such notable compositions as the Code of HAMMURABI, where the principal prose section was prefaced and concluded by means of poetic material. Exactly the same compositional technique can be seen in the book of JOB, where a prose prologue and epilogue enclose a large poetic section. The book of Daniel is yet another example of a unified and consciously constructed literary integer involving different linguistic components, and once the underlying compositional traditions are recognized, the need for postulating a diversity of authorship on this ground disappears.

III. Authorship and special problems. The question of the authorship of Daniel is closely linked with considerations of date, particularly since modern critical scholarship has been virtually unanimous in its rejection of the book as a 6th-cent. B.C. document written by Daniel. If the book was composed by an unknown author during the Maccabean period with the aim of encouraging faithful Jews in their resistance to the hellenizing policies of ANTIOCHUS IV Epiphanes (cf. 1 Macc. 2:59–60), as critics have long maintained, it must have been written about 165 B.C., and therefore could not possibly have been the work of Daniel (see MACCABEE). So diametrically opposed are these views of authorship that the problems they raise must be given some consideration.

The traditional opinion of authorship has maintained that the book was in its final form during or shortly after the lifetime of Daniel, and that both the historical experiences through which he passed and the visions received were of a genuine nature. In ascribing authorship to Daniel within this general period the traditional view does not overlook the possibility that Daniel may have had scribal assistance in the compilation of his work, especially if the finished product can be regarded in any sense as his memoirs. In any event, however, the traditional view could not place the extant form of the book later than half a century after the time of Daniel's death.

The critical view of authorship and date can be said to have begun with Porphyry, a 3rd-cent. A.D. neo-Platonic philosopher who took special issue with the leading tenets of Christianity. His comments on Daniel have survived only in quotation form, but show that his objections to the traditional view were based on the a priori supposition that there could be no predictive element as such in prophecy. Hence the predictions in Daniel relating to post-Babylonian kings and wars were not really prophecies so much as historical accounts, and therefore of a late date. In assigning the work to the time of Antiochus IV Epiphanes, Porphyry held that the author of Daniel had lied so as to revive the hopes of contemporary Jews in the midst of their hardships. As a result the book of Daniel contained a number of historical errors because of its distance in time from the original events.

This view has been reflected in one way or another ever since in rationalistic attacks upon Daniel. The shallowness of its basic philosophical presupposition is readily apparent from even a casual perusal of OT prophetic literature, where the speakers not only dealt with contemporary events but also pronounced upon happenings in the future, some of which had no particular relationship to the circumstances of their own time. The reason for this, stated simply, is that the Hebrew prophets would have had little sympathy for the modern antithesis between forthtelling and foretelling, if only because for them the future was inherent in the present in a special revelational manner.

Rather more serious attention should be paid to the suggestion of Porphyry that the author of Daniel committed specific historical errors. This allegation is curious, since modern critics have regarded him as an extremely talented Jew, and one who therefore could be expected to write authoritatively. Furthermore, no intelligent 2nd-cent. B.C. Jew could possibly have committed the kind of mistakes alleged if he had ever read the book of Ezra, which covered the history of the early Persian period. Nor would the Jews of the Maccabean age have recognized the book as canonical had it actually contained the kind of errors proposed, since they had access to the writings of such ancient historians as Herodotus, Ctesias, Berossus, and Menander, who preserved correct chronological and historical traditions. By contrast, however, 2nd-cent. B.C. Palestinians rejected such works as 1 Maccabees as being unworthy of inclusion in the Hebrew canon, which by this time had become closed by common consent. See MACCABEES, BOOKS OF.

Characteristic of the sort of historical error popularly supposed to be present in Daniel is the assertion that the reference in Dan. 1:1 can be regarded only as anachronistic, since it implies that Jerusalem had been captured in the third year of Jehoiakim (605 B.C.), and this in turn conflicts with other passages (Jer. 25:1, 9; 46:2) which spoke in the following year as though Jerusalem had yet to fall to the Chaldean armies. This apparent discrepancy of one year rests on a misunderstanding of chronological reckoning in antiquity. The Babylonian scribes used an accession-year system of computation, reckoning the year in which the king ascended the throne as the "year of the accession to the kingdom," and this was followed by the first, second, and subsequent years of rule. The Palestinian scribes, by contrast, tended to follow the nonaccession patterns of reckoning found in Egypt, in which the year when royal rule began was regarded as the first of the reign. (See CHRONOLOGY (OT).) Quite obviously, therefore, Jeremiah reckoned according to the current Palestinian pattern, while Daniel followed the one used in Babylonia. As a result, the fourth year of Jer. 25:1 is actually identical with the third year of Dan. 1:1. Both writers were clearly using systems of reckoning with which they were familiar, and which fully accorded with their different cultural backgrounds. It should also be noted that the reference in Daniel does not affirm that Jerusalem was destroyed in 605, but states only that Nebuchadnezzar took with him certain hostages to Babylonia as a token of good faith on the part of Jehoiakim.

Another supposed historical error on the part of the author has been seen in his use of the term *Chaldean* in an ethnic sense and in a restricted context to indicate a group of "wise men," a usage that does not occur elsewhere in the OT and that allegedly points to a late date of composition. See CHALDEA. This difficulty can be dismissed immediately when it is realized that the 5th-cent. B.C. historian HERODOTUS spoke consistently of the

Chaldeans, acknowledged their priestly office, and stated that some of their cultic procedures went back at least to the time of Cyrus. Furthermore, Assyrian annals employed the term (Akk. *kaldu*) in an ethnic sense; and under NABOPOLASSAR of Babylon (626–605 B.C.), a native Chaldean, the designation became extremely reputable, reflecting OT usage.

Further critical objections to the historicity of Daniel have been raised in connection with the relationship between BELSHAZZAR and NABONIDUS. In the book of Daniel the former was king of Babylon, whereas in contemporary CUNEIFORM writings it was Nabonidus who occupied the Babylonian throne (c. 555–539 B.C.). Obviously a contemporary writer would not have made so elementary a mistake, it is argued, and thus the book must be a late product. Babylonian historical sources show that Nabonidus came to power at a time of considerable unrest in the Chaldean period. Amel-Marduk (562–560), the successor of Nebuchadnezzar, was assassinated by Neriglissar (560–556), who then set out with an army to CILICIA in an attempt to stem the rising power of LYDIA. His son, Labashi-Marduk, reigned for less than a year before being overthrown by Nabonidus, who in turn marched to Cilicia and appears to have achieved some sort of political settlement between Lydia and the Medes. The latter then began to threaten Babylonia, and when its inhabitants refused to accept certain reforms proposed by Nabonidus, he promptly made his son Belshazzar coregent and left for Syria. He campaigned there and in N Arabia for a decade while the feud between himself and the Babylonian priesthood gradually simmered down.

About 544 B.C. political conditions in Babylonia made his return possible, but by then the country was weak and hopelessly divided politically. Against this historical background it was perfectly correct for the author of Daniel to speak of Belshazzar as "king," since he was in fact coregent, and to observe that Daniel was "the third highest ruler in the kingdom" (Dan. 5:29), the absent partner being Nabonidus. The reference in Dan. 5:18 to Belshazzar as a son of Nebuchadnezzar is also correct according to Semitic usage, since "son" often was used as the equivalent of "descendant." Nitocris, the mother of Belshazzar, was apparently the daughter of Nebuchadnezzar, which again supports the tradition contained in Daniel.

As far as incidental historical accuracy is concerned, the author was sufficiently well informed about 6th-cent. B.C. life in Babylonia to represent Nebuchadnezzar as being able to formulate and change Babylonian law with absolute sovereignty (Dan. 2:12–13, 46), while showing that Darius the Mede was powerless to alter the rigid laws of the Medes and Persians (6:8–9). Again he was quite correct in recording the change from punishment by fire in the time of the Babylonians (ch. 3) to punishment by being thrown into a lion's den under the Persians (ch. 6), since fire was sacred to ZOROASTRIANISM. Similarly, the author of the work knew precisely why the image of Nebuchadnezzar had been set up in the plain of DURA. Archaeological excavations have shown that this enterprising king undertook considerable restoration of ancient buildings during his reign, one of the more notable instances being at UR of the Chaldees. Nebuchadnezzar also instigated a thoroughgoing reformation of religious calendars and cultic practices, and from the evidence presented by the excavation of the temple at Ur it appears that the general tendency of his cultic reforms was in the direction of greater public participation in what hitherto had been rather esoteric sacrificial and other rites. The erecting of a large image in the plain of Dura served to establish general congregational worship by the public, with the king rather than the priesthood as the representative of the god. Substituting this form of worship, Nebuchadnezzar displaced the secret rituals performed by the priests and brought religion within the reach of the lowliest citizen in the empire.

All of the foregoing is of immediate significance for the 6th cent. B.C., but is of no relevance whatever for the Maccabean period. Critics of the traditional date and composition of Daniel have long employed the circumstances surrounding the insanity of Nebuchadnezzar as an indication of the unhistorical nature of the book, since such a mental affliction was supposedly not recorded in nonbiblical sources. The latter is by no means true, however, for three centuries after the time of Nebuchadnezzar a Babylonian priest named Berossus preserved a tradition that Nebuchadnezzar became ill suddenly toward the end of his reign (Jos. *Ag. Ap.* 1.20 §§145–46; cf. Euseb. *Praep. Ev.* 9.41.1). The garbled nature of Berossus's report lends strength to the view that the illness was a form of madness. In Mesopotamia this kind of affliction was dreaded above all others because it was thought to be the direct result of demon possession. Consequently, madmen were immediately deprived of normal social contacts lest they should cause others to be possessed, and the affliction in its various forms was treated with superstitious dread. For such an ailment to overtake a Babylonian king was unthinkable, but even if it occurred it could never have been recorded as such in the annals.

More than three centuries later only the most discreet of references to this calamity was deemed advisable, and this attitude contrasts markedly with the concise, objective Hebrew report in Dan. 4. That this latter described accurately a genuine though rare psychotic condition is evident from the way in which it is still seen occasionally today, and can be recognized clearly even from the Daniel narrative alone. The condition is a rare form of monomania known as *boanthropy*, in which the sufferer imagines himself to be an ox and behaves accordingly. The present writer has actually encountered one such case in a British mental institution, and despite the fact that the patient was receiving professional care he manifested all the physical attitudes described in Daniel, including the eating of grass and the drinking of rain water, these latter two items forming his entire diet. Some light may perhaps be thrown on the historical situation by a damaged tablet Sir Henry Rawlinson recovered from the period of Nebuchadnezzar. When translated it read in part: "For four years ... in all my dominions I did not build a high place of honor, the precious treasures of my kingdom I did not lay out. In the worship of Merodach ... I did not sing his praises ... nor did I clear out the canals." If this is a genuine contemporary record, it could well be a direct allusion to this embarrassing interlude in the reign of Nebuchadnezzar.

From the fourth QUMRAN cave came a papyrus scrap containing the "Prayer of Nabonidus" (4Q242 = 4QPrNab ar), and this discovery has prompted the suggestion that the disease described in Dan. 4 was wrongly attributed to Nebuchadnezzar evidently by another author writing long after the events described. The papyrus fragment in question preserved a prayer supposedly uttered by Nabonidus "the great king, (who) prayed when he was smitten with a serious inflammation by command of the most high God in the city of Teima." This affliction evidently occurred during the years when Nabonidus was in voluntary exile from Babylonia and was living in Arabia. The fragment recorded that Nabonidus confessed his sin when a Jewish priest from the exiles in Babylonia had been sent to him, and the priest then furnished a partial interpretation of the significance of the illness.

Scholars who have studied this material have supposed that the author of the papyrus had preserved an "older" tradition regarding Nabonidus, rather than Nebuchadnezzar, as the victim of illness (cf. M. Henze, *The Madness of King Nebuchadnezzar: The Ancient Near Eastern Origins and Early History of Interpretation of Daniel 4* [1999]). The substitution of the latter in the Daniel account was thought to have occurred long after the original story had been brought to Palestine, where recollections of Nabonidus soon faded. There are obvious difficulties in such a position, however. Precisely why the author of Daniel should have used the "Prayer of Nabonidus" as the basis for the fourth chapter of his book, and then altered the names, the locale, and even the nature of the disease itself, is extremely difficult to explain. Furthermore, there was already a strong historical tradition associating Nabonidus with Teimaʿ, and because of the brutality with which Nabonidus established himself at the site, it is highly unlikely that either he or the events themselves would be forgotten, particularly among the Arab tribes of the area. Again, while Nabonidus was undoubtedly strong-willed and self-assertive as well as being a man of culture and antiquarian tastes, there is no tradition extant that at any time described him as a madman, cruel though he may have been occasionally. Furthermore, the "Prayer of Nabonidus" contains pathological elements that are certainly unknown to modern medicine, whereas the account in Daniel describes a well-attested and readily-recognizable psychotic condition.

It seems clear that two very different traditions are involved. The Qumran scrap seems to preserve an account of some ailment, whether of a staphylococcal nature or not, that afflicted Nabonidus during his years at Teima‛, and because of certain unrealistic elements it can only be assigned to the realm of legend and folklore. By contrast, the account in Daniel is of an attestable clinical nature, and forms part of a larger tradition that associated madness with Nebuchadnezzar II. Compositions such as SUSANNA and BEL AND THE DRAGON show that the book of Daniel attracted a good deal of legendary material, and it may well be that the Qumran fragment is another hitherto undiscovered element of this apocryphal corpus.

However, in the view of the present writer, the "Prayer of Nabonidus" more probably constitutes a near contemporary of the apocryphal composition Prayer of Manasseh, written in the century between 250 and 150 B.C. and closely related to it in both form and content (see MANASSEH, PRAYER OF). There is clearly no connection between the "Prayer of Nabonidus" and the fourth chapter of Daniel, and it is therefore extremely difficult to see how the Qumran fragment can underlie the Daniel tradition in any sense. The fact that the "Prayer of Nabonidus" was first discovered at Qumran might well indicate that it originated during the Maccabean period, and it may possibly have been composed by the Qumran secretaries themselves. There is no single element in it that requires a date of composition significantly earlier than the Maccabean period, and it could possibly have been written as late as 100 B.C.

One of the most tenacious arguments against the historicity and traditional authorship of Daniel has involved the identity of DARIUS THE MEDE. Since this man is not mentioned as such by name other than in the book of Daniel, and the contemporary cuneiform inscriptions leave no room for a king of Babylon between Nabonidus-Belshazzar and the accession of Cyrus of Persia, his historicity has been denied on the ground that the events dealing with him in Daniel represent a mixture of confused traditions. However, because the narratives relating to Darius the Mede have all the appearances of a genuine historical record, it may be instructive to examine the evidence a little more closely. According to Dan. 5:30–31, Darius the Mede received the government on the death of Belshazzar, being made ruler of the Chaldeans (Dan. 9:1) at the age of sixty-two (5:31). He was accorded the title of "king" (6:6, 9, 25), and the years were reckoned in Babylonian fashion according to his reign (11:1). He appointed 120 subordinate governors of provincial districts under three presidents of whom Daniel was one (6:2). Darius was a contemporary of Cyrus the Persian, and during his rule Daniel came into even greater prominence than before.

Those who take the Daniel narrative as historical have made numerous attempts to identify Darius the Mede with persons mentioned in Babylonian cuneiform texts. Since he was a contemporary of Cyrus he clearly cannot be identified with Darius I, son of Hystaspes, who ruled over Babylonia and Persia from 521 to 486 B.C. Darius the Mede has also been identified with Cyrus the Great, who on his defeat of Astyages, king of Media, in 549 was accorded the title "king of the Medes" by Nabonidus of Babylon. Cyrus is known to have been in his early sixties when he conquered Babylon, and according to contemporary inscriptions he appointed many of his subordinates to positions of high office in the provincial government. Such a view would require that the phrase "and the reign of Cyrus" (6:28) be translated "in the reign of Cyrus," using two names for one person. This device is quite permissible linguistically, and would accord with the suggestion by D. J. Wiseman that Darius the Mede and Cyrus the Great should be regarded as alternative titles for the same individual, in exactly the same way as James VI of Scotland was known as James I of England. This theory is unfortunately weak in that nowhere was Cyrus named "son of Xerxes" (as Darius the Mede is identified in Dan. 9:1), though it may be, of course, that this title was a term used of the royal succession. However, even though Cyrus was considered the king of Media, he was again never described in contemporary inscriptions as "of the seed of a Mede."

Probably the best approach to the problem is to follow J. C. Whitcomb (*Darius the Mede* [1959]) and identify Darius the Mede with Gubaru the governor of Babylon and the "Regions beyond the River" under Cyrus. The Nabonidus Chronicle mentioned two persons connected with the fall of Babylon, namely Ugbaru and Gubaru, and faulty translation of the Chronicle since 1882 has tended to confuse their identities. It was on the basis of this misunderstanding that scholars such as H. H. Rowley (*Darius the Mede and the Four World Empires in the Book of Daniel* [1935]) assumed that they were actually one person, the Gobryas of Xenophon's *Cyropaedia*, who died after the fall of Babylon in 539 B.C. The translation of the Chronicle by Sidney Smith in 1924, however, distinguished between Ugbaru and Gubaru, and it is now apparent that the former, who was governor of Gutium and an ally of Cyrus, took a prominent part in the capture of Babylon and then died shortly afterward, presumably of wounds sustained in the battle. Whereupon the other victorious leader Gubaru, who with Ugbaru was apparently responsible for diverting the river Euphrates so that his soldiers could capture the city by infiltrating along the dried-up river bed, was appointed by Cyrus as the governor of Babylon. He appears to have held this position for fourteen years, and was mentioned in a number of cuneiform texts.

One of the Nabonidus tablets discovered at Haran referred to the "king of the Medes" in the tenth year of the reign of Nabonidus (546 B.C.), and while this text does not throw any light on the identity of Darius the Mede, it does at least show that the title was in existence after Cyrus had conquered Media, perhaps as the designation of a provincial governor. Certainly the evidence presented by the Nabonidus Chronicle would not permit Darius the Mede to be regarded as a "conflation of confused traditions" as Rowley maintained, but instead offers definite possibilities of the identification of Darius with a historical personage, namely Gubaru. Subsequent cuneiform discoveries may well clarify the situation completely.

At the end of the 19th cent., liberal scholars were fond of adducing as proof of a Maccabean date certain of the linguistic features found in Daniel. Thus, in 1891 S. R. Driver (*An Introduction to the Literature of the Old Testament*, 508) could pronounce quite confidently that "the Greek words *demand*, the Hebrew *supports*, and the Aramaic *permit* a date after the conquest of Palestine by Alexander the Great." This opinion was widely quoted, and H. H. Rowley in particular tried to substantiate these conclusions in some of his publications (e.g., *The Aramaic of the Old Testament: A Grammatical and Lexical Study of Its Relations with Other Early Aramaic Dialects* [1929]).

However, with more information concerning the history of the ARAMAIC LANGUAGE now on hand, the opinions of Driver and others have undergone sobering modifications. Certain Aramaic forms that originally were regarded as late in date have been discovered in the Ras Shamra texts of the Amarna Age (see UGARIT), and include specific ones found in the book of Daniel. As a spoken language Aramaic was already current in the 3rd millennium B.C. and was the dialect favored by LABAN (Gen. 31:47) in the following millennium. Of the four groups of Aramaic as established by linguistic research, Old Aramaic, the language of the N Syrian inscriptions from the 10th to the 8th centuries B.C., formed the basis for official Aramaic. This latter was already in use by government personnel during the Assyrian period (c. 1100–605 B.C.), and when the Persians gained control of the ANE it became the approved language of diplomatic and other communications. Even before the end of the Assyrian empire, Aramaic "dockets" were already being attached to cuneiform tablets to indicate names and dates connected with the texts as well as to give a summary of their contents. During the Hellenistic period, official Aramaic continued in use on dockets as well as on coins, papyri, and a variety of inscriptions.

Recent studies have shown that the Aramaic of Daniel was the kind that developed in government circles from the 7th cent. B.C. and subsequently became widespread in the ANE. The linguistic forms are also closely related to the language of the 5th-cent. B.C. ELEPHANTINE papyri from Egypt, as well as to the appropriate sections of Ezra. The Hebrew portions of Daniel have affinity with the linguistic forms of Ezekiel, Haggai, Ezra, and Chronicles, and not with the later linguistic characteristics of Ecclesiasticus as preserved in rabbinic quotations. Furthermore, it is now seen inadvisable to distinguish at all sharply between the eastern and western branches of the Aramaic language, as older scholars were accustomed to do, and this weakens even further the argument for a later rather than an earlier date of composition.

In addition, Persian loanwords in Daniel are consistent with an earlier date for the book instead of one in the Maccabean age. Thus the term *satrap*, once thought to be Greek, is now known to have been derived from the Old Persian *kshathrapan*, which also occurred in the cuneiform texts as *satarpanu*, from which the Greek form emerged. The Persian terms in Daniel are actually Old Persian in nature, that is to say, words that occurred specifically within the history of the language up to 300 B.C. To this extent at the very least the Aramaic of Daniel is decidedly pre-Hellenistic in nature and reflects clearly the classical period when the language was the *lingua franca* of the Persian empire. From the foregoing evidence it will be obvious that the kind of Aramaic used in Daniel is a forceful argument for an earlier rather than a later date of composition, and strongly supports the traditional view of authorship by Daniel in 6th cent. B.C. Babylonia.

The fact that Greek names were used for certain musical instruments in Daniel, translated in the KJV as "harp," "sackbut," and "psaltery" (Dan. 3:5 et al.) was formerly much in vogue as an argument for a Maccabean date for the writing of the book. However, this view no longer constitutes a serious problem, since archaeological discoveries have revealed something of the extent to which Greek culture had infiltrated the ANE long before the Persian period. It is now known that, despite their ostensible Greek nature, the instruments in question are of undoubted Mesopotamian origin. Thus the "harp" was one of the numerous Asiatic forerunners of the Greek *kithara*; the "sackbut" was most probably similar to, or derived from, the *sabitu* or Akkadian seven-stringed lyre, while the "psaltery" was the old Persian *santir* or dulcimer frequently portrayed on 1st-millennium B.C. reliefs in Assyria. (See further D. J. Wiseman et al., *Notes on Some Problems in the Book of Daniel* [1965].) See MUSIC, MUSICAL INSTRUMENTS IV.D.

In the light of the foregoing evidence it would appear that it is both unnecessary and undesirable for the authorship of the book of Daniel to be assigned to any other place and time than the Babylonia of the 6th cent. B.C. This being the case, there can be little objection to the view that the book was written by Daniel, whether with or without scribal assistance, during or immediately after the period of time the work purports to cover.

IV. Date. Because questions of authorship and historicity are closely connected with the dating of the book, the historical, archaeological, and linguistic evidence adduced in the previous section strongly confirms the traditional date assigned to Daniel. While the problems associated with Darius the Mede are not yet completely resolved, the situation is by no means as fictitious historically as Rowley and others have maintained. All the evidence to date indicates that Darius the Mede must once again be regarded as a historical personage, and it is not too much to hope that future cuneiform discoveries will vindicate his historicity and reveal his identity.

As far as the languages of the book of Daniel are concerned, the most recent studies place the Aramaic firmly within the tradition of chancellery usage from the 7th cent. B.C. onward, and indicate a positive *terminus ad quem* in the pre-Hellenistic period at the absolute latest. The Hebrew linguistic forms also accord with the traditions of the exilic and postexilic period as found in Ezekiel, Haggai, and Ezra, and not with a considerably later stage in the language. From this it would appear that the book emerged from a period in the 6th to 5th centuries B.C. rather than from the Maccabean age. Some liberal scholars have adduced as evidence for a Maccabean dating the fact that the name of Daniel was omitted from the list of noteworthy Israelites in the book of Ecclesiasticus (Sir. 44). Since the latter was in extant form by 180 B.C., it has been argued the omission implies that the author, Ben Sira, knew nothing of either Daniel or his book. Aside from any other considerations it is simply inconceivable that a person such as Daniel, whose prophecy had already attracted significant legendary accretions, would be entirely unknown to an erudite 2nd-cent. B.C. Jew, particularly if, as liberal critics claimed, the sagas of Daniel were on the point of being written and accepted with great enthusiasm by oppressed Jews. When the list of notables as preserved by Ben Sira is examined even superficially, it will be observed that not merely was the name of Daniel omitted but also those of Job, all the judges except Samuel, King Asa, Jehoshaphat, Mordecai, and even Ezra himself. Quite clearly an appeal to ignorance has to be abandoned in favor of some other principle of selectivity whose nature is unknown. There are, however, references to Daniel and his book in other documents that are at least 2nd-cent. B.C. compositions and attest to the familiarity of the Daniel tradition at that time (1 Macc. 2:59–60; Bar. 1:15—3:3; *Sibylline Oracles* 2.247 [*OTP*, 1:351]) .

Much of the most damaging evidence to the liberal assessment of the date of Daniel has been provided by the Qumran discoveries (see DEAD SEA SCROLLS). It is now clear that the sect originated in the 2nd cent. B.C. and that all its biblical MSS were copies, not originals. The nature of Jewish compositions aspiring to canonicity was that they were allowed to circulate for a period of time so that their general consonance with the law and the other canonical writings could become established. Once this had taken place, the works were accorded a degree of popular canonicity as distinct from a conciliar pronouncement. Under normal circumstances a moderate interval of time was required for this process, though some prophecies were doubtless recognized early for what they were by those who heard them. Nevertheless, the written form generally only gained acceptance as the Word after some time had elapsed, but once this happened it was transmitted with scrupulous care.

Daniel is represented at Qumran by several MSS in good condition as well as by numerous fragments, thus showing the popularity of the work. Since all of these are copies, the autograph must clearly be earlier than the Maccabean period. Two fragments of Daniel recovered from Cave 1 proved to be related paleographically to the large Isaiah scroll, and another was akin to the script of the Habakkuk *pesher*. If this relationship is as genuine as paleographers think, the liberal dating of Daniel will need radical upward adjustment, since the book of Isaiah was certainly written several centuries before the earliest date to which the large Isaiah scroll (1QIsa^a) can be assigned on any grounds. A Maccabean dating for Daniel has now to be abandoned, if only because there could not possibly be a sufficient interval of time between the composition of Daniel and its appearance in the form of copies in the library of a Maccabean religious sect.

Fragmentary copies of the book of Daniel (one of them dated to the late 2nd cent. B.C.) have been discovered in Qumran. It seems fatuous for scholars to abandon the Maccabean dating of certain Psalms that had long been regarded as demonstrably late, and yet adhere to it rigidly with regard to the book of Daniel. For the sake of consistency alone, if the "late" Psalms are to be assigned now to the Persian period, precisely the same should be done for the book of Daniel. That scholarly prejudice is largely involved is seen in the fact that critics can argue from the reference to JADDUA (Jos. *Ant*. 11.7.2) to an earlier rather than a later date for the list of high priests (Neh. 12:10, 22), and yet completely ignore or dismiss the tradition preserved in the next section (*Ant*. 11.8.5), which relates that after Jaddua had met Alexander the Great outside Jerusalem and had instructed him in the cultic procedures of Jewish sacrifice, the book of Daniel was shown to the conqueror. If one tradition concerning Jaddua is acceptable, logical consistency would again demand that another concerning the same individual be given at least some consideration.

From the foregoing evidence it can be stated that a Maccabean date for the book of Daniel as a whole is now precluded by the evidence. Most specialists today recognize that at least the material in the first six chapters is older, although mainstream scholarship continues to hold that the book did not reach its present form until the beginnings of the Maccabean period.

V. Place of origin. On the basis of a 6th-cent. B.C. date of composition, the place of origin is clearly Babylonia. Indeed on any dating sequence there can be no real question as to the Babylonian background of the work. There is no single element that is consistent with a Palestinian compositional milieu, and the book consistently breathes the air of the Neo-Babylonian and Persian periods. The city of Babylon itself seems the most probable place of compilation.

VI. Destination. Liberal scholars who have suggested a Maccabean origin for the book have thought that it was intended as a "tract for the times" to encourage oppressed Palestinian Jews as they resisted the program of hellenizing that Antiochus IV Epiphanes was imposing upon his realm. Since the work has been shown to belong properly to the 6th cent. B.C., the book can have been meant only for the exiles in Babylonia, evidently with the avowed purpose of showing that foreign captivity and a living faith in God were by no means as incompatible as some exiles imagined.

VII. Occasion. The contents of Daniel arose out of the experiences of the seer in the Babylonian court, and comprise memoirs and visions. The various chapters represent the outstanding occurrences in the life of Daniel, which covers fully the period of the exile in Babylonia. It is difficult to say whether the book was prompted by any specific occurrence, since it appears to be a straightforward record of notable events in the life of an outstanding servant of God. In the historical section the specific occasion was invariably one of pagan culture or superstition being confronted by the power of the Israelite God. In the visions the events of future times were the dominant concern, and whether these were occasioned by specific happenings in the life of Daniel or not is unknown.

VIII. Purpose. The overall aim of the book is to show the superiority of the Israelite God over the heathen idols of Mesopotamia. Daniel also makes it clear that, although the Babylonians had been the means of punishment for Israel, they also would pass from the historical scene. The visions go even further in predicting the time when the Messiah's work would begin, showing that in the latter days God would establish a permanent kingdom. Despite the fact that the chosen people would not remain unscathed throughout their existence, their destiny was bound up with that of the Messiah. A living faith in the power of God would be more than a match for whatever difficulties might arise, as exemplified in the life of Daniel himself.

IX. Canonicity. From its inception the work was apparently assigned to the third division of the Hebrew canon, the Writings (*Ketubim*), presumably on the basis that Daniel could not be regarded as a prophet in the sense of Isaiah or Ezekiel, since he was not the mediator of revelation from God to a theocratic community. This conviction evidently underlay the pronouncement of the TALMUD (*b. B. Bat.* 15a), which nevertheless testifies to the esteem in which Daniel was held. In the SEPTUAGINT version the book was placed among the prophetic writings following Ezekiel but preceding the Twelve, a position adopted by the English versions.

X. Text. The MT is in good condition, and the ancient versions do not suggest the presence of significant textual corruptions, although legendary accretions such as the Song of the Three Young Men and Bel and the Dragon formed part of some versions. Two distinct Greek translations are known: what may be called the Old Greek survives complete in only one Greek MS (plus fragments in other MSS) and in the Syro-Hexapla, whereas the version traditionally attributed to Theodotion is found in all other witnesses. See discussion under SEPTUAGINT IV.C.

XI. Content. The book can be analyzed as follows:

A. Daniel and his friends come to prominence in Babylon (Dan. 1:1–21).

B. The vision of the image recalled and interpreted (2:1–49).

C. Image-worship in the plain of Dura and its consequences for Daniel and his friends (3:1–30).

D. A vision of the impending illness of Nebuchadnezzar (4:1–37).

E. The explanation of the cryptic text and the fall of Babylon (5:1–31).

F. Daniel in the den of lions (6:1–28).

G. A vision of four great beasts and their significance (7:1–28).

H. A vision of future kingdoms (8:1–27).

I. Confession, followed by a vision relating to the coming of the Messiah (9:1–27).

J. A divine message is given to Daniel that serves to introduce the prophecies of chs. 11 and 12 (10:1–21).

K. The wars of Syria and Egypt and the sealing of the prophecy (11:1—12:13).

XII. Theology and interpretation. The theological standpoint of Daniel has much in common with that of EZEKIEL. God is viewed as a transcendent Being who by nature is superior to all the gods of the heathen. Because God is all-powerful, events work out according to a predetermined divine purpose, and this is consistent with 8th-cent. prophetic thought, which maintained that God was in firm control of the trend of events. In the same way Daniel thought of the messianic kingdom as the conclusion of the age, and as a matter for divine rather than human decision. Although the coming kingdom was contemplated in largely material terms, the concepts of resurrection in Dan. 12 are an advance on the ESCHATOLOGY of the preexilic prophets. The angelology of Daniel is similar to that of Ezekiel, and although somewhat vague on occasions it recognizes that angels possessed personalities and even names (see ANGEL). However, the angelology is by no means as elaborate as that of later Jewish APOCALYPTIC LITERATURE such as *1 Enoch*. The apocalyptic character of the visions should be distinguished carefully from oriental apocalypticism generally, since Daniel contains no DUALISM of the kind found in Zoroastrian religion and does not reflect an ethical passivity that would preclude Daniel from announcing divine judgment upon individuals or nations.

The apocalyptic sections of the book have been widely discussed, partly because of the interpretation to be assigned to the four kingdoms of Dan. 2, where critics have divided Medo-Persia into two separate empires, making the kingdoms Babylonia, Media, Persia, and Greece respectively. However, the history of the Median kingdom precludes such a division, so that the order of the empires would be Babylonia, Medo-Persia, Greece, and Rome. The identity of the fourth kingdom is important for the later visions of Daniel. It is quite different in nature from the "goat" (Dan. 8:5), and thus cannot represent Greece, as liberal scholars have maintained. Again, the "little horn" (8:9 KJV), representing Antiochus IV Epiphanes, is not the same as the "little one" (7:8), and is also different from the successor to the ten kings (7:24). The "little horn" emerging from the fourth beast was represented in conflict with the saints of God before the establishing of the divine kingdom (7:21).

Attempting to interpret the prophecies, some conservative scholars have seen the predictions concerning the image (Dan. 2:31–49), the four beasts (7:2–27), and the SEVENTY WEEKS (9:24–27) as culminating in the INCARNATION of Christ and the birth of the Christian church. On this view the stone (2:34–35) points to the coming of Christ, while the ten horns of the fourth beast (7:24), the little horn (7:8), and the concept of "time, two times, and half a time" (7:25) are interpreted symbolically. The messianic work is accomplished during a period of seventy sevens (9:24), presumably dating from the decree of Cyrus in 538 B.C., including the work of Ezra, and culminating in the advent and ascension of Christ. The death of the Messiah causes Jewish sacrifices to cease, and the one who "causes desolation" (9:27) is TITUS, who destroyed Jerusalem in A.D. 70.

Other conservatives have related the apocalyptic passages to the SECOND COMING of Christ rather than the incarnation, and have seen in the imagery of Daniel two successive forms of the Satan-dominated kingdom of men represented by the empires of Babylon, Medo-Persia, Greece, and Rome, the latter being protracted in some form until the second advent of Christ. This ends with the rise of the ten kings (2:41–44; cf. Rev. 17:12), who are destroyed by Christ at his second coming. The divine kingdom is then established (cf. Matt. 6:10; Rev. 20:1–6) and becomes a "great mountain," filling the whole earth (Dan. 2:35). Daniel 7:25 shows an advance in thought over Dan. 2, however, with the antichrist being introduced as the eleventh horn who persecutes the saints for "a time, and times and half a time" (i.e., three and a half years; cf. Dan. 7:6; 8:5; Rev. 12:14). One like a son of man (Dan. 7:13) achieves the ultimate destruction of the antichrist, the four kingdoms, and the ten kings. The seventy sevens of years is reckoned on this view from the decree of ARTAXERXES I in 444 B.C. to rebuild Jerusalem (Neh. 2:1–8) and concludes with the founding of the millennial kingdom (Dan. 9:24). A gap is held to separate the end of the sixty-ninth week from the beginning of the seventieth (9:62), since Christ set the abomination of desolation at the end of the present age (cf. 9:27; Matt. 24:15).

The millennial interpreters see in the seventieth week a seven-year period just prior to the second coming of Christ during which interval the antichrist arises and persecutes the saints of God. The transition from the purely historical situation represented by the Persian, Greek, Ptolemaic, and Seleucid regimes, culminating in the persecutions of Antiochus IV Epiphanes (Dan. 11:2–35a), is marked by the phrase "for it will still come at the appointed time" (11:35b), which introduces the specifically eschatological situation relating to the second coming of Christ. Some premillennial interpreters have seen the "king of the north" subduing the antichrist along with the "king of the south" before being destroyed himself (cf. 11:40–45; Ezek. 39:4, 17), but ultimately the antichrist recovers and begins his era of world domination (Dan. 11:44; cf. Rev. 13:3; 17:8). The great tribulation of three and a half years (Dan. 7:25) or 1,260 days (Rev. 12:6) ends with the bodily resurrection of those saints who have died in the tribulation (Dan. 12:2–3; cf. Rev. 7:9–14). After a short interval in which the temple is cleansed (Dan. 12:11), the fullness of the millennial kingdom is ushered in (12:12). (See also R. K. Harrison, *Introduction to the Old Testament* [1969], 1105–38.)

(Significant commentaries include J. A. Montgomery, *A Critical and Exegetical Commentary on the Book of Daniel*, ICC [1927]; E. J. Young, *The Prophecy of Daniel* [1949]; H. C. Leupold, *Exposition of Daniel* [1949]; R. D. Culver, *Daniel and the Latter Days* [1954]; L. F. Harman and A. A. DiLella, *The Book of Daniel*, AB 23 [1978]; A. Lacocque, *The Book of Daniel* [1979]; J. E. Goldingay, *Daniel*, WBC 30 [1988]; J. J. Collins, *Daniel*, Hermeneia [1993]; S. R. Miller, *Daniel*, NAC 18 [1994]; G. W. Buchanan, *The Book of Daniel* [1999]; T. Longman III, *Daniel*, NIVAC [1999]; K. O. Gangel, *Daniel*, Holman OT Commentary 18 [2001].

Note also R. D. Wilson, *Studies in the Book of Daniel*, 2 vols. [1917, 1938]; G. K. Beale, *The Use of Daniel in Jewish Apocalyptic Literature and in the Revelation of St. John* [1984]; A. S. van der Woude, ed., *The Book of Daniel in the Light of New Findings* [1993]; T. J. Meadowcroft, *Aramaic Daniel and Greek Daniel: A Literary Comparison* [1995]; J. J. Collins and P. W. Flint, eds., *The Book of Daniel: Composition and Reception*, 2 vols. [2001]; L. DiTommaso, *The Book of Daniel and the Apocryphal Daniel Literature* [2005]; and the bibliography compiled by W. E. Mills, *Daniel* [2002].)

R. K. Harrison

Danite dan′it. See Dan (person and tribe).

Dan Jaan dan-jay′uhn (דָּן יַעַן H1970, meaning uncertain). A locality somewhere between Gilead and Sidon (2 Sam. 24:6). According to the NIV, David's census takers "went to Gilead and the region of Tahtim Hodshi, and on to Dan Jaan and around toward Sidon." The NRSV (appealing to the obviously corrupt LXX, *eis Danidan kai Oudan*, "to Danidan and Oudan") translates, "they came to Dan, and from Dan they went around to Sidon." Others, on the basis of 1 Ki. 15:20 and 2 Chr. 16:4, emend the Hebrew *dnh yʿn* to *dnh wʿywn*, "to Dan and Ijon" (the town of Ijon was 9 mi. NNW of Dan (place)). Still others follow the Lucianic recension of the Septuagint (*heōs Dan*) and emend the Hebrew to *ʿd dn*, "to Dan" (see P. K. McCarter, *II Samuel*, AB 9 [1984], 505).

Dannah dan′uh (דַּנָּה H1972, possibly "stronghold"). A town of the hill country of Judah, near Socoh and Debir (Josh. 15:49). The exact location is unknown, but it must have been some 8–12 mi. SW of Hebron.

Daphne daf′nee (Δάφνη). A park or pleasure resort in a suburb of Antioch of Syria where the high priest Onias III took refuge when he fled from Menelaus (2 Macc. 4:33). Daphne was consecrated by Seleucus I to the royal gods and especially to Apollo (cf. Strabo, *Geogr.* 16.2.6). It was a beautiful precinct of temples and gardens with associated theaters and stadia, similar to Delphi and all other religious centers of the Greeks in which worship of the Olympian gods, ritual, drama, and sport were inevitably linked. Daphne became a haunt of pleasure seekers and merry-making Antiochenes and tourists, winning a worldwide reputation for vice and carnality. E. Gibbon gave a description of the place in *The History of the Decline and Fall of the Roman Empire* (vol. 2, ch. 23; see pp. 395–96 in the J. B. Bury ed. [1946]). Considerable archaeological work has been done at the site (cf. R. Stillwell, ed., *Antioch-on-the-Orontes: II. The Excavations 1933–36* [1938]).

E. M. Blaiklock

dappled. This English term is used by the NIV and other versions to render Hebrew *bārōd* H1353 in the description of some horses in Zechariah's vision (Zech. 6:3, 6). In the description of Jacob's flock, the same Hebrew word is rendered "spotted" by the NIV (Gen. 31:10, 12).

J. B. Scott

Dara dair′uh. See Darda.

Darda dahr′duh (דַּרְדַּע H1997 [in 1 Chr. 2:6, דָּרַע], derivation uncertain). One of the sons of MAHOL who were regarded as wise men (1 Ki. 4:31). The same group of names (plus that of Zimri) apparently occurs in 1 Chr. 2:6, although most Hebrew MSS here have "Dara" instead of "Darda." This latter text, however, purports to list the children of ZERAH son of JUDAH. The discrepancy is often explained by arguing that Mahol was the proximate father, while Zerah was a remote ancestor. Others believe that the phrase "sons of Mahol" in the Kings passage should be understood as "sons of dance" (Heb. *māḥôl* H4688) and thus as the designation of a musical guild serving in the temple. See also ETHAN.

daric dair′ik (אֲדַרְכֹּנִים H163). A Persian gold coin of great value (1 Chr. 29:7; Ezra 8:27; KJV, "dram"). See COINS; DRACHMA.

Darius duh-ri′uhs (דָּרְיָוֶשׁ H2003 [Aram. H10184]). In addition to DARIUS THE MEDE, this was the name of two Persian kings mentioned in Haggai, Zechariah, Ezra, and Nehemiah. See also PERSIA.

I. Darius I Hystaspes. Fourth ruler of the Persian empire (521–486 B.C.) after CYRUS, CAMBYSES, and Gaumata (cf. Dan. 11:2, which lists three kings *after* Cyrus and *before* the "richer" king, who is obviously XERXES). Darius I often is referred to as "Darius the Great" because of his brilliant achievements as restorer of the empire after Gaumata, the Pseudo-Smerdis, usurped the throne from Cambyses. The Achaemenid dynasty would probably have ended with Cambyses had not Darius—one of his officers, son of Hystaspes (a satrap), and great-grandson of Ariyaramnes (brother of Cyrus I)—retained the loyalty of the Persian army. Within two months he had killed Gaumata (522 B.C.) and during the next two years defeated nine kings in nineteen battles to secure his throne. His own account of these victories is recorded in the BEHISTUN INSCRIPTION, a trilingual CUNEIFORM text (Old Persian, Akkadian, and Elamite) carved on the face of a large rock.

In one of these campaigns a Babylonian usurper claiming the title Nebuchadnezzar IV was trapped with his followers within Babylon. After a long siege the city was taken and three thousand of its leading citizens were crucified as a warning to other potential rebels (Herodotus, *Hist.* 3.159). This helps to explain the amazing zeal of TATTENAI to obey a decree of Darius I about a year later to which the following warning was appended: "I decree that if anyone changes this edict, a beam is to be pulled from his house and he is to be lifted up

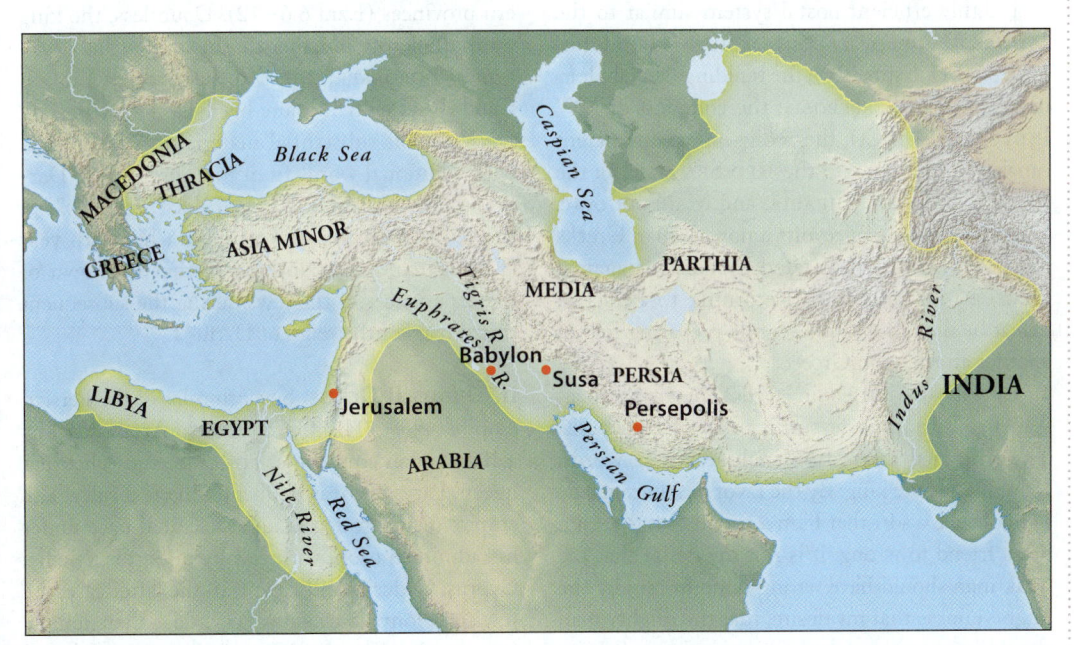

The Kingdom of Darius the Great.

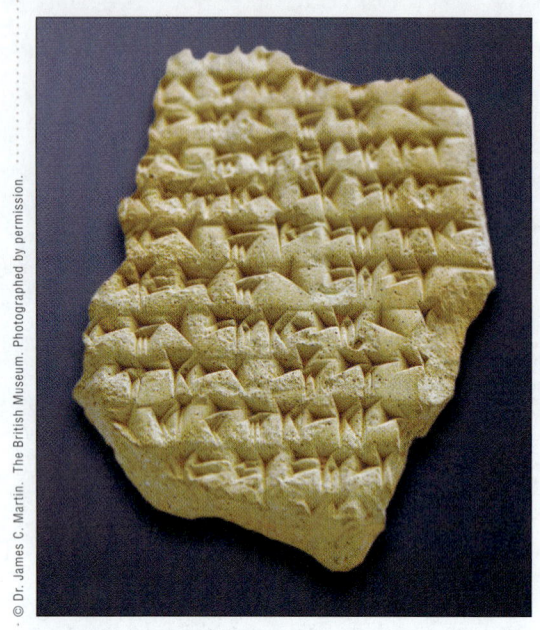

Clay tablet inscribed in Old Persian (Susa, 5th cent. B.C.) and recounting the achievements of Darius the Great (521–486).

and impaled on it. And for this crime his house is to be made a pile of rubble" (Ezra 6:11–13).

The remaining years of his reign were devoted to the reorganization of the empire into twenty satrapies and many provinces; the establishment of a highly efficient postal system similar to the 19th-cent. American pony express (Herodotus, *Hist.* 8.98; cf. Esth. 8:10); the building of a fabulous new capital at PERSEPOLIS; the conquest of NW INDIA (c. 514 B.C.); the redigging of an ancient canal from the NILE to the RED SEA (c. 513); the conquest of LIBYA, THRACIA, and MACEDONIA (c. 512); the crushing of revolts among Ionian Greeks (500–493); and the ill-fated expeditions against GREECE (493 and 490). Returning to Persia in defeat he died in 486 B.C. while preparing for yet another attack upon Greece.

Darius was buried in a rock-hewn tomb at Naqsh-i-Rustam, a few miles NE of Persepolis. The trilingual inscription includes these words: "Says Darius the king: By the favor of Ahuramazda I am of such a sort that I am a friend to right, I am not a friend to wrong; it is not my desire that the weak man should have wrong done to him by the mighty; nor is that my desire, that the mighty man should have wrong done to him by the weak" (for a somewhat different trans., see A. T. Olmstead, *History of the Persian Empire* [1948], 125).

Early in his reign, just after securing his throne, Darius I became God's instrument for encouraging the Jews to complete their second temple. In 520 B.C., Tattenai, the recently appointed Persian governor of W Euphrates provinces (formerly included in the realm of Darius the Mede), challenged the Jews who had started to build their TEMPLE through the encouragement of HAGGAI and ZECHARIAH (Ezra 5:1–3). Their explanation that Cyrus had given SHESHBAZZAR (= ZERUBBABEL?) official permission to build the temple was forwarded to Darius I with a request to investigate. Providentially the work was not halted during the long process of searching for Cyrus's decree (Ezra 5:5).

The transition of royal power from Cambyses to Darius I was so traumatic that it is a testimony to Persian efficiency that the document was ever discovered. An expanded form of the decree of Cyrus on a parchment scroll had been filed away in a branch library in the distant city of ECBATANA (Ezra 6:2). Darius I then proceeded to issue his own decree, commanding Tattenai to assist the Jews in their work on the temple and to provide expenses from the tribute that came from the western provinces (Ezra 6:6–12). Doubtless, the king was sufficiently polytheistic (in spite of his devotion to ZOROASTRIANISM) to suspect that Yahweh could either help or injure his dynasty (6:10).

With this substantial material assistance (and with additional words from the Lord during Darius's fourth year [518 B.C., cf. Zech. 7:1—8:23]), the Jews completed the temple in his sixth year (Feb/March, 516). Nothing further is known of the experiences of the Jews during the subsequent thirty years of the reign of Darius I.

II. Darius II Ochus. Seventh ruler of the Persian empire (423–404 B.C.), and son of Artaxerxes I by a Babylonian concubine. His cruel and scheming queen, Parysatis, was frequently the real ruler. The empire disintegrated at an accelerated pace under his administration, with revolts in Sardis, Media, Cyprus, Cadusia, and Egypt. In the latter case, the Jewish colony at ELEPHANTINE lost their temple (on an island in the Nile of Upper Egypt) and wrote desperate letters to Jerusalem and Samaria for help, all in vain.

It was probably during the reign of Darius II that Nehemiah went to Jerusalem the second time and found that many abuses had arisen (Neh. 13:6–11). Also, it was during his reign that the names of some Jewish priests were recorded (12:22). Some have insisted that this must have been Darius III Codomannus (335–331 B.C.), because the same verse mentions a high priest JADDUA, and JOSEPHUS states that Jaddua was high priest in 332 (*Ant.* 11.8.4). If we assume that Josephus was historically accurate at this point, he could have been referring to another high priest of the same name or to the same Jaddua at a very advanced age. The Elephantine papyri mention Jaddua's father Johanan as being high priest in 408 (cf. *ANET*, 492). Therefore, Jaddua could easily have been high priest in 404, especially since he was only five generations removed from Joshua (JESHUA, Neh. 12:10–11), who was high priest until at least 519 (Zech. 1:7; 6:11). Consequently, there is no valid reason for denying that this king was Darius II and that Nehemiah could have written this verse. (See A. T. Olmstead, *History of the Persian Empire* [1948], chs. 8–15, 26; R. Ghirshman, *Iran: From the Earliest Times to the Islamic Conquest* [1954], 139–88; E. M. Yamauchi, *Persia and the Bible* [1990], ch. 4; P. Briant, *From Cyrus to Alexander: A History of the Persian Empire* [2002], chs. 3–4, 14, 17–18.)   J. C. WHITCOMB

Darius the Mede. Ruler of Babylonia mentioned especially in the sixth chapter of Daniel. Immediately following the death of BELSHAZZAR in Oct. 539 B.C., Darius the Mede is said to have "received the kingdom" (Dan. 5:31, NRSV), probably having been made "king over the realm of the Chaldeans" (9:1, NRSV) by CYRUS the Great (1:21; 6:28). He is best remembered for the unalterable decree his officers tricked him into signing, which resulted in Daniel being cast into a den of lions (6:7–18). In contrast to NEBUCHADNEZZAR, this ruler was helpless to reverse his own decree, vividly illustrating the inferiority of the silver kingdom of Medo-Persia to the golden kingdom of Babylon in the matter of royal sovereignty. Compare Dan. 3:29; Esth. 1:19; 8:8, and the testimony of Diodorus Siculus (*Bibl. Hist.* 17.30) that Darius III (335–331) wanted to free a man he had condemned, but realized that "it was not possible to undo what was done by royal authority."

Darius the Mede is not to be confused with the later Persian monarch DARIUS I Hystaspes (521–486 B.C.), for the former was of Median extraction and his father's name was AHASUERUS (the Hebrew equivalent of XERXES, Dan. 9:1). Darius the Mede must have been born in the year 601/600, for at the fall of Babylon in 539 he was sixty-two (Dan. 5:31).

A major assumption of higher criticism has been that the book of Daniel was authored by an unknown writer of the Maccabean age (c. 164 B.C.) who mistakenly thought that an independent Median kingdom ruled by Darius the Mede followed the fall of Babylon and preceded the rise of Persia under Cyrus. (See H. H. Rowley, *Darius the Mede and the Four World Empires in the Book of Daniel* [1935], 12–60; cf. J. J. Collins, *Daniel*, Hermeneia [1993], 30–32.) Darius the Mede, however, is not depicted in the book as a universal monarch. His subordinate position (under Cyrus) is clearly implied in the statement that he "was made ruler [Heb. passive, *homlak*] over the Babylonian kingdom" (Dan. 9:1 NIV). Also, the fact that Belshazzar's kingdom was given to the Medes *and Persians* (5:28) and that Darius found himself incapable of altering the law of the Medes *and Persians* (6:15) renders the critical view untenable.

The early-20th-cent. publication of additional CUNEIFORM texts from this period has enabled one to understand much better the circumstances surrounding the fall of Babylon in 539 B.C. It seems quite probable that Darius the Mede was another name for Gubaru, the governor under Cyrus who appointed subgovernors in Babylonia immediately after its conquest ("Nabonidus Chronicle," *ANET*, 306, and cf. Dan. 6:1; he is not to be confused with Ugbaru, governor of Gutium, mentioned also in the Chronicle as the general under Cyrus who conquered Babylon and died three weeks later). This same Gubaru is frequently mentioned in cuneiform documents during the following fourteen years as "Governor of Babylon and the Region beyond the River" (i.e., the entire FERTILE CRESCENT). Gubaru thus ruled over the vast and populous territories of Babylonia, Syria, Phoenicia, and Palestine, and his name was a final warning to criminals throughout this area. (Cf. R. D. Wilson, *Studies in the Book of Daniel: A Discussion of the Historical Questions* [1917], 128–263; J. C. Whitcomb, *Darius the Mede: A Study in Historical Identification* [1963], 10–24; W. H. Shea in *AUSS* 20 [1982], 229–47; K. Koch, "Dareios, der Meder," in *The Word of the Lord Shall Go Forth*, ed. C. L. Meyers and M. P. O'Connor [1983], 287–99.) The fact that he is called "king" in the sixth chapter of Daniel is not an inaccuracy, even though he was a subordinate of Cyrus. Similarly, Belshazzar was called "king," even though he was second ruler of the kingdom under Nabonidus (Dan. 5:29). Nevertheless, many scholars continue to argue that Gubaru is nowhere called Darius and thus reject this identification. (For the view that the reference is to Cyrus, see D. J. Wiseman et al., *Notes on Some Problems in the Book of Daniel* [1965], 9–16.)

The book of Daniel gives more information concerning the personal background of Darius the Mede than concerning that of Belshazzar or even of Nebuchadnezzar; he is the only monarch in the book whose age, parentage, and nationality are recorded. Although he was a subordinate ruler like Belshazzar, it is evident that he ruled Babylonia with far greater zeal and efficiency than did his profligate predecessor; and even more important, he honored the God of Daniel (Dan. 6:25–27). See also DANIEL, BOOK OF, III. J. C. WHITCOMB

darkness. This English word is used primarily to translate Hebrew *ḥōšek* H3125 and Greek *skotia* G5028 and *skotos* G5030. The word first appears in Scripture as a description of the chaotic condition of the world before God created LIGHT (Gen. 1:2–3). The subsequent division between light and darkness resulted in "day" and "night." Darkness has a certain reality, being more than the absence of light (Isa. 45:7). The regular succession of darkness and light is under God's control, who can modify it as he wills. A day is lengthened to afford victorious Israel more time (Josh. 10:12–13), whereas darkness shrouds the scene of Christ's death (Matt. 27:45). Thick darkness plagued the Egyptians for three days (Exod. 10:22). Mines are characterized by darkness (Job 28:3), as is SHEOL (10:21–22; Ps. 88:11–13). Even darkness cannot hide from God, to whom all is light (Ps. 139:11–12). The blind are said to be in darkness (Isa. 42:7; 49:9).

Metaphorically darkness symbolizes distress (Isa. 5:30; 9:1), mourning (47:5), perplexity (Job 5:14), ignorance (Job 12:24–25; Matt. 4:16), and captivity (Ezek. 34:12). Statements made in secret are described as being spoken "in the dark" (Matt. 10:27). The judgment and terror of the day of the Lord are likened to darkness (Amos 5:18). In the spiritual sphere, darkness denotes sin and godlessness, everything that is opposed to God, including demonic forces (Isa. 9:1; 42:7). Darkness represents the condition of the spiritually unenlightened (Jn. 1:4–5), who are blinded by the power of SATAN (Acts 26:18). The eye which is evil fills the body with spiritual darkness (Matt. 6:33). In general, the world loves darkness rather than the reproof of the light (Jn. 3:19–20; cf. C. H. Dodd, *The Interpretation of the Fourth Gospel* [1953], 201–12). The unregenerate can even be directly called "darkness" (Eph. 5:8).

Evil spirits are the "cosmic powers of darkness," against which believers must be armed (Eph. 6:11–12 NRSV; NIV, "the powers of this dark world"). The wicked will be cast "outside, into the darkness" (Matt. 8:12; 22:13). Believers must beware lest they walk in darkness and mar their fellowship with God (1 Jn. 1:6). In the end, the darkness of the nations will be dispelled by the glory of Yahweh (Isa. 60:2, where "thick darkness" renders the Hebrew term *ʿărāpel* H6906, "cloud"; cf. Exod. 14:20 and 1 Ki. 8:12, and note also Rev. 21:23–25).

The expression "shadow of death" (known esp. from Ps. 23:4 and Isa. 9:2) renders the Hebrew word *ṣalmāwet* H7516, which evidently means "deep shadow, thick darkness" (e.g., Job 3:5; 10:21–22; Ps. 107:10, 14; see D. W. Thomas in *JSS* 7 [1962]: 191–200). The word "death" here functions as a superlative (cf. such English expressions as *deathly cold*). Accordingly, the NRSV renders Ps. 23:4, "Even though I walk through the darkest valley." This translation is not incorrect, but the psalmist may well have chosen the term because it would convey both a literal meaning (crossing a dangerous valley in the night) and a metaphorical one (the death that might result from such an event). Thus the traditional understanding of this verse as an allusion to death is probably correct, and in fact the NRSV rendering does not preclude such an allusion. H. M. WOLF

Darkon dahr´kon (דַּרְקוֹן H2010, meaning disputed). Ancestor of a group of "Solomon's servants" who returned from BABYLON with ZERUBBABEL and his associates (Ezra 2:56; Neh. 7:58). (On possible derivations of the name, see R. Zadok in *JQR* 71 [1980]: 107–17, esp. 115.)

dark saying. See RIDDLE.

darnel. See TARES.

dart. This English term is used by the KJV to render several Hebrew words referring to arrows or javelins (e.g., 2 Sam. 18:14; Prov. 7:23; cf. also Greek *belos* G1018, Eph. 6:16). The NIV and other translations use "dart" to render the rare Hebrew term *massāʿ* H5025 (only in Job 41:26). See ARMOR, ARMS.

dates. The Bible does not specifically mention this fruit, but the Hebrew term for PALM TREE (*tāmār* H9469; also Gk. *phoinix* G5836) refers to the *Phoenix dactylifera* or date palm. Moreover, the word *ʾešpār* H882 probably means "cake of dates" (so NIV, 2 Sam. 6:19; 1 Chr. 16:3; NRSV, "cake [loaf] of bread"). The fruit of the date palm was used to make HONEY as well as alcoholic drinks (see WINE AND STRONG DRINK). Because they were long-lasting, dried dates were handy to carry on long camel journeys across the deserts. Dates are borne in huge clusters that hang down among the leaves. This fruit is the main FOOD of some Arabian tribes.

W. E. SHEWELL-COOPER

Dathan day´thuhn (דָּתָן H2018, possibly "strong, warlike"). Son of Eliab and descendant of REUBEN. With his brother ABIRAM and another Reubenite, he joined the Levite KORAH in leading a rebellion of 250 chosen men against the leadership of MOSES and AARON (Num. 16:1, 12, 24–25, 27; 26:9). Moses specifically summoned Dathan and Abiram, but they refused to come. The next morning the glory of the Lord appeared to them all, the ground split apart, "and the earth opened its mouth and swallowed" the rebels and their families (16:31–32). Later Moses reminded Israel of this discipline of the Lord (Deut. 11:6; cf. also Ps. 106:17; Sir. 45:18; 4 Macc. 2:17).

W. G. BROWN

Dathema dath´uh-muh (Δαθεμα). A fortress in GILEAD where the Jews of that region found refuge from the Syrians (1 Macc. 5:9). They were besieged there by the SELEUCID forces until Judas MACCABEE and his brother Jonathan rescued them. The town lay a night's march from BOZRAH (vv. 28–29). Attempts to locate it have failed. Proposals include ʿAthaman (E of el-Muzerib), Tell Hamad (E of KARNAIM), and Tell er-Ramet (for the latter, see Y. Aharoni et al., *The Carta Bible Atlas*, 4th ed. [2002], map 190).

H. WOLF

daughter. The Hebrew term *bat* H1426 is used irrespective of age for a proximate circle of female relatives. Although applied to classes of females (e.g., "daughters [NIV, women] of Zion," Isa. 3:16 et al.), this use of the term is considerably less common than such constructions as "son/sons of." See BEN-. The word is compounded in some names: BATH RABBIM (daughter of a multitude), BATH-SHEBA (daughter of an oath), BATH-SHUA (daughter of abundance?). The word is often used figuratively, as in the sense of VILLAGE (Num. 21:25 et al.). In the NT the common Greek term for "daughter," *thygatēr* G2588, is used throughout (Matt. 9:18). See FAMILY.

W. WHITE, JR.

daughter-in-law. This English term may be used to render Hebrew *kallâ* H3987 (Gen 11:31 et al.), which can also be rendered "bride" (Isa. 49:18). It refers to a woman as being first under the authority of her own father and then of her father-in-law (representing the husband). The Levitical code explicitly prohibits sexual relations between a man and his daughter-in-law (Lev. 18:15; 20:12). The Greek term Greek *nymphē* G3811, which means primarily "bride" (Rev. 21:9 et al.), can also refer to a daughter-in-law (Matt. 10:35).

W. WHITE, JR.

David day´vid (דָּוִד H1858, possibly related to דוֹד H1856, "beloved"). The son of JESSE of BETHLEHEM and second king of Israel.

    I. The life of David
       A. His family
       B. The days before his kingship
       C. The reign of David
   II. David's influence on the history of Israel
       A. The estimate of David in Israel

B. The concept of the throne of David and its perpetuity
C. David and the worship in Israel
D. The influence of David's walk before God

III. David in the prophets
A. Isaiah
B. Jeremiah
C. The other prophets

IV. David in the NT
A. The Gospels
B. The Acts
C. The Epistles
D. The Revelation

I. The life of David

A. His family. The genealogy of David is given several times in Scripture (first in Ruth 4:18–22). He was a direct descendant of Judah, Perez, Hezron, Ram, Amminadab, Nahshon, Salmon, Boaz (the husband of Ruth), Obed (the son of Boaz and Ruth), and Jesse, his father (cf. 1 Chr. 2:5–16; Matt. 1:3–6; Lk. 3:31–33).

B. The days before his kingship.

1. The anointing of David. a. *God's choice made known.* When God determined to reject SAUL as the king of Israel, he sent SAMUEL with oil to ANOINT another: one of the sons of Jesse of Bethlehem. When Samuel arrived at Jesse's home, he had the sons of Jesse brought forward one by one. Samuel favored ELIAB, the eldest, but God showed him that he should not look on the outside but in the heart for truly kingly qualities. God passed by seven of the sons of Jesse until only the youngest, David, remained. David was then keeping the sheep of his father, and Jesse did not consider it important to bring him before Samuel. He was described as "ruddy, with a fine appearance and handsome features." When Samuel insisted and David was brought before him, God indicated that this was his choice. David was anointed that day, and the Spirit of the Lord came upon him mightily. It is not certain that his family understood at that time why he was anointed (1 Sam. 16:1–13).

b. *God's favor shown.* In the meantime God's Spirit departed from Saul and an evil spirit from God came and troubled him. On the advice of some to call a harpist to soothe him, one young man in the court recommended David as "skillful in playing, a man of valor, a warrior, prudent in speech, and a man of good presence" (1 Sam. 16:14–18 NRSV). Saul sent for David, thus giving him an early opportunity to see and know court life. Jesse sent David with a donkey loaded with bread, wine, and a kid. When he arrived before Saul, Saul loved him at first sight and made David his armorbearer. Saul sought and received Jesse's permission for David to stand before him. Whenever the evil spirit fell on Saul, David was at hand with his harp to soothe him. He undoubtedly composed many psalms in this period (16:19–23).

2. David's rapid rise and Saul's jealousy. a. *The victory over Goliath.* When the PHILISTINES gathered to do battle with Israel in the valley of Elah, GOLIATH, a giant of the Philistines, came out and threatened Israel. Jesse was by now quite old, and his three older sons were fighting with Saul. He sent David to the front to see how his sons were doing. He sent with him corn and bread for the brothers and cheeses for their captain. David went, leaving the sheep with a keeper and found his brothers in the camp. As he was talking with them, Goliath came out and threatened as before. When David heard Goliath's boasting, he was indignant. Eliab was disgusted with David for his interest in these matters and accused him of vain curiosity, but David gave his brother no heed. The men in the camp told David that Saul had promised to give his daughter and great riches to the slayer of Goliath.

David's words of indignation against Goliath reached Saul and Saul sent for him. When David assured Saul he would fight Goliath, Saul listened. David related to Saul how he had cared for the sheep and protected them against a lion and a bear. He gave all the glory to God for his victories over the wild beasts. He confessed that he believed the same God would now deliver him from Goliath. Saul was convinced and sent him out to face the giant. David rejected the use of Saul's armor and took those weapons with which he was familiar, his staff, some stones, and a sling—the weapons of a shepherd.

The Valley of Elah (looking E). David and Goliath met for battle at the Elah brook, identified at the lower part of photo by a line of shrubs growing along the ravine.

When Goliath saw this boy, he ridiculed and threatened him. David, not being afraid, affirmed his faith in God. He knew that God would give him the victory so that all might know that there is a God in Israel and that God's people might know that God does not save by sword and spear, but by his own strength. David ran to meet Goliath and killed him with the first stone. He then cut off Goliath's head with his own sword. Israel won the day in battle (1 Sam. 17:1–51).

b. *David before Saul.* (1) *Friendship with Jonathan.* David remained in Saul's court and a great friendship blossomed between him and Saul's son JONATHAN. The two made a covenant and Jonathan sealed it by giving to David his robe, apparel, sword, bow, and girdle (1 Sam. 18:1–4).

(2) *Popularity brings a negative reaction.* David behaved wisely before Saul and the people and was set over all of Saul's men. This pleased the people, but trouble developed because the women began to praise David more than Saul. Saul became jealous, seeing his throne threatened. He no longer trusted David and soon tried to kill him, so David fled. Now Saul's fear of David increased since it was evident that God was with the young man but no longer with Saul. He demoted David to captain over a thousand men, but still he conducted himself wisely and God was with him. This troubled Saul even more, for now all Israel and Judah loved David (1 Sam. 18:5–16).

(3) *Saul's plot to destroy David.* Though Saul offered MERAB, his eldest daughter, to David, he did not keep the bargain. She was given in marriage to someone else. Then MICHAL, a second daughter, was offered as bait to get David to fight the Philistines. David bargained for her for a dowry of one hundred foreskins of the Philistines. Saul, however, hoped that David would be killed in the attempt. David not only got the one hundred foreskins, but one hundred more, and Michal was given to him. Saul understandably feared David even more now and was his enemy. Yet David, acting wisely, grew more popular (1 Sam. 18:17–30).

Saul also tried to turn Jonathan against David. However, Jonathan warned David to avoid Saul and at the same time tried to persuade his father that David was good to the king. Saul assented for a short time and David was temporarily restored to the court. As soon as war began again, David's popularity rose and Saul was again aroused to jealousy. He tried to kill David in his bed while he slept, but Michal helped him escape (1 Sam. 19:1–17).

c. *David's flight from Saul.* David first went to Samuel at RAMAH, and together they fled to NAIOTH. When Saul heard he was hiding there, he sent a force to capture him. These men sent by Saul were made helpless when the Spirit of prophecy fell on them by Samuel's command. Saul, when he came personally to capture David, fell under the same power (1 Sam. 19:18–23).

David now fled from Naioth back to Jonathan, who found it hard to believe that his father really hated David but promised to find out the truth. The truth was that Saul did hate David. Jonathan himself was nearly killed by his father, who was now in a rage. The two young men then made a pact in which Jonathan expressed assurance that David would one day be king, and David promised to protect Jonathan's descendants forever. Then David fled (1 Sam. 20:1–42). He was now an outlaw and went first to Nob to get help from Ahimelech, the priest. He lied to Ahimelech, not telling the priest that he was fleeing from Saul. His lie later was fatal to Ahimelech. The priest gave him some of the holy bread and Goliath's sword, but Doeg, a servant of Saul, saw it all. David next fled to the king of Gath, but when he saw he was not welcome there, he feigned madness and escaped (21:1–15).

3. David's life as a fugitive. a. *The mustering of a force.* David went to the cave of Adullam and his family joined him there. Others in distress also came to David. Soon he had a fighting force of 400 men. All who came seemed to be of one mind with David in his cause (1 Sam. 22:1–2; 1 Chr. 12:16). From there David and his men went to Mizpah of Moab where he left his parents. Gad, the prophet, warned David to leave there and go to Judah, and thus he came to the forest of Hereth (1 Sam. 22:3–5). See Gad #2.

b. *Saul's hot pursuit.* Meanwhile Saul learned of David's maneuvers. He complained that his own men did not help him and that they failed to inform him that his own son was working against him. Doeg then volunteered information about the events at Nob. As a result, in his frustration, Saul had all the priests of Nob killed. One son of Ahimelech, Abiathar, escaped with the ephod and joined David (1 Sam. 22:6–23).

During this time, David took the city of Keilah from the Philistines, and Saul, hearing of this, came to Keilah to capture him. David learned from God that the people of Keilah would betray him, so he fled with some 600 men to the hill country of the wilderness of Ziph, where he hid in the woods. It was here that he saw Jonathan for the last time. When the Ziphites offered to help Saul capture David, David moved to Maon in the Arabah, S of the desert. Saul pursued and nearly caught David there on a mountain, but just as he was about to succeed, he received word to return and fight off an attack of the Philistines. Understandably David called the place Sela Hammahlekoth ("the rock of escape," 1 Sam. 23:1–29).

Next, David fled to En Gedi. Saul took 3,000 men to capture him there. When Saul went into a cave where David was hiding, David's men urged him to kill the king, but he refused, respecting God's anointed. He did cut off Saul's robe, and later even that bothered David's conscience. When Saul had left the cave, David showed from a distance how he had spared the king's life. Saul, under great stress and emotion, seemed to see his own wrong, and even confessed that he believed David would be king. The change, however, was not long-lasting (1 Sam. 24:1–22).

c. *David and Abigail.* At this time Samuel died and was buried at Ramah, and David went to the wilderness of Paran. There was a citizen of Maon named Nabal who had great possessions. Nabal was rich but also miserly and evil. David asked Nabal for some help for his men in return for the years his men had protected Nabal's sheep and shepherds. Nabal, instead, ridiculed David. Infuriated, David armed his men and started out to get revenge. Meantime, Abigail, Nabal's wife, who was both lovely and wise, heard of her husband's folly and went to meet David to make peace. She met him and pleaded for mercy, urging him not to blot his own good name by shedding innocent blood. She expressed confidence that God would bless David. Reacting favorably to her pleas, David spared Nabal and his sons, accepting her gifts. All this time Nabal was drunk and unaware of what had transpired. The next day, when he learned the truth, he was stricken and died. David later married Abigail. About the same time, Saul gave Michal, David's wife, to another man (1 Sam. 25:1–44).

d. *The end of the pursuit.* The Ziphites continued to aid Saul by reporting David's whereabouts. Again the king took some 3,000 men and went after him. This time David carefully followed Saul's progress by means of his own spies. One evening as Saul slept,

David and ABISHAI went into the camp where he lay. God had caused deep sleep to fall on all the camp. All David did was to take Saul's spear and water jug, though Abishai urged him to kill his enemy. When David had left the camp, he called to Saul and chided the royal commander, ABNER, for not guarding his master. Saul, realizing that a second time David had spared his life, seemed convinced that David meant no ill. He returned home and never pursued him again. David, however, distrusting Saul thoroughly now, fled to the Philistines and dwelt at GATH with the king ACHISH (1 Sam. 26:1—27:2).

e. *David as ally to Philistines.* Achish was impressed with David and gave him ZIKLAG as a home. David, while pretending to be his friend, raided Philistine towns in the neighborhood. He left no survivors to tell tales. He reported dutifully to Achish that he was raiding cities of Judah. In this period many men of Judah and Israel, including some of Saul's own people, joined David (1 Chr. 12:1-17). When the Philistines later prepared to war on Israel, Achish wanted to take David to battle with him but the war lords of the Philistines wisely refused him. David was forced to stay away from this battle providentially, for in it Saul and Jonathan would die (1 Sam. 28:1-2; 1 Chr. 12:19-22). Returning to Ziklag, David and his men discovered that the city had been raided and their families carried away. Bitterly they followed in pursuit; eventually they found the Amalekite raiders and destroyed them, recapturing their own families (see AMALEK). He sent gifts from the spoils to the elders of Judah to gain their favor. In this battle a principle was established by David whereby those who fought and those who guarded the supplies would share alike in the booty. From the incident at Ziklag, David had learned the value of leaving some men behind to guard the families (1 Sam. 30:1-31).

4. The death of Saul and Jonathan. a. *A word from Samuel.* Saul became afraid of the Philistines and perhaps had premonitions of his own death. He no longer had Samuel to consult and so he went to a medium at ENDOR for some word from Samuel of his own fate. He tricked her into attempting to call forth Samuel's spirit and surprisingly, to her and Saul, God obliged. Samuel foretold Saul's death (1 Sam. 28:3-25).

b. *The battle with the Philistines.* In battle the next day Saul and his sons were killed. Israel fled in confusion, leaving Saul's body behind. The Philistines, in mockery, hung his body and those of his sons on the wall at BETH SHAN. In an act of great devotion, the people of JABESH GILEAD bravely took the bodies from the wall and gave them proper burial. David later showed his appreciation to them for their kindness. Jonathan's nurse, on hearing of the defeat, picked up Jonathan's son MEPHIBOSHETH and fled, but the boy fell in flight and was permanently lamed (31:1-13; 2 Sam. 4:4).

C. The reign of David

1. The years in Hebron. a. *News of Saul's death.* While David was at Ziklag, news came from Saul's camp that Saul was defeated and killed. The newsbearer thought he was bringing good news. He even claimed to have killed Saul whom he had found in pain. He hoped for reward, but his reward was execution. David wanted no friend who despised the Lord's anointed. The fact that the newsbearer was an Amalekite did not help, of course. At this time David composed a beautiful lamentation over the memory of Saul and Jonathan. This first example of David's poetry in Scripture is representative of his great inspiration as seen in the psalms credited to him (2 Sam. 1:1-27).

b. *David anointed by the people.* At God's instruction, David went up to HEBRON and there was anointed king over Judah. He showed his character by honoring the men of Jabesh Gilead for their bravery and asked for their support. About the same time Abner took Saul's son ISH-BOSHETH and made him king over the rest of Israel. David remained at Hebron and Ish-Bosheth at MAHANAIM (2 Sam. 2:8-10).

c. *The war between the two houses.* Soon a showdown between David and Ish-Bosheth was inevitable, and the two armies met at GIBEON by the pool. David's men led by JOAB defeated Abner. In this battle Abner killed Joab's brother ASAHEL; Joab never forgot this deed (2 Sam. 2:12-32). From that time Saul's house weakened while David's increased in strength. David remained at Hebron seven and one-half years. In all, six sons were born to him there. Three of them, AMNON, ABSALOM, and ADONIJAH would later play significant roles in his life (2 Sam. 3:1–5; 1 Chr. 3:1–4a).

As Abner came to dominate Saul's house, Ish-Bosheth resented his power and accused him of taking Saul's concubines, an act tantamount to treason. Abner angrily sold out to David and sent to him word of his plans. David agreed to a meeting, providing he could have back Michal, Saul's daughter, as a wife. In the meeting, Abner agreed to a covenant that made David king of all Israel. Joab, who had been away at the time, pursued Abner on his return to Mahanaim and treacherously killed him. He had never forgiven Abner for killing his brother in battle. David, innocent of any guilt in this, openly condemned Joab. He lamented publicly for Abner that all Israel might know his own innocence (2 Sam. 3:6–39). Subsequently, Ish-Bosheth too was killed. His head was brought to David, but those seeking a reward were rewarded as the Amalekite had been—David had them executed (4:5–12).

d. *David firmly established*. Now the elders of Israel came and made covenant with David. He was anointed king of all Israel (2 Sam. 5:1–3).

2. David in Jerusalem. a. *The capture of the city*. To inaugurate his kingship, David desired to capture the city of JERUSALEM, a Jebusite city David had known from the days of shepherding his father's sheep (see JEBUS). He took the stronghold by entering through the tunnels that led out to the GIHON SPRING. Those tunnels and the spring are visible today. David increased the size of the city by building up a fill on the steep sides of the hill, called the MILLO (2 Sam. 5:6–10; 1 Chr. 11:4–9; NIV, "supporting terraces").

b. *David's wars*. In quick succession David conquered Israel's enemies. First he fought and defeated the Philistines. While the Philistines held Bethlehem, David unintentionally expressed a desire for water from the well there. Three brave men went in to get the water. When David saw their devotion, he poured out the water as an offering to God. Now David was victorious at BAAL PERAZIM, GEBA (NIV, Gibeon), and GEZER. Finally he took the chief city of the Philistines, Gath. During this time, HIRAM king of TYRE undoubtedly saw the wisdom of befriending David and sent him cedars to build his house in Jerusalem (2 Sam. 5:11–12, 17–25; 8:1; 21:15–22; 1 Chr. 11:15–19; 12:8–15; 14:1–2, 8–17; 20:4–8). David next turned to fight the Ammonites when the latter treated his ambassadors disgracefully. The king of AMMON, HANUN, hired the Arameans to fight against David. At MEDEBA, David beat them soundly (2 Sam. 10:1–19; 1 Chr. 19:1–19).

c. *David's sin*. The next spring, when David should have been in battle against Ammon, he sent Joab and remained at home. While Joab had RABBAH of Ammon under siege, David lusted after and finally seduced BATHSHEBA, the wife of a HITTITE soldier in his ranks named URIAH. She became pregnant. To cover his sin, David sought to have Uriah sleep with Bathsheba, hoping he would think she was pregnant by him. Uriah, however, proved a loyal soldier and would not go to his wife while his brothers fought in battle. Now David added sin to sin by plotting Uriah's death. He commanded Joab to put Uriah in the heat of battle and order a retreat, leaving him to the mercy of the Ammo-

The Kingdom of David.

nites. When news of Uriah's death came to David, he took Bathsheba as his wife (2 Sam. 11).

But God did not overlook David's actions. He sent NATHAN the prophet who put the finger of guilt on David. The king's immediate response was confession of his sin (cf. Ps. 51). Unlike Saul he could see his own faults. Though forgiven, David was told that his own house would display the sins he had sought to cover. Shed blood and sexual misconduct would blight his house. David went out to battle later and won over Rabbah, but it was for him a bitter victory (2 Sam. 12:1–31).

Among the nations captured by David were ARAM (SYRIA), Moab, Ammon, Philistia, Amalek, and Zobah. To crown his great victories, David composed a song of thanksgiving that is closely related to Ps. 18 (2 Sam. 8:13–18; 11:15–18; 1 Chr. 18:3–17; 2 Sam. 22:1–51).

d. *David's peace.* (1) *The moving of the ark.* During times of peace, David gave attention to other matters. He desired to move the ARK OF THE COVENANT to Jerusalem, for it had remained in KIRIATH JEARIM since Samuel's day. Because David did not heed the Mosaic law of instruction for moving the ark, one of the men transporting it was killed by God. After the ark rested for three months at the home of OBED-EDOM, David brought it into the city by the proper means. On that day there was a great celebration in Jerusalem and David composed a psalm of praise for the occasion. Rules and appointments were made for the care of the ark, and for the first time proper worship of God in Jerusalem was conducted (2 Sam. 6:1—7:29; 2 Chr. 13:1—17:27).

(2) *Plans for a sanctuary.* David was not content for the ark to remain in a tent. He desired to build a permanent structure. However, the Lord would not permit David to do this, and through Nathan told David that not he but his son would build God's house (2 Sam. 7:1–29).

(3) *David keeps his promise to Jonathan.* At this time David showed his faithfulness to the memory of his friend Jonathan by allowing the crippled Mephibosheth, Jonathan's son, to sit at David's own table, much as David once had sat at Saul's table with Jonathan (2 Sam. 9:1–13).

e. *David's family troubles.* (1) *Amnon and Tamar.* From this time David's sins of the past began to be seen in his own family. One of his sons born at Hebron, AMNON, fell in love with his half-sister, TAMAR. He seduced her and afterward cast her off. David knew of this evil but failed to discipline Amnon (2 Sam. 12:24–25; 13:1–22).

(2) *Absalom's revenge.* ABSALOM, the full brother of Tamar, seeing Amnon go unpunished, plotted revenge. After two years he had Amnon killed. David again displayed weakness, letting Absalom flee, and did not seek to gain his respect. Only after Joab insisted did David call Absalom back to Jerusalem. Even then David refused to see him. Absalom, a fiery individual, again took matters into his own hand and burned Joab's fields to get his attention. At Joab's insistence David finally received Absalom in the court (2 Sam. 13:23–29; 14:1–33).

(3) *Absalom's treachery.* Absalom in these years had grown to distrust his father and now plotted his overthrow. He told the people how much better he would run the kingdom if he were ruler. It worked to a degree and he was able to sow seeds of rebellion. After about four years Absalom was able to get enough of a following to try to take the kingdom for himself. He went to his home town, Hebron, and there was acclaimed king by his followers. AHITHOPHEL, David's counselor, sided with him (2 Sam. 15).

(4) *David's flight.* When David heard the news he fled Jerusalem with a small following. ITTAI and others went with him to show their support, but David would not permit the priest ZADOK to bring the ark. Among David's supporters was HUSHAI, a man whom David asked to remain in Jerusalem to attempt to foil the good counsel of Ahithophel. As they left the city, SHIMEI, a descendant of Saul, cursed David. David received this as a rebuke from

David captured the small city of Jebus (Jerusalem), located on the ridge in the foreground. (View to the S.)

God and did not punish Shimei. Absalom entered Jerusalem with Ahithophel at his side.

Ahithophel counseled Absalom wisely to pursue with a few men and attack David while he was weary and discouraged. But Hushai, David's friend, pretending loyalty to Absalom, counteradvised him to wait until he had mustered a large force. This would, of course, give David time to reorganize and also give the people time to come to David's aid. Absalom followed Hushai's advice and sealed his own doom. Hushai sent word to David of all that had transpired (2 Sam. 15:37—17:29).

(5) *The fall of Absalom.* When the battle was fought, David was not permitted to go. He pled for the troops to spare his son's life, but Joab ignored David's pleas and killed Absalom. When David received news of the victory, he was grieved by word of Absalom's death. Joab, in his brusque manner, rebuked David for his mourning on the day of victory, and David smiled before the people through a veil of tears. He was once again restored as king in Jerusalem (2 Sam. 18:1—19:43).

f. *Sheba's rebellion.* A short-lived attempt to rebel soon followed. SHEBA, a Benjamite, sought to lead the ten tribes away from David, but he failed. In the battle, Joab killed his rival AMASA, whom David had appointed as commander. Joab took command and put down the revolt himself (2 Sam. 20:1–22; cf. 19:13).

g. *Unsettled accounts.* In a series of acts David now sought revenge on Saul's house for the slaying of the Gibeonites. He killed seven descendants of Saul but spared Mephibosheth. David also had Saul and Jonathan buried in the family sepulchre of Kish, the father of Saul (2 Sam. 21:1–14).

h. *The census.* For some reason, David took a census of the people at this time. The Bible does not give the reason why it displeased God, but apparently the pride of David was involved. As a consequence of David's action in this matter, God determined to punish Israel. David was given three choices: seven years of famine, or three months of war, or three days of pestilence. He chose the latter and still seventy thousand were killed. When it seemed as though the whole city of Jerusalem would be destroyed, God stopped the angel of destruction as the latter stood on the threshing floor of ARAUNAH, which overlooked the hill on which the city of Jerusalem was built (2 Sam. 24:1–25; 1 Chr. 21:1–30).

i. *Preparation for the temple.* God sent Gad the prophet to instruct David to acquire the property belonging to Araunah (or Ornan, according to Chronicles). He did so and built an altar there. This field would be the future site of SOLOMON's temple, for which David made preparations before his death (see TEMPLE, JERUSALEM). He gave specific instructions, insisting that Solomon strictly abide by the law of Moses (1 Chr. 22:1–19). The various duties in the temple were preassigned to the Levites. David established the order for the temple services and appointed chiefs of the tribes to oversee the treasury. He publicly announced to the people that Solomon should be his successor, giving Solomon and the officers specific instructions on how to build the temple. On a closing day of ceremony, David made prayers of thanksgiving and offered many sacrifices (1 Chr. 23:1—29:22a).

j. *David's last days.* In his last days David was not to be spared trouble. Being very old, he was given a young virgin to warm his body. During this time, ADONIJAH, a son of David, sought to take over the kingdom. At the foot of the hill in Jerusalem, at a well called EN ROGEL, he tried to have himself made king. He succeeded in getting both Joab and Abiathar the priest to follow him, but Zadok and Nathan would not desert David's son Solomon.

Nathan and Bathsheba moved quickly and told David of the plot. David immediately ordered Solomon brought to the spring of Gihon, within earshot of En Rogel, and there had him publicly acclaimed king. The plan worked and all those following Adonijah fled, fearing David's wrath. David then charged Solomon before his death to be strong and keep the law of God.

After forty years as king, seven in Hebron and thirty-three in Jerusalem, David died and was buried in Jerusalem. Solomon reigned after him (1 Ki. 1:1—2:11; 1 Chr. 29:22b–30).

II. David's influence on the history of Israel

A. The estimate of David in Israel

1. Highly regarded among the people. Respect for the good name of David was great after his death. Solomon was careful that he cleared his father from all guilt in the ignominious death of Abner (1 Ki.

2:32-33). Solomon further showed his respect for his father in sparing the life of Abiathar though he had taken part in Adonijah's attempt to usurp the kingdom from Solomon. He spared Abiathar's life because he had always been faithful to David and had suffered with him (2:26). Solomon, by the same token, executed Shimei for having ill-treated David when Absalom was in rebellion (2:44–46).

The respect for David, however, extended far beyond the person and time of Solomon. Hiram was later kind to Solomon for David's sake (1 Ki. 5:1). And long after, JOSIAH is said to have sought after the God of David (2 Chr. 34:3). Even David's enemies respected him. It took the news of his death to embolden Hadad to leave his retreat in Egypt, where he had fled from David (1 Ki. 11:21). See HADAD (PERSON) #4. Later JEROBOAM, after leading a rebellion against David's grandson, and fearing greatly that the people would return to David's house, risked the wrath of God by forming a new worship to prevent the people from going to David's city (12:27).

2. Highly regarded in God's eyes. Similarly, God often expressed his own high regard for this servant. David, we are told, was hand-picked by the Lord to be over God's people (1 Ki. 8:16). Thereafter, the Lord was known by the people as the God of David (2 Ki. 20:5; 2 Chr. 21:12). God's favor can be seen in his promise of peace to David's seed forever (1 Ki. 2:33). This divine favor toward David is expressed in terms of both kindness and goodness (3:6; 8:66).

B. The concept of the throne of David and its perpetuity.
Solomon was established as the rightful successor to the throne before David died. Soon after his death, the concept of the throne of David was developed and became a permanent part of the COVENANT involving God's goodness to his people.

Solomon sat on David's throne, a gift to Israel from God (1 Ki. 3:6; 5:7). He was known for his great discretion and understanding, which was indicated early in his reign. He humbly acknowledged that God had raised him up to fulfill his promise to David. There was, however, much more to the concept of the throne of David than his successor-son. God had established David's throne forever (2:45). Solomon, recognizing this, sought for God's assurance as soon as he was made king. He desired that God would perform his whole promise to David, that there fail not an heir on the throne (8:25–26).

God clearly honored this promise through all the history of Judah. When it appeared, in the days of ATHALIAH, that the seed of David might be completely destroyed, David's spears and shields were used to put his descendant (JOASH) on the throne in spite of Athaliah's power (2 Ki. 11:10). Joash was made king on the basis of God's promise to David (2 Chr. 23:3). Later, in the days of HEZEKIAH the king and ISAIAH the prophet (2 Ki. 19:34), God determined to defend Jerusalem for David's sake.

Nevertheless, the promise of God to bless the throne of David was not unconditionally given. For David's throne to be blessed, the successors had to walk uprightly as David had done (1 Ki. 9:5). When Solomon failed to walk purely before God as David had walked, God determined to rend the kingdom and leave for David's seed only Judah (11:13). Yet, for David's sake, even this judgment would not take place in Solomon's day (11:12, 24). Later, though rent asunder, the throne of David remained a reality, and God was determined that David should always have a lamp before God in Jerusalem (11:36). This promise became a constant reminder of hope to God's people thereafter (15:4–5; 2 Ki. 8:19; 2 Chr. 21:7). Beyond the days

The emperor Hadrian quarried away much of the area in Jerusalem that once held the tombs of the kings of Judah from David to Hezekiah.

of trial gleamed the constant hope that David's seed would not be afflicted forever (1 Ki. 11:39).

The split-off tribes were, in essence, put under the same conditions for blessings as Judah. The perpetuity of Jeroboam's throne depended on his doing right as David had done (1 Ki. 11:38). But Jeroboam led the northern tribes away from the worship ordained by Moses and later is pictured as having led a revolt against God's will (2 Chr. 13:6–8). God clearly disapproved of Jeroboam's innovations in worship and forewarned, through an unnamed prophet, that a descendant of David would one day destroy the altar Jeroboam had built at BETHEL. That seed was to be JOSIAH (1 Ki. 13:2). This judgment underlines the temporal nature of the throne of Jeroboam in contrast with the eternal nature of David's throne.

To this day, the concept of the throne of David is alive in the hearts of the Jewish people who still await the birth of David's son, the MESSIAH. For Christians, of course, this promise is already fulfilled in Jesus Christ, who is David's Seed forever. (See section IV, below.)

C. David and the worship in Israel. Nowhere can the influence of David be seen more clearly and felt more strongly than in the worship of God's people in the temple that David had planned (2 Chr. 1:4).

1. David and the temple of Solomon. In a sense, this building rightly could be called the temple that David built. It was his desire to build it, and his influence was heavily felt in its construction, as to form and usage. Although David had desired to build the temple (1 Ki. 8:18) and God approved that desire, yet he would not permit David to do so (5:3; 8:18). Instead, God told him that Solomon was to build it (1 Ki. 5:5; 2 Chr. 6:10), and promised to put his name in it (1 Ki. 8:15, 24). Solomon was conscious of this promise at the dedication of the temple (2 Chr. 1:9). In the later history of Judah, the promise that God's name would be in the temple was highly regarded by the faithful (2 Ki. 21:7; 2 Chr. 33:7). The skills and devotion of David are seen throughout the construction of the temple. David had dedicated gold, silver, and vessels for the house of God (1 Ki. 7:51), which things Solomon brought in when the temple was completed (2 Chr. 5:1). For the construction itself, David had already provided skilled workmen (2:7).

2. David and the worship in the temple. David is said to have made the musical instruments that were used to praise God and give him thanks (2 Chr. 7:6). He also had written the words of praise for the temple worship (29:30), and to him are credited many of the psalms in the Bible that were used in worship by God's people. He also ordered the courses for the priests (8:14).

David's influence was felt in later years as much as it had been in the days of Solomon his son. JEHOIADA, the priest in the days of Joash, when a brief revival of true worship was observed, appointed officers of the house of the Lord under the hand of the priests, even as David had ordered (2 Chr. 23:18). Later, in the greater revival of Hezekiah's time, the musical instruments for God's house that David had ordered were again prescribed (29:25–27). Also the words of praise David had prepared for the temple worship were used by Hezekiah (29:30). It could be said in Hezekiah's day that not since the days of Solomon had there been such a worship in Jerusalem (30:26).

Still later in the last revival of the kingdom of Judah, in Josiah's day, once again the courses for the house of God and the singers followed the instructions of David (2 Chr. 35:4, 15). Finally, in the restoration in the time of Ezra and Nehemiah, this same respect for David's influence in worship can be seen. Temple worship was according to the order of David. The musical instruments used were still those specified by him, and the singing followed David's own teaching (Ezra 3:10; Neh. 12:24, 36, 45–46).

D. The influence of David's walk before God. David's walk before God is seen as an example of the integrity God demanded of all the kings of Israel. God, on numerous occasions, declared that David walked before him in integrity of heart. He was upright in all that God commanded, keeping his ordinances (1 Ki. 9:4). God showed great kindness to David for this conduct and made clear that the condition of God's continued blessing on his covenant with David depended on such behavior in his seed after him (2 Chr. 7:18). At first, Solomon walked in the statutes of David, but in the long run he failed to live up to those standards (1 Ki. 11:1). As a result Solomon caused all Israel to depart from David's righteous walk (11:33). In Israel, after the divided kingdom, Jeroboam was the first of a long list of kings who were described as not being like David, who had kept God's commandments and followed after God with the whole heart (14:8). Thus it became the standard of all the kings of Judah and Israel to be judged in the light of the works and heart of David before God (15:3, 11; 2 Ki. 14:3; 16:2; 18:3; 22:2; 1 Chr. 17:1–2; 2 Chr. 7:17–18; 28:1; 29:2; 34:2).

III. David in the prophets. In the prophetic writings, various expressions are used in connection with David.

A. Isaiah

1. The house of David. There are ten references to David in Isaiah. The first two are in the context of the threat of allied Aram and Israel against Jerusalem. At that time, the seed of David on the throne was the unworthy AHAZ. God's word in this time of danger to Jerusalem was addressed to the house of David (Isa. 7:2). When Ahaz refused to ask a sign of God as the Lord had commanded, then Isaiah, God's prophet, ignoring the king, spoke words of hope to the house of David (7:13). These words foretold the birth of the Christ by the virgin (7:14). The only other reference to the house of David occurs in 22:22, where ELIAKIM is spoken of as receiving the keys of the house of David on his shoulders. The phrase "house of David" is used several times in the historical books of the OT to designate the Davidic kingdom (1 Ki. 12:19–20, 26; 13:2; 14:8; 2 Chr. 10:16; 21:7; Neh. 12:37).

2. The throne of David. In Isa. 9:6, a passage that is clearly messianic, the prophet predicts the coming of a child who shall be called Mighty God and rule in peace on the throne of David. He will establish and uphold David's throne with justice and righteousness forever.

3. The tabernacle of David. Similarly, Isa. 16:5 is messianic and points to the same kingdom and throne. The future King is described as sitting in the tent of David in truth, seeking justice and doing righteousness.

In all three of the above categories one sees that the use of David's name in Isaiah relates to the future blessing on God's people. David's characteristics, noted in Kings and Chronicles after his death, are here shown to be a type of the more perfect King to come.

4. City of David. When Jerusalem was under siege it was described as the City of David, thus recalling the covenant of God with him (Isa. 22:9). The term "City of David" applied to Jerusalem is of frequent occurrence in Kings and Chronicles (1 Ki. 3:1; 8:1; 2 Ki. 8:24; 9:28; 2 Chr. 5:2; 8:11; et al.). See DAVID, CITY OF.

5. The sure mercies of David. God indicates his mercy on Jerusalem for David's sake (Isa. 37:35). This provokes the promise from God to defend the city in Hezekiah's day. Later (55:3), God spoke of the sure mercies of David as pertaining to his covenant with David and his seed.

The House of David Inscription discovered in 1994 at Tel Dan (basalt stela, 9th cent. B.C.). This unique monument, written in Aramaic, is part of a victory stela erected by an Aramean king (presumably Hazael) in which he, according to the usual interpretation of the text, claims to have killed Joram son of Ahab, king of Israel, and Ahaziah son of Jehoram, of the "house of David" (apparently the earliest extrabiblical occurrence of this expression).

6. The God of David. It follows then that long after the time of David, it was comforting to such a descendant as good King Hezekiah to have the Lord describe himself as "the God of your father David" (Isa. 38:5).

B. Jeremiah

1. The throne of David. This is Jeremiah's favorite term for the successors to David in Jerusalem (Jer. 13:13; 17:25; 22:2, 4, 30; 29:16; 33:17; 36:30). It is, in most contexts, simply used to describe the kings who followed David and perpetuated the kingdom. One passage (33:17) is in the context of a messianic prophecy relating the throne of David to the promise of God that a seed shall not fail David.

2. The house of David. Jeremiah uses this phrase to address the king on the throne (Jer. 21:12).

3. The righteous Branch of David. This term as used in Jeremiah clearly refers to the promised seed of David and heir to his throne (Jer. 23:5; 33:15). It is a messianic term: it undoubtedly refers to the ultimate fulfillment of the eternal seed of David, the Christ.

4. David as king. In accord with the above, David is described as the future king of Israel (Jer. 30:9). Jeremiah thus applies the term "David" to the Messiah himself.

5. Covenant with David. In the same context mentioned twice above, assurance was given that God would not break his covenant with David, promising that he would have a seed forever on his throne (Jer. 33:21).

6. Seed of David. In a way reminiscent of God's promise to Abraham, God spoke of the seed of David as immeasurable and sure of perpetuity, for David's descendants would rule as kings over the seed of Abraham, Isaac, and Jacob (Jer. 33:22, 26).

For the most part, then, Jeremiah's use of the name David is for messianic prophecy, relating the promise of God to David. The ultimate promise of God is to send his Messiah to save all of his people.

C. The other prophets.

Ezekiel always uses the name "David" with the idea of the servant of God in a messianic and eschatological sense (Ezek. 34:23; 37:24–25). In referring to King David, Hosea looks to the future when David will reign as king over God's people (Hos. 3:5); this also is an eschatological view. In one passage Amos refers to David's reputation as a musician (Amos 6:5). In another (9:11) he speaks of the tabernacle of David to be restored to its former glory. This latter passage comes at the end of the book, in the concluding section of hope for the future. Here a great contrast is seen between the messianic hope and the contemporary evil of Israel in Amos's day. Finally, Zechariah uses the term "house of David" five times in a passage that speaks of the restoration of glory to David's house in the latter days (Zech 12:7—13:1).

In all these prophets there is a continuation of the concept first seen in the life of David and immediately thereafter, that David's seed would be the channel of God's blessings on his people.

IV. David in the NT

A. The Gospels

1. Jesus the Christ as heir of David. It is notable that all the gospel writers seek to make clear the relation between the Lord Jesus and David. With great frequency they note this relationship by the term "the son of David," which is applied to Jesus. Thereby they show that Jesus is the fulfillment of the OT prophecies concerning the eternal kingdom of David. The great thesis of the Gospels is that Jesus fulfills exactly all of the conditions and promises of God's covenant with David, that a seed should never fail on his throne. Jesus is the seed of David and the eternal King whom God had promised (Matt. 1:1; 9:27; 12:23; Mk. 10:48; 12:35; Lk. 18:38–39; 20:41). Both Mark and John indicate that the Jewish leaders of Jesus' day fully expected the Christ to be the seed of David (Jn. 7:42; Mk. 11:10).

When Matthew began his gospel, he felt it important to establish this fact. In great detail he listed the generations of Jesus, showing that he was indeed the direct descendant of David (Matt. 1). Joseph was specifically called the son of David (1:20). Luke in a similar approach gathers together evidence for the fulfillment of God's promise to David in the coming of Jesus (Lk. 1:27, 32, 69; 2:4).

2. The city of David. One noticeable difference between the Gospels and the OT is the reference to the city of David in the NT. While in the OT this constantly refers to Jerusalem, in the NT it consistently refers to Bethlehem (Lk. 2:4, 11; Jn. 7:42).

3. The superiority of Christ over David. Most important in the whole matter of the NT concept of Jesus as the fulfillment of God's covenant with David is the lesson taught by the Lord to the PHARISEES. Jesus said to them that the Christ, while properly the son and heir of David, is most certainly shown, even in the OT, to be above and superior to David. He is indeed the Son of God. All three of the Synoptic Gospels record this most important lesson (Matt. 22:45; Mk. 12:35, 37; Lk. 20:41, 44).

4. Other references to David. Jesus refers to David in two more contexts. Once he uses an event in David's life to show the propriety of his disciples plucking and eating grain on the SABBATH (Matt. 12:3 and parallels). Elsewhere he speaks of David as the psalm writer who wrote in the Spirit (Matt. 22:43 and parallels).

We conclude then that the dominant Davidic theme in the Gospels is the complete fulfillment, in the coming of Jesus Christ, of all God had promised in reference to David and his kingdom.

B. The Acts

1. The superiority of Christ over David. This theme from the Gospels (see above) becomes a major theme in the early church. Both PETER and PAUL demonstrated that the prophecies about David were by no means fulfilled in David himself but *only* in Jesus Christ. They particularly stressed this in reference to the resurrection (Acts 2:29, 34; 13:36). Paul, furthermore, at Antioch of Pisidia when addressing the Israelites, spoke of David as the king and a man after God's own heart. However, he taught that only in Jesus Christ and his resurrection could we know the sure mercies of David that God had promised (Acts 13:16–34).

2. David as an inspired writer. In two places Luke makes mention of David as someone inspired by the Holy Spirit in the writing of the Psalms (Acts 1:16; 4:25).

3. The tabernacle of David. James, quoting Amos 9:11–12, which speaks of the tabernacle of David to be built again, relates the rebuilding of the tabernacle of David to the election of the Gentiles. The Gentiles were to have full part in David's kingdom as Amos had foretold (Acts 15:16–18).

C. The Epistles. In the Epistles also, Christ is demonstrated as being of the seed of David according to the flesh (Rom. 1:3; 2 Tim. 2:8). In several other passages mention is made of David: one in connection with forgiveness of sins as demonstrated in David's life and psalms (Rom. 4:6; Pss. 69 and 95 are specifically ascribed to David in Rom. 11:9 and Heb. 4:7), and another listing David as among the faithful of the OT period (Heb. 11:32).

D. The Revelation. The inheritance of David is spoken of as the key of David, which is described as being in Christ's hands (Rev. 3:7). In keeping with the Gospels and Epistles, the book of Revelation also clearly teaches that Jesus is the true fulfillment and ultimate application of all God's promises to David. As the "Root and the Offspring of David" (Rev. 22:16; cf. 5:5), Jesus is the eternal seed in whom all the promises and hopes pertaining to David's throne are to be found.

(Helpful works on David include J. Bosch, *David: The Biography of a King* [1966]; D. M. Gunn, *The Story of King David* [1978]; L. Rost, *The Succession to the Throne of David* [1982]; I. H. Weisfeld, *David the King* [1983]; W. Brueggemann, *David's Truth in Israel's Imagination and Memory* [1985]; J. W. Flanagan, *David's Social Drama* [1988]; R. C. Bailey, *David in Love and War: The Pursuit of Power in 2 Samuel 10–12* [1990]; J. Bright, *A History of Israel*, 4th ed. [2000], ch. 5; S. Isser, *The Sword of Goliath: David in Heroic Literature* [2003]; K. Bodner, *David Observed: A King in the Eyes of His Court*

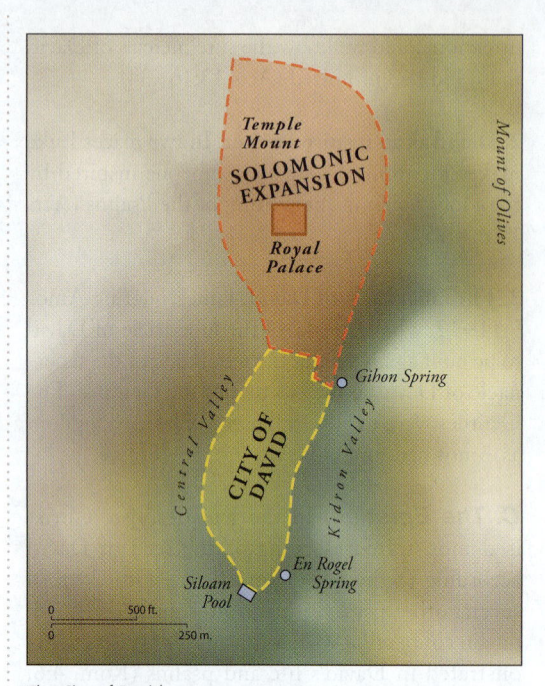

The City of David.

[2005]; K.-P. Adam, *Saul and David in der judäischen Geschichtsschreibung* [2007].)   J. B. SCOTT

David, City of. The oldest, or SE, portion of JERUSALEM, on the original Mount ZION, and equated with "the fortress of Zion" (2 Sam. 5:7). Such a mountain stronghold at Jerusalem dated back to patriarchal and Canaanite days (Gen. 14:18, SALEM; cf. Ps. 76:2). It occupied the sharply sloped ridge (about one-quarter mile) between the KIDRON Valley on the E and the Tyropoeon Valley on the W, to the N of their junction with the HINNOM Valley. The location was determined by the presence at its NE end, in the Kidron Valley, of the GIHON SPRING, which was the area's only perennial source for water. Earlier excavators had limited the City of David to the crest, barely 100 yards wide from a gate on the W (J. W. Crowfoot in 1927) to a wall and towers on the E (R. A. S. Macalister in 1923–1925); more recent archaeologists (e.g., K. Kenyon in 1961) have demonstrated that the main walls, from c. 1800 B.C. to the fall of Jerusalem in 586 B.C., were 50 yards more nearly toward the bottom of the slope, with houses crowding the ascents.

This city David captured from the Jebusites in 1003 B.C. (2 Sam. 5:7; see JEBUS), renamed it after himself, and settled in it, making it his capital (v. 9). His subsequent building projects included a palace (1 Chr. 15:1) and the MILLO (2 Sam. 5:6–10; 1 Chr. 11:4–9; NIV, "supporting terraces"), a word that literally means "a filling" and that may refer to massive 10th-cent. retaining walls with which the previous system of Canaanite terraces on the slopes was strengthened (K. Kenyon in *BA* 27 [1964]: 43). The ARK OF THE COVENANT was brought into the City of David (1 Chr. 15:1, 29); there it remained until 959 B.C., when SOLOMON removed it to the new temple he had built for it on Mount MORIAH to the N (1 Ki. 8:1; 2 Chr. 5:2). Solomon seems also to have constructed an acropolis or palace area, with casemate walls, on the crest of the City of David (Kenyon, 41). His palace for the daughter of Pharaoh was not there (1 Ki. 9:24), but between Moriah and Zion (?), because of the holiness of these places as caused by the presence of the ark (2 Chr. 8:11).

Scripture notes that within the City of David were buried David himself (1 Ki. 2:10), Solomon (11:43), most of the kings of Judah down to Jotham, d. 736 B.C. (2 Chr. 12:16; 14:1; 16:14; 21:1, 20; 24:25; 27:9), and other important figures such as JEHOIADA the priest (24:16). Certain "barrel vaults," now partly cut away, near the S end of the city may be their remains. King HEZEKIAH strengthened it before the Assyrian crisis of 701 B.C. (32:5) and brought water down its W side via his tunnel from Gihon (32:30) and thus included the Pool of SILOAM and the KING'S GARDEN at the southern tip within the walls (Neh. 3:15; Isa. 22:9–11). Babylon destroyed the city in 586 B.C.

NEHEMIAH's refortification in 444 B.C. probably embraced only the crest of the City of David, the walls of Crowfoot and Macalister (Neh. 3:15; 12:37). Later expansion was to the hill W of the Tyropoeon Valley, on which JOSEPHUS located (falsely) the "Tomb of David" (*War* 5.4.1) and to which, with the abandonment of the original City of David after A.D. 70, the name Zion was attached. The NT uses the phrase "city of David" with reference to BETHLEHEM (Lk. 2:11). (See J. Simons, *Jerusalem in the Old Testament* [1952], 60–64; M. Avi-Yonah, *Jerusalem* [1960]; N. Avigad, *Discovering Jerusalem* [1983]; Y. Shiloh in *IEJ* 34 [1984]: 57–58 and 35 [1985]: 65–67, 301–3.)   J. B. PAYNE

David, tower of. A famous fortress "built with elegance" on which hung "a thousand shields"; now unknown except as a symbol of strength (Cant. 4:4). The "Tower of David" in modern JERUSALEM, by Jaffa Gate, is only medieval, built on a Herodian substructure.

dawn. This English term, as a noun or a verb, can be used to render several words and expressions, especially Hebrew *šaḥar* H8840 (e.g., Job 38:12; KJV, "dayspring"). Some believe this word refers to the Amorite god SHAHAR. The light of dawn can be a symbol for truthfulness and discernment (Isa. 8:19–20). The Greek term *anatolē* G424 ("rising"), rendered "dawn" by the NRSV in Lk. 1:78, is a figurative reference to the coming of MESSIAH.

H. M. WOLF

day. The Bible includes a number of different uses of this word (Heb. *yôm* H3427, Gk. *hēmera* G2465). (1) It often refers to the hours of daylight between dawn and dusk (Gen. 1:5; 8:22; Acts 20:31; et al.). In OT times this period was divided into morning, noon, and evening (Ps. 55:17), or the time of the day might be indicated by the use of such expressions as sunrise, heat of the day, cool of the day, sunset, and the like. The Babylonians reckoned their days from sunrise to sunrise; the Romans, from midnight to midnight; the Greeks and the Jews, from sunset to sunset. The first mention in the Bible of a twelve-hour day is found in Jn. 11:9. The division of the day into twelve-hour periods came from the Babylonians.

(2) The concept of a legal or civil day—the period between two successive sun risings—goes back to the CREATION story (Gen. 1:14, 19) and is found throughout the Bible (Lk. 9:37; Acts 21:26). The only day of the week to which the Jews gave a name was the SABBATH; they used ordinal numbers for the days, although the day before the Sabbath was often called PREPARATION DAY (Matt. 27:62; Mk. 15:42; Lk. 23:54; Jn. 19:31, 42). The night was subdivided into watches—first, middle, and morning. The Romans had four watches. Acts 23:23 shows that the night also was divided into twelve hours.

(3) The word often is used in the sense of an indefinite period of time, such as the whole creative period (Gen. 2:4b NRSV; cf. NIV, "When the LORD God made …"), "the day of God's wrath" (Job 20:28), "the day of trouble" (Ps. 20:1 NRSV). The plural is sometimes used in the sense of "time," as in "the days of Abraham" (Gen. 26:18 NRSV; cf. also "the days of Noah," Matt. 24:37), or of the span of human life, as in "the days of Adam … were eight hundred years" (Gen. 5:4 NRSV; cf. "I will lengthen thy days," 1 Ki. 3:14 KJV). Note that the eternal God is called "the Ancient of Days" (Dan. 7:9, 13; see ETERNITY).

(4) Many times the word is used figuratively. Jesus said, for example, "As long as it is day, we must do the work of him who sent me. Night is coming, when no one can work" (Jn. 9:4; here "day" means the time of opportunity for service). The reason Jesus made this statement was that his disciples saw the light as they walked "by day" (11:9), and he himself claimed to be "the light of the world" (8:12). Paul called Christians "sons of the light and sons of the day," contrasting them with those who "belong to the night or to the darkness" (1 Thess. 5:5). When Paul wrote, "The night is nearly over; the day is almost here" (Rom. 13:12), he meant by "day" the time of eschatological salvation. There will be perpetual day in the final state of perfection (Rev. 21:25).

(5) There are special days set aside for, and belonging in a peculiar sense to, Yahweh, such as the SABBATH day (Gen. 2:3; Exod. 20:8–11), the PASSOVER (Exod. 12:14), and the Day of Atonement (Lev. 16:29–31; see ATONEMENT, DAY OF). On these days no labor was to be done and special rituals were observed.

(6) In both Testaments frequent mention is made of the DAY OF THE LORD and similar terms used to designate it. This is not a particular day, but a period of time at the end of history when God will bring judgment upon godless peoples and vindicate his name (Isa. 2:12; 13:9; Ezek. 7:7, 8; Matt. 24; 25; 2 Thess. 2:1–12). After this supernatural intervention of God in history, he will set up his eternal kingdom (Rev. 20–22), and all things will be consummated in Christ (Eph. 1:10).

(7) The phrase "the last days" seems to include in its broadest meaning the whole period from the cross to the SECOND COMING (Acts 2:17; 2 Tim. 3:1; Heb. 1:2; 2 Pet. 3:3–4). See ESCHATOLOGY.

S. BARABAS

day, Joshua's long. When JOSHUA and the Israelites began to conquer the hill country of Judah from the Canaanite tribes, the town of GIBEON made peace with the invaders. A coalition of petty kings—ADONI-ZEDEK of JERUSALEM, HOHAM of HEBRON, PIRAM of JARMUTH, JAPHIA of LACHISH, and DEBIR of EGLON, together with five chieftains of the AMORITES—met Joshua in battle at Gibeon (Josh. 10:1–10). There the Lord rained down

The sun rising over the village of el-Jib (biblical Gibeon).

hailstones and killed many of the enemy. Then Joshua, before Israel, prayed to God with a short poem: "O sun, stand still over Gibeon, / O moon, over the Valley of Aijalon" (10:12). The next verse, also in poetic form, states: "So the sun stood still, / and the moon stopped, / till the nation avenged itself on its enemies" (with a reference to the Book of JASHAR). It seems as though the parallelism connects the movement of sun and moon. According to the next verse, "There has never been a day like it before or since."

The long day is not mentioned anywhere else in Scripture and has been the subject of much debate. (For a summary of interpretations, see R. D. Nelson, *Joshua* [1997], 141–45; for an attempt to understand the passage within the framework of the theory of catastrophism, see D. Patten et al., *The Long Day of Joshua and Six Other Catastrophies* [1973]). The Scripture narrative undoubtedly means to be understood in the sense of a supernatural event, but the precise nature of the miracle is very difficult to determine. Because an actual change in the Earth's rotation would have had cataclysmic consequences, some suggest alternate explanations (e.g., did God cause the sunlight to continue in Canaan by means of light refraction?). The reference to the moon (over AIJALON, thus setting in the W?) as well as the sun standing still at midday ("the sun stopped in the middle of the sky") raises additional questions about the meaning of the text. Nevertheless, it is clear that the victory thus won by Israel was the direct result of the sovereign work of God. The short poem is a hymn of praise for God's providential provision. The mechanics of that action are not told, but only its result in a victory for the children of Israel. See BETH HORON, BATTLE OF. W. WHITE, JR.

day, last. See ESCHATOLOGY.

day, that. See DAY OF THE LORD.

day, third. See THIRD DAY.

Day of Atonement. See ATONEMENT, DAY OF.

day of Christ, day of Jehovah. See DAY OF THE LORD.

day of judgment. See ESCHATOLOGY.

day of the Lord. Also "day of Yahweh." Together with associated expressions, such as "the day of the wrath of Yahweh" and "that day," it designates God's decisive intervention in history for JUDGMENT. (Elsewhere decisive events are called "days," cf. "the day of Midian" in Isa. 9:4; "the day of Jezreel" in Hos. 1:11. Hebrew has no special word for "hour." See DAY.)

The phrase "day of the Lord" was evidently current in the time of AMOS in the 8th cent. B.C., indicating the time when Yahweh would avenge his people on their enemies. Amos turns it back upon those who use it, for the day will bring judgment upon sinful Israel as well (Amos 5:18–20; 6:3; 8:9; cf. chs. 1 and 2). Already Amos's vision of the day oscillates between battles, natural disasters, and supernatural calamities, but he ends on a note of hope. The day will usher in a new age (9:11–12, a passage interpreted Christologically in Acts 15:16–17).

The expression figures a great deal in subsequent prophecy. The theme of judgment is developed by Isaiah (cf. Isa. 2 and 22), but like other prophetic books it telescopes numerous themes together. Most prophets look forward to the day of the Lord, but there is a sense in which it was fulfilled in the fall of Jerusalem in 587 B.C. (Lam. 1:21; Ezek. 34:12). Sometimes the prophet foretells the impending judgment of a particular nation: Babylon (Isa. 13:1, 6, 9, 13); Edom (Isa. 34:8–9; 63:4); Egypt (Jer. 46:10; Ezek. 30:3–4); the Philistines (Jer. 47:4). Zephaniah, after describing the horrors of the day in great detail (Zeph. 1), mentions by name the surrounding nations (ch. 2; cf. 3:8) before announcing the judgment and restoration of Jerusalem (ch. 3). Obadiah announces that "the day of the Lord is near for all the nations" (Obad. 15), while Zech. 12–14 paints a vivid and detailed picture of the desolation of Jerusalem on that day. See eschatology; prophets and prophecy.

The day of the Lord is also associated with universal restoration, and in places it is connected with the Messiah. "In that day the Root of Jesse will stand as a banner for the peoples; the nations will rally to him, and his place of rest will be glorious. In that day the Lord will reach out his hand a second time to reclaim the remnant that is left of his people ..." (Isa. 11:10–11; cf. 61:2; Lk. 4:18–19). Isaiah looks forward to "the last days" of universal peace and prosperity, when the Lord shall judge between the nations (Isa. 2:2–4; cf. Mic. 4:1–3).

Malachi stresses the unbearable judgment and purging as well as the healing and joy that the day will bring (Mal. 3:2; 4:1–2). He also speaks of the messenger, Elijah, who will herald the day (Mal. 3:1; 4:5). The latter is identified with John the Baptist in the Gospels (Matt. 11:10; 17:10–13; Mk. 1:2; 9:11–13; Lk. 1:17, 76; 7:27). Joel's description of the day of the Lord might at first seem to refer to a plague of locusts (Joel 1:15; 2:1–2, 11), but the vision merges into one of cosmic, supernatural events and final judgment (3:14–21). Against the background of heavenly portents, the promise is given that "everyone who calls on the name of the Lord will be saved" (2:32), and God will pour out his Spirit "on all people" (2:28). Acts 2:17–21 sees the prophecy being fulfilled at Pentecost. Jeremiah speaks of "that time" and "those days" rather than of the day of the Lord (cf. Jer. 3:16–18; 4:11; 50:4). The thought seems to be the same. He announces that "the time is coming" when God will make a new covenant, by which he will write his law on men's hearts and fulfill the covenant promise: "I will be their God, and they will be my people" (31:31–34). See covenant, the new.

The expression is not found in Daniel, who speaks rather of "that time" when "Michael, the great prince who protects your people, will arise. There will be a time of distress such as has not happened from the beginning of nations until then. But at that time your people—everyone whose name is found written in the book—will be delivered. Multitudes who sleep in the dust of the earth will awake: some to everlasting life, others to shame and everlasting contempt" (Dan. 12:1–2; cf. 9:26; 10:14; 11:27, 35, 40; 12:4, 9, 13, where mention is also made of the "end"). The expression virtually disappears in late Jewish literature, which ceases to use the name of Yahweh. The terminology survives in a few passages, such as 2 Bar. 48:47; 49:2; 55:6. It is revived in the NT (2 Pet. 3:10, 12; Rev. 6:17; 16:14), where it is also connected with the return of Christ both in language and imagery (Matt. 24–25; Mk. 13; Lk. 17:22–31; 21; 1 Cor. 1:8; 5:5; 2 Cor. 1:14; Phil. 1:6, 10; 2:16; 1 Thess. 5:2; 2 Thess. 2:2). See second coming.

OT prophecy stresses the imminence of the day of the Lord. Men need to prepare for it without delay. God's justice and judgment are certain, as is his mercy. Sometimes prophetic utterances found partial fulfillment in particular events. But these are, in fact, foretastes or trailers of the decisive acts of God in the coming of Christ, the outpouring of the Spirit and Christ's return in final judgment and glory. (See L. Cerný, *The Day of Yahweh and Some Relevant Problems* [1948]; H. H. Rowley, *The Faith of Israel* [1956], 177–201; S. Mowinckel, *He that Cometh* [1956]; G. von Rad, "The Origin of the Concept of the Day of Yahweh," *JSS* 4 [1959]: 97–108; Y. Hoffmann, "The Day of the Lord as a Concept and a Term in the Prophetic Literature," *ZAW* 93 [1981]: 37–50; N. Wendebourg, *Der Tag des Herrn* [2003].) C. Brown

day's journey, day's walk. The distance that a person can normally travel in one day. It would necessarily vary with the terrain and the method of travel—whether on foot, with an animal, with a caravan; also whether the journey was made in leisure or in haste. HERODOTUS in one place says that he reckons a day's journey at 25 mi., but in another at 18 mi. (*Hist.* 4.101; 5.53). The Bible makes mention of a day's journey (Num. 11:31; 1 Ki. 19:4; Jon. 3:4; Lk. 2:44); of a three days' journey (Gen. 30:36; Exod. 3:18; 5:3; 8:27; Num. 10:33; Jon. 3:3); and of a seven days' journey (Gen. 31:23; 2 Ki. 3:9). It is said that LABAN and his relatives pursued JACOB from HARAN to GILEAD, a distance of 350 mi., in seven days, an average of 50 mi. a day (Gen. 31:23), but they would have been riding camels. See also SABBATH DAY'S JOURNEY. J. C. CONNELL

days, last. See ESCHATOLOGY.

daysman. This archaic term, referring to someone appointed to serve as arbiter (on a *day* fixed for trial), is used by the KJV to render Hebrew *môkiaḥ* (hiphil ptc. of *yākaḥ H3519*, "to rebuke, judge, settle dispute") in a passage where JOB expresses the longing for someone to mediate the conflict between God and himself (Job 9:33; NRSV, "umpire"; NIV, "someone to arbitrate"; cf. the use of the Heb. term in Isa. 29:21 et al.). That longing of the human heart was fulfilled in the INCARNATION. See also MEDIATOR.

dayspring. See DAWN.

day star. See MORNING STAR.

deacon, deaconess. The Greek noun *diakonos G1356* was a common term for "servant, assistant, messenger." It and its cognates (*diakonia G1355*, verb *diakoneō G1354*) are used with reference to table waiters (Lk. 22:26–27; Jn. 2:5, 9), royal servants (Matt. 22:13), service or ministry in general (Mk. 10:43–45 [Jesus]; Acts 1:17, 25 [apostles]; Rom. 11:13 [Paul]), and local Christian leaders, possibly an official title (Phil. 1:1; 1 Tim. 3:8, 12–13). In Rom. 13:4 the word is applied to secular rulers. See also MINISTRY; SERVANT; SLAVE.

I. Background. In Greek thought, service was considered unworthy of the dignity of free men (Plato, *Gorg.* 492b, "How can a man be happy when he has to serve someone?"), except when rendered to the state (Demosthenes, *Or.* 50.2 [*Against Polycles*]; Plato, *Leg.* 955). In Hellenistic times the term *diakonos* is applied to certain cult officials (MM, 149); more generally, EPICTETUS described the wise man as a servant of God (*Diss.* 2.22.69 et al., see *TDNT*, 2:82–83). JUDAISM viewed service much more positively, but the SEPTUAGINT used other terms to describe it (*diakonos* only in Esth. 1:10; 2:2; 6:1, 3, 5; Prov. 10:4; *diakonia* in Esth. 6:3, 5). The Suffering Servant of Isa. 40–53 (Heb. *ʿebed H6269*; see SERVANT OF THE LORD) is described in the SEPTUAGINT as "slave" (*doulos G1528*, Isa. 42:19) or "child" (*pais G4090*, 52:13). Some aspects of the OT concern for the POOR perhaps anticipate the charitable functions of the Christian deacon. The relationship of the SYNAGOGUE ruler to his attendant (rabbinic Heb. *ḥazzān*, cf. *hypēretēs G5677* in Lk. 4:20) shows certain similarities to the later correlation between the Christian BISHOP and his deacons, but the functions involved were very different and there is no evidence of any causal link between the two sets of offices.

II. Christ as deacon. The unique source of all Christian service, and its perfect prototype, is found in him who, being Lord, made himself servant (Rom. 15:8) and slave (Phil. 2:6). By his INCARNATION as the messianic servant of the Father and by his messianic suffering, Christ completely inverted the servant-master relationship and transvalued the dignity and honor of serving and suffering. Contrasting his own servant-role with both the power structures of Gentile authority and the ambitious strife of the disciples, he affirmed that "whoever wants to become great among you must be your servant, and whoever wants to be first must be slave of all. For even the Son of Man did not come to be served, but to serve, and to give his life as a ransom for many" (Mk. 10:43–45, cf. 9:35; Matt. 20:20–28). Luke, who places the episode in the table context of the Last Supper, concludes the account with the declaration of Christ, "But I am among you as one who serves" (Lk. 22:27). In the fourth gospel the same servant-nature of the Son is dramatically illustrated by his washing the disciples' feet prior to the Supper (Jn. 13:1–11; see FOOTWASHING).

All three Synoptic Gospels refer to the women who followed Jesus and ministered to him (Lk. 8:3; Matt. 27:55; Mk. 15:41); also Peter's mother-in-law, healed of her fever, arose and ministered to the disciples (Matt. 8:15; Mk. 1:31; Lk. 4:39). Whereas the master customarily dines before his servant and expects the required attentions as a matter of course (Lk. 17:8), at the final marriage feast the Master himself will seat his faithful servants at his table, don the apron of table service and wait upon them (Lk. 12:37; cf. Jn. 12:25–26). (Str-B, 2:257, mentions the curious rabbinic parallel that Rabban Gamaliel II astonished his fellow rabbis by rising and serving them at table, prompting Rabbi Jehoshua to comment that "Abraham was greater than he, and he served at table," while another confrere added, "God himself spreads the table before all men, and should not Rabban Gamaliel therefore arise and serve us?") In the judgment described in Matt. 25:31–46, the Son of Man will separate the sheep from the goats on the basis of service (cf. *diakoneō* in v. 44): the Son acknowledges those who ministered to him by feeding, clothing, sheltering, and visiting "one of the least of these."

From these teachings it becomes clear that all Christian service, and indeed the whole Christian life, is a participation by grace in the servanthood of the Son of Man. This diaconate-in-Christ marks the entire church; we are partakers in the communal life and in the corporate servanthood and suffering of the Suffering Servant (cf. Phil. 2:5–11; Col. 1:24–28). According to Rom. 12:7 and 1 Pet. 4:11, this service is a distinctive gift of the Spirit within the BODY OF CHRIST, along with (or manifested in) such SPIRITUAL GIFTS as encouragement, generosity, mercy, and hospitality.

III. Christian ministry. Throughout the NT the relevant Greek terms are consistently used in the broad sense implied in the above data; out of more than 100 occurrences, few even hint at the ecclesiastical office that later developed. The noun *diakonia* is used of financial aid (2 Cor. 8:4; 11:8; Rom. 15:25; see CONTRIBUTION), of beneficence (Acts 6:1), and of personal assistance with regard to temporal needs or in evangelistic and missionary efforts (Acts 19:22; 1 Cor. 6:15; 2 Tim. 4:11; Rev. 2:19). The title *diakonos* is applied to Christ (see above), the Twelve (Acts 1:17, 25), Paul (1 Cor. 3:5), Timothy (1 Thess. 3:2; 1 Tim. 4:6; Acts 19:22, with Erastus), Tychicus (Col. 4:7; Eph. 6:21), and Epaphras (Col. 1:7); more generally, it is applied to the minister of God (2 Cor. 6:4), of Jesus Christ (11:23), of the new covenant (3:6), of the gospel (Eph. 3:7, Col. 1:23), of the church (Col. 1:25). Thus the term alludes to an area of ministry that includes the apostle, missionary, evangelist, and prophet—in effect, all the varied forms of Christian ministry (1 Cor. 12:5; Eph. 4:12).

Some have seen in Acts 6 the initiation of the diaconate as a church office, since the passage introduces the significant distinction between the "ministry of the word" (*tē diakonia tou logou*, 6:4) and the "ministry of tables" (*diakonein trapezais*, 6:2). But the seven men chosen in this context are nowhere called "deacons"; PHILIP is in fact called an "evangelist" (21:8), and subsequent accounts emphasize the role of the seven in disputing, teaching, preaching, and baptizing.

The salutation of Phil. 1:1 seems to refer to the diaconate as a specific and relatively defined function within the congregation, closely associated with the bishop (or overseer), perhaps especially in administration of the contribution for which Paul thanks the Philippians. The same quasi-official use reappears in 1 Tim. 3:8–13, again closely linked to the bishop. The requisites for the choice of deacons fit those required for the administration of congregational funds and for house-to-house visitation, two functions typically ascribed to the deacon in patristic literature (Hippolytus, *The Apostolic Tradition* 9, 21, 23–25, 30). These two NT passages stand alone as instances of a more technical official sense of the term. Patristic literature illustrates the progressive definition of its official character, along with the gradual distinction of the bishop and presbyter to constitute a threefold ministry in which the deacon assists the bishop. See ELDER (NT).

IV. Deaconess. The Synoptic Gospels give curious emphasis to the ministry of certain women (see above). In Rom. 16:1 PHOEBE is described as a *diakonos* (RSV, "deaconess"; NRSV, "deacon"; NIV, "servant"), but the first clear indications of an office of "deaconess" appear only in the 3rd cent. It is highly doubtful that the verse refers to a specific and definite church office. The "women" of 1 Tim. 3:11 are probably the wives of deacons rather than deaconesses (cf. NIV). These passages, however, plus the role of WIDOWS indicated in 1 Tim. 5:3–16 and 1 Cor. 7:8, may point to the earliest origins of the development of the later office of deaconess. (See B. Reicke, *Diakonie, Festfreude und Zelos* [1951]; J. McCord and T. H. L. Parker, *Service in Christ* [1966]; H. von Campenhausen, *Ecclesiastical Authority and Spiritual Power in the Church of the First Three Centuries* [1969]; A. G. Martimort, *Deaconesses: An Historical Study* [1986]; N. Collins, *Diakonia: Re-interpreting the Ancient Sources* [1991]; A. Hentschel, *Diakonia im Neuen Testament* [2007]; *NIDNTT*, 3:544–49.) J. STAM

dead. The participial form of the Hebrew verb *mût H4637* ("to die") is the general OT word for "dead," applied to men or animal alike (Exod. 21:35). Occasionally, it can refer to a living person in a prospective sense, such as in God's warning to ABIMELECH that he was a dead man because of SARAH (Gen. 20:3; NIV, "You are as good as dead"). A leper is also called "one dead" (Num. 12:12 KJV; NIV, "a stillborn infant"). The phrase "dead dog" refers to a particularly worthless and lowly individual, sometimes an opponent of the king (1 Sam. 24:14; 2 Sam. 9:8; 16:9). Physical deformity or vile character can be involved in that expression. In several instances the term *rĕpāʾîm H8327* ("shades, departed spirits"; see REPHAITES) occurs parallel to "the dead" as the inhabitants of SHEOL (Ps. 88:10; Isa. 26:14). The etymology of this word is disputed (see *NIDOTTE*, 3:1174–76), but cognates are attested in Phoenician inscriptions and in Ugaritic literature. Note also the word *ʾôb H200*, which is usually rendered "medium, spiritist," but can also mean "spirit of the dead, ghost" (1 Sam. 28:8; Isa. 29:4).

Hebrew law had strict requirements relating to defilement through contact with dead bodies. The high priest could not go near the dead (Lev. 21:11); neither could a NAZIRITE during the days of his separation to Yahweh (Num. 6:6). Individuals who touched the dead were unclean seven days (19:11) and had to perform a purification ritual or face death (19:13). Hyssop dipped in water was sprinkled upon the defiled person and the place where the man died (19:18). See PURITY; UNCLEANNESS.

MOURNING for the dead was common. This practice involved donning of special apparel and anointing with oil (2 Sam. 14:2), weeping in a house of mourning, and eating and drinking for the dead (Jer. 16:5–8; 22:10). Ezekiel was forbidden to remove his shoes or cover his lips when his wife died (Ezek. 24:17). BURIAL of the dead was the usual custom (but note 1 Sam. 31:12). The dead are said to be forgotten (Ps. 31:12) and, in a sense, without knowledge (Eccl. 9:5). They do not praise the Lord (Ps. 115:17). Their abode is "the dark places" of Sheol (143:3). Glimpses of the RESURRECTION of the dead appear in the OT (Isa. 26:19; Dan. 12:2).

NT usage includes the idea of being spiritually dead in sin (*nekros G3738* in Eph. 2:1; cf. Matt. 8:22). Believers, however, are to be dead to sin (Rom. 6:11). This sense of "lifeless" or "inactive" is applied to unproductive faith (Jas. 2:26), to the sterile works of the law (Heb. 9:14), and to the church of SARDIS (Rev. 3:1). The RESURRECTION OF JESUS CHRIST and of the dead is a vital NT doctrine (1 Cor. 15:20, 52). See also DEATH. H. M. WOLF

dead, abode of the. See HADES; SHEOL.

dead, state of the. On the subject of the condition of those who have departed this life, divine revelation is progressive. By this is meant that there is development, not from error to truth, but from a little truth to more truth, although even in the NT there is little said by comparison with what is revealed on other subjects. See also DEATH; INTERMEDIATE STATE.

I. Old Testament. The revelation given by God on this matter in the OT is extremely meager. In the early chapters of Genesis man is threatened with death if he disobeys (Gen. 2:17), and when he does sin he is told that eventually he will die: "for dust you are / and to dust you will return" (Gen. 3:19). The fact of human death is recorded at the beginning of the genealogy in Gen. 5, but no more is said. The genealogy itself emphasizes the universality of death with its monotonous repetition "… and he died"; but on the other hand, an intimation of more glorious possibilities is given in the account of ENOCH, who "walked with God; then he was no more, because God took him away" (5:24). Further hints of some form of life after death have also been seen in the expression "gathered to his people" (e.g., 25:8) and in the words of the dying JACOB

(47:30). In the NT, it is suggested that ABRAHAM grasped the truth of a life beyond the grave (Heb. 11:11–16), but this is never positively stated in the patriarchal narrative itself.

The word SHEOL (Heb. *šeʾôl* H8619), the exegesis of which normally figures largely in discussions on the OT view of life after death, occurs first in Gen. 37:35 (also 42:38; 44:29, 31). This word occurs sixty-five times in the OT, and its etymology is in doubt. Most OT scholars, however, are in no doubt as to the derivation of the idea. They believe that Israel took over from her neighbors the ideas of the underworld and the afterlife that were fairly widespread in the ANE. According to this view, Sheol (cf. also ABADDON) is a deep pit far down in the earth, a place of darkness, where the "shades" of men (Heb. *rĕpāʾîm* H8327; see DEAD) have a vague shadowy existence, cut off from the land of the living, from all joys, and from communion with God (cf. *NIDOTTE*, 4:6–7). Sheol is therefore something to be dreaded and avoided for as long as possible. There are no moral distinctions in Sheol; good and bad are there together. Various Scriptures are used to substantiate this reconstruction, and those passages that express belief in some kind of moral distinction in Sheol, or where believers look for deliverance from Sheol, or even RESURRECTION, are either explained in other ways or are said to be among the latest parts of the OT and so to prepare the way for the development that is found in literature of the intertestamental period. (See W. Eichrodt, *Theology of the Old Testament* 2 [1967], 210–23.)

Some evangelical scholars, however, are unhappy about this account of the OT teaching. They feel that too much from the beliefs of Israel's neighbors is read into the OT, and while they in turn may be accused by others of attempting to read too much of the NT teaching into the OT, they believe that the OT and NT revelation in the afterlife is consistent. The following points need to be considered: (1) A distinction should be made between what is felt, feared, or even believed by godly people and what is positively revealed by God in his word. This principle needs to be treated with caution, but it is relevant. (2) The fear of death is sometimes to be explained in terms of fear of the unknown, about which nothing has been revealed, and/or fear of exclusion from the blessings of the COVENANT, which in the OT were given exclusively in terms of this life. (3) The word Sheol may not always have the same meaning. In some passages it is used abstractly to signify the state of death (e.g., 1 Sam. 2:6). In others it apparently has the meaning "the grave" (Gen. 35:20). In others it has the idea of "hell," the place of punishment (Deut. 32:22; Ps. 9:17) that speaks of God's anger burning to the depths of Sheol. (Cf. L. Berkhof, *Systematic Theology* [1941], 679–93; J. B. Payne, *The Theology of the Older Testament* [1962], 443–63.)

In Exod. 3:6 God is recorded as saying to Moses: "I am the God of your father, the God of Abraham, the God of Isaac and the God of Jacob." Jesus uses this passage to prove the resurrection: "He is not the God of the dead, but of the living, for all are alive to him" (Lk. 20:37–38 and parallels). With this may be linked a number of passages in which desire or hope of waking from death is expressed (Job 19:25; Pss. 16:11; 17:15; 49:14–15; 73:24), and those in which resurrection is definitely promised (Isa. 26:19; Dan. 12:2; and prob. Ezek. 37:1–14).

II. Apocryphal and apocalyptic writings of the intertestamental period. There are certain developments of belief in these writings, and while there is no complete agreement among them, one finds a number of trends, some of which may have been influenced by Persian or Greek ideas. Belief in the resurrection of the bodies of the righteous becomes more clear-cut, possibly due to the terrible sufferings and martyrdom during Maccabean times (see MACCABEE). More attention is also given to the intermediate state. Sheol (and its Greek equivalent HADES, *hadēs* G87) largely refers to the place to which the ungodly go at death while awaiting judgment, while PARADISE (*paradeisos* G4137, from a Persian word for a garden or pleasure ground, sometimes thought of as the "upper compartment" of Sheol) is used to denote the state of blessedness enjoyed by the souls of the righteous between death and resurrection. At the resurrection, the wicked are consigned to GEHENNA, while the righteous are raised to enjoy more fully the blessings of Paradise in terms of a new earthly Garden of EDEN or a more transcendent, heavenly hope. (See further D. S. Russell, *The Method and Message of Jewish Apocalyptic* [1964], 353–90.)

III. New Testament. In the NT the emphasis is on the resurrection and transformation of the bodies of the righteous, which will take place at the SECOND COMING of the Lord Jesus Christ, and the subsequent enjoyment of the presence of God and of Christ to all eternity (1 Cor. 15; Phil. 3:20–21; 1 Thess. 4:15–17; et al.). For the ungodly there will be a resurrection to JUDGMENT, resulting in WRATH, PERDITION, and the eternal punishment of the LAKE OF FIRE (Matt. 25:46; Jn. 5:29; 2 Thess. 1:7–10; Heb. 9:27–28).

On the matter of the state of the dead between death and resurrection, there is more reticence in the NT. From the point of view of those remaining on earth, it is a sleep (Acts 7:60; 1 Thess. 4:13, 15) and a time of "nakedness" in the disembodied state (2 Cor. 5:1–5). It means, nevertheless, being "at home with the Lord" (2 Cor. 5:8), being "with Christ," which is "better by far" and "gain" (Phil. 1:21, 23). In Rev. 6:9–11 there is a vision of the souls of the martyrs "under the altar," who ask how long it will be before their blood will be avenged. They are given a white robe and told to rest until the full number of their brethren is complete. (Cf. S. D. F. Salmond, *The Christian Doctrine of Immortality* [1901]; W. Strawson, *Jesus and the Future Life* [1959].)

Many have seen further revelation regarding the intermediate state in Jesus' parable of the rich man and Lazarus (Lk. 16:19–31; see LAZARUS AND DIVES). Most scholars, however, point out that the terms and ideas are all familiar Jewish ones and that "it is no purpose of the parable to give information about the unseen world" (A. Plummer, *A Critical and Exegetical Commentary on the Gospel according to Luke*, ICC, 5th ed. [1922], 393). The purpose seems to be that of showing the reversal of status in the messianic age, and the impossibility of altering that status once death has intervened. However, it might still be argued that the parable does teach the general truth that at death people have a foretaste (good or ill) of the state which will be eternally theirs at the Last Judgment.

Also relevant to the discussion are several other passages (Lk. 23:43; Acts 2:27–28; Eph. 4:8; 1 Pet. 3:18–20; 4:6). These have led some to believe that between his death and resurrection, the Lord visited paradise (the upper half of Sheol) and removed it and its inhabitants—the OT saints—into the presence of God. Some indeed have felt that the last two references justify saying that he went to hell and gave a second chance to certain lost souls by preaching the gospel to them. However, this has not been the position of historic Christianity, and the reader is referred to a detailed discussion in the commentaries on the passages. See also DESCENT INTO HADES. R. E. DAVIES

Dead Sea. An intensely saline lake occupying the southern end of the JORDAN Valley, called in Scripture the Salt Sea (Gen. 14:3; Num. 34:3, 12; Deut. 3:17; Josh. 3:16; 15:2, 5; 18:19), the Sea of the Arabah (Deut. 3:17; 4:49; Josh. 3:16; 2 Ki. 14:25), and "the eastern sea" (Ezek. 47:18; Joel 2:20). Other names include Bahr Lut (Arab. for "the Sea of Lot"), Lake Asphaltites (Jos. *Ant.* 1.9.1), and the Sea of Sodom (*b. Baba Batra* 74b).

The Dead Sea is a remarkable geographical feature and a pivot point of history. See PALESTINE. Filling a segment of the great Afro-Asian Rift

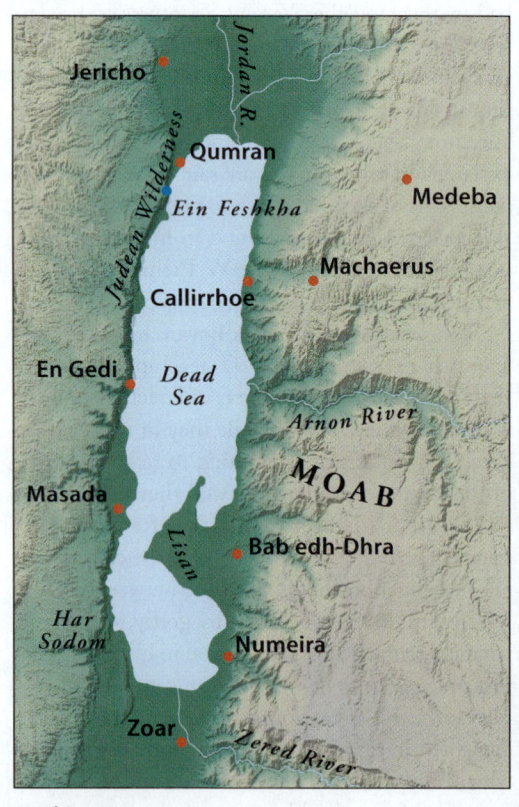

Dead Sea.

Looking E across the Dead Sea towards the mountains of Moab (modern Kingdom of Jordan).

Zone and the deepest of continental depressions, with a shoreline 1,300 ft. below the Mediterranean surface and a floor plunging 1,300 ft. deeper, it forms a sheet of greenish water extending almost 50 mi. from the muddy salt flats of the Jordan delta in the N to the scrubby marshland of the Sebkha in the S. Constricted by the mountain walls of Judea and Jordan, it is scarcely 11 mi. across at its broadest and narrows to 2 mi. where the Lisan or "Tongue" Peninsula divides the 294 sq. mi. of the deep northern basin from the 99 sq. mi. of the shallow southern basin. Yet this harsh lifeless sea is notable for its geological structure, its hydrology, its natural resources, and its role in biblical history.

I. Origin and structure. If the geological signs have been read right, the Dead Sea was initially formed when a Miocene "earth storm" trapped the fringe of the ancient Mediterranean (or "Tethys") between the walls of the subsiding Rift, and when the inland sea that once extended from the slopes of HERMON to the central ARABAH subsequently shrank into the residual water bodies of Huleh, Galilee, and the Salt Sea. The earth storm left its legacy of abrupt walls, plunging strata, and crustal weakness. Tethys left its deposits as the thick strata of hard limestone and soft chalk that form the Judean hills and cap the continental crystallines and "Nubian sandstones" of TRANSJORDAN, while the trace of fluctuating shorelines is left in elevated terrace and crumbling deposit. This is a gross oversimplification, for the pattern was complicated and modified by cross currents of crustal movement and climatic change—particularly the alternation of pluvial and arid phases that correlated with the advance and retreat of the European ice sheets.

During the three major pluvial periods the Dead Sea expanded to form terraces high in the walls of the Rift, while a simultaneous acceleration of erosion creased the valley slopes with WADIS and spread thick deposits across the valley floor— masses of gravel that choked the wadi exits, beds of rock salt and gypsum, shale and clay, sand and soft chalk, along with the ash gray or yellowish marls that form the Lisan peninsula and bleach the terrace lands of the Jordan. Subsequently exposed and eroded during arid phases, such marls crumbled into the intricate chaos of corrugated "badlands" that flank the GHOR, and the Jordan carved the jungled trench of the Zor. Crustal deformations depressed and tilted the northern basin of the Dead Sea, perhaps simultaneously upthrusting the mass of rock salt and gypsum that forms Mount Sodom (Jebel Usdum). The subsequent breaching of the Sodom-Lisan ridge and the flooding of the southern basin may well be events of historic times, hypothetically burying the Valley of SIDDIM with its ruined cities (cf. Gen. 14:3).

SODOM and GOMORRAH apart, instability is a recurrent feature of this structural "shatter belt." Intermittent earthquakes, submerged trees, a Roman road traced to the vanished Lisan crossing, the fording of this now deeper sill as late as 1846—all manifest the continuance of ancient crustal weakness. The faulting was complicated. Apart from the primary faults that shaped the Ghor, the downward pull of subsidence tilted the flanking strata into plunging monoclines, while diagonal "hinge faults" splintered the adjacent scarps to form the Plain of Moab and create zones of weakness subsequently deepened into the sawcut river gorges of the Moab scarp.

II. Springs and seepages. Crustal weakness also released a variety of subsurface materials. The rock salt of Mount Sodom, pressured and plastic, apparently exuded through broken cap rock, while springs—hot and cold, fresh and mineral—issued forth. Patches of greenery mark the sites of freshwater springs such as those of ZOAR and EN GEDI, while hot and sulphurous waters like those of Zerka Ma'in long have been accounted therapeutic. Submarine sources send salt water as well as fresh welling into the sea floor, contributing, moreover, such minerals as bromide and sulphur that exclude all but a modicum of bacterial life, and impart the distinctively bitter taste and nauseous smell of Dead Sea water. Exhalations of gas and seepages of petroleum and especially bitumen occur, the latter impregnating chalk and limestone to furnish trader and artisan with coal-like "Dead Sea stone" and welling to the sea's surface particularly after earthquakes; the "tar pits" (Gen. 14:10) may well have been bitumen seeps. In all likelihood—since volcanic eruption is geologically improbable—it was an earthquake accompanied by the explosive ejection of gas, bitumen, and rock salt that wrought destruction to Sodom and Gomorrah.

III. The salty sea. While the sea derives something of its saltiness from surface or subterranean springs along with sporadic runnels from Sodom rock salt, some salinity is added from the soils of the arid watershed. The four permanent streams that drain the rainier uplands of Moab—the 'Udhemi, Zerqa, Arnon, and Zered—along with countless intermittent wadis, all carry their quota of salts, while the Jordan, which supplies about 6,500,000 of the 7,000,000 tons of daily inflow, has a high content of sodium and magnesium chloride.

Nevertheless the salt sea would be fresh or only mildly saline had it an outlet: but the landlocked basin in a hot and arid climate forms a superb evaporating pan. The desert climate, accentuated by the rain shadow of the Judean uplands and the hot, gusty winds that pour downslope to the Ghor, is here intense. Scarcely four erratic inches of unreliable precipitation fall annually at the N end, while the S has less than two. Dry heat accelerates evaporation. Relative humidity is only 57%, average annual temperatures (though reduced by the inclusion of moderate winters and the marked nocturnal cooling of the desert) reach 77° in places, with individual days soaring to 124° in the almost nonexistent shade—to say nothing of fiercer heat in the glaring sunlight. True enough, occasional winds from the moderate N and regular onshore breezes generated particularly by the northern basin may temper the heat, but they also increase the evaporation. Though this is reduced by high barometric pressure and its own concomitants of light surface mists and high salinity, evaporation remains intense enough to balance the daily inflow of 7,000,000 tons and maintain a fairly constant level. There are seasonal and long term oscillations, of course, which render the 1963 mean of "1,308 ft. below" somewhat theoretical: winter levels seasonally rise some 10–15 ft. above those of summer, while cycles of relative wetness or drought in the Jordan catchment area—along with more hypothetical crustal deformations—may produce cumulative changes. The rising trend of recent centuries gave way to sinking shorelines after 1929, and measurements since 1900 record a rise of 37 ft. and a fall of 16 ft. Walled in to E and W, the shoreline perforce expands or contracts at its shelving ends, sometimes inundating the Sebkha for several miles.

IV. Mineral extraction. The work of extracting minerals is concentrated at these shallow ends. The western shore has long yielded "Dead Sea stone," and salt has been collected for distant markets and temple sacrifice from Sodom and the SW Lisan. Arabs and Romans inherited an ancient trade, and the MEDEBA mosaic depicts the passage of a salt-laden Byzantine vessel. Massive extraction awaited the rising demand for chemicals—especially fertilizers—and in the Mandate period the Dead Sea became a treasure trove. Apart from such crystallized minerals as gypsum (calcium sulphate) and common salt (sodium chloride), which veneer the lake floor, the water—surpassed only by Turkey's Lake Van—sustains a 25% concentration of mineral salts, rising to 30% in the shallow southern basin and to 33% at depth. The individual elements chlorine, potassium, and sodium are dominant (67%, 16%, and 10% respectively), while bromine, potassium, calcium, and sulphur are present in the small but essential amounts critical for combination into the immense tonnages of salts that saturate the sea—22,000,000,000 tons of magnesium chloride, 11,000,000,000 tons of common salt, 6,000,000,000 tons of calcium chloride, 2,000,000,000 tons of potassium chloride, 980,000,000 tons of magnesium bromide, and 200,000,000 tons of gypsum. Furthermore, the mass of Jebel Usdum preserves a vast residue of rock salt from a larger sea.

Initiated by the Palestine Potash Company at Kallia in 1929, extraction was expanded in 1934 to the subsidiary but ampler site of Sodom, now the focus of production. With the wreckage of Kallia behind the Jordanian lines, and with the Beersheba road completed in 1952, the present pattern took shape. A bromide factory built in 1955 has been merged with a revived and expanded "Dead Sea Works," rock salt quarried from Sodom, and a complex of evaporating pans extended around and into the water. The brine, conducted into pans, deposits common salt before evaporating to leave the carnallite which yields first potash and then bromine. With potash production multiplied four-fold between 1960 and 1965 and doubling again to 1,000,000 tons by 1971, with the addition of table salt refining, with natural gas delivered from the newly-discovered Arad field and with bromine-bottling established at Beersheba, a distinctive industrial complex has emerged.

V. Agricultural resources. By contrast, AGRICULTURE is uninviting. Even the BEDOUIN flocks find little sustenance in scanty grass and thorny scrub, which occasionally thickens into a scatter of acacia, and in ancient times, when irrigation agriculture was patchily intensive at wadi mouths, most of the region was apparently used only intermittently from peripheral upland settlements. Even the tangle of reed and tamarisk typical of wetter patches may cover soils of repellent saltiness, and "Dead Sea fruit" (*Calotropis procera*) is an appropriate metaphor—a ball of threads and air. Nevertheless, islands of greenery, often dominated by *spina Christi*, occur around fresh water springs, which (skillfully utilized) can sustain a varied range of crops and livestock.

A series of actual or potential settlement sites are aligned along the Dead Sea shores. Little significant development has characterized the eastern side, for (despite the ampler streams of Moab) cliffs crowd the shoreline to eliminate route ways, and the gorges that cleave the sandstone cliffs offer little in the way of level and cultivable land. Settlement, however, could lodge at the N end where the well-watered Plain of Moab gave Israel a base (Num. 22:1), at Callirrhoe (prob. ZERETH SHAHAR), and particularly in the fertile depression extending from the backslope of the Lisan Peninsula to the delta of the Wadi el-Ḥesa or ZERED. Though this oasis belt has a considerable potential for intensive and varied production, it lacks the essential stimuli of access to markets and cultural or historical conditioning: despite some cropping and grazing, it remains only patchily developed. However, the descent of five streams from the adjacent escarpment has suggested one hypothetical location for the five CITIES OF THE PLAIN.

The western shore, by contrast, is better developed: water supplies may be meager, but the mountains shelve less brusquely to the lake, and ancient route ways could not only thread the beach but also penetrate the Judean uplands from the three oases of ʿAin Feshka (near QUMRAN), En Gedi, and JERICHO. Jericho lay 8 mi. to the N, but springs such as ʿAin Feshka, ʿAin el-Ghuweir, ʿAin el-Turaba, and especially the splendid oasis of En Gedi enabled settlement to lodge along the shoreline. Three elevated springs sent water cascading from the cliffs to the sea, sustaining the irrigation settlement of HAZAZON TAMAR (En Gedi) in Abraham's day (Gen. 14:7; 2 Chr. 20:2): gracious with vineyards and gardens in Solomon's time (Cant. 1:14), it now nourishes a kibbutz, rich with tropical oasis crops.

VI. Historical role. Typically enough, En Gedi's backdrop is a barren chaos of crags and wadis that gave refuge before ever the fugitive David sought its fastnesses (1 Sam. 23:29), a barrenness reinforcing the general impression of lifeless shores around a lifeless sea. In Scripture the region is characteristically a scene of judgment or of battle. KEDORLAOMER overwhelmed the Palestinian kings and swept LOT into brief captivity (Gen. 14:12), and somewhere hereabouts—perhaps beneath the southern embayment—lay the cities whose destruction reverberated through history and prophecy. The eastern escarpment, seamed by the canyons of the ARNON and the ZERED, recalls the thrust and counterthrust of EDOM, MOAB, and Israel, as do the heights behind En Gedi (2 Chr. 20:2). The Moab rim gave Moses a glimpse of the Promised Land across the Rift, while the plains of Moab and Jericho witnessed the passage of the invader. The hot springs of Callirrhoe gave momentary relief to the dying HEROD, while among the opposing cliffs of Judea, the Qumran community meditated and wrote (see DEAD SEA SCROLLS). The fortress of MACHAERUS, traditional site of John's beheading, crested the eastern scarp, while the western shores were dominated by the outthrust mesa of MASADA, grimly reminiscent of the ZEALOTS' last stand as the temple lay in ruins. But, in a vision of messianic healing, the role of the Dead Sea changes. The harsh wadi of the Kidron fills with the fresh waters of healing that flow from the temple to the Sea, and though the marshes still yield their salt, the once lifeless waters now swarm with shoals of fish (Ezek. 47:9–10).

(See further W. F. Lynch, *Official Report of the United States Expedition to the Dead Sea* [1849]; G. A. Smith, *Historical Geography of the Holy Land* [1931]; F. M. Abel, *Géographie de la Palestine*, 2 vols. [1933–1938]; E. Orni and E. Efrat, *Geography of Israel* [1966]; Y. Aharoni, *The Land of the Bible: A Historical Geography*, rev. ed. [1979]; D. Baly, *Basic Biblical Geography* [1987]; *The Dead Sea: The Lake and Its Setting*, ed. T. M. Niemi et al. [1997].)

G. R. LEWTHWAITE

Dead Sea Scrolls. The popular name given to a collection of manuscripts belonging originally to an ancient religious community living near the DEAD SEA at QUMRAN. In the larger sense the designation Dead Sea Scrolls refers to all of the MSS found in numerous unrelated sites in the Judean desert in the area immediately surrounding the Dead Sea.

I. Early discoveries
II. Further explorations
III. Dating the scrolls
IV. Contents of manuscripts
V. The Qumran settlement
VI. The Qumran community
   A. Origins
   B. Community life
   C. Relation to Essenes
   D. Qumran and Christianity
VII. The scrolls and the Bible

I. Early discoveries. The exact date when the first MSS were found is uncertain, but is thought to have been early in 1947. A BEDOUIN goatherd searching for lost animals entered one of the caves in the limestone cliffs N of Wadi Qumran, a mile or so W of the NW corner of the Dead Sea and a little over 8 mi. S of JERICHO. There he stumbled upon several jars somewhat over 2 ft. in height and almost 10 in. wide, containing leather scrolls wrapped in linen cloth. These first scrolls, numbering seven in all, were removed from the cave in two lots. The first was smuggled to a BETHLEHEM cobbler and occasional antiquities dealer who subsequently sold them to the archbishop of the St. Mark's Syrian Orthodox Monastery in Jerusalem. The second lot was sold to another antiquities dealer along with jars from the cave and by December 1947 had made their way into the hands of the late E. L. Sukenik, a professor at the Hebrew University in Jerusalem. The lot held by the Syrians—who had become aware of the value of the scrolls—was not sold until July 1954 and was then reunited with the second lot.

Several scholars examined the scrolls during 1947, some of whom discredited the MSS as forgeries. But this original error was quickly rectified: Sukenik recognized the antiquity of the second lot of scrolls, and the first lot was taken by the Syrians to the American Schools of Oriental Research, where the acting director, J. C. Trever, realized their value and promptly photographed them, sending some prints to W. F. Albright, the eminent biblical archaeologist. The opinion of the latter that the scrolls represented the most important archaeological discovery ever made for the study of Christianity and Judaism has been amply confirmed by subsequent research.

By the time the value of the scrolls had become apparent, the Arab-Israeli war of 1948 made it impossible for the original cave (Cave 1) to be located and explored scientifically. However, this work was accomplished in 1949 by O. L. Harding of the Jordanian Department of Antiquities and R. de Vaux of the École Biblique in Jerusalem, who recovered several hundred fragments of biblical, nonbiblical, and apocryphal writings, many of which were unknown previously. The cave had served as a repository of a library comprising perhaps as many as 200 scrolls, although fragments of only 72 survived. This or another MS cave may have been discovered on an earlier occasion if a report of EUSEBIUS is correct that ORIGEN (c. A.D. 185–254) had employed a Greek translation of the Psalms recovered from a cave near Jericho. This may also have been the same library as the "little house of books" that a shepherd found near Jericho about A.D. 800, a discovery subsequently reported to the Nestorian Patriarch Timothy I.

The scrolls acquired by E. L. Sukenik included a fragmentary scroll of Isaiah (1QIsa[b]), the *War Scroll* (1QM), and a scroll containing a collection of *Thanksgiving Hymns* or *Hodayot* (1QH[a]). Following two preliminary publications in 1948 and 1949, the entire group was published posthumously in 1954 under the title, *The Collection of the Hidden Scrolls Which Are in the Possession of the Hebrew University*. The fragments recovered from the Qumran Cave 1 were published in 1955 by D. Barthélemy and J. T. Milik in the first volume of the series *Discoveries in the Judaean Desert* (Oxford University Press), which would eventually number almost 40 volumes.

M. Burrows, J. C. Trever, and W. H. Brownlee published the first lot of scrolls in two volumes in 1950 and 1951. These included a complete scroll of the book of Isaiah (1QIsa[a]), a commentary on the book of Habakkuk (1QpHab), and a document which Burrows styled the *Manual of Discipline* (1QS), because it contained the rules for community life at Qumran. One scroll, at first believed to be an apocalypse of Lamech, could not be opened at the time, and it was only in 1956 that the MS was unrolled and found to comprise an Aramaic paraphrase of early chapters of the book of Genesis; the document is now known as the *Genesis Apocryphon* (1QapGen).

In 1955 it was announced that the MSS originally in possession of the Syrian monastery had been acquired by the State of Israel. The two original lots from Cave 1 are now housed with other ancient documents in a museum known as the "Shrine of the Book" in Jerusalem.

The Dead Sea Scrolls were discovered in caves near Khirbet Qumran (excavated area left of the modern building). The site, close to the NW edge of the Dead Sea, lies by a ravine that leads to Wadi Qumran. (View to the W.)

II. Further explorations. Toward the end of 1951 some new MS fragments were found by bedouins in two caves of Wadi Murabbaʿat, about 11 mi. S of Cave 1 and 2 mi. W of the Dead Sea. Clandestine investigators anticipated the official excavation of the caves in 1952 and recovered several biblical MSS of the Masoretic textual variety, including a scroll of the Minor Prophets, potsherds inscribed in Greek and Hebrew, two Greek literary papyri in fragmentary condition, coins from the Second Jewish Revolt (A.D. 132–135; see WARS, JEWISH) that dated the occupational level accurately in the Roman period, and other less significant artifacts. Important sources for study of the Second Jewish Revolt against Rome were some papyrus letters in Hebrew, two of which were signed by rebel leader Simon BAR KOKHBA or his amanuensis and addressed to a certain Joshua ben Oalgola, apparently the commander of the military outpost at the Wadi Murabbaʿat. Caves in cliffs above Naḥal Ḥever, excavated in 1960, produced MSS from the same period.

Another important MS discovery was made in 1952 in the ruins of a monastery about 8 mi. NE of

Qumran Cave 1, where the first of the Dead Sea Scrolls were discovered.

Bethlehem at a site known as Khirbet Mird. These documents were later in date than those recovered from other sites, being assigned to a period between the 5th and 9th centuries A.D. The biblical MSS were of Christian rather than Jewish origin, written in both Greek and Syriac. The literary material from the Wadi Murabbaʿat, Naḥal Ḥever, and Khirbet Mird, though interesting and important archaeologically, is not directly related to the scrolls and fragments from Qumran.

From 1952, serious attempts were made to locate and explore other caves in the rugged terrain near the Wadi Qumran, the result of which has been that eleven caves were eventually discovered in the vicinity, yielding a varied assortment of MSS, fragments, pottery, and the like. The second Qumran cave (Cave 2), discovered in 1952, had already been looted by Taʿamireh bedouin tribesmen before the official archaeologists arrived, and only a few tiny fragments of MSS were found at the site. Cave 3, located about one mile north of Cave 1, contained the remains of 14 fragmentary Aramaic and Hebrew MSS written on parchment (animal skin) as well as a 12-column scroll embossed on copper. The latter had become oxidized and great technical difficulties confronted those attempting to unroll it. When finally opened and translated, the scroll was found to contain information relating to the locations of treasure hoards. The treasure has not been located and researchers still debate whether the scroll is the evidence of an ancient hoax or perhaps a detailed plan to hide the temple treasury that eventually fell into the hands of the Romans (A.D. 70). See further section IV, below.

Cave 4 proved to be the "mother lode." Located just W of Khirbet Qumran, it was discovered in 1952 and contained the remains of nearly 600 fragmentary MSS, including nearly all the biblical books (except, apparently, Esther), many familiar and unknown apocryphal writings, commentaries, liturgical texts, and other literary works. Caves 5–10, in the vicinity of Qumran, yielded less significant material, but Cave 11, discovered in 1956, contained four relatively complete scrolls as well as the fragmentary remains of another 27 MSS.

In addition to the early scroll publications by Burrows, Trevor, and Brownlee (1950), and the posthumous publication of Sukenik (1954), scholars have produced at the time of writing nearly fifty large volumes of scroll publications. Only two volumes of Cave 4 scrolls are still forthcoming; the first comprises the three Samuel MSS and the second some 34 fragmentary Aramaic texts (4Q550–4Q582). Most of the MSS and fragments from Caves 2–11 are preserved in the Rockefeller Museum (also known as the Palestine Archaeological Museum) in East Jerusalem.

III. Dating the scrolls. When reports were circulated concerning the antiquity of the scrolls and the early date assigned to those in the possession of Sukenik, many scholars were frankly incredulous, and almost immediately an acrimonious debate arose on the matter. Unfortunately it was conducted for the most part by those who knew of the discoveries only at second hand and who were unaware of corroborating archaeological evidence. Sukenik had assigned a date not later than A.D. 70 for the scrolls he had studied, and if this was correct it meant that the textual evidence for the Hebrew OT had been advanced by at least a millennium. They would thus be by far the oldest surviving Hebrew MSS, and of priceless value for the textual critic.

Many were aware that literary hoaxes had been foisted previously on unsuspecting biblical scholars, particularly in the 19th century. When it was announced that the original cave (Cave 1) had been rediscovered and excavated officially, the whole matter appeared in very different perspective. The problem of dating is basically fourfold in nature, involving (1) the date of composition of the literary works; (2) the date of the scrolls themselves, determined by paleography (handwriting analysis) and radiocarbon testing (carbon 14); (3) the date—again determined by radiocarbon testing—to be assigned to the linen in which some scrolls were wrapped; and finally, (4) the actual time the jars were deposited in the caves.

It is almost impossible to answer the first question satisfactorily with respect to most of the biblical material, with the exception of the *pesharim* or "commentaries" (see PESHER). For example, in the case of the book of Isaiah, the most complete of the extant MSS is 1QIsa^a: this scroll is assigned a paleographic date of 125 to 100 B.C. and a radiocarbon date of 201 to 93 B.C., and is at the most some 600 years subsequent to the draft form entrusted by Isaiah to his disciples (Isa. 8:16). The oldest of all the biblical MSS appears to be a scroll containing the texts of Exodus and Leviticus (4QExod-Lev^f or 4Q17), dated paleographically to the mid-3rd cent. B.C. The youngest MSS, such as 4QPs^f (4Q88), are from the middle of the 1st cent. A.D. The Habakkuk Commentary presents a twofold problem, since the commentary is obviously later in date than the book itself. If the commentary portion of 1QpHab is to be dated to the 1st cent. B.C., this then becomes the earliest external evidence for the text of the canonical book. The date of the pesher depends partly on the identification of the militant KITTIM, with which the sect was concerned, and which have been identified variously with the Seleucid forces of ANTIOCHUS IV Epiphanes (175–164 B.C.), the military might of Alexander Jannaeus (103–76 B.C.; see HASMONEAN II.C), or most commonly, the occupation forces of the Roman period in Palestine, from 63 B.C.

The date of composition of 1QS, 1QH^a, and 1QM has encountered as wide a range of scholarly opinion as that of the biblical documents. To what extent the contents of 1QH^a had been in circulation before the Christian era is hard to say, but it seems evident that the document discovered in Cave 1 was a copy of an earlier MS and not the original autograph. The Qumran scrolls, whether copies or originals, came from a general historical period beginning about 250 B.C. and ending with the abandonment of the Qumran site in A.D. 68. Burrows dated the MSS of 1QS to about 100 B.C., while assigning 1QM and 1QH^a along with the *Genesis Apocryphon* to the first quarter of the 1st cent. B.C. He has also maintained that 1QpHab was written during the last quarter of the 1st cent. B.C., and these estimates, based primarily upon paleographic evidence, have been shown to be remarkably accurate when correlated with subsequent archaeological discoveries and radiocarbon testing.

The potsherds excavated from Cave 1 belonged variously either to the Hellenistic period and were dated from the 1st cent. B.C., or to the Roman period of about the 3rd cent. A.D. The pieces of cloth removed from Cave 1 proved to be linen of local manufacture and were dated through radiocarbon testing. This procedure is based on the fact that every living organism contains a proportion of radioactive carbon 14, which is unstable and begins to degenerate when the animal or plant dies. The half life of a radioactive carbon atom is 5,500 years, and computation of the age of organic material can be achieved by reducing it to carbon through burning, and then measuring the carbon 14 residue by means of a highly sensitive radiation counter (there is naturally a small margin of error). W. F. Libby of Chicago, who had pioneered this method of dating, tested the flax from Qumran and announced that it had ceased to absorb carbon 14 in A.D. 33, with a plus or minus margin of 200 years, furnishing a complete range of from 168 B.C. to A.D. 233. Subsequent improvements in radiocarbon testing (Accelerator Mass Spectrometry), which have permitted the testing of minute amounts of material, eventually allowed even the scrolls themselves to be examined. Two separate tests conducted on more than 20 MSS at Zurich (1991) and Tuscon (1994–95) provided dates ranging from as early as 385 B.C to as late as 131 A.D., with most grouped around the last two centuries B.C. and the 1st cent. A.D. The median date thus obtained confirmed the antiquity of the scrolls, and needed only to be corroborated by archaeological discoveries at Khirbet Qumran.

The actual time when the jars and their contents were placed in the caves of Qumran for safety is not easy to establish. R. de Vaux maintained that the caves had formed an emergency storage place for the literature of the sectaries, and if this is so the jars could have been deposited on several occasions during the troubled period in which the Qumran sectaries lived. On paleographic grounds, it seems clear that all copies of the scrolls in Cave 1 had been made by the mid-1st cent. A.D. at the latest and thus it is most probable that the MSS were hidden just before community life at Qumran ended in A.D. 68 at the hand of the Roman army.

IV. Contents of manuscripts. The contents of the major scrolls can now be surveyed briefly, beginning with the large Isaiah MS (1QIsa^a). In surprisingly good condition, it comprises 54 columns of clear Hebrew script written on 17 sheets of leather stitched end to end. It measures 24 ft. in length and is about a foot wide. The text averages 29 lines to each column and is set out in clearly marked paragraphs and sections. Despite considerable handling in antiquity, there are only ten lacunae in the MS and about a dozen small holes, making restoration of the text comparatively easy. The activity of two different hands in the MS was proposed by Sukenik, and scribal errors had been corrected in numerous ways. Certain curious marginal symbols are present in the MS and may have served to divide up the prophecy for liturgical reading. The fairly numerous transcriptional errors in 1QIsa^a could have arisen from the MS being dictated, but aside from these the scroll lends impressive support to the Masoretic textual tradition. The orthography of 1QIsa^a exhibits certain phonetic characteristics that are less prominent in the MT; these comprise in part a contemporary phonetic spelling designed to facilitate reading without changing the traditional pronunciation. This particular deviation is valuable in enabling scholars to know the way in which Hebrew was enunciated just before the Christian era, and in showing that Hebrew persisted as a living language after the 2nd cent. B.C.

The more fragmentary Isaiah scroll from Cave 1 (1QIsa^b) ranges from Isa. 7:22 to 66:24, totaling about 20% of the overall contents of the book; most of the script could be deciphered only by infrared photography. The textual form of this scroll is even closer than 1QIsa^a to the Masoretic tradition, using older forms of spelling evidently current after the EXILE.

The most clearly written scroll of all is the Habakkuk Commentary (1QpHab), which consists of two parchment strips stitched together and measures 5 ft. by 7 in. As with the other scrolls, the letters are suspended from faintly ruled lines and the text is grouped in columns. Deterioration of the leather resulted in several lines being lost from the bottom of each column. Only the first two chapters of the canonical Habakkuk survive in the scroll, probably because the third, a poem, was unsuited to the exegetical aims of the sect. The commentator cited short sections of Habakkuk and then explained them eschatologically or allegorically in terms of the history of the Qumran community. The scroll writer used an interpretive methodology (now referred to as PESHER method) that focuses not on the historical meaning of the canonical prophecy of Habakkuk as proclaimed before the Babylonian exile, but rather on the fulfillment at the time of the Qumran sect from which the scroll originated. The opposition of a "wicked priest" and the ruthless Kittim were dominant concerns, for these two powers represented the spiritual and temporal opponents of the sectaries. Needless to say, their identification has provoked a good deal of contemporary discussion but very little agreement.

The so-called *Manual of Discipline* (1QS) or *Rule of the Community* was recovered in two separate sections, which when joined form a document about 6 ft. by 9.5 in. The script is remarkably clear and the style of writing is similar to that of the

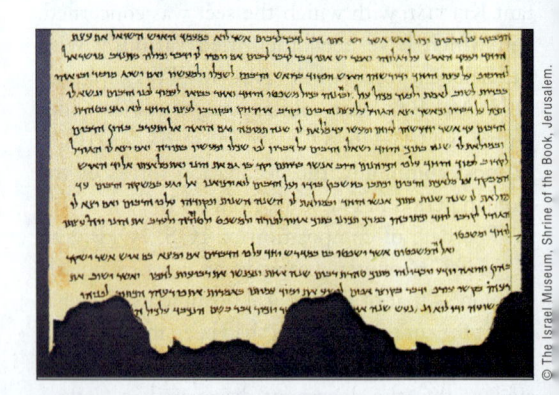

The *Community Rule* (1QS) from Qumran is also referred to as the *Manual of Discipline*. Shown here is the sixth column (out of eleven).

scribe who copied 1QIsa[a]. The text comprises 11 columns with about 26 lines to each column, the precise number determined by overlapping fragments found in Cave 4. This work is by far the most important source of information concerning the religious sect at Qumran. It begins with a statement of requirements from those aspiring to "enter into the covenant," and this is followed by a description of the ceremony of initiation. A section of the text deals with the Qumran doctrine of human nature, and this is followed by a list of community rules occupying five columns, concluding with a devotional psalm.

When Sukenik acquired the *Thanksgiving Hymns*, the material was in four separate portions, one of which was very difficult to unroll. Parts of the collection were badly decayed and needed infrared photography before becoming legible. The original document had comprised perhaps 28 columns of about 12 in. in height with up to 41 lines of script per column. The handwriting reveals the activity of two scribes and the collection of hymns numbers about twenty. They reflect two distinctive types of liturgical writing, namely "thanksgiving" hymns commencing with an act of praise to God ("I give thanks to you, O Lord") and "benedictory" compositions in which a formula of blessing opens the psalm ("Blessed are you, O Lord"). The collection shows many points of contact with Semitic traditions, and in the matter of the personal relationship existing between God and the worshiper they are particularly close to the thought of the Psalter. These poetic writings are probably the most original of the spiritual expressions to emerge from Qumran.

The last of the four scrolls originally acquired by the Syrian Metropolitan defied many attempts at unrolling, but its contents were finally revealed in 1954. The badly deteriorated state of the work suggested prolonged exposure to unfavorable climatic conditions, and reconstruction of the text has been extremely difficult. As already noted, preliminary scrutiny had suggested that the scroll was the long-lost apocryphal "Book of Lamech," but it proved instead to be an Aramaic version of several chapters from Genesis, dealing in paraphrase form and midrashic insertions with the lives of the PATRIARCHS. It was published in 1956 by N. Avigad under the title, *A Genesis Apocryphon* (1QapGen).

The text had been inscribed in a clear hand, but the ink had apparently reacted with the leather to produce holes in the scroll.

The scroll commonly known as the *War Scroll* (1QM) was originally issued by Sukenik under the title, *The War of the Sons of Light with the Sons of Darkness*. It was preserved in good condition, and when unrolled it was 9 ft. in length and almost 7 in. in width. The text had been written on four sheets in 18 columns, with the scant remains of another column from a fifth sheet completing the scroll. It deals in an eschatological manner with the prosecution of a war between Levi, Benjamin, and Judah ("the Sons of Light") on one side, and on the other, the enemies of Israel, including the Greeks, Philistines, Moabites, and Edomites ("the Sons of Darkness"). This forthcoming conflict is introduced by means of a short prologue, followed by a detailed series of directions for the conduct of the battle and several prayers to be uttered at intervals by the Sons of Light. Although more a blend of military

Fragments from a Qumran leather scroll of Exodus written with the older Hebrew script (4QpaleoExod[m] or 4Q22).

D

manual and liturgical handbook than apocalypse, the MS evidences an apocalyptic worldview similar to that of the later Christians and likewise complete with an age-ending ARMAGEDDON.

Three fragments of Daniel recovered from Cave 1 were found to have come from two different scrolls. Two of them are related paleographically to the large Isaiah scroll, while the other is very similar to the script of 1QpHab. Two pieces preserve portions of the same chapter of Daniel, while the third includes the point where the Aramaic section of Daniel begins. The text is in essence that of the Masoretes, and the chief differences have to do, like those of 1QIsa^a, with the spelling of words.

Other fragments from the Qumran area include some 33 MSS found in Cave 2, among which are portions of the Torah, the Psalter, Jeremiah, and Ruth. Half of the fragments are from nonbiblical MSS and were mainly apocalyptic or messianic in nature. From Cave 3, about a mile N of Cave 1, came the remains of 15 MSS. The most significant discovery in this cave is that of the *Copper Scroll*, which had escaped destruction when the cave roof collapsed in antiquity. This one scroll survived in two pieces, and originally the strips had been fastened together to form a sheet of metal about 8 ft. long and a foot wide. The complete oxidization of the metal made unrolling almost impossible, and it was only in 1956 that the copper was specially treated and cut into strips at the Manchester College of Technology. A textual loss of under 5% occurred in the process. The rolls contain a list of about sixty treasure caches, and describe their locations in various parts of ancient Judea, some of which have not been identified. An estimate of the value of the items detailed in the *Copper Scroll* has been placed as high as 26 tons of gold and 65 tons of silver. Such a vast hoard of wealth seems out of character with a sect that had renounced riches and established communal living as two of its most important regulative factors, and an explanation of the situation that is satisfactory to all scholars has not been forthcoming to date. Quite aside from the historical nature of this catalog, the text itself is of importance since it was written not in standard literary Hebrew but in a dialect that was known to scholars only in some Jewish religious treatises of which the MISHNAH (2nd cent. A.D.) was the oldest.

A great many fragments were recovered in 1952 from Cave 4 located near Khirbet Qumran. Over 600 scrolls had been stored there originally, about one-quarter of which were canonical in nature. Fragments of every OT book with the exception of Esther were represented in the cache, along with such apocryphal compositions as TOBIT and ECCLESIASTICUS, and the pseudepigraphic works *1 Enoch, Jubilees,* and the *Testament of Levi*. Most of the compositions were not previously known. To mention but a few: 4QMMT (a Hebrew acronym which translates, "Some of the Works of the Law") is important both for the early history of a significant Jewish text, the Mishnah, as well as background for Paul's discussion of works, law, and grace, which forms the backbone of the NT epistles to the Galatians and Romans. The *Messianic Apocalypse* (4Q521) is a key text for understanding the messianic consciousness of Jesus. The *Aramaic Apocalypse* (4Q246) contains the expression SON OF GOD a full century before the gospel writers used the title to describe Jesus' ministry. In addition, Cave 4 contained MSS that demonstrate a clear relationship to Cave 1, namely, 1QS (4Q255–262), 1QH^a (4Q427–432), and 1QM (4Q491–496).

Cave 5 contained some almost completely decomposed fragments of 25 MSS, including portions of Kings, Lamentations, and Deuteronomy,

Fragment from the *Mishmarot* scroll (4Q321), a calendrical text used in Qumran.

as well as an Aramaic eschatological work entitled *Description of the New Jerusalem*, which was also represented in other caves (1, 2, 4, and 11). Cave 6 contained 31 fragmentary MSS, including small portions of Genesis and Leviticus written in paleo-Hebrew script, sections of Kings, and 5 fragments of Daniel. Nonbiblical books are represented by some apocalyptic writings and a number of Aramaic compositions. Cave 7 is of note because it preserved 19 very fragmentary MSS, all written in Greek. Of the eleven caves at Qumran, Cave 7 is the only site that clearly suggests an organizing principle. This cave is significant also because some have suggested that perhaps as many as 6 of the MSS contain fragmentary remains of the NT (7Q4–10, 7Q15). This proposal has not gained wide acceptance; the fragments are far more likely from other Greek works such as *1 Enoch* (7Q4, 7Q8, and 7Q11–14). Caves 8–10 were found in the marl terrace to the south of Khirbet Qumran and combine for a total of 6 MSS and one ostracon.

The last cave to be found in the region of Qumran was Cave 11, discovered in 1956. It yielded several scrolls in a very good state of preservation, including a MS of Leviticus written in paleo-Hebrew and a Psalms scroll that includes hymns not contained in the traditional Hebrew text (MT), as well as a different order of presentation. Also notable was the recovery from the same cave of an Aramaic TARGUM of Job, which was probably composed in the 1st cent. B.C. The longest of all the nonbiblical scrolls, the *Temple Scroll* (11Q19), recasts legal portions of the Torah in the first person, as spoken by God to Moses (see TEMPLE SCROLL).

The fragments found in the caves of Wadi Murabbaʿat in 1952 comprised 2nd-cent. A.D. documents written in Hebrew, Aramaic, Greek, and later texts written in Latin and Arabic. Of these, probably the most important was a papyrus palimpsest inscribed in an archaic hand that seems to be earlier than the 6th cent. B.C. script of the LACHISH ostraca and was assigned by J. T. Milik to the 8th cent. B.C. It contains a short list of masculine names. Fragments of the Pentateuch, Isaiah, and an extensive Minor Prophets scroll were recovered from Murabbaʿat and exhibit close agreement with the consonantal basis of the MT. These have been dated to the late 1st and early 2nd cent. A.D.

Fragment 33 from the second column of a Qumran document known as *Daily Prayers* (4Q503 or 4QpapPrQuot).

Some additional light was thrown on the latter period with the recovery of a few Hebrew papyri written by Bar Kokhba to his forces positioned in the Wadi Murabbaʿat region. The fact that letters from Bar Kokhba were written in Hebrew is further proof of the fact that this language had survived into the Christian era as a living tongue.

In 1953 Belgian archaeologists found MSS fragments at Khirbet Mird, north of Bethlehem, which included Arabic, Greek, Syriac, and Christo-Palestinian material. The documents recovered, dating from the 7th to 10 centuries A.D., are later than those from either Qumran or Murabbaʿat.

In 1952 a fragmentary Greek text of the Minor Prophets came to light and was eventually determined to have come from a cave above Naḥal Ḥever. Additional fragments of the same scroll were found on site in 1961. It is written on leather in a beautiful uncial hand and contains portions of Micah, Jonah, Nahum, Habakkuk, Zephaniah, and Zechariah. Its age is debated, but editor E. Tov dates it to the latter half of the 1st cent. B.C. This scroll is of great value for the textual critic as it was based on the SEPTUAGINT and then revised using a Hebrew text very close to that of the later MT. Thus the antiquity of the Septuagint form of the Minor Prophets is established, as well as a type of revision that is attested in the later work attributed to Aquila, Theodotion, and Symmachus (2nd cent. A.D.).

Rounding out the important Judean desert discoveries, excavations at MASADA in 1963 uncovered fragments of Genesis, Leviticus, Deuteronomy, Ezekiel, and Psalms. Eight extrabiblical works were found as well, the most important being a large fragment of the *Songs of the Sabbath Sacrifice*, also found in 9 MSS at Qumran, and a 7-column fragment of the apocryphal work known as Ecclesiasticus. The latter is an important MS that dates to the 1st cent. B.C., only a century removed from the book's composition.

V. The Qumran settlement. While the Qumran area was being excavated officially in 1949 for additional MS evidence, the attention of the archaeologists was drawn to some ruins on a rocky plateau about one mile S of Cave 1. After preliminary soundings the excavation of the ruin or *khirbeh* was undertaken thoroughly in 1952, revealing the presence of a large complex of rooms. There was also a system of cisterns joined in antiquity by means of an aqueduct to Wadi Qumran. Of particular significance was the discovery of a number of jars, identical in size and shape with the jars recovered from Cave 1, establishing beyond question a link between the occupants of the ruins (known as Khirbet Qumran) and the MSS from Cave 1. These jars are rare or unattested at other archaeological sites in the area.

Although alternate theories have been proposed, the vast majority of researchers have concluded that a religious community once lived at the site and was responsible for the documents deposited in the nearby caves. On the basis of this association, Sukenik proposed that this community was the ESSENES, a group known from ancient sources (PLINY the Elder, JOSEPHUS) to have practiced a type of JUDAISM reflected in the scrolls and to have inhabited a site S of Jericho on the banks of the Dead Sea. A cemetery found adjoining the *khirbeh* contains mostly male skeletons, a fact that also conforms to the male orientation emphasized by the ancient sources and much of the MS evidence.

Subsequent campaigns at the site have uncovered the entire community complex. On the NW corner of the main structure was a large fortified tower, which had apparently been buttressed following a severe earthquake in 31 B.C. when it was damaged on the E side and on the SE corner. The principal community building was located N of the dining hall and kitchen. To the SW were four or five rooms that may have served as places of study and prayer. One of these, the so-called *scriptorium*, contained the remains of plaster benches which some have theorized were used by scribes as they sat to copy the scrolls. While this interpretation continues to be debated, the discovery of three inkwells—quite rare in Palestinian archaeological sites—makes it clear that writing of some kind took place at the site.

At the SE corner of the complex the excavators unearthed the remains of a workshop containing the tools used by the community members. A pottery kiln was also discovered nearby, indicating that the community was virtually self-supporting. Conduits and cisterns were in considerable evidence in the well-planned community settlement. From the abundance of cisterns and reservoirs it has been supposed that the religious sect placed a good deal of emphasis upon rites involving ceremonial washings. It is also true that the sheer physical needs of a community of perhaps as many as 150 persons would require the provision of ample supplies of water. It is thought that the community derived its principal staple commodities such as grain, vegetables, and meat from ʿAin Feshka, a date palm oasis lying about 2 mi. S. of the *khirbeh*, on the W coast of the Dead Sea.

De Vaux dated the sectarian settlement at Qumran in three periods of occupation which he named

View looking SE across the Qumran excavation and toward the Dead Sea (upper right corner).

Ia (130–100 B.C.), Ib (100–31 B.C.), and II (4 B.C. to A.D. 68). He found evidence that Period Ib ended with an earthquake and fire which initiated a 27-year abandonment of the site. Period II began in 4 B.C., and the presence of ash and arrow heads witnessed to a violent and fiery end at the hands of the Roman army in A.D. 68. Reevaluation of this scheme based on the evidence of the hundreds of coins found at the site has cast doubt on the existence of Period Ia and suggests that the period of abandonment was much shorter (likely in 9/8 B.C. or shortly thereafter; see J. Magness, *The Archaeology of Qumran and the Dead Sea Scrolls* [2002]). Less certain, but possible, is the supposition that the community came to an end not in A.D. 68, along with Jericho to the N, but five years later, at the same time as Masada to the S.

VI. The Qumran community

A. Origins. The general character of the Qumran sect has become evident through the MS discoveries, and particularly from the contents of the *Rule of the Community* (1QS). Although not all problems relating to the nature of this social group have been solved, it is clear that the sect comprised a group of priests and laymen pursuing a communal life of strict dedication to God. The mysteries of prophecy had been revealed to the founder, a priest described as the Righteous Teacher (lit., "Teacher of Righteousness"). An important feature of community life was the interpretation of Scripture in terms of the witness of the sect and reflection on the end of the age: the sect believed that the Righteous Teacher had been sent by God to announce the punishment that was to come upon Israel. According to the Habakkuk Commentary, the Teacher knew even more of the eschatological implications of this than did the prophet himself. Though ostensibly delayed, the end would come, but a remnant would survive. This remnant was the Qumran community, which had pleased God because of its fidelity to the Torah and its trust in the Righteous Teacher.

This general message was rejected flatly by the Wicked Priest and his followers, whose concerns, according to the scrolls, were apparently with matters other than spirituality and proper study of the Torah. This reference to the Wicked Priest was evidently to the office of high priest in Jerusalem, since the incumbent was spoken of as "ruling in Israel" and bearing the "true name." While a broad allusion to the high priesthood was doubtless intended, it seems clear that a specific clash between the Righteous Teacher and the Jerusalem high priesthood had occurred at some point in the early history of the sect, for the Habakkuk *pesher* speaks of the Wicked Priest persecuting the Righteous Teacher intent on doing the latter physical harm. The issue reached a climax on the Day of Atonement, when the Wicked Priest "pursued the Righteous Teacher to destroy him" (1QpHab XI, 5).

However, the persecuting Wicked Priest was himself to be condemned by God (1QpHab XII, 5) and in company with the "last priests of Jerusalem" was to be delivered into the power of the Kittim, the enemies of the last days. The commentary thought in even broader terms of the destruction of the whole nation by these Kittim, valiant and proud agents of divine anger in the last days. In the OT this name was used of the people of CYPRUS (Gen. 10:4; Isa. 23:1, 12; Jer. 2:10; Ezek. 27:6; et al.), and in the APOCRYPHA as a designation of Macedonians (1 Macc. 1:1). In later Jewish authors the name was applied cryptically to any victorious power regardless of the particular epoch, and this tradition may be reflected in 1QM, where the Kittim of Assyria are mentioned. However, the Kittim of 1QpHab can only be Romans, who accord with the description better than any other earlier imperial power. They came from distant maritime places, were under the command of a "guilty house," venerated their weapons of war, and sacrificed to their standards. This latter form of cult worship was apparently common in the 1st cent. B.C., when the Romans regarded the "eagles" as sacred objects and offered worship to them accordingly. Josephus recorded that this custom was still in existence in the 1st cent. A.D., for he described the way in which the Roman legions erected their standards near the east gate of the temple compound and offered sacrifices to them prior to storming the temple in A.D. 70.

If the Kittim can be identified with the Romans, it may be that 1QpHab describes the occupation of Judea under POMPEY in 63 B.C. In that event, the Wicked Priest may have been either Alexander

Jannaeus or Aristobulus II, although assured identification is difficult. Precisely who the Righteous Teacher might have been is even more uncertain. Two fragmentary *pesharim* also mentioned the struggle between the Righteous Teacher and the Wicked Priest. The *pesher* of Psalm 37 describes the divine mission of the Teacher and his task of occupying the Holy City and its Temple. The text of this fragment reports that the Wicked Priest had been sent to kill the Righteous Teacher and to slay "the upright of the way." In portions of a Nahum *pesher* are mentioned a certain Antiochus and also a man named Demetrius, "king of Javan" (Greece), presumably Demetrius III of Damascus who aided the Pharisees against their despotic ruler Alexander Jannaeus (103–76 B.C.). It is possible that the reference in the *pesher* to the Lion of Wrath "hanging up men alive" refers to the revenge of Jannaeus after a victory by Demetrius, but the cryptic use of terms in the *pesharim* makes this less than certain.

Against this background the sect would seem to have been a splinter group within Judaism, likely originating sometime following the reign of Antiochus IV Epiphanes (175–163 B.C.), separating themselves from the normative Judaism of the day under the charismatic leadership of the Righteous Teacher. Archaeological evidence affirms that they took up residence at Qumran only in the late 2nd cent. B.C.

B. Community life. For this topic the *Rule of the Community* is an invaluable guide to the organization of the sect, which comprised a group of priests and laymen following a communal existence in dedication to God. According to 1QS, those desirous of "entering into the covenant" had to comply with certain preliminary procedures, after which they were initiated on a probationary basis, only reaching full membership after three years. Each member was subsequently required to renew his pledge of obedience annually, when he was also reminded of those faults that could result in his expulsion from the brotherhood. The fifth column of 1QS supplies the rules for community government, from which it is evident that the sect was controlled by elders and priests for the purpose of engaging in biblical study and participating in a sacramental type of worship.

The sect clearly regarded itself as God's chosen, awaiting the establishment of divine rule on earth. The expectation of the apocalyptic Last Days loomed large in the thought of the community. The sectaries were required to follow their pattern of living according to the Torah until the coming of a prophet and two messianic figures styled "the anointed ones of Aaron and Israel," that is, a priestly and a royal messiah.

The *Rule of the Congregation* (1QSa), an appendix to 1QS, contains perhaps the clearest depiction of this bifurcated messianic hope. This document is the fulfillment of the expectations surrounding daily community meal which are detailed in *The Rule of the Community* (1QS). The members are assembled in order of seniority, and the presiding messianic priest is charged with blessing the bread and wine. Then the royal messiah arrives, takes his place at the table, and adds his blessing to the elements of the meal. This banquet was clearly apocalyptic in nature, yet at the same time had definite sacramental qualities. The ritual could be followed at any time ten community members reclined to dine; the sense of expectation of the events ushering in the divine kingdom is a prominent feature of the ceremony. For the sectaries, the kingdom would emerge after the Kittim of various countries had been conquered and Israel had emerged triumphant.

Ritual lustrations occupied a large place in the practices of the sect, and adequate amounts of water were provided for these purposes. The spiritual implications of such rites are stressed, making it clear that true repentance and submission to God alone determined whether or not a person was cleansed as a result of these ceremonies.

The Torah was studied day and night at Qumran, and sacred festivals were strictly observed. Theologically, the covenanters are believed to have held to a dualistic view of the universe in which the spirits of light and darkness, God and BELIAL, were placed in ethical opposition (see DUALISM). The struggle between them would be resolved only on the Day of Judgment, a theme elaborated in 1QM in the description of the ultimate victory of God in an apocalyptic battle between the offspring of light and darkness and for which the sect had to prepare. Despite their tendency toward dualism, the members stressed truth, justice, humility, and devotion, seeking by their disciplined life to acquire such virtues.

C. Relation to Essenes. Although in the first fifty years of scroll research nearly every Jewish group of antiquity was suggested as a solution to the lack of self-identification in the writings, the relation to ancient descriptions of the ancient Essenes has continued to be the most economical of the proposals. This determination has taken on a particular sense of certainty among scholars who have committed themselves to Qumran studies. The location of the group on the Dead Sea, the staged initiation procedure, ascetic lifestyle, conservative theological tenets, and strict adherence to a unique form of Judaism in the interpretation of biblical law all serve to underline this identification. (For a different viewpoint, see Y. Hirschfeld, *Qumran in Context: Reassessing the Archaeological Evidence* [2004].)

D. Qumran and Christianity. Some scholars have attempted to see in the Qumran community a distinct anticipation of Christianity, the most important areas being that of the Righteous Teacher as messianic figure and the organizational and quasi-sacramental practice of the group. Most scholars today agree, however, that the sectaries did not regard their founder as the Messiah, and their commitment to a strict adherence to biblical law has few parallels with early Christianity.

Suggestions that JOHN THE BAPTIST and Jesus may have received some training at the settlement are defensible only in the case of the former. John was of a priestly lineage, ministered in an area close to the Qumran site, and preached repentance of sins leading to baptism. John's ministry was characterized by Isa. 40:3, "A voice of one calling in the desert, / 'Prepare the way for the Lord ... '" (Matt. 3:3 and parallels). This ministry was also echoed as the mission of the Qumran community, although they likely punctuated the passage in the manner suggested by the Hebrew parallelism: "A voice of one calling: / 'In the desert prepare the way for the LORD; / make straight in the wilderness / a highway for our God.'"

There are, however, significant points of contact which clearly show that the messianic expectations surrounding Jesus and the Gospels' description of the world in which he lived give a historically accurate picture of the 1st cent. A.D. The scrolls evidence expectations for a messiah who would be called "Son of David," "Branch of David," "Son of God," and "firstborn." And significantly, the messianic mission was to be evidenced by healing the sick, raising the dead, and preaching good news to the afflicted. However, as confirmed by the expectations of the disciples, the world of the Dead Sea Scrolls hoped for a victorious military savior who would save them from the power of their enemies rather than dying at their hands. The latter development, evidenced in the Christian interpretation of such biblical passages as Isa. 53 and Ps. 22, are, despite occasional claims, not a part of the Dead Sea Scrolls messianic complex.

Although the apostle PAUL would have found much in Qumran theology to commend, he would not have agreed with their view of the importance of what might be termed "Jewish identity markers." In the NT epistles to the churches in Rome and Galatia he incorporated the expression "works of the law," which would include such issues as CIRCUMCISION and SABBATH observance (to what extent the phrase had broader application for him is a matter of scholarly debate). For Paul, a person did not come into closer fellowship with God through "works of the law," but rather by FAITH. In the Qumran text known as 4QMMT (a Hebrew acronym for "Some of the Works of the Law") the argument is the reverse: closer fellowship comes by "works of the law." Two important factors are to be noted: first, this is the only extant instance of the phrase "works of the law" in antiquity apart from Romans and Galatians; second, 4QMMT appears to evidence a theology very similar to that held by the group whom Paul calls "false brothers" (Gal. 2:4).

A date of A.D. 68 or 73 for the destruction of the Qumran site and the attendant deposition of the Qumran MSS allows for the prospect of NT materials in the library. A small but vocal group of scholars has been suggesting just such a possibility for a handful of Greek fragments found in Cave 7. If true, this would demonstrate that the Qumran community had direct contact with early Christians, or that Christians placed documents in the Qumran caves after the community had dispersed. If the former is accurate, well-established theories regarding the dating of the formation of the NT would also have to be reconsidered. However, the vast majority of scholars are convinced that the fragments in question—the largest of which measures only 2.75 x 1.25 in.—represent portions of a ms of *1 Enoch*.

VII. The scrolls and the Bible. While the Qumran discoveries are extremely valuable for the development of intertestamental Judaism and for biblical studies generally, they are particularly important for the text of the OT. See TEXT AND MANUSCRIPTS (OT). Among the 202 biblical scrolls found in the caves, all books in the Protestant-Jewish canon have been recognized with the exception of Esther. The fact that the Feast of PURIM is not present in the table of feasts celebrated by the community strongly suggests that the lack of evidence for Esther is not simply accidental. The books of Nehemiah and 1 Chronicles are also wanting among the fragments but are assumed to have been originally present in view of the existence of Ezra and 2 Chronicles. Of the Deuterocanonical books (Apocrypha), Tobit, Sirach (Ecclesiasticus), and the Epistle of Jeremiah were also discovered in the caves.

The Bible scrolls witness to both the antiquity and accuracy of the traditional Hebrew Bible (MT) as well as a surprising degree of variation. A study by E. Tov of the 202 biblical MSS shows that in the immediate pre-Christian period there were at least four groups or text types in existence, one of which was the precursor of the MT (47%), another being a text closely allied to that used by the SEPTUAGINT translation (5%), a third was related to the SAMARITAN PENTATEUCH (6%), while a fourth group is mixed and shows alignment to no known text type (47%). Earlier studies by Tov posited a fifth group which he termed Qumran Practice (21%). Determinative characteristics of this latter group—variant orthography (spelling) and morphology—are not sufficiently important to determine a text type, but are of significance in the determination of what texts may have been copied into the slightly idiosyncratic Hebrew of the community. Reflecting the number of MSS written in Qumran Practice, perhaps 20% of the library was copied at Qumran while 80% was added to the collection from the personal libraries of initiates.

The variety of text types at Qumran has suggested to most scholars that the form of the biblical text was still evolving and that the traditional Hebrew text (MT) that would eventually become the "received text" for normative Judaism and Protestant Christianity did not appear until the end of the 1st cent. A.D. at the earliest. The Bible scrolls from Masada and Murabbaʿat appear to verify this theory as they are textually much closer to the MT than the Qumran MSS. There may be, however, sociological reasons that would account for this fact apart from purely chronological issues. The variety observed especially in the Torah and Prophets from Qumran might witness to an acceptance in the Qumran community of variant spelling conventions, harmonizations, and other editing features that were spurned by rabbinic Judaism of the 2nd cent. A.D. and following. In other words, it is still unclear to some researchers whether the Qumran biblical MSS attest to final stages of evolution towards a "received text" (MT) or are the witness of a community which, while they evidence a conservative view of the authority of the text, allowed—as does much of Christendom of the 21st cent.—for a variety of expressions.

While much study of the Qumran biblical material is still needed, it is quite clear that neither the biblical nor the sectarian MSS present a threat to Christianity or Judaism as was rumored when the discoveries first came to light. They have confirmed much that was previously known about the Scriptures, but have also shown the desirability of a revision of certain theories cherished by some scholars. Not the least benefit is the stimulus given to the task of reconstructing as accurate a pre-Christian OT text as possible.

(See further J. T. Milik, *Ten Years of Discovery in the Wilderness of Judaea* [1959]; R. K. Harrison, *The Dead Sea Scrolls* [1961]; J. C. VanderKam, *The Dead Sea Scolls Today* [1994]; F. M. Cross, *The Ancient Library of Qumran*, 3rd ed. [1995]; M. O. Wise, M. G. Abegg, Jr., and E. M. Cook, *The Dead Sea Scrolls: A New Translation* [1996]; G. Vermes, *The Complete Dead Sea Scrolls in English* [1997]; M. G. Abegg, Jr., P. W. Flint, and E. C. Ulrich, *The Dead Sea Scrolls Bible* [1999]; G. Vermes, *An Introduction to the Complete Dead Sea Scrolls in English* [1999]; L. H. Schiffman and J. C. VanderKam, eds.,

Encyclopedia of the Dead Sea Scrolls, 2 vols. [2000]; E. Tov, *Textual Criticism of the Hebrew Bible*, 2nd ed. [2001]; J. Magness, *The Archaeology of Qumran and the Dead Sea Scrolls* [2002]; J. C. VanderKam and P. W. Flint, *The Meaning of the Dead Sea Scrolls* [2002]; G. J. Brooke, *The Dead Sea Scrolls and the New Testament* [2005]; J. H. Charlesworth, ed., *The Bible and the Dead Sea Scrolls*, 3 vols. [2006].)

R. K. HARRISON; rev. by M. G. ABEGG, JR.

deaf. The Bible speaks of deafness both in a literal and in a figurative sense. People insensitive because of sin are said to be deaf to the voice of God. ISAIAH, in anticipation of the spiritual awakening to be introduced by the coming of the MESSIAH, prophesied: "Then will the eyes of the blind be opened / and the ears of the deaf unstopped" (Isa. 35:5). He regarded deafness as a voluntary state that could be changed by choice, for he commands: "Hear, you deaf; / look, you blind, and see!" (42:18). Physical deafness was healed by Christ to seal his claims of messiahship, and also to illustrate that he healed spiritual deafness as well (Mk. 7:32–37). See DISEASE; HEALING.

D. A. BLAIKLOCK

death. The biblical terms for "death" are Hebrew *māwet* H4638 and Greek *thanatos* G2505, but other words and expressions are also used. Most books of the Bible have something to say about this topic.

I. Old Testament

A. Death is punishment for sin.
The first reference to death in the OT (Gen. 2:17), although not without its problems, nevertheless gives the basic orientation for the biblical understanding of death. Here death is punishment for SIN. This truth is seen further in the course of events: when Adam and Eve sinned, they were excluded from the Garden, the place of communion with God, also from access to the TREE OF LIFE, which would have prevented the onset of their dying (3:22–23), and are consigned to a life of pain and toil that will terminate in physical dissolution (3:16–19). Theological distinctions are usually made between physical death, spiritual death, and eternal death. In general these are valid, but from the passage it appears that death in its totality is the result of sin.

One must remember also that, in the biblical view, man is a psychosomatic unity. The whole person is the subject of death. In the history of the church some have felt that physical death, the dissolution of the body, was normal and natural, and that this is only reversed by a divine provision, as shown in the Genesis narrative by access to the tree of life. The majority of orthodox theologians, however, have rejected this idea. The rest of the biblical revelation, especially that of the NT, seems to run counter to it, although it is often said that with our present physical make-up death is a biological necessity.

B. Death is a fact of human experience.
It is certainly true that in much of the OT narrative death is recorded as a universal fact of human experience (cf. the genealogical table of Gen. 5, with its monotonous repetition, "and he died"), but this is not to say that the writers thought of death as "natural," or as something that was part of God's perfect will for human beings. It is indeed seen as inevitable in their present sinful and fallen state, but this is rather different. The bright exception of ENOCH (Gen. 5:24) gives an indication of something better and more desirable.

C. Death is something to be feared and avoided.
This element becomes clearer in considering the great number of places where the OT writers expressed their personal feelings, speaking of death as something to be feared and avoided at all costs (e.g., Pss. 6:1–5; 88:1–14; Isa. 38). It may be said that it is early death which is feared, and examples may be given of people dying "at a

Assyrian depiction of impaled victims. Later the Persians used impaling rods for the form of execution that came to be known as crucifixion.

good old age" (e.g., ABRAHAM, Gen. 25:8), with the sense of satisfaction that they have enjoyed their natural span and that they continue to live on in their posterity, accepting their death as something natural. On the other hand, Ps. 90 bears witness to the belief that even a full life span is short and is cut off because of God's wrath.

It is true, of course, that much of the abhorrence of death expressed by the OT writers may be due to fear and avoidance of the unknown, so little having been positively revealed in the OT on the state of the dead. It is also true that in view of this, it was felt that death would cut one off from enjoyment of the COVENANT blessings, which in the OT were given in terms of the land, the temple, the people, and length of days. Even this fact may be used to show that death was considered as unnatural, since it might possibly separate one from the living God, the God of the covenant, and therefore could not be part of God's original purpose for his creatures. If length of days is promised for obedience (Exod. 20:12) and is a sign of God's favor (Job 5:26), then the cutting off of those days, even when long, is an indication that death is something unnatural.

D. Death is not outside the control or rule of God. God can give escape from death (Ps. 68:20; Isa. 38:5; Jer. 15:20). He can restore the dead to life (1 Ki. 17:22; 2 Ki. 4:34; 13:21). He kills and makes alive, brings down into SHEOL and raises from there again (Deut. 32:39; 1 Sam. 2:6). He can take people to himself without their dying (Gen. 5:24; 2 Ki. 2:11). He can completely bring death to nothing and triumph over it by raising the dead (Isa. 25:8; 26:19; Ezek. 37:11–12; Dan. 12:2; Hos. 6:2; 13:14).

E. Death is not victorious. These last references introduce the hope expressed in the OT of victory over death. One or two of the verses may refer to a revival of national fortunes, but others speak quite clearly of a RESURRECTION from physical death, and to these may be added those which indicate a confidence in personal resurrection (e.g., Job 19:25–27; Pss. 16:9–11; 17:15; 73:23–26). This hope, however slight, is present in the OT, but finds its full flowering in the NT, which reveals Christ as the one "who has destroyed death and has brought life and immortality to light through the gospel" (2 Tim. 1:10).

II. New Testament

A. Death is the penalty for sin. The victory of Christ over death in his own resurrection from the dead and the consequences of this for believers is the theme that dominates the NT in all its parts, but this is set against the backdrop of death as the penalty for sin. See RESURRECTION OF JESUS CHRIST. PAUL traced back the entrance of death into the human race to the sin of the first man, ADAM (Rom. 5:12–21; 1 Cor. 15:22). Other NT writers, while not making this explicit connection, say nothing that would militate against it; they are concerned, as is Paul in the main, rather with the empirical facts of human beings in sin. Indeed, the responsibility of the individual is not diminished by his involvement in Adam's fall; for the individual "the wages of sin is death" (Rom. 6:23; cf. Ezek. 18:4, 20). This is death in its totality, contrasted with "eternal life" in the second part of the verse, and is elaborated and developed in different parts of the NT in the following ways:

1. Physical death. This is the result of the entrance of sin into the world through Adam. It is the lot of all human beings (Heb. 9:27), and through fear of it and what may follow it they are throughout their lives in bondage (Heb. 2:15; cf. Rom. 8:15).

2. Spiritual death. All people are by nature spiritually dead, that is, alienated by sin from God the source of life, insensible to divine things, unresponsive to his laws. This is clear from the words of Jesus (Matt. 8:22; cf. Lk. 15:32) as well as from the writings of Paul (Eph. 2:1–3; 4:17–19; Col. 2:13; cf. Jude 12).

3. Eternal death. Those who remain in spiritual death throughout their lives and do not believe on the Son of God die in their sins (Jn. 8:21, 24), remain under the wrath of God (3:36), and in the day of JUDGMENT will be consigned to a state of ETERNAL separation from God, called in Scripture the second death (Rev. 21:8).

B. Jesus Christ has risen from the dead and overcome death. This is the center of the NT message, and is witnessed to in every part of the NT. All four Gospels record Jesus' prophecies before the event (e.g., Mk. 8:31; 9:31; Jn. 2:19–22) and the event itself (Matt. 28; Mk. 16; Lk. 24; Jn. 20–21); it was the core of the apostolic preaching in Acts (e.g., Acts 2:24–36; 3:15; 17:31); and the Epistles and the Apocalypse all bear witness to its centrality (e.g., Rom. 1:4; 4:25; 1 Cor. 15:4–8; Heb. 13:20; 1 Pet. 3:21–22; Rev. 1:5). He holds "the keys of death and Hades" (Rev. 1:18); he has abolished death (2 Tim. 1:10); he has overcome the devil, who had the power of death (Heb. 2:14); he is the head of the new humanity, the firstborn from the dead (Col. 1:18); he has caused believers to be born anew to a living hope through his resurrection from the dead (1 Pet. 1:3). This last reference introduces the blessings that come to believers as the result of Christ's resurrection and triumph over death.

In the coming of Christ, and especially in his resurrection, the eschatological process has begun, and the life of the age to come has broken into this present age. Believers already partake of the life of the coming age (Jn. 3:36); for them the eschatological verdict has been passed. They have already passed from death—the condition of sinners in this age—to life (Jn. 5:25). Paul makes a similar point when he says that in Christ, who is the Second Adam or head of the new humanity, believers have died and risen again (Rom. 6:1–4; Col. 3:1–3) and therefore, although they still live in this world, their attitude to sin, the law, and the world is to be that of dead people (Rom. 6:11; Gal. 2:19, 20; 6:14).

In Christ their head believers partake of the life of the age to come, and physical death is for them a sleep (1 Thess. 4:15; cf. Acts 7:59). The sting of death has been removed (1 Cor. 15:56); it cannot separate from Christ (2 Cor. 5:8; Phil. 1:23) and so is not to be feared, and may even be desired (Phil. 1:21–23). At the SECOND COMING of Christ, believers' bodies will be changed, and all traces of sin, mortality, and death will be removed. Then death will be swallowed up in life (1 Cor. 15:52–57). At the judgment, death and HADES are said to be cast into the LAKE OF FIRE (Rev. 20:14), signifying that as God brings in the new heaven and new earth (Rev. 21), the last enemy, death (1 Cor. 15:26), is finally and irrevocably destroyed.

(Cf. L. A. Muirhead, *The Terms Life and Death in the Old and New Testaments* [1908]; R. H. Charles, *Eschatology: Hebrew, Jewish and Christian* [1913]; L. Morris, *The Wages of Sin* [1955]; R. Bultmann in *TDNT*, 3:7–25 and 4:896–99; L. R. Bailey, Sr., *Biblical Perspectives on Death* [1979]; L. Coenen in *NIDNTT*, 1:430–47; P. S. Johnston, *Shades of Sheol: Death and Afterlife in the Old Testament* [2002]; S. U. Gulde, *Der Tod als Herrscher in Ugarit and Israel* [2007].) R. E. DAVIES

death, second. This phrase is found only in the book of Revelation (Rev. 2:11; 20:6, 14; 21:8). It is characteristic of the repetitive and reciprocal nature of the structure of this book, wherein ordinal numbers play an important part. The phrase refers to the eternal JUDGMENT of God upon sin that occurs after physical DEATH (cf. Matt. 10:28; Lk. 12:4–5). It is therefore synonymous with other apocalyptic expressions, such as LAKE OF FIRE. The concept, expressed in various ways, is found in Jewish literature, and the TARGUM to Isa. 65:5–6 explicitly identifies "the second death" with the constant fire of GEHENNA. See HELL. W. WHITE, JR.

death of Christ. The NT writers had an absorbing interest in the death of Christ. This interest is principally interpretive; they were more concerned with the meaning of the event than with the circumstances that made up the event. Yet it is entirely misleading to suggest, as some moderns have done, that the faith of the apostolic Christians was indifferent to the historical reporting of the facts as they actually happened. The theology of the CROSS, first elaborated by PAUL, is by no means independent of the events recorded in the narratives of the Gospels. The death of Christ is both a fact and a doctrine; the two are inextricably bound together in the NT. As the doctrinal aspects of Christ's death are discussed elsewhere (see ATONEMENT; EXPIATION; PROPITIATION), more attention shall be given in this article to the historical circumstances surrounding this event.

Paul wrote to the Corinthians that he determined to know nothing among them "except Jesus Christ and him crucified" (1 Cor. 2:2). This emphasis is also reflected in the manner in which the Gospels report the story of Jesus' life. The spotlight focuses on the last few days of Christ's public ministry, leading up to his crucifixion. The evangelists considered his death the great purpose of his life; Jesus lived that he might die.

When Jesus first introduced the subject of his death (Matt. 16:21; Mk. 8:31; Lk. 9:22), it marked a turning point in his ministry. He spent less time with the multitudes and more with the Twelve; he spoke not only of the kingdom, but also of himself, especially the death he must die. The necessity of his death is not reported in a manner that presents Jesus as a helpless victim of overpowering opposition. Though the forces of evil that he faced were mighty, even in the last hour he could have summoned legions of angels to his rescue (Matt. 26:53). Rather, his own anticipation of his death testified to Jesus' sense of vocation and destiny as the one to fulfill the role of the suffering servant of the Lord. Hence, "As the time approached for him to be taken up to heaven, Jesus resolutely set out for Jerusalem"—a resolution that could not be daunted (Lk. 9:51–52).

His arrival at Jerusalem began the period known as Passion Week. (PASSION is a term used in ecclesiastical literature to describe the sufferings of the Lord, particularly the agony of GETHSEMANE and the cruel treatment by the Roman soldiers who finally crucified him.) Though he entered the city in triumph (Matt. 21:1–11 and parallels), his authority was soon challenged (21:23–27), and as opposition stiffened, the chief priests conspired to destroy him (26:1–5). JUDAS ISCARIOT, one of the Twelve, became surreptitiously involved in the conspiracy (26:14–16). While Judas plotted to betray his master for money, Jesus sent two disciples to a private residence with directions for preparing the PASSOVER, which he observed with his disciples. Jesus solemnly reminded them that he was soon to leave them, going so far as to identify the traitor, though the disciples were too incredulous and amazed to apprehend the significance of Judas's treachery.

In reporting this last meal with the disciples, the gospel writers emphasize not so much the Passover feast as such, but rather Jesus' unique handling of the bread and wine during and after the meal. See LORD'S SUPPER. We read, "While they were eating, Jesus took bread, gave thanks and broke it, and gave it to his disciples, saying, 'Take and eat; this is my body.' Then he took the cup, gave thanks and offered it to them, saying, 'Drink from it, all of you. This is my blood of the covenant, which is poured out for many for the forgiveness of sins'" (Matt. 26:26–28). Because he was soon to die, Jesus interpreted his death to his disciples. Here is illustrated how fact and meaning are united in the NT view of Christ's death. When they had finished eating, they sang a hymn (prob. the paschal hymns, Pss. 113–118 and 136) and went out to the MOUNT OF OLIVES. (At this point they lingered to talk, for John records a long farewell discourse concluding with the well-known intercessory prayer; see Jn. 13–17.) As Jesus spoke to them further of his impending death and their defection, the disciples—especially PETER—protested their steadfast loyalty, even producing weapons ready for his defense.

The following scene, in the Garden of GETHSEMANE, is so steeped in pathos that it has stirred Christians through the centuries, inspiring innumerable masterpieces of art and poetry. In these familiar environs, Jesus retreated with three of his closest disciples to pray. Though their eyes were heavy with sleep, the Lord was in an agony of spirit that seems to surpass in sheer intensity anything that he suffered subsequently. As he prayed that he might be delivered—"Father, if you are willing, take this cup from me"—he began to sweat "drops of blood" (Lk. 22:42–44). Some have interpreted this statement to mean that his perspiration was large and beady, but the assimilation to blood strongly suggests the color of red, and several instances have been cited of a bleeding of the pores of those suffering from intense emotional anguish. More important than the physical aspects of the Lord's suffering is his resolute submission to his Father's will, which he achieved in and through this severe trial—a resolution without which salvation could never have been achieved. "During the days of Jesus' life on earth, he offered up prayers and petitions with loud cries and tears to the one who could save him from death.... Although he was a son, he learned obedience from what he suffered and, once made perfect, he became the source of eternal salvation for all who obey him" (Heb. 5:7–9).

Having surmounted this crisis with the help of angelic comforters, the Lord rejoined his disciples as Judas Iscariot appeared with a band of temple guards to apprehend him. The Master was identified by a kiss (the verb here, *kataphileō* G2968, is thought by some to denote affectionate kissing; if so, this underscores the perfidious nature of his act). Without resistance, Jesus gave himself to his captors, though remonstrating with them because they had armed themselves as if they sought a dangerous criminal. Though Peter made a quixotic defense by striking off an ear of the high priest's servant with his sword (Jesus cured him with a touch), the entire company of the disciples soon dispersed into the night, leaving Jesus to his fate (Matt. 26:47–56 and parallels).

In reporting the arrest, John's gospel includes a detail not found in the synoptics: at the first encounter Jesus' would-be captors fell backward on the ground (Jn. 18:6). This was evidently intended to underscore the truth that Jesus was master of the situation even at the moment of his arrest, and is in keeping with the saying, "No one takes it [my life] from me, but I lay it down of my own accord" (10:18). (In this same vein, John also reported Jesus' answer to Pilate, when he claimed to have power to crucify Jesus: "You would have no power over me if it were not given to you from above," 19:11.)

Apprehended, Jesus was brought to the palace of the former high priest Annas, who vainly tried to extract a confession from him, and then sent him to Caiaphas, the high priest. Jesus was tried before the Sanhedrin, hastily assembled at daybreak (Matt. 26:57–75 and parallels; see Trial of Jesus). After great difficulty in securing competent and consistent witnesses against Jesus, Caiaphas finally adjured him respecting his messianic claims, and upon the strength of his avowal, accused him of blasphemy, the whole council concurring in the sentence of death. In this account of the trial before the Jewish authorities, the repeated denial of Peter counterpoints Jesus' indictment as a secondary theme, and underscores further the utter loneliness of the Lord in the hour of his extremity. Condemned by his compatriots, denied by his friends, the tragic element is heightened—if possible—as Judas the betrayer, in a paroxysm of remorse, confessed the innocence of Jesus, cast down the accursed silver on the pavement, and went out and hanged himself. The twisted conscience of the elders is revealed in their calloused indifference to Judas's confession and their careful use of the money so as not to offend legal scruple (27:3–10).

After many vile insults to his person, Jesus was led to Pilate to obtain legal sanction of the death sentence. The messianic issue appeared again, only now with a political twist: Jesus was accused of sedition. But Pilate showed himself reluctant to be involved, and having learned the defendant was from Galilee, engaged in the delaying tactic of sending Jesus off to Herod Antipas (see Herod V), who happened to be in Jerusalem during the Passover season. Herod received Jesus with overweening curiosity, having heard of his miracles; but when Jesus refused to break his silence, Herod sent him back to Pilate, having mocked him with the raiment of royalty (Lk. 23:8–12). The moment of truth had now come for Pilate. Compelled to adjudicate the case, yet convinced of the prisoner's innocence—his conscience being reinforced by a message from his wife—he sought to release Jesus as a common criminal according to the custom that dictated a gesture of clemency at the Passover season. Instead, the multitude clamored for the release of Barabbas, a notorious criminal; and Pilate having ceremoniously washed his hands before them, yielded to their demands, passed sentence upon Jesus, and left him to the abuse of the Roman soldiers (Matt. 27:15–30 and parallels).

As Jesus was led out of the city to Golgotha, where he was to be crucified, a passerby named Simon of Cyrene was pressed into the service of bearing his cross. Meanwhile Jesus, in somber accents that anticipated the imminent desolation of Jerusalem, bade the disconsolate women to weep for themselves and their nation rather than for him (Lk. 23:26–31). Having reached the place of execution, he was crucified between two criminals, with a prayer on his lips for his murderers. Though reviled by spectators, soldiers, and Jewish leaders, one of the thieves sued for mercy and was assured by Jesus with the well-known words, "Today you will be with me in paradise" (23:43). Having committed his mother to the care of John, and having given utterance in the language of Ps. 22 to his agonizing loneliness ("My God, my God, why have you forsaken me?" Matt. 27:46), he expired with a loud cry, "Father, into your hands I commit my spirit!" (Lk. 23:46). The veil of the temple was rent by an earthquake and the sun was darkened. The centurion in charge, awed by evidence of the supernatural, exclaimed, "Surely this mas was the Son of God" (Mk. 15:38).

Up to this point, the CRUCIFIXION was typically Roman—scourging, mocking, the garments becoming the spoil of the soldiers, the place of execution on an elevated spot outside the city, and the superscription over the head of the accused. At this juncture is introduced a concern to remove the body before sundown, a strictly Jewish matter; the Jews did not want the bodies on the cross during the SABBATH. They petitioned Pilate to hasten the death of the victims so that the bodies could be removed before sundown. The order was given, but they did not break Jesus' legs because he was already dead. A soldier, however, plunged his spear into Jesus' side (to make sure he was dead?) and water mingled with blood poured from the wound (Jn. 19:31–37).

The report of the crucifixion in the Gospels is characterized by reserve and sobriety, fitting for such an awful and solemn tragedy. It is assumed that the readers were familiar with the details. Inasmuch as crucifixion is unknown in the modern world, and because the event of Jesus' death has been idealized by the poetry and art of the centuries, some account perhaps should be given of the stark details.

Crucifixion appears to have been first used by the Persians as a form of execution, then by ALEXANDER THE GREAT (who crucified 2,000 Tyrians at one time), and then by the Carthaginians, whence it came to the Romans. It was commonly acknowledged the most horrible form of death, worse than burning. (A fire was sometimes built under the crucified to hasten death.) In the scourging that preceded the crucifixion, soldiers often used nails or pieces of bone to heighten the pain, which was sometimes so intense that the victim died under its duress. (Pilate had Jesus flogged before passing sentence—not so much from custom, it would seem, as to excite pity and procure immunity from further punishment, Lk. 23:22.)

The main stake forming the cross was secured in the ground in advance, and the condemned car-

Artistic rendition of the crucifixion of Jesus.

ried the crossbar with him from the place of incarceration to the place of execution. Lying on the ground, he was tied or nailed to the crossbar, and then raised up and fastened to the main post. The body of the victim was usually only a foot or two above the ground. Midway up the main post was a peg on which the weight of the body rested, and the feet were secured by tying or nailing. Sometimes a single nail secured both feet. At this point usually some drink was given to confuse the senses and deaden the pain (Jesus refused it, Matt. 27:34). A centurion with a band of soldiers was assigned to keep watch, because the lingering character of the death would allow a person to be taken down and recover, which sometimes happened. (It is reported that women among the Convulsionaires—an 18th-cent. religious sect in France—were crucified repeatedly, some remaining on a cross for three hours.)

The rapidity with which death overtook the Lord has been occasion for infidelity to suspect he only swooned, later to be revived by the coolness of the tomb. Others have sought to divine some unique fact in his medical history, such as a rupture of the heart due to the violence of the emotional stress under which he suffered. Still others have appealed to the voluntary surrender of his life implied in the expression, he "gave up his spirit" (Matt. 27:50; cf. Jn. 10:18, "I lay it [my life] down of my own accord"). Whatever theory one may adopt of the cause of Jesus' death, it is beyond all cavil that he died. Pilate expressly satisfied himself on this score by questioning the centurion (Mk. 15:44). It cannot be doubted that he suffered excruciating agonies before he was mercifully relieved by death. This most brutal and degrading form of execution devised by civilized man was abolished in the 4th cent. by the emperor Constantine, probably out of reverence for the sign under which he was said to have conquered. From this time on, the cross, the symbol of disgrace and degradation, became the chief symbol of the Christian faith.

There are two questions that have no direct bearing on the meaning of Christ's death, but that are nonetheless of such perennial interest as to warrant a brief discussion. One concerns the time of the arrest, trial, and crucifixion; the other, the responsibility for these events. As for the first question: did the crucifixion take place on the 14th of Nisan (April 6) or the day following? If the former date is chosen, not only is there a discrepancy between John and the synoptics as to the most important and conspicuous date in the life of Jesus, but also the last meal that Jesus ate with his disciples was not the Passover. This fact would cast doubts on the historicity of the synoptic accounts of the institution of the Lord's Supper and Jesus' own understanding of his impending death.

The technical aspects of this question are too large for an article of this scope. See CHRONOLOGY (NT). Suffice it to say that when John commented that the Jewish leaders did not enter the PRAETORIUM to remain undefiled and so eat the Passover (Jn. 18:28), or again, when the day of the trial was identified as the PREPARATION of the Passover (19:14), the term "Passover" need not be narrowly understood of the initial evening meal, but is flexible enough to include the entire feast of unleavened bread that followed the meal that Jesus celebrated with his disciples (see Jos. *Ant.* 17.9.3 and *War* 2.1.3; also Lk. 22:1). On such an interpretation, there is no discrepancy between John and the synoptics, who plainly teach that Jesus partook of the paschal supper. This supper occurred on Thursday evening, as we reckon time. That same Thursday night he was betrayed, seized by the Jewish authorities, and condemned by the Sanhedrin. Early Friday morning he was brought before Pilate, and before the day was over, that is before sundown, he had been condemned, crucified, and buried.

As for the question of responsibility for his death, the church has traditionally accused the Jews of the crime of deicide, for which they were supposedly accursed to all generations. Only the hollow eyes of prejudice could fail to see that this was a pious cloak to cover a deep-seated anti-Semitism. The canonical Gospels indeed indicate that Jesus' death was instigated by the Jews—which was inevitable under the circumstances—but it was made possible, approved, and carried out by the Roman authorities. It would seem, then, that neither Jews nor Gentiles can escape the reproach of complicity in this crime. It was the sin of all humanity against heaven, an evil that God has transformed into our salvation, so making his goodness to triumph over man's wickedness.

In saying all this, the theology of Christ's death is introduced, which is the primary, almost exclusive concern of the NT apart from the Gospels. The doctrine of the cross was first elaborated by PAUL, who was concerned not with the historical details, but with the salvation significance of the cross. Christ "became obedient to death—even death on a cross" (Phil. 2:8), and by this obedience to his Father's will he accomplished the sinner's salvation. Hence, wherever Paul went, he so preached Christ crucified as to placard him before the eyes of all who heard (Gal. 3:1). This word of the cross is God's wisdom, which is foolishness to human reason; but to those who are saved, it is the wisdom and power of God (1 Cor. 1:18–25). Paul wrote to the Galatians that if he were to proclaim CIRCUMCISION as the means of salvation, then the offense of the cross would be removed, but circumcision and the cross are mutually exclusive; therefore, he will glory in the cross that all glorying in self may be brought to nought (Gal. 5–6).

How is it that Christ's death on the cross is the decisive revelation of God in history? Because it is the means by which God is reconciled to sinners (Eph. 2:16; Col. 1:20; 2:14). The basis of the reconciling power in the death of Christ is the propitiatory power of the blood that he shed there (Rom. 3:21–26). Another way of putting it is to say that he canceled the bond that stood against us with its legal demands, nailing it to his cross (Col. 2:14). Paul told the Ephesians that they were brought near by the blood of Christ—near, that is, to God, from whom, as Gentiles, they were alienated, being "foreigners to the covenants of the promise" (Eph. 2:11–12). All of this has happened, ultimately, because God loved human beings even when they were sinners (Rom. 5:8). On the one hand, God loved the world (Jn. 3:16), and, on the other, the wages of sin is death (Rom. 6:23); therefore Christ died for us. This is the basic reason for the death of Christ. Historically, his death was due to the jealousy of the Jewish leaders, the treachery of Judas, the fear of the disciples, the vacillation of Pilate, the cruelty of the Romans; but on a different level, the cause of Christ's death is our sin and God's love. Sin involved human beings in death, and Christ could not deal with sin effectually, except as he took the consequences upon himself: "God made him who had no sin to be sin for us, so that in him we might become the righteousness of God" (2 Cor. 5:21).

The rest of the NT takes essentially the same view of Christ's death as is found in the epistles of Paul. Especially in Hebrews is this the case. Christ is set forth as a priest whose work is to bring sinners into fellowship with God. To do this he had to die, and to die, he had a body prepared for him (Heb. 10:5). The INCARNATION was for the purpose of atonement. And this atoning death was, so to speak, God's last word; he has nothing more in reserve. Christianity is final. Speaking of the cross of Christ, Watts wrote:

Here we behold God's inmost heart,
  Where grace and vengeance strangely join;
Here his whole name appears complete,
  His wrath, his wisdom, and his love.

Having known his "whole name" in the cross, Christians look forward to the day when, with people from every tribe and kindred and tongue and nation, they shall join in praise to the Lamb who was slain, who loved his own and loosed them from their sins by his blood (Rev. 1:5; 5:9). (For a classic treatment, see J. Denney, *The Death of Christ* [1951]; cf. also G. C. Berkouwer, *The Work of Christ* [1965], ch. 6; J. B. Green, *The Death of Jesus: Tradition and Interpretation in the Passion Narrative* [1988]; J. T. Carroll et al., *The Death of Jesus in Early Christianity* [1995]; S. McKnight, *Jesus and His Death: Historiography, the Historical Jesus, and Atonement Theory* [2005].) See also JESUS CHRIST IV.G. P. K. JEWETT

Debir (person) dee'buhr (דְּבִיר H1809, possibly "back room [of a shrine]"). King of EGLON, a member of the confederacy of five AMORITE rulers who opposed the town of GIBEON at the invitation of ADONI-ZEDEK, king of Jerusalem. The Gibeonites appealed to JOSHUA, and he and his army fought the Amorites in the Valley of AIJALON, where the sun stood still (see DAY, JOSHUA'S LONG). The five kings fled to a cave in MAKKEDAH, but they were captured and executed (Josh. 10:1–28).

Debir (place) dee'buhr (דְּבִיר H1810 [also דְּבִר], possibly "back room [of a shrine]"). **(1)** The more frequently mentioned Debir was located in the hill country of the SHEPHELAH to the W of Jerusalem. W. F. Albright (in AASOR 12 [1930–31] and subsequent vols.) identified it with Tell Beit Mirsim some 12 mi. SW of HEBRON (cf. *NEAEHL*, 1:177–80). However, insufficient topographical and archaeological evidence has come to light to support this contention. K. Galling (in *ZDPV* 70 [1954]: 135–41) proposed that the site might be modern Khirbet Rabud (8.5 mi. SSW of Hebron), especially since this location is near a set of naturally occurring springs of various altitudes (which accords well with the description in Jdg. 1:15, in the context of CALEB's granting of the request for land from Acsah, his daughter). Excavation of this site by Moshe Kochavy and others in 1968–69 has turned up much material from the period of the conquest, and this site is now generally accepted as biblical Debir. (See *NEAEHL*, 4:1252.)

The town's original name was Kiriath Sepher (*qiryat-sēper* H7963, "city of writing," Josh. 15:15), also known as Kiriath Sannah (*qiryat-sannâ* H7962, v. 49, but this form may be a textual corruption). The history of the town is woven throughout the narrative of the conquest and settlement of Canaan. It is first mentioned as a Canaanite royal town whose inhabitants, the Anakites (see ANAK), were destroyed by JOSHUA (10:38; 11:21; 12:13). The particular force involved was that under the command of Caleb (15:15–17; Jdg. 1:11–15). After the division of the land it became a regional center (Josh. 15:49) and is mentioned along with the other towns and villages of the Shephelah that were ceded to the tribe of JUDAH.

(2) A town or settlement near the Valley of ACHOR on the N boundary of the tribe of JUDAH (Josh. 15:7). Its precise location is unknown.

(3) A town in GILEAD located near the Jordan, within the territory of the tribe of GAD (Josh. 13:26). Its location is unknown. However, the MT reads, ʿad-gĕbûl lidbir (lit., "to the border to Debir"), which can be rendered "to the border of Lidbir" (so NJPS; cf. NRSV mg., "Lidebir"), and many scholars revocalize the name to read Lo DEBAR (some believe that Lidbir or Lidebir is the original name of Lo Debar).   W. WHITE, JR.

Deborah deb′uh-ruh (דְּבוֹרָה *H1806*, "honeybee"). (1) The nurse of REBEKAH, Issac's wife; she was buried under an oak at BETHEL, and the place was then named ALLON BACUTH, "The Oak of Weeping" (Gen. 35:8; cf. 24:59). Some scholars have suggested that this text confuses Rebekah's nurse with #2 below.

(2) An Israelite judge and prophetess (Jdg. 4). She is said to have been the wife of a certain LAPPIDOTH (the feminine form of this name in Heb. has been the subject of much speculation). Deborah is referred to as "a prophetess," the only judge thus described (4:4). She held court under a giant palm that stood between RAMAH and BETHEL and that came to be known as "the palm of Deborah" (v. 5). In the time of the oppression of the loosely knit tribes of Israel by King JABIN of HAZOR, Deborah summoned BARAK the son of Abinoam from KEDESH in NAPHTALI and gave him the command of the Lord to gather 10,000 soldiers from the tribes of Naphtali and ZEBULUN and marshal them at Mount TABOR. When Barak requested Deborah to go with them to the battle against Jabin and his host at the Wadi KISHON, she replied that God would deliver Jabin into the hand of a woman to be slain, thus rebuking the cowardice of the men of Israel. Jabin's military chief, SISERA, heard of the Israelite preparations for battle, and he obliged by setting off for the battlefield. When Deborah gave the command, the battle began. Israel was victorious, and Sisera fled the battlefield to be slain by JAEL, the wife of HEBER the KENITE. Thus was Deborah's prophecy fulfilled, and Sisera was put to death by a woman.

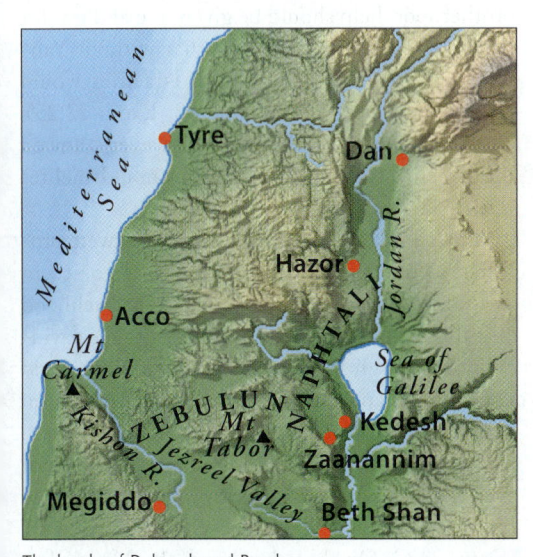

Giant date palm tree not far from the road connecting Ramah to Bethel. Deborah held court under such a tree.

The locale of Deborah and Barak.

The next chapter (Jdg. 5) contains the magnificent psalm known as the Song of Deborah. This piece of ancient poetry (13th cent. B.C.) is one of the oldest fragments of the Hebrew language in the Bible. It has beautiful lyric parallelism and contains many precise expressions drawn from older literature. It is difficult to translate and exegete because of its antiquity and obscurity. However, the joy of Israel's deliverance is stated gloriously in such lines as the following: "Wake up, wake up, Deborah! / Wake up, wake up, break out in song! / Arise, O Barak! / Take captive your captives, O son of Abinoam" (5:12). Note also the often cited words, "From the heavens the stars fought, / from their courses they fought against Sisera" (5:20). The victory of Yahweh's righteousness is inspired by the prophetess Deborah. Her psalm ends with the prayer, "So may all your enemies perish, O Lord" (5:31). (For a literary analysis of this poem, see M. D. Coogan in *CBQ* 40 [1978]: 143–66.)

(3) The paternal grandmother of Tobit; she raised him after his father's death (Tob. 1:8).

W. White, Jr.

debt. Money, property, or contract that one is bound to repay or perform for another; that which is owed or due and must be paid. A *debtor* is the person who owes another a debt or obligation. Figuratively, the word *debt* can refer to a sin or trespass.

The OT, particularly in Exodus and Leviticus, records detailed stipulations and limitations regarding debts, loans, interest, and contracts (see borrow; credit; interest). Abuse of the biblical regulations brought forth repeated admonition and condemnation from the prophets. Interesting word pictures regarding contracts and debts arose among the Israelites. The Mosaic legislation attempts to protect both lender and borrower through a system of pledges and guarantees. The ideas carry over into the NT, although the NT ethic is not so restricted and lacks detail.

It is to be expected that the OT ethic centers much on interest and usury, since these were the source of both profit and abuse. In Israel the system of lending and borrowing was not for big commercial enterprises, but to help private individuals who lacked everyday needs. Not the rich but the poor were in debt. When greed replaced concern in loans, the common people considered it unfortunate and a disgrace to be in debt because it placed the debtor at the mercy of the creditor. Yahweh, the God of mercy, would protect by manifold regulations the poor and downtrodden from the wicked oppressor. The OT legislation deals with interest and usury in such a way that both mercy and justice be done. Poverty was common in Israel, caused by over-population, high taxes, poor resources, and war. The payment of interest made lending and borrowing difficult and burdensome for both parties of a transaction in that one party had the power to charge exorbitant interest and the other could choose to default. After the exile a whole system of guarantees and limitations was developed to protect both debtor and creditor from each other. Later the rabbis worked out ways and means by which profit might be made from capital, but usury was forbidden.

The Pentateuch indicates that a first principle of lending and assuming debts is that such a transaction was pleasing to both God and man, since it gave the lender an opportunity to help a neighbor in need as an act of love. Lending to the poor was considered a good deed (Ps. 37:21). Since the borrower would pay back what he owed, he could receive help with thanks and respect. This is why Moses forbade an Israelite to take interest from a fellow Israelite. The idea was that in a brotherhood help should be given free and not for profit. The motive should be that without Yahweh's intervention in Egypt all Israelites would have been slaves (Lev. 25:35–38; Exod. 22:25). This doctrine of brotherhood, however, allowed the Israelite to lend on interest to non-Israelites (Deut. 23:19–20).

The poor who were forced to borrow were protected in other ways. It was not lawful to accept as surety objects that were a means of livelihood (see also pledge). A creditor could not take a widow's ox through foreclosure of a loan. One could not keep a man's garment overnight if it had been given as security for a loan (Exod. 22:26–27; Deut. 24:12–13). "Do not take a pair of millstones—not even the upper one—as security for a debt, because that would be taking a man's livelihood as security" (Deut. 24:6). On the other hand, the Mosaic law protected the lender through a complex system of security arrangements.

Pledges were of various kinds: money, movable property, garments, millstones, etc., which were surrendered to the lender at the time of the contract. Securities were not always equal to the value of money borrowed. The guarantee meant that the debtor upon his honor would pay his debts. Such contracts weighed heavily upon the borrower. When the lender took a pledge home with him, it was a visible token to everyone that the debtor would repay. (See the episode of JUDAH and TAMAR, Gen. 38:12–26.) Early in Judaism a debtor could pledge a son or daughter into the hands of a creditor—the value of their labor would be charged against the interest and the debt itself (2 Ki. 4:1–7). One could also give himself as a slave for surety of repayment, or he might be able to persuade a third party to be surety for him (Job 17:3; Prov. 6:1). The prophets and rabbis sometimes cautioned against this procedure (Prov. 22:26–27; 27:12–13). To alleviate the burden of the poor, debts were released every seven years during the SABBATICAL YEAR (Deut. 15:1–6), and seized property was restored during the JUBILEE YEAR (Lev. 25:28).

In spite of all the legislation, however, Israel did not follow the word of the Lord. The preaching of the prophets reveals that the abuse of all guarantees and pledges became a scourge of the people in later Judaism. During the days of NEHEMIAH, some Israelites were compelled to give up their sons to regain their vineyards (Neh. 5:1–13). Rates of interest became exorbitant, a social plague, and the poor debtor became helpless. All of Israel's neighbors oppressed the poor. The Hebrew word for "interest," *nešek* H5968, was likely associated with the verb "to bite" (*nāšak* H5966, Gen. 49:17), perhaps indicating the attitude toward loans, debts, and interest among the people. The lender would take his "bite" even before the borrower received a loaf of borrowed bread, but expected a full loaf in return. The term for interest also took on the meaning of "oppress" (Hab. 2:7).

The borrower gave his right hand in the transaction because it represented the power and honor to repay, as we in our culture raise our right hands when giving an oath. EZEKIEL describes the sins of Israel as if they had broken all the statutes of the law regarding debts and interest (Ezek. 18:8, 13, 17; 22:12). They abused the laws wholesale (2 Ki. 4:1–7). Hundreds of people were reduced to actual slavery (Isa. 50:1). Whereas the purpose of loans was really to help a person in need, naked commercialism killed all love and mercy, and both debtor and creditor cursed each other. Greece and Rome, too, were hard on people who defaulted on loans. Rome allowed a creditor to seize the debtor and place him in jail where he could never pay (cf. Jesus' parable of the debtor). (See E. Day, *The Social Life of the Hebrews* [1901], 175–95; R. de Vaux, *Ancient Israel* [1961], ch. 11.)

In the NT, Jesus and the apostles speak of debts, debtors, creditors, money-changers, interest, and other commercial practices that carried over from OT times (Lk. 7:41). This is evident from the Lord's imagery in the parable of the wicked servant (Matt. 18:23–35). "Be patient with me," pleads the wicked slave, "and I will pay back everything." But he himself refused to have patience with the servant under him and had him "thrown into prison until he could pay the debt" (cf. Lk. 12:57–59). Jesus speaks of a commercial system in the SERMON ON THE MOUNT: "Settle matters quickly with your adversary who is taking you to court. Do it while you are still with him on the way, or he may hand you over to the judge, and the judge may hand you over to the officer, and you may be thrown into prison. I tell you the truth, you will not get out until you have paid the last penny" (Matt. 5:25–26). Although Jesus nowhere condemns interest directly, and in spite of the implications in his parable of the pounds (Lk. 19:11–27) and the parable of the talents (Matt. 25:14–30), his use of commercial terminology should not be construed as an approval of all business activity. His words go beyond the OT law—he has contempt for money-making (Matt. 6:19–21). All such activity belongs to the kingdom of MAMMON. No one can serve two masters (6:24). The rich man ends in hell, but Lazarus is found in Abraham's bosom (Lk. 16:19–31). In general, Jesus is hard on the improper attitude toward WEALTH and oppression of the poor, just as in the OT ethic. The creditor forgives just as God does (6:14). God loves all people alike regardless of social and economic status (20:1–16). (See H. Daniel-Rops, *Daily Life in*

Palestine at the Time of Christ [1962]), 246–48; T. B. Maston, *Biblical Ethics* [1967], 62–85.)

The most prominent use of the debtor-creditor terminology in the NT, however, is to picture SIN and FORGIVENESS. A debt of sin is contracted by one who has offended his neighbor and sinned against him, and thereby has sinned against God. The words of the LORD's PRAYER, "Forgive us our debts [*opheilēma* G4052], as we also have forgiven our debtors" (Matt. 6:12), are easily understood against the OT commercial background. (This language may reflect the usage of ARAMAIC, where the term *ḥôbāʾ* often meant "sin"; cf. the TARGUM to Isa. 50:1.) Sin implies guilt that must be paid or canceled before man is free. The Christian has such redemption through Christ. The imagery is interpreted by the words which follow: "For if you forgive men when they sin against you, your heavenly Father will also forgive you" (v. 14). Other statements in the NT also take on meaning in the light of the OT. Jesus is "the guarantee of a better covenant" (Heb. 7:22). The HOLY SPIRIT is the guarantee of our inheritance (Eph. 1:14). Paul is a debtor to preach the gospel to both Greeks and non-Greeks (Rom. 1:14). Christians are debtors, but "not to the sinful nature, to live according to it" (Rom. 8:12). The Gentiles are debtors to those who shared the gospel with them (Rom. 15:26–27). The circumcised man is a debtor to keep the whole law (Gal. 5:3).

L. M. PETERSEN

Decalogue. See TEN COMMANDMENTS.

Decapolis di-kap′uh-lis (Δεκάπολις G1279, from δέκα G1274, "ten," and πόλις G4484, "city"). In Roman times, a large area mostly E of the JORDAN constituted by ten prominent Hellenistic towns. In such significance the term occurs in the Gospels (Matt. 4:25; Mk. 5:20; 7:31), PLINY the Elder (*Natural History* 5.16–17), and JOSEPHUS (*War* 3.9.7). It has often been thought that the original meaning of the area was political rather than geographical, signifying a league of ten towns possibly organized by POMPEY (cf. A. H. M. Jones, *Cities of the Eastern Roman Provinces*, 2nd ed. [1971], 259) or taking shape in the period between HEROD's domination of the area and Rome's stabilization of the eastern frontier in the early days of imperial rule. Some have argued that the area E of the Jordan and GALILEE, where nine of the ten allied communities were located, was exposed to the open and unpacified desert, and a military alliance was sound policy for a group of predominantly Greek cities, which in characteristic Greek fashion set some value on autonomy and political independence. However, there is no concrete evidence that such a league existed (cf. S. T. Parker in *JBL* 94 [1975]: 437–41; further discussion in M. A. Chancey, *The Myth of a Gentile Galilee* [2002], ch. 4).

The complex of Greek communities in eastern Palestine was a phenomenon of the Hellenistic diaspora, that deep penetration of the whole of the eastern Mediterranean by Greek immigrants that followed the conquests of ALEXANDER THE GREAT. Two of the ten Decapolis towns, PELLA and Dion, both Macedonian names, were probably founded by Alexander's own veterans in the mid-4th cent. B.C. Almost as ancient were Philadelphia (the site of RABBAH of the Ammonites and modern Amman, capital of Jordan) and GADARA. They were both important strongpoints by the end of the 3rd cent. B.C. Neither GERASA (whose extensive ruins are one of the great sights of Jordan) nor Hippos seems to have attained strength and eminence until Roman times. Most northerly of the ten towns, according to Pliny, was DAMASCUS, one of the most ancient of the world's cities. Josephus, however, seems to exclude Damascus, calling Scythopolis (see BETH SHAN) the largest of the ten.

A tradition of free government was established by the Greek immigrants, and though the cities lost such autonomy in the days of Maccabean domination (see MACCABEE), Pompey recognized the spirit of the territory when he established Roman control in 64–63 B.C. In the words of Josephus, he "restored the cities to their citizens." Josephus, in this connection, mentions Gadara, Pella, Dion, and Hippos; but Philadelphia also dates coinage by Pompey, and must therefore have been a recipient of his beneficence. Such freedom meant that the cities of the area elected their own councils, possessed the privileges of coinage and asylum, the right of property and administration in adjacent territory, and the right of association for defense and commerce. The area was nevertheless under the overall control of the governor of the province of SYRIA, who was empowered to supervise political administration, law, and foreign affairs, and to levy imperial taxes. It was a system typical of Rome's multilateral concept of government and the empire's readiness to adopt and adapt indigenous forms and patterns of rule and control.

The Greek communities of the Decapolis would undoubtedly have regarded Rome as protector and benefactor. From Rome's point of view, they strengthened the desert frontier where the great caravan routes and highways of trade bent around the inner curve of the FERTILE CRESCENT. Security was a pressing need. Information is fragmentary, but an inscription of A.D. 40 speaks of grave menace to the town of Hauran from BEDOUIN incursion from the desert. Rome's long effort to stabilize her vast frontiers, as well as the extreme vulnerability of the desert borders in the E, are facts that must be considered in the study of imperial history in Palestine.

Trade and commerce originally determined the pattern and progress of the Greek communities of eastern Palestine. The widest gateway to the Jordan Valley from the Mediterranean is the great fertile plain of ESDRAELON. Traffic to the territories E of Jordan and the Lake of Galilee necessarily passed between the high country to the S and the lake; hence the importance of the fortress of Beth Shan (or Scythopolis, its Greek name) and the inevitable association of the place with the ten towns that spread fanwise along the highways farther E. Scythopolis is the only one of the ten to lie W of the Jordan (and the only Decapolis site in modern Israel—so persistent is the shape of history in that ancient land). Scythopolis covered E-W communications between the sea and the Decapolis.

On the three roads that branch eastward from this nodal point, all the remaining cities of the Decapolis were situated, except for those that lie on the N-S route from Damascus to Arabia along the edge of the desert, which forms the terminal line of all the other highways. Across the Jordan, the cities of Gadara, Hippos, and Pella marked the beginning of the three roads. From Pella, a highway ran SE to Philadelphia through Gerasa. The central road ran from Gadara, NE by E to Raphana (prob. the same as RAPHON) and on to Kanatha, most easterly of the Decapolis cities, at the foot of Jebel Hauran. The third road ran N to Damascus. To these ten towns—Scythopolis, Pella, Dion, Gerasa, Philadelphia, Gadara, Raphana, Kanatha, Damascus, and Hippos—others joined themselves. Ptolemy, the geographer, listed eighteen names, omitting Raphana of the original ten. Abila and Kanata (a town apparently distinguished from Kanatha) are the most important additions.

Each of the Decapolis cities controlled surrounding territory and perhaps separated enclaves of land. This probably accounts for the confusion between the various readings "Gadarenes," "Gerasenes," or "Gergasenes" in the text of the Gospels (Mk. 5:1 and parallels). There is no reason why Gerasa should not have controlled a section of lakeside territory in an area geographically associated with Gadara. Generally, around Hippos was Hippene territory and villages, and around Gadara, Gadarene land. Gadara's long aqueduct reveals the extent to which the community of Gadara must have controlled territory necessary to its

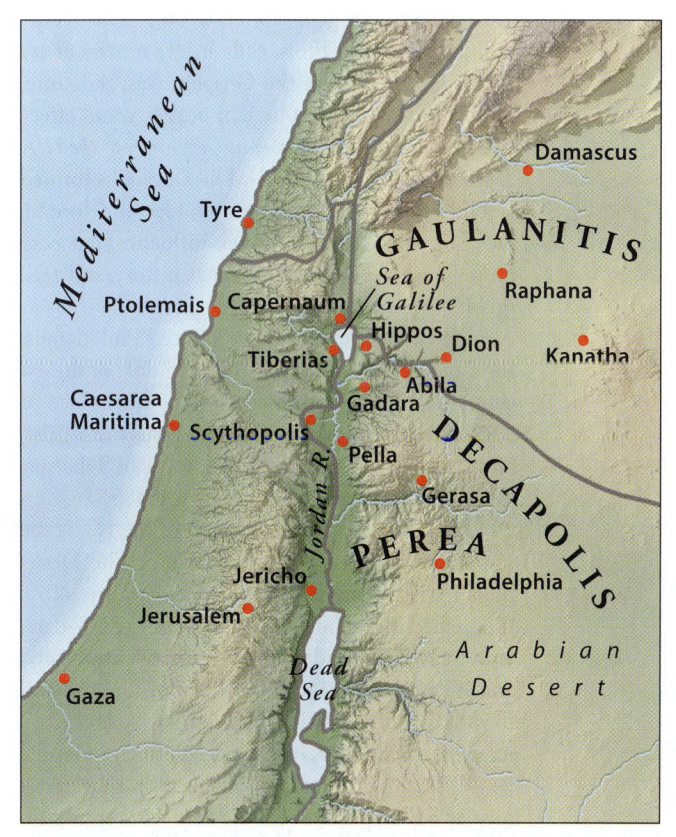

The Decapolis.

The uplifted hill of the Decapolis city of Hippos located on the eastern side of the Sea of Galilee. (View to the W.)

life, commerce, and convenience. G. A. Smith, the great Palestinian geographer, wrote, "The Decapolitan region, as Pliny calls it, *the borders of the Decapolis*, as styled in the Gospels, was, therefore, no mere name, but a sphere of property and effective influence" (*The Historical Geography of the Holy Land*, 25th ed. [1931], 403). The Decapolis formed a solid belt of territory along Galilee and Jordan, deeply permeated with Greek influence, but cosmopolitan by reason of commerce, history, and geographical position. Cultural life was as vigorous as commercial activity. Gadara produced Philodemus, the Epicurean philosopher, in the middle of the 1st cent. B.C. The same town was the birthplace of Meleager the epigrammatist, Menippus the satirist, and Theodorus the rhetorician, tutor of Tiberius. Gerasa was also renowned for its teachers.

Of chief interest to the student of the NT is the impact of the Decapolis on Galilee. "The Decapolis," writes Smith (*Historical Geography*, 407), "flourished in the time of Christ's ministry. Gadara, with her temples and amphitheaters, her art, games, and literature, overhung the Lake of Galilee, and the voyages of its fishermen." Across the lake, 5–8 mi. wide, the farmers of Galilee could see a Gentile world. That world had a bridgehead in their territory at Scythopolis; and the roads, converging on that center and radiating thence, must have exercised an attraction on many Jews. Perhaps the story of the prodigal (Lk. 15:11–32) illustrates the fact with the "far country" remote only in outlook and way of life. Swine, a Gentile food, was among the farmstock of the Gadarene territory, and the wanderer of the story, trapped and ruined by an alien society, may have been no more than a hard day's journey from home. Contact between the two areas was separated only by the tenuous barrier of the river and the lake. Large crowds from the Decapolis followed Christ at an early period of his ministry (Matt. 4:25). He visited the area when he returned from Tyre and Sidon, reaching the eastern shore of the lake through Hippos. The healed lunatic of Gadara, the first "apostle to the Gentiles," was sent to proclaim his blessing there (Mk. 5:20). The multitudes of the later visit (8:1) were the fruit of this witness.

The Jewish church withdrew to Pella at the time of the Great Rebellion and the siege of Jerusalem, A.D. 66–70. G. A. Smith concludes: "We cannot believe that the two worlds, which this landscape embraced, did not break into each other. The many roads which crossed Galilee from the Decapolis to the coast, the inscriptions upon them, the constant trade between the fishermen and the Greek exporters of their fish, the very coins—everywhere thrust Greek upon the Jews of Galilee. The Aramaic dialect had begun to fill with Greek words. It is hard to believe that our Lord and His disciples did not know Greek. But, at least, in that characteristic Greek city overhanging the Lake of Galilee [Gadara], in the scholars it sent to Greece and Rome, we have proof that the Kingdom of God came forth in no obscure corner, but in face of the kingdoms of this world" (*Historical Geography*, 407–8). E. M. BLAIKLOCK

deceit, deception. These and similar terms are used to render various words, such as Hebrew *mirmâ H5327* and Greek *dolos G1515* (e.g., Job 15:35; Mk. 7:22; for other semantically related words, see *NIDOTTE*, 5:53 and LN, 1:759–60). Deceit is the deliberate misleading or beguiling of another. Of course, it is always condemned in Scripture (cf. Jer. 23:26). It cannot be justified from 2 Cor. 12:16, for Paul was here employing irony and quoting the words of his critics. SATAN is the master of deception (cf. 1 Tim. 2:14; Rev. 20:8, 10), but no deceit was found on Christ's lips (1 Pet. 2:22). See also BEGUILE; LIE. K. L. BARKER

decision, valley of. This phrase, which occurs in only one verse (Joel 3:14), apparently refers to the Valley of Jehoshaphat (vv. 2, 12). The latter in turn seems to be a symbolical name of a valley near Jerusalem that is to be the place of God's ultimate judgment on the nations gathered to attack Jerusalem. Significantly, JEHOSHAPHAT had witnessed one of the Lord's historical victories over the nations (2 Chr. 20). The valley has been traditionally identified with the KIDRON, but the location remains a problem. Perhaps the solution is contained in Zech. 14:4, which indicates that when the Lord returns to the MOUNT OF OLIVES a great valley will be opened. Since Jehoshaphat's name means "Yahweh judges," possibly this newly opened valley is so named because of the Lord's judgment there. See JEHOSHAPHAT, VALLEY OF. K. L. BARKER

deck. As a verb, this word is used in the sense of "adorn, decorate" (e.g., Hos. 2:13, rendering Heb. *ʿādâ H6335*; Rev. 17:4 KJV, rendering Gk. *chrysoō G5998* ["to gild"]). As a noun, the word refers to the platform that extends from one side of a ship to the other, providing a floor for the space above and a roof for the space underneath (e.g., Ezek. 27:6, rendering Heb. *qereš H7983*). K. L. BARKER

deconstruction. See INTERPRETATION II.G.

decree. This English term can be used to translate a variety of Hebrew words, some referring to God's statutes (esp. *ḥōq H2976*, Exod. 15:25 and frequently; see LAW (OT) II), and others referring to an official edict or decision issued by a king (e.g., *maʾămār H4411*, Esth. 9:32; cf. Aram. *tᵉʿēm H10302*, Ezra 5:13 et al.; similarly Gk. *dogma G1504*, Lk. 2:1 et al.). The term is also used in the theological sense of God's sovereign plans and decisions, as when JOB says, "He carries out his decree [*ḥōq*] against me, / and many such plans he still has in store" (Job 23:14; cf. also Pss. 2:7; 105:10; see ELECTION; PROVIDENCE). J. C. CONNELL

Dedan dee´duhn (דְּדָן *H1847*, derivation unknown; gentilic דְּדָנִי *H1848*, "Dedanite"). **(1)** Son of RAAMAH and descendant of HAM through CUSH; his brother was SHEBA (Gen. 10:7; 1 Chr. 1:9). See NATIONS II.A.

(2) Son of JOKSHAN and grandson of ABRAHAM by KETURAH; his brother also is called Sheba (Gen. 25:3; 1 Chr. 1:32). The Asshurites, the Letushites, and the Leummites are said to have descended from him. Whether there is a connection between this Dedan and #1 above is uncertain, but many scholars posit a merging of ethnic traditions. See also #3 below.

(3) As a geographical and ethnic term, Dedan is mentioned several times in the prophets. The Dedanites (prob. viewed as descendants of #2 above) are said to lodge in the thickets of ARABIA and are referred to as being in caravans (Isa. 21:13, where the pl. form may be a gentilic). Dedan is mentioned in company with TEMA and BUZ as the object of God's wrath (Jer. 25:23). In the context of a prophecy against EDOM, the people of Dedan are warned of God's punishment to befall them (49:8). In a similar context, God's judgment against Edom includes all the territory from TEMAN to Dedan (Ezek. 25:13; in 27:15 the MT is usually emended to read RHODES). Finally, Dedan is mentioned with Sheba in a prophecy concerning GOG (Ezek. 38:13–14).

One can conclude therefore that the Dedanites were a people of Arabia who were closely associated with Sheba. Extrabiblical sources of antiquity indicate that Dedan also was an oasis on the trade routes of the peoples of Sheba, Tema, and Buz. The oasis of Dedan was known as ed-Dajan as late as A.D. 1200, and some ruins just N of modern al-ʿUla are to be identified as the most likely site, being located 50 mi. SW of Tema and 150 mi. E of the Red Sea in Central Arabia. (See J. Simons, *The Geographical and Topographical Text of the Old Testament* [1959], 21; J. Thompson, *The Bible and Archaeology* [1962], 201ff.; F. V. Winnett, "The Arabian Genealogies in Genesis," in *Translating and Understanding the Old Testament*, ed. H. T. Frank and W. L. Reed [1970], 171–96, esp. 190–91; G. Bawden in *Atlal: The Journal of South Arabian Archaeology* 3 [1979]: 63–72; I. Ephʿal, *The Ancient Arabs: Nomads on the Borders of the Fertile Crescent, 9th-5th Centuries B.C.* [1982], 14–15 et al.). J. B. SCOTT

dedicate. To set apart to God for a religious purpose. This English term can be used to render several Hebrew verbs, such as *qādaš H7727* ("to be holy," but in piel and hiphil, "to set apart as holy"; e.g., Lev. 27:14), *nāzar H5693* (hiphil "to separate oneself [as Nazirite]"; e.g., Num. 6:12), and *ḥānak H2852* (e.g., 1 Ki. 8:63). The word is rarely used in English versions of the NT, but the Greek verbs *hagiazō G39* ("to make holy, sanctify"; e.g., Jn. 17:17) and *enkainizō G1590* ("to renew"; cf. Heb. 10:20, NIV "opened") approximate its meaning. See also ANATHEMA; CONSECRATION; DEDICATION, FEAST OF; HOLINESS; NAZIRITE; SANCTIFICATION.

Dedication, Feast of. This phrase occurs once in the NT (Jn. 10:22) as a rendering of *ta enkainia G1589* (lit., "the renewals," a term first used in the LXX to render Heb. *ḥănukkâ H2853*, "dedication," Neh. 12:27; cf. Ezra 6:16–17). It refers to the Feast of Hanukkah, celebrated annually by the Jews for eight days to commemorate the cleansing of the TEMPLE in Jerusalem after it had been desecrated by the Syrians under ANTIOCHUS Epiphanes (1 Macc. 4:52–59; 2 Macc. 10:5). The restoration of the worship of God was effected by Judas MACCABEE about 165 B.C., three years after its defilement.

The Greco-Syrian Antiochus, in his excessive zeal to hellenize his realm, had persecuted the Jews, proscribed their religious observances, and erected

The *hanukkiah* is a special menorah with holders for nine candles. Eight candles correspond to the eight days of Hanukkah, and the middle candle is used to light the others.

an idolatrous altar on the altar of burnt offering in Jerusalem, where heathen sacrifices were then offered (1 Macc. 1:41–64; 2 Macc. 6:1–11; Jos. *Ant.* 12.5.4). The Maccabees raised the cry of revolt at Modein and ultimately overthrew the forces of Antiochus (JOSEPHUS gives a vivid account in *Ant.* 12.7.4). The feast falls on the twenty-fifth day of Kislev, which tallies with December (or late November; cf. Jn. 10:22, "It was winter"). Josephus designated it "The Feast of Lights"; it is also known as "The Feast of the Maccabees" and "The Feast of Illumination." The festival was characterized by the illumination of synagogues and homes. It was a time of joy and merriment, and no public mourning was permitted on this feast. Jewish tradition claims that Judas Maccabee found a cruse of oil that was sufficient for a day but lasted for eight.

The feast is still celebrated among the Jews today. The system of lighting is one light for the first day, and an additional one for each succeeding day of the festival. According to 2 Macc. 10:6–7, the feast was observed like the Feast of Tabernacles, with palms, branches, and the singing of psalms (see FEASTS). On this occasion, Ps. 30 (see title) was read in the ritual of the day (1 Macc. 1:41–64; 2 Macc. 6:10–11). In the celebration today, although work is allowed on these days, there is a prescribed festive ritual. The family solemnly gathers around the father as he lights the candles with a prayer of thanksgiving to God for the liberation of his people from the persecution of the oppressor. Presents and money gifts are distributed to the children. During the evening, games are played with the posing of riddles and exchange of jokes. In Europe the special table dish for the occasion was pancakes. (Cf. H. Schauss, *The Jewish Festivals* [1938], 208–36; S. Zeitlin in *JQR* 29 [1938–39]: 1–36; B. M. Edidin, *Jewish Holidays and Festivals* [1940], 87–103; J. VanderKam in *Journal for the Study of the Pseudepigrapha* 1 [1987]: 23–40.) C. L. FEINBERG

deep (the). As an adjective, the English term *deep* can be used to translate a number of words, such as Hebrew ʿāmōq H6678 (e.g., Prov. 18:4) and Greek *bathos* G958 (e.g., Lk. 5:4). The chief biblical usage, however, is as a noun, referring to a lake or sea. Of particular importance is Hebrew *tĕhôm* H9333, thought by some to be used mythologically of the waters of a nether world in Gen. 1:2 (cf. also ṣûlâ H7425 and its derivatives; see MYTH). This view sees a parallel to TIAMAT of the Babylonian creation story. Tiamat was the demon of chaos from whose split body MARDUK made the earth and sky. This Babylonian story, called ENUMA ELISH, has little if anything else in common with the biblical account.

It should be noted that *tĕhôm* is not used elsewhere in the OT of mythical subterranean waters. It is used repeatedly of the RED SEA through which Israel passed (Exod. 15:5, 8; Ps. 77:16; Isa. 51:10; Hab. 3:10). It is used also many times of the Mediterranean or the deep ocean in general (Gen. 7:11; Ps. 107:26; Jon. 2:5). In several poetic passages, it occurs in parallel to such words as *yām* H3542, "sea," and *mayim* H4784, "waters" (Job 38:16; Pss. 33:7; 135:6; Ezek. 26:19; 31:4, 15). The biblical cosmology does not picture any subterranean watery chaos (see COSMOGONY). Such terms as "the water under the earth" (Deut. 4:18, NRSV) refer only to waters below shore line, as the mention of fish in them clearly shows (see R. L. Harris in *ETSB* 5 [1962]: 11–17). Although *tĕhôm* and Akkadian *Tiamat* are etymologically related, the Hebrew term cannot be considered a direct borrowing from the latter (the Akkadian language lacks the laryngeal consonant *h*). It is far better to assume that the old Semitic root *thm* indicated "ocean," of which the Babylonian demon Tiamat was a personification. (See A. Heidel, *The Babylonian Genesis* [1951], 98–101; B. Anderson, *Creation versus Chaos: The Reinterpretaion of Mythical Symbolism in the Bible* [1987]; D. Tsumura, *The Earth and the Waters in Genesis 1 and 2* [1989]; D. T. Tsumura, *Creation and Destruction: A Reappraisal of the Chaoskampf Theory in the Old Testament* [2005]; *NIDOTTE*, 4: 275–77.)

The SEPTUAGINT regularly renders *tĕhôm* with Greek *abyssos* G12 (lit., "bottomless"), which thus about thirty times means merely the ocean and lakes. However, as the seas were the deepest things known to the ancients, the word gained a figurative sense and is used seven times in the book of Revelation of the bottomless PIT, the abode of evil spirits. It is possible that Lk. 8:31 also shows this usage. The only other reference (Rom. 10:7) uses this term of the place from which Christ was raised. Opinions will differ whether the reference here is to the grave (cf. R. L. Harris in *ETSB* 4 [1962]: 129–35) or to the underworld. See ABYSS; HADES; SHEOL. R. L. HARRIS

deer. At least three species of deer (family *Cervidae*) lived in Palestine during OT times, but they were probably not distinguished. It seems agreed that Heb. ʾayyāl H385 (fem. ʾayyālâ H387, "doe") applied to all three or at least to the larger two. Those once native to Palestine are the following:

(1) Red deer (*Cervus elaphus*). This species formerly had a wide distribution, living in all suitable wooded parts of Europe and SW Asia, and also in N Africa. Its range has been reduced, and with the destruction of forest it has sometimes become a moorland and mountain animal. Red deer were often preserved strictly as royal game, and with continuing protection they have survived even in industrialized lands. This animal stands 4–5 ft. at the shoulder and the stag has large spreading antlers with ten or even more points, which are shed and renewed annually, as with all deer. This species disappeared from Palestine early, perhaps several centuries before NT times. It became extinct in Iraq less than one century ago, and the nearest survivors are probably in Anatolia and Greece.

(2) **Fallow deer** are much smaller, standing only 3 ft. All deer are spotted at birth, but in this species the coats remain spotted at all ages, especially in summer. Their antlers are palmate. This deer has been used as a park animal for so long and introduced so often that its distribution is confused. In early times there were two species in the Middle East, both living in hill forests. They disappeared long ago, but one, known as the giant fallow deer (*Dama mesopotamica*), survives in the Zagros Mountains of Luristan, Persia. Both red and fallow deer are herd animals for most of the year and more likely to be obtainable in quantity.

(3) **Roe deer** (*Capreolus capreolus*) are smaller still, standing only about 28 inches, with short upright antlers. In contrast to the others, it is solitary and stays mostly under cover, coming out only to graze on field margins. As a result it exists almost unknown in many woodland areas, and recorded facts about it are scanty, but it has long been lost to Palestine. Although it was probably the commonest kind, it was rarely depicted in ancient art, whereas the others were often illustrated.

All deer make excellent eating when in good condition and, being ruminants, were clean meat to the Israelites. The first references to deer in the Bible are in literal contexts, and they imply clearly that animals were familiar and regularly eaten (cf. Deut. 12:22). The meat was available daily for SOLOMON's kitchen (1 Ki. 4:23), and it could be that he had a deer park where fallow deer were kept in readiness. Other references are figurative, suggesting graceful animals, sure-footed and swift (e.g., 2 Sam. 22:34). (Cf. F. S. Bodenheimer, *Animal and Man in Bible Lands*, 2 vols. [1960–72]; *FFB*, 20, 26.) See also FAWN; GAZELLE.   G. S. CANSDALE

Fallow deer.

defile. This English term has been used to render about a dozen biblical words, such as Hebrew *ṭāmēʾ H3237* (e.g., Gen. 34:5; cf. *NIDOTTE*, 1:365–76) and Greek *miainō G3620* (e.g., Heb. 12:15; cf. *NIDNTT*, 1:447–49). In the OT five kinds of defilement are mentioned: *physical* (Cant. 5:3); *sexual*, either moral (illicit intercourse, Lev. 18:20) or ceremonial (intercourse at forbidden times, Lev. 15:24; 1 Sam. 21:5); *ethical* (Isa. 59:3; Ezek. 37:23); *ceremonial*, that is, rendering oneself ritually unclean so as to be disqualified for religious service or worship (Lev. 11:24; 15:19; 22:6); and *religious*, often hard to distinguish from the ceremonial, but concerned more with the heart attitude toward Yahweh (Num. 35:33; Jer. 3:1; Mal. 1:7, 12). The Gospels show that by the time of Christ the rabbis had extended the rules regarding defilement into a complex and very burdensome system (Mk. 7:2; Jn. 18:28). In the teaching of Christ and the apostles, defilement is uniformly ethical or spiritual (Matt. 15:18; Mk. 7:19; Heb. 12:15). See also CLEAN; HOLINESS; PURITY; SANCTIFICATION; UNCLEANNESS.

S. BARABAS

degree. This English term (which once could mean "step") occurs frequently in the KJV as a rendering of Hebrew *maʿălâ H5092*, used, for example, of the steps in the stairway of AHAZ (2 Ki. 20:9–11; see DIAL). The phrase "song of degrees" is found in the titles of Pss. 120–34 (NIV, "song of ascents"); it probably indicates that these psalms were especially appropriate for pilgrims "going up" to Jerusalem to worship. See MUSIC, MUSICAL INSTRUMENTS VI.D. Applied to persons, the term *degree* refers to social or official rank (e.g., "high degree," 1 Chr. 17:17 KJV).

degrees, song of. See MUSIC, MUSICAL INSTRUMENTS VI.D.

Dehavite di-hay´vit. According to the KJV and other versions, the Dehavites (RV, "Dehaites") were a people group listed among those who were transferred to SAMARIA by the Assyrians (Ezra 4:9). According to some scholars, they were the ancient inhabitants of Dehistan or Daikh, E of the Caspian Sea. However, no satisfactory identification has been made. For this reason, G. Hoffmann (*Zeitschrift für Assyriologie* 2 [1887]: 54) made the plausible suggestion that the Aramaic word in question, *dehāwēʾ*, be vocalized *dĕhûʾ* (lit., "which he [they]," used in the sense "namely"). This proposal, which agrees with two MSS and with Codex Vaticanus, has been widely adopted, with the resultant translation, "the people of Susa, *that is*, the Elamites" (cf. NRSV; similarly NIV, "the Elamites of Susa").   K. L. BARKER

Deir ʿAlla, Tell. A site 22 mi. SSE of BETH SHAN, on the E side of the Jordan, and identified with biblical SUCCOTH. Here, in 1967, a text consisting of several plaster fragments was discovered. Dated to 700–750 B.C., it appears to have been written in Old ARAMAIC, though some scholars believe it is a form of Canaanite. This find has created great interest not only because of its linguistic significance, but because it purports to be an account of a seer named BALAAM son of Beor. The text is difficult to interpret, but it presents Balaam as seeing a vision of the gods in council. It is clear that several centuries after the incident recorded in Num. 22–24, Balaam was remembered in the Jordan Valley as an important religious authority. (See J. A. Hackett, *The Balaam Text from Deir ʿAllā* [1984]; *NEAEHL*, 1:338–42.)

deities. See GODS.

deity of Christ. The English term *deity* (meaning "the essential nature of being God") could be used to render several Greek terms, including *theiotēs* G2522 (Rom. 1:20; NIV, "divine nature") and *theios* G2521 (Acts 17:29 NRSV, though here the word refers to the divine *being* [cf. NIV] rather than to the divine *nature*). Especially significant is the use of *theotēs* G2540 in Col. 2:9, "For in Christ all the fullness of the Deity lives in bodily form." In all three of these passages the KJV uses the term GODHEAD. (Another English word, *divinity*, can be a synonym of *deity*, but it is also used sometimes in the less forceful sense of "godlike character.")

The clearest and fullest expression of the deity of Christ is found in the Nicene Creed, which was originally presented at the Council of Nicaea, A.D. 325. In the Anglican *Book of Common Prayer* the translation appears as follows: "… one Lord Jesus Christ, the only begotten Son of God, Light of Light, Very God of Very God, Begotten, not made." (See CREED.) The claims of JESUS CHRIST embrace the idea that what he teaches God himself teaches, that what he has done only God could do, and that in his full personality there is an absolute oneness with God. To assert himself in any way at all is to assert God. Anyone making the claims that Jesus Christ makes for himself must be either mad and perverted or his claims must be true. Since the former simply cannot stand in the light of other evidence available, one is forced to conclude that the latter is established. Jesus Christ is what he claims to be: "Very God of Very God." The character portrayed in the Gospels and reflected in the rest of the NT will not allow us to believe that the one "altogether lovely" is a deceiver or self-deceived (*Si non Deus, non bonus*—"If he is not God, he is not good").

In the NT he is expressly called God, as seen in the order of the words in Jn. 1:1, *kai theos ēn ho logos*, "and the Word was God." The absence of the article simply shows *theos* to be the predicate, and the predicate precedes the verb for emphasis: the LOGOS was not only with God, he was God. (Cf. also Jn. 1:18 and Rom. 9:15.) In Tit. 2:13 there is a careful declaration of his deity, "the glorious appearing of our great God and Savior, Jesus Christ." Moreover, the address of THOMAS, "My Lord and my God" (Jn. 20:28), goes unrebuked by Christ in the presence of the disciples, who given their Jewish heritage would have regarded such a statement as blasphemous unless true (see also Phil. 2:6; Col. 2:9; Heb. 1:8; 1 Jn. 5:20).

OT descriptions of God are applied to Christ. The descriptions, the support of oral tradition, the writers of the Gospels, Paul in his Jewishness: none of these could have allowed for the treatment of Christ as he appears in Scripture apart from their acceptance of the truth of deity (indignation was the normal and automatic reaction of the Jews to Christ's assertions of his relationship to the Father). Take, for example, the frequency of prophetic support in Matthew's gospel: "Prepare the way of the Lord" (Matt. 3:3; cf. also Jn. 12:41 with Isa. 6:1; Eph. 4:7–8 with Ps. 68:18; 1 Pet. 3:15 with Isa. 8:13). The NT writers move so easily from the OT God, whose name is ineffable, to Jesus' name that their point becomes self-evident.

As is attested in any systematic theology, other evidences of a scriptural support for the deity of Christ are legion. For example, Christ possesses the attributes of God: OMNIPOTENCE (Matt. 28:18; Rev. 1:8); OMNIPRESENCE (Matt. 28:20; Eph. 1:23); OMNISCIENCE (Matt. 9:4; Jn. 2:24–25; Acts 1:24; 1 Cor. 4:5); TRUTH (Jn. 14:6; Rev. 3:7); LOVE (Jn. 3:16); HOLINESS (Lk. 1:35; Jn. 6:69; Heb. 7:26). "In him was life" (Jn. 1:4; 14:6). He possesses the attributes of eternity (Jn. 8:58; Col. 1:17; Heb. 1:11; Rev. 21:6) or self-existence or immutability. The works of God are ascribed to him in such things as the creation of the world, the upholding of all things by his power, the raising of the dead, and the judging of the world. His name is associated with God's name upon a footing of equality. The titles of deity are applied to him. He is willing to receive the honor and worship that are due only to God, and his equality with God is expressly claimed. There may be reasons why the deity of Christ might be controverted, but such reasons cannot be drawn from any serious acceptance of Scripture. (See the standard works on systematic theology, e.g., by C. Hodge, A. H. Strong, L. Berkhof, M. Erickson. Note also W. Sanday, *Christologies Ancient and Modern* [1910]; H. R. Mackintosh, *The Doctrine of the Person of Jesus Christ* [1912]; G. C. Berkouwer, *The Person of Christ* [1954]; M. J. Harris, *Jesus as God* [1992].) See also CHRISTOLOGY.

Every person who has been saved and who has the assurance of communing with Christ is by the nature of the experience driven to give the Redeemer the highest place and bow before him in worship. "Jesus Christ is the same yesterday and today and for ever" (Heb. 13:8) is not only a description of Christ's eternal essence but is also a useful description of the unanimous report in every age and in every place of the presence of Christ. Christian experience, rather than speculation, compelled the formulation of the doctrine of Christ's deity. Indeed it may be said that one does not think so much of the attributes of God and then apply them to Christ as that he sees Christ and knows what God must be like. See also TRINITY. A. H. LEITCH

Dekar. See BEN-DEKER.

Delaiah di-lay´yuh (דְּלָיָה H1933, "Yahweh draws up"). **(1)** Son of Elioenai and a descendant of DAVID through SOLOMON (1 Chr. 3:24).

(2) A priest during the time of David who was the leader of the twenty-third division (1 Chr. 24:18). Some scholars believe that Delaiah here is the family name of a later priestly group.

(3) Son of Shemaiah; he was one of the officials in the court of JEHOIAKIM who heard BARUCH read JEREMIAH's scroll and urged the king not to burn the inspired prophecy (Jer. 36:12, 25).

(4) Ancestor of a family that returned from the EXILE but could not prove that they were Israelites (Ezra 2:60; Neh. 7:62; 1 Esd. 5:37 [KJV, "Ladan"]).

(5) Son of Mehetabel and father of Shemaiah; the latter was an opponent of Nehemiah (Neh. 6:10; see SHEMAIAH #19). Some believe this Delaiah is the same as #4 above. In any case, he is not to be confused with a son of SANBALLAT by the same name who is mentioned in the ELEPHANTINE papyri (see *ANET*, 492b) but not in the Bible.

W. G. BROWN

Delilah di-li´luh (דְּלִילָה H1935, meaning disputed). A woman of pagan extraction mentioned as the temptress of the judge SAMSON (Jdg. 16:4–20). No convincing Semitic etymology for the name has been forthcoming, and the comparison to Arabic *dall*, "coquettish," is quite fanciful; the name may be related to *dallâ H1929*, "[flowing] hair." (Some literary scholars suggest that *Delilah* would remind Hebrew readers of the word for "night" [*laylâ H4326*], contrasting with *Samson* [*šimšôn H9088*], which sounds like the word for "sun" [*šemeš H9087*].) The woman was presumably a PHILISTINE. She seems to be pictured in the story as a courtesan who was hired by her countrymen to lure Samson into compromising his personal strength and his position as judge in Israel. In antiquity, the lot of women was closed off and separated from that of the men of her community; the exceptions were usually bar maids and prostitutes such as RAHAB (Josh. 2:1). It is probable that Delilah was one of these footloose women who were severely restricted in Israel. (See further L. R. Klein, *The Triumph of Irony in the Book of Judges* [1988], ch. 7; J. M. Sasson in *Prooftexts* 8 [1988]: 333–39.) W. WHITE, JR.

deliver. Although this English term has several meanings (e.g., "to give birth to" and more commonly "to hand over"), a very important one in the Bible is "to save, rescue, set free." In this sense, it can render a variety of words, such as Hebrew *gāʾal* H1457 (e.g., Gen. 48:16), *nāṣal* H5911 (Deut. 32:39), and *yāšaʿ* H3828 (1 Sam. 9:16), as well as Greek *rhyomai* G4861 (Matt. 6:13) and *sōzō* G5392 (Jude 5). (See *NIDOTTE*, 1:789–94 and related articles; *NIDNTT*, 3:177–223.) These verbs (and their cognate nouns) have many applications, referring either to material and temporal deliverance or to spiritual and eternal salvation. In the NT "save" largely takes the place of "deliver" in the OT, and the emphasis is more on spiritual and eternal deliverance, although the latter is present in the OT.

God's people are said to be delivered from bondage (Exod. 6:6; NIV, "I will free you"), and the exodus from Egypt is frequently alluded to as the supreme demonstration of God's power on their behalf. See EXODUS, THE. God can rescue us from death, troubles, and distresses (Pss. 33:19; 34:6; 107:6, 13, 19; C. Westermann, in *The Praise of God in the Psalms* [1965], 64–81, maintains that even in psalms of individual petition or lament there is a movement from supplication to praise for expected deliverance). God rescued DANIEL from the den of lions and his friends from the fiery furnace (Dan. 3; 6). The MESSIAH delivers Israel (Isa. 59:20; Rom. 11:26). The Father delivers us from the evil one, from the power of sin, from eternal death (Matt. 6:13; Acts 16:31; Eph. 2:8; et al.). Thus, even the basic idea of spiritual REDEMPTION or SALVATION is deliverance, including deliverance from sin's penalty, power, and, eventually, presence. K. L. BARKER

deliverer. This English term in the OT is usually the translation of a participle with causative meaning, such as *môšîaʿ* H4635, lit., "one who saves" (e.g., Jdg. 3:9; for other verbs, cf. Pss. 7:2; 40:17). The words so used are from common roots and can refer to both physical and spiritual deliverance.

See DELIVER. In the NT one finds the noun *lytrōtēs* G3392, "ransomer," applied to MOSES' work of delivering God's people from Egypt (Acts 7:35; cf. Ps. 19:14 [LXX 18:15]; this word is not used in secular writings). Of special importance is Rom. 11:26, which promises that a deliverer (participle of *rhyomai* G4861, "to rescue, save") will come from ZION. This is taken by some to predict the salvation of national Israel. Others refer it to spiritual Israel. The quotation is from Isa. 59:20, where the Hebrew has *gōʾēl* (participle of *gāʾal* H1457, "to redeem"), a term often used in the OT to refer to a kinsman who redeems a relative from poverty or who avenges a relative's murder (see AVENGER OF BLOOD; GOEL). The word is elsewhere applied to God as the redeemer of the helpless (see REDEMPTION). R. L. HARRIS

Delos dee´los (Δῆλος, "visible, conspicuous"). KJV Delus. A small Aegean island, regarded as the center of the Cyclades, which derive their name from their encirclement of Delos. That they do so is apparent to anyone viewing the panorama of surrounding islands and sea from the 480-ft. summit of Mount Cynthus, the central rock knoll of the island. The island itself, barren of trees and uninhabited, is covered with the remarkable ruins of a Greco-Roman town.

Delos was reputed to be the birthplace of APOLLO and ARTEMIS, and from earliest recorded history the island was honored by song and dance. It was also the scene of a sacred festival that, as early as the 8th cent. B.C., attracted visitors from all parts of the AEGEAN world. The island was taken over by colonists of Greek stock as early as 1000 B.C., and was already famous as a place of Hellenic life by the time the *Odyssey* was written, in the 8th cent. History, in the stricter sense of the word, begins however in the 6th cent., when Pisistratus of ATHENS (560–527 B.C.) and Polycrates (who came to power in SAMOS in 540 B.C.) sought in turn to bring Delos within their spheres of control.

When the Persian fleet was on its way to Greece in 490 B.C., it respected the sanctity of Delos, and when, after the clash with Persia, the Greeks set up a maritime confederacy to protect their independence (in 478), Delos was chosen as the seat of the common treasury. When the Athenians boldly removed the treasury to Athens, Delos remained a member without tribute. Athenian control continued until the end of the disastrous war with Sparta that closed the 5th cent., when Athens lost her great naval power. A generation later (378–377) Athens led a revived maritime league and again controlled Delos. With Athens' final eclipse (in 314), her influence in Delos ended.

For the next century and a half, the island was administered by officials known as *hieropoioi*, with Ptolemaic Egypt and metropolitan Macedon, successor states of Alexander's empire, contending for power in the Aegean. Delos enjoyed the status and institutions of a city-state over this period. Monuments and inscriptions reveal the rivalries of the surrounding states—Egypt, Macedon, Pergamum, and Syria—under their Hellenistic kings, all of whom, however, seem to have respected Delian independence and the island's sanctity.

Early in the 3rd cent., Delos became the center of the Aegean grain trade. Foreign banking firms flourished and Italian names began to appear in Delian inscriptions. Delos lost her neutral status when she made the mistake of supporting Perseus of Macedon in his clash with Rome. Rome, after breaking Macedon, handed Delos to Athens, which had been shrewd enough to support the victor, and Athens replaced the whole Delian population by her own colonists (166 B.C.). Delos was made a free port to damage Rhodian trade, and the island rapidly became a cosmopolitan center of business commerce and the chief center of the slave trade in the central Mediterranean. It was one of the states to whom the Roman Lucius Calpurnius Piso appealed for protection of Jewish interests in the war with Antiochus VII (1 Macc. 15:15–24). When Mithridates of Pontus launched his great assault on Rome in 88 B.C., Archelaus his general massacred 20,000 Italians on Delos and the island failed to recover its commercial prosperity. The trade routes changed, and the place fell into the dereliction in which it is seen today.

The French began the archaeological investigation of Delos in 1873. Its mass of remains, buildings—public and private, sacred and secular—and its multitude of inscriptions have notably added to the knowledge of the Greek world and its culture. (See W. A. Laidlaw, *A History of Delos* [1933]; P. J. Hadjidakis, *Delos* [2003].)   E. M. Blaiklock

Deluge of Noah. See Flood, Genesis.

Delus. KJV Apoc. form of Delos (1 Macc. 15:23).

Demas dee´muhs (Δημᾶς *G1318*; possibly a shortened form of Δημήτριος or Δημάρατος). A companion of Paul first mentioned in the greetings sent from Rome to Colosse (Col. 4:14; Phlm. 24), but later marked for his desertion of Paul in his last imprisonment (2 Tim. 4:10). Paul speaks volumes in the few words applied to Demas: he "hath forsaken me, having loved this present world" (KJV). Demas had gone to Thessalonica, but whether this was his home and whether he continued to fall away or became a faithful preacher one cannot say. It is highly unlikely that he can be identified with the Demetrius of 3 Jn. 12 (cf. Don John Chapman in *JTS* 5 [1904]: 364ff.). Not lack of courage but a lust for materialism seemed to be his downfall.

L. Foster

Demetrius di-mee´tree-uhs (Δημήτριος *G1320*, "belonging to Demeter"). **(1)** The name of several Seleucid rulers, including Demetrius I Soter, who ruled from 164 B.C. until his death c. 150 (1 Macc. 7:1—10:52; Jos. *Ant.* 12.10.1–4 et al.; he was the son of Seleucus IV Philopator and the grandson of Antiochus the Great). His son, Demetrius II Nicator, assumed power c. 145 but lost it five years later, then ruled again 129–125 (1 Macc. 10:67—15:22; Jos. *Ant.* 13.4.3 et al.); it was this king who in the year 142 confirmed Simon Maccabee as high priest, thereby acknowledging Jewish independence. See also Hasmonean.

(2) A jeweler in Ephesus who raised a mob against Paul because the apostle's preaching had resulted in damage to the lucrative business of making silver shrines of the goddess Artemis (Acts 19:23–27). See silversmith. The name of one Demetrius, a warden of the Ephesian temple, has been found by modern explorers, but the suggestion that he was the same person as the one mentioned in Acts has not been widely accepted (on this matter and other questions regarding the text, cf. C. K. Barrett, *A Critical and Exegetical Commentary on the Acts of the Apostles*, ICC, 2 [1998], 922–23).

(3) A disciple whom the apostle John praised in his letter to Gaius (3 Jn. 12); it has been suggested that he was the bearer of the letter.

demon. This English word is derived from the Greek *daimōn* G1230, which was used of rather anonymous influences whether of a good or bad variety. When the concept of a supernatural spirit or intelligence subsequently developed in Greek circles, the word gradually acquired a malign connotation and was used as a general designation of malevolent powers; these were commonly assigned individuality and characteristic functions.

    I. Use in Greek thought
    II. Mesopotamian demons
    III. Egyptian demons
    IV. Demonism in the OT and Apocrypha
    V. Demonism in the NT

I. Use in Greek thought. The most common occurrence of *daimōn* in Homer was in connection with the idea of divinity, deity, or divine power, as contrasted with *theos* G2536, which denoted a god in person. Such a being was thus treated as a personification of the vague powers associated in the Greek mind with the activities of the major deities; in consequence they were thought to exert some influence upon human life. The term was also employed of an individual's genius, and thus of one's lot or fortune in life. In Hesiod the *daimōn* was sometimes regarded as one of the souls of men from the golden age who formed a connecting link between the gods and mortals. One result of this was that when *daimones* and *theoi* were mentioned in association with one another, the former were thought of as gods of inferior rank. Because the general fortunes of human life appeared to incline to a preponderance of evil, the term (in the sense of one's lot) acquired an increasingly malign connotation, especially at the hands of the Attic poets.

Despite this development, however, the term never completely lost its associations with the rather ill-defined powers believed to govern the circumstances of life, and for this reason the Greeks could think consistently of good as well as evil spirits. The latter were often thought of as ghosts, and it is interesting to note that the ghosts of heroes were commonly believed to be particularly dangerous, since for some unexplained reason they were capable only of working evil. The Greeks gave consistent credence to the idea of a guardian spirit that watched over an individual from his birth and that could be either friendly or malign in character. Quite independently of this, evil demons were represented as attaching themselves to an individual in order to insure his untimely end. A demon that was given the title of *alastōr* ("Avenging Deity") was credited with special powers of vengeance for the punishment of specific transgressions.

Among the Greek philosophers, Thales maintained that "all things are full of gods," and the Pythagoreans made this animism more specific by teaching that all the air was filled with souls, which they described in terms of demons and heroes. These disembodied entities were responsible for sending health and disease alike to both animals and men. Beneficial relations could be established with them through rituals of purification and expiation as well as by divinatory acts and omens. Heraclitus refined the popular concept of an indwelling, controlling deity by the remark that "character is each man's demon," while to Empedocles was credited the dubious distinction of describing the rehabilitation of wicked demons by means of various phases of reincarnation. Socrates gave the impression that he was not infrequently dissuaded from following a particular course of action through receiving a divine sign or warning, and this must have suggested to his hearers the operation of that kind of fate or destiny by which individual lives were popularly supposed to be controlled. Plato held that demons, which he identified with the souls of the dead as did his contemporaries, served as interpreters between the gods and men. Reflecting the thought of Heraclitus, he believed that the true guiding genius within each man was the soul, which was the gift of God. Aristotle had a rather less exalted view of the demonic situation, however, merely assenting to the popular theory that all men had demons that accompanied them consistently through life.

The most convinced exponents of demonism in ancient Greece were the STOICS, whose pantheism and fatalism enabled demons to be represented as experiencing human passions and emotions, pains and pleasures. Being composed of the same substance as the human soul, they enjoyed a permanent existence and were located in an area beneath the moon. Epicurus went to the other extreme in denying the very existence of demons, and maintained that even if they did exist they could not possibly communicate with human beings in any way (see EPICUREAN).

II. Mesopotamian demons. From their beginnings the Mesopotamian peoples were highly superstitious in character, due in no small measure to the influence of their natural environment and living conditions upon their religious projections. See MESOPOTAMIA. Whereas in Egypt the quiet, regular inundations of the NILE gave a sense of order and stability to life, in Babylonia the formulation of an ordered civilization was only the result of a prolonged struggle against the unpredictable and devastating floods to which the TIGRIS and EUPHRATES were subject. The Sumerians gave definition to the religious traditions of Mesopotamia, and in formulating the concepts that were to become normative for many centuries they took a low view of the significance of human life, regarding man as constituting little more than an afterthought of divine creativity. Sumerian mythology contained numerous allusions to the underworld gods or *anunnaki* and the seven evil *asakki* or demons, which also inhabited the nether regions.

Clay mask of the demon Humbaba, a monster mentioned in the Epic of Gilgamesh (from Sippar, c. 1800–1600 B.C.). An inscription on the back suggests that the entrails of an animal might be arranged in the shape of this face.

The demons were popularly held to be responsible for all the misfortunes that overtook men and were especially credited with causing the onset of DISEASE. In Mesopotamian thought sickness occurred when demons entered the apertures of the head and penetrated the internal organs. To forestall this activity it was necessary to resort to magical incantations, amulets, jeweled ornamentation, and the like. See MAGIC. The modern earrings and necklaces are survivals of an age when such adornments were endowed with magical power as a means of guarding the ears, nostrils, and mouth against invasion by disease demons. Thus Ea, the god of the waters, was especially invoked in incantations and spells, being venerated as the ally of humanity in its conflict with the malevolent forces of existence. Ea thus became the patron deity of those priestly orders that were trained in EXORCISM, the knowledge of spells, the formulating of incantations, and the interpreting of dreams and omens.

The spirits most dreaded by the Sumerians and their religious successors were the wraiths of those defunct persons who had not had the appropriate burial rites performed over them, or who had died under mysterious or violent circumstances. Such ghosts were popularly known as *etimmu*, and a special kind of exorcist-priest, the *ashipu*, was required to recite the proper incantations for dispelling their attacks. Such priestly activities involved a substitute for the sufferer, and the appropriate object, whether an animal, a clay image, or some other inanimate substitute, was regarded as being dead and already in the underworld. The offerings and rituals were made to the malign powers suspected of occasioning the disease, and when an incantation invoking such life-giving gods as Ea or Marduk had been pronounced, the sick person was regarded, often in an act of faith, as having risen from the dead, and by this means liberated from the malevolent power of the demon, ghost, or evil deity.

The Mesopotamians gave names to the demons they feared; some of the designations were those of actual diseases, while others were the names of hostile natural powers. One demon was known as Rabiṣu or "the croucher," because he was thought to lie in wait secretly for his enemies (cf. Gen. 4:7). Apparently the reason demons and evil spirits were given names was that the Sumerians and

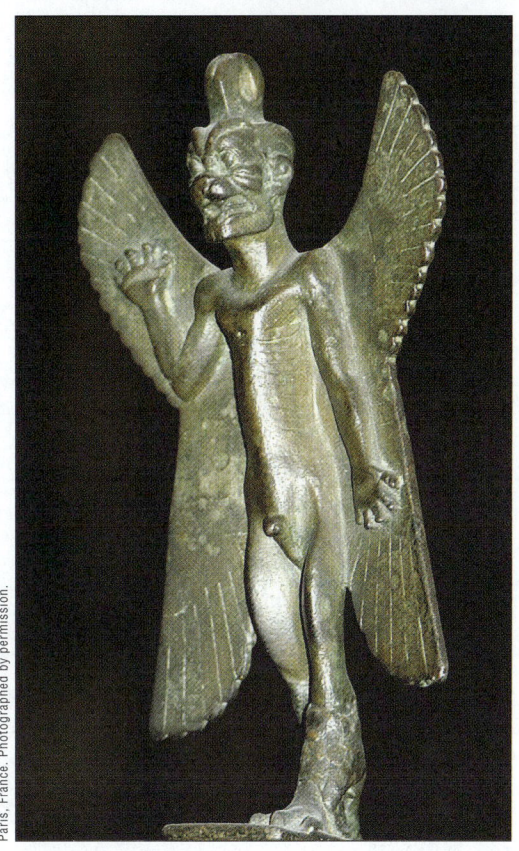

Bronze sculpture of an Assyrian demon (c. 1000 B.C.).

the Semites of Babylonia generally laid great stress on the belief in the magical power of names. If a demon was to be expelled, it was necessary for the exorcist-priest to know its name and use it properly in a conjuration or spell (cf. Mk. 5:9; Lk. 8:30). While the incidence of sickness was widely attributed to demons, almost any other kind of human activity could also be threatened by malign supernatural forces. For example, the laying of a foundation provided an occasion when demons could infiltrate the planned structure and bring about the subsequent collapse of the fabric. The Sumerian practice of making foundation deposits in all public and sacred buildings was marked by rituals designed to forestall the activities of the malevolent underworld powers and insure the stability of the structure against internal or external onslaught.

Among the Babylonians, Assyrians, and later Semitic peoples, there existed a great many non-human demons for whose creation mankind had no responsibility. The *asakki* of the Sumerians were known to the Babylonians as *utukku*, and were frequently mentioned in exorcism texts. Over the centuries the demons were accorded a realistic form, so that by the time of AsHURBANIPAL (669–627 B.C.) it was common for pictures or figurines of these evil powers to be made and employed for protective purposes. The *utukku* seem to have originated in the concept of ghosts, but in a developed form they were regarded as devils who lurked in the desert areas, ready to pounce upon the unwary or solitary traveler. A female demon named Lamashtu was an object of particular dread. The daughter of Anu, the Sumerian high god of heaven, she frequented mountainous regions or marshy areas looking for unprotected or straying children. Equally feared was the deity Namtar, the herald of death, who controlled sixty diseases that he was able to inflict at will upon mankind. Another deadly enemy of mankind who was associated with Namtar was Irra, the god of plagues, against whom many incantations were formulated. Another spirit of pestilence was named Ura, who was prominent in Babylonian apotropaic or protective tablets. These contained a representation of the deity in human form on one side, while on the other was inscribed an exorcist ritual or formula designed to discourage the attentions of the demon. Well-known among Semitic peoples of a later age was the Babylonian female demon Lilitu, who was in effect a *succuba*, a ghostly lecher who tempted men by means of sexual dreams. The Assyrian *ardat lili*, for whom there was also a male counterpart, was supposed to roam at night until she found an unmarried man with whom to mate.

III. Egyptian demons. As with other peoples of the ANE, the Egyptians believed in the presence of a multiplicity of demons against which the powers of magic had to be marshaled if everything was not to be blotted out by their malign influences. Despite a belief in demonic forces, the ancient Egyptians did not catalog their devils and evil spirits in the same way as so many other peoples did. Furthermore, such celestial phenomena as floods and storms, which elsewhere were regarded as the work of demons, were attributed by the Egyptians to the gods themselves. As in Mesopotamia, the incidence of disease was generally ascribed to demons, who would steal at night into the inert form of the sleeper to bring pain, fever, and perhaps even death. Powerful magical agencies in the form of charms and incantations were needed to combat such dreaded demonic influences.

Demons were also thought to inhabit the air itself, hence the need for periodic fumigation of temples and palaces, especially on the occasion of a funeral. More than any other demons, the Egyptians feared the disembodied dead, who in ghostly form could devise all sorts of malicious deeds against humanity. They could be held in check only by powerful magical spells, and in the *Book of the Dead* they were depicted as ready even to harm souls that had newly arrived in the nether world. Insofar as demons were named in Egyptian literature, they were described functionally by such epithets as "the cutter," "the archer," "the ripper," and so on, while specifically female demons were spoken of as "the lady of the sword thrusts," "she who is violent," and the like.

Because of the difficulty of distinguishing clearly in ancient Egyptian thought between a god and a demon, there is some ground for the view that the possession of a proper name served to identify a god as such. The situation is somewhat complicated by the fact that anonymous groups of demons were accorded superstitious veneration by sections of the populace from time to time, as well as by the process of development through which it was imagined that demons could become gods. Popular demonology in Egypt, however, manifested many of the characteristics found in the demonism of other nations, including the superstitious influence of days and horoscopes, the response of demons to chants, and the ability to control demons by the use of their correct names. Unlike the writings of the Babylonians, Egyptian literature never mentions demons who attacked children or who were wantonly bloodthirsty.

IV. Demonism in the OT and Apocrypha. In the earliest Hebrew sources there was no specific term equivalent to "demon," and in those cases where supernatural phenomena needed to be described, the words ʾēl *H446* and ʾĕlōhîm *H466*, commonly translated "God," were employed in the narrative. Thus an inspired man was a "man of God," that is, a godly man, an expression that found its counterpart in the Hittite phrase "man of the gods," that is, a seer. The word ʾĕlōhîm was frequently used in a descriptive sense of a formidable power, as in Gen. 30:8 ("*great* struggle") or Jon. 3:3 ("a *very important* city").

In the same neutral sense, the idea of a divine spirit possessing a person was employed to account for extraordinary phenomena such as the prophetic activities of Balaam (Num. 24:2) or Saul (1 Sam. 10:11; 19:20–23). The adjectival use of ʾĕlōhîm in connection with an evil spirit occurs in 1 Sam. 16:15–16, 23, but the English versions may be wrong in ascribing the provenance of the phenomenon to God. In actual fact, the use of the generic term for "god" was merely intended by the author to describe the evil spirit as "powerful" or "mighty," without any inherent demonism being conveyed. In the same way the outpouring of a positive spiritual endowment was described in Exod. 31:3; 35:31 by the expression *rûaḥ* ʾĕlōhîm or "impressive gifts," again incorrectly rendered in the English versions as "the Spirit of God." Possession by a powerful extraneous spirit was described by the same phrase in relation to the ecstatic activities of Saul (1 Sam. 10:6; 11:6). The exploits of Samson in the vineyards of Timnah (Jdg. 14:6) were attributed to the inspiration of the Lord, where the proper name YHWH may have been substituted for ʾĕlōhîm as an adjective (cf. Jdg. 13:25).

In view of the common ANE attribution of sickness to demons, it is important to notice that the diseases mentioned in the OT were related in their incidence to the activity of the one God, in line with the consistent monism of Hebrew thought. The plagues of Egypt came from the divine hand (Exod. 9:3), and even the calamities that overtook Job, including a loathsome disease (Job 2:7), were perpetrated by the adversary (Satan) with divine permission. Similarly the expression "convulsions have seized me" (2 Sam. 1:9 NRSV, but NIV "I am in the throes of death") has been claimed by some scholars to denote seizure or possession by an evil power, whereas in actual fact Saul was describing an attack of giddiness due to extreme emotional exhaustion. The occurrence of disease due to the activity of demonic powers has been wrongly inferred from the reference in Isa. 53:4, where the suffering servant was "powerfully smitten" (lit., "smitten by God") as part of his affliction. A plain reading of the Hebrew text makes it clear that this did not result from the activities of malign forces, even though his travails included the bearing of sicknesses and pains.

Yet the OT does contain some allusions to the popular demonology of pagan nations, particularly in the context of cultic worship. The plural of the term *šēd H8717* (Deut. 32:17, rendered in the LXX with *daimonion G1228*) referred to foreign gods (cf. Ps. 106:37), which need not have been specifically demonic in nature. In postbiblical Hebrew this word became the common designation of a malign spirit, and the reference in Deuteronomy may imply only the Assyrian *shêdu* or "guardian spirit." Another allusion to pagan gods occurs in Lev. 17:7, where the term *śāʿîr H8539* (lit., "hairy one," NIV, "goat-idols"; NRSV, "goat-demons") has been taken by some commentators as a reference to SATYRS. The same form usually means "goat," but in pagan thought the "hairy ones" were deemed to be sylvan gods or demons that inhabited waste places (cf. Isa. 13:21; 34:14; in 2 Chr. 11:15, the LXX renders the word with *mataios G3469*, "vain thing"). Goat worship, accompanied by depraved rituals, was prevalent in Lower Egypt, and was familiar to the Israelites of pre-exodus times. This was one form of worship from which God desired to preserve his people (cf. Josh. 24:14; Ezek. 20:7), hence the prohibition of offerings to satyrs.

In attempting to understand these terms, it is important not to regard late interpretations as necessarily identical in meaning with the original usage. While Arabic popular thought could envision a whole class of hirsute demons, all the OT references to "hairy ones" make it quite possible that the writers were speaking merely of wild goats or he-goats as objects of pagan veneration, not as spirits of the wilderness. While *šēd* could be given a demonic interpretation, its concrete use suggests a heathen deity rather than an indeterminate afflatus. Both Hebrew terms are specific rather than generic in nature, and thus an appropriate interpretation needs to take that fact into account.

Various demons referred to either by name or title in literature from the ANE are also mentioned in certain OT passages. There is a problem of interpretation, since the fact that all such allusions occur in poetic sections raises the question as to whether they are actually anything more than mere figures of speech. Isaiah refers to the familiar Akkadian female demon Lilitu by the Hebrew name of *lîlît H4327* (Isa. 34:14; LXX *onokentauros*, "satyr"; Vulg. *lamia*, "witch"). In Mesopotamian literature Lilitu appeared as an alluring female wraith who tempted men in sexual dreams, but by the 8th cent. B.C. she had tended to become confused in Palestine with the child-stealing hag Lamashtu. In popular thought LILITH was believed to be a night demon who prowled among ruins and lurked in desolate places, but despite this the name is not derived from the root for "night," as was once imagined. Instead it comes from the Sumerian term *lil*, meaning "wind."

Another demon familiar to ANE mythology was RESHEPH, who was mentioned in documents from such widely separated places as Mari, Ugarit, Egypt, Cyprus, and Carthage between the 19th and 4th centuries B.C. Resheph was the Canaanite deity of pestilence, and in both Ugaritic and Egyptian texts was associated with violent death. The pestilence as an agent of divine power is mentioned in Hab. 3:5 (*rešep H8404*), although there was no personification, despite the poetic nature of the passage. The term occurs also in Cant. 8:6, where it is used in the sense of "sparks" or "flames" (NIV, "blazing") rather than pestilence. In Ps. 76:3 it is employed to describe "flashing arrows," while in Ps. 78:48 it alluded to the destruction of herds by means of thunderbolts. What appears to be the threat of a febrile condition of high mortality is mentioned in Deut. 32:24, where the word carries overtones similar to those found in connection with Resheph in the Ugaritic texts. The idea of Resheph as a "searing flame" may have originated in Babylonia, where Girra was the god of fire as well as pestilence.

Since the foregoing references occur in poetic passages, it is difficult to imagine that they are anything more than thoroughly demythologized forms of literary allusion. The mention of Rahab (Job 9:13; 26:12; Ps. 89:10; Isa. 30:7; 51:9–10) has been interpreted as referring to a mythological dragon slain in primordial combat by God, although this explanation is doubtful if only because the meaning of the name is uncertain. See

Rahab (monster). The Septuagint translators were quite dubious about the allusion, omitting the word altogether in Isa. 51:9 and refusing to recognize it as a proper name in Isa. 30:7. In Job 9:13 and 26:12 it was translated by *kētos* ("sea monster") and was simply transliterated in Ps. 87:4. In this latter passage, as also in Isa. 30:9, the name was used figuratively of Egypt, with the implication that the proud nation would be humbled.

Some interpreters have seen further allusions to demonic influences in references to "the plague [*qeṭeb* H7776] that destroys at midday" (Ps. 91:6). The affliction in question may have been sunstroke, or possibly acute spinal meningitis, but the description is of a general nature, and although the LXX understands "the plague" as a demon (but not in Deut. 32:24; Hos. 13:14), there is no obvious personification in the Hebrew. While it is true that many ANE peoples regarded the onset of dizziness in the heat of the day as the result of demonic activity, the nature of the Hebrew expression makes it more probable that an empirical medical description, and not a demonic one, was being contemplated. Of a rather more substantial nature is the allusion in Ps. 91:5 to a phenomenon described as the "terror of night," which may reflect the universal dread of "things that go bump in the night." It is uncertain, however, from a straightforward reading of the verse, whether the terror is of an external order that produces fright, or of a purely internal kind due to the mild state of shock that accompanies an unexpected disturbance of sleeping patterns. Certainly there is insufficient evidence, particularly against a poetic background, for the assumption that the author had in mind one of the many malign spirits that in ANE demonology were popularly supposed to perpetrate their assaults under cover of darkness.

Yet another allusion to demonic powers has been seen in the reference to the "leech" (Prov. 30:15). The Hebrew term here (*ʿălûqâ* H6598) has generally been thought of as the equivalent of the late Arabic word for "leech," *ilgitu*. More romantic interpretations have argued from the late Arabic word *ʿaulaq* ("vampire, ghoul") to the view that the biblical reference was to a greedy demonic creature that fed with an insatiable appetite upon its victims. Again, it seems quite clear that poetic imagery alone is involved, and that the Hebrew sage was using metaphorical language to describe the relentless pressures exerted upon humanity by certain well-attested phenomena of nature and life. To regard the "leech" as an allusion to a vampire or some other demonic creature is to proceed far in advance of the available evidence.

A similar criticism can be entertained regarding what some have called "the seven evil spirits" in Deut. 28:22, where the children of Israel are warned that disobedience of the divine commands would cause God to smite them "with wasting disease, with fever and inflammation, with scorching heat and drought, with blight and mildew, which will plague you until you perish." Had this list originated from Mesopotamian sources, it could be argued that such terms as "wasting disease" and "fever" were the official names given to the demons thought to have occasioned the diseases, as with the celebrated Babylonian "Headache" series, where a specific disease was personified and addressed as though it were a spiritual being. The fact that the biblical utterance emerged from a specifically wilderness milieu prior to the entrance into Canaan emphatically repudiates any suggestion of either the presence or the influence of magic. Instead, Moses was promising the recalcitrant Israelites a variety of punishments that would affect their persons and their livelihood, and whose nature was already well known to them. To interpret these phenomena in demonic terms as though they were the Israelite counterparts of the agents of Irra, the Mesopotamian god of disease, is entirely fanciful and unwarranted by the evidence of the Hebrew text.

Another passage that has been wrongly interpreted in demonic terms is Job 18:14, where the wicked man is spoken of as being brought to "the king of terrors." Since this phrase occurs in a poetic section, it is best seen as a euphemism for death rather than as an allusion to Nergal, lord of the Babylonian underworld, or to Osiris, the ruler of the Egyptian dead. As a general observation it should be noted that such references to pagan mythology as do occur in the OT have themselves been thoroughly stripped of their pagan associations and appear largely as figures of popular thought or speech rather than as serious metaphysical concepts. Native to the OT Scriptures, however, was the idea of an "adversary" who was opposed to the outworking of the divine will. While OT references to his activities are few in number, they certainly depict them as being against the best interests of humanity. This character was most evident in the temptation and fall of man (Gen. 3:1–19), and illustrated further in the opposition presented to DAVID (1 Chr. 21:1) and the high priest Joshua (JESUA, Zech. 3:1–2). The book of Job describes the adversary as presenting himself before the Lord among the "sons of God," and shows that despite the inimical nature of his intentions, he was unable to carry out his plans without the permission of God. In this sense the book describes an experiment by Satan into the nature of disinterested virtue, and while it indicates that the evil that overtook Job was to some extent the responsibility of God, it also makes clear the fact that the operations of the adversary have never been free from all restraint.

During the period of the APOCRYPHA and PSEUDEPIGRAPHA, popular thought gave fuller expression to the concepts concerning good and evil spirits that had appeared in the canonical literature. This development was not uniform, for there are books such as Ecclesiasticus and Maccabees that contain almost no allusions at all to spiritual beings (cf. Sir. 48:21; 1 Macc. 7:41; 2 Macc. 11:6; 15:22–23). The Wisdom of Solomon makes no reference to demons or angels except in the description of the exodus (Wisd. 18:15), in which the divine word is spoken of as an active vengeful angel. Some of the APOCALYPSES carried the belief in good and evil spirits to great extremes, though a more moderate estimate appears in works such as Tobit and 2 Esdras, as well as in the *Testaments of the Twelve Patriarchs*, the *Apocalypse of Baruch*, and *Jubilees*. The author of the latter composition tended to attribute a spirit to the various natural forces (cf. *Jub.* 2.2; 10.5), while in the *Testaments of the Twelve Patriarchs* it is the immoral tendencies of human nature that are given demonic status. Seven "spirits of deceit" are enumerated, and to these wicked elements are subsequently added sleep and the human senses.

These evil forces led men into sin and then exacted retribution from them. In popular thought the demons became a distinct order of malign spirits operating under the control of BELIAL or Satan, the former term indicating an extremely wicked person (cf. Ps. 18:4). The apocalyptists generally thought of Satan and his allies as being overthrown by God and the powers of goodness before the new creation was ushered in (cf. *Test. Ash.* 1.9; 6.2; *Test. Dan* 1.6–7; *Test. Jud.* 13.3; 14.2; *Test. Levi* 19.1; et al.). This idea was also clearly formulated in the DEAD SEA SCROLLS, one section of the *Manual of Discipline* attributing all mortal plagues and difficulties to the "spirit of perversity" (1QS III, 22–24), whose control of evil forces was a continual embarrassment to the spirituality of the sons of light and righteousness (cf. 1QS IV, 12–13), but who would be vanquished at the dawn of the messianic age. This perverse spirit and his allies depicted in the Qumran writings have a great deal in common with the Iranian *druj* and the *daevas*, whose malign influences were greatly feared in Persia and elsewhere in the ancient orient.

Despite the impact of pagan thought, orthodox Jewish beliefs consistently challenged any dualistic tendencies that would cast doubt on the complete sovereignty and supremacy of God. In order to explain the ills that afflicted human beings, some writers thought of Satan as the archdemon who tempted man and led him astray (cf. Wisd. 2:4; *2 Enoch* 3.31). Such writers called Satan by his Greek name *diabolos G1333*, "devil," and identified him with the serpent of EDEN. In *1 Enoch* another view of the origin of evil involved a presentation of a theory of demonic beginnings. Devils, it was assumed, had at one time been angels who had rebelled against God and had caused mischief on earth by mating with human wives (cf. Gen. 6:1–4; Ezek. 28:13–17). Because matter was thought to be evil, following Iranian DUALISM, these spiritual beings had thereby corrupted themselves, and could only look forward to ultimate destruction by fire.

Further Persian influence is seen in the book of TOBIT, where a specific demon named ASMODEUS was regarded as a male counterpart of the Babylonian *succuba*. It is uncertain, however, whether the name is a variation of the demonic Shamedon, found in Palestinian Jewish midrashim, or whether it was actually a representation of the familiar Persian demon Aeshma. In any event, other aspects of the work exhibit clear traces of Persian demonology. Perhaps the most rational demonology in pre-Christian times occurred in the *Testaments of the Twelve Patriarchs* and the *Ascension of Isaiah*, where the evil propensities of man were personified and placed under the control of Beliar (a variant form of Belial). This avoided the fanciful practice of associating "fallen angels" with human mating procedures, and related most of the evil in the world to aberrant behavior.

During the intertestamental period most people, including the Jews of Palestine, believed that the world was full of supernatural agencies working for good or ill. Just as angels were able to accomplish beneficent deeds, so demons or devils were always at hand to perpetrate calamity, sickness, or misfortune. So pervasive had ANE superstitions become that Jews and Gentiles alike regarded the onset of disease as the work of demonic powers. In Israel, in particular, the physician was of comparatively low repute, since God was regarded as the dispenser of sickness and health alike. When superstitious beliefs in demons arose, the best the physician could do was to treat the patient by means of charms, incantations, and the like, which was a far cry from the nonmagical, empirical therapy of the Mosaic law.

V. Demonism in the NT. Whereas the subject of devils and demonism was not of particular interest to OT writers, there are many references to devils in the earliest Christian literature, and particularly in the Gospels. They were generally referred to by the term *daimonion* G1228, a diminutive form of *daimōn* but employed without any significant difference. In addition the term *diabolos*, already mentioned, was used to describe a "devil." As distinct from classical Greek thought, where *daimōn* was not infrequently employed in a good sense, the NT writers always thought of devils or demons as spiritual beings that were hostile to both God and men. The "prince" of these malign beings was accorded the name of BEELZEBUB, so that demons generally were regarded as his agents in human society (Mk. 3:22).

There were, however, a few instances (Acts 17:18; 1 Cor. 10:20; Rev. 9:20) where *daimonia* simply meant "pagan deities" rather than "demons." This was particularly the case when it concerned sacrificial meats offered to pagan gods, regarding which PAUL gave special attention (1 Cor. 10:20; cf. the teachings of Christ about the impossibility of serving God and MAMMON, Matt. 6:24; Lk. 16:13). Aside from this instance, there are few references to either demonism or demon-possession in the Epistles. In the Gospels the outbursts of demonic opposition to the work of God in Christ are most evident, and the evangelists depict Christ in continual conflict with evil forces. To expel demons was no easy matter, as the disciples discovered (Matt. 17:19; Mk. 9:28), and the recognition that Christ was able to accomplish this with apparent ease led his enemies to link him perversely with demonic forces instead of recognizing his divine origin (cf. Lk. 11:15; Jn. 7:20; 10:20). This association was quickly dispelled by Christ with the comment that a house thus divided against itself would soon fall (Lk. 11:17–18). This, in turn, led to the observation that if he by the "finger of God" was able to expel demons, then indeed the KINGDOM OF GOD was already present in contemporary society. Reporting the same incident, Matthew attributes the power of Christ in this area to the Spirit of God (Matt. 12:28).

Jesus shared his gifts of EXORCISM with his followers at the time of the mission of the Twelve (Lk. 9:1), where the disciples were given power and authority over all demons. Subsequently the Seventy (or Seventy-two) were sent out and on their return reported that even the demons were subject to them through his name (10:1–20). In NT times there was apparently no significant difference between

This coin from the 1st cent. A.D., with the LXF abbreviation and a running boar that symbolized the Tenth Roman Legion, can serve as a reminder of the legion of demons that Jesus sent into the herd of pigs.

demons, evil spirits, and unclean spirits, since in the case of the Gadarene demoniac the terms "unclean spirits" and "devils" were used interchangeably (8:27–29). In Lk. 11:24 the "unclean spirit" that went out of a man returned with seven other spirits of a more wicked though still kindred nature. Demons and evil spirits were regarded in the NT as one cause of disease (Mk. 1:23; 7:25), but it is interesting to note that such possession did not defile the sufferers either morally or spiritually, since they were not specifically excluded from the synagogue or the temple precincts. The possessing spirits were uniformly regarded as evil and had to be expelled on all possible occasions, for they were allies of Satan and thus hostile to God and man alike.

The nature of these references makes it clear that the evangelists did not treat evil as impersonal, a fact further substantiated by the intensely personal character of the temptations experienced by Christ (Matt. 4:1–11; Mk. 1:12–13; Lk. 4:1–13). Here as elsewhere the identity of the demonic force was revealed (cf. "Legion," Mk. 5:9; Lk. 8:30), and this was done to make evident its metaphysical reality as well as to confront it by an even more powerful force that also partook of a personal character. This force, expressed in the divine name, enabled the demons to be expelled (cf. Matt. 7:22).

The concept of the "power of the name" was widespread in antiquity, and was based on the assumption that the NAME was not only a personal designation but also represented an integral part of the personality of the bearer. The superior power inherent in the name of God was reflected by the psalmist (Pss. 20:7; 118:12), who entertained the defeat of pagan armies through divine intervention. In the time of Christ it was the custom in Jewish circles to commence a magical incantation against a demon with the words, "I conjure you by the name." This was reflected in Acts 19:13, where certain itinerant Jewish exorcists took it upon themselves to pronounce the name of the Lord Jesus over those who were possessed with evil spirits, using with entirely unexpected results the formula, "I adjure you by the Jesus whom Paul preaches." In the NT the only names of demons mentioned are Legion and the various designations of the "prince of the devils," namely Satan, Belial, and Beelzebub. The name "Legion" presents certain problems, because while it is given as the designation of the Gadarene demoniac (Mk. 5:9, 15; Lk. 8:30), it is clear that it is the large number of demons who are speaking and not the man himself. Perhaps the demons were unwilling to identify themselves and gave instead a collective name indicative of a large number, which would accord with the tradition of Matt. 12:45 and Lk. 8:2 that demons preferred to go about in groups. The "destroying one" (1 Cor. 10:10; NIV, "destroying angel") is not so much an evil demon as an avenging angel of God (cf. 2 Sam. 24:16), while the prince of the abyss (Rev. 9:11) named Apollyon (see ABADDON) was an angel also, not a devil in revolt against divine power.

In the Gospels the term *daimonia* is used to designate unclean spirits, although Luke prefers the expression *pneumata akatharta* (cf. Lk. 8:29; Acts 5:16; et al.). They are described as "seizing" and "tormenting" people (Mk. 9:28; Acts 5:16). Sometimes a person "had" them (*echō G2400*, Lk. 4:33), the result of which was physical disorders (Matt. 4:24; 9:32; Mk. 9:18; Lk. 11:14; et al.) or mental pathology (Matt. 11:18; Jn. 10:19–21; et al.). Although the descriptions of disease are framed for the most part in untechnical or popular language, there does seem to have been some attempt in the NT to differentiate between demon-possession and other forms of pathology. Neurasthenic conditions were allotted to the same general classification as demon-possession, and these were viewed in a somewhat different light from epilepsy and lunacy. Despite this, however, the thought of the day tended to attribute the same demonic etiological factors to both varieties of mental affliction. What is significant, however, is that in certain passages (Matt. 4:24; Mk. 1:32; Acts 5:16; 10:38) demon-possession was referred to as additional to the other kinds of diseases mentioned, which would imply that it had certain recognizable features of its own.

The ancient beliefs concerning the influence of the moon over certain types of mental conditions was reflected in the case of the epileptic boy (Matt. 17:14–18; Mk. 9:14–27; Lk. 9:37–42), whom Matthew described as "moon-struck" (*selēniazomai G4944*). The NRSV rendering of "epileptic," apart from describing one of the symptoms, furnishes no greater understanding of the pathological situation than does Matthew's popular terminology, and serves to illustrate some of the difficulties involved in understanding the recorded case histories in the Gospels. In this instance, for example, it is virtually impossible to say whether the boy was suffering from a true congenital epilepsy, from infantile idiopathic epilepsy, or from some deep emotional disturbance in the subconscious mind that resulted in epileptoid attacks. For this reason it is obviously quite arbitrary to assume that demon-possession was actually nothing more than a popular designation for epilepsy. In any event, modern scientific medicine has its own difficulties with epilepsy, since very little is actually known concerning the etiology of the clinical form. As a result it becomes extremely difficult on occasions for doctors to distinguish between the classical convulsive disease and glandular or emotional disturbances that may simulate it. See discussion of epilepsy under DISEASE.

Numerous forms of epilepsy have been described to date, including hereditary types and those that may have resulted from a cerebral tumor, an apoplectic stroke, or some injury to the brain tissue. Single convulsive attacks that give the appearance of genuine epilepsy can also be precipitated by deep emotional conflicts, to which the ancients were no less liable than their modern counterparts. If such attacks are brought into focus by means of a sudden shock that produces cerebral vasoconstriction with a rapid reduction in the oxygen content of the brain, an epileptiform seizure would take place. When speaking of emotional conflicts, one is attempting to designate certain processes of an ill-defined nature that operate deep within the uncharted recesses of the subconscious mind and that are thus not readily amenable to detailed clinical delineation. It is known, however, that the vital forces of the human personality function within this area of the mind, and that there is always a significant emotional or psychic element in most diseases, and not least in idiopathic mental afflictions. If such states are to be seen in terms of the evil, destructive powers found in the subconscious mind gaining the ascendancy over the positive forces for good in the human personality, it is possible to think of all mental disorders as being to some limited extent at least the result of temporary possession of the human mind by demonic influences, a situation that could conceivably become permanent. Indeed, in so far as specific clinical conditions can be identified as emotogenic, the same considerations could apply to a significantly wider range of human afflictions.

Because modern psychosomatic medical research has shown that attestable clinical disease can result from such metaphysical entities as suggestion, emotional conflicts, fear, and the like, it is no longer possible to dismiss as implausible the noxious effects that the various forms of evil, working through the personality of fallen man, can have upon individual and mental well-being. Indeed, Jesus viewed all disease in these general terms, and reemphasized the OT concept of the individual as "a living being" (Gen. 2:7), that is, a personality manifesting an essential unity of body and mind. He frequently saw the incidence of disease as the result of evil producing an imbalance within the individual personality, and his healings stressed that the will of the Father was for humanity to enjoy wholeness and salvation (Jn. 3:16; 10:10). So important was the human mind to Jesus that many of his teachings were formulated in a way that would help his followers to achieve inward peace (Matt. 11:29), as illustrated by the SERMON ON THE MOUNT.

Prominent NT cases of demon-possession include the Syrophoenician's daughter (Matt. 15:22; Mk. 7:25), the Gerasene demoniac (Matt. 8:28; Mk. 5:2; Lk. 8:27), the Capernaum madman (Mk. 1:23; Lk. 4:33), the blind and mute demoniac (Matt. 12:22; Lk. 11:14), and the young woman with divinatory insights (Acts 16:16). In the case of the little Syrophoenician girl, her mother described her acute condition as "suffering terribly from demon-possession" (Matt. 15:22; "possessed by an evil [unclean] spirit," Mk. 7:25), but aside from this there are no other clinical indications that would assist in determining precisely what constituted demon-possession. The Gerasene (Gadarene) demoniac(s) behaved as though a separate personality was speaking through the man's mouth and using his physical strength to destructive ends. His psychosis was deeply entrenched, and it has been suggested that his self-imposed name of Legion furnishes a hint as to the origin of the shock that precipitated his illness, namely some atrocity committed in the area by the Roman LEGION, possibly the massacre of children. Whether this is actually the case or not, the sufferer spoke as though possessed in the most literal sense, and the phenomena that accompanied his cure did nothing to dispel this notion in the minds of those who witnessed it. The Capernaum madman spoke as though he was a victim of multiple personality, and his convulsive interlude during the healing might have resulted from the discharging of long-repressed emotion in the subconscious mind. The narratives concerning the blind and mute demoniac are too vague to admit of pronouncements concerning the nature of the affliction, unlike those of the young woman with divinatory gifts, who seems in point of fact to have been little more than a fortune teller or soothsayer. While such individuals were popularly supposed to be "possessed," they certainly came into a different category from the mentally afflicted, since they were not diseased in any clinical sense. One interesting form of possession (Matt. 12:43–45) showed that the spirits were sometimes concerned with moral evil. Quite obviously people cannot effect their own moral reformation merely by expelling the "demons" within and leaving a spiritual vacuum. What is needed to sustain human efforts at reformation is the entrance of the Spirit of God.

Evidences of contemporary survivals of the biblical type of demon-possession have been described from oriental countries by medical and other missionaries. Generally the phenomenon assumed the form of characteristic personality possession, and when the individuals concerned had been exorcized, they subsequently led normal healthy lives. A modern psychiatrist would describe many cases of "possession" by quite different terms, which, however, prove to be no more meaningful than those of the Bible. The soundest approach to the situation is ultimately a theological one, which recognizes that because of the depravity of human nature the mind is peculiarly liable to the influence of evil. In imbalance this constitutes a form of possession, however mild, since the personality is then at the disposal of the powers of darkness to some extent.

(See further R. C. Thompson, *The Devils and Evil Spirits of Babylonia* [1903]; id., *Semitic Magic* [1908]; H. Kaupel, *Die Dämonen im Alten Testament* [1930]; J. Trachtenberg, *Jewish Magic and Superstition* [1939]; L. D. Weatherhead, *Psychology, Religion and Healing* [1951], 62–70; T. H. Gaster, *IDB* 1:817–24; J. W. Montgomery, ed., *Demon Possession* [1976]; G. Twelftree, *Christ Triumphant: Exorcism Then and Now* [1985]; C. F. Dickason, *Demon Possession and the Christian* [1987]; S. H. T. Page, *Powers of Evil: A Biblical Study of Satan and Demons* [1995]; C. Wahlen, *Jesus and the Impurity of Spirits in the Synoptic Gospels* [2004]; *DDD*, 235–40.)

R. K. HARRISON

Demophon dem′uh-fon (Δημοφῶν). A district governor in Palestine during the Maccabean era (2 Macc. 12:2; see MACCABEE). With him were mentioned three other governors, Timothy, Apollonius, and Hieronymus, who were in favor of the hellenizing policy of the SELEUCID regime. This brought them into conflict with the more orthodox segments of Judaism, provoking local disturbances.

R. K. HARRISON

Demotic. This term (meaning "of the people" or "popular") is applied to a simplified form of ancient Egyptian. See LANGUAGES OF THE ANE I.B. The *Demotic Chronicle*, written in that form of the language, is a document giving information about dates, feasts, and religious themes within the context of the political history of Ptolemaic Egypt (4th cent. B.C.). The term is also used to designate a form of Modern Greek based on everyday speech.

demythologization. See MYTH.

den, lions'. A phrase used various times in Dan. 6:7–24. The Aramaic word used here, *gōb H10129*, refers to a trenched-out "pit." The Babylonians and Assyrians kept lions captured in the marshlands as beasts for hunting and as pets. They are shown in the magnificent reliefs of the Neo-Assyrian rulers ASHURNASIRPAL II (884–859 B.C.) at Nimrud (CALAH) and ASHURBANIPAL (669–626 B.C.) at NINEVEH. The later Medo-Persian rulers continued this practice. The punishment described in Dan. 6 has not survived in visual representation, but the condemnation to a "trial by ordeal" has many precedents in Mesopotamian-Iranian law. When DANIEL was spared, his accusers were condemned to the same fate (Dan. 6:24). The dens in which lions crouch and feed are mentioned elsewhere as frightful places (Job 38:39–40; Amos 3:4; Nah. 2:11–12).

W. WHITE, JR.

Denarius coin with the image of Emperor Tiberius.

denarius di-nair′ee-uhs (δηνάριον *G1324*, from Lat. *denarius*). Plural *denarii* (di-nair′ee-i). A standard silver coin in the Roman Empire, roughly equivalent to the Greek DRACHMA. It was widely accepted as a day's wage for common laborers. The KJV translates the Greek term with "penny" (pl. "pence"). See COINS.

deny. This English term can be used to render several Hebrew words, such as the piel form of *kāḥaš H3950* (e.g., when SARAH denied that she had laughed, Gen. 18:15 NRSV; NIV, "lied"), the hiphil of *nāṭâ H5742* (e.g., of setting justice aside, Exod. 23:6; NRSV, "pervert"), *mānaʿ H4979* (e.g., when AGUR asks the Lord not to deny his requests, Prov. 30:7 NRSV; NIV, "refuse"), etc. In the NT it is usually the translation of the Greek verb *arneomai G766*, "to say no, reject, disown," which may be used in both negative contexts (such as PETER's denial or disowning of Jesus, Matt. 26:34, 70, et al.) and positive ones (we should deny ourselves, that is, set aside our self-interests, Matt. 16:24 et al.). Especially important are those passages that warn believers against denying the faith (e.g., 1 Tim. 5:8). See APOSTASY.

deposit. An individual in biblical times would sometimes leave a deposit either as security or for safekeeping. Since there were no banks or security houses in the ancient world, it would not be uncommon for an individual to deposit valuables with a friend or neighbor if he were going on a journey. Specific laws are spelled out in Exod. 22:7–13 and Lev. 6:1–7 concerning the protection of deposits (in Lev. 6:2 and 4 the NRSV uses "deposit" to render Heb. *piqqādôn H7214*; NIV, "something entrusted"). The person to whom goods or money are entrusted bears a heavy responsibility to watch over those goods. If it can be proven that he was negligent with that which he had been entrusted, then he is responsible to pay the owner in full. See also PLEDGE.

In the NT, the term *deposit* is sometimes used as the rendering of Greek *parathēkē G4146*, "property entrusted to another," used with reference to the GOSPEL, which has been given over to the apostles and disciples for their care, so that they might proclaim it faithfully (1 Tim. 6:20; 2 Tim. 1:12, 14). In addition, the NIV uses the phrase "a deposit, guaranteeing [what is to come]" to render Greek *arrabōn G775* (2 Cor. 1:22; 5:5; Eph. 1:14). See EARNEST.   G. GIACUMAKIS, JR.

depravity. Scripture uniformly traces voluntary transgression to its root cause in sinful human nature (cf. Prov. 4:23; Mk. 7:20–23). In biblical history human depravity assumes particular prominence in the ANTEDILUVIAN period (Gen. 6:5). It is characterized by potency ("great ... wickedness on the earth"), inwardness ("every inclination of the thoughts of his heart was only evil"), and invariability ("evil all the time"). The flood that human depravity called forth swept away sinners, but it could not eradicate depravity (cf. Pss. 14:1–4; 51:5; 58:3; see FLOOD, GENESIS). When JEREMIAH contended against an external observance of religion that did not arise from inward love of God, he emphasized the fact of human depravity (Jer. 17:9). In his conflict with the PHARISEES, our Lord drew attention to the innate perversity of the heart (Mk. 7:20–23; Jn. 3:6). According to the teaching of PAUL (Rom. 5:19) all human beings have depraved natures, for they all have imputed to them the SIN of ADAM, which carries with it "involvement in the perversity apart from which Adam's sin would be meaningless and its imputation an impossible abstraction" (J. Murray in *NBD*, 1107). With a chain of quotations from the Psalms, Paul proves that depravity is a deep-seated and universal moral perversity (Rom. 3:10–18).

Because men and women are depraved, they turn aside from God (Rom. 3:12). They are incapable of pleasing God, since even their "good" actions do not spring from the principle of love to God that finds expression in obedience to his law (8:7–8). Depravity is not partial, extending to part of mankind only, or only to part of the HUMAN NATURE. It is total. This description should not, however, be misunderstood. It does not mean that people are as thoroughly wicked as they could possibly become. Neither does it mean that the unregenerate sinner is lacking in an innate knowledge of God (1:19–21), or is without a conscience that distinguishes between good and evil (2:15–16). Nor does it imply that the sinner does not, and cannot, approve of virtuous character, or that he is incapable of kindness toward others (Lk. 11:13). It does mean that inherent corruption extends to every aspect of human nature. The sinner is depraved in *all* the faculties and powers of body and soul.

The implications of the biblical doctrine of depravity are far-reaching. First, since the sinner is incapable of spiritual good, SALVATION must be entirely of GRACE. In particular this means that we must be renewed in all our faculties by the HOLY SPIRIT. Second, evangelism and apologetics should proceed on the assumption that human reason is as corrupted as the will and the affections. While the truth of the gospel will be presented to the mind, there will be the awareness that without the enlightenment of the Holy Spirit the sinner remains in darkness (1 Cor. 2:14). Finally, in the realm of SANCTIFICATION, true HOLINESS will be defined not merely in terms of outward actions, but also in respect of the inward principles of positive desire for the glory of God and love of his commandments.   D. P. KINGDON

depth. See DEEP (THE).

deputy. This term meaning "a person empowered to act for another," is used occasionally in English Bible versions to designate, for example, an official appointed to function in lieu of a king (1 Ki. 22:47). The KJV also uses the term to render the Greek word *anthypatos* G478 (Acts 13:7 et al.), which is more accurately translated PROCONSUL.

Derbe duhr'bee (Δέρβη G1292, possibly from a dialectical word for the "juniper tree"; adj. Δερβαῖος G1291). A city situated in the southeastern part LYCAONIA, a region that was part of the Roman province of GALATIA. It was the most easterly locality visited by PAUL and BARNABAS on the journey in which they established the churches of southern Galatia. The reason for their pausing at this point is plain if Paul's Roman strategy is taken into account. To proceed further E would have taken them beyond the confines of the Roman province and into the territory of a client kingdom (Acts 14:6–7). Later, Paul and SILAS visited the place as they moved westward on the second journey through ASIA MINOR: coming from CILICIA, they reached Derbe first, then passed on to LYSTRA (Acts 15:40—16:1).

The site of Derbe has been a matter of considerable debate. The last chapter of W. M. Ramsay's study (*The Cities of St. Paul* [1908], 385ff.) discusses the matter at great length, but the precise locality seems to have been established in 1956 by M. Ballance at Kerti Hüyük, some 13 mi. NNE of Karaman, or Laranda, and 60 mi. SE of Lystra ("The Site of Derbe: A New Inscription," *Anatolian Studies* 7 [1957]: 147–51). Therefore, as F. F. Bruce remarks, the closing words of Acts 14:20 must necessarily mean that the following day Paul and Barnabas *set out for* Derbe: "Translations which suggest that the journey from Lystra to Derbe was completed in one day belong to the time before the location of Derbe was known" (*The Acts of the Apostles: The Greek Text with Introduction and Commentary*, 3rd ed. [1990], 325). Derbe must also have

The unexcavated site of Derbe. (View to the NW.)

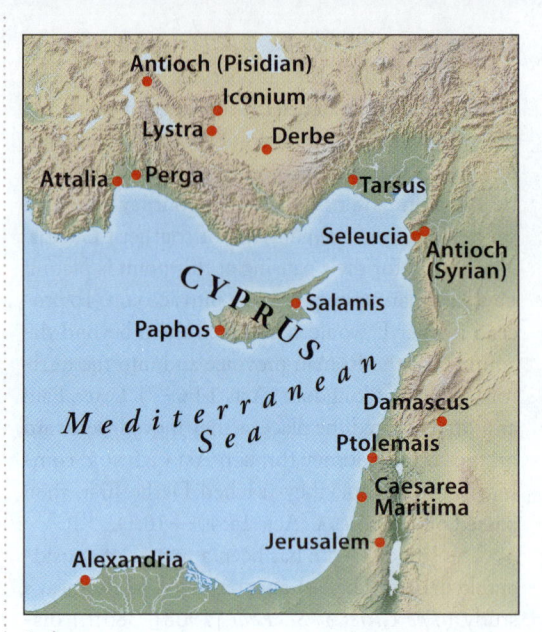

Derbe.

been on the route of Paul's third journey, but wins no mention in the later narrative of Acts.

Derbe has left no great mark on history. Amyntas, ruler of Galatia from 39 to 25 B.C., held the area as part of his domain, and Derbe must have passed with the rest of his territory into Roman hands in the year of his death (25 B.C.). From A.D. 41 to 72, it was dignified with the prefix Claudia, in recognition of its position as a frontier town of the province. This covered the period of the visits of Paul and the establishment of the Christian community in the area. Of that community, one GAIUS is known (Acts 20:4). He traveled with Paul, no doubt as one of the representatives of the Galatian churches in the deputation that carried monetary contributions for the poor of the Jerusalem church.

E. M. BLAIKLOCK

descent into Hades (hell). An alleged descent of Christ into HADES or HELL is an article in the doctrinal tradition of the entire Christian church. It is strange, however, that few doctrinal statements have had more research and less clarity of understanding than this single statement. Not only are the sources of tradition blurred, but Scripture passages thought to throw light on the doctrine are denied by some authorities as source material, and those used as support create problems in exegesis even to every single word. Because of these obscurities, some denominations do not now include "he descended into Hades" in their liturgical use of the APOSTLES' CREED.

I. The tradition. This particular expression does not appear in the early Roman Symbol but makes its first appearance in the Symbol of Aquileia by Rufinus. It appeared in the Fourth Sirmian Formula in A.D. 359, in the same year in the Formula of Nice, and again in Constantinople in 360. Its appearance in these creedal statements, however, reflected an earlier tradition, as it had already been mentioned by CLEMENT OF ALEXANDRIA, TERTULLIAN, JUSTIN MARTYR, and IRENAEUS. Thus there is a clear tracing to the apostolic period. The question still remains what was understood during the patristic period and in the early creedal statements. Was the descent made for the deliverance of the OT saints? Was it an offer of the gospel to those who had not heard it? Was it a victorious battle with SATAN who tried to restrain Christ? None of these questions is clearly answered, and in some such form they still remain.

The early church had hard questions about what had taken place between Christ's death and resurrection, questions akin to those reflected in the Thessalonian epistles regarding what would happen to those who died before Christ's SECOND COMING. Two problems were particularly difficult: (1) Where was Christ's spirit between death and resurrection? (2) What was the fate of those who had died before the gospel was preached? According to the climate of opinion of the day, Christ went to Hades (the abode of the dead) precisely because he was dead and buried. What, then, was he like there, and what did he do there? As far as can be known now, the beginnings of this doctrine of the church rest more in tradition, for which there are now no clear answers, than in biblical interpretation, which seems to have been a later development used to justify the tradition.

What can be understood of the nature of the abode of the dead in the day in which the tradition arose? There is the possibility of provisional judgment on the soul at death, awaiting the judgment of the last day, a provisional place of punishment (Lk. 16:23) known as GEHENNA (Matt. 5:22, 29–30) or the furnace of fire (13:42, 50), from which there is a possible transition to PARADISE before the last day, the latter view playing into Roman Catholic hands on their position on purgatory (see INTERMEDIATE STATE). What can be said then of a provisional state of salvation, as, for example, ABRAHAM'S BOSOM (Lk. 16:22) or the kingdom of heaven (Matt. 25:34; Lk. 13:29; 2 Tim. 4:18; 2 Pet. 1:11), or Jesus' words to the thief on the cross, "I tell you the truth, today you will be with me in paradise" (Lk. 23:43)? These questions are further aggravated in the preaching of PETER, for he applies to Jesus the words of Ps. 16:10, "For you will not abandon my soul to Hades, or let your Holy One experience corruption" (Acts 2:27 NRSV). Jesus had applied Isa. 61:1 to his own ministry, "He has sent me to proclaim release to the captives" (Lk. 4:18 NRSV), a statement understood by some as a reference to the prison house of Hades. (For a discussion of descents to the underworld in ancient thought, see R. Bauckham in *ABD*, 2:145–59.)

II. Exegesis. The basic text used in support of the *Descensus ad inferos* is 1 Pet. 3:19, with the wider context of vv. 17–22. Interestingly enough, the basic text does not expressly state (as does the Apostles' Creed) that Christ even descended into the realm of death, that is, Hades. Interest is restricted to two particular facts: (1) that Christ preached and (2) that his preaching was for "spirits in prison." Of significance in interpretation is the verb for preaching, *kēryssō* G3062, which is consistently used in the NT for the announcing of the KERYGMA, that is, the proclamation of the Christian gospel that Jesus is the Christ, that the Suffering Servant is the Lord. One can assume, therefore, that this is the content of the preaching to the "spirits in prison." Whether it was a message of judgment or release on this occasion is not even mentioned, and the reader is shut up to the single idea of the proclamation of the gospel. That Christ went in the spirit and not in the flesh seems perfectly clear from the context, although this raises serious questions for the Lutheran tradition, which insists on the ubiquity of Christ's body.

Apart from the message preached, there are intractable questions about the nature of "the spirits in prison." Although some light is shed on this issue by the reference to NOAH (1 Pet. 3:20) and to BAPTISM (3:21), the character of these "spirits" is so confusing that attempts have been made to evade the thrust of the passage entirely. J. Rendel Harris, for example, argues that v. 19 contains a textual error in which the name of ENOCH has been dropped out (cf. E. G. Selwyn, *The First Epistle of St. Peter*, 2nd ed. [1947], 197–98), and that the passage therefore refers to the apocryphal book of *1 Enoch* (relating to Gen. 6:1–4) with scriptural authority equal to that of Jude 14. Peter was trying to give support to Christians under the pressure of evil men, and reading Jude 6–16 one obtains the impression that there are no distinctions between angels and men, and that exceptionally evil persons often assumed superhuman proportions. The relevant passage is in *1 En.* 67.4—69.1 and especially 67.12, "This judgment wherewith the angels are judged is a testimony for the kings and the mighty who possess the earth." Although brilliant work has been done by Harris and supported by both Moffatt and Goodspeed, there is no real evidence at all for their conjectures. Selwyn (p. 360) makes out of this passage that Christ's death was a proclamation to the powers of evil: "And what St. Peter and St. Paul assert of these powers of evil, as the divine Master had asserted it before them, is that in Christ's death their end was sealed." This may well be true, but there is no evidence for such an interpretation of this passage.

The simplest meaning, although still an unsatisfactory one, is that the Lord, between his death and resurrection, descended into Hades, although Peter does not say so (Hades or SHEOL could be in this case a place of punishment or bliss or some such intermediate state) and preached to certain spirits in prison there. Possibly, judging from the context in 1 Peter, they could have been the fallen angels spoken of in Gen. 6:1–4 or, more likely, the spirits of that rebellious generation who perished in the flood. However, see SPIRITS IN PRISON.

III. Church doctrine

A. The Roman Catholic position. According to Roman Catholic doctrine, during the interval between his death and resurrection, Christ descended into hell in the soul, and not in the body.

The scene of the Descent is the forecourt of hell, the *limbus patrum*. The purpose of the Descent was to show his power and glory even in the underworld and to comfort and deliver the souls of the just held captive there, that is, take them to heaven.

Although this is the official position, the theologians of the church are still left with many unsolved problems: (1) If Jesus promised paradise to the thief on the cross, what is the relationship of paradise to his time in hell, or is one to assume that paradise is wherever Christ is? (2) Where was Jesus' abode during the forty resurrection days between his preaching in hell and his ascension? In other words, where was he when he was not manifested to his followers? (3) After the incarnation can one think of Jesus Christ apart from his humanity? If so, what was his nature when only his spirit descended into hell while his body lay in the grave? (4) Does the passage in 1 Peter refer at all to the doctrine of the Descent?

B. The Lutheran position. The Lutherans are faced with the difficulties of other doctrines as related to the Descent, such as the ubiquity of Christ's body and the problem of soul sleep. The Lutheran problem is intensified by the apparent discrepancies between the theological position and the popular discourses. Luther seems to give a definition in his Easter sermon of 13 April 1533 (Earl. ed., 19:40–54): "The Lord Christ—his entire person, God and man, with body and soul undivided—had journeyed to hell, and had, in person, demolished Hell and bound the Devil." Apparently in such a statement Luther has accepted ubiquity and dismissed its problems. In his exordium on this Easter discourse he commented, "And it pleases me well that, for the simple, it [*Descensus*] should be painted, played, sung or spoken ... and I shall be quite content if people do not vex themselves greatly with high and subtle thoughts as to how it was carried out" (ibid., 40). Regarding the problem of the whole person, it is typical of Luther to say, "Please God, the banner, doors, gate, and chains were of wood, or of iron, or did not exist at all." In short, Luther rather characteristically gives some affirmations and dismisses the explanations.

C. The Reformed position. Here there is a complete abandonment of Roman Catholic dogma.

What matters is that Christ really died: *vere mortuus est*. He died and was buried and therefore went to Hades, the abode of the dead. He really died. Calvin thought that the Roman Catholic idea that the souls of the dead are confined in a prison is a *fabula*. He regarded the whole approach as "childish" (*Institutes* [1559], 2.16.9). With AUGUSTINE and Aquinas, Calvin looked upon the Petrine passage as referring to the agonies of the soul in death, what Jesus was experiencing during the hours of his death. He did not attribute the Petrine passage to the *Descensus* at all. The possibility that there is preaching to the dead and an offer of salvation after death has no basis in Scripture nor in any sound tradition of the church in Reformed doctrine.

IV. The modern emphasis. The descent into Hades is merely another way of emphasizing the depth of Christ's humiliation and his total identification with the sufferings of man in death. Furthermore, it is one more way of saying what the creed already said by reaching a climax in the building up of phrases: crucified, dead, buried, descended into hell. The creedal phrase "descended into hell" does not come out of the NT at all but develops out of the proclamation of his death and his "resurrection from the dead." James D. Smart puts it well: "Perhaps, then, 'he descended into Hell' is meant to say to us that Jesus not only shared with us our death and burial, that strange and troubling end of our familiar life, but so bound himself into one with men that he knew the agony of man's utmost deprivation of life.... Hell is the existence of the man who is alone with himself with no way of access either to God or to his fellow man. The descent into hell, then, is Christ with man in hell, what no man could expect, what no man could deserve; the love of God reaching across the abyss that sin has made, bearing the pain and darkness of hell with man in order to deliver him to the brightness and joy of life with God.... [T]his at last it means: that in his death he conquered death and hell, finishing the battle that he had waged throughout his life" (*The Creed in Christian Teaching* [1962], 131; see also *ERE*, 4:654–63). A. LEITCH

desert. This term, like *wilderness* and *wasteland*, refers to a barren, desolate area. The word is most often used of dry and sandy regions that have little rainfall.

I. Geography and culture. Deserts are mentioned in numerous contexts throughout the Bible. In most places it is a mild desert receiving some RAIN during the winter season of the year. Rain falls at intervals from November to April, causing flooding at certain places because of the treeless soil, while the other six months it is extremely dry because of the *khamsin* or desert winds. The NEGEV in the S is the driest area, with only one to two inches of rain per year. GALILEE, to the N, is at the other extreme as far as rainfall is concerned, for it receives as much as forty inches of rainfall per year. The reason for such a contrast in climate is the location of PALESTINE between the Mediterranean Sea and the harsh desert areas to the E. The winds from each direction are "in conflict," thus causing such extremes in climate.

The desert has had a far greater influence on the life and culture of Palestine than has the SEA. This is because of the lack of good natural harbors along the Palestinian coast, whereas to the N along the Syro-Phoenician (Lebanon) coast there are a number of excellent natural harbors (see PHOENICIA). SOLOMON had to depend upon the Phoenicians to carry out his interests on the sea, for his own people and land were not accustomed to that way of life. There was continuous hostility between the inhabitants of the desert and those of the more fertile areas. The lure of the planted crops was more than a hungry BEDOUIN tribe could withstand. In other periods of time when peace was negotiated, active trade took place over the desert routes, bringing many goods from the S and E to Palestine. The open avenue of trade or conflict with the desert kept Palestine a Semitic territory. Down through the centuries the Semitic nomads would either settle in Palestine or otherwise influence the culture so that it remained Semitic in spite of the Mediterranean contacts (Y. Aharoni, *The Land of the Bible: A Historical Geography*, rev. ed. [1979], 11).

II. Biblical words. Several words in the Bible are rendered "desert" or "wilderness." The most common and inclusive term in the OT is *midbār* H4497, "uninhabited land." It includes not only the barren deserts of sand and rock, but also the steppe lands that can be classified as semidesert. These would be used for the grazing of sheep and goats at certain periods of the year. The words *ṣiyyâ* H7480 (e.g., Isa. 41:18; NIV, "parched ground") and *yĕšîmôn* H3810 (e.g., Ps. 78:40; NIV, "wasteland") tend to be a little more narrow in meaning, referring to very dry and waterless areas. Another term, *ḥorbâ* H2999, refers to a place of ruin and rubble (e.g., Lev. 26:33). Two additional words sometimes rendered "desert" or "wilderness" are better treated as proper names: ARABAH (the barren plain located in the southern part of the Jordan valley) and NEGEV (the great southern desert tucked between the Sinai peninsula to the W and the Arabah to the E).

In the NT, the standard term is Greek *erēmos* G2245, "desolate [area]." This term is used not so much to designate a dry region, but more in the sense of a solitary place. It occurs, for example, with reference to the area around BETHSAIDA on the eastern shore of the Sea of Galilee (Mk. 6:31–32), even though there was "plenty of grass in that place" (Jn. 6:10).

III. Allegorical uses. The desert is presented both in a positive and in a negative way in its relationship to Israel. At the beginning of the nation's history, the desert was where God showed his power and his love for Israel (Jer. 2–3; Hos. 13:5). DEBORAH sings praise to the God of SINAI and the desert (Jdg. 5:4–5), and likewise HABAKKUK as he speaks about God's deliverance of Israel (Hab. 3:2–7).

Aerial view of the Desert of Paran. (View to the NE.)

The wilderness, however, also is seen as a place of sin. The golden calf scene took place in the desert (Exod. 32:23; see CALF, GOLDEN). KORAH's rebellion took place there (Num. 16–17). At SHITTIM many of the Israelites identified with BAAL PEOR (Num. 25) and suffered the judgment of God. (See *NIDOTTE*, 4:520–28.) G. GIACUMAKIS, JR.

desire. There are many biblical words (and expressions) that can be translated into English as "desire," including Hebrew *taʾăwâ H9294* (e.g., Ps. 10:17) and Greek *epithymia G2123* (e.g., Gal. 5:16). (For other terms in this semantic field, see *NIDOTTE*, 5:57; *NIDNTT*, 1:456–61; *LN*, 1:288–96.) See also WILL (VOLITION). Practically the whole spectrum of underlying psychological meanings is covered by the wide range of the biblical vocabulary. This clearly shows how important a characteristic it is, especially as far as Scripture is concerned. (On the use of English "desire" in Eccl. 12:5, see CAPERBERRY.)

I. Craving. One aspect of this word is that of craving or covetousness (see COVET), which is condemned and prohibited in the tenth commandment (Exod. 20:17). GREED is seen as lying at the base of sin and social injustice (Mic. 2:1–2). The writers in Proverbs and Ecclesiastes indicate a number of times that ENVY and greed are never satisfied (Prov. 27:20; Eccl. 5:10). The psalmist expresses it as the "cravings" of the wicked (Ps. 10:3).

II. Love. Under the category of LOVE would come friendship (Ps. 133:1–3). Then there is the love/desire expressed between a man and a woman, so vividly described in the Song of Songs. In Ezek. 24:16 there is illustrated the love/desire between husband and wife. The expression of love or desire toward God is seen in Deut. 19:9 and Rom. 10:1.

III. Good or pleasure. This third aspect of the word *desire* involves delight or happiness in beauty and accomplishment. SOLOMON had accomplished his goal in the construction of the TEMPLE (1 Ki. 9:1). Solomon granted to the QUEEN OF SHEBA all she desired that was good for her and her country (2 Chr. 9:12). Handsomeness is called that which is desirable (Ezek. 23:6). The Suffering Servant of Isa. 53 is not beautiful that he be desired (Isa. 53:2).

IV. Natural desires. Included here are hunger (Ps. 145:16), protection and refuge (Ps. 7:1), sexual desire separate from a love relationship (Deut. 21:11). PAUL strongly stressed the conflict that takes place between the desires of the old nature without Christ and those of the new nature under the control of Jesus Christ (Rom. 7). With spiritual growth the desires under the control of Christ would supersede those of the old nature.

G. GIACUMAKIS, JR.

desire of all nations, the. This phrase is found only in Hag. 2:7, where the KJV reads, "And I will shake all nations, and the desire [NIV, desired] of all nations shall come" (Heb. *ûbāʾû ḥemdat kol-haggôyim*). The prophet predicts glory for ZERUBBABEL's temple greater in the future than in the present. The verse is often taken as a messianic prediction (cf. Zech. 3:8; 9:9; note also that Hag. 2:6 is quoted in Heb. 12:26–27). The RSV translates, "the treasures of all nations shall come in" (ASV similar), taking the verse to mean that the temple will be enriched by foreign gifts or tribute. This reading involves a revocalization of the singular *ḥemdat* (construct of *ḥemdâ H2775*) to the plural *ḥămudōt* so that it agrees grammatically with the plural verb *ûbāʾû* (such an interpretation is reflected in the plural LXX rendering, *ta eklekta*, "the choice ones"). Others argue that this kind of grammatical irregularity is attested elsewhere (cf. GKC §146; the NRSV reverts to the sing. "treasure"). It seems from the context that the prophet was looking to the distant future, and elsewhere he apparently refers to Zerubbabel symbolically as the MESSIAH (Hag. 2:22–23; cf. Zech. 6:12). Some believe that Hag. 2:7 refers not to the arrival of the Messiah, but to the coming of the leaders of the Gentiles to join in worship in the messianic age. R. L. HARRIS

desolation, abomination of. See ABOMINATION OF DESOLATION.

Dessau des´aw (Δεσσαυ). A village where the Jews joined battle with NICANOR, a general of ANTIOCHUS Epiphanes, in Maccabean times (2 Macc. 14:16; ERV, "Lessau," following Codex A, *Lessau*). The town was probably located in the hills N of Jerusalem, but the precise site is uncertain.

destiny. As a proper name, this term refers to a pagan god, MENI (*měnî H4972*), which is mentioned once along with Gad, "Fortune" (Isa. 65:11; the KJV mistranslates this verse). See GAD (DEITY). One may guess that there is some similarity with the STOIC theory of fate, but the fact that the founder of Stoicism, Zeno, was a Semite is insufficient ground for asserting any historical connection.

Pagan ideas of fate or destiny vary. In Greek mythology and in some popular forms of Islam, the hour of death is determined, and perhaps the place also, but the ordinary course of life is left to chance. Stoicism, more consistently, insisted that every event was determined. Sometimes fate is supposed to be a blind, purposeless force, rather than providence, foresight, and wise planning. Again, the Stoics, particularly in later times, asserted the wisdom and foresight of God.

Though the word *destiny* is seldom used in English Bible versions (NIV Eccl. 9:2–3 et al.), the idea, divested of pagan implications, is frequent in the Bible. God sees the end from the beginning. He has appointed a destiny for the Christian, for the unbeliever, for Israel, and for other nations. As the *Westminster Shorter Catechism* (Q. 11) says, "God's works of providence are, his most holy, wise, and powerful preserving and governing all his creatures, and all their actions." See ELECTION; FOREORDAIN; PROVIDENCE.　　　　　　　　　　G. H. CLARK

destroyer, the. A superhuman being, used as an instrument of God's WRATH in the execution of his judgment. It is difficult to say whether this is a good ANGEL used by God as an agent of destruction, or SATAN or one of his minions. If a good angel, God could use it to bring both blessing and destruction. In Exod. 12:23 (cf. Heb. 11:28), the term occurs in connection with the tenth plague of Egypt, the destruction of the Egyptian firstborn. In 1 Cor. 10:10, Paul warned against grumbling, as some Israelites did in the wilderness and thus "were killed by the destroying angel" (NIV, for *olothreutēs G3904*). It is thought by some that here Paul was referring to the fiery serpents God sent to bring death to the complaining Israelites.

With different terminology, the concept is found elsewhere. For example, the Lord sent an angel to smite the people by means of a plague because DAVID had made a census of the nation (2 Sam. 24:16). In HEZEKIAH's time in a single night an angel destroyed 185,000 men in the Assyrian camp (2 Ki. 19:35). The prophet EZEKIEL saw in a vision a number of angels executing judgment upon Jerusalem and Judah (Ezek. 9:5–7). The psalmist petitioned that the angel of the Lord would drive his enemies like dust before the wind (Ps. 35:5-6). The composer of Ps. 78:49 believed that angels could smite one's enemies upon God's command. In the OT APOCRYPHA, JEREMIAH warned that the angel of God who was with the Israelites would punish them if they apostatized (Ep. Jer. 6:5–7), and HELIODORUS was flogged by angels ("two young men") when he attempted to plunder the temple at Jerusalem (2 Macc. 3:26).　　　　　　　S. BARABAS

destroying locust. See LOCUST.

Destruction, City of. The future name of one of five cities in EGYPT that, according to Isaiah's prophecy, will in the last day "speak the language of Canaan and swear allegiance to the LORD Almighty" (Isa. 19:18). The Hebrew word for "Destruction" used here, *heres H2239*, is thought by many to be a scribal pun for an original *ḥeres H3064* ("sun"), which is in fact the reading of some Hebrew MSS (including one of the DSS) and a few versions. If so, the name City of the Sun would be a reference to HELIOPOLIS. See also SUN, CITY OF THE.

Deuel doo´uhl (דְּעוּאֵל *H1979*, possibly "known of God"). Father of ELIASAPH; the latter was a Gadite leader (Num. 1:14, 24–25; 2:14 [MT *rĕʿûʾēl*]; 7:42, 47). In all these passages the SEPTUAGINT reads *Ragouēl*, which some scholars believe reflects the correct spelling. See REUEL #2.

Deuterocanonical Books. See APOCRYPHA.

Deutero-Isaiah. See ISAIAH.

Deuteronomistic History. Over the past fifty years, biblical scholarship has come to a virtual consensus that the books of Joshua, Judges, Samuel, and Kings comprise a single history of Israel sharing a literary and theological unity that reflects selected aspects of the theology of the book of DEUTERONOMY. Viewing Deuteronomy as the introduction to the historical account of Joshua–Kings, scholars have called the entire collection the Deuteronomistic History (DH).

The narrative in Joshua-Kings clearly reflects particular aspects of the theological viewpoint of Deuteronomy. Practices forbidden in Deuteronomy are routinely condemned in Joshua-Kings: idolatry (e.g., Deut. 4:23–24; Josh. 24:19–23; Jdg. 2:11–14; 1 Ki. 16:30–33) and worship outside the place God designated—ultimately Jerusalem (e.g., Deut. 12:1–14; Josh. 22:1–34; 2 Sam. 15:25–29; 1 Ki. 3:2–3). The covenantal perspective of Deuteronomy—i.e., that Yahweh was the God of Israel and expected her obedience to the COVENANT made at SINAI—also permeates these historical books: covenant blessing for obedience and covenant cursing for disobedience (e.g., Deut. 28; Josh. 7:1–26; Jdg. 6:1–5 [cf. Deut. 28:38–42]; 1 Sam. 15:20–23; 2 Ki. 1:16–17). While there are other deuteronomistic themes and features, these have been the main items upon which the scholarly consensus for the existence of a DH has been focused.

The idea that the books of Joshua, Judges, Samuel, and Kings share many similarities of theology, theme, and content, and that they reflect the theology of Deuteronomy, is certainly not new. In Jewish and Christian traditions, Joshua through Kings have always been collected together under more general headings—the Former Prophets in Jewish tradition, and the historical books in Christian tradition. Julius Wellhausen, the father of the source-critical approach to the OT, had argued from the outset of his research for the existence of a redactor and source that reflected deuteronomistic concerns. He labeled the redactor the Deuteronomist (Dtr) and called the latter's source the "Deuteronomistic Source" (D-Source). The influence of this Dtr was believed to extend beyond the PENTATEUCH. Gerhard von Rad, for example, looked for traces of the D-Source (and other sources) in Joshua through Kings.

The current concept of a DH, however, takes scholarship in a different direction: it is a movement from parts to whole, from looking at the sources to looking at the redactor. The books of Deuteronomy through Kings are treated as a literary, theological, and redactional unity in order to identify the situation, original audience, and theological focus of the Dtr. The Dtr's situation, rather than the more ancient context of the sources themselves, provides the context for interpretation.

I. Terminology: deuteronomic versus deuteronomistic
II. The origins of the theory of a single Deuteronomistic History
III. The characteristics of the Deuteronomist's redaction, according to Noth
   A. Programmatic texts
   B. Linguistic details
   C. Unified and overarching theological perspective
   D. Common, overarching, "consistent" chronology
   E. Purpose
IV. Scholarly reaction to Noth
   A. General agreement with Noth's theory
   B. Modifications to and disagreements with Noth's theory
   C. View of the monarchy a key issue for distinguishing redactors
   D. Alternate viewpoints
V. The editorial process
VI. Who were the Deuteronomists and how did their theology evolve?
VII. Purpose and occasion
VIII. Differences between deuteronomic and deuteronomistic theology
IX. The implications for interpretation of books in the DH
X. Conclusions

I. Terminology: deuteronomic versus deuteronomistic. Too often scholars have used these two terms interchangeably, which has led to confusion. It is best to distinguish them. *Deuteronomic* (in the traditional sense of the use of this term) refers to the issues and theology of the book (or at least some original core) of Deuteronomy itself, whereas *deuteronomistic* refers to the perspective and theology of the entire DH (Deuteronomy through Kings), a tradition that developed over time, up to—and including—the EXILE. While the term *deuteronomistic* describes a theology that is drawn from a larger body of texts, it is actually more narrowly focused and selective than *deuteronomic*. Put another way, deuteronomistic theology has taken a subset of themes and features from deuteronomic theology and elaborated them. Deuteronomistic theology accents these features in a manner that is not equally the case in deuteronomic theology. For example, centralized worship (Deut. 12) became one of the four primary pillars of deuteronomistic theology—along with the condemnation of idolatry, the encouragement of covenant theology, and the caution of retribution theology—though it is not similarly prominent in the theology of the book of Deuteronomy itself. *Deuteronomistic*, then, is the label applied to the tradition of interpretation that shaped the DH.

II. The origins of the theory of a single Deuteronomistic History.

Martin Noth is credited with originating the hypothesis of a DH in 1943 (English trans., *The Deuteronomistic History* [1981]). He observed that certain sections of Deuteronomy through Kings seemed to exhibit similar linguistic, stylistic, and theological characteristics (for the list of programmatic texts, see below, III.A). On that basis he argued that these books were not several independent works that had been edited and developed as histories over a long period, but rather a single, coherent history (the DH) that was edited from a deuteronomistic perspective, during the exile, by a single redactor (the Deuteronomist—Dtr). Noth also argued that the sources used by the Dtr in producing the DH had previously existed only as independent traditions, not as *collections* of texts or books.

Noth proposed that what currently exists as the separate books of Deuteronomy through Kings were produced as a unified whole by the Dtr, who brought the independent traditions together for the first time and wove them into a coherent whole, joining sections together with "seams" of new material which the Dtr himself supplied. In this sense, Noth viewed the Dtr not simply as an editor, but as an author. Noth believed that the Dtr did not significantly alter the preexisting traditions he included in his DH, but left them largely unchanged. The Dtr's creative contribution was in the arranging of the traditional materials and in the seam material with which he joined them. Noth was also innovative in his argument that Deuteronomy was produced as an introduction to the history. In particular, Noth said that the Dtr created Deut. 1–4 not as an introduction to Deuteronomy but as an introduction to the entire history.

III. The characteristics of the Deuteronomist's redaction, according to Noth

A. Programmatic texts. According to Noth, the Dtr strategically placed speeches and narratives at critical points in his account of the history of Israel, reflecting the Dtr's overarching theological point concerning the meaning of that history. These speeches and narratives "look forward and backward in the attempt to interpret the course of events" (Noth, *Deuteronomistic History*, 18). These texts were located at crisis points in the narration of the DH (e.g., the death of Moses, the entry into the land, the death of Joshua, choosing a king in Israel, etc.).

According to Noth, the following speeches were written by the Dtr and placed in the mouth of significant historical characters: Moses' opening speech to Israel in the land of Moab (Deut. 1–4); Joshua's opening words to Israel (Josh. 1); Joshua's speech prior to the covenant renewal (Josh. 23); Samuel's speech at a subsequent covenant renewal in response to Saul's inauguration as king (1 Sam. 12); Nathan's oracle of God's covenant with David and David's prayer in response (2 Sam. 7); Solomon's prayer at the dedication of the temple (1 Ki. 8:14–66). In addition, Noth argued that the Dtr was the author of the following narratives: the roster of kings defeated by Joshua (Josh. 12); the theological framework for the book of Judges (Jdg. 2:6–3:6); the theological rationale for the fall of Samaria (2 Ki. 17:7–23).

Identifying these speeches and narratives as sharing a common theology and linguistic style as well as providing the DH with its overall organization and chronology, Noth argued that they were created by a single author, the Dtr, and that the deuteronomistic author used them as the glue to hold together the traditions that he had collected as a single literary unit.

B. Linguistic details. Noth argued that the Hebrew in the Dtr's speeches and narratives was consistently of the most simple sort: "The characteristics of ['Deuteronomistic'] style, its vocabulary, diction and sentence structure, are, therefore, undisputed; we need not consider them in detail. But we note that this linguistic uniformity in itself must at least suggest that the work is self-contained" (ibid., 18). They repeat throughout the Dtr's programmatic texts and are easily identifiable.

C. Unified and overarching theological perspective. In the subject matter and theological outlook of the speeches and narratives which he attributed to the Dtr, Noth perceived a "language and way of thinking [that] closely resembles those found in the Deuteronomic Law" (ibid., 17). The deuteronomistic passages exhibit "a simple and unified theological interpretation of history" (ibid., 20). The foundation and framework for the Dtr's theology was to be found in the covenant God had made with Israel at Sinai. For the Dtr, obedience to God's covenant commands, especially his command against idolatry, was essential to maintaining a relationship with God. Idolatry became *the* covenant-breaking sin (Deut. 4:23–24), and covenant retribution—blessing for obedience and cursing for disobedience—became the interpretative lens by which he understood and presented God's actions with respect to Israel. The Dtr was not interested in the specifics of cultic worship, but only in that place of worship—all worship was to happen in Jerusalem, and Jerusalem alone (e.g., 1 Ki. 3:2–3).

D. Common, overarching, "consistent" chronology. Noth argued that the Dtr used his inserted speeches and narratives to structure the DH into five periods. It was also the Dtr who placed chronological notices throughout the history. In 1 Ki. 6:1, for example, the announcement of 480 years from the exodus to the laying of the foundation for Solomon's temple is a note inserted by the Dtr. If other deuteronomistic notes regarding time spans (e.g., such and such a judge judged for so many years) are added together, the sum is very close to the figure of 480 (ibid., 34–44). The Dtr's five major historical periods are as follows:

1. The history of the Mosaic period (Deut. 1–34)
2. The occupation of the land W of the Jordan (Josh. 1—Jdg. 2:5)
3. The period of the "judges" (Jdg. 2:6—1 Sam. 12)
4. Saul, David, Solomon (1 Sam. 13—1 Ki. 11)
5. The period of the Kings of Israel and Judah (1 Ki. 11—2 Ki. 25)

E. Purpose. According to Noth, the Dtr's purpose in organizing and recounting the DH in the way he did was to explain to the Israelites why they were in exile and to berate them for their sin, which was the reason God had sent them there. The exile was their fault, not God's. It was a sort of theodicy—a defense of God's actions—but with a very pessimistic tone that gave no hope.

IV. Scholarly reaction to Noth

A. General agreement with Noth's theory. In the last fifty years, scholars have come to a remarkable consensus (an unusual degree of it in the scholarly world) on the foundational principles underlying Noth's theory of DH. Scholars almost universally agree on the following points: (1) Deuteronomy to 2 Kings together comprise a unity called the DH; (2) someone akin to Noth's Dtr brought together and organized preexisting traditions and provided connecting narratives between the traditions; (3) particular aspects of the theology of Deuteronomy shaped the telling of the history; (4) the DH is tendential, written with a purpose that reflects the exigencies of particular moments of crisis in the life of Israel—in other words, the DH was addressed to an audience later in time than the events recorded, in order to exhort that audience concerning their own moment in time; (5) the final redactional hand was exilic.

Scholars also agree that Noth was mistaken in his view that the Dtr's viewpoint in the history was strictly negative and that his only purpose was to further chastise an Israel suffering in exile. Many have argued that the final verses in 2 Kings—the signal exaltation of JEHOIACHIN (the king of Judah in exile) at the table of the Babylonian king EVIL-MERODACH—offer some sort of hope for the future of the exilic community.

B. Modifications to and disagreements with Noth's theory. On the particular details of Noth's theory there is much less agreement. Most scholars, contrary to Noth, believe there was more than one redactor of the DH, but they disagree with each other over how many redactors there were, and in what period(s) of time they worked. Was the primary redactional hand exilic or preexilic? Also, most scholars argue that the previously existing traditions collected and used by the Dtr were edited by the Dtr himself, which was more than Noth allowed for. Some even argue that portions of the DH were compiled and edited by deuteronomistically oriented editors prior to the point at which the Dtr brought them together.

The two scholars who have put forth the primary positions modifying Noth's are Frank Moore Cross and Rudolph Smend. Cross's challenge to Noth's theory is made on primarily chronological grounds. In 1972, Cross argued that there were two redactions of the DH and that the *primary* redaction was preexilic, done by a first deuteronomistic redactor (Dtr¹) at the time of king JOSIAH as propaganda for Josiah's reform. Cross perceived two themes that characterized the Josianic edition of the DH, one grounded in deuteronomic covenant theology and the other in the covenant with David. The first was conditional and exemplified by the judgment on Israel for the sins of JEROBOAM. The second was unconditional and recounted God's enduring faithfulness to his selection of David as king and the promises he had made to David. Cross allowed that a second editor (Dtr²) worked during the period of the exile to produce a much less significant redaction, which does not affect the primary thrust of the Josianic redaction. Dtr² was deemed inferior to Dtr¹ and added only minor notes, primarily the ending to complete the history and to show that the Josianic reform had failed. According to Cross, the terseness of Dtr²'s additions and his lack of theological reflection on the fall of Jerusalem demonstrate that his work was a minor redaction. Cross's position has been modified by his students and others who have followed him, though they have held to his overarching framework of a double-redaction theory.

At approximately the same time that Cross argued for his double-redaction theory, Rudolf Smend (1973) argued an approach that differentiated redactors and redactions, not on chronological grounds, but primarily on the basis of theological perspective. With Noth, Smend saw the entire DH as exilic, but he believed that there were three redactors responsible for the production of the DH. The first one, who was similar to Noth's Dtr, was labeled DtrG (or DtrH) by Smend. Two other redactors followed, one after the other. These redactors could be identified by how they each distinctively added to and shaped the DH. The second redactor (DtrP) added material on the role of the prophets shown through prophecy and the fulfillment of prophecy (e.g., the prediction and fulfillment about the death of AHAZIAH in 2 Ki. 1:16–17). The third redactor (DtrN) added the material emphasizing retribution—obedience to the law leads to receiving blessing and disobedience to the law leads to being cursed (e.g., the obedience of the people was essential for inheriting the land in Jdg. 2:20–23). In Smend's view, Israelite law was a later development, a response to the need to reform Israel.

C. View of the monarchy a key issue for distinguishing redactors. Fundamentally Noth, Cross, and Smend identified their various deuteronomistic redactors on the basis of the putative redactor's particular attitudes toward kingship. Noth believed that the Dtr's view of the monarchy was foundational to the Dtr's theology: "Dtr. thought that the rise of the monarchy was of fundamental importance; with hindsight afforded by the situation in his own time, he inevitably concluded that the monarchy had led the Israelite nation to destruction—a theme that he developed in his treatment of the history" (Noth, *Deuteronomistic History*, 77). For Noth's Dtr there was nothing good about kingship.

Cross identified his primary Dtr (Dtr¹) as preexilic because he perceived that the unconditional promises to David (2 Sam. 7) shaped the relatively positive treatment of the kings of Judah up to Josiah, who was the apex of Davidic descendants for Dtr¹. Concurrent with the positive view of David, and especially Josiah, there was a thoroughly negative view of the kings in the north, whose failures were grounded not in the promises to David—they were not his descendants—but in the conditionality of the Mosaic covenant, exemplified in their idolatrous worship. The recurring phrase "for David's sake," the use of David's faithfulness as a standard against which the kings of Judah were measured, and the very positive view of Josiah led Cross to propose his Dtr[1], who was using David in a positive manner in order to elevate Josiah's position and advance Josiah's reform.

Smend and his students have primarily identified their three redactors—DtrG, DtrP, and DtrN—on the basis of various attitudes toward kingship found in the DH. DtrG was perceived to be mildly negative about the monarchy; DtrP elevated the role of the prophet to one who almost universally condemned the monarchy; and DtrN took the innovative position (innovative for his moment in history, the late exile) of looking back to Davidic kingship as a basis for the future restoration of kingship.

To summarize, Noth identified a negative tone in the texts concerning kingship in the DH and believed that this negative tone shaped his Dtr's history. On the one hand, Cross ultimately agreed with Noth that the final redactor (Cross's Dtr[2]) was not positive in his view of kingship. On the other hand, Cross's Dtr[1] held a positive view of kingship, which Cross believed indicated a preexilic, Josianic redaction. Smend understood the positive view of kingship as pointing to a late exilic time.

D. Alternate viewpoints. W. Richter, A. Campbell, and others have argued, contra Noth, that some of the Dtr's traditional source material had already been compiled and theologically shaped in some sort of deuteronomistic fashion prior to the exile. Richter sees three separate deuteronomistic redactions of the book of Judges prior to Noth's Dtr. Campbell argues the existence of a pre-Dtr compilation, which he labels "the prophetic record." H. D. Hoffmann and J. Van Seters, on the other hand, while agreeing with Noth about one Dtr in the exile, have argued that deuteronomistic texts cannot be distinguished from predeuteronomistic texts, and that therefore the debate about pre-Dtr redactions is moot.

Provan and others go further and conclude that there is no DH as Noth proposed, but simply a set of independent books, each sharing a common deuteronomic source for the theology that shaped the recounting of the particular history in that particular book. From the perspective of the text-linguistics and literary analysis, each book has its own structural and theological coherence and integrity. "Particular books ... also appear quite different from each other in their particular theological emphases (cf., e.g., Judges with Kings). The construction of a 'Deuteronomistic theology' characteristically involves the blurring of all such subtleties, complexities and differences" (I. W. Provan, *1 & 2 Kings* [1997], 94).

Some have suggested that the idea of a DH falls prey to the assumption that all the writing of the Bible was generated by the crisis of the exile and was written only then or later. There is no doubt that Joshua, Judges, Samuel, and Kings show the influence of the theology and themes found in Deuteronomy. But the question of their overall unity remains a matter for continuing thought and exploration.

V. The editorial process. Part of what led Noth to posit the role of the Dtr in the formation of the DH was the recognition of logical and/or theological tensions among texts in the DH. One of the more celebrated inconsistencies concerns the monarchy; for example, 1 Sam. 8, the final section of ch. 10, and ch. 12 are deemed negative treatments of kingship, whereas chs. 9, 11, and 2 Sam. 7 (the covenant with David) are seen as positive. Noth accounted for this and other tensions by arguing that the Dtr used available source traditions as they were, that is, without editing them. The Dtr let seemingly contradictory texts stand together unchanged, and simply organized them into the DH, supplying his comments in connecting narratives, but not in the source traditions themselves.

Other scholars have unraveled the deuteronomistic editorial process and perceived tensions differently than Noth. While all agree that the editing process involved adding to, omitting from, and organizing traditional materials, there is a diversity of scholarly perspectives on the actual editorial activity in the DH, as follows: (1) one exilic author incorporated independent traditions without substantively editing the traditions themselves (Noth); (2) without omitting contrary voices, one or more editors added their variant voice to an existing tradition or redaction (Smend and Cross); (3) an earlier editor (or editors) had already compiled some of the traditions that were then used by a later deuteronomistic editor—with or without adaptation to the traditional materials (Richter and Campbell); (4) the work of the deuteronomistic editor cannot be distinguished from that of the editor of the preexisting traditions (Hoffmann and Van Seters). There are of course positions that suggest some combination of these perspectives. The tensions are there. The question is how to solve them.

VI. Who were the Deuteronomists and how did their theology evolve?

Almost all agree that Noth's Dtr did not create deuteronomistic theology, but that he worked within a long-standing tradition that had its roots earlier in the history of Israel. All agree that any exilic editing was attempting to explain the disaster of the exile in light of certain themes from deuteronomic tradition, themes that had become increasingly prominent during the course of Israelite history.

Most agree that by the time of the exile, deuteronomistic theology had existed in some form for generations and that it had its genesis in problems in the northern kingdom (Israel). Some (e.g., Nicholson) have argued that faithful prophets in the northern kingdom, who confronted apostasy in terms of the core deuteronomic concern of idolatry, originated deuteronomistic theology. After the fall of the northern kingdom (Israel) in 722 B.C., these northern prophets fled S to Judah and brought their anti-monarchical, anti-idolatry theology with them. The evidence for northern roots to the Dtr's theology is found in his negative view of northern kingship, defined by the sins of Jeroboam, which continue unabated through the entire period of the northern kingdom's existence: Jeroboam encouraged the people to worship at idolatrous shrines in DAN (PLACE) and BETHEL rather than at the temple in Jerusalem.

Some (e.g., M. Weinfeld) have argued that court scribes in the S preserved Israel's history and that deuteronomistic theology was at root a WISDOM theology—Israel would be known as a wise people on account of the law they had (Deut. 4:6–8). Others (e.g., von Rad) have argued that Levites (dispersed in various cities throughout the land) created deuteronomistic theology. R. E. Clements has argued that deuteronomistic theology simply originated as part of some reform movement, and that various reform movements through the generations took up the tradition and modified it for their contemporary situation.

In what location did the exilic Dtr(s) write: Babylon or Palestine? While there is no conclusive evidence for either locale, many suppose that the kind of access to sources required to produce the DH almost surely suggest someone living in Palestine.

VII. Purpose and occasion.

All are agreed that any deuteronomistic editorial activity was spawned by a particular crisis faced by the community of faith. Understanding the situation and its solution involved an appeal to reform by the means offered in deuteronomistic theology. The hypotheses about which specific crises occasioned the formation of the DH vary: the fall of the northern kingdom, the threat and attempt at reform in the period of Hezekiah, the reform of Josiah, or the aftermath of the exile itself. All these situations represent moments in time when the community of faith would surely have been seeking explanations and solutions that were rooted in covenant, law, and the book of Deuteronomy. As the various theories show, each period is a possible candidate for deuteronomistic redactional activity. The theological perspective was similar at any of these points: the community of faith failed to keep the law, summed up primarily in the sin of idolatry and failure to worship in Jerusalem alone. The problem was not that God's promises had failed or that he had been unfaithful, but that it was Israel who had failed and been unreliable.

VIII. Differences between deuteronomic and deuteronomistic theology.

The difference in deuteronomic and deuteronomistic terminology has already been briefly elaborated. The difference can be seen as one of accent. Deuteronomic theology shares with deuteronomistic theology the latter's main features: the condemnation of idolatry, the exhortation to worship only in the place of God's choosing (Jerusalem), the encouragement that God's covenant brings to his people, and the behavioral caution brought by an awareness of God's reward for obedience and punishment for disobedience. But these main features of deuteronomistic theology are integrated under broader and further reaching concerns in deuteronomic theology.

Deuteronomy 4 is arguably the key to understanding the theological orientation of the book, that is, deuteronomic theology. This passage argues that obedience begins with knowing and recalling who God is and what he has done. First and foremost Israel was to remember that since the beginning of time nothing like the exodus had ever happened, where a deity chose a people for himself in a most visible fashion. Indeed, the exodus was the event toward which God had been moving all history from the beginning in order to reveal himself (Deut. 4:32–35). God's people were to recall what God had done in the exodus (v. 9), learn to fear him and teach their descendants what he had done and to fear him (vv. 9–12). In the light of this knowledge that God had chosen them as his firstborn son, and in the fear of the Lord, they were to acknowledge him and obey him (vv. 39–40). Covenant, with its blessings and cursings, begins with "I am the Lord [Yahweh] your God, who brought you out of Egypt, out of the land of slavery" (5:6).

The centrality of the exodus, the movement from what God had done to what God required, and the command to teach Israel to fear God by proclaiming his past salvation are not listed among features attributed to the theology of the various Dtr's. Rather, reflecting on and applying Deuteronomy to those later situations when Israel had violated covenant, deuteronomistic theology accented the failures of Israel: their sin and covenant disobedience.

IX. The implications for interpretation of books in the DH. The idea that the books of Deuteronomy through Kings comprise a single literary unit impacts the interpretation of individual passages in these books in two ways. First, because interpretation begins with what the original audience should have understood, it makes a difference, for example, whether that audience was living during the period of Israel's exile in Babylon, or in Josiah's day, or in the period when David was king. The second implication is related to the first. Because in interpretation a passage is ultimately treated in the context of the whole of the corpus to which it belongs, a passage in a particular book will ultimately be understood differently if it is treated primarily as part of the entire DH rather than as primarily a part of that particular book alone.

For example, the introduction to Gideon in Jdg. 6:11–24 will be interpreted differently depending on the context. The framework of the entire DH, and therefore the situation in the exile, provides a different perspective than the more select context of an independent book of Judges, written perhaps during the early reign of David. Specifically, Gideon's first encounter with the angel of the Lord raises questions of his—or any judge's—fitness for leadership. For Israelites in exile, the application would be for the restoration of (kingly) leadership in Israel, whereas the application for Israelites in the period when David was first king would be to urge Israel to follow David and not Ish-Boseth, the son of Saul and king of the northern tribes for a time during David's early reign.

X. Conclusions. Noth's theory was relatively simple: in the exile, one author created one unified work out of diverse traditional material. The Dtr's theology was straightforward: idolatry was evil, and worship should take place in Jerusalem only. Failure on either count brought judgment on the people. Modification upon modification to Noth's theory has been made, but the scholarly consensus concerning the basic contours of the DH is still remarkable. Yet, the complexities of the redactors and the redactional process leave the scholarly community wrestling with the details of the theory.

(See R. Smend in *Probleme biblischer Theologie: Gerhard von Rad zum 70. Geburtstag*, ed. H. W. Wolff [1971], 494–509; F. M. Cross, Jr., in *Canaanite Myth and Hebrew Epic: Essays in the History of the Religion of Israel* [1973], 274–89; M. Noth, *The Deuteronomistic History* [1981]; T. E. Fretheim, *Deuteronomic History* [1983]; A. F. Campbell and M. A. O'Brien, *Unfolding the Deuteronomistic History: Origins, Upgrades, Present Text* [2000], 4–34; J. G. McConville, *Grace in the End: A Study in Deuteronomic Theology* [1993]; A. de Pury et al., *Israel Constructs Its History: Deuteronomistic Historiography and Recent Research* [2000]; R. F. Person Jr., *The Deuteronomic School: History, Social Setting, and Literature* [2002]; T. C. Römer, *The So-called Deuteronomistic History* [2005].) J. A. GROVES

Deuteronomy, Book of doo´tuh-ron´uh-mee. The fifth book of the Bible and traditionally one of the five books of MOSES (the PENTATEUCH or TORAH).

    I. Introduction
   II. Content
  III. Analysis
  IV. Authorship
      A. Critical views
      B. Traditional view
   V. Background
      A. Personal element
      B. Historical setting
      C. Geographical features
  VI. Later influence

I. Introduction. The English title of this book, meaning "second [*or* repeated] law," is derived from that of the SEPTUAGINT (Gk. *Deuteronomion*; Vulg. *Deuteronomium*). This title in turn is based on Deut. 17:18, where the Hebrew phrase for "a copy of this law" is incorrectly translated by the LXX as *to deuteronomion touto*, "this repetition of the law." Such a description, however, is not inappropriate, for the book does include, along with much new matter, a repetition or reformulation of a large part of the laws. In Hebrew literature the book (like the other books of the Pentateuch) was known from its opening words, "These are the words" (ʾēlleh haddĕbārîm), or simply, "Words" (*dĕbārîm*, pl. of *dābār H1821*).

II. Content. Deuteronomy claims to consist almost entirely of the farewell speeches of Moses addressed to the new generation that had grown to adulthood in the wilderness. The speeches are dated in the eleventh month of the fortieth year of wandering (Deut. 1:3), and it is stated that Moses wrote as well as spoke them (31:9, 22, 24). The three main discourses are preceded by a brief introduction (1:1–5) and followed by an epilogue (ch. 34) that narrates the death of Moses. The first discourse is chiefly historical and hortatory, reviewing the life of Israel in the wilderness from the mountain of Horeb or SINAI to the land of MOAB (1:6—4:43). This discourse contains a brief statement about setting aside three CITIES OF REFUGE on the other side of the JORDAN (4:41–43) and introduces the exposition of the law by Moses under the triple heading of testimonies, statutes, and ordinances.

The second discourse (Deut. 5–26) opens with an exposition of the TEN COMMANDMENTS and develops particularly the first commandment at great length (chs. 5–11). Next follow the laws that can be considered under the categories of ceremonial (12:1—16:17); civil (16:18—18:22); and criminal (19:1—21:9). This is followed by the miscellaneous laws pertaining to family and property (21:10—25:19).

The ceremonial laws treat place of worship (Deut. 12:1–28); idolatry (12:29—13:18; 16:21—17:7); clean and unclean food (14:1–21); tithes (14:22–29); remittance or release (15:1–18); setting aside of firstlings as holy (15:19–23); and holy seasons (16:1–17). The civil ordinances treat appointment of judges (16:18–20; 17:8–13); election of a king (17:14–20); regulations concerning the rights and revenues of priests and Levites (18:1–8); and rules concerning prophets (18:9–22). The criminal laws cover the manslayer and cities of refuge (19:1–14); false testimony (19:15–21); conduct of war (20:1–20); expiation of an undetected murder (21:1–9); and crime punishable by hanging (21:22–23).

The collection of miscellaneous laws covers such a variety of subjects as marriage with a female captive (Deut. 21:10–14); right of primogeniture

View from the summit of Jebel Musa looking SE up to the peaks of Jebel Katerina (St. Catherine's Mountain), the tallest mountain in Sinai.

(21:15–17); disobedient son (21:18–21); kindness to animals (22:1–4, 6–8); prohibition of various mixtures (22:5, 9–11); twisted cords on garments (22:12); punishment of unchastity (22:13–29); exclusion from the congregation (23:1–9); ritual cleanness in the camp (23:10–15); runaway slaves (23:16-17); temple prostitutes (23:18–19); exaction of interest (23:20–21); vows (23:22–24); use of neighbor's fruit and corn (23:25); remarriage after divorce (24:1–4); exemption of newly married men from war service (24:5); pledge (24:6, 10–13, 17–18); man-stealing (24:7); leprosy (24:8–9); wages (24:14–15); parents and children (24:16); treatment of strangers, orphans, and widows (24:17–22); excessive punishment (25:1–3); muzzling the laboring ox (25:4); levirate marriage (25:5–10); indecent assault (25:11–12); weights and measures (25:13–16); and the extermination of Amalek (25:17–19). The next section (chs. 26–27) presents the didactic applications of these laws, and ch. 28 is a declaration of the blessings and curses that will overtake the people, depending on whether they observe or neglect the prescribed statutes and ordinances.

The third discourse (Deut. 29–30) consists of a supplementary address, exhorting the people to accept the terms of the new covenant and promising them forgiveness in case of sin, if attended by wholehearted repentance. These three addresses are followed by a collection of miscellaneous materials, such as Moses' farewell, his deliverance of the law to the priests, his commission to Joshua, the Song of Moses, and the Blessing of Moses (chs. 31–33).

At least three elements—historical, legislative, didactic—can be traced through the book. The references to history are usually with a didactic aim. The legislative element tends directly to secure the national well-being. The tone of exhortation that runs through the earlier and later addresses pervades also the legislative portion. The laws are not systematically stated but are ethically expounded in order to set forth their relation to the theocratic principles laid down in chs. 5–11. The author's purpose is primarily hortatory; he is not a historian or jurist as much as he is a religious teacher.

The author wrote under a keen sense of idolatry and was deeply concerned to guard Israel against it by insisting earnestly on the debt of gratitude and obedience the nations owed to her sovereign Lord. Therefore, the truths on which he dwells are the divinity of the Lord, his spirituality (Deut. 4), his choice of Israel, and the love and faithfulness he has manifested toward it. From this is then deduced the need for Israel's loving devotion to him, an absolute repudiation of all false gods, a warm and spontaneous obedience to his will, and a generous attitude toward men.

Throughout Exodus–Numbers the Lord speaks to Moses; through Deuteronomy Moses speaks to the people. Here Israel's redemptive history is translated into living principles; Deuteronomy is more

Key locations from Deuteronomy.

commentary than history. The purpose is to arouse Israel's loyalty to the Lord and his revealed law. Deuteronomy clearly teaches that the relation of God to his people is more than law. The thought of the love of Israel toward her God, which is indeed laid down in the words of the Decalogue (Exod. 20:6; Deut. 5:10), is not explicitly required elsewhere in the Pentateuch, but in Deuteronomy it is earnestly insisted upon (Deut. 10:12; 12:1, 13, 22; 13:3; 19:9; 30:6, 16, 20). Appeals made to Israel to keep the commandments often are based on the recollection of God's might and of his terrible visitation, awe, fear; but the highest appeal is to the consciousness of his own free love (7:7, 8; 8:17; 9:4–6). Love indicating the people's affection and devotion to the Lord is again and again insisted upon as the true spring of all human action (5:10; 6:5; 7:8; 10:12, 15; 11:1, 13, 22; 13:8; 19:9; 30:16, 20).

The idea of Israel as "son" and of the Lord as "father" is set forth in Deuteronomy. The loving God had given Israel life by redemption from Egypt; he had reared and educated Israel in the wilderness (Deut. 8:2–3, 16; 14:2). These new Israelites, born and trained in the desert, were to inherit the blessings promised to their fathers. This intimacy emphasizes the demand that Israel should cleave to the Lord (11:22; 13:4) and not follow "other gods" (6:14–15; 7:4; 8:19–20; 11:16–17, 20; 30:17–18). Because Israel was holy, she was not to join other gods (7:6). This spirit of holiness was also expressed by observing love toward neighbor and charity toward the poor, widow, orphan, Levite, stranger (10:18–19; 24:17–21).

By means of the COVENANT, the Israelites became heirs of all the promises given to their fathers the PATRIARCHS (Deut. 4:31; 7:12; 8:18; 29:13). Israel was considered holy and peculiar, and especially loved by the Lord (7:6; 14:2, 21; 26:18–19; 28:9). They were indeed disciplined for their own good (8:2–5, 16), but also to be established as a special people, as the Lord's peculiar lot and inheritance (32:6, 9; 4:7).

The chief thought of Deuteronomy is the unique relation that the Lord, as a unique God, sustains to Israel as a unique people. The monotheism of Deuteronomy is very explicit: "Hear, O Israel: The LORD our God, the LORD is one" (Deut. 6:4). The LORD is the only God, and "besides him there is no other" (4:35, 39; 32:39), "he is God of gods, and Lord of lords" (10:17), "the living God" (5:26), "the faithful God, keeping his covenant of love to a thousand generations of those who love him and keep his commands" (7:9), who despises graven images and every species of idolatry (7:25–26; 12:31; 13:14; 18:12; 20:18; 27:15), to whom belong the heavens and the earth (10:14), who rules over all the nations (7:19), whose relation to Israel is near and personal (28:58).

Being such a God, he is jealous of all rivals (Deut. 7:4; 29:24–26; 31:16–17), and therefore all temptations to idolatry must be removed from the land, the Canaanites must be destroyed, along with their altars and images (7:1–5, 16; 12:2–3; 20:16–18). The other nations feared their gods, but Israel was expected not only to fear the Lord but also to love him and cleave to him (4:10; 5:29; 6:5; 10:12, 20; 11:1, 13, 22; 13:3, 4; 17:19; 19:9; 28:58; 30:6, 16, 20; 31:12–13). Israel was destined to enjoy the highest privileges because the people were partakers of covenant blessings; all others were strangers and foreigners, except when admitted into Israel by special permission (23:1–8).

III. Analysis. In recent years scholars have compared the covenant treaties (between suzerains and their vassals) in the ANE with the biblical material, and some have concluded that Deuteronomy, to a great extent, follows the classic covenant pattern consisting of the following sections: preamble, historical prologue, stipulations, curses and blessings, invocation of oath deities, direction for deposit of duplicate treaty documents in sanctuaries, and periodic proclamation of the treaty of the vassal people. M. G. Kline (*Treaty of the Great King* [1963]) has made a detailed comparison of Deuteronomy with this classic treaty structure and made the following outline of Deuteronomy: I. Preamble: Covenant Mediator (Deut. 1:1–5); II. Historical Prologue: Covenant History (1:6—4:49); III. Stipulations: Covenant Life (chs. 5–26); IV. Curses and Blessings: Covenant Ratification (chs. 27–30); V. Dynastic Disposition: Covenant Continuity (chs. 31–34). (For other approaches, cf. D. R. Hillers, *Treaty-Curses and the Old Testament Prophets* [1964]; M. Weinfeld, "The Loyalty Oath in the Ancient Near East," *Ugarit-Forschungen* 8 [1976]:

379–414; D. J. McCarthy, *Treaty and Covenant: A Study in Form in the Ancient Oriental Documents and in the Old Testament*, new ed. [1978].)

Stylistically, this comparison of the pattern of the international suzerainty treaty is noteworthy. Deuteronomy is an exposition of the covenant concept and reveals that God's covenant with his people is a proclamation of his sovereignty and an instrument for binding his elect to himself in a commitment of absolute allegiance. Ancient suzerainty treaties began with a preamble in which the speaker, the one who was declaring his lordship and demanding the vassal's allegiance, identified himself. The Deuteronomy preamble identifies the speaker as Moses (Deut 1:1), but Moses stands as the earthly, mediatorial representative of the Lord (v. 3), the heavenly Suzerain and ultimate Lord of this covenant. Following the preamble in the international suzerainty treaties there was a historical section, written in the I-thou style, which surveyed the previous relationships of lord and vassal. Benefits conferred by the lord upon the vassal were cited with a view to grounding the latter's allegiance in a sense of gratitude and fear. All these features characterize Deut. 1:6—4:49.

Following the historical section were the stipulations that constituted the long and crucial central section of the covenant. When suzerainty treaties were renewed, these stipulations were repeated, but with modifications, especially such as were necessary to meet the changing situation. So, in these Deuteronomy stipulations (Deut. 5:1—26:19) Moses rehearses and reformulates the requirements promulgated in the Sinaitic Covenant. Also, just as treaty stipulations customarily began with the fundamental and general demand for the vassal's absolute allegiance to the suzerain and then proceeded to various specific requirements, so Moses confronts Israel with the primary demand for consecration to the Lord (chs. 5–11) and then with the ancillary stipulations of covenant life (12:26).

The fourth standard division in the ANE suzerainty treaties included the curses and blessings. In Deuteronomy this section is found in chs. 27–30. The final section of the covenant document has as its unifying theme the perpetuation of the covenant relationship. This succession is provided for by the appointment and commissioning of Joshua as dynastic heir to Moses in the office of mediatorial representative of the Lord (ch. 31). Included are two other standard elements in the international treaties. One is the invocation of covenant witnesses, here represented chiefly by the Song of Witness (ch. 32). The other is the direction for the disposition of the treaty document after the ceremony (31:9–13). By way of notarizing the document, an account of the death of Moses is affixed at the end (ch. 34).

The implications of this comparative evidence for the questions of the antiquity and authenticity of Deuteronomy are far-reaching. The kind of document with which Deuteronomy has been compared did not originate in some recurring ritual situations. Where, either in monarchic or premonarchic times, except in the very occasion to which Deuteronomy traces itself, can a historical situation be found in which such a treaty document is most appropriate?

This literary structure of Deuteronomy also has important implications for the way in which, having once been produced, this document would have been transmitted to subsequent generations. By their very nature, treaties like Deuteronomy were inviolable. They were sealed legal documents; in fact, it was a practice to deposit such treaties in sanctuaries under the eye of the oath deities. In some of the extant texts there are examples of specific curses pronounced against anyone who would in any way violate the treaty inscriptions. Corresponding to these special stela curses is an injunction (Deut. 4:2): "Do not add to what I command you and do not subtract from it."

This extrabiblical evidence confirms and illuminates not isolated data in the book but the Deuteronomy treaty in its very structure. The evidence argues against the view that a long evolutionary process was required to produce a book like Deuteronomy.

IV. Authorship

A. Critical views. The traditional critical view (the Graf-Wellhausen hypothesis) claims that Deuteronomy (at least Deut. 12–26) was first published in 621 B.C. when Hilkiah found "the Book of the Law" in the temple during the eighteenth year of King Josiah (2 Ki. 22:8). This book was written, so the critics claim, for the express purpose of promoting a religious reform, to include the abolition of the HIGH PLACES, or local sanctuaries, supposed to have been perfectly legitimate up to that time, and to concentrate on the people's worship in Jerusalem. As a 7th-cent. B.C. literary creation reflecting the teaching of the 8th-cent. "ethical" prophets, Deuteronomy was accorded a position late in the evolutionary process that led, in Wellhausen's thought, from the primitive religion of the patriarchs through the henotheism of later times to the exalted monotheism of Deutero-Isaiah and the literature of the exilic and postexilic period. If, however, as the critics claimed, the author was a prophet whose object was a religious reformation, and his aim was to abolish the "high places," why does he not refer to them? If he wanted to centralize worship in Jerusalem, why not make it clear? Jerusalem is not even mentioned. Moreover, would a prophet of such oratorical and spiritual power as reflected in this book be afraid to proclaim his message openly, or prefer to remain unknown, write it in a book, and hide it in the temple?

Many cogent arguments have been raised against any critical view that would date the book in the 7th cent. B.C. and connect it with Josiah's reformation. The law book discovered by Hilkiah was recognized immediately as an ancient code (2 Ki. 22:13). Were they all deceived? Even Jeremiah (Jer. 11:3–4)? There were many persons who would have strong motives for exposing such a forgery. Also one wonders why a code formulated in Josiah's time would include such archaic and anachronistic references as the command to exterminate the Canaanites (Deut. 7:16, 22), and to blot out AMALEK (25:17–19), the last remnants of which were completely destroyed in HEZEKIAH's time (1 Chr. 4:41–43). It is especially remarkable that if the document was composed shortly before the reign of Josiah, there should be no anachronisms in it betraying a post-Mosaic origin. There are no allusions to schism between Israel and Judah, no hint of Assyrian oppression through exaction of tribute, nor any threat of Israel's exile to Assyria or Babylon, but rather to Egypt (Deut. 28:68). From a literary point of view it is well nigh impossible for a writer to conceal all traces of his age and circumstances, yet no Egyptologist has ever detected an anachronism in Deuteronomy.

Of course, the traditional critical view of the origin of Deuteronomy is an integral part of the documentary hypothesis (see PENTATEUCH); indeed, one might say that the question of Deuteronomy is the cornerstone of the documentary hypothesis. So the approach of the critics to the book of Deuteronomy is based on their attitude toward the origin and nature of the Pentateuch itself, as well as to the whole question of the development of Israelite religion. The classical critical approach to Deuteronomy was altered in various ways during the 20th cent. so that the origin of the book became among the most controversial problems with the critics. Serious problems raised by late-date theories have caused scholars to make various modifications that confuse and cancel each other. Almost every period has been advanced as the age in which the book was composed, while its authorship has been ascribed variously to Moses himself, to SAMUEL, or less specifically to prophetic, priestly, and other circles. As to its origin, it has been associated with such sanctuaries as Jerusalem, Shechem, and Bethel, or less precisely to northern Israel or Judah. A convenient survey of the evolution of these differing and conflicting theories of the critics may be found in E. W. Nicholson's *Deuteronomy and Tradition* (1967).

B. Traditional view. The traditional view of the Mosaic authorship of Deuteronomy is based on the teaching of the Bible itself as well as on Jewish and Christian tradition, which was in full accord until the advent of higher criticism. Deuteronomy is represented as emanating from Moses. Nearly forty times his name occurs, and in the majority of cases as the authoritative author of the subject matter. The first person is sometimes used (Deut. 1:16, 18; 3:21; 29:5). It is expressly stated that Moses taught Israel these statutes and judgments in order that they should obey them in the land they were about to enter (4:5, 14; 5:31). The book bears the message of one who is interested in Israel's political and religious *future*. A paternal mood runs throughout that marks it as Mosaic.

The Bible clearly indicates, "So Moses wrote down this law and gave it to the priests, the sons of Levi" (Deut. 31:9). "After Moses finished writing in a book the words of this law from beginning to end, he gave this command to the Levites who carried the ark of the covenant of the Lord: 'Take this Book of the Law and place it beside the ark of the covenant of the Lord your God. There it will remain as a witness against you'" (31:24–26). Here it is distinctly and emphatically stated that "Moses wrote down this law." The simplest explanation is that Moses "wrote" the legislation itself, namely chs. 12–26. An unbroken line of tradition assigns authorship to Moses; this was accepted by Jesus himself (Matt. 19:8) and generally by the NT writers.

The record of Moses' death is not as serious a problem as some would claim. It is not out of order, even today, for an editor to furnish addenda to an autobiography, giving an account of the author's death. It will be noticed that the book of Joshua is closed in the same way (see JOSHUA, BOOK OF). This appendix may have been attached to the document soon after the death of Moses, or it may be, as some suppose, that what is now the end of Deuteronomy was once the beginning of Joshua. The author of the appendix could have been JOSHUA, the intimate friend of the great lawgiver and his successor as the leader of Israel. He was the one above all others who should have pronounced the eulogy upon his master after his death. Notice the expressions "Moses the servant of the Lord" (Deut. 34:5) and "Moses the man of God" (33:1). Neither of these phrases is found in the preceding part of the Pentateuch, and it does not appear that Moses even assumed such titles for himself. It was a favorite method with Joshua, however, in speaking of his dead friend and leader. The phrase "Moses the servant of the Lord" occurs more than a dozen times in the book of Joshua and is found in both the narrative matter and the speeches attributed to the author. The other expression also was known to Joshua, for CALEB referred to "Moses the man of God" in addressing him.

V. Background

A. Personal element. The content of Deuteronomy contains what one would expect to find from the hand of Moses; the background reflects a Mosaic character. References to experiences that must have deeply stirred Moses' feelings crop up unexpectedly, such as "the house of bondage" (Deut. 5:6 KJV), the recalling of the attack by the Amalekites (25:17), the burden of judgment (1:9–18), the murmurings of the people (9:22–24), the material of which the ark of the covenant was made (10:3), the enemies they had overcome. The references to AARON (9:20; 10:6; 32:50) and MIRIAM (24:9) spring naturally from Moses but appear strange if merely inventions of a 7th-cent. B.C. prophet.

Throughout Deut. 12–26 Moses' name is absent, yet it is clearly assumed that he is the speaker. This is the more striking since his name is repeated no fewer than thirty-eight times in the narrative portions. His personality shines through by the intrusion here and there of the first person, especially in the phrase, "I command thee," sometimes with the addition of "this day" (e.g., 4:30 KJV). This is particularly the case in the remarkable passage 18:15–18, with its reference to the people's memory of Horeb in v. 16. One can well imagine this intrusion with its promise coming from the mouth of Moses; but otherwise it loses much of its point. It is not easy to conceive of it as a device of a reformer, or to see how it could serve his purpose.

The personal element again appears, quite unexpectedly, in Deut. 24:8, "In cases of leprous diseases be very careful to do exactly as the priests, who are Levites, instruct you. You must follow carefully what I have commanded them." The emergence of the first person in this verse is uncalled for, if not Mosaic. Then comes, "Remember what the LORD your God did to Miriam along the way after you came out of Egypt." How natural for Moses to call to mind his own sister's folly and punishment; how strange if simply used by one intent on the reform of the cult! Other incidents that must have deeply impressed Moses unexpectedly intrude into the law, such as the attack of the Amalekites (25:17) and the hiring of BALAAM to curse (23:4).

The number and character of reminiscences is a striking feature. The mode of their occurrence is frequently quite incidental, such as the frequent references to Egypt and the reference to Miriam. They convey the impression that they issue from an old man who rebuked the people for disobedience as if they were children, and who wished to display his concern that these younger hearers should "remember" and "not forget" his words, when he should be no longer there to guide (Deut. 4:9—6:7). There are also signs that the speaker has known the responsibility of leadership. He remembers the "ways" by which they traveled, the turnings, the treatment they received, the difficult crossings, and the places where water was attainable for the cattle. There are names of events, all of which stirred Moses' feelings deeply, the tempting (MASSAH), striving (MERIBAH), destruction (HORMAH), the burning (TABERAH), the graves of lust (KIBROTH HATTAAVAH), and the chastisement (MOSERAH). Is this combination of words pure accident, or is it not probable that these are the names Moses himself attached to the events? It is significant that Moses is never praised until after his death (34:10).

It should also be noted that these reminiscences found in Deuteronomy cover the whole period of Moses' life but never transgress that limit. The author remembers the "vegetable garden" artificially watered (Deut. 11:10), the plagues that fell on Pharaoh (7:18), his household (6:22), and his land (29:2). He also recalls the PASSOVER instituted in the month of ABIB (16:1), the departure "in haste" and "at even" (16:3, 6 KJV), and the destruction of Pharaoh's army in the RED SEA "to this day" (11:4 KJV), the proving at Massah (6:16; 8:3, 16; 9:22), and the attack by Amalek (25:17–19). Also remembered are the covenant in Horeb, the ten "words" and the "ark of acacia wood" (10:1–3), and Moses' prayer for Aaron (9:20). Also specific reference is made to the forty years in the wilderness (8:2, 19; 11:5), "vast and dreadful" (1:19), where were "venomous snakes and scorpions" (8:15), the MANNA (8:3, 16), the water from the "rock of flint" (8:15 KJV), the divine care (2:7; 8:3), and the judgment on DATHAN and ABIRAM (11:6). Also recalled are the stay in KADESH BARNEA (1:19–46), the pillar of fire, the pitching of the tents, the mission of the twelve spies, and the long journey around EDOM, MOAB, and AMMON. Note also the comment, "until you arrived here" (9:7), as the long wilderness journey terminated.

This is a formidable list when compared to the few references found in the prophetic writings. There is nothing to compare with this amount of detail in any of the speeches recorded in the historical books, and much less would have sufficed to provide the law with a "Mosaic" setting. These reminiscences contribute nothing to the alleged program of reform attempted at a late date. In Exodus it is related that Moses prayed for the people, but nothing is said about his prayer for Aaron. In

Moses and the Israelites may have looked for water in the canyon of Ein Avdat, centrally located in the Desert of Zin. (View to the SE.)

Deut. 9:20, however, we read, "And the LORD was angry enough with Aaron to destroy him, but at that time I prayed for Aaron too." Why should a late writer introduce this detail? Yet nothing could be more true if Moses were the author. Another reference (32:50) records Aaron's death, an event that must have left an indelible impression on his brother's mind, since they were both involved in the same trespass.

Could all these personal Mosaic features have been introduced by some reformer, priest, prophet, or Levite, in order to invest his collection of laws with a Mosaic dress? Is it probable that such an author would have succeeded in establishing a correspondence so natural, so close in manifold and minute particulars, and so profound? Or is it more reasonable to think that this result proceeds from a true historical connection between the book of the law and the man whose name it has always borne? If Deuteronomy is universally acknowledged to be a great book that exerted great influence, should it not also have a great author? Who can fill that place so worthily as the old and tried leader who brought the Israelites out of Egypt, shared their experiences, and laid the foundations of their faith?

B. Historical setting. The date of these discourses in Deuteronomy is plainly stated: it was the eleventh month of the fortieth year during the period of wandering imposed upon the people for their unbelief (Deut. 1:3, 35; 2:14). If one endeavors to picture the author living in monarchic or later days, one meets on every side baffling paradoxes; if, however, the author is speaking to Israel as they approach the Promised Land and are about to settle, the language is precisely what one would expect. The aim of the author is to protect the Israelite community against Canaanite influence. This danger is viewed as future, and not as in Hosea, where the people are already entangled with much idolatry. Deuteronomy speaks of "other gods ... you have not known" (13:2), even of "gods that recently appeared" (32:17). This is not the language of one addressing a degenerate Israel of a later age; it is language connected with entry into the land.

The historical setting, moreover, is explicit in "you will cross the Jordan" (Deut. 12:10) and "When you enter the land" (18:9), and implicit throughout. The campaign against the former inhabitants had still to be fought (20:17). The remembrance of the bondage in Egypt recurs frequently, and is treated as a recent experience in the living memory of some. Close connection with the immediate past is reflected in "Remember what the Amalekites did to you along the way" (25:17); the Israelites also are told to exclude the Ammonites and the Moabites from membership in the congregation "because they did not come to meet you with bread and water on your way" (23:4).

Two of the most frequent phrases in the book are, "Go in and take possession" (e.g., Deut. 1:8) and "the land the LORD your God is giving you" (e.g., 5:16). The occupation of the land by the Israelites had a primary place in the mind of the author. The language of promised blessings was for a people about to settle in a new land, not for a nation long established in Palestine. The gods of the Canaanites are described as those of "the nations whom you are about to dispossess" (12:2 NRSV; cf. vv. 29–30). This language is in striking contrast to Ezekiel, Haggai, or Ezra!

Where "tribes" are mentioned in Deuteronomy, they are separate entities but included in one whole. There is nothing to indicate a breach between N and S; Judah and Ephraim are not two kingdoms, and in fact are named only once, which is in the blessing (Deut. 33:7–17). The consistent address to "all Israel" assumes the unity of the nation; the people were addressed as a whole. For the period of the divided kingdom this was neither appropriate nor significant. Moreover, in Deuteronomy the election of Israel and the covenant at Horeb are always referred to as past events, but the inheritance of the land is always regarded as future. There is a national consciousness and a national religion, but as yet there is no central political organization. The contents are precisely suitable to the time and place (4:44–49). Anachronisms and discrepancies are not present in the text to reflect a "late" author.

It should also be noted that the primitive nature of the laws is suitable for a time when Israel first became a nation, but insufficient if viewed in relation to the needs of the 7th cent. B.C. These laws were to be executed by judges (Deut. 16:18), priests (17:9), and elders or "men of the town" (21:21), not by the king (contrast 2 Ki. 15:3–4). Note that the laws in Deuteronomy are issued with a tone of authority that seems to proceed from a great leader. The prophets plead, but this author commands (cf. 13:18; 19:9; 27:1). The theology of the Deuteronomic legislation is simple and unsophisticated; it shows no advance upon that of Moses and no difference from it. The same cannot be said of the theological outlook of Isaiah or his successors. Deuteronomy reflects the optimism of the Mosaic era: the promise of the fathers, the wonders in Egypt, the people's deliverance and the covenant at Horeb. Such a combination of qualities can scarcely be due to accident, nor does it wear the appearance of design. The laws laid down in chs. 12–26 exactly correspond to the background of the Mosaic era and not to any other. See also LAW (OT).

C. Geographical features. An analysis of the background data contained in Deuteronomy reveals geographical references too accurate for a Mosaic setting to be accidental. The account of the journeyings (Deut. 1–3) is altogether realistic and quite unlike an introduction later prefixed to a collection of old laws. The views described and the features of the Moabite country reproduced here reflect an eyewitness account. There is much geographical detail recorded, especially in the opening and closing chapters, but Palestine is always viewed from the outside. The minute accuracy of the description of the land of Moab and the journey to it is especially a striking feature. In contrast, Deuteronomy knows nothing of Zion or David, and even these omissions are significant. If Deuteronomy comes from a late period as critics have persistently asserted, why is there no mention of Jerusalem, or even Shiloh, where the tabernacle came to rest?

Deuteronomy contains numerous notices concerning nations with whom the Israelites had then come in contact, but who, after the Mosaic period, entirely disappeared from the pages of history, such as the accounts of the residences of the kings of BASHAN (Deut. 1:4). The observation is made (2:10) that the EMITES had formerly dwelt in the plain of Moab and that they were a great people, equal to the Anakites (see ANAK); this observation accords with Gen. 14:5. Deuteronomy gives a detailed account (2:12) concerning the HORITES and their relations to the Edomites. An account of the ZAMZUMMITES (2:20–21), one of the earliest races of Canaan, is given though mentioned nowhere else; the author apparently had some interest in them. All of this is most strange if viewed from a "late" period, but exactly what one would expect from Moses. Deuteronomy uses the appellation, "hill country of the Amorites" (1:7, 19–20, 44), but even in the book of Joshua, soon after the conquest of the land, the name is already exchanged for "hill country of Judah" (Josh. 11:21).

The book of Deuteronomy clearly reflects the personality of Moses, the historical setting of his age, and the geographical data one would expect.

VI. Later influence. The influence of Deuteronomy upon the later writings and history of Israel is great. Of all the books of the Pentateuch, Deuteronomy has been most used by the prophets,

Olive crushing vats carved into the surface near Heshbon in Moab. The author of Deuteronomy shows a clear awareness of Moabite geography.

simply because it is best calculated to serve as a model for prophetic declarations.

In the books of Joshua, Judges, 1–2 Samuel, and 1–2 Kings, there are sufficient references to reveal that Deuteronomy was known and observed. When JERICHO was taken, the city and its spoil were "devoted" (Josh. 6:17–18) in keeping with Deut. 13:15–18 (cf. Josh. 10:40; 11:12, 15 with Deut. 7:2; 20:16–17). When ACHAN trespassed, he and his household were stoned and burned with fire (Josh. 7:25; cf. Deut. 13:10; 17:5). When Ai was captured, the Israelites took for themselves only the livestock and plunder (Josh. 8:27 and Deut. 20:14); also note that the body of the king of Ai was taken down before nightfall from the tree on which he had been hanged (Josh. 8:29), which was required (Deut. 21:23; cf. Josh. 10:26–27). Joshua built an altar on Mount EBAL, "as Moses the servant of the LORD had commanded" (8:30–31), and he wrote thereon a copy of the law (Josh. 8:32), as Moses had instructed (Deut. 27:3, 8). Especially notice that the elders and officers and judges stood on either side of the ARK OF THE COVENANT between Ebal and GERIZIM (Josh. 8:33), as directed in Deut. 11:29; 27:12–13; and Joshua read to all the congregation of Israel all the words of the law, the blessings, and the curses (Josh. 8:34–35), in strict accord with Moses' orders (Deut. 31:11–12). Other references make it quite clear that Deuteronomy was known in the days of Joshua.

The book of Judges has references to Deuteronomy. The complete destruction of ZEPHATH (Jdg. 1:17) may be compared to Deut. 7:2; 20:16–18. GIDEON's elimination of the fearful and fainthearted from his army (Jdg. 7:1–7) should be compared to Deut. 20:1–9. The case of MICAH, who congratulated himself that the LORD would do him good seeing he had a Levite for a priest, is clear evidence that Deuteronomy was known in the days of the Judges (Jdg. 17:13; cf. Deut. 10:8; 18:1–8; 33:8–11).

The prophets of the 8th cent. were certainly aware of the book. Hosea alludes to bringing charges against priests (Hos. 4:4; cf. Deut. 17:12), removing landmarks (Hos. 5:10; cf. Deut. 19:14), and returning to Egypt (Hos. 8:13; 9:3; cf. Deut. 28:68), and mentions the Lord's tender dealing with Ephraim (Hos. 11:3; cf. Deut. 1:31; 32:10).

Amos also appears to have been familiar with the contents of Deuteronomy (cf. Amos 3:2 with Deut. 7:6; 9:12). Amos condemns Israel's inhumanity and adultery in the name of religion, and complains that the people are retaining overnight pledges wrested from the poor, which was distinctly forbidden (cf. Amos 2:6–8 with Deut. 24:12–15; 23:17).

The NT contains several references to, and some citations from, the book of Deuteronomy, and in these its Mosaic authorship and divine authority are generally assumed. In Heb. 10:28 the words of Deut. 17:6 are quoted as "Moses' law." Paul quoted Deut. 27:26 and 21:23 with the introduction: "It is written" (Gal. 3:10, 13), and similarly parts of the Decalogue (Rom. 7:7; 13:9; Eph. 6:2). In another passage (Rom. 10:6–9) he equated the words in Deut. 30:12–14 with the "word of faith" that he preached.

Jesus, in the hour of his temptation, three times quoted the words of Deuteronomy as authoritative (Matt. 4:1–11; Lk. 4:1–13). He called Deut. 6:4–5 the "first and greatest commandment" (Matt. 22:38), and described the Decalogue as "the commands of God" (Mk. 7:9–12; cf. 10:17–19) or as "the word of God" (7:13). In response to the question of the PHARISEES concerning DIVORCE, he described the permission for divorce under certain conditions given by Moses (Deut. 24:1) as the precept that Moses "wrote" (Mk. 10:5).

(Important commentaries include S. R. Driver, *A Critical and Exegetical Commentary on Deuteronomy*, ICC, 3rd ed. [1901]; G. von Rad, *Deuteronomy*, OTL [1966]; P. C. Craigie, *The Book of Deuteronomy*, NICOT [1976]; M. Weinfeld, *Deuteronomy 1–11*, AB 5 [1991]; E. H. Merrill, *Deuteronomy*, NAC 4 [1994]; J. H. Tigay, *Deuteronomy*, JPS Torah Commentary [1996]; C. J. H. Wright, *Deuteronomy* [1996]; W. Brueggemann, *Deuteronomy* [2001]; D. L. Christensen, *Deuteronomy 1:1—21:9*, rev. ed., WBC 6 [2001]; id., *Deuteronomy 21:10—34:12*, WBC 6A [2002]; R. D. Nelson, *Deuteronomy: A Commentary*, OTL [2002].

Among significant monographs, see G. T. Manley, *The Book of the Law: Studies in the Date of Deuteronomy* [1957]; E. W. Nicholson, *Deuteronomy and Tradition* [1967]; M. Weinfeld, *Deuteronomy and the Deuteronomic School* [1972]; J. G. McConville, *Law and Theology in Deuteronomy* [1984]; N. Lohfink,

Theology of the Pentateuch: Themes of the Priestly Narrative and Deuteronomy [1994]; B. M. Levinson: *Deuteronomy and the Hermeneutics of Legal Innovation* [1997]; J. Gary Millar, *Now Choose Life: Theology and Ethics in Deuteronomy* [1998]; P. A. Barker, *The Triumph of Grace in Deuteronomy* [2004]; and the bibliography compiled by W. E. Mills, *Numbers–Deuteronomy* [2002]; P. T. Vogt, *Deuteronomic Theology and the Significance of Torah* [2006].)

L. L. WALKER

devil. In the plural, this word is used by the KJV several times in the OT (Lev. 17:7 et al.) and frequently in the NT (Matt. 4:24 et al.). For these uses, see DEMON. Otherwise, the term occurs only in the NT, and only in the singular, as the rendering of Greek *diabolos* G1333, which means "slanderer" (the pl. of this Gk. word is used a few times to describe slanderous people). The devil is depicted as one inciting to evil (Matt. 4:1; 13:39; Jn. 13:2; et al.). Those under his control could be called children of the devil (1 Jn. 3:10; cf. Jn. 6:70; 8:44), and he is said to hold the power of death (Heb. 2:14). Though ruler of the world, he was defeated by the death of Christ and his resurrection (cf. Matt. 25:41; Rev. 2:10; 12:9; et al.; cf. *DDD*, 244–49). For detailed discussion see SATAN.

devoted (things). The Hebrew verb *ḥāram* H3049 and its cognate noun *ḥērem* H3051, which are used of dedicating something or someone to the deity either for sacred use or for utter destruction, occur about eighty times in the OT. The verb is usually translated "utterly destroy" or the like. The translation "devote" or "devoted," though less common, is more expressive of the meaning of the root. In Arabic the word *Ḥaram* is used for the consecrated area of the Dome of the Rock in Jerusalem (the word *harem* also comes from this root and implies that the quarters of the women in a polygamous society are private and forbidden to outsiders).

The overwhelming usage of the root refers to the destruction of the enemy in the total wars commanded in the conquest of Canaan, in the campaign against the Amalekites, and in similar situations. The enemy was put "under the ban," as it is sometimes expressed. An example is the city of JERICHO, which was thus devoted. All was to be destroyed except metals that could be purified by fire, for the Lord's treasury. Thus ACHAN in violating the ban actually stole from God.

There is another usage observable. Some passages (Lev. 27:21, 28, 29; Num. 18:14; Ezek. 44:29) refer to offerings dedicated to holy use, which are given to the priests. Leviticus 27:21 specifies that such a field shall be the priests' in perpetuity and shall not revert to the owner in the jubilee year (similar religious endowments are a part of Arabic law in some countries to this day). We read that every devoted thing "is most holy to the LORD" (27:28). A man may not exchange a different animal for a devoted thing, as may be done in the case of certain firstlings (27:26–27).

Devoted men are mentioned in Lev. 27:29 as certainly condemned to death. This does not refer to those persons consecrated to the Lord by a vow and serving as slaves in the temple (these are mentioned in vv. 1–8). Nor does it refer to the firstlings of men who were redeemed when God chose the tribe of LEVI as an equivalent (Num. 3:12). There is no vestige of early human sacrifice. Rather the devoted men who must be killed as directed in Lev. 27:29 are captives from the holy wars. These captives theoretically belonged to God. Yet such foreign captives could not serve in the holy precincts. Like AGAG and the Amalekites, they must be put under the ban (1 Sam. 15:3–33).

Before we judge Israel too harshly in this matter, or object to God's commandment, we should remember that misplaced mercy can result in the slaughter of the innocent (Ps. 106:34–38). It may further be observed that when JOSHUA conquered Canaan, he was carving out a homeland for his people from the Palestinian possessions of the Egyptian empire. In a sense, Israel had paid for Canaan many times over in blood and tears in Egypt. Remember Lincoln's second Inaugural Address, "If God wills … that every drop of blood drawn by the lash shall be paid by another drawn with the sword, … it must be said, the judgments of the Lord are true and righteous altogether." (Cf. R. de Vaux, *Ancient Israel* [1961], 251–65; G. F. Oehler, *Theology of the OT* [1883], 81–82; J. B. Payne, *Theology of the Older Testament* [1962], 329–30.) See also ACCURSED; BAN; CURSE; ANATHEMA; EXCOMMUNICATION.

R. L. HARRIS

devotion. This English term is used once by the KJV to render Greek *sebasma G4934*, "an object of religious worship" (Acts 17:23; cf. 2 Thess. 2:4). Modern versions occasionally use the word *devotion*, in the sense of "ardent and selfless dedication," to render a variety of biblical terms and expressions (e.g., NIV 2 Ki. 20:3; Job 15:4; Jer. 2:2; 1 Cor. 7:35; 2 Cor. 11:3).

devout. Dedicated to religious duties; displaying sincere piety. The term appears in English versions primarily in the writings of Luke as a rendering of Greek *eulabēs G2327* (e.g., Lk. 2:25, applied to SIMEON), *eusebēs G2356* (e.g. Acts 10:2, applied to CORNELIUS and his family), and the middle participle of the verb *sebō G4936* (e.g., Acts 13:43, applied to Jewish converts). The last Greek term is often used of "God-fearing" Gentiles (e.g., Acts 13:50; see PROSELYTE VIII.B.).

dew. In a dry climate, and in the hot season, dew plays an important part in WATER supply. Only on this basis can we understand ELIJAH's threat in 1 Ki. 17:1, "there will be neither dew nor rain." In areas where skies are normally clear in summer and cooling takes place at night, heavy dews are produced wherever moisture is present in the atmosphere (e.g., as a result of wind from the sea). On the Levant Coast dew is formed on twenty to twenty-five nights per month in summer. This dew will probably represent the vital difference between total barrenness and a vegetation cover. It may freshen up shrubs or plants sufficiently to offer at least a meager form of pasture for flocks, and it can even keep a person alive for limited periods: dew collection has been reported by several desert travelers when short of water.

Nowhere does the Bible more clearly reveal its environmental background than in the prominence given to the dew (Heb. *ṭal H3228*), particularly as a symbol of blessing. It is mentioned in Isaac's blessing of both JACOB and ESAU (Gen. 27:28, 39) and in MOSES' blessings of the tribes (Deut. 33:13, 28). In Prov. 19:12 the king's favor is likened to the dew, and in Hos. 14:5 God promises that he will be like dew in blessing his people. Conversely, the withholding of dew is a sign of divine displeasure (Hag. 1:10). J. H. PATERSON

diadem. This English term (from Gk. *diadēma G1343*, cf. NRSV Rev. 12:3 et al.), which usually refers to a CROWN as a symbol of royalty, is seldom found in Bible versions. The NIV uses it three times to render *nēzer H5694* (Exod. 29:6; 39:30; Lev. 62:3), and once to translate *ṣānîp H7565* (Isa. 62:3). Both Hebrew terms designate a headband or TURBAN.

dial. An instrument that shows the time of day by measuring the shadow. The term is used by the KJV and other versions to render the plural of Hebrew *maʿălâ H5092* ("ascent, step") in 2 Ki. 20:11 (also in the parallel passage, Isa. 38:8, where the text is a little different and difficult). According to this narrative, HEZEKIAH was given a sign to prove the authenticity of ISAIAH's prophecy that God would heal the king of his disease: "And Isaiah the prophet cried unto the LORD: and he brought the shadow ten degrees [*maʿălôt*] backward, by which it had gone down in the dial [*maʿălôt* again] of Ahaz" (so KJV; the NRSV, similarly, "and he brought the shadow back the ten intervals, by which the sun had declined on the dial of Ahaz"). The NIV translates more literally, "and the LORD made the shadow go back the ten steps it had gone down on the stairway of Ahaz," but even in this rendering it is apparent that the stairs in question functioned as a kind of sundial. One possibility is that "the device consisted of two sets of steps each facing a wall whose shadow fell upon the steps. As the sun rose, the eastern steps would be in the wall's shadow, which, as the day advanced, would grow shorter. On the other hand, during the afternoon, the steps facing west would more and more be in the shadow" (E. J. Young, *The Book of Isaiah*, 3 vols., NICOT [1965–72], 2:515n.). How the miracle was effected has been the subject of much speculation, but no one really knows. (On the reading of 1QIsa[a], see S. Iwry in *BASOR* 147 [Oct. 1957]: 27–33.)

Dialogue of the Savior. A Gnostic document preserved in the NAG HAMMADI LIBRARY (NHC III, 5). The work consists of a dialogue between Jesus and his disciples, but scholars believe it is a compilation of several distinct sources. Originally composed in Greek, perhaps around A.D. 250, it is preserved only in a 4th-cent. Coptic MS. The material consists of traditional sayings of Jesus with expansions and shows some similarities with the *Gospel of Thomas* (see THOMAS, GOSPEL OF). Some scholars argue that it also resembles the Gospel of John. (For an English trans., see *NHL*, 244–55.)

diamond. A pure carbon mineral that commonly occurs as octahedral crystals. Diamonds are the most desired of all the precious stones and the hardest naturally occurring substance known. They have been mined in INDIA from the earliest times, and this must have been the source of all famous diamonds of antiquity. It is uncertain whether the Bible refers to this mineral. The KJV uses "diamond" to render Hebrew *yāhălōm H3402*, a word of uncertain meaning (Exod. 28:18; 39:11; Ezek. 28:13; NRSV, "moonstone"; NIV, "emerald"), and one occurrence of *šāmîr H9032* (Jer. 17:1), which possibly means "emery" (NIV, "flint"; this Hebrew word also occurs in Ezek. 3:9 and Zech 7:12, where KJV has "adamant"). See ADAMANT; FLINT.

Diana di-an´uh. See ARTEMIS.

Diaspora di-as´puh-ruh. The scattering of the Jews beyond the boundaries of Palestine (when lower-cased, the word can refer to the dispersion of any group).

I. The term. The Greek word *diaspora G1402* ("dispersion"), though sometimes equated with Hebrew *gôlâ H1583* ("exile"), typically refers to a voluntary moving of the Jews to lands other than their own. It set them apart both from their kindred that remained at home and from the strangers among whom the transplanted Jews lived in other lands. The Hebrew term designates specifically the Jews who were moved by force, sometimes imprisoned. The descendants of such exiles were a large part of the diaspora of NT times. By the 1st cent. it was estimated that more Jews lived outside of Palestine (perhaps as many as three to five million) than lived in the homeland. In the NT, the Greek term is used of the Jewish scattering (Jn. 7:35) and also, in a derived sense, of Christians (Jas. 1:1; 1 Pet. 1:1).

The primary cause of the Diaspora was deportation of the Jews into EXILE by their enemies. The Assyrians took many people from SAMARIA to the E in 722 B.C., and the Babylonians took some from Jerusalem as early as 586. Later POMPEY took Jews to Rome as slaves. Being an industrious people, the Jews also went voluntarily to other lands where the opportunities in business and trade were better. The increasing population in Palestine kept pressure on the people there to look elsewhere, especially to the large cities in surrounding countries, for livelihood. These circumstances helped to create the Diaspora.

II. Geographic areas. Egypt had possibly the largest concentration of Jewish people outside Palestine in NT times. The Jews of Egypt, especially in ALEXANDRIA, came close to producing a religious center to rival Jerusalem. It was from Egyptian sources that the SEPTUAGINT came. Whether the Egyptian or Mesopotamian settlement came first has been debated, but unquestionably the scattering of the Jews to the E was quite early. The two main Jewish centers in Mesopotamia were at Nehardea and Nisibis. SYRIA was said by JOSEPHUS to have had the largest percentage of Jewish inhabitants in his day. The Jews of that country were primarily found at ANTIOCH OF SYRIA. There were thousands also at DAMASCUS. Judas MACCABEE and his brother Jonathan had brought settlements of Jews into the borders of Syria as a protection for Judea. The nearness of Syria to Palestine was enough to draw the enterprising Jews to its cities.

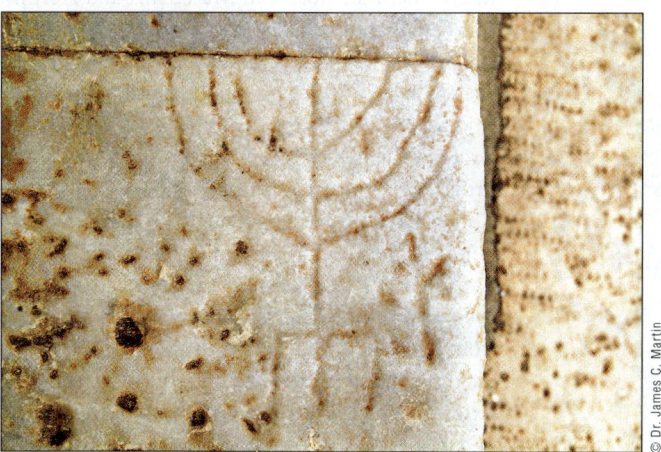

This menorah carved into the steps of a 2nd-cent. library at Ephesus is evidence of Jewish presence in Gentile lands.

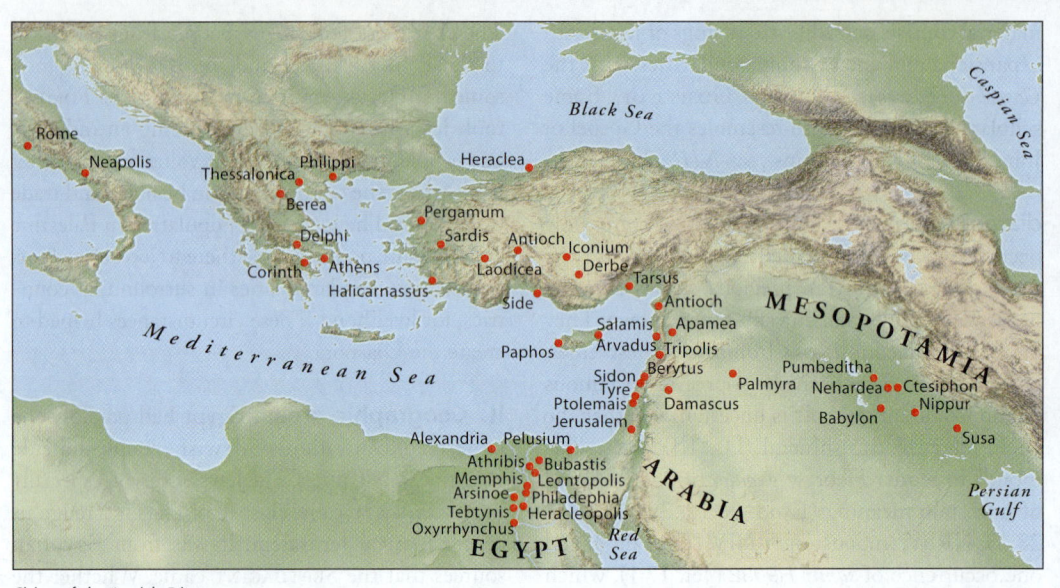

Cities of the Jewish Diaspora.

There is considerable evidence both inside and outside the NT for the presence of Jews in Greece and Asia Minor. PHILO JUDAEUS preserved a letter from Herod Agrippa I (see HEROD VII) to the Emperor CALIGULA that besought him to grant religious and civic freedom to the Jews in PAMPHYLIA, CILICIA, and a greater part of ASIA MINOR as far as BITHYNIA; also in Boeotia (the area just to the NW of Attica), Thessaly (farther N), MACEDONIA, and CORINTH. The Jews seem primarily to have been in these areas because of trade opportunities. A major trade route ran through Cilicia to Syria and Palestine. Other trade routes in Macedonia and ACHAIA collected Jews also. In addition, there is evidence that ANTIOCHUS III, to help insure peace, transferred to Asia Minor 2,000 Jewish families loyal to him.

Jews were dispersed throughout Italy. Cicero wrote of them with hate and fear (62 B.C.). TIBERIUS Caesar persecuted the Jewish settlement in Rome. CLAUDIUS Caesar sought to drive the Jews out of Rome and forbade their assembling in their synagogues. The Jews seem to have been in Rome even prior to the deportation of Pompey's captives from Jerusalem (63 B.C.). Jewish settlements populated the islands of the Mediterranean as well. The letter of Agrippa I to Caligula mentioned CYPRUS and CRETE as possessing Jews in considerable numbers. Cyprus seems to have been the home of BARNABAS, and TITUS was associated with Crete.

PAUL found well-established SYNAGOGUES throughout Asia Minor. This was true also in Macedonia and Achaia. Habitually, he began his work among his own people in each new location.

III. Characteristics. In many lands the Jews were given places of trust and enjoyed social freedom. Often they were entrusted with military positions and, because of their loyalty, even commanded armies. They became high officials in government also.

Most Jewish settlements were autonomous in affairs that were strictly their own. In many places they had equal or almost equal rights with the strangers among whom they lived. In religious affairs the Jews of the Diaspora were devoted to their ancestral faith. When persecution came upon the Jews away from Palestine, it was nearly always because of some religious fanaticism, as it was judged by the authorities of the nations where they lived. Tiberius Caesar hated the Jews because he believed that the Jews considered their religion to be above all other religions.

In most instances the Jews of the Diaspora enjoyed freedom of religion. This seems to have been the policy of Antiochus III. The Roman government considered Judaism as *religio licita*, a licensed or legitimate religion. The Jews, therefore, did not have to appear in court on the SABBATH; and when the distribution of public dole fell on a Sabbath, the Jews were permitted to draw their relief the next day. Although some Jews served in military forces with distinction, the Jews as a whole in Asia Minor were exempted from military service because of their peculiar food laws and Sabbath observance.

The scattered Jews maintained strong ties with JERUSALEM and the TEMPLE. Frequent pilgrimages were made to Jerusalem for the religious festivals. Gifts of money were sent regularly to the temple. A half-shekel was expected from the Jews of the Diaspora, but no doubt many people sent much more. Nearly every country had a collection point where the gifts were gathered, awaiting the annual journey to Jerusalem. Mithridates, king of PONTUS in Asia Minor, confiscated on the island of Cos 800 talents of silver that the Jews had collected in Ionia for the temple. Pomponius Flaccus, a Roman governor of Asia Minor, confiscated on another occasion 100 gold pounds that had been gathered for the temple from Apamea, Laodicea, Pergamum, and Adramyttium. It was especially the treasure from the Diaspora that made the temple in Jerusalem rich and beautiful.

Some of the Jews of the Diaspora obtained Roman CITIZENSHIP. In the NT, PAUL would serve as an example. How Jews came by such citizenship is not known precisely. Paul apparently inherited his. Some, no doubt, were able to purchase Roman citizenship. Other Jews were apparently rewarded with it for distinguished military service to the Caesars.

According to some scholars, proselytizing was another characteristic of the Jews outside Palestine (see PROSELYTE). The translation of the OT into Greek (see SEPTUAGINT) had enabled them to communicate their religion to the people among whom they lived. The high ethical content and monotheism of Judaism combined to appeal to a considerable segment of the pagan world. God-fearers stood in large numbers on the fringe of Judaism, while many other Gentiles entered fully into it.

IV. Contributions. If it had not been for the Diaspora, there would have been no LXX. The Diaspora also gave rise to a significant body of literature, including some of the books that are part of the APOCRYPHA and PSEUDEPIGRAPHA. It is thought also that the SYNAGOGUE had its rise in the Diaspora.

V. Influence. Jews in foreign lands were inevitably influenced by the cultural and religious environment that surrounded them. Many scholars have felt that angelology and demonology among the Jews were doctrines especially indebted to the Diaspora. However that may be, it is unquestioned that there was a considerable effort made to adjust Judaism to the thought world of the Greeks; witness Philo of Alexandria, who was a foremost leader in the hellenizing process.

Some have suggested that the seeds of Jewish legalism were sown in the Diaspora. In the times of captivity it was not possible to carry out the Levitical requirements of sacrificial worship. The concentration of the synagogue was, therefore, directed toward the letter of the law. After the return to Palestine the preoccupation with legal observance and interpretation continued in Pharisaism. On the other hand, the Diaspora also had an influence in the direction of personal religion. The conviction of sin was quickened; personal piety grew; spiritual elements in religion were emphasized. A universal outlook, a cosmopolitan view, came to Judaism through the mingling of Jews with people of other heritages.

VI. Significance. The Diaspora was indispensable to the spread of Christianity. The Judaism of the scattered was sometimes more open to change than was the religion of the homeland. The presence of communities of Jews across the Mediterranean world made it possible for early Christian missionaries to move quickly from one area to another, preaching a message for which the people of the synagogues had a basic preparation, not to mention the large number of Gentile God-fearers who were ready to hear the gospel. The LXX was also invaluable to the spread of Christianity because it was the Scriptures of the early churches. The messianic expectation of the Jews of the Diaspora had prepared to a certain extent the whole civilized world for the message of Christ.

(See further A. Causse, *Les disperses d' Israel* [1929]; R. H. Pfeiffer, *History of New Testament Times* [1949]; *HJP*, rev. ed. [1973–87], 3/1:1–176; M. Goodman, ed., *Jews in a Graeco-Roman World*

[1998]; M. Williams, *The Jews among the Greeks and Romans: A Diasporan Sourcebook* [1998]; E. S. Gruen, *Diaspora: Jews amidst Greeks and Romans* [2002]; J. M. G. Barclay, ed., *Negotiating Diaspora: Jewish Strategies in the Roman Empire* [2004].)

H. L. DRUMWRIGHT, JR.

Diatessaron dī'uh-tes'uh-ron (from Greek διά *G1328* + τέσσαρες *G5475*, "by means of four"). The name traditionally given to a harmony of the Gospels, compiled by Tatian, a Christian apologist from MESOPOTAMIA who lived in ROME in the mid-2nd cent., until returning to the E in A.D. 172. The work consists of one continuous narrative that omits apparent doublets and smooths out discrepancies. In one ancient source, it is called *Diapente*, "by means of five." Both terms belong to Greek music theory, meaning perfect fourth and perfect fifth respectively, these harmonies being most highly esteemed. Hence the work is defined as the "perfect harmony." It has also been suggested that the use of *Diapente* may signify Tatian's inclusion of apocryphal material from a fifth source, together with the four canonical Gospels.

It was probably composed in Syriac, but an early Latin rendering may have been made in his lifetime. It is unlikely that its original language was Greek, as some have argued. The one certain Greek fragment known appears to be a retranslation from Syriac. The Diatessaron has not survived in its original form, but a partially preserved Syriac commentary upon it by EPHRAEM SYRUS (d. 378) was edited in 1963 and is the most direct source. An Armenian translation has preserved the whole commentary. An Arabic version of the harmony is known in several MSS. These two form the primary sources of knowledge, but may be supplemented from many others. A Persian adaptation is known, and the harmony has left its mark in the E on the Armenian, Georgian, and Palestinian Syriac versions of the Gospels (see VERSIONS OF THE BIBLE, ANCIENT). Its influence can also be seen in the source of these versions (the Old Syriac Gospels), as well as in quotations by Syriac Fathers and in MANICHEAN literature. In the W, stemming from the early Latin translation mentioned, there are marked traces in the Old Latin Gospels, in Latin harmonies adapted to the text of the VULGATE, and in vernacular harmonies in Old High German, Middle High German, Medieval Dutch, Middle English, and the Medieval Tuscan and Venetian dialects of Italian.

This astoundingly wide influence bespeaks Tatian's literary skill and popular devotional appeal. The harmony even in the remotest sources bears traces of the extreme ASCETICISM that forbade both sexual experience and the partaking of meat and wine (see ENCRATITES). Some ancient references even assert that Tatian omitted the gospel genealogies of Jesus, although many of the sources have them. Three sure signs of Diatessaric influence upon any document are the assertion that both Joseph and Mary were of Davidic descent; that a great light shone on the Jordan at Jesus' baptism; and that Jesus looked on the rich young ruler "lovingly."

(See further C. Peters, *Das Diatessaron Tatians* [1939]; L. Leloir, *Le témoignage d'éphrem sur le Diatessaron* [1962]; B. M. Metzger, *The Early Versions of the New Testament: Their Origin, Transmission, and Limitations* [1977], 10–36; W. L. Petersen, *Tatian's Diatessaron: Its Creation, Dissemination, Significance, and History in Scholarship* [1994]; N. Perrin, *Thomas and Tatian: The Relationship between the Gospel of Thomas and the Diatessaron* [2002].)

J. N. BIRDSALL

diatribe. This English term (from Gk. *diatribē*, which had various meanings, including "conversation, lecture") is commonly used today in the sense of "bitter denunciation," but in literary studies refers to a rhetorical style. Broadly used, the word may indicate a moral discourse; more specifically, it may refer to the use of an artificial dialogue by which a writer (often with sharp language) interacts with an imaginary opponent. Several passages in the epistles of the NT are thought to reflect this technique (e.g., Rom. 2:1–6, 17–24; Jas. 2:14–25). (See S. K. Stowers, *The Diatribe and Paul's Letter to the Romans* [1981].)

Diblah dib'luh (דִּבְלָה *H1812*, possibly "lump, cake [of pressed figs]"). KJV Diblath. An unknown city mentioned in a prophetic oracle of judgment (Ezek. 6:14). Because the Hebrew consonants *d* (ד) and *r* (ר) can be easily confused, many scholars emend the text to read RIBLAH (cf. NRSV), a reading attested as a variant in Codex Petropolitanus.

Diblaim dib′lay-im (דִּבְלַיִם *H1813*, apparently dual form of דְּבֵלָה *H1811*, "lump, cake [of pressed figs]"). The father of GOMER, the unfaithful wife of the prophet HOSEA (Hos. 1:3). According to some, Diblaim was her hometown. A few scholars interpret the name allegorically (e.g., a reference to her cheap price as a prostitute or to the raisin cakes used in the worship of BAAL).

Diblathaim. See ALBON DIBLATHAIM and BETH DIBLATHAIM.

Dibon dī′bon (דִּיבוֹן *H1897*, derivation uncertain). (1) A Judean town toward the S, inhabited in the time of NEHEMIAH by members of the tribe of JUDAH (Neh. 11:25), which seems to be the same as DIMONAH (Josh. 15:22), possibly modern Khirbet edh-Dheiba.

(2) A city in MOAB, E of the DEAD SEA and N of the ARNON River, to which reference is first made in the OT in describing Israel's victory over SIHON of the Amorites (Num. 21:30). Dibon, together with the whole area, was given to the tribes of GAD and REUBEN (Num. 32:3, 34; Josh. 13:9), and although Dibon was built (i.e., rebuilt) by Gad (Num. 32:34) and, therefore, was sometimes called Dibon Gad (Num. 33:45–46), it was part of the territory of Reuben (Josh. 13:17).

Subsequently Israel did not keep continuous possession of Dibon, as is evidenced by Moabite control of the surrounding area under EGLON (Jdg. 3:12–14), the conquest of the area by DAVID (2 Sam. 8:2), and Moab's rebellion (2 Ki. 1:1; 3:4–5). Furthermore, in ISAIAH's time (Isa. 15:2), and later in that of JEREMIAH (Jer. 48:18, 22) this town, with others, was counted under the control of Moab (in Isa. 15:9 there appears to be a play on words, since DIMON resembles the Hebrew term for "blood").

Moab as a political state seems to have been destroyed by NEBUCHADNEZZAR. Later Dibon was probably under Jewish control, as suggested by a coin of the HASMONEAN ruler Hyrcanus II (63–40 B.C.) found there. The city is not mentioned in the NT, but that the town flourished from before the time of Christ through the Arabic period is attested by the presence there of Hellenistic, Nabatean, Roman, Byzantine, and Arabic sherds and coins, there being only a few literary references to the place in these periods, one in EUSEBIUS, who says that Dibon was a very large village (*kōmē pammegethēs*, *Onomasticon* 76.17–22).

The modern Dhiban, located a few miles N of the Arnon Valley on the road to KERAK, adjoins the ancient tell of Dibon, where the MOABITE STONE was found in 1868. The discovery indicates that this was Moab's capital (cf. 2 Ki. 3:4–5). Dibon was the original name; the Moabite king MESHA

Excavations at this tell near modern Dhiban reveal the ruins of ancient Dibon.

in rebuilding it gave at least a part of it the name Qarhoh (*ANET*, 320), a title that did not endure.

Archaeological excavation of Dibon was undertaken by the American Schools of Oriental Research between 1950 and 1956 in the following campaigns (directors are noted): 1950–1951, Fred V. Winnett; 1952, W. L. Reed; 1952–1953, A. D. Tushingham; 1956 and 1965, W. H. Morton (see the summary by Morton in *Studies in the Mesha Inscription and Moab*, ed. A. Dearman [1989], 239–46). These excavations were of particular interest because Dibon was a Transjordanian tell that had been occupied during most of the history of the region; it could thus give a cross section of the country's archaeological history. The site, elevation about 2,134 ft. above sea level, consists of two mounds: one is occupied by the modern village, Dhiban; the other (to the NW, connected by a saddle) is the ancient tell, Dibon, six acres in size. The SE section of the latter mound probably was the area where Mesha built his royal addition to Qarhoh. There are no springs in the area.

Some conclusions derived from the seasons of excavation thus far are: the identification of Dhiban with Dibon of the Omri-Ahab-Mesha period (c. 850 B.C.) is certain; the site was occupied in the Early Bronze period; and the city was important during the medieval and early Arab, Byzantine, Roman, Nabatean, and Iron II periods. Caution must be used in drawing conclusions concerning the absence of strata that could be associated with the Maccabean, Hellenistic, Persian, and Late or Middle Bronze periods because of the restricted areas of the excavations at Dibon; a hundred cisterns already found verify the statement of the Moabite Inscription on the need for such objects. That Dibon was an agricultural center is illustrated in the discovery of grain, ovens, and storage jars for grain. (See *NEAEHL*, 1:350–52.)

W. H. Mare

Dibon Gad. See Dibon #2.

Dibri dib´ri (דִּבְרִי *H1828*, possibly "talkative"). A man of the tribe of Dan whose daughter Shelomith married an Egyptian (Lev. 24:11). Shelomith's son blasphemed "the Name" (of God) and was stoned (vv. 10–23).

dictionaries. See Bible dictionaries and encyclopedias.

Didache did´uh-kee (Διδαχή *G1439*, "teaching"). A writing of the early church, usually included among the Apostolic Fathers.

I. The text. The full title of the document, according to the Greek MS which is the primary text, reads, "The Teaching of the Lord by the Twelve Apostles to the Gentiles." It was quoted, perhaps as Scripture, by Clement of Alexandria in his *Miscellanies* (1.20). However, Eusebius classed it among the *nothoi* (spurious books) in his *Ecclesiastical History* (3.25.4), and Athanasius said that it was not in the canon but among the books "to be read by those who newly join us" (*Festal Letter* 39). The last western indication of it before modern times seems to be a trace in Pirminius (d. 753). It is listed in the *Stichometry of Nicephorus* (c. 850) as a rejected book. It appears to have dropped out of learned discussion after that time. But in 1873 Philotheos Bryennios, metropolitan of Nicomedia, found the text of the *Didache* in a MS dating from 1056. He published it in 1883 and quite a sensation was created, as it appeared that it might be from a very early period of the church. This MS still provides the basic Greek text. There is a nearly complete variant Greek text in the Apostolic Constitutions and a fragment in Oxyrhynchus Papyrus No. 1782, both from the 4th cent.

Two Latin versions of some of the material in the first part of the *Didache* are in existence, one dating from the 9th or 10th cent. and the other, much more extensive, from the 11th cent. E. J. Goodspeed of the University of Chicago considered this second Latin MS, preserved at Munich and known as *De doctrina apostolorum*, to be the original form of the *Didache*. This, however, does not seem to be quite the best way to solve the problem. There are also Coptic, Georgian, Ethiopic, and Arabic versions of parts or most of the text.

II. Content. Broadly considered, the *Didache* may be divided into four sections as follows: the description of the two ways (chs. 1–6); directions for worship, including baptism and the Eucharist (chs. 7–10); directions concerning officers and the conduct of congregational affairs (chs. 11–15); eschatology (ch. 16). These subjects are of intense interest if the *Didache* is an early document as it appears to be (see section IV, below).

The description of the two ways is a document by itself. It forms the first part of the *Didache* and the last part of the so-called *Epistle of Barnabas* (see BARNABAS, EPISTLE OF). This concept, of course, is an ancient one (cf. Deut. 30:15). It may also be found in the OT prophets (Jer. 21:8). The QUMRAN *Manual of Discipline* presents a similar concept (1QS III, 13 to IV, 26). In the *Didache* the contrast is life/death as it is in the OT. In *Barnabas* and the Qumran *Manual* it is light/darkness. There are other forms of the contrast. Because of the close similarity between the two patristic documents, it has been thought by some that Barnabas borrowed from the *Didache* (e.g., F. X. Funk, O. Bardenhewer) or, more frequently, the *Didache* from *Barnabas* (e.g., R. H. Connolly, F. C. Burkitt, J. A. Robinson, J. Muilenburg). It is more likely that both took the idea from a third source circulating in the Greek-speaking Jewish DIASPORA. This view has found considerable favor. (For further discussion, see J. A. Robinson, *Barnabas, Hermas and the Didache* [1920]; J. Muilenburg, *The Literary Relations of the Epistle of Barnabas and the Teaching of the Twelve Apostles* [1929].)

The contrast between the two ways is an ethical one. It is set forth in a form for use in teaching catechumens. It clearly reflects the moral instruction of the OT. There is a section in the *Didache* (1.3–6), which does not correspond to anything in the *Barnabas* text, where the background is clearly that of the SERMON ON THE MOUNT. It is not obvious that the writer was using the text of Matthew or Luke. Probably some earlier form, perhaps oral, was the source.

One of the areas of greatest interest dealt with by the *Didache* is WORSHIP, since it appears that there was early information concerning BAPTISM and the LORD'S SUPPER. Chapter 7 is devoted to baptism. Catechetical instruction is stated to be presupposed. Fasting is to precede the baptism (7.4). The formula of baptism is trinitarian: "in the name of the Father and of the Son and of the Holy Spirit" (7.1). Cold running water was preferred, and immersion is probably the assumed mode. An alternate mode was pouring (7.3).

The common word for the Lord's Supper in the early church was EUCHARIST (*eucharistia* G2374, "thanksgiving"), and this term is used in the *Didache* (9.1; 10.7; 14.1). It has been thought (e.g., by Gregory Dix, *The Shape of the Liturgy* [1945], 90ff.; F. E. Vokes, *The Riddle of the Didache* [1938], 177–207) that the section beginning at 9.1 describes an AGAPE meal and ch. 14 the Eucharist proper. It is more likely that chs. 9 and 14 represent an observance where the Eucharist and the agape meal are still celebrated together, while ch. 14 refers to a Sunday celebration of the Eucharist alone. Other interpretations are possible and have been defended.

Assuming, as most likely, the suggestion just made, it may be noted that the thanksgiving prayers (9.2–4) are in the order cup-bread while the order "eat … drink" (9.5) follows and may well refer to the action. The cup-bread order, however, occurs in Lk. 22:17–19 (parts of vv. 19 and 20 are omitted by the Western text) and in 1 Cor. 10:16. The strong emphasis upon thanksgiving and triumph in the prayers is noteworthy. The Eucharist is restricted to the baptized. Knowledge and holiness are stressed. The enjoyment of food and drink as gifts of God is noted. The celebration of the Eucharist is appointed for each Lord's Day (14.1). The use of the word "sacrifice" (*thysia* G2602) in this connection is not to be understood as a reference to the death of Christ. The word was a common description of prayers, alms, and gifts in the usage of the time. It is the "sacrifice" of the people to which reference is being made.

The prescriptions for conduct are, of course, influenced by the OT law and by Jewish development of that law. There is to be mutual oversight of, and assistance to, one another in the community (15.3). Love and prayer for others are commanded (2.7). Division is to be avoided (4.3). Gifts to others are commended (1.5; 13.3–4). Hospitality is proper, both toward the leader (11.4) and toward the ordinary stranger (12.1–2). Food is restricted. It may not include that offered to idols (6.3), and fasting is to be practical (8.1). The presumption throughout appears to be that the community is a relatively poor one economically. The members are not influential in this world. They are subject to the temptations to be quarrelsome that often afflict such groups (15).

The official titles used in the document are apostle (11.3–6), prophet (10.7; 11.3–11; 13.1–4; 15.2), teacher (11.2; 15.2), bishop (15.1), and deacon (15.1). The first three are applied to itinerant individuals whose stay in the community is expected to be very short. The possibility that a prophet might wish to remain is provided for, however, and is welcomed (ch. 13). In such a case prophets are to be as high priests to the community (13.3). The bishops and deacons, on the other hand, are thought of as the resident equivalents of the traveling prophets and teachers, and are to be honored by the group (15.2).

The return of Christ in the future is expected (16.8). The hour is unknown (16.1), but there will be indications of its approach. False prophets and corrupters will increase in number, and the allegiance of some people will change (16.3). An individual claiming to be the Son of God will arise whose evil and deceptive actions will mislead (16.4). The coming itself will be preceded by a sign extended in the sky, a trumpet peal, and the resurrection of the saintly dead (16.6–7). The visible coming will follow and, according to the Georgian version, the last judgment (16.8). It behooves Christians to be watching and ready (16.1).

III. Place of origin. It is impossible to be dogmatic about the locale where the *Didache* was written. It seems likely that it did not originate in a large city where the stay of a traveling prophet or apostle might be expected to be longer than is contemplated (11.5; cf. 12.2). The reference to mountains (9.4) may reflect the environment. Possibly it contained warm baths or springs (7.2). Syria is perhaps as likely a place of origin as any, in the light of these considerations.

IV. Date. Speculation concerning the date has ranged over a wide period. It is clear that the references to church officers presuppose a relatively early state of affairs when traveling apostles and prophets were not too rare. There is no indication of a monarchical episcopate. The eucharistic practices seem comparatively primitive. While, therefore, speculation has ranged over the period from about A.D. 50 to the early 3rd cent., a date between A.D. 70 and 110 is to be preferred.

(See further R. Knopf, *Die Lehre der zwölf Apostel, die zwei Clemensbriefe* [1920]; J.-P. Audet, *La Didachè: Instructions des Apôtres* [1958]; R. A. Kraft, *Barnabas and the Didache*, vol. 3 of *The Apostolic Fathers*, ed. R. M. Grant [1965]; W. Rordorf and A. Tuilier, *La Doctrine des Douze Apôtres = Didachè: introduction, texte critique, traduction, notes, appendice, annexe et index*, 2nd ed [1998]; K. Niederwimmer, *The Didache: A Commentary*, Hermeneia [1998]; H. van De Sandt and D. Flusser, *The Didache: Its Jewish Sources and its Place in Early Judaism and Christianity* [2002]; A. Milavec, *The Didache: Faith, Hope, and Life of the Earliest Christian Communities, 50–70 C.E.* [2003]; id., *The Didache: Text, Translation, Analysis, and Commentary* [2003]; M. Del Verme, *Didache and Judaism: Jewish Roots of an Ancient Christian-Jewish Work* [2004].) P. WOOLLEY

Didascalia apostolorum. A Christian writing dealing with matters of church order, probably composed in SYRIA in the early 3rd cent. Originally written in Greek, it has survived in a Syriac translation and partially in Latin. Much of the work was incorporated into the first part of the APOSTOLIC CONSTITUTIONS AND CANONS. (English trans. in S. Brock and M. Vasey, *The Liturgical Portions of the Didascalia* [1982].)

didrachma di-drak′muh (δίδραχμον *G1440*). A double DRACHMA (Matt. 17:24 KJV mg.; NIV, "the two-drachma tax"; NRSV, "the temple tax"). Although the ancient two-drachma coin was no longer used by NT times, the term could still refer to that coin's monetary value. It was equivalent to a Jewish half shekel (about the wage of a common laborer for two days' work), the amount required annually as a temple tax. See also COINS.

Didymus did′uh-muhs (Δίδυμος *G1441*, "twin"). This designation, another name for the apostle THOMAS, appears only in the Gospel of John (Jn. 11:16; 20:24; 21:2). The form *Thōmas G2605* appears to be a genuine Greek name (BDF, §53), but it coincides with the ARAMAIC word for twin (*tĕʾōmāʾ*; cf. Heb. *tôʾămîm H9339*, Gen. 25:24; 38:27; Cant. 4:5; 7:3). Some however believe that the Greek form is a transliteration of the Aramaic word and that the Greek equivalent, Didymus, was used among Greek-speaking friends of Thomas. The theory that Jesus gave him this name because of his twofold nature, divided between doubt and faith, seems to be pure invention. More likely the designation refers to the simple fact that Thomas was a twin. L. FOSTER

die. See DEATH.

Diklah dik'luh (דִּקְלָה *H1989*, "date palm"). Son of JOKTAN and descendant of SHEM through EBER (Gen. 10:27; 1 Chr. 1:21). The names of Joktan's thirteen sons appear to refer to S Arabian tribes, but the places associated with them (Gen. 10:30) are difficult to identify. Suggested locations for the tribe of Diklah include the Yemenite coastal plain and the area of Ṣirwaḥ; the latter was an important city in the early kingdom of the SABEANS, and the surrounding region was known for its palm groves. (Cf. J. Simons, *The Geographical and Topographical Texts of the Old Testament* [1959], 136; *ABD*, 2:198–99.) G. G. SWAIM

Dilean dil'ee-uhn (דִּלְעָן *H1939*, possibly "protrusion"). A town in the Judean SHEPHELAH (Josh. 15:38). It was in the same district as LACHISH, but its precise location is not known (one suggestion is Tell en-Najileh).

dill. An aromatic herb (*Anethum graveolens*) native to Eurasia and common in Palestine, where it is found growing wild or in modern gardens as a cultivated plant. It has yellow flowers and looks like parsley when growing. The seeds can be used for flavoring bread and cakes. (They are used in Great Britain as a salad, but in Scandinavia as the flavoring for new boiled potatoes; dill is often put into jars of pickles.) It is certainly the herb referred to by Jesus when he rebuked the PHARISEES for rigorously tithing the smallest things while ignoring important acts of obedience (Gk. *anēthon G464*, Matt. 23:23; KJV, "anise"). Some versions use "dill" also as a rendering of Hebrew *qeṣaḥ H7902* (Isa. 28:25, 27 NRSV; NIV, CARAWAY). See CUMMIN.
 W. E. SHEWELL-COOPER

Dimnah dim'nuh (דִּמְנָה *H1962*, perhaps related to דֹּמֶן *H1961*, "refuse"). A town within the tribal territory of ZEBULUN, assigned to the Levites descended from MERARI (Josh. 21:35). No such place is otherwise attested, and many believe it is a scribal error for *rimmōn* or *rimmōnâ* (cf. 19:13; 1 Chr. 6:77). See RIMMON (PLACE) #2.

Dimon di'muhn (דִּימוֹן *H1904*, derivation unknown). In his oracle against MOAB, ISAIAH says, "Dimon's waters are full of blood, / but I will bring still more upon Dimon— / a lion upon the fugitives of Moab / and upon those who remain in the land" (Isa. 15:9). Because there is no other reference to such a city in Moab, many scholars follow a text from the DEAD SEA SCROLLS (1QIsa[a]) and the VULGATE in reading DIBON (cf. NRSV), assuming either a textual corruption or a deliberate play on the Hebrew word for "blood" (*dām H1947*). Others, however, point out that Dimon, as the harder reading, is more likely to be original (cf. H. Wildberger, *Isaiah 13–27: A Continental Commentary* [1997], 109); that there may be a connection between Dimon and MADMEN (Jer. 48:2); that Dibon was mentioned earlier (Isa. 15:2; no other place is mentioned twice in the passage); and that it is possible to identify Dimon with Khirbet Dimneh (7.5 mi. N of KIR HARESETH; cf. J. Simons, *The Geographical and Topographical Texts of the Old Testament* [1959], 436–37 §1261).

Dimonah di-moh'nuh (דִּימוֹנָה *H1905*). A city of the NEGEV, near the Edomite border, belonging to the tribe of JUDAH (Josh. 15:22). It is generally thought to be the same place as the DIBON of Judah occupied by the Jews in the period of the return from EXILE under NEHEMIAH (Neh. 11:25). The exact site is not known, but some identify it with modern Khirbet edh-Dheiba, about 2 mi. NE of ARAD.

Dinah di'nuh (דִּינָה *H1909*, possibly "justice" or "[female] judge"). The daughter of JACOB and LEAH (Gen. 30:21; 34:1–31; 46:15). During an inspection of the land and a visit with the pagan women, Dinah was criminally assaulted by SHECHEM, son of the ruler HAMOR, stated to be a HIVITE. Subsequently Jacob and the brothers of the victim returned and listened to a proposal of marriage and settlement presented by the Hivites on behalf of Shechem. The sons of Jacob agreed to the plan but insisted that the Hivite males submit to the rite of CIRCUMCISION. After the rite had been performed upon all the Hivites and the strangers in their midst, but while the wounds were sore and debilitating, two of Dinah's brothers, SIMEON and LEVI, took their weapons and slew all the males. Apparently the ravished sister was by this time married to Shechem, because they took her from his house (34:26), then despoiled all the rest of the village. For this act of wanton revenge the brothers Simeon and Levi were cursed in Jacob's final blessing (49:5–7), where it is said of them that "their swords [*or* plans] are weapons of violence."

Many interpreters, both Jewish and Christian, have suggested that Dinah was careless in her behavior or even that she was at fault in this incident, but the biblical narrative passes no judgment on her. In recent scholarship, Gen. 34 has become a focus of discussion regarding the alleged patriarchal bias and androcentrism of the Bible. (For an anthropological study, see J. Pitt-Rivers, *The Fate of Shechem or the Politics of Sex* [1977]; cf. also R. Parry, *Old Testament Story and Christian Ethics: The Rape of Dinah as a Case Study* [2004].) W. WHITE, JR.

Dinaite di′nay-it. According to the KJV, the Dinaites were an ethnic group that, with others, complained to the Persian monarch ARTAXERXES against the Jewish rebuilding of the TEMPLE (Ezra 4:9). This rendering follows the MT, *dināyēʾ*, but most scholars revocalize this Aramaic word to *dayyānayyāʾ*, "judges" (from *dayyān* H10171).

Dinhabah din′huh-buh (דִּנְהָבָה H1973, derivation disputed). The capital city of BELA, who was king of EDOM in the period before the Israelite monarchy (Gen. 36:32; 1 Chr. 1:43). Its location is unknown.

dinner. See FOOD; MEALS.

Diognetus, Epistle to di-og′ni-tuhs (Διόγνητος). An apologetic work of the early church, usually included among the APOSTOLIC FATHERS. It is a brilliant, lucid exposition of Christianity by an unknown author. A Diognetus who served as the tutor of the emperor MARCUS AURELIUS (*Meditations* 1.6) may be the assumed recipient of the epistle, but even this is not certain. Written in a rhetorical Greek style, the letter seeks to demonstrate the foolishness of IDOLATRY. It also accuses Judaism of unnecessary sacrifices and of ridiculous observances. In contrast, Christian character is praised. The INCARNATION brought a revelation of God's truth. God "gave his own Son as ransom for us" (*Diog.* 10.2). Chapters 11–12 are by a different hand, perhaps Hippolytus or Melito. The main body of the work probably dates from the late 2nd or early 3rd cent. The suggestion (advanced by P. Andriessen in 1946) that it is the lost *Apology* of Quadratus is not likely. The only pre-Reformation MS of the text was destroyed by fire in 1870, but copies of it had earlier been made. (See H. G. Meecham, *The Epistle to Diognetus* [1949]. For the view that the author of this work was none other than POLYCARP, see C. E. Hill, *From the Lost Teaching of Polycarp* [2006].) P. WOOLLEY

Dionysia di′uh-nish′ee-uh (Διονύσια). A series of festivals that honored DIONYSUS, the god of wine. The first of the feasts was the Oschophoria in the month of Pysanepsion (October to November), which celebrated the ripening of the grapes. The running of races, making of processions, and singing of choruses were climaxed by a sacrifice and banquet. The smaller Dionysia was held in the month of Poseideon (December to January) and celebrated the first tasting of the new wine. A solemn procession to the altar of the god was climaxed by a sacrifice, followed by dancing and dramas. The Lenoea was the feast of the vats held in ATHENS in the month of Gamelion (January to February) at Lenaeon, the oldest and most sacred shrine of Dionysus. The feast was notable for its meal provided at the public expense, after which a procession was made to the tragedies and comedies. The Anthesteria was observed for three days in the month of Anthesterion (February to March) and celebrated the opening of the casks of new wine. The most important feature was the symbolic marriage of the wife of the high priest of Dionysus to that god. The great urban Dionysia was held for six days in the month of Elaphebolion (March to April). Processions and singing were climaxed by three days of performances of the new tragedies, comedies, and dramas. H. L. DRUMWRIGHT, JR.

Dionysius the Areopagite diʹuh-nishʹee-uhs airʹee-opʹuh-gīt (Διονύσιος ὁ Ἀρεοπαγίτης *G1477* ["of Dionysus"] + *G741* ["of the Areopagus"]). A convert of PAUL in ATHENS who was apparently a member of the council of the AREOPAGUS (Acts 17:34). He is one of a number of prominent men who are mentioned by Luke as converts (13:12; 19:31; 26:32; 28:7). Little else is known about him except by traditions that cannot be verified. According to Suidas he was born at Athens and studied there and in Egypt. While he was in Egypt he observed the eclipse that took place at the time of the crucifixion and theorized that God was suffering. He then returned to Athens and became a person of influence. EUSEBIUS (*Hist.* 3.4.10; 4.23.3), quoting a later Dionysius who was bishop in CORINTH, states that Dionysius the Areopagite was the first bishop of Athens.

Accounts vary concerning his death. One tradition is that he was martyred at Athens under DOMITIAN. Another indicates that he came to Rome and was then sent to Paris by Clemens I, where he was beheaded on the martyr's mount (Montmartre). He is often identified with St. Dennis, the patron of France. (Christian and Neoplatonic writings of three or four centuries later were attributed to him, such as *On the Celestial Hierarchy, On the Ecclesiastical Hierarchy, On the Divine Names, On the Mystical Theology*. These were widely read and influential throughout the Middle Ages. Many commentaries were written on them from the 9th cent. on. The real author may have been the monophysite Peter the Iberian, 411–491. See E. Honigmann, *Pierre l'Ibérien et les écrits du Pseudo-Denys l'Aréopagite* [1952]; W. Volker, *Kontemplation und Ekstase bei Ps.-Dionysius Areopagita* [1958].)   A. RUPPRECHT

Dionysus diʹuh-niʹsuhs (Διόνυσος). Also called Bacchus. The god of an ecstatic and emotional cult, which appears to have reached GREECE from Thrace (THRACIA). The cult satisfied that strange and somewhat terrifying urge in human nature that found expression also in the "dancing madness," which periodically invaded Europe from the 14th to the 17th cent. and even appropriated to its mass excitement perverted forms of Christianity (other examples include the "Shakers," the Jewish Hasidim, the Muslim dervishes, and the Siberian shamans).

Mythology made Dionysus the son of ZEUS and Semele (a mortal mother), snatched unborn from his mother's womb when Semele was incinerated before the burning glory of Zeus that she had insisted on seeing. The babe was born in due time from his divine father's thigh, in which he was sewn. Myths clustered around the young god's name, the most famous of which forms the theme of Euripides' last and strangest tragedy, the *Bacchae*, a drama which, rightly viewed, is a moving and horrifying study of the worship of Dionysus as the tragedian encountered it in its northern homeland in his final years.

The Dionysiac myths are of little account. They are accretions around a form of primitive worship of vast antiquity that came to Greece from ancient times and found new forms and adaptations as society grew more sophisticated and civilized. The drama, tragedy, and comedy, but especially the former, had their primitive roots in the worship of Dionysus, and the Attic Dionysiac festivals produced their final splendid fruit in the magnificent theater of Aeschylus, Sophocles, and Euripides (see DIONYSIA).

Beneath the mass of MYTH and the final shape of the ritual, it is possible to see the worship of a vegetation spirit, and the FERTILITY CULT so frequently associated with such deities, in primitive religion. Dionysus was "the Power of the Tree," the "Blossom-bringer," the "Fruit-bringer," the "Abundance of Life." His domain was, as E. R. Dodds (*Bacchae* [1944], x) puts it, "Not only the liquid fire in the grape, but the sap thrusting in a young tree, the blood pounding in the veins of a young animal, all the mysterious and uncontrollable tides which ebb and flow in the life of nature." The tidy-minded Romans turned this ancient deity into the jolly Bacchus, the wine god with his reveling nymphs and satyrs—theme of Titian and Rubens—and turned *orgia* (from Gk. *orgia*, "secret rites") into "orgies," not the ecstatic acts of the transforming and horrible devotion that they were in their primitive context of nature worship and religious "possessions." (See further W. F. Otto, *Dionysus: Myth and Cult* [1965]; W. K. C. Guthrie, *The Greeks and their Gods* [1950]; C. Seltman, *The Twelve Olympians and Their Guests* [1952], ch. 13.; M. P. Nilsson, *The Dionysiac Mysteries of the Hellenistic and Roman Age*

[1957]; C. Kerenyi, *Dionysos: Archetypal Image of Indestructible Life* [1976]; *DDD*, 252–58.)

E. M. BLAIKLOCK

Dioscorinthius di´uhs-kuh-rin´thee-uhs (Διὸς Κορίνθιος). This name is found just once, in the APOCRYPHA (2 Macc. 11:21). It is used to date a letter that Lysias, deputy of ANTIOCHUS Epiphanes and later regent of his successor Antiochus Eupator, wrote to the Jews. The date is given as the twenty-fourth day of Dioscorinthius (in the year 165–164). The name is otherwise unknown. There are several possible explanations. (a) It may mean the month Dios (or Dius) in the Macedonian calendar, equated with the Jewish month Marheshwan by JOSEPHUS (*Ant.* 1.3.3). The addition of *-corinthios* remains unexplained. (b) Latin MSS of the passage have the variants *Dioscoridos*, a name not otherwise known as the name of a month, and *Dioscurus*, the third month of the Cretan year (the latter is supported by P. Katz in *ZNW* 51 [1960]: 15). (c) Another suggestion is that it was an intercalary month such as the Babylonians and Jews found it necessary to insert every two or three years, because they realized that the lunar year fell eleven days short of the solar year (see *IDB*, 1:486–87).

F. FOULKES

Dioscuri di´uhs-kyoor´i (Διόσκουροι *G1483*, "sons of Zeus"). The twin patrons of distressed seamen in Greek and Roman mythology; their names were Castor and Pollux. Traditionally the sons of ZEUS by Leda, to whom he appeared as a swan, they were also considered to be the children of Tyndareus, king of Sparta, where they were said to have ruled and had been buried. They were especially worshiped by the Dorian Greeks. Castor was a great charioteer and Pollux a boxer. When Pollux was offered immortality by Zeus, he chose to share death with Castor, who had been killed in a fight. As the patrons of sailors, they were identified with the two highest stars of the constellation Gemini (Twins), and they were also said to appear during electrical storms in the form of St. Elmo's fire. (See R. Harris, *The Cult of the Heavenly Twins* [1906]; *DDD*, 258–59.)

PAUL sailed from MALTA to PUTEOLI on an Alexandrian ship that had the mark of the Dioscuri (Acts 28:11; NRSV, "the Twin Brothers"; NIV, "the twin gods Castor and Pollux"). This was probably the name of the ship, which carried a symbol of the gods on the masthead, or as the figurehead.

A. RUPPRECHT

Diotrephes di-ot´ruh-feez (Διοτρέφης *G1485*, "nourished by Zeus"). The lone biblical reference to this churchman is 3 Jn. 9, where he is reprimanded for his failure to receive the representatives sent by the author, John. Evidently he had opposed a former letter from John, had maligned the apostle, and had refused to grant hospitality to the brethren, urging that all others of the congregation do likewise (v. 10). John characterizes him as someone "who loves to be first." Diotrephes probably held an office in the church and abused his authority. In any case, he clearly tried to exercise dominance over the congregation. (See A. J. Malherbe in *God's Christ and His People*, ed. J. Jervell and W. A. Meeks [1977], 222–32.)

L. FOSTER

Diphath di´fath. See RIPHATH.

discernings of spirits. The charismatic gift of determining the genuineness of allegedly divine messages and works (1 Cor. 12:10 KJV, rendering *diakriseis pneumatōn*; NIV, "distinguishing between spirits"). It was recognized, not only in Christianity but also among other religious groups, that supernatural acts and utterances might come from evil as well as good sources. There was consequent need for a means of discerning the motivating spirits. The early church was plagued by false prophets (1 Jn. 4:1), as Jesus and Paul had warned (Matt. 7:15; Acts 20:28–31). The outcome of predictions (Deut. 18:22; see PROPHETS AND PROPHECY III) or the evidence of fruit (Matt. 7:15–16) could not always be waited for, and God's true message must be quickly recognized and heeded (1 Thess. 5:19–21).

The apostle John, in his first epistle, applies a confessional test: the spirit in question must make a commitment to the orthodox belief in the deity and humanity of Christ (1 Jn. 4:1–3; cf. v. 15). Further, there must be submission to apostolic authority (vv. 5–6), and the letter as a whole stresses the need for evidence of Christian moral character. In 1 Cor.

12–14 the concern is for edifying ministry. With free participation, only the divine charismatic gift of discerning of spirits could provide the needed control. Therefore the gift of discernment was given. Many regard this gift, like apostleship, as temporary to meet this early church peril only (e.g., J. F. Walvoord, *The Holy Spirit* [1954], 188). It supplied, in gifted persons, what was later available through a completed NT, an authoritative standard. Not the gifted only, however, but all believers must exercise discernment to some degree, then as now (1 Cor. 2:14, 15; 1 Jn. 2:20, 27; 4:1–6; cf. Phil. 1:10). See also SPIRITUAL GIFTS. W. L. LIEFELD

discernment. See WISDOM.

discharge. See DISEASE.

disciple, discipleship. The idea of discipleship is very old, and common among the Greeks (*mathētēs* G3412, "disciple," occurring over 250 times in the NT; fem. *mathētria* G3413, only in Acts 9:36). Though words for "disciple" or "student" rarely occur in the OT (*talmid* H9441, 1 Chr. 25:8; *limmud* H4341, Isa. 8:16; 50:4), discipleship was a prominent feature of later JUDAISM. It always involved a teacher-student relationship. Discipleship of course denoted the learning process (the terms derive from verbs meaning "to learn," Gk. *manthanō* G3443 and Heb. *lāmad* H4340), but it also involved adopting the philosophy, practices, and way of life of the teacher (cf. Xenophon, *Mem.* 1.6.3). Physical proximity of the student to his teacher was also implied, although there are instances when discipleship was extended to include pupils separated from their masters by centuries (Dio Chrysostom, *Homer and Socrates* [*Or.* 55], 3–5; note that in Jn. 9:28 Jews contemporary with Jesus call themselves disciples of Moses).

Discipleship is also a prominent and important concept in the NT. JOHN THE BAPTIST had his disciples (Matt. 9:14), as did the PHARISEES (22:16) and even PAUL (Acts 9:25). Most often, however, the word *disciple* is used in the NT to denote the relationship between Jesus and his followers. In its widest sense it included all those who believed on him (Jn. 8:30–31), or who came to learn from him (Matt. 5:1–2). At one time these disciples were many (Lk. 6:17) and included a cross section of society from sinners to scribes (Matt. 8:18–22; Mk. 1:16–20; 2:13–15; Lk. 6:14–16; Jn. 19:38). Many of these were from GALILEE, but not all (Jn. 7:3). The word also was used more narrowly, referring to some or all of Jesus' intimate circle of friends (Matt. 10:1; 11:1; Lk. 9:54; Jn. 6:8), a frequent synonym for the Twelve. All of Jesus' disciples were learners required to "abide" in his word (Jn. 8:31–32). This meant not only that they were to listen to what he said, but also that they were to adopt his teaching as their way of life (Lk. 6:40; Jn. 15:7–8).

Jesus' teachings covered many topics, but the whole of it was summarized in one commandment, LOVE (Jn. 13:34); and although discipleship had many facets it was summed up in a single concept—obedience to this command (13:35). Many heard Jesus speak, but because his teaching was radical, and at times too difficult to accept (Jn. 6:60), the majority of disciples defected (6:66). Consequently, much of what he taught about such topics as his death and resurrection (Matt. 16:21), the end of the age (Mk. 13), love, the Father, and the Holy Spirit (Jn. 14–16), was given only to the inner circle (6:68). See ETHICS OF JESUS; JESUS CHRIST VI.

Discipleship was initiated by Jesus (Matt. 4:19, an exception being Lk. 9:57), and involved a commitment to his person even more than to his teaching. (Note that to criticize Jesus' disciples was to criticize Jesus, Mk. 2:18, 23, 24, and to remove the teacher was to destroy the community of disciples, Mk. 14:27, 50.) This is not to say that his disciples were unconcerned with what he taught. They probably memorized much of his teaching, as was customary for disciples to do, and no doubt were responsible for passing on this teaching as the tradition of the church (1 Cor. 15:1–3).

The idea of physical adjacency inherent in the word *disciple* also applied specifically to Jesus' associates. It was this idea that placed such radical demands on any one desiring to be his disciple. An itinerant RABBI, Jesus was constantly on the move. To be his disciple was in a literal way to be his follower. (The verb "to follow" [*akoloutheō* G199] occurs about eighty times in the Gospels, and exclusively describes the relationship between the earthly Jesus and his companions. The word "follower" became a synonym for "disciple.") This meant, therefore, that every disciple in the strict sense had to leave his occupation (Mk. 1:18–19), his father and mother (10:29), everything (10:28), take up his cross and go forward even to death (Matt. 10:38). For the disciple was not above his teacher (10:24), and what would happen to the teacher could also happen to the taught (10:25; Lk. 6:40). See also EDUCATION.

The expression "disciple of Jesus" was also used less strictly. It described those who were his disciples secretly (Jn. 19:38), and by implication those who were not at all physically adjacent to him (cf. Mk. 9:38–40; 5:18–19). This looser concept of disciple may have made it possible for the writer of Acts to use it as a general term for "Christian" (Acts 9:25 and 19:1 are the only exceptions), the original idea of being an intimate companion of the earthly Jesus now almost forgotten.

Surprisingly, the word *disciple* never appears a single time in the NT outside of the Gospels and Acts. It is also instructive to discover that the verb "to follow" occurs only twice outside of them to describe the relationship between the risen Lord and his adherents (Rev. 14:4; 19:14). Apparently, therefore, because the writers of the epistles saw in the meaning of the words *disciple* and *follower* a disciple-teacher relationship no longer possible in the new era, they dropped them from their vocabulary lest those requirements for the disciples of the earthly Jesus—to leave one's trade, his father and mother, etc.—be universalized and made general requirements for those who would believe on him now as the exalted heavenly Lord. See also DISCIPLINE.

The word *disciple* was revived, however, in the writings of the early subapostolic church, and given much the same meaning as that in Acts, *Christian*. IGNATIUS, however, employed it almost exclusively to denote those who became martyrs for the sake of Christ (*Trall.* 5:2; *Eph.* 1–2). (See B. Gerhardsson, *Memory and Manuscript* [1964]; E. Best, *Following Jesus: Discipleship in the Gospel of Mark* [1981]; M. Hengel, *The Charismatic Leader and His Followers* [1981]; M. J. Wilkins, *Discipleship in the Ancient World and Matthew's Gospel* [1995]; *TDNT*, 4:390–461; *NIDNTT*, 1:480–94.) G. F. HAWTHORNE

discipline. This English word derives from Latin *disciplīna*, "learning, training" (cf. *discipulus*, "pupil," and *discere*, "to learn"). The Hebrew term *mûsār* H4592 can be variously rendered "correction, chastisement, education, warning." Greek *paideia* G4082 in classical literature is strictly a positive term ("the rearing of a child [*pais* G4090], education, learning, culture"), but in the SEPTUAGINT, as a rendering of the corresponding Hebrew word, it begins to take on as well the negative sense of "punishment." Paul counsels: "Fathers, do not exasperate your children; instead, bring them up in the training and instruction [*paideia kai nouthesia*] of the Lord" (Eph. 6:4). He states that the commendable conduct of the Lord's servant is to correct or instruct (verb *paideuō* G4084) his opponents with gentleness (2 Tim. 2:25). And in his climactic admonition to Timothy, he wrote, "All Scripture is God-breathed and is useful for teaching, rebuking, correcting and training [*paideia*] in righteousness" (2 Tim. 3:16).

In the negative sense, the OT speaks only of punishment by "the discipline of the LORD" (Deut. 11:2) and by parents. Consequently, the following may be observed. Punitive discipline is administered by someone in authority and in position of responsibility. It is introduced biblically with the Mosaic law as punishment for its violation (Lev. 26:23; Deut. 4:36; 11:2; cf. Exod. 20:20). In a liturgy on divine judgment the psalmist quotes God in saying, "You hate discipline, / and you cast my words behind you" (Ps. 50:17 NRSV). Centuries later, when national Israel was on the brink of disaster, facing the impending judgment of the Babylonian captivity, its apostasy was recalled: "This is the nation that did not obey the voice of the LORD their God, and did not accept discipline" (Jer. 7:28 NRSV). Means of divine discipline included plagues, pestilence, poverty, wild beasts, crop failure, property, destruction, famine, sword, captivity, fear, pining, disease, desolation, and death (Lev. 26:14–39).

Most references to discipline occur in Proverbs. The writer admonishes: "My son, do not despise the LORD's discipline" (Prov. 3:11). He points out that "the corrections of discipline are the way of life" (6:23); that "Whoever loves discipline loves knowledge" (12:1); and that one should not hate discipline (5:12), for the wicked "will die for lack of discipline" (5:23). Several passages deal specifically with parental discipline (13:24; 19:18; 22:15; 23:13; 29:17). In the end, "Stern discipline awaits him who leaves the path" (15:10).

In the NT, discipline is primarily of a positive nature and is associated with love rather than law (however, see also EXCOMMUNICATION). Jesus' life and teachings, and that of his dedicated followers, elevated discipline to an essential and desirable means of achieving the highest goals. Jesus' willingly self-imposed deprivations and sacrifices constitute the noblest forms of discipline (Lk. 9:58; Phil. 2:1–8). The same spirit is manifest in his teachings concerning self-denial and bearing the cross (Matt. 10:37–38; Lk. 14:25–33).

Significantly and appropriately, Jesus' specially selected twelve men were called "disciples." They were learners under the great Teacher, having accepted his invitation: "Take my yoke upon you and learn from me" (Matt. 11:29). They had matriculated in his school and committed themselves to his discipline, the education required for their high calling. See DISCIPLE, DISCIPLESHIP. Following this precedent, self-discipline became a chief characteristic of dedicated Christian workers. After the resurrection, and the new power given on PENTECOST, Christ's followers committed themselves to learning the sacred writings and to teaching others. PAUL admonished TIMOTHY: "Train yourself to be godly" (1 Tim. 4:7; cf. v. 16; 2 Tim. 2:15). The writer of Hebrews mentions discipline six times, all in one chapter, in the punitive manner of its OT use. He begins with the exhortation, "My son, do not make light of the Lord's discipline" (Heb. 12:5, quoting Prov. 3:11), and concludes, "No discipline seems pleasant at the time, but painful. Later on, however, it produces a harvest of righteousness and peace for those who have been trained by it" (Heb. 12:11). Though discipline is delegated in part to institutions (home, school, church, government), it is ultimately in the hands of God. (See R. de Vaux, *Ancient Israel* [1962], 147–50; *NIDOTTE*, 2:279–82; *TDNT*, 5:596–625; *NIDNTT*, 1:494–503.) See also CRIMES AND PUNISHMENTS; EDUCATION.   G. B. FUNDERBURK

Discipline, Manual of. See DEAD SEA SCROLLS IV.

Discourse on the Eighth and Ninth. Modern title given to a HERMETIC dialogue in which the teacher (Hermes Trismegistus) guides his pupil into a spiritual experience of the eighth and ninth spheres surrounding the earth. This tractate is preserved only in a 4th-cent. Coptic MS in the NAG HAMMADI LIBRARY (NHC VI, 6); the original Greek is thought to be as early as the 2nd cent. The document places emphasis on secret knowledge and gives expression to a sharp DUALISM between body and soul that negates the physical world. (For an English trans., see *NHL*, 321–27.)

discus. Throwing the discus was an athletic exercise practiced by the Greeks and an important event in the Greek athletic festivals. It is frequently mentioned by Homer, and the discus thrower was a subject of Greek artists, Myron's *Discobolus* being world famous, though the original is lost. There is no mention of discus or discus throwing in the canonical books of the Bible, but it is referred to in the APOCRYPHA as an indication of the degree of hellenization promoted by the high priest, JASON, who set up a place of exercise under the citadel (2 Macc. 4:14). See MACCABEE.   C. E. DEVRIES

disease. An abnormal condition of part or all of the body, with a characteristic group of symptoms. (For a brief description of the development of medical care to cope with diseases in biblical times, see PHYSICIAN; see also HEALING AND HEALTH; MEDICINE.) It is likely that the Hebrews were subject to the same diseases that are prevalent in the semitropical climate of the Middle East today. However, in many cases the Bible only mentions symptoms, such as fever, hemorrhage, discharge, or itch, and one can only surmise what the disease entity was. In this article, the diseases of the Bible are listed in alphabetical order and then briefly described. (These descriptions are very general in nature and are not intended as a substitute for authoritative, up-to-date discussions.)

Alcoholism. WINE was a very common drink in biblical days, much as coffee is now. In a country like Israel, dysentery of several kinds was endemic, and drinking water easily contaminated. Wine was a safe drink because of its alcoholic content. The Bible speaks favorably of wine in several places.

When Isaac gave Jacob his blessing, he said, "May God give you ... an abundance of grain and wine" (Gen. 27:28). Then, of course, we have the record of Jesus miraculously changing a huge volume of water into wine. Some scholars seek to show that the wine was really only grape juice. This is improbable, since grape juice would quickly spoil with temperature and living conditions as they were in biblical days. Wine was definitely wine as we know it today, and it was a good thing for the people of that day.

However, it is also true that some Hebrews used wine to excess and got themselves and others in trouble. The Bible repeatedly speaks favorably of wine, but warns frequently and emphatically against its excessive use. There seems to be a strange chemistry in the bodies of certain people that produces a strong craving for alcohol. They start drinking it in normal manner with their food, or socially, but are unable to control themselves and go on to excess. Drinks such as whiskey were probably unknown to the Jews, but excessive wine drinking can do just as much damage as other forms of alcohol intake, destroying the brain, liver, and other organs.

In modern times alcoholism is looked upon as a disease and is treated as such. In biblical days it was considered a moral problem. Chronic alcoholism is an amazingly stubborn ailment. Persons who seem to have recovered from it show relapses after months or years in seventy-five percent of such cases. Christian faith is of enormous help. Several chronic alcoholics have been instantaneously cured of alcoholism by simply accepting Jesus as their Savior and Lord. Undoubtedly there were cases like that in the old days when alcoholics returned to sincere Yahweh worship. Medication, counseling, institutional training, and Alcoholics Anonymous are valuable, but none are as effective as that mysterious experience known as "rebirth."

Atrophy. Job speaks of one of his afflictions with the expression, "he has shriveled me up" (Job 16:8 NRSV; the meaning of the Hebrew verb is uncertain, and NIV translates, "You have bound me"). The impression received of Job's physical troubles is that he was assailed with several ailments, one of which was atrophy. The disease most likely to make Job "shrivel up" (if that is the correct rendering of the Hebrew) might be muscular dystrophy. This is a condition in which the muscles refuse to absorb the food brought to them by the blood. Food intake may be adequate, with digestion and absorption from the gastro-intestinal tract normal, but when the food gets to the muscles it is not adequately absorbed by them. As a result the muscles grow increasingly thinner and weaker. As an example we may think of a child with muscular dystrophy being picked up by a parent. In a normal child, the muscles in its shoulders, chest, back, and hips give it some solidity; but when a youngster with muscular dystrophy is picked up, he may unexpectedly slide through a parent's arms like a slippery eel, because there is so little muscular structure left. The brain is not involved, but the body in an advanced case would be much as Job described himself.

Another reference to atrophy is found in Lk. 6:6, which says that Jesus healed a man's right hand that was withered (Gk. *xēros* G3831, lit., "dry"). This time the atrophy could have been due to injured nerves paralyzing the hand. Another likely cause is polio meningitis. Polio is caused by a virus—an organism so small that it is not even visible with an ordinary high-power microscope. The tiny virus is found primarily in the mouth and pharynx, and in the lower bowel. Food contaminated by fecal material may contain the polio virus, and this is the principal method by which it is spread. The germ is picked up by the small bowel and travels to the central nervous system. Sometimes the disease is so mild that it is not even diagnosed except during an epidemic. At other times paralysis of almost every degree may occur and be permanent. Polio is more frequent in tropical climates than farther N, and it must have been a common ailment in biblical days. The man with the withered hand may very well have had polio years earlier, with just the single hand permanently affected by it. When paralyzed muscles are not used, withering or atrophy inevitably occurs. Thanks to devoted scientists—and the goodness of God—vaccines have been developed that are amazingly effective in protecting people against polio. As with smallpox, polio is now almost unheard of in our country. See also PARALYTIC.

Baldness. Jews usually had a luxuriant growth of hair on head and chin. It was a source of pride to them. Foreign neighbors of Israel sometimes shaved their scalps and chins as a sign of mourning

(Isa. 15:2), but the Israelites were strictly forbidden to follow this practice (Deut. 14:1). Unavoidable baldness was considered regrettable, and sometimes disgraceful. There were, and still are, many reasons for baldness. Perhaps the greatest is an inherited tendency. Wearing a heavy or tight hat can interfere with the flow of blood to the scalp. Advanced and debilitating diseases can be the causative factor in baldness, as also simple old age. However, the two most common causes were seborrheic dermatitis, a fungus infection with a dirty mess of greasy, yellowish crusts, and tinea capitis (ringworm of the scalp). See also separate article on BALDNESS.

Blindness was common in Egypt, Israel, and the Arabian countries. Poverty, unsanitary conditions, brilliant sunlight, excessive heat, blowing sand, accidents, and war injuries were some of the factors involved, but the main cause was ignorance of infectious organisms. The blindness from birth spoken of in the Bible was probably ophthalmia neonatorum (gonorrhea of the eyes). This has been the prime cause of infantile blindness for centuries. Women often harbor gonorrheal diplococci in the vagina, even though they may be totally unaware of the infection. At birth, as the baby makes its passage down from the uterus, it may get some of the germs in its eyes. The conjunctiva of a baby is an ideal breeding place for gonococci, and in about three days the baby's eyes run with pus. In many cases permanent blindness results. In modern practice, antiseptic drops are placed in the infant's eyes immediately after birth, and the infective organisms that may be present are destroyed.

The other frequent cause of blindness was trachoma. The infecting organism is a virus. I have treated scores of Navajo Indians with this disease, and it was a pitiful sight to see them come in with their bleary, itching, painful eyes. Some of them had an apron of tissue, called a pannus, growing down over the cornea. Many older people had badly deformed eyelids, and some were blind. Today's sulfa drugs provide an easy and complete cure, but in former days it was a devastating illness.

Boil. It is likely that this term, as used in the Bible, covered many types of skin diseases, such as pustules, simple boils, carbuncles, abscesses, and infected glands. Boils, as we know them today, are usually caused by staphylococci. These germs are normally present on the surface of the skin, and do no harm unless there is some kind of injury to the skin, allowing the germs to get inside and proliferate. The body reacts with its defense of leucocytes, and in the battle that ensues germs, leucocytes, and debris may form a painful pocket of pus that we call a boil. If the boil is single and comes to a head, it ruptures and recovery follows.

A carbuncle is much like a collection of boils in a limited area. The infection runs deeper than an ordinary boil and has several openings. It is commonly located in the back of the neck. It usually covers an area several inches in diameter, and sometimes is fatal. An abscess may be minor, but frequently is deep, involving important structures of the body, such as muscles, lungs, brain, liver, spleen, kidney, bowel, and appendix. Hezekiah's boil (2 Ki. 20:7 = Isa. 38:21) must have been a carbuncle or deep abscess, as his life hung in the balance when he was afflicted with it. Job's boils (Job 2:7 KJV) were superficial, or they would have resulted in his death. The boils of the sixth Egyptian plague (Exod. 9:8–11) probably were extremely painful superficial boils.

Cholera. See below under *pestilence*.

Consumption. This word is used by some English versions to render Hebrew *šaḥepet H8831*, which appears only twice in the Bible (Lev. 26:16; Deut. 28:22; NIV, "wasting disease"). In both instances it is included in a list of disasters that would befall the people of Israel if they rejected their God. Efforts have been made to limit its meaning to tuberculosis or malaria, but it is more likely to refer to the whole group of wasting diseases, including especially dysentery (see below) in its several forms.

Blind man asking for donations at the mosque in Hebron.

Deafness may be partial or complete, and it may affect only one ear or both. There are several general areas that may be involved in deafness. The first of these is the external ear canal. With the sand, dust, and drying heat of the ANE, there must have been many cases in which the ear canal became plugged with wax and dirt, producing a serious degree of deafness. Undoubtedly many persons suffered deafness much of their lives because of dirty ears. Infections of the external ear canal were also common in tropical and semitropical countries.

The middle ear is another frequent source of trouble. This little chamber with its three tiny ossicles—the malleus, incus, and stapes—forming a little chain from the ear drum to the window of the cochlea, and the Eustachian tube coming into it from the pharynx, serves an important function in hearing. The area may become infected by organisms coming through a ruptured ear drum, or through the Eustachian tube. Severe deafness may also be due to the ossicles becoming rigidly solidified to each other following an infection.

The inner ear is the third possible location of trouble. It is called the cochlea because it resembles a snail shell. It is really an extension of the auditory nerve. Infection of the cochlea or tumors of the auditory nerve and hearing center of the brain are uncommon, but severe when they occur.

Demon possession. It is undeniably true that in biblical days diseases in general were ascribed to the presence of evil spirits in the patient, although not so much in Israel as in other countries. See DEMON. Violent episodes, such as might occur with insane persons, or those with severe attacks of epilepsy, strengthened belief in demon possession. Demon possession may simulate or cause diseases such as epilepsy, insanity, or aphasia, but it is distinguished from these in the Bible (see Matt. 4:24; 17:15; Mk. 9:17–27). Not every case of illness that Jesus cured was attributed to demonic influence, but certain instances were definitely so identified (see below under *epilepsy*).

Dropsy is an abnormal accumulation of serous fluid in the tissues of the body or in one of the body cavities. If it is locked in the structure of the tissues, it is usually called edema. It is commonly seen due to a faulty heart or diseased kidneys. There is bloating of the face. Arms and legs may be greatly swollen and have a doughy appearance. Liver disease from alcoholism can fill the abdomen with gallons of fluid. The abdomen feels as hard as a drum, and pressure of the fluid against the diaphragm makes it difficult for the patient to breathe. If the fluid is drawn off with a hollow needle, it gives only temporary relief and the abdomen soon fills up again.

Dumbness may refer to total inability to speak (mutism), or to inability to speak clearly and coherently (aphasia), as was the case with the "deaf man who had an impediment in his speech" (Mk. 7:32 NRSV; NIV, "could hardly talk"). Dumbness in the sense of mutism may be due to stubborn uncooperativeness, to severe depression because of an external calamity (Ps. 38:13), to extreme fright (as seen in SAUL's companions, Acts 9:17), to hysteria, or to a lesion of the brain. A person born completely deaf may be mute for a long time because he is unfamiliar with sounds. However, the organs of speech may be normal, so that with proper training the person can learn to speak (as in the well-known story of Helen Keller). The dumbness of sheep (Isa. 53:7) was not due to inability to make a sound, but is considered to be a token of submission. Idols were called dumb (1 Cor. 12:2) because they had no life in them. They were unable to hear, speak, or act.

Dwarfism. Also called *nanism*. Dwarfs seem normal at birth, but early in life it is noted that linear growth is abnormally slow, and after the tenth year it may stop entirely. This retardation in growth may have various reasons. One is a deficiency of the pituitary gland. This small gland near the base of the brain has various important functions, and one is to manufacture a growth hormone. When the supply of this hormone is insufficient, dwarfism results; if it is excessive, gigantism may result. Human growth hormone is almost impossible to obtain and extremely costly, but when used in cases of dwarfism due to deficiency of this hormone, it really stimulates growth. Thyroid extract seems to fortify its effectiveness. Dwarfism may be an inherited characteristic, as in the pygmies of Africa. It may also be due, and often is, to such deficiencies as rickets, poor absorption of food from the small bowel, chronic kidney disease, and malformations of the heart. Physical normalcy was demanded of Hebrew priests, and therefore dwarfs were barred from priestly duties (Lev. 21:20).

Dysentery was a very common ailment among the people of the ANE. It was due primarily to three types of organisms—amebae, bacteria, and worms. In some cases the body adjusted itself to the invading organism, and there would be only sporadic attacks of diarrhea. But often it was very severe, and at times so bad it was called malignant dysentery. Plague is the most striking example of such malignancy. The stools consisted mainly of mucus, pus, and blood. It was accompanied by severe abdominal pain, and frequently high fever. Passage of stools was painful with dysentery because of the irritating effect of the excretions. Hemorrhoids developed, and at times there was a prolapse of the lower part of the colon, as was the case with JEHORAM (2 Chr. 21:18–19). There was also rapid loss of weight, and death might ensue within a few days. PUBLIUS "was sick in bed, suffering from fever and dysentery" (Acts 28:8), and we can readily appreciate his gratitude when God healed him.

Epilepsy. This term comes from Greek *epilēpsis*, "a seizing, seizure." This seizure may be very light, such as a twitch of the face or hands, or even a recurring sharp but brief abdominal pain, and is then known as *petit mal*. The really alarming attacks are called *grand mal*. The patient suddenly falls down, loses consciousness, starts shaking all over with convulsions, chews his tongue, and foams blood from his mouth. The fit lasts from five to twenty minutes. Epilepsy, in some form, is a very common disease, with an estimated average occurrence of one in every two hundred persons. Hippocrates gave a good description of it about 400 B.C. Like many of his contemporaries, he considered it due to possession by some god or DEMON. Sometimes it was called the "sacred disease"; at other times "possession by demons." The NT refers to epilepsy with the term *selēniazomai* G4944 (lit., "to be moonstruck"). In Matt. 4:24 this malady is listed as one of a group of diseases. In Matt. 17:15 a man asks Jesus to have mercy on his son: "He has seizures and is suffering greatly. He often falls into the fire or into the water." Jesus ordered the demon out, and the boy was healed.

The cause of epilepsy is obscure. It may be inherited. If just one party in a marriage has epilepsy, their offspring will probably not have it; but if there is epilepsy in the person or family of both individuals, the danger of one or more of their children inheriting the disease is very great. Other causes are brain injury from accident, tumors on the brain, hardening of the arteries, etc. With modern sedatives, the attacks can be almost completely eliminated, but no effective medical treatment was available in biblical days.

Fever refers to bodily temperature distinctly higher than normal. Our bodily temperatures are beautifully controlled under normal circumstances by an inner mechanism that keeps the temperature at about 98.6 degrees Fahrenheit. The controller of this mechanism is a small gland called the hypothalamus, located near the center of the brain. It sends its commands to the liver, heart, lungs, muscles, fat, skin, sweat glands, and other organs, and has them work in unison to keep the body temperature within approximately one degree of the normal 98.6. This temperature control system is another evidence of the supreme intelligence, wisdom, and power of God in creation.

Disease may overwhelm this mechanism. When an infecting organism enters the body, a tremendous battle goes on, involving millions of cells, with the body trying desperately to defeat the invading organism. This increases the metabolism of the body, and fever results. Usually the body wins and the temperature returns to normal. With extremely severe sickness, the temperature may rise to as high as 108 degrees, and death may ensue. PETER's mother-in-law had a high fever (Matt. 8:14–15 and parallels). It might have been due to flu, pneumonia, or an intestinal disease. It is assumed that malaria was common in the ANE and that this may have been the cause of her high fever. However, the Bible does not say, and trying to identify the disease is pure speculation.

Fiery heat. This expression is used in Deut. 28:22 (NRSV), "The LORD will afflict you with ... fiery heat and drought" (NIV, "scorching heat"). Is this affliction related to the high fevers associated with diseases mentioned in the same text, or to heat stroke, or perhaps to the failure of harvest due to excessive heat? Possibly to all three. The temperatures in Israel ran very high in summer, and although the people were acclimatized to heat—enabling them to work in temperatures that would kill someone from a cooler climate—the blazing sun could injure with heat stroke. Heat stroke is characterized by body temperatures that rise very high—106 and 107 degrees Fahrenheit, together with cessation of sweating, and with unconsciousness. It is not difficult to envisage the distress of people in a hot country, with successive years of drought, and the dangers related to the necessity of hard, physical labor in the hot sun. The boy who cried, "Oh, my head, my head" and then died (2 Ki. 4:19) undoubtedly had an attack of heat stroke.

Headache. See above, under *fiery heat*.

Hemorrhage. In Lk. 8:42–48 we have the account of a woman who had a flow (KJV, "issue") of blood for twelve years. Was this rectal or vaginal bleeding? In a primitive, semitropical country like Israel, there were many cases of bloody diarrhea and dysentery. The woman's trouble may have been a recurrent or chronic attack of one of these. It is generally assumed, and probably correctly so, that it was vaginal bleeding. If so, we would like to know approximately how old she was. If forty years or less, she might have been concerned not only about the unpleasantness of her condition, plus the loss of strength and weight, but also about the fact that she was unable to bear children (see BARRENNESS).

It is not likely that she had a continuous flow of blood, since she lived twelve years with it. More likely it was a frequently recurring experience. A common cause of this condition would be hormone imbalance. Her ovaries could have been secreting too much estrogen. Her menstrual periods would then have been prolonged and profuse, or they might have occurred more than once a month. It has been suggested that fibroid tumors were the cause of her trouble. Many women have such tumors—most of the time without abnormal bleeding. Much depends on the location and size of the tumors. They may occur on the outer surface of the uterus. They may be smaller than marbles or larger than grapefruit. Another frequent location is within the muscular walls of the uterus, expanding the uterus until at times it fills the pelvis like a wedge. In such cases constipation or distressing frequency in passing urine may be experienced, as well as heavy bleeding. Other fibroids grow just beneath the mucosa on the inner walls of the uterus. Sometimes these appear as finger-like polyps that may be the forerunner of carcinoma.

Carcinoma must be expected in every case of chronic vaginal bleeding. The focus of the disease is usually in the cervix of the uterus. The cervix becomes ragged and cancer may develop in this area, spreading later to the body of the uterus and neighboring glands. It is not likely that the woman healed by Jesus had cancer, however. If that were the case, she would probably have died before twelve years went by.

Impediment of speech. This physical difficulty is mentioned in Mk. 7:32, "and they brought to him a deaf man who had an impediment in his speech." *Aphasia* is such an impediment and it appears in many forms. For example, some persons are at a total loss for words when they smell something and want to give expression to their reaction. Others have the same experience when it concerns tasting food. Others have what is called amnesic aphasia. They cannot recall certain words that ordinarily are completely familiar to them. Then there are those with motor aphasia—people who know what they want to say but cannot utter the words because the muscles of mouth and face refuse to respond. Persons with gibberish aphasia speak words and phrases that make no sense. People who stutter also have a real impediment of speech.

There are impediments of speech due to abnormalities of the face or mouth, such as a severe tongue tie, or hare lip, or a face that is badly scarred. A rather common impediment of speech is auditory aphasia. Persons who were born deaf, or became deaf in early childhood—perhaps as a complication of measles—do not know what speech sounds like, and, excepting in rare cases, either do not try to talk at all, or speak with difficulty and lack of clarity. This was probably the case of the man who was healed by Jesus, as it is recorded that he was also deaf.

Indigestion. PAUL writes to TIMOTHY, "Stop drinking only water, and use a little wine because of your stomach and your frequent illnesses" (1 Tim. 5:23). The digestive processes of the body are more evidence of the wonderful way the Lord has fashioned us. As soon as food enters the mouth, digestion starts. Our saliva contains an enzyme called *ptyalin* that starts the digestion of carbohydrates. When the food gets to the stomach, some of the carbohydrate digestion continues, but proteins get the major attention and are broken up by pepsin and hydrochloric acid. After the stomach has completed its job, the partly digested food seeps through the pylorus into the duodenum and small intestine. Here several additional digestants get to work, including secretions from the liver and pancreas. Millions of villi — like microscopic hairs — extend from the inner surface of the bowel, absorb the digested food, and pass it on to the blood and lymph vessels.

Many people feel that they have to use a whip to this system, and so add pepper, hot sauce, or chili to their food. Some of these are powerful additives. WINE is not nearly as strong as chili, but the alcohol in it is a stimulant, and its sugar content also has a tonic effect. So Paul advises Timothy to use a little of it instead of water. The word "little" is interesting. Paul did not want to give the impression of advocating substantial use of wine. Timothy was evidently not strong physically. Paul does not say why. Improper diet and nervous strain may have been factors. At all events, Timothy did not have an ulcer of the stomach or duodenum, for then wine would have been contraindicated.

Infirmity. According to Jn. 5:5 (KJV), a man at the pool of BETHESDA "had an infirmity [*astheneia* G819] thirty and eight years" (cf. also v. 7). *Infirmity* is a word with a very broad meaning and may refer to any disease of the body or any abnormality in its structure. The implication seems to be that something had happened to him thirty-eight years previously leaving him with a residual incapacity so severe that he was unable to compete successfully with other diseased or handicapped people in getting into the healing pool of water. This malady could well have been a paralysis dating back to an attack of polio in his youth. In many cases of polio both legs are left completely and permanently paralyzed. Other extremities and organs of the body may also be involved. If his infirmity had been a continuous illness, it would in all probability have run its course in far less than thirty-eight years and ended in either recovery or death. See also separate article on PARALYTIC.

Inflammation. Deadly germs, especially streptococci and staphylococci, are always present on the surface of our bodies. Surgeons are well aware of this, and before they perform a major operation they must scrub their hands with a stiff brush and plenty of soap to get them as free as possible of these germs. The first defense against these organisms is the skin itself. Skin consists of several layers of cells packed closely together and gives excellent protection against germs. If that skin is bruised or cut, germs immediately get in and start multiplying. They promptly encounter a second line of defense: leucocytes (white cells) go to war with the invaders. Leucocytes are so called because, when looked at through a microscope, they appear transparent, in contrast with the iron-laden red blood cells. They are of various types, and each kind has its own job to do. Leucocytes are always present in the body by billions (a tiny cube 1 mm. in size contains about 5,000,000 red cells and 6,000 leucocytes). These leucocytes are constantly on patrol throughout the body. They are present in every organ and even in the stroma between the cells of body structures. They are continuously on the watch for foreign invaders and for any debris that may be floating along.

After a bruise or cut, the leucocytes attack invading organisms. Most of the time they win their battle with relative ease and the patient does not take his injury seriously. Sometimes, when the invaders are particularly virile or numerous, they win the first battle. The call goes out immediately for additional leucocytes held in reserve in bone marrow. Within hours, the leucocyte army will not only be doubled, but new ones by the billions will go into production. At the site of infection, some leucocytes will absorb the invaders by a process known as phagocytosis. Microscopic examination has shown that a single leucocyte will absorb (eat) as many as 20 invaders, and some have been seen to engulf up to 100 of them. The germs are digested by the leucocytes and unwanted remnants are excreted. As a result of this struggle, there will be inflammation with localized heat, swelling, and pain. A pocket of pus may result from the debris of battle. The leucocytes can be aided by allowing the pus to escape. As healing takes place, other leucocytes (trash collectors) take the debris away. Liver and spleen are the principal organs for filtering the unwanted material from the blood. Some of it is used to manufacture new cells (recycling), and the balance goes primarily to the kidneys for excretion. The inflammation may be localized, as in a single boil, or appear in multiple lesions, as predicted in Deut. 28:27 and experienced by Job.

Insanity is an unpleasant term. Many persons think of it in the words of Prov. 26:18—"like a madman shooting / firebrands and deadly arrows." It is, however, an illness of degrees, and is the result of a defect in part or all of the brain. Insanity (lunacy, dementia) may be unrecognized in its early stages. It may start with a loss of mental alertness, loss of energy, difficulty in remembering, especially concerning recent events, or the patient may have trouble connecting words so they make sense. He may become lost easily, show poor judgment, become depressed, gloomy, anxious, irritable, and fearful that someone is trying to hurt him (paranoia). He fails to take care of himself and may have to be given nursing care. His trouble may lead to total disorientation.

There is a form of dementia called Alzheimer's disease. It can start in middle life and is the result of gradual deterioration of the cerebral cortex. It is characterized by disorder in gait, disorientation, and hallucinations. Death usually occurs in from five to eight years. This disease is of special interest because the deterioration of the brain is similar to that seen in senility.

What brings on insanity? Perhaps the greatest factor is heredity. In some cases excessive use of drugs such as barbiturates, alcohol, marijuana, and heroin may have caused the damage to the brain. Certain illnesses, such as syphilis, pernicious anemia, epilepsy, malaria, plague, and typhoid fever may be responsible. Arteriosclerosis, cerebral hemorrhage, and injury are relatively common causes. The madness predicted in Deut. 28:28 will result from inability of the people to cope with overwhelming disaster (the Heb. word there, *šiggāʿôn* H8714, is also used in 2 Ki. 9:20 and Zech. 12:4). See also above under *epilepsy* and separate articles on LUNACY and MADNESS.

Issue of blood. See above under *hemorrhage*.

Itch. A severe itch is another of the curses with which the Lord threatened Israelites who departed from the faith (Deut. 28:27). Itch is a discomfort with which the inhabitants of the subtropical ANE were thoroughly familiar. The chief culprit in producing itch is a tiny mite known as *Sarcoptes scabiei*, and the disease it generates is known as *scabies*. The female in the scabies family is the one who does all the hard work. She digs through the upper layer of skin and makes a burrow for her home. The burrow is short—just a small fraction of an inch—but it is a definite characteristic of scabies. A clever dermatologist, with the aid of a magnifying glass, can pull the mite out of its burrow.

While in that burrow, the scabies mite causes intense itching, especially at night. The victimized person scratches desperately to relieve the itching, frequently digging through the skin and starting serious infection. The mite has a few favorite spots for burrowing. They include the inner surface of the wrist, the lower abdomen, and the glans penis. The scabies mite is stubborn and may exist for years (seven-year itch) in unclean, untreated individuals. It is prevalent in time of war and has been known to seriously handicap soldiers.

Lice also can make life miserable with their itching. There are three well known types—the head louse, the body louse, and the crab (or pubic) louse.

Leprosy was greatly feared by the Israelites, not only because of the physical damage done by the disease, but also because of the strict isolation laws applying to leprosy, making the patients feel like feared outcasts of society. It was in 1873 that a Norwegian by the name of G. Armauer Hansen discovered a bacillus he called *Myobacterium leprae*, which he found in nearly all cases of leprosy, and abundantly so in severe cases. The more euphonious term of "Hansen's disease" is now commonly used instead of leprosy. However, it is important to note that the Hebrew and Greek terms translated "leper" or "leprosy" seem to designate a variety of skin disorders, not necessarily "Hansen's disease" (see E. V. Hulse in *PEQ* 107 [1975]: 87–105).

Leprosy appears in two principal forms. The first, and by far the more dangerous, is called *lepromatous*; and the other, more benign type, is designated as *tuberculoid*. Both start with discoloration of a patch of skin. This patch may be white or pink. It is most likely to appear on the brow, nose, ear, cheek, or chin. I have seen one case of beginning leprosy with a whitish patch on the side of the abdomen. The patient said he felt no pain whatever when the skin in this patch was repeatedly pierced by a needle.

Leprosy colony near Bethany in 1905.

In the lepromatous type of leprosy, the patch may spread widely in all directions. Portions of the eyebrows may disappear. Spongy, tumor-like swellings grow on the face and body. The disease becomes systemic and involves the internal organs as well as the skin. Marked deformity of hands and feet occurs when the tissues between the bones deteriorate and disappear. Often the sensory nerve endings no longer respond to heat or injury, and the unwary patient may be subject to further destruction of his limbs before he realizes his danger.

Leprosy is a long-lasting disease. Untreated cases may be sick with lepromatous leprosy from ten to twenty years, death occurring from the disease itself or from an intercurrent invasion of the weakened body by tuberculosis or some other disease. The tuberculoid type is less severe. As stated, it starts with a change of skin color in a localized area. More such patches may follow and each patch is characteristically surrounded by a low ridge. However, the tuberculoid type of leprosy tends to be limited and even untreated cases heal completely in from one to three years.

One interesting phenomenon in both the lepromatous and tuberculoid types is that they have recurrent periods of exacerbation and subsidence. During the period of exacerbation the lepromatous cases suffer fever, pain, and prostration. This flare-up may last for hours, days, or weeks, and it is during these periods that the disease is most contagious. So far as we know, the Hebrews had no cure for leprosy other than divine intervention. In modern times, there are very effective medicines available, and leprosy patients are usually not isolated. See also MEDICINE IV.

Lunacy; madness. See separate articles on LUNATIC and MADNESS. See also above under *insanity*.

Obesity. According to Jdg. 3:17, 22, the Moabite king EGLON "was a very fat man," and when EHUD, an Israelite judge (leader), plunged his sword into the king's belly, "the fat closed in over it." Surgeons who have had to cut through two to four inches of fat to get into an abdomen can easily understand what happened to Eglon. Moreover, excessive fat is located not only in a thick, greasy layer between the skin and muscles, but also in the abdomen with its thick mesentery and abundance of fat around the organs.

The principal causes of obesity are heredity, glandular disturbance, nervous worry, and big appetite. Another is the desire for prestige. In countries where food was scarce and an adequate diet difficult to obtain, it was a source of pride to a person if he and the members of his family had full faces and protuberant abdomens. Once while I was in China, and in conversation with a language teacher, the teacher became enthusiastic in describing his wife, who he said was very fat and he was so proud of it. Fatness could be important in a country where the ability to obtain adequate food was uncertain, and the person might have to call on his reserves of fat, much as a camel uses the fat in his hump. In modern times we have been alerted to the dangers of obesity with respect to our hearts, varicose veins, arteriosclerosis, arthritis, diabetes, possible surgery, and the number of years we shall live. Diet and reasonable exercise are the ingredients of relief.

Old age is a disease if it is regarded as a gradual decrease in vitality, finally ending in death. There is a marvelous reconstruction process going on in our bodies at all times. Old cells are constantly being replaced by new ones, and it has been estimated that a person acquires almost a complete set of new cells every seven years; but the replacement cells are not all perfect. Until we reach about twenty-two years of age, the new cells are fully as good, even better, than the ones they replace. After that age limit, replacement still goes on vigorously, but the new cells are somehow defective and become increasingly so as old age creeps up with decreasing muscular strength, vague aches and pains, loss of teeth, defective eyesight and hearing, forgetfulness, and other familiar handicaps.

Clay models of diseased body parts such as eyes and ears have been discovered at the Asklepieion in Corinth. They date to the 4th cent. BC.

Prior to NOAH's time, people lived up to almost a thousand years. In later biblical times, the average life span was much shorter than it is now. Look up the records of the lives of the kings of Judah and Israel, and note at what age most of them died! Today we may be grateful if our lives have been free from serious diseases and we may slowly, almost imperceptibly, move to the day of our transition.

Palsy. See separate article on PALSY.

Pestilence is a word used frequently in the Bible. A striking example is DAVID's sin in connection with the census, as a result of which 75,000 of his people died by a pestilence that lasted three days (2 Sam. 24:15). Amos 4:10 speaks of "pestilence after the manner of Egypt" (NRSV). Plague is the disease most likely referred to. It was endemic in Egypt and along the Mediterranean Coast of Palestine. In severe outbreaks of the disease, death usually occurred within three days of the first appearance of symptoms.

Some biblical scholars have suggested that cholera might be implicated, but according to P. B. Beeson and W. McDermott (*Textbook of Medicine* [1971]), "Prior to the nineteenth century, cholera was unknown outside India." If cholera did exist in the land of Israel, it certainly would fit under the heading of pestilence. It is commonly transmitted by contaminated drinking water or by food that had been grown in fields fertilized with human excrement. It is endemic in India and oriental countries. It is characterized by a terrific diarrhea, with adult patients passing up to thirty quarts of liquid bowel movement in one day. Patients drink great quantities of water, if they can get it. In modern times, early treatment cures almost every case; but when patients are not treated, the death rate in adults is about seventy percent. See also separate articles on PESTILENCE and PLAGUE.

Scabies. See above under *itch*.

Scurvy. This word is used by the NRSV to render Hebrew *gārāb H1734*, one of the afflictions with which the Lord threatened to punish the Hebrews if they failed to serve him (Deut. 28:27; NIV, "festering sores"). The Hebrew term is used to cover almost any kind of obnoxious eruption, and it is pure speculation to limit its meaning to any single skin disease, or even to one definite symptom. According to Lev. 21:20, priests were not allowed to perform their ceremonial duties if they were deformed in any way or had such a disease. Similarly, sacrificial animals had to be in prime condition, and certainly with no scurvy or scabs (Lev. 22:22).

Skin diseases. See above under *boil*, *itch*, *leprosy*, *scurvy*. See also separate articles on SCAB; SORE; TETTER.

Starvation. In the ANE, periods of drought were common, and when they continued for successive years they were disastrous. We need think only of the experience of the Egyptians and JOSEPH. The drought was so bad that Joseph induced the Egyptians to pay for their food with their personal wealth, then with their livestock, next with their land, and finally with their freedom, making them all slaves of the pharaoh.

The craving of a hungry person can be extreme. Within the brain there is a small portion of tissue known as the hypothalamus. This organ has control of appetite and sends out agonizing sensations of hunger when the food intake is seriously inadequate.

Experience of soldiers in concentration camps, such as the men captured by the Japanese at Bataan during World War II, show to what extremes men will go to get a morsel of food when they are being starved. Civilized people have even been known to resort to cannibalism. If a mother had a baby, she prepared her afterbirth as food. Parents will eat their children in extremities of hunger, and men will eat one of their comrades if he succumbs during a desperate search for food in a desert, or the sea, or when caught in a siege (see Deut. 28:53).

When the intake of calories is less than the body needs for its metabolism, reserve body fat is first used. When this is largely exhausted, the proteins will be called on. Meanwhile, of course, the body is gradually weakening until it dies, either from starvation itself or from an intercurrent disease that has gotten a foothold in the weakened body. If water is easily obtainable, a healthy man may live from thirty to forty days without food. With no water, he will be gone in less than half that time.

Tetter. See separate article on TETTER.

Trachoma. See above under *blindness*.

Tumor. See separate articles on TUMOR and PLAGUE.

Ulcer. See separte article on TUMOR.

Worms are perhaps as ubiquitous and prolific as any animals on earth. Certainly the Israelites had plenty of them while living under rather primitive conditions in a semitropical country. The variety of them is almost unbelievable. Some of the main groups are tapeworms, flukes, roundworms, hookworms, ascariases, threadworms, and our old nemesis, the pinworm. Authorities say that there are over a half million identifiable species.

The tapeworm gets into the body when a person eats food infected with them. The worm has three or four suckers, and with these attaches itself to the upper part of the small bowel. The worms are flat, like a ribbon, and grow in segments. They are all bisexual (hermaphrodites). In the small bowel they allow themselves to be swished back and forth by the liquid food. As long as there is plenty of food coming down from the stomach, the bowel does not mind the floating ribbon of tapeworm enjoying a share. It is interesting to note that the tapeworm absorbs food through the covering of its body. It has no mouth. It would be the same as if we were able to smear peanut butter on our abdomen and have it absorbed directly through the skin.

There are beef, pork, and fish tapeworms. They grow to be ten or more yards long and some live twenty-five years. Segments of the tail break off, and some of these segments are loaded with eggs. They may reach a farmer's fields when included in fertilizer and grow on the plants that the cattle eat. The embryos penetrate the muscles of the cattle. People eat the infected meat and a new life cycle begins. It should be noted here that with tapeworms, as well as with other species of worms, the body can well tolerate a few of them, but when they overpopulate they can cause serious illness and even death.

Flukes are the small worms that our soldiers had so much trouble with in Vietnam. Somehow the eggs of flukes penetrate snails. The flukes multiply rapidly, get into water, and attach themselves with suckers to anyone sloshing through the water. They dig through the skin, enter the blood stream, and reach the lungs. Ultimately they land in the veins of the liver, intestine, and bladder, where they may do permanent damage. It is estimated that one-fourth of the population of Africa is infected by these flukes. In Israel, Iraq, and Iran, they are endemic. Irrigation is a big help to the flukes and their snails. When the Aswan Dam was being built in Egypt and irrigation started, the pools of water came alive with flukes and started an epidemic.

Pinworms are one of our commonest worms and are well known in the Middle East also. They have an interesting life cycle in that the female pinworm migrates to the anus, usually during the night, and deposits her eggs. She then causes intense itching of the anus, and sometimes of the vagina also. The normal reaction is to scratch. Eggs get under finger nails and next day into the food, to start life all over again in the intestine. Surgeons operating for appendicitis occasionally find the appendix filled with pinworms.

The *Ascaris lumbricoides* is the large roundworm found in human beings, and it has been estimated that one in every four people of the world have it. The Ascaris has a daily output of about 200,000 eggs. It has a dangerous habit of forming bridges across the lumen of the bowel and thus occasionally causing intestinal obstruction.

The hookworm sucks blood from the small bowel and causes anemia. It grows rapidly in warm, moist soil. It is able to climb stems of grass as high as three feet. Like some other worms, if they are able to reach the skin of man, they penetrate it and travel with the blood stream to the lungs. Then, in some strange way, they are able to squeeze through the walls of the alveoli of the lungs, climb up the bronchi, go down the esophagus, and reach their favorite home in the bowel.

The guinea worm often is mentioned in a discussion of mid-Eastern worms. It is not as prolific as some of the others, but has an interesting life. The worm is found in shallow wells or pools used for drinking water, and thus gets into the human body. As is more often the case, the male is small and not very important except for copulation and fertilizing eggs. The female grows until she may be a yard long. To discharge her larvae she works her way through the body till she reaches the buttocks or thighs. There she secretes a little toxin from her head and raises a vesicle. When the top is rubbed off this vesicle, she lets go of her larvae and hopes they will safely get to drinking water again. It is important to pull the long worm out of the body. This is done by grasping her head end and winding her on a stick, an inch or two a day, until she is completely dislodged. If, during this process, the yard long worm is broken and the remaining part cannot be found, a serious infection may take place.

(See W. A. Dorland, *The American Illustrated Medical Dictionary* [1951; 28th ed., 1994]; A. C. Guyton, *Textbook of Medical Physiology* [1966; 11th ed. with J. E. Hall, 2006]; D. Brothwell and A. S. Sandison, eds., *Diseases in Antiquity* [1967]; H. C. Kee, *Medicine, Miracle and Magic in New Testament Times* [1986]; B. Palmer, ed., *Medicine and the Bible* [1986]; R. Jackson, *Doctors and Diseases in the Roman Empire* [1988]; M. D. Grmek, *Diseases in the Ancient Greek World* [1989]; H. Avalos, *Illness and Health Care in the Ancient Near East: The Role of the Temple in Greece, Mesopotamia, and Israel* [1995]; M. D. Grmek, ed., *Western Medical Thought from Antiquity to the Middle Ages* [1998]; H. Avalos, *Health Care and the Rise of Christianity* [1999]; R. North, *Medicine in the Biblical Background* [2000]; J. K. Howard, *Disease and Healing in the New Testament: An Analysis and Interpretation* [2001]; C. Roberts and K. Manchester, *The Archaeology of Disease*, 3rd ed. [2005].)   R. H. POUSMA

dish. This English term may be used to render several Hebrew words, especially *kap* H4090, which literally means "palm [of the hand]" but can also refer to objects that have a comparable shape (e.g., Exod. 25:29; 37:16; Num. 4:7; 7:14). In the NT it is used to render Greek *paropsis* G4243 (e.g., Matt. 23:25–26) and other terms. See also BOWL; PLATE.

Dishan di'shan (דִּישָׁן H1915, possibly "mountain goat" or "ibex"). Seventh son of SEIR and chief of a HORITE clan (Gen. 36:21, 28, 30; 1 Chr. 1:38, 42 [in the latter reference the MT reads "Dishon"]). Dishan had both a brother and a nephew called DISHON, and some argue that the two forms are variant spellings of the same name, thus reflecting some kind of confusion in the genealogies (in the three Genesis references, the LXX reads *Risōn*).

Dishon di'shon (דִּישׁוֹן [also דִּישֹׁן and דִּשֹׁן] H1914, possibly "mountain goat" or "ibex"). **(1)** Fifth son of SEIR and chief of a HORITE clan (Gen. 36:21, 26 [MT, "Dishan"], 30; 1 Chr. 1:38, 41b). See DISHAN.

(2) Son of ANAH and grandson of Seir the Horite (Gen. 36:25; 1 Chr. 1:41a); his sister OHOLIBAMAH became ESAU's wife.   D. H. MADVIG

Dismas. Alternate form of DYSMAS.

dispensation. The act of dispensing or administering; an arrangement whereby something is managed. In theology, it usually refers to God's ordering of the world's affairs in general, or to the unfolding of God's purposes for humanity, or more specifically to a period of time during which a particular divine arrangement is at work.

I. Definition

A. Scriptural use.
The English term *dispensation* is used by the KJV four times to render Greek *oikonomia* G3873. In three of those passages (1 Cor. 9:17; Eph. 3:2; Col. 1:25) it refers to the commission PAUL was given so that the GOSPEL of divine GRACE might be dispensed to others. The fourth passage (Eph. 1:10, but also 3:9, where KJV trans-

lates differently) uses the term more broadly of God's plan of SALVATION (3:2 shows the conceptual connection between these two uses of the term). This Greek noun is also used in Lk 16:2–4 with regard to the "management" or "stewardship" of a business (cf. in the same passage the term *oikonomos* G3874, "manager" or "steward"), and in 1 Tim. 1:4 with the possible meaning of "training" (see BDAG, 698, meaning #3).

C. C. Ryrie (*Dispensationalism Today* [1965], 26), on the basis of Lk. 16, observes four pertinent features: (1) Two parties are involved, one who delegates duties and one whose responsibility is to fulfill those duties. (2) There are specific responsibilities involved in the arrangement. (3) A steward may be called to account for his administration of his stewardship. (4) A change may be made if there is unfaithfulness in the arrangement. Some writers see this passage as illustrative of Paul's use of the term when he speaks of the divine administrations of God manifest in his program on earth.

B. Theological definition. Based on the above use of the word in Scripture, theologians have given further definition to the word in its use as describing the unfolding of God's program on earth. Although the term *dispensation* is used by most, there are substantial differences in the use of the term. The major division is between covenant theology and dispensationalist theology.

The covenant theologian sees the COVENANT of grace as the overriding unity of Scripture and uses the concept of a dispensation to speak of the manifestations of that covenant. Charles Hodge, for example, asserts that there are four dispensations after the FALL—Adam to Abraham, Abraham to Moses, Moses to Christ, and Christ to the end. These dispensations are simply the outworking of the covenant of grace (*Systematic Theology*, 3 vols. [1871–73], 2:373–77). Others, such as Louis Berkhof, more typically speak of only two dispensations—the old and the new. An alternative approach for this concept in covenant theology is to speak of the old covenant and the new covenant without recognizing either as a dispensation. This approach is demonstrated by J. O. Buswell (*A Systematic Theology of the Christian Religion*, 2 vols. [1962–63]). The common characteristic among covenant theologians is that any change of administration is seen only as an aspect of the unifying covenant of grace. Thus its emphasis is soteriological, and the change is more that of anticipation in the old and accomplishment in the new than it is an actual change of administration.

In contrast to this methodology, dispensationalism develops its understanding of the progress of revelation as a series of dispensations or arrangements with human beings that God has set forth in the course of history. The *Scofield Reference Bible* (1909) has been the primary popularizer of this approach. Scofield defines a dispensation as "A period of time during which man is tested in respect of obedience to some specific revelation of the will of God" (p. 5). Scofield then distinguishes seven such dispensations in the Scriptures. Other dispensational writers have not emphasized the time period aspect in their definition and have placed their emphasis on the nature of the arrangement. For example, Ryrie defines a dispensation as "A distinguishable economy in the outworking of the plan of God" (*Dispensationalism Today*, 29). H. A. Ironside has stated, "There are various economies running through the Word of God. A dispensation, an economy, then, is that particular order or condition of things prevailing in one special age which does not necessarily prevail in another" (*In the Heavenlies: Practical Expository Addresses on the Epistle to the Ephesians* [1937], 67).

II. Historical uses of the word. The distinctions made by theologians today are not necessarily characteristic of the use of the word down through church history. According to Ryrie, the earliest use of the word is by JUSTIN MARTYR, who distinguished the programs of God while noting the uniformity of God's righteousness. He also speaks of the present dispensation (*Dialogue with Trypho* 42). Berkhof identifies IRENAEUS's three covenants as dispensations, but Irenaeus himself does not refer to them as such. He does refer to dispensations and speaks of the Christian dispensation. AUGUSTINE uses the word with some frequency and states in one place: "The divine institution of sacrifice was suitable in the former dispensation but is not suitable now.... There is no variableness with God, though in the former period of the world's history he enjoined one kind of offerings, and in the latter period another, therein ordering the symbolical actions pertaining to the blessed doctrine of true religion in harmony with the changes of successive epochs without any change in himself" (*To Marcellinus* 138.5, 7).

Among post-Reformation writers who used the term in developing their understanding of Scripture is Pierre Poiret (1647–1719), who wrote *The Divine Economy*. Poiret identified seven dispensations; although differing from the contemporary forms, they include one before the flood, one from the flood to Moses, and so on (the millennium will be the final dispensation). Jonathan Edwards published a volume in 1699 entitled, *A Complete History or Survey of All the Dispensations*. He includes four dispensations since the fall, but considers the millennium to be a spiritual fulfillment in the Christian dispensation (2:720). Isaac Watts identifies five dispensations and defines the terms as follows: "Each of these dispensations may be represented as different religions, or at least, as different forms of religions, appointed for men in several successive ages of the world" (*The Works of the Reverend and Learned Isaac Watts*, 6 vols. [1753], 2:625).

There is, therefore, a variety of uses of the term down through the centuries, preceding the modern period. If there is a uniformity of description of the dispensations in this list, it would probably have two common characteristics: (1) God has worked in varying ways with people and (2) these ways are identified with successive time periods in God's sovereign plan.

III. The current debate. The modern discussion about the nature of a dispensation grows out of the development of systematic theology since the Reformation. With the return to the Word and to evangelical theological growth, theology became much more systematic. Luther's and Calvin's work became respectively Lutheranism and Calvinism and were gradually organized into full-scale theologies.

Out of Calvinism developed covenant theology with its organization of the progress of revelation around the covenants of works and grace. Within the covenant of grace, the change of administration was noted as the old and new covenants or sometimes dispensations. This concept was intended to help organize and explain the differences that are found in the old and new covenants with reference to the manifestations of salvation. The Reformation also brought a return to prophetic study, and there is a rise of belief in premillennialism that was characteristic of some post-Reformation groups. As was illustrated in Pierot and Watts above, this approach was sometimes organized into a dispensational scheme.

In the 19th cent., a member of the Plymouth Brethren, John Nelson Darby, began the process of systematizing and organizing these dispensational approaches into a systematic theology. His system, known as *dispensationalism*, came to be a significant force in American Christianity. Ryrie defines it as follows: "Dispensationalism views the world as a household run by God. In this household God is dispensing or administering its affairs according to his own will and in various stages of revelation in the process of time. These various stages mark off the distinguishably different economies in the outworking of his total purpose and these economies are the dispensations. The understanding of God's differing economies is essential to a proper interpretation of his revelation within those various economies" (*Dispensationalism Today*, 31).

Therefore, the modern discussion revolves around the proper use of the term theologically. The dispensationalist does not object to the covenant theologian's use of the word, but believes that this approach has not done full justice to the differences and development of the various dispensations. The covenant theologian usually objects strongly to using the concept of the dispensations as the foundation for the unity of the Scriptures.

The primary objection to this latter use is the claim that dispensationalism teaches two ways of salvation. A footnote to Jn. 1:17 in the *Scofield Reference Bible* is usually cited at this point: "The point of testing is no longer legal obedience as a condition of salvation, but acceptance or rejection of Christ with good works as a fruit of salvation." While the clear implication is that salvation in the OT is by works, not faith, contradicting the principle of faith, Buswell has well pointed out that this approach is not unique to dispensationalism but is also implied by Hodge and Calvin (see Hodge, *Systematic Theology*, 1:316). There is a sense in which the covenant of works faces the same problem. It implies that sinners at one time could merit salvation by their works. While there are passages that may be interpreted to suggest the possibility of salvation by works (e.g., Lk. 10:28; Rom. 2:6; Jas. 2:14–26), it is clearly taught in Scripture that salvation is by faith alone. Therefore, later dispensationalists have rejected the inference of Scofield and insist that the various arrangements of the dispensations should be viewed as manifestations of saving faith rather than of obedience as a condition of salvation.

A second major objection to the dispensationalist structure is that it makes dispensations into time periods rather than stewardship arrangements. While it is admitted that the word *oikonomia* refers to the arrangement, there is a close connection between an arrangement and the time in which it is in effect. Many dispensationalists, however, do not include the time factor in their definition.

A third major criticism of dispensationalists' use of the term is that it divides the Bible into time periods and fails to see the unity of Scripture. L. Berkhof has stated, "Since the dispensations do not intermingle, it follows that in the dispensation of the law there is no revelation of the grace of God, and in the dispensation of Grace, there is no revelation of the law as binding on the New Testament people of God" (*Systematic Theology* [1941], 291–92). While there may be a validity to this criticism in some statements made by dispensationalists, most theologians holding this position state that in the progress of revelation there is unfolded the will of God in various economies. Rather than being terminated as a principle they grow or evolve into the next economy. The resulting process is like stair steps, with each arrangement building on the preceding one, sometimes borrowing from it and usually adding to it. Thus, while there is always a manifestation of the grace of God, the dispensationalist states that the contemporary age is characterized by *grace* while the previous one is better described by the term *law*.

Another criticism is the contention that dispensationalism is recent in church history, divisive within the church, and by implication in error. While there is some validity to this argument especially in the life of Darby (see Clarence B. Bass, *Backgrounds to Dispensationalism* [1960], 48–99), the implications of such arguments are not necessarily valid. The Protestant Reformation too could be viewed as both recent and divisive. The key is that theology must be evaluated for its scriptural support in a primary sense and for its impact in a secondary sense.

IV. The number of dispensations

A. Covenant theology. In this position the number of dispensations is widely varied. Buswell accepts none while Berkhof and most others accept two; Hodge contends that there are four in the old covenant and one in the new. The actual number really does not significantly affect the system.

B. Dispensational theology. From this perspective the number of dispensations varies somewhat, although the seven held by the *Scofield Bible* are the most common. Some minimize the early ones and combine conscience and human government, while others make the tribulation a separate dispensation and then the total may be more than seven. The crucial concern that characterizes dispensationalism's approach is a threefold distinction: (1) God's program for Israel in the past, particularly the law, (2) God's present program for the church, and (3) the future manifestation, which is the millennium. Usually this scheme is accompanied by a belief that the church will be raptured before the tribulation, further distinguishing the church age.

C. Ultradispensationalism. There is a distinctive branch of dispensationalism that further distinguishes the dispensations and is sometimes called Bullingerism after one of its early leaders, E. W. Bullinger. It is sometimes called the Grace Gospel Fellowship or the Worldwide Grace Testimony. While there is considerable difference among the adherents, their consistent tenet dispensationally is that they distinguish at least two dispensations in the current church age. They identify a Jewish church early in the book of Acts and then a separate Gentile church later on. They often reject water baptism, but usually observe the Lord's Supper.

DISPENSATION

Their definition of a dispensation usually includes a strong emphasis on the aspect of time as well as the emphasis on the stewardship or economy involved.

D. Recent developments. Since the initial publication of this encyclopedia, some writers have attempted to articulate the distinctives of dispensationalism in fresh ways. Often referred to as "progressive dispensationalism," this new approach seeks to do greater justice to the continuity between the old and new covenants while still recognizing the differences between the two dispensations. Similarly, the contrast between Israel and the church is maintained, but to a lesser degree than has been the case in classic dispensationalism. Several other theological and hermeneutical modifications are made. (See esp. C. A. Blaising and D. L. Bock, *Progressive Dispensationalism* [1993], and the response by Ryrie in the 1995 ed. of his book, now entitled simply *Dispensationalism*).

(In addition to the titles already mentioned, influential dispensationalist works include L. S. Chafer, *Dispensationalism* [1936]; E. Sauer, *From Eternity to Eternity* [1954]; J. D. Pentecost, *Things to Come* [1958]. Critics of dispensationalism include O. T. Allis, *Prophecy and the Church* [1945]; G. E. Ladd, *Crucial Questions about the Kingdom of God* [1952].)

H. P. Hook

CHART OF REPRESENTATIVE DISPENSATIONAL SCHEMES

Pierre Poiret 1646–1719	John Edwards 1639–1716	Isaac Watts 1674–1748	J. N. Darby 1800–1882	James H. Brookes 1830–1897	James M. Gray 1851–1935 (Pub. 1901)	C. I. Scofield 1843–1921 (Pub. 1909)
Creation to the Deluge (Infancy)	Innocency / Adam fallen Antediluvian	Innocency / Adamic (after the Fall)	Paradisaical state (to the Flood)	Eden / Antediluvian	Edenic / Antediluvian	Innocency / Conscience
Deluge to Moses (Childhood)	Noahic / Abrahamic	Noahic / Abrahamic	Noahic / Abrahamic	Patriarchal	Patriarchal	Human Government / Promise
Moses to Prophets (Adolescence) / Prophets to Christ (Youth)	Mosaic	Mosaic	Israel— under law under priesthood under kings	Mosaic	Mosaic	Law
Manhood and Old Age	Christian	Christian	Gentiles / Spirit	Messianic / Holy Ghost	Church	Grace
Renovation of all things			Millennial	Millennial	Millennial	Kingdom
					Fullness of times / Eternal	

Adapted from *Dispensationalism Today* by Charles C. Ryrie, © 1965 Moody Press. Used by permission.

Dispersion. See DIASPORA.

dispute, dissension. See CORINTHIANS, FIRST EPISTLE TO THE; HERESY; SECT; UNITY.

distaff. A stick used to hold FLAX or WOOL fibers during the process of SPINNING. One of the virtues of a noble woman is that "In her hand she holds the distaff [*kîšôr* H3969] / and grasps the spindle [*pelek* H7134] with her fingers" (Prov. 31:19; the two terms are reversed in the KJV, and it is possible that the first term refers to the whorl or disk at the bottom of the spindle [cf. *HALOT*, 2:473]). A woman when spinning would hold the distaff under her left arm. She would take the long fibers from the distaff and attach them to the notch in the end of the spindle, which was a shaft 9–12 inches long and tapered on both ends. Near the bottom of the spindle was a whorl. This was a circular weight of clay, stone, or some other heavy material with a hole in the center to allow it to be placed on the spindle. The whorl provided momentum to keep the spindle turning smoothly when it had been twirled between the thumb and forefinger. Additional fibers would be added and twisted into thread as the spindle rotated. When the thread became so long that the spindle reached the ground, it would be wound around the spindle and the process repeated until the spindle was full. D. H. MADVIG

distinguishing spirits. See DISCERNING OF SPIRITS.

Dives di'veez. The name traditionally given to the rich man in the parable of the rich man and Lazarus (Lk. 16:19–31). Actually, his name is nowhere given in the parable, but the Greek term for "rich" (*plousios* G4454) corresponds to Latin *dives* (cf. Vulgate), and the latter began to be used as the man's name as early as the 2nd cent. (Irenaeus, *Against Heresies* 2.34.1). See LAZARUS AND DIVES. J. B. SCOTT

divination. The practice of consulting beings (divine, human, or departed) or things (by observing objects or actions) in the attempt to gain information about the future and such other matters as are removed from normal knowledge.

I. Classification of types. The above definition suggests the need for distinguishing between what might be termed *personal* (or intuitive) and *impersonal* methods. The term *divination* suggests that a divine Being provides the information. Seers, the Pythia who uttered the oracle at Delphi, and mediums who consult the dead, all are said to receive messages from a personal source or in a subjective way. Other methods, sometimes called "artificial" or "automatic," are gathered from impersonal things like the flight of birds, a sneeze, or the casting of lots.

Divination is related to MAGIC, but is distinct from it mainly in that the latter attempts to produce certain effects while the former seeks knowledge. Nevertheless practitioners of one might also engage in the other. Note the various practices and practitioners listed together in Deut. 18:10–11 (cf. 2 Chr. 33:6) that were a threat to Israel.

II. Methods of divination

A. Chresmology refers to prognostication by seers and through oracles. Also known as soothsaying and fortune-telling (cf. Acts 16:16), it is a form of divination to the extent that information is sought out. The OT indicates that PROPHETS were formerly called seers and were consulted to ascertain God's will (1 Sam. 9:9). However, seers, like prophets, could be false, and Mic. 3:7 links them with diviners, to whom God refuses an answer. Oracles were messages from a deity (the word could also be applied to the place or person who transmitted them).

B. Oneiromancy is the practice of predicting the future through the interpretation of DREAMS, which were thought to convey divine messages (cf. the interpretations given by JOSEPH and DANIEL). An ancient dream analyst, Artemidorus, who itinerated from city to city plying his trade, has left a vivid account of his practice. Sometimes one would sleep in a temple (incubation) hoping for a dream from the resident deity. The god of healing, ASCLEPIUS, was thought especially communicative in this regard. Aelius Aristides, a hypochondriac orator, has related in his *Sacred Discourses* how Asclepius instructed him regarding treatment.

C. Astrology was an ancient means which gained in popularity, especially in the Hellenistic period. On the assumption that the planets and stars were in harmony with earth and mankind, the character and fate of an individual, or even a whole nation, were determined through a horoscope based on the signs of the Zodiac (see ASTROLOGY).

D. Necromancy was consultation with the DEAD. This was done through a medium, who received messages through a "familiar spirit." This method receives severe condemnation in the Bible (Lev. 19:31; 20:6, 27; Deut. 18:10; 2 Chr. 33:6; Isa. 8:19–20). King SAUL, who had banished mediums and wizards, nevertheless in desperation consulted the medium at ENDOR, an act for which he was judged by God (1 Sam. 28:9–19; 1 Chr. 10:13–14).

E. Haruspicy refers to the study of the entrails of animals, especially their livers (*hepatoscopy*); it was a means of impersonal divination used widely from the Babylonians to the Romans. Since the liver was at one time considered the seat of life and since sacrificial animals were used, hepatoscopy was a religious practice.

F. Augury was the analysis of the movements of animals, and especially of birds.

G. Omens and portents were of many kinds (including the previous two items). A portent was an omen of great or supernatural character, such as earthquakes or heavenly phenomena. Typical omens were involuntary human actions, as a cough or hiccup, the actions of animals, or other impersonal occurrences. (Divination by human signs is called *cledonomancy*.) Since one who had decided on a course of action would be more affected by contrary omens, these, and especially portents, frequently took on a negative character.

H. Mechanical means. These would include (1) *hydromancy*, divination by water (see below on Joseph and the cup); (2) *pyromancy*, the observation of fire, and (3) *cleromancy*. The latter includes the use of plates or rods drawn at random (*sortilege*), the interpretation of the position of objects such as rods or arrows (*rhabdomancy*), and, in general, any casting of lots, or of dice, drawing straws, etc.

It will be observed that, in general, the above methods range from the personal (seer and oracle) to the completely impersonal (lots). Yet, even omens were considered to convey the mind of God (cf. Prov. 16:33; Acts 1:26).

III. History. Divination and magic are known from early times among many cultures. The OT reflects the situation in contemporary cultures: Moabite (Num. 23:23), Philistine (1 Sam. 6:2), and Babylonian (Isa. 44:25). Egyptian magicians sought to duplicate the acts of MOSES and AARON (Exod. 7:8–13, 22; 8:7, 18). Apparently Joseph learned divination performed by observing water in a cup (Gen. 44:1–5, 15), although the Hebrew also may be understood in a way that attributes wisdom to Joseph concerning (rather than by means of) the cup in question. The ability to interpret dreams is attributed to Joseph (Gen. 37:5–11; 40:5–19), but this is understood to be a revelation from God (40:8), not a duplication of pagan techniques.

Divination in ancient Greece was originally not as much a religious function as in some other cultures. The seer was a familiar figure. Dreams and omens were of great importance throughout Greek history. The latter were especially sought with regard to a tentative course of action. Astrology, introduced from Babylonia, was accepted by many because of its claim to scientific accuracy. It made great gains after the unification of the world in the Hellenistic period and the decadence of formal religion and philosophy, which made its claim to cosmic unity and its offer of personal guidance attractive.

Oracles were offered not only at the famous shrine of APOLLO at Delphi, but also at that of ZEUS at Dodona (the oldest shrine) and others. At Delphi the Pythia, the prophetess, sat on a tripod over a steaming fissure and communicated the oracle, which usually had to be interpreted by the "prophets" there. The ambiguity of many of these oracular interpretations is well known.

It will be noted from the above that the Greeks practiced both personal and impersonal divination. Often the personal involved "possession" by a deity, or "enthusiasm." This type did not find ready acceptance at Rome. Cleromancy, especially sortilege, haruspicy, and various omens were popular. Augury was used to determine times for official functions that were "auspicious" (from *auspicium*, divination by the flight of birds). Such practices, though widely used, were, like astrology, spurned by some Romans. Nevertheless, they had their influence, as did the SIBYLLINE ORACLES, which had full acceptance.

IV. Divination in the Bible. First it must be noted that there are several apparent occurrences of divination in both the OT and the NT. The case of JOSEPH has been mentioned. DANIEL's interpretation of dreams is attributed to the revelatory power of the true God (Dan. 2:17–23). LABAN claimed to have superior knowledge as a result of enchantment or divination (Gen. 30:27). BALAAM found that such methods were powerless against Israel (Num. 23:23; 24:1). The servants of the Aramean king BEN-HADAD watched for an omen (1 Ki. 20:33 NRSV). In the case of a woman suspected of adultery, Num. 5:11–31 provides for a procedure that could be considered either divination or perhaps more precisely a means of judgment. GIDEON's use of the fleece (Jdg. 6:36–40) is probably to be classed with God's provisions of signs to confirm his revealed will, rather than as a means of divination. (Shortly afterward, Gideon also heard of someone's dream which indicated his forthcoming victory [7:13–15].) The incident in 1 Sam. 14:7–12 may be of the same nature. EZEKIEL provides a description of the devices used by the king of Babylon, arrows, teraphim (images), and liver (Ezek. 21:18–23). The use of arrows by JONATHAN (1 Sam. 20:20–22) and by JOASH (2 Ki. 13:15–19) was not for divination as some have maintained.

It is not known how the URIM AND THUMMIM were used. It is suggested that they were two stones or other objects, possibly inscribed on opposite sides with the words Urim and Thummim. They were kept in the breastpiece attached to the EPHOD worn by the high priest (Exod. 28:30). Moses gave directions for its use (Num. 27:21), and David employed it, asking questions that required a positive or negative answer. These answers are preceded by the words, "And the LORD said ..." (1 Sam. 23:9–12).

There is no further mention of this device until postexilic times (Ezra 2:63; Neh. 7:65).

In the NT, the casting of LOTS in Acts 1:26 is related without further comment. God indicated his will to PAUL in an unspecified way through a prophet (16:6–10; 21:10–11). Paul exorcised a "spirit of divination" who had possessed a girl (16:16–18 NRSV). Luke describes Simon the magician, whose figure reappears in early Christian literature as the antagonist SIMON MAGUS (Acts 8:9–13). In Acts 13:6–11 we are introduced to ELYMAS, called a *magos G3407*, a word used also to describe the Persian wise men and astrologers (Matt. 2:1; see MAGI), clever people and magicians in general, or any scoundrel one might suspect or accuse of evil practices. This word and *goēs G1200* ("sorcerer") were frequently employed in postapostolic times as invectives against practitioners who were not of one's own religious persuasion. They are found in JOSEPHUS, the church fathers, and other literature. The Jewish TALMUD contains accusations implying that Jesus had employed sorcery.

From time to time in Jewish history, cabalistic (i.e., secret or occult) practices have been followed, but, except for certain periods, divination has been rare in Judaism and likewise in Christianity. The church has on occasion risen to oppose allegedly magical practices, and the Salem witch hunts are especially notorious. In the latter part of the 20th cent., occult practices began to flourish, requiring a fresh application of biblical teaching.

It bears repeating that the Scriptures forbid divination and magic. The major passages include Lev. 19:26, 31; 20:6; Deut. 18:9–14; Isa. 8:16–20; 44:24–28; Jer. 14:13–16; 27:8–11; Ezek. 13:6–9, 23. These references, given here in their full contexts, contain not only warnings against divination, but also affirmations that God speaks through his own true prophets.

(For further information, cf. Cicero, *On Divination*; A. Bouché-Leclercq, *Histoire de la divination dans l'antiquité* [1872–82]; M. Summers, *The History of Witchcraft and Demonology* [1926]; M. Summers, *The Geography of Witchcraft* [1927]; H. S. Lea, *Materials Toward a History of Witchcraft* [1939]; K. Seligmann, *The History of Magic* [1948]; R. La Roche, *La Divination* [1957]; R. H. Robbins, *The*

Encyclopedia of Witchcraft and Demonology [1959]; R. Alleau, *Histoire des sciences occultes* [1965]; R. Flaceliere, *Greek Oracles* [1965]; A. Jeffers, *Magic and Divination in Ancient Palestine and Syria* [1996]; R. M. Berchman, ed., *Mediators of the Divine: Horizons of Prophecy, Divination, Dreams, and Theurgy in Mediterranean Antiquity* [1998]; L. Ciraolo and J. Seidel, eds., *Magic and Divination in the Ancient World* [2002]; F. Rochberg, *The Heavenly Writing: Divination, Horoscopy, and Astronomy in Mesopotamian Culture* [2004]; S. I. Johnston and P. T. Struck, eds., *Mantikê: Studies in Ancient Divination* [2005].) W. L. Liefeld

divine, diviner. See divination.

Diviners' Oak. The RSV rendering of ʾēlôn mĕʿônnîm (Jdg. 9:37; KJV, "the plain of Meonenim"; NRSV, "Elon-meonenim"; NIV, "soothsayers' tree"). This tree was evidently in a prominent place, possibly on a small rise. The translation "Diviners" is based on the Hebrew term's derivation from the verb ʿānan H6726, which in the poel stem can mean "to practice soothsaying." The existence of a tree in Canaan used for augury is not surprising in view of the widespread practice of divination. (See also Moreh.) W. L. Liefeld

divinity of Christ. See deity of Christ.

division. See Corinthians, First Epistle to the; heresy; sect; unity.

divorce. A legal term for the act of removing the obligations of a marriage contract. Most societies have made some provision for the dissolution of a marriage when it does not prove satisfactory. Normally a divorce also allows the parties involved to contract a subsequent marriage.

Knowledge of the practice of divorce among the ancient Hebrews is sketchy. The primary references to divorce in the law (Deut. 22:18–29; 24:1–4) are "case laws" referring to particular situations. No general law on divorce is present. Only Deut. 24:1 alludes to the procedure to be followed. Several biblical stories recount divorces (Gen. 21:8–14; Jdg. 14:19–20; 15:2, 6; 1 Sam. 18:12–17). Much discussion has focused on whether Deut. 24:1–4 refers to divorce because of adultery or for some lesser reason of incompatibility. However, since the law called for adultery to be punished by death (Deut. 22:22), the latter is likely. Of course, Hebrew men in some cases probably used divorce as a merciful response to an unfaithful wife (Matt. 1:19).

Hebrew marriage was a legal contract binding a man and a woman and their families to perform certain socially prescribed roles. The contract covered the lifetime of the contracting parties; the male as senior partner, however, appears to have had the right of preparing a "certificate of divorce" (*sēper kĕritût*) and thereby terminating the arrangement. It is important to realize that divorce is essentially a sociopolitical concept. Religion has been concerned primarily with challenging its abuse and with ministering to the suffering it causes. Religiously, divorce, as Jesus later explained, lay outside God's will. Politically, it had to be allowed. A reading of OT laws concerning marriage and divorce suggests the importance of responsibility in one's family life.

The basic ethical questions asked by Christians in discussions of divorce are: (1) Is a Christian ever justified in seeking a divorce? (2) Once divorced, may a Christian remarry? Jesus' own teachings on the subject of divorce appear in Matt. 5:27–32; 19:3–12 (and parallels, Mk. 10:2–12; Lk. 16:18). The first passage appears in the Sermon on the Mount. Here Jesus is depicted as going beyond Moses, making even more strict demands. The issue for interpretation is whether Christ was giving a "new law" for Christians or stating the extent of God's perfect will for mankind so that all might realize they are sinners in need of God's grace. Is this law or hyperbole? The second passage records Jesus' response to a rabbinical question concerning possible "justifiable" grounds for divorce. (The background to this dialogue may have been the tradition that Rabbi Shammai restricted divorce to cases of adultery, whereas Rabbi Hillel allowed divorce for most grievances.) Here Jesus declares that marriage forges a unity between the couple. To dissolve this unity is contrary to God's will. Again, law or hyperbole?

In the history of Christian ethical thought, two different approaches to ethics have been taken: (1) casuistry; (2) law/grace. The casuistic approach — resolving specific ethical cases by interpreting principles and doctrines — has been the more popular one. It sees Jesus as a new lawgiver. His teachings on divorce are the law for Christians. This law is normative and is to be applied to marital problems occurring in the life of individual Christians. The exceptive clause ("except for marital unfaithfulness," Matt. 19:9) has been variously interpreted when applied to problems of justifying divorce under certain circumstances. Examples include subsequent discovery of premarital unchastity, extramarital sex relations, and failure to perform marital responsibility. In Roman Catholic ethics this process becomes very elaborate. So-called situation ethics is also casuistic. It glosses over Jesus' teaching on divorce and focuses on the law to love. The situationalist may justify divorce in a specific case as being "the loving thing to do." Essentially the casuistic approach seeks to determine if justifiable cause for a divorce action by a Christian can be found. This approach is often condemned on two grounds: (a) it is legalistic and devoid of the grace proclaimed in the gospel; (b) it eases one's conscience allowing a person to feel justified without suing for God's forgiveness.

The alternate approach finds Jesus' teachings to be an attack on the "cheap grace" of the PHARISEES and their casuistry. Jesus' teachings on the commandments of God (Matt. 5:17–48) radicalize them, removing any justification for one's doing less than the ideal. The Christian measures his actions by the ideal. Anything less is sin. Sin can be atoned only by the gracious forgiveness of God. Specifically, divorce is not the will of God; it is evil. Divorce hurts the husband and wife, the children, the families, the church, and the community. The damage of divorce is irreparable. To divorce a woman, Jesus taught, is to brand her as unfaithful. If a man marries a divorcee, he becomes suspect. This approach finds no "justification" for divorce.

Subsequently, when the Pharisees challenged Jesus' authority to go beyond the commands by appealing to Moses, he responded that Moses was simply accommodating God's perfect will because of the sinfulness of the people. Moses was giving laws for the state; and the laws of the state can never be as demanding as those of the faith. This approach questions either the authenticity or the common understanding of the exception clause (Matt. 5:32 and 19:9) on the grounds that it does not appear in Mark and Luke. How does a radical ethic respond to those situations where divorce appears to be the "lesser evil," where divorced people wish to remarry,

This papyrus written in Aramaic is a *get* or certificate of divorce, found at Wadi Murabbaʿat and dated to A.D. 111.

or where a divorced person wishes to hold a place of leadership in the church? Here the emphasis shifts from law to grace. Although divorce is always wrong, God is gracious and will forgive (1 Jn. 1:9). God forgives; Christians forgive; divorce is not the unpardonable sin. This approach to Christian ethics counsels repentance and faith.

Two passages from PAUL, the "Pauline Privilege" (1 Cor. 7:12–15) and the qualifications for bishops (1 Tim. 3:1–7), should also be mentioned. The first is sometimes interpreted to mean a Christian can divorce an unbelieving spouse without sinning. The latter is interpreted as disqualifying divorced men from the ministry and the diaconate. Both interpretations are questionable.

In summary, the emphasis in the Bible is on contracting a successful marriage. At best, divorce is not in keeping with God's will. The family today is in a state of flux, undergoing many changes. Christians must hold fast to the "one flesh" concept and see divorce as a disruption of this relationship. Christ was right when he said that divorce was caused by the "hardness of our hearts."

(See further R. Patai, *Sex and Family in the Bible and the Middle East* [1959], 112–21; D. S. Bailey, *Sexual Relations in Christian Thought* [1959], 32–97, 103–10, 211–29; O. Piper, *The Biblical Views of Sex and Marriage* [1960], 140–51; M. and R. Kysar, *The Asundered: Biblical Teachings on Divorce and Remarriage* [1978]; C. S. Keener, *And Marries Another: Divorce and Remarriage in the Teaching of the New Testament* [1991]; R. F. Collins, *Divorce in the New Testament* [1992]; D. Instone-Brewer, *Divorce and Remarriage in the Bible: The Social and Literary Context* [2002]; W. Heth and G. Wenham, *Jesus and Divorce*, updated ed. [2002].)

G. E. FARLEY

Dizahab diz´uh-hab (די זָהָב *H1903* [from Aram. relative pronoun די *H10168* and Heb. זָהָב *H2298*, "gold"], possibly "possessor of gold"). Also Dizahab. A locality listed along with PARAN, TOPHEL, LABAN, and HAZEROTH to specify the place where MOSES delivered the messages of the book of Deuteronomy to Israel (Deut. 1:1). The exact location of Dizahab has not been established. Earlier identifications with Minaʾ edh-Dhahab and ME-ZAHAB (Gen. 36:39) are no longer accepted.

The context suggests a location in the E of the ARABAH. The other locations named provide no assistance since they are also unknown. The name itself has been explained in Jewish tradition as having some connection with the golden calf destroyed by Moses. Another suggestion is that it was an area abounding in gold. The latter has led to the possible identification with edh-Dheibeh (cf. M. Seligsohn in *Jewish Encyclopedia* [1925], 4:628).

D. H. MADVIG

Docetism doh´suh-tiz´uhm (from δοκέω *G1506*, "to seem"). The view, associated with GNOSTICISM, that Jesus did not have a physical body and thus only appeared to die on the cross. This opinion appeared so early in the history of Christianity that there is an answer for it in 1 Jn. 4:2 and 2 Jn. 7. The Docetae or Docetists held that the body of Christ was not real flesh and blood but only a hallucination or a phantasm, deceptive and passing; that Christ's body was purely spiritual and therefore took up nothing even in the body of the Virgin of true human nature. This heresy developed easily and rapidly in one form or another because of the pagan philosophic emphasis of the time that matter is inherently evil (see DUALISM). This being so, it was blasphemous to maintain that the spiritual Christ could have, in any sense at all, a physical body. Basilides, an early Gnostic, held to a relatively human Christ with whom the divine *nous* ("mind" or immaterial essence) became united in baptism, but his followers became true Docetae. Hippolytus gave an early account of the whole system of this sect and attached to the movement the names of Saturninus, Valentinus, MARCION, and the MANICHEANS. Distinction should be observed in that Docetae denied the *reality* of Christ's human body, whereas the Apollinarians denied the *integrity* of Christ's human nature. In the case of the Apollinarians there was a human nature in body and soul, lacking mind or spirit.

A. H. LEITCH

doctor. This English term (from Latin *doctor*, "teacher") is used by the KJV to render the Greek noun *didaskalos G1437*, "teacher" (only in Lk. 2:46; cf. also "doctor of the law" for *nomodidaskalos G3799*, Lk. 5:17; Acts 5:34). See LAWYER; SCRIBE; TEACHER. The NIV uses the term *doctor* in its modern sense of PHYSICIAN to render *iatros* G2620 (Matt. 9:12 and parallels; Col. 4:14).

Doctrina Addaei. The *Doctrine of Addai*, a Syriac account of the origins of Christianity in EDESSA, related to the ABGAR legend recorded by EUSEBIUS (see also THADDAEUS, ACTS OF). Messengers sent by Abgar to the governor of SYRIA report the deeds of Jesus on their return. Abgar sends a letter, to which Jesus gives a verbal reply (in Eusebius, it is a letter): he cannot come himself but will send a disciple. The king's envoy also paints and takes home a portrait of Jesus (in the *Acts of Thaddaeus*, a towel imprinted with his likeness). After the ascension, THOMAS sends Addai, one of the Seventy, who heals Abgar, makes converts, and builds a church. His deeds are said to have been recorded by the king's scribe and placed in the official records, but references to "the Old and New Testaments," to Acts, and to the Epistles of Paul, and especially to the DIATESSARON, show that the document belongs to a later date (c. A.D. 400: W. Bauer, *NTAp* [1963–65], 1:438). An interesting feature is an account of the finding of the true cross by Protonice, wife of the emperor Claudius (cf. the story of Helena, mother of Constantine). The Syriac text was edited by G. Phillips, *The Doctrine of Addai, the Apostle* (1876; English trans. in G. Howard, *The Teaching of Addai* [1981]).   R. McL. WILSON

doctrine. This term is used frequently by the KJV to render the Greek terms *didaskalia* G1436 (e.g., 1 Tim. 1:10) and *didachē* G1439 (e.g., Acts 2:42), both of which mean "teaching" (the usual rendering in modern versions, except in the Pastorals), usually emphasizing the *content* of what is taught. In the Greek world, teaching implied the communication of knowledge; for the most part it had a clear intellectual character. Among the Jews, especially in the OT, teaching served not simply to communicate religious truth, but rather to bring the one taught into direct confrontation with the divine will. What is taught are the commandments; what is expected is obedience. Thus MOSES is taught what he should do (Exod. 4:15), and he in turn teaches Israel the commandments (Deut. 4:1, 5, et al.), which they likewise are to teach to their children (Deut. 6:1, 6, 7, et al.). Therefore, although a "doctrine" of the unity of God or of divine election is presupposed in OT teaching, such teaching is primarily instruction in the divine will.

For the most part the NT use corresponds more to the OT idea than to the Greek. That is, teaching usually implies the content of ethical instruction and seldom the content of dogmas or the intellectual apprehension of truth. For example, in the Pastoral Epistles "sound doctrine that conforms to the glorious gospel" is contrasted with all kinds of immoral living (1 Tim. 1:9–11; cf. 6:1, 3; Tit. 1:9; 2:1–5, 9–10). Also the later work entitled DIDACHE (*The Teaching of the Twelve Apostles*) is a manual of ethical instruction and church discipline with scarcely any theological content.

In the NT this usage is strengthened by the relationship of *didachē* to *kērygma* G3060, "preaching." It was by means of the KERYGMA that sinners were brought to faith in Christ (1 Cor. 1:21); and the content of that *kerygma* included the essential data of the Christian message: the life, work, death, and resurrection of Jesus Christ as God's decisive act for the sinner's salvation (cf. Acts 2:14–36). Those who responded to the preaching would then be instructed in the ethical principles and obligations of the Christian life (2:42).

This relationship may be seen throughout the NT. Thus Jesus "preaches" the in-breaking of the KINGDOM OF GOD (Matt. 4:17; 11:28). Sinners are called to decision by his mighty words and deeds. But his teaching, which astonished the crowds for its authority, was replete with ethical demands (cf. the sixfold "You have heard that it was said … But I tell you" in Matt. 5:21–45). So also PAUL in his epistles often followed the kerygmatic content of his gospel with its ethical demands. Such demands were seen as the inevitable corollary of response to the *kerygma*. One may note, therefore, that "doctrine" in contemporary parlance would derive from the content of the *kerygma*.

However, since ethical instruction or obedience to the divine will in the NT is so closely related to response to the preaching with its "doctrinal" content, it is not surprising that teaching itself eventually came to include the essential data of the faith. Thus "the elder" uses *didachē* to refer to the truth of the INCARNATION, belief in which, of course, should eventuate in love (2 Jn. 9–10). This latter meaning of "teaching," as including the essential beliefs of the Christian faith, ultimately prevailed in the early church and continues in vogue today. (See further *TDNT*, 2:135–65; C. H. Dodd, *The Apostolic Preaching and Its Developments* [1936]; D. M. Stanley in *CBQ* 17 [1955]: 216–28; E. F. Harrison in *BSac* 119 [1961]: 118–28; J. I. H. McDonald, *Kerygma and Didache* [1980].)

G. D. FEE

Documentary Hypothesis. See PENTATEUCH.

Docus doh'kuhs. KJV Apoc. form of DOK (1 Macc. 16:15).

Dodai doh'di (דּוֹדַי H1862, "beloved"). Apparently a variant of DODO. Dodai the AHOHITE, one of DAVID's military officers, was in charge of the division for the second month (1 Chr. 27:4). He was probably the same person identified as the father of Eleazar, one of David's famous warriors (2 Sam. 23:9 [where the *Ketib* is *ddy*, *Qere dôdô*]; 1 Chr. 11:12 [*dôdô*]; NRSV reads "Dodo" in both verses).

Dodanim doh'duh-nim. See RODANIM.

Dodava doh'duh-vuh. KJV form of DODAVAHU.

Dodavahu doh'duh-vay'hyoo (דֹּדָוָהוּ H1845, "beloved of Yahweh"). KJV Dodavah. The father of the prophet ELIEZER of Mareshah, who condemned JEHOSHAPHAT king of Judah for his alliance with AHAZIAH of Israel and foretold the destruction of his navy (2 Chr. 20:37).

Dodo doh'doh (דּוֹדוֹ H1861, "[his] beloved"). **(1)** Grandfather of TOLA; the latter was a judge (leader) in ISSACHAR (Jdg. 10:1).

(2) Father of ELEAZAR; the latter was one of DAVID's famous warriors (2 Sam. 23:9; 1 Chr. 11:12; in these verses NIV reads "Dodai"). Apparently the same as DODAI the Ahohite (1 Chr. 27:4).

(3) Father of ELHANAN; the latter was one of David's famous warriors (2 Sam. 23:24; 1 Chr. 11:26).

doe. The female of a DEER. English Bible versions use this term sometimes to render the feminine Hebrew noun *ʾayyālâ* H387 (e.g., Gen. 49:21; KJV, "hind").

Doeg doh'ig (דֹּאֵג H1795, possibly "anxious"). An Edomite who served King SAUL as head shepherd (1 Sam. 21:7; 22:9, 18, 22; Ps. 52 title [here spelled דּוֹאֵג]). The rabbinical commentators point out that Doeg must have been a proselyte or a Jew who once came from EDOM to the SE of Israel; otherwise he could not have entered the sanctuary. The conversation between Doeg and Saul about the support rendered by AHIMELECH to DAVID, leading finally to the slaughter of the priests by Doeg himself, must have been a celebrated incident, as it was recorded in Ps. 52 and became the subject of discussion in Talmudic tradition. The latter, for example, refers to Doeg as "a mighty man in Torah" (*b. Sanh.* 106b; see *Soncino Talmud*, Seder Nezikin 3:726); the rabbis also interpreted the variant spelling as an inclusion of an implied curse. The basis for so much legend is found in the assumption that Ps. 52, which decries the misuse of gifts of wisdom, applied to Doeg. The narrative about this rather obscure personage lends much to the outline of the history of David's reign. It is most evident that the atrocities of Saul's dominion made the people of Israel more than ready for a change in dynasty and fulfilled SAMUEL's warning about the harsh and selfish treatment a king would bring to Israel (1 Sam. 8:10 et al.).

W. WHITE, JR.

dog. To the Israelites all dogs were utterly unclean. In Palestine and Egypt then, as in parts of the E today, the dog was a scavenger and did in larger towns what hyenas helped do in the villages and outside the walls; though classified as a carnivore, it lived on refuse of all kinds and thus was a potential carrier of many diseases, either mechanically or as a vector. The statement that the dogs (Heb. *keleb* H3978) ate JEZEBEL after she had been thrown off the city wall and killed (2 Ki. 9:30–37; cf. v. 10) may suggest that throwing dead bodies to the dogs was not totally unusual (even contact with a corpse was ritually defiling, Lev. 22:4). That the dog was so highly esteemed in Egypt (it was considered a desirable goal for the human soul after death and was associated with Anubis, the jackal god) may have also affected the attitude of the Hebrews.

Terra-cotta plaque of a man leading a dog (Old Babylonian, 2000–1600 B.C., from Borsippa). Dogs were already domesticated at the time of Abraham.

The Israelites, however, were exceptional in this regard. The dog was the first animal to become domesticated, and already in early Egypt it was developed into many useful forms, especially in the hunting field. There is ample evidence that Stone Age humans enlisted dogs as helpers in many parts of the world. Opinions differ slightly, but it is generally agreed on anatomical and behavioral grounds that the WOLF is the ancestor of all domestic dogs, which are known collectively as *Canis familiaris*. The association began when humans lived by hunting, but its development must be a matter for conjecture. From clearing up the remains of a kill and taking refuse from around the encampment there could come a closer cooperation leading to defending the area of their owners against other groups, and hence to assuming proper guard duties, herding, assisting in the hunt, etc.

Dog remains have been found in the earliest JERICHO stratum, while in Egypt at least three breeds can be distinguished in predynastic material, and a much wider range in the Old Kingdom. A type like the greyhound was firmly established prior to 3,000 B.C. Dogs were regarded just as highly in Mesopotamia, where a big hunting mastiff was in use in the earliest Babylonian period (3rd millennium B.C.). Development of different forms went on continuously, with certain types being fixed as they became useful, especially in herding stock and in many forms of hunting. (See further K. Z. Lorenz, *Man Meets Dog* [1954]; F. E. Zeuner, *A History of Domesticated Animals* [1963], ch. 4; *FFB*, 21–22.)

Because of Israel's attitude most dogs were semi-wild, like the pariahs that still haunt districts in India and other countries. Such dogs were descended from individuals that had "gone wild," when they soon lost any breed characteristics and reverted to a general type. Several possible exceptions can be found in the biblical record. In speaking of the dogs of his flock (Job 30:1), JOB can be referring only to sheep dogs, but it is not certain that Job was an Israelite. The figurative expression "mute dogs, they cannot bark" (Isa. 56:10) certainly suggests that it was the custom to keep guard dogs; they were probably sheep dogs, since the preceding verse calls upon the "beasts of the field" to "come and devour." Most contexts, both literal and figurative, portray the dog as contemptible, whether as a filthy scavenger or as an animal that "returns to its vomit" (Prov. 26:11, quoted in 2 Pet. 2:22 [Gk. *kyōn* G3264]), which is one of several proverbs in which it features. The word *dog* can be an abusive term (1 Sam. 17:23), but also a self-deprecating description of humility (2 Sam. 9:8). In Deut. 23:18 the Hebrew word is used as a technical term, perhaps a euphemism, for a male temple prostitute, perhaps echoed by Rev. 22:15, which lists those who must remain outside the Holy City.

Especially significant is the incident of the SYROPHOENICIAN woman (Matt. 15:26–27; Mk. 7:27–28; here the diminutive *kynarion* G3249 is used, referring to young dogs or, more probably, to small pet dogs allowed to enter a Gentile house). Since the dog was regarded by the Jews as ritually impure (see UNCLEANNESS), the term had a theological connotation when applied to GENTILES, who were of course outside God's covenant unless they joined his people Israel. Thus Jesus' comment that it would not be right to take the food that belongs to the children (the Israelites) and toss it to the dogs (the Gentiles) reflects the truth that he had been "sent only to the lost sheep Israel" (Matt. 15:24). Interestingly, PAUL refers to the Judaizers as "dogs" (Phil. 3:2). Although they were Jews, they opposed the gospel of grace by insisting that the Gentile Christians be circumcised and adopt Judaism. The apostle in effect suggests that, by their activity, the Judaizers are the ones who have placed themselves outside God's COVENANT and who therefore must be regarded as Gentiles. G. S. CANSDALE

dogma. A doctrine; an ecclesiastical teaching or body of principles to be believed. The Greek noun *dogma G1504*, which is of infrequent occurrence in the NT, originally signified "an opinion" or "a judgment." It came to mean "a judgment given with authority" and so "a decree." Thus it refers to imperial decrees in Lk. 2:1; Acts 17:7 (cf. Heb. 11:23, where a minor textual variant uses it of a decree of Pharaoh). It is used also of religious decrees, specifically the commands of God as expressed in the Mosaic law (Eph. 2:15; Col. 2:14). To this realm also belongs the verb *dogmatizō G1505* (middle voice, "to submit oneself to ordinances"), used once in the NT (Col. 2:20). The noun is used in Acts 16:4 of the decrees of the COUNCIL OF JERUSALEM (the verb *dokeō G1506*, "to seem [good]" is from the same root and is used in the account of the council's proceedings, 15:22, 25, 28). It may have been due to its use at such a council that it came to be employed widely by the early fathers with reference to official doctrinal pronouncements of the church, which is the meaning the English word normally bears today. It is found in this sense in IGNATIUS (*Magn.* 13), fairly often in ORIGEN, and frequently from the Council of Nicaea onward. G. W. GROGAN

Dok dok (Δωκ, corrupted to Δαγων in Jos. *Ant.* 13.8.1). KJV Docus. A small fortress built (or rebuilt) by Ptolemy, the son of Abubus and son-in-law of Simon MACCABEE. The name of the ancient city survives in modern ʿAin Duq, a spring about 3 mi. NW of JERICHO. The ancient site is identified with nearby Jebel Qarantal. Simon and his sons Mattathias and Judas, in making a circuit of the cities of the country, were received at Dok by Ptolemy. After they had banqueted and become drunk, Ptolemy's men who were lying in wait arose and killed them (1 Macc. 16:15). Dok was one of several fortresses guarding the routes into the central mountain region. D. H. MADVIG

dolphin. See SEA COW.

dominion. This English term is used to render a variety of words and expressions, such as Hebrew *memšālâ H4939* (e.g., Mic. 4:8, in parallel with *mamlākâ H4930*, "kingdom, kingship, sovereignty") and Greek *kyriotēs G3262* (e.g., Eph. 1:21). Several forms of dominion are mentioned in the Bible, including: (1) God's rule over the universe (Ps. 22:28); (2) man's dominion over nature given to him by God (Gen. 1:26; Ps. 8:6); (3) Christ's eschatological rule (1 Cor. 15:24–28; 2 Thess. 2:8); (4) the saints' eschatological rule with Christ (2 Tim. 2:12; Rev. 3:21); (5) the believer's freedom from the dominion of sin (Rom. 6:9, 14; 7:1). See also AUTHORITY; KING, KINGSHIP; POWER.
S. BARABAS

Domitian duh-mish'uhn. When the popular TITUS died at the untimely age of forty-two (A.D. 81), after only two years and a few months as emperor, he was succeeded by his thirty-year-old brother Domitian (born A.D. 51), whom neither Titus nor their father VESPASIAN had expected to be called to the task. Domitian (whose full name was Titus Flavius Domitianus) was no trained soldier like his two predecessors, and he came to office, a despised younger brother, embittered by his elders' contempt, a resentment all the deeper for his keen intellect. He was shrewd enough to note the parallel of his case with that of TIBERIUS, who succeeded the first emperor, AUGUSTUS, after being similarly passed by, humiliated, and embittered. The documents of Tiberius were his favorite reading (Suetonius, *Dom.* 20) and played some part in bringing out the worst in Domitian. It is difficult to ascertain the truth behind the distortions of writers such as Juvenal, TACITUS, SUETONIUS, and PLINY the Younger, who belonged to, or spoke for, the upper section of Roman society, on whom the prince vented his spite.

Sensitive about his absence of military glory, a conspicuous advantage in his two predecessors, Domitian ordered an attack on the Chatti of the Main Valley, and celebrated his victory in a great triumphal celebration. The campaign salutarily removed an awkward salient in an essential frontier. It revealed, too, that Domitian, like Augustus and CLAUDIUS, had a faculty for picking able men.

Roman historiography is Rome-centered and aristocratic. It failed to record in detail that the provinces were content and well governed at the time when the pathological fears and suspicions of

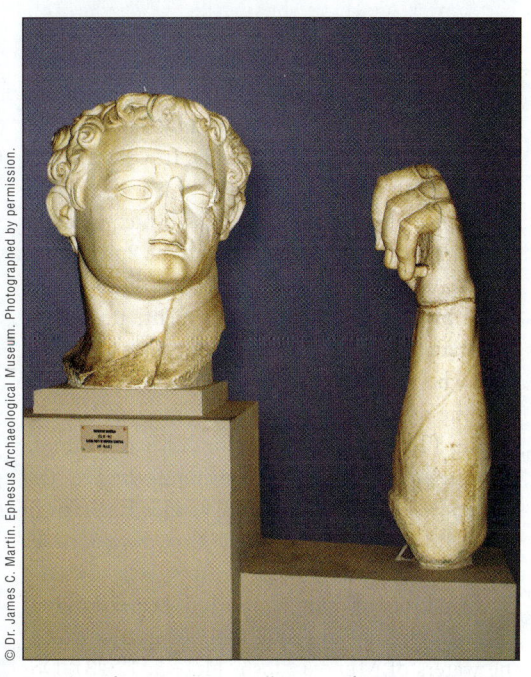

Remains of a seven-meter tall statue of Emperor Domitian found in Ephesus in a temple dedicated to him.

Domitian were reviving in Rome the hated cult of delation—that pernicious system of the common informer and the law of treason that so played into his hands. Both Tacitus (*Agr.* 45.2) and Pliny (*Pan.* 48) spoke with horror of those days when aristocracy and senate were decimated by the jealous suspicions of the prince.

Among Domitian's victims were the Christians. He was heir to a policy and legislation established by NERO and sporadically pursued under Vespasian and Titus, both of whom had links with Palestine and entertained some fear of any movement initiated there. But Domitian, with a sharp eye for treason and enthusiastic for the Caesar-cult (see EMPEROR WORSHIP), justly ranks with Nero as a systematic persecutor. According to IRENAEUS (*Haer.* 5.30.3), the Apocalypse of John was written during the reign of Domitian and reflected the emperor's anti-Christian attitude. Suppression extended to the family of the emperor, so high had Christianity penetrated. It seems even to have destroyed Domitian's arrangements for the succession. Domitian was murdered in the year 96, after a plot supported by his wife, who felt the insecurity of her own position. The abiding significance of his somber fifteen years as emperor is that a sharp advance was made toward complete autocracy and monarchy. (See W. M. Ramsay, *The Church in the Roman Empire* [1893], ch. 11; E. M. Blaiklock, *The Century of the New Testament* [1962], 116–26; H. Bengtson, *Die Flavier: Vespasian, Titus, Domitian: Geschichte e. röm. Kaiserhauses* [1979]; B. W. Jones, *The Emperor Domitian* [1992]; P. Southern, *Domitian: Tragic Tyrant* [1997].)   E. M. BLAIKLOCK

donkey. See ASS, DONKEY.

door. Ancient doors usually were made of wood, sometimes sheeted with metal as in the case of city gates or in large public buildings. Sometimes they were made of one slab of stone or, rarely, a single piece of metal. Hinges on doors, as known today, were unknown; instead, doors turned on pivots set in sockets above and below. The sockets were made of stone or, sometimes, of metal. In Egypt, the hinge consisted of a socket of metal with a projecting pivot, into which two corners of the door were inserted. A wide doorway had a pair of folding doors (Isa. 45:1; Heb. *delet* H1946), which could be bolted with bars of wood (Nah. 3:13) or of metal (Isa. 45:2; Ps. 107:16; NIV, "gates"). The temple doors were two-leaved (1 Ki. 6:34). Doors were provided with a bolt (2 Sam. 13:17) or with lock and key (Jdg. 3:23). The doorway consisted of three parts: the threshold or sill, the doorposts at the side, and the lintel. Doorways often were highly ornamented (Isa. 54:12; Heb. *šaʿar* H9133, "gate") and inscribed with sentences of Scripture in literal accordance with the law of Moses, "Write them on the doorframes of your houses and on your gates" (Deut. 11:20). The word is also used metaphorically, as in Jn. 10:7, "I am the door" (Gk. *thyra* G2598; NIV, "gate"); Acts 14:27, "he had opened the door of faith to the Gentiles"; and Rev. 3:20, "I stand at the door and knock." See ARCHITECTURE; GATE.   S. BARABAS

doorkeeper. A person who guarded the entrance to public buildings, temples, city walls, etc. The NIV uses this term a number of times, for example, with reference to those who guarded the ARK OF THE COVENANT (1 Chr. 15:23 [Heb. *šōʿēr* H8788]; NRSV, "gatekeepers"). To be a lowly doorkeeper of the temple is preferred to a life of wickedness (Ps. 84:10 [*sāpap H6214*]). The Greek word for "doorkeeper" or "porter" (*thyrōros G2601*) occurs in three passages in the NT. The doorkeeper of a rich man's house is mentioned by Jesus as an example of one who watches faithfully (Mk. 13:34; NIV, "the one at the door"). A doorkeeper might guard the entrance of a sheepfold (Jn. 10:3; NIV, "watchman"). A maid kept the door of the courtyard of the high priest the night Jesus was on trial (18:16–17; NIV, "the girl on duty … at the door"). D. H. MADVIG

Dophkah dof´kuh (דָּפְקָה *H1986*, meaning disputed). A place where the children of Israel encamped on their journey from the RED SEA to SINAI (Num. 33:12–13). Some scholars identify it with Serabit el-Khadim, where the Egyptians carried on mining, and where the famous "Sinaitic Inscriptions" were found (dating from about 1525 B.C. and written in a Semitic hieroglyphic alphabet). J. Simons (*Geographical and Topographical Texts of the Old Testament* [1959], 252 §428) suggests that the name be read *mapqâ*, because Mafqat is the name of the turquoise mined there as well as the name of the district. D. H. MADVIG

Dor dor (דּוֹר *H1888*, variant דֹּאר *H1799* [only Josh. 17:11], "generation" or "dwelling"; LXX Δωρ, but Δωρα in 1 Macc. 15:11 et al. [KJV "Dora"]). A fortified city on the coast of Palestine, S of Mount CARMEL, c. 8 mi. N of CAESAREA. The surrounding hilly area was known as NAPHOTH DOR (Josh. 11:2; 12:23; 1 Ki. 4:11; cf. Josh. 17:11). It was settled in very ancient times by PHOENICIA because of the abundance of shells along the coast which were the source of a rich purple dye. Late in the 2nd millennium B.C., Dor was inhabited by the Tjekker, one of the SEA PEOPLES. The city is mentioned in the Egyptian story of Wen-Amon, an emissary of Pharaoh who stopped there on his way to Phoenicia. The site of Dor is identified with modern Khirbet el-Burj (Tel Dor), N of Tanturah. (See J. Simon, *The Geographical and Topographical Texts of the Old Testament* [1959], 272, 418–19, 433; E. Stern in *The Land of Israel: Cross-roads of Civilization*, ed. E. Lipiński [1985], 169–92.)

The king of Dor supported JABIN king of HAZOR in his unsuccessful battle against JOSHUA at the waters of MEROM (Josh. 11:2–5; 12:23). Dor was one of the cities within the borders of Issachar and Asher that were assigned to Manasseh, although Manasseh was unable to capture it. In later years, when it was captured, its Canaanite inhabitants were subjected by Israel to forced labor (Josh. 17:11–13; Jdg. 1:27–28). Dor is listed also among cities possessed by descendants of Ephraim

Dor was an important harbor along the Mediterranean Sea used by Phoenicians and Israelites during the period of the Israelite monarchy. (View to the S.)

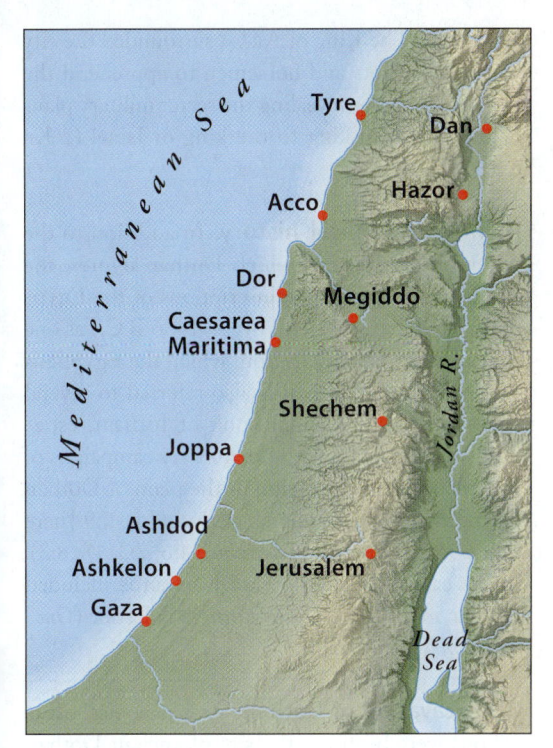

Seaports on the Mediterranean.

(1 Chr. 7:29). Dor and the neighboring territory were made the 4th administrative district by SOLOMON (1 Ki. 4:11).

TIGLATH-PILESER III (744–727 B.C.) conquered Dor and established an Assyrian governor over it. In 219 B.C. the city was besieged by ANTIOCHUS the Great. He did not capture Dor, however, for rumors of an approaching Egyptian army caused him to agree to a truce. The Phoenician cities were subject to the Ptolemies until c. 200 B.C., when they were taken by the Seleucids who made Dor and several other cities independent (see SELEUCIA). In 139 B.C. the usurper TRYPHO fled to Dor when he was pursued by Antiochus VII (1 Macc. 15:10–25; KJV, "Dora"). The city was rebuilt, made free, and made a part of the province of Syria by POMPEY in 64 B.C. (See *NEAEHL*, 1:357–72.) D. H. MADVIG

Dora dor´uh. KJV Apoc. form of DOR (1 Macc. 15:11 et al.).

Dorcas dor´kuhs (Δορκάς *G1520*, "gazelle," corresponding to Aram. טָבְיְתָא or טְבִיתָא). A feminine name not uncommon to both Jews and Greeks, used in the NT to denote the Christian woman of JOPPA who died and was raised from the dead by PETER (Acts 9:36–43). Her ARAMAIC name was TABITHA, which has the same meaning as Dorcas. While Peter was healing AENEAS at LYDDA, about 10 mi. distant from Joppa, the ailing Dorcas died. She was held in high esteem for her outstanding service to others (and her example has inspired the founding of numerous "Dorcas societies" in congregations today). She was described as a *mathētria G3413*, the only citation in the NT where the feminine form of "disciple" is used. On the occasion of her death, two men were sent to Lydda to summon Peter. When Peter arrived, the body already had been washed for burial and placed in an upper room. The widows were mourning and, in deep appreciation, were showing the handiwork of Dorcas as they displayed the garments she had made, perhaps for these very individuals. Like Jesus (Matt. 9:25), Peter sent everyone out, then knelt and prayed. Upon the command to arise, Dorcas responded; and she was presented to the others alive. Because of this miracle many believed in the Lord. (See B. Witherington, *Women in the Earliest Churches* [1988], 149–51.) L. FOSTER

Dorymenes dor-im´uh-neez (Δορυμένης). The father of a certain Ptolemy who was one of the officers chosen by LYSIAS to lead a campaign against Judah (1 Macc. 3:38; 2 Macc. 4:45; prob. also the governor of Coelesyria and Phoenicia, 8:8).

Dositheus doh-sith´ee-uhs (Δοσίθεος [in LXX Esther, Δωσίθεος]). (1) A man who said he was a Levite and who carried the Letter of Purim to Egypt (Add. Esth. 11:1; Rahlfs 10:3l).

(2) A captain under Judas MACCABEE (2 Macc.12:19, 24).

(3) A horseman under Judas Maccabee who almost captured the SELEUCID general GORGIAS (2 Macc. 12:35).

(4) Son of Drimylus; he was an apostate Jew who saved the life of King PTOLEMY IV Philopator (3 Macc. 1:3).

Dositheus, Apocalypse of. See SETH, THREE STELES OF.

dot. This English term is used by the RSV to render Greek *keraia* G3037 (KJV, "tittle") in two of Jesus' statements: "Not an iota, not a dot, will pass from the law until all is accomplished" (Matt. 5:18); "But it is easier for heaven and earth to pass away, than for one dot of the law to become void" (Lk. 16:17). The Greek word literally means "horn" but is used of any "projection." In the context of writing, it can be applied to an accent, a diacritical mark, or a small part of an individual letter. Note, for example, the stroke that distinguishes similar Hebrew letters, such as *daleth* (ד) from *resh* (ר) and *beth* (ב) from *kaph* (כ). Accordingly, the NRSV renders, "one stroke of a letter"; NIV, "the least stroke of a pen."

The *iota* is the smallest letter in the Greek alphabet and here it may refer to the *yod* (י), the smallest letter of the Hebrew (and Aramaic) alphabet. The expression "not an iota, not a dot" signifies the tiniest details. It is used by Jesus to emphasize the enduring and unchangeable nature of the law of God (i.e., the Torah, the OT). Similar statements are found in Jewish tradition asserting that a *yod* could not be removed from the law, and that the world would be destroyed if one mark that distinguishes similar letters were removed (A. Edersheim, *The Life and Times of Jesus the Messiah*, 2 vols. [1899], 1:537–38).

D. H. MADVIG

Dothaim doh´thay-im (Δωθαιμ). KJV Apoc. form of DOTHAN (Jdt. 4:6; 7:3, 18; 8:3).

Dothan doh´thuhn (דֹּתָן H2019, according to some, "two wells," but most scholars dispute that the ending is a dual form [cf. GKC §88c]). A prominent town about 5 mi. S of the JEZREEL Valley and identified with modern Tel Dotan, some 11 mi. NNE of SAMARIA.

I. In biblical history. The city of Dothan was a focal point in an event of the earlier days of JOSEPH (c. 1900–1800 B.C.). His father, JACOB, sent him to inquire about the well-being of his brothers, and he found them at Dothan, pasturing their flocks (Gen. 37:13–17). They put Joseph in a pit, and subsequently sold him to a passing caravan of Ishmaelites, who took him to Egypt. A thousand years later (c. 850 B.C.), the prophet ELISHA lived at Dothan. The King of ARAM surrounded the city with his chariots and horsemen to apprehend the prophet, who was revealing the secret military plans of the Aramean king to the king of Israel (2 Ki. 6:8–14).

II. In extrabiblical history. In addition to the two biblical events in which Dothan figures, the city is mentioned in the inscriptions of the Egyptian king THUTMOSE III (1490–1436 B.C.) as one of the Palestinian towns from which the Egyptians exacted tribute. Dothan is also referred to several times in the apocryphal book of JUDITH, especially in connection with the military campaigns of HOLOFERNES in the region of the plain of Dothan during the intertestamental period (Jdt. 3:9 [here Gk. *Dōtaia*, elsewhere *Dōthaim*]; 4:6; 7:3, 18; 8:3). In the early Christian period, EUSEBIUS included Dothan in his list of place names in Palestine (*Onomasticon* 76. 13–15).

III. Excavation of Dothan. Archaeological excavations were begun at the site of ancient Dothan in 1953 by J. P. Free and his wife, and the Dothan expedition staff. (See the report for the first season in *BASOR* 131 [Oct. 1953]: 16–29; subsequent reports were published in issues 135, 139, 143, 152, 156, 160). A deep sounding the first season at the top of the slope of the mound showed that Dothan began about 5,000 years ago (3000 B.C.),

Dothan.

and, though destroyed and rebuilt many times, was a thriving town in every main period of biblical and ANE history from 3000 B.C. through NT times, with evidence of occupation in Byzantine times (c. A.D. 300–500) and the Arabic period (600–1100) and Crusader times.

The city of Dothan during the thousand years (3000–2000 B.C.) leading up to the patriarchal period was well attested by seven levels of occupation containing Early Bronze Age sherds (3000–2000 B.C.). This evidence in the deep sounding of the first season implied the destruction and rebuilding of seven towns over this thousand-year period, and parallels other such rebuilding and destruction, "when the Amorite was in the land," as found at other northern Palestinian sites, including MEGIDDO and BETH SHAN. A heavy city wall surrounded the city in this period, still surviving to a height of 16 ft. after it was uncovered. It probably was 25 ft. high in biblical times. It measured 11 ft. thick at the base and 9 ft. thick in the upper surviving part.

In the patriarchal period (2000–1600 B.C., Middle Bronze Age), we uncovered ten rooms of a heavily built citadel, with walls 4 ft. thick (ninth season, 1964). The citadel abutted against the inside of the heavy city wall, near the gateway area. This heavy construction reflected the days of minimal central power and the need for individual defense on the part of each Palestinian city. Outside the wall in this gateway area we uncovered a wide stairway (13 ft.) leading up to the city wall. In patriarchal times, water was doubtless carried up these stairs from the well a few hundred feet down the slope in the plain of Dothan. This was the city of Dothan of Joseph's time, represented by two Middle Bronze Age levels in our archaeological stratification.

The Late Bronze Age (1600–1200 B.C.) was abundantly attested by two main levels that yielded thousands of potsherds from Late Bronze pottery. The citadel of the Middle Bronze period appeared to have suffered partial destruction in the late 17th or the 16th cent. B.C., and after repairs, to have continued in use into the Late Bronze period. One of the striking discoveries from the Late Bronze period was a tomb on the W slope of the mound, cut into the bedrock of the hill on which Dothan was built. It began as a family tomb about 1300 B.C. or shortly thereafter, and continued in use between 200 and 300 years. In it were found nearly 600 clay lamps and nearly 600 pyxis oil juglets, implying the burial of approximately that number of people. With this number of burials, there was a considerable amount of bones. Over eighty skeletons could be separately identified the first main season of the tomb project, and about the same number the second season.

Years later the roof of the tomb had partially collapsed, and tons of bed rock lay on the bones and objects. In places there were several inches of "bone material," compressed together without individual bones being particularly recognizable, but representing numerous skeletons. This tomb (Tomb 1) yielded over 3,200 pottery objects—lamps, pyxis jars, craters, bowls, jugs, and almost every type of vessel used in later Late Bronze and earlier Iron I times. Also over 200 bronze objects came from the tomb: daggers, spear points, chisels, and even a bronze lamp in the shape of a typical spouted pottery lamp. All objects of this type would have been familiar to GIDEON and the other judges who lived in the period either side of 1200 B.C.

The Iron I period (1200–1000 B.C.), parallel to the later part of the period of the judges, was represented by two levels. The tomb continued in use during the earlier part of this period, and when it was full, another tomb was carved out next to it (Tomb 2), discovered during the eighth season (1962). It yielded 500 objects similar to many

Tel Dotan (looking SE).

found in Tomb 1. These two tombs yielded five pottery lamps that had seven spouts on each lamp, attesting to the earlier date of the concept of the sevenfold light, a notion formerly downdated to about 600 B.C. by the Wellhausen school and subsequent followers.

The Iron II period (1000–600 B.C.) paralleled the period of the Israelite monarchy and yielded four main levels. The lowest of these represented the Solomonic period (c. 1000–900 B.C.) and contained a large well-built structure that appeared to be the local "administrative building." In one room we found the remains of 96 small storage jars, all the same size, likely standard measures for collecting taxes in oil and other commodities at this local "county seat." This evidence of administrative procedure parallels the biblical implications of Solomonic governmental organization. The heavier walls of the "administrative building" were about 4 ft. thick. Two drains served the building, providing better sanitation facilities than existed in Elizabethan England nearly three millennia later.

The level representing the third city of Dothan in the days of the biblical kings, dating to about 725 B.C., was likely the city destroyed at about the same time that the city of SAMARIA was taken by the Assyrian army (2 Ki. 17:5–6). The fourth city of this period, dating about 700 B.C., continued into the 7th cent. Many of the houses of this period had plaster-covered courtyards. The excavation at Dothan and other sites shows that hydraulic lime plaster first came into general use in the 10th cent. B.C., probably due to the progressive planning and inventiveness of the Solomonic regime.

We have not found a distinct level of the Persian period (c. 500–300 B.C.), but some Persian pottery and metal bowls have come to light. Perhaps it was a small settlement, reflecting the desolation of the exilic and postexilic period, and covered only a part of the mound that has not been excavated.

The Hellenistic period is well attested (c. 300–50 B.C.). The higher part of the mound yielded house walls and sherds, including a number of Rhodian jar handles having stamped inscriptions datable to this period. During the eighth and ninth seasons house walls from the Roman period were uncovered. One sherd bore a stamp with the letters SC, standing for *Senatus consultus*. This is a reversal of the usual Lat word order, *Consultus senatus* (senate consulted), implying approval of the Roman senate, and tying in with the Roman rule over Palestine at this time.

The higher part of the mound yielded Byzantine walls, sherds, and glass (A.D. 300–600); also Arabic period sherds (A.D. 600–1100), and on the highest part of the mound the remains of a medieval fortress-palace (12th–14th cent. A.D.). We uncovered 25 rooms of this structure around a courtyard. Five other adjacent depressions imply five more courtyards; if each of them has 25 rooms, we have a medieval feudal-type structure with 150 rooms for the retainers, the servants, and the rest of a feudal-type retinue. Arabic sherds abound on top of the mound. The Venetian coin of about A.D. 1600 has been mentioned, and the modern village of about ten houses on the lower slope.

Shepherds still come from southern Palestine to the region of Dothan to water and pasture their flocks, as they did 4,000 years ago in the days of Joseph's brothers. Some doubt has been expressed on the biblical record of shepherds traveling out of "the vale of Hebron" 80 mi. or more to the Dothan area. One spring week-end we counted 90 flocks on the road from Jerusalem to the Dothan area; many came from the region between Hebron and Jerusalem. (For a recent and tentative stratigraphy, see W. G. Dever in *ABD*, 2:226–27; cf. also *NEAEHL*, 1:372–74.)

J. P. FREE

Douay Version. See VERSIONS OF THE BIBLE, ENGLISH.

double-minded. This English expression is used in Bible versions to render Greek *dipsychos* G1500 (from the adverb *dis* G1489, "twice," and the noun *psychē* G6034, "soul, mind"), which occurs twice (Jas. 1:8; 4:8). Although the word (as well as derivatives) is used in postapostolic writings, especially referring to the indecision of accepting Christianity or believing specific Christian doctrine, its first attested occurrence is in the letter of James, who may have coined the term (but see S. S. C. Marshall in *Studia evangelica* 6 [1973]: 348–61). What he means by this word he makes clear with a further description: James is referring not simply to someone who experiences personal doubts, but to the one who is "unstable in all his ways" (cf. the description of the ungodly as people who speak with "a double heart" in Ps. 12:2 NRSV [NIV, "deception"]; the same Heb. expression is found in 1 Chr. 12:33). Set in context with an admonition to pray (Jas. 1:5–6), it would be understood that the essence of prayer is the turning over of the entire mind to God. A person cannot pray while facing in two directions. We face God when we pray, thus prayer is the elimination of the double mind. James's second use of the term is likewise set in an admonition to draw near to God. The answer to the double mind with its wavering loyalties, indecision, divided interests, and impurity was the rededication of the whole personality to Christ. (The synonymous term *dignōmōn* is used in *Did.* 4.2 and *Barn.* 19.7. Cf. also the references to "double-faced" [*diprosōpos*], "two tongues," and "double sight/hearing" in *T. Ash.* 3.1; *T.Benj.* 6.5–6.) See DOUBLE-TONGUED; SINCERE.

H. L. DRUMWRIGHT, JR.

double-tongued. An expression used to render Greek *dilogos* G1474 ("two-worded"), which occurs only once in the NT (1 Tim. 3:8 NRSV). The phrase "not double-tongued" (NIV has the clearer rendering, "sincere") designates one of the qualifications of a deacon: he must not be someone who says one thing at one time and something else at another time (or perhaps who says one thing but means another). In extrabiblical literature, the term means "repeating." The similar word *diglōssos* ("bilingual, interpreter") occurs with the sense "deceitful" in the SEPTUAGINT (e.g., Prov. 11:13) and elsewhere. Note especially *Did.* 2.4, "Do not be double-minded or double-tongued [*dignōmōn oude diglōssos*], for double-tonguedness [*diglōssia*] is the snare of death." See DOUBLE-MINDED; SINCERE.

dough. A mixture of flour with water or, sometimes, olive oil; it was kneaded in a wooden trough usually by hand, but also, when a large quantity was to be kneaded, by foot (Heb. *bāṣēq* H1302 in Exod. 12:34, 39; 2 Sam. 13:8; Jer. 7:18; Hos. 7:4; Gk. *phyrama* G5878 figuratively in Rom. 11:16; 1 Cor. 5:6–7; Gal. 5:9). It was made chiefly from wheat and barley, but occasionally from beans, lentils, millet, and spelt (Ezek. 4:9). It is not certain whether there was a class distinction between those who ate BREAD made from wheat and barley. A little bit of LEAVEN (dough left to sour from the previous baking) was placed in the dough to cause it to rise—for leavened bread. For the PASSOVER, only UNLEAVENED BREAD could be used. Some salt was sprinkled in the dough, for both leavened and unleavened bread. After the dough was sufficiently kneaded, it was put aside to allow it to rise, and then it was baked in one of a variety of ovens that were then used. See also FOOD.   S. BARABAS

dove, pigeon. In English these two terms (referring to any of various birds of the family *Columbidae*) are largely interchangeable, although *dove* is used especially of small wild pigeons, while *pigeon* often refers to a wide variety of rock doves seen in public places. The most common Hebrew term for "dove" is *yônâ* H3433 (Gen. 8:8–12 et al.); another word, *tôr* H9367, appears mostly in Leviticus in conjunction with the former term (Lev. 1:14 et al.; in these cases, the NIV renders *tôr* "dove" and *yônâ* "young pigeon"; the NRSV has "turtledove" and "pigeon" respectively). A third term, *gôzāl* H1578, "young of a bird," apparently refers to a dove in one passage (Gen. 15:9; its only other occurrence refers to the young of an eagle, Deut. 32:11). The common Greek term is *peristera* G4361 (Matt 3:16 et al.; in Lk. 2:24 [quoting Lev. 12:8], it appears in conjunction with *trygōn* G5583, NRSV "turtledove").

Palestine today has at least six members of this family: rock, ring, and stock doves of the genus *Columba;* turtle, collared, and palm doves of the genus *Streptopelia* (see TURTLEDOVE). The last of these has become common and widespread in Israel since the 1950s with the extension of farming. It seems likely that *yônâ* applies in particular to the rock dove and generally to all three *Columba* species. These are generally blue-gray and distinctly larger than the other three, which are mostly rufous and vinaceous. These birds are wholly vegetarian, taking seeds, fruits, and green stuff.

The rock dove is the sole ancestor of all domestic pigeons and has a wide range in Europe, Asia, and N Africa. It nests on cliff faces, and when town pigeons use ledges of high city buildings they revert to wild habits. It is likely that it was domesticated independently in several different areas. It is featured on monuments in the earliest dynasty of ancient Egypt, and the first record of the pigeon being used as a table bird is in the fourth dynasty c. 2500 B.C. It has been universally regarded as good for food and was probably first domesticated for that purpose, later becoming important for sacrifices. It is recorded that four pigeons were dispatched in different directions to announce the coronation of RAMSES III (1204 B.C.), but it is unlikely that they were taking messages. Although it is implied that pigeons were trapped (Hos. 7:11–12), the "young pigeons" offered by the poor were likely domestic stock; most breeding colonies were inaccessible.

The term *dove* occurs often in figurative contexts, some of which merit comment for their natural history allusions. The statement "Be like a dove that makes its nest / at the mouth of a cave" (Jer. 48:28) describes precisely their habitat in the NEGEV today, from where they must fly large distances to find food and water. King HEZEKIAH, in recalling his illness, says, "I cried like a swift or thrush, / I moaned like a mourning dove" (Isa. 38:14). Many doves have a plaintive note, and the Hebrew *yônâ* possibly comes from a root meaning "to lament, mourn" (*ʾānâ* H627). Their courtship displays make doves an obvious symbol of love (Cant. 1:15 et al.). Because the ancients believed that the dove had no bile, it was considered a peaceful bird, especially suitable for sacrifices; it thus also became a symbol of Christian virtue (cf. Matt. 10:16). The name JONAH is the same as the Hebrew word for "dove"; and the name of Job's daughter, JEMIMAH (Job 42:14), is thought to come from another root that has the same meaning in Arabic. (See G. R. Driver in *PEQ* no vol. [1955]: 129–30; P. Arnold, *Birds of Israel* [1962]; *FFB*, 23–24).

G. S. CANSDALE

dove's dung. This phrase is used by the KJV and other versions to render Hebrew *ḥărê yônîm* (= *ḥărāʾîm* H2989 plus *yônâ* H3433), which is the KETIB reading in 2 Ki. 6:25, "As the siege continued, famine in Samaria became so great that a donkey's head was sold for eighty shekels of silver, and one-fourth of a kab of dove's dung for five shekels of silver" (NRSV; similarly LXX, *koprou peristerōn*). The QERE is *dibyōnîm* H1807, possibly a euphemism meaning "flux." Some scholars interpret the phrase literally, assuming that the material was used either as food or as fuel (cf. T. R. Hobbes, *2 Kings*, WBC 13 [1985], 79; JOSEPHUS, in *Ant* 9.4.4. §62, speculated that it was used in place of salt).

Others, however, argue that the term refers to a cheap vegetable. According to one tradition, it designates the bulb *Ornithogalum umbellatum*. Also known as "bird's milk" or "bird's dung," the plant is known today as Star of Bethlehem (*FFB*, 24). The bulbs have to be roasted or boiled before eating. There is some Akkadian evidence, however, that the phrase "dove's dung" was used of the seeds of the carob and that it was thus a colloquial way of referring to inedible husks (cf. NIV, "seed pods"; M. Cogan and H. Tadmor, *II Kings*, AB 11 [1988], 79; cf. also J. A. Gray, *I and II Kings*, OTL, 2nd ed. [1970], 518n., who follows Cheyne in emending to *ḥărûbîm*).

dowry. Money (or property) given by a bride to her husband at marriage. The word is used by the KJV several times to render Hebrew *mōhar* H4558, but this term refers to the compensation a husband pays to the bride's family, that is, a sum given to the father of the bride for her economic loss to the family. It is thus better translated "marriage present" or "bride-price" (Gen. 34:12; Exod. 22:17; 1 Sam. 18:25); this compensation could be paid in service (Gen. 29:18). In addition, both the KJV and the NRSV use "dowry" to translate *zēbed* H2273, "gift," which occurs only once (Gen 30:20). Finally, *šillûḥîm* H8933 ("dismissal") is used in the sense of "parting gift" (Mic. 1:14) and appears to mean "dowry" once (1 Ki. 9:16 NRSV; the NIV has "wedding gift").

doxology. An ascription of praise or glory to God in song or prayer (from Gk. *doxa* G1518 "glory, praise, honor"). Although the word does not occur in the Bible, doxologies were uttered by angels to shepherds the night Jesus came into the world (Lk. 2:14) and by "the whole crowd of disciples" the day Jesus rode triumphantly into Jerusalem on Palm Sunday (Lk. 19:37–38); the book of Revelation speaks of doxologies by angels around the throne in heaven (Rev. 5:13) and by "a great multitude in heaven" (Rev. 19:1–31). In the OT all five books of the Psalter end with a doxology, the last comprising a whole psalm in which "praise" appears thirteen times (Pss. 41:13; 72:18–19; 89:52; 106:48; 150:1–6).

The LORD'S PRAYER is traditionally concluded with the doxology: "For thine is the kingdom, and the power, and the glory, for ever. Amen" (Matt. 6:13 KJV; it does not appear in some old Greek MSS); a similar statement is found in 1 Chr. 29:11. Paul uses doxologies sparingly as well as briefly, not as a set formula but as the spontaneous outburst of his soul at spiritual peaks (Rom. 11:36; 16:27; Eph. 3:21; 1 Tim. 1:17). The longest and most comprehensive doxologies in the NT, frequently used as benedictions by pastors, are in Heb. 13:20–21 and Jude 24–25.

In Christian liturgy the *Gloria Patri* (an ancient hymn also known as the Lesser Doxology and beginning with the words, "Glory be to the Father …") and the hymn widely known as "The Doxology" (composed by Bishop Thomas Ken, 1637–1711, "Praise God, from whom all blessings flow …") are sung every Sunday in a host of churches all over the world. G. B. FUNDERBURK

drachma drak´muh (דַּרְכְּמוֹנִים *H2007*; δραχμή *G1534*, lit., "a handful"). In the OT it refers to Persian gold coins (Ezra 2:69; Neh. 7:70–72; KJV, "dram"; NRSV renders DARIC [cf. BDB, 204], but see *HALOT*, 1:232). The Greek term referred originally to a unit of weight; in the NT it is used only of a Greek silver coin, roughly equivalent in value to a DENARIUS (Lk. 15:8–9). In one passage (Acts 19:19), the NIV uses "drachma" also to render *argyrion G736*, which means "silver, money, silver coin." See also DIDRACHMA; COINS.

Silver coin worth four drachmas, minted at Seleucia-on-the-Tigris. Obverse: King Antiochus III (222–187 B.C.) with diadem. Reverse: the god Apollo.

drag, dragnet. See NET.

dragon. This English term is used in some Bible versions to render Hebrew *tannîn H9490* (NIV, "monster") in passages that speak of cosmic combat (Job 7:12; Ps 74:13; Isa. 27:1; 57:9; Ezek. 29:3; 32:2; the Heb. word can also mean "snake," Exod. 7:9 et al.). In the book of Revelation it stands for Greek *drakōn G1532* and designates SATAN (Rev. 12:3–17; 13:1–11; 16:13; 20:2). (Cf. J. Day, *God's Conflict with the Dragon and the Sea: Echoes of a Canaanite Myth in the Old Testament* [1985]; *DDD*, 265–67.) See also LEVIATHAN; MYTH; RAHAB (MONSTER).

Dragon, Bel and the. See BEL AND THE DRAGON.

Dragon's Spring (dragon well). See JACKAL WELL.

dram. See DARIC; DRACHMA.

draught house. This phrase is used by the KJV to render the plural of Hebrew *mahărāʾâ H4738*, "latrine" (2 Ki. 10:27, where the *Qere* is *môṣāʾôt*, apparently a euphemism). In abolishing BAAL worship from Israel, JEHU demolished the temple of BAAL and converted it into a cesspool; such an action was the utmost desecration (cf. Ezra 6:11; Dan. 2:5). D. H. MADVIG

drawer of water. An expression used by the KJV and other versions with reference to a lowly servant class (Deut. 29:11; Josh. 9:21–27; NIV, "water carrier"). Drawing WATER was a menial task often performed by women (Gen. 24:13; 1 Sam. 9:11). Sometimes it was assigned to young men (Ruth 2:9). It may have been customary to subject defeated enemies to this service as Israel did to the Gibeonites (Josh. 9:21–27). The well or spring was usually located outside the city walls. The water was carried into the city in water pots or goatskins by the drawer of water or on donkey back. Drawers of water are listed as the lowliest of those entering into covenant with God (Deut. 29:11). D. H. MADVIG

dream. A series of thoughts, images, or emotions occurring during sleep. Erich Fromm defines *dream* as a meaningful and significant expression of any kind of mental activity under the condition of sleep.

I. Psychological description. Dreams seem to be the reappearance of thoughts that have, in some form or other, been formed in our minds. They are portions of our former conceptions and impressions revived and randomly reassembled. Henri Bergson conceives of a dream as being the direct link between sensation and memory, and as being constructed around what we have seen, said, desired, or done; thus the elaboration of dreams depends on memory images collected and preserved in the unconscious since earliest childhood. The same faculties function when we dream as when we are awake, but in one instance they are tense and in the other relaxed. The fullness of our mental life is available in our dreams, but with a minimum of tension, effort, or movement.

II. The importance of dreams. Doubtless the primary function of the dream is that of the "guardian of sleep." Though a person be in a state of sleep, stimuli are still present and registering on the human nervous system. Various stimuli, simple and/or complex, single and/or mingled, may prompt certain memory images or perceptions that the mind associates with those stimuli. These stimuli the unconscious mind puts together, producing the dream, and thus allows the person to continue in a sleeping condition, and not awake to consciousness.

Dreams attest to the infinite bounds of the human mind. They are a forceful suggestion of the manifold and extensive possibilities within the mind and soul waiting to be called forth. Of this arresting quality of dreams much has been written. "The slumber of the body seems to be but the waking of the soul.... It is the litigation of sense, but the liberty of reason; and our waking conceptions do not match the fancies of our sleep" (Sir J. Browne). "Dreams, these whimsical pictures, inasmuch as they originate from us, may well have an analogy with our whole life and fate" (Goethe). "Dreams have a poetic integrity and truth.... Their extravagance from nature is yet within a higher nature. They seem to suggest to us an abundance and fluency of thought not familiar to the waking experience.... A skillful man reads his dreams for his self-knowledge; yet not the details, but the quality" (Emerson). "We are not only less reasonable and less decent in our dreams but we are also more intelligent, wiser, and capable of better judgment when we are asleep than when we are awake" (Fromm).

Dream analysis is the fundamental technique of psychoanalysis. The free associations that occur within the unconscious as revealed in the dream are seen as guides to the person's motivational schema and underlying dynamics. Ideas, images, and events occurring in the dream may be interpreted as symbols of repressed anxieties, fears, or wishes. Such is suggested not only by the analysts, but by playwrights such as Goethe: "Inasmuch as they originate from us, [dreams] may well have an analogy with our whole life and fate." (For a detailed treatment, see S. B. Noegle, *Nocturnal Ciphers: The Allusive language of Dreams in the Ancient Near East* [2007].)

III. Views held by ANE culture. Ancient Eastern peoples, especially the Jews, held dreams in high regard; they noted them and sought out those who professed or were known to explain and interpret them. Dream interpreters were highly esteemed, as witnessed in the Egyptians during the time of JOSEPH (Gen. 40–41). A. L. Oppenheim (*The Interpretation of Dreams in the Ancient Near East* [1956], 84) observes that in the ANE "dream-experiences were recorded on three clearly differentiated planes: dreams as revelations of deity that may or may not require interpretation, dreams that reflect, symptomatically, the state of mind, the spiritual and bodily 'health' of the dreamer, which are only mentioned but never recorded, and thirdly, mantic dreams in which forthcoming events are prognosticated." (For a detailed treatment, see S. B. Noegel, *Nocturnal Ciphers: The Allusive Language of Dreams in the Ancient Near East* [2007].)

IV. Dreams in the OT. The Bible views the origin, and thus the importance, of dreams as being of three kinds: natural (Eccl. 5:3, 7), divine (Gen. 28:12), and evil (Deut. 13:1–2; Jer. 23:32). The major use of the word in the OT (Heb. *ḥălôm H2706*) is as a medium of a message from God (e.g., to Abimelech, Gen. 20:3; to Jacob, 31:10–11; to Laban, 31:24; to prophets, Num. 12:6; to Solomon, 1 Ki. 3:5; cf. Job 33:14–18). Another use concerns the prophetic function, the foretelling of events, including: the dreams JOSEPH related to his brethren (Gen. 37:5–11); the Egyptian baker's and butler's dreams and the interpretations by Joseph (40:5–22); Pharaoh's dream (41:1–32); GIDEON's encouragement in the Midianite camp from hearing a Midianite relate his dream of Gideon's forthcoming victory (Jdg. 7:13–15); NEBUCHADNEZZAR's dream of world empires (Dan. 2:1–45); Nebuchadnezzar's "tree" dream (4:4–28); DANIEL's dream of the four winds, the great sea, and the four great beasts (7:1–28). The Israelites were instructed to show discernment concerning dreams and interpreters, for they may be evil (Jer. 23:28). They were not to place them above the commandments of God (Deut. 13:1–5). The word is employed also as a figure of speech, an expression to denote what is fleeting or unbelievable or vain (Job 20:8; Pss. 73:19–20; 126:1; Isa. 29:7–8).

V. Dreams in the NT. All six occurrences of the Greek word *onar* G3941 ("dream") in the Gospels are found in Matthew and concern the person of our Lord Jesus. Through a dream, an angel spake to Joseph about Mary's conception of the Christ child by the Holy Ghost (Matt. 1:20–23); the MAGI were warned concerning HEROD (2:12); Joseph was warned to flee with the child and Mary to Egypt (2:13); an angel told Joseph to return to Israel from Egypt (2:19–20); Joseph was warned that Archelaus (see HEROD IV) reigned over Judea in place of his father Herod so that he (Joseph) withdrew to Galilee (2:22); the wife of PILATE suffered over Jesus and her husband to have nothing to do with Jesus, "that righteous man" (27:19). The only other passage in the NT using this word is a direct quotation of Joel 2:28 (Acts 2:17; however, note also the term "dreamers" in Jude 8). See also TRANCE; VISION.　　　　　　　　　　　　　J. M. LOWER

dress. The Bible gives considerable information as to articles worn by men and women. Sometimes the Hebrew, Aramaic, and Greek terms are clear as to the exact nature of the items, and at other times there exists doubt as to the specific shape, size, or character of the articles.

I. Descriptions in which terms for several articles of dress occur together. Several passages give descriptions of dress to be worn (including ornaments) in which a number of terms for articles of apparel are to be found together. These and other terms are found scattered throughout the Scriptures. Two NT passages are instructive as to the ancient practice of wearing outer and inner garments. In Matt. 5:40 the word *chitōn* G5945, "tunic" (inner garment) occurs first because in the legal case described the defendant was to relinquish this indispensable piece of clothing besides the more easily accessible *himation* G2668, "cloak." In Lk. 6:29, however, the order of words is reversed because in a robbery situation the outer garment would logically be stolen first, and then the inner.

Fully dressed men are described in Dan. 3:21 as being attired in "robes, trousers, turbans and other clothes," but the meaning of the Aramaic words here is uncertain. In Ezek. 16:8–14 Jerusalem is presented in the figure of a woman regally attired as a bride. She is pictured as clothed "with an embroidered dress," "fine linen," and "costly garments" (v. 10). She is shod "with leather sandals" (v. 10) and has a "beautiful crown" on her head (v. 12). She also is pictured as adorned with jewelry, such as arm bracelets, a necklace, a nose ring, and earrings (vv. 11–12). Another passage, Isa. 3:18–24, presents a fairly long list of clothing and ornamental items, and

Red granite head of Pharaoh Amenophis III with double crown (from Thebes, 1390 B.C.). Headwear was used as a sign of authority and power.

materials for beautifying, among which are finery for the ankles, headbands, crescents, pendants, bracelets, veils, headdresses, armlets, sashes, and so on (some of the words are difficult to translate).

When ABRAHAM's servant went to NAHOR in Mesopotamia to obtain REBEKAH as a bride for ISAAC, he gave her a gold nose ring, arm bracelets (vv. 22, 47), jewelry of silver and gold, and clothing (Gen. 24:22, 47, 53). The dress of the high priest AARON and his sons was to some extent specialized. In Exod. 28:4 it is said to have included a BREASTPIECE, an EPHOD, a robe, a tunic, a turban, and a sash (Exod. 28:4, 39; Lev. 8:7; 16:4). For Aaron's sons were made the tunic, the girdle, and a hat or cap that was different from that of the high priest (Exod. 28:40; 29:9; 39:28; Lev. 8:13). The kind of dress worn by Jesus and his disciples can be deduced from the instructions given by Jesus to the Twelve and to the seventy as they went out on their preaching missions (Matt. 10:5–15; Lk. 9:1–6; 10:1–12). Finally, Rev. 18:16 pictures Babylon as a woman in her finery with her fine linen garments dyed with purple and scarlet and adorned with gold ornaments, precious stones, and pearls. See also CLOTH and separate articles for individual items. For military dress see ARMOR, ARMS.

II. General terms for garments of men and women.
Some of the terms included in the passages mentioned above can also refer to clothing in general rather than to distinguish individual garments. One such widely used OT term is Hebrew *beged H955*, which indicates a garment or robe of any kind. It is used for the garment of the poor and needy (Job 22:6), including the widow (Deut. 24:17) and the prophet (2 Ki. 4:39), but also the elaborate and costly robes of the wealthy (Esth. 4:1; Zech. 14:14) and royal robes of princes and kings such as DAVID, AHAB, and JEHOSHAPHAT (1 Sam. 19:13; 1 Ki. 1:1; 2 Chr. 18:9). Likewise, the term can refer to the filthy, torn clothes of lepers (Lev. 13:45, 47) and to the holy garments of the priests (Hag. 2:12) and the high priest (Exod. 28:2). The word is used prophetically for the garments of Christ, which were to be divided among the soldiers (Ps. 22:18; cf. Jn. 19:24). It is used also for the clothing of the ordinary human being (Ps. 102:26; Prov. 25:20; Joel 2:13).

Another common term, *śimlâ H8529*, also is used in the general sense of garments as in the instructions to RUTH to put on her "best clothes" (Ruth 3:3) and in the reminder to Israel that in the wilderness wandering their clothing did not wear out (Deut. 8:4). The Lord is pictured as one who gives the sojourner clothing as well as food (Deut. 10:18), and these garments are such as a man would cover himself with at night (Exod. 22:26; cf. Gen. 9:23). JACOB instructs his household to change their garments (Gen. 35:2), and DAVID, following the death of the child born to him and BATHSHEBA, "changed his clothes" (2 Sam. 12:20). This term can be used to refer to a captive woman's clothing (Deut. 21:13), but can also indicate the garments both of men and women (22:5). Such garments could be used to hold various objects, such as military spoil (Jdg. 8:25), a sword (1 Sam. 21:9), and kitchen equipment (Exod. 12:34). This word by metathesis becomes *śalmâ H8515*, and as such is used as a general term, for example, in reference to the clothes of the Gibeonites (Josh. 9:5) and the well-preserved garments worn by the Israelites following the exodus (Deut. 29:5).

Additional Hebrew words used as general terms include *mad H4496* (Jdg. 3:16; Ps. 109:18; with reference to soldier's garments, 1 Sam. 17:38; 18:4; 2 Sam. 20:8), *kĕsût H4064* (of a woman's clothing, Exod. 21:10; of a "covering" used to keep a man warm at night, 22:26–27; Job 24:7), and *maklûl H4815* (a beautiful or choice garment, Ezek. 27:24).

In the NT *himation* can be used generally for clothing (as well as specifically for the outer

Various forms of ancient dress are apparent in this Assyrian relief.

garment), as seen in reference to an old garment (Matt. 9:16; Mk. 2:21; Lk. 5:36; Heb. 1:11; cf. Ps. 102:26), to clothing (in the plural, Matt. 27:35; cf. Jn. 19:24; Ps. 22:18), and to various pieces of clothing contributed as covering for the colt upon which Jesus rode and for the road upon which he traveled (Matt. 21:7–8; Mk. 11:7–8; Lk. 19:35–36). The *ependytēs G2087* (Jn. 21:7) can mean just "clothes" or possibly "outer garments."

III. Individual articles of clothing for the body

A. Materials used. Clothing could be made of sackcloth (Jon. 3:6) or of costly materials (Gen. 24:53; Esth. 4:4; Zech. 14:14; Rev. 18:16), and the material itself might be made of sack or coarse hair (*saq H8566*, 1 Ki. 21:27; 2 Ki. 6:30) or of fine linen as in the case of priestly garments (Lev. 6:10; 16:4) and the fine linen garments given by Pharaoh to JOSEPH (Gen. 41:42; cf. also Ezek. 16:10; Rev. 18:12, 16).

Sometimes garments were made of especially fine fabric (Ezek. 16:10, 13). Garments of such materials would be known as "soft raiment" (Lk. 7:25 KJV). The OT instructed that garments should not be woven out of two different materials (Lev. 19:19), such as wool and linen (Deut. 22:11), materials from the different animal and plant kingdoms. Some garments would contain special adornments, as the collar on Aaron's robes (Ps. 133:2), the embroidered or checker work on his coat (Exod. 28:4, 39), and tassels, as indicated in the instructions regarding the cloak of the common Israelite (Deut. 22:12). Garments ordinarily seem to have been white (Eccl. 9:8; Jn. 20:12; cf. Rev. 3:5, 18; 4:4; Matt. 17:2), but they were also dyed purple and scarlet (2 Sam. 1:24; Prov. 31:22; Rev. 18:16), and were black in the case of mourning (Rev. 6:12; cf. Herm. *Vis.* 4.1.10). Sometimes garments were scented with perfume as in the case of those of kings (Ps. 45:8) and brides (Cant. 4:11).

B. Men's garments. Men's outer garments could be designated by the previously discussed terms *beged* (see Isa. 36:22; 37:1 where Hezekiah and his men rend their clothes) and *śalmâ* (a new garment with which the prophet Ahijah clothed himself and which he tore into twelve pieces, 1 Ki. 11:29–30). A different Hebrew word, *měʿîl H5077*, is used in the OT to indicate an "exterior garment" or "robe" worn over an inner tunic or coat. It was like the *qumbaz* of modern Palestine, being a long and loosely fitting robe, probably sleeveless, worn over all other garments. It was worn by men of rank such as kings and princes (Saul and Jonathan, 1 Sam. 18:4; 24:5), foreign rulers (Ezek. 26:16), David (1 Chr. 15:27), prophets (as Samuel, 1 Sam. 15:27), and scribes (Ezra 9:3). The term is used of the high priest's "robe of the ephod," made of blue (Exod. 28:31; 39:22); around the hems were alternatively colored pomegranates and golden bells, and an opening at the top by which it could be pulled over the head (Exod. 39:22–26).

As already pointed out, the NT term *himation* could refer not only to clothing in general but also to the outer garment, "the cloak," in contrast to the *chitōn*, the inner garment, "the coat" or "tunic." It means "cloak" in Matt. 9:20, where we are told that a woman "touched the edge" of Jesus' garment, and in the passage where Jesus tells his disciples to sell their cloaks and buy a sword (Lk. 22:36). The purple robe that the soldiers put on Jesus was an outer garment (Jn. 19:2), and at the wedding supper of the Lamb, Christ's outer robe is to be inscribed with the title "King of kings and Lord of lords" (Rev. 19:16). Those who stoned STEPHEN laid aside their cloaks to free their arms for their task (Acts 7:58). The tearing of the cloak was a sign of grief (14:14).

The *peribolaion G4316*, a covering something like a cloak or robe, is pictured as perishable in comparison with the eternal God (Heb. 1:12). The *stolē G5124*, a long-flowing robe, was evidently something like the outer *himation* but of superior quality, being the best robe put on the prodigal son (Lk. 15:22); it is worn by triumphant saints (Rev. 7:14) and angels (Mk. 16:5). Scribes are characterized as walking around in these long robes (12:38). In contrast, the *chitōn* was worn next to the skin (cf. Matt. 5:40; Lk. 6:29), and was the seamless garment of Jesus for which the soldiers cast lots (Jn. 19:23–24). DORCAS had made numbers of these articles (Acts 9:39).

The principal Hebrew word to designate the inner garment was the *kuttōnet H4189*, the ordinary clothing worn by men and women next to the skin, as seen in the garments of skin worn by ADAM and EVE (Gen. 3:21). It was the cloth inner garment rent as a sign of extreme grief (2 Sam. 15:32). It had a mouth or collar (Job 30:18), and at least in some cases reached to the ankles and had sleeves (Gen. 37:3, 23, 32). These tunic-type garments, as pictured in the Beni-Hasan painting of about 1890 B.C. (*ANEP*, 3), are sleeveless, draped over one shoulder, and about calf-length. This type of garment was also worn by the high priest (Lev. 16:4) and by the priests generally (Exod. 29:8; 40:14). The *miknās H4829* ("undergarments") was a special priestly linen piece of clothing worn next to the skin to cover the body from the loins to the thighs (Exod. 28:42); it was to be used by the priest when removing ashes from the altar of burnt offering (Lev. 6:10) and by the high priest on the Day of Atonement (Lev. 16:4). A special garment was the *ʾadderet H168* ("mantle, cloak") worn by ELIJAH the prophet (1 Ki. 19:13, 19; 2 Ki. 2:8, 13–14), evidently an insignia of his office (cf. Zech. 13:4), and also by the king of NINEVEH (Jon. 3:6). Such a distinctive kind of mantle, a beautiful and costly one from Shinar, was that which tempted ACHAN (Josh. 7:21, 24).

Accessories in addition to clothing included waistcloths or belts, which were made of leather or linen (2 Ki. 1:8; Jer. 13:1); this article would be loosened at night (Isa. 5:27). Soldiers would use a belt or girdle to which was attached a sheath with its sword (2 Sam. 20:8). Adam and Eve made themselves a "girdle" or "loin covering" (Gen. 3:7), though the same word is used of the belt worn by the warrior (1 Ki. 2:5). A sash was worn by the priests (Exod. 28:4, 40) and also by a high official (Isa. 22:21). The NT mentions belts made of leather (worn by John the Baptist, Matt. 3:4; Mk. 1:6) or of gold (Rev. 1:13); they were used to bind parts of the body (Acts 21:11) and to hold up the long flowing garments for ease in traveling (1 Pet. 1:13). Money could also be kept in them (Matt. 10:9; Mk. 6:8).

C. Women's garments. The general Hebrew terms for clothing could be used also for women's garments (*beged*, Deut. 24:17; *śimlâ*, Deut. 22:5; Isa. 4:1; *lebûš*, 2 Sam. 1:24; Ps. 45:14). The inner tunic, the *kuttōnet*, was worn by women (Eve, Gen. 3:21; the king's daughter, 2 Sam. 13:18–19), and could be put off at night (Cant. 5:3). The *sādîn H6041*, a kind of "linen wrapper," is included in a list of women's lingerie (Isa. 3:23). In the NT, the regular Greek terms for outer and inner garment are also used of women's clothing (*himation*, Acts 9:39; 1 Tim. 2:9; 1 Pet. 3:3; *chitōn*, Matt. 10:10; Acts 9:39). As to accessories, the women's sash is mentioned in Isa. 3:24, presumably being similar to that worn by men.

IV. Footwear. The normal covering for the foot was the SANDAL (Heb. *naʿal H5837*), as in reference to the footwear of the Israelites in the wilderness journey (Deut. 29:5) and those worn out, patched ones of the Gibeonites (Josh. 9:5; cf. 1 Ki. 2:5), which evidences the general practice of wearing some sort of protective covering for the bottom of the foot. Sandals were removed in mourning (Ezek. 24:17, 23) and when standing on holy ground (Exod. 3:5; Josh. 5:15; Acts 7:33). Evidently there were other times, however, when a person would not wear sandals (Matt. 3:11 [*hypodēma G5687*]; Mk. 6:9 [*sandalion G4908*]; Lk. 10:4). They were taken off when sleeping (Acts 12:8). The sandal was bound on the foot by means of a thong (Gen. 14:23; Isa. 5:27; cf. Mk. 1:7). Another Hebrew word for footwear was the *seʾôn H6007* (prob. a loan word from Akk. *šēnu*, "[leather] shoe, sandal"), but its one OT use in Isa. 9:5 refers to a soldier's "boot." Women, too, wore sandals, as evidenced by Cant. 7:1 and Ezek. 16:10, in the latter case the footwear being of leather. In the Beni-Hasan painting (*ANEP*, 3) men are shown in thonged sandals but the women in shoes with a white border around the top, completely covering the foot and coming up over the ankle.

V. Headwear. Some kind of TURBAN was worn by the bridegroom (Isa. 61:10; NRSV, "garland"), by priests (Exod. 39:28; Ezek. 44:18), and by elegant women (Isa. 3:20). It could be worn as a sign of joy (Isa. 61:3; the opposite of mourning, Ezek. 24:17, 23). Other terms are used for the turban of the priest and high priest (Exod. 28:4, 37, 39–40; 29:9; Lev. 8:9, 13). This headwear may have been conical in shape (cf. *ANEP*, 46, 47, 61, 355). Women wore various kinds of headdress (Isa. 3:20, 23), a face-veil (Gen. 24:65; 38:14, 19), and a wide or large veil that evidently was to cover the upper part of the body (Cant. 5:7; Isa. 3:23). A tiara is mentioned

This portrait on limewood painted with encaustic dates to c. A.D. 55–70 and depicts a woman dressed in a tunic and cloak, wearing gold ball earrings, gold necklace with a pendant, and snail curl hairdo.

in the Apocrypha (*mitra*, Jdt. 16:8), but the Greek word does not occur in the NT.

VI. Ornaments. Ornaments worn with clothing included the finger RING, used as a symbol of authority (Gen. 41:42; Esth. 3:10; 8:2) and also as an instrument to seal official documents (Esth. 3:12; 8:8). A seal or signet was hung by a cord around the neck (Gen. 38:18), and also worn on the right hand (Jer. 22:24). A "gold ring" (Job 42:11) was the customary golden earring of the Ishmaelites (Jdg. 8:24–26), and was worn by men and women (Exod. 32:2–3); but it was also used as a woman's ornamental nose-ring (Gen. 24:47; Isa. 3:21; Ezek. 16:12). Rings are mentioned in the NT only twice (Lk. 15:22; Jas. 2:2).

Beyond the above, women were adorned with a number of ornaments (2 Sam. 1:24; Jer. 2:32), including jewels of silver and gold (Gen. 24:53; 1 Tim. 2:9). The bracelet worn on the wrist (Ezek. 23:42) or arm (Gen. 24:22, 30; Num. 31:50; Ezek. 16:11), and the chain for the neck (Ezek. 16:11), among others, were important items of adornments. Royalty wore crescent-shaped ornaments (Jdg. 8:26; as did women, Isa. 3:18) and also armlets (2 Sam. 1:10; cf. Num. 31:50; Isa. 3:20). See also JEWELS AND PRECIOUS STONES as well as separate entries on the individual items mentioned in this article. (Cf. L. Bonfante and E. Jaunzems in *Classical Civilizations of the Mediterranean*, ed. M. Grant and R. Kitzinger [1988], 3:1385–1413; V. H. Matthews, *Manners and Customs in the Bible* [1988], 117–21, 233–35; P. J. King and L. E. Stager, *Life in Biblical Israel* [2001], 259–80; D. Collon in *CANE*, 1:503–15.)   W. H. MARE

dried grapes. This item is included in the proscribed list of foods for NAZIRITES (Num. 6:3; NIV, "raisins"). All products of the VINE, even the seeds and the skins, were forbidden to the Nazirite during the time of his separation (v. 4).

Drimylus drim´uh-luhs (Δρίμυλος). Father of a certain Dositheus who saved the life of King PTOLEMY IV Philopator (3 Macc. 1:3).

drink. This English term, both as a noun and as a verb, renders a number of Hebrew and Greek terms that are used in the Scriptures in various ways. (1) In the literal and ordinary sense, many passages speak of the bodily consumption of fluids such as water, wine, grape juice, milk, and vinegar (even this activity is to be done to God's glory, 1 Cor. 10:31). (2) The language may be symbolic of the spiritual expression of one's faith in God (Isa. 32:6; Jn. 6:54–55; 7:37; 1 Cor. 10:4). (3) It can also be symbolic of Christ's acceptance of God's will (Jn. 18:11) and of the disciples' participation in Christ's suffering (Matt. 20:22–23). (4) Drinking wine is the means by which Christians participate in the sacrament of the LORD's SUPPER (Matt. 26:27; 1 Cor. 10:21; 11:25). (5) The act of "giving drink" is an indication of Christian love and compassion (Matt. 25:35–46). (6) Drink can symbolize the reception of God's judgment and wrath (Job 21:20; Ps. 75:8; Rev. 14:10). (7) It can represent as well the sinners' participation in all kinds of evil practice (Job 15:16; Prov. 4:17; 26:6). (8) The expression "drink blood" is symbolic of blood slaughter against one's enemies (Ezek. 39:18). (9)

The word can be used also to describe the process by which the earth is watered by the rain from heaven (Heb. 6:7). J. B. SCOTT

drink offering. See SACRIFICE AND OFFERINGS.

dromedary. See CAMEL.

dropsy. See DISEASE.

dross. That which is removed from metal through the smelting process; the waste matter. The Bible makes reference to the dross of SILVER on a few occasions (Prov. 25:4; Isa. 1:22, 25 [parallel to "impurities" or "alloy"]; Ezek. 22:18–19). In each case dross is a symbol of moral corruption (cf. Ps. 119:119), sometimes describing the wickedness of Israel (Ezek. 22:18). The KJV phrase "silver dross" in Prov. 26:23 (MT, *kesep sigim*) is usually emended to "like glaze" (*kspsgym* [vocalization uncertain], based on Ugar. *spsg*, "whiteness, white glaze"; see H. L. Ginsberg in *BASOR* 98 [April 1945]: 21 n. 55, and W. F. Albright's comments on pp. 24–25). Subsequent research, however, has challenged this emendation, and the TNIV restores the traditional rendering, "silver dross" (see discussion in B. K. Waltke, *The Book of Proverbs: Chapters 15–31*, NICOT [2005], 341–42 n. 42). H. M. WOLF

drought. An extended period of abnormally low rainfall. Any community whose habitat embraced a semi-arid region on the desert's fringe would certainly be painfully aware not only of the value but also of the variability of rainfall amounts that is characteristic of such a region. Rainfall maps of Israel reveal deviations from long-term mean of over one hundred percent in individual years. When successive subnormal years occur (cf. 1 Ki. 17:1), famine results. Numerous Bible passages see drought as evidence of God's withholding blessing from his people. See PALESTINE; RAIN. J. H. PATERSON

drum. See MUSIC, MUSICAL INSTRUMENTS IV.B.

drunkenness. There are many evidences in Scripture that alcoholic intoxication was one of the major social evils of ancient times. This was true of all nations in the ANE and the Mediterranean world, including Israel. Drunkenness was common among all classes, but especially among the rich and the members of the nobility (1 Sam. 25:36; 2 Sam. 13:28; 1 Ki. 16:9; 20:16). The prophet AMOS said that God would bring judgment upon the wealthy women of SAMARIA for oppressing the poor and enticing their husbands to drink with them (Amos 4:1). The fact that ELI suspected HANNAH, the mother of SAMUEL, of being inebriated while she was engaged in prayer near the tabernacle (1 Sam. 1:13–14) shows that intoxication was not unknown even in that holy place. Isaiah wrote of priests and prophets in his own time, that they reeled and staggered with strong drink and that their minds were confused with WINE (Isa. 28:7).

The effects of strong drink are vividly described in the OT. There are frequent references to the unsteady gait of drunkards (Job 12:25; Ps. 107:27; Isa. 19:14; 24:20). Drunkards stagger in their vomit (Isa. 19:14); they are given to quarrelsomeness and brawling (Prov. 20:1; 23:19–35); they begin to drink early in the morning and continue until late hours, till wine inflames them (Isa. 5:11); their minds are confused with drink (28:7); their understanding is taken away (Hos. 4:11); they neglect their duties (Prov. 31:4–5); they think they are heroes (Isa. 5:22); they end their days in poverty (Prov. 21:17; 23:20–21) and in woe and sorrow (23:29–32).

Among the better known cases of drunkenness in the OT are the following: NOAH (Gen. 9:21), LOT (19:33, 35), NABAL (1 Sam. 25:36), URIAH (who was made drunk by DAVID, 2 Sam. 11:13), AMNON (13:28), ELAH king of Israel (1 Ki. 16:9), and BEN-HADAD king of Aram with thirty-two allied kings (20:16). Priests were forbidden to drink wine and strong drink while on duty in the sanctuary (Lev. 10:9). NAZIRITES were expected to abstain from intoxicating beverages during the period of their vows (Num. 6:3–4). The Scriptures contain other strong injunctions against strong drink (Lev. 10:9; Deut. 21:20; Lk. 21:34; 1 Cor. 5:11; Gal. 5:21). Some references to drunkenness are metaphorical (Job 12:25; Isa. 19:14; Jer. 23:9; Ezek. 23:33; 39:19; Nah. 3:11). S. BARABAS

Drusilla droo-sil´uh (Δρούσιλλα G1537). A diminutive or pet name for Drusa, chosen no doubt by Herod Agrippa I (see HEROD VII) for his youngest daughter, who happened to be born in A.D. 38 when the mad CALIGULA, recently made emperor, was mourning the sudden death of his twenty-two-year-old sister Drusilla. Herod Agrippa, a companion of Caligula, was in Rome at the time. Drusus, son of TIBERIUS, had also been a protector of the young Jewish prince. It was probably in A.D. 53 that Drusilla, in her sixteenth year, was married to Azizus of Emesa, a small principality in the N of SYRIA that included Palmyra (TADMOR). A year later, FELIX, who was CLAUDIUS's unprincipled freedman and that emperor's notorious appointee to the procuratorship of Palestine, persuaded the beautiful Drusilla to leave her husband (Jos. *Ant.* 20.7.2 §§141–44). She became Felix's third wife (Suetonius, *Claud.* 28), and in that role appears briefly in the story of Paul's imprisonment at CAESAREA (Acts 24:24–27). According to JOSEPHUS, who was at the time a member of VESPASIAN's household, Drusilla's son by Felix, named Agrippa, died in the eruption of Vesuvius on 24 August 79. Whether his widowed mother died with him is not known. Josephus's account is ambiguous. E. M. BLAIKLOCK

dualism. In philosophy and theology, the view that the universe fundamentally consists of two (eternal) antagonistic entities, one good and the other evil; usually, these are identified respectively with the spiritual and the physical. Dualism has been adopted, to some degree, by numerous religions and schools of thought, including ZOROASTRIANISM, a number of Greek thinkers (see GREEK PHILOSOPHY AND RELIGION), GNOSTICISM, and Far Eastern religions to this day. In contrast, the Bible affirms the inherent goodness of the one God and of the physical world he created (Gen. 1:31). A dualistic viewpoint can have a direct effect on ethics, sometimes leading to the extreme forms of ASCETICISM (on the assumption that since the physical body is bad, it must be punished so that the spirit can flourish) and blatant immorality (since only the spirit is good, it does not matter what one does with the body). See also BODY; CREATION.

dugong. See SEA COW.

duke. This English word is used by the KJV to render Hebrew *ʾallûp H477* ("head of a thousand"), applied to the tribal chiefs of EDOM until the time of MOSES (Gen. 36:15–43; Exod. 15:15; it also renders a word for "prince" in Josh. 13:21).

dulcimer. See MUSIC.

Dumah (person) doo'muh (דּוּמָה H1874, possibly "silence" or "enduring"). Sixth son of ISHMAEL and presumed founder of an Arab community (Gen. 25:14 [cf. v. 16]; 1 Chr. 1:30). Dumat al-Jandal appears to identify with the biblical Dumah as the capital of a district known as al-Jauf. The site is a large oasis in N central Saudi Arabia, half way between the head of the Persian Gulf and the Gulf of AQABAH. Royal Assyrian and Babylonian inscriptions from the 7th and 6th centuries refer to the destruction of the Adummatu, which may be a reference to the descendants of Dumah. (See F. V. Winnett, "The Arabian Genealogies in Genesis," in *Translating and Understanding the Old Testament*, ed. H. T. Frank and W. L. Reed [1970], 171–96, esp. 193–96; I. Ephʿal, *The Ancient Arabs* [1984], 16, 116–25.)

Dumah (place) doo'muh (דּוּמָה H1873, possibly "silence" or "enduring"). (**1**) A town in the hills of JUDAH (Josh. 15:52). Eusebius's *Onomasticon* refers to a town of this name. It is usually identified with the present Khirbet ed-Deir Domeh, located some 10 mi. SW of HEBRON. See also RUMAH.

(**2**) A place that is the subject of a prophetic oracle (Isa. 21:11). Because the next words mention SEIR, some believe that the reference is to EDOM (the reading of two Heb. MSS; cf. also LXX, *Idoumaia*). Others point to the Arabian locations in the following verses (DEDAN and TEMA) and argue that this Dumah is to be identified with #1 above. (See H. Wildberger, *Isaiah 13–27: A Continental Commentary* [1997], 328–29.) H. JAMIESON

dumb, dumbness. See DISEASE.

dung. In modern usage, this term refers to manure, the excrement of animals. In some Bible versions it is sometimes used also of human waste (e.g., KJV and NRSV at 2 Ki. 18:27 [NIV, "filth"]; Ezek. 4:12, 15 [NIV, "excrement"]). Various Hebrew words can be thus rendered. One of them, *pereš H7302*, is used specifically of the waste parts of a sacrificed animal; because this waste (NIV, "offal") is unclean, it is to be burned outside the camp (Exod. 29:14 et al.). The Greek word *skybalon G5032* ("dung, filth, refuse") is used by Paul to characterize his personal achievements in comparison with the greatness of knowing Christ (Phil. 3:8; KJV, "dung"; NIV and NRSV, "rubbish"). See also DOVE'S DUNG; DUNG GATE.

dungeon. This English term is used a number of times in Bible versions, usually as a rendering of Hebrew *bôr H1014*, "pit" (e.g., Gen. 40:15; Exod. 12:29). ISAIAH uses the term in a figurative sense, saying that the MESSIAH would "release from the dungeon those who sit in darkness" (Isa. 42:7). See PRISON. S. BARABAS

Dung Gate. One of the gates of JERUSALEM in NEHEMIAH's day. From this gate Nehemiah surveyed the broken walls of Jerusalem in the night (Neh. 2:13). It was located between the VALLEY GATE and the FOUNTAIN GATE and was repaired by a certain MALKIJAH (3:13–15). It was near this gate that Nehemiah had the dedication of the wall when it was completed (12:31). Many scholars believe that the Dung Gate is to be identified with the POTSHERD GATE, which apparently led to the rubbish dump in the HINNOM VALLEY, S of the city (Jer. 19:2; 2 Ki. 23:10). (Cf. J. Simons, *Jerusalem in the Old Testament* [1952], 123–24). See JERUSALEM II.D.2 and III.A.

Dura door'uh (Aram. דּוּרָא *H10164*). A plain somewhere in the province of ancient BABYLON, in which King NEBUCHADNEZZAR erected his golden image (Dan. 3:1). The common Akkadian name *dûru* (from which the Aramaic comes) means "circuit, walled place" and was common in Mesopotamian geographical names (this meaning of the word evidently prompted the LXX to translate the name by *peribolos*, "enclosed area"). Of the three most likely identifications for the place, the first, near CARCHEMISH (Polybius, *Hist.* 5.48), was not a part of provincial Babylon, and the second, located beyond the TIGRIS not far from Apollonia (ibid., 5.52) is too far from the capital Babylon. Rather, the place may more likely be identified with the mounds or tells of Dura, a few miles to the S of the city of Babylon. (See J. A. Montgomery, *A Critical and Exegetical Commentary on the Book of Daniel*, ICC [1927], 197, 199.) W. H. MARE

Dura-Europos door'uh-yoor-oh'puhs. This (modern) compound name refers to an ancient Mesopotamian city, halfway between ALEPPO and Baghdad; the site is the modern village of Shiliyeh in Syria, on the W bank of the EUPHRATES. Although the city is not mentioned in the Bible, it is the site of significant archaeological discoveries, especially an ancient SYNAGOGUE with extensive wall paintings that constitute important evidence of early Jewish art. (See C. Hopkins, *The Discovery of Dura-Europos*, ed. B. Goldman [1979]; M. H. Gates in *BA* 47 [1984]: 166–81.)

dust. The first mention of dust (Heb. *ʿāpār H6760*) in the Bible is at the creation of ADAM (Gen. 3:16, 19; cf. 1 Cor. 15:47). Dust was thrown upon the head as a sign of MOURNING (Josh. 7:6; cf. Rev. 18:19), but could serve to indicate abundance collectively (Gen. 13:16). Jesus instructed his disciples to shake the dust (Gk. *koniortos G3155*) off their feet when leaving a home or town that would not welcome them; this act was clearly a sign of judgment (Matt. 10:14 and parallels; cf. Acts 13:51).

dwarfed. This term is used by the NIV to render Hebrew *daq H1987* ("scanty, thin, lean") in one passage that lists the physical handicaps that disqualify a descendant of AARON from offering sacrifices (Lev. 21:20; NRSV, "dwarf"). The word is used of thin cows and ears of corn (Gen. 41:3–7), of small, fine manna (Exod. 16:14), of dust (Isa. 29:5), and of a mere whisper (1 Ki. 19:12). Although the exact meaning in Leviticus is disputed, the idea of "withered" fits best (cf. BDB, 201). H. WOLF

dwelling. This frequent term (also *dwelling place*) translates a number of words from the biblical languages. It is not always clear whether the location or the structure in which one dwells (tent or house) is in view. It can refer to ZION as the habitation of God (*môšāb H4632*, Ps. 132:13) and to his dwelling place in HEAVEN (1 Ki. 8:30). The term *miškān H5438* often denotes the particular wilderness TABERNACLE where God chose to abide (Exod. 25:9 et al.; cf. Gk.

skēnōma G5013 in Acts 7:46). When it does not refer to this building, it is sometimes parallel to "houses" (Ps. 49:11) or "tents" (Jer. 30:18). Several other Hebrew terms are used with similar meaning. In the NT, Paul uses the Greek word *oikētērion G3863* with reference to the Christian's future heavenly dwelling (2 Cor. 5:2), and its synonym *katoikētērion G2999* to describe believers as "a dwelling in which God lives by his Spirit" (Eph. 2:22). H. Wolf

dye. A substance used to color materials. The actual dyeing process is not described in the Bible. Dyed materials are mentioned as early as the time of the exodus. Material for the TABERNACLE is described as "blue, purple and scarlet yarn" (Exod. 26:1, 31). Josephus described the TEMPLE materials as "woven of four stuffs, byssus as a symbol of the earth, whence the flax grows; purple, the sea which was dyed with the blood of fishes; hyacinth, the air; and scarlet, the fire" (*Ant.* 3.7.7). Dyeing, with its infinite possibility in color variations, had its secret formulae. Not until Hellenistic times were many of the secrets used in the dye industry recorded. All ancient crafts were family affairs, and the best techniques and materials were trade secrets. With the rise of the new science of chemistry in the Hellenistic period, the secret formulae were made known.

The dye used must have a natural affinity for the cloth used, or a mordant must be added to make the color fast. Wool, the most common cloth in biblical times, was easy to dye. Natural WOOL came in a variety of colors, running from white and yellow through tans and browns. By the use of different dyes on these various wools it was possible to make the "many-colored robes" (Ps. 45:14 NRSV). LINEN was more difficult to dye, but it was used in the tabernacle (Exod. 35:6) and the TEMPLE (2 Chr. 2:7). Cotton was easy to dye. Its home was INDIA and by the time of ESTHER it may have been used in PERSIA (Esth. 1:6 NRSV; the NIV has "linen"). Cotton did not appear in Palestine until the intertestamental period. Some silk was dyed before it left the Far E for ANTIOCH OF SYRIA, while some was dyed in Mediterranean cities. Fine leather also was dyed.

The most important RED used in dyeing ran from a brilliant hue to a SCARLET (Isa. 1:18). It was produced from cochineal insects. A cheaper commonly used dye was secured from the root of the madder plant. The best BLUE dye was that extracted from the molluscs *Purpura* and *Murex*, which flourished on the Phoenician coast. The expensive garments that symbolized rank and nobility were dyed PURPLE from the secretion of the mollusc. During intertestamental times indigo came into Palestine from India. Yellows were made from safflower, turmeric, and pomegranate. The dominant color of cloth described in the NT is purple (Mk. 15:17; Lk. 16:19; Jn. 19:2, 5; Acts 16:14). The Greek term *porphyra G4525* refers back to the purple shellfish, then to the purple dye obtained from the mollusc, and finally the cloth or clothing dyed purple. When the apostle PAUL went to PHILIPPI, LYDIA from THYATIRA, "a dealer in purple cloth" (Acts 16:14), was one of the first to respond to the gospel.

The best example of dye works in Palestine comes from Tell Beit Mirsim (c. 12 mi. SW of HEBRON). Six dye plants have been excavated by archaeologists, but it is estimated that approximately thirty installations had been constructed at the site. The size of the vats indicates that thread rather than CLOTH was dyed. H. Jamieson

Vat of scarlet dye, used in coloring thread for making carpets.

dysentery. See DISEASE.

Dysmas diz´muhs (Δυσμᾶς). Also Dismas, Demas. A name given in later apocryphal accounts to the repentant thief described in Lk. 23:39–43. The Greek *Acts of Pilate* (9.5) uses it to name the thief on the right, while the unrepentant thief on the left is called Gestas. Syrian sources give the names as Titus and Dumachus respectively. (Cf. J. K. Elliott, *The Apocryphal New Testament* [1993], 176–77, 218, 220.) L. Foster

Edomite cult stand (7th–6th cent. B.C.) discovered at ʿAin Ḥuṣb (biblical Tamar).

E. An abbreviation for ELOHIST; it is used (along with D, J, and P) to designate one of the supposed sources of the PENTATEUCH, according to the Documentary Hypothesis.

eagle. The eagle (referring to the imperial eagle, *Aquila heliaca*, or the golden eagle, *A. chrysaetus*) is mentioned in the OT more frequently than the other BIRDS OF PREY. Its position at the head of the Levitical table (*nešer H5979*, Lev. 11:13) suggests great size, a feature implied in several contexts (e.g., Exod. 19:4, "I carried you on eagles' wings"). Other attributes are swiftness and strength (cf. Jer. 49:22). It is said to fly high in the heavens, making its "nest among the stars" (Obad. 4).

These facts would apply to either eagles or VULTURES, and Palestine is rich in these birds. Eagles include the following: imperial, golden, spotted, lesser spotted, Bonelli's, booted, tawny, Verraux's, short-toed, and white-tailed. There are black-bearded, griffon, and Egyptian vultures. The context in Mic. 1:16 ("Make yourselves as bald as the *nešer*") suggests the griffon vulture, whose head is covered with short creamy down, giving the appearance, at a distance, of being bare. The Greek term *aetos G108* clearly refers to the vulture in Matt. 24:28 (= Lk. 17:27), "Wherever there is a carcass, there the vultures will gather." In the book of Revelation, the word apparently refers to the eagle (Rev. 4:7 et al.).

Few people today, other than experienced naturalists, can distinguish between these birds, usually seen at great distances and heights, where color cannot be distinguished. The Hebrew and Greek terms can thus be taken as embracing them all. Several figurative passages reflect interesting beliefs. The comment that an eagle "stirs up its nest" (Deut. 32:11) implies that a hen eagle deliberately disturbs the young, persuades them to take off, and then catches them on her wings if need be, but this has little basis in fact. Young birds spend long periods alone at the nest, especially as they grow older. Between eight and twelve weeks, according to species, the juvenile becomes fully feathered and begins flapping and exercising its wings, finally becoming airborne. The proverb that riches "fly off to the sky like an eagle" (Prov. 23:5) may be connected with an ancient belief that the eagle disappeared into the sun every ten years, to dive down into the sea, like the sun, and emerge refreshed. PLINY the Elder wrote of the eagle forcing her young to look straight against the sun's beam (*Nat. Hist.* 10.3 §10).

The biology of eagles in Palestine is too varied to treat. About three species breed in tall trees or, more often, on cliffs. The others are passing migrants or winter visitors. They feed mostly on live prey, which ranges from young deer to reptiles and insects. (See G. R. Driver in *PEQ* no vol. [1955]: 5–20; *FFB*, 82–85.) G. S. CANSDALE

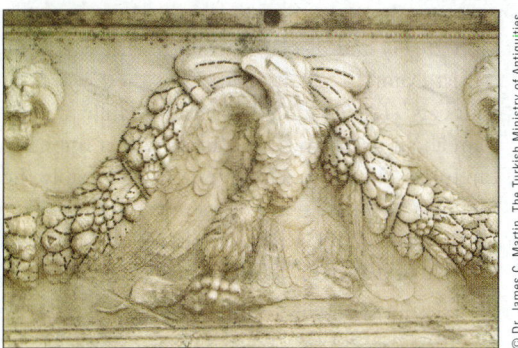

Relief of an eagle on a sarcophagus discovered in Antioch of Syria.

Eanes ee´uh-neez. KJV Apoc. variant of MAA-SEIAH (1 Esd. 9:21).

ear. The vital organ of hearing. While the Bible often refers to the ear in the physical sense, more frequently the use of the term (Heb. *ʾōzen* H265, Gk. *ous* G4044) involves understanding and obedient response. The tip of the right ear of the priests was touched with blood during their consecration (Lev. 8:23–24). A servant who spurned freedom to continue in the service of his master had his ear bored with an awl to signify his continual subservience (Exod. 21:6). Cutting off ears was a feared practice of the enemy (Ezek. 23:25). PETER's severing of the ear of the servant in the garden marks the only occurrence of *ōtion* G6065 (the diminutive of *ous*), signifying the outer ear (Matt. 26:51; Mk. 14:47).

Several idioms are worth noting. "To incline the ear" means "to give attention" (Ps. 88:2). "To uncover someone's ear" denotes "to reveal to someone" (1 Sam. 20:2; 2 Sam. 7:27). "Uncircumcised" ears are deaf to moral and spiritual instruction, not delighting whatever in the word of God (Jer. 6:10; Acts 7:51). Likewise, people with healthy ears sometimes do not hear (Jer. 5:21) or are prevented from hearing spiritually (Isa. 6:10, quoted in Matt. 13:15 et al.). "Ears that hear" is an expression that indicates obedience (Prov. 20:12; 25:12), whereas one who "stops his ears" from listening to an evil plot declares that he wants no part of it (Isa. 33:15). At the hearing of disastrous news, ears tingle (1 Sam. 3:11; 2 Ki. 21:12).

While idols cannot hear (Ps. 135:17), God's ears are not heavy (Isa. 59:1–2). God is said to open ears with the result that people gain understanding (Job 29:11) and display obedience (Isa. 50:4–5). Christ exhorted the disciples, "Put these words in your ears" (Lk. 9:44; NIV, "Listen carefully to what I am about to tell you"), a command that implies a careful and heart-searching response. Probably the "digging" of David's ears refers to this same capacity to respond to God's voice (Ps. 40:6; NIV, "my ears you have pierced"). Occasionally, the phrase "in the hearing of" equals "in the presence of" (1 Chr. 28:8; Lk. 4:21). H. WOLF

early rain. See RAIN.

earnest. As a noun, this English term is used by the KJV in the NT to render *arrabōn* G775, a word that came into Greek from a Semitic language, perhaps from the vocabulary of Phoenician traders; it is related to Hebrew *ʿērābôn* H6860, "pledge" (used in Gen. 38:17–20 and rendered by the LXX with *arrabōn*). Right down to modern Greek, where *arrabōn* can refer to an engagement ring, the word is used for a pledge in a contract.

In a derived sense an *arrabōn* in a commercial transaction came to be a down payment, as in the modern hire-purchase system (some good examples are given in MM). Both meanings, "pledge" and "first installment," are involved in each of the three NT uses of the word. Paul speaks of God's gift of the HOLY SPIRIT as the pledge and foretaste of what the Christian will enjoy later (2 Cor. 1:22; the NIV renders the word with a descriptive phrase, "a deposit, guaranteeing what is to come"); significantly the word SEAL is also used in the context. Similarly, we are told that the Holy Spirit is the earnest of that fullness of life which the Christian will enjoy after the dissolution of his earthly "tent" (5:5). The promised Holy Spirit is also described as an earnest or deposit that assures our future INHERITANCE (Eph. 1:14). The earnest, therefore, is a pledge or deposit guaranteeing that the larger and final gift will be bestowed. F. FOULKES

ear of grain. Also, *head of grain*. The seed-bearing spike of a cereal plant. See GRAIN.

earring. Earrings have been a popular ornament from the remotest antiquity, and they are mentioned frequently in the OT (Heb. *nezem* H5690, used also of NOSE JEWELS). They were often regarded as amulets or talismans (cf. Gen. 35:4), as they still are in the E. Among all oriental peoples, except the Hebrews and Egyptians, earrings were in general use by both sexes; but Exod. 32:2 shows that at least in the time of MOSES they were also worn by Israelite boys. In the W they have been largely female ornaments, but not exclusively so. The Ishmaelites customarily wore gold earrings (Jdg. 8:24–25). Prior to the 4th cent. B.C., Greek statues had the ear lobes perforated so that earrings might be hung from them. Usually they were made of gold or silver. S. BARABAS

earth. This English term, referring to the physical world in contrast to HEAVEN, usually renders Hebrew *ʾereṣ H824* (Gen. 1:1 and often, but the word can also be translated "land" or "country"; cf. *NIDOTTE*, 1:518–21) and Greek *gē G1178* (Matt. 5:5 et al.; cf. *NIDNTT*, 1:517–26). See WORLD.

earth, circle of the. A phrase used once in the Bible to emphasize God's greatness: "He sits enthroned above the circle of the earth, / and its people are like grasshoppers" (Isa. 40:22). The word for "circle," *ḥûg H2553*, is combined with "heaven" in another passage, where it appears to mean "vault" or "dome" (Job 22:14). Finally, we read that God "drew a circle on the face of the deep" (Prov. 8:27 NRSV). This last reference, especially, suggests a boundary, and some would treat the "circle of the earth" as a protective wall or mountains guarding the earth from the foreboding waters around it. Such an interpretation, however, imposes too much upon the term, which has a less precise meaning, more like "horizon" (cf. NIV). The view that the meaning is "sphere" may likewise be reading something into the word.

earth, four corners of the. This expression, referring figuratively to "the whole world," occurs twice in English Bible versions (Isa. 11:12 [NIV, "four quarters of the earth"]; Rev. 7:1). The Hebrew phrase is found also in Ezek. 24:16, where it refers to the country of Israel and is thus better translated "the four corners of the land." A more general phrase, "the corners [edges, ends] of the world," occurs in three other passages (Job 37:3; 38:13; Isa. 24:16). Similar expressions are found elsewhere. They generally allude to the outer limits of a vast expanse.

earth, new. See ESCHATOLOGY III; HEAVENS, NEW.

earth, pillars of the. Although the KJV and other versions use this phrase only once (1 Sam. 2:8; NIV, "the foundations of the earth"), there are two other passages that speak of the earth as having pillars or columns (Heb. *ʿammûd H6647*, Job 9:6 [God can make them tremble]; Ps. 75:3 [God can keep them steady]). It is possible that many people

This Byzantine graffiti on plaster at the Church of the Annunciation in Nazareth represents the gospel being taken to the four corners of the earth.

in the ANE thought of the world as supported by literal columns, but this language clearly became conventional (cf. even today such expressions as "the sun rose") and was used in poetic and metaphorical texts not to describe the physical world but to exalt God's greatness.

earthen vessels, earthenware. See POTTERY.

earthquake. A shaking of the earth's crust resulting from the release of stored elastic strain energy; this release is caused by the sudden deformation of a region of the earth that has been in a state of stress. The destruction with which earthquakes are commonly associated is caused by seismic waves that travel outward in all directions from a focus where fracturing or faulting has occurred. The focus of most major earthquakes, and those causing most destruction, is less than 25 mi. below the earth's surface. However, earthquakes as deep as 420 mi. have been recorded.

EARTHQUAKE

About 50,000 earthquakes annually are noticed without the aid of instruments, and about 100 of them are intense enough to cause substantial damage if their centers are near regions of habitation. The great majority of these earthquakes occur in well-defined zones, particularly in the circum-Pacific belt and in the Transalpine belt, which stretches from Burma across southern Asia through Iran and Turkey, to Bulgaria, Greece, and Italy. Another seismic belt corresponds with the ocean ridge system together with the apparently connected E African Rift Valley, the Levantine rift including the JORDAN Rift Valley and the region of the RED SEA. All these major seismic regions can be related to major features of the earth's crust and in particular to the margins and relative motions of "plates" of the lithosphere in the order of 30–60 mi. thick and up to several thousands of miles across.

There is considerable evidence suggesting that the present Mediterranean Sea represents only a remnant of a large ocean that once existed between Eurasia and Africa. The high seismic activity of the region is related to the general northward movement of the African and Arabian plates, together with the relative motions of two rapidly moving plates that generally correspond with the regions of Greece/Aegean Sea and western Turkey. These regions and those of eastern Turkey and Iran are seismically active throughout. Very destructive earthquakes have occurred in modern times in Iran and Turkey, while 60,000 and 45,000 people, respectively, died in earthquakes in CILICIA in A.D. 1268 and in CORINTH in A.D. 856. Hence the region of Mesopotamia, with which the beginnings of human activity in the ANE is so closely associated, and the region of the Pauline journeys have been and are both subject to considerable earthquake activity, some of it very destructive (Acts 16:26).

While the Mediterranean region is essentially one of crustal compression, the region from the Red Sea down to the E African Rift Valley is one of extension, with three crustal plates meeting at the southern end of the Red Sea. The faulting and release of strain energy as these plates have moved (and are still moving) relative to one another, and parted, has resulted in considerable seismic activity. While this is largely concentrated SE of the Holy Lands, the Jordan Rift Valley represents part of a related very large fault zone that stretches northward from the entrance of the Gulf of AQABAH for over 683 mi. to the foot of the Taurus ranges.

The geological evidence indicates that there has been, in the region of the present DEAD SEA, 67 mi. of left-hand shear movement (cf. Zech. 14:4) during the last c. 60 million years. This is associated with the separation of the Arabian peninsula from the African continent. The rifting took place in two main stages, but this major crustal dislocation, with the associated earthquake phenomena, has been moving from c. 60 million years ago to the present, and is still active both on the major faults and also the complex set of associated faults. Hence the inhabitants of the region have been familiar with the earth shaking (cf. Ps. 68:8; Isa. 13:13; Hag. 2:6), with even the mountains that were regarded as symbols of permanence being affected (Ps. 46:3).

The earthquakes during the twenty-seventh year of the reign of King UZZIAH must have been severe (Amos 1:1; Zech. 14:5), while the earthquakes at the time of the crucifixion and resurrection of Jesus Christ had marked effects (Matt. 27:54; 28:2). Earthquakes figure prominently in indications of the nature of things to be (e.g., Matt. 24:7; Mk. 13:8; Lk. 21:11; Acts 8:5; Rev. 6:12; 11:13; 16:18). Other catastrophic events, such as landslips of

Maktesh Gadol is a large crater located in the Desert of Zin that was formed through seismic activity in the area that caused the geology to buckle or push up. Subterranean erosion then caused the uplift to collapse, forming the existing crater. (View to the NE.)

unstable sediments, triggered off by earthquake activity, could explain the background to the story of SODOM and GOMORRAH (Gen. 19:24). Certainly one of the chief geological characteristics of Palestine has been its proneness to earthquakes. (See further P. Kearey and F. J. Vine, *Global Tectonics*, 2nd ed. [1996]; E. A. Keller and N. Pinter, *Active Tectonics: Earthquakes, Uplift, and Landscape*, 2nd ed. [2002].) D. R. BOWES

east. Possibly because it is the direction in which the sun rises, the E was the point of orientation for many (but not all) ANE peoples, including the Israelites. The primary Hebrew term for "east" is *qedem H7710* (lit., "in front"). In the NT, the common Greek term used is *anatolē G424* (lit., "rising"). See also WEST.

east, children (people) of the. The Hebrew phrase *bĕnê-qedem* (NIV usually, "eastern peoples") evidently describes nations located to the E of Palestine. The term *Qedem* already occurs in the Egyptian *Romance of Sinuhe* (c. 1900 B.C.) as a vague term for a region near Canaan where bedouins were seen (*ANET*, 19; N. H. Sarna, *Genesis: The Traditional Hebrew Text with JPS Translation* [1989], 173, thinks there was a specific territory named Kedem). In Gen. 29:1 we are told that JACOB journeyed to the territory of the people of the E in PADDAN ARAM (northern MESOPOTAMIA; see 28:2–7). The phrase is used in the book of Judges to designate Arabs who joined the Midianites and the Amalekites in fighting Israel (Jdg. 6:3, 33; 7:12; 8:10; cf. Jer. 49:28; Ezek. 25:4, 10). JOB is described as the "greatest man among all the people of the East" (Job 1:3); some think that northern ARABIA, EDOM, or MOAB provides the setting of the book, a location that fits Isa. 11:14 also. P. K. Hitti (*History of the Arabs*, 7th ed. [1960], 43) affirms that Arabia in general was the home of the children of the E. In a more general sense, eastern peoples (along with the Egyptians) were known for their wisdom (1 Ki. 4:30), and the wise men (MAGI) who visited the young child Jesus were also from the E (Matt. 2:1–12). See also EAST COUNTRY. H. M. WOLF

east country. According to Genesis, ABRAHAM sent the children of his concubines to this region (Gen. 25:6; NIV, "the land of the east"). It lay probably to the SE of Palestine, including part of ARABIA. MIDIAN was one of the sons involved (v. 2). See also EAST, CHILDREN (PEOPLE) OF THE.

Easter. The KJV uses this term to render Greek *pascha G4247* only in Acts 12:4; in all other instances it correctly renders the word as PASSOVER. The name *Easter* is related to *Eastre*, a Teutonic spring goddess, to whom sacrifices were offered in April (cf. Bede, *De ratione temporum* 15). The pagan festival probably gave way to the Christian celebration of the RESURRECTION OF JESUS CHRIST.

It is held by some that the annual celebration of the Lord's resurrection was observed in apostolic times. They see an intimation of Easter in 1 Cor. 5:7–8, which is very doubtful, however. The earliest written evidence for such a festival appears in the "paschal controversy" over the correct date for "the feast of the Savior's passover," which apparently began with the discussions between POLYCARP, bishop of Smyrna, and Anicetus, bishop of Rome (Euseb. *Eccl. Hist.* 5.23–25). It is likely, therefore, that by the middle of the 2nd cent. this festival was generally observed throughout the Christian church. J. C. CONNELL

eastern people. See EAST, CHILDREN (PEOPLE) OF THE.

eastern sea. This term (Heb. *hayyām haqqadmônî*, "the sea in front") occurs in three eschatological passages: Ezek. 47:18; Joel 2:20; Zech. 14:8. In the last two it is contrasted with "the western sea" (*hayyām hāʾaḥărôn*, "the sea behind"), which clearly refers to the Mediterranean (cf. Deut. 11:24; 34:2; see GREAT SEA), and so most scholars interpret "the eastern sea" as a reference to the DEAD SEA, which could be viewed as an eastern boundary. However, some scholars suggest that these terms do not refer to geographical entities but rather reflect APOCALYPTIC language, indicating cosmic (primeval, mythological) extremes, that is, the uttermost east and west (see M. Lubetski in *ABD*, 2:249–50).

East Gate. Among those who helped repair the walls of Jerusalem was a certain Shemaiah who is described as "the guard at the East Gate" (*šōmēr šaʿar hammizrāḥ*, Neh. 3:29). It was situated between the Horse Gate at its N and the Muster Gate at its S (3:28, 31; NIV, "Inspection Gate"), but its precise location is uncertain. See Jerusalem II.D.2. Presumably, this is the same as a temple gate that existed during Hezekiah's reign, for a Levite named Kore is given the title, "the keeper of [the one] to the east" (*haššōʿēr lammizrāḥâ*, 2 Chr. 31:14; cf. 1 Chr. 26:14). In addition, the book of Ezekiel uses comparable expressions to refer to one (or more?) of the gates of the future temple (e.g., *šaʿar bêt-yhwh haqqadmônî*, Ezek. 10:19 et al.); indeed, the prophet saw "the glory of the Lord [entering] the temple through the gate facing east" (43:4). (The KJV incorrectly has "east gate" in Jer. 19:2; modern versions render it Potsherd Gate.)

east wind. A scorching wind, known as the *sirocco*, which in Palestine and Egypt blows in from the desert most often in May and October. It withers vegetation (Gen. 41:6; Ezek. 17:10) and dries up fountains and springs (Hos. 13:15). Sometimes it destroys houses (Job 1:19) and ships (Ps. 48:7; Ezek. 27:26). By an E wind God drove back the waters so that the Israelites could cross the sea on dry land (Exod. 14:21). God used an E wind to bring judgment (Isa. 27:8; Jer. 4:11–12; 18:17). "God provided a scorching east wind" to afflict Jonah (Jon. 4:8). In the NT, there is a reference to the "northeaster," a violent wind in the Mediterranean that drove Paul's ship off course (Acts 27:14; see Euroclydon).   E. Russell

eating and drinking. See food; meals.

Ebal ee´buhl (עֵיבָל H6507, possibly from a root meaning "stout"). **(1)** Son of Shobal and grandson of Seir the Horite (Gen. 36:23; 1 Chr. 1:40).

(2) Variant of Obal (1 Chr. 1:22 KJV and other versions, following MT).

(3) The name of a mountain. See Ebal, Mount.

Ebal, Mount ee´buhl (עֵיבָל H6506, possibly from a root meaning "stout"; LXX Γαιβαλ but Josephus Ἥβηλος [*Ant.* 5.1.19 §69], Vulg. *Hebal*). A 3,080-ft. mound of rock with little vegetation N of the valley of Shechem. It is opposite Mt. Gerizim, and the two mountains form a steep embankment on the sides of the valley, which runs E and W. The Mount of Ebal was the scene of the reading and reaffirmation of the law before the encampment of Israel by Joshua and the priests and elders (Josh. 8:30–35). This event was a renewal of the

Looking NW toward Mount Ebal.

blessing (pronounced on Mt. Gerizim) and the cursing (on Mt. Ebal), as commanded by Moses prior to the entrance into Canaan by the Israelites (Deut. 11:29–30; the command was reiterated in 27:4–9). These mountains and the highlands S of Esdraelon were divided between the tribes of Manasseh and Ephraim. Omri, the king of the rebellious ten northern tribes, built his capital at Samaria, which was later used as the name for this whole hilly region. During the period of Assyrian conquest all these cities and the areas around Ebal were depopulated and the inhabitants carried off to Mesopotamia. New Semitic peoples were deported to Samaria, and the resultant fused culture with vestiges of the Jewish religious practice is called Samaritan.

Numerous small incidents have occurred in this area between the inhabitants and the invaders who periodically passed through these hills. The view from the summit of Mount Ebal was frequently praised by 19th-cent. travelers. Its height of almost 1,500 ft. above the valley proper makes it an excellent observation post, a fact not lost on the innumerable armies who crossed this land. The Muslims hold that the severed head of John the Baptist is buried here, and a small memorial building was erected over the traditional site in the Middle Ages. There are also ruins of early orthodox churches and what may have been monastic settlements that once stood on both Gerizim and Ebal. Excavations at the site of ancient Shechem have shown that the area was inhabited from the middle of the 4th millennium B.C., but received its greatest impetus to growth during the era of Israelite kingship at Samaria. In 1980, archaeologists discovered what appears to be a 1200 B.C. cultic site (possibly an altar for burnt offerings) on the S side of the mountain. (See *ABD,* 2:255–58; *NEAEHL,* 1:375–77.)

W. White, Jr.

Ebed ee´bid (עֶבֶד H6270, "slave, servant"; perhaps short form of עַבְדִּיאֵל H6280, "servant of God"). **(1)** Father of Gaal; the latter was an Israelite who led a revolt against Abimelech (Jdg. 9:26–35).

(2) Son of a certain Jonathan and descendant of Adin; accompanied by fifty men, he was among those who returned from the exile (Ezra 8:6; according to 1 Esd. 8:32, he was accompanied by 250 men and his name was Obed [KJV, "Obeth"], but Codex B has *Bēniōnathou* [therefore, "Ben-Jonathan"] rather than *Ōbeth Iōnathou*).

K. L. Barker

Ebed-Melech ee´bid-mee´lik (עֶבֶד־מֶלֶךְ H6283, "servant of the king"). TNIV Ebed-Melek. An Ethiopian (Cushite; see Cush) in the court of Zedekiah who received permission to rescue Jeremiah from a miry dungeon (Jer. 38:7–13). Because he risked incurring the wrath of Jeremiah's opponents, God said to him: "I will save you; you will not fall by the sword but will escape with your life, because you trust in me" (39:15–18). He is identified as a eunuch, probably referring to his official status. In addition, the term *Ebed* ("slave") was employed in Akkadian circles to designate a class of court official hired usually for a specific purpose, in contrast to the older patriarchal institution of elders or tribal heads (cf. 1 Ki. 1:9). As a proper noun, "Ebed-Melech" is known from Assyrian and Nabatean sources.

R. K. Harrison

Eben-Bohan. See Bohan.

Ebenezer eb´uh-nee´zuhr (אֶבֶן הָעֵזֶר H75, "stone of help"). **(1)** The scene of two defeats of the Israelites by the Philistines (1 Sam. 4:1–11). In the first battle, the Israelites lost 4,000 men, and in the second, 30,000. In the second battle, the ark of the covenant was taken by the Philistines and taken to Ashdod (5:1); also Eli's sons, Hophni and Phinehas, were killed. The precise location of Ebenezer is debated: some identify it with ʿIzbet Ṣarṭa, about 13 mi. E of Joppa (cf. M. Kochavi and A. Demsky in *BAR* 4/3 [Sept.-Oct. 1978]: 19–21; on an important ostracon found there, see W. H. Shea in *AUSS* 28 [1990]: 115–25); others had earlier suggested Majdel Yaba, NE of Joppa.

(2) Ebenezer also was the name given by Samuel to the stone set up by him between Mizpah and Shen to commemorate a later Israelite victory over the Philistines (1 Sam. 7:12). It is not certain whether this is a place different from #1 above. The writer may have intended a symmetry between this victory and the earlier defeat. "The Israelites were attacked at Ebenezer in the first battle and routed; in the second battle they harry the Philistines as far as Ebenezer. So the former state of affairs is exactly restored" (P. K. McCarter, Jr., *I Samuel*, AB 8 [1980], 149).   A. C. Schultz

Eber ee´buhr (עֵבֶר *H6299*, perhaps "traveler" [from עָבַר *H6296*, "to cross over"]; Ἔβερ *G1576*). **(1)** A descendant of Shem (through Arphaxad and Shelah) and an ancestor of Abraham (Gen. 10:21–25; 11:14–17; 1 Chr. 1:18–25); included in Luke's genealogy of Jesus Christ (Lk. 3:35 [KJV, "Heber"]). Practically nothing is known of him. Interest attaches to the name, which is derived from the same root as the name ʿibrî *H6303*, "Hebrew" (Gen. 14:13 et al.). See Habiru; Hebrew.

(2) Son of Abihail; he was one of seven relatives from the tribe of Gad who occupied the region E of Gilead (1 Chr. 5:13 [KJV, "Heber"]; cf. vv. 10, 14).

(3) Son of Elpaal and descendant of Benjamin (1 Chr. 8:12).

(4) Son of Shashak, also a Benjamite (1 Chr. 8:22 [KJV, "Heber"]).

(5) A priest who returned from the exile; he was the head of Amok's family (Neh. 12:20).

(6) A place or a people group mentioned by Balaam in one of his oracles: "Ships will come from the shores of Kittim; / they will subdue Asshur and Eber, / but they too will come to ruin" (Num. 24:24). The name Kittim (Cyprus) could be used generally with reference to people from the W (cf. W. F. Albright in *JBL* 63 [1944]: 207–33), while Asshur refers to Assyria or its people. The oracle, therefore, may allude to an apocalyptic battle between western and eastern forces. Some scholars think that Eber here refers to "the region across [the river Euphrates]," possibly N Syria, not far from Assyria. Others prefer to see here an allusion to Abraham's ancestor (see #1 above) and thus to the Hebrews themselves (e.g., P. J. Budd, *Numbers*, WBC 5 [1984], 271).   R. L. Harris

Ebez ee´biz (אֶבֶץ *H82*, derivation unknown). KJV Abez. A town located in the territory of Issachar (Josh. 19:20), which occupied the greater part of the fertile plain of Esdraelon (on the basis of the LXX reading *Rebes*, some emend the MT to *rēbeṣ H8070*, "resting place"). The actual location of Ebez is unknown, but suggestions include ʿAin el-Ḥabuṣ and an unnamed site 9 mi. N of Beth Shan.
        R. K. Harrison

Ebiasaph i-bi´uh-saf. Alternate form of Abiasaph.

Ebionites ee´bee-uh-nīts. A term used to describe certain Judaeo-Christian groups in the early centuries of Christianity. Although some early sources (e.g., Tertullian) suggested that these sects took their name from an individual with the supposed name of Ebion, it is more likely that the term and title (from Heb. *ʾebyôn H36*, "poor") was at first one of reproach indicating their stress upon poverty and asceticism, partially as a literal interpretation of Matt. 5:3.

I. Ebionite sects. The origin of these sects is shrouded in mystery. It is clear from early Christian literature and especially Acts, however, that certain Judaizing tendencies manifested themselves from the very first in the Jerusalem church (cf. Acts 15; Gal. 2). See Judaizer. After the fall of Jerusalem in A.D. 70 and again when Hadrian destroyed the city after the Bar Kokhba rebellion, A.D. 132–35, Jewish Christianity lost its standing in Jerusalem, and the church there came under the control of a Gentile bishop. It is known from the writings of the fathers that at least two Jewish Christian groups were known: one heretical in its Christology and resentful of Gentile Christianity, the other friendly to (though distinct from) Gentile Christianity and orthodox in its view of Christ. (See Justin, *Dial.* 47; Irenaeus, *Haer.* 1.26.2; 3.21.1; 5.1.3; Tertullian, *Praescr.* 33; Hippolytus, *Haer.* 7.34; 9.13–17; Epiphanius, *Pan.* 30. This material is brought together in A. F. J. Klijn and G. J. Reinink, *Patristic Evidence for Jewish-Christian Sects* [1973].)

It is possible to distinguish three Judaeo-Christian groups sometimes loosely referred to as "Ebionites": (a) the so-called Nazarenes, who accepted the supernatural birth of Jesus without developing a Christology such as that of Chalcedon; (b) Pharisaic Ebionites, who recognized Jesus as Messiah but denied his virgin birth and hated Paul; (c) Gnostic or Essene Ebionites, who tended toward a docetic Christology (cf. *ERE*, 5:140–41; see Docetism).

As the early Christian sources indicate, generally the Ebionites were known for two doctrines: adherence to the Jewish law (at least for Jews if not for Gentiles) and a tendency to interpret the Person of Christ as merely a man on whom the Holy Spirit descended at his baptism. The exact relationship of the Ebionites to the Dead Sea Community and/or the Essenes, as well as to the older sect known as the Recabites, is still a matter of conjecture, although some scholars have tended to see basic similarities if not some type of direct relationship. (See H. J. Schoeps, *Jewish Christianity: Factional Disputes in the Early Church* [1969].)

II. The Gospel of the Ebionites. Only Epiphanius (d. A.D. 403) describes a distinctive gospel used by this sect; modern scholars refer to it as the *Gospel of the Ebionites*, but the patristic evidence is ambiguous and even contradictory. Sometimes this writing is identified with or confused with either the *Gospel to the Hebrews* or the *Gospel of the Nazarenes*. The meager traces of this document in the extant quotations of Epiphanius are peculiar in their stress upon vegetarianism in the NT accounts of John the Baptist and Jesus. (For further information, including an English translation of these quotations, see *NTAp*, 1:166–71.) See also Apocryphal New Testament I; Hebrews, Gospel of the; Nazarenes, Gospel of the.   D. Lake

Ebla ebʹluh. An ancient city in N Syria, identified with modern Tell Mardikh, about 40 mi. S from the city of Aleppo. Ebla, with its surrounding towns and villages, was the largest in the region. At its height, the city reached a size of 140 acres with a population of perhaps 15,000 to 20,000. It flourished in the middle of the 3rd millennium B.C., but remained a center of some influence well into the 2nd millennium. For this reason scholars have related this latter emergence of Ebla to the cities of nearby Mari and Alalakh and their cuneiform archives of the 18th–17th centuries B.C. However, its period of greatest interest lay some 600 years before that time. Texts from 3rd-millennium Mari also mention Ebla in this earlier era.

I. Excavation. Since 1964 P. Matthiae has excavated at Tell Mardikh, an impressive mound chosen for its dominance of the surrounding region. Within a few years, he had concluded that this site was to be identified with Ebla. This was based on its mention in other sources, such as those from Mari to the E and Alalakh to the W. With the discovery of texts at Ebla itself, this identification was confirmed. The most exciting discovery occurred as the archaeologists were digging the royal palace. In 1975, Matthiae uncovered thousands of cuneiform tablets and fragments in a room near to the throne room. These included some 1,757 texts that were whole or nearly complete, nearly 5,000 fragments with at least ten lines of writing, and many thousands of smaller fragments. Wooden shelving covered the walls of the room, and the cuneiform tablets were apparently stacked upright in rows leaning against the walls. The wood had disintegrated but the remaining piles of tablets found on the floor of the archive room by the excavators revealed a systematic pattern.

The tablets dated to the 24th and 23rd centuries B.C. With the passing of three decades, a sufficient amount has been learned about the texts to conclude that most are administrative (about 80 per cent). These could contain accounts of textiles and metals, tax deliveries, and temple offerings. Many of these included detailed listings for each month. These were then transferred into summaries on smaller tablets that would be stored permanently in the archive room. Labels were found that summarized the contents of groups of tablets and their information. Some describe the movement of tablets and their contents in a manner that indicates the process was ongoing when it was suddenly cut short by the violent destruction of the city.

There were also some lexical texts, a number of letters, a few literary compositions, and one or two treaties. Although two international teams of scholars have been at work on the decipherment, translation, and publication of these texts, much remains to be done on all fronts. A major part of the problem is the nature of the script used to write the texts, namely, cuneiform. The ancient scribes employed many hundreds of different signs in writing. Some of these resemble signs already identified from texts found in contemporary ANE archives. Further, the identification of a given sign does not guarantee the correct reading. There are multiple values for some signs and sometimes not even the values that are known are appropriate for the Ebla syllabary. However, many appear to be drawn in new and unexpected ways. The resultant difficulties in reading the signs have made progress on translation slow and difficult, especially for the more literary and diplomatic texts. Unfortunately, these are the ones often of most interest.

II. History and religion. The absence of royal inscriptions means that little of certainty can be known about the sequence of kings and historical events at Ebla between 2400 and 2250 B.C. The administrative documents reveal only two persons with the title "king of Ebla." These are Igrish-Halam and Irkab-Damu. A certain Ishar-Damu may also have reigned as a king, according to one document. In addition, on a list of offerings to dead kings, some nine kings precede Irkab-Damu: Igrish-Halam, Adub-Damu, Kum-Damu, Ishar-Malik, Enar-Damu, Badamu, Ibidamu, Agur-Lim, and Abur-lim. A longer list of offering recipients begins with these kings and adds another fifty names to the list (tablet TM [Tell Mardikh] 74.120; see A. Archi, ed., *Eblaite Personal Names and Semitic Name-Giving* [1988], 212–13). These may be tribal chiefs from various places within the kingdom who were locally venerated.

At the end of the reign of the last apparent ruler of Ebla, Ishar-Damu, the site was destroyed by fire. The cause of this event is not known but many scholars assume that the most likely explanation was the growing empire of Sargon of AKKAD. Ebla was rebuilt and reappears in Ur III texts from the end of the 3rd millennium. Archaeology attests a flourishing city at the site during the period of 1800–1600, and it is reasonable to assume that families such as those of the patriarchs of Gen. 12–36 knew of its existence. It was destroyed by the HITTITES from Anatolia (ASIA MINOR) around 1600, in the same events that brought about the end of the Old Babylonian dynasty at that city. In the following centuries HURRIAN poets from places not far from Ebla remembered the city in poems and associated it with their chief god, Teshub.

The economic texts and titles demonstrate a complex bureaucracy with taxation and labor requirements for the citizens of Ebla as well as those living in the surrounding towns and farms. Some of these systems were borrowed from earlier forms attested to the S in Sumerian culture (see SUMER), while others were innovative. As in the contemporary Old Kingdom of EGYPT, the economy was centrally controlled in a manner that placed the royal family at the apex. Not only the king, but both male and female members of the royalty played a prominent role in the economy and politics of the kingdom. Beneath the king and the royal family were many officials, religious, military, and civil, who ensured the functioning of the state. In this respect, the organization anticipated the bureaucracies of later Syrian states such as Alalakh and UGARIT, as well as the structure that flourished under King SOLOMON (cf. 1 Ki. 4).

In such a system villages and towns could be inherited or sold, according to the wishes of the king or to whomever he gave them (1 Ki. 9:11, 16). However, Ebla as an epitome of increased urbanization (i.e., city building) in Syria in the 3rd millennium, a fact attested as well by the extensive palace and government architectural remains at the site, also needed to deal with the remnants of small town and tribal society. Therefore, the clan and tribal elders, along with members of leading families, played a significant role in the administration of the kingdom of Ebla.

Ebla appears as an early example of a north Syrian population and power center that survived in a generally inhospitable climate in comparison with its distant neighbors in the EUPHRATES flood plain to the E and S. Therefore, it depended on the control of a large area of pasturing flocks and for growing what crops the limited rain would allow. Its hegemony extended over other smaller urban centers which, while retaining an element of independence in their own affairs, ceded to Ebla such matters as grazing rights and agreements to allow goods to circulate freely.

The king lists mentioned above demonstrate that former rulers were regarded as worthy of receiving sacrifice and therefore in some sense divine. In addition to a sacrificial cult, there is evidence of divination practices, to determine favorable times and actions. The deities of Ebla were numerous and included names that may be recognized in the Bible: BAAL, Dagan (DAGON), and RESHEPH. In addition, some names such as Adamma, the earth mother, remind us of the same form of a Hebrew word used in Gen. 1–3 to identify the ground or soil from which the man was created. The practice of a sacrificial cult to dead kings, the use of divination, and the multiplication of deities were all condemned in the Bible (Exod. 20:3; Deut. 18:11).

III. Relation to the Bible. Soon after the discovery of these texts, amazing claims were made regarding their relation to accounts in the Bible. For example, some claimed that the cities of the plain in Gen. 14 were named on one text. From hindsight, these observations appear to have been premature. No text has ever been published substantiating such claims. The town and city names identified so far can be located in the region around Ebla, in northern Syria. The disappointments raised by these early pronouncements, the difficulty of translation, and the recent scholarly tendency to discount any authentic biblical records before 1000 B.C. led to a lack of interest in the study of the Ebla texts for comparative purposes. In part, this is reasonable because the Ebla texts, themselves extending over perhaps three generations, date centuries before anyone would place even the figure of ABRAHAM. Therefore, it cannot be expected that direct parallels with biblical events would occur.

Further, earlier claims that Ebla lay at the center of a vast empire must now be rejected. It was perhaps the most significant city state of its time and is of interest in its own right. However, it had no direct or explicit relation to any events in the Bible. Before Abraham, the narratives of Gen. 1–11 do not betray any direct parallels. There has been no creation story or flood account published from the Ebla texts, nor do the smaller narratives of the fall (ch. 3), the son of God and daughters of men (6:1–9), and the tower of BABEL (12:1–9) resemble anything from this ancient site. Moreover, the scene of activity in the remainder of Genesis as well as the other early literature of the Bible is for the most part set hundreds of miles to the S in Palestine. Even the occasional focus to the N involves regions other than Ebla. There is little in the way of direct connection. Rather, one must look at certain personal names and a few general matters of culture and religion that are addressed in later biblical texts for similarities, let alone insights.

Ebla's role in illuminating the Bible may be more productive from the standpoint of language and vocabulary. Insofar as its language, Eblaite, may be grouped within the W Semitic family of languages, it remains one of the earliest of such languages yet discovered (however, some scholars believe that Ebalite should be identified as E Semitic; see LANGUAGES OF THE ANE II). Linked with contemporary languages found in texts from Mari and N Babylonia, it may form the background for the development of biblical Hebrew. Ebla itself is found in N Syria, in the general region that the Genesis records suggest that the PATRIARCHS remembered as their ancient homeland (Gen. 24:10–15; 28:1–5), a view also expressed by many of the names in Abraham's genealogy that can be associated with place names in the region (11:10–32). However, even here caution must be exercised. Earlier attempts to associate Ebrium, king of Ebla, with EBER in Gen. 10:24 must be rejected. Ebrium was an important official but probably not the sovereign of the city. In addition, it is not certain that the roots behind Ebrium and Eber are related, so the names themselves may be different.

Clear examples of linguistic affiliation may be found in the title that officials at Ebla use, such as *malikum* and *šapiṭum*, evidently cognates of Hebrew *melek* H4889, "king," and *šōpēṭ* (from *šāpaṭ* H9149), "judge, leader." Then there are the similarities in custom. Notice has been made of a ritual text from Ebla that seems to make use of an animal such as a goat to convey cultic defilement away from the people. This has been compared to Lev. 16 (cf. I. Zatelli in *VT* 48 [1998]: 254–63). A law found in a treaty at Ebla that forbids the cursing of a deity or a king recalls Exod. 22:28. Later in the treaty laws mandate serious fines (fifty rams) for homicides (unpremeditated) that may occur as a result of fights that arise at public gatherings during religious festivals (perhaps this was expected to appease blood vengeance, unlike the biblical use of CITIES OF REFUGE in Deut. 19 and Josh. 20). Comparisons of this sort may be found in later Semitic archives, such as Mari, Ugarit, and Alalakh. However, the Ebla evidence projects this common culture that the patriarchs shared back into a period centuries earlier than previously thought. Therefore, there is no longer any doubt that the patriarchs, despite their nomadic lifestyle, continued a much older and sophisticated culture.

In addition to general parallels in terms of vocabulary, the personal names of people in the Ebla texts preserve many similarities with names found in the earliest chapters of the Bible. For example, the name ADAM occurs in the Ebla texts as a personal name (or part of one) as well as a name of a deity. This is interesting because later on the name of Adam ceases to be used. By the time of Israel's monarchy it is never used within or outside the Bible. This remains true until the Hellenistic period, when its reappearance reflects the reemergence of the biblical name. Therefore, its more frequent occurrence in the earliest of W Semitic texts, such as those at Ebla, attests to the antiquity of the name. Other personal names of Gen. 1–11, and the elements within them, also occur at Ebla. These include names such as EVE, NOAH, JABAL, JUBAL, and HARAN. In particular, Noah and Haran are unusual names whose early attestations in the Ebla texts of the 3rd millennium are not found so frequently in later millennia. Therefore, they testify to the authentic antiquity of these names in the narratives and genealogies of the first eleven chapters of Genesis.

Future research and analysis of the Ebla texts may yield new comparisons and insights into the Bible. However, it is certain that future research into these ancient tablets will yield important new insights into the life and culture of the 3rd millennium West Semitic world. (See further G. Pettinato, *Ebla: A New Look at History* [1991]; C. H. Gordon et al., *Eblaitica: Essays on the Ebla Archives and Eblaite Language*, 4 vols. [1987–2002]; R. D. Biggs in *ABD*, 2:263–70; L. Milano in *CANE*, 2:1219–30.)

R. S. HESS

ebony. In his oracle against TYRE, the prophet EZEKIEL says that traders paid this great city "with ivory tusks and ebony" (*hobnim H2041*, Ezek. 27:15). The reference is surely to the *Diospyros ebenum* (or *D. ebenaster*), a large tree of the family *Ebenaceae* that produces a hard and durable timber. The outside is soft and white, but the central part or heart of the trunk is hard and black. This central portion is often only two feet in diameter. (The *Diospyros* can be a date tree or date plum, called *D. lotus* in W Asia; it is not the date palm [see PALM TREE].) Ezekiel is referring to the luxury importations from Ceylon and India to Palestine, for it is undoubtedly from these countries that the ebony came. Ebony polishes well and even today is used for carvings of elephants and the like. It is obvious that IVORY and ebony were used together by the ancients just as they are today in the E. The pure white ivory goes well as a contrast to the jet-black, polished ebony.

W. E. SHEWELL-COOPER

Ebron ee'bruhn (עֶבְרֹן *H6306* [not in NIV]). KJV Hebron. A town located in the territory allotted to ASHER (Josh. 19:28 NRSV). A few Hebrew MSS, however, read ʿabdôn *H6278*, and this variant has been followed by the NIV; see ABDON.

R. K. HARRISON

Ebronah i-broh'nuh. KJV form of ABRONAH.

Ecanus i-kay'nuhs. KJV Apoc. form of ETHANUS (2 Esd. 14:24).

Ecbatana ek-bat'uh-nuh (Aram. אַחְמְתָא *H10020*, possibly "citadel"; some MSS of LXX Ezra 6:2, Ἀμαθα, but elsewhere Ἐκβάτανα). KJV Achmetha. Ecbatana was the Greek name of the capital of the empire of the Medes (see MEDIA), and later one of the capitals of PERSIA and of the PARTHIANS (the Old Persian name of the city was Hangmátana, "the place of assembly"). Ecbatana is mentioned several times in the apocryphal books. In TOBIT it was the home of Reguel and Sarah his daughter (Tob. 3:7 et al.). It was fortified by the Median king Arphaxad in his war against NEBUCHADNEZZAR (Jdt. 1:1–2, 14), and to it ANTIOCHUS Epiphanes IV fled shortly before his death (2 Macc. 9:1–3). The site is occupied today by Hamadan, Iran, on the plain near the NE foot of Mount Alvand, c. 175 mi. SW of Teheran. The city owed its importance to its strategic location on the caravan route from Mesopotamia to the Persian plateau. The pleasant summer climate accounts for its popularity as a resort city.

According to the Greeks (Herodotus, *Hist.* 1.96), Ecbatana was founded by the half-legendary Deioces the Mede c. 678 B.C., who also established the Median dynasty, but scholars question the

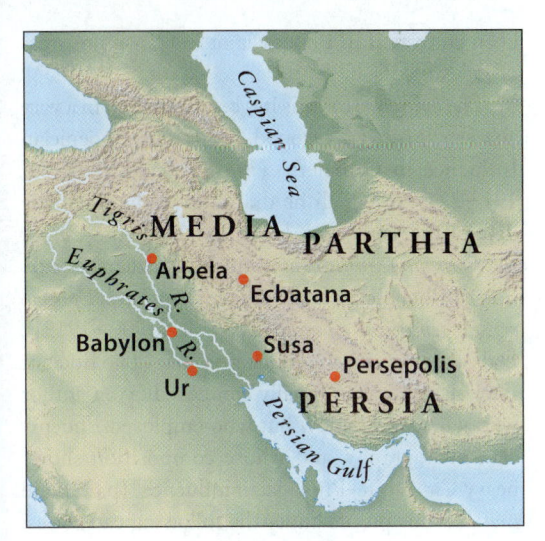

Ecbatana.

with the name of Darius I, and also column bases of Artaxerxes II. These indicate that Darius I and ARTAXERXES II built palaces in Ecbatana. The so-called tomb of ESTHER and MORDECAI shown today in Hamadan is probably the tomb of the wife of the Sassanid king, Yazdegird (A.D. 399–420). (See A. T. Olmstead, *History of the Persian Empire* [1948], 29–30, 37–38, 162; A. L. Oppenheim, *Ancient Mesopotamia* [1964], 134, 394; C. H. Gordon, *The Ancient Near East* [1965], 255, 281–82; E. M. Yamauchi, *Persia and the Bible* [1990], ch. 8.)

A. C. SCHULTZ

accuracy of this tradition. The Median empire may have been established by Phraortes, the son of Deioces, who built Ecbatana to check the advance of the Assyrians. A description of the city is given by Herodotus (ibid.) and Polybius (*Hist.* 10.27). It was surrounded by seven concentric walls, the inner walls rising above the outer, since the city was on a hill. Each wall was of a different color. The citadel was also a treasure house, the city famous for its luxury and splendor. Ecbatana was captured by CYRUS the Great of Persia from Astyages in 550 B.C., and he made it his summer residence. According to Ezra 6:2 (= 1 Esd. 6:23), the imperial records of the time of Cyrus were kept here, and here DARIUS found the decree of Cyrus authorizing the rebuilding of Jerusalem. It was taken from the last Achaemenid by ALEXANDER THE GREAT in 330 B.C. He destroyed the walls and looted the palaces.

Ecbatana became the summer capital of the Parthian kings, maintaining its traditional reputation, but under the Sassanids it declined. After the Islamic conquest, the modern city of Hamadan took its place. The ruins of the ancient citadel of Ecbatana lie outside the present city, and on the slope of Mount Alvand are Achaemenid inscriptions. Modern Hamadan stands on most of the ancient city, which prevents extensive archaeological excavations of the site. In 1923, two foundation plaques of silver and gold were found, inscribed

Ecclesiastes, Book of i-klee´zee-as´teez. One of the WISDOM books of the OT, though it belongs to a special genre of philosophical discourse of which there are no other extant examples in ANE literature. In the Hebrew Bible it is included among the Five Scrolls (*Megilloth*, along with Ruth, Song of Solomon, Lamentations, and Esther) and bears the title Qoheleth (also Koheleth), from the Hebrew word *qōhelet* H7738, which appears in the opening statement and elsewhere in the book (Eccl. 1:1–2, 12; 7:27; 12:8–10). This term has been interpreted in various ways, such as "someone who calls [or speaks in] an assembly [*qāhāl* H7736]" and "a collector of sayings," but it is often rendered "teacher" or "preacher." The SEPTUAGINT translates it with Greek *Ekklēsiastēs* (lit., "a member of the assembly"), a word that was taken over into Latin in the VULGATE translation and thence into English.

    I. Authorship and time of composition
   II. Other internal evidences as to authorship
  III. Doctrinal message of Ecclesiastes
  IV. Outline of the contents of the book
   V. Final summation

I. Authorship and time of composition. The book purports to have been composed by "the son of David, king in Jerusalem" (Eccl. 1:1), that is, by SOLOMON. Since it consists of a review of his life-long search for truly valid goals in human existence, it would have been a product of his old age, c. 940 B.C. The Solomonic authorship of this book, however, is regarded by most modern authorities as purely fictional, composed by some unknown later author upon the basis of the experiences and insights of the historic Solomon. On the basis of supposed allusions to the misfortunes of the Israelite nation down through the Babylonian EXILE, as well as on allegedly late characteristics of language, Ecclesiastes has been assigned a 5th-cent. date by such conservative authors as E.W. Hengstenberg, F. Delitzsch, H.C. Leupold, and E. J. Young, and 3rd-cent. or later by liberal scholars.

These allegations of spuriousness (or fictional character) are not justified by the objective evidence. Some scholars admit that "Linguistically the book is unique. There is no question that its language has many striking peculiarities" (J. Muilenberg in *BASOR* 135 [Oct. 1954]: 21). In other words, it differs from all other books of the OT of whatever age; it equally differs from all known intertestamental Hebrew works, such as ECCLESIASTICUS (which, however, has been greatly influenced by it) and the Qumran sectarian literature (see DEAD SEA SCROLLS). No significant resemblances can be made out with the extant pre-Christian Hebrew literature of any period in respect to vocabulary, grammar, or style. It is quite as dissimilar to 5th-cent. productions (e.g., Zechariah, Ezra, Nehemiah, Esther, and Malachi) as to any writings of the pre-exilic period. This poses an insuperable difficulty to those who, like Delitzsch and Young, date the book around 430, or to W. J. Beecher (in *ISBE* [1929], 2:896), who puts it at around 400 B.C. The earliest MS fragments come from Qumran Cave 4 and date from the 2nd cent. B.C., and so there is no possibility of dating it after the sectarian period (to whose writings it is altogether dissimilar).

The true explanation for the peculiar language and style of Ecclesiastes is to be found in its genre. As in ancient Greek literature, the dialect or style in which each genre (such as the epic, the elegiac, the love poem, etc.) was first brought to classic perfection became a binding convention upon all who would in later ages compose in that genre, so also in ancient Semitic and Egyptian circles a peculiar style became conventional for each genre. It so happens that there are no other surviving examples of the genre to which Qoheleth belongs (the philosophical disquisition), and there is no literary parallel with which to compare it. The book, however, has a noteworthy affinity to early Canaanite and Phoenician characteristics. It is thus likely that Solomon, if he was the true author, wrote in a genre that had been cultivated in Phoenicia or in Canaanite areas of Palestine itself.

The evidence for this has been gathered in a very able article by M. J. Dahood, "Canaanite-Phoenician Influence in Qoheleth" (*Bib* 33 [1952]: 30–52, 191–221), in which he draws upon the linguistic data of the 14th-cent. Ugaritic tablets, the *Corpus inscriptionum semiticarum*, and M. Lidzbarski's edition of Phoenician and Punic inscriptions (*Ephemeris für semitische Epigraphik*, 3 vols. [1900–1915]). Dahood comes to the conclusion that "The Book of Ecclesiastes was originally composed by an author who wrote in Hebrew but who employed Phoenician orthography, and whose composition shows heavy Canaanite-Phoenician influence" (p. 32). He marshals his proofs under the following categories: (1) orthography, (2) inflections, pronouns, and particles, (3) syntax, and (4) lexical borrowings or analogies.

A. Orthography. Under Phoenician spelling he lists many instances of variants (differences between the MT and the ancient versions of Ecclesiastes) that are most easily accounted for by an original text in which no vowel letters were written (final consonants used as vowels were introduced into Heb. spelling at least by late 8th cent., judging by the SILOAM Inscription). Thus it was possible to supply differing final vowels affecting the number and gender of verbs. For example, the MT of Eccl. 1:13 reads *naʿăśâ* ("was made") whereas some of the versions reflect the reading *naʿăśû* ("were made"); similarly in 1:16, where MT has *hāyâ* ("was"), but the versions appear to read *hāyû* ("were"). These variants indicate that the original author spelled the words without the final letter (thus *nʿś* and *hy*), which was the normal Phoenician spelling until the 3rd cent. B.C. or later, and that later readers could interpret those words as ending in either *-ā* or *-ū*. In medial position, notice 3:16, which reads *haṣṣedeq* ("the righteousness") in MT, but *haṣṣaddiq* ("the righteous one") in the versions.

B. Inflections and particles. As for inflections, Phoenician uses the *-t* ending even for feminine nouns in the absolute state; so there are nouns like *mattat* H5522 ("gift," Eccl. 3:13; 5:18), as in a 7th-cent. Phoenician inscription from Ur (ibid., 46).

Egyptian craftsman making alabaster vessels. "What does man gain from all his labor at which he toils under the sun?" (Eccl. 1:3).

Even more distinctive are prepositions with the same ending, such as ʿal-dibrat ("with regard to") in 3:18; so Phoenician uses ʿlt as well as ʿl for "upon." As for the relative pronoun še- (or ša- H8611, which occurs 67 times in Ecclesiastes) alongside ʾăšer H889 (89 times), it is very close to the Phoenician ʾš ("who, what"). It occurs elsewhere in the OT largely in writings containing N Israelite elements. Closely related is the combination mah-šše- ("whatever," 1:9; 3:15; et al.), which appears as mʾš in the 9th-cent. Kilamuwa Inscription. The same inscription also uses the interrogative "who?" (m or my) five times in the sense of "whoever"; compare this with the four occurrences in Ecclesiastes (1:9; 3:15; 5:9; 9:4) where the same indefinite interrogative appears—a far higher ratio than in any other OT book.

As for the definite article ha-, "the," its sporadic and irregular use conforms perfectly with Phoenician usage, where ʾyt, the sign of the accusative, often precedes a noun lacking the article (contrary to the rule in Heb. grammar), just as Qoheleth often uses ʾēt before an anarthrous noun. Alternatively, he leaves out the article before an adjective modifying a definite noun—which is also good Phoenician usage. (This cannot be explained as a translation from a late Aram. original that no longer used the emphatic state -ā for definite nouns only; it is now known from the 1st-cent. *Genesis Apocryphon* that even by that period the emphatic was still restricted to definite nouns.) As for particles, the conditional ʾillû H467 ("if," Eccl. 6:6) is found in the 11th-cent. Ahiram Inscription spelled as ʾl; hence it is not to be regarded as derived from Aram. ʾillāʾ, as some have argued.

C. Syntax. The peculiar combination of infinitive absolute plus the independent pronoun (e.g., wěšabbēaḥ ʾănî, "And I praised," Eccl. 4:2) occurs four or five times in Qoheleth and only once elsewhere in the OT (cf. the combination qtl ʾnk in the Karatepe Phoenician inscription, as well as in the even earlier TELL EL-AMARNA correspondence [EA, 113:40–42]). Even the use of the independent personal pronoun as a linking verb, which occurs quite often in Qoheleth (e.g., Eccl. 3:13), is shown to be a Phoenician usage, as well as Aramaic and Mishnaic Hebrew. For example, the 5th-cent. Yehawmilk Inscription states that "he was a righteous king" (kmlk ṣdq hʾ).

D. Lexical affinities. Ecclesiastes uses ʾādām H132 for "man" in the nongeneric sense (contrary to normal Heb. practice); cf. the Azitawadda 9th-cent. inscription, which uses ʾdm five times and ʾš (Heb. ʾîš H408) only once. The characteristic phrase "under the sun" occurs in no other ancient NW Semitic language except Phoenician (cf. the inscriptions of Tabnit and Eshmunazar at Sidon). Even the term rěʿût H8296 ("a striving, chasing, desire"), which occurs seven times in Qoheleth and is usually explained as a borrowing from Aramaic, occurs in Punic inscriptions: once meaning "decree, decision," once meaning "pleasure, good will." An unusual pair of verbs occurs in Eccl. 10:18: "If a man is lazy, the rafters sag [mākak H4812]; / if his hands are idle, the house leaks [dālap H1940]." It is most significant that these two verbs occur nowhere else in combination except in Ugaritic (*UT*, 68:17). The distinctive climax series "seven ... eight" occurring in Eccl. 11:2 (nowhere else in OT except Mic. 5:5) appears at least six times in Ugaritic literature (*BASOR* 76 [Dec. 1939]: 5–11). The distinctive phrase *šemen rôqēaḥ* occurs nowhere else besides Eccl. 10:1 ("perfumer's oil," NRSV) and in *UT*, 120:5. But the noun *rqḥ* ("perfumer") occurs at least five times in Phoenician and Punic inscriptions. It is unknown in Aramaic, although *ruqqû* appears in Akkadian as "compound ointment."

Dahood's article closes with an impressively large assortment of mercantile terms (e.g., *yitrôn H3862*, "gain," Eccl. 1:3 and frequently; *ḥesrôn H2898*, "deficit," 1:15). This evidence confirms still further the theory that the genre to which Qoheleth belongs was borrowed from a Phoenician prototype. Nor should it be forgotten (although Dahood does not discuss this) that Israel in the age of Solomon was more deeply involved in international trade than at any other time in its history, before or since (1 Ki. 9:26–28; 10:28–29). (Dahood attempts to retain an early postexilic date on the basis of a theory that a substantial colony of Jews took refuge in Phoenicia after the fall of Jerusalem in 587 B.C., and that the unknown author composed Ecclesiastes there; but there is not a shred of historical evidence for any such colony, and it seems unlikely that a Phoenician subject to Nebuchadnezzar's authority—apart from a revolt by Tyre resulting in the complete destruction of its mainland city—would have dared to harbor refugees from the wrath of the Chaldeans subsequent to the assassination of Gedaliah. All the refugees of whom there is any recorded knowledge fled southward to Egypt.)

In view of the prominence of the Red Sea port of Elath during Solomon's reign, there is every reason to believe that he had extensive contacts with India. He might therefore have borrowed such terms as *pardēs H7236* ("park") and *pitgām H7330* ("official decision") from Sanskrit rather than from Persian (which is rather closely related to Sanskrit, the classical language of India). The verb *šālaṭ H8948* ("to have dominion, authority") is alleged to be postexilic, but the Hyksos invaders of Egypt called their ruler by the title *Salitis* (derived from the same root) back in the 18th cent. B.C., long before the time of Moses. As for the argument that the term *zĕmān H2375* ("appointed time," Eccl. 3:1) appears outside of Ecclesiastes only in Esther and Nehemiah, it is also true that it was used in Akkadian as *simānu* (similarly, Arab. *zamanun* and Ethiopic *zaman*). It was a Pan-Semitic word and therefore provides no evidence for a post-Solomonic date, especially since the same meaning is elsewhere in Ecclesiastes always expressed by the classical Hebrew *ʿēt H6961* (cf. 3:1–8).

II. Other internal evidences as to authorship.

Apart from linguistic factors, there are other internal evidences used by opponents of Solomonic authorship to indicate a later date of composition. Thus there are said to be such obvious anachronisms as to alert any Hebrew reader to the fictional character of this work. The Preacher declared that he had attained more wisdom than "all who were over Jerusalem before me" (Eccl. 1:16 NRSV). Since the only Hebrew king before Solomon in Jerusalem was his father David, the statement must point to a long succession of Jewish kings before Ecclesiastes was actually written. But this argument overlooks the fact that the author is not referring to kings who preceded him in Jerusalem, but rather to "wise men" or sages who were practitioners of the various genres of wisdom literature (cf. 1 Ki. 4:31, which states that Solomon excelled even Heman, Calcol, and Darda, doubtless outstanding scholars who flourished in pre-Israelite Jerusalem, a city of notable influence and prestige from the days of Melchizedek and Adoni-Zedek centuries before). A second anachronism

Flat limestone sundial with a triangular fin. "There is a time for everything" (Eccl. 3:1).

is alleged in Eccl. 1:12, where the author says that he *was* king in Jerusalem, a statement thought to imply that Solomon was no longer king (and therefore dead) at the time this book was written. It should be pointed out, however, that the Hebrew form *hāyîtî melek* can also mean "I became king," a perfectly natural explanation for an elderly king to give when recollecting the commencement of his reign.

Solomonic authorship is supposedly excluded by the nonroyal viewpoint of the author. Instead of speaking of himself as the ruler of the land, he occasionally expresses sentiments implying disapproval of, or even hostility toward, the king. See, for example, Eccl. 10:17: "Blessed are you, O land whose king is of noble birth / and whose princes eat at a proper time— / for strength and not for drunkenness" (cf. also 4:13; 10:20). In dealing with passages such as these, however, it should be understood that the author is writing as a philosopher, not as the head of a government, or even as a propagandist in his own behalf. As a keen observer of world history, both past and current, he would have been well aware of the existence of gluttonous, intemperate, stubborn, or misguided kings in other countries, or of the unhappy consequences to their subjects under such a rule. Just as at a later age the Roman emperor MARCUS AURELIUS composed his *Meditations* not as a piece of government propaganda but (esp. after the introductory book 1) as a STOIC philosopher, so also Solomon, as a scholar of wide renown, wrote this remarkable treatise on the true values of life in order to persuade others to settle for nothing less than obedience to the revealed will of God. In order to illustrate his various points, he drew upon familiar experiences and vicissitudes common to the ANE in recent and contemporary history: the downfall of the rich and proud, the sudden elevation of the ignoble and lowly to positions of prominence and honor.

It is quite pointless and futile to attempt to discover in these illustrations covert allusions to the national downfall of Judah in 587, the miseries of the Babylonian exile, or the penury that prevailed in the days of EZRA and MALACHI. The author is dealing with the misfortunes and hardships that befall mankind generally as individuals rather than as nations. Sentiments such as, "But better than both / is he who has not yet been, / who has not seen the evil / that is done under the sun" (Eccl. 4:3), point to the injustice and calamity that all too often infects society and assaults its hapless victims at all periods in human history. Even though prosperity and peace prevailed during most of Solomon's reign, his recollection of the harrowing experiences of his father during ABSALOM's revolt, and his knowledge of the tides of invasion and bloodshed that had always characterized the history of the ANE, all served to give him a realistic understanding of the afflictions of mankind. Indeed it was these afflictions that posed the anguished questions of meaning and value without which the adventure of life made little sense. One concludes, then, that there is nothing in the sentiments expressed or the attitudes assumed in the text of Ecclesiastes to preclude Solomonic authorship. The so-called allusions to exilic and postexilic conditions are incapable of demonstration, nor are they at all inappropriate to a 10th-cent. setting. Neither in this area nor in the linguistic phenomena of the book can a convincing case be made out for non-Solomonic authorship.

III. The doctrinal message of Ecclesiastes.
The basic theme of Qoheleth is the ultimate futility of a life based upon earthly ambitions and desires. Any worldview that does not rise above the horizon of human goals is doomed to meaninglessness and frustration. To view personal happiness or enjoyment as life's greatest good is sheer folly in view of the transcendent value of God himself as over against his created universe. Happiness can never be achieved by pursuing after it, since such a pursuit involves the absurdity of self-deification: "The hearts of men, moreover, are full of evil and there is madness in their hearts while they live, and afterward they join the dead" (Eccl. 9:3). The final judgment upon all self-seeking, autonomous human effort and pursuit after meaning and permanent achievement is: "Vanity of vanities" (KJV), that is, complete futility. Transient mortals must realize that they are mere creatures, and that they derive importance only from their relationship to the almighty Creator: "I know that everything God does will endure forever; nothing can be added to it and nothing taken from it" (3:14).

In other words, Ecclesiastes is really intended to be a tract for the conversion of the self-sufficient intellectual; it compels him to discard his comfortable, self-flattering illusions and face honestly the instability of all those materialistic props on which he attempts to base his security. At the end of the road for the "hard-headed" materialist lies death and physical dissolution. Only as one finds a new meaning for life in surrendering to the sovereignty of God and faithful obedience to his will in moral conduct can one find a valid principle and goal for responsible human living. There may be many aspects of God's will that man does not yet understand, nevertheless he must submit to it with unrebellious trust, and gratefully receive and enjoy the mercies of food and clothing and material comforts as he may apportion them to us (Eccl. 3:11–13). It is from this perspective that the so-called EPICUREAN passages (like 2:24) are to be understood; they do not exalt mere hedonism to the status of absolute value (as some interpreters have imagined), but rather they exhort men to a wholehearted appreciation and enjoyment of God's material bounties, even while they recognize them as possessing only temporal and conditional value.

As for the alleged pessimism of the book's teaching, with its recurrent reminder of the inevitability and universality of death, these elements too must be interpreted in the light of the overall purpose of the book, as defined above, and also in the light of the immediate context. Thus in the case of Eccl. 4:2, "And I declared that the dead, / who had already died, / are happier than the living, / who are still alive," this is no rejection of the worthwhileness of life as such. The preceding verse makes it clear that if a person's life is to consist of nothing but oppression, calamity, and sorrow, then it would have been better never to have been born at all. Or again, the query in 6:8—"What advantage has a wise man / over a fool? / What does a poor man gain / by knowing how to conduct himself before others?"—is to be put in focus with the main thrust of the book: apart from God and his holy will, the life of no individual (whether educated or uneducated, rich or poor) has any ultimate meaning, but ends in futility. If a person's relationship to the Lord is what it should be, then it will be well with him. "Although a wicked person who commits a hundred crimes may live a long time, I know that it will go better with those who fear God, who are reverent before him" (8:12 TNIV).

It should be added that the Preacher lays great stress upon the importance of this life as the only arena of opportunity and accomplishment before one steps off the stage into the eternity of the life beyond. From this standpoint it is true that "Anyone who is among the living has hope—even a live dog is better off than a dead lion!" (Eccl. 9:4). The following verse is no affirmation of soul-sleep ("the dead know nothing") but rather a warning that the DEAD have no longer any expectation of a personal future with opportunities of choice for or against God, or between good and evil, such as they had prior to the grave. Nor do they have any knowledge of what goes on "under the sun," that is, upon earth, while they wait in SHEOL for the day of judgment. (In Solomon's time, of course, it would have been premature to reveal anything clear about the glories of heaven, since access to these glories for believers was largely delayed until the triumph of Christ's resurrection.) All of these considerations, then, are intended to point people away from the specious and pretended values of this life (personal enjoyment, happiness, success, or materialistic achievements) to the one true and abiding value: fellowship with God and living in obedience to his will. Plainly this is the resolution to which the author wishes to drive his readers, for he ends by saying: "Now all has been heard; / here is the conclusion of the matter: / Fear God and keep his commandments, / for this is the whole duty of man" (12:13).

It is only by dint of deleting from the text of Ecclesiastes the verses that speak of obedience to God and trust in him that rationalist critics are able to construe the book as a pessimistic manifesto of skepticism which somehow found its way into the OT canon despite its heresy. No plausible motivation can be made out for the reworking of an originally Bible-rejecting book in order to make it acceptable to the believing community through the insertion of occasional pious-sounding verses. Such a theory is totally without objective foundation, and a mere product of the inventive imagination of modern higher criticism.

(Since the initial publication of this encyclopedia, debate regarding the message of Ecclesiastes has remained vigorous. For the view that a distinction should be made between, on the one hand, Qoheleth himself as a skeptic, and on the other, the author of the prologue and epilogue as an orthodox wisdom teacher, see the summary in T. Longman III and R. B. Dillard, *An Introduction to the Old Testament*, 2nd ed. [2006], 279–84. See also the recent commentaries and monographs listed at the end of this article.)

IV. Outline of the contents of the book. The book is composed of four main discourses and a conclusion.

First discourse: The vanity of human wisdom (Eccl. 1:1—2:26)
  A. Basic thesis: mere human effort and achievement are futile (1:1–3)
  B. Thesis demonstrated (1:4—2:26)
    1. Futility of the cycle of human life and history (1:4–11)
    2. Ultimate uselessness of human wisdom and philosophy (1:12–18)
    3. Enjoyments of pleasure and wealth are empty (2:1–11)
    4. Even the wise must eventually die (2:12–17)
    5. Heritage of diligent industry left to undeserving heirs (2:18–23)
    6. Duty of contentment with God's gracious providences (2:24–26)

Second discourse: Appreciate the divine laws governing life (3:1—5:20)
  A. The attitude compelled by realities of life and death (3:1–22)
    1. A proper time appointed for each activity and experience (3:1–9)
    2. God is the only guarantor of abiding values (3:10–15)
    3. Punishment and death appointed for all the unrighteous (3:16–18)
    4. Death is, however, universal for man and beast (3:19–20)
    5. Unsure of the life beyond, make the best of this present life (3:21–22)
  B. The disappointments of earthly life (4:1–16)
    1. Cruelty and misery may afflict this life (4:1–3)
    2. Disadvantages even to success, and penalties for laziness and greed (4:4–8)
    3. Life's trials faced better by partners than by loners (4:9–12)
    4. Even success in politics is unstable (4:13–16)
  C. Futility of the self-seeking life (5:1–20)
    1. Folly of false sacrifices, vain words, broken promises (5:1–7)
    2. Sure retribution for oppressors; disappointment for the greedy (5:8–17)
    3. Contentment comes from thankful enjoyment of God's gifts (5:18–20)

Third discourse: No satisfaction in earthly goods or treasures (6:1—8:17)
  A. The inadequacy of worldly attainments (6:1–12)
    1. No lasting satisfaction in wealth or large family (6:1–6)
    2. No real satisfaction for either the worldly wise or the foolish (6:7–9)
    3. No real point to life apart from God (6:10–12)
  B. Prudent counsels for a sin-corrupted world (7:1–29)
    1. True values emerge in the face of sorrow and death (7:1–4)
    2. Pitfalls of cheap gaiety, dishonest gain, short temper (7:5–9)
    3. Wisdom is better than wealth in coping with problems (7:10–12)
    4. Both good fortune and ill come from God (7:13–14)
    5. Self-righteousness and immorality both lead to disaster (7:15–18)
    6. Great advantages to wisdom, but sin is universal (7:19–20)
    7. Be unconcerned at base malice toward yourself (7:21–22)
    8. Man by mere wisdom cannot attain spiritual truth (7:23–25)
    9. Worst of all evils is an evil woman (7:26)
    10. But all have fallen from original goodness (7:27–29)

C. Coming to terms with an imperfect world (8:1–17)
  1. Wise to respect governmental authority (8:1–5)
  2. God's law operates despite sorrows and death (8:6–9)
  3. The esteemed, unpunished wrongdoer will finally meet God's judgment (8:10–13)
  4. Life's injustices may encourage shallow hedonism (8:14–15)
  5. But God's ways are inscrutable to man (8:16–17)

FOURTH DISCOURSE: GOD WILL DEAL WITH INJUSTICES IN THIS WORLD (9:1—12:8)
  A. Death is inevitable for all (9:1–18)
    1. Death inevitable for both evil and good; moral insanity of man (9:1–3)
    2. At death all moral choice and knowledge of this life terminate (9:4–6)
    3. The godly must use opportunities of this life to the full (9:7–10)
    4. Success is uncertain, life span unpredictable even for the worthy (9:11–12)
    5. Yet wisdom, though unappreciated, succeeds better than force (9:13–18)
  B. The uncertainties of life and the baneful effects of folly (10:1–20)
    1. Even a little folly ruinous; be prudent before princes (10:1–4)
    2. Reversals of fortune and sad retribution for sin (10:5–11)
    3. Empty talk and misdirected effort mark a fool (10:12–15)
    4. Moral responsibility vital for nations and men (10:16–19)
    5. Contempt for authority brings sure retribution (10:20)
  C. The best way to invest a life (11:1—12:8)
    1. Kindness returns with blessing to the benefactor (11:1–2)
    2. To alter or fathom God's laws of nature is beyond human wisdom (11:3–5)
    3. Wisest course is cheerful diligence and industry (11:6–8)
    4. There is ultimate retribution for youth spent in seeking pleasure (11:9–10)
    5. Start living for God early before the infirmities of old age (12:1–8)

CONCLUSION: LIFE'S MEANING IN THE LIGHT OF ETERNITY (12:9–14)
  A. Qoheleth's purpose to teach the meaning and duties of life (12:9–10)
  B. These admonitions more valuable than all literature of this world (12:11–12)
  C. God's will comes first, for his judgment is final (12:13–14)

V. Final summation. Ecclesiastes presents itself as the matured and chastened wisdom of a king who has learned from experience the futility of living for any other purpose than the glory of God. He has come to realize what a poor bargain it is for a man to gain the whole world but to lose his own soul. He had been personally favored with unlimited wealth and power to test all that the world had to offer. He enjoyed the finest education and an unrivaled reputation for wisdom (Eccl. 1:16). His riches were immeasurable (2:8); he was surrounded with hosts of servants (2:7); his opportunities for carnal pleasure knew no restriction (2:3); he could afford the most extensive building projects and look with pride on their accomplishment (2:4–6). Yet in the end these false avenues to life's highest good led only to a vanished satisfaction and a sense of personal emptiness: all was "vanity," futile meaninglessness. In the end this son of David was driven back to the lessons and insights of his early upbringing, and he had to recognize that only in God can a person find real significance and lasting satisfaction. It was therefore this legacy that Solomon wished to leave behind him for his willful, headstrong people, and also for all people of subsequent generations who earnestly search for life's highest good. Paradoxically, it is not found in this life at all, but rather in God and the supernal realm of his perfect will.

(Significant commentaries include E. W. Hengstenberg, *Commentary on Ecclesiastes* [1860]; F. Delitzsch, *Commentary on the Song of Songs and Ecclesiastes* [1877]; A. L. Williams, *Ecclesiastes* [1922]; R. N. Whybray, *Ecclesiastes*, NCBC [1989]; J. L. Crenshaw, *Ecclesiastes*, OTL [1987]; R. E. Murphy, *Ecclesiastes*, WBC 23A [1992]; D. A.

Garrett, *Proverbs, Ecclesiastes, Song of Songs*, NAC 14 [1993]; C. L. Seow, *Ecclesiastes*, AB 18C [1997]; T. Longman, *The Book of Ecclesiastes*, NICOT [1998]; N. Lohfink, *Qoheleth: A Continental Commentary* [2003]; T. Krüger, *Qoheleth: A Commentary* [2004]; E. S. Christianson, *Ecclesiastes through the Centuries* [2007]. Among important monographs, see H. L. Ginsberg, *Studies in Koheleth* [1950]; R. Gordis, *Koheleth: The Man and his World* [1955]; J. A. Loader, *Polar Structures in the Book of Qohelet* [1979]; C. F. Whitley, *Koheleth: His Language and Thought* [1979]; M. V. Fox, *Qohelet and His Contradictions* [1989]; id., *A Time to Tear Down and a Time to Build Up: A Rereading of Ecclesiastes* [1999]; D. Rudman, *Determinism in the Book of Ecclesiastes* [2001]; D. B. Miller, *Symbol and Rhetoric in Ecclesiastes: The Place of Hebel in Qohelet's Work* [2002]; A. Schoors, *The Preacher Sought to Find Pleasing Words: A Study of the Language of Qoheleth*, 2 vols. [1992–2004]; M. A. Shields, *The End of Wisdom: A Reappraisal of the Historical and Canonical Function of Ecclesiastes* [2006]; and the bibliography compiled by W. E. Mills, *Ecclesiastes/Song of Solomon* [2002].)

G. L. Archer

Ecclesiasticus, Book of i-klee′zee-as′ti-kuhs. The longest book of the Apocrypha and one of the most important in that group. It is known also as the Wisdom of Jesus the Son of Sirach (= Jeshua ben Sira) or simply as Sirach (cf. the occasional Latin form, *Siracides*). The title in Rahlfs's edition of the Septuagint, following Codex Vaticanus, is *Sophia Sirach* (Wisdom of Sirach). The Latin term *Ecclesiasticus* (from Gk. *Ekklēsiastikos*, "of the church") was given to the book as early as the 3rd cent., probably in recognition of the superior worth of the book for reading in the church among those writings that did not hold canonical status (i.e., which were not a part of the Hebrew OT). The early church fathers referred to the book as the "most excellent" or (literally) "all virtuous" Wisdom (*Panaretos Sophia*). However, the title Ecclesiasticus may also have been given to the book because it was early placed alongside the book Ecclesiastes, and a similar title was deemed suitable.

    I. Author
   II. Date
  III. Place and language
  IV. Purpose
   V. Content
  VI. Theological teaching and importance
 VII. Canonicity
VIII. Text

I. Author. The generalizing title Ecclesiasticus obscures the fact that the author of the book is known to have been Jesus the Son of Sirach (as the alternate title correctly recognizes). Among the Apocrypha, this is the only book that includes the author's name in the actual text. He writes, "Instruction in understanding and knowledge I have written in this book, Jesus the son of Sirach, son of Eleazar, of Jerusalem, who out of his heart poured forth wisdom" (Sir. 50:27 RSV; the Gk. is ambiguous, and the NRSV renders, "Jesus son of Eleazar son of Sirach"). There is considerable textual difficulty concerning the names mentioned, and particularly noteworthy is the fact that one Hebrew ms apparently ascribes the book to "Simon the son of Jeshua, son of Eleazar, son of Sira." This same ascription (but in two forms, one omitting reference to Eleazar) occurs in the colophon of the ms. Probably the Hebrew ascription of the book to Simon is the result of the importation of Simon's name from 50:1 and is to be regarded as erroneous. The Greek mss are unanimous in their ascription of the book to "Jesus the son of Sirach" both in 50:27 and in the colophon.

More important, however, is the reference to the author of the book contained in the prologue; this

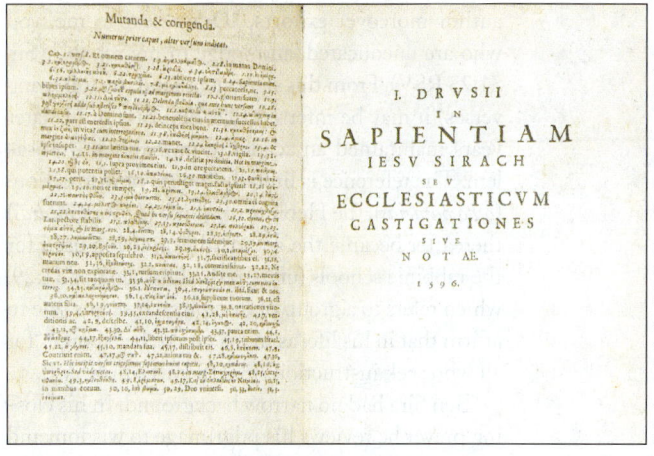

A 1596 edition of the book of Ecclesiasticus.

prologue was written by the Greek translator, who was also the grandson of the author. The translator narrates as follows: "So my grandfather Jesus, who had devoted himself especially to the reading of the Law and the Prophets and the other books of our ancestors, and had acquired considerable proficiency in them, was himself also led to write something pertaining to instruction and wisdom, so that by becoming familiar also with his book those who love learning might make even greater progress in living according to the law" (NRSV).

Who was this Jeshua ben Sira? Nothing is known of him beyond what can be deduced from the book that he authored. Due to the length of the writing, along with the comparatively generous number of personal references that it contains, one knows a fair amount about the author. Ben Sira, as he may be called, seems almost certainly to have been a scribe, that is to say, a professional student of the Scriptures. This is evident not only from what the translator indicates concerning his grandfather's serious study of the Scriptures, but also from the contents of the book. In particular, Ben Sira's glowing description of the calling of a scribe (Sir. 38:24—39:11) could be seen as a veiled autobiographical sketch of his own life work, of which the present book is but an embodiment.

The calling of a scribe was not simply to study, but rather to practice the law and especially to teach (cf. Ezra 7:10). Ben Sira was also a teacher. This would have been clear from the character of the book alone—obviously the product of a heart concerned with and experienced in teaching. The author moreover exhorts, "Draw near to me, you who are uneducated, and lodge in my school" (Sir. 51:23 RSV). From this statement (and the following verses) it may be inferred that Ben Sira in his later years maintained an academy, probably in Jerusalem. The reference is literally "house of instruction" (*oikō paideias*), the Hebrew of which (*bêt hammidrās*) thereafter became the standard expression used for the rabbinic schools (cf. also the Heb. text of 51:29, which refers to a group of disciples). It seems safe to affirm that in his life, as in his books, he labored "for all who seek instruction" (33:18 [v. 17 in RSV]).

Ben Sira had no narrow background. In his closing prayer he reviews his pilgrimage to wisdom and understanding. He refers to travels undertaken in his youth (Sir. 51:13), which recalls an earlier mention of how an educated man gains understanding particularly by travel experience, as he himself could personally testify (34:9–12). It may even be that he traveled as an adviser on diplomatic missions, which as he suggests was at times the duty of the scribe (39:4). Along with his thorough knowledge of the Scriptures, Ben Sira reveals in his writing a great wealth of knowledge, which may be called "worldly wisdom"—that wisdom common to the sages of antiquity. One may suggest that he was not only widely traveled, but also well-read (parallels to Euripides, Theognis, and Aesop have been seen).

With regard to religious stance, Ben Sira is most often described as a precursor of the SADDUCEES. Whereas his book does reveal some of the traits of the later Sadducees, it is quite appropriate also to see the book as propounding the classical ideals of the PHARISEES. In the discussion of the actual teaching of the book (see below), more information will be found concerning the religious viewpoint of Ben Sira.

II. Date. In contrast to other books of the Apocrypha, both the author of Ecclesiasticus and also the nearly exact date of the book is known. The evidence comes from the prologue supplied by the translator. This translator, whose name is unknown but who was the grandson of the author, says that he emigrated to Egypt in the thirty-eighth year of the reign of Euergetes. Two Egyptian kings bore the surname "Euergetes," PTOLEMY III and Ptolemy VII, but the former reigned some twenty-five years, whereas the latter reigned no less than fifty-three years. Obviously, the Euergetes referred to by the translator must be Ptolemy VII, whose reign began in 170 B.C., thereby putting the date of the translator's emigration at about 132. This being the case, the date of the book is most probably to be put in the early decades of the 2nd cent. B.C. Since the book reveals no knowledge whatsoever of the catastrophic events that occurred in 168 at the instigation of ANTIOCHUS IV, such a conclusion is confirmed, and the scholarly estimates of the date of the book almost all fall between 200 and 180.

Another piece of evidence that bears directly on the date of Ecclesiasticus is the reference to "the high priest, Simon son of Onias" (Sir. 50:1;

see ONIAS #2 and SIMON ##10–11). The following description of his work and ministry in the sanctuary is given in the past tense, and there are suggestions that it was written after the death of Simon (cf. "in his life ... in his time," 50:1; a prayer for peace to prevail among Simon's sons is found in the Heb. text of 50:23–24). Some confusion exists concerning the identity of this individual: is it Simon I (cf. Jos. *Ant.* 12.2.5; 12.4.1) or Simon II (ibid. 12.4.10; 12.5.1)? Next to nothing is known of Simon I, surnamed "the Righteous," who is said to have flourished about 300 B.C. This sparseness of data, combined with the fact that, according to the MISHNAH, Simon the Righteous mediates between the Great Synagogue of Ezra and Antigonus of Socho (about 180 B.C.), thus occupying a span of more than two centuries, has led some to the conclusion that Simon I is a mythical rather than a historical personage. In any event, if Simon I did flourish about 300 B.C., he was too early to have been the Simon referred to by the grandfather of our translator (who, as indicated, emigrated to Egypt in 132). Simon II, on the other hand, seems to have been high priest from about 220 to about 195 and, by virtue of the coincidence with the chronological data already reviewed, is almost certainly the Simon referred to by Ben Sira. This being the case, a date of shortly after 195 B.C. for the writing of the book is very probable.

III. Place and language. Other matters concerning Ecclesiasticus are known with certainty (more than for any other book of the Apoc.). Ben Sira says that he lived in Jerusalem (Sir. 50:27), and it was doubtless there also that he maintained his academy and ultimately committed his teaching to writing. Although it is not specifically stated in the prologue, Ben Sira's grandson probably came to Egypt from Palestine. Perhaps he brought the book with him, which he later felt compelled to translate.

It is certain that Ben Sira wrote his masterpiece in Hebrew. The unnamed translator asks the readers' indulgence for the imperfections of his work, adding a sentiment common to translators: "For what was originally expressed in Hebrew does not have exactly the same sense when translated into another language." He further remarks that the Law, the Prophets, and "the rest of the books" in Greek all exhibit the same type of inevitable discrepancies with the original. The task of Ben Sira's grandson, then, is parallel to the work accomplished by the translators of the LXX in making available Hebrew writings to a Greek-speaking public.

Prior to 1896, scholars knew Ecclesiasticus only through the Greek and Syriac versions, which served as the basis for subsequent translations. However, in that year and succeeding years, significant portions of the Hebrew text were identified among the materials excavated from the Cairo GENIZA. More recently, fragments of the Hebrew text have been discovered at Qumran. The net result is that today approximately two-thirds of the entire book in its original language has been acquired. Considerable debate has centered on the question of the authenticity of this Hebrew text, and a number of important scholars have argued that it is merely a retranslation of the Greek versions. Clearly it is a very corrupt text, but it appears to be representative of the original product of Ben Sira. (Even the opponents of the authenticity of the recovered text, however, allow that Ben Sira must originally have written his work in Hebrew.)

IV. Purpose. Ben Sira's purpose is immediately apparent upon a perusal of Ecclesiasticus. Like the great wisdom writer who authored PROVERBS, Ben Sira seeks to provide his reader with instruction in wisdom by the compilation of various epigrams and sayings designed to inculcate righteousness, or

Fragments of the Wisdom of Sirach (Ecclesiasticus) were discovered in the Qumran caves.

obedience to the law. Indeed Ben Sira somewhat immodestly regards himself as standing at the end of a long line of writers who upheld the teachings of the law. Thus he writes: "I was the last to keep vigil; I was like a gleaner following the grape-pickers; by the blessing of the Lord I arrived first, and like a grape-picker I filled my wine press" (Sir. 33:16–17; cf. 24:33). Ben Sira's book serves as a complete guide to right thinking and right conduct.

There is perhaps a subsidiary motive in the author's mind as he emphasizes in one of the climactic sections of his book that Wisdom has made her dwelling place in Israel (Sir. 24:8–12) and as he equates Wisdom with the law of Moses (24:23). In all of this, Ben Sira may be speaking to his brethren who were weakening under the constant temptations of HELLENISM. He exhorts that they should not be ashamed "of the law of the Most High and his covenant" (42:1–2). Throughout the book the exhortations to the standards of conduct set by the law may be taken as countering an opposite tendency provoked by the hellenizing influences of the day. This still remains secondary, for what argument there may be against Hellenism remains always tacit. Ben Sira's purpose is better taken as that which is so readily apparent from the content of the book. This is summed up beautifully by the translator in his prologue when he writes that "by becoming familiar also with his book those who love learning might make even greater progress in living according to the law."

V. Content. There is virtually no organization in the contents of Ecclesiasticus, and no progression of thought is apparent in the book. A few proverbs and sayings will often cluster around a common subject, but beyond this rather natural occurrence, the materials are set in no particular structure. Instead, as in the case of the book of Proverbs, the author allows himself to dart from subject to subject in a seemingly haphazard fashion. It has been suggested that the contents of the book may well consist of the notes that were used by Ben Sira in teaching at his academy.

Because of the lack of intrinsic structure in the book, it is difficult to suggest a meaningful outline of its contents. There are some natural divisions in the last ten chapters of the book formed by material that is different in character from the preceding portion of the book. The first of these (Sir. 42:15–43:33) is a panegyric on the glory of God as seen in the works of creation and ends on the futility of ever adequately recounting the greatness of his works, for as the author concludes, "let the final word be: 'He is the all'" (43:27). The following section (44:1–50:21) reviews the history of the great men of Israel, ending with a great tribute to Simon the high priest, the son of Onias. This is followed by a general doxology and prayer (50:22–24), an odd proverb (50:25–26), and a concluding postscript identifying the author and encouraging the reader (50:27–29). The book seems naturally to end here, yet there is added an excellent thanksgiving hymn (51:1–12) and a final poem on the pursuit of wisdom (51:13–30; an acrostic in the Heb.).

In addition to the divisions found toward the end of the book, however, a number of writers have found a major division in the main portion of the book, although the latter seems at first glance to consist only of random collections of proverbs and wisdom sayings. The division has been made largely on the basis of the long poem on wisdom, which begins in Sir. 24:1. Since this is parallel to the long discourse that opens the book (1:1–20), and these two are by far the longest poems on wisdom, it has been suggested that the second opens a second volume of the same work. (It should be noted that the book of Proverbs also begins with a long treatise on wisdom, chs. 1–9.) To some extent this conjecture may find support in the remarks that follow the second poem on wisdom. Ben Sira likens his work to the watering of a garden, but he says, "my canal became a river, and my river a sea" (24:31), perhaps implying that his work grew to unexpected proportions. He continues, "I will again make instruction shine forth like the dawn" (24:32) and "I will again pour out teaching like prophecy" (24:33), affirmations that may well refer to a renewed activity of composition.

Perhaps a simple outline is best for a book of this nature, and the following may be suggested:
Prologue (usually not given verse enumeration)
  A. Instruction in wisdom, part one (Sir. 1:1—23:27)
  B. Instruction in wisdom, part two (24:1—42:14)

C. The glory of God in his works (42:15—43:33)
D. The glory of God in his servants (44:1—50:21)
E. Concluding remarks (50:22–29)
F. Thanksgiving hymn (51:1–12)
G. On the pursuit of wisdom (51:13–30)

Bypassing the translator's prologue, one may devote some comments to the contents of the two main sections, which, although essentially undistinguishable, are discussed separately for the sake of convenience. The opening poem on wisdom can be regarded as setting the tone of the whole book and not merely that of the first section alone. Ben Sira writes, "All wisdom is from the Lord, and with him it remains for ever" (Sir. 1:1). He proceeds to argue eloquently that because this is true, wisdom can mean only one thing for man: the fear of the Lord. To fear the Lord is not only the beginning of wisdom (cf. Prov. 1:7) and its root, but also its perfection and crown. To fear the Lord is to keep his commandments; therein lies wisdom (Sir. 1:26–27). A large proportion of the remaining teaching of the book grows out of this basic premise. In addition to the traditional Jewish piety that derives from this reverence for the law, Ben Sira includes considerable proverbial wisdom that bears no special relation to the law.

Much of the material, then, is hortatory, calling the reader to keep the commandments. Negatively, this means to keep oneself from sin. The reader is exhorted to beware of evil (Sir. 4:20; 17:14), and to flee from sin "as from a snake" (21:2). Although the Lord is merciful, his mercy must not be presumed upon, for he also knows wrath (5:6; 16:11). The Lord knows all that a man does, and nothing can be hid from him (17:15–20). Moreover, judgment is sure to come despite all present appearances to the contrary (16:12–14; 17:23). Consequently, only the fool presumptuously boasts, "I sinned, yet what has happened to me?" (5:4). The punishment of the ungodly is severe (7:17), and the end of the road for the sinner is "the pit of Hades" (21:10). A man ought therefore to examine himself before judgment comes (18:20); for if he remembers the end of his life, he will never sin (7:36).

It is within this basic framework that Ben Sira sets his teachings concerning the avoidance of specific sins. To give some examples, the wise man does not set his heart on wealth (Sir. 5:1), does not slander (5:14), does not fall into the snare of a loose woman (9:1–9), is not angry (10:6) or proud (10:18), avoids evil desires, gluttony, and lust (23:6), does not lie (20:24–26), swear (23:9–11), speak foul language (23:13), or fall victim to sexual sins (23:1–27). On the positive side, Ben Sira exhorts his readers to find wisdom by honoring their parents (3:1–16; 7:27–28), by humility (3:17–20; 10:7–9), charity to the poor and the wronged (4:1–6; 7:32–33), sincerity in speech (5:9–13), almsgiving to the devout (12:1–7), and self-control (18:27–33). These are examples drawn at random, but they help to catch the tenor of the book.

Significant religious teaching is found in the following emphases of the first section. Ben Sira speaks clearly of the sovereignty of the Lord. Everything, both good and bad, comes from the Lord (Sir. 11:14). Despair and rejoicing should be minimized because the Lord can easily turn the tables (11:21–28). Moreover, death is inevitable (14:17–19). The right attitude is to bow before the sovereignty of God and accept what he brings (2:4). At the same time, a man cannot say that the Lord is responsible for his sinning, for as Ben Sira writes, "If you choose, you can keep the commandments, and to act faithfully is a matter of your own choice" (15:15). The greatness of the Lord defies expression (18:1–7), and his work of creation is both great and good (16:26—17:14). Man, however, is insignificant, like a grain of sand or a drop of water by comparison (18:8–10).

Also to be found throughout these chapters is wisdom of a more common, proverbial type, which also has its place in the good life as understood by the author. Ben Sira expounds on the qualities of true and false friendship (Sir. 6:5–13; 12:8–12), good government (10:1–4), the right use of silence (20:1–8), and the disagreeableness of a fool (22:7–15). Although he cautions against an undue harshness of self-discipline ("If one is mean to himself, to whom will he be generous?" 14:5), he urges the strict disciplining of children (7:23; 22:3–6). It is right to give heed to the wisdom of the elderly (8:8–9), and one does well to keep virtuous companions (9:13–16) and avoid those who are not of like mind (13:1–2). Not only ought one to keep clear of the ungodly (12:13–18), but one ought also to avoid giving hospitality to strangers (11:34). Among his counsels, one of the most interesting is to refrain from seeking answers to questions that transcend the limits of human understanding (3:21–24). A host of other wise sayings are to be found throughout the chapters of this first division of the book. They are pithy and often employ a characteristic poetic parallelism. In addition to the long opening passage praising wisdom, there are other, shorter, passages devoted to the praise of wisdom (e.g., 4:11–12; 6:18–22; 14:20–27).

The content of the second main section of the book (Sir. 24:1—42:14) is very similar to what has just been described. Again a wide variety of subjects is discussed, and these are connected only in the loosest fashion. The opening poem on wisdom (ch. 24) is particularly noteworthy. Wisdom is personified and made to speak in the first person (cf. Prov. 8). She speaks of herself in the most exalted language and invites all to come and partake of her fruit. Those who do will return for more of her delights (Sir. 24:21). After this passage spoken by personified Wisdom, Ben Sira makes the striking assertion that this Wisdom is nothing other than the law: "All this is the book of the covenant of the Most High God, the law that Moses commanded us as an inheritance for the congregations of Jacob" (24:23; cf. 19:20). The material that follows contains motifs already familiar from the first section. Thus, "Fear of the Lord surpasses everything" (25:11), and the man who has gained wisdom accordingly guards against what is unpleasing to the Lord, such as sin in business (27:2), anger and hatred (27:30), sins of the tongue (28:13–21, 25–26), and love of money (31:5–9). Readers are directed to consider the end of their lives as an incentive to keep the commandments (28:6). Justice is sure to come from the Lord who will repay each person according to his deeds (35:12–20). Offerings and sacrifices are important, but they must be offered by the righteous who keep the law (35:1–3). Emphasis is given to the sovereignty of the Lord in all his acts. As a potter molds his clay, so does the Lord order the ways of men (33:13). Inequality (33:12) and death (41:3–4) are the results of his pleasure. At the same time, Ben Sira laments, "From a woman sin had its beginning, and because of her we all die" (25:24); and elsewhere, "O inclination to evil, why were you formed to cover the land with deceit?" (37:3).

There is even more teaching of the proverbial wisdom type in this second section of Ecclesiasticus than in the first. Ben Sira advises on a great variety of matters, including lending and sureties (Sir. 29:1–7), table etiquette for a guest (31:12–18), the proper use of wine (31:25–30), correct behavior at a party (31:31), the treatment of slaves and servants (33:24–31), dreams and divinations (34:1–8), and friendship (37:1–6). Ben Sira's teachings in these and other similar areas have an attractiveness to them, being based on the two foundations of consideration for others and moderation in all things. As in the first section, again the reader is exhorted to be strict with his children (30:1–2). Whereas a good wife is praiseworthy (cf. 36:24), nothing is worse than an evil wife (25:16). In the end, however, Ben Sira's view of woman is decidedly pessimistic (cf. 42:12–14).

In one interesting passage, the reader is exhorted to make proper use of physicians and medicines in time of illness (Sir. 38:1–8). A helpful section follows on the place of grief for the dead: it is proper for a season but is not to be prolonged, since by it, "you do the dead no good, and you injure yourself" (38:21). Ben Sira knows the value of positive thinking and exhorts his reader to be glad and to rejoice, for so is his life best lived (30:21–25). Particularly significant is the lengthy discussion of the occupation of the scribe as contrasted with that of other occupations, which, though necessary, do not afford the leisure that is the *sine qua non* of the contemplative life (38:24—39:11). Also noteworthy is the prayer for national restoration (36:1–17), which is complete in itself and exactly analogous to the similar prayers of other books of the intertestamental period. Special mention is in order for the hymn of praise to God found in 39:13–35. Stylistically, attention should be called to the numerical proverbs of ch. 25, and the "better than both" comparisons of 40:18–27.

The remaining sections of the book, which are quite different in nature from the preceding, have already been described above and need not be elaborated upon.

VI. Theological teaching and importance. It must first be made clear that not only is Ecclesiasticus not a theological treatise, but it also does not systematize or in any other way set in order, or even attempt to harmonize, its theological teaching. Whereas it contains no small amount of such material, that teaching is largely incidental to the immediate purpose of the author, and often the exhortations of the book presuppose rather than delineate the underlying theological truth.

Ecclesiasticus stands solidly in the mainstream of orthodox Judaism. Ben Sira's God is the God of the Torah, the Creator who is transcendent in his glory, whose sovereignty rules the universe, and whose holiness and righteousness are absolute. God has entered into covenant relationship with Israel, especially endowing her with wisdom in the form of the law. In this identification of wisdom with the law (Sir. 24), Ben Sira makes an apparently original contribution to traditional Judaism. There is no question in Ecclesiasticus concerning the specially privileged position of Israel, and Ben Sira can make his voice heard in strongly nationalistic tones (cf. 36:1–17). Nonetheless, the emphasis in his book is clearly upon personal piety. The individual who possesses wisdom is the one who heeds the commandments of the law. In all of this, Ben Sira reflects his thorough acquaintance with and dependence upon not only the Torah, but also the prophets and, particularly, the Psalms.

As far as moral ability is concerned, Ben Sira acknowledges the existence of an evil inclination within human beings, yet insists that it is possible for a person to keep the law (Sir. 15:15). The sovereignty of God and the free will of human beings stand in tension through the whole of the book. Man inevitably sins, and consequently every individual is deserving of punishment (8:5). Salvation, however, is possible because the Lord is merciful and forgives the sins of those who turn to him (2:11; 5:7; 17:24).

A number of the theological emphases of Ecclesiasticus have been regarded as reflecting, anachronistically, a Sadducean viewpoint. In his book, Ben Sira reveals a great love for the priesthood, the temple, and the sacred rituals performed there. When reviewing the history of God's work through the famous men of Israel, Ben Sira gives more than a proportionate amount of space to those entrusted with the priesthood. AARON, with whom the priestly lineage begins, is given a glowing tribute that takes more space than that given to ABRAHAM, ISAAC, JACOB, and MOSES combined (45:6–22). Similarly, PHINEHAS the son of Eleazar is given a prominent place among the great of Israel because of his importance for the priesthood (45:23–24). Most impressive in many ways, however, is the praise showered upon the high priest Simon son of Onias, whom Ben Sira describes in his priestly functions on the Day of Atonement with the vividness of an admiring eyewitness (50:1–21). Similarly, the temple is of great significance for Ben Sira (cf. 24:10; 36:13–14), as are also the religious festivals of Israel (33:7–9).

Further, Ecclesiasticus contains no hint of the doctrine of the RESURRECTION of the dead. Rewards and retribution are experienced in this life only. SHEOL (HADES) is the abode of the dead where nothing occurs (cf. Sir. 17:27; 41:4; 14:16), though in the Greek version of Ecclesiasticus this view is modified somewhat (after 19:17, a Greek interpolation speaks of "the fruit of the tree of immortality" [v. 19 in KJV]). The only "immortality" acknowledged by Ben Sira is found in the memory of a name of good repute (cf. 44:8–15). Since the attention of Ecclesiasticus is constantly focused on the present life, when the wicked prosper and the righteous suffer—a paradoxical situation for this viewpoint—Ben Sira counsels that circumstances may change quickly and thus it is not prudent to make such judgments prior to the death of the persons in question (11:21–28). The problem, however, remains, and many passages indicate that Ben Sira was not unaware of it.

The conservatism of Ben Sira in these viewpoints, reflected also in his conception of the aristocratic scribe (38:24) and in his penchant for biblical phraseology throughout the book, has been taken as indicative of a Saducean orientation. Whereas one does not properly speak of Sadducees before the post-Maccabean age, it is clear that Ben Sira does anticipate certain of their characteristic doctrines. It is, however, an oversimplification simply to categorize Ben Sira as a proto-Sadducee. In his book, he carefully counterbalances his emphasis on temple ritual with forceful assertions of the necessity of personal righteousness. He can speak like the prophets in this regard: "The Most High is not pleased with the offerings of the ungodly; and he is not propitiated for sins by a multitude of sacrifices" (34:23 [v. 19 in RSV]; cf. 35:8–9 [vv. 6–7 in RSV]). Ben Sira exhibits an interest in the prophetic tradition at least equal to, if not greater than, his interest in the priestly tradition. In his "praise of great men" he seems to stress that it is prophetism that serves as the significant linking factor in the history of Israel (cf. 46:1; 47:1; 48:1, 8, 13).

These facts, when combined with the orthodox theology of Ecclesiasticus, make it possible to view Ben Sira as the forerunner of Pharisaic Judaism. Certainly, the juristic nature of the traditional wisdom with which Ben Sira expounds and supplements the law anticipates and parallels the oral tradition handed down in rabbinic Judaism, which was later to be codified in written form in the MISHNAH. The particular significance of Ecclesiasticus lies in its position in the literary history of Israel. The last, and perhaps the greatest of the wisdom books, it presents the culmination of the wisdom tradition. At the same time, it stands immediately prior to, and in many ways as the clear precursor of, both Sadducean and Pharisaic Judaism.

Mention must be made of one other important fact about Ecclesiasticus. Within the prologue, important information is found concerning the state of the CANON in the 2nd cent. B.C. The translator once speaks of his grandfather who devoted himself to the reading of "the Law and the Prophets and the other books of our ancestors," and a little later again refers to "the Law itself, the Prophecies, and the rest of the books," suggesting that by 132 B.C. the OT canon had already taken its threefold division (cf. Lk. 24:44). Within Ecclesiasticus are intimations of a threefold division of canonical writings (e.g. 38:34—39:1, "law," "wisdom," and "prophecies"; cf. 44:3–5), and in his praise of famous men (chs. 44–49), Ben Sira follows closely the order of their appearance in books of the Hebrew Bible, although there are some strange omissions in the list (esp. Daniel and Ezra).

VII. Canonicity. Ecclesiasticus was among the books that found their way into the SEPTUAGINT and thus gained currency, particularly in the early church. It was never accepted as canonical by the Jews, although it was often quoted, and it exercised considerable influence on the later rabbinic literature. A number of parallels to Ecclesiasticus in the NT, especially in Matthew and James (see APOT, 1:294–95), also testify to the early influence of the book. The patristic writers often quote from Ecclesiasticus, and on occasion refer to the book as "Scripture," but in these early centuries, although the book seems to have enjoyed a quasi-canonical status, it did not receive technical recognition of canonicity until AUGUSTINE and certain church councils of the late 4th and early 5th cent. formally accepted the book as canonical. JEROME, however, clearly set Ecclesiasticus apart from the canonical books (i.e., those of the Heb. canon). The book became an established part of the Roman Catholic canon following the decision taken at the Council of Trent in the 16th cent. Protestants, although highly esteeming Ecclesiasticus, receive it only as a book of the Apocrypha.

VIII. Text. The textual evidence for Ecclesiasticus constitutes a fascinating and difficult puzzle for scholars. There are three primary witnesses to the text: the Greek of the LXX (a translation done by Ben Sira's grandson), the Syriac of the Peshitta (made originally from the Heb. rather than the LXX), and the fragmentary Hebrew MSS (about two-thirds of the book extant) from the magnificent finds of the Cairo GENIZA. There are a number of secondary witnesses in the form of versions (Old Latin, Syriac, Coptic, Ethiopic, Arabic, Armenian, Georgian, and Old Slavonic) that for the most part derive from the LXX, but which may occasionally show the influence of other primary witnesses.

Not only is there question concerning the relationship of the three primary witnesses, but there is debate also concerning the history of various textual representatives within each of the three recensions. Among the Greek MSS, great divergencies in text are discovered (transpositions, interpolations, and omissions). Basically, the Greek MSS have been separated into two categories, some going back to an earlier (original?) Hebrew text, and others apparently to a later recension of that text. The Syriac Peshitta seems also to have been influenced by the hypothetical later Hebrew recension.

Perhaps most confusing of all, however, are six Cairo Hebrew MSS that date from about the 11th or 12th cent. (on the recently discovered sixth MSS, see A. A. Di Lella in *Bib* 69 [1988]: 226–38). These MSS reveal numerous secondary readings in common with the second group of Greek MSS and the Syriac. Do these secondary readings indicate that the Hebrew MSS depend to some extent upon the hypothetical Hebrew recension that seems to have influenced certain of the Greek MSS, or are they "retroversions," that is, retranslations into Hebrew of certain readings of the Greek or Syriac witnesses? Whereas the latter explanation has been popular, others have persuasively argued for the former (e.g., A. A. Di Lella, *The Hebrew Text of Sirach: A Text-Critical and Historical Study* [1966]; H. P. Rüger, *Text und Textform im hebräischen Sirach* [1970]). It is striking that the fragments of Ecclesiasticus found at QUMRAN seem to bear a text form similar to that of Cairo MS A. If a relationship to Qumran could be ascertained, the reliability of the Cairo MSS would be established. The difficulty in solving the textual problem posed by Ecclesiasticus is thus compounded by what appear to be various signs of reciprocal influence among the three primary witnesses.

The text of the major Greek witnesses is available in the standard printed editions of the LXX, but preference should be given to the critically reconstructed text of J. Ziegler (*Sapientia Iesu Filii Sirach*, Septuaginta 12/2 [1965]). The Hebrew is available in a reconstruction by M. S. Segal (*Sepher Ben-Sira Ha-shalem* [1953]) and in a more recent edition by P. C. Beentjes (*The Book of Ben Sira in Hebrew: A Text Edition of All Extant Hebrew Manuscripts and a Synopsis of All Parallel Hebrew Ben Sira Texts* [1997]; cf. the brief discussion by L. F. Hartman in *CBQ* 23 [1961]: 443–51; and the monograph by B. G. Wright, *No Small Difference: Sirach's Relationship to Its Hebrew Parent Text* [1989]). The modern English versions usually follow an eclectic text, indicating more important variants in accompanying notes.

(See further W. O. E. Oesterley, *The Books of the Apocrypha* [1915], 321–48; R. H. Pfeiffer, *History of New Testament Times with an Introduction to the Apocrypha* [1949], 352–408; P. W. Skehan and A. A. Di Lella, *The Wisdom of Ben Sira*, AB 39 [1987]; D. J. Harrington, *Invitation to the Apocrypha* [1999], ch. 6; D. A. deSilva, *Introducing the Apocrypha: Message, Context, and Significance* [2002], ch. 7; D. J. Harrington, *Jesus ben Sira of Jerusalem: A Biblical Guide to Living Wisely* [2005].)   D. A. HAGNER

eclipse. The obscuring of one celestial body by another (from an observer's perspective). For someone observing from the earth, a solar eclipse occurs when the moon passes between the sun and the earth, thus blocking sunlight; a lunar eclipse occurs when the earth passes between the sun and the moon, thus blocking moonlight. For possible references to eclipses in the Bible, see ASTRONOMY II.B. Significant eclipses in the past aid scholars in identifying historical dates and establishing CHRONOLOGY.

ecstasy. See PROPHETS AND PROPHECY IV.H.

ecumenism. As a theological term, *ecumenism* (from Gk. *oikoumenē* G3876, "inhabited world") refers to the unity and universality of the Christian faith and the church. The mutual concepts of UNITY and universality are rooted in OT teachings regarding the COVENANT and cult WORSHIP but come to fullest expression in the NT doctrine of the CHURCH. (More generally, the term can refer to a modern movement promoting unity among Christian denominations or even among diverse worldwide religions.)

I. OT concepts of covenant universality and cultic unity. Ecumenism as both universality and unity are clearly observable in the context of OT BIBLICAL THEOLOGY. Israelite particularism sometimes obscures the broader concepts of the "world" and "nations," but the evidence clearly points to a profound universalism in the OT, as follows.

(1) Creation and the genealogical Table of NATIONS in Genesis clearly place God's COVENANT people within the broader framework of universal world history (cf. Gen. 1; 2; 5; 10).

(2) The Abrahamic Covenant not only calls attention to Israel's elective soteriology but includes "all the families of the earth" (Gen. 12:1–3; 17:1–8).

(3) God's covenant with Israel at SINAI implies a redemptive particularism as well as a universal priesthood. Yahweh calls Israel to be "a kingdom of priests and a holy nation" (Exod. 19:5–6). Indeed,

the record of OT history portrays Israel's failure to serve in this servant ministry, as Yahweh's priestly CONGREGATION among the nations.

(4) During the monarchy of DAVID there is a growing consciousness of a universal mission, as may be seen from several Davidic psalms (Pss. 9:11; 18:49; 57:9). Even more pronounced is SOLOMON's dedication of the TEMPLE, for he prayed that it might become a place of universal worship of Yahweh (1 Ki. 8:41–53).

(5) The fact that the prophetic literature consistently contains sections in which judgment is pronounced upon foreign nations and salvation is promised to them also confirms the deep-seated universalism implicit in the structure of Israel's faith (cf. Amos 1:3—2:3; Isa. 13–28; Jer. 46:51).

(6) Also one may trace in the exilic and postexilic prophets an equal emphasis upon Israel's universal mission to the nations. What Israel had failed to be, her dispersion among the kingdoms of the world was to accomplish (cf. Jer. 18:7; Ezek. 3:6; 47:22; Mal. 1:11).

(7) Finally, what are we to conclude about the numerous cases of Gentile participation in Israel's history as well as the examples of faith found among non-Israelites? Note the "mixed crowd" that came out of Egypt with Israel (Exod. 12:38 NRSV); the protection of the alien (Deut. 10:19); RAHAB the Canaanite harlot (Josh. 2); the whole story of RUTH and her contribution to the Davidic line; ITTAI (2 Sam. 15:21); and NAAMAN (2 Ki. 5).

This universalism must not hide the equally obvious fact of Israel's uniqueness and particular ELECTION. This particularism is vital and essential to the covenant relationship of Yahweh and Israel: "Now if you obey me fully and keep my covenant, then out of all nations you will be my treasured possession" (Exod. 19:5; cf. Deut. 7:6–16). The Deuteronomic idea of Yahweh's choosing a "place where his name will dwell" served during the monarchy to justify the establishment of a central sanctuary where not only Israel but all nations would come to worship (cf. Deut. 12; 14:23–25; 15:20; 16:1–16; 17:8, 10; 18:6; 23:16; 31:11; esp. 33:27). History has recorded the elaborate growth of cultic ceremony and ritualism that developed around the temple. The centralizing of Israel's worship in Jerusalem was intended to provide the unity of Israel's covenant relationship with Yahweh. The division of the monarchy in 931 B.C. and the increase in the worship of BAAL in both the southern and northern kingdoms indicates the failure of cultic centralization as well as unity based upon a single sanctuary. With the exilic DIASPORA and the development of the synagogue, Israel had to find her unity in the recovery of that essential spirituality of God's covenantal relationship; hence, later Judaism turned to the Shema (Deut. 6:4–6) as a theological basis for her oneness before God. The debate over a centralized sanctuary never ceased in JUDAISM, and echoes can still be heard in Jesus' discussion with the woman at the well in SYCHAR (cf. Jn. 4).

The concept of unity was vital to OT ESCHATOLOGY. (1) In the prophetic writings there are repeated references to Zion as the source of man's knowledge of God and salvation. "In the last days / the mountain of the LORD's temple will be established / as chief among the mountains; / it will be raised above the hills, / and all nations will stream to it. / Many peoples will come and say, / 'Come, let us go up to the mountain of the LORD, / to the house of the God of Jacob. / He will teach us his ways, / so that we may walk in his paths.' / The law will go out from Zion, / the word of the LORD from Jerusalem" (Isa. 2:2–3; cf. Isa. 56:6–8; 66:18–21; Mic. 4:1–5).

(2) EZEKIEL's apocalyptic vision of a new temple (Ezek. 40–48) points again to the cult as the center of Israel's faith, worship, and unity. Although Ezekiel warns against bringing "foreigners uncircumcised in heart and flesh" (44:7), his enlarged vision of the boundaries of the land obviously includes other nations (47:21–23).

(3) Jeremiah's prophecy of a "new covenant" engraved on the human heart speaks of a spiritual unity transcending all institutions and legal prescriptions (Jer. 31:31–34). It is the same "new covenant" that forms the basis for unity as well as universality in the NT church as the BODY OF CHRIST (cf. Heb. 8:8–12; Matt. 26:17–29; Mk. 14:12–25; Lk. 22:28–30). See COVENANT, THE NEW.

(4) And ultimately, not only in the cultic unity of Israel's worship but in Israel herself—both old and new Israel—as the "people of God," there is to be seen both continuity and unity (cf. Gal. 6:13–16). This can account for the prophetic interpretation

of Israel's return to Palestine as a united kingdom (cf. Jer. 31–34; Ezek. 36–37). Paul's discourse on Israel in Rom. 9–11 also points to the continuing role of Israel in God's *Heilsgeschichte* (salvation history), but it is a role in which all nations will also play a part. It is here that eschatology blends with ecumenism as both universality and unity (cf. Rev. 7:1–17).

II. World and church in the NT. In the NT, the term *oikoumenē* should be viewed in the light of the more frequent term *kosmos G3180*, which speaks of a divinely created world of order and humanity, of an ordered and organic society controlled by the "evil one," and of a world redeemed through Jesus Christ. (Cf. Matt. 4:8; 5:14; 26:13; Mk. 8:36; Jn. 1:9–10, 29; 3:16–19; 4:42; 12:31; Acts 17:24; Rom. 1:18, 20; 11:15; 1 Cor. 1:20–21; 2 Cor. 5:19; Gal. 4:3; 1 Jn. 2:15–17.) Although the longer ending of Mark is of questionable textual authority, there can be no doubt that the mission of the church is coextensive with the universal redemption of Jesus Christ (cf. Mk. 16:15; 2 Cor. 5:14–21). The kingdom of the world becomes the kingdom of Christ (Rev. 11:15).

The NT draws a distinction between the church as a metaphysical spiritual reality transcending all historical institutional forms and the church as a local institution (for the latter, see Acts 8:1; 9:31; 11:22, 26; 12:1; Rom. 16:1; 1 Cor. 1:2; 1 Thess. 1:1). All local congregations, however, depend for their existence upon the metaphysical, spiritual reality of the church as the body of Christ. At the same time, the church always assumes and manifests itself in the reality of institutional societies who bear a distinctively Christological character. Paul's Ephesian letter presents the clearest examples of the NT idea of the church. Speaking of Christ, the apostle says that "God placed all things under his feet and appointed him to be head over everything for the church, which is his body, the fullness of him who fills everything in every way" (Eph. 1:22–23; cf. Col. 1:15–29). The last phrase points not to Christ alone but to Christ and his church (cf. Eph. 2:19–22; 3:1–12; 5:21–33; 2 Cor. 12:12–13; Rom. 12:3–8).

Ecumenically speaking, the church transcends all historical, institutional, and geographical expressions, but is, nevertheless, manifested in all local assemblies called into being by the preaching of Jesus as the Christ (cf. Acts 2:14–47). The pastoral nature of the NT literature reveals the tension of the churches always being called to be *the* church.

III. Conclusions: unity, universality, and institutionalism. *Unity.* In later Christianity the term *catholic* came to designate the unity as well as the universality of the church and is one of the clearest indications that ecumenicity soon became a concern of the postapostolic church. (Note the third article of the APOSTLES' CREED.) IGNATIUS (d. c. A.D. 107) is the first to use the term to distinguish a true church that holds to the apostolic doctrine of Christ from all other institutions founded upon heresy. The NT stress upon unity among Christians is almost too obvious to require illustration. Note, however, Christ's promise to build his church, not churches (Matt. 16:18). Christ's high-priestly prayer in Jn. 17, to which ecumenicists have always appealed, is a prayer that the unity of Christians will serve apologetically the spread of the gospel (Jn. 17:20–26). Earlier in the fourth gospel, Christ is presented as saying "there shall be one flock and one shepherd" (10:16). Paul's repeated emphasis, wherever the church is defined as the body of Christ, is upon her essential oneness in Christ (cf. 1 Cor. 12:12–13; Rom. 12:3–8; Eph. 4:1–16). He confronts the schism of the Corinthian church with the rebuke, "is Christ divided?" (1 Cor. 1:13). (See J. H. Maude in *ERE*, 3:258–61.)

Universality. Christ's great commission is a call to a worldwide mission (Matt. 28:19–20; see COMMISSION, GREAT). The nineteen hundred years of church history is confirmation of the church's ecumenical mission and its partial fulfillment. Yet even in the 1st cent. Paul expressed his "ambition to preach the gospel where Christ was not known," and he hoped that before his life was over he might travel as far as Spain—considered then to be one of the utmost western points of the world (cf. Rom. 15:20, 28). In Acts 1:8, the church's mission is coextensive with "the ends of the earth."

Institutionalism. The themes of unity and universality have more recently raised the question of a united, universal institution that can lay claim to being "Christ's church." No NT evidence can support any attempt to construct a monolithic institution. There is indeed clear evidence that the church in the NT period was institutional in nature, with a Christological, apostolic foundation, with ministerial offices, with a liturgical structure, and with a membership concept capable of ecclesiastical discipline. But there is no evidence that a centralized organization with headquarters in Jerusalem, Antioch, or Rome ever existed in the 1st cent. or was projected for future centuries. (Cf. Matt. 18:15–20; Acts 2:37–47; 6:1–6; 14:23; 20:17, 28–32; 1 Cor. 5:1–13; 10:14–22; 11:17–34; Eph. 2:20; 4:1–16; Phil. 1:1; 1 Tim. 3:1–16; Tit. 1:5–9.) The unity of the early church and the unity that the church in all ages is called to demonstrate is her confession of Jesus as Lord, and her members as servants for Jesus' sake (2 Cor. 4:1–6).

(See further E. Brunner, *The Misunderstanding of the Church* [1953]; L. Newbigin, *The Household of God* [1953]; J. D. Murch, *Co-operation Without Compromise* [1956]; T. F. Torrance, *Conflict and Agreement in the Church*, 2 vols. [1959]; B. Vassady, *Christ's Church: Evangelical, Catholic, and Reformed* [1965]; G. Fackre, *Ecumenical Faith in Evangelical Perspective* [1993]; H. Meyer, *That All May Be One: Perceptions and Models of Ecumenicity* [1999]; M. VanElderen, *Finding a Voice: Communicating the Ecumenical Movement*, new ed. [2001].)

D. M. LAKE

Ed ed (עֵד H6332, "witness"). An altar built by the Reubenites and the Gadites (and the half-tribe of Manasseh) who settled E of the JORDAN, as a witness of their loyalty to the God of Israel and to the tribes W of the river (Josh. 22:34 KJV). See GAD, TRIBE OF; MANASSEH, TRIBE OF; REUBEN. The name Ed appears to be missing in the MT (also in the LXX, but see Syriac and a few Heb. MSS), therefore the KJV has "Ed" in italics on the basis of the explanation in the second part of the verse: "And the children of Reuben and the children of Gad called the altar *Ed:* for it *shall be* a witness between us that the LORD *is* God" (the NRSV and NJPS supply "Witness" rather than "Ed"). The NIV, however, interprets the explanation as the name itself: "… gave the altar this name: A Witness Between Us that the LORD is God."

Edar ee´duhr. KJV alternate form of EDER (only Gen. 35:21).

Eddias i-di´uhs. KJV Apoc. form of IZZIAH (1 Esd. 9:26).

Eddinus ed´uh-nuhs (Εδδινους). One of the temple singers who participated in the PASSOVER celebrated by King JOSIAH (1 Esd. 1:15 NRSV); the KJV and others identify him with JEDUTHUN (cf. 1 Chr. 35:15).

Eden (person) ee´duhn (עֵדֶן H6360, prob. "delight"). Son of Joah and a Levite from the descendants of GERSHON during the time of HEZEKIAH (2 Chr. 29:12). He is probably the same man who faithfully assisted KORE in distributing the contributions made to the temple (31:15).

Eden (region). See BETH EDEN.

Eden, Garden of ee´duhn (עֵדֶן H6359, prob. "delight"; less likely related to Akk. *edinu*, "open field, steppe" [cf. A. R. Millard in *VT* 34 [1984]: 103–6). A beautiful and fertile place where God "put the man he had formed" (Gen. 2:8).

I. Location. Three major possibilities have been suggested for the location of Eden: (a) Armenia, (b) Babylonia, or near the head of the Persian Gulf, and (c) near the N Pole. The last of these may be dismissed quickly, inasmuch as about all it can adduce by way of support is that evidence of tropical flora in the frozen N has been discovered as fossil remains. Babylonia also seems unlikely, because the river-pattern described in Gen. 2:10–14 does not agree with this claim. At least two of the streams mentioned here (the TIGRIS and the EUPHRATES) are known to have been in days of old, as they are to this day, near to one another and springing from the Armenian highlands. With regard to the PISHON and the GIHON, the conjecture has been offered, among others, that they are the Indus and the Nile, but positive identification cannot be established.

Since no such set of four rivers deriving from one major stream can be identified anywhere, it is likely that some major topographical change, such as might have been wrought by the great flood, may have taken place. See FLOOD, GENESIS. (The reverse often occurs that a number of streams in confluence combine to make one stream. The subdividing of a stream is, as far as is known, to be found only in deltas, which is not what is being described here.) The only helpful fact left is that the Tigris and Euphrates still originate in the same general area, as well as do some minor streams (such as Araxes and Murat) that would come close to making up the original four mentioned in the text. To try to make of the Pishon and the Gihon two of the canals that in days of old connected the Tigris and the Euphrates does not seem a happy solution of the problem. These canals originated at a much later date.

II. Description of the garden. The scriptural emphasis in reference to the garden seems to lie in the fact that it constituted a flawless background for human beings who were themselves flawless. It had many tokens of divine goodness and favor made accessible for the first parents. Among these tokens "trees" are mentioned first (Gen. 2:9), all manner of them "pleasing to the eye and good for food." Of particular moment are two special trees, the TREE OF KNOWLEDGE (of good and evil) and the TREE OF LIFE. These may well have been the center of the garden, as they certainly were in their intrinsic importance to mankind. In addition to many types of trees there were numerous animals, representative perhaps of all major classes of the creatures that had been created on the sixth day (1:24–25). It should also be noted that the garden lay "in the east, in Eden." Thus Eden appears as a larger territory within whose confines the garden was located. Hebrew readers would naturally have understood the statement from their perspective, that is, E of Palestine.

That the garden was well-watered is indicated by the statement about the one river and its four headwaters. In biblical language almost always abundance of water is the major physical blessing. At the same time the care of the garden provided a suitable occupation for the first parents, but since nature had not been yet "subjected to frustration" (Rom. 8:20), the work assigned was neither too much nor too little. Lastly, everything points to the possibility that the climate was temperate, for clothing apparently was not a physical necessity. It is not to be wondered that the Garden of Eden became the symbol or epitome of beauty and perfection, to which the following passages bear witness: Isa. 51:3; Ezek. 28:13; 31:9, 16–18; Joel 2:3.

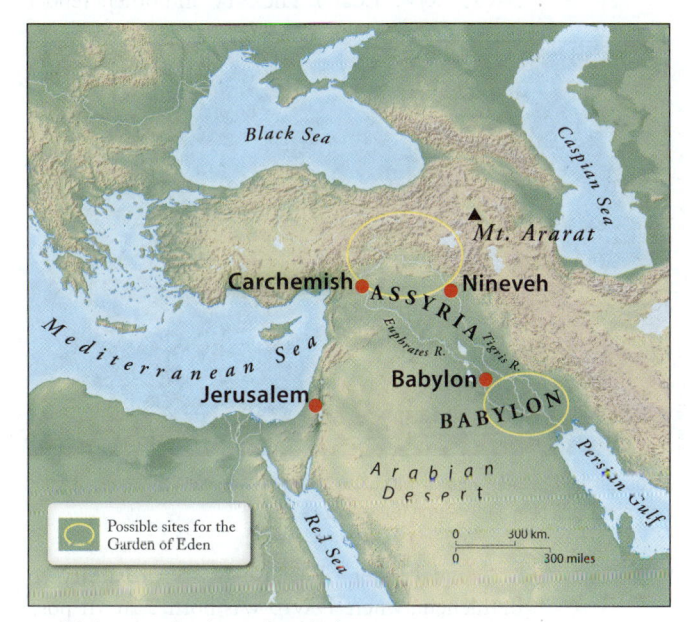

Possible locations for the Garden of Eden.

II. The later history of the garden. At first it must be remembered that cherubim (see CHERUB) were stationed to the E of the garden to prevent the entrance of man (Gen. 3:22). It was also a matter of tradition that CAIN's place of dwelling lay to the E of the garden. From there on, everything is wrapped in silence. There is always the possibility that the garden continued to exist and was the place of the manifestation of the Lord's presence until the time of the flood; if so, the cherubim involved upheld the throne of the Almighty. See also PARADISE. (For a detailed study, see H. N. Wallace, *The Eden Narrative* [1985].) H. C. LEUPOLD

Eder (person) ee′duhr (עֵדֶר *H6374* [1 Chr. 23:23; 24:30] and עֶדֶר *H6376* [8:15], derivation uncertain). **(1)** Son of BERIAH and descendant of BENJAMIN (1 Chr. 8:15; KJV, "Ader").

(2) Son of MUSHI and descendant of LEVI through MERARI (1 Chr. 23:23; 24:30).

Eder (place) ee´duhr (עֵדֶר *H6375* [Josh. 15:21] and מִגְדַּל־עֵדֶר *H4468* [Gen. 35:21], derivation uncertain). **(1)** The "tower of Eder" was located between BETHLEHEM and HEBRON, where JACOB pitched his tent after RACHEL's death, and where REUBEN cohabited with BILHAH (Gen. 35:21–22 NRSV; KJV, "Edar"). The NIV and others render it "Migdal Eder." Because of its proximity to Bethlehem, where DAVID was born, MICAH possibly refers to it ("watchtower of the flock") and to OPHEL ("stronghold of the Daughter of Sion," where David's palace stood in Jerusalem) as symbols of the royal house of David (Mic. 4:8).

(2) A town in the NEGEV district within the tribe of JUDAH (Josh. 15:21), identified by some with el-ʿAdar, c. 5 mi. S of GAZA on the right bank of the Wadi Ghazzeh. Some MSS of the SEPTUAGINT, however, have either *Ara* (Codex B) or *Arad* (several Lucianic cursives), suggesting that ARAD is probably the correct reading (cf. Y. Aharoni, *The Land of the Bible: A Historical Geography*, rev. [1979], 117).   J. REA

Edes ee´deez. KJV Apoc. form of IDDO (1 Esd. 9:35).

Edessa i-des´uh. An ancient city in NW MESOPOTAMIA, between the TIGRIS and EUPHRATES Rivers; today it is Şanlı Urfa, in SE Turkey, near the border with Syria (not to be confused with Edhessa in N Greece). Also known as Orhay (Syr. *ʾUrhay*) and Antioch Callirrhoe, it became prominent as the capital of Osroëne in Hellenistic and Roman times. According to an apocryphal tradition, one of its kings, ABGAR V, was converted in the 1st cent. by Jesus' disciple Addai (THADDAEUS). Certainly the gospel reached Edessa before the end of the 2nd cent., and the city became the major center of Syriac-speaking Christianity. Important Christian literature, including probably one or more Syriac versions of the Bible, originated in Edessa. The best-known Syriac theologian, EPHRAEM SYRUS, did most of his work there in the 4th cent. The city fell to the Muslims early in the 7th cent. (See F. C. Burkitt, *Early Eastern Christianity* [1904]; J. B. Segal, *Edessa the "Blessed City"* [1970]; W. S. McCullough, *A Short History of Syriac Christianity to the Rise of Islam* [1982]; H. J. W. Drijvers in *JJS* 36 [1985]: 88–102.)

edict. See DECREE.

edification. The Greek noun *oikodomē G3869* ("a building" or "the act of building") as well as its cognate verb *oikodomeō G3868* ("to build") occur sometimes in the NT in a literal sense (Matt 23:29; 24:1). More frequently they are used in the metaphorical sense. Christ spoke of building his church (Matt. 16:18), and Paul of the building up of character in Christians (e.g., 2 Cor. 10:8; 13:10; Eph. 4:12, 16). The apostle describes the church as a building (1 Cor. 3:9; Eph. 2:21), and talks of erecting it on the proper foundation (1 Cor. 3:10, 12, 14). Paul says to the Corinthians that when they come together, each one making a contribution (hymn, instruction, revelation, etc.), all is to be done "for edification" (14:26; NIV, "for the strengthening of the church"). He is anxious that Christians mature, that they grace Christ's cause, that they become well-founded in the faith.

The Puritans stressed edification, and influenced John Wesley (1703–91) in the matter. Wesley wrote a sermon on "The Means of Grace," in which he treated prayer, Scripture searching, and the Lord's Supper as the chief means of being built up in the faith. Elsewhere he added fasting and Christian conference (fellowship) to these three primary means of growth in grace (cf. J. K. Grider, *Taller My Soul: The Means of Christian Growth* [1964]).   J. K. GRIDER

Jacob pitched his tent near a watchtower somewhere near this area at Eder between Bethlehem and Hebron (Gen. 35:21–22).

Edna ed′nuh (Εδνα, from עֶדְנָא H6363, "delight"; cf. Adna; Adnah; Eden). Wife of Raguel (Tob. 7:2–3); their daughter Sarah became the wife of Tobias son of Tobit (7:9–16; 10:10–13). Edna prepared the marriage chamber and comforted Sarah. She accepted Tobias as a son-in-law, and her farewell to the departing couple is touching; in turn, she received the blessing of Tobias. In the Vulgate she is named Anna, which is also the name of the wife of Tobit. J. P. Lewis

Edom ee′duhm (אֱדוֹם H121, "red"; gentilic אֱדוֹמִי H122, "Edomite"). A name that can refer to Esau (alluding to the red vegetable soup he received in exchange for his birthright, Gen. 25:30), to the land of his descendants (32:3; 36:20–21, 30), or to the Edomites collectively (Num. 20:18–21; Amos 1:6, 11; Mal. 1:4).

I. The territory of Edom. The land that was occupied by the Edomites was a rugged mountainous area, stretching S from the Brook Zered (Wadi el-Hesa, which formed the boundary with Moab) to the Gulf of Aqabah for nearly 100 miles, while to the E and W extending up to 40 miles across the Wilderness of Edom. Although the terrain was inhospitable, there were several good cultivable areas (Num. 20:17–19). Edomite territory generally has been divided into three areas, the first of which was the northern section, embracing Bozrah and Punon (modern Feinan). It comprised a rough rectangle about 15 mi. wide and 70 mi. long, extending S from the Brook Zered. This area ranged in elevation from about 5,000 ft. above sea level at Bozrah to nearly 5,700 ft. near Teman (modern Tawilan), where the S limit was marked by the escarpment overlooking the Hismeh Valley. This quadrangle formed the fortified area of Edom in antiquity, being dotted with a series of strong points, particularly on the exposed E frontier. In biblical times the king's highway passed along the E plateau after ascending the Wadi Laban, and then passed S near to Tophel, Bozrah, and Dana until it descended into the Hismeh Valley. Sela, the capital of Edom, lay to the W of the king's highway on the massive plateau of Umm el-Biyara, which towers 1,000 ft. above Petra (the Greek form of Sela).

The second principal area of Edom, the outlying district, comprised the region S of the Hismeh Valley as far as the Gulf of Aqabah, which was under Edomite control though not settled. Those portions of the Arabah involved were valuable for their iron and copper mines, and constituted an important source of wealth for the Edomites who worked them.

The mountains of Edom. (View to the E.)

In addition, trading routes connecting Mesopotamia and Egypt passed through the S extremity of this region, thus contributing further to the Edomite treasury. A third area of land, to the W of the Arabah, was occupied by nomadic tribes sometimes loosely associated with the Edomites (Gen. 36:11–12), but were never actually under firm Edomite control. It was through this area that the Israelites passed just prior to the conquest of Canaan.

II. Its history and population. Archaeological investigations reveal that the land was occupied before the time of Esau, since from the 23rd to the 20th centuries B.C. there was a thriving civilization in the locality, after which the land remained uninhabited until the 13th cent. B.C., apart from bands of roving bedouin. Whether the invasion of Kedorlaomer (Gen. 14) was responsible for the depopulation of the area or not is hard to say, but it is probable that Esau and his sons absorbed the original Horite settlers (14:6) when they came to Mount Seir (36:5–8). The Horites already had some tribal chiefs ruling the country (36:29–30), and Esau took the daughter of one of these chiefs for a wife (36:2, 25). The descendants of Esau were also tribal chiefs (36:15–19, 40–43), and no doubt took over Horite functions in this respect (cf. Deut. 2:12, 22).

Esau had already occupied Edom when JACOB returned from HARAN (Gen. 32:3; 36:6–8; Deut. 2:4–5), and the Edomites were well established in the country and living by a monarchic pattern prior to the exodus period, having apparently abandoned the system of tribal chiefs. Unfortunately all inscriptions and written records of the Edomites have perished, and it is necessary to depend on Egyptian, Hebrew, and Assyrian sources for information about them.

In this connection the mention of Edom and Seir occurs in the records of two pharaohs, MERNEPTAH (c. 1225–1215 B.C.) and RAMSES III (c. 1198–1167), as being their tributaries, but caution has to be exercised in assessing this claim. Hebrew records (Gen. 36:31–39; 1 Chr. 1:43–51) indicate that the Edomites possessed kingship long in advance of the Israelites, thus further attesting to the antiquity of that particular social pattern in Edom. The Edomites were also mentioned in the 13th cent. B.C. Papyrus Anastasi VI of Egypt (*ANET*, 259) in connection with the passing of shepherd tribes from Edom to the lush pasturelands of the NILE delta and again in TELL EL-AMARNA

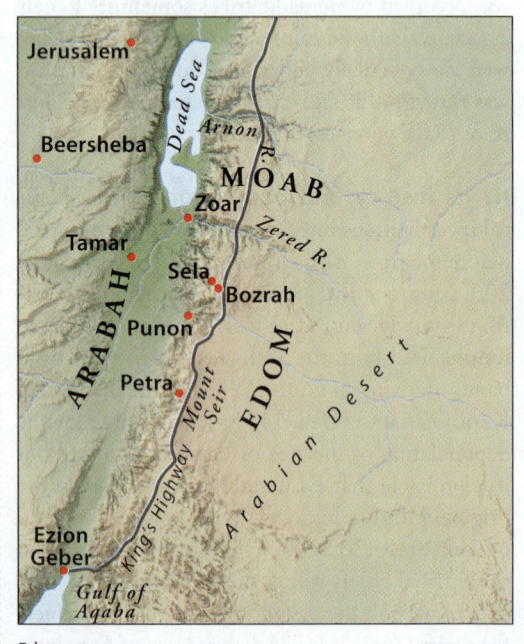

Edom.

letter 256 (*ANET*, 486), dated about 1400, where Edom (*Udumu*) was described as one of the enemies of a Jordanian prince. In view of the constant OT emphasis on the closeness of racial relationship between Israel and Edom, it is probable that originally the Edomites came from ARAM. However, at an early period they intermarried with the Canaanites (the "Hittites" of Gen. 26:34) and probably also with the native Horites of Seir (36:20–30), whom they absorbed (Deut. 2:12), thus making Edom a composite entity. (On the Edomite king list, see J. R. Bartlett in *JTS* NS 16 [1965]: 301–14; E. A. Knauf in *ZAW* 97 [1985]: 245–53.)

Despite the discourtesy of being refused permission to travel through the country by the king's highway, the Israelites were forbidden to hate their Edomite brothers (Deut. 23:7–8). In the time of JOSHUA the tribe of JUDAH was allocated territory reaching to the borders of Edom (Josh. 15:1, 21), though not violating Edomite territory. During the time of the conquest and settlement there was no recorded contact between Israel and Edom. Two centuries later, SAUL was in conflict with the Edomites (1 Sam. 14:47), although some of them were in his service (1 Sam. 21:7; 22:9, 18). It fell to DAVID to subdue the country and place garrisons throughout the land (2 Sam. 8:14), a defeat that was made more decisive when JOAB, the Israelite commander, conducted a six-month campaign designed to eradicate all male Edomites (1 Ki. 11:15–16). However, some warriors escaped the slaughter, for a certain Hadad, a royal prince, fled to Egypt and was subsequently a source of annoyance to SOLOMON (11:14–22). See HADAD (PERSON).

The subjugation of Edom marked an important stage in the economic growth of the kingdom under Solomon, for not merely did he secure control of the rich caravan trade by this means, but also made possible the exploitation of the COPPER and IRON mines of the territory. Solomon also built a port at EZION GEBER on the Gulf of Aqabah that served as the terminal point for his RED SEA trading vessels to OPHIR and ARABIA (1 Ki. 9:26; 2 Chr. 8:17). Archaeological excavations show that, on a new site about 2.5 mi. W of Aqabah (Elath), there was constructed a copper and iron smeltery in the time of Solomon. Situated between the hill country of Sinai and Edom, it was ideally located for the purpose, since it received the full force of the N winds howling down the Arabah rift-valley. The ore for the blast furnaces was obtained locally, and was probably processed by slave labor.

In the time of JEHOSHAPHAT (870/869–848 B.C.), Edom joined AMMON and MOAB in an attack upon Judah (2 Chr. 20:1), but the allies subsequently came to blows (20:22–23). Jehoshaphat tried to use the port facilities at Ezion Geber, which he apparently reconstructed after they had burned down in the preceding century; but his fleet was wrecked by the strong winds (1 Ki. 22:48; 2 Chr. 20:36–37). At this period Edom was governed by a deputy who functioned as king (1 Ki. 22:47). He was under the control of Judah, and joined the coalition between Israel and Judah in an attack on MESHA, king of Moab (2 Ki. 3:4–27).

Edom rebelled in the time of JEHORAM (848–841 B.C.), cutting off, sacking, and occupying Ezion Geber (2 Ki. 8:21). Although Jehoram defeated the Edomites in battle, he failed to subjugate them, and Edom became independent for some forty years. AMAZIAH (796–767) invaded Edom, slew 10,000 warriors in the valley of Salt, and captured Sela their capital (14:7; 2 Chr. 25:11, 12). UZZIAH (767–740/39) his successor completed the conquest and restored the port at Elath (2 Ki. 14:22), but in 735 Edom regained its freedom from Judah, apparently by allying with Israel and Aram, and carried captives away from the southern kingdom (2 Ki. 16:6; 2 Chr. 28:17). Judah never recovered Edom; Assyrian inscriptions show that in 732 TIGLATH-PILESER III compelled Kaush-Malaku, king of Edom, to become his tributary, a state of affairs that lasted for a century with virtually no interruption.

The heavy tribute required of Edom diminished its prosperity considerably, resulting in a general decline of the kingdom and quiet acceptance of Babylonian suzerainty in 604 B.C. The Edomites allied with NEBUCHADNEZZAR when he overthrew Jerusalem in 587, and were overjoyed at the destruction of their traditional foes (Ps. 137:7; Lam. 4:21–22; Obad. 10–16). Some Edomites subsequently occupied S Judah and made HEBRON their capital, thus forming the IDUMEA of the postexilic era. During the 5th cent. B.C., Edom proper came under Arab control, and by the 4th cent. it had been overrun by the NABATEANS, who entered the land from the S and E, making Petra their capital city. While some Edomites moved to Idumea, others apparently remained and were absorbed by the Nabatean Arabs.

Known Idumean history commenced with the Maccabean revolt, part of the military success of Judas MACCABEE comprising a victory over the Idumeans in the Akrabattene in 164 B.C. (1 Macc. 5:1–5; Jos. *Ant*. 12.8.1). John Hyrcanus occupied all Idumea about 120 and compelled its people to adopt Judaism (Jos. *Ant*. 13.9.1; 15.7.9). When the Romans took over Palestine, the Edomites naturally fell under their jurisdiction, one result being that from Idumea came Antipater as governor of the country in the year 63. His son, HEROD the Great, founded in 37 B.C. the final dynasty of Palestinian rulers, and after the destruction of Jerusalem in A.D. 70 the Idumeans disappeared from history, thus ending the varied career of the Edomites. Ironically, the descendants of those who had exulted over the fall of Jerusalem in 587 B.C. were among its staunchest defenders against Rome in A.D. 66–70.

III. Edom in the OT. The traditional antagonism between Edom and Israel had its roots in the relations between Esau, identified with Edom, and Jacob, representing Israel (Gen. 36:1). In Gen. 27:11 there is perhaps a play on words in the description of Isaac as "smooth" (*ḥālāq H2747*) and Esau as "hairy" (*śāʿîr H8537*), since Mount HALAK, standing on the S border of Israel, faced the Edomite boundary of Seir (Josh. 11:17; 12:7), but this may be entirely accidental. The bitter hatred of Edom for the Israelites was severely censured by almost all the prophets of Judah. Amos condemned the Edomites for their brutal practices in war and mentioned an otherwise unrecorded border conflict (Amos 2:1) in which the Moabites burned the bones of an Edomite king to powder, thus inflicting the greatest possible personal insult upon a corpse. The whole of the prophecy of OBADIAH is given over to a bitter denunciation of Edom and a prediction of its destruction. The principal point at issue in this prophecy was the sense of betrayal felt by the Judeans when blood relatives, albeit hereditary enemies, turned upon them in the time of crisis that saw the fall of Jerusalem in 587 B.C., and aided the common enemy.

The memory of this tragic occurrence was perpetuated by the psalmist (Ps. 137:7), who prayed for retribution for such a dastardly act. A prophetic oracle in JEREMIAH (Jer. 49:7–22) reflects much the same sentiments as Obadiah in predicting the desolation of Edom, a theme that also occurs in Isa. 11:14; 34:5–17; Ezek. 35:1–15. The book of MALACHI was particularly emphatic as to the divine choice of Jacob and the uncompromising rejection of Esau as a medium of revelation (Mal. 1:2–4). On the other hand, ZEPHANIAH and ZECHARIAH did not include Edom among those people who were to be punished by destruction, and in the Torah provision was made for the admission of Edomites into the community of Israel (Deut. 23:7–8). If the characters in the book of JOB, which has as its setting a locale in the Arabian desert E of Palestine, were in fact Edomites, the author of this work had clearly risen far above purely national sentiments in making them the vehicles of divine revelation in the vital area of human experience involving suffering. Nevertheless, of all the neighbors of Israel, Edom, as a nation, was the only one who was not extended any promise of mercy from God.

(See further F. Buhl, *Geschichte der Edomiter* [1893]; N. Glueck, *The Other Side of the Jordan*, rev. ed. [1970], 138–67; J. F. A. Sawyer and D. J. A. Clines, eds., *Midian, Moab and Edom: The History and Archaeology of Late Bronze and Iron Age Jordan and Northeast Arabia* [1983]; J. R. Bartlett, *Edom and the Edomites* [1989]; P. Bienkowski, ed., *Early Edom and Moab: The Beginning of the Iron Age in Southern Jordan* [1992]; K. G. Hoglund in *Peoples of the Old Testament World*, ed. A. J. Hoerth et al. [1994], 335–47; B. Dicou, *Edom, Israel's Brother and Antagonist: The Role of Edom in Biblical Prophecy and Story* [1994]; D. V. Edelman, ed., *You Shall Not Abhor an Edomite for He Is Your Brother: Edom and Seir in History and Tradition* [1995].)

R. K. HARRISON

Edrei ed′ree-i (אֶדְרֶעִי *H167*, possibly "strong," if related to Aram. אֲדְרָע *H10013*, "arm, force"). **(1)** A residence city of OG king of BASHAN (Deut. 1:4; 3:10; Josh. 12:4; 13:12). It was built on a bluff overlooking a southern fork of the YARMUK River, along the S boundary of Bashan near the eastern desert. Here Og could watch for invaders from the S or from the E. MOSES defeated Og in a pitched battle outside Edrei, which was then destroyed (Num. 21:33–35; Deut. 3:1–6). The ruins were included in the allotment to the Makir clan of the tribe of MANASSEH (Josh. 13:31). Edrei is identified with modern Derʿa, a town of 5,000 in southern Syria, c. 60 mi. S of DAMASCUS and 30 mi. E of the JORDAN. The site has ruins going back to Early Bronze times as well as a remarkable subterranean city of numerous streets, shops, rooms, and cisterns, probably from the Hellenistic or Roman period.

(2) A fortified city allotted to the tribe of NAPHTALI, near KEDESH in Upper GALILEE (Josh. 19:37), possibly modern Tell Khureibeh. It is probably the same as ʾitrʿ, #91 in the campaign list of THUTMOSE III at Karnak (*ANET*, 242; Y. Aharoni, *The Land of the Bible: A Historical Geography*, rev. ed. [1979], 162).

J. REA

education in biblical times. Several Hebrew verbs in the OT are used of learning and instruction, such as *ḥānak H2852*, "to train, dedicate" (Prov. 22:6, "Train a child in the way he should go"; from this root is derived the Modern Heb. word for "education," *ḥinnûk*), *lāmad H4340*, "to learn" (Deut. 4:10; piel "to teach," Jdg. 3:2; from this root is derived the term TALMUD), *yāsar H3579*, "to teach, correct" (Prov. 9:7), and *yārâ H3723*, hiphil "to throw, direct, teach" (1 Sam. 12:23). From these verbs are derived various relevant nouns, such as *môreh H4621*, "teacher, instructor" (Prov. 5:13), *limmud H4341*, "student, disciple" (Isa. 8:16), *mûsār H4592*, "discipline, correction, instruction" (Prov. 1:2), and especially *tôrâ H9368*, "direction, instruction, teaching, law" (Deut. 1:5; Prov. 1:8). (Cf. the entry "Learning/teaching" in *NIDOTTE*, 5:117–18.)

Because repetition was at the heart of learning, the verb for "repeat," *šānâ H9101* (cf. also *šānan H9112* in Deut. 6:7), came to be used in postbiblical Hebrew for "to study, teach" (with special reference to the MISHNAH, a noun derived from the same verb). Its ARAMAIC cognate *tĕnê* (or *tĕnāʾ*) is the origin of the term *Tanna* (pl. *Tannaim*), "teacher," applied to the sages quoted in the Mishnah. More generally, teachers were referred to with the term *rab H8042* (which in the Bible means "commander, chief officer," from the word for "great") or derived forms, such as *rabbî* ("my master"), *rabbān* (a heightened title), Aramaic *rabbāʾ*, etc.

This usage is reflected in the NT, where the term RABBI is translated *didaskalos* G1437, "teacher" (Jn. 1:38; "rabboni" in 20:16). Jesus is described as TEACHER about fifty times in the Gospels, and he is frequently said to have taught (verb *didaskō* G1438, e.g., Matt. 7:29; cf. the noun *didachē* G1439, "teaching," Jn. 7:16). He taught the multitudes (Mk. 2:13); he taught in the synagogue (1:21). He also taught his disciples (Matt. 5:1–2). The Greek term for DISCIPLE, *mathētēs* G3412 (from the verb *manthanō* G3443, "to learn," Matt. 11:28) occurs over 200 times in the Gospels. Having been taught by Jesus, his disciples were told to teach others also, making them disciples (Matt. 28:19–20). (For other terms, see *NIDNTT*, 1:480–94; 3:759–81.)

  I. Introduction
 II. Jewish education in OT times
    A. Origin and aims
    B. Development
    C. Characteristics
    D. Synagogue
    E. Schools and academies
    F. Personnel
    G. The place and use of the law
    H. Educational symbols, principles, and methods
    I. The Qumran sect
    J. The Diaspora
    K. Conclusion and criticism
 III. Hellenistic education
    A. Origin, development, and aims
    B. Characteristics
    C. Influence on Jewish education
    D. Conclusion
 IV. The education of Jesus
  V. The education of the apostles
    A. The Twelve
    B. Paul
 VI. Education in the church in holiness and maturity

I. Introduction. The purpose of this article limits investigation to the development of education in Israel and the early church. But it will be necessary to say a few words about the background out of which Israel's educational ideals developed.

Educational systems had evolved as early as the 3rd millennium B.C., and there are a number of school texts dating from about the year 2500. From these documents we learn of numerous schools for scribes in ancient SUMER. In them literary works were copied and studied. The study was connected with the training for the needs of the temples, palace courts, and the administration of the empire. Education of this kind was voluntary and costly, and pupils were drawn from the upper class. Subjects studied were botany, zoology, geology, geography, mathematics, languages, and other cultural studies. The schools were staffed by a professor and his assistants who gave regular classroom tuition. A teacher was referred to as "father" and he referred to his pupils as "sons." (See M. Civil, "Education (in Mesopotamia)," *ABD*, 2:301–5. Note also D. M. Carr, *Writing on the Tablet of the Heart: Origins of Scripture and Literature* [2005], which compares the educational currricula of both Mesopotamia and Egypt with the alphabetic cultures of Israel and Greece.)

The profession of the scribes was highly regarded also in ancient EGYPT. Other occupations are compared unfavorably with it. Such was the prestige of this profession that a severe discipline and single-minded study could be required of those who intended to enter it. The scribal school was attached to the temple and was called the "House of Life." Study was divided into two sections, elementary and higher education. The elementary education consisted of the learning of WRITING (calligraphy), the study of ancient literature, and the copying of texts. At the end of this educational period, students transferred either to the government administration or to the priesthood. If to the former, they received a higher education in the duties of office, composition, geography, and natural science. If to the priesthood, their study was in theology and medicine.

Three points of contact or similarity with Israel may be mentioned here. First, education was connected with the TABERNACLE or the TEMPLE. At an early age, SAMUEL was dedicated to God's service and was brought to the tabernacle, where he ministered to the Lord and was educated by ELI the priest. The incident raises the question as to whether there was a school attached to the sanctuary, even

Stela of a scribe named Dedu-Sobek and his family (from the period of the 12th dynasty in Egypt). The duties of a scribe included teaching.

in those early days. Many OT scholars now claim that around the cultic shrines in Israel there were schools of PRIESTS who were responsible for the transmission of the law, both oral and written. If such was the case, it is a parallel situation to what took place in Egypt and the ANE.

Second, notice the class of men known as SCRIBES in Israel. They are to be compared with the scribes of Egypt and the ANE, where such officials played an important part in the administration of the nation. They were friends, philosophers, and guides to the kings and leaders of the nation of their time. In Israel there is little evidence for the existence of a scribal class until the exilic and postexilic period of history. Prior to this, the stage had been dominated by such figures as MOSES, the judges, the kings, the prophets, and the priests. It may be that the scribal functions were carried out by some of these officials. Indeed, it has been suggested that Moses learned a great deal about the scribal activities in the course of his education in Egypt.

It was not until the time of the EXILE, however, that the scribes came to the fore in Israel. EZRA is described as a *sōpēr* H6221 ("scribe, teacher") who was "well versed in the law of Moses, which the LORD, the God of Israel had given" (Ezra 7:6). This description seems to assume that the institution of scribes, though not a special class, had been in existence for some time. Some officials carried out secretarial functions in the king's court and in the administration of the nation (cf. 2 Sam. 8:17; 1 Chr. 24:6; 27:32; 2 Chr. 24:11; 26:11; 34:13; Jer. 36:26). Other scribes also were occupied in the transmission of the law (Jer. 8:8). Initially it is possible that the priests combined scribal functions with their teaching duties. The later priesthood, however, developed in a different direction. The upper class became involved in politics, and other priests and Levites were involved in the intricacies of temple worship. Biblical scholarship and exposition passed over into the hands of a special class of scribes. Ezra the scribe, who was a priest, marks the development of this new profession (Ezra 7:6, 11; Neh. 8:4, 9, 13). From the time of Ezra onward, the scribes were a special class of biblical scholars, exegetes, official teachers, and spiritual leaders.

Third, there was apparently contact with the background of the ancient world in the reference to a teacher as "father" and the pupil as "my son" (Prov. 2:1 et al.). It is probable that the scribes were the "wise" of Proverbs who collated the Wisdom Literature of the OT and became the educators of Israel.

II. Jewish education in OT times

A. Origin and aims. Educational ideas and practice begin with the birth of the nation. OT scholarship has long recognized a double origin for Israel: the first began with the call of Abraham and the second with Moses and the exodus. The Israelites were called to understand themselves as the people of God and to come to know how they should serve the Lord who had called them. Thus the primary aim of all the educational activity was religious (Gen. 18:19). The goal was to train the young to know and serve the Lord (Deut. 6:7; Prov. 1:7) so that throughout their life they would not depart from this way (Prov. 22:6). Thus religious education centered its attention on the TORAH (God's law or instruction) and aimed at educating the Jews for living. It was not merely an education to make a living but was concerned with persons and the forming of their character. Knowing was not divorced from being and doing, and good character was seen to result from a right relationship with God through the study of the Torah. The primacy of the Torah embraced the whole of life from the cradle to the grave. One was never too old or too young to learn. It embraced every aspect of life also. From the time of Ezra onward, the life of the Jews was Torah-centric. They became known as "the people of the Book." It was this that separated them from all other people.

It may be said that the Jewish aims in education were almost exclusively religious, sometimes neglecting cultural development. In later JUDAISM, the preoccupation with the Torah developed, at least in some circles, into a legalistic approach and even into a form of self-righteousness (cf. Lk. 18:9). In spite of this narrowness, Jewish educational aims succeeded where the systems of SPARTA, ATHENS, and ROME failed. The latter were unsuccessful because of faulty aims. The system of Sparta may be said to have aimed at the obliteration of the individual in the service of the state. The aim in Athens may be said to be the training of the individual in the service of culture. In Rome, the training of the individual was in the service of the state. The aim in Israel, however, was the training of the individual in the service of God. Rome, Sparta, and Athens failed at a moral level. Their systems did not contain the faith capable of challenging indifference and superficiality. Therefore, they lost their sense of direction and failed. It has been said that "the Graeco-Roman world was decaying and dying from the dearth of true educational ideals" (W. M. Ramsay, *The Education of Christ: Hillside Reveries* [1902], 66). Jewish education never lost its sense of direction. Its intention was not education in academic and technical knowledge, but education in holiness (Lev. 19:2). Though the people of Israel often forgot the ideals, there were always priests, prophets, scribes, sages, rabbis, and teachers to remind them. God and not man was the center; righteousness, not self-interest, was the aim (Exod. 19:6).

B. Development. The Jewish educational system was the result of a long and gradual development from a simple origin to a complex organization as it appears in NT times. Throughout the OT period there was nothing like a state educational system. Generally speaking, the boys were taught the necessary skills of AGRICULTURE by their fathers, and the girls were taught domestic skills by their mothers. But as education in Israel meant education in living and serving God, attention must be drawn to the necessity of reading and understanding the law; hence the question of literacy in OT times. Throughout the ANE, as early as the beginning of the 3rd millennium, writing was a sign of civilization. In the 2nd millennium ALPHABETS were developed with a resulting increase of literacy. As yet, few documents from the preexilic period have been found in Palestine, but many thousands have been discovered in neighboring territories. It is reasonable to assume that its proximity to other cultural centers enabled Israel to share the art of writing throughout all the periods covered by the OT. Throughout the whole of the OT period there were individuals in Israel who could read and write. Moses read the Decalogue (Exod. 24.12, cf. 17:14; 34:27; Num. 24:4; Deut. 30:10; Josh. 8:31), and his assistants apparently were literate officials (Num. 11:16). During the wandering in the wilderness, the priests wrote down curses (5:23). Samuel wrote down the rights and duties of kingship (1 Sam. 10:25). David wrote letters to Joab (2 Sam. 11:14). Solomon wrote to Hiram, king of Tyre (2 Chr. 2:1–10). Scribes recorded lists of persons (1 Chr. 24:6). The prophet Isaiah wrote (Isa. 8:1); Jeremiah dictated his teaching to his secretary Baruch (Jer. 36:27).

It is impossible to say what proportion of the population was taught to read and write. E. W. Heaton (*Everyday Life in Old Testament Times* [1957], 178–79) suggests that only a small percentage would have been literate. Isaiah distinguishes the literate and illiterate (Isa. 29:12), and he mentions a child's writing (10:19). Isaiah was in close touch with the aristocratic circle of the court, and his casual reference cannot be used as the basis for a sweeping generalization. Far more significant of the general state of affairs is the fact that when an Israelite borrowed money he did

EDUCATION IN BIBLICAL TIMES

Akkadian school text listing personal names, each beginning with the same cuneiform sign (c. 2250 B.C., prob. from Girsu).

not write an I.O.U., but gave a garment in pledge (Deut. 24:13). The garment had no security value and probably was used as a symbol of indebtedness by the illiterate.

It is quite certain that some boys were taught to read and write, and it is possible that evidence of their writing exercises has survived. The rough scribbling known as the GEZER Calendar has been plausibly interpreted as a student's effort, and in 1938 someone noticed the first five letters of the Hebrew alphabet scratched in their conventional order on the vertical face of a step of the royal palace at LACHISH. This inscription has been dated in the early part of the 8th cent. B.C. It has been suggested that it was written by a boy who was just learning his alphabet. G. R. Driver has suggested that Isa. 28:10 ("precept upon precept, line upon line" [NRSV]) is a reference to a child's spelling lesson. It also has been suggested that the Israelite teacher had his boys repeat, in turn, the letters of the alphabet.

It seems likely that increasing numbers of Israelites became literate as time passed. Those who could not write but needed to transact official business simply made their mark. This was done by placing one of the letters of the alphabet at the foot of the script (Job 31:35). Another method of signing a document was to seal it. Such evidence as we have would suggest that prior to the monarchy and during the monarchy, education of a formal nature was only for the few. Such teaching was done in Hebrew, in the homes by the parents. In the exilic and postexilic periods, education expanded its scope to many more individuals and was carried out in ARAMAIC as well as Hebrew. Such teaching continued to be done in the home, but also in schools and by specialized individuals such as the scribes. With the coming of the Greeks in the 4th cent. B.C., the Greek language also was used in Israelite education. Thus, we notice a development in Israelite education from teaching in the home to a developed school system. It should be noted that from the first, nurses or guardians or teachers *in loco parentis* were employed among the higher classes (see Ruth 4:16; 2 Sam. 4:4; 2 Ki. 10:5; Isa. 49:23).

Some scholars believe that there is evidence of literacy, even among the peasants, by the 10th cent. B.C., that is, during the early monarchy; thus it has been suggested that though literacy was not universal (Isa. 29:11) it was widespread (see Deut. 6:9; 17:18–19; 27:2–8; Josh. 18:4, 8–9; Jdg. 8:14; Isa. 10:19). The SILOAM inscription, the LACHISH letters, and the ELEPHANTINE papyri show widespread writing of daily affairs. Further, the development of the cursive script indicates a broadening use by the masses. (1 Macc. 1:56 indicates that copies of the Torah were in houses, and other Jewish literature shows a high degree of literacy in the days of the second commonwealth.)

With the development of literacy a change in the aims of education can be detected. The fundamental aim in Israelite education was religious, but one can distinguish two separate emphases. One was the transmission of a historical heritage.

Israelites were requested to teach their history (Exod. 12:26–27; 13:7–8, 14; Josh. 4:21–22). They were required to remember to teach the ordinances (Deut. 4:9–10; 6:20–21; 7:17–19; 32:7). The aim was to transmit an ethical heritage (Gen. 18:19; cf. Exod. 20:1–17). Of course, ethical injunctions were aimed at producing a good and just society (Lev. 19). Social justice is linked with the HOLINESS of God (Amos 2:6–7). The fear of the Lord is to lead to a good life (Prov. 9:10). In fact, WISDOM is equated with life itself (8:35). In the Wisdom Literature, the emphasis shifts to instruction in ethical conduct of life. Here the instruction in daily existence finds many parallels in the literature of the ANE. There is instruction, for example, concerning the sex life (5:3–21). Again and again the stress is laid on the need for instruction for the good life. This is the purpose of education, to instruct in righteousness (1:2–4). The need for the continuity of this instruction remains life-long (1:5).

C. Characteristics.

The most important characteristic of Jewish education was its whole religious ethos and intention. Consequently, the system lacked scientific character. We find nothing of physics, chemistry, biology, psychology, and the other natural sciences. But the Hebrews knew many practical TRADES and skills: building, mining, metallurgy, wood, and stone work (Exod. 35:30–35). The point of significance is that there were no schools to teach these trades; rather, they were learned in apprenticeships. As far as we know, there were no schools of music, architecture, sculpture, painting, arts, or the theater. The place that MUSIC plays in the WORSHIP in Israel suggests that at least this art must have been developed by systematic instruction, but evidence is lacking. Most of the cultural arts here mentioned were associated with the heathen religions and were developed in Greek and Roman culture.

Just as the Jewish educational system ignored the arts, so it ignored also the development of PHILOSOPHY. Philosophic origins presuppose a culture alien to that of Israel. Philosophy originated in a humanistic society that believed in the power of human intellect. Such a presupposition is foreign to the Jewish dependence on divine REVELATION. The whole of Israel's religion, worship, and educational practice was based on the firm belief that God had revealed himself to Moses and to the prophets. It was this historical revelation that was to be communicated in the educational process. (See further F. H. Swift, *Education in Ancient Israel to 70 A.D.* [1919]; N. Drazin, *History of Jewish Education from 515 B.C.E. to 220 C.E.* [1940]; J. Pedersen, *Israel: Its Life and Culture*, 2 vols. [1926–40]; G. H. Blackburn, *Aims of Education in Ancient Israel* [1966]; J. L. Crenshaw, *Education in Ancient Israel: Across the Deadening Silence* [1998]; A. Lemaire, "Education (Ancient Israel)," in *ABD*, 2:305–12.)

D. Synagogue

1. Origin and development. There is no account of the origin of the SYNAGOGUE in the OT, the APOCRYPHA, or the NT. In spite of this lack of information, most scholars feel sure that the synagogue developed as an institution during the exile in BABYLON. In the OT, the only possible reference to synagogues is Ps. 74:8 (*môʿădê-ʾēl*, "meeting places of God"). The SEPTUAGINT uses the Greek word *synagōgē* G5252 on many occasions, but it refers to the whole assembly of Israel, not to the institution of the synagogue (as it frequently does, however, in the NT).

Although the origin of the synagogue is uncertain, its significance can hardly be overestimated. It was this institution that gave Judaism its character. Prior to the exile, WORSHIP in Israel had been centered on the TEMPLE and on the sacrificial cultus. With the destruction of the temple, this focal point was removed. For the exiles even worship at Jerusalem was an impossibility. It seems that the synagogue arose as a place for instruction in the Scriptures and prayer. There are scholars who consider that the exile does not mark the origin of the synagogue but a modification in its functions, worship becoming from then on the principal, though far from the only, purpose, with administrative functions falling into the background. Other scholars have suggested that Ezek. 14:1 ("Some of the elders of Israel came to me and sat down in front of me"; cf. 20:1) provides a probable basis for the origin of the synagogue. After A.D. 70, some interpreted Ezek. 11:16 ("Yet will I be to them as a little sanctuary" [KJV]) to mean that in the worldwide

DIASPORA, Israel would have a synagogue in miniature to replace the lost temple. One may conclude that from a shadowy origin the synagogue developed into the characteristic institution in Judaism by NT times.

One of the few synagogues that date to the period of the Gospels is this one at Gamla (NE of the Sea of Galilee; view to the SW). The small room at the bottom left of the photo may have been used as a Bet Midrash (school) where the rabbis would have taught the Torah to their disciples.

2. Function. In every place in the ancient world where there was a community of Jews, there was a synagogue. In the synagogue there was no altar. The reading of the Torah and prayer took the place of sacrifice. The synagogue became the center of a new social and religious life. The temple had centered God's presence in one place. Now there were synagogues throughout the Diaspora wherever ten adult male Jews were found, bringing God's presence to the people wherever they were. Worship, education, and the government of the community were the purposes the synagogue fulfilled. The purposes of worship and education often were carried forward in one activity, because in the synagogue worship took on the character of instruction.

According to the MISHNAH (*m. Meg.* 4:3), the service of the synagogue consisted of five parts: (a) The reading of the Shema, that is, Deut. 6:4–9; 11:13–21; Num. 15:37–41. (b) The recitation of synagogue prayers (such as the Eighteen Benedictions, though this form may be later than the NT period); at the heart of these prayers is the theme of the restoration of Israel to the land of the fathers and the return of the glory of God to the temple, rebuilt in Jerusalem. (c) The reading from the Law. (d) The reading from the Prophets. (e) The benediction. Because many people could not understand Hebrew, a paraphrase of the lessons was given in Aramaic and an exposition and exhortation drawn from it. This part of the service came after the reading in Hebrew and preceded the benediction. It has been suggested that this is a later practice. NEHEMIAH seems to refer to this practice when he writes, "They read from the Book of the Law of God, making it clear and giving the meaning so that the people could understand what was being read" (Neh. 8:8). The synagogue provided a mass system of adult education in which the Torah was studied weekly. With the destruction of the temple in the 6th cent. B.C., the synagogue came into prominence and it became the most enduring and widespread institution in Israel after the exile. Under its influence, all Jews became students of the law, and without the synagogue they would have perished.

E. Schools and academies. The text of the OT suggests that the prophets were responsible for the first schools in Israel. The prophets' educational role is quite plain from the beginning. They look back to Moses as their founding figure, as the prophet par excellence (Deut. 34:10). He embodied the prophetic ideal: "The Lord your God will raise up for you a prophet like me [i.e., Moses] from among your own brothers. You must listen to him" (18:15). The prophets were considered teachers of Israel as a whole. By the time of the beginning of the Israelite kingdom, there was a prophetic profession (cf. 1 Sam. 10:5, 10; 19:20). The "sons of the prophets" (1 Ki. 20:35 et al.) were the disciples who were taught by the prophets. Later on there is clear evidence of the prophets teaching their disciples (1 Ki. 19:16; 2 Ki. 2:3–8; 4:38; Isa. 8:16). The prophets transmitted knowledge to their disciples, and an aspect of that teaching touched on matters of health (2 Ki. 4:38–41; cf. the practice in Egypt, where theology and medicine were combined; see MEDICINE). As may be expected from a tradition that had its roots in a Mosaic prototype, the teaching of the prophets centered on the Torah, the law, taking into account the question of a relevant interpretation for the times in which they lived.

The development of schools in the more formal sense is related to the growth of the synagogue. If there is some uncertainty as to the time of the origin of the synagogue, the same is true of the origin of the school system in Israel. It does not seem likely that such a system was in operation in the time of the exile. More likely is the suggestion that the development took place under Hellenistic influence, therefore in the 4th cent. B.C. or later. During the second commonwealth, as already mentioned, literacy was widespread, books of the law being found in many houses (see 1 Macc. 1:56–57). Rabbinic literature attributes a compulsory school system to the PHARISEES during the 1st cent. B.C. The Pharisees were the popular party c. 76–67 B.C. Simon ben Shetach (75 B.C.) taught people systematically. He decreed that children should attend school (*bêt hassēper*, "the house of the book," i.e., the Torah, with the explanation and the oral law).

The first elementary school was probably in Jerusalem, with the institution spreading to the urban centers at a later time. Joseph ben Gamala (c. A.D. 65) tried to make elementary education universal and compulsory by endeavoring to provide teachers in all provinces and allowing children to enter the school at the age of six or seven. Instruction was given in reading, and the Torah was studied both in its written and oral form (i.e., both the Bible and the traditions codified in the Mishnah). The curriculum in the elementary school was basically the Hebrew Bible and Jewish tradition. Scientific and political ideas were embedded incidentally in the OT, which was studied in Hebrew (Aramaic in parts of Ezra and Daniel). Some apocryphal books were in Greek, and the OT itself was translated into this language (see SEPTUAGINT), but Hebrew continued as the language for scholarly study. In the Jewish Diaspora there was more emphasis on the study of the Greek language and hence more contact with Greek culture, but the difference between Palestinian and Hellenistic Judaism must not be overemphasized. Elementary education concluded about the age of fifteen, and promising students could then go on to secondary school. By NT times there was a strong attempt to make elementary education universal for all Jews wherever they were.

Academies of the rabbis were the secondary schools for promising students. The academy was called "the house of study" (*bêt hammidrāš*; cf. Sir. 51:23). It seems probable that the elementary schools studied the OT and the oral law (see below, G.1). In the secondary schools the rabbis conducted theological discussions, and these discussions now have been written down and constitute the TALMUD. Each house of study was conducted by a great teacher (e.g., HILLEL and Shamai). These academies had more sanctity even than the synagogue (*b. Meg.* 26b–27a). Under the leadership of the rabbi, students discussed the interpretation of the Torah and its application. These discussions became the basis of normative Judaism. Paul was educated in the academy of the Pharisee GAMALIEL, who was the grandson of Hillel and was probably the leading teacher of the time. A mention of the men of the great assembly or the Great Synagogue in the Mishnah is probably also a reference to the academies (see SYNAGOGUE, GREAT).

Under the wing of the synagogue, elementary and secondary schools grew up. The elementary school normally operated in or near the synagogue building, and the rule of the synagogue was normally the teacher's. The secondary school or the academy normally operated apart from the synagogue in the temple precincts or in the teacher's own house. Through the influence of these three institutions—the synagogue, the elementary school, and the academy—all Jews became students of the law, and these institutions more than anything else made the Jews the people of the Book.

F. Personnel

1. God. In the ancient world there was no such thing as a "secular culture." God or gods were presupposed in Greek and Roman civilization just as much as in the Hebrew civilization. Nevertheless, there were important differences between the Hebraic approach to knowledge and the Greco-Roman approach. The Hebrews believed that all truth came from God the Creator, Judge, and Redeemer, who revealed to man the knowledge necessary for his own welfare. Human welfare was thought to be dependent on a satisfactory relationship to God. For the Greeks and Romans, the human mind had the potential power for the discovery of truth. Therefore, they stressed the development of reason, and this led to the study of science and philosophy.

The Hebrew approach to education arose from their understanding of revelation. If human beings were to have knowledge, it was only because God had revealed himself to them. Consequently, God was the primary educating figure in Israel. He is called "your Teacher" (Isa. 30:20 NRSV), and as such the prophet considers that people should consult him for knowledge rather than idols or the dead (Isa. 8:19). As the Teacher, he calls on his people to listen to him, "O my people, hear my teaching; / listen to the words of my mouth" (Ps. 78:1). And because God is the ultimate Teacher, it is considered impertinent to ask who has taught him (Job 21:22; Isa. 40:13–14). The content of the instruction given by the Lord is the Torah: "Let me understand the teaching of your precepts; / then I will meditate on your wonders" (Ps. 119:27). But teaching the Torah includes telling "the next generation / the praiseworthy deeds of the LORD, / his power, and the wonders he has done" (Ps. 78:4). The teaching of the Torah and God's activity in history are inseparably linked together.

The method God used in teaching his people was a form of DISCIPLINE (Deut. 8:3, 5). The future hope was that the people would be taught by God (Isa. 54:13; see also Jer. 31:31–34). The Torah was not taught directly by God. He communicated the Torah through Moses, priests, and prophets (see below). The Lord remained the prototype of the teacher, but the law was communicated to Israel through Moses (Deut. 4:1, 5); and through Moses, Israel is commanded to educate the coming generations (4:9–10). While God remained the source of knowledge and revelation, and the prototype of teacher in Israel, he commanded others to carry out the teaching and communicated knowledge through them. Not only did he command but he also inspired them to teach (Exod. 35:31–35). When false prophets declared their message, they were upbraided because God had not revealed knowledge to them. He had not commanded them; he had not inspired them; therefore no heed was to be paid to their teaching (see Jer. 14:14; Hab. 2:18–19).

2. The family. The OT evinces a clear, high regard for children in Israel. Children were regarded as the most precious gift of the Lord (Job 5:25; Pss. 127:3; 128:3–4). Happiness could not be understood without children (see Zech. 8:5). The Lord himself was regarded as the prototype of the loving father (Ps. 103:13), and Israel was his son (Hos. 11:1). It is natural that care was taken in bringing up children. Training began at an early age (Isa. 28:9). Prior to the exile, with few exceptions, children were trained in the home by the parents. Exhortations to teach were intended for families (Gen. 18:19; Deut. 11:19; Prov. 22:6), though later they were interpreted as an exhortation concerning formal education. The primary importance of the FAMILY was never forgotten in Israel's educational system. The family never gave up its responsibility. The parents' responsibility to teach the children provided preliminary requirements such as literacy.

But the system, whether domestic, elementary, or rabbinic, was always devoted to the elaboration of duty toward God, that is, the exposition of the law. The aim was the perfect application of the law. It was Abraham's duty to instruct his whole household (Gen. 18:19). The duty of every father was to instruct his children (Exod. 10:2; 12:26–27). The essence of what was taught was summed up in the Shema (Deut. 6:4–9), which was to be taught to the children. The importance of this transmission is indicated in Ps. 78:3–6 and Prov. 4:3–4. It would seem that this kind of education began as soon as the child could speak, and one may perhaps describe the nature of the instruction as the culture of memory. The place of the development of memory in the educational system of Israel is of primary importance. The purpose of the instruction was that the children may grow up to know and remember, and consequently obey, the law.

In the family situation, children were trained in their everyday duties (1 Sam. 16:11; 2 Ki. 4:18), and artistic training was given at least in some cases (Jdg. 21:21; 1 Sam. 16:15–18; Ps. 137; Lam. 5:14). Girls learned household crafts presumably from their mothers (Exod. 35:25–26; 2 Sam. 13:8). During the second commonwealth, the schools were intended only for boys. Girls learned their household skills at home (Prov. 31:13–31). If there were no sons, girls did the work of the sons (Gen. 29:6; Exod. 2:16). Some women received a relatively good education and consequently became leaders

(Jdg. 4:4–5; 2 Ki. 22:14–20). In Proverbs mothers appear to be of equal importance as fathers in their teaching responsibilities (Prov. 1:8; 6:20). Women were among "the wise," the "teachers" of the Wisdom Literature. LEMUEL, the king of Massa, was taught by his mother (Prov. 31:1). Among the higher classes, evidently nurses (guardians or teachers) were used *in loco parentis* (Ruth 4:16; 2 Sam. 4:4; 2 Ki. 10:5; Isa. 49:23). The instance of Samuel's education by Eli should be noted, but this may be an exception for the period. The rule in ancient Israel was education by the family, that is, by the father and to some extent by the mother, though we have noted exceptions to this rule.

3. The place of Moses. In Judaism, there was no more prominent teaching figure than MOSES. In fact, Moses was the ideal of each class of Israelite leader or teacher. His importance arises from his relationship to the law. The Jews recognized that the law was given through Moses, but not only this, the law became known as the law of Moses (see Num. 12:6, 7; Neh. 9:14; Dan. 9:11). Afterwards, Israel's hope became bound up with the expectation of a new Moses, a prophet like him whom the Lord God would raise up, and to whom the people of Israel would hearken (Deut. 18:15, 18). The prophecy concerning the new covenant (Jer. 31:31–34) probably arises out of the expectation of the new Moses who would usher in a new covenant that would be effective. In the OT, Moses is characteristically described by God as "my servant" (see Num. 12:7 et al.). With this in mind, it is possible that the SERVANT OF THE LORD (Isa. 42; 49; 50:4; 53) is the fulfillment of the hope of a prophet like Moses. The servant is given as a covenant to the people (Isa. 42:6). He publishes the law (42:4) and brings out the prisoners from the dungeon and captivity (42:7). His role appears to be modeled after the role of Moses. Moses offered to give his life for the people of Israel when they sinned. The Servant, in fact, gives his life for the people (see Isa. 53:5).

4. The priests. Initially the priesthood was rooted in Moses' office (Exod. 4:10–17; see PRIESTS AND LEVITES). AARON was to act as Moses' mouth. He was Moses' brother and thus a Levite (4:14). The function indicated was to communicate to the people the knowledge of God. The primary task of the priesthood, therefore, was to teach the law of Moses (Lev. 10:8–11; Deut. 31:9–13; 33:10; Mal. 2:6–7). In the course of teaching the Torah, they were to preserve it (Deut. 17:8–9). As the custodians of the law, the priests kept a copy in the temple (31:9). The custodians of the law at times failed in their duties. Not only did they fail to teach the law, they failed to keep it themselves (Ezek. 22:26). The writings of the prophets are studded with critiques of the function of the priesthood in Israel. Again and again, one finds the criticism that the priests who should have taught the law had failed to do so (2 Chr. 15:1–6; Ezek. 7:26; Hos. 4:6; Zeph. 3:4; Mal. 2:6–8). The priesthood, which was in essence a teaching office, failed to fulfill this function, and Israel was without a teaching priest (2 Chr. 15:3). It is not surprising that when the priesthood forgot to teach the law, the law was forgotten and lost. Evidently this was the situation prior to the rediscovery of the book of the law in the time of King JOSIAH (2 Ki. 22:8). The priests became involved in politics and the worship of the temple. Their work as expounders and teachers of the law became overlooked. Consequently, the need arose for a special class of men to carry out these tasks.

It is possible that from the beginning, the teaching functions of the priesthood were restricted to trained members of this class, though Lev. 10:11 indicates that the sons of Aaron were to teach Israel, and the prophets seem to presuppose that all priests shared in the teaching office (Mal. 2:6–7). At least some Levites were also instructed to teach (Deut. 33:10; 2 Chr. 35:3). Priests were not to be paid for their instruction (Mic. 3:11). Instruction was carried out by the priest visiting a town (2 Chr. 17:8–9), gathering the people together, and expounding the Torah (Deut. 31:10–13; 2 Chr. 17:8–9). This practice continued after the return from the exile (Ezra 8:15–20; Neh. 8:7–9). The teaching was carried on by those skilled in the art of exegesis.

By the time of the return from the exile, there was a body of teaching that was the property of the priesthood, and its exposition was one of the most important functions of the priests and Levites. Ezra was a priest (Ezra 7:1–5; Neh. 8:2), but he evidently was a member of a section of the priesthood with special knowledge and ability to teach the Torah

(Ezra 7:6, 10). When Ezra came from Babylon he brought with him a copy of the Torah and, with the assistance of teaching Levites, expounded it to the assembly of returned exiles (Neh. 8:1-9). The purpose of this instruction was probably to refresh the memories of the teaching Levites. The instruction was carried out from a wooden pulpit (8:4). During the second commonwealth, the Torah was expounded on Mondays and Thursdays, these being the market days when there would be a congregation. Later on, a three-year consecutive cycle of readings was worked out for the Torah. Thus a major program of adult education was initiated.

It is possible that some priests combined scribal and teaching duties. If this is so, they were the ancestors of the scribes of the second commonwealth who were the custodians of the Torah and its interpreters. Our knowledge of Ezra, the priest, who was also a scribe, fits in with this theory (Ezra 7:6-11; Neh. 8:4, 9, 13). From Ezra's time, the scribes were a special class of biblical scholars, exegetes, official teachers, and spiritual leaders in Israel. The scribes were the predecessors of the doctors of the law from Maccabean times to about A.D. 200. The scribes and the doctors of the law adapted biblical exegesis to meet the requirements of the time, and from their teaching the Mishnah developed. The aim of these teachers was to pass on their heritage to an ever-increasing number of disciples. As Moses was the originator of the priesthood, so also the scribes looked back to Moses as "the great scribe of Israel." With the coming of Ezra, the scribe and priest, began the development of the scribal schools, an institution that had greater impact on Israelite education than any other.

5. The king. The teaching function of the kings is often overlooked in thinking of education in Israel. David's songs had a considerable instructional effect in Israel. The sons of David, the kings of Israel, were responsible for keeping the law as a condition for sitting on his throne (Ps. 132:12). JEHOSHAPHAT caused his princes to be sent throughout the land of Judah teaching the people in all the cities (2 Chr. 17:7-9). The wisdom of Solomon became a proverb throughout the ancient world so that even the QUEEN OF SHEBA came to test his wisdom (1 Ki. 10:1-13). The kings were not often competent for the teaching task, however. More often than not, they disregarded the law in their own lives and led the nation to sin against God.

6. The prophets. The role of the PROPHETS also has its origin in the office of Moses (Deut. 18:15, 18; 34:10; Hos. 12:13). Moses is thought of as the prophet par excellence, with whom the Lord spoke face to face. The activity of the prophets was largely bound up with teaching the law and bringing out its meaning in the current situation (see Isa. 1:10; 8:16, 20 and esp. Zech. 7:12). The activity of ELIJAH the prophet is depicted as a return to Moses; in his journey to Horeb, the mount of God, Elijah comes to know the true meaning of his mission (1 Ki. 19).

The prophets were the critics of evil government, standing fearlessly before kings to declare to them the errors of their ways, as Elijah did before King AHAB (1 Ki. 17 et al.). The prophets were also the friends of wise government, strengthening the kings who sought to lead the people in the way of the Lord, as Isaiah did with King HEZEKIAH (2 Ki. 19). The prophets criticized injustice in the social behavior of the people (see Amos). They condemned the infidelity of Israel in forgetting Yahweh (see Hosea). They denied adamantly the false hope that because of Jerusalem and the temple, Israel never would be enslaved by the enemy. The message of the prophets was one of judgment and doom on a nation that had strayed from the law of God. The message of judgment and doom was itself bound up with the message of the law (Deut. 30).

The message of the prophets, however, was not one of ultimate doom: God in his covenant love would not permanently cast off his covenant people (see Hosea). Ultimately, he would find a way of redeeming them. In the new act of redemption, Israel would return to him as their Lord. Consequently, an important aspect of the message of the prophets was one of returning unto the Lord, a message of REPENTANCE (Joel 2:12-14). The message of repentance was, itself, a message of hope (Isa. 40 et al.). The message of the prophet involved an inspired interpretation of the law of Moses and of the historical situation in which they lived. During the first commonwealth, it was the prophets that kept the people true to their historical heritage. The prophets were to the first commonwealth what the scribes and the doctors of the law were to the second. Of course, there is a great difference in that the prophets spoke with direct divine authority, whereas the scribes and the doctors of the law offered their words as varying interpretations of the law of Moses (cf. Mk. 1:22).

7. The sages. Moses is also the prototype of the wise man in the OT (Deut. 4:5–6; cf. Acts 7:22). The class of wise men in Israel is related in its origin to the wise men of other nations. When the prophets ceased to proclaim the word of the Lord in their inspired and penetrating manner, the need arose for those who could give guidance in the everyday matters of life. It was in this area that the sages played their part in educating Israel. This practical WISDOM appears in the Wisdom Literature of Israel. Practical or worldly wisdom does not always harmonize with the economy of God. Consequently, there are occasions in the OT when the prophets came into conflict with the professional wise men (Isa. 29:13–14; Jer. 8:8–9). On these occasions, what was put forward as practical wisdom was evidently "worldly wisdom."

Just as the prophets faced the problem of preaching a message to those who would not heed them (cf. the experience of Jeremiah), so also the wise men found that people were more ready to pursue a course of folly than to heed a course of wisdom (Prov. 5:13). Although their wisdom was not always heeded, the sages were nevertheless effective in building up a philosophy of education and a pedagogical system. Through them, education previously carried out with little planning or consistency was worked into a systematic whole.

G. The place and use of the law. The Jews had one textbook, the Scriptures. The Scriptures were made up of the OT canonical books. The body of writings known as the PSEUDEPIGRAPHA had no official recognition in the schools, though it had a wide circulation in private homes. One should recognize that the development of these written records was gradual and covered a long period.

1. Oral law. According to Jewish tradition, God gave the law to Moses in both a written and an oral form, and the latter was transmitted by word of mouth through many generations. The oral law was eventually committed to writing around A.D. 200 in a work known as the MISHNAH, which in effect contains the debates and legal decisions of rabbis ("the tradition of the elders," Mk. 7:3) from about the 1st or 2nd cent. B.C. to the 2nd cent. A.D. To a large extent, these rabbinic materials consist of discussions regarding the proper interpretation of the Torah, that is, its application to daily life. Subsequent discussions are embodied in the TALMUD, the more comprehensive written form of the sayings of the rabbis. Thus, in considering the place of the law in Jewish education in biblical times, one must take into account the development of oral law as well as written law.

A few miles NW of Nazareth lies the city of Sepphoris, where Judah the Prince codified the Mishnah (Jewish oral law) around A.D. 200. (View to the NE.)

2. Written law. The written TORAH dates from the time of Moses and gradually developed into a greater body of writings. The Hebrew word *tôrâ* H9368 has a number of different senses. It can be used to describe the TEN COMMANDMENTS. This is the narrowest sense. In a broader sense, the Torah or law can describe the five books of Moses, the PENTATEUCH. In a more general sense, Torah can describe the whole of the OT. Torah may even be used to include the oral Torah of the Mishnah and the Talmud. The most basic study concerned the written law, and certain passages of it received special attention. Of these passages, the great Shema is the best known. The passage begins with the Hebrew word *šāmaʿ* H9048 ("hear"), "Hear, O Israel: The LORD our God, the LORD is one" (Deut. 6:4).

Torah also has the sense of teaching or instruction. The commandments were instruction about the way to live. Torah in the wider sense was instruction concerning the meaning and implication of these commandments. The prophets' message was Torah because they applied to their own day the meaning of the teaching of the law of Moses. By the end of the biblical period, the Jews had as their canonical writings the whole OT but continued to give emphasis to the teaching of the Pentateuch. In Jewish education, reading and writing were only a means to the end of understanding the Torah. Other subjects were incidental to the teaching of the law. Ideas of science, politics, and medicine were embedded incidentally in the Torah. With this emphasis on teaching the Torah, education took the form of the culture and development of memory, which is so important for the preservation of oral tradition.

The scattering of the Jews throughout the ancient world in the dispersion also brought about the need for the translation of the Scriptures into Greek. This need may be viewed from two points of view. First of all, Jews who lived in the dispersion came under Hellenistic influence more strongly than their fellow countrymen in Palestine. Many of them understood Greek better than they did either Hebrew or Aramaic. Second, the scattering of the Jews brought the Jewish faith to the people of the ancient world. The *Letter of Aristeas*, purporting to be written by a certain Aristeas to his brother Philocrates during the reign of PTOLEMY Philadelphus (285–246 B.C.), relates how Philadelphus appealed to the high priest in Jerusalem for a copy of the Hebrew Scriptures for his royal library (see ARISTEAS, LETTER OF). The result was that the high priest sent seventy-two elders to ALEXANDRIA with an official copy of the law. The seventy-two made independent Greek translations that miraculously corresponded to what we now know as the SEPTUAGINT. The story has legendary accretions, but it seems likely that the Pentateuch was translated in Egypt in the reign of Ptolemy Philadelphus. The remaining books were probably translated piecemeal at a later date, most of them by the 1st cent. B.C. Subsequently the name Septuagint (LXX) was extended to cover all the books of the OT and also the APOCRYPHA.

H. Educational symbols, principles, and methods. The FEASTS of the Jews served to solidify national consciousness in a manner that many other races are never able to achieve except in time of war. Festivals were national holy days as well as holidays. Through them the Jews realized their dependence on God in providing food and protection. In the time before Ezra, the festivals were most important for education, and they remained so even after the establishment of schools. The law required a father to explain great festivals to his son (Exod. 13:8; Deut. 4:9; 6:20–21). Through participation in the festivals, the children would learn their meaning, and in this way the festivals became a part of life indelibly etched upon their minds. The festivals were unique opportunities for teaching the young the great truths of the Jewish faith. They provided a dramatic, vivid, and intrinsically interesting way of teaching. It was a far more effective means of teaching than by abstract ideas and philosophical principles. In this way, the dealings of God with

Boy reading the Torah at his Bar Mitzvah, a very important occasion in his Jewish training when he passes into manhood.

his people were effectively brought to attention by religious ceremony. All festivals were colorful and intensely interesting. The child was always at the heart of each one. This is the genius of the Jewish people. They placed the child at the center of life, and by the educational media they developed, insured that the Jewish history and Jewish religion was passed on to succeeding generations.

The most important of the holy days was the SABBATH. One reason for its importance was its frequent repetition, week by week. In ceasing from their labors, the Jews indicated their faith in God to supply all their needs. The Sabbath was a day in which faith was expressed, a day of rejoicing in the Lord, a day of meeting for worship, a day of learning, a day of instruction. In a sense, the whole of the covenant faith was gathered together and symbolized in the Sabbath observance.

There were seven important festivals during OT times, a further one being added during the intertestamental period. Each of these festivals symbolized an aspect of Jewish faith. The first of the festivals was the Feast of Unleavened Bread (Exod. 23:15), preceded by the PASSOVER (Lev. 23:5), which commemorated the deliverance from Egypt (Exod. 10:2). It was one of three annual festivals and it occurred on the fourteenth day of the first month. The second of the festivals was the Feast of Weeks. It is also called the Feast of Harvest, the Day of the Firstfruits (Exod. 23:16; 34:22; Num. 28:26). This feast later became known as PENTECOST because it was celebrated on the fiftieth day from the Sabbath beginning the Passover. This festival marked the Jewish dependence on God for the harvest. The third festival was the Feast of the Tabernacles or the Feast of Booths. It is also called the Feast of the Ingathering (Exod. 23:16; 34:22; Lev. 23:34, 39; Deut. 16:13). The fourth was the Sabbath, which is regarded as a feast in Lev. 23:2–3. The fifth, the Feast of the Blowing of Trumpets (Num. 29:1). The sixth, the Day of Atonement (Exod. 30:10; Lev. 23:26–31; see ATONEMENT, DAY OF). The seventh was the Feast of PURIM, described in Esth. 9. This feast commemorated the remarkable deliverance from the intrigues of HAMAN. It was a day of feasting and gladness. The feast that was instituted after the completion of the OT literature was the Feast of DEDICATION, commemorating and celebrating the cleansing of the Jerusalem temple by Judas MACCABEE in 164 B.C. after its desecration by ANTIOCHUS Epiphanes. It is also called the Festival of Lights (the feast is mentioned in Jn. 10:22).

The TABERNACLE, and later the TEMPLE, embodied much educational symbolism. The structures themselves symbolized the place where God's presence was to be located. Within the structures there were several items of notable symbolic value. First of all, one notices the geography of these buildings. The Holy of Holies in its separation from the meeting places of the people symbolizes the holiness of God in his separation from all sinfulness. The furniture reminded the Jews of the exodus history, and also of the problem of sin and the means of ATONEMENT. The temple stood for the presence of God with his people made possible by the overcoming of sin by way of atonement.

The prophets used symbolical methods to emphasize the meaning of their message to the people. Such symbolism is described as the prophetic "sign." The method was to enact the meaning of the word declared. An instance of this is given in Isa. 8:1–4, where the Lord tells ISAIAH to take a large tablet and write upon it in common characters, and also to give his children certain names that bear out the prophetic message. JEREMIAH is told to buy a linen waistcloth and cause it to be spoiled even before its first wash, to show how the Lord will spoil the pride of Judah (Jer. 13:1–11). The prophet went about with a wooden set of yoke bars on his neck to show how the people will be led into slavery by NEBUCHADNEZZAR (28:13). When the false prophet HANANIAH broke the wooden yoke bars to show how the Lord would break the power of Nebuchadnezzar, Jeremiah then took yoke bars of iron to reinforce the point that the people really would be led into bondage. The prophet EZEKIEL is told, "I have made you a sign to the house of Israel" (Ezek. 12:6). Ezekiel proclaimed his message of destruction and doom on Jerusalem by means of symbolic actions. He ate bread and drank water, trembling in fearfulness, symbolically portraying the destruction coming on Jerusalem and the fear that it would bring. He proclaimed the destruction of Jerusalem by drawing a picture of Jerusalem on a piece of clay, and shattering it in pieces to show how Jerusalem would be razed to the ground.

At a domestic level, other symbolical articles were used, such as the zizith or TASSEL (Heb. *ṣiṣit* H7492, Num. 15:39–41; Deut. 22:12), the PHYLACTERY (Exod. 13:1–10; Deut. 6:4–9; 11:13–21), and the mezuzah, an inscription on the doorframe (Heb. *mĕzûzâ* H4647, Deut. 11:20).

The basic principle of Israelite education was to begin at an early age (Ps. 8:2; Prov. 22:6; Isa. 28:9). Second, it seems to be suggested that the morning was the best time to teach, when the student is fresh (Isa. 50:4). No doubt the lack of adequate lighting facilities influenced this judgment. Third, it is suggested that the subject matter should be presented to the child gradually, at a level that can be understood by the child at that stage (28:10, 13). This leads to the fourth point, that education should proceed from the known to the unknown. Fifth, the problem of forgetting is recognized, and thus the necessity for relearning is prominently in view (Exod. 13:3; 20:8; 32:13; Num. 15:39; Deut. 4:9; 5:15; 9:7; 24:9; et al.).

Oral instruction took precedence over all other methods (Deut. 5:1; Prov. 1:8; Isa. 1:10; 50:4). Hence the frequent exhortation to "hear," because the most important method of instruction was oral. Emphasis was placed on the need to remember. Consequently there was a strong emphasis on the culture of memory in the Israelite situation. The development of memory also led to the development of means that could present the teaching in a memorable form, such as mnemonic devices for memory (cf. Prov. 31:10–31, where each new section begins with the next letter of the alphabet). Memory is also helped by the use of the parable, the oracle (Num. 23:7), the analogy (1 Sam. 10:12), the riddle (Ezek. 17:2), and the story with the vivid moral (2 Sam. 12:1–10). Written instruction played an important part in Israelite education (Deut. 31:19; Ps. 119:18; Prov. 22:20; Isa. 30:8), but even the written forms suggest the importance of the oral history of the teaching (Prov. 1:8).

The importance of dramatic instruction via the various festivals and institutions has already been noted. The prophets evidently used symbolical methods also to emphasize the point of their message. They used PROVERB and PARABLE (Jer. 31:29; Ezek. 12:22–23; see also Mk. 4 for the use of parables by Jesus, and cf. Isa. 28:23–29; Hos. 12:10).

Instruction also was given in a catechetical form, that is, by means of a question and answer. The use of rhetorical questions appears in various passages (e.g., Deut. 6:20; Jer. 15:11–21; Amos 3:3–8; Mic. 6:6–8). Variation of method is used in the OT (cf. Heb. 1:1). God spoke to Moses face to face, he spoke to the prophets in visions and dreams, he spoke through omens and the casting of the lot, he spoke through nature and in the normal events of daily life. He spoke in the events of history, he spoke through the priest, the prophet, and others who were his servants. His voice was to be heard through conscience, and his will to be known through the law.

Instruction and DISCIPLINE are inseparably linked together (Deut. 8:5; Prov. 23:12–14; cf. Eph. 6:4). The latter was considered to be an integral part of the former. Discipline was considered as a means by which the love of God fulfilled its purpose in the life of his people (Isa. 54:8; Jer. 31:18–20). When God disciplined Israel, it was to bring Israel back to himself (Prov. 3:11, 12; cf. Heb. 12:5–11). Discipline, or chastisement, is to be regarded as a mark of God's love and concern in instructing those whom he loves (Ps. 94:8–13). Chastisement is at times fruitless (Jer. 4:22; 5:3; Amos 4:6–12). In these instances the chastisement has a penal emphasis (Ezek. 21:8–17; Amos 4:6–12). Discipline as a means of carrying out instruction leads to an incentive of reward and punishment. Rewards and punishment are an inducement to good behavior and hard work (Isa. 52:13; 53:12). As the Lord used the means of discipline as an incentive for Israel to learn so the wise teacher in Israel used discipline with his students.

I. The Qumran sect. The discovery of the DEAD SEA SCROLLS has provided much information about a community that evidently broke with mainstream Judaism over the question of a legitimate high priest. The interests of the sect were largely APOCALYPTIC. They were concerned with the end time when God would destroy evil and reinstate his people. Their value judgments were strict, and on the whole they were an inward-looking community. The purpose of the discussion of the sect at this point is to draw attention to the place of Scripture in the life of Judaism. At the heart of the buildings of the Qumran sect there was a scriptorium, a building that was occupied for the purpose of copying and transmitting the sacred texts of Scripture. Most of the texts are in Hebrew, though there are some Aramaic and Greek documents. In addition to the canonical OT writings, there are some documents, such as the *Manual of Discipline* and various biblical commentaries, that are peculiar to the Qumran sect. In these documents, the sect's own distinctive teaching is put forward.

J. The Diaspora. The difference of the Judaism of the Diaspora from that of Palestine is one of degree and not of kind. It is a mistake to think that the Judaism of Palestine wholly rejected Hellenistic influence. There is clear indication of Hellenistic influence, even in such a nationalistic group as the Qumran sect. Greek was a widely spoken language in Palestine. The difference in degree is that some Jews in the dispersion lost touch altogether with their native Aramaic and Hebrew. Many more Jews in Palestine were aware of the meaning of Aramaic and Hebrew than were the Jews of the dispersion. The Jews of the dispersion were more acutely aware of Hellenistic influence. Philo Judaeus of Alexandria, for example, was fully aware of Hellenistic philosophical ideas and expressions. (See A. Mendelson, *Secular Education in Philo of Alexandria* [1982].)

K. Conclusion and criticism. Jewish education was primarily religious education, based on the belief that God had revealed himself. It was education that presupposed revelation at every point. Thus philosophy played no real part in its system. As its system was almost exclusively religious, apart from elements of science and other studies that incidentally were taught in the process of teaching religious knowledge, Jewish education lacked scientific character. It neglected culture, but in spite of this it succeeded where Greek and Roman educational systems failed. The aim was the perfect application of the law.

Paul gives a critique of the system as one who has been inside it, a student of the law at the feet of Gamaliel. He gives two lines of attack. First, he draws attention to the status of Christ in relationship to the law, a status of superseding the law. Second, he draws attention to the fact that the law could not achieve its aims anyway. The NT writers did not disparage the law itself and the high ideal of educational responsibility it inspired in Jewish minds (Rom. 2:17–20). They were convinced, however, that the covenant was fulfilled and that the perpetuation of a system of Judaism would be a case of arrested educational development, unnecessary to those who had graduated to God's household. Further, pride in the law was an anachronism condemned because Gentile was as likely as Jew to live up to the ideals of the law, for the law sets up goals without the means of achieving them (2:14–15; 7:13–24). Pride in the law encouraged contempt for others (2:17–24; Jas. 1:26; 3:14–16). See law (NT).

III. Hellenistic education. By "Hellenistic" is meant the later Greek empire beginning with Alexander the Great and including the Greco-Roman empire. It has been said that the Greeks first learned culture themselves and then they taught the ancient world. Consequently, in the Greco-Roman period, Hellenistic culture was the culture of the then known world. Of course, there were variations from place to place according to the local traditions. Hellenism is to be described as a cultural, military, and political phenomenon.

A. Origin, development, and aims. The educational system of Hellenism had its roots in Sparta and Athens. In Sparta, the aim of education may be described as the obliteration of the individual in the service of the state; in Athens, the training of the individual in the service of culture. From Sparta, the emphasis on the development of physical attributes and the training for warfare; and from Athens, the emphasis on the development of

Hellenistic education is illustrated by this student's tablet with a Greek inscription. It is made of wood and covered with wax.

culture, carried over into Hellenistic education. The Greeks produced their philosophers of education, and perhaps the most important of these was Plato. One of his many books, *The Republic*, gives a detailed account of the aims, ideals, and methods of education. Plato was a student of Socrates, whom we know only through the writings of Plato. One of the most important students of Plato was Aristotle. With regard to the theory of knowledge, Aristotle rejected Plato's approach, and his reaction has been likened to "a colt that kicks his mother." In due course, Aristotle became tutor in the court of Philip of Macedon. At this stage he began a relationship with Alexander the Great, then thirteen years old, a relationship that was to last about eight years. His influence on Alexander cannot be doubted. From Aristotle onward, the study of philosophy and the natural sciences went hand in hand. See GREEK RELIGION AND PHILOSOPHY.

The importance of Alexander in the spread of Hellenistic culture cannot be overemphasized. Alexander has been described as the apostle of Hellenism. Through his exploits, Hellenistic culture was spread throughout the then known world. Even when the Greeks finally bowed the knee to the strength of Rome, the Romans showed themselves to be the heirs of Greece, adopting and exploiting Hellenistic culture. In the Greco-Roman age, the spread of the Greek language, religion, education, and philosophy continued throughout the ancient world.

In its early stages, Greek education was for the aristocratic class only. The ideals that students sought to attain were those of strength, courage, skill with weapons, and music. These were the Greek virtues. Goodness was described in aesthetic rather than moral terms. The Greek school system presupposed that every attribute of mind, body, and soul, properly disciplined, is good and worthy. In Greek thinking, in its pure form, there is no room for ASCETICISM. The aim was the development of personality, and from this point of view it may be described in terms of humanism. The educational ideal required both intellectual and physical effort. The physical effort is not to be understood in terms of labor (which was for the servile class), but in terms of athletic prowess. See ATHLETE.

Girls received no education outside the home. For boys, the first five years of life were spent with their mothers. Elementary schools took up the years from six to fifteen. During these years, they undertook the basic learning programs. The years from sixteen to eighteen were spent in the GYMNASIUM (from Gk. *gymnazō*, lit., "to train naked," then more generally "to exercise"), and activities were basically physical exercise, music, and dancing, though literature, the sciences, and politics also were studied. The aim of the gymnasium was to prepare persons fit for citizenship. This kind of education was restricted to citizens who were native-born. The years nineteen and twenty were spent in military service by those who were eligible for this undertaking.

In cities that lost their citizenship in the Roman empire, the original purpose and military nature died out in the gymnasiums. They became rather "liberal arts colleges" for the sons of aristocrats. The training became somewhat like that of a university. Athens, TARSUS, and ALEXANDRIA were cities famous for their "universities," where the ultimate in study was either philosophy or rhetoric. By the NT period, philosophy had given way to rhetoric as the primary subject. Schools were open to foreigners as well as natives. The aim that Plato had outlined of preparing scholars for citizenship was now lost. Instead, these universities or schools equipped a few wealthy unoccupied young men to enjoy their own leisure time. (See further G. Compayré, *The History of Pedagogy*, 2nd ed. [1899]; W. Barclay, *Educational Ideals in the Ancient World* [1959]; M. L. Clarke, *Higher Education in the Ancient World* [1971]; S. F. Bonner, *Education in Ancient Rome from the Elder Cato to the Younger Pliny* [1977]; R. Cribiore, *Gymnastics of the Mind: Greek Education in Hellenistic and Roman Egypt* [2001]; J. T. Townsend, "Education (Greco-Roman Period)," in *ABD*, 2:312–17.)

B. Characteristics. Hellenistic education was characterized by the belief that man's mind discovered truth. The system stressed the development of reason. This led to the study of science and philosophy. Due to the skepticism of later philosophers and the recognition of the power of persuasive speech, philosophy gave way to rhetoric as the "queen of the sciences." Aesthetic qualities like beauty and symmetry were applied standards rather than moral ideals such as those we find in Judaism.

C. Influence on Jewish education.

Scholars have recognized Hellenistic influence on the development of the later Wisdom Literature among the Jews; some even think it doubtful that there would have been such a body of literature had there been no contact with Hellenism. This influence brought about an interest in the more practical affairs of living and the development of a pedagogical system. It is also doubtful whether the Jews would have developed their school system had Hellenism not suggested this system to them.

Second, there was an extensive development of writings in the Greek language among the Jews. Notable among these is the SEPTUAGINT, the translation of the OT and Apocryphal books into Greek. The need for such a translation indicates the inroads that Hellenistic thought had made into Jewish ways of thinking (see C. H. Dodd, *The Bible and the Greeks* [1935]). Along the same line was the influence of Hellenistic thought in the writings of PHILO JUDAEUS (1st cent. A.D.). He shows himself to be one thoroughly acquainted with the popular ideas of Hellenism. JOSEPHUS, the Jewish historian, was acquainted with Hellenistic culture. PAUL (Saul of Tarsus) also seems to have had contact with Hellenistic culture. It is possible that as a citizen of TARSUS, "no mean city," Paul received a Hellenistic education. However, it is more likely from the evidence of the Acts of the Apostles that he received a traditionally Jewish, Pharisaic education at the feet of Gamaliel.

D. Conclusion.

For all the wealth of cultural appreciation that Hellenistic education brought, the fact that the Greek standard was aesthetic rather than moral must be regarded as a fundamental weakness. By the NT period, the Greeks admired the accomplishment of rhetoric as the apex of achievement. Paul was aware of this and critiqued a system that gave pride of place to the art of rhetoric. His critique arises out of an involvement in the Hellenistic educational system. Paul also had his rival platform. He gave lectures in "the lecture hall [*scholē* G5391] of Tyrannus" in Ephesus (Acts 19:9). Thus the question is raised: did Paul have a full classical training? It is more likely that he moved to Jerusalem at an early age for rabbinic training. His skill in rhetoric was probably acquired in action. There were others who could be considered professionals, such as APOLLOS (Acts 18:24, 28; cf. 1 Cor. 1:17; 2:1–4; 3:2; 4:19, 20; 2 Cor. 11:5; Col. 2:4, 8).

Paul himself was ridiculed on occasions (2 Cor. 10:10; 11:6). He was plunged into a competition for status, and it is in this context that the boasting passages that are so hard to reconcile with the rest of his teaching are to be understood. They make sense in the contemporary professional etiquette, while at the same time parodying the system. Among the nobility, there was a cult of glory. Winning glory was the aim of public life, and the assurance of immortality. Public figures defined their own glory for posterity. Self-magnification became a feature of Hellenistic higher education. To Paul's mind, such glorification of man was anathema. Even pride in the law was now excluded.

Yet, in this context, the apostle was entitled to boast (1 Cor. 15:31; 2 Cor. 7:4, 14). The boasting passages are in fact an attack on the Hellenistic system of education. Paul now boasts in his humiliation (2 Cor. 6:4–10; 10:9—12:13). There is a new design for the glorification of human beings in the sufferings and glory of Christ (4:7–17; Phil. 2:3–11). The death of Christ is the sole object of boasting (Gal. 6:14). The person who is a Christian has rejected the world and thus shares in the passion and glory of Christ through the resurrection. Worldly boasting is excluded for the "new man" in Christ Jesus. Paul specifically rejects the power of persuasive speech as the prime test of human cultivation (1 Cor. 1:17—2:5). In the place of this system, Paul draws attention to the need for personal morality, for a system where the standard of personal goodness is the test for the claim to wisdom. Neither the service of the state nor the service of culture could make a total claim on man. Paul's critique placed the revelation of God in Christ, Christ crucified, at the heart of any system of education.

IV. The education of Jesus.

There is little knowledge of how Jesus was educated, but the following may be said with a great deal of certainty. It is apparent that Jesus was born to a God-fearing family. Joseph is described as a righteous man, Mary as a pious young woman. See JOSEPH #11; MARY, MOTHER OF JESUS. This family undoubtedly lived up to its responsibilities of teaching the young child Jesus the matters of the Law and the Prophets. Jesus' education probably consisted of what he was taught by his mother and father, supplemented by the teaching of the local synagogue school. What he knew of the Scriptures he learned in these situations. He did not attend any of the academies of the great rabbis, as indicated in the question asked by the Jews, "How did this man get such learning without having studied?" (Jn. 7:15). While it is true that Jesus belonged to the royal line of David, his family seems to have been poor, of the peasant class (Lk. 2:24; cf. Lev. 12:6, 8). Jesus learned a trade, that of a builder, following in the footsteps of Joseph. Jesus did make trips to Jerusalem with his family, attending the temple, and on one occasion he astounded his elders with his learning (Lk. 2:47). It was his custom to go to the synagogue (4:16).

Jesus' education consisted of the teaching he received in the synagogue services, and also what he learned from those trips to Jerusalem on the great festival occasions. (See A. Edersheim, *The Life and Times of Jesus, the Messiah* [1883]; A. C. Bouquet, *Everyday Life in New Testament Times* [1956].) But all of this does not explain Jesus' teaching and authority. Of course, one may assume that he meditated long on the Scriptures of the OT. When all this has been said, however, it should be recognized that the origin of his teaching is not to be found in the home, the synagogue, or the temple. Again and again Jesus was to claim, "My teaching is not my own. It comes from him who sent me" (Jn. 7:16). See JESUS CHRIST.

V. The education of the apostles

A. The Twelve. None of the twelve apostles appear to have been learned men originally. Andrew, Peter, James, and John were fishermen; Levi (Matthew) was a tax collector; others have unknown backgrounds. It seemed unlikely that any of these men would have had very good formal education. The best that can be expected would be that they were educated in their homes and sent to primary school, that they attended the synagogue, and perhaps, on rare occasions, had trips up to Jerusalem to the temple for the great festivals. They were, by and large, uneducated, common men. Having called these men to follow him, Jesus taught them. They would have heard Jesus' teaching to the multitudes. Above and beyond this, Jesus at times taught his own disciples secretly, apart from the multitudes (Mk. 4:10–34). Thus one must take into account the effectiveness of Jesus, the great Teacher. The evidence suggests that his teaching had great effect, so that after Peter and John had been instrumental in the healing of the lame man at the gate of the temple and had occasion as a consequence to bear witness to Jesus, Luke records the following: "When they saw the courage of Peter and John and realized that they were unschooled, ordinary men, they were astonished and they took note that these men had been with Jesus" (Acts 4:13). Of course, it should not be forgotten that along with the effectiveness of Jesus' teaching, there was the new power of the Holy Spirit, effective in and through the lives and teachings of Peter and John. See JOHN THE APOSTLE; PETER.

B. Paul. PAUL grew up as a PHARISEE, receiving a full Pharisaic education. Though Paul was a Roman citizen, born in Tarsus (Acts 16:37; 21:39; 22:25–29), it seems almost certain that his real home was Jerusalem, where he sat at the feet of Rabbi GAMALIEL, the doctor of the law and member of the SANHEDRIN (22:3). Gamaliel represents the liberal wing of the Pharisees, the school of HILLEL, as opposed to the more conservative group, the school of Shammai. Gamaliel intervened on behalf of the apostles with a persuasive speech at their trial (5:33–40). It is of significance that Paul, author of most NT books, was educated by one of the leading (if not *the* leading Jewish teacher) of his time. It is

Saul of Tarsus (Paul) probably sat at the feet of Gamaliel here at this rabbi's teaching staircase located at the southern wall of the temple mount.

ironic, to say the least, that the student, unlike his teacher, pursued a course of persecuting the church (9:1–2), only to be converted through an encounter with the living Christ. Of all the church leaders of the NT times, it seems probable that Paul was the most adequately equipped from an intellectual point of view (cf. Gal. 1:14).

VI. Education in the church in holiness and maturity. In NT times, the church did not create any special educational system for teaching children. It used the existing institutions in both the Greek and Jewish worlds. That Christians continued to do so for some time is supported by what is known of Julian "the Apostate," who in the 4th cent. attempted to drive out Christianity and restore paganism. Julian required that those who shared in Hellenistic education should also subscribe to its ideology. His action made it virtually impossible for Christians to be involved in Hellenistic education and raised the question of a separate educational system. This problem falls outside the period under consideration.

In the period of the early church, leaders were drawn from those whose educational qualifications were taken for granted. The church made heavy educational demands on its members. One may say that the church was not out of touch with the need for education; it was creating a new need for it. While accepting the formal education of existing institutions, the church in its life and order constituted a substitute schooling. An awkward dualism of religion and education began to grow up. Such a dualism led, of necessity, to a criticism of educational systems from a religious standpoint. Already in the NT both the Jewish and the Hellenistic patterns of thought are criticized, the rivalry between them is condemned, and members are challenged to a new way of life that is superior to both (Eph. 2:11–22; cf. Acts 20:21; Rom. 1:14–16; 2:9–11; 10:12; 1 Cor. 1:21–24; 12:13; Gal. 3:28; Col. 3:11). (See E. A. Judge, "The Early Christians as a Scholastic Community," in *Journal of Religious History* 1 [1960–61]: 4–15, 125–37.)

The new way of life in Christ was dependent to some extent on a teaching-and-learning relationship. The specific training of children, however, is nowhere catered for or implied in the church as such. The church was concerned with adult education or "higher education" in Christ, education that presupposed the existing educational systems but discounted their end product in favor of the new man (Eph. 4:11–16; Col. 2:2–7). The church had its officials whose tasks were primarily educational in function (Rom. 12:6–8; 1 Cor. 12:4–10, 27–31; Eph. 4:11; 1 Tim. 3:1–13; Tit. 1:7–9; 1 Pet. 4:11). The way the aims of these functions should work out in the church is expressed in Eph. 4:8–16 and may be set out in the following three points.

(1) *Spirituality* (1 Cor. 2:4; cf. Gal. 3:14). Christ in his ascension poured out his Spirit on all who believed (Jn. 7:39). At the heart of the church's educating task was the need to keep the centrality of faith in Christ crucified and risen. Those who drifted away from their faith in Christ could not hope to grow into the new man in Christ.

(2) The believer who had received the Spirit (and the Spirit's gift of ministry) was to grow up, through the fellowship of the church and the ministry it brought to him, into *maturity* in Christ (Eph. 4:13). This maturity was marked by a sharing in the fellowship of the church and appreciation of its teaching.

(3) The ideal was *love*. The mark of the Spirit in Christians and the sign of their growth and maturity is loving action. Consequently, it is evident that the church rejects both the Greek and the Jewish ideals. The goal is not simply private goodness in moral or aesthetic terms, but mutual service of the members of the body. The diversity of individual roles is recognized as the diversity of the gifts of the Spirit and cooperation in the power of the Spirit is emphasized. In this new body, the fellowship of the church, there is the recognition that each believer is equipped by the Spirit and is responsible for ministering his gifts within that fellowship. Each member has an educational role in building up the body until it comes to full maturity. Each member is called to a "mutual responsibility in interdependence in the body of Christ." A. W. MORTON

Eduth. See MUSIC VI.B.

Egerton 2, Papyrus. Name given to four small PAPYRUS fragments discovered in 1934 (an additional fragment was subsequently identified).

Dating to about A.D. 150, they represent the oldest noncanonical Christian text that has survived. Also known as the Unknown Gospel, these fragments contain parts of several accounts, such as a dispute between Jesus and the Jewish leaders regarding the interpretation and authority of MOSES, a story about the healing of a leper, and others. The relationship between this text and the canonical Gospels is disputed, as are its purpose and scope. (See C. H. Dodd in *BJRL* 20 [1936]: 56–92; D. F. Wright in *Gospel Perspectives* 5, ed. D. Wenham [1985], 207–32; J. D. Crossan, *Four Other Gospels: Shadows on the Contours of the Canon* [1985].)

egg. The OT makes several references to eggs (Heb. *bêṣâ H1070*). The PENTATEUCH, for example, contains an injunction not to take a mother bird with her eggs or her young, but the young only (Deut. 22:6–7); and the book of JOB speaks of the ostrich leaving her eggs on the ground to be warmed by the sun (Job 39:14). Other references are found in metaphorical contexts (Isa. 10:14; 59:5; cf. also the NIV in Job 6:6; Isa. 34:15; Jer. 17:11). In the NT, Jesus refers to the absurdity of thinking that a father would give a scorpion to a son who asked for an egg (*ōon G6051*, Lk. 11:12).

Wild birds' eggs were first gathered for food (Deut. 22:6). By NT times eggs of domesticated fowl were a staple of diet. A bird's egg consists of the yolk, in which is the germ of life, surrounded by the white, an albuminous substance, and a calcareous shell that protects the contents yet can be broken by the chick when it is ready to emerge.

E. RUSSELL

Eglah eg´luh (עֶגְלָה *H6321* "heifer-calf"). A wife of DAVID who bore him his sixth son, Ithream, at HEBRON (2 Sam. 3:5; 1 Chr. 3:3).

Eglaim eg´lay-im (אֶגְלַיִם *H104*, possibly "[two] drops"). A town on the border of MOAB (Isa. 15:8). Its site is uncertain. EUSEBIUS mentions a place named Agallim, 8 mi. S of Areopolis (Rabba), which would be along the northern border. Others identify Eglaim with Khirbet el-Gilime, NE of er-Rabba (cf. J. Simons, *The Geographical and Topographical Texts of the Old Testament* [1959], §1259). Y. Aharoni suggests Mazraʿ, an oasis on the shore of the DEAD SEA, NE of the Lisan peninsula (*The Land of the Bible: A Historical Geography*, rev. ed. [1979], 35). See also EN EGLAIM.

J. REA

Eglath Shelishiyah eg´lath-shi-lish´uh-yuh (עֶגְלַת שְׁלִשִׁיָּה *H6326*, "the third Eglath [heifer-calf]"). An unidentified town near ZOAR mentioned in prophetic oracles of judgment on MOAB (Isa. 15:5 [LXX *damalis trietēs*, "a three-year-old heifer"]; Jer. 48:34 [LXX *Aglath-salisia*]). The KJV takes the words as a metaphorical description of Zoar (and Horonaim), "an heifer of three years old."

Eglon (person) eg´lon (עֶגְלוֹן *H6323*, "young bull"). An obese king of MOAB who early in the judges period occupied territory W of JORDAN near JERICHO. The military campaign of this king was assisted by neighboring AMMON, which attacked an area to the E of the JABBOK River (Num. 21:24; Josh. 12:2; 13:10, 25; Jdg. 11:13, 22), and also by the desert bedouin Amalekites (see AMALEK). The exploits of Eglon resulted in the occupation of the City of Palms (Jdg. 3:13), but since this site (Jericho) had been destroyed in the previous century (if not earlier) by JOSHUA, the 12th-cent.-B.C. Moabite occupation doubtless involved the subjection of the surrounding territory, including BETHEL. The Israelites were dominated by the Moabites for eighteen years, after which God raised up EHUD to deliver Israel from this humiliation (Jdg. 3:21). Ehud brought the annual tribute to Eglon, gaining a private audience, and when the obese king stood up to receive the tribute, Ehud inflicted a fatal abdominal wound upon him. (See B. Halpern, "The Assassination of Eglon: The First Locked-Room Murder Mystery," in *BRev* 4/6 [Dec. 1988]: 32–41, 44.)

R. K. HARRISON

Eglon (place) eg´lon (עֶגְלוֹן *H6324*, "young bull"). An AMORITE town in the western SHEPHELAH. The contention of W. F. Albright (*BASOR* 15 [Oct. 1924]: 7–8) that Eglon be identified with Tell el-Ḥesi (c. 16 mi. NE of GAZA) enjoyed general acceptance for much of the 20th cent.; the ancient name was thought to be preserved at nearby Khirbet ʿAjlan, to where the town had been moved by Byzantine times (Euseb. *Onomasticon* 48.18). It should be noted that the earlier archaeological excavations of that area by W. M. F. Petrie (*Tell el Hesy* (*Lachish*) [1891], 18–20) and F. J. Bliss (*A Mound of Many Cities, or Tell Hesy Excavated* [1898]) were the genesis of modern ARCHAEOLOGY in Palestine. Eight distinct levels were uncovered dating from the Early Bronze III to the Persian Periods. More recent work, however, suggests that Eglon should be identified with Tell ʿAitun, 11 mi. WSW of HEBRON (cf. A. F. Rainey in *BASOR* 251 [Summer 1983]: 1–22, esp. pp. 9–10).

The earliest mention of Eglon is the reference to ʿq̓y in the Egyptian execration texts (G. Posener, *Princes et pays d'Asie et de Nubie* [1940], no. E-58). The cuneiform tablet discovered at Tell el-Ḥesi is contemporary with the Late Bronze texts from TELL EL AMARNA (EA, 333). The letter describes the high treason that was brewing at nearby LACHISH and JARMUTH against the pharaoh. The king of Jerusalem took action against his subjects the Gibeonites (see GIBEON) because they had made a pact with Joshua. The Amorite kings of Jarmuth, Hebron, Lachish, and Eglon were called upon for assistance (Josh. 10:3–6). The Israelites came to the rescue of the Gibeonites and defeated the Amorites. Subsequently, the five kings were captured (10:23), and during the campaign in S Palestine, the city of Eglon was conquered (10:34–37; 12:12). It was assigned to the inheritance of the tribe of JUDAH, in the second district of the SHEPHELAH region (15:39).   A. F. RAINEY

Egnatian Way. See VIA EGNATIA.

Egrebeh, Egrebel i-gree´buhl. See ACRABA.

Egypt ee´jipt. A country in the NE corner of Africa, including the NILE delta and valley, with their flanking deserts. In antiquity, it extended from the Mediterranean Sea to the first cataract of the Nile (to the second cataract in modern times). In the Table of NATIONS, Egypt (Heb. *miṣrayim* H5213) is listed as one of the sons of HAM and as the ancestor of seven people groups (Gen. 10:6, 13–14 = 1 Chr. 1:8, 11–12 NRSV; the NIV follows KJV in rendering "Mizraim").

   I. Natural conditions
     A. The setting
     B. Topography
   II. Population and languages
     A. Population
     B. Languages and scripts
   III. Names of Egypt
   IV. Chronology
     A. Basis of Egyptian chronology
     B. Outline table of Egyptian dates
   V. Historical survey
     A. Predynastic Egypt
     B. Archaic Egypt
     C. Old Kingdom
     D. Rise and fall of the Middle Kingdom
     E. New Kingdom
     F. The Third Intermediate and Late Periods
   VI. Egyptian literature
     A. Historical outline
     B. Egyptian literature and the OT
   VII. Egyptian religion
     A. The gods of the Egyptians
     B. Worship and cult
     C. Funerary beliefs

I. Natural conditions

A. The setting. The Nile in past ages carved out a long gorge or valley northward to the Mediterranean across the African tableland; the successive phases of the process can be seen in the terraces visible in the cliffs that border the valley. Not until the valley floor had been filled with alluvial mud could there be a long, narrow strip of human settlement in the valley "flood-plain" on either river bank, and that only in the last eight thousand years or so. The delta, formerly a bay of the sea, was formed by alluvial mud at the same time, and this region early consisted in large measure of low-lying marshland, gradually and progressively reclaimed during the course of Egypt's long history. Desiccation of the Sahara steppe land forced early hunters into the Nile valley, and they became its first settlers.

The course of the Nile is hindered by six outcrops or "cataracts" of granite. Eroded less easily than the Nubian sandstone or the limestone that succeeds it northward some 70 mi. N of Aswan, these cataracts limited ancient Nile navigation. The first is at Aswan, and the others are counted southward to the sixth, about 70 mi. N of Khartum in the Sudan. Now flooded by the new High Dam at Aswan, the valley between the first and second cataracts was Lower Nubia; southward is Upper Nubia. Nubia was the biblical CUSH, and its history was closely bound up with that of Egypt.

Within Egypt proper, the Nile valley is rarely more than 12 mi. wide. Green vegetation flourishes as far as the life-giving waters reach, but immediately beyond, all is desert, a change so sharp that one may stand with one foot on the cultivation and one on the sand. On the modern political map of Africa, the Arab Republic of Egypt occupies a large rectangle almost 384,000 sq. mi. in extent, but about 96% of that terrain is desert, so that 99% of Egypt's population live on and from the 4% of usable land in valley and delta. Hence HERODOTUS's famous dictum about Egypt being the gift of the Nile, especially as the rainfall is of the slightest: about 7.5 inches at Alexandria, an inch at Cairo, and nil at Aswan apart from very occasional showers or cloudbursts. Until the advent of modern regulation, the Nile created and renewed the fertility of Egypt by its annual flood or "inundation," derived from the rains and melting snows of equatorial Africa and Ethiopia. These waters brought down a vast quantity of silt that was deposited as virtually a layer of new soil. The Nile begins its rise in June/July, subsiding after October. The abundance of the inundation determined that of the crops, and thus prosperity or famine (cf. JOSEPH); modern dams are designed to retain a reserve of water and so guarantee the supply.

The long narrow valley and broad spreading delta stand in striking contrast, forming two Egypts,

The Nile River (looking W).

Upper (valley) and Lower (delta). The pharaonic monarchy effectively began with the uniting of these two lands under one rule, but the ancient Egyptians never forgot the duality of their country: the pharaohs were always "King of Upper and Lower Egypt" and "Lord of the Two Lands." This conception affected the administration both in its ceremonial titles and in its practical divisions (e.g., separate viziers for S and N). The only feasible site for a capital of such a bipartite land is at the region of junction of the two areas—in the district where Cairo now stands as successor to ancient MEMPHIS only a few miles across the river. Some 40 mi. S of Cairo, but on the W bank, is the natural depression of the Fayum, connected to the Nile by a long water channel. From at least the 12th dynasty, the Fayum served as a reservoir, and by irrigation became (and is) a garden province. Farther W in the Sahara desert, a string of oases owes its existence to wells of artesian water, used since pharaonic times.

Within her valley and delta, Egypt had one splendid highway, the Nile itself. Her deserts largely protected her from external invasions for much of her early history, but access routes across the Sinai isthmus and through the E desert to the RED SEA, plus contacts S up the Nile and W along the Libyan coast all provided scope for Egypt both to give and to receive cultural stimuli.

B. Topography. Within the two broad divisions of Upper and Lower Egypt, the land was divided anciently into provinces or *nomes*. While various of these (esp. in Upper Egypt) may have originated as petty chiefdoms in prehistoric times, the organization of the nomes first clearly emerges during the Old Kingdom (3rd millennium B.C.) and continued to develop thereafter. As early as the 12th dynasty (1900 B.C.), Upper Egypt was already divided into the later canonical number of twenty-two such provinces (P. Lacau and H. Chevrier, *Une chapelle de Sésostris Ier à Karnak* [1956]). The more gradual development of the delta can be seen in the recognition of only a dozen Lower-Egyptian nomes in the 12th dynasty, the full twenty provinces being established finally only in the 2nd cent. B.C. under the Ptolemies.

The ancient Egyptians took their geographical orientation from the S, not N, hence Aswan was in the first Upper-Egyptian nome; it was early a frontier post (first cataract) with Nubia, and a staging post when Nubia was under Egyptian control. A hundred miles to the N (some 300 mi. S of Cairo), the spectacular monuments at Luxor preserve the memory of ancient THEBES in the fourth nome, most magnificent of Egypt's capitals during the empire age (c. 1550–1085 B.C.), with the Karnak and Luxor temples of the god Amun, and the tombs of its pharaohs in the Valley of the Kings. Some 50 mi. farther N (8th nome) stood Abydos, holy city of OSIRIS, the Egyptian god par excellence of the dead and of the afterlife, sacred (even before Osiris) from the earliest times. Among the cities farther N in Middle Egypt, suffice it to name Hermopolis (15th nome), the seat of Thoth the god of learning, to the SE of which AKHENATEN established his city for the worship of the solar disc (whence came the TELL EL-AMARNA tablets), and also Heracleopolis (20th nome), opposite the Fayum and seat of the 9th and 10th dynasties.

The territory of Memphis (biblical Noph), the administrative capital, counted as the first nome of Lower Egypt, and was probably founded by the very first pharaohs; across the Nile, just N of modern Cairo once stood HELIOPOLIS (biblical On), city of the sun god RE. Farther N was Bubastis (biblical PI BESETH), famed for its cat goddess and festival, while the NE delta contained administrative centers such as Pi Ramesse (see RAMESES) and its successor Tanis (ZOAN), on or near the main route to Palestine. The delta could boast of other renowned cities: Busiris (sacred to Osiris), Mendes, and especially Sais, an ancient city from which later came the 26th dynasty of NECO and HOPHRA. Out on the NW shore of the delta, PTOLEMY I and his successors made ALEXANDRIA their capital, developing ALEXANDER THE GREAT's new foundation into a vast city of Hellenistic culture where only a village (Rakoti) had stood before. Egyptian society was (as now) predominantly rural, and her ancient cities were not dense industrial communities, but groups of settlements with garden lands among and between them.

Detailed study of the ancient geography and topography of Egypt is very complex, especially as the courses of the delta branches of the Nile have varied in number and location at different historical epochs. Ancient Egyptian sources mention three main arms and classical writers distinguish seven, while today only two main streams function, from and between which a network of lesser channels, canals, and drains run and intersect. (On earliest conditions, see W. C. Hayes, *Most Ancient Egypt* [1965], and R. Said, ed., *The Geology of Egypt* [1990]. Generally, see J. Ball, *Contributions to the Geography of Egypt* [1939]. On ancient topography, Sir A. H. Gardiner, *Ancient Egyptian Onomastica*, 2 vols. [1947], is a mine of information, more careful than the vast compendium by H. Gauthier, *Dictionnaire des noms géographiques*, 7 vols. [1925–1931], and the later survey by P. Montet, *Géographie de l'Égypte Ancienne*, 2 vols. [1957]. On classical sources, cf. J. Ball, *Egypt in the Classical Geographers* [1941]. For the interrelation of land, culture, and history, see H. Kees, *Ancient Egypt: A Cultural Topography* [1961].)

II. Population and languages

A. Population. The ultimate origins of those earliest settlers who first colonized the Nile valley remain uncertain. The predynastic (i.e., prehistoric) Egyptians who developed the beginnings of settled culture in the Nile valley show African affinities. On the eve of the formation of a literate and united kingdom in the country, N Egyptian cemeteries of that epoch retain traces of people showing slightly different physical characteristics (e.g., in cranial capacity), the so-called "Giza race." These are thought by some to have been newcomers who infiltrated from W Asia, fused with the existing stock, and promoted the rapid flowering of what is known as typically Egyptian culture of the pharaonic period. However, certainty on the point is not attainable. From the Old Kingdom onward, the Egyptians show from their statues, reliefs, and paintings their own distinctive type, a physical form that has persisted ever since (despite all invasions), so that the Egyptians of today are the lineal descendants of their ancient predecessors, notwithstanding the transition through three civilizations in the interim.

B. Languages and scripts

1. Languages. The language of the ancient Egyptians had a complex origin and very long history. It was basically an African language, which linguists used to place within the so-called "Hamitic" family. It is now regarded as one of the branches of the Afroasiatic (Afrasian) family, and within that family it is most closely related to the Semitic and Berber languages (the latter spoken in Morocco and other NW African countries; see LANGUAGES OF THE ANE I.B). The independent personal pronouns, for example, are very similar to those of the best-known Semitic languages, and cognates in vocabulary can be readily recognized. The links between ancient Egyptian and other African languages are less easy to establish clearly (partly due to lack of ancient African texts), but useful work is being done in this field (cf. I. M. Diakonoff, *Afrasian Languages* [1988]; R. Hetzon in *The World's Major Languages*, ed. B. Comrie [1990], 645–53). Ancient Egyptian was already established by the time of the earliest inscriptions.

The main phases of the Egyptian language may be summarized as follows. *Old Egyptian* is the relatively terse form of the 1st to 8th dynasties in the 3rd millennium B.C. (Archaic period and Old Kingdom); apart from tomb inscriptions, the main source for this phase is the Pyramid Texts (see the sections on literature and religion, below), which show the most archaic forms of the tongue (see E. Edel, *Altägyptische Grammatik*, 2 vols. [1955–64]). *Middle Egyptian* was probably the spoken language of the early Middle Kingdom (11th–12th dynasties, c. 2100–1800 B.C.) and is the "classical" phase of the language—it was thus used for formal writings of every kind (esp. literary) not only in the Middle Kingdom but also throughout the New Kingdom (even with Late-Egyptian current), and well on into the late period, even till the Greco-Roman age in a modified form. (See A. H. Gardiner, *Egyptian Grammar*, 3rd ed. [1957]; R. O Faulkner, *A Concise Dictionary of Middle Egyptian* [1962]; A. Loprieno, *Ancient Egyptian: A Linguistic Introduction* [1995]; J. P. Allen, *Middle Egyptian: An Introduction to the Language and Culture of Hieroglyphs* [1999]). *Late Egyptian* was the vernacular of the New Kingdom (the empire established in the 16th cent.), but had begun to develop before that period (with traces back to the 18th cent.). With Akhenaten of the late 18th dynasty, Late Egyptian came to be used regularly in written documents, especially of current business, administration, etc.; literary and religious texts also were composed in Late Egyptian from the Ramesside age onward, alongside the Middle-Egyptian literature. *Demotic* ("popular"), really the name of a script, is the term applied to "later" Late Egyptian; it is attested in documents from the 7th cent. B.C. into the Roman epoch. It was always principally the language of business and daily life, but literary and religious works in Demotic joined the existing Middle and Late Egyptian traditions (A. Erman, *Neuägyptische Grammatik*, 2nd ed. [1933]; F. Junge, *Late Egyptian Grammar: An Introduction*, trans. D. Warburton [2001]).

Coptic was the final phase of Egyptian, as it came to be used in Byzantine Egypt. It developed among native Christian writers, especially for translating the Bible and Greek church literature. Coptic has survived in Egypt into modern times as the liturgical language of the Coptic or indigenous church (cf. the use of Latin at Rome), while the everyday tongue of modern Egypt is Arabic. Coptic exhibits several dialects, Sahidic (J. M. Plumley, *Introductory Coptic Grammar* [1984]; B. Layton, *A Coptic Grammar, with Chrestomathy and Glossary: Sahidic Dialect* [2000]) and Bohairic (A. Mallon, *Grammaire copte*, 4th ed. [1956]) being the most important. (All dialects are usefully outlined in W. C. Till, *Koptische Dialektgrammatik*, 2nd ed. [1961].)

2. Scripts. The oldest Egyptian script consists of hieroglyphs, by origin pictorial signs (see WRITING). Such signs may be used (i) to stand for the object depicted (ideogram or word sign); (ii) to represent the consonants of the word for the object depicted, giving the sign a phonetic value that can allow it to be used to write other words; and (iii) as a "determinative" appended to a phonetically spelled word to indicate its general class. (See N. M. Davies, *Picture Writing in Ancient Egypt* [1958]; P. Wilson, *Hieroglyphs: A Very Short Introduction* [2004].)

However, almost as early as the hieroglyphs themselves, there appeared abbreviated or "cursive" forms of them. Writing more rapidly with a reed pen and carbon ink upon papyrus, or making jottings on limestone flakes or on potsherds ("ostraca"), the scribes soon developed running, even

Hieroglyphs of the Egyptian pharaoh Mernephtah (c. 1200 B.C.) from Memphis.

ligatured forms based on the hieroglyphs but no longer pictorial. This form of book-script we call *hieratic*. It was the usual script for all documents (literary or otherwise) on papyrus, while the hieroglyphs remained the monumental script on stone and wood. Both scripts were used to write Old, Middle, and Late Egyptian, right on into the days of the Roman empire, that is, for about 3,000 years. (See G. Möller, *Hieratische Paläographie*, 2nd ed., 4 vols. [1927–36]; S. Wimmer, *Hieratische Paläographie der nicht literarischen Ostraka der 19. und 20. Dynastie* [1995].)

In the 8th cent. B.C., there was developed a "shorthand" version of hieratic, now termed *demotic*, and which has given its name also to the still later form of Late Egyptian expressed in this script. This, too, continued into Roman times. With the advent of Christianity in the valley of the Nile, the need arose for ordinary people to be able to read the Scriptures. For this, the old scripts were much too cumbersome with their hundreds of signs and groups. After some experimentation ("Old Coptic"), the Egyptian Christians took over the Greek alphabet, adding to it seven letters to represent sounds not covered by the Greek letters. Because this is the only form of Egyptian that shows the vowels, it is of philological importance.

During the course of Egyptian history, various foreign loan words entered the language, especially in the highly international age of the 14th–13th centuries B.C.; these are mainly Semitic. Such attestations of W Semitic vocabulary are of great value for the study of Hebrew and its cognate languages. Occasionally, Egyptian words appear in CUNEIFORM, for example, in the Amarna tablets. In the Coptic of Christian Egypt, a large body of Greek vocabulary was taken over, plus a sprinkling of Latin and further Semitic terms.

Southward from Egypt, the Nubian kingdom and civilization of Meroë adopted Egyptian hieroglyphs, modified them to write the Meroitic tongue, and eventually developed its own cursive script. This kingdom flourished from the 6th cent. B.C. to the 4th cent. A.D. However, Meroitic is not yet fully deciphered; it would have been the mother tongue of CANDACE's officer (Acts 8:27).

III. Names of Egypt. The ancient Egyptians had several terms for their homeland: *Kemyt*, the "black land" (as opposed to the desert, the "red land"), *Tawy* the "Two Lands" (Upper and Lower Egypt), and *Ta-meri*, a term of uncertain meaning. The English name *Egypt* derives from Greek *Aigyptos G131*, which in turn derives from Egyptian *ḥ(t)-k͗-ptḥ*, "Mansion of the *ka*-spirit of [the god] Ptah," a name for Memphis, the ancient capital. (Cf. A. Gardiner, *Ancient Egyptian Onomastica*, 2 vols. [1947], 1:124.) This term, already attested in the Amarna letters of the 14th cent. B.C. as *Hikuptah*, shows the use of a city name for the land. Conversely, the Arabic name of the land, *Maṣr* or *Miṣr*, also stands for Cairo, successor to Memphis. This Arabic term for Egypt is that attested in the older Semitic languages, including Akkadian (*Muṣri*; cf. P. Garelli, "Musur," in *DBSup* 5 [1957], cols. 1468–74; and H. Tadmor in *IEJ* 11 [1961]: 143–50), Ugaritic (*Mṣrm*), and biblical Hebrew (*miṣrayim*, which may mean "[two] boundaries" [cf. *HALOT*, 1:625], perhaps alluding to Upper and Lower Egypt).

Throughout the OT, *miṣrayim* stands for Egypt virtually without exception, despite sporadic attempts in the past to refer some passages to a Musri near SE Anatolia (ASIA MINOR). By Muṣri, the Assyrian sources for their part usually mean Egypt, and sometimes a land N of ASSYRIA; its use for N ARABIA is dubious (cf. *ANET*, 279 n. 9, for references). The only OT passages that have been seriously attributed to a northern Muṣri are the references to Solomon's horse and chariot trade with Miṣrayim and KUE (1 Ki. 10:28–29 = 2 Chr. 1:16–17). That Kue is CILICIA seems clear, but then Miṣrayim could hardly be a near neighbor of Kue if Solomon's traders were to act between them. If the trade was between Egypt to the S (producing chariots) and Kue in the N (horses), then Solomon was ideally placed to be middle man between the two.

IV. Chronology

A. Basis of Egyptian chronology

1. Introduction. Ancient Egypt shows a continuous history for almost 3,000 years down to the Roman conquest (31 B.C.), a span rivalled only by MESOPOTAMIA. Current knowledge of that history varies in accuracy and detail from period to period in relation to the available sources, and the accuracy of Egyptian chronology is similarly conditioned, as a compact survey of the basic evidence will make clear.

Before the decipherment of the hieroglyphs, the principal source of Egyptian chronology was the epitome of dynasties and kings based on the *History of Egypt*, written in Greek by the Egyptian priest Manetho (3rd cent. B.C.), who divided the long line of kings into thirty "dynasties" or families. This basic framework has largely stood the test of modern knowledge of firsthand Egyptian sources opened up by decipherment of the hieroglyphs, and so it is still retained today. However, it has been found convenient to group the dynasties into larger units, corresponding to the main divisions of Egyptian history, the whole now being prefaced by the predynastic (and in practice, prehistoric) period.

Thus, the three most brilliant and best understood epochs of Egyptian history are termed the Old Kingdom (3rd–6th dynasties, 3rd millennium B.C.), the Middle Kingdom (11th–12th dynasties, early 2nd millennium), and the New Kingdom or Empire period (18th–20th dynasties, late 2nd millennium). Before the Old Kingdom came the formative Protodynastic or Archaic Period of the 1st and 2nd Dynasties. Between the Old and Middle Kingdoms, then between the Middle and New Kingdoms, come respectively the First and Second Intermediate Periods (7th–10th and 13th–17th dynasties), obscure periods of internal weakness. After the New Kingdom, the Late Period covers the 21st to 30th dynasties and Persian rule prior to Alexander the Great (i.e., c. 1085–332). The 21st to 24th dynasties are sometimes termed the "Third Intermediate Period" because of conditions reminiscent of the earlier Intermediate Periods; the 26th dynasty saw an archaizing "renaissance" until overwhelmed by the Persian empire. After Alexander the Great, the Ptolemies ruled until supplanted by Rome. Between the limits of prehistory and Alexander, the profile of Egypt's history may be set out thus:

Archaic Period
Old Kingdom
First Intermediate Period
Middle Kingdom
Second Intermediate Period
New Kingdom
Late Period

2. Sources and limits of Egyptian dates. Besides the excerpts from Manetho preserved in defective versions by later writers, there exist also Egyptian king lists from the New Kingdom. Despite its pitifully damaged state, the most valuable of these is the Turin Papyrus of Kings, which once listed nearly all the kings of Egypt, from the mythical dynasties of gods and spirits and the first human dynasties down to the time of RAMSES (also spelled Ramesses) II, giving lengths of reigns and of groups of dynasties, etc. It thus preserves, for example, a figure of 955 years for the first eight dynasties, and gives 143 (136 + 7) years for the 11th dynasty, besides the reigns of many individual kings. Other lists give simply the names of kings in order, often omitting obscure periods; such are the lists of Sethos I and Ramses II in their temples at Abydos, and from the tomb of Tjenuna at Saqqara. A list of THUTMOSE (Tuthmosis) III from Karnak (now in the Louvre) merely gives groups of selected kings. For the first five dynasties, one must add the limited but vital evidence of the Palermo Stone and other fragments from the same or a similar monument that once contained a record of all the years of the kings of the 1st to 5th dynasties, with notes of events (mainly religious).

At all periods, we possess monuments dated by the regnal years of individual pharaohs; these furnish at any rate minimum figures for reigns in default of other evidence. Genealogies of officials in which successive generations served different kings can be very helpful, especially in the Late Period (21st–25th dynasties). Synchronisms between Egyptian pharaohs and the rulers of states in W Asia in the 2nd and 1st millennia B.C. afford valuable cross-checks on dates of both areas.

Finally, there are some "external" means of control upon Egyptian dates. The carbon 14 method is of limited utility, mainly for the prehistoric epoch. ASTRONOMY is more serviceable for the historical period. The Egyptian calendar was 365 days long, and so ended a day too early every four years (no leap year). Thus, after some 700 years the calendar-seasons fell in the wrong natural seasons (calendrical summer in natural winter, etc.), and after some 1,453 years the calendar would coincide with nature's seasons again. The proper starting point of the Egyptian calendar happened to coincide with the "heliacal" rising of the Dog Star, Sothis (Sirius). Thus, mentions of such risings of Sothis in terms of dates of the moving calendar are of great value in helping to fix the date B.C. of such references within narrow limits. Lunar dates can be useful, if they are known to fall within a limited general time span. (See R. Krauss, *Sothis- und Monddaten: Studien zur astronomischen und technischen Chronologie Altägyptens* [1985].)

This kind of evidence has made it possible to date the 12th dynasty closely to 1991–1786 B.C. (a Sothic rising, plus lunar dates), and so the 11th dynasty with 143 years before it at c. 2134–1991. A similar Sothic datum is attested for Amenophis (Amenhotep) I in the early 18th dynasty. Taken as observed at Thebes, this seems to indicate a date of c. 1551 for the start of the 18th dynasty, while lunar data for Thutmose III would place his reign in 1490–1436. This allows good dates for the dynasty to the death of Amenophis III in about 1364. This dynasty would end by either 1315 or 1301 at the latest, depending on the date adopted for Ramses II, and affected by the vexed question of a possible coregency of Amenophis III and Akhenaten.

In the 19th dynasty, lunar data indicates that the redoubtable Ramses II reigned either 1304–1238 or 1290–1224 B.C. (a margin of only fourteen years), but intensive attempts to decide finally between the two dates have proved fruitless, because the Egyptian and ANE data contain ambiguities not yet eliminated; new material is needful. After Ramses II, the next generally agreed fixed point was not reached until the beginning of the 26th dynasty in 664 (not 663); from the Persian conquest (525) onward, Egyptian dates are well enough tied in with the rest of antiquity to cause little difficulty beyond details.

However, between Ramses II and 664 B.C. it is possible to suggest that Shoshenq I (biblical SHISHAK), who raided Palestine in the fifth year of REHOBOAM of Judah, did so about 925, and so reigned c. 945–924; some set these dates about a decade later. Shoshenq's line, the 22nd dynasty, ended with Osorkon IV, who was probably the Shilkanni mentioned by Assyrian documents of SARGON II in 716, which sets an upper limit for the rule of the 25th dynasty in Egypt. With this outline framework and a large body of scattered facts, it is then possible to produce reasonable dates for the 20th to 25th dynasties that rarely exceed a decade or so in margin of error.

Between the end of the 12th dynasty (1786) and the beginning of the 18th (c. 1551) there are some 235 years for the 13th to 17th dynasties of the difficult Second Intermediate Period. However, the 13th dynasty can be allowed 153 years for its sixty kings during 1786–1633, ruling most of Egypt until c. 1650. The 14th dynasty was a minor line local to the NW delta, not affecting general chronology. Similarly, the "16th dynasty" consists of local HYKSOS chiefs subject to the main 13th dynasty and Hyksos kings. The 15th or Hyksos dynasty itself had six rulers for 108 years (Turin Papyrus); and, being expelled in about the eleventh year of Ahmose I of the 18th dynasty, it probably ruled most of Egypt during c. 1648–1540 until the last decade.

Going back beyond the 11th dynasty (from 2134), there is the Turin Papyrus figure of 955 years for the 1st to 8th dynasties, which may be fairly correct. The length of the 9th/10th dynasties is not really known, nor the length of their overlap with the 11th dynasty. If the 9th and 11th dynasties competed for the kingship immediately from the end of the old 8th dynasty, then 955 years before 2134 would set the start of the 1st dynasty at c. 3089—say c. 3100 in round figures. If the 11th dynasty was founded only some years after the 9th dynasty took over from the 8th, then the whole set of dates for the 1st to 8th dynasties would have to be raised by the amount of that interval. Conversely, if the 400 years or so usually allotted to the

1st and 2nd dynasties proved to be excessive, then the beginning of the 1st dynasty would have to be correspondingly lowered somewhat. Thus, for the 3rd to 8th dynasties, there is several decades' margin of error; for the 1st and 2nd, up to a century or more.

PREDYNASTIC PERIOD (prehistoric age)	c. 4000: Taso-Badarian Period
	c. 3700: Naqada I Period
	c. 3500–3000: Naqada II Period
ARCHAIC PERIOD (formative age)	c. 3000–2700: 1st–2nd dynasties
OLD KINGDOM (age of pyramids)	c. 2700–2160: 3rd–8th dynasties
FIRST INTERMEDIATE PERIOD	c. 2160–2010: 9th–10th dynasties (overlaps 11th dynasty)
MIDDLE KINGDOM (classical period)	c. 2106–1963: 11th dynasty
	c. 1963–1786: 12th dynasty
SECOND INTERMEDIATE PERIOD	c. 1786–1550: 13th–17th dynasties (overlapping reigns)
	Hyksos rule (c. 1648–1540)
NEW KINGDOM (age of empire)	c. 1550–1295: 18th dynasty
	Thutmose I (c. 1505–1492)
	Hatshepsut (senior coregent, c. 1479–1457)
	Thutmose III (c. 1479–1425)
	Akhenaten (c. 1352–1336)
	c. 1295–1186: 19th dynasty
	Sethos (Seti) I (c. 1294–1279)
	Ramses II (c. 1279–1213)
	c. 1186–1069: 20th dynasty
	Ramses III (c. 1184–1153)
THIRD INTERMEDIATE PERIOD (age of disunity)	c. 1069–945: 21st dynasty
	c. 945–715: 22nd–23rd dynasties
	Shishak (= Shoshenq I, c. 945–914)
	So (= Osorkon IV [?], c. 730–715)
	c. 727–715: 24th dynasty
	c. 780–656: 25th dynasty (Kushite period)
	Tirhakah (= Taharqa, 690–664)
LATE PERIOD	664–525: 26th dynasty (Saite revival)
	Psammetichus I (664–610)
	Nec(h)o II (610–595)
	Hophra (= Apries, 589–570)
	525–404: Persian rule ("27th dynasty")
	404–343: 28th–30th dynasties
	343–332: Persian rule ("31st dynasty")
HELLENISTIC AND LATER PERIODS	332–30: Alexander and the Ptolemies
	30 B.C. to A.D. 395: Roman rule
	A.D. 395–641: Byzantine rule
	A.D. 641: Islamic conquest

B. Outline table of Egyptian dates. The major periods of Egyptian history may be dated as follows (all dates B.C. unless noted otherwise).

(For a more detailed and updated table, see K. A. Kitchen, "Egypt, History of (Chronology)," in *ABD*, 2:328–30. For a recent collection of specialized articles, see E. Hornung et al., eds., *Ancient Egyptian Chronology* [2006].)

V. Historical survey. (For general treatments of ancient Egyptian history as a whole, see J. H. Breasted, *A History of Egypt*, rev. ed. [1909], a fundamental but dated work; J. A. Wilson, *The Burden of Egypt* [1951=*The Culture of Ancient Egypt*, 1956]; W. C. Hayes, *The Sceptre of Egypt*, 2 vols. [1953–59]; A. H. Gardiner, *Egypt of the Pharaohs* [1961]; É. Drioton and J. Vandier, *L'Égypte*, 4th ed. [1962], well-documented; E. Hornung, *Grundzüge der ägyptischen Geschichte* [1965]; *The Legacy of Egypt*, ed. S. R. K. Glanville, rev. ed. [1972]; B. G. Trigger et al., *Ancient Egypt: A Social History* [1983]; relevant chapters in *CAH*, rev. ed., vols. 1–5 [1970–92]; W. J. Murnane in *CANE*, 2:691–717, a clear and up-to-date summary with useful bibliography; *The Oxford History of Ancient Egypt*, ed. I. Shaw [2000]; *The Oxford Encyclopedia of Ancient Egypt*, ed. D. B. Redford, 3 vols. [2001]; B. J. Kemp, *Ancient Egypt: Anatomy of a Civilization*, 2nd ed. [2006]. Most historical sources are in J. H. Breasted, *Ancient Records of Egypt*, 5 vols. [1906–7].)

A. Predynastic Egypt. In Upper Egypt, the first settled societies are known as Badarian (earliest phase, Tasian). These people practiced agriculture, lived in villages (huts or tents), and made pottery (some, very fine), having flint tools and some use of copper. They had already developed some concept of an afterlife, as indicated by the furnishings of their modest burials. The following period, Naqada I (or Amratian), had some contacts abroad with S Arabia, Iran, and Mesopotamia, possibly passing via Wadi Hammamat in the eastern desert and down the Red Sea. The final period of Egyptian prehistory, Naqada II (or Gerzean), witnessed great changes by its end. By now, regular townships existed, some walled (e.g., at Naqada itself). Graves and their furnishings increased in elaboration. During this age at the latest the Egyptian language crystallized. And before the end of Naqada II, cultural influences from Mesopotamia had a tangible impact, inspiring the Egyptians to use cylinder seals, undertake monumental brick architecture, and above all produce their own form of writing—the hieroglyphs. By the end of the period, Upper Egypt had become a unified kingdom, and another kingdom had rule over at least part of the Delta. (See further W. C. Hayes, *Most Ancient Egypt* [1965]; K. R. Weeks, *An Historical Bibliography of Egyptian Prehistory* [1985]; F. A. Hassan in *CANE*, 2:665–78.)

B. Archaic Egypt (1st and 2nd dynasties, c. 3000–2700 B.C.). Traditionally, Egyptian history begins with the union of the Two Lands under King Menes from Upper Egypt, conquering the delta kingdom and founding a new capital at Memphis for the 1st dynasty to rule all Egypt. It is likely that the Menes of late tradition is the King Narmer of contemporary monuments. This king dedicated a superb, shield-shaped "palette" bearing triumphal scenes that show him wearing the crowns of Upper and of Lower Egypt—perhaps direct evidence of his actually uniting the two Egypts under his rule. Seven other kings, his descendants, continued the dynasty, a period of tremendous advance in early civilization. At Abydos, each king had at this holy place a tomb surrounded by graves of the nobles of the court, well back on the desert edge, and also—rather nearer the town—an imposing "funerary palace" (possibly with provision for his continuing cult) itself surrounded in turn by the graves of palace servitors. The stela or tombstone of the fourth king, Wadji (or, "Djet"), is in beauty of execution the noblest monument of its kind.

At Saqqara, on the desert edge to the NE of Memphis the new capital, magnificent brick tombs were built, combining a burial with a superstructure having a "palace-façade." These were probably the tombs of great men of the realm who served the king at Memphis. Several scholars have suggested that some of these Saqqara tombs were the real royal tombs, the Abydos tombs being a species of cenotaph, but this is far from certain. (On the significance of these series of tombs, see B. J. Kemp in *JEA* 52 [1966]: 13–22, and in *Antiquity* 41 [1967]: 22–32.) The physical furnishings of all these tombs—both at Abydos and at Saqqara—illustrate the great strides made in the applied arts: fine vases of the hardest stones, fantastically carved slate dishes, fragments of beautiful furniture employing ivory, ebony, etc., a full range of copper tools and vessels, and free use of gold (usually plundered long since).

The evidence of clay sealings and of bone and ivory labels once attached to goods deposited in the tombs bear witness to a rapidly developing and elaborate state administration already in the 31st to 29th centuries B.C. One may perceive the functioning of a treasury, state bureaus for provisions, the existence of various royal estates and institutions as economic units, and so on—all of it 2,000 years before David and Solomon had to organize their state administration. Only in contemporary Sumer do we have written evidence for a parallel elaboration of civilized life, but the mute evidence from Asia Minor, Syrian, and Palestinian town sites, with palatial and military architecture, organized material wealth, and so forth, is enough to hint that, this early, much of the future biblical world already had highly organized societies.

Under the 2nd dynasty, progress was for a time halted by internal dissensions, possibly epitomized in the figures of the falcon god Horus and the god Seth of Ombos (both of Upper Egypt). These troubles were probably ended by a King Khasekhem who perhaps took the modified name Khasekhemwy ("the two powers are manifest") as symbol of a reconciliation. The Palermo Stone preserves some records of the first two dynasties, but mainly of religious ceremonies and the founding of buildings. The date-lines of the ivory and bone labels "date" their years within the king's reign by reference to such events plus the royal name. The data on these labels plus the once continuous enumeration of such years and events on the Palermo Stone are the nearest approach to historical annals for this early epoch. (See further W. B. Emery, *Archaic Egypt* [1961].)

C. Old Kingdom (3rd–8th dynasties, c. 2700–2160 B.C.). The rapid progress of the early dynasties, consolidated by Khasekhemwy, had laid the foundation for Egypt's first and most vigorous period of greatness, an age epitomized for many by the PYRAMIDS that are her most enduring monuments. The 3rd dynasty is dominated by the figures of Pharaoh Djoser and his minister Imhotep. At Saqqara they built the Step Pyramid, the world's first great building of stone, originally nearly 200 ft. high. It stood in a vast enclosure, nearly 600 yards long by over 300 wide, which contained besides the pyramid a whole series of special buildings for the royal cult in perpetuity, all with an external finish of the finest limestone masonry. Doubtless that cult was celebrated with rituals of matching elaboration, precursors of the later attested Pyramid Texts. Imhotep was celebrated early by the Egyptians as an author, probably of Egypt's first wisdom book (cf. later allusions, e.g., ANET, 432a, 467a), and by the Greeks as a healer and identified with ASCLEPIUS. Further step pyramids were built by Djoser's successors, but were all unfinished because of the premature deaths of most of these kings.

True pyramids came into fashion only with the 4th dynasty; its founder, Snofru, built two at Dahshur. His son Cheops (Khufu) built the Great Pyramid (originally 481 ft. high) at Giza opposite the area of modern Cairo. Khephren built the Second Pyramid and was probably responsible for the carving of the Sphinx, a large specimen of a common royal/divine guardian figure in Egyptian sculpture. The Third Pyramid, of Mycerinus, was much smaller but was expensively sheathed in granite. The step pyramids may have given tangible expression to the concept of a stairway to heaven (cf. distantly Jacob's ladder Gen. 28:12, and the Mesopotamian temple towers). The true pyramid was a solar symbol, reminiscent of the *benben* stone of the sun god RE of HELIOPOLIS, and perhaps symbolized the rays of the sun as a ramp upon which the king might ascend to

The Saqqara Step Pyramid (looking SE).

heaven. The divine pharaoh ruled supreme but in due course had to yield in authority to the sun god, to whom he was subordinated theologically as Son of Re. This began in the 4th dynasty, but reached full expression in the 5th dynasty when the kings built not only pyramids but also separate solar temples in their vicinity. (See further A. Fakhry, *The Pyramids* [1961]; I. E. S. Edwards, *The Pyramids of Egypt*, rev. ed. [1985]; A. Siliotti, *The Illustrated Guide to the Pyramids* [2003].)

Throughout the 4th to 6th dynasties, the pharaohs sent expeditions S into Nubia, establishing a foothold at the second cataract, and also in the N maintained trade relations with Byblos in Phoenicia to procure timber of the class of "cedar of Lebanon." In the 6th dynasty, movements of peoples in the ANE caused pressure on Egypt's Palestinian frontier; and so, under Pepi I, the dignitary Uni led five expeditions into Palestine to ward off this threat, the fifth of these being an amphibious operation.

In internal politics, the increasing elaboration of administration meant that the pharaoh delegated ever more authority to his ministers and officials. In the 4th dynasty the chief ministers had often been members of the royal family, but from the 5th dynasty onward this ceased to be so. The steady fragmentation of power and the economic drain of tax-exempt royal endowments for temples attached to pyramids and gifts of land for the funerary cults of officials all combined to reduce the effective power of the kings, especially in the 6th dynasty. In Upper Egypt, the provincial governors became hereditary local rulers with an increase in real local authority at royal expense. To counterbalance this trend, the pharaohs appointed special governors of the S as "overlords" for the local rulers, but this measure eventually proved inadequate. The end came with the reign of Pepi II, who acceded as a boy of six and reigned for ninety-four years; for the latter part of his overlong reign, the aged king was probably helpless to halt the centrifugal forces in the realm. (On matters of administration, see further W. Helck, *Untersuchungen zu den Beamtentiteln des ägyptischen Alten Reiches* [1954]; K. Baer, *Rank and Title in the Old Kingdom* [1960]; H. Goedicke, *Königliche Dokumente aus dem Alten Reich* [1967]; N. Strudwick, *The Administration of Egypt in the Old Kingdom* [1985].)

The internal peace and security of Egypt under a strong and effective administration headed by the vizier and other ministers made possible the full development of all the civilized arts. Architecture was represented not only by the vast surfaces of the pyramids, but also by the sumptuous royal temples attached to them. Choice and costly granites and alabaster were often employed for pillars and paving, and their walls were increasingly decorated with superbly executed scenes in delicate low relief, usually painted, and mainly of ritual subjects. The tombs of the great nobility each consisted of a massive rectangular structure of stone over a burial shaft and pit; in the 5th and 6th dynasties, funerary chapels within these massifs (called *mastabas*) were brilliantly decorated with scenes in relief of daily life, etc., for the other-worldly benefit of the owner, but vividly preserving the life of the epoch. Statuary in the round reach heights of excellence unrivaled at any later period in world history before the works of the Greeks. (See W. S. Smith, *Egyptian Sculpture and Painting in the Old Kingdom*, 2nd ed. [1949], and *Art and Architecture in Ancient Egypt* [1958]; D. Arnold, *When the Pyramids Were Built: Egyptian Art of the Old Kingdom* [1999]; F. Tiradritti, *Ancient Egypt: Art, Architecture and History* [2002].)

So much ability and brilliance in practical and visual arts did not lack counterparts in the intellectual realm, although the evidence is much more fragmentary. The gods of Egypt were already served in temples with elaborate rituals. From the time of King Unas (end of the 5th dynasty), the inner chambers of the royal pyramids were inscribed with a vast series of spells, magical rituals, and religious texts now known collectively as the "Pyramid Texts," the oldest major corpus of religious literature yet known. They served magically to insure the protection and well-being of the pharaoh in the afterlife (cf. also the section on literature, below, for their evidence on early literary form). Another famous document, the *Memphite Theology*, probably originated in the Old Kingdom; it shows the first known formulation of a *logos*-type concept. Of quite another order were the "Instructions" or wisdom books composed by leading dignitaries of the monarchy from Imhotep of the 3rd dynasty to Ptahhotep of the 5th (see the section on literature, below). In their day, these were the quintessence of the "wisdom of the

Egyptians," and inculcated the rules for a successful and "integrated" life within the society and service of the pharaoh. They aimed also at "good style" in their mode of literary expression (so, Ptahhotep). Then, especially in the 6th dynasty, we have the biographical tomb inscriptions of high officials, giving glimpses of history (e.g., Uni) associated with their personal achievements. Royal decrees in favor of temples exhibit the official style.

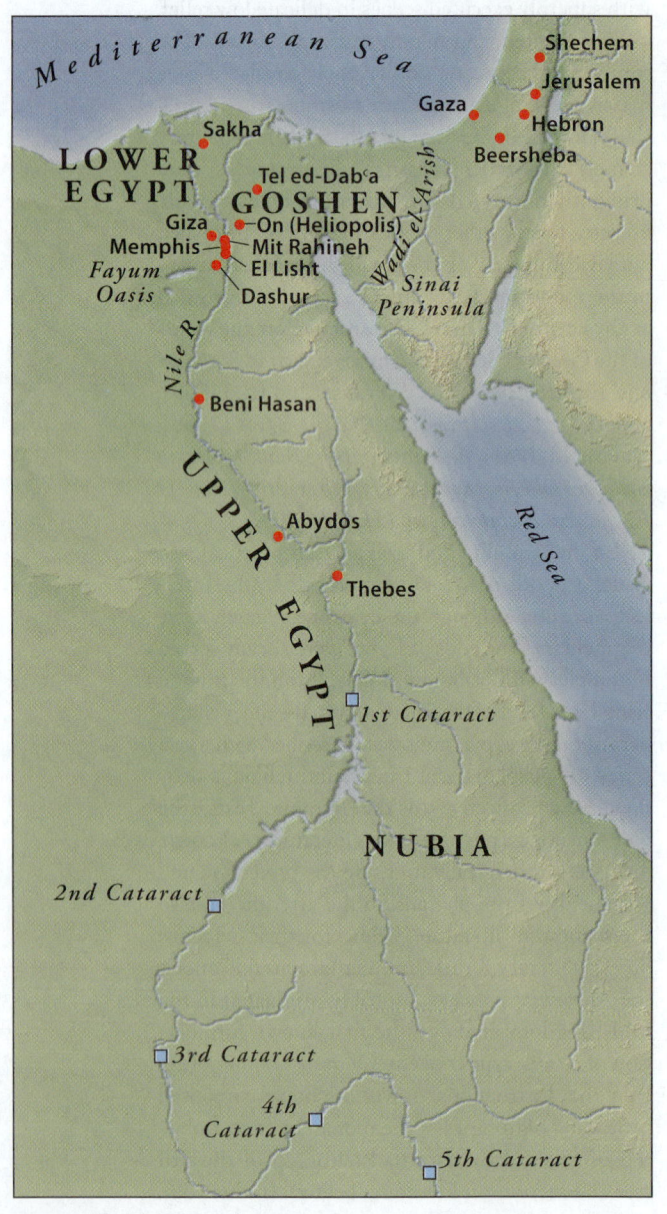

Egypt at the time of Abraham (Middle Kingdom Egypt).

Having arisen, flourished, and passed away long before Abraham was born, this brilliant age (and its parallels abroad) is of value in several respects from the viewpoint of biblical studies. Like the Archaic Period, it serves to underline the fact that the biblical world was not merely the dim haunt of savages prior, say, to the Hebrew monarchy or the Babylonian exile. Such conception is false, even 1,000 years before Abraham. The wealth of pictorial matter contributes to our understanding of ordinary daily life and custom in the biblical world, and the literature provides material toward a really factual history of literary style in the biblical world as a setting for OT literature. (For a brief but reliable survey, with many illustrations, see A. J. Spencer, *Early Egypt: The Rise of Civilisation in the Nile Valley* [1993].) The 7th and 8th dynasties show a rapid series of brief reigns without any notable undertakings. The pharaohs at Memphis were still recognized in Upper Egypt, if rather nominally, as shown by their temple decrees from Coptos.

D. Rise and fall of the Middle Kingdom

1. First Intermediate Period (9th–10th dynasties, c. 2160–2010 B.C.). When the throne fell vacant, a prince from Middle Egypt (Heracleopolis), Khety I, founded a new line (9th–10th dynasties), but the order ran into difficulties in both N and S. From Palestine, Asiatics penetrated the delta and added to unrest in the towns, while in the S the princes of Thebes established a rival line of kings—the 11th dynasty—in southern Upper Egypt from c. 2106. This period of internal stress came to an end only when the Theban King Mentuhotep II (Nebhepet-re) reunited all Egypt by about 2030, so ushering in the Middle Kingdom proper. However, this tense age produced (or inspired) noble literature: the earnest questings about life and death in the *Dispute of a Man with His Soul* (*ANET*, 405–7), the demand for social justice reflected in the ornate rhetoric of the *Eloquent Peasant* (*ANET*, 407–10), and the royal wisdom of the *Instruction* [of Khety III?] for King Merikara (*ANET*, 414–18, including the advice, "More acceptable is the character of one upright of heart than the ox [i.e., sacrifice] of the evildoer" [p. 417b; cf. 1 Sam. 15:22]).

2. Middle Kingdom proper (11th–12th dynasties, 2106–1786 B.C.). The 11th dynasty ended with the great Mentuhotep's second successor. Into the vacant kingship stepped the latter's former vizier as Amenemhet I to found the 12th dynasty, establishing a new administrative center (Ithettawy) just S of Memphis itself. In the pseudoprophecy of Neferty, he had himself portrayed as a promised deliverer of Egypt from her ills, and announced a program of internal prosperity and external security, thus inaugurating the deliberate use of literature for political and social propaganda. He undertook correspondingly vigorous measures for two decades, but was almost assassinated on the eve of appointing his son Sesostris I as coregent. In the *Instruction of Amenemhet I* (*ANET*, 418–19) the old king set out the achievements of his reign, casting bitter odium on his ungrateful assailants. Thereafter, the dynasty stood on a firmer footing, and Egypt again knew an age of peace, effective government, and considerable prosperity. Some kings, such as Amenemhet III, took particular interest in irrigation and developed the Fayum province. New wisdom books (see the section on literature, below) inculcated loyalty to the throne, or exalted the role of the scribes upon whom the success of the administration rested (*Satire of the Trades*).

Nubia was brought under firm control as far as the second cataract and beyond, with trade posts in the third cataract region. Trade and gold mining interests were safeguarded through massive mudbrick forts of medieval proportions. Egypt also had intimate contact with W Asia, especially through Byblos (GEBAL), whose princes by the end of the 12th dynasty were writing their names in Egyptian hieroglyphs, and thereafter full-length inscriptions also. The EXECRATION TEXTS of the 12th/13th dynasties, for cursing the pharaoh's enemies, throw vivid light on the political geography of Syria-Palestine in the age of the PATRIARCHS, including references to Jerusalem and Shechem, and the land of Damascus under the term Upe. They show the division of Canaan into city-states and tribal areas much as is presupposed by the narratives of Gen. 12–26. Sesostris III raided Palestine as far as Shechem (cf. *ANET*, 230).

A close guard was kept by use of forts on Egypt's Sinai frontier, and important centers were

Statuette of Pharaoh Amenemhet I, founder of the 12th dynasty (c. 1963 B.C.).

established in the E delta, especially near modern Qantir (see RAMESES; HYKSOS). One may note, as a background parallel to the men appointed to escort Abraham out of Egypt (Gen. 12:20), those appointed to conduct the Egyptian fugitive Sinuhe back into Egypt (*ANET*, 21b). The well-known tomb scene at Beni Hasan of the magnate Khnumhotep welcoming "37 Asiatics" into Egypt under Sesostris II is the classic pictorial background for the Egyptian journeys by Abraham and Jacob (Gen. 12; 46–47). (See further G. Posener, *Littérature et politique dans l'Égypte de la XII*ᵉ Dynastie [1956]; D. Franke in *CANE*, 2:735–48.)

3. Second Intermediate Period (13th–17th dynasties, 1786–1550 B.C.). The great 12th dynasty had ended with a queen. The 13th dynasty (c. 1786–1633) saw a rapid succession of kings. At first, Egypt remained outwardly powerful, but real power now resided with the viziers, not the throne;

"Asiatics" (mainly W Semites) increasingly came into Egypt, partly as slaves and in many occupations. Some Semites probably gained a foothold as local rulers in the E delta, and eventually one of them overthrew the reigning pharaoh, banishing the 13th dynasty to Thebes and the S. Thus was established the 15th (Hyksos) dynasty, a line of six kings that lasted 108 years, from c. 1648 to c. 1540. Historical data for this whole epoch are very meager. The settlement of Joseph and his family in Egypt may perhaps be placed around 1700, that is, late 13th dynasty passing over into the Hyksos period. A Brooklyn papyrus of c. 1740 sheds light on the prison system of the day; and of about seventy servants of an official listed elsewhere on this document, over forty bear names of good Semitic origin like Joseph himself (a Menahem, a Shipra, et al.). Joseph (Gen. 39:2–4) began as a domestic, Egyptian *ḥery-per*, "in the house," and like some of these he rose to become steward or "overseer of the house" (*imy-ra per*).

The interpretation of DREAMS was the subject of special textbooks; in the British Museum, Papyrus Chester Beatty III is a New Kingdom copy of a work probably much earlier than Joseph's day. Horses were known in Egypt from about the 18th cent. (skeleton from the Middle Kingdom fort, Buhen), and as horses were used for chariotry *before* being ridden as cavalry, this is probably indirect evidence for some knowledge of the chariot in Egypt just before Joseph's time. The keeping of cattle (see GOSHEN) was a matter of interest to the pharaohs in the delta (Gen. 47:6), including in texts of barely a century or so later (*ANET*, 232b and n. 5). Utterly dependent on the Nile flood, Egypt always feared famine while blessed oftener with rich harvests. (See further J. Van Seters, *The Hyksos: A New Interpretation* [1966]; J. Vergote, *Joseph en Égypte* [1959]; P. Montet, *L'Égypte et la Bible* [1959]; S. Quirke, *The Administration of Egypt in the Late Middle Kingdom* [1990].)

E. New Kingdom (18th–20th dynasties)

1. The 18th dynasty (c. 1550–1295 B.C.). Ahmose I (c. 1550–1525) completed the work of his elder brother King Kamose in ejecting the Hyksos rulers from Egypt, and in the process invaded Palestine. The first major step toward an empire was taken by his second successor, THUTMOSE I (c. 1504–1492), who reached the river EUPHRATES in N SYRIA, and as far as the fifth cataract of the Nile in Upper Nubia. After the premature death of her husband Thutmose II (c. 1492–1479), Queen Hatshepsut (1479–1437) ruled Egypt during the minority of her stepson Thutmose III (1479–1425). Her reign was remarkable mainly for works of peace: a great

Egypt at the time of the exodus (New Kingdom Egypt).

trading expedition down the Red Sea to Punt (SE Sudan), her superb W Theban funerary temple at Deir el-Bahri, a shrine at Karnak, etc., but she did not hesitate to repress rebels in Nubia. After her death, the now mature Thutmose III conducted no less than sixteen campaigns in W Asia, turning Syria-Palestine into an Egyptian province.

The wealth, religious influences, and captured peoples from Canaan entered Egypt, while Egyptian artistic canons penetrated Syria-Palestine, during the ensuing period. Thutmose III was also a great builder of temples and an energetic administrator. His immediate successors maintained Egypt's power, and made marriage alliance with the strong N Mesopotamian state of MITANNI. Thus Amenophis (Amenhotep) III (c. 1390–1352) had a reign of peace and hitherto unparalleled magnificence, still reflected by his buildings (e.g., the temples of Luxor and Soleb, and the "Colossi of Memnon," sole relic of his funerary temple in W Thebes). Babylon and Mitanni courted Egypt for gold.

Tensions between the monarchy and the priesthood of Amun (see AMON #4), god of Thebes, broke out openly under his son Amenophis IV, who, under the name AKHENATEN, proclaimed the sole worship of the sun god manifest in the solar disc as Aten, abolishing the other gods (esp. Amun) and disbanding their priesthoods. Akhenaten built himself a new capital (Akhet-Aten, "Horizon of the Aten"), now El Amarna, in Middle Egypt; part of his diplomatic correspondence with Babylon, Mitanni, and the Syrian city-states was found there in 1887, becoming known as the TELL EL-AMARNA tablets or letters. Along with HITTITE annals and the archives from UGARIT in PHOENICIA, these tablets shed a brilliant light on conditions in Canaan in the 14th cent., on the eve of the Hebrew exodus and conquest. During Akhenaten's preoccupation with the Aten, a war between the Hittite and Mitannian empires lost Egypt her N Syrian possessions, while Palestine lapsed into some disorder.

With the deaths of Akhenaten and his brother Smenkhkara, the throne came to the young prince later known as Tutankhamen, famous principally for the splendors of his burial-equipment, discovered almost intact in the Valley of the Kings in W Thebes. As he died prematurely without heir, his queen appealed to the Hittite King Suppiluliuma I for a son of his to become pharaoh as her husband. But the over-wily Hittite delayed, so that his younger son then was murdered on his way into Egypt when the plan became known. Instead, the aged retainer Ay reigned briefly, until the general Haremhab took in hand the renewal of Egypt's now neglected internal administration.

Egypt reached the zenith of her political power and wealth in this epoch. Under the king, two viziers served for Upper and Lower Egypt and a viceroy ruled Nubia as a separate province. In Syria-Palestine, the city states continued to be ruled by their own local dynasties, but on oath of allegiance to the pharaoh who regulated the succession in these states. A large and usually reasonably effective administrative organization supported these and other departments of state. A standing army was the nucleus of Pharaoh's forces. The increasingly splendid temples of the gods enjoyed rich endowments in land and settlements in Egypt and abroad, and a goodly share of the spoils of conquest. In these temples, the priesthoods performed complex rituals, often of great length, both daily and for the great periodical festivals (See further G. Steindorff and K. C. Seele, *When Egypt Ruled the East*, 2nd ed. [1957]; D. B. Redford, *History and Chronology of the Eighteenth Dynasty of Egypt* [1967]; K. A. Kitchen in *Chronique d'Égypte* 43/86 [1968]: 313–24. Note also several specialized works by W. Helck, such as *Zur Verwaltung des Mittleren und Neuen Reiches* [1958], *Materialen zur Wirtschaftsgeschichte des Neuen Reiches*, 6 vols. [1961–65], and *Die Beziehungen Ägyptens zu Vorderasien im 3 und 2. Jahrtausend v. Chr.*, 2nd ed. [1971].)

2. The 19th dynasty (c. 1295–1186 B.C.). From Haremhab, the throne passed to a military colleague, Paramesse, who reigned a brief sixteen months as RAMSES (Ramesses) I (c. 1295–1294) but was succeeded by his able son Sethos (Seti) I (c. 1294–1279). Sethos I immediately set about the reconquest of Syria-Palestine, and thus collided head-on with the Hittites, not unsuccessfully. At home, he undertook the vast hypostyle Hall of Columns in the Karnak temple of the god Amun at Thebes, and built a temple in Abydos now famed for its exquisite colored reliefs. He also began building works in the delta and was probably a pharaoh of the Hebrew oppression. His son Ramses II (1279–1213) doggedly fought on against the Hittites, the pyrrhic Battle of Qadesh being his most famous encounter (see KADESH ON THE ORONTES). Eventually, both powers made peace in Ramses II's twenty-first regnal year by a treaty later sealed by dynastic marriages. Within Egypt, Ramses II erected and adorned more temples than any other pharaoh. His were the great rock temples of Abu Simbel in Nubia (two of half-a-dozen shrines), the Ramesseum (funerary temple) in W Thebes, much at Karnak, a great court at Luxor temple, and the residence city of Raamses in the E delta. It was perhaps in his reign that the exodus occurred. (See further K. A. Kitchen, *Pharaoh Triumphant: The Life and Times of Ramesses II, King of Egypt* [1982]; summary in *CANE*, 2:763–74.) His successor MERNEPTAH (1213–1203) beat off a massive Libyan invasion of Egypt, after a brief campaign in W Palestine on which his forces encountered some Israelites (cf. the "Israel Stela," *ANET*, 376–78). Merneptah's successors were short-lived and insignificant.

The 19th dynasty was perhaps the most cosmopolitan age in Egyptian history, and was a fitting backdrop for the oppression, MOSES, and the exodus (see EXODUS, THE). Official intercourse between major and minor states of the ancient world was at its height, following on from the 18th dynasty. At every level of Egyptian society, foreigners—especially from Syria-Palestine—filled a multitude of roles in the main centers, whether in the E delta, in Memphis, or in Thebes. Ever since the expulsion of the Hyksos, a steady stream of prisoners of war had flowed into Egypt, used to help cultivate the fields and man the workshops of the state institutions and of the great temples; such slaves could also be found in small numbers in Egyptian households.

In the early 18th dynasty, the veteran warrior Ahmose son of Abana lists nineteen such slaves in his tomb at El Kab (Upper Egypt), one woman bearing the good Akkadian name Ishtar-ummi (K. Sethe, *Urkunden der 18. Dynastie*, 2nd ed., 5 vols. [1927–30], 1:11). At the other end of the scale, Amenophis II (c. 1427–1400) lists vast numbers of captives from Syria from his (and his father's?) campaigns there: e.g., 3,600 ʿApiru, 15,200 Shasu (semi-nomads), 36,300 people of Hurri (Horites, Syria-Palestine), 15,070 people of Nukhasse (in N Syria), and so on (cf. *ANET*, 247). These people often were installed in special settlements, for example at Thebes, "a settlement of Thutmose IV with Syrians (who were) spoils of his Majesty from Gezer," attached to the king's funerary temple in W Thebes (*ANET*, 248a). Such people were used on building projects, like the biblical Hebrews in the brickfields (Exod. 1:14).

The tomb chapel of the vizier Rekhmire under Thutmose III contains the famous painting of Egyptians, Semites, and others making bricks. In addition, an ostracon of that same official deals with building works, referring to the hauling of stone, causing to mold bricks, and to various personnel including thirty Hurru (Syrians) among others (Sethe, *Urkunden der 18. Dynastie*, 1174–75). Under Ramses II, the chief of militia and of royal works, named Amenemone, had charge of "the soldiers and the ʿApiru who drag stone for the great pylon" of a building of Ramses II at Memphis (Papyrus Leiden 348; translated by R. A. Caminos, *Late-Egyptian Miscellanies* [1954], 491, 494; cf. G. A. Gaballa and K. A. Kitchen in *Chronique d'Égypte* 43/85 [1968]: 263–69). In the Anastasi Papyri of this general period, one official noted his work people "making their quota of bricks daily" (Caminos, 106), while another had to complain, "there are neither men to make bricks nor straw in the neighborhood" (ibid., 188), scenes reminiscent of Exod. 5.

Furthermore, a close surveillance was kept of the days worked, as is exemplified by jottings on ostraca from W Thebes concerning work on the royal tombs there. Such journals of work took special note of days worked and days "idle," in some examples even for individuals by name and giving the reasons for their absences from the job—"ill," "eye trouble," "brewing (beer)," or plain "idle." And religious holidays for festivals (cf. Exod. 5:1, 3, 8) occur as "offering to the god" (so, Ostracon British Museum 5634, of the fortieth year of Ramses II). Such references occur in many other similar documents (K. A. Kitchen, *Ancient Orient and Old Testament* [1966], 157 nn. 17–19). When such a close check was kept on Egyptian workmen, one cannot expect foreign slaves to escape from equally close oversight.

However, the brickfields and building sites did not account for all Semites in Egypt, whether

Hebrews or not. The abilities of BEZALEL and OHOLIAB (Exod. 31:1–11) and the early career of Moses indicate otherwise. Such foreigners could be employed in all manner of callings (e.g., shepherds, weavers, brewers, wine merchants, porters, soldiers, and ships' captains), including also craftsmen. One finds shipbuilders, stonemasons, coppersmiths, and goldsmiths (see W. Helck, *Die Beziehungen Ägyptens zu Vorderasien im 3. und 2. Jahrtausend v. Chr.* [1962], 372–73, § V, for references). Some Hebrews may have reached such employments. Higher up the scale, besides foreigners serving as priests (ibid., 373–74, § VI), one finds scribes high and low, high stewards of the Kings Sethos I and Ramses II (Horites, in two cases), and cupbearers who were the trusted confidants of several pharaohs (e.g., Ben-Ozen [from Rock-of-Bashan!] under Merneptah, one Baal-mahir under Ramses III, and a Pen-Hasuri ["he of Hazor," ibid., 369]). One also notes foreign couriers coming and going over the E Delta frontier between Egypt and S Palestine (*ANET*, 258b). Si-Montu, a son of Ramses II, married the daughter of a Syrian sea captain called Ben-Anath (W. Spiegelberg in *Recueil de travaux* 16 [1894]: 64), while a daughter of Ramses II bore the corresponding name Bint-Anath, "daughter of [the goddess] Anath."

In Ramesside Egypt, the learned scribes prided themselves on their knowledge of Canaanite, as in the *Satirical Letter* of this period (*ANET*, 477b); at a humbler level, a father reproached his son for making blood brotherhood with "Asiatics" while in the delta (see J. Černý in *JNES* 14 [1955]: 161ff.). This extraordinarily rich background for the mingling of Semites and Hurrians (Horites), etc., with Egyptians in Egypt, and at all levels from court to slaves, is a fitting backcloth for the early career of a Moses—taken up by a minor princess in a delta harem of the reigning pharaoh, and brought up in an Egyptian and Semitic milieu. Like him, other Asiatics were brought up in "district harems," for example, in the Fayum (see S. Sauneron and J. Yoyotte in *Revue d'Égyptologie* 7 [1950]: 67–70).

This upbringing carries the implication that a person in Moses' position would undergo an Egyptian royal education, no mean equipment in its day. (Cf. H. Brunner, *Altägyptische Erziehung* [1957], for details of Egyptian education.) As a scribe, a Moses would be able easily to learn the 26 or 30 letters of the W Semitic alphabet. Apart from the Sinai texts of c. 1500 B.C., other brief epigraphs in alphabetic script are known, for example, one mentioning ꜣmht, "maidservants," on an ostracon from the Valley of the Kings at Thebes, far distant from Palestine or the delta; and, significantly, all these are homely, everyday inscriptions, not recondite. In this context, the picture of a literate Moses is no fantasy—and the Hebrews would have known the ways of Canaan in Egypt itself, long before they ever set out for the Promised Land. (See further D. B. Redford, *Egypt, Canaan, and Israel in Ancient Times* [1992].)

3. The 20th dynasty (c. 1186–1069 B.C.). Siptah, last king of the 19th dynasty, was a short-lived puppet ruler, enthroned by the Syrian "king-maker," the chancellor Bay. After the deaths of Siptah and the dowager Queen Tewosret, one Setnakht briefly took the throne, founding the 20th dynasty and restoring internal order in Egypt again. His

The Ramesseum, located near ancient Thebes (Luxor), portrays the crowning achievements of Ramses III throughout.

son Ramses III was the last great pharaoh of the empire. While SEA PEOPLES in the E Mediterranean basin and other folk moving overland brought final destruction to the Hittite empire and to the old order of Amorite and Canaanite states in Syria, Ramses III was able in three campaigns to beat off both the Libyans and their allies in the W (years 5, 11) and the Sea Peoples on his NE (year 8) in a dramatic land and sea conflict in S Palestine and at the mouths of the Nile, so saving Egypt from invasion. His inscriptions (e.g., in his great funerary temple of Medinet Habu in W Thebes) contain the first known mention of the Philistines outside the pages of the OT.

The peace and prosperity so hard won by Ramses III were transitory, ebbing away with the decay of administration, increase of graft and venality among officials, and spiraling inflation, causing great hardship to the ordinary people. His life ended with a harem conspiracy, and none of his successors—Ramses IV to XI—was able to stop the rot. In this period there first came into the open under Ramses IX a series of notorious tomb robberies in W Thebes, from which not even the sacrosanct bodies of the pharaohs were exempted. Under these later Ramses, Thebes (and in some measure, Upper Egypt) was increasingly dominated by virtually a dynasty of high priests of Amun, until Amenhotep was displaced by the military commander Herihor in a coup d'état. Ramses XI then endeavored to stabilize the internal situation through the introduction of a "Renaissance" era whereby he as pharaoh had as his direct subordinates Herihor ruling Upper Egypt and Nubia, and one Smendes ruling Lower Egypt. Herihor also became high priest of Amun in Thebes, a dignity that remained hereditary in his family for another 130 years or more. With the death of Ramses XI, the empire formally came to an end, and the accession (c. 1069) of his northern deputy Smendes marks for us the beginning of the Late Period.

No age is better known by documents and by visual remains than is the New Kingdom; special mention should be made of the great war reliefs and topographical lists in the Theban temples, so valuable for Syro-Palestinian geography, and of the amazing wealth of scenes of official and daily life still brilliantly preserved in many of the more than 400 tomb chapels of nobles and officials at Thebes. Both literary and nonliterary papyri and ostraca throw a flood of light on literature, religion, and society in the Egypt of the general period of the exodus.

F. The Third Intermediate and Late Periods

1. The 21st dynasty (c. 1069–945 B.C.). In an age of decline, the only outstanding kings were Psusennes I and Siamun. This dynasty reigned in the delta with Tanis (ZOAN) as its capital, while Thebes in the S was in the hands of Herihor's descendants as military governors and high priests of Amun. They ruled almost a state within a state, acknowledging the overlordship of Tanis as long as the latter allowed their regional hegemony. Egypt's internal division and impotence ruled out any expansionist policy abroad, and helps to explain her modest international role in the age of the later judges and of Saul, David, and Solomon.

The first link between Egypt and the OT at this epoch is afforded by 1 Ki. 11:18–22. After DAVID's commander JOAB had devastated EDOM, the young prince Hadad was spirited away to Egypt by his retainers. See HADAD (PERSON). He there grew up, married a pharaoh's sister-in-law, and had a son who was "brought up in the royal palace." At the death of David (c. 970), Hadad returned to Edom; hence, one may place his period of residence in Egypt within roughly 990–970, which in the 21st dynasty would run from late in the reign of Amenemopet through the brief six years of Osochor, well into the reign of Siamun. His Egyptian wife was perhaps, then, a sister-in-law of either Osochor or Siamun. The TAHPENES of 1 Ki. 11:19–20 seems simply to be the Hebrew transcript of the Egyptian phrase for "queen," *ta-ḥem(t)-pa-nesu* (giving Hebrew consonants *thpns*), and not to be a proper name (cf. B. Grdseloff in *Revue de l'histoire juive en Égypte* 1 [1947]: 88–90; differently, W. F. Albright in *BASOR* 140 [Dec. 1955]: 32).

The provision assigned to young Hadad and his retainers—a house, food allowance, and land (1 Ki. 11:18)—agrees with known Egyptian custom. A thousand years earlier, the courtier Sinuhe on his return from Syria-Palestine was assigned the house of a former courtier plus some ground, and meals were brought to him from the palace "three and four times a day" (cf. *ANET*, 22). In the New Kingdom, it was normal for members of the royal family (as Hadad became, by marriage) to have a personal estate (*per*), including princes (references in W. Helck, *Materialen zur Wirtschaftsgeschichte des Neuen Reiches*, 6 vols. [1961–69], 2:201–14), and foreigners who entered Egypt by marriage, like the Mitannian queen of Amenophis III (ibid., 212). Some inscriptions of the 21st and 22nd dynasties show that the pharaohs and high priests sometimes built up such estates by purchase (A. H. Gardiner in *JEA* 48 [1962]: 57–69; G. Legrain and A. Erman in *Zeitschrift für ägyptische Sprache* 35 [1897]: 12–16, 19–24).

Again the notice that Hadad's son GENUBATH "lived with Pharaoh's own children" (1 Ki. 11:20) reflects long-standing Egyptian usage, whereby the sons of officials were educated along with the royal princes at court. In the Old Kingdom, one may refer to the example of Ptah-shepses who married a king's daughter (cf. J. H. Breasted, *Ancient Records of Egypt* 1 [1906], §§ 256–57). In the Middle Kingdom, in his *Instruction*, Khety, son of Duauf, imparts his wisdom to his son while en route to the palace school (*ANET*, 432b and n. 1), and the official Ikhernofret was reminded of his royal training (*ANET*, 329b). In the New Kingdom, references to this youthful status early in the lives of officials (as ḫrd-n-kʾp, "pages") are very common. At that period, the sons of Syrian kinglets subject to Egypt were taken as hostages to Egypt and kept at court much as were Hadad or Genubath (cf. W. Helck, *Beziehungen Ägyptens zum Vorderasiens im 3. und 2. Jahrtausend v. Chr.* [1962], 366 nn. 73–76).

SOLOMON, in the early years of his reign (cf. A. Malamat in *JNES* 22 [1963]: 9–17), married the daughter of a pharaoh who gave GEZER as a dowry (1 Ki. 3:1; 9:16; et al.). The pharaoh concerned was probably Siamun of the 21st dynasty, from whose reign a broken relief found at Tanis shows him smiting an Asiatic who holds an Aegean-looking weapon. It has therefore been suggested that Siamun had conducted a "police action" in neighboring Philistia, and perhaps also had taken Gezer then, so thereafter giving it as dowry when making the marriage alliance with his powerful Hebrew neighbor.

2. The 22nd–24th dynasties (c. 945–715 B.C.). At the death of Siamun's successor Psusennes II in c. 945, the obvious candidate for the vacant throne was Shoshenq, Great Chief of the Mashwash (Libyans), whose eldest son had married the daughter of Psusennes II, and who himself seems to have had a royal mother. As founder of the 22nd dynasty, Shoshenq I obtained a firm grip on the government of all Egypt, bringing Thebes under his effective control by appointing there as high priest his second son. At the head of a reunited Egypt, Shoshenq (SHISHAK) in due course planned to deal effectively with his powerful neighbor in Palestine. He harbored such political refugees as JEROBOAM son of Nebat (1 Ki. 11:40); and when Solomon died, Shoshenq allowed Jeroboam to return to Palestine to precipitate the schism of the Hebrew kingdom (1 Ki. 12:2).

The divided realm of Rehoboam and Jeroboam was no match for Shoshenq when he invaded Palestine in Rehoboam's fifth year (c. 925); a broken stela from the Karnak temple suggests that a border incident gave Shoshenq his cue to launch an attack (cf. B. Grdseloff, *Revue de l'histoire juive en Égypte* 1 [1947]: 95–97). The reality of Shoshenq's campaign is graphically illustrated by his great triumphal relief on the S wall of the Karnak temple of Amun at Thebes, naming many towns in Palestine (Epigraphic Survey, *Reliefs and Inscriptions at Karnak* 3 [1954], plates 3ff.), and by a fragment of a stela of his that was actually found at MEGIDDO (cf. C. S. Fisher, *The Excavation of Armageddon* [1929], figure on p. 13). However, though his booty was rich (1 Ki. 14:26), Shoshenq's triumph was short lived; he probably died even before his great Karnak sculpture was completed.

Later Egyptian adventures in Palestine in this period were less successful. "Zerah the Cushite" (2 Chr. 14:9) was probably an Egyptian army commander of Nubian origin who under either Osorkon I or Takeloth I endeavored to emulate Shoshenq's success, but in vain (see ZERAH #6). Later pharaohs of the 22nd dynasty had neither the ability nor the political power of Shoshenq. By the time of Osorkon II (c. 860 B.C.), the inner unity of the state was already prejudiced by the ambitions of the high priests in Thebes—again hereditary, but among rival branches of the reigning dynasty.

Osorkon II seems to have returned to the more modest foreign policy of the 21st dynasty in similar circumstances of inner political weakness, and so to have made an alliance with Israel. A presentation vase of this pharaoh was found long since in the Omride palace at Samaria (G. A. Reisner, C. S. Fisher, and D. G. Lyon, *Harvard Excavations at Samaria 1908–10* [1924], figure on 1:247).

Such an alliance would best explain how it was that, rather later on in history, Israel's last king (HOSHEA) sent to "So, king of Egypt" for help against Assyria in about 725 B.C. By this date, the Egyptian monarchy had already split into two, with twin lines of pharaohs at Tanis and Bubastis (22nd dynasty) and at Leontopolis (23rd dynasty), and further subkings were beginning to emerge in Middle Egypt at Heracleopolis and Hermopolis. These further changes had been heralded and accompanied by bitter civil wars in Upper Egypt, sparked by rival claims on the high priesthood of Amun at Thebes (cf. R. A. Caminos, *Chronicle of Prince Osorkon* [1958], passim). No pharaoh of Egypt in 725 could possibly aid the luckless Hoshea against Assyria, and his appeal to So (2 Ki. 17:4) seems to have gone unanswered. So may be an abbreviation for Osorkon, in this case the powerless Osorkon IV last king of the 22nd dynasty (cf. K. A. Kitchen, *The Third Intermediate Period in Egypt* [1973], 182, 372–76). It is unconvincing to interpret this name as "Sais," W delta capital of the prince Tefnakht (so H. Goedicke in *BASOR* 171 [Oct. 1963]: 64–66). A few years later, the impotence of Osorkon IV was well illustrated by his having to buy off SARGON II of Assyria from the Egyptian border by the gift of twelve large horses in the year 716 (cf. S. Tadmor, *Journal of Cuneiform Studies* 12 [1958]: 77–78).

During the period c. 730–715 B.C., two new powers arose on the Nile to contend for the mastery of Egypt. In the N, Tefnakht, prince of Sais, built up a kingdom in the NW delta, and briefly claimed kingship (c. 727–720), and his son Bekenranef was sole king of the 24th dynasty for five or six years (720–715). From Nubia, the prince Piankhi had raided Egypt c. 728, and his successor there, Shabako, invaded Egypt in 715 and eliminated the hapless Bekenranef, thereby uniting Egypt and Cush under the 25th dynasty.

3. The 25th dynasty (c. 780–656 B.C.). Shabako was neutral toward Assyria, extraditing rebels when this was requested of him by the Assyrian king, in 712; clay sealings of Shabako from Nineveh suggest further contacts. His successor Shebitku changed to a more ambitious and so more aggressive policy. It was probably he who sent his younger brother TIRHAKAH (then aged about twenty or so) in 701 to oppose the Assyrian forces led by SENNACHERIB against HEZEKIAH of Judah. The title "king of Cush" accorded to Tirhakah at this juncture in the biblical narratives (2 Ki. 19:9; Isa. 37:9) is his eventual title (with the kingship of Egypt) from the year 690, but it is used by the biblical writers after that date for identification purposes. See CUSH. This is a prolepsis of exactly the same nature as is used in Tirhakah's own inscriptions (e.g., Kawa Stela IV, lines 7–8). That Tirhakah was only about nine years old in 701 (as some have suggested) is ruled out by the fact that his father Pinkhi had died within 717–713 (extreme dates), and probably in 716 (see Kitchen, *Ancient Orient and Old Testament* [1966], 82–84 and note 29, and with fuller background, *Third Intermediate Period*, passim).

Tirhakah's intervention failed, but Hezekiah survived. Egypt and Cush were no match for Assyria, and as king, Tirhakah experienced two disastrous Assyrian invasions of Egypt in 671 and 666/665. Finally, his successor Tanwetamani (or Tanutamon) involved Egypt in a further Assyrian invasion that resulted in the sack of Thebes in 664/663—an event that echoed round the ancient world, and decades later furnished the prophet NAHUM with an appropriate analogy when he proclaimed the fall of Assyria in her turn (Nah. 3:8–19). The pharaohs from Cush had indeed proved to be a broken reed (2 Ki. 18:21; Isa. 36:6).

4. The 26th dynasty, Saite Revival (664–525 B.C.). Like Tefnakht half a century before, a prince of Sais in the delta—Psammetichus I—arose to gain control of Egypt, and this time without a Nubian rival. Within eight years of 664, the sage Psammetichus succeeded in gaining full control of the delta, winning over the shipmasters of Heracleopolis who ruled Middle Egypt, and finally obtaining recognition in Thebes and the S, installing his daughter as "God's Wife of Amun" (cf. Caminos in *JEA* 50

[1964]: 71–101). Like Shoshenq I, Psammetichus succeeded in reuniting Egypt internally, but with far more lasting success, resulting in a period of great prosperity. Under the new dynasty, Egypt looked increasingly for inspiration to her august past, especially to the Pyramid Age of 2,000 years before, and archaic modes were in fashion. Psammetichus established a force of Greek mercenaries as the core of his army and encouraged Greek traders. Abroad, Psammetichus I and Neco II supported the waning Assyria against the emerging power of Babylon, as if to keep a balance of powers in W Asia. When Neco II marched N to support Assyria against Babylon in 609, Josiah of Judah delayed him sufficiently to seal Assyria's fate, but at the cost of his own life (2 Ki. 23:29).

Egypt's attempt to replace Assyria as overlord of Palestine was defeated at the Battle of Carchemish in 605, when the Babylonians ousted the Egyptians and took over the region (Jer. 46:2). In 601, in a further clash, Egypt so severely mauled the Babylonian army that it had to retire for eighteen months for a refit, and thereafter Neco II remained neutral. In Judah, however, Jehoiakim then rebelled against Babylon, perhaps hoping for Egyptian aid (not forthcoming), but in 597 Nebuchadnezzar II took Jerusalem, and deported the new king, Jehoiachin, to Babylon. In Egypt, Psammetichus II maintained the policy of neutrality in regard to Palestine, but his less cautious successor Hophra encouraged Zedekiah in his fatal new rebellion against Babylon in 589/8, yet without affording the Judeans any real help. Later, as prophesied by Jeremiah (Jer. 46:13–26), and attested by a Babylonian text, Nebuchadnezzar II duly marched against Egypt, but perhaps came to some agreement with the new King Amasis (Ahmose II), who had displaced Hophra. Henceforth, both powers were more concerned to ward off the rising threat posed by Media. However, in 525 Cambyses of Persia took Egypt just as earlier Cyrus had taken over Media and swallowed Babylon.

5. Later Egypt. Under Cambyses and Darius I, Persian rule was fair if firm, and these two kings were given pharaonic titles (27th dynasty). Hankering for their lost independence, the Egyptians revolted just before the death of Darius. They brought upon themselves the wrath of Xerxes I. Henceforth, Egypt was treated as a rebellious province, under a much less liberal regime. In turn, the Egyptians rebelled time and again, until at last during the years 400–341 B.C. they achieved a precarious independence under the kings of the 28th to 30th dynasties. Often in alliance with Greeks (either Athens or Sparta, depending on the varying shifts in Greek politics), Egypt held off her vast foe until finally overwhelmed by the might of Artaxerxes III in 341, to be ruled again by the Persians for nine years until Alexander the Great, who on his arrival in 332 was hailed as a liberator.

Jewish communities in Late Period Egypt dated from the early 26th dynasty, when Jeremiah was carried off by his countrymen to Tahpanhes (Daphnai) in the NE delta (Jer. 42–43). Under the Persian regime there was a Jewish mercenary force acting as garrison on Elephantine Island opposite Aswan (first cataract). They had their own local temple, and the papyri from their settlement form the major part of the Aramaic documents for the period (c. 480–400). Egyptian independence from c. 400 may have brought this group to an end.

After the death of Alexander the Great in 323, one of his generals, Ptolemy son of Lagus, assumed the rule of Egypt. He became king as Ptolemy I in 305, founding a long dynasty. The Ptolemies ruled as a Hellenistic Greek monarchy, based on Alexandria, and ruled Egypt simply as an estate for their own wider ends. Initially, their efficient organization brought renewed prosperity, but the later decay of their administration fostered unrest among the Egyptians. With the defeat of Antony and Cleopatra, Egypt passed under Roman rule in 30 B.C., and thereafter remained part of the Roman and Byzantine empires for seven centuries until the Islamic conquest in A.D. 641/642. From the 3rd and 4th centuries A.D., Egypt was predominantly a "Christian" land, its indigenous church—still extant—being known as the Coptic church. Monasticism found its first roots in Christian Egypt (St. Antony); the most notable native leader was Shenoute. (For further information on the Late Period, see G. Posener, *La première domination perse en Égypte* [1936]; F. K. Kienitz, *Die politische Geschichte Ägyptens vom 7. bis zum 4. Jahrhundert vor der Zeitwende* [1953]; M. F. Gyles, *Pharaonic Policies and Administration, 663 to 323 B.C.* [1959]; N. Lewis, *Life in Egypt under Roman Rule* [1983]; K. A. Kitchen, *The Third Intermediate Period in Egypt*, 2nd ed. [1986]; A. K. Bowman, *Egypt after the Pharaohs: 332 BC–AD 642, from Alexander to the Arab Conquest* [1986]; R. S. Bagnall, *Egypt in Late Antiquity* [1993]; R. S. Bagnall and D. W. Rathbone, eds., *Egypt from Alexander to the Early Christians: An Archaeological and Historical Guide* [2005]; J. Bingen, *Hellenistic Egypt: Monarchy, Society, Economy, Culture* [2007].)

VI. Egyptian literature. Ancient Egypt produced one of the world's first great treasuries of literature. What is extant has been preserved and recovered only in part, and much remains to be fully understood, but it is of merit and value both in itself and as background for biblical study.

Egyptian relief and ancient writings in the tomb (mastaba) of Ptah-Hotep, a priest during the 5th dynasty (c. 2400 B.C.).

A. Historical outline

1. Third millennium B.C. a. *Old Kingdom* (2700–2200 B.C.). The oldest literature is religious, namely the Pyramid Texts. (The material was first published by K. Sethe, *Die altägyptischen Pyramidentexte*, 4 vols. [1908–22], and *Übersetzung und Kommentar zu den altägyptischen Pyramidentexte*, 4 vols. [n.d.]; an English version is given by R. A. Faulkner, *The Ancient Egyptian Pyramid Texts*, 2 vols. [1969]. See now J. P. Allen, *Ancient Egyptian Pyramid Texts* [2005].) These are a vast corpus of material inscribed in the funerary chambers of the kings of the 6th dynasty, following the example of Unis at the end of the 5th dynasty. These rituals and spells were for the benefit of the dead pharaoh (see the section on religion below). Despite their early date (extant copies of c. 2350–2180 resting on older originals), these texts already exhibit a wide range of literary forms, appropriate to poetry, for example. These forms are then attested in Egyptian literature for 2,000 years thereafter, as well as independently in other ANE literature and in the OT.

The use of parallelism of thoughts in consecutive lines and also of converse concepts (so-called "synthetic" and "antithetic" parallelism) occurs in its simplest forms, with many detailed variations, and runs to four-line groupings and even six and eight-line constructions with variations. See HEBREW POETRY II. These stylistic modes of the 3rd millennium are as artistically "advanced" as anything to be found in Proverbs or the Psalter and have nothing Hellenistic or even postexilic about them. The literary device of CHIASM, where elements are varied in the order A-B, B-A, is to be found, sometimes with subtle internal variations, again providing an immense time-perspective as background to the flowering of OT literature (on the style of these texts, see O. Firchow, *Grundzüge der Stilistik in den altägyptischen Pyramidentexten* [1953]). An almost equally famous religious effusion that originated in this period is the so-called *Memphite Theology*, known from a copy of the 8th cent. B.C. This is remarkable mainly for its "advanced" concepts (early *logos* formulation) at so distant an epoch (*ANET*, 4–6).

Wisdom literature in Egypt traditionally began with Imhotep in the time of Djoser and the Step

Pyramid (c. 2680), but his *Instruction* has yet to be recovered. Fragments are known for those of Kairos (uncertain) to Kagemni, and of Hardjedef, a son of Cheops (builder of the Great Pyramid). Happily, the *Instruction of the Vizier Ptah-hotep* (c. 2400; *ANET*, 412–14) is preserved complete in two Middle Kingdom versions. Other literary traces occur in the autobiographies of officials in their tombs. That of Uni cites a victory hymn over his Palestinian foes; it shows a very simple poetic structure exactly like that of Ps. 136 (but with the refrain coming first in each couplet; see *ANET*, 228). Sometimes the Old Kingdom tombs of the nobles preserve snatches of songs of the common folk (*ANET*, 469b).

b. *First Intermediate Period* (2200–2030 B.C.). The noblest product from this troubled age was doubtless the *Dispute of a Man with His Soul*, especially its moving poems on death and disillusion. (For translations, cf. *ANET*, 405–7, and R. O. Faulkner in *JEA* 42 [1956]: 21–40, plus the very important comments by R. J. Williams in *JEA* 48 [1962]: 49–56, and E. Brunner-Traut in *Zeitschrift für ägyptische Sprache* 94 [1967]: 6–15.) The *Eloquent Peasant*, a plea for social justice put into the mouth of a peasant, shows the same A-B-A structure of prose prologue, a cycle of highly poetic speeches, and prose epilogue as does JOB (cf. *ANET*, 407–10). Since the badly preserved *Discourse of Sisobk* appears to have had this pattern also, the A-B-A structure is evidently a proper literary form of high antiquity, and attempts to divorce the authorship of the speeches from the prologue and epilogue in Job are revealed as entirely arbitrary from a purely literary viewpoint. The *Instruction for King Merikara* (cf. *ANET*, 414–18) is also notable.

2. Second millennium B.C. a. *Middle Kingdom and Second Intermediate Period* (2134–1551 B.C.). In this, the classical age of the Egyptian language, there emerges a fine group of short stories. Finest of all is the autobiography of *Sinuhe*, a courtier of Amenemhet I, who fled to Syria at his master's death (*ANET*, 18–22). The *Shipwrecked Sailor* is a nautical fairy tale. Middle-Egyptian stories about the Old Kingdom include the tale of King Neferkara and General Sisenet, and the *Tales of the Magicians* set at the court of Cheops. Field sports feature in the *Sporting King* and the *Pleasures of Fishing and Fowling*. Wisdom literature is represented by propagandistic works of great skill. Apart from the pseudonymous *Prophecy of Neferty* (*ANET*, 444–46), one may notice Khety's *Satire on the Trades* other than that of scribe (to encourage "civil service" recruitment, *ANET*, 432–34), and the *Instruction of Amenemhet I* to justify his regime against would-be assassins (*ANET*, 418–19). The *Instructions of Sehetepibra* and the *Instructions of a Man to His Son* inculcated loyalty to the throne as the path of wisdom. Religious literature included long hymns to the Nile, Osiris, and Min, as well as to King Sesostris III; less "literary" is the great corpus of Coffin Texts, spells for safety and benefit in the afterlife.

b. *The New Kingdom* (1551–1070 B.C.). Literature was greatly enriched under the empire. New stories included the *Foredoomed Prince*, from a world of fairy tales like that of more modern times; the *Tale of the Two Brothers* (a mythical fantasy); and an allegory, the *Blinding of Truth*. The *Capture of Joppa* foreshadowed *Ali Baba and the Forty Thieves*, while the *Adventures of Wanamun* in Syria (c. 1075) is probably a historical report, but has literary merit. Many other narrative fragments exist, including two "ghost-stories." Complete is a ribald treatment of Osirian mythology in the *Contendings of Horus and Seth*. Wisdom literature was enriched by the *Instructions* of various individuals, such as Aniy (*ANET*, 420–21), Amennakht (a priest), Amenemhet, and above all Amenemopet, which is so often correlated with Proverbs (see below). A series of other fragments also survive, especially a text written in praise of ancient writers (*ANET*, 431–32).

New in this age is a delightful series of collections of lyric love poems, somewhat reminiscent of the SONG OF SOLOMON in style and language. Besides mythological items, religious texts include the great hymns to Amun (Amon-Re; e.g., *ANET*, 365–69), and Akhenaten's beautiful hymn to the Aten (solar disc; *ANET*, 369–71). Of some merit are the stately triumph hymns of such pharaohs as Thutmose III, Amenophis III, and Merneptah (*ANET*, 373–78), and the touching hymns of penitence of humbler folk, a testimony to the meaning of religion to individuals in the late 2nd millennium (cf. some Psalms) on a personal level (cf. B. Gunn in *JEA* 3 [1916]: 81–94). However, the so-called *Book of the Dead* is merely a collection of spells for the afterlife; and various "illustrated" guidebooks through the Netherworld were inscribed in the tombs of the pharaohs (Books of Gates, of Caverns, of What is in the Netherworld, et al.).

3. First millennium B.C. Most of the preserved (and original) literature of this Late Period is in demotic, dating from the 6th cent. B.C. to the Roman age. Stories include the *Cycle of Pedubastis* and *Egyptians and Amazons*, romances based on the rivalries of local princes in the 8th/7th centuries, and the *Stories of the High Priests of Memphis*, famous magicians (esp. Khamwese, a son of Ramses II). Wisdom is well represented by the *Instruction of Onkhsheshonqy*, the *Papyrus Insinger* and variants, and works preserved in the Louvre and Brooklyn museums. Among hieroglyphic inscriptions, a 22nd-dynasty priest, Nebneteru, gives his ideals and counsels (H. Kees, *Zeitschrift für ägyptische Sprache*, 74 [1938]: 73–87, esp. 78ff.; corrections in 78 [1962]: 24–26), while the priest Petosiris (c. 300 B.C.) may in his "wisdom" even have been influenced by Hebrew (G. Lefebvre, *Le tombeau de Petosiris*, 3 vols. [1923–24]).

B. Egyptian literature and the OT

1. Direct links. Real examples of direct contact have yet to be substantiated. Akhenaten's solar monotheism was essentially little more than the recognition of the beneficent, life-sustaining force of the sun, and offers no basis for Mosaic or ethical monotheism (cf. the section on religion below). The incident in the *Tale of the Two Brothers*, where a youth is wrongly accused by a woman with designs on him is similar in plot to that of Joseph and Potiphar's wife, but it occurs in a wholly different milieu. Such banal sins are only too well attested in reality (in Egypt as elsewhere) to have any bearing on direct literary connection.

A more promising link between the OT and Egyptian literature seemed to be between the Egyptian *Instruction of Amenemopet* and parts of the book of Proverbs (cf. such studies as that of D. C. Simpson in *JEA* 12 [1926]: 232–39). Dependence has been argued both ways. An ostracon of Amenemopet of the 21st dynasty (c. 1070–945) would seem to exclude Egyptian dependence on the Hebrew, while a proper critical study of both works in the *total* context of ANE wisdom literature (instead of in isolation) shows that there is no adequate basis for making the Hebrew Proverbs dependent on Amenemopet. The closest points of comparison are far too often banal or merely such as have equally good parallels in other ANE wisdom writings, while some comparisons fail because they are inexact in form, content, or both.

2. An objective background for OT literature. In this role, alongside the literatures of Mesopotamia, the Hittites, Canaan, and others, that of Egypt is of the utmost value and offers a vast field of study. A few examples and references must suffice to illustrate this theme (cf. already above, the example of literary forms illustrated by the Pyramid Texts).

a. *Literary criticism*. The attempts to find a variety of different hands in the composition of the Pentateuch and Joshua-Judges must fall under the gravest suspicion in the light of Egyptian and allied literatures. With its criteria of double names of deity, humans, clans and places, synonyms in vocabulary, appeals to style, etc., and to supposedly "primitive" and "advanced" concepts, this mode of analysis was produced in the 18th cent. and fully developed in the 19th, when at first no objective control from directly comparable sources was available. After such material did become available (late 19th cent. onward), its help was neither sought nor properly utilized. Yet, the same kind of "phenomena" can be found in these literatures as in the OT and are therefore quite meaningless for analysis, which should carry a sharp danger warning in OT study. Similar criticisms apply also to the methods of study used in FORM CRITICISM (*Gattungsforschung*) and oral tradition (TRADITION HISTORY), with equally drastic implications. Only when OT criticism can proceed from the extant structure of OT literature, in comparison with real modes of composition and attested structure clearly exhibited by the rest of the biblical world, will a realistic, objectively based and constructive biblical criticism become possible. (See provisionally, K. A. Kitchen, *Ancient Orient and Old Testament* [1966], 112–46 and references.)

b. History and forms of literary categories. A good example of the application of the data of Egyptian and allied literatures to OT study can be drawn from the wisdom literature, especially in relation to the book of PROVERBS. As it stands, Prov. 1–24 (with a second collection in chs. 25–29) is labelled as Proverbs of Solomon; this section includes a full title with name and rank of the author in the third person, with prologue and discourses (chs. 1–9), a subtitle (10:1), and then the main body of maxims. It has been commonly suggested that chs. 1–9 are the latest part of the whole work, of the 4th to 3rd centuries B.C., partly because of supposedly "advanced" concepts (e.g., personification, as of wisdom), partly on the longer sentence structure, etc. According to this view relatively little even of chs. 10–24 need be attributed as far back as Solomon's time.

However, such assumptions, analyses, and datings are not supported by the comparative criteria offered by ANE, and especially Egyptian, wisdom literature. Thus, a title with author's name in third person plus rank occurs as normal practice in almost a score of Egyptian wisdom books, at all periods from Old Kingdom to Late Period; and such titles are to be taken seriously. The literary pattern of main title plus discourses, then subtitle and maxims, is precisely the pattern presented by Ptahhotep back in the late 3rd millennium, by Khety son of Duauf in the early 19th cent., and as late as Onkhsheshonqy in about the 4th cent. B.C. Variety in sentence length and structure, moreover, is palpably worthless for dating purposes as late as Solomon's time: when one observes the length and elaboration of both discourses and maxims in Ptahhotep in the 3rd millennium along with the one-line proverbs of Onkhsheshonqy 2,000 years *later*, "evolution" here stands on its head (or, rather, is simply inapplicable and irrelevant).

Personification belongs not to Hellenism but to the ANE from the 3rd millennium onward (cf. K. A. Kitchen in *Tyndale House Bulletin* 5/6 [1940]: 4–6). This and various other aspects may suffice to indicate that Prov. 1–24 (and chs. 25–29 originally separate) represents a well attested unitary literary form, with nothing later, and much earlier, than Solomon. (For further information on Egyptian literature, see H. Grapow, *Bildliche Ausdrücke des Aegyptischen* [1924]; G. Lefebvre, *Romans et contes égyptiens* [1949]; *Handbuch der Orientalistik* 1/2, ed. B. Spure [1952]; E. Brunner-Traut, *Altägyptische Märchen*, 2nd ed. [1965]; A. Erman, *The Ancient Egyptians: A Sourcebook of their Writings* [1966]; H. Brunner, *Grundzüge einer Geschichte der Altägyptischen Literatur* [1966]; R. B. Parkinson, *Voices from Ancient Egypt: An Anthology of Middle Kingdom Writings* [1991]; J. Assmann et al., "Egyptian Literature," in *ABD*, 2:378–99.)

VII. Egyptian religion

A. The gods of the Egyptians. Fundamentally, Egyptian religion was very local in its practice and horizons. The Egyptians in each district tended to worship principally their particular local deities rather than some greater figure of national or cosmic scope. As was commonly the case in ancient paganism, the gods of Egypt were in large measure the personifications of the powers of nature (e.g., fertility), and of natural phenomena (e.g., the Nile) and their supposed attributes (e.g., of falcon gods, bull gods, etc.). Some were cosmic (sun god), and some were the embodiments of certain concepts (e.g., Maat, goddess of "truth" and right order).

Insofar as various animals, plants, etc., were respected as symbols of natural powers and of mysterious forces, these in turn were considered as manifestations of the deities concerned, even as vehicles of their presence—a role that came to be shared by statues and other images, and by sacred animals (like the Apis bull of Ptah at Memphis,

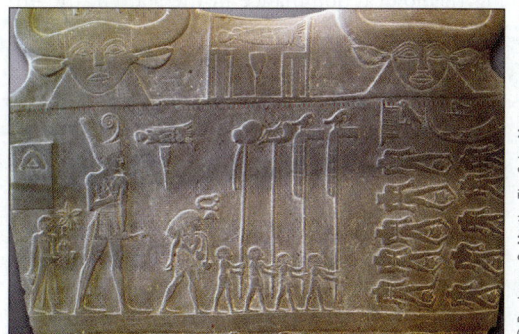

King Narmer (1st dynasty, c. 3100 B.C.), founder of Memphis, the first capital of united Egypt, attributed his victories over the people of the Nile delta to the goddess Hathor, whose features included the horns, ears, and neck of a cow.

for example). This affected the representations of Egyptian gods in art. As early as the Old Kingdom, the gods came to be conceived in basically human form. Some, like Ptah or Osiris, were shown commonly in entirely human form. Others, by a kind of iconographic shorthand, appeared in human form, except for their heads, which are shown as the characteristic heads of the animals connected with particular deities concerned. Anubis appears with the head of a jackal, Sobk with that of a crocodile, Horus and Re commonly with that of a falcon, Thoth with that of an ibis, etc. Sometimes, they might appear in more than one form: Amun of Thebes was generally in purely human guise, but could have a ram's head.

Among local gods, Amun of Thebes represented the hidden powers of nature, and his close relative Min of Coptos embodied virility and fertility, especially human and animal. At Memphis, Ptah was the artificer, patron of craftsmen, the Egyptian Vulcan, while the falcon headed Sokar was a local god of the dead and of new life (soon identified with Osiris). In Middle Egypt, Thoth was a god of wisdom and letters, and linked with moon worship. Further S, Hathor of Dendera was a goddess of love. The goddesses Bast of Bubastis and Sekhmet at Memphis respectively represented beneficent powers and the menace of pestilence among other things.

Among gods who had a far-reaching impact, beyond merely local appeal, RE and OSIRIS were by far the most important. Re the sun-god had his main cult center at HELIOPOLIS (On). He early became closely associated with the kingship, reaching theological dominance in the state in the 4th and 5th dynasties, outrivaling Ptah of Memphis, the administrative capital. His cult also affected the forms of Egyptian temple cult generally. His impact on the monarchy is indicated by the title "Son of Re," adopted by nearly every pharaoh from the 5th dynasty to the Roman period, some 3,000 years in all. In the 18th dynasty, Akhenaten endeavored to make a special form of sun worship the sole religion of Egypt. Re also affected life in the hereafter—the dead could sail over the heavens by day with him in his sacred boat, and also by night through the nether world, rising daily with him on the eastern horizon. During the Old Kingdom, the rise to prominence of Osiris provided an alternative afterlife, and in later days (by the New Kingdom) there was even a theological construction of Re and Osiris as the risen sun by day and the night sun preceding rebirth, respectively.

The worship of Osiris perhaps came nearest to a universal religion in all Egypt prior to the impact of Christianity. He was a funerary god who, in the Old Kingdom, became identified with Khentamentyu ("Chief of the Westerners"), the local funerary god at Abydos in Upper Egypt, a place hallowed long previously by tombs of the earliest kings. Osiris was the lord of the netherworld and of the afterlife therein, modeled partly upon earthly Egypt—his followers could sow and reap bountiful harvests, and enjoy the pleasures they formerly had on earth. He held the promise of a continued existence in this afterworld, and also became identified with the Nile, whose rise annually brought new life to the land.

An important aspect of the cult of Osiris was its "family" nature. His wife was the goddess Isis, a resourceful character as wife and mother of their son Horus, who avenged his father and supplanted their foe Seth in mythology. Here Egypt found a religion that offered something after death in terms that appealed to both men and women. Already accepted into the Pyramid Texts by the late Old Kingdom, the triumph of Osiris was complete from the advent of the Middle Kingdom, c. 2000 B.C., and Abydos became one of the most sacred and famed cities of Egypt. Many hundreds of memorial stelae in the world's museums (esp. Cairo) exhumed from its sands since the 19th cent. bear mute witness to the wish of countless Egyptians to have their names there in the presence of the "great god." In the Late Period, the influence of Osiris on other cults was most noticeable; even the great imperial god, Amun of Thebes in the 21st to 26th dynasties, saw his precinct at Karnak dotted with twenty or more little shrines to various forms of Osiris. Still later, the cult of Osiris (esp. as Serapis) and Isis penetrated the Greco-Roman world, and that religion competed with MITHRAISM and early Christianity, reaching far across Europe and throughout the Roman empire.

The Nile god, Hapi, was also venerated throughout Egypt and at all periods (esp. in relation to agriculture), but he never received great temples. His worship was more often marked by seasonal riverside ceremonies, those at Memphis and Heliopolis (later, at Cairo) surviving even into modern times (the "Night of the Drop" on the traditional feast for the beginning of the annual rise of the Nile). However, besides the local cults and gods such as Re and Osiris with a wider appeal lasting for millennia, the history of Egyptian religion shows also the wax and wane of other gods, conditioned by political changes. Under the earliest dynasties in the Old Kingdom, Ptah of Memphis shared in the central importance of that city, but then was overshadowed by the sun god Re. The *Memphite Theology* from this age probably represents Ptah's claim (against Re) to the role of supreme god and creator of all else.

By the late Old Kingdom, Osiris was gaining ground so much as even to invade the domain of Re, that is, royal theology; and as noted above, furnished the Egyptians with their most powerful hope in the afterlife from the Middle Kingdom onward, such that in the New Kingdom, theological accommodation even reckoned Re and Osiris as forms of each other. Amun of Thebes well illustrates the fluctuating fortunes of a god and his city. His importance first arose when in the Middle Kingdom he became Amon-Re (with a more universal scope) and was favored by the 12th dynasty, itself of S Egyptian origin. It was only with the all-conquering Theban pharaohs of the 18th dynasty that Amun of the hidden forces of nature became also king of the gods and virtually god of the empire, with the biggest temples ever seen. However, the disproportionate prominence of Amun and his priesthood in the state was felt as a menace by the monarchy, culminating in the deposition of Amun and the other gods in favor of the sun god by Akhenaten. However, Akhenaten's solar monotheism was shallow and (as noted above) concentrated largely on the beneficent and life-sustaining force of the sun in nature; it had no moral tone or philosophical basis. The epithet "living in truth" (Maat) merely reflected Akhenaten's claim that his way, not that of the old gods, was true to the right order of the cosmos. There is here no adequate source for the emphatic moral and social monotheism of a Moses or a Sinai covenant.

In the 19th and 20th dynasties, the Ramessides curbed the power of Amun by favoring him as one of a trinity of gods: Amun of Thebes, Re of Heliopolis, and Ptah of Memphis. One or two remarkable texts even syncretistically seek to identify the three as aspects of one great deity (cf., e.g., A. H. Gardiner, *Hieratic Papyri in the British Museum, 3rd Series*, 1 [1935], 28–37), a fact that shows a high level of religious thinking and speculation already in the 13th cent. B.C. In this light, the revealed monotheism of the OT need hardly wait until after the Babylonian exile to be expressed or formulated. In the Late Period (cf. above), Amun's fame outside of Thebes waned with the eclipse of empire, Ptah similarly resumed the main role of local artificer and god of Memphis, and Re continued traditionally as part of the theology of kingship. Osiris and Isis with their son Horus enjoyed the greater general popularity, while the gods and goddesses of the delta received more prominence with that achieved by the delta cities under Lower Egyptian kings in the later dynasties.

Finally, each PHARAOH must be reckoned among the gods. He was their representative on earth, and among the Egyptians a man who moved in the world of the gods. The living king counted as Horus, and the dead ruler(s) as Osiris; a new king received an unchallengeable right of succession at least partly by virtue of giving proper burial to his predecessor in filial fashion, as did Horus for Osiris. (For valuable outlines, see H. Frankfort, *Ancient Egyptian Religion* [1951]; J. Černý, *Ancient Egyptian Religion* [1952]; E. F. Wente, "Egyptian Religion," in *ABD*, 2:408–12. Fuller and well documented are J. Vandier, *La religion égyptienne* [1949]; H. Kees, *Der Götterglaube im alten Ägypten*, 2nd ed. [1956], and *Totenglauben und Jenseitsvorstellungen der alten Ägypter*, 2nd ed. [1956]; S. Morenz, *Ägyptische Religion* [1962; ET 1984] and *Gott und Mensch im alten Ägypten* [1964]; H. Bonnet, *Reallexikon der ägyptischen Religionsgeschichte* [1952] is invaluable. For the early periods [e.g., Pyramid Texts], cf. J. H. Breasted, *Development of Religion and Thought in Ancient Egypt* [1912]. For an up-to-date handbook, see F. Dunand and C. Zivie-Coche, *Gods and Men in Egypt: 3000 BCE to 395 CE* [2004]. Among treatments of religious themes, see the important work by J. Assmann, *Death and Salvation in Ancient Egypt* [2005].)

B. Worship and cult. The Egyptian temple was the house of its god in quite a literal sense. The basis of the cult was the daily ritual. This was modeled on ordinary life. In the morning, the god in his sanctuary was awakened with the morning hymn, his shrine was opened, his cult image ritually purified and dressed, and offerings presented to it (breakfast). At midday and later, lesser services of offering were celebrated. The god might give oracles, receive visitors (other gods embodied in their cult images), or himself go in procession to some other temple. His life had its necessities and duties, so to speak, as did the king or a householder.

The cult so celebrated was the preserve of the priests; there was no lay congregation to witness or share in the rites. This element is illustrated and emphasized by the form of Egyptian TEMPLES, best known from New Kingdom examples. The whole sacred precinct was shut in by massive mud-brick walls, pierced by one or more massive gateways. Within the area stood not only the temple of the god (and perhaps shrines of associated deities) but also the dwellings of the priests, the storehouses for offerings, quarters for livestock for offerings, temple gardens and trees, and the sacred lake—source of holy water and setting for dramatic rites.

The temple itself would often be approached along an avenue lined with sphinxes on either side, leading to a great gateway between two flanking towers of inward sloping form, broader than high—the whole being termed a *pylon*. Such an entrance might be preceded by obelisks and colossal royal statues; beyond it, one commonly entered an open court with colonnades. Beyond this, the privileged entered the temple proper, perhaps through a second pylon, into a great "hypostyle" hall of columns, with a central nave higher than the rest, allowing of clerestory lighting. Thereafter, one would pass through successive halls and rooms (each with its role), into ever-increasing darkness, whose mystery was heightened by rising floor levels, lower roofs, and in the dim light, the gleam of gold and glow of rich colors from painted reliefs of the king performing ritual acts. Finally came the sanctuary containing the shrine of the god, its doors bolted and sealed, guarding the cult image within. Around were sanctuaries of co-templar gods, and storerooms for the treasures and paraphernalia of the cult. The spectacle of the outwardly powerful Egyptian gods actually dependent in some measure on the food offerings presented to them (and on images of the rites, should human agents fail) stands in striking contrast with the God of Israel (and, a fortiori, of the NT), self-sufficient and sustaining all else, whose offering rites in tabernacle and temple were aimed at the benefit of his worshipers, with didactic role concerning sin and atonement and reconciliation.

Excluded from the great temples, the populace frequented lesser shrines or oratories at the gateways of the vast major precincts. Their main contact with the great gods came only on high days of festival, when the gods went forth in glittering array on stately processions. The splendor of the festivals culminated under the empire; suffice it to mention some great Theban festivals. On the Feast of Opet, Amun sailed on the river from Karnak to Luxor temple, accompanied by joyous crowds along the river bank (cf. W. Wolf, *Das schöne Fest von Opet* [1931], Luxor scenes). On the Feast of the Valley, Amun's golden barge took him to W Thebes across the river to the funerary temples of the pharaohs, while the Thebans offered to their own ancestors and made holiday at the tomb chapels, brilliantly painted venues for the feasting (cf. S. Schott, *Das schöne Fest von Wüstentale* [1953], on rites). Both at Memphis and at Thebes, the rich festival of Sokar-Osiris attracted the multitude to see the fantastically formed golden boat of Sokar borne around the walls of town or temple, and to the necropolis (G. A. Gaballa and K. A. Kitchen in *Orientalia* 37 [1968]: 1–76). Herodotus reported on the feasts of the delta, and the temples of Edfu and Dendera give much detail on feasts in the Ptolemaic age.

Both the ordinary rituals and the festival rites of Egypt far outstrip in complexity anything to be found in the rituals of the Hebrew Pentateuch. Even on an "evolutionary" basis (inherently erroneous), therefore, it would be unrealistic to make the relatively simple Hebrew rituals as late as the Persian age; by Egyptian standards, they would be more than prepatriarchal, let alone Mosaic! (On priests, cf. S. Sauneron, *The Priests of Ancient Egypt*, new ed. [2000]; H. Kees, *Das Priestertum im ägyptischen Staat* [1953–1958], and *Die Hohenpriester*

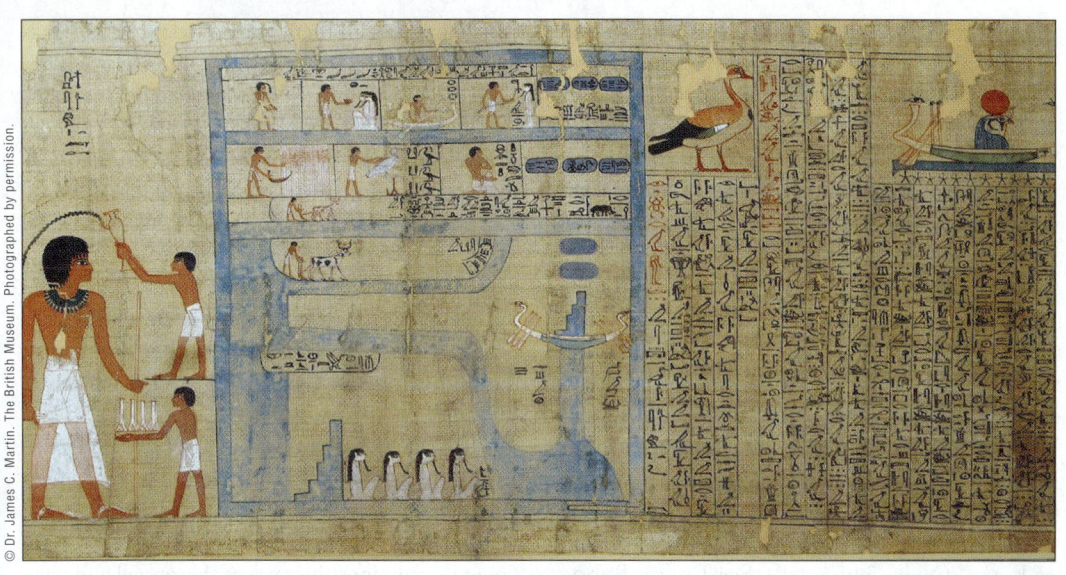

An early example of the *Book of the Dead* on papyrus, produced by a scribe named Userhat (from Thebes, c. 1450 B.C.).

des Amun von Karnak von Herihor bis zum Ende der Äthiopenzeit [1964], completing G. Lefebvre, *Histoire des grands prêtres d'Amon de Karnak* [1929]. On Egyptian temple cult, cf. H. W. Fairman in *BJRL* 37 [1954]: 165–203. On festivals, cf. S. Schott, *Altägyptische Festdaten* [1950], and C. J. Bleeker, *Egyptian Festivals* [1967].)

C. Funerary beliefs. Belief in an afterlife was a leading feature of Egyptian religion at all periods, but as already seen was not a unity—solar and Osirian hereafters offered either the company of Re across the heavens or else the netherworldly realm of Osiris on a more earthly model. In either case, the body was a material abode for the soul, hence the efforts to preserve it (mummification) and the use of statues to preserve a likeness even if the body perished. Insofar as the afterlife reflected earthly conditions, tomb pictures magically could supply the wants of the deceased, and the tomb was his eternal house, to be appropriately furnished with goods that would be magically effective—hence the wealth of Egyptian burials, a famed target of tomb robbers. While the *Book of the Dead* included a moral element in a form of judgment of the dead, the impact of this was weakened by resort to MAGIC. To the materialistic nature of Egyptian eschatology we owe a great deal of our knowledge of that civilization. K. A. KITCHEN

Egypt, Brook (Wadi) of. The SW border of the Promised Land (Num. 34:5), of the tribe of JUDAH (Josh. 15:4, 47), of SOLOMON's kingdom (1 Ki. 8:65; 2 Chr. 7:8), and later of JUDEA (2 Ki. 24:7; Isa. 27:12). Ezekiel refers to it simply as "the brook" or "the wadi" (*naḥălâ* H5711, Ezek. 47:19, 48:28). The biblical evidence places this WADI westward from GAZA (cf. Josh. 15:47) and KADESH BARNEA (cf. Num. 34:4–5).

Not to be confused with "the river of Egypt" (the NILE, but see EGYPT, RIVER OF), the Wadi of Egypt has usually been identified with Wadi el-ʿArish, reaching the Mediterranean at the town of el-ʿArish some 90 mi. E of the Suez canal and almost 50 mi. SW of Gaza. Local geography is thought to support this identification—only scrub and desert W of el-ʿArish, but cultivable terrain eastward therefrom, claimed by Judah (cf. A. H. Gardiner in *JEA* 6 [1920], 115; B. Rothenberg et al., *God's Wilderness* [1961], 21 end, 32 [plate 9], 57). More recently, however, some scholars have identified it with Naḥal Besor, which is farther N (see N. Naʾaman in *Tel Aviv* 6 [1979]: 68–90; cf. P. K. Hooker in *History and Interpretation: Essays in Honour of John H. Hayes*, ed. M. P. Graham et al. [1993], 203–14).

The name "Brook of Egypt" is found in Akkadian as *naḥal muṣur*, mentioned by SARGON II of Assyria in 716 B.C. (*ANET*, 286; H. Tadmor in

Journal of Cuneiform Studies 12 [1958]: 77–78). He settled people in its "city," the Arzâ(ni) or Arṣâ (classical Rhinocorura), which ESARHADDON's texts place on the Brook of Egypt (*ANET*, 290); the form of the name is phonetically comparable with modern (el-)ʿArish, but some think it refers to Yurza (cf. *ABD*, 2:321). In any case, the "Brook of Egypt" probably should not be confused with SHIHOR, the old Pelusiac and easternmost arm of the Nile (never a wadi; see further discussion in *NBD*, s.v. "Egypt, River of," 302–3). K. A. KITCHEN

Egypt, river of. The phrase "the river of Egypt" renders Hebrew *nĕhar miṣrayim*, which occurs only once (Gen. 15:18). It may refer to the NILE (Heb. *hayĕʾōr*, lit., "the river"), although many scholars believe it is the same as "the Brook [*naḥal*] of Egypt" (Num. 34:5 et al.). See EGYPT, BROOK (WADI) OF. The NIV also uses "the river of Egypt" to render Hebrew *yĕʾōr miṣrayim*, which occurs twice (Amos 8:8; 9:5; NRSV, "the Nile"; cf. the plural form in Isa. 7:18).

Egyptian, the. An unnamed individual mentioned in the context of PAUL's arrest and removal from the temple precinct (Acts 21:38). In the narrative the Roman officer asked Paul if he was not a certain Egyptian who was attempting a revolt against Rome. This man was supposed to have led his 4,000 dagger-bearers or *Sicarii* (Greek *sikarios G4974*, see ASSASSINS) into the wilderness. JOSEPHUS (*Ant.* 20.8.6 §§168–72; cf. *War* 2.13.5 §§261–63) apparently refers to the same Egyptian, "a man who declared that he was a prophet and advised the masses of the common people to go out with him to the mountain called the Mount of Olives.... For he asserted that he wished to demonstrate from there that at his command Jerusalem's walls would fall down, through which he promised to provide them an entrance into the city." The revolt was quelled by FELIX; 400 were killed and another 200 taken prisoner, but the Egyptian himself escaped. The precise identification of this agitator is unknown. During the years of Roman imperial occupation of Palestine, many such revolutionaries appeared and were brought to judgment by the legions. The last revolt in A.D. 66 engaged the *Sicarii* and their leaders, and there is strong evidence to associate them with the defense of MASADA in A.D. 73 (see WARS, JEWISH; ZEALOT). They were the most violent and terroristic of the many national sects that appeared among the Jews under Roman domination. (See R. A. Horsley and J. S. Hanson, *Bandits, Prophets, and Messiahs* [1985], esp. pp. 167–72.) W. WHITE, JR.

Egyptians, Gospel of the. ORIGEN (*Hom. Luc.* 1; text in *NTAp*, 1:44–46) makes mention of a *Gospel of the Egyptians* among other apocryphal books, but two distinct works are known under this title.

(1) CLEMENT OF ALEXANDRIA quotes from such a work in *Stromateis* 3, where he is concerned with questions of marriage and sexual morality over against the views of the ENCRATITES and other groups. In so doing he mentions their use of this gospel and gives a few extracts from a dialogue between Christ and Salome. (A fragment of this dialogue is quoted also in the pseudonymous homily known as *2 Clement* [12.1–2], but whether the other noncanonical sayings in *2 Clement* also derive from the *Gospel of the Egyptians* is by no means certain.) A further quotation occurs in Clement's *Excerpta ex Theodoto* (67), and according to Hippolytus (*Haer.* 5.7.8–9) the book was used by the Naassenes. Epiphanius (*Pan.* 62.4) mentions its use by the Sabellians, but gives no information of its character. The evidence is not sufficient to provide a basis for conclusions about the nature, content, and structure of the book, but it must go back to the 2nd cent. and seems to have been of a Gnostic, or at any rate, Encratite character. Clement quoted it *against* the Encratites, but had to read his own interpretation into the text. While he clearly places it on a lower level than the canonical Gospels, there is no sign that he entirely disapproved of it. W. Bauer believed that it was the gospel of Gentile Christians in Egypt, while the *Gospel of the Hebrews* was that used by the Jewish Christians, but other scholars have contested this suggestion. Parallels in the Coptic *Gospel of Thomas* have led to the suggestion that the *Gospel of the Egyptians* was one of its sources, but this again remains uncertain. (For the texts and further discussion, see *NTAp*, 1:209–15.) See also APOCRYPHAL NEW TESTAMENT I; HEBREWS, GOSPEL OF THE; THOMAS, GOSPEL OF.

(2) Completely different is a document contained in the NAG HAMMADI LIBRARY in two different Coptic versions from a Greek original (NHC III, 2 and IV, 2). Both versions have the title "Sacred Book of the Great Invisible Spirit," but Codex III also has in the colophon the title, *Gospel of the Egyptians*. The description of the heavenly world from its opening pages has been translated and discussed by A. Böhlig (*Le Muséon* 80 [1967]: 5ff.). It begins with a description of the great invisible Spirit and of the emanations (Father, Mother, Son) that proceed from him. The appearance of Barbelo and various points of agreement with the *Apocryphon of John* (see JOHN, APOCRYPHON OF) suggests a connection with the Barbelo-gnostic sect. (English trans. in *NHL*, 208–19.) R. McL. WILSON

Ehi ee´hi (אֵחִי *H305*, derivation uncertain). Sixth son of BENJAMIN and grandson of JACOB (Gen. 46:21). Some scholars regard Ehi as an abbreviated form of AHIRAM (Num. 26:38). According to others (e.g., O. Eißfeldt in *BHS*), the four-name series "Ehi and Rosh, Muppim and Huppim" (*ʾḥy wrʾš mpym wḥpym*) in the Genesis passage is a scribal corruption of an original three-name series, "Ahiram and Shupham and Hupham" (*ʾḥyrm wšwpm wḥwpm*; cf. Num. 26:38–39).

Ehud ee´huhd (אֵהוּד *H179* [in 1 Chr. 8:6, MT has אֵחוּד *H287*], possibly "where is the glory?" or short form of אֲחִיהוּד *H310*, "my brother is majesty" [see AHIHUD]). **(1)** Son of Gera and descendant of BENJAMIN. Ehud, a left-handed hero, led the revolt against the Edomite King EGLON, who early in the period of the judges had subjugated Israel for eighteen years (Jdg. 3:15–31; 1 Chr. 8:6; in v. 3, "Gera and Abihud" [*grʾ wʾbyhwd*] is probably a scribal mistake for "Gera, father of Ehud" [*grʾ ʾby ʾhwd*]). Before taking the annual tribute to Eglon, Ehud fashioned a thirteen-inch double-edged dagger which he carried on his right thigh for convenience, being left-handed. Having publicly paid the tribute, he seized an opportunity through a ruse to speak privately to Eglon and slew the unsuspecting king. Gaining time by locking the body in the private chamber, Ehud escaped through a window and marshaled the W Jordanian Israelites to prevent 10,000 Moabite soldiers from fleeing homeward, thus insuring peace for eighty years. Some scholars have seen in the deliverance narrative two closely interwoven accounts, but such a view does nothing to clarify or enhance the narrative, which possesses its own genuine motifs typical of the exploits of heroes in the E Mediterranean Heroic Age. While Ehud is not specifically described as a "judge," the characteristic introduction and conclusion to the narrative (Jdg. 3:12–15a, 28–30; 4:1) indicate that the compiler of the book clearly regarded him as such. See JUDGES, PERIOD OF.

(2) Son of Bilhan and descendant of BENJAMIN (1 Chr. 7:10). R. K. HARRISON

Eker ee´kuhr (עֵקֶר *H6831*, possibly "root" or "offspring"). Son of Ram and descendant of JUDAH (1 Chr. 2:27).

Ekrebel ek´ruh-buhl. KJV Apoc. form of ACRABA (Jdt. 7:18).

Ekron ek´ruhn (עֶקְרוֹן *H6833*, possibly "barren place"; gentilic עֶקְרוֹנִי *H6834*, "Ekronite"). The northernmost of the five major PHILISTINE cities; it became a border town in the tribal territory allotted to the tribe of JUDAH. It was not taken by the Israelites before the death of JOSHUA (Josh. 13:3; 15:11, 45–46) but was acquired later (Jdg. 1:18). Elsewhere it is said to belong to Dan (Josh. 19:43, though here the text possibly allows the rendering "Timnah of Ekron"; cf. Y. Aharoni, *The Land of the Bible: A Historical Geography*, rev. ed. [1979], 312); and JOSEPHUS also mentions Ekron

View looking NE toward the ancient site of Ekron.

in his account of the press of the Danites by the Philistines (*Ant.* 5.3.1 §177). See DAN (PERSON AND TRIBE).

Though Ekron is said to have been taken by Judah at the beginning of the period of the judges (Jdg. 1:18), the Philistines continued to dominate it through that period and during the monarchy. While the ARK OF THE COVENANT was in Philistine possession, after being at ASHDOD and at GATH, it was sent to Ekron (LXX reads "Askalon": 1 Sam. 5:10; 6:16), where its presence caused panic and from which it was returned with gifts to the Israelites at BETH SHEMESH and eventually came to KIRIATH JEARIM (5:10–12; 6:16; 7:1). SAMUEL is said to have restored Israel's territory from Ekron to Gath (7:14); again the Philistines were driven back to the gates of Ekron following the death of GOLIATH (17:52).

The god of Ekron was BAAL-ZEBUB, whom the ailing King AHAZIAH (c. 850–849 B.C.) wished to consult regarding the possibilities of his recovery. The king's action brought stern denunciation from ELIJAH (2 Ki. 1:2–3, 6, 16). Destruction was threatened Ekron by the prophets in their oracles against the Philistines (Jer. 25:20; 32:20; Amos 1:8; Zeph. 2:4; Zech. 9:5, 7). Gath had by this time disappeared from the Philistine list, leaving only a group of four cities. Zechariah promised that, like the Jebusites, Ekron would be incorporated into Israel.

According to SENNACHERIB'S own account (*ANET*, 287–88), when Padi king of Ekron was imprisoned by HEZEKIAH in 701 B.C., Sennacherib both forced his release and compelled Hezekiah to cede Judean territory to him. Sennacherib arrived at Ekron on his way S after taking ELTEKEH and TIMNAH. Later, tribute was taken from Ekron by both ESARHADDON and ASHURBANIPAL (*ANET*, 291, 294). After the destruction of Jerusalem in 587 B.C., Ekron is unmentioned until the Maccabean period, at which time (147 B.C.) Alexander Balas gave the city as a prize for services to Jonathan MACCABEE (1 Macc. 10:89). The city continued on to Crusader times.

The identification of the site of Ekron was long disputed. EUSEBIUS (*Onomasticon* 22.9–10) mentions Ekron as a large Jewish village between Azotus (ASHDOD) and Jamnia (JABNEEL, Jabneh), to the E of the route between these two towns. JEROME (*PL*, 23:915) suggests that some identify it with *turrim Stratonis* (CAESAREA), a view that is now completely rejected. E. Robinson (*Biblical Researches in Palestine, Mount Sinai and Arabia Petraea*, 3 vols. [1841], 3:22–24) identified Ekron with the village of ʿAqir, but the latter (situated in a level plain 4 mi. E of Jabneel and 12 mi. NE of Ashdod) has neither a tell nor potsherds from the required 1,500-year period of occupation. R. A. S. Macalister (*The Philistines: Their History and Civilization* [1911], 64–65, 74–76) attempted a distinction between northern Ekron (the Danite town), which he thought might be ʿAqir, and a second Ekron (in Judah), for which he proposed Dhikerin, a location between MARESHAH and Ashdod where there are caves and cisterns from antiquity. Qatra, a hill 3 mi. SW of ʿAqir, with a tell and remains from the Greco-Roman period, was favored by W. F. Albright (in AASOR 2–3 [1923]: 1–7) as fitting the description of Eusebius; the site would lend itself to the strong fortifications expected in a major Philistine city (this identification is also favored by R. Boling in *Biblical and Related Studies Presented to Samuel Iwry*, ed. A. Kort and S. Morschauser [1985], 23–32, esp. 30).

In the late 1950s, however, J. Naveh identified Ekron with Khirbet el-Muqannaʿ (Tel Miqne), located S of the SOREK valley, about 20 mi. SE of JOPPA (see *IEJ* 8 [1958]: 87–100, 165–70). This identification has been generally accepted. Philistine sherds are to be found on the surface. The city existed from the Iron Age to the Persian period, and at its height of development would have covered 40 acres, which makes it the largest Iron Age city yet found in Palestine. Sections of the wall and the city gate can be traced out. There are springs of water in the area sufficient to support a sizable town. (For an account of later excavations, see S. Gitin and T. Dothan in *BA* 50 [1987]: 197–222; *NEAEHL*, 3:1051–59.) J. P. LEWIS

El el (אֵל *H446*, etymology disputed; ancient Semitic term for deity, cf. Assyr. *ilu*, Ugar. *il*). Largely poetic designation of the one and only true God of Israel. It is often used with the definite article, although no such article is needed to define the true God (Num. 12:13). But the term, which possibly means "strength" (cf. the infrequent noun ʾēl *H445*, Gen.

31:29 et al.), can be applied more generally (e.g., to angels, Ps. 29:1). Just as the word *god* in English can be used of the true God or of false gods, so this word in Hebrew may refer to heathen gods, usually meaning idols (Exod. 15:11; 34:14; Isa. 43:10). The same root is used in the Ugaritic mythology (see UGARIT) as the name of the chief god of the Canaanite pantheon, although *Il*, father-god of the pantheon, played a role of lesser importance than such hero gods as BAAL (see M. H. Pope, *El in the Ugaritic Texts* [1955]; *DDD*, 274–80). Critics posit the idea that the Hebrew ancestors worshiped clan deities who bore this element in their names. Old Phoenician and Ugaritic literature uses the feminine form of this word for the goddesses of the pantheon. The Bible wholly avoids this feminine usage of the word because the Hebrew religion had no mythological concept of a goddess. The heathen goddesses are named in the Hebrew Bible (e.g. ASHTORETH, 1 Sam. 7:3). *El*, however, is often combined with other terms to create epithets (*ʾēl šadday*, *ʾēl ʿelyôn*, et al.) that express God's numerous attributes. See ELOAH, ELOHIM; GOD, NAMES OF, II.   E. B. SMICK

Ela ee´luh (אֵלָא *H452*, possibly from אֵל *H446*, the Semitic term for deity). Father of SHIMEI; the latter was one of the twelve governors in charge of providing for King SOLOMON's household (1 Ki. 4:18; KJV, "Elah").

Eladah el´uh-duh. KJV form of ELEADAH.

Elah ee´luh (אֵלָה *H462*, possibly "oak" or a variant of אֵלָא *H452* [see ELA]; cf. Noth, *IPN*, 38, 90). **(1)** One of the Edomite chiefs descended from ESAU (Gen. 36:41; 1 Chr. 1:52). Some believe that the word should be taken as a place name and identified with ELATH (cf. *ABD*, 2:423).

(2) Son of CALEB and descendant of JUDAH (1 Chr. 4:15).

(3) Son of BAASHA and fourth king of Israel (1 Ki. 16:8–14). He succeeded his father in the twenty-sixth year of ASA of Judah, reigned in TIRZAH, and was assassinated in the following year (vv. 10, 15). The note "two years" (v. 8) indicates that his reign covered more than a full year. This short period was long enough for him to show his adherence to his father's religious policy, in defiance of the prophecy of JEHU son of Hanani (v. 1), but he seems to have lacked his father's energy and leadership. It is recorded that he met his death while carousing at the home of his chamberlain in Tirzah, though the army was at the time laying siege to the PHILISTINE city of GIBBETHON.

(4) Father of HOSHEA; the latter became the last king of Israel (2 Ki. 15:30; 17:1; 18:1, 9).

(5) Son of Uzzi and one of the first Benjamites to resettle in Jerusalem after the EXILE (1 Chr. 9:8).

(6) KJV form of ELA.   J. LILLEY

View looking SW through the dry streambed of the shrub-lined Wadi Elah, where David and Goliath met for battle.

Elah, Valley of ee´luh (אֵלָה *H463*, possibly "oak" or "terebinth"). A valley in the SHEPHELAH, generally identified with Wadi es-Sanṭ ("Valley of the Acacia"), about 18 mi. WSW of JERUSALEM. The area is rich in ACACIAS, TEREBINTHS, and OAKS. It was the scene of the combat between DAVID and GOLIATH (1 Sam. 17:2, 19; 21:9). Coursing through the valley is a watercourse (or WADI, as the Arabs call it), which runs in the period of the rains only. The bottom of the watercourse is covered with small stones, the kind David might have used for his sling. — A. C. SCHULTZ

Elam (person) ee′luhm (עֵילָם *H6521* [*H6520* for #1 below], derivation uncertain). **(1)** Son of SHEM, grandson of NOAH, and eponymous ancestor of the Elamites (Gen. 10:22; 1 Chr. 1:17). See ELAM (PLACE).

(2) Fifth son of Meshelemiah and descendant of LEVI through KORAH; like his father, he and his brothers were Levitical gatekeepers in the time of DAVID (1 Chr. 26:3).

(3) Son of Shahach and descendant of BENJAMIN (1 Chr. 8:24). Some identify him with #4 below.

(4) The eponym of a clan from which 1,254 persons returned to Palestine with ZERUBBABEL after the EXILE (Ezra 2:7; Neh. 7:12; 1 Esd. 5:12). An additional 70 members of this family, headed by Jeshaiah son of Athaliah, returned with EZRA (Ezra 8:7; 1 Esd. 8:33). Still another member of this family, Shecaniah son of Jehiel, suggested to Ezra that those Israelites who had married foreign women put away these wives and their children (Ezra 10:2–4). Six of the men of this family put away their foreign wives (10:26; 1 Esd. 9:27).

(5) A man referred to as "the other Elam" also had a family of 1,254 who returned from the exile (Ezra 2:31; Neh. 7:34; cf. also 1 Esd. 5:22 RSV and see CALAMOLALUS). Because the number of family members is the same as that of #4 above, some scholars identify the two individuals as one.

(6) One of the chiefs who are said to have sealed the covenant with NEHEMIAH (Neh. 10:14). Some scholars identify him with #4 above.

(7) A priest who participated in the dedication of the walls of Jerusalem in Nehemiah's time (Neh. 12:42). — A. C. SCHULTZ

Elam (place) ee′luhm (עֵילָם *H6520*; Aram. gentilic עֵלְמָי *H10551* [Ezra 4:9] and Gk. gentilic Ἐλαμίτης *G1780* [Acts 2:9], "Elamite"). The biblical designation of both a people and a country in the southern area of the Iranian plateau in the Zagros mountains E and NE of the valley of the TIGRIS (approximately equivalent to the present Iranian province of Khuzistan). The name derives from the Elamite *Ha(l)tamti*, from which derives the *Elamtu* of the Assyrians and the Babylonians as well as the *Elymais* of the Greeks. It has often been referred to also as Susiana because SUSA (modern Shush) was the capital of Elam for a period (cf. Dan. 8:2; on the need to distinguish between Susa and Elam, see F. Vallat in *CANE*, 2:1023–24). Scholars are not agreed in regard to the relationship of the language of the Elamites to the other LANGUAGES OF THE ANE, but it is not Semitic. The earliest stage of the language, going back to the 4th millennium, is written in a script not yet completely deciphered. Toward the end of the 3rd millennium, the language was written in CUNEIFORM, which in turn gave way at the end of the 6th cent. B.C. to the Elamite adaptation of the writing of the Achaemenid Persians. (Cf. E. Reiner in *Keilschriftforschung und die Geschichte Vorderasiens* [Handbuch der Orientalistik 1/2], ed. B. Spuler [1969]; F. Grillot-Susini, *Éléments de grammaire élamite* [1987]; *CANE*, 4:2162–64, 2178.) The history of the Elamites is known largely from the records of other peoples, thus breaks in its continuity are inevitable.

I. Early history. The biblical record traces the Elamites back to Elam son of SHEM (Gen. 10:22; 1 Chr. 1:17). Scholars classify them as non-

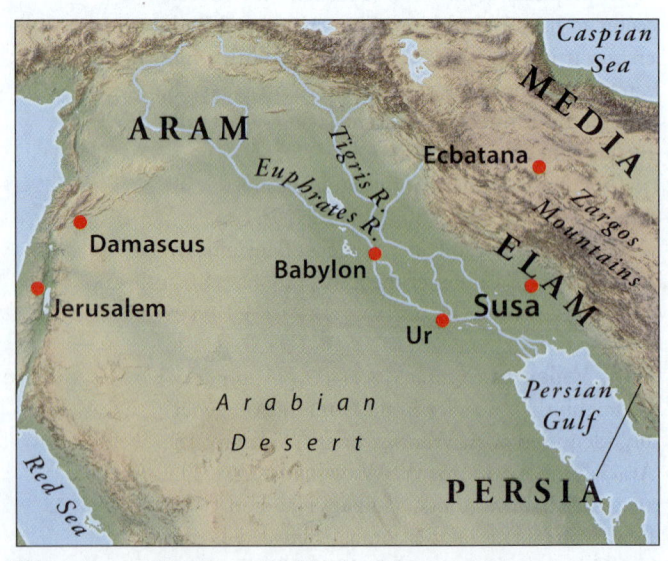

Elam.

Semitic Caucasians. Archaeology and anthropology shed no particular light upon Elamite origins, but it is clear that Elam was influenced by the Jemdet Nasr culture during the later period of the 4th millennium B.C. The dependence culturally of Elam upon MESOPOTAMIA that began in this early period lasted through her entire history. Elam's earliest appearance in Mesopotamian records shows it in subjection to a Sumerian king, Eannatum of Lagash in 2450 B.C. This further strengthened the influence that the culture of SUMER had upon the Elamites. Elamite dependence upon Mesopotamia continued after hegemony in the Tigris-Euphrates valley shifted from the Sumerians to the Akkadians under Sargon of AKKAD (2360–2305). It was in this period that the Elamites appropriated the Sumero-Akkadian cuneiform script with which they produced their inscriptions on clay tablets and stone. Elamites from Susa participated in the building of the temple of Gudea of LAGASH (c. 2000).

With the decline of Akkadian power Elam gained her freedom and established an independent dynasty. But the third dynasty of Ur (see UR OF THE CHALDEES) eventually gained control of much of Elam and dominated many of the country's cities. However, the Elamites were eventually able to reassert their independence and to destroy their oppressor's capital city, carrying back to Elam the last king of the dynasty of Ur, Ibbi-Sin (c. 2030 B.C.). The destruction of Ur by the Elamites is bewailed in a Sumerian lamentation text.

At this time of Elamite history, the rulers of the country were known as "governors" and not as kings in the Mesopotamian sense of the term. The rulers of Elam were actually feudal lords, considered to be representatives of Inshushinak, god of Susa. A unique cultural form appeared in this period that served to determine the method of the transition of power from one ruler to another to the end of Elamite history. This was the principle of matrilineal succession: the throne was hereditary through women so that the new ruler was the son of a sister of a member of the previous ruler's family. The quality of the succession was somewhat protected by the regulation that the successor was expected to have had some experience as viceroy, usually at Susa.

The power of Elam spread into Mesopotamia under King Kutir-Mabug, who made Rim-Sin king of Larsa and through him controlled S Babylonia as far N as BABYLON. Larsa fell to the First Amorite Dynasty of Babylon under HAMMURABI (c. 1728–1686 B.C.), who made Elam a province of his empire, according to his records, in the thirtieth year of his reign. The empire of Hammurabi's dynasty fell before the Kassite invasion (c. 1600), and Elam was delivered from Babylonian domination. For the next 300 years practically nothing is known about Elam. In the last quarter of the 14th cent. the Kassite Kurigalzu III claims to have conquered Elam.

II. The classical period. This period begins c. 1200 B.C., when Elam again gained independence and reemerged as an international power. A succession of capable kings expanded Elamite power, and an invasion of Babylon in 1160 destroyed Kassite domination. Babylon was made a satellite of Elam. Throughout the empire scores of temples were built and dedicated to Elamite deities, and tribute flowed into Susa the capital. Archaeological excavations at Susa have disclosed that the Elamites plundered several Babylonian cities. Among the trophies found at Susa were the stela of the Code of Hammurabi and the victory stela of Naram-Sin. Many of the captured monuments were set up in the courts of important city temples and dedicated to the gods of Elam. These Elamite successes were abruptly ended by Nebuchadnezzar I, who captured and plundered Susa (c. 1130 B.C.) and once more made Elam subject to Babylon. And once again for nearly 300 years nothing is known of Elamite history.

The Babylonian Chronicle mentions Elam as an independent state in 742 B.C., and it is described in the same way in the inscriptions of the Assyrian kings TIGLATH-PILESER III (745–727) and SARGON II (722–706). The Assyrians demonstrate great diplomatic skill in playing the various claimants to the Elamite throne against each other. Elamite inscriptions begin with Shutruk-Nahhunte II (717–681) and are an important supplement to the Assyrian inscriptions. The Elamites cooperated with the Babylonian rebel MERODACH-BALADAN against SENNACHERIB (705–681), which resulted only in Elam becoming a refuge for the rebellious Babylonians humiliated by the Assyrians. Sennacherib was unable to gain a decisive victory over Elam. In at least one battle the Elamites inflicted a defeat upon the Assyrians.

The struggle between the two powers continued until the later years of the reign of the Assyrian ASHURBANIPAL (633–619). Ashurbanipal defeated King Teumman, and in one of his reliefs shows the defeated Elamite monarch's head dangling from a tree in the palace garden where he and his queen are feasting with other nobles. Ashurbanipal placed a puppet upon the throne of Elam but he proved disloyal, with the result that in 640 the Assyrian monarch invaded Elam, sacked Susa, and deported many of the population to SAMARIA. Elam as an independent nation thus comes to an end. At the rise of the Persian empire (550), Elam was made a satrapy paying tribute to the Achaemenid kings. See PERSIA. Susa was maintained as an important city and was used as the king's residence for three months of the year. It was widely known for the beauty of its halls and palaces. The city was mentioned by Greek writers such as Arrian, Ctesias, and Herodotus.

III. Elam in the Bible. Elam, the progenitor of the Elamites, with ASSHUR, ARPACHSHAD, LUD, and ARAM, was a son of SHEM (Gen. 10:22). In Gen. 14:1–17 KEDORLAOMER, king of Elam, is described as the overlord of three other Mesopotamian kings. Cuneiform tablets discovered at MARI indicate that in this period Elamite mercenaries served in the armies of the kings of Mesopotamia and that Elamites traveled as emissaries as far as ALEPPO and HAZOR, which may help to understand Gen. 14. It is impossible on the basis of present knowledge to synchronize adequately the rulers of the Mesopotamian cities and the Elamite kings.

Elam is listed among those nations that attacked Jerusalem and is described as a land of archers (Isa. 22:6; Jer. 49:35). It also is listed with the Medes (see MEDIA) among the attackers of Babylon under CYRUS (Isa. 21:2, 9). Elam is mentioned as one of the places to which Israelites were exiled (Isa. 11:11). Jeremiah lists Elam with the nations that will be forced to drink the cup of the wrath of God (Jer. 25:25; cf. 49:34–39). Ezekiel numbers Elam among the nations over whose graves a lamentation shall be chanted (Ezek. 32:16, 24). The Elamites are listed among the peoples settled in Samaria by the Assyrians (Ezra 4:9–10). Cyrus (Isa. 44:28; 45:1) was from the Elamite province of Anshan. The episodes recorded in the book of ESTHER occurred at Susa, the ancient capital of Elam, in the reign of AHASUERUS the Persian, who is generally identified as XERXES I. In Acts 2:9 the Elamites are said to have been present, along with PARTHIANS, Medes, and others, in Jerusalem on the day of PENTECOST. (See further G. C. Cameron, *History of Early Iran* [1936]; E. Herzfeld, *Iran in the Ancient Near East* [1941]; P. Amiet, *Elam* [1966]; F. Vallat, *Suse et l'Elam* [1980]; E. Carter and M. W. Stolper, *Elam: Surveys of Political History and Archaeology* [1984]; *CANE*, 2:1001–33.) A. C. SCHULTZ

Elasa el′uh-suh (Ελασα, from Heb. אֶלְעָשָׂה H543, "God has made"; see ELASAH). KJV Eleasa. The place where Judas MACCABEE lay encamped when BACCHIDES advanced upon him in 160 B.C. (1 Macc. 9:5). In the ensuing battle, Judas was killed. The site has often been identified with Khirbet Il'asa, near BETH HORON, but others prefer Khirbet el-'Aššī, just SE of present-day Ramallah (so J. A. Goldstein, *I Maccabees*, AB 41 [1976], 373, who discusses several topographical and textual problems in the narrative).

Elasah el′uh-suh (אֶלְעָשָׂה H543, "God has made"; see also ELEASAH). (**1**) Son of SHAPHAN; he and Gemariah son of Hilkiah were entrusted with a letter from JEREMIAH to the exiles in Babylon (Jer. 29:3).

(**2**) One of the descendants of PASHHUR who agreed to put away their foreign wives (Ezra 10:22; the parallel in 1 Esd. 9:22 reads "Salthas" [KJV, "Talsas"; RSV, "Elasah"]). D. H. MADVIG

Elath, Eloth ee′lath, ee′loth (אֵילַת H397 [Deut. 2:8; 2 Ki. 14:22; 16:6] and אֵילוֹת H393 [1 Ki. 9:26; 2 Chr. 8:17; 26:2], possibly "grove of [palm] trees"). The NIV renders "Elath" consistently. A town on the northern end of the Gulf of AQABAH (also known as the Gulf of Elath, the NE arm of the RED SEA). Many believe it is the same as EL PARAN (Gen. 14:6). Some have also speculated that the

Ancient Elath lay at the N end of the Gulf of Aqabah. (View to the E.)

name Elath may have been given to the settlement by the Edomite chief ELAH (Gen. 36:41).

The town is mentioned along with EZION GEBER in connection with the wilderness travels of the Israelites through MOAB (Deut. 2:8). Because of its strategic position, Elath was an asset to any nation. The first mention of the place after the exodus states that "King Solomon also built ships at Ezion Geber, which is near Elath in Edom, on the shore of the Red Sea" (1 Ki. 9:26; cf. 2 Chr. 8:17; David had earlier subdued the Edomites, 2 Sam. 8:14). Later, in the time of JEHOSHAPHAT, the ships were wrecked at Ezion Geber (1 Ki. 22:48; 2 Chr. 20:35–37). There is no deep harbor, and the strong northerly winds coming down the ARABAH make its use as a port difficult.

The Edomites apparently captured Elath when they rebelled against King JEHORAM (2 Ki. 8:20), for AMAZIAH is said to have rebuilt the city and restored it to Judah (2 Ki. 14:22). His son, King UZZIAH (Azariah), apparently completed the rebuilding (2 Chr. 26:2), but under the reign of AHAZ the town was lost to the Arameans (NRSV by conjecture reads "Edom" rather than "Aram"), and the Edomites reoccupied it (2 Ki. 16:6). There is evidence that Elath continued to play an important role long after OT times. The site is thought to be a short distance SE of Tell el-Kheleifeh, which is widely identified with Ezion Geber. The modern Israeli town of Eilat shares the same general locale, but the Jordanian town of Aqabah may be covering the ancient biblical site. (See N. Glueck, *Rivers in the Desert* [1959], 157–63; G. D. Pratico in *BASOR* 259 [Summer 1985]: 1–32.)   R. L. ALDEN

El-Berith el´bi-rith´ (אֵל בְּרִית *H451*, "God of the covenant"). A god worshiped at SHECHEM, in whose temple some of the Shechemites took refuge when ABIMELECH destroyed the city (Jdg. 9:46; KJV, "the god Berith"). It is possibly an alternate name for the god BAAL BERITH.

El Bethel el-beth´uhl (אֵל בֵּית־אֵל *H450*, "the God [of] Bethel"). The name that JACOB, after his return from PADDAN ARAM, gave to the altar he erected at BETHEL, "because it was there that God revealed himself to him when he was fleeing from his brother" (Gen. 35:7).

Elcia el-ki´uh. KJV Apoc. form of ELKIAH (Jdt. 8:1).

Eldaah el-day´uh (אֶלְדָּעָה *H456*, possibly "God has called"). Son of MIDIAN and grandson of ABRAham through KETURAH (Gen. 25:4 [cf. vv. 1–2]; 1 Chr. 1:33). The names of Keturah's sons and grandsons appear to function as the clan names of various ARABIAN tribes.

Eldad el′dad (אֶלְדָּד *H455*, possibly "God has loved" or "God is friend"). One of the seventy elders chosen to assist MOSES in leading the Israelites (Num. 11:26–27; possibly the same person as ELIDAD, 34:21). When Moses found that the discontent of the people, on the journey from Sinai toward Canaan, was hard to bear, he was commanded to choose seventy elders who would share the burden of administration (11:16–17). The elders gathered at the TABERNACLE, and the Spirit of the Lord came upon them and they prophesied. Two of those chosen, Eldad and Medad, remained in the camp, yet they received the same Spirit of prophecy (some argue that these two were not among the seventy; cf. the discussion in M. Noth, *Numbers: A Commentary*, OTL [1968], 90). JOSHUA was indignant because these two prophesied in the camp rather than at the tabernacle, but Moses refused to forbid them, remarking that he wished all the Lord's people were prophets (11:28–29). The imparting of some of the Spirit that was upon Moses indicates that the endowment of the leadership abilities was due to the direct operation of the Spirit of God. The prophesying, which occurred only once, appears to have been an outward sign of this spiritual gift. There is little clue as to the precise nature of the activity, but it is commonly held that it was a form of ecstatic experience (cf. 1 Sam. 19:23–24; cf. J. Lindblom, *Prophecy in Ancient Israel* [1962], 100–102; W. Eichrodt, *Theology of the Old Testament* [1967], 2:50–54). See ELDAD AND MEDAD (MODAD), BOOK OF; PROPHETS AND PROPHECY. G. GOLDSWORTHY

Eldad and Medad (Modad), Book of. All we know about Eldad and Medad is that they were among the seventy elders who were appointed by MOSES and who prophesied after the Spirit of God rested on them (Num. 11:26–27). See ELDAD. Nevertheless, a rich tradition grew up around them, and a pseudepigraphic work appeared that was purported to be the written transcript of their prophecies in the manner commonly known

An elder reads from the liturgies of the Feast of Shevuot (Pentecost) at the Western Wall of the temple mount.

from the various apocalypses of the post-Persian era. The only citation we have from this book is found in the 2nd-cent. Christian work, *Shepherd of Hermas* (*Vis.* 2.3.4): "'The Lord is near those that return [to him],' as it is written in the Book of Eldad and Modat [*en tō Eldad kai Mōdat* (Codex A has *Mōdad*)], who prophesied to the people in the wilderness." The Palestinian Targumic traditions have more extensive details on the story of Num. 11:24–29 and add several phrases about what was said by Eldad and Medad. *Targum Pseudo-Jonathan* has the phrase, "The Lord is close by them who are in the time of trial," and the context would indicate that they prophesied about the coming of GOG and MAGOG at the end time of Israel. W. WHITE, JR.

elder (OT). In Israel, the elders (Heb. *zāqēn* H2418, from the word for "beard," *zāqān* H2417) were adult men who gathered in popular assembly, or as a kind of council in every village. They also served as local rulers. Usually they were the heads of families, but probably were selected also on the basis of age, wisdom, ability, respect, or prowess. It is difficult to determine if the officials (Heb. *śar* H8569) were equivalent to the elders (see Num. 22:7, 14; Jdg. 8:6, 14 16; and cf. Job 29:9 with Prov. 31:23). Pharaoh had his elders (Gen. 50:7), and so did the Midianites and Moabites (Num. 22:7), and the Gibeonites (Josh. 9:11). The Greeks and Romans also had elders. A modern equivalent is the sheik of Arabia. (Cf. *NIDOTTE*, 1:1137–39.)

The origin of the elders in Hebrew history goes back to the nomadic period in the life of Israel before the occupation of Palestine, with the roots of the office probably in the individual home within the clan. The elders were already recognized as a part of the community during the period of bondage in Egypt (Exod. 3:16; 4:29). It was the elders (obviously the heads of the houses) who were instructed concerning the observance of the first PASSOVER in Egypt whereby the people might escape death (12:21). They were particularly associated with religious leadership (24:1, 9), including the offering of sacrifices (Lev. 4:15). Seventy elders were selected to share with Moses the burden of the people and were given part of the Spirit that rested on Moses (Num. 11:16–17). Elders are often mentioned alongside the priests (1 Ki. 8:3). There is one mention of elders of the priests (2 Ki. 19:2).

The elders served in various capacities. A principal function was to serve as judges in disputes or to dispense justice as they sat in the gates of the city (Deut. 22:15). The prophets demanded that respect for justice at the gate be shown (Amos 5:10–12; Zech. 8:16) and charged that the elders had become corrupt in their administration of justice. As members of what amounted to a popular court, the elders were not to bear false witness, accept gifts, or follow the majority in defiance of justice. Their responsibility was to condemn the guilty and acquit the innocent. Each town had its own elders (Deut. 19:12), who determined if a criminal should be turned over to the avenger to die, thus depriving him of the protection of the CITIES OF REFUGE. They determined whether a rebellious son should be stoned to death, and they participated in the execution of the sentence (21:18–21). They also adjudged the validity of a husband's charge that his bride was not a virgin (22:15). They settled cases concerning LEVIRATE LAW when a man did not want to marry his deceased brother's wife (25:7–10). The elders also served as witnesses to commercial transactions (Ruth 4:4) and as military leaders (Josh. 8:10; 1 Sam. 4:3).

Elders were involved in the selection of kings of the nation. They demanded that SAMUEL appoint for them their first king (1 Sam. 8:4–5) and participated in the anointing of DAVID as king over all Israel after the death of SAUL (2 Sam. 3:17; 5:3). It is most likely that it was the elders who gathered at SHECHEM after the death of SOLOMON to receive certain assurances from REHOBOAM before recognizing him as king. They apparently did not acknowledge the right of automatic succession by inheritance (1 Ki. 12). When JEZEBEL plotted the death of NABOTH, she wrote the elders and nobles of JEZREEL to provide false witnesses in order that NABOTH might be stoned to death (1 Ki. 21:8–11). Through the wise counsel of the elders, JEREMIAH's life was saved by remembering the prophecies of MICAH (Jer. 26:16–19). Elders were included among those carried into EXILE (Jer. 29:1; Ezek. 8:1).

Nothing is said about the organization of the councils of the elders of the tribes. Their number probably depended on the size of the local community; there were seventy-seven at SUCCOTH (Jdg. 8:14). It is quite unlikely that there was a council of elders of the entire nation selected from the elders of the various tribes. The elders seemed to occupy a continuing place of importance throughout the history of Israel, from their sojourn in Egypt to the postexilic period, when mention was made that they gave orders to assemble the people to deal with the question of foreign marriages (Ezra 10:8). The elders were able to survive the collapse of the royal institutions.

In the MARI archives of the 18th cent. B.C. down to the royal correspondence of the SARGON dynasty in the 8th, the elders appear as representatives of the people and defenders of their interests, but without administrative functions. In the HITTITE empire, the elders did control municipal affairs and settled local disputes in cooperation with the commander of the garrison. The Phoenician towns had their elders also, as nonbiblical documents attest for Byblos (GEBAL) and TYRE. (See J. Pedersen, *Israel: Its Life and Culture*, 2 vols. [1926–40]; R. de Vaux, *Ancient Israel* [1961]; H. Reviv, *The Elders in Ancient Israel: A Study of a Biblical Institution* [1989]; T. M. Willis, *The Elders of the City: A Study of the Elders-Laws in Deuteronomy* [2001].)   F. B. HUEY, JR.

elder (NT). The Greek term *presbyteros* G4565 (lit., "older person, old man," sometimes transliterated "presbyter"), which occurs over seventy times in the NT, designates three different groups: (a) In a few passages (e.g., Lk. 15:25; Acts 2:17) it refers to older individuals comparatively speaking. (b) Almost half of the occurrences (e.g., Matt. 15:2; Acts 4:5) refer to the religious-political leaders of JUDAISM. (c) The remaining references are to an ecclesiastical office in the apostolic period.

The Christian notion of church eldership has its roots in the history of Israel. See ELDER (OT). Sometime during the postexilic period, the office of elder became a regular position in the Jewish SYNAGOGUE. In the tractate *Sanhedrin* of the MISHNAH, the duties of this office are clearly outlined. The council of elders was responsible for the government of the Jewish community. In Jerusalem, the SANHEDRIN, a council composed of seventy-one elders, acted as the supreme court for all Judaism. In addition, the discoveries at QUMRAN have revealed a covenant community in which the office of elder functioned in much the same sense as it did in mainstream Judaism, and there are some parallels between that community and early Christianity (cf. B. Reicke in *The Scrolls and the New Testament*, ed. K. Stendahl [1957], 143–56). The *Manual of Discipline* (1QS VI, 8) speaks of the elder as being second in rank behind the priests. See DEAD SEA SCROLLS.

In the Lukan apostolic history, the Christian office of elder appears for the first time in Acts 11:30. The reference here is to the leaders of the church in JUDEA for whom a collection had been taken in the church at ANTIOCH OF SYRIA. Later we are told that PAUL appointed elders in every church (14:23). The exact nature of this apostolic ordination or appointment is not described except to imply that prayer and fasting were a part of the ritual. We may assume that this unexplained appearance, in contrast to the selection of the seven in Acts 6, implies a rather natural transition from the synagogue structure of Judaism to the organization of the early church (cf. 2:46).

The question over which Christians have been divided throughout the centuries is the relationship of the office of elder to the total ministry of the church. First, it should be noted that in several important ecclesiological passages the office of elder is not specifically mentioned. The offices of DEACON and BISHOP, as well as elder, are noticeably omitted in 1 Cor. 12:4–11, 28–30 (possibly "those with gifts of administration" in v. 28 refers to a sort of ruling elder). In a somewhat more definitive listing of church offices in Eph. 4:11, PASTORS and TEACHERS are among the titles used to describe these leaders. Second, the PASTORAL EPISTLES refer to only two offices: overseers or elders and deacons. In 1 Tim. 3:1–13, the text uses *episkopos* G2176 ("overseer, bishop") and *diakonos* G1356 ("servant, deacon"), whereas Tit. 1:5–9 seems to use the terms *episkopos* and *presbyteros* almost interchangeably. In the letter to the church at PHILIPPI, the salutation mentions only "overseers and deacons" (Phil. 1:1), and it should be noted that both terms are plural.

Two questions are raised by the NT evidence. First, what is the significance of the plurality of elders in the NT church? Second, what is the relationship of bishop or pastor to the office of elder? (1) In regard to the first question, it should be observed that two possible explanations are available. On the one hand, the existing structure of the synagogue with its plurality of elders is paralleled by the NT church organization. Even in Judaism there was a "head of the synagogue" (Heb. *rōʾš hakkĕneset*, Gk. *archisynagōgos* G801; see RULER OF THE SYNAGOGUE). The plurality in this case would not forbid the predominant leadership of one elder. There is in later church history a traceable development from a plurality of elders to a presiding bishop to an episcopal hierarchical structure. The nature of the early NT Christian assemblies, which often worshiped in the homes of the members, may also help to explain the plurality of elders. In other words, in a given community there might be a number of elders, each one responsible for the care of a particular congregation that met in his home or in the home of some other Christian in the congregation. Clear examples of this are found in the NT itself (cf. Rom. 16:3–5).

(2) As to the latter question, it already has been noted that by the time the Pastoral Epistles were written, the terms "bishop" and "elder" were used interchangeably (cf. 1 Tim. 3; Tit. 1). But even earlier in Paul's ministry (cf. Acts 20:17–38), when the apostle met with the elders of the Ephesian church, those two terms, plus the notion of "pastoring" or "shepherding," seem to be identified (cf. Acts 20:17 and 28). The idea of the elders serving as shepherds of the flock and overseeing the administration of the church helped to distinguish the title of the office from its practical functions. In other words, the term *elder* originally designated those who were naturally as well as spiritually older or more mature. Note that Paul makes specific mention that no one is to be admitted to the office of elder or bishop who is a "recent convert" or novice (cf. 1 Tim. 3:6). The other terms—pastor or shepherd and bishop or overseer—refer to the functions of this office in the church. An elder is, therefore, an older, spiritually more mature male member of the church who is responsible for the administration of the congregation. In this latter case, it is instructive that PETER refers to himself as an elder (1 Pet. 5:1). In the later postapostolic writings of the church, there is clear evidence that the offices of pastor or bishop and elder were the same (cf. *Didache* 10.6). See also CHURCH GOVERNMENT IN THE APOSTOLIC AGE.

Finally, it should be noted that the term also has a decidedly eschatological signification. In the Revelation of John, a select group is given the title "twenty-four elders," and they are called to share in the eschatological structure of redemption (Rev. 4:4, 10; 5:5–14; 7:11–13; 11:16; 14:3; 19:4). NT commentators have not been agreed as to the precise reference of these twenty-four elders but it may be suggested that this title points again to the Jewish (OT and rabbinic) origin of the office as well as to the dynamic relationship of Israel and the Church. The doubling of the number twelve may point to that spiritual unity that shall be fulfilled eschatologically and ecclesiologically in the final age.

(See further H. B. Swete, ed., *Essays on The Early History of the Church and the Ministry* [1921]; K. E. Kirk, ed., *The Apostolic Ministry* [1946]; W. Michaelis, *Das Ältestenamt der christlichen Gemeinde im Lichte der Heiligen Schrift* [1953]; R. A. Campbell, *The Elders: Seniority within Earliest Christianity* [1994]; R. T. Beckwith, *Elders in Every City: The Origin and Role of the Ordained Ministry* [2003]; B. Merkle, *The Elder and Overseer: One Office in the Early Church* [2003]; *TDNT*, 2:608–22; 6:651–81; *NIDNTT*, 1:188–201.) D. LAKE

Elead el´ee-uhd (אֶלְעָד *H537*, "God has testified"). Son of EPHRAIM (or possibly son of SHUTHELAH [#1] and grandson of Ephraim); he and EZER (prob. his brother), while raiding the livestock in GATH, were killed by the men of the city (1 Chr. 7:21). The passage has been interpreted variously (see discussion in KD, *Chronicles*, 139–41; cf. also G. N. Knoppers, *I Chronicles 1–9*, AB 12 [2004], 456 and 464–65). This tragedy in the family moved Ephraim to call his next son BERIAH, an allusion to the Hebrew word for "calamity" (v. 23).

Eleadah el´ee-ay´duh (אֶלְעָדָה *H538*, "God has adorned"). KJV Eladah. Son or, more probably, descendant of EPHRAIM; it is possible that his father's (as well as his son's) name was TAHATH (1 Chr. 7:20; the referent of the repeated phrase "his son" is ambiguous).

Elealeh el´ee-ay´luh (אֶלְעָלֵה *H542* and אֶלְעָלֵא *H541* [only Num. 32:37], possibly "God ascends"). A city in TRANSJORDAN on the S boundary of the region known as GILEAD. It lay over a mile NNE of HESHBON, almost due E of the northern tip of the DEAD SEA. It is identified with the modern site of el-ᶜAl. This region was disputed territory throughout the OT period. It was conquered by the Israelites as they occupied Transjordan, and Elealeh and surrounding towns were given to the tribe of REUBEN (Num. 32:3). They were rebuilt and given Israelite names (32:37–38). The Moabites soon reoccupied the area, and the territory was in dispute between AMMON and MOAB (Jdg. 11:13–33). Upon the death of AHAB (c. 850 B.C.), MESHA of Moab revolted; the territory thus became Moabite and remained so throughout the prophetic period. Elealeh and Heshbon are mentioned in both Isaiah's and Jeremiah's oracles of judgment on Moab (Isa. 15:4; 16:9; Jer. 48:34).

F. W. BUSH

The tabernacle furniture carried by the Kohathites included the seven-branched candlestick (menorah), the table for the showbread, and the incense altar.

Eleasa el´ee-ay´suh. KJV Apoc. form of ELASA (1 Macc. 9:5).

Eleasah el´ee-ay´suh (אֶלְעָשָׂה H543, "God has made"; see also ELASAH). (1) Son of Helez and descendant of JUDAH (1 Chr. 2:39–40).

(2) Son of Raphah and descendant of SAUL through JONATHAN (1 Chr. 8:37; 9:43).

D. H. MADVIG

Eleazar el´ee-ay´zuhr (אֶלְעָזָר H540, "God has helped"; Ἐλεάζαρ G1789; see also ELIEZER). (1) Son of AARON and ELISHEBA (Exod. 6:23). Two of Eleazar's brothers, NADAB and ABIHU, were killed when they offered "unauthorized fire before the LORD" (Lev. 10:1–11). Eleazar, the oldest remaining son, married a daughter of Putiel, otherwise unknown (Exod. 6:25). Eleazar evidently had the primogeniture rather than his younger brother, ITHAMAR. He succeeded in the high priestly office after his father's death (Num. 20:25–28; Deut. 10:6). Eleazar supervised the Kohathites (see KOHATH), who carried the ARK OF THE COVENANT and the holy furniture upon their shoulders on the march (Num. 3:30–32). He was also charged with the oversight of the TABERNACLE and its furniture, the oil, the incense, etc. (4:16). His brother Ithamar was over the Gershonites and Merarites (see GERSHON; MERARI), who transported the tabernacle curtains, boards, etc. (4:28, 33).

Eleazar was prominent after the rebellion of KORAH, DATHAN, and ABIRAM (Num. 16). He was the first appointed to prepare holy water from the ashes of the red heifer (19:4), and he served as high priest to JOSHUA (27:19–21). His son PHINEHAS carried the trumpets and other articles to battle in TRANSJORDAN (31:6). With Joshua, Eleazar divided the land of Palestine by lot (34:17; Josh. 14:1; 17:4). In later days, his son Phinehas evidently wore the mantle (Josh. 22:13; Jdg. 20:28). This line of priests is traced in the genealogies down to EZRA (1 Chr. 6:1–15; Ezra 7:1–5). For a time, and for reasons that are not clear, the descendants of Ithamar superseded those of Eleazar in the tabernacle of SHILOH. The priest ELI was of the house of Ithamar, but because of the wickedness of his house, his line was rejected.

In David's day the chief men of Eleazar's line were numbered sixteen to Ithamar's eight (1 Chr. 24:4). See PRIESTS AND LEVITES.

(2) Son of ABINADAB; he was consecrated to keep the ARK OF THE COVENANT after it was brought back from Philistia (1 Sam. 7:1).

(3) Son of Dodo the Ahohite and one of David's first three "mighty men" (2 Sam. 23:9; 1 Chr. 11:12). See discussion under SHAMMAH #4.

(4) Son of Mahli and descendant of LEVI through Merari; the text records twice that he died without sons (1 Chr. 23:21–22; 24:28). His daughters married the sons of his brother KISH.

(5) Son of Phinehas and a priest of the time of Ezra (Ezra 8:33; 1 Esd. 8:63; prob. the same as the temple singer mentioned in Neh. 12:42).

(6) One of the descendants of Parosh who agreed to put away their foreign wives (Ezra 10:25; 1 Esd. 9:26).

(7) A Jewish scribe who, at the age of ninety, became a martyr for refusing to eat pork (2 Macc. 6:18–31; 3 Macc. 6:1, 16; 4 Macc. 1:8 [and often in this book]).

(8) Son of MATTATHIAS, surnamed Avaran (1 Macc. 2:5; 6:43; apparently also 2 Macc. 8:23, but see ESDRIS).

(9) Father of a certain Jason; the latter was one of the ambassadors that Judas MACCABEE sent to Rome (1 Macc. 8:17).

(10) Father of Jeshua (usually referred to as Jesus ben Sirach), author of the book of ECCLESIASTICUS (Sir. 50:27 NRSV, which follows the Heb. text; the Gk. text is ambiguous, but possibly means "Jesus son of Sirach, son of Eleazar").

(11) Son of Eliud, included in Matthew's GENEALOGY OF JESUS (Matt. 1:15).

Note further that KJV reads "Eleazar" elsewhere in the APOCRYPHA (1 Esd. 8:43; 9:19; see ELIEZER) and that JOSEPHUS mentions as many as nine other men who bore the same name. Special importance attaches to the high priest Eleazar, son of Simon the Just (see J. C. VanderKam, *From Joshua to Caiaphas: High Priests after the Exile* [2004], 157–67), and to one of the leaders in the first Jewish revolt against Rome (see WARS, JEWISH; ZEALOT). R. L. Harris

Eleazurus el´ee-uh-zoor´uhs. KJV Apoc. form of ELIASHIB (1 Esd. 9:24).

election. The English term *elect*, when used as a verb (Heb. *bāḥar* H1047 and Gk. *eklegomai* G1721, both meaning "to choose, select"), denotes the action whereby an individual or group is chosen for a specific purpose. As an adjective (cf. Heb. *bāḥîr* H1040, Gk. *eklektos* G1723), it is used to characterize the individual or group chosen. The corresponding substantive is *election* (*eklogē* G1724). Though the verb can be used with reference to human action (cf. Lk. 10:42; 14:7; Acts 6:5), yet it is with God's action we are concerned when we use these terms. It is particularly upon the differentiation involved for human beings that thought is focused, and Scripture is permeated with this emphasis.

I. Theocratic election. Israel as a people was chosen by God for special favor and privilege and set apart from all the nations of the earth (Deut. 4:37; 7:6–7; 10:15; 14:2; 1 Ki. 3:8; Pss. 33:12; 76:1–2; 105:6, 43; 135:4; Isa. 41:8–9; 43:20–22; 44:1–2; 45:4; cf. also Gen. 18:19; Exod. 2:25; Jer. 31:3–4; Hos. 11:1; Amos 3:2; Mal. 1:2). With respect to this election the following considerations are to be noted.

A. It proceeded from God's love. The election of Israel originated in God's love, and this love was not constrained by any eminence in might or righteousness belonging to the people. Israel was "the fewest of all peoples," and it was also a rebellious and stiff-necked nation (Deut. 4:37; 7:6–8; 9:4–13). It was, therefore, of his own sovereign good pleasure that God loved them and took delight in them. Election arose from the free determinations of his loving will.

B. It was unto separation. The goal of election was separation from all other nations so that Israel might be holy and a people for God's own possession (Deut. 14:2; Pss. 33:12; 135:4), a people formed for himself to show forth his praise (Isa. 43:1, 7, 21). Repeatedly in the history of Israel it had been declared through prophets and demonstrated in the events of providence that Israel had not only been chosen to show forth God's praise but had also been increased, preserved, and restored for his name's sake (Exod. 9:16; 32:9–14; Ps. 106:8, 47; Isa. 43:25; 48:9–11; 63:12–14; Ezek. 36:21–24).

C. It was unto obedience. Another purpose of election was obedience in the bond of COVENANT fidelity (Exod. 19:4–6; 20:2–17; 24:7; Lev. 18:4–5; 19:2–4; 20:7, 8; Deut. 14:1–2; Ps. 147:19–20). Israel's privilege could never be divorced from the corresponding obligations nor from the curses incident to unfaithfulness (Deut. 27:1–26; Amos 3:2).

D. It became specialized. The election became more specialized in reference to certain tribes and persons for distinct functions and prerogatives (Num. 16:5; Deut. 18:1–5; 1 Sam. 10:24; 2 Sam. 6:21; 2 Chr. 6:6; Ps. 78:68).

E. It did not guarantee the eternal salvation of all who were comprised in it. Of itself, therefore, it is to be distinguished from the more specific and particularized election that is unto and commensurate with SALVATION. This principle was exemplified in the OT (cf. 1 Ki. 19:18; Ps. 95:8–11; Isa. 1:9; 10:22–23). It is made more perspicuous in the NT. "They are not all Israel, that are of Israel" (Rom. 9:6 ASV; cf. 9:7–13; 11:7–10; Heb. 4:2–7). There are, however, two important observations to be made.

(a) Though the ethnic election did not insure salvation, it is not to be depreciated. "What advantage then hath the Jew? or what is the profit of circumcision? Much every way: first of all, that they were intrusted with the oracles of God" (Rom. 3:1, 2 ASV). To Israel pertained "the adoption, and the glory, and the covenants, and the giving of the law, and the service of God, and the promises" (Rom. 9:4 ASV). The election of Israel was the channel through which God was pleased to administer his saving grace and in the fullness of time fulfill his redemptive purpose for all nations (cf. Gen. 12:3; 22:18). Within this context Christ came (Rom. 1:3; 9:5; Gal. 4:4).

(b) The ethnic election must not be dissociated from the particular election that is unto salvation. Within the context of the former there were always those who were elected to salvation, and the blessings and privileges dispensed in terms of the ethnic election provided the means through which particular election came to expression and achieved its purpose. Furthermore, at the center of the administration which constituted the ethnic election was "the election of grace" (cf. Rom. 11:5) insuring the salvation of those who were the children of God and the true seed (cf. 9:7–8). This is verified in the history of the OT by the faithful in all generations.

II. Messianic election. This subject refers to the election of Christ (Ps. 89:19; Isa. 42:1; 1 Pet. 2:4, 6; cf. Isa. 28:16; Lk. 23:35). The Father's witness to Christ on the occasion of the baptism by John (Matt. 3:17; Mk. 1:11; Lk. 3:22) and also at the transfiguration of Jesus (Matt. 17:5; Lk. 9:35) bears directly on this election. The words "in whom I am well pleased" should be taken to mean "on whom my good pleasure has come to rest," and the word "chosen" in Lk. 9:35 points to this conclusion. The Father's good pleasure rested on the Son for messianic appointment and investiture. The various passages cited above are in distinctly messianic contexts—chosen out of the people for kingly rule (Ps. 89:19), elect as Servant (Isa. 42:1; cf. Ps. 2:6) and as the living chief cornerstone and sure foundation (Isa. 28:16; 1 Pet. 2:4, 6). This implies that the election must be conceived of within the economy of salvation and is concerned with the office to which the Son of God is appointed in order to bring to fruition God's saving purpose. We have no warrant to assume or affirm that Christ's election is the precondition of the election of men and women unto salvation even though, as will be noted, the latter was election in Christ (Eph. 1:4). It is, however, of paramount significance that God the Father is the author of both and thus Christ and the elect are all of one (Heb. 2:11).

III. Soteric election. Though closely related to the foregoing aspects, election to salvation is distinct. It is distinct from Israel's ethnic election in that it insures the salvation of its objects; and it is distinct from Christ's election in that the latter is not to salvation but to office for the accomplishing of salvation. In the OT much emphasis falls on ethnic election. In the NT ethnic election recedes to the background and the terms *elect* and *election*, when the action of God in reference to men is in view, are used with few exceptions (cf. Acts 13:17; Rom. 11:28) of the election unto life and salvation. The revelatory data establish its characterizing features.

A. Eternal. Paul is explicit to this effect: the election in Christ was "before the foundation of the world" (Eph. 1:4 ASV). The same is implied when Paul says that God "saved us, and called us with a holy calling, not according to our works, but according to his own purpose and grace, which was given us in Christ Jesus before times eternal" (2 Tim. 1:9 ASV). Whether the concluding clause refers to the "calling" or to the "grace" (the latter alternative is distinctly to be preferred), we are, in any case, pointed to God's eternal counsel; and the analogy of Paul's teaching (Eph. 1:4, 9; cf. Rom. 9:11) would require that this counsel include election. We cannot think in terms of ETERNITY because we are creatures and are temporally conditioned. But we must think of eternity, and it is of faith to believe that the fountain from which salvation emanates is the eternal purpose of God. All the other features of election cannot be properly construed except as they are related to its origin in the mystery of God's eternal will.

B. Sovereign. To suppose that election is constrained by or grounded in any differentiating quality or condition in human beings themselves would contradict the pervasive emphasis of Scripture upon the good pleasure of God. When Paul speaks of election in Christ before the foundation of the world, he explicates this still further as predestination in love unto adoption, and then informs us of that in accordance with which election and predestination took place: it is "according to the good pleasure of his will" (Eph. 1:4 ASV). These terms are sufficient to express God's sovereign determination as the explanation, but the apostle is not content. He reiterates the thought and piles up expressions that obviate the possibility of intruding a human factor as the conditioning element. Predestination, he repeats, is "according to the purpose of him who worketh all things after the counsel of his will" (v. 11 ASV).

The same accent on the pure sovereignty of God appears elsewhere in Paul. In meeting the objection that the differentiation impugns the justice of God, he appeals to the word of God to MOSES: "I will have mercy on whom I have mercy, and I will have compassion on whom I have compassion" (Rom. 9:15 ASV; cf. Exod. 33:19) and concludes: "So then it is not of him that willeth, nor of him that runneth, but of God that hath mercy" (Rom. 9:16 ASV). God's sovereign will is compared to the right of the potter over the clay in order to show, not that God deals with people as clay, but that God in his dealings with them has the right to differentiate and does so as the potter makes one vessel unto honor and another to dishonor (9:19–24). It may not be pleaded that this is only Pauline doctrine. The same principle of God's sovereign good pleasure appears in the teaching of our Lord and is predicated of the Father and of Jesus himself: "Yea, Father, for so it was well-pleasing in thy sight ... and he to whomsoever the Son willeth to reveal him" (Matt. 11:26–27 ASV). It is thus of the essence of the NT doctrine of election to characterize it as unconditional, and this means that the source and cause reside in God's sovereign good pleasure alone.

C. Gracious. That election is all of grace is implicit in its sovereign character. In addition to the emphasis upon the good pleasure of God, the Scripture expressly defines election as gracious. It is "the election of grace" (Rom. 11:5 KJV), and the ultimate design is stated to be the praise of the glory of God's grace (Eph. 1:7; cf. v. 12). GRACE and MERCY are correlative in the plan and execution of salvation, and when the apostle says that the election is "of God that hath mercy" (Rom. 9:16 KJV) and that he makes known "the riches of his glory upon vessels of mercy, which he afore prepared unto glory" (Rom. 9:23 ASV), the reference to mercy accentuates the gracious character. In the history of revelation this feature is verified in none more than in the choice of JACOB. All the circumstances converge to point up sovereign grace as opposed to any determining factor belonging to Jacob or to his conduct (cf. Rom. 9:11–13). In the theocratic election, Israelites were repeatedly reminded that they were not chosen because of their might or righteousness. In particular election, the choice of the foolish, weak, base, despised things of the world and the things that are not is to the end that no flesh should glory before God (1 Cor. 1:27–29; cf. Jas. 2:5). The eternal fount of salvation is the grace exhibited in its actual possession (cf. Eph. 2:8–10).

D. Immutable. "The purpose of God according to election" (Rom. 9:11 KJV) cannot mean less than electing purpose, and it is this that is said to stand. The thought is the security and inviolability of the purpose entailed in election. Various considerations show that the end contemplated in election cannot fail of realization. (a) When Jesus said that the days of tribulation would be shortened for the sake of the elect, the implication is that the elect must be saved (Matt. 24:22; Mk. 13:20). The gathering of the elect from the four winds, from one end of heaven to the other, at Jesus' coming in glory (Matt. 25:31; Mk. 13:27) is the assurance given by Jesus himself that at the end the elect will be gathered to him by a ministry that belongs to the people of God as the heirs of salvation, the ministry of the angels (cf. Matt. 18:10; Lk. 16:22; Heb. 1:14). (b) Since election involves determinate purpose, it is impossible to conceive of this purpose as defeated, and the purpose must be one correspondent with the grace of election itself. This is the tenor of various passages—elected to be holy (Eph. 1:4), predestinated unto adoption (1:5), chosen unto salvation (2 Thess. 2:13). The purpose according to which calling takes place (Rom. 8:28) is the one that issues in glorification (8:30). (c) The security of the elect is the theme of Rom. 8:33–39. The triumphant conclusion of vv. 38–39 is continuous with—and the climax to—the series of questions that begins with: "who shall lay anything to the charge of God's elect?" (v. 33). (d) The "vessels of mercy" (9:23) are, by reason of the context, to be identified with the elect (cf. v. 11) and they are said to be "afore prepared unto glory" in contrast with the "vessels of wrath fitted unto destruction" (v. 22 ASV).

E. In Christ. The only place where this feature is expressly intimated is Eph. 1:4. Much debate has arisen respecting the import of this thought. Since there are no parallel passages to shed light on the precise meaning, we shall have to be content with the unanswered questions that we are disposed to ask. Christian faith is resigned to the unsolved mysteries with which revelation confronts us. Election in Christ is, however, a datum of revelation to be received, and obscurity respecting certain implications should not be allowed to eclipse the truths and relationships involved of which we do know.

God the Father is the subject of election; it is his distinguishing action and he is the one who initiates the whole process of salvation. That the ultimate source resides in the Father is the sustained witness of Scripture, and faith is greatly impaired if this principle is not recognized and appreciated. But this action of the Father may not be dissociated from Christ nor conceived of apart from him. How the action of the Father relates itself to Christ we are not able to define; this belongs to his unsearchable counsel. Nevertheless it is of the essence of our faith in the Father's electing grace to know that in the fount of salvation the elect were never contemplated apart from Christ, that UNION WITH CHRIST was constituted in the decree of election. The people of God prize the mediation of Christ in all phases of redemption accomplished and applied. They should also prize the relation to Christ constituted in eternal election.

The election in Christ, as shown above, must be construed in messianic terms and as relevant to the economy of salvation. This economy has its source in election, and election is unto the salvation of its objects. It would be proper, therefore, to infer that Christ is contemplated in his messianic identity when it is said that the elect were chosen in him. Election must not be thought of apart from the salvation which it insures, and salvation is inconceivable apart from Christ. One must conclude that election in Christ and the election of Christ are correlative and therefore not only to be conjoined in our thought but intrinsically inseparable by reason of the terms in which Scripture enunciates them.

No phase of salvation is more basic or central than union with Christ. REDEMPTION once wrought is efficacious because the redeemed died with Christ and rose with him (Rom. 6:2–6). At the inception of salvation in possession is the call of the Father into the fellowship of Christ (1 Cor. 1:9). It is in Christ we have the FORGIVENESS of sins and are justified (Rom. 8:1; Eph. 1:7). In him we are given an INHERITANCE and in him sealed with the HOLY SPIRIT as the earnest of the inheritance (Eph. 1:11–14). In Christ believers die, and they are dead in Christ (1 Thess. 4:14, 16). In Christ they will be resurrected (1 Cor. 15:22). Together with Christ they will be glorified (Rom. 8:17). Election in Christ before the foundation of the world is the ASSURANCE given us that this union with Christ in all its aspects and in the richness of its grace has its source in a union constituted before times eternal. All spiritual blessing bestowed is in accordance with this election in Christ and flows from it. No spiritual blessing can be regarded as the precondition of election in Christ; every such blessing is its fruit.

The pivotal passage (Eph. 1:4) has no precise parallel. It may be that Rom. 8:29 expresses what is intended by election in Christ. If this is so, then "predestinated to be conformed to the image of his Son" defines the import of "in Christ," and the purpose of the latter is to inform us that election had not been conceived of or determined by God the Father except in terms of the end to which it was directed, namely, conformity to the image of the Father's only begotten. It can be said that this concept would provide a sufficient reason for the terms of Eph. 1:4. In any case, Rom. 8:29 informs us of what is implied in the election in Christ. Even if it is not intended as definition, no other text is comparably rich in setting forth what is involved. For conformity to the image of God's Son that he might be the firstborn among many brethren is the highest conceivable destiny for creatures.

F. Obligations. All of God's revealed counsel comes to us with demand. The kind of demand is determined by the specific content of what is revealed and by the relation we particularly sustain to God. It might be supposed that only believers should be concerned with election and that to unbelievers this truth of election is sealed. It is true that unbelievers cannot know themselves as elect of God, and it would be presumption for them to entertain the faith of their election or the conviction of their nonelection. But the truth of God's electing grace is revelation given to all to whom the gospel comes. Unbelievers should be stirred by concern to use the God-appointed means for their salvation to the end that through repentance and faith they may come to know that they are elect of God. Election should be encouragement rather than discouragement to sinners seeking salvation. Election assures them that God does save and that the grace which saves is the same grace that has its fountain in election. Furthermore, the free overture of grace in Christ to all without distinction comes from God's electing grace. Hence, it is a grave error to maintain that election either as to its truth or in its proclamation has no relevance to unbelievers. No part of God's counsel may be withheld from men. The obligations incident to election have special reference to believers, as follows.

1. They are to make their election sure (2 Pet. 1:10 KJV). This does not mean that they are to make it sure by effecting it, by causing it to be. It is God who elects, and no human agency enters into it or contributes to it. To make it sure means to make certain that it is a fact pertaining to ourselves. How this is to be done the Scripture makes plain. It is significant that a certain order is observed: "make your calling and election sure." Though calling is likewise an act of God and of God alone, it is an act addressed to us and comes within our experience. See CALL. Calling and election are always conjoined (Rom. 8:28–30; 2 Tim. 1:9), and from the certainty of our calling we may be assured of our election. Paul also indicates this order of thought (1 Thess. 1:3–4). It was from the "work of faith and labor of love and patience of hope," that he knew of the election of the saints, not by some esoteric or mystical insight into the hidden mysteries of God. The same process applies in the sphere of self-examination. Our thought proceeds upstream. Only from the fruit may we be assured of the ultimate root in divine election. Perplexity and confusion result from neglect of this order of human inquiry and faith.

2. The assurance of election should evoke gratitude and humility. Salvation is all of grace, and this grace takes its origin from the sovereign good pleasure of God the Father in the counsel of his will from eternal ages. This truth should fill the believer with adoring amazement that he should have been chosen in love for life everlasting. Election constrains the praise of the glory of God's grace (Eph. 1:6, 12, 14), and to make it the occasion for presumption or pride is to turn the grace of God into lasciviousness. "The thought of election should drive ransomed sinners to incessant doxologies and thanksgivings, as it does Paul" (J. I. Packer in *NBD*, 309). The fruit of gratitude is not license but constant care to "prove what is the good and acceptable and perfect will of God" (Rom. 12:2 ASV), to be "sincere and void of offence unto the day of Christ" (Phil. 1:10 KJV; cf. Col. 3:12).

3. The certainty of election imparts to the believer a sense of security. Bound up with election is the immutable purpose of God. In this resides the security of God's people, and nothing will separate them from the love of God in Christ Jesus (cf. Rom. 8:33–39). The praise of God's grace is intensified the more believers rely upon the faithfulness and power of God. His counsel stands fast and is the guarantee that the final issue will correspond with the love that election reveals.

IV. Election to office. In the NT, as in the OT, there is election to specialized functions. It is to be distinguished from election to salvation in two respects. First, election to salvation is specifically the action of God the Father, as has been noted repeatedly, whereas election to special office appears as that exercised by Christ (Lk. 16:13; Jn. 6:70; 15:16, 19; Acts 9:15; an exception is Acts 15:7, where Peter, by implication, is represented as chosen to bring the word of the gospel to the Gentiles).

Second, election to office is not *necessarily* concomitant with election to salvation. The choice of JUDAS ISCARIOT shows this truth. Judas's loss points up the necessity of observing the distinction because his loss is not to be construed as defeat of the election of grace or as an exception to the security it entails. The case of Judas likewise warns us that endowments for office are not of themselves the guarantee of salvation. The words of our Lord also advise us (Jn. 17:12; 18:9) that the example of Judas is not the rule in the institution of Christ. The rule is what we find in Jn. 15:16, 19, namely, that those chosen to office are not of the world and bear the fruit that abides (cf. also 17:16).

V. Elect angels. The angels that kept their first estate (cf. Jude 6) are called the elect angels (1 Tim. 5:21). See ANGEL. Election in their case differs from election as it pertains to human beings. These angels never sinned, and so their election was not to salvation or redemption but to preservation and confirmation. Although they perform manifold functions in connection with the salvation of sinners, their election was not in Christ nor were they predestinated to the unsurpassable glory designed for the elect of mankind (cf. Rom. 8:29; Heb. 2:5, 10–16). But the services they perform for the heirs of salvation (Heb. 1:14) are bound up with the confirmation they enjoy by reason of election. The elect of mankind in deriving untold blessing from the ministry of angels should know that this ministry the angels perform in gratitude to God for the election of which they are partakers. See also FOREKNOW; FOREORDAIN.

(For a more detailed treatment of election, see J. Calvin, *Institutes* 3.21–24; G. Zanchi [J. Zanchius], *The Doctrine of Absolute Predestination Stated and Asserted*, 2nd ed. [1779]; A. Booth, *The Reign of Grace* [1949], 53–97; H. H. Rowley, *The Biblical Doctrine of Election* [1950]; B. B. Warfield, "Predestination," in *Biblical and Theological Studies* [1952], 270–333; G. C. Berkouwer, *Divine Election* [1960]; P. K. Jewett, *Election and Predestination* [1985]; W. W. Klein, *The New Chosen People: A Corporate View of Election* [1990].)   J. MURRAY

elect lady. This title (Gk. *eklektē kyria*) occurs in the salutation of 2 Jn. 1 (NIV, "To the chosen lady"). It has been understood to identify a Christian woman, the acquaintance of the Elder who wrote the letter. Her sister may have been his hostess at the time he wrote. "Lady" in Greek was sometimes a proper noun, and some have thought it should have been transliterated ("To the elect Kyria"; cf. the name of GAIUS in 3 John). It is more likely that the reference was a figure of speech referring to the church to which the letter was addressed, as also the closing reference to "sister" would be understood as a designation for a Christian community. The symbolism of the church as a mother and its members as children may be hinted in 1 Pet. 5:13 also. The election of God's people was a prominent idea in the OT, and the figure of the messianic community as a woman bearing children may likewise be understood in Gal. 4:25 and Rev. 12.

H. L. DRUMWRIGHT, JR.

El Elohe Israel el-el´oh-heh-is´ray-uhl (אֵל אֱלֹהֵי יִשְׂרָאֵל H449, "God is the God of Israel"). The name of a confessional altar erected by JACOB, who appropriated the Canaanite deity name EL for use as one of the designations of the true God (Gen.

33:20). When the patriarch returned from PADDAN ARAM with his family, he purchased a portion of a field from the sons of HAMOR, on which he had camped (33:18–19) and on which he erected the altar. This Canaanite family ruled Shechem, which made it possible for Israel to have a permanent shrine here. See SHECHEM (PLACE). This later proved useful when the Israelites took the land under JOSHUA (Josh. 24:32).   E. B. SMICK

El Elyon el'el-yohn' (אֵל H446, "God," and עֶלְיוֹן H6610, "high, highest"). A name of God used especially in Genesis and the Psalms. When ABRAHAM paid tithes to MELCHIZEDEK, this is the name by which the latter worshiped God (Gen. 14:19–20). This priest, who was "like the Son of God" (Heb. 7:3), said to Abraham, "Blessed be Abram by God Most High, / Creator of heaven and earth. / And blessed be God Most High, / who delivered your enemies into your hand." The name occurs exactly in this form again in Ps. 78:35, but there are other Psalms where *Elyon* is combined with *Yahweh* or *Elohim* (see Pss. 7:17; 47:2; 57:2; 78:56). Frequently, *Elyon* (the Highest) is used by itself as a name for God (Num. 24:16; Deut. 32:8; 2 Sam. 22:14; Pss. 9:2; 18:13; 21:7; 46:4; 50:14; 73:11; 83:18; 87:5; 91:1, 9; 92:1; 107:11; Isa. 14:14; Lam. 3:35, 38). The sons of *Elyon* (Ps. 82:6) are either rulers of this earth (cf. Gen. 6:2) or they are the angel-princes of the heavenly sphere. The SEPTUAGINT renders the Hebrew expression with *hypsistos* G5736, "highest," a term also used by the NT writers (Mk. 5:7 et al.; it occurs mostly in Luke-Acts). (Cf. *DDD*, 293–99.) See also GOD, NAMES OF.   E. B. SMICK

elements, elemental spirit. These and similar English terms are used by the NRSV and other versions to render Greek *stoicheion* G5122 (in the NT always pl. *stoicheia*). The NIV uses "basic principles" or "principles" (Gal. 4:3, 9; Col. 2:8, 20; TNIV, "elemental spiritual forces"), but also "elements" (2 Pet. 3:10, 12) and "elementary truths" (for *ta stoicheia tēs archēs*, Heb. 5:12).

Various meanings are associated with this word in ancient religion and philosophy. It meant "one of a row," that is, anything standing in a series, such as the letters of the alphabet. It aptly described the rudiments ("ABCs") of a system of knowledge or religion, which is probably its meaning in Hebrews. This "logical-pedagogical" sense also may apply to the Galatian and possibly the Colossian passages.

A natural extension of the word was to the elemental substances of the world, which is its probable meaning in 2 Peter. In later times the heavenly bodies and signs of the Zodiac also were so designated. However, the evidence for this use is probably too late to allow its consideration, in spite of the references to "new moons" in Col. 2:16 and to calendar observances in Gal. 4:10.

The term also came to designate personified beings or "elemental spirits." These could be simply personifications of natural forces, or could be individualized as demons or, possibly, as angels. See ANGEL; DEMON. Recent scholarship has tended to interpret the language of Col. 2:8, 20 in this way. Some interpreters have so understood Gal. 4:3, 9 as well.

Discussions on the above options usually include some of the following considerations and assumptions. The context of the Galatians passage deals with the Jewish law. The idea of bondage to the elements parallels that of bondage to the law. The description of the elements as "weak and miserable" (Gal. 4:9; KJV, "weak and beggarly") may be compared to PAUL's statements regarding the weakness of the law, thwarted by human nature (e.g., Rom. 8:3). Therefore, the elements could here signify the rudiments of the law. (See H. N. Ridderbos, *Commentary on Galatians* [1953], 152–53; A. J. Bandstra, *The Law and the Elements of the World* [1964]. According to J. L. Martyn, *Galatians*, AB 33A [1997], 404, Paul shifts from the traditional pairs of elements—earth/air, fire/water—to those "listed in 3:28, emphatically the first pair, Jew and Gentile, and thus the Law and the Not-Law.") If the modifying phrase "of the world" (Gal. 4:3) is taken to refer to the astral or spirit sphere, it is conceivable that the angels (3:19) are the elemental spirits who transmitted the law and hence have held sinners in bondage (so B. Reicke in *JBL* 70 [1951]: 259–76). However, nowhere does Scripture say that angels tyrannize human beings.

The meaning of the term in Colossians may or may not be equivalent to that in Galatians (cf. E. Schweitzer in *JBL* 107 [1988]: 445–68). The interest in laws, rituals, astral phenomena, and seasons could have applied to either Jewish or Gentile heretics. The interpretation of the elements in Colossians as spirit beings may be supported by the reference to angels (Col. 2:18) and to "powers and authorities" (2:15, cf. v. 10; for this view, see esp. C. E. Arnold, *The Colossian Syncretism: The Interface between Christianity and Folk Belief at Colossae* [1996], ch. 6). The reference to the "new moon" may suggest reverence of spirits behind the heavenly bodies. Similarities between the heresy of Colossians and later Gnostic speculations renders it possible that Gnostic intermediary powers are alluded to here (see GNOSTICISM). It also must be noted, however, that much of the language of Colossians applies to Jewish custom (2:11, 14, 16). It may be argued also that the Christian has not "died" to angels or other spirits but to the law (2:20). The interpretation is, therefore, still open to debate (see further J. D. G. Dunn, *The Epistles to the Colossians and to Philemon: A Commentary on the Greek Text*, NIGTC [1996], 149–50). W. L. LIEFELD

Eleph ee´lif. KJV form of HAELEPH.

elephant. Elephants are not mentioned by name in the OT or the NT, but references to them are found in 1–3 Maccabees (Gk. *elephas*, e.g., 1 Macc. 6:30–37), and the biblical writers were certainly familiar with IVORY (e.g., 1 Ki. 10:18; Rev. 18:12). Extinct forms of elephant roamed Palestine during the Pleistocene period, but the nearest natural occurrence of the Asiatic elephant was in the upper reaches of the EUPHRATES, where it was exterminated by hunters late in the 1st millennium B.C. Although other teeth, especially of hippopotamuses, are sometimes used, true ivory comes only from elephant tusks, which are a pair of highly modified upper incisors. Ivory has been highly prized since the dawn of civilization and put to a wide range of ornamental uses, and these articles provide valuable archaeological material today. Most of the ivory used in Palestine and Syria came from the western race of the Asiatic elephant, now extinct, but supplies also came from INDIA by sea to BABYLON, via the Persian Gulf, or to ELATH, via the Gulf of AQABAH. The African elephant provided even heavier tusks, usually taken to Palestine overland via DEDAN in ARABIA, but routes were also developed across the Sahara, and merchants carried ivory, skins, and even live animals of various kinds, through the Roman era. (See F. S. Bodenheimer, *Animals and Man in Bible Lands*, 2 vols. [1960–72]; H. H. Scullard, *The Elephant in the Greek and Roman World* [1974].) G. S. CANSDALE

Elephantine el´uh-fan-ti´nee (Ἐλεφαντίνη, "Elephant place," translation of the older Egyptian name, *Iebew*, which later Aramaic papyri reproduced as יב). A settlement on an island in the NILE River, opposite ancient SYENE, with the modern name of Geziret Aswan (the "Island of Aswan"). It is best known because of certain papyri (see PAPYRUS) of the 5th cent. B.C. that were found there and that provide very important information about ancient ARAMAIC and about Jewish society in EGYPT.

I. Geographical location. Elephantine, known as "Yeb the fortress" (E. G. Kraeling, *The Brooklyn Museum Aramaic Papyri* [1969], 2.2 et al.), was located at the southern frontier of ancient Upper Egypt on a narrow palm-studded island in the NILE. It was just below the site of the modern Aswan High Dam. On the E bank was Syene, from whose quarries came the sought-after red granite (cf. the mineral name, *Syenite*). It served as a terminal port

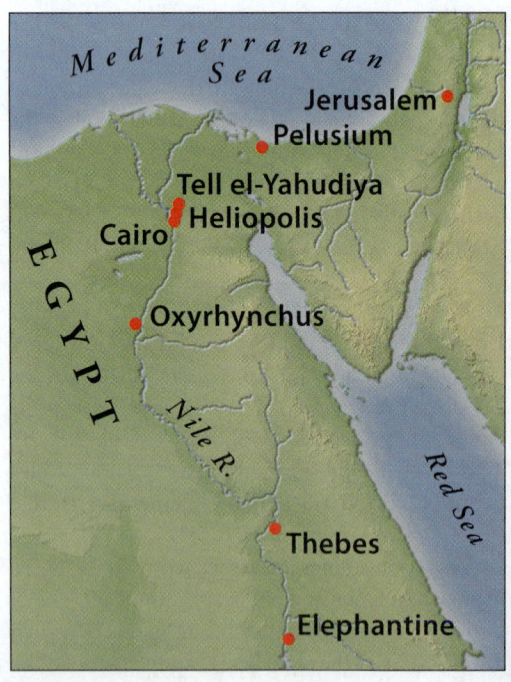

Cities of the Jewish Diaspora in Egypt.

for deep-water boat traffic because of the first cataract just above it (cf. the phrase "boatsman of the waters" [ibid., 12.20] for the importance of such workers in this territory in the Persian period).

II. Biblical references. Although Elephantine is not mentioned in the Bible, it is probably to be included in the reference to Syene (Ezek. 29:10; 30:6), just as HERODOTUS in referring to stone from Elephantine (*Hist.* 2.175) must have included Aswan where the stones were quarried. Two biblical names, SANBALLAT and JOHANAN (Neh. 2:10; 12:22; 13:28), are mentioned in the Elephantine Papyri (Kraeling, *Brooklyn Papyri*, 30.18, 29).

III. Archaeological finds and excavations. It was not until 1893 and later that significant quantities of Aramaic papyri and OSTRACA appeared, chiefly from Elephantine. Most of these are now published: Kraeling's edition includes the papyri purchased by C. E. Wilbour at Aswan in 1893; the edition of A. Cowley (*Aramaic Papyri of the Fifth Century B.C.* [1923]) includes the collections of J. Euting, H. Sayce, A. Cowley, and E. Sachau.

Excavations at Elephantine have been conducted by the French (beginning in 1902); the Germans (1906–1908); the Fathers of the Pontificio Istituto Biblico in Rome after World War I; and the Egyptian government (1932 and 1946). Among building structures excavated were the Temple of Khnum (of the 4th to the 2nd centuries B.C.) and an earlier mud-brick temple, the latter excavated by the Egyptians in 1948. These excavations have not produced conclusive evidence regarding the exact location of the 6th–5th cent. B.C. Jewish temple of Yahu that seems to have been located near an earlier temple of Khnum. (Cf. B. Porten in *JAOS* 81 [1961]: 38–42.)

IV. Early Egyptian history of the area. Elephantine was established as a fortress possibly as early as the 3rd dynasty, but surely so by the 6th dynasty, when powerful princes of Egypt resided there. During the periods of Egyptian history from the time when Nubia was subservient to Egypt (c. 1550–700 B.C.) down to the period of Persian domination (6th–5th centuries B.C.), Elephantine undoubtedly played an important part as a frontier military post against enemies and desert tribesmen and as a fortress for keeping open the trade routes to the S. The space was cramped at Elephantine, but a supplementary fort at Syene provided more adequate room there for social activity, so it is no wonder that inhabitants owned houses in both places, considering themselves as being both of Yeb and Syene (*Brooklyn Papyri*, 11).

Elephantine Island.

V. Background and history of the Jewish colony. When the Elephantine 5th-cent. B.C. Aramaic papyri were written, a Jewish group was already established with houses, families, and a temple dedicated to their God, Yahu, being a part of a military organization in service to the Persians, as is evidenced by letters addressed to such as "my brethren Yehoniah and his colleagues, the Judean garrison" (Cowley, *Aramaic Papyri*, 21.1; cf. also 22.1; 24.33). That the Jewish colony was well established at Elephantine before 525 is proved by the Bagoas letter's reference to the temple's existence before CAMBYSES invaded Egypt (ibid., 30). It was probably founded early in the reign of Pharaoh Apries (= HOPHRA, 588–566 B.C.) or later, the Egyptians evidently being friendly at that time to the erection of such a temple. Later, when the Jewish garrison served under the Persians, the Egyptian attitude must have changed, as they destroyed the temple in 410 B.C. (ibid., 30). That the Yahu structure was subsequently rebuilt has been shown by its mention of being in existence in 402 (Kraeling, *Brooklyn Papyri*, 12.18–19). The colony and its temple evidently came to an end in the reign of Nepherites I (399–393).

Aside from the Elephantine papyri, Aramaic-speaking Jews of Egypt have left only a little trace of their existence. There is a fragment of about 300 B.C. referring to Jewish persons (Cowley, *Aramaic Papyri*, 82) and a long papyrus of approximately the same time that includes Jewish and Greek names and mentions a Johanan the priest (ibid., 81), suggesting the presence of a temple, a possible successor to the one at Elephantine. In the 1st cent. A.D. there may have been Jews in the Elephantine area (Philo, *Flaccus* 43).

VI. Religious beliefs and practices of the Jewish colony. Aramaic religious syncretism seems to have been at work in the religious life at Elephantine, exampled by the listing, along with Yahu, of such other gods as Eshembethel and ʿAnathbethel (Cowley, *Aramaic Papyri*, 22). It has been noted that the component *bethel* ("house of God") in those names may be taken simply as a personification of El's house (in heaven) and as a substitute expression for EL. The Jewish colony did accommodate itself to the gods of the area, as is shown in the use of the polytheistic formula, "may the gods desire your welfare" (ibid., 21.2 et al.).

In spite of these compromises and tendencies to syncretism, the worship of Yahu, the God of Palestine, is seen in the use of the phrases "God in heaven" (Cowley, *Aramaic Papyri*, 38.2–3; 40.2; cf. Dan. 2:19, 44, where the same phrase is used) and "Yahweh of Hosts" (on an ostracon found by C. Clermont-Ganneau), which show the relationship of the colony to Jerusalem and its worship. It is quite possible that the colony observed the SABBATH (C-G ostracon 204, 152, 186), and it seems certain that they observed the Feast of Unleavened Bread and possibly also the PASSOVER (Cowley, *Aramaic Papyri*, 21).

(For other editions of the texts, see G. R. Driver, *Aramaic Documents of the Fifth Century B.C.*, 3rd ed. [1965]; B. Porten and A. Yardeni, *Textbook of Aramaic Documents from Ancient Egypt: Newly Copied, Edited and Translated into Hebrew and English*, 4 vols. [1986–99]; B. Porten et al., *The Elephantine Papyri in English: Three Millennia of Cross-Cultural Continuity and Change* [1996]; note also the detailed article by Porten in *ABD*, 2:445–55.)

W. H. MARE

Eleusis i-loo´sis (Ἐλευσίς). A town 14 mi. NW of ATHENS; it lies on a bay opposite the island of Salamis. A wealthy and independent town in the 8th and 7th centuries B.C., Eleusis later became a part of the city-state of Athens. It was the seat of the cult of the goddess Demeter and her daughter Persephone. Numerous archaeological remains of all periods from the Mycenaean period to Roman times survive. Most important are the temple and sacred precinct of the mystery cult. The ceremony connected with this cult was elaborate and aimed at stirring the emotions and promoting a feeling of purification and regeneration. Little is known of the rite, but it is likely that part of it involved the elevation of a sheaf of wheat, which symbolized death and rebirth. See MYSTERY RELIGIONS.

A. RUPPRECHT

Eleutherus i-loo´thuh-ruhs (Ἐλεύθερος, "free"). A river (modern Nahr el-Kebir) flowing from the LEBANON Mountains across PHOENICIA to the Mediterranean Sea. It marked the northern limit of two expeditions by Jonathan MACCABEE (1 Macc. 11:7; 12:30). Today it marks the N boundary between Lebanon and Syria.

Eleven, the. This term (Gk. *hoi hendeka*) is used in Luke–Acts with reference to the eleven apostles of Jesus who remained after the death of JUDAS ISCARIOT (Lk. 24:9, 33; Acts 2:14; cf. Matt. 28:16; Mk. 16:14; Acts 1:26). The use of the Greek definite article sets them apart as a group who retained their continuity with the Twelve. After the choice of MATTHIAS (Acts 1:26), they became "the Twelve" again (Acts 6:2; cf. Rev. 21:14). Listing the resurrection appearances of Jesus, PAUL wrote of "the Twelve" though there were at that time only eleven (1 Cor. 15:5).

E. RUSSELL

Elhanan el-hay´nuhn (אֶלְחָנָן H481, "God has been gracious"). **(1)** Son of JAARE-OREGIM, from BETHLEHEM; he was a member of DAVID's army in the wars against the PHILISTINES at GOB who slew GOLIATH the Gittite, the shaft of whose spear is said to have been like a weaver's rod (2 Sam. 21:19; KJV conjecturally reads "*the brother of* Goliath"). In Chronicles, however, the father of Elhanan is said to be JAIR, and his victim is Goliath's brother, LAHMI (1 Chr. 20:5). Various explanations have been proposed. (a) There were two separate giants named Goliath, one slain by David and one by Elhanan, or else *Goliath* is a generic name for a class of giants. (b) In Samuel, "Jaare-Oregim" is a scribal error for "Jair" (note that the last word in the verse is *ʾōrĕgîm*, "weavers") and the phrase "the brother of" has fallen out of the text. (c) In Chronicles, "Bethlehemite" (*bêt hallaḥmî*) was changed to "Lahmi the brother of" (*ʾet-laḥmî ʾăḥî*) in order to harmonize with Samuel (or "to reconcile two different claims found in Samuel"; see G. N. Knoppers, *I Chronicles 10–29* AB 12A [2004], 736). (d) A story originally dealing with Elhanan has been transferred to David, whose victim previously had been anonymous. (e) According to a tradition preserved by JEROME and in the TARGUM, David and Elhanan are identical, and some scholars have argued that *David*, rather than being a personal name, is a throne name (cf. J. Bright, *A History of Israel*, 4th ed. [2000], 192); although this solution is plausible, the alleged support for it from the occurrence of *dawidum* in the MARI texts (see V. Pákozdy in *ZAW* 68 [1956]: 257–59) has been generally abandoned.

(2) Son of Dodo, from Bethlehem; he was one of David's Thirty who ranked next to the Three (2 Sam. 23:24; 1 Chr. 11:26). A few scholars have identified him with #1 above. J. P. LEWIS

Eli ee′li (עֵלִי *H6603*, possibly "lofty" or "[God/Yahweh] is high"). The (high) priest at SHILOH during SAMUEL's youth (1 Sam. 1–4); he ruled Israel for forty years (4:18). Eli is a tragic figure of whom comparatively little is known. An old man with faithless sons, he raised the child Samuel as a temple servant. Eli is remembered for his ineffective protests against the sins of his sons, HOPHNI and PHINEHAS. Because of this failure the boy Samuel was called to pronounce Eli's doom and the removal of his family from the priestly office (3:11–14; cf. 2:27–36). Finally when the army in distress called for the ARK OF THE COVENANT to be used as a talisman of success in battle, Eli's two sons who bore it were killed, and the ark was captured. On hearing the bad news, Eli, a heavy man, fell off his seat by the city gate and died of a broken neck. He was ninety-eight years old.

The wilderness TABERNACLE had been pitched in Shiloh for many years (Josh. 18:1; Jdg. 18:31).

Eli was a descendant of AARON's son ITHAMAR, as one learns from the notation concerning his successor AHIMELECH (1 Sam. 22:20; 1 Ki. 2:27; 1 Chr. 24:3; cf. differently 2 Esd. 1:2). Eli's descent is not given in 1 Chr. 6, because after the judgment on Eli's family the priestly line was reckoned through Aaron's other son ELEAZAR. In David's day, after the slaughter of the house of Ahimelech (1 Sam. 22:18–20), it is noted that the priests descended from Eleazar outnumbered those from Ithamar, two to one (1 Chr. 24:4).

The sins of the sons of Eli included both sacrilege and immorality. They paid little attention to the proper ritual of the sacrifices and less to their meaning; they used the priestly office merely for livelihood (1 Sam. 2:12–16). The sordid story includes their sin with "the women who served at the entrance to the Tent of Meeting" (2:22). The words may suggest that Hophni and Phinehas had introduced into the tabernacle worship the sacred prostitution so common at the surrounding Canaanite shrines. In any case, their sin "was very great" (2:17).

There was also a better side to Eli. He exhorted HANNAH to godliness and blessed her for her faith. He doubtless had much to do with raising Samuel and did better with him than with his own sons. He presided over the tabernacle in Shiloh a long time. Archaeological investigation indicates that Shiloh was destroyed close to 1050 B.C., which is just the time of Eli's death. The tragedy of Shiloh was remembered until JEREMIAH's day (Jer. 7:12).

R. L. HARRIS

Eli, Eli, lama sabachthani ee′li ee′li lah′muh suh-bak′thuh-ni. A Semitic phrase meaning, "My God, my God, why have you forsaken me?" It comes from Ps. 22:1 and was quoted by Jesus on the cross; it occurs transliterated into Greek in Matt. 27:46 and Mk. 15:34. In Matthew, according to most MSS, the divine name (including the personal possessive suffix "my") is transliterated as *ēli*, which corresponds with the Hebrew form in Ps. 22 (*ʾēlî*), whereas Mark (and a few important MSS of Matthew; cf. NIV) has *elōi*, which seems to reflect an Aramaic form (*ʾĕlāhî*, but hebraized to *ʾĕlōhî*). The interrogative pronoun "why" can be either Hebrew (*lāmâ*) or Aramaic (*lĕmâ*; the Gk. MSS have variously *lema*, *lima*, and *lama*). The verb (plus suffix) *sabachthani*, however, can only be Aramaic (*sĕbaqtanni*, "you have forsaken me"; the Heb. MT has ʿ*ăzabtānî*). It is generally agreed that Jesus' mother tongue was ARAMAIC and that he naturally would have expressed himself with it at this time of suffering. If the original form in Matthew was *ēli*, it may be that the evangelist used it to make clearer why the people listening to Jesus thought he was crying out to Elijah; it is also possible, however, that someone speaking in Aramaic might use Hebrew terms for God.

The statement is of great theological significance for understanding the self-revelation of Jesus, who quoted from a messianic Psalm as his death was quickly approaching. The cry of the dying Messiah in the passion narratives highlights the mystery of Christ's two natures: the just covenant God was pouring judgment on his coeternal Son, the divine Suffering Servant. The sinless Christ was thus experiencing a separation from the Father that should have been the lot of sinners. "For you know the grace of our Lord Jesus Christ, that though he was rich, yet for your sakes he became poor, so that you through his poverty might become rich" (2 Cor. 8:9; cf. 5:21). See CHRISTOLOGY; CRUCIFIXION; DEATH OF CHRIST; JESUS CHRIST; TRINITY.

Eliab i-li´uhb (אֱלִיאָב *H482*, "my God is father"). (1) Son of Helon and a leader from the tribe of ZEBULUN, heading a division of 57,400 (Num. 2:7; 10:16). He was among those who assisted MOSES in taking a census of the Israelites (1:9) and who brought offerings to the Lord for the dedication of the TABERNACLE (7:24–29).

(2) Son (or descendant) of PALLU son of REUBEN. Two of Eliab's sons (or descendants), DATHAN and ABIRAM, were among the leaders who joined the Levite KORAH in his rebellion against Moses and Aaron in the wilderness and subsequently suffered judgment (Num. 16:1, 12; 26:8–9; Deut. 11:6).

(3) Son of Nahath and descendant of LEVI through KOHATH; he was also an ancestor of SAMUEL the prophet (1 Chr. 6:27). He is apparently the same as ELIEL (1 Chr. 6:34) and ELIHU (1 Sam. 1:1).

(4) Eldest son of JESSE whose physical appearance made him attractive to SAMUEL as a candidate for king but who at the Lord's prompting was passed in favor of his brother DAVID (1 Sam. 16:6;

1 Chr. 2:13). Eliab, who served SAUL in the Valley of ELAH when Goliath challenged the army, was angry at David for coming to the battle (1 Sam. 17:13, 28). He also was the father of ABIHAIL, wife of REHOBOAM (2 Chr. 11:18). On the assumption that ELIHU is a variant name, many scholars believe Eliab was the brother of David who later became an officer over the tribe of JUDAH (1 Chr. 27:18).

(5) A warrior, third in rank among the Gadite officers, who served DAVID at ZIKLAG (1 Chr. 12:9). These Gadites "were brave warriors, ready for battle and able to handle the shield and spear. Their faces were the faces of lions, and they were as swift as gazelles in the mountains" (v. 8).

(6) A Levite, listed among those who sang and who played lyres and harps when the ARK OF THE COVENANT was transferred, as arranged by David (1 Chr. 15:18, 20; 16:5).

(7) Son of Nathanael and ancestor of JUDITH, from the tribe of SIMEON (Jdt. 8:1, *Eliab*; cf. 9:2).

J. P. LEWIS

Eliada i-li´uh-duh (אֶלְיָדָע *H486*, "God knows"). (1) Son of DAVID; he is listed among those children born after David took concubines and wives in Jerusalem (2 Sam. 5:16; 1 Chr. 3:8). His original name was probably BEELIADA ("Baal [= the Lord] knows," 1 Chr. 14:6) and was later changed when the term BAAL became distasteful because of its associations with IDOLATRY.

(2) Father of REZON (1 Ki. 11:23; KJV, "Eliadah"); the latter seized DAMASCUS and became SOLOMON's adversary (vv. 24–25).

(3) A skilled soldier and a commander of 200,000 archers from BENJAMIN during the reign of JEHOSHAPHAT (2 Chr. 17:17). The large numbers in this passage (well over one million soldiers residing in Jerusalem) seem impossibly high. Some argue that the word for "thousand" (ʾ*elep H547*) should be "leader" (ʾ*allûp H477*), in which case Eliada commanded 200 specially trained soldiers. Alternatively, the term ʾ*elep* came to indicate a military unit of varying sizes (see discussion of this term under NUMBER II.B and NUMBERS, BOOK OF, VII.A). Others believe that the Chronicler deliberately uses hyperbole to indicate divine favor.   G. H. LIVINGSTON

Eliadas i-li´uh-duhs. See ELIOENAI #5.

Eliadun i-li′uh-duhn. KJV Apoc. form of ILIADUN (1 Esd. 5:58).

Eliah i-li′uh. KJV form of ELIJAH (only 1 Chr. 8:27; Ezra 10:26).

Eliahba i-li′uh-buh (אֱלִיחְבָּא *H494*, "God hides"). A Shaalbonite (i.e., from SHAALABBIN) and one of the "Thirty," DAVID's elite guard (2 Sam. 23:32; 1 Chr. 11:33).

Eliakim i-li′uh-kim (אֶלְיָקִים *H509*, "God raises up," i.e., "may God deliver" [cf. JEHOIAKIM]; Ἐλιακίμ *G1806*). (1) Son of HILKIAH and palace administrator under King HEZEKIAH (2 Ki. 18:18—19:7; Isa. 36:3—37:7; called "Jehoiakim" in Bar. 1:7 [KJV, "Joachim"]). Eliakim, with two others (Shebna and Joah), was selected to negotiate with the besieging Assyrian army in 701 B.C. The trio objected to the Assyrian commander's use of Hebrew instead of Aramaic in the public conference, but to no avail. After hearing the repeated demands that Jerusalem surrender, they relayed the message to the king with great sorrow, and the king in turn sent these officials to inquire of the prophet ISAIAH. Contrasted with SHEBNA, Eliakim receives very high commendation from the Lord: "He will be a father to those who live in Jerusalem and to the house of Judah. I will place on his shoulder the key to the house of David; what he opens no one can shut, and what he shuts no one can open. I will drive him like a peg into a firm place; he will be a seat of honor for the house of his father" (Isa. 22:20–24). See also KEYS, POWER OF THE.

(2) Son of JOSIAH and one of the last kings of Judah (2 Ki. 23:34–37 et al.). See JEHOIAKIM.

(3) One of the priests who, with their trumpets, participated in the dedication of the wall of Jerusalem under the leadership of NEHEMIAH (Neh. 12:41).

(4) Son of Abiud, included in Matthew's GENEALOGY OF JESUS CHRIST (Matt. 1:13).

(5) Son of Melea, included in Luke's GENEALOGY OF JESUS CHRIST (Lk. 3:30).

D. H. LIVINGSTON

Eliali i-li′uh-li. KJV Apoc. form of ELIALIS (1 Esd. 9:34).

Elialis i-li′uh-lis (Ελιαλις [as emended by Rahlfs; most MSS Ελιαλι]). KJV Eliali. One of the descendants of Bani who agreed to put away their foreign wives and children (1 Esd. 9:34; he is not mentioned in the parallel, Ezra 10:34–37).

Eliam i-li′uhm (אֱלִיעָם *H500*, "God is [my] kinsman"). (1) The father of BATHSHEBA, who became David's wife (2 Sam. 11:3; in 1 Chr. 3:5 he is called AMMIEL [note that the two names have the same meaning, but with the components reversed]). The fact that Bathsheba is identified first as Eliam's daughter and then as URIAH's wife may indicate that Eliam was a person of some significance. According to some scholars, this Eliam should be identified with #2 below (see *ABD*, 2:460, and cf. *b. Sanh.* 69b and 101b).

(2) Son of AHITHOPHEL of Gilo and a member of DAVID's Thirty, the military élite of the nation (2 Sam. 23:34). This man is also called AHIJAH ("my brother is Yahweh") the Pelonite (1 Chr. 11:36).

G. H. LIVINGSTON

Eliaonias i-li′uh-oh-ni′uhs. KJV Apoc. form of ELIEHOENAI (1 Esd. 8:31).

Elias i-li′uhs. KJV NT form of ELIJAH.

Eliasaph i-li′uh-saf (אֶלְיָסָף *H498*, "God has added"). (1) Son of DEUEL (or REUEL) and a leader of the tribe of GAD, heading a division of 45,650 (Num. 2:14; 10:20). He was among those who assisted Moses in taking a census of the Israelites (1:14) and who brought offerings to the Lord for the dedication of the tabernacle (7:42–47).

(2) Son of Lael and the leader of the Levitical clan descended from GERSHON during the time of MOSES (Num. 3:24). The Gershonites were responsible for the care of the TABERNACLE (vv. 25–26).

G. H. LIVINGSTON

Eliashib i-li′uh-shib (אֶלְיָשִׁיב *H513*, "God has restored"). (1) A priest chosen during the time of DAVID to head the eleventh of the twenty-four courses of priests who took turns serving in the sanctuary (1 Chr. 24:12).

(2) A high priest during the time of NEHEMIAH who helped to rebuild the SHEEP GATE (Neh. 3:1,

20–21). Reference is made to his son Joiada and to a grandson who married SANBALLAT's daughter (13:28). This Eliashib may be the same priest who incurred NEHEMIAH's displeasure because he made a temple storage area into special living quarters for TOBIAH (13:4–9). He may also be the father (grandfather?) of a certain Jehohanan (Johanan) who provided a room for EZRA's mourning (Ezra 10:6; 1 Esd. 9:1 [KJV, "Eliasib"]; cf. Neh. 12:10–11 [where "Jonathan" should perhaps be read "Johanan"], 22–23), but this identification is tied to the disputed question regarding the date of Ezra's mission (see E. M. Yamauchi in *EBC*, 4:582; J. C. VanderKam, *From Joshua to Caiaphas: High Priests after the Exile* [2004], 49–53).

(3) A singer among the Levites during the time of Ezra (Ezra 10:24; 1 Esd. 9:24 [KJV, "Eleazurus"]). He pledged to put away his foreign wife and children when commanded to do so.

(4) One of the descendants of Zattu who agreed to put away their foreign wives (Ezra 10:27; 1 Esd. 9:28 [KJV, "Elisimus"]).

(5) One of the descendants of Bani who agreed to put away their foreign wives (Ezra 10:36; 1 Esd. 9:34 [KJV, "Enasibus"]).

(6) Son of Elioenai and descendant of DAVID through ZERUBBABEL (1 Chr. 3:24).

G. H. LIVINGSTON

Eliasib i-li′uh-sib. KJV Apoc. form of ELIASHIB (1 Esd. 9:1).

Eliasis i-li′uh-sis (Ελιασις). One of the sons of Bani who agreed to put away their foreign wives (1 Esd. 9:34; he is not mentioned in the parallel, Ezra 10:34–37).

Eliathah i-li′uh-thuh (אֱלִיאָתָה *H484*, אֱלִיָּתָה *H517*, "God has come"). Son of HEMAN, the king's seer (1 Chr. 25:4). The fourteen sons of Heman, along with the sons of Asaph and Jeduthun, were set apart "for the ministry of prophesying, accompanied by harps, lyres and cymbals" (v. 1). The assignment of duty was done by lot, and the twentieth lot fell to Eliathah, his sons, and his relatives (25:27). D. H. MADVIG

Elidad i-li′dad (אֱלִידָד *H485*, possibly "my God has loved" or "my God is friend"). Son of Kislon, from the tribe of BENJAMIN (Num. 34:21). He was one of the leaders chosen by God to divide the land of Canaan on the W side of the Jordan for the inheritance of the ten tribes. Elidad may be the same as ELDAD, who together with Medad prophesied in the camp of Israel (Num. 11:26–27). J. B. SCOTT

Eliehoenai i-li′uh-hoh-ee′ni אֱלִיהוֹעֵינַי *H492*, "to Yahweh are my eyes [looking]"). **(1)** Son of Meshelemiah, a Levite (1 Chr. 26:3; KJV, "Elioenai"). Meshelemiah and his seven sons were Korahites (i.e., descendants of LEVI through KORAH) appointed as doorkeepers in the time of DAVID.

(2) Son of Zerahiah and descendant of PAHATH-MOAB; he was at the head of two hundred men who returned from the EXILE with EZRA (Ezra 8:4 [KJV, "Elihoenai"]; 1 Esd. 8:31 [KJV, "Eliaonias"]).

J. B. SCOTT

Eliel i-li′uhl (אֱלִיאֵל *H483*, "my God is God"). **(1)** Son of Toah; he was a descendant of LEVI through KOHATH and an ancestor of SAMUEL the prophet and of HEMAN the musician (1 Chr. 6:34). He is probably the same as ELIAB (1 Chr. 6:27) and ELIHU (1 Sam. 1:1).

(2) One of the family heads in the eastern half of the tribe of Manasseh (1 Chr. 5:24; see MANASSEH, TRIBE OF). He and others are described as "brave warriors, famous men, and heads of their families. But they were unfaithful to the God of their fathers and prostituted themselves to the gods of the peoples of the land" (vv. 24b–25).

(3) Son of Shimei; Benjamite family head who lived in Jerusalem in David's day (1 Chr. 8:20; cf. v. 28).

(4) Son of Shashak; another Benjamite family head who lived in Jerusalem in David's day (1 Chr. 8:22; cf. v. 28).

(5) A MAHAVITE included among David's mighty warriors (1 Chr. 11:46).

(6) One of David's mighty warriors (1 Chr. 11:47, apparently different from Eliel the Mahavite, v. 46).

(7) A warrior, seventh in rank among the Gadite officers who served David at ZIKLAG (1 Chr. 12:9). These Gadites "were brave warriors, ready for battle and able to handle the shield and spear. Their faces were the faces of lions, and they were as swift as gazelles in the mountains" (v. 8). It is possible that this Eliel is the same as either #5 or #6 above.

(8) A descendant of HEBRON and one of the Levitical leaders whom David brought together when the ARK OF THE COVENANT was transferred to Jerusalem (1 Chr. 15:9, 11).

(9) One of the temple supervisors under CONANIAH, who was in charge of the contributions during the reign of HEZEKIAH (2 Chr. 31:13).

J. B. SCOTT

Elienai el´ee-ee´ni (אֱלִיעֵנַי H501, short form of אֶלְיְהוֹעֵינַי H492, "to Yahweh are my eyes [looking]"). Son of Shimei; a Benjamite family head who lived in Jerusalem in DAVID's day (1 Chr. 8:20; cf. v. 28).

Eliezar. See ELIEZER.

Eliezer el´ee-ee´zuhr (אֱלִיעֶזֶר H499, "my God is [my] help"; Ἐλιέζερ G1808; see also ELEAZAR). **(1)** A servant (prob. the chief servant) in the household of Abram who was due to receive the inheritance if the latter had no sons (Gen. 15:2-3; see ABRAHAM). The text presents some difficulties. The phrase "the one who will inherit my estate" (KJV, "the steward of my house"; NRSV, "the heir of my house") renders Hebrew *bēn-mešeq bêtî*, lit., "the son of possession [?] of my house," an otherwise unknown expression. Moreover, the description "Eliezer of Damascus" (which some think distinguishes him from other servants of the same name) renders a phrase that has a peculiar word order, *dammeśeq ʾĕlîʿezer*, lit., "Damascus Eliezer" (for a discussion of possible explanations, see V. P. Hamilton, *The Book of Genesis: Chapters 1–17*, NICOT [1990], 420–22). There appears to be a wordplay between *mešeq* and *dammeśeq*, and some think there is also an allusion to the battle related in Gen. 14:14–16 (it has even been noted by rabbinic writers that the numerical value of the Heb. letters in "Eliezer" is 318). Whatever may be the precise explanation of 15:2, the following verse makes the meaning explicit, and the Lord's response is equally clear, "This man will not be your heir, but a son coming from your own body will be your heir" (v. 4). Eliezer was most likely the unnamed servant of Gen. 24 who was sent to get a wife for ISAAC from among Abraham's people. If so, he was a devout man of faith.

(2) The second son of MOSES by ZIPPORAH (Exod. 18:4; 1 Chr. 23:15). The name was given to him by Moses with this explanation, "My father's God was my helper [*ʿēzer* H6469]; he saved me from the sword of Pharaoh." Eliezer had only one son, Rehabiah, "but the sons of Rehabiah were very numerous" (1 Chr. 23:17). One of Eliezer's descendants was in charge of all the treasuries of the gifts that DAVID and the heads of the families of Israel had dedicated to God (26:25–26).

(3) Son of BEKER and grandson of BENJAMIN (1 Chr. 7:8).

(4) One of the priests appointed to blow the trumpet when David transferred the ARK OF THE COVENANT to Jerusalem (1 Chr. 15:24).

(5) Son of Zicri and chief officer of the tribe of REUBEN in David's day (1 Chr. 27:16).

(6) Son of Dodavahu and a prophet in JEHOSHAPHAT's time (2 Chr. 20:37). He was from MARESHAH and predicted the destruction of Jehoshaphat's fleet because the king had made alliance with AHAZIAH.

(7) One of a group of leaders sent by EZRA to Iddo to get attendants for the house of God (Ezra 8:16; the name is given as "Eleazar" in 1 Esd. 8:43 KJV [NRSV, "Eliezar"]).

(8) One of the descendants of JESHUAH who agreed to put away their foreign wives (Ezra 10:18; the name is given as "Eleazar" in 1 Esd. 9:19 KJV [NRSV, "Eliezar"]).

(9) One of the Levites who agreed to put away their foreign wives (Ezra 10:23; the parallel list in 1 Esd. 9:23 has "Jonah" at this point).

(10) One of the descendants of Harim who agreed to put away their foreign wives (Ezra 10:31; the parallel in 1 Esd. 9:32 has "Elionas").

(11) Son of Jorim, included in Luke's GENEALOGY OF JESUS CHRIST (Lk. 3:29).

J. B. SCOTT

Elihoenai el´ee-hoh-ee´ni. KJV form of ELIEHOENAI (Ezra 8:4).

Elihoreph el´uh-hoh´rif (אֱלִיחֹרֶף H495, possibly "my God rewards" or "Autumn God"). Son of Shisha and a chief official during SOLOMON's reign; he and his brother AHIJAH functioned as secretaries (1 Ki. 4:3; see SCRIBE). The suggestion that the Hebrew text indicates a title rather than a personal name (cf. J. A.

Montgomery, *A Critical and Exegetical Commentary on the Book of Kings*, ICC [1951], 113–17) requires emendation and has little in its favor. J. B. SCOTT

Elihu i-li′hyoo (אֱלִיהוּא *H491*, short form אֱלִיהוּ *H490*, "my God is he"). **(1)** Son of Tohu and ancestor of the prophet SAMUEL (1 Sam. 1:1). He is apparently the same as ELIAB (1 Chr. 6:27) and ELIEL (1 Chr. 6:34).

(2) One of the commanders from the tribe of Manasseh who deserted SAUL to join DAVID's army (1 Chr. 12:20).

(3) Son (or relative) of Shemaiah and grandson (or descendant) of OBED-EDOM (1 Chr. 26:7). This family of Korahites (see KORAH #3) belonged to one of the divisions of gatekeepers (v. 1).

(4) A brother of David who became an officer over the tribe of JUDAH (1 Chr. 27:18). Many scholars believe he should be identified with ELIAB, David's eldest brother (1 Sam. 16:6 et al.).

(5) Son of BARAKEL the Buzite and one of the friends who reasoned with JOB (Job 32:2; see BUZ). He became angry with Job's arguments and the failure of his three friends to respond to those arguments. Thereupon he launched into a speech in which he insisted that suffering has a disciplinary purpose (Job 32:6—37:24). G. H. LIVINGSTON

Elijah i-li′juh (אֵלִיָּהוּ *H489* and אֵלִיָּה *H488* [2 Ki. 1:3 et al.], "my God is Yahweh"; Ἠλίας *G2460*). KJV NT, Elias. Five men in the OT and APOCRYPHA are known by this name. **(1)** The famous 9th-cent. prophet who served in the northern kingdom in the reigns of AHAB and his son AHAZIAH (see below). **(2)** Son of Jeroham and descendant of BENJAMIN; he is listed among the heads of families who lived in Jerusalem (1 Chr. 8:27; KJV, "Eliah"). **(3)** One of the descendants of Harim who agreed to put away their foreign wives (Ezra 10:21). **(4)** One of the descendants of Elam who agreed to put away their foreign wives (Ezra 10:26; KJV, "Eliah"). **(5)** Son of Hilkiah and ancestor of JUDITH (Jdt. 8:1; KJV, "Eliu"). The rest of this article deals only with the prophet Elijah.

One of the outstanding heroes of the Bible, Elijah was prominent in Jewish prophetic expectations. In NT times, representatives of religious officialdom were sent to question JOHN THE BAPTIST concerning his identity and asked him if he was Elijah (Jn. 1:21, 25). Elijah's importance in God's plan for the ages is apparent from his predicted reappearing before "that great and dreadful day of the LORD" (Mal. 4:5) and from his presence with MOSES and the Lord upon the Mount of TRANSFIGURATION, where the three talked about the Lord's sacrificial death (Matt. 17:1–13; Mk. 9:2–13; Lk. 9:28–36).

I. Identity and personal characteristics. Nothing is known of Elijah's family and little of his geographic origin. The Bible states clearly that he was from GILEAD (1 Ki. 17:1), so he certainly lived at some time in TRANSJORDAN. He was also known as "the Tishbite," which indicates his association with a place named TISHBE, whether in NAPHTALI or E of the Jordan. (The MT of 1 Ki. 17:1 apparently means, "the Tishbite, from the settlers [*mittōšābê*] of Gilead" [cf. KJV], an unusual description; modern versions, following LXX, treat the unusual Hebrew word as a proper name, "from Tishbe.")

Elijah often is regarded as a wilderness dweller, probably because of his Transjordanian connections, his directed seclusion at the brook KERITH, his identifying apparel ("a man with a garment of hair and with a leather belt around his waist," 2 Ki. 1:8), and his NT associations with John the Baptist. His simple attire and diet did not prevent him from moving in more sophisticated circles, and he had repeated opportunities to address the king in person. Elijah was a man of great physical endurance; his feat of running before the chariot of AHAB from Mount Carmel (see CARMEL, MOUNT) to the entrance of JEZREEL demonstrates his excellent physical condition. His unhesitating devotion to the Lord made him a bold spokesman for what is right; he did not turn aside from vigorous denunciation of the actions of the hostile king, nor did he cringe before the fanatic opposition of the priests of BAAL.

The human side of Elijah is evidenced in his flight from the vindictive JEZEBEL, when she sent him the message that she would take his life. The combination of zealous bravery and human failure gives added weight to the power of prayer exemplified in this man of God; he was "a man just like us," but he "prayed earnestly" and God answered him

(Jas. 5:17–18). Elijah was not only an enthusiastic religious leader; he was also an ardent patriot, and his energetic service for God was coupled with a sincere concern for the nation of Israel. He also had strong interests in education; he continued the schools of the prophets founded by SAMUEL and he instructed Elisha in their administration. The "company [*lit.*, sons] of the prophets" regarded him with respect and affection. When he and ELISHA left JERICHO to cross the JORDAN, fifty of the sons of the prophets accompanied them and stood at some distance from them as the two crossed the river (2 Ki. 2:7). When Elisha returned alone, the group at Jericho insisted that fifty men be sent to look for him (vv. 16–18), though they had known that he was to be taken away.

II. Career and mighty works. The biblical account introduces Elijah with a dramatic and sudden appearance before King AHAB (1 Ki. 17:1), to whom he declared that there would be neither dew nor rain except at the prophet's word. After making this prediction, he was directed by the Lord to hide himself by the brook Kerith (possibly Wadi Yabis), E. of the Jordan, where he was supplied morning and evening with bread and meat carried by ravens. When the waters of the brook dried up, he was divinely commanded to go to ZAREPHATH (modern Sarafand, between TYRE and SIDON), where a widow was to feed him.

Arriving at Zarephath, Elijah found a widow whose supplies of meal and oil were nearly exhausted. He requested that she first bake a cake for him and later for herself and her son, and explained that this supply of flour and oil would last until the rains returned (1 Ki. 17:8–16). When the widow's son became ill and died, the widow blamed Elijah for her loss, but he took the boy to his room, prayed, and stretched himself upon the child's body three times. When the boy returned to life, Elijah presented him to the mother, who then recognized the divine mission of the prophet (17:17–24).

After three rainless years the Lord instructed Elijah to present himself before Ahab. On his way the prophet met OBADIAH, a man of faith who was in charge of the king's palace, and told him to inform the king that he had come. Ahab came to meet Elijah and greeted him as the "troubler of Israel" (1 Ki. 18:17), but he replied that it was Ahab who troubled Israel, because he had forsaken the Lord and followed BAAL. He further challenged Ahab to bring to Mount Carmel the 450 prophets of Baal and the 400 prophets of ASHERAH who were subsidized by Jezebel, the queen.

Those prophets assembled as directed, along with many of the people, and God's prophet proposed a test to determine who was the true God. The prophets of Baal were to prepare a meat offering and Elijah was to do the same; the god who answered by fire and consumed the offering would be God. The efforts of the Baal worshipers proved to be ineffectual, and Elijah mocked them as they tried to induce Baal to receive their offering. Finally he took charge, repaired an old altar of the Lord, prepared his offering, and instructed the people to pour four jars of water on it three times, so that the water soaked the prospective offering and everything about it. When he prayed, God answered with fire from heaven and consumed the offering, the wood, the altar, and even the dust and water about the altar. Then he commanded that the false prophets should be seized and slain, so they were put to death by the KISHON Valley.

Elijah next announced to Ahab that a great rain was about to fall. The prophet went to the top of Carmel and prayed. He ordered his servant to go look toward the sea, and upon the servant's seventh trip of inspection a small cloud was seen. Ahab was told to make ready his chariot before the rain

After confronting the prophets of Baal, Elijah fled to Horeb. The cypress trees at the bottom of the photo mark the traditional site of Elijah's spring. (View to the SW.)

stopped him. The sky grew dark, and soon wind and a heavy downpour arrived, but Elijah ran all the way to the entrance of Jezreel in front of Ahab's chariot and ahead of the storm (1 Ki. 18:41–46).

When Jezebel heard of the death of the false prophets, she swore vengeance on the prophet, who decided to flee, going S to BEERSHEBA and into the wilderness. Overcome by fatigue and strain, he despaired of life, but an angel provided food and drink for him and encouraged him to go on to Mount Horeb in SINAI, where he found shelter in a cave. While Elijah was at Sinai, the Lord spoke to him and, after sending a powerful wind, an earthquake, and a fire, revealed himself to the prophet in "a gentle whisper." The Lord told him to anoint HAZAEL to be king over Damascus, JEHU to be king of Israel, and ELISHA son of Shaphat to be Elijah's successor in the prophetic office. Elijah found Elisha plowing with twelve yoke of oxen. He cast his mantle upon the younger man, who immediately acknowledged the call but requested the privilege of bidding his parents farewell (1 Ki. 19:1–21). The appointments of Hazael and Jehu were not carried out in the time of service of Elijah, but were left for the ministry of Elisha (see 2 Ki. 8:7–15; 9:1–10). (See A. J. Hauser and R. Gregory, *From Carmel to Horeb: Elijah in Crisis* [1990].)

Sometime later, when Ahab coveted the vineyard of NABOTH to the point of frustration and illness, his wicked Tyrian wife arranged to gain the property by means of false charges that resulted in the execution of Naboth. Ahab went to take possession of the vineyard, but he was confronted by the fearless Elijah, who both accused Ahab of murder and predicted the violent deaths of Ahab and Jezebel. (Cf. A. S. Peake, *Elijah and Jezebel* [1927].) Ahab gave indication of repentance and the Lord informed the prophet that because of Ahab's changed attitude the predicted evil would be delayed (1 Ki. 21:1–27; when Jehu became king he used this prophecy as a basis for the annihilation of all of the relatives of Ahab, 2 Ki. 10:10, 17).

After the death of Ahab, his son AHAZIAH succeeded him. The new king accidentally fell from an upper room of his palace and was seriously injured. To learn of his prospects for recovery, he sent messengers to inquire of BAAL-ZEBUB. Elijah intercepted the messengers and sent them back with the prediction that the ruler was soon to die. Ahaziah determined from a description of the prophet that he was dealing with Elijah and he sent a contingent of fifty men to arrest him. Elijah responded to the demand of the captain of the group by having fire from heaven destroy the would-be captors (cf. Lk. 9:54, NIV mg.). A second unit suffered the same fate, but when a third captain arrived he pleaded for his life and the Lord directed Elijah to go with him in safety. The prophet personally gave to the king the prediction that he would not recover.

Although Elijah's ministry was almost exclusively concerned with the northern kingdom, the Chronicler records an incident that affected the Kingdom of Judah. When JEHORAM, the son of JEHOSHAPHAT, made high places and led Judah astray, Elijah sent him a letter informing him that

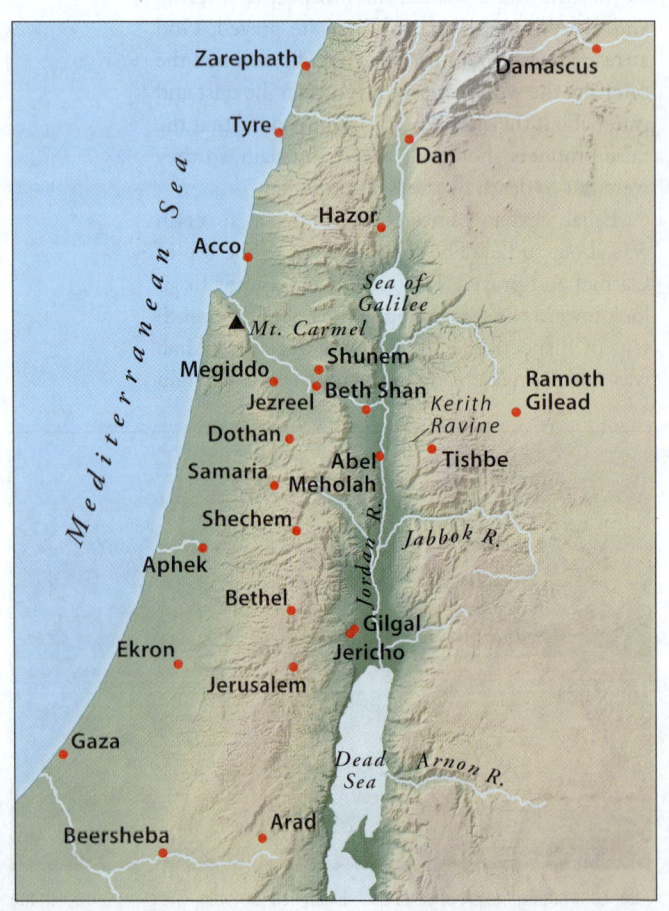

The ministry of Elijah and Elisha.

catastrophe would occur to the nation and to him because of his apostasy (2 Chr. 21:12–15).

III. The translation of Elijah.

When the time came for Elijah to be taken up to heaven, he and Elisha were engaged in their duties with the schools of the prophets, going from Gilgal to Bethel and to Jericho. At Gilgal and Bethel, Elijah asked Elisha to stay behind, but Elisha swore that he would not leave him. The sons of the prophets and Elisha knew that Elijah was to be taken away by the Lord. Leaving Jericho the two prophets crossed the Jordan miraculously; Elijah struck the water with his mantle, and the waters parted to make a way for them. He asked the younger man what he wanted as a favor from him. Elisha requested a double portion of the spirit of his master, and Elijah replied that the petition would be granted if Elisha saw him as he left. Suddenly they were separated by a chariot and horses of fire; a whirlwind caught up Elijah as Elisha watched and cried, "My father! My father! The chariots and horsemen of Israel!" (2 Ki. 2:1–12).

Elisha picked up the fallen mantle of his master, recrossed the Jordan, and went to Jericho, where the sons of the prophets remarked, "The spirit of Elijah is resting on Elisha" (2 Ki. 2:15). They kept urging that a search be made for Elijah; Elisha reluctantly permitted fifty men to go, but they returned without finding him.

IV. Significance of Elijah.

The life of Elijah centers on the conflict between the worship of the Lord and the religion of Baalism. There were many Baals in Israel, but during Ahab's time the prominent one was the deity of TYRE (prob. Baal-Melqart). Ahab married Jezebel, the daughter of ETHBAAL, king of Tyre and Sidon; she persecuted the prophets of the Lord (1 Ki. 18:3, 13; 19:10, 14), and promoted the cult of Baal in Israel (18:19). The drought indicated the impotence of Baal, a supposed nature-god, while the survival of Elijah showed God's power to care for his own, even at Zarephath, in the home territory of Baal-Melqart. The contest on Mount Carmel brought the nation of Israel to a place of decision, and the subsequent flight of Elijah took him to the scene of earlier revelation at Mount Horeb. The Naboth affair demonstrated the superior moral content of revealed religion, and the encounter between Ahaziah and Elijah showed that there was a God in Israel superior to Baal-Zebub of Ekron. Elijah was throughout the man of God, the prophet and the spokesman of God, and his life testified to the reality and power of the one true God.

The figure of Elijah is prominent in later Scriptures (for Jewish views more generally, see 1 Macc. 2:58; 4 Ezra 7:109 [= KJV 2 Esd. 7:39, "Helias"]; Sir. 48:1–12; cf. A. Wiener, *The Prophet Elijah in the Development of Judaism: A Depth-Psychological Study* [1978]). MALACHI foretold that Elijah would appear again before the day of the Lord (Mal. 4:5); this prediction has both NT and future fulfillment (cf. Rev. 11:6). The annunciatory angel declared to ZECHARIAH that his son, JOHN THE BAPTIST, would go before the Lord "in the spirit and power of Elijah" (Lk. 1:17). In response to some misguided questions, John denied that he was Elijah (Jn. 1:21, 25), probably because he did not see in his own ministry the significance that others were suggesting. Jesus, however, spoke of John as "the Elijah who was to come" (Matt. 11:14; 17:10–13; cf. further R. E. Brown, *The Gospel according to John I-XII*, AB 29 [1966], 47–49). Jesus himself was regarded by some of the Jews as Elijah (Matt. 16:14; Mk. 6:15; 8:28), and when he cried out "Eli" ("my God") on the cross, the bystanders thought he was calling Elijah (Matt. 27:46–49; Mk. 15:34–35).

In his ministry Jesus used the example of Elijah's reception by the widow of Zarephath to illustrate the scarcity of faith within Israel (Lk. 4:25–26). Moreover, Elijah appeared as a participant in the scene of the TRANSFIGURATION, when he and MOSES discussed with the Lord the "departure" that Jesus was to accomplish at Jerusalem (Lk. 9:31). On this occasion PETER suggested that three tabernacles should be built for Jesus, Moses, and Elijah (Matt. 17:4; Mk. 9:5; Lk. 9:33). PAUL, arguing for the principle of a REMNANT of Israel, referred to the 7,000 faithful worshipers in the time of Elijah (Rom. 11:2). The two witnesses of Rev. 11 are not mentioned by name, but the powers ascribed to them (see v. 6) are those of Moses and Elijah.

(In addition to the works mentioned in the body of the article, see F. Krummacher, *Elijah the Tishbite* [1838]; J. M. Lowrie, *Translated Prophet* [1868]; R. S. Wallace, *Elijah and Elisha* [1957]; L. L. Bronner, *The Stories of Elijah and Elisha* [1968];

G. Hentschel, *Die Elijaerzählungen: zum Verhältnis von histor. Geschehen u. geschichtl. Erfahrung* [1977]; R. B. Coote, ed., *Elijah and Elisha in Socioliterary Perspective* [1992]; R. B. Dillard, *Faith in the Face of Apostasy: The Gospel according to Elijah and Elisha* [1999]; *TDNT*, 2:928–41; *NIDOTTE*, 4:572–78.

C. E. DeVries

Elijah, Apocalypse of. Two pseudepigraphic works are known by this title. **(1)** One of them, sometimes referred to as *Apocalypse of Elijah (H)* and as *The Book of Elijah*, has survived in Hebrew, but whether it was originally composed in this language is uncertain. (For an edition of the text see A. Jellinek, *Bet ha-Midrash*, 2nd ed. [1938], 3:65–68; English trans. in G. Buchanan, *Revelation and Redemption: Jewish Documents of Deliverance from the Fall of Jerusalem to the Death of Nahmanides* [1978], 426–41; the fundamental study is M. Buttenwieser, *Die hebräische Elias-Apokalypse* [1897].) It purports to record eschatological secrets (e.g., future wars between Rome and Persia, the defeat of Gog and Magog, the resurrection of the dead, et al.) revealed to Elijah by the archangel Michael on Mount Carmel. It is a composite work put together possibly as late as the 7th cent., but some of its contents probably go back to the 3rd cent. Some think that an early form of this work was the text to which Origen (*Commentary on Matthew* 27:9) attributed Paul's quotation in 1 Cor. 2:9. (Cf. also the allusion by Epiphanius in *Pan.* 42.)

(2) A second and more important document, known as *Apocalypse of Elijah (C)*, was written originally in Greek c. A.D. 250 (perhaps earlier), but has survived only in Coptic (except for a small Greek fragment). It appears to combine Jewish and Christian traditions going back to the 2nd cent. or even the 1st. (See G. Steindorff, *Die Apokalypse des Elias* [1899]; J. M. Rosentiehl, *L'Apocalypse d'Elie* [1972]; English trans. with full introduction by O. S. Wintermute in *OTP*, 1:721–53.) The work is not written in typical apocalyptic form. It begins with a homiletical introduction on the need for fasting, followed by various predictions, such as the coming and eventual destruction of the Antichrist, the return and subsequent martyrdom of Elijah and Enoch, the persecution of believers, and the establishment of a millennial kingdom.

Elika i-liʹkuh (אֱלִיקָא *H508*, possibly short form of אֱלִיקָם, "God has arisen" [cf. *HALOT*, 1:56], but see J. D. Fowler, *Theophoric Personal Names in Ancient Hebrew* [1988], 142). A Harodite (see Harod) included among the Thirty, David's elite military force (2 Sam. 23:25; his name is omitted in the parallel list in 1 Chr. 11:27).

This oasis, Wadi Gharandel, may be the location of ancient Elim. (View to the N.)

Elim ee´lim (אֵילִם H396, "oaks" or "terebinths"). The second recorded stopping place of the Israelites on their journey from the RED SEA to SINAI (Exod. 15:27; 16:1). The exodus narrative recounts that they journeyed from the Red Sea to MARAH, and from there to Elim, where there were twelve springs of water and seventy palm trees. A similar description of the place is given in Num. 33:9–10. The exact location of this oasis is not certain, for it depends upon the location of Sinai. If the traditional identification of Mount Sinai in the lower part of the peninsula is correct, Elim is likely to be one of the oases in the wadis along the main route into that area (see I. Beit-Arieh in *BAR* 15/3 [1988]: 28–37). The place now known as Wadi Gharandel (55 mi. SE of Suez) is frequently suggested. Another proposal is ʿAyun Musa (9 mi. SE of Suez). The suggestion that the name Elim is a masculine variation of the feminine form Eloth (= ELATH, a location at the top of the Gulf of AQABAH) does not accord with the evidence of Num. 33:35, which indicates that this area was reached much later on the journey. (See J. Simons, *The Geographical and Topographical Texts of the Old Testament* [1959], 252–53.) G. GOLDSWORTHY

Elimelech i-lim´uh-lek (אֱלִימֶלֶךְ H497, "my God is king"). TNIV Elimelek. An Ephrathite from BETHLEHEM and the husband of NAOMI (Ruth 1:2). Because of a famine in their homeland, Elimelech took his family to sojourn in MOAB. After his death, his sons MAHLON and KILION married Moabite women, RUTH and ORPAH respectively. These two sons died also, and Naomi returned to Judah with Ruth. A man named BOAZ, being of the same clan as Elimelech (Ruth 2:1, 3) and having the right of kinship, purchased from Naomi the land formerly belonging to Elimelech. He also married Ruth, the daughter-in-law of Elimelech (Ruth 4:3, 9). From this marriage came DAVID, a great-grandson of Ruth and Boaz. By marriage, Ruth the Gentile was brought eventually into the line of promise from Abraham to Christ (Matt. 1:5; see GENEALOGY OF JESUS CHRIST). J. B. SCOTT

Elioenai el´ee-oh-ee´ni (אֶלְיוֹעֵינַי H493, "to Yahweh my eyes [look]"; short form of ELIEHOENAI). (1) Son of Neariah and postexilic descendant of DAVID through SOLOMON (1 Chr. 3:23–24).

(2) A clan leader from the tribe of SIMEON during the days of King HEZEKIAH (1 Chr. 4:36). His family and other Simeonite clans "increased greatly," and so they migrated to GEDOR "in search of pasture for their flocks." Subsequently they destroyed the Hamites and other inhabitants of the land (vv. 41–43).

(3) Son of BEKER and grandson of BENJAMIN (1 Chr. 7:8).

(4) Descendant of Pashhur; he was among the priests who put away their foreign wives (Ezra 10:22; 1 Esd. 9:22 [KJV, "Elionas"]). He may be the same as #6 below.

(5) One of the descendants of Zattu who agreed to put away their foreign wives (Ezra 10:27; called "Eliadas" in 1 Esd. 9:28).

(6) A postexilic priest who, with his trumpet, participated in the dedication of the wall of Jerusalem (Neh. 12:41). He may be the same as #4 above.

J. B. SCOTT

Elionas el´ee-oh´nuhs. (1) KJV Apoc. form of ELIOENAI (1 Esd. 9:22).

(2) One of the descendants of Annan who had married foreign women (1 Esd. 9:32; the parallel in Ezra 10:31 has ELIEZER).

Eliphal i-li´fuhl (אֱלִיפָל H503, "God has judged"). Son of Ur and one of the Thirty, DAVID's military elite (1 Chr. 11:35). Some scholars believe that the text has suffered scribal corruption and that his original name was ELIPHELET, as in the parallel list (2 Sam. 23:34). See discussion under AHASBAI.

Eliphalet i-lif´uh-lat. KJV alternate form of ELIPHELET.

Eliphaz el´i-faz (אֱלִיפַז H502, derivation disputed, possibly "God is victorious"). (1) Firstborn of ESAU; his mother was ADAH the HITTITE, and his sons became chiefs in EDOM (Gen. 36:4, 10–12, 15–16; 1 Chr. 1:35–36).

(2) An Edomite from TEMAN (or TEMA) and one of the friends who visited JOB to "sympathize with him and comfort him" (Job 2:11). Eliphaz may have been the eldest and the leader of the three friends (cf. 42:7–9). He was the first to address Job and is marked out by the courtesy with which he spoke (chs. 4–5). Like his friends, he took for granted that

Job must have committed some major sin, for only so could he explain his sufferings. But dominated, as he was, by a dream he had had of man's sinfulness before God (4:12–21), he tried to make it as easy as possible for Job to repent. In his second address (ch. 15) one senses the note of irritation caused by Job's rejection of his advice; the colors are darkened, and the applicability to Job heightened. The third address (ch. 22) is in many ways the bitterest of all addressed to Job, for Job had virtually denied the basis of his theology: without evidence, Eliphaz accuses him of all the worst sins according to the concepts of the time, but even then his kindliness breaks through in a final offer of hope.

H. L. ELLISON

Elipheleh i-lif′uh-luh. KJV form of ELIPH-ELEHU.

Eliphelehu i-lif′uh-lee′hyoo (אֱלִיפְלֵהוּ H504, possibly "may God distinguish him"). KJV Elipheleh. A Levite and one of the gatekeepers assigned to be a musician when DAVID made preparation to transfer the ARK OF THE COVENANT to Jerusalem (1 Chr. 15:18). He is called one of the brothers of the "second order" (NRSV; NIV, "next in rank") who followed HEMAN, ASAPH, and ETHAN. Eliphelehu and some others "were to play the harps, directing according to *sheminith*" (v. 21; see MUSIC VI.C).

E. B. SMICK

Eliphelet i-lif′uh-let (אֱלִיפֶלֶט H505, "my God is deliverance"; in 1 Chr. 14:5, אֶלְפֶּלֶט H550; cf. also PALTIEL). **(1)** Son of DAVID, listed as the last of eleven children born to him in Jerusalem (2 Sam. 5:16; KJV wrongly, "Eliphalet" [a pausal Heb. form affects the vowel]). His mother's name is not given, but the Chronicler includes him as the last of thirteen sons who were not born of a concubine (1 Chr. 3:8; see v. 9); another passage lists him as the last of thirteen children born in Jerusalem (14:7; KJV, "Eliphalet").

(2) Son of David, listed among the thirteen children born to him in Jerusalem not from a concubine (1 Chr. 3:6); he is elsewhere called "Elpelet" (14:5; KJV, "Elpalet"). Because his name (as well as Nogah) is not included in the parallel list in the MT (2 Sam. 5:16; but see P. K. McCarter, Jr., *II Samuel*, AB 9 [1984], 148), some scholars doubt his existence. Others suggest scribal corruption in Samuel and speculate that this Eliphelet died at an early age and that a later child (see #1 above) was named after him. (See the chart and discussion in J. W. Flanagan, *David's Social Drama: A Hologram of Israel's Early Iron Age* [1988], 348; J. B. Payne in *EBC*, 4:338.)

(3) Son of Ahasbai, from Maacah, and one of the Thirty, David's military elite (2 Sam. 23:34). Some scholars believe that he is the same as ELIPHAL son of Ur (1 Chr. 11:35). See discussion under AHASBAI.

(4) Third son of Eshek and a descendant of SAUL through JONATHAN (1 Chr. 8:39).

(5) A son or descendant of Adonikam who, with Juel, Shemaiah, and sixty other kindred, returned from Babylon with EZRA (Ezra 8:13).

(6) One of the sons or descendants of Hashum who had married foreign women (Ezra 10:33).

J. B. SCOTT

Elisabeth i-liz′uh-buhth. KJV form of ELIZABETH.

Eliseus el′uh-see′uhs. KJV NT form of ELISHA.

Elisha i-li′shuh (אֱלִישָׁע H515, "God is salvation" [cf. ELISHUA]; Ἐλισαῖος G1811). Son of Shaphat and the prophet who succeeded ELIJAH.

I. Origin, call, and early ministry. Elisha was born to a family that lived in ABEL MEHOLAH (possibly on the W side of the Jordan and about midway between the Dead Sea and the Sea of Galilee). Elisha's name appears for the first time in 1 Ki. 19:16, as the one Elijah was ordered to anoint as his successor. Elisha served primarily in the northern kingdom, from the latter part of the reign of AHAB into the rule of JOASH (roughly 850 to 800 B.C.).

The call of Elisha to the prophetic office was given by the prophet Elijah and was acted out in the manner characteristic of many of the OT prophets. As he passed by Elisha, Elijah cast his mantle upon him. Elisha immediately ran after Elijah and said that he would follow him as soon as he had said farewell to his parents. Like many other biblical heroes, Elisha was a man who was close to the soil. At the time of his call he was plowing with twelve yoke of oxen (1 Ki. 19:19; cf. 1 Sam. 11:5). Before leaving with Elijah, he made a feast for the people by butchering two of the oxen. While Elijah's ministry continued, Elisha served him (1 Ki. 19:21), much as JOSHUA had assisted MOSES. Elisha's name does not reappear in the narrative until 2 Ki. 2:1, which marks the beginning of the account of Elijah's ascension to heaven and prefaces the active role of Elisha as the full successor to Elijah.

Elisha accompanied the older man as he made his rounds to the prophetic schools ("sons of the prophets"). The two men went from GILGAL to BETHEL and JERICHO. At Gilgal and Jericho, Elijah tested the younger man by requesting him to stay while the old prophet went on, but Elisha swore that he would not leave his master. At Bethel and Jericho the sons of the prophets asked Elisha if he knew that the Lord would take Elijah away from him that day; Elisha knew it well. The two men proceeded to the Jordan, which they crossed by a miraculous parting of the waters. Beyond the river, Elijah asked what Elisha wanted as a favor from him. Elisha requested a double portion of the spirit of the older man; Elijah answered that this petition would be granted on the condition that Elisha saw him as he was being taken from him. While they walked and conversed, they were separated by a chariot of fire and horses of fire; Elijah was taken up by a whirlwind as the younger man watched.

II. The prophetic ministry of Elisha. Elisha was now the full-fledged successor of his master and he proceeded with the same type of ministry, serving the schools of the prophets, helping the needy, performing miracles, giving advice to the king, and acting as a spokesman for God. It has been remarked that the miraculous works of Elisha are double the number performed by his predecessor, thus indicating that he had, in fact, been endowed with a double portion of the spirit of Elijah. The deeds and miraculous works of Elisha are as follows.

The parting of the Jordan (2 Ki. 2:13–14). Upon the disappearance of Elijah, Elisha tore his own clothes into two pieces and took up the fallen mantle of Elijah. Returning to the river Jordan he faced his first crisis. With the cry, "Where now is the LORD, the God of Elijah?" he struck the waters with the mantle and the waters parted. When he came to Jericho the sons of the prophets recognized that the spirit of Elijah rested on him. They met him and did obeisance to him, but they insisted that he send a group to look for Elijah.

The purifying of the spring (2 Ki. 2:19–22). The people of Jericho complained to Elisha about the quality of the water, so he threw a bowl of salt into the spring and declared that the Lord had changed the fountain. The account states, "the water has remained wholesome to this day," and Elisha's

View across the Harod Valley toward Mt. Moreh. To the far left is the village of Shunem (at the SW base of Mt. Moreh), where the Lord used Elisha to raise the widow's son.

Fountain is still an important source of good water for the people around Jericho.

The cursing of the children (2 Ki. 2:23–24). While going from Jericho to Bethel, Elisha was mocked by small boys who made fun of his bald head. He "called down a curse on them in the name of the LORD. Then two bears came out of the woods and mauled forty-two of the youths."

The defeat of Moab (2 Ki. 3:1–27). JEHORAM king of Israel, JEHOSHAPHAT king of Judah, and the king of EDOM joined in a military campaign against MESHA king of MOAB. Marching through the wilderness of Edom, the armies found no water and were near despair. Jehoshaphat wished to consult a prophet of the Lord and was informed that Elisha was present. At first Elisha refused to counsel Jehoram, but after listening to a minstrel the prophet was empowered by the Lord to predict that the land would be filled with water and that the allies would defeat the Moabites (vv. 16–19). The next morning the prediction was fulfilled.

The widow's oil (2 Ki. 4:1–7). A poor widow complained to the prophet that a creditor was about to enslave her two children. When Elisha learned that the woman owned only a jar of oil, he instructed her to borrow many empty vessels from her neighbors, and then to go into her house with her sons and fill all of those vessels from the single jar of oil, so that she could pay her debts and live on the income from the oil.

The Shunammite's son (2 Ki. 4:8–37). A wealthy woman of SHUNEM proposed to her husband that they should build on their house a room for the prophet's use. In return for this kindness, Elisha foretold that in about a year the childless couple would have a son. A few years later this child suddenly became ill and died. The woman went to Mount Carmel to see "the man of God" (v. 25), who sent his servant, GEHAZI, to place the prophet's staff upon the face of the child, but this had no effect (vv. 29–31). Elisha then came to the house, prayed, and stretched himself upon the body of the child, who regained life and was presented again to his mother.

The poison pot (2 Ki. 4:38–41). During a famine, the prophet came to Gilgal and ordered his servants to prepare food for the sons of the prophets. When one of the men in ignorance placed some poisonous wild gourds into the cooking pot, Elisha threw meal into the mixture and the contents of the pot became harmless.

The multiplying of the loaves and grain (4:42–44). A man from BAAL SHALISHAH brought twenty barley loaves and some heads of grain, which Elisha told his servant to set before a hundred men. Though the servant protested, he finally obeyed and there was food enough and some left over.

The healing of Naaman (2 Ki. 5). NAAMAN, the commander of the Syrian army (see ARAM), was a leper (see DISEASE). A captive Israelite girl who served in Naaman's household suggested to his wife that the prophet in SAMARIA could heal Naaman. The king of Aram sent Naaman to Israel, with a letter of introduction to the king of Israel. The Israelite king panicked, but Elisha heard of the problem and cured the commander's leprosy by having Naaman dip seven times in the Jordan River. Naaman then acknowledged the God of Israel, but Gehazi could not resist requesting a reward for the healing and was punished by becoming a leper.

The floating ax head (2 Ki. 6:1–7). While constructing new buildings near the Jordan for the sons of the prophets, one of the men lost the head of a borrowed ax in the water. The prophet threw a stick into the water and the ax head floated and was recovered.

Divine espionage (2 Ki. 6:8–10). On several occasions when the Arameans and Israelites were at war, Elisha saved the Israelite king by warning him of the location of the Aramean army.

The Dothan episode (2 Ki. 6:11–23). The Arameans attempted to capture the prophet at DOTHAN, but the Lord protected him with chariots of fire. When the Lord struck the soldiers blind, Elisha brought them to Samaria, where they recovered their sight. Upon Elisha's advice, the king of Israel made a great feast for them and then released them.

Famine and feast in Samaria (2 Ki. 6:24—7:20). Under siege by the army of BEN-HADAD of Aram, Samaria suffered such famine that cannibalism was resorted to by several women. When the king proposed executing Elisha, the prophet foretold that there would be an abundance of food the next day. During the night the Arameans fled in disarray and four lepers discovered that the Aramean camp was forsaken; they reported the good news to the city, whose inhabitants soon enjoyed abundance.

The Shunammite's property (2 Ki. 8:1–6). During a seven-year famine in Israel, the Shunammite woman sojourned in Philistia, and upon her return wished to recover her house and land. The woman and her son arrived to make appeal to the king while Gehazi was relating her earlier story to that ruler, who secured the restoration of her property.

Elisha and Hazael (2 Ki. 8:7–15; cf. 1 Ki. 19:15). Ben-Hadad became ill and sent Hazael to the prophet to inquire about his recovery. Elisha's answer indicated that Hazael would become king of Aram; Hazael smothered his ailing master and seized the throne.

Elisha and Jehu (2 Ki. 9:1–3; cf. 1 Ki. 19:16). Elisha sent one of the sons of the prophets to Ramoth Gilead to anoint Jehu to be king of Israel.

Elisha and Joash (2 Ki. 13:14–19). During his final illness the prophet signified in a symbolic prophecy that Joash would defeat the Arameans.

The raising of a dead man (2 Ki. 13:21). Even after his death, a miracle is attributed to Elisha: a corpse hastily thrown into the grave of the prophet came to life when the body touched Elisha's bones. The unusual character of this and other miracles of Elisha has led many to regard the prophet's life as legendary. His deeds, however, may be a clue to the distinctive historical context in which he ministered.

Elisha is referred to once in the Apocrypha: "When Elijah was enveloped in the whirlwind, Elisha was filled with his spirit. He performed twice as many signs, and marvels with every utterance of his mouth. Never in his lifetime did he tremble before any ruler, nor could anyone intimidate him at all" (Sir. 48:12). In the NT Elisha is mentioned only once also: while preaching at Nazareth, the Lord used Elisha's healing of Naaman as an example of the scarcity of faith within Israel (Lk. 4:27). However, several features of Jesus' ministry have notable parallels with that of Elisha (cf. the raising of the son of Nain, Lk. 7:11–17, with that of the Shunammite's son, 2 Ki. 4:8–37; Nain and Shunem were in close proximity, on either side of Mt. Moreh).

(See further C. Geikie, *Old Testament Characters* [1888], 331–49; R. S. Wallace, *Elijah and Elisha* [1957]; L. L. Bronner, *The Stories of Elijah and Elisha* [1968]; R. B. Coote, ed., *Elijah and Elisha in Socioliterary Perspective* [1992]; R. B. Dillard, *Faith in the Face of Apostasy: The Gospel according to Elijah and Elisha* [1999].)   C. E. DeVries

Elishah i-lī′shuh (אֱלִישָׁה H511, meaning uncertain). Son or descendant of Javan and progenitor of a nation known by the same name (Gen. 10:4; 1 Chr. 1:7; Ezek. 27:7). Since Javan is the Hebrew word for the Greeks, Elishah is to be associated with them. Elishah and the other descendants of Javan are called "the maritime peoples" (*ʾiyyê haggôyim*, lit., "the coasts [or islands] of the nations," Gen. 10:5), and Tyre is said to have imported blue and purple dyes "from the coasts of Elishah" (Ezek. 27:7). Its association with Greece and Kittim (Cyprus) would seem to indicate a location in the area of the N Mediterranean. Josephus identified them with the Aeolians, an ancient people of Greek stock. Some have identified Elishah with Carthage in N Africa, because of the similarity between Elishah and Elissa (a Tyrian princess said to have founded Carthage). Many identify Elishah with Alashiya, one of the islands (prob. Cyprus) affected by the invading Sea Peoples (see *ANET*, 29, 262; *HALOT*, 1:54; *CANE*, 3:1435–36, 1447). Most probably Elishah in the Bible refers to the inhabitants of the islands of the Aegean Sea. Its close association with Javan, as well as its dye industry, which would necessitate close proximity to the sea, seem to support this general identification.   T. E. McComisky

Elishama i-lish′uh-muh (אֱלִישָׁמָע H514, "my God has heard"; cf. Shemaiah). (1) Son of Ammihud of the tribe of Ephraim (Num. 1:10). He was selected to help Moses as a representative from his tribe in the taking of the census. He is later described as "the leader of the people of Ephraim," with a division numbering 40,500 (2:18). In that capacity he brought his tribe's offering on the seventh day of the dedication of the altar (7:48–53). He was in command of the Ephraimite camp in the march through the wilderness (10:22). From 1 Chr. 7:26–27, one learns further that he was the father of Nun and grandfather of Joshua.

(2) Son of David, listed among eleven children born to him in Jerusalem (2 Sam. 5:16). His mother's name is not given, but the Chronicler includes him as one of the thirteen sons who were not born of a

concubine (1 Chr. 3:8); another passage lists him as one of thirteen children born in Jerusalem (14:7).

(3) Another son of David, listed among the thirteen children born to him in Jerusalem not from a concubine (1 Chr. 3:6 NRSV, following the MT); the NIV, on the basis of two Hebrew MSS and the parallels (2 Sam. 5:15; 1 Chr. 14:5), reads ELISHUA. See also ELIPHELET #2.

(4) Son of Jekamiah and descendant of JUDAH through PEREZ (1 Chr. 2:41). JEROME suggested that this Elishama is the same as #5 below.

(5) The grandfather of a certain ISHMAEL who killed GEDALIAH, the governor of Judah after the fall of Jerusalem (2 Ki. 25:25; Jer. 41:1).

(6) A royal secretary (see SCRIBE); he was one of the officials in the court of JEHOIAKIM who heard BARUCH read Jeremiah's scroll and urged the king not to burn the inspired prophecy (Jer. 36:12). Later the scroll was put in his chamber, where it remained until it was taken to be read to the king (36:20–21).

(7) A priest sent by JEHOSHAPHAT to teach God's book of the law in Judah (2 Chr. 17:8).

J. B. SCOTT

Elishaphat i-lish′uh-fat (אֱלִישָׁפָט *H516*, "my God has judged"; cf. JEHOSHAPHAT). Son of Zicri and one of five commanders of units of a hundred who helped JEHOIADA depose ATHALIAH and enthrone JOASH (2 Chr. 23:1).

Elisheba i-lish′uh-buh (אֱלִישֶׁבַע *H510*, "my God is [*or* makes] an oath" or "my God is abundance"). Daughter of Amminadab and wife of AARON (Exod. 6:23). Her brother NAHSHON was leader of the tribe of Judah (Num. 1:7; 2:3), so Elisheba was a Judahite. She bore four sons, one of whom, ELEAZAR, succeeded Aaron as high priest (Num. 20:25–28).

Elishua el′uh-shoo′uh (אֱלִישׁוּעַ *H512*, "God is salvation" [cf. ELISHA]). Son of DAVID, listed among eleven children born to him in Jerusalem (2 Sam. 5:16); another passage lists him as one of thirteen children born in Jerusalem (1 Chr. 14:7). Apparently the same son is called ELISHAMA in the MT of 1 Chr. 3:6, but this is probably a transcriptional error (note that "Elishama" occurs again in v. 8); thus the NIV reads "Elishua" here too on the basis of two Hebrew MSS and the parallel passages.

Elisimus i-lis′i-muhs. KJV Apoc. form of ELIASHIB (1 Esd. 9:28).

Eliu i-li′yoo. KJV Apoc. form of ELIJAH (Jdt. 8:1).

Eliud i-li′uhd (Ἐλιούδ *G1809*). Son of Akim, included in Matthew's GENEALOGY OF JESUS CHRIST (Matt. 1:14–15).

Elizabeth i-liz′uh-buhth (Ἐλισάβετ *G1810*, from Heb. אֱלִישֶׁבַע *H510*; see ELISHEBA). Wife of the priest ZECHARIAH and mother of JOHN THE BAPTIST (Lk. 1:5–7, 13, 24–25, 36, 40–45, 56–60). Like her husband, Elizabeth was of Aaronic descent; indeed, she had the same name as AARON's wife, ELISHEBA (Exod. 6:23). She and her husband are described as "upright in the sight of God, observing all the Lord's commandments and regulations blamelessly" (Lk. 1:6). Her BARRENNESS was a great trial to them, until an angel appeared to Zechariah and told him that in spite of their age, their prayer would be answered; moreover, their son would be the forerunner of the MESSIAH. The story is reminiscent of similar answers to prayer in the OT (see SARAH; HANNAH).

Elizabeth is called a "relative" of MARY, MOTHER OF JESUS (Lk. 1:36; Gk. *syngenis G5151*), but the term is too broad to indicate the precise nature of the relationship. When Mary came to visit her, the babe leaped in the womb of Elizabeth and, through the HOLY SPIRIT, Elizabeth told Mary how greatly blessed she was and expressed her amazement that God should honor her with this visit from the mother of her Lord. A few Old Latin MSS and other witnesses have "Elizabeth" (rather than "Mary") in v. 46, thus ascribing the MAGNIFICAT to her (this weak textual variant is accepted by some scholars; see *ExpTim* 41 [1929–30]: 266–67 and 42 [1930–31]: 188–90). S. BARABAS

Elizaphan, Elzaphan el′uh-zay′fan, el-zay′fan (אֱלִיצָפָן *H507*, short form אֶלְצָפָן *H553* "[my] God has hidden [*or* treasured *or* protected]"; cf. ZEPHANIAH). **(1)** Son of Uzziel and the leader of the Kohathites in the wilderness (Exod. 6:22 [Elzaphan]; Num. 3:30); the families descended from KOHATH "were responsible for the care of the ark" and the furniture of the TABERNACLE (v. 31). After NADAB and ABIHU offered unauthorized fire,

Elizaphan and his brother MISHAEL were directed by MOSES to take their relatives away from the sanctuary (Lev. 10:4 [Elzaphan]). His descendants are mentioned during the reigns of DAVID (1 Chr. 15:8) and HEZEKIAH (2 Chr. 29:13).

(2) Son of Parnach and the leader from the tribe of ZEBULUN who assisted Moses in dividing the land into future inheritance portions for each tribe (Num. 34:25). E. B. SMICK

Elizur i-li′zuhr (אֱלִיצוּר H506, "my God is a rock"). Son of Shedeur and the leader of the tribe of REUBEN who assisted MOSES in taking a census of the Israelite community (Num. 1:5). He commanded a division numbering 46,500 (2:10; 10:18), and he brought the offering of his tribe on the fourth day of the dedication of the altar (7:30–35).

Elkanah el-kay′nuh (אֶלְקָנָה H555, "God has taken possession" or "God has created"). A common name, especially among Levites descended from KORAH. In particular, several ancestors of the prophet SAMUEL, including his father, bore the name Elkanah. Because of ambiguities (and possible scribal corruptions) in the genealogical lists, some of the identifications are uncertain. After a discussion of the list in 1 Chr. 6:22–28 (MT vv. 7–15), C. F. Keil concludes that the enumeration "is not a continuous list of one Kohathite family, but contains only fragments of several Kohathite genealogies" (KD, *Chronicles*, 124; on the incongruities in the genealogy see G. N. Knoppers, *I Chronicles 1–9*, AB 12 [2004], 426–28).

(1) Son or descendant of Korah and head of a Levitical clan (Exod. 6:24; see v. 25). He may be the same as #2 below.

(2) Son of Assir and grandson of Korah; father (or ancestor) of Ebiasaph (1 Chr. 6:23). He is probably the same as #3 below.

(3) Father or ancestor of Amasai and Ahimoth (1 Chr. 6:25); he is also described as the son of Joel (v. 36).

(4) Son of AHIMOTH and grandson or descendant of #3 above (1 Chr. 6:26; Ahimoth must be the same as Mahath, v. 35).

(5) Son of Jeroham, descendant of #4 above, and father of Samuel (1 Chr. 6:27, 34). Elsewhere he is described as a "man from Ramathaim, a Zuphite from the hill country of Ephraim," and thus "an Ephraimite," not by descent but by virtue of the tribal territory where he lived (1 Sam. 1:1; the KJV has "Ramathaim-zophim"; see RAMAH #3). Elkanah had two wives: the favorite HANNAH, who was barren, and PENINNAH (1:2). Aside from those who had a royal claim, Elkanah is the only man in the Samuel–Kings narrative to have more than one wife—probably an indication of his wealth and social standing. He was also a godly man who made it a habit to visit the sanctuary in SHILOH every year (1:3). Hannah, brought to tears by Peninnah's taunting, prayed to God for a son whom she would return to the Lord. God answered her petition and she bore Samuel, who after being weaned was given to ELI the priest (1:28). Later Hannah bore to Elkanah other sons and daughters (2:20–21). Elkanah's great-grandson, HEMAN, became a leading musician in DAVID's day (1 Chr. 6:33).

(6) One of the two Levites who were appointed doorkeepers for the ARK OF THE COVENANT when it was transferred by David to Jerusalem (1 Chr. 15:23).

(7) One of several Korahite warriors who joined David at ZIKLAG (1 Chr. 12:6; cf. vv. 1–2). Some argue that Korah here is the name of a locality in the tribe of Benjamin (see BENJAMIN, TRIBE OF).

(8) A high official during the reign of AHAZ of Judah, described as second to the king in authority (2 Chr. 28:7). Because the people of Judah were unfaithful, the Lord allowed PEKAH king of Israel to inflict heavy casualties on the army of AHAZ. During the conflict Elkanah, along with a prince and another official, was killed by an Ephraimite warrior named Zicri.

(9) Grandfather or ancestor of Berekiah; the latter is listed among those Levites who first resettled in Jerusalem after the return of the Babylonian captivity (1 Chr. 9:16).

Elkiah el-ki′uh (Ελκια, from Heb. חִלְקִיָּה H2759; see HILKIAH). Son of Ananias and ancestor of JUDITH (Jdt. 8:1; KJV, "Elcia").

Elkosh el′kosh. See ELKOSHITE.

Elkoshite el′kosh-it (אֶלְקֹשִׁי H556). A term used to identify NAHUM the prophet (Nah. 1:1). It presumably refers to a town named Elkosh (cf. NRSV). Various identifications have been proposed, including (a) a site in GALILEE called Helcesaei or Elcesi, according to JEROME; (b) Al-Qush, a town in Mesopotamia N of Mosul near the TIGRIS River, where a so-called "tomb of Nahum" is found; (c) modern Beit Jibrin (ancient Eleutheropolis), a site about half-way between JERUSALEM and GAZA; (d) CAPERNAUM, which means "village of Nahum." There is no credible evidence to support any of these suggestions.   J. B. SCOTT

Ellasar el'uh-sahr (אֶלָּסָר *H536*, derivation uncertain). A kingdom ruled by Arioch, one of the allies of KEDORLAOMER, king of ELAM, in his raid on the Jordan valley in the time of ABRAHAM (Gen. 14:1). Earlier scholars, who considered the identifications of these kings as reasonably firm, believed that Arioch was the same as Eri-aku, king of Larsa (an important city in S MESOPOTAMIA). Further studies weakened this confidence, and some scholars argue that Ellasar should be identified with ASSHUR. For further discussion, see ARIOCH.   A. C. BOWLING

elm. This English term (referring to the *Ulmus campestris*) is used by the KJV once to render Hebrew ʾēlâ *H461* (Hos. 4:13). Modern versions more properly translate it "terebinth" (*Pistacia terebinthus*). See also OAK; POPLAR; TEREBINTH.
                                W. E. SHEWELL-COOPER

Elmadam el-may'duhm (Ἐλμαδάμ *G1825*; most MSS, Ἐλμωδάμ). KJV Elmodam. Son of Er, included in Luke's GENEALOGY OF JESUS CHRIST (Lk. 3:28).

Elnaam el-nay'uhm (אֶלְנַעַם *H534*, "God is pleasantness"). The father of Jeribai and Joshaviah, two of the mighty men of DAVID's army (1 Chr. 11:46); they are mentioned in a list of sixteen warriors (vv. 41b–47) beyond the military elite known as the Thirty (vv. 10–41=2 Sam. 23:8–39).

Elnathan el-nay'thuhn (אֶלְנָתָן *H535*, "God has given"; cf. NETHANEL). **(1)** Father of Nehushta, who was the wife of King JEHOIAKIM and the mother of King JEHOIACHIN (2 Ki. 24:8). It is often thought that this Elnathan is the same as #2 below.

(2) Son of ACBOR and an official during the reign of Jehoiakim (this king was possibly Elnathan's son-in-law; see #1 above). Elnathan and others were sent by the king to Egypt to bring back the prophet URIAH, who was then executed (Jer. 26:22). Elnathan was also one of the officials to whom was read JEREMIAH's scroll and who urged the king not to burn it, but to no avail (36:11–26). Elnathan's father was probably the Acbor who, with others, was commissioned by King JOSIAH to consult the prophetess HULDAH (2 Ki. 22:12–14).

(3) Three men named Elnathan—two of them described as leaders and the other one as wise (NIV, "men of learning")—are said to have been part of a group of eleven sent by EZRA to search for Levites (Ezra 8:16; cf. 1 Esd. 8:44 [LXX v. 43], which has only two names, *Elnatan* and *Ennatan* [KJV, "Alnathan" and "Eunatan"]). Because it seems unlikely that three different persons in a relatively small group would bear a name that is otherwise not frequent, some scholars suspect textual corruption. According to one view, the last two names, "Joiarib and Elnathan," should be omitted, following 1 Esdras (cf. "Jarib and Elnathan" earlier in the verse). If so, the group consisted of nine men, all of whom are described as "wise leaders" (*rāʾšîm mĕbînîm*).

Eloah, Elohim i-loh'uh, el'oh-him (אֱלוֹהַּ *H468*, אֱלֹהִים *H466*, prob. related to אֵל *H446* [see EL]). Two Hebrew names for God. The term *Eloah* occurs almost sixty times, mostly in poetic sections of the OT (e.g., Deut. 32:15, 17; Job 3:4 [and very frequently in this book]; Ps. 18:31; Dan. 11:37–39; et al.). The plural form *Elohim* is however the standard term, occurring over 2,200 times. When used for God in the OT, *Elohim* is most emphatically singular in meaning (e.g., Deut. 4:35, 39; 1 Ki. 8:60; 18:39; Isa. 45:18), and there is real probability that the Hebrews looked on it as a "plural of majesty." (The 14th-cent. B.C. Ugaritic literature appears to use a comparable plural when referring to a single deity; cf. M. Dahood, *Psalms I*, AB 16 [1966], XXIV and 43 et al. For the view that the ancient Canaanite term *ilānu* should be viewed as a "concretized abstract plural," see J. S. Burnett, *A Reassessment of Biblical Elohim* [2001], ch. 2. See further *DDD*, 285–88 and 352–65.) Often but not always when referring to the true God, the definite article is employed with the word in Hebrew, perhaps with the overtone, "the Mighty One."

The word *Elohim* is frequently used also to refer to heathen gods (Exod. 18:11; 20:23; 1 Sam. 4:8; 2 Ki. 18:33; et al.); less frequently it refers to a heathen god in the singular (e.g., Dagon, 1 Sam. 5:7; Chemosh, Jdg. 11:24; Baal, 1 Ki. 18:24). There are a number of references where the word can be rendered "magistrates," "judges," or "rulers." Noteworthy are Exod. 21:6, where a slave is said to be brought before "God" (NRSV) or perhaps "the judges" (NIV) to have his ear pierced, and Exod. 22:28, which possibly may be translated, "You shall not revile the magistrates [*ělōhîm*] or curse the ruler of your people" (cf. 1 Ki. 21:13). Other passages should be studied in this light (cf. 1 Sam. 2:25 and Jdg. 5:8). It is quite clear that the "sons of Elohim" are the angels in Job 1:6; 2:1; 38:7 (see Angel); the use of the same phrase in Gen. 6:2, 4 is controversial (the present writer takes it as a reference to dignitaries; see Sons of God). The NT follows the Septuagint in rendering *Elohim* as "angels" (Heb. 1:6, quoting Ps. 97:7). See God, names of II.

E. B. Smick

Elohist el′oh-hist. A designation (abbreviated "E") for the author or editor of one of the sources supposedly used in the redaction of the Pentateuch. This source is thought to have stemmed from the northern kingdom in the 8th cent. B.C.; it is characterized by the use of the common Hebrew term for God, Elohim.

Eloi, Eloi, lama sabachthani. See Eli, Eli, lama sabachthani.

Elon ee′lon (אֵילוֹן H390, "terebinth"; gentilic אֵלֹנִי H533). (1) A Hittite and father of Basemath, who married Esau (Gen. 26:34). Elsewhere (36:2) Elon's daughter is called Adah. In the latter passage the name Basemath is given to the daughter of Ishmael so that apparently two of Esau's wives were named Basemath. Perhaps the Hittite was given an alternate name to distinguish the two wives. For further discussion, see Basemath.

(2) Son of Zebulun; he was among those who came to Egypt with Jacob (Gen. 46:14). From him sprang the Elonite clan (Num. 26:26).

(3) A judge in Israel from the tribe of Zebulun; he ruled Israel ten years until his death and was buried in Aijalon (Jdg. 12:11 – 12).

(4) A city on the border of the inheritance of Dan between Ithlah and Timnah (אֵילוֹן H391, Josh. 19:43). It is probably the same as Elon Bethhanan, which was part of Solomon's second administrative district (1 Ki. 4:9). The town was on the coastal plain, E of Joppa (cf. Jdg. 19:46). Its precise location is uncertain, though some have identified it with Khirbet Wadi ʿAlin (just E of Beth Shemesh; cf. J. Simons, *The Geographical and Topographical Text of the Old Testament* [1959], 200, 349). J. B. Scott

Elon Bethhanan ee′luhn-beth-hay′nuhn (אֵילוֹן בֵּית חָנָן H392, "terebinth of the house of grace"). A town in the territory of Dan that was part of Solomon's second administrative district (1 Ki. 4:9). The Septuagint understands the passage as referring to two distinct places (*Ailōn heōs Baithanan*), and some modern scholars take the same approach (cf. N. Naʾaman, *Borders and Districts in Biblical Historiography: Seven Studies in Biblical Geographic Lists* [1986], 115). Others believe that Elon Bethhanan is an alternate name for Elon.

Elon-bezaanannim ee′luhn-bi-zay′uh-na′nim. See Zaannannim.

Elon-meonenim ee′luhn-mee-on′uh-nim (אֵילוֹן מְעוֹנְנִים H471 + poel ptc. of עָנַן H6726). A place mentioned once in the Bible (Jdg. 9:37 NRSV, NJPS; the NIV renders the words as common nouns, "soothsayers' tree"). See Diviners' Oak.

Eloth ee′loth. Alternate form of Elath.

Elpaal el-pay′uhl (אֶלְפַּעַל H551, "God has made"). Son of Shaharaim and descendant of Benjamin (1 Chr. 8:11; five sons of Elpaal are listed in vv. 12 – 13). Some scholars believe that the Elpaal included later in this genealogy (v. 18, which mentions another group of sons) is a different individual. Otherwise, one of the two passages (or both) may list descendants within a large Elpaal clan.

Elpalet el-pay′lit. KJV form of Elipelet. See Eliphelet #2.

El Paran el-pay′ruhn (אֵיל פָּארָן H386, "terebinth of Paran"). A place described as the southernmost point of the campaign of Kedorlaomer against the HORITES in the mountains of SEIR (i.e., EDOM); it is said to be on the edge of the wilderness (Gen. 14:6). The name PARAN refers to a wilderness area in the E central region of the SINAI peninsula whose eastern boundary was the Wadi ARABAH in the N and the Gulf of AQABAH in the S. Since the mountains of Seir (the modern Jebel esh-Sharah range) extend to the SW as far as the Gulf of Aqabah, "El of Paran" on the edge of the desert (of Paran), situated at the southern limit of the mountains of Seir, exactly describes the position of ELAT, the seaport on the northern tip of the gulf (note that both names contain the same initial element *ʾēl*, from *ʾayil H381*, "[mighty] tree" or "terebinth"). It is very likely that El Paran was the ancient name of Elat. F. W. BUSH

Elpelet el-pee'lit. Alternate form of ELIPHELET.

El-roi el-roi'. The NRSV rendering of Hebrew *ʾēl rŏʾî H446 + H8024* (Gen. 16:13; NIV, "the God who sees me"; RSV, "a God of seeing"). It is the name that HAGAR gave to the Lord, whose protection she experienced when fleeing from Sarai (SARAH). For that reason, a spring where the angel appeared to her was named BEER LAHAI ROI ("the well of the Living One who sees me"). (See *DDD*, 291–92.) M. R. WILSON

El Shaddai el-shad'i (אֵל שַׁדַּי *H446 + H8724*, derivation disputed). Also El Shadday. Transliteration of an epithet of God used in the patriarchal narratives and as an archaism in many poetic passages of the OT. The term is usually translated "God Almighty" (Gen. 17:1; 28:3; 35:11; 43:14; 48:3; Exod. 6:3; Ezek. 10:5). These are prose passages where the full term El Shaddai is used. In many other passages (Gen. 43:25; Num. 24:4, 16; Ruth 1:20–21; Pss. 68:14; 91:1; Joel 1:15 [cf. Isa. 13:6]; Ezek. 1:24; Job 5:17 [and thirty times more in Job]) the single element Shaddai is used and is translated "the Almighty." This rendering, which goes back to the SEPTUAGINT (Gk. *pantokratōr G4120*), is somewhat dubious, since it appears to be based on a Hebrew root (*šādad H8720*) that means "to deal violently with, to devastate." Some critics believe it refers to a tribal deity, a high god worshiped by the PATRIARCHS, who allegedly were not true monotheists. They usually point to Deut. 32:17 or Josh. 24:2, which record the fact that the Israelite ancestors served other gods "beyond the River [Euphrates]." The Genesis account, however, emphatically states that ABRAHAM turned from this false religion to worship the true and only God. One of his many descriptive epithets was El Shaddai, a meaning of which one cannot be absolutely sure, although W. F. Albright makes a strong case for the meaning, "God of the mountain(s)" (*JBL* 54 [1935]: 180–93). The name Shaddai is sometimes used as a divine element in proper names (cf. Zurishaddai, Num. 7:36) and is attested in Egyptian documents (cf. W. F. Albright, *From the Stone Age to Christianity*, 2nd ed. [1957], 243). See also ALMIGHTY; EL; GOD, NAMES OF, III. E. B. SMICK

Elteke. See ELTEKEH.

Eltekeh el'tuh-kuh (אֶלְתְּקֵא *H558* and אֶלְתְּקֵה *H559*, derivation disputed). A town in the territory of DAN (Josh. 19:44). It was assigned to the Kohathite Levites (21:23; NRSV, "Elteke"). The Assyrian king SENNACHERIB destroyed the town in 701 B.C. on his way to TIMNAH and EKRON (*ANET*, 287–88). The decisive battle between the Assyrians and Egyptians was fought nearby, and it is probable that the forces defeated by Sennacherib consisted of Jews along with Ekronites and Egyptians. A natural place for these allies to meet and take their stand would have been on the high road between Ekron and Jerusalem. The precise location of Eltekeh is uncertain. Some have identified it with Khirbet el-Muqannaʿ (Tell Miqne), though this site is now usually thought to be Ekron (however, see R. Boling in *Biblical and Related Studies Presented to Samuel Iwry*, ed. A. Kort and S. Morschauser [1985], 23–32, esp. 30). Another possibility is Tell esh-Shallaf, some 11 mi. SSE of JOPPA. C. L. FEINBERG

Eltekon el'tuh-kon (אֶלְתְּקוֹן *H560*, derivation uncertain). A town given in the hill country of the tribe of JUDAH (Josh. 15:59). The precise location has not been determined, but one possibility is Khirbet ed-Deir, c. 4 mi. W of BETHLEHEM.

Eltolad, Tolad el-toh'lad, toh'lad (אֶלְתּוֹלַד *H557*, תּוֹלָד *H9351*, possibly "[place of] request for a child"). A town in the NEGEV, part of the southernmost territory of the tribe of JUDAH (Josh. 15:30; cf. v. 21). Eltolad was later assigned to the tribe of SIMEON (19:4); the alternate name Tolad (1 Chr. 4:29) appears to be a shortened form. The precise location of the town is unknown, but presumably it was near BEERSHEBA, where an ostracon bearing the name Tolad has been found (Y. Aharoni, *Beersheba* I [1973], 71–73).

Elul ee′luhl (אֱלוּל *H469*, prob. derived from the Babylonian *Elūlu* [*Ulūlu*], the month of purification). The sixth month (August-September) in the Jewish CALENDAR (Neh. 6:15; cf. *Eloul*, 1 Macc. 14:27).

Eluzai i-loo′zi (אֶלְעוּזַי *H539*, "God is my strength"; cf. UZZIEL). One of the ambidextrous Benjamite warriors who joined DAVID while he was in exile from SAUL at the Philistine city of ZIKLAG (1 Chr. 12:5; cf. v. 2).

Elymais el′uh-may′uhs (Ἐλυμαΐς, gentilic Ἐλυμαῖος, "Elymean"). A term used by Greek writers to refer to the western part of ELAM in the southern Iranian plateau; for a time, SUSA was its capital. "The number and chronology of the kings of Elymais are uncertain since the only sources are their coins, but inscriptions from Tang-i Sarwak reveal that the population was Aramaic-speaking" (R. N. Frye, *The Heritage of Persia* [1963], 216; see also id., *A History of Ancient Iran* [1984], 273–75). The name occurs in the APOCRYPHA (Tob. 2:10; note also the reference to a certain Arioch as king of the Elymeans in Jdt. 1:6 [contrast Gen. 14:1]). According to 1 Macc. 6:1, "King Antiochus was going through the upper provinces when he heard that Elymais in Persia was a city famed for its wealth in silver and gold." Since no such "city" is known, the text should probably be corrected to read: "that in Elymais in Persia there was a city" (cf. J. A. Goldstein, *I Maccabees*, AB 41 [1976], 308). K. L. BARKER

Elymas el′uh-muhs (Ἐλύμας *G1829*, derivation disputed). Also named BAR-JESUS; a Jewish magician and false prophet whom PAUL met on his first missionary journey (Acts 13:6–12). Elymas was in the retinue of Sergius PAULUS, the Roman proconsul of CYPRUS who is described by Luke as "an intelligent man" and who summoned Paul and Barnabas to appear before him so that he might hear what they had to say (there were at the time many traveling teachers and philosophers, some of whom acquired a great reputation and eventually were asked to teach). Bar-Jesus, which means "son of Jesus [Joshua]," was a member of the proconsul's court and probably had considerable influence over him. Ancient literature abounds in stories of men skilled in the lore of the occult who became favorites of men in power. Juvenal (*Sat.* 6.562; 14.248) and Horace (*Sat.* 1.2.1), for example, mention Chaldean astrologers and impostors who were probably Babylonian Jews. It must not be assumed that such men were necessarily cheap frauds, like gypsy fortune tellers. Often they were the men of science of the day, better acquainted than most people of their time with the powers and processes of nature, but also learned in the strange skills of the Median priests.

Afraid that he might lose his influence over Sergius Paulus if the proconsul were persuaded of the truth of the Christian religion, Elymas spoke against Paul and Barnabas and sought to turn the proconsul from the faith. Paul, filled with the Spirit, looked intently upon him and told him that because he had opposed the truth of God he would become blind and be unable to see for a time. Immediately Elymas lost his sight; and when Sergius Paulus saw what befell the magician, he believed, "for he was amazed at the teaching about the Lord" (Acts 13:12). Some have suggested that Elymas should be identified with a certain Atomos, a Cyprian Jew mentioned by JOSEPHUS; this man was a magician who helped the procurator FELIX to win Drusilla, the wife of Aziz of Emesa, away from her husband (*Ant.* 20.7.2 §142; note in Acts 13:8 the variant *Etoimas* attested by Codex D).

The name Elymas has created considerable discussion. After referring to the man as Bar-Jesus (Acts 13:6), Luke says abruptly, "But Elymas the sorcerer [*magos G3407*] (for that is what his name means) opposed them" (v. 8). Some scholars have attempted, without success, to establish a connection (etymological or semantic) between the two names. Instead, the term Elymas is generally thought to be derived from a Semitic root (cf. Arab. ʿ*alim*) signifying "wise" or "one who has insight [into the future]" and thus roughly equivalent to *magos*. The likelihood is that Bar-Jesus gave himself the name or the title Elymas because he claimed the powers of the Median priests. See MAGI; SIMON MAGUS. (For other suggestions, see BDAG, 320; *ABD*, 2:487.) S. BARABAS

Elymean el′uh-mee′uhn. See ELYMAIS.

Elyon. See EL ELYON.

Elzabad el-zay′bad (אֶלְזָבָד *H479*, "God has granted"). **(1)** The ninth of eleven Gadite army officers who joined DAVID while he was at ZIKLAG in exile from SAUL (1 Chr. 12:12). These men are described as "brave warriors, ready for battle and able to handle the shield and spear. Their faces were the faces of lions, and they were as swift as gazelles in the mountains" (v. 8).

(2) Son of Shemaiah, grandson of OBED-EDOM, and a gatekeeper from the Korahites (1 Chr. 26:7; cf. v. 1). See KORAH. Elzabad and his brothers are described as "leaders in their father's family because they were very capable men" (v. 6).

Elzaphan el-zay′fan. Short form of ELIZAPHAN.

Emadabun i-mad′uh-buhn (Ημαδαβουν). According to 1 Esd. 5:58 (LXX v. 56), "the sons of Jeshua Emadabun" (*hoi huioi Iēsou Ēmadaboun*) were among the Levites who participated in the rebuilding of the TEMPLE under the better known leader also named JESHUA (KJV omits "Jeshua [Jesus]" and reads, "the sons of Madiabun"). The Greek appears to regard Emadabun as a surname to distinguish this individual from the more prominent Jeshua, though some have interpreted the text to mean that only one Jeshua is in view and that Emadabun was his son. The name is absent from the parallel passage (Ezra 3:9, unless it corresponds to Henadad).

Emar ee′mahr. Also Imar. An ancient city in N SYRIA, not mentioned in the Bible. The site is known today as Tell Meskene, about 60 mi. E of ALEPPO, on the middle EUPHRATES RIVER. Although the existence of Emar is attested as early as the 3rd millennium B.C., the city was abandoned at some point (prob. because of the meandering changes of the river) and in the 14th cent. it was rebuilt nearby. Emar became an important center of the HITTITE empire, but was destroyed early in the 12th cent. The archaeological remains are rich and shed considerable light on the Late Bronze Age. (For an English trans. of selected texts recovered at Emar, see W. W. Hallo and K. L. Younger, eds., *The Context of Scripture*, 1 [1997], 427–43; see also M. W. Chavalas, ed., *Emar: The History, Religion, and Culture of a Syrian Town in the Late Bronze Age* [1996]; M. R. Adamthwaite, *Late Hittite Emar: The Chronology, Synchronisms, and Socio-Political Aspects of a Late Bronze Age Fortress Town* [2001].)

Emathis em′uh-thuhs (Εμαθις). Apoc. form of ATHLAI (1 Esd. 9:29).

embalming. The treatment of a corpse with various substances to preserve it from decay. The Egyptians invented embalming. They believed that the state of the soul in the afterlife was directly dependent upon the preservation of the body. The Hebrews, however, did not practice the art of embalming. Laws concerning the touching of dead bodies prevented the Hebrews from being innovators in medicine and human anatomy (cf. Num. 5:1–4; 19:11–22). These laws, in part, reflect Hebrew repugnance of Egyptian religion. See EGYPT VII.

The only clear examples of embalming in the Bible are those of JACOB and JOSEPH (Gen. 50:2–3, 26; the Heb. verb is *ḥānaṭ H2846*, prob. unrelated to a verb of the same form in Cant. 2:13). These are exceptional cases primarily due to the prestige of the persons and the necessity of preservation of the bodies until BURIAL in their homeland of Canaan. After Jacob was embalmed he was carried by his sons to the patriarchal burial area E of MAMRE, the cave of MACHPELAH (50:13–14). (See TOMB.) Joseph's interment at SHECHEM, however, was delayed several centuries until after the exodus (Exod. 13:19; Josh. 24:32). Joseph's age at death, 110 years (Gen. 50:26), was viewed by Egyptians as the ideal span of life for a man.

For the method of embalmment, one is particularly dependent upon two Greek historians, Diodorus Siculus (*Bibl. Hist.* 1.91) and Herodotus (*Hist.* 2.86–89). Genesis indicates forty days were required for the physicians to embalm Jacob, whereas seventy days seems to have been the usual length of time. According to Herodotus, the

This Egyptian relief from Alexandria depicts embalming methods.

embalmers offered three methods that differed in elaboration and cost. In the cheapest method, the intestines were cleared out with a purgative and then the body was placed in natron for seventy days. In the second type, the body was soaked in natron after cedar oil was injected at the anus, thus dissolving the stomach and intestines.

The most elaborate method, mummification, called for the removal of the brain and all internal organs except the heart. The abdominal cavity was then washed out and filled with spices. Next, the body was soaked in natron for seventy days. It was then washed and wrapped from head to foot with bandages of linen cloth smeared with gum. Finally, relatives took the corpse, placed it in a wooden coffin of human shape, and left it upright against the wall of the burial chamber.

(See P. Montet, *Everyday Life in Egypt* [1958], 300–330; J. Vergote, *Joseph en Égypte. Génèse chap. 37–50 à la lumière des études égyptologiques récentes* [1959]; L. Cottrell, *Life under the Pharaohs* [1960], 221–36; B. Mertz, *Temples, Tombs and Hieroglyphs* [1964], 64–113; A. J. Spencer, *Death in Ancient Egypt* [1982]; C. Andrews, *Egyptian Mummies*, 2nd ed. [1998]; R. G. Mayer, *Embalming: History, Theory and Practice*, 3rd ed. [2000]; A. T. Chamberlain and M. Parker Pearson, *Earthly Remains: The History and Science of Preserved Human Bodies* [2001]; F. Dunand and R. Lichtenberg, *Mummies and Death in Egypt* [2006]; R. N. Jones in *ABD*, 2:490–96.) M. R. WILSON

embroidery. Decoration on cloth by means of ornamental needlework. Embroidered work, chiefly using geometric patterns and stylized motifs, is well attested in sculptured and painted scenes from the ancient world. The relevant Hebrew terms are *rāqam H8387* (ptc. "embroiderer, weaver of colored fabrics," Exod. 26:36 et al.) and *riqmâ H8391* ("embroidery, many-colored fabric," Ps. 45:14; Ezek. 16:10; et al.). The latter term can also be used of the varied sheen of the eagle's feathers (Ezek. 17:3) and of multicolored stones (1 Chr. 29:2). Embroidery is well attested in the background cultures of the OT, and may be expected to appear in Hebrew crafts also. The expressions denoting the raw materials used by the embroiderer ("blue, purple and scarlet yarn and finely twined linen," Exod. 26:36) apparently refer to thread and yarn suitable for embroidery, since they can be used of products of spinning (35:25). It should be noted, however, that some of these terms occur in contexts where they could be taken as denoting woven cloth as well as spun thread (e.g., 39:22). In one passage a distinction is made between the embroiderer and the weaver (*ʾārag H755*, 35:35; see WEAVING).

Other Hebrew terms have been thought to refer to embroidery (cf. KJV, Exod. 28:4, 39), but the evidence is ambiguous (see also FILIGREE). The type of skillful work mentioned in Exod. 26:31 refers to the TABERNACLE hangings decorated with cherubim and to some of the priestly garments (28:6). It has been suggested that the passage refers to more original designs (*HDB*, 1:699) in contrast to the stereotyped, geometric patterns of typical "embroidery." On the other hand, some of the rabbis—perhaps with no more real evidence—thought that it referred to decorative weaving in which the design showed on both sides (*JE*, 5:148). It has also been suggested that the pomegranates on the hem of the high priest's garment (Exod. 28:33; 39:24) were appliqué work (*NBD*, 315). It is equally possible that they were hanging ornaments of a braided or plaited sort that, like the golden bells, hung from the hem. The meanings of these terms remain unclear for lack of decisive or even reasonably clear attestation.

In the OT, embroidery symbolizes luxury and lucrative commerce (Ps. 45:14; Ezek. 27:16). As early as the Song of DEBORAH, embroidered goods were prized as spoils of war (Jdg. 5:30). Most of the references to embroidered goods in the OT are to the tabernacle and the priestly garments. The curtain for the gate of the court and the curtain for the door of the tabernacle were both embroidered (Exod. 27:16; 26:36), whereas other hangings are described differently (26:1, 31). The high priest's girdle was embroidered (28:39), and other garments were woven (28:4). (See H. F. Lutz, *Textiles and Costumes among the Peoples of the Ancient Near East* [1923]; M. S. and J. L. Miller, *Encyclopedia of Bible Life* [1944], 353–55.) See DRESS. A. BOWLING

Emek Keziz ee′mik-kee′ziz (עֵמֶק קְצִיץ *H6681*, "valley of Keziz" or "plain of gravel"). Also Emek-keziz. A town on the E boundary of the tribe of Benjamin (Josh. 18:21; KJV, "the valley of Keziz"). See BENJAMIN, TRIBE OF. The site is unidentified, but it was presumably to the SE of the tribal territory, near JERICHO.

emendation. See TEXT AND MANUSCRIPTS (OT).

emerald. A rich and yellow-green to deep-green variety of BERYL, a beryllium aluminum silicate. It is one of the most valuable of all gem stones and owes its beauty to its color and transparency (Rev. 4:3, *smaragdinos G5039*; 21:19, *smaragdos G5040*; the NIV uses "emerald" also to render Heb. *yāhălōm H3402*, a word of uncertain meaning, Exod. 28:18; 39:11; Ezek. 28:13). "Fire," such as shown by diamond, is lacking. The best emeralds are deep grass-green in color and free from flaws, although unflawed emeralds are rare, and large unflawed emeralds are unknown. Many crystals contain feathery inclusions, while in some the color is variable, due to a small proportion of chromium. Emerald mines were worked 2,000 years ago near the RED SEA, in Egypt, with hundreds of shafts sunk, some to 850 ft.; however, the stones were not of fine gem quality. All the fine emeralds today come from mines in Colombia, which were worked by the Spaniards. They occur in calcite (calcium carbonate) veins that cut across black shales. D. R. BOWES.

emerod. See TUMOR.

Emim ee′mim. See EMITES.

Emites ee′mits (אֵימִים *H400*, "terrors, frightening ones"). Also Emim (KJV superfluous English pl., "Emims"). Early inhabitants of an area E of the DEAD SEA who were defeated in the time of ABRAHAM by KEDORLAOMER and his allies (Gen. 14:5; NRSV, "Emim"; NIV, "Emites"). Their descriptive name was given to them by the Moabites, who subsequently occupied that territory (cf. Y. Aharoni, *The Land of the Bible: A Historical Geography*, rev. ed. [1979], map 7, facing p. 140). See MOAB. The Emites are described as "a people strong and numerous"; apparently they had some connection with the Anakites (see ANAK) and REPHAITES, who were regarded as GIANTS (Deut. 2:10–11).

Emmanuel. See IMMANUEL.

Emmaus i-may′uhs (Ἐμμαοῦς *G1843*). A Judean village that was 60 stadia (about 7 mi.) from JERUSALEM; the risen Jesus appeared to two disciples who were on their way to this town (Lk. 24:13; CODEX SINAITICUS and some other MSS give the distance as 160 stadia, almost 20 mi.). The location of the village is uncertain (its direction from Jerusalem is not stated), and several sites, ranging 4–20 mi. away from Jerusalem, have been suggested, as follows.

(1) El Qubeibeh, 7 mi. NW of Jerusalem; its connection with Emmaus, however, goes back only as far as the times of the Crusaders, who had found

nearby the place Castellum Emmaus, an ancient Roman fort. In 1878 the Franciscans found here remains of a basilica dating to Crusader or, possibly, Byzantine times.

(2) Only 4 mi. to the W of Jerusalem is the modern Qaloniyeh (Qalunyah, Lat. *Colonia*), often identified with an Emmaus at which Vespasian is said to have settled 800 soldiers (*Ammaous,* Jos. *War* 7.6.6 §217). According to JOSEPHUS, the town was 30 stadia from Jerusalem (some MSS say 60 stadia, but this variant may be an assimilation to the text in Luke). Qaloniyeh is equated with Motza in rabbinic literature (*b. Sukkah* 45a; cf. *m. Sukkah* 4:5; see also MOZAH), and some have argued for a linguistic correspondence between Motza and Emmaus (see J. Wilkinson, *Jerusalem as Jesus Knew It: Archaeology as Evidence* [1978], 162–64, which includes a very helpful map). It has also been suggested that Luke's distance of 60 stadia refers to the round trip (e.g., J. A. Fitzmyer, *The Gospel according to Luke X-XXIV,* AB 28A [1985], 1562, which provides important bibliography).

(3) At about 20 mi. W of Jerusalem on the Jaffa road is an Emmaus where Judas MACCABEE in 166 B.C. defeated Gorgias (*Ammaous,* 1 Macc. 3:40, 57; 4:1–15; a fortress was built there, 9:50). In the 3rd cent. A.D. the name was changed to Nicopolis, and the modern designation is ʿAmwas (ʿImwas; cf. *NEAEHL,* 2:385–89). EUSEBIUS (*Onomasticon* 90.16) and other early writers identified it with the Emmaus mentioned in Luke. This site, however, seems to have been a large city (the seat of a toparchy, Jos. *War* 3.3.5 §§54–55) rather than a village. Moreover, its distance from Jerusalem is too great, unless the variant reading in Luke, 160 stadia, be accepted (with the resultant problem of having the two disciples traveling a very arduous 40 mi. in one day from and to Jerusalem). It is possible that the variant reading arose because of the patristic identification of Emmaus with Nicopolis-ʿAmwas (cf. *HJP,* rev. ed. [1973–87], 1:512–13 n. 142).

(4) Abu Ghosh, about 9 mi. W of Jerusalem, also known as Kiryat el-ʾEnab, makes claim to having been Emmaus, for a Crusader church was built over a Roman fort which contains an inscription indicating that part of the Tenth Legion was stationed there. This place seems to be too far from Jerusalem to be identified with biblical Emmaus.

Less likely suggestions include el-Khamsa (over 60 stadia SW of Jerusalem) and Artas (S of Bethlehem, where Roman baths have been found). None of the proposed sites can be confirmed. (See further F.-M. Abel in *RB* 34 [1925]: 347–67; J. A. Grassi in *CBQ* 26 [1964]: 463–67.) W. H. MARE

Emmer em´uhr. KJV Apoc. form of IMMER (1 Esd. 9:21).

Emmor em´or. KJV NT form of HAMOR.

emperor. In modern usage an emperor rules an area larger than a single kingdom. In Roman law and custom two significant ideas are found. However dictatorial he may have been, the emperor was thought of as exercising *imperium* (i.e., the properly delegated authority to command in behalf of the state); in contrast, kings ruled by virtue of personal legitimacy or personal authority. In addition, the emperor was the one declared ruler or *imperator* by the Roman armies (this custom clearly contradicts the spirit of the first idea). Most historic European "emperors" traced the legal origins of their title from the Roman emperors. None of these distinctions is significant for biblical usage. CYRUS, NEBUCHADNEZZAR, and CAESAR all are referred to as "king" (Ezra 1:1; Dan. 3:9; Jn. 19:15). Moreover, in contrast to the rich theological connotations of KING in Scriptures, no theological concepts are attached to the office of emperor. Christ as ruler is "King of kings" (Rev. 19:16) rather than "Emperor." See also EMPEROR WORSHIP; ROMAN EMPIRE.
A. BOWLING

emperor worship. The worship of the Roman emperor as a divine being—the cause and occasion of the tragic rift between the empire and the church—began spontaneously in the eastern provinces, was recognized by AUGUSTUS and TIBERIUS, and was progressively promoted by their successors as a political measure. Such a cult had manifest usefulness as a cementing and unifying force in the 1st cent., as the principate struggled to stabilize the frontiers and establish cohesion in the Mediterranean world. "The imperial cultus," wrote J. Moffatt, "was instinctive rather than deliberate, developing out of certain germs within the ancient mind, such

Coin minted following the death of Augustus in A.D. 14. The rays radiating from the figure are meant to indicate divinity.

as the blend of religion and patriotism among the Persians, and the worship of the Ptolemies which shocked the pious Plutarch. Its primary aim was to foster patriotism by providing a symbol of the solidarity and unity of the Empire" (*EGT*, 5:307).

The cult, as the words quoted indicate, found origin and form in the E. From earliest times, the rulers of EGYPT had been regarded as incarnations of deity and accorded divine honors and worship. When the Ptolemies, on the breakup of ALEXANDER THE GREAT's vast empire, took control of Egypt, they were regarded as the successors of the pharaohs, and similarly were honored by the Egyptian people. The Caesars were no more than the successors of the Ptolemies (see CAESAR; PTOLEMY). Nor was it difficult for similar concepts of a divine ruler to find place in SYRIA and ASIA MINOR. The idea was indigenous. "Distance," writes Moffatt in the passage already quoted, "lent enchantment to the provincial view of the emperor. Any sordid traits or idiosyncracies retired into the background before the adoration felt for the divinity which hedged this unseen, powerful figure who was hailed with a mixture of servility and real gratitude as 'the Saviour,' 'the Peace,' or the lord of men. Asia became a hotbed of the cult" (ibid., 308).

In PERGAMUM, in many ways the Asian headquarters of the cult, the worship of ROME, and of Caesar as its incarnate deity, colored the city's life.

The first temple of the cult was located at Pergamum as early as 29 B.C., and provided a motif for Pergamene coinage for over a century. A second temple was built in honor of TRAJAN before A.D. 100, and a third for Severus a century later. Only the first temple functioned when the apocalyptic letter was written to Pergamum (Rev. 2:12–17), but its ritual and worship were sufficient to make the presence of the imperial power very real in the city, and were for Christians shockingly oppressive. When the imagery of the letter speaks of "the words of him who has the sharp, double-edged sword," and of those who live "where Satan has his throne," it has this confrontation between Christianity and Caesarism in full view.

Ancyra served as cult-center for GALATIA, as Pergamum did for Asia. Through all the provinces of the great peninsula, provincial assemblies maintained the cult, and special officials (e.g., the ASIARCHS of EPHESUS) saw to its proper ordering and maintenance. An extant letter of PLINY the Younger, governor of BITHYNIA at the end of the first decade of the 2nd cent., showed the cult in its political operation. Pliny, a kindly but legally minded man, had found his province in the grip of Christianity. Doubtless pressed hard by the temple wardens of the cult whose shrines were empty, and the guild of butchers whose sacrificial meat was finding no purchasers, the governor, following the lamentable anti-Christian legislation that had been on the imperial statute books since NERO or VESPASIAN, proceeded to suppression.

Pliny writes: "Those who denied they were, or had ever been, Christians, who repeated after me an invocation to the gods, and offered adoration, with wine and frankincense, to your image, which I had ordered to be brought for that purpose, together with those of the gods, and who finally cursed Christ—none of which acts, it is said, those who are really Christians can be forced into performing—these I thought it proper to discharge. Others who were named by that informer at first confessed themselves Christians, and then denied it; true, they had been of that persuasion but they had quitted it, some three years, others many years, and a few as much as twenty-five years ago. They all worshipped your statue and the images of the gods, and cursed Christ" (*Letters* 10.96–97).

Here is a vivid picture of the imperial cult in operation against a minority who were regarded as dissident and "tampering with the established processes of life: challenging, rebuking" (E. M. Blaiklock, *The Christian in Pagan Society* [1951], 15). This, in fact, was the usefulness that the emperors saw in the cult, and why they gave its spontaneous appearance in the E instinctive welcome and official encouragement. Nor must the sufferings of a Christian minority under its impact obscure the fact that the empire, or the principate as it is more correctly called, avoiding the dual sense of the word empire, brought manifold blessings to the eastern provinces. Cicero's letters from Cilicia and his orations against Verres are indication enough of the exploitation and misgovernment that was common in the provinces during the last turbulent century of the Roman republic. The emperors brought peace and at least some semblance of stable government. Hence, the natural adoration of him whose rule had brought such blessings. The whole system of worshiping a man must be seen in its ancient context of ruler-worship in the ANE, of the cult of heroes in GREECE, and against the background of a popular theology without the advantage of the Christian or even the Jewish idea of a transcendent God.

So far the worship of the emperor in the eastern stronghold of the cult has been the major theme. In Rome, the myth of a deified ruler was invented in the 4th cent. B.C. under Greek influence, and there are instances, as Roman power spread through the Greek world, of Roman officials receiving divine honors. See ROMAN RELIGION. In the city itself, such notions became prominent only in the 1st cent. B.C. and were concerned mainly with the thought of the deification of the virtuous dead. Julius CAESAR, who had tasted the adulation of the E, accepted divine honors in his lifetime, and was deified after his assassination. Augustus, preoccupied in avoiding his adoptive uncle's mistakes, was canny about such honors in the W, ready though he was to exploit the instinctive adoration of the E. He allowed altars, not temples, to be set up to his "genius," associated with the worship of *Dea Roma*, the deified spirit of Rome.

In literature, Virgil, Horace, and others of the poets of the Golden Age, spoke commonly of the prince in a manner associated with divine things and the hero-cults. They shared, after all, the common gratitude for the gift of peace that Augustus's subtle diplomacy, clever leadership, and immense prestige had brought. The very name Augustus, bestowed by the Senate on Octavian, was indication of this drift of thought. The successors of Augustus shared his hesitation about frank acceptance in Italy of divine appellatives and formal worship. The Greeks and the provinces had no reserve, and the gradual growth of absolutism, together with the spread in the W of eastern cults, finally established Caesar worship with its full ritual throughout the Mediterranean world. The cult in no way fulfilled a religious need. It was never more than a tribute of flattery, a demonstration of gratitude, a symbol of patriotism or subjection, and as such a vastly important political force.

(See further L. R. Taylor, *The Divinity of the Roman Emperor* [1931]; G. W. Bowersock in *Self-Definition in the Greco-Roman World*, ed. B. F. Meyer and E. P. Sanders [1983], 171–82; S. R. F. Price, *Rituals and Power: The Roman Imperial Cult in Asia Minor* [1984]; D. Fishwick, *The Imperial Cult in the Latin West*, 3 vols. [1987–2005]; I. Gradel, *Emperor Worship and Roman Religion* [2002]; M. Bernett, *Der Kaiserkult in Judäa unter den Herodiern und Römern* [2007].) E. M. BLAIKLOCK

emptied. See KENOSIS.

En en (עֵין, construct form of עַיִן H6524, "eye" or "spring"). A word compounded with various other terms to form place names, such as EN GEDI, EN ROGEL, etc. Note similarly the use of Arabic ʿAin to form numerous compounds.

Enaim i-nay'im (עֵינַיִם H6542, possibly "[two] eyes" or "double spring"). A town "on the road to Timnah"; at its entrance TAMAR, disguising herself as a prostitute, seduced her father-in-law JUDAH because he had not given her as a wife to his son SHELAH (Gen. 38:14, 21). Enaim is widely regarded to be the same place as ENAM, but some, following the Syriac and the Vulgate, have thought that the Hebrew phrase *bĕpetaḥ ʿênayim* means "at the crossroads" or the like (KJV, "in an open place"; NEB, "where the road forks in two directions"). See also TIMNAH.

Enam ee'nuhm (עֵינָם H6543, "[place of] the spring"). A town in the SHEPHELAH within the tribal territory of JUDAH (Josh. 15:34); probably the same place as ENAIM. The location is uncertain, though various sites have been suggested, including Khirbet Beith Ikka, some 5 mi. SE of BETH SHEMESH. W. WHITE, JR.

Enan ee´nuhn (עֵינָן H6544, possibly "spring"). Father of AHIRA; the latter was a leader in the tribe of NAPHTALI (Num. 1:15; 2:29; 7:78, 83; 10:27).

Enasibus i-nas´uh-buhs. KJV Apoc. form of ELIASHIB (1 Esd. 9:34).

encampment by the sea. The night before God's miraculous destruction of the Egyptian chariot force in the RED SEA, the Israelites were instructed "to encamp by the sea," more specifically, near PI HAHIROTH, MIGDOL, and BAAL ZEPHON (Exod. 14:2). As in the case of other sites of the early exodus, the location of this encampment is dependent upon the interpretation of the route taken by the Israelites. A northern route would place it on Lake Sirbonis, while a southern route would locate it on the present Red Sea, and a central route on one of the lakes in between. See EXODUS, THE. A. BOWLING

enchanter. A person who influences people or things through charms and spells (see MAGIC AND SORCERY). The work of the enchanter is universal. Although the practice of divination and similar arts was forbidden to the Hebrews (Deut. 18:10–11), the OT shows acquaintance with several kinds of enchantments, including SNAKE CHARMING (Eccl. 10:11; Jer. 8:17; cf. also Isa. 3:3). The Hebrew verb *ḥābar* H2489 ("to bind") is used with its cognate noun *ḥeber* H2490 ("company," but also "enchantment, spell") to mean "bind with a charm, cast a spell, enchant" (Deut. 18:11; Ps. 58:5; Isa. 47:9, 12). Other relevant terms include *naḥaš* H5728 (Num. 23:23; 24:1; NIV, "sorcery") and *ʾaššāp* H879 (Dan. 1:20; 2:2; cf. Aram. *ʾāšap* H10081, 2:10 et al., from Akk. *[w]āšipu*). A. BOWLING

Encratites en´kruh-tits. Derived from the Greek word for "self-control" (*enkrateia* G1602), this term is applied to Christians in the early church who adopted an extreme form of ASCETICISM. The earliest description we have comes from IRENAEUS (*Haer.* 1.28; see *ANF*, 1:353):

> Springing from Saturninus and Marcion, those who are called Encratites (self-controlled) preached against marriage, thus setting aside the original creation of God, and indirectly blaming Him who made the male and female for the propagation of the human race. Some of those reckoned among them have also introduced abstinence from animal food, thus proving themselves ungrateful to God, who formed all things. They deny, too, the salvation of him who was first created. It is but lately, however, that this opinion has been invented among them. A certain man named Tatian first introduced the blasphemy. He was a hearer of Justin's, and as long as he continued with him he expressed no such views; but after his martyrdom he separated from the Church, and, excited and puffed up by the thought of being a teacher, as if he were superior to others, he composed his own peculiar type of doctrine. He invented a system of certain invisible Aeons, like the followers of Valentinus; while, like Marcion and Saturninus, he declared that marriage was nothing else than corruption and fornication.

Little more is known about the Encratites (cf. Euseb. *Eccl. Hist.* 4.28–29), and they probably never formed a well-defined or organized sect; the church fathers seem to use the term as a general title for various heretical groups, including the EBIONITES and the Gnostics (see GNOSTICISM).

encyclopedias. See BIBLE DICTIONARIES AND ENCYCLOPEDIAS.

end of the world. This phrase is used by the KJV and other versions to render Greek *synteleia tou aiōnos* (NIV, "end of the age"), which is distinctive of Matthew (Matt. 13:39–40, 49; 24:3; 28:20; in Heb. 9:26 with the pl. *tōn aiōnōn*; the same idea is expressed simply by *telos*, "end," in Matt. 24:13–14). It refers to the miraculous and catastrophic events that will close history and open the eternal age. See ESCHATOLOGY.

Most ideas associated with the end of the world in the OT appear as relatively subordinate details to God's future work in restoring his chosen people to the Promised Land. The gradual emergence of these details is an instructive example of progressive revelation. The miraculous character of some of these events shows that the restoration of God's people is not merely another event within history, but rather that it marks the apocalyptic end of history.

Some of these events are: (1) catastrophes in nature (Joel 2:30; Zech. 14:4); (2) judgment upon the nations, particularly those who have persecuted God's people (Joel 3:9–12; Obad. 15–16; Zech. 14:12–15); (3) restoration to a world of miraculous prosperity (Hos. 2:22; Joel 3:18; Amos 9:11–15), political peace (Isa. 2:3–4; Mic. 4:3), and peace within nature (Isa. 65:23–25); (4) judgment followed by God's personal rule (Obad. 21; Dan. 2:44); (5) restoration to a sinless state (Zeph. 3:11–13; Zech. 14:20, 21); and (6) resurrection to immortality (one relatively late passage only, Dan. 12:2–3).

As an examination of the passages referred to above shows, OT apocalyptic eschatology was the end product of a gradual development that began well before the exile (see APOCALYPTIC LITERATURE). It is, therefore, erroneous to suppose that such a viewpoint emerged only as the disappointed Hebrews of the exile deserted history for an "other-worldly" hope. Rather, apocalyptic eschatology can be viewed as a normal outgrowth of the older Hebrew confidence in God's working within history.

NT eschatology retains the ideas listed above and adds some new ones: (1) seen from one perspective, the end of the world had already begun with Christ's appearance as a sacrifice (Heb. 9:26), though other aspects of the end are clearly future; (2) even the preaching of the gospel can be regarded as only a preliminary for the end (Matt. 24:14); (3) a distinction is made between the events introducing the earthly MILLENNIUM and the events introducing the eternal age (only Rev. 20–21); (4) the end is associated with the personal return of Jesus Christ to earth (Matt. 24:29–30); (5) a total, catastrophic dissolution will end the present world and make room for a new, eternal earth (2 Pet. 3:7–10; Rev. 21:1). See SECOND COMING. A. BOWLING

Endor en′dor (עֵין־דּוֹר H6529 [also עֵין־דֹּאר and עֵין־דֹּר], perhaps "spring of habitation" or "source of generation"). Also En-dor. A town in the tribal territory of ISSACHAR allotted to MANASSEH (Josh. 17:11). Apparently, the Manassites did not drive out all the Canaanites from Endor at the time of the conquest (17:12). According to Ps. 83:9–10, the town was near the river KISHON and thus a part of the battlefield of the JEZREEL Valley; it was the scene of the defeat of JABIN and SISERA by BARAK. Endor is perhaps most famous because here King SAUL sought the help of a medium (see FAMILIAR SPIRIT) in the uncertain hours before his final battle (1 Sam. 28:7).

The precise location of Endor is disputed. It was earlier identified with the historical Endur (Indur), 4 mi. S of Mount TABOR and 6 mi. SE of NAZARETH, on the N slope of Little Hermon (Nebi Dahi), where there are several ancient caves. Archaeological work has failed to confirm this site, however, and many scholars now favor Khirbet Ṣafṣafeh, about 2 mi. farther N. Others argue for a site S of the plain of Jezreel. (See O. Margalith in *ZAW* 97 [1985]:109–11; D. V. Edelman in *ABD*, 2:499–501.) A. C. SCHULTZ

En Eglaim en-eg′lay-im (עֵין עֶגְלַיִם H6536, "spring of [two] heifers"). Also En-eglaim. This place is mentioned only in the APOCALYPTIC vision of Ezek. 47:1–12, where the prophet describes a future river flowing from the temple to the E and emptying into the (Dead) Sea so that "the water there becomes fresh" (v. 8), making it possible for large numbers of fish to live in it. Then he adds, "Fishermen will stand along the shore; from En Gedi to En Eglaim there will be places for spreading nets" (v. 10). EN GEDI lies on the W shore of the DEAD SEA, close to the half-way point, so many scholars have sought to locate En Eglaim to its N (e.g., at ʿAIN FESHKA, near QUMRAN). Others believe that En Eglaim is viewed in this passage as opposite En Gedi, that is, on the E shore. Support for this view is claimed from a Hebrew document found in the Judean desert and dated to the 2nd cent. A.D. which mentions a place named *mḥwz ʿgltyn* ("the harbor town of Eglatain") apparently in Moabite territory (see J. Starcky in *RB* 61 [1954]: 161–81, esp. 167). The further suggestion that En

Eglaim is the same as EGLAIM (*ABD*, 2:501) seems dubious on linguistic grounds. More plausible, but still speculative, is its identification with EGLATH SHELISHIYAH (*ISBE* rev. [1979–88], 2:81).

Enemessar en′uh-mes′uhr (Ενεμεσσαρος). An Assyrian king during whose reign TOBIT was taken captive (Tob. 1:2, 16, KJV; NRSV, "Shalmaneser"); when he died, he was supposedly succeeded by SENNACHERIB (1:15). Because Sennacherib's father was SARGON II (really an adopted title, Akk. *šarru-kēn*, "the king is legitimate"), some have argued that the name Enemessar reflects either this title or Sargon's personal, but otherwise unknown, name. The VULGATE, however, reads *Salmanassar*, that is, SHALMANESER V, who immediately preceded Sargon on the throne. Because a corruption from Greek *Salamanasar* (CODEX VATICANUS reads *Samenassar* in 2 Ki. 17:3; cf. also 18:9) to *Enemessaros* is plausible, some scholars believe that the book of Tobit, inaccurately, refers to Shalmaneser.

enemy. One who feels or behaves in a hostile manner. Various Hebrew words may be translated "enemy," especially ʾōyēb H367 (Gen. 22:17 and very frequently; cf. *NIDOTTE*, 1:365–71), *ṣar* H7640, "oppressor" (e.g., Gen. 14:20), and the participle of *śānēʾ* H8533, "to hate" (e.g., Gen. 24:60). In the NT it is almost always the rendering of Greek *echthros* G2398 (cf. *NIDNNT*, 1:553–57).

Enmity among human beings, resulting in murder, is one of the first recorded results of the FALL (Gen. 4:5–8), but will someday be removed (Mic. 4:3–4). Enmity is opposed to LOVE, a basic ethical principle even in the law (Lev. 19:18; love is commanded even for the resident FOREIGNER, v. 34). The enmity of nature toward humanity is also a result of the fall (Gen. 3:17–18). The future will include reconciliation of the parts of nature with one another, as, for example, in the case of reconciling the enmity between the animals (Isa. 65:25).

Those who oppose God's purposes (even among his chosen people, Lam. 2:4; Isa. 1:24–25) can become enemies of God. The Scriptures hint that their hatred of God is self-destructive (Isa. 26:11c, lit., "the fire of your enemies will consume them"). God's vengeance on his enemies is coming (Jer. 46:10), and they must be destroyed when God reigns (Ps. 97:1, 3).

The OT principle of revenge (Lev. 24:19–21) seems to sanction revengeful enmity (see VENGEANCE). On the other hand, revenge may have been a necessary, though unpleasant, expedient for maintaining public order in the absence of central governmental authority. Also, the OT principle prevented the act of revenge from becoming disproportionately larger than the original crime. The revenge could not exceed in degree the crime or hurt committed. As such, the principle of revenge would not have been an unconditional warrant for personal hatred. In personal relations, the OT attitude is expressed in the warning not to rejoice in the enemy's misfortunes (Prov. 24:17) and in the command to return the enemy's lost goods (Exod. 23:4–5).

Hatred toward the national enemy is expressed in strong poetical terms (e.g. Ps. 137:8–9). See HATE. This hatred in behalf of the nation and God's purposes should not be confused with personal hatred. Concerning the national enemy, when the people are in God's will, their enemies are God's enemies (Gen. 12:3; Exod. 23:22), and God gives victory (Lev. 26:3, 8; Ps. 44:5). But when they become God's enemies through sin, God fights for their enemies (Jer. 21:4–6). God even raises up enemies against his sinning people (Isa. 9:11). But the enemy thus raised up should not glory in his own power since he is merely God's tool (Deut. 32:27; Isa. 37:22–29). Israel sometimes complained that God had delivered them to their enemy without reason (Ps. 89:38–45).

The NT specifically and unequivocally commands love both for the stranger (Lk. 10:29–37) and for the hostile enemy (Matt. 5:38–44). The message of Christ, however, may produce enmity (Matt. 10:34–36). Theologically, enmity with God has been universalized and used to describe fallen mankind (Rom. 5:10). RECONCILIATION, then, views salvation as making enemies of God into friends of God (cf. 2 Cor. 5:18–20). See also WRATH. A. BOWLING

Eneneus i-nen′ee-uhs (Ενηνιος). KJV Enenius. An Israelite mentioned among leading individuals who returned from Babylon with Zerubbabel (1 Esd. 5:8 NRSV; the RSV has "Bigvai" [cf. Ezra 2:2; Neh. 7:7]).

Water springs in the canyon at En Gedi.

Enenius i-nen´ee-uhs. KJV Apoc. form of ENE-NEUS.

En-gaddi en-gad´i. KJV Apoc. from of EN GEDI (Sir. 24:14).

En Gannim en-gan´im (עֵין גַּנִּים H6528, "spring of gardens"). **(1)** One of the towns in the second district of the tribe of JUDAH (Josh. 15:34). Beyond the fact that it was in the SHEPHELAH (lowland) and probably not far from ZANOAH and JARMUTH, there is no indication of its site. The identification with the modern Beit Jemal is dubious.

(2) A town in the tribal territory of ISSACHAR; it was one of the Levitical cities given to the Gershonites (Josh. 19:21; 21:29). The parallel passage has ANEM, which is probably the same place (1 Chr. 6:73). En Gannim had earlier been identified as modern Jenin (but see BETH HAGGAN). Other proposals include ʿOlam, some 8 mi. SE of Mount TABOR (W. F. Albright in *ZAW* 44 [1926]: 231–32), Khirbet Beit Jann, about 6 mi. W of the S tip of the Sea of Galilee (adopted tentatively by Y. Aharoni, *The Land of the Bible: A Historical Geography*, rev. ed. [1979], 434), and, perhaps most likely, Khirbet ed-Dir, some 5 mi. SW of the Sea of Galilee.

En Gedi en-ged´i (עֵין גֶּדִי H6527, "spring of young goat"; cf. Arab. *ʿAin Jidi*). Also En-gedi. A spring and associated streams that issue from beneath the limestone cliffs on the W side of the DEAD SEA at a temperature of 80°F. It lies almost due E of HEBRON and apparently was also known as HAZAZON TAMAR (2 Chr. 20:2), which suggests the presence of palm trees; if so, these as well as its vineyards (Cant. 1:14) disappeared after the Muslim occupation. En Gedi belonged to the territory of the tribe of Judah (Josh. 15:62; see JUDAH, TRIBE OF). Because of the oppressive heat of the Dead Sea valley, there can never have been any large population here; it is called a small town by JOSEPHUS (*War* 4.7.2 §402). The "Desert of En Gedi" (1 Sam. 24:1; cf. 23:29), figuring in the story of DAVID, is one of the bleakest parts of the Wilderness of Judah (JESHIMON). When the nations of AMMON, MOAB, and EDOM tried to invade Judah through En Gedi in the time of JEHOSHAPHAT (2 Chr. 20:1–2), it was presumably because they hoped to achieve a tactical surprise by attacking one of the few weak spots on Judah's eastern flank. Once warning had been given, failure was inevitable. En Gedi is mentioned again in the prophet's vision of the transformed Dead Sea (Ezek. 47:10; see EN EGLAIM). (For archaeological data, see *NEAEHL*, 2:399–409.) H. L. ELLISON

engine. This English term is used by the KJV twice in the OT (2 Chr. 26:15; Ezek. 26:9). According to the first passage, King UZZIAH made engines

(Heb. *ḥiššābôn* H3115, "device, invention"; NIV and NRSV, "machines") "for use on the towers and on the corner defenses to shoot arrows and hurl large stones." (The LXX renders the Hebrew word with Greek *mēchanē*; cf. also 1 Macc. 6:51–52 et al.). Y. Yadin believes that the passage does not refer to a specific catapult or firing device, as there seems to be no evidence that such a machine existed anywhere at this time, but rather to a wooden device with shields in the fortification of the walls to protect those who were shooting arrows and throwing stones (*The Art of Warfare in Biblical Lands* [1963], 16–18, 313–16, 326–27). They protected the defenders of the city so that they could stand upright and use their weapons with comparative safety and freedom of movement. These are pictured in Assyrian reliefs.

The second passage (Ezek. 26:9) uses the Hebrew *qĕbōl* H7692, found only here. It is a technical term for some kind of siege device, probably a BATTERING RAM (for which Hebrew elsewhere uses *kar* H4119, e.g., Ezek. 4:2). The siege engine mentioned in 1 Macc. 13:43–44 (Gk. *heleopolis*) was probably a large, portable tower that included battering rams; the usual term is *krios* (2 Macc. 12:15). A typical battering ram, the kind used by the Assyrians, was mounted inside of a mobile device about 15 ft. long and half as high. It was suspended by a rope in the center so that it could be swung. The ram was used to strike at the cracks between the stones and when forced into the cracks it was then pushed back and forth to dislodge the stones. On the front of the unit was a turret adding another 9 ft. to the height from which the assailants could shoot arrows or direct operations. The unit was mounted on four or six wheels for mobility. (Cf. C. Singer, ed., *A History of Technology*, 5 vols. [1957–65], 2:698–703, 715–17.) See ARMOR, ARMS III.C.   C. P. WEBER

English Bible Versions. See VERSIONS OF THE BIBLE, ENGLISH.

engraving. The art of cutting letters or designs into a hard surface, such as metal, stone, and wood. This English term usually renders the Hebrew verb *pātaḥ* H7338 (piel stem). The names of the tribes of Israel were engraved on two onyx stones fastened to the high priest's EPHOD (Exod. 28:9–11; 39:6–7; cf. Zech. 3:9), and attached to his turban was a plate of gold that had the words "Holy to the LORD" engraved on it (28:36–37). Designs were engraved as decorations on the bronze stands of Solomon's TEMPLE (1 Ki. 7:31, 36). A broader term, *ḥāraš* H3086 (often "to plow, work"), can also be used for the art of engraving (Jer. 17:1, where NIV renders this verb and *kātab* H4180 ["write"] respectively as "inscribed" and "engraved"). The TEN COMMANDMENTS are said to be engraved on the two tables of stone (ptc. of *ḥārat* H3100, a root that occurs only in Exod. 32:16; cf. *entypoō* G1963 in 2 Cor. 3:7). Other terms are used elsewhere (e.g., Job 19:23–24; Isa. 49:16).

The inscribing could be accomplished with an "iron tool" (Job 19:24; Jer. 17:1; the latter passage also speaks of a "flint point," which could refer to a different chisel or to some kind of diamond or emery point on the iron stylus). Files, wheels, and drills were also used, and grinding was accomplished with the aid of an abrasive. The finest engraving is often referred to in Scripture as that of signet rings (see SEAL; the archaeologist confirms this verdict. (See J. H. Middleton, *The Engraved Gems of Classical Times* [1891]; C. Singer, ed., *A History of Technology*, 5 vols. [1957–65], 1:189–90, 648–49, 663–681.)   C. P. WEBER

En Haddah en-had'uh (עֵין חַדָּה H6532, possibly "spring of gladness"). Also En-haddah. A town in the tribal territory of ISSACHAR (Josh. 19:21). It is usually identified with the modern village of el-Ḥadatheh, about 6 mi. WSW of the S tip of the Sea of Galilee, or the nearby Tell el-Karm (cf. Z. Kallai, *Historical Geography of the Bible* [1986], 195–96).

En Hakkore en-hak'uh-ree (עֵין הַקּוֹרֵא H6530, "spring of the one who calls" or "spring of the partridge"). Also En-hakkore. The spring where SAMSON drank after slaughtering the Philistines at LEHI; upon drinking from it, "his strength returned and he revived" (Jdg. 15:19). Attempts to locate this site, presumably in Judah, have been unsuccessful.

En Hazor en-hay'zor (עֵין חָצוֹר H6533, "spring of Hazor [enclosure]"). Also En-hazor. A fortified city included in the assignment to the tribe of NAPHTALI (Josh. 19:37). The precise location of this town (not to be confused with the royal city of HAZOR) is unknown, although one possible site is the modern town of ʿAinitha in S Lebanon (cf. Y. Aharoni, *The Land of the Bible: A Historical Geography*, rev. ed. [1979], 162; perhaps the same as ʿny, no. 86 in the list of THUTMOSE III).

G. GIACUMAKIS, JR.

enlighten. This English verb is used relatively few times in the Bible (similar expressions include "bring/give light," "shine," et al.; cf. Job 33:30; Ps. 19:8). Of special significance is the use of the Greek verb *phōtizō* G5894. Writing to the church in EPHESUS, PAUL says, "I pray also that the eyes of your heart may be enlightened in order that you may know the hope to which he has called you, the riches of his glorious inheritance in the saints, and his incomparably great power for us who believe" (Eph. 1:18; contrast SATAN's work of blinding the mind, 2 Cor. 4:4). JOHN THE BAPTIST proclaimed that the MESSIAH is the "true light that gives light to every man" (Jn. 1:9), and Jesus himself more than once claimed to be the LIGHT of the world (8:12; 9:5).

In one of the most difficult passages in the NT, the author of Hebrews says, "It is impossible for those who have once been enlightened, … if they fall away, to be brought back to repentance" (Heb. 6:4–6; cf. 10:26, 32). Ancient writers understood the language of enlightenment here as a reference to BAPTISM (e.g., Justin, *1 Apol.* 61.12); modern expositors debate whether or not this statement describes REGENERATION (see also PERSEVERANCE). True enlightenment is the intellectual and moral effect produced upon a person by the reception of the Christian REVELATION. It is not a mere intellectual illumination or understanding of divine truth, for this spiritual insight manifests itself in ethical action. Christians are "sons of light and sons of the day," as Paul puts it (1 Thess. 5:5).

J. C. CONNELL

Enlil en´lil. Also Ellil. One of the gods worshiped in MESOPOTAMIA. Especially revered in SUMER, he was referred to as Father Enlil, the Great Mountain (see *ANET*, 573–76, for these and other epithets). He was said to be the son of An, the consort of Ninlil, and the father of various other gods, such as Nergal and Ninurta. A major temple, Ekur, was erected in his honor at NIPPUR. (See H. Behrens, *Enlil und Ninlil: ein sumerischer Mythos aus Nippur* [1978].)

En Mishpat en-mish´pat (עֵין מִשְׁפָּט H6535, "spring of judgment"). A place to which KEDORLAOMER and his allies went in the course of their military campaign; it is identified as KADESH (Gen. 14:7).

enmity. See ENEMY.

Ennatan. See ELNATHAN #3.

Enoch ee´nuhk (חֲנוֹךְ H2840, possibly "dedicated" or "initiated" [see HANOCH]; Ἐνώχ G1970). **(1)** Son of CAIN and father of Irad; Cain named a city after him (Gen. 4:17–18).

(2) Son of Jared, descendant of SETH, and father of METHUSELAH (Gen. 5:18–24; 1 Chr. 1:3). It is said of him that he "walked with God; then he was no more, because God took him away" (Gen. 5:24), clearly a reference to his being taken to heaven without dying (cf. ELIJAH's experience, 2 Ki. 2:11). His name is included in Luke's GENEALOGY OF JESUS CHRIST (Lk. 3:37). A hero of faith, he is known as a man who pleased God (Heb. 11:5), while Jude 14–15 refers to a tradition that Enoch prophesied against ungodly men (cf. ENOCH, BOOKS OF).

The same Hebrew name is rendered HANOCH elsewhere (Gen. 25:4; 46:8–9; Exod. 6:14; Num. 26:5; 1 Chr. 1:33; 5:3).

E. B. SMICK

Enoch, Books of. Several APOCALYPTIC writings are ascribed to ENOCH son of Jared and father of METHUSELAH (Gen. 5:18–24). Enoch's translation to heaven gave rise to the belief that he must be knowledgeable concerning secrets about the future.

I. First Enoch. Also known as the *Ethiopic (Apocalypse of) Enoch* or simply as the *Book of Enoch*. It is a lengthy and composite work of 108 chapters, compiled in five sections or "books" that probably correspond, at least in part, to the author's sources. The whole was provided with an introduction and conclusion. It is possible to define further the structure of the book in the light of continuing study of the QUMRAN material.

A. Contents. The first five chapters serve as a kind of introduction to the whole work and especially its major themes of rewards and punishment, the end of the world, and the final judgment. Book I (chs. 6–36, often called the Book of the Watchers) is concerned largely with angels and the universe. Chapters 6–11, thought to come from a book attributed to Noah (see NOAH, APOCALYPSE OF), suggest that the fall of angels occurred because of the marriage of the SONS OF GOD with the daughters of men (cf. Gen. 6:1–2). The angels in turn taught human beings the various arts and skills of civilization, and mankind became corrupted and godless. God then pronounced judgment on mankind and on AZAZEL, who led them astray. In chs. 12–16, Enoch has a vision and, while he intercedes passionately on behalf of the fallen angels, he is finally instructed to predict their utter doom. In chs. 17–36, he is escorted by the angels of light on various tours throughout the earth, to the place of punishment of the fallen angels, to SHEOL, to the tree of life, to Jerusalem with its mountains, rivers, and streams, and to the Garden of Righteousness.

Book II (chs. 37–71) is composed of three parables or similitudes. Each parable is quite lengthy (compared to a parable of the Gospels, for example), and each is primarily concerned with the triumph of righteousness over wickedness. The first parable (chs. 38–44) deals with the impending judgment of the wicked, the abode of the Righteous and Elect One, the four archangels, and certain astronomical and meteorological secrets. The second parable (chs. 45–57) is concerned mainly with the Elect One or SON OF MAN sitting in judgment. He is not pictured as a human being but rather as a majestic heavenly being possessing absolute dominion over the world of men and of angels. The third parable (chs. 58–71) speaks of the blessedness of the saints, the measuring of paradise, and the judgment of the kings and mighty ones; it also gives the names and functions of the fallen angels.

Book III (chs. 72–82) is the so-called Book of the Heavenly Luminaries. It is an almost purely scientific treatise, showing virtually no interest in ethical questions. The author seeks to construct a uniform astronomical system from the data of the OT and argues that the measurement of time should be solar rather than lunar. Interestingly, however, the author's solar year is 364 days, though he is aware of the 365¼ day year. In ch. 80, however, the interest suddenly becomes ethical, and it is stated that in the last days the heavenly bodies as well as the earth will suffer serious disorders.

Book IV (chs. 83–90) consists of two lengthy dream-visions predicting the future history of Israel. Chapters 83–84 give the first dream-vision, which, in the view assumed by the author, predicts the flood as a judgment upon the world (see FLOOD, GENESIS). The second dream-vision encompasses chs. 85–90 and, after recounting the history from the beginning to the time of Enoch, goes on to predict the history of the world to the founding of the messianic kingdom. This history is given using a wide array of symbolism. Thus, oxen appear to symbolize the patriarchs; sheep, the true house of Israel; preying beasts and birds, the heathen; a sheep with a great horn, possibly Judas MACCABEE; and a white bull with great horns, the MESSIAH. The dream-vision ends with the new Jerusalem, the conversion of the Gentiles, the resurrection of the righteous, and the establishment of the messianic reign. The fact that the history as understood from the symbols goes no further than the Maccabean period is an indication of the date of this part of the work.

Book V (chs. 91–105, known as the Epistle of Enoch) is a work that includes exhortations for the righteous and maledictions for the wicked. The structure of this section is difficult, even though the theme is much the same as the rest of the work. A notable feature here is the Apocalypse of Weeks found in 93:1–10 (cf. 91:12–17). The history of the world from Enoch's time and on is divided into ten weeks of unequal length, each seemingly marked by some special event. Thus, the first is marked by Enoch's birth, the third by Abraham's call, and the seventh by the publication of Enoch's writings. In the eighth week the righteous will gain the victory over their oppressors. In the ninth week the world will be made ready for destruction. In the tenth and endless week a new heaven will be ushered in.

The conclusion of the work occupies chs. 106–8. This section relates the increase of sin after the flood until the messianic reign and then returns to the theme of rewards for the righteous and punishment for the wicked.

B. Texts and versions. Until the discovery of the Dead Sea Scrolls, the text of *1 Enoch* was best preserved in the Ethiopic MSS, more than forty of which are known (the earliest, however, goes back only as far as the 15th cent., perhaps the 14th). Most of these contain the complete work, sometimes together with certain biblical or apocryphal books. Within this group of MSS, two text types seem to be distinguishable.

Portions of the book have also been preserved in Greek. Two MSS dating from the 8th cent. or later were discovered in 1886–87 in a Christian grave at Akhmim, Egypt, and preserve chs. 1:1—32:6 and 19:3—21:9. Three MSS are known, including a 4th-cent. fragment among the Chester Beatty Papyri. In addition, some quotations from Enoch (esp. from 106:1–18) are preserved in Latin.

The scrolls from Qumran now appear to provide the best representatives of the original text of *1 Enoch*. About ten fragmentary MSS of the work in Aramaic were found in Cave 4 (cf. J. T. Milik, *The Books of Enoch: Aramaic Fragments of Qumran Cave 4* [1976]). Five of these correspond roughly to Book I and Book IV of the work. It appears that these sections together with the last chapters of the book once formed a separate work. Book III, the astronomical section, is represented by four Aramaic MSS that provide a more intelligible text than any others available to this time. The beginning of Book V is represented by one MS. It may have circulated as a separate work as well. Support for this suggestion comes from the fragmentary Chester Beatty papyrus. The fact that there are no fragments of Book II may be due to accident, or it may be that this too was a separate composition not known to the Qumran community; it is even possible that those chapters were composed after NT times (see summary by J. C. VanderKam, *The Dead Sea Scrolls Today* [1994], 37–39).

C. Date. Because the book is a composite work it is necessary to speak of "dates" rather than "date," and scholars are not agreed concerning them. R. H. Pfeiffer (*History of New Testament Times* [1949], 76–77) proposed the following dates (all B.C.):

Introduction, 150–100
Book I, c. 100
Book II, 100–80
Book III, 100–80 (but Apocalypse of Weeks 163)
Conclusion, 100–80.

It is now believed, however, that significant portions are pre-Maccabean in origin. On the other hand, Book II (Similitudes) is thought by some to be a later Christian document.

D. Language. Generally, experts in the field agree that the original language of *1 Enoch* was Semitic, though it is uncertain whether it was Hebrew or Aramaic. R. H. Charles (*APOT*, 2:171–77) assigned chs. 1–5 and 37–105 to Hebrew, and chs. 6–36 to Aramaic. Such a bilingual phenomenon is attested elsewhere (cf. the biblical books of Daniel and Ezra). The book has a distinctly poetical element, and this fact has been of considerable assistance in the editing of the work.

E. Influence. The book of *1 Enoch* exerted a strong and widespread influence on both Jewish and Christian literature. It appears that the writers of the *Testaments of the Twelve Patriarchs*, the *Assumption of Moses*, *2 Baruch*, and *4 Ezra* quoted from it. There appears also to be literary dependence between the book of *Jubilees* and *1 Enoch*, though it is not possible to be certain at all points which way the dependence runs. Charles suggested that for the earlier sections of *1 Enoch*, the writer made use of *Jubilees*, while in the later sections the dependence was reversed (this problem is linked with the question of dating). After the 2nd cent. A.D. Jewish literature took little notice of *1 Enoch*.

Parallels with *1 Enoch* from practically every section of the NT can be cited, though it is probably going too far to say that every NT writer must have been familiar with the book. Perhaps the most familiar reference is the famous passage in Jude 14–15. In addition to this apparent literary dependence, however, many of the concepts familiar to us from the NT appeared either first or most prominently in *1 Enoch*. These include the spiritual nature of the messianic reign, as well as the titles used to refer to the Messiah, such as "The Righteous One," "The Elect One," and "The Son of Man." The NT concepts of Sheol, resurrection, and demonology also bear striking similarities to those of *1 Enoch*.

Much of the early patristic literature shows acquaintance with *1 Enoch*. Barnabas and Tertullian, for example, seem to rate the work almost as highly as Scripture. Gnostic and apocryphal literature also make use of the book. However, by the 4th cent. A.D. the book had fallen into considerable disfavor in the W, and JEROME declared it to be an apocryphal work. Its use evidently continued for a longer time in the E. (See further R. H. Charles, *The Book of Enoch: Translated anew from the Editor's Text, with Introduction, Commentary, Critical Notes, and Appendices* [1912]; M. A. Knibb and E. Ullendorf, *The Ethiopic Book of Enoch*, 2 vols. [1978]; M. Black, *The Books of Enoch or 1 Enoch: A New English Edition with Commentary and Textual Notes* [1985]; E. Isaac in *OTP* 1:5–89; G. W. E. Nickelsburg, *1 Enoch*, Hermeneia, 2 vols. [2001–]; G. Boccaccini, Gabriele, ed., *Enoch and Qumran Origins: New Light on a Forgotten Connection* [2005]; D. R. Jackson, *Enochic Judaism: Three Defining Paradigm Exemplars* [2004].)

II. Second Enoch. Also known as the *Slavonic (Apocalypse of) Enoch* and the *Book of the Secrets of Enoch*. This work is known to us only from some twenty MSS written in Old Slavonic. These appear to fall into two recensions of different length.

A. Contents. *Second Enoch* is basically an account of Enoch's travels through the seven heavens; it includes certain revelations given to him and Enoch's exhortations to his children. The revelations are concerned with creation and the history of mankind. In the beginning God created the world out of nothing. He also created seven heavens with all the angelic hosts and mankind as well. Just as God performed his creative work in six days and rested the seventh, even so the history of the world would span 6,000 years and it would then rest for 1,000 years. After this, an eternal day of blessing would begin.

The souls of men were created before the world began, and also a place either in heaven or in hell for the future habitation of each soul. The soul was created good, but because of free will and because of the soul's habitation in the body, sin appeared in spite of the instruction man had received regarding the Two Ways. Men will therefore have to face judgment, and only the righteous will escape the hell prepared for sinners. The ethical teaching of the book is in many respects noble. Man should work and be just, charitable, unavenging, and humble. Above all, he should fear God.

B. Language, place of writing, author, date. At least a part of the book was originally written in Greek. The evidence is threefold: the name Adam is derived from the initial letters of the Greek words for the directions E, W, S and N; the chronology of the LXX is followed; the text of the LXX is used as over against the Hebrew; and the Greek of ECCLESIASTICUS and of WISDOM OF SOLOMON are evidently used. Some portions of the book, however, were most probably Hebrew in origin.

The place of writing of the book is thought to be Egypt, possibly in ALEXANDRIA. This is argued from the typically Hellenistic and Philonic speculations the book contains, the lack of messianic teaching typical of the OT, the appearance of monstrous serpents that are typically Egyptian, and the syncretistic character of the creation account. The author must have been a Hellenistic Jew with syncretistic tendencies.

On the question of dating, the fact that the *Testaments of the Twelve Patriarchs* makes use of passages from *2 Enoch* implies a pre-Christian date for those portions. The use of Sirach, *1 Enoch*, and the Wisdom of Solomon implies a date after 30 B.C. The fact that the temple is still standing in *2 Enoch* implies a date before A.D. 70. Most scholars, in fact, prefer an early Christian date (e.g., A.D. 1–50) for the composition of this book.

C. Influence. The book seems to have exercised considerable influence upon both Jewish and Christian literature. Its presence is felt in the *Book of Adam and Eve*, the *Apocalypse of Moses*, the *Apocalypse of Paul*, the *Sibylline Oracles*, the *Ascension of Isaiah*, and the *Testaments of the Twelve Patriarchs*. IRENAEUS and ORIGEN both show traces of its influence, as does the *Epistle of Barnabas*. Many passages of the NT can be cited for the similarity of their thought and expression with *2 Enoch*. (See further R. H. Charles and W. R. Morfill, *The Book of the Secrets of Enoch* [1896]; English trans. of both recensions by F. I. Andersen in *OTP*, 1:91–221.)

III. Third Enoch. Also known as the *Hebrew Enoch* or the *Rabbinic Enoch*. This work follows, to some extent, the *Slavonic Enoch* and is attributed to Rabbi Ishmael, a prominent figure in the Bar Kokhba rebellion. In this book, Rabbi Ishmael ascends through six heavens to meet Enoch (who is referred to as "Metatron") in the seventh. Here Enoch discusses some events of his own life and the life of Adam. The work reflects some of the traditions of *2 Enoch*, and it is probably these that were originally in Hebrew. The date is hotly disputed, but probably no earlier than the 6th cent. A.D. (See further H. Odeberg, *3 Enoch* [1928]; English trans. and extensive introduction by P. S. Alexander in *OTP*, 1:223–315.)

H. G. Andersen

Enoch (place) ee′nuhk (חֲנוֹךְ *H2840*, possibly "trained" or "initiated" or "follower"; Ἐνώχ *G1970*). A city that Cain built and named after his son Enoch (Gen. 4:17).

Enos ee′nuhs. Alternate form of Enosh.

Enosh ee′nosh (אֱנוֹשׁ *H633*, "man"; Ἐνώς *G1968*). KJV Enos (except 1 Chr. 1:1). Son of Seth and grandson of Adam; it is noted that at his birth "men began to call on the name of the Lord" (Gen. 4:26; on the apparent discrepancy between this statement and Exod. 6:3, see God, names of, II). At the age of 90 years, Enosh became the father of Kenan; he had other sons and daughters and died at 905 years (Gen. 5:6–11). Because his name means "man," he may represent a new Adam (ʾādām *H134*, "man, mankind"), that is, a humanity revived by the birth of Seth and preserved after the flood. Enosh is included in the Chronicler's genealogy (1 Chr. 1:1) and in Luke's genealogy of Jesus Christ (Lk. 3:38, where many English versions have "Enos," a spelling that reflects the Gk. form). (See S. D. Fraade, *Enosh and His Generation: Pre-Israelite Hero and History in Postbiblical Interpretation* [1984].)

C. P. Weber

En Rimmon en-rim′uhn (עֵין רִמּוֹן *H6538*, "spring of Rimmon [pomegranate]"). Also En-rimmon. A village resettled by the people of Judah after the exile (Neh. 11:29). Its identification is uncertain, but many scholars believe it is the same as Rimmon (place), a city in the Negev (Josh. 15:32; 19:7; 1 Chr. 4:32; in these three passages, the two names "Ain" and "Rimmon" perhaps should be read as one, "En Rimmon"). It may have marked the extreme S of Judah in postexilic times (if Zech. 14:10 refers to the same town).

H. L. Ellison

En Rogel en-roh′guhl (עֵין רֹגֵל *H6537*, prob. "spring of the fuller"; see Fuller). A spring S of Jerusalem, just below the junction of the Hinnom and Kidron Valleys, on the boundary between the tribes of Benjamin and Judah (Josh. 15:7; 18:16). It was here that Jonathan and Ahimaaz, two of David's spies, stayed during Absalom's rebellion (2 Sam. 17:17). From that point just S of the city of David they could report to David what a maidservant told them, since they themselves could not enter the city. The spring was mentioned again as the coronation site during the attempted usurpation of the kingdom by Adonijah, who sacrificed animals at a site near En Rogel known as the Stone of Zoheleth (1 Ki. 1:9).

Today En Rogel is connected with Bir Ayyub (The Well of Job), where a gasoline-powered pump brings up the water that in olden times came up of itself. The one other source of water in E Jerusalem, ʿAin Sitti Maryam (Spring of the Lady Mary) or the Virgin's Fountain, has also been a suggested identification but is a less likely candidate (the latter is now thought to be the Gihon Spring of 1 Ki. 1:33 et al.). (See J. Simons, *Jerusalem in the Old Testament* [1952], 48–49.) See also Jackal Well.

R. L. Alden

The spring of En Shemesh lies at the base of the ridge that leads to Bethany, home of Mary, Martha, and Lazarus. (View to the W.)

enrollment. See CENSUS.

En Shemesh en-shem´ish (עֵין שֶׁמֶשׁ *H6539*, "spring of Shemesh [sun]"). Also En-shemesh. A spring on the boundary between the tribes of BENJAMIN and JUDAH (Josh. 15:7; 18:17). It is usually identified with modern ʿAin Ḥoḏ, about 2 mi. E of JERUSALEM on the way to JERICHO in the Jordan Valley. It is sometimes referred to as the "Spring of the Apostles." G. GIACUMAKIS, JR.

ensign. See BANNER.

En Tappuah en-tap´yoo-uh (עֵין תַּפּוּחַ *H6540*, "spring of Tappuah [apple tree]"). Also known as En-tappuah. A settlement on the boundary between the tribes of EPHRAIM and MANASSEH, near the town of TAPPUAH (Josh. 17:7; cf. v. 8).

Enuma Elish en-*oo*´muh-el´ish. The opening phrase and title of the most important Mesopotamian cosmological myth. The text was usually written on seven tablets in the Babylonian dialect of Akkadian (see LANGUAGES OF THE ANE II.A) and used as the ceremonial epic in the New Year's ritual at the great temple of Esagila in BABYLON. The standard version of the narrative dates from the 1st millennium B.C., but the true provenience of the epic is controversial. The text has been recovered by the excavations at NINEVEH, ASSHUR, and Kish, and several editions and many translations have been published.

The contents of the tablets are as follows. Tablet I: the initial coming into being of the most primitive forces and gods; the rage of the sea goddess TIAMAT. Tablet II: Tiamat and her monsters gird for battle against the gods who take MARDUK (in some versions ASSHUR) as their champion. Tablet III: the assembly of the gods decrees the outcome of the impending battle and the glory of Marduk. Tablet IV: Marduk prevails over Tiamat in a gruesome struggle and dissects the cadaver. Tablet V: Marduk constructs the cosmos and the cosmological order from the remains of Tiamat. Tablet VI: Tiamat's captive henchman, Kingu, is slain and dissected, and his blood used to make mankind. Tablet VII: a list of the magical names of Marduk to which is attached a short epilogue.

The text has been proposed by the followers of the pan-Babylonian school of critics as the true source of the biblical story of CREATION. A brief survey of the two narratives will show that they are only superficially related and that the biblical account is of a considerably higher order of thought. The epic of Enuma Elish is of low literary quality in comparison with other eloquent texts, such as GILGAMESH, Ludlul Bel Nemeqi, and the like. (See A. Heidel, *The Babylonian Genesis*, 2nd ed. [1951]; *ANET*, 60–72, 501–3; A. L. Oppenheim, *Ancient Mesopotamia* [1964], 177–203, 264ff.; W. G. Lambert, *Enuma Elish: The Babylonian Epic of Creation, the Cuneiform Text* [1966].) W. WHITE, JR.

envy. A feeling of displeasure and ill will because of another's advantages or possessions. The English word may render Hebrew *qinʾâ H7863*, "passion," which is often used in the good sense of "zeal," less frequently in the negative sense of "envy" (e.g., Job 5:2; verb *qānāʾ H7861*, "to be envious, arouse jealousy," e.g., Gen. 26:14). Both the Psalms and Proverbs warn against the temptation of becoming envious of evil persons when they seem to prosper in spite of their wrongdoing (Pss. 37:1; 73:2, 3; Prov. 3:31; 23:17; 24:1, 19). The author of Ecclesiastes observes that men are driven to work and to develop their skills when they envy the prosperity of their neighbors (Eccl. 4:4). The OT abounds in examples of the evil effects of envy—among them JACOB and ESAU, RACHEL and LEAH (Gen. 30:1), JOSEPH and his brothers, HAMAN and MORDECAI. (See *NIDOTTE*, 3:937–40.)

In the NT "envy" usually renders Greek *phthonos G5784*, which uniformly has a negative meaning, "ill will, envy" (cf. R. C. Trench, *Synonyms of the New Testament*, 9th ed. [1880], 86–90; LN, 1:760–61; *NIDNTT*, 1:557–58). For example, envy is said to have led to the crucifixion of Jesus (Matt. 27:18), and it is listed with the worst of sins by Jesus and by Paul (Mk. 7:22; Rom. 1:29; Gal. 5:21). Christians are warned against it (Gal. 5:26; 1 Pet. 2:1). James uses the term in a very difficult statement, "the spirit he caused to live in us envies intensely [*pros phthonon epipothei*]" (Jas. 4:5 NIV). There is much to be said for the alternate rendering, "he jealously longs for the spirit he has caused to dwell in us" (TNIV), perhaps an allusion to Exod. 20:5. (For a full discussion, see P. H. Davids, *The Epistle of James: A Commentary on the Greek Text*, NIGTC [1982], 162–64.) See also COVET; JEALOUSY. S. BARABAS

Epaenetus. See EPENETUS.

Epaphras ep´uh-fras (Ἐπαφρᾶς *G2071*, prob. a contracted form of Ἐπαφρόδιτος *G2073*, "charming"). A native of COLOSSE and founder of the Colossian church, who was with PAUL when he wrote COLOSSIANS (Col. 1:7–8; 4:12–13; Phlm. 23; not to be confused with EPAPHRODITUS, a member of the Philippian church, Phil. 2:25; 4:18). Epaphras may have been Paul's convert. As Paul's representative he had evangelized Colosse (Col. 1:7) and the neighboring towns of LAODICEA and HIERAPOLIS (4:13) during Paul's Ephesian ministry (Acts 19:10). His visit to Paul in Rome and his report concerning conditions in the churches of the Lycus Valley caused Paul to write Colossians (Col. 1:7–9).

Paul's high esteem for Epaphras is seen in the terms he applies to him: "our dear fellow servant," "a faithful minister of Christ on our behalf" (Col. 1:7), "a servant of Christ Jesus" (4:12), and "my fellow prisoner" (Phlm. 23). Because the last term is also applied to ARISTARCHUS (Col. 4:10), the probable meaning is that Epaphras and Aristarchus alternated in voluntarily sharing Paul's imprisonment (cf. J. D. G. Dunn, *The Epistles to the Colossians and to Philemon: A Commentary on the Greek Text*, NIGTC [1996], 347–48). The unique distinction of Epaphras is Paul's praise of him for his fervent intercession for the churches in the Lycus Valley (Col. 4:12–13). (See H. S. Seekings, *The Men of the Pauline Circle* [1914], 147–53; H. C. Lees, *St. Paul's Friends* [1918], 146–59; D. E. Hiebert in *BSac* 136 [1979]: 54–64.) D. E. HIEBERT

Epaphroditus i-paf´ruh-di´tuhs (Ἐπαφρόδιτος *G2073*, "handsome, charming"). A member of the church at PHILIPPI who brought an offering to PAUL when the apostle was imprisoned in Rome (Phil. 2:25–30; 4:18). His Greek name (corresponding to the Lat. *Venustus*, "belonging to Venus," called Aphrodite by the Greeks) was common and indicates a non-Jewish origin. It was also common in a contracted form, EPAPHRAS, but there is no reason to identify Epaphroditus with the Epaphras from Colosse (Col. 1:7; 4:12).

Epaphroditus was an esteemed member of the Philippian church; that he was an officer is not certain. He was commissioned to deliver the church's offering to Paul (Phil. 4:18) and to stay and help him (2:25, 30). Addressing the Philippians, Paul calls him "your messenger, whom you sent to take care of my needs," thus commissioned to serve Paul on their behalf. He became dangerously ill at Rome "for the work of Christ." His sickness possibly came from exposure on the trip, but more probably from overexertion in fulfilling his commission at Rome, "risking his life to make up for the help you could not give me."

After his slow recovery, Paul felt it best to send him back home. Epaphroditus was distressed because of anxiety for him at Philippi and longed to return. Paul sent him back with the letter to the PHILIPPIANS and asked them to receive Epaphroditus "in the Lord with great joy." (For the view that the Philippians expected Epaphroditus to stay with Paul so that TIMOTHY could go to Philippi, and that the apostle was thus concerned about how the church might receive Epaphroditus, see M. Silva, *Philippians*, BECNT, 2nd ed. [2005], 138–40.) Paul's description of Epaphroditus as "my brother, fellow worker and fellow soldier" indicates his own high esteem of him. (Cf. H. S. Seekings, *The Men of the Pauline Circle* [1914], 157–64; H. C. Lees, *St. Paul's Friends* [1918], 192–209; A. T. Robertson, *Types of Preachers in the New Testament* [1922], 230–38; R. A. Culpepper in *RevExp* 77 [1980]: 349–58.) D. E. HIEBERT

Epeiph ee´fif (Επιφι). Also Epiphi. Eleventh month of the Egyptian year, approximately August in the 3rd cent. B.C. (the corresponding date in the Julian calendar slipped by one day every four years). It is mentioned in 3 Macc. 6:38, which records that the Jews in Egypt, under the Egyptian monarch PTOLEMY IV Philopator (222–204 B.C.), were registered during the forty days from 25 Pachon (the ninth month) to 4 Epeiph. The purpose of this registration was their destruction, which was scheduled for 5–7 Epeiph, but they were spared through a series of miraculous events (vv. 17–29).

C. P. WEBER

Epenetus i-pee′nuh-tuhs (Ἐπαίνετος *G2045*, "praised"). Also Epaenetus. A Christian in ROME affectionately greeted by PAUL as "my dear friend" and "the first convert [*lit.*, the firstfruits] to Christ in the province of Asia" (Rom. 16:5; KJV, "Achaia," reflecting an inferior variant reading). Such senior Christians naturally assumed positions of leadership in the church. That Epenetus was an accepted leader is implied in Paul's mention of him immediately after PRISCILLA AND AQUILA. It is not stated that Epenetus was the personal convert of Paul; he may have been won by Priscilla and Aquila before Paul returned to EPHESUS (Acts 18:27). This mention of Epenetus has been used to support the claim of an Ephesian destination for Rom. 16, But the mention of more than twenty others with no known Ephesian connections blunts the claim.

D. E. HIEBERT

ephah (measure) ee′fuh. See WEIGHTS AND MEASURES III.B.

Ephah (person) ee′fuh (עֵיפָה *H6549*, "darkness"). (1) Son of MIDIAN and grandson of ABRAHAM and KETURAH (Gen. 25:4; 1 Chr. 1:33). Ephah was thus the eponym of a prominent Midianite tribe, apparently inhabiting NW ARABIA and famous for its camels (Isa. 60:6 [ʿêpâ *H6548*]; cf. I. Ephʿal, *The Ancient Arabs: Nomads on the Borders of the Fertile Crescent, 9th-5th Centuries B.C.* [1982], 216–17, 230–32; E. A. Knauf, *Midian* [1988]). See also HANOCH.

(2) A concubine of CALEB who bore him three sons; she is mentioned in the genealogy of JUDAH (1 Chr. 2:46).

(3) Son of JAHDAI included in the genealogy of Judah (1 Chr. 2:47). The mention of Jahdai and his sons is abrupt, but apparently there was some connection between them and Caleb (cf. vv. 46, 48). See also #2 above.

E. B. SMICK

Ephai ee′fi (עֵיפַי *H6550* [*Ketib*, עוֹפַי], "my darkness" or "my bird"). An inhabitant of NETOPHAH (a city or group of villages near BETHLEHEM) whose sons were army officers under the authority of GEDALIAH, governor of Judah after the destruction of Jerusalem by the Babylonians (Jer. 40:8; the parallel passage, 2 Ki. 25:23, reads differently; see TANHUMETH). Gedaliah and his officers were subsequently murdered (Jer. 41:1–3).

G. GIACUMAKIS, JR.

Epher ee′fuhr (עֵפֶר *H6761*, "[kid of] gazelle"). (1) Son of MIDIAN and grandson of ABRAHAM and KETURAH (Gen. 25:4; 1 Chr. 1:33). Epher was thus the eponym of a Midianite tribe in NW ARABIA (cf. Gen. 25:6). There may have been more than one clan of Midian, or the name may be used broadly of different peoples. Some who were the descendants of Abraham were helpful to Israel (Exod. 3:1), while others became bitter enemies (Num. 31:2–12; Jdg. 6:1–6). (See E. A. Knauf, *Midian* [1988].) See also HANOCH.

(2) Son of EZRAH and descendant of JUDAH (1 Chr. 4:17).

(3) One of the heads of families in the half-tribe of MANASSEH at the time of TIGLATH-PILESER III (1 Chr. 5:24; cf. v. 26). These leaders are described as "brave warriors, famous men," but also "unfaithful to the God of their fathers" (v. 25).

E. B. SMICK

Ephes Dammim, Pas Dammim ee′fiz-dam′im, pas-dam′im (אֶפֶס דַּמִּים *H702*, "border of Dammim [blood]"; פַּס דַּמִּים *H7169*, perhaps a short form). Also Ephez-dammim, Pas-dammim. A site in the territory of JUDAH between SOCOH and AZEKAH where the PHILISTINES encamped and near which DAVID defeated GOLIATH (1 Sam. 17:1; 1 Chr. 11:13; cf. 2 Sam. 23:9 NIV). Some have conjectured that the deep red color of the soil gave rise to the concept of blood, but it is more probable that the site was so named because of the number of battles fought there between Israel and the Philistines. The site was near the Valley of Elah (see ELAH, VALLEY OF), but the precise location is uncertain. Proposed identifications include Beit Faṣed (SE of Socoh) and, more likely, Damun (about 4 mi. NE of Socoh).

C. L. FEINBERG

Ephesians, Epistle to the i-fee′zhuhnz. One of the so-called PRISON EPISTLES of the apostle PAUL. According to most Greek MSS and other ancient testimony, this letter was written to the Christians in EPHESUS (Eph. 1:1). The words "in Ephesus," however, are omitted by the earliest and best texts: P[46], CODEX SINAITICUS, and CODEX VATICANUS, with some additional support. Many scholars believe that the phrase was incorporated from an early marginal gloss and that the original writing did not include an address, TYCHICUS having the responsibility to introduce the letter personally to those for whom it was intended (cf. 6:21; Col. 4:7).

If so, the letter was written generally to the "saints" in the province of ASIA. When the need arose to identify the letter more specifically with a church center, Ephesus was chosen because of its proximity to the region involved and its importance as the chief city of Asia. Instrumental in the assignment may have been the fact that Paul apparently had written no other letter to this important city, even though he had carried on an extensive and prolonged mission in its environs (cf. Acts 19:8, 10). It is possible that when the letter was read at Ephesus, the church simply appropriated it and was responsible for introducing the marginal gloss into the text. When one considers the prestige enjoyed by a church that had been a recipient of a letter from an apostle, such an eventuality cannot be excluded.

The reference to Tychichus and to the apostle's "chains" (Eph. 6:20) identifies this letter with others written by Paul probably during his (first) Roman imprisonment (cf. Phil. 1:12–14; Col. 4:18; Phlm. 9). Its close relationship in subject matter to COLOSSIANS fixes rather closely the time of its composition (A.D. 60–62). The epistle focuses upon the CHURCH, triumphant and exalted, in which Christ's reconciling activity is being demonstrated. Because of modern ecumenical concerns, Ephesians has assumed a dominant place in the life and study of the Christian community.

   I. Authorship and canonicity
  II. Arguments against the genuineness of Ephesians
     A. Vocabulary
     B. The relationship of Ephesians to other Pauline epistles
     C. Style
     D. Subjective questions
 III. Origin and destination
 IV. Content and organization
  V. Outline of Ephesians
 VI. Theology of the epistle
     A. Church
     B. Holy Spirit

I. Authorship and canonicity. The author of the letter identifies himself as Paul, the apostle to the Gentiles (Eph. 1:1; 3:1). In a genuinely Pauline manner, he makes frequent personal references to himself and his activities, incorporating these statements into the body of his argument (cf. 3:3–4, 7, 13–14; 4:1, 17; 5:32; 6:19–20). The vocabulary, subject matter, and general theological approach are admittedly Pauline. Moreover, the external attestation for the knowledge and use of the book as a genuine Pauline writing in the ancient church is wholly positive. Some scholars feel they can detect its influence on 1 Peter and Acts. Strong reminiscences of it are to be found in most of the APOSTOLIC FATHERS; POLYCARP, for example, includes an explicit citation of its text. It is found also in the writings of the heretical schools as well as in the Apologists of the 2nd cent. Although IRENAEUS is the first to cite it as Pauline, it is clear that this was the common understanding of the church. As such, it is included in the MURATORIAN CANON, in MARCION's statement of books to be accepted (though under the name of the Epistle to the LAODICEANS), and in every subsequent list of Pauline writings. Its authorship was never disputed in the ancient church, nor was its place in the canon ever challenged.

Aerial view of Ephesus, showing the excavation area with the theater and the Cardo, main street of the city. (View to the E.)

With the rise of critical studies in the 18th cent., however, its authenticity became suspect. The title Epistle to the Ephesians served to compromise its integrity. That Paul could have written such an impersonal letter, devoid of personal references to people with whom he had labored three years, was deemed incredible. Moreover, it was judged an absurdity that Paul would write to the Ephesians in terms of "mutual hearsay" (cf. Eph. 1:15, "ever since I heard about your faith in the Lord Jesus and your love for all the saints"; 3:2, "you have heard about the administration of God's grace that was given to me for you"). The whole tenor of the letter showed that it was written by someone who had no firsthand acquaintanceship with the recipients. For these early critics, who had no reason to be suspicious of the words "in Ephesus" at 1:1 (the earliest MSS had not yet come to light), there could be only one conclusion: Paul had not written this letter.

Building on this seemingly secure conclusion, critics began to look for other evidence of the inauthentic character of this epistle. Singled out were the extraordinarily close relationship of Ephesians to Colossians, the verbose and unusually long sentences of Ephesians, the peculiar phrase, "holy apostles and prophets" (3:5; cf. 2:20), and the presence of many "non-Pauline" words.

Just at the time when the spurious nature of the epistle seemed beyond question, however, new MS discoveries and textual studies showed that the letter had not been addressed to the church at Ephesus. This meant that the primary evidence for deciding against the authenticity of Ephesians was no longer valid. The problem became then whether the arguments dependent upon the vocabulary, style, and internal inconsistencies were sufficient to reject an epistle that had the strongest possible external and internal attestation to Pauline authorship. On this question critical scholarship became divided. English scholars generally defended it, German scholars with a few notable exceptions rejected it, and American scholars appeared on both sides of the issue.

What tends to complicate the debate are several factors. (1) Among the critics who reject the authenticity of the epistle there is some disagreement concerning the basis for their rejection. (2) Some of the arguments advanced are mutually exclusive (e.g., many scholars who reject Ephesians accept the genuineness of Colossians, yet the arguments against Ephesians advanced by others would make Colossians inauthentic as well). (3) Arguments that have been shown to be invalid (such as those based on vocabulary statistics) continue to be presented against Ephesians; in such instances it appears that some critics depend on the number of objections that can be raised rather than on the decisive value of any given argument.

II. Arguments against the genuineness of the epistle

A. Vocabulary. One of the older but more persistent arguments advanced against the genuineness of the letter is the number of "non-Pauline" words it contains. F. W. Beare (in *IB*, 10:598) states it this way: "There are, to begin with, an extraordinarily large number of *hapax legomena* — eighty-two words not found elsewhere in the Pauline letters." G. Johnston (in *IDB*, 2:109) uses the same argument: "Linguistic considerations alone are not decisive; yet note that Ephesians has about a hundred non-Pauline words, of which some forty are unique in the NT." Every writing of Paul, however, including the brief note to Philemon, has a number of "non-Pauline" words. Some of these occur nowhere else in the NT (commonly called *hapax legomena*), whereas others, though they occur elsewhere in the NT, do not appear in any other Pauline writing.

Out of the total vocabulary of Ephesians (529 words), 95 are "non-Pauline" (the statistics do not include the PASTORAL EPISTLES, since many critics question their genuineness also). The number indeed appears imposing. Romans, however, has 292 non-Pauline words; 1 Corinthians, 283; 2 Corinthians, 207; and Galatians, with a vocabulary of 526 words, has an identical number of 95 non-Pauline words. Moreover, Philippians, with 84 non-Pauline words out of a total vocabulary of 448, has a higher percentage than Ephesians. Yet these letters are accepted as Paul's by virtually all scholars. Every study of non-Pauline vocabulary supports the Pauline authorship of Ephesians (see P. N. Harrison, *The Problem of the Pastoral Epistles* [1921]; J. Schmid, *Der Epheserbrief des Apostels Paulus* [1925]; and the very sophisticated study of K. Grayston and G. Herdan, "The Authorship of the Pastorals in the Light of Statistical Linguistics," *NTS* 6 [1959]: 1–15; note also the present author's own investigation, G. W. Barker, *A Critical Evaluation of the Lexical and Linguistic Data Advanced by E. J. Goodspeed and Supported by C. L. Mitton in a Proposed Solution to the Problem of the Authorship and Date of Ephesians*, unpub. Harvard Univ. thesis [1962]).

A study by E. J. Goodspeed (*The Meaning of Ephesians* [1933]) sent the argument based on vocabulary in a new direction, based not on the number of non-Pauline words but on the more frequent appearance of these words in writings of the tenth decade of the 1st cent. In a limited investigation he has shown that 31 of the 32 non-Pauline words studied in Ephesians reappear in Acts, Revelation, Hebrews, and 1 Peter, writings dated by him in the tenth decade. This served to confirm Goodspeed's thesis that Ephesians was written by a disciple of Paul sometime around A.D. 90. Goodspeed failed, however, to test his findings from Ephesians by similar studies of unchallenged Pauline writings. If he had done so, he would have found that Galatians, for example, has 61 words that met his criteria, 56 of which reappear in the same four writings as is true of Ephesians. Moreover, they occur with even greater frequency (433 instances to 235). The same is true of 1 Corinthians, Romans, 2 Corinthians, and Philippians. All that Goodspeed discovered was an unusual trait of a *genuine* epistle, not a proof of inauthenticity.

It has been alleged that an unusually high number of non-Pauline words in Ephesians reappear in the writings of the early church fathers, again supporting a late date for Ephesians. The facts, however, prove to be contrary. In comparable studies, Ephesians shows proportionately fewer words that appear either in the Apostolic Fathers or the Apologists than does Galatians or Romans. If the Apostolic Fathers alone are compared, Ephesians shows proportionately fewer such words than 1 Corinthians or Philippians. However, non-Pauline writings show a vast difference in this respect. Ephesians has the identical statistical pattern of the genuine epistles of Paul. That such a pattern could have been effected deliberately or unconsciously by an imitator seems wholly unreasonable.

The appearance of certain "key" terms not before encountered in Paul is cited as an argument against Ephesians. Specifically noted are the phrase *en tois epouraniois* ("in the heavenly realms," Eph. 1:3 et al.) and such words as *diabolos* G1333 ("devil," 4:27; 6:11), *eusplanchnos* G2359 ("compassionate," 4:32), and others. However, there is nothing especially noteworthy about this. Of a total Pauline vocabulary of 2,177 words, over half (1,203) occur in only one epistle, and inevitably included are key terms. In Romans, Paul uses key words that never appear elsewhere among the Pauline epistles (e.g., *apeitheō* G578, *dikaiōma* G1468, *apistia* G602, et al.). Nonetheless these words become common terms in the later literature.

B. The relationship of Ephesians to other Pauline epistles. It has been alleged that Ephesians reads as a "mosaic," implying that it is "shot through" with expressions from earlier Christian writings (cf. E. Käsemann in *Studies in Luke-Acts*, ed. L. Keck and J. L. Martyn [1966], 289). Goodspeed finds that out of 618 phrases in Ephesians, 550 have unmistakable parallels in the other Pauline letters either in "word or substance." Although C. L. Mitton (*The Epistle to the Ephesians* [1951]; see also *ExpTim* 67 [1955–56]: 195–98) concedes that Goodspeed has overstated the case, he still finds 250 phrases in Ephesians that have parallels in other Pauline writings—an amount far in excess of a genuine Pauline epistle. Neither Goodspeed nor Mitton, however, exercised the same care to discover in their test book, Philippians, parallels to other Pauline epistles as they did with Ephesians. They include verbatim parallels between Ephesians and the other Paulines, 6 consisting of a single word, 28 phrases of two words, 18 of three, and 12 of four. Of the 12 parallels consisting of more than five words, 7 occur in Colossians, 2 are citations from the OT, 2 more are formulae (benedictions), and one consists of a standard Pauline introduction formula.

On the other hand, approximately one half of the parallels between Philippians and the other Pauline letters are overlooked. If one counts the number of words in Ephesians that occur in phrases that have exact verbal correspondence with other Pauline writings, the total amount will be 148. If one makes a similar count of Philippians, the corresponding total will be 129. Considering the difference in length between the two books, the results are negligible. Moreover, if one subtracts the Colossians parallels from both books, Philippians is left with 122 instances of verbatim likenesses compared to 115 in Ephesians. The evidence indicates that although there is a remarkable relation between Ephesians and Colossians, there is nothing at all unusual concerning the relation of Ephesians to the other Pauline epistles.

C. Style. It has been long observed that the style of Ephesians is remarkably unlike that of the other Pauline letters. There is a predilection for overly long conglomerate sentences, synonyms heaped one upon another, and endless genitival connections. Although the phenomena can be paralleled elsewhere in Paul (cf. Ernst Percy, *Die Probleme der Kolosser- und Epheserbriefe* [1946]), such Semitic, syntactical phenomena occur four times as often in Ephesians as in all other epistles of the Pauline corpus (cf. K. G. Kuhn, "Der Epheser im Lichte der Qumrantexte," *NTS* 7 [1960]: 334–35). The style is variously described as "Hymnic-liturgical" (Goodspeed), "Meditative-doxological" (Käsemann); and "Liturgical-prayerful" (M. Barth). Yet the stylistic phenomena in Ephesians cannot alone be used to decide the issue of its genuineness. The familiar Pauline phrases are clearly in evidence, and the pattern of thought is admittedly Pauline. What distinguishes Ephesians from the other epistles is not so much the presence of that which is non-Pauline as it is the concentrated use of the Pauline language of worship.

D. Subjective questions. Other questions are raised by those who doubt the authenticity of this epistle. Would Paul have written two letters so much alike as Colossians and Ephesians? Would he have employed the same words (e.g., *mystērion* G3696 or *oikonomia* G3873) but have given them new meanings? Would he have referred to the apostles as "holy," or to the church as built upon the apostles and prophets? Could he have conceived of the church as "universal," believed that Christ descended into Hades, or refrained from mentioning the parousia?

The problem with these questions, however, is their subjective character. By their very nature, they defy objective analysis. Their answers depend heavily on our own prejudices of what we think would be appropriate for Paul in a given situation. There is no possibility of determining from a 20th-cent. viewpoint what Paul could or could not have thought or written. It is just as difficult to enter the thought-world of "baptizing for the dead" (1 Cor. 15:29), being transported "to the third heaven" (2 Cor. 12:2), or "delivering someone over to Satan" (1 Cor. 5:5). If any of these references had occurred in Ephesians they would most certainly have constituted additional evidence for the presence of ungenuine Pauline utterances.

In summary, the internal considerations, where they can be reduced to objective, statistical data, clearly support Pauline authorship. The external data are early and weighty, and have always been recognized as tipping the scales heavily toward genuineness. What remains are those differences of style, mood, word usage, and point of view that confront us for the first time in this letter. Most critics will acknowledge that no one illustration of difficulty from this material would by itself be sufficient to cause us to question the genuineness of the writing.

It is this situation that demands confronting the well-known question that Cadbury has so aptly framed: "which is more likely, that an imitator in the first century composed a writing ninety or ninety-five percent in accordance with Paul's style or that Paul himself wrote a letter diverging five or ten percent from his usual style?" (H. J. Cadbury, "The Dilemma of Ephesians," *NTS* 5 [1958–59]: 91–102, esp. 101). The force of Cadbury's question becomes even more formidable if one allows that the circumstances that brought forth this particular letter are undeniably different from what was true of the other Pauline letters, and that they require both differences in style and subject matter.

III. Origin and destination. At the beginning of his ministry, Paul was almost totally consumed in establishing and maintaining his churches. Little time was left to him for anything else, especially for "writing theology" or publishing treatises on baptism or church government. When he wrote at all during this period, his letters were limited to that which was critical for the mission and thus they are relatively easy to fix as to occasion, date, and purpose. They abound in personal allusions and make frequent reference to the local situation.

Toward the end of Paul's life, this situation changed. His arrests grew more frequent, and the amount of time he spent in prison became a primary factor. He was arrested at Ephesus and probably imprisoned. He gained his freedom, but was arrested in Jerusalem. Two long years were spent in prison at CAESAREA followed by two more years at ROME. Although prison itself represented no new experience for Paul (cf. 2 Cor. 11:23), the curtailment of his freedom for such extended periods was new. Particularly hard to bear was the fact that contact with his churches was limited to that maintained through intermediaries who came to visit him.

If Paul lost something by being cut off from personal contact with his churches, he was to some extent compensated by the opportunity he gained for reflecting upon the Christian mission as it had developed and as to its future. In such a review Paul could not have avoided certain conclusions: (1) the mission of the church in the world was going to involve a longer time than was originally supposed; (2) the time could not be far distant when the apostles and their associates would no longer be available to lead the church; (3) God's plan from the beginning must have anticipated this fact; (4) there were mysteries in God's dealing with Jews and Gentiles yet to be understood.

Paul's attention was inevitably drawn to the consideration of these questions, and the so-called prison correspondence logically includes some refinement of the apostle's thinking on these subjects. Also the epistles of this period understandably bear less of the personal touch. Large sections of the writings seem to have been predigested. More of it seems to have originated out of the life and worship of the Christian community. If the above is assumed, it is understandable why a reconstruction of events leading to the publication of Ephesians must indeed be tenuous. Apart from the reference to Tychicus (Eph. 6:21) and Paul's imprisonment (3:1), Ephesians is void of any objective clue as to occasion. What may be concluded concerning the occasion is largely dependent upon what can be inferred from a study of the subject matter, and the style and language of the text. Two elements relating to Ephesians, however, demand special attention and must be included in any such reconstruction.

In the first place, a significant number of hymns (e.g. Eph. 1:3–12, 20–23; 2:4–10, 14–18), creedal confessions, and stereotyped liturgical formulas are included in the text (cf. G. Schille, *Liturgisches Gut in Epheser* [1953]). It is the presence of this material in the letter that tends to transform it from prose (an epistle) to liturgical poetry (a tract). Either the subject matter has caused the author to elevate his style (which accounts for the inclusion of worship elements in it), or the author included elements of worship because he meant his tract to be used by worshiping communities in a special context (cf. Goodspeed and Mitton).

Those who opt for the latter possibility are impressed with the value of the writing for the newly baptized. The opening prayer reads like a benediction given before a baptismal service, ch. 2 is practically a baptismal homily, and chs. 4–6 include catechetical instructions particularly pertinent for the newly baptized. The very tone of the epistle acts to instruct the believer concerning membership in the church. Kirby offers a more sophisticated reconstruction of the baptismal elements, seeing in the letter a Christianized form of the renewal of the covenant. Others suggest that the baptismal liturgy is not primarily meant for the instruction of catechumens but to recall to the readers their own baptism: the liturgy in which they participated, the confession they made, the hymns they sang, and the exhortation to which they gave heed.

Building on this commitment, the author was anxious that his readers press on until all "reach unity in the faith and in the knowledge of the Son of God" (Eph. 4:13). In any instance, it seems likely that the liturgical style of the letter was not accidental (i.e., an expression of the peculiar style of the author). Either the writer chose this style deliberately because it furnished the best context for the materials he was using, or else it was dictated by the tastes of the community to which he was writing and the use to which it would be put.

In the second place, Ephesians has a distinct relationship to Colossians. The reference to Tychicus in both letters and the overlapping of vocabulary, style, and subject matter makes it clear that the origin of Ephesians cannot be explained apart from that of Colossians. The usual explanation is that Paul first wrote Colossians as a polemical epistle and then adapted portions from it for use in Ephesians. A close study of specific texts, however, makes this solution doubtful. The fact is that although there are passages where Colossians appears to offer the more original statement, there are no less than twenty-five passages where the converse is true. Equally difficult is the fact that words and phrases in Colossians are used in different combinations and with quite different meanings in Ephesians. That the same author within a limited time span should have composed *de novo* two letters to the same area with such startling alterations seems incomprehensible. A different solution is demanded.

One possibility is that the Ephesian letter was already in process of preparation when the Colossian controversy arose. Paul had been utilizing his time in prison to collect from the community appropriate hymns, prayers, and confessions, which he intended to work over into a general tract meant to instruct catechumens among the churches of Asia. These plans were interrupted, however, by the crisis in the Lycus Valley triggered by a fresh invasion of Gnostic type speculation (see GNOSTICISM). An unwholesome ASCETICISM was being advocated in the church along with false teaching concerning the person of Christ and his place in the cosmos. The issue was serious enough to require an immediate and specific response from Paul.

A letter was prepared and addressed to the church at Colosse. Because Paul had saturated his mind with the worship language and speculative thought of the area in preparation of his Ephesian tract, it was inevitable that he would draw upon this ready reservoir for his epistle to the Colossians. Many of the same words and phrases that later appear in Ephesians are used, although here in a more specifically "Pauline" formulation. Afterward, when Paul hastened to complete the Ephesian tract so that it could be sent along with Tychicus, certain overlappings of subject material occurred. Some of the things mentioned in Colossians were included in Ephesians, but in a more expanded form, whereas others were referred to only cursorily. The difficult problem, then, of the differences between Colossians and Ephesians in word usage and phraseology can be accounted for in this reconstruction by the following: (1) the difference of purpose of the two letters; (2) the result of adapting language drawn from worship materials to an epistolary style; (3) the utilization by Paul of some worship materials that he collected from the churches but had not necessarily authored.

IV. Content and organization

The first main division (Eph. 1:3—3:21). The epistle begins with a simple preface (1:1–2) and moves directly to a beautiful DOXOLOGY or hymn of praise to God (1:3–14). In it Paul thanks God the Father for all those ways he has blessed us in Christ: that from the beginning God (1) chose us to stand in his presence (v. 4), (2) destined us for sonship (v. 5), (3) redeemed us through the blood of Christ (v. 7), (4) forgave us our trespasses (v. 7), and (5) revealed to us the mystery of his own divine will (v. 9). Most of all, he rejoices that the time has come when the eternal plan of God set forth in Christ for the world is to be accomplished, which is: *to bring into union everything and everybody, earthly and heavenly, through Christ Jesus.* This latter statement (v. 10) provides the climax to the hymn and at the same time introduces the theme of the epistle.

Paul proceeds by showing that God's plan is already prevailing among Jews who believe, as well as among Gentiles who, having received the same "guarantee" of the HOLY SPIRIT, are now awaiting with their Jewish brethren the full manifestation of their mutual inheritance (1:11–14). He then continues with the main body of his exposition, which is framed as a "prayer meditation" concluding at the end of ch. 3. He prays that his readers might have wisdom to understand the significance of God's plan as it relates to them. Especially does he pray that they lay hold of the hope that God has now given them, that they be open to receiving the riches that are part of the new inheritance, and, above all, that they experience the greatness of God's power available to them. Paul states that this power is identical to that which raised Jesus from the dead, established him at God's right hand, and gave him dominion over everything including the church (1:15–23). Paul continues by showing that this power provides similar benefits to his followers (2:1–10). Though they were dead in trespasses and sins, God has made them alive, elevating them in Christ to God's right hand in the heavenlies, and giving them dominion by manifesting the Father's workmanship in their lives.

In the next section (2:11–22), the prayer formulation momentarily gives way to admonition and instruction: they are not to forget their former status as Gentiles, when they were strangers to the covenant of promise and without God. They are to compare that situation with their present circumstances as members of the household of God. They are to remember that it was only their relation to Jesus Christ that reversed their status. By joining them together to his body on the cross, Christ broke down the wall that shut them out, brought peace between them and the Jews, and reconciled both to the Father. Now together, they constitute a new worshiping community, banded together and growing into a holy temple, a dwelling place of God in the Spirit.

The prayer that Paul began at 1:15, and amplified by a discourse on God's power and what it has availed for them as Gentiles, is resumed in 3:1. As soon as he takes up this prayer, however, he interrupts it with an account of his own ministry. He explains how his understanding of God's mysterious intention to make Gentiles fellow-heirs and members of the same body has functioned in his own life. He also makes clear that this understanding of the MYSTERY is the one he shares with the apostles and prophets. In spite of the primacy that is accorded apostles and prophets in this text, Paul declares that it is the church, not the apostolate, which is to be the sign of the manifold wisdom of God to the principalities and powers in heavenly places. Paul concludes his prayer meditation with a series of moving petitions on behalf of his readers (3:14–19) and ends with a doxology (3:20–21).

The second main division (4:1—6:24). In the practical section of Ephesians, Paul offers simple words of admonition to guide believers in each of the four spheres in which they live their lives: in the church they are to maintain unity; in society, to practice purity; in the household, to manifest love and respect; and against Satan and the powers of darkness, to exercise strength.

Paul exhorts his readers to unity (4:1–16) by appealing that they maintain the kind of conduct that will give evidence of their Christian commitment. This means that the individual Christian will give himself to the practice of humility, gentleness, patience, and loving forbearance, and will be actively engaged in maintaining the spirit of unity in the BODY OF CHRIST. To support this commitment to unity, Paul cites the sevenfold oneness unique to the Christian faith. He then discusses individual gifts and their function, showing that diversity of service is not a contradiction to unity, but a necessary means of achieving it.

Paul began his practical exhortation by challenging his readers to walk worthily of their calling (4:1). He continues this theme in the exhortation to purity (4:17—5:20), which contrasts the Christian life to pagan values. The key term for his admonition is *walk*, which occurs four times in the section: "walk not as other Gentiles" (4:17); "walk in love" (5:2); "walk as children of light" (5:8); and "walk circumspectly, not as fools, but as wise" (5:15 KJV; in these passages, the NIV and other versions translate "live"). The section includes important appeals relating to the Holy Spirit (4:30; 5:18), as well as ethical instructions on how to treat fellow Christians (4:25–26; 4:32; 5:19).

To members of households, Paul gives an exhortation to love and respect one another (5:21). He asks them to realize unity through willing subjection to one another as to the Lord and by practicing self-sacrificing love. Husbands and wives are told that marriage is a symbol of the relation that exists between Christ and his church (5:21–33). Children are reminded of the OT commandment to honor their parents, and slaves and masters are warned of their responsibility to manifest Christ in their dealings one with the other.

Finally Paul exhorts his readers to exercise strength against the evil forces in the world (6:10–20). Although the appeal to be armed with God's weaponry is couched in personal terms, as if in individual encounter, the section continues the concern for oneness by asking the believers to make supplication for each other and for all the saints.

Conclusion (6:21–23). The letter's conclusion is as brief as its introduction, with a simple reference to Tychicus and a benediction.

V. Outline of the epistle

  I. The salutation (Eph. 1:1–2)
  II. The teaching (1:3—3:21)

A. A hymn of praise and thanksgiving for the revelation of God's eternal plan in Christ (1:3–14)
  1. The plan required that God
     a. elect us in Christ before the world began (v. 4)
     b. adopt us in him as children (v. 5)
     c. redeem us through his blood (v. 7)
  2. It provided that all things earthly and heavenly become united in him (v. 10)
  3. It resulted in Jews as well as Gentiles receiving the Holy Spirit, a guarantee of a mutual inheritance yet to be received (11–14)
B. Prayer meditation (1:15—3:21)
  1. That they have wisdom to understand the majesty of God's plan (1:17) and the mighty power by which God will effect it (1:19—2:10). This power worked in Christ in that it
     a. raised him from the dead (v. 20)
     b. gave him dominion over everything (v. 21)
     c. made him head over the church (v. 22)
     This power works also for the believers (2:1–10) in that it
     a. makes them alive from the death through sin (v. 1)
     b. raises them with Christ in the heavenly places (v. 6)
     c. bestows on them the riches of God's grace (v. 7)
     d. creates them anew to good works (v. 10)
  2. That they remember how God's plan has already worked for the Gentiles (2:11–22) in that it
     a. removed their alienation (vv. 11–14)
     b. made them with the Jews one new man (v. 15)
     c. gave them access to the Father through the Spirit (v. 18)
     d. made them into a holy habitation of the Father (v. 21)
  3. That they understand Paul's relation to the plan and not become discouraged at his sufferings on their behalf (3:1–13). This plan
     a. came to him by revelation (v. 3)
     b. required that Gentiles become fellow heirs with the Jews (v. 6)
     c. made him a minister to Gentiles (v. 7)
  4. That they come to spiritual fullness (3:14–19)
  5. Benediction (3:20–21)
III. The application (4:1—6:24)
  A. Exhortation to promote unity in the church (4:1–16)
    1. The need for consecration (4:1–6)
    2. The matter of diverse gifts (4:7–16)
  B. Exhortation to a life of purity in the world (4:17—5:20)
    1. A contrast with paganism (4:17–24)
    2. The new lifestyle (4:25—5:7)
    3. Light against darkness (5:8–14)
    4. Closing appeal (5:15–20)
  C. Exhortation for love and respect among members of Christian households (5:21—6:9)
    1. Wives and husbands (5:21–33)
    2. Children and parents (6:1–4)
    3. Servants and masters (6:5–9)
  D. Exhortation to put on God's armor against spiritual enemies (6:10–20)
  E. Final greetings and benediction (6:21–24)

VI. Theology

A. Church. The doctrine most extensively treated in the epistle is that of the CHURCH. Three images are used to describe it: the BODY OF CHRIST (Eph. 1:23; 4:3–16), the bride of Christ (5:22–23), and the temple of the Holy Spirit (2:19–22). In Ephesians the concept that best defines the church is the body, of which Christ is head. The addition of this latter phrase represents a development in Paul's way of thinking and speaking of the church. It appears elsewhere only in Colossians, where it has obvious connections with Paul's statement on CHRISTOLOGY. If Christ is head over the cosmos, the fullness of him who fills all things, the preeminent One exercising dominion over all things, then he is head also over the church. Christ's leadership over the church has special consequences that Paul is concerned to work out in Ephesians. For the church is also Christ's body. Its existence as his body is dependent on the death of his body on the cross and the renewed life from the Father by which he rose from the dead. In this body he also ascended to the Father.

The community of believers who have received his renewed life by the Holy Spirit constitute his body on earth. Yet, because he fills this body with his own life, he transforms its existence from one that is only earthly to one that is "heavenly" (i.e., in the heavenlies). This does not mean that the church no longer lives an empirical life in this world. It is concern with this life in the world that caused Paul to write most of his letters to the churches. But it does mean that the ultimate origin and destiny of the church can no longer be found in the temporal sphere, but rather in that which is hidden in the eternal purposes of God; and what God has made known is that the church, Christ's own body, was selected from before the ages to be the fullness of him who fills all things.

What Paul envisions as the mission of the church extends beyond reconciliation of Jew and Gentile, beyond the healing of the fundamental divisions within humanity, beyond even the overcoming of the alienation that cuts off sinners from God. It is the cosmos itself for which God has designed the church. It is his purpose to combine through the church all things that exist—heavenly and earthly, temporal and eternal. All are the object of the church's existence, the beneficiary of the divine grace that flows from its head. Through the church even the angelic powers ("principalities and powers in the heavenly realms") are to be brought to know the wisdom of God.

Therefore, Christ loves the church and labors over her that she may become a vessel worthy to fulfill the purposes of God. The apostle also suffered on her behalf that she may achieve maturity. Believers also play a part in all this. They are the body of Christ, who with the head constitute the single entity with which the Father has to do. Only as the members are filled from the head can the body grow and come to its full stature as the body of Christ. To assist the body in its growth, Christ bestows upon it gifts—apostles, prophets, evangelists, pastors, teachers—who promote the training of the individual members for service so that each one may be able to fulfill his function. As each contributes a particular activity according to the gift he or she has received, the body increases. Because it enjoys a common life derived from its head, it grows together in love and so serves the Lord.

B. Holy Spirit. Although there is not much new presented in Ephesians on the HOLY SPIRIT, there

Reconstructed street of Ephesus. (View to NW.)

is a significant summing up of the Spirit's relation to the believer. The Spirit is given to Christians when they believe (Eph. 1:13, where "seal" is often understood as a reference to BAPTISM), and his presence assures them of their share in the INHERITANCE from the Father (1:14; 5:5). He enlightens the mind to make believers wise toward God (1:17); furnishes access to the Father (2:18); indwells the community, enabling it to become a holy temple of the Lord (2:22); makes the believer strong with the might of God (3:16); gives revelations to the apostles and prophets (3:5); and constitutes part of the oneness and unity of the believers (4:4). Exhortations are also advanced in Ephesians concerning the Holy Spirit. Christians are admonished not to grieve the Spirit (4:30), urged to be filled with the

Spirit (5:18), and instructed to pray as those led by the Spirit (6:18).

(Among many significant commentaries on this letter, note the following: T. K. Abbott, *A Critical and Exegetical Commentary on the Epistles to the Ephesians and to the Colossians*, ICC [1897]; B. F. Westcott, *Saint Paul's Epistle to the Ephesians* [1906]; J. A. Robinson, *St. Paul's Epistle to the Ephesians* [1923]; F. Foulkes, *The Epistle of Paul to the Ephesians* [1963]; J. Gnilka, *Der Epheserbrief* [1971]; M. Barth, *Ephesians*, AB 34, 2 vols. [1974]; F. F. Bruce, *The Epistles to the Colossians, to Philemon, and to the Ephesians*, NICNT [1984]; A. T. Lincoln, *Ephesians*, WBC 42 [1990]; R. Schnackenburg, *Ephesians: A Commentary* [1991]; E. Best, *A Critical and Exegetical Commentary on Ephesians*, ICC [1998]; P. T. O'Brien, *The Letter to the Ephesians* [1999]; J.-N. Aletti, *Saint Paul, Épître aux Éphésiens* [2001]; J. Muddiman, *A Commentary on the Epistle to the Ephesians*, BNTC [2001]; H. W. Hoehner, *Ephesians: An Exegetical Commentary* [2002]. Among specialized studies, in addition to those mentioned in the article, see C. C. Caragounis, *The Ephesian Mysterion: Meaning and Content* [1977]; C. E. Clinton, *Ephesians: Power and Magic* [1989]; E. Best, *Essays on Ephesians* [1997]; N. A. Dahl, *Studies in Ephesians* [2000]; T.-L. N. Yee, *Jews, Gentiles, and Ethnic Reconciliation: Paul's Jewish Identity* [2005].) G. W. BARKER

Ephesus.

Ephesus ef′uh-suhs (Ἔφεσος G2387, perhaps "desirable"). A major city at the mouth of the Cayster River, between the Koressos Range and the sea, on the W coast of ASIA MINOR. Like all the river valleys around the great blunt end of the Asian continent's westward protrusion, that of the Cayster was a highway into the interior, the terminal of a trade route that linked with other roads converging and branching out toward the separated civilizations of the E and the Asian steppes. This was why Ephesus was chosen by the early Ionian colonists from ATHENS as a site for their colony. The Greeks called a colony an *emporion* G1866 ("a way in," then "trading place, market") because their concept of such a settlement was that of a gateway by which an active self-governing community could tap the trade and resources of a foreign hinterland. Ephesus filled the role precisely.

By NT times, however, the great days of Ephesus' trade were long past. Like her rival MILETUS, similarly located at the end of the Maeander Valley 30 mi. to the S, Ephesus had difficulty with her harbor, the essential gateway to the sea. Deforestation was mankind's ancient folly, and no part of the Mediterranean world suffered worse than Asia Minor. The quest for timber and charcoal, the result of overgrazing, and the destructiveness of the Mediterranean goat, eternally nibbling and trampling the regenerating forest, denuded the hinterland. Topsoil slipped from the bare hillsides reft of their cover, streams became swamps, and the storm waters reached the sea laden with silt that choked the harbors. The harbor works of Ephesus may be traced today 7 mi. from the sea. Where once a sheltered gulf and waterway formed a safe haven for ships, there is now a reedy plain. Sir William Ramsay, most factual of archaeologists, speaks in awe of the "uncanny volume of sound" which, in his day at the turn of the 20th cent., greeted the evening visitor to the desolate levels where Ephesus once harbored her ships.

She was, nonetheless, over many centuries, fortunate in her engineers. The winding Maeander was silting up the harbor of Miletus as early as 500 B.C., and when that city suffered irreparable damage in the Persian suppression of the great revolt of the Ionian Greek cities, the choking up of her waterway passed beyond repair. It was Ephesus' opportunity, and a succession of rulers promoted the maintenance of the harbor facilities that the increased volume of trade and traffic demanded. The kings of PERGAMUM, most dynamic and powerful of the lesser successor states of ALEXANDER THE GREAT's divided empire, did much for Ephesus, and when the Romans inherited the kingdom of Pergamum by the will of its last ruler, Attalus III, they continued the policy of promoting Ephesian trade. The Romans assumed the legacy of Pergamum in 133 B.C. and used Ephesus as the proconsul's seat. The city was proud of its title, "the Landing Place," found on a coin as late as the 3rd cent. of the Christian era. It is, perhaps, not without significance that the same coin bears the image of a small oar-propelled boat, an official's "barge," not the deep-hulled merchantmen that mark the city's pride in her sea-borne trade on the coins of earlier centuries. PAUL's ship made no call there in A.D. 57. DOMITIAN, at the end of the 1st cent., appears to have been the last ruler to attempt to repair the harbor of Ephesus, but trade had obviously declined two centuries before. By the time of Justinian, five centuries later, the battle with sand, silt, and mud was lost, and Ephesus was falling to ruins in a swampy terrain. Justinian, to be sure, built a church to Saint John on the site, in part compensation perhaps for the looting of the columns from the temple of ARTEMIS for St. Sophia in Byzantium, where they may still be seen in the vast basilica. It is significant that the church of Saint John gave its name to the place. JOHN THE APOSTLE was called in Greek *Hagios Theologos*—"The Holy Theologian." This was corrupted into *Ayasoluk*, the modern Turkish name for the village that stands near the site of ancient Ephesus.

Deepening economic depression and decline must have been a feature of Ephesus' life over the last cent. B.C. The city turned, as any anxious community might in such circumstances, to the equivalent of her tourist trade. Multitudes came to visit the temple of Artemis, a cult that requires explanation. When the son of Codrus, last king of ATHENS, founded the city, he placed his colonists near the shrine of an ancient Anatolian goddess whom the Greeks, following the religious syncretism common in the ancient world, called after their own goddess Artemis. This was perhaps in the 10th, 11th, or 12th cent. B.C., so uncertain are dates in this borderland of legend and history. The cult thus recognized was that of a nature-goddess, associated with carnal fertility rituals, orgiastic rites, and religious prostitution. The peculiar feature in the case of Ephesus was that the cult was associated with a meteoric stone, the image *diopetēs* (lit., "that fell from Zeus," Acts 19:35). Lost somewhere among the ruins, or concealed in the surrounding countryside by its last devotees, the cult-object possibly still exists. Charles Seltman, with some plausibility, suggests that it is actually a strange stone object, at present in the Liverpool City Museum (*Riot in Ephesus; Writings on the Heritage of Greece* [1958], 86–87). Other elements over the course of centuries intruded into the worship, and the final

Figure of Artemis, goddess of the Ephesians (c. A.D. 150).

form of the cult-image of Artemis of Ephesus was a strangely ornamented female figure, shrine and basket on head, a veil decorated with beasts, long necklaces, embroidered sleeves, legs sheathed with empaneled animals, and with multiple breasts, or, as some suggest, an apron covered with clusters of grapes or dates, sign and symbol of Artemis's role as the nourishing spirit of nature. (See A. Bammer, *Das Heiligtum der Artemis von Ephesos* [1984].)

It was Croesus of neighboring Lydia (he reigned from 564 to 546 B.C.) who promoted the construction of the first temple to Artemis. Fragments of the columns that he donated, inscribed with his name, are in the British Museum. At the time, Croesus's was the largest of Greek temples, and perhaps was some consolation for the loss of her independence, for it was Croesus who made Ephesus subject to Sardis. She was never, in fact, independent again. This temple, first sign of the international importance of the Artemis cult of Ephesus, stood right through the Persian imperial dominance of the Aegean coast of Asia Minor. It was maliciously burned in 356 B.C. on the very night, the makers of omens later noted, that Alexander the Great was born of Olympias in distant Macedon.

Alexander, into whose control Ephesus passed in 334 B.C. at the beginning of his mighty "drive to the East," contributed largely to the new temple, which was destined to be a shrine of unrivaled splendor and to rank as one of the wonders of the world. It endured until the Goths sacked the city in A.D. 263. The ruins have been identified in a marsh, 1.5 mi. NE of the city, after the discovery of Ephesus' main boulevard in 1870. It is said that the building was four times the size of Athens' magnificent Parthenon. Pheidias, Praxiteles, and Apelles all adorned it. It was widely depicted on coins. The general impression left with the archaeologist and historian, who peer into the crowded past of the great city, is that Demetrius the silversmith was not unjustified in his claim that "all Asia and the world" (Acts 19:27 NRSV) reverenced the Ephesian Artemis. As the silversmith by implication admitted, the temple was the core of Ephesus' commercial prosperity. Around the great shrine, to which worshipers and tourists poured from far and near, tradesmen and hucksters found a living, supplying visitors with food and lodging, dedicatory offerings, and the silver souvenir models of the shrine that the guild of Demetrius was most interested in making and selling.

The temple was also a treasury and bank, in which private individuals, kings, and cities made deposits. Xenophon, the Athenian, described such a deposit with the "sacristan of Artemis," together with a testamentary deposition regarding the disposal of the money in the event of his not surviving the campaign ahead of him. Paul was, in fact, assaulting a stronghold of pagan religion, together with the active life and commerce associated with a vast heathen cult, in a key city of the central Mediterranean and a focal point of communication. Ephesus was also a seat of proconsular power from which the whole province of Asia could be influenced. Churches arose significantly during his stay in the three cities of the Lycus Valley—Laodicea, Colosse, and Hierapolis—in spite of the fact that Paul did not visit these centers. Radiation along the lines of communication from a point of active life accounted for such foundations. All the seven churches mentioned in the apocalyptic letters (Rev. 2–3) were no doubt established during the same period of apostolic ministry. "A great door for effective work has opened to me," wrote Paul, "and there are many who oppose me" (1 Cor. 16:9).

The preaching of Christianity in the school of Tyrannus was hitting the Artemis cult hard, so

The Bouleuterion, a theater-shaped structure in Ephesus where the civil leaders met to discuss politics and economics.

hard that the turnover in dependent trades was visibly showing the adverse effects. A riot ensued, so vividly and ironically described in Acts 19. The story is a strong, clear light on the manner in which the new faith was cutting across established forms and patterns of pagan life in the 1st cent. So it came about that Paul "fought wild beasts in Ephesus" (1 Cor. 15:32). He caught up a phrase of Plato from his student days in Tarsus. Plato likened the mob to wild animals. It was a dangerous situation. A fine street ran through the city from the harbor wharves at the river mouth to the great theater where the level land began to rise toward Mount Pion, a boulevard of some beauty and lined by fine buildings and columned porticoes. It was the main artery of Ephesian life, destined in later years to be even more richly adorned.

Led by the silversmiths, the mob poured down this highway. Codex Bezae sometimes supplies a detail that has a ring of authenticity, and this unorthodox ms adds a phrase to Acts 19:28 that may, in one flash, give a glimpse of the excited scene. Inflamed by the speech of the rabble-rouser Demetrius, delivered no doubt in the meeting house of the silversmith's guild, the audience, says Beza's text, poured "into the street." It is surely the great central boulevard that is mentioned. The noisy group swept along with them the flotsam of the town, the idlers, the visitors, the mob of any great eastern city, and flowed toward the common place of assembly—the theater on the low hillside. The greater part, says Luke in one ironical phrase, "did not even know why they were there" (19:32).

It was a perilous situation, not only for Paul and his little party, but also for the Jews at large, who had every reason to fear a pogrom. The Jews had a large colony at Ephesus, and considerable privileges (Jos. *Ant.* 24.10.12, 25). They had much to lose; hence the venture of a certain Alexander whom the Jews pushed to the front, doubtless to make sure that their community as a whole was not blamed for the revolutionary views of the rabbi from Tarsus. At the sight of Alexander, who had taken some risk by his public appearance, the crowd broke into their chant, a rhythmic din that they kept up for two hours.

It is, as W. M. Ramsay says, "the most instructive picture of society in an Asian city at this period that has come down to us.... In the speech of Demetrius are concentrated most of the feelings and motives that, from the beginning to the end, made the mob so hostile to the Christians in the great oriental cities" (*St. Paul the Traveller and Roman Citizen*, 11th ed. [1896], 277, 280). It required all the political art of the *grammateus* G1208, no mere "town-clerk," but the city's leading official and obviously a most able man, to restore quiet and order (see CLERK, CITY). One phrase in his clever speech would appear to date the incident with some precision. If anything illegal had been done to rouse the just resentment of the silversmiths' guild, he said "there are proconsuls" (Acts 19:38). The historian Tacitus tells how Agrippina, the vicious mother of the Emperor Nero, had Junius Silanus, the proconsul of Asia, poisoned (*Annals* 13.1). Silanus was a great-grandson of the Emperor Augustus, and was thus considered a menace to her son, whom Agrippina had thrust forward to the succession by all manner of intrigue and crime. The murder was committed by two men, a Roman knight and a freedman who held the post of steward of the imperial estates in Asia. If the two villains assumed temporary proconsular power, the plural of the official's speech is accounted for; otherwise it is without explanation. This assumption would fix the date of the incident at A.D. 54.

Another phrase in the story is illuminating. Why did the Asiarchs seek to protect Paul? These

This theater in Ephesus, seating 25,000, was the site of a public hearing after the silversmith Demetrius incited the other craftsmen against Paul for opposing the worship of the idol Artemis of the Ephesians (Acts 19:29).

officials were members of a corporation, built on the model of an earlier Greek institution, and charged with the maintenance and protection of the Caesar cult (see EMPEROR WORSHIP) in Asia. It would appear probable that there was a measure of rivalry between those in charge of the newer ritual, a cult that was not yet deeply founded in Ephesus, and the custodians and champions of the vast commercialized worship of Artemis. Perhaps the Asiarchs, not yet aware of all the implications of Christianity, and as yet unhampered by any anti-Christian legislation, were not disturbed by damage to their rivals. Paul's Roman CITIZENSHIP may have weighed a little with the officers of Caesar. Whatever happened, Paul was rescued and, perhaps under some official pressure, withdrew before the irate guildsmen had the opportunity to file a formal indictment. It may also have been a consideration that weighed with Paul—that such an indictment would have had scant chance of a just hearing before such scoundrels as Publius Celer and the freedman Helios, if indeed they held brief authority in the city at the time.

It is possible from the NT to gain some idea of the progress of the Ephesian church. Although there is not the intimate insight into the doings and problems of the Ephesian Christian community, as the Corinthian epistles give, the NT provides a series of glimpses of considerable interest. First, there is the vivid story already examined. Another incident is the apostle's advice to the elders. He passed along the Asia Minor coast three or four years after the riot in Ephesus. He invited the leaders of the church to meet him at Miletus (had he given some promise to the Asiarchs not to return to Ephesus?). Paul conversed with them, and from the intimacy of almost three years' experience, warned the little community of tensions to come. That the trouble came is evident from John's letter to the Ephesian church (Rev. 2:1–7), most probably written when Domitian's persecution was raging.

John's letter was one of seven addressed to the Asian circuit, and prudently couched in the style of Jewish apocalyptic literature Ephesus, as was proper, was the first church addressed, and the subject matter sheds light on the city, and its church, a generation after its founding. Three years of Paul's teaching in the school of Tyrannus, the nature of which may be partly glimpsed from Paul's own letter to the Ephesians, had laid a firm basis for growth. There was much for which John could commend the Ephesian Christians; their toil, endurance, discernment, and vigor. Their lapse from first ardor and enthusiasm was due, according to Ramsay's famous thesis, to an infiltration of the Christian minority by the weariness of a civic community that had passed its prime and was living on its fading splendor.

It was natural enough in the religious capital of Asia that the sect of the NICOLAITANS should be in evidence. Of this group it is fair to assume that they were Greeks who saw in their own cults a measure of true revelation, a position that might have arguments to commend it, but who carried this belief to the point of advocating unwise compromise with the debased forms of those cults in such prominence around them. Perhaps, too, they saw in the Caesar-cult only a harmless ritual of loyalty, and not an issue of man-worship on which a Christian need stake life and livelihood. Ephesus, taught by two apostles, rejected all accommodation with paganism and those who advocated the softer policy.

The question remaining is this: Was John too rigid, too extreme? Need the church, for instance, for the sake of a pinch of incense, have been exposed to the bitterness of persecution? History gives the answer. Those who accepted John's rigid rule came through that persecution refined and strengthened. They became the forefathers of all true Christianity. They laid in their suffering the foundations on which all true religion has since built. To compromise would ultimately have set Christ where Emperor Severus ultimately placed him—in a chapel along with the images of Jupiter, Augustus, and Abraham. "The historian," writes Sir William M. Ramsay, "must regard the Nicolaitans with intense interest, and must deeply regret that we know so little about them.... At the same time he must feel that nothing could have saved the infant church from melting away into one of those vague and ineffective schools of philosophic ethics except the stern and strict rule that is laid down here by St. John. An easygoing Christianity could never have survived; it could not have conquered and trained the world; only the most convinced, resolute, almost bigoted adherence to the most uncompromising interpretation of its principles could have given the Christians the courage and self-reliance that were needed. For them to hesitate or to doubt was to be lost" (*The Letters to the Seven Churches* [1904], 300).

The last glimpse of Ephesus in the NT reveals an aging church in need of an infusion of new life, hence, the closing detail of imagery in the apocalyptic letter (Rev. 2:1–7). Coins of Ephesus sometimes show a date palm, sacred to Artemis, and the symbol of the goddess's beneficent activity. "To him who overcomes I will give the right," recorded John, "to eat from the tree of life." The church, however, did not survive. IGNATIUS, writing a generation later, still accorded the church high praise. It became a seat of bishops, where a notable council was held as late as A.D. 431. Then came a long decline. The coast, with continual soil erosion of the hinterland, became malarial. The Turks came with ruin for Asia. The church died with the city. The "lampstand" (cf. 1:20) was removed from its place. (See C. Foss, *Ephesus after Antiquity: A Late Antique, Byzantine, and Turkish City* [1979].)

Archaeology, none the less, has shown that the prestige and magnificence of the city long outlived its declining usefulness as a seaport. Ramsay, broadly correct in his main thesis of Ephesus' decline, dates its disastrous impact too early. Under CLAUDIUS in the middle of the 1st cent. and under TRAJAN at the beginning of the 2nd, the great theater was remodeled. Under Claudius the monumental Marble Street was built. Nero gave Ephesus a stadium. Domitian widened and beautified the great central boulevard. Adorning continued till the days of the Gothic raid in A.D. 263. It is obvious that Paul's vision had picked one of the strategic centers of the world.

(See further E. M. Blaiklock, *The Christian in Pagan Society* [1951] and *The Cities of the New Testament* [1965]; A. H. M. Jones, *Cities in the Eastern Provinces*, 2nd ed. [1971]; E. Yamauchi, *The Archaeology of New Testament Cities in Western Asia Minor* [1980], ch. 7; C. J. Hemer, *The Letters to the Seven Churches of Asia in Their Local Setting* [1986], ch. 3; R. E. Oster, *A Bibliography of Ancient Ephesus* [1987]; H. Koester, ed., *Ephesos, Metropolis of Asia: An Interdisciplinary Approach to Its Archaeology,* *Religion, and Culture* [2004]; P. Trebilco, *The Early Christians in Ephesus from Paul to Ignatius* [2004].)

E. M. BLAIKLOCK

Ephlal ef′lal (אֶפְלָל *H697*, derivation uncertain). Son of Zabad and descendent of JUDAH in the line of JERAHMEEL (1 Chr. 2:37).

ephod (garment) ee′fod. A close-fitting, armless outer vest of varying length, but generally extending down to the hips. In the OT the Hebrew word *ʾēpōd H680* refers almost exclusively to a priestly garment, or one used in the worship of God. In the Old Assyrian texts of the 19th cent. B.C. and the Ugaritic texts of the 15th, the word appears as *epadu* or (fem.) *epattu* (Ugar. *ʾipdk*), and apparently denoted a close-fitting garment which some interpret as "rich vestment" (cf. R. de Vaux, *Ancient Israel* [1961], 350), but others as a more ordinary garment (W. F. Albright in *Old Testament Commentary*, ed. H. C. Alleman and E. E. Flack [1948], 147). The feminine form *ʾăpuddâ H682*, "close-fitting garment," also occurs, but without cultic connotations (Exod. 28:8; 39:5; Isa. 30:22).

In the Mosaic Code the ephod is given special prominence as part of the high priest's vestments. It was fastened around the waist with a beautifully woven waistband (Exod. 28:27–28), and held together at the top by shoulder-pieces (28:12) set with onyx stones engraved with the names of the twelve tribes. The ceremonial BREASTPIECE containing twelve gem stones inscribed with the names of the twelve tribes was attached to a set of rings on the ephod. This breastplate also contained the sacred lots known as URIM AND THUMMIM (although some authorities equate them with the twelve gems on the breastplate just mentioned).

Less elaborate ephods were worn by the rest of the priesthood, especially when officiating before the altar (1 Sam. 2:28; 14:3); these are simply described as ephods of linen and probably lacked any extensive ornamentation. Even a young acolyte like SAMUEL (1 Sam. 2:18) wore such an ephod. A special veneration was accorded the high priestly type of ephod to such an extent that in the time of the judges GIDEON (Jdg. 8:27) had a replica fashioned from the gold and precious stones stripped from the Midianite warriors slain by his troops in the war. MICAH the Ephraimite is said to have made an ephod for use in the worship of his silver idol, along with his images of the household gods (Jdg. 17:5).

The high priestly ephod in the TABERNACLE was apparently mounted on a model of some sort or otherwise displayed in a prominent position in the sanctuary. Probably because of the Urim and Thummim attached to it, the ephod was considered of great value, especially at crises when important decisions had to be made. When DAVID needed to know in advance whether the people of KEILAH whom he had befriended would hand him over to King SAUL, he had ABIATHAR consult God by means of the ephod (1 Sam. 23:9–12). Presumably this was done by means of the Urim and Thummim, just as in the earlier instance when Saul by that means found out that JONATHAN was the one who had transgressed his ban on eating food before victory (14:18, reading "ephod" with LXX, rather than "ark," which must have been kept at KIRIATH JEARIM at this time). The Urim and Thummim were drawn as "yes" or "no" answers (v. 41), eliminating the wrong choice between two alternatives.

It would appear that even in the northern kingdom ephods were made for cultic purposes in the temples of Israel (Hos. 3:4). Whether these were made of woven cloth set with gold and gems, or whether they were like Gideon's of old (Jdg. 8:26–27) is not clear from the evidence. No mention is made of an ephod after the fall of Jerusalem in 587 B.C. There is no evidence that a new ephod was made for the high priest after the restoration from Babylon, although it may safely be assumed that this was done in conformity with the Mosaic Law. (See Jos. *Ant.* 3.7.3 §162; *War* 5.5.7 §233; J. Morgenstern, *The Ark, the Ephod and the Tent of Meeting* [1945]; *NIDOTTE*, 1:476–77.) G. L. ARCHER

Ephod (person) ee′fod (אֵפֹד H681, possible meaning, "ephod"). Father of Hanniel; the latter was a leader in the tribe of MANASSEH appointed to help distribute the land of Canaan among the tribes (Num. 34:23; cf. v. 18).

ephphatha ef′uh-thuh (ἐφφαθά G2395, Gk. transliteration of a Semitic form meaning "be opened"). This word was spoken by Jesus—looking "up to heaven and with a deep sigh"—to a deaf mute in the DECAPOLIS (Mk. 7:34). "At this, the man's ears were opened, his tongue was loosened and he began to speak plainly" (v. 35). This passage is one of the rare occasions when a biblical author saw fit to quote from an original Semitic language the exact word Jesus used. After quoting the foreign word, Mark immediately translates it (*dianoichthēti*, "be opened," pass. impv. of *dianoigō* G1380). The use of this term (hardly a secretive word of magic), along with Jesus' touching and spitting (v. 33), may suggest the special difficulty and thus greatness of the miracle (cf. R. H. Gundry, *Mark: A Commentary on His Apology for the Cross* [1993], 384).

Scholars have debated whether the Semitic word is HEBREW or ARAMAIC. If Hebrew, the form was probably *hippātaḥ* (2nd masc. sing. impv. nifal of *pātaḥ* H7337 [cf. Isa. 35:5], a form that is apparently pronounced *affeta* in Samaritan Heb.; cf. I. Rabinowitz in *JSS* 16 [1971]: 151–56, with response by S. Morag in *JSS* 17 [1972]: 198–202). Since Aramaic was almost surely Jesus' mother tongue and the commonly used language by Jews in GALILEE and surrounding areas, most scholars interpret *ephphatha* as representing the Aramaic form ʾ*eppataḥ* (a contraction of ʾ*etpětaḥ*, 2nd masc. sing. ethpeel). According to others, it represents an apocopated form of Aramaic ʾ*eppětaḥaʾ* (3rd fem. pl., "[your eyes] be opened"; cf. G. Dalman, *Grammatik des jüdisch-palästinischen Aramäisch*, 2nd ed. [1927], 278n.; see further F. L. Horton in *ZNW* 77 [1986]: 101–8).

In the Roman Catholic Church, the Ephphatha ceremony refers to a part of the baptismal rite in which the priest pronounces that word as he touches the ears and mouth of the person being baptized.

Ephraemi Syri Rescriptus. See CODEX EPHRAEMI SYRI RESCRIPTUS.

Ephraem Syrus. Also Ephrem. The most important biblical exegete and theologian of the ancient Syriac church, and the author of hundreds of hymns. Born c. A.D. 306 in Nisibis, Ephraem moved to EDESSA in 363, where he wrote most of his extant works, and died ten years later. He led an austere life and was a prolific author, writing mainly in poetic form. He is especially known for his commentaries on Genesis and on the DIATESSARON, as well as for his refutations of various heresies. (See W. S. McCullough, *A Short History of Syriac Christianity to the Rise of Islam* [1982], 57–61; S. [P.] Brock, *The Luminous Eye: The Spiritual World Vision of Saint Ephrem* [1992]; bibliography in *ODCC*, 551.)

Ephraim (person and tribe) ee′fray-im (אֶפְרַיִם H713, derivation uncertain, but by popular etymology, "doubly fruitful"; gentilic אֶפְרָתִי H718, "Ephraimite" [the form can also mean "Ephrathite"; see EPHRATH]). The younger of two sons born to JOSEPH and ASENATH in Egypt; his older brother was MANASSEH (Gen. 41:50–52; 46:20). He was also the ancestor of the tribe that bears his name. Ephraim was born during the seven years of plenty so that his boyhood years overlapped with the last seventeen years of JACOB, who had migrated to Egypt. In this way Ephraim had opportunity to learn of the patriarchal promises and blessings directly from Jacob.

After Jacob exacted an oath from Joseph that he would bury him in Canaan (Gen. 47:27–31), Jacob adopted the two sons of Joseph as his own (48:1–5). Jacob's favorite wife had been RACHEL, whose son Joseph had been favored above all other sons until he was sold as a slave to POTIPHAR in Egypt. By adopting Manasseh and Ephraim as his own sons, there were three tribal representatives of Rachel—BENJAMIN, Ephraim, and Manasseh. Joseph, who had been considered dead by Jacob, now had a double representation. Ephraim was chosen by Jacob for the greater blessing even though he was not Joseph's firstborn. Overruling Joseph's objections, Jacob placed his right hand on Ephraim and allotted to him a greater blessing and prosperity than he did to Manasseh. The patriarch gave his blessing in the name of the God before whom Abraham and Isaac walked, and the God who had shepherded Jacob throughout his whole lifetime. Although Jacob was about to die in Egypt, he expressed before Ephraim the firm belief that future generations would realize and experience the fulfillment of the promises to possess the land of Canaan (48:8–20). (The clans descended from Ephraim are listed in Num. 26:35–36; the parallel genealogy in 1 Chr. 7:20–27 has some unexplained differences.)

Ephraim and Manasseh were allotted a particular plot of real estate in Canaan that is described as "the ridge of land I took from the Amorites with my sword and my bow" (Gen. 48:22). This could hardly refer to the involvement of SIMEON and LEVI with SHECHEM which displeased Jacob exceedingly (ch. 34). Jacob did purchase some land from the sons of HAMOR, Shechem's father (33:19). Abraham may have previously purchased some land at this place when he erected an altar at Shechem after arriving in Canaan (12:7–8). If so, this may have been referred to by STEPHEN (Acts 7:16). Since Jacob identifies this portion or ridge of land as being obtained by conquest, the possibility exists that this adventure by Jacob is noted only here in the biblical account. Joseph was ultimately buried in the vicinity of Shechem (Josh. 24:32). In Jn. 4:5–6 the tract of land Jacob presented to Joseph's descendants is identified as being near SYCHAR. Four centuries later the tombs of the twelve patriarchs were known to be at Shechem according to JEROME. This likely would have included Ephraim since his tribe was so prominent in Israelite history.

In subsequent history the tribe of Ephraim had a very prominent position. In Israel's encampment around the TABERNACLE, Ephraim was the leader of the western camp supported by the tribes of Manasseh and Benjamin (Num. 2:18–24). Among the twelve spies sent into Canaan, JOSHUA represented the tribe of Ephraim (Num. 13:8) and later was appointed as the successor of MOSES (Deut. 31:7). Joshua and ELEAZAR the high priest had the responsibility to divide the land of Canaan among the tribes of Israel.

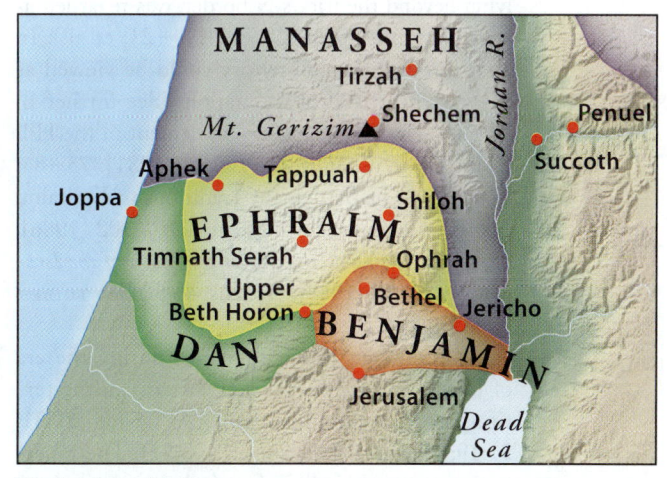

Tribal territory of Ephraim.

EPHRAIM (PLACE)

The Ephraimites received an allotment of land between the Jordan River and the Mediterranean Sea, with the tribes of Benjamin and Dan to the S and one half of the tribe of Manasseh to the N (Josh. 16:5–9; see EPHRAIM, HILL COUN-

Broad regional view of the topography of Ephraim.

TRY OF). The S boundary extended from the Jordan and JERICHO westward approximately 10 mi. N of JERUSALEM, but included Upper and Lower BETH HORON as it continued to the sea. On the N, Ephraim was bounded by the brook KANAH and the city of TAANATH SHILOH, where the boundary turned southward to ATAROTH and passed near Jericho on to the Jordan. It is clear, however, that historically the name Ephraim was applied to a much larger region (cf. 17:14–18). For example, the central city of Shechem, though apparently lying beyond the tribe's N border, was regarded as an Ephraimite town (20:7; 21:20–21; et al.). In any case, Ephraim's territory could be viewed as the very heartland of the nation. (See further B. Mazar, "The Early Israelite Settlement in the Hill Country," in *BASOR* 241 [winter 1981]: 75–85; Z. Kallai, "The Settlement Traditions of Ephraim: A Historiographical Study," in *ZDPV* 102 [1986]: 68–74; I. Finkelstein, *The Archaeology of the Israelite Settlement* [1988], esp. chs. 4–5.) See TRIBES, LOCATION OF.

The religious center for Israel during the era of Joshua and the judges was SHILOH in the territory of Ephraim (Josh. 18:1; 22:12; Jdg. 18:31; 21:19; 1 Sam. 1:3, 9, 24; 2:14; 3:21). The tabernacle was erected in Shiloh by Joshua and remained there until the ARK OF THE COVENANT was taken by the PHILISTINES after the sons of ELI took it into the battlefield (1 Sam. 4:1–11). Scholars are of the opinion that the city of Shiloh was destroyed at this time (cf. Jer. 7:12). There is no indication that the ark was returned to Shiloh.

The Ephraimites were involved in civil strife in the days of Gideon (Jdg. 8:1–3) and in the period of JEPHTHAH's leadership (12:1–6). During the Davidic and Solomonic era the tribe of JUDAH with its leading city Jerusalem emerged as the leading tribe, but at Solomon's death a secession was led by an Ephraimite, JEROBOAM I, who became the first king of the northern kingdom. During the two centuries that this kingdom existed it was frequently identified as Ephraim, reflecting the fact that this was the most powerful tribe in opposition to Judah. In the books of Chronicles, Isaiah, Hosea, and other prophets, the name Ephraim is commonly used for the northern kingdom.

Ephraim is to be reunited with Judah in the messianic kingdom. The schism introduced by Jeroboam I is to be healed when the ruler of the Davidic family will rule over both Judah and Ephraim, according to the prophet Ezekiel in his message concerning the final kingdom (Ezek. 37). S. J. SCHULTZ

Ephraim (place) ee′fray-im (אֶפְרַיִם H713 [see EPHRAIM (PERSON AND TRIBE)]; Ἐφραίμ G2394). A town that was near BAAL HAZOR (the place where ABSALOM kept his sheepshearers, 2 Sam. 13:23). This town is often identified with OPHRAH (P. K. McCarter, Jr., *II Samuel*, AB 9 [1984], 330, 333, even emends the text to read "Ophrah"; against the identification, see W. F. Albright in *AASOR* 4 [1924]: 124–33). Ophrah, in turn, is usually thought to be the same as EPHRON (PLACE) and the NT village of Ephraim (modern et-Ṭaiyibeh, 13 mi. NNE of JERUSALEM), where Jesus once stayed with his disciples (Jn. 11:54). It is possible, however, that 2 Sam. 13:23 refers not to a town at all but to the tribal territory of Ephraim (cf. NIV, "near the border of Ephraim"). See also APHAIREMA.

Ephraim, forest of. This expression occurs only once with reference to the scene of the defeat of ABSALOM (2 Sam. 18:6; KJV, "wood of Ephraim") but is referred to implicitly elsewhere (Josh. 17:15).

Opinions differ as to whether the latter refers to the expansion by the house of JOSEPH eastward into TRANSJORDAN (K. Budde in *ZAW* 7 [1887]: 123–24; C. E. Burnes, *Israel's Settlements in Canaan* [1919], 20ff.) or to settlement in the forested sectors of the Ephraimite hill country itself. Two details in Josh. 17:15 support the first view: (1) the reference to the land of the REPHAITES indicates an area in Transjordan; (2) "the forest" is placed in juxtaposition with "the hill country of Ephraim," which was clearly in Cisjordan, the area W of the Jordan. The proximity of the forest of Ephraim to MAHANAIM (2 Sam. 17:27), formerly ISH-BOSHETH's Transjordanian capital (2 Sam. 2:8–9), firmly establishes this location. (The Lucianic MSS of the LXX read "the forest of Mahanaim" at 2 Sam. 18:6, possibly to modernize or clarify its location.) Originally this territory was granted to "the house of Joseph—to Ephraim and Manasseh" (Josh. 17:17). Ephraim later lost this woodland E of Jordan to JEPHTHAH and the Gileadites (Jdg. 12:1–15). Although the Hebrew word translated "forest" (*ya'ar H3623*) has various meanings (D. Baly, *The Geography of the Bible* [1957], 83, 93), it probably has the normal significance of the English: note that Joshua commands the people to "clear land" (Josh. 17:15) and that Absalom's rebellion ended with his head caught in a tree.   B. K. WALTKE

Ephraim, hill country of. The Hebrew phrase *har-'eprāyim* (KJV, "mount Ephraim"), which occurs more than thirty times in the OT (Josh. 17:15; Jdg. 3:27; 1 Sam. 1:1; et al.), denotes not a single mountain but the hill country in central Palestine occupied by the tribe of EPHRAIM and extending N into the territory of MANASSEH. It was more fruitful than the hill country of JUDAH, especially on its western slopes, and it was one of the few areas where the Israelites were able to establish themselves after the conquest under Joshua. For this reason the two main sanctuaries in the period of the judges, BETHEL and SHILOH, were within its borders. At its highest point, the plateau rises to over 3,000 ft. This section "is built of Cenomanian limestone, resistant to erosion and weathering into the fertile *terra rossa*; hence its extensive vegetation and the dense habitation which followed deforestation" (Y. Aharoni, *The Land of the Bible: A Historical Geography*, rev. ed. [1979], 29). See also PALESTINE III.A.   A. E. CUNDALL

Ephraim Gate. A northward-facing gate of OT JERUSALEM (it exited to the ridge route and thus led to the hill country of Ephraim). We read that, during the reign of AMAZIAH king of Judah, Jehoash (JOASH) king of Israel invaded the southern kingdom and "broke down the wall of Jerusalem from the Ephraim Gate to the Corner Gate—a section about six hundred feet [*lit.*, four hundred cubits] long" (2 Ki. 14:13; 2 Chr. 25:23). This statement has led many to infer that the Ephraim Gate was 600–650 ft. E of the CORNER GATE (however, see D. C. Liid in *ABD*, 2:556; cf. the contrasting maps in D. Bahat, *The Illustrated Atlas of Jerusalem* [1990], 30–31 and in *NBD*, 559). In times of NEHEMIAH, the square by the Gate of Ephraim was one of the places where the Israelites built booths to celebrate the Feast of Tabernacles (Neh. 8:16). Later, at the dedication of the walls, one of the processions went N to the BROAD WALL and turned E "over the Gate of Ephraim, the Jeshanah Gate, the Fish Gate, the Tower of Hananel and the Tower of the Hundred" (12:39). Some have identified the Ephraim Gate with the JESHANAH GATE (Old Gate) and others with the FISH GATE, but both of these proposals are doubtful. (See further J. J. Simons, *Jerusalem in the Old Testament* [1952], 226–81, 447–58.)

Ephrain ee'fray-in. KJV alternate form of EPHRON (only 2 Chr. 13:19).

Ephrath, Ephrathah ef'rath, ef'ruh-thuh (אֶפְרָה *H714* and *H715*, אֶפְרָתָה *H716* and *H717*, "fruitful"; gentilic אֶפְרָתִי *H718*, "Ephrathite" [the form can also mean "Ephraimite"; see EPHRAIM]). **(1)** A city or area associated with BETHLEHEM. The precise connection is uncertain, but it is possible that Ephrathah was originally independent and later absorbed into Bethlehem. ELIMELECH and his family were "Ephrathites from Bethlehem" (Ruth 1:2); the same description is applied to JESSE, the father of King DAVID (1 Sam. 17:12; the KJV has Ephrathite also in 1 Sam. 1:1 and 1 Ki. 11:26, where modern versions more correctly have Ephraimite). The two places are identified in the compound form "Bethlehem Ephrathah" (Mic. 5:2). On the way to Ephrath (the spelling used in Genesis), BENJAMIN was born and his mother RACHEL died and was buried (Gen. 35:16–20; 48:7).

It should be noted, however, that the burial place of Rachel is elsewhere set in the tribal territory of Benjamin (1 Sam. 10:2; cf. Jer. 31:15), whereas Bethlehem was in JUDAH (the LXX adds Ephrathah to the towns of Judah in Josh. 15:59). Since Gen. 35:16 indicates that there was "some distance" between Bethlehem and Ephrath, the parenthetical references in Gen. 35:19 and 48:7 often have been regarded as late and inaccurate glosses. Some therefore believe that Genesis refers to a different Ephrath/Ephrathah somewhere to the N. Moreover, in Ps. 132:6 Ephrathah (if not a different area) is associated with JAAR (prob. KIRIATH JEARIM, on the border between Benjamin and Judah). A plausible solution is that Ephrathah referred originally to a relatively large area extending from the Benjamin/Judah border to the S as far as TEKOA, and that Bethlehem was thus a village within this region. "As Israel's tribal structure gave way to the monarchy along with the rise of Ephrathah's most famous family as the dynasty, Ephrathah became more and more identified with Bethlehem, its royal village" (L. M. Luker in *ABD*, 2:558). It has been argued further that Ephrathah was originally the name of a Judahite clan descended from #2 below.

(2) The second wife of CALEB son of HEZRON; her firstborn was HUR, whose descendants included Kiriath Jearim and Bethlehem (Ephrath in 1 Chr. 2:19; Ephrathah in 2:50; 4:4). There may be a reference to her also in 2:24, where the RSV (following the LXX) translates, "After the death of Hezron, Caleb went in to Ephrathah, the wife of Hezron his father, and she bore him Ashhur, the father of Tekoa" (the MT reads differently; see CALEB EPHRATHAH).

Ephrem. See EPHRAEM SYRUS.

Ephron (person) ee´fron (עֶפְרוֹן H6766, possibly "dust" or "fawn"). Son of Zohar; he was the HITTITE from whom ABRAHAM purchased a burial place for SARAH his wife in MACHPELAH (Gen. 23:7–20). The study of the transaction between Abraham and Ephron is a study in oriental shrewdness and politeness. Apparently Ephron was willing to sell the land for a good price, yet he did not initially state the price. Rather, depending on Abraham's knowledge of propriety, he offered at first to give away the land (23:11). Even when Abraham properly insisted on paying for it, Ephron did not offer to sell the land, but slyly stated the value he put on the property (23:13–15). Abraham, understanding that this was the asking price, responded by purchasing it at that price.

The field formerly owned by Ephron had a cave and several trees (Gen. 23:17). Sarah was buried there, and later Abraham (25:9). Machpelah served as the burial place also for ISAAC and REBEKAH, and for JACOB and LEAH (49:29–32; 50:13). Today a large stone structure covers the cave and marks the spot in HEBRON where the field of Machpelah was. Visitors may see the interior of the building but are not shown the cave.   J. B. SCOTT

Ephron (place) ee´fron (עֶפְרוֹן H6767, possibly "[place of] dust" or "fawn"). **(1)** Mount Ephron (Josh. 15:9) probably refers to a range near KIRIATH JEARIM that served to describe the N boundary of the tribe of JUDAH. The site has not been identified, but one possibility is el-Qastel, about 5 mi. WNW of Jerusalem.

(2) A town that, along with BETHEL and JESHANAH, was taken from King JEROBOAM of Israel by King ABIJAH of Judah (2 Chr. 13:19). This Ephron, thought to be the same as OPHRAH and NT Ephraim (Jn. 11:54), is usually identified with modern eṭ-Ṭaiyibeh, about 13 mi. NNE of JERUSALEM. See discussion under EPHRAIM (PLACE).

(3) A "large and very strong" town in GILEAD. When Judas MACCABEE was leading the Jews of that area on their way to the land of Judah, the inhabitants of the city would not allow him to go through. In response, Judas captured Ephron and killed every male (1 Macc. 5:45–52; 2 Macc. 12:27–28; Gk. *Ephrōn*).

Epictetus ep´ik-tee´tuhs (Ἐπίκτητος, "acquired"). A popular and influential STOIC philosopher. Born c. A.D. 50, Epictetus was a slave during his youth in ROME. After being set free, he became a teacher of philosophy, eventually setting up a school in NICOPOLIS, where he died c. A.D. 130. His vigorous and practical teaching attracted many listeners, including eminent citizens and officials. Among them was Arrian, one of the most distinguished writers of his day, who took it upon himself to record Epictetus's lectures. These were published under the title *Discourses* or *Dissertations* (*Diatribai*) in eight books, four of which have survived (the *Manual* or *Encheiridion* is a summary of this material).

Instead of using a high literary style (the Atticistic Greek found in his own writings), Arrian sought to preserve the colloquial character of his teacher's lectures. For this reason, the *Discourses* of Epictetus provide one of the most important sources for the living Koine of the time and shed considerable light on the language of the Greek NT, especially the letters of Paul. (Cf. D. S. Sharp, *Epictetus and the New Testament* [1914]; more broadly based and fundamental is A. Bonhöffer, *Epiktet und das Neue Testament* [1911]. Some scholars have argued that the *Discourses* are basically Arrian's own work; at the other extreme, it has been suggested that Epictetus himself composed this material.) See also Greek language.

Although Epictetus shows familiarity with the technical aspects of Stoic teaching, his own emphasis is on the need for moral progress. Making a basic distinction between that which is under our control (namely, "the power to make correct use of external impressions," *Diss.* 1.1.7) and that which is not (everything outside one's "own governing principle," 1.3.1), Epictetus describes true progress as the act of "withdrawing from external things" and focusing attention on one's "own moral purpose, cultivating and perfecting it so as to make it finally harmonious with nature" (1.4.18; trans. W. A. Oldfather in LCL). Although he does not clearly distinguish between the divine being(s) and nature, Epictetus often speaks of God (Zeus) in personal terms and urges submission to his will (cf. 1.6.37–43). See also Greek religion and philosophy II.C.

Many Christians in the early church and in subsequent centuries have viewed the teachings of Epictetus as corresponding to those of Jesus and the NT, but the differences are far more profound than are the apparent parallels. Throughout his lessons (e.g., when he urges his readers "to desire each thing exactly as it happens," 1.12.15), Epictetus gives expression to a strong fatalistic streak. Because he has no solution for sin, he refuses to accept its reality: serenity is achieved, in effect, by responding to evil as though it did not exist (cf. 1.18.5–16; 3.18.1–4; 4.7.1–5). Nevertheless, Epictetus has much wisdom to offer, expressed in a provocative and entertaining style. (See further J. Bonforte, *The Philosophy of Epictetus* [1955]; J. C. Gretenkord, *Die Freiheitsbegriff Epiktets* [1981]; A. A. Long and D. Sedley, *The Hellenistic Philosophers* [1987]; A. A. Long, *Epictetus: A Stoic and Socratic Guide to Life* [2002]. For a new English trans. with introduction and commentary, see R. F. Dobbin, *Epictetus: Discourses Book I* [1998].)

Epicurean ep´i-kyoo-ree´uhn (Ἐπικούρειος *G2134*, from Ἐπίκουρος, Epicurus, meaning "helper, ally"). A prominent philosophical school in the Greco-Roman period. The Epicureans are mentioned in Acts 17:18, along with the Stoics. Luke gives no information on their views, except that they rejected the idea of a bodily resurrection. See Greek religion and philosophy II.C.

I. Moral reputation. Epicurus founded the school in Athens about 300 B.C. In a sense he effected a reform of the earlier school of Cyrenaics, whose crass slogan is partially quoted in 1 Cor. 15:32, "Let us eat and drink [and be merry], / for tomorrow we die." Contrasted with the licentiousness of the Cyrenaics, the Epicureans as judged by Greek or generally human standards advocated a fairly pure morality.

In a letter preserved by Diogenes Laertius, Epicurus states: "By pleasure we mean the absence of pain in the body and of trouble in the soul. It is not an unbroken succession of drinking bouts and of revelry, not sexual love, not the enjoyment of fish and other delicacies of a luxurious table, which produce a pleasant life; it is sober reasoning, searching out the grounds of every choice and avoidance, and banishing those beliefs through which the greatest tumults take possession of the soul." Epicureanism included even a strain of asceticism: "Sexual intercourse has never done a man any good, and he is lucky if it has not harmed him. Nor will a wise man [except in unusual circumstances] marry and rear a family" (Diogenes Laertius, *Lives of Eminent Philosophers* 10.118–19).

II. Hedonism. Although the Epicureans identified the aim of life as pleasure, for "No pleasure is

This bust of Epicurus (c. 341–270 B.C.) is a Roman copy of a lost Greek original dating to the 2nd cent. B.C. or even earlier.

a bad thing in itself," yet to call them hedonists, etymologically correct as it may be, is misleading. They recognized that "the means which produce some pleasures bring with them disturbances many times greater than the pleasures." More profoundly, the Epicureans defined pleasure, not as the titillation of the senses, but as the absence of pain, the avoidance of trouble, and freedom from annoyances. It was this aim to avoid everything disturbing and to achieve tranquillity of mind that motivated their views both on religion and on physics. These two subjects, with the Epicureans as with other schools in the history of philosophy, were closely related.

III. Religion, source of evil. The greatest disturber of tranquillity of mind and the most prolific source of all evils is the belief that the gods punish evildoers. Lucretius (94–55 B.C.), a Roman Epicurean, wrote, "Most often it is religion itself that inspires impious and criminal acts" (e.g., the sacrifice of Iphigenia by her father). The fear of the gods disturbs man in his dreams. The thought of punishment in a life beyond the grave tortures him all his days.

Therefore the fundamental principle for a happy life is, "Nullam rem e nilo gigni divinitus umquam" ("nothing ever comes about by divine power," Lucretius, *De rerum natura* 1.150). Confirmation of this principle is later stated: "That the world has by no means been created by divine power is clear from the fact that it contains so many flaws"; for example, "so much of its surface is uninhabitable, the remainder requires hard labor to produce food, the human infant is helpless, the man is harassed by wild beasts, disease, and early death" (2.180; 5.195ff.). In spite of this last reference to early death, death itself is not an evil. This principle must be understood, for otherwise the thought of extinction might be as disturbing as the thought of a future life. He enjoins: "Accustom thyself to believe that death is nothing to us.... A right understanding that death is nothing to us makes the mortality of life enjoyable, not by adding to life an illimitable time, but by taking away the yearning after immortality.... Foolish, therefore, is the man who says he fears death, not because it will pain him when it comes, but because it pains him in the prospect. Whatsoever causes no annoyance when it is present, causes only a groundless pain in the expectation. Death, therefore, the most awful of all evils, is nothing to us, seeing that, when we are, death is not come, and, when death is come, we are not."

IV. Atoms and freedom. All that remains, according to the Epicurean, is to frame an acceptable physics that will see mankind through the present life. If all natural phenomena can be plausibly explained in terms of atoms moving through empty space, the last reason for fearing the gods is gone. Such explanations the Epicureans give of sunlight penetrating the air, of images in mirrors, of the sun and moon, of thunder and lightning, and of many other things, but especially of sensation and reason—all in terms of atoms moving through empty space. These explanations need not be the absolute truth. All that is needed to show that no divine purpose rules nature is to give a materialistic account that is possible.

More important than many of these details is the theory of free will. Two opposing theories would make life miserable. First, if God had planned the universe and determined everything, nothing would be in our power and ethics would be impossible. Second, if all the atoms were always mechanically determined, as Democritus taught, the same unacceptable conclusion would follow. The physical theory is that the atoms generally move in straight lines, but sometimes for no cause whatever swerve just a little. Hence human beings, that is, bodies composed of atoms, can sometimes, for no cause whatever, move in opposition to the laws of mechanics. This is free will.

Hence, nature is to a limited extent under human control: "The future is not wholly ours nor wholly not ours, so that neither must we count upon it as quite certain to come, nor despair of it as quite certain not to come.... Destiny, which some introduce as sovereign over all things, [man] laughs to scorn, affirming rather that some things happen of necessity, others by chance, others through our own agency. For he sees that necessity destroys responsibility and that chance and fortune are inconstant; whereas our own actions are free.... Exercise thyself in these and kindred precepts day and night ... then never, either in waking or in dream, wilt thou be disturbed" (Lucretius, *De rerum natura* 10.124, 133–34).

(See further C. Bailey, *The Greek Atomists and Epicurus* [1928]; N. De Witt, *Epicurus and His Philosophy* [1954]; id., *St. Paul and Epicurus* [1954]; J. M. Rist, *Epicurus: An Introduction* [1972]; A. A. Long and D. Sedley, *The Hellenistic Philosophers*, 2 vols. [1987]; P. Mitsis, *Epicurus' Ethical Theory: The Pleasures of Vulnerability* [1988]; T. O'Keefe, *Epicurus on Freedom* [2005]; *OCD*, 532–34.)

G. H. CLARK

epigraphy. The study of INSCRIPTIONS; see also WRITING.

epilepsy. See DISEASE.

Epiphanes i-pif′uh-neez (ἐπιφανής G2212, "evident, manifest, notable"). A title meaning "[God] Manifest" and adopted by several Hellenistic kings, among whom the best known is ANTIOCHUS IV.

Epiphanius ep′i-fay′nee-uhs. Born in Palestine c. A.D. 315, Epiphanius founded a monastery in Judea while he was still a young man. He was a vigorous defender of orthodoxy as well as an efficient leader, and in 367 he was elected Bishop of SALAMIS (Constantia) in CYPRUS. During his career Epiphanius became involved in several doctrinal controversies. He died at sea in a voyage in 403. The author of several works, Epiphanius is best known for a treatise entitled *Panarion* (also called *Refutation of All Heresies*). Although not reliable in every respect, this work is one of the most important historical sources for our knowledge of most heretical movements in the early church. (See J. F. Dechow, *Dogma and Mysticism in Early Christianity: Epiphanius of Cyprus and the Legacy of Origen* [1988]; P. R. Amidon, *The Panarion of St. Epiphanius, Bishop of Salamis: Selected Passages* [1990]; A. Pourkier, *L'hérésiologie chez Epiphane de Salamine* [1992].)

epiphany i-pif′uh-nee. This English term (from Gk. *epiphaneia G2211*) can be used generally of any manifestation or even of a sudden realization. More specifically, it refers to a supernatural revelation or to the appearance of a divine being. When capitalized, it designates the Christian feast (January 6) that celebrates the visit of the MAGI because at that time the divine nature of Jesus was manifested to the Gentiles. In the Christian churches of the E, it celebrates the baptism of Jesus (when his messianic office was made manifest); this was its original significance, which can be dated to the 3rd cent.

Epiphi ep′i-fi. See EPEIPH.

epistle i-pis′uhl. This term (from Gk. *epistolē G2186*, "message, commission, letter") in English usage normally refers to a literary composition that is written in the form of a letter. Since the "epistles" of the NT are real pieces of correspondence (not published literary works), most modern versions translate the Greek word as LETTER.

I. Differentiations. Preserved documents in epistolary form "might more accurately be classified as public orations, philosophical treatises, political tracts, or moral exhortations ... [and] have all the marks of having been written for general publication" (O. J. F. Seitz in *IDB*, 3:115). Robinson notes that "An epistle is a work of art; a letter is a piece of life.... One is like the carefully finished photograph which does you justice; the other is like a snapshot which shows you as you are." The letter is less formal, more personal and direct than is the epistle. Indeed, some of Paul's letters, especially ROMANS, bear certain epistolary characteristics, as does HEBREWS. Few letters, in the technical sense, are found in the OT canonical books (see 2 Sam. 11:14–15; 1 Ki. 21:8–9; 2 Ki. 19:14; Jer. 29).

II. Composition and delivery. The NT letters were the earliest form of Christian literature. They were written on sheets of PAPYRUS with a reed pen and ink, then rolled or folded, tied, and often sealed for privacy and authentication (2 Ki. 21:17; Esth. 3:12; 8:8; Dan. 12:4; Rev. 5:9). Such letters were sometimes written on waxed tablets with a stylus, mainly for economy since they could be erased. As the official Roman postal service (*cursus publicus*) was not open to private correspondence, the Christians employed members of the churches as carriers (Acts 15:22; 2 Cor. 8:16–23; Phil. 2:25; Col. 4:7–8). While the NT letters were written, under divine guidance, in response to specific needs of individuals or churches (1 Cor. 7:1), it may be questioned whether the authors were ever aware

THE EPISTLES IN BRIEF

Title	Date (approx.)	Place of writing	Destination
Romans	57	Corinth	Church in Rome
1 Corinthians	55	Ephesus	Church in Corinth
2 Corinthians	56	Macedonia	Church in Corinth
Galatians	49 or 55	Antioch or Ephesus	Churches in Galatia
Ephesians	61?	Rome?	Churches in Asia Minor
Colossians	61?	Rome?	Church in Colosse
Philippians	62?	Rome?	Church in Philippi
1 Thessalonians	51	Corinth	Church in Thessalonica
2 Thessalonians	52	Corinth	Church in Thessalonica
Philemon	61?	Rome?	Philemon
1 Timothy	63	Macedonia?	Timothy
2 Timothy	64	Rome	Timothy
Titus	63	Macedonia?	Titus
Hebrews	68?	Unknown	Jewish Christians
James	48?	Jerusalem?	Christians of Dispersion
1 Peter	55?	Rome?	Christians of Dispersion
2 Peter	67?	Rome?	Christians of Dispersion
1 John	87?	Ephesus?	Christians of Asia Minor
2 John	87?	Ephesus?	"Elect Lady"
3 John	87?	Ephesus?	Gaius
Jude	Unknown	Unknown	Christians of Dispersion

that they were writing for all time and Christendom (2 Tim. 3:16).

III. Classifications. Twenty-one of the twenty-seven NT books are letters. In addition, the contents of two brief letters are included in Acts (Acts 15:23–29; 23:26–30), and seven in Revelation (Rev. 2:1—3:22); the latter are, Seitz thinks, "simply literary introductions to a book which is itself cast in an epistolary framework" (*IDB*, 3:115). Together they constitute more than one third of the NT. Christianity is unique in that of all the other sacred books of the world, not one is composed of letters.

Four persons or groups of persons were usually involved in a NT letter: the writer, the secretary (AMANUENSIS), the carrier, and the readers. It is considered, traditionally, that Paul was the author of thirteen of the NT letters. James wrote one; Peter, two; John, three; Jude, one; and one (Hebrews) is anonymous. Paul's letters may be classified as follows: (1) eschatological (1–2 Thess.), (2) soteriological (Gal., Rom., 1–2 Cor.), (3) Christological (Col., Eph., Phil.), (4) ecclesiological (1–2 Tim., Titus), and personal (Philemon). James is ethical; Jude is polemical; 1–2 Peter are pastoral; 1–3 John are pastoral; and Hebrews is largely polemical.

IV. Structure and value. Structurally the NT letters closely resemble their Hellenistic counterparts (cf. A. Deissmann, *Light from the Ancient East* [1911], 217–38). Paul's general practice is typical. (1) He begins with personal greetings, which sometimes include Christian friends or coworkers present with him, or possibly his secretary, which in some cases may account for his use of the first person plural. His introductory greetings normally set the keynote for the entire letter. (2) He offers thanksgiving to God for his Christian readers. (3) Prayers for the spiritual, and sometimes temporal, welfare of his readers usually follow. (4) He treats the principal concerns of his readers, often including a doctrinal discussion of their problems that may have been raised in previous communications (see 1 Cor. 7:1). (5) A practical or ethical section follows in which he applies to their needs the doctrinal principles set forth. (6) A benediction, personal messages, and salutations are sometimes included (Rom. 16). (7) A brief autograph, in part for authentication, closes the letter (Gal. 6:11; 2 Thess. 3:17).

The far-reaching influence of the NT letters on subsequent Christian literature is evinced by the writings of the 2nd cent. Not all of the 1st-cent. Christian letters survived (1 Cor. 5:9; Col. 4:16). From the beginning these NT letters were received by the church as divinely inspired messages along with the OT Scriptures (2 Pet. 3:15–16). (See further W. G. Doty, *Letters in Primitive Christianity* [1973]; J. L. White, ed., *Studies in Ancient Letter Writing* [1982]; J. L. White, *Light from Ancient Letters* [1986].)   C. W. CARTER

Epistle of the Apostles. See APOSTLES, EPISTLE OF THE.

epistles, apocryphal. Interest in the apostles generally took the form of apocryphal Acts, relating their travels, miracles, and martyrdoms, rather than of letters forged in support of some doctrinal position. An exception is the *Epistle of Pseudo-Titus*, in praise of virginity (see PSEUDO-TITUS, EPISTLE OF). Jesus left nothing in writing, but EUSEBIUS preserved an apocryphal correspondence with King ABGAR of Edessa. The *Letters of Paul and Seneca* are clear propaganda, the *Epistle to the Laodiceans* is forged to fill a gap in the Pauline Corpus, and the *Epistle of the Apostles* (*Epistula Apostolorum*) is largely an alleged account of revelations given by the risen Jesus (see LAODICEANS, EPISTLE TO THE; APOSTLES, EPISTLE OF THE). Other letters are to be found in the CLEMENTINE LITERATURE and in such documents as the *Acts of Paul*. (For a list of additional pseudepigraphic letters that have not survived, see *NTAp*, 2:31–32.) See also APOCRYPHAL NEW TESTAMENT and separate articles.
R. McL. WILSON

Epistles, Catholic (General). See CATHOLIC EPISTLES.

Er uhr (עֵר H6841, "watcher" or "protector"; Ἤρ G2474). **(1)** Firstborn son of JUDAH by his Canaanite wife, the daughter of Shua (Gen. 38:3). Er married TAMAR, but the Lord slew him for some unnamed wickedness before he had any children

(Gen. 38:6–7; 46:12; Num. 26:19; 1 Chr. 2:3). Tamar was then given to his brother ONAN (Gen. 38:8).

(2) Son of Shela and grandson of JUDAH, thus nephew of #1 above (1 Chr. 4:21).

(3) Son of a certain Joshua, included in Luke's GENEALOGY OF JESUS CHRIST (Lk. 3:27).

R. L. ALDEN

Eran ihr´an (עֵרָן *H6896*, "watcher" or "protector"; gentilic עֵרָנִי *H6897*, "Eranite"). Son of SHUTHELAH and grandson of EPHRAIM; eponymous ancestor of the Eranite clan (Num. 26:36; on the basis of the LXX and other versional evidence, some scholars emend the Heb. text to ʿēden). The parallel passage (1 Chr. 7:20) does not mention Eran.

J. B. SCOTT

Erastus i-ras´tuhs (Ἔραστος, "beloved"). A common Greek name, occurring in the NT with reference to two (or possibly three) companions of PAUL. (1) A helper of Paul, sent along with TIMOTHY to MACEDONIA while the apostle remained in the province of ASIA for a while longer (Acts 19:22). He is very likely the same Erastus whom Paul left behind at CORINTH (2 Tim. 4:20); some think he may be a different individual.

(2) A man described as "director of public works" in Corinth (the city from which ROMANS was written) and who sent greetings to the Christians in ROME (Rom. 16:23; NRSV, "city treasurer"). He was apparently the steward or manager (Gk. *oikonomos G3874*) of the property or financial affairs of the city. Such officials were generally slaves or freedmen, though often wealthy. It is debated whether the title reflects high social status (G. Theissen, *The Social Setting of Pauline Christianity: Essays on Corinth* [1982], 75–83) or the humble position of a city-owned slave (H. J. Cadbury in *JBL* 50 [1931]: 42–58). In 1929, archaeologists uncovered at Corinth a 1st-cent. Latin inscription reading, "Erastus, commissioner for public works [*aedile*], laid this pavement at his own expense." That he was the Erastus of Romans is possible, but not probable (see the discussion by D. W. J. Gill in *TynBul* 40 [1989]: 293–301; A. D. Clarke discusses "Another Corinthian Erastus Inscription" in ibid. 42 [1991]: 146–51). It has also been suggested by some that the Erastus of Romans may be the same as #1 above; it is unlikely, however, that a city official (esp. if he was a city-owned slave) would have been able to travel with Paul.

D. E. HIEBERT

Erech ee´rik (אֶרֶךְ *H804*; Akk. *Uruk*). TNIV Uruk. The second of the cities founded by NIMROD (Gen. 10:10). In times of the Assyrian empire, Erech was one of the cities whose inhabitants were deported to SAMARIA by King ASHURBANIPAL (Ezra 4:9–10). Erech, or Uruk, was one of the oldest, largest, and most important cities of ancient SUMER. The site is located at modern Warka, c. 160 mi. S of Baghdad. Originally the city was on the W bank of the EUPHRATES River but the river now lies some distance to the E of the site.

The original village, known as Kullab, was founded by the Ubaid people c. 4000 B.C., and the founder of Erech's semi-mythical "First Dynasty" was Meskiaggasher. Uruk was the capital of the mythical hero-king GILGAMESH. From c. 3600 to 3000, the city was the central power in MESOPOTAMIA. It was here also that the earliest known WRITING system (proto-cuneiform) came into use. From the time of HAMMURABI it became part of Babylonia and shared its fortunes and misfortunes. Erech was a chief center for the cult of Anu and Inanna, among the foremost Babylonian deities. There is perpetual reference to the city in Assyrian and Babylonian literature, and commercial documents to 200 B.C. attest its continued prosperity. See ASSYRIA AND BABYLONIA. Later in history—

This stone, discovered in 1929, was placed by Erastus, the commissioner for public works at Corinth, at his own expense. Some think he is the same Erastus who sent greetings to the Christians in Rome (Rom. 16:23).

perhaps Assyrian times, certainly by the PARTHIAN period—it became a sort of national necropolis. The site was abandoned soon after A.D. 600.

The site of Erech was first excavated by William K. Loftus in 1850 and 1854 (see his work, *Travels and Researches in Chaldaea and Susiana* [1857]). German expeditions conducted excavations several times during the 20th cent. These revealed city walls c. 6 mi. in circumference, encircling c. 1,100 acres; two ZIGGURATS; and several temples from the late 4th and early 3rd millennia B.C. Also found were hundreds of pictographic tablets, seals, etc. The library found contained many documents on religious practice, some dating as late as 70 B.C. Excavations also revealed remains of canals in the immediate area of the city, while the site itself was flanked by two large streams and intersected by many canals. Poetical references imply that the city and surrounding area were regarded as once quite fertile, a contrast to the desolation of the area now.

(See further H. W. Eliot, *Excavations in Mesopotamia and Western Iran* [1950]; S. Lloyd, *The Archaeology of Mesopotamia: From the Stone Age to the Persian Conquest* [1984]; P.-A. Beaulieu, *The Pantheon of Uruk during the Neo-Babylonian Period* [2003]; G. Algaze, *The Uruk World System: The Dynamics of Expansion of Early Mesopotamian Civilization*, 2nd ed. [2004].) L. L. WALKER

Eri ee´ri (עֵרִי *H6878*, "watcher" or "protector"; gentilic עֵרִי *H6879*, "Erite"). Son of GAD, grandson of JACOB, and eponymous ancestor of the Erites (Gen. 46:16; Num. 26:16).

Eridu. One of the most ancient cities of Mesopotamia, modern Tell Abu Shahrain in SE Iraq. The earliest excavated level dates to about the middle of the 6th millennium B.C. Sumerian literature (see SUMER) refers to it as existing even prior to the great flood (cf. *ANET*, 43). Many levels of temple mud-brick architecture have been discovered, as well as a massive ZIGGURAT that was constructed c. 2100 B.C. (See F. Safar et al., *Eridu* [1981].)

eruption. See DISEASE.

Esaias i-zay´yuhz. KJV NT form of ISAIAH.

Esarhaddon ee´suhr-had´uhn (אֵסַר־חַדֹּן *H675*, from Akk. *Aššur-aḫ-iddin*, "Ashur has given a brother"; in the LXX called Ασορδαν [2 Ki. 19:37; Isa. 37:38] and Σαχερδονος [Tob. 1:21–22; KJV, "Sarchedonus"]). Also Esar-haddon. King of ASSYRIA 681–669 B.C.

I. Sources. The principal events of Esarhaddon's reign are listed in the Babylonian Chronicle, the Esarhaddon Chronicle for the years 681–667 B.C., and numerous royal inscriptions. Copies of his treaties with TYRE and others have been recovered. The OT names him as son and successor to SENNACHERIB (2 Ki. 19:37; Isa. 37:38; some have identified him with "the great and noble Osnappar" of Ezra 4:10 NRSV, but the latter is probably ASHURBANIPAL).

II. Family. Sennacherib was murdered by one or more of his sons (see ADRAMMELECH and SHAREZER) in Tebet 681 B.C. (2 Ki. 19:36–37; 2 Chr. 32:21; Isa. 37:37–38). This may have been in revenge for having nominated Esarhaddon—whose name implies that he was not the eldest son of the Aramean wife of Sennacherib, Naqiya-Zakutu—as crown prince. The wife of Esarhaddon (d. 673) bore him twin sons, Ashurbanipal and Shamash-Shumukin, whom in May 672 he had designated respectively crown prince of Assyria and of Babylonia, doubtless in the hope of avoiding internecine struggle similar to that experienced at his own accession. A daughter he gave in marriage to the Scythian chief Bartatua.

III. Rule. Esarhaddon's first task was to rally popular support, pursue the rebels into the mountains to the N, and execute the nobles who had aided them in NINEVEH. This led to further operations to keep the northern trade routes open and to check the incursions of the CIMMERIAN tribesmen (679 B.C.). In the E, the Median chiefs (see MEDIA) were tamed by frequent raids and the imposition of vassal treaties watched over by local Assyrian garrisons. Farther S, the Elamites (see ELAM) continued to stir up the Babylonian tribes. Esarhaddon raided their territory and deported prisoners to other sites (Ezra 4:9–10). With clever diplomacy he installed Na'id-Marduk of Bīt-Yakin, a son of the rebel MERODACH-BALADAN, as local governor and secured long and loyal support.

Esarhaddon was now free to devote his attention to EGYPT, which was the source of intrigue within the Syrian and Palestinian city-states. He raided the Bit-Adini area (cf. Isa. 37:12; see BETH EDEN) and the Arabs (676 B.C.). SIDON was besieged and a treaty made with Baʿal of TYRE. Tribute was received from thirteen kings of the E Mediterranean islands and coast and twelve kings of the mainland including Tyre, Sidon, EDOM, MOAB, GAZA, ASHKELON, EKRON, GEBAL, ASHDOD, Beth-Ammon, and MANASSEH (Akk. *Menasi*) of Judah. There is as yet no mention in the Assyrian texts of Manasseh's deportation to BABYLON (2 Chr. 33:11), though Esarhaddon, who had been viceroy there while crown prince, was then engaged in reconstruction of the city after its sack by his father and may have called in tributaries to help. An 8th-cent. letter found at Nineveh records "10 mana of silver sent by the men of Judah" about this time. The terms imposed by Esarhaddon on his vassals, including Manasseh, are known from texts found at Nimrud (CALAH). They had to assent to ASSHUR as their god and to teach their children obedience to him and Assyria. Any deviation from the terms was punished by the threat of invasion and deportation. It is not surprising that the prophets and historians considered his reign as more than unusually evil (2 Ki. 21:9).

In 675/4 B.C., Esarhaddon sent two expeditions against Egypt itself, having taken the city of Arzani on the border some years before and neutralized Tyre by siege works and made conciliations with the tribes of N ARABIA. TIRHAKAH (2 Ki. 19:9) retreated to Nubia (see ETHIOPIA), and MEMPHIS fell. Assyrian control of the NILE delta was by means of puppet governors. The first campaign ended by the Assyrians withdrawing with much loot "before a great storm." Soon, however, local intrigue at Nineveh must have encouraged Tirhakah to stir up open revolt in Egypt itself. It was at HARAN, while on the way to suppress this rebellion, that Esarhaddon fell sick and died (10 Marheshvan 681) and was succeeded by Ashurbanipal.

IV. Building. Esarhaddon built a new palace-fortress at Kar-Esarhaddon near Asshur and in SE Calah. Temples were restored also at Nineveh, Nippur, Babylon, and other cities. (See R. Borger, *Die Inschriften Asarhaddons, Königs von Assyrien* [1956]; D. J. Wiseman, "The Vassal-Treaties of Esarhaddon," *Iraq* 20 [1958]: 1–99 [cf. *ANET*, 534–41]; *CAH*, 3/2, 2nd ed. [1991], 38–47, 122–41; B. N. Porter, *Images, Power, Politics: Figurative Aspects of Esarhaddon's Babylonian Policy* [1993]; F. Reynolds, ed., *The Babylonian Correspondence of Esarhaddon* [2003].)　　　　　　　　　　　D. J. WISEMAN

Esau ee´saw (עֵשָׂו H6916, derivation uncertain, but by popular etymology, "hairy"; Ἠσαῦ G2481). Son of ISAAC and REBEKAH, and elder twin brother of JACOB. At their birth, "The first to come out was red, and his whole body was like a hairy [Heb. *śēʿār* H8552] garment; so they named him Esau" (Gen. 25:25). He was also named EDOM, meaning "red" (25:30). As Esau grew up, he became an outdoors man who enjoyed hunting. He would bring venison home to his father and became his father's favorite. At the same time his brother Jacob won the favor of his mother by remaining indoors and learning to work in the house.

On one occasion Esau returned from the hunt to find his brother cooking some red stew (see LENTIL). Famished, Esau asked for some of the stew, but Jacob took advantage of the situation by asking Esau's BIRTHRIGHT in exchange. Esau, reasoning that his birthright would be meaningless if he were to die of starvation, sold his birthright (Gen. 25:29–34). Although Jacob took advantage of his brother's weakness, Esau is censured for the little value he placed on the birthright (v. 34; Heb. 12:16–17). He did not trust God to provide for him in his need (cf. Mal. 1:2–3; Rom. 9:13).

Esau showed his lack of concern for the COVENANT promises by marrying two local girls who were not related to the people of ABRAHAM (Gen. 26:34–35; 36:1–2). The mixed marriages caused grief to Esau's parents, particularly his mother. When Isaac was old and feeble, he decided to confer his blessing on Esau, his firstborn and favorite son. Rebekah, however, determined to fool her husband into blessing Jacob instead. Esau was sent out to find the game his father enjoyed eating. Rebekah, in the meantime, placed Esau's clothes on Jacob and induced him to go to his father with the meat that she had prepared, to get the blessing intended for Esau. The deception was successful. Jacob received the blessing meant for Esau, and Esau was angered. He planned to kill Jacob, but Jacob—with his mother's aid—fled to the ancestral home in northern MESOPOTAMIA, where he married and began to raise his family.

With the principal blessing given to Jacob, Esau had to be content with a lesser one. He would continue to be a man of the open spaces, and while he would be subject to his brother, the time would come when he would regain his independence (Gen. 27:39–40; cf. 25:23, quoted in Rom. 9:12). This statement reflects the fact that the Edomites, descendants of Esau, were subject to Israel during times of Israelite strength. In Israelite weakness, however, Edom became an independent state. Jacob remained in N Mesopotamia twenty years, and on his way back he sought means of appeasing Esau. Esau, however, had prospered in the region of Mount SEIR (Heb. *śēʿîr* H8541, Gen. 32:4; Josh. 24:4) during Jacob's absence. They had an amicable reunion, after which Jacob went on to Canaan, and Esau back to the region of Edom. The biblical account of Jacob and Esau seeks to show that the line of promise went from Abraham to Isaac to Jacob-Israel, and that the later Israelites are the descendants of Jacob. Esau, who lost his birthright and blessing, forfeited the rights of the firstborn. He had, however, a prosperous life in the region of Mount Seir. A full account of his descendants is given in Gen. 36 (cf. also Deut. 2:4–5 et al.; 1 Chr. 1:34–35).   C. F. PFEIFFER

eschatology es´kuh-tol´uh-jee. The doctrine of the last things (from Gk. *eschatos* G2274, "last," and *logos* G3364, "word, discourse, subject"). This term designates the teaching from Scripture concerning the final consummation of all things. It is assumed throughout Scripture that history is the scene of God's redemptive activity and is therefore moving toward a new order when SIN and evil will be overcome, so that God will "become all in all." It is hardly possible to overestimate the importance of eschatology to Christian faith: life without FAITH is empty, and faith without HOPE is impossible. If the "eschatology" of modern science—death for the individual, death for the species, death for the entire system of wheeling suns that we call the universe—is the only truth by which we can live, then indeed "let us eat, and drink, and be merry, for tomorrow we die." The Christian, however, does not believe that DEATH is the last word. For him the RESURRECTION OF JESUS CHRIST has robbed death of its victory and brought hope and IMMORTALITY to light. It is the content of this hope that the Christian doctrine of eschatology sets forth.

  I. Eschatology of the OT
     A. The eschatology of the people of God
     B. The eschatology of the individual
  II. Eschatology of the Apocrypha and Pseudepigrapha
     A. Introduction
     B. The afterlife
     C. The Messiah and his kingdom
     D. The resurrection
     E. The judgment
  III. Eschatology of the NT
     A. Introduction
     B. The teaching of Jesus
     C. Events leading up to the second coming
     D. The second advent
     E. The resurrection of the dead
     F. The intermediate state
     G. The Last Judgment
     H. The divine retribution: hell
     I. The final consummation: heaven
     J. The millennium
     K. Concluding observations

I. Eschatology of the OT

A. The eschatology of the people of God.

In the OT one may distinguish between individual and national eschatology; the latter, in many passages, being enlarged to embrace not only Israel, but the Gentile nations as well. As the hope of Israel is the predominant eschatological note in the OT, the discussion of eschatology will begin from the broader perspective of an eschatology of the people of God.

The hope of God's chosen people is the fundamental strand of OT teaching regarding the future. Eschatology is the climax of the history of Israel's salvation. God, who led the fathers out of Egypt and gave them the Promised Land, will eventually triumph over all his and their enemies; he will secure to his people complete fellowship with himself, and eventually establish his dominion over the whole earth. Thus the promise made to ABRAHAM, "all peoples on earth will be blessed through you" (Gen. 12:3), ultimately will be fulfilled. (If instead of "be blessed," one translates "bless themselves" [cf. RSV]—i.e., wish upon themselves the same blessings enjoyed by Abraham and his seed—it makes little difference in the ultimate meaning.)

The fact that this hope is the consummation of history does not mean that it is something human beings will achieve by their own efforts or that they can even calculate when and how it will come about. It is rather the coming of Yahweh, who will miraculously intervene and create all things new, that makes possible the full realization of the COVENANT promises. For the most part, the prophets tended to depict this age of final SALVATION after the analogy of God's former acts of salvation history; the glorious future of Israel would be continuous with current history as they knew it. As time went on, more and more stress was laid on the qualitative difference between the present historical order and the new age of eschatological fulfillment. This is particularly true of DANIEL and the later apocalyptic writers.

1. The day of the Lord. Perhaps the most characteristic formula in the OT to describe the eschatological drama is "the DAY OF THE LORD." The term *day* can be used for a time of battle (cf. "the day of Midian," Isa. 9:4 NRSV; NIV, "the day of Midian's defeat"). In popular parlance, the day of the Lord is the time (not necessarily a literal day) when Yahweh will interpose on behalf of his people to save them from their enemies and alleviate the miseries that burden their lives. It is the time when the remnant, loyal to Yahweh, shall be delivered (Isa. 6:13; Amos 9:9). It is the day when he shall pour out his Spirit on all flesh and all who call on the name of the Lord shall be delivered (Joel 2:28–32).

This does not mean—and the prophets make the point clear—that the day of the Lord is a time of salvation alone. On the contrary, when the Lord shall visit the righteous with salvation, he shall also discomfit the wicked with JUDGMENT: "Woe to you who long / for the day of the LORD! / Why do you long for the day of the LORD? / That day will be darkness, not light. / It will be as though a man fled from a lion / only to meet a bear, / as though he entered his house / and rested his hand on the wall / only to have a snake bite him. / Will not the day of the LORD be darkness, not light— / pitch-dark, without a ray of brightness?" (Amos 5:18–20). The reason the day of the Lord is a day of doom is that the God who saves is also a God of HOLINESS who punishes the rebellious sinners, and Israel had thus sinned (Amos 4:12). Before the EXILE, the note of judgment predominated, though the note of salvation shone through (Isa. 1:25–26; Hos. 2:16–17), especially in the latter part of ISAIAH. After the exile, the theme of salvation took the ascendancy, especially in the book of EZEKIEL.

Often the day of the Lord is given wider scope to include the Gentile nations along with Israel in the realization of the divine purpose. Sometimes nations were used as instruments of God's judgment on Israel (Assyrians, Babylonians, Persians), although they too would be judged in turn by the Lord (cf. the prophecies against the nations in Isaiah, Jeremiah, Ezekiel, Amos, Nahum, and Habakkuk). As in the prophecies concerning Israel, salvation was also the purpose of God toward the nations. The reign of God shall be extended until all the earth is full of his glory (Isa. 2:2–3; 42:4; 60; Jer. 12:14–16; 16:19–21; Ezek. 16:53–54; Mic. 4:1–5). These events will come to pass in the "last days" (Isa. 2:2; Jer. 48:47; Hos. 3:5).

In Daniel's prophecy of the four kingdoms, these kingdoms were broken in pieces by a massive stone cut out of the mountains without hands (Dan. 2:44–45), which was to become a great mountain to

Ketef Hinnom tombs (Jerusalem, 6th cent. B.C.). The doctrine of resurrection is one of the concerns of eschatology.

Parchment MS of an apocalyptic work entitled Vision of Daniel, discovered in the Cairo Genizah.

fill the whole earth (v. 34), symbolizing God's everlasting kingdom. In the same vein is the beautiful prophecy of Malachi, "My name will be great among the nations, from the rising to the setting of the sun" (Mal. 1:11). Although the Gentiles shall be made fellow heirs of Israel's salvation, the Hebrew nation will still prevail. Israel will inherit the Gentiles (Isa. 54:3). "Then the sovereignty, power and greatness of the kingdoms under the whole heaven will be handed over to the saints, the people of the Most High" (Dan. 7:27). The nations will do homage to Israel: "They will bow down before you / and plead with you, saying, / 'Surely God is with you, and there is no other; / there is no other god'" (Isa. 45:14; cf. Isa. 49:23).

Though the day of the Lord is principally concerned with God's coming to mankind for salvation or judgment, it is also a time when the order of *nature itself* will be shaken with great convulsions. Scenes of gloom and dissolution are not uncommon in the prophets (Isa. 2:12–15; chs. 13–14; Hos. 10:8; Joel 2–3; Amos 5:18; Zeph. 1). Along with these terrifying visions, there are those that picture a new paradisiacal order in which "the wilderness will rejoice and blossom" (Isa. 35:1). "The wolf will live with the lamb, / the leopard will lie down with the goat / ... The cow will feed with the bear, / ... and the lion will eat straw like the ox. / ... They will neither harm nor destroy / on all my holy mountain, / for the earth will be full of the knowledge of the LORD / as the waters cover the sea" (Isa. 11:6–9). The involvement of the order of nature in the eschatological drama, set forth in rapturous poetic language, expresses the essential truth that the physical world was created for humankind and, therefore, shares in the judgment and renewal that is his final prospect. The ancient Hebrews knew nothing of the Greek concept of salvation by flight from the body and the world of which man is a part.

When the prophets speak of the day of the Lord, they regard it as near, as an especially threatening judgment (Isa. 13:6; Joel 1:15; 2:1). Of course, its exact time was known to no one; because it was a free act of God, it was not predictable as some event in the natural course of things. A presentiment of its nearness was awakened by the moral lapses and seemingly incorrigible apostasy of the people. Man's insensibility to the divine majesty seemed so frightful that the Lord must surely intervene (Isa. 13; Joel 1:2).

In this regard it should be noted that some prophecies were actually fulfilled, at least in part, by the proximate sequel of events. In the war with Aram and Ephraim (743/33), for example, Isaiah predicted the defeat of the enemy though the hostile threat remained to Judah (Isa. 7:5–7, 16; 8:4). In the siege of Jerusalem by SENNACHERIB (701), he prophesied its collapse (37:33–35). It was especially the threat of NEBUCHADNEZZAR that tended to give historic definition to the visions of eschatological doom. The eschatological dimension is actualized in the ensuing events, so that some scholars speak of the captivity and exile of Israel as an "actualizing" eschatology. Similarly, the RESTORATION of Israel was not only a future hope but, in a limited way, a present reality in the person of CYRUS, the king of the Persians (Isa. 41:2–3, 25; 44:28; 45:1; et al.). This proximate fulfillment of the prophetic visions of judgment in the calamities that overtook Israel from the northern hords, and of salvation in the restoration under Cyrus of Persia, gave meaning to the sense of imminence that informed much of the eschatological vision of the prophets.

2. The messianic hope. The messianic hope is an important element of OT doctrine, though the figure of the MESSIAH did not have the central place in OT eschatology that Jesus had in the eschatology of the NT. The redeemer in whom the pious of the OT hoped was God (Ps. 3:8), and if the Messiah is a redeemer, or a savior, it is because of his divine nature.

The word *messiah* means "anointed." In the OT the Hebrew term (Heb. *māšiaḥ* H5431) is applied to the priests, but especially to the kings, and it is this latter usage of royalty that has left the most pronounced traces in the eschatological hope of the Jewish people. By virtue of the oil of anointing, which symbolized his investiture with the Spirit of God, the king was a sacred person, consecrated as Yahweh's vicegerent in Israel. See ANOINT. From the time of NATHAN's oracle, the hope of Israel was fixed on the dynasty of DAVID (2 Sam. 7:12–16). With the humiliation of that dynasty by the Babylonians, though the faith of Israel was severely tried, it survived in the hope of a future king who would be the true SERVANT OF THE LORD, bringing justice, light, and deliverance to all nations (Isa. 42:1–4, 6–7), and extending the covenant of God to all the earth.

Visions of this coming Servant are delineated in a section of Isaiah sometimes known as the "Servant Songs" (Isa. 42:1–7; 49:1–6; 50:4–9; 52:13—53:12). In these passages is a certain fluid movement between the thoughts that either the nation of Israel or some individual is the Servant. The corporate personality progresses toward the individual, as the prophecies progress, which justifies the classic Christian application of these Servant prophecies to the person and work of Jesus Christ. The mission of the Servant is expressly described thus: "It is too small a thing for you to be my servant / to restore the tribes of Jacob / and bring back those of Israel I have kept. / I will also make you a light for the Gentiles, / that you may bring my salvation to the ends of the earth" (Isa. 49:6; part of this verse was quoted by Simeon, Lk. 2:32).

Another prophecy that belongs to the messianic strand of OT eschatology is Dan. 7, which refers to one coming with the clouds of heaven "like a son of man, coming with the clouds of heaven" and receiving "an everlasting dominion" (vv. 13–14). SON OF MAN appears to have been the most common self-designation used by Jesus. It must be remembered that the OT does not clearly coordinate all these categories—"seed of David," "Servant of the Lord," "son of man"—as is done this side of the INCARNATION. But they all, even if ambiguous at times, have their place in the eschatological hope of Israel.

3. The restoration of Israel. The interpretation of Israel's hope of restoration to its own land is difficult to achieve from a Christian perspective. It is, however, a prominent feature of OT prophecy. Just as the judgment of God upon his people was never separated, in the prophetic vision, from the historical event of the exile, so the salvation of the people was never separated from the historical event of the return to the land. God said "to the north, 'Give them up!' / and to the south, 'Do not hold them back.' / Bring my sons from afar and my daughters from the end of the earth" (Isa. 43:6). Restored to the land, the people would enjoy everlasting felicity and righteousness, together with all earthly blessings (Amos 9:11–15). In the eyes of the nations they were in truth the people of God (Isa. 43:3).

There can be little question of the meaning of similar prophecies of restoration to the land. Though the essential element was the spiritual beatitude of the righteous through God's making his abode in their midst, nonetheless this noble vision involved an external condition of the people in the glorified land of Canaan. If the final meaning of the OT is revealed in the NT, what shall be made of the fact that the latter says nothing of the restoration of Israel to the land? Paul, the only NT writer to discuss Israel's future in detail (Rom. 9–11), deals only with the spiritual aspect of the promises made to the fathers. For Paul, the salvation of Israel is that they shall be grafted back into the olive tree into which the Gentiles have been grafted, through faith in Christ (Rom. 11:13–36). It seems best, therefore, to take the many prophecies of restoration to the land as having their literal fulfillment in the return under EZRA and NEHEMIAH, when the temple and city of Jerusalem were restored; and to construe their final fulfillment in terms of those blessings of a heavenly land, secured to all God's people in Jesus Christ. The present-day return of Israel to Palestine should indeed give one pause; yet it is difficult to see in this interesting development a clear fulfillment of prophecy, as long as the Israelis remain a nation in unbelief and their prosperity in the land is more a tribute to their technological ingenuity than to any divine, supernatural act of eschatological redemption.

B. The eschatology of the individual. As can be seen from the above, the central themes of OT eschatology—the advent of God, his judgment of the nations, and establishment of the final kingdom of righteousness—are themes that concern mankind as a whole. What of the individual? Is a person's life, no matter how prolonged and blessed, cut off by death? Do we live only in the memory of our descendants? Is the state of beatitude only for those living in "that day" when God shall create new heavens and a new earth?

It is difficult for the Christian to understand the limited place that is given in the OT to the individual, and the emphasis on the solidarity of the larger unit of the household, of the tribe, of the nation, and of the race. In the OT, the happiness of the upright consisted in a long life in the land that the Lord had given them, and their hope in a pious and numerous seed that should live after them. Yet the Israelites did not suppose that the individual became extinct at death; from earliest times they possessed a belief in the shadowy existence in SHEOL.

The Hebrew term *šĕʾôl* H8619 refers to a subterranean region, or pit, where the dead subsist in a shadowy and attenuated form; it is only a feeble reflection of life on earth. Though under God's dominion (Ps. 139:8; Amos 9:2), God has withdrawn his Spirit from the denizens of that forgotten land, so that they lack energy and the vital spirit of life, being consigned to a flaccid and vacuous existence as shades. The abode of the dead is called "silence" (Ps. 94:17); "the land of forgetfulness" (Ps. 88:12); the dead know nothing (Eccl. 9:5). Death levels all to a common fate; it brings them to a state where the wicked cease from troubling and the weary are at rest (Job 3:17). SAMUEL complained at being "disquieted" by the medium of ENDOR (1 Sam. 28:15). The most threatening aspect of death for the righteous is the fear that they will be cut off from God. "For in death there is no remembrance of you; / in Sheol who can give you praise?" (Ps. 6:5 NRSV; cf. Isa. 38:18).

The OT teaches that both the righteous and the wicked go to Sheol, and the factor of REWARD and RETRIBUTION is not the paramount consideration. Yet it would be too much to say that the same fate awaits the righteous as the wicked, who perish under the bane of the divine displeasure. "The wicked shall depart to Sheol" (Ps. 9:17 NRSV), and the proud and haughty shall be brought down to Sheol, to the pit (Isa. 14:15; Ezek. 32:23). Scholars have frequently seen the penal character of Sheol also in Ps. 49 and 73. On the other hand, the fervent prayer, "Let me die the death of the righteous, / and may my end be like theirs!" (Num. 23:10), would seem to imply more than a desire for a prolonged and happy old age on earth.

It seems not too much to say, then, that the hope of the righteous is for a deliverance from Sheol, and that, as time went on, the deliverance was seen to imply a RESURRECTION. The flesh of the righteous shall rest in hope, because God will not leave their soul in Sheol, but rather show them the path of life, the joy of divine presence, and the pleasures at God's right hand (Ps. 16:9–11, cf. Pss. 17:15; 49:15; 73:24). JOB raised the question, "If a man dies, will he live again?" (Job 14:14). In the light of this question, it is plausible to translate the strong affirmation of faith in Job 19:25–26 as involving the vision of God "from the flesh." Isaiah 26:19 strikes a clear note of resurrection, and in EZEKIEL's vision of the valley of dry bones (Ezek. 37:1–14) the element of individual resurrection surely cannot be excluded.

Jesus alluded to this site, the Hinnom Valley (Gehenna), in connection with the eschatological prophecy of Isa. 66:24 (cf. Mk. 9:48). (View to the SE.)

Finally, in Dan. 12:2 for the first time the resurrection of the wicked, as well as the righteous, is affirmed: "Multitudes who sleep in the dust of the earth will awake: some to everlasting life, others to shame and everlasting contempt." The implication this prophecy contains concerning the judgment of the wicked is found as early as Isa. 66:24, "And they will go out and look upon the dead bodies of those who rebelled against me; their worm will not die, nor will their fire be quenched, and they will be loathsome to all mankind." This threat to the wicked, together with the hope of the righteous that God will receive them to glory (Ps. 73:24), summarizes the limits of personal eschatology in the OT.

II. Eschatology of the Apocrypha and Pseudepigrapha

A. Introduction. The APOCRYPHA and PSEUDEPIGRAPHA consist of extracanonical books written from the beginning of the 2nd cent. B.C. to the close of the 1st cent. A.D. Some do not touch upon the eschatological theme; others dwell upon it in great detail. Whereas many writings in the intertestamental period follow the basic perspective of the OT and conceive of the eschatological fulfillment of the divine purpose as continuous with this present age, others are strongly APOCALYPTIC, postulating two distinct and separate ages: (a) the present evil age under the sway of SATAN, and therefore beyond redemption, and (b) the eternal age to come, under divine dominion. Describing this eschatological hope, these books indulge in vividly imaginative representations, characterized by an increased emphasis on the individual and the afterlife. Many of these representations are developed from the OT, others reflect Babylonian, Persian, and even Greek influence. Although often conflicting with the teachings of the NT, and far from uniform within themselves, these documents constitute a nexus between the eschatology of the OT and the NT, with its heightened emphasis on the individual and its extensive use of imagery.

B. The afterlife. The realm of the dead is Sheol, a dreary, subterranean chamber in the earth. In the postexilic literature it became a temporary rather than permanent abode, especially for the righteous, who will leave it at the resurrection (*Pss. Sol.* 14.6–7; 2 Macc. 7:9; 14:46). In those sources that limit the resurrection to the righteous alone, Sheol is thought of as a place of punishment for the wicked who remain incarcerated there. The author of 2 Maccabees wrote that Judas MACCABEE prayed for his fellows who had fallen in battle, and who were presently in Sheol (2 Macc. 12:43–45). This passage has been used as a proof text for the Roman Catholic doctrine of prayers for the dead in purgatory, though Sheol and purgatory are by no means the same.

When Sheol is thought of exclusively as a place of punishment for the wicked, the abode of the righteous is sometimes thought of as PARADISE. According to the *Apocalypse of Moses* 33.4, when Adam died his soul was taken to paradise. In like manner, in the *Testament of Job*, Job was taken by the angel of death to the throne of God's glory, to where his children had preceded him. In Bar. 21:23–24; 30:2; 2 Esd. 7:95, the souls of the righteous go to heavenly "treasuries" or chambers, awaiting the resurrection, whereas the souls of the wicked descend into Sheol.

C. The Messiah and his kingdom. In the intertestamental literature the Messiah is sometimes presented as a passive ruler over a transfigured Israel (*1 En.* 83–90); at other times he is a warrior who slays his enemies with his own hands (*Sib. Or.* 3.652–660), or by the word of his mouth, ruling in justice and holiness (*Pss. Sol.* 17.27, 31, 37–41). In *1 En.* 37–70 he is the supernatural ruler and judge of all mankind, the most sublime view found outside the canon.

As for the Messiah's kingdom, it is sometimes eternal, on a transformed earth (*1 En.* 1–36), inaugurated by a resurrection and a final judgment; at other times it is of temporary duration, followed by these events (*1 En.* 91–104; *Pss. Sol.* 17–18; *Jubilees, Assumption of Moses,* et al.). In some of the literature of this period (2 Esdras = 4 Ezra), no mention is made of a messianic kingdom. Many of the intertestamental books reiterate the OT promise that Israel will return from the dispersion to her own land.

D. The resurrection. Because it is only just that the righteous dead should share in the messianic kingdom, the idea of a resurrection became important in the literature between the Testaments. It is generally conceived of physically, the soul coming from Sheol, or some other place, to be united with the body. Sometimes it is general—both the righteous and the wicked are raised (*Apoc. Moses* 41.3). God will fashion human bodies just as they were in life, so that they may be recognized (*Sib. Or.* 4.179–80; *2 Bar.* 50). Sometimes the resurrection is limited to the righteous, as in certain parts of the *Testaments of the Twelve Patriarchs*; for example, the affirmation that the godly alone will be raised, especially the martyrs (*Test. Judah* 25.4), which seems to be the thought also of 2 Macc. 7:9.

As for the nature of the resurrected body, the maimed and broken limbs of the martyrs will be restored. According to *1 En.* 62.15–16, the bodies of the righteous will be clad in garments of glory. In *2 Bar.* 50 is expressed the quaint notion that in the general resurrection, human bodies will be exactly as in life; but that the bodies of the righteous will gradually change until they surpass the angels and are like the stars in glory, whereas the wicked, observing this wondrous transformation, will see their own bodies waste away and decay.

E. The judgment. The judgment is sometimes conceived realistically, that is, as involving the destruction of the wicked by the Messiah or the saints; sometimes forensically, that is, as a court decision based on human works. The former view is analogous to the OT prophets, the latter to the pattern of Dan. 7:9–10, where the Ancient of Days, seated on a throne, judges out of open books (cf. *1 En.* 47.3; 90.2–27; 2 Esd. 7:33). In some of the sources (*Test. Job* 5.10–11; *1 En.* 10.6; 16.1), fallen angels as well as men are judged. The judge is either God or the Messiah, and the judgment takes place either at the beginning of the messianic kingdom or at its close; or, if no such kingdom is expected, at the end of the world. Rewards and punishments according to one's just deserts are impartially meted out. The ungodly are consigned to some place of eternal torment, generally in the lower parts of the earth, where they are plagued by fire and sometimes eaten by worms. The righteous, on the other hand, enter into paradise, which is either heaven or a renewed and transformed earth. There they will have rest from oppression and death, and enjoy the presence of God, or of the Messiah, forever. (See further C. Rowland, *The Open Heaven: A Study of Apocalyptic in Judaism and Early Christianity* [1982].)

III. Eschatology of the NT

A. Introduction. In eschatology, as in all other matters, the NT grows out of the OT. It also reflects the intertestamental period, insofar as this period is marked by a development of thought that is consonant with the basic thrust of the NT.

According to the NT, the INCARNATION is the fulfillment of the OT promise of salvation. This fulfillment is of such a nature that it anticipates a final consummation that is still future. The historic work of Christ (his life, death, and resurrection) may be called a "realized" eschatology, yet it is only a partial realization that anticipates a final fulfillment at the SECOND COMING of Christ, an event that is still in the future. According to the writer of Hebrews, the "last days" of which the prophets spoke, are here (Heb. 1:2). As the promise of the Spirit (Joel 2:28) has been fulfilled in the outpouring of PENTECOST, those who have the Spirit of Christ have already experienced the "powers of the age to come" (Heb. 6:5). Therefore, the final eschatological hope of the return of Christ is not merely a hope, as though it were altogether a future event; it is a hope that has already become a historical reality. It is the consummation of what was already accomplished in the first coming, especially in the RESURRECTION OF JESUS CHRIST from the dead.

This dialectic of an ETERNAL LIFE that is already a historical reality, and yet remains a future hope, permeates the entire NT. It is a past reality that the apostles have seen with their eyes, looked upon, and touched with their hands (1 Jn. 1:1); yet they confess that they still walk by faith, not by sight (2 Cor. 5:7), and that only "when he appears, we shall be like him, for we shall see him as he is" (1 Jn. 3:2). In the resurrection of Christ and the quickening by his Spirit are the first fruits of the heavenly order; believers are those upon whom the "end of the ages has come" (1 Cor. 10:11). At the same time, the "last day" still lies in the future; Christians are still looking for the Savior (Phil. 3:20) and confess that beyond this world there is a world to come (Eph. 1:21).

B. The teaching of Jesus. What Jesus taught concerning the future is a matter of dispute. The older liberal school believed that the eschatological pronouncements attributed to Jesus in the Gospels are not to be taken seriously. They viewed these pronouncements as the product of the Jewish-Christian community that adapted Jewish apocalyptic theories to Christian needs. If indeed Jesus did use such terms, it was an accommodation to his contemporaries, and we must construe them in a way that is consonant with the basic ethical principles at the core of his teaching. In such a view, a literal acceptance of the PAROUSIA robs it of its true meaning. Because Christ comes as judge not finally in the last day, but always in the providential moments of life, the "coming" of Christ as judge provides an impulse to moral conduct. Christ's eschatological language may be viewed as a picture of the truth of his present and continued judgment of mankind, not a description of actual future events. Even the imagery of coming in the clouds is not too much for the splendor of this thought of a present and perennial judgment.

In the school of "consistent eschatology," associated mainly with Albert Schweitzer, the opposite view is taken. Jesus is interpreted as an apocalyptist for whom eschatology was anything but a peripheral matter of accommodation. Jesus regarded himself as fulfilling the role of Daniel's "Son of Man" who would come in the clouds of heaven and set up the glorious kingdom of God on earth. This interpretation of the data of the Gospels has been credited with "rediscovering" eschatology in the Christian message. However, according to Schweitzer and his disciples, Jesus taught that these events were to occur in the lifetime of the generation then living. Obviously things did not turn out this way and, according to this viewpoint, Jesus died a disillusioned martyr, when his expectation of the imminent end of the world failed to materialize. His apostles clung to the hope he would soon return in glory, but the delay of the parousia gradually compelled a major adjustment in the theology of the church. In this process of adjustment, Jesus was metamorphosed into the Christ of dogma, having little to do with the man who lived in history.

The modern "form critical school" gives little support to this view. It is doubtful, according to Rudolf Bultmann, that one can know much about Jesus beyond the fact that he heralded the coming kingdom by calling men to repentance. For Bultmann, not only did the kingdom *not* come in Jesus' lifetime, but there is no way of saying it will ever come, except for the vertical act of God in each individual life, whereby the moment becomes "existential," resulting in one's living "authentically."

The view that is most faithful to the text of the Gospels accords with the general position outlined in the introduction to this article. Jesus believed that the eschatological teaching of the OT prophets received its fulfillment in his life and ministry. He began his ministry, therefore, by proclaiming that the KINGDOM OF GOD was about to be realized among men. "Repent, for the kingdom of heaven is near" (Matt. 3:2). In fact, in the person of Jesus, the kingdom was already present. (One plausible translation of Lk. 17:21 is "the kingdom of God is in the midst of you.") At the same time, there is a sense in which the kingdom was not fully realized in Jesus' own lifetime, but remains a future hope. The day is yet coming when all people will be judged, and their final destiny determined (Matt. 11:21–23; Lk. 10:13–15). We are admonished to prepare for the day that shall usher in the glorious kingdom (Mk. 13:33–37; Lk. 12:42–46). There is in Jesus' teaching respecting the kingdom both present reality and future expectation.

As the Messiah, Jesus looked upon himself as the mediator of the kingdom to God's people, both in its present form and in its glorious consummation. As for the time of the consummation, the question of its imminence is indeed central. The view that Jesus was mistaken in this matter is by no means the only plausible reading of the evidence. The verses giving the greatest difficulty are those in which Jesus said that some would "not taste death before they see the kingdom of God come with power" (Mk. 9:1; Lk. 9:26–27), or until they see the "Son of Man coming in a cloud with power and great glory" (Lk. 21:27–33; cf. Matt. 16:27–28; 24:34).

The context in which these sayings are given is important to their understanding. When the disciples pointed out the magnificent temple structure, Jesus predicted that the day would come when there would not be one stone standing upon another in that vast edifice. The startled disciples drew the conclusion that such a catastrophe could mean nothing less than the end of the world. "Tell us," they urged, "when will this happen, and what will be the sign of your coming [*parousia G4242*] and of the close of the age?" (Matt. 24:3). In a discourse sometimes referred to as the Little Apocalypse, Jesus answered this question the way it was put; that is, he wove together into a single tapestry a grand apocalyptic scene, made of two strands: on the one hand, the destruction of Jerusalem, and on the other, his own coming in the clouds "with power and great glory."

To account for this procedure, it must be remembered that he was uttering a prophecy, and that prophetic perspective involves what has been called a "timeless sequence," a telescoping of events that, in their fulfillment, may be chronologically separated from each other. (The prophets of the OT, for example, spoke of the coming of the Messiah without distinguishing between his coming in humiliation and his coming in glory.) As an artist imposes a three-dimensional landscape on a two-dimensional canvas, so Jesus spoke of the fall of Jerusalem and the final judgment of the evil world system as *one* event—which they are theologically but not chronologically. He did this, not only because he spoke prophetically, but because the lesser event—the fall of Jerusalem—is a paradigm of the greater event, the fall of this sinful world order, when God shall judge the wicked and vindicate the righteous at the end of the age. Had nothing happened in Jesus' generation corresponding to his prophecy, then one would have every reason to believe that nothing ever would, and that Jesus made a fatal mistake. But because Jerusalem and the temple were destroyed in A.D. 70, believers are confirmed in their faith that this prophecy, so strikingly fulfilled in miniature, will one day be fulfilled in the larger theater of world history. Therefore, the eschatological hope of the second advent, essential to the Christian faith, is grounded in the teaching of Jesus himself, and this teaching is by no means an illusion.

C. Events leading up to the second coming. The second advent is really a whole complex of events, some of which precede, some of which follow, the appearing of Christ in glory. The events leading up to the parousia should not be used to predict the time of Christ's coming, as some have vainly done. Indeed, Jesus said that no one, except the Father, knows the day or hour of his return (Mk. 13:32). Though one cannot know the times and seasons that the Father has fixed by his own authority (Acts 1:7), yet the NT has much to say about the manifestation of evil prior to the coming of the Lord, an evil that will be intensified as the time of the end draws near. Although hope is already a reality in this age, yet it is an evil age (Gal. 1:4). Living in an era that is under the power of Satan, Christians are to beware of false messiahs (Matt. 24:5) and antichrists (1 Jn. 2:18, 22; 4:3; 2 Jn. 7). Jesus compared the time of the coming of the Son of Man to the days of Noah (Lk. 17:26–27), and Paul warned that "evil men and impostors will go from bad to worse" (2 Tim. 3:13).

As early as the book of Daniel, this demonic principle of evil, opposed to Christ and his kingdom, an evil that will especially characterize the end time, begins to take on personal embodiment. Daniel's prophecy of the "little horn" (Dan. 7:8, 23–26) is perhaps a veiled, apocalyptic reference to ANTIOCHUS Epiphanes, typifying some evil eschatological personage who will appear at the end of the age. Jesus warned of "the desolating sacrilege" (Matt. 24:15 NRSV; NIV, "the abomination that causes desolation"; Dan. 11:31; 12:11), and Paul spoke of "the man of lawlessness" who will be revealed in his own proper time. This individual is a "man doomed to destruction" who "will oppose and will exalt himself over everything that is called God or is worshiped, so that he sets himself up in God's temple, proclaiming himself to be God" (2 Thess. 2:3–4).

This same figure may be the subject of the visions of evil in Rev. 13, which describes two beasts appearing, one coming up out of the sea, the other out of the land; the former representing world empire, the latter religious apostasy. Both were empowered by the dragon, who symbolizes the devil. (This evil triumvirate—beast, false prophet, dragon—comprises a sort of demonic counterpart to the Trinity.) Many interpret both the first "beast" in Revelation and the "man of lawlessness" in Paul as a political ruler of great power, appearing at the end of the age, who will use apostate religion to serve his blasphemous ambition to be worshiped as

God (Rev. 13:8, 12), following the example of the ancient Roman emperors. Not only will he impose economic sanctions on all who will not submit to this sacrilege (Rev. 13:16–17), but he will also threaten a general and ruthless persecution against all the godly. Thus the church of the end time, as in the 1st cent., will be a martyr church sealing its witness with its own blood. This dire threat of persecution has often been seen as a fulfillment of Jesus' prophecy of a time of "great tribulation" (Matt. 24:21 KJV), which will be shortened for the elect's sake (v. 22).

This time of bold defiance of heaven and persecution of the saints is also pictured in Revelation as a time of divine judgment upon the wicked that shall culminate in the final destruction of Satan and his emissaries. Under the symbolism of trumpets and bowls, the seer of the Revelation sets forth the plagues and disasters with which God, in his wrath, shall vex and destroy the beast and those who worship him (Rev. 8; 9; 14; 16). Against these terrible visitations of heaven the people of God will be protected, being sealed as his own (7:1–8) and beatified by martyrdom (7:9–17).

Other interpreters look upon these predictions of eschatological evil in personal categories, as fulfilled throughout Christian history. In such a view, there is no one ANTICHRIST par excellence, nor one period that may be designated *the* tribulation, at the end of the age. All who are opposed to Christ and his church, from NERO and his successors in ancient times to Hitler and Stalin in modern times, and any in the future who shall emulate their example, are a manifestation of the principle of antichrist, and the church that they persecute is the church in "tribulation."

D. The second advent. The event climaxing the judgments in which "this age" will end, bringing in the full salvation of the righteous in the "age to come," is the advent of Christ. Revealed from heaven with his mighty angels in flaming fire, the Lord Jesus will inflict vengeance upon those who do not know God nor obey the gospel. At the same time, he will be glorified in his saints and will "be marveled at among all those who have believed" (2 Thess. 1:7–10). The event is often described in terms that reflect the OT usage of the "day of the Lord" (Acts 2:20; 1 Thess. 5:2; 2 Pet. 3:10). Whether it be called "the day of God" (2 Pet. 3:12) or "the last day" (Jn. 6:39–40, 44, 54, et al.) or just "that day" (Matt. 7:22 et al.), there can be no doubt that the figure of the glorious Christ will be at the center of this final revelation of God. The NT phrases "the day of the Lord Jesus" (1 Cor. 5:5; 2 Cor. 1:14), "the day of our Lord Jesus Christ" (1 Cor. 1:8), "the day of Jesus Christ" (Phil. 1:6), and the "day of Christ" (Phil. 1:10; 2:16), all designate the time of the second advent.

Besides the general term *day* are several other technical terms used in the NT to describe the coming of Christ for the second time (Heb. 9:28). The most common is *parousia* G4242 (1 Cor. 16:17), which means "presence" in the sense of a "becoming present" or "arrival." It is used in Hellenistic Greek of the visit of a ruler. So Jesus will "visit" this earth by way of a personal presence. Christ's appearance also is called an *apokalypsis* G637, that is, a "revelation" or "unveiling" (1 Cor. 1:7). Then will be manifest the glory that he now has, being exalted at the Father's right hand. A third term is *epiphaneia* G2211, from which comes the English word EPIPHANY, meaning "appearance." In 2 Thess. 2:8 is a reference to the "epiphany of his parousia," which is difficult to interpret because of the closeness of the meaning of the two terms. Some have suggested that the two terms denote two distinct events, but there is nothing in the context to suggest

The ruins of the temple dedicated to Emperor Domitian in the city of Ephesus, where was located one of the seven churches addressed in the book of Revelation.

that the *parousia* is a secret event separate in time from the *epiphany*. The two terms seem rather to be related as dawn to noon day, the epiphany being the full realization of the parousia. Scholars sometimes translate the phrase "the manifestation of his coming" (NRSV) or "the splendor of his coming" (NIV).

Even the most cursory review of the language with which the NT describes the return of Christ shows how impossible it is to construe Christ's second advent as a slow, sure, spiritual conquest, in which the ideals of Jesus will yet win universal assent and his Spirit dominate the world, as in the older liberal theology (cf. Douglas C. MacIntosh, *Theology as an Empirical Science* [1927], and William Adams Brown, *Christian Theology in Outline* [1906]). Rather than a tendency of history toward an ideal, the second coming is presented as an event, like in kind to the resurrection and ascension. The difference is that in his resurrection and ascension, Christ "was not seen by all the people, but by witnesses [the apostles] whom God had already chosen" (Acts 10:41). When he returns a second time, it will be a public event: "every eye will see him" and "all the peoples of the earth will mourn because of him" (Rev. 1:7). It will be a *glorious* coming: people "will see the Son of man coming in clouds with great power and glory" (Mk. 13:26, and parallels). It will be *personal*: the same Jesus (Acts 1:11) who walked with his disciples in Galilee and Judea, will come again to take his own to himself (Jn. 14:3).

E. The resurrection of the dead.

Though even the wicked will be raised when Christ comes (Jn. 5:28, 29; Acts 24:15; Rev. 20:12–13), resurrection is principally set forth in the NT as a blessing, that is, the redemption of the BODY from the power of death and the grave. The apostolic proclamation of the resurrection is based on the fact of Jesus' resurrection. It is he who, by his resurrection, "has destroyed death and has brought life and immortality to light through the gospel" (2 Tim. 1:10).

The new age manifests itself not only in Jesus' resurrection, but also in the new life that believers experience in him (Rom. 6:4; Eph. 2:5–6; Col. 3:1–3), which makes the CHURCH an eschatological community. This new order of existence, however, is preliminary and anticipatory; it is a life that will be fully realized only in the resurrection at the parousia. Jesus is "the firstfruits of those who have fallen asleep" (1 Cor. 15:20), and "we know that when he appears, we shall be like him" (1 Jn. 3:2). There is this confident hope because many have already been delivered from death to life: "We know that we have passed from death to life, because we love our brothers" (1 Jn. 3:14). "And if the Spirit of him who raised Jesus from the dead is living in you, he who raised Christ from the dead will also give life to your mortal bodies through his Spirit, who lives in you" (Rom. 8:11). Then shall this mortal put on immortality, this corruption shall put on incorruption, and death shall lose its sting and be swallowed up in victory (1 Cor. 15:53–54).

The resurrection is not a reanimation of the FLESH, a view that contradicts 1 Cor. 15:50 ("flesh and blood cannot inherit the kingdom of God"). Rather, the new body will be "spiritual" (1 Cor. 15:44; some would translate "Spiritual," that is, a body that has been given new life by the HOLY SPIRIT). The paradoxical expression "spiritual body" suggests that in the life to come, the mode of existence will be neither wholly similar nor wholly dissimilar to the present mode. The body is the mark of creaturehood, the outward principle of a person's individuality. The Christian hope is not escape from the body, as a prison house of the soul, but deliverance from this mortal body of flesh and blood, to be clothed in a glorious body like that of the Lord Jesus Christ.

The concept of a bodily resurrection is a prime illustration of how the gospel was foolishness to the Greeks. Busying themselves collecting mental bric-a-brac, the Athenians indulged Paul with condescending curiosity concerning the new gods he was setting forth; but when he propounded the idea of a resurrection of the body, they walked away mocking (Acts 17:32). This pagan incredulity has been given a new impetus by modern "scientism," the view that the realm of natural causality defines the possibilities of reality. Dead bodies just do not rise. It should not be supposed that resurrection means the reassemblage of the same atoms in the same molecular pattern that existed when the body was laid in the grave. Though such a concept is implied in some of the Jewish apocalyptic literature, the NT does not speculate on the "how" of

After decomposition of a body in the tomb, the bones were sometimes placed in an ossuary to await the resurrection.

the resurrection. Paul admitted that he was telling a MYSTERY (1 Cor. 15:51) when he spoke of such things in answer to the questions, "How are the dead raised? With what kind of body will they come?" (v. 35). He used the apt figure of a germinating seed to illustrate continuity with a difference. Yet, this is merely a picture drawn from nature.

Perhaps another illustration from nature may illumine the mystery of man's resurrection in a small way. In the Middle Ages, an indestructible "bone of immortality" was postulated as the nexus between the body of this life and that which would rise from the grave in the last day. By contrast, modern science teaches that the body cells, including its solid bony frame, not only turns to dust in death, but even in life perishes without a trace. In a relatively few years, the human body is renewed completely. When a person looks at a picture of a young child, he or she may say, "This is I," for there is continuity at the physical level; the pattern of the hair, the pigmentation of the skin and eyes, even such individual factors as a birthmark, all underscore the sameness of the person according to his or her bodily nature. Yet the body of the child in the photo is not "literally" the same body; it is an entirely different body, several times removed from the present one. If this continuity in change can be maintained in this life, who is to say that death is such a radical destruction of the body that it cannot be overcome by the power of God?

The Christian doctrine of the resurrection rests not on any analogy of nature, but on the fact of the resurrection of Christ, which is without analogy, a setting aside of that fundamental law of entropy that has marked the entire system of nature with the sign of death. "And if Christ has not been raised, our preaching is useless and so is your faith" (1 Cor. 15:14); "you are still in your sins" (v. 17), and "those also who have fallen asleep in Christ are lost" (v. 18). But, knowing that Christ has risen and become the "firstfruits of those who have fallen asleep," there is hope that when he comes, all Christians shall share his resurrection, for if God raised his crucified Son, will he not raise his people by the same Spirit?

At the moment of the resurrection, those who are alive shall be changed "in the twinkling of an eye, at the last trumpet" (1 Cor. 15:52) and all together shall be "raptured," that is, "caught up … to meet the Lord in the air. And so we will be with the Lord forever" (1 Thess. 4:17). The wicked, on the other hand, supposing they are safe, shall be surprised as by a thief in the night (Matt. 24:42–43) and overtaken by the sudden destruction that shall come upon them (1 Thess. 5:2–3). Though they be working in the same field, grinding at the same mill, even sleeping in the same bed with the righteous (Matt. 24:41; Lk. 17:34–35), they shall be left behind, as were the sinners in NOAH's day (Matt. 24:38–39), and the inhabitants of SODOM, when LOT departed from the doomed city. Then the wheat shall be separated from the tares (Matt. 13:24–30, 36–43), and the sheep from the goats forever (Matt. 25:32–33).

F. The intermediate state. What is the state of the dead who await the voice of the Son of Man at the last day (Jn. 5:25)? For the writers of the OT, as pointed out earlier, the dead did not cease to exist, but entered a shadowy existence in the undifferentiated silence of the nether world. Removed from the presence of the living God, the righteous devoutly hoped that God would not abandon them to Sheol, but give them to know the joy of life in his presence (Job 19:25–26). It was not until the inauguration of the NT age and the resurrection of Christ that this hope was given a clearer definition. Even in the light of NT revelation, however, the question of whether the dead must await the resurrection before they enjoy the conscious fellowship of God, or whether they will "sleep" until the powerful summons awakens them from death, is hard to answer with certainty.

The idea of "soul sleeping," originally held by certain sects of the Anabaptists and by the Socinians, has been revived in modern times by various groups of Millennial Dawnists and Adventists, and is even suggested by such a critically trained scholar as Oscar Cullmann. Paul's pithy statement, to be "away from the body and at home with the Lord" (2 Cor. 5:8), an expression pregnant with hope for all Christians, is understood to reflect an immediacy of sequence in the consciousness of the individual only. When a Christian closes his eyes in death, the next moment, as far as he is concerned, he will be with the Lord, though countless millennia may have intervened. Thus the basic structure of the NT—death followed by resurrection—is preserved; at the same time, the postponement of the resurrection, until the parousia, is also maintained.

Such a view also makes possible a more consistent application of the NT emphasis on the unity of the person. Traditionally, because of the interval of time between death and the resurrection, it has been taught that the SOUL continues in a disembodied form, intermediate between its present and its final state. This view is not without its difficulties, because it lends itself so readily to a more Greek than biblical mode of conception. The Greeks, suspicious of the body as evil, conceived salvation as the liberation of the soul from its fleshy prison house, that it might ascend to its proper element (see DUALISM). They believed in IMMORTALITY, but not in resurrection. So concerned have some contemporary biblical scholars been to escape this Greek way of thinking, and to stress the biblical concern with the redemption of the whole person, including the body, that they have affirmed that the resurrection takes place immediately upon death. The obvious teaching of the NT, that the resurrection occurs for all at the last day, is construed as a mark of our temporal perspective. When one steps over the line in death, he shall see how, *im nunc aeternum* (in the eternal now), being present with the Lord at the moment of death, and meeting him in the air at the parousia, are different ways of speaking of a simultaneous event.

Another suggestion is that in the INTERMEDIATE STATE a body is given in anticipation of the resurrection body. The soul, though it has not yet been given a resurrection body, is not disembodied at death. This view is based on Paul's statement: "Meanwhile we groan, longing to be clothed with our heavenly dwelling, because when we are clothed, we will not be found naked. For while we are in this tent, we groan and are burdened, because we do not wish to be unclothed but to be clothed with our heavenly dwelling, so that what is mortal may be swallowed up by life" (2 Cor. 5:2–4). How such an "interim" body would function, however, no one can say. If it is a glorious body, then what is the need of a final resurrection? If it is not, what is the advantage over our present mortal existence?

The church, as a whole, has taught that while one awaits the resurrection of the body, death does not extinguish consciousness. If absent from the body, I—the essential self—am at home with the Lord (2 Cor. 5:8), even though I must await the final resurrection to experience the redemption of the body. This seems to be the best, but by no means the only possible view, since it is most compatible with the fragmentary and somewhat disparate statements of the NT. In truth, the early Christians, knowing of Christ's resurrection, and assuming he would soon return to deliver them in like manner from death, were not much concerned with the interval between death and the resurrection. Sometimes they spoke of the dead as "sleeping" (1 Cor. 11:30; 15:20, 51; 1 Thess. 4:14); sometimes as present with the Lord (2 Cor. 5:8), from the analogy of the Lord's own word to the penitent thief, "Today you will be with me in paradise" (Lk. 23:43). Those who are persuaded of "soul sleeping" punctuate this passage in a different manner: "Truly I say to you today, you will be with me in paradise." On such a reading, the fellowship in paradise, which Jesus promised, is yet future, awaiting the voice of the archangel and the trump of God. But because "today" for the thief was his death day, and since the early Christians recalled these words of Jesus in the full knowledge of this fact, it seems they must have related "today" to the paramount concern of the man's death; otherwise "today" becomes mundane and superfluous.

In like manner, it seems impossible to suppose that STEPHEN's final prayer (Acts 7:59), "Lord Jesus, receive my spirit," refers to some indefinite future, when his spirit would be awakened out of the sleep of death. Why should the heavens have opened upon him in the last moments of life (v. 56), only to close upon him again in death? Rather one must suppose that he joined the "spirits of the righteous made perfect" (Heb. 12:23 TNIV); that he was the first of many "souls of those who had been slain because of the word of God" who cry out to the Lord from beneath the altar (Rev. 6:9; cf. 20:4); that he entered into that blessed rest, a rest not from consciousness, but from labor (Rev. 14:13), which is laid up for the people of God (Heb. 4:9).

G. The Last Judgment

1. Introduction. God is the sovereign Lord of history, who reveals himself not only as redeemer, but also as judge. He took vengeance on Pharaoh and the gods of Egypt; he rained down fire on the Sodomites; he scattered Israel among the nations for their sins. In the OT, the "day of the Lord" was a day of God's judgment of the wicked, a day of darkness and gloom.

The somber note of judgment looms large in the teaching of Jesus, who prophesied that the day would soon come when Jerusalem would be destroyed utterly (Matt. 24 and parallels), the city in which the awful cry was heard, "Let his blood be on us and on our children!" (Matt. 27:25). In a uniquely dark and sobering passage, Paul expressed the conviction (though he did not live to see the fall of Jerusalem) that a Damocles' sword was hanging over the head of his fellow-Jews "who killed the Lord Jesus and the prophets and also drove us out. They displease God," but his wrath "has come upon them at last" (1 Thess. 2:15–16).

The Jews, however, are under the judgment of God to no greater degree than the Gentiles. The same fate awaits the heathen who rage and imagine vain things against the Lord and his Anointed. Perhaps the most awesome vision in the Apocalypse is that of the fall of Babylon the great, symbol of the godless world order concentrated in the state and dominated by Satan (Rev. 17:1—19:4). Culminating a series of bowl judgments upon the unrepentant and godless (Rev. 16:2–21), the thinly veiled allusions to Rome leave little doubt as to the proximate reference of the vision. But as in the prophecy of the fall of Jerusalem, so here, the implications go beyond history to a final, eschatological denouement.

2. Christ the final Judge. The one who shall administer this judgment is Jesus Christ. The day will come in which God "will judge the world with justice by the man he has appointed" (Acts 17:31; 10:42). That "day when God will judge everyone's secrets through Jesus Christ" (Rom. 2:16 TNIV) will be the time of the parousia. "When the Son of Man comes in his glory, and all the angels with him, he will sit on his glorious throne" and judge the nations, separating the sheep from the goats (Matt. 25:31–36). At the end of the age, "the Son of Man will send out his angels, and they will weed out of his kingdom everything that causes sin and all who do evil. They will throw them into the fiery furnace.... Then the righteous will shine like the sun" (Matt. 13:41–43).

Overpowering pictures of this last judgment are drawn by John the seer. In one passage, the picture is in the realistic, dynamic terms of battle action. Seated on a white horse at the head of a great army, One whose name is "Faithful and True" rides forth to judge the wicked in righteousness. From his mouth proceeds a sharp sword with which he smites the nations. His robe is dipped in blood and he treads the winepress of the fury of the WRATH of God (Rev. 19:11–15). In another passage, the judgment is forensic in character. The judge is seated on a great white throne before which the dead stand to receive sentence, according to what is recorded in the books and according to whether or not their names are written in the "book of life" (Rev. 20:11–15).

3. The standard of judgment: grace and works. Even in this life, by virtue of God's justifying grace, Paul could declare that there is no condemnation to those who are in Christ Jesus (Rom. 8:1). Everyone who believes in Christ is justified from all things—something the law of Moses could not accomplish (Acts 13:39). By contrast, he who believes not is already condemned (Jn. 3:18). Therefore, when the day of judgment dawns, the wicked, already accused by an evil conscience, will call to the mountains to fall on them and cover them from the wrath of the Lamb (Rev. 6:16). Believers, however, will be "confident and unashamed before him at his coming" (1 Jn. 2:28; cf. 4:17).

There are some pressing questions that such a representation evokes. For one, if JUSTIFICATION by faith has this eschatological implication; if being now justified assures one that he shall be saved from the wrath of God (Rom. 5:9); if no one can bring a charge against God's elect, or condemn him for whom Christ died (Rom. 8:33); is not the final judgment evacuated of all meaning? Does the believer not have a pass into the heavenly city? How then can Paul say that all must appear "before the judgment seat of Christ" to receive good or evil according to what they have done in the body (2 Cor. 5:10)? One must not make a bagatelle of such a solemn statement in the name of grace, as though only to non-Christians is it appointed once to die and after this the judgment (Heb. 9:27). Whereas the Christian, as a citizen of the heavenly country, has a "scroll" (John Bunyan) and wears a "wedding garment" marking him as an invited guest to the marriage supper of the Lamb, there is surely an awesome accounting that he must render for the manner in which he has lived his life. Whereas grace and works are mutually exclusive principles in justification, grace does not exclude good works. Good works are the fruit of grace, and he whose life has been unfruitful will give answer for his lack of stewardship. The NT does not offer cheap grace.

In 1 Cor. 3:10–15, Paul uses the figure of a building to illustrate this truth. The foundation is Jesus Christ (grace), but on this foundation each believer builds a superstructure (works). Let him take care how he does his work. If he builds with "gold, silver, [and] costly stones," his work will stand the fire of judgment, but if he uses "wood, hay or straw," his works in that "Day" will be burned; "he himself will be saved, but only as one escaping through the flames" (1 Cor. 3:15). The importance of good deeds is also evident in the parable of the sheep and the goats: in the judgment the King will tell the righteous that by visiting those in prison, helping those who were sick, clothing the naked, and feeding the hungry, they did it as to him (Matt. 25:34–36). Without such credentials, it will do no good to call him "Lord! Lord!" for not everyone who does so "will enter the kingdom of heaven, but only he who does the will of my Father" (Matt. 7:21).

In the judgment scene of Rev. 20, this dualism of grace and works seems to be the key to understanding the distinction between the "books" and the "book." "Books were opened" and the dead were judged by what is written in them; that is, by what they have done. But there is another book, called the BOOK OF LIFE, and to have one's name written in that book is salvation. This book sometimes is called "the Lamb's book of life" (Rev. 21:27). To say that the book belongs to the Lamb is to say that one's attitude to Christ, "the Lamb of God, who takes away the sin of the world!" (Jn. 1:29), is decisive in the judgment. On the assumption that all are sinners and cannot be justified by the works of the law (Rom. 3:23; Gal. 2:16), the NT consistently stresses that salvation is for those who confess Christ. "Whoever acknowledges me before men, I will also acknowledge him before my Father in heaven. But whoever disowns me before men, I will disown him before my Father in heaven" (Matt. 10:32–33; cf. 11:21–24). To the anxious inquiry of the Philippian jailer, "What must I do to be saved?" the answer is given, "Believe in the Lord Jesus" (Acts 16:30–31; cf. Rom. 10:9).

What is to be said of those who have never heard the name of Jesus Christ? "How can they believe in the one of whom they have not heard?" (Rom. 10:14). Because they could neither acknowledge nor deny the Christ, the only standard by which they can be judged is the light of nature. They stand condemned, Paul argued, because they willfully suppressed the knowledge of the truth, worshiped the creature rather than the Creator, and did what they knew to be worthy of death (Rom. 1:18–23). One must not suppose that the offense of those who never heard the gospel is the same as of those who deny Christ. It is a basic principle of Scripture that responsibility is commensurate with knowledge. "But the one who does not know and does things deserving punishment will be beaten with few blows" (Lk. 12:48; cf. Acts 17:30, where reference is made to the Gentile ignorance that God overlooked in the past). The degree of guilt that a person has before his Maker, only God the Judge can finally ascertain, but surely to whom less opportunity is given, of him less shall be required.

H. The divine retribution: hell. It is the common doctrine of many churches that the issue of the last judgment is not alike for all people. The righteous will be acquitted, but the wicked and impenitent will be condemned to everlasting separation from

God in HELL (the common translation of Gk. *geenna G1147*; see GEHENNA). Some have sought to soften this doctrine by affirming that the wicked are annihilated. The biblical terms of "perdition," "corruption," "destruction," "death," that describe the fate of the lost are thought to suggest the cessation of being (cf. Ps. 37:20, "they will vanish— vanish like smoke"). Such punishment is "eternal" only in the sense that those who are annihilated never get over it. Whereas this doctrine seems to palliate the severity of the traditional view, it is by no means certain that such is the case.

> Thus repulsed, our final hope
> Is flat despair; we must exasperate
> Th' Almighty Victor to spend all his rage,
> And that must end us, that must be our cure,
> To be no more: sad cure! for who would lose,
> Though full of pain, this intellectual being,
> Those thoughts that wander through eternity,
> To perish rather, swallowed up and lost
> In the wide womb of uncreated night,
> Devoid of sense and motion?
> *Paradise Lost* 2.142–43.

Annihilation is not only theologically dubious, but exegetically untenable. The NT writers measure the misery of the wicked and the bliss of the righteous with the same terms. We read of "eternal" fire (Matt. 18:8; 25:41), "eternal" punishment (Matt. 25:46), "everlasting" destruction (2 Thess. 1:9), "eternal" sin (Mk. 3:29). The fire is "unquenchable" (Matt. 3:12); the worm "does not die" (Mk. 9:48); the smoke of torment "rises for ever and ever" (Rev. 14:11). There is a lake of fire and brimstone, where the devil and his emissaries shall be tormented day and night "for ever and ever" (20:10; cf. 14:11). This same phrase, "for ever and ever," is used of the reign of the saints by the same author in the same book (22:5). The conclusion seems inescapable, therefore, that the punishment of the wicked extends interminably.

For many, such a doctrine is unthinkable. Some suppose not only that the wicked do not perish eternally, but that in addition finally all sinners will be restored to God's fellowship, because God's nature is LOVE. The recrudescence of universalism in the contemporary literature is marked by an appeal to the Scripture that says "God is love" (1 Jn. 4:8), as though retributive justice were incompatible with love. But Scripture also has much to say about the holiness and justice of God, who is a "consuming fire" (Heb. 12:29). In fact, love without justice is sentimental. As for the Scripture that speaks of the "restoration of all things" (Acts 3:21 ASV), it should probably be understood of the restoration of *conditions* in which persons live (conditions lost by sin), rather than of the restoration of every individual to fellowship with his Maker.

There are, however, some striking statements on the universal scope and efficacy of the ATONEMENT in the NT. Christ took away the sins of the *world* (Jn. 1:29); drew *all* men to himself (12:32); propitiated the sins of the *whole* world (1 Jn. 2:2); in Christ shall *all* be made alive (1 Cor. 15:22); in Christ the *world* is reconciled to God (2 Cor. 5:19). It is a fundamental rule of hermeneutics that such universal language should be interpreted in context; and always, faith in and obedience to Christ as Lord is the context for enjoying the saving benefits of his work. There is no warrant, therefore, for understanding such universal statements of Scripture as giving any hope for the salvation of those who willfully reject the claims of Christ and die in unbelief.

To be sure, the redeemed will number men and women from *all* nations, tribes, peoples, and tongues (Rev. 7:9); the *whole world*, and not Israel only as in the OT, is embraced in God's redemptive purpose. This is not to say that every individual of mankind will be made alive in Christ and reconciled to God.

But it is commonly objected, granted that God is not only loving but holy, that it would be an intolerable miscarriage of justice that any person who has sinned threescore years and ten should suffer the consequences everlastingly. It must be remembered, however, that hell is not a place of passive suffering (as in some of Dante's visions), but rather a state of active rebellion. "Better to reign in hell than serve in heaven," said Satan. By the lives they have lived, the wicked have said, "Better to serve Satan than God," even if it be in hell. The character that one chooses in this life is irrevocably confirmed in the life to come. Sinners who chose a life without fellowship with God would prolong their lives indefinitely if they could. Can they then justly complain of hell that it is just that—life without God forever? This is not to imply that the denizens of hell will be happy with their lot. They will neither be happy in hell nor aspire to heaven. Hell is frustration, the reality behind the myth of Prometheus and the rolling stone. And this restlessness is the opposite of the "eternal rest" laid up for the people of God.

I. The final consummation: heaven. As the Scripture employs terrifying figures in speaking of the fate of the wicked ("worm," "gnashing of teeth," "darkness"), it uses equally evocative figures in speaking of the bliss of the righteous. Theologians have called this bliss HEAVEN because Scripture uses the term to describe the abode of God (Deut. 26:15); to dwell with God is man's highest beatitude. Heaven is the place where God is; and the final hope of God's people is to dwell with him, that he may be their God and they his people, in unbroken fellowship.

Heaven is set forth in Scripture under many figures. It is the "Sabbath-rest" (Heb. 4:9) lost in the first creation by human sin and restored by him who said, "Come to me ... and I will give you rest" (Matt. 11:28); it is the "wedding supper of the Lamb" (Rev. 19:7–9), marriage feasts being supremely joyous occasions in biblical times; it is a lovely home, a "mansion in the sky." "In my Father's house," said Jesus, "are many dwelling places" (Jn. 14:2 NRSV). Heaven is a land, that "better country" of which the author of Hebrews wrote (Heb. 11:13–16); it is a bright, white, opalescent "city," with golden streets, pearly gates, and jasper walls; a perfect cube in measurement (Rev. 21:9–10); it is "Paradise Regained," a new EDEN without a serpent and with the "tree of life" (Rev. 22:1–5). In this new order, God shall reign supreme. All his and man's enemies—sin, Satan, and death—shall be overcome (Rev. 20:10–11; 1 Cor. 15:26). His people, living and reigning with him, will enjoy eternal life. This is the "kingdom of God," or the "kingdom of heaven," consummated (Matt. 25:34, 46; Mk. 10:17, 24).

The kingdom, foretold by the prophets of old, was "near" in the person of Jesus (Matt. 4:17). God is still delivering those who believe in Christ from the dominion of darkness, transferring them "to the kingdom of the Son he loves" (Col. 1:13). When Christ comes the second time, he will bring in this kingdom "with power." "Then the King will say to those on his right, 'Come, you who are blessed by my Father; take your inheritance, the kingdom prepared for you since the creation of the world'" (Matt. 25:34). At the end of the age, all evildoers having been gathered out, "the righteous will shine like the sun in the kingdom of their Father" (Matt. 13:42).

It is difficult to know how literally scriptural representations of this glorious kingdom should be interpreted. The OT prophetic vision of the consummation involves a large degree of continuity with the present order of creation. Having beaten their swords into plowshares and their spears into pruning hooks, "every man will sit under his own vine / and under his own fig tree, / and no one will make them afraid" (Mic. 4:4; cf. Isa. 11:1–9). In the NT, also, is the teaching that the natural order, having been cursed for human sin (Gen. 3:17–19), will be delivered and receive "the glorious freedom of the children of God" (Rom. 8:21). If we believe in the resurrection of the *body*, there must be some analogy of a physical and outward sort between the present and the final state of things. If one may use the account of Jesus' appearances in his glorified humanity as a paradigm of what is to come for all believers, it is plain that he did not appear to the disciples as a disembodied spirit, for he ate and drank with them (Acts 10:41), though his bodily presence belonged to another order of existence. (All of his recorded appearances, including the last one when he was "taken up" from them [1:9], contain this element of mystery, a bodily form of existence that transcends all earthly limitations.)

Along with this continuity implied in a bodily form of existence, Scripture stresses discontinuity, a radical difference between this world and the world to come, so much so that the latter may be called a *new* heaven and a *new* earth (Isa. 65:17; 66:22). The Bible ends on this note of the radically new. "I saw," wrote John, "a new heaven and a new earth, for the first heaven and the first earth had passed away" (Rev. 21:1). Pointing in this direction of radical change, one may interpret the reiterated vision of cosmic convulsions, characteristic especially of apocalyptic literature. In the last days, wonders shall be wrought in the heavens above and signs in the earth beneath. The sun shall be turned to darkness, and the moon to blood (Acts 2:19–20; cf. Joel 2:28–32). The Apocalypse speaks of lightnings, thunder, and earthquakes, so great that the islands flee away and the mountains are not found (Rev. 6:12–14; 8:5; 11:19; 16:18–21). Perhaps the most graphic picture of all is in 2 Pet. 3:10, which speaks of the heavens passing away with a loud noise, the elements dissolving in a fervent heat, and the earth with its works being burned up.

Theologians have mediated these pictures of continuity and discontinuity between a mere glorification of the present world order and a completely new creation *ex nihilo*. The biblical words *regeneration* and *restitution* are suggestive of a mediating position. In Matt. 19:28, Jesus referred to the "regeneration" (*palingenesia G4098*; NIV, "renewal") when the Son of Man shall sit on his glorious throne. Peter, preaching in the portico of Solomon in the temple, spoke of the "restitution" (*apokatastasis G640*) of all things at the time Christ shall return (Acts 3:21).

J. The millennium. When thinking of the relation of this world to that which is to come, some scholars and students of Scripture posit a transition period, a manifestation of the kingdom more glorious than the present, called the MILLENNIUM, but not as glorious as what shall finally be. Millennialists tend to construe prophetic visions of a future glorious age of this world as referring to this millennial kingdom, making the passages that speak of a radically new order to refer to the final state, that kingdom of glory when God shall be "all in all" (1 Cor. 15:28).

Postmillennialists—who hold that Christ will return at the end of the millennium—construe the prophetic vision of a future golden age on earth largely in spiritual terms. The gospel of the kingdom will gradually permeate society like leaven (Matt. 13:33; Lk. 13:21) until men and nations shall own Christ as Lord, and justice and peace shall prevail in all the earth. As far as the *natural* order of things is concerned, the millennial age is really coterminous with the present. It is only at the close of this era of peace and righteousness that the glorious Christ shall be revealed.

Premillennialists, by contrast, have no such sanguine hope for the future accomplishments of the church in human society. Far from accepting the gospel, this world will remain evil until Christ himself returns visibly to inaugurate his millennial kingdom. Giving many of the OT prophecies that speak of a coming glorious kingdom a more literal reading than postmillennialists would do, they believe that Christ will return to this world, bind Satan so that he can deceive the nations no more, and reign in a glorified Jerusalem with the resurrected saints for a thousand years (Rev. 20:1–6). At the close of this period, Satan will be loosed to gather the nations to war for the last time. Both he and they shall be overwhelmed in catastrophe (vv. 7–10). Then they who had no part in the "first resurrection" (v. 5) shall be raised to judgment and condemnation, after which the Son will turn over the kingdom to the Father (1 Cor. 15:24). A threefold view of the kingdom—as manifested in this church age, followed by the millennium, culminating in the final state—is corroborated in the minds of many students of Scripture by the structure of 1 Cor. 15:23–28. The age began with the resurrection of Christ; it will be terminated by the resurrection of the righteous at his return; and will end when he shall deliver the completed kingdom of the Father. The premillennial view has a classic pedigree, being found in the thought of many of the ancient church fathers. Though it has had no place in the official theology of Roman Catholicism, nor appreciable influence in the mainstream of Protestant thought, there have been distinguished individual scholars and groups of Christians committed to some form of millenarian doctrine in all ages, including the present.

K. Concluding observations. Whether the consummation shall be attained by the triumph of the gospel (postmillennialism) or by the personal reign of Christ (premillennialism), or whether this present evil age shall be terminated and the new heaven and new earth ushered in by an immediate act of God, without analogy in history (amillennialism), it is the common confession and hope of all Christians that God shall be all in all at last. Although it is natural that the factor of human blessedness should be emphasized, it is not such a bliss that is central in the data of Scripture nor in the doctrine of Christian hope. The *summum bonum* is to "glorify God and to enjoy him forever" (*Westminster*

Shorter Catechism). The beatific vision is a vision of God. "Whom have I in heaven but you?" asked the psalmist (Ps. 73:25). One sees the caricature of S. Freud (*Future of an Illusion* [1928]) in representing Christian hope as the projection of a muted desire for happiness, which desire, being frustrated in this life, is transferred to the world to come. The goal of Christian aspiration is not "pie in the sky bye and bye," but rather *soli Deo gloria*; and when God shall be glorified in all his saints, then man will have reached the end of redemptive history, and spoken the last word of Christian doctrine.

It is, perhaps, because some unwittingly make human happiness, rather than the glory of God, an end in itself, that the question is so often asked, "How can the redeemed be happy in heaven when there is a hell?" Should they not rather ask, "How could the redeemed be happy in heaven, if those who hate God are there?" It assumes that no one can enjoy God unless he can enjoy his neighbor. Is it not true, rather, that they cannot enjoy their neighbor unless they enjoy God? Was the psalmist altogether wrong when he said, "Do I not hate those who hate you, O LORD? … I count them my enemies" (Ps. 139:21–22)?

It is preoccupation, too, with the bliss of the creature rather than the glory of the Creator that has led to the oft-repeated charge that the Christian heaven is a boring place. To sit on a cushion and play a harp forever would indeed be monotonous. Such a view overlooks the fact that the great throne scene of Rev. 4:1—5:14 presents a different picture. The center of the scene in the book of Revelation is God, adored by his creatures who praise him in a deafening diapason of sound. Heaven, for the Christian, is to hear the "four living creatures" sing "Holy, holy, holy is the Lord God Almighty" (Rev. 4:8), and to join their gratitude and adoration. Additional comment should be made about the "words" that the church, following the example of inspired prophets and apostles, has used to express the Christian doctrine of hope. The modern debate over theological language—"God talk"—has an obvious, if not basic, application to the eschatological statements that are made by theologians. It is alleged that the modern scientific view of time, space, and causality has rendered traditional eschatology meaningless. With a prescientific view of the "three-decker" universe, one can picture Christ's coming in glory on the clouds, surrounded with angelic legions, to summon the dead with trumpet sound. Through the eyes of Einstein, a heaven of angels above, a hell of demons beneath, and a world in the middle as the stage for the awesome drama of the resurrection and judgment at the end of time is unthinkable, it is alleged.

The problem is much older than the age of modern science; natural science may have sharpened the problem, but it did not create it. Philosophy always has been offended by a personal view of God, a God who revealed himself in the massive form of historical events. If the doctrine of Christian hope be rejected, it is rejected because a philosophy of reality has been chosen that excludes the possibility of such hope. Such a philosophic choice does not rest upon science. Science is not a philosophy; it is a method of knowing the world of objects. Revelation, on the other hand, is concerned with the disclosure of God, who is not objective at all, but personal—the One who says, "I am." The language and thought categories of science are inadequate to describe even the mystery of *human* personality. How much less, then, should one expect an adequate description, in scientific terms, of the ultimate personal revelation of God at the last day.

It is no wonder, then, that anyone who shuts himself up to the method of science will have no time for a "glorious appearing of our great God and Saviour, Jesus Christ" (Titus 2:13). Why should anyone shut himself up to a method of knowledge that makes him a mystery even to himself? The Christian theologian grants the inadequacy (not the meaninglessness) of all human language about God and the world to come, an inadequacy that will be overcome only in the consummation of all things, when faith shall become sight. In the meantime, giving up the rational autonomy of philosophy, he rests in a truth given by revelation, not discovered by reason. He believes to understand (*fides praecedit intellectum*).

(See further R. H. Charles, *A Critical History of the Doctrine of the Future Life* [1899]; L. S. Chafer, *The Kingdom in History and Prophecy* [1915]; G. Vos, *Pauline Eschatology* [1934]; H. H. Rowley, *The Relevance of Apocalyptic* [1941]; E. Brunner, *Eternal Hope* [1954]; H. Quistrop, *Calvin's Doctrine of Last Things* [1955]; J. D. Pentecost, *Things* to Come [1958]; O. Cullmann, *Immortality of the Soul or Resurrection of the Dead* [1958]; E. Brunner, *Dogmatics*, 3 vols. [1950–62], 3:339–444; K. Heim, *The World: Its Creation and Consummation* [1962]; K. Stendahl, ed., *Immortality and Resurrection* [1965]; G. C. Berkouwer, *The Return of Christ* [1972]; L. J. Kreitzer, *Jesus and God in Paul's Eschatology* [1987]; N. M. de S. Cameron, ed., *Universalism and the Doctrine of Hell* [1992]; M. Erickson, *A Basic Guide to Eschatology: Making Sense of the Millennium* [1998]; D. L. Bock, ed., *Three Views on the Millennium* [1999].) P. JEWETT

Esdraelon ez´druh-ee´luhn (Εσδρηλων, Gk. form of Heb. יִזְרְעֶאל H3476, "God will sow"). A lowland that transects the central ranges of PALESTINE separating the hills of GALILEE and SAMARIA. It is popularly known as "the Emek" (from Heb. *ʿēmeq* H6677, "valley"). The name Esdraelon occurs only in the APOCRYPHA (Jdt. 1:8; 3:9; 4:6; 7:3), but it corresponds to the Valley of JEZREEL (Josh. 17:16; Jdg. 6:33; cf. the "fertile valley" of Isa. 28:1, 4), and forms the setting for several passages of Scripture. In broadest usage, Esdraelon may include the whole plain from the sea to the Jordan, but a stricter terminology excludes both the Acco plain and (less emphatically) the valley eastward from Jezreel. It thus denotes the central triangle of lowland, approximately 15 mi. along each side, with its apices at the KISHON Gorge, Jenin (BETH HAGGAN), and Mount TABOR.

I. Structure. Esdraelon was formed by subsidence at the center and faulting at the periphery, and defined to the SW by the relatively continuous limestone scarp extending from Carmel (see CARMEL, MOUNT) to GILBOA and on the NW by the analogous if somewhat lower limestone escarpment of the NAZARETH ridge. But the NE limits are less regular, since clear-cut fault lines are replaced here by lowland salients that isolate the limestone dome of Tabor—keystone of a vanished geological arch—and the basaltic mass of Mount MOREH. A slight volcanic "causeway" divides the eastern from the western plain, but the basins themselves are largely infilled with alluvial loams stripped from the encircling rim of limestone and basalt, and by the dark organic soils of former swamplands.

II. Roads and passes. Enclosed within its triangle of hills, Esdraelon had its exits and its entrances, strategic keys to the FERTILE CRESCENT. Cutting from E to W across the grain of Palestine, the Emek opened a vital passage from the Mediterranean to the Jordan—the easiest lowland corridor in the length of the Syrian ranges. The western gate, guarded by ancient HAROSHETH, followed the ravine of the Kishon between the abrupt scarp of Carmel and the Galilean hills, whereas the eastern gate, properly the Valley of Jezreel, linked Esdraelon with BETH SHAN and the fords of the Jordan.

But this E-W traverse gained added significance from its connections with N-S routeways. Since the forests and swamps of SHARON and the brusque promontory of Carmel impeded coastal movement, the "way of the Sea" turned inland for easier passage through the Samarian hill country to Esdraelon. Avoiding hard limestone uplands, the two westerly roads followed channels etched into softer chalk and reached the plain at JOKNEAM and MEGIDDO respectively, whereas the two easterly passes, following down-faulted valleys, emerged at TAANACH and IBLEAM.

Esdraelon Valley (also called the Jezreel Valley).

Valley of Esdraelon looking ENE toward Mt. Tabor and the Nazareth ridge.

Each route had its particular advantages. The Jokneam road provided lower and more direct access from Sharon to PHOENICIA; the Ibleam road, linking SAMARIA to Jezreel and the Jordan, was in constant use; and the Taanach route, though somewhat difficult, was an acceptable alternative to Megiddo should strategy dictate. The Megiddo route was crucial. Uniquely combining the chalk depression of the Wadi ʿAra with dry basaltic causeway, it carried the main route from Egypt across the Esdraelon marshlands and the fords of the Kishon to the Tabor gate—a further focus for traffic. For though the hills W of Tabor were not impassable and the narrow Wadi Bira led occasional traffic eastward to the Jordan, it was the easier Tabor gate that led most naturally to GALILEE and SYRIA.

III. Settlement.

Highway towns and mercantile wealth apart, Esdraelon was less significant for settlement. Its drainage retarded by narrow gorge and basalt barrier, the Kishon broadened sporadically into malarial marsh and waterlogged soils. Ancient settlements—long Canaanite rather than Israelite—clustered on the marginal lines of hills and springs, whereas the plains were grazed in patchy and seasonal fashion. The drier Valley of Jezreel was better tilled, and Megiddo sent wheat to Egypt. Since 1920, however, planned colonization with eradication of malaria, drainage, well-drilling, and intensive cultivation have transformed the Emek into a rich mosaic of farmland and settlement.

IV. A pattern of violence.

Esdraelon, nevertheless, has been more noted for the arts of war than those of peace. Long before THUTMOSE III hailed the fall of Megiddo as "the capture of a thousand towns," the strategic implications were clear. The tale continued with SISERA's defeat and GIDEON's victory (Jdg. 5:19–21; 6:33), SAUL's last battle and SOLOMON's chariot fortress (1 Sam. 31; 1 Ki. 9:15), JEHU's relentless pursuit of AHAZIAH and the downfall of JEZEBEL and JOSIAH (2 Ki. 9:20–24, 37; 23:29). When John bore witness to the final triumph of Christ, it was Har Megiddo (ARMAGEDDON, Rev. 16:16) that loomed in the Apocalyptic vision.

(See further G. A. Smith, *Historical Geography of the Holy Land*, 25th ed. [1931], ch. 19; (British) Naval Intelligence Division, Geographical Handbook Series, *Palestine and Transjordan* [1943]; E. Orni and E. Efrat, *Geography of Israel*, 3rd ed. [1971], see index s.v. Jezreel; Y. Aharoni, *The Land of the Bible: A Historical Geography*, rev. ed. [1979], 22–24 et passim).

G. R. LEWTHWAITE

Esdras, First ez´druhs (Εσδρας, Gk. form of Heb. עֶזְרָא H6474, "help"). A narrative work, usually listed as the first book of the OT APOCRYPHA, and covering the period from King JOSIAH to EZRA. In the Latin VULGATE, where 1–2 Esdras correspond to the canonical Ezra–Nehemiah, it is designated 3 Esdras and included as a kind of appendix (it is placed after the NT along with the Prayer of Manasseh, 4 Esdras, Psalm 151, and the *Epistle* to the Laodiceans). The book is sometimes referred to as the "Greek Ezra" to distinguish it from the canonical Ezra in Hebrew and from the *Apocalypse of Ezra* in Latin (see ESDRAS, SECOND). The author of 1 Esdras is unknown.

I. Literary character. The similarity of 1 Esdras to the canonical books of 2 Chronicles (the last two chapters), Ezra (nearly all), and Nehemiah (Neh. 7:73b—8:12) is obvious. Most of the book can be regarded as a free Greek rendering of the Hebrew narrative, but the precise relationship between its text and the SEPTUAGINT version of the canonical books is debated (cf. R. H. Pfeiffer, *History of New Testament Times with an Introduction to the Apocrypha* [1949], 236–50; S. Jellicoe, *The Septuagint and Modern Study* [1968], 290–94). There are noticeable changes in literary usage; in addition, 1 Esd. 3:1—5:6 represents a unique section, having no parallel in the OT.

Among the types of literary characteristics are the following: (1) omissions (cf. 2 Chr. 35:11) and additions (1 Esd. 1:23–24); (2) word changes (e.g., "commandment" in 1 Esd. 1:6 for "word" in 2 Chr. 35:6 NRSV); (3) frequent elimination of the conjunction "and"; (4) transposition of phrases (e.g., "in Jerusalem to the Lord" in 1 Esd. 1:1 for "to the LORD in Jerusalem" in 2 Chr. 35:1); and (5) change or addition in thought (e.g., "according to their divisions" in 1 Esd. 1:2 for "to their duties" in 2 Chr. 35:2; cf. also 1 Esd. 5:60 with Ezra 3:10).

There is nothing in 1 Esdras which corresponds to Neh. 1:1—7:73a, nor is the name of Nehemiah mentioned in the narrative concerning the reading of the law (cf. 1 Esd. 9:49 with Neh. 8:9). Ezra is mentioned as "chief priest and reader" in 1 Esd. 9:39, the only place where the title occurs; Neh. 8:2 calls him "the priest." Possibly this detail was intended to show the prominence of Ezra in his role as spiritual leader of the RESTORATION period.

II. Date. Due to the close relation of 1 Esdras to the canonical books of 2 Chronicles, Ezra, and Nehemiah, the latter dating from the late 5th cent. B.C., and also some apparent dependence on the book of DANIEL in the LXX (cf 1 Esd. 4:58–60 with Dan. 2:20–23), translated in the 3rd and 2nd centuries B.C., the *terminus a quo* would be sometime in the 2nd cent. B.C. As the book is used by JOSEPHUS (*Ant.* 11.5.1–5), the *terminus ad quem* would be c. A.D. 90. Various dates have been suggested, ranging from c. 150 to 50 B.C.

III. Content. The historical range extends from Josiah's celebration of the PASSOVER (1 Esd. 1:1–24) to Ezra's role as leader of the people in Jerusalem (9:37–55). An annotated structural outline follows:

(1) 1 Esd. 1:1–58 (cf. 2 Chr. 35–36). Josiah's Passover; his battle with Pharaoh NECO and resulting death; and the Babylonian invasion of Judah fulfilling Jeremiah's prophecy.

(2) 1 Esd. 2:1–15 (cf. Ezra 1:1–11). CYRUS's decree allowing the Jewish captives to return to Jerusalem to rebuild their TEMPLE.

(3) 1 Esd. 2:16–30 (cf. Ezra 4:7–24). Letter from Persian officials in SAMARIA to ARTAXERXES asking that construction of the Jewish temple be stopped, and the granting of the request.

(4) 1 Esd. 3:1—5:6 (no OT parallel). Story of King DARIUS and three of his court guards. The third guard was ZERUBBABEL, who showed the greatest wisdom and was granted permission to return and rebuild Jerusalem.

(5) 1 Esd. 5:7–73 (cf. Ezra 2:1—4:6). The roster of returning Jews and the beginning of the restoration of the temple in the days of Cyrus.

(6) 1 Esd. 6:1—7:15 (cf. Ezra 5:1—6:22). HAGGAI and ZECHARIAH urge the building to continue in the second year of Darius, and after some delay, the temple is completed in the sixth year (515 B.C.).

(7) 1 Esd. 8:1–67 (cf. Ezra 7:1—8:36). The return of Ezra and his companions to Jerusalem with a commission from the Persian King Artaxerxes. He was to administer, rebuild, and teach.

(8) 1 Esd. 8:68–90 (cf. Ezra 9). Ezra's prayer of confession.

(9) 1 Esd. 8:91—9:36 (cf. Ezra 10). Repentance on the part of the people, and Ezra's reforms, including judgment against mixed marriages.

(10) 1 Esd. 9:37–55 (cf. Neh. 7:73—8:12). Ezra reads the law to the people, and the Levites carry on the work of instruction.

IV. Attitude toward the law. The book speaks of the law as given by MOSES (1 Esd. 1:11; 5:49;

7:6, 9; 9:39). The expression "the book of Moses" occurs four times and "the law of Moses" once. Further, according to 9:39, the law of Moses "had been given by the Lord God of Israel." In addition, obedience to the law was an assumed practice. Offerings were made in accordance with its directions (1:10, 11; 5:49; 7:6–9). Its words were considered a reason for rejoicing and a directive for daily life (9:37–41, 46–47, 49–55). After a long period of neglect and disobedience, this prevailing attitude toward the law seems to have been due in great measure to the work and influence of Ezra. According to W. F. Albright, Ezra's greatest importance "probably lay in the field of cultic reform than in that of political action" (*The Biblical Period from Abraham to Ezra* [1963], 94). The law was established as "the normative rule of Israel's faith."

V. The story of Darius and the youths. While little background is supplied here for the story (1 Esd. 3:1–3), Josephus (*Ant.* 11.3.1) adds a number of details that shed a different light on the incident. Among other things, the latter reveals that "there had been an old friendship between him [Zerubbabel] and the king [Darius]."

The three wise sayings concerning what is strongest—wine, the king, and women, but, above all, truth—supply interesting insights into differing views on life, a common theme in Jewish WISDOM writings. Wine, said the first guard, is strongest, for it distorts the mental processes of those who consume it, causing them to do foolish and harmful things; often one will reverse his normal attitudes toward his friends and his obligations. The king is the strongest, averred the second man: he is absolute, bearing rule over even the strongest men (obedience to the king is described by a relatively rare word, *enakouō*, "to listen," 1 Esd. 4:3, 10); every subject's life is at his disposal, an apt description of the oriental monarch. The third guard, Zerubbabel, first named women as the strongest, yet concluded that "truth is great, and stronger than all things" (4:35). His argument for the former may be reduced to a simple syllogism: kings and wine are both great, but women as mothers bear the men who conquer and who grow grapes; therefore, women are strongest. Similarly, his praise of truth followed this approach: women, along with wine and the king, are unrighteous, but there is no unrighteousness in truth; therefore, truth is strong and prevails for ever.

The people responded to his analysis, "Great is truth, and strongest of all!" (1 Esd. 4:41; this saying has become proverbial in its Latin form, *magna [est] veritas et praevalet*). At this, Darius proclaimed Zerubbabel the wisest and promised him anything he wished, and that he would be called his "Kinsman" (4:42). (See further J. Myers, *I and II Esdras*, AB 42 [1974]; D. J. Harrington, *Invitation to the Apocrypha* [1999], ch. 12; Z. Talshir, *1 Esdras: From Origin to Translation* [1999]; id., *1 Esdras: A Text Critical Commentary* [2001]; D. A. deSilva, *Introducing the Apocrypha: Message, Context, and Significance* [2002], ch. 13.)   W. M. DUNNETT

Esdras, Second (see ESDRAS, FIRST). A Jewish APOCALYPTIC work (thus sometimes called the *Apocalypse of Ezra*), included among the books of the APOCRYPHA. The title 2 Esdras—which comes from the opening verse and has been traditionally used in English versions since the Geneva Bible—can be confusing. This book should be clearly distinguished from 2 Esdras in the SEPTUAGINT (a book that corresponds to the canonical Ezra–Nehemiah). In the Latin VULGATE it is called 4 Esdras, and printed editions place it as an appendix after the NT. Contemporary scholarship usually refers to this book as *4 Ezra*. Written originally in Hebrew (according to some, Aramaic), the work survives mainly in Latin translation, but versions in Syriac, Ethiopic, and other languages are also available. Many writers regard the first two chapters, as well as the last two, to be Christian interpolations (these sections are sometimes called 5 Ezra and 6 Ezra, respectively).

I. Literary character. While set in a Persian context (2 Esd. 1:1–3), where the prophet EZRA received divine communication during the reign of Artaxerxes, the book is mainly an APOCALYPTIC or revelatory work on the order of Dan. 7–12. It is made up of seven visions (2 Esd. 3:1—5:20; 5:21—6:34; 6:35—9:25; 9:26—10:59; 11:1—12:51; 13:1–58; 14:1–48) containing judgment against "Babylon" (Rome).

	OT Ezra	OT Nehemiah	Paraphrase of 2 Chr. 35–36; Ezra; Neh. 8, with an original story	A Latin pseudepigraph (apocalyptic)
LXX	Ἔσδρας β		Ἔσδρας α	
Vulg.	1 Esdras	2 Esdras	3 Esdras	4 Esdras
Many later Latin MSS	1 Esdras		3 Esdras	2 Esdras (chs. 1–2) 4 Esdras (chs. 3–14) 5 Esdras (chs. 15–16)
Great Bible, 1540	1 Esdras	2 Esdras	3 Esdras	4 Esdras
39 Articles, 1562	1 Esdras	2 Esdras	3 Esdras	4 Esdras
Geneva Bible, KJV, et al.	Ezra	Nehemiah	1 Esdras	2 Esdras

In words reminiscent of the prophet HABAKKUK, the writer of 2 Esdras wrestled with the problem of evil: "How long and when will these things be? Why are our years few and evil?" (2 Esd. 4:33; see also 6:59; cf. Hab. 1:2). Even when the angelic informant offered an explanation, Ezra showed his bewilderment (2 Esd. 4:10–12). Much of the message is conveyed by symbolism. Outstanding are the fifth and sixth visions, where (1) an eagle with twelve wings and three heads was encountered by a lion (11:1, 37) and (2) a man-like figure who rose from the sea and flew with the clouds of heaven was opposed by an innumerable multitude (13:3, 5).

II. Date. There is fairly general agreement that the main body of this work (2 Esd. 3–14) was composed near the end of the 1st cent. A.D., and that chs. 1–2 and 15–16 (which show affinities with the Gospels and Revelation and also contain anti-Jewish sentiments) were added later, probably sometime during the 3rd cent. The main reason for rejecting the Persian setting and placing the book in the Christian era is the interpretation of the eagle vision (11:1—12:51) as a symbol of the Roman empire (with apparent allusions to VESPASIAN, TITUS, and DOMITIAN). The destruction of Jerusalem, not by the Babylonians in the 6th cent. B.C. but by the Romans in A.D. 70, appears to be the true setting for the book.

III. Content. As indicated above, there are nine parts in the book, made up of an introduction and conclusion with seven visions:

(1) 2 Esd. 1:1—2:48. The genealogy of Ezra and the record of the commands he received from the Lord to deliver the people of Israel (notice 1:4; 2:33, 42). This section is sometimes referred to as *5 Ezra*.

(2) 3:1—5:20. At Babylon, thirty years after the fall of Jerusalem, Ezra saw the contrast between the destruction of his city and the affluence of Babylon. He was perplexed over the seeming injustice, but was assured that God would solve the problem justly.

(3) 5:21—6:34. Seven days later he received a vision concerning the scattering of Israel among the nations ("O Lord, why hast thou … scattered thine only one among the many?"). Much of the discussion sounds similar to the book of JOB, and the solution to the problem seems to echo the book of Revelation (on the former, see 5:35–55; on the latter, 6:17–24).

(4) 6:35—9:25. This is the longest vision. Eight days after the previous vision he spoke "in the presence of the Most High." Perplexity over the contrast between the many who will perish and the few who will be saved dominates this section. The judgment of mankind is vividly described. (Section 7:36–105, appearing in brackets in modern editions, is found in many ancient MSS but is missing from the Vulgate and the KJV. It is the opinion of some that theological reasons were involved in the latter, for these verses strongly prohibit prayer for the dead, e.g., v. 105.)

(5) 9:26—10:59. Ezra saw a woman mourning because her son had died. Then he saw a city

of huge foundations. The vision was explained as follows: the woman was the heavenly Zion (10:44; cf. Rev. 21:9–10); her son was the earthly city (2 Esd. 10:46); and his death was the destruction that befell Jerusalem (10:48).

(6) 11:1—12:51. An eagle, having twelve wings and three heads, arose from the sea. He reigned over the earth, but was soon countered by a lion who uttered the words of the Most High against him. The interpretation identified the eagle as the fourth kingdom of Daniel's vision, and the lion as the MESSIAH who shall destroy the enemies of the Lord.

(7) 13:1–58. Seven days later Ezra saw "something like the figure of a man" arising from a stormy sea, and the man "flew with the clouds of heaven," language similar to Dan. 7:13. Opposed by a great multitude, the man sent forth fire from his mouth and burned them all up. The man was the Son of the Most High (2 Esd. 13:32) who shall destroy the wicked and gather the people of Israel from their dispersion.

(8) 14:1–48. In this final vision the prophet was commissioned to write for forty days, then would be taken to live with the Son until the times were ended. He wrote ninety-four books; twenty-four were to be made public; seventy were to be kept secret for the wise among the people. The former represented the Hebrew canon (five, the Law; eight, the Prophets; eleven, the Writings); the latter probably allude to apocalyptic books. The Holy Spirit, sent into him as a cup full of fiery water, enabled him to write.

(9) 15:1—16:78. This final section, added in the 3rd cent. A.D., consists mainly of warnings of divine judgments against the nations. Egypt, Arabia, Parthia (Carmania), Babylon, Asia, and Syria are mentioned by name. God's elect shall be delivered from the days of tribulation. This section is sometimes referred to as *6 Ezra*.

IV. Theology.
Second Esdras shares in common with other Jewish apocalypses a concern for the future. This concern is backed by a variety of affirmations about God and man, and by an expectation of the appearance of the Messiah (or, a Messiah) and the kingdom of God, along with a variety of beliefs about resurrection and judgment. Some of these conceptions in this book are the following:

A. God. The favorite title is "the Most High" (at least 68 times, RSV text), followed by "Lord" (at least 60 times, RSV). There are various combinations, in addition, such as "Lord God" (4), "the Lord Almighty" (6), and "the Mighty One" (5). The name God occurs some 21 times. One interesting variant may be noted. "Most High" does not occur in 2 Esd. 1–2, 15–16, the "interpolated" sections of the book. On the other hand, the title "Lord" (with combinations) is found many times (at least 43 out of 70) in these same chapters.

B. Man. God allowed the nations to exercise free will unhindered (2 Esd. 3:8). Man's ungodly nature showed itself because of his evil heart (3:20). ADAM's sin resulted in a permanent moral disease, the good departing and the evil remaining (3:22). The idea of original sin showed itself in Adam (4:30; cf. 4:33, 38, 39; 7:22–25, 46–48). Human understanding is limited (4:1–2), and man cannot understand God's ways (4:11). When he is questioned he is unable to fathom the depths (4:1–12; 5:33–40).

C. Resurrection and judgment. There is strong affirmation of a RESURRECTION of the body at the end time (2 Esd. 2:16; 7:32). The new age will soon dawn, after evil has been punished (4:26–32). The day of judgment is like a time of threshing (4:30). No one knows when this time will come (4:51–52), but God has already determined the length of the age (4:36–37; cf. Sir 36:8), and has prepared the judgment (2 Esd. 7:70).

D. Messiah. He is God's son who shall reign for 400 years, then die (2 Esd. 7:28–29). He appears as a lion who shall destroy the wicked nations (12:31–32), and as a man arising from the sea and flying with the clouds of heaven (13:3, 25–26). Once again he is declared to be God's Son (13:32, 37, 52), and shall stand victoriously on Mount Zion (13:35–38).

E. Kingdom. There is to be a temporary earthly kingdom (2 Esd. 7:26–44), preceded by certain signs (6:20–24). A city shall be established (8:52; 10:27, 41–44), the heavenly Zion. After 400 years, this kingdom shall end (7:28–29). Then comes the new age, characterized by resurrection, judgment, and "the paradise of delight" (7:31–32, 36).

While many of the lines are not clearly defined, one point is made often—the solution to the prevailing state of evil and the fate of both the good and the bad is the day of judgment, when all shall be made right by the Most High. (See further G. H. Box, *The Ezra-Apocalypse* [1912]; J. Myers, *I and II Esdras*, AB 42 [1974]; A. L. Thompson, *Responsibility for Evil in the Theodicy of IV Ezra* [1977]; M. E. Stone, *Features of the Eschatology of IV Ezra* [1989]; T. W. Willett, *Eschatology in the Theodicies of 2 Baruch and 4 Ezra* [1989]; T. A. Bergren, *Fifth Ezra: The Text, Origin, and Early History* [1990], dealing with 2 Esd. 1–2; M. E. Stone, *Fourth Ezra*, Hermeneia [1990]; B. W. Longenecker, *2 Esdras* [1995]; T. A. Bergren, *Sixth Ezra: The Text and Origin* [1998], dealing with 2 Esd. 15–16; A. Hamilton, *The Apocryphal Apocalypse: The Reception of the Second Book of Esdras (4 Ezra) from the Renaissance to the Enlightenment* [1999]; D. J. Harrington, *Invitation to the Apocrypha* [1999], ch. 16; D. A. deSilva, *Introducing the Apocrypha: Message, Context, and Significance* [2002], ch. 17; English trans. with notes in *OTP*, 1:517–59.)

W. M. DUNNETT

Esdris ez′dris (Εσδρις, Gk. form of Heb. עֶזְרָא *H6474*, "help"). An army officer at the time of Judas MACCABEE (2 Macc. 12:36; KJV, "Gorgias," reflecting a LXX textual variant). All that is said about him is that he and his men became fatigued after fighting for a long time. However, some scholars suggest that Esdris is the same as a certain Eleazar mentioned earlier (8:23, possibly Judas's brother, see ELEAZAR #8) and even the same as AZARIAH (a commander who disobeyed Judas, 1 Macc. 5:55–62). Since all three names are derived from the same Hebrew root (ʿzr), the sources may reflect some confusion. (See J. A. Goldstein, *I Maccabees*, AB 41 [1976], 80; id., *II Maccabees*, AB 41A [1983], 446–47.)

Esebon es′i-bon. KJV Apoc. form of HESHBON. It appears in the phrase "all them of Esebon," rendering Greek *pantas tous Esebōnitas* (lit., "all the Heshbonites," Jdt. 5:15).

Esebrias es′i-bri′uhs. KJV Apoc. variant of SHEREBIAH (1 Esd. 8:54).

Esek ee′sik (עֵשֶׂק *H6922*, "dispute"). An artesian well dug by the servants of ISAAC in the valley between GERAR and BEERSHEBA (Gen. 26:20; the LXX renders the name with *Adikia*, "offense, wrong"). Rather than quarrel with the native herdsmen, Isaac moved on, digging two more wells before he established an undisputed claim. The site is unknown.

Eshan ee′shuhn (אֶשְׁעָן *H878*, possibly "support"). KJV Eshean. A town in the tribal territory of JUDAH (Josh. 15:32). It is mentioned as part of a group of towns in the hill country and presumably was not far from HEBRON, but its precise location is not known.

Esh-Baal esh-bay′uhl (אֶשְׁבַּעַל *H843*, "man of the Lord" or "the Lord exists"). An alternate form of ISH-BOSHETH, son of King SAUL. While this form occurs only twice (1 Chr. 8:33; 9:39), it was probably his original name, later changed by scribes when the name BAAL became too closely associated with idolatry.

Eshban esh′ban (אֶשְׁבָּן *H841*, derivation uncertain). Son of Dishon and descendant of SEIR the HORITE (Gen. 36:26; 1 Chr. 1:41).

Eshcol (person) esh′kol (אֶשְׁכֹּל *H866*, "cluster [of grapes]"). TNIV Eshkol. An AMORITE, brother of MAMRE and ANER, who apparently resided near HEBRON (Gen. 14:13, 24). All three were allies of ABRAHAM when LOT was rescued from KEDORLAOMER. According to some scholars, the names of all three brothers refer to localities. See ESHCOL (PLACE).

Eshcol (place) esh′kol (אֶשְׁכּוֹל *H865*, "cluster [of grapes]"). TNIV Eshkol. The valley or WADI where the twelve spies found a cluster of grapes so huge that it required two men to carry it (Num. 13:23–24; 32:9; Deut. 1:24). The site is unknown, but some think it should be associated with ʿAin-

Vineyard N of the Valley of Eshcol.

Eshkali, a spring c. 2 mi. N of HEBRON. The vineyards in this general area still produce delicious grapes. — R. C. RIDALL

Eshean esh′ee-uhn. KJV form of ESHAN.

Eshek ee′shik (עֵשֶׁק H6944, possibly "strong" [cf. *HALOT*, 2:897]). Son of Eleasah and descendant of BENJAMIN through SAUL (1 Chr. 8:39; cf. vv. 33 and 37). Some of his descendants "were brave warriors who could handle the bow" (v. 40). According to G. N. Knoppers (*I Chronicles 1–9*, AB 12 [2004], 486), the reference to Eshek and his sons represents an updating of the Benjamite genealogy found in 9:35–44 (and paralleled in 8:29–38).

Eshkalonite esh′kuh-luh-n*it*. See ASHKELON.

Eshkol. TNIV form of ESHCOL.

Eshtaol esh′tay-uhl (אֶשְׁתָּאוֹל H900, "[place of] inquiry"; gentilic אֶשְׁתָּאֻלִי H901, "Eshtaolite" [1 Chr. 2:53]). A town in the SHEPHELAH, always mentioned with ZORAH; though apparently allotted to the tribe of JUDAH (Josh. 15:33), it is also listed as one of the cities of DAN (19:40–41). Some harmonize the passages by assuming that the most northerly part of Judah's district was given up to the tribe of Dan on the second division of the land by JOSHUA (cf. KD on the former passage). A. Alt, followed by most modern scholars, proposed that the Judean town list in Josh. 15:21–62 is based on a later administrative apportionment by the Judean monarchy (A. Alt in *Palästinajahrbuch* 21 [1925]: 100–116=*Kleine Schriften zur Geschichte des Volkes Israel*, 3 vols. [1953–59], 2:276–88; F. M. Cross and G. E. Wright in *JBL* 75 [1956]: 202–26; Z. Kallai-Kleinmann in *VT* 8 [1958]: 134–60; Y. Aharoni in *VT* 9 [1959]: 225–40).

When the Danites' attempt to occupy the Shephelah region around Zorah and Eshtaol encountered stiff opposition from the AMORITE cities there (Jdg. 1:34–35), the Danites of Zorah and Eshtaol played a principal role in relocating the tribe in Leshem (Josh. 19:47; Jdg. 18:2, 8, 11). In the genealogy of Judah (1 Chr. 2–4), the sons of its various clans are mentioned along with the names of their respective settlements in such a way that a clansman becomes the father of the place occupied; accordingly it can be determined that Judeans from KIRIATH JEARIM, descendants of Hur, probably replaced the Danites in both Zorah and Eshtaol (1 Chr. 2:50–53). It was between Zorah and Eshtaol that the Spirit of God began to stir SAMSON, a Danite; he was also buried there (Jdg. 13:24–25; 16:31). The site is identified with the modern village of Ishwaʿ (more precisely, the nearby site of Khirbet Deir Shubeib; see Z. Kallai, *Historical Geography of the Bible* [1986], 368), about 14 mi. W of Jerusalem.   B. K. Waltke

Eshtemoa, Eshtemoh esh´tuh-moh´uh, esh´tuh-moh (אֶשְׁתְּמֹעַ *H904*, אֶשְׁתְּמֹה *H903* [only in Josh. 15:50, possibly a scribal corruption], "[place of] hearing," i.e., where an oracle is heard). **(1)** Son of Ishba and descendant of Judah (1 Chr. 4:17). The genealogical connection is not stated, but he was possibly related to Caleb (cf. v. 15). Some have suggested he is the same as #2 below (the text may have suffered scribal corruption). Since these genealogical lists are partly personal and partly topographical, it is possible to regard Ishbah as founder or leader of the town of Eshtemoa; see #3 below.

(2) A Maacathite, described as descending from Hodiah's wife, and included in the genealogy of Judah (1 Chr. 4:19). He may have been an inhabitant of Maacah or a descendant of Caleb's concubine by the same name (cf. 2:48).

(3) A town in the hill country of Judah (Josh. 15:50); it was later ceded to the Levites (21:14; 1 Chr. 6:57; cf. A. Alt, *Kleine Schriften zur Geschichte des Volkes Israel*, 3 vols. [1953–59], 2:306–15). It was one of the cities where David had friends who were elders of Judah and to whom he sent part of the booty taken from the Amalekites after his raid upon Ziklag (1 Sam. 30:26–28). Eshtemoa is identified with modern es-Semuʿ, some 9 mi. SSW of Hebron. (See *NEAEHL*, 2:423–26.)

B. K. Waltke

Eshton esh´ton (אֶשְׁתּוֹן *H902*, perhaps "effeminate" or "uxorious"). Son of Mehir and descendant of Judah (1 Chr. 4:11–12). The family is described as "the men of Recah," but their genealogical connection with other Judahite families is not stated.

Esli es´li (Ἐσλί *G2268*). Son of Naggai, included in Luke's genealogy of Jesus Christ (Lk. 3:25).

Esora i-sor´uh. KJV Apoc. form of Aesora (Jdt. 4:4).

espousals. This English term, meaning "betrothal" or "wedding," is used by the KJV in two passages (Cant. 3:11; Jer. 2:2); in the second reference, "the love of thine espousals" means "your love as a bride" (so NRSV and other versions). See marriage.

Esril es´ril. KJV Apoc. form of Azarel (1 Esd. 9:34).

Esrom es´rom. KJV NT form of Hezron.

Essene Gate. See Essenes, Gate of the.

Essenes es´eens (Ἐσσηνοί, Ἐσσαῖοι). A Jewish religious group that flourished between the 2nd cent. B.C. and the 1st cent. A.D. Although not mentioned by the NT writers, the Essenes formed an important school of thought in the time of Christ.

   I. Name
  II. Literary sources
     A. Josephus
     B. Pliny the Elder
     C. Philo
     D. Hippolytus
 III. Essene history
 IV. Essene life

I. Name. The meaning of the name Essene has been much debated. The eastern Aramaic term *ḥsyʾ*, "pious," has been suggested as a possible origin, but this root does not occur with such a meaning in Jewish (western) forms of Aramaic. Other proposed derivations include Greek *hosios* ("holy"; also *isos*, "equal") and Hebrew *ḥāsîd* ("pious" [see Hasideans]; also *ʿāśâ*, "to do [the law]," *ʿāšîr*, "noble, powerful," et al.). As early as Philo Judaeus, its etymology is obscure. This confusion is understandable if, as seems probable, the name Essene was never used by the sect itself as a descriptive term.

II. Literary sources. Josephus described the Essenes as the third of the "philosophies" or schools of religious thought in contemporary Judaism, but apart from his testimony there are further descriptions of Essene beliefs and customs in his older Jewish contemporary, Philo, as well as another from the Roman author Pliny the Elder. A later account furnished by Hippolytus (fl. A.D. 200) was based on Josephus, though certain sections were apparently derived from independent sources.

A. Josephus. Though it is recognized that this author, who lived c. A.D. 37–100, tended on occasions to modify strict historical fact for apologetic and other purposes, it is nevertheless true that his description of the Essenes gives evidence of being factual and based upon first-hand knowledge. His earliest account of the sect (*War* 2.8.2ff.) was in the compilation made shortly after the fall of Jerusalem in A.D. 70, and there are several references to the Essenes in various parts of his other works, along with a shorter version in his *Antiquities* (13.1.5) written about the year 90.

In his autobiography, Josephus recorded that, as part of his study of the Jewish culture, he had joined a wilderness sect headed by a certain Bannus, with whom he stayed for three years before returning to Jerusalem and joining the PHARISEES. Whether or not Josephus was ever actually an Essene novitiate, as he seems to imply, must remain a matter of some doubt, particularly in the light of Essene admission regulations. The fullest account of the Essenes that Josephus furnished appears in his *Jewish War*. Here this third philosophical sect was depicted as espousing a stricter discipline than the Pharisees or SADDUCEES, and a greater sense of fellowship. They rejected worldly pleasures as evil, but regarded continence and the control of the passions as virtuous acts. The Essenes rejected matrimony, preferring instead to train the young offspring of others and mold them to their own patterns of life. While not forbidding marriage for others, they felt that their own attitude was the only legitimate safeguard against the lasciviousness and infidelity of women generally.

Josephus continued to describe the communal life of the Essenes, which was based on the premise that the possession of riches was abhorrent. Those who joined the sect were required to bring their assets for the enrichment of the group as a whole, so that there would be no appearance of either poverty or riches in the community. Their common affairs were managed by stewards appointed for the purpose, whose sole aim was the well-being of the whole group. The Essenes apparently did not form a separate community, preferring instead to mingle with society at all possible levels. They were to be found in every large city, and were evidently well-received by the Jewish populace as a whole.

Essene piety had made a great impression upon Josephus, for he spoke at considerable length of their habits of worship and devotion. They began their day before dawn with an act of prayer, and following this the members of the sect pursued the various secular avocations for which they were fitted, being noted for the conscientious and diligent discharge of their duties. At noon they bathed in cold water and, having reassembled in the communal dining room, they partook of a simple meal after grace. They then returned to work, and in the evening repeated the procedure of washing and eating.

The strict discipline of the group was indicated by the absence of strife or disturbance, and the only things permitted of the members' free will were acts of help to the needy and attitudes of compassion. While mercy was not allowed to usurp justice, the sect was noted for its fidelity, integrity, and humanity, and such characteristics seldom made acts of strict justice necessary. Admission to this group was by way of an initial one-year novitiate, during which the beginner was expected to manifest the qualities to which the sect aspired. If he was deemed a suitable candidate, he was required to undergo a further two-year period of testing, after which he was formally admitted to Essene society. At this point the candidate took oaths of fidelity and piety toward God and justice toward men, after which he was allowed to partake of the communal food as a fully accredited member of the group.

The strictness of Essene discipline was evident in the penalties prescribed for major transgressions. The offenders were banished from the sect and, being bound by oaths not to partake of common food, frequently came to the point of starvation before they were taken back into the group, often out of sheer compassion. Communal life was under the control of a number of elders, who prescribed strict decorum in public meetings.

According to Josephus, the Essenes believed that, whereas the body was mortal, the soul was immortal. This gave a certain Platonic aspect to their teachings; that the body constituted the prison house of the soul, from which the latter was released at death to wing upward to the heavens. Cessation from work, and worship on the SABBATH day, were matters of punctilious observance in Essene society, and their veneration of MOSES, their legislator, required them to indulge in careful study and practice of the TORAH. Some Essenes were renowned for their insights into OT prophecy and for their ability to foretell events still in the future.

Josephus noted that one order of the Essenes diverged from the general tradition on the sole issue of MARRIAGE. This group used the married state for the procreation of offspring rather than for sexual pleasure, in the belief that by refraining from marriage the other Essenes were depriving themselves of the "principal part of human life," namely, the prospect of lineal succession. They supported their position by the unshakeable argument that if everyone was to be of the same mind as the majority of the Essenes, the whole race of mankind would disappear.

In his *Antiquities,* Josephus furnished a more concise account of Essene teachings and habits of life, in which they were described as holding to a belief in the immortality of the soul and the necessity for ascribing all things to God. They were independent of the temple cultus to a considerable extent, and because they deemed certain of their own rites to be of purer quality than those of the temple priests, they were excluded from the common court of the temple. Despite this situation the Essenes were renowned for the fact that their virtue and righteousness exceeded that of the scribes and Pharisees, and at the time that Josephus was writing they showed every indication of continuing in that fashion. For him, this notable mark of spirituality was the direct product of communal living.

B. Pliny the Elder. Another 1st-cent. A.D. author who commented on Essene life and behavior was the Elder Pliny. This man was a fellow soldier of VESPASIAN, and was perhaps with the Tenth Legion in A.D. 68 when it marched down the JORDAN valley. In his *Natural History,* completed in the year 77, he included a topographical description of the W side of the DEAD SEA, beginning with JERICHO and ending with the mountain fortress of MASADA, which protected the S border of JUDEA. This narrative mentions a religious community that lived near a palm tree oasis, and it may be that this was the group at QUMRAN which cultivated crops at the oasis of ʿAIN FESHKA. (See DEAD SEA SCROLLS.) Pliny described its location in general terms as being "on the W side of the Dead Sea," but N of EN GEDI, and spoke of the community as "the solitary tribe of the Essenes," which was noteworthy for its renunciation of women and worldly goods. Pliny was impressed by the remarkable manner in which world-weary postulants flocked to the community seeking to follow the strict rule of life that the Essenes required of their members. Although the passage is obviously rhetorical in style, the general identification of the Qumran locality with some kind of Essene community is quite apparent.

C. Philo. In the writings of Philo, the Alexandrian Jew (c. 20 B.C. TO A.D. 52), there is still more information about the Essenes in general, occurring in two of his works, *Hypothetica* (11.1–18) and *Quod omnis probus liber sit* (12–13). These works, apparently based on a common literary source, were probably written in Egypt before A.D. 50, and the factual descriptions that Philo has preserved can be taken as constituting valuable information about Palestinian Essenism in the early decades of the Christian era. However, his narratives need to be assessed critically, since Philo had apologetic interests in mind when writing about the Essenes. His attitude was governed by moralistic considerations, for he was utilizing his own people as an example to support the hypothesis that virtue had not vanished entirely from the contemporary Hellenistic scene.

He computed the number of Essenes in Palestinian Syria in excess of 4,000, as Josephus did at a later period. Pliny suggested that their name had been derived from the Greek *hosiotēs*, "holiness." This designation he attributed not to the prosecution of cultic observances but to the resolve of the Essenes themselves to serve God devoutly and to sanctify their minds. Philo commented on the preference of the Essenes for life in villages rather than in cities, since the latter were much more likely to corrupt and deprave the person who was seeking to lead a sincere spiritual life. He also noted their diligence with respect to manual labor, and marveled at the way in which they had deliberately divested themselves of all personal wealth and property, esteeming frugality and contentment as constituting an abundance of riches. Equally significant for Philo was the pacifist attitude adopted by the Essenes, who neither manufactured nor traded in weapons of WAR. In harmony with this rejection of the military arts was the disavowal of any form of SLAVERY, since they believed in the free exchange of services and held that the owners of slaves outraged the law of the equality of individuals.

The Essenes laid great emphasis on their ancestral laws, which had been mediated by divine REVELATION and were of supreme importance for faith and behavior. According to Philo, the Essenes observed the ethical precepts of the Torah strictly, manifesting their love for God in a variety of ways, including consistent religious purity, abstinence from oaths, a love of virtue, freedom from bondage to material possessions, self-mastery, frugality, humility, and contentment. Their respect for their fellows was manifested in deeds of love and charity, in their avowed sense of the equality of individuals, and in their notable spirit of fellowship. The communal life of the Essenes was particularly significant in that it was emulated nowhere else in actual practice. Their clothes and meals were held in common possession, and the wages each person earned were put into the community treasury so that all might benefit as the need arose. The sick were cared for by those who were well, and the cost of treatment was met from the monetary reserves of the group. The elderly members of the community were accorded the respect due to their age, and in their declining years they were maintained in dignity and contentment.

Like Josephus, Philo stressed the place given in Essene circles to the study of Scripture and the manner in which they were instructed on the SABBATH day. The Essenes abandoned all work at that time and proceeded to sacred locations called "synagogues," where they were arranged in rows according to seniority, the younger ones sitting below their elders. In process of divine worship someone read a passage of Scripture, and after this another individual who was particularly competent in this area would expound after an allegorical manner anything in the section that was not clearly understood. Philo noted that the Essenes were trained in piety, holiness, justice, and domestic and civil conduct. They summarized their beliefs and practices under three headings, namely, love of God, love of virtue, and love of men.

In a later work, the *Hypothetica*, Philo again commented on the diligence and industry of the sect. He mentioned the common ownership of goods and money, and remarked upon their general insistence on a rule of celibacy for their members, on the ground that women and children tended to distract the community from its avowed aim of the pursuit of goodness and truth. Women who were mothers were believed to be a particularly serious menace, since they would stoop without any qualms to use their children as a means of imposing their will upon others in a fashion that would disrupt the spiritual unity of the group.

In a treatise entitled *On the Contemplative Life*, Philo devoted considerable attention to the activities of another religious group that bore some slight resemblance to the Essenes. Known as the *Therapeutae*, this community flourished in Egypt for some two centuries prior to the beginning of the Christian era. The Therapeutae were organized on a monastic basis, but were actually recluses who occupied their time in prayer, meditation, and the study of their sacred writings, only assembling for divine worship as a community on Sabbath days and sacred occasions. According to Philo, the Therapeutae prayed twice daily, at dawn and dusk, and spent the remainder of the day in meditation, reading the OT and interpreting it allegorically.

Qumran Cave 12. The Dead Sea Scrolls discovered in the caves near Khirbet Qumran have been connected to the Essenes by many scholars.

In addition to this kind of study, they composed hymns and psalms in the solitude of their cells. On the weekly day of worship, the Therapeutae assembled in order of seniority and listened to a discourse given by one of the elders of the sect, subsequently returning to their cells for meditation and study. Women formed part of this monastic group, and were subjected to the same conditions of life as the men. Self-control formed the basis of their philosophy of life, which in other respects, however, was not as rigorous as that of the Palestinian Essenes, due to climatic and other factors. Although the Therapeutae may represent a late development of a pre-Christian Jewish sect that was perhaps the progenitor of the Essenes, they may be of quite independent origin. Nevertheless, the similarities between the Essenes and the Therapeutae warrant some consideration of the latter in any estimate of Palestinian Essenism.

D. Hippolytus. The evidence of a Christian writer, Hippolytus (c. 170–235), can be adduced as an important supplement to the testimony of Josephus and Philo concerning the Essenes. In a treatise entitled *The Refutation of All Heresies*, he commented on the attribute of mutual love and concern that characterized Essene behavior. In describing those who renounced matrimony, Hippolytus noted that they did not admit women to their company under any considerations, even when they presented themselves as postulants and gave evidence of a desire to participate in community life on the same basis as that of the male members of the sect. They did, however, adopt young boys and train them in the ways of the Essenes, although they did not forbid them to marry should they desire to do so at a later time.

The usual regulations concerning wealth were evident in the observations of Hippolytus. While the Essenes despised riches, they were by no means averse to sharing their goods with those destitute persons who came to them for help. On joining the order the novitiates were required to sell their properties and present the proceeds to the head of the community, who was responsible for distributing them according to individual need. Hippolytus noted what must have been a rather distinctive practice in ancient Palestine, namely, the abstention of the sect from the use of oil, on the ground that for them it constituted defilement to be anointed.

The decorum of the sect was governed by strict rules of behavior, which apparently impressed Hippolytus as much as earlier writers. The Essenes lived and worked under the control of elders and overseers, and were required to live lives of rigorous self-discipline. Disorderly behavior was not tolerated in any form, and swearing was a particularly serious matter, since whatever anyone said in this respect was deemed to be more binding than an oath. Swearing invariably lowered the individual concerned in the esteem of the community, and diminished his reliability as a credible person.

The account of the initiation requirements furnished by Hippolytus was similar to that of other writers on the subject. There were some differences in detail, however, as for example in the observation that, during the initial one-year novitiate, those desiring admission to the sect lived in a house apart from the community meeting place, although they partook of the same food and observed the identical rules of life. Hippolytus appears to have thought in terms of a two-year probationary period rather than the three-year period indicated by Josephus. This latter author was evidently the source of much of the information that Hippolyptus furnished about the nature of the oaths which the initiate was required to swear on being admitted to the order, the various sects into which the Essenes were divided, and the theological tenets to which they adhered.

However, it is quite possible that Hippolyptus was also using another source of information, since there are certain significant differences between his description of the Essenes and that of Josephus. For example, Hippolytus regarded the ZEALOTS and the Sicarii (see ASSASSINS) as subordinate groups of Essenes, and in his description of Essene religious practices he omitted all references to the supposed worship of the sun at dawn as part of the morning devotions of the sect. Furthermore, whereas Josephus attributed to the Essenes as a whole the traditional Hellenic belief that the body formed a prison for the soul from which death was the only release, Hippolytus stated that the Essenes held to a belief in the RESURRECTION of the body as well as in the immaterial and immortal nature of the soul, maintaining in addition that both would be reunited in the day of judgment. In view of these divergences, it may be that Hippolytus was drawing upon a source of information that was closer to the real facts of the situation than the one Josephus employed.

III. Essene history. Because of the rather spare amount of available material, any attempt at the reconstruction of Essene history must be rather tentative in nature. Furthermore, because of the difficulties attached to interpreting some of the source material, one can hardly speak of a scholarly consensus on the matter. However, there are good reasons for assuming that the Essenes originated among the HASIDEANS (the "loyal ones," 1 Macc. 2:42; 7:13). These people were zealous for the Jewish law at a time when Hellenistic ideas and patterns of life were flooding into Palestine early in the 2nd cent. B.C.

This situation took a critical turn during the rule of SELEUCUS IV (187–175 B.C.), the son and successor of ANTIOCHUS the Great, when a dispute between the high priest ONIAS III and Simon, the commander of the temple guard, nearly resulted in the plundering of the temple treasury by Seleucus, who was anxious to pay off some of the debts Antiochus had incurred during his struggle against the Romans. The entire incident accentuated the tension in Judea between the more orthodox Jews and those who had succumbed to the wiles of HELLENISM. The latter strongly favored Seleucid ideals, and were led by Simon and his brother Menelaus, while the more orthodox segment of Jewry remained loyal to Onias III and looked to Egyptian hegemony for support. They resisted the encroachments of Hellenism vigorously, realizing that their traditional religious beliefs had nothing in common with the skepticism, irreligion, and moral degeneration of Hellenic culture.

When Joshua, the younger brother of Onias III, became the leader of the hellenizing party in Jerusalem and adopted the Greek name JASON, he prevailed upon ANTIOCHUS IV Epiphanes, who had succeeded Seleucus IV in 175 B.C., to depose Onias and appoint himself as high priest. This was agreed to on condition that Jason achieved the hellenizing of Jerusalem as quickly as possible, a task to which Jason lent every effort. In protest against this trend the Hasideans became involved in outbreaks of violence, some of which were directed at the temple priesthood.

Hostilities flared up again in 168 B.C. at a time when Antiochus Epiphanes had determined to eradicate Judaism and colonize Judea with people of Hellenic sympathies. Accordingly a royal decree was promulgated requiring all that was characteristic of Judaism to be removed. The temple was profaned, the sacred books of the law were burned, and the sacrificial worship of Judaism was prohibited, being replaced by pagan Greek rites in which the people were compelled to participate on pain of death. Many of the Hasideans would have preferred to withdraw to the wilderness rather than clash openly with the Syrian regime, but the implacable hostility of the hellenizing party gave them little choice.

Numerous Hasideans perished in the massacres of 167 B.C., and when active resistance crystallized at Modein under the leadership of MATTATHIAS, the surviving Hasideans threw in their lot with his guerrilla forces and fought with Judas MACCABEE, the son of Mattathias. Following the success of the Maccabean revolt and the establishing of a treaty by which LYSIAS guaranteed the restoration of Jewish liberties (1 Macc. 6:59), the nation entered a new phase of development in which the allies of the revolution began to vie with one another in a struggle for control of the new state. While a strong hellenizing party still remained in Judea, the majority of the people gave firm support to the Maccabees, who became increasingly designated by their family name of HASMONEANS, and who ultimately emerged as the dominant political party, with avowed nationalistic aims.

In the course of this struggle for power there emerged the three major religious or theocratic groups known as the Sadducees, the Pharisees, and the Essenes. They had in common the spiritual aspirations of the Maccabean revolt, namely a national existence for the Jews as a separate entity in the Gentile world, and a strict observance of the Mosaic law. The Sadducees were a priestly group, being well represented in the most influential ecclesiastical circles, and they enjoyed the favor of the Hasmonean rulers until the reign of ALEXANDRA Salome (76–67 B.C.), who preferred the Pharisees, the second major party in Judea.

These latter had won popular support under John Hyrcanus I (134–104 B.C.), but their political fortunes were uncertain until the time of Alexandra, after which they maintained a dominating position in the SANHEDRIN. The Pharisees and Essenes alike seem to have developed from rival groups of earlier revolutionary Hasideans, and it may be that the real division between them occurred about 141 B.C., when a formal decree was issued in Judea that recognized SIMON MACCABEE as hereditary high priest and governor of the Jewish people (1 Macc. 14:41). The many similarities between the Pharisees and the Essenes can thus be explained in terms of their common origin.

The Pharisees certainly constituted the majority party, however, and their determined pursuit of political aims in Judea disenchanted the Essenes, who despaired of the human situation and saw the only form of salvation in terms of divine eschatological intervention. Jewish tradition depicted the Essenes as being active in Jerusalem to the time of Aristobulus I (104–103 B.C.), as mentioned by Josephus (*War* 1.3.5; *Ant.* 13.11.1–2), but by the time Alexander Jannaeus died in 76 B.C., the Essenes had made a sharp break with Hasmonean interests, and were increasingly critical of the political aims and pursuits of the other parties in Judea. They withdrew to a large extent from public life, and this action coincided with the decline of Hasmonean fortunes when Aristobulus II came to the throne in 67 B.C.

A series of abortive attempts by the Hasmoneans to overthrow the Herodian dynasty may well have favored the pietistic aspirations of the Essenes, particularly in the time of HEROD the Great (37–34 B.C.). The chief political difficulty faced by this ruler was the opposition of the populace to his claim to be the legitimate ruler of Judea, and he offset this partly by the backing of the Roman military power and partly by conciliating such anti-Hasmonean elements in the nations as the Essenes. In an astute political move, Herod excused the Essenes, along with some of the Pharisees, from the oaths of loyalty imposed upon the Jews in the early period of his rule, thereby giving the Essenes an unprecedented degree of religious freedom. Quite possibly they returned to Jerusalem, having doubtless obtained an assurance from Herod that their peculiar legal concepts would not be flouted by the temple priesthood. Most probably it was at this time that the Essenes carried out their program of missionary expansion, which saw the founding of Essene communities in all the villages and small towns of Judea. The only hint of their presence in Jerusalem was the designation given to an entrance through the S wall of the city, the "Gate of the Essenes" (Jos. *War* 5.4.2; see ESSENES, GATE OF THE).

Certainly the friendly relations that existed between Herod and the Essenes had become well known by the time of Josephus (*Ant.* 15.10.5), although there is little doubt that the group generally looked with disfavor upon the doings of Herod the Great. Be this as it may, at least one Essene was employed in the royal court as late as the period immediately after the death of Herod (*Ant.* 17.13.3). In A.D. 66, at the outbreak of the war with Rome, one of the Jewish generals was an Essene named John, and Josephus recorded that many of the Essenes were martyred by their Roman captors (*War* 2.8.10). The remainder may have offered sporadic resistance to Rome until the revolt of BAR KOKHBA was crushed in A.D. 135, but precisely what part they played is unknown, though Bar Kokhba himself may have been an Essene. Ultimately the Essenes were doubtless assimilated by the Jewish Christians or some other Jewish group that may have survived the Second Jewish Revolt.

A religious group that flourished in the same general period as the Essenes and had close affinities with them was the ancient sect known as the Covenanters of Damascus. The existence of this group became known through the exploration of a Cairo synagogue GENIZAH or storeroom in 1896. Some of the MSS recovered were subsequently published under the title, *Fragments of a Zadokite Work* (also known as the *Damascus Document*), a document that narrated the fortunes of a band of priests in Jerusalem who seemed to have been deposed as part of a reform movement (see ZADOKITE FRAGMENTS). They named themselves the "Sons of Zadok," and under the leadership of a person known as the "Star" they moved to a location styled "Damascus," which may or may not be the historic city of that name, where they organized what came to be known as the party of the New Covenant.

This sect indulged in a monastic pattern of life, and under the guidance of a notable leader described as the "Righteous Teacher" it flourished as a criticism of the secular and political aspirations of the Pharisees, and to a lesser extent, of the Sadducees also. Despite this, however, the sect maintained a close contact with the temple at Jerusalem, as the *Zadokite Fragments* indicate, for the members maintained that Jerusalem was their holy city and the temple their proper sanctuary. Their affinities with the Essenes appeared evident from their insistence upon fidelity to the law of Moses, the necessity for repentance as a prerequisite to entering the covenant community, an emphasis upon upright behavior, humanitarian concerns, and other matters dear to the Essene mind.

When archaeologists were excavating the Qumran caves, they unearthed some MS fragments from the sixth cave (6Q) that were found to be equivalent to a portion of the *Zadokite Fragments*. This discovery was augmented still further by the recovery from the fourth cave (4Q) of seven fragmentary MSS that also contained sections of the same document. Taken together, these sources would seem to point to a close relationship between the religious group known to have produced the Qumran MSS and the sect responsible for the drawing up of the *Zadokite Fragments*. Because of the close similarity of religious ideals, many scholars have regarded the two orders as identical in nature, and have suggested that the Damascus community had probably lived at Qumran for about seventy-five years prior to the end of the first occupational period, after which they moved to Damascus.

Many of those who regard the Damascene Covenanters as Essenes have maintained that they probably returned to Jerusalem under some kind of concordat in the reign of Herod the Great, and that they subsequently returned to Qumran after his death, but there is no proper evidence for this supposition. There is also some doubt as to whether the sectaries of the *Zadokite Fragments* were actually Essenes, in view of their emphasis upon animal sacrifice (CD XIII, 27; XIV, 1). They were doubtless related to the Hasidim movement, but evidently regarded themselves as the true sons of Zadok. Their tenets had elements in common with the Sadducees, though they differed from them in their belief in immortality (CD V, 6), the advent of the Messiah (CD II, 10), and the recognition of prophecy and the Hagiographa. Along with the Pharisees they acknowledged the existence of heavenly beings (CD VI, 9; IX, 12), divine predestination (CD II, 6, 10), and free will (CD III, 1–2; IV, 2, 10). On the other hand, they forbad divorce (CD VII, 1–3), and held that the Pharisees defiled the temple through what they considered were sexual irregularities (cf. CD VII, 8–9).

The excavation of a ruined settlement at Qumran and its subsequent association with the MSS and fragments recovered from nearby caves led to a study of the nature of the religious community which had inhabited the site. One of the scrolls, the *Community Rule* or *Manual of Discipline* (1QS), furnished most of the information concerning the structure and organization of the Qumran sect. Apparently it arose as part of the Hasidean movement and crystallized after the time of Antiochus IV Epiphanes, when the high priesthood as well as the civil and military power came under Hasmonean control.

The *Copper Scroll*, almost 8 ft. long, has detailed descriptions of numerous treasures and may have functioned as a treasure map for the Essenes.

The *Copper Scroll* was discovered in Qumran Cave 3.

Under the leadership of a "Righteous Teacher," the Qumran sectaries withdrew to the Judean wilderness in protest against the "epoch of wickedness" and organized themselves as a covenant group to prepare the way for the divine coming in the New Age.

Characteristic of their attitude was an avowed refusal to recognize the Jerusalem priesthood, and in the Habakkuk Commentary specific mention is made of a Wicked Priest, most probably a Hasmonean, who manifested a particularly serious degree of hostility toward the community and its leader. Apparently the sect prepetuated a framework of Zadokite priests and Levites who would be available for the conduct of proper and legitimate sacrificial worship in Jerusalem once the unworthy priesthood had been dispossessed. The general historical background for this movement is that of the Maccabean and subsequent eras, including the period of Herod the Great. Some scholars think that the Qumran group, which they regard as Essene in nature, moved their sphere of operation to Jerusalem, only to return to Qumran after the death of Herod.

From 1QS it appears that the Qumran sectaries lived a communal life of strict dedication and obedience to God. While members of both sexes were allowed to join the group, an exacting novitiate of one year was required, and if the postulant met the stipulations of the group at the end of the second year, he was enrolled as a member of the order (1QS VI, 22–23) after an elaborate ceremony (1QS I, 18ff.). Each subsequent year the members were required to renew their pledges of loyalty to the ideals of the group (1QS II, 19ff.), and delinquent members were reminded of their obligations (1QS V, 20ff.). Ritual lustrations and quasi-sacramental meals were given great prominence at Qumran, and the sectaries appear to have avoided all unnecessary contact with the outside world, preferring to live and work as a self-sustaining group, unlike the Essenes who mingled freely with society.

The Qumran sectaries devoted specific parts of the day and night to meditation and study of the law. In the interpretation of the latter they were considerably stricter than the most severe Pharisees, and according to their exposition of Scripture, given in apocalyptic terms, they themselves were to play a prominent part in realizing the coming of the New Age. Specific guidance about the latter had been given by God to the Righteous Teacher, who bestowed this esoteric knowledge upon his disciples. However, their expectations were not fulfilled in the hoped-for manner, since their settlement was destroyed in the war of A.D. 66–73, over two decades after the founding of the Christian church.

Many scholars have identified the sect of the *Zadokite Fragments* with the Qumran group and have regarded both as Essene. However there are some significant differences between Essene and Qumranic practices that merit notice. The Qumran sectaries evidently did not regard themselves as Essene in nature, since the word *Essene* appears nowhere in the DSS. Whereas the Essenes had groups in every village and town in Judea and mingled freely with secular society, the Qumran sectaries adopted a separatist policy and had no dealings whatever with those who stood outside their own group. Neither the Damascus nor the Qumran covenanters distrusted women, unlike most Essenes, but were in accord with the minority Essene segment that approved of marriage. The Essene novitiate appears to have lasted for about three years, whereas at Qumran it probably did not exceed two years in length. The Essenes were strictly pacifist by nature, but the Qumran sectaries were not, if their military scroll (1QM) is a true indication of their attitudes. The Qumran fellowship did not address the sun at dawn, as did the Essenes in the report of Josephus, though the author may have been referring to only one quasi-Essene group, the Sampsaeans, who followed this custom.

These differences will be sufficient to show that despite the elasticity of the term *Essene* in the pre-Christian era, the Qumran group can be thus regarded only in the most general sense, and may actually be nearer in nature to certain cave sects flourishing in the 1st cent. B.C. For some scholars, consequently, it is difficult to place the Qumran covenanters firmly within the stream of Essene history (more recently, the controversial book by Y. Hirschfeld, *Qumran in Context: Reassessing the Archaeological Evidence* [2004], has argued that the archaeology of the relevant sites does not support an Essene connection). For others, "The correspondence of geographic location and the extensive similarity of community structure make overwhelmingly probable the identification of Qumran, and of the *Rule of the Community*, as 'Essene'" (J. J. Collins in *ABD*, 2:625).

IV. Essene life. A brief summary from known sources of the Essene way of life can now be attempted. The vast majority of Essenes were scattered about the smaller settlements of Judea, avoiding the larger cities because of their contamination by Gentile elements. Strict observance of the purity laws in the Torah was a feature of Essene behavior, being matched by an equal emphasis on purity of life. They were notable for their communal ownership of property, which arose from their abhorrence of worldly wealth, and also for their hospitality to other members of their own sect. A strong sense of mutual responsibility characterized the Essene communities, in which the needy were given every care. Life was authoritarian in nature, with everything, apart from personal acts of mercy and charity, being governed by those in charge of the brotherhood. Admission to Essene groups was preceded by a period of testing for about three years, and when a candidate had proved his suitability he had to take solemn oaths of piety and obedience. Subsequent violation of these oaths could, and most frequently did, result in expulsion from the group.

Daily worship was an important feature of community life, beginning with prayer at dawn, and on holy days and sacred seasons special rites were observed. The sacrifices offered at such times took place within the confines of the various Essene communities, since their emphasis upon special conditions of purity prevented them from participating actively in the worship of the cultus at the Jerusalem temple. However, it was their practice to send to the temple certain things they had dedicated to God. One aspect of Essene daily worship was the study of their sacred scriptures, a task to which special expression was given on the Sabbath. Scriptural study on such occasions was a communal affair, as with many other features of Essene life, with the group assembling in their meeting hall or "synagogue," according to seniority.

The method of biblical study consisted of a reading, followed by an exposition of the passage by some learned secretary. Philo recorded that the Essenes studied their sacred writings with a view to finding out their symbolic meaning, in the belief that the divine promises to the prophets of Israel were being fulfilled in their own day. In this connection some of the *pesharim* or commentaries (see PESHER) from the Dead Sea community are illuminating, particularly if the Qumran sect was related in some way to the Essenes, since the authors of these writings commented on the text of some specific prophecy, and then proceeded to interpret what was written in terms of events that were either contemporary or expected to occur in the very near future.

The question of marriage appears to have split the Essenes into major and minor divisions, with the former section insisting on vocational celibacy as a feature of community life and the latter permitting marriage as a primary means of perpetuating the sect. Though the majority did not condemn marriage in principle, they avoided it because of its deleterious effects on community life. Because the Essenes thought of themselves as Israelite warriors fighting a holy war, as in the time of Moses and Joshua, marriage was deemed unsuitable for a long-term volunteer (cf. Deut. 23:9–14). Despite their strict behavior there is no doubt that they exerted a profound spiritual influence over Jewish life at the beginning of the Christian era.

(See further R. K. Harrison, *The Dead Sea Scrolls* [1961], 72–101; A. H. Jones, *Essene: The Elect of Israel and the Priests of Artemis* [1985]; T. S. Beall, *Josephus' Description of the Essenes Illustrated by the Dead Sea Scrolls* [1988]; G. Vermes and M. D. Goodman, *The Essenes According to the Classical Sources* [1989]; G. Stemberger, *Jewish Contemporaries of Jesus: Pharisees, Sadducees, Essenes* [1995]; L. Cansdale, *Qumran and the Essenes: A Re-evaluation of the Evidence* [1997]; G. Boccaccini, *Beyond the Essene Hypothesis: The Parting of the Ways between Qumran and Enochic Judaism* [1998]; M. Lönnqvist and K. Lönnqvist, *Archaeology of the Hidden Qumran: The New Paradigm* [2002].)

R. K. HARRISON

Essenes, Gate of the. A gate in JERUSALEM (not mentioned in the Bible) that was S of the Hippicus Tower, near a place named Bethso, and at the point where "the most ancient wall" changed orientation (Jos. *War* 5.4.2 §§140–45). It was probably on the SW hill of the city; there may have been an Essene quarter near it. (See R. Riesner in *ABD*, 2:618–19.)

Esther es′tuhr (אֶסְתֵּר H676, possibly from Akk. ISHTAR [meaning uncertain] or from Pers. *stāreh*, "star"). A Benjamite woman whose name is immortalized in the book that bears her name (see ESTHER, BOOK OF). Her cousin, MORDECAI, adopted her on the death of her parents (Esth. 2:7). She was also named HADASSAH, meaning "myrtle." It is uncertain which of the two names was original. If it was Esther, then Myrtle could have been a descriptive title, but since the name Hadassah is mentioned first, the probability is that this was the original name. Some have thought that her Persian playmates, who did not understand Hebrew, approximated a strange name to one with which they were familiar.

The book of Esther relates how she was chosen to succeed VASHTI as queen. Out of a large number of virgins, she was the one to find favor with King XERXES. At first Mordecai told her to conceal her Jewish ancestry, but later he warned (or blackmailed) her that she would not escape

Susa, the capital of Xerxes, is the setting for Esther's story.

the massacre of the Jews that HAMAN was planning, and consequently she agreed to do what she could with the king. However, she insisted that the Jews in the city should fast, and presumably pray, for her.

She appeared before the king unbidden, which could have meant death for her, but the king received her kindly. She invited the king and Haman to dinner, where she had evidently planned to disclose Haman's schemes, and, if the story had been fiction, we should have heard that she now did so. For some unexplained reason she did no more than repeat her invitation for the next night. One may assume that her courage failed her at the first dinner. On the second occasion, she exposed Haman's plot. The king was angry and went out of the room. When he returned he found Haman leaning over Esther to beg for mercy, and the king thought the worst. Haman was taken out and hanged.

Esther and Mordecai then obtained the king's permission to avert the massacre. Since the original decree could not be directly reversed, they authorized the Jews to defend themselves on the day of the massacre on the 13th day of Adar. In this way, the edge of the decree was turned, since it was unlikely that the local authorities would now support the massacre, as they would otherwise have done. In SUSA, where Esther lived, she asked permission for the Jews to kill their enemies on the following day as well, and it appears that on this day the Jews took the initiative for revenge instead of merely defending themselves (Esth. 9:15–16).

The Bible shows how God used Esther and Mordecai to deliver his people in an emergency. It is not known how long either of them remained in power, but certainly Esther was not the mother of any subsequent heir to the Persian throne. Her name does not occur in secular records. According to HERODOTUS (*Histories*) and Ctesias (*Persika*), the name of the chief wife of Xerxes, both before and after his expedition to Greece, was Amestris, who may well be identified with Vashti. Since Esther did not actually become queen for four years after the incident of chapter one (Esth. 1:3; 2:16)—Xerxes was occupied with arranging and accompanying his disastrous expedition against Greece—it is likely that Xerxes retained Vashti (Amestris?) as his wife during this time. He might

Esther probably saw these capitals of the columns from the audience hall at Susa. Originally built during the reign of Darius I, they were still in use at the time of Xerxes.

well have continued to do so if she had not brutally mutilated a woman with whom she suspected her husband was having an affair. Rather than risk the vengeance of Xerxes, she probably withdrew for the time, leaving him to choose his new wife, and waiting her time to come back into favor and power once more. J. S. WRIGHT

Esther, Additions to. Considered part of the APOCRYPHA, the Additions to Esther consist of six passages (107 verses) inserted into the Greek text in various places. It is generally assumed that the Hebrew was translated into Greek by an Egyptian Jew, possibly living in Jerusalem, no later than 114 B.C. Whether all the additions were present in the text at the time of the translation is a matter of debate. All the Greek recensions and the Old Latin version contain the additions in their proper place. When JEROME produced his Latin translation (the VULGATE), he removed these passages because they did not appear in the Hebrew, and he placed them at the end of the book with explanatory notes indicating where they should be inserted. Subsequent editors removed the notes. Finally, when Stephen Langton (d. 1228) divided the Latin Bible into chapters, he numbered the additions, which had been placed at the end of the book, in consecutive order. This practice was followed by Luther and the English versions (in the JB, these additions are in the text, but are printed in italicized type).

I. Content. The six passages making up the Additions to Esther are identified by letters. Each passage may be briefly summarized.

Addition A (Add. Esth. 11:2—12:6) is a dream of Mordecai in which two great dragons appear ready to fight. A tiny spring grew into a great river when the righteous nation cried to God. Mordecai later overheard two eunuchs plotting against the king. He reported them and was rewarded by appointment to a high office. All this precedes the canonical Esth. 1:1.

Addition B (Add. Esth. 13:1–7) is the text of the edict of Ahasuerus (Greek has Artaxerxes) against the Jews. It is to be inserted after Esth. 3:13.

Addition C (Add. Esth. 13:8—14:19) gives the prayers of Mordecai and Esther. It follows Esth. 4:17.

Addition D (Add. Esth. 15:1–16) is an elaboration of Esth. 5:1–2 and should be inserted before 5:3. This passage describes the anger of the king at Esther's intrusion, but God changed the king's heart and attitude toward Esther.

Addition E (Add. Esth. 16:1–24) gives the text of the edict of Ahasuerus in behalf of the Jews. This passage follows Esth. 8:12.

Addition F (Add. Esth. 10:4—11:1), which follows Esth. 10:3, is the interpretation of Mordecai's dream. The two dragons are Mordecai and Haman, and the tiny spring is Esther. The "lots" of Purim are two destinies, a "lot" for the Jews and a "lot" for the Gentiles.

II. Purpose. From the content of the Additions, the following conclusions may be drawn: (1) the author wanted to strengthen the religious element in the book and so inserted the prayers; (2) the trustworthiness and historical accuracy of the text are enhanced by the exact words of the two royal edicts; (3) the author tried to improve on the story by including sections D, A, and F; (4) if Esth. 9:20—10:3 is an addition (cf. L. H. Brockington, *A Critical Introduction to the Apocrypha* [1961], 49–53), then there is an attempt to harmonize the record with current usage.

III. Language. Most scholars believe the Additions were written originally in Greek. Roman Catholic scholars have usually held they were all translated from Hebrew or Aramaic originals. L. B. Paton (*A Critical and Exegetical Commentary on the Book of Esther*, ICC [1908], 31–34, 41–47) argued that there is no evidence for the existence of Semitic originals for any of the additions. C. C. Torrey (in *HTR* 37 [1944]: 1–40) claimed that the original language was Aramaic, that most of the Additions (A C D F) were part of the original text, and that our canonical Hebrew is a late abridgment. Debate has continued on these matters. It is generally agreed that Additions B and E (and esp. the latter) were composed in Greek; the other Additions may be translations of a Semitic source, but the evidence is regarded as inconclusive by some scholars (cf. K. H. Jobes, *The Alpha-Text of Esther: Its Character and Relationship to the Masoretic Text* [1996], 25–28).

IV. Date. The date of the Additions cannot be determined with accuracy. The little evidence there is points to a date near the time of the translation into Greek, around 100 B.C.

V. Discrepancies. The many discrepancies introduced by the Additions make it difficult to accept them as original parts of the text. The attitude of Esther toward the king in Esth. 2:15–18 is not at all the same as that given in Add. Esth. 14:15–16. The irrevocable edict of Esth. 1:19 and 8:8 is revoked in Add. Esth. 16:17. Haman is hanged in Esth. 7:10 but crucified in Add. Esth. 16:18. Only the Jews are to keep PURIM according to Esth. 9:20–32, but all Persians are instructed to keep it in Add. Esth. 16:22. Other contradictions are found when Esth 2:16–19 is compared with Add. Esth. 11:3—12:1; 2:21–23; Esth. 6:3–4 with Add. Esth. 12:5; Esth. 3:5 with Add. Esth. 12:6; Esth. 5:4–8 with Add. Esth. 14:7; and Esth. 3:1 with Add. Esth. 16:10. (See also J. A. F. Gregg in *APOT* 1:665–671; R. H. Pfeiffer, *History of New Testament Times with an Introduction to* *the Apocrypha* [1949], 304–12; B. M. Metzger, *An Introduction to the Apocrypha* [1957], 55–63; C. A. Moore, *Daniel, Esther, and Jeremiah: The Additions*, AB 44 [1977]; D. J. Harrington, *Invitation to the Apocrypha* [1999], ch. 4; D. A. deSilva, *Introducing the Apocrypha: Message, Context, and Significance* [2002], ch. 5.) R. E. HAYDEN

Esther, Book of. One of the historical books of the OT in the English Bible. In the Hebrew Bible, it is found among the KETUBIM (Writings) and grouped with the Five MEGILLOTH (Scrolls). Each of the Megilloth was associated with one of Israel's principal feasts, and Esther was read at the Feast of PURIM.

  I. Background
 II. Unity
III. Authorship and date
 IV. Purpose
  V. Canonicity
 VI. Special problems
VII. Contents
VIII. Theology and morals

I. Background. It is now established that the AHASUERUS mentioned in Esth. 1:1 (KJV and other versions) is the king of PERSIA usually known as XERXES I (486–465 B.C.). The Hebrew form of his name, *ʾăḥašwērôš H347*, corresponds to the Persian *Khshayarsha*, and the SEPTUAGINT translator, without the benefit of access to Persian inscriptions, quite reasonably identified the name with ARTAXERXES (cf. also Jos. *Ant.* 11.6.1). The Persian equivalent of this name, however, is *Artakhshathra*, which is not close to the Hebrew form in this book. If the king had been Artaxerxes I (464–424), he would have married Esther in the year when he sent EZRA to Jerusalem (Esth. 2:16; Ezra 7:8), and Esther would presumably have been the queen in NEHEMIAH's day (Neh. 2:1, 6). The only serious alternative to Xerxes is Artaxerxes II (404–359). This identification was urged by J. Hoschander (*The Book of Esther in the Light of History* [1923]) and A. T. Olmstead (*History of Palestine and Syria* [1931], 612–14). The Hebrew form for Artaxerxes, however, is quite different (*ʾartaḥšastāʾ H831*). Moreover, Plutarch's *Life of Artaxerxes II* allows little room for the story of Esther. This king was dominated by the queen mother, Parysatis, who poisoned his wife, Stateira, in the fourth year of his reign (cf. Esth. 1:3). Plutarch relates that Artaxerxes afterward married two of his own daughters.

If Xerxes is the king, it is possible to bring together the biblical and secular records. In the third year of his reign, he called together all the leading men to discuss a campaign against Greece (Herodotus, *Hist.* 7.8), where his father, DARIUS, had been defeated at Marathon in 490 B.C. This assembly could correspond to the one described in Esth. 1, which took place in the third year (1:3). Although the search for Vashti's successor begins at this time, Xerxes does not marry Esther until the seventh year (2:16). In the intervening period he was occupied with the Greek campaign, taking four years to collect his armies (Herodotus, *Hist.* 7.21). He was ultimately defeated by the Greeks at Salamis in 480. The biblical dating indicates that he married Esther on his return. HAMAN's plot against the Jews took place in the twelfth year, which means that the biblical story ends about 473. There is no record of how long MORDECAI and Esther remained in power.

It has been objected that Herodotus and Ctesias speak of Amestris as queen; she was certainly the wife of Xerxes before 482, for in this year their son, the later Artaxerxes I, was born. Amestris was queen mother (i.e., the widow of the former king) during the reign of Artaxerxes I. She also was with Xerxes during part at least of his Greek campaign, and Herodotus (*Hist.* 9.108–12) relates an appalling incident at Saris. Xerxes had an affair with his

Artistic representation of the Persian guard at the Susa palace where Esther lived.

daughter-in-law, and Amestris ordered that the woman's mother (whom she thought responsible) be horribly mutilated.

This incident may be linked to the Esther story, if Amestris is Vashti. Xerxes would have taken at least one wife with him, and, although he had deposed Vashti from being queen during his drunken stupor, he retained her as his wife for the time being. Her mutilation of the woman's mother would have led to her falling out of favor, or even to temporary banishment, and, on his return, Xerxes was ready to take Esther as his new queen. Amestris was clever enough to wait her time and work her way back into favor, perhaps taking advantage of a reaction against Esther and Mordecai after the Jews had killed so many of their enemies. We do not know what happened to Esther eventually.

II. Unity.
The only section in the Hebrew which some believe to break the unity is Esth. 9:20—10:3. This is largely a section that shows how the previously recorded facts of history gave rise to the specific observance of the Feast of PURIM. The historical narrative has shown what actually happened on certain vital days, whereas this section tells how Mordecai selected two of these days for special observance. The recapitulation (Esth. 9:24–25) is intended as no more than a summarizing of the main facts, and cannot fairly be said to be out of harmony with the main body of the book.

The LXX contains 107 extra verses, and these are printed together in many editions of the APOCRYPHA, where the material is numbered as additional chapters attached to the end of the book (see ESTHER, ADDITIONS TO). In fact, the additional material consists of six sections that are to be inserted at various points in the narrative. The actual order of the whole book in the LXX, if one brings together the numberings in the Bible and in the Apocrypha, is as follows: Add. Esth. 11:2—12:6; Esth. 1:1—3:13; Add. Esth. 13:1—7; Esth. 3:14—4:17; Add. Esth. 13:8—15:16; Esth. 5:1—8:12; Add. Esth. 16:1—24; Esth. 8:13—10:3; Add. Esth. 10:4—11:1. These additions appear to be orthodox correctives that, for example, introduce the name of God, absent from the Hebrew. The opening words of Add. Esth. 11:1 state that Dositheus and Ptolemy brought the Letter of Purim in the fourth year of Ptolemy and Cleopatra. This would be 114 B.C., and could be the year when these Greek additions were made. It should be noted that there is a second Greek version of Esther, thought at one time to be the Lucianic recension but now referred to simply as the Alpha-Text, that also includes the Additions. Its relationship both to the LXX and to the MT has been the subject of considerable discussion (see esp. K. H. Jobes, *The Alpha-Text of Esther: Its Character and Relationship to the Masoretic Text* [1996]).

III. Authorship and date.
The book is anonymous. Such references as it contains to writing are to the official court records (Esth. 2:23; 6:1; 10:2) and to what Mordecai wrote when he "recorded these things" and set down the regulations for Purim (9:20, 23, 29–32). It is possible that Mordecai himself was the author. His omission of the name of God would be accounted for if he wished to have his book inserted among the court records. There is no reason to regard Mordecai as a devout man, though he was certainly a strong nationalist. If he is to be identified with Matakas, who is mentioned by Ctesias (F. Jacoby, *Die Fragmente der griechische Historiker* [1923–58], IIIc, 688, F.13 [p. 464]), he had plundered the temple at Delphi on Xerxes' behalf when others refused to do so. He would have been glad at the opportunity to insult a Gentile god. It is possible that a later author used the Persian chronicles when he wanted to write the story of the origin of Purim, and, since the official records would naturally not speak of the Jewish god, the Jewish copyist chose to let them stand as they were.

Various periods have been suggested for the writing of the book. It must have been in circulation for some time before the LXX translation appeared toward the end of the 2nd cent. B.C., but neither Esther nor Mordecai is listed in Sir. 44–50 (180 B.C.). Many believe that it was written under the stress of the persecutions in the time of the Maccabees in the middle of the 2nd cent. It is, however, difficult to account for the total omission of the name of God if the book were composed by an enthusiastic Jew at such a time.

One further suggestion must be noticed, namely, that this book derived from a cultic story that centered in a conflict of deities, namely ISHTAR (Esther) and

Marduk (Mordecai), who were both deities of Babylon, and Humman (Haman) and Mashti (Vashti), deities of Elam. Since some Jewish exiles, such as Daniel and his friends, bore Babylonian names, it is quite possible that Mordecai's name is the equivalent of the common Babylonian personal name, Mardukaia, which contained the name of Marduk, and Esther's name could be linked with Ishtar also. This is not to say that the story was originally cultic. The real objection to the cultic theory is the unlikelihood that the Jews would use a polytheistic Babylonian tale as a ground for a Jewish festival of deliverance; there is no evidence for Purim ever being other than a Jewish feast that the Jews might have adopted.

The earliest postbiblical reference to the Feast of Purim (2 Macc. 15:36) records the victory of Judas Maccabee in 161 B.C. on the thirteenth day of the twelfth month, which is said to be on "the day before Mordecai's day." The date of 2 Maccabees is probably the first half of the 1st cent. B.C. Presumably the book of Esther was known by that time.

IV. Purpose. The apparent purpose of the book is to relate the origin of the Feast of Purim. The narrative gives the historical occasion, the reason for the dates, and the origin of the name (the latter is connected with the Ass. *pûru*, used for a small stone suitable for the casting of lots, Esth. 3:7; 9:24, 26). It is evident, however, that the book serves other religious purposes as well (see below, section VII).

V. Canonicity. The book is included in the third division of the Hebrew Scriptures (the Writings), and is grouped with Ruth, the Song of Songs, Ecclesiastes, and Lamentations, as one of the Five Scrolls. It was one of the books to which the rabbis gave special consideration as to whether it should continue to be counted among the inspired books. The chief argument against it was that it instituted a new festival as obligatory, whereas the law of Moses was believed to have laid down all the festivals. According to the Jerusalem Talmud (*y. Megillah* 70d), the solution found was that the book was revealed to Moses on Sinai, but not written until the time of Mordecai. See also CANON (OT).

VI. Special problems. Most commentators hold that the author had access to information about the Persian court, even though he may have written much later than the period in which he sets his story. Thus references to the plan of the palace correspond with what archaeologists have discovered at Susa. Although this structure was built by Artaxerxes II, he was restoring a palace that had been destroyed earlier. Another palace completed by Xerxes at Persepolis was based on the same general pattern (A. T. Olmstead, *History of the Persian Empire* [1948], 272–73; 422–23). The curtains and hangings in the courtyard (Esth. 1:6) would be attached to the pillars that have been found; the colors of white and blue (1:6; 8:15) were favorite Persian colors. The practice of reclining at the feast (1:6), the inner council of Seven (1:14), the difficulty of access to the king (4:11), the ban on entering the palace in mourning (4:2), the honoring of a favorite by dressing him in royal robes (6:8), the use of couriers for taking important messages (3:13)—these incidental touches are all true to facts that are known from Herodotus and other writers. One therefore approaches problems with a bias favoring the historicity of the book. The following objections may be noted:

(a) Herodotus and Ctesias make no mention of Esther or Vashti, but Amestris appears as queen and later as queen mother. Vashti and Amestris, however, could be the same person (see above, section I).

(b) The writer is so confused over the time scale that he views Mordecai as one of the original captives in 597 B.C. (Esth. 2:5–6), which would make him more than 100 years old. The text, however, could equally refer to his great-grandfather, Kish, the relative pronoun being attached to the last name in the series (2 Chr. 22:9; Ezra 2:61).

(c) Esther 1:1 mentions 127 provinces, whereas Herodotus (*Hist*. 3.89) speaks only of 20 satrapies. Inscriptions of Darius vary between 21 and 29 provinces. There is no doubt that the larger regions, whether called satrapies or provinces, were divided into smaller units, and the small unit of Judah is regularly designated by the same word as is used in Esth. 1:1 (*mĕdînâ H4519*).

(d) According to Herodotus (3.84), the king had to choose his wife from one of seven families. It is not clear from Herodotus whether this was a permanent rule or merely a temporary agreement to satisfy the six other conspirators besides Darius, who had dethroned the previous usurper. Certainly Darius himself married other wives besides one from the seven, and his son Xerxes, who succeeded him, was not the son of this wife.

(e) If Purim had really been instituted by Mordecai, why is it not mentioned until it occurs as "Mordecai's day" in 2 Macc. 15:36? Why are not Mordecai and Esther included in the praise of famous people in Sir. 44–49? However, it is difficult to see where it could have been mentioned in extant literature. In Ezra's day, it would not yet have established itself on an equal footing with the Mosaic festivals, and the book of Ezra does not mention even all of these. One cannot argue too much from the silence of Ben Sirach in Ecclesiasticus, since he also omits Ezra. As a Wisdom writer, he was not especially concerned with individual festivals, and he may not have approved of Mordecai's methods nor of Esther's marriage to a pagan king.

The above are the chief objections that have been brought against the historicity of the book. One cannot here consider subjective objections based on opinions of whether such and such an incident is likely. There is therefore no adequate reason for rejecting the book's presentation of itself as genuine history. (See further J. S. Wright in *New Perspectives on the Old Testament*, ed. J. B. Payne [1970], 37–47.)

VII. Contents. *Chapter 1.* The Persian king at a seven-day feast at Susa for all his chief men deposes queen Vashti for refusing to come in and display her beauty before the men.

Chapter 2. Esther, the adopted daughter of a Jew named Mordecai, is chosen as Vashti's successor. Mordecai discovers a plot to murder the king and passes on the information to Esther, with the result that the plot is foiled.

Chapter 3. Mordecai offends Haman, the new vizier, through refusing to bow down to him, and Haman plans his revenge by massacring all the Jews in the empire. Experts cast the lot (*pur*) to fix a lucky day for the massacre, and a date is chosen eleven months ahead. Haman sends decrees for the massacre throughout the empire.

Chapter 4. Mordecai persuades Esther to intervene, and she explains how dangerous it could be for her to approach the king unbidden. She agrees, on condition that the Jews in Susa fast, and presumably pray, for three days.

Chapter 5. Esther approaches the king and invites him and Haman to dinner. When they come, she repeats the invitation for a second dinner next day (did her courage fail her?). Haman's happiness is marred by Mordecai's refusal to honor him, but his wife suggests that he build a gallows and obtain the king's permission to hang Mordecai in the morning.

Chapter 6. The king, suffering from insomnia, reads the records of his reign and finds that Mordecai had not been rewarded for revealing the plot against him. He makes Haman lead Mordecai in honor through the city the next day.

Chapter 7. At the second dinner, Esther reveals the plot against the Jews and names Haman. The king hangs him on the gallows prepared for Mordecai.

Chapter 8. The king puts Mordecai in Haman's place, and authorizes him to write further decrees allowing the Jews to resist on the day of the massacre.

Chapter 9. The Jews take advantage of this and kill any enemies who attack them. Esther obtains permission for the Jews in Susa to attack their enemies on the next day also. Mordecai then institutes the Feast of Purim on the fourteenth and fifteenth days of the month Adar, which had been days of rejoicing after the abortive massacre on the thirteenth.

Chapter 10. A summary of the greatness of the king and of Mordecai.

VIII. Theology and morals. The absence of the name of God in the narrative does not mean the absence of the hand of God. The whole book traces how the right person was in the right place at the right time. This did not happen automatically, but Esth. 4:16 shows that fasting, which would include prayer, was part of the working out of God's plan. One is not bound to approve of the extra massacre that Mordecai ordered in Susa, including the hanging of Haman's sons (9:13–15). Mordecai was a strong nationalist and a brave man, but his concealment of his Jewish ancestry at first (2:10) may indicate that he was more opportunistic than devout. Moreover, it has been argued that even the character of Esther suffers from moral ambiguity. For the Jews of the DIASPORA, God may have indeed seemed hidden on account of the nation's apostasy. Possibly the author's aim was not so much to give historical information about the origins of Purim, but to encourage the exiled nation with the assurance that the Lord was still at work.

(Significant commentaries include L. B. Paton, *A Critical and Exegetical Commentary on the Book of Esther*, ICC [1908]; C. A. Moore, *Esther*, AB 7B [1971]; J. G. Baldwin, *Esther*, TOTC [1984]; M. Breneman, *Ezra, Nehemiah, Esther*, NAC 10 [1993]; F. W. Bush, *Ruth, Esther*, WBC 9 [1996]; J. D. Levenson, *Esther: A Commentary* [1997]; K. H. Jobes. *Esther*, NIVAC [1999]; A. Berlin, *Esther: The Traditional Hebrew Text with the New JPS Translation* [2001]; L. C. Allen, *Ezra, Nehemiah, Esther*, NIBCOT 9 [2003]. See also S. B. Berg, *The Book of Esther: Motifs, Themes, and Structure* [1979]; D. J. A. Clines, *The Esther Scroll: The Story of the Story* [1984]; M. V. Fox, *Character and Ideology in the Book of Esther* [1991]; M. V. Fox, *The Redaction of the Books of Esther: On Reading Composite Texts* [1991]; T. S. Laniak, *Shame and Honor in the Book of Esther* [1998]; S. W. Crawford and L. J. Greenspoon, eds., *The Book of Esther in Modern Research* [2003].)

J. S. WRIGHT

Etam ee′tuhm (עֵיטָם *H6515*, possibly "place of birds of prey"). **(1)** Son (or descendant or clan) of HUR included in the genealogy of JUDAH (1 Chr. 4:3–4). The reading "These were the sons of Etam" is an emendation based on the SEPTUAGINT and the VULGATE (the latter has *stirps*, "progeny"). The Hebrew text reads, "these the father [*ʾăbî*] of Etam," which is obviously corrupt. Other suggestions include the conjecture "These are the families of Abi-Etam" and the view that "father" here (as elsewhere) indicates the lord or founder of a town. If the latter is correct, then it refers to #2, below.

(2) A town near BETHLEHEM and TEKOA that REHOBOAM fortified after the secession of the ten northern tribes (2 Chr. 11:6; cf. also the LXX addition to Josh. 15:59, which some scholars consider original). JOSEPHUS (*Ant.* 8.7.3) relates that Etam was a very pleasant place c. 50 furlongs (less than 6 mi.) from JERUSALEM, situated in fine gardens "and abounding in rivulets of water." He also states that SOLOMON was accustomed to take a morning drive in his chariot to Etam. According to the TALMUD, the spring of Etam supplied water for the TEMPLE at Jerusalem. This fact probably explains the ancient aqueduct that extends 7 mi. from Jerusalem to three large Hellenistic Roman reservoirs S of Bethlehem, now known as the "pools of Solomon." The lowest pool is fed by a stream called ʿAin ʿAṭan (today Bethlehem gets water from ʿAin ʿAṭan by pipe line).

The aqueduct was constructed before the Christian era and antedates the Roman period. Pontius PILATE probably used it as the last section of his great conduit that brought water into Jerusalem from a distance of either two hundred or four hundred furlongs (cf. Jos. *Ant.* 18.3.2 with *War* 2.9.4). This action aroused the fury of the populace because Pilate had used the sacred money (CORBAN) for public welfare. Apparently the Jews believed that money once dedicated to Yahweh could never be employed for a secular purpose. Etam is generally identified with the nearby Khirbet el-Khokh, only c. 2 mi. SW of Bethlehem. (See H. J. Kraus in *ZDPV* 72 [1956]: 152–62.)

(3) A village in the tribal territory of SIMEON (1 Chr. 4:32). The site is unknown today. Some identify it with #2 above, others with ʿAitum (c. 11 mi. WSW of HEBRON). It was probably located between the NW NEGEV and the Simeon-Judah boundary.

(4) The "rock of Etam" refers to a cliff somewhere in W JUDAH where SAMSON took refuge after slaughtering many PHILISTINES (Jdg. 15:8, 11). This cliff has not been identified. Some believe that it was near #2 above, but the most likely site is ʿAraq Ismaʿin in Wadi Ismaʿin, 2.5 mi. ESE from ZORAH.

R. C. RIDALL

eternal. This English word is often the rendering of Hebrew ʿ*ôlām H6409*, which refers to "duration," both of antiquity and futurity. The term takes color from its context. To speak of a "slave forever" (Deut. 15:17 NRSV) manifestly limits the word to the duration of a human lifetime (cf. NIV). To refer to "the everlasting hills" (Gen. 49:26 NRSV) also obviously limits the word to the geological age of a feature of the landscape (but NIV renders "age-old hills"). On the other hand, when the word is applied to God, his abiding acts, his covenants, promises, and laws, it clearly signifies the eternal and everlasting in the literal and absolute sense of the term. The word often refers simply to a long time; for example, the possession of Canaan (Gen. 17:8); the throne of DAVID (2 Sam. 7:16; 1 Chr. 17:14; in these two contexts we may have a messianic extension of the promise); or Jewish rites and privileges (Exod. 12:14, 17; Num. 10:8). (See further *NIDOTTE*, 3:345–51.)

The Greek adjective *aiōnion G173* is derived from the noun *aiōn G172* ("age") and bears the basic meaning, in consequence, of "belonging to time in its duration," that is, "constant, abiding, eternal." It was found in this meaning in classical Greek, such as Plato (*Rep.* 2:363d), "the fairest reward of virtue being, in their estimation, an everlasting carousal." Biblical and ecclesiastical Greek used the word commonly (in the LXX it is the standard trans. of the Heb. ʿōlām).

In the NT, its most common application is to *zōē G2437*, "life" (Matt. 19:16 et al.). The frequency of its use in Johannine contexts is notable. The significance mingles future and present, for "eternal life" in Christian belief is not only a life of endless duration, but a quality of life in which the possessor shares in God's eternal being by faith. In a careful essay, William Barclay examines the word *aiōnion* in classical and NT contexts, with full analysis of the meaning and its spiritual applications (*More New Testament Words* [1958], 24–32). Eternal life, as he points out in conclusion, were it a mere duration, could become the burden which Tithonus, in the deeply meaningful Greek myth, found it to be. "Life is only of value when it is nothing less than the life of God—and that is the meaning of eternal life." It necessarily follows that it has no termination.

Other NT connections with the adjective include such words as "fire" (Matt. 18:8; 25:41; Jude 7), "punishment" (Matt. 25:46), "destruction" (2 Thess. 1:9), "sin" (Mk. 3:29), "judgment" (Heb. 6:2), "salvation" (5:9), and others. (See further *NIDNTT*, 3:826–33.) A rare word in NT contexts, but common enough at all stages of classical Greek from Homer onwards, is *aidios G132* (Rom. 1:20; Jude 6). See also ETERNITY; IMMORTALITY; LIFE; PUNISHMENT, ETERNAL.

E. M. BLAIKLOCK

eternity. Infinite time, without beginning or end; a timeless state.
  I. Biblical data
  II. Theological analysis
  III. Philosophy of time
  IV. Augustine's view
  V. Some modern views
  VI. Practical application

I. Biblical data. According to Isa. 57:15, God is "the high and lofty One that inhabiteth eternity, whose name is Holy" (KJV). This is the only verse in which the word *eternity* occurs in the KJV. The same Hebrew word ʿ*ad H6329* is found elsewhere, as in Isa. 9:6, "Everlasting Father, Prince of Peace." The most frequent relevant terms in the Bible are Hebrew ʿ*ōlām H6409* and Greek *aiōnion G173* (see ETERNAL; for a detailed study of other Hebrew terms, see G. Brin, *The Concept of Time in the Bible and the Dead Sea Scrolls* [2001]). In addition to these instances of the words *eternal* or *everlasting*, the Bible has much to say about the nature of God. From this other material, even more than from the lexical occurrences, one must learn what eternity means.

The simplest teaching of Scripture is Ps. 90:2, "Before the mountains were born / or you brought forth the earth and the world, / from everlasting to everlasting you are God." This is a denial that God ever began to exist in time. On the surface the words seem to ascribe to God never-ending duration. Involved of course is the divine creation of the world at a point of time in the finite past; practical lessons concerning the certainty of the COVENANT are implied, but the nature of God himself is here characterized as one of infinite duration. See GOD, BIBLICAL DOCTRINE OF.

Both the OT and the NT contain ANTHROPOMORPHISMS and other metaphorical language. God is said to have ears and eyes, and the mountains skip like rams. Metaphorical language is not unusual. Literature and ordinary conversation make frequent use of figures of speech. Therefore, when God is described as one who exists through all time, and is also described as a temporal being, one must determine whether these are figurative anthropomorphic expressions.

Geerhardus Vos notes that the prophets represent God as dwelling in heaven, unlimited by space, and yet they also say that he dwells in Zion and that Canaan is his land. Then Vos continues, "The same relation applies as between Jehovah and time. In popular language, such as the prophets use, eternity can only be expressed in terms of time, although in reality it lies altogether above time" (*Biblical Theology: Old and New Testaments* [1948], 263). One must therefore look beyond the metaphorical expressions.

II. Theological analysis. Time and temporality is usually connected with change and motion. Things in time have a beginning, they develop in stages, and come to an end. But the Bible teaches that God is immutable: "the heavens are the work of your hands. / They will perish, but you remain; / ... your years will never end" (Heb. 1:10–12). The idea of immutability helps us to understand eternity, for if God is immutable, if he has no beginning or end, if he does not change or move, can one say he exists in time? Is not another mode of existence—eternity—necessary? In a discourse on the "Eternity of God," Charnock says: "Time hath a continual succession.... We must conceive of eternity contrary to the notion of time; as the nature of time consists in the succession of parts, so the nature of eternity is an infinite immutable duration. Time began with the foundation of the world; but God being before time, could have no beginning in time. Before the beginning of the creation and the beginning of time, there could be nothing but eternity ... for as between the Creator and creatures there is no medium, so between time and eternity there is no medium (S. Charnock, *Existence and Attributes of God* [1873], 280–82).

That God is not in time seems harder for some people to understand than that he is not in space. No Christian conceives of God as bounded by space, even though space be infinite in extent. Contrariwise, space is in God, or, at least, "In him we live and move and have our being." Even when one says he has his being in God, the literal spatial meaning is not intended. We are not in God as we are in New York or Chicago.

Because it is recognized that God is not in space, and because it is usually supposed that space and time are in some way analogous, it should not be so surprising that God is not in time either, even though time be infinite. Of course, if time and space are not infinite, it is more obviously necessary to maintain that God is not in time. The reason is that if time began at the creation of the world, one must not suppose that God began to exist; therefore he must have an eternal existence outside of time.

III. Philosophy of time. The line of argument begins to clarify that in large measure the discussion of eternity is really an investigation of time. What is time? What a theologian or philosopher says of time will color his view of eternity.

Aristotle said that time is the measure of motion. Bodies move through space, and the number of motion is time. For Aristotle, the physical world always existed; motion never began and will never end; therefore time never began and will never end. In such a view, a god can be both temporal and everlasting, if he were a physical object or were in some way dependent on a BODY. Nontemporal eternity could be asserted of a mathematical theorem or abstract concept, for truth is not a body and does not change. Aristotle's god—the unmoved mover, a pure form, free of all matter—can also be called eternal. Although a Christian cannot accept Aristotle's concept of God, he might accept the definition of time. In this case, God would be called eternal, for obviously the biblical God could not be

This artistic motif in the Church of the Annunciation in Nazareth depicts the Trinity along with the apostles and all believers in Jesus gathering to spend eternity together.

subject to the numbering, or the numerable aspect, of physical motion.

Aristotle will suffice as an example of pagan antiquity. Before considering any Christian thinker, it would be wise to examine a non-Christian philosopher of modern times. Immanuel Kant defined space and time as the two a priori forms of sensory intuition. His meaning can be explained briefly as follows: Ordinary or empirical intuitions, such as the sensations of blue, loud, rough, bitter, acrid, vary from person to person. But all men see everything as in space, and their ideas all change in time. Because the contents of experience are so varied, whereas space and time are the same, it follows that the knowledge of space and time cannot be derived from experience. The history of British empiricism, which made the attempt and failed, supports this conclusion. As a priori forms independent of experience, space and time are not only infinite (as no object of experience can be), but they are also universal and necessary, forming the basis of the necessary truths of mathematics, none of which sort can be learned empirically. Therefore, concludes Kant, space and time are the innate, or as he calls them, the a priori forms of intuition. The contents of experience are poured into the mind, as hot jelly is poured into a jelly glass, and they take the shape of the mind. It is similar to the ordinary phenomenon of perspective on a profounder level. One sees parallel lines converging in the distance. This convergence is due to the mind: it is the way one sees. So too, trees and rocks are in space because that is the way one sees, and sensations follow one another in time because that is the way one arranges them.

A Christian, however, cannot accept Kant's philosophy in toto any more than he can Aristotle's. If he accepts Kant's theory of time, consistency will require him to make God nontemporal. God has no optic nerves, no tongue, no tympanum. God has no sensations. Therefore God, though he may know things as they are in themselves, cannot impose time on them by seeing them. Nor can man impose time on God, because God is not a sensory object to be seen. His status may then be called eternal.

IV. Augustine's view. Secular philosophers, such as Aristotle and Kant, paid no attention to the Christian doctrine of CREATION; on the other hand, Christian theologians usually pay little attention to the nature of time. Hence their ideas of eternity are confused or at least incomplete. AUGUSTINE, however, the great philosopher-theologian of the 5th cent., tried to work out a systematic theory. Rejecting pantheism and emanationism, Augustine asked how God could create the world, time, and change out of nothing, though he himself is immutable. God must be immutable, because if he changed he would become either better or worse, and both are impossible for a perfect Being. The Bible attributes a beginning to created things (Gen. 1:1). Because time is somehow connected with change, it too must have been created and must have had a beginning. No time could have preceded the world, for a preceding time would require God to choose one moment rather than another for the act of creation, and this would have been irrational. But if time began at creation, God himself, because immutable, because unchanging, is eternal, and with respect to him there is no before or after.

Human misunderstandings of eternity arise through the illegitimate comparison of two heterogeneous types of duration. These two modes are based on two types of being: created, changing being, and uncreated, changeless being. Because human beings know virtually nothing about the being of God, they naturally have an incomplete idea of eternity. Human possibilities are largely confined to one's own changing being and time. Time itself, continued Augustine, is difficult enough to understand. Aristotle, brilliant though he was, misunderstood it, for time can be neither motion itself nor its numerable aspect. The same motion can occur in different lengths of time, and those motions are measured by something that is not an attribute of motion. Thus, Augustine spends several pages in his *Confessions* refuting Aristotle.

Augustine's own view begins with the admitted fact that human beings can and do measure time. But they cannot measure what is not present to them. Hence they could not measure past time unless, strangely, it were present. A physical past, such as a motion yesterday, cannot be present. It is past and gone; but the human mind can make the past present intellectually. Human beings remember. The existence and continuity of time, therefore, are the work of the human spirit. It is the nature of mind to preserve a series of past events in the present. Augustine's words are, "In thee, O my spirit, I measure time .... The impression that passing things leave in thee remains when they are gone. It is that present impression that I measure, not the past things. It is that impression that I measure when I measure time. Therefore either that impression is itself time, or I do not measure time" (*Confessions* 11.27).

By thus making time depend on perception and memory—a view roughly similar to that of Kant—Augustine preserves the doctrine that God is eternal. An omniscient Being could not have a series of perceptions one after another, for such a series implies that the mind does not know something and later perceives and knows it. But OMNISCIENCE means that the divine Mind is never ignorant of anything. He neither loses an idea he once had nor gains one he previously did not know. Therefore there can be no temporal succession in God's knowledge. He is not subject to the form of time. Finite beings, who know and do not know, are temporal; but the infinite and omniscient God is eternal.

V. Some modern views.
Contemporary theologians also discuss eternity and time, but it is not clear that they have improved upon the great thinkers of the past. For example, F. R. Tennant produced a massive analysis of time, but "we still lack a theory as to the nontemporal serial order which manifests itself in time" (*Philosophical Theology* [1930], 2:138), and if he does not bluntly deny that God is timeless, at least he denies creation.

Oscar Cullmann, *Christ and Time* (1950), has a chapter entitled "Time and Eternity." It is short and disappointing. The book might better have been called *Christ and History*, for it contains no theory of time, and it is unclear whether or not he thinks that God is eternal. Cullmann makes a sound observation when he remarks that the Scripture nowhere discusses time and eternity in any philosophical manner. As was said earlier, the nature of eternity must be gathered by implication from what the Scripture teaches about God's immutability, independence, and sovereignty. The explicit message of Scripture, instead of stating these implications, uses the idea of eternity for the practical purpose of engendering in the worshipers truth and confidence in God. (See further A. G. Padgett, *God, Eternity and the Nature of Time* [1992]; W. L. Craig, *Time and Eternity: Exploring God's Relationship to Time* [2001]; G. E. Ganssle, ed., *God and Time: Four Views* [2001]; W. Achtner et al., *Dimensions of Time: The Structures of the Time of Humans, of the World, and of God* [2002].)

VI. Practical application.
Because God is eternal, his decrees must be eternal, for he could never have existed without thinking or willing them. He can accomplish his decrees because he is almighty, but he could not be almighty without being eternal. A being who is at times ignorant could not be almighty. See OMNIPOTENCE.

What confidence could we have in any of God's attributes, such as his mercy, wisdom, righteousness, goodness, and truth, unless he were immutable, eternal, and almighty? How could we entertain hope of a resurrection unless God were everlasting? How could we rely on God's covenant, if he were not eternal? The covenant is founded on the eternity of God: "Because God wanted to make the unchanging nature of his purpose very clear to the heirs of what was promised, he confirmed it with an oath. God did this so that, by two unchangeable things in which it is impossible for God to lie, we who have fled to take hold of the hope offered to us may be greatly encouraged" (Heb. 6:17–18).

In times of distress, decline, or apostasy, the doctrine of the eternity of God provides assurance and comfort. The God who never was born cannot die; and although declension and unbelief may corrupt the visible church, the eternal God has said, "I will build my church, and the gates of Hades will not overcome it" (Matt. 16:18). The concept of eternity, the philosophical theories of time, and the carefully extended implications from Scripture may seem to be too technical and far removed from a living religion, but what part of Christianity would remain if God were not eternal?   G. H. CLARK

Etham ee´thuhm (אֵתָם H918, possibly "fort"). The first encampment of the Israelites after leaving SUCCOTH at the time of the exodus (Exod. 13:20; Num. 33:6–7). Its precise location is unknown, but it was on the edge of the wilderness of SHUR (Exod. 15:22), a portion of which was known as the wilderness of Etham (Num. 33:8). Probably it was N of Lake Timsah and formed part of the Egyptian fortifications guarding their eastern frontier (cf. the reference to MIGDOL, "watch-tower," Num. 33:7). The strength of these defenses caused the Israelites to detour S, which led Pharaoh to imagine that they were trapped between the wilderness and the sea (Exod. 14:1–3). (For the view that Etham is a variant of PITHOM, see M. Görg in *ABD*, 2:644.)

A. E. CUNDALL

Ethan ee′thuhn (אֵיתָן *H420*, "long-lived"). **(1)** Son (or descendant) of ZERAH and grandson (or more distant descendant) of JUDAH (1 Chr. 2:6, 8). Because the other sons (or descendants) of Zerah included HEMAN, CALCOL, and DARDA, many scholars identify this Ethan with #2 below. According to C. F. Keil (KD, *Kings*, 56), this passage in 1 Chr. 2 is clearly not concerned with providing "genealogical exactness"; rather, "certain persons and households of [Zerah's family] who had gained historical renown are grouped together without any more precise account of their lineal descent."

(2) A wise man described as an EZRAHITE to whom SOLOMON was compared (1 Ki. 4:31). In this verse Solomon is also said to be wiser than "Heman, Calcol and Darda, the sons of Mahol." According to many scholars, the expression "the sons of Mahol" refers to members of a musical guild and should therefore be translated "the singers" or "the musicians" (see DARDA; MAHOL). In addition, Ps. 89 is attributed to "Ethan the Ezrahite" and Ps. 88 to "Heman the Ezrahite." It is possible that the term Ezrahite is equivalent to "descendant of Zerah" and that therefore this Ethan is the same as #1 above. It has also been argued, however, that the term really means "native" and was used of non-Israelite inhabitants of Canaan (W. F. Albright, *Archaeology and the Religion of Israel*, 5th ed. [1968], 127, 210). If so, the connection (if any) between this Ethan and the son (or descendant) of Zerah becomes more difficult to determine.

(3) Son of Zimmah, descendant of LEVI through GERSHON, and ancestor of ASAPH (1 Chr. 6:42–43; cf. v. 39).

(4) Son of Kishi (or Kushaiah), descendant of LEVI through MERARI, and a musician who served at the left hand of HEMAN (1 Chr. 6:44; 15:17, 19). Heman, ASAPH, and Ethan had the responsibility of sounding the bronze cymbals. Some have thought that this Ethan was the same as #1 above and that both Ethan and Heman were Levites incorporated into the Judahite family of Zerah, but the evidence for such a connection is not strong (see KD, *Chronicles*, 59–61). It has also been argued by many that this Ethan is the same as JEDUTHUN (16:41–42 et al.). G. N. Knoppers suggests that "members of two different tribes claimed Heman and Ethan among their ancestors. The appearance of these well-known names in two different lineages may reflect competing ancestral claims" (*I Chronicles* 1–9, AB 12 [2004], 303).

Ethanim eth′uh-nim (אֵתָנִים *H923*, "ever-flowing [streams]"). The seventh month in the Hebrew religious CALENDAR (later called TISHRI), corresponding to late September and early October (mentioned only in 1 Ki. 8:2, dating SOLOMON's transferral of the ARK OF THE COVENANT to the TEMPLE). The name was borrowed from the Canaanite calendar. The Hebrew word occurs elsewhere as a common noun with reference to rivers that flow the year round, and Ethanim was the month when all but permanent rivers were dry, preceding the early rains.

C. P. WEBER

Ethanus i-thay′nuhs. One of five scribes trained to "write rapidly" and commissioned to record the apocalyptic vision of EZRA on "many writing tablets" (2 Esd. 14:24).

Ethbaal eth-bay′uhl (אֶתְבַּעַל *H909*, "with [him is] BAAL"). The king of SIDON whose daughter JEZEBEL was married to King AHAB of Israel (1 Ki. 16:31). The Bible says nothing more about him, but the ancient historian JOSEPHUS, citing Menander of Ephesus, mentions a drought (cf. 1 Ki. 17) that occurred during the reign of Ethbaal (*Ithōbalos*, with variant spellings, Jos. *Ant.* 8.13.2 §324). He states further that Ethbaal built the cities of Botrys in PHOENICIA and Auza in LIBYA. Elsewhere (*Ag. Ap.* 1.18 §§123–24), Josephus again quotes Menander, who states that Ethbaal was a priest of Astarte (see ASHTORETH), that he killed his predecessor on the throne, Phelles, and that he then went on to reign for thirty-two years.

Ether ee′thuhr (עֶתֶר H6987, perhaps "[place of] fragrance"). A town in the SHEPHELAH within the tribal territory of JUDAH (Josh. 15:42); it was later given to the tribe of SIMEON (19:7; cf. v. 1). Ether is commonly identified with Khirbet el-ʿAter, some 4 mi. NE of LACHISH (see Y. Aharoni, *The Land of the Bible: A Historical Geography*, rev. ed. [1979], 261, 353, 434). Because the Simeonite towns are associated with the NEGEV (19:8), some believe that there were two distinct towns and that the Ether in the latter passage should be identified with Khirbet ʿAttir (see JATTIR), about 8 mi. N of BEERSHEBA (but see Z. Kallai, *Historical Geography of the Bible* [1986], 381 n. 105, 386). Some scholars have argued that Ether (and possibly also TOKEN in the parallel, 1 Chr. 4:32) should be emended to, or is an alternate form of, ATHACH (cf. *HALOT*, 2:906).

ethics in the Old Testament. The terms *ethics* and *morality* derive from Greek and Latin roots that mean "custom." This indicates that in a general sense ethics has to do with that which is in accord with custom. The ethics of any given culture are related to the accepted custom of the majority in that culture. It has to do with questions such as "What to do?" "How do I act?" "What is right?" "What is wrong?" "Why is it right?" and "Why is it wrong?" These and many other questions are addressed in one form or another by the study of what is called *ethics*. What is at stake are the fundamentals of human conduct and how they are played out in daily life.

By contrast, biblical ethics in general and OT ethics in particular are rooted in God. Rather than being based on the opinion of the majority or on the accepted norms of any given society, the biblical text urges the people of God to begin with God. In this context, God is primarily understood as the ultimate King of all and the Judge of all the earth. OT ethics begins with God. Thus, ethics in the Hebrew Bible is God-centered and not human-centered. At its foundation, it has much more to do with God's demands and requirements and less so with human habits and accepted custom. The legitimization of conduct originates in God, who is understood as the universal Judge of all creation. As such, it is important to understand the holistic view of reality present in ancient Israel. For the people of God, worship and religion were not separate from cultural behavior. The Western rift between the so-called "religious" and "secular" was not part of ancient Israelite society. Moral precepts and religious teaching were intimately related and were based on the redeeming work of God.

I. God as the ultimate standard. The highest ethical standard resides in the person of God. The measure of what is good can be found in God's HOLINESS and his perfect will (Exod. 33:19; Rom. 12:2). As D. Bonhoeffer has suggested, one has to examine constantly what is God's will (*Ética* [1968], 24–27). It is not about one's own personal knowledge of good and evil, but about the living will of God. As such, it is clear that the Israelites considered God and his will as absolutely holy. God represents the ultimate standard for HOLINESS and justice. In this regard, though there may be some exceptions in the WISDOM Literature of the OT, ethical teachings were expressed as commands. These were not the result of philosophical argumentation, but rather were the specific injunctions expressed by God himself.

Perhaps the most clear-cut command regarding this ethical dimension of holiness is found in Lev. 11:44–45: "I am the LORD your God; consecrate yourselves and be holy, because I am holy … I am the LORD who brought you up out of Egypt to be your God; therefore be holy, because I am holy." The ideal for every human being is to imitate God. This is the ethical demand par excellence. And to imitate God means to imitate his holiness. God's holiness is expressed in various ways throughout the Hebrew Bible. At times his holy character is signaled by "faithfulness, fidelity" (Heb. *ʾĕmûnâ* H575; see FAITH). At others God is "faithful love, loyal love" (*ḥesed* H2876; see LOVINGKINDNESS and cf. E. Voth, "Hesed," *Encuentro y Diálogo* 2 [1984]: 1–15). God's character also embodies justice (*ṣĕdāqâ* H7407; see RIGHTEOUSNESS). These then are the more practical expressions of God's holiness that each human being must imitate. By imitating God, the end result is a transformation of the human heart. There is a shift from a self-centered universe to a God-centered universe.

Finally, a word must be said about a key phrase in the Leviticus passage quoted above. The injunction to be holy because God is holy is set within the context of liberation: "I am the LORD who brought you up out of Egypt to be your God." It is most interesting to note that both here and in the introduction to the Decalogue (Exod. 20:2), the reality of liberation is present. More about this will be said later. Suffice it to say here that one must be careful not to decontextualize the Hebrew Bible's ethical demands from the context of redemption.

II. Human dignity. It is impossible to deal with all the areas of OT ethics within the parameters of this article. One would have to cover matters such as the meaning of creation, covenant, Deuteronomic formulas, sexual conduct, justice, the role of the king, and many more. (See LAW (OT); TEN COMMANDMENTS; and separate articles on individual topics.) Selection becomes a must. Therefore the concept of human dignity will be the focus of our discussion and other matters will be touched upon as they relate to this more overarching concern.

It would be a mistake to reduce OT ethics to a series of laws, rules, precepts, prohibitions, and demands. OT ethics proposes what can be understood as "relational ethics" or "ethics of relationships." Many have observed that the ethical codes of the OT are primarily concerned with right relationships. The various laws and regulations are not primarily interested in building a restrictive wall or a wall of containment based on abstract ideals that control human conduct. On the contrary, they are primarily concerned with the building and development of relationships. C. Dempsey (*Hope Amid the Ruins: The Ethics of Israel's Prophets* [2000], 20) has commented that "the preservation and continuation of right relationships become the reason for and the fruit of an ethical approach to life that flows not from sole obedience and adherence to law, but rather from first being in right relationship with God and all creation." A right relationship with God and thereby a right relationship between human beings is the concern of the ethical demands present in the Hebrew Bible. It is in this sense that we can speak of human conduct being conformed to the will of God.

For these relationships to develop it is essential to consider the high value that is placed on human dignity. In one way or another the ethical demands have as their background the creational reality. Every human being has been created in the image and likeness of God (see IMAGE OF GOD). Any historical reality that diminishes, restricts, or violates that essential reality represents an attack on God's will. OT ethical teaching seeks to redeem, if necessary, or safeguard, if possible, the creational gift that every human being without distinction has received from God. That is why the issue of human dignity is so crucial to an understanding of OT ethics. (Cf. J. L. León, "Fundamentos de la dignidad humana y de los derechos humanos en el Antiguo Testamento," *Revista bíblica* 1 [1999]: 45–69.)

The Sinaitic Covenant, with the Decalogue as its focal point, represents one body of literature in the OT where the dignity of the human being is a major concern. The Decalogue itself can be seen as a document which addresses the more fundamental relationships of human life. It deals with the sanctity of God as well as with the sanctity of life, matrimony, family, property, and truth. In this regard Hebrew Bible scholarship has recognized for some time that in order to adequately understand the demands of the Decalogue it is necessary to do so in the context of creational theology (Gen. 1–2). The God who expresses his will through these ethical demands is the same God who created the human beings of whom he expects said ethical conduct. See CREATION. As such, these ethical demands, though expressed in another place and at another time, transcend time and place and are applicable to all human beings on planet earth.

As one considers these ethical demands one must not fail to recognize the background that is present in the Hebrew Bible. When Yahweh establishes his covenant with the people of Israel he is being faithful to the promises made to ABRAHAM in the past (Gen. 12:1–3). These promises were about creating a people that would possess a land. Therefore the background to the establishing of the ethical code is the action of Yahweh on behalf of this nation. The action was one of liberating the people from slavery in Egypt, of making it possible for the slaves to become a people with rights to a land, and by extension to live in freedom. The God of the ethical demands is the God of freedom from oppression. He is also the God who frees a people from the land of oppression, accompanies the people on the road, and leads them to a better land. As mentioned above, this is the context that cannot be ignored when considering the ethical demands of the God revealed in the OT.

Once the people are liberated, they need norms and regulations in order to learn to live in harmony with each other in accordance with the COVENANT established by God with them. Therefore this historical reference to the liberation from oppression in Egypt is critical. The God who liberates, who redeems his people, now gives them ethical guidance so that they may continue to live as a free people. In other words, the underlying motive is to restore their human dignity, their freedom, and to help them avoid falling into slavery again. In this sense, one can suggest that ethics in Israel originates in the gift of liberation. Israel must learn to obey the law (law understood in its wider and holistic sense) not in order to be saved, but precisely *because* it has been saved. If you will, obedience to the commandments in the Deuteronomic sense is the only adequate response befitting the liberated people. That is why it is so important to remember the introduction to the Decalogue. If one decontextualizes the Decalogue from its context of liberation, one violates the very essence of the ethical demands made by a liberating God who affirms human dignity. At the same time, the people who are liberated from oppressive slavery in Egypt are invited by way of the covenant to a new and freeing bondage characterized by a relationship with God and with each other.

The Decalogue, as the source for understanding the ethical demands in the Hebrew Bible, points toward the way of freedom and redemption. Its purpose is firmly rooted in God's desire to preserve a redeemed community. The commandments are given after the liberation from Egypt and they point the way toward a life of freedom within the context of a covenant relationship with God. That relationship with God and with each other is possible when human dignity is restored to its creational intent, and OT ethics has everything to do with this restoration.

III. The "other." The idea of an OT ethic of relationship presupposes the existence of the "other." It is interesting to note that whether in the Sinaitic Covenant or in the Deuteronomic Code or in the Holiness Code, the "other" is generally referred to as the alien, the widow, the orphan, the poor. Of course these are categories that point beyond their own personal realities since they are the examples of those who are most marginalized and ignored. OT ethics refuses to give a blind eye to that reality. Paraphrasing E. Levinas (*Du sacré au saint* [1977], 21), the other human being awakens me from my spontaneous sleep-walking, cracks the peaceful and innocent imperialism of my perseverance on self (*me, myself, and I*). My freedom is not the final word, I am not alone. Without announcing her/himself, the Other, the Neighbor, enters my life, naked-faced, exposed. This intrusion, this mess, is my birth to ethics (scruple).

The relational core of OT ethics demands the recognition that the "other" indeed exists. The sanctity of life proclaimed throughout the ethical codes demands that the "other" be recognized and treated with dignity. The Levitical injunction, "love your neighbor as yourself" (Lev. 19:18), which was later incarnated by Jesus Christ, is the basis upon which the wider biblical code of ethics is supposed to be practiced. The commandments, given in a context of liberation, depend on the practice of love. For it is love that transforms the mere avoidance of evil into an active practice of that which is good. There is a fundamental difference between avoiding the doing of evil and the active doing of good as an ethical principle. This active and intentional desire for that which is good is possible when LOVE is present in the recognition of the "other." It is within this framework that the ethics of the OT stand as an indictment against all discrimination, marginalization, and oppression of any human being. No matter how disturbing, dangerous, ugly, different the "other" might be, the ethical call is to recognize Jesus in every human being (Matt. 25:31–46).

Therefore, be it in the Decalogue or in the other ethical codes present in the OT, we find a deep concern for the correct development of relationships on the human level. They must be developed on an equal level and they must be just. All relationships must ultimately reflect God's character and his holiness.

IV. Justice. The prophet MICAH challenged the people of Israel, and by extension all of the human race when he proclaimed: "He has showed you, O man, what is good. / And what does the LORD require of you? / To act justly and to love mercy / and to walk humbly with your God" (Mic. 6:8). From the very birth of Israel, the ethical concern was that justice be practiced at all levels of the society. The Deuteronomic demand is, "Follow justice and justice alone, so that you may live and possess the land the LORD your God is giving you" (Deut. 16:10). Two of the primary elements that God promised Abraham, life and land, are predicated upon the practice of justice. The classical prophetic literature informs us that injustice was prevalent in Israelite society. When the holy will of God is ignored or rejected, injustice shows its ugly face. The ethical demands given by God to the Israelites that would enable them to live in freedom, to live in their own land, are the key to correct relationships on the human level. However, the sense of maintaining and nurturing a right relationship with God and with one another was not always a priority among the Hebrew people. It is for this reason that both the Deuteronomic literature and the prophetic literature are concerned with the issue of justice as an ethical demand. Justice as promise or as obligation appears in the Scriptures at least 800 times—a clear indication of its significance for Israelite society.

If indeed imitating God as the Holy One is the key to knowing what is right and wrong, and by extension, knowing what is a right relationship with God and with each other, then one could argue that in order to live out this reality and to maintain it, there has to be justice. In this sense, justice can be considered the engine for ethical conduct. In fact, some would argue that the presence of justice is the basis for all ethics. The undeniable reality of the "other" demands an ethic of relationship that is based on justice.

Justice in a general sense has first of all to do with human rights. Every human being has rights. Common sense suggests that it is ethically incorrect to deprive others of that which belongs to them. At the same time, if there is a "right" that one possesses, then there is an obligation. The "other" has the same obligation to honor the "right" possessed by her/his fellow human being. It is evident then that justice, much like ethics, is social. It is not an abstract reality, nor something that exists in a vacuum. Justice, or injustice, is always practiced in a social framework. This is very similar to the relational emphasis found in the Sinaitic Covenant in general and the Decalogue in particular. Justice is always present in the context of "my rights versus yours," "my rights versus the rights of society," etc.

In a more particular sense, we now turn our attention to justice as it is understood by the PROPHETS of the Hebrew Bible. There is general consensus that the prophet's understanding and grasp of justice is rooted in the stipulations and requirements already stated in the covenant. What the prophet does is contextualize the ethical demands of the covenant for a new and different situation. However, the prophets being nurtured by the covenant find an inseparable relationship between justice and holiness. In Lev. 19:2 and 15 we have a key ethical teaching that was embraced passionately by the prophets: "Speak to the entire assembly of Israel and say to them: 'Be holy because I, the LORD your God, am holy.... Do not pervert justice; do not show partiality to the poor or favoritism to the great, but judge your neighbor fairly.'"

The prophets of Israel saw and experienced much injustice in their time. This ultimately meant that there was a serious lack of relational ethics within the Israelite society. Thus many of the Israelites became the prey of others who were more powerful. As has been the case throughout human history, it is usually the weak, the disenfranchised, the widow, the orphan, the poor, the alien, and so forth, who suffer in flesh and blood the reality of injustice. It is this reality that moves the prophet to proclaim an ethical message that exposes, denounces, and confronts social injustice not merely as a violation of the accepted law of the land, but as a direct and blatant affront to the holiness of God. The prophet ISAIAH brings to light the injustice against the weak and the oppressed (Isa. 1:15–17; 58:1–7), but he does so in relationship to the holiness of God. For the prophet, the exercise of justice is not merely a matter of human rights. That is only a first step towards true biblical justice. The deeper concern is for the restoration of human dignity whereby the person is restored in a holistic way and is able to live in šālôm *H8934* ("wholeness, well-being"). The ethical demand of the prophet with relationship to justice was that a context had to be created where human beings could truly live out the meaning of šālôm.

The prophetic cry for justice also exposes the corruption of the judges. The entire justice system in ancient Israel had become corrupt. The powerful were able to bribe the judges so that the weak were treated unfairly in the courts of law (Amos 5:12; Mic. 7:3; Isa. 5:23; Jer. 22:3; Ezek. 45:9). The prophets knew the ethical demands present in the covenant (Deut. 1:16–18; 15:4–5) and they expected the judges to obey the stipulations set forth in the ethical code revealed by God. Once again we see that in the final analysis the proclamation is theocentric—God is the measure and the standard for ethical behavior.

Finally, the prophet issues a call against GREED and the unbridled desire to accumulate. This of course is directed to all, rich and poor, powerful and weak alike (Isa. 5:8; Jer. 5:27–28; 6:13). Greed will in one way or another affect the "other." The OT ethic does not accept the practice of greed, be it expressed by the accumulation of land so that there is no living space left for others, or the hoarding of natural resources, or any other way that impinges on the well-being of others.

To conclude, it is quite clear that the ethical demand for justice is also framed within the context of relationship. There is a deep concern for teaching the relationship between the holiness of God and the just treatment of others. As mentioned above, any type of practice that dehumanizes a person, be it through discrimination, oppression, or violation of human rights, is ethically unacceptable and it becomes an affront to the holiness of God and his creational purposes. As such, the ethical demands of the OT are just as relevant today as they were in the times of ancient Israel. These demands should be applied personally, religiously, politically, and structurally at all levels and for all time.

(See further B. C. Birch, *Let Justice Roll Down: The Old Testament, Ethics, and Christian Life* [1991]; W. Janzen, *Old Testament Ethics: A Paradigmatic Approach* [1994]; M. Weinfeld, *Social Justice in Ancient Israel and in the Ancient Near East* [1995]; G. J. Wenham, *Story as Torah: Reading the Old Testament Ethically* [2000]; C. S. Rodd, *Glimpses of a Strange Land: Studies in Old Testament Ethics* [2001]; J. Barton, *Understanding Old Testament Ethics: Approaches and Explorations* [2003]; J. W. Rogerson, *Theory and Practice in Old Testament Ethics* [2004]; C. J. Wright, *Old Testament Ethics for the People of God* [2004]; J. Jensen, *Ethical Dimensions of the Prophets* [2006].)

E. VOTH

ethics of Jesus. Widely lauded, and variously interpreted, the ethics of Jesus constitute not only a standing reproach of human sin and moral weakness but also a vivid picture of the kind of people his followers should and can be. See also JESUS CHRIST VI.B.

   I. Interpretation
      A. Major schools of thought
      B. Principal factors involved
      C. Pointers to proper interpretation
   II. Contents
      A. Negative teaching
      B. Positive teaching
   III. Sanctions

I. Interpretation

A. Major schools of thought

1. Absolutist. A number of interpreters have understood the ethics of Jesus in ways that emphasize the absolute nature of its demands. Though their ideas vary, they have in common that they take the teaching with the utmost seriousness. Yet, for the most part, they fail to relate it in its rigor to life here and now. The following summary may be noted.

(a) The view characteristic of Lutheran orthodoxy is that the ethical teaching is intended not so much as a guide to life but as a means of bringing us to REPENTANCE for our failure to live up to it. (b) The interim-ethic view put forward by J. Weiss and A. Schweitzer is that the rigor of Jesus' ethics was conditioned by his conviction that the eschatological coming of the KINGDOM OF GOD was imminent. The severity of his teaching is explained by the theory that it was intended only as "emergency regulations" for the brief interim period prior to its coming. (c) The extreme dispensationalist interpretation insists that the SERMON ON THE MOUNT, at least, is the ethics of the future kingdom of God, which is to be established on earth subsequent to the SECOND COMING (though it is conceived as having a secondary application to the Christian here and now). (d) Superficially similar to the foregoing is the view held by M. Dibelius and others that the teaching is a declaration of the divine will, unconditioned by any consideration of expediency. As such, however, it is designed to shock people into action. (e) R. Bultmann asserts that the stark demands of Jesus constitute an existential call for decision. (f) Finally, there is the view expounded by scholars such as H. Windisch, and more recently by J. Knox, that the teaching was intended to be rigorous and that its severity should be taken seriously. It must be interpreted faithfully, and applied absolutely and universally. Of those who have attempted to practice it in its full rigor, the most celebrated is L. Tolstoi.

2. Modified. Other interpretations have, in one way or another, modified the ethical teaching of Jesus. Early in the history of the church, for example, the idea of the "double standard" was applied to Jesus' ethics. According to this view, whereas the basic commands apply universally, the advice given over and above these commands is relevant only to those who voluntarily apply them to themselves. Less is therefore expected of the rank and file than of those who, for instance, embrace the "religious" vocation.

Martin Luther, although strenuously repudiating the idea of a double standard, nevertheless argued strongly for the idea of "two realms," in only one of which the rigorous teaching applies—the spiritual realm, by which he understood the sphere of personal relationships. In the temporal realm, that of the Christian-in-relation, special guidance is not needed. The law of the land and the natural law provide all the guidance that is needed.

In other ways the ethical teaching has been toned down. Some have so emphasized the figurative, and especially the hyperbolic, nature of the language in which the teaching was given, as to modify it more or less drastically. Others have interpreted it in the light of the general tenor of Scripture, and have thereby reduced its severity. Some have simply toned it down to make it more practicable.

3. Reinterpreted. Remaining to be considered are methods of interpretation that view the teaching in a wider light than that cast by the words themselves. Some regard Jesus' teaching as commanding or forbidding not merely the particular acts specified, but also any other action of a similar kind. This application of the teaching in terms of acts tends to focus attention on the external side of morality. Others see the particular acts commanded or forbidden as representing the outworking of inner attitudes. These, it is held, should be embodied not only in the acts specified but also in others. This view has a similar effect to the previous one, but focuses attention on the inner attitude rather than on the outer act.

B. Principal factors involved

1. The setting. It is impossible to abstract the ethical teaching of Jesus from its total setting without seriously distorting it. T. W. Manson has shown that the idea of ethics as an autonomous discipline of thought is unbiblical (*The Teaching of Jesus: Studies in Its Form and Content*, 2nd ed. [1935], 285–87). It is important therefore to give attention to some aspects of the religious setting of the ethics of Jesus—law, eschatology, and gospel.

a. In relation to the law. Jesus came not to destroy the LAW but to fulfill it (Matt. 5:17–18). This means, on the one hand, that he endorsed it. This he did, first, by yielding to it an obedience that was unique. Not only in moral matters but also in its wider connotation, Jesus abode by the law (Matt. 17:27; 23:23; Mk. 14:12). Second, he endorsed its teaching, subsuming all under the twofold head of love to God and neighbor (Matt. 22:37–40).

On the other hand, since to fulfill includes in its meaning "to bring to fullness of completion" (F. J. A. Hort, *Judaistic Christianity* [1894], 15), Jesus reinterpreted and reapplied as well as reinforced the law. On his own authority, he rejected scribal interpretations not only of ceremonial matters, such as the SABBATH (Mk. 2:23–28; 3:1–6; Lk. 13:10–17; 14:1–6), FASTING (Mk. 2:18–22), and ceremonial PURITY (Matt. 15:1–20; Mk. 7:1–23; Lk. 11:37–41), but also of moral issues (Matt. 5:21–47). Furthermore, he reinterpreted the role of law in such a way as to elevate its moral principles to a position of eminence greater even than that accorded to them in the OT. He set aside the principle of ceremonial purity (Mk. 7:15, 18–23), stripped away the traditions of men that served to obscure the moral demands of the law (Matt. 15:3–9), and asserted the primacy of moral requirements within the law as a whole (Matt. 12:1–8; cf. 23:23).

In the light of the insistence of the prophets on the worthlessness of ceremony apart from obedience to the moral law, and indeed on the primacy of the latter over the former, this emphasis is not altogether novel. But attention has been drawn by J. I. Packer to the new "depth of exposition" and "stress in application" in the ethical teaching of Jesus (*Our Lord's Understanding of the Law of God* [1962], 9ff.). The former—seen in the obligation to love enemies and to forgive and love others as oneself—arises from the fuller revelation of the character of God in the person of Jesus himself. The latter—seen in the stress on qualities of character such as humility, meekness, and generosity, rather than on externally correct behavior alone—reflects the positive functions of the new covenant that Jesus had come to establish, in contrast to the largely negative functions of the old covenant. See COVENANT, THE NEW.

The newness of the teaching of Jesus should not be overstated. Even the antitheses of Matt. 5:21–48 are concerned with correcting the rabbinic oral law (see MISHNAH) and drawing out the implications of the provisions of the moral law. W. D. Davies describes them in terms of exegesis rather than antithesis. Deeply rooted in the law and the prophets, the ethical teaching of Jesus consists of authoritative pronouncements that draw out the deepest implications of the law of God in the light of a fuller revelation of the character of God. As such, they constitute a moral demand of the highest order, even though—as will be noted later—they are not to be thought of merely in terms of legal requirements.

b. In relation to eschatology. Various approaches have been developed under this subject. (1) The theory known as *consistent eschatology*, associated with J. Weiss and A. Schweitzer, marked a vigorous reaction against the depreciation of the eschatological element in the teaching of Jesus that was prevalent at the beginning of the 20th cent. In sharp contrast to the Ritschlian view of scholars such as A. Harnack, who maintained that the eschatological element was merely formal, the shell within which lay the kernel of the moral teaching, it was asserted that "the whole of ethics lies under the concept of repentance—penitence for the past and the determination to live henceforward liberated from everything earthly in expectation of the messianic kingdom" (Schweitzer). A rigorist ethic, such as Jesus taught, could be relevant only for the short interim period of life to be lived under "emergency regulations" before the apocalyptic coming of the kingdom.

This theory, as Dean Inge pointed out, "makes Christ a psychological monster and his character an insoluble enigma." The early church did not so understand his teaching, doubtless remembering his parting words (Matt. 28:18–20). Furthermore, it has been argued that the ethical teaching is not always directly colored by eschatological considerations. Indeed, as C. W. Emmet has pointed out, "where the contents of the teaching might be regarded as determined by the eschatological outlook, the eschatological motive is conspicuously absent" (*Expositor*, 8th ser., vol. 4 [1912]: 429). As already noted, the ethics of Jesus are deeply rooted in the ethical teaching of the OT. See ETHICS IN THE OLD TESTAMENT.

(2) A reaction against consistent eschatology, referred to as *realized eschatology*, is based upon those statements and parables in the Gospels that indicate that the KINGDOM OF GOD has come in the person and work of Jesus. The ethical teaching is therefore set in the context, not of the interim period prior to the coming of the kingdom, but of the kingdom itself.

This view is a necessary corrective to consistent eschatology, avoiding much of the naïveté of the Ritschlian presentation of the ethics of Jesus. For it asserts that divine initiative has been put forward in the coming of Jesus, which has fulfilled the scriptural prophecies. Nevertheless, it fails to do adequate justice to the evidence presented in the Gospels that shows that Jesus spoke in terms of the second advent. Not even the modification of this view indicated by the revision of the term "realized eschatology" to "inaugurated eschatology" can deflect the cutting edge of this criticism.

(3) A view sometimes known as *futurist eschatology* and held by some dispensationalists asserts that

the ethical teaching of the Sermon on the Mount, if not the ethical teaching of Jesus as a whole, is related to the future millennial kingdom to be set up on earth after the second advent (see MILLENNIUM). It would seem, however, that this presentation too fails to do justice to the scriptural data. Only strained exegesis can deny the force of Matt. 12:28, which asserts that the kingdom of God "has come." The references in the sermon to the malevolent activity of persecutors (5:11–12, 44) and the whole context of life in a mixed society cannot be accommodated to the millennial kingdom. The proffered explanation that there is a secondary reference to the life of the Christian in contemporary society is more ingenious than convincing.

(4) Though none of the above-mentioned views commends itself as adequate, each contains some element of truth. Taken together, these point the way to an understanding of the relation between the ethics of Jesus and the kingdom of God. There is surely a sense in which the ethic is rooted in the idea of the kingdom as an eternal fact, independent of all earthly contingencies—nothing less than the sovereignty of God. This explains its absoluteness and the magnitude of its demand: "Be perfect, therefore, as your heavenly Father is perfect" (Matt. 5:48).

At the same time, "realized eschatology" has some contribution to make to the understanding of the teaching. It is evident that it was given for action here and now. Attested by significant signs, the presence of the King was a sure indication that the kingdom of God had come. As the teacher par excellence, Jesus expounded with the full weight of his divine authority the moral principles of the kingdom to those who recognized him for what he was. It is equally clear, however, that the consummation of the kingdom was—and is—still future. Present in the world and dynamically active among people, the kingdom has not yet filled the sphere of human society, and there are inadequate grounds for believing that it will do so, apart from direct divine intervention. Therefore, Jesus' ethics can best be interpreted in terms of the dynamic concept of God's rule that has already manifested itself in his person, but will come to its consummation only as a result of new eschatological action (cf. G. E. Ladd, *Jesus and the Kingdom* [1964], 274–300). See also ESCHATOLOGY.

c. In relation to the gospel. There are many who see the ethical teaching of Jesus as the heart, if not the sum and substance, of the Christian message. This has been particularly true of liberal Protestantism, as exemplified in A. von Harnack and the exponents of the "social gospel."

A necessary corrective to this view has been provided by the distinction drawn by C. H. Dodd between *kērygma* G3060 ("preaching") and *didachē* G1439 ("teaching")—even if the distinction has been overdrawn at times. See KERYGMA. Religion and ethics, though closely linked, are not to be confused, still less identified. Just as OT ethics had a religious basis and law was a function of covenant, so in the NT ethics and religion are not to be confused, for teaching followed the preaching of the gospel. Does the teaching of Jesus bear out the contention—which needs to be raised not only against liberal Protestantism but also against the New Morality adherents—that Christian ethics is essentially ethics for disciples? There are clear indications that it does.

Attention must be drawn, in the first place, to the fact that the ethical teaching of Jesus is essentially personalistic. He taught on the basis of his own authority ("I say to you"), called men and women to follow him, and evoked a response on the basis not of compulsion nor even of compliance with legal requirements, but of loving and glad obedience to himself (Jn. 14:15). In his teaching, the phrases "because of righteousness" and "because of me" are interchangeable (Matt. 5:10–11). Although he taught moral imperatives and his very precept of LOVE was formulated as a command (Jn. 13:34), and despite the fact that he took his stand on the Mosaic law, yet he was no mere lawgiver, a new Moses and no more. Whereas the law of Moses derived its sanction from the fact that it was also the law of God, the law of Christ (Gal. 6:2) stands in its own right in dynamic relationship to his person.

Furthermore, in his ethical teaching, Jesus called for a radical transformation of character. "Repent and believe the good news" (Mk. 1:15) was his first command, and response to it was, and is, the essential prerequisite. Since he taught that the human heart is the source of moral defilement (Matt. 15:19–20), it is hardly surprising that he called for the transformation of character at its source

(12:33). The tree must be made good if its fruit is to be good.

The ethical teaching of Jesus in the SERMON ON THE MOUNT is clearly set in a context of grace. Addressed to disciples, the ethical demands are preceded by the BEATITUDES, which far from being rewards promised for virtuous behavior, are compelling expressions of divine grace. True, the form critics see this context as the work of the early church; J. Jeremias (*The Sermon on the Mount* [1961]), for example, regards the sermon as an early Christian catechism in which scattered sayings of Jesus were gathered together in what he agrees is a context of grace. Such a setting is, however, in perfect harmony with the general setting of the ethical teaching, which—as the ethics of the kingdom—is the ethics of the new covenant, the way of life of the people of God, and the ethics of the new heart and the new spirit. Only those who have repented and committed themselves to discipleship, those who are the followers of Jesus—as T. W. Manson points out in *Ethics and the Gospel* (1960)—are the proper objects of his teaching.

2. The form. *a. Literary.* There is no evidence to suggest that the ethical teaching of Jesus was delivered systematically. Certainly in its recorded form it bears the character of scattered sayings; even the Sermon on the Mount is not an ethical treatise. Furthermore, since the sayings were often given in response to questions on particular issues, or in the context of situations in life, they express "with dazzling finality one aspect only of eternal truth, and that the aspect which on the particular occasion needed to be emphasized" (S. Cave, *The Christian Way* [1949], 45). It is patently obvious that the teaching thus given was frequently expressed in figurative language. Metaphor and hyperbole, together with simile, parable, and paradox, were used with great effect to give force to the teaching. One may attempt to rationalize a camel going through the eye of a needle, but the speck and the log or the gnat and the camel cannot be interpreted literally—nor can the command to cut off the offending hand or foot, or to pluck out the eye that causes sin.

It is a cardinal principle of literary interpretation, biblical as well as secular, that due attention should be paid to the literary form employed. This is not to say that the meaning is to be toned down, but that it should be understood in accordance with the mode in which it is expressed. It is therefore necessary to recognize metaphor, hyperbole, and the rest, and to interpret accordingly, without in any way lessening the intended force of the teaching. Not always is it easy, especially for occidentals, to recognize oriental use of figurative language. L. Dewar's suggestion (in *An Outline of New Testament Ethics* [1949], 52–53) that the teaching should be interpreted metaphorically when to understand it literally involves a *reductio ad absurdum* remains a subjective criterion. Nevertheless, despite the difficulties, it is clear that just as "seventy times seven" is not to be understood mathematically, so the command to pray in secret is not to be understood so as to forbid public prayer.

b. Didactic. Not only the literary form of the teaching needs to be taken into account; what

The stained-glass windows within the Church of Beatitudes contain the statements of blessing from the Sermon on the Mount.

might be called the didactic form must also be recognized. The suggestion made by C. A. Anderson Scott (*New Testament Ethics* [1930]) that the ethical injunctions fall into different categories is worthy of serious consideration. He discerned that a single commandment—love to God and neighbor—underlies the ethical teaching as a whole. Alongside this mandate are numerous examples that serve to illustrate specific ways in which love may come to expression. The sayings about turning the other cheek, giving the cloak as well as the coat, going the second mile, and giving to all who ask, are therefore illustrations of the length to which love is prepared to go in typical situations. It would clearly run contrary to the general tenor of the teaching of Jesus to interpret such sayings merely as legal requirements to be interpreted literally and obeyed formally. Rather, they would seem to be examples of the kind of response that those obedient to the command to love will be prepared to give in provoking circumstances. The guidance provided by such examples must, however, be balanced by other guidance given. For example, it can hardly be disputed that there are circumstances in which we are expected not to "give" (cf. Matt. 7:6).

In addition to the mandate and examples, Anderson Scott finds *consilia* that he regards as sayings giving urgent advice to particular people in particular circumstances. They are, therefore, not to be taken as necessarily incumbent upon everyone. Jesus' command to the rich young ruler to sell his possessions and give all to the poor was addressed to him personally in the light of his particular spiritual condition and is not to be generalized. This distinction should not be confused with the distinction between basic commands incumbent upon all and additional advice that is voluntary. The latter distinction has served only to produce a double standard with its concomitant, the acquisition of merit for going beyond obedience to the commands laid upon all. The former approach is an aid to seeing more clearly the central thrust of Jesus' ethical teaching and the kind of practical application that may be given to it.

The emphasis upon love as the central and governing factor in Jesus' ethics is sharply distinct from the view maintained by exponents of a relative morality who advocate that "love" is the guide to moral decisions. For the love of Jesus' teaching is the love of the Father, which demands religious expression as well as ethical activism; there is no religionless ethic in the Gospels.

C. Pointers to proper interpretation. The ethical teaching of Jesus was clearly intended to be taken seriously. With all the weight of his messianic and divine authority, Jesus reasserted the fundamental moral principles of the Law and the Prophets. In doing so he focused OT imperatives with a new intensity, showing that these extended to thought as well as act, to motive as well as deed. With striking clarity, he revealed the moral demands of the kingdom of God that was now active in his person, and he portrayed with bold strokes the character as well as the conduct appropriate to his followers. Couched in pictorial and vivid language of the Orient, its interpretation calls for a proper understanding of its literary and didactic form. Furthermore, the Christian who reads it in the Gospels as part of the completed revelation of Scripture is duty bound to interpret it in the light of the overall teaching of Scripture.

II. Contents

A. Negative teaching. The ethics of Jesus includes his forthright denunciation of evil. The call to repent (Mk. 1:15), to deny the self (Mk. 8:34), and to follow Jesus involves the repudiation of one way of life in favor of another. By comparison with the teaching of PAUL, little is said in condemnation of sexual sins, which were probably a greater problem in pagan societies. See ETHICS OF PAUL; SEX. Nevertheless, enough is said to show that Jesus regarded as fundamentally evil such things as fornication, adultery, and licentiousness (Mk. 7:21–23), and, in addition, lustful desire (Matt. 5:28).

Theft, murder (including the angry thought or word, Matt. 5:22), and malicious acts of any kind are also condemned, as also is slander or abusive speech (Mk. 7:21–22). A number of attitudes and dispositions also find their place in Jesus' denunciation of evil. These include thoughts that are mental processes calculated to expedite malicious acts—covetousness (the insatiable desire to have more), deceitfulness, jealousy, arrogance, and moral insensibility (7:21–22).

Some of the sins denounced by Jesus can only be described as sins of a religious complexion. Religious observances undertaken in such a way as to foster pride received his condemnation (Matt. 6:1–5; 23:5–7). Nor did he spare the hypocrisy evident among the PHARISEES (Matt. 23). Modern research shows that the Pharisees were, by and large, as outwardly righteous as they claimed to be, and this information has caused some to question the rightness of Jesus' denunciation of them. Their hypocrisy, however, lay not so much in conscious deception as in the moral blindness and self-righteousness that blinded their sensibilities. Theirs may not have been conscious hypocrisy, but it was hypocrisy nonetheless.

B. Positive teaching

1. Personal ethics. In his summary of the law, Jesus provided also a summary of his positive ethical teaching. This is found in the command to love God and neighbor (Matt. 22:37–39) and in the Golden Rule (7:12). Despite parallels in JUDAISM, such teaching was nonetheless unique. Here alone, love to God and love to neighbor are specifically linked together and related to each other. Furthermore, the command to love is given unprecedented preeminence in the teaching of Jesus. Rabbi AKIBA may have quoted the OT (Lev. 19:18) as the summation of the teaching of the law, but he saw it as standing alongside the rest of the law, both written and oral. HILLEL may have used the Golden Rule, but only in its negative form. Moreover, Jesus radicalized love by revealing love in its fullest meaning—not only in his teaching, but also in his life. In particular, he universalized the meaning of love by specifically extending the term *neighbor* beyond the bounds of those who have a claim upon us (Lk. 10:29–37; cf. Matt. 5:43–47). This he demonstrated in his own life through his compassion.

Love to God is a command that is absolute and unqualified. It involves all the heart, soul, and mind. Such a love overrides all other claims and demands the subordination of every lesser love. By comparison, therefore, love for father and mother, wife and children, brothers and sisters, is hatred (Lk. 14:26; cf. Matt. 10:37). Since no one can serve two masters, the love and service of God entails lack of concern for material possessions and prospects. Such things are to be regarded as expendable items in the service of the kingdom of God, and their supply is not to be a matter of excessive concern, but can safely be left in the Father's hands (Matt. 6:19–34; Lk. 12:13–34).

Love for neighbor is inseparably linked with love for God, though it is no substitute for it. In Jn. 15:12 Jesus indicates the extent to which love must go in the context of the fellowship of Christ. Love in the ethical teaching of Jesus is not merely a sentiment of affection; indeed, sentiment is not of primary importance. The parable of the Good Samaritan and the injunctions to do good without counting the cost (Matt. 5:42; Lk. 6:38) show that in essence it is the performance of good to others.

One manifestation of love especially emphasized by Jesus is readiness to forgive others their trespasses (Matt. 6:12–15; 18:21–35; Mk. 11:25; Lk. 11:4; 17:3–4). This element is to be viewed not as the cause but as the result and the assurance of having received divine FORGIVENESS. It is to be exercised without limitation of any kind, though its effect will be conditioned by the degree of willingness on the part of the offending party to receive it. A forgiving spirit combines with the attitudes of humility, meekness, and service as characteristic of the true disciple of Jesus. The meek who inherit the earth (Matt. 5:5) have a capacity to absorb evil and to overcome it with good (5:38–41; Lk. 6:27–29). Anderson Scott has suggested that most of Jesus' injunctions can be grouped under two headings— "Do not press for your rights," and "Do more than your duties."

2. Social ethics. That there is little explicit social teaching in the Gospels is not necessarily because Jesus had a foreshortened view of the future. It does indicate that Jesus was more concerned with the fundamental matter of personal ethics than with the construction of a blueprint or even the enunciation of principles designed to lead to the transformation of society. This is not surprising if he did not come to establish the kingdom in its fullness and if its consummation still awaits his second coming. It is not without significance that attempts to give full form to the kingdom of God on earth have unfailingly ended in disillusionment.

ETHICS OF JESUS

A Roman coin with the image of Emperor Tiberius. The Pharisees inquired about the ethics of Jesus by asking him if it was proper to pay taxes to Caesar (Matt. 22:15–22).

At the same time, since the kingdom is at work in the world, its presence must make itself felt, even as the presence of salt and light cannot be hid (Matt. 5:13–16). This should be true at the physical and material levels of ministry as well as the spiritual, even as the presence of the kingdom in the person of Jesus touched all levels of human need. Granted that Jesus held aloof from political and military affairs, he nevertheless enunciated general principles of love and service within the community of his disciples (Mk. 9:33–37; 10:35–44) and to any who are in need (Lk. 10:30–37), and made pronouncements on several specific issues within the field of social ethics.

a. Duty to the state. The question raised by the Pharisees and Herodians regarding the payment of taxes was clearly designed as a trap to ensnare Jesus (Matt. 22:15–22). His answer not only defeated their purpose but also clearly revealed the duty of his followers to discharge such debts as they owe to the state as well as those they owe to God. In this way Jesus distinguished the secular and the sacred without dividing them, and united the two spheres in which disciples have to live without unifying them (R. V. G. Tasker, *The Gospel according to St. Matthew*, TNTC [1961], 210). Possible tension between the twofold duty was not resolved by this pronouncement, but the implication is clear that duties to the state must not take precedence over duties owed to God, and it can hardly be doubted that Peter and John acted in accordance with this principle (Acts 4:18–20).

b. Marriage and divorce. Another testing question prompted the teaching of Jesus on this subject (Matt. 19:3–9; Mk. 10:2–12; cf. Matt. 5:31–32; Lk. 16:18). Again he avoided involvement in current wrangles, this time by taking his questioners back to the creation ordinance (Gen. 2:24), thus showing MARRIAGE to be a lifelong union not to be dissolved by man. In answer to a rejoinder, he explained the Mosaic concession as necessitated by human "hardness of heart." If Matthew's account is compared with Mark's, it may be seen that further teaching on the subject was given "in the house" in reply to questions from the disciples. The Matthean exception was therefore given to the disciples rather than to the Pharisees. This averts the force of the argument that Jesus would hardly have allowed himself to become embroiled in the Hillel-Shammai controversy by aligning himself with one school—the stricter—that argued that divorce was permissible only in the case of unchastity in the wife.

Some scholars, usually anxious to preserve the absolute indissolubility of marriage, deny the dominical authority of the Matthean exception—but without any objective evidence. Those who accept its genuineness differ in their interpretation of the meaning of *porneia* G4518 (NIV, "marital unfaithfulness"). Some regard it in the light of its use elsewhere in the NT (1 Cor. 5:1) as referring to "marriage" contracted within the prohibited degrees (incest), or understand it to mean prenuptial unchastity. In both these cases, the indissolubility of marriage can be maintained, since in neither case can the "divorce" envisaged be understood as other than a declaration of the nullity of the "marriage" from the beginning. On the other hand, a considerable number of scholars—evangelicals among them—take *porneia* to mean postmarital unchastity, and therefore envisage a situation where the marriage bond is so ruptured as to be beyond repair. In such circumstances, divorce and remarriage are not to be regarded as constituting adultery. If this seems to be a striking conclusion, so too is the recognition of the equal rights of the sexes regarding divorce (Mk. 10:12). Here is something without parallel in Judaism.

Jesus indicated, in reply to the disciples' further question, three categories of those who are exempt from the divine plan for men and women (Matt. 19:12). These may be paraphrased as (1) those constitutionally unfitted for marriage, (2) those involuntarily prevented from marrying, (3) and those who refrain from entering that state to give themselves unreservedly to the work of the kingdom of God. This is however, no elevation of celibacy over marriage, but a statement anticipatory of Paul's aphorism that each person "has his own special gift from God" (1 Cor. 7:7 RSV).

III. Sanctions. The ethical teaching of Jesus is far more than good advice. It is authoritative to the highest degree, and its authority involves sanctions. The most striking of these is the appeal to REWARDS and penalties of an eschatological nature. Rewards are offered for enduring persecution (Matt. 5:12), practicing love (Matt. 6:14; Lk. 14:13–14; 18:22), humility (Lk. 14:10–11), and renunciation (Mk. 10:29–30). Rewards appear to be offered as a quid pro quo and are sometimes graduated according to the extent to which a duty is performed (Lk. 19:17, 19). Punishment is similarly threatened and sometimes graduated (12:47–48).

It has often been pointed out that all this serves to underline the gravity of moral choices, and some have asserted that the rewards offered by Jesus are the inevitable issue of goodness, just as victory is the reward for success in battle. The prominence given by Jesus to the theme of reward still seems reminiscent of Judaism, with its tendency to think of virtue as meritorious.

The problem is eased by noting that Jesus promised rewards only to those who were prepared to follow him from some other motive. The righteous will be astonished by their reward (Matt. 25:31–46); the reward will far outweigh any claim that might conceivably be made (20:1–16); and in fact the most faithful service represents no more than our duty (Lk. 17:7–10). "Reward, in fact, is not reward, but grace" (K. E. Kirk, *The Vision of God* [1931], 144). The essence of the reward is the kingdom itself (Matt. 5:3, 10) and the privilege of discipleship (Lk. 14:26–27, 33), so it is hardly likely to appeal to the self-centered. Kirk's further suggestion that the prominence of the idea of reward is a warning against undue emphasis on "duty for duty's sake" that can only lead to self-satisfaction and pride, is also worthy of notice.

The eschatological element is prominent in the sanctions of Jesus' ethics, and it will not do to regard this element as purely formal, as does A. N. Wilder (*Eschatology and Ethics in the Teaching of Jesus*, rev. ed. [1950]). Since Jesus' ethic is that of the kingdom of God that awaits its final consummation, the life of the disciple is to be lived in the light not only of his first advent but also of his second. The "futurist" eschatology of the Gospels, as well as the "realized" element, is ethical through and through. The Olivet Discourse has as its primary object the exhortation to spiritual and moral watchfulness (Matt. 24–25). The pure will of God lies at the heart of the matter, but this is related by Jesus not only to the past revelation of that will in the Law and the Prophets and to its present manifestation in his person and mission, but also to the future consummation when "he will reward each person according to what he has done" (16:27).

(See further T. Walker, *The Teaching of Jesus and the Jewish Teaching of his Age* [1923]; T. W. Manson, *The Teaching of Jesus* [1931]; W. Manson, *Jesus the Messiah* [1943]; C. H. Dodd, *Gospel and Law* [1951]; H. Windisch, *The Meaning of the Sermon on the Mount* [1951]; P. Ramsey, *Basic Christian Ethics* [1952]; A. M. Hunter, *Design for Life* [1953]; C. F. H. Henry, *Christian Personal Ethics* [1957]; T. W. Manson, *Ethics and the Gospel* [1960]; J. Knox, *The Ethic of Jesus in the Teaching of the Church* [1961]; W. D. Davies, *The Setting of the Sermon on the Mount* [1964]; A. N. Wilder, *Eschatology and Ethics in the Teaching of Jesus*, rev. ed. [1978]; R. W. Longenecker, *New Testament Social Ethics for Today* [1984]; W. Schrage, *The Ethics of the New Testament* [1987]; A. E. Harvey, *Strenuous Commands: The Ethic of Jesus* [1990]; D. Cook, *Living in the Kingdom: The Ethics of Jesus* [1992]; W. C. Spohn, *Go and Do Likewise: Jesus and Ethics* [1999]; G. H. Stassen and D. P. Gushee, *Kingdom Ethics: Following Jesus in Contemporary Context* [2003]; R. Brawley, ed., *Character Ethics and the New Testament* [2007].)

H. H. ROWDON

ethics of Paul. The letters of PAUL are often perceived as theological treatises (see PAULINE THEOLOGY), but in fact they are pastoral documents intended to address specific problems in the churches to which they were sent. As such, the apostle's writings are a major source of ethical Christian teaching.

I. Introduction
II. Theological basis of Paul's ethics
   A. Hope anchored on God's redemptive act in Christ—the eschatological framework of Paul's ethics
   B. Faith as obedient appropriation of God's grace in Christ—the structure of Paul's ethics
   C. Love as the fulfillment of the law—the linchpin of Paul's community ethics
   D. Life in the Spirit—the empowerment for ethics
III. The shape, sources, and substance of Paul's ethics
   A. Conformation to the image of Christ
   B. The Old Testament
   C. Hellenistic moral teaching
IV. Conclusion

I. Introduction. Paul's teaching of JUSTIFICATION by faith raises acutely the ethical question, why be good? It would be easy for Paul's opponents to conclude that he was advocating lawless behavior (Rom. 3:8). If one can break the law and still have salvation, then does GRACE not undo ethics and provide excuse for sin? Even some of Paul's converts misunderstood him—rather badly, if not perhaps conveniently—to mean that "all things are lawful" (1 Cor. 6:12; 10:23) and turned freedom into moral license, while others continued to live in a way that was indistinguishable from their former pagan lifestyle. Furthermore, Paul's teaching about Christ's imminent return and the end of the present world order might have led some believers to downplay ethical concerns.

The actual content of Paul's letters, however, leaves us in no doubt regarding the apostle's moral earnestness. Paul wrote on diverse ethical topics such as personal character formation, sexual ethics, family lives, community relationship, work, stewardship of wealth, and attitude towards outsiders and secular authorities. He was adamant that "the unrighteous will not inherit the kingdom of God" (1 Cor. 6:9–11; Gal. 5:19–24; Eph. 5:5), and he urged his converts to live upright, ethical lives that contrast starkly with their former pagan lives (2 Cor. 6:14—7:1; Rom. 12:1–2; 13:12–14; Eph. 4:17–32). He was appalled, dismayed, and outraged at any behavior that was unworthy of their calling as God's people. He excoriated those who confessed God but lived ethically corrupt lives (Tit. 1:16; cf. 2 Cor. 12:20–21; 13:5). In fact, a substantial portion of Paul's letters was devoted to affirming and clarifying the ethical implications of his gospel, as they were attacked, abused, misunderstood, or disobeyed.

But Paul's ethical exhortations are not merely reactionary. They are also rooted in his gospel. The goal of God's redemptive grace is "to redeem us from all wickedness and to purify for himself a people that are his very own, eager to do what is good" (Tit. 2:14). Therefore, ethical instruction, or *parenesis* (see below), is a regular feature of Paul's letters. Sometimes it is concentrated in a section following the theological exposition of his gospel (Rom. 12:1—15:13; Gal. 5:1—6:10; 1 Thess. 4:1—5:22; Col. 3:1—4:6; Eph. 4:1—6:20); sometimes it is interwoven throughout the letter (1–2 Corinthians; Philippians; the Pastorals). Moreover, even the most theological passages in Paul's letters were often suffused with, if not motivated by, ethical concerns (e.g., Rom. 6; 8; 1 Cor. 15; Phil. 2).

II. Theological basis of Paul's ethics. Paul never formulated a comprehensive ethical system. Much of his moral teaching was in the form of concrete response to specific pastoral situations. Moral issues were discussed sometimes only because there was misunderstanding or disobedience. In addition, Paul's emphasis on the role of the HOLY SPIRIT in Christian conduct gave his ethical exhortation a spontaneity that eschewed detailed regulations such as those found in QUMRAN and rabbinic writings—and even in the OT to some extent.

However, the absence of a systematized code of conduct does not mean that Paul's injunctions are unprincipled, unreflective, or inconsistent. The genius of the apostle is that he does not treat moral problems symptomatically, but perceives with great insight their underlying spiritual causes, and accordingly handles them in the light of fundamental principles of the gospel. Hence the permanent value of his instruction: as the authority of Paul's moral teaching is inextricably bound up with that of his gospel, it cannot be casually disregarded because of changing historical contexts and cultural norms. It continues to instruct us even when details of the original situation which evokes Paul's response are no longer clearly known.

One cannot hope to understand Paul's moral reasoning without seeing its theological grounding. At the same time, Paul's theology is intensely practical, constantly aiming to shape the behavior of his churches. It is not rightly comprehended unless it translates into righteous living. Therefore, to examine Paul's ethic is to wrestle with his theology, and vice versa. In the following we will explore some major features of the theological basis of Paul's ethics. We will relate Paul's theological principles to the three interlocking cardinal Christian virtues: hope, faith, and love. Then we will address various aspects of the life in the Spirit.

A. Hope anchored on God's redemptive act in Christ—the eschatological framework of Paul's ethics.

Paul's ethics—like his theology—is thoroughly eschatological (see ESCHATOLOGY). It is framed, informed, and dominated by two epochal events. The first is the death and resurrection of Jesus Christ, which signaled the end of the present age, a period characterized by the flesh, bondage, sin, and death; at the same time it inaugurated the new age, characterized by the Spirit, freedom, righteousness, and life. The second event is Christ's impending return at the consummation of the new age, which will bring about God's ultimate triumph over all the evil forces of the present age and the believers' final inheritance of the future kingdom in holiness and righteousness (1 Thess. 3:13).

Christians live in the overlap of the present age and the age to come. Baptized and united with Christ in his death and resurrection, they have already participated in the world to come. So great is the contrast with the present age, that Paul employs the terminology of "new creation" (2 Cor. 5:17) to describe the new life of faith and moral renewal, both the personal and the corporate level. Christians are created in Christ for good works (Eph. 2:10). They are renewed in the image of God in righteousness and holiness (Eph. 4:22–24; Col. 3:9–10).

Crucial to this experience is the Holy Spirit, whom God provided as an eschatological sign, a foretaste and guarantee of the future consummation (2 Cor. 1:22; 5:5; Rom. 8:23; Eph. 1:14), bridging the righteousness already received (Gal. 3:2–9) and the righteousness eagerly expected (Gal. 5:5). The Spirit represents God's presence in the believers, both individually and as a community (1 Cor. 3:16; 6:19). By the Spirit God's people are "reborn," "renewed" (Tit. 3:5), and "transformed" into the very likeness of the Lord (2 Cor. 3:18). As they wait for the consummation, the Spirit supplies various gifts and ministries to assist them in their life together (see 1 Cor. 1:7; 12:4–11; Eph. 4:12).

How does this eschatological framework inform Paul's ethics? We may note four principles: (1) By uniting with the crucified Christ, our attachment to the world—as well as the world's power over us—is irrevocably severed (Gal. 6:14). Our true "citizenship is in heaven," from which we "eagerly await a Savior ... the Lord Jesus Christ" (Phil. 3:20). Therefore, in the here and now, we must set our minds on that heavenly realm where Christ reigns and where our lives truly belong (Col. 3:1–2). There is a tension, however, between our heavenly life and earthly existence. Our new life is hid with Christ in God, to be fully revealed only in the eschaton (vv. 3–4). In the meantime, the present created order and earthly obligations (e.g., marriage, gender roles, parenthood, work, and respect for authorities) remain in force.

As life in ADAM still coexists with life in Christ, moral perfection is not possible (cf. Phil. 3:12–14). We need constant reminder to put off the "old self" (lit., "old man," the singular perhaps alluding to Adam, Col. 3:9; Eph. 4:22) and to desist from sin (Rom. 6:12–13). While we live "in the body" (lit., "in the flesh," Gal. 2:20; 2 Cor. 4:11), there is always the danger of indulging the "sinful nature" (lit., "flesh," Gal. 5:13).

In Paul's eschatological scheme, life in Adam is life under the dominion of SIN. Sin is more than the transgression of God's law; it is also a power that enslaves those who belong to the present evil age, with the result that they are bound to transgress the law (Rom. 7:14–20). But those who are in Christ are set free from sin and the law, and thus from that old order with its elemental spirits and enslaving regulations (Col. 2:20). Just as sin is more than breaking commandments, so power over sin is far more than the ability to keep a set of moral codes. With the life-giving Spirit as the guiding principle in the life of the believer, there is a freedom and spontaneity to Paul's ethics that will not reduce righteous behavior to a list of dos and don'ts (cf. 2 Cor. 3).

(2) Since the present world is passing away, there is little point in scrambling for new social positions (1 Cor. 7:17–24, 29–31). Paul applies this principle to MARRIAGE: Christian couples should maintain sexual relationship in marriage (vv. 1–7); those widowed and unmarried need not seek marriage (vv. 8–9); those who are married should not leave their spouses (vv. 10–11); those with non-Christian spouses should try to maintain their marriage, unless the latter determine to leave (vv. 12–16); those who are single or engaged should preferably remain unmarried (vv. 25–38). Paul does qualify his recommendations in view of a person's desire and opportunities (cf. his comments on the slave's opportunity to gain freedom, v. 21). His chief concern is not to insist that Christians must remain in their present status but to set them free for wholehearted devotion to God whatever their present social location.

(3) The sociopolitical order of this age will be swept away by God's eschatological judgment and is even now already heading for its destruction (1 Cor. 2:6; 11:32). Paul shows little interest in "social ethics," and his fullest treatment of the subject of government can be regarded as quietist (Rom. 13:1–7; cf. 1 Tim. 2:2; Tit. 3:1). He does not criticize the SLAVERY system and is prepared to send ONESIMUS, a runaway slave, back to his master. He does not consider it the Christian's duty to correct the social injustice of the day or to curb its immorality, let alone to impose Christian morality on pagans (1 Cor. 5:9–10). Paul's ethical appeal is always directed to the Christian community. Nevertheless, Paul still holds the world accountable to God's moral standard—and hence desperately in need of the gospel. In this regard, Christians can and do impact the world indirectly through their evangelism and character. Hence there is a definite emphasis on the Christians' virtuous behavior to command public respect and to avoid putting obstacles in anyone's path (2 Cor. 6:3; 1 Cor. 9:12; Col. 4:5–6; 1 Thess. 4:12; 1 Tim. 3:7; 6:1; Tit. 2:5, 8; 3:2, 8).

On the other hand, Paul's eschatology renders inoperative those distinctions and conflicts that typically divide humanity in his world: Jews and Gentiles, slave and free, male and female (Gal. 3:28). In Christ there is a new social reality that transcends these social boundaries. Within the believing community, Paul's insistence on Gentiles' being accepted without first becoming Jews, or his stress on the kinship of masters and slaves in the Lord, is a social stand that is every bit as radical and courageous as that of the most progressive civil right leaders. The present sociopolitical order is destabilized from within, thus preparing the way for radical social changes, such as the withering away of slavery.

(4) Finally, the "endurance of hope" is directly connected with "work of faith" and "labor of love" in the transformation of the Thessalonians' lives (1 Thess. 1:3 NRSV). Hope inspires faith and love (Col. 1:5) and upright moral behavior (Rom. 13:11–13; 2 Thess. 2:16–17). In the light of resurrection hope, the Corinthians are to shun bad company, to stop sinning, and to labor for the Lord (1 Cor. 15:33–34, 58). In short, instead of leading to moral quietism, the expectation of the end makes Paul's ethic more intense and urgent, more fully governed by the thought of the judgment seat of Christ (2 Cor. 5:9–10; cf. Rom. 2:1–16; 14:10–12; 1 Cor. 3:8–17; 11:27–32; Phil. 3:14; 1 Thess. 3:13; 5:1–11, 23; 2 Tim. 4:8).

B. Faith as obedient appropriation of God's grace in Christ—the structure of Paul's ethics. FAITH initiates our UNION WITH CHRIST and sustains the whole process of our conformation to Christ's image. Faith has to do with the righteousness that characterizes the Christian life from first to last (Rom. 1:17; also cf. Gal. 3:6–9 with Gal. 5:5). It is never merely a momentary intellectual assent, but a steadfast, obedient reliance on God's grace in Christ which leads to transformed lives. We who have received salvation by grace through faith are "God's workmanship, created in Christ Jesus to do good works" (Eph. 2:10). While faith is not a work, it inevitably issues in good works through love. Moreover, Paul not only speaks affirmatively of "work produced by faith" (1 Thess. 1:3) and the "law of faith" (Rom. 3:27 NRSV), but can even describe the goal of his ministry as leading to the "obedience of faith," a key phrase that frames the presentation of his gospel to the Roman Christians (Rom. 1:5; 16:26 NRSV). Thus a life of faith is a life that is radically separated from sin and oriented to righteousness.

Yet God's grace is always prior in salvation. Without the new creation the new life is impossible. Therefore Paul does not simply urge people to be good; he reminds them that they are people who have been transformed by God's grace and who should live in a way that is worthy of such grace (Phil. 1:27; Eph. 4:1; Rom. 12:1). Their conduct should flow from their identity, working out what God has worked in them (Phil. 2:12–13). This movement from what God has done to how we ought to respond is often summed up under the rubric "indicative and imperative" in discussions of Pauline ethics. Ethical injunctions, or imperative statements, are based upon indicative statements of the Christian's new identity. A clear example is found in Rom. 6:1–14, where the primarily indicative statements of vv. 2–10 are followed by imperative statements in vv. 11–14: as our old self was crucified with Christ so that the body of sin might be destroyed (indicative), we must consider ourselves dead to sin and must not let sin exercise dominion in our mortal bodies (imperative). If we "live by the Spirit, let us keep step in the Spirit" (Gal. 5:25). Similarly, we are exhorted to cleanse out the old leaven because we really are unleavened (1 Cor. 5:7 NRSV).

The very necessity of ethical exhortation makes it clear that living out the new life in Christ does not come automatically. The imperative statements are not, however, a realistic corrective to the high-flying ideals of the indicative statements. Nor do they represent a progress from the indicative whereby the believer becomes more and more sanctified (the indicative already portrays the pinnacle of the believer's new life). Rather, the coexistence of indicative and imperative is a reflection of the eschatological tension between the already of the new creation and the not-yet of the final consummation. For Paul, the Christian has already and truly died to sin and does in fact live by faith, in the Spirit, as a new creation. Yet in the overlapping of the ages, the power of sin, death, and the flesh is still operative. Hence there is also a sense in which this dying and living has not yet been completed. Our obedience, though significant, will always be imperfect. The imperative therefore represents neither a correction nor a completion, but an obedient appropriation and outworking of the indicative. On the basis of grace, we are to live out, by faith, with the enabling of the Holy Spirit, the life of the future in the present age, in which our obedience is constantly threatened by hostile powers. Moral rectitude is consonant with our holy status. Moral carelessness increases the dissonance between our present existence and our true status, and may eventually cast doubt upon the genuineness of our status in Christ (1 Cor. 10:12; 2 Cor. 13:5).

C. Love as the fulfillment of the law—the linchpin of Paul's community ethics.
Life in the new age is primarily life in the new community, the CHURCH. The bulk of Paul's ethical exhortation has to do with the common life of the church, for it is God's purpose "to purify for himself a people that are his very own" (Tit. 2:14). Christians are to do good to all people, including strangers and enemies (Rom. 12:13–14), but especially to the household of faith (Gal. 6:10; cf. 1 Thess. 3:12; 5:15). LOVE seeks the common good of the body of Christ and binds it in the mutual sharing of suffering and honor. So basic is brotherly love to Christian existence that—in language echoing the theme of the new covenant in Jer. 31:31–34 and Ezek. 36:26–27—Paul says the Thessalonians do not need instruction about brotherly love since they have been God-taught to love one another (1 Thess. 4:9). Yet, to underscore the absolute importance of the subject, Paul exhorts them in the very next verse to abound even more in such love!

Since love is the primary characteristic of God (cf. the Trinitarian benediction of 2 Cor. 13:14), love for the brethren is at the very core of Paul's community ethic, the linchpin that holds everything together. Love is the greatest virtue and the perfect bond (Col. 3:14). It heads the list of the fruit of the Spirit (Gal. 5:22). It is "the most excellent way" (1 Cor. 12:31), the absence of which renders even the most spectacular charismatic and virtuous acts utterly valueless (13:1–3).

This law of love can be seen as the overarching principle and goal of Paul's ethical instruction (1 Tim. 1:5). "Faith working through love" characterizes life in the new creation and expresses how God's commandments are to be kept (cf. Gal. 5:6 with Gal. 6:15 and 1 Cor. 7:19). In Rom. 13:9–10, reminiscent of Jesus' own teaching, Paul sums up his ethical instruction with the words of Lev. 19:18: "Love your neighbor as yourself." He explains that love is the fulfillment of the law because love does no wrong to a neighbor. It leads to those spiritual qualities of life against which there is no law (Gal. 5:22–23). Therefore it is the believer's duty to pursue love (1 Cor. 14:1), to do all things in love (16:14), to walk in love (Eph. 5:2), to be devoted to one another in brotherly love (Rom. 12:10), and to owe nobody anything except love (13:8).

The principle of love applies straightforwardly to issues of personal relationships, such as not taking advantage of one's brother (1 Thess. 4:3–10) or loving one's wife as Christ loves the church (Eph. 5:25, 28–29). It also applies to less obvious problems, such as the limitation of one's freedom in communal relationships (1 Cor. 8–10) or the appropriate use of SPIRITUAL GIFTS in corporate worship (1 Cor. 12–14, esp. 14:1–4). Love seeks not what is rightful or beneficial to oneself, but what builds up the community. Indeed, true freedom is found not in self-indulgence or self-elevation but in becoming slaves to one another in love (Gal. 5:13; 1 Cor. 9:19; Phil. 2:3–4). Though Paul recognizes the tremendous spiritual benefit "to depart and be with Christ," he refuses to put that before his responsibility to others. In order to serve the Philippian Christians, even heaven can wait (Phil. 1:21–24)! Again, like Jesus, Paul is especially concerned about love for the weaker brethren (1 Cor. 8:7–13; 12:22–26; Rom. 14:13–16; cf. Matt. 18:6, 10; 25:40, 45). He urges believers not to do anything that might lead the weak into sin or force them to act contrary to their convictions to obey God, even though such convictions are based on deficient knowledge.

While love fulfills the law, it does not make commandments and exhortations superfluous, for they are concrete expressions of love that give shape and substance to the call to love. Nevertheless, love cannot be reduced to carrying out specific good deeds. In 1 Cor. 13:3, Paul can imagine resolute altruism and self-sacrifice without love, for these may stem from a desire for self-aggrandizement. Love involves the motives and affections of the heart, and is something other than, or more than, merely doing deeds that conform externally to what appears loving.

D. Life in the Spirit—the empowerment for ethics. Paul never summons us to live a moral life on the basis of our own abilities. The power of the HOLY SPIRIT is the only means by which we can do God's will. In fact, "life in the Spirit" is perhaps a better designation than "ethics" for Paul. How does the Holy Spirit lead us to righteous living?

While the Spirit's operation is ultimately unfathomable and far exceeds our conscious effort, we are never passive agents in the process of moral transformation. The Spirit does not absolve us of responsibility but engages our hearts and minds and wills to the fullest extent. Instead of replacing human freedom, the Spirit enhances it by fulfilling its potentiality in our intellect, will, and emotion.

(1) Paul does not conceive of life in the Spirit apart from the renewal of the mind. The depraved and futile minds of the pagan lead to all kinds of wickedness and rejection of God (Rom. 1:28–32; 1 Cor. 1:21; Eph. 4:17–19), but the believers' minds are renewed and empowered to discern God's will, to assess what is good, pleasing, and perfect, and to be like God in true righteousness and holiness (Rom. 12:2; Eph. 4:23–24). While knowledge without love only puffs up, love needs to be conjoined with knowledge and discernment to produce the fruit of righteousness (Phil. 1:9–10). The Spirit who enables love is the same Spirit who supplies "spiritual wisdom and understanding" so that we may know and do what is pleasing to God (Col. 1:8–10; cf. 1 Cor. 2:12; 12:8). The minds controlled by the Spirit "have their minds set" on spiritual things (Rom. 8:5–6).

The renewed mind is a crucial part of the new covenant in which God's law is written on people's hearts by the Spirit. See COVENANT, THE NEW. The knowledge of God's will is more than something that can be read off from a law code. It requires Spirit-enabled sensitivity. When Paul discussed a marriage problem in 1 Cor. 7:39–40, he explicitly referred to the Spirit as the source of his opinion. More important, Paul believes that as Christians are enabled by the Spirit to perceive the truth of God's redemptive actions, they would or should logically live the kind of lives for which the gospel saves us. Therefore, though Paul occasionally exerts his authority as an apostle and issues commands, he mostly prefers to draw others to Christ by exhortation, persuasion, and gentleness (1 Thess. 2:7–11; 2 Cor. 12:1–6; 13:10). Even when he has to use commands or threats of punishment, he insists that he is speaking to sensible people who can judge what is right (1 Cor. 10:15; 11:13, 27–31). His constant aim is that one must test what is the will of God and live accordingly (1 Thess. 5:21; 1 Cor. 14:29; Eph. 5:10; 5:15). Without the renewed mind this is impossible.

(2) Life in the Spirit also consists of constant resolve and efforts to "keep in step with the Spirit" (Gal. 5:25). Paul's frequent use of athletic and combat motifs in his moral exhortation underscores the struggle involved in living the Christian life (Phil. 3:13–16; 1 Cor. 9:24–27; Gal. 5:7; Col. 1:28–29; 1 Tim. 4:7–8; 2 Tim. 4:7–8; Gal. 5:17–18; cf. Rom. 8:13–14; Phil. 1:27–28; 2:25; Eph. 6:10–18). Paul writes of the war between the flesh and the Spirit (Gal. 5:17) and is concerned that believers may grow weary and even give up in doing good (cf. Gal. 6:5, 9; 1 Cor. 15:58).

However, Paul does not accept moral stalemate or constantly living in willful sin as an option, let alone an inevitability, as though the Spirit were not sufficient for righteous living. Paul's point is the opposite: through Christ and the Spirit, the power of sin and the weakness of the flesh are defeated. God's people are freed from the power and inescapability of sin, so they must actively take their side with the Spirit as they are caught up in a cosmic moral war against the flesh. Flesh has nothing specifically to do with physicality or sexuality. Nor are flesh and Spirit coexisting anthropological entities that oppose each other. Rather, the war between flesh and Spirit expresses the contrast between the old human order of existence in rebellion against God and the new order in which God's Spirit is powerfully and redemptively at work. Unlike non-Christians who are totally enslaved by the flesh, believers have crucified the flesh and can overcome the flesh and kill the sinful passions by walking in, and being led by, the Spirit, who enables the new life of righteousness (Gal. 5:16, 18, 24; Rom. 8:4–13).

(3) The biggest problem with morality is not so much knowing what to do, nor even being able to do it, but rather desiring to do it. Living a life that is pleasing to God is not just a matter of logical thinking or unswerving resolve, but also something that touches our deepest emotional being. For Paul, the most powerful stimulus and support for ethical living is a heart warmed by the Spirit with thankfulness to God.

Through the Spirit, believers can appreciate the boundless love of Christ which surpasses knowledge (Eph. 3:16–19). God's wonderful love, expressed through Christ's death for us, his enemies, becomes an experienced reality as it is richly poured into our heart by the Spirit. It undergirds the development of character and endurance in the face of difficulties (Rom. 5:3–8), making us "more than conquerors through him who loved us" (8:26–39, esp. v. 37). The sheer wonder of God's love and mercy casts the whole of the Christian life into a context of glowing gratitude and impels us toward ethical actions (cf. 1 Jn. 4:11, 19). Just as thanksgiving, resulting in sacrifice and offerings in response to God's goodness and mercy, was central to OT worship (e.g., Pss. 35:18; 50:23; 54:6; 69:30–33; 95:1–2; 100:4–5; 145:8–10; Isa. 12:1–6; Jon. 2:9), so NT believers are to "offer [their] bodies as living sacrifices, holy and pleasing to God" in view of his mercy (Rom. 12:1; cf. 1 Cor. 6:20). Pauline morality is thus a covenant morality, in which the gracious invitation of God leads to the grateful response of the people. It would be an exaggeration to say that, for Paul, religion is grace and ethic is gratitude—but probably not by much.

Perhaps in reaction to a kind of crass debtor's ethic which says "God has done x and y for me, so I owe him a favor to do x and y for him in return," it is becoming fashionable in recent scholarship to downplay the role of gratitude in Pauline ethics. But this is to ignore the fact that the subject of thankfulness or thanksgiving is mentioned more frequently by Paul than by any other Hellenistic writer, pagan or Christian. Virtually all of Paul's letters begin with a thanksgiving for what God has done for, in, or through the believing community.

Moreover, the numerous references in Paul's letters to the love of God or Christ are surely meant to evoke an emotional response of gratitude. Paul sees ingratitude as the fundamental human rebellion that produces idolatry, the vice that leads to all moral vices (Rom. 1:21–32). Over against this, Christians are to be characterized by thankfulness (Col. 2:7; 3:15; 4:2; 1 Thess. 5:18). Thanksgiving is not only a natural element of worship (1 Cor. 14:16–17; Col. 3:16; Eph. 5:19–20), it must also be an overarching principle of Christian conduct: "Whatever you do, whether in word or deed, do it all in the name of the Lord Jesus, giving thanks to God the Father through him" (Col. 3:17; cf. 1 Cor. 10:31; 2 Cor. 4:15; Eph. 1:12; also 1 Pet. 4:11). Paul even calls down a curse on anyone who has no love for the Lord (1 Cor. 16:22)!

There is little doubt that gratitude is what provides the fire and drive of Paul's own life and ministry. What Paul proclaims, he has first experienced. The love of Christ so overwhelms him that he no longer lives for himself but only for Christ (2 Cor. 5:14; Gal. 2:20); he is deeply conscious that he is what he is because of the grace of God, and this grace sustains him through all hardship and enables him to work more diligently than all the other apostles (1 Cor. 15:10; cf. 2 Cor. 4:1).

Thankfulness also results in imitation of God and the effort to please God (Eph. 5:2). The importance of thankfulness for Christian conduct can be clearly seen in Paul's teaching about the sharing of possessions (2 Cor. 8–9). At the heart of Paul's appeal to the Corinthians for generosity stands thankfulness to the immeasurable generosity of God. Christian generosity is not the result of a legal demand (8:8). The highest possible incentive to be generous is found in the example of Jesus Christ himself, whose sacrificial death on our behalf is the supreme act of generosity that makes us truly rich (8:9; cf. Phil. 2:6–8). It is unthinkable that those who experienced such generosity could be stingy in their collection for the saints. But, in the last analysis, Paul's focus is not on the givers at all. His main concern is that the collection will lead to the overflowing "in many expressions of thanks to God" (2 Cor. 9:12), and he concludes his argument with an exuberant paean of thanksgiving to God for his "indescribable gift" (9:15).

III. The shape, sources, and substance of Paul's ethics.

The attention we have given to the theological principles underlying Paul's ethical teaching serves to emphasize that the specificity and newness of his ethics lies primarily not in its content but in its redemptive historical context and the transforming power of the Spirit in motivating and enabling obedience to God. Paul's theological perspective does not necessarily dictate a totally new ethos and ethic or provide a distinctive source of moral knowledge. In fact, much of Paul's ethical instruction is drawn from his Jewish and Hellenistic cultural backgrounds and appears conventional and uncontroversial. Nevertheless, Pauline morality is not simply a matter of doing the same things as non-Christians but from a different perspective. As we have pointed out above, Paul's theological convictions, such as the eschatological framework and the centrality of love, do lead to a certain distinctiveness in the content and emphases in moral actions. It remains for us to outline some key influences on the substance of his ethical instruction and to indicate in what major ways these are modified or qualified by his theological principles.

A. Conformation to the image of Christ.

Paul's vision of the Christian life is the continual transformation into the image of Christ (2 Cor. 3:17–18; Rom. 8:29; Col. 3:10; cf. 1 Cor. 15:49; Phil. 3:21; Col. 1:15). Put simply, "to live is Christ" (Phil. 1:21). This involves not only "learning Christ" (Eph. 4:20), living our lives for Christ (2 Cor. 5:15; Rom. 14:7–9) and under the law of Christ (1 Cor. 9:21; Gal. 6:2), but also letting Christ live in our lives (Gal. 2:20). There are three key aspects to this kind of living.

(1) We are accountable to the Lord for the way we live. Putting on Christ is opposite to gratifying sinful desires (Rom. 13:14). Paul can talk about his "way of life in Christ Jesus" that agrees with his teaching (1 Cor. 4:17). His use of the phrase "in Christ" or "in the Lord" often implies a certain attitude or course of action. "In Christ" he is constrained to speak with truthfulness and sincerity (Rom. 9:1; 2 Cor. 2:17; 12:19). "In the Lord Jesus Christ" he commands and urges believers to work and earn their bread (2 Thess. 3:12). Christians are to welcome one another "in the Lord" (Phil. 2:29; Rom. 16:2; cf. Phlm.

20). Our bodies are "for the Lord" (1 Cor. 6:13), and union with a prostitute is unthinkable for one who has united himself with the Lord (vv. 15–17). The Lordship of Christ also dominates all levels of human relationship in the Christian community (Col. 3:18—4:1; Eph. 5:21—6:9; Phil. 4:1).

(2) As we are united with Christ, we must act like him. With other NT writers, Paul considers Christ to be a model for imitation (cf. Jn. 13:3–17; 1 Pet. 2:21). There is no agreement on how much Paul knew or cared about the details of character and conduct of Jesus prior to his passion. What is hardly disputed is that Paul saw Jesus' death on the cross as the supreme disclosure of the pattern of loving, sacrificial obedience that becomes paradigmatic for our own obedience and loving actions. In particular, he stressed Jesus' humiliation and self-giving love, his voluntary subordination of personal interest to the needs and well-being of others. Thus whenever Paul mentions Christ as an example to follow, there is almost always reference to the unity and benefit of the church (Col. 3:10–11; Phil. 2:1–11; 1 Cor. 10:31—11:1; Rom. 15:1–3, 7; 2 Cor. 8:8–9; Eph. 4:32—5:2; 5:25–28).

As one who patterned his life after Christ, Paul also presented himself as a model to his churches. He recalled how he, though free and belonging to no man, had made himself a slave for the sake of others (1 Cor. 9:19), showing what it meant in practice to follow Christ, who self-sacrificially took the form of a slave. In fact, Paul considered his own life an embodiment and authentication of the gospel (2 Cor. 4:10–12; 1 Thess. 2:8). He also held up the life and work of his coworkers such as TIMOTHY and EPAPHRODITUS (Phil. 2:19–30) as exemplary. For Paul, many aspects of a life in conformity to Christ—however imperfectly lived and still on a pilgrimage (Phil. 3:12–14)—were more easily caught than taught. Through imitating him and those following the apostolic pattern, his churches would join him in imitating Christ (1 Thess. 1:6; 1 Cor. 11:1; Phil. 3:1, 7). They, too, might become models in turn (1 Thess. 1:7). Because of the importance of modeling, Paul held leaders to a standard that was nothing short of model Christian existence (1 Tim. 3:2–13; Tit. 1:5–9).

(3) Scholars debate strongly how much of Paul's ethic is shaped by Jesus' ethical teaching. Paul's explicit references to Jesus are so heavily focused on his death and resurrection that questions are legitimately raised about his interest in Jesus' pre-passion ministry. In view of the paucity of his explicit quotations of Jesus to deal with moral dilemmas or disputes in his churches, it seems difficult to claim that Jesus' teaching plays a significant role in Paul's ethics. In fact, as Paul deals mainly with Gentile believers standing on this side of the cross and sees everything in the light of Jesus' death and resurrection, the lack of exact or substantial correlation between his teaching and that of Jesus, whose earthly ministry is largely confined to Jews, would not be surprising.

Nevertheless, it would be a mistake to minimize the influence of Jesus' ethical teaching on the apostle. Paul's appeals to certain dominical traditions indicate that he can assume a fair degree of knowledge in his churches regarding Jesus. That he has a repertoire of ethical teachings coming from Jesus seems to be borne out by the statement that he has no word of the Lord regarding the unmarried (1 Cor. 7:25), implying that he does have Jesus' teaching on other subjects. It is arguable, though hard to prove, that Paul seldom quotes Jesus explicitly in his parenesis because Jesus' teaching is for the most part presupposed and uncontroversial, and hence an allusion or echo is sufficient. Thus in Rom. 12–14, even though Paul never quotes Jesus, there are quite a number of very probable echoes of his teachings (cf. Rom. 12:14 ["bless those who persecute you"] with Matt. 5:44 and Lk. 6:27–28; Rom. 12:17–21 ["do not repay anyone evil for evil ... overcome evil with good"] with Matt. 5:39–42; Rom. 12:18 ["Live at peace with everyone"] with Mk. 9:50; Rom. 13:7 ["Give everyone what you owe him: If you owe taxes, pay taxes"] with Mk. 12:14, 17; Rom. 14:10, 13 ["Why do you judge your brother?"] with Matt. 7:1; Rom. 14:13 ["not to put any stumbling block ... in your brother's way"] with Matt. 18:6; Rom. 14:14 ["nothing is unclean in itself"] with Matt. 15:11 and Mk. 7:15).

When Paul does cite Jesus' teaching explicitly, it is perhaps because he feels he is going beyond that teaching in some significant way. Thus in his discussion about divorce in 1 Cor. 7:10–16, he quotes Jesus' authority and distinguishes between the Lord's teaching and his own. In 1 Cor. 9:14 he quotes Jesus' teaching that the workman is worthy of his wages but explains why he does not accept the Corinthians' financial support, in apparent disregard of such teaching.

There are probably echoes of Jesus' teachings in Paul's epistles that are not recorded in the Gospels (1 Thess. 4:17; cf. Acts 20:35). After all, the Gospels do not contain all of Jesus' teachings (Jn. 21:25). We must also remember that when Paul wrote his letters the four Gospels had not been written yet, and hence he could not have cited from a well-known and codified form of Jesus' sayings with the same ease as he could have cited from the OT Scriptures. Finally, as a faithful Jew, Jesus himself would have relied heavily on the OT for his ethical teaching. It is noteworthy that the love commandment from Lev. 19:18, which Paul particularly emphasized as an overarching ethical principle (Rom. 13:8–10), was one that was important to Jesus as well (Matt. 22:39–40). In this way, Paul's reliance on the OT to provide ethical norms was a continuation of Jesus' practice. And it is to the OT Scriptures that we now turn.

B. The Old Testament. Paul expects his converts to observe a standard of ethics that is largely derived from Scripture, however informed and transformed it is by the Christ event (see ETHICS IN THE OT). Given Paul's impressive Jewish credentials (Phil. 3:5; Gal. 1:14; 2 Cor. 11:22), this is hardly surprising. Paul always regards the law as holy and perfectly good (Rom. 7:12). His stricture against the law is not directed to the law per se, but to the tendency to rely on it and attribute to it what only God's gracious act in Jesus Christ can achieve. Even as he insists that Christ has freed believers from the law in its temporary, constrictive, and condemning function (Gal. 3:11, 22–25; 4:1–5), he never repudiates the law as God's holy will for right and wrong. On the contrary, the objective of God's saving action in Christ was the fulfillment of the righteous requirements of the law by those who live according to the Spirit (Rom. 8:4)! The same Paul who speaks of discerning the will of God with reference to the renewal of the mind (12:2) can also speak of knowing God's will and discerning what is best with reference to one's being instructed from the law (2:18). In other words, the renewed mind has the same objective as the law—the doing of God's will.

When forced to think, Paul can be very creative. But on many ethical issues he can simply base his moral judgments on ready-made OT examples and commands as self-evidently normative. In fact, writing to the Corinthians—most of whom were non-Jews—he asserts that the OT is written "for us, upon whom the ends of the ages have come" (1 Cor. 10:11; cf. Rom. 15:4; 1 Cor. 9:9–10). Likewise, even for Gentiles, ABRAHAM is "our forefather" (Rom. 4:1) and a model for faith; the wilderness generation of Israel is "our forefathers" (1 Cor. 10:1) and a paradigm of unfaithfulness. Paul also takes for granted that sexual immorality, idolatry, lying, swindling, coveting, and the like are wrong per se, as these are already condemned in the OT. He frequently uses the characteristic OT metaphor of daily conduct as the "walk" of life. He scatters items of OT prohibitions in his vice lists. In particular, the vice list in 1 Tim. 1:9–11 bears striking resemblance to the Decalogue. In Rom. 13:8–10, he lists the prohibitions from the TEN COMMANDMENTS against adultery, murder, stealing, and coveting as part of the law that love fulfills, and sums up all commandments with the OT injunction that one must love one's neighbor as oneself (Lev. 19:18). Against the surrounding Greek culture, the fundamental OT concept of God as the benevolent creator leads Paul to a high view of the material world. The body, food, work, sex, marriage, and so on are not to be deprecated, but are to be used to the glory of God (1 Cor. 6:20; 10:26, 31; 1 Tim. 4:3–4). The benevolence and impartiality of God also exclude pride and boasting (1 Cor. 3:21; 4:7).

Of course, Paul could not have bypassed centuries of Jewish interpretive traditions and approached the OT with a *tabula rasa*. Paul's moral teaching has much demonstrable similarity with rabbinic writings and Jewish wisdom and apocalyptic literature in the Hellenistic era. But the fact remains that it is the Scriptures—not the sages or other Jewish traditions—to which Paul made his most conscious, direct, and frequent appeal in providing the authority for his own teaching. The OT is the God-inspired manual for "training in righteousness" that will thoroughly equip the believer for every good work (2 Tim. 3:16).

Unfortunately, the OT as a continuing norm for Christian conduct is not all that Paul has said about the law. What creates confusion for interpreters is that Paul does proclaim freedom from certain requirements of the law such as CIRCUMCISION and the dietary rules. By excluding such requirements, the "law" under which Paul sees himself (1 Cor. 9:21) cannot be exactly identical to God's law as found in the OT. Though Paul never explains clearly why some laws are not to be followed and why others are, he seems to work with a common-sense distinction between laws meant just for Jews to preserve their Jewish identity (ceremonial laws) and laws meant for everyone who wants to worship the God of Israel (ethical laws). Already in Jewish DIASPORA literature before Paul, certain fundamental laws, such as those regarding the worship of the true God and sexual ethics, were thought to be universally applicable and were given much more prominent places than the distinctive Jewish observances such as circumcision and dietary laws. Paul's vision of the new humanity in Christ, comprising Jews and Gentiles, leads him to take the further step of abrogating peculiar Jewish boundary-marking requirements. However, there is no hint that Paul forbids Jewish Christians to continue in observing them, and he is himself willing to subject to such requirements for the sake of winning the Jews (1 Cor. 9:20).

Paul also makes a distinction between the letter and the Spirit (2 Cor. 3:6–7; Rom. 2:29; 7:6). He even appears to cite Moses against Moses in contrasting the righteousness by the law and the righteousness by faith (Rom. 10:5–8). This implies that the mere outward fulfillment of the written code is not the same as the deeper obedience that can be achieved only by faith in Christ with the help of the Spirit. Therefore, while God's ethical expectations have not changed substantially, the believer's means and motivation for meeting them have. The law which functions as the authoritative guidance for God's people cannot be the law before Christ or the law without Christ, but only the law understood and lived out in the light of all that Christ represented and accomplished. In this sense, we are under the law of Christ. As a result, Paul often supplies Christological reasons as he reiterates OT commands. Even the commonplace OT prohibitions of idolatry and sexual immorality are supported by Paul with reference to Christ and the Spirit (e.g., 1 Cor. 6:9–17; 10:14–22; 1 Thess. 4:7).

C. Hellenistic moral teaching. Whether directly or through the mediation of Hellenistic Judaism, Paul is familiar with Hellenistic parenetic materials, especially those of STOIC and CYNIC origins. In a broad sense, *parenesis* refers to a popular ancient rhetorical and literary style that loosely strings together conventional moral exhortations of an eclectic nature, or even to any admonition of a general ethical content. The parenetic style is reflected, for example, in Rom. 12:9—13:10. Within the span of some twenty verses, Paul jumps back and forth between the believers' intra-community relationships (12:9–13, 15–16; 13:8–10) and relationships with unbelievers (12:14, 17–21) and the state (13:1–7). He moves quickly through a variety of themes, drawing upon the OT, Jewish, and Greek ethical and wisdom sayings, and the Jesus tradition without any obvious order. Moreover, Paul's general exhortations would seem applicable to any Christian community (cf. also 1 Thess. 5:15–18).

Understood in a narrower sense, and especially when couched in epistolary forms, parenesis usually carries a gently persuasive tone and involves the interplay of three key elements: models, maxims, and memory. Young people are encouraged to imitate models of virtue. Parents and teachers, who are more experienced than their audience, are expected to fit that bill. As noted above, imitation is an important aspect of Paul's ethical instruction. We may further note Paul's emphasis on the father/children relationship (in Christ) between himself and his churches (1 Cor. 4:14–16; 1 Thess. 1:6; 2:7–8, 11) as the context of imitation. As the young are reminded of their prior knowledge about the models and their teaching, they are to act accordingly (1 Thess. 2:9–10; 4:1–2; Phil. 3:1; 4:9).

Since the models only supply the contours of a virtuous life, the parenesis is filled out by maxims, which cover common themes of friends, parents, money, greed, reputation-seeking teachers, attitude to superiors, etc. The topics discussed need not reflect actual inadequacy or vices among the readers, but are included for the sake of reinforcement or reminders because of their perceived importance by the writer.

The maxims are often arranged antithetically. It can be a summary statement like "Hate what is evil; cling to what is good" (Rom. 12:9; 1 Thess. 5:21–22) or more elaborate virtue and vice lists. The passage on the "works of the flesh" in Gal. 5:19–21 is in the form of a traditional vice list, and the "fruit of the Spirit" (5:22–23) is a list of virtues. Likewise, vice and virtue lists are given in Col. 3:5–14 and Eph. 4:17–32. The lists can also occur alone rather than antithetically (cf. Rom. 1:29–31; 1 Cor. 5:11; 6:9–10; 2 Cor. 12:20–21; Phil. 4:8). Related to the virtue lists is the delineation of qualifications and characteristics of good leaders and officials. Paul uses this form prominently in the PASTORAL EPISTLES (1 Tim. 3:2–13; Tit. 1:5–9), perhaps because they are addressed to leaders of established churches (Acts 16:1; Gal. 2:3). Paul expects the kind of life and behavior described to be approved by society (1 Tim. 3:7). Paul likewise uses a related form, the "household codes" (*Haustafeln*), which specify the responsibilities of various members of the household toward one another (Col. 3:18—4:1; Eph. 5:21—6:9; 1 Tim. 5:1–8; Tit. 2:1–10; cf. 1 Pet. 2:18; 3:1–7).

Besides similarity in form, there is considerable overlap in content. Certain items in Paul's vice lists, such as greed or drunkenness, were widely condemned. The "excellent and praiseworthy" items in Phil. 4:8 were generally admired. Some themes in Paul's teaching on brotherly love (such as harmony and unity, sharing of possessions, and promoting one another's honor) can be paralleled in the well-developed Greco-Roman ethic for kin. Paul even writes about self-control (1 Cor. 7:5; 9:25–27) and contentment (Phil. 4:11–12) with the terminology of Stoic philosophers, who sought complete self-sufficiency as the greatest virtue.

Consistent with his belief that God is the creator of all people, Paul has no qualm drawing on Greco-Roman ethical norms. People everywhere have enough intuitive grasp of God's moral standards that they can be said to "know God's righteous decree" (Rom. 1:32). Gentiles are held accountable to God because they have CONSCIENCE as moral guidance and can "do by nature things required by the law" (2:14–15; cf. 1:28; 1 Cor. 11:4, 14). Again, "conscience," and especially (conformity to) "nature," are prominent Stoic themes.

Paul's borrowing from Hellenistic moral teaching has been used to argue that when Paul first founded his churches, he offered little moral direction because of his belief in the imminent return of Jesus. The delay in Jesus' return, though, forced Paul (or his disciples writing in his name) to retreat to a conventional bourgeois ethic, with no significant connection with the proclamation of the gospel. This view is difficult to sustain. Paul does not simply tack ready-made parenetical material onto his letters unreflectively. The diversity of Paul's ethical lists indicates that his parenesis, even when conventional, is often conditioned by specific situations in his congregations.

More important, while Paul follows the form of Hellenistic moral teaching, his content and emphases are often very different, shaped as they are by his gospel. For example, Paul's condemnation of idolatry and sexual immorality stands strongly against the prevailing belief and conduct of the Greco-Roman world. While he utilized the Stoic criterion of what is "fitting" in denouncing homosexual acts, many Stoics would have found his use of such a concept very unusual to say the least. Scarcely less striking is Paul's emphasis on humility. Pagan moralists valued human nobility. A "lowly" attitude (Rom. 12:16) could be highly regarded as a virtue only in light of a God who humbled himself and became a slave. Likewise, the exaltation of love—especially love for the weak—as the greatest virtue is distinctively Pauline.

Paul's insistence on the believers' oneness and equality in Christ (Gal. 3:28) also shapes his household codes in the direction of reciprocity, while Hellenistic philosophers are usually more narrowly concerned about the duties of the subordinate to their superior. Similarly, Paul's emphasis on social virtues and vices can be contrasted to the more individualistic focus of Hellenistic exhortation. Finally, while Paul takes his moral norms from traditional sources, he conceptualizes them very differently. For Paul, the primary criterion for virtue is not conformity to nature (as Stoics teach) but conformation to Christ. For a Stoic, self-sufficiency can be achieved by tapping on one's inner resources, while Paul's sufficiency comes from Christ (Phil. 4:13).

Paul exhorts Christians to carry out their rather traditional responsibilities within the household with repeated use of phrases such as "in the Lord" and "as to the Lord." Furthermore, he is concerned to underscore the eschatological dimension of his parenesis (Rom. 13:11–14; 1 Tim. 6:11, 15; Tit. 2:11–14). He labels his list of virtues "fruit of the Spirit," and the vices, "work of the flesh."

IV. Conclusion. Paul's moral exhortation is integrally related to his theological understanding. It is distinctive primarily in its eschatological context, Christological motivation, and Spirit empowerment. Ethical behavior is the result of, and the grateful response to, God's gracious and truly epoch-making saving act in Christ's death and resurrection. United with Christ by faith and indwelt by the Spirit, Christians are given a new understanding, empowerment, and motivation for meeting all of God's righteous requirements as revealed in the law and actualized in love, especially the kind of love that is patterned after Christ's self-sacrificial love on the cross.

Perhaps Paul has not forged a whole new ethic at the level of material norms. But one can only catch so much of morality in norms. The more morality is understood not just in the "what" but also in the "why" and "how" of behavior, the more the specificity and genius of Paul's ethic stands out, and the more we—despite changed and ever changing historical contexts and cultural values—can learn from the great apostle in delineating our own moral vision that is consonant with faith, hope, and love.

(See further V. P. Furnish, *Theology and Ethics in Paul* [1968]; P. Richardson, *Paul's Ethic of Freedom* [1979]; T. J. Deidun, *New Covenant Morality in Paul* [1981]; V. P. Furnish, *The Moral Teaching of Paul: Selected Issues*, 2nd ed. [1985]; J. P. Sampley, *Walking between the Times: Paul's Moral Reasoning* [1991]; B. S. Rosner, ed., *Understanding Paul's Ethics: Twentieth Century Approaches* [1995]; D. G. Horrell, *Solidarity and Difference: A Contemporary Reading of Paul's Ethics* [2005]; F. Blischke, *Die Begründung und die Durchsetzung der Ethik bei Paulus* [2007]. Note also the bibliography under PAULINE THEOLOGY.) A. CHEUNG

Ethiopia ee´thee-oh´pee-uh. A country referred to also as Nubia, located S of EGYPT, in what is now N Sudan (but modern Ethiopia, known as Abyssinia prior to the 20th cent., lies farther S and E). Ethiopia is often associated with Egypt in the Bible (e.g., Ps. 68:31; Isa. 20:3–5; Ezek. 30:4–5) and is identified as being S of SYENE (Aswan, Ezek. 29:10), the southernmost important city of Egypt (cf. Herodotus, *Hist.* 2.29). The name comes from Greek *Aithiopia* (understood to mean "[land of the] burnt-faced people"; gentilic *Aithiops G134*, "Ethiopian"), which the ancient Greeks applied generally to any region far to the S. The SEPTUAGINT uses this term to render Hebrew *kûš H3932* (gentilic *kûšî H3934*, "Cushite"; see CUSH), and for that reason many English versions translate the Hebrew term as "Ethiopia." The NIV transliterates "Cush, Cushite," but uses "Ethiopian" twice (Jer. 13:23; Acts 8:27).

I. History. The first historical reference to an Ethiopian in the Bible is the incident of the Cushite slave who carried to DAVID the news of ABSALOM's death (2 Sam. 18:21–23, 31–32). There were Ethiopian mercenaries in the army of SHISHAK, a Libyan king of Egypt (see LIBYA), when he invaded Palestine about 918 B.C. (2 Chr. 12:3). An attack on Judah by Ethiopians and Libyans (2 Chr. 14:9–15), led by ZERAH the Ethiopian, was repulsed by King ASA (913–873 B.C.). These attackers may have been mercenaries in the Egyptian army settled in southern Palestine by Pharaoh Shishak. Possibly these mercenaries are also the Ethiopians near the Arabs (2 Chr. 21:16), though some scholars think the reference is to the close contact of the S Arabians with Africans across the RED SEA.

Ethiopian MS of the Bible (18th cent. A.D.).

ETHIOPIA

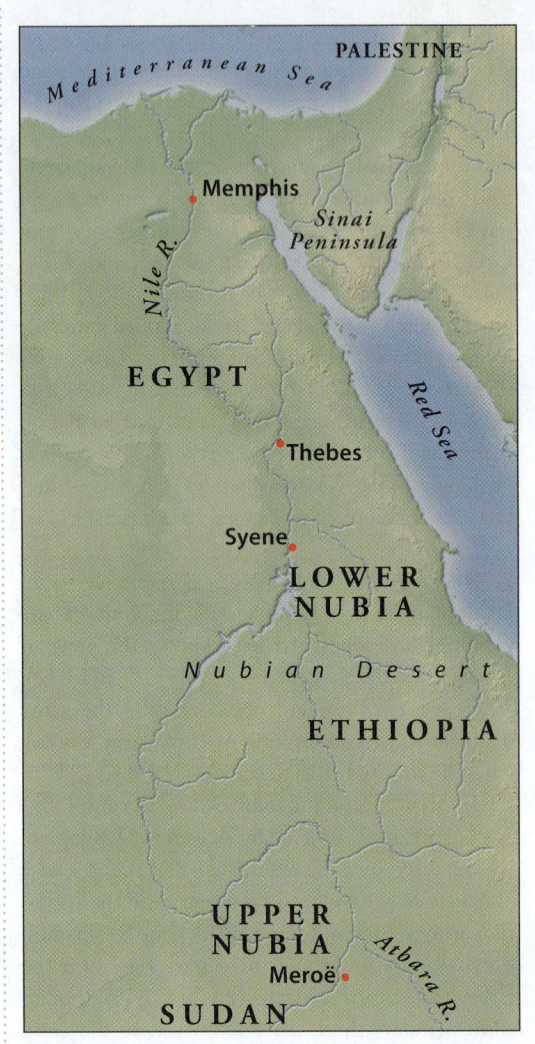

Ethiopia.

According to 2 Ki. 19:9 (= Isa. 37:9), the Cushite king TIRHAKAH attempted to check SENNACHERIB's invasion of Palestine in the time of King HEZEKIAH. The Assyrians mockingly called Tirhakah "a bruised reed" (2 Ki. 18:21 KJV) and defeated him at ELTEKEH. In Egypt, Tirhakah was again defeated by the Assyrian king ESARHADDON and retired to Ethiopia. These defeats may be referred to by Isaiah (Isa. 20:3–5). Tirhakah ruled about 689–664 B.C. as the third and last Pharaoh of the 25th (or Ethiopian) dynasty of Egypt. The Ethiopian control of Egypt under this dynasty explains why Ethiopia was called the "strength" of THEBES, Egypt's southern capital (Nah. 3:9). This brief Ethiopian empire included Egypt for about fifty years. Tirhakah's nephew and successor as king of Ethiopia, Tanut-Amon, was defeated by the Assyrian king ASHURBANIPAL, who destroyed Thebes in 663 (Nah. 3:8).

The *Letter of Aristeas* 13 states that Pharaoh Psammetichus II (593–588 B.C.) used Jewish mercenaries in his campaign against Ethiopia, an incident also mentioned by HERODOTUS (*Hist.* 2.161). He, or a Pharaoh soon after, settled a Jewish garrison on ELEPHANTINE Island to guard the border between Egypt and Ethiopia.

EBED-MELECH, who secured JEREMIAH's release from the cistern (Jer. 38:7–13), was an Ethiopian eunuch who held a high position in the household of King ZEDEKIAH of Judah (597–587 B.C.). He believed in God, and Jeremiah promised that he would be safe in the coming capture of Jerusalem (39:15–17).

King Ahasuerus of Persia (usually identified with XERXES, 486–465 B.C.) included Ethiopia at one extreme of his empire (Esth. 1:1; 8:9; cf. also Add. Esth. 13:1; 16:1); DARIUS I of PERSIA also mentions Ethiopia in his list of provinces. The Ethiopians who were to follow ANTIOCHUS Epiphanes, king of the N, or Syria (175–163 B.C.), after his conquest of Egypt (Dan. 11:43), may have been mercenaries in his army; the exact meaning, however, is uncertain in this context.

Sibylline Oracles 5.194 mentions the capture of Syene by the Ethiopians. This comment may refer to an expedition into Egypt sent by an Ethiopian queen with the title Candace in 24 B.C. (Strabo, *Geogr.* 17.1.54).

The NT mentions "Candace the queen of the Ethiopians" (Acts 8:27). CANDACE was a Nubian royal title, probably corresponding to "queen mother." The queen who ruled at Meroë (then the Ethiopian capital) with this title at that time was Amantitere (A.D. 25–41). That her treasurer should visit Jerusalem and have an interest in Isaiah is not surprising in the light of Jewish contacts with Nubia. Some have suggested that he was a proselyte or even a Jew. See ETHIOPIAN EUNUCH.

II. Features. The Bible several times refers to "the rivers of Cush" or Ethiopia (Isa. 18:1; Zeph. 3:10), presumably the NILE, the Blue and White Niles, and the Atbara. The papyrus boats used on these rivers (Isa. 18:2) are pictured in Egyptian reliefs and paintings, and they are still used in modern Ethiopia. The merchandise of Ethiopia (Job 28:19; Isa. 45:14) included the topaz as a precious product of that land. Egyptian records list among the imports from Ethiopia: gold, precious stones, incense, ebony, ivory, ostrich feathers and eggs, leopard skins, greyhounds, cattle, gazelles, bows, shields, and slaves. Isaiah calls the Ethiopians "tall and smooth-skinned" (Isa. 18:2). Not only are some of the Sudanese tribes tall, but they also have little body hair and very smooth skin. Jeremiah implies that the Ethiopian's skin is black (Jer. 13:23). The prophet also lists Ethiopians with shields among the soldiers of the Egyptian army (46:9); small wooden models of shield-bearing Nubian soldiers have been found in Egyptian tombs.

III. Prophecies about Ethiopia. Some prophecies predicted that Jewish exiles in Ethiopia would return to Palestine (Isa. 11:11; Ps. 87:4). Isaiah expected that Persia would take Ethiopia as reward, poetically called a ransom, for freeing the Jewish captives (Isa. 43:3). Several passages speak of coming judgment on Ethiopia (Isa. 20:3–4; Ezek. 30:4–5, 9; Zeph. 2:12). Ezekiel includes Ethiopians among the forces of GOG that will attack Israel in the end times (38:5). *Sibylline Oracles* 3.320 evidently misunderstood the geography of the Ezekiel passage and misplaced Gog in Ethiopia. According to Amos 9:7, God is concerned with the Ethiopians as with Israel. Other passages (Ps. 68:31; Isa. 45:14; Zeph. 3:10) mention the conversion of the Ethiopians and their inclusion in the kingdom of God.

(See further E. A. W. Budge, *A History of Ethiopia, Nubia, and Abyssinia* [1928]; T. Säve-Söderbergh, *Ägypten und Nubien* [1941]; A. J. Arkell, *A History of the Sudan* [1955]; E. Ullendorff, *Ethiopia and the Bible*, rev. ed. [1988]; D. N. Edwards, *The Nubian Past: An Archaeology of the Sudan* [2004]; D. B. Redford, *From Slave to Pharaoh: The Black Experience of Ancient Egypt* [2004].)

J. ALEXANDER THOMPSON

Ethiopian eunuch. A convert of the evangelist PHILIP (Acts 8:27–40). The ethnic term "Ethiopian" (Gk. *Aithiops* G134) was applied in Roman times to the area of E Africa, S of Egypt. and beyond the mountains of the second cataract. See ETHIOPIA. The Acts account states that this man was "an important official" (Greek *dynastēs* G1541, "lord, ruler, vizier") of CANDACE, the queen of the Ethiopians. Candace was a name used frequently by the African queens of the island of Meroē, but the specific ruler is difficult to identify (the name appears on monuments as hieroglyphic, *kntky*).

The practice of emasculation was widespread throughout the ANE, and such men served as chamberlains in the royal HAREM. It is most unlikely that this man was a Jew because EUNUCHS were forbidden to enter the congregation of Israel (Lev. 21:20; Deut. 23:1). However, there is no doubt that after the Persian settlement of military colonies of Jews in the area of Meroe, numbers of "Godfearers" (Acts 10:2 et al.) sprang up around the local synagogue. The Ethiopian eunuch was probably the treasurer or minister of trade and so traveled widely and could well have known either Hebrew or Greek sufficiently to read the Isaiah scroll. The purpose of the story is to present the oneness of all races and tongues in confession of Christ.

Further investigation into the early history of the missionary spread of the gospel shows that both Judaism and Christianity were more widely distributed at an earlier period than has usually been accepted. The apparent faith of the Ethiopian in the OT prophecy is very important to the understanding of the current interpretation of Isaiah in the apostolic age. It is abundantly clear that the Ethiopian understood the passage in Isa. 53:7–8 as referring not to the people of Israel but to a unique personage, possibly the prophet himself. Philip interpreted the passage to refer to the life and atonement of Christ. The story in the Lukan narrative comes immediately after the events of the scattering of the church under Paul's persecution, the preaching of Philip in Samaria, and the general missionary expansion of the gospel in concentric patterns out from Jerusalem. The fulfillment of this plan is seen in the eunuch's case as the gospel's outreach beyond the borders of the Roman empire to a black man of the African world. The story logically sets the stage for the conversion of the least likely candidate of all, PAUL the persecutor, and through him the presentation of the message of Jesus to the

Gentiles. Historical evidence indicates that it was through such singular converts that the national churches were planted and the universal spread of the message continued.　　　　　　W. WHITE, JR.

Ethiopic language. See LANGUAGES OF THE ANE II.D.

Ethiopic Versions. See VERSIONS OF THE BIBLE, ANCIENT, IV.

Eth Kazin eth-kay´zin (עֵת קָצִין *H6962* [occurring only in the locative form, עִתָּה קָצִין], from עֵת *H6961*, "time," and קָצִין *H7903*, "ruler"). KJV Ittah-kazin. A town on the NE boundary of the tribal territory of ZEBULUN (Josh. 19:13). Its location is unknown, but apparently it was N of GATH HEPHER and S of RIMMON (PLACE); a possible site is Kefr Kenna, some 4 mi. NE of NAZARETH.

Ethma eth´muh. KJV Apoc. variant of NOOMA (1 Esd. 9:35; same as NEBO in Ezra 10:43).

Ethnan eth´nuhn (אֶתְנָן *H925*, possibly "gift"). Son of Asshur (by his wife Helah) and descendant of JUDAH (1 Chr. 4:7; cf. v. 5). Some believe Ethnan may be the name of a town, possibly ITHNAN in S Judah (Josh. 15:23).

ethnarch eth´nahrk (ἐθνάρχης *G1617*, from ἔνος, "a body of people," and ἄρχω, "to rule"). The Greek term appears after the Hellenistic expansion under ALEXANDER THE GREAT and has various meanings. Usually it was the title of a governor of a town or county who ruled for an overlord of a different race or culture than the subjects. Unfortunately, none of the classical historians of the Hellenistic age give its origin. It is used by Strabo and is also found in the APOCRYPHA (1 Macc. 14:47; 15:1–2, where the title is applied to the high priest Simon as a representative of Syria). The chiefs of the seven districts of Roman Egypt bore the title, as did the princes of the Bosporus under Caesar AUGUSTUS. Moreover, after the death of HEROD the Great, his son Archelaus (Matt. 2:22) was appointed ethnarch of Judea by Augustus (Jos. *Ant.* 17.11.4 §317).

The term is used in the NT only once, with reference to the governor of DAMASCUS under King ARETAS (2 Cor. 11:32). PAUL, in recounting his narrow escape from the city, uses this peculiar title of Greek origin. The incident mentioned here appears to be identical to the one narrated in Acts 9:22–26. In the latter text, it is the Jews who waited night and day to kill the apostle. The two texts, however, complement each other; the ethnarch of Damascus could have acted in response to Jewish involvement. Some have argued that the governor himself may have been a Jew, as suggested by the use of the term for Jewish magistrates in the communities of the DIASPORA (e.g., Jos. *Ant.* 14.7.2 §117). More likely, he was the prince of a NABATEAN tribe under the authority of Aretas, who was at the time in control of Damascus. According to J. Taylor, Paul's expression is elliptical, for the apostle uses a title referring to the governor's tribal authority "while having in mind rather his royal function, for which his other title of *stratēgos* would have been more appropriate" (*RB* 99 [1992]: 719–28, esp. 724; see also M. E. Thrall, *A Critical and Exegetical Commentary on the Second Epistle to the Corinthians*, ICC [1994–2000], 2:767–70).
　　　　　　　　　　　　　　W. WHITE, JR.

Ethni eth´ni (אֶתְנִי *H922*, "gift"). Son of Zerah, descendant of LEVI through GERSHON, and ancestor of ASAPH (1 Chr. 6:41). In a somewhat parallel list (see v. 21), JEATHERAI is identified as the son of Zerah, and some emend the text to read "Ethni." Both lists, however, appear to have gaps in them.

Eubulus yoo-byoo´luhs (Εὔβουλος *G2300*, "good counsel"). A Christian who, along with others (CLAUDIA, LINUS, and PUDENS), was a friend of the apostle PAUL during his second Roman imprisonment and who sent greetings to TIMOTHY (2 Tim. 4:21). Apparently a member of the Roman church, Eubulus is otherwise unknown (there is likely no connection between him and a Corinthian presbyter by the same name mentioned in the apocryphal *Acts of Paul* 8.1.1). His Greek name, found frequently in papyri and inscriptions, may imply that he was a Gentile by birth.

Eucharist yoo´kuh-rist (εὐχαριστία *G2374*, "thankfulness, thanksgiving"). The Greek verb *eucharisteō* *G2373* and its cognates occur frequently in the

NT denoting grateful acknowledgment of benefits received especially through the bounty and goodness of the Lord. For this reason, the term *Eucharist* in ancient times came to be applied to the LORD'S SUPPER, probably because of the giving of thanks by the Lord at the time of institution, as he gave his disciples the bread and the cup (cf. Mk. 14:22; 1 Cor. 11:23–24). It first appears as a designation of the communion meal c. A.D. 110 in the letters of IGNATIUS (*Phld.* 4; *Smyrn.* 7). Later in the 2nd cent., IRENAEUS wrote that after the consecration the bread "is no longer common bread, but the Eucharist, consisting of two realities, earthly and heavenly" (*Haer.* 4.18.5). Because of this usage, early liturgies made the thanksgiving, next to the reception of the elements, the most significant part of the celebration, and this no doubt promoted the general adoption of the name. Gratitude for salvation was reflected generally in the prayers and hymns associated with the celebration of the Lord's Supper. (See *ODCC*, 566–69.) P. JEWETT

Euergetes yoo-uhr´juh-teez (Εὐεργέτης *G2309*, "well-doer, benefactor"). In the prologue to ECCLESIASTICUS, Ben Sira's grandson dates his work of translation at the time when he went to Egypt "in the thirty-eighth year of the reign of Euergetes," that is, PTOLEMY VIII (145–116 B.C.). The term was a title of honor borne by some rulers as well as by important citizens whose contributions to society were generally recognized (cf. Lk. 22:25 and see BENEFACTOR).

Eugnostos, Letter of *yoog*-nos´tuhs. Also known as *Eugnostos the Blessed*. A Gnostic document preserved in the NAG HAMMADI LIBRARY (NHC III, 3; a different version in V, 1). Composed in the form of a religious epistle, it describes an invisible, heavenly region that is the dwelling of the Father and three androgynous beings: Immortal Man, Son of Man, and Savior. The document, probably written in Egypt before A.D. 100, may have been the source for a similar, but heavily Christianized tractate, the *Sophia Jesu Christi* (NHC III, 4; also Berlin Gnostic Codex 8502, 3), composed in the form of a dialogue between Jesus and the disciples. (For a parallel English translation of the two works, see *NHL*, 220–43.)

Eumenes yoo´muh-neez (Εὐμενής, "well-disposed"). A king to whom the Romans allotted much of the territory previously held by ANTIOCHUS III (1 Macc. 8:8). The reference is to the king of PERGAMUM, Eumenes II Soter (197–158 B.C.), son of ATTALUS I. Eumenes became the most powerful ruler in ASIA MINOR and brought Pergamene influence to its peak, but toward the end of his reign he fell out of favor with the Romans. (See E. V. Hansen, *The Attalids of Pergamon*, 2nd ed. [1971]; R. E. Allen, *The Attalid Kingdom: A Constitutional History* [1983]; *CAH*, 8, 2nd ed. [1990], 324–34.)

Eunatan yoo-nay´tuhn. KJV Apoc. form of ELNATHAN (1 Esd. 8:44).

Eunice yoo´nis (Εὐνίκη *G2332*, "good victory"). The daughter of LOIS and mother of TIMOTHY (2 Tim. 1:5). Eunice's husband was a Gentile (Acts 16:1), but she was Jewish, as was also her mother. Timothy had not been circumcised (see CIRCUMCISION), undoubtedly because his father was a Gentile, but he was brought up by his mother and his grandmother in the Jewish faith. Paul wrote of Timothy that from a child his mother had taught him to know the holy Scriptures (2 Tim. 3:15). Eunice, her mother Lois, and Timothy were probably converted to Christianity during PAUL's first missionary journey at LYSTRA, where the apostle had been stoned and left for dead. On his second missionary journey, when he returned to Lystra, Paul was evidently so impressed with the fervency of Timothy's spirit that he decided to take him along. Paul said that Timothy witnessed his persecutions and afflictions at Lystra (2 Tim. 3:11). Without doubt the young missionary had a very remarkable mother. (On the question whether Timothy would have been considered Jewish through a matrilineal principle, see the articles by S. J. D. Cohen and C. Bryan, respectively in *JBL* 105 [1986]: 251–68 and 107 [1988]: 292–94. Cf. also F. M. Gillman, *Women Who Knew Paul* [1989].) S. BARABAS

eunuch. A male officer in the court or household of a ruler, and often one who had been castrated. The Hebrew term is *sārîs H6247*, probably a loan word from Akkadian *ša rēši*, "he of the head" (a shorter form of *ša rēš šarri*, "he of the head of the king"), indicating a courtier or confidant (cf. RAB-SARIS). The meaning "castrated one" was secondary, arising from the preference of rulers for such men in offices that involved contact with the women of their households. It is therefore improbable that all those designated with the term *sārîs* in the OT were eunuchs, but in most cases it is not possible to decide by other than the probabilities of the context whether the meaning "official" or "eunuch official" is more appropriate. There are passages in which the sense "eunuch" seems unlikely (e.g., Gen. 37:36; 40:2; 1 Ki. 22:9; 2 Ki. 8:6; 1 Chr. 28:1; Jer. 52:25), whereas in others it seems probable (Esth. 1:10; 2:3 et al.; Isa. 39:7). (See K. A. Kitchen, *Ancient Orient and Old Testament* [1966], 165–66; *NIDOTTE*, 3:288–95. On the question whether NEHEMIAH was a eunuch [cf. the Gk. MSS at Neh. 1:11], see E. M. Yamauchi in *ZAW* 92 [1980]: 132–42.)

Men who had been emasculated were not permitted to enter the assembly of the Lord (Deut. 23:1), yet Isaiah assures eunuchs who are faithful to God's covenant that they will be given "a memorial and a name better than sons and daughters" (Isa. 56:4). Jesus made a distinction between those who are eunuchs (*eunouchos* G2336) in a physical sense and those who make themselves eunuchs (NIV, "have renounced marriage") for the sake of the kingdom (Matt. 19:12). See also ETHIOPIAN EUNUCH.   T. C. MITCHELL

Euodia yoo-oh´dee-uh (Εὐοδία G2337, "prosperity"). KJV Euodias (wrongly interpreting it as a masculine name). A Christian woman in PHILIPPI whom PAUL asked to be reconciled to SYNTYCHE (Phil. 4:2). Clearly both were influential Christians in the Philippian church, where women were prominent from the beginning (Acts 16:12–15; cf. F. X. Malinowski in *Biblical Theology Bulletin* 15 [1985]: 60–63). The cause of their disagreement, whether doctrinal or personal, is unknown, but obviously it had become chronic. Paul's impartial appeal for reconciliation implies that both were responsible for the estrangement. He realized that outside help was needed and asked his "loyal yokefellow" to assist "these women who have contended at my side in the cause of the gospel" (Phil. 4:3; see YOKEFELLOW).   D. E. HIEBERT

Euodias yoo-oh´dee-uhs. KJV form of EUODIA.

Eupator yoo´puh-tor (Εὐπάτωρ, "[born] of a noble father"). The surname of ANTIOCHUS V (reigned 163–162 B.C.), who as a boy succeeded his father Antiochus IV Epiphanes (175–163 B.C.) on the Seleucid throne (1 Macc. 6:17; 2 Macc. 2:20; et al.).

Euphrates yoo-fray´teez (פְּרָת H7310 [Akk. *Purattu*, from Sum. *bura-nuna*, "the great river"]; Εὐφράτης G2371 [Old Pers. *Ufrâtu*; modern names, *Fra Su, Shatt el Fara*). The longest river of W Asia. It rises in the mountains of ARMENIA in modern Turkey, heads W as if to reach the Mediterranean, then swings in a wide bow in SYRIA, eventually joins the TIGRIS to become the Shatt el-Arab, and empties into the Persian Gulf. The Euphrates is some 1,780 mi. long, considerably longer than its companion stream, the Tigris, with which it is often linked in discussion of MESOPOTAMIA (a name that means, "the land between [or in the midst of] the rivers"). Among its tributaries are the Balikh and the Khabur, which are associated with the Euphrates in locating ARAM NAHARAIM (cf. Gen. 24:10; this was the region where LABAN lived and where the city of HARAN was situated, 11:31). The ruins of many ancient cities are found along the river in Iraq; among them are Sippar, Babylon, Kish, Nippur, Uruk (modern Warka, biblical Erech), Larsa, Ur, and Eridu. Geological and archaeological investigations leave the problem of the ancient coastline unsettled.

In the Bible the Euphrates is called "the river Euphrates," "the great river, the river Euphrates," or simply "the River." The Euphrates is named as one of the four streams into which the river of the Garden of Eden divided (Gen. 2:14; see EDEN, GARDEN OF). In the covenant God made with ABRAHAM, the river Euphrates was designated one of the boundaries of the Promised Land (Gen. 15:8; cf. Deut. 1:7; 11:24). Before the conquest of Canaan, the Lord again referred to the Euphrates as one of the borders of the Land of Promise (Josh. 1:4). In his final address to Israel, JOSHUA stated that the fathers of the nation had lived "beyond the River," where they served other gods, but God took Abraham "from the land beyond the River" and brought him to Canaan (Josh. 24:2–3, 14–15). During the monarchy

The Euphrates River in N Mesopotamia. (View to the NE.)

David defeated Hadadezer the king of Zobah when the latter "went to restore his control along the Euphrates River" (2 Sam. 8:3; 1 Chr. 18:3).

Isaiah refers to Assyria as an instrument of judgment against Israel, "a razor hired from beyond the River" (Isa. 7:20), and speaks of a threshing and ingathering of Israel from the river Euphrates to the brook of Egypt (27:12). It was to Carchemish on the river that Pharaoh Neco went to aid the Assyrians in an unsuccessful battle against the Babylonians (2 Ki. 23:29; 24:7; 2 Chr. 35:20). In the prophecy of Jeremiah concerning Egypt, the Euphrates is mentioned three times in connection with this defeat of Egypt (Jer. 46:2, 6, 10). The Euphrates is referred to by name four times in an acting prophecy that Jeremiah was commanded to perform against the pride of Judah and Jerusalem (Jer. 13:4–7). The prophet was instructed to have Seraiah throw into the Euphrates a stone-weighted document of a prophecy against Babylon, as a symbol that Babylon was to sink and never rise again (51:63).

The genealogical section of 1 Chronicles states that a descendant of Reuben "occupied the land up to the edge of the desert that extends to the Euphrates River" (1 Chr. 5:9). The river was the boundary between Mesopotamia and Syria-Palestine in the Persian period, and the satrapy of the region of Syria-Palestine was called "Beyond the River" (Ezra 4:10–11 et al.; Neh. 2:7 et al.; NIV, "Trans-Euphrates"). The Euphrates is also mentioned in the book of Revelation: a command was given to release "the four angels who are bound at the great river Euphrates," and subsequently "the sixth angel poured out his bowl [of wrath] on the great river Euphrates" (Rev. 9:14; 16:12). (See E. Techen, *Euphrat und Tigris* [1934]; M. G. Ionides, *The Regime of the Rivers Euphrates and Tigris* [1937]; R. McC. Adams, *Heartland of Cities: Surveys of Ancient Settlement and Land Use on the Central Floodplain of the Euphrates* [1981]; D. H. French and C. S. Lightfoot, eds., *The Eastern Frontier of the Roman Empire*, 2 vols. [1989].) C. E. DeVries

Eupolemus yoo-pol′uh-muhs (Εὐπόλεμος, "skilled in war"). Identified as "son of John son of Accos," Eupolemus was a Jewish ambassador who, along with Jason son of Eleazar, was sent to Rome by Judas Maccabee "to establish friendship and alliance" (1 Macc. 8:17; 2 Macc. 4:11; cf. Jos. *Ant.* 12.10.6 §§415–19). The Romans agreed and sent back a treaty (1 Macc. 8:21–32).

Many scholars believe that this Eupolemus is also the Jewish historian who wrote a work known as *On the Kings in Judea* (see Clement of Alexandria, *Strom.* 1.153.4; cf. also 1.141.4). No mss of this work are extant, but several sections, one of them substantial, have been preserved by Eusebius in book 9 of his *Praeparatio evangelica* (see chs. 26, 30–34, 39; for this material Eusebius is dependent on Alexander Polyhistor's work, *On the Jews*). The lengthiest fragment outlines Hebrew history from Moses to the united monarchy and focuses on the building of Solomon's temple. (For an English trans. of the fragments, see *OTP*, 2:861–72.) Elsewhere (*Praep. ev.* 9.17) Eusebius attributes another quotation to Eupolemus, but this material (as well as an anonymous brief citation in 9.18.2) is now assigned by scholars to an unknown "Pseudo-Eupolemus" (see *OTP*, 2:873–82).

Eurakylon, Euraquilo yoo-rahk′i-lon, yoo-rahk′wi-loh. See Euroclydon.

Euroclydon yoo-rok′li-don (Εὐροκλύδων). The KJV name for the wind that aroused a storm and caused Paul's shipwreck at Malta (Acts 27:14; see ships IV). This reading, which is based on the later Greek mss, would refer to a SE wind that stirs up the waves (from *ho Euros*, "the E [or SE] wind," and *klydōn*, "wave"; cf. also the form *Euryklydōn* [from *eurys*, "broad"], that is, a wind that stirs far-reaching waves). The earliest mss, however, have *Eurakylōn G2350*, a sailor's term compounding Greek *Euros* ("E wind") with Latin *Aquilo* ("N wind"). Thus modern translations usually render it "northeaster" (some versions transliterate "Eurakylon" or "Euraquilo"). Such a word suits the local situation on the S coast of Crete, where a southerly breeze often gives way to a NE gale. "Blowing down from Mount Ida, the wind would be very dangerous to a ship with one large sail; if it did not capsize her, it would probably drive her to the Syrtes [sandbars off the Libyan coast]. The same wind is well known today in the Mediterranean world as the *grigal* or *gregale*" (F. F. Bruce, *The Acts of the Apostles: The Greek Text with Introduction and Commentary*, 3rd ed. [1990], 518; see also J. Smith, *The Voyage and Shipwreck of St. Paul* [1880], 119ff., 287ff.; C. J. Hemer in *JTS* n.s. 26 [1975]: 100–111, and in *TynBul* 36 [1985]: 79–109). J. C. Connell

Eusebian Canons. A system of ten tables containing references to parallel passages (i.e., sections numbered consecutively) in the Gospels. Prepared by Eusebius of Caesarea, these became extremely useful and were often included in NT mss. These tables are reproduced in the introduction to the Nestle-Aland *Novum Testamentum Graece* (in the inner margin of the text of the Gospels, numerical references to the tables are included; see also B. M. Metzger and B. D. Ehrman, *The Text of the New Testament: Its Transmission, Corruption, and Restoration*, 4th ed. [2005], 38–39).

Eusebius yoo-see′bee-uhs (Εὐσέβιος, "reverent, religious"). Although this name was borne by several figures in early church history, greatest importance attaches to Eusebius of Caesarea (c. A.D. 260–340). Trained according to the teachings of Origen, he became Bishop of Caesarea in 315 and was widely regarded as the most erudite Christian leader of his time. In 324 he was condemned for supporting Arius, but was soon reinstated by the Council of Nicaea. Eusebius is best known for his *Ecclesiastical History*, which even today is the primary source for the history of the Christian church during the first two centuries of its existence. He wrote several other historical works, as well as apologetic and theological treatises (e.g., *Preparation for the Gospel* and *Demonstration of the Gospel*), commentaries on the Psalms and Isaiah, and a very important work on biblical topography (the *Onomasticon*). (See D. S. Wallace-Hadrill, *Eusebius of Caesarea* [1960]; R. M. Grant, *Eusebius as Church Historian* [1980]; C. Luibhéid, *Eusebius of Caesarea and the Arian Crisis* [1981]; G. F. Chesnut, *The First Christian Histories: Eusebius, Socrates, Sozomen, Theodoret, and Evagrius*, 2nd ed. [1986]; R. Steven Notley and Ze'ev Safrai, eds., *Onomasticon: The Place Names of Divine Scripture, Including the Latin Edition of Jerome / Eusebius, Translated into English and with Topographical Commentary* [2005].)

Eutychus yoo′tuh-kuhs (Εὔτυχος *G2366*, "fortunate"). A young man at Troas who fell from a window seat during a prolonged discourse by Paul late in the evening (Acts 20:7–12). Eutychus was a common name, and some have speculated that he was a slave who had worked hard all day. He had taken a seat in the open window and, overcome by irresistible drowsiness (note Luke's reference to the "many lamps" in the room, v. 8), sank into a deep sleep and "fell to the ground from the third story and was picked up dead" (v. 9). Having embraced him, Paul quieted the tumult with the assuring words, "his life is in him" (v. 10 NRSV). The presence of the lad alive at dawn greatly comforted the group (v. 12).

Efforts have been made to break the natural meaning of a restoration from the dead. That Eutychus only appeared to be dead is contrary to the precise language used by Luke, who was an eyewitness of the event ("we," v. 8; contrast 14:19, "thinking he was dead"). Paul's act of embracing the body is not the act of one investigating a case of apparent death; it clearly recalls the actions of Elijah (1 Ki. 17:21) and Elisha (2 Ki. 4:34). (See W. M. Ramsay, *St. Paul the Traveller and the Roman Citizen*, 14th ed. [1896], 290–91; R. O. H. Lenski, *Interpretation of the Acts of the Apostles* [1934], 819–28; C. K. Barrett, *A Critical and Exegetical Commentary on the Acts of the Apostles*, ICC, 2 vols. [1994–98], 2:950–56.)   D. E. Hiebert

evangelist. A preacher of the gospel (Gk. *euangelistēs G2296*, "one who announces good news" [*euangelion G2295*]). The word appears three times in the NT. Philip is the typical example of an evangelist (Acts 21:8). He conducted a successful evangelistic campaign in Samaria and subsequently converted and baptized the Ethiopian eunuch, sending him back home with the gospel (8:4–40). Philip was a deacon, one of "the Seven" elected by the Jerusalem church to serve the widows (6:5), and was not an apostle. But he was an evangelist, for "he preached the good news of the kingdom of God and the name of Jesus Christ" (8:12). Thus whoever is "a bringer of good tidings" is an evangelist. God himself may be regarded as an evangelist, for he "announced the gospel in advance to Abraham" (*proeuangelizomai G4603*, Gal. 3:8). And so were the announcing angel (Lk. 2:10), Jesus himself (20:1), and the apostles and early converts in general (Acts 8:4).

Paul admonished Timothy to "do the work of an evangelist" as a ministerial duty (2 Tim. 4:5). Primarily, the work of the evangelist is to "proclaim good tidings" in new areas. It is the vanguard of Christianity, announcing the good news of the kingdom and of Christ where it has not been heard before. Paul, like Philip, did this kind of work, as did Timothy and other traveling Christians. They planted Christianity (cf. 1 Cor. 3:6), then moved on to other virgin soil. The preacher-pastor and teacher were to shepherd and teach the flock, while the evangelist went from place to place enlisting new converts. Later, the authors of the four Gospels were called "evangelists" because they were the first to proclaim the good news through writing.

The vocation of the evangelist is distinct. Paul said that Christ gave the church special gifts: "some to be apostles, some to be prophets, some to be evangelists, and some to be pastors and teachers, to prepare God's people for works of service, so that the body of Christ may be built up" (Eph. 4:11). Divine wisdom foresaw the growth of the church and consequent need for workers of diversified gifts (1 Cor. 12:28). Special talent is needed for pioneer proclamation of the gospel, founding new missions, and building new churches. The evangelist is endowed with appropriate spiritual gifts to unlock pagan, heathen, and sinful doors and admit the saving Christ. See also ministry IV.C.

G. B. Funderburk

Eve eev (חַוָּה *H2558*, "life" [by popular etymology]; Εὔα *G2293*). The first woman, wife of Adam. Already in the summary of creation it is stated that there were two sexes ("male and female he created them," Gen. 1:27). But when Eve was brought to her husband by the Creator, Adam made the pronouncement: "she shall be called 'woman,' [ʾiššâ *H851*] / for she was taken out of man [ʾîš *H408*]" (Gen. 2:23)—not a precise etymology, but a clever play on words (the first term is not derived from the second, cf. *NIDOTTE* 1:537–38). The name "Eve" originated in the experience of the fall, when God had laid disabilities on the tempter, on Adam, and on his wife. Then it became apparent to Adam that the life of mankind was tied up with his wife, and he called her *ḥawwâ*, a form that may bear some relation to *ḥāyâ H2649* ("to live"). This too is an instructive play on words, aiding the memory, not a scientific etymology. She was called "Eve" because she was to be "the mother of all the living."

I. Her relation to Adam. Just before the creation of Eve, Adam was assigned the task of giving meaningful names to all creatures in the garden. As they came to him by pairs, it became obvious that they all had mates, but not he. Adam felt his lone station keenly. He was to appreciate the gift of a "helper suitable for him" (Gen. 2:18). So now he had a counterpart, as did the other creatures. It is apparent that Eve served to supplement the life of Adam. To this the thought is added that the purpose of having two persons united in marriage is procreation (1:28). It is also broadly indicated that the sex relationship was uniquely pure, for though naked the first parents felt no shame.

II. Her share in the fall. The occasion for the fall came from without, not from some native defect. By the blandishments of the tempter, Eve let herself be led to the point where she overstepped the limitation laid upon her. Alone, she took the direction of affairs into her own hands and became guilty of a gigantic fiasco. In the revulsion of feeling against the tempter, Eve shared in the antipathy that was indicated by the Lord as an enduring consequence—"enmity," lasting enmity that was to exist between her and the tempter from this time forth, being carried on through the ensuing generations by the daughters of Eve (Gen. 3:15). As a continual reminder of all this, a certain burden was laid upon Eve—pain in childbearing, and being perennially attached to her husband, who from this time forth was to rule over her (v. 16).

III. Historical fact or figure of speech? Is the creation of woman (Gen. 2:21–25) to be accepted as an exact description of an actual event? Or must one regard the whole incident as too crude to be thought of as having transpired according to the letter? At least three approaches have arisen as a result of such questions: (1) the woman was actually formed from the rib of man; (2) the whole experience was a vision informing man as to the actual relation of the woman to the man; (3) analogous to this, what is written is an allegory for our instruction. Though substantial arguments may be adduced for each of these views, the first still deserves the preference as being most in harmony with the whole tenor of the account. What the Lord did involves an instructive symbolism to the effect that woman is to be regarded as a full equal to man in companionship. Partly for this reason, attempts to establish a root meaning for *ḥawwâ* after the Aramaic word for "serpent" (*ḥiwyāʾ*) prove futile. Also, all attempts to make the text set forth Eve as an intended correlate to MARY MOTHER OF JESUS introduce much into the text that is not actually there.

IV. NT teaching. Eve is mentioned twice in the NT. "Just as Eve was deceived by the serpent's cunning" (2 Cor. 11:3) is apparently a passing reference to show how easily a fall may occur, and with serious consequences. The second reference occurs in a controversial passage where Paul, urging women to be submissive, argues as follows: "For Adam was formed first, then Eve. And Adam was not the one deceived; it was the woman who was deceived and became a sinner" (1 Tim. 2:11–14). According to some scholars, Paul here appropriates arguments, found elsewhere in Jewish writings, for the superiority of man on the basis of temporal precedence and of woman's greater susceptibility to sin. According to others, Paul is less concerned with chronology than with what the chronology implies (the woman was created to be a help to man); moreover, the man sinned willfully, whereas the woman was deceived (with implications regarding the function of teaching). Still others believe that the author is refuting a false teaching (perhaps the view that the man originates in the woman, or simply that traditional roles needed to be challenged). It is likely that the specific situation in EPHESUS has some bearing on the meaning of this passage, but our imperfect knowledge of that historical context makes a precise analysis difficult. (See G. W. Knight III, *The Pastoral Epistles: A Commentary on the Greek Text*, NIGTC [1992], 138–44; I. H. Marshall, *A Critical and Exegetical Commentary on the Pastoral Epistles*, ICC [1999], 452–67.)

H. C. LEUPOLD

Eve, Gospel of. A *Gospel of Eve* is mentioned only by EPIPHANIUS (*Pan.* 26.2–3 [GCS, 1:277–78]), who also gives the only certain quotation. On a high mountain, the narrator (unidentified) sees two figures and is thus addressed: "I am you and you are I, and where you are, there am I; and I am sown in all things. And whence you want, you gather me, and in gathering me you gather yourself." The mountain setting recalls some Gnostic gospels, as does the formula, "I am you and you are I," often found in Gnostic, Hermetic, and magical texts. (See *NTAp* [1963], 1:241–43.) R. McL. Wilson

evening sacrifice. A daily offering that, with the morning sacrifice, constituted the continual burnt offering; it consisted of a yearling lamb without blemish, flour, oil, and wine (Exod. 29:38–42;

Stone altar at the Israelite temple in Arad. Each evening a lamb was to be offered as a whole burnt offering by the Israelites.

Num. 28:3–8). The observance was important in the history of Israel (2 Chr. 13:11 et al.). See SACRIFICE AND OFFERINGS III.D.2. C. P. Weber

everlasting. See ETERNITY; PUNISHMENT, ETERNAL.

Evi ee′vi (אֱוִי H209, perhaps "desire" or "shelter"). One of the five kings of MIDIAN slain by the Israelites (Num. 31:8). This was apparently an act of retribution, for earlier the Lord had said to MOSES, "Treat the Midianites as enemies and kill them, because they treated you as enemies when they deceived you in the affair of Peor" (Num. 25:17–18). The incident is recalled in Joshua, where the kings are said to be allies of SIHON (Josh. 13:21). The name ʾwy is attested in other Semitic languages and may be derived from a place name, perhaps near PETRA (see E. A. Knauf, *Midian* [1988], 166–67).

evil. This English term is usually the rendering of Hebrew *ra'* H8273 in the OT. Appearing about 800 times with its cognates, it refers to what is physically undesirable and what is morally bad. Rotten figs are "evil" in the sense of "harmful," as are poisonous herbs (2 Ki. 4:41) and a "ferocious" beast (Gen. 37:20). The child prophesied by Isaiah would reject the "wrong" and choose the right (Isa. 7:15). Individuals are sometimes described as "wicked" in the sight of the LORD (Gen. 38:7; Deut. 4:25; Ps. 51:4). The same is true of the counterpart words of the NT, especially *ponēros* G4505 with its cognates (e.g., Matt. 6:23; Mk. 7:23; of physical evil only twice in Matt. 7:17–18; Rev. 16:2) and *kakos* G2805 and cognates (e.g., Matt. 24:48; Mk. 7:21).

Natural or physical evil occurs when undesirable natural occurrences tend to frustrate human life. Examples of such evils are earthquakes, storms, and disease. Accidents are usually thought of as instances of natural evil, although they often happen as a result of improper human decisions. A psalmist complained, "For troubles without number surround me" (Ps. 40:12). Jeremiah asked, "Why is my pain unending / and my wound grievous and incurable?" (Jer. 15:18). Natural evil has presented a difficult dilemma for believers in God. If God is God, they ask, why do the wicked often flourish like the green bay tree while the righteous salt their bread with tears? Leslie Weatherhead confesses, "The subject of pain has haunted my thinking ever since I began to think for myself at all" (*Why Do Men Suffer?* [1936], 9). John S. Whale has called it "this notorious problem which has vexed thought and tried faith in every age of human history" (*The Christian Answer to the Problem of Evil* [1939], 13).

In response to evil, some have been embittered, "pan-diabolistic" pessimists (Buddha, Schopenhauer, Joseph Wood Krutch). Others have been optimists of some sort (Neo-Platonists, Spinoza, Calvin, Mary Baker Eddy), agreeing in general with Robert Browning, who said, "God's in his heaven—all's right with the world" ("Pippa Passes"), and with Alexander Pope, who announced, "One truth is clear, Whatever is, is right" (*Essay on Man*). Some would call themselves meliorists (esp. E. S. Brightman) and say that both good and evil are real and that men should become coworkers with God to rout evil and enhance what is beneficial to men.

It might well be that an adequate conception of the INCARNATION would furnish a pointer on this problem. Perhaps Christ, who holds the solution of moral evil, is also the locus of solution for the abysmal mystery of natural evil. His enfleshment surely implies that materiality as such is not evil. His healings suggest that diseases are not necessarily the direct will of the Father. Since the Father is to unite all things under Christ (Eph. 1:10); since there is to be "a new heaven and a new earth" (Rev. 21:1); and since "the whole creation has been groaning as in the pains of childbirth right up to the present time" (Rom. 8:22)—along with our groaning "inwardly as we wait eagerly for our adoption as sons, the redemption of our bodies" (8:23)—it is evident that through Christ the harbingers of redemption from all evil (natural as well as moral), which may now be experienced, are one day to be complete, when all things will be put in subjection to Christ "so that God may be all in all" (1 Cor. 15:27–28). See also SIN; SUFFERING.   J. K. GRIDER

evil eye. This phrase, as a literal rendering of the corresponding Hebrew and Greek idioms, is used by the KJV both in the OT, where it can refer to such qualities as hostility, lack of compassion, stinginess (Deut. 15:9; 28:54–56; Prov. 23:6; 28:22), and in the NT, where it refers to envy (Matt. 20:15; Mk. 7:22; cf. Matt. 6:22–23; Lk. 11:34). The expression is not used directly in the Bible in the superstitious sense of an eye that is supposed to be capable of harming, or even killing, living beings by looking at them (whether the damage is intentional or not). This belief, however, was widespread in ancient times and has continued up to the present, although it seems never to have spread to the western hemisphere. Methods of defense against effects of the evil eye included the wearing of charms (the camels' ornaments of Jdg. 8:21, according to some), repeating of oaths, and obscene gestures. A person might be held in suspicion of evil intentions if observed watching children or farm animals. The effects of the evil eye were believed to be rooted in envy so that when one expressed his admiration for animals or children he would often say, "God bless them," or its equivalent, so that his motivations would not be questioned. (See F. T. Elworthy, *The Evil Eye* [1895].)   C. P. WEBER

Evil-Merodach ee′vuhl-mer′uh-dak (אֱוִיל מְרֹדַךְ H213, from Akk. *Amēl-Marduk* [originally *Awīl-Marduk*], "man [*or* servant] of MARDUK"). Son and successor of NEBUCHADNEZZAR II as king of the Neo-Babylonian empire, c. 562–560 B.C. According to 2 Ki. 25:27–30 and Jer. 52:31–34, in the first year of his reign he released JEHOIACHIN, former king of Judah, from prison, even honoring him above all the other vassal kings in Babylon. It is noteworthy that administrative documents found at Babylon and containing lists of ration issues (oil), refer to a Yakukinu of Yakudu (= Jehoiachin of Judah; see *ANET*, 308). According to Berossus and the canon of Ptolemy, Evil-Merodach was assassinated by his brother-in-law, Neriglissar (prob. the NERGAL-SHAREZER who appears as a Babylonian officer, Jer. 39:3, 13), who then took the throne. (See R. H. Sack, *Amel-Marduk: 562–560 B.C.* [1972].)   K. L. BARKER

Evil One, the. See SATAN.

evil spirit. See DEMON.

Evodius, Homily of i-voh′dee-us. A Coptic writing claiming to be from Evodius, bishop of Rome (traditionally, he was bishop of Antioch) after Peter. The writer testifies that he, along with Peter, John, and others, was an eyewitness to the death of Mary and her assumption seven months later. (Cf. F. Robinson, *Coptic Apocryphal Gospels* [1896], 44–89; M. R. James, *The Apocryphal New Testament* [1924], 194–98; W. H. C. Frend in *The Modern Churchman* 43 [1953]: 23–28; J. K. Elliott, *The Apocryphal New Testament* [1993], 695–97.) See also ASSUMPTION OF THE VIRGIN.   C. P. WEBER

evolution. See COSMOGONY; CREATION.

ewe. See SHEEP.

exaltation of Christ. The Greek verb translated "exalt" (*hypsoō* G5738) and its cognates are used with reference to Christ several times (Acts 2:33; 5:31; Phil. 2:9; Heb. 7:26; note also Isa. 52:13 LXX). The same Greek term is translated "lift up" in the Gospel of John, where the reference is to the CRUCIFIXION of Christ (Jn. 3:14; 8:28; 12:32, 34); however, John clearly intends to communicate that Jesus' death is intimately connected with his glorification (cf. 7:39; 12:23–28; 13:31–32; et al.).

The terms *humiliation* and *exaltation* are commonly used in theology to denote the two states of Christ the mediator. The former extends from Christ's conception to his burial and marks the period of his INCARNATION, where the "form of the servant" was the dominant feature of his life on earth. The latter starts with the resurrection and includes his ascension, his session at the right hand of the Father, and his glorious second coming. While some have attempted to interpret Christ's humiliation and exaltation as applying to either his divine or his human nature, it appears wisest to view both states in reference to Christ's performance of his mediatorial office. It is along this line that Phil. 2:5–11 can receive the most natural interpretation.

There has been some question whether Christ's DESCENT INTO HADES belongs to the exaltation of Christ, as commonly asserted in the Roman Catholic, Eastern Orthodox, and the Lutheran traditions. The major support for this approach—and for the view that the statement of the APOSTLES' CREED, "he descended into hell," refers to a specific transaction performed by Christ between death and resurrection—is found in 1 Pet. 3:19–20. But to build such a heavy inferential superstructure of doctrine upon a passage so manifestly obscure and of which no one appears to be able to give a truly satisfactory interpretation (cf. B. Reicke, *The Disobedient Spirits and Christian Baptism* [1946]) seems precarious in the extreme. Those who view the "descent" as a stage of Christ's exaltation frequently assume that he went to proclaim his victory to OT believers so that they might share in the full benefits of his redemption (cf. Eph. 4:8–10). But this picture does not fit well with the "spirits in prison, who disobeyed ... in the days of Noah," about whom Peter is speaking. One may perhaps conclude that the doctrine of the "descent into hell" rests on a fragile basis and that it is not of primary importance to determine whether it belongs to the humiliation or the exaltation of Christ. (Cf. F. Pieper, *Christian Dogmatics* 2 [1951], 314–20; H. Bavinck, *Gereformeerde Dogmatiek*, 3rd ed., 3 [1917], 459–69.) See SPIRITS IN PRISON.

The RESURRECTION OF CHRIST is the first notable stage of his exaltation (Acts 2:32; Rom. 1:4). By the resurrection not only was Christ's body reanimated (as had been the case, e.g., for LAZARUS), but his whole human nature was constituted incorruptible, glorious, powerful, and spiritual; that is to say, adapted to the purpose of the Spirit (1 Cor. 15:42–45).

In the ASCENSION OF CHRIST we see a perfecting of the glory inaugurated by the resurrection. In entering heaven Christ, the mediator, initiates a new form of relationship with his people, and prepares their ultimate reunion with him (Jn. 14:2–3). Then, in the session at the right hand of God (Ps. 110:1; Matt. 22:44 and parallels; 26:64 and parallels; Acts 2:33–36; 5:31; 7:55–56; Rom. 8:34; Eph. 1:20; Col. 3:1; Heb. 1:3, 13; 8:1; 10:12; 12:2; 1 Pet. 3:22; Rev. 3:21; 22:1), Christ exercises his kingly rule (Eph. 1:20–22), sends the Holy Spirit to his own (Jn. 14:26; 16:7), and pursues the ministry of intercession (Rom. 8:34; Heb. 7:25; 9:24; 1 Jn. 2:1; et al.). See OFFICES OF CHRIST.

At the SECOND COMING the ascended Lord will return to bring to completion his redemptive work, raise the dead, judge mankind and the angels, fulfill his union with his church as the heavenly bridegroom, and inaugurate his eternal reign.

R. NICOLE

excellent, most. The title "most excellent" (Gk. *kratistos G3196*, superlative of *kratys*, "strong" [cf. *kratos G3187*]) is found four times in the NT. It may have been the official rendering of the Latin *vir egregius*, which meant "a man of equestrian rank," that is, one of the knights who came in order after senators in ROME. The title was applied to FELIX (Acts 23:26; 24:3) and to FESTUS (Acts 26:25), both of whom were governors of Judea. In addition, the term could be used more generally as a courtesy title in addressing one honored for his position, such as THEOPHILUS (Lk. 1:3). Some have argued that the author of Luke–Acts addressed an apology for Christianity to an influential Roman governor, but the social standing of Theophilus is debated. (See L. Alexander, *The Preface to Luke's Gospel: Literary Convention and Social Context in Luke 1:1–4 and Acts 1:1* [1993], 132–33, 188–200.)

F. FOULKES

excommunication. The temporary or permanent exclusion of an individual from fellowship with a religious group.

I. Jewish practice. Under the old covenant excommunication was represented by the BAN (*ḥērem* H3051), which was placed on those who, by violating the Mosaic law, put themselves outside the COVENANT relationship (e.g., Exod. 30:33; Lev. 17:4). There is reference to the threatened excommunication of those Israelites who did not come to Jerusalem in obedience to EZRA's proclamation (Ezra 10:8).

In the NT there are references to Jewish discipline in relation to the SYNAGOGUE (Lk. 6:22; Jn. 9:22; 12:42; 16:2). There were different degrees of discipline, ranging from a temporary ban on contact with fellow Jews to the death penalty. The power to excommunicate seems generally to have been vested in the SANHEDRIN. (See A. Edersheim, *The Life and Times of Jesus the Messiah* [1891], 2:183–84.)

II. In the teaching of Christ. The Lord clearly recognized the place of church discipline (see CHURCH VIII.C). He gave his apostles, and through them the church, the power of BINDING AND LOOSING (Matt. 16:19; 18:18). He indicated the procedure that should be followed in the case of offending brethren. There must first be personal admonition, but if that does not have the desired effect, there must be further admonition in the presence of witnesses. Should this not succeed, then the church must be notified. If the offender refuses to listen to the church, there is no alternative but excommunication (Matt. 18:15–17).

III. In the apostolic era. There are several passages in the NT that refer to the exercise of discipline (1 Cor. 5:2, 7, 13; 2 Cor. 2:5–7; 2 Thess. 3:14–15; 1 Tim. 1:20; Tit. 3:10). In the church at CORINTH there had been a moral breakdown that was tending to cause scandal throughout the city. To its shame, the church had taken no action, and it was therefore giving the impression that it condoned the sin that had been committed. PAUL called upon the church to act. The phrase "hand over to Satan" occurs twice (1 Cor. 5:5; 1 Tim. 1:20) in the NT. It probably means simply to put out of fellowship and to consign to the pagan world, which is regarded as SATAN's domain. Some scholars have suggested that the infliction of some physical disease or disability might also be involved. A warning of possible physical consequences to those who partake of the LORD's SUPPER unworthily was given by the apostle Paul (1 Cor. 11:30).

Being deprived of Christian fellowship, the offender loses any false sense of security he might otherwise enjoy by being allowed to remain in fellowship with the church. He must be brought to see the heinousness of the sin he has committed, and at the same time the world in general must be made aware that blatant sin cannot be tolerated within the Christian church. Opinions vary as to the meaning of the Pauline phrase "the destruction of the flesh" (1 Cor. 5:5 NRSV). The underlying thought may be that the offender, having been cut off from Christian fellowship, will become acutely conscious of his sin and guilt and repent for what he has done. Subsequently, Paul makes reference to an action taken by a majority vote of Corinthian church members, which resulted apparently in a change of heart on the part of the offender. The apostle asks that the church shall now regard the matter as closed and restore the disciplined member to full fellowship (2 Cor. 2:5–11).

It seems that in the early church excommunication was exercised on both moral and doctrinal grounds. In the church at Corinth, the offense to which reference has already been made was one of incest. Paul intimates in his first letter to Timothy that he had excommunicated HYMENAEUS and ALEXANDER because of their false teaching (1 Tim. 1:20). A schismatic spirit was also regarded as an occasion for exclusion from the privileges of church fellowship (Tit. 3:10). In the messages to the seven churches in the book of Revelation, the church of EPHESUS is commended because it did not tolerate evil men, while the churches of PERGAMUM and THYATIRA are reproved because they did not take effective action against heretical teachers or heathen abominations in their midst. The purpose behind the exercise of church discipline is both to safeguard the purity of the church itself and to bring home to the offender his need to repent. Those who are called upon to enforce such discipline must always be aware of their responsibility to restore the guilty party if and when there is true repentance.

It is not absolutely clear from the NT what precise form excommunication took in every case. It would seem, however, that by the time the Pastoral Epistles were written (1 Tim. 5:19–20), a more or less regular method of procedure had been adopted based on the Lord's own teaching on the subject. Formal excommunication meant not only the severance of formal links with the local fellowship, but exclusion from the church life generally. Church members were counseled not to eat or enjoy social intercourse with one who had been excommunicated (1 Cor. 5:11; 2 Thess. 3:14–15). At the same time they had a continuing responsibility to admonish and exhort the erring brother to repent. It is not to be assumed that someone who has been excommunicated ceases to be in "a state of grace." It is clear that the apostle Paul fully expected to see the disciplined offender numbered among the Lord's people "on the day of the Lord" (1 Cor. 5:5).

Whereas the exercise of church discipline is open to abuse (cf. 3 Jn. 9–10), the necessity for it remains. The Puritan preacher John Owen (*Works* [1862], 15:512) defined discipline as "the due exercise of that authority and power which the Lord Christ, in and by his word, has granted unto the church for its continuance, increase and preservation in purity, order and holiness, according to his appointment." Historically there has been considerable discussion whether the exercise of such discipline is vested in church officers or in the church itself as a corporate body. It is clear that when private remonstrances fail to achieve the necessary result, the church must concern itself; and even though church officers may act on behalf of and in the name of the church, it is the corporate body that must assume ultimate responsibility for action taken. Church discipline must be seen not merely as a safeguard to the purity of the church, but also as a necessary means of promoting the glory of God. Those who are called upon to enforce it must themselves be sure that their motives are right and that the ultimate redemptive aim is not overlooked. (Cf. J. Bannerman, *The Church of Christ* [1869], 2:186–200; D. D. Bannerman, *The Scripture Doctrine of the Church* [1887], 144–46, 176–88, 201–3.) See also ANATHEMA. G. W. KIRBY

Execration Texts. Egyptian texts inscribed on bowls and figurines, dating mainly from the Middle Kingdom period (approximately 20th–18th cent. B.C.) and consisting of formal curses pronounced on the enemies of Egypt and on evil forces (for a sample from the Berlin texts, see *ANET*, 328–29). The shattering of the pottery was thought to break the power of these opponents. The texts list a large number of foreigners, including rulers in the environments of Canaan, but their significance for our understanding of the history of Palestine is debated. See also INSCRIPTIONS.

execution. The OT makes a clear and precise distinction between murder—the illicit and violent killing of a human being (Exod. 20:13)—and the legal, moral act of slaying a criminal by the duly constituted authority (Gen. 9:6 et al.). Several cases of execution, or legal deprivation of life, are mentioned in the OT (2 Chr. 25:2–4 et al.). Criminals were to be either stoned (Deut. 13:10) or hanged (Deut. 21:22). But strict prohibitions against vendetta were in force (24:16). Several executions at the hands of the authorities are mentioned in the NT (Matt. 14:10 et al.). CRUCIFIXION was the Roman method of execution. See CRIMES AND PUNISHMENTS. W. WHITE, JR.

exegesis. The critical analysis and explanation of texts. See INTERPRETATION.

Exegesis on the Soul. A Christian-Gnostic treatise, in the form of a hortatory narrative, preserved in the Nag Hammadi Library (NHC II, 6). The document survives in a 4th-cent. Coptic MS, apparently the translation of an early 3rd-cent. Greek original. The narrative, interspersed with biblical quotations, describes the fall and salvation of the soul by portraying it as a female that was originally an androgynous virgin alone with the Father, then fell into a body and prostituted herself, but finally repented and was restored. (See M. Scopello, *L'Exégèse de l'âme. Nag Hammadi Codex II,6* [1985]; English trans. in *NHL*, 190–98.)

exile. The enforced removal of people from their native country. (The Heb. terms *gôlâ* H1583 and *šĕbî* H8660 and their cognates are used more or less interchangeably in the sense of "exile" and "captivity." See *NIDOTTE*, 5:595–96. Cf. also

Gk. *aichmalōsia* G168 and *metoikesia* G3578.) When exile is imposed upon an individual, the choice of the place of banishment is usually left to the person exiled. However, when exile is the lot of groups of people, the place of banishment is imposed. The deportation of communities was usually practiced in the ancient world for political reasons, frequently to destroy the power of a nation considered an enemy or to colonize an area in which it was desirable, for various reasons, to create a cultural fusion. Sometimes several reasons for the imposition of exile upon a people operated at once. There are two instances of the Israelites being taken into exile referred to in the Bible. The first was the Assyrian exile in the 8th cent. B.C.; the second the Babylonian exile two centuries later.

I. The Assyrian exile. The first deportation of Israelites recorded in the OT (2 Ki. 15:29) occurred in 734 B.C. under the Assyrian monarch TIGLATH-PILESER III (745–727 B.C.). He marched against PEKAH of Israel and REZIN of Aram because they had made war against his vassal, King AHAZ of Judah, and he punished Israel by carrying some of them into exile (2 Ki. 16:7–9). The captives of this deportation to Assyria were of the tribes of Naphtali, Reuben, Gad, and the half-tribe of Manasseh (1 Chr. 5:26). The second deportation by the Assyrians took place after the destruction of the northern kingdom and its capital SAMARIA in 722 after a three-year siege (2 Ki. 17:1–6). It was SHALMANESER who began the siege, but his successor finally took the city. Assyrian inscriptions recording this event indicate that 27,290 people were taken captive and deported, some to the Assyrian province of GOZAN in MESOPOTAMIA and others to MEDIA. At the same time, colonists from other Assyrian provinces were settled in Samaria and neighboring areas to take the place of the Israelites deported. The intermarriage of these provincials and the Israelites who remained in the land resulted in the hybrid SAMARITANS of later biblical history.

The exiles were transplanted mostly to depopulated areas in the provinces of HALAH, Gozan, and Media, as well as in NINEVEH, and apparently were permitted to live fairly normal lives. The only record of them is contained in the book of TOBIT, which indicates that some of the captives were loyal to Yahweh. Others were submerged or amalgamated into the Assyrian population. The problem of the so-called Ten Lost Tribes has been greatly exaggerated. The Assyrian figure of 27,290 captives shows that only a fraction of the Israelite population was deported and that the tribes were not "lost" in the sense implied by the term. The destruction of the northern kingdom of Israel was due, according to HOSEA and AMOS, to the moral and spiritual degeneration of the country and not to the might of Assyrian military power, as great as that was.

II. The Babylonian exile. The people of the southern kingdom were subjected to various deportations by the Babylonians under NEBUCHADNEZZAR, who adopted the Assyrian policy toward conquered peoples. The first incident of this kind took place in 608 B.C. when, after the battle of CARCHEMISH, NEBUCHADNEZZAR advanced to Jerusalem. He spared King JEHOIAKIM, who had rebelled against him, but carried off several of the princes of Judah, among whom were DANIEL and his friends (Dan. 1:1–7).

JEREMIAH mentions three deportations (Jer. 52:28–30). The first of these took place in 597 after another conquest of Jerusalem by Nebuchadnezzar (2 Ki. 24:1–16). The Babylonian monarch had come to Jerusalem to punish King Jehoiakim for renouncing allegiance to Babylonia, but before the siege of the city ended, the king's son JEHOIACHIN had succeeded to the throne of his father. Nebuchadnezzar ordered the exile of Jehoiachin and his mother along with the most distinguished men of the country, together with the treasures of the tem-

Assyrian relief from the time of Tiglath-Pileser III (c. 728 B.C.) depicting captives being taken into exile. Panel from a palace in Nimrud.

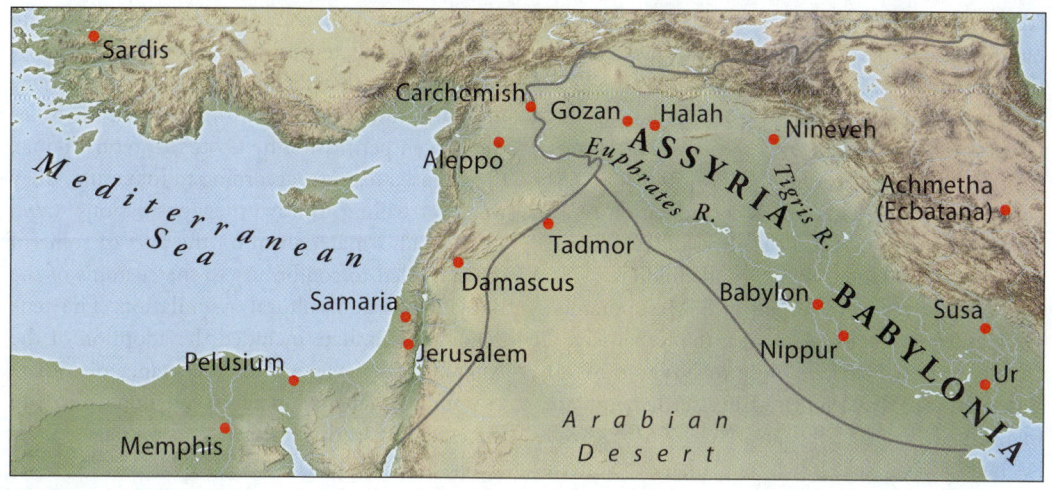

Assyrian and Babylonian exiles.

ple and the royal palace. Among the captives was the prophet EZEKIEL, who dates the chronology of his book according to the date of this captivity. Evidence of this phase of the exile has been found by German archaeologists in the form of CUNEIFORM tablets that list, among the people receiving rations of grain, "Yakin [Jehoiachin], king of Judah," and five of his sons, together with other Hebrews.

The second deportation recorded by Jeremiah took place eleven years after the first. In 586 B.C. ZEDEKIAH, who was placed on the throne by Nebuchadnezzar to succeed Jehoiachin, took an oath of fealty to the Babylonian monarch (Ezek. 17:13). He soon began to give evidence of disloyalty to Nebuchadnezzar, who again took action against the Hebrews. The Babylonian monarch set up headquarters at RIBLAH on the ORONTES, from which he directed the campaign against Jerusalem. The siege of the city lasted from 10 January 587 to 9 July 586, when the Babylonians were able to breach the city wall built in the days of Hezekiah (2 Chr. 32:5). The flight from the city by Zedekiah and his entourage was intercepted, and he was brought to Nebuchadnezzar at Riblah. He was forced to witness the execution of his sons, after which his eyes were put out, and he was taken in chains to Babylon. Approximately eighty distinguished leaders of the Jerusalem community, among them the high priest Seraiah, were taken to Riblah and executed upon the orders of Nebuchadnezzar. On 1 August 586, NEBUZARADAN, the captain of Nebuchadnez-zar's bodyguard, commanded that the TEMPLE be destroyed and its treasures further confiscated. The royal palace and the city were set on fire, and the survivors (except the poorest of the land) were taken into captivity (2 Ki. 24:20—25:21; Jer. 39:1–10).

Nebuchadnezzar then appointed GEDALIAH as governor of Judea. He exercised his office in MIZPAH until he was treacherously assassinated by a certain ISHMAEL, who had been a fugitive in AMMON and who objected to Gedaliah's apparent cooperation with the Babylonians. This new rebellion by the Israelites led to the third deportation recorded by Jeremiah, and took place in the year 581. Some of the remaining Hebrews of strong anti-Babylonian feeling fled to Egypt, forcing Jeremiah, who had been given special consideration by Nebuchadnezzar, to accompany them (2 Ki. 25:22–26; Jer. 40–44).

The statements in regard to the number of captives taken to Babylonia are confusing. Jeremiah gives the total carried away in his three deportations at 4,600 (Jer. 52:28–30). How this figure was arrived at is not clear, but it could be a reference to individuals of a specific class only. The number of those exiled in 597 is said in this passage to be 3,023 instead of the 8,000, as in 2 Ki. 24:15–16. In this second reference, it is stated that 7,000 fighting men and 1,000 craftsmen and artisans were exiled. William F. Albright (*The Biblical Period from Abraham to Ezra* [1963], 85) suggests that the difference in these figures "may be partly due to the fact that the latter was only a conjectural estimate, but may also be partly due to the heavy mortality of the starving and diseased captives during the long desert trek to Babylonia." George Adam Smith (*Jerusalem: The Topography, Economics and History from the Earliest Times to A.D. 70* [1908], 2:268) concludes on the basis of his consideration of all the figures involved that the captives did not exceed a total of 70,000 men, women, and children.

The captives were settled in S Mesopotamia. Ezekiel mentions "Tel Abib near the Kebar River" (Ezek. 3:15), which was close to NIPPUR, SE of BABYLON (see TEL ABIB). Other settlements are mentioned in Ezra 2:59 and Neh. 7:61, as well as Bar. 1:4 (cf. Ezek. 1:3; Ezra 8:15, 17). Western Semitic proper names have been found in inscriptions from Nippur, confirming that some of the exiles were settled there. Various reasons have been given for the location of the exile in Babylonia. One view is that Israel, having originated in that area (Gen. 11:28; Josh. 24:2), was sent back home by God as a husband sends his unsatisfactory wife back home. One opinion in the rabbinic literature is that Babylonia, being a low-lying country, becomes a symbol of the nether world from which Israel was rescued (cf. Hos. 13:14). Some believe that the northern and southern kingdoms were exiled to different places so that the two groups of captives might each derive some comfort from the other's misery.

The exiles were under royal protection and generally may be described as being under liberal internment rather than in a concentration camp. Some of the captives were used to supply labor for Nebuchadnezzar's many building projects, at least in the beginning of the exile. Some of them enjoyed special prerogatives. They could own their homes and land, and enjoy the produce of their gardens (Jer. 29:4–7; Ezek. 8:1; 12:1–7). This would enable them to provide for some of their physical needs. Some of the captives apparently made an adequate living in other ways (Zech. 6:9–11) and even entered business in the "city of merchants," as BABYLON was known (Ezek. 17:4, 12). The Hebrew banking house of Murashu appears in the inscriptions. The lists of captives receiving rations includes, along with the Hebrew names, the skilled trades in which some of them worked.

According to Jer. 29:5–7, the Israelites were able to accumulate wealth. Many were so successful financially that they were able to send money to Jerusalem (Bar. 1:6–7, 10), and when the exiles were given permission by CYRUS to return home, they refused because, according to JOSEPHUS, "they were not willing to leave their possessions" (*Ant.* 11.1.3). This materialism on the part of some of the exiles led to conformity to the customs of the Babylonians and cultural assimilation. The tendency to assimilate included the adoption of the ARAMAIC language and the acceptance of IDOLATRY and participation in pagan ceremonies, even to the extent of sacrificing their sons on pagan altars (Ezek. 14:3–5; 20:31).

Socially, the Israelites were apparently permitted complete freedom. They married, established families as they pleased, and kept in touch with Jerusalem (Jer. 29:6). They met in assemblies and these occasionally were religious gatherings. It was probably on such occasions that those faithful to Yahweh found the opportunity for worship, fellowship, and the renewal of faith that served to keep alive the vision of restoration to their homeland. It was at these gatherings that Ezekiel emphasized the promises of the return and revived their confidence in the Law and the Prophets (cf. Ps. 137). The high festivals of the Israelites could not be observed in captivity, but there were observances of solemn prayer, fasting, and penance (Zech. 7:3–5). Observances not dependent upon the high festivals related to the temple were practiced. These included the observance of the SABBATH, the practice of CIRCUMCISION, and praying with the face turned toward Jerusalem (1 Ki. 8:48–50). It is in this context that Ezekiel's emphasis upon personal responsibility and individual morality and spirituality appears (Ezek. 18:20–32; 36:26–27).

This loyal core of Israelites surrounding Ezekiel formed the nucleus of those that returned to their homeland and provided the enthusiasm and leadership for the restoration. A harbinger of freedom to come for the Israelites was the release of King Jehoiachin from imprisonment. According to 2 Ki. 25:27–30, he was freed by EVIL-MERODACH, king of Babylonia in 560 B.C. Jeremiah had prophesied that the captivity would last seventy years (Jer. 25:12; 29:10; cf. 2 Chr. 36:21). One way, among others, that this period may be calculated is from the time of the destruction of the temple in 586 to the time of its reconstruction and dedication in 516.

In 538, the Persian king Cyrus destroyed the Babylonian empire and in the same year issued a decree permitting the Jews to return to their native land (Ezra 1:1–4; 6:3–5). These accounts of the edict of Cyrus have been confirmed by archaeology. The response of the exiles to the possibility of return was not widespread. Some were prosperous and comfortable in exile, whereas conditions in the homeland were unsettled, the journey long, dangerous, and expensive. The first group to return, under the leadership of ZERUBBABEL, governor of Judea and son of Jehoiachin's oldest son SHEALTIEL, laid the foundations of the new temple.

The second group of returnees, under the leadership of EZRA, scribe and reformer, set out for Jerusalem in the seventh year of ARTAXERXES, 457 B.C. He gathered the people at the AHAVA River, a group of about 1,800 men, or 5,500 to 6,000 men and women besides 38 Levites and 220 servants of the temple from CASIPHIA (Ezra 8). Then in 444 came NEHEMIAH, cupbearer to Artaxerxes and later governor of Judea, to rebuild the wall of Jerusalem (Neh. 1–13). Ezra and Nehemiah, invested with royal power, were able in spite of great difficulties to establish the postexilic Jewish community. It was in this period that it became common for an Israelite to be called a "Jew" (*yĕhûdî* H3374, "Judean," from *yĕhûdâ* H3373, "Judah"). From the list given in Neh. 7:5–73, it appears that the whole Jewish community numbered 42,360 men, or 125,000 people.

The skepticism with which the biblical accounts concerning the exile were regarded by some earlier scholars has been dispelled by archaeological reconstruction of the ANE. The position of C. C. Torrey, S. A. Cook, G. Holscher, W. A. Irwin, and others, that there never occurred a Babylonian exile and consequently no return to Judah, not only denied the validity of the biblical historical narratives but also the prophetic messianism that was based in large measure upon these events. Such biblical books as Ezekiel, Jeremiah, Ezra, and Nehemiah were, according to this view, largely a fabrication of later writers. All this has changed. Archaeological discoveries, such as the OSTRACA from LACHISH and explorations in the areas concerned, have revealed evidence for the destruction of the cities of Judah by the Babylonians at the time required by biblical chronology. The royal archives of Nebuchadnezzar supplement the evidence from Judah in giving support to the credibility of the biblical history.

III. The effects of the exile. The cause of the exile was apostasy from God and his COVENANT. The Israelites had consistently rejected the message of the PROPHETS and persistently continued in their sin and idolatry. The prophets constantly warned the Israelites against trusting in their own wisdom and power. The exile was interpreted by the prophets as divine judgment that would eventuate in restoration and a revelation of God's eternal love for Israel (Isa. 54:9–10; Jer. 31:3–6). It is the primary historical incident upon which biblical messianism is based. Among the results of the exile for Israel was a more profound comprehension of the law of Moses and the prophetic writings as important for the Jews as a people. There came also a clearer grasp of the universality and SOVEREIGNTY OF GOD—that Yahweh is one and there is no god beside him. This faith remained so unshakable that it withstood the influence and fascination of Greek culture in spite of Hellenism's effects upon some other areas of Judaism and the rest of the Mediterranean world.

(See further J. Gray, *Archaeology and the Old Testament World* [1962], 180–98; P. R. Ackroyd, *Exile and Restoration* [1968]; T. M. Raitt, *A Theology of Exile: Judgment/Deliverance in Jeremiah and Ezekiel* [1977]; N. P. Lemche, *Ancient Israel: A New History of Israelite Society* [1988], ch. 5; R. Albertz, *Israel in Exile: The History and Literature of the Sixth Century B.C.E* [2003]; R. P. Carroll in *ABD*, 3:567–76.)

A. C. SCHULTZ

Exodus, Book of. The second book of the Bible and traditionally one of the five books of MOSES (the PENTATEUCH or TORAH).
    I. General features
       A. Name
       B. Relation to the rest of the Pentateuch
       C. Unity and authorship
       D. General structure
       E. Principal emphasis

II. Historical background
III. Contents
IV. Miracles
V. The legal sections of Exodus
   A. General remarks
   B. Relation to the law codes of other nations
   C. The originality of the laws
   D. Types of law
   E. Survey of the legal sections
   F. Laws given before Sinai
   G. The Decalogue
   H. The covenant code
   I. Regulations for the tabernacle and for the establishment of the priesthood
   J. The laws of Exod. 34
   K. The Sabbath

I. General features

A. Name. In the Hebrew Bible, this book is usually referred to as *Shemoth*, taking its title (as do the other books of the Pentateuch) from the opening words, *wěʾēlleh šěmôt* ("And these are the names [of]"), since it begins with the names of the patriarchs who had gone down into Egypt. The English designation is taken from the SEPTUAGINT title, *Exodos*, "departure" (from Egypt), which accurately describes the first thirteen chapters of the book.

B. Relation to the rest of the Pentateuch. The narrative of Exodus is closely connected with that of GENESIS, for it carries forward the history of the descendants of the patriarchs from the point where it ended in Gen. 50, even though considerable time intervened between the death of JOSEPH and the first events of Exodus (Exod. 1:6–14), during which the people of Israel had been brought into a position of servitude. After describing the departure from Egypt, the book tells of the giving of the law and the building of the TABERNACLE. The rules for SACRIFICE that naturally follow make up the first part of LEVITICUS. Exodus is not so much an independent book as a somewhat arbitrarily delimited portion of the middle section of the Pentateuch; the division between Exodus and Leviticus is similar to that between 1 and 2 Samuel or between 1 and 2 Kings.

C. Unity and authorship. From a very early time, Jewish tradition held that the entire book was written by MOSES. Only within the last two centuries or so has its origin been questioned by any considerable number of writers, but many modern scholars deny the Mosaic authorship as a result of the spread of the critical theories which, beginning with Genesis, were extended to the Pentateuch and today are widely taught.

Mosaic responsibility for the contents of the book is strongly indicated. Twice the book states that God told Moses to write (Exod. 17:14; 34:27), and once it says that Moses wrote (24:4). Christ declared that Moses wrote (Jn. 5:46–47), and he ascribed Exod. 20:12 and 21:17 to Moses in Mk. 7:10. In Mk. 12:26 Jesus referred to "the book of Moses." Although this latter usage does not in itself prove that Christ considered that Moses had written the entire book, it fits the common tradition and clearly affirms the Savior's regard for the historical accuracy and inspiration of Exod. 3.

The book of Exodus occupies a prominent place in the history of the higher criticism, an issue discussed primarily in the article on the PENTATEUCH (which includes a treatment of Exod. 6:3, one of the cornerstones of the documentary theory). Here it should be noted that those who follow the theories of Julius Wellhausen in general have differed greatly in their interpretations of the book of Exodus. Certain followers of the documentary theory attribute considerable historicity to the career of Moses, whereas others almost completely deny it.

D. General structure. The book is almost equally divided between narrative and legal sections. The first nineteen chapters are entirely narrative, except for short legal sections in Exod. 12:14–27, 42–49; 13:1–16. The remainder of the book is largely law, except for ch. 24, which describes the adoption of the covenant, and chs. 32–34, which describe the people's rebellion, Moses' intercession, and the renewal of the covenant.

E. Principal emphases. The book has four principal emphases. The first is REDEMPTION from the oppressive power of PHARAOH. This is greatly stressed as conditioning the mind of the Israelites for all future ages and establishing a permanent debt of gratitude to the One who delivered them from bondage. It also typically stresses the great importance of redemption from slavery to sin in the life of every one who is redeemed through Christ, who is typified by the PASSOVER lamb (Exod. 12:1–14). The second great emphasis is the establishment of God's COVENANT (19:1—24:18). This covenant is based upon the fact that God, having redeemed his people, has a right to expect their allegiance and loyalty. It refers back to the redemption upon which it is based (19:4–6; 20:2; 22:21; 23:9, 15). The people whom he has redeemed have become his covenant people. He promises them protection and continuing oversight, whereas they, in turn, are obligated to obey his righteous law. The third great emphasis is LAW. Declaration of the covenant begins with the great summary of the moral law in the TEN COMMANDMENTS, and then goes on to present various laws important for the lives of those who are to be a holy nation and a people peculiarly devoted to God. The fourth great emphasis is WORSHIP. This is touched on in ch. 3 (vv. 5–6), and in the rules for the Passover in ch. 12, which would place vividly before the minds of succeeding generations the nature of God's redemption and every individual's need for personal participation. It is primarily handled in chs. 25–31, which describe the arrangements for the building of the tabernacle and the setting apart of the priests, and in the account of the actual construction of the tabernacle in chs. 35–40.

II. Historical background.

The first twelve chapters of the book mainly describe occurrences in EGYPT during the latter half of the 2nd millennium B.C., while the events related in the remaining chapters take place in the Sinaitic peninsula. Although there is much in the book that reflects the background of Egyptian life and history, there is little that specifically indicates the precise time of the events. The king of Egypt is called either "Pharaoh" or "the king of Egypt." In no instance is an Egyptian monarch mentioned by name. The statement in Exod. 1:8 that a new king arose "who did not know about Joseph" strongly suggests that the expulsion of the HYKSOS occurred between the death of JOSEPH and the birth of MOSES, and makes it easy to see why the new king would have an unfriendly attitude toward those whom he connected with the Hyksos, who were also Asiatics and who had held Egypt in unwelcome subjection for a considerable time.

The problem of dating the oppression and the exodus has been much discussed, but the data are insufficient for a final decision. See EXODUS, THE II. Though much relevant archaeological material has been found, further discoveries are needed. The names of the two store cities, PITHOM and RAMESES (Exod. 1:11), have been advanced as proof that the events described could not have occurred until the 19th dynasty, because the first kings bearing the name of Rameses (see RAMSES) belonged to that dynasty. It would not be at all impossible that the original names should have been changed in the text to those that were known later, just as it might be said that the Dutch founded New York in 1626, even though the city did not receive this name until its conquest by the English in 1664, having been previously known as New Amsterdam. That the kings by the name of Ramses did not reign until the 19th dynasty does not necessarily prove that a city might not have been named Rameses at a previous period, for worship of the god RE (or Ra) was prominent in most periods of ancient Egyptian history, and the ending *-mss* is common in personal names. Whereas evidence of the names is therefore not conclusive proof that the events described did not occur until the 19th dynasty, the lack of

It was probably in this area of the Nile River that Pharaoh's daughter went to bathe and found the infant Moses in a basket. View from the pharaonic palace at Qantir, looking E toward Tell el-Dabᶜa (prob. biblical Rameses).

The mother of Moses placed her infant son into a reed basket similar to this mummy coffin used to bury infants.

archaeological evidence of previous occupation at the probable sites of both store cities constitutes important evidence in this direction.

The Egyptian oppression is described as very severe. Some have thought that this indicates the Egyptians' mobilization of great multitudes of people to build the colossal PYRAMIDS. This is not relevant, however, as the pyramids must have been standing at least a thousand years before the time of the exodus. Nonetheless, there is abundant evidence from the period of the 18th and 19th dynasties of the harshness shown by Egyptians toward slaves and foreigners. The hieroglyphic sign representing a foreigner is a picture of a bound man with blood flowing from a wound in his head. This sign is used even in connection with the names of honored foreign kings with whom treaties were being made. Egyptian hatred of foreigners and severe Egyptian oppression of slaves is well evidenced and fits precisely with the events set forth in the early portion of Exodus.

Sometimes the historicity of the exodus and of the deliverance at the RED SEA has been questioned on the ground that they are not mentioned in the known remains of ancient Egypt. This objection rests on a misconception of the nature of Egyptian archaeology. Most of the day-to-day ephemeral records of ancient Egypt, and the remains of the homes of the people, are largely beneath the water table in the delta of the NILE, which was the region where most of the people lived. Although the extant remains of ancient Egypt are very extensive, they consist largely of burial places and monuments erected in the desert to celebrate Egyptian achievements and victories. Defeats such as the departure of the Israelites and the failure of Pharaoh to recapture them would hardly result in the erecting of monuments.

At one time it was thought that the date of the exodus could be ascertained by determining which Pharaoh had drowned. The relevant passage, however, does not necessarily indicate that the king was drowned, but that he suffered a considerable defeat that included the sinking of his chariots and his host, and the drowning of his chosen captains (Exod. 15:4). An argument that Pharaoh himself perished has been built on 15:19, which says that "the horse of Pharaoh went in with his chariots and with his horsemen into the sea" (KJV). The form here translated "horse," however, is identical with that used in 14:9 and 23, where it clearly is used as a collective and refers to a cavalry.

There is much yet unknown about the historical background of the book of Exodus, but it can safely be said, though the dates of the events are not yet certain, that there is no reasonable ground for denying that the book could have been written by a contemporary.

III. Contents

A. Preparation for deliverance from Egypt (Exod. 1:1—4:28)
  1. The oppression (1:1–22)
    a. List of tribes (1:1–7)
    b. Bondage (1:8–14)
    c. Attempted killing of children (1:15–22)
  2. Preparation of God's representative (2:1–22)
    a. Moses' childhood (2:1–10)
    b. Premature attempt at deliverance (2:11–14)
    c. Flight (2:15–22)
  3. Moses' divine call (2:23—4:28)
    a. Divine compassion for Israel (2:23–25)
    b. The burning bush (3:1–6)
    c. The divine promises (3:7–22)

d. Moses given divine credentials (4:1–9)
  e. Help for Moses' weakness (4:10–17)
  f. Return to Egypt (4:18–23)
  g. Neglect of circumcision remedied (4:24–26)
  h. Aaron provided as an associate (4:27–28)
 B. The actual deliverance (4:29—12:36)
  1. First Attempts (4:29—7:13)
   a. The people's hopes raised (4:29–31)
   b. Oppression intensified by withholding straw (5:1–18)
   c. Moses rejected by Israel but encouraged by God (5:19—6:13)
   d. Ancestry of Moses (6:14–27)
   e. Divine encouragement continued (6:28—7:5)
   f. Pharaoh rejects the evidence of miracles (7:6–13)
  2. The ten plagues (7:14—11:10)
   a. Water turned to blood (7:14–25)
   b. Frogs (8:1–15)
   c. Lice (8:16–19)
   d. Swarms of insects (8:20–32)
   e. Pestilence on the livestock (9:1–7)
   f. Boils on man and beast (9:8–12)
   g. Hail (9:13–35)
   h. Locusts (10:1–20)
   i. Darkness (10:21–29)
   j. Death of firstborn predicted (11:1–10)
  3. The Passover instituted (12:1–28)
  4. Death of firstborn experienced (12:29–30)
  5. Pharaoh's permission for hasty departure (12:31–36)
 C. The journey to Sinai (12:37—19:2)
  1. Departure from Egypt (12:37—14:4)
   a. The journey commenced (12:37–42)
   b. Permanent regulations for Passover (12:43–51)
   c. Firstborn consecrated to the Lord (13:1–16)
   d. Avoidance of the Egyptian military route (13:17–20)
   e. Divine leading (13:21—14:4)
  2. Pharaoh's attempt to reconquer Israel (14:5—15:21)
   a. Israel pursued and fearful (14:5–12)
   b. Miraculous passage through the sea (14:13–22)
   c. Egyptian disaster (14:23–31)
   d. The song of victory (15:1–21)
  3. Wilderness experiences (15:22—19:2)
   a. Bitter water sweetened at Marah (15:22–26)
   b. Quails and manna given (15:27—16:36)
   c. God provides water (17:1–7)
   d. Amalek attacks (17:8–16)
   e. Jethro visits and advises (18:1—19:2)
 D. The divine covenant established (19:3—24:11)
  1. Preparation for the covenant (19:3–25)
  2. Declaration of the moral law (20:1–17)
  3. The people's fear (20:18–21)
  4. Miscellaneous commands (20:22—23:19)
  5. Divine promises (23:20–33)
  6. Ratification of the covenant (24:1–11)
 E. Commands on the mount (24:12—31:18)
  1. Moses ascends the mount (24:12–18)
  2. Directions for building the tabernacle (25:1—27:21)
  3. Directions for the priesthood (28:1—29:46)
  4. Further instruction (30:1—31:18)
 F. Interlude: the golden calf (32:1—33:23)
  1. Relapse into idolatry (32:1–6)
  2. The Lord's anger (32:7–10)
  3. Moses' advocacy (32:11–14)
  4. The people punished (32:15–29)
  5. Moses' intercession (32:30—33:23)
 G. The covenant reestablished (34:1—35:3)
 H. Construction and erection of the tabernacle (35:4—40:38)
  1. Offerings and workers provided (35:4—36:7)
  2. The parts of the tabernacle (36:8—38:20)
  3. The cost of the tabernacle (38:21–31)
  4. Garments for the high priest (39:1–31)
  5. The tabernacle completed and set up (39:32—40:33)
  6. Divine manifestation of approval (40:34–48)

IV. Miracles.

Exodus describes one of the few periods in biblical history when God chose to work a substantial number of MIRACLES. Long sections of the Bible contain no account of any such incident. The purpose of a miracle is to show that a greater than human power, namely the power of God, is involved, and to establish God's authority in the presence of doubt or apostasy.

The modern distinction between supernatural and providential acts is not specifically indicated in Scripture. The English word *miracle* is generally used to indicate an act that involves direct use of supernatural power, but there is no such distinction in the Hebrew and Greek words that are used. In both Testaments, the words sometimes translated "miracle" are frequently used in connection with actions in which no supernatural power is involved and may be rendered "sign." For example, the KJV uses "miracle" to render the Hebrew word *ʾôt H253* in Num. 14:22, but the same term is translated "sign" and used with reference to the continuing observance of the Sabbath in Exod. 31:13 and 17. See SIGN. It would require divine omniscience to draw an exact line between what God does providentially with forces he has already established in the world, and what he does by introducing new supernatural forces. Use of the word *miracle* does not necessarily mean that a supernatural power is directly involved; it points to a sign that could rightfully be accepted by an observer as evidence that divine activity was present regardless of whether this activity was exerted through acts of PROVIDENCE or through direct intervention of supernatural power.

The first miracle recorded in Exodus is the incident of the BURNING BUSH (Exod. 3:2). Moses saw a flame of fire coming out of a bush and yet the bush was not consumed. There is no way of knowing whether God created something entirely new to produce this impression upon Moses or whether he made an unusual use of forces that he had already established in his universe. The account is very brief. All that is certain is that something occurred that Moses had never seen before and that he correctly considered it to be extremely remarkable.

This was soon followed by a group of miracles given to Moses to enable him to prove to the Israelites that God had really sent him (Exod. 4:1–9). The first of these was the turning of his staff into a serpent. This was evidently a complete surprise to Moses, since Moses fled before it. Then God performed a new miracle by enabling Moses to seize it by the tail, whereupon it again became a rod. This double miracle was later used for the purpose of convincing both the Israelites and the Egyptians that Moses actually spoke for God (4:30; 7:10).

The second sign given to Moses for this purpose is described in Exod. 4:6–7. Moses was permitted, after putting his hand into his bosom, to withdraw it leprous as snow, and then, replacing it in his bosom, to pull it out completely recovered. If the Israelites should still fail to be convinced, a third sign was promised in 4:9. Moses would be enabled to take water from the river and pour it on the dry land, and it would immediately become blood. All of these miracles, those given to Moses as signs to show the Israelites or the Egyptians, and the burning bush to attract Moses' attention, were quite beyond Moses' understanding and gave him, as well as those before whom he later showed them, clear evidence of divine intervention.

The next group of miracles consisted of the ten plagues of judgment upon Egypt. See PLAGUES OF EGYPT. It is interesting to notice that every one of these, with the possible exception of the tenth, consists of something that might naturally occur in the land of Egypt. There are, however, four unique features that set them apart as extremely unusual events and thus give definite proof of the action of supernatural power and wisdom. These unique features are: (1) intensification, whereby the phenomenon was extremely severe; (2) acceleration, whereby all these great plagues occurred within a comparatively short space of time; (3) specification, whereby the land of GOSHEN was exempted from certain plagues; and (4) prediction, whereby Moses was able to foretell when the plague would occur. In the tenth plague, it was not unnatural for many children to die very suddenly from unexplained causes. The miraculous element was that the firstborn of every family in Egypt would be killed. God gave an important lesson by not simply sparing the Israelites because they were Israelites, but because they obeyed God's order for a lamb to be slain for each household and the blood to be placed upon the two side posts and on the upper door posts of the houses. This indicated that every family was under sentence of death for its sin, and that only when the blood of the lamb was shed and appropriated could punishment be escaped.

The third group of miracles was connected with the wilderness journey. Near the outset of the journey God allowed the people of Israel to become hemmed in by the sea in a place where they could easily be attacked, with no possibility of escape. Then he made it possible for them to cross over the sea on dry land, after which he brought back the waters so that when the Egyptians tried to cross they were drowned. It has been suggested that a ledge may have crossed this body of water a few feet below the surface. When Moses stretched out his hand over the sea, "the LORD drove the sea back with a strong east wind and turned it into dry land," thus dividing the water (Exod. 14:21). Deep water would remain on both sides, constituting a wall of protection against attack. Whereas it is possible that God introduced some new force other than the one mentioned in the Scripture, the specific statement about the E wind forcing the sea back strongly indicates his providential use of forces he had already placed in the earth: God caused these forces to become operative just when they were needed to perform his purpose and to display his power.

Another supernatural element in the wilderness journey was the pillar of cloud by day and fire by night by which God led the people (Exod. 14:19–20). The movement of the cloud in the direction desired, or its standing still in obedience to the Lord's will, manifests the strong supernatural element involved. See PILLAR OF FIRE AND CLOUD.

On two occasions during the portion of the wilderness journey described in Exodus, God miraculously provided water. There was sufficient water at MARAH, but the people could not drink it because it was so bitter (Exod. 15:23). God showed Moses a tree, which, when cast into the waters, made them sweet. At REPHIDIM (17:1–7) there was no water at all for the people to drink. God told Moses to smite a rock with his staff. When he did so, water flowed out. This may have been a new supernatural creation, or God may have chosen to cause a great underground stream gradually to burrow its way into the rock, perhaps over a period of years, so that when Moses struck it, an opening could be made through which an abundant supply of water would force its way. (A similar event, recorded in Num. 20:2–13, occurred later.)

Another aspect of God's miraculous care during the wilderness journey was his provision of food. After the sweetening of the water at Marah, the people soon began to fear starvation and to long for the "pots of meat" in Egypt (Exod. 16:1–3). Unlike the longer account in Num. 11:31–35 regarding the provision of meat through QUAILS and of the serious epidemic that followed, Exod. 16:11–13 includes only a brief mention of quails being provided. Here is no suggestion that a supernatural act of creating birds was involved. Quails are known to travel in large flocks only a few feet above the ground. God caused them to migrate in great numbers just at this time, and at a height at which they could easily be struck and brought down. The passage devotes more attention to the provision of the MANNA. This may have been a direct creation of God or a supernatural intensification and miraculous increase of a natural product of the area. Somewhat similar materials have been noted in this region, which crystallize at night and fall from trees to the ground. These partial parallels fall far short of what God provided for the Israelites. It would seem that he did indeed "rain down bread from heaven" (16:4; cf. Pss. 78:24; 105:40).

A remarkable supernatural event is described in Exod. 20, which relates that God spoke the TEN COMMANDMENTS audibly so that the words could be understood by Moses and the listening crowd.

This oasis (Bir Mara) has been identified by some with biblical Marah.

This struck terror to the hearts of the people; they begged that further revelations be transmitted through Moses rather than directly from God. The wording in Exodus is not absolutely explicit that the people could understand the words beyond the mere sound of thunder, but Deut. 5:24 makes it clear that the words were actually heard and understood. It is also stated that the Ten Commandments were originally written with the finger of God on tablets of stone (Exod. 31:18; 32:16). The original tablets were broken (32:19). God commanded Moses to prepare new tablets on which the commandments would be written (34:1, 27–28).

Exodus describes one of the great periods of miraculous divine intervention in the Scripture, yet it contains very few occurrences of other types of miracles, such as the raising of the dead by Elisha, or the walking on the water by Christ—incidents that would seem necessarily to involve the sort of creative power that God used in forming the universe in the first place. Many of its miracles may have been the use of forces that God implanted in nature and prepared long before the time of the exodus, but became operative at precisely the time when God willed that they should occur and in response to the action of Moses, his divinely appointed leader. It is absolutely clear that whether the miracle was of direct supernatural intervention or natural forces under a work of providence, in either case every one of them was definitely an evidence of the presence and activity of God.

V. The legal sections of Exodus

A. General remarks. In Genesis, the only legal sections in the Bible are the short commands contained in the various covenants with Adam, Noah, Abraham, Isaac, and Jacob, including the law of circumcision (Gen. 17:10–14). Such laws were given in connection with promises of divine blessing to God's people. A new emphasis is found in Exodus. Every legal section in this book is firmly based upon a great past event—the redemption of the people from Egyptian bondage. As a sign of gratitude for what God has done, his people took upon themselves the obligation of carrying out his will. Therefore Exodus presents far more extensive and detailed legal sections than any previously given.

There is a second reason why the legal sections in Exodus are so much longer than those in Genesis. Exodus describes God's dealings not with a few individuals, but with an entire nation. If multitudes are to live together in orderly fashion, detailed regulations for the conduct of the people in many situations are necessary. The laws of Exodus have two purposes: (1) to regulate the relationship of the redeemed to God; (2) to establish order and justice in the relationship of the redeemed with one another.

B. Relation to the law codes of other nations. In the 19th cent. many critics declared that the laws of the Pentateuch could not possibly have been written as early as the time of Moses, since life was then much too primitive for such advanced laws. Then in 1901 the Code of Hammurabi was discovered in Mesopotamia. It was at once apparent that the laws of the Pentateuch are not too complex to have been written at so early a date, for the laws of the Code of Hammurabi, written centuries earlier, are far more complex. Since that time, still earlier Mesopotamian legal documents have been found. An extensive Hittite law code from Asia Minor has also been discovered. Egyptian records contain references to the great scrolls of Egyptian law, but no portion of these laws has yet been recovered.

As a result of these discoveries, the critical argument was reversed, and it was suggested that much of the law of Moses had been taken over from the Code of Hammurabi or from other ancient codes. Closer examination shows this view also to be unfounded. The laws in the Pentateuch that have direct relationship to individual laws in any of these codes are comparatively few. The Code of Hammurabi is strictly a secular code and has little to say about religious matters, except for particular privileges or responsibilities of the priestly class. In contrast, fully half of the laws of the Pentateuch are concerned with specifically religious matters. Much of the Pentateuch includes regulations for sacrifice and for annual festivals or other religious services, matters that the Code of Hammurabi does not touch. (For further discussion, see below, section D.)

C. The originality of the laws. According to the Pentateuch, the laws of Exodus were given to the people by God through Moses in the wilderness. The greater portion of these laws has no precise counterpart in anything else that has been discovered in the ancient world. The secular portion has definite contacts with laws that have been found from earlier times. This does not in any way cast question upon the authenticity of the laws as given by Moses or upon the validity of their claim to represent God's will for his people.

It is necessary to note the nature of God's REVELATION. Everything that can be known with certainty about eternal things, about the origin of the universe, about its ultimate destiny, and about the future of individual persons or God's will for them, requires direct revelation from God, as he alone knows these matters. Everything of this sort that is contained in the Bible is a direct revelation, and could not otherwise be made known to us.

The case is somewhat different regarding the divine teaching about people's relationships with one another. When the Israelites left Egypt, their minds were not blank concerning laws of human relations. The effects of many judicial enactments and customary observances become part of the outlook of every individual by the time he or she becomes an adult. Many matters are settled by customary procedure of the area in which a person lives, by the ideals that are expressed, and by the results of law cases that come to one's attention. After the Israelites left Egypt, there was no reason to expect that a completely new legal system of relationship between human beings should be introduced. It was necessary at that point only to state those principles and precepts that were most urgent and vital, in order that the life of the Israelites should show forth the justice and kindness of the God who had redeemed them.

D. Types of law. Although many of the laws of Exodus treat secular matters, it is impossible to divide these laws sharply into religious and secular categories. All were based upon the covenant obligation to the Lord, who had redeemed his people from bondage, and to whose righteous law they therefore owed obedience. Many laws were concerned exclusively with ritual or with an individual's relation to God; even most of the secular laws have a religious tinge or at least a humanitarian attitude such as is not usually found in the laws of other nations of the time.

In a famous article entitled "The Origins of Hebrew Law," published at Leipzig in 1934, Albrecht Alt suggested that light could be thrown on the origin of OT laws by dividing them into two types that he called apodictic and casuistic (for an English trans. of this article, see his *Essays on Old Testament History and Religion* [1966]). He pointed out that about half of the laws in what is sometimes designated as the Book of the Covenant (Exod. 20:22—23:33) are casuistic in form, in contrast to the other half. By *casuistic* Alt meant laws that treat specific situations and formulate the judgment that should be given under various conditions. These laws generally begin with the particle *kî H3954* ("if") introducing a description of the general situation. This is sometimes followed by one or more occurrences of the particle *ʾim H561* (also translated "if"), which introduces the more specific situation plus a statement of the appropriate penalty or action (contrast 21:2 with v. 3). Such laws give the impression of having been developed through actual cases. In the codes from Mesopotamia and in the Hittite code, this is the most common type of law.

The other type, called *apodictic*, refers to laws that are categorically stated, usually without a penalty, as in the Ten Commandments, but also including those legal statements that simply end with such a phrase as "he shall be put to death" or that are preceded by the words "cursed be he who…" In view of the great similarity of form between the casuistic laws in the Pentateuch and those in the codes of the highly developed nations of Mesopotamia or Asia Minor, Alt suggests that the casuistic law in the Pentateuch was taken over from the Canaanites, but that the apodictic law, in contrast, had a specifically Israelite origin.

This view of the difference of origin of the two types of law is flatly denied by G. E. Mendenhall in his article "Covenant" (in *IDB*, 1:714–23), where he declares that such a distinction can no longer be taken as an evidence of a different origin, since he finds laws of both types not only in the covenant code of Exod. 21–23, but also in the Hittite treaties and laws from Asia Minor.

In any event, derivation of these laws from the inhabitants of Palestine must be recognized as entirely conjectural, since no non-Israelite code has yet been found in that area. The Israelites were doubtless familiar with this type of law from their experience in Egypt; moreover, the patriarchs who came out of Mesopotamia must certainly have had wide acquaintance with it. Some of these laws are very similar to laws in one of the Mesopotamian or Hittite codes, while others are strikingly different. The arduous labors of Moses in judging the people are alluded to in Exod. 18:13–26. From such labors, a body of precedents would naturally emerge. There is no evidence that the Bible claims to set forth a complete code for this sort of judgment. Doubtless many issues were decided on the basis of equity and of precedent.

In Exodus, casuistic law is not grouped by itself as distinct from apodictic law. Most of the law in the book, outside of Exod. 21–24, is apodictic law. In these chapters, the two types of law are about equally intermixed. The purpose of the section is not to provide a complete code for all situations, but to produce an impression of the sort of conduct that the people were expected to maintain, while giving specific guidance in a few common types of legal situations and constantly stressing the necessity of complete loyalty to the true God, utter abandonment of all fealty whatever to false gods or idols, and careful observance of the principles of benevolence and humanitarianism that God desires in his people.

E. Survey of the legal sections. The principal legal sections of Exodus, some of which shall be discussed in more detail below, are as follows:
(1) The law of the Passover (Exod. 12:1–27, 43–49)
(2) The firstborn set apart (13:1–16)
(3) The law of the manna (16:16, 23–33)
(4) The Decalogue (20:1–17)
(5) The "Book of the Covenant" (20:22—23:33)
(6) Regulations for the tabernacle and the priesthood (25:1—31:17)
(7) The laws of Exod. 34:10–26
(8) Renewed emphasis on the Sabbath (35:1–3)
(9) Orders to establish the tabernacle and the priesthood (40:1–15)

F. Laws given before Sinai. Before the solemn and rather lengthy presentation of God's law at Sinai, three briefer legal passages occur in Exodus. The last of these, which regards the manna, was directly tied to the immediate need to regulate the collection and use of this food. The other two legal sections that precede the experiences at Sinai did not similarly fill a definite immediate need in connection with the progress of the Israelites toward the Promised Land. On the contrary, they would seem rather to slow up and hinder this progress.

The nine great plagues had been completed, and the effect upon Egyptian determination to hold the Israelites in bondage must have been tremendous. When the last and most terrible plague occurred, the Egyptians did not merely permit the Israelites to leave; they urged them to go quickly (Exod. 12:31–33). Later events proved that Pharaoh and his leaders soon regretted this decision and set out to recapture the Israelites to bring them back (14:5–9). Under these circumstances, from a human viewpoint, it must have seemed advisable at the time of the tenth plague that the Israelites should leave as quickly as possible. Yet in the midst of these circumstances the Lord gave explicit and full orders for the ceremony of the Passover (12:3–13), and, in addition, took time to lay down permanent regulations regarding the future keeping of this great annual festival and the setting apart of the FIRSTBORN (12:43–49; 13:1–16). Only one conclusion is possible. More important than deliverance from bondage was the impression of great concepts upon their minds and hearts and the setting up of regulations whereby this impression would be continued and reinforced in subsequent years.

Therefore, the Passover had further lessons to stress in addition to the one great purpose of remembering the deliverance. Although the tenth plague forced Pharaoh to let the people go, it was also important to impress upon the Israelites that they too could not escape God's wrath except through a sacrifice. Nor would one sacrifice do for the nation. Each family must have its own lamb; the sacrifice was necessary. A lamb must be provided and be slain as a substitute for the sinful family. Each family was responsible before the Lord. It was necessary to interrupt the procedure of leaving Egypt to initiate this great ceremony in careful detail and, beyond that, to lay down regulations for its continuous observance in future years.

G. The Decalogue. The TEN COMMANDMENTS, which are contained in Exod. 20:2–17 and repeated with slight differences in Deut. 5:6–21, stand apart from all other legal sections of the OT. Their importance is stressed in a very special way. An introductory passage (Exod. 19) describes the stirring events that prepared human minds to realize the tremendous importance of what was about to occur. It is clearly implied in Exod. 20:18–19, and explicitly stated in Deut. 5:4, that God spoke these words so that all the people could hear. All other commandments in the Bible were given through individual prophets, such as Moses. The Ten Commandments were spoken directly to the nation as a whole.

In addition, the Ten Commandments were "inscribed by the finger of God" on tablets of stone (Exod. 31:18; 32:16; Deut. 9:10). The original tablets did not last long, but were broken as a result of Moses' hot anger when he saw the people turned away in the worship of the golden calf (32:19). Thereupon God told him to hew new tablets on which the words would again be written (34:1, 4, 28). When Moses repeated these laws in his farewell address, he emphasized that some of those present had personally heard them divinely proclaimed at Sinai (Deut. 5:3–4). The importance of a particular group of laws could hardly be stressed more emphatically.

The Ten Commandments summarize the ethical law. All are stated in absolute form. There is little detailed explanation. Thus stealing is forbidden, but the nature of private property, which such a law assumes, is not spelled out in detail. Murder is forbidden, but the difference between murder and justifiable homicide is left for separate explanation later (Exod. 21:12–14).

The Sabbath commandment in Exodus and Deuteronomy contains hortatory statements of why it should be obeyed, and also specific detail as to its application in particular circumstances. The command regarding parents is called by PAUL in the NT, "the first commandment with a promise" (Eph. 6:2). Such elements are notably lacking in other portions of the Ten Commandments. No specific penalties are mentioned in any of them. Infraction of the command on coveting would be impossible for human beings to punish, since it is an internal, spiritual matter.

Most legal sections of Exodus include some provisions that are civil law rather than moral law; that is, they relate to particular circumstances that might be subject to change. Nothing of this nature is found in the Ten Commandments. Nor do these commandments include any details of ritual or ceremonial law. (Some critics have suggested that a ritual decalogue preceded the ethical decalogue of Exod. 20.)

It has been questioned whether the Ten Commandments in the present form represent exactly the form in which they were originally given. The difference in wording between the Sabbath command in Exod. 20:8–11 and its counterpart in Deut. 5:12–15 suggests that the command was originally either longer so as to include all that is in both forms, or shorter, being thus presented only in bare outline. To those who believe in the plenary inspiration of the Scripture, it would seem more likely that the full commandment included every word of both sections rather than that it was originally given in shorter form. J. Wellhausen and other critics have held that the Ten Commandments represent an advanced form of law which could hardly have come into existence until the time of the later Israelite kingdom. Subsequently, other critics have taken the view that the commandments in a much shorter and more primitive form originated in the time of Moses.

There have been various modes of enumerating the commandments. The listing of JOSEPHUS (*Ant.* 3.6.5) shows that he followed the arrangement now common in most non-Lutheran Protestant churches and in the Greek church. This arrangement was followed by JEROME and Gregory Nazianzen. The TALMUD takes the introductory statement (Exod. 20:2) as the first "Word," and then combines the command on worshiping no other God with that against idolatry to form the second commandment. This is not as strange as it may appear, since the Hebrew noun translated "commandment" in Exod. 34:28 (also Deut. 4:13; 10:4) is the common term for "word" (*dābār H1821*); thus the Ten Commandments might also be called "the Ten Words."

AUGUSTINE adopted a different mode of enumeration: he took as the first commandment the combination that the Talmud calls the second commandment, and then secured the number ten by considering the coveting of a man's wife as the ninth commandment and the coveting of the house or other property as the tenth commandment. This arrangement is generally followed by the Roman Catholic church and by most Lutheran divines, but strikes an obstacle in that Exod. 20:17 (in contrast to Deut. 5:21) mentions coveting the house first and coveting the wife, second.

There has been discussion as to the arrangement of the commandments on the tablets. Augustine suggested that the first three were on the first tablet, and seven on the second. Calvin suggested that four were on the first and six on the second. PHILO JUDAEUS and Josephus explicitly held that five were on each tablet. Others have thought that the two tablets refer to two copies of the law (cf. M. G. Kline, *Treaty of the Great King* [1963], 17–19). There is no scriptural evidence on which to make a decision among these different views.

H. The covenant code. It is customary among Bible scholars to call the section from Exod. 20:22 to 23:33 "the Covenant Code" or "The Book of the Covenant." The latter title would seem to imply that this was the section read to the people by Moses, as described in Exod. 24:7, when they agreed to obey "the book of the covenant." It seems more likely, however, that the actual covenant consisted of the Ten Commandments, and that this portion was a further explanation and enlargement of the duties that would rest upon the people, rather than the actual constitution referred to in that verse, particularly in view of the reference to the Ten Commandments in 20:22.

This section consists of laws that were particularly important to present to the people at this stage of their religious life, at a time when they were looking forward to life in Canaan as the people of God (cf. Exod. 3:12). Consequently its laws look forward to Canaan and imply at many points a settled life in the land that the Lord would give them, and at the same time include provisions applicable to the situation during the time when they would still be in the wilderness. It had not yet been revealed that their unfaithfulness at KADESH BARNEA would result in a forty-year period of wandering, though God knew this would happen, and he so regulated the laws that they would be applicable to both situations.

These laws divide naturally into certain sections. They begin with a reiteration of the warning against idolatry—a very important warning since they were so soon to fall into the sin of worshiping the golden calf. This is followed by specific regulations for worship in the wilderness. As the community moved through the wilderness, it would be necessary to construct an altar at each place where sacrifice would be offered. General regulations for the type of altars are given (Exod. 20:24–26).

A long section follows that is mostly secular rather than specifically religious. It stresses humanitarian principles in the relation of master and servant, lays down rules for preservation of property, gives laws of compensation for personal injuries, prescribes regulations for the preservation of property rights, and then proceeds to declare specific commands against immorality, bestiality, spiritism, unkindness to the weak or the oppressed, and so forth.

Interspersed among these regulations, particularly toward the latter part, are comparatively simple rules for the general direction of the ritual and religious life of the people. Three annual feasts are presented and their importance is stressed. Avoidance of the Canaanite rite of boiling a kid in its mother's milk is ordered. The principle of the SABBATICAL YEAR is laid down. The commands to avoid any relationship to false gods or to any false type of sacrifice are stressed, and the weekly SABBATH is emphasized.

A particularly important ordinance is the law of ASYLUM, given in its first brief form in Exod. 21:12–14. According to the view associated with J. Wellhausen, this was the first stage in a development. Such an interpretation, however, is quite unnecessary. It should be noticed that it is not here said that the altar is the place of asylum. It is rather declared that a murderer is to be executed, and he is not to be safe even at such a holy place as the altar. Only the person who is guilty of accidental homicide is to be protected. The words "he is to flee to a place I will designate" could have found fulfillment during the time in the wilderness through some special arrangement by Moses. After the conquest of Canaan, it was fulfilled by the establishment of the CITIES OF REFUGE.

It was not the purpose of the secular portions of the Covenant Code to provide a complete set of laws for all the different types of problems that might arise, but merely to give an indication of the type of judgment to be made in certain common situations. In the main, they were a reiteration of principles already known. It contained a few specific ordinances that were vital for immediate application and presented the general attitude that God's people would be expected to maintain after entering Canaan. The purpose of this law, as far as the secular portions are concerned, was to illustrate the high moral principles and benevolent attitudes the Lord desired in the conduct of his people. (For another vital characteristic of the Covenant Code, note the discussion above in section D, "Types of law.")

I. Regulations for the tabernacle and for the establishment of the priesthood. During the first period of forty days and forty nights during which Moses remained on the mount, the Lord gave him instructions for the establishment of the permanent system of Israelite WORSHIP. Plans for the building of the TABERNACLE were set forth in precise detail. Four times it was stressed that everything about the tabernacle must be built exactly in accordance with the pattern that God had caused Moses to see in the mount. The language used (Exod. 25:9, 40; 26:30; 27:8) raises the question whether the revelation was simply given in words, or whether Moses actually was shown a model of the complete tabernacle.

The great emphasis laid on precise details of worship in these chapters and later on in the Pentateuch is in striking contrast to the very meager detail regarding divine service for the Christian in the NT. The difference is that when the NT worship was instituted, Christ already had been crucified and raised from the dead. The great central facts of the Christian religion had occurred and had been clearly explained. The ceremonies of the Christian religion looked back to something already fully known. Since a variety of forms could remind the hearer of these vital matters, there was no longer the same need to stress precise forms of worship.

In the OT, on the other hand, everything looked forward to the great events that God intended to bring about through the INCARNATION and the ATONEMENT. All this was seen by the OT believer through a glass darkly. Therefore it was necessary that the forms be strictly observed; otherwise the ceremony might fail to accomplish its purpose, or might even have the opposite effect of suggesting things that were not God's intention at all.

The details in the establishment of the tabernacle meant much to the Israelite believer. Its place in the very center of the camp during the wilderness journey would constantly remind him of the place that God should occupy in the life of the nation and of every individual member. The daily sacrifices (Exod. 29:38–42) would remind the Israelites that their sin constantly needed expiation and that nothing that they themselves could do would provide a permanent atonement. Perfect salvation could be secured only by that to which the sacrifices looked forward as they pointed to the DEATH OF CHRIST. The place of the great brazen altar in the outer courtyard barring the entrance to the tabernacle stressed the fact that only through atonement could anyone have access to God. The laver emphasized the requirement of holiness without which no one could see the Lord.

The first part of the tabernacle, with the altar of INCENSE and the table of SHOWBREAD, demonstrated the importance of the worship of God's people and the need of constant appropriation of the Bread of Life (which the NT identifies as Christ, John 6:35). The veil between the holy place and the holy of holies showed how sinners were unable to approach God until a new and living way was opened. In the

This Egyptian wooden box (with the deity Anubis on top) may be similar in appearance to the ark of the covenant made by Moses.

holy of holies, the ARK OF THE COVENANT represented the throne of God and his abiding presence with his people. This ark would contain reminders of the time in the wilderness, such as the tablets of stone to emphasize the importance of the moral law in any relation between God and man, and the pot of manna to show God's marvelous provision in the wilderness journey and the fact of his constant presence with his people. All these matters were presented to Moses in his first period in the mount, and the necessity of carrying out the details with complete accuracy was emphasized.

J. The laws of Exod. 34. After the covenant had been ceremonially established (Exod. 24) and Moses had gone up to the mount for forty days to receive the plans for the tabernacle, the apostasy of the golden calf occurred. See CALF, GOLDEN. Moses condemned the terrible apostasy of the people who had already fallen into idolatry, and God visited severe punishment upon those involved. Then God promised that he would renew the covenant and make it possible for the tablets that Moses had broken (32:15–19) to be replaced by a new set containing the basic law. Between the promise that the tablets would be replaced (34:1) and the statement that such tablets were actually prepared (34:27–28) is an interesting section in which a number of the previous laws are repeated in a different order. In this section, stress is laid on the covenant that God was renewing, and on his wonderful promises to bring his people into the Promised Land. Some of the most important of the Ten Commandments and of the religious ordinances of the Book of the Covenant are repeated, but none of its secular or casuistic laws.

When still a young man, the poet Goethe suggested that the laws of this section were the original Ten Commandments written on the two tablets. Julius Wellhausen accepted this idea, though admitting that Abraham Kuenen, his important coworker in the development of the documentary theory, resolutely denied it. C. A. Briggs (*The Higher Criticism of the Pentateuch* [1893]) presented the view as definite fact and maintained that the "ritual decalogue" of Exod. 34 was later displaced by the "ethical decalogue" of Exod. 20. However, H. Gressmann (*Mose und seine Zeit* [1913]) and R. H. Pfeiffer (*Introduction to the Old Testament* [1941]) strongly opposed it, insisting that Exod. 34 represents a later, rather than an earlier, form. Subsequently, many critical scholars have been inclined to believe that the Ten Commandments, although in a more simplified form, actually go back to the Mosaic period.

An apparently conclusive objection to the view that this is the primitive Decalogue is that it contains not ten laws but either twelve or thirteen, depending upon how they are divided, and that hardly any two scholars agree as to which of these twelve or thirteen should be designated as later insertions to secure the number ten, which is specifically mentioned in Exod. 34:28. The laws of this chapter, however, are in no sense an earlier form of the Ten Commandments, but were simply a reiteration for the particular needs of the situation of some of the laws previously given, including some of the Ten Commandments and also some sections of the Book of the Covenant.

K. The Sabbath. Unless it be the commands against compromising with false gods or falling into idolatrous practices, no feature of the law is more repeated in Exodus than that of the maintenance of the weekly SABBATH. This was stressed in the wilderness when the manna was first given by a special supernatural arrangement concerning the times when the manna would come (Exod. 16:22–30). It could not be gathered at all on the Sabbath. If more than enough for the day was gathered on any day except Friday, it would spoil during the night. On Friday, however, a double amount was given, and it would remain fresh for two days. Thus the importance of the Sabbath was stressed. Neither here nor in Exod. 20:8 was the Sabbath presented as something new, but as something that must be faithfully observed.

In the Ten Commandments, the Sabbath commandment is strongly emphasized (Exod. 20:8–11), and the people were reminded that its validity rests upon the arrangement followed in the CREATION of heaven and earth (20:11). In the midst of the Book of the Covenant, 23:12 again urges observance of the Sabbath. In the period on the mount, when the directions for worship were being given, 31:12–17 emphasizes the importance of Sabbath observance and again mentions its relation to the creation. In the laws particularly emphasized after the punishment for the apostasy of worshiping the golden calf, 34:21 urges Sabbath observance, and 35:1–3 stresses this aspect of the life of the Israelites. Thus in the early part of this nation's experience, after its deliverance from Egyptian bondage, emphasis is given to the importance of maintenance not merely of the day of rest that man needs, but also of the ceremonial provision that pointed forward to the goal of divine rest God provides for his people (Heb. 4:9–10).

(Significant commentaries include J. G. Murphy, *Exodus* [1866]; M. Noth, *Exodus*, OTL [1962]; U. Cassuto, *A Commentary on the Book of Exodus* [1967]; B. Childs, *The Book of Exodus*, OTL [1974]; J. I. Durham, *Exodus*, WBC 3 [1987]; N. H. Sarna, *The JPS Torah Commentary: Exodus* [1991]; T. Fretheim, *Exodus* [1991]; B. Jacob, *The Second Book of the Bible: Exodus* [1992]; D. E. Gowan, *Theology in Exodus: Biblical Theology in the Form of a Commentary* [1994]; P. Enns, *Exodus*, NIVAC [2000]; C. Houtman, *Exodus*, 4 vols. [1993–2002]; W. H. C. Propp, *Exodus*, 2 vols., AB 2–2A [1999–2006]; D. K. Stuart, *Exodus*, NAC 2 [2006]. See also J. Plastaras, *The God of Exodus: The Theology of the Exodus Narratives* [1966]; D. Patrick, *Old Testament Law* [1985]; H. Bloom, ed., *Exodus* [1987]; M. Vervenne, ed., *Studies in the Book of Exodus: Redaction, Reception, Interpretation* [1996]; G. Larsson, *Bound for Freedom: The Book of Exodus in Jewish and Christian Traditions* [1999]; M. R. Hauge, *The Descent from the Mountain: Narrative Patterns in Exodus 19–40* [2001]; J. K. Hoffmeier, *Ancient Israel in Sinai: The Evidence for the Authenticity of the Wilderness Tradition* [2005]; and the bibliography compiled by W. E. Mills, *Exodus* [2001].) A. A. MacRae

exodus, the ek′suh-duhs (from Gk. ἔξοδος *G2016*, "a going out"). The departure of the Hebrew people from Egypt under Moses.

I. Route

A. The main biblical data. The main starting point of the Israelites is given as the city of Rameses (Exod. 12:37; Num. 33:5), from which was named "the district of Rameses" (Gen. 47:11), identical at least in part with Goshen (cf. Gen. 47:6). Thence, they moved to Succoth (see Pithom) for their first camp (Num. 33:5; implied by Exod. 12:37 plus 13:20; cf. the phrasing of Num. 33:6), and thereafter to Etham on the edge of the wilderness (Exod. 13:20; Num. 33:6).

Then the Hebrews were instructed to turn back from the wilderness-edge (i.e., instead of continuing eastward), so that the Pharaoh might be taught a sharp lesson for seeking to subdue them (Exod. 14:1–4). Having so turned, their next camp was between Migdol and the sea (Exod. 14:2, the sea later qualified in 15:22 as "the sea of reeds," i.e., the Red Sea of the English versions). This was also before Pi Hahiroth and Baal Zephon, by the sea (14:2, 9; Num. 33:7). Having proceeded from W to E without encountering a "sea" previously, they would "turn back" either N or S somewhat, from the wilderness edge, and so come to a "sea" and the neighborhood of the three places named. In the Pharaoh's eyes, they were "wandering around the land in confusion, hemmed in [to Egypt] by the desert" (Exod. 14:3).

At this juncture came the crossing through the wind-divided waters of the "sea" (Exod. 14:21–22), which brought the Israelites back eastward into the Desert of Shur (15:22) with waterless travel for three days to Marah. Significantly, this wilderness is identified as that of Etham (Num. 33:8)—so, coming here a second time, the Hebrews had made a circuit. Schematically, their route would appear as one of the following (route A if they turned northward; route B if southward):

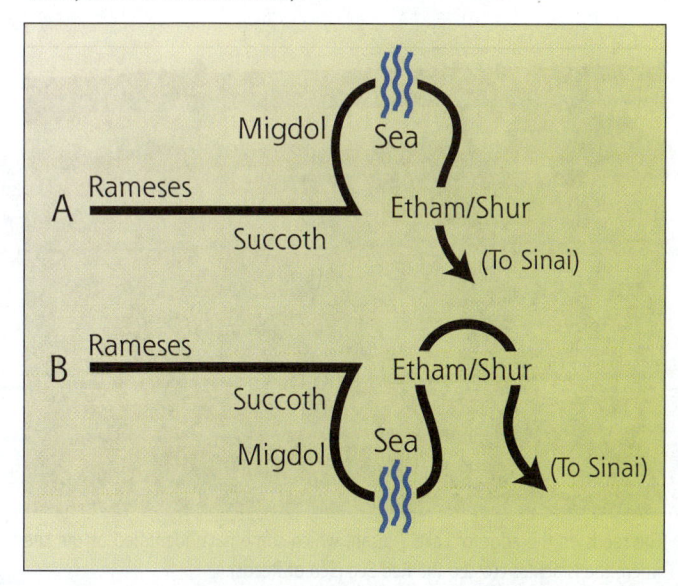

They were explicitly kept away from the road to the land of the PHILISTINES (i.e., the direct route from Egypt to GAZA near the Mediterranean coast), and so would have to take a more southerly route within the SINAI peninsula. On this consideration, pattern A is more meaningful than B, as A permits the Hebrews simply to continue in a southeasterly direction for Sinai, while B would land them back on the forbidden N coast route unless they further performed a sharp U-turn (not reflected by the narratives) to bring them back S again for Sinai.

B. Topographical background evidence.
The starting point, Rameses, would seem beyond any reasonable doubt to have been located either at Tanis (ZOAN) or near Qantir (17 mi. SSW of Tanis). Although Tanis has hitherto been the more popular identification, Qantir would appear to be preferable on both archaeological and topographical grounds. None of the quantity of Ramesside monuments at Tanis were actually found in place — all had been reused by later kings who appear to have brought them as quarry-material from elsewhere. At Qantir, evidence of palaces, the houses of high officials, temples, and houses for military personnel has been found of a kind that is clearly not brought from elsewhere or (like a well of RAMSES II) is definitely *in situ*. Geographically, Rameses in Egyptian documents stood on the "Waters of Ra" in a fertile district — true of Qantir, but not of Tanis.

Therefore, with a high degree of probability, one may place Rameses as the starting point of the exodus in the district of Qantir-Khatana. This identification fits well with the general location of the land of Goshen, which was also in some measure the "district of Rameses" (Gen. 47:6, 11). This latter phrase itself corresponds in some degree to the Egyptian name of the city, namely *Pi-Ramessē*, "Estate/domain [not merely 'house'] of Ramses" — that is, the whole territory attached to the king's city, itself named after him. Among other tasks unspecified, the Hebrews in this area had to labor on the building of both Rameses and Pithom (Exod. 1:11), and so it seems in order to infer that Pithom should also be within reach of Goshen and Rameses. Pithom is most probably to be sought in the Wadi Tumilat, either Tell el-Maskhuta (with Succoth) or westward therefrom at Tell el-Rotab. The latter possibility in particular would place Pithom quite near the S end of Goshen, while Rameses at Qantir would be at its N end, Goshen itself extending along the territory on the E of the Waters of Ra (Bubastite-Pelusiac, the eastern arm of the NILE). A location of Rameses at Tanis would perhaps be too far N to fit these requirements, and would extend the first day's march of the Hebrew multitude to up to 50 mi., an unconvincingly high figure.

From a Rameses at Qantir, two routes lay before the Hebrews, a fact perhaps reflected by an inscription of an earlier epoch (12th dynasty) from near Qantir and mentioning the settlement Ro-waty, "Mouth of the Two Roads," that is, the place where these roads diverged. (Text in S. Adam, *Annales du Service des Antiquités de l'Égypte* 56 [1959]: 216, 223 and pl. 9; cf. H. Kees, *Mitteilungen, Deutschen Archäol. Instituts, Kairo* 18 [1962]: 1–13, and J. Van Seters, *The Hyksos: A New Investigation* [1966], 141.) The first road thence was the main route to Palestine going NE to Qantara and ancient Sile (Tjaru) and so by the way of the land of the Philistines to Gaza and Canaan, but this approach was forbidden to the Hebrews (Exod. 13:17). The second way was to go SE from the Qantir district across uncultivated semi-desert terrain that extended between the main Palestine route in the N and the Wadi Tumilat on the S (cf.

The reeds on the edge of Lake Timsah, which some have identified as the site where the Israelites crossed the Red Sea (Sea of Reeds).

frontispiece map of K. Baedeker's *Egypt: Handbook for Travellers* [1908], for the terrain). This would bring the Hebrews to Succoth (Tell el-Maskhuta) near modern Ismailia, and then eastward into the wilderness proper and to Sinai. This was "the way of the wilderness" expressly taken by the Hebrews (13:18; NIV, "the desert road"), and so too, according to Papyrus Anastasi V, by two Egyptian slaves pursued from the delta-residence to Succoth and beyond (cf. *ANET*, 259b). Hebrew Succoth corresponds well to Egyptian Tjeku; at Tell el-Maskhuta, this would make a first day's march of some 20 mi. from just E of Qantir as Rameses.

The second day's march was perhaps briefer (perhaps 15–18 mi.), probably ENE toward the desert, now E of the Suez Canal and the El-Gisr ridge, and so to the wilderness proper, named Etham or Shur. Etham is a name that lacks any convincing identification in the Egyptian texts. It can hardly be Egyptian *Khetem* (ḫtm, "fort"; the Heb. ʾaleph represents a different sound, much weaker than Egyptian ḫ); nor is it the ʾIdm of Papyrus Anastasi VI, 55 (*ANET*, 259a; Heb. *t* appears in Egyptian as *t*, not *d*, and ʾIdm is most likely EDOM). However, within the biblical data, the tacit equation of Etham with Shur (Exod. 15:22 plus Num. 33:8) is a useful indication. For the wilderness of Shur was also on the main routes into Egypt from Palestine, that is, on that from Gaza, el-ʿArish, and via Qantara into Egypt, and that which branched off S to pass into Egypt via Ismailia and Wadi Tumilat. (See Gen. 25:18; 1 Sam. 15:7; and esp. 27:8.) Thus, the wilderness of Shur/Etham (Etham referring to its western edges?) extended N-S from the Mediterranean to about the latitude of Lake Timsah by Ismailia, and W-E from about the el-Gisr ridge (and Suez Canal) perhaps much of the way toward el-ʿArish and the "Brook of Egypt." This means

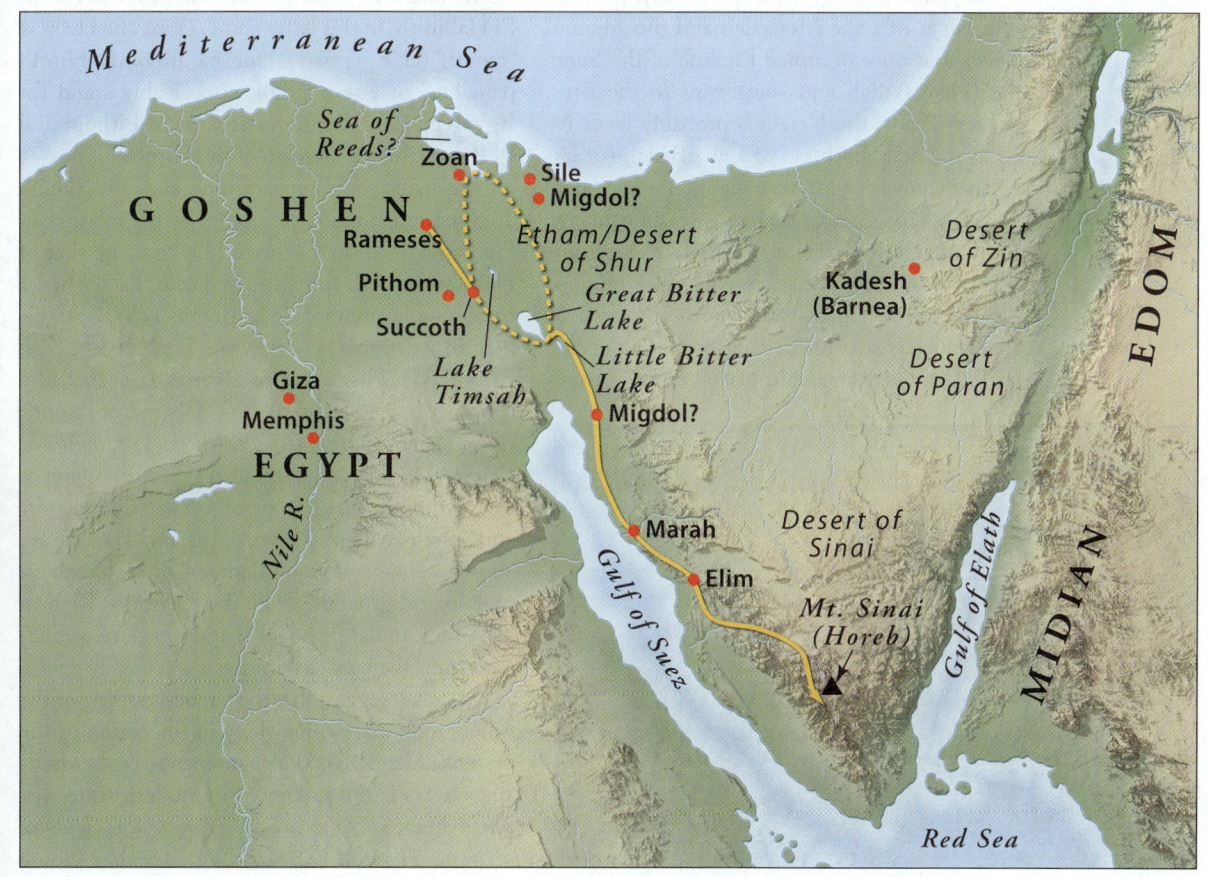

Possible Routes of the Exodus.

that when the Israelites doubled back from the wilderness, went along by the "sea," and crossed it only to return to this same wilderness, they more probably did so northwards from Ismailia rather than from S of it, as they thereafter went on to Sinai (scheme A, above, rather than B).

Therefore, it is possible to suggest that when the Hebrews "turned back" (Exod. 14:2) from Etham, they did so by going back NNW, then N (and not SSW and S, toward Suez). If so, then Migdol, Pi Hahiroth, and Baal Zephon would be nearer to Qantara in the N than to Suez in the S. The *yām sûp* (13:18 et al.) would not be the RED SEA of today; this is no problem, as the Hebrew term *sûp* G6068 corresponds to Egyptian *twf*, "papyrus," and should here be rendered "sea of reeds" (for a different view, see B. F. Batto in *BAR* 10/4 [July–August 1984]: 56–63). The Sea of Reeds would appear to be water bordered by reed-swamps in which papyrus might grow; this would fit in with the SE edges of Lake Menzaleh and the adjoining lakes that once occupied the line of the Suez Canal (Lake Ballah and southward to the Bitter Lakes). Thus, the Israelites probably went N as far as the neighborhood of Lake Ballah (or its pre-Canal equivalent). If Baal Zephon is the later TAHPANHES (and Greek *Daphnai*), as is quite likely, its location at Tell Defenneh (barely 8.5 mi. from Qantara) would be compatible with the situation of the Hebrews. The best-attested occupation of Tell Defenneh is later (26th dynasty, 7th–6th centuries, B.C.), but Ramesside-period remains were found there. A later Phoenician papyrus speaks of "Baal-zephon and all the gods of Tahpanhes" (N. Aimé-Giron, *Annales du Service des Antiquités de l'Égypte* 40 [1941]: 433ff.). Migdol would then be an Egyptian fort on the desert land W of Lake Ballah, so far unidentified, and could not be the Migdol of the prophets, nearly 18 mi. NE of Qantara, far out on the wrong side of the "sea." The name is a common Semitic word for "fort, watchtower," taken over by the Egyptians in the New Kingdom, and there was a plurality of such places.

Pi Hahiroth cannot be closely identified geographically at present, but may be attested in Egyptian sources as Pa-ḥir, "the ḥir-waters" (a canal or lake). In Papyrus Anastasi III (2.9), Pa-ḥir is set in parallel with SHIHOR (old Pelusiac Nile-arm), producing natron and flax (ibid., 3.4; see *ANET*, 471, "*the Her canal*"). It therefore had salt marshes and fresh water lands in common with the Sea of Reeds, and was probably near Shihor, as was true of Pi Hahiroth. In this latter name, *Pi* may be Hebrew "mouth" (cf. Egyptian *ro*) for "mouth of the Ḥiroth [canal?]," or else it might conceivably stand for Egyptian *Pi(r)*, "house/estate," as in Pithom and Pi Beseth, hence "domain of the Ḥiroth."

The name could appear simply as *haḥirōt* (Num. 33:8; no emendation needed). For the relation of Hebrew Ḥiroth to Egyptian Ḥir, compare that of Hebrew Succoth to Egyptian Tjeku. Pa-ḥir had a royal temple vineyard under Sethos I (W. Spiegelberg in *Zeitschrift für ägyptische Sprache* 63 [1923]: 28; VI, 31). His successor Ramses II even had a daughter named Hent-pa-ḥir ("Mistress of Pa-ḥir"; cf. G. Lefebvre, *Annales du Service des Antiquités de l'Égypte* 13 [1914], 202:XXIII; the Pi-Qerehet of Naville, the Pi-Hathor of Clédat, and the *Hr* and *Phrt* canals of Papyrus Anastasi III, 2:7 are all unacceptable as equivalents of Pi Hahiroth on philological grounds, while the Pa-ḥrn or Pa-ḥrm of Wadi Tumilat is too far S and too close to Succoth to fit the exodus narrative).

One may suggest that the famous crossing of the waters took place somewhere in the region of the present Lake Ballah; the phenomenon of the winds and waters is not unknown in modern times (cf. Ali Shafei, *Bulletin de la Société Royale de Géographie d'Égypte* 21 [1946]: 278 and figs. 10–11). Going on SE and S from such a crossing, the Hebrews

Some think that Jebel Serbal was the Bible's Mount Horeb (Sinai).

under Moses would then find themselves back in the Desert of Shur and Etham. Three days later (or, on the third day?) they reached Marah, which on such a time scale might well be as far S as the traditional ʿAyun Musa, some 9 mi. SE of Suez, on the Sinai side of the Gulf.

Naturally, the foregoing suggestion of a possible route of the exodus remains in some degree tentative (cf. P. Enns in *DOTP*, 272–80), but it will serve to show how well the extant biblical data fit into the background setting as they stand; one has no need of an appeal to documentary hypotheses to solve the problem, like the one offered in a well-documented study by H. Cazelles (in *RB* 62 [1955]: 321–64).

II. Date

A. Introduction. During the late 19th cent. and the first half of the 20th cent., many dates were suggested for the Hebrews' departure from Egypt. Two in particular have enjoyed some prominence. An "early" date for the exodus placed that event in the mid-18th dynasty under Amenophis II c. 1440 B.C., reckoning his predecessor THUTMOSE III as pharaoh of the oppression; the initial conquest of Canaan under JOSHUA then came c. 1400 (in the time of Amenophis III). The main basis of this scheme was a linear interpretation of the 480 years between the exodus and the building of Solomon's TEMPLE (1 Ki. 6:1). A "late" date for the exodus commonly placed it in the 19th dynasty under MERNEPTAH, with RAMSES II as pharaoh of the oppression; the conquest of Palestine would then have begun c. 1200 or later. The starting point was the place name RAMESES (Gen. 47:11; Exod. 1:11). However, neither view today seems really satisfactory; instead, one may suggest an intermediate solution, covering most of the data. No totally complete solution is yet possible, because of the lack of fully adequate data. Other famous events of ANE history are equally difficult to date definitively for much the same reason, so the biblical student is in good company here.

B. Data and background

1. Specific OT data. The biblical accounts do not name the Egyptian kings involved with the Hebrews, but merely refer to them as PHARAOH. One more specific datum is the names of the "store-cities" in Exod. 1:11, Pithom and Rameses. If these can be located, archaeological light on their history would help, and in the second case the very name Rameses (usually spelled Ramses or Ramesses) is that used by some eleven to thirteen kings of Egypt. Of these kings, RAMSES III to XI (and still later, Ramses-Psusennes) can be set aside: all reigned later than c. 1200 B.C. and too late for any reasonable date for the exodus. They are also later than the so-called Israel stela, attesting the presence of the Hebrews in Palestine in the late 13th cent. (see below), and this also excludes Ramses-Siptah. Ramses I reigned only sixteen months, so one is left only with Ramses II. He reigned sixty-six years and did build and adorn towns and temples named after himself, and is the only likely candidate to be the king reflected in the Hebrew place name Rameses. But what is the connection between the two? If this town can be located, was he really its builder, or did he, as some have suggested, merely rename an earlier foundation (assuming also that the "second" name came into Hebrew tradition, if not at the exodus then much later on)?

PITHOM lay somewhere in the Wadi Tumilat, in the SE delta. There are two possible sites: Tell el-Maskhuta and Tell el-Rotab. Whichever is correct, the result archaeologically is the same. Chance finds as well as regular excavations have produced virtually nothing before the 19th dynasty at either site (see the lists in B. Porter and R. L. B. Moss, *Topographical Bibliography of Ancient Egyptian Hieroglyphic Texts, Reliefs and Paintings*, 4 [1934], 53–55). Impressive monuments of Ramses II and later times came from both sites. Hence, it would be more natural for the Hebrews to be engaged on work at Pithom (whichever be its site) under Ramses II, when major monuments were installed there, than under the 18th-dynasty kings who appear to have manifested almost no interest in the Wadi Tumilat region (Porter and Moss have only some usurped traces at Gebel Hassa).

The situation for RAMESES is similar. The two possible sites are either Tanis or Qantir, with archaeological and geographical data increasingly favoring the latter, as noted above (section I). Again, the remains recovered from both locations tell a similar story. Relics from the Middle Kingdom and the HYKSOS age are followed by nothing else until the mass of monuments of the 19th and 20th Ramesside dynasties (see again Porter and Moss, 13–26 [Tanis]; 9–10, 26–27 [Qantir area, plus "Horbeit" monuments really from Qantir]; cf. L. Habachi, *Annales du Service des Antiquités de l'Égypte* 52 [1954]: 514–26). So many of the Ramesside works are original (usurpations being from the Middle Kingdom) that one cannot support the theory that Ramses II had merely usurped those of the 18th dynasty, for at neither Tanis nor Qantir was there anything of consequence from that epoch for him to usurp. It would appear that Sethos I began the new residence city, but that Ramses II took it over and by his vast works made it his own in fact as well as in name. The appellation of "store-cities" applied to Pithom and Rameses was probably very apposite. Each stood on a main route from Egypt to Palestine, and at Rameses the "Horbeit" stelae (so miscalled) show the existence there of military contingents, requiring arsenals and stores. Rameses was at once a summer residence, a base for military campaigns, and an administrative center alongside Memphis and Thebes.

In relation to Pithom and Rameses, there is good reason to place the exodus no earlier than the early years of Ramses II, that is, after either 1304 or 1290 B.C., the two alternative dates for that king's accession. The term "district of Rameses" (Gen. 47:11) is not an anachronism, because it is not put into the mouth of either Joseph or his pharaoh but is the phrase of the later *narrator*—a point frequently overlooked. If that narrator were a Moses in the 13th cent., the phrase in question would be entirely appropriate, a definition of Goshen in terms meaningful to his contemporaries. The use of the term *pharaoh* for the king, without personal name appended, is current usage precisely in the Ramesside age and soon thereafter; but from the 22nd dynasty onward, the usage of *pharaoh* plus personal name (cf. Pharaoh NECO) came increasingly into fashion.

2. Other external data. The other limiting datum comes from outside the OT, from Egypt itself: the so-called Israel stela (cf. *ANET*, 376–78 and refs.). This inscription is dated to the 5th year of MERNEP- TAH, successor of Ramses II, that is, to either 1234 or 1220 B.C. (depending on the latter's date). Its main theme is to commemorate Merneptah's great victory in smashing a massive Libyan invasion of Egypt, but at the end he also claimed that the Hittites were pacified, Canaan purged, Ascalon conquered, Gezer held, Yenoam made as if non-existent, Israel destroyed as without seed (either grain or offspring), and Palestine (Khuru) left as like a widow. These names are specific and concrete, not just vague boasts, and would seem clearly to place Israel squarely in W Palestine (by Merneptah's 5th year). These names would reflect a brief Palestinian campaign of Merneptah before his Libyan war. These apparently clear inferences and the data on which they are based have been doubted by some, but doubts of Merneptah's veracity can be discounted in the light of a less famous monument. On a stela in the temple of Amada in Nubia, Merneptah has a specially elaborate titulary, calling himself in parallel clauses "Binder of Gezer" and "seizer of the Libyans." Again, GEZER should reflect a specific event. "Seizer of Libya" is a clear allusion to Merneptah's Libyan victory, and so one may legitimately expect an equally real exploit to appear in the parallel clause—here, the capture of Gezer in Palestine, and so a campaign there in the course of which the Egyptian forces happened to brush with some Israelites, these already being in W Palestine.

Occasionally, skepticism has been expressed as to whether the name on the Israel stela is actually Israel and not some other people or place, such as JEZREEL. Such doubts are totally unjustified, and this interpretation is highly improbable in view of the close correspondence to the Egyptian term and the Hebrew word for "Israel" (cf. K. A. Kitchen in *TynBul* 17 [1966]: 90–92). Hence, one may suggest that the initial phase of the conquest under Joshua could not well have begun any later than shortly before 1234 or 1220 B.C. Thus, the exodus, the wilderness sojourn of forty years, and the beginning of the conquest are best located, based on available evidence, within the seventy years between 1304–1234 or 1290–1220.

Some further indirect confirmation of this result may perhaps be drawn from reliefs of Ramses II in the Luxor temple at THEBES, illustrating a campaign in MOAB. He records the capture of *"Bwtrt* in the land of Moab" (perhaps the later Raba-Batora), and of *Daibon* (i.e., DIBON of MESHA stela fame; see K. A. Kitchen in *JEA* 50 [1964]: 47–70, especially 50, 53, 55, 63–67, 69–70). It is far easier to assume that Ramses II raided Moab before the Hebrews entered that area, than to envisage the pharaoh's forces bursting into a district already populated by Israelite tribes (e.g., Dibon northwards; cf. Num. 21:21–31 et al.). The OT has no trace of such an event, nor does Ramses mention Israelites (as his son did, later) along with Moab and SEIR. As the tradition of "all Israel" is both ancient and persistent (cf. K. A. Kitchen in *TynBul* 17 [1966]: 85–88), it is hard to justify the skepticism of R. Giveon (in *Fourth World Congress of Jewish Studies: Papers* 1 [1967], 194) concerning the application of the term "Israel" to the Transjordanian tribes, although the Egyptians certainly could have used more generalized or traditional terms like Shasu or Asiatic.

C. Exodus and conquest

1. Wilderness sojourn. For the travels of Israel in the wilderness, there exists only the biblical account. There seems no warrant for doubting the reality of the forty years, first because it is made up of lesser specific amounts (e.g., thirty-eight years in Deut. 2:14, plus short spans in the book of Numbers), and secondly because the purpose of this period was expressly to allow a new generation to grow up in place of the one that had rebelled (Num. 14:21–23; 32:9–13; Deut. 2:14). So, forty years before the lowest possible date for Joshua's initial campaigns gives 1274 or 1260 B.C. as the terminal date for the exodus. Similarly, forty years below the highest possible date for the exodus gives 1264 or 1250 as the highest date for Joshua's opening campaigns. With Ramses II acceding in 1304, the exodus would fall within c. 1304–1274, and the initial conquest c. 1264–1234. On the 1290 date for Ramses II, the exodus would fall within c. 1290–1260, and the conquest would begin within c. 1250–1220. The generalized round figures of c. 1280 for the exodus and c. 1240 for the beginning of Joshua's wars would not be too far out in either case.

2. Data in Palestine. With these results one may correlate the Palestinian evidence. In TRANSJORDAN, the early Iron Age kingdoms of Edom and Moab seem to have become real entities politically, ringed with forts, from c. 1300 B.C. onward, in contrast to the earlier conditions with the area mainly left to nomadic tribes and occasional settlements on some routes (cf. N. Glueck, *The Other Side of the Jordan* [1970], and further references in Kitchen, *Ancient Orient*, 43 n. 40 and 61 n. 16). Thus, for Edom and Moab to oppose Israel (Num. 20:14–21; Jdg. 11:17), one would prefer the Hebrew passage of Transjordan to occur after c. 1300.

In W Palestine, the evidence for several sites would seem to agree with this result. This is so at Tell Beit Mirsim, LACHISH (Tell ed-Duweir), BETHEL (Beitin), Tell el-Ḥesi, and especially HAZOR (Tell el-Qedah). The final destructions at Canaanite Lachish could represent the exploits of CALEB after Joshua's campaigning. An important point is the change of culture visible when some of these sites were reoccupied (cf. Kitchen, *Ancient Orient*, 66 and 68 nn. 37, 45). In this picture, only AI and JERICHO appear to cause real difficulty. But there is no proof that et-Tell (destroyed c. 2400 B.C.) is Ai rather than Beth-Aven (see J. M. Grintz in *Bib* 42 [1961]: 201–16), and the real Late Bronze Age town of Ai may yet await discovery. At Jericho, heavy denudation of the long-unoccupied mound has apparently destroyed nearly all of the Late Bronze levels, along with much of the Middle Bronze. Hence, the Palestinian evidence is incomplete but is not incompatible with the other data.

D. Wider aspects. The 430 years between Jacob's entering Egypt and the date of the exodus (Exod. 12:40–41), if they be reckoned back from roughly 1280 B.C., would set Joseph and Jacob at c. 1700, in the period of the late 13th dynasty leading into the Hyksos period. Such a date would be feasible on independent grounds (patriarchs with early 2nd-millennium background; Egyptian conditions then). The 480 years of 1 Ki. 6:1 does not so obviously correspond with the 300 or more years from c. 1280 to c. 970.

However, 480 years is not *the* biblical figure, but only one biblical datum alongside others. Adding up the available figures in Exodus to 1 Kings gives not 480 but 553 years plus three unknown amounts, whereas DAVID's genealogy in the book of RUTH seems short for the period involved. The genealogy of ZADOK the high priest (1 Chr. 6:3–8) of ten generations would fit well into the roughly 300 years here envisaged. A short genealogy like David's may be selective. A larger total like the 553 years may contain partly overlapping items (e.g., judgeships), and the 480 be a portion of it. It is instructive to compare from Egypt the 500-odd years of dynasties 13 to 17 that are known to fit into the 240 years or so between the 12th dynasty (ended in 1786) and the early years of the 18th dynasty (c. 1550). Only Jdg. 11:16 does not readily fit into the picture here suggested, but it requires further study.

Attempts to utilize references to the HABIRU have proved rather sterile, because the term is too wide, ranging in ancient sources from c. 1800 to 1150, over the whole area of Mesopotamia, Asia Minor, Syria-Palestine, and Egypt; and conditions in the TELL EL-AMARNA tablets do not correspond with those in the book of Joshua, and so throw no direct light on the conquest period.

(An outline review of older views will be found in C. de Wit, *The Date and Route of the Exodus* [1960]. A 15th-cent. date is defended by J. J. Bimson, *Redating the Exodus and Conquest* [1978]. For a compact but fully documented treatment of the date of the exodus, see K. A. Kitchen, *Ancient Orient and Old Testament* [1966], 57–75, summarized and updated in *ABD*, 2:700–708. See also E. S. Frerichs and L. H. Leonard, eds., *Exodus: The Egyptian Evidence* [1997]; J. K. Hoffmeier, *Israel in Egypt: The Evidence for the Authenticity of the Exodus Tradition* [1997]; K. A. Kitchen, *On the Reliability of the Old Testament* [2003]; J. K. Hoffmeier, *Ancient Israel in Sinai: The Evidence for the Authenticity of the Wilderness Tradition* [2005]; J. H. Walton and P. Enns in *DOTP*, 258–780.)   K. A. KITCHEN

exorcism. The act of expelling an evil spirit from a person (see DEMON). The English term derives from the Greek verb *exorkizō* G2019, "to adjure, to put someone under oath" (Matt. 26:63); the cognate term *exorkistēs*, "exorcist," which is not attested prior to the NT, occurs there only once (Acts 19:13; this verse also uses the verb *horkizō* G3991, "adjure" [NIV, "command"]).

The concept of possession by a god or evil spirit is ancient. The Babylonians, Egyptians, and Greeks have left ample evidence. Various physical illnesses and states of frenzy were attributed to possession. Formulas of exorcism of definable types are found in ancient incantation texts. Exorcists employed such formulae, sometimes saying a specific magical word thought to have extraordinary power, and occasionally using magical objects. The demon was addressed by name if possible, as it was characteristic of ancient thought that to know the name of such a being was to control him. The exorcist might also invoke the name of a favorable deity. This was in contrast to the practice of Jesus, who performed exorcisms with a touch or word of command, without invoking the name of another. (It should be noted that often in Greek literature the term *daimōn* G1230 can refer to a divine power or to a person's "genius" in a good sense.)

The OT reflects God's opposition to evildoers, but in only one case is there anything like an exorcism. This was by MUSIC rather than command, the release of SAUL from an evil spirit when DAVID played for him (1 Sam. 16:14–23). In two further instances (18:10; 19:9) this therapy did not prevent possession. Instances of recorded demonic activity in Jewish literature increase in the Hellenistic period. Exorcism is described in the book of TOBIT (Tob. 6:7, 16–17; 8:3). King SOLOMON acquired a reputation as an exorcist in the writings of JOSEPHUS (*Ant.* 8.2.5) and, later, in the TALMUD. Josephus testifies that he saw Solomon's methodology used effectively. Jesus' words in Matt. 12:27 imply the existence of Jewish exorcists, and some itinerant ones are mentioned in Acts 19:13.

The NT narratives assume two things, the reality of demon possession and the victory of Christ over SATAN and the demon world. Although there have undoubtedly been numerous cases of alleged demon possession throughout history which, along with reputed exorcisms, may be attributed to suggestion or insanity, the cases in the NT cannot be dismissed without radical implications for NT history and theology. Several passages speak of the eventual doom of Satan and his angels (Matt. 25:41; 2 Pet. 2:4; Jude 6). The actual victory was accomplished by Christ (Jn. 12:31; Col. 2:15; 1 Jn. 3:8), who once spoke of Satan's defeat in connection with the casting out of demons (Lk. 10:18). When Jesus was accused of performing exorcisms by the power of BEELZEBUB, he stated that these acts were accomplished against Satan, in the power of the HOLY SPIRIT, the "finger of God," and as an expression of the KINGDOM OF GOD (Matt. 12:22–28; Lk. 11:14–20). The various instances of Jesus' expulsion of demons cannot be understood in isolation, or merely as acts of mercy to release oppressed people, although such was also the case. All was part of the great conflict against the powers of evil, in which conflict the disciples were commissioned. Whereas the text of Mk. 16:17 is uncertain, the earlier commands to the disciples are clear (Mk. 3:14–15; 6:7; and parallels).

This confrontation with demons occurred at the very beginning of his ministry (Mk. 1:23–27, 32–34; Lk. 4:33–37, 40–41). Mark distinguishes between exorcism and the healing of merely physical diseases, and notes that the demons obeyed the authoritative command of Christ. In a similar passage, Matthew says the act was performed "with a word" (Matt. 8:16). The woman bound by Satan was released simply by the laying on of Jesus' hands (Lk. 13:10–16). The Lord's disciples, however, needed to invoke the name of Christ (Lk. 10:17; so Paul in Acts 16:16–18). The daughter of the SYROPHOENICIAN woman was healed at a distance, which rules out psychological suggestion as an explanation of Jesus' exorcisms (Matt. 15:21–28). In the case of the GERASENE demoniac (Lk. 8:26–39), Jesus asked the demon's name, but it is not stated that this is related to his control of the demons. The demons on expulsion entered swine. Instances of such transference are also described in earlier, nonbiblical sources. In another case of violent behavior (Mk. 9:14–29), the disciples were unable to perform the exorcism. Here Jesus stressed the need of strong faith and prayer (also fasting, according to some MSS) on the part of the exorcist.

The various apocryphal "Acts" (see APOCRYPHAL NEW TESTAMENT III), JUSTIN MARTYR, TERTULLIAN, ORIGEN, and JEROME provide evidence of the continuing involvement of early Christians in this activity. The apologists of the 2nd–3rd centuries cited cases of exorcism to prove the power of Christ and the compassion of his followers. During the course of church history, matters of possession, witchcraft, etc., had great importance. Near the end of the 15th cent., James Sprenger and Heinrich Kramer compiled their code of the practices of the church against such evils, the *Malleus maleficarum*. The next century saw the *Flagellum demonum*, and in the 17th cent. there appeared the *Thesaurus exorcismorum* and the *Rituale romanum*. The latter, based on some of the preceding material, has been revised and published through the present time by the Roman Catholic Church. In the rites of that church, exorcism has become a preventative measure (for example, warding off demons from a baptism), as well as a curative one.

In conclusion, it should be stressed that the expulsions performed by Jesus are not called exorcisms in the NT, and that in contrast to typical exorcisms in pagan and even Jewish literature they were devoid of magical formulae, devices, and invocations. Our Lord's authoritative commands were an expression of his victory. (See further J. L. Nevius, *Demon Possession* [1894]; M. F. Unger, *Biblical Demonology* [1952]; R. H. Robbins, *The Encyclopedia of Witchcraft and Demonology* [1959]; K. Koch, *Occult Bondage and Deliverance* [1970]; J. W. Montgomery, ed., *Demon Possession* [1976]; G. Twelftree, *Christ Triumphant: Exorcism Then and Now* [1985]; C. F. Dickason, *Demon Possession and the Christian* [1987]; S. H. T. Page, *Powers of Evil: A Biblical Study of Satan and Demons* [1995]; C. Wahlen, *Jesus and the Impurity of Spirits in the Synoptic Gospels* [2004].)   W. L. LIEFELD

expiation. This word is not used in the KJV, but the RSV uses it in a number of passages, including three verses where the KJV has PROPITIATION (Rom. 3:25; 1 Jn. 2:2; 4:10; both NRSV and NIV render "sacrifice of atonement" or "atoning sacrifice"). The term *expiation* is preferred by some theologians in these passages on the grounds that it avoids the idea—alleged to be contained in *propitiation*—that God must be appeased (cf. C. H. Dodd, *The Bible and the Greeks* [1935], 82–95). It is argued that the rendering "expiation" correctly interprets the action of the Hebrew verb *kāpar* H4105 (piel stem *kipper*, "to cover," possibly "wipe away"), commonly translated in the SEPTUAGINT by *hilaskomai* G2661 (usually in its compound form, *exilaskomai*). There is no real ground linguistically or theologically for altering "propitiation" to "expiation." Expiation (the covering or forgiveness of sin) is a necessary element in the work of SALVATION, but it is not an alternative to propitiation.

Expiation deals with sin and guilt in such a way that propitiation is effected, and thus the pardoned sinner is restored to fellowship with God. The act of propitiation, therefore, is directed toward God, while the act of expiation is directed toward human beings in their state of sin and guilt. Wherever the action of expiation is present, the action of propitiation is always implied. By expiation the guilty person, or rather the offense which renders him guilty in the sight of God, is covered from the eyes of the holy God who looks upon him in righteous judgment. This is, of course, no fiction, as though God were prevented from seeing what is really there. The sin is dealt with so effectively that it no longer remains as the object of God's condemnation.

The OT presents this action of covering in several ways, usually expressed in English versions as "make atonement." Normally it was the priests who made ATONEMENT by the offering of sacrifice. The range of its application can be seen in the account of Yom Kippur (Lev. 16), when atonement was made for the sins of the people (vv. 30, 33), but also "for the Most Holy Place, the Tent of Meeting and the altar" (vv. 20, 33), presumably because these also were defiled through the contact of sinners (see ATONEMENT, DAY OF). The verb *kipper* is used frequently of the effect of the blood of the sin offering (4:18–20, 30–31, et al.) and of the trespass or guilt offering (5:6, 16–18), and even of the burnt offering (1:4; 14:20; 16:24). The latter has been regarded as purely a worship offering, but it is clear from these passages that all blood sacrifice had an expiatory value. "Underlying all these offerings there is the conception that the persons offering are covered by that which is regarded as sufficient and satisfactory by Jahweh" (BDB, 498; for the view that the Heb. word involves both ransom and cleansing, see J. Sklar, *Sin, Impurity, Sacrifice, Atonement: The Priestly Conceptions* [2005]).

The biblical presentation of the process of expiation shows that, according to divine revelation, sin against the holy God merits death, and that this judgment can be removed only if satisfaction is made to the requirements of God's justice by the death of another, usually an animal, in the place of the sinner. Atonement is made for the person, that is, his or her sin is expiated by death. This fact appears even in instances where the animal sacrifices are not offered. In Exod. 32:30–32 MOSES was willing to give up his own life in place of the people to make atonement for their sin, although in fact his intercession proved sufficient. PHINEHAS (Num. 25:10–13) "made atonement for the Israelites" by putting to death the leaders of this guilty action, thus turning aside God's wrath and stopping the plague he had inflicted on them. (For a discussion of other nonsacrificial passages where *kipper* is used, see Leon Morris, *The Apostolic Preaching of the Cross* [1955], 143–50.)

While the OT stresses the substitutionary character of the offerings by which expiation for sin is made, the phrase "make atonement for" combines the ideas of expiation and propitiation. Both actions are essential for restoring the guilty to fellowship with the holy God. In the NT the atoning sacrifice of Christ also includes both factors. Therefore the RSV rendering "expiation" is inadequate to express the full import of the reconciliation effected by Christ's death and resurrection. Propitiation, by pointing to the Godward aspect, also inevitably includes the manward expiatory value of his saving work. (See *NIDOTTE*, 2:689–710; *NIDNTT*, 3:148–66.)

J. C. CONNELL

extortion. The act or crime of obtaining what belongs to another by such means as coercion, intimidation, blackmail, and fraud. It has been said that as soon as two people met, they began to trade and also to take advantage of each other. Numerous passages of Holy Scripture condemning fraud and extortion of various kinds indicate that even the people of God often became guilty of exploiting others. God himself forbids all types of stealing and fraud, including extortion (Exod. 21–23). The prophet EZEKIEL warns that God will deal justly with an extortioner (Ezek. 18:18) and states that such crimes were common in his day: "The people of the land practice extortion and commit robbery; they oppress the poor and needy and mistreat the alien, denying them justice" (Ezek. 22:29). The psalmist preached that those who place confidence in extortion and robbery follow a vain hope (Ps. 62:10).

Extortion through excessive INTEREST, or usury, is particularly hit hard to prevent the exploitation of a fellow Israelite's misfortune (Lev. 25:35–36; Deut. 23:19). The TALMUD and the rabbis called usury the "abomination of abominations" and likened it to murder. The OT has no patience with the plea that the extortioner is within the law; legally or illegally, it is always wrong. One common form of extortion was to trick a man into a huge loan or pledge, then foreclose and force him to become a slave (Lev. 25:39, 47). Insolvency was the common cause of people being reduced to slavery in Israel. It was not unknown that a husband would falsely accuse his new wife of not being a virgin to obtain the marriage payment (Deut. 22:29). Much extortion went on along the caravan routes. Leaders of brigands would force merchants to pay tribute not to be robbed.

Jesus aimed charges of extortion, fraud, and robbery against the people of his day, particularly some of the PHARISEES, in the sharpest terms their ears could bear: "Woe to you, scribes and Pharisees, hypocrites! for you cleanse the outside of the cup and of the plate, but inside they are full of extortion [Gk. *harpagē* G771, 'seizure, greed'] and rapacity" (Matt. 23:25 RSV; cf. Lk. 11:39; 18:11). JOHN THE BAPTIST counseled repentant tax collectors and soldiers: "Don't collect any more than you are required to.... Don't extort money and don't accuse people falsely—be content with your pay" (Lk. 3:13–14). The final stroke is given by PAUL: "nor thieves nor the greedy nor drunkards nor slanderers nor swindlers will inherit the kingdom of God" (1 Cor. 6:10). (Cf. R. de Vaux, *Ancient Israel* [1961], 172–73; H. Daniel-Rops, *Daily Life in Palestine at the Time of Christ* [1962], 219–21.) See also CRIMES AND PUNISHMENTS; GREED. L. M. PETERSEN

eye. The organ of vision. The Hebrew term for "eye" (*ʿayin* H6524) usually appears in the dual form and is the basic component of many idiomatic expressions, some of which can be traced back to Sumerian. The common usage is of sight proceeding out from the eyes (Gen. 13:10 et al.). The eye often is used as the symbol of understanding (3:5 et al.). A period of sorrow and a loss or diminution of the understanding as in old age is symbolized as a dimming of the eyes (Job 17:7 et al.). Often "eyes" is used in poetic parallelism to "ears" (Isa. 6:10 et al.). In other references, it is in parallelism with "soul" or "body" (Ps. 31:9).

Canopic jar lids made of alabaster with the image of Tutankhamen highlighting his eyes.

In the NT, the word *ophthalmos* G4057 appears throughout. It too is the basis of various idioms, such as "an evil eye" (one who looks with ENVY or JEALOUSY, Matt. 6:23 KJV) and "in the twinkling of an eye" (1 Cor. 15:52). Another Greek term is *omma* G3921; a poetic term from Homer on, it is often used for the insight of intuition, "the eyes of the soul." This relatively rare term appears in the NT only in two contexts that involve the healing by Christ of blind men (Matt. 20:34; Mk. 8:23). On the phrase "An eye for an eye and a tooth for a tooth," see LEX TALIONIS. W. WHITE, JR.

eye, diseases of the. See DISEASE.

eyelids of the morning. This phrase is the KJV's literal rendering of Hebrew *ʿapʿappê-šāḥar*, which occurs twice in the OT (Job 3:9; 41:18; NRSV, "eyelids of the dawn"). The expression seems to refer to the gradual appearance of sunlight culminating in sunrise itself (thus NIV, "the rays of dawn"). Some scholars have suggested that this language derives from the notion of the god SHAHAR as a gigantic figure whose eyelids cover the whole earth.

eye of a needle. See NEEDLE.

eye paint. A substance made of mineral or other powder and used by women in ancient times for beautifying the eyes. The Hebrew term for this kind of paint is *pûk* H7037 (sometimes translated "turquoise" or "antimony"). JEZEBEL put paint in her eyes to allure Jehu (2 Ki. 9:30), and Jeremiah depicted Jerusalem as a prostitute that shades or enlarges her eyes with paint (Jer. 4:30). Using a different term (the unique verb *kāḥal H3949*), Ezekiel also represents Jerusalem, under the name Oholibah, as a prostitute that paints her eyes (Ezek. 23:40). It should not be inferred that eye paint as such had a negative connotation: the word *pûk* appears also in the name of Job's third daughter, Keren-Happuch (Job 42:14), which means literally "horn of [eye] paint," that is, a box for cosmetics (the eye paint powder before mixture with water was kept in a horn or slender reed, or in a jar).

Eye paint was used to enhance the beauty of women by "enlarging" the eyes (Jer. 4:30 NRSV), that is, making them stand out brightly by outlining them and projecting the line to the outer edge of the eye. The gray or black mineral could also be applied to the eyebrows. Note the sculptor's bust of the Egyptian Queen Nefertiti, from Tell el-Amarna (*ANEP*, no. 404). The material used for the eye paint mentioned in the OT was probably the powdered minerals galena and/or stibnite. The galena was a lead ore (lead sulphide PbS), of bluish gray color and metallic luster. The stibnite was an antimony trisulphide (Sb_2S_3) of lead gray color and brilliant luster, a substance the Romans called *stibium*. This mineral was listed as a part of Hezekiah's tribute to Sennacherib in the latter's annals (*ANET*, 288). (See R. J. Forbes, *Studies in Ancient Technology*, 8 vols. [1955–64], 9:160–66.)

W. H. Mare

eyesalve. This term is used by the KJV to render Greek *kollourion G3141* (a diminutive of *kollyra*, "little cake"), which appears in the context of the address to the church at Laodicea (Rev. 3:18 [NIV simply, "salve"]; many mss have the variant spelling *kollyrion*). Some scholars have seen a connection between the use of this term and the existence of a famous school of medicine in Laodicea (associated with the temple of the Phrygian god Men Karou). The ancient physician Galen, using the term *kollyrion*, speaks of a medicine for the eyes made from Phrygian stone and in the form of a tabloid (*De sanitate tuenda* 6.439). Since Laodicea was a well-known city in the region of Phrygia, W. M. Ramsay argued that Galen was referring to a "Phrygian powder" mentioned by Aristotle, and that this medicine came from Laodicea (see *The Letters to the Seven Churches of Asia* [1904], 417, 419). This inference, though plausible, cannot be confirmed (cf. D. E. Aune, *Revelation 1–5*, WBC 52 [1997], 260).

eyeservice. This term, used by the KJV and other versions, is a literal rendering of the Greek noun *ophthalmodoulia G4056*, which appears twice in nearly identical phrases (Eph. 6:6; Col. 3:22). Such a compound form, possibly coined by Paul himself, vividly describes insincere service, that is, work done to impress masters (or employers) "when their eye is on you" (NIV).

eyewitness. Someone who has personally witnessed an event and can verify its truthfulness. One Greek term with this meaning (*autoptēs G898*) is used by Luke to support and insure the authenticity of his narrative (Lk. 1:2). A close synonym (*epoptēs G2228*) is used by Peter similarly to designate himself and the other disciples who witnessed the majesty of Christ and who can testify that Christians have not followed "cleverly invented stories" (2 Pet. 1:16). This second term is attested in both pagan and Christian writers of the Greco-Roman period who describe the deity as one who "watches over" human beings (e.g., *1 Clem.* 59.3).

Ezar ee´zuhr. KJV alternate form of Ezer (only 1 Chr. 1:38 in some editions).

Ezbai ez´bi (אֶזְבָּי *H256*, meaning uncertain). Father of Naari; the latter is listed among the Thirty, David's military elite (1 Chr. 11:37). The parallel passage at this point has, instead of "Naari son of Ezbai" (*naʿăray ben-ʾezbāy*), "Paarai the Arbite" (*paʿăray hāʾarbî*, 2 Sam. 23:35; some mss of the LXX here read *huios Asbi*). These differences, like others in the lists, reflect textual confusion, but scholars do not agree regarding the original form. Some prefer the reading of 2 Samuel, citing the place name Arab (Josh. 15:52) or emending the text to "Arkite" (cf. Gen. 10:17; 1 Chr. 1:15; see P. K. McCarter, Jr., *II Samuel*, AB 9 [1984], 493).

E. L. Ackley

Ezbon ez´bon (אֶצְבֹּן *H719*, possibly related to Arab. *ʾaṣaba*, "to be bald" [*HALOT*, 1:81]). **(1)** Fourth son of GAD (Gen. 46:16); apparently the same as OZNI in the parallel passage (Num. 26:16).

(2) Son of BELA and grandson of BENJAMIN (1 Chr. 7:7). Since the longer genealogy for Benjamin (ch. 8) is quite different, some have argued that the shorter genealogy (7:6–12) really belongs to ZEBULUN, but this suggestion requires significant textual emendation.

Ezechias, Ezecias, Ezekias ez´uh-ki´uhs. KJV alternate forms of HEZEKIAH (inconsistent transliterations of Gk. *Hezekias G1614*). The form "Ezekias" occurs several times in the APOCRYPHA (Sir. 48:17 et al.; 2 Macc. 15:22) and in the NT (Matt. 1:9–10); "Ezechias" occurs twice (1 Esd. 9:14; 2 Esd. 7:40) and "Ezecias" once (1 Esd. 9:43 [9:110]).

Ezekiel i-zee´kee-uhl (יְחֶזְקֵאל, H3489, "God strengthens"; cf. HEZEKIAH, JEHEZKEL, JEHIZKIAH). Son of Buzi, descendant of ZADOK, and a major Hebrew prophet during the EXILE (Ezek. 1:3). Like ZECHARIAH (Zech. 1:1; Neh. 12:12, 16) and JEREMIAH (Jer. 1:1), Ezekiel was unusual in that his work combined the offices of prophet and priest; the Levitical influence is especially apparent in the last section of his prophecy (Ezek. 40–48). He was reared in Jerusalem and perhaps had already entered upon the work of the priesthood when he was taken with other captives, including King JEHOIACHIN, to Babylonia into exile by NEBUCHADNEZZAR in 597 B.C.

The problem concerning the age of Ezekiel when he was taken into exile has been a matter of discussion, but it is most probable that he was twenty-five years old at the time. The opening statement of his prophecy, "In the thirtieth year ... as I was among the exiles," appears to be a reference to his age at the time of his call into the prophetic ministry, which in the following verse is dated in "the fifth year of the exile of King Jehoiachin," who was also among the captives of the 597 B.C. deportation (Ezek. 1:1–2). The summons to take up the prophetic ministry thus came to Ezekiel in 592. Both JOHN THE BAPTIST and JESUS CHRIST began their public ministry at the age of thirty (Lk. 3:23).

As a member of the Zadokite family, Ezekiel was among the aristocracy taken into captivity by Nebuchadnezzar (2 Ki. 24:14). The prophet therefore built the chronology of his prophecy on the years of Jehoiachin's abduction (Ezek. 1:2; 33:21; 40:1). His last dated prophecy is in the year 570, the twenty-seventh year of Jehoiachin's captivity (29:17), and indicates that Ezekiel exercised his prophetic office for at least twenty-two years, his first prophecy having been announced in 592.

Ezekiel's prophetic ministry falls into two major periods. The first included the years 592–586, during which the prophet's message—directed toward Jerusalem—consisted of reiterated warnings and symbolic actions designed to bring Judah to repentance and back to her historic faith in God. The second period, which began with the year of the destruction of Jerusalem and the temple by Nebuchadnezzar, included the years 586–570. In the course of these years, Ezekiel was a pastor to the exiles and a messenger of comfort and hope (Ezek. 33–48). Thirteen years of silence separated the two periods of active prophesying, the last prophecy of the first period having been delivered in April 585 (32:17). He was not heard from again until April 572 (40:1). It has been suggested that Ezekiel returned to Jerusalem before the city fell, but there is no real evidence for this proposal. He was in Babylonia when the city fell (cf. 33:21–22).

The years of Ezekiel's captivity were the most severe years of Judah's history. The period of Assyrian domination of Judah actually began in 722 when the Assyrian SARGON took SAMARIA and destroyed the northern kingdom, and although Judah remained an independent nation, she was forced to pay tribute to the Assyrians. With the rise of Babylonian power under Nebuchadnezzar in 605 through the battle of CARCHEMISH, the position of Judah rapidly grew worse. In that year, DANIEL was in the group taken into captivity by the Babylonians. This was the first deportation, which was followed by another one in 597, when Nebuchadnezzar again invaded Judah and took the young king Jehoiachin and many of the leading citizens as captives to Babylonia (2 Ki. 24:14–17). Among the captives of this deportation was Ezekiel. The third deportation of Judean captives to Babylonia by Nebuchadnezzar was in 586, the year of the destruction of the city of Jerusalem, the temple, and the kingdom of Judah. Thus Ezekiel's life

EZEKIEL

Glazed brick reliefs of the lion, the sacred animal of the goddess Ishtar, from the procession street in Babylon (6th cent. B.C.). It was from Babylon that Ezekiel prophesied to Israel.

paralleled the years of the greatest crisis of Israel's history.

In Babylonia, Ezekiel was a member of a colony of captives in or near TEL-ABIB on the KEBAR River (Ezek. 1:1), which was probably the arm of an extensive system of canals (3:15). Ezekiel was married (24:16–18) and lived in his own house (3:24; cf. 8:1). On the fifth day of the fourth month in the fifth year of his exile (592 B.C.), he was summoned in a vision to be a prophet of God (1:1—3:11). His description of this vision is full of mysterious imagery designed to demonstrate the OMNIPOTENCE, OMNIPRESENCE, and OMNISCIENCE of God as these attributes are related to the ministry of Ezekiel and the future of Judah. Ezekiel was commissioned to summon the rebellious nation to hear the word of the Lord. Another vision followed in which the prophet was given a scroll with writing on both sides. He was told to eat the words, "words of lament and mourning and woe" (2:10), and he found them "as sweet as honey" to the taste (3:3). He was informed that he would meet resistance (3:4–11), and he then went to the exiles and sat among them overwhelmed. He proceeded to prophesy the inevitability of Jerusalem's destruction for its persistence in sin.

It is interesting to contrast Ezekiel's inaugural vision with the experiences of Isaiah and Jeremiah. The lips of ISAIAH were cleansed and then he received an audible and verbal communication from the Lord (Isa. 6:6–10). JEREMIAH first heard the Lord addressing him. The Lord then touched his mouth in an act symbolizing the delivering of his words to the prophet (Jer. 1:4–10). For Ezekiel, however, the words for the people were written in advance, and he "ate" the written words (Ezek. 2:10).

Ezekiel emphasized the doctrine of personal responsibility for sin in the most vigorous terms. "The soul who sins is the one who will die" (Ezek. 18:4). The message of Ezekiel in this respect constituted an important turning point in the prophetic message. With the destruction of the nation, the emphasis on national responsibility gave way to an emphasis on individual responsibility.

To a greater degree than other prophets, Ezekiel enforced his spoken message from the Lord by various symbolic acts. These symbolic acts were enacted words, and they were assumed to have in themselves divine effectiveness. He drew a plan of besieged Jerusalem upon a brick (Ezek. 4:1–3). He lay prostrate on one side and then on the other for several days (4:4–8). He shaved himself with a sword and then divided the hair (5:1–17). Many such dramatic symbolic acts enhanced the effectiveness of the prophet's message. After the destruction of Jerusalem, Ezekiel's prophecy became predominantly a message of consolation. Fully aware of the weaknesses of God's chosen people, the prophet centered Israel's messianic hope in them, describing in glowing terms their religious, moral, political, and economic future.

Aside from Ezekiel's influence upon the NT, especially the imagery of Revelation (see REVELATION, BOOK OF), he exerted great influence upon the later development of Jewish thought. He is sometimes referred to as the father of JUDAISM. The subject of personal IMMORTALITY, the doctrine of the RESURRECTION, and the emphasis upon the law in Judaism were all profoundly influenced by Ezekiel. His visions, frequently mysterious, affected considerably the development of Judaism's APOCALYPTIC thought as well as the medieval mysticism of the Cabala. The prophet figures prominently in the mural paintings of the synagogue of DURA EUROPOS completed in A.D. 255 (the synagogue was removed and reconstructed as part of the national museum in Damascus, Syria). Some rabbis of the school of Shammai regarded Ezekiel as only an apocryphal book because they thought it contradicted the Mosaic law. See also EZEKIEL, BOOK OF.

A. C. SCHULTZ

Ezekiel, Apocryphon of. A pseudepigraphic work attributed to the prophet EZEKIEL and usually dated between 50 B.C. and A.D. 50. Four brief quotations of little significance preserved in the patristic literature are thought to come from this book. JOSEPHUS (*Ant.* 10.5.1 §79) comments that Ezekiel wrote two books, and it is assumed that one of them is the work that EPIPHANIUS refers to as Ezekiel's "own apocryphon" (*Pan.* 64.70.5–17 [GCS, 2.515]). Epiphanius goes on to quote a substantial extract from the book, namely, a parable about a lame man and a blind man that illustrates God's righteous judgment (a similar story is preserved in the TALMUD; see *b. Sanh.* 91a-b). According to some scholars, the fragments that have survived do not come from an independent document, but rather from an expanded (perhaps Christianized) form of the OT book. (For an English trans. of the relevant materials, see *OTP*, 1:487–95; for greater detail, J. R. Mueller, *The Five Fragments of the Apocryphon of Ezekiel: A Critical Study* [1994]; M. E. Stone et al., *The Apocryphal Ezekiel* [2000].)

Ezekiel, Book of (see EZEKIEL). The third book among the Major Prophets of the OT.

  I. The historical background of the book
     A. The fall of the northern kingdom of Israel
     B. The destruction of Assyria
     C. The fall of Jerusalem
     D. The captivity
 II. History of Ezekiel studies
     A. Early attitudes
     B. Twentieth-century critical studies
     C. The locale of Ezekiel's activity
III. Text, integrity, style, and canonicity
     A. Condition of the text and its integrity
     B. The style of Ezekiel
     C. The problem of canonicity
 IV. Division and contents
  V. Teaching
     A. Ezekiel's concept of God
     B. Ezekiel's concept of Israel
     C. The freedom and responsibility of the individual before God
     D. The kingdom of God in its final glory
 VI. The NT use of Ezekiel
     A. Quotations from Ezekiel in the NT
     B. Ezekiel's influence on John
VII. Ezekiel in the history of Judaism
     A. His influence upon the mysticism of Judaism
     B. His influence upon the cult of Judaism

I. The historical background of the book.

The ministry of EZEKIEL took place in one of the great critical periods of history. His book presents a clear picture of a definite historical situation because the events of his day made a profound impression upon him. He makes allusions to contemporary events known to us from extrabiblical sources. In addition to general summaries of history (e.g., Exod. 20:5–29), Ezekiel refers to specific historical events, frequently dating accurately an incident or an oracle in accordance with his chronological system, which is based upon the years of the Babylonian captivity. From his situation in BABYLON as one of the captives, Ezekiel describes the destruction and restoration of Israel.

A. The fall of the northern kingdom of Israel.

The northern kingdom fell in 722 B.C. with the destruction of SAMARIA by the Assyrians, who had grasped the hegemony of the ANE. The Assyrians invaded Judah also but were unable to take Jerusalem. In the reign of ASHURBANIPAL (669–633 B.C.) the Assyrian empire began to disintegrate. The Babylonians under King NABOPOLASSAR led a coalition of the Medes, Persians, and Scythians against the Assyrians and in 612 destroyed NINEVEH. Amid the battle, the last king of the great Assyrian dynasty, Sin-sharishkun (627–612) lost his life. The Assyrian army, however, was mustered by Ashuruballat, an army officer, for the final struggle. See ASSYRIA AND BABYLONIA.

At the same time there was a revival of power in Egypt, and Pharaoh NECO, because of the growing Neo-Babylonian menace, decided that alliance with Assyria was the best way to accomplish his own ambitions for Egypt. It was necessary for Neco to march his army northward through Judah, to which JOSIAH (639–608) king of Judah objected. Over JEREMIAH's objections Josiah attempted to stop Neco at MEGIDDO, and in the battle Josiah lost his life (2 Ki. 23:29). Judah was now a vassal state of Egypt, and Neco placed Josiah's son Shallum, called JEHOAHAZ, on the throne (Jer. 22:10–12; Ezek.

19:2–4). He proved to be unsatisfactory for the purposes of Neco, and after three months as king Jehoahaz was deported to Egypt. Neco now placed JEHOIAKIM (608–597), an older son of Josiah, on the throne of Judah (2 Ki. 23:31–36).

B. The destruction of Assyria. The Egyptians joined the Assyrians for the final battle against the coalition led by the Babylonians for the hegemony of the ANE. At CARCHEMISH in 605 B.C. on the EUPHRATES River, the Egyptians and Assyrians were defeated by NEBUCHADNEZZAR, who had succeeded his father as king of Babylonia (Jer. 46:2). World hegemony now belonged to the CHALDEANS, and Jehoiakim became a vassal of Nebuchadnezzar (2 Ki. 24:1). The Babylonians marched upon Jerusalem to discourage Jehoiakim's tendency to be disloyal to Nebuchadnezzar. The result was the first deportation of captives to Babylon, among whom was DANIEL, Ezekiel's younger contemporary. The spiritual life of Judah suffered under the leadership of Jehoiakim, who persecuted the prophets (Jer. 36:1, 9, 28–32). His inclinations to revolt brought Nebuchadnezzar to Jerusalem again in 597, but apparently before the arrival of the Babylonians' punitive expedition, Jehoiakim died ignominiously and was buried with "the burial of a donkey" (Jer. 22:18–19).

Jehoiakiam was followed on the throne by his son JEHOIACHIN (also Coniah or Jeconiah), who three months later surrendered to Nebuchadnezzar (2 Ki. 24:8–17; Jer. 22:24–30; Ezek. 19:5–9). The Babylonians humiliated Jerusalem and deported several thousands of the influential of the population to Babylonia. Among these exiles were Jehoiachin and Ezekiel, and the prophet dated his prophecies by the years of this captivity (Ezek. 1:2). As a member of the exilic community, where Jehoiachin still bore the title of king, Ezekiel avoided a chronology for his oracles based upon the years of King ZEDEKIAH (597–586), Jehoiachin's successor.

Nebuchadnezzar made Mattaniah, Jehoiachin's uncle and third son of Josiah, king of Judah in the place of Jehoiachin, and his name was changed to Zedekiah (2 Ki. 24:17—25:7; Ezek. 19:11–14). He proved to be spiritually and administratively incapable of handling well a difficult situation and was induced by the pro-Egyptian party in Jerusalem to break his oath of fealty to Nebuchadnezzar. He joined a coalition of anti-Babylonian nations (Jer. 27:1–11; Ezek. 17:13–15), news of which reached Nebuchadnezzar, who summoned Zedekiah to Babylon in the fourth year of his reign (Jer. 51:59). Judah, caught between the opposing forces of the two superpowers of the ANE, was in an extremely difficult position with the pro-Egyptian and the pro-Babylonian parties each putting pressure on the king. Zedekiah vacillated for a while but finally yielded to the demands of the pro-Egyptian party and joined the rebellion against Nebuchadnezzar (2 Ki. 24:20). The Babylonian army appeared again at the gates of Jerusalem.

C. The fall of Jerusalem. The Babylonian siege of the city lasted a year and a half (2 Ki. 25:1–3) and culminated in the razing of the city and the plundering and burning of the TEMPLE. By the time JERUSALEM fell, famine had reduced the beleaguered city to desperate straits (Jer. 37:21; Lam. 2:4). Zedekiah, giving up all hope, tried to escape by fleeing in the direction of the wilderness, only to fall into the hands of the troops of Nebuchadnezzar. Ezekiel presents a symbolical portrayal of the king's flight. Zedekiah was brought before Nebuchadnezzar, who was encamped at RIBLAH, and there the Babylonian passed sentence upon the Judean king. He was made to witness the execution of his sons and then was blinded and brought in chains to Babylon. The prophecies of Ezekiel (Ezek. 12:13) and Jeremiah (Jer. 34:2–5) were fulfilled. In 586 B.C. Zedekiah joined Jehoiachin in the captivity.

D. The captivity. Even as king of Judah appointed by Nebuchadnezzar, Zedekiah was in a rather anomalous situation. Jehoiachin had gone into captivity in 597 B.C., but there were some who believed that he would shortly return to occupy the throne of Judah (Jer. 28:3–4, 11). Jehoiachin himself may have believed in the possibility of his restoration, prompting Jeremiah's warning that this would not take place (Jer. 22:24–30). It may be that the Babylonians preserved Jehoiachin in Babylon against the possibility of his return to Jerusalem. In captivity he retained the title of king and he was called "Yaukin" in official Babylonian records. In recently published tablets from the archives of Nebuchadnezzar dating c. 592, "Yaukin king of

Judah" and five of his sons are listed among the recipients of food rations from the royal supplies. Three jar handles stamped with the inscription "Belonging to Eliakim, steward of Yauqin" found at BETH SHEMESH and Kiriath Sepher may suggest the hope of his return. Jehoiachin was released from prison by EVIL-MERODACH son of Nebuchadnezzar in 560, the thirty-seventh year of his captivity (2 Ki. 25:27). It appears obvious that generally Jehoiachin was regarded as the legitimate king of Judah, with Zedekiah acting as regent until the time of the imminent return of the exiles.

According to Jer. 29:4–7, the exiles as a whole were able to rise above the slavery and serfdom that was the lot of some of the captives. Many were able to build their own houses, plant their own vineyards, and raise their own crops. Others were successful in the business and commercial affairs of the country. Records recovered from the ruins of the city of NIPPUR show the names of many Jews connected with the influential banking house of Murashu and Sons. According to Ezra 2:68–69, some of these successful Jews made substantial contributions to the return from Babylonia under ZERUBBABEL. The prosperity of the Jews in the Babylonian captivity (Heb. *gôlâ* H1583) explains why comparatively few took advantage of the opportunity to return to their homeland.

According to 2 Ki. 24:14, there were 10,000 captives in the 597 B.C. deportation. There are some difficulties with the figures regarding the number of the exiles involved (cf. Jer. 52:28–30), but it has been estimated that nearly 50,000 Jews were captives in the three deportations imposed by Nebuchadnezzar. They were settled in colonies where they were permitted a reasonable degree of liberty. The principal colony appears to have been at TEL ABIB, by the River KEBAR, a canal mentioned in Babylonian sources as *nāru kabari*, which passed through Nippur, a city SE of Babylon. Ezekiel lived in the colony at Tel Abib, and his home became a meeting place of the elders of the exiled community (Ezek. 3:24; 8:1; 14:1; 20:1). In the course of a profound theophany (1:4–28) he was commissioned to be God's messenger to the Jews of the captivity (2:3).

The visions of the prophet, his allegories, symbolic actions, apocalyptic imagery, and the interpreting angel have led to attempts on the part of some scholars to demonstrate that Ezekiel was psychopathic. He has been described as being a victim of paranoid schizophrenia or even catatonia (E. C. Broome in *JBL* 65 [1946]: 277–92). C. G. Howie (*The Date and Composition of Ezekiel* [1950], 69–84) gives an adequate answer to these views and concludes that Ezekiel "was a mystic by nature with a sensitive, artistic imagination which brought forth some of the best-known visions and symbolic figures of speech in Biblical literature" (p. 84). The deviations of Ezekiel from his contemporaries and other prophets are accounted for by his peculiar genius. See PROPHETS AND PROPHECY.

II. The history of Ezekiel studies

A. Early attitudes. Shortly after the formation of the OT CANON, some Jewish scholars raised doubts about the book of Ezekiel. It was thought that Ezekiel at some points contradicted the PENTATEUCH. Benedict Spinoza in the 17th cent. suggested that parts of Ezekiel's work had been lost and that what remained suffered from corruption. In the 18th cent., G. L. Oeder suggested that two books comprise Ezekiel (Ezek. 1–39 and 40–48). Only the first of these, according to Oeder, belongs to the prophet Ezekiel. In the 19th cent., Leopold Zunz held that the entire book was spurious and was written around 400 B.C. In the early 20th cent., Hugo Winckler advocated the idea that Ezekiel was a composite work of the early Persian period. A. B. Davidson, however, offered what was at the time the representative opinion of scholarship: "The Book of Ezekiel is simpler and more perspicuous in its arrangement than any other of the great prophetical books. It was probably committed to writing late in the prophet's life, and, unlike the prophecies of Isaiah, which were given out piecemeal, was issued in its complete form at once. The prophecies are disposed upon the whole in chronological order ..." (*The Book of the Prophet Ezekiel* [1916], iv).

B. Twentieth-century critical studies. In the beginning of the 20th cent., critical opinion changed radically. Liberal literary criticism advocated the redactional character of the book, leading to attempts to determine the amount of authentic Ezekielian material. In 1924 Gustav

Hölscher published his *Esechiel: Der Dichter und das Buch*, which was a milestone in the history of biblical criticism. It presented an entirely new view of both the prophet and his book and maintained that of the 1,273 verses in the book only 170 could be attributed to Ezekiel. According to Hölscher, 5th-cent. priestly redactors were responsible for most of the book. They added all the legalistic and ritual material, which completely transformed the prophet's original oracles and made of him a teacher of the law instead of a simple messenger of the people. The Ezekiel presented in the prophecy never existed, but was a fiction invented by the priestly editors of the book.

V. Herntrich (*Ezechielprobleme* [1932]) held that Ezekiel prophesied in Palestine and that a redactor was responsible for adding the material related to the Babylonian background. The most radical critical position was that of Charles C. Torrey, who in 1930 published his *Pseudo-Ezekiel and the Original Prophecy*. Torrey's view was that the book came from a writer who lived c. 200 B.C. and that the prophet Ezekiel never existed as a historical person. The book is a pseudepigraphon presenting a fictitious Ezekiel who is imagined to have lived in the reign of MANASSEH. The Babylonian setting is the result of still later editing, according to Torrey.

In the United States, William A. Irwin of the University of Chicago published *The Problem of Ezekiel* (1943), which was an attempt to build a critical theory upon the results of his predecessors in liberal biblical criticism. Irwin considered the substance of the book to be Hellenistic. Of the 1,273 verses in the prophecy, only 251 are genuine in whole or in part, the proportions of originality varying from complete genuineness down to a bare remnant of not more than a word or two. About eighty per cent of the book is spurious, according to Irwin. From Irwin's methods, the prophecy emerges as a patchwork of many authors, consisting of commentaries and explanations of the commentaries written over a period of several centuries. However, the prophet Ezekiel appeared as a truly prophetic personality after his genuine oracles had been disentangled from the spurious later additions.

Opposed to the opinions of critics such as the foregoing during this period were scholars who took a more conservative view. C. G. Howie (*The Date and Composition of Ezekiel* [1950]) supports the substantial correctness of the traditional view of Ezekiel and disputes the idea that the book is a composite work. Georg Fohrer (*Die Hauptprobleme des Buches Ezechiel* [1952]) also considered the major part of the book as being authentic and that whatever editing took place in the course of the history of the text did not essentially affect its content. He supports the idea of a Babylonian setting for the prophetic activity of Ezekiel. H. H. Rowley (*The Book of Ezekiel in Modern Study* [1953]) also rejected the conclusions of the popular liberal critical position and emphasized that the major content of the book belongs to the prophet.

The historical accuracy of Ezekiel has also been attacked. C. C. Torrey denied that there had been a destruction of Jerusalem and Judah by Nebuchadnezzar, which meant also that the biblical account was mistaken in its history of the captivity. This denial of the Chaldean invasion with its destruction of Judah and the resulting captivity meant also that the biblical account of the RESTORATION was false. Consequently Ezra, Nehemiah, and Jeremiah were also viewed as unreliable history along with Ezekiel. The denial of the historical accuracy of the account of what is perhaps one of the most important periods in Israel's history was also by implication of tremendous theological significance. Much of the messianic message of the prophets is built around the events of the destruction of Jerusalem and the temple, the Babylonian exile, and the restoration.

Archaeological researches have confirmed many aspects of the historical background of Ezekiel's book. The destruction of the cities of Judah by the Chaldeans has been confirmed by the evidence of inscriptions and pottery. The LACHISH ostraca recreated vividly the military campaign of the Babylonians in Judah just before they destroyed Jerusalem. Excavations in Babylon have uncovered ration lists of captives receiving grain from the supplies of Nebuchadnezzar among whom are many Jews. The fact that "Yaukin [Jehoiachin] king of Judah" and five of his sons are mentioned several times in the lists is a remarkable attestation to the biblical records of the *gôlâ*. Even Torrey's contention that specialists and skilled workers like gardeners were not taken captive to Babylonia as indicated in the biblical records has been refuted by the mention of such workers in the ration lists.

Archaeological reconstruction of this period has come also to the support of the reliability of the record in Jeremiah, Ezra, and Nehemiah. In addition, there is extrabiblical evidence of the return of the captives to Jerusalem. William F. Albright says, "The substantial historicity of the Edict of Cyrus (Ezra 1:2–4; 6:3–5) in 538 has been confirmed by modern archaeological discoveries" (*The Biblical Period from Abraham to Ezra* [1963], 87). All of this has contributed to a return on the part of the critical school to a more conservative position in regard to the origin of the book.

This tendency has continued during the last decades of the 20th cent. The influential scholar Walther Zimmerli, though skeptical in important respects, used a form-critical approach to argue for the genuineness of the prophetic style of the book. Moreover, recent emphasis on a literary approach has demonstrated that Ezekiel is characterized by far greater unity than some scholars had admitted (see, e.g., L. Boadt, *Ezekiel's Oracles against Egypt* [1980]).

C. The locale of Ezekiel's activity. The problem of the locality of Ezekiel's prophetic activity is closely related to some of the aspects of the preceding discussion. The traditional position, based upon the book itself, is that the place of Ezekiel's ministry was Babylonia, in Tel Abib beside the River Kebar (Ezek. 1:1). It was there that the heavens were opened and Ezekiel saw visions of God. Contrary to this view is the opinion of many of the critical school that Ezekiel prophesied in Jerusalem. This judgment rests upon the idea that many of the detailed descriptions of the religious, cultural, and political situation in Jerusalem are so vivid and realistic as to require that the writer was a personal eyewitness to the events and scenes described (Ezek. 8; 11:1–13).

Scholars who believe that Ezekiel spent his entire ministry in Judea hold that a later editor added the materials that reflect a Babylonian setting. On the other hand, these same materials indicate to other scholars that the period of the prophet's ministry was divided between the two places, first in Jerusalem and later in Babylonia.

C. C. Torrey, James Smith, and Volkar Herntrich held to the Palestinian ministry of Ezekiel, while Alfred Bertholet advocated the view that both areas were involved as the locale of the prophet's activity. The arguments involved in this problem are somewhat subjective in character, and it is not impossible that the entire prophetic activity of Ezekiel took place in Babylonia.

There was close contact between the exiles in Babylonia and the Jerusalem community. Consequently it was not impossible for a prophet in Babylonia to deliver prophecies and perform symbolic actions for the instruction of the people in Judah. If Ezekiel and Jeremiah were in Jerusalem together, one would expect to find some indication of it not only in the books of Jeremiah and Ezekiel, but also in the biblical historical records of the period.

III. Text, integrity, style, and canonicity

A. Condition of the text and its integrity. The MT of Ezekiel reflects scribal errors produced in the course of its transmission through the centuries, a phenomenon to which all ancient documents were subjected. Fortunately the SEPTUAGINT, as well as other versions, parallel texts, and general textual evidence have made possible reasonably reliable restoration of many passages (cf. the recent work by L. J. McGregor, *The Greek Text of Ezekiel* [1985]). Hölscher and Irwin determined what they conceived to be the original and true text by means of a preconceived key to the genuine Ezekielian material. Their method was based upon what they judged to be Ezekiel's literary style, and deviations from that style were expunged from the text and declared to be spurious. Emendations were made in the text to suit the requirements of the presuppositions.

A clumsy text does not necessarily indicate an irregularity or deviation from the smoothness of a preconceived style or a nonoriginal expression. The subjective character of the process is well described by Herbert G. May: "Literary and Historical criticism is not an exact science. The scholar can only be as honest as possible in considering and weighing all the facts.... There is one further warning: in a book as difficult as that of Ezekiel it is inevitable that Biblical scholars should have been much influenced by their total conception of the development and character of Hebrew religion and history" (*IB*, 6:45).

B. The style of Ezekiel. The various literary types in the book reflect the antithetical characteristics of the prophet's personality, his seemingly contradictory moods determining the wide variations of his style, as expressed sometimes in vivid poetry and at other times in ordinary prose. Ezekiel's poetic nature is reflected in his effective use of the dirge (*qînâ H7806*), as in the beautiful lament over the banished princes of the royal house (Ezek. 19:1–14). Perhaps the greatest poetry in the book is that of the allegories of the whelps (19:2–9) and of the ship Tyre (27:3–9, 25–36). The description of the ship Tyre is so true to life that it is one of the most important literary sources of our knowledge of ancient navigation. The image of Jerusalem as a foundling child (16:1–63) is as beautiful as any to be found in prophecy. Ezekiel's prose style is generally without particular distinction, but is lucid and adequate to convey his message. There is some Akkadian influence in the prophet's Hebrew, but Aramaic influence is more pronounced.

Frequently repeated typical words and phrases give support to the idea of the literary unity of the book: "walking in my statutes" (eleven times), "my sabbaths" (twelve times), "As I live, says the Lord God" (thirteen times), "countries" (twenty-four times), "idols" (forty times), "Then they will know that I am the Lord" (fifty times). These Ezekielian words and phrases appear in every part of the book, indicating its literary homogeneity and suggesting a single author for the prophecy. The book thus bears the stamp of a single mind in its phraseology, its imagery, and in its process of thought, which is developed on a plan so perspicuous and comprehensive that the evidence of literary design in its composition is unquestionably clear.

C. The problem of canonicity. The book of Ezekiel became a part of the Hebrew canon, but in the days of the rabbis Shammai and Hillel questions arose in regard to some of the canonical books. Among these was Ezekiel together with Esther, Proverbs, Ecclesiastes, and Song of Solomon. The actual point at issue was not the standing of the book of Ezekiel in the canon, a status that was taken for granted, but the use of the book for liturgical purposes and in public readings. There is no clear evidence that there was an attempt to remove Ezekiel from the canon. The Talmud indicates that because of supposed contradictions to the Torah in Ezek. 40–48, it was thought that the use of the book in public was not desirable (*b. Ḥag.* 13a). It was anticipated that the difficulties would be solved by Elijah upon his return. It was also thought that the beautiful vision at the beginning of the prophecy would be profaned through public use or through its study by any person under thirty years of age.

Eventually, after burning 300 jars of oil in the course of his nightly researches, Hananiah ben Hezekiah was able to find a satisfactory solution for the so-called contradictions. Others continued to be dissatisfied, however, and some have speculated that this situation contributed to carelessness in the transmission of the book, resulting in the unusual number of corruptions in the present text. The so-called contradictions between the last part of the book and the Torah are the basis of much of the radical criticism concerning Ezekiel, which presumes that Ezek. 40–48 is a description of the revival of the Mosaic rituals. On the contrary, it is possible to see in these chapters not a revived Mosaism but a description of a future temple with its own ceremonies—an interpretation that accounts for the differences.

IV. Division and contents. In its general theme the book of Ezekiel resembles Isaiah, the first part having to do with judgment, the second with blessing. In its structure the forty-eight chapters of Ezekiel may be divided into four sections indicating the contents of the book. Within the general structure, the order of the material is, on the whole, chronological.

    A. Prophecies against Israel (Ezek. 1–24).
      1. Ezekiel's call and commission (1:1—3:15). At the River Kebar the prophet has a vision of the glory of God and his call to prophesy to a "rebellious house" (2:5–8; 3:26–27; 12:2–25) and to act as a guide to Israel. There is vivid description of the divine chariot, which occupies a prominent place in the book (3:23; 8:4; 43:3).

2. Oracles against the people of Israel (chs. 4–24).
   a. Oracles of symbolic actions describing the coming siege and destruction of Jerusalem and the exile (chs. 4–5).
   b. Prophecies against the mountains of Israel and the land of Judah (chs. 6–7).
   c. The prophet's vision of the destruction of Jerusalem and the departure of the glory of the Lord. It contains a description of the conditions in the city at the time (chs. 8–11).
   d. Oracles of symbolic actions of the exile (ch. 12).
   e. Oracles against false prophets (ch. 13).
   f. Oracles against idolaters (14:1–11).
   g. Discourse on personal responsibility (14:12–23).
   h. Allegories concerning Jerusalem; the city symbolized as a vine and as an unfaithful wife (15:1—16:52).
   i. Prophecies concerning the doom and restoration of Israel (16:53–63).
   j. Allegories concerning the kings of Judah, together with remarks on personal responsibility (chs. 17–19).
   k. Discourse on Israel's apostasy and a prophecy of restoration (ch. 20).
   l. Swords of the Lord and Nebuchadnezzar (ch. 21).
   m. Description of the sins of Jerusalem and Israel (ch. 22).
   n. Allegory of the two sisters Oholah and Oholibah, symbolical of Samaria and Jerusalem (ch. 23).
   o. Allegory of the pot; death of Ezekiel's wife (ch. 24).
B. Prophecies against foreign nations (chs. 25–32).
   1. Against Ammon, Moab, Edom, Philistia (ch. 25).
   2. Against Tyre, represented in its wealth and beauty as the anointed cherub on the mountain of God, with a prophecy of blessing to Israel (26:1—28:19).
   3. Against Sidon (28:20–26).
   4. Against Egypt (chs. 29–32).
C. Prophecies of restoration (chs. 33–39).
   1. The prophet as a watchman (33:1–9; cf. 3:16–27).
   2. Discourse on individual responsibility (33:10–20).
   3. Ezekiel's muteness (33:21–22; cf. 3:22–27; 24:25–27).
   4. Reaction of Ezekiel's audience (33:23–33).
   5. Prophecy against the false shepherds of Israel (ch. 34).
   6. Prophecies against Edom because of her support of the Babylonians in their attack upon Judah (ch. 35).
   7. Renewed prophecies concerning the restoration of the land and people of Israel (ch. 36).
   8. Vision of the valley of dry bones prophesying Israel's resurrection (37:1–14).
   9. Oracles of the two sticks and the restoration of Israel and Judah (37:15–28).
   10. Prophecies against Gog of Magog (chs. 38–39). These chapters describe the final assault upon the kingdom of God by the nations of the world under Gog from the land of Magog, and their destruction on the mountains of Israel in a great demonstration of the might of Yahweh to all the ends of the earth.
D. Ezekiel's vision of the ideal theocracy of messianic times with its restored land and temple (chs. 40–48).
   1. The temple (40:1—44:3).
      a. Ezekiel's preparation for the vision (40:1–4).
      b. The temple wall, courts, gates, chambers for the priests, and altar (40:5–47).
      c. The Holy Place, the Holy of Holies, interior decoration of the temple and its general dimensions (40:48—41:26).
      d. Two three-story buildings N and S of the temple containing the chambers for the priests (42:1–14).
      e. Measurements of the whole temple area (42:15–20).

f. The glory of Yahweh returns to the temple after having departed from it for a time (43:1–12; cf. 10:19; 11:23).
  g. The altar for the burnt offerings (43:13–27).
  h. The eastern gate (44:1–3).
 2. The priesthood (44:4—45:17).
  a. The statutes of the Levites (44:4–14).
  b. Regulations for the Zadokite priests (44:15–31).
  c. A specific area reserved sacred for the temple, the priests, the Levites, and the prince (45:1–8).
  d. The duties of the prince (45:9).
  e. Correct weights and measures (45:10–12).
  f. Taxes paid to the prince for the support of the temple (45:13–17).
 3. The temple ritual (45:18—46:24).
  a. Two semiannual atonement ceremonies for the temple at the beginning of the first (March-April) and seventh (September-October) months (45:18–20).
  b. The Passover Feast observed in spring (45:21–24) and the Feast of Tabernacles celebrated in autumn (45:25).
  c. Sabbath and New Moon (46:1–7).
  d. Regulations for entrance into the sanctuary (46:8–10).
  e. The meal offering (46:11).
  f. The prince's freewill offering (46:12).
  g. The daily burnt offering in the morning (46:13–15).
  h. Regulations for the tenure of land (46:16–18).
  i. Regulations for the temple kitchens (46:19–24).
 4. The holy land (chs. 47–48).
  a. The life-giving stream (47:1–12). Flowing out of the temple mount, it transforms the desert into a paradise and the Dead Sea into a fresh-water lake abounding in fish.
  b. The borders of the land of Israel, W of the Jordan River (47:13–20).
  c. Aliens in Israel may acquire land in the country (47:21–23).
  d. The seven tribes north of the temple (48:1–7).
  e. The area between the tribes of Judah and Benjamin is sacred for the affairs of the temple (48:8–22).
  f. The five tribes S of the temple (48:23–29).
  g. The twelve gates of the city (48:30–35). The gates are named after the twelve tribes of Israel, and the name of the city will be, "The Lord is there."

The central point of Ezekiel's prophecy is the destruction of Jerusalem. In the period before 586 B.C., the prophet's principal purpose was to preach the importance of REPENTANCE and to demand a change in the people's way of life; to warn them that their confidence that the Egyptians could save them from defeat at the hands of the Babylonians was mistaken (17:15–17; cf. Jer. 37:7); and to assure them that their city and temple were to be inevitably and quickly destroyed. In the period after Jerusalem was destroyed, however, Ezekiel's main purpose was to comfort the exiled Hebrews by promises of eventual deliverance and restoration to their homeland, and to encourage them by assurances of future abundant blessings. His prophecies against foreign nations were delivered between these two periods, most of them having been spoken during the interval between the revelation to Ezekiel that Nebuchadnezzar had laid siege to Jerusalem (24:2) and the reception of the news that the Babylonians had taken it (33:21). The periods at which the prophecies on these various subjects were delivered are usually carefully noted in relation to the chronology of the exile.

V. Teaching. A study of the teaching of Ezekiel's prophecy places him among the greatest of the Hebrew prophets. He gave definite and clear expression to the great theological concepts that were at the heart of the preaching of all his predecessors in the prophetic office.

A. Ezekiel's concept of God. Fundamental to an understanding of Ezekiel's theology is his concept of God. It is the GLORY of God that is first drawn to our attention by the prophet. The vision

Ezekiel envisioned life-giving waters flowing into the Dead Sea so that there would be places for fishermen to cast their nets (Ezek. 47:8–10).

by the River Kebar, which formed the introduction to the call of Ezekiel to the prophetic office, was "the appearance of the likeness of the glory of the Lord" (Ezek. 1:28). Here Yahweh is described as the absolute ruler of all creation, over which he sits enthroned. The vision is in the form of a divine throne-chariot and appears as a great cloud and fire coming from the N. The chariot is borne by four living creatures in the form of men, each of whom "had four faces and four wings.... Each of the four had the face of a man, and on the right side each had the face of a lion, and on the left the face of an ox; each also had the face of an eagle"— representing the whole living creation (1:6, 10; cf. vv. 22–28). These figures appear again in Rev. 4:7. The vision symbolized the transcendence of God, his omnipotence, omnipresence, and omniscience. It represented the constant and diverse manifestation of God's power in the world, and Ezekiel gives it a greater emphasis than any of his predecessors.

This concept of God enters profoundly into the fiber of the prophet's teaching and is woven into every aspect of his theology.

The key to the ministry of the exiled prophet was that the glory of God could be revealed in the plains of Babylonia as clearly as on the hills of Judea. He experienced it again in the plains of Babylonia (Ezek. 3:23). By the power of the Spirit he beheld it in the temple together with "the utterly detestable things the house of Israel is doing" in its very presence (8:3–6). He saw it leaving its accustomed place on the cherubim as the command was given to destroy the sinful city (9:3; 10:4) and eventually deserting the polluted place, which had become unfit for its presence (10:18–19; 11:22–23). In still another vision Ezekiel saw the glory of God return to the restored city and temple. Again "the glory of the Lord entered the temple" and he heard the voice saying, "this is the place of my throne and the place for the soles of my feet. This is where I will live among the Israelites forever" (43:2–7; 44:4).

This abiding sense of the glory of God has its counterpart in the title by which Ezekiel is led to speak of himself. He is the "son of man," a weak and mortal representation of fallen humanity, conscious of his limitations before the presence of the glory of God (Ezek. 2:1). This indicates that Ezekiel is conscious of the fact that Yahweh is a moral being with the attributes of jealousy, anger, pity, etc., but he consistently insists that the activity of deity must be self-centered; that is, the purpose of all his dealings with human beings, whether in judgment or in mercy, is a revelation of his own Godhead. The constantly recurring declaration (more than fifty times) is "You will know that I am the Lord" (6:7). It is a doctrine to which the prophet attaches the utmost importance.

Ezekiel has much to say about the name of the Lord, Yahweh, which is the correlative of his glory (see God, names of). "I am the Lord" (*'ănî yhwh*, Ezek. 6:7) is the constantly reiterated claim in the prophecy. All of Yahweh's dealings with Israel have been, are, and will be "for the sake of my name." The acts of God are designed to reveal his one immutable nature. Israel had deserved nothing but destruction in the wilderness, but he spared them for his name's sake, to "keep it from being profaned in the eyes of the nations" (20:9, 14, 22). Nor is it for any merit on the part of Israel that she will be returned from the exile: "It is not for your sake, O house of Israel, that I am going to do these things, but for the sake of my holy name" (36:22). Both the redemption of Israel and the judgment of the nations are examples of the sovereign expression of divine grace in accordance with the immutable character of the divine nature.

Closely related to the ideas of the glory and the name of the Lord in Ezekiel's prophecy is the concept of his HOLINESS. The phrase "show myself holy" appears repeatedly as an expression of Yahweh (Ezek. 20:41; 28:22, 25; 36:23; 38:16, 23; 39:27). His holiness is his essential deity. Contemporary usage of the term "holy" has lost its original and proper comprehensive sense. The Hebrew root from which the verb (*qādaš* H7727) is derived seems to denote "separation." It represents God as distinct from human beings and separate from the CREATION he has brought into being. The term comes to signify the separation of God from everything that is finite, imperfect, and sinful. It is not a merely negative concept: it is used as an appropriate epithet for his deity, not to express any specific attribute, but rather to refer to the general idea of the Godhead. It includes the whole essential nature of God in its moral reference. Yahweh swears by his "holiness" or by "himself" without distinguishing between them (cf. Amos 4:2; 6:8). Among non-Israelite peoples, when the term was used with the word "god" or "gods," it was merely an otiose epithet, "the holy gods," with no more meaning than "the gods" (cf. Dan. 4:8–9, 18; 5:11, 14; cf. the Inscription of Eshmunʿazar, *ANET*, 662). Ezekiel uses the epithet of Yahweh, who is the Holy One of Israel, or "the Holy One in Israel" (39:7).

The term is applied also to anything that belongs to the sphere of the Holy One in Israel or has come into his presence (cf. Exod. 3:5; Num. 16: 37–38) or that belongs to him. Hence his arm, his Spirit, his temple are "holy," as are his city, people, land, etc. The word in this sense is applied to persons, places, and things set apart for his service, and are holy by virtue of that consecration or separation to God. It expresses not a quality but a relation. Things and men that were God's shared his "holiness" but they could be "profaned," such as his sabbaths or his holy princes (7:22, 24; 20:16).

When Yahweh reveals himself as that which he is, he "sanctifies" himself. Consequently to "magnify" or "glorify" himself or set his glory among the nations are acts that "sanctify." It is said of the destruction of GOG: "Thus will I magnify myself, and sanctify myself [*hitqaddišti*, NIV "show ... my holiness"]; and I will be known in the eyes of many nations, and they shall know that I am the LORD" (38:23 KJV; cf. 28:22; 36:23; 38:16). In the same manner people "sanctify" Yahweh when they acknowledge what he is or ascribe to him his true nature: Yahweh is "sanctified" in the eyes of the nations by the restoration and defense of his righteous people Israel (36:23; 38:16).

B. Ezekiel's concept of Israel. Yahweh reveals himself through Israel to the nations. The statement, "for the sake of my name I did what would keep it from being profaned in the eyes of the nations" (Ezek. 20:9, 14, 22), is used in reference to Israel and its destinies. It is an expression of Ezekiel's philosophy of history. History, especially that of Israel in the context of world history, is Yahweh acting for his own name's sake. Yahweh's concern for his own name was the origin of Israel's history and accounts for its course and future promise; otherwise she would have been

An artist's reconstruction of the temple described in Ezekiel's vision.

destroyed because of her iniquities. The thrust of the prophet's idea is indicated by the fact that he who is God over all in the highest monotheistic sense is Yahweh, God of Israel. He has become historically God of Israel to begin his revelation of himself to the nations, and will continue in this revelation until he is known to all the earth. Consequently Yahweh cannot destroy Israel, for such an action would invalidate or obliterate the revelation already made (20:9, 14, 22; cf. Deut. 9:28). Thus Ezekiel views Yahweh as inseparably linked with the destinies of Israel. In spite of the frequent apostasies of the people, Yahweh's revelation proceeded until the nation had to be punished and forced into exile. Among the nations, according to Ezekiel, this event was interpreted as a setback that reflected the weakness of Yahweh. They said, "These are the Lord's people, and yet they had to leave his land" (Ezek. 36:20).

In this way the name of Yahweh was profaned, the heathen gained a false impression of the God of Israel, and knowledge of him was obscured. The adverse effect of the captivity included not only the nations but also many in Israel who did not understand what happened. This effect will be eliminated when the final lesson of history is revealed (Ezek. 39:23). Since the honor of Yahweh is historically identified with the destinies of his chosen people, the ultimate disclosure of his deity can be effected only by the restoration of this nation to its Promised Land under conditions that reflect the holiness and glory of Yahweh. The same principle involved in the temporary exile of Israel becomes the surety of Israel's final redemption. Yahweh's recovery of his people from the lands of the Diaspora restores the prestige of his name among the nations and emphasizes the profound moral principles of his reign (39:23). At the same time it reaffirms and clarifies to Israel the historic truths that had been the subject of the preaching of the prophets in the past (20:42–44; 36:11, 37; 39:28–29).

Ezekiel is consequently led to a doctrine of salvation that is profoundly monergistic. Everything proceeds on the basis of the sovereign irresistible grace of God. It melts the hard hearts of the people, brings them to repentance, and endows them with a new spirit motivating them to walk in his statutes and to do his will (Ezek. 6:9; 11:19; 20:43; 32:14).

C. The freedom and responsibility of the individual before God. A prominent idea in Ezekiel is the doctrine of the responsibility of the individual soul before God. He had been anticipated in his teaching by Jeremiah (Jer. 31:29–30) but propounds it with an emphasis that is peculiarly his own. The idea of the corporate responsibility of the covenant community, in which people were being punished for the sins of their ancestors, was a common tradition in Israel (see corporate personality). In some respects this was an easy deduction on the part of people chosen by God to live in a particular land. It is in this connection that Ezekiel affirms the following principle: "The soul who sins is the one who will die. The son will not share the guilt of the father, nor will the father share the guilt of the son. The righteousness of the righteous man will be credited to him, and the wickedness of the wicked will be charged against him" (Ezek. 18:20). On the other hand, the presence of the righteous will not avail to save a sinning nation from punishment: "even if these three men—Noah, Daniel and Job—were in it, they could save only themselves by their righteousness" (14:14).

The sense of personal responsibility was a matter of great concern for Ezekiel in his own work. The nature and limits of his responsibility were defined for him at the beginning of his prophetic ministry, and again when he began the second period of his work. It was made clear to the prophet that although he was responsible for the proclamation of the revelation vouchsafed to him, he was not responsible for its success or failure (Ezek. 3:16–19; 33:1–6).

The idea of personal responsibility is inseparably related to the concept of faith as personal fellowship between the believer and God, a concept that was part of the thinking of all the prophets in regard to their own relation to Yahweh. Jeremiah had anticipated Ezekiel also in the doctrine that this is the character which true faith must assume in the experience of all people. It was Ezekiel who developed the principle most logically that neither a person's sins nor hereditary guilt can prevent the work of divine grace in the life of the penitent sinner (Ezek. 18). Spiritual action thus takes place at the center of life. Yahweh will reign ultimately because in his people there will be a new heart and a new spirit (cf. 11:19; 18:31; 36:26). This will be the creation of Yahweh himself.

D. The kingdom of God in its final glory. The final section of Ezekiel's prophecy is in many respects the most remarkable part of the book (Ezek. 40–48). In the form of a messianic prophecy, Ezekiel describes a politico-religious constitution by which his fundamental concept of holiness is expressed in the regulation of the details of the life of the redeemed community. These chapters are separated by an interval of twelve or thirteen years from the last of the other prophecies. Foregoing prophecies described the redemption and restoration of the land and the people (chs. 33–37). This section presents a description of the condition of the people in the experience of the promised redemption. The background of this picture is formed by the first thirty-nine chapters of the book. The concluding statement of the foregoing section is, "I will no longer hide my face from them, for I will pour out my Spirit on the house of Israel, declares the Sovereign LORD" (39:29).

The controlling idea is that of Yahweh's presence in visible glory in his sanctuary in the midst of his people, together with a suggestion of the obligations this relation involves on the part of Israel. The Israelites are a righteous people who know that Yahweh is their God and who are led by his Spirit. There is no indication in the passage how salvation is to be attained simply because the people have realized it and live in the consciousness of redemption. This accounts for the supernatural elements in the record with which the natural elements are commingled. It is important to realize that the commingling of these two elements is common in all of the prophets where descriptions of the ultimate destiny of Israel are concerned. It is also important to understand that the natural and supernatural features of the prophecy are to be taken literally.

One should hesitate to conclude, as some do, that the supernatural features of the account, such as the change in the physical condition of the area in and around Jerusalem (cf. Jer. 31:38; Zech. 14:10), and the effects of the river that issues from the temple bringing fertility to the region and life to the waters of the Dead Sea (cf. Zech. 14:8; Joel 3:18), are merely symbolical representations of future spiritual existence just because there are natural features in the description such as the people living in their natural bodies, living on the natural produce of the earth, and enduring physical death. The restoration described by Ezekiel is more than the natural restoration that took place under Zerubbabel, Ezra, and Nehemiah at the close of the Babylonian captivity. Like that prophesied by Isaiah (Isa. 60), Ezekiel's restoration involves the final state of the people and the world. The final perfect kingdom could be realized only through Yahweh's personal presence among the redeemed, when the tabernacle of God would be with them. The final words of Ezekiel's book are: "And the name of the city from that time on will be: THE LORD IS THERE" (Ezek. 48:35). The name of the new Jerusalem proclaims that God dwells with his people, the difference between life and death.

One also must guard against the tendency to emphasize the supernatural elements in Ezekiel's description, such as the life-giving stream which issues from the temple mount, the personal presence of Yahweh, etc., and conclude that the whole passage is merely an allegory representing the spiritual perfection characteristic of the church in the Christian age. The literalness and reality of the prophetic program described here are quite clear. The temple is real, as are the ceremonies and those who serve him. Sacrifices and offerings are thought of as continuing when Israel is redeemed and the kingdom is Yahweh's by the greatest prophets (Isa. 19:19, 21; 60:7; 66:20; Jer. 33:18). The sacrifices and rituals are not practiced in order to secure redemption, as some scholars suggest, but in order to memorialize and conserve the redemption which in the restored kingdom has already been effected. They are ceremonies of the worship of Yahweh and personal edification, for although the people are redeemed, righteous, and led by his Spirit, they are still subject to the weaknesses of their human nature. The people are not perfect but err from inadvertency. These errors of inadvertency were recognized and confessed in the acts of worship involved in the ceremonies.

The priestly character of the institutions prescribed by Ezekiel is due in some respects to the fact that the prophet himself was a priest, but more importantly to the suitability of the priestly concept of holiness to be the principle of a theocracy that was to be the reflection of the essential character of Yahweh and the relation of his people to him.

VI. The NT use of Ezekiel

A. Quotations from Ezekiel in the NT. There are several references and quotations from Ezekiel in the NT. The words "Whoever will listen, let him listen" (Ezek. 3:27) may possibly be the source of similar phrases in the Gospels and Revelation (cf. Matt. 11:15; Mk. 7:16; Lk. 14:35; Rev. 13:9; et al.). The solemn warning that judgment must begin at the house of God (1 Pet. 4:17) has its origin in Ezek. 9:6. It appears to some interpreters that 2 Cor. 6:16 contains a combination and condensation of Ezek. 37:27 and Lev. 26:11–12, and that 2 Cor. 6:18 is dependent upon Ezek. 36:28.

B. Ezekiel's influence on John. Ezekiel is more closely related to the Gospel of John and the Revelation, as indicated by a definite literary as well as doctrinal kinship. Gog and Magog of Ezek. 38:2–21 and 39:1–11 are the basis of the prophecy in Rev. 20:8, representing the forces of Satan ultimately destroyed by God.

The vision of God in Ezek. 1:22–28 is reflected in various places in the Apocalypse. John says that the voice of Christ "was like the sound of rushing waters" (Rev. 1:15; 19:6; cf. Ezek. 1:24). Other elements of this vision appear in Rev. 4:3, 6. The figure of the life-giving stream (Ezek. 47:1–12) flowing from the throne of God, regenerating the land with which it comes in contact, is used by John in Rev. 22:1–2. In the Revelation passage the flowing river brings healing to everything it touches and the trees along its banks yield their fruit every month as they do in the vision of Ezek. 47:12. John's vision of the holy city, the new Jerusalem (Rev. 21:10–27), is anticipated in great measure by Ezek. 48:15–35. In both visions the dimensions of the city are carefully described. (See B. Kowalski, *Die Rezeption des Propheten Ezechiel in der Offenbarung des Johannes* [2004].)

The Gospel of John contains several allusions to Ezekiel. Jesus' statement to NICODEMUS that "no one can enter the kingdom of God unless he is born of water and the Spirit" (Jn. 3:5) is reminiscent of the promise in Ezek. 36:25–27. Another passage, Ezek. 34:11–31, with its concept of a good shepherd, unquestionably influenced John. The prophet presents the Messiah as a shepherd who seeks out his sheep, protects and feeds them. Jesus uses the same figure to describe his own work (Jn. 10:1–39; the dependence of this passage on the Greek version of Ezek. 34 is especially clear). Ezekiel's influence upon John is again seen in the account of the useless vine (Ezek. 15:2–6; Jn. 15:1–5). John uses the idea of Ezekiel's vine to emphasize his own lesson. (See G. T. Manning, Jr., *Echoes of a Prophet: The Use of Ezekiel in the Gospel of John and in Literature of the Second Temple Period* [2004].)

VII. Ezekiel in the history of Judaism.
Ezekiel exerted important influence upon the development of JUDAISM. In some respects he shares with EZRA the reputation of being the father of Judaism. He prophesied in the transition period between the preexilic faith of an established covenant people and the postexilic faith of this same people, now a legal community in a strange land. In this period of devastation and change, the prophet contributed to the safeguards that were to protect the Israel of the future against the heathenism that had brought about the destruction of the nation.

A. His influence upon the mysticism of Judaism. Ezekiel's influence upon the mysticism of Judah is the result of his visions. His visions initiated that tendency in the life of Israel, resulting in the production of an extensive APOCALYPTIC LITERATURE chiefly between the 2nd cent. B.C. and the 2nd cent. A.D. He influenced as well the development of the later mysticism of the Cabala. There is, however, an important difference between Ezekiel's apocalyptic writing and that of the later apocalyptic writing of Judaism. These later writers borrowed Ezekiel's style, but were not inspired as to the origin, content, and delivery of their message. Consequently these apocalyptic writings were not considered canonical.

B. His influence upon the cult of Judaism. Of particular interest and significance in the influence of Ezekiel is his exposition of the temple and its ceremonies. A priest as well as a prophet, he emphasized ritualism (but not at the expense of moral values), laying the foundations for its eventual prominence in Jewish life. The direction given by the prophet in regard to the cult was followed in succeeding generations. He was the forerunner of that Judaism which developed around the temple cult and ceremonial minutiae. The moral and spiritual influence of Ezekiel upon Judaism was equally important. The doctrines of personal immortality, bodily resurrection, and the importance of the law in Judaism were all profoundly influenced by Ezekiel. The prophet, upon the basis of the lessons of the past with its many examples of Israel's apostasy, tribulations, and exile, insists that the future restoration depends upon Israel's observance of the will of Yahweh and strict adherence to the laws expounded by its legitimate religious leaders.

(Significant commentaries on Ezekiel include P. Fairbairn, *An Exposition of Ezekiel* [1851]; G. A. Cooke, *A Critical and Exegetical Commentary on the Book of Ezekiel*, ICC [1937]; W. Eichrodt, *Ezekiel*, OTL [1970]; W. Zimmerli, *Ezekiel*, Hermeneia, 2 vols. [1979–83]; M. Greenberg, *Ezekiel*, AB 22, 3 vols. [1983–]; W. H. Brownlee, *Ezekiel 1–19*, WBC 28 [1986]; L. C. Allen, *Ezekiel 20–48*, WBC 29 [1990]; D. I. Block, *The Book of Ezekiel*, NICOT, 2 vols. [1997–98]; I. M. Duguid, *Ezekiel*, NIVAC [1999]; M. S. Odell, *Ezekiel* [2005]. See also K. W. Carley, *Ezekiel among the Prophets: A Study of Ezekiel's Place in Prophetic Tradition* [1975]; P. Joyce, *Divine Initiative and Human Response in Ezekiel* [1989]; I. M. Duguid, *Ezekiel and the Leaders of Israel* [1994]; T. Renz, *The Rhetorical Function of the Book of Ezekiel* [1999]; A. Mein, *Ezekiel and the Ethics of Exile* [2001]; R. L. Kohn, *A New Heart and a New Soul: Ezekiel, the Exile and the Torah* [2002]; S. L. Cook and C. L. Patton, eds., *Ezekiel's Hierarchical World: Wrestling with a Tiered Reality* [2004]; T. J. Betts, *Ezekiel the Priest: A Custodian of Tôrâ* [2005]; J. Robson, *Word and Spirit in Ezekiel* [2006]; and the bibliography compiled by W. E. Mills, *Ezekiel* [2002].)   A. C. SCHULTZ

Ezekiel the Tragedian. A Jewish Hellenistic author who lived in the 2nd cent. B.C., probably in ALEXANDRIA. He apparently wrote several Greek tragedies, but the only one that survives (mainly in a partial but substantial quotation by EUSEBIUS, *Praep. ev.* 9.28–29) is a drama known as the *Exagōgē* ("leading out"), based on the story of the exodus. The work is of considerable importance for our knowledge of dramatic literature in the Hellenistic period (most of which has not survived). Moreover, it is the only extant Jewish play from antiquity, merging biblical material with Greek culture, and giving witness to an early understanding of the exodus narrative. (English trans. in *OTP*, 2:803–19; see also H. Jacobson, *The Exagoge of Ezekiel* [1983].)

Ezel ee´zuhl (אֶ֫צֶל H262, possibly "departure"). The name of a stone, otherwise unknown, near which DAVID was supposed to wait for JONATHAN (1 Sam. 20:19). On the basis of the SEPTUAGINT (which has the demonstrative pronoun *ekeino*, "that"), many scholars emend the Hebrew text from *hā'āzel* (pausal form with definite article) to *hallāz* H2137 ("this"; cf. NRSV, "remain beside the stone there"). In addition, the LXX has the transliteration *ergab* instead of the Greek word for "stone," so some scholars further emend the Hebrew *hā'eben* ("the stone") to a hypothetical *hā'argāb* (presumably "the heap," from *regeb* H8073, "clod"), resulting in the translation "wait beside that mound" (P. K. McCarter, Jr., *I Samuel*, AB 8 [1980], 333, 337; cf. also RSV, "remain beside yonder stone heap").

Ezem ee´zuhm (עֶ֫צֶם H6796, "bone" [signifying "strength"]). KJV also Azem (in Joshua). One of the southernmost towns of JUDAH in the NEGEV (Josh. 15:29); it was among the towns later assigned to the tribe of SIMEON (Josh. 19:3; 1 Chr. 4:29). The location of Ezem is unknown, but a popular suggestion is Umm el-ʿAzam, 12 mi. SE of BEERSHEBA (cf. J. Simons, *The Geographical and Topographical Texts of the Old Testament* [1959], 144); others believe it should be located N of Beersheba (cf. *IDB*, 2:213).

E. L. ACKLEY

Ezer ee´zuhr (אֵ֫צֶר H733, perhaps "treasure" [only #1 below]; עֵ֫זֶר H6470, "help"). **(1)** Son of SEIR the HORITE in the land of EDOM; he is mentioned sixth among the chiefs of the Horites (Gen. 36:21, 27, 30; 1 Chr. 1:38 [here KJV editions since 1628 have "Ezar"], 42).

(2) Father of Husha and a descendant of JUDAH (1 Chr. 4:4). His place in the genealogy is unclear.

(3) Son (or grandson) of EPHRAIM who, with his brother Elead, was killed by the men of GATH (1 Chr. 7:21). See discussion under ELEAD.

(4) The chief of the mighty men of GAD, who came to DAVID in ZIKLAG when David fled from SAUL (1 Chr. 12:9). The Gadites are described as "brave warriors, ready for battle and able to handle the shield and spear. Their faces were the faces of lions, and they were as swift as gazelles in the mountains" (v. 8).

(5) Son of JESHUA and ruler of Mizpah; he was a Levite who repaired a section of the walls of Jerusalem in the days of NEHEMIAH (Neh. 3:19).

(6) A priest listed among those who assisted Nehemiah in the dedication of the rebuilt walls of Jerusalem (Neh. 12:42).   E. L. ACKLEY

Ezerias ez´uh-ri´uhs. KJV Apoc. form of AZARIAH (1 Esd. 8:1).

Ezias i-zi´uhs. KJV Apoc. form of UZZI (1 Esd. 8:2).

Ezion Geber ee´zee-uhn-gay´buhr (עֶצְיוֹן גֶּבֶר H6787, meaning uncertain). A city located on the N end of the Gulf of AQABAH, banked on the E by the hills of EDOM and on the W by those of PALESTINE. The site, Tell el-Kheleifeh, is 2.5 mi. NW of modern Aqabah (biblical ELATH) in Jordan, and about the same distance SE of Eilat in Israel. Some scholars, however, believe that the offshore island known as Jezirat Faraun ("Pharaoh's Island," now Coral Island) is the probable site (see A. Flinder in *BAR* 15/4 [July-August 1989]: 30–43).

The Bible mentions Ezion Geber as one of the stations along the route of the Israelites as they journeyed toward the plains of MOAB (Num. 33:35–36; Deut. 2:8). In the reign of SOLOMON the city was of great commercial significance as the port where he built his fleet of ships and manned them with Phoenician sailors. The ships sailed to OPHIR and brought back gold, almug wood (ebony?), silver, ivory, apes (perhaps baboons), and peacocks (1 Ki. 9:26–28; 10:11, 22; 2 Chr. 8:17). No further mention is made of the city until JEHOSHAPHAT joined with AHAZIAH to build a fleet there. The ships were wrecked in port and the venture was frustrated (1 Ki. 22:48–49; 2 Chr. 20:35–37).

The history of the city was recovered through the archaeological excavations of Nelson Glueck after F. Frank, a German explorer, discovered the insignificant mound of Tell el-Kheleifeh and identified it as Ezion Geber in 1934. The mound was about 700 ft. from the gulf (perhaps on the

Pharaoh's Island may have been the site of Ezion Geber. (View to the SE toward the border with Jordan and Saudi Arabia.)

ancient shore-line). In 1938 and subsequent years Glueck excavated the city and confirmed Frank's earlier identification (see N. Glueck, *The Other Side of the Jordan*, rev. ed. [1970], ch. 4). He identified four cities built upon one another. The first was dated in the Solomonic period. Built upon virgin soil, the city indicated a carefully laid out complex suggesting no gradual growth, but rather development at one time according to a preconceived plan. He based the claim for the Solomonic date upon a comparison of the structure of the main gate of Ezion Geber I and that of Stratum IV at MEGIDDO (dated by P. L. O. Guy as belonging to the Solomonic period) and the one at LACHISH (also dated in the 10th cent. B.C.). Solomon was the only king in the period to possess the wealth, the power, and the peaceful circumstances for such a building project. As for the earlier mention of Ezion Geber (Num. 33:35–36; Deut. 2:8), these probably had reference to a few mud huts eastward of the later city.

Referring to Ezion Geber as the "Pittsburgh of Palestine," Glueck originally believed the city to be a refinery for the copper and iron that were mined from the near-by mines of the ARABAH. There were flues and air ducts in the floor and walls of the first city, and the location of the city was such, he felt, as to derive the maximum benefit of the winds that rushed through the corridor of the Arabah. B. Rothenberg (in *PEQ* 94 [1962]: 44–56) challenged this view on the basis of the failure of the excavations to turn up either the clay crucibles that would have been used in smelting or the slag from the refining process. Besides, the location seems to have been the best for the least number of sand-storms and at the same time have the availability of drinking water. Rothenberg points out that the finds and ground plans indicate that the city was a large storehouse for grain and supplies for caravans and a fortress guarding the southern approaches on both sides of the gulf. Glueck abandoned his earlier ideas about this being a copper refinery (see *BA* 28 [1965]: 70–87). The smelting was done near the mines. (For further questions about Glueck's identification, see G. D. Pratico in *BAR* 12/5 [1986]: 24–35.)

The first city was sacked and burned probably by SHISHAK c. 925 B.C. The Bible mentions his campaign into Palestine (1 Ki. 14:25–26; 2 Chr. 12:1–9), and a topographical list preserved in the Amon temple at Karnak includes Edomite names, indicating that the strategic location at Ezion Geber would probably have been included. The city was rebuilt by Jehoshaphat of Judah (c. 860), who imitated Solomon by building a fleet there. A few years later the Edomites revolted during the reign of Jehoram (2 Ki. 8:20–22) and burned it. The third city was rebuilt after Azariah (UZZIAH) recovered it from the Edomites (2 Ki. 14:22; 2 Chr. 26:2), and it was renamed Elath. A seal of JOTHAM, his successor, was found in the third level (cf. *BASOR* 163 [Oct. 1961]: 18–22). This level is the best preserved, with many walls standing almost at their original height.

When REZIN and PEKAH formed the Aramean-Israelite coalition and invaded Judah, the Edomites regained Elath (Ezion Geber) and drove AHAZ's troops from the city (2 Ki. 16:6, "Edomites then moved into Elath and have lived there to this day").

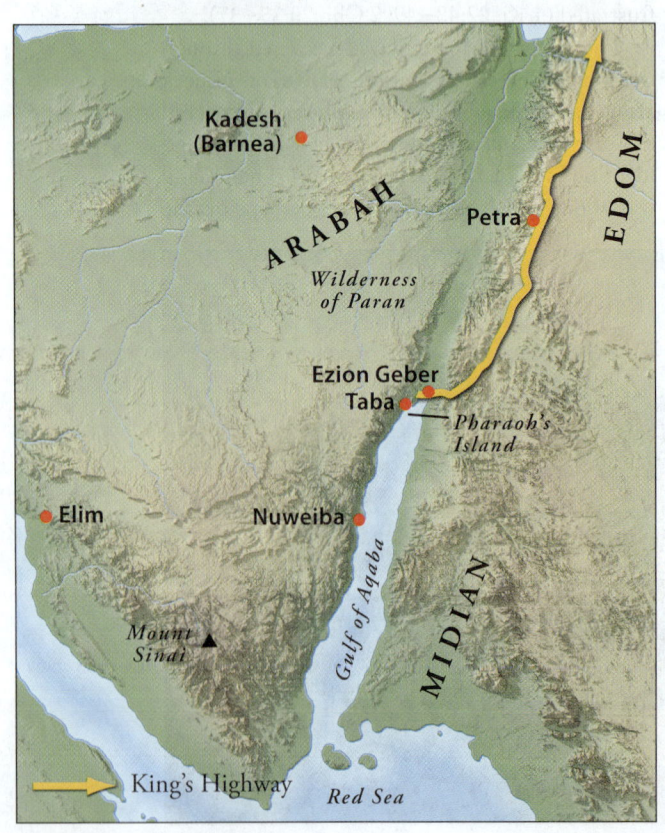

Ezion Geber.

The final phases of the city from the 7th to the 4th cent. B.C. saw the continued flourishing of trade, evidenced by Aramaic ostraca and sherds of black-figured Attic ware. The city was destroyed in the 4th cent. and was never rebuilt. The NABATEANS later built a port city at the N end of the gulf, but it was located at the site of the present day Aqabah.

W. B. COKER

Eznite ez′nit. See ADINO.

Ezora i-zor′uh (Εζωρα). Ancestor (or clan leader) of six men who agreed to put away their foreign wives (1 Esd. 9:34; the name does not occur in the parallel passage, Ezra 10:40).

Ezra ez′ruh (עֶזְרָא H6474, "help"; see also EZRAH). Son (meaning prob. "descendant") of SERAIAH and one of the most prominent leaders in postexilic Israel; his priestly genealogy is carried back to AARON (Ezra 7:1–5; 1 Chr. 6:3–15; the Ezra mentioned in Neh. 12:1 is a different person [see AZARIAH #24]). Described as a scribe or "teacher well versed in the Law of Moses" (Ezra 7:6), Ezra led back some 1,750 men, perhaps a total of 5,000 people, in a second return from BABYLON. It seems clear that Ezra wrote the book bearing his name (see EZRA, BOOK OF). The last two verses of 2 Chronicles are identical with two of the opening verses of Ezra, and according to Jewish tradition Ezra wrote Chronicles also (cf. W. F. Albright, *Yahweh and the Gods of Canaan* [1968], 182).

Ezra's return is dated in the seventh year of ARTAXERXES (Ezra 7:7). The usual view has been that this was Artaxerxes I and the date therefore about 457 B.C. More recently the view has been advanced that he returned in the seventh year of Artaxerxes II, that is, 398. The matter is adequately discussed in J. S. Wright's monograph, *The Date of Ezra's Coming to Jerusalem* (1947). The arguments for the late date are not conclusive. The first point concerns the walls of Jerusalem (4:12–16). Part of this chapter (4:7–23) refers to opposition in the days of an Artaxerxes, but the rest of the context refers to the times of CYRUS around 539. It is most logical to say that this chapter includes a synopsis of the opposition met by the Jews both in building the temple in 516 and in the efforts to build the wall under Artaxerxes I. In any case, the reference to work on a wall that was later stopped must relate to events before the completion of the walls by NEHEMIAH in the twentieth year of Artaxerxes I, about 444. It is quite likely that Ezra, who returned with 5,000 people and much treasure, had secured permission to build the walls and had made a beginning. But the opposition made the work cease until Nehemiah came in 444 with a new building permit. This may explain how Nehemiah finished his work in so short a time—fifty-two days—for Ezra had already done much. (Incidentally, this view suggests that Daniel's sixty-nine sevens of years [Dan. 9:25] should begin with Ezra's return at about 457. The period would end about A.D. 26 with the beginning of Jesus' public ministry.)

The only other argument of consequence for a late date of Ezra concerns the mention of ELIASHIB, who was high priest in 444 B.C. (Neh. 3:1). He was the father of a JEHOHANAN associated with Ezra (Ezra 10:6); and the ELEPHANTINE papyri mention

Column capital from the palace of Xerxes, during whose time some of the inhabitants of Palestine lodged an accusation against the people of Judah and Jerusalem (Ezra 4:6).

a high priest Jehohanan in 408. The problem is not serious. Ezra's marriage reform of Ezra 10 has no date given. Jehohanan could have been made high priest at some subsequent time and lasted in office until 408. Or there may have been two Eliashibs and two Jehohanans. It was the custom to name a boy for his grandfather. Three such successive Sanballats are now known! The traditional order of Ezra and Nehemiah is still satisfactory.

Of Ezra's political office very little is known, but he clearly had influence at court. He was given a blank check by the king and authority to appoint officers (Ezra 7:21–26), but is not called a governor as was Nehemiah. His faith is shown by refusing a military guard for his caravan (8:22). Nehemiah emphasizes Ezra's scribal activity. Actually, Ezra was a priest of the line of ZADOK and would be expected to teach the law (cf. Neh. 8). Ezra and Nehemiah led the two processions at the dedication of the walls (Neh. 12:36–40).

Ezra was prominent in postbiblical Jewish tradition. In an apocryphal work (2 Esd. 14), he is said to have rewritten and published the twenty-four books of the Hebrew canon, which had been burned during the captivity (see ESDRAS, FIRST; ESDRAS, SECOND; EZRA IN THE PSEUDEPIGRAPHA). In the tradition he dictated the books rapidly under special divine enablement. (See H. H. Schaeder, *Esra der Schreiber* [1930]; A. C. Welch, *Post-Exilic Judaism* [1934]; H. L. Ellison in *EvQ* 53 [1981]: 48–53; O. Margalith in *ZAW* 98 [1986]: 110–12.) See also RESTORATION.   R. L. HARRIS

Ezra, Apocalypse of. See ESDRAS, SECOND; EZRA IN THE PSEUDEPIGRAPHA.

Ezra, Book of. One of the historical books of the OT, included among the KETUBIM (Writings) in the threefold canon of the Hebrew Bible.
   I. Background
   II. Authorship
   III. Date
   IV. Canonicity
   V. Special problems
   VI. Content and outline

I. Background. The books of Ezra and NEHEMIAH originally were regarded by the Jews as a single work, and a general introduction must treat them together. Moreover, the opening verses, when compared with the closing verses of CHRONICLES, show that Ezra-Nehemiah continues the Chronicler's history.

After recounting the history of the monarchy and the temple until the EXILE, the writer passes over the period when the temple lay in ruins and the key men in Judah were in Babylonia, then records the predicted return—leading to the rebuilding of the temple through ZERUBBABEL (of the line of DAVID) and JESHUA (of the line of AARON). He describes the establishment of the new Jewish community during the period 538–433 B.C. The Jews came under the Persian empire when CYRUS (Ezra 1:1–8) conquered Babylon in 539. Subsequent kings were CAMBYSES (530–522), Gaumata (or Pseudo-Smerdis, a usurper, 522), DARIUS I (522–486, Ezra 5–6), XERXES I (or Ahasuerus, 486–465, Ezra 4:6; also Esth. 1:1 et al.), ARTAXERXES I (464–424, Ezra 4:7–23; 7:1—10:44; the whole of Nehemiah's work belongs to this reign). Some suppose that Ezra himself belongs to the reign of Artaxerxes II.

II. Authorship. Style and approach, as well as the verbal link already noted, suggest that the compiler of Chronicles and Ezra-Nehemiah is the same person. In much of the book he is a compiler, since he makes extensive use of documents and often inserts them word for word. Thus the authorship must in the first instance be applied to the individual documents, as follows.

A. Memoirs of Ezra. These are written in the first person singular (Ezra 7:27—9:15), preceded and followed by third person narratives (7:1–26; ch. 10) that could be based on a record made by Ezra himself; or, since they incorporate a verbatim decree and legal affairs, these memoirs could come from the temple archives. See EZRA.

B. Memoirs of Nehemiah. These are in the first person singular (Neh. 1:1—7:5; 12:27–43; 13:4–30).

C. Aramaic documents. ARAMAIC was the diplomatic language of the day. The following documents are mentioned: (1) A letter of complaint to Artaxerxes I about the rebuilding of the city walls, and his reply (Ezra 4:8–24); chronologically this probably comes immediately before Neh. 1, which refers to a recent destruction of the walls (Ezra 4:23; Neh. 1:3). (2) A letter to Darius I and his reply (Ezra 5:1—6:18); the whole incident is appropriately related in Aramaic. (3) The official authorization of Artaxerxes (Ezra 7:12–26).

D. Lists. Listings of names are included under various categories. (1) Returned exiles, perhaps including some who came at later dates (Ezra 2; cf. Neh. 7). (2) Those who returned with Ezra (Ezra 8:1–14). (3) Those who had married pagan wives (Ezra 10:18–43). (4) The builders of the wall and the sections where they worked (Neh. 3). (5) The leaders who set their seal to the covenant (Neh. 10:1–27). (6) The allocation of the people in Jerusalem and neighborhood (Neh. 11). (7) Lists of priests and Levites down to JADDUA (Neh. 12:1–26); this may be the Jaddua who was high priest in the reign of Darius II (338–331 B.C.). These lists would have been filed in the temple archives.

E. Narrative. It is not possible to say how much of the remaining narrative comes from the Chronicler himself, and how far he drew upon oral or documentary sources. The temple staff would naturally hand down oral and documentary records of the first return and rebuilding of the TEMPLE, and there would also be background material in the temple to supplement the memoirs of Ezra and Nehemiah.

III. Date. The latest name mentioned in Ezra –Nehemiah is Jaddua, who was probably the high priest in the reign of Darius III (338–331; Neh. 12:11, 22). This need not mean that the Chronicler compiled his work at that late date. Copyists on the temple staff would tend to keep a simple list of this kind up-to-date.

Since the Chronicler writes on the assumption that the Priestly Code was in force all through the monarchy, scholars who hold that the source labeled P (the priestly source of the PENTATEUCH) was introduced by Ezra, and then later incorporated into the previously existing codes, naturally place the Chronicler sufficiently long after Ezra for this to be possible. Those who date Ezra's coming in 398 B.C. place the compilation of Chronicles and Ezra–Nehemiah in the last part of the 4th cent., although some hold that further additions were made after this. If, however, the Pentateuch in its present form existed from the time of MOSES, we are free to postulate any reasonable date for the compilation of the books after about 430.

The identity of the compiler must remain unknown, but it could have been Ezra himself. He had the ability and aptitude as a student-scribe, and, as priest, he had access to the temple records (Ezra 7:1–6). Talmudic tradition (*b. Baba Bathra* 15a) regards Ezra as the writer of Chronicles and of Ezra–Nehemiah up to his own day, though it suggests that Nehemiah completed the work.

IV. Canonicity. In the Hebrew Bible, Ezra –Nehemiah is placed in the third group of books (the Writings), which were the last to be recognized as inspired Scriptures. See CANON (OT). Illogically it precedes Chronicles, but this may be because it covered an entirely new field, whereas Chronicles was parallel with Samuel and Kings, and so might be read as a supplement. For its relationship with 1 Esdras of the Apocrypha, with its confusion of people and dates, see ESDRAS, FIRST.

V. Special problems. There are two historical periods about which scholars have queried the biblical account, and it will be convenient to consider these separately, and deal with the first here, and the other in the article NEHEMIAH, BOOK OF.

The Chronicler is said to be in confusion over the rebuilding of the temple. Ezra 3:10 says that the foundation was laid in 536 B.C. by ZERUBBABEL and JESHUA. The work was hindered and lapsed until 520, when, through the preaching of HAGGAI and ZECHARIAH, it was taken up again and completed by 516 (Ezra 6:15). On the other hand, according to Haggai's own words, the foundation was laid in 520 (Hag. 2:18). Some suppose that only a small number returned in 537, and were content to worship on the ruined site of the temple. A fresh party of enthusiasts came with Zerubbabel, Jeshua, Haggai, and Zechariah, in 520, and laid the foundation.

The whole weight of national psychology is against this view. It is the enthusiasts who flock back in large numbers as soon as the doors are opened, without waiting for seventeen years, although even enthusiasts can be diverted by intense opposition from building the temple to building their own houses and scraping a living for themselves (Hag. 1:4, 9–11). The statement in Hag. 2:18 does not necessarily mean that the foundation had only just been laid in 520, but this interpretation is probable. If so, with so little having been done since 536, the enthusiasm of the Jews would be kindled by a fresh foundation ceremony. This would not be unusual, since Akkadian and Hittite rituals exist for founding and repairing temples, and mention more than one foundation stone in different parts of the building (cf. *ANET*, 339–40, 356).

In Ezra 3:8 Zerubbabel lays the foundation, but in 5:16 this is said to be the work of SHESHBAZZAR, who is spoken of there as though he were dead, whereas Zerubbabel is still alive. The Jews (5:13–17) were trying, however, to identify a missing document that they hoped would be in the Persian archives. This document was the authorization given to Sheshbazzar, who had been appointed governor (1:8), and it would be useless to look for one with the name of Zerubbabel, although Zerubbabel had actually been the prime mover. The statement that the work had been going on ever since (5:16) is purely diplomatic, since, if they had admitted that they had stopped building, the answer would have been, "If Cyrus really gave you permission, why did you stop?"

There are variant versions of Cyrus's decree in Ezra 1 and 6. But the public decree of ch. 1, with Cyrus's acknowledgment of Yahweh, is paralleled by extant inscriptions in which Cyrus acknowledges the Babylonian god MARDUK in speaking to the Babylonians. The filed decree in 6:1–5 is naturally formal and contains maximum dimensions of the temple for which Cyrus was prepared to make a grant.

There is, then, no inconsistency between individual sections of the book of Ezra, nor between Ezra and Haggai or Zechariah. An interesting link may be found between the letter of complaint to Darius in Ezra 5, which might have resulted in the work being stopped, and the great mountain (Zech. 4:7) that was blocking Zerubbabel's completion of the temple.

VI. Content and outline

A. Cyrus authorizes the return of the Jews under Sheshbazzar and gives them their temple treasures (Ezra 1:1–11; it is known that he allowed other captive peoples to take back their idols).

B. A list of those who returned, classified under various heads (Ezra 2:1–70).

C. The altar is set up for regular offerings; later the foundations of the new temple are laid (Ezra 3:1–13).

D. Many non-Jews, including the semipagan inhabitants from the N (cf. 2 Ki. 17:33–41) offer to help, but are refused; they then hinder the work (Ezra 4:1–4).

E. The compiler brings together subsequent occasions of opposition, but has dated them carefully as happening in the reigns of Xerxes I and Artaxerxes I (Ezra 4:5–23). There is no mention of building the temple but only of building the city and the walls. Artaxerxes orders the work to cease, and the enemies use violence to stop it.

F. The author takes up the story again (Ezra 4:24—5:17; the opening words refer back to 4:5). Haggai and Zechariah, who may have been infants at the original return, urge the people to take up the building again; the authorities make a formal protest, and are referred to the decree of Cyrus.

G. The decree is found in the Persian archives, and Darius orders the work to proceed (Ezra 6:1–22). The temple is finished in four years (516), and now returned Israelites, and others of the northern kingdom who had not gone into exile, are allowed to celebrate the Passover, once they have broken with everything pagan.

H. There is a gap between the years 516 and 458, when Ezra is sent by Artaxerxes I to investigate and enforce the operation of the Jewish law in the province of Judah (Ezra 7:1–28).

I. Ezra's journey, with another group of exiles and gold and silver for the temple (Ezra 8:1–36).

J. Ezra's prayer of anguish after hearing of mixed marriages with pagan peoples (Ezra 9:1–15).

K. The people unitedly investigate all the alleged cases of foreign marriages and agree that the Jews in such marriages should put away their pagan wives (Ezra 10:1–44; the decision was almost unanimous, v. 15). In all probability with the Jews being a minority group, the parents and families of the wives would secure proper alimony for them.

(Significant commentaries include L. Batten, *A Critical and Exegetical Commentary on the Books of Ezra and Nehemiah*, ICC [1913]; W. Rudolph, *Esra und Nehemia*, HAT, 1/20 [1949]; F. C. Fensham, *The Books of Ezra and Nehemiah*, NICOT [1982]; H. G. M. Williamson, *Ezra-Nehemiah*, WBC 16 [1985]; J. Blenkinsopp, *Ezra-Nehemiah*, OTL [1988]; M. Breneman, *Ezra, Nehemiah, Esther*, NAC 10 [1993]; L. C. Allen, *Ezra, Nehemiah, Esther*, NIBCOT 9 [2003]. See also C. C. Torrey, *Ezra Studies* [1910]; J. Stafford Wright, *The Date of Ezra's Coming to Jerusalem* [1947]; T. C. Eskenazi, *In an Age of Prose: A Literary Approach to Ezra-Nehemiah* [1988]; K.-J. Min, *The Levitical Authorship of Ezra-Nehemiah* [2004]; J. Pakala, *Ezra the Scribe: The Development of Ezra 7–10 and Nehemia 8* [2004]; and the bibliography compiled by W. E. Mills, *Ezra-Nehemiah* [2002].) J. S. WRIGHT

Ezra, Fourth. See ESDRAS, SECOND.

Ezra, pseudepigraphic books of. In addition to *4 Ezra* (see ESDRAS, SECOND), several pseudepigraphic works are attributed to EZRA, but their date and provenance are very uncertain. Apocalypses in various languages (including Armenian, Ethiopic, Greek, Latin, and Syriac) bear his name. Among them are the *Greek Apocalypse of Ezra* (the most substantial of these works), the *Questions of Ezra* (preserved only in Armenian, possibly its original language), the *Revelation of Ezra* (Latin), and the *Vision of the Blessed Ezra* (an original Greek work preserved only in Latin). (English trans. of these four documents in *OTP*, 1:561–604; see also *ABD*, 2:728–31.)

Ezrah ez´ruh (עֶזְרָה *H6477*, "help"). KJV Ezra. A descendant of JUDAH who had four sons (1 Chr. 4:17). His precise place in the genealogy is not indicated (see discussion in G. N. Knoppers, *I Chronicles 1–9*, AB 12 [2004], 352–56).

Ezrahite ez´ruh-hit (אֶזְרָחִי *H276*). A descriptive term applied to ETHAN (1 Ki. 4:31; Ps. 89 title) and HEMAN (Ps. 88 title). The term has traditionally been understood as equivalent to "descendant of Zerah." However, W. F. Albright (*Archaeology and the Religion of Israel*, 5th ed. [1968], 127, 210) proposed that it means "aborigine, member of a pre-Israelite family," and this interpretation has been followed by many. G. G. SWAIM

Ezri ez´ri (עֶזְרִי *H6479*, "my help"). Son of Kelub; he was an official in charge of those who farmed the royal lands during the reign of DAVID (1 Chr. 27:26). Ezri is included in a list of twelve administrators who were "in charge of King David's property" (v. 31).

Harbor at Fair Havens on the south coast of Crete (view looking SE).

fable. A literary genre in the form of a short story embodying a moral and making use of animals, birds, or inanimate things as persons or actors. (The KJV uses the word "fable" several times in a different sense to render Gk. *mythos G3680* [1 Tim. 1:4 et al.]. See MYTH.) Fables were well known in ANE literature, especially in Sumerian and Akkadian writing. According to R. C. Trench (*Notes on the Parables*, 14th ed. [1882], 1–5), a principal difference between a fable and a PARABLE is that the former tries to inculcate maxims of prudential morality (e.g., industry, foresight, caution), while the latter teaches spiritual virtues.

There are two fables in the OT. In the first (Jdg. 9:8–15), JOTHAM, standing on Mount GERIZIM and speaking to the people of SHECHEM in the valley below, tried to show them the folly of choosing as king a worthless fellow like his brother, who had just murdered seventy sons of GIDEON. The trees of the forest asked an olive tree, a fig tree, and a vine, to rule over them, but they all refused, saying that they were too busy serving the community to waste their time waving their branches over their fellows. Finally they chose a useless bramble (representing his brother ABIMELECH), a dangerous choice, for conflict would result in the destruction of all in the forest fire.

In the other OT fable, Jehoash (JOASH) king of Israel indicated that he would demean himself if he agreed to fight AMAZIAH king of Judah, who had challenged him. "A thistle in Lebanon sent a message to a cedar in Lebanon, 'Give your daughter to my son in marriage.' Then a wild beast in Lebanon came along and trampled the thistle underfoot" (2 Ki. 14:9). Amaziah was not dissuaded, and in the battle that followed he was roundly defeated.

Some OT prophets employ illustrations that approach the status of fable, like Isaiah's poem about the vineyard (Isa. 5:1–7), and Ezekiel's poems concerning the lioness and her whelps (Ezek. 19:2–9), the vine (19:10–14), and the great eagle (17:3–10). S. BARABAS

face. This term (which renders primarily Heb. *pānîm*, pl. of *pāneh H7156*, and Gk. *prosōpon G4725*) can refer not only to the front of a human head (e.g., Gen. 4:5; Jas. 1:23) but also to that of animals (Gen. 30:40 NRSV), the seraphim (Isa. 6:2), and the living creatures around the throne (Rev. 4:7). In a figurative sense, the Bible speaks of the face of God (Num. 6:25–26) and of Christ (2 Cor. 4:6), and the term can also refer to the surface of inanimate objects, like the waters (Gen. 1:2 NRSV), the earth (1:29), the moon (Job 26:9), and the sky (Matt. 16:3 KJV). Both the Hebrew and the Greek term can refer to the whole person (2 Sam. 17:11 [NIV, "you yourself"]; 2 Cor. 1:11). It should also be noted that the Hebrew word for "nose" (*ʾap H678*, e.g., Gen. 19:1) may stand for the whole countenance.

The face reflects feelings. "Cain was very angry, and his face was downcast" (Gen. 4:5). "A happy heart makes the face cheerful" (Prov. 15:13). The face was covered in mourning (e.g., DAVID after ABSALOM's defection and death, 2 Sam. 19:4; cf. also Esth. 7:8; Gen. 38:15), although "his face is covered with fat" suggests prosperity and arrogance (Job 15:27). MOSES hid his face in reverence (Exod. 3:6) but put a veil on his face when addressing the people to dim the radiance received while talking with God (34:29–35).

To seek the face is to desire an audience (Ps. 105:4), but to turn away or hide the face is rejection (13:1), or to forsake the house of God (2 Chr. 29:6); and to harden the face is to promise no

513

This crystalline limestone image of the face of Thutmose III (15th cent. B.C.) was found in 1964; subsequently, Egyptologists realized that it was part of a bust discovered in 1907.

appeal (Prov. 21:29; NIV, "put up a bold front"). Ruth fell on her face in humility and astonishment (Ruth 2:10). Favors are granted when the face is lifted up (Num. 6:25), but to spit in the face was a grave insult (Matt. 26:67). Determination was evident when Christ set his face to go to Jerusalem (Lk. 9:51; NIV, "resolutely set out").

Much is said about the face of God. It means God himself or his GLORY in its fullest, which could not be seen by Moses before he received the TEN COMMANDMENTS (Exod. 33:20). When JACOB said, "I saw God face to face" (Gen. 32:20), he was referring to the relationship of closest intimacy he felt because of his wrestling with the man by the ford of JABBOK and the blessing given to him. "No one has ever seen God" (Jn. 1:18) face to face but "the knowledge of the glory of God" is seen in the face of Christ (2 Cor. 4:6). "Speaking face to face" suggests that God shows his attributes even though not in their completeness, yet his servants are promised that they shall see his face (Rev. 22:4) when they approach the throne of God in the new Jerusalem. Note that the term for SHOWBREAD (the bread kept in the ARK OF THE COVENANT, Exod. 25:30; NIV, "bread of the Presence") means literally "bread of [God's] face." On the other hand, God hides his face when angry (Job 13:24), sets his face against the wicked for evil (Jer. 44:11), and hides his face from sin, both to show his displeasure with it (Ps. 27:9) and to show he has forgiven it (51:9).

R. L. MIXTER

fair. This English term is used in the KJV primarily in the sense of "beautiful" (e.g., Gen. 6:2); in the NIV it usually means "just" (e.g., Col. 4:1). See BEAUTY; GOOD; RIGHTEOUSNESS.

Fair Havens (καλοὶ λιμένες G2816, from καλός, "good," and λιμήν, "harbor"). A bay near LASEA on the S coast of CRETE, about 5 mi. E of Cape Matala (Acts 27:8). PAUL, in the custody of a centurion, sailed W from CNIDUS on an Alexandrian grain ship. The weather forced them to sail on the S side of Crete. They passed Cape Salome, the eastern tip of the island, and took refuge at Fair Havens. Since Fair Havens was only an open bay, the centurion, the captain, and the owner of the ship decided to attempt to reach PHOENIX, a harbor farther to the W. Failing, they drifted in the open sea for fourteen days until the shipwreck at MALTA.

A. RUPPRECHT

fairs. This English term (now obsolete, but related to the noun *fair*, "market, exhibition") means "wares, merchandise" and is used by the KJV to render Hebrew ʿizbônîm H6442, which occurs seven times, but only in one passage (Ezek. 27:12–33).

faith, faithfulness. These two concepts are central to biblical thought. They deal with the relationship between God and human begins. They are in some respects correlative, for human faith is that which responds to and is sustained by God's faithfulness. In other respects there can be a progression of thought, for faith on the part of a person should lead to faithfulness. Again, the idea of faith can move from the subjective attitude of trustfulness to "the faith"—that which God has revealed objectively through deed and word and sign in order that it should be trusted. Associated closely with the two nouns is the adjective *faithful* and the verbs to have *faith in, trust, believe*. In some parts of the Bible the verb is more prominent than the noun. As always in the Scriptures, the divine initiative is emphasized or assumed, and the fact that the living God is willing to enter into relationship with his creatures, and has shown them that he is worthy of their trust, is what gives biblical faith its distinctive character. Faith as it is demonstrated in the OT is a necessary but incomplete preliminary to its full possibility through Christ in the NT.

    I. Faith and faithfulness in the OT
        A. Terminology
        B. Theological presentation
    II. Faith and faithfulness in Judaism
        A. The Apocrypha and Pseudepigrapha
        B. Philo
        C. Qumran
        D. The rabbis
    III. Faith and faithfulness in Greek thought
        A. Classical
        B. Hellenistic
    IV. Faith and faithfulness in the NT
        A. Terminology
        B. The usage of the NT writers
        C. Faith and faithfulness in NT theology

I. Faith and faithfulness in the OT

A. Terminology. The primary Hebrew terms for "faith" and "faithfulness" are derived from the root ʾāman H586 (the verb is used only in the niphal and hiphil stems). An original meaning connected with "firmness, stability" leads to the idea of "trust, constancy," which is prominent in the OT. The related word AMEN, which is used frequently in the OT and NT, shows the confident affirmation associated with the verb. In the niphal conjugation ("to be stable, prove oneself reliable"), the verb may be used of God (Deut. 7:9) or of his servants (Num. 12:7). It can be extended to witnesses (Isa. 8:2; Jer. 42:5) and to a city (Isa. 1:21, 26). It can be used of testimony (Ps. 19:8) and of promises (2 Chr. 1:9).

This verb is used slightly more frequently in the hiphil conjugation, which has the active sense "to believe, trust." Although the verb may be used absolutely ("I believed," Ps. 116:10), it is more common for it to rule a clause (introduced by *kî H3954*, "that," as in Exod. 4:5) or a prepositional phrase.

The prepositions (*bĕ- H928* and *lĕ- H4200*, with no discernible difference in meaning) are linked with God (Gen. 15:6; Isa. 43:10), with men (Exod. 4:1; 19:9), or with things (usually words or messages, 1 Ki. 10:7; Ps. 106:12).

Derived from the verb are two nouns found often in the OT: *ʾĕmet H622* and *ʾĕmûnâ H575*. Generally speaking, these are connected more with the passive sense ("to be reliable, faithful") than with the active ("to believe, trust"). They may refer to the faithfulness of God (Pss. 25:10; 36:5) or to that of his servants (Josh. 24:14; 1 Sam. 26:23). There seems to be little difference between the two nouns, which function as key words of Hebrew religion. They are especially prominent in the Psalter. (See further *NIDOTTE*, 1:427–33.)

A different verb is *bāṭaḥ H1053*, which is used sixty times in a secular sense, as against fifty-seven in a religious context. As an important devotional word it has a special place in the Psalter, where it is found thirty-seven times. Its sense is that of "feeling secure." This feeling may be unjustified (Jdg. 18:7, 27, where the word is used of an unsuspecting city) or misplaced (trusting in human strength, Jer. 17:5; or in idols, Ps. 115:8). In its positive sense, it is that attitude to God which acknowledges him as the believer's own God (Ps. 31:14). The cognate noun (*beṭaḥ H1055*) has the sense of safety or security, and it can likewise be used of a true or false security. (See further *NIDOTTE*, 1:644–49.)

Other relevant terms include *ḥāsâ H2879*, "to take refuge," used predominantly in a religious sense in the Psalter (e.g., Ps. 7:1), as well as several words that denote hope (such as *qāwâ H7747* and its cognates). Of even greater importance is the word *ḥesed H2876*, which denotes the COVENANT relationship between God and his people (see LOVINGKINDNESS). It was the covenant which formed the heart of Israel's religion and which gave faithfulness and faith their fullest opportunity for expression.

B. Theological presentation. The idea of a *faithful* God in whom human beings should put their *faith* is absolutely fundamental to OT religion. It will be possible here only to outline some areas in which this concept is represented, even where none of the "faith" words actually appear.

1. Creation and providence. The faithfulness of God who has made the world and all that is in it, who orders it regularly and provides for his creatures, is abundantly illustrated in a nature psalm such as Ps. 104. It is a demonstration of the fact that all is under the control of a God who can be relied upon. This produces in the believing beholder a response of exultation in his might and majesty. See CREATION; PROVIDENCE.

2. Redemption. The whole sweep of God's REDEMPTION in the OT, from the call of ABRAHAM to the establishment of the people in their own land with a place for his name to dwell in, was evidence of his faithfulness (Exod. 33:1; 1 Ki. 8:56). The central point of this redemption was the exodus, which is a supreme example of the faithful God in action (Exod. 15:1–17; see EXODUS, THE). The response of the people when God had delivered them was to believe in Yahweh and his servant Moses (14:31). The mighty acts of God had to be kept in remembrance for future generations. One way in which this was done was through the PASSOVER service (12:24–27). Another was through the recitation of creedal forms (Deut. 26:5–9; cf. 6:20–24). It was intended that these should lead people of every age to faith in the redeeming God (Ps. 77; Mic. 6:3–5). In addition, there were psalms that were devoted entirely to the exodus period, such as Ps. 105, which lays great emphasis on the faithfulness of God, and Ps. 106, which stresses the unfaithfulness of the people. In Ps. 136 the idea of Yahweh's faithfulness in redemption is linked to his faithfulness in creation, and both are cause for praise that "his love [*ḥesed*] endures forever." When God delivers his people again from captivity, this is further evidence of his faithfulness in action, calling for a response of trust from them (Isa. 40–55 passim).

3. Promises and signs. In the OT God is not represented simply as doing things in history. He also is shown to promise them by word and by symbolic deed. The most important instance of God's promises in the OT is found in the story of Abraham. From Gen. 12:1–3 onward, the unlikely promises of God to Abraham of a land and descendants were slowly but surely, against all the odds, being fulfilled. The greatness of Abraham was found in the fact that he "believed the Lord, and he credited it to him as righteousness" (Gen. 15:6). Faith in the God of the impossible brought Abraham into a new relationship with him, which, of course, also needed obedience (faithfulness) as its outworking (22:15–18). The intellectual, the moral, and the spiritual aspects of faith all can be seen intertwined in his character. The faithfulness of God is written large upon his page of history.

The other particular instance where we note the faithful fulfillment of God's promises is in the establishment of the Davidic house (1 Ki. 8:1–66). This truth was something clung to even in the nation's darkest hour, but inevitably with a new dimension added to it (Jer. 33:14–26). The PROPHETS had to look ahead through history to a more glorious age when the MESSIAH would come. There were many other cases when the prophets interpreted the times and spoke predictively in the name of Yahweh, and he performed what he said he would. In every such case they required a response of faith in their hearers.

In addition to the faithfulness of God shown in words that came true, there were signs as visible words. Notable signs were performed in preparation for the exodus so that people might believe that God was in action redeeming his people (Exod. 4:1–5). On occasion a person could receive guidance from Yahweh by a special sign (Jdg. 6:36–40). These were to give people confidence, provided that

Dragnet fishermen at the Sea of Galilee. God's faithfulness to creation is evident in the provision of food for his creatures.

their attitude to him was right (Isa. 7:3–17). If they did not believe, they could not be established.

4. The covenant. The focus of God's faithful dealing with his people and their response to him is in the covenant relationship he established with them. A covenant was a binding obligation between two parties, and in the case of a covenant in which Yahweh was involved, it was always he who took the initiative and who was the dominant partner in the relationship. The basic terms of a covenant were, "I will be your God and you shall be my people"—it was a corporate relationship to him out of which various obligations sprang. The covenant with Noah included promises of blessing to his descendants and to all flesh (Gen. 6:18; 9:9–17). The covenant with Abraham was based on the promises of God, with the seal of circumcision as a reminder of divine undertaking and human obligation (17:1–14). The covenant with the people of Israel after the exodus was linked with that made with Abraham (Exod. 2:24); it was sealed with blood and included the stipulation of obedience on the part of the people (24:7–8). Under JOSHUA the people renewed the covenant with promises of obedience (Josh. 24:24–25). God made a covenant with DAVID and his descendants (2 Sam. 7:12–17), and the way in which this demonstrated his faithfulness is brought out most strikingly in Ps. 89.

The fact that Yahweh had entered into covenant with his people in these different ways was the basis for much exhortation to the people to be true to him. The book of DEUTERONOMY constantly dwells upon his faithfulness and the obligations of the covenant nation. The penalties of unfaithfulness also are brought home. Most of the prophets seem to have had the idea of the covenant somewhere in their thought, but in HOSEA the theme of God's loyalty and man's disloyalty is absolutely basic to the whole book. The northern kingdom went into captivity because of its failure to observe the covenant (2 Ki. 17:15–38), and the southern kingdom had to reform itself drastically when reaffirming the covenant under JOSIAH (2 Ki. 23:1–4). It was JEREMIAH's great achievement that he saw that outward reform could not go far enough and that unfaithfulness to an outward covenant was unavoidable. Hence the dramatic new spiritual prospects opened up through his prophecy of the new covenant (Jer. 31:31–34). See COVENANT, THE NEW.

The religion of the OT was dominated by the LAW. No Israelite could conceivably be ignorant of the fact that he was under obligation to be faithful to God. Yet, at its best, Israel saw that law was not legalism and that the claims of God for their complete loyalty were based upon his prior action in loyalty to his obligations freely entered into by the divine promise (Exod. 20:1–3). But when Yahweh had revealed himself in the way that he had, the call to obedience could never be divorced from the invitation to faith.

5. Personal. The main thrust of the OT is concerned with God and his people as a whole, but it would be wrong to infer that there was no such thing as individual, personal faith. That is abundantly illustrated at all periods of Israel's history. The personal faith of Abraham, Moses, David, or Elijah is something real and important as well as the national faith. The PSALMS afford abundant examples of trust in Yahweh through thick and thin. They often are couched in tones of deep personal devotion. God's faithfulness is the one thing which can be relied upon, and it is under the shadow of his wings that human beings take their refuge (Ps. 36:5–7).

So we see the connection between faith and faithfulness in the OT. The God who acts gives signs and promises, and enters into relationship with his people. People are utterly dependent upon him and are called upon to acknowledge that dependence and to obey his will. The covenant is the undergirding of the nation's life and in his personal life "the righteous will live by his faith" (or faithfulness, Hab. 2:4). Any confidence in anyone or anything to the exclusion of God is condemned (Ps. 146), yet there is an overflowing of the concept of faithfulness in our dealings with others (2 Sam. 2:5). The prophets were insistent that relationship with God must lead to just dealing with neighbors, and the psalmist sees that the person who dwells with God and is truly established is the one who can be relied upon in all his dealings with others (Ps. 15). Behind it all is the character of the God of the covenant whose faithfulness was proclaimed in the great congregation (Ps. 40:9–10).

II. Faith and faithfulness in Judaism

A. The Apocrypha and Pseudepigrapha. While these writings drew freely upon their OT heritage, there can be seen an increasing institutionalization of the idea of faith and faithfulness. In particular, the observance of the law was closely involved with it (Sir. 32:24). The defense of the law and institutions of Israel as an expression of faith is found movingly portrayed in the struggles of Judas MACCABEE and his followers. In the DIASPORA there grew up an emphasis upon the greatness of the God of Israel as opposed to the pointless polytheism of the nations. This is shown particularly in some sections of the WISDOM OF SOLOMON. There also was developed the absolute use of the term "the faithful" (*hoi pistoi*) as the pious, contrasted with unbelievers inside and outside Judaism (Wisd. 3:9–15). In these processes there was some movement also toward a concept of faith that was more intellectual and less a matter of personal trust. In the APOCALYPTIC books faith was much more connected with the future and therefore in some respects would be better described as HOPE. In the coming eschatological judgment, it is the faithful remnant who will be vindicated.

B. Philo. PHILO JUDAEUS's understanding of the OT was influenced greatly by his knowledge of Greek philosophy, in particular that of Plato. As a Jew he believed in the greatness of the one God, but rather than seeing him as active in history he sought him through withdrawing from the world. The phenomenal world was essentially insubstantial, and true security could be found only in a mystical relationship with the ultimate reality in God. To him we owe the description of faith as "the queen of virtues."

C. Qumran. There is considerable emphasis in the Qumran documents upon the faithfulness of God (see DEAD SEA SCROLLS). The community, inevitably as a group within a larger whole, thought of itself as a faithful remnant. As with many other groups in later Judaism, their stress was not so much upon an active personal trust in God as in a loyal obedience to his commandments. Among their writings, the Habakkuk Commentary emphasizes both faith in the Teacher of Righteousness (esp. in the truth of his teachings) and in God's vindication of them.

D. The rabbis. What was true of the Apocrypha and Pseudepigrapha, as far as the institutionalizing of faith is concerned, was even more marked in the case of much of the rabbinic literature. Faith is connected closely with obedience, and prominence is given to the keeping of the law with the many subtle interpretations preserved in the "tradition of the elders" (see MISHNAH). There were among the rabbis men of personal trust in the living God, but it became fatally easy for this element to be obscured by a misplaced emphasis upon the TORAH, including the oral law.

III. Faith and faithfulness in Greek thought

A. Classical. There is a clear interrelation between the ideas of faith and faithfulness in the vocabulary of classical Greek. Both the adjective *pistos* G4412 and the noun *pistis* G4411 can be used in an active or a passive sense and thus may refer either to trusting or to being worth trusting. The verb *pisteuō* G4409 could express trust in persons or things. There was nothing necessarily religious about these terms, although they could be used in the area of religion. But none of the words standing by themselves would immediately suggest a religious significance.

B. Hellenistic. In the postclassical period, *pisteuō* became one of the words that could be used regularly to denote belief that there were gods. At the same time *pistis* began to acquire a flavor of piety, for the belief in the existence of gods naturally extended to a recognition that they had some claims upon human allegiance. Likewise there followed the belief in certain theological propositions, with particular reference to the invisible world and man's relationship to it. The word group really came into its own when there was competition among various religions and each proclaimed the necessity of faith in the truth for which it claimed to stand. The concept might vary in its intellectual or moral content, but in the MYSTERY RELIGIONS it was seen as the way of illumination and salvation. While there are clear differences in the object and nature of faith between Hebrew and Greek writings, *pistis* and its cognates were ready-made for the SEPTUAGINT translators when they wished to render the ʾmn word group into Greek

IV. Faith and faithfulness in the NT

A. Terminology.
There is no need to emphasize the centrality of the concept of faith in the NT. The words that are used to express it are almost always those of the *pistis* group (in contrast, *alētheia* G237, though often used in the LXX to render ʾĕmet and ʾĕmûnâ, always denotes "truth, genuineness" in the NT). The verb *pisteuō* often has a nontechnical sense even in religious contexts (note the various syntactical constructions in Mk. 13:21; Jn. 8:24; 1 Cor. 13:7; it is most frequently found with the dative of the thing or of the person, Jn. 2:22; 4:21). More important is the technical sense of Christian believing that it developed. It could be used with the dative of faith in God (Acts 16:34), in Christ (Jn. 8:31), and in his name (1 Jn. 3:23). There were various prepositional uses, of which the most important is *eis* G1650 followed by the accusative (Jn. 2:11), but *epi* G2093 also is found with the accusative (Rom. 4:5) and with the dative (1 Tim. 1:16). In addition, the verb may be used absolutely (Jn. 1:7), and the participle became a technical term for Christians (1 Thess. 1:7).

The noun *pistis* is used only rarely in the NT of human fidelity (Tit. 2:10) and of divine faithfulness (Rom. 3:3). In the great majority of cases it means human faith in God. It is one of the great "theological virtues" (1 Cor. 13:13). The noun can be further defined by the use of the objective genitive or by several prepositions. (Some scholars have argued that the expression *pistis Christou* should be understood as a subjective genitive referring to the faith or faithfulness of Christ, but that is very unlikely, since in the NT the names Christ and Jesus Christ never function as the subject of the verb *pisteuō*. Cf. M. Silva in *Justification and Variegated Nomism*, ed. D. A. Carson et al., 2 vols. [2001–2003], 2:217–48.) Faith may be in God (Mk. 11:22), in Christ (Rom. 3:22), in his name (Acts 3:16). It also may be in objects, such as his blood (Rom. 3:25) or the gospel (Phil. 1:27). The word also may be used in an objective sense of the doctrine which is to be believed (Jude 3).

The adjective *pistos* also may be used both technically and nontechnically, and in both active and passive senses. It is commonly used of the reliability of servants or stewards (1 Cor. 4:2). God is supremely the One in whom confidence may be placed (1:9), but his word and his promises are also reliable (Rev. 21:5). Statements of Christian truth also may be trusted (1 Tim. 1:15). When the adjective is used in the active sense to mean "believing," it is only as a technical term (Jn. 20:27). It also can be used almost as the equivalent of "a Christian" (Acts 16:1).

Negative terms include the verb *apisteō* and its cognates, used of unbelief and unfaithfulness (e.g., Lk. 24:41; Acts 26:8; Rom. 3:3; 1 Pet. 2:7). The adjective *apistos* G603 can refer to a non-Christian (1 Cor. 6:6). Finally, the compound *oligopistos* G3899, "of little faith," is a word found only in the Synoptic Gospels (Matt. 6:30 et al.). (See further *NIDNTT*, 1:593–606.)

B. The usage of the NT writers

1. The Synoptic Gospels. *God's faithfulness.* God is portrayed in the Synoptics mainly under two figures—as King and as Father. Each of these concepts is associated in some way with the idea of his faithfulness. The KINGDOM OF GOD comes not out of the blue, but because the time is fulfilled (Mk. 1:15). The first two chapters of Luke's gospel give a vivid picture of people who were waiting for God to fulfill his promises made under the old covenant (Lk. 2:25, 38). Those who see the beginning of the fulfillment rejoice in his faithfulness. The MAGNIFICAT (1:46–55) is a song of praise to God who "has helped his servant Israel, / remembering to be merciful / to Abraham and his descendants forever, / even as he said to our fathers" (1:54–55). The BENEDICTUS (1:68–79) likewise is a celebration of the faithfulness of God, who has acted "to show mercy to our fathers / and to remember his holy covenant, / the oath he swore to our father Abraham" (1:72–73). The opening chapters of Matthew's gospel also commemorate the faithfulness of the Lord, who fulfilled what he had spoken through the prophets (Matt. 1:22–23). This theme of fulfillment of Scripture is found elsewhere in the Gospels, but it is a particular emphasis which is found throughout Matthew.

When God is spoken of as Father, there is conveyed the idea of his faithfulness in loving and providing for his children. This theme is particularly brought out in the SERMON ON THE MOUNT (with parallels in Luke). It is the Father who in his faithful providence "causes his sun to rise on the evil and the good, and sends rain on the righteous and the unrighteous" (Matt. 5:45). It is he who is faithful in rewarding those who do his will (6:4, 6, 18). It is he who feeds the birds of the air and clothes the grass of the field—how much more will he provide for his human children! The realization of this truth should lead us to trust him in a way that will banish worry. Faith will mean taking his providence seriously and putting his claims first (6:25–34). It is absurd to suppose that human parents with all their sinfulness would fail to give their children what they really needed. How much more is this true of the heavenly Father (7:7–11)!

Human faith. The response of men and women to the arrival of the reign of God in their midst in the person of Jesus Christ was to be that they should "repent and believe the good news" (Mk. 1:15). Here faith is shown to be dependent upon the divine initiative. The kingdom comes whether people hear or whether they forbear, but the claim which it makes is faith. This faith is centered in the GOSPEL, the good news of God's redeeming action. There is therefore at least to some extent an intellectual content to faith. Its moral content is emphasized by its close association with repentance.

The MIRACLES of Jesus were signs of the coming of the kingdom of God. In some cases faith was a necessary prerequisite for their performance by Jesus (Mk. 2:5; 5:34; 10:52) and also for the FORGIVENESS that was associated with many of the healing miracles. He was astonished at the unbelief of his own countrymen (6:5–6). During a storm on the Sea of Galilee, Jesus rebuked the disciples for their lack of faith in his ability to exercise the power of the Creator in stilling the storm (4:35–41). The same power that he had to heal was also available to those who had faith in God, for "Everything is possible for him who believes" (9:23–24). The command of Jesus is, therefore, "Have faith in God." Where there is such faith, the results of believing prayer will be remarkable (11:22–24). The moral and intellectual sides of faith are seen to stand together.

Distant shot of the Herodium (view to the SE). To construct this palace-fortress, Herod had to build a mountain. Referring to a different elevation, Jesus once said, "If anyone says to this mountain, 'Go, throw yourself into the sea,' and does not doubt in his heart but believes that what he says will happen, it will be done for him" (Mk. 11:23).

The unexpected faith of some whom Jesus commended warmly (Lk. 7:9) was in marked contrast to the unbelief of professed believers. The chief priests were aware that they had not believed JOHN THE BAPTIST (Mk. 11:30–31). Jesus asserted that they would not believe him if he told them that he was the Christ (Lk. 22:67). They mockingly suggested that they would believe if he would come down from the cross (Mk. 15:32). Even the disciples were slow to believe all that the prophets had spoken (Lk. 24:25). Yet God had given them the MYSTERY of the kingdom of God, whereas others were taught in parables to confirm them in their blindness (Mk. 4:11–12). Luke emphasizes that the purpose of Satanic activity is to prevent men from believing and being saved (Lk. 8:12).

An interesting and significant feature of the Gospels is the portrayal of the faith that Jesus had in God. This is illustrated well by the way in which he addressed God as his Father. He could use the intimate word ABBA and show complete dependence upon him and his will (Mk. 14:36). In a famous saying, similar in thought and style to John's gospel, he reveals the complete mutual trust between the Son and the Father, as well as the possibility of others entering in some measure into that unique relationship. "No one knows the Son except the Father, and no one knows the Father except the Son and those to whom the Son chooses to reveal him" (Matt. 11:27; Lk. 10:22). It is because of this relationship that he can tell his disciples to pray, "Our Father." The faith of believers in a trustworthy God is nowhere better expressed than in the LORD'S PRAYER (Matt. 6:9–13; Lk. 11:2–4). In Matthew it is set in the context of teaching about the heavenly Father, who knows his children's needs and who forgives their sin even as they are of a forgiving disposition themselves. Here one sees clearly the personal and moral connotations of faith in God (Matt. 6:7–8, 14–15).

There is not revealed in the Synoptic Gospels the fullness of Christian faith, for that was essentially something which came after the RESURRECTION OF JESUS CHRIST and PENTECOST. The faithfulness of God revealed in the OT is given a new dimension with the coming of Jesus Christ, and the practice of a new intimacy with him is inaugurated through the life of his Son.

2. John's gospel and epistles. These books are here treated together because even scholars who question their common authorship recognize that they belong to the same school of thought and that the concept of faith in them is similar.

God's faithfulness. The only use of a word from the *pistis* group ascribed to God is in 1 Jn. 1:9, where he is said to be "faithful and just and will forgive our sins." The word for "true" (*alēthēs G239*) is sometimes used of God in the Johannine writings and its meaning is often not far from that of faithfulness (Jn. 3:33; NIV, "truthful"). The fulfillment of Scripture, a theme common in the synoptics, is also found in John (13:18; 17:12; 19:24, 28, 36–37). God is portrayed as the author and unseen director of the whole drama in which Jesus is the leading actor. Yet there is relatively little that stresses directly God's faithfulness. It is rather assumed, in contrast to faith in God, which is made vividly explicit throughout the gospel.

The nature of faith. There are numerous other words that are used alongside *pisteuō* and that help us to obtain a clearer understanding of its meaning. The noun *pistis* is not found in the Gospel of John at all and occurs only once in the Johannine epistles (where the victory that overcomes the world is described as "our faith," possibly meaning "our creed," 1 Jn. 5:4). The reason John did not use the word *gnōsis G1194*, "knowledge," is generally understood to be that the Gnostics had made it their own. It is less easy to see why *pistis* is not used. It may be that the increasing application of it to "the faith" would have made its use somewhat misleading when John wrote. It also is possible that the use of the verb gives a more vivid representation of a dynamic relationship.

Faith is connected with knowledge. There is no question of knowledge being a stage of perfection beyond mere faith. Both are concerned with the divine origin of the mission of Jesus (*ginōskō G1182*, "to know," in Jn. 7:17; 17:8; *pisteuō* in 11:42; 16:27–30; 17:8, 21). Both are ways of reaching the truth (8:32; 14:1) and of apprehending that Jesus is the Christ (6:69; 11:27). Faith can help people to know, but never to know in such a way that they do not need faith. Faith is also connected with OBEDIENCE, for the believer is contrasted with the one who does not obey the Son (3:36).

There are some metaphorical expressions that seem to be illustrative of faith. Believing is said to be the same as "receiving" Christ (Jn. 1:11–12; 5:43–44). It also can be said to be "coming to" Christ (6:35; 7:37–38). Further, it is associated closely with loving him (16:27), and indeed is connected in some way or other with all the leading ideas of John's gospel.

The object of faith. There are a number of occasions when the verb *pisteuō* is used without an object and the sense must be something like "become a disciple" (Jn. 1:7, 50; 4:42, 53; 6:47; 19:35). Far more common, however, is the use of the verb with the preposition *eis* and having Jesus as its object (2:11; 3:16, 18, et al.). This construction is unknown in secular Greek, and of the forty-five occurrences in the NT, thirty-seven are in John or 1 John. The expression undoubtedly suggests not only intellectual credence, but also moral commitment to the person of Christ and is absolutely central to Johannine thought. There are also a number of places where the verb is followed by a *hoti* ("that") clause describing something about the person and mission of Christ that should be believed. People were to believe "that I am he" (8:24; 13:19; NIV, "I am the one I claim to be"); that he was the Christ (20:31; as MARTHA acknowledged, 11:27); that he and the Father mutually indwelt each other (14:11); and that he came from the Father (11:42; 17:8; as the disciples confessed in 16:27, 30).

Faith in Jesus also could be described as faith in his name (Jn. 1:12; 2:23; 3:18). This language no doubt has reference to his character, but also, it is likely, to his ownership. It may emphasize the sense of allegiance and obligation that faith in him brings. There are also references to believing in the words of Jesus (2:22; 4:21; 14:11). The believing of Moses in the OT is linked with believing him (5:46). Faith in Jesus was the gateway to faith in God the Father (5:24; 14:1).

The basis of faith. As such tremendous importance is attached to faith in John's gospel, the evangelist emphasizes the solid foundation that any faith in Jesus will have. The concept of evidence (*martyria* G3456, "witness") is referred to frequently as something that leads the way to faith. John the Baptist came for the purpose of bearing "witness to testify concerning that light, so that through him all men might believe" (Jn. 1:7). Jesus had greater testimony than that of John to lead people to faith. There was the evidence of his deeds and the evidence of his Father himself, but their disbelief of Jesus showed their failure to receive the Father's word (5:30–40). In the First Epistle of John it is stated that there is divine as well as human testimony to Jesus as the Son of God. It is meant to lead men to believe in him. Those who do not are making God a liar by refusing to believe the evidence he has given (1 Jn. 5:6–12). Jesus likewise gives his own testimony, which men do not receive (Jn. 3:11).

In John, faith is related to both seeing and hearing. Seeing the Son was the natural preliminary to believing as far as his contemporaries were concerned (Jn. 6:40), but it was possible to see and not to believe (6:36). Seeing the Father directly was not possible, but believing was the gateway to eternal life (6:46–47). Faith would lead on to seeing the glory of God (11:40). The faith of THOMAS in the risen Christ was based upon sight, but Jesus pronounced a great benediction upon those who did not see and yet believed (20:29). The idea of sight varies between the literal and the metaphorical. In the former sense it may or may not be the prelude to faith. In the latter, believing is seeing. Hearing can likewise be a purely natural process, not leading on to faith (6:60–65). Those who do not hear God's word in the words of Jesus cannot come to believe (8:43–47). On the other hand, people may hear his word and believe the Father who sent him, and they find not judgment and death, but life (5:24).

On several occasions John describes the immediate cause of belief. Many of the SAMARITANS from SYCHAR believed in Jesus because of the testimony of the woman whom he met at the well, though in the end the ground of their faith was his word rather than hers (Jn. 4:39–42). Jesus prayed not only for his disciples but "for those who will believe in me through their message" (17:20). It was not only the spoken word that had this effect; it was also the acted word. His disciples were urged to believe because of the works he had done (14:11).

Some of the works were described as SIGNS. They were not only miracles on the physical level but also dramatic illustrations of the spiritual life Jesus brought. They were therefore meant to bring people to believe in Jesus (Jn. 2:11, 23; 4:50,

53), though often they were the cause of conflict (11:45–47; 12:9–11). No more than in the Synoptics is Jesus willing to provide mere wonder-working as a basis for faith (4.48).

The result of faith. The first consequence of faith mentioned in the fourth gospel is becoming sons of God (Jn. 1:12). This meant that believers could to some extent enter into the same relationship Jesus had with his Father which is so integral a part of this gospel, though the words for faith and faithfulness are not used to describe it. People may be said to receive light (12:36) and satisfaction (6:35; 7:37–38). By far the most frequent picture, however, is that of ETERNAL life, or as it is often called, simply LIFE. The loving purpose of God was that the believer should have eternal life (3:15–16; 6:40). Those who believe have eternal life here and now (3:36; 6:47; 1 Jn. 5:13). The evangelist's purpose in writing with a selection of the signs that Jesus did was to invoke faith in Jesus as Christ and Son of God and so to lead sinners to life in his name (Jn. 20:31).

The blessedness of faith is contrasted with the wretchedness of unbelief. The believer is not condemned, but the unbeliever is already condemned (Jn. 3:18). The believer has passed from death to life and does not come into judgment, but those who have done evil do (5:24, 29). Unless men believed, they would die in their sins (8:24), and sin was essentially unbelief in him (16:9). There is a paradox in the gospel between the great universal "whoevers" (3:15–16; 6:40; 11:26; 12:46) and the inability of some to believe in fulfillment of prophecy (12:37–43), because they are not "of God" (8:45–47) and do not belong to Jesus' sheep (10:25–26).

The development of faith. It is interesting to note the ebb and flow of faith as it is dramatically revealed in John's gospel. The first person said to "believe" is NATHANAEL, who confessed Jesus as Son of God and King of Israel, but had greater things to see than that Jesus had seen him under the fig tree (Jn. 1:45–51). After the sign at the wedding at CANA, Jesus' disciples believed in him, but as yet with imperfect faith (2:11). Many believed in his name when he had cleansed the temple, but Jesus knew them and the nature of their faith well enough not to commit himself to them (2:23–25). The inability of the religious leaders to believe earthly things prevented them from believing heavenly things (3:12). The Samaritans, however, believed in him and confessed him to be "the Saviour of the world" (4:39–42). The official whose son Jesus healed not only believed his word but "believed" with his household (4:46–53). "The Jews" could not believe because they were too concerned with prestige, and they did not even really believe Moses (5:44–47). Those who saw the feeding of the 5,000 only saw and did not believe (6:36).

Even some of Jesus' disciples did not believe (Jn. 6:64), but PETER spoke for the Twelve when he said, "We believe and know that you are the Holy One of God" (6:69). This faith was not shared during the ministry by his brothers (7:5). Many believed as he spoke about his origin and destination (8:30–31), but others would not believe him when he was telling the truth (8:45–47). The blind man whom he healed said, "Lord, I believe," though not at first knowing who the SON OF MAN was (9:35–38). "The Jews" would not and could not believe the evidence that he was the Christ (10:24–26), but at the other side of the Jordan many who remembered what John the Baptist had said about him believed in him (10:40–42).

The death of LAZARUS provided a special opportunity for his disciples to believe (Jn. 11:15), and before he was raised MARTHA confessed, "I believe that you are the Christ, the Son of God, who was to come into the world" (11:27). After the raising of Lazarus many of the Jews believed in him (11:45), so that the chief priests and PHARISEES were afraid that everyone would believe in him (11:48). The miracle continued to lead many to faith (12:11). Many others, however, did not believe despite the signs (12:37), or if they did believe in him they were afraid to admit it (12:42–43). The disciples in the last week of the ministry needed to be told to believe the mutual indwelling of Father and Son (14:10–11), though they believed that he had come from God (16:30; 17:8). The fullness of faith could not come until the resurrection (2:22), and it was the BELOVED DISCIPLE who was the first to see the empty tomb and believe (20:8). Only after the resurrection did THOMAS address Jesus in terms of adoring wonder as "My Lord and my God!" (20:26–29). His was the first adequate confession of faith.

Human faithfulness. John also speaks about holding on to one's faith. Only those who continued in his word were truly Jesus' disciples (Jn. 8:31). They were to "abide" or remain in him and keep his commandments (15:1–11). Their faithfulness to each other was described as LOVE, which was derived from his prior love for them and was the mark of true discipleship (13:34–35; 15:12).

3. The Acts of the Apostles. *God's faithfulness.* This theme is emphasized in two ways in the book of Acts. In the first place, what God has already done in Christ is proof of his faithfulness. The apostolic KERYGMA is grounded upon the fact that he has been faithful to his promises. The INCARNATION showed this truth, as PAUL indicated when he spoke in the synagogue at ANTIOCH OF PISIDIA: "From [David's] descendants God has brought to Israel the Savior Jesus, as he promised" (Acts 13:23). His suffering and death fulfilled Scripture and showed the PROVIDENCE of God without excusing the guilt of the human agents (2:22–24; 3:18; 13:27–29). The apostles brought "the good news: What God promised our fathers he has fulfilled for us, their children, by raising up Jesus," thus giving us "the holy and sure blessings promised to David" (13:33–34; cf. 26:6–8).

The resurrection was one of the great pieces of evidence of God's faithfulness and is described as an "assurance" or "pledge" (*pistis*) of future judgment (Acts 17:31). The other was the presence and the power of the HOLY SPIRIT. The outpouring of the Spirit was the gift promised by the Father to those who repent, that is, all those God calls to himself (1:4; 2:33, 38–39). And the return of Christ in due time would mark the restoration of "everything, as he promised long ago through his holy prophets" (3:21).

The second way God's faithfulness is stressed is through his present activity, which is seen to overrule the life of the church and the progress of the Christian mission. It was he who "added to their number daily those who were being saved" (Acts 2:47). His angel guided PHILIP to the ETHIOPIAN EUNUCH (8:26–40) and released Peter from prison (12:6–11). His Spirit sent out BARNABAS and Saul on their missionary journey (13:1–4), guided the COUNCIL OF JERUSALEM (15:28–29), and led the apostles into Europe (16:6–10). He guided Paul on his dangerous and roundabout journey to Rome (19:21–22; 23:11; 27:21–26). There are also two occasions when Paul is recorded as mentioning the faithfulness of God as the Creator and Judge who "has not left himself without testimony: He has shown kindness by giving you rain from heaven and crops in their seasons; he provides you with plenty of food and fills your hearts with joy" (14:17; cf. 17:24–31).

Human faith. This theme is, if anything, even more prominent a theme in Acts than God's faithfulness, to which it is the response. The verb *pisteuō* often is used without an object in the sense of believing the *kerygma* and so becoming a Christian (Acts 2:44; 4:4, 32; et al.; cf. also the adjective *pistos*, 10:45; 16:1, 15). The verb sometimes is followed by a noun to indicate in whom people believed—the Lord (9:42; 14:23; 18:8), the Lord Jesus Christ (11:17; 16:31; cf. 10:43; 19:4; 22:19), or God (16:34). The response seems to have been superficial only in the case of SIMON MAGUS (8:13). The commitment to Christ might have as a prelude believing the Scriptures (24:14; 26:27) or believing an evangelist (8:12). The initial act of faith needed to be succeeded by a constant trust in the promises of God (27:25).

The noun *pistis* does not occur frequently. It can be used absolutely (Acts 6:5; 11:24; 14:9, 27; 15:9) or with reference to Christ explicitly (3:16; 20:21; 24:24; 26:18). It also has the meaning "the faith"—the body of Christian doctrine (6:7; 13:8; 14:22; 16:5). So we see that the lively exercise of faith is dependent upon an objective act of God. Faith is connected with REPENTANCE (11:21; 20:21) and has moral consequences (24:24–25). It leads to FORGIVENESS (10:43; 26:18), cleansing (15:9; see PURITY), and JUSTIFICATION (13:39). It was the result of God's calling (13:48) and was due to his grace (18:27). It was accompanied by the gift of the Spirit (10:43–44; 11:17; 19:2). It might be induced by a miracle (5:14; 13:12), by the Scriptures (17:12), or by the preaching of the gospel (4:4; 18:8). It sometimes involved healing (3:16; 14:9). Its natural outcome was a common purpose with other believers (2:44; 4:32) and joy (16:34). Some outstanding disciples can be described as "full of faith" (Stephen in 6:5; Barnabas in 11:24).

The agora at Paphos. By the faithful leading of the Holy Spirit, Paul and Barnabas were brought to this city, where Sergius Paulus received the gospel.

None of the words of the *pistis* group are used to describe human faithfulness, but this idea is found in relation to God when the verb *prosmenō* **G4693** ("to remain") is used (Acts 11:23; 13:43). Loyalty to God and to the Christian brotherhood is implicit throughout the book and perhaps finds clearest expression in the incident involving Ananias and Sapphira (4:32—5:11).

4. The Pauline epistles. Neither Paul the man nor his writings can possibly be understood unless we grasp the meaning of faith to him. Ever since his encounter with the risen Christ on the road to Damascus, the whole of his thinking and his life were dominated by the ideas of the faithfulness of God and the need for a responsive human faith. If there is a systematic treatment of these themes only in Romans, their living reality bursts forth spontaneously again and again in the varied pastoral situations which he deals with in all his epistles. His entire doctrine of salvation, his entire theology, could be summed up under the heading of faith, but we shall have to concentrate on the passages where the *pistis* words or closely associated ideas are present.

God's faithfulness. This truth is the solid foundation upon which all else in Pauline theology is built (Rom. 3:3). The adjective *pistos* is used six times with reference to God or Christ. God is faithful in fulfilling his promises (2 Cor. 1:18). He is faithful in continuing to work in, and thus preserve, those whom he has called to himself (1 Cor. 1:9; 10:13; 1 Thess. 5:24; 2 Thess. 3:3). Even "if we are faithless, he will remain faithful, for he cannot disown himself" (2 Tim. 2:13). It is because he is faithful that there are "trustworthy sayings" about his work that deserve "full acceptance" (1 Tim. 1:15; 3:1; 4:9; 2 Tim. 2:11; Tit. 3:8). Christian teaching as a whole can be described as "the trustworthy message" (Tit. 1:9).

We find also in Paul a fair number of references to *eleos* **G1799**, "mercy." This is the Greek word that the LXX normally uses to render Hebrew *ḥesed*. In the Gospels its main uses are in the twice-repeated quotation of Hos. 6:6 (Matt. 9:13; 12:7) and in the opening chapter of Luke, where it occurs five times (Lk. 1:50–78). Paul uses it as a greeting, alongside "grace" and "peace" (1 Tim. 1:1; 2 Tim. 1:1) and also as a benediction (Gal. 6:16). Its chief use as noun or verb (*eleeō* **G1796**) is, however, in Rom. 9–11. In these chapters Paul shows how God's faithfulness has been demonstrated despite the unfaithfulness of Israel. The word of God had not failed (Rom. 9:6). There was no injustice with God, for "it depends not on human will or exertion, but on God who shows mercy" (9:16 NRSV). He has not rejected his people (11:1). The gifts and call of God are irrevocable (11:29). The purpose of God is "that he may have mercy on them all" (11:32).

Another important subject illustrating the faithfulness of God is that of his promises. This is dealt with especially in Rom. 4 and Gal. 3–4, where the story of Abraham is in mind. Abraham was "fully persuaded that God had power to do what he had promised" (Rom. 4:21), and the promise was guaranteed to all his descendants (4:16). Christians, "like Isaac, are children of promise" (Gal. 4:28).

Faith and the gospel. Christian faith begins as a response to the *kerygma*. "God was pleased," says Paul, "through the foolishness of what was preached [the *kerygma*] to save those who believe" (1 Cor. 1:21). He expresses the main thrust of the *kerygma* as the CROSS (1:17, 18, 23, 24). The resurrection also was something that had to be believed, for if it were not true, both *kerygma* and faith would be futile (1 Cor. 15:14). The relationship of faith to the gospel is dealt with more fully in Rom. 10:8–17. With relentless logic Paul shows that salvation depends on calling upon God, which depends on faith, which depends on the preaching of the gospel. "Faith comes from hearing the message, and the message is heard through the word of Christ" (10:17). Faith is defined further as confessing with the lips that Jesus is Lord and believing in the heart that God raised him from the dead (10:9). Faith then involves an intellectual acceptance of and a moral response to the *kerygma*, and it is the means by which salvation is experienced (1:16). It is connected with obedience to God's command to repent (1:5; 10:16; 16:26; Gal. 3:2; 2 Thess. 1:8). It is established by the power of God rather than human wisdom (1 Cor. 2:5), but there was still a need of human preachers (Rom. 10:14–15; 1 Cor. 3:5; 15:11). Yet underlying all the human activity involved was the conviction that faith was due to grace—that it was a gift of God (Eph. 2:8).

Faith and justification. While Paul uses a number of different figures parallel to one another in order to express the new relationship with God that is entered by Christian faith, the chief figure is that of JUSTIFICATION. It means declaring a person to be in the right, giving the believer a right standing with God. In the case of sinners that can be done only through faith in the Christ and his work of redemption. It is something achieved by the grace of God and is a gift to be received by faith (Rom. 3:21–26). Faith that leads to justification is the correlative of grace. GRACE means divine action from sheer undeserved love, and faith therefore is humble and thankful acceptance of something unearned. Because sinners prefer to earn things in order to have something to pride themselves upon, Paul is insistent that the principle of faith understood thus is utterly opposed to the principle of works—of earning salvation by good deeds. This was a particular temptation for Jews who kept the law of Moses and had higher moral standards than their contemporaries (Rom. 3:27–31; 9:30–33; 10:1–8; Gal. 2:16; 3:10–14; Eph. 2:8; Phil. 3:9). While Paul could in one sense regard the law as a custodian "until faith should be revealed" (Gal. 3:23–26), he was concerned to show that, far from overthrowing the law by this faith, he was in fact upholding it (Rom. 3:31).

In order to show the importance of faith even in the OT, he goes back behind Moses to Abraham. The faith principle can be found working in his case, for Abraham "believed the LORD, and he credited it to him as righteousness" (Gen. 15:6; cited in Rom. 4:9; Gal. 3:6). This act took place before circumcision was instituted (Rom. 4:10) and four centuries before the law was given (Gal. 3:17). Religion in Abraham's case was a matter of promise. Abraham believed these divine promises, and through him they were made to his descendants. Those descendants need now to be redefined in terms of the ones who share the faith of Abraham (Rom. 4:11–12; Gal. 3:29; 4:28). For Abraham did not just believe promises, he believed also in God as one "who gives life to the dead and calls things that are not as though they were" (Rom. 4:17). The equivalent for Christians therefore is to "believe in him who raised Jesus our Lord from the dead," for Jesus "was delivered over to death for our sins and was raised to life for our justification" (4:24–25).

This then is the heart of the gospel that had such power in the life of Paul and others, for in it "a righteousness from God is revealed, a righteousness that is by faith from first to last, just as it is written, 'The righteous will live by faith'" (Rom. 1:16–17;

citing Hab. 2:4; cf. Gal. 3:11). The emphasis of the prophet may well have been more on the continuing relationship of faithfulness than on the initial saving act of faith, but the principle is the same—faith is the only way to receive righteousness and life.

Faith and relationship. Justification by faith means not only accepting a doctrine but also commitment to a person. It is trusting him who justifies the ungodly (Rom. 4:5). While the verb *pisteuō* is generally used by Paul absolutely (it is however followed by *eis* in Rom. 10:14; Gal. 2:16; Phil. 1:29), the noun *pistis* is made more specific on a number of occasions by being explicitly related to God (1 Thess. 1:8) or to Christ (Rom. 3:22, 26; Gal. 2:16, 20; 3:22, 26; Eph. 1:15; 3:12; Phil. 3:9; Col. 1:4; 2:5; 1 Tim. 3:13; 2 Tim. 1:13; 3:15). Close to the center of Pauline thought is the idea of "faith-union" with the Lord, an idea expressed by the phrase "in Christ" (see UNION WITH CHRIST). It is in him that we become children of God through faith (Gal. 3:26). The Holy Spirit also is received through faith (Eph. 1:13; Gal. 3:5, 14).

The life of faith. BAPTISM is the sign of beginning the new life of faith (Col. 2:11–12; cf. Gal. 3:26–27), and wherever it is spoken of, faith is assumed to be present. But faith needs to grow (2 Cor. 10:15). There may be deficiencies in it that need to be made up (1 Thess. 3:10), and the aim should be fullness of faith (Rom. 4:20; 1 Thess. 1:5). Christians "live by faith, not by sight" (2 Cor. 5:7). Having faith will lead to action (1 Thess. 1:3). The faith of a community may become something that is widely known (Rom. 1:8; Eph. 1:15; Col. 1:4; 1 Thess. 1:8; Phlm. 5). Faith will bring confidence about death (1 Thess. 4:14) and may be associated with hope (1 Cor. 13:13). There are some members of the church who may have special gifts of faith (12:9), but a loveless faith of this kind is useless (13:2). Faith also is involved in the question of religious scruples (see Rom. 14, where weak faith signifies over-scrupulousness; cf. Paul's comments on conscience, 1 Cor. 8:1–13; 10:23–30).

Human faithfulness. The adjective *pistos* is used simply for believers, without distinction being made between beginning and continuing in faith. It has the specific meaning of *trustworthy* when referring to stewards of the gospel (1 Cor. 4:1–2) and ministers (Eph. 6:21; Col. 1:7; 4:7). Paul can believe himself to be reckoned trustworthy by the Lord (1 Cor. 7:25; 1 Tim. 1:12) and to have had the gospel entrusted to him (passive of *pisteuō*, 1 Tim. 1:11; Tit. 1:3). He urges TIMOTHY to find trustworthy people to teach others (2 Tim. 2:2). The idea of continuing steadfastly in faith is found also as an important theme (1 Cor. 16:13; 2 Cor. 1:24; 2 Thess. 1:4), though the word used for this concept is more often *hypomonē G5705*, "patient endurance" (Rom. 15:4–5 et al.). Faithfulness needs also to be shown to others, as it is part of the fruit of the Spirit (Gal. 5:22). Faith in Christ is linked with love (Eph. 1:15; 3:17; 6:23; 1 Thess. 1:3; 3:6; 2 Thess. 1:3). Faith and love are two of the "theological virtues" (cf. 1 Cor. 13:13). Paul sums up the relationship of the two by speaking of "faith working through love" (Gal. 5:6 NRSV).

The faith. On some occasions Paul refers to "the faith" as the body of Christian belief, though it is not always possible to be sure whether *pistis* is being used in this objective sense. It may be referred to as something to obey (Rom. 1:5). Paul was described by Christians in Judea as "preaching the faith he once tried to destroy" (Gal. 1:23). It is possible that the objective sense is intended elsewhere (2 Cor. 13:5; Col. 1:23; 2:7), though in all these cases it may refer to the subjective exercise of faith. It is most common in the PASTORAL EPISTLES, though there again it is not always clear which usage is involved. There is the mystery of the faith (1 Tim. 3:9) and "the truths of the faith" (4:6). It is possible to depart from the faith or to deny it (4:1; 5:8; 6:10) or to miss "the mark as regards the faith" (6:21 NRSV). There are a number of other possible references (1 Tim. 1:2, 19; 3:13; 6:12; 2 Tim. 3:8; 4:7; Tit. 1:4, 13; 2:2; 3:15).

The negative words for unbelief are also found in Paul, mainly in Romans and the Pastoral Epistles, but the adjective *apistos* is used fourteen times in the Corinthian letters.

5. The epistle to the Hebrews. *God's faithfulness.* This theme is first introduced when the writer shows that God can be relied upon to punish sin under the new covenant even more than under the old (Heb. 2:1–4). He would not overlook their work and love in dealing with the readers (6:10). Emphasis is laid upon God's swearing an oath when making the promise to Abraham. There were therefore "two unchangeable things [the promise and the oath] in which it is impossible for God to lie," and this assurance provides "an anchor for the soul, firm and secure" (6:18–19). The new covenant is better than the old because it is enacted on better promises, and it shows God's loving and forgiving relationship to his people (8:6–13). The certainty of judgment for willful sin is balanced by the promises and rewards of God for the faithful (10:26–39). Even the suffering that the saints had to endure was evidence of the faithfulness of God (12:3–11). The kingdom he offered was unshakable (12:25–29). It was the God of peace who had saved them through the death and resurrection of Christ, who would equip them to do his will (13:20–21). This theme is perhaps best summarized in the phrase "he who promised is faithful" (10:23; cf. 11:11).

Human faith. Our response of faith is dependent upon Christ, who was himself "a merciful and faithful high priest in service to God" (Heb. 2:17). If Moses was faithful as a servant, Jesus was faithful as a son (3:1–6). He was therefore the surety of a better covenant (7:22). He was the pioneer and perfecter of our faith (12:2). In response, believers are to hold fast their confidence and glory in their hope (3:6). Holding their first confidence firm to the end was the only way to escape from the unbelief that was characteristic of the people of the first exodus who failed to enter God's promised rest (3:7—4:7). This faith involved "sharing in Christ" (3:14). Sinners could draw near with confidence to the throne of grace to receive mercy and help (4:16).

When upbraiding his readers for their immaturity, the writer regards repentance from dead works and faith toward God as elementary Christian teaching (Heb. 6:1). He wants them "to imitate those who through faith and patience inherit what has been promised" (6:12) and urges them to seize the hope set before them by God's promises (6:13–20). Again he exhorts the readers "to draw near to God with a sincere heart in full assurance of faith" and to hold fast the confession of their hope without wavering (10:22–23). They were not to throw away their confidence but to have faith and keep their souls (10:35–39), and to reinforce his point he quotes Hab. 2:3–4 (rather more in its context than does Paul).

Chapter 11 of this letter is one of the classical NT passages on faith. It begins with a definition: "Now faith is being sure of what we hope for and certain of what we do not see" (Heb. 11:1). It is the means by which there is present experience of realities that are either future in time or unseen as belonging to the spiritual sphere. It is something found in the OT and necessary for divine approval (11:2–6). It means trusting the God who made the world out of nothing (11:3) and who rewards those who seek after him (11:6). Faith of this quality, which believes in God's power to bring the invisible to life and acts upon that belief even when it means suffering and shame, is now abundantly illustrated from the OT. Noah (11:7), Abraham and Sarah (11:8–19), Isaac, Jacob, and Joseph (11:20–22), Moses (11:23–28), and a multitude of others, all displayed a faith whereby they "saw him who is invisible" and endured to the end. The saints of the old covenant could not in this life receive the true fulfillment of the promises—that is available to us in Christ (11:39—12:2). Our faith is to show itself in faithfulness to others (13:1–6). The readers must imitate the faith of their leaders in the faithful Jesus Christ, who is "the same yesterday and today and for ever" (13:7–8).

6. The epistle of James. This epistle includes a good number of references to the faithfulness of God. It is he who gives wisdom to all those who ask him (Jas. 1:5) and who grants the crown of life that he has promised to those who love him (1:12). Every good endowment and every perfect gift comes from him, and he "does not change like shifting shadows" (1:17). It is he whose mercy triumphs over judgment (2:13). His coming is certain though delayed (5:7–9). He will answer the prayers of the righteous (5:15–18).

Human faith or faithfulness must be tested to produce steadfastness (Jas. 1:3). When it is exercised in prayer it must be without doubting (1:6), and it can be used for the healing of the sick (5:15). Our faith in Christ must be held without partiality (2:1), for God has chosen the poor in the world to be rich in faith (2:5). Most significant, however, is the discussion of the relationship between faith and works (2:14–26). James insists that faith cannot save a person unless it has action to back it up. Even

Abraham, the great type of justification by faith in the OT, was justified by his action of offering Isaac. At first sight this seems to be a contradiction of Pauline teaching, but closer examination suggests that this is not likely. Faith is in this passage mere intellectual belief, such as the demons have. Paul would never deny that such faith would need to be proved real by actions. Works are not treated as a way of earning salvation, as Paul treats them when setting them against faith. Justification also seems to be used rather differently, in the sense of outward vindication rather than of receiving a right relationship with God. It is quite probable that James was refuting perversions of Pauline teaching, but he does not seem to answer any known Pauline letter point by point. It is a healthy reminder that faith is no isolated part of religious experience, but has to determine all the actions of a person.

7. The epistles of Peter and Jude. In the First Epistle of Peter we see emphasis laid on the faithfulness of God in the face of persecution of the church. It is he who chose and destined Christians (1 Pet. 1:2). It was his mercy that gave them new birth, and a safe INHERITANCE for which they were preserved. Because of this the outcome of their faith would be the salvation of their souls (1:3–9). God's plan before the creation was revealed for their sake, and this should produce faith and hope in him (1:20–21). Their response of faith was obedience to the truth, and they were born through the dependable message of the gospel (1:22–25). The prophecy of Isa. 28:16 is invoked to show that the believer will not be let down by God. The calling and mercy of God achieve this, and unbelievers are destined to fall (1 Pet. 2:6–10). Christ left an example of entrusting "himself to him who judges justly" (2:21–23). Whenever there is unjust suffering, they must remember that "the eyes of the Lord are on the righteous, / and his ears are sensitive to their prayer" (3:12; citing Ps. 34:15). The fiery ordeal of persecution is something to be accepted with joy because it means sharing the glory of Christ (1 Pet. 4:12–14). Those who suffered according to God's will were to do what is right and "entrust their souls to a faithful Creator" (4:19 NRSV). Because God cared for them and would provide them with strength and exalt them in the end, they were to trust him with all their cares and anxieties (5:6–11). They were to resist the devil and remain firm in their faith (5:9). The epistle ends with a note that Peter regards Silvanus (see SILAS), through whom he has written, as a "faithful brother," who would presumably transmit his message reliably in writing (5:12).

In 2 Peter faith is said to be something precious received "through the righteousness of our God and Savior Jesus Christ" (2 Pet. 1:1). Faith is treated as something that needs to be supplemented by virtue and various other qualities (1:5). According to Jude, "the faith" was something that "was once for all entrusted to the saints" and had to be defended (Jude 3). It could be described as "your most holy faith" (Jude 20). Throughout the two epistles the need for steadfast faith and faithfulness is set against the background of widespread apostasy and the faithfulness of God. The judgment would come as promised (2 Pet. 3:8–10) and God was "able to keep [them] from falling" (Jude 24).

8. Revelation. The greeting in this book invokes grace from God "and from Jesus Christ, who is the faithful witness" (Rev. 1:4–5). He is described in a similar way again as "the Amen, the faithful and true witness" (3:14), and later the man on the white horse "is called Faithful and True" (19:11). His words therefore are trustworthy and true (21:5; 22:6). His witnesses are likewise to be faithful to death, as ANTIPAS was (2:10, 13). Those who are in the army of the Lamb are "called, chosen and faithful" (17:14). This faithfulness means not denying the faith of Christ (2:13) but rather obeying "God's commandments and [remaining] faithful to Jesus" (14:12). Faith therefore is very much linked with endurance (2:19; 13:10). This is what would be expected in a writing to churches undergoing persecution. Likewise there is the sense of the reliability of God, whose victory and vindication of his people is sure.

C. Faith and faithfulness in NT theology.
The NT sees God's faithfulness in a new way, for many of the promises made in the OT have been fulfilled, and God has so acted that there is little doubt that the others will be fulfilled also in due course. While the idea of God's faithfulness

in creation and providence is given a new depth through the life and ministry of Christ, it is essentially his faithfulness in redemption that is central to NT thought. What the OT could only look forward to, the NT could look back upon. Things had come to their culmination in the life, ministry, death, and resurrection of Christ and in the gift of the Holy Spirit. The new covenant of forgiveness and the personal knowledge of God had come into its own. The faithful God had acted decisively for the redemption of the world.

The gospel was therefore good news, to be believed and acted upon by all. The *kerygma* recited the mighty acts of God and called sinners to repentance and faith on the basis of the divine initiative. So people of every nation, believing the facts of redemption on divine testimony, abandoned themselves completely to the love and mercy of God. In the face of opposition and persecution, they stood fast by the unshakable realities of the gospel and proved in the depths of human experience that God keeps faith.

(See further W. H. P. Hatch, *The Pauline Idea of Faith* [1917]; id., *The Idea of Faith in Christian Literature* [1920]; J. G. Machen, *What Is Faith?* [1925]; C. H. Dodd, *The Bible and the Greeks* [1935], 42–75; id., *The Interpretation of the Fourth Gospel* [1953], 151–86; G. C. Berkouwer, *Faith and Justification* [1954]; J. Murray, *Redemption Accomplished and Applied* [1955], 106–16; J. Barr, *The Semantics of Biblical Language* [1961], 161–205; R. Bultmann and A. Weiser, *Faith* [1961]; A. Dulles, *The Assurance of Things Hoped For: A Theology of Christian Faith* [1994]; L. Newbigin, *Proper Confidence: Faith, Doubt, and Certainty in Christian Discipleship* [1995]; E. O. Springsted, *The Act of Faith: Christian Faith and the Moral Self* [2002]. Note also the bibliographies under OLD TESTAMENT THEOLOGY and NEW TESTAMENT THEOLOGY.) R. E. NIXON

faithfulness. See FAITH, FAITHFULNESS.

falcon. This English term is used by the NIV to render Hebrew ʾayyâ *H370* (Job 28:7; so also NRSV), a word elsewhere translated "black kite" (Lev. 11:14 et al.). The NIV uses it also to render *dayyâ H1901* (Deut. 14:13; Isa 34:15), apparently a general term referring to various unclean BIRDS OF PREY (see also BUZZARD; HAWK; KITE; VULTURE; and cf. *FFB*, 40–41). The falcon (*Falco peregrinus*) is among the commonest birds of prey; Palestine has about ten species. These include peregrine and lanner, about 18 in. long; also kestrel and lesser kestrel, hobby and red-legged falcon, 11–14 in. long. These take only living prey; the biggest catch birds up to the size of a rock dove, but others take small rodents, lizards, and insects. About half breed in Palestine; the others are migrants. G. S. CANSDALE

fall, the. A term used with reference to the first SIN of ADAM and EVE, who through disobedience fell from the state of integrity in which God had created them and thus brought a curse upon themselves and their descendants.

I. The occasion. Adam and Eve did not themselves originate the thought that came to fruition in their disobedience to God's commandment. They were subjected to suggestion and solicitation in the form of TEMPTATION. The direct instrument of this temptation was the serpent (Gen. 3:1). The narrative seems to indicate that the serpent belonged to the category of the beasts of the field. The presence and agency of a literal serpent may not be denied. Furthermore, the curse pronounced (3:14) implies a being to which its terms could apply. Behind the serpent was the activity of SATAN (cf. Jn. 8:44; Rom. 16:20; 2 Cor. 11:3; 1 Jn. 3:8; Rev. 12:9; 20:2). The information given in Gen. 3 is not complete and must be supplemented by subsequent revelation. The later revelation confirms the earlier and assures us that from the beginning of fallen human history there was the sinister craft and power of the archenemy.

The focus of the temptation was direct assault upon the veracity and integrity of God (Gen. 3:4–5). It was not an impeachment of God's knowledge nor merely a denial of his power. The tempter accused God of deception and deliberate falsehood. God, it was alleged, perpetrated a lie in order to preserve his own exclusive possession of the knowledge of good and evil. Herein lies the diabolical character of the allegation. The design was the destruction of human integrity by the breakdown of belief in the integrity of God. The way of integrity is unreserved and unrelenting trust in God and the giving to him of the SOVEREIGNTY and finality that are exclusively his.

II. The cause. Temptation was the occasion; it was not the cause. To be subjected to temptation is not sinful for the tempted. Embrace and acquiescence constitute sin. So it was with our first parents. Eve succumbed to the solicitation of the tempter, and Adam to that of Eve.

The strategy of the tempter was to direct his solicitations to the woman. The silence of Scripture compels reserve concerning the reason. In the case of Eve, however, one is justified in tracing the process by which she came to the point of overt disobedience to the divine prohibition. Acquiescence in the allegation of the serpent and defection from God's word cannot be postponed beyond the point when she "saw that the fruit of the tree … was desirable for gaining wisdom" (Gen. 3:6). This demonstrates that the tempter had gained her trust; she accepted as true what was a blasphemous assault upon the veracity of God and came to regard the tree as desirable in the direction that contravened the divine prohibition. She served the creature rather than the Creator. Her failure to recoil with revulsion from the tempter's "You will not surely die" (3:4) is evidence that defection had already taken place and that she exemplified the invariable psychology of sin that overt action proceeds from the inward disposition of the heart (cf. Prov. 23:7; Mk. 7:21–23; Jas. 1:14–15). The eating of the forbidden fruit was the expression of an inward movement of apostasy at the instance of satanic beguilement. In the case of Adam there was a difference; he was not deceived (1 Tim. 2:14). What the movement of his thought was cannot be defined. But the same principle must hold that the actual volition cannot be divorced from precedent disposition of mind and heart.

The prohibition imposed upon Adam and Eve (Gen. 2:17) was for the purpose of proving the ultimate criterion of faith in God, unquestioning obedience to God's commandment. In the prohibition were epitomized the sovereignty, authority, wisdom, goodness, justice, holiness, and truth of God. Transgression was no trivial offense; it was assault upon God's majesty, repudiation of his sovereignty, doubt of his goodness, dispute with his wisdom, contradiction of his veracity. All along the line of God's perfections it was what all sin is, the contradiction of God. Hence its gravity and the corresponding liabilities.

III. The consequences

A. Subjective. The human dispositional complex was radically altered. The pivot on which this revolution turned was the changed attitude to God (Gen. 3:7–10). Adam and Eve were made for the presence and fellowship of God and in the presence of God would have found their supreme delight. Now they flee from God's face; shame and fear took possession of their heart. "Everyone who does evil hates the light, and will not come into the light for fear that his deeds will be exposed" (Jn. 3:20).

B. Objective. God changed his relation to man. The reason for the rupture between them was human sin, but the rupture was not one-sided. After Gen. 3:9 an aspect of God's character is disclosed that previously (2:17) had been threatened to be in exercise but had not been manifested, and it appears in reproof, condemnation, curse, and retribution (3:14–19, 23–24), the echoes of divine WRATH. At the outset is the lesson that sin not only involves our changed attitude to God but also his changed attitude to us, not only our estrangement from God but also his alienation from us.

C. On creation. The fall was an event in the human spirit. It did not consist in physical disturbance or maladjustment, yet it drastically affected the physical and nonspiritual. "Cursed is the ground because of you" (Gen. 3:17). "The creation was subjected to frustration" (Rom. 8.20). Man was the crown of CREATION, and with his fall came the bondage of corruption for all over which he was to exercise dominion. Only with the consummation of redemption will the cosmos be released from the curse incident to human sin (cf. Rom. 8:19–23; 2 Pet. 3:13).

D. On humanity. The sequel to the fall of Adam and Eve is the catalogue of sins in the unfolding history of mankind—envy, malice, murder, polygamy, violence. The result was cumulative, and human wickedness was great on the earth (Gen. 6:5), so that the earth became "filled with violence" (6:13). History shows that Adam's fall was not an isolated event but affected the whole race. Scripture reveals the reason and specifies the kind of solidarity existing between Adam and posterity explanatory of this consequence. Adam was not only the father of all mankind but he was also by divine institution the representative head: "one trespass resulted in condemnation for all people ... through the disobedience of the one man the many were made sinners" (Rom. 5:18–19 TNIV). As all died in Adam (1 Cor. 15:22), so all sinned in Adam (Rom. 5:12, 15–16). All mankind is reckoned as participating with Adam in his sin and therefore in the depravity which his sin entailed. This is the biblical explanation of universal sin, condemnation, and death, and no other validation of the involvement of the human race in sin is necessary or justifiable.

E. Death. The threat pronounced upon eating of the forbidden fruit was, "you will surely die" (Gen. 2:17). The fulfillment of this threat is eloquently stated in Gen. 5 in the repeated formula: "and he died." Notwithstanding the longevity of the patriarchs, they could not escape this appointment (cf. Heb. 9:27). The disintegration following in the wake of the fall, exemplified in the respects specified above, enters also into the constitution of man and separates the elements of his being (cf. Gen. 3:19; Eccl. 12:7). The biblical witness is unequivocal that DEATH took its origin from the trespass of Adam, that it is the wages of sin and not the debt of nature (Gen. 2:17; 3:19; Rom. 5:12; 6:23; 1 Cor. 15:22).

IV. Historicity. Much has been written in support of the thesis that Gen. 3 is MYTH or legend, not history but story, portraying what happens to all men and women but not an account of a unique, once-for-all series of events at the beginning of human history. Adam, it is alleged, is everyone. We all sin as Adam sinned. This might appear to be an acceptable and effective way of maintaining the biblical doctrine that all have sinned, but the position is fraught with fallacies.

A. It is not true that all sin as Adam. There is a radical difference between Adam and posterity. We all come to be as sinners; Adam and Eve did not. The beginning of our sinfulness was not by voluntary defection and transgression as in the case of our first parents, but by divinely constituted solidarity with Adam in his sin. As a consequence we are shapen in iniquity and conceived in sin (cf. Ps. 51:5); we are "by nature children of wrath" (Eph. 2:3 NRSV). We are dead in trespasses and sins not by acquisition but by IMPUTATION to us of Adam's sin and by generation. So the position in question fails to correspond with the total witness of Scripture and to assess the human situation in sin and misery.

B. If we are all Adam, then the uniqueness of Adam as the first man is denied. The parallel between Adam and Christ (Rom. 5:12–19; 1 Cor. 15:21–22, 45–49) belongs to the way of salvation and to the integrity of the gospel. This parallel provides the antithesis between the way in which sin, condemnation, and death came to reign and the way righteousness, justification, and life come to bear upon us. The former was by Adam, the latter is by Christ. Therefore Adam and Christ sustain unique and incomparable relations to human beings. The preservation of both the parallel and the antithesis requires that Adam should be as real

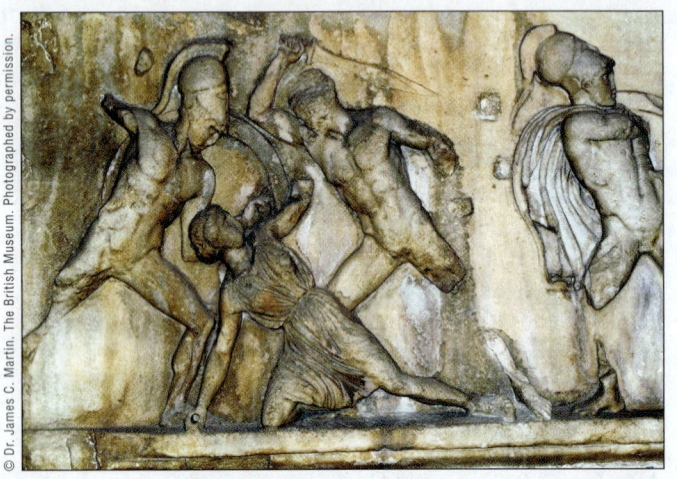

The fall into sin brought with it many horrible consequences, including the pain of war as depicted in this Greek battle scene. (Amazon frieze from the Mausoleum at Halicarnassus, 4th cent. B.C.)

and unique in his historical identity as was Christ. To aver that Gen. 3 is story but not history, that we are all Adam and we all sin as Adam, destroys the particularity of Adam and undermines what belongs to our history in sin and redemption.

C. NT allusions assume the historicity of Gen. 2 and 3.
In Matt. 19:5–6 (= Mk. 10:7–8) reference is made to Gen. 2:24, and the actual terms of the latter are quoted. The reference to the transgression of Adam (Rom. 5:14) clearly indicates that the one man mentioned in v. 12 is none other than Adam and the one trespass of the one man (cf. vv. 15–19) is the first sin of Adam. In 1 Cor. 15:45–49 there is distinct allusion to Gen. 2:7. In 1 Tim. 2:13 there is reiteration of the principle stated in Gen. 2:20–23, and in the following verse there is explicit appeal to Gen. 3:1–6, 13. These examples suffice to show that in the esteem of our Lord and of the apostle Paul the accounts given in Genesis could be appealed to for what they purported to be. We cannot dissociate the doctrine set forth in such passages from the premises on which the inspired teachers proceeded in enunciating the doctrine. Not only is the historical character of the early chapters of Genesis involved in the question, but also the authenticity and relevance of the NT allusions and appeals to them. (See further J. Murray, *The Imputation of Adam's Sin* [1959]; G. C. Berkouwer, *Man: The Image of God* [1962], 119–93; J. G. Machen, *The Christian View of Man* [1965], 161–72, 208–19; M. Shuster, *The Fall and Sin: What We Have Become as Sinners* [2004].)

J. MURRAY

fallow deer. See DEER.

fallow ground. Land that is left idle for a season after plowing and harrowing, so that weeds and insects are killed while the soil regains its fertility. The term is used by the NRSV and other versions to render Hebrew *nîr* H5776 (Jer. 4:3; Hos. 10:12; NIV, "unplowed ground"); the Heb. word occurs also in Prov. 13:23, "field"). In addition, the expression "lie fallow" (for Heb. *šāmaṭ* H9023, NIV, "lie unplowed") is used in Exod. 23:11, which discusses the law of the SABBATICAL YEAR, prescribing one year of rest every seven years for cultivated soil. Such a custom was practiced by other nations as well. Evidently Israel failed to obey this dictum during much of its history (Lev. 26:34–35).

H. M. WOLF

false apostle. Reference to false apostles occurs only in 2 Cor. 11:13 (*pseudapostolos* G6013). The reason for PAUL's harsh judgment of these leaders was twofold. First, they led the Corinthian Christians astray from their "sincere and pure devotion to Christ" (2 Cor. 11:3) and preached "a Jesus other than the Jesus we preached" (v. 4). Second, they said Paul was an inferior (v. 5) and unskilled apostle (v. 6) who received "outside" support from MACEDONIA (vv. 7–9). These false teachers boasted of their special religious prerogatives as Jews (v. 22). These items show they lacked the apostolic virtues and message.

They were counterfeit apostles, but not from the circle of the apostles or apostolic men. Rather, they were members of the Judaizing party whose activity in the early churches gave the occasion for Paul's classic defense of his gospel and apostleship in the letter to the GALATIANS (see JUDAIZER). In the narrative of Galatians, PETER and JAMES figure prominently, but not as opponents of Paul. The Judaizers claimed the authority of James (Gal. 2:12), but these claims were false (Acts 15:24). One should compare the language of 2 Cor. 11 with Gal. 1–2 and Acts 15, noting especially "false brothers" in Gal. 2:4 and 2 Cor. 11:26 (cf. also Rev. 2:2). (See M. E. Thrall in *JSNT* 6 [1980]: 42–57, and the response by S. E. McClelland in 14 [1982]: 82–87.) See also CORINTHIANS, SECOND EPISTLE TO THE.

J. C. DEYOUNG

false Christ. One who makes a spurious claim to be the MESSIAH. Jesus cautioned against such impostors (*pseudochristos* G6021, Matt. 24:24; Mk. 13:22). A false messiah is distinct from an ANTICHRIST. The former is an impersonator or impostor, usurping the title or allowing others to herald him as such. The latter, mentioned only by John (1 Jn. 2:18, 22; 4:3; 2 Jn. 7), indicates not impersonation as much as opposition by one who is against Christ (J. A. Broadus, *Commentary on the Gospel of Matthew* [1886], 488; R. C. Trench, *Synonyms of the New Testament*, 10th ed. [1886], 107). He opposes Christ by doctrines about his person and work that are contrary to truth, as in the Gnostic heresies (see GNOSTICISM). Antichrists active in John's day (1 Jn. 2:18, 22) were characterized by the same spirit as the supreme antichrist, whose career will be just before Jesus Christ returns (2 Thess. 2; Rev. 13:1–10).

Christians view Jesus of Nazareth as the genuine Messiah of Israel who, though rejected at his coming, will come again with blessing for all who receive him, including Jews. Evidence for his authenticity sets him apart from false christs. When he claimed to be God (Jn. 5:17; 10:30, 37; 14:9; cf. Isa. 7:14; 9:6; Mic. 5:2), he displayed the character and works of God (Matt. 9:6; 25:31). He was recognized as God by those who spent their lives proclaiming him as such (Matt. 14:33; 16:16–17; Col. 2:9), and he never disappointed them. He fulfilled many prophecies pointing to one who would be God and man (Isa. 9:6; Mic. 5:2) and reaching down to the precise time when he came (Dan. 9:25–26). He died (Isa. 53), then arose as verified by many evidences (Ps. 16:10; Matt. 28; 1 Cor. 15; et al.).

False christs have differed from one another in several ways: (1) in motives, some seeking prestige, others deliverance from oppression, or clever mockery; (2) in methods, some using violence, others appealing to fasting, prayer, and a miracle that failed to occur as announced; (3) in line of messiahship, some proposing to be the Messiah of the house of David (2 Sam. 7:4–16), others of the house of Joseph as an Ephraitic messiah; (4) in claims, certain ones heralding themselves out of self-deception or to exploit the hopes of the people, others being announced by followers and riding the crest of popular opinion, still others claiming to be forerunners or prophets, with Messiah himself to be manifested on some date or by some miracle; (5) in influence, some swaying Jews in Palestine, some in different lands, some in several countries; (6) in emphasis, certain ones being religious reformers, some political messiahs, others both; (7) in end, some vanishing to unknown places, some fading into obscurity, others being put to death by armies, royal power, or their own disappointed but wiser followers; (8) in beliefs after their deaths, some being rejected as impostors by certain of their group, others supposedly rising from the dead but without any substantial evidence, still others expected to reappear in the future.

A few examples may be cited. (1) THEUDAS (c. A.D. 44; Acts 5:36) promised to divide the Jordan for his followers to cross. They massed for a miracle, but Roman troops massacred many and took others captive. (2) BAR KOKHBA (c. 132) was named "son of a star" in expectation that he would fulfill Num. 24:17. He led a Jewish rebellion, conquering Jerusalem for three years, where he was hailed as king and messiah. The Romans retook Jerusalem and he was later slain at BETHER, a stronghold, with five to six hundred thousand followers. (3) Moses Cretensis (c. 440) assumed the name "Moses" on the island of CRETE, capitalizing upon a Talmudic computation of Messiah's date. Many Jews gathered at his assurance that the sea would open for a march dry-shod to Palestine. Some leaped into the water and were drowned. "Moses" vanished from the scene. (4) David Alroy (c. 1160), a Persian Jew, led a revolt against the Muslims. His death is obscured by different traditions, and his movement came to nought. (5) Asher Lammlein (1502), a rabbi in Italy, claimed to be a forerunner, with Messiah to appear if people would fast, pray, and give alms. A pillar of cloud and fire would lead them to Palestine. Then Lammlein disappeared. (6) Sabbethai Zebi (1626–1676) took the title "king of the kings of the earth" in Smyrna, attracting many Jewish followers. Later, he defected to the Muslim faith under charges by the Turkish government. He was beheaded. Some of his group claimed to be Messiah after him.

Other notable names include Menahem (A.D. 60s), Julian (529), Serene (720), David el-David (1199), Abraham ben Samuel Abulafia (1240–1292), Nissim ben Abraham (1290s), Moses Botarel (1393), David Reubeni (1525), Isaac Luria (1534–1572), Hayyim Vital Calabrese (1543–1620), Abraham Shalom (1574), Mordecai Mokiah (1680), Jacob Frank (1726), and Moses Hayyim Luzzatto (1707–1747). (See the index of names in H. Graetz, *History of the Jews*, 6 vols. [1891–1898]; note also A. H. Silver, *A History of Messianic Speculation in Israel from the First through the Seventeenth Centuries* [1927].)

J. E. ROSSCUP

false prophet. Moses ordered the death of any prophet advocating the worship of another god (Deut. 13:1–4). See PROPHETS AND PROPHECY. During the monarchy, false prophets were often in the majority in the court of Israel. The 800 prophets of AHAB openly advocated the worship of BAAL and ASHERAH (1 Ki. 18:20). Later, 400 prophets, influenced by a lying spirit, assured Ahab of victory at RAMOTH GILEAD, only to be contradicted by MICAIAH, the true prophet (22:6–23). Frequently, lying prophets told the leaders what they wanted to hear (Jer. 5:31; Lk. 6:26). JEREMIAH inveighed against those who claimed to be receiving visions from God, but who counseled rebellion against Babylon (Jer. 27:9). Two false prophets by the name of Zedekiah and Ahab were cursed because of their evil advice (29:21–23). Testing the prophets should have been a constant practice.

In the NT false prophets were plentiful (1 Jn. 4:1, *pseudoprophētēs G6021*) and were compared with wolves in sheep's clothing (Matt. 7:15) and false teachers (2 Pet. 2:1). The false prophet BAR-JESUS was smitten with blindness by PAUL (Acts 13:6, 11). Christ warned of false prophets whose miracles would deceive many in the end (Matt. 24:24; Mk. 13:22). In Rev. 13:12–14 and 19:20, the master false prophet is described. He will support the beast through powerful signs before his destruction. H. M. WOLF

false testimony, false witness. Bearing false testimony, particularly in court, is banned in the OT laws (Exod. 20:16; 23:1; Deut. 5:20), and the false witness is subject to the penalty he intended to inflict on the accused (Deut. 19:16–21). Twice God is said to hate false witnesses (Prov. 6:19; Zech. 8:17). Jeremiah condemns those who swear falsely, even though they say, "As surely as the LORD lives" (Jer. 5:2). Note also the warning against taking the Lord's name in vain (Exod. 20:7). See LIE; OATH.
H. M. WOLF

familiar spirit. This term is used by the KJV to render Hebrew *ʾôb H200*, which modern versions usually translate "medium." The Hebrew word appears to refer to the spirit of a dead person, which a medium, in the form of magic known as necromancy, claimed to summon to consultation (Deut. 18:11; see DIVINATION). In necromancy, in which the dead were consulted about the future, it was believed that either a spirit dwelt in the controlling medium (Lev. 20:27), who was most commonly a woman, or that the medium had fellowship with a spirit from whom she could receive information. The word "familiar" in this phrase has the sense of belonging to one's family, and so to oneself; ready to serve one as a servant.

Mediums seem to have deceived their inquirers by speaking in a thin weak voice, as though it came from the ground or from a bottle (Isa. 8:19; 29:4). The SEPTUAGINT generally represents them as ventriloquists. Nothing is known of their method of procedure. The Mosaic law forbade the consulting of familiar spirits, and mediums were commanded to be put to death (Lev. 19:31; 20:6, 27; Deut. 18:11).

King SAUL put away the mediums early in his reign, but, greatly worried about the outcome of his last battle, he consulted the witch of ENDOR and asked to speak to the prophet SAMUEL (1 Sam. 28:3, 7–9; 1 Chr. 10:13). It appears that Saul was told by the witch that she saw Samuel, and Saul himself entered into the conversation with the prophet. King MANASSEH also fell into the sin of consulting mediums (2 Ki. 21:6; 2 Chr. 33:6); but his grandson JOSIAH put them out of the land (2 Ki. 23:24). Belief in the possibility of communing with the spirit of the dead was common in ancient heathendom. The GILGAMESH Epic, Tablet XII, gives evidence of it; and Acts 16:16–18 tells of a slave girl who was a medium and brought her owners much gain by her divination. S. BARABAS

family. The fundamental unity of human SOCIETY and the center of God's COVENANT activity.

I. Family in the OT. The OT teaching about the family is embodied in the first chapters of the TORAH. The CREATION of God was in a world-order and in a family-order. In the OT, family relationships are concentric: husband and wife form the nucleus of the circle, the children lie in the next circle, then the grandparents, cousins, and the like. This principle is clear in the terminology. Each term is applicable beyond the mere immediate definition to the set of relations that the term represents; for example, the term DAUGHTER may be applied to a number of other individuals aside from one's own female offspring, or it may be applied to any number of females who are in a specific law-relationship to the "father."

A. Terminology. The OT often uses the common Semitic term for "house" (Heb. *bayit* H1074) with reference to the household or family (cf. Ruth 4:11 [NIV, "home"]; 1 Chr. 13:14; 2 Chr. 35:5, 12; Ps. 68:6). The most frequently occurring term for this concept, however, is *mišpāḥâ* H5476 (e.g., Exod. 12:21). This noun, though applicable to the family, actually embraces the whole range of meanings from "clan" (10:5) through "species" (8:19) to "consanguinity" (24:38; cf. NRSV, "kindred"). The term appears some 300 times in the OT, the highest frequency being in NUMBERS, where it stands for the "clans" of the tribes of Israel (notice esp. the expression *lĕmišpĕḥōtām lĕbêt ʾăbōtām*, Num. 1:20 et al.; NIV, "according to the records of their clans and families"; NRSV, "in their clans, by their ancestral houses").

B. The creation ordinances and the law. The initial statement of the relationship of man and woman in the Scripture is given in the narrative of the creation account. In the section that begins the creation of the world-order (the creation ordinances, Gen. 2:4—5:1), the form of human family life is set forth. The unity of male and female in the MARRIAGE bond is set down on two levels, the fulfillment of man's need for companionship and the sexual relationship for the procreation of the race (2:18; 3:20; 4:1–2). There is no question throughout the rest of the Bible that the monogamy of the Garden of Eden is the situation to be considered "normal" because it is the ordained law of marriage (Mk. 10:6–9). This relationship was not to supersede the relationship to God (Deut. 13:6–10; Matt. 19:29; Lk. 14:26) nor was it binding upon either party when separated by death (Matt. 22:30 and Mk. 12:25, on the analogy of many OT passages).

This complete reliance upon the monogamous law-order was an inherent part of the Israelite worldview and from that source has continued to be a mark of Western civilization. Regardless of all evolutionary and psycho-analytic theories of explanation, the monogamous, lifelong relationship is that which is the nature of human beings. In view of this principle, the creation ordinance is walled about with several other sets of strictures, the Decalogue (Exod. 20:14, 17), the Levitical laws (Lev. 18:6–18; 20:14–21; 21:7–15), and customs such as the DOWRY. To the positive statement of the text and the illustration in the history of the creation there are added the various negative restrictions. It was correctly assumed by the rabbis that for every negative commendation or commandment the contrapositive statement also was true. Thus the negative statements concerning the family relationships have equally binding positive obligations.

C. Cultural developments. The OT is primarily a continuous narrative of the history of the covenant people of God. It begins with the Adamic covenant, continues through the patriarchal and tribal periods, and ends with the rise and fall of the Israelite monarchy. There is a definite temporal progression, and the various changes in the cultures of the ANE—the development from mesolithic to neolithic, from bronze to iron, and from food-getting nomads to food-producing township settlements—all have their impact on the covenant people. In such an arrangement, the place and structure of the family underwent certain alterations. Some of these are insignificant, some positive, and some absolutely contrary to the covenant and the law-order itself.

In the patriarchal period several incidents, such as the story of LOT and his antagonism to the rampant sexual immorality of his surroundings (Gen. 19:4–11), show the resistance of the covenant people to the family notions of their contemporaries. Ultimately, however, as Israel became a settled and inde-

Colossal statues made of hard limestone and representing Amenophis III, Queen Tyi, and their daughters. From the temple of Midine, Habu (18th dynasty).

pendent political entity, these cross-cultural forces worked upon the family associations of the Jews. (For a discussion of family life in Egypt, Mesopotamia, Hittite culture, and Canaan, see the chapters on private life in *CANE*, Part 4. Note further E. B. Cross, *The Hebrew Family* [1927]; M. Burrows, *The Basis of Israelite Marriage* [1938]; E. Neufeld, *Ancient Hebrew Marriage Laws* [1944]; J. Pedersen, *Israel: Its Life and Culture*, 2 vols. [1926–40], 1:46–60; J. Leipoldt, *Die Frau in der antiken Welt und im Urchristentum* [1954], 69–114; A. van Selms, *Marriage and Family Life in Ugaritic Literature* [1954]; R. de Vaux, *Ancient Israel* [1961], 19–64; L. G. Perdue et al., *Families in Ancient Israel* [1997].)

1. Polygamy. The greatest single erosion of the creation order of marriage, the polygamous relationship, appears early in the patriarchal narrative: "Lamech married two women" (Gen. 4:19). The subsequent events of the families of Abraham, Isaac, and Jacob frequently follow what is now known to have been the customs of the other Semites of the time. Analogies frequently have been drawn between patriarchal customs and the family laws of BABYLON, NUZI, and Hatti (see HITTITES). The concubinage of a servant girl to her mistress's husband is a specific type of polygamy widely practiced in the ANE and also recorded in the patriarchal period (16:1–4; 30:1–5, 9–13). One result of this practice was the expansion of the family to include not only the man and his wife and their children, but also uncles, aunts, cousins, servants, concubines, slaves, travelers, employees, and even prisoners of war.

All of these people came under the family covenant of ABRAHAM (Exod. 20:10 et al.). In light of this, the rite of CIRCUMCISION was performed on all males born in a Jewish house (Gen. 17:23–27). One important factor of Jewish polygamy is the preservation of the dignity and rights of the CONCUBINE and her offspring. Nowhere does the OT provide for the elaborate caste systems commonplace in Mesopotamian descriptions of family relationships. Even a female prisoner had to be treated as a bride in binding marriage (Deut. 21:10–13), and captives, whether man, woman, or child, could not be sold into slavery. The offspring born to wives were to have no better inheritance than those born to concubines or slaves merely because of their inferior status. Since the polygamy of the ruling and dominating families greatly increased the degree of consanguinity, and other males were either slain or forced into monogamy, the children of Israel were in a few generations a separate entity from the other nations round about them.

Since the polygamous marriage of two individuals in separate families was in effect a covenant between the families, this also tied the few major strains of inheritance even more tightly together so that the families or clans not only grew larger numerically, but they were also more tightly related (Gen. 34:8–22). Aside from some specific instances, the extent of polygamy or bigamy in the OT is small, and in the books of Samuel, Kings, and Chronicles there is no reported polygamy on the part of commoners who lived during the age of the monarchy of Israel. Even though polygamy was accepted as a reality, and legislation concerning it was ordained (Deut. 21:15–17), yet the actual situations in which it occurred are hardly shown to be happy and are forthrightly declared to be the sources of continual bickering, envy, and other sins.

On the other hand, the monogamous relationship is praised and lauded (Prov. 5:15–19; 31:10–31). In fact, the worship of the one and only true God of Israel is presented in terms of marital devotion and fidelity (Isa. 50:1; 54:6–8; 62:4, 5; Jer. 2:2), while idolatry and heterodoxy are painted in images of harlotry, bigamy, and incest (Hosea). A woman had no legal status in Israel and had to be under the legality or protection of either her father or husband; if neither was living, then under a kinsman-deliverer (see GOEL), described in great detail in the book of RUTH. In effect, the woman was subservient to the male member of the family (a common Heb. term for "husband" is *baʿal* H1251, "master, lord"; e.g., Exod. 21:22). Thus the woman was in a subordinate position in the family as declared in the law-ordinance (Gen. 3:16); however, the husband or kinsman was absolutely responsible for the rights and treatment of his female family members. In the case of the payment of the "bride price," some girls were actually sold (31:15), an unfortunate outcome of the system.

The need to retain the family title to land in an agrarian society and similar customs in the nations around them seem to have induced the Jews to accept the relationship of the LEVIRATE LAW, whereby a man was expected to marry the wife of a brother who had died (Deut. 25:5–10). Even these somewhat contrived matches appear to have been monogamous. In fact, it is doubtful that the family holdings would have been of much value if too many inheritors were forthcoming. The levirate marriage was easily brought about, as brides were usually chosen and grooms arranged, although true love often developed between the partners. Love was not the primary motivation, which was familial not personal to begin with, the goals being clan preservation and children. As with most neolithic agricultural people, wealth was measured in the number of sons a man possessed for tilling and herding and the number of daughters for marrying and thus bearing more generations (Ps. 127, which in light of Ruth 4:11 et al. refers entirely to one's children).

2. Fatherhood, motherhood, childhood. In the participant tribalism of a small agricultural village in Palestine, the ages and groups of the members of the village appear to have acted in concert in most of the common tasks. The dress and activities of each group were defined strictly, as were the times of their activities. Fatherhood was assumed to be the prerogative of the mature male, and there is some evidence that the marriage of older men (35–55) to younger women (13–18) tended to lower the birth rate. However, PROSTITUTION also is noted in the OT, and it apparently had no relation to the marriage bonds (Gen. 38:14). Motherhood was construed as the natural outcome of wedlock, and the plight of the barren woman is greatly lamented (see BARRENNESS). The notion of male infertility is nowhere advanced. Motherhood was accompanied by an increased security that no other wife or concubine would be necessary to the husband. Although restrictions are placed upon the times of sexual relations, nothing is indicated about the frequency, and the OT is much more frank about the female response than have been some recent societies (cf. 3:16).

Childhood is nonexistent as a class or separate period. While very young children are considered noncombatants (Deut. 20:14), and while pleas are made for infants (Jon. 4:11), children who are old enough to talk are held responsible for their deeds and frequently judged (2 Ki. 2:24). Progress toward manhood was marked by skill and wisdom. Primogeniture (see FIRSTBORN) was strictly observed for both sons and daughters (Gen. 25:24–26; 25:24–34; 29:26; 38:27–30); however, the father had the right to assign the BIRTHRIGHT to any son he signified (49:3–4). Because of the immediate tribalistic nature of life, most children grew up worldly wise and old before their years. While children were suckled up to three or four years old, they were considered mature at a very early age, boys at thirteen (the bar mitzvah), and girls at their first menstrual cycle. During their early years boys were kept with the women, but later on allowed to sleep in the father's quarters, while girls were kept close to their mother's activities.

The HAREM, long a feature of the ANE, does not appear until the wealth and opulence of the monarchy. Israelite girls were allowed a great deal of freedom in the small farming communities that predominated in the period of the conquest and the early kings of Israel. After the TELL EL-AMARNA Age (15th century B.C. and thereafter), when no one nation of the Eastern Mediterranean held sway over the many petty kingdoms, political marriages and courtly concubinage became commonplace. It was during this time that SOLOMON and his successors built their elaborate harems and fostered many sons and daughters who were raised from infancy in the women's apartments to rule the kingdom someday. It was in this period of decadence that Israel began its final decline; almost all of the creation ordinances and the Levitical precepts were ignored, and Israel went first through captivity and finally into the DIASPORA.

II. Family in the NT. The only family actually portrayed in the NT is that of Jesus, and then only scarcely and occasionally. It is clear, however, that while a vast stable of princes and princelings had been enforced by the Hellenistic and Roman rulers, the common people still followed the OT family tradition. The father was still the head, the wife concerned with motherhood, and the children raised in the community obligations. The one significant change seems to have been in the growth of the SYNAGOGUE and the rabbinate, which provided a modicum of participation and EDUCATION for Israelite boys throughout the country. To some extent this development may have been in self-conscious opposition to the zeal for education caused by HELLENISM and the paganizing schemes of the Hellenistic rulers. Be that as it may, it had a great effect upon the Jewish family. (For discussions of family life in the Mediterranean world, see M. I. Rostovtzeff, *The Social and Economic History of the Hellenistic World*, 3 vols. [1941]; B. Rawson, *The Family in Ancient Rome: New Perspectives* [1986]; R. Garland, *The Greek Way of Life: From Conception to Old Age* [1990]; B. Severy, *Augustus and the Family at the Birth of the Roman Empire* [2003].)

As with all urbanization, the growth of Roman age towns caused more and more breakdown in the old extended family. The visit of Mary and the subsequent trip to Bethlehem show some of this shearing of the older clan ties (Lk. 1:36–40; 2:4). For one thing, there is a marked change in the terminology applied, and the many difficult semisocial clan determinations that marked the OT pattern are no longer in use. The Greek terminology is more precise, analytical, and directly individualistic; no remnant of the ancient concentricity remains.

A. Terminology. Expressions such as "the house and line of David" (Lk. 2:4) reflect the Hebrew background of the NT. A frequent Greek term is *oikia* G3864, "house," which from Attic classical literature was used in the sense of "family" (Matt. 13:57; Mk. 6:4; Jn. 4:53; et al.). Less frequent is Greek *patria* G4255, "family, clan, relationship," which occurs three times in the NT (Lk. 2:4; Acts 3:25; Eph. 3:15). More often than in the OT, the relationships of individuals within the family are stressed, and the terms for father, mother, husbands, wives, and children are thus foremost.

B. Jesus' teaching about the family. Much of Christ's instruction concerning the family is simply reiteration of the creation ordinances, with the added responsibility of motivation (Matt. 5:27–32). However, the family is used as the pattern for the FORGIVENESS, LOVE, and LONGSUFFERING of God. In fact the use of the endearment, "Our Father," is one of the most profound insights into the nature of God revealed through Jesus' teaching. It is clear that monogamy is uppermost, and the bond of love is central in such discourses (Matt. 18–20).

The family as covenant and the covenant members as a family are two themes repeated in the illustrations Christ gives (Matt. 19:13–15). The institution of the new covenant with its central rite of the EUCHARIST expanded the availability of the ritual outside of the male members of the family. (See COVENANT, THE NEW.) However, the concept of corporate or "household" salvation certainly is represented in the gospel narratives. It also is important that some of our Lord's miracles were concerned with families, their sorrows, and their relationships (Matt. 8:1–15; 9:18–26; 15:21–28; 17:14–20; Mk. 1:30–31; 5:21–43; 7:24–30; 9:14–29; Lk. 4:38–39; 7:1–10; 8:40–56; 9:37–43; Jn. 2:1–11; 4:46–54; 7:11–17; 11:1–46; 21:6–11).

C. The apostolic and epistolary teaching about the family. The concept of the family was so easily extended that the apostles apparently used it in their preaching to describe, not only the Israel of the theocracy, but also the CHURCH of Christ. Specific instructions concerning the family are given in terms of husband and wife (1 Cor. 7:1–28; 11:3; Eph. 5:22–33; Col. 3:18; 1 Tim. 5:8; 1 Pet. 3:1–7). Of special emphasis is the subject of the subjection of the woman to her husband. This theme is repeated in a number of Paul's epistles and in 1 Pet. 3:1–7.

The dissolution of the family in the later Roman republic and early empire was probably a recurrent problem in the churches. The relation of children to parents is far less prominent than in the OT (Rom. 1:30; 2 Tim. 3:2; and the exhortations of Eph. 6:1–4; Col. 3:20–21; 1 Tim. 4:12). In the three Johannine epistles the figure of the child is brought to its fulfillment with the repetition of the apostolic love for the church in terms of family endearment (1 Jn. 3:10 et al.). The legal position of children, inheritance, adoption, illegitimacy, and naming all are used as figures of the application of the ATONEMENT in the Epistles (Gal. 4:5; Eph. 1:5; Phil. 4:3; Heb. 12:8; 1 Pet. 1:4; et al.).

D. The family in the early church. The fact that the first churches were in private homes as that uncovered at DURA-EUROPOS, and that the initial converts were usually family groups, gave a specific character to the family image of Christianity (Acts 16:31 et al.). Symbols of Jesus, such as the Good Shepherd, the murder of the innocents, and the scenes of Jesus' childhood, are all extant in early Christian art.

In the subapostolic book *Shepherd of Hermas*, there were collected some folk stories of the childhood of Jesus (see HERMAS, SHEPHERD OF). Of all Christian concepts, that of its application to the family as a unit seems to have been the most appealing. Even the love of Christ for the church is stated as the love of a husband for his wife. This image of the bridegroom and the bride is used in the final apocalyptic visions of the New Jerusalem (Rev. 18:23; 21:2, 9; 22:17). (Cf. J. W. van Henten and A. Brenner, eds., *Families and Family Relations as Represented in Early Judaisms and Early Christianities: Texts and Fictions* [2000]; P. Balla, *The Child-Parent Relationship in the New Testament and Its Environment* [2003]; K. M. Campbell, ed., *Marriage and Family in the Biblical World* [2003].) See also CHILD; DIVORCE; MARRIAGE; WOMAN.   W. WHITE, JR.

famine. An acute and prolonged food shortage (Heb. *rāʿāb* H8280 and Gk. *limos* G3350, both of which can also be translated "hunger"). In lands dependent on seasonal rainfall, failure of the RAIN or its coming at an inappropriate time means the failure of crops and pasturage. In PALESTINE there were two rainy seasons, the "early rain" in October-November and the "latter rain" in March-April. The OT also mentions famines caused by the destruction of the food supply by hail (Exod. 9:23–25, 31–32), insects (Exod. 10:15; Joel 1:4; Amos 4:9), or by the human agency of invasion (Deut. 28:51) or siege (2 Ki. 6:25). Famines in EGYPT, as in the time of JOSEPH, were caused by the failure of the annual overflowing of the NILE, due ultimately to lack of rain in the interior. Famine often was accompanied by widespread DISEASE (1 Ki. 8:37; Jer. 14:12; 21:9; Lk. 21:11).

In the Bible famine is never regarded as a mere accident of nature, for God is the Creator and Ruler of all natural powers. Famines form part of God's ordering of the lives of his people, as with the journeys of ABRAHAM and ISAAC to Egypt (Gen. 12:10) and the meeting of NAOMI with RUTH (Ruth 1:1). By means of a famine God raised Joseph to a position of authority in Egypt and brought all the families of Israel into that land (Gen. 41–47). The usual stated purpose of famine, whether actual or threatened, was the judgment of God: to warn (1 Ki. 17:1), correct (2 Sam. 21:1), or punish his people or the heathen (Jer. 14:12, 15). Jesus predicted famines as a sign of the end of the age (Matt. 24:7; Mk. 13:8; Lk. 21:11).

Scripture tells of many famines, among them those in the time of Abraham (Gen. 12:10), Isaac (26:1), Joseph (chs. 41–47), Ruth (Ruth 1:1), David (2 Sam. 21:1), Elijah (1 Ki. 17–18), Elisha (2 Ki. 4:38; 6:24—7:20), Zedekiah (2 Ki. 25:3), Claudius (Acts 11:28)—the last probably being the one mentioned by JOSEPHUS (*Ant.* 20.2.5), who also gives one of the most vivid descriptions of the terrible effects of famine in a besieged city in his account of the Roman siege of Jerusalem (*War* 5.10.3). The prophet Amos used the word in a figurative sense when he predicted "a famine through the land— / not a famine of food or a thirst for water, / but a famine of hearing the words of the LORD" (Amos 8:11). (For a discussion of famines within the context of climatology and historical events, see W. H. Shea in *ABD* 2:769–73.)

J. C. CONNELL

fan. This English term is used by the KJV a few times to render the Hebrew verb *zārâ* H2430, "to winnow" (Isa. 41:16 et al.; cf. also *mizreh* H4665, "winnowing fork," 30:24), and the Greek noun *ptyon* G4768, "winnowing fork" (Matt. 3:12 = Lk. 3:17. The latter is used figuratively to describe the judging activity of Christ as he separates the wheat from the chaff (cf. Jer. 15:7). The Hebrew verb also can refer to the scattering of powder (Exod. 32:20) or to the dispersion of the nation Israel (Ezek. 36:19). In Jer. 51:2, the KJV uses "fanners" to render *zrym* (apparently vocalizing it *zōrîm*, ptc. of *zārâ*; similarly NRSV, "winnowers"); the NIV renders it "foreigners" (accepting the MT vocalization *zārîm*, plural of *zār* H2424).   H. M. WOLF

farmer. One who tills the soil. In the OT, the Hebrew noun *ʾikkār* H438 is used generally for one who raises crops in fear of drought (Jer. 14:4); in terms of OCCUPATION, the farmer is mentioned along with the SHEPHERD (31:24). Other contexts,

Modern farmer still using an ancient technique for plowing his field.

however, more specifically describe the farmer as a plowman with a team (Jer. 51:23) or a worker in the vineyard (Amos 5:16; cf. 2 Chr. 26:10). The corresponding Greek term, *geōrgos G1177*, occurs generally in the NT for one who grows crops (2 Tim. 2:6; Jas. 5:7). In the parable of the wicked tenants (Matt. 21:33–41 and parallels), the farmer is a vinegrower (cf. Jn. 15:1). See also AGRICULTURE; TRADE. M. R. WILSON

farthing. This term (which in the earlier currency of England was worth one fourth of a penny) is used by the KJV to render Greek *kodrantēs G3119* (= Lat. *quadrans*, the smallest Roman coin, Matt. 5:26; Mk. 12:42; cf. Lk. 12:59 [KJV, "mite"]) and *assarion G837* (= Lat. *assarion* [or *as*], the next smallest, Matt. 10:29; Lk. 12:6). Modern versions typically use English *penny* to translate these terms. See COINS.

fasting. The act of abstaining from food, especially for religious purposes.

I. In the OT

A. Psychology of fasting.
Abstinence from food and/or drink in times of distress is practiced among many peoples. In Scripture, refusal to eat when under violent emotions such as jealousy, anger, and vexation is illustrated in several passages. HANNAH would not eat when provoked by her rival (1 Sam. 1:7); JONATHAN in anger abstained from eating when his father cast the spear at him because of his relationship with DAVID (20:34); AHAB refused food because he could not have NABOTH's vineyard (1 Ki. 21:4). This type of abstinence has nothing to do with religious fasting.

Religious abstinence is mentioned first in connection with MOSES, who refrained from eating forty days and nights while on Mount SINAI (Exod. 34:28; cf. Deut. 9:9) and also after his breaking the tables of stone (9:18). Fasting in Scripture often is accompanied by the putting on of sackcloth and ashes. This self-affliction seems to have as its basic psychology the desire to say to the Deity, "I am penitent; I am not high and mighty. You need not afflict me further." Perhaps also an appeal to divine pity is involved. The one case where a specific motive is supplied is that of DAVID: "While the child was still alive, I fasted and wept. I thought, 'Who knows? The LORD may be gracious to me and let the child live'" (2 Sam. 12:22). There is the humbling of oneself before God: "Have you noticed how Ahab has humbled himself before me? Because he has humbled himself, I will not bring this disaster in his day" (1 Ki. 21:29).

B. Occasions of fasting

1. Day of Atonement. By the law, "afflicting one's soul" (Lev. 16:29; Num. 29:7; cf. KJV; the NIV has, "you must deny yourselves") from morning until evening is strictly demanded on the Day of Atonement (see ATONEMENT, DAY OF). The penalty for infraction is to be cut off from the community (Lev. 23:27–32). While neither the verb nor the noun for fasting (Heb. *ṣûm H7426* and *ṣôm H7427*) occurs in this section of the PENTATEUCH, "to afflict one's soul" equals "to fast." This fast was observed by the QUMRAN community according to its calendar (CD VI, 19), though the Wicked Priest is said "to cause them to stumble on the Day of Fasting" (1QpHab XI, 8).

The rabbis ruled that one could not eat a quantity as large as a date on this day, and enacted other privations. According to the MISHNAH (*m. Yoma* 8:1), on the Day of Atonement it is forbidden to eat, or drink, or bathe, or anoint oneself, or wear sandals, or to indulge in conjugal intercourse. When the day fell on a SABBATH, the duty to fast took precedence over the normal manner of Sabbath observance (*m. Menaḥot* 11:9).

Since this fast par excellence (cf. Philo, *On Special Laws* 1.186; 2.193ff.; *Life of Moses* 2.23; Jos. *Ant.* 14.16.4; 17.6.4) came in the fall of the year, it might be used to indicate that the winter season was at hand (e.g., "by now it was after the Fast," Acts 27:9). The Romans considered that sailing was hazardous after September 11; it ceased altogether on November 11, not to be resumed until March 10 (Vegetius, *De re militari* 4.39; Caesar, *Bell. gall.* 4.36; 5.23). Some rabbis considered travel on the sea to be possible from Passover to the Feast of Tabernacles (Str-B, 3:771).

2. Times of distress. In addition to the Mosaic fast, Israelites abstained from food without specific commandment on numerous other occasions in time of distress. Some were communal affairs while others were acts of the private individual.

a. *War or the threat of it.* Israel fasted at BETHEL in the war against the Benjamites (Jdg. 20:26); at MIZPAH in the PHILISTINE war (1 Sam. 7:6); SAUL had not eaten all day and all night before his visit to the medium of ENDOR (1 Sam. 28:7–20). Fasting might be imposed upon warriors in a campaign (Jdg. 20:26; 1 Sam. 7:6), though the evidence is insufficient to conclude that it always was demanded. Saul issued a curse on the man who ate before evening that he might take vengeance on his enemies the Philistines. JONATHAN's breaking his father's injunction would have cost him his life had not the people intervened (1 Sam. 14:24–45).

b. *Sickness.* DAVID fasted and wept for his son while the boy was ill, but when the boy died, he, contrary to the expectations of his servants, washed and anointed himself, went to the house of the Lord, and then ordered food (2 Sam. 12:16–20). The psalmist also mentions fasting for sick friends (Ps. 35:13).

c. *Mourning.* The men of JABESH GILEAD fasted seven days for Saul (1 Sam. 31:13; 1 Chr. 10:12); David and the people fasted for Saul and Jonathan (2 Sam. 1:12); and the custom of fasting in mourning is considered normal behavior (12:21).

d. *Penitence.* Calamities were considered manifestations of divine anger. Acts of penitence were therefore the way to end them. Perhaps in this light is to be interpreted the fast requested by JEZEBEL at which the fate of Naboth was decided (1 Ki. 21:9–13). Ahab fasted—not in vain—after being threatened by ELIJAH for having taken Naboth's life and vineyard (21:27). The general fast at the communal reading of the law by EZRA was an act of penitence (Neh. 9:1). After the destruction of the TEMPLE in A.D. 70 and sacrifice was no longer possible, fasting was allied in the rabbinic view with sacrifice (*b. Ber.* 17a). As a means of expiation it was preferred by some over almsgiving (*b. Ber.* 32b), while others placed its value in the accompanying almsgiving (*b. Ber.* 6a). Neither fasting nor confessing sufficed, unless they were accompanied by a practical amendment of conduct (*b. Taʿanit* 16a).

e. *Impending danger.* JEHOSHAPHAT fasted when threatened by EDOM (2 Chr. 20:3). JEHOIACHIM proclaimed a fast in the ninth month of his fifth year (Jer. 36:9). Ezra led a fast when seeking the favor of God toward his return from EXILE (Ezra 8:21)—a journey likely to be fraught with many dangers, but for which he did not wish to ask for mounted guards. NEHEMIAH fasted when he heard of the state of Jerusalem (Neh. 1:4). The Jews fasted when they heard that HAMAN had obtained the king's decree against them (Esth. 4:3); ESTHER and MORDECAI fasted before she went before the king (4:16), and the establishment of PURIM is said to deal with fasts and lamentations (9:31). The onset of a LOCUST plague might occasion a fast in which all members of the community—people, elders, children, and even the bride and bridegroom—participate (Joel 1:14; 2:15).

f. *Commemoration of calamities.* During and after the exile special fasts were observed on the days calamities had befallen Jerusalem (*m. Taʿanit* 4:6). The tenth of the fifth month was the burning of the temple (cf. Jer. 52:12–13); the second day of the seventh month was the murder of GEDALIAH (2 Ki. 25:23–25; Jer. 41:1–3); on the tenth day of the tenth month was the beginning of the siege of Jerusalem (2 Ki. 25:1); and on the ninth day of the fourth was its fall (25:3–4). An inquiry by men of Bethel concerning the validity of these fasts in the fifth and seventh month brought a reply from ZECHARIAH that obedience, justice, and kindness rather than fasting were significant in the sight of the Lord (Zech. 7:1–14). The fasts were to be seasons of joy (8:19).

g. *Drought.* By the 1st cent. a fast was the preferred method of appealing to the Lord for rain.

If the fall rains did not make their appearance in due time, first individuals voluntarily fasted, but if this action was ineffective, a communal fast of three days was proclaimed. If no rain fell, three more days were proclaimed, and, if necessary, seven more days to make a total of thirteen. These were of increasing severity. At first eating and drinking after nightfall, washing oneself, anointing oneself, putting on of sandals, and marital intercourse were permitted. In the second period these were prohibited, and in the last period shops were closed except on Mondays after dark and on Thursdays. The *shofar* was blown (*m. Taʿanit* 1:5ff.). The individual could not disassociate himself from the community at such times and refuse to fast (*b. Taʿanit* 11a). These customs and other Jewish fasting practices are the subject of extended treatment in the Mishnah.

3. Preparation for revelation. In the cases of Moses (Exod. 34:28; Deut. 9:9, 18) and Daniel (Dan. 9:3), fasting was engaged in as a preparation for receiving revelation.

C. Length of fasts. A fast was often for one day (Jdg. 20:26; 1 Sam. 14:24; 2 Sam. 1:12; 3:35) from sunrise to sunset, and after sundown food would be taken. Or a fast might be for one night (Dan. 6:18; Aram. *ṭĕwāt* H10297). The fast of Esther continued three days, day and night, which seems to be a special case (Esth. 4:16). Jesus also is said to have fasted day and night (Matt. 4:2). At the burial of Saul the fast by Jabesh Gilead was seven days (1 Sam. 31:13; 1 Chr. 10:12). David fasted seven days when his child, born after his illicit affair with Bathsheba, was ill (2 Sam. 12:16–18). Prolonged fasting brought on weakness (Ps. 109:24; cf. 1 Sam. 28:20). Moses' fast for forty days (Exod. 34:28; Deut. 9:9), Elijah's (1 Ki. 19:8), and Jesus' (Matt. 4:2; Lk. 4:2) are the longest recorded in Scripture. A mild form of fasting might involve abstinence from wine, flesh, and dainty food, and from anointing oneself for an extended period, such as three weeks (Dan. 10:2–3).

D. Participation of beasts in fasting. The unusual custom practiced in Nineveh, including animals in a fast (Jon. 3:7), is also attested for Jews (Jdt. 4:10–13).

E. Display in fasting. Fasting lent itself to external show and it is this feature of the practice that the prophets attack. The most vigorous attack is that made by Isaiah in response to people who complain that they have fasted and God has not noticed (Isa. 58:3). In contrast to the external display of bowing one's head like a rush and spreading sackcloth under oneself (58:5), the fast pleasing to the Lord is to loose the bonds of wickedness, to let the oppressed go free, to share bread with the hungry, to bring the poor into one's house, and to cover the naked (58:6–7). Joel called for a rending of hearts and not of garments (Joel 2:13). The Lord refused to heed the fast of Jerusalem in her degradation (Jer. 14:12).

II. In the apocryphal writings. The Apocrypha and Pseudepigrapha extol the merits of fasting. Judith fasted each day of the week except on Friday, the Sabbath, and certain feast days (Jdt. 8:6). This fast extending through all the days of her widowhood is considered an extraordinary act of piety. Jeremiah and others fasted (2 Bar. 5:7). Ezra fasted in preparation for receiving visions (4 Ezra 6:31; cf. 9:24). Fasting in times of danger is attested for the Maccabean period (1 Macc. 3:47; 2 Macc. 13:12). Reuben (*T. Reub.* 1.10) and Judah (*T. Jud.* 15.4) fasted in penitence. Simeon fasted two years because of his hatred for Joseph (*T. Sim.* 3.4). Joseph fasted during the seven years he was tempted by Potiphar's wife (*T. Jos.* 3.4; 4.8; cf. 10.1). Benjamin was born after his mother had fasted twelve days (*T. Ben.* 1.4). Fasting makes atonement for sins of ignorance (*Pss. Sol.* 3:8). Prayer, fasting, almsgiving, and righteousness are jointly praised in Tobit (Tob. 12:8). But if one fasts and sins again, his humiliation is unprofitable (Sir. 34:26).

III. In the NT. John the Baptist taught his disciples to fast often (Mk. 2:18; Lk. 5:33). Though Jesus fasted in the wilderness (Matt. 4:2; Mk. 1:13), fault was found with him and his disciples for failure to fast. To this objection Jesus replied that his disciples would fast when the bridegroom was taken from them (Matt. 9:14–15; Mk. 2:18–19; Lk. 5:33–35).

In what appears to be a paranomasia ("they disfigure [*aphanizousin*] their faces to show [*phanōsin*]"), Jesus castigated insincere fasting of hypocrites whose mournful faces were to be seen by others (Matt. 6:16). In the cases of almsgiving and praying, they received that which they sought, namely, the praises of men. He charged the washing of the face and the anointing of the head that the fast not be seen of men but of God who sees in secret (6:17–18).

The claim of the PHARISEE in the parable that he fasted twice in the week is in excess of any demand made of him (Lk. 18:12), but is paralleled in the 2nd-cent. document *Didache* (8.1), which exhort Christians to fast on Wednesday and Friday, as contrasted to the fast on Monday and Thursday of the Jews. The Babylonian TALMUD (*b. Taʿanit* 12) also attests the custom of fasts on Monday and Thursday; the pious might fast more often (Jdt. 8:6). A late source reports that Jews refrained from fasting on Sunday because of the Nazoreans (*b. Taʿanit* 27b).

PRAYER and fasting frequently are associated together. ANNA served God with fasting (Lk. 2:37). Certain demons could be cast out only by fasting (according to the Majority Text at Matt. 17:21 = Mk. 9:29); PAUL fasted following his vision on the road to DAMASCUS (Acts 9:9). CORNELIUS had been fasting before he received his vision (10:30, Maj. Text). The sending of BARNABAS and Saul out on the first missionary journey was preceded by fasting (13:2–3). Jews of Jerusalem pledged themselves not to eat until they had killed Paul (Acts 23:12, 14; we are informed in *m. Nedarim* 5:6 and 9:1–2 that such vows were not considered binding in cases where they could not be carried out). Those on the ship with Paul in the storm abstained from food for fourteen days (27:33). A couple may abstain from conjugal relations by consent to give themselves to fasting (1 Cor. 7:5, Maj. Text). Paul claims to be approved to the church in fasting (2 Cor. 6:5) and lists as one of his sufferings "in fastings often" (11:27 KJV). These last passages may be cases of abstinence due to the unavailability of food (cf. *nēstis* G3765, Matt. 15:32). Other than these cases, there is nothing in the NT Epistles about fasting.

IV. In the 2nd-cent. church.
In addition to the biweekly fasts mentioned above, baptismal ceremonies were preceded by a fast in which the one being baptized, the person performing the baptism, and other members of the community who were able participated (*Didache* 7.4). The *Epistle of Barnabas* allegorizes fasting as it does the other demands of the law (*Barn.* 3.1ff.), and the author of *2 Clement* (16.4) regards fasting as better than prayer. Hermas calls fasting "keeping a station," but proclaims the good life as the real fast pleasing to the Lord (*Sim.* 5.1). He speaks of a fast in which only bread and water are eaten and the money that otherwise would be spent is saved to be spent on charity (*Sim.* 5.3). (See further G. F. Moore, *Judaism in the First Centuries of the Christian Era: The Age of the Tannaim*, 3 vols. [1927–30], 2:55ff., 257ff.; Str-B, 4:77–114; J. Pedersen, *Israel: Its Life and Culture*, 2 vols. [1926–40], 2:11–12, 454–58; J. F. Wimmer, *Fasting in the New Testament* [1982]).

J. P. LEWIS

fat, fatted. The first reference to fat in the Bible is in Genesis: "Abel brought fat portions [pl. of *ḥēleb* H2693] from some of the firstborn of his flock. The LORD looked with favor on Abel and his offering" (Gen. 4:4; see ABEL). According to the Mosaic law, all the fat of sacrificed animals belonged to the Lord and was burned as an offering to him, "a pleasing aroma" (Lev. 3:14–16; 7:30). The fatty portions are specified in Lev. 3–7 as the fat of the entrails, of the kidneys, and of the liver, and also the tail of the sheep. The fat had to be offered on the day the animal was sacrificed (Exod. 23:18). It is sometimes asserted that the eating of any fat was forbidden to the Israelites; however, the prohibition did not apply to animals slain solely for food, but only to specified parts of sacrificed animals (Deut. 12:15, 16, 21–24). A "fatling" (e.g., 2 Sam. 6:13 NRSV) was a young animal fattened for slaughter (cf. the references to "fatted" calves, 1 Sam. 18:24; Lk. 15:23; et al.). The word *fat* is sometimes used in a figurative sense to signify the best part of anything, for example, "the fat of the land" (Gen. 45:18), "the fat of wheat" (Ps. 81:16 lit.; NIV, "the finest of wheat"). (Note that the KJV also uses the now archaic terms *fat* and *winefat* with the meanings "vat" and "winepress"; see Joel 2:24; 3:13; Isa. 63:2; Mk. 12:1.) See SACRIFICE AND OFFERINGS.

S. BARABAS

fate. This English term, in the general sense of "outcome" or "what befalls," is used occasionally by Bible versions to render various Hebrew words or expressions (e.g., *ḥēleq* H2750, "portion," Job 27:13 NIV; *miqreh* H5247, "event, fortune," Eccl. 2:14 et al.). See DESTINY; ELECTION; FOREORDAIN; PROVIDENCE.

father. A male parent or ancestor (Heb. *ʾāb* H3; Gk. *patēr* G4252).

I. The patronymic system. Both the OT and the NT offer ample proof that the Jewish FAMILY life was patronymic or paternal in nature. As the name implies, the patronymic system traces kinship through males who play the dominant role in the family and in society (Num. 1:22; 3:15). Evidence is not lacking that the patronymic system supplanted an earlier maternal kinship system. This more primitive system is reflected in Gen. 36, where the "generations" of ESAU are traced through his wives, and in the book of RUTH, where LEAH and RACHEL are recognized as the women responsible for building the house of Israel (Ruth 4:11). See WOMAN.

Wherever the paternal system is found, both rank and property descend through the father. In general, ethnologists agree that the development of private property and the taking over by men of the chief functions of production have been the major influences in the development and extension of father power and a paternal family system. With the development of the paternal family organization among the ancient Hebrews went a steady increase in the power of the head of the family—the patriarch—over wives, children, slaves, and immigrants ("the alien within your gates," Exod. 20:10).

II. Paternal privileges. In early times the Hebrew children, like their mothers, were almost completely under the authority of the father. In the rude days of the patriarchs, the controls extended even to life and death rights over them. This was made clear by ABRAHAM's attempt to sacrifice his son ISAAC as a burnt offering. However, quite early in their history the Israelites were forbidden by Mosaic law to burn their children upon the altars of MOLECH (Lev. 18:21). The power of the patriarchal father was restricted in two other situations: he was not allowed to make his daughter a prostitute (19:29) and he was not allowed to sell her to a foreigner. The father had the authority to give his children in MARRIAGE as he saw fit. He had also the authority to sell children as slaves but only to fellow countrymen (Exod. 21:7–9). See CHILD.

The Hebrew children owed their parents the utmost respect and reverence, coupled with the most scrupulous obedience. The Mosaic law required that the child who smote or cursed his father should be put to death (Exod. 21:15, 17). The stubborn or gluttonous son was condemned to be stoned by his fellows after the father and the mother had testified against him before the elders of the people of Israel (Deut. 21:18–21). The Jewish household included slaves and many times even strangers sojourning among them who placed themselves under the protection of the patriarch. For all practical purposes such FOREIGNERS were

Father and son at the Western Wall in Jerusalem celebrating the Feast of Tabernacles.

treated as members of the family as long as they remained in the household and under the control of its head.

In the Talmudic period (see TALMUD) the father was permitted to contract for the marriage of his daughter only before she reached the age of puberty. After reaching the legal age the daughter had the privilege, if she wanted, to refuse to carry out the contract. In such a case the contract became null and void. In this respect the Talmudic law was more advanced than the marriage laws of Greece and Rome. The strict rules established by the patriarchal father for his family continued to have restrictive effects upon the decisions of his children even after they reached the legal age, and therefore limited the complete application of the Mosaic law.

III. Parental responsibilities. The Jewish household was a closely knit social, religious, and economic organization. The Hebrew home had also other very important functions. The family was the only educational institution for the training of the children until the time of Christ. The parents, particularly the father, served as the chief teachers of their children (Deut. 4:9; 6:7; 31:13; Prov. 22:6; Isa. 28:9). The father was expected to exercise rigid control and discipline over his children (Prov. 13:24; 19:18; 22:15; 23:13). The religious exercises taking place in the home, coupled with the instruction offered to the children, were probably the most significant influences in the establishment of the strong ties and solid foundations of the Jewish family.

The Babylonian TALMUD establishes the fact that the father was obligated to circumcise his son, to redeem him, to teach him the books of Moses, to find a wife for him, and to teach him a trade as a means of livelihood. The father continued to exercise great and decisive influence over the lives of his children even after they were married. (See E. P. Barrows, *Sacred Geography and Antiquities* [1872], 469–81; W. Goodsell, *A History of Marriage and the Family* [1939], 1–80.)   P. TRUTZA

fatherhood of God. The special relationship of authority and care between God and (1) his Son Jesus Christ and (2) his people.

I. Father of his people. One of the most frequent comparisons in the OT is that between the father/child and the God/Israel relationship. This concept is expressed in terms of a father's love for his children (Ps. 103:13), his discipline of the children he loves (Deut. 8:5; Prov. 3:12), and God's desire that his chastised children return to him (Jer. 3:22; 31:20). In contrast to the timeless, nonhistorical character of the divine fatherhood concept in the FERTILITY CULTS, the OT doctrine is expressed in terms of God's dealing in history with his people, particularly in the exodus (Hos. 11), although occasionally a more general understanding can be seen, as in the Lord's being "father to the fatherless" (Ps. 68:5). Although the fatherhood relation extends to the entire nation, it is concentrated in a particular way in the Davidic royal line and its perpetual rule (2 Sam. 7:11–16) and in the person of the MESSIAH to come (Ps. 2:7). Perhaps the prophetic utterance in Mal. 2:10 speaks of the future extension of the fatherhood to all the world; however, the book is distinctly addressed to Israel (1:1).

II. Father of Jesus Christ. Jesus identifies himself as being the Son of the Father. While the Jews correctly understood this as a claim to deity (Jn. 5:18; 10:30, 33; 19:7; see DEITY OF CHRIST), Jesus himself also related his sonship to that which was enjoyed by those "to whom the word of God came" (10:35). While the followers of Christ are also sons of the same Father, it is noteworthy that the expression "our" Father is never used by Christ, but rather the deliberate "my Father and your Father" (20:17); the "Our Father" of the Lord's Prayer (Matt. 6:9) is not prayed by Christ himself, but is instruction to the disciples as to how they are to pray (cf. Christ's continual reference to "your" father).

III. The responsibility of children. Jesus' messianic work is described in terms of his filial relationship to his Father. Both the task given him (Jn. 17:4) and the authority to perform it (3:35) come from the Father, as well as the people given him as the reward for his obedience (17:24, cf. 10:29). The disciples' attitude to God's children should be the same as God's (cf. the rebuke to the elder brother in Lk. 15:31–32). Their prayers should be confident ones, for their Father is more generous than a human one (Matt. 7:9–11; Lk. 11:11–13).

While the NT doctrine of the new birth (see REGENERATION) would seem to provide the basis for the sonship of believers, more explicit teaching is in the realm of ADOPTION (Rom. 8:14, 15; Gal. 4:6), whereby it is the HOLY SPIRIT who makes us sons, and it is also through him that we recognize that sonship. The Christian life is a life of responsibility before our Father (1 Pet. 1:17) but also a life of blessing and praise to the Father who has given us all things (2 Cor. 1:3; 2 Thess. 2:16; 1 Pet. 1:3).

(See further T. J. Crawford, *The Fatherhood of God* [1868]; R. S. Candlish, *The Sonship and Brotherhood of Believers* [1872]; G. Vos, *Biblical Theology* [1948], 381–97; H. Ridderbos, *The Coming of the Kingdom* [1950], 232–84; G. Schrenk and G. Quell in *TDNT*, 5:945–1022; J.-B. Metz and E. Schillebeeckx, eds., *God as Father?* [1981]; D. Tennis, *Is God the Only Reliable Father?* [1985]; J. Koessler, *God Our Father* [1999]; D. Tasker, *Ancient Near Eastern Literature and the Hebrew Scriptures about the Fatherhood of God* [2004].)   D. C. DAVIS

fatherless, the. The CHILD depends upon his FATHER to fill the many needs of his life. The relation of father and son appears to be, in the divine PROVIDENCE, a provision greatly needed to secure the survival of the fatherless. Yet, there are the ORPHANS, deprived of the care and protection of a father.

In biblical times, as often today, the fatherless were considered the most helpless and pitiable members of the human society. No clear-cut evidence is presented in the Scripture record in regard to established institutions founded for the purpose of defending their interests and caring for their needs, but God has made provision for them (Deut. 14:29; 24:19–21; 26:12; 27:19). God proclaims himself, in a special way, as a "father to the fatherless" (Ps. 68:5) and their helper (10:14). The Scriptures reiterate again and again warnings given by God to those who mistreat the fatherless. The orphan is generally coupled with the WIDOW in the Scripture. God's protection is equally extended over both. Oppression against them is forbidden (Deut. 16:14; 24:17, 19, 21; 26:12–13). In the Talmudic period to give proper care to the orphans was commended as the most praiseworthy act.   P. TRUTZA

Fathers, Apostolic. See APOSTOLIC FATHERS.

father's house. In the OT, while the word "house" by itself basically means a dwelling in which people live, in conjunction with "father" it indicates at least a FAMILY home (Gen. 12:1; 31:14, 30; 1 Sam. 18:2), that is, the head of a family and his dependents, a household. The term "father's house" (*bêt-ʾāb*) can also refer to the head of a family, his sons and their wives and children, and the slaves (Gen. 46:31; Exod. 12:3). This expression (esp. in the pl. form) was also used of the clans or main divisions of each TRIBE (Exod. 6:14; Num. 3:15, 20; 7:2; NRSV, "ancestral houses"; NIV, "families"), and even for the whole tribe (17:2). (See R. de Vaux, *Ancient Israel* [1961], 19–23.)

In the NT, the phrase *oikos patros* may refer to a home (Lk. 16:27; Acts 7:20), but in Jesus' lips "My Father's house" means the TEMPLE (Lk. 2:49; Jn. 2:16). Jesus' well-known statement, "In my Father's house are many rooms" (Jn. 14:2), may be a reference to HEAVEN, but some take the expression to mean God's household or family (the CHURCH).

J. C. CONNELL

fathom. See WEIGHTS AND MEASURES I.G.

fatling. See FAT, FATTED.

fauchion fam´chuhn. This obsolete English word (also spelled *falchion* and referring to a medieval broad-bladed, short, and curved sword) is used by the KJV APOCRYPHA to render Greek *akinakēs*, "short [straight] sword," which occurs only twice (Jdt. 13:6; 16:9).

fauna. In this article, the sources of evidence for animals mentioned in the Bible are surveyed from three perspectives. The first section discusses ancient material provided by explorers and archaeologists, as well as textual and philological evidence. The second surveys the fauna and FLORA of these areas today, treated regionally and considered in the light of history. Finally, because the area has been radically affected by human activities that in some cases have left no sign of the original vegetation, this issue is discussed in some detail historically, after considering, and rejecting, the theory that the widespread deterioration of flora might be due primarily to climatic worsening since biblical times. Many species are mentioned here, but their fuller description is found in individual articles.

   I. Sources of information about earlier fauna
      A. Ancient material
      B. Biblical evidence
  II. Natural regions
      A. Desert
      B. Sand dunes
      C. Lowlands and plains of Sharon and Esdraelon
      D. Rift valley
      E. Hill country
      F. Transjordan hill country
      G. Marshlands
 III. Results of human interference
      A. Climatic change or human damage?
      B. General effect of human occupation
      C. The Fertile Crescent
      D. Palestine
      E. Modern developments
      F. Results of introducing new plants and animals
      G. Conclusions

I. Sources of information about earlier fauna. Any description of the fauna of PALESTINE in the biblical period must be based clearly on reconstruction. This section considers the sources of literary and other recorded information on which this is based.

A. Ancient material. Data provided by the paleontologist largely refer to older faunas that probably lived in climatic conditions so different that they are of only academic interest. Archaeological material is becoming much more relevant now that animal remains have been examined more critically by modern methods. In particular, the work of the late F. E. Zeuner was invaluable for its treatment of bones found in human contexts, especially because he sought to differentiate wild animals from the modified forms domesticated from them. It is fortunate that much of his work concerns Palestine and nearby lands. By its nature this material is limited largely to three groups: (1) Domestic animals. (2) Wild animals, especially game, whose meat was

There have been recent efforts to reestablish a herd of oryx, a kind of desert antelope, in Israel.

eaten and whose bones, horns, and antlers were used for making weapons and tools. (3) Other animals connected with superstition or religion. The great volume of dated and localized pictorial and written material resulting from excavations is an equally useful source of data. Prehistoric cave drawings are of less importance here than elsewhere.

B. Biblical evidence. The Bible itself provides not only the names of numerous animals, many from roots of known meaning, but also considerable information about them, whether stated explicitly or to be deduced from the context. It is unrealistic, however, to search the Scriptures for anything in the nature of a "check-list" of animals once found in Palestine. By and large the animals are present as an integral part of the life of ordinary people. Thus the frequency with which an animal is mentioned in the Bible, with its range of names, is a good indication of its importance, whether economic or ceremonial (e.g., sheep, with about 400 occurrences, and cattle, with over 450, far outnumber any other species, wild or domesticated). Biblical animals are largely confined to: (1) Domestic stock and clean wild animals used for food. (2) Animals that were a danger or nuisance to human life, stock, crops, or other possessions, ranging from lions to clothes moths. (3) Familiar animals seen along roadsides, around houses, etc., including swallow, raven, and sparrow. (4) A special class of unclean animals forbidden as food. As is explained in more detail where these are discussed individually, this prohibition was not just arbitrary, but was in many cases based on sound hygiene not understood or properly practiced for another 3,000 years.

There is little difficulty in identifying (1) and (2), for many are mentioned often, or occur in meaningful contexts; (3) contains a wide variety of animals, mostly rather small, not all of which can be named with certainty; (4) includes most of the doubtful names, given in what amounts to little more than two bare lists. Even here there are exceptions: the Hebrew term *peres* H7272 (from *pāras* H7271, "to break"), translated VULTURE (Lev. 11:13), is a good example of the help given by philology. Listed among unclean birds, it is clearly a bird of prey; the name "bone-breaker" precisely describes the habits of the black vulture and bearded vulture. Such ease of naming is exceptional. Some names have no known root meaning and are not known in any modern cognate form; further, they appear only in these lists. It should be noted that it is unsafe to rely on modern Hebrew, in which some names have been given to entirely different animals. Animals mentioned mainly in figurative contexts, in poetical, wisdom, and prophetic books, are sometimes difficult to identify, but in most cases tentative suggestions can be made.

II. Natural regions. Although "Palestine" as such no longer exists, it is a useful term for the area where much of the biblical story was set. For a period after World War I it covered present Israel and all land W of the Rift Valley and Jordan; it is in this rough sense that it is used here. The topography is such that the regions into which this area is divided are fairly clearly demarcated; they are primarily geographical and botanical, aspects that are treated in greater detail elsewhere (see PALESTINE). These factors, in turn, determine the potential fauna, though geographical and faunal regions seldom coincide exactly, and humans have had such an overwhelming impact on both flora and fauna that natural boundaries are sometimes completely masked. (Denis Baly, *The Geography of the Bible* [1957], defines these regions well.) The object of this discussion is to relate what is seen today with the original flora and fauna.

A. Desert

1. Description. Much of S and E Palestine consists of DESERT and near desert. Surface varies from deep sand through gravel to more or less bare rock; topography from steep escarpments to almost level plains; and altitude from far below sea level to rather over 2,000 ft. above sea level. Rainfall, mostly from 2 to 8 in., usually occurs in a few winter storms violent enough to cause local flooding, especially in the loess areas where the soil surface quickly forms an impervious skin, but a year often passes with no rain at all in one part of the desert or another. There is no closed cover, yet few large areas are entirely without trees or shrubs, which can draw moisture from deep in the soil, while most wadis are lined with specialized woody plants.

Some soil is potentially fertile, especially the loess, and quickly becomes temporarily covered with grass and flowering plants after rain. This is the only fresh green stuff available to the domestic stock around the desert edge, and the BEDOUINS' intimate local knowledge allows them to make full use of it. Even in the hills around the DEAD SEA, the centuries-old, well-trodden grazing tracks of sheep and goats are plainly visible at all seasons, though perhaps used only for a short period once a year. The desert is subject to great ranges of temperature, both diurnal and annual. In summer the ground surface temperature by day would be lethal to small animals, whose activity is therefore confined to the night; winter nights can be too cold, and animals may then be active in late evening and early morning. Within the desert there are some areas where no animals can live, and the average density of animal life is low everywhere.

Griffon vulture soaring above Israel.

2. Large mammals. Gazelles and desert oryx are the only large wild animals able to survive in such surroundings; they are big and fast enough to travel far in search of food and they stand high enough to keep above the fierce ground heat. The pale coat gives some degree of camouflage and also reduces absorption of sun heat, while with their specialized physiology they seldom need to drink water, getting most of their moisture from their food. They are few in number and are reckoned in many square miles per head. The Nubian ibex—one of the mountain goats—is at home on some of the desert hills, including those on the W of the Dead Sea around En Gedi, where it is now protected. Only camels can serve as beasts of burden in desert conditions. Thorny plants provide food when they are allowed to range freely, but camels need occasional access to water, and if they are used on long, heavily loaded stages, they must be well fed.

3. Small mammals. These are more numerous and varied. The Egyptian jerboa, known in World War II as the desert rat, lives a similar life to that of the unrelated kangaroo rat of the California and Arizona deserts, spending the day in burrows where the lower temperature and higher relative humidity give more moderate conditions, and coming out at night in search of seeds, fruits, and succulent roots. Other small rodents—several species of gerbils, jirds, and sand rats—also live in dry habitats but are more typical of the desert edge, with rainfall above 8 inches.

4. Carnivores. With their possible prey so scarce, carnivores are even more rare, and the only true cat seems to be the caracal, or desert lynx; a very small pale variety of the leopard lives near, rather than in, the actual desert. The fennec fox, with huge ears, is a true desert form, smaller than the ordinary fox but with the same omnivorous habits. The slow-moving Arabian hedgehog is well known; it feeds mostly on invertebrates and small reptiles.

5. Birds. The griffon and black vultures and lammergeier, or bearded vulture, are in a special position. Very small numbers serve to scavenge a great area of desert, which they survey while cruising or soaring slowly from several thousand feet. Precise identification is not possible, but large birds of prey high overhead would have been a familiar sight to the Israelites on their desert wanderings. In the migration seasons these included eagles, vultures, and buzzards; for the rest of the year mostly vultures. Migrant birds are without doubt the most conspicuous animals of the desert, the large ones usually flying high overhead, the smaller ones traveling in shorter spells and stopping where possible for food and water. Like the quail, which still flies N in numbers, these migrants are travelers across the desert rather than residents in it. In contrast, the rock dove, from which domestic pigeons are descended, nests on desert cliffs, flying far each day to find food and water. See bird migration.

6. Reptiles. Although the total numbers are low and their distribution patchy, the desert has a surprisingly large range of reptiles, none very big and most of them carnivorous. They include one plant-eating lizard, the uromastyx or spiny-tailed lizard. Having little or no internal means of regulating body temperatures, reptiles are even more restricted in their periods of activity; they must spend both the burning day and the cold parts of the night safely underground, where only a few inches from the surface the temperature range is much reduced. It is likely that some desert snakes are almost independent of water, obtaining all necessary moisture from their victims. The sand boa, a constrictor, lives in sandy desert and has a typical "swimming" motion to bury itself. At least four vipers are widely distributed, including two whose bites can be fatal to man (see serpent). All are highly adapted to a desert life, with a movement known as "sidewinding"; the same method of progressing over loose sand has been developed independently by the American sidewinders, which are desert rattlesnakes. Most snakes probably take a range of prey, but it seems that they depend to some extent on the casualties from the flocks of small migrant birds that pass N between February and May, and S again in late summer and autumn. Some desert reptiles go into a resting state, called estivation, in the hottest weather. Many species of snake can survive without food for many months.

7. Dead Sea. This is true desert, physiologically, for the high mineral content of the water (about 25%)

makes it useless for drinking, and no form of life is known to exist in it.

8. Large oases. Within the desert are large oases with ample underground water (e.g., Yotvata) or with piped spring water (e.g., En Gedi). The irrigated fields and orchards form an artificial habitat and attract fauna not typical of the surrounding desert.

B. Sand dunes. A feature of the Mediterranean coast, from around GAZA to beyond modern Haifa, is a discontinuous belt of rather mobile sand dunes, up to a few miles in width and up to 150 ft. high. These should not be confused with true desert dunes, which seldom carry vegetation. The coastal dunes enjoy reasonable rainfall but form a quasi-desert habitat, for until a layer of soil is formed water cannot be retained and only specialized plants thrive. The typical animals are those of the less extreme sandy desert—especially the small rodents, whose tracks and entrances to burrows are seen widely, for such areas can support a denser population. Hedgehogs are also typical, the E and W species meeting somewhere in this area. As on similar coasts in other parts of the world, the dunes are to a large extent the result of human activity, destroying woody cover and making movement of sand easier. Man is now reversing this process by fixing these dunes and thus re-creating a habitat more favorable to both agriculture and animal life generally.

C. Lowlands and plains of Sharon and Esdraelon. Much of this region is potentially fertile and has been farmed in varying degrees since the dawn of history. See ESDRAELON; SHARON. In modern times all suitable parts have been so intensively occupied that little or no trace of their original cover now remains. Enjoying a fair, though sometimes marginal, rainfall and once covered with forest, scrub, and marshland, they are now a complex of settlements, orchards, and fields, mostly irrigated. The woodlands were the home of DEER, notably fallow and roe deer, and possibly red deer also, but these were driven out long ago and the nearest survivors today are in Persia and Turkey. LIONS hunted here, though not as much as in the broken hill country and lower ground beyond. Bird life is likely to be more numerous today, for farms and orchards often support a richer and larger bird fauna than virgin woodlands. Many birds are resident and they are small rather than large; migrants pass through but are less obvious, for they are traveling on a broad front and have more cover. Dense beds of milk thistles often fill road verges and odd corners left fallow, providing food for many goldfinches and cover for other small birds. It is likely that most animals familiar to the shepherds of the hill country also went down to the plains at some seasons.

D. Rift valley. From the Huleh area nearly to JERICHO is a semi-tropical tract with many plants more typical of the NILE Valley, including PAPYRUS. The lake fish most in demand is the *Tilapia*, a genus of cichlid well represented in Central Africa, where it is one of the main food fishes of the great lakes. The deeply cut valley itself is lined in parts with almost impenetrable jungle in which wild boar, fishing cats, and perhaps other large animals survive, but little is known of this area today, for much of it is along a frontier where naturalists are not encouraged.

E. Hill country. Much of the biblical narrative is set in the hills—from GALILEE in the N through SAMARIA to beyond BETHLEHEM. The rainfall generally is above 24 in., though it decreases rapidly on the E or leeward side. In the N large oaks can grow, but are now rare; over much of the area the natural climax is scrub, with taller trees growing in pockets of deeper soil. The olive is the most common planted tree.

1. Mammals. This region once provided a wide range of animal life, for it offered both browsing and grazing, while the rock formation gave shelter for mammals as varied as the brown bear and Syrian rock hyrax—the CONEY. Deer were the most important wild ungulates, with the Palestine gazelle. The former have long been lost; the Palestine gazelle was able to survive in drier country to the S and, under protection, has made a good recovery, living in fair numbers through the Judean hills and even on the Plain of Esdraelon, where it takes little notice of tractors working in the fields. Bears and lions are extinct here, but the striped hyena and wolf linger in small numbers. The leopard once hunted in these hills and still just survives in the Jordan Valley. Smaller carnivores are locally common—fox, jackal, mongoose, and badger—and on a day's journey through these hills it is not unusual to see a run-over corpse on the road. Mole-rats push up small heaps in irregular lines wherever the soil is deep enough, but never appear above ground.

2. Birds and insects. The rock partridge is heard daily at some seasons but prefers running to flying and is seldom seen. The varied cover in the hills makes it the home of many perching birds, and the smaller migrants go through without being obvious. The resident Palestine jay and hooded crow are often seen and heard, the latter waiting on the roadside to pick up small road casualties. The larger resident birds of prey are now rare and the main scavenger is the conspicuous black and white Egyptian vulture, which still frequents garbage heaps outside towns. The harvester ant is busy throughout spring gathering food supplies to store underground; the trail of husks, removed before storage and thrown out, marks the entrance clearly.

3. Snakes. The largest venomous snake—Palestine VIPER—is found in the hills, as well as in most habitats other than true desert. Reaching a length of over 4 ft. and thickness of 1 in., it must be treated with respect. It is considered responsible for more human casualties than any other snake, largely because it lives in inhabited areas.

4. Domestic stock. SHEEP and GOATS have always been the main stock in the hills, the latter causing serious damage to vegetation by their browsing habits. They may even climb trees to get what they cannot reach from the ground. The rolling hills in N Galilee are more suited to CATTLE raising. The hills are not really CAMEL country, but camels are still kept in small numbers as beasts of burden and for farm work in a few Arab areas, notably in Samaria, around Nazareth, and in the Druse district of N Israel, where they look strangely out of place in the green countryside.

F. Transjordan hill country. To the E, beyond Jordan, are further ranges of hills and broad plateau—the country of AMMON, EDOM, and MOAB. These are distinctly drier than the western hills, which make the winds drop much of their rain, but the highest points are much higher—above 5,000 ft. above sea level—and the general conditions are more extreme, with the desert adjacent. In early times both lions and leopards were well known, though it is hard to speak with certainty of their prey. The land perhaps suited the Persian race of fallow deer, which lived in poor scrub and dry woodlands. The onager was at the extremity of its range here and was still fairly common in a few places over a century ago, though now extinct (see WILD ASS). Perhaps it came only to the edge of the hills from which the lions would hunt; in Africa zebras are their favorite prey, and this could have been true of the closely related onager. Great numbers of sheep were kept in Ammon and Moab, as is suggested by the tax that MESHA king of Moab paid annually—100,000 lambs and the wool of 100,000 rams (2 Ki. 3:4–5). If the land could support such numbers, however skillfully managed, there had presumably been many wild ungulates, preyed on by suitable carnivores. Much of this area was camel country, though perhaps around rather than up in the hills, and these provided the basic transport for the traders whose routes ran straight through these lands.

G. Marshlands. There were once considerable areas of marshland: some, perhaps all, resulting from human activity around the former Lake Huleh, which also had much open water; on the plains of Sharon and Esdraelon; and near the coast N of Haifa. The first was kept permanently wet by the lake through which the Jordan flowed, but the other areas perhaps dried out in part in summer. All have now been drained and reclaimed, but they once formed major barriers to invading armies and were a serious menace to health, for the most important insect living there was the *Anopheles* mosquito, carrier of malaria.

1. Mammals. These marshes made a suitable habitat for the fishing cat. Frogs of several kinds and water tortoises were common. When the wild boar was driven out of other parts, the marshes made a safe retreat, and its main stronghold today is around the Huleh Valley and in the dense jungle lining the lower Jordan.

2. Birds. Above all, the marshes were breeding grounds for many water-loving birds, especially members of the heron family. They are also refuges for countless waders (shore birds), ducks, terns, and herons on the N and S migrations, and provide winter quarters for vast numbers of coots and ducks. A group of brackish water fishponds on the coast midway between Haifa and Tel Aviv, reclaimed from useless marsh, is now a wild life sanctuary, and during spring migration it is alive with birds headed for their breeding grounds in all parts of Central, E, and N Europe.

III. Results of human interference. Large areas of Palestine and adjacent lands have become degraded through centuries of ill treatment and erosion; the FLORA was impoverished and the fauna diminished. In some parts, both town and country, humans have used the ground so completely that no traces of original cover remain. As a direct result, the status of many animals has changed radically; a few are known, on good historical evidence, to have been exterminated from the area as a whole or from large parts of it. This change is largely quantitative, but to some extent qualitative also. Human action alone explains the position in the occupied areas; is this also true as a whole?

A. Climatic change or human damage? Only one other factor need be considered here—the climate. Has this perhaps become less favorable since the biblical period? If so, it would greatly complicate the assessment of conditions, say, 4,000 years ago, for the earlier potential would have been different; it could have included some species not on the present list, that is, those which live in more moist conditions; and excluded others, namely, those which demand drier conditions. One school of thought claims that destruction of tree cover has an adverse effect on climate, especially on rainfall, while the planting of trees improves it. It is true that land with good woody cover makes better use of available water; also that forest on a hill top may sometimes just cause a cloud to shed rain, but this effect is so marginal as to be negligible. It has also been claimed—by those who cannot regard Palestine with its present climate as even potentially "flowing with milk and honey"—that there has been a long-term swing to a drier climate; some are also mystified that the N NEGEV was successfully occupied for at least two long periods, widely separated.

However, all evidence is against any significant climatic change, so that the vegetation of the various regions is still potentially what it was when the patriarchs first saw Canaan. The massive reduction in area and quality of cover is due solely to human action, direct and indirect. Regarding the Negev, botanists and agriculturalists have reconstructed the NABATEAN earthworks at Avdat, abandoned c. A.D. 100, and used their specialized system of irrigation to establish farms and orchards, which suggests that the rainfall is no less now than it was then. Unchanged climate presupposes an unchanged climax vegetation; the fauna, dependent on this, is thus potentially the same. This somewhat simplifies the interpretation, even though human influence through the ages has been destructive and complex. This will now be discussed in sections.

B. General effect of human occupation. With the advance of civilization and rapid increase of population, human occupation has now become the overriding factor in nearly all parts of the world and at an increasing pace, but this process began very early, especially in the lands around Palestine. Humans affect animal life mainly in two ways. First, by occupying land, turning forest and scrub into farm, and raiding much larger areas for fuel, they so changed the habitat that many animals moved out; some because there was no room for them, others because they would not tolerate interference. In general, the larger species are most adversely affected; smaller kinds may be helped by human activity and become much more numerous as a result, some even becoming pests that must be controlled.

Second, humans took direct action against various animals, either killing them or driving them away. These fall into several classes: (1) The browsing and grazing animals, such as antelopes, cattle, and wild horses, which were competitors with domestic stock. Many of these, and others also, were good for food or desired as trophies or totems, and were therefore hunted or trapped. (2) Beasts of prey—wolf, bear, lion, etc.—which are potential enemies to man himself and his livestock. (3) Animals, other than predators, that are dangerous to life and health, for example, venomous snakes and a wide range of noxious insects. The total result is to reduce seriously the range of many animals that were once widespread. For instance, within historic times the lion was found through much of SW Asia but is now reduced to a small group of some 200 in the Gir Peninsula of India. The aurochs, ancestor of the main cattle stock, disappeared for good early in the 17th cent., and the wild forebears of both kinds of camels were probably lost soon after these were domesticated.

C. The Fertile Crescent. Since the dawn of civilization man has been busy exploiting and destroying his environment, but the impact has varied from country to country and in the course of time. In MESOPOTAMIA, for instance, long periods of comparative peace allowed the development of great cities and cultures, based on efficient AGRICULTURE. Much of the wild flora and fauna disappeared and, in time, widespread desiccation caused irreversible degradation of the habitat. This latter did not occur in Egypt, where the Nile periodically renewed the fertility of the land as well as watered it. The larger fauna survived only in regions, such as mountains and deserts, which were self-protecting, and in hunting reserves that the kings established and guarded carefully for their own pleasure.

D. Palestine. As a whole this area enjoyed no such period of prolonged peace, the longest apparently beginning toward the end of David's reign and lasting through most of Solomon's (before the Hebrew invasion, the land had been owned by a patchwork of tribes and nations, and it is doubtful if occupation was ever complete). Century after century saw unrest and guerrilla warfare, or massive campaigns. Except perhaps for the valley of Esdraelon, few parts were used intensively, and throughout this time the wild fauna was probably less affected than in most nearby lands. Several successive periods of deportation and scattering, with big resultant casualties, kept the population low, and Palestine continued to be a troubled area, under Greek and then Roman rule, until well into the Christian era. It seems likely that through most of these periods much of the natural vegetation remained untouched and was a sanctuary for wild animals, with comparatively little change in the fauna from the days of the Judges until the time of the Crusades.

If this hypothesis is true, the wild life that the biblical writers from Moses onward knew was richer and much more prolific than what is there today, and it came much closer to the everyday lives of the ordinary people. A limited area would be under cultivation at any time; flocks and herds were led over wide areas to find grazing, but they were always controlled and protected against both predators and raiders from other tribes. Under such conditions the hillside soil remained stable and safe, with little or no serious erosion. Between the rise of Islam and the end of the 19th cent., the damage was far greater than in all the preceding centuries, though it is hard to know just when this serious change began. The damage had three main causes:

(1) Livestock, especially goats, ranged uncontrolled and destroyed vegetation of all kinds, leaving steep hillsides exposed to fierce winter rain storms, which quickly removed the thin layer of soil that had been built up slowly over many centuries. This lack of control continues in many Arab countries today; in places along the Israel/Jordan border in spring, the noticeably green vegetation on the one side, where goats must always be tethered, is in marked contrast to the brown of the exposed soil on the other.

(2) Many trees, within and outside the farmed areas, were cut for firewood, charcoal, and timber, with similar effect. During one period of Turkish rule a tree tax was imposed, which the Arabs avoided simply by cutting down their trees.

(3) As soil deteriorated, the unit yield dropped and larger areas had to be brought into cultivation, including some of the steeper slopes. This would have been reasonably safe if conservative methods of farming had been used, with plowing only along the contours, but this principle was not generally understood, though the Phoenicians had early practiced it, and the usual result was progressive erosion. The farming of hillsides in Upper Galilee

was a factor in filling much of Lake Huleh with silt and so creating swamps that were drained during the 1950s.

In such comparatively hot countries, where the variable rainfall mostly comes in heavy storms in winter and spring when the ground has least natural cover, these changes can be almost irreversible. The position can be restored only by long, painstaking effort, in contour-plowing and planting, which is highly expensive in labor, for such work can hardly be mechanized.

E. Modern developments. The 20th cent. introduced several new factors that complicated the situation still further. The first two are direct and the others indirect in their effects.

(1) High-powered rifles brought danger to larger desert animals that had previously been approachable only with great difficulty. Fast motorized transport, and the advent of great wealth from oil, made things much worse, and within a few years the desert oryx was high on the world list of threatened species. The Palestine and Dorcas gazelles were greatly reduced.

(2) The creation of the state of Israel attracted zoologists and naturalists from countries with a tradition of wild life conservation that was entirely new. The establishment of sanctuaries and nature reserves, with a more humane national attitude, has made Israel an area where animal life of all kinds is less harassed than it has been for a long time, and the gazelles are now safe again; but this factor cannot help the oryx, of which the nearest is well over 1,000 mi. away in S ARABIA. In some other states the official attitude to wild life is changing somewhat, but this cuts right across the Arab philosophy, which includes little thought for wild animals, large or small, except as something that Allah has provided for them to eat—and will go on providing. This disregard for wild life has added markedly to the more indirect damage that the fauna has suffered in recent centuries.

(3) The extensive tree-planting programs in forests, roadside shelter-belts, and orchards, as well as the introduction of irrigated cultivation over large areas, have created new habitats and conditions that have allowed many species, especially birds, to improve their status radically. For instance,

With retractable pads and claws, Blanford's fox is well adapted for climbing on rocks.

the palm dove, once a largely African species, has spread so widely and become so numerous that it is locally a pest and seems to be driving out the turtle dove. The African bulbul has also come from the S and moved into gardens and orchards, being useful to humans when it catches insects to feed its young, but doing damage later to ripening fruit.

(4) Land reclamation programs have been started, often with international help. The object is to restore woody cover to eroded hillsides, though often with introduced species of trees that are expected in time to produce a more useful crop than the native scrub. The end result can thus be different from the original climax vegetation, but always more favorable to most forms of animal life than the degraded cover which it replaces. The draining of Lake Huleh is a different type of reclamation that has resulted in a major change of land usage; the area remains useful as a resting and feeding place for migrants, but it is no longer a habitat fit for the larger wild animals and great flocks of water birds that once lived there.

(5) Intensive arable farming has resulted in serious plagues of rodents, especially voles. These have often been attacked with permanent poisons such as thallium; the dead and dying animals have been taken by birds and beasts of prey, and these in turn have died, to be eaten with fatal results by jackals, hyenas, vultures, and other scavengers. Before the danger was realized, the breeding population of some of the animals concerned had been reduced to about 10%. Many years of protection will be needed to restore the situation fully. A similar chain of damage has been started by the use of resistant insecticides.

F. Results of introducing new plants and animals. There is still another way in which man has affected the fauna of Palestine—by the deliberate introduction of plants and animals from other lands. Among the former should be listed crops of most kinds, few of which are truly native; these are an integral part of agriculture, the general effect of which has been discussed. This is true also of domesticated animals; even if they are derived from once local species, their impact on the land is quite different, and this, too, is a concomitance of farming. Introduction of exotic wild animals has been on a more limited scale than in many temperate countries, where this practice has sometimes resulted in catastrophic damage, first to the vegetation and then to native animals. Such few as can be cited for Palestine are quasi-domesticated and of these only the carp is worth discussion. This cultured form has been kept in fishponds for many centuries (see FISH, FISHING). It is now the basis of an intensive fish-breeding industry in great complexes of artificial ponds, especially in the Jordan Valley. Occasional escapees find their way down into the Lake of Galilee, where they are caught by net fishermen; the carp fills a man-made niche, and its introduction is unlikely to affect adversely either other fish or animals of other classes, if only because it is edible and valuable, and therefore worth controlling.

G. Conclusions. The above are probably the most important factors that have combined to produce the changed and impoverished flora and fauna that a visitor to the Holy Land sees today. The birds, especially the small migrants, have changed least of all. The larger mammals have been reduced to a tiny remnant, seen only by the energetic enthusiast but in places responding to protection. Livestock continue to be the most conspicuous animals, but even here a major change is taking place. Intensive animal husbandry is putting cattle and sheep, and even chickens, more or less permanently into stalls or under cover, especially in the desert settlements such as Yotvata and En Gedi, while the tractor is steadily replacing the donkey, horse, and camel in all parts for work in the fields, and the bicycle and car are taking over for personal transport.

(See further H. B. Tristram, *The Natural History of the Bible*, 9th ed. [1898]; F. S. Bodenheimer, *Animal and Man in Bible Lands*, 2 vols. [1960–72], which includes detailed references to classical authors; F. E. Zeuner, *A History of Domesticated Animals* [1963]; D. L. Harrison, *Mammals of Arabia*, 3 vols. [1964–72]; United Bible Societies, *Fauna and Flora of the Bible*, 2nd ed. [1980], 1–86; M. Goren, *Fresh Water Fishes of Israel: Biology and Taxonomy* [1983]; J. Clutton-Brock, *A Natural History of Domesticated Animals*, 2nd ed. [1999]; and the extensive article by E. Firmage, "Zoology," in *ABD*, 6:1109–67.)   G. S. CANSDALE

favor. See GRACE; MERCY.

fawn. A young DEER. The term can render Hebrew ʿōper H6762, which is twice used figuratively of a woman's breasts (Cant. 4:5; 7:3 [KJV, "roes"]; the same Hebrew word is usually rendered "young stag" in its other occurrences, 2:9, 17; 8:14). The English word is sometimes supplied in modern versions to clarify the meaning of the text (e.g., Job 39:1 NIV). It is also a possible translation in an uncertain passage (Gen. 49:21 NIV and NRSV).

fear. Several Hebrew words are translated "fear" in the OT, especially the verb yārēʾ H3710 and its cognates. The corresponding Greek verb is *phobeomai* G5828. These words, as in common parlance, are used in many ways, all of which fall into two categories: one beneficial, and the other baneful. Hence, fear is either friend or foe. In its natural sense, innate fear serves as an alarm system, or an arousal, alerting one to impending danger. Consequently, the threatened may prepare for the appropriate reaction—to fight, to flee, or to freeze. Fear of this character is nature's asset. Contrarily, if fear is not soon expelled, it sinks into the subconscious mind where it becomes *phobia*, an unhealthy condition. In modern scientific experiments with primates and children, psychologists have learned that the principal sources of innate fear are darkness, loss of support, strange things, sudden noises, and snakes. (See L. D. Weatherhead, *Psychology and Life* [1935], 213–37; D. O. Hebb, *A Textbook of Psychology* [1960], 64–97.) All these are potentially beneficial or harmful, and all are found in the Bible either factually or figuratively. Numerous other objects of human fear may be added to this list, both from everyday life and the Bible. In the Scriptures clear distinction is made between what we should and should not fear.

I. Beneficial fear—the fear of God. The most prevalent use of fear in the Bible is the fear of God. Next to that is the fear of God's people. The former is the reverential or awesome side of the fear spectrum. This fear is friend.

A. As religion of God's people. The majesty and holiness of God cannot but incite fear. "God comes in awesome majesty. / The Almighty is beyond our reach and exalted in power; / in his justice and great righteousness, he does not oppress. / Therefore, people revere him [*yĕrē'ûhû*]" (Job 37:22–24 TNIV). Anything of magnitude that dwarfs us by contrast incites fear in us. As we gaze into a deep canyon, or into limitless stellar space, or across a boundless ocean, we sense a feeling of awesome fear. How much more is this effect in the presence of God who is vastly greater than all these. As the psalmist meditated on this contrast, he was amazed that God would be mindful of him (Ps. 8:1–4). Similarly, God's HOLINESS transcends the human character with like effects (Isa. 6:5). Naturally then, the phrases "the fear of God" and "the fear of the Lord" occur frequently in the Bible, particularly in the OT. The Hebrew deity was awesome, so naturally the Israelites were constantly called on to "fear the LORD your God and serve him" (Deut. 10:20; note that "serve" helps to define "fear"). The admonition was an instrument with two edges, rewards and restraints.

"The fear of God" is synonymous with religion, and therefore rewarding. It was considered so as early as ABRAHAM's day. When that patriarch misrepresented his wife SARAH to ABIMELECH, he gave as his reason, "I said to myself, 'There is surely no fear of God in this place'" (Gen. 20:11). The fear of deity was an integral part of primitive and pagan religion. Even God was called the FEAR OF ISAAC (31:42). In advising MOSES to appoint subordinate judges to share the judicial burden, his father-in-law, JETHRO, recommended that he select "capable men from all the people—men who fear God" (Exod. 18:21). Proselytes in the NT were called "God-fearing," as CORNELIUS (Acts 10:2) and PAUL's congregation in ANTIOCH OF PISIDIA (13:26).

"The fear of God" was required in the following ways: by keeping his commandments (Exod. 20:20); by serving him and keeping his statutes (Deut. 6:13, 24); by hearkening to his voice (1 Sam. 12:14); and by worshiping in his temple (Ps. 5:7). Moses' strict injunction to Israel was, "fear your God" (Lev. 19:14b). Furthermore he said, "The LORD commanded us to obey all these decrees and to fear the LORD our God, so that we might always prosper and be kept alive" (Deut. 6:24). From early times rewards were promised for Yahweh worship.

God's blessings on those who fear him are numerous, mentioned frequently throughout the Bible. SATAN asked the Lord, "Does Job fear God for nothing?" and in answering his own question declared that God had "put a hedge around him" (Job 1:9–10). And ELIPHAZ asked Job, "Is not your fear of God your confidence?" (4:6 NRSV). The psalmist said, "But the eyes of the LORD are on those who fear him / ... to deliver them from death / and keep them alive in famine" (Ps. 33:18–19). In the WISDOM Literature it is stated: "The fear of the LORD adds length to life" (Prov. 10:27); "The fear of the LORD is a fountain of life" (14:27; cf. 22:4; Pss. 61:5; 119:37–38). One of the most familiar proverbs is, "The fear of the LORD is the beginning of wisdom" (Prov. 9:10; Ps. 111:10; cf. Prov. 1:7; 15:33). DAVID summarized religious benefits in two statements: "He fulfills the desire of those who fear him" (Ps. 145:19); "How great is your goodness, / which you have stored up for those who fear you" (31:19; cf. 34:9).

Isaiah's prophetic description of the MESSIAH was that "he will delight in the fear of the LORD," and "the fear of the LORD is the key to his treasure" (Isa. 11:3; 33:6c). MALACHI prophesied in the words of the Lord, "But for you who fear my name the sun of righteousness shall rise, with healing in its wings" (Mal. 4:2 RSV). And one psalmist sang, "Surely his salvation is near those who fear him" (Ps. 85:9).

Another benevolent work of the fear of God is its restraining force. Constantly the Israelites were warned of the consequences of wrongdoing. Moses taught, "And now, O Israel, what does the LORD your God ask of you but to fear the LORD your God, to walk in all his ways, to love him, to serve the LORD ..." (Deut. 10:12). One Hebrew philosopher said, "through the fear of the LORD a man avoids evil" (Prov. 16:6). Clearly, all these references to the fear of God mean the Yahweh religion, worship and service of God. Consequences of failure to do so are clearly stated, as in the major categories of infidelity, injustice, and insincerity.

Since spiritual infidelity, or APOSTASY, mothers a multitude of sins, the penalty was death: "Then all Israel will hear and be afraid, and no one among you will do such an evil thing again" (Deut. 13:11; cf. 17:13; 21:21; 28:58–59, 67). JOSHUA (Josh. 24:14) and SAMUEL (1 Sam. 13:14) and all the prophets uttered similar warnings. Judicial injustices were sternly warned against by King JEHOSHAPHAT and governor NEHEMIAH by appealing to the fear of God (2 Chr. 19:5–11; Neh. 5:6–15). And the psalmist warned, "Therefore, you kings, be wise; / be warned, you rulers of the earth. / Serve the LORD with fear / and rejoice with trembling" (Ps. 2:10–11; cf. 90:11). ISAIAH warned against insincerity, those who "honor me with their lips, while their hearts are far from me, and their fear of me is a commandment of men learned by rote" (Isa. 29:13 RSV). The extreme penalty was paid by ANANIAS and SAPPHIRA for insincerity, and "Great fear seized the whole church" (Acts 5:11).

B. As reflected on God's people. God said to NOAH and his sons, "The fear and dread of you will fall upon all the beasts of the earth and all the birds of the air, upon every creature that moves along the ground, and upon all the fish of the sea; they are given into your hand" (Gen. 9:2). It is doubtless the IMAGE OF GOD reflected in the countenance and personality of human beings that incites fear in lower creatures (Ps. 139:14). Consequently, Eliphaz told Job that he "need not fear the beasts of the earth" (Job 5:22).

Moreover, God's people are feared by wicked people. As the Israelites began the conquest of Canaan, God said, "This very day I will begin to put the terror and fear of you on all the nations under heaven" (Deut. 2:25; cf. 11:25). And the harlot RAHAB confessed to the spies "that a great fear of you has fallen on us" (Josh. 2:9). Soon the tribal kings "feared greatly" Joshua's army (10:2 RSV). Note also ABSALOM's rebellion (2 Sam. 17:10); Jews in Persia (Esth. 9:2); mariners and JONAH (Jon. 1:1–16); and HEROD and the Jewish rulers (Matt. 14:5; 21:46; Mk. 12:12).

II. Baneful fear—the fear of evil. The other side of the ledger of fear is deficit. This fear is harmful to those who fear, and in turn makes them a source of fear. This fear is man's foe. It debilitates, disorganizes, demoralizes, and destroys.

A. As it affects the wicked. The wicked person is destroyed by his fears. Some wise man said, "The wicked man flees when no one pursues" (Prov. 28:1). Numerous records confirm this. When CAIN was exiled, he was seized with a fearful dread that "whoever finds me will kill me" (Gen. 4:14). He had slain and was afraid someone would slay him. Likewise, Herod's guilt fears haunted him after he beheaded JOHN THE BAPTIST (Matt. 14:1–2). In dreadful hallucinations one fears all kinds of evil, destitution, desolation, and destruction (see Job 5:21; Isa. 7:25; 8:6; Rev. 18:10, 15). In ELISHA's day the Aramean army fled, panic-stricken, in the night, "for the LORD had caused the Arameans to hear the sound of chariots and horses and a great army" (2 Ki. 7:6). Later, Isaiah encouraged HEZEKIAH with God's promise, "Listen! I am going to put such a spirit in him that when he hears a certain report, he will return to his own country" (2 Ki. 19:7). Fear itself is a destructive enemy. "What the wicked dreads will overtake him" (Prov. 10:24). Isaiah said, God will "bring their fears upon them" (Isa. 66:4 RSV). Fear disorganizes the wicked. When BELSHAZZAR saw a man's handwriting on the wall, "His face turned pale and he was so frightened that his knees knocked together and his legs gave way" (Dan. 5:6). Fear also paralyzes. When the angel rolled away the stone from the sepulchre, "for fear of him the guards trembled and became like dead men" (Matt. 28:4 RSV).

B. As it affects the godly. No matter how it works, "Fear of man will prove to be a snare" (Prov. 29:25). It takes its toll among good people. It disqualified men from fighting the holy wars. Moses left instructions for the officers to ask, "Is any man afraid or fainthearted? Let him go home" (Deut.

20:8). And when GIDEON screened men to fight the Midianites, he said, "Anyone who trembles with fear may turn back" (Jdg. 7:3). The good are sometimes stricken with fear as with a dreadful disease. Job said, "What I feared has come upon me; / what I dreaded has happened to me" (Job 3:25). False perception can replace faith with fear. When Jesus came to his disciples at night on the stormy sea, they "were terrified … and they cried out for fear" because they thought he was "a ghost" (Matt. 14:26).

Christian freedom has been threatened from the beginning by fear of the wicked. JOSEPH of Arimathea "was a disciple of Jesus, but secretly because he feared the Jews" (Jn. 19:38); parents of the healed blind man declined testimony (9:22); and the Twelve hid behind closed doors (20:19). Punishment and judgment are causes of fear for all (Deut. 28:67; Heb. 10:27, 31).

III. Banishing fear—freedom from fear. By precept and example Jesus taught his disciples to make conquest of their fears. It can be done.

A. By the presence of God. David said triumphantly, "I fear no evil, for you are with me" (Ps. 23:4). Long before this, God had said to Abraham, "Do not be afraid, Abram. I am your shield, your very great reward" (Gen. 15:1). To Isaiah he said for Israel, "Fear not, for I have redeemed you … Do not be afraid, for I am with you" (Isa. 43:1, 5; cf. Zeph. 3:15; Jn. 12:15). Divine visible presence, after the first startling moments, always dispelled fears (Exod. 3:6; Lk. 1:30; 2:10; Matt. 14:27; 17:6–7). Moreover, God's unseen presence hovers over his own and protects them. Elisha had at his command a mountain covered with "horses and chariots of fire" (2 Ki. 6:17). And Jesus had in reserve "more than twelve legions of angels" (Matt. 26:53).

B. By perfected love. The "fear of God" in the OT yielded to the "love of God" in the NT. Though the awesome nature of God will never diminish, his Fatherly LOVE was manifested through Jesus. His tenderness has replaced terror. Consequently, John could give the Christian antidote for fear: "There is no fear in love. But perfect love drives out fear, because fear has to do with punishment. The one who fears is not made perfect in love" (1 Jn. 4:18). The Christian should have no fear of hunger, nakedness, sickness, suffering, wicked people, death, nor judgment. All have lost their power of fear in the love of Christ. "Do not be afraid, little flock, for your Father has been pleased to give you the kingdom" (Lk. 12:32). (See E. S. Jones, *Abundant Living* [1942], 68–88; *NIDOTTE*, 2:527–33; *NIDNTT*, 1:621–24.)   G. B. FUNDERBURK

Fear of Isaac. This expression (Heb. *paḥad yiṣḥāq*) appears twice in Scripture (Gen. 31:42, 53; in the latter passage, "the Fear of his father Isaac"). It is generally thought to be a name for God, pointing to his protective care and power, which inspires terror in his enemies. Some scholars have argued that the term *paḥad* H7065 here has a different meaning, such as "kinsman" or "thigh." The latter sense is established elsewhere (Job 40:17, *paḥad* H7066), and such a meaning would presumably be related to oath-making (cf. Gen. 24:2, where a different word is used; see M. Malul in *VT* 35 [1985]: 192–200). These alternative interpretations have not become widely accepted (see *ABD*, 2:779–80; *DDD*, 329–31).

feasts. This English term is often used in Bible versions without distinction for both private and public celebrations, but Hebrew typically reserves *mišteh* H5492 for the former and uses other words for the latter.

I. In the OT

A. Private feasts. The social life of ancient Israel provided many joyous occasions that were celebrated with feasts: weddings (Gen. 29:22; these celebrations might extend seven days, Jdg. 14:10, 12, 17), the weaning of a child (Gen. 21:8), the birthday of a king (40:20), and the arrival of or approaching departure of guests (19:3; 26:30). Sheepshearing was also a joyous season, and the first sheared wool went to the sanctuary (Deut. 18:4; cf. Gen. 38:12; 1 Sam. 25:4–11, 36; 2 Sam. 13:23–27). JOB's children took turns holding feasts in their respective homes (Job 1:4–5). In a monarchy, the feast could be a state occasion that extended to the whole court (2 Sam. 3:20; cf. Esth. 1:3–8; Dan. 5:1); the queen might entertain the king (Esth. 5:4, 14; 7:2, 7). SOLOMON celebrated his dream with a feast (1 Ki. 3:15), and XERXES celebrated his finding of a new queen (Esth. 2:18).

Ancient Hebrews were not ascetics. Often feasts demanded no specific occasion other than gladness (Job 1:4–5; Isa. 5:12). It was a severe restriction upon participation in social life imposed by the Lord on JEREMIAH when he forbade him to go to the house of feasting (Jer. 16:8).

B. Communal feasts. For public, religious celebrations, the common Hebrew terms are *mō‘ēd* H4595 ("appointed time"; also "assembly" and "meeting-place") and *ḥag* H2504 ("round dance, festival gathering, pilgrim-feast"). MOSES and AARON in Egypt requested of PHARAOH permission to celebrate a feast in the desert (Exod. 5:1). After the exodus the communal festivals were seasons of rejoicing (Deut. 16:14). In early Israel, at the yearly feast in SHILOH, the girls danced in the vineyard (Jdg. 21:21). ELKANAH annually attended the feast at Shiloh (1 Sam. 1:3). Later there were processions at the house of the Lord with songs and shouts (Ps. 42:4). There was the ever-present danger that drinking might result in drunkenness (cf. ELI's suspicions in 1 Sam. 1:13–15). Abuse of the festivals and false trust in their efficacy brought forth denunciations from the PROPHETS (Isa. 1:12–14). The communal festivals of Israel may be considered in temporal categories: weekly, monthly, annual, and periodic.

1. Weekly festival—The Sabbath. The seventh day, sanctified by the Lord at creation (Gen. 2:1–3), but possibly not observed until the time of the exodus, is listed among the festivals (*šabbāt* H8701, Exod. 16:23; Lev. 23:1–3). The SABBATH commemorated both the Lord's rest at CREATION and the deliverance from servitude to Egypt (Deut. 5:12–15). It was a sign between Yahweh and Israel (Exod. 31:17; Ezek. 20:12, 20).

The Sabbath was observed by strict cessation of work from sunset until sunset (Exod. 20:12–13; Neh. 13:15–22), so that kindling a fire (Exod. 35:3) and picking up sticks (Num. 15:32–33) were punishable by death (Exod. 31:14; 35:2). Each person was to remain in his own place (Exod. 16:29; Lev.

Lighting of the Sabbath candles.

23:3). Forming an analogy from the distance used to measure pasture lands (Num. 35:4–5), the rabbis defined the Sabbath day's journey to be limited to 2,000 cubits (about 3,000 ft.; cf. Acts 1:12; Jos. *War* 5.2.3). The topic of movements on the Sabbath is treated at length in the MISHNAH, tractate ‘*Erubin*.

Some Jews of the Maccabean period allowed themselves to be massacred on the Sabbath rather than to profane it by self-defense, but later MATTATHIAS and those who followed him permitted self-defense on the day (1 Macc. 2:38–41; see MACCABEE). Some Jews would not negotiate for peace on the Sabbath (Jos. *War* 4.2.3). The extent of permitted activities was a point of dispute between Jesus and the PHARISEES. The latter permitted defiling the Sabbath when human life was in danger. Jesus contended that lesser cases of human need as well as animal need took precedence over the Sabbath (Matt. 12:1–14). The QUMRAN sectaries denied the right to aid suffering beasts on the Sabbath (CD XI, 13–14).

Special offerings were made on the Sabbath (Num. 28:9, 19), and the twelve loaves of SHOWBREAD were placed on the table in the Holy Place (Lev. 24:5–8). The title of Ps. 92 has the description, "A song. For the Sabbath day." It was a day of holy convocation (Lev. 23:3), but only after the rise of the SYNAGOGUE are instruction and worship activities attested as a prominent part of Sabbath observance (cf. Lk. 4:16, 31; Acts 13:14; 18:4).

Despite its restrictions, the Sabbath was a joyous occasion (2 Ki. 4:23; Isa. 58:13–14), the cessation of which in the EXILE was considered a punishment from God (Lam. 2:6; Hos. 2:11). The prophets called for proper Sabbath observance (Isa. 56:4; Jer. 17:19–27).

2. Monthly festival—the New Moon. At the beginning of the month special offerings were demanded by the law (Num. 28:11–15; cf. Ezra 3:5); there was also a blowing of trumpets (Num. 10:10; Ps. 81:3). This New Moon festival was usually referred to simply with the Hebrew word for "month" (*ḥōdeš* H2544; e.g., 1 Sam. 20:5). The observance was prominent in the period of the kings. An accidental uncleanness excused one from attending, as did a conflict with a "daily feast." One might visit a holy man on that day (2 Ki. 4:23). DAVID's arrangements for the Levites included service on the New Moon (1 Chr. 23:31). A cessation of activity, not demanded in the law, seems to have been observed with laxity in AMOS's day (Amos 8:5).

This day is included with others in prophetic denunciations of abuses of religious observances (Isa. 1:13–14). The exile brought a temporary cessation (Hos. 2:11 [Heb. 2:13]) but the festival continued to the end of the OT period (Neh. 10:33) and formed a part of EZEKIEL's temple description (Ezek. 45:17) and of ISAIAH's picture of the new heaven and earth (Isa. 66:22, 23). In Pauline thought, New Moon festivals and "sabbaths" are mere shadows of good things to come (Col. 2:16–17).

3. Annual festivals. Three annual seasons, requiring the appearance of all males at the sanctuary, dominated the Israelite religious year: Passover, Weeks, and Tabernacles (Deut. 16:16). These occasions, called "festivals to the LORD" (Exod. 12:14; Lev. 23:39, 41; et al.), were times in which freewill offerings were made (Deut. 16:16–17). Some aspects of the seasons were celebrated at night (Isa. 30:29). These days were of course interrupted by the exile (Hos. 9:5). Several other special occasions—the Day of Atonement, the New Year, Purim, and Hanukkah (the last two postexilic in origin)—are also discussed below.

a. *Passover (pesaḥ H7175).* The PASSOVER commemorated the final plague in Egypt: the firstborn of the Egyptians died, but the Israelites were spared by the blood on the doorpost (Exod. 12:11, 21–27, 43–48). Thereafter the event was observed as a feast to the Lord (12:14). The second Passover was observed in the wilderness of Sinai (Num. 9:1–5).

Passover fell in the first month (ABIB, Deut. 16:1; the first month is called NISAN in postexilic times, Neh. 2:1; Esth. 3:7), on the fourteenth day at evening (Lev. 23:5). The victim was selected on the tenth day of the month (Exod. 12:3) and after slaughter on the fourteenth was boiled and eaten (Deut. 16:7). Neither the uncircumcised person nor the hired servant could eat (Exod. 12:48). None of the lamb should be left over on the following morning (34:25). Special sacrifices were made to the Lord (Num. 28:16–25). The unclean person observed the corresponding day in the second month (9:10–13).

This night was followed by seven days that made up the Feast of Unleavened Bread (*ḥag hammaṣṣôt*, Exod. 34:18–19; Lev. 23:6; cf. Exod. 12:31–34; Acts 12:3; Lk. 22:1). On the first and the seventh of these days no servile work was to be done, and special offerings were made upon them all. The Passover was observed at GILGAL when JOSHUA brought Israel into Canaan (Josh. 5:10–12). The reforms of HEZEKIAH and JOSIAH were characterized by elaborate Passover celebrations (2 Ki. 23:21–23; 2 Chr. 30:1–27; 35:1–19). Passover and Unleavened Bread were observed by the Jews of ELEPHANTINE (*ANET*, 491).

The liturgy of the Passover celebration is the subject of minute elaboration in the Mishnah tractate *Passover*. Despite the assertion of *Jubilees* 49.16 that one cannot eat the Passover outside the sanctuary, Jesus ate with his disciples in a private house as was the custom of the times (cf. *m. Passover* 5; 8:13). In addition to the pilgrimage to Jerusalem, this festival retained some features of a home celebration that reasserted themselves after the fall of Jerusalem. The Passover meal was eaten at home with bitter herbs, successive cups of wine, the blessings and reciting of the Psalms. Whether a roast was eaten or not varied from community to community (*m. Passover* 4:4). The need for each individual to feel personally that he was brought out of Egypt was stressed.

During NT times large crowds, including Greeks, attended the celebration (Jn. 12:20; Jos. *War* 6.9.3). Jesus was a participant in the celebration

(Lk. 2:42; Jn. 2:13; 6:4; 11:5) and was himself crucified during the Passover season (Jn. 13:1). PETER's imprisonment and deliverance was also at this season (Acts 12:3). In Pauline thought the feast is treated figuratively when Christ our Passover lamb is said to have been sacrificed and when the disposing of the LEAVEN is allegorized to signify the casting out of insincerity (1 Cor. 5:7).

b. *Weeks* (*ḥag šābuʿōt*; LXX *heortē hebdomadōn*, but called *pentēkostē* ["fiftieth"], PENTECOST, in the APOCRYPHA and the NT). This one-day festival, also called the Feast of Harvest (Exod. 23:16) and "the day of firstfruits" (Num. 28:26), is named from the fact that its date is set by counting from the Sabbath of Passover to the morrow after the seventh sabbath, thus fifty days (Lev. 23:15–16; cf. Tob. 2:1, "the feast of Pentecost which is the sacred festival of the seven weeks"). Two loaves of bread and seven lambs one year old, one bullock, and two rams made up the special offering of the day. No laborious work was to be done. A free-will offering was to be made, and there was to be rejoicing with family and with the unfortunate classes of the community: the Levite, widow, orphan, and sojourner (Deut. 16:9–12).

A memorial significance was given to the Feast of Weeks by later rabbis when they designated it as the time the law was given at Sinai (*b. Pesaḥim* 68b), but the connection is not made in Scripture. The book of *Jubilees* puts all the covenants it can find in the OT on the day of the Feast of Weeks, and the Qumran Community celebrated the renewal of the covenant during that festival as well.

An ambiguity in the instructions for the day was the occasion of debate between the PHARISEES and the SADDUCEES. The former argued that "Sabbath" (Lev. 23:16) means the first day of Passover without regard to the day of the week (*m. Ḥagigah* 2:4). Thereby for them Pentecost could fall on any day of the week. The Sadducees (Boethusians) argued that "Sabbath" has its regular meaning in the passage and thereby Pentecost must fall on the first day of the week (cf. *m. Menaḥot* 10:3; *m. Ḥagigah* 2:4).

The outpouring of the Spirit took place on Pentecost (Acts 2), and thereby the day acquired additional meaning as the beginning day of the church. Paul hoped to extend his stay in EPHESUS until Pentecost (1 Cor. 16:8), but sought to be in Jerusalem at that season in a later year (Acts 20:16).

c. *Booths* or *Tabernacles* (*ḥag hassukkôt*) or *Ingathering* (*ḥag hāʾāsip*). This festival fell on the fifteenth of the seventh month, five days after the Day of Atonement, and occupied seven days (Exod. 23:16–17; 34:22). The first and eighth days were days of rest. Branches of palm trees, leafy branches, and willows, along with choice fruit (Lev. 23:40), were used to make the booths in which the Israelites dwelt seven days—"so your descendants will know that I had the Israelites live in booths when I brought them out of Egypt" (23:43). There was rejoicing with family, servants, widows, orphans, Levites, and sojourners in the community (Deut. 16:13–15). Special sacrifices for this season totaled seventy bulls. Each seventh year there was the public reading of the law (31:9–13).

The returned exiles observed this feast under DARIUS (Ezra 3:4), at which time EZRA read the law and led the people in acts of penitence. The celebration is said to be different from anything done since the days of Joshua (Neh. 8:13–18). ZECHARIAH envisions all nations coming up to Jerusalem year by year to keep the Feast of Tabernacles (Zech. 14:16–19). The punishment for those who neglect it is that upon them no rain shall fall, but in the case of Egypt the inundation of the NILE would fail.

Jesus participated in the Feast of Tabernacles (Jn. 7). JOSEPHUS calls it the holiest and greatest of the Hebrew feasts (*Ant.* 8.4.1). Both he (*Ant.* 3.10.4; 13.13.5) and the Mishnah (*Sukkah*) enlarge

A *sukkah* made from palm fronds. The Israelites built such shelters during the Feast of Tabernacles or Booths (Sukkoth).

upon the customs of the later observance, one chief feature of which was a libation of water drawn from the fountain of SILOAM. This practice furnishes a likely background for Jesus' discourse on living water (Jn. 7:37–39).

d. *The Day of Atonement* (*yôm hakkippurim*; see ATONEMENT, DAY OF). This holy celebration fell on the tenth day of the seventh month, TISHRI (Lev. 23:27–32; Num. 29:7–11). Its ritual, which included the expiation for the priest and for the people and the sending away of the goat for AZAZEL, is described in Lev. 16:8, 10, 26. It was a day of rest and fasting.

e. *New Year*. One of the most debated questions in modern study is whether or not there was a New Year's Day celebration in ancient Israel. Beginning with an analogy with the Babylonian *Akitu* festival, which fell in the spring of the year and celebrated the renewal of creation and kingship of MARDUK, some scholars postulate that Israel's God was crowned annually at the "New Year Feast of Yahweh." S. Mowinckel (*The Psalms in Israel's Worship* [1962], ch. 5) argued that the "enthronement psalms" (Pss. 47, 93, 96–99), in which the expression "Yahweh reigns" prominently occurs, were a part of the liturgy of that special day. Out of these concepts it is thought that Israel's messianic and eschatological thought developed. It is argued that JEROBOAM introduced a festival in the eighth month, similar to the one held in Judah, in order that the people not be attracted to Jerusalem (1 Ki. 12:32).

Opponents of the theory point out the difficulty of explaining how a spring festival got shifted to fall. The Pentateuch points to Nisan as the beginning of the year (Exod. 12:2). There were special offerings on the first of the seventh month, a convocation was held in which no laborious work was done, trumpets were blown, and an offering was made to the Lord (Lev. 23:24–27; Num. 29:1–6), but the text says nothing specific about the New Year's day. The postexilic gathering on the first of the seventh month is not said to be a day of high feast (Neh. 8:1), and the one occurrence of *rōʾš haššānâ* in Scripture (Ezek. 40:1) describes a vision on the tenth of the month and not one on the first. The observance of such a feast also goes unmentioned in the Apocrypha, Josephus, and PHILO JUDAEUS, but is the subject of a Mishnah tractate (*Roš Haššanah*). (See further N. H. Snaith, *The Jewish New Year Festival* [1947].)

f. *Purim* (*pûrim*). This festival has its origin in the deliverance wrought by ESTHER (Esth. 9:16–28) and falls on the fourteenth of ADAR (February-March) for those in villages and unwalled towns, and on the fifteenth for those in fortified cities (Esth. 9:18–19; Jos. *Ant*. 11.6.13). The name is explained as coming from the "lot" (*pûr* H7052) that HAMAN planned to cast to destroy the Jews. The observance of the festival is first attested by 2 Macc. 15:36, where it is called the "Day of Mordecai." There is no mention of any religious observance connected with the day. In later tradition the book of Esther was read in the synagogue amidst rejoicing, and food and presents were sent to friends (see the Mishnah tractate *Megillah*). See also PURIM.

g. *Hanukkah* or *Dedication* (*ḥănukkâ* H2853 [cf. Neh. 12:27]; in Apocr., *ho enkainismos tou thysiastēriou* [1 Macc. 4:56]; in the NT, *ta enkainia* G1589 [Jn. 10:22]). Following the victories of Judas MACCABEE in 167 B.C., a celebration of eight days commemorating the rededication of the TEMPLE, whose worship had been interrupted three years, was instituted (1 Macc. 4:41–59; 2 Macc. 10:6–8). The festival begins on the 25th of Kislev (November-December), and one additional candle is lighted each day until a total of eight is reached (*b. Sabbath* 21b). Josephus calls it "Lights" (*phōta*, *Ant*. 12.7.7). There was no partial or total abstention from ordinary occupation nor was there a holy convocation at the beginning and end. Jesus was once in Jerusalem at this season (Jn. 10:22). (Note also the institution of NICANOR's day on the thirteenth of Adar, commemorating the Jewish victory over this SELEUCID general, 1 Macc. 13:51–52.) See also DEDICATION, FEAST OF.

4. Periodic festivals. a. *Sabbatical year* (*šabbāt šabbātôn* [Lev. 25:4], "Sabbath of rest"). Each seventh year brought a cessation of agricultural activity and a release from debt. That the land might have its required rest, exile was threatened for neglect of the observance (Exod. 23:10–11; Lev. 25:1–7; Deut. 15:1). At the Feast of Booths during that year there was the public reading of the law (Deut. 31:10–13). See also SABBATICAL YEAR.

b. *Year of Jubilee* (šĕnat hayyôbēl). At the Day of Atonement of the forty-ninth year, the sounding of a trumpet (a ram's horn, *yôbēl* H3413) marked the onset of the JUBILEE YEAR as a period of freedom in the land. Property returned to its original owners. There was a price adjustment in sales in view of its approach. Sowing and reaping was forbidden (Lev. 25:8–17). The pseudepigraphic book of *Jubilees* is built around this custom, but uses a different system of calculation from that in Scripture. (For detailed discussions of Jewish feasts, see G. F. Moore, *Judaism in the First Centuries of the Christian Era: The Age of the Tannaim*, 3 vols. [1927–30], 2:40–54; R. de Vaux, *Ancient Israel* [1961], 468–517.)

II. In the NT

A. Jewish festivals. Allusions to the Sabbath, Passover, Unleavened Bread (Matt. 26:17; Mk. 14:1; Lk. 22:1; Jn. 7:2), Feast of Tabernacles, Dedication (Jn. 10:22), and Pentecost (Acts 2) may be seen under the appropriate heading in the above discussion. The parents of Jesus observed Passover when he was a child (Lk. 2:42), and during his public ministry Jesus may have attended as many as four Passovers (Jn. 4:45; 5:1; 6:4; 12:1; Greeks would come to it, 12:20). Pilate had a custom of releasing a prisoner at the feast (Matt. 27:15; Mk. 15:6).

The festivals were sources of figurative interpretation for the NT writers. Christ our Passover lamb has been sacrificed (1 Cor. 5:7–8). Sabbaths, New Moon celebrations, and festival days are mere shadows of good things to come (Col. 2:16–17). The epistle to the Hebrews allegorizes the rest of the people of God to be the eternal rest (Heb. 4), and the ceremony of the Day of Atonement forms the basis for the presentation of the work of Christ as our High Priest (Heb. 8).

THE JEWISH SACRED YEAR

	MONTH	SPECIAL DAYS
Nisan	(April)	14 — Passover 15 — Unleavened Bread 21 — Close of Passover
Iyar	(May)	
Sivan	(June)	6 — Feast of Pentecost — seven weeks after the Passover (Anniversary of the giving of the law on Mt. Sinai)
Tammuz	(July)	
Ab	(August)	
Elul	(September)	
Tishri	(October)	1 & 2 — The Feast of Trumpets, Rosh Hashanah, beginning of the civil year 10 — Day of Atonement 15–21 — Feast of Tabernacles
Marheshvan	(November)	25 — Feast of Lights, Dedication, Hanukkah
Kislev	(December)	
Tebeth	(January)	
Shebat	(February)	
Adar	(March)	14 — The Feast of Purim

B. Other special occasions.
Jesus denounced the Pharisees for seeking the uppermost seats at feasts (Matt. 23:6; Mk. 12:39; Lk. 20:46). Levi (MATTHEW) entertained Jesus and his friends at a great feast after he was called to discipleship (Lk. 5:29). Jesus suggested that the poor rather than the rich should be invited when one gives a feast (Lk. 14:13). Jesus attended the marriage feast in CANA (Jn. 2:1–11). In CORINTH, because of food sacrificed to idols, a problem faced Christians as to whether or not they could attend a meal given by an unbeliever. Paul grants the right to go and eat whatever is set out asking no questions for conscience' sake (1 Cor. 10:27). Certain characters with heretical tendencies are said to be blots in the "love feasts" (Jude 12).

C. The marriage feast.
The MARRIAGE feast wedding banquet is the background theme of several parables of Jesus: the ten virgins (Matt. 25:1–13), the marriage of the king's son (22:2–14), and the great supper (Lk. 14:15–24). Jesus compared his relation to the disciples to that of the bridegroom and his friends (Matt. 9:15; Mk. 2:19; Lk. 5:34); while John the Baptist spoke of himself as only the friend of the bridegroom (Jn. 3:29). The book of Revelation climaxes with the invitation to the marriage supper of the Lamb (Rev. 19:9). The background for this concept was laid in the prophets (Isa. 25:6) and is closely related to the MESSIANIC BANQUET of rabbinic thought at which the righteous would dine on behemoth and leviathan. A disciple's exclamation, "Blessed is the man who will eat at the feast in the kingdom of God" (Lk. 14:15), called forth the parable of the great supper. The universality of the gospel may be expressed in terms of a feast in which many from the E and the W will eat with Abraham, Isaac, and Jacob (Matt. 8:11; Lk. 13:29). The entire Christian life may be called a feast (1 Cor. 5:8).

D. The eschatological feast.
In the prophets already appears the figure of speech in which God's judgment on a people as a sacrificial banquet is expounded (Isa. 34:5–8; Ezek. 39:17–20). This inversion of the concept of a banquet in the Apocalypse, when the birds are invited to enjoy the great supper of God, is the counterpart of the messianic banquet (Rev. 19:17–21).

J. P. LEWIS

feet, washing of. See FOOTWASHING.

Felix fee´liks (Φῆλιξ *G5772*, from Lat. *felix*, "fruitful, fortunate"). Antonius Felix was a freedman of Antonia, the mother of the emperor CLAUDIUS, and brother of the same prince's freedman and favorite, Pallas. (On the question of Felix's full name, see F. F. Bruce in *JSNT* 1 [1978]: 33–36, and C. J. Hemer in *JSNT* 31 [1987]: 45–49.) A social reject through the formative years of his life, Claudius had fallen into the company of the freedmen of the imperial household, and it was inevitable that they should play a large part in the affairs of the principate, a situation that naturally roused the aristocratic scorn of such writers as TACITUS. It was the influence of Pallas which secured the appointment of Felix to the governorship of JUDEA.

Tacitus's dislike for both freedmen betrayed him into carelessness over detail in two vital chapters of the *Annals* (12.53–54). Felix would naturally have been appointed to the governorship of Judea after the recall of Ventidius Cumanus in A.D. 52. Tacitus, probably misinformed, and finding closer research in such a context distasteful, seems to suggest some overlap between two procuratorships with Felix in authority in SAMARIA and Cumanus in GALILEE. There is certainly a discrepancy between the account in Tacitus and that given by JOSEPHUS (*War* 2.12.; *Ant.* 20.8.5), a discrepancy which ampler detail might easily remove.

Unreliable though Tacitus's account is, it is worth examining in some detail for the lurid light

Coin minted during the procuratorship of Antonius Felix.

it throws on Felix's character and reputation. After some acid comment on honors paid by the Senate to Pallas, Tacitus proceeds in his next chapter (*Annals* 12.54) to show how Felix found protection from the consequences of his corruption and misrule under his powerful brother's shadow. The Jews, says the historian, were still in a state of excitement and resentment over CALIGULA's narrowly averted plan to defile Yahweh's temple with his own statue. The situation was wantonly exploited by Cumanus in Judea and Felix in Samaria. The pair of scoundrels had connived at an almost open conflict between the rival communities, claiming a share in the loot.

The situation so cynically permitted got out of hand, and savage repression by both governors provoked the intervention of Quadratus, the governor of SYRIA, and in consequence the nearest commander with sufficient military strength at his disposal to impose a forcible solution on the distracted area. It was a further illustration of the difficulties that beset the Romans' persistent attempt to hold Palestine with the token force based at CAESAREA, and of the fumbling and too often corrupt rule of the minor officials who filled up the sorry list of procurators. Quadratus himself was heavily impeded by circumstances. Hesitating to deal with the influential Felix, the legate placed the full blame on Cumanus, with the result that Felix succeeded to the vacant procuratorship. Details and dating may remain uncertain, but Tacitus's laconic account is illustration vivid enough of another comment he made concerning Felix as a governor. He described him in the *Histories* (5.9) as "a master of cruelty and lust who exercised the powers of a king in the spirit of a slave." Such is the truth that emerges from the garbled story.

According to Josephus, Cumanus was sole procurator in A.D. 48, and Felix in 52, which is an oversimplification. It is a fair guess that Felix, by his brother's favor, exercised some commission in Palestine under Claudius, and perhaps used his position to entangle Cumanus in administrative difficulties and replace him. Such was the stage-setting of corruption and misrule in Palestine in the decade before the savage outbreak of the Great Rebellion. The state of the country under the rule of Felix is illustrated by the fact that the military commandant of the Jerusalem garrison found it necessary to provide an escort of 470 troopers to secure the safe convoy of one political prisoner down the guerrilla-ridden mountain road from Jerusalem to Caesarea. The countryside must have been in a state of near anarchy.

In Luke's account of the examination of PAUL by Felix in the Roman garrison town, the procurator appeared true to form. With him was DRUSILLA, the Herodian girl whom he had enticed from her royal husband, Aziz of Emesa. Felix's disregard for Roman justice and his avarice are visible in the story. Such was the scoundrel before whom the apostle to the Gentiles preached of "righteousness, self-control and the judgment to come" (Acts 24:25), and who put the consideration of such matters off until a more convenient time. NERO recalled Felix in 57 or 58. Dates again become a difficulty. Nothing is known of his subsequent fate. (See further *HJP*, rev. ed. [1973–87], 1:458–66.) E. M. BLAIKLOCK

felloe. Variant form of *felly*, which refers to the rim of a wheel supported by spokes. It is used by the KJV once in connection with the wheels of the ten bronze stands in the temple (1 Ki. 7:33; NIV, "spokes").

fellow fel´o. This English term (meaning "man, companion, peer") is used in Bible versions to render several words and expressions, such as Hebrew *rēa'* H8276 (e.g., Exod. 2:13 KJV; the NIV and NRSV clarify, "fellow Hebrew"). The term can be used in expressions of contempt; for example, it sometimes renders the simple Greek pronoun *houtos* G4047, "this [one]" (Matt. 9:3 et al.). It also occurs frequently as an adjective in combination with various nouns (e.g., "fellow worker" for *synergos* G5301, Rom. 16:3; "fellow servant" for *syndoulos* G5281, Col. 4:7; et al.). W. H. JOHNSON

fellowship. The meaningful Greek term *koinōnia* G3126 ("association, communion") and its cognates stand for one of the most powerful concepts in the Scriptures. They apply first of all to participation in a person or project and a "common" spirit. Christians are "participants [*koinōnoi*] in the divine nature" (2 Pet. 1:4 NRSV). Fellowship in the family of God comes after the new birth (2 Cor. 5:17; 1

Jn. 3:9; see REGENERATION). Christians partake of Christ (Heb. 3:14), and of the HOLY SPIRIT (6:4; in Hebrews a different term is used, *metochos G3581*). True fellowship results in mutual LOVE (Jn. 13:34). A "common salvation" (Jude 3) and a "common faith" (Tit. 1:4) characterize true Christians.

The significant KJV rendering "communicate" (for *koinoneō G3125*, Gal. 6:6) touches the heart of the Christian spirit: those who are taught in the Word of God are admonished to exercise their sense of community or fellowship sharing. This was an essential strength of the early Christians. Although a minority movement, they shared the strength of belonging to each other and to God.

The notion of *koinonia* can have negative aspects as well. A Christian has no genuine "fellowship" with an unbeliever, whose nature is different (2 Cor. 6:14–16). Pagan ceremonies are not a part of true *koinonia* (1 Cor. 10:20–22). Christians should have no "fellowship" with unfruitful works of darkness (Eph. 5:11 KJV).

True NT *koinonia* is rooted in a depth of fellowship with God as Father (1 Jn. 1:3, 6). The FATHERHOOD OF GOD has significance for those who are in the family of God through the new birth. Christians must continue to walk in the light to enjoy this fellowship. They are called to fellowship with the Son (1 Cor. 1:9). The LORD'S SUPPER is a symbol of this inner fellowship (10:16). Fellowship with the Spirit is a blessing of Christians (2 Cor. 13:14). The true *koinonia* is not only earthly, but continues and is consummated in heaven (Rev. 21:1–4). (See *NIDNTT*, 1:635–44.) See also COMMUNION; COMMUNITY OF GOODS; CONTRIBUTION.

W. H. JOHNSON

fellowship offering. See SACRIFICE AND OFFERINGS IV.C.

felspar. Also *feldspar*. The most important group of rock-forming minerals. The rendering "green felspar" is used by the NEB in a few passages for the rare Hebrew word *bāreqet H1403* (Exod. 28:17; 39:10; *borqat H1404* in Ezek. 28:13), which refers to BERYL or EMERALD. The feldspars are aluminosilicates of potassium, sodium, calcium, or barium and are generally white, gray, or pale shades of orange-red. Green feldspar is generally a variety of the potassium feldspar, microcline. It is referred to as amazon stone or amazonite and is sometimes cut and polished as an ornamental stone. Amazon stone occurs in the Ilmen Mountains and at other points in the Urals, in Italy, and in the gem-bearing pegmatites of Madagascar.

female. See WOMAN.

fence. This English term is used frequently by the KJV, especially in the expression "fenced city," which is better rendered "fortified city" (Num. 32:17 et al.). The NIV uses "fence" only once to render Hebrew *gādēr H1555* ("stone wall") in Ps. 62:3, where the psalmist speaks of his oppressors as a "leaning wall" and a "tottering fence," that is, ready to fall over. See HEDGE; WALL.

ferret. Incorrect KJV rendering of Hebrew *ănāqâ H652*, "gecko" (Lev. 11:30). See LIZARD.

ferry boat. Term used once by the KJV to render the noun *ăbārâ H6302*, which means "ford" or "crossing" (2 Sam. 19:18). Because the Hebrew expression is unusual (lit., "And the crossing crossed to cross [i.e., to bring over] the king's household"), the KJV translators either misinterpreted the noun or rendered the clause freely, "And there went over a ferry boat to carry over the king's household" (cf. NIV, "They crossed [apparently reading *ābĕrû* instead of *ābĕrâ*] at the ford to take the king's household over").

Fertile Crescent. A stretch of land beginning at the Persian Gulf, extending NW through the TIGRIS and EUPHRATES River Valley, continuing W to the NE coast of the Mediterranean Sea, turning S through CANAAN, and (popularly) including the NILE River Valley. The region described forms an arc or crescent and is indeed very fertile, although the outlying area is barren. The earliest records of civilization come from this region (see SUMER), and it was the center of civilization until the age of GREECE. EGYPT at the western tip, as well as ASSYRIA AND BABYLONIA in the E, developed in power and influence, while the coastland at the E end of the Mediterranean developed commercially, but was often subjected to invading armies from

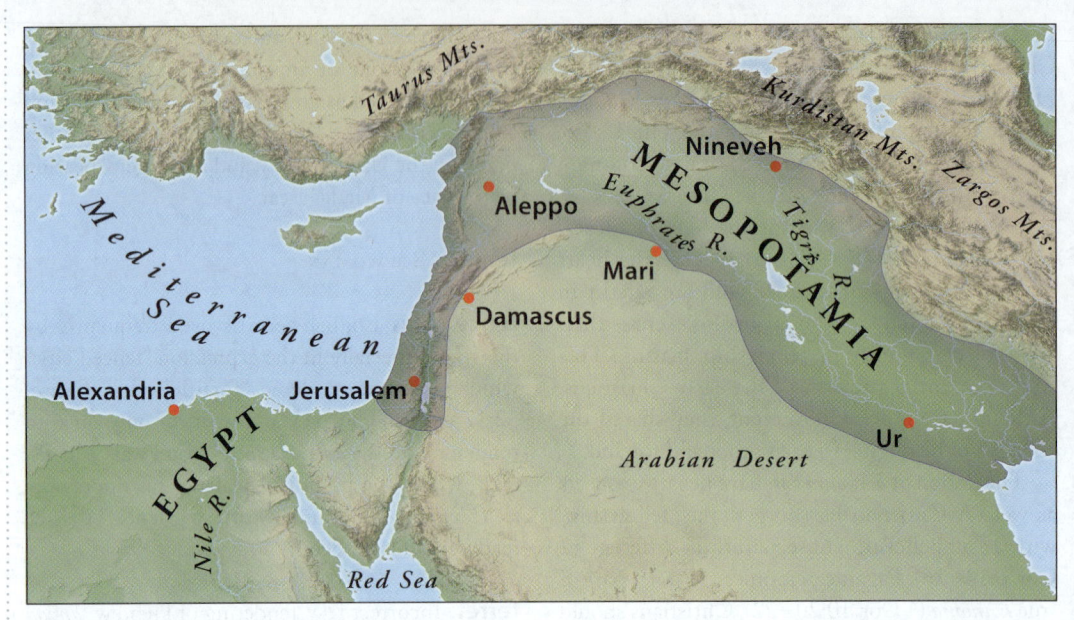

The Fertile Crescent.

either end. It is in this crossroads of humanity that God chose to place his people Israel and later to send his Son. See also MESOPOTAMIA.

C. P. WEBER

fertility cults. Since the classic work of James G. Frazer at the beginning of the 20th cent. (e.g., *Adonis, Attis, Osiris*, 3rd ed. [1914]), it has been widely held that a number of cults promoted the fertility of men, animals, and crops by celebrating the MYTH of a dying-and-rising god with rites of mourning and of later jubilation. The god was believed to typify the death and renewal of vegetation. A "sacred marriage" between the god, represented by the king, and the goddess, represented by a hierodule (temple slave or prostitute), also was believed to promote the fertility of the land. The sacred prostitution of Astarte (see ASHTORETH) and of Aphrodite also was directed to this end.

In EGYPT, OSIRIS was supposedly killed by his brother Seth but later revived by his wife Isis. From the Egyptian empire to the Ptolemaic period, Osiris was associated with germinating grain. The Egyptian dead also were identified with Osiris as the prototype of "resurrection." In MESOPOTAMIA the Sumerian god Dumuzi (the Akk. TAMMUZ) was originally a king of ERECH deified as the consort of the goddess Inanna (the Akk. ISHTAR). Although the text of the myth, "Inanna's [or Ishtar's] Descent to the Netherworld," is missing, it has been widely assumed that the goddess descended in order to resurrect her lover. Laments for Tammuz are well known, as are some "sacred marriage" love songs. In the Greco-Roman period the youthful ADONIS, beloved of Aphrodite, was mourned in Byblos (GEBAL) in LEBANON. Adonis was slain by a boar in midsummer. Seeds sown in pots, known as "the gardens of Adonis," were cast into the sea or in wells. In ASIA MINOR, Attis, the consort of Cybele, met death by castration. The priests of Cybele, the famous Magna Mater, were castrated men. (See P. Borgeaud, *Mother of the Gods: From Cybele to the Virgin Mary* [2004].)

In Greece the figure representing the dying vegetation was the goddess Persephone or Kore, whose abduction into HADES was mourned by her mother Demeter. Mysteries of Kore were celebrated at ELEUSIS. Some scholars have suggested that similar mysteries promising immortality were celebrated for various dying-and-rising gods, and further, that the RESURRECTION OF JESUS CHRIST and the preaching of PAUL are in some measure dependent upon these mysteries. See GREEK RELIGION AND PHILOSOPHY; MYSTERY RELIGIONS; ROMAN RELIGION.

The only explicit reference to any of these gods is found in Ezek. 8:14: "Then he brought me to the entrance of the north gate of the house of the LORD, and I saw women sitting there, mourning for Tammuz." The Jewish month of June-July still is called Tammuz, but this name no doubt lost its original significance (just as in English we no longer associate Thursday with the Norse god Thor). The "plants of pleasantness" in Isa. 17:10 (NIV, "finest plants") have been interpreted by some as "Adonis gardens," and Hos. 7:14 has been considered to refer to ritual wailing for grain.

Other scholars have gone further in seeing the fertility-cult background as the key to the interpretation of a number of books of the OT. They argue that the Canaanite fertility cult was transmitted to Israel when the prophets exalted Yahweh as the god of the sacred marriage in place of BAAL. They interpret the imagery of Yahweh and Israel as his bride as being derived from the fertility cult. T. Meek (in *IB*, 5:94–96) comments on Canticles as a Tammuz liturgy, and T. H. Gaster (*Thespis*, 2nd ed. [1961], 37–39, 44–48) sees in numerous psalms and in JOEL the seasonal pattern of God's victory over his cosmic foes. Indeed, H. G. May (in *AJSL* 48 [1932]: 73–98) went so far as to derive the concepts of immortality, of the suffering servant, and of the FATHERHOOD OF GOD from the fertility-cult background of popular Hebrew religion. (See E. M. Yamauchi in *ETSB* 4 [1961]: 80–88, and in *JBL* 84 [1965]: 283–90.)

In the NT, Paul warned the Corinthians against the defilement of their bodies in relation with the sacred prostitutes of Aphrodite. Paul's harsh words of Gal. 5:12 concerning the JUDAIZERS may have been an allusion to the self-mutilation of the priests of Cybele. JEROME reports that HADRIAN (A.D. 135) deliberately desecrated the birthplace of Jesus at BETHLEHEM by consecrating it to the worship of Adonis/Tammuz. Many scholars from Reitzenstein to Bultmann have compared the resurrection of Christ to the resurrection of such figures as Attis, Adonis, or Osiris, and have attributed some of Paul's teachings to a dependence upon pagan mysteries.

Subsequent research has tended to undermine seriously the Frazerian thesis of a generically similar series of fertility cults, on the one hand, and the thesis of the dependence of Christianity upon the pagan mysteries, on the other hand. Studies by S. N. Kramer (*The Sacred Marriage Rite* [1969]) indicate that no CUNEIFORM text speaks explicitly of the resurrection of Dumuzi/Tammuz. A fragmentary passage does imply that Tammuz spent half the year in the underworld with his sister taking his place for the other half year. H. Frankfort (*Kingship and the Gods* [1948], ch. 15) has pointed out that Osiris is not a "dying" god but a "dead" god: he reigns as the mummy-clad king of the dead.

P. Lambrechts (e.g., *Annuaire de l'Institut de Philologie et d'Histoire Orientales et Slaves* 13 [1953]: 207–40) has shown that the evidence for the deity and the resurrection of both Attis and Adonis do not antedate the late 2nd cent. A.D. G. Wagner (*Pauline Baptism and the Pagan Mysteries* [1967]) has demonstrated that in many cases the alleged mysteries of the fertility gods are dubiously attested, and that Christianity is not dependent upon the pagan mysteries. (Cf. also B. M. Metzger, "Methodology in the Study of the Mystery Religions and Early Christianity," in *Historical and Literary Studies: Pagan, Jewish and Christian* [1968], 1–24; A. Bonanno, ed.,

Marble statuette of Aphrodite, Greek goddess of beauty, love, and fertility (3rd–2nd cent. B.C.). Paul warned the Corinthians about the worship associated with this deity.

Archaeology and Fertility Cult in the Ancient Mediterranean [1986].)

E. M. YAMAUCHI

festal garments. The NRSV rendering of Hebrew *ḥălîpôt běgādîm* in a few verses (Jdg. 14:12–13, 19 [*ḥălîpôt* by itself]; the RSV had used the same translation also in Gen. 45:22 [*ḥălîpôt śĕmālōt*] and 2 Ki. 5:5, 22–23). The expression means literally "changes [i.e., sets] of clothes" (from *ḥălîpâ* H2722 and *beged* H955 [or *śimlâ* H8529]), but the contexts suggest costly gifts and thus possibly special garments.

festivals. See FEASTS.

Festus, Porcius fes´tuhs, por´shuhs (Φῆστος G5776 [from Lat. *fēstus*, "festal, joyful"], Πόρκιος G4517 [a Roman clan name]). Roman governor in JUDEA. Of Porcius Festus's life prior to his appointment as governor nothing is known. The date is variously given as A.D. 57, 58, 59, and 60. The discrepancy can manifestly be much narrowed (see CHRONOLOGY [NT] II.G). The time of the year is nowhere mentioned, nor is any gap specified between official nomination and his taking office. Months of traveling time are also involved. If the date were more certain, it would provide valuable aid toward a firmer chronology for PAUL.

Festus died early in his tenure of office, so the one glimpse afforded of him is the scene of his examination of Paul at CAESAREA and his consultation with Agrippa II (Acts 24:27—26:32; see HEROD VIII). It is an interesting view of a minor Roman governor at work in a most difficult situation. Festus, a welcome contrast (according to JOSEPHUS in *Ant.* 20.8.9; 20.9.1) to his vicious predecessor, Antonius FELIX, and to the equally corrupt Albinus who succeeded him in the procuratorship, had inherited a load of trouble from Felix's maladministration. There was a shocking breakdown of law and order in the countryside, and open armed hostility between the rival factions in the hierarchy. It was the first foreshadowing of the fearful internecine strife that was to add unprecedented venom to the ordeal of the coming rebellion, now a brief six or seven years away.

Festus knew that he could not afford to alienate or offend any collaborating elements in the Jewish population, and the problem presented him by the priestly elements who were determined to be rid of Paul must be weighed and appreciated in this context. Any perceptive governor could see that tension in Palestine was fast mounting toward some sort of climax. Herein lay the difference between Festus's position and that of PILATE some thirty years before, when the same hierarchy had sought to do away with an obviously innocent man. Events had seriously deteriorated in Palestine. Nor was Festus damagingly compromised by past mismanagement of the difficult Jews, as Pontius Pilate was. He was nonetheless under orders to do his utmost to contain an explosive situation, and, in the light of this, A. P. Gould's contention that "Paul's appeal to Caesar is the lasting condemnation of Festus" is without validity.

More fortunate than Pilate in his similar conflict of duties and considerations, Festus was offered a way of escape by the prisoner's own action. He offered Paul an acquittal on the major and relevant charge of sedition, and added the proposal, not unreasonable in normal times from the point of view of the occupying power, that the ex-Pharisee should face a religious investigation before his coreligionists. It was a crisis for Paul. Perhaps with fuller information and sharper apprehension than the procurator's, Paul saw the peril of the situation in Judea, the deepening anarchy, and the looming crisis. He cut the knot, to Festus's relief, by the exercise of his Roman citizen's right of an APPEAL to Caesar. Festus was obliged by law to accept the appeal, and did so with alacrity. It solved his major problem, Paul's security.

On the other hand, as a new arrival in Palestine, Festus was unfamiliar with Jewish law and religion. He had a career to make, and the lucidity and correct terminology of a document over his signature addressed to Rome's highest court might have been a matter of deep concern to him. Hence, the eagerness with which Festus availed himself of the aid of Agrippa II, an able man, an indispensable ally of Rome in the mounting difficulties of her rule, and a person with a close acquaintance with both Judaism and Christianity. To honor where convenient the old Herodian house was also a policy as old as AUGUSTUS himself. Nowhere else in the records of 1st-cent. history is so authentic a description of the empire in political action to be found. (See further E. M. Blaiklock, *The Century of the New Testament* [1962], ch. 6; A. N. Sherwin-White, *Roman Society and Roman Law in the New Testament* [1963], 48–70; *HJP*, rev. ed. [1973–87], 1:467–68 [see also n. 42 on pp. 465–66]; C. K. Barrett, *A Critical and Exegetical Commentary on the Acts of the Apostles*, ICC [1994–98], 2:1116–18.) E. M. BLAIKLOCK

fetters. This English term is used in Bible versions to render several terms, such as Hebrew *kebel* **H3890** (Ps. 105:18), which refers to foot shackles, as does Greek *pedē* **G4267** (Mk. 5:4; NIV, "irons on his feet"). The dual of Hebrew *nĕḥōšet* **H5733** ("bronze") could be used of fetters binding the two limbs (Jdg. 16:21; 2 Sam. 3:34). Other Greek and Hebrew terms seem to have more general application (see BOND; CHAIN). Two typical types of fetters seen in sculptured figures are the shackles for the feet, connected by a short rope that limited the victim's length of stride, and hand shackles connected to the neck by a short rope. A. BOWLING

fever. See DISEASE.

field. This English term can be used to translate a variety of words in the Bible, especially Hebrew *śādeh* **H8441** (e.g., Gen. 2:5) and Greek *agros* **G68** (e.g., Matt. 6:28). Both of them mean an unenclosed tract of ground, whether for pasture or tillage, and varying in size, though the Hebrew term can be used with reference to the territory of a people (Gen. 14:7; Ruth 1:6). It is sometimes contrasted with what is enclosed, whether a vineyard (Exod. 22:5), a garden, or a walled town (Deut. 28:3, 16). In some passages the word implies land remote from a house (Gen. 4:8) or a settled habitation (24:27).

The separate plots of ground were marked off not by fences but by stones, which might easily be removed (Deut. 19:14). Flocks and herds therefore constantly had to be watched. Fields sometimes received names after remarkable events, as HELKATH HAZZURIM ("the field of daggers," 2 Sam. 2:16, using a different Hebrew word, *ḥelqâ* **H2754**, "plot"), or from the use to which they may have been applied, as "Fuller's Field" (Isa. 7:3 NRSV) and "potter's field" (Matt. 27:7). S. BARABAS

Field of Blood. See AKELDAMA.

fiery serpent. This expression is used by the KJV to render Hebrew *nāḥāš śārāp* (**H5729 + H8314**), referring to the desert VIPERS that attacked the Hebrews in the wilderness as they journeyed around MOAB (Num. 21:6, 8 [*śārāp* alone, referring to the image]; Deut. 8:15). Their bite was cured miraculously when the victim looked at the bronze serpent made by MOSES on that occasion (see NEHUSHTAN; SERPENT). The context suggests a poisonous viper living in the desert regions near biblical Moab. Some believe it is the same as Hebrew *ʾepʿeh* **H704** (e.g., Isa. 30:6), which is, in turn, identified by many with *Echis carinata*, the desert viper (cf. *IDB*, 4:289).

In other usages, the term *śārāp* refers to legendary creatures (the flying serpents of Isa. 14:29; 30:6) or supernatural angelic beings (the SERAPHS of Isa. 6:2–7). This raises the possibility that the term is used in Num. 21:6 not because it normally designated a particular kind of snake, but rather to emphasize the supernatural, miraculous character of the plague. A. BOWLING

fig. The fig tree is *Ficus carica*; its fruit is a succulent, enlarged hollow receptacle, containing the flowers inside (the flowers are not seen unless the fruit is cut open). Hebrew *tĕʾēnâ* **H9300** can refer both to the tree (e.g., 1 Ki. 4:25) and to the fruit (Num. 13:23), whereas Greek uses *sykē* **G5190** for the fig tree (Matt. 21:19) and *sykon* **G5192** for the fig itself (Matt. 7:16). The fruit can be referred to also with Hebrew *bikkûrâ* **H1136** (Isa. 28:4) and *pag* **H7001** (only Cant. 2:13) and with Greek *olynthos* **G3913** (only Rev. 6:13). The land of Palestine was described as "a land with wheat and barley, vines and fig trees" (Deut. 8:8).

The fig is first mentioned in Gen. 3:7, when ADAM and EVE pulled off the leaves in order to make a semblance of a covering. Again and again the fig tree is used by God to indicate the prosperity of the Jewish nation (1 Ki. 4:25; Mic. 4:4). Figs were made into cakes (*dĕbēlâ* **H1811**, 1 Chr. 12:40); ABIGAIL gave 200 cakes of figs to DAVID in HEBRON (1 Sam. 25:18). HEZEKIAH was cured of his illness by a *dĕbēlâ* of figs being laid on the boil, presumably a lump used as a poultice (2 Ki. 20:7; Isa. 38:21). The falling or the destruction of figs is used in the Bible to indicate the Lord's judgment (cf. Isa. 34:4; Jer. 5:17; 8:13; Hos. 2:12; Joel 1:7). Our Lord condemned a fig tree at PASSOVER time on the MOUNT OF OLIVES (Mk. 11:13; Matt. 21:19). This tree should have borne early ripe figs. The Lord would have known whether the tree should have been cropping.

There are today in the Holy Land both cultivated varieties of figs and wild figs. Most modern Israeli gardens contain a trained fig tree. Looked after, it can be 30 ft. tall and strong; growing wild, it will straggle uncontrolled over the rocks and stony places. Figs are shaped generally like pears, though there are rounder varieties. At the farthest end from the stalk there is a small aperture through which a pollinating insect, called the fig wasp, may go. When the ripened fig is eaten, the little somewhat gritty seeds are "felt"—these are indeed the true fruits. The fig is the receptacle that holds them.

In the E, the fig tree produces two definite crops of fruits per season. The normal winter figs ripen in May and June and the summer figs in late August and September. Sometimes, one crop overlaps the other. The baby fruit buds are usually seen in February before the leaves appear in April each year. It is possible to pick fruits over nine or ten months of the year in Palestine. In Europe, and especially in Great Britain, the baby figlets are killed during the winter, and so the first crop is never produced. Fig trees have lived for over 400 years. In the days of PLINY the Elder, there actually were six known varieties.

Young fig trees growing in the drier regions need to be mulched with dung (cf. Lk. 13:8). Even today in Palestine fig trees grow in the corners of vineyards. Fig trees must have grown well in BETHPHAGE, which means "house of figs." A fig tree produces masses of large green leaves and gives ample welcome shade in a hot country. This is the reason one finds a fig planted next to a well. The thick dark shade keeps the water cool. (See *FFB*, 118–19.) See also FLORA (under *Moraceae*).

W. E. SHEWELL-COOPER

figure. This English term is used variously in Bible versions to render several words, such as Hebrew *dĕmût H1952*, "likeness" (Ezek. 8:2). The expression "figure of speech" can translate Greek *paroimia G4231*, "proverb, parable" (Jn. 10:6; cf. also *parabolē G4130* in Heb. 9:9; 11:19 KJV). Special interest attaches to the use of "figure" in the KJV to render Greek *typos G5596*, a term that has a wide range of meanings, such as "mark" (Jn. 20:25), "pattern" (Acts 7:44), and "example" (1 Tim. 4:12). The most important and characteristic usage is in the sense of an event or personage who fulfills a prophetic prefigurement. Such a connotation is involved, for example, in PAUL's statement that ADAM "was a pattern of the one to come" (Rom. 5:14). The English cognate *type* often has been used to translate this usage (cf. NRSV). The compound form *antitypos G531*, "that which corresponds [to something else]," is also rendered "figure" by the KJV (Heb. 9:24; 1 Pet. 3:21).

From such terms, along with the notion of prophetic prefigurement, the whole elaborate system of hermeneutics known as TYPOLOGY was developed. Although the roots of such figurative views were developed in the later Platonic academy, they grew and flourished in the medieval period. The complex exegesis of the Roman Church sought for manifold levels of meaning in the text of the Scriptures. The "types" of Christ, Mary, and others are shown in church art and celebrated in hymns. This interpretation survived the Reformation and appealed to pietist and romanticist alike, and so they have become part of the inheritance of various groups in the modern age. See also INTERPRETATION.

W. WHITE, JR.

figured stone. This phrase is used by the NRSV to render Hebrew *maśkît H5381* in two passages (Lev. 26:1 [with *ʾeben H74*, "stone"]; Num. 33:52). From contextual usage, the word probably refers to religious images carved in relief on flat surfaces (cf. NIV, "carved stone," "carved image"). These, along with other pagan cult objects, were proscribed and to be destroyed. The same Hebrew word is rendered "image" in Ezek. 8:12 (NIV, "idol"), which speaks of idolatrous pictures carved or scratched on walls (cf. v. 10). Such contexts recall numerous religious-magical relief figures on walls of Egyptian tombs and temples, Babylonian boundary markers with reliefs of protective deities and their symbols, and, most specifically, the N Syrian practice of carving mythological scenes on upright stone slabs (cf. W. F. Albright, *Archaeology and the Religion of*

These figures of Amun and Mut from Karnak are examples of figured stone.

Israel [1941], 160). The Hebrew word is also used with other meanings elsewhere (Ps. 73:7; Prov. 18:11; 25:11). See also CARVING; GRAVEN IMAGE; IDOLATRY.   A. BOWLING

figurehead. A carved figure on the prow of a ship. The term is used in connection with the Alexandrian ship on which Paul sailed toward Rome, which had as its insignia the DIOSCURI, that is, Castor and Pollux, the twin sons of ZEUS who were "good luck" deities of sailors (Acts 28:11). There is some uncertainty whether the Greek word (*parasēmos* G4185) should be taken as an adjective (which usually has the negative sense "marked falsely") or, more likely, as a noun meaning "distinguishing mark" (see C. K. Barrett, *A Critical and Exegetical Commentary on the Book of Acts*, 2 vols. [1994–98], 2:1227–28).

filigree. Delicate ornamental work in fine wire, usually GOLD or SILVER. Archaeological finds have demonstrated that filigree work was produced throughout the ANE. Egyptian funerary jewelry provides some of the best examples, with intricate wire reproductions of divine symbols inlaid with glazed beads and semiprecious stones. Although the evidence is less than conclusive, biblical scholars generally agree that some of the settings of the high priest's garments were of gold filigree (*mišbĕṣôt* H5401). These are the settings for the two onyx stones of the shoulder pieces of the EPHOD (Exod. 28:11–14; 39:6), the two settings on the shoulder pieces for the chains that connected the shoulder pieces with the BREASTPIECE (28:13–14, 25; 39:16–18), and the settings for the twelve precious stones of the breastpiece (28:20 [here the pual ptc. of *šābaṣ* H8687]; 39:13). The Hebrew term appears in one other passage, apparently referring to gold thread brocade (Ps. 45:13).   A. C. BOWLING

fillet. This English term is used by the KJV to render Hebrew *ḥāšûq* H3122, referring to the bands or rings binding the pillars of the TABERNACLE, probably close to the capitals (Exod. 36:38). The fillets for the pillars of the court were overlaid with silver (38:10–12, 17, 19), while those for the door pillars were of gold (36:38). The root of the Hebrew word is obscure. The cognate term *ḥiššuq* H3140 means "spoke [of a wheel]" (1 Ki. 7:33), and some contend that the fillets were in reality rods connecting the tops of the pillars, which supplied greater stability and from which the curtains were suspended. There is no solid evidence that rods instead of bands are intended; Exod. 26:32, 37 says nothing about the curtains hanging from rods, whereas hooks are explicitly mentioned. If "bind" or "clasp" (rather than "connect") is indeed the basic idea, the "ring" concept is more suitable (cf. M. Noth, *Exodus* [1962], 217). Perhaps the hooks were attached to the fillets on the pillars. (The KJV has the word "fillet" also for Hebrew *ḥûṭ* H2562 in Jer. 52:21, referring to a "line" used to measure the circumference of the pillars.)   H. M. WOLF

filth. This English word and its cognates are used variously in Bible versions to render several terms, such as Hebrew *ṣōʾâ* H7363, which refers specifically to excrement but is used figuratively of spiritual pollution (e.g., Isa. 4:4). Similarly, Greek *rhyparia* G4864 ("dirt") can mean "moral filth"

(Jas. 1:21). The Scriptures often use such terms to convey the great depravity of sin and its effects. See also CLEAN; UNCLEANNESS.

fine flour. See BREAD II.

fine linen. See LINEN.

finer. KJV term for "refiner, smith" (Prov. 25:4). See REFINE.

finery. This English term, rarely used in Bible versions, renders Hebrew *tipʾeret H9514* ("ornament, splendor") in a passage that describes the beauty of the necklaces, bracelets, and other items that adorned the upper-class women of Jerusalem (Isa. 3:18). God promises that he will replace these luxuries with articles of shame when he judges the city. The NIV uses it also to render *ʿēden H6358* once (2 Sam. 1:24; NRSV, "luxury").

fines. See CRIMES AND PUNISHMENTS III.E.

finger. Although the fingers (Heb. *ʾeṣbaʿ H720*; Gk. *daktylos G1235*) are an extension from the palm, they often stand for the whole hand. Note the parallelism in "your hands are stained with blood, / your fingers with guilt" (Isa. 59:3) and "Praise to the LORD, / who trains my hands for war, / my fingers for battle" (Ps. 144:1). A rare dominant hereditary trait was the possession of extra fingers and toes, such as of the man of great stature at GATH (1 Chr. 20:6).

Priests used a finger to sprinkle the sacrificial blood (Lev. 4:6 et al.). The fingers were used in conversation, as in most cultures, to add to the expression of the mouth: the scoundrel "winks with his eye, / signals with his feet / and motions with his fingers" (Prov. 6:13). Accusation was made, and still is, by pointing (Isa. 58:9). In addition, the finger could be used as a unit of measure (Jer. 52:21). Much of a person's wealth could be carried in rings on his fingers.

REHOBOAM stressed the severity of his yoke upon the people by following the counsel of his young advisers to say, "My little finger is thicker than my father's waist" (1 Ki. 12:10). Jesus complained that the scribes and PHARISEES laid burdens on men's shoulders, even though they themselves were "not willing to lift a finger to move them" (Matt. 23:4). According to the textually uncertain story of the woman taken in adultery, Jesus wrote on the ground with his finger; possibly the writing was a sentence of conviction (Jn. 8:6). Jesus healed a deaf man by putting his fingers into the man's ears (Mk. 7:33). THOMAS refused to believe that Jesus had risen unless he could put his "finger where the nails were" (Jn. 20:25; cf. v. 27).

Special interest attaches to the anthropomorphic expression, "the finger of God," a striking way of referring to God's power (see ANTHROPOMORPHISM). The Egyptian magicians said, after one of the plagues of MOSES which they could not duplicate, "This is the finger of God" (Exod. 8:19), meaning, "This is beyond the power of man to do; it is supernatural; God must be backing Moses and Aaron." The TEN COMMANDMENTS are said to have been written by the finger of God, that is, by some supernatural process, and not by any human hand (Deut. 9:10). The psalmist says that the heavens are "the work of your fingers" (Ps. 8:3), suggesting not only God's power, but also his creative skills. In a miracle God made the fingers of a man's hand to appear and write on the plaster of the wall, pronouncing doom on BELSHAZZAR (Dan. 5:5).

In a very important passage, Jesus is quoted as saying that he was driving out demons "by the finger of God" and that these miracles indicated the arrival of the KINGDOM OF GOD (Lk. 11:20). In the parallel passage in Matthew the words are "by the Spirit of God" (Matt. 12:28). It is possible that Luke preserved the Semitic figure and that Matthew interpreted it so as to bring out clearly the connection between this miracle and his earlier reference to the Holy Spirit (v. 18, citing Isa. 42:1; cf. D. L. Bock, *Luke*, BECNT, 2 vols. [1994–96], 2:1079 n. 21; for a different view, see J. Nolland, *Luke 9:21—18:34*, WBC 35B [1993], 639–40). In either case, Jesus was claiming to have divine power and to inaugurate God's reign in fulfillment of the OT promises. R. L. MIXTER

finger of God. See FINGER.

fining pot. KJV rendering of *maṣrēp H5214* (Prov. 17:3; 27:21; NIV, "crucible"), a melting pot used for refining metals. See REFINE.

fir. This English term (which refers to various evergreen trees of the genus *Abies*) can be used to render several Hebrew words. In the KJV it is normally the translation of *bĕrôš* H1360 (e.g., 1 Ki. 5:8; NIV, "pine"; NRSV, "cypress"). The NIV uses it to render *bĕrôt* H1361, which occurs only once (Cant. 1:17; NRSV, "pine"), and *tidhār* H9329, which occurs twice (Isa. 41:19; 60:13; NRSV, "plane"). Some believe that one or more of these terms refer to the Aleppo pine (*Pinus halepensis*), a tree that grows to a height of 60 ft., bearing short, stalked cones. Able to withstand considerable periods of drought, it is certainly abundant in the hilly areas of Palestine, where its wood is considered almost as valuable as cedar. Other possibilities are *Pinus tinaster* (which grows to a height of 120 ft. and is an important resin-producing tree), *Pinus brutia* (with dark and whorled branches), *Juniperus phoenicea*, and *Cupressus sempervirens* (cf. *FFB*, 162–65). See CYPRESS; JUNIPER; PINE.   W. E. SHEWELL-COOPER

fire. This word is usually the translation of Hebrew *ʾēš* H836 or Greek *pyr* G4786.

I. Instrument of service. Fire was used domestically for cooking, heating, and lighting (cf. baked cakes, Gen. 18:6). On the night of the exodus the Israelites were instructed to eat meat "roasted over the fire" (Exod. 12:8–9). One of the cereal offerings was to be "new grain roasted in the fire" (Lev. 2:14; see SACRIFICE AND OFFERINGS). And when Jesus appeared to his disciples in Galilee after his resurrection, "they saw a fire of burning coals there with fish on it" (Jn. 21:9).

ISAIAH, in rebuking unfaithful Israel, exclaimed, "Here are no coals to warm anyone; / here is no fire to sit by" (Isa. 47:14). When Jesus was before CAIAPHAS, "It was cold, and the servants and officials stood around a fire they had made to keep warm. Peter also was standing with them, warming himself" (Jn. 18:18). And the natives of MALTA "built a fire" for Paul and his shipwrecked fellowmen "because it was raining and cold" (Acts 28:2).

A third domestic service of fire was to give LIGHT. This is reflected in Jesus' parable of the woman who lost her valuable coin: "Does she not light a lamp, sweep the house and search carefully until she finds it?" (Lk. 15:8). Jesus compared his disciples to a lamp that "gives light to everyone in the house" (Matt. 5:15). Fire was used also occupationally, as in processing crude METAL ore: it served the dual purpose of burning out dross and melting the ore to be molded or minted for useful purposes (cf. Exod. 32:24; Num. 31:2–23; Ezek. 22:18–20).

II. Instrument of destruction. Fire was employed as the ultimate means of destroying property and people. In the conquest of Canaan, JOSHUA and the Israelite army burned the cities of JERICHO, AI, and HAZOR, wholly sacrificing the first to God, and they burned the chariots of the Canaanite coalition (Josh. 6:24; 8:19; 11:9, 11). They also killed and burned the whole family of ACHAN (Josh. 7:24–25). Later the men of Judah captured Jerusalem "and set it on fire" (Jdg. 1:8). King NEBUCHADNEZZAR tried to burn the three young Hebrews, SHADRACH, MESHACH, AND ABEDNEGO (Dan. 3:19–28).

Human sacrifice by fire was an ancient practice in some primitive religions. It may have some correlation with ABRAHAM's aborted effort to sacrifice ISAAC (Gen. 22:1–14). It was at times practiced by the Canaanites, for MOSES warned the Israelites not to imitate them: "They even burn their sons and their daughters in the fire as sacrifices to their gods" (Deut. 12:31). He further commanded, "Do not give any of your children to be sacrificed [*lit.*, to make them pass (through fire)] to Molech," one of the heathen divinities (Lev. 18:21). MOLECH (Milcom) was made the national god of the Ammonites, resulting in the contamination of SOLOMON's religion (1 Ki. 11:5–7). Later, Kings AHAZ and MANASSEH both sacrificed their sons to Molech (2 Ki. 16:3; 21:16). In the days from Ahaz to Manasseh, Molech worship was centered in the Valley of HINNOM, where a huge pyre stood (TOPHETH, Isa. 30:33); on it children were sacrificially burned. JOSIAH had it destroyed (2 Ki. 23:10). This place of lowest human degradation served Jesus as a symbol of hell, which he called GEHENNA (Matt. 5:29; NIV, "hell").

III. Emblem of divine presence. Though literal fire is a natural phenomenon, it has a quality of mystery, a factor invariably associated with deity. Consequently, it was an emblem of divine presence to the Hebrews. In the first Scripture reference to fire, as Abraham made sacrifice, "a smoking firepot with a blazing torch appeared and passed between the pieces" (Gen. 15:17). Fire was an emblem of divine presence to Moses in the burning bush; to Israel in the "pillar of fire"; and to Moses and Israel on Mount Sinai when the law was given (Exod. 3:2; 13:21; 19:18). ELIJAH called down fire to consume two contingents of soldiers; and he was taken to heaven by "a chariot of fire and horses of fire" (2 Ki. 1:9–12; 2:11). ELISHA asked God to open his servant's eyes to see the mountain "full of horses and chariots of fire" (2 Ki. 6:17). The most consistent expectancy of God's presence was at the altar at the time when burnt offerings were made. There are more than a hundred references to altar fires in the OT, including laws governing burnt offerings. There are singular instances of divine fire consuming sacrifices offered by Aaron, David, Solomon, and Elijah (Lev. 9:24; 1 Chr. 21:26; 2 Chr. 7:1; 1 Ki. 18:38). Also, a guest angel made a holocaust with the meals offered by GIDEON and MANOAH (Jdg. 6:21; 13:20).

IV. Symbol of divine punishment.

The metaphorical meaning of fire as the WRATH of God is used abundantly throughout the Bible. God's wrath, like fire, was both purifying and punitive. As fire in cooking destroys the harmful enzymes, making food more edible and tasty, and in smelting it burns out the dross and refines the metal for use, so God's wrath conditions man for better use. In Moses' song, God said, "a fire has been kindled by my wrath" (Deut. 32:22). Through JEREMIAH he warned, "my wrath will break out and burn like fire" (Jer. 4:4; cf. 15:14). EZEKIEL spoke of "the fire of my wrath" (Ezek. 22:21 NRSV). ZEPHANIAH said, "In the fire of his jealousy / the whole world will be consumed" (Zeph. 1: 18). And NAHUM warned, "His wrath is poured out like fire" (Nah. 1:6). Moses told the Israelites, "For the LORD your God is a consuming fire, a jealous God" (Deut. 4:24). The invariable use of fire in this sense is punitive, whether literal or figurative. SODOM and GOMORRAH were destroyed by "sulfur and fire from the LORD" (Gen. 19:24 NRSV). Fire from the Lord consumed 250 rebellious Levites who were making unauthorized offerings (Num. 16:35).

The unquenchable fire, the final reward of the wicked, was proclaimed by the prophets and emphasized by Jesus and John. Isaiah declared, "their worm will not die, nor will their fire be quenched" (Isa. 66:24; cf. Ezek. 20:47). John said that the one who was coming after him would baptize the people "with the Holy Spirit and with fire" and that he would "clear his threshing floor, gathering the wheat into the barn and burning up the chaff with unquenchable fire" (Matt. 3:11–12; cf. "tongues of fire" in Acts 2:3). Jesus himself said, "Every tree that does not bear good fruit is cut down and thrown into the fire" (Matt. 7:19), and stated that his mission was "to bring fire on the earth" (Lk. 12:49). Jesus solemnly warned people not "to go into hell, where the fire never goes out" (Mk. 9:43).

G. B. FUNDERBURK

fire, lake of. See LAKE OF FIRE.

fire, pillar of. See PILLAR OF FIRE AND OF CLOUD.

firebrand. This English term occurs seldom in the OT, being used variously to render several Hebrew words, such as *zēq H2415*, referring to some kind of flaming missile (only Prov. 26:18; for other Hebrew words, see Job 41:19 NIV; Isa. 7:4; 50:11 NRSV).

fire offering. See SACRIFICE AND OFFERINGS.

firepan. A container for carrying live or dead coals. The Hebrew term (*maḥtâ H4746*) refers to objects that had three different functions in the SACRIFICE and WORSHIP of the OT. (1) Firepans were used to carry coals to and from the ALTAR of burnt offering (Exod. 27:3; 38:3; Num. 4:14). (2) The containers could also be used in combination with the snuffers of the golden lampstand (see CANDLESTICK, GOLDEN), probably as receptacles to catch the pieces of burned wick (Exod. 25:38; 37:23; Num. 4:9; KJV, "snuff dishes"; NIV and NRSV, "trays"). (3) Finally, the Hebrew term could refer to a CENSER (Lev. 10:1; 16:12; Num. 16:6; et al.). In some passages it is difficult to determine which of these specific usages is meant (1 Ki. 7:50; 2 Ki. 25:15;

2 Chr. 4:22; Jer. 52:19), although firepans for carrying coals are probably intended (esp. in the latter case, where the terms in the list are the same as in Exod. 27:3; 38:3; Num. 4:14). F. W. BUSH

firkin fuhr´kin. A unit of capacity (approx. 9 gallons). The term is used by the KJV once to render Greek *metrētēs* G2445 (Jn. 2:6). See WEIGHTS AND MEASURES III.C.

firmament. The traditional rendering in the English versions for Hebrew *rāqiaʿ* H8385, a difficult word that seems to suggest beaten metal plate (cf. the verb *rāqaʿ* H8392, piel "to hammer out," Exod. 39:3 et al.; however, the qal is simply "to spread out," used of divine creation in Ps. 136:6; Isa. 42:5; 44:24. The Hebrew word is used only with reference to the sky (Gen. 1:6–8 et al.), viewed apparently as an "expanse" (NIV) or "vault" (RSV) or "dome" (NRSV). Numerous authors have assumed that the use of this term indicated a specific system of ANE COSMOGONY involving a hollow concavity of the celestial sphere. While Genesis does indicate that the firmament was formed to separate the mass of waters and divide them into two layers, little can be inferred from that. The name God gave to the firmament was *šāmayim* H9028, "heaven" or "sky" (Gen. 1:8). The SEPTUAGINT rendered *rāqiaʿ* with Greek *stereōma* G5106 ("solidity, foundation, firmness, steadfastness"; cf. Col. 2:5), which was in turn rendered *firmamentum* by JEROME in the VULGATE, and thus "firmament" in the KJV. The firmament is mentioned always in the context of CREATION: nine times in the Genesis account, but also in the Psalms and the Prophets (Pss. 19:1; 150:1; Ezek. 1:22–26; 10:1; Dan. 12:3). It seems probable that the Hebrew term reflects everyday experience in the human perception of nature: the firmament is thus simply the place where God put the sun, moon, and stars, and where birds fly (Gen. 1:14–17, 20). (See detailed discussion in R. C. Newman, *The Biblical Firmament: Vault or Vapor* [2000].) W. WHITE, JR.

first and last. See ALPHA AND OMEGA.

firstborn. This term (Heb. *bĕkōr* H1147; Gk. *prōtotokos* G4758) normally means the oldest son (Exod. 6:14; 11:5). He enjoyed prerogatives over his brothers, like receiving the father's blessing (Gen. 27:1–4, 35–37), preferential treatment by the father (43:33), respect as leader among the brothers (37:22), and a double portion of the INHERITANCE, twice what any other son received (Deut. 21:17). The firstborn might barter away his rights, as did ESAU (Gen. 25:29–34), or forfeit them for misconduct, as did REUBEN by incest (35:22; 49:3–4; 1 Chr. 5:1). The Lord claimed the firstborn of humans and animals for himself (Exod. 13:1–16). Such animals were sacrificed, while the sons were redeemed, since God did not tolerate child sacrifice as in heathen customs (13:11–15). Levites as a group were designated for special service to the Lord in lieu of the firstborn (Num. 3:12–13; 8:16–18). (See R. deVaux, *Ancient Israel* [1961], 41–42; *NIDOTTE*, 1:658–59.) In the NT, Jesus is called the firstborn son of Mary (Lk. 2:7), who was a virgin before his birth, but who had other sons after him (Mk. 6:3; cf. Jn. 7:5).

Sometimes the meaning is figurative, denoting priority or supremacy. Israel was God's "firstborn son" (Exod. 4:22; Jer. 31:9). As the firstborn son had special priority, so Israel was privileged over other nations. Christ is the "firstborn" of the Father (Heb. 1:6), having preeminent position over others in relation to him. He is "firstborn among many brothers" (Rom. 8:29), that is, sovereign above those related to him in the new creation. He is "the firstborn of all creation" (Col. 1:15 NRSV), a statement misunderstood by the Arians of the 4th cent. and modern-day Jehovah's Witnesses, who make him a created being and not God. The proper meaning is that Christ, truly God, stands in a relationship of priority or sovereignty over all creation (see, e.g., J. B. Lightfoot, *Saint Paul's Epistles to the Colossians and to Philemon* [1879], 146–47).

This second meaning is correct because: (1) Christ is himself creator of all (Col. 1:16); (2) he is prior to all, having existed before creation (v. 17), and also supreme over it; (3) only this view that he is God would combat the Gnostic error Paul answers, for they made Christ only a created emanation from God, and such a concession by PAUL would play into their hands; (4) rabbis called God himself "firstborn" as the supreme being, the "firstborn of the world" (R. Bechai, cited by Lightfoot, 147); (5) Paul claims the fullness of deity for Christ elsewhere (2:9; Tit. 2:13). Paul further says that Christ is "firstborn from among the dead" (Col. 1:18; cf. also John in Rev. 1:5). Certain others arose from the dead before Jesus did, but they later died again. He was first to rise bodily from the grave to immortality, and he is also the one supreme over those in this class. He is the FIRSTFRUITS of the RESURRECTION (1 Cor. 15:20). (Cf. *NIDNTT*, 1:664–70.) See also BIRTHRIGHT; COLOSSIANS, EPISTLE TO THE; DEITY OF CHRIST; FAMILY; GNOSTICISM. J. E. ROSSCUP

first day of the week. See LORD'S DAY.

firstfruits. This term (Heb. *bikkûrîm* H1137, also *rēʾšît* H8040; Gk. *aparchē* G569 [LXX often *prōtogenēma*]) is used both literally, referring to the fruit that is gathered first during the HARVEST, and figuratively.

I. Literal. Just as the FIRSTBORN of humans and cattle were sacred to the Lord, so also the first production of a vineyard (Lev. 19:23–25) and the first of the annual production of grain, wine, olive oil, sheared wool (Exod. 23:16; 34:22; Deut. 18:4), and the first of coarse meal (Num. 15:20–21), of honey, and of all the produce of the land (2 Chr. 31:5; cf. Prov. 3:9) were the Lord's. An offering of new grain was presented to the Lord on "the day of firstfruits," that is, the Feast of Weeks or Pentecost (Num. 28:26; cf. Exod. 23:16; 34:22; see FEASTS). In a few passages (Exod. 23:19; 34:26; Ezek. 44:30), the two Hebrew terms mentioned above occur in a combined expression, but no clear distinction appears to be made. The priest benefited from the firstfruits (Num. 18:12). The offering was brought in a basket to the sanctuary for presentation (Deut. 26:1–11).

Firstfruits of twenty barley loaves and of fresh ears of grain supplied ELISHA with resources to feed a hundred men (2 Ki. 4:42). Firstfruits were given to priests in HEZEKIAH's time (2 Chr. 31:5) and pledged in NEHEMIAH's day (Neh. 10:35). Officials were appointed to oversee store chambers in which to store them (Neh. 12:44; 13:31). The firstfruits were included in EZEKIEL's plans for worship (Ezek. 44:30; 48:14).

Though the NT has no provision for the paying of firstfruits, the community from which the DIDACHE arose paid firstfruits of the winepress, threshing floor, oxen, sheep, bread, newly opened jars of wine and oil, money, clothes, and all possessions to the prophets as being the high priests; in the absence of prophets, they gave the firstfruits to the poor (*Did.* 13.3).

II. Metaphorical. The OT custom lends itself naturally to becoming a metaphor for that which is first and best. The term is used only metaphorically in the NT. The way for such a use may have been prepared by JEREMIAH, who calls Israel the firstfruits of God's harvest (Jer. 2:3; cf. Hos. 9:10; *1 Clem.* 29.3). Paul, speaking of the Jewish people, says that what is "offered as firstfruits is holy," possibly referring to Jewish Christians (Rom. 11:16; cf. Num. 15:20–21 and see T. R. Schreiner, *Romans*, BECNT [1998], 600). For James, Christians are the firstfruits of God's creatures (Jas. 1:18), and in Rev. 14:4 those who follow the Lamb are described as "firstfruits to God and the Lamb." Christ is the firstfruits of them that slept (1 Cor. 15:20, 23; cf. *1 Clem.* 24.1); EPENETUS was the firstfruits in ASIA (Rom. 16:5; NIV, "the first convert to Christ"); and the household of STEPHANAS, the firstfruits in ACHAIA (1 Cor. 16:15; cf. *1 Clem.* 42.4). The present blessings experienced by believers are the firstfruits of the HOLY SPIRIT (Rom. 8:23), an indication of that which is to come. In the *Epistle of Barnabas* (1.7), prophecy is said to give the firstfruits of the taste of things to come. (See J. Pedersen, *Israel: Its Life and Culture*, 2 vols. [1926–40], 2:300ff.; *NIDNTT*, 3:415–17.) See also SACRIFICE AND OFFERINGS. J. P. LEWIS

fish. The common Hebrew term for "fish" is *dāg* H1834 (also *dāgâ* H1836). In the NT, Greek *ichthys* G2716 is the standard term, but the diminutive *ichthydion* G2715 occurs twice (Matt. 15:34=Mk. 8:7), and John prefers *opsarion* G4066 (for fish about to be eaten; in classical writers it may also mean "cooked food").

Fishing remains to this day a very important part of Israel's life and economy, as it has been from biblical times. In 2000, the total fish catch, both freshwater and marine, was 5,818 tons.

I. Species available. The Hebrew terms, though always translated "fish," may also cover shellfish,

Tilapia are mouthbreeders, protecting their eggs and young by taking them into their mouths.

crustaceans, etc., and even sea mammals. The words for "fish" are not used in the food laws of Lev. 11:9–12 and Deut. 14:9–10. The latter is more concise, "Of all the creatures living in the water, you may eat any that has fins and scales." This rule excludes all aquatic invertebrates, some of which are tasty and nutritious, but can easily cause food poisoning; also marine mammals, of which the dugong was once common in the RED SEA (see SEA COW) and the monk seal rare in the Mediterranean; sharks, which are cartilaginous fish with rough skin but no scales; and eels, including moray eel, which was later a favorite Roman food. The catfish (*Clarias lazera*) of Galilee might also have been avoided, but this still left several excellent eating lake fishes, in particular the *Tilapia* species. Known as St. Peter's fish, it is now too expensive for any but the luxury trade. These fish are mouthbreeders, of a family well known to aquarists—*Cichlidae*. The barbels (*Barbus canis* and *B. longiceps*) are also native to these waters. In modern times the gray mullet (*Mugil cephalus*) from the brackish estuary waters of the Mediterranean has been successfully introduced. The small fishes of Matt. 14:17 and 15:36 cannot be identified but can be assumed to have come from the lake. Many small fish are salted and dried, and either stored for future use or used for eating as described. The most common is the lake sardine (*Acanthobrama terrae sanctae*), of which large quantities are canned.

II. Fishing method

A. Nets. The *cast net* (*amphiblēstron* G312, Matt. 4:18) is usually taken to be the net thrown by hand. It is circular, with small weights around the perimeter, and thrown so as to fall flat on the surface, enclosing a shoal. It is still used widely in Africa and parts of Asia; also occasionally on the lake for benefit of tourists! It is uneconomical where labor is expensive.

The *gill net* is perhaps the best modern equivalent of *diktyon* G1473 (Matt. 4:20), and is still used for catching medium-sized tilapia and other species. Long nets, supported on floats, hang near the surface, usually through the night, and are hauled up the following day. This net is used in a passive way and takes fish only of one approximate size; the smaller pass through and the larger cannot insert their heads. This is mostly used well out in the lake and at sea, and fish are brought ashore by boat.

The term *sagēnē* G4880 refers to the *drag net*. As described figurative in Matt. 13:47–48, this would better fit a modern seine net several hundred yards long, which is taken by boat around a semicircle and then both ends are hauled in to the shore. All kinds and sizes of fish were taken and then sorted. Much time ashore was occupied with net maintenance including washing (Lk. 5:2), spreading and drying (Ezek. 47:10), and mending (Matt. 4:21). Much of this work is now greatly lightened by using artificial (drip-dry) filaments and machine-made nets. See also NET.

B. Hook and line. Isaiah speaks of the fishermen "who cast hooks [*ḥakkâ* H2676] into the Nile" (Isa. 19:8). The Hebrew term is found elsewhere (Job 41:1; differently in Hab. 1:15). Although the contexts are figurative, such technical terms confirm that the method was general. Jesus' words to Peter,

Fishermen in the early 20th cent. pulling in a drag net.

"go to the sea and cast a hook; take the first fish that comes up" (Matt. 17:27 NRSV), could refer to a baited hook or to another method still used by children in Galilee. A large triangle of sharp unbaited hooks, perhaps two inches across, tied on a long cord, is thrown into a shoal and snatched, sometimes hooking a fish. A watersnake may be caught by mistake, a problem perhaps alluded to in Jesus' comment, "Which of you fathers, if your son asks for a fish, will give him a snake instead?" (Lk. 11:11).

C. Fish spear. Referring to the CROCODILE, God says to JOB, "Can you fill his hide with harpoons / or his head with fishing spears?" (Job 41:7). This method, however, was more often used in shallow water for taking fish. Fish-spearing from a PAPYRUS raft is illustrated in a painting in the tomb of Simut at Thebes c. 1500 B.C. In spring the large tilapia are vulnerable to such weapons when they enter the reed beds to spawn, but in such areas they are usually taken undamaged in trammel nets. See also OCCUPATIONS.

III. Fishing regions

A. Inland Palestine. Through much of its history, Israel had control over the whole Lake of Galilee, but this body of water has little mention in the OT, and nothing is said about its fish. In the Gospels, largely because much of the Lord's ministry was based on its shore, it is important, and the word for "sea" (*thalassa G2498*) was commonly applied to it (see GALILEE, SEA OF). At least seven disciples were fishermen, and lake fishing receives special emphasis. Except for the carp (*Cyprinus carpio*), which may escape from fishponds and reach the lake, where they grow big, and the gray mullet (see above), the species are the same as when PETER took them. Including those already listed, there are at least twenty-five species.

Intensive cultivation, with manuring, in parts of the Jordan Valley makes nutrient salts available in the drainage water, and fish growth should be faster. Since World War II much research has been done and modern methods introduced, including production of fry. For much of its passage through Upper Galilee, the JORDAN is fast-flowing and unsuitable for fishing. The yield from this river and others, subject to rapid rise and fall, would have been very small. Until about 1950 the Lake of Huleh, though partly silted up, was still a useful fishing ground; this is now drained, but the fishponds that ring the reclaimed area much more than make up for the loss.

B. Marine. Varying lengths of the Mediterranean coastline were occupied by the Israelites, but they were never a seafaring people and most maritime shipping mentioned in the OT and NT was foreign-owned. Any fishing they did was probably close inshore. "Men from Tyre who lived in Jerusalem were bringing in fish and all kinds of merchandise and selling them in Jerusalem on the Sabbath to the people of Judah" (Neh. 13:16). This was presumably sea fish from the Phoenician coast, and because of distance it must have been preserved by salting, drying, smoking, etc. For several reasons, especially the narrow coastal shelf with shallow water, the Mediterranean is generally poor fishing ground, and even with modern methods its potential is low. Half of the catch is sardines. At several periods, especially during the reigns of SOLOMON and JEHOSHAPHAT, Israel had access to the Red Sea, where a range of tropical fish is found, but these could have been only of local value.

C. Egypt. The Israelites looked back from the desert and longed for the fish they had enjoyed in Egypt (Num. 11:5). The NILE fish were killed by the first plague, and this was enough to pollute even a river of such great volume. The Nile has always been a major source of food, and various methods of fishing are illustrated in ancient Egyptian art. The dense population of lower Egypt and its intensive cultivation greatly increased the area of channels available for fish, as well as making the water more fertile. Over 100 species are recorded for lower Nile, many of them edible, including carp, perch, and cichlids. This fauna has changed little since OT times.

D. Fishponds. The SONG OF SOLOMON contains a reference to "the pools of Heshbon" (Cant. 7:4). The old Moabite city of HESHBON is in TRANS-

JORDAN, more or less level with the N point of the DEAD SEA, and excavation has revealed remains of pools and conduits, so the Hebrews probably practiced some form of fish farming. This was known early in other lands; fishponds have been found in ancient Mesopotamia and Egypt, and they are illustrated in Assyrian reliefs. Romans became experts and developed methods of raising several species of sea fish including mullet, wrasse, and, above all, moray eels. This work needs a high degree of skill. The Romans also made fresh water ponds in occupied countries, and the monks' "fish-stews" of Europe were their successors. There is no evidence about the fish kept in these ponds in Palestine. Fish-farming has become an important industry in modern Israel, where the climate allows a fairly long growing season. It produces mostly carp and much of it for the Passover market. This is an ideal pond fish, which probably originated in E Europe, but it was not used extensively for this purpose until the Middle Ages. (See *FFB*, 26–27.)

IV. Figurative use. Of various Hebrew words for "net," at least three refer to types of fish nets, and all contexts are figurative (e.g., of evil intent, "each hunts his brother with a net," Mic. 7:2). Fishing imagery is used to give warnings of judgment: "The time will surely come / when you will be taken away with hooks, / the last of you with fishhooks" (Amos 4:2). The metaphors are different in the NT: "I will make you fishers of men" (Matt. 4:19). The kingdom of heaven is compared to a drag or seine net (13:47). The fish became a symbol in early Christian art, almost a code word, because Greek *ichthys* (ΙΧΘΥΣ) spelled out the initials of a simple creed, *Iēsous Christos theou huios sōtēr*, "Jesus Christ, God's Son, Savior."

V. Fish in worship. God expressly forbids making an image of fish (Deut. 4:18). The fishtailed deity shown on coins found at ASHKELON is identified with ATARGATIS the fish goddess, whose cult originated in SYRIA and was spread by merchants. It does not seem to have been practiced by the Israelites at any stage. The often repeated statement that DAGON (1 Sam. 5:2–7) was a fish deity has no strong foundation. G. S. CANSDALE

Fish Gate. An entrance on the N wall of JERUSALEM. King MANASSEH is said to have "rebuilt the outer wall of the City of David, west of the Gihon spring, as far as the entrance of the Fish Gate and encircling the hill of Ophel" (2 Chr. 33:14). After the EXILE, "The Fish Gate was rebuilt by the sons of Hassenaah. They laid its beams and put its doors and bolts and bars in place" (Neh. 3:3; see HASSENAAH). It was apparently located between the JESHANAH GATE and the Tower of HANANEL, and one of the choirs proceeded past it at the dedication of the walls (12:39). It presumably obtained its name from a fish market nearby (cf. 13:16). Elsewhere it is mentioned with the Mishneh or SECOND DISTRICT of the city (Zeph. 1:10).

The majority of scholars in the past held that the Fish Gate stood at the N end of the Tyropoeon (Central) Valley in the NW wall of the city (so J. Simons, *Jerusalem in the Old Testament* [1952], 291 n. 3, though M. Avi-Yonah, in *IEJ* 4 [1954]: 242, identified it with the EPHRAIM GATE). Later excavations, however, have indicated that the wall did not extend to the N end of the valley until about the 1st cent. B.C., and so the Fish Gate was likely near the NW corner of the temple mount (see N. Avigad, *Discovering Jerusalem* [1980], 54; D. Bahat, *The Illustrated Atlas of Jerusalem* [1990], maps on pp. 30, 31, 36). F. W. BUSH

fishhook. This English term is used by the NIV and other versions to render Hebrew *ḥakkâ* H2676 once (Job 41:1; cf. also in v. 2 the word *ḥôaḥ* H2560, which usually means "thorn, thistle"). The Hebrew word occurs in two other passages (Isa. 19:8; Hab. 1:15), where it is translated simply "hook," though the reference is certainly to fishing. In addition, the expression *sîrôt dûgâ* (H6106 + H1855), meaning literally "thorns for fishing," is properly translated "fishhooks." This method of fishing was widely used in the ancient world, although it was not an important industry in Palestine. See FISH.

fish pool. The KJV rendering of Hebrew *bĕrēkâ* H1391 (Cant. 7:4), which simply means "pond, pool."

fitches. This English term (which in modern usage refers to the polecat, a mammal of the weasel family) is used by the KJV in the sense of "vetch," an herb (Isa. 28:25, 27; Ezek. 4:9). In the first passage it renders Hebrew *qeṣaḥ H7902*, which possibly refers to the black CUMMIN (see also CARAWAY). In the second it mistakenly renders Hebrew *kussemet H4081*, which refers to a grain (elsewhere translated "rie" by the KJV, Exod. 9:32; Isa. 28:25b; see SPELT).

flag. This English term, in the sense of a plant that has long leaves, is used by the KJV in three passages, rendering Hebrew words that are better translated "reed" or "rush" (*sûp H6068* in Exod. 2:3, 5; Isa. 19:6; *ʾāḥû H286* in Job 8:11).

flagon. A large vessel used for holding liquors. The NRSV uses it several times, usually to render Hebrew *qaśwâ H7987* (NIV, "pitcher" or "jar"; Exod. 25:29 et al.; in Esth. 1:8 the NRSV translates freely). Both the NRSV and the KJV have it once as the rendering of the synonymous term *nēbel H5574* (Isa. 22:24). In addition, the KJV uses it wrongly several times (2 Sam. 6:19; 1 Chr. 16:3; Cant. 2:5; Hos. 3:1) to translate *ʾăšîšâ H862*, which really means "raisin cake."

flagstaff. Term used by the NIV and other modern versions to render *tōren H9568* in one passage where God warns the people that they will flee until they are left "like a flagstaff on a mountaintop, / like a banner on a hill" (Isa. 30:17). The Hebrew term apparently could refer to poles of various kinds, for in its other two occurrences it clearly means "mast [of a ship]" (Isa. 33:23; Ezek. 27:5).

flask. A small container, usually with a narrow neck. The term is occasionally used by English versions, for example, to render Hebrew *pak H7095* ("small jug, vial"), which occurs in two passages (1 Sam. 10:1; 2 Ki. 9:1, 3), or Greek *angeion G31*, used once with reference to jars of oil (Matt. 25:4 NRSV).

flat nose. The KJV translation of Hebrew *ḥārum*, used only once to describe one of the conditions that rendered a man unfit for priestly service (Lev. 21:18). This term, not used elsewhere, can be understood as an adjective or as the passive participle of a verb *ḥāram H3050*, possibly meaning "to split, perforate" (cf. the postbiblical refs. in M. Jastrow, *A Dictionary of the Targumim* . . . [1903] 1:503, and note the name HARUMAPH; G. R. Driver, in *JTS* 32 [1931]: 251, argued that the verb occurs in Isa. 11:15). Some believe the word refers to the condition that often accompanies a cleft palate. The NRSV renders it, "one who has a mutilated face"; NIV simply, "disfigured."
F. W. BUSH

flax. Although this term is applied to any of the plants of the genus *Linum*, it usually refers specifically to *Linum usitatissimum*, which grows 2–4 ft. high and bears beautiful blue flowers (there are occasionally white varieties). Flax has been cultivated from very ancient times for its textile fiber, from which LINEN cloth is produced. The plants were grown until they were ripe, when they were pulled up whole and laid out to dry. To lose a crop of flax was serious, and could be one of God's punishments (Hos. 2:9). The capsules of flax are called *bols*, and the bolled flax is the mature flax, ready for harvesting and drying. Bundles of flax are soaked in water for three or four weeks, a process that causes what is called *retting* (i.e., the fibers separate, and it is only then that the threads can be combed). The usual Hebrew term for "flax" is *pēšet H7324* (e.g., Josh. 2:6; cf. the cognate *pištâ H7325* in Exod. 9:31), which can also be rendered "linen" (e.g., Lev. 13:47–48). The corresponding Greek term is *linon G3351*, used especially of products made from flax, such as a lamp-wick (Matt. 12:20, citing Isa. 42:3) and linen garments (Rev. 15:6). (See *FFB*, 119–21.)

Flax was certainly grown in Palestine before the arrival of the Israelites, for RAHAB hid the two spies under the stems of flax she had drying on the flat roof of her house (Josh. 2:1, 6). The cloth made from local-grown flax would have been welcomed by the Jews, whose clothes, after their long trek, might have been wearing out. SOLOMON congratulates a good wife who separates the fibers of the flax and makes fine linen (Prov. 31:13). It appears that white cloth and thin white linen were made in Israel (Isa. 19:9). The Egyptians knew about growing flax. PHARAOH gave JOSEPH fine linen robes (Gen. 41:42), and after the Israelites had escaped from Egypt and had "plundered the Egyptians"

(Exod. 12:36), they were able to make fine linen priestly garments for AARON and his sons (Lev. 16:4). Solomon knew the value of linen and seems to have made it a state monopoly. Linen was used also as sails for yachts (Ezek. 27:7). In the NT, linen towels and napkins are mentioned (Jn. 11:44; 13:4). Linen also was used for the wrappings of dead bodies (Mk. 15:46). Of course, the best linen was used for wrapping the body of our Lord, while the church—the bride of the risen Lord—is arrayed in fine linen (Rev. 19:8), and the angels themselves are robed in "clean, shining linen" also (15:6).

W. E. SHEWELL-COOPER

flea. This term (referring to *Pulex irritans*) occurs in the Bible only twice as the rendering of Hebrew *parʿōš* H7282 (1 Sam. 24:14; 26:20; some scholars emend the latter verse to "my soul" on the basis of the LXX). These are metaphorical passages in which DAVID refers to himself as a small and insignificant insect being pursued by King SAUL. Fleas (*Pulex* and *Ctenocephalides* species) belong to a small and highly specialized insect family. The adults are bloodsuckers, and each species normally concentrates on one host. The larvae are not parasitic but live on rubbish, so that human species thrive where there is dirt. In the dry conditions of Palestine, fleas often swarm and may be regarded with indifference by the local folk. Besides causing much discomfort, fleas can transmit several diseases, in particular bubonic PLAGUE.

G. S. CANSDALE

fleece. The coat of wool freshly sheared from a SHEEP. It is the rendering of the cognate terms *gēz* H1600 (which can also refer to mown grass, Ps. 72:6; Amos 7:1) and *gizzâ* H1603 (both nouns derive from the verb *gāzaz* H1605, "to shear, cut," Gen. 31:19 et al.). GIDEON requested that a fleece be covered with morning dew while the ground remained dry (and then the opposite) as a sign that God intended to deliver Israel through him (Jdg. 6:36–40). The first wool from the shearing is specified as one of the FIRSTFRUITS due to the Levitical priests (Deut. 18:4). Job could testify that he had warmed the needy "with the fleece from my sheep" (Job 31:20).

F. W. BUSH

fleet. See SHIPS.

flesh. This term, which refers literally to bodily tissue and to animal meat, is often used figuratively in the Bible and plays a significant role in theological formulations.

I. In the OT. The usual Hebrew word for "flesh" is *bāśār* H1414 (Gen. 2:21 and frequently), though another noun, *šeʾēr* H8638, occurs with the same meaning in several poetic passages (cf. esp. the parallelism of the two words in Prov. 5:11). In addition, the KJV uses "flesh" to render *ṭibḥâ* H3186 ("meat, slaughtering") in one verse (1 Sam. 25:11). (See *NIDOTTE*, 1:777–79; 4:17–18.)

A. Literal usage. The word *bāśār* has cognates in other Semitic languages, and the meaning embraced such concepts as flesh and blood or a family relationship by blood. Its earliest connotation may have been that of the flesh immediately beneath the skin, but this is uncertain. In common usage the word signified the soft muscular tissues of the BODY, both of people (e.g., Gen. 2:21; 2 Ki. 5:14) and of animals (Gen. 41:2; Deut. 14:8). Such organic bodies were still regarded as flesh even when dead (1 Sam. 17:44), and only lost their characteristics when they returned to the earth in the form of dust (Eccl. 12:7). All OT writers based their concept of flesh in a literal sense on the words of Gen. 2:7 and 7:22, which describe flesh as the clay (the "dust" of the English versions) from the ground which had been made to live as the result of divine creativity. Animal flesh alone could be used for food (9:4; 40:19; et al.), and the hygienic prescriptions of the Mosaic law (Lev. 11:2–47) made a careful distinction between animals and birds which were fit for food and those which, because of their particular eating habits, were unsuitable for human consumption.

Although the term *šeʾēr* was far less frequently used in the OT, it was nevertheless of considerable antiquity (cf. Akk. *šīru*). Some have thought that, in distinction from *bāśār*, this word referred to the inner organic tissues of the body that were richly supplied with blood vessels and therefore bled profusely when seriously damaged. In actual biblical usage, however, *šeʾēr* too denoted the body or flesh in general (Prov. 11:17 KJV; Mic. 3:2), or the whole constituent human being (Ps. 73:26;

Prov. 5:11). With reference to the animal creation, it also denoted meat to be used as food (Exod. 21:10; Ps. 78:20, 27).

B. Metaphorical use. Aside from their purely literal incidence, these terms were generally employed in *synecdoche* as a means of referring to the human body either partially or as a whole. Synecdoche is a rhetorical form based on contiguity and, as the Greek name implies, involves the understanding of one element or concept simultaneously with another. Thus the individual can be substituted for the class, the more general for the less general, the concrete for the abstract, and so on. In this sense the word "flesh" could denote humanity in a comprehensive sense, and by extension the expression "all flesh" could include the animal creation (Gen. 6:13 [NIV, "all people"]; Lev. 17:14 [NIV, "every creature"]).

Similarly, the concept of "flesh" served as an acceptable substitute for the human personality, since the body constituted its spatio-temporal extension (Job 19:26; Ps. 16:9). This use was thoroughly consistent with the tradition of creativity, for we are told that God breathed the living breath into the clay he had fashioned into human shape and that thereby man became a *nepeš ḥayyâ* (Gen. 2:7). This expression is usually rendered "living soul" or "living being," but the true emphasis of the Hebrew is not so much upon "soul" or "existence" as upon the fact that, by virtue of special creativity, man is an integrated living personality. See SOUL. For this reason the ancient Hebrews found no difficulty whatever in attributing emotional or psychosomatic functions to bodily organs other than the brain (whose workings were unknown to them), because the fact that the individual constituted an integrated personality meant that psychic and somatic functions necessarily interpenetrated one another at the various levels of existence.

This realization, which was expressed widely and in differing ways in the OT writings, has formed the basis of modern psychosomatic medical research. It need occasion no surprise, therefore, to discover that under this figure of rhetoric the "flesh" could be used to designate the personality in its total reaction to life (Ps. 63:1), where the psalmist parallels the idea of the soul thirsting with the flesh fainting. By extending the psychosomatic concept in a particular direction and fixing it upon one of the internal organs that gave vitality to the "flesh" or personality, it was possible in poetic thought to conceive of the "heart and flesh" singing for joy (84:2). By contrast, the heart of the psalmist had been stricken within him, so that his knees became weak with fasting and his body gaunt with hunger (109:23–24). Because of his physical appearance his enemies knew that he was enduring emotional and spiritual affliction. The author of LAMENTATIONS complained that the outpouring of divine anger had made his flesh and his skin waste away and had broken his bones (Lam. 3:4), implying that affliction had brought his entire personality to a low level of expression.

The term *flesh* was used also in this same figurative sense as a euphemism for parts of the human body that were associated with sexual activity. The reference to the normal menstruation of the female is directed to the functioning of the womb (Lev. 15:19). In another reference to a bodily discharge (15:2–3, 7), the term *bāśār* alludes to the male genitalia (cf. also Ezek. 16:26; 23:20) and to a venereal secretion, as contrasted with the benign emissions (15:16–18). Such euphemisms are seen also in the substitution of "hands" and "feet" for the male or female genitalia (e.g., Deut. 28:57; possibly also Ruth 3:4; 1 Ki. 15:23; Isa. 6:2; et al.). The circumcising of the "flesh" is a more familiar way of

The reckless lifestyle of the sinful flesh is often pictured on Greek drinking vessels that were used at orgies.

avoiding a direct reference to the *membrum virile* (Gen. 17:14 et al.).

A second figurative use of the term "flesh" involved another rhetorical device, *metonymy*, which is somewhat different from synecdoche. Instead of naming the thing itself, metonymy describes it in terms of some significant accompaniment or adjunct; whereas in synecdoche the name substituted is generally cognate in meaning, in metonymy the meaning is often less closely related to the substituted term. In the latter figure the instrument can do duty for the agent, the container for the thing contained, the maker for the thing made, the name of a passion for the object of desire, and so on. By using this figure, the Hebrews could think of "flesh" in terms of natural or family relationships. Thus ADAM spoke of his helpmeet as specifically "bone of my bones and flesh of my flesh" (Gen. 2:23), and the brothers of JOSEPH expressed the same sentiment (37:27). The combination *šĕʾēr bĕśārô* was employed to express the concept of a somatic relative (Lev. 18:6; 25:49), while *šĕʾēr* was used to designate both sides of family descent (18:12–13). Under the patriarchal system, the unit of natural relationship could reach beyond the family to include the township (Jdg. 9:2) or the people as a whole (2 Sam. 5:1).

C. Theological implications. Although the term *flesh* frequently denotes the vitality of individual personality, there are several instances where human flesh is associated with weakness and frailty. Mortal nature can be implied by the word (Gen. 6:3; cf. Job 34:15), and God is said to withhold his judgment on the ground that human beings were only flesh after all (Ps. 78:39). Flesh as weakness is compared unfavorably with spirit as strength (Isa. 31:3), and the reputed strength of the king of Assyria is described as a mere "arm of flesh," in contrast with the mighty power of God (2 Chr. 32:8). On occasions the use of the expression "all flesh" has direct implications of weakness, for example, when humanity is compared to grass that is frail, short-lived, and easily consumed (Isa. 40:6; cf. Pss. 37:2; 90:5; 103:15). The dependence of "all flesh" upon God for day-to-day sustenance is also emphasized (Ps. 136:25).

From the comprehensive concept of "flesh" as representative of the people (2 Sam. 5:1), it is possible to argue toward the use of *bāśār* along the lines of CORPORATE PERSONALITY. This is by no means out of harmony with other aspects of OT thought, since the COVENANT relationship between God and Israel was based upon this general concept. Consequently, the forgiveness of national sins of inadvertence could be entertained in the Hebrew sacrificial system just as readily as ATONEMENT could for individuals, both procedures not uncommonly involving animal flesh.

The OT theology of human personality, noted above, is of a dynamic order that emphasizes the psychophysical unity of human nature. Although this "flesh" was regarded in the OT as generally weak, there is no single element in Hebrew thought that corresponds to the NT view of the "flesh" as the central principle of fallen humanity. While the flesh for the Hebrews was frail, it was not regarded as sinful, and the nearest approach to the idea of moral weakness seems to be in Ps. 78:39. Salvation for EZEKIEL, however, constituted that regeneration which would replace a stony heart with one of flesh (Ezek. 36:26), and this language contains the idea that the flesh is perverted. (See further A. R. Johnson, *The Vitality of the Individual in the Thought of Ancient Israel* [1964], 37–38; H. W. Wolff, *Anthropology of the Old Testament* [1974], 26–31.)

II. In the NT. There are three basic ways in which the Greek word *sarx* G4922 is used in the NT. At the one extreme are those passages where no negative moral judgment is implied and where the word therefore bears no connotation of evil at all. At the other extreme are those places where a negative moral judgment is made and *sarx* becomes descriptive of the baser nature or is defined as being simply sinful. Bridging the two extremes is a set of uses where the flesh is not represented as sinful per se, but tends in that direction because of its weakness. See HUMAN NATURE.

A. Flesh as not sinful. There are three subdivisions here, and in none is sinfulness implied. First, *sarx* is seen as the physical substance from which human beings are made. The basic and most obvious use is when the meaty or fleshy parts of the body are in view (Rom. 2:28; Col. 2:13; Jas. 5:3; Rev. 19:21), and here flesh may even be distinguished from bones (Lk. 24:39). Men share this with animals, which also are fleshy, but PAUL is careful to say that it is not the same kind of flesh (1 Cor. 15:39). An extension of this idea is where *sarx* describes the body as a whole, physically considered (1 Cor. 15:39; 2 Cor. 7:5; Gal. 6:12–13; Col. 2:1). The flesh is a person's contact with the world at large and other human beings. The term may also be used to describe the physical substance one has inherited from his parents or what unites him with others of like descent (Rom. 4:1; 9:3, 8; Heb. 12:9). Jesus is said by Paul to be united with his ancestors in this way as well (Rom. 1:3; 9:5).

Second, taking the idea of physical substance one step farther, the term *sarx* is used to define humanity as such; that is, corporeality (flesh) and humanity are made to coincide. This idea is not wholly different from the above, but it looks at flesh from the side of humanity rather than as the vehicle in which humanity resides. Flesh becomes in fact an aspect of humanity as such. Here *sarx* becomes a commonplace designation for a human individual or for mankind in general (Mk. 13:20; Lk. 3:6; Acts 2:17; Rom. 3:20; Gal. 2:16). The term is more or less synonymous with person or human being (Jn. 17:2), and the expression "flesh and blood" means human beings (1 Cor. 15:50; Gal. 1:16). Here, too, Jesus is said to take part in our common humanity (Jn. 1:14; 1 Tim. 3:16; Heb. 10:20; 1 Jn. 4:2).

Because our essential being is corporeal, the term *sarx* may be used to set humanity apart from beings who are not physical, but spiritual, whether it be God (Matt. 16:17), or a spirit in the abstract (Lk. 24:39), or spirits concretely (demonic or otherwise, Eph. 6:12). Also, while we are alive we are described as being in the flesh, but after we are gone we no longer have fleshly existence and are presumably as the angels, that is, spiritually existent, until the RESURRECTION of the body (1 Cor. 7:28; Phil. 1:24; Heb. 5:7).

Third, there is the symbolic use of the word *sarx* made by Jesus in Jn. 6:51–56, where eating his flesh means participating in the benefits of his death. In this passage Jesus says that he is the living bread and the one who eats of it shall live forever. He defines that bread as his flesh which is to be given for the life of the world. He then affirms that his flesh, like the living bread, must be eaten in order for a man to live. All of this points symbolically to a genuine participation in the benefits of Christ's self-offering.

B. Flesh as weak. Although the above category implies no necessary or inherent weakness, it tends in that direction. In other passages the flesh is explicitly called "weak" (Matt. 26:41), although the spirit might be willing; that is, the flesh is not always a fit medium through which the higher element of the person may act. The law which tells us of God's requirements is weak not in itself, but because of the flesh (Rom. 8:3); the flesh simply does not cooperate. The flesh is subject to physical infirmity (Gal. 4:13) or may more comprehensively designate the whole person as weak (Rom. 6:19). The flesh is mortal (2 Cor. 4:11), and what is born of flesh (Jn. 3:6)—that is, what is human only— is irreversibly so. It can never be more than it is. The flesh gives rise to pride when one glories in the externals related to it (Phil. 3:4). The flesh is unavailing and ineffectual when it comes to spiritual warfare (2 Cor. 10:3) and cannot add to what God has done by his Spirit (Gal. 3:3). In none of this is there necessarily sin, but the weakness of the flesh is that it cannot, in its present state, fight off temptations and lusts and therefore is the place where sin may make its malevolent entrance into human lives.

C. Flesh as sinful. In this category a negative moral judgment is made. Here the term is used to define a person's lost condition before the life-giving Spirit of God makes his entrance (in the relevant passages, the NIV often uses "sinful nature" to render *sarx*). See HOLY SPIRIT. When we were "in the flesh" we were lost (Rom. 7:5; 8:5–8). Akin to this, in Paul's ALLEGORY concerning HAGAR and SARAH to be "born after the flesh" is to be lost (Gal. 4:29). Because Paul has used the word *sarx* to mean being lost, he is careful to point out that the Christian is not in the flesh, but in the Spirit (Rom. 8:9). A lost person is in the flesh and dominated by sin, thus the ideas of sin and flesh may blend together. The flesh becomes the baser side of a person, defining either the impulse to sin itself or at least the seat of it (Rom. 7:18, 25; 8:5b, 12–13; Gal. 5:17–19; 6:8; 1 Pet. 3:21; 2 Pet. 2:10, 18; 1 Jn. 2:16). See SIN.

In this sense of base nature, the flesh as it were lurks about seeking a chance to break loose and wreak havoc on us (Gal. 5:13). An extension of this correlation of sin and flesh is seen in passages where *sarx* is virtually equated with sin (Jude 23), or where by extension the word functions like an adjective meaning sinful and qualifies other ideas. Hence one may have a fleshly body (*tou sōmatos tēs sarkos*, Col. 2:11) or a fleshly mind (Rom. 8:7; Col. 2:18). The cognate adjectives (*sarkikos* G4920 and *sarkinos* G4921) are used in this way as well, meaning "base" or "sinful" (e.g., Rom. 7:14; 1 Cor. 3:1; 1 Pet. 2:11). Indeed, the flesh may be defined as simply "sinful" (Rom. 8:3). Here too Paul is careful to say that the Christian is not dominated by the flesh. Just as the believer is not in the flesh (8:9), so he has crucified the flesh with its affections and desires (Gal. 5:24). In this connection it is significant that Paul nowhere says the flesh will be resurrected; for him it is the body that will be raised to newness of life (e.g., 1 Cor. 15:44). This is because *sarx* connoted sin to Paul and the word *body* was a more neutral term. The flesh, human fallen nature, will not be raised again.

What is the connection between the conception of flesh as an earthly substance and flesh as debased? The link seems to be sin. Flesh is not sinful per se as made by God, but now, as fallen, the flesh is sinful because all human beings are de facto sinners. It is through the flesh that sin makes its most dramatic entrance (lust), and hence flesh and sin may become almost synonymous terms; but it must be remembered that the mind may generate desires that are sinful too (Eph. 2:3), and that there is uncleanness of the spirit, as well as of the flesh (1 Cor. 7:1). However, the Christian is freed from bondage to the flesh, for although the flesh is contrary to the Spirit attempting to prevent believers from doing what they would (Gal. 5:17), it is fighting a losing battle. To walk in the Spirit is not to do the desire of the crucified flesh (5:16), because we are no longer debtors to the flesh (Rom. 8:12) but alive through the Spirit and heirs of God destined to be glorified together with Christ (8:16–17). (Cf. E. de Witt Burton, *Spirit, Soul and Flesh* [1918]; J. A. T. Robinson, *The Body* [1952], 11–33; W. Barclay, *Flesh and Spirit* [1962]; R. Jewett, *Paul's Anthropological Terms* [1971]; J. W. Cooper, *Body, Soul, and Life Everlasting: Biblical Anthropology and the Monism-Dualism Debate*, rev. ed. [2000]; *NIDNTT*, 1:671–82.)

R. K. Harrison (OT); W. A. Elwell (NT)

fleshhook. KJV rendering of *mazlēg* H4657, "[meat] fork," one of the sacrificial implements used in the TABERNACLE and the TEMPLE (Exod. 27:3; 38:3; Num. 4:14; 1 Chr. 28:17; 2 Chr. 4:16; in these passages the MT pointing reflects a different form, *mizlāg*). What appears to be the same device is described as a three-pronged instrument used to remove meat from a boiling pot (1 Sam. 2:13–14).

flesh pot. This term is used by the KJV once in a passage where the Israelites complain that, when living in Egypt, they used to sit around pots of meat eating whatever they wanted (Exod. 16:3). These pots (Heb. *sîr* H6105) were large metal kettles used not only for cooking meat (2 Ki. 4:38; Ezek. 11:3), but also for boiling water (Jer. 1:13) and for washing (Ps. 60:8).

flint. An opaque black, gray, brownish-black, or smoky brown variety of very fine grained silica (silicon dioxide) possibly with some hydrated silica. Flint, which is allied to CHALCEDONY, is not as hard as many gem stones (Ezek. 3:9, Heb. *ṣōr* H7644), but is harder than steel and is used as an abrasive. It commonly occurs as hard, tough, structureless nodules (cf. Isa. 50:7, Heb. *ḥallāmîš* H2734), particularly in chalk deposits which, to a large extent, consist of calcareous remains of minute organisms, together with varying proportions of detrital sandy (siliceous) and clayey material. The concretionary nodules of flint represent the redeposition, from percolating ground water, of silica derived from the solution of small scattered sponge spicules, originally scattered through the chalkstone. The nodules tend to be found mainly along bedding planes in the CHALK where there was some detrital silica.

This is the case for the flint nodules occurring in the chalks and chalky limestones of northern SAMARIA, parts of W GALILEE, and over large areas E of the JORDAN Rift Valley. In Jordan, particularly, the relatively soft chalkstone has been eroded away, mainly by the wind, and has left the hard impervious nodules as residual flint gravels. Flint fractures into shell-like shapes as the result of either a blow or under thermal action (heat or frost). The flakes, which at their edges may be pale gray or yellowish-brown, afford sharp cutting edges. Because of this, and the hardness of the material, flint was extensively used by prehistoric humans for weapons and tools. (See E. S. Dana, *A Textbook of Mineralogy*, 4th ed. [1932], 472–73; E. M. Blaiklock, ed., *The Zondervan Pictorial Bible Atlas* [1969], 438–52.)

D. R. Bowes

float. This English term is used by the KJV to render two Hebrew words for "raft," each of which occurs only once (1 Ki. 5:9; 2 Chr. 2:16).

flock. A group of animals; the word is used in the Bible especially of small cattle, that is, SHEEP or GOATS that are herded together. The most frequent Hebrew term is *ṣōʾn H7366* (Gen. 4:2 et al.), but *ʿēder H6373*, which can include larger cattle, is also common (29:2–3 et al.). In the NT, the cognate Greek terms *poimnē G4479* (Matt. 26:31 et al.) and *poimnion G4480* (Lk. 12:32 et al.) are used without any discernible difference in meaning. All these terms are often used figuratively. The nation of Israel is described as the flock of God, the object of his special care (e.g., Ps. 77:20; Isa. 40:11; Zech. 10:3). Jesus reassures his disciples by addressing them with the phrase "little flock" (Lk. 12:32), and he describes himself as the Good Shepherd of the one flock (Jn. 10:14–16). Both PAUL and PETER viewed the church as a flock that needs tending by spiritual shepherds (Acts 20:28–29; 1 Cor. 9:7; 1 Pet. 5:2–3 [v. 4 refers to Jesus as the Chief Shepherd]). See SHEPHERD.

flog. To beat with a whip or rod. The term can be used to render several Hebrew and Greek words, such as *nākâ H5782* (hiphil, "to strike"; e.g., Deut. 25:2; Prov. 17:26) and *mastigoō* (e.g., Matt. 10:17; Jn. 19:1). See also CRIMES AND PUNISHMENTS III. C; SCOURGE.

flood. This English term can be used to render a variety of words, such as Hebrew *šipʿâ H9180* (Job 22:11) and Greek *plēmmyra G4439* (Lk. 6:48). The Genesis Flood is referred to with the terms *mabbûl H4429* and *kataklysmos G2886* (see FLOOD, GENESIS). Floods have been part of the many vast cycles of nature throughout all of the years of earth's geological history. These cycles may be seasonal annual rainfall or melting of winter snows, or sporadic and unpredictable, caused by great hurricanes and monsoon storms. There are also massive seacoast floods caused by high winds and tides. As man began to build his centers of living near the great river systems and ocean ports, and as the population increased, the incidence of landslides, tsunami waves, and cycles of flooding became disasters.

Flash floods are sudden violent bursts of water surging down narrow mountain valleys or desert gullies previously dry. They occur in mountainous areas where high slopes are relatively bare of vegetation, but do not generally last long. The illustration of Jesus concerning the men who built their houses on rock and sand and then passed through a flood is probably an allusion to this phenomenon (Matt. 7:24–28; Lk. 6:46–49). Tsunamis are low seismic sea waves, generated by earthquakes. The energy wave can travel across oceans, fastest in deepest water, up to 600 mph. One of the earliest such waves recorded wiped out cities of Crete, Greece, and other Aegean seaports after the eruption of Santorini volcano about 1500 or 1400 B.C. (See W. G. Hoyt and W. B. Langhein, *Floods* [1955]; L. B. Leopold, M. G. Wolman, and J. P. Miller, *Fluvial Processes in Geomorphology* [1964]; A. N. Strahler, *The Earth Sciences*, 2nd ed. [1971].)

W. U. Ault

Flood, Genesis. The great deluge that occurred during the days of NOAH, recorded in Gen. 6–9 and mentioned frequently elsewhere in the Bible.
    I. The biblical account
        A. Reason
        B. Date
        C. Place
        D. Ark
        E. Animals
        F. Cause
    II. Sumerian, Babylonian, and other traditions
    III. Interpretations

IV. Theories to explain the cause of the flood
   A. Canopy theory
   B. Rapid melting of glacier ice
   C. Fountains of the deep (isostasy)
V. Evidence cited for the flood
   A. Universal language
   B. Flood traditions
   C. Diluvia
VI. Catastrophism vs. uniformitarianism
   A. Unconformities
   B. Aeolian deposits
   C. Redbeds
   D. Rain
   E. Evaporite deposits
   F. Fossil sequence
   G. Mass extinctions
   H. Coal
   I. Cyclothems
   J. Age of fossil fuels
   K. Sediments
   L. Serious flaw
   M. Geologic time table
VII. Conclusions

I. The biblical account. The biblical account of the deluge at the time of Noah is found in Gen. 6–9. The relative amount of space in Scripture and details given for this event in human history seem to underline its importance. In the NT it is cited as a significant event. (The reader is referred to the important treatments of the flood presented by A. Heidel, *The Gilgamesh Epic and Old Testament Parallels* [1946], and B. Ramm, *The Christian View of Science and Scripture* [1954].) We accept the Genesis account of the flood as factual and true, a historical event; but we cannot interpret, explain, or add to the words given in Genesis without introducing uncertainty. Many theories have been advanced to explain specific aspects of the flood and thus make the account fit a particular interpretation. Some of these theories can be briefly evaluated on the basis of established archaeological and geological data.

A. Reason. The reason for the flood was that "the earth was corrupt in God's sight and was full of violence" (Gen. 6:11). But "Noah was a righteous man, blameless among the people of his time" (6:9), and God commissioned him as a preacher of righteousness to warn the people (2 Pet. 2:5), and to prepare a large ark to preserve human and animal life during the flood (see ARK OF NOAH).

B. Date. The date when the flood occurred is not known. Many conservative Christian writers believe, based on archaeological remains, that the deluge took place "long before 4000 B.C." (e.g., M. F. Unger, *Introductory Guide to the Old Testament* [1951], 194; Ramm, *Christian View*, 233). The genealogical methods used for computing dates are at best only estimates, having uncertainties of perhaps thousands of years (see ANTEDILUVIANS). It appears that most writers on the subject would place Noah between 5,000 and 15,000 years ago, but without satisfactory basis. Fifteen thousand years would cover the recessional stages of melting and flooding of the last continental ice sheets, but not the human migration into North and South America.

Layers of fine sediment from a flood of very limited extent have been found at several ancient cities of MESOPOTAMIA. In archaeological literature we find the use of the terms "pure river silt" and "clean uniform clay" to apply to the 8-ft. layer of river sediment at Ur dating from the mid-Ubaid Period, and later "evidences of a large flood" at Shuruppak during the Jemdet Nasr Period, and still later a "layer of sediment" (or "similar stratum" compared to that at Ur) 1.5-ft. thick at Kish and "some distance above the Jemdet Nasr Period." Hence these terms applied to flood sediment must be taken in the general sense to indicate their fine-grained size and not in the technical sense to distinguish between silt and clay or to indicate composition. J. Finegan (*Light from the Ancient Past* [1946], 24) suggests that the flood at Shuruppak or Kish may be the one referred to in the Sumerian King List. G. A. Barton (*Archaeology and the Bible*, [1937], 41) indicates that "there is no real proof" that either of the sediment layers (Ur or Kish) were deposited at the time of the Genesis Flood. In fact, the evidence from pottery examined by Frankfort has shown that the two "inundations were not even in the same century." He concludes that there is "no evidence that these deposits ... mean more than that for a time the Euphrates and Tigris changed their beds and flowed for a time over parts of Ur and Kish that had previously been inhabited."

Some so-called "Pre-Flood Seals" and "Pre-Flood Tablets" found at Fara and Ur, and at Kish respectively beneath layers of silt are most likely older than the silt, but whether they pre-date Noah is open to question. Ramm (*Christian View*, 233) indicates that there are four such "flood deposits" separated in time by about 600 years, therefore they "cannot be cited as evidences of Noah's flood." They cannot be used to date the flood.

So far, we know of no bonafide materials, either archaeological or geological, that are known with certainty to derive from the flood of Noah. This must not be construed to mean that we do not believe the flood to be a historical event, but rather that we have not found or recognized any flood remains evidencing it. Any material evidence, if it can be produced, could and would be studied by varied physical and chemical analytical techniques. For example, any particular sediment or sedimentary rock frequently has characteristics revealing information concerning the source rock and its proximity, and the processes of weathering, erosion, transportation, and deposition of the sediment. These factors are varied and diverse as represented by the present day accumulation of sediment.

Archaeologists have discovered several ancient historical records of the flood from Sumerian and Babylonian sources in Mesopotamia. These show remarkable similarities to the Genesis account and are discussed later. Frequent stories about finding Noah's ark have all proven fictitious, and even recent expeditions to Mount Ararat (Ağri Daği), variously given as 16,254 to 16,946 ft., have produced no convincing evidence. Berossus reported that "the vessel being thus stranded in Armenia, some part of it yet remains in the Corcyraean Mountains." According to Gen. 8:4, the ark "came to rest on the mountains of Ararat." G. F. Wright (*ISBE* [1929], 2:821) indicates that this is some indefinite place in the highlands of Armenia and not Mount Ararat.

A few writers, not geologists, appeal to terrace gravels and unconsolidated sediments as evidence of flood deposits, but this is untenable. None of the terrace gravels are known to correlate worldwide, and the more recent ones date throughout 1.6 million years of the Pleistocene Epoch. The divisions of the Pleistocene Epoch are discussed more fully later. Any organic materials such as plant debris, humic soil layers, or wood from the ark could be reliably dated by radiocarbon.

C. Place. Essentially all writers concur that Noah lived in Mesopotamia and built the ark there. The Sumerian King List, indicating ruling cities before and after the flood in Mesopotamia, lends strong support (Barton, *Archaeology*, 317). If the date for Noah is placed too far back, the Persian Gulf would have been nonexistent as a gulf. It would simply have been an extensive lowland traversed by the confluenced TIGRIS and EUPHRATES Rivers and subsequent tributaries. During the prolonged Wisconsin Ice Age of perhaps 40,000 years or more, when vast ice sheets covered some 6 million square miles of North America and Eurasia, sea level was about 330 ft. lower than today. In its last stages the North American ice sheet had several advances with periods of retreat (melting back) in between. The last glacial maxim, the Tazewell, occurred at c. 17,000 BP (before present) and the last readvance, the Cochrane, at c. 8,000 BP.

Consequently, before 17,000 BP and possibly until 8,000 BP, mankind likely inhabited extensive areas of the continental shelf that are now below sea level. Areas like the Persian Gulf should be fruitful areas to explore for buried remains of early humans. However, even the oldest Sumerian flood stories refer to cities in postglacial Mesopotamia and not to an extended lowland area as discussed above. A possible exception may be a Babylonian cuneiform text that reads, "Dumuzi the hunter (?), whose city is *among the fishes*, ruled 100 years" (Barton, *Archaeology*, 318). This statement, it might be noted, does not prove, but fits well with, a date for Noah and the flood within the last 8,000 years.

D. Ark. Noah was commanded to make an ark of GOPHER wood, with three decks and rooms, covered inside and out with pitch, with a roof, and finished "to a cubit above," and with dimensions: 300 cubits long, 50 cubits wide, and 30 cubits high (Gen. 6:14–16 NRSV). The gopher wood is thought to be CYPRESS, which the Phoenicians used for their ships, as did ALEXANDER THE GREAT to build his fleet at Babylon (Ramm, *Christian View*, 229). The ark was essentially a rectangular box with one door. Apparently the roof was to be finished to within a cubit of the walls, leaving an opening all around for ventilation (Heidel, *Gilgamesh Epic*, 234). The length of the cubit is uncertain, since there were long and short cubits, royal cubits, Egyptian cubits, and Talmudic cubits, with lengths ranging from eighteen to twenty-five inches. The legal cubit of the Talmudists was twenty-two inches (see WEIGHTS AND MEASURES I.A.). Regardless of which cubit was used, the ark was built with dimensions perfect for floating, the approximate ratios of which have been copied by modern ships (Ramm, 230). Covering the ark within and without pitch (see BITUMEN) would make it waterproof with a flexible covering.

E. Animals. The animals, birds, and creeping things coming into the ark to Noah, all in pairs and some by sevens, was nothing less than a miracle. Taxonomists report that there are presently about 4,500 species of living mammals and 8,650 species of living birds. There are some, but comparatively few, species of each that are known to have become extinct in the last few thousand years (V. J. Stanek, *The Pictorial Encyclopedia of the Animal Kingdom* [1962], 7; R. F. Pennak, *Collegiate Dictionary of Zoology* [1964], 302; J. L. Austin, *Birds of the World* [1961], 11).

F. Cause. The flood waters are attributed to RAIN and to factors not understood. The windows (or sluice gates; NIV, "floodgates") of heaven were opened, and all the springs of the great deep burst forth (Gen. 7:11). If the waters covered the highest mountains as they stand today, it would require some eight times as much water as presently existing on earth. There were certainly high mountain ranges at the time of the flood because the highest mountain ranges of today were uplifted many millions of years ago—the Alps and Himalayas around 35 million years ago, the Rockies and Sierra Nevada about 80 million years ago, and the Andes about 10 million years ago. Hence, it is highly improbable that, due to any normal natural process, the elevations of ocean floor and the highest mountain peaks at the time of the flood a few thousand years ago were different from present elevations by more than a few feet. Conjectures on the meaning of "windows of heaven" and "fountains of the deep" are no more than theories and must be recognized as such until substantiating evidence is discovered. We can say with confidence that there is no adequate source of subterranean waters. Water has a specific gravity of one, which is about one-third that of average crustal rock. The oceans and continents have been traversed by gravity surveys sufficient to make this generalized statement. No such subterranean reservoirs have been found.

II. Sumerian, Babylonian, and other traditions. Remarkable supporting evidence for the Genesis Flood comes from ancient clay tablets found in Mesopotamia. Below is a comparison showing some of the similarities and differences between the several sources. Barton (*Archaeology*, 317–36) gives a translation and comparison of the Babylonian accounts. Wright (*ISBE* [1929], 2:823–24) compares the Genesis and Babylonian accounts, which are ably summarized by Ramm (*Christian View*, 247–48). Similarities: (1) The deluge is a divine punishment for man's wickedness. (2) The ark floats inland in Mesopotamia. (3) Both

Cuneiform tablet (c. 1635 B.C.) containing the *Epic of Atrahasis*, one form of the Babylonian flood story.

accounts agree in general regarding the collecting of animals for preservation, but the Babylonian account does not mention the number seven for clean animals. (4) Birds are sent out in both accounts, but the order in Genesis is a raven and a dove (twice), while in the cuneiform the dove and raven are reversed and a swallow is added. (5) Both accounts mention an altar after the flood, but the Babylonian account is polytheistic. (6) The accounts both agree in indicating that the human race will not again be destroyed by a flood.

The differences are: (1) The cuneiform inscription is polytheistic, while Genesis is monotheistic. (2) The different names used are not reconcilable at present. (3) The dimensions of the ark in Genesis are reasonable, being similar to the dimensions of modern shipping, while those given by the cuneiform text and by Berossus are not reasonable. The cuneiform gives 140 x 140 x 140 cubits, and Berossus gives the length as 5 stadia (3,000 ft.) and the width as 2 stadia (1,200 ft.). (4) In the cuneiform text, the deluge results from a quarreling among the gods, and the survivors escape through a mistake, which angers the god Bel. In Genesis the holiness, justice, and mercy of God is evident even in his punishment of the wicked. (5) Both accounts indicate rain as a source of water, but the biblical account gives "fountains of the deep" and the Babylonian tablet indicates a raging sea and wind. (6) The Babylonian tablet relates the slaughter of animals for food, a mast and pilot for the ship, and the lading of the ship with silver and gold. (7) The duration of the flood in the Bible is a year and seventeen days, while in the Babylonian tablet it is fourteen days.

III. Interpretations. The church generally has held to a belief in a *universal* flood. According to this view, all the high mountains of the world were covered by liquid water at the same time, and all terrestrial living beings perished as a result. Many Christians, however, including conservative scholars, hold to a nonuniversal deluge (that is, limited to a locality or region).

Arguments commonly presented in defense of a universal flood are the following: (1) The apparently universal language of the biblical account; according to Gen. 7:19–22, "all the high mountains under the entire heavens were covered. The waters rose and covered the mountains to a depth of more than twenty feet. Every living thing that moved on the earth perished—birds, livestock, wild animals, all the creatures that swarm over the earth, and all mankind. Everything on dry land that had the breath of life in its nostrils died." (2) The universality of flood legends among all people, attributed to the descent of all races from Noah. (3) The worldwide distribution of diluvia deposits. (4) The sudden death of many woolly mammoths frozen in Alaskan and Siberian ice; an inferred milder climate to support the necessary flora for food in contrast to frozen conditions which prevail presently; and the reported observation that these animals died by choking or drowning and not by freezing. (5) The so-called depletion of the species claimed by "flood geologists," who argue that there are fewer species living today compared to the number evidenced in rock strata and attributed to the flood.

Those who hold that the flood was less than universal do so because of the seemingly insurmountable physical problems involved: (1) The amount of water needed to cover Mount Everest would be about eight times as much as that presently on the earth, and there is no known source for such an amount of water, and no way of getting rid of the water afterward. (2) The unique distribution of animals (e.g., the kangaroo in Australia, Tasmania, and New Guinea [Wallabies]) and the problem of getting them to Mesopotamia and back again without populating other parts of the world. (3) The practical logistics of housing so many species of mammals (4,500), and birds (8,650), and other terrestrial life in a three-story ark about one acre in floor plan (3 acres total), and caring for them for one year. Since Scripture records the flood as a natural-supernatural occurrence and not as a pure and gigantic multiple miracle, these interpreters argue, it is only logical to assume that the practical problems presented by a universal flood indicates that such an interpretation is incorrect and not intended by the inspired account. Indeed, other Scripture references suggest that such universal language expressions should not be taken in the absolute sense (see discussion below).

Several nonuniversal flood interpretations have been suggested: (1) That all the highest mountains were not covered by liquid water but perhaps were covered by snow and ice, or were simply not meant to be included. (2) That the flood was universal only with respect to mankind; if so, (a) the flooding covered lowlands worldwide and the habitation of mankind was limited to these lowlands, or (b) the flooding was limited to the Mesopotamian area, as was the distribution of mankind. (3) That the entire record must be interpreted phenomenally (that is, on the basis of what is derived from the senses): the flood was local, even though spoken of in universal terms from what was observable to Noah and his family; similarly, the destruction of living beings was local, though spoken of in universal terms.

These interpretations involve many assumptions and must each be viewed only as theories of interpretation. The various factors involved will be discussed in the next section.

IV. Theories to explain the cause of the flood.

Since the account of the flood in Genesis is simple and brief, there are numerous unanswered questions. Many of these may remain unanswered indefinitely, but they have generated numerous theories. It is important to remember that essentially all discussion to explain the *cause* of the flood consists of theories that are not to be considered on a par with the data from the inspired Scriptures. By INSPIRATION we mean that under God's guidance the original autographs of the Scriptures were factual and accurate within the intended meaning of the writer. The Genesis account describes historical persons, places, and physical phenomena. The favored viewpoint (interpretation) should be one that appears to have the best agreement with Scripture and with information derived from our present knowledge of the physical universe. Theories propounded in a way that shows disregard for basic knowledge or that consist of conjecture having little or no basis in fact should be labeled, perhaps, as science fiction. A number of theories that cluster around the miraculous are of this type, because they assume physical phenomena that have no basis in fact.

There is a sense in which the whole phenomenon of the flood was supernatural, for God said to Noah, "I am going to bring floodwaters on the earth" (Gen. 6:17). However, the deluge is not called a miracle in Scripture. It is stated in terms of physical phenomena seemingly emanating from the earth alone. Writers who hold to a universal flood are driven to postulate miraculous phenomena for the source of the water and its subsequent removal from the earth; or they postulate a miraculous change in the height of the mountains and depth of the ocean basins. Ramm ably reminds us that much of the weight of evidence for a local flood view stems from showing the imponderable difficulties of a universal flood (*Christian View*, 240).

We must emphasize that it is not a question of what God can or cannot do. The question is rather, "What *did* God do?" Those who hold to a local flood view believe in the OMNIPOTENCE of God as much as those who hold to a universal flood. The difference is not one regarding the inspiration of the Scripture but rather its interpretation. The problems arising from the universal flood, and the resulting questions of interpretation, have prompted writers to postulate various supposed physical phenomena to effect the universal flooding of the earth, or to associate the worldwide flooding of all lowlands (or lands to a certain arbitrary elevation) with the rapid melting of continental glaciers at the end of the Wisconsin Ice Age.

A. Canopy theory. The canopy theory and ice-lens theory are similar in that they suggest a source of flood water that is beyond the atmosphere, and these both suffer from the same problems. The former postulates that the earth was initially enveloped by a layer of water or water vapor beyond our atmosphere, supposedly formed during the early (prob. high-temperature) history of the earth. This canopy of water was the source for the water that flooded the earth. The ice-lens version is similar, suggesting that the water required to flood the earth initially existed as an ice lens or perhaps a satellite (moon) of the earth. This ice mass was broken up and precipitated on earth causing the great ice age (vast continental glaciers) and the flood.

We are reminded that to envelop the earth with water to a depth to cover Mount Everest (elevation 29,028 ft.) would require some eight times as much water as presently on earth. Even if there were naturally existing extraterrestrial sources of water precipitated on the earth by some physical phenomena, the subsequent removal of the water would be a stupendous miracle, for there is no known existing mass of water above the atmosphere today. Water in the atmosphere comprises only 0.001% of the total water on earth.

Both the canopy and ice-lens theories propose the precipitation on earth of presumably fresh water. This would greatly dilute the world's oceans and could be verified in several ways. If this were the case, then geochemical studies of marine water and marine organisms predating the flood would be expected to differ from those of today. Precipitation is substantially different isotopically from sea water. Oxygen in precipitation is isotopically lighter in mass by about 0.7% in the mid-latitudes and by 3% in the Arctic. Hydrogen in precipitation is lighter by about 7% in mid-latitudes and by 30% in the Arctic. Although no isotopic study has been directed solely at the problem of possible recent dilution of the oceans, there is ample oxygen isotopic data available on marine samples from the present back millions of years. The study of paleotemperature (ancient temperature) measurements is possible because of the verification that certain marine organisms build their shells of carbonate in which the oxygen composition is isotopically in equilibrium with that of the ocean water and is temperature dependent. Also, the hydrogen and oxygen isotopic data on ancient brines (trapped residues of ancient sea water) is typically that of present-day oceans. The geochemical data has shown no evidence of a large dilution—say a dilution of times eight or even a dilution of times three or times two—a few thousand years ago.

Keil and Delitzsch consider the problem of the great amount of water needed and that possibly the loftiest mountain peaks were not covered, then mention the view that Gen. 7:19, like Deut. 2:25 and 4:19, is a rhetorical expression which is not of universal application (KD, *Pentateuch*, 1:146). However, they maintain that even if mountain peaks higher than Ararat (there are more than forty) were not covered, we must regard the flood as universal because the few peaks uncovered would be insignificant in comparison with the surface covered, and no human beings could exist upon these mountains covered with perpetual snow and ice. Their suggestion does not help the problem much, since over three times as much water as is present on earth would still be required.

Some writers suggest that there were no high mountains on earth at the time of Noah. Such a suggestion cannot be taken seriously, because the Himalayas and Alps were uplifted gradually from the Tethyan geosyncline in post-Eocene time over many millions of years beginning about 35 to 40 million years ago. Most other major mountain ranges are much older. The ice-lens or ice-planet suggestions apparently were conceived first because of the requirement of much water to effect the flood, and secondly as a result of assuming that the ice age was a catastrophic event of "extreme suddenness" (D. W. Patten, *The Biblical Flood and the Ice Epoch* [1966], 101ff.). It is rather ill conceived, making numerous assumptions without established evidence, and the theory does not account for the disposition of the excess water after the flood. The theory is especially inadequate in that it ignores most of the evidence for the glacial periods.

1. Ice ages. There was not just one glacial period—precipitated suddenly a few thousand years ago and lasting for one year—when continental glaciers covered much of the northern part of continents in the northern hemisphere, but there is adequate evidence that there have been four periods of extensive continental glaciation throughout much of the Pleistocene Epoch (the last 1.6 million years). The continental ice sheets slowly spread outward and generally southward from the several areas of snow accumulation on each of the northern continents. In North America the place of major snow accumulation was the vast area around Hudson Bay. These phenomena of snow accumulation, changing to glacial ice under pressure and spreading outward from areas of accumulation, are well known, being presently observed in the interiors of Greenland and Antarctica and in numerous valley glaciers under study in the high mountain ranges.

The continental glaciers each took thousands of years to advance, lasted for tens of thousands of years, and took several thousand years to retreat (melt back). The last major ice sheet in North America is called the Wisconsin. Along most of its southern front it did not advance as far S as the much earlier and successively older Illinoian, Nebraskan, and Kansan ice sheets did. During the Wisconsin period there were subperiods covering thousands of years when the glacier was receding followed by minor readvances. R. W. Fairbridge ("The Changing Level of the Sea," in *Scientific American* [May 1960], 70–79) gives data on some of these subperiods of readvance—Tazewell (about 17,000 BP, before present), Carey (about 15,000 BP), Valders (10,500 BP), and Cochrane (8,000 BP). Just prior to the Valders subperiod the glacier had retreated from the area around Two Creeks, Wisconsin, on the shore of Lake Michigan so that a black spruce forest had grown there. This spruce forest was pushed over, buried, and preserved by the fine glacial sediment about 11,300 BP (see W. S. Broecker and W. R. Farrand, "The Radio-carbon Age of the Two Creeks Forest Bed, Wisconsin," in *Geological Society of America Bulletin*, 74 [1963]: 795–802).

2. Climatic change. Another assumption made for the canopy theories is that the earth's climate abruptly changed at the time of the flood from widespread subtropical to temperate over most of the earth to that of the ice ages (Patten, *Biblical Flood*, 110). This assumption ignores the dates and great length of time shown for the repeated buildup and advance of continental glaciers, as already discussed, and also the various ages of the flora remains cited as evidence for change in climate. Repeatedly in the past there were long periods of widespread subtropical conditions, but one cannot at random claim one of these as evidence and ignore the time aspect of when such conditions prevailed.

The last interglacial (Sangamon or Riss-Würm), with mean temperatures of about 75°F (24°C), prevailed for thousands of years prior to approximately 40 or 50 thousand years ago. Present-day mean temperature is about 30°F. These interglacial periods did not come on abruptly, but the change happened over thousands of years, as evidenced by ocean-bottom sediments and the dating by the thin varve layers of glacial lake sediments formed during recession of the glaciers. Many of the widespread climatic changes of the past took place over millions of years. For example, the gradual change that occurred during the Miocene and Pliocene Epochs of the Tertiary Period covered some twenty-five million years.

3. Mammoth extinctions. The extinction of woolly mammoths, which are found frozen in the glacial ice and permafrost areas of Alaska and Siberia, have been cited by nonscientific writers as evidence of a sudden catastrophe which deep-froze the whole population with fresh grass still in the mouths and undigested food in the stomachs. It is alleged that this is evidence of an abrupt change in climate.

Again, important data have conveniently been omitted. The woolly mammoth, mastodon, woolly rhinoceros, and other associated animals are cold-weather animals native to the colder latitudes. J. Drumm (*Mammoths and Mastodons: Ice Age Elephants of New York* [1963], 7, 121) indicates that the woolly mammoth "had heavy fur and a layer of fat beneath the skin, both adaptations of extreme cold." Contrary to popular opinion, the mammoth carcasses were "not as fresh as quick-frozen meat." Its remains have been found associated with typical tundra plants and animals. The Beresouka mammoth, discovered in northern Siberia near the Beresouka river in 1899, had undigested food in its stomach—"remains of grasses, sedges, the alpine poppy and buttercup." Scientific opinion places the extinct mammoth within their usual arctic habitat and attributes each death and burial to normal accidents such as falling over a cliff or into a crevass, caught in a blizzard or a mud flow, etc., in situations where they were quickly frozen and preserved.

Drumm (ibid.) also estimates the mammoth population in late Pleistocene prior to extinction as about 50,000. The woolly mammoth has been extinct so long that no mention of it is known from the legends of living people, but paleolithic man left drawings of it on the walls of a cavern at Combarelles, France. Beside the nearly complete Beresouka carcass, about fifty others less complete have been found frozen in Alaska and Siberia (C. O. Dunbar and K. M. Waage, *Historical Geology*, 3rd ed. [1969], 35). Radiocarbon dates of the carcasses show that they lived and died 11,450–39,000 BP. Significantly they did not all die at the same time but over a period of time, 37,000 years or longer, and the most recent one over 10,000 years ago.

TABULATED CHRONOLOGY OF THE FLOOD	
1. The making of the ark (Gen. 6:14)	
2. Collection of the animals (7:9)	7 days before the rain started
3. Fountains of the great deep were broken up and the windows of heaven were opened (7:11)	2nd month, 17th day in Noah's 600th year
4. Rain (7:12)	40 days and 40 nights
5. All the high hills covered (7:19)	
6. Water prevailed upon the earth (7:24)	150 days
7. Water returned from off the earth (8:3)	150 days
8. Ark rested upon the mountains of Ararat (8:4)	7th month, 17th day
9. Waters decreased (8:4)	
10. Tops of mountains seen (8:5)	10th month, 1st day
11. Noah waited (8:6)	40 days
12. Noah sent forth raven and a dove; dove returned (8:7–9)	
13. Noah waited (8:10)	7 days
14. Noah sent forth dove again (8:10); dove returned with olive branch (8:11)	7 days
15. Noah waited (8:12)	7 days
16. Noah sent forth dove which did not return (8:12)	7 days
17. Noah removed covering; face of the ground was dry (8:13)	1st month, 1st day, Noah's 601st year
18. Earth dried; Noah left ark (8:14)	2nd month, 27th day

Chart uses KJV terminology.

The existence of frozen mammoth carcasses that are 39,000 years old is strong evidence that the north tundra regions of the earth have remained frozen and therefore have not been covered by a flood during this time. Such evidence would appear to be fatal to Patten's theory, for he postulates that the ice age came suddenly, froze the mammoths, and caused a worldwide flood. However, he does not explain how the mammoths remained frozen during a year-long flood that was violent, with huge tidal waves that transported all types of sediment but left all the mammoths and associated animal remains undisturbed in their cold habitat. K. Kowalski, discussing possible causes of the extinction of mammoths, calls attention that this animal's adaptation to cold climate preclude life in the present southern steppes of Eurasia with their warm dry summers (in *Pleistocene Extinctions*, ed. P. S. Martin and H. E. Wright, Jr., [1967], 356–57). The present-day tundra N of the Arctic Circle, with its long polar nights and abundant winter snowfall, is very different from the steppe-tundra of the late Pleistocene with no polar night and possibly light snowfall.

In summary, the extraterrestrial ice theory as the cause of the flood, as presented by Patten, is invalidated by (1) the existence of more than one period of glaciation in the Pleistocene Epoch; (2) the duration of the Wisconsin period of glaciation for 40,000 years or more; (3) the duration of the combined periods of glaciation during the Pleistocene Epoch (perhaps as much as 1.6 million years); (4) the evidence of extensive glaciation during the latter part of the Paleozoic era, namely, the Permian period (200 to 300 million years ago) and also during the Huronian time of the Precambrian era (some 600–700 million years ago); (5) the existence of widespread subtropical and temperate climate numerous times in the past, the last being about 60,000 years ago (there is the existence of widespread subtropical and temperate climate changes); and (6) the fact that the supposed catastrophic mass extinctions by freezing at a recent date do not accord with the data.

B. Rapid melting of glacier ice. There is much evidence that during maximum glaciation (greatest extent of continental glaciers) the world mean sea level was over 300 ft. lower than it is today. If the Greenland and Antarctic ice caps were to melt completely, sea level would rise another 300–400 ft. During maximum glaciation much of the presently submerged continental shelf areas were dry-land coastal regions inhabited by humans. It has been suggested by Fairbridge that a period of relatively rapid melting of the glaciers and flooding of the extensive coastal regions accompanied by torrential rains could have generated the numerous flood stories among many peoples. Data is also cited to indicate that the mean sea level rose during some oscillations of the glaciers at approximately 30 ft. per century. The greatest and fastest rise was about 6,000 BP, and the highest mean sea level was about 10–12 ft. higher than at present.

In the absence of any other confirming evidence, the above should be taken only as a suggestion. We do not know the date of Noah's flood, or that the human population inhabited only the coastal regions at that time. Fossil man, Australopithecines to Homo sapiens, seems to have ranged far inland. Furthermore, an appeal to worldwide flooding to generate the numerous flood stories implies that all of mankind today did not derive from Noah.

C. Fountains of the deep (isostasy). Another theory that has been suggested to explain the mechanism of flooding of the earth is that the ocean floor was uplifted and the continental masses, especially the mountain ranges, sank. Isostasy or isostatic equilibrium is the geologic phenomenon that describes the various segments of the earth's crust, for example, the deep ocean floors or parts of continental masses as floating more or less independently in the plastic (or hot and viscous) mantle of the earth. The principle can be illustrated by barges in a river. When loaded, they float lower than when unloaded. Also, even though two identical barges were loaded with the same weight, if one were loaded with solid rock having a density of 3.3 and another with somewhat more bulky rock having a density of 2.8, then the bottom of the barges would each float at the same level in the water but the load of the second barge would stand at a higher elevation. Illustrating still further, if the second barge had a much heavier load than the first in addition to being more bulky (lower density), then its lower surface would float lower and its upper surface higher than that of the first barge. This is precisely the comparison that geophysical data indicates between the crust of the earth in the ocean basin and the continents. The few miles of water (low density) added to the dense basaltic rock composing the ocean floor averages a higher density than the very thick crustal plates consisting mostly of low-density granitic and sedimentary rock. As mountain ranges are slowly unloaded by erosion, they continue to rise.

The isostatic adjustment of the earth's crust to loading is a slow response because of the viscosity of the mantle substratum. Parts of the continent, where unloaded of their burden of glacial ice 8–10,000 years ago, are still rising measurably (adjusting isostatically). Thus to suggest that the ocean floors rose and the mountains sank without any known physical cause and within a few months' time would invoke nothing less than a gigantic miracle. It is evident that the highest mountain ranges, such as the Himalayas, Alps, Andes, and Rockies, could not have been depressed several miles independent of the continents and raised again without leaving telltale fault trenches and gouge (ground-up rock) zones. To suggest that the convection cells in the earth's mantle, proposed by geophysics on much evidence, localized selectively and greatly speeded up by a factor of a billion or more, is again suggesting nothing less than a worldwide miracle.

Again we remind the reader that there is no known scientific evidence that would allow us to expand on the meaning of "fountains of the deep."

There certainly are no vast atmosphere reservoirs or subterranean reservoirs of water beneath the floor of the oceans. Seemingly the simplest miracle would be to create and then remove the additional water required for the year-long flood. But the Scriptures nowhere call the flood a miracle, or indicate that God created much water for this occasion, or that the continents and mountains sank beneath the waters. Rather, we are told that the waters rose and prevailed exceedingly until the high hills and mountains were covered.

V. Evidence cited for the flood

A. Universal language. The universal expressions in the biblical account are not sufficient proof for a universal flood in face of the inherent problems and absence of any confirmatory evidence. Similar language is used elsewhere (e.g., 1 Ki. 18:10; Job 37:3; Ps. 22:17; Matt. 3:5; Jn. 4:39; Acts 2:5) but not pressed for universality. Did literally all countries of the world come to Egypt to buy grain (Gen. 41:57)? Did the American Indians live in fear because of Joshua's conquest of Canaan (Deut. 2:25)? Our attitude must be one of desiring to know all the facts in the case by weighing all the evidence before drawing our own conclusions, rather than being committed immovably to a position. If we are seeking truth we will be willing to change when the facts warrant it.

B. Flood traditions. Stories of a flood (or floods) are widespread among many peoples. This is generally taken as evidence that all people of the earth descended from Noah. The deluge was so impressive that they carried the story with them as they spread out over the earth, changing and corrupting the story down through the millennia. Ramm (*Christian View*, 242) points out that flood stories are not found in some areas, such as Japan, Egypt, and other parts of Africa. But Wright (*ISBE* [1929], 2:822) and F. A. Filby (*The Flood Reconsidered* [1970], 52) discuss many flood legends, among them traditions from China, Siberia, Kamchatka, the Americas, and Africa. Filby concludes that "there is no other story of an ancient event in all the world so widely accepted," and the cumulative weight of evidence is "that the present human race has spread from one center and even from one family" (ibid). However, even if such accounts are taken as evidence for the universal destruction of mankind in the flood, they cannot be interpreted to indicate the extent of inundation of the high mountains without making assumptions about the distribution of antediluvian man. It must also be admitted that there is no proof that the traditions all refer to the same flood.

C. Diluvia. Over a hundred years ago, worldwide *diluvia* (unconsolidated alluvial deposits) were cited as proof of Noah's flood. Such views were held by the then prominent geologist William Buckland in his *Reliquiae diluvianae* (Relics of the Deluge, 1823), as well as by zoologist Georges Cuvier and others. Buckland, however, recanted his views in 1836 because of closer study of these geologic materials that had been quite unspecifically designated. Unconsolidated stream and glacial alluvial deposits of widely differing ages had been erroneously grouped together. Many streams will leave valley terrace gravels, as do glacial lakes during the retreating stages of the glacier and high sea level stands of former interglacial warm periods.

VI. Catastrophism vs. uniformitarianism.
J. R. Moore ("Charles Lyell and the Noachian Deluge," *JASA* 22/3 [1970]: 107–15) helpfully reviews the debate between catastrophic and uniformitarian viewpoints of geology during the 19th cent. He wisely counsels writers that to understand the history of the warfare of the past "is valuable both as a warning to avoid repeat performances and as an aid to better understanding of the present debate." (See also D. A. Young, "Scripture in the Hands of Geologists," *WTJ* 49 [1987]: 1–34, 257–304.)

Catastrophists variously attributed certain types of rock strata to Noah's flood. With the development of many analytical techniques and ensuing detailed studies of geological strata, numerous sedimentary phenomena are recognized, none of which indicate a universal flood. The times of formation of the various strata in question also are known to represent not one point in time but many geologic epochs and periods over thousands and millions of years. Today no qualified geologists hold to the catastrophic viewpoint, essentially because there is no evidence for it.

Some recent writers on the flood take an antiuniformitarian position, but it is significant that none are geologists. They do not seem to realize that an antiuniformitarian position, to be valid, requires them to demonstrate, in the cause-and-effect relationship of the physical and chemical laws of the universe, the variability which they propose. In nearly every case such a writer, after disclaiming uniformity, will then proceed to present a scheme which, to make it plausible to the reader, employs the uniformity of cause and effect in the natural phenomena he proposes. To every Christian the nature of the Judeo-Christian God of Scripture, in whom is no variableness, neither shadow of turning, should not only fit well with the uniformitarian concepts but would seem to demand them. In fact, if it were not for uniformity of cause and effect in nature, it would be impossible to recognize a miracle (an act of the supernatural). We conclude that the nonuniformitarian view is incorrect and that such writers are inconsistent. The Christian should intuitively accept uniformitarian principles as the usual course of nature because a belief in miracles and the supernatural requires it.

Flood geology, otherwise known as catastrophic geology, is an attempt by some to explain all the geologic formations as due to the flood of Noah (see esp. H. M. Morris and J. C. Whitcomb, Jr., *The Genesis Flood* [1966]). Basically it is an attempt to claim all the great thicknesses (many miles) of sedimentary strata as physical evidence for the flood. The writings of these nongeologists exhibit a basic lack of understanding of even the fundamental principles of geology. J. L. Kulp ("Deluge Geology," *JASA* 2/1 [1950]: 1–15) and Ramm (*Christian View*, 179–188) have reviewed a number of basic points that completely invalidate the flood geology approach. Many types of geologic features could not have formed under water, others could not have formed in a short period of time, and countless other features show varied, sequential, and definite space and time relationships that require varied environments and much time. A few of these are the following.

A. Unconformities. Essentially all erosional unconformities, whether formed on horizontal strata of marine origin or on formerly horizontal strata that have been tilted at an angle or folded and faulted, are formed by subaerial erosion. This is subsequently covered by a different sequence of horizontal strata frequently deposited after the region in question has again become covered by marine waters. An example of this is the early Paleozoic

Some believe that the layers of sedimentary rock found in places like the Timna Nature Reserve in N Sinai may provide evidence from the time of the Genesis Flood.

strata, the Tapeats sandstone of Cambrian age, which overlies the Grand Canyon Series of late Precambrian age. The early Paleozoic strata in the Colorado Plateau show a gradual ingress of the sea from W to E on a time scale of millions of years.

B. Aeolian deposits. Thick deposits of wind-blown sand showing beautiful cross bedding, such as the Navajo sandstone of Zion National Park and the Windgate and Entrado sandstones, give evidence of extensive deserts prevailing during the Triassic and Jurassic periods when these thick wind-blown sands were deposited. The Silurian and Permian were also periods when widespread deserts prevailed in North America.

C. Redbeds. Subaerial exposure of sediments during deposition in the near shore environment, produced on fluviatile floodplains, or by migrating shorelines due to fluctuations in sea level or continental elevations, results characteristically in redbeds. Good examples of this are the extensive Devonian redbeds of the Catskills, the Triassic redbeds of the ancient fault troughs of the eastern United States, and the Old Red Sandstone of Great Britain.

D. Rain. The flood of Noah is sometimes coupled with the assumption, on the basis of Gen. 2:5, that there was no rain before the flood. That there were hundreds of millions of years of rain throughout the history of the earth is evident from the existence of rivers, flood-plains, glaciers, fresh water lakes, water erosion and transportation of sediments, and many others, among them fossil raindrop imprints in formerly soft mud now preserved in sedimentary rock.

E. Evaporite deposits. The sequences of sedimentary strata from Silurian and Permian periods contain extensive beds of salt. Noteworthy are the Silurian salt deposits of western New York (aggregate thickness, 250 ft.), the Silurian and Devonian of eastern Michigan (aggregate thickness of Silurian alone is 1,600 ft.), the Delaware and Midland Basins of the Permian period in New Mexico and Texas (which precipitated nearly 2,000 ft. of anhydrite and salt in the Castile formation and 2,400 ft. in the overlying Salado formation), and enormous Permian salt deposits in Kansas and Jurassic anhydrite deposits in the Williston Basin on the northern Great Plains. Similar salt deposits are found in other parts of the world. There is no way that these precipitate beds of salt could be intercalated with other basin strata in a submarine environment of a great flood. Rather, salts are precipitated from saline water, which is saturated because of intense aridity and evaporation, and the thick layers are evidence of continual but limited inflow of sea water from the ocean. Interlayering of halite, sylvite, cancrinite, and other salt and potash evaporite minerals is controlled by slight variations in geochemical conditions (temperature, pH, etc.). It is calculated that to produce the Permian salt of Kansas, Texas, and New Mexico alone (3×10^{13} tons) would require the evaporation of 22,000 cubic miles of sea water of normal salinity (Dunbar and Waage, *Historical Geology*, 301).

F. Fossil sequence. The sequence of fossils in the strata of the world or in the stratigraphic column in any one region simply cannot be explained on the basis of a one-year flood. The fossil species are not hopelessly mixed. Rather, many index fossils distinctive of a given geologic period have been recognized and used successfully by geologists around the world. Different brachiopod species, for example, which are index fossils for different periods, may have distinctive morphological features but be quite similar in shape and size. There is no way that these fossils could be selectively winnowed out of worldwide flood waters and deposited in their respective strata; they must have lived at different times and were buried where they lived. Likewise, Cenozoic mammals and birds are not found in the Mesozoic strata, and Mesozoic reptiles (dinosaurs) are not found in the Cenozoic strata. On the other hand, fossil flora and faunal assemblages in a given stratum often allow one to deduce a picture of paleoclimatic conditions distinctive to and consistent with the marine, littoral, or terrestrial environment.

G. Mass extinctions. It is repeatedly and erroneously claimed by some writers that the mass extinctions of animals all occurred simultaneously a few thousand years ago during the flood. Fossil evidence does not show a mass extinction several thousand years ago. Rather, there have been extinctions throughout geologic times since the Cambrian, but some periods are characterized by extensive extinctions of many species. Noteworthy are the Permian about 225 million years ago and the Cretaceous about 65 million years ago. It is erroneously claimed by some that the woolly mammoth, mastodon, woolly rhinoceros, saber tooth tiger, and others were wiped out simultaneously in a common world cataclysm which left many carcasses frozen in tundra and glacial ice. As already mentioned, the paleontologic data show that of about fifty such carcasses found, they were entombed from 11,450 to 39,000 years ago. In fact, radiocarbon dates indicate that most of the woolly mammoths died before 30,000 years ago (though some survived longer in certain locales). The time element completely vitiates the catastrophic ice or flood theory with respect to the mammoths.

H. Coal. Kulp ("Deluge Geology") cites characteristics of coal formation that would preclude it from being formed in a worldwide flood. There is much evidence that the vegetative matter grew right where it accumulated.

I. Cyclothems. The coal beds of the Pennsylvania period throughout Pennsylvania, Ohio, Indiana, and Illinois show cycles of deposition. The organic matter collected where it grew in great swamps much like it does today forming peat, which under suitable conditions of arrested decay and burial can form coal. In eastern Ohio tree roots and stumps in some coal beds are still in place in the underclay in which they grew. Typically, after a long period of accumulation (about 100 ft. of vegetative matter will form 1 ft. of coal and some coal beds are many feet thick), the swamp would be inundated and the layer of peat would be covered by sediments that formed shale, limestone, or sandstone in sequence. About 100 such cycles of deposition, cyclothems, are recognized in eastern Ohio. This alternation, from terrestrial swamps to near shore sandstone or shale deposition to marine limestone environment and back again repeatedly, rules out flood geology as a reasonable possibility. Cannel coal, formed almost entirely from pollen accumulation in open water patches of the swamp, gives evidence of lengthy selective accumulation.

J. Age of fossil fuels. If any deposits of coal, petroleum, asphalt, oil shale, or black organic shales were formed within the last 40,000 years from plants or animals still living at the time of formation, then the deposit could be dated reliably by radiocarbon. Anyone who proposes a recent origin for any of these deposits should diligently try to verify the assumed age by dating them.

K. Sediments. Flood geology cannot explain how the proposed gigantic tidal waves could fill the Rocky Mountain seaway (Cordilleran geosyncline of the Cretaceous, which subsequently uplifted to form the Rocky Mountains) with billions of km^3 of sediments from the W, and the Appalachian geosyncline (Paleozoic trough that uplifted to become the folded Appalachians) with terrestrial sediments from the E, and at the same time not scatter the terrestrial sediments into the ocean basins. The fact that continents were not denuded of even their loose sediment demonstrates the nonexistence of such hypothetical gigantic tidal waves. The Genesis account does not give the faintest suggestion of tidal waves; rather, Noah and the ark appear to quietly ride out the flood.

Furthermore, Genesis seems to indicate the existence of the Tigris and Euphrates Rivers in Mesopotamia before and after the flood. Thus even transient geomorphological features like river systems and regolith (loose rock material) survived the flood with no demonstrable change. Another serious question to be faced by advocates of the various flood theories is what would happen to all the neritic (shallow) marine life, for example, immobile coral and bottom dwellers, if suddenly the depth of water were increased by several miles, and that by the addition of nonmarine or fresh water. Both the increased pressure and decreased salinity would have a devastating effect on marine life. There is no evidence of such a recent massive extinction or decimation of the population.

L. Serious flaw. Perhaps the most serious flaw exhibited in flood geology treatment is the incompatibility with the scientific method. To hold to the flood geology theory of catastrophism in the face of all the evidence to the contrary, much data and analytical techniques must be rejected, even though they can be demonstrated repeatedly by observation and measurements. Clearly this is not an objective approach. An objective approach allows and demands that we change our interpretations when established data warrant it.

M. Geologic time table. A geologic time table of many consistent data-points over 3,000 million years (or 4,500 million years including meteorites and lunar rock samples) has been obtained on geological materials by several independent, established radioactive methods. This is confirmed by many research scientists in numerous countries around the world. No one has been able to alter the rates of radioactive decay by physical, chemical, or radiation techniques. It appears that God, the Creator, has provided us with a built-in geochronometer with which to unravel the time problems of the universe. These indicate that the solar system is about 4500 million years old which is compatible with Genesis in that it gives no age—"In the beginning"—and with our eternal God who existed even before he created time.

VII. Conclusions. In conclusion, the predominance of qualified Christian scholarship appears to favor a local flood interpretation because of the lack of evidence for, as well as the problems attendant on, a universal flood. There is no lack of writers who propose a catastrophic universal flood. However, they present little that is new, and no data that are convincing. The serious Bible student will not seek to support the physical aspects of Bible history with pseudoscience. In the final analysis the true interpretation of the biblical flood account will fully accord with true science. At this time we may favor one viewpoint over another but must seek continually to integrate all the pertinent data that seem well established. (For a more up-to-date and detailed treatment see D. A. Young, *The Biblical Flood: A Case Study of the Church's Response to Extrabiblical Evidence* [1995].) W. U. AULT

floor. The most common use of the word *floor* in the Bible is in the term "threshing floor" (Heb. *gōren* H1755, Gen. 50:10–11 and often; Gk. *halōn* G272, Matt. 3:12; Lk. 3:17). It refers to a flat platform of stone or clay often in the open to insure the blowing wind for WINNOWING. Either walking animals or dragging sleds were used to separate the grain from the stock. Other Hebrew terms may be rendered "floor," such as *qarqaʿ* H7977, "floor, bottom" (Num. 5:17 et al.) and *ṣēlāʿ* H7521, "side, wing [of building], story" (1 Ki. 6:8). G. GIACUMAKIS, JR.

flora. The Linnean Society of Burlington House in London, probably the oldest Botanical society in the world, says that there are in the plant world 111 natural orders. Although *natural order* may correspond to *family*—that is, "a group of one or more genera, having close natural affinity"—the term is "usually applied to a group of families nearly related to one another" (Royal Horticultural Society, *Dictionary of Gardening* [1951]; several editions through 2001). The *genera* (sg. *genus*), in turn, are groups of *species* with common structural characters, which may be supposed to have derived in the remote past from some common ancestor. The main characters on which reliance is placed in defining genera are found in the flower, fruit, and seed. The number of species in a genus may be extremely large, or may be only one, so much structurally isolated from its nearest relative as to stand by itself. The name of the genus in designating a plant is placed first and invariably has a capital initial letter.

In this article, the rules of the Royal Horticultural Society's *Dictionary* have been adhered to (for a more recent official taxonomy see J. McNeill et al., *International Code of Botanical Nomenclature* [2006]). The correct Latin names have been given in each case, as far as the writer can ascertain them; the generic name has been given, together with the species, and in some cases, the common English name as well. Of the 111 natural orders recognized by the Linnean Society, some fifty-four are found in the Bible, either in the OT or NT, while a few appear in the APOCRYPHA. It must be remembered that the Bible is largely a Middle Eastern book, and therefore the natural orders that are included are those normally found in that part of the world. In order to cover the whole flora of the Bible methodically and intelligently, the natural orders are first listed by classification, then discussed in alphabetical order.

(For illustrative drawings and further information, see W. B. Shewell-Cooper, *Plants, Flowers, and Herbs of the Bible* [1977], and the United Bible Societies handbook, *Fauna and Flora of the Bible*, 2nd ed. [1980], referred to below as *FFB*. Both M. Zohary, *Plants of the Bible* [1982], and F. Nigel Hepper, *Baker Encyclopedia of Bible Plants* [1992], include numerous color photographs. See also I. Jacob and W. Jacob, "Flora," in *ABD*, 2:803–17. For a more comprehensive treatment, see M. Zohary et al., *Conspectus florae orientalis: An Annotated Catalogue of the Flora of the Middle East*, 5 fascicles [1980–90]. Note that the scientific identifications included in *HALOT* depend heavily on J. Löw, *Die Flora der Juden*, 4 vols. [1924–34], which is a fundamental work, but not always correct.)

Classification of biblical plants
1. Cereals
    a. Barley (Gramineae)
    b. Beans (Leguminosae)
    c. Lentils (Leguminosae)
    d. Millet (Gramineae)
    e. Wheat (Gramineae)
2. Fruit trees
    a. Almond (Rosaceae)
    b. Apple (Rosaceae, Solanaceae)

c. Fig (Moraceae)
   d. Mulberry tree (Moraceae)
   e. Nuts (Anacardiaceae, Juglandaceae)
   f. Olive tree (Elaeagnaceae; Oleaceae)
   g. Palm tree (Palmaceae)
   h. Pomegranate (Punicaceae)
   i. Sycamore (Moraceae)
   j. Vine (Vitaceae)
3. Vegetables and gourds
   a. Cucumber (Cucurbitaceae)
   b. Endive (Compositae)
   c. Garlic (Liliaceae)
   d. Leek (Leguminosae, Liliaceae)
   e. Onion (Liliaceae)
4. Flax (Linaceae)
5. Flavors and condiments
   a. Anise (Umbelliferae)
   b. Fitches (Ranunculaceae)
   c. Mint (Labiatae)
   d. Mustard (Cruciferae)
   e. Saffron (Iridaceae)
   f. Salt (Chenopodiaceae)
6. Balms, drugs and incense
   a. Aloes (Liliaceae)
   b. Balm (Zygophyllaceae)
   c. Cane, calamus, sweet cane, sweet calamus (Gramineae)
   d. Cassia (Compositae)
   e. Cinnamon (Lauraceae)
   f. Galbanum (Lauraceae)
   g. Henna (Lythraceae)
   h. Myrrh (Burseraceae, Cistaceae)
   i. Spikenard, nard (Valerianaceae)
   j. Spices (Leguminosae)
7. Costly timbers
   a. Algum, almug timber (Leguminosae)
   b. Ebony (Ebenaceae)
   c. Gopher wood (Pinaceae)
8. Forest trees and shrubs
   a. Acacia tree, acacia wood (Loranthaceae)
   b. Bay tree (Lauraceae)
   c. Box tree (Buxaceae)
   d. Bush, thornbush (Compositae)
   e. Cedar (Pinaceae)
   f. Fir, fir tree (Pinaceae)
   g. Juniper (Leguminosae)
   h. Laurel (Lauraceae)
   i. Hyssop (Labiatae)
   j. Mallow (Chenopodiaceae)
   k. Myrtle (Myrtaceae)
   l. Oil tree, wild olive (Elaeagnaceae)
   m. Oak (Fagaceae)
   n. Pine (Pinaceae)
   o. Storax tree (Styracaceae)
   p. Terebinth, turpentine tree (Anacardiaceae)
   q. Willow (Salicaceae)
9. Lilies and roses (Amaryllidaceae, Apocynaceae, Iridaceae, Liliaceae, Nymphaeaceae, Ranunculaceae, Rosaceae)
10. Reeds and rushes
    a. Cattail (Typhaceae)
    b. Flag, meadow, reeds (Butomaceae)
    c. Reeds (Gramineae)
    d. Rush, papyrus, bulrushes (Cyperaceae)
11. Thorns and thistles
    a. Brier (Rosaceae)
    b. Thistle (Compositae)
    c. Thorn (Compositae)
12. Weeds and nettles
    a. Cockle (Caryophyllaceae)
    b. Nettle (Acanthaceae, Cruciferae, Urticaceae)
    c. Tares (Gramineae)
    d. Wheel, rolling thing, whirling dust (Compositae, Cruciferae)
13. Wormwoods and poisons
    a. Bitter herbs (Rutaceae)
    b. Gall, hemlock (Cucurbitaceae)
    c. Wormwood (Compositae)
14. Hedges and fences
    a. Brambles, thorns (Rosaceae)
15. Other plants
    a. Caper (Capparidaceae)
    b. Mandrake (Solanaceae)

Acanthaceae. The only plant possibly mentioned in this natural order is the *Acanthus syriacus*, a common WEED in Palestine, growing strongly and having spiny leaves (*ḥārûl* H3017, variously translated "nettle, undergrowth, weed," Job 30:7; Prov. 24:31; Zeph. 2:9). The Hebrew term, however, may refer to one or more species of the genus *Urtica* (see *FFB*, 152–53). Other suggestions include chick pea, wild artichoke, and vetchling.

Amaryllidaceae. In this natural order, only one plant is probably mentioned: the *Narcissus tazetta*, called today a Polyanthus Narcissus (*ḥăbaṣṣelet H2483*, traditionally translated ROSE, Cant. 2:1 [of Sharon]; Isa. 35:1). It is yellow and very sweet smelling, is plentiful in the SHARON Plain, and grows on the hills around JERUSALEM and JERICHO. Alternate identifications are the CROCUS (cf. NIV and NRSV in Isaiah), the asphodel, and the red tulip (see *FFB*, 150–51).

Anacardiaceae. There are three trees that may be grouped in this natural order: (1) *Pistacia lentiscus*, a shrubby, evergreen dwarfish tree that produces a scented gum from its branches when pierced (*ṣŏrî H7661*, usually translated "balm," Gen. 37:25 et al.). The Hebrew word may refer to the *P. mutica* (mastic resin) or to the *Balanites aegyptiaca* (see *FFB*, 93–94). (2) *Pistacia terebinthus palaestina* (turpentine tree), an oak-like, deciduous tree, growing 20–24 ft. high, which produces almost invisible flowers, followed by pretty, red fruits; when the branches are pierced, a Cyprus turpentine oozes out. This species may be mentioned in the OT (*ʾēlâ H461*, usually rendered OAK or TEREBINTH, Gen. 35:4 et al.), but many believe that the Hebrew term refers to an unspecified stately tree (*FFB*, 182–83; see also below under Fagaceae). (3) *Pistacia vera*, a spreading tree that can grow to a height of 30 ft.; it bears light-colored nuts, containing greenish-yellow kernels sweet to the taste. These may be the "pistachio nuts" of Gen. 43:11 (*boṭnâ H1063*), but some argue that they are rather the fruit of the *P. terebinthus palaestina* (cf. *FFB*, 165; *HALOT*, 1:121).

Apocynaceae. The Apocrypha makes mention of the *rhodon*, "rose" (Sir. 24:14; 39:13). This is probably the *Nerium oleander*, a beautiful flowering shrub that grows up to 12 ft. tall, bearing masses of white or pink flowers. These are often double, and it is claimed for this reason that they have a rose-like look. The leaves are evergreen, but they are poisonous. See also below under Cruciferae (1).

Araliaceae. Only one plant is included under this natural order, the *Hedera helix* (*kissos*, 2 Macc. 6:7; cf. 3 Macc. 2:29). No one doubts that this is the common English or British ivy, which was plaited into wreaths and often worn on the head like crowns by those who were to go in procession in the temple. As a plant, the ivy was dedicated to the wine god, Bacchus (DIONYSUS), by the Greeks. Today the plant has lost its heathen connotation.

Burseraceae. A natural order of 13 genera and 320 species, all of which are shrubs and trees which grow in the tropics only. The flowers are generally small and unisexual, the fruits are capsules or drupes, and most of the species produce resins or balsam. The MYRRH mentioned in Scripture (*mōr H5255*, Exod. 30:23 et al.; *smyrna G5043*, Matt. 2:11 et al.) undoubtedly came from the plant normally called *Commiphora*, but the present writer is not certain to which particular species this refers. *Commiphora abyssinica* (also *C. africana*) is a small, thorny tree from which myrrh is obtained; both the wood and the bark produce a strong scent. It is often said that the myrrh came from *Commiphora myrrha*, which was called *Balsamodendron myrrha* many years ago and subsequently renamed *Canarium*—from *canari*, the Malayan name. (See *FFB*, 147–49.) See also below under Cistaceae. Note further that the Bible may refer to the *Commiphora opobalsamum* (or *Balsamodendron opobalsamum*; cf. *HALOT*, 1:163) with the term *bōśem H1411*, usually rendered "spice" (Exod. 25:6 et al.; see *FFB*, 177).

Butomaceae. The plant found in this natural order is *Butomus umbellatus*, mentioned in connection with Pharaoh's dream (Gen 41:2, 18; also Job 8:11). The word used here (*ʾāḥû H286*) is apparently Egyptian and not truly Hebrew and would appear to be a reed grass or flowering rush. This plant, growing in the marshy sides of the NILE, would be eaten by the cattle. (See *FFB*, 125–26.)

Buxaceae. In this natural order is found only *Buxus longifolia*, the BOX TREE, a slender, hardy evergreen, which may grow 20 ft. high (Isa. 41:19; 60:13 KJV; possibly also Ezek. 27:6). The wood is hard and polishes well, and so is much used for carving, wood engraving, furniture, and the like. Because this tree is not found in Palestine today, it has been argued that it could not have been there in biblical days, and many scholars think the word refers to the CYPRESS (cf. NIV). It is far more sensible to believe that the box trees were so popular and coveted that they became extinct in that country.

Capparidaceae. The word rendered "desire" in Eccl. 12:5 (*ʾăbiyyônâ H37*) refers literally to the CAPERBERRY, the fruit of the *Capparis spinosa* (or *C. sicula*), which was regarded as an aphrodisiac. The common caper is found growing profusely in many parts of Palestine, and especially on the hilly slopes round about Jerusalem. It can cover ruins like ivy, or it can spread over the ground. Not only are the berries picked, pickled, and used in the kitchen, but the little unopened flower buds are also popular when pickled in vinegar. (See *FFB*, 102).

Caryophyllaceae. Only one possible plant is mentioned from this natural order: *Agrostemma githago*, the corn COCKLE, a common weed in Palestine. It can grow 2–3 ft. tall and be a great nuisance; the blooms, much like those of the campion, may be white, red, or purple. The KJV translates *boʾšâ* H947 with "cockle" (Job 31:40), but this Hebrew word may simply refer in general to foul WEEDS (cf. NRSV) or specifically to darnel (*Lolium temulentum*; cf. *FFB*, 195).

Chenopodiaceae. The only plant in this natural order is *Atriplex halimus*, a kind of saltwort related to the spinach, also known as sea purslane and sea orache (Heb. *mallûaḥ* H4865 [from *melaḥ* H4875, "salt"], Job 30:4; the NRSV renders it MALLOW, while the NIV more generally "salt herbs"). It is naturally found round about the DEAD SEA (*FFB*, 136–37). There are incidentally over twenty species of *Atriplex* in Palestine. Some scholars, however, believe that the Hebrew word refers to a species of fig-marigold.

Cistaceae. There are three possible entries under this natural order: the rockroses *Cistus salvifolius*, *C. creticus*, and *C. villosus*. It all depends on how one understands the word *lōṭ* G4320 (Gen. 37:25; 43:11; NIV, "myrrh"; NRSV, "resin"). This scented product could indeed have come from one of the flowering rockroses. The name *ladanum* is given to the gummy, dark-brown, blackish substance that will ooze out of the foliage and little stems of the cistus plants (*FFB*, 149). This gum is very fragrant. It is collected by drawing a piece of material over a bush, and the substance sticks to the cloth and can afterward be removed. It is wondered whether *Cistus creticus* really ought to go into this list, as it is not predominantly Palestinian.

Compositae. There are eight possible plants that can be included in this natural order. (1) The first is *Anthemis palaestina*, the chamomile, with its aromatic leaves and daisy-like little flowers. It is very common in Palestine, where the plants are in flower from February to May and June; they are dried like hay, and can be burned. According to some, this is the plant referred to by Jesus when he said that "not even Solomon in all his splendor was dressed like one of these" (Matt. 6:28; Lk. 12:27). The Greek word *krinon* G3211 occurs in nonbiblical Greek literature with reference to the LILY (*Lilium candidum* or *L. chalcedonicum*; see below under Liliaceae), which is the traditional rendering, but the term is probably used generically of beautiful flowers. Suggestions include crocus, gladiolus, and especially anemone (*FFB*, 135–36; bibliography in BDAG, 567). See also below, under Ranunculaceae (1).

(2) *Artemisia herba-alba* (or *A. judaica* or *A. absinthium*), the wormwood, mentioned in various passages (*laʿănâ* H4360, used only figuratively of bitterness, Deut. 29:18 et al.; *apsinthos* G952 Rev. 8:11). All wormwood has an acrid smell and the leaves taste bitter. The ancient Jews thought the plants to be poisonous. *Herba-alba*, which has a camphor fragrance, is the most common species in Palestine, but one cannot be absolutely sure to which species Scripture refers. See also below under Cucurbitaceae (1).

(3) It is thought that the THISTLES mentioned in some passages (*dardar* H1998, Gen. 3:18; Hos. 10:8; other terms elsewhere) are a reference to the star thistle, *Centaurea calcitrapa*. Some identify it as a subspecies of *C. pallescens* (*HALOT*, s.v.). The problem here is that one cannot obviously be sure of the species, let alone the genus. There are other thistles found in Palestine today, such as *C. iberica* and *C. verutum*.

(4) The BITTER HERBS (pl. of *mārōr* H5353) to be eaten during PASSOVER (Exod. 12:8; Num. 9:11) may be chicory, *Cichorium intybus*. It could as easily be the *C. endivia*, the "endive," which is much used as a salad today. In Great Britain, roots of chicory are forced in heat and in the dark, in order to produce the golden chicons used as a salad. In Palestine, the leaves of both these plants would be eaten as growing, and this is why they were described as tasting bitter. The bitterness is removed today by blanching, which is the etiolation of the leaves by keeping out the light. Some believe that the reference is to a species of *Centaurea*. (See *FFB*, 98.)

(5) The next plant to be found in this natural order is *Saussurea lappa*, that is, the orrisroot (Ps. 45:8; see CASSIA). The plant is a perennial with strong roots, and looks like a thistle when growing,

often 6 ft. high. (See *FFB*, 104–5.) See also below, Lauraceae (1).

(6) The *Gundelia tournefortii* is best described as a prickly, milky herb with headlets of six to seven flowerets. The leaves are leathery, thick, and rigid, having prominent veins; the plants usually are easy to find around Nazareth and Jerusalem, and near the sea of Tiberias. This is one of the plants thought to be the *galgal H1650*, "rolling thing" (Ps. 83:13; Isa. 17:13; NIV, "tumbleweed," but NRSV, "whirling dust"), because it is thistle-like and can curl up into a ball so that it rolls in the wind. It collects sometimes in the hollows or dips. (See *FFB*, 187–88.)

(7) *Notobasis syriaca* is a very common Palestinian plant found growing on the roadsides and in the fields. The stems are erect and branching, the leaves are glabrous above and hairy below, and they are edged with spines. The flowerets are tubular. This is one of the thistle-like plants that may find a place in Scripture, being perhaps the THORN mentioned in some passages (e.g., Job 31:40; Isa. 34:13).

(8) *Xanthium spinosum* is the burrweed or clot burr found at the roadsides, bearing tripartite, green leaves, wedge-shaped at base, with strong yellow spines. This may be the plant referred to by the term *qimmôś H7853* (Prov. 24:31; Isa. 34:13; Hos. 9:6). The clot burr is very prickly. The plants are usually 3 ft. tall and produce tiny green flowers at the top of the stems. See also below under Cruciferae (3).

Cruciferae. It seems that three plants mentioned in the Bible can be included in this natural order. (1) The "rolling thing" already referred to (Ps. 83:13; Isa. 17:13; see above under Compositae 6), and even the "rose" (Sir. 24:14; 39:13; see above under Apocynaceae), could be the *Anastatica hierochuntica*. This tumbleweed of Palestine is known in Great Britain as the resurrection plant. It grows flat on the ground and, after flowering and seeding, curls up to form a hollow ball. Later, the stem breaks in two and the ball rolls away in the wind. As it travels it sows the seeds it contains. This spreads the weed everywhere. Thousands may be seen in Palestine, rolling about and traveling at a fast rate in gales. (2) The MUSTARD mentioned in the NT (*sinapi G4983*, Matt. 13:31) is probably the *Brassica nigra*. In Palestine the plant was grown for the oil it produced and not for the yellow condiment so much used today. This annual plant normally grows 4 ft. high, but the writer has seen in Palestine plants growing to a height of 15 ft. (see further *FFB*, 145–46). (3) The third plant in this natural order is *Sinapsis arvensis* or charlock, which may be the nettle or thorn referred to by the Hebrew term *qimmôś H7853* (Prov. 24:31; Isa. 34:13; Hos. 9:6; but see above under Compositae 8). A very common weed in fields of wheat, it looks like mustard, has yellow flowers, and grows about 3 ft. high.

Cucurbitaceae. (1) The *Citrullus colocynthis* may be described as a clambering plant like a squash or marrow, bearing round, orange-like fruits, with a very hard skin. This wild vine is a very common plant in Palestine; the fruits look tempting, but when eaten are found to be extremely bitter, having purgative and even poisonous qualities (see *FFB*, 124–25). These are probably the GOURDS that were put into a pot of stew, causing sickness in the company of the prophets (*paqquʿōt H7226*, 2 Ki. 4:29). Some have thought that the Hebrew term *rōʾš H8032* (also spelled *rôš*), which is used of POISON generally, including the venom of snakes, may in some passages refer to this fruit (e.g., Ps. 69:21; Hos. 10:4; but see *FFB*, 167–68).

(2) A second plant found in this natural order is the CUCUMBER, *Cucumis sativus* (possibly *C. chate* or *C. melo*; Heb. *qiššuʾâ H7991*, only Num. 11:5; cf. *miqšâ H5252*, Isa. 1:8; Jer. 10:5). It is said that cucumbers were much eaten, being easy to grow and cheap, by the children of Israel when in bondage in Egypt. Whether the cucumbers they ate were the normal ones grown today, or the *C. chate*, the present writer cannot tell. This species has been described as being somewhat variable in shape; the fruit being fusiform, or cylindrical, and a foot long or more. It develops a woody rind and is picked before it reaches the ripe state, and is then cooked and eaten (information supplied by Sir George Taylor, Director of the Royal Botanic Gardens, Kew, England; see also *FFB*, 112–13).

Cynomoriaceae, sometimes called **Balanophoraceae.** *Cynomorium cocineum* is a parasitic plant found in the salt marshes and in the sand dunes, as well as in the Plain of Jericho toward the Dead Sea. It bears a crimson petal-like leaf called a spathe, which makes it very conspicuous. One biblical passage speaks of people eating the root of the BROOM tree (Job 30:4), but since this is poisonous, some have thought that the reference here is to the root of *Cynomorium*. See also below under Leguminosae (4).

Cyperaceae. The only plant found under this natural order is *Cyperus papyrus*, which was almost a menace along the sides of the Nile in biblical days; it was also the BULRUSH from which the PAPYRUS writing material was made (*gōmeʾ* **H1687**, Exod. 2:3; Job 8:11; Isa. 19:6; 58:5). These rushes are said to have grown as high as 16 ft. and could be 3 in. thick. It is no wonder when they were growing in a mass that they could hide little MOSES floating in his basket made with the same reeds.

Ebenaceae. There is little doubt that the EBONY (*hobnîm* **H2041**) mentioned in Ezek. 27:15 is *Diospyros ebenum* (according to *HALOT*, 1:237, *D. mespiliformis*). This is the best of many kinds of ebony. Large trees can be produced whose heart wood is usually jet black, though occasionally streaked brown or yellow. It is extremely heavy and strong (see *FFB*, 117). The *Diospyros lotus* (sometimes called *D. ebenaster*) or date plum also is found in this natural order, but in the present writer's opinion is not the tree referred to in Scripture.

Elaeagnaceae. Though in this natural order there are three genera and about forty-five species, the only one that seems to appear in the Bible is the oleaster, *Elaeagnus angustifolia* (*E. hortensis*; cf. *HALOT*, 4:1569, s.v. שֶׁמֶן, sect. C), apparently referred to with the expression ʿēṣ-šemen, lit., "wood of oil" (1 Ki. 6:23 et al.; others think it refers to the Aleppo PINE, see below under Pinaceae). The oleaster is a deciduous tree growing some 20 ft. high, with spiny branches and narrow, oblong leaves. The flowers are yellow within and silver without, and the fruits are yellowish, oval, with silvery scales (see *FFB*, 157–58). They are mealy and sweet. Some writers have called this tree the wild olive, but this does not mean that it is truly related to *Olea europaea* (see below under Oleaceae).

Fagaceae. OAKS are mentioned repeatedly in English Bible versions, though the five Hebrew terms involved seem to refer generically to strong or stately trees (ʾ*ayil* **H381**, Ps. 29:9 et al.; ʾ*ēlâ* **H461**, Gen. 35:4 et al.; ʾ*ēlôn* **H471**, 12:6 et al.; ʾ*allôn* **H473**, 35:8 et al.; ʾ*allâ* **H464**, only Josh. 24:26; these words are all related to ʾ*ēl* IV **H445**, "power, strength"; cf. also the Hebrew names for God, EL and ELOAH, ELOHIM). It is difficult to know for certain which oaks were grown in Palestine at the time, but there is little doubt that the list included the valonia oak, *Quercus aegilops*, which produces the largest acorn cups and acorns of any species. The tree is widely spread in the Eastern Mediterranean region. It undoubtedly includes also the kermes oak, or grain

Bulrush reeds.

tree, so called because it is the host plant of the kermes insect (*Chermes ilicis*), which produces a remarkable scarlet dye. The leaves are thick, hard, and prickly; the acorns solitary on a short stalk, more than half enclosed in the cup. This is the most pleasing of the dwarf evergreen oaks. (See further *FFB*, 154–55, 182–83.)

There is a variety of *Coccifera* called *Pseudococcifera* also found in Palestine, and it is said that Abraham's oak tree at Mamre was this variety. The holm tree, *Quercus ilex*, could also be included because it is a native of the Eastern Mediterranean, being an evergreen tree of good size, often 40–50 ft. high. The acorns are usually 0.75 in. long, produced two or three together on a short stalk. There has been a suggestion that *Quercus lusitanica* should be included, but this is a native of Spain or Portugal; a variety, *infectoria*, is found in Asia Minor, but the only tree the writer has seen is small and elegant, with grayish foliage, and does not therefore seem to fit in with the biblical descriptions. Occasionally (see esp. Isa. 6:13; Hos. 4:13), the term ʾēlâ is rendered "terebinth"; see above under Anacardiaceae (3).

Gramineae. This natural order concerns the family of grasses, which includes 400 genera and 5,000 species at least. They are all monocotyledons. The starch seeds, sometimes also rich in protein, make a number of species of this natural order valuable food for man and beast. The leaves of some other species are used today for their fiber and for paper making. The following plants belonging to this natural order are mentioned in Scripture.

Women bundling wheat stalks.

(1) *Andropogon aromaticus* (also known as *Calamus aromaticus*) is probably referred to in some passages with the common Hebrew term for "cane," qāneh H7866 (the "calamus" of Cant. 4:14 et al.; see also AROMATIC CANE). This is the ginger grass of the E that all kinds of cattle love to eat. The foliage, when cut, smells of ginger; it also tastes of ginger, while from the grass may be obtained a ginger-oil. Some believe that the same term in Isa. 43:24 (NIV, "fragrant calamus") is *Saccharum officinarum*, a strong growing perennial grass, looking something like sweet corn, maize, or mealies. It certainly was not made into sugar until perhaps the 7th cent., but it may have been sucked and chewed by the Israelites as a kind of "sweet" or "candy." The sweetening of drinks in biblical times was undoubtedly by the addition of honey. (See *FFB*, 173.)

(2) A second plant is probably the *Arundo donax*, the REED mentioned in various passages (again qāneh H7866, 2 Ki. 18:21 et al.; kalamos G2812 in Matt. 11:7). It is the giant reed or Persian reed, which can grow to a height of 18 ft. and was used for fishing rods, walking sticks, and even musical instruments.

(3) The common BARLEY is *Hordeum distichon* (*H. sativum*, according to *HALOT*, 3:1346, śĕʿōrâ H8555, Exod. 9:31 et al.; krithē G3208, Rev. 6:6). The spring-sown barley is *H. vulgare*; the winter-sown barley, *H. hexastichon*. BREAD made from barley was considered food for the poor, hence the poor boy who had two small fish and five small barley loaves (krithinos G3209, Jn. 6:9, 13). GIDEON being poor also is compared to a cake of barley (Jdg. 7:13). Today, barley is made into beer, but it was not so in biblical days. Barley is an easy crop to grow in the E because it puts up with drought better than wheat, and it is ready for harvest four weeks earlier than wheat as a rule. (See *FFB*, 95–96.)

(4) *Panicum miliaceum* is the old Latin name for the true European MILLET (dōḥan H1893, only Ezek. 4:9 [possibly also pannag H7154 in 27:17]). This bears a very small grain. The grass itself does not grow more than 2 ft. high. In biblical days it was used for food, but today it is almost entirely bird seed. Large fields of millet are still grown in Palestine in some parts. According to some, the Hebrew term refers to the *Sorghum vulgare*, a millet widely grown in warmer countries under such

names as *durra*, Indian millet, Egyptian rice corn, Tunis grass (used for forage), and the Kaffir corn (it may be the reed mentioned in Matt. 27:48; Mk. 15:36). (See *FFB*, 141–42.)

(5) The *Triticums* are the wheats found again and again in Scripture: GRAIN (Gen. 40:2), bread and wheat and flour (Exod. 29:2), WHEAT (Jdg. 6:11), roasted or parched grain (1 Sam. 17:17). As in the case of barley, there is winter-sown as well as spring-sown wheat, both *Triticum aestivum* (*ḥiṭṭâ* H2636, Gen. 30:14 et al.; *sitos* G4992, Matt. 3:12 ct al.). There is also bearded wheat, *T. compositum*; one-grained wheat, *T. monoccum*; and Egyptian wheat, *T. tungidum*. Today in Palestine, *T. durum* and *T. vulgare* are grown almost entirely. Wheat has always been one of the most important crops of Palestine, and has been called "the staff of life." (See *FFB*, 195–97.)

(6) *Lolium temulentum* is an annual, called the bearded darnel and sometimes referred to as TARES, which is found in the fields of grain around Jaffa and Jericho (*zizanion* G2429, Matt. 13:25 et al.; see *FFB*, 194–95). See also WEEDS, and above under Caryophyllaceae.

Iridaceae. This is a family of some 57 genera and over 800 species. Most are tuberous or rhizomatous plants of great importance to the gardener. (1) The *Iris pseudacorus* is the yellow flag iris, which grows 3 ft. high and is found in Europe as well as in the Middle E. The flowers are bright yellow and almost scentless. There were numerous irises grown in Palestine, but this species is the one that grows by the water side, and so fits the full description in Sir. 50:8, "like lilies by a spring of waters" (the other species grow largely on the hillsides). However, see below under Liliaceae.

(2) The SAFFRON (*karkōm* H4137, only Cant. 4:14) is probably the blue-flowered *Crocus sativus*, saffron crocus. This was grown in very large quantities in Saffron Waldon, Essex, for the saffron powder used to flavor cakes and puddings (400 crocus stigmas are needed to produce one ounce of saffron powder). Other identifications include *Curcuma longa* (cf. *HALOT*, 2:498) and *Carthamus tinctorius*. (See *FFB*, 174–75.)

Juglandaceae. The name of this natural order is derived from *Jovis glans* (Jupiter's acorn). There are sixteen species, all of them deciduous trees bearing walnuts, the common walnut being *Juglans regia* (*ʾĕgôz* H100, only Cant. 6:11). This tree will grow to a height of 65 ft. Not only are the nuts much prized but the wood is classed as one of the best timbers; it is much used for furniture. *Juglans regia* is not indigenous to Palestine, but must have been introduced long before Solomon's time. The beautiful shade as well as the fragrant leaves and delicious nuts the trees give would have been much beloved by Solomon's relatives and friends. (See *FFB*, 192–93.)

Labiatae. This natural order contains 160 genera and 3,000 species, only two of which are mentioned in thc Bible. Curiously enough, though, the family is widely distributed—particularly so in the Mediterranean region. It is a natural order that contains most of the culinary herbs like marjoram, thyme, savory, rosemary, sage, basil, horehound, and so on.

(1) *Mentha longifolia* (*hēdyosmon* G2455, Matt. 23:23 = Lk. 11:42) is the common house or hairy MINT, which grows 3 ft. high and has pale purple flowers. Why some have suggested this could be *Mentha sativa* the present writer cannot understand; it is doubted whether this plant (really a cross of *M. arvensis* with *M. spicata*) was in existence in NT times. (See *FFB*, 143–44.)

(2) The HYSSOP (*ʾēzôb* H257, Exod. 12:22 et al.; *hyssōpos* G5727, Jn. 19:29; Heb. 9:19) is *Origanum maru* or *O. syriacum*, a shrubby plant, growing about 40 in. high with erect, stiff, hairy branches and long, hairy, thick leaves. The flowers are purplish, being borne in oblong spikes. It is quite common in Palestine and Syria.

Lauraceae. This family includes 45 genera and 1,000 species, mostly tropical and subtropical trees and shrubs, usually evergreen—all parts being aromatic. Only two species are found in the Bible. (1) The *Cinnamomum cassia* (*qiddâ* H7703, Exod. 30:24 and Ezek. 27:19), sometimes used as an adulterant in the true CINNAMON (*C. zeylanicum*), was certainly imported, probably from Ceylon. The genus *Cinnamomum* includes about 40 species of evergreen trees, all of which would seem to be natives of SE Asia. (See *FFB*, 104–5.) See also above, Compositae (5).

(2) *Laurus nobilis* is the bay laurel or sweet bay, an evergreen aromatic tree, growing often 60 ft. high,

and native to Palestine. The flowers are small and greenish-yellow, often inconspicuous. The leaves are dark, shining green. It certainly is an easy tree to grow, and a very leafy one. Some think that the bay laurel is referred to in Ps. 37:5 (NIV, "flourishing like a green tree in its native soil"), but the text is difficult and often emended (cf. NRSV, "towering like a cedar of Lebanon," following the LXX). Others believe this tree is mentioned in Isa. 44:14 (Heb. ʾōren H815; NIV, "pine"; NRSV, "cedar").

Leguminosae. This natural order includes trees, shrubs, perennial and annual plants, diverse in habit. There are about 430 genera and some 7,000 species. On their roots, these plants have nodular outgrowths formed by bacteria that have the power of using the free nitrogen in the air. The plants therefore benefit, and further, the nodules may be left behind for the benefit of crops that are to follow. Thus the "legume" plant may be said to enrich the soil at no cost to itself. There appear to be eight plants in this natural order mentioned in the Bible.

(1) The first one is *Acacia nilotica*, one of the plants that, according to some critics, may be the answer to the miracle of the BURNING BUSH (*sĕneh* H6174, Exod. 3:2–4; Deut. 33:16). See also below, under Loranthaceae.

(2) *Astragalus tragacantha* is probably the plant referred to as "spices" (*nĕkōʾt* H5780, Gen. 37:25; 43:11; NRSV, "gum"). It is an evergreen shrub, much branched and very thorny, and growing only 3 ft. high as a rule. Some believe that the Hebrew word refers to the *Astragalus gummifer* or to the resin from the rockrose. It has also been suggested that the *A. tragacantha* is referred to with the Hebrew word *bōśem* H1411 (Exod. 25:6 et al.; cf. *FFB*, 178), but see above under Burseraceae.

(3) *Cercis siliquastrum* is the Judas tree, which can grow to 40 ft., but is usually smaller. The blood-like flowers, purply-red or rose, are produced directly on the trunk and branches, giving the idea of the tree "bleeding." Although not mentioned directly in the Bible, this is the tree from which JUDAS ISCARIOT is supposed to have hung himself (Matt. 27:5).

(4) *Genista raetam*, also called *Reata raetam*, is the white BROOM or juniper bush—very graceful indeed. The white sweet-pea-scented flowers are followed by pods about 0.4 in. long. The bush may grow to 10 ft. high in Palestine, so it could have given ELIJAH plenty of shade (*rōtem* H8413, 1 Ki. 19:4–5; also Job 30:4; Ps. 120:4). (See *FFB*, 100.)

(5) *Lens esculenta* is the LENTILS mentioned in Gen. 25:34 (*ʿădāšîm* H6378), when JACOB gave ESAU a soup, or when BARZILLAI brought food to DAVID (2 Sam. 17:28; see also 23:11; Ezek. 4:9). This is a vetch-like annual plant, 12–18 in. high, which produces pale-blue-colored, sweet-pea-like striped flowers, followed by pods containing one pealike seed that splits up into the lentils known and used today. (See *FFB*, 134; illustration on p. 133.)

(6) *Pterocarpus santalinus*, the red sandalwood, is presumed to be the ALMUG TREE (*ʾalmuggîm* H523, 1 Ki. 10:11–12; spelled differently in 2 Chr. 2:8; 9:10–11). The name comes from Greek *pteron*, "wing," and *karpos*, "fruit," because the pods are surrounded by broad wings. *Pterocarpus draco* is the dragon gum tree and *Pterocarpus indicus* is the burmese rosewood. Since no one quite knows where OPHIR is, it is difficult to pinpoint the species of tree referred to, but it may well be the red sandalwood. It has been argued, however, that the word refers to the *Juniperus phoenicia*, which is native to LEBANON (*FFB*, 88).

(7) *Trigonella foenum-graecum* (from *treis* meaning "three," and *gony*, "angle," because the flowers have a triangular appearance) is the annual fenugreek, which was eaten as a salad by the Egyptians and Israelites. The plant grows up to 2 ft. high, quite erect, and produces tiny white flowers. Years ago this plant was used in medicine and as a vegetable. It may be the LEEK referred to in Num. 11:5 (*ḥāṣîr* H2946), but most scholars believe the Hebrew word (to be distinguished from another word of the same form, *ḥāṣîr* H2946, "grass") refers to *Allium porrum*; see below, under Liliaceae (2).

(8) *Faba vulgaris* is undoubtedly the bean mentioned in 1 Sam. 17:28 and Ezek. 4:9 (*pôl* H7038). Its synonym is *Vicia faba*, the broad bean. It bears white flowers with large blue-black spots on them. The pods are large and thick, often 7–8 in. long. It has been widely cultivated for years. (See *FFB*, 97.)

Liliaceae. This is a large natural order, containing over 200 genera and 2,000 species distributed all over the world. Most of the species are perennials and bulbous. (1) The ONION, *Allium cepa*, is said to have come originally from PERSIA. The Israelites longed for the onions of Egypt when they were on the march to the Promised Land (*bāṣāl H1294*, Num. 11:5). The Egyptians' onions even today are among the best, since they ripen so well in that country. The city of Ashkelon (from which the word *scallion* is derived) also developed a reputation for fine onions. (For this and the next two items, see *FFB*, 159–60.)

(2) *Allium porrum* is the LEEK; it should now be called *Allium ampeloprasum porrum*. This is a plant whose main stem is blanched when it can be 2 ft. or more long and one inch across. This is also the pot leek, which is stouter and shorter, say, 1 ft. of ivory white stem, 2 in. or more thick. The nomadic Hebrew longed for these vegetables too in the wilderness (*ḥāṣîr H2946*, Num. 11:5). Leeks make good soup, and are said to be good for the throat. See also above, under Leguminosae (7).

(3) *Allium sativum* is the GARLIC, another of the Egyptian vegetables that the Israelites missed (*šûmîm H8770*, Num. 11:5). The garlic plant produces oblong ovate offsets around the planted bulb or clove. This is an extremely popular vegetable worldwide. It is claimed that garlic is the only plant containing freely assimilable sulphur. It is used medicinally for this reason, and if planted around peach trees prevents an attack of the leaf curl disease. The Talmud speaks of the value of garlic and recommends the bulbs for seasoning dishes.

(4) The cultivation of ALOES goes back to the earliest of days. There are over 200 species, 110 of them being found in Africa. The aloe mentioned in the OT is probably *Aquilaria agallocha*, also known as eaglewood (*ʾăhālôt H189*, Cant. 4:14 et al.). Its fragrance is secreted when the wood partially decays. In the one NT mention (*aloē G264*, Jn. 19:39), the reference is to *Aloë succotrina*. This plant was first introduced into Great Britain in 1697. It was lost in the intervening years and rediscovered in 1905 in Cape Province, South Africa, by the well-known amateur botanist Rudolf Marloth. The stem can be 4 ft. long, and the flowers on the top are pale red. The leaves are thick and tapered; they are pale or glaucous, sometimes blotched toward the base. (See *FFB*, 90–91.)

(5) Biblical references to the LILY (Heb. *šûšan H8808*; Gk. *krinon G3211*) may well include several species. Some believe that Cant. 2:1 ("I am ... a lily of the valleys") refers to the *Hyacinthus orientalis*, the common hyacinth, a very graceful plant that is certainly indigenous to Palestine, found largely in the rocky parts. It is much grown today in its various forms. More likely identifications are *Lilium candidum* and *L. chalcedonicum*. The former is the Madonna or white lily, whose flowers are pure white, rarely tinged with purple. The length of the stem varies from 2 to 5 ft. The flower is known to have grown in the E in biblical days. The *L. chalcedonicum* produces bright scarlet flowers, olive brown at the base. The stems are stiff, and 3–4 ft. long. *L. candidum* would be a poor claimant for inclusion but for the fact that in 1925 the first of the wild candidum lilies was discovered by students—and subsequently others were found growing. It seems likely that the red *L. chalcedonicum* is the plant referred to in Cant. 5:13, "His lips are like lilies, / dripping with myrrh" (cf. Moffatt's translation: "his lips are red lilies, breathing liquid myrrh"). A plant of great beauty, it may have been rare in the Holy Land, but there is little doubt that it was known then. In fact, it is catalogued at the Royal Botanic Gardens at Kew, England, as a Palestinian plant. (See *FFB*, 134–36.) With regard to NT passages, see above under Compositae (1).

(6) *Ornithogalum umbellatum* is commonly called the Star of Bethlehem, because of its starry white satiny flowers, has bulbs 1.5 in. thick, and the stems are often 1 ft. high. The writer has seen it growing in Palestine and in the Maltese Islands. It is a very close relation to the popular South African Chincherinchee, *Ornithogalum thyrsoides*. Its name comes from Greek *ornis* (bird) and *gala* (milk). The flowers are supposed to resemble the white excreta of birds when seen growing in stony places, and some therefore think that the DOVES' DUNG of 2 Ki. 6:25 were the baked bulbs of this plant being sold in the famine (*FFB*, 24).

(7) *Tulipa* is named after the Turkish word for "turban," which the flower is said to resemble. It is a genus of over 100 species of bulbs, and a special classification was made by Sir Daniel Hall (*The Genus Tulipa* [1940]). *Tulipa montana* or *T. ursoniana*, which some claim is mentioned in the Bible (*ḥăbaṣṣelet H2483*, Cant. 2:1, "I am a rose of Sharon"), has solitary flowers opening nearly flat. They are crimson-scarlet with a small, black blotch.

The stems are about 5 in. long, the bulb about 0.75 in. thick. A more likely candidate is *T. sharonensis*, which has a solitary wide bell as a flower, dark scarlet in color, with a dark olive blotch, narrowly margined yellow. The stem is 6 in. long, and the bulb 1 in. thick. This is undoubtedly a native of Palestine, and probably the only tulip that is. Other suggestions include the narcissus (e.g., *Narcissus tazetta* and *N. jonquilla*, both with yellow flowers) and the *Asphodelus* (a member of the lily family with clusters of white, pink, or yellow flowers). (See *FFB*, 150–51.)

Linaceae. This natural order of 9 genera and over 150 species is found all over the temperate and warm regions of the world. These are mostly trees and shrubs, several of which are very ornamental. The only biblical species is *Linum usitatissimum*, known as the common FLAX. It is an annual about 18 in. high, with an erect stem. The flowers are of a beautiful blue color. Varieties have been chosen for their value as fiber in the making of linen, and incidentally for the oil content of the seeds, known as linseed oil. From flax has come the oldest of fibers that make very good LINEN. It presumably is the main vegetable material used for cloth in biblical days. It was common enough for the flax to be blanched on the flat roofs of houses in Palestine, as RAHAB was doing when she was visited by the spies in JOSHUA's days (Josh. 2:6, Heb. *pēšet H7324*; in the NT, the Gk. term used is *linon G3351*, e.g., Rev. 15:6). (See *FFB*, 119–21.)

Loranthaceae. A family of evergreen shrubs and herbs usually with berry-like fruits. There are 21 genera and over 700 species, but only one is possibly mentioned in Scripture. Some suggest that the burning bush (*sĕneh H6174*, Exod. 3:4) was the crimson-flowered plant *Loranthus acaciae*, or strap-flowered acacia. This is a parasitic plant found growing on acacias in Palestine. The claim is that the flame-like blossoms looked like fire to MOSES when growing on a bush—a rather unlikely explanation, since Moses would probably have been familiar with this plant. See also above, under Leguminosae (1).

Lythraceae. A family of 21 genera and 50 species, found everywhere except in the colder regions. They may be herbaceous perennials, shrubs, or trees. The only plant of this genus found in the OT is *Lawsonia inermis*, the HENNA plant, a shrub growing to a height of 10 ft., bearing rose-colored flowers in panicles (*kōper H4110*, Cant. 1:14; 4:13; KJV wrongly, "camphire"). There is a white variety and a species called *miniata*, which bears cinnabar-red flowers. The latter was not seen in Palestine. This plant is always cultivated in the E for the production of a dye. Even today, the leaves are imported into Europe for the making of cosmetics. (See *FFB*, 127–28.)

Moraceae. A family of 55 genera and over 1,000 species, most of them trees and shrubs, but including some plants whose stems contain milky juice, found in the tropics. (1) The *Ficus carica* is the common FIG mentioned again and again in the OT and NT (Heb. *tĕʾēnâ H9300*, Gen. 3:7 et al.; Gk. *sykē G5190*, Matt. 21:19 et al.). The fruit was considered part of the staple diet of the Israelites (Mic. 4:4; Zech. 3:10). (2) The *Ficus sycomorus*, also known as *Sycomorus antiquorum*, is the SYCAMORE fig tree of the Bible (*šiqmâ H9204*, 1 Ki. 10:27 et al.; *sykomorea G5191*, Lk. 19:4). It is sometimes called the mulberry fig; it certainly is not what we today call the sycamore (*Platanus occidentalis* or buttonwood; *Acer pseudoplatanus* or sycamore maple). (3) The *Morus nigra* is the common or black MULBERRY. This can grow to a height of 30 ft. with fruit clusters 1 in. long, dark red, subacid and sweet. It is grown in some countries for the fruit, but in Great Britain for the beauty of the leaf and trunk. It is a tree indigenous to W Asia. The fruit of the

Fig tree.

black mulberry is mentioned once in the Apocrypha (*moron*, 1 Macc. 6:34), and the tree itself is probably mentioned once in the NT (*sykaminos* G5189, Lk. 17:6, although this term is used by the LXX to render Heb. *šiqmâ*, "sycamore"). The KJV, probably incorrectly, uses "mulberry tree" to render the Hebrew term *bākāʾ* H1132, "baka-shrub" or "balsam tree" (2 Sam. 5:23–24; 1 Chr. 14:14–15). (See *FFB*, 118–19, 144–45, 179–81.)

Myrtaceae. A natural order of some 70 genera and 2,800 species, usually growing in subtropical and tropical areas. The shrubs or trees are invariably aromatic and evergreen, and the flowers are usually showy. *Myrtis communis* is the common MYRTLE, a densely-leaved shrub with downy shoots that can grow 15 ft. tall (*hădas* H2072, Neh. 8:15 et al.). The solitary flowers are small and white and scented when bruised. These are followed by a purple-black berry, half an inch long. The myrtle is quite a common tree in Palestine. The leaves, flower petals, and fruits are all used in perfumes. Myrtle is a symbol of peace and justice to the Jews. Biblical references to "leafy trees" (Lev. 23:40 et al.) are thought by some to be descriptions of the myrtle. (See *FFB*, 149–50.)

Nymphaeaceae. This is the family of water plants. There are 8 genera and over 60 species found almost everywhere in the world except the Arctic regions. The flowers of this family are as a rule striking and beautiful. *Nymphaea lotus* (also *N. alba*), the Egyptian lotus or "water lily," also known as "the bride of the Nile," is the only species possibly mentioned in the Bible, if that is the plant in view when some of the ornaments of the temple are described (1 Ki. 7:19, 22; 2 Chr. 4:5; see LILYWORK). The flowers, which open on four nights only, are large and scentless; the leaves are large and flat. See also below under Rhamnaceae (2).

Oleaceae. This natural order contains 21 genera and nearly 400 species, generally speaking in subtropical areas, or certainly in warm temperatures. Some genera include plants of economic value like the fraxinus. Most others are ornamental. There is only one plant to be included here: *Olea europaea* is the well-known OLIVE, a round-headed, much branched tree often 40 ft. tall. The flowers are small and white, while the berries are oval green or black, containing one long seed each. This plant is mentioned repeatedly in Scripture, from the olive leaf plucked by Noah's dove (*zayit* H2339, Gen. 8:11) to Paul's parable of the olive tree (*elaia* G1777, Rom. 11:17–24). The tree is used as a picture of the Jewish nation (e.g., Jer. 11:16). It is the symbol of prosperity, blessing, strength, and beauty (cf. Ps. 52:8; Hos. 14:6). Kings were anointed with olive oil (1 Sam. 10:1). It can even be an instrument for healing (Jas. 5:14). Since olive wood is not useful for building, it is possible that the wood used for the doors of the inner sanctuary (1 Ki. 6:31–33) came from the narrow-leaved oleaster, *Elaeagnus angustifolia*, sometimes called wild olive. (See *FFB*, 156–58.)

Palmaceae. A natural order of 150 genera and over 1,100 species, found in the subtropics and tropics. The palms are of great importance economically, and it is said that all human wants are met by members of this natural order: food, building materials, ropes, baskets, wax, oil, alcoholic drinks, betel nuts for dyeing, and so on. The *Phoenix dactylifera* is the PALM TREE or date palm, a well-known tree in Palestine in the olden days (*tāmār* H9469, Exod. 15:27 et al.; *phoinix* G5836, Jn. 12:13; Rev. 7:9). Almost every part of the date palm is valuable: the fruit, the stones, the leaves, the trunk, the crown, the branches. The custom in the E is to cut off the male inflorescence and hang it in the top of a female tree to insure complete fertilization. The date palm, which can grow some 80 ft. high, stands out often in the plain, especially as at the apex of this straight up-and-down tree there is a beautiful large cluster of deeply serrated and feathery leaves. ABSALOM's beautiful sister was called TAMAR, because the palm stood for elegance and grace in the estimation of the Hebrews of her day. (See *FFB*, 160–62.)

Pinaceae. A natural order of 24 genera and over 300 species, all of which are found in the temperate regions of the world. The family contains many trees of great economic importance, all of them conifers. (1) *Pinus pinea* is the stone PINE or umbrella pine, a tree that will grow 80 ft. high, with a long, clean trunk. The cones are produced singly or two or three together, egg-shaped, and 5–6 in. long. These take three years to mature. The seeds found in the cones are large, and contain an edible kernel (in South Africa these are called Donna Ball "pits"). The root system is not very extensive, and many trees are blown over. Often called *Apinus pinea*, this tree is much grown in Palestine and may be the "green pine tree" referred to in Hos. 14:8. However, the meaning of the Hebrew term (*bĕrôš* H1360, also 1 Ki. 5:8 et al.) is disputed and perhaps more likely refers to (2) *Pinus halepensis*, the Aleppo pine or Jerusalem pine. This tree grows to a height of 60 ft., and the young shoots are gray with a glaucous bloom to them. The cones are short-stalked and point backward on the branches. Others think the word refers to the CYPRESS (cf. NRSV) or to the *Juniperus phoenicea* (*HALOT*, 1:155). See further below. (3) *Pinus brutia* is not a separate species, as was thought in the past (cf. the Royal Horticultural Society's *Dictionary*), but is a variety of *P. halepensis*. Its branch system is less dense, and the cones on the branches point forward. This pine will withstand long periods of drought and is an excellent tree for places that are too dry for most conifers. Some believe it is referred to with Hebrew *tidhār* H9329 (only Isa. 41:19; 60:13; NIV, "fir"; NRSV, "plane"). (See *FFB*, 162–65.)

(4) *Cedrus libani* (also *C. patula*) is the CEDAR of Lebanon, growing up to more than 100 ft. high. The cones are barrel-shaped, 4 by 2.5 in. wide. They are beautiful trees and the timber is first-class. In the OT, cedars are mentioned in numerous passages (*ʾerez* H780). BALAAM in his prophecy spoke of "cedars beside the waters" (Num. 24:6); at the building of the Palace of the Forest of Lebanon by Solomon, cedars were used (1 Ki. 7:2), as they were when the second temple was built (Ezra 3:7). The tree is often mentioned in the Psalms and in the Prophets (e.g., Ps. 104:16; Isa. 44:14; Ezek. 17:22; Zech. 11:1–2). According to some scholars, the trunks of the cedar are not long enough for building, so other evergreens have been proposed, such as the *Abies cilicia* or FIR (so *HALOT*, 1:86), the *Juniperus oxycedrus*, and the *Sabina phoenicia* (see *FFB*, 108). See further below.

(5) *Tetraclinis articulata* is a tender evergreen tree that seldom grows taller than 30 ft., with erect, feathered branches divided into a fine spray. It bears solitary cones at the ends of the shoots. Its synonyms are *Callitris quadrivalvis* and *Thuja articulata*. The wood is yellow or red, quite fragrant, and is often marked prettily. It is used in making furniture for this reason. From its trunk exudes a hard resin called sandarac, which is made into varnish. This is the thyine wood mentioned in Rev. 18:12 (*thyinon* G2591), that is, the sandarac tree, sometimes known as the CITRON tree or even citrus tree, though it has nothing to do with oranges and lemons.

(6) *Cupressus sempervirens* (var. *horizontalis*) is the Mediterranean CYPRESS, an evergreen tree now used for ornamental purposes when young. The tree grows like a pyramid but when old it spreads. It is interesting to note that the juvenile leaves and the older ones are quite dissimilar. There are two main forms, one very erect, 150 ft. high, and the other spreading. The wood, which can be quite fragrant, is useful for furniture. An oil may be distilled from the leaves and shoots. This is very possibly the tree from which planks were cut to make the ark (*gōper* H1729, only Gen. 6:14; see ARK OF NOAH; GOPHER WOOD). The same tree may be referred to elsewhere (*tĕʾaššûr* H9309, Isa. 41:19 et al.; *tirzâ* H9560, only 44:14). Noah's example, incidentally, was followed by ALEXANDER THE GREAT, who also built his ship from the cypress wood. (See *FFB*, 115–16, 123.)

(7) *Juniperus* is a genus containing almost 50 species of hardy or half-hardy shrubs and trees, nearly all of them growing in the northern hemisphere. The one species found in the southern hemisphere is the sharp cedar, *Juniperus oxycedrus*. This is a tree that grows up to 30 ft. high, with prominently angled branches, and bearing globose half-inch wide cones, reddish-brown when ripe. An essential oil, which is said to have medicinal properties, is distilled from the fragrant wood of this tree; it is known as cade oil. Either this tree or the *Juniperus phoenicia* is probably referred to by Hebrew *ʿarʿār* H6899 (Jer. 17:6; NIV, "bush"; perhaps also 48:6 by slight emendation). Some believe that *J. phoenicia* is also referred to by Hebrew *ʾalmuggîm* H523; see above, under Leguminosae (6).

(8) *Juniperus sabina* is known as the savin. It is a shrub that may grow to 15 ft. in height, and the branches are divided into fine sprays. A strong odor is released when a shoot is bruised; this comes from what is known as an oil gland. This oil, which can be distilled, is said to have diuretic properties. The cones look waxy-white. *J. sabina* is said to grow well

in Palestine, but there are no apparent references to it in the Bible.

Platanaceae. This natural order contains only one genus, *Platanus* (sometimes *Plantanus*) *orientalis*. There are six or so species that bear unisexual flowers. The fruits are one-seeded nutlets, packed into round balls. This *Platanus orientalis*, known as the oriental plane, grows to a height of 100 ft. (cf. Sir. 24:14). The fruit balls it bears may be anything from two to six on a pendulous stalk. The tree is extremely long-lived and well known in Palestine, growing chiefly in the valleys and plains. The Hebrew term is ʿ*ermôn* *H6895* (Gen. 30:37; Ezek. 31:8; KJV, "chestnut tree"), derived from a root meaning "naked." Even in London, where these trees are grown abundantly, large pieces of bark are constantly peeling off, leaving the trunk underneath looking white or bare.

Punicaceae. There is only one genus with two species, both of which are deciduous small trees or shrubs. The most popular species is *Punica granatum*, the POMEGRANATE, a very popular fruit in Palestine, where it ripens well. The present writer has seen it growing to a height of 30 ft., bearing beautiful scarlet flowers 1.25 in. across, followed by yellow and crimson fruits, which may be as wide as 3.5 in. This fruit is mentioned frequently in the OT (Heb. *rimmôn* *H8232*). The beautiful little colored pomegranates decorated the hem of the robe of the high priest (Exod. 39:26). The Israelites took a poor view of the fact that there were no pomegranates growing in the wilderness (Num. 20:5). SAUL at one time stayed under a pomegranate tree (1 Sam. 14:2). Pomegranates were carved to beautify the temple (1 Ki. 7:18). The beauty of the pomegranate is reflected in the Song of Solomon (Cant. 4:13 et al.). Pomegranates, promised by God to his people (Deut. 8:8), were regarded as a definite blessing. They are certainly very sweet and delicious to eat on a hot day in Palestine, especially when picked straight from the tree. (See *FFB*, 168–70.)

Ranunculaceae. This is a very large family containing 48 genera with something like 1,300 species. They can be shrubs or herbs, and nearly all of them have acrid sap, some of which can cause blisters when handled. (1) The *Anemone coronaria* is found in this natural order. It grows today very popular cut flowers—red, blue, violet, or yellow. Anemones undoubtedly grew wild in Palestine in our Lord's time, and especially on the Mount of Olives, and were therefore most probably the lilies to which he referred as being more beautiful than "Solomon in all his splendor" (*krinon* *G3211*; Matt. 6:28; Lk. 12:27). (See *FFB*, 135–36.)

(2) The second plant in this large order is *Nigella sativa*, commonly called the nutmeg flower or black CUMMIN; it must not be confused with the annual plants called devil-in-the-bush or love-in-the-mist. The black cummin was cultivated for its aromatic seeds, which even today are used in the E for flavoring curries. It is almost certainly the plant referred to with the Hebrew word *qeṣaḥ* *H7902* (only Isa. 28:25, 27; KJV, "fitches"; NRSV, "dill"; NIV, "caraway"). (See *FFB*, 153–54.)

Rhamnaceae. Closely related to the Vitaceae family, this natural order includes 40 genera and 500 species, the great majority of them found in the tropics. (1) *Paliurus spina Christi* (also *P. bergatus*) is a shrub growing to a height of 10 ft. as a rule. It bears greenish-yellow flowers and interesting fruits which are 1 in. wide and look like a wide-brimmed hat. This shrub will grow in any ordinary soil and loves full sunshine. The Royal Horticultural Society *Dictionary* says that it is one of the legendary trees from which the crown of thorns was made (Matt. 27:29; Jn. 19:2; cf. also *HALOT*, 4:1562, s.v. *šāmîr* *H9031*, Isa. 5:6 et al.). Other suggestions are *Zizyphus spina Christi* (see below) and *Poterium spinosum* (*FFB*, 185). See CROWN OF THORNS; THORN.

(2) *Zizyphus* is a genus of approximately 40 species of evergreen or deciduous shrubs and trees, living in the warm, temperate, or tropical regions. The flowers are invariably small and greenish or yellow. Two species that possibly are mentioned in the OT are *Z. lotus* (*ṣeʾĕlîm* *H7365*, Job 40:21–22), a deciduous small tree with tiny flowers and ovoid-roundish yellow fruits, and *Z. spina Christi*, an evergreen with ovate, oval leaves and minute woolly flowers in short clusters. The fruit in this case is black, half an inch wide, and when ripe is edible. This thorny shrub undoubtedly grows happily throughout Palestine, and could therefore be the plant referred to with various terms in some passages (e.g., Jdg. 8:7; Isa. 9:18; Matt. 7:16).

(3) The thorns mentioned elsewhere (e.g., Gen. 3:18; Ps. 58:9; Prov. 15:19; Isa. 10:17; Hos. 2:6) may

well be those of the buckthorn. There is a species, *Rhamnus palaestina* (often called *Rhamnus punctata*, var. *palaestina*), that grows to a height of 5–6 ft. It has evergreen leaves and extremely thorny branches.

Rosaceae. This family includes some 90 genera and 2,000 species found all over the world. (1) The *Prunus amygdalus communis*, often quoted as being mentioned in the OT, is really *Prunus communis* (also *Amygdalus communis*), the ALMOND, a tree that will grow in the E to a height of 20 ft. (*šāqēd* H9196, Gen. 43:11 et al.; also *lûz* H4280, only 30:37). It produces 2-in.-long velvety fruits, containing smooth stones in which are the almonds. (See *FFB*, 89–90.)

(2) Some claim that *Prunus armeniaca* (or *Armeniaca vulgaris*) should be included here. This is the apricot, a tree that will grow 30 ft. high. It produces white or pinkish flowers, followed by delicious yellow fruits, tinged with red. The only reason to mention it is that there are those who claim that the tree in Gen. 3:6 was an apricot.

(3) *Rosa phoenicia* is a strong climbing rose with hooked prickles and white flowers, 2 in. across. It came to Great Britain from Syria in 1885, and the Royal Horticultural Society's *Dictionary* thinks that it may have been one of the parents of the damask rose. This species of rose should be included here because of two possible references in the APOCRYPHA (2 Esd. 2:19; Wisd. 2:8).

Hollyhocks growing near the precipice of the Arbel cliffs in Galilee. (View to the N.)

(4) *Rubus* is a genus of some 400 species and contains all the members of the bramble family—raspberries, blackberries, boysenberries, and so on. The *Rubus sanctus* is usually called the Palestinian bramble, and is closely related to *Rubus ulmifolius*, a semievergreen, spreading shrub, with downy, purply stems, covered with broad spines. The flowers are rosy-red, but the fruits are of no value for food. These, it is thought by some, may be the thorns and briers mentioned in some passages (e.g., Jdg. 8:7; Isa. 7:25; 9:18). Others think *R. sanctus* was the burning bush (*FFB*, 186); see also above under Loranthaceae. Some writers of the 1800s used the label *R. fruticosus*, which was a comprehensive Linnaean term for brambles. Today, however, this so-called species has been split up into many other species and even varieties.

Ruscaceae. T. W. Sanders (*Encyclopaedia of Gardening* [1955]) states that *Ruscus aculeatus* is in the natural order *Ruscaceae* or *Liliaceae*. The genus *Ruscus* itself includes four evergreen subshrubs with creeping root stocks. The species thrive in shady places. *R. aculeatus* is the "butcher's broom," found all round the Mediterranean region; it is really lovely when covered with red berries. Unfortunately, there seem to be more male forms than female, and so the brilliant, berried types are seldom seen. *R. aculeatus*, an extremely prickly and stiff plant, is well-known in Palestine and can be seen around Mount Carmel. It has been suggested that this plant is referred to by one of the Hebrew terms for "thorn" (*sillôn* H6141, Ezek. 2:6; 28:24; the Arabs apparently refer to it with the cognate word *sullāʾ*). In Ezek. 2:6, the word is combined with *sārāb* H6235, usually rendered "brier" and perhaps a reference to the closely related *R. hyrcanus*, but the text is problematic and some scholars emend it.

Rutaceae. This is a family of 100 genera and 900 species, most of which are found in South Africa and Australia. They are usually shrubs or trees, and several of them are useful because they yield oil. *Ruta chalepensis* (also *R. angustifolia*) is a subshrub, growing to 2.5 ft. and bearing yellow half-inch-wide flowers. It is well-known in the Mediterranean regions, including Palestine. Some believe this is the RUE to which our Lord referred when he spoke about the Pharisees' tithing their herbs (*pēganon* G4379, Lk. 11:42). A more likely candidate is *R. graveolens*, called the herb of grace, an acrid evergreen shrub, semi-woody, growing to a height of 3 ft. with erect shoots. The flowers are 0.75 in. wide, and of a rather dull yellow color. The leaves have a very strong odor, and in Great Britain are often used in claret cup. (See *FFB*, 174.)

Salicaceae. This is a family of two genera only, but with 330 species, all of which are shrubs and trees. The flowers are catkinlike and generally appear before the leaves. A distinction needs to be made between the POPLAR (genus *Populus*), which produces catkins that hang, and the WILLOW (*Salix*), whose catkins hold themselves upright. Three Hebrew terms are relevant here: *libneh* H4242, KJV "poplar" (Gen. 30:37; Hos. 4:13); ʿărābâ H6857, KJV "willow" (Lev. 43:40; Job 40:22; Ps. 137:2; Isa. 15:7; 44:4), and *ṣapṣāpâ* H7628, KJV "willow" (Ezek. 17:5).

The last of these terms undoubtedly refers to the willow, of which several varieties are possible. The word, still used today, suggests that the reference is to *Salix safsaf*, which is a common Palestinian willow. It is a tree with reddish-brown branches, which loves the water and is happy growing in the upper parts of the Jordan for this reason. Some believe it is also the tree mentioned in several other passages (Job 40:22; Isa. 15:7; 44:4). *Salix acmophylla* is another species found in Palestine that likes to grow near water and was once thought to be a variety of *safsaf*. The branches are reddish, and the catkins erect, oblong, and cylindrical. Mention should also be made of other varieties. *Salix alba* is the white willow with pendulous branches of beautiful shape. The young shoots are silky and the catkins often 2 in. long. The weeping willow is *S. babylonica*, which may grow 50 ft. high, with its branches hanging down, and looking extremely beautiful in the winter as well as in the summer (cf. possibly Ps. 137:1–2).

The term ʿărābâ, however, may refer to the poplar. Some have claimed it is the balsam poplar, *Populus tacamahaca*, but this seems to be a N American tree and not one known in Palestine. More likely, the reference is to the Euphrates poplar, *P. euphratica*, a high tree that has oblong leaves similar to those of the willow. It grows on the banks of many rivers in the Middle E, including the Jordan. The word *libneh*, apparently derived from the Hebrew root for "white," is considered by some to be the *P. alba*, a species that likes to grow in wet places. Its leaves are green above and snowy white beneath, and the shoots would therefore suit the schemer Jacob well (Gen. 30:37; see also Hos. 4:13). Others, however, identify this term with the storax tree, *Styrax officinalis*; see below, under Styracaceae. (See *FFB*, 170, 178–79.)

Solanaceae. A natural order of 70 genera and 1,800 species, rarely trees. Large numbers of the family are of importance economically, such as the potato, the tomato, the capsicum, the aubergine, and even tobacco. (1) *Lycium europaeum* (also *L. mediterraneum*) is the boxthorn, and within the genus there are 100 species of shrubs, usually thorny. Most of them bear bright red fruits profusely. *L. europaeum* is a rambling, spiny shrub, bearing globose fruits, and is found in the Mediterranean region. It is apparently mentioned twice in the OT (ʾāṭād H353, Jdg. 9:14–15; Ps. 58:9; cf. also the name ATAD in Gen. 50:10–11). (See *FFB*, 184–86.)

(2) The *Mandragora officinarum* (also *Atropa mandragora*, according to *HALOT*, 1:215) is the MANDRAKE or devil's apples. There are three species of perennials within this genus, none very beautiful. All of them, however, seem to have legends and magical powers attached to them because its root resembles a human body. The Royal Horticultural Society's *Dictionary* states that *M. officinarum* is the mandrake of Gen. 30:14–16 (*dûdāʾîm* H1859). It is claimed to be the original love apple (Cant. 7:13). (See *FFB*, 138–39.)

(3) The Hebrew term *ḥēdeq* H2537, "brier" (Prov. 15:19; Mic. 7:4), is probably *Solanum incanum* (or *S. coagulans*), the Palestinian nightshade, sometimes called the Jericho potato. It is found on roadsides and in waste places in the Lower Jordan Valley and around Jericho, and is extremely prickly. The fertile flowers produce yellow berries. (See *FFB*, 184.)

Styracaceae. This natural order contains 6 genera and about 80 species of trees and shrubs. Most of these are found in Mexico, Texas, Java, or Japan, but *Styrax officinalis* is definitely popular in the Mediterranean region. This is a small tree or shrub that can grow to a height of 20 ft., bearing pendulous clusters of fragrant white flowers. It is known to have grown in Asia Minor, and even today is easy to find in Palestine in the lower hills. The stems, when punctured, yield an aromatic resin known as STORAX, which is possibly referred to by the term *nāṭāp H5753* (only Exod. 30:34; NRSV, "stacte"; NIV, "gum resin"; cf. Gk. *staktē*, which occurs here and elsewhere in the LXX). According to other scholars, however, the Hebrew word may refer to such plants as *Commiphora opobalsamum* (see above, under Burseraceae), *Cistus salvifolius* (see above under Cistaceae), and *Pistacia lentiscus* (see above, under Anacardiaceae).

On the other hand, the *Styrax officinalis* or storax tree is thought by some to be equivalent to *libneh* (generally rendered "poplar"; see above, under Salicaceae). Finally, it has been claimed that the sweet spice called ONICHA (*šĕḥēlet H8829*, only Exod. 30:34) is the *Styrax benzoin*, which grows wild in Sumatra and produces a resin called benzoin with which friar's balsam is made. The present writer doubts that there would have been an export from Sumatra to Palestine in biblical days.

Tamaricaceae. This natural order comprises 4 genera and 100 species of small trees or shrubs, usually heath-like, often found by the seaside or in desert places. The TAMARISK mentioned in the Bible (ʾēšel *H869*, Gen. 21:33; 1 Sam. 22:6; 31:13) is probably *Tamarix aphylla* (alternate names *T. articulata, T. orientalis*, et al.). It is a small tree or bush, some 20 ft. high, bearing pink flowers one-eighth of an inch across (*FFB*, 182; illustration on p. 181). Some have suggested that the shrub underneath which HAGAR put her child (Gen. 21:15) could be the *T. aphylla*, because bushes of this species now grow in the desert where it is thought she was wandering. The tamarisks certainly grow in sandy soil. The shrub is unlikely to have been the species *T. tetrandra*, a glabrous shrub, growing 12–15 ft. high, with tiny pink flowers packed into cylindrical spikes, usually 2 in. long. The rendering "tamarisk" by the NRSV at Isa. 44:4 appears to be a conjecture (reading *kĕbin* instead of MT, *bĕbên*; the word *bin* [= Aram. *bināʾ*] is a postbiblical term for tamarisk).

Typhaceae. A natural order of one genus and possibly 15 species, all of them being marsh plants. The flowers are closely crowded with the male blooms above and the female blooms below. The biblical plant (*sûp H6068*, Exod. 2:3 et al.) is probably the small reed mace, *Typha angustata*, which grows 4 ft. high, producing dark green leaves half an inch or so wide, convex beneath and channeled above toward their base (see also RED SEA; REED). The flower spikes are brown. The reed mace is sometimes called *cattail*, but the true cattail is *Typha latifolia*, growing 8 ft. high. This, it is claimed, is the reed or staff (*kalamos G2812*) with which our Lord was smitten (Mk. 15:19) and the reed put into our Lord's hand as an imitation scepter (Matt. 27:29). Whether *T. latifolia* grew in the Holy Land at that time, however, the writer has been unable to discover. (See *FFB*, 171.)

Umbelliferae. This natural order has approximately 180 genera and 1,400 species. Most of these grow in the northern temperate regions, but some are distributed in the Middle E. The flowers are invariably produced in compound umbels, hence the name of the natural order.

(1) *Peucedanum graveolens* is an annual with yellow flowers in a large umbel. It was originally called *Anethum graveolens* and is still found under this name in some books. This is undoubtedly the DILL mentioned by Jesus (*anēthon G464*, Matt. 23:23; KJV, "anise"). The plant is grown for its seeds, which are used in a similar way to caraway seeds. Dill water given to babies comes from the distillation of this seed. (See *FFB*, 117; illustration on p. 116.)

(2) *Coriandrum sativum* is an annual that grows about 18 in. high. The name comes from the word *coris*, a bug. This alludes to the unpleasant odor of the leaves. The flowers are pale mauve or white and the fruits globose. The seeds are used in flavoring sweets or candy, in bread, mixed spices, some curry powders, and alcoholic drinks like gin. The seeds smell unpleasant when unripe, but the odor disappears when they are dried. The seed is mentioned in the Bible merely because manna was likened to it (*gad H1512*, Exod. 16:31; Num. 11:7). The plant, however, was and is grown in Palestine. (See *FFB*, 110–11.)

(3) *Cuminum cyminum*, the CUMMIN, is a half-hardy annual herb with aromatic fruits that are used in flavoring. It produces a pink or white flower, grows 1–2 ft. high, and is known to have been popular in the Mediterranean region. To the uninitiated, it is a member of the "carrot family," and the seeds are larger than those of the caraway.

They were and are still used in Palestine as a spice or flavoring. Cummin is mentioned both in the OT (*kammōn H4021*, Isa. 28:25, 27, describing the farmer's work of plowing, planting, and harvesting) and in the NT (*kyminon G3248*, Matt. 23:23, where Jesus speaks of the Pharisees' tithing small things but neglecting important matters). (See *FFB*, 114–15.)

(4) Though *Ferula* is a genus of about 80 species of herbaceous perennials, only one appears to be mentioned in Scripture: *F. galbaniflua*, whose gum is called GALBANUM (*ḥelběnâ H2697*, only Exod. 30:34; LXX, *chalbanē*, also Sir. 24:15). This plant bears yellow flowers on short, thick stalks, and the little fruits that follow are oblong and elliptic. The special gum exudes from the lower part of the stem, as well as from the bases of the leaf stalks. An incision is made in the young stem 3 in. above ground level, and as a result, a milky juice appears which in a short time hardens and becomes the galbanum used commercially as an anti-spasmodic in medicine, as well as for certain varnishes. It is not known for certain whether this plant grew in Palestine, or whether the galbanum was imported from Persia. (See *FFB*, 123; illustration on p. 122.)

Urticaceae. This is a natural order of over 40 genera, containing 500 species, the great majority of them tropical shrubs, trees, and herbs (Lat. *urtica*, from *ūrō*, "to burn," refers to stinging nettles). The perennial nettle is *Urtica dioica*, and the dwarf annual nettle is *U. urens*. A third species, *U. caudata*, is found in waste places in Palestine, having erect branching stems; it bears small, greenish flowers. And a fourth, *U. pilulifera*, is also found on waste ground round about Jericho and Jerusalem, where it is commonly known as the Roman nettle. As these four nettles are found in Palestine, it is wondered whether they are those referred to in some OT passages (*ḥārûl H3017*, Job 30:7 et al., but see above, under Acanthaceae; *qimmôś H7853*, Isa. 34:13 et al., but see above, under Compositae 8 and Cruciferae 3). (See *FFB*, 152–53.)

Valerianaceae. In this natural order there are 8 genera and 350 species. The flowers are usually numerous but small, and they are often showy. The only biblical plant that seems to fall into this natural order is the *Nardostachys* (from *nardos*, "fragrant shrub," and *stachys*, "spike"), a genus of two species. *Nardostachys jatamansi*, the ancient nard or SPIKENARD (*nērd H5948*, Cant. 1:12; 4:13–14; *nardos G3726*, Mk. 14:3; Jn. 12:3), bears rose purple flowers in a small terminal panacle. The plant was not grown in Palestine, but was imported in sealed alabaster boxes as a delicious perfume. It is found growing in the cold, dry upper areas of the Himalayan mountains, and was given the name JatamanSee—spelled in this way by the Hindus in their country. It is the roots and woolly, young stems that are carefully dried and made into an ointment or perfume. (See *FFB*, 151–52.)

Vitaceae. A natural order of 11 genera and 450 species of shrubs, most of which are climbers. These are widely distributed in the subtropical and tropical regions. The flowers are small and regular, but sometimes unisexual. The fruit is a berry. If the "wild vine" mentioned in the Bible (Jer. 2:21; cf. Isa. 5:4) is the ornamental type, then *Ampelopsis orientalis* is probably the species referred to, since it grows in Palestine and Syria, bearing tiny, red fruits resembling red currants. Its synonym is *Vitis orientalis* because it was thought at one time to be a member of the VINE genus. The true grapevine is *Vitis vinifera* (*gepen H1728*, Gen. 40:9–10 et al.; *ampelos G306*, Matt. 26:29 et al.), said to have been originally a native of the Caucasus region, and it was certainly known to Noah (*kerem H4142*, "vineyard," Gen. 9:20). The fruits are oval or globose, amber-colored, or black with a blue bloom. (See *FFB*, 188–92.)

Zygophyllaceae. A family of 26 genera and 250 species, all of which grow in the warmer regions. Rarely are they annuals, occasionally are they herbs, but usually they are subshrubs or shrubs. Generally speaking, the flowers are solitary, though occasionally there are two together. The fruit is generally a capsule, hardly ever a drupe or berry. *Balanites aegyptiaca* has hermaphroditic, green flowers. The leaves are woolly, and the plants as a whole are found in desert places, especially between Jerusalem and Jericho. It has been thought by some that the BALM mentioned in the OT (*ṣŏrî H7661*, Gen. 37:25 et al.) refers to the resin or gum from this plant. It is commonly known as the Jericho balsam, because it grows abundantly in the desert areas around Jericho, often 12–15 ft. tall. The fruits of this shrub are boiled for the sake of the oil content, which is said to possess healing properties, hence the text, "Is there no balm in Gilead?" (Jer. 8:22; cf. 46:11; 51:8). The Douay Bible renders, "Is there no rosin in Gilead?" and for this reason, soon after it was published, this version was known as the Rosin Bible. Other possible identifications of the biblical balm are *Pistacia lentiscus*, *P. mutica*, and *Silphium terebinthinaceum*; see above, under Anacardiaceae. (See *FFB*, 93–94.) W. E. SHEWELL-COOPER

Florilegium flor´uh-leej´ee-uhm. This Latin term, meaning "flower-culling," is used to name a fragmentary QUMRAN document (4QFlor or 4Q174) that consists of quotations gathered from various biblical books, followed by short interpretative comments. Although brief, this document is an important example of sectarian biblical hermeneutics (cf. G. J. Brooke, *Exegesis at Qumran: 4QFlorilegium and Its Jewish Context* [1985]). See DEAD SEA SCROLLS. The term can also be used in a general way to refer to any anthology of biblical citations. See TESTIMONIA.

flour. See BREAD II.

flower. There are several different Hebrew words used for flowers in the OT (esp. *ṣîṣ H7488*, Num. 17:8 et al., and *peraḥ H7258*, 8:4 et al.); the NT uses the common Greek term (*anthos G470*, Jas. 1:10–11; 1 Pet. 1:24). Today, botanists and horticulturalists are careful to give all flowering plants Latin names that describe properly the genus, the species, and sometimes the strain or variety as well. In biblical times, flowers were given local names, which could mean very different plants from district to district. Even today, the London plane tree, for instance, means quite a different tree in Scotland.

It is curious, some people say, that flowers are mentioned so little in Holy Writ, but in Palestine there were usually no gardens as we have now, merely farm fields to grow crops in, and groves of trees around the houses to provide shade. Even today in agricultural Spain there are no gardens around farm workers' houses. Further, flowers were not used in vases in the home in Palestine in those days — there were no occasional tables for bowls of blossoms — and no large windows through which the sun could shine. There were undoubtedly plenty of wild flowers, but these would have been taken for granted and hardly even noticed. It is claimed that in the plains and on the mountains could be found 500 different species of wild flowers that are now actually grown in Great Britain, and another 500 species in addition that are indigenous to Palestine also.

Our Lord, as he preached, must have stood on mountain sides, which were carpeted with thousands of wild flowers of all kinds. In fact, this is what he may have had in mind when he said, "Consider the lilies" (Matt. 6:28=Lk. 12:27 NRSV), using the word LILY to cover all the beautiful varieties of flowers at his feet. Some specific flowers are mentioned, for which see separate articles. See also FLORA. W. E. SHEWELL-COOPER

flute. See MUSIC IV.C.

flux, bloody. See DISEASE.

fly. Technically, this term is applied to members of the order *Diptera* (two-winged), which are true flies, but it is given to many other insects also (dragonfly, firefly, sawfly, etc.). One Hebrew term, ʿ*ārōb H6856*, occurs only in connection with the fourth Egyptian plague (Exod. 8:21–31; Pss. 78:45; 105:31). Flies of many kinds abound in Egypt; some of them are biting and blood-sucking, and become a pest because of their numbers. There is nothing in the context to identify the kind, or perhaps kinds, of flies concerned, but the fact that the insects were *on* the people suggests that they may have been biting flies such as *Stochomys calcitrans*. Some commentators see a connection between the fourth and sixth plagues, with the fly serving as the vector for a skin disease, perhaps a modified form of the anthrax that struck the cattle in the fifth plague.

A second Hebrew word, *zĕbûb H2279*, occurs in the name BAAL-ZEBUB (1 Ki. 1:2–3, 6, 16) and by itself only twice. In Eccl. 10:1 the context is proverbial: most ointments were scented with spices and other perfumes, and unless covered they attracted flies, which quickly drowned in the greasy base, causing it to spoil. In Isa. 7:18 the prophet predicts a foreign invasion by using figurative language that underscores God's sovereign power over the nations: "In that day the LORD will whistle for flies from the distant streams of Egypt and for bees from the land of Assyria."   G. S. CANSDALE

foal. The young of a horse, donkey, or zebra. In the Bible it can be used as a contextual rendering of Hebrew *ʿîr* H6554, "donkey" (Gen. 49:11 NRSV) or as the translation of *bēn* H1201, "son [of a donkey]" (Zech. 9:9, cited in Matt. 21:5, Gk. *huios* G5626).

fodder. Feed for livestock. It was usually mixed from that which remained after a crop had been harvested and threshed (*mispôʾ* H5028, Gen. 24:25 et al. [cf. the verb form in Jdg. 19:21]; *bĕlîl* H1173, Job 6:5 et al.). One passage, Isa. 30:24, may indicate the practice of salting the mixture in order to fulfill the animals' salt needs.   G. GIACUMAKIS, JR.

fold. A pen in which to keep SHEEP or GOATS. Folds were used chiefly as a protection from wild beasts at night. They consisted of a walled enclosure, preferably near water, and often with a small tower inside. Sometimes flocks of more than one shepherd were kept overnight in the same fold, with one shepherd taking care of the animals. In the morning the sheep would be carefully counted when the shepherds came to reclaim their FLOCKS. The word "fold" is used in some versions to render several Hebrew words, especially *nāweh* H5659, which more properly means "pasture" (Jer. 23:3 et al.; cf. also *miklāʾ* H4813, "pen," Hab. 3:17 et al.). In the NT it can be used to render *aulē* G885, usually "courtyard" (in the sense "pen," only Jn. 10:1, 16).
S. BARABAS

folly. Lack of good sense or WISDOM; foolish behavior. In the Bible the concept has a strong moral and spiritual connotation.

I. In the OT. Folly is the opposite of godly wisdom. It is not imbecility, insanity, or error. It is wrong-headedness. It has to do with practical insights into the nature of things that lead to success or failure in life. Wisdom and folly in the Bible rest on the principle of adjustment to a higher law for a practical purpose. Folly involves rejection or disregard of the revealed moral and spiritual values on which life is based. The fool sins against his own best interests and rejects God (Ps. 14:1). This general idea is expressed with various terms.

A common word, especially in Proverbs, is *ʾiwwelet* H222, which conveys the idea of moral badness. The fool is hasty (Prov. 14:29), self-sufficient (12:15), impervious to instruction (15:5), given to unrestrained anger (17:12), and stupid in his persistence in evil (26:11). The most frequent word for folly, however, is *kĕsîlût* H4070 (derived from a root that may indicate thickness, sluggishness, or plumpness). The slow, self-confident person is ignorant (Eccl. 2:14), thoughtless (Prov. 10:23; 17:24), contentious (18:6), indolent (Eccl. 4:5), and brutish (Ps. 49:10). Disregarding moral ideals, he is a victim of stupidity.

Most common outside the Wisdom Literature is the term *nĕbālâ* H5576, attributed to a wicked person as an evil character, shamelessly immoral. The word is often associated with base and unnatural lewdness and can be rendered "disgraceful thing" (Gen. 34:7; Deut. 22:21; Josh. 7:15). ISAIAH describes in detail the destructive attitudes and conduct of such wicked people (Isa. 32:6). ABIGAIL spoke of her husband, NABAL, as "this man of Belial" (i.e., "wicked, worthless"), "for as his name is, so is he" (1 Sam. 25:25 KJV). Several other terms convey similar ideas (cf. Job 4:18; 24:12; Eccl. 2:12; Prov. 1:22). (For a study of the semantic field, see T. Donald in *VT* 13 [1963]: 285–92. Note also S. A. Mandry, *There Is No God! A Study of the Fool in the Old Testament* [1972]; *NIDOTTE*, 1:306–9; 2:678–80; 3:11–13.)

II. In the NT. As folly in the OT accounts is so deeply rooted in the human mind and heart that only the revealed law could extirpate it, so in the NT the sinner is a victim of folly until the gospel dawns on him (Rom. 2:20; Tit. 3:3–5). The highest wisdom is revealed in the gospel. Sinful people are so radically wrong in their relation to the moral world that they decry the gospel as foolishness (*mōria* G3702, 1 Cor. 1:21–25). Yet it is their only hope of becoming wise. Terms for folly include *anoia* G486, "without understanding" (2 Tim. 3:9; this can express itself in rage, Lk. 6:11); *asophos* G831 (Eph. 5:15); and *aphrosynē* G932, "without good judgment" (moral, Mk. 7:22; intellectual,

1 Cor. 11:1, 17, 21). (For a full list of relevant Gk. terms, see LN, 1:385–88; note also *NIDNTT*, 3:1023–26.)

W. T. DAYTON

food. That which is eaten to provide the nutrients that maintain the BODY; used also figuratively of that which sustains the SOUL.

  I. Literal
    A. Food supplies
    B. Food of animals
    C. Food for humans
    D. Food availability
    E. Food of special periods
    F. Food preparation
    G. Food prices
    H. Eating habits
    I. Prohibited foods
    J. Clean and unclean food
    K. Food offered to idols
    L. Sharing food
    M. Life and food
  II. Metaphorical

I. Literal

A. Food supplies. Despite recurrent droughts (2 Ki. 4:38; Jer. 14:1, 4–6; Hag. 1:11), hail (Hag. 2:17), other calamities (Amos 4:6–10) with resulting famines (Gen. 12:10; 26:1; 41:25–31; 1 Ki. 18:2; 2 Ki. 4:38), and periodic want brought on by the ravages of war (2 Ki. 6:25), Palestine was to the biblical writers a land "flowing with milk and honey" (Exod. 3:8, 17; Num. 13:27; et al.), in which food could be eaten without want (Deut. 8:7–9; Josh. 24:13; Jdg. 18:10). The description left by Sinuhe, a fugitive from Egypt c. 1920 B.C., is in agreement: "Figs were in it, and grapes. It had more wine than water. Plentiful was its honey, abundant its olives. Every (kind of) fruit was on its trees. Barley was there, and emmer. There was no limit to any (kind of) cattle.... Bread was made for me as daily fare, wine as daily provision, cooked meat and roasted fowl, besides the wild beasts of the desert, for they hunted for me and laid before me, besides the catch of my (own) hounds. Many ... were made for me, and milk in every (kind of cooking)" (*ANET*, 19–20).

Scarcity was a warning or a punishment from God sent upon his unfaithful people (Lam. 4:9, 11; Amos 4:6). According to ECCLESIASTICUS the necessities of life include salt, wheat flour, milk, honey, the blood of the grape, and oil (Sir. 39:26). The land produced a variety of food stuffs.

B. Food of animals. The Lord supplies his creatures their proper food in due season (Ps. 104:27–28)—a grace attributed in the Egyptian hymn of Ikhnaton to his god Aton. For the carnivorous such as the lion, there is flesh (Dan. 6:24; 7:5; Nah. 2:12); for the wolf, there is prey (Ezek. 22:27); for the scavenger, there is carrion (Jer. 16:4; 19:7; 34:20; Ezek. 32:4); and the dog returns to his vomit (2 Pet. 2:22). For the plant eaters there is herbage (Jer. 14:6); for the ox there is grass (Dan. 4:15, 25; 5:21) and straw (Job 6:5; Isa. 11:7; 65:25). Swine feed on the carob pod (Lk. 15:16); horses on barley and straw (1 Ki. 4:28); the birds eat seed (Matt. 13:4); and the locust devours plants (Joel 1:4).

C. Food for humans

1. Plant foods. *Cereal grains.* The fields of Palestine produced WHEAT (Gen. 30:14; Ezek. 4:9; et al.), BARLEY (Ruth 1:22; 2:23), MILLET (Ezek. 4:9), and SPELT (Exod. 9:32; Isa. 28:25; Ezek. 4:9). Corn (Indian maize) was unknown to the biblical world; the term is used by the KJV in the sense of the cereal GRAIN. In times of FAMINE, grain was obtained in Egypt (Gen. 41:49), where FLAX, barley, wheat, and spelt were produced (Exod. 9:31–32). Grain might be shelled out as one went through the fields (Deut. 23:25; Matt. 12:1). One of ELISHA's friends brought fresh grain to the prophet (2 Ki. 4:42–44). When harvested, grain was ground into flour made into BREAD, which was the staff of life (cf. Isa. 3:1 KJV). There are more than 200 references to bread in Scripture. Bread is often a synonym for food in general. Bread was at times baked on coals (1 Ki. 19:6), first on one side, and then properly turned over to bake the other (Hos. 7:8).

A subsistence diet consisted of bread and water (Gen. 21:14; 1 Ki. 18:13; 22:27). In times of famine children cry for bread and wine (Lam. 2:12). Both wheat bread and barley bread were used. In numerous cases barley bread (Jdg. 7:13; 2 Ki. 4:42) or barley cakes (Ezek. 4:12) are encountered. It was from five barley loaves that Jesus fed the

Almonds ready for picking.

5,000 (Jn. 6:9, 13). Millet and spelt also could be used for bread (Ezek. 4:9). Cakes baked for the QUEEN OF HEAVEN formed a part of a Canaanite cult (Jer. 7:18). Grain might be parched and eaten (Lev. 23:14; Josh. 5:11; Ruth 2:14; 1 Sam. 17:17; 25:18; 2 Sam. 17:28). The diet of the laborer at noon might consist of parched grain and wine (Ruth 2:14). Grain might be crushed and spread out to dry as was done over the well where AHIMAAZ and JONATHAN were hidden (2 Sam. 17:19; Prov. 27:22).

Nuts and vegetables. JACOB sent to PHARAOH a present of produce of the land that included pistachio NUTS and ALMONDS, along with BALM, HONEY, SPICES, and MYRRH (Gen. 43:11). The wilderness generation complained over lack of CUCUMBERS, MELONS, LEEKS, ONIONS, and GARLIC, which they had enjoyed in Egypt (Num. 11:5). Later generations in Palestine doubtless ate many of these, including BEANS and LENTILS (2 Sam. 17:28) as well as cucumbers (Isa. 1:8; Jer. 10:5). There were the bitter HERBS of PASSOVER (Exod. 12:8; Num. 9:11) and the garden plants: MINT, DILL, and CUMMIN (Matt. 23:23). A dinner of herbs might suffice for the poor (Prov. 15:17; Rom. 14:2). In times of want the carob POD, ordinarily used for cattle (*m. Šabbat* 24.2), might be eaten. There was also sweet calamus from a distant land (Jer. 6:20; see AROMATIC CANE).

Fruits. The grape (see VINE) produced WINE and VINEGAR (Ruth 2:14) as well as raisins (Num. 6:3; 1 Sam. 25:18; 1 Chr. 12:40; Hos. 3:1). Fresh grapes might be eaten while passing through a vineyard (Deut. 23:24). The spies brought a large cluster of grapes borne on a pole between two of them (Num. 13:23). Sour grapes set the teeth on edge (Jer. 31:30; Ezek. 18:2). Wine, which cheers "gods and mortals" (Jdg. 9:13 NRSV) and makes glad the human heart (Ps. 104:15), might lead to intoxication, as it did in the case of NOAH (Gen. 9:21), LOT (Gen. 19:33, 35), and NABAL (1 Sam. 25:37). It is therefore a mocker (Prov. 20:1). The butler squeezed the grapes into Pharaoh's cup (Gen. 40:9–11). The NAZIRITE refused all products of the grape (Num. 6:1–4; Jdg. 13:4, 14; Jer. 35:5–6). RAISIN CAKES were eaten frequently (1 Sam. 25:18; 30:12; 2 Sam. 16:1); they were also used in Canaanite worship (Hos. 3:1). In the NT that which comes from the grape is referred to as "fruit of the vine" (Matt. 26:29).

The OLIVE was perhaps eaten both green and ripe as today, though this is not specifically stated. Olives were beaten into oil (Exod. 27:20). The FIG was eaten fresh (Jer. 24:1–2) and dried (1 Sam. 25:18; 30:12; 1 Chr. 12:40). The first fig of the season was a special delicacy (Isa. 28:4; Jer. 24:2; Hos. 9:10; Mic. 7:1; Nah. 3:12). Every man under his vine and fig tree with none to make them afraid is considered the ideal state (Mic. 4:4). Dried figs were used for boils (2 Ki. 20:7; Isa. 38:21) and also eaten on journeys (1 Chr. 12:40). The POMEGRANATE (Exod. 28:33; Num. 13:23; 1 Ki. 7:20; Cant. 6:11; 8:2; Joel 1:12) and the APPLE (Prov. 25:11; Cant. 2:5; 7:8; 8:5; Joel 1:12) were available. The PALM TREE (Jdg. 4:5; Ps. 92:12; Joel 1:12; Jn. 12:13) and the SYCAMORE (Amos 7:14) are mentioned in Scripture but no reference is made to their fruit as food. Summer fruits of unspecified variety are often mentioned (Jer. 40:10–12; Amos 8:1).

2. Animal products. *Flesh.* In the KJV "meats" is a term for food in general and is not limited merely to FLESH. For the Israelite, the domesticated animals supplied meat. The mother and offspring were not to be slaughtered on the same day (Lev. 22:28). The kid of the SHEEP (2 Sam. 12:3) or GOAT was a preferred dish (Gen. 31:38; 37:31; Lev. 4:23, 28; Lk. 15:29). The stalled ox (Prov. 15:17; cf. Amos 6:4; Hab. 3:17) or the fatted calf was reserved for slaughtering on special occasions (1 Sam. 28:24; Matt. 22:4; see CATTLE). For such a celebration over the return of the prodigal the elder brother objected (Lk. 15:30). After the EXILE there was a SHEEP GATE in Jerusalem doubtless so named because the sheep market was near (Neh. 3:1).

NIMROD is said to have been a mighty hunter (Gen. 10:9). A variety of wild game existed to be hunted (cf. 27:3; KJV, "venison"). Deuteronomy lists seven varieties (Deut. 14:5; cf. Lev. 17:13). There was the WILD GOAT, the IBEX, the mountain sheep (Deut. 14:5), the ROEBUCK, the GAZELLE, the HART (Deut. 12:15), and the ANTELOPE (Deut. 14:5; Isa. 51:20).

In the wilderness the people missed the FISH they had enjoyed in Egypt (Num. 11:5). Fish could be found in Galilee and in the sea (Jer. 16:16; Eccl. 9:12; Ezek. 47:10; Neh. 13:16; Matt. 4:18; Lk. 11:12); in postexilic times fish were sold in the FISH GATE (Neh. 3:3). No specific species are mentioned except good and bad (Matt. 13:48) or big and small (Jon. 1:17; Mk. 8:7; Jn. 21:11). Dried fish were available (Neh. 13:16). Peter, Andrew, James, and John were fishermen prior to their being called to discipleship (Matt. 4:18, 21). The 5,000 were fed fish (Matt. 15:34; Mk. 6:38). The fish net formed the basis of one of Jesus' parables (Matt. 13:47–50).

From the insect family four types of LOCUSTS were eaten (Lev. 11:22–23; cf. Matt. 3:4). Various fowl also provided food (1 Ki. 4:23), including the PARTRIDGE (1 Sam. 26:20; Jer. 17:11), the QUAIL (Exod. 16:13; Num. 11:32), the PIGEON (Lev. 12:6 et al.; see DOVE), the TURTLEDOVE (Gen. 15:9 et al., NRSV), and the SPARROW (Matt. 10:29; Lk. 12:6). After the Persian period, CHICKENS became available (female, Matt. 23:37; male, 26:34).

Dairy products. Milk from cows, goats, and sheep was used by the Israelites (Deut. 32:14; Prov. 27:27) and kept in skins (Jdg. 4:19). Use of camel milk also may be inferred (cf. Gen. 32:15). CURDS (KJV, "butter," Gen. 18:8 et al.) and CHEESE (1 Sam. 17:18 et al.), as well as EGGS (Deut. 22:6–7; Lk. 11:12; et al.), were also eaten. It should be also noted that HONEY, both wild and domestic, was known (Gen. 43:11; 1 Sam. 14:25–26; Matt. 3:4; et al.), though it was forbidden in offerings to God (Lev. 2:11).

3. Condiments. Food was seasoned with SALT (Ezra 6:9; 7:22; Job 6:6; see also COVENANT OF SALT). Salt was obtained by evaporation, and for this the DEAD SEA furnished an inexhaustible supply (Ezek. 47:11). Not always pure, there was the possibility of its becoming mixed with foreign matter until it lost its power (Matt. 5:13). Lot's wife became a pillar of salt (Gen. 19:26). All cereal offerings required salt (Lev. 2:13), and Ezekiel prescribed it for all other offerings (Ezek. 43:24; cf. Mk. 9:49 KJV). Elisha cast it into the spring to make the water suitable for use (2 Ki. 2:20–21). Use of pepper is not mentioned in Scripture, but the condiments MINT, DILL, and CUMMIN (Matt. 23:23), CORIANDER seeds (Exod. 16:31; Num. 11:7), and MUSTARD (Matt. 13:31; 17:20; Lk. 13:19; 17:6) made food more palatable.

D. Food availability. One is not to suppose that all this abundance was available at all times and places. Patriarchal fare was doubtless scant. For guests there was bread freshly baked, curds, milk, and the slaughtered young calf (Gen. 18:6, 8). Jacob, on the other hand, dined on bread and pottage of lentils, and for this Esau sold his birthright (25:34); at other times there might be other pottage to make a meal (2 Ki. 4:38). Roasted grain and wine (Ruth 2:14) or bread and wine (Gen. 14:18) might make up the meal of the ordinary person. Victory in battle occasioned feasting from the supplies of the vanquished.

Settled life in Palestine brought a greater variety of foods. Abigail brought to David and his men two hundred loaves, two skins of wine, five sheep ready dressed, five measures of parched grain, a hundred clusters of raisins, and two hundred cakes of figs when David was fleeing from Saul (1 Sam. 25:18). Ziba brought two hundred loaves of bread, one hundred clusters of raisins, one hundred summer fruits, and a skin of wine to David as David fled from Absalom (2 Sam. 16:1). At David's return Barzillai brought to him wheat, barley, meal, parched grain, beans and lentils, honey, curds, sheep, and cheese from the herd (2 Sam. 17:28–29). Solomon's daily supplies included fine flour, meal, oxen, pasture-fed cattle, sheep, harts, gazelles, roebucks, and fatted fowl (1 Ki. 4:22–23). Tables of the rich were more luxurious than those of nomads and included "choice lambs and fattened calves" (Amos 6:4). An army on the march might have bread, a cake of figs, and clusters of raisins (1 Sam. 30:12). Jesse sent to his sons parched grain and bread, and cheeses to the commander (1 Sam. 17:17–18). Foreign trade added to the variety of foods. TYRE trafficked in wheat, olives, early figs, honey, oil, and balm (Ezek. 27:17).

E. Food of special periods. ADAM in Eden was granted permission to eat of every green plant and of the fruit of all trees except for the TREE OF KNOWLEDGE (Gen. 1:29; 2:16–17). At the time of the flood, Noah took into the ark all kinds of food for himself and for the animals (6:21). Afterwards he was informed that eating flesh was permitted (9:3). Some scholars conclude from this text, and from the silence of Scripture on this topic in the earlier chapters, that early humans until the time of the flood were vegetarian.

When Israel hungered in the wilderness, the Lord supplied MANNA, which was gathered to the extent of one omer per person (Exod. 16:16, 22). Manna was white and tasted like wafers made of honey (16:31). It could be ground, baked, and boiled to make cakes that tasted as cakes of oil (29:23; Num. 11:7–8). Manna continued through the forty years until Israel crossed Jordan and came to Gilgal (Josh. 5:12). Paul describes manna as spiritual food (1 Cor. 10:3). When the people desired meat, the Lord supplied quail (Exod. 16:13; Num. 11:31; Ps. 105:40).

Under the law the PRIESTS ate of the SACRIFICES (Exod. 29:27–28; Lev. 2:3, 10; 6:16–18; Deut. 18:1) and of the SHOWBREAD (Lev. 24:9; 1 Sam. 21:6; Matt. 12:4). Some portions of certain offerings were consumed by the offerer (Lev. 7:15, 19–20; 2 Chr. 25:14); the TITHE was consumed before the Lord (Deut. 12:17; 14:23), as were the FIRSTBORN from the herds and flocks (15:19).

ELIJAH was fed bread and meat by the ravens when he was at the brook KERITH (1 Ki. 17:6). DANIEL and his companions in BABYLON refused the king's delicacies and wine, eating vegetables and drinking water instead (Dan. 1:8–16). During the time of exile, when laws of clean and unclean could not be observed, unclean food was eaten (Ezek. 4:13; Hos. 9:3). JUDITH carried wine, oil, parched grain, a cake of dried fruit, and fine bread when she went to HOLOFERNES's camp (Jdt. 10:5). Judas MACCABEE and his companions lived on what grew wild, in order to escape defilement (2 Macc. 5:27). Also to avoid ceremonial uncleanness JOSEPHUS and his companions lived on figs and nuts (Jos. *Life* 3). The food of JOHN THE BAPTIST was locust and wild honey (Matt. 3:4). Jesus and his disciples bought food from time to time as they journeyed (Jn. 4:8; 13:29).

F. Food preparation. Though royal houses may have had male bakers (Gen. 40:16) and both male and female cooks (1 Sam. 8:13), and though some lesser figures like Samuel had cooks (9:23), the division of labor with the Israelites made food preparation the woman's work (Gen. 18:6; 1 Sam. 8:13; Prov. 31:15; see COOKING). TAMAR took dough, kneaded cakes, baked them, and served them to AMMON (2 Sam. 13:8). Flour must be ground daily, and the cessation of the sound of the grinding of the mill is the end of a civilization (Eccl. 12:4; Jer. 25:10; Matt. 24:41; Rev. 18:22). Since it was necessary for the continuance of life, the upper millstone

Figure of an ancient Egyptian woman grinding grain with a hand mill.

could not be taken as a pledge for DEBT (Deut. 24:6). Dough consisting of flour and water kneaded in kneading troughs and baked in an oven to make bread formed the staff of life (Isa. 3:1). When baked in haste, it was unleavened bread (Gen. 19:3; Deut. 16:3) but when baked with LEAVEN, which was formed from a bit of sour dough left from a previous baking, it was the more usual bread. Bread was sometimes baked on coals (1 Ki. 19:6). In Jerusalem the bakers had a special street in Jeremiah's day (Jer. 37:21).

Meat was boiled in pots (1 Sam. 2:13; Ezek. 24:3–5) or roasted (1 Sam. 2:15; Prov. 12:27); the roasted lamb at Passover was eaten with unleavened bread and bitter herbs (Exod. 12:8, 9). There are six different names for the types of pots or caldrons used in boiling. Water was first boiled and the meat added (Ezek. 24:3–5) with salt. The broth left over also was eaten (Jdg. 6:19; Isa. 65:4). Fish were broiled on coals (Lk. 24:42; Jn. 21:9).

G. Food prices. One knows little of the exact prices of food in ancient times. One seah (about 7 liters) of fine flour and two of barley sold for a shekel (about 11.5 grams of silver, 2 Ki. 7:1, 16). In times of want a donkey's head brought eighty shekels of silver (6:25). Two sparrows sold for a penny ("assarion," Matt. 10:29). In the vision of the Apocalypse, a quart of wheat is worth a denarius (a day's wage), the price also of 3 quarts of barley (Rev. 6:6). The MISHNAH gives some information about prices (*m. Menaḥot* 13:8).

H. Eating habits. Early Israelites probably sat on the ground while they ate while the host might stand by to serve (Gen. 18:8). Isaac sat when he ate (27:19), as did Jacob's sons (37:25), the Levite and his concubine (Jdg. 19:6), Saul (1 Sam. 20:5, 24), and Samuel (1 Sam. 9:22). Those fed by the miracle of the Lord sat on the ground (Jn. 6:10). Tables were used quite early. ADONI-BEZEK had seventy captive kings at his table (Jdg. 1:7; cf. Ps. 23:5). In NT times crumbs fell to the dog under the table (Matt. 15:27; Mk. 7:28). Jesus sat at a table when MARY anointed him (Jn. 12:2). The guests at ESTHER's banquet, however, reclined on couches (Esth. 7:8). Reclining on the left elbow was a normal posture in NT times (Jn. 13:23). It is likely that the guests dipped food from the common dish. The PHARISEES were strict in demanding, for ritual reasons, the prior washing of hands (Mk. 7:3). A blessing said over food was also an established custom in the 1st cent.

The OT has no reference to a meal earlier than noon; however, too much should not be made of the silence. The disciples of Jesus ate an early morning meal on the seashore after a night of toil (Jn. 21:12). The main meals were at noon and in the evening. Peter argued that the apostles could not be drunken at nine o'clock (Acts 2:15). The custom of two meals probably goes back to Scripture: "At twilight you will eat meat, and in the morning you will be filled with bread" (Exod. 16:12). The ravens brought Elijah food in the morning and evening (1 Ki. 17:6). In Egypt there was a mid-day meal (Gen. 43:16), as there was among laborers in Palestine (Ruth 2:14). It was at the sixth hour (noon) that Jesus rested at the well in SAMARIA while his disciples went to buy bread (Jn. 4:6). Peter's intended noonday meal was being prepared when messengers from CORNELIUS arrived (Acts 10:9–10). This meal is called "dinner" (*ariston* G756, Matt. 22:4; Lk. 11:38; 14:12). Supper came after the work was done (Ruth 3:7; Jdg. 19:16–21). In some cases it might be prepared by a servant who had previously done field work all day (Lk. 17:7–8). This meal has no special name in the OT, but in the NT it is referred to as *deipnon G1270* (Jn. 12:2; 13:2; 21:20; 1 Cor. 11:20).

I. Prohibited foods. In Eden every herb and tree yielding seed was for food (Gen. 1:29), and only the fruit of the tree of knowledge of good and evil was forbidden (2:16, 17; 3:1–3). See EDEN, GARDEN OF. Prohibitions of eating of the sinew of the hip (not otherwise attested in the OT) are traced to Jacob's wrestling with the angel (Gen. 32:32). Josephus thought this to be the broad sinew or sciatic nerve (*Ant.* 1.20.2). In Rabbinic legislation, a punishment of forty stripes is meted out to the transgressor (*m. Ḥullin* 7.1,3).

Under the law, food regulations dealt with meat and not with vegetable products. There is no basis either in Scripture or in Rabbinic literature for JUSTIN MARTYR's accusation (*Dialogue* 20) that certain vegetables are prohibited. Recabites and

Nazirites abstained from the produce of the vine (Num. 6:2; Jdg. 13:14; Jer. 35:5–6), and Josephus speaks of a certain Bannus who was a vegetarian (*Life* 2), but these are exceptional cases. The argument that early humans were vegetarian is based on the prior silence of Scripture connected with the specific permission to eat meat given to Noah (Gen. 9:3).

The eating of blood, prohibited in the days of Noah (Gen. 9:4) and prohibited by the law (Lev. 19:26; Deut. 12:16, 23–25; 15:23; 1 Sam. 14:34), was further prohibited in the apostolic letter (Acts 15:20, 29). Flesh of an animal found dead (Lev. 7:24; Deut. 14:21), flesh of an animal torn by beasts (Exod. 22:31; Lev. 7:24; 22:8), and a limb torn from a living animal are forbidden foods. The eating of FAT (Lev. 3:16–17; 7:23) and the fat tail (Exod. 29:22; Lev. 3:9) is prohibited and carried the death penalty when this food was a part of a sacrifice (7:25). These parts belonged to the Lord (Gen. 4:4; 1 Sam. 2:16; 2 Chr. 7:7). After the exile, eating "the fat" is commended (Neh. 8:10 [NIV, "choice food"]; cf. Isa. 25:6). Deuteronomy prohibits the taking of the mother bird and eggs and young ones at the same time. The mother bird is to have her freedom (Deut. 22:6–7).

J. Clean and unclean foods. Laws regarding CLEAN and unclean animals, already in part alluded to in the days of the patriarchs (Gen. 7:2–3), are the most significant regulations of the law in matters of food. These laws deal with quadrupeds, fish, birds, and insects (Lev. 11:1–27; Deut. 14:3–21). For quadrupeds, only those which have parted hoofs and chew the cud are edible. The camel, the rock badger, the hare, and the swine are specifically rejected by name (Lev. 11:4–8; Deut. 14:8). It is specifically stated that swine's flesh is an abomination (Isa. 65:4; 66:3, 17).

Of fish, those which have fins and scales are edible (Lev. 11:9–12). Of birds, a list of twenty are specified that are to be rejected (11:13–19). Of insects, the ones that have legs and leap may be eaten. The locust and grasshopper are specifically mentioned as being edible, while other flying, swarming, and crawling things are rejected (11:20–23). Distinctions in food broke down in times of want (Ezek. 4:13).

Peter in his vision rejected the command to eat animals not conforming to these categories (Acts 10:12–15). Jesus is said to have done away with distinctions concerning foods (Mk. 7:19). These were regulations of the old covenant that have lost their significance (Heb. 9:10) and cannot confirm the faith (13:9). The effort to try to connect these regulations of the law with modern laws of hygiene breaks down when applied in details. It has no more to commend it than the earlier allegorical exegesis of the same laws.

The rabbinic prohibition of eating milk and meat at the same time is based on an exegesis of the command not to "cook a young goat in its mother's milk" (Exod. 23:19; 34:26; Deut. 14:21; cf. *m. Ḥullin* 8.4). Ugaritic discoveries have, from a reconstructed text (C. H. Gordon, *Ugaritic Manual* [1955], 52.14), called attention to a similar practice on the part of the Canaanites to that forbidden in Scripture.

K. Food offered to idols. A special problem with food faced the early Christians when they asked whether or not they could eat food previously offered to idols. The apostolic letter enjoined abstinence "from food sacrificed to idols" (Acts 15:29). When questioned about this issue, PAUL answered that food does not commend one to God. The KINGDOM OF GOD is not meat and drink. One may eat what he is disposed to—whatever is sold in the market (1 Cor. 10:25)—without asking questions for conscience' sake; but if the eating causes a brother to stumble then the Christian abstains for the sake of his brother's conscience (Rom. 14:13–23; 1 Cor. 8:1–13). See IDOLATRY III.

L. Sharing food. Sharing one's food with the hungry was demanded by John the Baptist as a sign of repentance (Lk. 3:11). In the OT JOB claims this trait among his virtues (Job 31:17). Those who are hungry are to be fed (Matt. 25:35–36). The duty extends to the hungry enemy (Prov. 25:21; Rom. 12:20). Faith that refuses to feed the hungry brother or sister is dead faith (Jas. 2:15–17).

M. Life and food. As important as it is, food is not the chief ingredient of life: "man does not live on bread alone but on every word that comes from the mouth of the LORD" (Deut. 8:3; cf. Matt. 4:4; Lk. 4:4). Failure of food should not destroy faith in God (Hab. 3:17–18). Life is more than food (Matt. 6:25, 32; Lk. 12:22, 30). (See further H. N. and A. L. Moldenke, *Plants of the Bible* [1952]; A. C. Bouquet, *Everyday Life in New Testament Times* [1954], 69–79; D. R. Brothwell and P. Brothwell, *Food in Antiquity: A Survey of the Diet of Early Peoples*, expanded ed. [1998].)

II. Metaphorical. The basis for a metaphorical use of food is laid in the prophets when Isaiah rebukes those who spend their substance for that which does not satisfy (Isa. 55:1–2). Food is a frequent metaphor in the NT. Jesus' comparison of himself to the bread of life (Jn. 6) is the chief figurative use of food in Scripture. As Israel ate manna in the wilderness, so Christ gives of himself to believers so that they may eat of his flesh and drink his blood and have life. The one eating this food shall never want.

In answer to the question of whether anyone had given him anything to eat, Jesus answered that his food was "to do the will of him who sent me and to finish his work" (Jn. 4:34). This, of course, did not imply that he could dispense with earthly food. Continuing the metaphor, the new believer is to desire the pure milk of the word (1 Pet. 2:2). Elementary teaching is milk for babes, while advanced matters are solid food for the mature (1 Cor. 3:2; Heb. 5:14). The preservative power of salt illustrates the powers of the disciple in the world (Matt. 5:13; Mk. 9:50). Its seasoning power is a figure of the proper choice of speech (Col. 4:6). The one who overcomes will "eat from the tree of life" (Rev. 2:7).　　　　　　　　　　　　J. P. LEWIS

fool. See FOLLY.

foot. The lowest extremity of the leg. References to the feet of God (e.g., Exod. 24:10; Ps. 18:9; Isa. 60:13–14; Heb. *regel H8079*) are of course figurative, for a spirit has no flesh or bones. However, the reference to the hands and feet of the resurrected Christ reveals that he still possessed a body (Lk. 24:39; Gk. *pous G4546*).

Great care was needed for the feet in the ANE. Since people wore SANDALS or went barefoot, the washing of feet showed needed and refreshing hospitality (Gen. 18:4; see FOOTWASHING). This was the lowest task of servants, performed by the youngest or least skilled upon the part of the body most likely to be defiled. Christ's example in washing his disciples' feet showed both HUMILITY and complete devotion (Jn. 13:5). A widow in the early church washed the feet of saints (1 Tim. 5:10). Undoing the latchet of a sandal was an equivalent task. By contrast, the disciples shook the dust off their feet to predict judgment on unhearing and inhospitable towns and villages (Matt. 10:14).

The feet of the Israelites were miraculously preserved during the long journey in the wilderness (Deut. 8:4). Feet suggest movement: "the feet of him who brings good tidings" (Isa. 52:7 RSV). Angels guard the feet of those who make the Most High their dwelling so that they will not strike their feet against a stone (Ps. 91:9–12). Taking off the shoes was not only proper before entering a house, but also in the presence of God (Exod. 3:5). The Preacher instructed, "Guard your steps [*lit.*, feet] when you go to the house of God" (Eccl. 5:1). In a striking hyperbole, Jesus commanded, "And if your foot causes you to sin, cut it off. It is better for you to enter life crippled than to have two feet and be thrown into hell" (Mk. 9:45).

To bare the foot in public expressed MOURNING (Ezek. 24:17) or SHAME (Deut. 25:9), but to take off a sandal and give it to another confirmed a transaction of redemption and exchange (Ruth 4:7). The phrase translated literally by the KJV as "Saul went in to cover his feet" (1 Sam. 24:3) is a euphemism (cf. modern versions, "to relieve himself"). A wicked man could communicate by scraping or tapping with his feet (Prov. 6:13).

A learner might sit at the feet of his teacher, as Mary did (Lk. 10:39), yet no believer should discriminate against the poor by asking them to sit at his feet (Jas. 2:3). In the BODY OF CHRIST, a foot should not envy the hand (1 Cor. 12:14–15). JAIRUS fell at the feet of Jesus in humility, respect, and supplication (Mk. 5:22). Feet were embraced or kissed in adoration (Lk. 7:38). Egyptian monuments picture conquerors treading on the vanquished as a method of insult, and the Lord promised to trample the Assyrian under foot (Isa. 14:25). JOB expressed his consistent behavior with the expression, "My foot has held fast to his steps" (Job 23:11 NRSV), while the psalmist prayed, "May the foot of the proud not come against me" (Ps. 36:11). R. L. MIXTER

footman. This term is used by the KJV a dozen times, usually to render Hebrew *ragli* H8081, "foot soldier" (1 Sam. 4:10 et al.), distinguished from the soldier who rides on horseback or in a chariot. In the Pentateuch, however, the Hebrew word is apparently used to contrast between adult men and children (Exod. 12:37; Num 11:21). The KJV also uses the word "footman" twice to render other Hebrew expressions (1 Sam. 22:17 ["guard"]; Jer. 12:5 ["foot-runner"]). G. GIACUMAKIS, JR.

footstool. A low stool for supporting the feet. The word is used in a literal sense only twice (*kebeš* H3900, 2 Chr. 9:18, of SOLOMON's throne, which had a footstool of gold; and *hypopodion* G5711, Jas. 2:3 [NIV, "by my feet"]). The thirteen other times the word is used are figurative, and in all of them it is God who makes use of the footstool, with the NT references being OT quotations or allusions. The ARK OF THE COVENANT, and by implication the temple where it resides, is called God's footstool (1 Chr. 28:2; Pss. 99:5; 132:7; Lam. 2:1). However, a house cannot contain God, who says, "Heaven is my throne, / and the earth is my footstool" (Isa. 66:1, quoted in Acts 7:49; cf. Matt. 5:35). In addition, the enemies of the Messianic King will be subdued and made a footstool for his feet (Ps. 110:1; quoted in Matt. 22:44; Mk. 12:36; Lk. 20:43; Acts 2:35; Heb. 1:13; 10:13). S. BARABAS

The lower steps of the royal seat at the Iron Age gate of Dan. When judging the Israelites from this platform, the king would place a footstool beneath his feet.

footwashing. Though never a major Hebrew rite, the washing of hands and feet of the priests did have a place in the Mosaic ritual (Exod. 30:17–21). It may indeed be that all ablutions of the Bible are ritual rather than sanitary, though they rise out of assumed sanitary practices (R. de Vaux, *Ancient Israel: Its Life and Institutions* [1961], 460). Guests ordinarily were offered water and vessels for washing the feet (Gen. 18:4; 19:2; 24:32; 43:24; Jdg. 19:21). As a special act of affection or humility, the host or hostess might even wash a guest's feet (1 Sam. 25:41). A "sinful woman" spontaneously and gratefully served the Lord in this way (Lk. 7:36–44).

At the Last Supper the Lord, taking a towel and basin during the meal (Jn. 13:4–10), proceeded to wash the disciples' feet and to wipe them with the towel. It was not to observe a custom, for the disciples were mystified by it. Jesus must have intended to communicate something distinctive. HUMILITY, however, was not the only, or even the main, lesson Jesus was seeking to teach: "A person who has had a bath [*louō* G3374] needs only to wash [*niptō* G3782] his feet; his whole body is clean" (v. 10). The precise meaning of this statement is disputed (depending partly on whether a distinction is intended by the two verbs and whether the phrase *ei mē tous podas*, "except the feet," is textually sound; see D. A. Carson, *The Gospel according to John* [1991], 464–66). Nevertheless, it is clear that Jesus was giving this act the symbolic significance of spiritual cleansing. (See also H. Weiss in *NovT* 21 [1979]: 298–325.)

Whether or not footwashing is a church ordinance (cf. vv. 14–15) must be decided on the basis of three criteria: (1) Was it instituted by Christ? (2) Is it universal? (3) Does it have permanent application? A number of smaller denominations developing out of the "left wing of the Reformation" (to use R. Bainton's phrase) believe it to be an ordinance, citing 1 Tim. 5:10 in addition to Jn. 13. The National Fellowship of Brethren Churches has sought to develop a cogent theology and defense of it as an ordinance (see H. A. Hoyt, *This Do in Remembrance of Me* [1947]; C. F. Yoder, *God's Means of Grace* [1908, repr. 2000]). Several arguments have been advanced against this view, such as the silence of Acts and the Epistles, and the observation that "baptism and the Lord's Supper cannot be understood to command something *other* than a ceremony" (see W. Grudem, *Systematic Theology: An Introduction to Biblical Doctrine* [1994], 962). R. D. CULVER

forbearance. Restraint and leniency in the face of provocation. In its religious meaning, forbearance or PATIENCE is characteristic of the God of biblical revelation. Yahweh, the God of Israel, was extremely patient with the perverse and recalcitrant people he had elected. In their wickedness he bore with them (*māšak H5432*, "to extend, prolong, protract," Neh. 9:30). In different language, he proved himself "compassionate and gracious, slow to anger, abounding in love" (Ps. 103:8). Thereby he revealed and exercised his forbearance, that is, his disposition to hold back or restrain his WRATH and to delay the divine punishment that must eventually fall upon all SIN not covered by REPENTANCE and ATONEMENT.

God's forbearance is not an easy and indifferent "tolerance" of sin. For sin God has only negations. Neither will God absolve the unrepentant sinner. The final judgment will call all people into account and seal their destiny for good or ill. But in this age, in the day of grace, he is LONGSUFFERING. Not only is he slow to punish, but also unwilling, even in the face of opposition and alienation, to withdraw his overtures toward peace or cancel his invitation to be reconciled.

God's forbearance is celebrated in the NT no less than in the OT. Jesus hinted both at it and at his kinship with the Father when he asked, "O unbelieving generation.... How long shall I put up with you" (*anechomai G462*, Mk. 9:19). In particular, the apostle Paul proclaims this truth in his letter to the Romans, where he teaches that God has shown forbearance and patience (*anochē G496, makrothymia G3429*) for a number of reasons: to show his wrath (upon sin), to make known his power, to disclose the riches of his glory for the vessels of mercy, and principally, to lead sinners to repentance (Rom. 2:4; 3:25; 9:22). The same is declared by the apostle Peter: faced with the scoffers' question, "Where is this 'coming' he [Christ] promised?" (2 Pet. 3:4), Peter answered, "The Lord is not slow in keeping his promise, as some understand slowness. He is patient [*makrothymeō G3428*] with you, not wanting anyone to perish, but everyone to come to repentance" (3:9).

Christians who wish to lead a life worthy of their calling are obliged, in imitation of their Lord, to forbear one another in love, with all lowliness, meekness, and patience (Eph. 4:2). That is, they are to exercise calm patience under provocation, avoid resentment and retaliation, be slow to judge and punish, and be ever ready to forgive (Phil. 4:5; Col. 3:13; 2 Tim. 2:24). See FORGIVENESS. H. STOB

ford. A shallow place in a stream where it may be crossed on foot. Fords were of great importance in OT times because of the absence of bridges, which were first built in large numbers by the Romans. Scripture often mentions the fords of the JORDAN, which could be crossed in many places (*maʿbārâ H5045*, Josh. 2:7; Jdg. 3:28; 12:5–6). The principal ford across this river seems to have been at JERICHO (Josh. 2:7; Jdg. 3:28; 2 Sam. 19:15). In time of flood, when the melting snows of the Lebanon mountains caused the Jordan to overflow its banks, it was impossible to cross the Jordan (Josh. 3:15). Near the DEAD SEA the Jordan is about 100 ft. wide and 5–12 ft. deep.

The crossing of the Jordan is mentioned in connection with JACOB (Gen. 32:10), GIDEON (Jdg. 8:4), DAVID (2 Sam. 10:17; 17:22), ABSALOM (17:24), and others. Under the leadership of JOSHUA, the Israelites crossed the Jordan on dry land, not by fording it since it was then in flood, but by a tremendous miraculous act of God. Jesus crossed the Jordan on numerous occasions when he journeyed between GALILEE and JERUSALEM by way of PEREA instead of passing through SAMARIA. Mention is also made in Scripture of the ford of the river JABBOK (*maʿăbār H5044*, Gen. 32:22) and the fords of the river ARNON (Num. 21:13; Deut. 2:24; Isa. 16:2; cf. also the noun *ʿăbārâ H6302*, 2 Sam. 15:28 [*Ketib*]; 17:16 [with many MSS]; 19:18 [see NIV]). S. BARABAS

forecast. This word is used in the KJV twice to render the Hebrew verb *ḥāšab H3108*, more properly translated "to plot, devise" (Dan. 11:24–25).

forehead. This term (Heb. *mēṣaḥ H5195*) is used with a literal sense in a number of passages. For example, AARON was instructed to wear the plate of pure gold on his forehead (Exod. 28:38);

DAVID struck GOLIATH on the forehead (1 Sam. 17:49); leprosy broke out on the forehead of Azariah (UZZIAH, 2 Chr. 26:19–20; a different term, *gibbēaḥ H1477*, indicates "forehead baldness," Lev. 13:41–42). Figuratively, the hardness of the forehead indicates determination or defiance (Isa. 48:4; Ezek. 3:8–9; cf. also Jer. 3:3 [NIV, "brazen look"]).

In the expression, "He will crush the foreheads of Moab" (Num. 24:17; cf. Jer. 48:45), the term used is *pēʾâ H6991*, properly "side [of head]," that is, "temple." And in the command that the Israelites should write God's instructions on the forehead (Exod. 13:9 et al.), the expression "between the eyes" is used. It was no doubt intended in a figurative sense, but around the time of the Babylonian captivity the Jews began to interpret it literally and to make leather boxes that held strips of parchment with the biblical text; these boxes were then fastened to the forehead and left arm (see PHYLACTERY).

In the NT all the occurrences of the term (Gk. *metōpon G3587*) are in the book of Revelation, mainly referring to the figurative or literal marks, seals, or names found on the foreheads of those who are servants of God as well as those who reject God (Rev. 7:3; 9:4; 13:16; 14:1; 20:4). The forehead is also where Babylon, mother of prostitutes, has her name written (17:5; cf. Jer. 3:3).

G. GIACUMAKIS, JR.

foreigner. Someone who is not a citizen, dwelling in another country either as a temporary guest, perhaps for purposes of trade, or as a permanent resident alien. The relevant Hebrew words are translated in a variety of ways but are not easily distinguishable in meaning. The term *nokrî H5799* (cf. also *bēn nēkār*, "son of a foreign land") is usually rendered "alien" or "stranger" by the KJV, but "foreigner" in modern translations (Deut. 14:21; Job 19:15; Ps. 69:8; Lam. 5:2). Two other terms, *gēr H1731* and *tôšāb H9369* (KJV, "sojourner"), are sometimes used together in the same passage with no apparent semantic difference (Lev. 25:35; 1 Chr. 29:15; Ps. 39:12), though it has been suggested that in some contexts the latter indicates an individual less assimilated to Israelite society and attached to someone else's household (cf. Exod. 12:44–45; Lev. 22:10). An additional term, *zār H2424*, has a broad range of meanings, such as "outsider" and "unauthorized," but can also refer to a foreigner (e.g., Isa. 1:7).

There were strangers among the Israelites from the first. A "mixed multitude" went up from Egypt with Israel (Exod. 12:28 KJV); after the conquest, Israelites and Canaanites dwelt side by side. The latter were never totally exterminated. The historical books frequently make mention of resident aliens, such as URIAH the Hittite. A whole clan or tribe might be sojourners in Israel, as for example the people of GIBEON (Josh. 9:22–27) and of BEEROTH (2 Sam. 4:2–3, verb *gûr H1591*). SOLOMON's census shows that the number of aliens in the land of Israel was quite considerable (2 Chr. 2:17). The word *foreigner* was applied also to the patriarchs in Palestine (Gen. 23:4; 26:3) and to Israelites making their home for a time in other lands (Gen. 47:4; Exod. 2:22; Ruth 1:1).

Foreigners in Israel enjoyed certain limited religious and civic privileges and were subject to certain laws. They could offer sacrifices (Lev. 17:8; 22:18–19), but were not permitted to enter the sanctuary unless they were circumcised (Ezek. 44:9). They could take part in the three great annual religious festivals attended by all Israelite males (Deut. 16:11, 14). They were not permitted to eat of the PASSOVER unless they were circumcised (Exod. 12:43, 48), and the Passover prohibition of the use of leaven applied also to them (Exod. 12:19). Like the Israelites, they were forbidden to work on the

Relief of a Hittite woman carrying a child. The Hittites were among those people whom the Lord considered to be foreigners.

Sabbath and on the Day of Atonement (Exod. 20:10; 23:12; Lev. 16:19; Deut. 5:14; see Atonement, Day of); and like them also they were stoned to death for reviling or blaspheming God's name (Lev. 24:16; Num. 15:30). They heard the law read to all the people in the sabbatical year (Deut. 31:10–13).

In general, there was one law for both foreigner and native (Exod. 12:49; Lev. 24:22), and in legal actions aliens were entitled to the same justice as the Israelites (Deut. 1:16) and were liable to the same penalties (Lev. 20:2; 24:16, 22). Israelites were warned not to oppress foreigners, since they themselves had once been strangers in the land of Egypt (Exod. 22:21; 23:9; Lev. 19:33–34). Foreigners were to be loved and treated like native Israelites (Lev. 19:34; Deut. 10:19), for God loves them (Deut. 10:18) and watches over them (Ps. 146:9; Mal. 3:5). Needy foreigners were to be given assistance (Num. 35:15; Deut. 10:19). They were to share in the special triennial tithe (Deut. 14:29) and in the produce of the sabbatical year (Lev. 25:6), as well as in the gleanings of the olives, grapes, and grain at the time of harvest (Lev. 19:10; 23:22; Deut. 24:19–21). They were entitled to asylum in the cities of refuge (Num. 35:15; Josh. 20:9). It was forbidden to oppress them when they labored as hired servants (Deut. 24:14). Like the Israelites, they were forbidden to eat blood (Lev. 17:10, 12), but, unlike them, they might eat animals that had died a natural death (Deut. 14:21). Israelite laws of sexual morality applied to them as well (Lev. 18:26).

Although there were certain prohibitions of marriage between foreigners and Israelites, these restrictions were frequently ignored (Gen. 34:14; Exod. 34:12, 16; Deut. 7:3; Josh. 23:12). However, the OT gives several striking examples of foreigners, such as Ruth, being fully integrated into the religious life of Israel (cf. F. A. Spina, *The Faith of the Outsider: Exclusion and Inclusion in the Biblical Story* [2005]).

Foreigners naturally suffered some obstacles. They could not take part in the deliberations of the clan, tribe, or nation. The law prohibited a foreigner from becoming a king of Israel (Deut. 17:15). They had to pay interest for money they borrowed (15:3; 23:20); and when, during the Jubilee Year the debts of Israelites were canceled, theirs were not (15:3), and when Hebrew slaves were freed, they remained in bondage (Lev. 25:45–46). Ezekiel, however, foresaw the time in the messianic age when they would share in all the blessings of the land with God's own people (Ezek. 47:22).

In the NT, several Greek words are used with the sense "foreigner" or "stranger," such as *allogenēs* G254 (Lk. 17:18, describing the Samaritan) and *allotrios* G259 (Heb. 11:34 et al.). The most common term, however, is *xenos* G3828 (Acts 17:21 et al.). Paul describes Gentiles as "foreigners to the covenants of the promise" (Eph. 2:12); when they come to Christ, however, they are "no longer foreigners and aliens [*paroikos* G4230], but fellow citizens with God's people" (v. 19). On the other hand, Peter refers to his readers as "aliens and strangers [*parepidēmos* G4215] in the world" (1 Pet. 2:11). See also barbarian. S. Barabas

foreknow. To have knowledge of something before it occurs. Although the Greek verb *proginōskō* G4589 can be used in the general sense of possessing prior information (Acts 26:5; 2 Pet. 3:17), both it and the substantive *prognōsis* G4590, "foreknowledge," have a specific theological usage that focuses on God's unique knowledge (Acts 2:23; Rom. 8:29; 11:2; 1 Pet. 1:2, 20).

In the sense of cognition, God's foreknowledge belongs to his omniscience and embraces all persons and things. Scripture throughout teaches God's all-comprehending prescience and knowledge. Nothing is hid from him (e.g., Job 28:23–24; 37:16; Pss. 44:21; 139:1–4; Isa. 46:9–10; 48:2–5; Jer. 1:5; 1 Cor. 2:10–11; 1 Jn. 3:20). There is no ground for dispute respecting God's foreknowledge in this sense. An implication, however, is liable to be overlooked. If God foresees all that comes to pass, then with God there is no uncertainty of occurrence. Hence, certainty respecting all that comes to pass is involved in foreknowledge no less than in foreordination (see foreordain), and foreknowledge provides no escape from the certainty that foreordination asserts and determines. It is of biblical faith to believe that for God there are no contingent eventualities, and believers should be assured that all the circumstances of their life are well known to him who is their God and Savior.

The crucial questions respecting foreknowledge arise in connection with those passages that expressly deal with salvation. There can be no question but that the phrases "those he foreknew" (Rom. 8:29) and "the foreknowledge of God the Father" (1 Pet. 1:2) are predicable of the elect and of those only. The former passage introduces a chain of events that issues in glorification, and those embraced in this chain are designated as "God's elect" (Rom. 8:31 NRSV). In 1 Pet. 1:1 also those concerned are called "elect." The question is: What is the import of "foreknew" and "foreknowledge" and, more particularly, what relation does the former sustain to predestination (Rom. 8:29) and the latter to election (1 Pet. 1:1–2)? It is widely maintained that the foreknowledge in these texts is the prescience of God, his foresight of faith or, more accurately, his foresight of certain persons as believing. Whom God foresees as believing he predestinates and elects to salvation.

If this were the intent of PAUL and PETER, it would not be unworthy of them and not contrary to the general tenor of biblical teaching. God's foresight of all persons and actions is, as noted, biblical doctrine, and he foresees his people as believing. There is, however, an important consideration, derived from Scripture teaching, to be kept in mind. FAITH itself is not an act or activity of human autonomy; it is not something of which sinners are capable. It is a gift of God. This was the teaching of the Lord expressly (Jn. 6:37, 44–45, 65) and by implication (3:3–8). It is Paul's teaching (Rom. 8:5–9; Eph. 2:8–10; Phil. 1:29) and Peter's (2 Pet. 1:1). Hence the faith God foresees is the faith he has determined to give. To use the Lord's language, the faith God the Father foresees is the coming to Christ which is the result of his own effectual drawing (Jn. 6:44), of the learning which he imparts (6:45), and of his own giving (6:65). Foresight of faith, therefore, does not eliminate the sovereign differentiation that God causes to be in his saving operations; it throws one back on God's sovereign will to work effectually to the exercise of faith. No escape from the sovereignty of God's will in salvation is provided by this view of foreknowledge.

The most significant passage (Rom. 8:29) requires further examination and the relevant considerations indicate that a different interpretation from that discussed above should be adopted. (1) It is to be noted that Paul says "whom he foreknew" (NRSV). The persons in view are the object of the verb "foreknew" and they are the object without any qualification or further characterization. The view that supposes foresight of faith or foresight of persons as believing is required to supply a characterization that the apostle himself does not add. Unless there is a compelling reason for this addition, one has no right to append it. We must ask the question: Is there a meaning of the word "foreknew" that can properly belong to it and that avoids the necessity of importing something without warrant in the text itself? If such a meaning can be found, a meaning supported by Scripture usage, then an interpretation based upon the need for a qualifying importation is ruled out. This alternative is valid. There is ample evidence for an interpretation in which "whom he foreknew" is intelligible and appropriate without further explanation.

(2) "Foreknow" is a compound in which the word "know" is the main ingredient. The first part in English, as in Greek, indicates simply that the knowing is beforehand. So it is necessary to focus attention on the term "know" and determine its precise force. It is used frequently in Scripture in the sense of simple cognition. It is used also often with a richer meaning in which the thought of distinguishing affection and will enters. When "know" is used in this sense, there is differentiation in the word itself. The instances are numerous in both Testaments (e.g., Gen. 18:19; Exod. 2:25; Ps. 1:6; Jer. 1:5; Hos. 13:5; Amos 3:2; Matt. 7:23; 1 Cor. 8:3; Gal. 4:9; 2 Tim. 2:19; 1 Jn. 3:1). The distinguishing connotation lies on the face of this usage. "Know" means to know with distinguishing regard, affection, and purpose and comes to be synonymous with love. This is all the more apparent in the OT when the distinction inherent in the word "know" is expressed by the word "love" (cf. Deut. 4:37; 7:8, 13; 10:15; 23:5; 1 Ki. 10:9; 2 Chr. 9:8; Jer. 31:3; Hos. 11:1; 14:4; Mal. 1:2). The inference is inescapable that "to know" is the same as "to love"—with the distinguishing affection and purpose which this term frequently conveys in Scripture. Hence, "to know beforehand" is to know with peculiar regard and love from before the foundation of the world (cf. Eph. 1:4), and

"foreknew" (Rom. 8:29) can have the persons as direct object with no further qualification.

(3) Corroboration is found in Eph. 1:4–5. That there is an identity of theme in the two passages needs no demonstration. When Paul says, "In love he predestined us to be adopted as his sons," he intimates that predestination is conditioned by love and springs from it. When foreknowledge is interpreted, as the analogy of Scripture and the terms of the passage dictate, Rom. 8:29 expresses the same relationship with the additional emphasis upon the coextensiveness of this love and predestination to be conformed to the image of God's Son. There is no duplication of thought in either passage. The love focuses attention upon the electing grace, the predestination upon the high destiny to which those embraced in electing love are appointed. The order of thought is similar to Eph. 1:4, where election in Christ is said to be to the end of being holy and without blame. Electing love is not fruitless affection. It always moves to a goal commensurate in magnitude with the love that impels.

(4) The idea of mere foresight of faith does not comport with the governing thought of Rom. 8:28–30. The accent in this passage falls upon God's determinate action, upon his monergism. It is God who predestinates, calls, justifies, and glorifies, and this emphasis appears in confirmation of the assurance of v. 28 and in elucidation of the purpose in accordance with which those concerned are called. Foresight, however true of God it is in itself, suggests a passivity out of agreement with the total thrust of the context. Only the efficient action involved in electing love measures up to this requirement. It is not the foresight of what will be but the foreknowledge that causes to be.

These considerations show that in this crucial passage "foreknowledge" as applied to God is not to be construed in terms merely of prescience, and so one may not proceed on the assumption that in other instances this diluted sense obtains. In Rom. 11:2 the reference to the people whom God foreknew is most appropriately taken of the people of Israel as a whole after the pattern of 11:28. Every consideration would point to the conclusion that the choice of Israel in love is in view. The notion of mere prescience is obviously inadequate. Although the full force of the distinguishing love of Rom. 8:29 cannot be applied to 11:2, yet the same basic meaning obtains, namely, the love on God's part by which Israel had been chosen and set apart (cf. Deut. 4:37 et al., as cited earlier). What is in view is the theocratic election of Israel, and Paul is assuring us that the love animating this election has abiding relevance and is the guarantee that Israel has not been finally rejected. This instance is additional evidence for the pregnant force of "foreknow."

In 1 Pet. 1:20—"foreknown indeed before the foundation of the world" (ASV)—"foreknown" is contrasted with "manifested" and, in reference to Christ, the distinction is between design from eternity and realization in the fullness of the time. It is apparent that the notion of "foreseen" before the foundation of the world falls short of Peter's intent. The thought is that Christ was chosen and provided before the world began, but was manifested in the end of the times. If the idea expressed by "foreknown" does not rise to that of "foreordained" (cf. KJV), the difference is scarcely perceptible (NRSV, "destined"; NIV, "chosen"). In any case, this instance shows that "foreknow" can properly express the thought of the ordination and appointment of God's design and counsel.

Before proceeding to the discussion of the substantive (*prognōsis*), it is necessary to take account of two other verbs: *prooraō G4632* (Gal. 3:8) and *problepō G4587* (Heb. 11:40). In the former passage, it is possible that nothing more than foreseeing is expressed (cf. Acts 2:25, 31). However, if "the Scripture" is personified and in reality means God, the verb might well mean "determine beforehand" after the pattern of 1 Pet. 1:20. The second verb, which means more literally "foresee," is clearly used in the sense of "provide" (Heb. 11:40). The interest of this passage is to show that a term closely corresponding to "foreknow" and, like foreknow, one that may express simply the thought of foreseeing, can be and is used with a much more active connotation, thus furnishing evidence parallel to the distinctly determining force of "foreknow" as demonstrated above.

The usage respecting the verb "foreknow" in each instance where God is the subject demonstrates that in the NT the term possesses an active and ordaining force that the English equivalent would not of itself readily suggest. This must be borne in mind in dealing with the two instances of the substantive "foreknowledge." The meaning of the verb creates strong presumption that the same force is present in the noun. It should be noted that Acts 2:23 is distinctly similar to 1 Pet. 1:20, for the predetermining counsel of God respecting Christ is the thought in both passages. Note also that 1 Pet. 1:2 is similar to Rom. 8:29, because foreknowledge conditions election in the former as it conditions predestination in the latter. This parallelism is a factor not to be discounted.

In Acts 2:23 there are several considerations bearing upon the interpretation of "foreknowledge." (1) The term indicates that the counsel of God involved in the CRUCIFIXION of Christ was prior to the event. The analogy of other passages (Eph. 1:4; 1 Pet. 1:20) would require that this priority was eternal, before the foundation of the world.

(2) The words with which foreknowledge is conjoined, "determinate counsel" (*hōrismenē boulē*; NIV, "set purpose"), denote the immutable purpose and decree of God. Stronger terms to express predetermination could not be found. It may not be argued that appeal to God's foresight of the crucifixion and of all the circumstances associated with it would be inappropriate in conjunction with the emphasis upon determinate counsel. Foreknowledge could relevantly draw attention to God's eternal omniscience in order thereby to assert that the efficient decree was made in the light of comprehensive knowledge of events and implications. But this notion of foreknowledge does not take proper account of the construction. It was, Peter says, "by the determinate counsel and foreknowledge" that Jesus was delivered, and the agency or instrumentality that is exercised *by* the determinate counsel is applied also to the foreknowledge. This implies for the foreknowledge an efficiency comparable to that of the fixed counsel. The mere notion of prescience does not possess this quality. The thought requires an active, determining element of which prescience falls short (cf. Rom. 8:29). It is not simply conjunction of counsel and foreknowledge that the text mentions but a conjunction of determining decrees, and foreknowledge for this reason requires the strength of foreordination. It may not be objected that there is virtual duplication of ideas. It is characteristic of Scripture to emphasize something by adding a virtual synonym. Here, however, this is not necessarily the case. Foreknowledge points to the *pre*-ordination, while determinate counsel indicates the immutable decree.

(3) It is significant that the writer of 1 Pet. 1:20 is the speaker in Acts 2:23. The determinate force of the verb "foreknow" in the former is an index to the meaning of the noun in the latter. Since the two passages deal with God's counsel respecting Christ, conclusive evidence would have to be available if differentiation on the question at issue were to obtain. This evidence does not exist. As maintained above, the considerations point to an identity in respect of active, determining will.

(4) It would not be legitimate to press unduly the analogy of Acts 4:28. It is conceivable that the terms of 4:28 were intended to express foreordination in a way that 2:23 does not. Yet, since other considerations evince that foreknowledge in 2:23 carries the force of foreordination, it is not possible to discount the unequivocal terms of 4:28 in interpreting 2:23. They both reflect on the same subject. Peter is the speaker in the one case; he is closely associated, if not the actual spokesman, in the other. There is proximity in the literary composition. It would be natural to regard them both as enunciating the same doctrine. If so, the foreknowledge of 2:23 would have to perform the service of "foreordained to come to pass" in 4:28.

It must be concluded, therefore, that the exegetical considerations claim for "foreknowledge" the same determinant force as is apparent in the use of the verb "foreknow." What is to be said for 1 Pet. 1:2? (1) If one proceeds on the assumption that "according to the foreknowledge of God the Father" is taken with the words "elect sojourners" (v. 1, *eklektois parepidēmois*), then the foreknowledge of God is to be regarded as conditioning election and causally prior to it. As indicated earlier, the similarity to Rom. 8:29 is apparent. The considerations adduced in connection with the Romans passage against the notion of mere prescience would be equally valid: foreknowledge here is not qualified any more than "foreknew" in Romans, and the pregnant meaning applies as much to "knowledge" as it does to the word "know."

(2) In 1 Pet. 1:2 there is another factor pointing to the active force of foreknowledge. The

foreknowledge of God the Father is coordinated with "the sanctifying work of the Spirit" and "sprinkling of the blood of Jesus Christ" (KJV). Foreknowledge is the source or, at least, the pattern of election; sanctification is the sphere within which it comes to effect or the means by which it is operative; and sprinkling of the blood of Christ is the end to which it is directed. One cannot think, therefore, of foreknowledge in less efficient terms than sanctification of the Spirit and sprinkling of Christ's blood. There is in this case what has been apparent in other contexts, namely, the active force that foresight does not possess. It is this quality that imparts to the foreknowledge of God the Father the efficiency in reference to election which the construction would lead one to expect. Foreknowledge is itself causally operative and determining.

(3) Since the predetermining character of "foreknow" and "foreknowledge" is necessary in the other instances, one should expect the same meaning in 1 Pet. 1:2, and, unless compelling reasons for exception should exist, the analogy of usage would throw its weight in favor of the same interpretation.

The upshot then is that "foreknow" and "foreknowledge," when applied to God in Scripture, designate much more than what belongs to the attribute of omniscience. In each instance these terms refer to God's determining will, and though each passage views this will from the aspect appropriate to its own context, yet the terms take on the strength of "foreordain" and "foreordination" and in some cases express the same thought. It is also significant that they are used only in reference to what falls within the sphere of salvation. In terms of Scripture usage, foreknowledge does not designate God's all-inclusive determining will, but his will as it concerns the provisions and objects of saving purpose. See also ELECTION; FOREORDAIN; SOVEREIGNTY OF GOD.   J. MURRAY

foreordain. The Greek verb *proorizō G4633*, "to determine beforehand," is applied in Scripture to both persons and events. As applied to persons it means to appoint to a fixed destiny; as applied to events, to make certain their occurrence. In every instance in the NT, God is the subject. In four cases (Rom. 8:29, 30; Eph. 1:4, 11) the predestination of the elect to the glory of ADOPTION and of conformity to the image of God's Son is in view, in the two other cases (Acts 4:28; 1 Cor. 2:7), the predetermination of what has come to pass. To foreordain and to predestinate are synonymous, but the former is more appropriate for events, the latter for persons. See ELECTION; FOREKNOW.

Although *proorizō* occurs infrequently, that to which it refers is pervasive in both Testaments. In the OT the thought is expressed in terms of God's undefeatable purpose (Job 23:13–14; Ps. 33:11; Prov. 16:33; Isa. 14:24–27; 37:26). In the NT other terms indicate the extent to which it is permeated with the conception of God's foreordaining, sovereign, and all-controlling will: *boulē G1087* (Acts 2:23; 4:28; Eph. 1:11), *thelēma G2525* (Acts 21:14; Rom. 1:10; 15:32; Gal. 1:4; Eph. 1:5), *eudokia G2306* (Matt. 11:26; Eph. 1:5, 9), *eudokeō G2305* (Gal. 1:15), *prothesis G4606* (Rom. 8:28; 9:11; Eph. 1:11; 2 Tim. 1:9). Two passages, Acts 2:23 and 4:28, are particularly instructive. They show conclusively that the sinful acts of human beings are embraced in the determinate counsel of God and occur in accord with what his counsel foreordained to come to pass. Yet this effective foreordination in no way curtails or interferes with the responsibility and guilt of the perpetrators of iniquity. It is in the indictment of the people of Israel with the crime of the crucifixion that the reference to God's COUNSEL and foreknowledge occurs. Both agencies are present, but the differentiation in respect of PURPOSE must be maintained. See SOVEREIGNTY OF GOD.

J. MURRAY

forerunner. This English term occurs once in the KJV and other versions as the rendering of Greek *prodromos G4596* (Heb. 6:20; NIV, "who went before us"). Although used primarily of military forces that "rush ahead," or of special guides of the army who "attack suddenly," the Greek word is used also in a metaphorical sense for any precursor. The author of HEBREWS uses it of Jesus as having entered the Holy of Holies (cf. Exod. 26:33–35; 40:20–21) ahead of us and on our behalf. This meant that the ancient order of priests which started with MELCHIZEDEK (Gen. 14:17–20) now came to its fulfillment and completion in the last priest, the messianic priest-sacrifice. Christ is therefore the precursor of all believers, who may now enter into the presence of Yahweh himself (Rom. 8:15; Gal. 4:6). W. WHITE, JR.

foresail. The principal sail hung to the front mast of a vessel (Gk. *artemōna G784*, Acts 27:40). See SHIPS.

foreship. The KJV rendering of Greek *prōra G4749*, which refers to the front section of a SHIP (Acts 27:30; NIV, "bow").

foreskin. The prepuce, a fold of skin that covers the glans of the penis (Heb. *ʿorlâ H6889*, Exod. 4:25 et al.; Gk. *akrobystia G213*, Acts 11:3 et al.). The rite of CIRCUMCISION, which was to take place on the eighth day after birth, consisted in cutting the foreskin, an act that symbolized the COVENANT God made with ABRAHAM and his descendants (Gen. 17:11–14). Its spiritual significance is made explicit by MOSES: "Circumcise, then, the foreskin of your heart, and do not be stubborn any longer" (Deut. 10:16 NRSV; cf. Jer. 4:4; 9:25; Rom. 2:25–29; Col. 2:13). In the NT, the Greek term is used mainly in a figurative sense, meaning either "[the state of] uncircumcision" (e.g., Gal. 5:6) or "uncircumcised people" (e.g., Eph. 2:11; this usage may have originated among Greek-speaking Jews as a slur against GENTILES).

forest. This English term is used primarily to render Hebrew *yaʿar H3623* (Deut. 19:5 et al.). Several forests are named, such as the forest of ARABIA (Isa. 21:13, prob. a very general designation), the forest of Ephraim (2 Sam. 18:6; see EPHRAIM, FOREST OF), and the forest of HERETH in Judah (1 Sam. 22:5). Special importance attaches to the forest of LEBANON, by far the biggest one in the Syro-Palestinian region. It was near TYRE and ran almost parallel to the seacoast, NE through SYRIA. Some 100,000 lumberjacks worked solidly for fifty-five years in these forests to provide sufficient cedar for SOLOMON's temple, palaces, and treasure house. Millions of feet of lumber floated down from Tyre to JOPPA, and from there were transported to Jerusalem. This forest not only grew cedars, but firs and almug trees as well. The House (or Palace) of the Forest of Lebanon (1 Ki. 7:2 et al.) refers to an armory or treasure house King Solomon built in or near Jerusalem. This was an imposing building that was so named because it included three rows of fifteen cedar pillars, which must have resembled a forest (see PALACE).

There is evidence that in ancient times great forests covered Syria and Palestine, but by the time the Israelites occupied the land, much of the forest land had been ruined by human greed. It is, for instance, believed that there was a date palm forest in the Jordan Valley from Lake GENNESARET to the

The forested area on the lower flanks of Mount Gilboa.

Dead Sea. Even in the days of JOSEPHUS (c. A.D. 37–95), there was a forest of date palms near Jericho, 7 mi. long. There must have been kermes oak forests, even if small, in the mountainous regions of Palestine. It is on this oak (*Quercus coccifera*) that the scale insect lives which produces the SCARLET dye used by the Israelites.

Various statements, such as "every animal of the forest is mine" (Ps. 50:10) and "wickedness ... sets the forest thickets ablaze" (Isa. 9:18), seem to refer to forests as a whole, and not to any particular one. God warned the Israelites, "When you lay siege to a city for a long time, fighting against it to capture it, do not destroy its trees by putting an ax to them, because you can eat their fruit. Do not cut them down. Are the trees of the field people, that you should besiege them?" (Deut. 20:19). The cutting down of forests invariably leads to soil erosion and often to a desert. Such unprotected soil dries out, and is blown or washed away. The sole reference to a forest in the NT is in a figurative passage concerning the corrupting power of speech (Jas. 3:5, Gk. *hylē G5627*). W. E. SHEWELL-COOPER

foretell. This verb is used rarely in English Bible versions (e.g., Mk. 13:23 KJV). See PROPHETS.

forfeit. To surrender, or be deprived of, the right to something. This English verb is used a few times in Bible versions, for example, "he who angers him [the king] forfeits his life" (Prov. 20:2, rendering Heb. *ḥāṭāʾ H3148*, "to sin, incur guilt"; cf. Hab. 2:10). Especially well known is Jesus' saying, "What good will it be for a man if he gains the whole world, yet forfeits his soul?" (Gk. *zēmioō G2423*, "to suffer loss," Matt. 16:26 = Mk. 8:36 = Lk. 9:25).

forge. The KJV uses this term twice to render Hebrew *ṭāpal H3260*, which really means "to smear," figuratively, "to besmear" (Job 13:4; Ps. 119:69). No Hebrew or Greek term in the Bible has the precise meaning "to forge," though occasionally modern versions use this English verb in appropriate contexts (e.g., the NIV at Gen. 4:22; Isa. 44:12). Allusions to the forging of METALS are found in various passages, as when JEREMIAH compares the Judeans to "bronze and iron" having impurities and needing the refining process of God (Jer. 6:27–30; cf. also Isa. 48:10; Ezek. 22:18–22). Likewise in the apocryphal book of ECCLESIASTICUS a number of references are noticed concerning the forging of metals (Sir. 31:26; 38:28). G. GIACUMAKIS, JR.

forget. See REMEMBER.

forgiveness. The act of pardoning or setting aside punishment and resentment for an offense. A variety of words are used to express this concept, such as Hebrew *nāśāʾ H5951*, "to lift" (Gen. 50:17 et al.), and *sālaḥ H6142*, "to forgive" (Exod. 34:9 et al.), Greek *aphiēmi G918*, "to send away, set free" (Matt. 6:12 et al.), and *charizomai G5919* (2 Cor. 2:7 et al.). (See *NIDOTTE*, 3:160–63; 259–64; *NIDNTT*, 1:697–703.)

I. Human and divine forgiveness. In the Bible there are instances of both human and divine forgiveness. This does not mean, however, that there is a basic difference between them. God is self-existent and eternal, while man is dependent and temporal, but both are personal beings and as such are similar in their attitudes and actions. Therefore Jesus could teach his disciples to pray, "Forgive us our debts, as we also have forgiven our debtors" (Matt. 6:12), and could conclude the parable of the unmerciful servant with the statement, "So my heavenly Father will also do" (Matt. 18:35 NRSV).

II. God's greater readiness to forgive. Though according to the Bible there is a close parallel between human and divine forgiveness, God is acknowledged as far more forgiving than man. The clearest OT statement to this effect is that of Isa. 55:8–9: "'For my thoughts are not your thoughts, / neither are your ways my ways,' / declares the LORD. / 'As the heavens are higher than the earth, / so are my ways higher than your ways / and my thoughts than your thoughts.'" These words are often taken to point to God's otherness, to his remoteness and inscrutability; but read in their proper context, they point to something far more comforting and thrilling. Immediately preceding them is one of the most striking assurances of God's pardon in all the Bible, and as an explanation of its truth the passage states that his thoughts and ways are higher than ours. They evidently are that because they are truer, nobler, better, wiser, and morally and spiritually more exalted. When injured or wronged, human beings tend to bear a grudge and seek revenge; they are apt to insist on their rights and demand restitution. Not so God: he will show mercy and abundantly pardon.

This greater readiness of God to forgive is exemplified by Jesus. When PETER asked him, "Lord, how many times shall I forgive my brother when he sins against me? Up to seven times?" Jesus responded, "I tell you, not seven times, but seventy-seven times" (Matt. 18:21–22). It is also clearly evidenced by the wonderful truth declared in Jn. 3:16 and confirmed by the cross. In the light of this truth, all human readiness to forgive fades into relative insignificance.

III. Distinctiveness of the biblical teaching of God's forgiveness.

It is noteworthy that divine forgiveness is distinctively a biblical concept. Zoroaster of PERSIA had a high ethical concept of God but knew little of his redeeming love and mercy (see ZOROASTRIANISM). According to him there was no hope for the wicked, who in crossing "The Bridge of the Separator" fell off it into hell (see J. H. Moulton, *Early Religious Poetry of Persia* [1911], 71). Hinduism believes in the inexorable law of Karma, according to which a person's deeds, both good and bad, work themselves out in one life after another. The only escape from the wheel of reincarnations is found in becoming wholly apathetic or in attaining insight into some allegedly releasing truth. Buddhism, too, has its law of Karma and knows of no such divine forgiveness as that set forth in the Bible. The idea is present in Islam, but not as prominent as in Judaism and Christianity. It is in the Bible that it comes to its own; and subsequently it has remained an important feature of the Hebrew-Christian tradition, one that for its adherents lifts this tradition above all other religions and marks it as definitely superior.

IV. Instances of forgiveness in the Bible

A. Human. In the OT ESAU forgives JACOB (Gen. 33:1–17); JOSEPH, his brothers (45:1–15; 50:15–21); MOSES, the people of Israel (Exod. 32:11–14, 30–33) and his sister (Num. 12:11–13); DAVID, ABSALOM and SHIMEI (2 Sam. 14:21, 33; 19:18–23); SOLOMON, ADONIJAH (1 Ki. 1:52f.). In the NT Jesus and Peter speak of forgiving others (Matt. 6:12–15; 18:21–35; Mk. 11:25; Lk. 17:3–4). PAUL forgives—and also enjoins the church at CORINTH to forgive—a member who has caused pain to the others (2 Cor. 2:5–11). In COLOSSIANS, among the attributes of the new nature that believers are to put on, forgiveness is highlighted: "Bear with each other and forgive whatever grievances you may have against one another. Forgive as the Lord forgave you" (Col. 3:13; cf. Eph. 4:32).

In some of these instances no specific term signifying forgiveness is used, but the attitude and deed are there, though not in every case to an equal degree nor always for the same reason. Esau's forgiveness of Jacob seems quite genuine and wholehearted, prompted by Jacob's evident recognition of guilt and his humility and goodwill. Joseph's forgiveness is likewise genuine. But Solomon's forgiveness of Adonijah is definitely conditional—likely for political reasons—and when in Solomon's opinion he oversteps the bounds laid down, he is executed (1 Ki. 2:22–25). Jesus characteristically expects a believer's forgiveness to be from the heart and counsels Peter never to stop forgiving his brother.

B. Divine. As in the case of human forgiveness, divine forgiveness in the Bible is often implied

View over the excavated storage rooms in the Fayum (looking NW). At the time of the patriarchs, the Egyptian administrative center was located here, where mud-brick pyramids were in use. Joseph's act of forgiving his brothers may have occurred at Fayum.

rather than explicitly stated. In the story of the FALL, judgment is pronounced upon ADAM and EVE and they are expelled from the Garden of Eden; but ABEL presently appears as one accepted by God. ENOCH some generations later walks with God. NOAH is singled out as a righteous man, and after the flood, ABRAHAM becomes the friend of God and a COVENANT is established with him.

In instances where it is explicitly mentioned, divine forgiveness is variously motivated and conditioned. There are a number of factors that are said, or assumed, to affect God's attitude. One is human weakness (Pss. 78:38–39; 103:12–14; Amos 7:2–3); another, ignorance (Lk. 23:34; Acts 17:30); a third, circumstances beyond one's control (Num. 30:5, 8, 12); a fourth, the presence of those who do justice and seek truth in sinful communities (Jer. 5:1, 7); a fifth, sufficient chastening (Isa. 40:2); and a sixth, God's reputation. In Num. 14:20 God's pardon is granted after Moses' manifest zeal for the glory of his name and God's apparent interest in it. It is true that in this case the pardon seems incomplete: those receiving it will not see the Promised Land (14:21–25). But the purpose achieved by it points to an important feature of divine forgiveness. A similar purpose is found elsewhere: "For the sake of your name, O LORD, / forgive my iniquity, though it is great" (Ps. 25:11); "O Lord, listen! O Lord, forgive! O Lord, hear and act! For your sake, O my God, do not delay, because your city and your people bear your Name" (Dan. 9:19). The persons uttering these prayers clearly expect God to find the highest reason for his forgiveness within himself. They assume that it is both his nature and his glory to forgive.

This truth is in accord with a further characterization of God's motive in forgiving. "We do not make requests of you because we are righteous, but because of your great mercy," says DANIEL just before the prayer quoted above. Here the prophet indicates an important reason for God's forgiveness. The Lord is merciful, compassionate (Ps. 78:38), and abounding in steadfast love (86:5). Justice would warrant his rejecting, disowning, and punishing the sinner; love prompts him to forgive (Exod. 34:7; Num. 14:18; Neh. 9:16–17; Pss. 86:5; 103:11–12; Mic. 7:18–20; Jn. 3:16).

V. Who is forgiven and what. From the preceding it is obvious that it is the sinner in every instance who is forgiven, whether by God or by others. In no case does a human being forgive God. The presupposition throughout is that God is holy and righteous and never in need of forgiveness, while all people are sinful and in need of it. Were God in need of forgiveness he would be subject to a principle higher and more perfect than himself, which is inconceivable, for then he would not be truly God. But humans, not animals or unconscious objects, are in need here. Forgiveness in any meaningful sense of the word presupposes guilt, and guilt presupposes understanding, moral consciousness, and responsibility. As agents endowed with these qualities, human beings are repeatedly guilty of injury and wrong done to others and of offense given to God. Consequently bad attitudes, evil intentions, and perverse deeds on their part call for forgiveness. Admittedly, these attitudes, intentions, and deeds may largely be what they are because of what a person is due to intelligence, disposition, experience, and training, as the latter in turn may be influenced by heredity and environment. Yet insofar as they are not forced upon us but willingly accepted, insofar as we approve them and knowingly identify ourselves with them, we are responsible for them. To this extent, we are not helpless victims but guilty agents. It is on this supposition that the Bible judges people according to their endowments, opportunities, and knowledge (Matt. 11:20–24; 25:14–30).

The analysis of the human situation and of the need for forgiveness is not yet complete. Underlying and informing our various evil attitudes, intentions, and deeds is apt to be a deeper factor that requires attention. Moses commanded, "Love the LORD your God with all your heart and with all your soul and with all your strength" (Deut. 6:5); there is a second commandment: "love your neighbor as yourself" (Lev. 19:18). "All the Law and the Prophets," Jesus said, "hang on these two commandments" (Matt. 22:40). The very essence of SIN in all its forms and the real determinant of the wrong one does to a neighbor would seem to be, primarily, the violation of the former and, secondarily, the violation of the latter.

In pride, we cherish ourselves, and our ability and worth, supremely rather than God; in greed, material wealth; in sensuality, bodily desires. In all of them we subordinate our neighbors. As a result, their rights and opportunities are trampled on and curtailed. "My people have committed two sins: / They have forsaken me, / the spring of living water, / and have dug their own cisterns, / broken cisterns that cannot hold water" (Jer. 2:13). This was true not only of ancient Israel, but also is true today, and it is what must be forgiven. Basically sin and human wrong are a matter of living by a wrong scale of values. This scale must be changed to achieve a harmonious, meaningful life; living by it we must be forgiven, if we are to be reconciled with God and our neighbors (see V. Taylor, *Forgiveness and Reconciliation: A Study in New Testament Theology* [1952], 3).

It has been said that nature does not forgive. Physical, mental, and social consequences of human deeds work themselves out according to dependable processes. We should observe, however, that even the consequences of evil deeds may in God's providence serve higher ends for those who know they have been forgiven. God ordained and ordered nature, and by anticipation, he has correlated its events with the exigencies of various human situations. Not only this: the influence of God's Spirit in human lives can also counteract the effects of sin in them. Furthermore, a changed and forgiven person can in dependence on the same processes mentioned above initiate a new and better series of consequences. Nature in a sense may not forgive, but it will respond to new endeavor.

Jesus speaks of BLASPHEMY against the Spirit as a sin that will not be forgiven (Matt. 12:31–32; Mk. 3:28–30; Lk. 12:10). Calvin holds that they alone are guilty of this sin "who, with evil intention, resist God's truth, although by its brightness they are so touched that they cannot claim ignorance" (*Institutes of the Christian Religion* 3.3.22, Battles trans. 1:617). One might ask, Resist God's truth to what extent? With what degree of evil intention and knowledge? The nature of this sin cannot perhaps be precisely stated in one short sentence. Certainly Calvin's characterization of it is not perfect, let alone complete. It would seem that the UNPARDONABLE SIN presupposes such spiritual perversity and blindness that neither the truth of God appeals nor does its true light appear. It may also presuppose such indifference as cares not for forgiveness or such hostility as flippantly derides what is holy. At all events, this sin apparently implies a situation in which true repentance never eventuates. He who truly desires forgiveness and would sincerely repent, need not fear that he has committed it. See HOLY SPIRIT III.B.

VI. Conditions of forgiveness

A. Human. The foregoing notes that there were different reasons why people in the Bible forgave others. A question is, Are there any conditions according to the Bible that offending persons must meet if they are to expect forgiveness? Some passages do not speak of any. When Peter asked how many times he should forgive his brother, Jesus responded without reference to any condition the offender must meet (Matt. 18:21–22). The parable that follows Jesus' answer to Peter clearly implies that forgiveness is being sought; and in a comparable passage (Lk. 17:3–4) REPENTANCE is specified as a condition. Moreover, though repentance on the part of the offender is not always mentioned, in some of the instances cited above it was evidently present. It may be concluded that a person must forgive if the offender repents; we should certainly repent when we are the offenders, and should in any case be ready to forgive. Should we ever forgive the impenitent offender who knowingly has done wrong? Doubtless we should as far as personal offense or injury are concerned, though not as far as violation of moral principle goes. It was obviously an absence of personal offense and his compassion for his spiritually blind persecutors that made STEPHEN pray the notable prayer he did (Acts 7:60).

B. Divine. As in the case of human forgiveness, so in the case of God's forgiveness, some passages of Scripture do not expressly mention repentance as a ground or condition (Pss. 65:3; 85:2; 86:5; 103:3, 10; Isa. 46:12–13; Jer. 31:31–34; 33:1–18; Ezek. 36:16–38; Mic. 7:18–20; Acts 13:38–39; Eph. 1:7; Col. 1:14; 2:13; 1 Jn. 2:2). In other passages repentance is clearly called for (Lev. 26:14–45; 1 Ki. 8:46–50; 2 Chr. 7:14; 30:18–19; Pss. 32:3–5; 51; Isa. 1:27–28; 55:6–7; chs. 59–61, esp. 59:20; Jer. 18:7–11; 26:3; Lam. 3:42; Ezek. 18:31–32; Zech. 1:3; Mal. 3:7; Matt. 4:17; Lk. 13:3, 5; Acts

5:31; 8:22; 1 Jn. 1:9). Omission of repentance in the first instances may be explained by the fact that in these it was either understood, or God was not so much forgiving sin as achieving other ends (Ezek. 36:20–23, 32, 35–36, 38). He also may have been moving his people to repentance by his action (36:31).

On this question of the condition, or conditions, required for forgiveness, recent and contemporary theologians differ. Karl Barth represented an extreme position. He held that all of life apart from God's own action in it falls under the judgment that it is sin. Christians live solely by God's forgiveness. Even repentance has been made for them (*Dogmatics in Outline* [1959], 149–52). Paul Tillich spoke of the unconditional character of the divine act in which God declares him who is unjust just. Transcending justice destroys in a person what must be destroyed, if reuniting love is to reach its aim. This which must be destroyed is the hubris of trying to conquer the evil in one's being as such, and to reach reunion with God by one's own good will. Such hubris, said Tillich, avoids the pain of surrendering one's own goodness to God's sole activity in a reunion with him, a surrender that occurs in the person who accepts the divine acceptance of himself, the unacceptable. The courage of this surrender is the central element in the courage of faith (*Systematic Theology* [1963], 3:226).

Emil Brunner emphasizes the need of repentance as a condition of forgiveness (*The Divine-Human Encounter* [1943], 98ff., 149ff.), a view shared by Rudolf Bultmann, Frederick C. Grant, H. R. Mackintosh, Ernest F. Scott, Vincent Taylor, and Benjamin B. Warfield, as well as the *Westminster Confession of Faith* (ch. 15). Nor does Brunner stop here. Instead he goes on to take exception to a one-sided advocacy of the doctrine of forensic JUSTIFICATION. He says, "God not only *declares*, he *creates* a new man.... We not only believe in the new man, but in faith we put him on" (p. 101). Repentance for him entails condemning the old man within and putting him off; it means accepting the death of Jesus Christ as a divine judgment upon oneself (pp. 101, 151).

Herman Bavinck of the Netherlands, like Brunner, underscored the requirement laid down in the Bible for God's forgiveness. Specifically, he held that regeneration, faith, and conversion are conditions for the forgiveness of sins and other benefits of the covenant of grace (*Gereformeerde Dogmatiek* [1930], 4:160). One's entry into the kingdom of heaven depends on them (p. 202). But, unlike Brunner, he adhered to a rather strict theory of forensic justification. The forgiveness of sins is not brought about by faith nor gained by man's endeavors. It is found completely in Christ, precedes faith, and is accepted only by faith (pp. 201–2). All works are excluded from the faith that is reckoned as righteousness (p. 168). G. C. Berkouwer, of the Free University of Amsterdam, seems in substantial agreement with him, except that he significantly distinguishes between works of the law and works of faith in the writings of Paul (*Faith and Justification* [1954], 104ff.). For him, however, these works of faith give form to faith; they show its nature, rather than themselves constituting part of the basis of God's acceptance of man.

From the foregoing, the diversity of thought on this question is evident. Yet it is clear that repentance as a condition of forgiveness of sin has been, and is, widely recognized, and that it is well supported scripturally. It is also clear in the Bible that with the advent of Jesus Christ repentance as a condition is definitely associated with his suffering and death. To his disciples on the day of his resurrection Jesus said, "This is what is written: The Christ will suffer and rise from the dead on the third day, and repentance and forgiveness of sins will be preached in his name to all nations" (Lk. 24:46–47). "The blood of Jesus ... purifies us from all sin" (1 Jn. 1:7). "He himself [Christ] bore our sins in his body on the tree" (1 Pet. 2:24; cf. Acts 2:38; 13:38–39; 26:18; Rom. 5:8–11; 1 Pet. 1:18–19; 3:18; 1 Jn. 2:1, 12; 3:5).

How are such passages to be understood? In the light of them, Brunner is doubtless right when he sees the death of Jesus Christ as a divine judgment upon oneself; and one may add a judgment which the truly penitent person, when confronted with it, will accept as his due and thus be assured of God's forgiveness. The sinner can by faith take the cross of Christ into his life, he can identify himself with Christ on the cross, and so be crucified with him (Gal. 2:20). He can die to sin that he may live to righteousness (1 Pet. 2:24), the righteousness that

Christ has shown but that the sinner admittedly has failed to achieve and will never achieve fully. In this way he rejects his sinful self and returns to the Shepherd and Guardian of his soul (2:25); he is healed by Christ's wounds and brought to God (2:24; 3:18).

A further condition of God's forgiveness is found in another teaching of Jesus which he stated explicitly on at least three occasions. The first statement occurs in the SERMON ON THE MOUNT. After formulating the LORD'S PRAYER, Jesus says, "For if you forgive men when they sin against you, your heavenly Father will also forgive you. But if you do not forgive men their sins, your Father will not forgive your sin" (Matt. 6:14–15). Equally clear and unqualified is his comment at the close of the parable of the unmerciful servant, referred to earlier in this article. This servant refused to forgive his fellow servant a debt, though his master had forgiven him a much greater one. His master thereupon revoked his cancellation of the debt and delivered him to the jailers until he should pay in full. Jesus then added, "This is how my heavenly Father will treat each of you unless you forgive your brother from your heart" (Matt. 18:35). The third statement is found in Mk. 11:25: "And when you stand praying, if you hold anything against anyone, forgive him, so that your Father in heaven may forgive you your sins." The import of this teaching of Jesus is plain: there is a direct correlation between our forgiving others and our being forgiven by God. This requirement, however, does not indicate that our salvation is a reward for good works; rather, it focuses on the genuineness of one's repentance. A person who seeks forgiveness but does not forgive others hardly knows what he is asking for and is not worthy of it.

Ethically, too, repentance is required for receiving the forgiveness of God. God is holy and righteous. His "eyes are too pure to look on evil" (Hab. 1:13). Because he is self-existent and the great Creator and Upholder of all, including the highest principles of reality and life, personal offense given him by human beings can hardly be distinguished from moral violation. In view of this, for him to forgive without requiring repentance would be like condoning sin or being indifferent to it. It would also mean that he is not treating human beings as the responsible moral agents he has made them. God accepts the unacceptable, but only as the unacceptable repents, that is, acknowledges God's righteous judgment of him in Christ and commits his life wholly to God. See also GRACE; RECONCILIATION.

(See further A. Ritschl, *The Christian Doctrine of Justification and Reconciliation* [1900], 38–79; D. White, *Forgiveness and Suffering* [1913]; B. B. Warfield, *The Plan of Salvation* [1915]; H. R. Mackintosh, *The Christian Experience of Forgiveness* [1927]; F. H. Wales, *The Forgiveness of Sins* [1940]; P. Lehmann, *Forgiveness, Decisive Issue in Protestant Thought* [1940]; R. Bultmann, *Theology of the New Testament* [1951], 1:22–26, 33–40, 72–74, 85, 114–21, 135–44, 270–85; J. G. Emerson, Jr., *The Dynamics of Forgiveness* [1964]; E. A. Blum, *The Forgiveness of Sins* [1985]; K. Scheiber, *Vergebung: Eine systematisch-theologische Untersuchung* [2006].)

P. H. MONSMA

fork. This term occurs in English Bible versions as the rendering of various words, especially Hebrew *mazlēg* H4657, "[meat] fork," which refers to one of the sacrificial implements used in the tabernacle and the temple. BEZALEL, the chief architect of the TABERNACLE, was also a skillful metal artificer, and among the implements he made for it were bronze forks. DAVID provided gold to make implements, including forks, for the TEMPLE, and HIRAM made some of bronze (Exod. 27:3; 38:3; Num. 4:14; 1 Chr. 28:17; 2 Chr. 4:16; in these passages the MT pointing reflects a different form, *mizlāg*). What appears to be the same device is described as a three-pronged instrument used to remove meat from a boiling pot (1 Sam. 2:13–14). A WINNOWING fork is referred to with Hebrew *mizreh* H4665 (Jer. 15:7) and Greek *ptyon* G4768 (Matt. 3:12; Lk. 3:17), both of which are used figuratively of God's judgment.

form criticism. The analytical study of the "forms" assumed by various categories of tradition, especially in its oral, preliterary phase. The German word *Formgeschichte* ("form history") suggests, as the English term does not, a study of the history of the tradition as revealed by the development of its "forms." While the word *Formgeschichte* in the field of biblical criticism does not appear to have been current before the publication of M. Dibelius's *Die Formgeschichte des Evangeliums* in 1919, the discipline itself was not new. The similar term *Formengeschichte* occurs in the subtitle of E. Norden's *Agnostos Theos* (1912): "Inquiries into the *history of the forms* of religious language." As far as the Gospels are concerned, A. Menzies anticipated some of the most characteristic features of the form-critical approach in *The Earliest Gospel* (1901).

The pioneer of form criticism in biblical study was H. Gunkel, who applied it to biblical literature as early as 1895 in his *Schöpfung und Chaos* (a comparison of Gen. 1 and Rev. 12). Gunkel's most fruitful application of this method (already used to analyze the literature of the heroic ages of Greece and Northern Europe) was to the Psalter, which he classified according to its *Gattungen* ("literary types"), assigning to each *Gattung* its life-setting — a life-setting almost invariably to be found in Israel's worship (*Die Psalmen*, 4th ed. [1926], and *Einleitung in die Psalmen* [1933], completed by J. Begrich). It is perhaps no accident that M. Dibelius had his interest in comparative religious study first aroused by Gunkel. (Cf. also G. M. Tucker, *Form Criticism of the Old Testament* [1971]; J. Barton, *Reading the Old Testament: Method in Biblical Study* [1984], ch. 3.)

I. Classification. The main classification of gospel material naturally recognizes the distinction between narratives and sayings. The terminology of classification differs from one form critic to another, but outstanding categories of narrative in the Gospels are (a) pronouncement stories (paradigms, apophthegms), (b) miracle stories (in which healing narratives are prominent), (c) stories about Jesus (e.g., the baptism, temptation, and transfiguration narratives). Notable categories of sayings are (a) wisdom sayings, (b) prophetic and apocalyptic sayings, (c) community rules, (d) "I" sayings, (e) parables. There are other ways of classifying the gospel material, and whichever way is adopted, a fair amount of overlapping is inevitable.

One important result of classification and cross-classification of the material is that a messianic picture of Jesus is consistently yielded: "We can find no alternative tradition, excavate as we will in the successive strata of the Gospels" (C. H. Dodd, *History and the Gospel* [1938], 103). Especially on the European continent, form critics warn scholars not to conclude that this picture goes back into the conditions of the actual ministry of Jesus; many of them hold that this study can take one back only to the Christ of the primitive early church preaching. Classification in itself, however, is not of prime importance; more important are two things closely connected with it in the history of form criticism: the theory of the composition of the synoptic tradition (propounded by K. L. Schmidt and adopted by many colleagues and successors) and the quest for the life-setting.

II. Composition. K. L. Schmidt's thesis in *Der Rahmen der Geschichte Jesu* (1919) was that the synoptic tradition consisted originally of isolated units, brought together by Mark in such a way as to form a consecutive narrative with the aid of "editorial cement" that lacked historical value of its own. The passion narrative, admittedly, did exist as a connected record from earliest days, partly because of its being repeatedly recalled in the cult (cf. 1 Cor. 11:26), but otherwise material simply did not exist to make a coherent life of Christ, or even a continuous account of his ministry, possible. C. H. Dodd ("The Framework of the Gospel Narrative," *ExpTim* 43 [1931–32]: 396–400) argued that the "editorial cement" in Mark, when considered in isolation from the units of tradition it joined together, presented an independent outline of the gospel story, comparable to outlines that can be discerned in some of the epistles and the speeches of Acts (e.g., Acts 10:37–42). Dodd's argument has not found much acceptance outside Britain, but it cannot be easily refuted.

III. Life-setting. In form-critical terms, the life-setting usually means the setting in the life of the primitive Christian community that determined the preservation of certain elements in the tradition about Jesus and the form in which they were preserved. An interest in this life-setting should not preclude an interest in the earlier setting in the ministry of Jesus. Although the possibility of establishing this earlier life-setting except in a handful of instances is widely denied, it should not be given up too quickly. W. Manson, for example, gave cogent reasons for believing that the setting given in Mk. 11:20–24 to Jesus' saying about mountain-removing faith corresponds to the original historical and geographical setting (*Jesus the Messiah* [1943], 29–30).

But in its more extreme formulations the doctrine of the life-setting rules that if a saying or action ascribed to Jesus in the Gospels reflects the post-Easter faith of the church, it should be regarded as a creation within the church, and that no saying or action ascribed to him can confidently be taken as authentic if a parallel saying or action is elsewhere ascribed to a Jewish rabbi. It is unlikely that the church never took over some of Jesus' historical teaching and it is equally unlikely that Jesus never said or did anything comparable to the word or action of some rabbi; nor need one take too seriously the insistent view that in such cases the burden of proof lies on those who maintain the authenticity of the gospel tradition.

Yet the life-setting approach helps one to appreciate the circumstances of the church's worship and witness within which the gospel tradition (Johannine as well as synoptic) was molded and transmitted, and in so far as form criticism makes it possible to move back from the setting in the early church to the setting in the ministry of Jesus (e.g., by removing, as it sometimes does, a later Hellenistic layer that has overlain an earlier Palestinian layer), it makes its own special contribution to the understanding of the Gospels and appraisal of the works and words of Jesus. See BIBLICAL CRITICISM IV.

(Important studies include V. Taylor, *The Formation of the Gospel Tradition* [1933]; R. H. Lightfoot, *History and Interpretation in the Gospels* [1935]; R. Bultmann, *The History of the Synoptic Tradition* [1963]; C. K. Barrett, *Jesus and the Gospel Tradition* [1967]; K. Koch, *The Growth of the Biblical Tradition: The Form-Critical Method* [1967]; N. Perrin, *Rediscovering the Teaching of Jesus* [1967]; D. E. Aune, *The New Testament in Its Literary Environment* [1987]; E. V. McKnight in *The New Testament and Its Modern Interpreters*, ed. E. J. Epp and G. W. MacRae [1989].) F. F. BRUCE

former rain. See RAIN.

fornication. This English term, which generally refers to sexual intercourse between persons not married to each other, is used by the KJV and other versions a few times in the OT (e.g., "commit fornication" for the Heb. verb *zānâ H2388* in Ezek. 16:26), but primarily in the NT to render the Greek noun *porneia G4518* (usually translated "sexual immorality" in the NIV). Out of seven lists of evils in the writings of PAUL, this Greek word is included in five of them (1 Cor. 5:11; 6:9; Gal. 5:19; Eph. 5:3; Col. 3:5) and is first on the list each time. Because the term can be applied to various situations, its meaning must be determined by the context of each passage.

(1) In 1 Cor. 7:2, Paul appears to warn *unmarried* people about the temptation to commit sexual immorality. It is possible that in 1 Thess. 4:3 as well *porneia* refers to voluntary sexual intercourse of an unmarried person with anyone of the opposite sex. In four other passages fornication is used in a list of sins that includes ADULTERY (*moicheia G3657*, Matt. 15:19; Mk. 7:21; 1 Cor. 6:9; Gal. 5:19). Since adultery involves a married person, the meaning of *porneia* in these passages too may well be restricted, involving voluntary unchastity of unmarried people, although some scholars take it in a general sense, that is, sexual immorality without specific reference to marital status, as in (3) below.

(2) In two passages (Matt. 5:32; 19:9), the term is apparently used as a synonym of adultery, though some scholars think that even here it refers to premarital unchastity (possibly during the period of betrothal), and others believe it has to do with the incestuous relationships prohibited in Lev. 18 (perhaps also in Acts 15:20, 29; 21:25; for a discussion of the Matthean "exception clause," see D. A. Carson in *EBC*, 8:413–18).

(3) The word can be used in a very general sense referring to all forms of unchastity (Jn. 8:41; Rom. 1:29; 1 Cor. 5:1; 6:13, 18; 2 Cor. 6:17; 12:21; Eph. 5:3).

(4) Finally, *porneia* can refer to harlotry and PROSTITUTION (e.g., Rev. 2:14, 20–21), especially in a figurative sense (14:8 et al.). (Further discussion in D. R. Mace, *Hebrew Marriage* [1953], 221–67; W. G. Cole, *Sex and Love in the Bible* [1959], 230–67; H. J. Miles, *Sexual Understanding before Marriage* [1971], 204–6.) See also DIVORCE; MARRIAGE; SEX. H. J. MILES

fort, fortification. These and similar terms are used to render a variety of Hebrew words, especially *mibṣār H4448* (Num. 13:19 et al.). Every town and city in the ANE was normally encircled by ramparts and defended by TOWERS and fortified GATES. Reports describing the large fortified cities of the Canaanites struck fear into the Israelites; and after their conquest of these towns, they rebuilt the broken defenses and improved them where they could. The walls of a city were usually of large dimensions, anywhere from 15 to 25 ft. thick; and often there were two or even three of them. Some of them were well over 25 ft. in height. They were made of rough or cut stone, with the upper courses made of brick, or even wood. Walls were rendered less assailable by having a trench, or fosse, dug around them.

TOWERS or bastions were built at the corners and other places on the wall where attack was to be apprehended (Zeph. 1:16; 2 Chr. 14:7). These towers protruded from the walls for some feet so that the defenders of a besieged city could assail the attackers with available weapons. Since gates were an obvious point of weakness, most towns had no more than one or two. The gates were ordinarily of two leaves, and for greater security against fire were often overlaid with bronze (Ps. 107:16; Isa. 45:2). No city could hold out for long without a supply of WATER, so it was of prime importance that a town be built where an abundance of water was available. Sometimes long tunnels were made to a source of water outside the walls. The Bible in a number of places tells of fortifications which the kings of Israel and Judah erected to protect their chief cities. SOLOMON, for example, fortified JERUSALEM, MEGIDDO, HAZOR, and GEZER (1 Ki. 9:15); REHOBOAM fortified fifteen cities in Judah (2 Chr. 11:5–12); and ASA fortified GEBA and MIZPAH (1 Ki. 15:22). (See R. de Vaux, *Ancient Israel* [1961], 229–40.) See also CITY. S. BARABAS

Large gates like this one at Arad protected fortified towns from unauthorized entry.

Fortunatus for´chuh-nay´tuhs (Φορτουνᾶτος *G5847*, from Lat. *fortunatus*, "blessed, fortunate"; both the Lat. and Gk. forms occur in papyri and inscriptions). A prominent member of the Corinthian church, mentioned only in 1 Cor. 16:17 (some MSS also insert it in v. 15). He is named second in a three-man delegation that brought a letter from the church to PAUL at EPHESUS (cf. 7:1 and see CORINTHIANS, FIRST). Their presence "refreshed" Paul, giving him the desired contact with that church. They apparently returned with the letter that we call 1 Corinthians (cf. the subscription in many MSS). Some forty years later, Clement of Rome mentions a Fortunatus who was part of the Roman delegation to Corinth (*1 Clem.* 65.1). The commonness of the name and the time lapse make identification unlikely. D. E. HIEBERT

fortune. See DESTINY.

fortune-telling. See DIVINATION.

forty. A frequently mentioned NUMBER in the Bible, often having symbolical significance. It was used as the approximate time span of a generation and to designate an extended period of testing, repentance, vigil, or punishment. It is associated with important new developments in the unfolding drama of redemption (such as the flood, the exodus, Elijah and the prophetic era, the life of Christ, and the birth of the church). For example, at the time of NOAH it rained for forty days, and the waters subsided for an equal period (Gen. 7:4, 12, 17; 8:6). MOSES was forty years old when he visited his brethren (Acts 7:23), was forty years in MIDIAN (7:29–30), was on the mount forty days (Exod. 24:18), and prayed for Israel for forty days (Deut. 9:25). The Israelites wandered forty years in the wilderness (Num. 14:33; 32:13). DAVID and SOLOMON each reigned forty years (2 Sam. 5:4; 1 Ki. 11:42). JONAH called on NINEVEH to repent within forty days (Jon. 3:4). Jesus fasted in the desert forty days (Matt. 4:2) and remained on earth forty days after his resurrection (Acts 1:3).

S. BARABAS

Forum of Appius for´uhm-uhv-ap´ee-uhs (Ἀππίου Φόρον *G716* + *G5842*). The forum was the public square or marketplace of an ancient Roman city, and the Forum of Appius was a traveler's stop on the APPIAN WAY, about 40 mi. S of ROME, where PAUL was met by Roman Christians on his way to the capital under guard (Acts 28:15). It was also the northern terminus of a canal that ran through the Pontine marshes to Feronia, providing public transportation in boats towed by mules (Strabo, *Geogr.* 5.233). Horace (*Sat.* 1.5) vividly described the Forum as an unsavory place crammed with boatmen, innkeepers, and wayfarers, who cheat, carouse, and quarrel, the disturbance compounded by the gnats and frogs of the marshes.

A. RUPPRECHT

foundation. The basis on which something stands or is supported. As many as ten Hebrew words (several of them derived from the verb *yāsad H3569*, "to lay the foundations of") can be used with this meaning. The usual Greek word for "foundation" is *themelios G2529*, but in the common phrase "the foundation of the world" the term used is *katabolē G2856* (e.g., Matt. 13:35; NIV, "the creation of the world"). (See *NIDOTTE*, 2:474–75; *NIDNTT*, 1:660–63.)

The ancients of course understood the necessity of sinking the foundations of a house down to the bedrock (cf. Lk. 6:48–49; see ARCHITECTURE; HOUSE). The foundation of Solomon's TEMPLE consisted of large (12 x 15 ft.), costly, and carefully dressed blocks of stone (1 Ki. 5:17). Babylonian records show that the laying of a foundation was sometimes accompanied by human sacrifice; such sacrifice is probably suggested in 1 Ki. 16:34, where it is said that HIEL laid the foundations of JERICHO "at the cost of his firstborn son Abiram, and he set up its gates at the cost of his youngest son Segub."

In both the OT and the NT the word is used metaphorically. It often refers to God's immovable creation (e.g., Ps. 104:5 [*mākôn H4806*]). It is also used of the ultimate basis on which life rests (Job 4:19 [*yĕsôd H3572*]; Ps. 11:3 [*šēt H9268*]; et al.), particularly the MESSIAH (Isa. 28:16 [*mûsād H4586*], quoted in Rom. 9:33 and 1 Pet. 2:6). Indeed, the CHURCH is built upon the foundation of the apostles and prophets, with Christ as the CORNERSTONE (Eph. 2:20).

S. BARABAS

Foundation Gate. This name occurs only in the account of JOSIAH's coronation (2 Chr. 23:5, *šaʿar hayĕsôd*; LXX has "the middle gate" here and in Jer. 39:3); in the parallel passage it is called SUR (2 Ki. 11:6, *šaʿar sûr*, LXX, "the gate of the ways"). The similarity in Hebrew between יסוד and סור suggests a textual error, but it is not possible to determine the original form of the name. The location of this gate is unknown; it was probably on an inner perimeter, close to the temple and the palace (some have thought it was the same as the HORSE GATE, where ATHALIAH was put to death, 2 Ki. 11:16; 2 Chr. 23:15).

W. H. MARE

fountain. A source of fresh running WATER; a spring. In a country like PALESTINE, which depends largely on RAIN for water, there are usually three sources from which rainwater may be obtained: springs, WELLS, and CISTERNS. All three were used from the earliest recorded times. The most common Hebrew word for fountain or spring is *ʿayin H6524* (lit., "eye"), and it is used in many compounded place names, such as EN GEDI, EN RIMNON, etc. Other terms include *maʿyān H5078* and *māqôr H5227*. In the NT, especially in the book of Revelation, the Greek word *pēgē G4380* is used.

Springs or fountains were essential to life, and the early settlements in Palestine usually clustered around a spring. Fortified cities (see FORT) grew up beside them, and often enclosed the spring in order to insure an ample supply of water in case of siege. In the war with the PHILISTINES, the Israelite army camped by the fountain in JEZREEL, where there was abundant water for their forces (1 Sam. 29:1), and the Samaritan woman encountered Jesus at the well of JACOB near SYCHAR when she went to replenish the supply for her household (Jn. 4:6). The term is often used figuratively. God is described as "the spring of living water" (Jer. 17:13), and the expression "fountain of life" is directly associated with the Lord and with the WISDOM he gives to those who fear him (Ps. 36:9; Prov. 10:11; 13:14; 14:27; 16:22). M. C. TENNEY

Fountain Gate. One of the entrances to JERUSALEM, mentioned after the EXILE (*šaʿar hāʿayin*, Neh. 2:14; 3:15; 12:37). Located in the SE section of the wall restored after the return, it was apparently adjacent to "the steps of the City of David on the ascent to the wall," and near "the house of David" and "the Water Gate on the east" (12:37). It may have been associated with a pool at the end of a canal that carried the overflow from the Pool of SILOAM (see *ABD*, 2:853). A Bronze Age tower recently excavated may have been part of the Fountain Gate (see D. Bahat, *The Illustrated Atlas of Jerusalem* [1990], 20, with reconstruction on p. 22 and map on p. 36).

foursquare. KJV term for "square" (Exod. 27:1 et al.; Rev. 21:16).

fowl. The usage of this English word has changed radically since the time of the KJV, when it was a common term for birds generally. Today it has a few specialized uses, such as referring to the domesticated CHICKEN or to birds used for FOOD or hunted as game. The NIV and other modern translations use it only once to render Hebrew *barbur H1350*, a word of undetermined meaning (only 1 Ki. 4:23). See FAUNA and separate articles on individual birds.

fowler. One who traps and hunts wild birds. In ancient times birds were caught or killed in many different ways—with decoys, traps, nets, snares, lures, bait, slings, bows and arrows, bird lime smeared upon branches, birdcalls, and setting dogs. Birds were a favorite food, especially in EGYPT. The Egyptians were expert at killing, preserving, and preparing for the table all kinds of birds. Even today countless birds migrate N and S across PALESTINE in the spring and fall, preferring to fly over land rather than across the Mediterranean (see BIRD MIGRATION). Birds were used for food, as caged pets, and for sacrifice. In the Mosaic legislation it was forbidden to take the mother bird with the eggs or young, lest the species should become exterminated (Deut. 22:6–7). The Hebrew word for "fowler" (*yāqûš H3687*) is used in the OT in a metaphorical sense to represent evil men who set snares to catch the unwary and bring them to moral and spiritual ruin (Pss. 91:3; 124:7 [ptc. of *yāqaš H3704*]; Prov. 6:5; Jer. 5:26; Hos. 9:8). J. L. KELSO

fox. The Hebrew term for fox (*šûʿāl H8785*) is sometimes rendered JACKAL (cf. NIV and NRSV, Lam. 5:18; Ezek. 13:4). Foxes (*Vulpes nilotica* and *V. flavescens*) and jackals (*Canis aureus*) are alike in size and form, and can easily be confused (*FFB*, 31–32). Three species of fox live in PALESTINE and EGYPT: the red fox, which is found in a number of forms over much of the old world, and two desert species, with large ears, the better known of these being the small fennec fox. Foxes are largely nocturnal, especially in hot dry country, and spend the day safely and comfortably in their holes, or earths, as the Lord pointed out (Gk. *alōpēx G273*, Matt. 8:20 = Lk. 9:58). Their fondness for fruit, especially grapes, is mentioned (Cant. 2:15).

The story of SAMSON in Jdg. 15:4–5 has caused considerable comment. The action was certainly far from humane, as were many things done by him and his enemies, but the effect of releasing 150 pairs of foxes (prob. jackals, which would be more easily caught in numbers) in ripe corn would be devastating. A similar cruel custom is recorded in Roman times when foxes with torches tied to their tails were hunted in the circus at the feast of Ceres. Brer fox has appeared in stories and fables since Greek and Roman times, but in Palestine and Iraq the jackal usually takes its place. In these stories the fox is cunning and crafty, and the Lord used this metaphor in one of his rare critical comments when he referred to Herod Antipas (see HEROD V) as "that fox" (Lk. 13:32). See also HYENA.

G. S. CANSDALE

frame. This English term, as a noun or as a verb, and with various meanings, is used in English versions to render a number of Hebrew and Greek terms. It is especially common in the book of Exodus, where it corresponds to Hebrew *qereš H7983*, "plank, board," used in connection with the wooden framework of the TABERNACLE (Exod. 26:15–29; 36:20–34; et al.). Among other meanings, note its use to render Hebrew *ʿōṣem H6798* (a collective

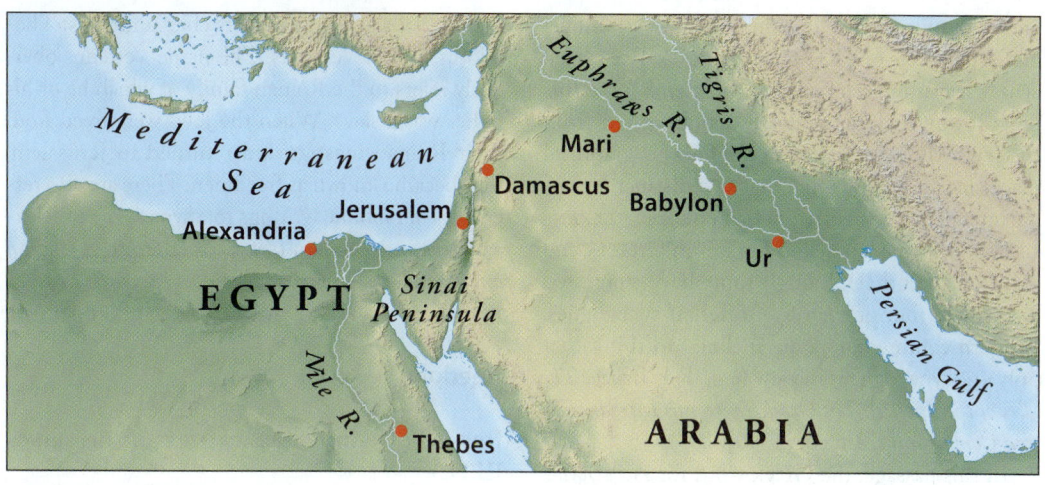

Arabia was the source of frankincense.

noun, "bones") in Ps. 139:15, "My frame was not hidden from you / when I was made in the secret place." In the NT, the KJV uses the verb "frame" as a translation of Greek *synarmologeō G5274*, "join together" (Eph. 2:21), and *katartizō G2936*, "prepare, form" (Heb. 11:3).

frankincense. An aromatic gum resin derived from trees of the genus *Boswellia*. There are various species from which gum may be obtained: *B. carterii* (or *B. sacra* Flückiger*—*this is the Arabian frankincense tree), *B. frereana*, *B. papyrifera*, and *B. thurifera*. The gum is collected during the summer; it is customary to peel the bark back first, and then to make a deep cut with a sharp knife. Boswellia trees are related to turpentine trees (see TEREBINTH); the star-shaped flowers are pure white or green, tipped with rose. The tree has leaves similar to the mountain ash. The Hebrew word for frankincense, *lĕbōnâ H4247* (usually translated INCENSE by NIV), derives from a root meaning "white" (the Gk term, *libanos G3337*, is a borrowing from the Semitic name). When the gum first exudes from the bark, it is of an amber color; later when removed from the tree, the resin produces a white dust on its surface. The gum, when warmed and burned, produces a sweet, pleasant odor.

Frankincense was an important part of the grain offerings (Lev. 2:1–2 et al.). Along with MYRRH and other spices, it was a highly valued perfume (Cant. 3:6; 4:6, 14; in the latter passage, "all trees of frankincense" [NRSV] may indicate several species of Boswellia trees). The Israelites imported frankincense from ARABIA; it was produced near Saba (SHEBA; cf. Isa. 60:6; Jer. 6:20). It was one of the gifts brought to the infant Jesus by the MAGI (Matt. 2:11). It is also mentioned in connection with the fall of apocalyptic Babylon (Rev. 18:13). (See G. Van Beek in *JAOS* 78 [1958]: 141–51, and *BA* 23 [1960]: 69–95; N. St. J. Groom, *Frankincense and Myrrh: A Study of the Arabian Incense Trade* [1981]; *FFB*, 121–22; *ABD*, 2:854.)

W. E. SHEWELL-COOPER

Frankish Versions. See VERSIONS OF THE BIBLE, ANCIENT, V.

freedman. This term, referring to an emancipated SLAVE, is used by the NIV and other versions to render Greek *apeleutheros G592*, which occurs only once in a figurative sense: "For he who was a slave when he was called by the Lord is the Lord's freedman; similarly, he who was a free man [*eleutheros G1801*] when he was called is Christ's slave" (1 Cor. 7:22). (See A. M. Duff, *Freedmen in the Early Roman Empire*, 2nd ed. [1958].) See also FREEDMEN, SYNAGOGUE OF THE; LIBERTY.

Freedmen, Synagogue of the. When STEPHEN began to perform wonders among the people, he was opposed by "members of the Synagogue of the Freedmen (as it was called)—Jews of Cyrene and Alexandria as well as the provinces of Cilicia and Asia" (Acts 6:9; KJV, "Libertines"). The Greek syntax leaves unclear whether the members of this SYNAGOGUE in Jerusalem are distinguished from the Jews who were native to the four geographical places listed. It is possible that two distinct groups are intended (freedmen from CYRENE and ALEXANDRIA on the one hand, and Jews from CILICIA and ASIA on the other), though some have suggested as many as four or even five different synagogues. Modern commentators are inclined to think that only one synagogue is in view (e.g., F. F. Bruce, *The Acts of the Apostles: The Greek Text with Introduction and Commentary*, 3rd ed. [1990], 187).

In this passage, the Greek word for FREEDMAN is not *apeleutheros G592* but the Latin loanword *Libertinos G3339*, and it has been suggested that the individuals involved descended from Jews who had been captured by POMPEY in 63 B.C. and sent to Rome (cf. *HJP*, rev. ed. [1973–87], 2:428 n. 8). Whatever the precise composition of this group, it is evident that it consisted of Hellenistic or DIASPORA Jews like Stephen himself. They apparently opposed him on theological grounds, but unable to withstand the wisdom by which he spoke, they hired false witnesses who accused him of speaking blasphemous words against Moses and God. As a result, a mob gathered and he was arrested and accused before the council.

The Synagogue of the Freedmen has been linked by some to a 1st-cent. inscription that mentions the building of a synagogue by its chief and priest Theodotus, son of Vettenus. The name Vettenus obviously refers to the Roman family of which he or his father was a slave. When the Jews were freed from their Roman masters and returned to Jerusalem, they became known as freedmen. There are also references in rabbinic writings to a synagogue of Alexandrians in Jerusalem (see C. K. Barrett, *A Critical and Exegetical Commentary on the Acts of the Apostles*, ICC, 2 vols. [1994–98], 1:324). J. B. SCOTT

freedom. See LIBERTY.

freewill offering. See SACRIFICE AND OFFERINGS III.D.3.

fret. This English verb, in its common intransitive meaning "to be vexed, troubled," appears rarely in modern versions (the NIV and NRSV, e.g., use it to render the hithpael of *ḥārâ H3013*, which occurs only in Ps. 37:1, 7–8; Prov. 24:19). The word, however, had a broader meaning in the time of the KJV, which uses it to render various Hebrew terms. Note, for example, the expression "a fretting leprosy" (Lev. 13:51–52, rendering *māʾar H4421*, ptc., "hurtful"; NIV, "a destructive mildew"), as well as the meaning "become annoyed, angry" (Isa. 8:21, rendering *qāṣap H7911*).

friend, friendship. Besides references to friendship in various forms, such as HOSPITALITY, the term *friend* occurs frequently in the Bible. Although the word can be used as a simple term of familiar, kindly address (Gk. *hetairos G2279*, Matt. 20:13; 22:12), it usually means a well-disposed acquaintance, dependable companion, or helpful neighbor (Heb. *rēaʿ H8276* and cognates, Gen. 38:20; Jer. 6:21; Gk. *philos G5813*, Lk. 11:5–8; 14:10; 15:6, 9), a political adherent (1 Sam. 30:26; 2 Sam. 3:8; 15:37; 1 Ki. 4:5; Jn. 19:12), or a person dear as one's own soul (Deut. 13:6 KJV). There are false friends as well as true ones (Prov. 18:24); friends who fail one (Job 6:14, 27; Lam. 1:2; Zech. 13:6) as well as friends who prove faithful (Ps. 35:14; Prov. 17:17; Jn. 15:13). There are those who are selfish (Prov. 19:4–7) and those who seek the welfare of others (27:6, 10).

Perhaps the most notable instance of human friendship in the Bible is that of DAVID and

This Greek inscription from a 1st-cent. synagogue in Jerusalem says that a certain Theodotus son of Vettenus, priest and synagogue ruler, built this structure for reading the Torah and teaching the commandments, and as lodging for the needy. Some have thought that this may be the Synagogue of the Freedmen mentioned in Acts.

JONATHAN (1 Sam. 18:1–4; 19:1–7; 20:1–42; 2 Sam. 1:25–26). According to some scholars, Paul's epistle to the PHILIPPIANS exhibits the formal characteristics of Greco-Roman "letters of friendship" or "family letters" (e.g., G. D. Fee, *Paul's Letter to the Philippians*, NICNT [1995], 1–14). The highest friendship the Bible speaks of is friendship with God (esp. Abraham's, 2 Chr. 20:7; Isa. 41:8 [ptc. of ʾāhab H170, "to love"]; Jas. 2:23), whose direct opposite, enmity with God, is friendship with the world (Jas. 4:4, *philia G5802*). (See H. Black, *Friendship* [1903]; S. Dodds, *Friendship's Meaning and the Heart of God in Nature* [1919], 7–43; *NIDOTTE*, 3:1144–49; *NIDNTT*, 2:547–51.)

P. H. MONSMA

fringe. See TASSEL.

frog. The only OT mention of this common amphibian is in connection with the second plague in Egypt (Heb. *ṣĕpardēaʿ H7630*, Exod. 8:2–15; Pss. 78:45; 105:30), which finds an echo in the only NT occurrence (Gk. *batrachos G1005*, Rev. 16:13). Many species are found in the marshes and rivers of the Middle E and the Nile Valley, the most common being *Rana esculenta*, the edible or green frog (another possibility is *R. punctata*, a spotted frog; see *FFB*, 33). It is sometimes known as the river frog because it stays in water most of the year and not only in the breeding season. It reaches a length of about 3 in. Many people dislike the cool moist feel of a frog's skin, but the reaction of the Egyptians was far more severe, because to them the frog was also unclean. This plague followed closely on the first, by which the NILE had become gravely polluted, possibly causing the frogs to leave the water and invade the houses. The magicians could produce frogs by sleight of hand, but could not drive away the plague that God had sent. In the hot dry air frogs quickly became dehydrated and died, the result being physically unpleasant as well as abhorrent. It is ironic that frogs are useful in keeping down insects, such as caused the following plagues.

G. S. CANSDALE

frontlets. This term is used by the KJV to render Hebrew *ṭôṭāpōt H3213*, "sign, emblem," used only three times (Exod. 13:16; Deut. 6:8; 11:18). In the first reference, Moses says to the Israelites that the PASSOVER was to remind them of their deliverance by God from Egypt, and was to have the same value as marks upon the hand and the FOREHEAD. In the other two references, the Israelites are instructed to affix the commandments on their hands and foreheads. It appears that the injunction was intended to be taken metaphorically, but in later times the Jewish people understood it literally and wrote four passages of the law (Exod. 13:1–10, 11–16; Deut. 6:4–9; 11:13–21) on small bits of parchment, which they enclosed in little boxes. These were worn, bound on the arm and brow, at morning prayer. See PHYLACTERY.

S. BARABAS

frost. This term (or *hoarfrost*) is used primarily to render Hebrew *kĕpôr H4095* (Exod. 16:14 et al.). Another term, *qeraḥ H7943*, "ice," can also refer to frost (cf. Jer. 36:30), as does the unique word *qippāʾôn H7885* (Zech. 14:6, *Qere*). More doubtful is the term *ḥănāmal H2857* (only Ps. 78:47), which the NRSV renders "frost," but which may mean "flood" (*HALOT*, 1:334) or "sleet" (NIV). The climate of Palestine is widely divergent from the hills around the Sea of Galilee to the desert of the southern SINAI. Although SNOW is rare and scattered, it does fall in the higher elevations. Frost will develop rapidly from the drop of temperature caused by the convection currents over the desert. Violent HAIL, swirling snow showers, and frozen DEW all are features of the variable climate. See PALESTINE V.

W. WHITE, JR.

fruit. This term appears numerous times in the Bible, almost always as a rendering of either Hebrew *pĕrî H7262* or Greek *karpos G2843*, but note also such words for "produce" as *yĕbûl H3292* (Lev. 26:4 et al.), *tĕnûbâ H9482* (Deut. 32:13 et al.), and *genēma G1163* (Matt. 26:29 et al.), as well as the Greek compounds *akarpos G182*, "unfruitful" (Matt. 13:22 et al.), and *karpophoreō G2844*, "to bear fruit" (v. 23).

The word *fruit* often is used both literally and figuratively. Figurative examples include "the fruit of your womb" (Deut. 28:4), "the fruit of the righteous is a tree of life" (Prov. 11:30), "his fruit is sweet to my taste" (Cant. 2:3), "they shall eat the fruit of their labors" (Isa. 3:10 NRSV), "the fruit of the Spirit" (Gal. 5:22), "the fruit of the light" (Eph. 5:9), "the fruit of righteousness" (Phil. 1:11), "the fruit of lips that confess his name" (Heb. 13:15).

In an Eastern country, the fruits grown are those indigenous to the area. The most important fruit tree is probably the VINE, which is mentioned again and again from Gen. 9:20 to Rev. 14:19. The OLIVE is almost as important, and occurs first in Gen. 8:11, when a dove brought an olive leaf to NOAH, and continues to Rev. 11:4, where two olive trees are described. The FIG is the third claimant; it is first mentioned in Gen. 3:7, when ADAM and EVE used fig leaves to cover themselves, and last in Rev. 6:13, which speaks of useless figs being shed. These three fruit trees are all used in parabolic form to describe the Jewish people (Ps. 80:8; Jer. 11:16; Lk. 13:6–9).

Other kinds of fruit mentioned include the APPLE (prob. an apricot), the MELON, the DATE, and the POMEGRANATE (the reference to MULBERRY trees in the KJV, 2 Sam. 5:23–24 and 1 Chr. 14:14–15, is probably incorrect). The ALMOND could be included, though it is really the seed of a fruit. The BALM (Gen. 37:25 et al.) probably comes from the fruit of the *Balanites* tree. There are two species of MYRRH that bear oval, plum-like fruits. The CUCUMBER is a fruit, though we classify it as a vegetable (Num. 11:5). The NUTS grown in SOLOMON'S garden (Cant. 6:11) also may be regarded as fruits. The MANDRAKE plant (Gen. 30:14–16) bears a yellow fruit like a large plum, called by the Arabs "devil's apples." It may be that other fruits were grown by Solomon (cf. Cant. 4:16, "choice fruits"); it is believed that he collected fruit trees from many different parts of the world.

The expression "does not produce good fruit" (Matt. 3:10; Lk. 3:9) may refer to seedling trees that bear quite useless fruit. Some fruits ripen early in the summer and must be eaten immediately (Isa. 28:4), while the term "summer fruit" (Amos 8:1–2 NRSV) refers to the last of the ripened fruits at the end of the season. W. E. SHEWELL-COOPER

fruits, first. See FIRSTFRUITS.

fuel. This term is used in Bible versions a few times, primarily to render two Hebrew words that mean "food [for fire]" (ʾoklâ H433, Isa. 9:5, 19;

Both wood and dried animal dung were used as fuel for heating and cooking.

maʾăkōlet H4409, Ezek. 15:4, 6; 21:32). The fuels of antiquity all were derived from vegetable hydrocarbons. Woods and barks were burned along with rushes, straw, twigs, sticks, thorn bushes, chaff, and roots. The only animal material was dung, which burned slowly and gave off a detestable odor. The process of making charcoal certainly was discovered by the beginning of the 2nd millennium B.C., as it was used to gain the necessary temperature for the smelting of copper and the alloys needed to make bronze. The richer homes and temples utilized charcoal, and the braziers upon which it was burned were probably imported (Lev. 11:35; Jer. 36:22–23). See COAL. W. WHITE, JR.

fulfillment. To deal fully with all that is involved in the idea of fulfillment would require a study of several broad theological themes, because it is a key concept of Christian thought. It will be possible here only (1) to indicate the various Hebrew and Greek words that represent the idea and to bring out their significance; (2) to show the relationship between PROMISE and fulfillment and to bring into focus the relevance of the OT; (3) to analyze the various types of fulfillment illustrated in the Bible; and (4) to note the special NT teachings on this subject.

I. Terminology. The main Hebrew words used are the verbs *mālēʾ* H4848 ("to be full, to fill") and *kālâ* H3983 ("to finish"). The former is frequently translated in the SEPTUAGINT with *plēroō* G4444, which also conveys the idea of fullness. This verb is also common in the NT, which in addition uses the compounds *anaplēroō G405* and *ekplēroō G1740* (in the sense "fulfill," only Matt. 13:14 and Acts 13:33 respectively). Like the second Hebrew verb, several Greek forms—*teleioō G5457* (Jn. 19:28), *teleō G5464* (Acts 13:29), and *synteleō G5334* (Acts 13:29)—indicate completeness. In the OT, note also the use of the verb *bōʾ H995*, "come [to pass]" (Josh. 21:45 et al.). (See *NIDOTTE*, 2:939–41; *NIDNTT*, 1:733–41.)

II. The relation of promise to fulfillment. Fulfillment presupposes previous prediction, and it is essential to understand the nature of the prediction to appreciate the significance of the fulfillment. The OT concentrates the promises in the COVENANT relationship and in the messianic hopes. The OT was in fact forward-pointing and takes on its true meaning only in the light of the consummation found in the NT. The OT is to the NT as promise is to fulfillment. The apostle PAUL makes much of the promises made to ABRAHAM (Rom. 4). These promises he clearly sees to have been fulfilled in Christ. It was the glory of Abraham's faith that it staggered not at the difficulties inherent in the fulfillment, because he was convinced of the inviolability of the promise. This is typical of the OT revelation. It was never represented as being complete in itself. There was always something more glorious to follow.

The early Christian appeal to OT citations is a striking reminder of the importance of the idea of fulfillment for primitive Christian theology (see QUOTATIONS IN THE NT). The Acts speeches are full of such citations and so are the Gospels. Moreover, in the Epistles there are frequent appeals to the OT, and various formulae of citation are employed to bring out the nature of fulfillment.

The essential link between the Testaments is never more clearly seen than under this concept. It is fundamental to the scriptural presentation of God that he must keep his promises. The Scripture cannot be broken (cf. Jn. 10:35), and for this reason fulfillment is certain. It was no more than might be expected. However, fulfillment did confirm the faith of those who either at the time or else later recognized that some former prediction of God had come to pass. It was this sense of thrilling fulfillment that gave to primitive Christianity a remarkable air of joyfulness. The age to come had arrived. Promise had merged into fulfillment.

III. Various types of fulfillment. The idea of fulfillment will clearly vary according to the nature of the prediction. For the sake of clarity some classification of these types is necessary. (1) The first class consists of cases of *immediate fulfillment*. An example from the OT is seen in the prediction of the prophet AHIJAH that JEROBOAM's wife would suffer the loss of her child as soon as she arrived home (1 Ki. 14:12). A NT example is the withering of the fig tree at the command of Jesus (Mk. 11:12–14; cf. Matt. 21:18–19), or the prediction of PETER's denial a few hours before it happened (Matt. 26:34, 75).

(2) The second class consists of cases of *delayed fulfillment*. Under this classification there are two main groups: those instances where fulfillment has already taken place, and those where as yet the promises remain unfulfilled. The former group gives assurance that the latter will yet be fulfilled. Under the former group must be classed all those messianic predictions that found their fulfillment in Jesus Christ, for instance, the seed that would bruise the serpent's head (Gen. 3:15) and the SERVANT OF THE LORD passages in Isaiah. In these cases the delay in fulfillment spanned many centuries, and yet there was no hesitation in the minds of Christians that Jesus was the perfect fulfillment of all the ancient predictions. Examples of prophecies yet to be fulfilled are numerous. In the OT there are various prophecies relating to Israel that are as yet unfulfilled, though others have seen remarkable fulfillment in the modern reconstitution of the nation of Israel. In the NT there are many eschatological predictions that await fulfillment at the end of the age.

(3) The third class consists of cases of both *immediate and delayed fulfillment*. It is important to recognize this class, since it has occasioned most difficulty in the interpretation of prophetic utterances. A notable illustration is the eschatological discourse in Mk. 13, where the predictions of Jesus received a partial fulfillment in the fall of JERUSALEM, but will be consummated only at the PAROUSIA. The line of demarcation between the immediate and the future was not clearly defined

for the original hearers, but subsequent events have shown the words to possess a double aspect. Sometimes an event that had originally a specific local significance is symbolic of a deeper fulfillment later, as for instance Isa. 7:14.

(4) A fourth class comprises cases of what might be called *extended fulfillment*. Where a prediction, after a brief interval of time, has a fulfillment that adequately satisfies the prediction, it may yet receive a further application in a sense different from its original significance. Thus in the NT some OT predictions not normally considered to be messianic are applied to the times of Christ. The prophecy of the slaughter of the innocents (Matt. 2:17–18) had a different meaning in its original context (Jer. 31:15). This process will explain many of the OT citations used in the NT. They had a meaning that was hidden from the people originally addressed, but that was nevertheless a true fulfillment. In these cases the recognition by Christians of the fulfillment of an ancient prediction was regarded as an important feature of God's dealing with them.

IV. Fulfillment in the NT. The early Christians were deeply impressed with the fact that the salvation events centered in Jesus Christ were fulfillments of Scripture. "According to the Scriptures" was a fixed part of the primitive preaching and tradition (cf. 1 Cor. 15:3–4). The Gospels contain many instances of events that are said to have happened in fulfillment of OT TESTIMONIA. This is particularly true in Matthew's gospel, where a group of twelve testimonies are introduced with some such formula as "This was to fulfill what was spoken." These formulae may at first give the impression that the people concerned with the action were acquainted with the fact that prophecy was being fulfilled, but the citations are for the most part the evangelist's own commentary on the events. It was in retrospect that the details in the life of Jesus were fulfillments (cf. Matt. 12:17–21). But one of the key factors in the interpretation of fulfilled prophecy was the conviction that all things were planned, working toward a climax. This conviction undoubtedly came from Jesus himself. When he appeared to the disciples after the resurrection, he said, "This is what I told you while I was still with you: Everything must be fulfilled that is written about me in the Law of Moses, the Prophets and the Psalms" (Lk. 24:44). This was the cue for their understanding of the OT.

There is ample evidence that Jesus was conscious of the processes of fulfillment both in his life and his death. When JOHN THE BAPTIST asked whether Jesus was the Coming One, Jesus in reply echoed the words of Isa. 35:5–6, and when JUDAS ISCARIOT shared the same dish with him at the supper table, Jesus stated that the SON OF MAN was going as it is written of him (Mk. 14:21). At the commencement of the ministry in Luke's story, Jesus read a passage of Scripture in the synagogue and then declared that Scripture had been fulfilled in their hearing (Lk. 4:21). This consciousness stayed with him throughout his public ministry. In John's gospel this idea is most clearly expressed. Jesus was sent to fulfill a divine mission. He was moving toward a specific "hour" that would climax his work (Jn. 2:4; 4:21–23; et al. [NIV, "time"]). All the evangelists are convinced that the death and resurrection of Jesus occurred in fulfillment of Scripture, and this is equally apparent in the speeches in Acts. It is through the Scriptures that Jesus is revealed to be the long promised MESSIAH.

It is in the Acts and especially in the Epistles that the theological importance of fulfillment is fully brought out. It formed an integral part of the primitive KERYGMA. Was it developed in the Epistles? It is clear from the repeated refrain in 1 Cor. 15:3–4, that the apostle PAUL took it from earlier tradition. The frequency with which he cited Scripture shows that it became an integral part of his theological outlook. This may best be illustrated from the most theological of his writings, the epistle to the ROMANS. He begins by noting that God had promised the gospel beforehand in the Scriptures. The gospel was itself fulfillment. The theme of the whole epistle is founded on an OT quotation, Hab. 2:4. The argument of the epistle is frequently buttressed from Scripture (Rom. 3). The promise is prominent in ch. 4, and the ADAM motif in ch. 5. The discussion in chs. 9–11 is impregnated with the problems of fulfillment and is frequently supported by the appeal to Scripture. Also in the ethical section (chs. 12–15), Scripture is repeatedly quoted under the formula, "It is written" (cf. 14:11; 15:9–12, 21). The closing DOXOLOGY (16:25–27) refers to the prophetic writings. What is true of this epistle is true of Paul's approach generally. The same is true for the other NT Epistles. HEBREWS may be described as an epistle of fulfillment, as the superiority of the new order over the old is developed. In 1 Peter some of the major ideas of the book of Exodus are shown to have their fulfillment in Christ.

The NT makes clear that the present age will reach its consummation in the fulfillment of the promise of the *eschaton* (the last time; see ESCHATOLOGY). The return of Christ is predicted (Matt. 25:31; Mk. 8:38), and the details given show that the event is still future. The *eschaton* will be a time of judgment (Jn. 12:48), but in the mercy of God judgment is delayed. Although the present period is a time of partial unfulfillment, the end is certain. It will be a time of great glory for the Son of man and for his people. His kingdom will be established and all the promises concerning it will be fulfilled. (See further W. J. Beecher, *The Prophets and the Promise* [1905]; R. V. G. Tasker, *The Old Testament in the New Testament* [1947]; O. Cullmann, *Christ and Time* [1950]; W. G. Kümmel, *Promise and Fulfillment* [1961]; G. von Rad, *Old Testament Theology* [1965], 2:319–87; additional bibliography under NEW TESTAMENT THEOLOGY and OLD TESTAMENT THEOLOGY.) D. GUTHRIE

fuller. One who cleans, shrinks, and thickens newly shorn wool or cloth. In ancient times the fuller often also dyed cloth. The Hebrew word for "fuller" (the ptc. of the verb *kābas* H3891, "to full, wash") is related to a root meaning "to tread," suggesting what was chiefly involved in the fuller's art. Before material could be used for a garment, it was necessary first to free it from the oily and gummy substances that adhered to the raw fiber. This was done by first washing the material with some cleansing substance like white clay, putrid urine, or nitre made from the ashes of certain plants that grew in Egypt (SOAP was unknown in ancient times). The material was then washed free from the alkali by many changes of clean water or by boys treading on it in a running stream. After that it was placed in the sun to dry and bleach. Because of the odors given forth in the process of fulling, the fuller's shop was usually outside the city.

There was an area called the Fuller's Field just S of Jerusalem, near the aqueduct of the Upper Pool (2 Ki. 18:17; Isa. 7:3; 36:2; NIV, "Washerman's Field"); in this area, the fullers may have used the water available at EN ROGEL, a name that probably means "fuller's spring" (cf. *ABD*, 2:859). In Mal. 3:2 God is compared to a refiner's fire and to the soap of fullers or launderers. In the NT, the corresponding Greek word is used only once (*gnapheus* G1187, Mk. 9:3 KJV), where the garments of Jesus at the time of his transfiguration are described as being whiter than any fuller on earth could whiten them. (See R. J. Forbes, *Studies in Ancient Technology*, 8 vols. [1955–64], 4:81–89.) J. L. KELSO

fuller's soap. See SOAP.

fullness of time. This expression (*to plērōma tou chronou*, Gal. 4:4) indicates the "right" or "proper" time for Christ's advent. The expression does not mean the "full term" of prenatal human life ("born of woman"), but rather the right time chosen by the Father ("God sent forth"). This "right time" was determined by God's plan of redemption and prepared for by historical developments: the completion of the OT era and messianic expectation, as well as cultural, political, and religious factors in the Roman world. These developments provided fertile soil for the ministry of the MESSIAH, the founding of the church, and the rapid spread of the gospel. Paul's language, however, calls attention to the theme of eschatological FULFILLMENT: Jesus' coming marks "the last days" when God's promises are coming to pass. (See H. N. Ridderbos, *When the Time Had Fully Come: Studies in New Testament Theology* [1957].) See also ESCHATOLOGY; PLEROMA. J. C. DEYOUNG

furlong. This English term is used by the KJV to render Greek *stadion* G5084, "stade" (Lk. 24:13 et al.), equivalent to one-eighth of a Roman mile. See WEIGHTS AND MEASURES I.G.

furnace. This term is used to translate a variety of words, especially Hebrew *kûr* H3929, which refers to a furnace for smelting METALS (Prov. 17:3; 27:21). In the Bible the word is used only in the metaphorical sense of SUFFERING permitted by God in punishment or discipline. The deliverance of Israel from Egypt was like being taken from the midst of an iron-smelting furnace (Deut. 4:20; 1 Ki. 8:51; Jer. 11:4). God told Israel that he had refined them in the furnace of affliction (Isa. 48:10). Another term, *tannûr* H9486, is rendered variously "firepot" (e.g., Gen. 15:17), "furnace" (e.g., Ps. 21:9), and especially "oven" (e.g., Exod. 8:3); while the rare term *kibšān* H3901 is rendered "kiln" by the NRSV in two passages (Exod. 9:8–10; 19:18; "furnace" in its other occurrence, Gen. 19:28). See OVEN.

In the NT, Greek *kaminos* G2825 is used with reference to HELL, the destiny of those who are finally impenitent (Matt. 13:42, 50; Rev. 9:2), but elsewhere in Revelation the feet of Christ are described as "like bronze glowing in a furnace" (Rev. 1:15). Refined bronze is a hard metal, symbolizing the crushing power of Christ when he deals with his enemies. Note also the term *klibanos* G3106, "oven" (Matt. 6:30=Lk. 12:28; NIV, "fire").

It will be seen that almost always the word *furnace* occurs in the Bible in a metaphorical sense of God's punishment or of his tempering the human character. Furnaces were used for smelting iron from the ore; melting and refining gold, silver, brass, tin, and lead; firing pottery and other ceramic products; firing bricks; and making lime. The metal industry flourished as early as 2000 B.C. Many mining and smelting camps along the edge of the ARABAH have been found. The largest was at Meneʾiyyeh, c. 21 mi. N of the Gulf of AQABAH. There was another at Khirbet en-Nahas, 52 mi. farther N.

The largest COPPER mine in the whole of the ANE was found at Tell-el-Kheleifeh (EZION GEBER), at the S end of the Wadi Arabah. It was built in the 10th cent. B.C., most likely by SOLOMON, who also built a fleet of merchant ships there for carrying on trade. The shelter was oriented so that the strong prevailing wind from the N would blow into the flues, making the use of bellows unnecessary. Charcoal was used for fuel. This smelter was in use up to the 5th cent. B.C. A number of smelting furnaces have been discovered in Palestine itself, some used to smelt copper, others IRON. Four were found at Tell Jemmeh, two at Ain Shems, and others at Ai and at Tell Qasile near Tel Aviv. (See further N. Glueck, *The Other Side of the Jordan* [1940], chs. 3–4; R. J. Forbes, *Studies in Ancient Technology*, 8 vols. [1955–64], 6:66ff.; C. Singer et al., eds., *A History of Technology* [1954], 391–97, 577; G. E. Wright, *Biblical Archaeology* [1962], 135–37.)

S. BARABAS

Furnaces, Tower of the. See OVENS, TOWER OF THE.

furniture. The common Hebrew term *kĕlî* H3998 has the very general meaning of "article" or "[useful] object," and thus can be translated with a wide variety of terms, depending on the context ("vessel, instrument, equipment, baggage, jewelry," etc.). It is properly rendered "furniture" or "furnishings" in some passages, such as the accounts of the building of the TABERNACLE (Exod. 25:9 et al.; cf. also Num. 3:8; 1 Chr. 9:29; et al.), but English Bible versions differ in many specific instances. In the NT, the Greek verb *strōnnyō* G5143, "to spread," is used in the sense of "to furnish" in one context (Mk. 14:15=Lk. 22:12).

Household furniture in biblical Palestine was very simple. Handwoven curtains separated the men's and the women's quarters. Beds were found only in the homes of the wealthy; the average person

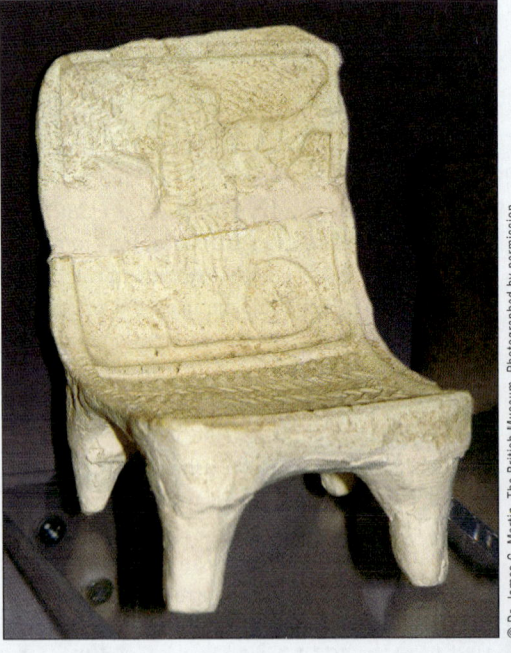

This terra-cotta model of a chair was discovered at Ur (2000–1750 B.C.).

used sleeping mats, which were rolled up when not in use. Since houses were primarily a place for sleeping, and people spent most of their time out of doors, there was little furniture in the house. Mats spread on the bare floor served in place of tables and chairs. Sometimes stone or wooden benches, covered with carpet, were placed along the walls. With the wealthy it was different, as evident in the denunciation of the grandees of SAMARIA by the prophet AMOS, who, he said, luxuriated in beds of ivory and lazily stretched themselves upon couches (Amos 3:12; 6:4). (Cf. M. S. and J. L. Miller, *Encyclopedia of Bible Life* [1944], 246–52; P. J. King and L. E. Stager, *Life in Biblical Israel* [2001], 63–64.)

S. BARABAS

furrow. The long trench made by a PLOW in its path. The term is found in English Bibles mainly as a rendering of Hebrew *telem H9439*, which occurs five times (Job 31:38; 39:10; Ps. 65:10; Hos. 10:4; 12:11; note also *maʿănâ H5103* in 1 Sam. 14:14; Ps. 129:3). In addition, the KJV uses it to render other Hebrew terms that have different meanings (Ezek. 17:7, 10; Hos. 10:10). The furrow was usually made with a single-handled wooden plow pulled by an animal. IRON was available after DAVID's period, but wood continued to be used in many instances. See AGRICULTURE.

G. GIACUMAKIS, JR.

future life. See ESCHATOLOGY; IMMORTALITY; LIFE.

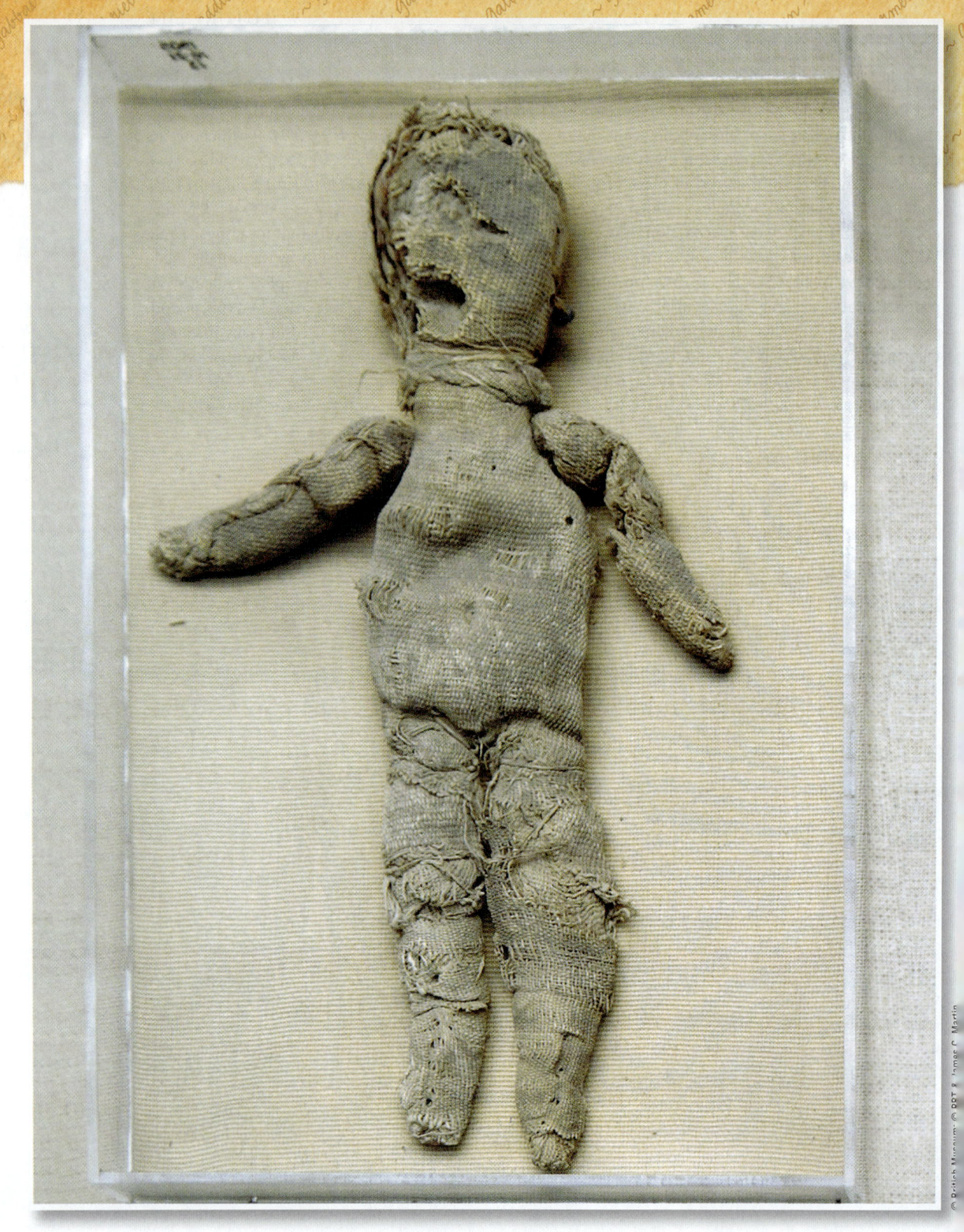

As in modern times, children during the Roman period played games with toys. This rag doll was discovered in Egypt.

G

Gaal gay´uhl (גַּעַל H1720, possibly "beetle" or "loathing"). Son of Ebed and leader of a revolt against Abimelech son of Gideon (Jdg. 9:26–41). Gaal and his relatives had moved into Shechem and had gained the trust of the city's inhabitants. While they were having a banquet, Gaal and the Shechemites became drunk and scoffed at Abimelech. In the midst of their revelry, Gaal boasted that with adequate support he could overthrow Abimelech. When Zebul, the ruler of Shechem, heard this, he sent word to Abimelech urging him to quell the rebellion at once. He advised Abimelech to set an ambush around the city during the night. The next morning, as Gaal and Zebul stood in the city gate watching, they saw the troops of Abimelech arise from hiding and approach the city. Zebul challenged Gaal to make good his boast to overthrow Abimelech. Gaal and his men were defeated and driven from the field, and they were repulsed from the city by Zebul. The next day Abimelech captured Shechem, destroyed it, and sowed it with salt. This was seen by the Scripture writer as the just judgment of God on the Shechemites who supported Abimelech in the assassination of his seventy brothers (cf. vv. 56–57). D. H. Madvig

Gaash gay´ash (גַּעַשׁ H1724, "quake"). A name used to identify a mountain and its ravines. Mount Gaash is described as being in the hill country of Ephraim and just S of Timnath Serah, where Joshua was buried (Josh. 24:30; Jdg. 2:9). The ravines are referred to as the area from which Hiddai, one of David's mighty men, came (2 Sam. 23:30; 1 Chr. 11:32 [Hurai]). The precise location is unknown, but it must have been approximately 20 mi. SW of Shechem and 15 mi. NW of Jerusalem. J. B. Scott

Gaba gay´buh. KJV alternate form of Geba (representing the Heb. pausal form; Josh. 18:24; Ezra 2:26; Neh. 7:30).

Gabael gab´ay-uhl (Γαβαηλ, "God is lofty"). (1) Ancestor of Tobit (Tob. 1:1).

(2) A relative of Tobit who lived in Rages of Media; he is described as brother (Tob. 1:14) or son (4:20) of Gabri (Gabrias). Tobit left ten talents of silver with Gabael for safekeeping. Later, having been prevented by political conditions from recovering the money himself, Tobit sent his son Tobias to get it. Gabael returned the money and attended Tobias's wedding (4:1; 5:3, 6; 9:1–6).

D. H. Madvig

Gabatha gab´uh-thuh (Γαβαθα). According to Addition A in the Greek texts of Esther, included at the very beginning of the book, Gabatha and Tharra (Teresh) were two eunuchs whom Mordecai overheard plotting against King Ahasuerus (Xerxes). Mordecai informed the king, the traitors were executed, and the incident was noted in the royal records (Add. Esth. 12:1–6 = Esth. 1:1 [1$^{m\text{-}r}$] in Rahlfs, *Septuaginta*). The name Gabatha corresponds to Bigtha (also Bigthan and Bigthana) in the Hebrew text (1:10; 2:21; 6:2).

Gabbai gab´i (גַּבַּי H1480, possibly "[tax] gatherer"). One of the leaders from Benjamin who volunteered to settle in Jerusalem after the return from the exile (Neh. 11:8). Because the Hebrew clause *wĕʾaḥărāyw gabbay sallāy*, "and after him [NIV, and his followers], Gabbai, Sallai," makes poor sense in context, many scholars emend the first word to *wĕʾeḥāyw*, "and his brothers" (cf. NRSV, following some MSS of the LXX). Other scholars, in addition, emend the last two words to *gibbôrê ḥayil*, "men of valor" (cf. *BHS* and ESV).

Gabbatha gab´uh-thuh (Γαββαθα G1119; possibly from Aram. גבתא, a word of uncertain meaning). The ARAMAIC (KJV, "Hebrew") name for "the Stone Pavement" (Gk. *Lithostrōtos* G3346), an unknown location in JERUSALEM where PILATE judged Jesus (Jn. 19:13). Attempts have been made to equate Gabbatha with various terms, such as the Greek transliteration *Gabath* (which JOSEPHUS says means *lophos*, i.e., "ridge, crest"; see *War* 5.2.1 §51), Latin *gabata*, "platter," hence a dish-shaped area (C. C. Torrey in *ZAW* 65 [1953]: 232–33), Aramaic *gabtāʾ*, "hill" (see M. Jastrow, *Dictionary of the Targumim* ... [1903], s.v. *gûbtāʾ*), and so on (for other suggestions, cf. C. K. Barrett, *The Gospel according to St. John*, 2nd ed. [1978]), 544–45).

The fact that Gabbatha lay outside the PRAETORIUM (governor's residence, Jn. 19:9, 13) would indicate either the palace of HEROD in the W part of Jerusalem or the fortress of ANTONIA in the E. The latter, at the NW corner of the TEMPLE area, has been favored by the identification at this spot of 2,500 square yards of pavement, beneath the present church of the Dames de Sion, as belonging to the fortress. The stone slabs are over one yard square and one foot thick, some still bearing marks suggestive of Roman soldiers' games (see L. Vincent, *Jerusalem de l'Ancien Testament* [1959], 216–21). However, more recent work indicates that this pavement was not built prior to A.D. 70, and so Gabbatha should probably be identified with a podium that apparently stood on the E side of HEROD's palace (see *ABD*, 2:862). At Gabbatha, Pilate sat on the *bēma* G1037, "judicial bench" (v. 13), and ultimately acceded to the pressure of the Jewish leaders, delivering Jesus to them for crucifixion (v. 16). J. B. PAYNE

Modern reconstruction of the Herodian palace in Jerusalem. The Gabbatha or Stone Pavement where Pilate judged Jesus may have been located here.

Gabdes gab´deez. KJV Apoc. form of GEBA (1 Esd. 5:20).

Gabri, Gabrias gay´bri, gay´bree-uhs (Γαβριας, possibly "[strong] man of Yahweh"). The brother or father of a certain GABAEL with whom TOBIT deposited ten talents of silver (Tob. 1:14 [NRSV, "Gabri"]; 4:20 [NRSV, "Gabrias"]; CODEX SINAITICUS reads *Gabri* in both passages).

Gabriel gay´bree-uhl (גַּבְרִיאֵל H1508, "[strong] man of God" or "God is my warrior"; Γαβριηλ G1120). The name of a supernatural messenger seen by DANIEL in a vision (Dan. 8:16; 9:21; maybe by implication in chs. 10–12 also). In the apocryphal and mystical Jewish writings, this ANGEL is joined with MICHAEL THE ARCHANGEL (Dan. 10:13, 21; 12:1), as well as with URIEL and RAPHAEL, around the throne of God. In the pseudepigraphic book of *1 Enoch*, the character and position of Gabriel are defined in terms of the Jewish folklore. In the Aramaic TARGUM he is written back into several accounts of the OT and is the angel credited with the finding of JOSEPH's brothers, the burial of MOSES, and the slaughter of the Assyrian armies of SENNACHERIB. It is not clear what the exact sources of these embellishments may have been, but it is highly possible that they were, in fact, aspects of the Persian demi-gods derived from the elaborate hierarchy of the Iranian pantheon. The simplicity of the account in Daniel is a far removed step from the involved tales of the rabbis.

The angel Gabriel plays a role in the Lukan account of the INCARNATION, as he is the messenger who announces the birth of JOHN THE BAPTIST to his father, the priest ZECHARIAH, in the temple (Lk. 1:19), as well as the birth of the MESSIAH to the Virgin Mary (1:26; see MARY MOTHER OF JESUS). His action in both places and the acceptance of his message are similar to the appearance recorded in Daniel. He indicates his authority as one who stands in the presence of the Almighty and thus follows his bidding and bears divine authority for his message. The mythical encrustation of the ages has not dimmed the simple narrative of the angelic announcement, and the Scripture envisions no such creature as the artists of the Renaissance often depicted, a half-man and half-bird derived from late Greek sculpture. A most interesting aspect is the rarity with which such heavenly visitations are mentioned in the Bible, and in each of the four cases mentioned, the incidents are directly connected to the fulfillment of the messianic promise. Speculations on the mechanism and details of these angelic announcements have troubled the church throughout the ages. W. WHITE, JR.

Gad gad (גָּד *H1514*, "fortunate"). (1) Seventh son of JACOB. See GAD, TRIBE OF.

(2) A prophet, or seer, who served DAVID. When David sought refuge for his father and mother in MOAB, during the time he was hunted by SAUL, Gad instructed him to leave his stronghold and return to Judah (1 Sam. 22:5). Gad also figures during David's reign. After conducting an ill-advised census of the people, David became conscience-stricken and confessed his sin to the Lord. The next day Gad brought David a message from the Lord. He was to choose one of three punishments— three years of famine, three months of defeat at the hand of his enemies, or three days of pestilence. David chose to suffer by pestilence, and 70,000 men perished. God relented just as the angel of the Lord was standing on the threshing floor of ARAUNAH (Ornan the Jebusite, 1 Chr. 21:15). Gad directed David to build an altar to the Lord on that very spot. After David had offered sacrifices, the plague was stopped (2 Sam. 24:10–25; 1 Chr. 21). In addition, Gad is said to have written a document recording the life and activities of David (1 Chr. 29:29) and to have assisted the king in establishing arrangements for the temple musicians (2 Chr. 29:25). D. H. MADVIG

Gad (deity) gad (גַּד *H1513*, "fortune"). A Semitic god of good fortune, mentioned with MENI (Isa. 65:11; modern versions usually render these two names respectively as "Fortune" and "Destiny"). Some scholars find a reference to this deity in LEAH's naming of Gad, her son through ZILPAH (Gen. 30:11). The popularity of the worship of this god among the Canaanites may be reflected in the place names BAAL GAD (Josh. 11:17; cf. 12:7; 13:5) and MIGDAL GAD (15:37; cf. also the personal names GADDI and GADDIEL, Num. 13:10, 11). Gad has sometimes been equated with the Babylonian god MARDUK and with the planet Jupiter. See also DESTINY; GAD, TRIBE OF. D. H. MADVIG

Gad, river (valley) of. According to the KJV, the commanders in charge of David's census encamped "in Aroer, on the right side of the city that *lieth* in the midst of the river of Gad, and toward Jazer" (2 Sam. 24:5; ASV, "the Valley of Gad"). This rendering is problematic, however. Recent versions have a comma after the word "river" or "valley" (NIV, "gorge") and translate the rest of the verse, "toward Gad and on to Jazer" (NRSV; similarly NIV, "and then went through Gad and on to Jazer"; see S. R. Driver, *Notes on the Hebrew Text of Samuel*, 2nd ed. [1913], 373–74).

Gad, tribe of gad (גָּד *H1514*, "fortunate"; gentilic גָּדִי *H1532*, "Gadite"). One of the tribes of Israel, named after its ancestor Gad, seventh son of JACOB. Gad was the first-born of ZILPAH, LEAH's maid (Gen. 30:10–11); his younger full brother was ASHER. He was born to Jacob in Paddan Aram, during the seven years he was working to pay LABAN for his second wife, RACHEL. When Gad was born, Leah exclaimed, "What good fortune!"—whence his name (the KJV rendering, "a troop cometh," is based on a different text, following the *Qere*). See also GAD (DEITY). Nothing is known of the life of Gad, except that he had seven sons at the time when he went with Jacob and his family down to Egypt to sojourn (Gen. 46:16; cf. Num. 26:15–16). Jacob's deathbed blessing to him

GAD, TRIBE OF

Tribal territory of Gad.

was, "Gad will be attacked by a band of raiders [*gād gĕdûd yĕgûdennû*], / but he will attack [*yāgud*] them at their heels" (Gen. 49:19). The tribe would be subject to attacks by raiding parties (prob. the Ammonites) but Gad would emerge victorious.

I. The tribe of Gad in the wilderness. At the first census (Num. 1:24–25), males twenty years old and upward fit for military service numbered 45,650. This is out of a total for Israel of 603,550 (vv. 44–46), which number did not include the tribe of Levi. At the end of their wanderings in the wilderness, the Gadites numbered 40,500, a substantial decrease (26:15–18). The number of non-Gadite Israelites during the same period increased slightly, the total (including Gad) being 601,730 (Num. 26:51; see also 1 Chr. 5:18). The leader of Gad at the beginning of the wilderness wanderings was ELIASAPH son of Deuel (Num. 2:14 [MT Reuel]; 10:20). He was appointed to assist MOSES in the first census (1:14) and later brought the representative offering from the Gadites for the dedication of the altar (7:42–47).

In the encampment, Gad was a member company of the camp of REUBEN, which camped to the S of the Tent of Meeting. Reuben camped next to the Tent of Meeting followed by SIMEON, with Gad on the outside (Num. 2:10–14). In the marching formation, the camp of JUDAH led, followed by the Gershonites and Merarites, who carried the TABERNACLE. Then came Reuben, Simeon, and Gad, followed by the Kohathites carrying the holy things, and then the rest of Israel (10:11–21). When Moses sent men to spy out the land of Canaan, the representative from Gad was GEUEL son of Maki (13:15).

II. The time of the conquest. After the defeat of SIHON, king of the AMORITES, and OG, king of BASHAN, the Gadites, along with the Reubenites, who were very rich in cattle and needed grazing land, saw that this land of GILEAD (in TRANSJORDAN) was good for cattle, and they requested from Moses that it be given to them as their INHERITANCE (Num. 32:1–6). The request was granted upon the promise that their fighting men accompany the children of Israel over the JORDAN River, and help to drive out the inhabitants of Canaan until the task was done (32:28–32). Moses later said of Gad, "Blessed is he who enlarges Gad's domain! / Gad lives there like a lion, / tearing at arm or head. / He chose the best land for himself; / the leader's portion was kept for him. / When the heads of the people assembled, / he carried out the LORD's righteous will, / and his judgments concerning Israel" (Deut. 33:20–21). The relationship of Reuben and Gad probably stemmed from their position at the S of the tabernacle, where Gad was part of the camp of Reuben. The other member, Simeon, received his inheritance to the W of the Jordan as the southernmost of the tribes (Josh. 19:1–9).

After the death of Moses, just before crossing the Jordan, JOSHUA reminded the two and one-half tribes (Reuben, Gad, and the half-tribe of Manasseh) that the men of war were to accompany the rest of Israel W of the Jordan (Josh. 1:12–18). When the children of Israel passed over the Jordan before the conquest of JERICHO, the armed forces of these tribes who went with them, leaving their children behind, amounted to about 40,000 (4:12–13).

After the defeat of AI, the Israelites stood by Mount GERIZIM and Mount EBAL for the blessing and the curse (Josh. 8:33–35), according to the words of Moses (Deut. 27:11–14). Gad and Reuben were among those designated for Mount Ebal. When the land had been conquered, Joshua officially released the Gadites to return home (Josh. 22:1–6). They crossed back over the Jordan with the Reubenites and the half-tribe of Manasseh and built an altar of great size by the Jordan. When the rest of the Israelites heard of it, they gathered together to make war with the two and one-half tribes. Then Reuben, Gad, and the half-tribe of Manasseh explained that this was not an altar for worship of false gods but was a witness that these tribes belonged with the commonwealth of Israel and were always to be included in the worship of the Lord. The explanation pleased the rest of the Israelites and a civil war was prevented (ch. 22).

III. Tribal inheritance. In the wilderness, Gad had been a part of the standard of the camp of Reuben on the S side of the Tent of Meeting (Num. 2:10, 14). This association continued when they asked Moses for an inheritance to the E of the Jordan (32:1–5). Moses granted to them (and to the half-tribe of Manasseh) the former kingdoms of Sihon and Og (32:33). At this time, the land was not divided into tribes, but the Manassites settled in the N (32:39–42), and the Reubenites and Gadites settled in the S (32:34–38). The locations of the towns belonging to Gad and Reuben mentioned here show that at that time their allotments intermixed. For example, Gad "built up" DIBON and AROER (v. 34), which were near the S border of Reuben (the ARNON River, Deut. 3:12, 16), opposite from the territory later given to Gad and actually listed as cities given to Reuben (Josh. 13:16–17). MESHA, king of MOAB at the time of AHAB, referred to the inhabitants of ATAROTH (Num. 32:34) as Gadites, indicating that they continued to occupy this town, deep in Reubenite territory, after tribal boundaries were fixed (*ANET*, 320). Moses listed the territory of Manasseh separately but that of Gad and Reuben together (Deut. 3:12–18). The latter included the area E of the Jordan from Kinnereth (Galilee) to the Salt Sea.

The whole area of the two and one-half tribes is delineated a second time (Josh. 12:1–6; 13:8–13). The border on the W was the Jordan; on the S, the Arnon; to the N, the border of GESHUR and MAACAH; and to the E, apparently the border of AMMON (to the JABBOK River). Joshua described the inheritance of Gad individually (13:24–28). The border in the N was from the S tip of the Sea of Kinnereth eastward with Manasseh as a border, including RAMOTH GILEAD (a city of refuge, 20:2). On the W was the Jordan. The border on the S was Reuben, just to the N of HESHBON (13:26), which belonged to Reuben (v. 17) but is listed as a Levite city from the tribe of Gad (Josh. 21:39; 1 Chr. 6:81). To the E were the Ammonites, the border being E of Aroer (Josh. 13:25; near Rabbah, modern Amman; not Aroer on the Arnon, v. 16).

Israel's possession E of the Jordan, especially that of Gad and Manasseh, was called GILEAD, a geographical term not clearly defined. At times Gilead was used in place of the tribal name (Jdg. 5:17). The cities for the Levites from the tribe of Gad were Ramoth, Mahanaim, Heshbon, and Jazer (Josh. 21:8, 38, 39; 1 Chr. 6:63, 80, 81). Of these, Ramoth in Gilead was a city of refuge (Deut. 4:43; Josh. 20:8). See TRIBES, LOCATION OF, I.B.

IV. The time of Saul and David. During the reign of SAUL, when the PHILISTINES oppressed Israel, some of the Israelites crossed the Jordan and migrated to the land of Gad (1 Sam. 13:6–7). The two and one-half tribes are tied together again in 1 Chr. 5. They produced an army of 44,760 and defeated the Hagrites "because they trusted in" God (vv. 18–21). If this is the same event as v. 10, it happened during the reign of Saul, who, because of lack of trust, was losing his battles.

When DAVID was in exile at ZIKLAG building up a following of trained fighting men, there came Gadites to join him: "They were brave warriors, ready for battle and able to handle the shield and spear. Their faces were the faces of lions, and they were as swift as gazelles in the mountains" (1 Chr. 12:8; cf. Deut. 33:20). BANI the Gadite was one of David's thirty mighty men (2 Sam. 23:36).

The Reubenites, Gadites, and the half-tribe of Manasseh are listed together as sending a contingent of 120,000 armed men to David's coronation (other tribes were listed individually). Gad is included in the numbering of the children of Israel by JOAB at David's command (24:5). David appointed Jerijah (JERIAH), chief of the Hebronites, along with his brethren, 2,700 men of ability, to the oversight of Transjordan, including the Gadites, for matters "pertaining to God and for the affairs of the king" (1 Chr. 26:29–32). A number of these men had been found in Jazer in Gilead and were perhaps formerly from Hebron. (See further R. H. Dornemann, *The Archaeology of the Transjordan in the Bronze and Iron Ages* [1983]; N. Halpern, *The Emergence of Israel in Canaan* [1983].)

V. Later history. During the time of Israel's monarchy, the Gadites are not usually referred to separately but share in the history of Gilead. When HAZAEL, king of Aram, defeated the Israelites, he took much of Transjordan, including the territory of Gad (2 Ki. 10:32–33); Ramoth Gilead had fallen earlier (2 Chr. 22). The region was probably restored under JEROBOAM II (2 Ki. 14:23–28), but the two and one-half tribes were taken captive by TIGLATH-PILESER III (744–727) and were transplanted into parts of his kingdom (1 Chr. 5:26).

Later, the Ammonites moved into the Gadite territory (Jer. 49:1).

Gad is included in the division of the land mentioned in the RESTORATION (Ezek. 48:27) and also as the name of one of the gates of the city (48:34). Among the 144,000 Israelites sealed are 12,000 Gadites (Rev. 7:5). C. P. WEBER

Gadara, Gadarene gad´uh-ruh, gad´uh-reen (Γάδαρα [not found in NT], Γαδαρηνός *G1123*). Gadara was a city of TRANSJORDAN, about 6 mi. SE of the southern end of the Sea of Galilee, and one of the cities of the DECAPOLIS. Its inhabitants, the Gadarenes, were predominantly non-Jewish.

I. The Gospels. The only NT reference to the Gadarenes is the account of the healing of two demoniacs and the drowning of the swine in the Sea of Galilee (Matt. 8:28). The parallel passages, which mention only one demoniac, refer to the same episode, but they use the term "Gerasenes" (Mk. 5:1; Lk. 8:26; cf. v. 37). In all of these references there are textual variants, reflecting some difficulty in the identification of the place (see D. L. Bock, *Luke 1:1—9:50*, BECNT [1994], 782–84). This problem of harmonization is resolved if one remembers that each reference is to the country (*hē chōra*) of the Gadarenes-Gerasenes. The

Gadara, one of the Decapolis cities, was a few miles SE of the Sea of Galilee. (The lake is visible on the top right.)

geographical and historical sources suggest that the area designations probably overlapped; Gadara was the chief city of the immediate area, whereas Gerasa may have referred to a wider area, including the lesser city of Gadara. Matthew gives a specific reference to the Gadarenes, Mark and Luke a more general reference to Gerasenes. The third reading, "Gergesenes," although it has poor MS evidence and obviously is a late, confused effort to harmonize the synoptic texts, yet gives the best location for the incident near the village of Gergesa. Although topographical maps show hills all along the SE shore of the Sea of Galilee, geographers who visited the area say the only place to locate the drowning swine incident is a strip of steep coastline near Gergesa, the present-day Kersa (see GERASENE).

II. History. JOSEPHUS gives additional information regarding Gadara. In the HASMONEAN wars, Alexander Jannaeus took the city after a ten-month siege and demolished it (*Ant.* 12.3.3; *War* 1.4.2). After the Roman conquest it was rebuilt by POMPEY in 63 B.C. (*War* 1.7.7) and made a "free" city. Gabinius made it the capital of one of the five districts of occupied Palestine. HEROD the Great received it as a gift from AUGUSTUS in 30 B.C. (*Ant.* 15.7.3; *War* 1.20.3). Herod ruled it harshly and was sustained in his policy by the emperor (*Ant.* 15.10.3). At Herod's death it was annexed to SYRIA (*Ant.* 17.11.4; *War* 2.18.1). During the rebellion of A.D. 68–70 it fell quickly to VESPASIAN, who burned it and plundered the countryside (*War* 3.7.1). Rebuilt again, it flourished, as coins from the city show, until the year 240. It had a Christian church from the 2nd cent. and was the seat of a bishop from 325 until the Moslem conquest.

III. Archaeology. Gadara is identified today as Muqeis, or Umm Qeis, overlooking the S valley of the YARMUK River. The ruins are extensive, including remnants of two amphitheaters, a basilica, a temple, colonnades, large residences, and an aqueduct, all showing the size, beauty, and importance of the city. Another Gadara is mentioned by Josephus as "the capital of Perea" (*War* 4.7.3), but he may have confused it with Gerasa. (See W. A. Thomson, *The Land and the Book* [1882], 333–38, 353–59; M. F. Unger, *Archaeology and the New Testament* [1962], 139–41;

U. Wagner-Lux and K. J. H. Vriezen, "Gadarenes," in *ABD*, 2:866–67.) J. C. DEYOUNG

Gaddah. See HAZAR GADDAH.

Gaddi gad´i (גַּדִּי H1534, possibly "my [good] fortune" or short form of GADDIEL [see also GADI]; Γαδδι). **(1)** Son of Susi, a leader of the tribe of MANASSEH, and one of the twelve spies whom MOSES sent from the wilderness of PARAN to spy out the land of Canaan (Num. 13:11).

(2) The surname (possibly a nickname) of John, son of MATTATHIAS and eldest brother of Judas MACCABEE (1 Macc. 2:2; KJV, "Caddis"). With his brothers, John Gaddi took part in the Jewish struggle for independence in the 2nd cent. B.C.; he was killed on a mission to the NABATEANS (9:35–42).
D. H. MADVIG

Gaddiel gad´ee-uhl (גַּדִּיאֵל H1535, possibly "my fortune is God"). Son of Sodi, a leader of the tribe of ZEBULUN, and one of the twelve spies whom MOSES sent from the wilderness of PARAN to spy out the land of Canaan (Num. 13:10).

Gader. See BETH GADER.

gadfly. This English term is used by the NIV and other versions to render Hebrew *qereṣ* H7976, which occurs only once in a metaphorical passage alluding to NEBUCHADNEZZAR (Jer. 46:20; KJV, "destruction"; others, "mosquito"). Gadflies include both botflies (*Oestridae*) and horseflies (*Tabanidae*). They approach their victims, such as livestock, with a loud hum and inflict painful bites. Nebuchadnezzar came from the N upon Egypt in 568–567 B.C. and brought disaster on the nation.
K. L. BARKER

Gadi gay´di (גַּדִי H1533, possibly "my [good] fortune" or short form of GADDIEL; see also GADDI). The father of MENAHEM, king of Israel (2 Ki. 15:14, 17). It should be noted that in extrabiblical sources the name Gaddiyahu ("my fortune is Yahweh") is once found abbreviated to Gad(d)i because the scribe ran out of writing space (see N. Avigad, *Hebrew Bullae from the Time of Jeremiah: Remnants of a Burnt Archive* [1986], 39–41).

Gadite gad′it. See GAD, TRIBE OF.

Gaham gay′ham (גַּחַם H1626, possibly "bright flame"). Son of NAHOR (brother of ABRAHAM) by his concubine REUMAH (Gen. 22:24).

Gahar gay′hahr (גַּחַר H1627, derivation uncertain). The ancestor of some temple servants (NETHINIM) who returned with ZERUBBABEL from exile in BABYLON (Ezra 2:47; Neh. 7:49; called "Geddur" in 1 Esd. 5:30; for possible etymologies of the name, see R. Zadok in *JQR* 71 [1980]: 112).

Gai gi (גַּיְא H1628, "valley"). According to some, Gai was the name of a place mentioned together with EKRON as the limit to which the Israelites chased the PHILISTINES after the victory of DAVID over GOLIATH (1 Sam. 17:52 ASV; KJV, "the valley"). Although some MSS of the SEPTUAGINT read *Gai*, the preferred reading is *Geth*, on the basis of which the NIV and other modern versions emend the Hebrew text to read *gat* H1781 (see GATH).

D. H. MADVIG

gain. This English term, as a noun or as a verb, is used variously in Bible translations to render a number of words and expressions, such as Hebrew *beṣaʿ* H1299, "[unjust] profit" (e.g., 1 Sam. 8:3), and *qānâ* H7864, "to acquire, buy" (e.g., Prov. 15:32), Greek *porismos* G4516, "[means of] gain" (e.g., 1 Tim. 6:5–6), and *kerdainō* G3045, "to acquire" (e.g., Matt. 25:16–17), and so on. Of special significance in the OT is Qoheleth's use of the noun *yitrôn* H3862, "advantage, benefit"; for example, "What does man gain [*lit.*, what is the advantage to man] from all his labor / at which he toils under the sun?" (Eccl. 1:3). In the NT, Jesus warns that it is no real profit for us to gain the whole world if we forfeit our soul (Matt. 16:26 and parallels). The apostle PAUL asserted, "For to me, to live is Christ and to die is gain [*kerdos* G3046]" (Phil. 1:21); he considered all his achievements "loss" and "rubbish" so that he might gain Christ (3:8).

Gaius gay′yuhs (Γάϊος G1127, from Lat. *Gaius* [for *Gavius*, from *gaudeo*, "rejoice"], a very common name often abbreviated *C.* for *Caius*). **(1)** A Macedonian Christian; as a travel companion of PAUL, he and ARISTARCHUS were seized by the mob during the Ephesian riot (Acts 19:29).

(2) A Christian from DERBE, listed among those waiting for Paul at TROAS (Acts 20:4; Codex D has "from Doberius" [a town in MACEDONIA], prob. to identify him with the Macedonian Gaius in 19:29). The men mentioned here were apparently the delegates assigned by the churches to go with Paul to Jerusalem with the collection (see CONTRIBUTION).

(3) A Christian in CORINTH; one of two men whom Paul names as having been baptized by him, contrary to his usual practice (1 Cor. 1:14, 17). He is doubtless the same as the Gaius who provided hospitality for Paul when he wrote ROMANS from Corinth on the third journey (Rom. 16:23). That he was host also to "the whole church" implies that the Corinthian church met in his spacious home. Tradition has made him the bishop of THESSALONICA, and some would identify him with Titius Justus (Acts 18:7; see E. J. Goodspeed in *JBL* 69 [1950]: 382–83).

(4) The addressee of John's third epistle (3 Jn. 1). The apostle had a deep affection for him, commended him for his hospitality, and desired his continued support for missionaries (vv. 2–8).

(5) Gaius Julius Caesar Germanicus, Roman emperor. See CALIGULA.

D. E. HIEBERT

Galaad gal′ay-uhd. KJV Apoc. form of GILEAD (Jdt. 1:8 et al.).

Galal gay′lal (גָּלָל H1674, possibly "tortoise"). **(1)** One of the Levites who resettled in JERUSALEM after the EXILE (1 Chr. 9:15). He is not identified in any other way.

(2) Son of JEDUTHUN and grandfather of OBADIAH (Abda); the latter is listed among the Levites who resettled in Jerusalem after the exile (1 Chr. 9:16; Neh. 11:17). Since Jeduthun was a prominent temple musician (1 Chr. 16:42 et al.), it is likely that both this Galal and #1 above, as well as the other Levites mentioned in the passage, had the same profession.

Galatia guh-lay′shuh (Γαλατία G1130). The word bears two senses in ancient history and geography: (a) a general geographical area and (b) a Roman

PROVINCE. In its first and ethnic meaning, it signifies the kingdom of Galatia in the northern part of the inner plateau of ASIA MINOR, made up of parts of a territory formerly known as CAPPADOCIA and PHRYGIA (see S. Mitchell, *Anatolia: Land, Men, and Gods in Asia Minor*, 2 vols. [1993], esp. ch. 2). The name derives from the fact that this area was occupied by GAULS, a Celtic people. In one of the final movements of the 2,000-year-old folk-wanderings of the Indo-European tribes, some Celts crossed the Hellespont at the unwise invitation of Nicomedes I, king of BITHYNIA (who was seeking allies in a civil war), and penetrated the Asia Minor peninsula in 278 B.C. After a typical period of raiding and plundering, the nomad invaders were finally pinned and contained in a tract of high territory extending from the Sangarius to a line E of the Halys. This was the achievement of ATTALUS I of PERGAMUM in 230 B.C. From this tribal area the Celts continued their petty harassment of their neighbors, and after the battle of Magnesia in 190 B.C., which marked the beginning of Roman interest and dominance in Asia Minor, the republic inherited the Gallic problem.

ROME sent Manlius Vulso to subdue the tribesmen, and he did so with effectiveness in a campaign of 188 B.C. With typical Roman diplomatic skill, the republic was able to use the Galatians as a check on the dynamic kingdom of Pergamum, and also to retain their allegiance when Mithridates of PONTUS launched his strong attacks on Rome in Asia Minor. Galatia, as a tribal region, was organized on a Celtic pattern, and three ethnic groups—Tolistobogii, Tectusages, and Trocmi—occupied separate areas with distinct capitals (Pessinus, Ancyra, and Tavium respectively). Each tribe was divided into four septs or wards, each under a TETRARCH. The combined council of the three tribes had provision for periodic meetings and retained collective jurisdicition in cases of murder. So coherent was their community that its Celtic character survived into the empire, and JEROME is evidence for their retention of their Gallic speech into the 5th century. Part of POMPEY's organization of Asia in 63 B.C. appears to have been the establishment of a paramount ruler in Galatia. Deiotarus, tetrarch of the Tolistobogii of W Galatia, was of considerable help to Pompey in the third Mithridatic War. He was rewarded by Pompey in 64 B.C. with part of neighboring Pontus, and twelve or thirteen years later received from the senate of Rome the district of Lesser Armenia and the kingship over the area of his control, together with the resultant royal title.

Cities visited by the apostle Paul in Galatia.

The Galatian king naturally followed Pompey in the civil war between the latter and Julius CAESAR, and was deprived of his territorial acquisitions by Caesar on his victory. In 45 B.C. he was accused before Caesar of various acts of insubordination, and was defended by the great orator Cicero, whose speech for the accused survives. Deiotarus had prudently befriended Cicero's son, during the orator's governorship of CILICIA. After Caesar's assassination in the following year, Deiotarus regained control of his lost territory and bought recognition from Antony. He supported Brutus and Cassius in the renewed civil war, again a wrong choice, but one hardly to be avoided when the "tyrannicides" lay across his communications with Rome. By a timely desertion to Antony at PHILIPPI, Deiotarus retained his kingdom, and in 42 B.C., after murdering a rival tetrarch, he acquired all of Galatia and associated regions. These details of petty history are important because they mark the course of the evolution of the ethnic region of Galatia into the multiracial Roman province, and the freedom with which Rome habitually varied frontier lines to suit administrative expediency.

Deiotarus died in 40 B.C. and was succeeded by his secretary, Amyntas, who had commanded the Galatian auxiliaries of Brutus and Cassius at Philippi and had shared in, or prompted, the desertion of the Galatian contingent to Antony. The following year Antony rewarded Amyntas with a Galatian kingdom that ultimately included parts of Lycia, Pamphylia, and Pisidia. Amyntas accompanied Antony to Actium when Antony and Octavian clashed in the final phase of the civil strife that saw the end of the Roman republic, and history repeated itself. A Galatian prince was, by force of geographical and political circumstances, on the wrong side. Again, a timely desertion, this time before the actual armed clash of Actium's decisive naval battle, won the favor of the victor. Octavian, soon to emerge from the long strife as the emperor Augustus, confirmed Amyntas in all his royal possessions.

Amyntas died in a campaign against unruly highlanders on the mountainous southern marches of his realm. It was in 25 B.C. that Augustus, engaged in the long task of establishing the Roman peace and organizing its frontiers, seized the opportunity to convert Amyntas's realm—augmented by parts of Phrygia, Lycaonia, Pisidia, and possibly Pamphylia—into a province called Galatia. The

The Roman region of Galatia near Pisidian Antioch. (View to the NW.)

precedent of including slices of contiguous territory under Galatian control had been set by Pompey. Augustus's principate merely adapted, adopted, and applied precedents that had been established at least since the days of the great Pompey. Portions of Paphlagonia and Pontus were afterward incorporated into the province, which was normally governed by a praetorian legate until A.D. 72. In this year Cappadocia and Lesser Armenia were included in the Galatian provincial boundaries, and the augmented province was placed under consular legate. A later reorganization saw Galatia again reduced, and under Diocletian the province had shrunk almost to the old ethnic area of the original Galatian tribal lands. The chief cities in the 1st century were Ancyra and Antioch of Pisidia. Within the province of Galatia were also the other towns visited by Paul in his fruitful first journey into Asia Minor—Iconium, Lystra, and Derbe, all of which included large populations of Romans and other Italian expatriates, Greeks, and Jews.

The precise reference of the name Galatia is of some importance in NT studies and involves a modern controversy that cannot be said to be completely resolved. It is beyond question from the full account given in Acts 13–14 that Paul visited urban centers in the southern part of the province and established Christian communities there. On the very slender evidence of Acts 16:6, some have contended that he also visited N Galatia, the habitat of the Celtic stratum of the population, and also established churches there. These scholars argue that it was to these churches, marked by their volatile, excitable, Celtic congregations, that Paul addressed the strictures of his letter "to the Galatians" (see, e.g., J. L. Martyn, *Galatians*, AB 33A [1997], 15–17; note also the reference to Memnon in BDAG, 187).

The opening clause of Acts 16:6, of which so much is demanded, runs in KJV: "Now when they had gone throughout Phrygia and the region of Galatia...." W. M. Ramsay (e.g., *The Church in the Roman Empire before A.D. 170*, 5th ed. [1897], ch. 4) cogently demonstrated that the clause described a single area and is to be rendered "the Phrygian Galatic region." Roman provinces were administratively cut into "regions." Rome's tampering with ancient boundary lines, noted above, was a feature

Paul would have traveled past Lake Egirdir in the Roman province of Galatia on his way to Pisidian Antioch. (View to the NW.)

of her government and organization in Asia Minor. Part of the one-time kingdom of Galatia was incorporated in the province of Galatia as it was constituted after the death of Amyntas. Another part belonged to the province of AsIA. It is reasonable then to interpret the opening clause of the verse under discussion as a reference to the section of Phrygian territory that was included in the new province of Galatia. This is an interpretation clearly supported by the rest of the verse concerning the constraint felt by the apostle not to extend at that time his activities into the neighboring province of Asia but rather move westward from Pisidia.

This is not the proper place to discuss Acts 18:23, where the same geographical expression is encountered in reverse. R. J. Knowling has a lucid and sufficient comment upon it (see *EGT*, 2:341, where he quotes periodical literature relevant to the controversy; A. Souter has a brief clear statement in *HDB*, 277; broader discussion in C. J. Hemer, *The Book of Acts in the Setting of Hellenistic History* [1989], chs. 6–7; Mitchell, *Anatolia*, ch. 15). At any time epigraphy, in a rich archaeological field, may provide evidence that will remove all perplexity. In the meantime, while the brevity of Luke's account of Paul's activity over considerable tracts of his ministry, and even his occasional complete silence, may be granted, it seems clear that the Galatian churches known to the NT were those founded in the more sophisticated and multiracial parts of the province. Such foundations were certainly consonant with Paul's obvious Gentile strategy. Christian communities may have been established in the northern Celtic reaches of the province at a comparatively early date, but if so their foundation must have been due to unrecorded diffusion from the more civilized S, and not to the personal penetration of the ethnic area by the apostle.

Many scholars therefore agree that the Galatians addressed in Paul's famous letter were the southern communities of his own planting, and it would follow that the "churches of Galatia," of which Paul makes mention to the Corinthians (1 Cor. 16:1), were the same group. Did Paul ever use the term Galatia in other than its Roman sense? He was a self-conscious Roman citizen and used language from that point of view, not in a parochial sense. He may even be observed rejecting an available alternative term and turning a Latin word into Greek (cf. ILLYRICUM, Rom. 15:19). The Galatians to his mind could not be the inhabitants of an ethnic area. They were the inhabitants of a province, and in his context the whole body of Christians from that area, regardless of race. It is on historical grounds rather than linguistic, and on the fact that there is no clear evidence either of a visit to

N Galatia, or a facet of Pauline policy which would make such a visit likely, that it may be assumed with some confidence that the Galatians addressed were the Christian communities of Pisidian Antioch, Iconium, Lystra, and Derbe.

It remains to mention the listing of Galatians among those to whom the first general epistle of PETER is addressed. The bearer of the letter obviously moved in a southward bending curve from E to W through the northern half of Asia Minor, the long deep tract of territory N of the Taurus Range. Facilities for travel were abundant, and the fact that church communities in Pontus, Galatia, Cappadocia, Asia, and Bithynia were addressed reveals the active Christian life apparent in the peninsula. Nothing, however, can be deduced about the pattern of Galatian Christianity, for however deeply the faith may have penetrated northern ethnic Galatia, an epistle couched in terms so general—a circular, in fact—cannot be supposed to have omitted the strong Christian communities in the multiracial southern province. E. M. BLAIKLOCK

Galatians, Epistle to the guh-lay'shuhnz. A letter addressed by the apostle PAUL to the Christian churches in GALATIA.

    I. Introduction
   II. The author
  III. The historical background
  IV. The Judaizers
   V. Destination and readers
  VI. Date and place of writing
 VII. Theme and purpose
VIII. Contents and outline
  IX. Characteristics and special features

I. Introduction. The epistle to the Galatians is one of Paul's greatest and most important letters. It contains in substance what the apostle taught: the gospel he had received by divine REVELATION (Gal. 1:12). Many have characterized the letter as a "short Romans"; indeed, the latter can in some ways be regarded as an expansion of Galatians. A comparison of the two epistles reveals that they are similar in theme and contents. Both teach boldly the Pauline doctrine of JUSTIFICATION by faith and the ethical imperatives that are the fruit of the gospel of love.

Influential Christians have esteemed Galatians highly. It has been the source of strength and guidance for many. For the reformers of the 16th cent., it was Galatians, more than any other single book, that became the manifesto of freedom and revival of biblical truth. The epistle was a favorite of Martin Luther. In it he found strength for his own faith and life and an arsenal of weapons for his reforming work. He said of the letter: "The Epistle to the Galatians is *my own little epistle*. I have betrothed myself to it; it is my Katie von Bora" (his wife). Luther lectured on Galatians extensively, and his *Lectures on Galatians* [1535] did much to expound the dominant theme of the Reformation, the doctrine of justification by *faith alone*, to the common people.

William M. Ramsay, the famous English scholar, described Galatians in this manner: "It is a unique and marvelous letter, which embraces in its six short chapters such a variety of vehement and intense emotion as could probably not be paralleled in any other work" (*A Historical Commentary on St. Paul's Epistle to the Galatians* [1900], 474). F. Farrar had this estimate of the letter: "It was the manifesto of emancipation.... The words scrawled on those few sheets of papyrus ... were to wake echoes which should 'roll from soul to soul, and live for ever and for ever'" (*The Life and Works of St. Paul*, 2 vols. [1880], 2:139). Another scholar has said that this letter is "the pebble from the brook with which the Reformers smote the papal giant of the Middle Ages" and that it was the cornerstone and battle cry of the Protestant Reformation. Merrill C. Tenney writes, "Few books have had a more profound influence on the history of mankind than has this small tract, for such it should be called. Christianity might have been just one more Jewish sect, and the thought of the Western world might have been entirely pagan had it never been written. Galatians embodies the germinal teaching on Christian freedom which separated Christianity from Judaism, and which launched it upon a career of missionary conquest. It was the cornerstone of the Protestant Reformation, because its teaching of salvation by grace alone became the dominant theme of the preaching of the Reformers" (*Galatians: The Charter of Christian Liberty* [1954], 15).

It is true that the letter, because of its extremely high doctrinal content, its apologetic nature, and

Excavations of the gate complex and Cardo (main street) at Antioch of Pisidia, which was incorporated into the Roman province of Galatia.

its lack of poetic beauty, has not always been well known or highly favored in some eras of the church's history, but since the Reformation it has come into its own and has been recognized particularly for what it meant to the early church. Its bold succinct definition of the beloved gospel *in terms of people* in the third chapter was like an ancient "shot heard around the world," and its note of freedom has struck the inner cords of millions of oppressed hearts. No words on human worth and equality and the universality of Christianity have ever matched these: "Now that faith has come, we are no longer under the supervision of the law. You are all sons of God through faith in Christ Jesus, for all of you who were baptized into Christ have clothed yourselves with Christ. There is neither Jew nor Greek, slave nor free, male nor female, for you are all one in Christ Jesus" (Gal. 3:25–28).

The church of the Protestant Reformation has always prized its doctrinal contents, especially its mighty statement and defense of justification by faith alone and its glorious defense of spiritual LIBERTY against any form of legalism. It has always been an impregnable citadel against any attack on the heart of the gospel: salvation by grace through faith. "All who rely on observing the law are under a curse, for it is written: 'Cursed is everyone who does not continue to do everything written in the Book of the Law.' Clearly no one is justified before God by the law, because, 'The righteous will live by faith.' The law is not based on faith; on the contrary, 'The man who does these things will live by them.' Christ redeemed us from the curse of the law by becoming a curse for us" (Gal. 3:10–13). In short, in Galatians we meet for the first time the great Pauline teaching of justification by faith which has helped people to understand the love of God and the person and work of Jesus Christ.

II. The author. Except for a few extremely radical scholars, no one has ever attacked the genuineness of Galatians, that is, that the letter came from the apostle Paul. Biblical scholars both ancient and modern attest to the Pauline authorship, and today most writers on Galatians no longer discuss the matter. The obvious reason is that from every possible consideration—ancient attestation, the literary style, the doctrinal content, the historical background, literary analysis—the letter leaves no room for doubt. Everyone admits that, if there ever lived a man like Paul who is known from other books he wrote, then Galatians must have come from him.

George G. Findlay once said: "No breath of suspicion as to the authorship, integrity, or apostolic authorship of the Epistle to the Galatians has reached us from ancient times" (*The Epistle to the Galatians*, Expositor's Bible 20 [1902]). The great scholar J. B. Lightfoot wrote: "Its every sentence so completely reflects the life and character of the Apostle of the Gentiles that its genuineness has not been seriously questioned" (*The Epistle of St. Paul to the Galatians*, 10th ed. [1898], 57). The external testimony of the ancient church leaders to the Pauline authorship of Galatians is unambiguous. One of the earliest church fathers, Clement of Rome, refers to the letter in his writings (see CLEMENT, EPISTLES OF). POLYCARP and Barnabas (see BARNABAS, EPISTLE OF) knew of Galatians, as did Hermas (see HERMAS, SHEPHERD OF) and IGNATIUS. Even MARCION, who excluded entire blocks of the NT writings from his early canon, placed the letter on his choice list and refers to it by title. JUSTIN MARTYR uses the third chapter of the letter to interpret the OT in the light of Paul's doctrine. Both the faithful and the heretics assume it was written by Paul. Early Gnostic interpreters used the epistle. IRENAEUS, TERTULLIAN, and CLEMENT OF ALEXANDRIA quote the letter and refer to Paul as the author.

The internal evidence is just as strong and certain as the witness from without. Most important, the author of the letter courageously calls himself "Paul, an apostle—sent not from men nor by man, but by Jesus Christ and God the Father" (Gal. 1:1). And in the body of the letter an almost unprecedented statement of Pauline authorship is found:

Pisidian Antioch, probably the site of one of the churches to which Paul sent Galatians, was a large city that needed to import its water supply via this aqueduct.

"I, Paul, tell you that if you let yourselves be circumcised, Christ will be of no value to you at all" (5:2). All of the personal and historical references in the first two chapters fit perfectly into the mission activity and life of Paul recorded in Acts. The letter exhibits the mind and fervor, logic and style of Paul in every detail. His doctrine of freedom in Christ (5:1) is like that emphasized in other of his writings. His contention against the law as a way to salvation and his love of faith and justification are unmistakably Pauline.

Parallels in his other letters are easily found, such as the reference to ABRAHAM's faith (Gal. 3:6; Rom. 4:3–5), his concern about the Jew-Gentile dilemma (Gal. 2:14; Eph. 2:4–19), his comments on CIRCUMCISION (Gal. 2:12; 5:2–6; 6:12–16; Rom. 4:9–12), his teaching regarding the HOLY SPIRIT (Gal. 5:16–25; Rom. 5:5), or his ethical teaching based upon the gospel of faith and freedom (Gal. 5:13–23; Col. 3:1–11), all of which match the teaching, and often the phraseology, of Paul exactly. A forger could not have imitated the mind and style of the Pauline teaching and parenesis, or placed himself into the Galatian situation with the feeling and understanding of the apostle. The burning church issues of the middle of the 1st cent., when Paul traversed the old Roman world, are those prominent in the epistle. How could another writer have placed antithesis between two great leaders of the time, PETER and Paul? Those few critics who have placed the writing of Galatians after the death of Paul did the same with such great letters as 1 and 2 Corinthians and even Romans—a view that cannot be considered worthy of solid NT scholarship.

III. The historical background. Paul's personal experience in his conversion is directly related to the question of the epistle: faith or works? Obviously this is why he writes with such fervor and conviction in absolute categories. Assuming that he was converted about A.D. 32 and wrote Galatians in 48 or 49, he had more than fifteen years of spiritual preparation for his missionary treks and epistolary efforts. He speaks of his conversion and defends his doctrine of salvation by faith before the crowd at the temple in JERUSALEM (Acts 22:1–21; cf. 9:1–19) and before King Agrippa in CAESAREA

(26:1–32; see HEROD VIII). In both addresses, before both friend and foe, his purpose is to offer his conversion as the greatest proof of his discipleship and the truth of his doctrine that sinners are saved by faith and not by works. In his first letter to TIMOTHY he described his conversion in glowing terms of grace as the epitome of the validity of the gospel he expounded and defended so magnificently in Galatians (1 Tim. 1:13–16). Indeed, his most effective use of his conversion experience in behalf of the gospel of grace is in Galatians itself (Gal. 1:11–17).

For Paul it all began on the DAMASCUS Road, and there was no road back. He penned Galatians to plead with all Christians to take only the Damascus Road—any other road leads to "another gospel." These events preceding the writing of Galatians help explain the letter itself and make it clear that only such a man could have written it. He is alone with his Lord in ARABIA, perhaps for several years, meditating, thinking, dialoging, preparing (Gal. 1:13–17). The urge to tell others move him to return to Damascus, probably around A.D. 34. It is enemy territory now—former friends make the fiercest enemies. A plot to take his life in Damascus causes him to seek shelter in Jerusalem (Acts 9:26–28; Gal. 1:18). It was a short visit of two weeks and his enemies tried to kill him once more, but his brethren whisked him away to Caesarea, where he boarded a ship and made his way to his home town of TARSUS (Acts 9:29–31; Gal. 1:21–24). All of this strife for the new convert against his former "friends" makes up the marrow of the Galatian letter and gives it the light and heat of newfound freedom in Christ. The years spent in Tarsus and other parts of CILICIA—on the fringe of the Galatian area into which he pushed on his first missionary journey—comprised more spiritual and mystical preparation for the road ahead.

Always the brethren know of Paul's whereabouts and of his fervor for Christ. It is probably true that he preached and defended this gospel in Cilicia between the years 36 and 43 because later the COUNCIL OF JERUSALEM sent communications to the Gentile brethren in ANTIOCH OF SYRIA and Cilicia (Acts 15:24). And in Acts 15:41 Luke writes that Paul was going to strengthen the churches of SYRIA and Cilicia. His first journey took him much farther W, so he must have witnessed in this area during his so-called "silent years." All the while the pressure between the (gospel of) "freedom" preachers and the "legal" preachers was building up until it reached the heated pitch of the Galatian polemic.

According to an accepted order of events, however, the first missionary journey intervened (Acts 13:1—14:28). The church in Antioch of Syria was growing tremendously. The Jerusalem brethren asked BARNABAS to journey to Antioch and to assist and lead the work. More workers were needed, and Barnabas went to Tarsus to get Paul and brought him to Antioch. Paul worked in Antioch with Barnabas (11:26) and other leaders in the city (13:1). There developed a famine in Jerusalem, and Paul and Barnabas were asked to take a collection of food and grain to the brethren in that city. After a few weeks in the Holy City, they made their way back to Antioch to resume the work there. John Mark went with them (12:24–25; see MARK, JOHN). The gospel of freedom should not be contained—it is for all people. Then we are told that the Holy Spirit himself instructed the young church: "Set apart for me Barnabas and Saul for the work to which I have called them." With fasting and prayer the church "placed their hands on them and sent them off" (13:2–3).

The first mission odyssey began—a portent of many more to come. John Mark joined the mission group. They left from SELEUCIA and sailed to CYPRUS. Astounding events in SALAMIS and PAPHOS! The power of the gospel of freedom

The temple of Augustus at Antioch of Pisidia. Paul wrote Galatians to believers who lived under Roman rule.

was felt by Roman officials and magicians. Luke describes one of the great gospel events of ancient times: "When the proconsul saw what had happened, he believed, for he was amazed at the teaching about the Lord" (Acts 13:1–13). They left the island and headed for the mainland of Asia Minor. PERGA in PAMPHYLIA, ANTIOCH OF PISIDIA—the strategy was to visit the cities and towns, the heavily populated areas. Christ has freed all people, and all must hear the good news (13:38–39). They preached the KERYGMA: Jesus is the MESSIAH, fulfiller of the OT. Many believed in the risen Lord. John Mark left the expedition at Pamphylia and returned home—perhaps the work was too difficult and free for the young Jerusalemite. Preaching in the synagogues of Antioch gave rise to opposition because of Jewish law. The extent of the inner division was beginning to be felt outwardly: the Jews "were filled with jealousy" and "stirred up persecution against Paul and Barnabas" (13:45, 50).

ICONIUM up in the hill country was next, and again the Jews stirred up opposition. Then came LYSTRA, where the apostle was stoned. Although DERBE was a receptive city, the ministry of Paul and Barnabas in the province of Galatia was in general characterized by opposition (Acts 14:1–22). More opposition surfaced when false teachers came into the Galatian churches and preached circumcision (Gal. 5:6–12). They must be counteracted, for it takes only a little leaven to spoil the whole group (5:9). "You, my brothers, were called to be free" (5:13). This was the real issue, which carried over into the Apostolic Council (Acts 15; see COUNCIL OF JERUSALEM). Against this foil Galatians was written and finds its meaning.

IV. The Judaizers. Almost without exception, biblical interpreters believe that the letter was written primarily to counteract the activities of the JUDAIZERS in Galatia. The term is derived from Greek *ioudaizō* G2678, "to live like a Jew." It is a religious designation rather than a national description. Bible students have called these opponents of the early Christian missionaries Judaizers because of their fundamental belief that Gentiles should live like Jews; that is, follow the Mosaic Law and Jewish customs and traditions after they became Christians. The implications of their insistence upon Jewish ceremonial law for the young Christian church, both theologically and socially, were volatile and divisive indeed.

The situation was brought about, on the one hand, by the teaching of Jesus himself on the law, the doctrine of grace and of God's love for all; and, on the other, by the mixture of Jews and Gentiles in the early Christian churches. It was one thing to preach grace to Jews only (and it may be assumed that Jewish Christians may have misunderstood the requirements of the kingdom even as they worshiped Christ); it was quite another task to preach the gospel of Christ and freedom to Jews and Gentiles in the same congregation, especially if it were still in the Jewish synagogue. After all, the Jewish person had been circumcised, he knew the glory of Israel, he knew the pride of Judaism with its one God and high morality; but the poor Gentile, what did he have? The Jew could easily summarize it for him: false gods, fornication, immorality, drunkenness, etc.

Surely (they thought), it was not enough just to give up these practices and simply believe—that was really cheap grace—but if one really wanted to be a Christian, like Jesus himself, he should really be a Jew first and then both a Jew and a Christian. No doubt many early Gentile Christians attempted to imitate their Jewish fellow believers, or at least tried not to offend them, but when it came to CIRCUMCISION, especially since Paul and Barnabas said it was not necessary, the reluctance for a Gentile to accede became strong indeed. The tension was highlighted by the fact that the first churches in Palestine were Jewish and by Paul's method of going to the Jewish synagogues as their first contact for preaching the gospel in a new area (cf. Rom. 1:16, "first for the Jew, then for the Gentile"). In these synagogues were also "devout converts to Judaism" (Acts 13:43) as well as God-fearers, that is, Gentiles who were "proselytes of the gate" and not fully converted to Judaism or involved in the synagogue, but who liked its high moral character and monotheism. These "fringe people" were made to order for the new church. While emphasizing that all the OT was preparatory to the Messiah and the new kingdom (cf. 13:26–41), Paul made it plain that the gospel was no addendum to Judaism, no mere supplement to the law, but the end and fulfillment of the law and, in some respects, the antithesis to it. The new kingdom would go beyond the boundaries of Israel, not just nationally but also theologically and socially. Even though Jesus the Messiah came from David's line, now "everyone that believes is freed from everything from which you could not be freed by the law of Moses" (13:39 RSV).

The doors of the new church were thrown open to everyone—to Jews, Jewish proselytes, Gentiles, publicans, sinners—and everyone had direct access to God through Christ by faith. Paul was saying out loud what for so long had been in the scrolls and parchments of the OT, in PENTECOST, in Jesus' ministry, in the calling of publicans as apostles; and he was practicing it in a new social situation. As a result large numbers of people of all kinds, Gentiles and slaves, came into the church without circumcision, not through the synagogue, not by doing all the laws and customs of the OT, but directly. These people came in "Just as I am, without one plea"; they took the apostles at their word. But this was too much for Jews who had grown up in JUDAISM, and their true thoughts and attitudes began to come to the surface. No one wanted to deny a Gentile the privileges of membership, but surely there was more to it than just believing. Was not the OT from Moses by God's will? Were all God's covenants, rites, symbols, his relationship to the commonwealth of Israel, and everything else to be discarded just because Christ came? Were the ancient people of God, the children of Abraham, simply to disappear from history?

It is not surprising, then, that strong-minded Jewish people became vigorous Judaizers. They came from within the new church. It appears from their activities in Acts that they were not from the congregations or synagogues in the mission churches, but men from other churches who followed Paul about and tried to undo his work. While they were primarily of Jewish origin, it is not impossible that there may have been some misguided Gentile PROSELYTES among them who had gone through the demands of Judaism and were circumcised when they joined the Christian church and wanted all other Gentiles to do the same. It was easy for them to operate in the church, which was in the stage of transition from a Jewish nationalistic group to one that was Gentile.

The Judaizers may have reasoned that they did not come to destroy Paul's work or the gospel, but to complete it (Gal. 3:3). The Messiah's coming, in their view, only culminated and sanctified the OT. The Sabbath and circumcision and all the other ordinances were by no means obliterated. They were covenants between God and his people forever. Christ never freed men from the law; he confirmed it. Faith alone, without circumcision, without the law, would leave Christianity incomplete. In fact, Paul and his coworkers were false apostles and were not telling the full truth: the other apostles had never spoken against the law, so Paul was the only libertine. Would not his teaching result in moral tragedy, in every dangerous and immoral act? Would faith not lead to license instead of liberty? Their attack upon Paul, therefore, may be considered threefold: (1) they challenged his apostolic authority; (2) they claimed that Paul's message was an incomplete gospel; (3) they argued that this message would lead to immorality (cf. Rom. 3:1–5; 6:1).

In Galatians Paul answers this threefold attack. He knew that they were striking at the very heart of the gospel. They wanted to be "Old Testament Christians," true Israelites who believed in the coming Messiah and kept all the law besides. It is possible that a Judaizer might do all the things demanded by the law, including circumcision, and that as long as he did not think he was thereby especially pleasing God by these acts it would do no harm. But what about demanding all this of a Gentile before he could be considered a good Christian? This was the burning issue. It was fought by Judaizers supposedly on theological or scriptural grounds. In their view, apparently, faith was not enough to make certain of God's grace and salvation. Besides accepting Jesus Christ as the Messiah, a new convert also should join the Jewish nation and observe its Mosaic laws and customs, generally epitomized in the refusal to eat with Gentiles (Gal. 2:11–14; 4:10). The Christian therefore must be saved by faith *and* works, faith *and* Judaism, grace *and* law on an equal basis.

In the Jerusalem church the Judaizing tendency had not become an issue because the Christians there were all of Jewish origin and had been circumcised before coming to faith in Christ. Perhaps they even continued in their old ways. In Antioch and in Asia Minor, however, the situation was different. In the mission fields the Gentiles often outnumbered the Jews. In their teaching and preaching, Barnabas and Paul had not insisted upon circumcision since faith made a person a member of the kingdom (Gal. 3:26). To do anything else would have destroyed God's universal grace and supplanted faith with works. It would have meant that Jewish people who became Christians had somewhat of a head start over all Gentiles and that the Gentiles had a built-in handicap before God.

The entire letter to the Galatians is actually constructed around this argument. Paul says the Christian does not have the choice of a "both-and," but it is an "either-or"—the choice lies only between grace or law, faith or works, Moses or Christ (Gal. 5:2–6). For Paul the mixing of a tiny requirement of human obedience to any law shakes the foundation of salvation by grace alone. GRACE excludes all works, not just highly publicized public deeds, but the most insignificant private deed if motivated for salvation by works. Any and all works in the doctrine of salvation were of the devil and destroyed the sinner's only hope and comfort for certainty in salvation. The heart of Christianity for Paul is God's free grace in Christ Jesus, and anything else is a sword thrust into the heart of Christianity. This is why Paul's thermometer rose so high against these false teachers: not only because their doctrine was a perversion of the gospel, but because it sounded so reasonable and natural to Jewish Christians, who in turn wished to impose these impossible demands upon Gentile Christians.

The Judaizing trap is an ancient snare. Many Christians in the past have fallen into it and no doubt many more will. It is difficult to find the proper place and distinction between law and gospel. Faith alone does not mean "no works" (cf. Gal. 5:13–26), but it does mean that only the gospel saves—not laws, customs, or ceremonies. Paul ends Galatians with a comment on this key point. Both Jew and Gentile have joined Christ and the one new church, on an equal basis: "Neither circumcision nor uncircumcision means anything; what counts is a new creation. Peace and mercy to all who follow this rule, even to the Israel of God" (6:15–16). The name Israel had to be redefined for both parties. Messiah had come.

V. Destination and readers. The epistle opens with the words, "To the churches in Galatia" (Gal. 1:2). It is the only Pauline epistle specifically directed toward a group of churches (unless one regards EPHESIANS as a circular letter). Who were the "Galatians"? Where were these churches located? Answers to these questions have caused a great deal of discussion in the past half century and have influenced scholars in determining the date and the readers of the letter.

The name GALATIA was used for centuries to designate the territory in the N and central part of ASIA MINOR to which a large number of Gauls migrated (or invaded) from Europe about 275 B.C. (compare Lat. *Gallia*, Gaul). By 230 B.C. the territory assumed rather fixed boundaries, and these Gauls, or Galatians, lived in this small kingdom, had their own government, and developed their own customs. In 25 B.C. the territory was taken over by the ROMAN EMPIRE and made a Roman PROVINCE. King Amyntas (36–25 B.C.) was the last ruler of this old Galatian territory, but before his death he added some parts of PHRYGIA, PISIDIA, LYCAONIA, and even Isauria (S of LYSTRA) to his small kingdom. The Romans added several other adjacent territories to old Galatia, combined that area with the territory to the S, and named the whole entity *Galatia*. It is possible, then, that in Paul's day there were two "Galatias," the first being the old Galatia in the northern part of Asia Minor and the second being the reorganized province. Although Bible students speak of N Galatia and S Galatia, one should not be misled by the terms as if there was a Galatia in the N and another Galatia in the S: the new province included both the old Galatia and the southern territory.

The important question for the letter to the Galatians is: In what way did Paul and Luke use the term? Was Paul referring to the old territory of Galatia proper or was he using the term in the Roman provincial sense? Or to put the question in a more specific manner, was the apostle referring to unnamed churches in the old territory of Galatia in the N, or was he referring to the churches of such towns as Derbe, Lystra, and Iconium, which he founded on his first missionary journey? The answer to this question is significant, as it relates to the people to whom the letter was addressed, the date, and the historical setting. If the epistle was not written until Paul visited the northern Galatian territory on his second or third journey, and thus long after the Apostolic Council, the epistle would have been composed at a relatively late date and addressed to unknown readers. If, on the other hand, the term Galatia refers to the cities he visited on the first missionary journey, it is possible to date the epistle early, even considering it the earliest letter the apostle wrote.

The first view has been called the North Galatian Theory. It was ably defended by Lightfoot in his great commentary on Galatians, arguing that Paul's initial visit to Galatia took place during the second journey when he traveled through the region of Phrygia and Galatia (Acts 16:6). This view holds that Paul visited such towns as Pessinus, Ancyra, and Tavium, and finally reached Troas after a long journey. On his third journey, he made a similar tour (18:23).

Today, however, many scholars give greater weight to the South Galatian Theory. The distinguished British archaeologist and historian William M. Ramsay championed this view, believing that "the churches in Galatia" were those founded on the first missionary journey and that they were later revisited on other journeys (Acts 16:1–6; 18:23). According to him and his followers, moreover, Galatians was written to these churches prior to the Apostolic Council. Several considerations undergird the hypothesis: (1) It has been shown that Paul in his writings generally uses provincial names of Roman districts or provinces, never the territorial identification (Achaia, Macedonia, Illyricum, Dalmatia). (2) If Paul wrote the letter after the Apostolic Council, it seems strange that he makes no appeal to the significant decisions at that meeting, an authority he could easily have used in his defense of the gospel against the Judaizers. The fact that the council is not mentioned probably means it had not taken place; and if so, the only churches Paul had founded in Galatia were those in the S during his first journey. (3) Paul's activities up to the time of writing, as we have seen, can be more easily explained if the letter was written early. One can also explain Paul's altercation with Peter (Gal. 2:11–14) with greater ease if this took place before the first church council. (4) Barnabas is mentioned in the letter as a person well known to the readers, but he was with Paul only on the first missionary journey as far as is know. (5) In 1 Cor. 16:1, where Paul speaks of having instructed the churches of Galatia regarding the collection, he evidently has in mind the southern section, because a representative from Derbe was part of the delegation (Acts 20:4). (6) There is no clear evidence that Paul founded churches in N Galatia—much less that Judaizers visited this area.

For these and others reasons most interpreters (at least among English-speaking scholars) have accepted the South Galatian Theory. It seems probable that after the first missionary journey, when Paul returned to Antioch of Syria, he was informed of the trouble the Judaizers were causing in the churches he had recently founded. He immediately sat down and wrote to these churches the firm and passionate letter which we know as Galatians. (One should note, however, that although an early date for Galatians requires a southern destination, the reverse is not the case. A southern destination makes possible, but does not necessitate, an early date. As noted below, some scholars believe that the letter was addressed to the churches founded during the first journey, but that it was written after the Apostolic Council, probably during the third journey. Cf. M. Silva, *Interpreting Galatians: Explorations in Exegetical Method*, 2nd ed. [2001], ch. 7.)

Some hold that Paul was opposing two sets of opponents in the letter; not only a Jewish or Judaizing tendency but also a Gnostic element. They say certain antignostic statements (cf. Gal. 4:8–11; 5:19–21) quite clearly suggest such a setting (see W. Marxsen, *Introduction to the New Testament* [1970], 50–54). There is clear evidence of Jewish-Gnostic tendencies in the early church, so it may well be true that both elements, and perhaps even a combination of the two, were represented in the Christian communities of Galatia. Most scholars, however, believe that a Judaizing presence sufficiently accounts for the data.

VI. Date and place of writing. The identification of the recipients of this letter has a bearing on the date and place of writing. Those who advocate the North Galatian Hypothesis have usually assigned the letter to the period of Paul's stay in EPHESUS during the third missionary journey (perhaps a few months before Romans was written from CORINTH). Others who hold this theory believe that it may have been written during the second missionary journey about A.D. 52. Scholars who support the South Galatian Theory, on the other hand, generally place the writing of the letter just before the Apostolic Council and place it in Antioch of Syria, though some of them believe it was written during the second or third missionary journeys and choose Corinth or Ephesus as the place of writing. All things considered, it seems best to date Galatians at about A.D. 48 just prior to the Apostolic Council.

According to this view, Paul wrote the letter on the eve of the council in order to take care of the emergency in Galatia. It is possible that Paul did not know such a council would be held, nor would he know its outcome. Peter's speech in Acts 15:7–11 may also take into consideration the views stated in Galatians. It is granted that not all of the evidence demands the writing of the letter before the Apostolic Council, and some of the problems in chronology are difficult. However, the argument that Gal. 2:1–10 refers to the Apostolic Council is not overwhelming, and if Paul was detailing his visits to Jerusalem, it seems unlikely that he would have excluded specific mention of that meeting.

VII. Theme and purpose. The theme of Galatians is freedom from the law as the way to salvation. In this it partakes of the objective of the great letter to the Romans. Another way of asking the major question of the letter is: What is the place of the law in Christian theology? Is Christian salvation a question of faith *and* works, or faith *without* works? No one denied that the law was given by God and that it was divine. But did the new Pauline emphasis on grace and faith wipe out the law completely? Paul's answer is negative, and his statement of the relationship between law and gospel in the letter becomes a dominant leitmotif. The law has its place in God's plan, but it is not the old legalistic approach. The law tells us what sin is, and if there is no law one cannot transgress law. See LAW (OT).

Furthermore, for Paul the law drives a person to despair and causes him to throw himself upon the grace of God in one great act of faith. The honest legalist knows from experience that he can never completely obey the law for God and that the law only condemns. Only grace and faith give true life and liberty. In this letter, then, the apostle's great theme is Christian liberty, which brings praise to the grace of God.

The Judaizers attempted to answer this question of the law and the gospel by opting for a legalistic system. Their argument was subtle and rational. If a Jew became a Christian, naturally he must bring Judaism with him into the Christian faith. Was not the Jew there first? Was not the law from God? It was so simple. A Jew must always remain a Jew. On the other hand, if a Gentile wished to become a disciple of Christ, he had to become a Jew to qualify. Were not all of God's promises, even of the Messiah, promised to Jews alone? Christianity, like Judaism, was for Jews only. This was a new kind of slavery, worse than the old. It also faced a person with demands he could not meet. What hopes the poor Gentiles had were dashed to pieces. Everything in the letter is gathered about the theme of freedom in the grace of God, whether it be Paul's own biography, his altercation with Peter, the works of a Christian (Gal. 2:19–21), the case of Abraham, the desires of the flesh and the compulsion of the Spirit, the doctrine of love, or forgiveness (6:15). In some way, each issue of the epistle has something to do with this theme.

The purpose of the letter is knotted to the theme. Paul wished to combat legalism and the Judaizers. Legalism always has, and always will, take the heart out of Christianity and transplant a heart made of stone. Only the Spirit gives life. The heart of Christianity is God's free grace in Jesus Christ. Let the law do the honorable work of showing people their sin, but do not let it save them from sin. Paul's purpose was to keep the new kingdom from being another Jewish sect—he preached a universal gospel of grace intended for all (Gal. 3:26). The Judaizers were not only teaching coercion to the Mosaic law, but also a works' righteousness. Paul wished to keep the new Christian converts true to the gospel of freedom which Christ had taught and confirmed on the cross. His letter to the Galatians, as it did in Galatia, has blocked the path of many who since then would change Christianity into a new paganism or another type of Judaism. It stands as a challenge to all who would take away the grace of God, the truth of the gospel, and joy and freedom that goes with it!

(The understanding of Galatians outlined above has been vigorously challenged since the initial publication of the present encyclopedia. E. P. Sanders, in his influential work *Paul and Palestinian Judaism: A Comparison of Patterns of Religion* [1977], argued that Judaism cannot be fairly characterized as legalistic and that its view of sin and grace was not substantially different from Paul's. Building on the work of Sanders, J. D. G. Dunn, in several of his writings, such as *Jesus, Paul and the Law: Studies in Mark and Galatians* [1993], has proposed that "works of the law" in Paul is a reference not to the requirements of the law in general but to the specific items—such as circumcision and food laws—that distinguished Jews from Gentiles. The resulting interpretation of Galatians is that Paul was attacking the Jewish attitude of ethnic superiority, not the view that one may gain personal salvation by obedience to the law. For a response to this so-called "new perspective" on Paul, see S. Westerholm, *Perspectives Old and New on Paul: The "Lutheran" Paul and His Critics* [2003], and D. A. Carson et al., eds., *Justification and Variegated Nomism*, 2 vols. [2002–2004].)

VIII. Contents and outline. The contents of the letter to the Galatians must compel the Christian's personal attention. This is not just a theological or polemical essay on which the reader, like a Greek debater, may take either side without impunity. The subject matter of this treatise of the gospel involves all persons and their eternal salvation or judgment. The news of the Judaizers' success caused great turmoil and even tempestuous anger in the apostle's heart. He divided his wrath between the Judaizers for preaching such heresy and the Galatians for believing it. It is not only that the Galatians would lose their liberty; they would lose their God and his eternal salvation in Jesus Christ. Justification by faith rather than by works must stand at all costs.

The first two chapters of the letter form a defense of Paul's apostolic authority. The best way to illustrate his point is to relate his own activities and show that the gospel came by revelation from God and not from Paul or even the other apostles, for if one apostle can be attacked, all may be attacked. So certain is he of the gospel's freedom that he even opposed the respected and renowned apostle Peter about his vacillation between Jews and Gentiles.

The second major section of the letter (Gal. 3–4) is freighted with Paul's defense of the gospel—teaching the positive truth to oppose error. He sets forth his doctrine of justification by faith to refute the Judaizers and as a vehicle of the Spirit to bring the Galatians back from their apostasy. The Galatians themselves knew they did not receive salvation by keeping the law—few of them had ever followed any law. The same is true, Paul says, of the great heroes of the OT, particularly Abraham, the father of the Jews. The purpose of the law was never to save, but rather to convince sinners that their salvation is from God.

In ch. 5 the apostle defends the other end of the valley: he fights off the antinomian who would say, "Yes, Paul, let us teach faith and not law and works—what do you have then? Have you not opened the very floodgates of sin and human desire? If there is no law and everyone is free, will not immorality, hate, murder and every other human passion run wild so that the last situation is worse than the first?" Paul carefully illustrates that on the contrary, the gospel, like a beautiful tree, brings forth fruits of the Spirit of every kind. Good works do not make a good person, but a good person does good works. This is true liberty—doing the will of the Spirit of God from the compulsion of the gospel. There are, Paul says, many fruits of the flesh, but the Christian is under grace and empowered by the Spirit of God himself to do good, a much greater power than any human attitude or desire. At the end of the letter the apostle takes the pen from the scribe and attests the truth of the document by inscribing his own name in his own hand.

The letter may be outlined as follows:

A. *Introduction* (Gal. 1:1–5)
   1. The writer and the addressees (1:1–2)
   2. The apostolic greeting (1:3–5)
B. *The apostle Paul defends Christian liberty by defending his apostolic authority* (1:6—2:21)
   1. Paul's defense forms the purpose and occasion of the letter (1:6–7)
   2. Paul was never a mere man-pleaser (1:8–10)
   3. He received his gospel directly by revelation from Christ himself and not from men (1:11–20)
   4. The time he spent in Syria and Cilicia shows that the Christians of Judea did not know him personally (1:21–24)
   5. Paul's dealings with the other apostles and with the Judaizers shows his gospel is true (2:1–10)
   6. His rebuke of the apostle Peter should convince all of his sincerity (2:11–16)
   7. Paul's personal testimony of his apostleship and doctrine (2:17–21)
C. *The apostle Paul defends and explains the doctrine of justification by faith alone* (chs. 3–4)
   1. Paul admonishes the Galatians again (3:1–5)
   2. Paul cites the example of Abraham's faith to recall the foolish Galatians (3:6–9)
   3. Paul explains justification by faith by speaking of Christ being made a curse (3:10–14)
   4. Paul speaks of justification under the picture of the covenant or testament (3:15–18)
   5. The apostle inserts a statement in his argumentation about the purpose and use of the law (3:19–25)
   6. Paul offers a summary argument that unites all believers into one, not under law, but in the gospel of Christ (3:26–29)
   7. Paul speaks of justification by faith under the picture of an heir (4:1–7)
   8. Paul inserts another rebuke to the Galatians for leaving the doctrine of justification (4:8–11)
   9. A personal appeal (4:12–20)
   10. The allegory of the two sons (4:21–31)
D. *The apostle Paul relates the doctrine of justification by faith to the Christian life* (5:1—6:10; Paul's definition of good works and defense of the gospel against immorality)
   1. Paul restates his reasons the Galatians should hold fast to the doctrine of justification (5:1–12)
   2. The apostle states his definition of law and good works for the justified person (5:13–26)
   3. Individual responsibility for ethical growth (6:1–10)
E. *Concluding remarks of the letter to the Galatians* (recapitulation, 6:11–18)
   1. Paul says he wrote the letter personally (6:11)
   2. He speaks once more about the problem in Galatia, comparing the false teachers and himself (6:12–15)
   3. Parting words (6:16–18)

IX. Characteristics and special features. The entire letter is "special" and a "feature event" in Christianity. For a clear understanding of Christianity there is no better introduction than Galatians. It is highly doctrinal but yet extremely personal. The gullibility of the Galatians for such patent error is a personal affront to the apostle, who had been God's instrument in bringing the gospel to them. Almost a third of the letter is a statement of personal biography. Paul himself was an object lesson of the gospel and often uses this method (cf. 1 Tim. 1:1–12). Not even the casual reader can overlook the fervor of personal faith (cf. esp. the personal pronouns in Gal. 2:19–20).

The epistle is a sharp defense of the Christian faith. "The tone of the book is warlike. It fairly crackles with indignation though it is not the anger of personal pique but of spiritual principle. 'Though we, or an angel from heaven, should preach unto you any gospel other than that which we preached unto you, let him be anathema' (Gal. 1:8), cried Paul as he reproved the Galatians for their acceptance of the legalistic error" (Tenney). Paul was answering those who challenged him on two counts: The truth of the gospel and Paul's right to preach it.

The letter is also highly emotional. Words run like a torrential mountain stream. He begins sentences that he does not have time to finish; he quotes his words to another apostle but then flies aloft in a soliloquy as he dwells on what Christ had done for his own person. He talks to his readers as if he were on a great stage with his readers personally before him. One time he can be angry and heated, at other times pleading and conciliating. He speaks of the glory of Christ and his doctrine, but also of the beauty of the fruits of the Spirit. He asks question after question, which he proceeds to answer himself.

The letter shows the sensitivity of one who has experienced the depths of God's grace. He speaks of love fulfilling the whole law and walking in the Spirit as in a peaceful verdant valley. Yet he can trumpet forth with such dicta as this: "Do not be deceived: God cannot be mocked. A man reaps what he sows. The one who sows to please his sinful nature, from that nature will reap destruction; the one who sows to please the Spirit, from the Spirit will reap eternal life" (Gal. 6:7–8). The letter to the Galatians shows beautiful eloquence and deep pathos. It manifests wrath against false teachers, tenderness with respect to the erring, and urgent pleading to the faithful. The heart of the gospel is found in its substance and in the life of freedom it advocates. The letter is most valuable for the full understanding of the Word of God. Scarcely another epistle emphasizes the "alone" of "by grace alone" and "through faith alone" as does Galatians. No presentation of the gospel can equal this letter in the force with which it presents the powerful claim of the pure grace of God.

Another special feature of this great letter is that it deals directly with basic concerns of men and women in their relationship to God and their life on earth. It reveals the basic human nature in that we tend to turn from truth to untruth because deception seems more delectable than truth (Gal. 1:6–9); it points up the basic premise upon which someone is received by God, namely the grace of God in Christ (2:11–21); it shows the all-sufficiency of Christ's atonement for the sins of all and the gift of salvation through his saving work (2:15–16); it reveals that God chooses to give his gospel through others whom he has called to be his ambassadors (2:6–10); it teaches the relationship between legal requirements and the gospel of freedom and human responsibility (2:17–21); it exhibits a brief but profound statement and understanding of the doctrine of justification by grace through faith (2:15–16); it shows a proper use and understanding of the OT (3:15–18; 4:21–31); it speaks in no uncertain terms about the equality of all people under God in Christ (3:23–29); the unity of the church is emphasized repeatedly (5:6); it teaches the work of the Spirit and his power in the lives of believers (5:6–25); its admonition to forgiveness is held up as a basic fruit of the gospel (6:1–5); in short, the letter teaches the basic elements of Christianity in brief and unforgettable form. See also ETHICS OF PAUL; PAULINE THEOLOGY.

(Significant commentaries include J. B. Lightfoot, *St. Paul's Epistle to the Galatians*, 10th ed. [1890]; E. de Witt Burton, *A Critical and Exegetical Commentary on the Epistle to the Galatians*, ICC [1921]; H. N. Ridderbos, *The Epistle of Paul to the Churches of Galatia*, NICNT [1952]; H. D. Betz, *Galatians: A Commentary on Paul's Letter to the Churches in Galatia*, Hermeneia [1979]; F. F. Bruce, *The Epistle to the Galatians: A Commentary on the Greek Text*, NIGTC [1982]; R. Y. K. Fung, *The Epistle to the Galatians*, NICNT [1988]; F. Mussner, *Der Galaterbrief: Auslegung*, HTKNT 9, 5th ed. [1988]; R. N. Longenecker, *Galatians*, WBC 41 [1990]; F. J. Matera, *Galatians*, SP 9 [1992]; J. D. G. Dunn, *The Epistle to the Galatians*, BNTC [1993]; T. George, *Galatians*, NAC 30 [1994]; L. Morris, *Galatians: Paul's Charter of Christian Freedom* [1996]; J. L. Martyn, *Galatians: A New Translation with Introduction and Commentary*, AB 33A [1997]; B. Witherington, *Grace in Galatia: A Commentary on St. Paul's Letter to the Galatians* [1998];

A. M. Buscemi, *Lettera ai Galati: Commentario esegetico* [2004].

Among many important monographs, see B. H. Brinsmead, *Galatians: Dialogical Response to Opponents* [1982]; J. M. G. Barclay, *Obeying the Truth: A Study of Paul's Ethics in Galatians* [1988]; C. H. Cosgrove, *The Cross and the Spirit: A Study in the Argument and Theology of Galatians* [1989]; G. W. Hansen, *Abraham in Galatians: Epistolary and Rhetorical Contexts* [1989]; G. Howard, *Paul: Crisis in Galatia*, 2nd ed. [1990]; I.-G. Hong, *The Law in Galatians* [1993]; R. B. Hays, *The Faith of Jesus Christ: The Narrative Substructure of Galatians 3:1—4:11*, 2nd ed. [2002]; M. D. Nanos, *The Irony of Galatians: Paul's Letter in First-Century Context* [2002]; Y.-G. Kwon, *Eschatology in Galatians: Rethinking Paul' Response to the Crisis in Galatia* [2004]; D. F. Tolmie, *Persuading the Galatians: A Text-Centered Rhetorical Analysis of a Pauline Letter* [2005]; T. A. Wilson, *The Curse of the Law and the Crisis in Galatia: Reassessing the Purpose of Galatians* [2007].) L. M. Petersen

galbanum gal'buh-nuhm. An aromatic gum, and one of four perfumes blended to produce a holy incense (Heb. *ḥelbĕnâ* H2697, Exod. 30:34; cf. also Gk. *chalbanē* in Sir. 24:15). Galbanum is the brownish gum or resin of the *Ferula galbaniflua*, a Mediterranean herbaceous perennial. It has thick stalks, yellow flowers, and fern-like green foliage. The gum exudes from the lower part of the stem. When collected, galbanum is found in both irregular and symmetrical drops. It may be yellowy-green or lightish brown, and has a musky, pungent smell. The particular value of galbanum is the fact that it "holds" the scent of a mixed perfume, and allows of its "distribution" over a long period. (Cf. *FFB*, 123, with illustration on p. 122.) See FLORA (under *Lauraceae*). W. E. Shewell-Cooper

Galeed gal'ee-ed (גַּלְעֵד H1681, "[stone] heap of witness"). The Hebrew name that Jacob gave to the heap of stones erected as a memorial to the covenant of reconciliation and nonaggression between himself and Laban, his father-in-law (Gen. 31:47–48). Laban called the heap of stones Jegar Sahadutha (*yĕgar śāhădûtāʾ* H3337, Aram. for "heap of witness"), and it was also known as Mizpah (*miṣpâ* H5207, "watchtower," v. 49). Jacob and Laban sealed their covenant with a communal meal (v. 46, 54). The erection of a stele or stone-heap as a memorial of some important event or treaty was common in the history of Israel (cf. Gen. 28:18; Josh. 4:3, 9; 22:21–34). Some have identified Galeed with Khirbet Jelʿad, S of the Jabbok River, but others think the incident took place before Jacob crossed the river on his way S. This story perhaps provides the reason why this territory in Transjordan has been named Gilead (cf. Gen. 31:25).

D. H. Madvig

Galgala gal'guh-luh. KJV Apoc. form of Gilgal (1 Macc. 9:2).

Galilean gal'uh-lee'uhn (Γαλιλαῖος G1134, from Heb. גָּלִיל H1665, "Galilee"). The name applied by both Jews and Gentiles to the inhabitants of Galilee, the portion of Syria-Palestine N of the Plain of Esdraelon and the Valley of Jezreel, and spreading E to the shores of the Lake of Galilee and W to the Mediterranean Sea. This area was little settled by the Jews after the return from the exile. John Hyrcanus and his successors, such as Alexander Jannaeus (see Hasmonean), conquered this area and incorporated its mixed population of Arameans and Hellenistic peoples into the Jewish state. Under the Hasmoneans, many Jews from the S migrated and settled in Galilee and thus became Galileans. Later, anti-Roman movements flourished among the hill people of this area; the revolutionary leader and founder of the Zealots was himself called Judas of Galilee. Josephus distinguishes between northern and southern Galilee (*War* 3.3.1 §§35–40). The inhabitants of this area always were considered somewhat inferior by their southerly countrymen in Judea. Josephus, however, who was of Galilean descent himself, described the Galileans as "fighters from the cradle and at all times numerous, and never has cowardice afflicted the men or a declining population the country" (*War* 3.3.2 §42, trans. G. A. Williamson [1959]). At one point Josephus was, in fact, the governor of Galilee.

It was to these people that John the Baptist and Jesus Christ had preached, and from this group the first circle of our Lord's disciples were drawn and his closest apostles chosen. Apparently

JOSEPH was from a family that had migrated from BETHLEHEM in JUDEA to Galilee, as shown by his return there with Mary upon the command of Caesar AUGUSTUS (Lk. 2:4). Since farming, herding, and fishing were the common callings of the country folk of Galilee, their experiences are apparent in Jesus' parables. In all four of the Gospels, and in Acts, it is clear that Galileans were easily distinguishable to their fellow Jews by their speech. The classic passage is, of course, the accusation by the bystanders against Simon PETER and his denial (Mk. 14:70; Lk. 22:59; cf. also Acts 2:7). The characteristic of this speech was no doubt its vocabulary, accent, and syntax. The direct speeches of Jesus Christ recorded in the Gospels (Mk. 5:41; 15:34), as well as the Aramaisms that were translated into Greek, leave little doubt that our Lord's mother tongue was this same Galilean ARAMAIC. After the Roman overthrow of the Jewish state in A.D. 70, many Jews and Jewish Christians fled from Jerusalem to Galilee, thus making the Galileans a center of the Jewish culture. Interest in Galilee and the Galileans was renewed after the introduction of the now discredited "Galilean Hypothesis" by the romantic author E. Renan (*La vie de Jesus* [1863]). (See R. Vale in *JSJ* 18 [1987]: 209–26; S. Freyne in *ABD*, 2:876–79.)

W. WHITE, JR.

Galilee gal'uh-lee (גָּלִיל *H1665*, used with the definite article and meaning "the circuit, the district"; Γαλιλαία *G1133*). The geographical area in PALESTINE bounded on the N by the Litani (Leontes) River, on the W by the Mediterranean Sea to Mount Carmel (see CARMEL, MOUNT), on the S by the northern edge of the Plain of ESDRAELON (though at times the plain itself is included), and on the E by the JORDAN valley and the Sea of Galilee.

I. Ancient boundaries. Little information is available to determine the boundaries of Galilee during OT times. The term is first employed during Israel's conquest of Canaan. In the hill country of NAPHTALI, the town of KEDESH is said to be in Galilee (Josh. 20:7; 21:32; 1 Chr. 6:76). During the kingdom period, Galilee appears to encompass the territory of Naphtali (2 Ki. 15:29), the tribal area of ASHER (provided CABUL is the same city in 1 Ki. 9:11–13 and Josh. 19:27), and possibly the tribal district of ZEBULUN (Isa. 9:1). It may be concluded that the OT Galilee is substantially the same as in the definition given above.

In the intertestamental period, Maccabean literature includes the Plain of Esdraelon in Galilee (cf. 1 Macc. 5:35; 10:30; 12:47, 49). Josephus describes Galilee as being bordered by PHOENICIA and SYRIA, bounded on the N and W by Tyrians, to which Mount Carmel belonged, on the S by SAMARIA and SCYTHOPOLIS as far as the Jordan River, and on the E by the TRANSJORDAN (*War* 3.3.1 §§35–40). The region of Galilee in the NT appears to encompass this same area (Matt. 4:13–15, 25; 28:16; Mk. 1:28; 3:37; Lk. 8:26; 17:11).

II. General description. The region of Galilee is approximately 60 mi. long from N to S and 30 mi. wide from W to E. Of all the regions of PALESTINE, Galilee contains the coolest, most picturesque, and lushest mountainous district. The terrain is diversified, containing volcanic and limestone hills with alluvial fertile plains. It has been compared with portions of the Carolina and Virginia piedmont. The entire region is watered by springs, heavy mountain dew, and an annual precipitation of about 25 inches.

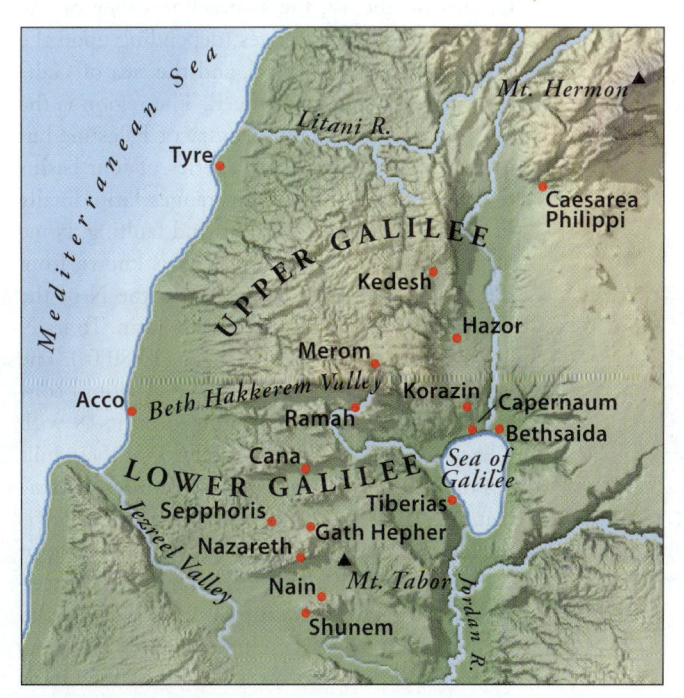

Upper and Lower Galilee.

The Plain of Magdala on the NW shore of the Sea of Galilee, with Mount Hermon and the volcanoes of Gaulanitis in the background. (View to the NE from the Arbel cliffs.)

A. Lower Galilee. The natural and historic boundaries of Lower Galilee include the fault of Esh-Shaghur (present Acre-Safed highway) to the N, the Mediterranean Sea from Acco to Mount Carmel on the W, the Esdraelon Valley or the Carmel and GILBOA ranges (depending upon the historical period) to the S, and the Sea of Galilee and Jordan Valley to the E. The region is the most level of all the hill country of Palestine but is divided into sections by a series of four basins that bisect its low mountain ranges latitudinally E to W through cross folding and faulting. None of the names of these four valleys is known from the Bible. The basins begin just to the N of the NAZARETH ridge with the Turʿan basin. To its N lies the steep slope of Jebel Turʿan (1,780 ft.). The larger basin of Sahl el-Baṭṭuf (Beth Netufa) constitutes the second basin, bordered on its N with hills to the height of 1,710 ft. North of these hills lies the Halazun (Sakhnin) basin with Jebel Kammana (1,950 ft.) rising to its N. The last valley is the long and narrow Esh-Shaghur basin (Plain of er-Ramah or Beth Hakerem), which abuts a steep slope that rises almost vertically 1,500–2,000 ft. to the mountain plateau of Upper Galilee. The most distinct landmarks in Lower Galilee are the Horns of Ḥaṭṭin, Mount TABOR, and the Hill of MOREH.

The Plain of Esdraelon, often considered the southern portion of Lower Galilee, is the largest valley bisecting the central mountain range of Palestine and the only one that joins the coastal plain with the Jordan Valley. This valley is known as the Valley of ARMAGEDDON (named after the site of MEGIDDO, Rev. 16:16), where the great battle of the last times will be fought. Its length from Mount Carmel to BETH SHAN (Scythopolis) is about 30 mi., and its greatest width about 15 mi. The fertility of this valley is compared with the delta areas of the Tigris-Euphrates, Nile, and Mississippi. This is due to the decomposition of volcanic deposits, basaltic subsoil, and the many springs. Two ancient valleys combined to make this larger one. The Valley of JEZREEL, named for the capital of the Omride dynasty, which sits on a spur of Mount Gilboa, formed approximately an equilateral triangle of sides 20 mi. long, the vertices being JOKNEAM to the W, TABOR to the E, and IBLEAM to the S. The eastern end of the Plain of Esdraelon was called the Valley of Beth Shan.

The Plain of Acco (Acre; Plain of Asher) on the Mediterranean coast from Carmel to the Ladder of Tyre crosses the western end of Lower and Upper Galilee. It was ASHER's allotment, but the tribe never possessed it entirely. The 10-mi.-wide section in Lower Galilee lay between Mount Carmel and Acco (Acre), composed mostly of marshes and sand dunes. The stream KISHON flowed through it, coming from and connecting it to the Plain of Esdraelon.

B. Upper Galilee. Upper Galilee differs from Lower Galilee in many ways. While the mountain elevation of Lower Galilee remains below 2,000 ft., the highest peaks of Upper Galilee surpass 3,000 ft., Jebel Jermuk the highest at 3,900 ft. From these high mountains N of the Esh-Shaghur basin, the mountain plateau of Upper Galilee slopes to about 1,500–1,800 ft. above sea level in the N before dropping into the gorge of the Litani (Leontes; Kassimiyah) River, which separates Upper Galilee from the Lebanese mountains. This mountain plateau is not uniform as in Lower Galilee and is not divided by a series of valleys. It is composed of bare ridges of hard Cenomanian limestone and flat-topped mountains of softer Senonian chalk. Rugged contours, broken by many peaks, divide the area into natural pockets. Most people feel that this area was more wooded in the past than it is today. Rainfall is heavy and consistent, helping to create small rivers: the major ones are the Ga'aton, Keziv, Amud, and Litani.

The upper Jordan Valley forms the eastern sector of Upper Galilee. The valley begins at the biblical site of IJON (c. 1,800 ft. elevation), initially bounded on the W by the Litani River and on the E by Mount HERMON (c. 9,100 ft. elevation). This valley, fertile and well-watered, is probably the land or valley of MIZPAH (Josh. 11:3, 8), which formed the OT border between Israel, Phoenicia, and Aram. It extends approximately 9 mi. to the area of ABEL BETH MAACAH and DAN (PLACE), where it rapidly descends to about 300 ft. elevation. Here, at Dan and Banias, two of the spring sources of the Jordan River are located. All the sources of the Jordan join together about 5 mi. S of Tell el-Kady. During biblical times they flowed through a marshy valley about 10 mi. to a small Lake Huleh, blocked in by masses of basalt. Today this marsh and lake have been drained and form the fertile Huleh Valley. Just S of this lake the Jordan River reaches sea level and continues to flow for another 10 mi. through a rocky basalt gorge (hills stand more than 1,200 ft. above the stream) to the Sea of Galilee situated about 685 ft. below sea level. This sea, approximately 13 mi. long and 7.5 mi. wide, is nestled between the hills of Lower Galilee on the W and the plains of Bashan on the E.

As in Lower Galilee, the plain of Acco forms the western region of Upper Galilee. It runs along the coast from Acre to the Ladder of Tyre (Rosh Haniqrah) for about 20 mi., its average width being 2 mi. The shore is rocky and without sand dunes, offering no natural harbors of any significance.

III. Ancient history. Though the records are scanty concerning the occupation of Galilee prior to Israel's conquest of Canaan, there are traces of settlement and occupation as early as the Chalcolithic and Early Bronze ages (c. 4000 to 2000 B.C.) at such sites as Megiddo and Beth Shan. The Egyptian EXECRATION TEXTS of the 20th and 19th centuries B.C. curse certain towns in the Galilean area of Palestine (e.g., Acco, Achshaph, Beth Shan; possibly Kedesh and Beth Shemesh). Later Egyptian control over this region is demonstrated by the campaign lists of THUTMOSE III, RAMSES II, et al. Subsequent loss of control by Egypt and the confusion among the Palestinian city states is evidenced in the TELL EL-AMARNA letters (c. 14th cent. B.C.) of Egypt.

A. Tribal divisions. Israel gained initial supremacy in Galilee through JOSHUA's victory over the Canaanite league at the Waters of MEROM (Josh. 11:1–11). JABIN, the king of HAZOR, was the leader of this alliance. Galilee was apportioned among four tribes (19:10–39): Asher received western Galilee with the coastal plain of Acco; Issachar settled in the eastern part of the Jezreel Valley and the hills to its N; Zebulun inherited the central part of Galilee between the Plain of Esdraelon and the Sahl el-Battut Valley; Naphtali occupied a large area in eastern and central Galilee. Archaeological surveys demonstrate that the Israelite settlement occurred in the largely unsettled interior regions of Lower and Upper Galilee, though Upper Galilee is not a region that enters much into biblical history. None of these four tribes (except perhaps Issachar) succeeded in driving the Canaanites out of their district (Jdg. 1:30–33). During the apostate and anarchic period of the judges, DEBORAH and BARAK, with men from the tribes of Zebulun and Naphtali, defeated the Canaanite oppression by swooping down from Mount Tabor and claiming victory at the Kishon River in the Plain of Esdraelon (Jdg. 4). GIDEON removed the Midianites' and Amalekites' tyranny by his surprise attack against them near the Hill of Moreh (ch. 6). Neither victory was permanent.

B. Kingdom period. SAUL, the first king of Israel, unified the tribes and thereby brought Galilee and the VIA MARIS (the major trade route) under his control. The balance of power soon shifted to the PHILISTINES, who proceeded to shut up the Israelites in the hill country. DAVID freed Israel from the Philistine threat and made Israel the leading nation of the region. Galilee came under David's control. In payment for helping to construct the TEMPLE, SOLOMON offered HIRAM of TYRE twenty cities in Galilee. When Hiram examined those towns, he was not pleased with them and appears to have returned them to Solomon (1 Ki. 9:10–14; 2 Chr. 8:1–2).

Following the division of the nation into the kingdoms of Israel and Judah, ASA king of Judah summoned BEN HADAD I, the Aramean, to aid him in his fight against Israel by invading Galilee. Ben Hadad promptly wasted the land of Naphtali and the whole circle of Kinnereth (1 Ki. 15:20). Galilee continued as an area of conflict between Israel and ARAM (Syria). OMRI and AHAB recovered the territory lost by Israel, but parts were lost again by JEHU to HAZAEL (2 Ki. 10:32). Hazael continued his battles with JEHOAHAZ of Israel (13:22). Finally JEROBOAM, the son of JOASH, king of Israel, delivered the region of Galilee for a short time (14:25). With the invasion of the Assyrian king TIGLATH-PILESER III in 734 B.C., the chief cities of Galilee passed into his hands (15:29; 16:7). Though some Israelites still remained in Galilee after this attack (2 Chr. 30:10–11), the Israelite period of dominion over Galilee ended quickly with SAMARIA's fall to ASSYRIA in 722 B.C. The kingdom of Israel, including the region of Galilee, was assimilated by Assyria. "Galilee of the Gentiles" (Isa. 9:1) probably referred to the mixture of Jews and Gentiles then living in that area.

C. NT times. Following the Babylonian captivity, information about the history of Galilee is sparse, though the area was continually inhabited. It was ruled by Babylon, Persia, Greece, and the Seleucid empire until the Maccabees conquered parts of it and began the process of Jewish resettlement. Jews were already in Galilee in 165 B.C. when SIMON MACCABEE brought numbers of them to live in Judea (1 Macc. 5:14–23). Josephus (*Ant.* 13.11.3 §§318–19) recounts Aristobulus I's conquest of ITUREA, and most scholars think that Galilee was treated similarly to Iturea in that both were Judaized.

Under Rome, HEROD the Great was made military commander of Galilee in 47 B.C. He subdued the various bands of thieves that plagued the country (Jos. *Ant.* 14.9.2 §§158–60). When Herod ascended the throne in 37 B.C., a period of peace and prosperity came to Galilee that continued until the banishment of his son Antipas in A.D. 40. At Herod's death in 4 B.C., Galilee fell to Antipas, who made his capital at TIBERIAS on the western shore of the Sea of Galilee, naming it after the emperor.

Herod Antipas ruled Galilee throughout most of Jesus' life. Jesus was born in BETHLEHEM of Judea, was raised in NAZARETH of Galilee, and made CAPERNAUM at the N end of the Sea of Galilee the headquarters of his ministry. There was a considerable Jewish population in Galilee at this time, which would explain, in part, Christ's following there. Most of his ministry was around the Sea of Galilee. The SERMON ON THE MOUNT, his TRANSFIGURATION (though no mountain has been identified with certainty for this event), nineteen of his thirty-two parables, and twenty-five of his thirty-three recorded miracles occurred in Galilee. The Messiah received his warmest welcome in Galilee, but the Jews from the S regarded the northern Jews with some contempt, feeling that nothing good could come out of Nazareth (Jn. 1:46; 7:52) and that a claim of a Messiah from Nazareth could hardly be taken seriously (Matt. 21:11). Late in Jesus' Galilean ministry, when opposition had increased, he spent considerable time in Upper Galilee.

Galilee was added to the territory of Herod Agrippa I in A.D. 40. ZEALOTS were arising in Galilee, some found among the disciples of both John the Baptist and Christ. Also in the year 40 the emperor CALIGULA ordered Petronius, the governor of Syria, to erect the emperor's statue in the temple at Jerusalem. Thousands of Jews gathered for forty days at Tiberias and Ptolemais in protest of this proposed sacrilege. Such reactionary pressure caused Petronius to give up the idea. Agrippa I died in 44, and parts of Galilee came under the dominion of Herod Agrippa II until the end of the 1st cent. As Rome continued to administer the remainder of Galilee, the Galileans struggled for independence. With VESPASIAN's invasion around the year 70, the whole area came under Roman rule, and after Herod Agrippa II's death in the year 100, Galilee was joined to the Roman province of Syria.

When Jerusalem fell in A.D. 70, Galilee became the seat of Jewish learning. The MISHNAH was compiled and written in Tiberias followed later by the composition of the Palestinian TALMUD. Later Tiberias became a major center of the Masoretes' work of preserving the OT text. The SANHEDRIN likewise moved to Sepphoris and then to Tiberias.

IV. Transportation.

The major trade route from Damascus to Egypt is called the VIA MARIS (the Way of the Sea). From Egypt this route enters Galilee from the SW through the pass of the Wadi ʿAra at Megiddo (alternative passes were at Taanach and Jokneam). At Megiddo the road branches. One way runs NW to the plain of Acco along the Phoenician coast to Anatolia. The second artery moves E to Damascus between the Hill of Moreh and Mount Tabor to Kinnereth on the NW corner of the Sea of Galilee, then N to Hazor, where one branch of it continues due N to Ijon and the other branch crosses the main ford of the Jordan River about 2 mi. S of Hazor and continues to Damascus. The third route leaves Megiddo heading E to Beth Shan, past Ashtoreth, the capital of Bashan, and joins the King's Highway to Damascus. Canaanite fortresses guarded this route: Hazor in the N; Beth Shan at the junction of the Esdraelon and Jordan valleys; Ibleam in the Esdraelon valley; and Megiddo, Taanach, and Jokneam at the passes leading S.

Most minor routes throughout Galilee run E-W following the E-W basins crossing Lower Galilee. N-S traffic is most difficult due to the many ranges and faults that run in every direction in Upper Galilee. Roads in Galilee usually follow the spurs rather than the valleys when climbing on to the mountain plateau, because a WADI leaving a plateau usually becomes a steep valley, often impassable. The main road from Acco (Ptolemais) to Tiberias went just N of Sepphoris across Lower Galilee, joining the Nazareth-Tiberias road. Another significant artery ran through Upper Galilee from Tyre to Abel Beth Maacah at the base of Mount Hermon. This highway system put the region of Galilee in contact with the entire ANE.

V. Flora and fauna.

The Galilean hills are considered to have been heavily forested in early times with an abundance of trees: olive, fig, oak, walnut, cedar, cypress, balsam, fir, pine, sycamore, bay, mulberry, and almond. The valleys were fertile and well-watered. Wheat was abundant in the upper Jordan Valley; pomegranates thrived near Mount Carmel; and the grapes of Naphtali were famous. Grains were plentiful. The major fauna of Galilee is FISH. At least twenty-two species have been classified from the streams and the Sea of Galilee.

VI. Settlement patterns.

Galilee was open and easily accessible to the outsider. Yet Upper Galilee and portions of Lower Galilee with their rugged terrain made sections of the area easily fortified and naturally defensible. Almost any group could defend itself. As a result many varied groups did survive. The population became heterogeneous, with Jews, Arameans, Itureans, Greeks, and Phoenicians living together. Upper Galilee gave the northern portion of Palestine an area of escape during troubled times.

Josephus reports that Galilee was densely populated (*War* 3.3.2 §43, though his claim that even the smallest villages had 15,000 inhabitants has to be an exaggeration). This could help explain the crowds that followed Jesus. In the valleys the villages often kept to the edges of the basin or up the slopes due to flooding in winter. In Lower Galilee two subregions proved less attractive to habitation than any other: (a) the SW area between the present Nazareth-Sheparam road and the Jezreel valley; (b) the SE region from Tiberias to the N edge of the Beth Shan valley which includes four steep scarps. Neither area is easy to cultivate nor has ever been thickly populated. The more notable cities of Galilee have been Kedesh, Hazor, Korazin, Bethsaida,

Capernaum, Beth Shan (Scythopolis), Nazareth, Megiddo, Jokneam, Ibleam, Acco (Ptolemais), Sepphoris, Jotapata, Cana, Nain, Aczib, and Tiberias. Sepphoris and Tiberias were Roman administrative centers in Galilee, Sepphoris being located about 4 mi. NW of Nazareth. The NT does not record Jesus' presence in either of these two cities. The men of Galilee were known to be courageous (Jos. *War* 3.3.2). OT notables were Barak, Gideon, Jonah, and Elijah. Eleven of Jesus' twelve apostles were Galileans.

(See further G. A. Smith, *The Historical Geography of the Holy Land*, 25th ed. [1931], ch. 20; D. Baly, *Geography of the Bible* [1957], 184–92; S. Abramsky, *Ancient Towns in Israel* [1963], 174–250; Y. Aharoni, *The Land of the Bible: A Historical Geography*, rev. ed. [1979], passim; S. Freyne, *Galilee from Alexander the Great to Hadrian: A Study of Second Temple Judaism* [1980]; W. Bosen, *Galiläa als Lebensraum und Wirkungsfeld Jesu: Eine zeitgeschichtliche und theologische Untersuchung* [1985]; S. Freyne, *Galilee, Jesus and the Gospels: Literary Approaches and Historical Investigations* [1988]; E. M. Meyers, ed., *Galilee through the Centuries: Confluence of Cultures* [1999]; J. L. Reed, *Archaeology and the Galilean Jesus: A Re-examination of the Evidence* [2000]; M. A. Chancey, *The Myth of a Gentile Galilee* [2002]; id., *Greco-Roman Culture and the Galilee of Jesus* [2005].)

R. H. ALEXANDER

Galilee, Sea of. A harp-shaped lake in the JORDAN Valley due E of Lower GALILEE and Acre bay (see Acco), just N of the intersection of the YARMUK and Jordan Rivers, and W of the plains of BASHAN. Also called Sea of TIBERIAS (Jn. 6:1; 21:1), Lake of GENNESARET (Lk. 5:1; cf. 1 Macc. 11:67), and simply "the sea" (*thalassa G2498*, Matt. 8:24, 32; Mk. 2:13; Jn. 6:16–17; et al.). The OT refers to it as Sea of KINNERETH (Num. 34:11 et al.).

I. Setting. To many, the focal point of the whole region of Galilee is the Sea of Galilee. It lies E of Lower Galilee in the great Jordan Rift Valley, about 60 mi. N of JERUSALEM. The mountains of Upper Galilee rise NW of it to a height of about 4,000 ft. above sea level, while the hills immediately E and W of the lake ascend abruptly to heights of about 2,000 ft. above sea level. This creates a sharp drop of approximately 2,650 ft. from the mountain tops down to the lake's surface, where the foot of the hills often abuts the lake. The main formation of the surrounding terrain is limestone overlaid with volcanic lava, broken at times with an outcropping of basalt. The high tablelands of BASHAN, HAURAN, and GAULANITIS to the E of the lake are composed of black basalt and some diorite. Since the Sea of Galilee is located in the Jordan rift, it has been subject to destructive earthquakes.

Three major valleys adjoin this lake: a plain formed by the northern entrance of the Jordan River, another one at its southern exit, and the plain of GENNESARET to the NW. The upper Jordan Valley begins at the biblical site of IJON (c. 1,800 ft. above sea level) near the foot of Mount HERMON, which towers about 9,100 ft. above sea level and can be observed easily from the southern shore of the Sea of Galilee. This fertile and well-watered valley (prob. the land or valley of MIZPAH in Josh. 11:3, 8) spreads approximately 9 mi. S to the region of ABEL BETH MAACAH and DAN (PLACE), where it rapidly drops about 300 ft. in elevation. The major spring sources of the Jordan River are located in this area. Two smaller streams that feed the Jordan, the Bareighit and the Hasbani, form a small waterfall near Metullah as they leave this plain and drop to the Huleh Valley. The two major streams of the Jordan, the Banyasi and the Liddani, spring up close to one another at Banias and Tell el-Qady respectively, considered the locations of the later towns of CAESAREA PHILIPPI and Dan.

Aerial view of the Sea of Galilee (looking SE).

These four streams join together about 5 mi. S of Tell el-Qady and flow through the marshes of the valley approximately 10 mi. to the small Lake Huleh. A few miles S of this lake the Jordan River reaches sea level and drops at a rate of about 60 ft. per mile for another 10 mi. through a rocky basalt gorge to the small plain that enters the Sea of Galilee situated about 685 ft. below sea level. The Jordan River is the major source of water in this lake. At the southern tip of the lake, the Jordan exits through a broad fertile valley that has been heavily populated from ancient times to the present. The Yarmuk River flows into the Jordan from the E about 7 mi. S of the lake. The plain of Gennesaret, with its average width of one mile, enters the lake from the NW.

II. Description. Looking down upon the Sea of Galilee from the heights of Safed, the lake looks harp-shaped (the Hebrew name Kinnereth may be derived from a word meaning "lyre"), with the bulge to the NW, and is deep blue. It is truly a beautiful sight. The ancient rabbis used to say that the Lord had "created seven seas, but the Sea of Galilee is his delight." It reminds one of a Scottish loch surrounded by barren hills. The surface of the lake is set anywhere from 680 to 695 ft. below sea level. The fluctuation is due to seasonal and annual climatic variation, but most Israelis fix its norm at 685 ft. below sea level. From the entrance of the Jordan at the N to the southern tip of the lake is normally taken to be about 13 mi., though again opinions vary from 12 to 15 mi. The width in the N of the lake at its greatest distance between el-Mejdel on the W to the mouth of the Wadi Semak on the E is usually understood to be 7.5 mi., though variations in this width range from 5 to 8 mi. Opinions concerning the sea's depth fluctuate from 80 ft. in the more shallow areas to a maximum of 160 ft. The lake's circumference is a little over 32 mi., while the average quantity of clear sweet water in it is estimated at 4,562 cubic meters. Around most of the lake the beach is pebbly with a scattering of small shells. Several hot mineral springs are found on the shore, two of the more notable ones located at et-Tabgha in the NW corner and ʿAin el-Fuliyeh about 2 mi. S of modern Tiberias. The climate is tropical due to the low elevation, having temperatures that range higher than the uplands.

As a result of this climate and the fertility of the soil in the plains surrounding the lake, the region is most productive. The harvesting of wheat and barley crops takes place about one month earlier

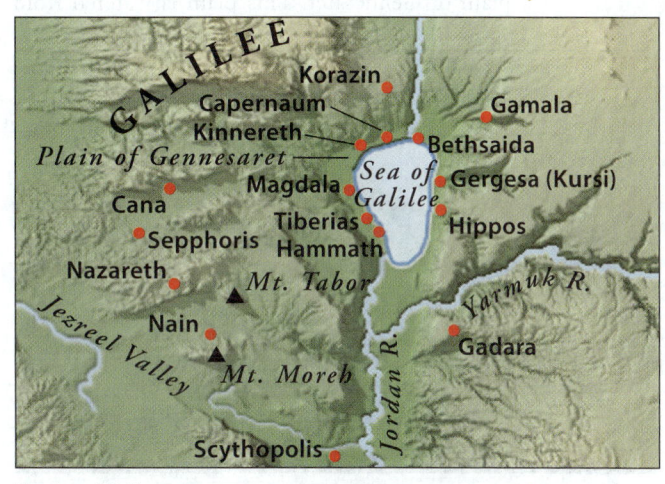

The Sea of Galilee.

than in the hill country. Wild flowers and oleanders fringe the shoreline.

The territory around the lake is varied and interesting. Moving E from the entrance of the Jordan past the site of Bethsaida, the mountain slope of the high plateau of Bashan drops almost vertically into the sea. This is broken only by the Wadi Semak entering the lake due E of Magdal. The ancient site of Gergesa (see Gerasene) was perhaps located near the mouth of the wadi. Approximately 3 mi. S of Semak, located high above the present town of Ein Gev, lie the ancient ruins called Sussita, probably the site of the Decapolis city named Hippos. The ribbon of plain between the coast and the mountains broadens into the Jordan Valley to the S as one reaches the S end of the lake. Six miles SE of the lake, on the other side of the Yarmuk River, lies the ancient site of Gadara. Somewhere in this SW portion of the Sea of Galilee the event of the swine rushing headlong into the lake occurred (Mk. 5:1–20), though the exact location is much debated.

The Jordan Valley S of the lake is considered the most fertile plain among those touching the sea. The Jordan exits from the lake on the W side of this valley, just S of the ruins of the ancient city of Khirbet Kerak. The ribbon type plain on the E is found once again on the western shore running

8.5 mi. N. The Roman capital of Tiberias, built on the slope of the western hills, is located near the northern end of this narrow plain shortly before it intersects the mile-wide fertile and well-watered plain of Gennesaret. This plain is watered from the W by the Wadi el-Ḥamam, which contains the ancient site of ARBELA high on its S rim overlooking the plain. Magdal lies on the S side of this plain near the lake. Moving N toward the Jordan's entrance there is a shallow vale through which a road to the N passes shortly before arriving at et-Tabgha with its hot springs. Two miles farther Tell Hum displays the well-preserved ruins of the 3rd-cent. A.D. synagogue of CAPERNAUM. Within the next 2 mi., the entrance of the Jordan River is reached.

The Jordan River flows into the Sea of Galilee from the N. (View to the SW toward Tiberias.)

III. Products. The small valleys around the Sea of Galilee have fertile alluvial soil, enjoy hot climates, and are well watered. These conditions produce abundant crops of wheat, barley, figs, grapes, and vegetables. Concerning the region's fertility, Josephus declares: "One may call this place the ambition of Nature, where it forces those plants that are naturally enemies to one another to agree together: it is a happy contention of the seasons, as if each of them laid claim to this country, for it not only nourishes different sorts of autumnal fruits beyond men's expectation, but preserves them a great while. It supplies men with the principal fruits—grapes and figs continually during the ten months of the year, and the rest of the fruits, as they ripen together through the whole year" (*War* 3.10.8 §§518–19). Arbela was noted for its linen. FISH was the major commodity from the lake, being found in great abundance and in over twenty-two different species. The best fishing was at the N end of the lake where the Jordan enters. Among the apostles, Peter, Andrew, John, and James were fishermen.

IV. Commerce. Commercially the major industries of the region surrounding the Sea of Galilee were agriculture, dyeing, tanning, boat-building, fishing, and the curing of fish. From the latter the lake gained fame throughout the Roman world. Major routes of trade passed by or over this lake. The eastern branch of the VIA MARIS touched the NW corner of the sea at the plain of Gennesaret. This was the major route from Egypt to Damascus and Mesopotamia. The produce from the mountain plateau to the E of the lake often was shipped across the lake on its way to the Mediterranean. The hot mineral springs along the lake's shore brought multitudes to be healed. Mineral baths are still offered today.

V. Population. The area immediately surrounding the Sea of Galilee is considered to have been the most heavily populated region of Galilee throughout history. Some maintain that in NT times there were nine cities around the lake, each said not to have a population less than 15,000. Such cities included Tiberias, Magdala, Korazin, Bethsaida, Hippos, Capernaum, Gadara, and Kinnereth (G. A. Smith, *The Historical Geography of the Holy Land*, 25th ed. [1931], 289). The fertile wellwatered valleys and warm climate were probably the major cause for this dense population. Ruins of palaces, hippodromes, theaters, and baths built by the Greeks and Romans found on the lake's shores also indicate a large population during the time of Christ. The eastern side of the sea was largely Gentile and constituted part of the region known as the Decapolis.

VI. Storms. The position of the lake in the Jordan rift below sea level with the high mountains to the E and W creates a natural condition for storms. The cool air masses from the mountain heights rush down the steep slopes with great force causing violent eruptions of the lake. Such tempests are not infrequent and are extremely dangerous to small craft.

VII. Biblical history. It is noticeably strange that this fertile and beautiful lake is mentioned in the OT only with respect to the land's borders. The Sea of Kinnereth forms part of the eastern boundary of the land the Lord gave to Israel (Num. 34:11; Josh. 12:3). Elsewhere (Josh. 13:27) it is referred to as the NW boundary of the land allotted to the Gadites. See GAD, TRIBE OF. Apart from these references, the OT is silent concerning this lake.

In contrast, the Sea of Galilee is one of the most important centers of NT events. The headquarters of Jesus' Galilean ministry was on the N shore at Capernaum. Peter, Andrew, and Philip were residents of Bethsaida, a town that Jesus often visited, and one of the towns along with Korazin and Capernaum that he cursed for rejecting his ministry. John and James, the sons of Zebedee, were fishermen upon the Sea of Galilee. In light of the fact that the medicinal mineral springs made the lake a resort for invalids, it is interesting that Christ performed ten out of his thirty-three recorded miracles beside this sea, many of them miracles of healing (Mk. 1:32–34; 3:10; 6:53–56). Most of his time was spent in the NW part of the lake between Tiberias and Capernaum. It is never recorded, however, that Jesus entered the capital at Tiberias, which Herod Antipas had constructed and patterned after the Greek *polis*.

Jesus and his disciples often walked through the grain fields of Gennesaret. Christ drew many illustrations for his gospel message from these fields and the activity of the lake (the parable of the wheat and tares; the parable of the sower; being fishers of men; casting the net into the sea; et al.). On a hill near this lake he preached the SERMON ON THE MOUNT (Matt. 5–7). On its shores he multiplied the loaves and fishes to feed 5,000 (Matt. 14:13–21) and healed demoniacs (Mk. 5), lepers (Lk. 5:12–16), and Peter's mother-in-law (Lk. 4:38). On its waters he walked (Mk. 6:45–52). He calmed the storms on this lake (Mk. 4:35–41). Certainly the Sea of Galilee was geographically central to Christ's ministry.

HEROD the Great ruled over this region from 37 B.C. until his death, when his son, Herod Antipas, began to govern the area. Antipas moved his capital to Tiberias, and from there he ruled over this territory throughout most of the life of Christ. Galilee

Aerial view of the Sea of Galilee (looking N).

was added to the realm of Herod Agrippa I in A.D. 40, and when he died in A.D. 44, parts of the Sea of Galilee came under the jurisdiction of Herod Agrippa II until A.D. 100.   R. H. ALEXANDER

gall. This English term is used in Bible versions with two different meanings, both of which are related to the sense "bitterness." (1) It may refer to a bitter or poisonous herb, comparable to HEMLOCK and WORMWOOD. The KJV uses it a number of times to render Hebrew *rō'š H8032*, which modern versions usually translate "poison" or the like (e.g., Deut. 29:18; Ps. 69:21; Jer. 8:14). According to some, this word refers to the inner pulp of the *Colocynth*, possibly the same as the "vine of Sodom" (Deut. 32:32; see VINE, VINEYARD). The belief that the gall comes from the poppy, whose juice is certainly bitter, is also feasible. A solution of poppy heads in water could describe the phrase *mê-rō'š*, "water of gall" (Jer. 8:14; 9:15). However, the Hebrew word was perhaps used generally of any poisonous or semipoisonous bitter herb grown in Palestine at that time. In addition, most translations use "gall" to render Greek *cholē G5958* in Matt. 27:34, referring to the substance that was mixed with the wine given to the Lord; this Greek term probably means nothing more than "something bitter" (see below).

(2) The word *gall* can also be used in the sense of "bile," the emulsive fluid secreted by the liver and stored in the gallbladder. This secretion can cause extreme bitterness and disgust, when by mistake left inside a cooked hare or rabbit. The figurative biblical usage of the word suggests a despairing or hopeless predicament, reflecting the ghastly taste of the gall bile. The word renders Hebrew *mĕrērâ H5354* (Job 16:13; cf. 20:25 NRSV for Heb. *mĕrōrâ H5355*, NIV, "liver") and Greek *cholē G5958* (Acts 8:23, lit., "in the gall of bitterness").

W. E. SHEWELL-COOPER

gallery. This term is used by many Bible versions to render Hebrew *ʾattîq H916*, an architectural term of uncertain meaning referring to some sections of the TEMPLE that EZEKIEL saw in a vision (Ezek. 41:15–16; 42:3, 5). This feature is not mentioned in the description of SOLOMON's temple. Some have compared the structure of Ezekiel's building, apparently with terraces or recessed upper stories, with the design of the Babylonian ZIGGURAT or stage-tower temple. Others think the term refers to passages or streets. (The KJV uses the English word also to render the rare term *raḥaṭ H8111* in Cant. 7:5; NIV and NRSV, "tresses.")

K. L. BARKER

galley. A long and low seagoing vessel, propelled by sails and oars, or by oars alone. The term is used only once (Isa. 33:21) to render Hebrew *ʾŏnî H639*, a collective term for "fleet" (e.g., 1 Ki. 9:26–27; contrast *ʾŏniyyâ H641*, "a unit of a fleet," i.e., a single ship). Obviously, the reference is to galleys propelled by oars and used primarily as warships. The passage teaches that the Lord is Jerusalem's defense. She will be like a great city protected by river-canals, into which no hostile SHIPS ("galleys") may venture. Thus, the galley of antiquity could be either a small or large vessel and was usually manned by oarsmen (Ezek. 27:8). It is of interest to observe that the Hebrew root under discussion is attested as a Canaanite gloss in the TELL EL-AMARNA Letters (*anaya*, EA, 245:28).

K. L. BARKER

Gallim gal'im (גַּלִּים *H1668*, "heaps"). A village in BENJAMIN, N of JERUSALEM, near GIBEAH of SAUL and ANATHOTH; Palti (PALTIEL) son of Laish, to whom Saul gave his daughter, was from Gallim (1 Sam. 25:44; Isa. 10:30). A town by the same name is also included by the SEPTUAGINT in a list of cities of Judah SW of Jerusalem (Josh. 15:59 [Rahlfs, v. 59a]; it is possible that this portion of the verse was inadvertently omitted from the Heb. Bible in the process of textual transmission).

K. L. BARKER

Gallio gal'ee-oh (Γαλλίων *G1136*). Lucius Junius Gallio Annaeanus was PROCONSUL of ACHAIA in A.D. 51–52 or 52–53, in residence at CORINTH (Acts 18:12–17). The son of the rhetorician L. Annaeus Seneca and brother of the famous philosopher SENECA, he was born Marcus Annaeus Novatus at Cordova in Spain. Adopted by the rhetorician L. Junius Gallio, whose name he thus bore, he was trained by him for administration and government. Gallio was a notably affable man. Seneca dedicated his treatise *De vita beata* to him, and in the preface of the *Naturales quaestiones* describes him as a man universally beloved.

An inscription from Delphi shows that he was proconsul of Achaia after the 26th acclamation of CLAUDIUS as emperor. Therefore, his term of office was in 51–52 or 52–53. According to PLINY the Elder (*Nat. Hist.* 31.33), the climate of Achaia made him ill. He went to Egypt after his term of office to recover from a lung hemorrhage. He then returned to Rome and became *consul suffectus* early in the reign of NERO. He was involved with his brother in a conspiracy to overthrow Nero, and, though temporarily pardoned, he was soon thereafter either forced to commit suicide or was put to death by order of Nero (Dio Cassius, *History* 62.25; Suetonius, *Rhetoric*).

While Gallio was residing at Corinth as proconsul of Achaia, a Jewish mob dragged the apostle PAUL before the rostrum and charged him with persuading the people to worship God contrary to law. Gallio, concerned primarily with Roman law, dismissed the case as a matter among Jews without letting Paul defend himself. Even when the mob seized SOSTHENES, the ruler of the synagogue, and beat him in front of the rostrum, Gallio did not exercise his prerogatives. This mention of Gallio's proconsulship in Acts is one of the few firm chronological details that allow us to synchronize Paul's ministry with extrabiblical history. Accordingly, we can confidently date the apostle's 18-month stay in Corinth during his second missionary journey within the period A.D. 50–52. (Cf. K. Haacker in *BZ* 16 [1972]: 252–55; C. Hemer in *Pauline Studies: Essays Presented to Professor F. F. Bruce on his 70th Birthday*, ed. D. A. Hagner and M. J. Harris [1980], 3–18, esp. 6–9; J. Murphy-O'Connor in *JBL* 112 [1993]: 315–17.) See also CHRONOLOGY (NT).

A. RUPPRECHT

gallon. See WEIGHTS AND MEASURES III.

gallows. A wooden structure used for execution by hanging. The term is used by Bible versions in the book of Esther to render Hebrew ʿēṣ *H6770*, "tree, wood" (Esth. 2:23 et al.; cf. also Gen. 40:19). See also CRIMES AND PUNISHMENTS III.

Gamad. See GAMMAD.

Gamael gam´ay-uhl (Γαμηλος). A descendant of ITHAMAR who affixed his seal to NEHEMIAH's covenant (1 Esd. 8:29; called DANIEL in the parallel lists, Ezra 8:2; Neh. 10:6).

Gamaliel guh-may´lee-uhl (גַּמְלִיאֵל *H1697*, "God is my completion [or reward]"; Γαμαλιήλ *G1137*). (1) Son of Pedahzur and a leader of the tribe of MANASSEH who was chosen to aid in the wilderness census and to bring the tribe's offering (Num. 1:10; 2:20; 7:54, 59; 10:23).

(2) A famous Jewish sage who advised moderation in the treatment of the apostles and who had earlier been PAUL's teacher (Acts 5:34; 22:3). He was one of the prominent TANNAIM or teachers whose rulings are mentioned in the MISHNAH. Known as Rabban Gamaliel the Elder, he was reportedly the grandson of none other than HILLEL, but this and other similar traditions cannot be confirmed. He is sometimes confused with his grandson, Gamaliel II, a very influential rabbi at the end of the 1st cent. The legal actions of Gamaliel I have to do with such matters as the invalidation of a bill of divorcement through a duplicity of names and the extension of the SABBATH prohibition on journeys of mercy. According to the Mishnah, "When Rabban Gamaliel the Elder died, the glory of the Law ceased and purity and abstinence [*pryšwt*, "separateness"] died" (*m. Soṭah* 9:15).

Gamaliel's precise opinion in regard to the early Christian church has been the subject of much debate in ecclesiastical circles. A tradition (in the *Clementine Recognitions*) that Gamaliel embraced Christianity toward his death in A.D. 70 is totally without foundation. Considering that the few mentions of Gamaliel in the Mishnah are inconclusive, it does appear that each of his enactments was liberalizing and humanitarian in its underlying motive, and this accords well with the speech quoted in Acts and with Paul's favorable mention of him as a man held in the highest esteem by the Jews. It may well be that Paul mentioned his name as a veiled suggestion that in his own case the policy of Gamaliel be adopted by the crowd. It is noteworthy that Paul casts no aspersions on the ability or insight of Gamaliel in regard to the law of Judaism. Yet he assumes that such a teacher's pupil would feel no compunction about persecuting the new and thriving "way." Paul does not again mention Gamaliel, as his new-found faith had irrevocably broken off his association with the Jewish sage. (See *HJP*, rev. ed. [1973–87], 2:367–68; on Gamaliel II, pp. 372–73.)

W. WHITE, JR.

game. Wild animals hunted for sports or food. The Hebrew term *ṣayid H7473* (Gen. 25:28; 27:3–7 et al.; KJV, "venison") refers to wild game of any kind. Game hunting apparently was not a popular Hebrew pastime, but was carried out mostly for reasons of hunger or the depredations of wild animals. However, men such as ISHMAEL (21:20) and ESAU (25:27) were renowned for their hunting skills. Game consisted chiefly of partridge, gazelle, and hart meat (Deut. 12:15), along with roebucks in the time of SOLOMON (1 Ki. 4:23).

R. K. HARRISON

games. Though many amusements, entertainments, diversions, and games were known in the ANE, there are few references to them in the Bible. In interpreting the activities of the ancients, it is often difficult to distinguish sacred and secular, ritual and amusement. Furthermore, entertainment ranged from the enjoyment of fine arts to the sadistic pleasure of the physical torture of captives or slaves, from the refined performances in the Greek theater to the cruel gladiatorial contests of Rome. Since material is considerable from antiquity concerning amusements—but little relating directly to the Bible—it is best to sketch ancient amusements generally and to note relevant Bible passages.

I. Children's games. Children love to play. The prophet ZECHARIAH described prosperity and peace as a time when "The city streets will be filled with boys and girls playing there" (Zech. 8:5). Children's active games are depicted on Egyptian tomb walls from the period of the Old Kingdom, for example, in the mastabas of Ptahhotep and Mereruka. Though often the scenes are difficult to interpret and the hieroglyphic legends are enigmatic in a number of instances, the activities can be described with some certainty—wrestling bouts, gymnastic games, and other exercises involving agility. Archaeological excavations have unearthed dolls and simple mechanical toys of several kinds from Egyptian burials. A number of balls have been found, and it is probable that most of these were for children's play. Children also engaged in games of make-believe. Jesus described the unresponsive and stubborn generation to which he ministered as being "like children sitting in the marketplaces and calling out to others: 'We played the flute for you, and you did not dance; we sang a dirge, and you did not mourn'" (Matt. 11:16–17).

II. Active sports. It appears that in Palestine hunting and fishing were means of livelihood rather than recreation. As a shepherd, DAVID defended his flock against incursions of predatory animals, killing marauding bears and lions by hand (1 Sam. 17:34–36); but this was performed from duty, not for amusement. On the other hand, kings and nobles of Egypt and Assyria hunted dangerous animals for diversion; reliefs, paintings, and inscriptions tell of their hunting exploits. Wealthy officials in Egypt participated in fishing or waterfowling for fun. Their sport, pursued in the marshy areas of the river, was termed *shmh-ib*, "distraction of heart," equivalent to "recreation," or "enjoyment." The most sporting type of waterfowling was done with a throwstick, or even with bow and arrow; but birds were also captured with a clapnet. Fishing was usually represented as a form of harpooning or spearing, but sometimes in tomb art the owner is shown using hook and line; bowfishing also is represented in ancient Egypt.

Swimming was practiced, apparently as a practical skill and not as a recreation. In the Bible, swimming is mentioned (Isa. 25:11; Ezek. 47:5), but not as an amusement. Competitive athletics existed from very early times, but found its greatest development in the Greek games (see ATHLETE). WRESTLING, in particular, was well known; evidence for it comes from both Mesopotamia and Egypt. In Egypt hundreds of wrestling groups are shown in the tomb art. Running, boxing, rowing, archery, and singlestick, or wandfighting, were also known. Participation often appears to be associated with the military or religion, and little of competitive sport could be called amusement for the participants. There is evidence from Medinet Habu and elsewhere that such competitions were performed to entertain the king and officials, or as part of the celebration of religious-political festivals.

In the OT, runners are mentioned as bearers of messages for the army or the king (cf. 2 Sam. 18:19–23). JOB lamented, "My days are swifter than a runner" (Job 9:25). The psalmist speaks of "a champion rejoicing to run his course" (Ps. 19:5). Swiftness of foot was a desirable manly quality, and the passage from the Psalms indicates that pleasure was derived from the exercise of strength in running.

DANCING and various acrobatic or rhythmic movements were associated with religious ritual, festivals, and even funerals. MIRIAM and the Israelite women played timbrels and danced after the Israelites crossed the sea (Exod. 15:20). Dancing was associated with the occasion of the worship of the golden calf at Mount SINAI (1 Cor. 10:7; see CALF, GOLDEN). When the ARK OF THE COVENANT was brought to JERUSALEM, "David danced before the LORD with all his might" (2 Sam. 6:14). Social dancing was unknown, and dances involving persons of both sexes are not depicted.

Various forms of ball playing were practiced in Egypt; women are shown taking part in such games at Beni Hasan. Possibly there was even a form of ritual in which a ball was struck with a stick or club. Playing ball is not mentioned in the Bible, though a reference to a ball appears (Isa. 22:18).

The Royal Game of Ur (found with other boards in graves dating to c. 2600 B.C.) was apparently one of the most popular games of the ancient world. Two players competed to race from one end of the board to the other.

III. Sedentary or inactive games. Sedentary games are widely evidenced throughout the ANE, especially board games of various kinds. Beautiful gaming boards and boxes have been found, as well as informal playing squares crudely scratched on flat rock surfaces. Playing draughts appears in the *Book of Gates* and is represented in the funerary art. Scenes at the High Gate of Medinet Habu show Ramses III and female members of his family indulging in such play. The representation of the playing board is found even in hieroglyphic writing as the biliteral sign *mn*.

Dice were used for determining moves in certain board games. The casting of lots is often referred to in the Bible, but always as a means of making decisions, whether of identity, procedure, or possession. Roman soldiers who crucified Jesus cast lots for his seamless tunic (Matt. 27:35; Mk. 15:24; Lk. 23:34; Jn. 19:23–24; Ps. 22:18).

IV. Spectator or passive amusements. The ancients were apparently more inclined to participate than to watch, but one may suppose that there were many spectators who observed religious ceremonies and royal festivities, with their attendant entertainment. The Philistines who congregated at the temple of Dagon in Gaza called for Samson to be brought to provide entertainment for them (Jdg. 16:25, 27).

People enjoyed hearing stories told, and eloquent speeches were appreciated, as in the Egyptian story of the Eloquent Peasant (cf. Ezek. 33:32). The NT Athenians took an avid interest in telling or hearing something new (Acts 17:21). Magicians amused people in ancient Egypt, as the Papyrus Westcar shows, but the Egyptian magicians mentioned in the Bible were involved in serious matters (cf. Gen. 41:8; Exod. 7:11, 22; 8:18–19). Magicians in Babylon were also mentioned at the time of Daniel (Dan. 1:20; 2:2, 27). See magic.

Throughout the ANE, banquets were held for entertainment. Many banquet scenes are shown in the Egyptian tombs, and many references to feasts appear in the Bible. Participants enjoyed abundant food and drink—sometimes to excess—and were entertained by dancers and musicians. Such entertainment was common at Egyptian banquets, and it is evident that Salome's dancing at the celebration of Herod's birthday pleased the viewers (Matt. 14:6; Mk. 6:22).

Music was an important diversion of antiquity. The ancients, like their modern descendants, were well aware of melody and rhythm. The beat of the drum or the clapping of hands, the playing of flute, trumpet, or stringed instruments, and the use of the human voice are clearly represented in the tomb art and well documented in the biblical literature (cf. Ezek. 33:32). Music was, of course, important in religious ceremonies and at affairs of state, but it was common at private parties and even in the solitude of the shepherd's care for his sheep. David provided music for Saul as an amusement, a therapy, and even as a spiritual exercise (cf. 1 Sam. 16:18, 23).

The hellenization of the ANE introduced many Greek amusements. Hippodromes, stadiums, and theaters sprang up as Greek culture pervaded the lands of the Bible. The NT missionary efforts enlarged the immediate geography of the biblical narrative and widened its cultural horizons as well. Paul alluded to the Greek athletic games (e.g., 1 Cor. 9:24). He also declared that the apostles had been made "a spectacle [*theatron* G2519, "theater"] to the whole universe, to angels as well as to men" (4:9). In the same epistle he also mentioned the Roman amusement of watching fights with wild animals (15:32).

The pagan world of the NT period was as absorbed with amusements as is the present age. The Christians were acquainted with the culture of their time, but they did not occupy themselves with it unduly, nor did they become engrossed in its less desirable features. (See further E. Falkener, *Games*

Ancient and Oriental [1892]; I. Lexova, *Ancient Egyptian Dances* [1935]; C. DeVries, *Attitudes of the Ancient Egyptians toward Physical-Recreative Activities* [Ph.D. dissertation, 1960]; P. Valavanis, *Games and Sanctuaries in Ancient Greece* [2004]; D. G. Kyle, *Sport and Spectacle in the Ancient World* [2007].) C. E. DE VRIES

Gammad gam'uhd (assumed name of a site, based on the gentilic גַּמָּדִים H1689, "Gammadites"). Also Gamad. In his poetic description of TYRE, EZEKIEL says, "Men of Arvad and Helech / manned your walls on every side; / men of Gammad / were in your towers" (Ezek. 27:11; KJV, "Gammadims"; LXX, *phylakes*, "guards"). The context suggests that the reference is to a city in PHOENICIA, otherwise unknown. Some have proposed an identification with Kumidi (modern Kamid el-Loz, N of Mt. HERMON; cf. map 11 in Y. Aharoni, *The Land of the Bible: A Historical Geography*, rev. ed. [1979], 173) or with *Qmd*, a town mentioned in Pharaoh Seti's lists and thought to be on or near the coast N of Byblos (so Aharoni, *Land of the Bible*, 178; for other suggestions, see W. Zimmerli, *Ezekiel*, Hermeneia [1979–83], 2:246).

Gammadim. See GAMMAD.

Gamul gay'muhl (גָּמוּל H1690, perhaps "benefit" or "weaned"). A leader of the Levites, appointed by lot as the head of the twenty-second course of priests during DAVID's time (1 Chr. 24:17). See also BETH GAMUL.

gangrene. Decay of bodily tissue. The term (Gk. *gangraina* G1121) is used figuratively of heretical teaching, compared to a spreading ulcer (2 Tim. 2:17). Some have thought that King ASA suffered from gangrene in his feet (1 Ki. 15:23).

Gar. KJV Apoc. variant of GAS (1 Esd. 5:34).

garden. A garden was the biblical setting for such important events as the entrance of SIN into the world (Gen. 3), Jesus' agony (Matt. 26:36–46), and Jesus' burial and resurrection (Jn. 19:41). God planted the first garden (Gen. 2:8); complete irrigation was provided (2:10), and God himself loved walking there in the cool of the day (3:8). See EDEN, GARDEN OF. Kings liked gardens. AHAB, for instance, wanted to make a scented garden of herbs near his palace, and his wife had NABOTH murdered so that he could have his wish (1 Ki. 21:1–16). AHAZIAH fled down the garden path and through the orangery or head gardener's house and so escaped (2 Ki. 9:27), but JEHU followed him and killed him. MANASSEH had a garden in Jerusalem and was buried there (2 Ki. 21:18). SOLOMON waxed lyrical about gardens (Cant. 4:15; 4:16; 6:2; cf. Eccl. 2:5). A well-watered garden is used to express joy, peace, and satisfaction (Jer. 31:12), while a fruitless life is described as "a garden without water" (Isa. 1:30). Foreign potentates delighted in watered gardens. ESTHER saw the beautiful courtyard gardens of King XERXES (Esth. 1:5); the king found that a walk in his gardens calmed him when he was angry (7:7). W. E. SHEWELL-COOPER

garden, king's. See KING'S GARDEN.

gardener. This term is used only two or three times in Bible versions to render different Greek terms (cf. Lk. 13:7 NRSV; Jn. 15:1; 20:15). By inference, however, gardeners are mentioned elsewhere in the Bible. ADAM and EVE were gardeners tending the Garden of Eden. CAIN became a gardener growing vegetables and fruits when ABEL was a farmer. Gardeners tended the groves or gardens of a nature-loving heathen god, BAAL (2 Ki. 10:19–23). PAUL was a tentmaker, but he may have been a keen amateur gardener also, for he had some knowledge of grafting (Rom. 11:17–24).
 W. E. SHEWELL-COOPER

garden of God. See EDEN, GARDEN OF.

Gareb (person) gair'ib (גָּרֵב H1735, "scabby"). An ITHRITE warrior included in DAVID's elite group, the Thirty (2 Sam. 23:38; 1 Chr. 11:40). The Ithrites were a clan from KIRIATH JEARIM (1 Chr. 2:53). Some scholars have emended the MT vocalization from *hayyitrî* to *hayyattirî*, "the Jattirite," that is, a native of the village of JATTIR (cf. S. R. Driver, *Notes on the Hebrew Text of the Books of Samuel*, 2nd ed. [1913], 372).

Gareb (place) gair'ib (גָּרֵב H1736, "scabby"). A hill in or near Jerusalem. JEREMIAH prophesied that God's city would be rebuilt "from the Tower of Hananel to the Corner Gate. The measuring line will stretch from there straight to the hill of Gareb and then turn to Goah" (Jer. 31:38–39). Because the Tower of Hananel was on the N wall (though its precise location is uncertain), with the Corner Gate apparently guarding the NW approach to Jerusalem, some traditions locate Gareb on the W side of the city and Goah farther S, but these sites have not been identified. See Jerusalem I.C.3.

G. G. Swaim

Garizim gair′uh-zim. KJV Apoc. form of Gerizim (2 Macc. 5:23; 6:2).

garland. This term is used by the NIV to render Hebrew *liwyâ H4292*, "wreath," which occurs only twice in a metaphorical sense, indicating honor and joy (Prov. 1:9; 4:9). The NRSV uses it a few additional times as a rendering of various other words (e.g., Heb. ʿăṭārâ H6498, Prov. 14:24 et al.; Gk. *stemma G5098*, Acts 14:13). See also crown; wreath.

garlic. KJV "garlick." This vegetable is mentioned only once in the Bible as one of the pleasant food varieties from Egypt that the Israelites longed for in the wilderness (*šûmîm H8770*, Num. 11:5). Though the passage refers to the garlic grown in Egypt, there is no doubt at all that this crop subsequently was grown in the Holy Land and was used in cooking. The bulbous perennial garlic is *Allium sativum*. When planted, it produces a number of smaller surrounding bulbs (cloves). Garlic has been used medicinally as a digestive stimulant, and its juice as an antiseptic.

W. E. Shewell-Cooper

garment. See dress.

Garmite gahr′mit (גַּרְמִי H1753, perhaps from גֶּרֶם H1752, "bone"). A gentilic, used only to identify a Judahite named Keilah, whose genealogical connection to the descendants of Judah is not specified (1 Chr. 4:19). Since no town by the name "Gerem" or the like is anywhere mentioned, some have speculated that the description "Garmite" may have referred to his bony or strong appearance.

garner. This noun, meaning "granary" or "barn," is used a few times in the KJV (Ps. 144:13; Joel 1:17; Matt. 3:12; Lk. 3:17), but not in the NIV and other modern versions. The verb *to garner* ("to gather and store") is used occasionally in recent translations (e.g., Isa. 62:9 NRSV).

garnet. A common and widely distributed accessory rock-forming mineral, particularly in micaceous schists and in some igneous rocks. The NEB uses "purple garnet" to render Hebrew *nōpek H5876*, referring to a semiprecious stone (Exod. 28:18; 39:11; Ezek. 27:16; 28:13; the NIV and NRSV identify it as turquoise). The color of garnet varies greatly, being dependent upon the varying proportions of calcium, magnesium, manganese, aluminum, chronium, and titanium present. It is used as a gemstone, particularly the deep red magnesium-aluminum variety *pyrope* and the brownish red to deep red iron-aluminum variety *almandine*, in which the color sometimes inclines to purple. Two other varieties also show purple color: (1) the manganese-aluminum variety *spessartite*, which is generally dark hyacinth red to brownish red, but sometimes with a tinge of violet, and (2) the magnesium-iron-aluminum variety *rhodolite*, which shows delicate shades of pale rose-red and purple. See also jewels and precious stones.

D. R. Bowes

garrison. A military post (or the troops assigned to it), often in a strategic frontier area, primarily for defensive purposes. Larger military units would be needed for an offensive drive. Garrisons were placed by the Philistines in the Judean region of Israel (*maṣṣāb H5163*, 1 Sam. 14:1–15; NIV, "outpost"). Once David brought these garrisons under his control, he then placed his own garrisons in Aram and Edom (*nĕṣîb H5907*, 2 Sam. 8:6, 14). See also army.

G. Giacumakis, Jr.

Gas gas (Γας). A servant of Solomon, mentioned as the ancestor of some temple servants (Nethinim) who returned from Babylon (1 Esd. 5:34; KJV, "Gar"). This name is omitted in the parallel passages (Ezra 2:57; Neh. 7:59).

Gashmu gash′myoo. KJV alternate form of Geshem (Neh. 6:6).

Gaspar gas´pahr. In late Christian tradition, the name of one of the MAGI who traveled to BETHLEHEM (Matt. 2:1–12).

Gatam gay´tuhm (גַּעְתָּם H1725, derivation uncertain). Son of Eliphaz, grandson of ESAU, and head of an Edomite clan (Gen. 36:11, 16; 1 Chr. 1:36).

gate. The entrance into a palace, camp, temple, etc., but especially into a CITY. Although the principal purpose of city gates was to make possible entrance and exit through its walls and to make the city secure, they also had other public functions in the economy of the state. Gates were the civic centers of the city. Since the city dwellers worked on farms outside the city walls, everyone passed through the gates every day. It was there, in an open square by the gate, that people met their friends or discussed news (Gen. 19:1; 23:10; 34:20; 2 Sam. 15:2; Neh. 8:1; Ps. 69:12). The gate was the market place of the town (2 Ki. 7:1) and the center of gossip (Ps. 69:12).

It was at the gate that the elders of the city sat for the administration of justice. See ELDER (OT). The Mosaic law, for example, directed that rebellious sons be brought before the elders of the city at the gate (Deut. 21:19). The manslayer had an opportunity to present his cause before the elders of the city of refuge at the entering in of the gate (Josh. 20:4). BOAZ consulted the elders of BETHLEHEM at the gate concerning RUTH's property (Ruth 4:1).

It was at the gate, moreover, that kings sat to meet with their subjects and made legal decisions. When DAVID heard of the death of ABSALOM, he sat at the gate and the people came before him to express their sympathy (2 Sam. 19:8). The king of Israel, joined by the king of Judah, sat at the entrance of the gate of SAMARIA and had the prophets prophesy before them (1 Ki. 22:10). ZEDEKIAH sat at the BENJAMIN GATE when he was told that JEREMIAH had been dropped into a cistern by his enemies (Jer. 38:7). When Jerusalem fell to the Babylonians, all the princes of Babylon came and sat in the middle gate (39:3). HEZEKIAH brought his military commanders together in the square at the gate of the city and told them not to despair over the threatened siege of Jerusalem (2 Chr. 32:6). The priests and prophets sometimes delivered their discourses, admonitions, and prophecies at the gate (2 Ki. 7:1; Neh. 8:1, 3; Jer. 17:19–20; 36:10).

The first legal transaction on record in the Bible, that of ABRAHAM's purchase of the cave of MACHPELAH as a burial place for SARAH, was completed at the gate of the city of HEBRON (Gen. 23:10, 18). Criminals condemned to death were punished outside the gates of the city (1 Ki. 22:10; Acts 7:58). Assyrian sculptures give numerous examples of

The entrance to the Israelite city of Dan was guarded by a massive gate complex (dating to the Iron Age).

execution by impalement outside the city walls and of burying outside the city gates. The dead were buried beyond the gates (Lk. 7:12; Heb. 13:12).

Gates consisted of two halves (Isa. 45:1) and were usually made of plain wood, perhaps studded with nails, or of wood covered with sheets of copper or iron (1 Ki. 4:13; Ps. 107:16; Isa. 45:2; Acts 12:10). Occasionally gates were made of a single slab of stone, like the doors leading into the tombs of the kings near Jerusalem, which consisted of a single stone 7 in. thick. They were secured by strong locks of brass, iron, or wood (Deut. 3:5; 1 Sam. 23:7; 1 Ki. 4:13; 2 Chr. 8:5; Ps. 147:13). The keys for gates (cf. Isa. 22:22) were large, sometimes more than 2 ft. in length.

Since the gates of a city were the weakest point of its defenses, they were strengthened by TOWERS (2 Chr. 14:7; 26:9; 32:5; Ps. 48:12). Usually there was an outer and an inner gate, with rooms for the keepers at the sides, and often a room above the gate (2 Sam. 18:24, 33). The width of the principal gate was about 13–14 ft. The other gates were low and narrow, permitting the entrance only of pedestrians or a single donkey. Gates were of course closed and guarded at night (Josh. 2:5, 7; Neh. 7:3).

In the Bronze Age, the city walls had only one or two gates, seldom more. In the Iron Age the gates were more numerous. A number of Bronze Age and Iron Age gates have been preserved, notably at GEZER and MEGIDDO. The city of BABYLON, which was 40 mi. in circuit, had one hundred bronze doors. JERUSALEM had fifteen, each with a different name. The great wall surrounding the TEMPLE at Jerusalem had nine gateways, with a massive two-storied gate-house over each one. One of them, called BEAUTIFUL GATE, was built entirely of Corinthian brass (Acts 3:2, 10).

The word *gate* often is used in a figurative sense. It frequently signifies the city itself, as when God promised Abraham that his posterity should possess the gate of his enemies (Gen. 22:17), meaning that they should have power or dominion over hostile cities. To "possess the gate" was to have dominion over the city (24:60). To sit at the city gates "among the elders of the land" was a high honor (Prov. 31:23), whereas crushing "the afflicted at the gate" was synonymous for judicial corruption (Prov. 22:22 NRSV; cf. Job 31:21).

Reconstruction of the massive cedarwood gate from the palace of Shalmaneser III (859–824 B.C.) at Balawat.

The gate is also a symbol of strength, power, and dominion (Ps. 24:7; 87:2; Isa. 60:18). Gates are pictured as howling and languishing, lamenting and mourning in time of a city's calamity (Isa. 3:26; 14:31; Jer. 14:2). Mention is made of the gate of HEAVEN (Gen. 28:17); the gate of the Lord (Ps. 118:20); the gates of DEATH (Ps. 9:13); the gates of SHEOL (Isa. 38:10); the gates of HADES (Matt. 16:18). When Jesus contrasted the wide gate and the narrow gate (Matt. 7:13), he had in mind the broad main gate at the entrance into a city and the small ones that allowed only pedestrians and single animals to pass through. (See M. Avi-Yonah, *Views of the Biblical World* [1960], 2:94, 107, 221, 262; 3:137, 151; R. de Vaux, *Ancient Israel* [1961], 152–55, 166–67, 233–34.) S. BARABAS

Gate, Beautiful. See BEAUTIFUL GATE. Similarly, EAST GATE; GUARD, GATE OF; VALLEY GATE; etc.

gate between the two walls. This gate is mentioned only three times in the OT (*šaʿar bên hahōmōtayim*, 2 Ki. 25:4; Jer. 39:4; 52:7). All three references are in the same context: JERUSALEM was under siege by NEBUCHADNEZZAR's army in 587 B.C., and ZEDEKIAH and his army fled eastward by night through "the gate between the two walls" to the Jordan Valley. One of the identifying factors about this gate is its location near the "king's garden," which in Neh. 3:15 is said to be near the Pool of SILOAM (Shelah). This pool at the southernmost part of Jerusalem lay between the main city wall and an outer wall. Several scholars have identified this gate with Nehemiah's FOUNTAIN GATE. Others believe it is the same as the POTSHERD GATE (Jer. 19:2), which in turn should probably be identified with the DUNG GATE (Neh. 2:13) at the extreme S end of the City of David.   G. GIACUMAKIS, JR.

Gath gath (גַּת *H1781*, "winepress"; gentilic גִּתִּי *H1785*, "Gittite"). One of the five cities of the PHILISTINES, the others being GAZA, ASHDOD, ASHKELON, and EKRON; they were all located on or near the coast of S Palestine, and each was ruled by its own king (Josh. 13:3; 1 Sam. 6:17). Gath was an old Canaanite city, and among its inhabitants, who were called Gittites (2 Sam. 6:10–11; 15:18–19, 22), were the Anakites, a people of extraordinary height who lived in the hill country of Palestine generally (see ANAK). The Anakites were destroyed by the Israelites in the general campaign under JOSHUA (Josh. 10:36–39; 11:21–22), but a remnant was left in Gaza, Ashdod, and Gath (11:22). Like all towns of any importance in ancient times, Gath was a walled city (2 Chr. 26:6).

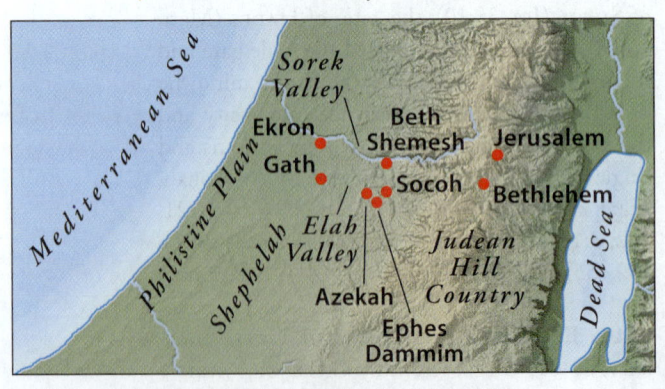

David of Bethlehem fought Goliath of Gath at the Valley of Elah.

Early in the history of Israel, the men of Gath slew some Israelites for raiding their cattle (1 Chr. 7:21; 8:13). When the Philistines captured the ARK OF THE COVENANT, they kept it successively in Ashdod, Gath, and Ekron, and then sent it back to Israel after many of the Philistines had died (1 Sam. 5:6–10; 6:17). In the days of SAMUEL, the Philistines took cities from the Israelites, but after they were routed at EBENEZER the cities were restored (7:14). However, the Philistines continued to be a source of trouble for the Israelites in the lifetime of Samuel (1 Sam. 9:16; 10:5; 13:3, 5, 19; 14:21; 17:1; 23:27). The giant GOLIATH, who was slain by DAVID, was one of the Anakites from Gath (17:4, 23; 2 Sam. 21:20, 22; 1 Chr. 20:5–8). Among some Anakites from Gath slain by David and his servants was a man with six fingers on each hand and six toes on each foot (2 Sam. 21:18–22; 1 Chr. 20:6–8). When the Philistines saw that their champion Goliath was dead, they fled from the pursuing Israelites to their own cities as far as Gath and Ekron (1 Sam. 17:52).

During the years of David's flight from King SAUL, he twice took refuge in Gath. On the first occasion, to save his life he feigned madness (1 Sam. 21:10–15; Ps. 56:1); on the second, he was accompanied by his wives and 600 followers, and was kindly received by ACHISH the king, who gave him the city of ZIKLAG in which to live (1 Sam. 27:1-28:2; 29). The likelihood is that for this favor David rendered Achish personal service in war (28:1). David's lament over the death of Saul and JONATHAN mentions the Philistine cities Gath and Ashkelon (2 Sam. 1:20). The OBED-EDOM to whom David entrusted the safe-keeping of the ark is referred to as a Gittite (6:10–11), but it is not known whether he was a follower of David from Gath or whether he was a native of the Levitical city of GATH RIMMON and therefore a Kohathite Levite (Josh. 21:24–25). David defeated the Philistines sometime during his reign—it is not certain exactly when—and took from them the city of Gath and its villages (1 Chr. 18:1). When David fled from Jerusalem after he had heard of ABSALOM's conspiracy to seize the throne, 600 Philistine followers from Gath accompanied him, and also ITTAI the Gittite, who shared the command of the army with JOAB and ABISHAI and who refused to

Goliath came from the Philistine city of Gath, probably modern Tell eṣ-Ṣafi, located on the ridge in the foreground of this photo.

accept David's kind invitation to dissociate himself from him (2 Sam. 15:18–22; 18:2, 5).

It is said in 1 Ki. 2:39–42 that two of the servants of SHIMEI, who had insulted David with gross language when David fled from Absalom, ran away to Gath and that Shimei pursued them there and brought them back, although he had been ordered by SOLOMON not to leave Jerusalem under any circumstances. Solomon's son REHOBOAM restored the fortifications of Gath (2 Chr. 11:8–10), which had either been destroyed by David or allowed to fall into disrepair. HAZAEL, king of SYRIA (ARAM), captured Gath during the reign of Jehoash (JOASH, 2 Ki. 12:17), but Jehoash later recaptured the city from Hazael's son BEN-HADAD. UZZIAH, king of Judah, made war on the Philistines and broke down the walls of Gath (2 Chr. 26:6), indicating that the Philistines must have retaken it from the Israelites.

In 715 B.C. SARGON II, king of ASSYRIA, brought a heavy defeat upon Ashdod and Gath. This attack, instigated by EGYPT, sought to include PALESTINE, JUDAH, EDOM, and MOAB in an anti-Assyrian league. It is not known whether Gath was then destroyed; but for some reason the later prophets omit it in the lists of Philistine cities (Amos 1:6–8; Zeph. 2:4–6; Jer. 25:20; Zech. 9:5). The city drops out of history, and its very location is a matter of dispute. Scripture indicates a site in the SHEPHELAH, not far from the border of Hebrew territory and from Ekron in N Philistia. Various places have been proposed as its location, including Tell Sheikh Ahmed el-ʿAreini, some 15 mi. E of Ashkelon (see W. F. Albright in *AASOR* 2–3 [1923]: 7–12) and Tell esh-Shariʿah, which is farther S (see G. E. Wright in *BA* 29 [1966]: 70–85, esp. 80). The most widely accepted site, however, is Tell eṣ-Ṣafi, c. 25 mi. SSE of JOPPA (see Y. Aharoni, *The Land of the Bible: A Historical Geography*, rev. ed. [1979], 271; *NEAEHL*, 4:1522–24, s.v. "Zafit, Tel"; *SacBr*, 154–56). This northerly location places Gath within a few miles of Ekron (Tell Miqne), with which it was closely associated (e.g., 1 Sam. 17:52).

There were several other places in Palestine with the name of Gath, since the culture of the vine was a major occupation in ancient Israel. Some of these, such as GATH HEPHER (2 Ki. 14:25) and GATH RIMMON (Josh. 19:45; 21:24–25; 1 Chr. 6:69), have an additional distinguishing element, but often the name stands alone, and it is difficult to decide exactly which Gath is meant. For example, a town mentioned outside the Bible and known as Gath Padalla (modern Jett, some 12 mi. NW of Samaria) is identified by some with the Gath of 1 Chr. 7:21 (see also GITTAIM). S. BARABAS

Gath Hepher gath-hee′fuhr (גַּת חֵפֶר H1783, "winepress by the [water] pit"). KJV, Gittah-hepher.

A border town of the tribe of ZEBULUN, to the E, next to the territory of NAPHTALI (Josh. 19:13); it was the home of the prophet JONAH (2 Ki. 14:25). The town is probably to be identified with Khirbet ez-Zurra‛, about 3 mi. NE of NAZARETH. Nearby, to the N, is the modern village of Meshhed, the traditional site of Jonah's tomb. Archaeological evidence for the occupation of this site during the time of Jonah has been found. JEROME reported visiting this tomb in his lifetime.

J. B. SCOTT

Gath Rimmon gath-rim´uhn (גַּת־רִמּוֹן *H1784*, "winepress by the pomegranate tree"). **(1)** A town in the territory of DAN (Josh. 19:45). It was one of four cities from this tribe allotted to the Levites descended from KOHATH (Josh. 21:24; 1 Chr. 6:69), and it may have been one of the CITIES OF REFUGE (see 1 Chr. 6:67 NRSV; cf. NIV note). Gath Rimmon is usually identified with Tell Jerisheh, 4.5 mi. NE of JOPPA and just S of the Yarkon River.

(2) A town of the one-half tribe of MANASSEH, W of the Jordan, and one of two cities from this tribe allotted to the Kohathite Levites (Josh. 21:25; LXX, *Iebatha*). Some have identified this Gath Rimmon with modern Rummaneh, NW of TAANACH, but many scholars believe that the text is the result of a scribal error (repeating the name of the Danite town in the previous verse) and so emend it to BILEAM, found in the parallel passage (1 Chr. 6:69).

J. B. SCOTT

Gaulanitis gawl´uh-ni´tis (Γαυλανῖτις, from Heb. גּוֹלָן *H1584*, "enclosure"). A district E of the Sea of Galilee, from Hippos in the S to Seleucia in the N. The name derives from the ancient town of GOLAN (LXX *Gaulōn*), located by archaeologists about 18 mi. E of the Sea of Galilee near the modern Arab town of Sheikh Sa᾽d. MOSES had designated Golan as one of three CITIES OF REFUGE in BASHAN, E of the Jordan, for the Manassites (Deut. 4:41–43). Under JOSHUA this status continued, and the descendants of GERSHON were assigned to the city (Josh. 20:8; 21:27; 1 Chr. 6:71). Undoubtedly Golan was the chief city of the district S of Mount HERMON settled by the tribe of Manasseh.

Neither the city of Golan nor the district of Gaulanitis is expressly mentioned in the NT, although there is an interesting parallel between Acts and JOSEPHUS. The latter describes a certain revolutionary leader named JUDAS as being from Gaulanitis (*Ant.* 18.1.1), whereas Luke identifies him as a Galilean (Acts 5:37). Elsewhere, however, Josephus also calls him a Galilean (*Ant.* 20.5.2; *War* 2.8.1); Judas was probably born in Golan and active in Galilee. Neither source confuses Galilee with Gaulanitis.

During the Herodian dynasty, the area of Gaulanitis was inherited by Philip after the death of HEROD the Great in 4 B.C. and continued as a part of his tetrarchy until A.D. 34. Philip's capital was BETHSAIDA, rebuilt and renamed Bethsaida Julias for the daughter of AUGUSTUS Caesar. Jesus traveled freely in this area (Mk. 6:45; 8:22, 27). It passed to the rule of Agrippa I in A.D. 37 until his death in 44. In the year 53, Agrippa II received it and continued to hold it until the Jewish revolt began in 66. The area was subject to the early campaign of the Romans against the Jewish revolutionaries (Jos. *War* 4.1.1). The land is part of the E Jordan plateau country and the soil is fertile. During the time of Christ the area was heavily populated. (See *HJP*, rev. ed. [1973–87], 1:336–39.)

J. C. DEYOUNG

The plateau of Gaulanitis is sprinkled with burial mounds that date before the time of Abraham. (View to the SE.)

Gauls gawlz (from Lat. *Galli*). An ancient name for the inhabitants of the land area from the Atlantic Ocean to the Rhine River and extending from the English Channel to the Pyrenees and extended W of the Alps. It was applied by the classical peoples to the Germanic tribes of the region. They were subdivided as early as the 1st cent. B.C. by Julius

CAESAR and other authors into Belgae, Celtae, and Aquitani. Their presence was known far earlier, although it was not specified. As wave after wave of Indo-European peoples migrated across the steppes of Eurasia during the 3rd and 2nd millennia into northern Greece, the Danube Valley, and the forests and coastal plains of modern Germany and France, they often brushed the borders of the great river valley civilizations of the ANE. They may have been included in the peoples mentioned by such names as TOGARMAH (Gen. 10:3). The scarce remnants of their languages are Germanic and show similarity to the Gothic dialects of the Danube Valley. Their art, as known from excavations of old Roman sites in Northern Europe, shows grotesque zoomorphic figures and finely wrought designs related to the Persian and Sarmatian art of the Indo-Iranian plateau. They are mentioned in the APOCRYPHA (under the name *Galatai*) as having been defeated by the Romans (1 Macc. 8:2) and the Macedonians (2 Macc. 8:20; cf. *ABD*, 2:911–12). See also GALATIA. W. WHITE, JR.

gauze, garments of. This expression is used by the NRSV and other versions to render the plural of Hebrew *gillāyôn* H1663 in one passage (Isa. 3:23). The term here has traditionally been understood as referring to a tablet of polished metal (thus KJV, "glasses," and NIV, "mirrors," following the Tg. and the Vulg.; cf. the clear meaning of "tablet" or "scroll," possibly made of PAPYRUS, in the word's only other occurrence, 8:1). The immediate context of Isa. 3:23 is a criticism of the women of Zion and includes a statement that the Lord will take away the articles of clothing with which they beautify themselves. Some scholars therefore see here a reference to delicate attire (cf. LXX v. 22; *HALOT*, 1:193, renders the Hebrew word, "papyrus garments"). Others emend the text (cf. H. Wildberger, *Isaiah 1–12: A Commentary* [1991], 155). G. GIACUMAKIS, JR.

Gaza gay´zuh, gah´zuh (עַזָּה H6445, "strong"; gentilic עַזָּתִי H6484, "Gazite" [Josh. 13:3, KJV "Gazathites"; Jdg. 16:2]). KJV also Azzah (Deut. 2:23; 1 Ki. 4:24; Jer. 25:20). The southernmost of the five chief cities of the PHILISTINES in SW Palestine, the others being ASHDOD, ASHKELON, EKRON, and GATH.

GAZA

I. Location. Ancient OT Gaza was located about 50 mi. SW of JERUSALEM and about 3 mi. inland from the Mediterranean Sea. The town was about 12 mi. S of Ashkelon and on the important caravan and military route that extended to the SW and then W through the sands close to the Mediterranean Sea to Pelusium and the NILE delta. Through Gaza, military expeditions were made from EGYPT to PALESTINE, SYRIA, and the countries of MESOPOTAMIA. It was vital, in any military campaign, for opposing enemies to hold this city as a rest area to or from the desert.

II. Geographical characteristics. OT Gaza lay on and about a hill some 100 ft. above a fertile plain. It was a natural location for a city because of fifteen fresh water wells that provided for adequate agricultural produce and the physical needs of a large population. It was inevitable that this town should develop as a trade center for caravans and a place where armies could restock their water supplies.

III. The earliest history of Gaza. The earliest OT reference (Gen. 10:19), which goes back to the pre-Abrahamic period, describes the territory of the Canaanites as extending from SIDON in the N to GERAR and Gaza in SW Palestine. Other early inhabitants of Gaza and the S end of Palestine, evidently prior to the time of MOSES, were called AVVITES (Deut. 2:23; cf. vv. 19–23). Later, in JOSHUA's day, the Avvites together with the Canaanites were still associated with S Palestine, but the Philistines were then in control of Gaza and the surrounding area (Josh. 13:3–4).

IV. Early extrabiblical references to Gaza. The annals of THUTMOSE III present Gaza as an important town, which this pharaoh and his Egyptian army seized and at which he stayed on his first campaign into Palestine involving the battle of MEGIDDO (1468 B.C.; see *ANET*, 235). Compare also the Taanach Letter No. 6, written to a prince Rewašša by an Egyptian official, Amenophis, who mentions his being in the town of Gaza, *Hazati* (see W. F. Albright in *BASOR* 94 [April 1944]: 24–27; Albright conjectures that this Egyptian official may have been a later pharaoh, Amenophis II). A little later in the 15th–14th cent. B.C., during this period of Egyptian domination of Palestine including the Gaza-Ashkelon area, one of the TELL EL-AMARNA letters, although not mentioning Gaza, refers to nearby Ashkelon in such terms as to reflect on the greater importance of the nearby official Egyptian residence at Gaza (*ANET*, 490, no. 320). Another Amarna letter mentions Gaza as well as the whole land as loyal to Egypt, although there was trouble from the advancing ʿApiru (*ANET*, 489, no. 289; the term could possibly refer to the Hebrews, see HABIRU). After the conquest of Palestine under Joshua, there was still much land to be subdued (Jdg. 2:20—3:1). The Egyptians c. 1200 B.C. could speak of still having influence over Gaza and other places S of Canaan (see Papyrus Anasti I, of the late Nineteenth Egyptian Dynasty, *ANET*, 478).

V. Gaza and Israel. According to the first biblical reference mentioning Israel's contact with this Philistine town (Josh. 10:41), Joshua in his conquest defeated all of S Palestine, including the area from KADESH BARNEA to Gaza. Another comment (11:22) adds that the ancient Anakites (see ANAK) in Israel were destroyed except in certain cities, including Gaza, which were really in the control of the Philistines (13:3). This town was allotted to the tribe of Judah (15:47), which then had the responsibility of trying to conquer it (Jdg. 1:18–19). Judah did not succeed because the Midianites, Amalekites, and others made attacks at will on Israel as far as Gaza (6:4), and in the time of SAMSON, the Philistines were well in control of the town (ch. 16). Samson had made inroads on Philistine power (chs. 14–15), eluding and humiliating his Gazite enemies by ripping off the doors of the gate of their city and carrying them off to HEBRON (16:1–3), but evidence of complete Philistine control of Gaza was their humiliation of Samson in the prison at this city (16:21).

Later mastery of the city and area by the Philistines is evident when the king of Gath and the other Philistine rulers sent the captured ARK OF THE COVENANT back to Israel with a trespass offering of gold (1 Sam. 6:17). In the time of the united monarchy, SOLOMON most likely had the mastery over even a border area such as Gaza (1 Ki. 4:24). AMOS (mid-8th cent. B.C.) pronounced the Lord's condemnation on Gaza because its inhabitants had conquered whole communities and delivered them as slaves to EDOM (Amos 1:6–7).

In the time of Assyrian ascendancy, TIGLATH-PILESER III (744–727 B.C.), in connection with his campaigns against Syria and Palestine (733–732), told how he received tribute of gold, silver, antimony, linen garments, etc., from a number of cities, including Gaza and its king Hanno (*ANET*, 282). Hanno eventually fled to Egypt and returned with the Egyptians to fight against SARGON II (721–705 B.C.) in a battle S of Gaza (c. 721–720). Following defeat he was deported to the city of ASSHUR (*ANET*, 283–85). Gaza became Assyrian, but the Philistines were still in the region, for a little later HEZEKIAH king of Judah, in rebellion against Assyria, "defeated the Philistines, as far as Gaza and its territory" (2 Ki. 18:8).

A few years later another Assyrian king, SENNACHERIB (704–681), made a campaign against the cities of Judah and conquered them (701 B.C., 2 Ki. 18:13), and when he threatened HEZEKIAH and Jerusalem, the Lord overthrew his army (18:17—19:35). In arrogant boasting in his annals, Sennacherib told of shutting up Hezekiah in Jerusalem "like a bird in a cage," and how he took away sections of Judah and gave them to Sillibel, king of Gaza, and to other Philistine rulers (*ANET*, 288). Sil-Bel king of Gaza (possibly the same ruler or a successor) and other rulers from the seacoast were forced to furnish building materials for the palace of ESARHADDON (680–669) at NINEVEH (*ANET*, 291), and to ASHURBANIPAL (668–633); the same

Gaza.

Philistine king is said to have brought heavy tribute and in submission kissed the Assyrian king's feet (*ANET*, 294). With this background in mind, ZEPHANIAH (638–608) prophesied the overthrow of Gaza and the area (Zeph. 2:4–7), which came about in stages in the succeeding centuries, as under Alexander Jannaeus (96 B.C.; see HASMONEAN).

JEREMIAH speaks of Pharaoh conquering Gaza (Jer. 47:1), as does also HERODOTUS (*Hist*. 2.159), who mentions Pharaoh's conquest of "the great Syrian city of *Kadytis*" (i.e., Gaza). This event took place in connection with Pharaoh NECO's military expedition in 609 B.C. across Syria to fight the Babylonian king NEBUCHADNEZZAR, conqueror of Assyria (Jer. 46:2; cf. 2 Ki. 23:29; 2 Chr. 35:20; Jos *Ant*. 10.5.1). Jeremiah also prophesied that Nebuchadnezzar would conquer Gaza and all the land of the Philistines (Jer. 25:20), words that were fulfilled, as witnessed to in the inscriptions of Nebuchadnezzar (605–562); the king of Gaza and others were ordered to carry on official duties in the Babylonian court (*ANET*, 307–8). (For the reading "Gaza" in 1 Chr. 7:28 KJV, see AYYAH.)

VI. Gaza in postexilic and intertestamental times.

Despite the conquests already mentioned, Gaza and the Philistines maintained some power and influence, as is indicated by Zechariah's prophecy against them (Zech. 9:5–6). In the time of the Persian invasion, Polybius (*Hist*. 16.22a) tells how brave the people of Gaza were. Later, under the Persians, the city with the help of Arab-hired soldiers (Arrian, *Anab*. 2.26–27) resisted a two-months' siege by ALEXANDER THE GREAT (332 B.C.) before finally falling to him (Diodorus Siculus, *Bibl. Hist*. 17.48; Jos. *Ant*. 11.83; Polybius, *Hist*. 16.22a), after which it became more and more a Greek city (Josephus calls it *polis Hellēnis, Ant* 17.11.4; *War* 2.6.3). In subsequent years Gaza became the possession at times of Syria and then of Egypt. A few years prior to the Maccabean revolt, Gaza came more permanently under the control of Syria, following the victory of ANTIOCHUS the Great at Panias (198 B.C.; cf. Polybius, *Hist*. 16.22a).

In Maccabean times Gaza surrendered to Jonathan MACCABEE (1 Macc. 11:61–62). Later, after the city had requested help from PTOLEMY of Egypt against Alexander Jannaeus and that help failed, Alexander made a one-year seige against Gaza, conquered it, and slaughtered its people (96 B.C.; Jos. *Ant*. 13.3). In a real sense Alexander made Gaza *erēmos*, or deserted, a fact so indicated by ancient writers (Jos. *Ant*. 14.5.3; Strabo, *Geogr*. 16.2.30). Under POMPEY, who conquered Syria c. 63 B.C., Gaza, such as it was, received its freedom (Jos. *Ant*. 14.4.4) and about six years later was rebuilt under the order of the Roman general Gabinius (*Ant*. 14.5.3). In 30 B.C. Gaza came under the control of HEROD the Great (*Ant*. 15.7.3; *War* 1.20.3), but after his death it reverted to the province of Syria (*Ant*. 17.11.4; *War* 2.6.3), as the imperial coins of Gaza, which begin to show up after Herod's death, demonstrate.

VII. Gaza in NT times and later.

The only NT mention of this city is Acts 8:26 in reference to the wilderness road "that goes down from Jerusalem to Gaza." A problem arises as to how the word *erēmos* G2245, "desert," is to be handled: whether to refer it to the word "road" (so most versions) or to the name Gaza, with the meaning "deserted [i.e., old] Gaza." Strabo (*Geogr*. 16.2.30) had an understanding that Gaza had remained deserted after its destruction by Alexander the Great, whom he seems to have confused with Alexander Jannaeus.

Diodorus Siculus (*Bibl. Hist*. 19.80) spoke of an old Gaza. Some think there was a new Gaza built a bit S of the old city as maintained by some ancient geographers (see *HJP*, rev. ed. [1973–87], 2:101), and that Josephus's inclusion of Gaza as among coastal towns (*Ant*. 14.4.4) also refers to this new city. The old Gaza no doubt became inhabited again after Alexander Jannaeus's destruction, since it lay on the main caravan road (cf. also Diodorus Siculus, *Bibl. Hist*. 19.80, and Arrian, *Anab*. 2.26–27), and it and the new Gaza may well have continued together even into the NT period. It does not seem, likely, however, that the old Gaza would then be called "desert" in Acts on account of its condition over a hundred years before. Rather, since the "road" is emphasized in this passage, it seems better to refer the concept "desert" to it, pointing out that it is the road that leads over to the desert way to Egypt.

In A.D. 66, Gaza was attacked and destroyed by the rebellious Jews (Jos. *War* 2.18.1), but evidently only partially, for Gaza coins show up during the years 68–74 (*HJP*, 2:101–2). In the 2nd and 3rd centuries, the city prospered as a center of Greek culture, and the church only after hard struggles firmly established itself there at about 400. From 635 on, except for a brief time during the Crusades, Gaza was in Arab hands, until the late 1960s. The modern city of Gaza rests on the old site, thus no significant archaeological work has been possible. (See further G. A. Smith, *The Historical Geography of the Holy Land*, 25th ed. [1931], 133–38; *HJP*, 2:98–103; Y. Aharoni, *The Land of the Bible: A Historical Geography*, rev. ed. [1979], passim; *ABD*, 2:912–21.)

W. H. MARE

Gazara guh-zay′ruh. See GEZER.

Gazathite gay′zuh-th*i*t. See GAZA.

gazelle. Comprising about twelve species, gazelles are medium-sized antelopes inhabiting dry grasslands and desert; they extend from central Africa through Palestine and India to the Gobi Desert of Mongolia. The usual Hebrew term is *ṣĕbî* H7383 (Deut. 12:15 et al.; more rarely, the alternate forms *ṣĕbiyyâ* H7386, *ṣābāʾ* H7373, *ṣĕbāʾâ* H7374); the KJV renderings "roe" and "roebuck" are not correct. The Greek name (*dorkas* G1520, cf. Acts 9:36 and see DORCAS) is still found in the scientific name of *Gazella dorcas*, one of the two species found in W Palestine today. The other, much more common, is the Palestine gazelle (*G. arabica*); this is one of the smallest, standing just over 2 ft. at the shoulders. Gazelles are usually of pale brown or sandy color, often with a dark line along the side demarcating the almost white underparts. (See *FFB*, 33–34.) This provides good camouflage, but their main defense is speed, and all four figurative passages outside SONG OF SOLOMON refer to this distinctive. In Song of Solomon the word is used as a symbol of grace and beauty (Cant. 2:9 et al.; note that the homonym *ṣĕbî* H7382 means "beauty, glory"), and the name today still suggests these attributes.

At one time gazelles, widely distributed in Palestine, were common enough to provide a useful amount of meat. This is clearly implied in Deut. 12:15 and 22, where it is mentioned almost as a standard commodity. When ISAAC asked ESAU to go and kill some game (Gen. 27:3; KJV, "venison"), this could have meant any wild game, but since he lived in the BEERSHEBA area—the gateway to the NEGEV—a gazelle would be the most likely target for Esau's arrow. Gazelle meat is sometimes rather dry but good enough for eating.

The spread of cultivation reduced the numbers of gazelles progressively, though the creatures are not unduly worried by human presence and will feed around or even in farms and close to tractors if allowed to do so. Wealth allowed desert hunting for sport in cars, quickly reducing numbers to the danger point. In some countries there is still little or no control, but with protection by game laws and reserves in Israel, stocks have recovered and their survival is much more hopeful. See also DEER.

G. S. CANSDALE

Palestinian gazelle.

Gazer gay′zuhr. KJV alternate form of GEZER (2 Sam. 5:25; 1 Chr. 14:16).

Gazera guh-zee′ruh. KJV Apoc. form of GEZER (1 Macc. 4:15 et al.) and GAZZAM (1 Esd. 5:31).

Gazez gay′ziz (גָּזֵז H1606, possibly "[sheep] shearer" or "born at shearing time"). **(1)** Son of CALEB by his concubine Ephah (1 Chr. 2:46). But this individual may be the same as #2 below.

(2) Son of Haran, grandson of Caleb, and nephew of #1 above (1 Chr. 2:46). Some have thought that the words "Haran was the father of [*lit.*, begat] Gazez" are an explanatory addition to the previous statement, in which case there was only one person by this name, Caleb's grandson.

Gazite gay′zit. See GAZA.

Gazzam gaz′uhm (גַּזָּם H1613, possibly "caterpillar"). Ancestor of some temple servants (NETHINIM) who returned to Jerusalem with ZERUBBABEL (Ezra 2:48; Neh. 7:51; called "Gazera" in 1 Esd. 5:31).

Geba gee′buh (גֶּבַע H1494, "hill"). KJV also Gaba (representing the Heb. pausal form; Josh. 18:24; Ezra 2:26; Neh. 7:30). A city in the territory of the tribe of BENJAMIN (Josh. 18:24); it was assigned to the Levites (Josh. 21:17; 1 Chr. 6:60). SAUL and JONATHAN may have encamped there when the PHILISTINES were at MICMASH (1 Sam. 13:16; the NIV, however, regards Geba here and in Jdg. 20:10, 33 as a spelling variant of GIBEAH; cf. the maps and text in C. G. Rasmussen, *Zondervan NIV Atlas of the Bible* [1989], 111–12). It was possibly in Geba also that DAVID began to smite the Philistines (2 Sam. 5:25; NIV, GIBEON, following LXX and 1 Chr. 14:16). ASA built a fortress in Geba with stones from RAMAH (1 Ki. 15:22; 2 Chr. 16:6). JOSIAH defiled the high places where the priests had burned incense from Geba, the N limit of JUDAH, to the S limit, BEERSHEBA (2 Ki. 23:8).

Geba is coupled with Ramah in the lists of those returning from BABYLON (Ezra 2:26; Neh. 7:30), and it is one of the cities where Benjamites lived after the EXILE (Neh. 11:31) and from which singers came and sang at the dedication of the temple (12:29). It was one of the stopping points of the Assyrian army on its approach to Jerusalem (Isa. 10:29). Geba is to be identified with modern Jebaʿ, c. 6 mi. NNE of Jerusalem, and 2 mi. E of Ramah. (On the possible textual confusion of Geba with Gibeah and Gibeon, see A. Demsky in *BASOR* 212 [Dec. 1973]: 26–31. J. M. Miller in *VT* 25 [1975]: 145–66 argues that all references to Geba and Gibeah refer to the same place, Jebaʿ. Cf. also P. Arnold in *ABD*, 2:921–22.) J. B. SCOTT

Gebal gee′buhl (גְּבַל H1488, "boundary"; gentilic גְּבָלִי H1490, "Gebalite" [KJV, "Giblite"]). **(1)** A non-Israelite town or region associated with such nations as EDOM, MOAB, and AMMON (Ps. 83:7); it was probably in TRANSJORDAN, SE of the Dead Sea.

Looking S toward the hilltop on which the ancient site of Geba once stood.

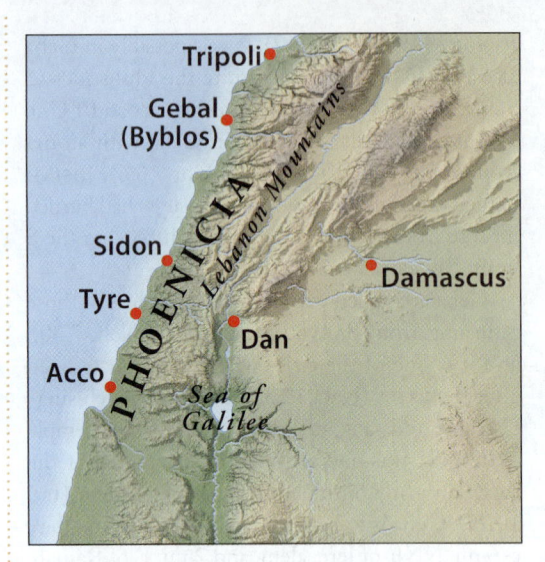

Gebal (Byblos).

(2) A city in PHOENICIA on the Mediterranean Sea; modern Jebeil (Jubayl), 18 mi. NNE of Beirut. It was called Gubla by the Assyrians and Babylonians, while the Greeks and the Romans knew it as Byblos (because the city was a major exporter of writing material, the Gk. word *byblos* came to mean "[papyrus] scroll"). Once a flourishing port and trading center, its most valuable export was pine and cedarwood from LEBANON. The city was also noted for shipbuilding and stonecutting. Excavation began in 1921 at Gebal by Pierre Montet, later joined by Maurice Dunand. The work has revealed successive layers of occupation. Traces of ancient magnificence in the ruins of its wall, castle, and temple were uncovered. It is one of the oldest towns in the world; occupation of the site has been traced to Neolithic times. By the latter half of the 5th millennium B.C., villages were in existence all over W Asia, including Gebal. Remains have been found of a people in late Chalcolithic GEZER and Gebal of small, slender, bony structure, long-headed, and delicate of feature. They lived in rectangular or circular huts, used silver for personal ornaments, and buried their dead in large earthen pots.

Late in the 4th millennium, as the protoliterate culture flourished in MESOPOTAMIA, there was widespread cultural exchange. Even at that early period, EGYPT was in contact with Gebal. Seal impressions found there suggest that a major route of exchange lay through Palestine and Syria. In c. 2800 B.C., fire swept through the city, causing a setback in its progress, but it was reconstructed on an even grander scale. It was at this time that Egypt was experiencing her great classic flowering—the Old Kingdom period. She had not yet organized an Asiatic empire, but was already protecting her commercial interests there with military force. Gebal was virtually a colony during this period, supplying the cedars of Lebanon, which were of vital importance to Egypt. The temple of Baaltis in Gebal received votive offerings in great quantities from Egypt all through the Bronze Age.

Before the end of the third millennium, Canaanites in Gebal had developed a syllabic script modeled on the Egyptian hieroglyphics (see ALPHABET; WRITING). A number of these inscriptions on copper have been found. The names of the kings at the end of the 3rd millennium indicate that the rulers were Semites, probably AMORITES. At the beginning of the 2nd millennium, the most prosperous period of Egyptian history was about to begin—the Middle Kingdom period. During the twelfth dynasty, Egypt enjoyed prosperity that was rarely matched in all her history. Most of Palestine and S Phoenicia were under Egyptian control at this time. Gebal was an Egyptian colony. Objects found in tombs there bear the cartouches of rulers of the twelfth dynasty. The native princes wrote their names in Egyptian characters and vowed their loyalty to the Pharaoh. As the Middle Kingdom was coming to an end (c. 1797 B.C.), the twelfth was followed by the weak thirteenth dynasty. There was a brief revival under Neferhotep I (c. 1740–1729), when nominal authority was exercised over Gebal. During this period MARI reached its zenith (1730–1700) under Zimri-lim and had widespread trade with many cities, including Gebal.

Gebal is mentioned in the TELL EL-AMARNA documents. King Rib-addi of Gebal sent more than fifty letters to the king of Egypt proclaiming his allegiance and complaining of imminent invasion by the HABIRU. At the beginning of the reign of RAMSES II (c. 1290–1224), Gebal was a border fortress for the Egyptian province of Canaan and in 1194 was destroyed by the SEA PEOPLES in their march on Egypt. A period of extreme Egyptian weakness followed c. 1080, so that Gebal, which was almost as Egyptian as Egypt herself, received the royal representative Wen-Amon with mockery and insolence, demanding cash for the trees he had been sent to acquire for constructing a sacred barge.

The sarcophagus of Ahiram of Gebal (c. 1000) was discovered with inscriptions of a Phoenician type script. These inscriptions use the twenty-two consonants found also in the Hebrew alphabet and are written from right to left. The Gebalites were considered master builders and able seamen (1 Ki. 5:18; Ezek. 27:9). Their land is mentioned as one of those that were not conquered by the Israelites (Josh. 13:5).

Gebal paid tribute to several Assyrian kings during their era of domination, including Ashurnasirpal II (883–859), Tiglath-Pileser III (745–727), Sennacherib (705–681), Esarhaddon (681–669), and Ashurbanipal (669–627). The Gebalites also were dominated in turn by the Babylonians, Persians, Greeks, and Romans. The remains of a castle built by the Crusaders in the 11th cent. A.D. are there. (See M. Noth, *The Old Testament World* [1966], 213–14; M. Dunand, *Byblos: son histoire, ses ruines, ses légendes*, 3rd ed. [1973]; M. Sagieh, *Byblos in the Third Millennium B.C.* [1983]; A. Nibbi, *Ancient Byblos Reconsidered* [1985].) F. B. Huey, Jr.

Geber gee´buhr (גֶּבֶר H1506, "man, strong one"). Son of Uri and one of the twelve district governors who supplied provisions for Solomon and the royal household; he was in charge of the twelfth district in Gilead (1 Ki. 4:19). Some have thought that this passage is a duplication of the sixth district (v. 13), but Geber may have been responsible for the southern parts of Gilead; see Ben-Geber.

Gebim gee´bim (גֵּבִים H1481, "pits"). A village of the tribe of Benjamin mentioned only in the poetic listing of the conquests of Assyria (Isa. 10:31). The passage mentions Gebim between Madmenah and Nob, but none of these locations has ever been confidently identified. The context also mentions Anathoth, which was 2.5 mi. NE of Jerusalem, so Gebim was probably in that vicinity. Eusebius (*Onomasticon* 74.1–2) identifies Gebim with a town named Geba (Gk. *Gēba*), modern Khirbet et-Tell,

by the Wadi el-Jib (see J. Simons, *The Geographical and Topographical Texts of the Old Testament* [1959], 175 n. 158), but there is no evidence that he is in fact correct. W. White, Jr.

gecko. See Lizard.

Gedaliah ged´uh-li´uh (גְּדַלְיָהוּ H1546, "great is Yahweh"). (**1**) Son of Jeduthun and a temple musician under David (1 Chr. 25:3, 9).

(**2**) Son of Ahikam, grandson of Shaphan, and governor of Judah after the fall of Jerusalem to the Babylonians (2 Ki. 25:22–26; Jer. 40:6—41:18). His family's political moderation, shown by his father's protection of Jeremiah, probably made him acceptable to the Babylonians (Jer. 26:24). Mizpah, his headquarters during his two-month rule, served as a rallying point for various groups of Hebrew soldiers and nobility. He avoided political intrigue in rejecting the scheme of Johanan son of Kareah to murder Ishmael son of Nethaniah. He, many Jewish leaders, and the Babylonian garrison were assassinated by Ishmael. Gedaliah's partisans, fearing Babylonian reprisals, then fled to Egypt, forcing Jeremiah the prophet to go with them. The events associated with his death made it impossible for a Jewish community to survive in Palestine under Babylonian control. The Jewish community, in effect, disappeared until the return of new leadership from Babylon. Jewish tradition recognizes the importance of his death in remembering its anniversary as a fast day. A contemporary seal, with the inscription "of Gedaliah who is over the house," has been found at Lachish.

(**3**) Son of Pashhur; he was one of the officials who opposed Jeremiah and put him in a cistern (Jer. 38:1–6).

(**4**) A descendant of Jeshua son of Jozadak, listed among the priests in Ezra's time who agreed to put away their foreign wives (Ezra 10:18).

(**5**) One of the descendants of Pashhur who agreed to put away their foreign wives (1 Esd. 9:22 NRSV [KJV, "Ocidelus"]; the parallel passage has Jozabad, Ezra 10:22).

(**6**) Son of Amariah and grandfather of the prophet Zephaniah (Zeph. 1:1). A. Bowling

Geddur ged´uhr. See Gahar.

Gedeon ged´ee-uhn. KJV Apoc. and NT form of GIDEON.

Geder gee´duhr (גֶּדֶר H1554, "stone wall"; gentilic גְּדֵרִי H1559, "Gederite"). A Canaanite city conquered by the Israelites (Josh. 12:13). It is listed after DEBIR and before ARAD, which may indicate a location either in the SHEPHELAH or in the NEGEV, but the site has not been identified. One of DAVID's officials, BAAL-HANAN the Gederite (1 Chr. 27:28), was apparently from this town.

Gederah gi-dee´ruh (גְּדֵרָה H1557, "stone-walled pen"; gentilic גְּדֵרָתִי H1561, "Gederathite"). (1) A town within the tribal territory of JUDAH located in the SHEPHELAH (Josh. 15:36; NIV regards Gederah and GEDEROTHAIM as the same place). Together with NATAIM, Gederah is listed as inhabited by clans of skilled craftsmen who served as potters for the king (1 Chr. 4:23; KJV has "plants and hedges" for "Netaim and Gederah"). Its location is unknown, although various sites have been proposed.

(2) A town in the tribal territory of BENJAMIN. We know of this village only because one of the Benjamite warriors who joined DAVID at ZIKLAG was named JOZABAD the Gederathite (1 Chr. 12:4). Some have identified this Gederah with modern Jedireh, a short distance from GIBEON.

A. BOWLING

Gederathite gi-dee´ruh-thit. See GEDERAH.

Gederite gi-dee´rit. See GEDER.

Gederoth gi-dee´roth (גְּדֵרֹת H1558, "stone-walled pens"). A town in the tribal territory of JUDAH located in the SHEPHELAH (Josh. 15:31). In the time of AHAZ, Gederoth was one of several towns occupied by the PHILISTINES (2 Chr. 28:18). Gederoth was no doubt located near the Judah-Philistia border, but the precise site is unknown.

A. BOWLING

Gederothaim gi-dee´ruh-thay´im (גְּדֵרֹתַיִם H1562, "[two] stone-walled pens"). A town in the tribal territory of JUDAH located in the SHEPHELAH (Josh. 15:36). It is the last name in a list of fifteen towns that were part of the tribe's third administrative district, but the text speaks of "fourteen towns and their villages." The NIV rendering treats Gederothaim as an alternate name for GEDERAH, thus bringing the total to fourteen. The SEPTUAGINT attempts to solve the problem by translating Hebrew wĕhaggĕdērâ wĕgĕdērōtāyim as *kai Gadēra kai hai epauleis autēs*, "and Gederah and its sheep pens." If Gederothaim is a distinct town, its location is unknown.

Gedi. See EN GEDI.

Gedor gee´dor (גְּדוֹר H1529 and H1530, "wall"). (1) A town in the tribal territory of JUDAH located in the hill country (Josh. 15:58). It is usually identified with Khirbet Jedur, 7.5 mi. NNW of HEBRON. According to many scholars, the description "Penuel was the father of Gedor" (1 Chr. 4:4) means that PENUEL founded or was an early inhabitant of this Judahite city. It is also possible that the Gedor mentioned later in the passage (v. 18) refers to the same town and that JERED was another important figure associated with it.

(2) A town in a valley settled by Simeonites but earlier inhabited by Hamites and Meunites (1 Chr. 4:39; cf. vv. 40–41). It is described as a land very spacious and peaceful, with good pasture. The location is unknown, and some scholars, following the SEPTUAGINT, emend the name to GERAR.

(3) A town in the tribal territory of BENJAMIN and the home of JOELAH and ZEBADIAH, two of the warriors who joined DAVID at ZIKLAG (1 Chr. 12:7). Attempts have been made to identify this Gedor with #1 above or with Khirbet Gadeirah, N of el-Jib. Other scholars believe the text is corrupt.

(4) Son of Jeiel and descendant of BENJAMIN; his brother NER was the grandfather of SAUL (1 Chr. 8:31; 9:37).

J. B. SCOTT

Ge Harashim gi-hair´uh-shim (גֵּיא חֲרָשִׁים H1629, "valley of the craftsmen"). Also Ge-harashim. The genealogy of the Judahite clan of KENAZ refers to a certain JOAB as "the father [*i.e.*, founder] of Ge Harashim. It was called this because its people were craftsmen" (1 Chr. 4:14; KJV, "valley of Charashim"). The same Hebrew expression (with a slight spelling variation), referring probably to the same area, occurs in a list of places where the Benjamites resettled after the EXILE: "... in Lod and Ono, and in the Valley of the Craftsmen" (Neh. 11:35). Its association with LOD and ONO points toward identification with one of the valleys bordering the Plain of SHARON. Proposed sites include Wadi esh-Shellal, Sarafand el-Kharab, and Hirsha; such identifications imply that this Judahite clan may have lived just outside the boundaries of Judah. A. BOWLING

Gehazi gi-hay´zi (גֵּיחֲזִי H1634, possibly "valley of vision"). The young servant of the prophet ELISHA. The strengths and weaknesses of his character are readily apparent in the three passages where he is mentioned by name. (He may also be the unnamed servant in 2 Ki. 4:43 and 6:15–17.)

Gehazi is first mentioned in the story of the wealthy Shunammite woman (2 Ki. 4:8–37; see SHUNEM). His master, Elisha, had been provided a chamber by this woman and was desirous of repaying the favor in some way. Gehazi perceptively alerted Elisha to the fact "she has no son and her husband is old" (v. 14). Elisha predicted the birth of a son, and his words were fulfilled the following spring. When the child had grown up, he died one day of a head ailment (vv. 18–20). Immediately, the Shunammite woman, in bitter distress, rushed up to Elisha at Mount Carmel. Gehazi was rebuked by Elisha for trying to thrust her away after she caught hold of the prophet's feet. Gehazi was then sent on ahead to Shunem with Elisha's staff to place on the woman's son. The child, however, did not come to life until the prophet arrived, prayed, and lay upon him (vv. 32–35).

Unlike the incident above, a second story pictures Gehazi as a man of covetousness and distrust (2 Ki. 5:20–27). After Elisha had cleansed NAAMAN the Aramean of leprosy and refused the gifts offered him in appreciation, Gehazi deceitfully sought the reward. He overtook Naaman's chariot and, by fabricating a story in Elisha's name, deceitfully got for himself "two talents of silver in two bags, with two sets of clothing" (v. 23). The sagacious prophet, however, knowing of the incident, harshly rebuked the deception of his servant by issuing a curse: "Naaman's leprosy will cling to you and to your descendants forever" (v. 27). It should be noted that this affliction was probably not what we today call "leprosy" (see DISEASE).

In a final account (2 Ki. 8:1–6), while Gehazi related to the king the great things Elisha had done, the Shunammite woman appeared with her son. She had returned from PHILISTIA after a seven year famine. When Gehazi attested the identity of both, she requested of the king restoration of her house and land. This, the king granted, along with all the produce her fields had yielded since she had been gone. (See L. Bronner, *The Stories of Elijah and Elisha as Polemics against Baal Worship* [1968], ch. 6.) M. R. WILSON

Gehenna gi-hen´uh (γέεννα G1147, from גֵּי־הִנֹּם, "Valley of Hinnom"; Aram. גֵּיהִנָּם). In the Greek NT, this name refers to the final place of punishment of the ungodly and is usually translated "hell." The word derives from the Hebrew phrase for "the Valley of [Ben] Hinnom," identified with the Wadi er-Rababi, just S and to the W of JERUSALEM. It is first referred to as marking the boundary between the inheritance of the tribes of JUDAH and BENJAMIN (Josh. 15:8; 18:16). During the reigns of AHAZ and MANASSEH, human sacrifices were offered at TOPHETH in this valley (2 Chr. 28:3; 33:6), but later JOSIAH in his reforms desecrated the place and thus prevented any further use of the valley for that purpose (2 Ki. 23:10). JEREMIAH announced that the name of the valley would be changed to the Valley of Slaughter because when the Lord judged Judah for her sins, the number of dead would be so great that they would be thrown into the valley to lie there without burial (Jer. 7:31–32).

In later times the valley seems to have been used for burning refuse, and also the bodies of criminals. From about the 2nd cent. B.C., it came to be thought of as the place of final punishment for the enemies of God. This arose either from the earlier associations or from Jeremiah's prophecy or from the later practice just referred to. The book of *1 Enoch* is the earliest witness to this use of the name (but cf. even in the OT itself, Isa. 30:33; 66:24). In later thought, Gehenna was thought of as the eschatological fire of HELL, still probably considered as a place (esp. in rabbinic thought), but now no longer locally outside Jerusalem. The term is used in the NT in this sense. J. Jeremias (in *TDNT*, 1:657–58) stresses the sharp distinction in the NT, as in pre-NT Judaism, between HADES and

Looking E into the Hinnom Valley, from which the name Gehenna derives.

Gehenna: the former receives the ungodly only for the intervening period between death and resurrection, while the latter is their place of punishment after the last judgment. In later JUDAISM, Gehenna was viewed as purgatorial by some rabbis (e.g., according to *Sifre Deut.* 45, if intercession is made for someone in Gehenna, he is taken out; see E. E. Urbach, *The Sages: Their Concepts and Beliefs*, 2nd ed. [1979], 1:510).

Apart from Jas. 3:6—where the tongue, compared to a fire that sets on fire the whole cycle of nature, is said to be itself set on fire by Gehenna— the remaining eleven occurrences are all in the Synoptic Gospels. In the SERMON ON THE MOUNT, Jesus warned that even mental or verbal infringements of the commandments render one liable to Gehenna (Matt. 5:20), and he said: "It is better for you to lose one part of your body than for your whole body to be thrown into hell" (5:29, reiterated in v. 30). He also held out the threat of Gehenna to anyone who "causes one of these little ones who believe in me to sin," and repeated the warning already quoted (Matt. 18:6–9; Mk. 9:42–47). On another occasion he told his disciples to fear none but God, who alone is able to cast both body and soul into Gehenna (Matt. 10:28; cf. Lk. 12:5).

The last two occurrences are found in our Lord's vigorous denunciation of the PHARISEES (Matt. 23). In the first one (v. 15), he accuses them of so indoctrinating any PROSELYTE that they cause him to become twice as much a "son of Gehenna"—i.e., someone fit and doomed for hell—as themselves. Later (v. 33) he concludes: "You snakes! You brood of vipers! How will you escape being condemned to hell?" (See further A. Edersheim, *The Life and Times of Jesus the Messiah*, 2 vols. [1886], 2:280–81, 791–96; Str-B 4:1029–1118; R. A. Stewart, *Rabbinic Theology* [1961], 157–60; L. R. Bailey in *BA* 49 [1986]: 187–91; *NIDNTT* 2:208–9; for a comparison between Matthew and Luke in their use of the term, see C. Milikowsky in *NTS* 34 [1988]: 238–49.)   R. E. DAVIES

Geliloth gi-li′loth (גְּלִילוֹת *H1667*, "circles [of stone]," thus "circuit, territory"; cf. GALILEE). **(1)** An area on the SE boundary of the tribe of BENJAMIN, near EN SHEMESH and facing the Pass of ADUMMIM (Josh. 18:17). In the corresponding description of the NE boundary of JUDAH, possibly the same place is referred to as GILGAL (15:7). The precise location is unknown. Some have thought that Geliloth refers to a general region, not a specific site. Cf. #2 below.

(2) A place "near the Jordan in the land of Canaan" where "the Reubenites, the Gadites and the half-tribe of Manasseh built an imposing altar"

(Josh. 22:10–11). Many believe, however, that the phrase *gĕlîlôt hayyardēn* in this passage is not a place name but should rather be translated "the region near the Jordan" (cf. NRSV).

gem. See JEWELS AND PRECIOUS STONES.

Gemalli gi-mal′i (גְּמַלִּי H1696, derivation uncertain, possibly a short form of GAMALIEL). The father of AMMIEL, a Danite; the latter was one of the ten spies sent by MOSES into the Promised Land (Num. 13:12).

Gemara guh-mah′ruh (Aram. גְּמָרָא, from גְּמַר, "to finish, know well, memorize [the law]"). This term refers in general to the learning of (Jewish legal) tradition or to the tradition itself. More specifically, it designates that part of the TALMUD containing discussions and expositions of the oral law, which had been codified in the MISHNAH (the latter consisting of legal expositions and applications of the written law). The material found in the Mishnah was developed in oral form over many generations of TANNAIM and was not written down until about A.D. 200. The Gemara, in turn, was developed by the AMORAIM mainly during the 3rd–5th centuries in TIBERIAS and BABYLON. The Mishnah and Gemara together make up the Talmud (both in its Palestinian and Babylonian forms).

Gemariah gem′uh-ri′uh (גְּמַרְיָה H1701 [Jer. 29:3] and גְּמַרְיָהוּ H1702, "Yahweh has fulfilled"). **(1)** Son of a certain HILKIAH; he was an emissary to NEBUCHADNEZZAR from King ZEDEKIAH charged with the task of carrying JEREMIAH's message to the captive Jews (Jer. 29:3).

(2) Son of SHAPHAN the royal secretary; he was one of the officials who urged King JEHOIAKIM not to destroy the scroll of Jeremiah (Jer. 36:10–12, 25). It was from Gemariah's room, in the upper courtyard of the temple, that BARUCH read the words of Jeremiah to the people (v. 10). His brother AHIKAM was also an important functionary, and his son MICAIAH was the one who reported the reading of the scroll by Baruch (v. 13). The name "Gemariah son of Shaphan," almost certainly referring to the same individual, survives in a seal impression dated to the time of the destruction of Jerusalem (Y. Shiloh, *Excavations at the City of David: I, 1978–1982* [1984], 20).

genealogy. A record listing the descendants of a person or family. The Bible contains numerous genealogies.

I. Introduction. Genealogies have various uses in the unfolding story of redemption. Inasmuch as history necessarily clusters around great individuals, the connected history of God's dealings with his people involves listing persons in their connections with others of various ages. Genealogies and chronologies form the connecting link from early days to the end of the biblical period. Usually other ancient histories are partial and piecemeal. By means of genealogical records, God has given a connected history from Adam to Christ.

Genealogies also have lesser uses in the sacred record. God's blessings were often passed on in the family line, and these genealogies express the COVENANT connections of ancient Israel. Military duty was by families. Certain offices, such as the priesthood, the Levitical work, and the kingship, were hereditary, and genealogies trace the perpetuation of these offices. Also, land tenure in Israel was carried on chiefly through male descent. Genealogies therefore certified the title to ancestral holdings. Finally, in a tribal or semitribal community, a person's genealogy was his identification and means of location. It was comparable to the addresses of modern houses. People today are located by country, state, city, and street. In a similar way, ACHAN, for example, was identified as of the tribe of Judah, the family of Zerah, the household of Zabdi, the son of Carmi (Josh. 7:17–18). Such a brief genealogy gave only the first two or three and the last two or three links of the man's ancestry.

II. Principal genealogies of Scripture. The ancient history of the race is compressed into the first chapters of GENESIS. Except for a few incidents, this history consists of the listing of famous men and nations. There are two genealogies before the flood (Gen. 4–5) and two after (Gen. 10–11). These genealogies have been the subject of much study because of their importance and their position at the head of Bible history.

The lists in Gen. 5 and 11 are obviously similar, giving the line from ADAM to NOAH and from Noah to ABRAHAM. Each chapter gives the age of a man at the birth of his son and the years that remained to him thereafter. Each genealogy consists of ten links followed by a family of three sons who were not triplets, though the record refers to them as born at the same time. It is natural to believe that these genealogies are schematic, naming only the chief men in easily memorizable form. That they are true genealogies, giving the descent of the ancients, there is no reason to doubt. It will be considered later whether or not they are complete. These genealogies are compared by some to the lists recorded on Sumerian tablets of the kings who reigned before and after the flood. There is no similarity in names. The reigns of the Sumerian kings are extremely long; those after the flood progressively shorter until the last few reigns are nearer the normal. The last links name a king or two who are historically known. Some have held that the biblical lists derive from the Sumerian and thus are legendary. It seems just as possible to believe that both lists derive from the ancient tradition of the race and represent early tradition. The biblical tradition is much more believable and by God's PROVIDENCE and INSPIRATION has preserved the true outlines of the past.

The genealogies in Gen. 4 and 10 are different from those in chs. 5 and 11. The one in ch. 10 is frequently called the Table of Nations, tracing the expanding migrations of the various sons of Noah and their successors. It can be shown that these successors are not given in straight genealogical lines. These are colonizations of peoples rather than merely lists of descendants. For instance, the "sons" of Ham (10:6) include the Ethiopians, Egyptians, Libyans (probably), and Canaanites, a wide variety of peoples. The Canaanites themselves included SIDON, a city; HETH, progenitor of the Indo-European HITTITES; the AMORITES, a Semitic people (see SEMITE); and others. That CANAAN begot Sidon his firstborn is not intended to be a reference to sonship, but an indication that the city Sidon was peopled early in the history of the land of Canaan. The chapter is aptly called "the earliest ethnological table in the literature of the ancient world" (*New Scofield Reference Bible* [1967], 15). See NATIONS.

Actually this difference between Gen. 10 and 11 may be reflected in the Hebrew wording. In the former passage (e.g., 10:8), the Hebrew verb *yālad H3528* occurs in the qal stem, which usually means "bear" rather than "beget" (the latter is more commonly expressed with the causative hiphil, as in 11:10). It is used figuratively of Moses begetting Israel (Num. 11:12) or God bearing Israel (Deut. 32:18), or God begetting the Messiah (Ps. 2:7). When applied to people, the verb in this form apparently is used of general relationships, as expressed in the Table of Nations of Gen. 10, and not necessarily of literal fatherhood.

The same remarks apply to Gen. 4:17–22. The so-called genealogy of CAIN includes doubtless some names of individuals who are progenitors of races and craftsmen, and who founded cities bearing their own names. The comparison with Gen. 10 and the fact that the same Hebrew verb form is used in both cases makes it apparent that the list of names in Gen. 4 also includes peoples and movements.

In the rest of the PENTATEUCH there are many shorter genealogies. These genealogies usually first present a brief reference to the worldly descendants, followed by a more detailed history of the godly line. ABRAHAM's family outside of ISAAC is given very briefly in Gen. 25. This is followed by the family of Isaac (25:19). The chief men in the family of ESAU are listed in ch. 36, followed by the family of JACOB in ch. 46. Part of this genealogy of Jacob is repeated (Exod. 6:14–25), but the family of LEVI is expanded there to give the genealogy of MOSES, son of AMRAM, son of KOHATH, son of Levi. It is clear that Kohath was actually one of Levi's three sons and head of a clan. Amram was probably Moses' own father (not a more distant ancestor) and head of a household. There must have been intervening links between Kohath and Amram because by Moses' day the Levites numbered 22,000 males (Num. 3:39). Many generations must have intervened. But the ancestry of Moses given in Exod. 6 places him within the tribe of Levi.

The history of the time of the judges is given in a chronological rather than genealogical format. See JUDGES, PERIOD OF. The judgeship was not hereditary but charismatic: God individually called the judges to their tasks. The period of the judges is spanned by one brief genealogy—that at the end of

Cuneiform tablet containing the genealogy of the Hammurabi dynasty (prob. from Sippar, 17th cent. B.C.). It lists the names of the kings of Babylon down to Ammiditana.

the book of RUTH. Actually Ruth is a book belonging in the time of the judges, and in old Hebrew listings it was counted as a part of Judges. In Ruth 4:18–22, the line of Ruth's husband, BOAZ, is traced back to PEREZ, the son of JUDAH, and onward to DAVID the great king. This genealogy, repeated in Chronicles and the NT, is our only record of the detailed ancestry of Israel's chief monarch. This genealogy is incomplete, however. It speaks of NAHSHON, the chief prince of Judah in Moses' day (Num. 2:3), as father of SALMON and grandfather of Boaz, whereas Ruth 2:1 says Boaz was of the family of ELIMELECH. Clearly there were other intervening links between Nahshon and Boaz and probably more than two links between Boaz and David.

For the history of the monarchy, the only genealogy of any extent is that of King DAVID, whose line is traced in the books of Kings through eighteen generations to the captivity. The genealogy of the high priests is not given in the histories, though it was known and is given in the collected genealogies of Chronicles. The genealogies of the PROPHETS are not given, for like that of the judges, their office was charismatic and not hereditary.

The remaining genealogies of any consequence in the OT are those of EZRA (Ezra 7:1–5) and Joshua (JESHUA) the high priest (Neh. 12:10–11), and those remarkable lists of names in 1 Chr. 1–9 where many previous genealogies are brought together and others are added. The genealogy in 1 Chr. 1 comes straight out of Genesis, usually quoted directly from the early lists. Following this are genealogies of the twelve tribes as far as they are preserved, in this order: Judah, Simeon, Reuben, Gad, Levi, Issachar, Benjamin, Naphtali, Ephraim, Asher, and Benjamin. Dan and Zebulun, tribes of the extreme N, are missing, though some have surmised that the second mention of Benjamin is a copyist's mistake for Zebulun (this is, however, questionable).

These tribal genealogies are, naturally enough, strong on the ancestries of famous people. David's line is traced down to six or seven generations beyond the captivity (1 Chr. 3:9–24). SAMUEL's line is given twice (6:22–30 and 6:33–38; cf. 1 Sam. 1:1; 8:2). The line of AARON is traced down through ELEAZAR to David's time (1 Chr. 6:50–53) and also to the captivity (6:3–15), whence it is taken on to Ezra in Ezra 7:1–5. The line of SAUL is also given briefly (1 Chr. 8:33–40). Curiously, nothing is known about Moses' descendants. His sons GERSHOM and ELIEZER are mentioned only once (Exod. 18:3–4).

Many of the names and the incidental references to habitation and family events are found only in CHRONICLES. The author (who prob. wrote c. 400 B.C.) obviously had access to ancient books of genealogies. Such books are referred to in Neh. 7:5, 64 and Ezra 2:62. It is quite possible that the author of Chronicles (Ezra or Nehemiah?) copied out of the book that NEHEMIAH had found. As is to be expected, some of the names are slightly different from those in the older lists. In some cases there may have been alternate names for a man. In other cases the names have suffered slightly in copying. This precise copying of names and numbers was notoriously difficult.

In American culture, detailed genealogies are seldom kept, but in other societies they are extensively preserved. The writer has had students from Korea and from India who possessed family records back forty generations and felt this to be not unusual. He has talked with an Arab in Jerusalem who named his child Edessa because his ancestors suffered in the persecutions of Edessa (3rd cent.). Such genealogies were kept even more in ancient times. A man living in China claims to be the seventy-seventh in direct descent from Confucius. In tribal cultures and in the settled life of ancient nations, such genealogies were apparently common.

The genealogies of Christ are recorded in Matt. 1 and Lk. 3. JOSEPH and Mary (see MARY MOTHER OF JESUS) were probably well aware of their ancestry. The two lists differ after the mention of David, and some have found here a contradiction. Others have suggested that the genealogy in Matthew is that of Joseph; the one in Luke is of Mary (cf. the excellent treatment of Luke's genealogy in John Lightfoot's commentary, *Horae hebraicae et talmudicae* [1859]). It appears that Mary is enigmatically referred to as the daughter of HELI in the TALMUD (quoted by Lightfoot; also in Str-B, 2:155). Joseph apparently was the son-in-law of Heli. But the genealogy of Joseph in Matthew loses its point, for Joseph was not the biological father of Jesus.

Comparison with Chronicles, however, will indicate that Matthew's list is not a true genealogy: Matt. 1:12 says SALATHIEL begat ZERUBBABEL, whereas 1 Chr. 3:19 shows that Salathiel died without children and Zerubbabel was actually his nephew. This was uncommon in the usual type of genealogy, but it was frequent in lists including men who claimed the title to a throne. If the kingly line ran out, the nearest male relative assumed the title. Thus the "genealogy" in Matthew is a list of the heirs to the throne of Judah. Joseph had that title and passed it on to his foster son, Jesus. It has further been pointed out that Joseph had the title to the throne of Judah, but being descended from JEHOIACHIN he could not reign, as he lay under Jeremiah's curse (Jer. 22:30). Jesus as the foster son received Joseph's title to the crown, but being born of the virgin Mary he escaped Joseph's curse. (For other views, cf. J. G. Machen, *The Virgin Birth of Christ* [1930], 204–9; see also GENEALOGY OF JESUS CHRIST.)

III. Genealogies incomplete. As mentioned above, it is clear that many OT genealogies are incomplete. There are four links from Levi to Moses (Exod. 6:16–20), but the descendants of Levi in Moses' day were 22,000 males (Num. 3:39). The genealogy from EPHRAIM, Levi's nephew, to Joshua seems to show eighteen links (1 Chr. 7:20–27). In the NT Matt. 1:1 names just three links from Christ to Abraham. The full genealogy, or list of kings (Matt. 1:2–17), omits the names of Ahaziah, Joash, and Amaziah and also Jehoiakim, in contrast to the lists of kings in the OT. The genealogy of Ezra (Ezra 7:1–5) has only five links from 456 B.C. back to ZADOK, David's high priest in about 960 B.C. Obviously, only the more famous men are mentioned.

These facts are necessary to know before drawing conclusions about the genealogies in Gen. 5 and 11. Attention already has been called to their schematic form. The assumption that the postdiluvian genealogy is complete leads to some strange results. For example, the years given from the birth of a father to the birth of his son total 292 years from the flood to the birth of Abraham and 467 years to his death. SHEM lived 502 years after the flood. Noah lived 350 years after the flood, and thus he would have been a contemporary of Abraham. ARPHAXAD, Shem's son, also lived until Abraham was 148 years old. Yet the record of Abraham says nothing about any contact with these ancient worthies. The record implies that Noah and his sons were long gone before Abraham was told to leave his kindred and start fresh in Canaan. Also the numerous peoples pictured as recolonizing the world (Gen. 10) could hardly have repopulated and spread so widely in ten generations. It is far easier to realize that Gen. 11 is incomplete. It is also held that some of these names are actually family or clan names.

Furthermore, any view that holds the flood to have destroyed all human beings on the earth must place the flood earlier than 292 years before Abraham, who lived about 2000 B.C. There is a record, practically continuous, of Egyptian dynasties going back to almost 3000 B.C.—that is, about 1,000 years before Abraham. The city of JERICHO in the Jordan valley shows many layers of mud-brick going back long before 3000, which any destructive flood would surely have washed away. The genealogy of Gen. 11 is clearly incomplete. The one found in

Gen. 5 is likely incomplete also. The date of 4004 B.C. assigned to creation by Ussher in the 17th cent. is wrong. He assumed these genealogies were complete.

Actually the genealogies in Gen. 5 and 11 may be considered as links in the ancient tradition of mankind. Some consider a GENERATION about thirty years long. From another viewpoint a generation is the period from birth to death—nearer seventy years or longer. From the latter viewpoint the time from Abraham back to the flood would be at least the sum of the lives of these patriarchs, about 2,263 years. Probably the flood was still earlier. See FLOOD, GENESIS. There seems to have been an abrupt change of climate about 9000 B.C. that would fit the genealogies well enough if the flood was connected with that event.

(See further P. W. Crannel, *ISBE* [1929], 2:1183–96; J. O. Buswell Jr., *A Systematic Theology of the Christian Religion* [1962], 1:325–43; R. R. Wilson, "The Old Testament Genealogies in Recent Research," *JBL* 94 [1975]: 169–89; M. D. Johnson, *The Purpose of the Biblical Genealogies: With Special Reference to the Setting of the Genealogies of Jesus*, 2nd ed. [1988]; R. B. Robinson, "Literary Functions of the Genealogies of Genesis," *CBQ* 48 [1986]: 595–608; T. Hieke, *Die Genealogien der Genesis* [2003].) R. L. HARRIS

genealogy of Jesus Christ. The Davidic ancestry of Jesus Christ is an accepted fact in the NT (Matt. 21:9; Mk. 10:47–48; Rom. 1:3). Apart from the two genealogies in Matthew and Luke, little attempt is made elsewhere to emphasize this point—it simply is presented rather as historical truth. JOSEPH, the legal father of Jesus, "belonged to the house and line of David" (Lk. 2:4). Along with other Jews of his time, Joseph treasured his family records. Genealogical registers were kept with great care, because they figured in legal matters concerning property, marriage, and religion (see GENEALOGY). Centuries ago, as in the days of EZRA and NEHEMIAH, such lists were kept and supervised (Ezra 2:62; 8:1; Neh. 7:5). In Joseph's case, his membership in the line of DAVID had messianic overtones (Jer. 23:5–6; Ezek. 34:23).

The two genealogies of Jesus (Matt. 1:1–17; Lk. 3:23–38) should be taken with seriousness. Both present him as a descendant of David and make clear that Joseph was the legal, not the actual, father of Jesus. Matthew traced the line from ABRAHAM and David in forty-one links to Joseph, whereas Luke reversed the official method and worked back from Joseph to David, Abraham, and all the way to Adam, employing 77 names. The slightest comparison of the two genealogies reveals striking differences. The most difficult of these is the fact that both lists trace their line through Joseph, yet none of the names from David to Joseph coincide. The apparent discrepancy between the lists has always constituted a severe problem to interpreters.

I. The genealogy in Matthew. Certain distinctive features stand out in Matthew's genealogy. Two high points in OT revelation figure prominently in the list—David and Abraham, both men being partners to God's covenants with Israel. Matthew intended that the pedigree of Jesus stand out sharply at the very beginning of his gospel, and it holds the first place of honor. His genealogy is structured in three sets of fourteen generations each. He arrived at this scheme through selection and omission in accord with OT practice. The device served to aid the memory, and indicated the main line of descent without sacrificing accuracy. Matthew may have chosen the number fourteen because it matches the numerical value of David's name in Hebrew letters, but this is no more than a theory. See MATTHEW, GOSPEL OF, V.

Another peculiar feature of Matthew's list is the inclusion, almost incidentally, of four women: RAHAB was a Canaanite from JERICHO, RUTH was from MOAB, and TAMAR and BATHSHEBA were famous chiefly for their participation in public scandal. Quite apart from the character and nationality of these women, the very occurrence of their names in an official Jewish genealogy is a distinct feature. Undoubtedly, Jesus was known by his enemies as the son of an illegitimate union. He was known as the son of Mary, not Joseph (Mk. 6:3), which in a male society was a dishonorable title. Later Jewish tradition developed the malicious rumor. Therefore, Matthew, desiring to offset the gossip, inserted with some relish the names of some OT characters whose reputations were not beyond reproach, but who were instrumental in the messianic line.

In Jesus' case, however, the rumors arose to counteract the miraculous character of his birth by a virgin. Jesus is presented in Matthew's genealogy as a legal male descendant of David through adoption by Joseph, and heir to the Davidic throne.

II. The genealogy in Luke. The Lukan genealogy is less official in form. It is not placed at the beginning of the gospel, but is tucked away in the third chapter, after the baptism of Jesus. The order is inverted, proceeding backward in time from Joseph to Adam, and includes almost twice as many entries. The most startling feature of the list is its total dissimilarity to Matthew's in the period between Joseph and David, with only two names common to both (other than Joseph and David), namely, Shealtiel and Zerubbabel. Luke traced Jesus' line through Nathan, son of David, and named Heli as grandfather of Jesus, whereas Matthew traced his line through Solomon, the royal son of David, and named Jacob as grandfather. See LUKE, GOSPEL OF.

III. Two solutions to the discrepancy. Attempts have been made from earliest times to resolve the apparent contradiction. Assuming no colossal mistake in either gospel, two primary explanations are possible. Either both lists are properly those of Joseph but reckoned in a different way, or one is the family tree of Mary, not Joseph. Annius of Viterbo (c. 1490) proposed that whereas Matthew gives the legal descent through Joseph, Luke presents the physical descent through Mary—an approach that can be traced back to the 5th cent. A.D. Certainly, Mary is the chief figure in the birth narrative of the third gospel, and she herself belonged very probably to the house of David (Lk. 1:27; 2:4). The Greek definite article, used in the list for every other entry, is noticeably absent from the name of Joseph (3:23), which leads to the interpretation that the list proper begins with Heli, not Joseph. Joseph's name is introduced into the list parenthetically only to fill in the gap between Jesus and his grandfather Heli. The text would read then: "Jesus, being the son (as it was supposed, of Joseph) of Heli, etc."

If so, Luke's list would be the register of Mary's family, beginning with Heli her father. This theory is attractive, but suffers from the suppression of Mary's name in the list. It is, however, clearly possible, and would provide a simple solution to the problem of the double genealogy. The fact that Mary was related to ELIZABETH, a daughter of Aaron, is not an insuperable difficulty if we suppose this relationship came through the mother rather than the father. The main weakness is in the failure of Luke to make this point explicit if that was his intention. The theory could be strengthened by supposing that Mary had no brothers, and that Joseph became the son and heir of Heli by virtue of his marriage to Mary.

The second possible explanation considers the Lukan genealogy to be the family tree of Joseph, as Matthew's is. Both Matthew and Luke stress that Joseph was of the house of David (Matt. 1:16; Lk. 1:27; 2:4). It is natural to suppose that both writers intended to provide Joseph's ancestry. Matthew's purpose was to trace the line of official succession to the Davidic throne, whereas Luke's informal aim was to enumerate the actual physical ancestors of Joseph back to David. This solution was originally proposed by Julius Africanus (c. A.D. 220) in a letter to Aristides, as reported by EUSEBIUS (*Eccl. Hist.* 1.7). Julius believed that the law of LEVIRATE marriage could be invoked to remove the tension between the two lists—that Joseph was really the son of Heli, with Heli and Jacob as uterine brothers, born of the same mother but of different fathers. If either one had married the widow of the other, Joseph could be reckoned in that sense a son of either.

A neat twist can be put on the theory by identifying the two grandfathers of Joseph (Matthan in Matthew, and Matthat in Luke). In that case, Heli might have married the widow of a childless Jacob and begotten Joseph, in which case Joseph would be the actual son of Heli, but the legal heir to Jacob. In both lists, then, the ancestry of Jesus is traced through Joseph, his legal father. Because Matthew wished to present the successive heirs to David's throne, he began with David's ancestry and worked forward to Jesus. Because Luke wished to record the actual line of physical descent, he began with Joseph and worked backward through his actual ancestors. The chief weakness of the second explanation is the series of coincidences required to make it function.

GENEALOGY OF JESUS CHRIST

THE TWO GENEALOGIES

Matthew	Both	Luke	Matthew	Both	Luke
—	—	1 Adam	(21) Ozias	—	40 Joseph
—	—	2 Seth	(22) Joatham	—	41 Juda
—	—	3 Enos	(23) Achaz	—	42 Simeon
—	—	4 Cainan	(24) Ezekias	—	43 Levi
—	—	5 Maleleel	(25) Manasses	—	44 Matthat
—	—	6 Jared	(26) Amon	—	45 Jorim
—	—	7 Enoch	(27) Josias	—	46 Eliezer
—	—	8 Mathusala	Jehoahaz	—	—
—	—	9 Lamech	Jehoiakin	—	—
—	—	10 Noe	*omitted*	—	—
—	—	11 Sem	(28) Jechonias	—	47 Jose
—	—	12 Arphaxad	(Jehoiachin)	—	—
—	—	*Cainan*	Zedekiah	—	—
—	—	13 Sala	*omitted*	—	—
—	—	14 Heber	—	—	48 Er
—	—	15 Phaleg	—	—	49 Elmodam
—	—	16 Ragau	—	—	50 Cosam
—	—	17 Saruch	—	—	51 Addi
—	—	18 Nachor	—	—	52 Melchi
—	—	19 Thara	—	—	53 Neri
—	(1) Abraham ...20	—	—	(29) Salathiel ...54	—
—	(2) Isaac ...21	—	—	(30) Zorobabel ...55	—
—	(3) Jacob ...22	—	(31) Ahiud	—	*Rhesa*
—	(4) Juda(s) ...23	—	(32) Eliakim	—	56 Joanna
—	(5) Phares ...24	—	(33) Azor	—	57 Juda
—	(6) Esrom ...25	—	(34) Sadoc	—	58 Joseph
—	(7) Aram ...26	—	(35) Achim	—	59 Semei
—	(8) Aminadab ...27	—	(36) Eliud	—	60 Mattathias
—	(9) Naasson ...28	—	(37) Eleazar	—	61 Maath
—	(10) Salmon ...29	—	—	—	62 Nagge
—	(11) Booz ...30	—	—	—	63 Esli
—	(12) Obed ...31	—	—	—	64 Naum
—	(13) Jesse ...32	—	—	—	65 Amos
—	(14) David ...33	—	—	—	66 Mattathias
(15) Solomon	—	34 Nathan	—	—	67 Joseph
(16) Roboam	—	35 Mattatha	—	—	68 Janna
(17) Abia	—	36 Menan	—	—	69 Melchi
(18) Asa	—	37 Melea	—	—	70 Levi
(19) Josaphat	—	38 Eliakim	(38) Matthan	(38) Matttha(n)(t) ...71	71 Matthat
(20) Joram	—	39 Jonan		Matthan and Matthat may be the same	72 Heli
Ahaziah	—	—			
Joash	—	—	(39) Jacob		
Amaziah	—	—		(40) Joseph ...73	—
omitted	—	—		(41) Jesus ...74	

Adapted from *A Guide to the Gospels* (1948) by W. Graham Scroggie. Names follow KJV spelling.

Other approaches have been suggested, and a final solution to so intricate a question may never be found. Enough is known, however, to show that the apparent discrepancy between the two genealogies is not insoluble. (See A. T. Robertson, *A Harmony of the Gospels* [1922], 259–62; J. G. Machen, *The Virgin Birth of Christ* [1930], 203–9; E. Stauffer, *Jesus and His Story* [1960], 22–25; M. D. Johnson, *The Purpose of the Biblical Genealogies: With Special Reference to the Setting of the Genealogies of Jesus*, 2nd ed. [1988]; D. L. Bock, *Luke*, BECNT [1994–96], 1:918–23; *DJG*, 253–59.) C. H. PINNOCK

general. This term, referring to a high-ranking military officer, occurs rarely in Bible versions. The NRSV, for example, uses it once in the OT to render Hebrew *śar* H8569, "chief, commander" (Jdg. 4:7; cf. also 1 Chr. 27:34 KJV), but also several times in the APOCRYPHA (e.g., to render Gk. *archistratēgos*, "chief commander," Jdt. 2:4 et al.). The word is occasionally used in the NT as a translation of Greek *chiliarchos* G5941, meaning literally "commander of a thousand," but used in Roman times of military TRIBUNES who led COHORTS consisting of about 600 men, and also more generally of high-ranking officers (e.g., NIV Rev. 6:15; 19:18). See ARMY.

General Epistles. See CATHOLIC EPISTLES.

generation. A group of related persons who belong to the same stage in the line of descent. The word can also refer to a body of individuals who happened to be born about the same time, and especially to contemporaries who share social and cultural traits. The biblical words rendered "generation" correspond closely, but not fully, to the English term.

The Hebrew noun *dôr* H1887 has a broad range of meaning: it may refer to a period of time as well as to the individuals who live during an age (this word has no reference to the concept of "begetting"). In particular, such phrases as *dôr wādôr* (lit., "an age and an age") means "eternity, forever." The same phrase occurs in the texts from UGARIT. The word is used (usually in the sing.) of many generations to come, as well as of a specific living generation, such as the one that died in the wilderness (Deut. 2:14). The average length of a generation is often assumed to be forty years, for in the wilderness all Israelites over twenty died within that time. This reckoning measures not the period from a person's birth to his children's birth (more like thirty years), but a lifetime sixty years or more (apparently the meaning of Gen. 15:16). The forty-year span of various rulers (David, Solomon, four of the judges) is thought by some to be a round number, but the same number in the MOABITE STONE has been shown to be an accurate figure (F. M. Cross and D. N. Freedman, *Early Hebrew Orthography* [1952], 39–40). A second Hebrew term, *tôlēdôt* H9352 (from *yālad* H3528, "to bear, beget"), can refer not only to "contemporaries" (e.g., Gen. 6:9), but also to a line of "descendants" (5:1), and even to a "[family] history" (2:4; 25:19; 37:2). See GENEALOGY.

In the NT, the Greek noun *genea* G1155 is usually translated "generation" but can also be rendered in other ways (e.g., NIV "kind," Lk. 16:8; "time," Acts 15:21). It is used in the genealogy of Matt. 1. Many times Jesus speaks of the faithless and perverse generation that opposed him (Matt. 17:17 et al.), where the reference is taken by some to be the Jewish nation. A special problem is raised by Jesus' statement, "this generation will certainly not pass away until all these things have happened" (Matt. 24:34 and parallels). Some understand the term in a strictly temporal sense and claim that Christ mistakenly expected the end in his own time. Others argue for the meaning "race, clan, nation," and hold that the verse predicts the continuation of the Jewish people until Christ's return. Still others believe that the statement has no temporal reference at all but rather stresses the certainty of Christ's words: "people such as these [i.e., sinful humanity] will not pass away until all these things have taken place." This assurance thus corresponds precisely to the next statement: "Heaven and earth will pass away, but my words will never pass away" (v. 35; cf. H. Ridderbos, *The Coming of the Kingdom* [1962], 498–503; for additional interpretations, see D. L. Bock, *Luke*, BECNT [1994–96], 2:1688–93).

R. L. HARRIS

generosity. See BOUNTY; CONTRIBUTION; KINDNESS.

Genesis, Book of. The first book of the Bible, traditionally attributed to the authorship of MOSES.

The English title is derived from that used in the SEPTUAGINT, *Genesis* (Gk. for "origin, beginning"). In the Hebrew Bible it bears the title *bĕrēʾšît* ("in the beginning"), which is the first word in the text. If indeed Moses wrote this book (see below), he probably did so in the Sinaitic peninsula or in the Plains of MOAB. The time of writing depends on one's view of the date when the Israelites left Egypt. See EXODUS, THE, II. No definite occasion for writing the book can be fixed. Its purpose is nowhere stated in the OT, though it could be surmised that the book was written to lay the groundwork for the remaining books of the PENTATEUCH.

   I. The importance of the book
  II. Outline
 III. Author
  IV. Unique problems
   V. Theology of Genesis
  VI. Content

I. The importance of the book. Many have waxed eloquent in singing the praises of this, the first book of the Bible, and justly so. It contains first of all great theology and has been rightly labeled as "the starting point of all Theology" (C. T. Fritsch, *Genesis*, The Layman's Bible Commentary 2 [1959], 13). It gives a basically adequate answer to the question how the world originated, how humankind originated, how sin came into the world, how man and woman fell from grace, how God gave the hope of redemption to fallen sinners, how sin spread, how a great judgment was visited upon the sinful world in the flood, how a remnant of the human race was providentially saved, how the human race again spread abroad still proudly asserting itself. All this is presented from a theological point of view. The rest of the book deals with the unique preparations that were made to let redemption grow out of one branch of the human family under the guidance of the Father of all mankind.

Aside from its theological importance there is its importance as great literature. Genesis compares favorably with other works of literature that give their own national version of creation and the flood. The skill of the author in portraying God's activity in the guidance of history is inimitable. The charm with which the important characters of sacred history are set forth has entranced young and old through the ages. The manner in which the tale keeps moving from one climax to another is most effective. From the standpoint of good literature, the book has never lost its appeal through the ages.

Of the many things that could yet be said in praise of the importance of Genesis, one should note especially its rare combination of depth and simplicity. Subjects most vital to men and women, involving their deepest needs and aspirations, are dealt with in an almost childlike simplicity, which allows the young mind to catch the essence of the divine revelation with comparative ease. Like all inspired Scripture, the first book in the series is still the stream through which the lamb can wade and through which the elephant must swim.

One fact stressing the extreme importance of this book is yet to be noted, and that is the frequent references to it made both by the rest of the OT and by the NT. True, many of the references made by the OT writers are not explicit, but they are there and they stand out. To mention one summarizing example from the NT, Lk. 24:27 represents the risen Lord as tracing back messianic prophecy to Moses and all the prophets. Genesis can hardly be set aside in a reference so broad.

II. Outline. No one outline can do full justice to the contents of Genesis. It is almost immediately apparent to anyone who takes the book in hand that Gen. 1–11 comprise a separate unit, even as do chs. 12–50. Various terms have been used to cover this difference, such as "Primeval History" and "Patriarchal History" (Fritsch, *Genesis*, 17). For that matter, an outline may be used that is actually presented by the book itself: it comprises ten headings, built on the Hebrew word *tôlēdôt* H9352 (2:4; 5:1; 6:9; 10:1; 11:10, 27; 25:12, 19; 36:1; 37:1), which in these passages is most aptly translated "history" (see GENERATION). So ten histories are offered by the book, some dealing with important characters (Terah, Isaac, Jacob, Joseph), some dealing with important categories, like heaven and earth or the sons of Adam and of Noah; others with minor characters, like Ishmael and Esau. This outline is the most effective, although it does not penetrate into the depth of issues involved; but it does emphasize that God guided the history of mankind through his dealings with individual characters that he felt free to use for the good of the rest of humanity.

Interesting is another approach suggested by H. Frey (*Das Buch der Anfänge*, 8th ed. [1977]), who finds four major subjects treated: The Book of Beginnings (Gen. 1—11); The Book of Faith (chs. 12—25); The Book of Struggle (chs. 26—35); and The Book of Guidance (*Führung*, chs. 36—50). Still other outlines may have their validity, for it is extremely difficult to press the rich contents of so striking a book as Genesis into the mold of an outline that may be helpful. Usually an outline catches some important feature of the contents and fails to do justice to other features.

III. Author. According to the common critical view, the books of the PENTATEUCH are the result of various sources that have been skillfully woven together by an unknown editor (commonly called the Redactor, and referred to as R). Toward the end of the 19th cent., the major sources were designated J (characterized by its use of the divine name Yahweh, sometimes spelled Jahweh), E (which preferred the divine name Elohim), D (marked by material that is both hortatory and legal in character, as such material appears in Deuteronomy), and P (setting forth the kind of material that priests would cultivate and cherish, such as the provisions of Lev. 1–16).

Subsequently it began to appear to scholars that even past the Mosaic age it would be far more likely for a nation like Israel to preserve the record of its experiences not in books, such as might be kept in a literary age, but in living tradition that was passed on by word of mouth from generation to generation. Attention was directed to tradition as the major source of Israel's history. This feature should have set aside the entanglement with the problems of the written sources, but the latter were kept and operated with as having achieved relative validity. It was not realized that people cannot operate with both approaches simultaneously. But it must be admitted that with this shift of emphasis the richness of the traditions of Israel began to be studied and appreciated as never before.

In the meantime, the search after sources had produced findings that gave even the adherents of these hypotheses some serious misgivings. For example, the P source had been broken down into various components (labeled P^g, P^1, P^2, P^3). Similar additional subsources were discovered for J and the rest—an obviously impossible array of documents that even the most astute ingenuity of scholarship could hardly accept seriously. The minor sources were dismissed and new reconstructions of at least JEDPR were attempted.

The inadequacy of this approach again became evident in that entirely new sources were demanded on every side. The original J had been broken up into two: J^1 had little in common with J^2, except for the use of the divine proper name Yahweh. So the label L (Lay Source, chiefly championed by O. Eissfeldt) was suggested as a helpful substitute for J^1. It was also found necessary to bring another new source into the picture labeled N (nomadic stratum). In addition, M. Noth felt that there was quite a bit of evidence for the similarity that is rather obvious when J and E are viewed side by side; and so he advocated a G source (*gemeinsame Grundlage*—common foundation) for both. A bit earlier, scholars like Robert H. Pfeiffer had postulated an S (Seir) source. Some appeared on the scene advocating that a K (Kenite) source is also clearly in evidence. Other critics, however, roundly rejected the validity of the newest sources, arguing that such proliferation defeats its own purpose and only causes confusion. One writer from this camp ventures the assertion that recourse to other than the basic standards like JE and P "has proved to be so much tilting at windmills."

Source-critical studies devoted little attention to the contents and message of Genesis. A thorough and much used textbook of introduction to the OT, for instance, devotes about 150 pages to critical problems and only casually touches upon a few matters of interpretation, indicating the meaning and value of the contents of the books treated. In the 1950s, the general editor of *IB* pointed out: "For fifty years no full-scale commentary has been produced in the English language on the whole Bible." During these "fifty years" source criticism had its day and dominated all Pentateuchal studies. Meager were the fruits it produced in constructive interpretation.

This leads to the other side of the question: If the critical approach has yielded so little fruit and has so many obvious weaknesses with its theory of multiple authorship, what has the conservative approach to offer by way of substitute? Answer: The possibility of Mosaic authorship advocated in a number of forms. We admit freely, to begin with, that nowhere in the Bible is there a direct and unmistakable claim maintaining the Mosaic authorship of Genesis in particular. But a number of factors point in this direction. That Moses wrote at least certain portions of the books that were traditionally ascribed to him may be noted (see Exod. 17:14; 24:4, 7; 34:27; Num. 33:2). In Leviticus at least thirty-five times expressions are used like, "And the LORD spoke unto Moses (and Aaron)." If the exact words of the Lord are referred to, the measure of probability is high that they were committed to writing as soon as received (cf. also Deut. 1:1). Unusually important are those passages that bear reference to written material dating from Moses (17:18; 27:1–8; 31:9, 24).

It could be argued feasibly that if Moses resorted to writing in the cases just referred to, he may well have written the rest of the framework that surrounds these portions written by him. It also appears feasible that the material from Exodus to Deuteronomy demands some such substructure as Genesis. Moses could well have sensed this need and taken steps to provide such a broader base, using such materials as were accessible at the time, in the form of ancient traditions that had been well preserved. Such an approach to the problem has as much to commend it as the hypothetical results of modern criticism.

When passages like Jn. 5:46–47 (in which Jesus refers to the "writings" of Moses) are presented, they cannot be dismissed casually with the statement: "Jesus was not at the time discussing the authorship of the Pentateuch." It all depends on how far one cares to extend the authority of the words of Jesus. That he incidentally combined with his statement a claim that Moses wrote these books could indeed have been done in the interest of reassuring his followers on this additional important question for years to come. It may be true that "Moses" in this context could mean the writings commonly attributed to Moses. It is equally true that it might be a pronouncement on the authorship of these writings. One may still say: "No reason has yet been produced which categorically requires that the belief in the Mosaic authorship should be abandoned" (E. F. Kevan in *The New Bible Commentary*, ed. F. Davidson [1953], 75). We hold the theory of Mosaic authorship of Genesis to be just as feasible as the theory of source analysis.

One need not deny that, in compiling Genesis, Moses used available documents or solid traditions currently in circulation. Nor is it unreasonable to hold with the Bible Commission of the Roman Catholic Church (1906) that though Moses was the author of the Pentateuch, he may have employed qualified persons as secretaries to work under his direction for the compiling of certain source materials (cf. H. Yunker, *Echter Bible* [1958]). Allowance may even be made for post-Mosaic editorial additions or alterations of a later date. By this we mean that the names of towns as they are listed here and there in Genesis may have been changed to agree with the names held at a later date, a perfectly legitimate modernizing. Aalders goes further in advocating that someone else may have compiled the work "at a comparatively later date" (prob. during the early days of the monarchy) but will have "made use of the extensive Mosaic literature together with some pre-Mosaic material" (G. C. Aalders in *The New Bible Commentary*, ed. F. Davidson [1953], 34).

IV. Unique problems. Quite a number of unique problems are encountered when one enters upon a study of Genesis. Almost the first to stare the student in the face is the problem of the apparent conflict between the modern worldview and that of this book. The difference of approach could even be magnified to the point where the two viewpoints are regarded as utterly irreconcilable. However, one need not be unduly alarmed at the prospect. It is now commonly conceded that obviously the writer of the Genesis CREATION account cannot have had the intention of providing a scientific theory cast in modern terms. He was so guided by the Spirit of INSPIRATION that he set forth basic truths of REVELATION in terms that were precise enough as to the truth conveyed, but yet were elastic enough to allow for the possibility of present-day scientific approaches that have been well established.

The emphasis in the account of Genesis lies upon the omnipotence and mercy of the Creator. A God

This Sumerian wall plaque from Ur (c. 2500 B.C.) depicts a priest and worshipers, some of whom carry animal offerings. Abraham came out of a society that new only polytheism.

who can be loved and worshiped is represented in action in a manner calculated to bring people to their knees as they behold what God did to bring this world and mankind into being. The time factor involved is certainly a subject of secondary importance. In fact, in the manner in which the account is written, it is quite clear that certain processes that may have required the lapse of a large measure of time are allowed for. Without a question the well-ordered nature of God's creation as well as the wisdom with which all things were made, all stand forth rather prominently. Many scientists can gratefully accept Genesis and many theologians gladly accept the numerous validated findings of science.

Of an entirely different nature are the instances in the Scripture that seem to fail to fit smoothly into the picture of interpretation. There is the question of the historical character of the old patriarchs: Did Abraham, Isaac, and Jacob actually live and do the things recorded here? Did these events actually take place in their lives? That they were uniquely led by divine PROVIDENCE is rather apparent. But does an unusual measure of providential leading make an account unhistorical? More of God's overruling power may have been manifested in one person's life than in another. Besides, ARCHAEOLOGY has done valiant service in demonstrating in the record of the lives of the patriarchs that the background of these lives corresponds precisely with the state of affairs that prevailed in these lands as archaeology retraces these records. M. F. Unger remarks, "The great service archaeological research is performing in this early period of Biblical history is to demonstrate that the picture of the patriarchs as presented in Genesis fits the frame of contemporary life.... Today archaeology compels a more general respect for the historical quality of the patriarchal stories." He adds that it "has had a momentous role in dealing a fatal blow to radical theories and in compelling a greater respect for the historical worth of the patriarchal narratives" (*Archeology and the Old Testament* [1954], 120; see also G. E. Wright, *Biblical Archaeology* [1957], ch. 3).

A matter that could cause the careful reader of Genesis some measure of difficulty is the fact that after one has read the largely narrative account of this book, the style of the record becomes so radically different in vocabulary and subject matter as one gets into material such as Exod. 21–23. Could one and the same writer be found to have such diversity of style as is here in evidence? A still different style appears as one explores the material of Deuteronomy. But is not this difficulty alleviated by the simple observation that at these points a change of subject matter is to be found? The writer is no longer telling how God dealt with the patriarchs, but is recounting laws that he set forth for the guidance of the nation. Style and vocabulary had to change under such circumstances. So, too, they had to change again when Moses, before his end, addressed touching admonitions to the nation he had guided for so many years, as is the case in much of the material that goes to make up Deuteronomy.

How about the question of sources? Is not the argument convincing that J largely and almost exclusively used the name Yahweh for the divine being, whereas E used Elohim? Cannot this speak strongly in favor of a clear separation of these two sources? No easy solution to the problem involved has yet been offered by either side in the argument. Criticism can hardly offer a valid parallel where a writer of the Mosaic period can be shown to have known only one name for the Deity. Besides, the obvious fact that names are to be used according to their meaning is totally ignored in this case. Observe, by way of a good parallel, the fine distinction that the NT makes in the use of the two names "Jesus" and "Christ." Add to this the many exceptions where J uses Elohim and E uses Yahweh.

Is there not a large measure of agreement among critics as to the major issues of source analysis? First of all, issues of this sort are not settled by majority vote. The majority often has been wrong. Besides, a large number of passages can be cited from the pen of critics admitting many unsolved problems. A. Bentzen admits that "the present situation concerning the question of the Pentateuch … is rather in suspense. Especially among the scholars of the younger generation there exists a definite scepticism toward the Documentary Hypothesis" (*Introduction to the Old Testament* [1958], 2:23). E. Nielsen, writing as a representative of an oral tradition theory, objects to the older literary criticism: "One can and must doubt whether the method by which literary criticism *finds* difficulties in the text and afterwards *solves* them is the right one. In other words one may doubt the correctness of the fundamental view and the methods of literary criticism" (*Oral Tradition* [1954], 94). Observe also how many findings are couched in cautious terminology, using frequently words such as "could" and "might." Somewhat striking besides is the fact that after many sources have been detected by the methods of criticism there are still certain materials left over that cannot be traced to any of the sources or redactors with which scholars operate (e.g., Gen. 14; Exod. 15:1–19; 19:3–8; Deut. 32).

Attention also should be drawn to the fact that when the theology of Genesis is set forth, the custom prevails to present not the theology of the book as a whole but to fragmentize it into the separate theologies of J, E, P, etc. The total impact of the book is lost, and the hypothetical theologies of unidentified writers are emphasized. The form in which the book has providentially come down to us is ignored, though the editor, or redactor—whoever he may have been—may have been highly praised by the present-day writer for his skill in organizing. It is not the theology of Genesis that is offered, but the hazy theologies of J, E, and P.

There is another unwholesome trend that may be observed in dealing with the book as a whole, namely, extreme skepticism regarding the history of the early patriarchs. It is taken for granted that one cannot accept as facts the things set forth as having been experienced by the fathers of old. Their encounter with the divine being in assumed human or angelic form, their providential deliverance from danger, the overwhelming instances of divine providence particularly in the life of Joseph—all these are thought to tax belief beyond what confidently may be accepted. Subjective feelings are not the final measure of miracles.

V. Theology of Genesis. On the doctrine concerning God, some distinct points of view emerge and some features obviously are missing. A full-rounded concept of God could hardly be conveyed by one brief book, especially since the doctrine of God also was subject to more abundant revelation as time went on. The God who does appear in Genesis is sole and supreme monarch of the universe and of his people. A latent monotheism is to be discovered in the book. It is a long while until statements like Deut. 6:4 can appear, but Genesis prepares for them. It is equally obvious that this God of the patriarchs is omnipotent: he can create whatever he is pleased to bring into being, and he does all his work by the use of his potent word. He knows all things, though this fact is hinted at rather than fully revealed. He knows of the hiding of our first parents in the garden, and of Sarah's secret laughter in the tent. He is present also far from the ancestral home, as Jacob to his amazement discovers (Gen. 28:16); he is omnipresent.

In his workings God is supremely wise, for all things that he creates bear the stamp of being most excellently adapted to their designed use and purpose. An integrated universe comes into being from his hands. At the same time concern for the well-being of his creatures leads him to give abundant evidence of his deep mercy and love, especially toward those creatures who are the crown of his creation. This God reveals himself to his children. Some measure of mystery surrounds the manner in which he does it. The sacred writers were not told how REVELATION in days of old came from God to human beings, at least not as far as the mechanics of the method were concerned. God did at times appear (one may not be able to say precisely in what guise), and in these theophanies he spoke understandably to the chosen recipients of his revelation (see THEOPHANY). Sometimes his message was conveyed in the stillness of the night in a dream (Gen. 31:11); sometimes the mysterious agent "the angel of the Lord" functioned on such occasions (again 31:11). These experiences on the part of the patriarchs were real and do not savor of an overly lively display of religious credulity.

A rather clear picture of who and what human beings are also begins to appear in the context of this book. They are creatures, made according to a preconceived design, with a material as well as a nonmaterial side to their being. They are from the outset creatures that have a free will, for they can assent or refuse temptation. God's image is stamped upon man, male and female. True, what the IMAGE OF GOD precisely embraces is nowhere defined, but it is asserted with emphasis that this belongs to his native endowment (Gen. 1:27). Equally mysterious is the somewhat representative character of the first man ("in Adam all die," 1 Cor. 15:22). He is the first of human beings in more than the mere sense of numerical priority. Again this representative character is not set forth in so many words. See ADAM.

This man is represented from the outset as a superior being as he comes forth as God's handiwork, free from the taint of SIN. Being led by the tempter, he allows himself to aspire to be like God, and rises in proud disobedience against the express will of his Creator, taking of the fruit "whose mortal taste brought death into the world and all its woe." The immediate consequences of this willful act are seen to be an unwholesome fear of God, a desire to shun his presence, and a sense of shame, together with many other distortions of what had been a "good" character. See FALL, THE.

Sin's capacity for rapid growth is indicated by the record that tells how the first son of our first parents, CAIN, slew his own brother ABEL in cold blood. In fact, as the record points out, sin rages up and down through the world, filling it with violence, even to the point where the Creator himself had to use drastic means to curb this monstrous evil. See FLOOD, GENESIS. When a new development sets in and people increase in numbers, soon they are defying the basic ordinance of the Almighty and are building a rallying point in the form of a huge tower. See BABEL. That sinners stand in need of help from on high is, by this account, represented negatively rather than positively. It soon becomes obvious that sin again is reaching horrible dimensions when the abnormal development of Canaanite sexual depravity comes to light, or when the incident of SODOM and GOMORRAH throws its lurid light on the pages of Sacred Writ.

That there is a GRACE mighty to save also soon becomes apparent. For hardly had Adam fallen, even before his well-deserved punishment is appointed, when strong evidence appears that God will not deal with men and women after their sins in ruthless justice, nor reward strictly according to their iniquities. He gives a rich promise, as Gen. 3:15, rightly interpreted, clearly shows. It is promised that one capable of breaking the power of the evil one will in due time appear, born of a woman. An incidental trace of the unmerited grace that God will make operative is to be found also in this, that the Creator provides garments for these children of his whom he had to oust from the blessed garden of Eden (3:23). In a similar manner God's attitude toward fallen man is indicated by the RAINBOW in the sky after the great deluge, which was a token of grace indicating a stable world order not again to be visited by a flood. In fact, God's undeserved goodness found solid expression finally in the COVENANT that he made freely with ABRAHAM, not because of Abraham's superior merit but because of the Lord's abounding favor (Gen. 15).

So there are to be found the basic elements of redemption even at this early date: GRACE on the part of God; FAITH on the part of his people. For Gen. 15:6 plainly states that when Abraham

This mud-brick gate provided access into the city of Laish (Dan) and dates to the time of Abraham.

believed the Lord's promises, "he credited it to him as righteousness," a passage that figures prominently in the upbuilding of PAULINE THEOLOGY (Rom. 4:3, 9, 22–23). Genesis comes close to saying that a sinner is justified by faith apart from the works of the law. See JUSTIFICATION.

It may also be noted that some clear thoughts on the subject of JUDGMENT are set forth in this early record. Abraham knows God as the fair and unimpeachable judge of all the earth (Gen. 18:25). There are no soft notions of an indulgent father of mankind, but a sense of the necessity of divine justice visiting sin's consequences upon the guilty—thoughts like this are strongly underscored by incidents like the destruction of Sodom (19:1–28).

Even more strongly the concept of divine PROVIDENCE is maintained and exemplified. In that food is expressly provided in creation for human needs, divine providence shows its face. The unique manner in which the patriarchs are guided and guarded in their ways conveys the same thought. In fact, perhaps nowhere in Scripture is the evidence of providential guidance exemplified more prominently than in the narrative that centers on JOSEPH.

VI. Content. The account of creation as given in the first two chapters of Genesis has something majestic about it. Being sanctified prose, it still reads almost like a great epic poem. It moves in solemn cadences to a great climax in the record of God's SABBATH, having just before recorded the sublime story of the creation of man. At the same time, in words coming from the lips of the divine Creator, it maps out with surprising effectiveness God's mandate to man, male and female, to exercise dominion over all created things (Gen. 1:28). Adam and Eve had rare duties and rare prerogatives and a nobel destiny outlined for them by God. They were not left to their own devices to determine what their Creator expected of them. Still the mandate was given with such latitude of movement that God could hardly have stressed man's moral accountability more heavily.

In the second chapter, God's work of creation—how it proceeded and what it involved—is more fully unfolded. These details could have been inserted at their proper place in the time sequence of the first chapter, but that would have interrupted the marvelous progression that is so evident in the initial description. There was something of lowliness in the story of Adam—he was fashioned "from the dust of the ground" (Gen. 2:7). This element, so effectively disclosed at this point, counterbalances the story of the high dignity that marked the previous chapter's account. All this in spite of the fact that man had the distinct imprint of the image of God in his being.

Woman's position over against man is also more fully outlined in the account of Gen. 2:21–25. What had previously been stated all too briefly ("male and female he created them," 1:27) is now expanded in a report also most instructive and helpful. There is no clash between these two accounts. They obviously are intended to supplement one another. See EVE.

For Adam's moral growth and development God had in deep wisdom provided two trees (Gen. 2:9) with important directives in regard to the TREE OF KNOWLEDGE. One must regard their nature as being almost sacramental. The full possibilities of the TREE OF LIFE have not been perpetuated in the traditions relative to this second tree. One still gains the impression that nothing needful for man's future development had been omitted.

Basic for the understanding of human nature is some instruction about the origin of evil. This is provided in Gen. 3. Many questions are left unanswered, perhaps because the mystery of iniquity is too great for human beings to fully comprehend it. The record of the fall reveals some basic guidelines that dare never be overlooked. Adam, as he came from the hand of God, was without moral deficiency. Sin did not originate from within man. A personal tempter brought it into the world. Man let himself be beguiled by the mysterious serpent. At a much later time it is made obvious that in the last analysis this tempter was none other than SATAN (Rev. 12:9). It is impossible to determine why the tempter is not more clearly identified.

Man and woman were not cursed as a consequence of the fall, although grievous burdens were laid upon them lest they forget the deep tragedy of the whole experience—that the ground is cursed and brings forth thorns and thistles; toilsome labor and death are to be their lot. But the case is not hopeless. In some strange way Adam was enlightened to see that, from the woman, life would come for mankind; for he designates his wife by the name Eve, which means "life." Further indications of hope for fallen mankind appear also in that one born of woman is to administer a crushing defeat ("crush the head") to the tempter in the course of time, a promise reiterated in Rom. 16:20. Additional evidence of God's merciful attitude appears in his having made personal provision for clothing those who had now become aware of a certain shameful nakedness (Gen. 3:21).

Something of a deeply mysterious nature also surrounds the tree of life. It was for man's own good that he was barred from access to this tree. For to have partaken of it would have meant irremediable involvement in the state of sin and so the loss of the hope of redemption (Gen. 3:22). The chapter has the memorable close that shows cherubim guarding the entrance to the garden of Eden lest man eat of the second forbidden tree and be caught in the toils of hopeless death.

In Gen. 4 the slaying of ABEL shows what horrible potentialities lie in sin. At the same time, this fratricide was the first step in the direction of separating the human race into two groups—the beginning of the sharp antithesis—church and world. Those who were the lineal descendants of CAIN (properly called "Cainites") from this point on are seen to live a life immersed in this world and its delights and pursuits. In the seventh generation from Adam this group reached a more intense development of worldly values (nomadism, music, mastery of metals, 4:20–24). On the other hand SETH (4:25–26) was the ancestor among whose descendants the worship of the Lord flourished—public worship even at this early date. The people of this group may be designated as "Sethites." The table of ancestry of the Cainites is given in 4:17–25, and the line of descent of the Sethites is presented in ch. 5. Both groups must be noted if one is to understand how the history of the nations unfolds.

Of the successive stories that cover the material of Genesis, the first "story"—that of heaven and earth—runs from Gen. 2:4 to 4:26. It is rightly designated as being the story of heaven and earth because the interests of both areas are deeply involved in these two. The second story—that of Adam—runs from 5:1 to 6:8, and indicates in its closing remarks how especially the Sethites forfeited their identity by letting their children intermarry with the godless Cainites. (For discussion, see SONS OF GOD.) From that point on, corruption grew so fast it was not long before only one righteous man was left on the face of the earth—NOAH.

This then leads to the story of Noah (Gen. 6:8–9:29), a period of history dominated by the lone figure of this venerable patriarch. Within this section is contained the record of the universal flood, telling particularly how God mercifully spared Noah and his family in the days when he wiped out all living creatures that were left outside the ark. The rainbow as token of God's covenant mercy overarches this story and brings it to a gracious conclusion.

That we may not forget that all human families, as far as we are able to detect, stem from the stock of Noah, the next story—Gen. 10:1–32—gives the genealogies of the sons of Noah and so traces the whole human family back to a second common ancestor. In spite of their ancestral unity, it was not long before a new rift in the races of mankind developed as a result of man's manifest disobedience to the command of the Lord in that they refused to keep spreading abroad on the face of the earth and sought to concentrate their strength and accomplishments about the great tower as rallying point. The mysterious confusion of tongues resulted, which helped to make obvious how deeply divided sinners had become from one another in spite of their common ancestry. This confusion could well have been allowed by the Almighty in order to prevent the consolidation of future opposition to the divine will.

The story found in Gen. 11:10–32 (the descendants of SHEM) makes it obvious that the writer is aiming to concentrate on some part of the family of Shem, and that he knew well how the families of the earth were integrated. With ch. 12 (beginning actually with 11:27), there is the special history of the chosen race, although this story is captioned as being that of TERAH. In some way, perhaps as a prominent figure among his contemporaries, Terah could at first have outranked ABRAHAM, but there can be no doubt that the Abraham story runs from 11:27 to 25:11. Terah seems to have died comparatively early and to have vanished from the scene at HARAN. In contrast, the story of the call of Abraham (12:1–3) is of the utmost importance. It is, of course, basic for the understanding of the sacred history that follows. It towers above the accompanying narratives, though we are not even told in what manner God appeared to Abraham. It is stated that in a surprising act of faith, Abraham obeyed the call.

In Gen. 12:10–20 we have the account of Abraham's sojourn in EGYPT with SARAH. It becomes apparent that though Abraham may have manifested surprising courage of faith in accepting the challenge of his call, yet he was far from being a perfect saint. Recent discoveries, however, relieve Abraham of some of his alleged weakness. It appears that in the HURRIAN society of Mesopotamia there remained traces of a fratriarchal organization. The other marriage and inheritance laws and customs of the patriarchs also have been brilliantly illustrated by the Hurrian culture evidenced by the documents from NUZI. There are marriage documents from Nuzi in which a wife, unrelated by blood to her husband, is adopted into the status of sistership. This legal status of sistership for a wife brought with it certain rights and protections characteristic of the upper classes of society. The HITTITES, it appears, did not recognize this peculiar custom. Apparently the wife-sister relationship was expected to give a woman a status that would make her free from improper approaches and thus make her husband safe in an unfriendly land. Abraham claimed this protection for both her and himself. It did not work in Egypt where Hurrian law was not followed. God in his providence preserved Sarah and Abraham anyway. Abraham tried it again in GERAR with the same result (possibly he also tried it elsewhere with a more positive outcome). ISAAC later tried it again, probably before a different PHILISTINE king, with no better success. The whole strange situation is seen to be in accord with Nuzi law and good ethics in the early patriarchal times (see E. A. Speiser, *Oriental and Biblical Studies* [1967], 68–72; some scholars have raised questions about this understanding of the Nuzi data).

Abraham's nephew, LOT, had associated himself with Abraham in the departure from UR of the Chaldeans. Nevertheless, as later developments show, his family did not constitute good material for incorporation with the chosen race. A separation had to take place. It ultimately appears that Lot gravitated toward Sodom, finding a certain attraction there. Some remarks (e.g., Gen. 13:13; 15:16) indicate that an unusual measure of depravity was beginning to prevail in that area of Canaan. There were more facets to Abraham's character than we might first suppose. He even filled the role of a deliverer from the perils of war, and as a warrior of no mean ability himself. He displayed fine family loyalty for his nephew, going to battle for him (ch. 14).

The following chapter records how God made a covenant with Abraham, promising him many descendants and also revealing to him that before better days came, a troubled and painful future awaited his descendants down in the land of

The patriarchs in Palestine.

Egypt. The shift of location down into Egypt did not come upon Abraham's descendants as a total surprise. Both the stay in that land and the affliction there incurred, together with the disclosure that God would ultimately deliver the nation—all these coming events were communicated already to Abraham. In this connection the sacrifice that was made according to 15:7–11, 17 is merely the record of the sacrifice by which the covenant was sealed in a formal fashion. The "smoking firepot" and "flaming torch" (15:17) constitute one single picture and symbolize light, the symbol of God's presence. God himself indicated by this sign that he personally had entered into a compact with Abraham. All this involved symbolic language, which in those days was readily understood.

The next section (Gen. 16) introduces a time of waiting. The fulfillment of God's promises did not come quickly. The period of waiting was a time of testing of the faith. Only under due tensions will faith grow and mature. This period of waiting extended over a number of decades. Under such circumstances people are inclined to resort to devices that are calculated to help God along. In the last analysis such devices are questionable and give evidence of a lack of faith. In this case they gave rise to family tensions, jealousy, friction, estrangement. HAGAR bore a son, but he was not to be a child of promise. Abraham still had to wait quite a number of years before the true son appeared. Though the procedure followed was sanctioned by prevailing customs of that day, it still did not meet with divine approval nor conform to the original promise God had given.

In the next chapter (Gen. 17) further promises were given to Abraham, but nothing more. Faith subsists on promises. It was even indicated to this venerable patriarch approaching the age of one hundred years that a number of nations would trace back the beginning of their existence to him. For the present, Abraham had to content himself with a unique sign of the covenant—CIRCUMCISION. At least two constructive thoughts must be associated with this rite: one, the removal of impurity, and second, the sanctifying of life at its source, which rightly may be classed as a thought involving messianic implications. In the obedience of faith, Abraham sees to it that he and his whole household take the obligations of this half-sacramental rite upon themselves. At the same time, Abraham learns that ISHMAEL will not rank as the son of promise. He will achieve some distinction as a son of Abraham. The promised one must be waited for, until the time is ripe in the Lord's sight.

A high point in the relationship of the two contracting partners in the covenant is reached in Gen. 18. The Lord condescends to meet with Abraham as an intimate friend, sharing food with him and sharing some of his divine secrets of judgment, as a person would with a confidential associate. A major catastrophe is about to occur near Abraham's home. God would have him know what it is and what it involves, and he comes in a special visit to apprise the man of what is about to take place. Abraham appears to good advantage. Being a man of faith, he is not self-centered. Impending calamity rouses deep sympathy on Abraham's part and shows him to be bold in prayer and much concerned about the well-being of others. Abraham's prayer for Sodom and Gomorrah is not petty haggling, but intercession at its best.

The sequel (Gen. 19) deals with ugly things. Sin has made tremendous inroads into the lives particularly of the Canaanites. Sin in its more repulsive forms is in evidence. It is not to be wondered at that the Almighty himself, through his angels, takes the desperate situation in hand, and thereby sets up a severe warning for all the inhabitants of the land. Homosexuality in its grimmer aspects, venting its spite on helpless strangers, is the particular sin in which the iniquity of these people found its expression. For the sake of the intercessory prayer of a righteous man, the Lord spares at least those few persons in the city who may be less infected by this basic immorality. Even in that family group one member perishes, Lot's wife, one who takes divine commandments somewhat lightly and is disobedient to a clear divine warning. The conclusion of the chapter indicates how one family that was saved had been infected by the unholy example of the surroundings in which the family had lived for a few years.

The episode recorded in Gen. 20 is not a doublet of the similar one that had transpired earlier (12:10–20); the location, the characters involved, and the details of the two are quite different from one another. The opening account of the next chapter gives indication how great the happiness was that reigned in the household of Abraham at the birth of the son long promised. The name of Isaac in itself already alludes to laughter; and the laughter referred to in this connection does not reflect amusement but rather joy unspeakable over the fact that God had so faithfully kept his promise. When the two sons of Abraham grew up and failed to get along well together, this led to the dismissal of the son of the slave woman. Though her expulsion was divinely sanctioned, God compensated to her what she had to forfeit and gave to Ishmael also the hope of a challenging future, all for the sake of his servant Abraham.

One of the best-known stories of the OT is found in Gen. 22. It should be noted in particular that the idea of offering a son to the Lord in a physical sacrifice on an altar did not originate with Abraham. God, however, does not follow mere whimsies in dealing with his people. It may well be that Abraham needed to be put to the test in this way, that he might become aware of the danger of loving this child of his old age more than even the Lord himself. He had to face the issue squarely: Whom did he love the most, the Lord or Isaac? Hard though the test was, the Lord did not suffer Abraham to be tested above that which he was able. That God provides (v. 14) in the most difficult emergencies was the point that particularly impressed Abraham. He had virtually made the spiritual sacrifice of his son to the Lord. At the same time, this episode may be regarded as a standing protest against child sacrifice: such offering is not willed by God. It also must be obvious that this sacrifice has messianic overtones. God was willing to offer his own Son for the saving of mankind (Rom. 8:32). There is much about this chapter that still perplexes the children of God. It has unplumbed depths.

An overly detailed account of the transactions connected with the purchase of a burial ground when Sarah died seems to be what Gen. 23 presents. Possession of the land of Canaan was an item that loomed up large in the thinking of all Israelites from the time when first God promised this land to Abraham. Why should he not want at least token possession in the case of his wife's place of burial? Viewed thus, the incident takes on increased importance as the act of a man of faith. With quiet dignity Abraham goes through all the necessary legal transactions to acquire at least this much of the soil of the land.

The tale of Gen. 24 could be viewed as a somewhat romantic one charmingly told. It is far more than that. Perhaps there was hardly a woman to be found in the land who was not in some manner infected with loose and ungodly Canaanite thinking and immoral idolatry. To have secured a wife for Isaac from this type of stock would have imperiled the faith and the morals of the descendants of Abraham. With fine discretion Abraham commissions the servant of his house (Abraham was by this time, no doubt, too old to undergo the rigors of journey to Mesopotamia) and instructs him on the subject of the issues involved in this transaction. The servant was a man worthy of so fine a master and carried out his commission in the spirit in which it was given. Rebekah's prompt acceptance could well have been regarded as token that the servant's prayer at the well had been answered.

Abraham's marriage to Keturah (Gen. 25:1) is a matter of historical record. Everything relating to the great father of the people of Israel is important. Most likely this marriage was entered upon after the death of Sarah. The children of this marriage are the fathers of the nations that had been foretold as coming from Abraham's line (17:5). At this point the Ishmael story is woven into the

View of the SW corner of the Machpelah, an imposing structure built by Herod the Great over the traditional burial cave of the patriarchs.

narrative. As a descendant of Abraham, Ishmael is important; aside from that he merits brief attention (25:12–18). Then comes the beginning of the Isaac story (25:19—35:29), covering a major section of the book of Genesis. In the Isaac story, however, Isaac stays pretty much in the background, being overshadowed in the first part of it by Abraham, as long as his father still lived, and then yielding place to his more famous son, JACOB. All this is partly due to the fact that Isaac was an ordinary person, pushed into the background by characters more important and more aggressive than he. Besides, it was the nature of the man Isaac to be unaggressive and somewhat phlegmatic by disposition. He stayed put quietly, inaugurated no new policies, hardly did an original thing. He perhaps never asserted himself.

Two sons are born of Isaac, one of them uniquely a child of promise (Gen. 25:23). These twins also present quite a contrast, being radically different in disposition from one another (vv. 25–34). In the brief sketch given they are effectively set off one against the other. JACOB should not be unduly blamed for acquiring the BIRTHRIGHT of the firstborn. Preeminence had been promised him before his birth (v. 23). Furthermore ESAU displayed little of a sense of appreciation of higher values in that he so readily disposed of his prerogative, selling his birthright. Such a sale of a birthright was not unique; an instance is recorded in the Nuzi texts, where a birthright was sold for three sheep (C. F. Pfeiffer, *The Biblical World* [1966], 423). It becomes quite obvious on reading the chapter that Jacob was the man who was better suited for outstanding leadership in the family.

The next chapter contributes some scenes from Isaac's life. None are particularly striking; some are similar to those found in Abraham's life. He repeated his father's procedure when he dwelt near GERAR (later in the land of the PHILISTINES) by claiming his wife as his sister. The grace of God watched also over Isaac. He had a dispute about wells with some of the shepherds of the general area, just as did his father, but he remained in the pattern of life established by his father. In connection with his move to BEERSHEBA we read of the one instance in his life when the Lord appeared to him and renewed the promises that had in the previous generation been granted to Abraham (Gen. 26:23–25). Isaac, for all that, enjoyed the great respect of his neighbors, and even of kings, and must have been more of a prominent figure than is sometimes supposed (26:26–33). That he too was a man of faith goes without saying.

In Gen. 27 we read how Isaac blessed his sons. Though in no sense can one condone the deception that Jacob and Rebekah planned to perpetrate, it should be noted from the outset that every participant in the action was more or less at fault. Jacob's fault already has been conceded. Rebekah was the originator of the deception practiced. Isaac, no doubt, knew of the word spoken by the Lord (25:23), but chose to try to invalidate it because of his favorite Esau. Esau on his part acted as though he had never sold his birthright. Out of all this moral confusion and deception came a result that was in harmony with the Lord's will in regard to the matter. Overruling providence controlled the final issue. The man of God's choice was given the better blessing and was thereby marked to all intents and purposes as the man that carried the line of promise in this chosen family.

In the light of the entire outcome in this instance, Isaac clearly confirmed the blessing that he had unintentionally at first bestowed upon Jacob (Gen. 28:4). Nothing less than the ultimate murder of his brother was in Esau's mind, yet he refrained from committing it while his parents were still alive. No other course was left open for Jacob than to leave the land, not in headlong flight, but in an adventure to which his parents consented. There is good ground for believing that Jacob by this time was truly repentant of his misdeed in the matter of securing his father's blessing. For this reason God appeared to him with gracious promises for reassurance and guidance in the well-known BETHEL incident, marked by the ascending and descending of angels on a ladder. They served as symbols of God's providence and protection and served to comfort a lonely, homesick, and penitent sinner. Jacob had not realized that God's providence would manifest itself away from the familiar setting of the ancestral home. He had never fully comprehended the meaning of God's OMNIPRESENCE. The words of the vow (vv. 20–22) are not an expression of mercenary bargaining of a shrewd man cautiously looking out for his own advantage. Jacob is merely reiterating the promises that the Lord had just made to him (v. 15). Jesus refers to this incident in a manner that shows that the passage also foreshadowed his own intimate communion with his heavenly Father (Jn. 1:51). It still must be noted that Jacob vowed to establish a shrine to mark the spot of his memorable experience.

One of the lovely biblical romances is presented at the beginning of Gen. 29. It was love at first sight at the well. To have seven years pass like seven days marks a man deeply in love. At this point it becomes obvious that LABAN is a crafty fellow who will stop short at nothing where his own material advantage is at stake. Crafty Jacob has a craftier prospective father-in-law. They are matching wits continually. He who has so subtly deceived his brother must learn what it means to be deceived. So divine retribution goes to work to correct Jacob's wayward propensities. In spite of all the craftiness of sinners, the Almighty keeps the situation totally under his control. Divine providence overrules human craft and cunning.

There is another unpleasant side to the matter. Jacob became a bigamist. True, it was by accident rather than by design. Nowhere in the narrative is a word of censure spoken on Jacob's bigamy, but in its own way the sacred record shows how sinful and unwholesome such a situation could become. It resulted in family intrigues and petty bickerings; in lack of family discipline and petty jealousies; in fact, in an entirely unwholesome atmosphere. That spiritual values had to be pushed into the background under such circumstances is obvious. Besides, on a broader scale tensions were building up between Jacob's family and Laban's. Mistrust and manifold connivings were the order of the day, until the situation became unbearable. Jacob had to leave Mesopotamia and return to the land of promise. He received divine sanction for the return. Providence was able to retrieve some good from the unwholesome ways of men. It should yet be noted that the significant names that were given by the mothers to the twelve sons of Jacob indicated that a spark of faith still was glowing beneath the surface of things.

As the family grew so did the flocks grow in size so as to become very large. Jacob resorted to a number of devices to get the advantage over his father-in-law in the matter of acquiring the newborn stock. It is not said that the devices employed produced results, but it is indicated that it pleased the Lord to let Jacob rather than Laban acquire wealth of herds. All this tended to increase the feelings of rivalry and jealousy that prevailed between the two camps (Gen. 30).

Finally, the situation became unbearable for Jacob (Gen. 31). God intervened on Jacob's behalf and approved of his return to the land of his fathers. His wives were entirely on his side, for their father had treated their husband shamefully. Again, quite cleverly Jacob took advantage of a situation that allowed him to make the most of the distance between the two herds. As soon as word was brought to Laban, he set out on an expedition calculated to exact revenge. Again the Lord intervened and forbade Laban from resorting to any punitive measure. He smoothly played the part of the father-in-law who had been deprived the opportunity to take affectionate leave of his daughters and grandchildren.

One thing Laban could charge against those who had fled: some one of their number had taken Laban's household gods (see TERAPHIM). No one except RACHEL knew that it was she who did it. According to the witness of the Nuzi documents, possession of the household deities guaranteed the right to the ancestral inheritance. By a clever ruse (not entirely honest), Rachel prevented her father from discovering the offender and the gods; and all this gave rise to a burst of indignation on Jacob's part that relieved feelings long pent up. This explosion seemed to clear the atmosphere and led at least to some kind of half-amicable settlement between the two parties. When a heap of stones was raised to commemorate the agreement, Laban still implied, in a memorable word, full of suspicion and mistrust, that Jacob was a man who could under no circumstances be trusted (Gen. 31:49) and had to be restrained by solemn oaths and pledges. For the sake of peace, Jacob entered upon the prescribed agreement and the matter was regarded as settled.

The tension of the narrative builds up in Gen. 32. A report came to Jacob that Esau was approaching with 400 men, gathered, beyond a doubt, for the purpose of executing the revenge that Esau

This statue was found in a small private chapel dedicated to the deity Hendursag (Ur, c. 1750 B.C.). If it represents a god, it may be similar to the household idols that Rachel took from her father's home (Gen. 31:19).

© Dr. James C. Martin. The British Museum. Photographed by permission.

the one for whom the gifts were intended, a wise move of appeasement. By sending these gifts, one after the other, the calculated impact of the act was reinforced. Should Esau prove hostile, some of the groups involved might have effected an escape. As night approached, Jacob brought the remainder of his herds and personnel across the ford of the river. Then he had recourse to desperate prayer, wrestling with a mysterious man (apparently the angel of the Lord) through a good part of the night. No one will ever completely understand the mysterious encounter involved. Somehow Jacob knew that his opponent was God and insistently sought his blessing. Men rightly believed in those days that he who encountered God face to face must die (Exod. 33:20). When Jacob named the place Peniel (Gen. 32:30, "face of God"), he commemorated the fact that he had survived the experience of direct encounter with God. See Penuel (place).

The event took an entirely unexpected turn (Gen. 33). Beneath a hard surface there dwelt in Esau's character a soft emotional nature. At the sight of his brother all thoughts of revenge were dispelled. The brothers embraced, kissed, and wept. The hour of extreme danger was past. God had also intervened and had somehow moved Esau's heart and directed it toward kindliness. Esau would have established closer bonds of fellowship, but the more sober Jacob recognized the somewhat unstable emotional character of his brother and contented himself with the reconciliation that had been effected. This episode of sojourn in Mesopotamia is brought to an effective close by the erection of an altar at the point of entrance into the land of promise, an altar commemorating God's grace and protective care. From this point on, a number of highly revealing incidents are reported that indicate the course that events are taking.

The first of these was the rape of Dinah (Gen. 34), an incident that indicates how carefree Jacob's children moved about among the Canaanites, seemingly unaware of the moral contamination that Canaan represented. Dinah associated with the women of the land and paid the price. A young Canaanite prince violated her, after which he was ready to enter upon matrimony. An agreement was reached with the family of Hamor, but treachery lurked behind it all. The brothers of Dinah were

had vowed to take after he lost the paternal blessing. Jacob could not begin to muster an equal force, though he had a goodly number of shepherds. Humanly, Jacob was almost at his wit's end. Then it was that Jacob was granted a vision of a host of angels at Mahanaim near the confluence of the Jordan and the Jabbok. This host never apparently went into action, but the angels were revealed as indicating the protective resources that the Lord could have put into action for Jacob.

Repeatedly Jacob resorted to prayer, but he also resorted to careful precautionary measures to appease his brother, setting up sizable numbers of sheep, oxen, camels, and donkeys as a gift for Esau. He who in such situations submitted gifts to another acknowledged the superior position of determined to take thoroughgoing vengeance on all the people of the town. Suddenly, the sons of Jacob appear in a very unfavorable light—they are murderers, truce-breakers, men given to waging bloody feuds. They are not at all men worthy of the caliber of their ancestor Abraham. They are beginning to represent a high state of deterioration. It is becoming apparent that Israel as a tribal group cannot continue to stay in Canaan without paying the price of total moral corruption. Something like the bondage in Egypt is imperative. Jacob's sons executed a horrid blood-bath, recklessly endangering their own family safety, and giving themselves a bad name. Minority groups that they were, they could easily have been exterminated if the native Canaanites had banded together for purposes of reprisal. Jacob freely admits that possibility as he rebukes his sons for their rash and wanton murder. Divine providence, undeserved though it was, watched over the group, for God had high purposes in mind for this race.

Jacob had made a significant vow at the time when he was about to leave the borders of the land of promise (Gen. 28:22). God helped him remember and fulfill his vow, establishing a sanctuary at Bethel (35:1–15). At the same time, God explicitly laid his promises, formerly made to Abraham and Isaac, upon Jacob, the bearer of the line of promise. The change of name to ISRAEL was confirmed at this time. Before the permanent settlement in Canaan took place, BENJAMIN was born and Rachel died at his birth, to Jacob's great grief. In one brief statement inserted at this point (v. 22), it is indicated that even the firstborn of the sons of Jacob had become infected with typical Canaanite immorality, committing incest with a secondary wife of his father. Jacob returned to the ancestral home and found his father still alive, but Rebekah had died. In a way she paid the price for her participation in Jacob's treachery to gain the father's blessing, for she never lived to see Jacob again after he left the land. Not long after this, Isaac also died.

The whole of Gen. 36 is concerned with the story of Esau, whose descendants, the Edomites, would later display a very unbrotherly attitude toward the Israelites. Israel, however, kept alive the sense of kinship with this chapter. From this point (37:1), the intriguing Jacob story runs to the end of

This 1905 photo shows the traditional tomb of Rachel near Bethlehem.

the book. Jacob, however, is overshadowed somewhat by his illustrious son JOSEPH. Still, Jacob is always behind the scene and the controlling factor in most of that which is done. Just because Joseph informed on his brothers in his earlier youth, he cannot be quickly written off as a cheap tattletale or a spoiled young man. In his attitude toward his brothers he did betray a measure of immaturity and indiscretion. On the other hand, Jacob's preference for Joseph can easily be understood. Most of the brothers had displayed a lack of spiritual character. The evidence about Joseph indicates that he had godly qualities from his youth. God chose to reveal the future to the young boy, and Jacob recognized his spiritual kinship with this son. The "richly ornamented robe" (37:3) possibly marked Joseph as his potential successor. Jacob erred in the manner in which he went about this disclosure. Without a doubt Joseph was a brilliant young man of admirable character, but his brothers being what they were, one could hardly have expected them to take any different attitude toward him than they did.

The brothers of Joseph had rashly penetrated into the very area of danger not too far removed from the city of SHECHEM. Fearing for their safety, Jacob dispatched Joseph to check on them, little dreaming that Joseph would thereby be exposed to danger. In fact, it amazes the reader that the great-grandchildren of father Abraham should be capable of thinking in terms of murder of their brother just because they were jealous of him. On beholding him approaching, they planned to dispose of him. REUBEN, the firstborn, had enough sense of right and wrong left to advocate at least a cooling-off period. He hoped to liberate his brother later. JUDAH proposed to sell him to traders so that he could be brought to the slave-market in Egypt, hardly a kindly alternative. With a certain callousness the brothers sent Joseph's special robe dipped in blood to their father, utterly deceiving him and causing him untold grief. He who had excelled in deceit in his younger years is now deceived by his own sons, and the experience is painful.

While Joseph faced a precarious future in Egypt, strange and unholy things were marking the careers of his brothers back in Canaan (Gen. 38). The narrative furnishes a typical example of the growing moral degeneracy of the family, especially in the case of Judah, who became involved, though in a sense unintentionally, with his own daughter-in-law. The ugly mess is described in all its repulsiveness. While Joseph languished in prison, his brothers were corrupting themselves. To have been exposed to this type of Canaanite corruption could have ruined the family. Going down to Egypt, or something similar, had become a necessity.

Joseph's career began at the lowest rung of the ladder. He was at first only a common slave, but he seems to have had such unusual gifts of administration and such perseverance in the faithful use of them that his master, POTIPHAR, soon discovered what a rare treasure he had in Joseph. Besides, the obvious blessing of the Lord was also in evidence. Joseph became master, or steward, of Potiphar's household (Gen. 39:3–4). A sudden danger confronted the good-looking young man—his master's wife became enamored of him. That Joseph's adherence to the ancestral religion was more than something learned by rote became apparent. In the hour of temptation, Joseph disclosed the deep wellspring of his whole life in the word: "How then could I do such a wicked thing and sin against God?" (39:9). Love spurned turns to hate. Joseph, entirely in the right, is libelled, thrown into prison (slaves had no legal rights), and allowed to languish there for years. God seemed to have forgotten him, but Joseph had not forgotten God. He served him just as faithfully in prison as he did when he was a free man. The prison warden recognized faithful service, and put him in charge of all prison administration. The whole experience served indirectly to prepare Joseph for the sudden rise to high position that was presently to occur.

While Joseph was busy with the affairs of the prison, quite unexpectedly a new avenue of activity opened up to him—the gift of DREAM interpretation (Gen. 40). The royal butler and the royal baker, both officials of the royal household, but languishing in prison for reasons unknown to us, had dreams in the same night. Without his design or plan, Joseph unexpectedly began to function as interpreter (cf. 37:5–11), and the sequel proved that his interpretation was entirely correct. A glimmer of hope seemed to appear on the scene for a moment, for Joseph pleaded with the butler to remember him when liberated. The butler readily promised—and promptly forgot his promise.

PHARAOH had two dreams which God used to convey knowledge to one farther removed from him (Gen. 41). When the news of the dreams spread, the butler was suddenly reminded of his promise and hastened to the king to inform him of Joseph's ability. Joseph is speedily summoned for appearance in court. He interpreted the dreams with such obvious authority that the correctness of his interpretation was immediately apparent to all. Important is Joseph's confession in this connection: "God will give Pharaoh a favorable answer" (v. 16 NRSV). Joseph's loyalty to the Lord had not wavered. He offered suggestions for the king to proceed in the existing situation. With amazement the king admitted the brilliant helpfulness of the suggestions given, and, after brief consideration, appointed Joseph as national food administrator. At once he launched into his new career with becoming zeal and energy. He inaugurated a policy of grain reserves to be accumulated during the impending seven years of plenty. In all the busy whirl of activity, home and the ancestral family are not forgotten (vv. 50–52). The seven years of plenty passed swiftly, only a few verses in the record being given to the subject. Against this broad backdrop of history play the events in the lives of that little group up in Palestine that constitute the family of Joseph.

The thread of the narrative of the family of the chosen people is resumed (Gen. 42). The famine was not limited to Egypt, but affected Canaan too. The news of Egyptian grain supplies reached Jacob's ears. Necessity compelled him to send his sons down to the old granary of the nations—Egypt. Almost at once upon entering the land, they encountered Joseph, never even remotely aware of his identity. Joseph followed a course of procedure with the object of discovering whether they were the same cruel, impenitent rascals that he had found them to be back in their homeland. When the collective prison sentence was pronounced, Reuben, speaking for all, reminds them how they merited just what they are now receiving because they mistreated Joseph near Dothan. Joseph was deeply moved to discover that a change for the better seemed to have taken place. One night in prison sufficed for present purposes; only Simeon was remitted to prison as hostage for them all. When the money given for the grain was found in the bag of one of their number on the way home, they all saw the hand of God in what was happening to them. The corrective measures were beginning to bear their fruit. That Simeon did not return added to Jacob's grief, which was still further enhanced by the prospect of not being able to go down to Egypt unless their youngest brother was brought along.

The grain brought from Egypt was consumed, and a second journey to Egypt became imperative (Gen. 43). The whole plan of Joseph was designed for the rehabilitation of the brothers, not as subtle revenge, which was farthest of all from Joseph's thoughts. When Jacob at first remonstrated, being unwilling to risk sending Benjamin along, it was Judah who pledged his life for Benjamin's and finally persuaded his father to take the hard step involved. Upon arriving in Egypt, the brothers found a situation created by Joseph that put them to the test as to whether they would sacrifice one of their number selfishly for their own safety (ch. 44). Once they had sacrificed Joseph to their unscrupulous ambitions. Would they now do the same with regard to Benjamin? The missing cup incident brought them all back to Egypt to the food administrator. Benjamin appeared to be guilty. Would they give him up and save their own lives? Judah stepped into the breach. In a deeply moving speech, he volunteered to stay behind in prison, if only Benjamin were allowed to go home. Twenty years earlier such an attitude would have been impossible.

The carefully designed plan had fully achieved its purpose (Gen. 45). Joseph had to reveal himself to his brothers, who immediately were filled with grave apprehensions. Joseph, however, pointed out the providential side of all that had transpired. The existence of a future nation, to which God had assigned a most important role, was being safeguarded. Steps were promptly taken to move Jacob and his household into the protective care of Joseph. God had answered the prayer of his servant, renewing his promise to Jacob and guaranteeing his return to Canaan in due time (ch. 46). Ample provision was made for the family of Jacob by assigning to it the good pasture land of Goshen. Everything was made official by presenting Jacob at Pharaoh's court. The next two chapters indicate that the physical needs of the family were amply guaranteed for the duration of the famine. Some account of how the famine was met in Joseph's administration follows quite properly at this point. Briefly the successive steps taken were disclosed: money was exhausted; cattle were sold for grain; and finally the Egyptians, on their own suggestion, were compelled to sell themselves and their lands. These measures were not tyrannical but a matter of desperate necessity. Jacob finally died as he had lived his last years, by the light of God's promises.

Jacob's blessing of his children at his deathbed is recorded in Gen. 49. He turned prophet before his end and spoke by divine enlightenment. Outstanding among the blessings was the word applicable to

Excavation of storehouse ruins at Hawara dating to the time of Joseph's rise to power in Egypt.

Judah (vv. 8–12), which refers to a somewhat vague figure ("until he comes to whom it belongs"). This implies that the qualities of leadership, inherent in the tribe of Judah, shall blossom forth in one individual to perfection. The alternate translation "until Shiloh comes" may indicate that in this man Judah's strivings come to rest (see SHILOH III). Reuben (vv. 3–4) was passed by; so were Simeon and Levi (vv. 5–7). Preeminence was appointed for Judah.

The last chapter of the book relates that after Jacob's death a memorable meeting of the twelve sons took place. The eleven were still apprehensive that Joseph had merely postponed the revenge that he might take upon his brothers until the father had passed from the scene. But nothing was farther from Joseph's thoughts than revenge. The full scope of God's dealings is beautifully described in the momentous word, "You intended to harm me, but God intended it for good to accomplish what is now being done, the saving of many lives" (Gen. 50:20). Joseph passed from the scene reassuring his people that God would remember them. In token of faith that it would be so, Joseph exacted a promise of his brothers that when they should leave for the true homeland they would take his bones along for burial. On the note of faith and hope rests this first biblical book, a solid foundation stone of all of God's later revelation to men.

(Important commentaries include J. Skinner, *A Critical and Exegetical Commentary on Genesis*, ICC, 2nd ed. [1930]; H. C. Leupold, *Exposition of Genesis* [1942]; G. von Rad, *Genesis: A Commentary*, rev. ed. [1972]; U. Cassuto, *Commentary on Genesis*, 2 vols. [1964]; B. Vawter, *On Genesis: A New Reading* [1977]; G. Coats, *Genesis with an Introduction to Narrative Literature* [1983]; C. Westermann, *Genesis*, 3 vols. [1984–86]; N. M. Sarna, *Genesis: The Traditional Hebrew Text with New JPS Translation* [1989]; G. J. Wenham, *Genesis*, WBC 1–2, 2 vols. [1987–94]; V. Hamilton, *Genesis*, NICOT, 2 vols. [1990–95]; B. K. Waltke and C. J. Fredricks, *Genesis: A Commentary* [2001]; J. H. Walton, *Genesis*, NIVAC [2001]; K. Mathews, *Genesis*, NAC 1A–1B, 2 vols. [1996–2005]. Among numerous monographs and anthologies, note J. P. Fokkelman, *Narrative Art in Genesis* [1975]; D. A. Garrett, *Rethinking Genesis: The Sources and Authorship of the First Book of the Pentateuch* [1991]; H. C. White, *Narration and Discourse in the Book of Genesis* [1991]; J. Van Seters, *Prologue to History: The Yahwist as Historian in Genesis* [1992]; R. S. Hess et al., eds., *He Swore an Oath: Biblical Themes from Genesis 12–50* [1994]; T. L. Brodie, *Genesis as Dialogue: A Literary, Historical, and Theological Commentary* [2001]; A. Wénin, ed., *Studies in the Book of Genesis: Literature, Redaction and History* [2001]; C. M. Kaminski, *From Noah to Israel: Realization of the Primaeval Blessing after the Flood* [2004]; C. J. Collins, *Genesis 1–4: A Linguistic, Literary, and Theological Commentary* [2005]; and the bibliography compiled by W. E. Mills, *Genesis* [2000].)

H. C. LEUPOLD

Genesis Apocryphon. An ARAMAIC document found in QUMRAN CAVE 1 (1QapGen ar; also 1Q20). See DEAD SEA SCROLLS. Dated to the 1st cent. B.C. or shortly after, it contains an interpretative rewriting of the Genesis story somewhat similar to that found in the book of JUBILEES. The surviving fragments cover approximately the same ground as Gen. 5–14, but with significant expansions. LAMECH, NOAH, and ABRAHAM play the role of narrators. The document is of great importance both as an early witness to the character of Jewish Palestinian Aramaic and as evidence of biblical INTERPRETATION in NT times. (See R. T. White, *The Qumran Genesis Apocryphon: A Review* [1988]; J. A. Fitzmyer, *The Genesis Apocryphon of Qumran Cave I (1Q20): A Commentary*, 3rd ed. [2004].)

Geneva Bible. See VERSIONS OF THE BIBLE, ENGLISH.

genizah guh-nee´zuh, guh-neet´suh (postbiblical Heb. גְּנִיזָה, "removal, storehouse"; cf. biblical Heb. גֶּנֶז H1709, "treasury"). Also *geniza*. A place in a SYNAGOGUE set aside for the storage of unwanted written and printed material of a religious nature. These items are called *Shemot* ("Names") because they contain the name of God and cannot be abused. They consist of worn-out, heretical, and otherwise unfit books, MSS, and even scraps of paper. Generally, the accumulated material is periodically removed and buried in a cemetery (also called *genizah*), sometimes with a pious person. During the 19th cent., many old and important

MSS, including biblical texts, were discovered and removed from the Ezra Synagogue near Cairo (cf. P. E. Kahle, *The Cairo Geniza*, 2nd ed. [1959]). See ZADOKITE FRAGMENTS; TEXT AND MANUSCRIPTS (OT) IX.   C. P. WEBER

Gennaeus gi-nee′uhs (Γενναίος, "noble"). KJV Genneus. Father of a certain Apollonius who served as a Syrian governor during the reign of ANTIOCHUS V; he is mentioned as one of several officials who did not let the Jews live in peace (2 Macc. 12:2).

Gennesaret gi-nes′uh-ret (Γεννησαρέτ G1166, derivation uncertain, possibly from Heb. כִּנֶּרֶת H4055). A small plain located on the NW side of the Sea of Galilee. The name should be associated primarily with an area mentioned in two NT references as the place where Jesus landed when he crossed the lake after feeding the 5,000 (Matt. 14:34; Mk. 6:53). Sometimes, however, the name is not restricted to the district, for Luke once refers to the Sea of Galilee as the Lake of Gennesaret (Lk. 5:1; cf. *Gennēsar*, 1 Macc. 11:67; Jos. *Ant.* 18.2.1 [*Gennēsaritis*]; *War* 3.10.7; see GALILEE, SEA OF). In this usage, the name of the lake derives from the name of the plain. A small town in the area also bore the name Gennesaret (see KINNERETH). E. G. Kraeling, on the basis of the ARAMAIC name and JOSEPHUS, thinks the short form *Gennesar* (found in some NT MSS) would have been current in NT times (*Rand McNally Bible Atlas* [1956], 375). The Arabs call the little plain el-Ghuweir.

The plain borders on the NW shore of the Sea of Galilee between CAPERNAUM and MAGDALA. It is less than 4 mi. long, running N and S along the shore, and about 1 mi. wide. The land is level, rising gently from the Sea of Galilee, which is 650 ft. below the Mediterranean. Hills rise sharply on three sides. The main road from Capernaum to TIBERIAS runs through close to the sea shore.

During the time of Christ, Gennesaret was regarded as the garden spot of Palestine. Josephus (*War* 3.10.8) eloquently described the beauty and fertility of the land. The soil was rich like that of the NILE delta. The climate ranges from hot to temperate. Plenty of water for irrigation was available from streams flowing out of the surrounding hills and from several flowing springs. The land produced an abundance of wild trees and flowers, as well as important crops such as grapes, figs, olives, walnuts (Josephus), rice, wheat, vegetables, melons. The rabbis spoke of this plain as "the Garden of God" and a "paradise."   J. C. DEYOUNG

Gennesaret, Lake of. See GALILEE, SEA OF.

Gentile. This English term (derived from late Lat. *gentīlis*, "pagan"; cf. Vulg. Acts 19:10) occurs occasionally in Bible versions as a rendering of

This oval-shaped hill marks the site of ancient Gennesaret. (View to the E.)

Hebrew *gôy* H1580, "people, nation" (pl. *gôyim*, e.g., Isa. 42:6), but more frequently it translates Greek *ethnos* G1620, "nation, tribe" (Matt. 4:15 et al.). See NATIONS. The Hebrew term was originally a general expression that stressed political and social affiliations rather than bonds of kinship, and thus was used of "nations" in the widest sense. The list of the descendants of NOAH (Gen. 10:2 et al.) showed the affinity of all ANE nations, but with the description of the offspring of ABRAHAM the OT narratives found it desirable to make a distinction between them and other contemporary peoples. This, however, was not undertaken in any narrow or exclusive sense (cf. 12:2; 18:18; 22:18; 26:4). When the Israelites entered into a special relationship with God in the COVENANT at SINAI (Exod. 19:6), they became conscious of nationhood, and thereafter the sense of uniqueness and separation as the people of God was brought to bear upon all their relations with neighboring peoples (cf. 34:10; Lev. 18:24, 25; Deut. 15:6).

The way in which the blessings of the covenant between God and Israel would permeate the lives of other nations was outlined in Deut. 28:1–14. This passage continued the spiritual traditions of the promise of God to Abraham (Gen. 12:1–3), whereby those nations that had been living under a curse would receive blessing through the influence of the newly chosen people. The reflexive form of the verb "will be blessed" (Gen. 12:3; niphal of *bārak* H1385, RSV, "shall bless themselves") suggests that the nations will not blend their separate identities in a common form of humanity, but that each will receive the blessing suited to its character and destiny. This motif was well understood in the ANE and is exemplified in such OT narratives as the blessings bestowed upon the sons of JACOB (Gen. 49:1–27), or the benediction of MOSES upon the Israelites (Deut. 33:2–29).

The benefits mentioned in Deut. 28:1–14 were conditional upon the adherence of the Hebrews to the ideals of the Sinai covenant; but given this situation, Israel could expect to be promoted to a place of prominence among the nations. Once the latter saw that the Israelites exemplified divine holiness, they would become subservient, and in the period of the universal peace that would follow, all the benefits of prosperity would be poured out upon mankind. No political or social imbalance of the kind that would allow one nation to prosper at the expense of another would be permitted (cf. Mic. 4:1–4), and in this general sense the nations would be pursuing their own way of life under the auspices of a covenant relationship.

The Mosaic tradition of a nation chosen out of all the peoples and fitted for the role of ministering priests for the whole of mankind found responsive echoes in the monarchy (cf. 1 Ki. 8:41–43), the preexilic period (Isa. 19:24–25; Jer. 4:2), and the postexilic era (Zech. 8:13; 9:9–10). This high ideal was virtually nullified by the trends of Hebrew history from the time of JOSHUA onward, which show that covenant holiness was seldom at the forefront of Hebrew thinking. So pervasive were Gentile customs that the Hebrews ultimately succumbed to their allurements, and with the disavowal of the covenant relationship came threats of punishment for Israel. Between 722 and 525 B.C., the Hebrew people shared the curse of the nations by being scattered in captivity among them. From then on, the only hope of realizing the ancient ideal of the Torah lay in the survival of a faithful minority of Israelites who would return to their homeland and try to revive the historic spiritual mission of Israel to the world.

The threat of contamination by paganism in the Greek period led the Jews to adopt a rigorous, exclusive attitude toward non-Jewish peoples, so that by the time of Christ the term *Gentile* had become one of scorn. Yet the Gentiles had a place in prophecies relating to the kingdom, whether as the conquered who would enhance Israelite glory (Isa. 60:5–6), or as themselves seeking the Lord (11:10) and worshiping him (Mal. 1:11), when the MESSIAH came to illumine them (Isa. 42:6) and bring salvation to the world (49:6). In this tradition the Gospels hailed the work of Jesus as fulfilling the promise to Abraham (cf. Lk. 2:32), and the Savior himself began his ministry in "Galilee of the Gentiles" (Matt. 4:15; cf. 12:18–21; Lk. 2:32). Jesus said that his disciples would witness to the Gentiles (Matt. 10:18; cf. 24:14), and he made clear that the evangelistic and baptismal commission of the primitive church was for all the nations (Matt. 28:19–20; Mk. 16:15; Lk. 24:47; Acts 1:8). The apostle PAUL saw in Christ's atonement the outpouring of the blessings of Abraham on the Gentiles (Gal. 3:14).

Through Israel's neglect of her spiritual mission to the world, the riches of God came to the Gentiles (Rom. 11:11–12) and would be mediated through them. (See H. H. Rowley, *The Missionary Message of the Old Testament* [1944]; J. Jeremias, *Jesus' Promise to the Nations* [1958].)   R. K. HARRISON

Gentiles, Court of the. The large outer portion of Herod's TEMPLE complex. Gentiles were allowed in this area, but not beyond it, and tablets were placed at the entrances to the inner courts warning foreigners not to enter (see *HJP*, rev. ed. [1973–87], 2:284–85; cf. Acts 21:27–29). The walls and porticoes of the court gave shade from the hot sun, and it was a common gathering place (similar to a park) and a thoroughfare. Paved with marble, it was also used for business such as selling sacrificial animals and money exchange. This area was probably the place from which Christ drove those engaged in such business (Matt. 21:12 and parallels).
C. P. WEBER

gentleness. See HUMILITY; MEEKNESS.

Genubath gi-ny*oo*′bath (גְּנֻבַת *H1707*, possibly "foreigner" [another proposed meaning, "thief," seems very unlikely]). Son of HADAD, an Edomite prince (1 Ki. 11:20). When the country of EDOM was invaded by DAVID's army under the leadership of JOAB, Hadad, who was still a boy, fled to Egypt. In time, he married a sister of Queen TAHPANES, and out of this union Genubath was born. The child was raised by Tahpanes and lived with PHARAOH's children in the royal palace.

geography of Palestine. See PALESTINE.

Geon gee′on. KJV Apoc. form of GIHON (Sir. 24:27).

Georgian Version. See VERSIONS OF THE BIBLE, ANCIENT, V.C.

Gephyrun gi-fi′ruhn. The ASV rendering of Greek *gephyroun*, a textually uncertain word found in CODEX ALEXANDRINUS at 2 Macc. 12:13, but missing in most MSS of the SEPTUAGINT. The KJV, understanding this term not as a proper noun but as the infinitive of *gephyroō*, renders it "to make a bridge." Among several textual variants, *gephyrais* is found in one MS (see R. Hanhart, *Maccabaeorum liber II*, Septuaginta 9/2, 2nd ed. [1976], ad loc.); this form was adopted in A. Rahlfs's *Septuaginta*, and on that basis the NRSV renders, "with earthworks." J. A. Goldstein (*II Maccabees*, AB 41A [1983], 439) has proposed that the term *gephyroun* is an alternative spelling for Ephron (described in v. 27 with language similar to that of v. 13), that an early scribe intended to include that spelling in v. 27 but by mistake wrote it at v. 13 (prob. on the margin), and that later the notation was moved into the text itself.

ger guhr. This transliteration of Hebrew *gēr H1731*, "alien, stranger" (Gen. 15:3 et al.) is used sometimes in the field of biblical studies, but not in standard English versions. See FOREIGNER.

Gera gee′ruh (גֵּרָא *H1733*, possibly short form of גֵּר *H1731* ["sojourner"] plus a divine name, thus "client of [deity]"; cf. *HALOT*, 1:201). Although this name is widely attested outside the Bible, it does not occur in the scriptural account of Israel outside the tribe of BENJAMIN, where it was borne by several men. Unfortunately, the genealogical lists of this tribe have suffered greatly in the course of transmission and can be correlated only partially. It is possible that "son of Gera" in some of the passages below means "belonging to the clan of Gera."

(1) Fourth son of Benjamin and grandson of JACOB (Gen. 46:21 [the LXX regards Gera as grandson of Benjamin through Bela]; the name is missing from the parallel list in Num. 26:38–41). See BEKER #1.

(2) Second son of BELA and grandson of Benjamin (1 Chr. 8:3; the name is missing from the parallel list in 7:7). Some scholars emend the MT (lit., "and Gera and Abihud") to "and Gera and [= that is] the father of Ehud." See the next three entries.

(3) Seventh son of Bela and grandson of Benjamin (1 Chr. 8:5; the name is missing from the parallel list in 7:7). Since it is very unlikely that two sons of Bela were given the same name, some scholars believe that the text has been corrupted and that this Gera was the son of Ehud; see #4 below.

(4) Third son of Ehud (1 Chr. 8:7). This text too is emended by some scholars.

(5) The father of EHUD, the Israelite judge (Jdg. 3:15). This Gera may be the same as #2 above, and his son Ehud may be the same individual mentioned in ##3–4 above.

(6) The father of SHIMEI (2 Sam. 16:5; 19:16, 18; 1 Ki. 2:8). Shimei was a Benjamite from BAHURIM who belonged to the clan of SAUL and who cursed DAVID when the latter was fleeing from ABSALOM.

gerah gee´ruh. The smallest unit of weight in Israel. See WEIGHTS AND MEASURES IV.D.

Gerar gee´rahr (גְּרָר *H1761*, meaning uncertain). A town and probably also a district S of GAZA and SW of the southern border of Canaan near the Mediterranean Sea (Gen. 10:19; 20:1–2; 26:1, 6, 17, 20, 26; 2 Chr. 14:13–14; cf. also LXX 1 Chr. 4:39–40, perhaps correctly for MT GEDOR; 2 Macc. 13:24 probably refers to a different and unidentified town). In its first occurrence in Genesis, Gerar is used as a reference point marking the southern end of the territory of the Canaanites.

ABRAHAM and SARAH are said to have dwelt in Gerar (in the district between KADESH and SHUR), where they came in contact with its king, ABIMELECH (Gen. 20:1–2). This same ruler, or another in the royal line who also had the title Abimelech (cf. the use of CAESAR in this way), is called king of the PHILISTINES in a similar encounter that ISAAC and his wife REBEKAH had with him (Gen. 26:1, 6–11; cf. also 26:26). Following these experiences, Isaac encamped in the valley of Gerar (26:17), probably the present Wadi esh-Shariʿah, where Isaac dug wells and experienced difficult relations with the herdsmen of the area (26:20). Centuries later, ASA king of Judah, with the help of God, routed Ethiopian invaders and pursued them to Gerar and plundered that whole region (2 Chr. 14:13–14).

Although the Philistines did not occupy this area until several hundred years after Abraham (who lived about 1900–1800 B.C.), for clarification the Genesis account speaks of Abimelech both as king of Gerar (Gen. 20:1–2), the common name of the place, and as king of the Philistines (26:1), meaning that he was king over a part of the area later called PHILISTIA, or that he was ruler over ancestors of the people who were later called Philistines. The district of Gerar was known in the intertestamental and early Christian centuries; it appears on the late 6th-cent. MEDEBA map.

The town Gerar should probably be identified with Tell Abu Hureireh (Tel Haror), about 9 mi. SE of Gaza and 17 mi. NW of BEERSHEBA. This site has been excavated and shows a long period of occupation, including that part of the Middle Bronze period (1800–1600 B.C.) when the patriarchs lived. (See E. D. Oren et al. in *BASORSup* 24 [1986]: 57–87; summary by E. D. Oren in *ABD*, 2:989–91.)

W. H. MARE

Gerasene ger´uh-seen (Γερασηνός *G1170*, gentilic of Γέρασα [Jos. *War* 2.18.1 §458 et al.]). An inhabitant of Gerasa, a city in TRANSJORDAN, situated about 35 mi. SE of the S end of the Sea of Galilee (see GALILEE, SEA OF). Gerasa was one of the cities of the DECAPOLIS. The NT references (Mk. 5:1; Lk. 8:26; cf. v. 37) describe Jesus' healing of the demoniac "Legion" and the drowning of the swine in the Sea of Galilee (cf. Matt. 8:28 and see M. W. Newheart, *"My Name Is Legion": The Story and Soul of the Gerasene Demoniac* [2004]). The Greek MSS preserve three variant spellings of the name in each gospel. The best text in Matthew reads "Gadarenes" (see GADARA), but in Mark and Luke, "Gerasenes" (some MSS preserve "Gergesenes" and "Gergustenes").

I. Gergesa. This town (Gk. *Gergesa*) is not to be confused with either Gerasa or Gadara. Gergesa is located, with relative certainty, midway along the E bank of the Sea of Galilee; Gadara is about 6 mi. SE from the S end of the Sea of Galilee; and Gerasa is another 30 mi. to the SE.

The fact that Matthew places the healing of "Legion" in the "region of the Gadarenes," whereas Mark and Luke place it in the "country of the Gerasenes," may be explained on the historical grounds that geographical boundaries overlapped, and on the exegetical consideration that "region" embraced a wide area around the cities. Further, the conclusion seems warranted that in some MSS there was confusion of Gerasa, with the more likely site for the miracle being near Gergesa. In any event, the apparent differences in the texts probably led to the substitute reading "Gergesenes," which was suggested by a study of the geography of the area. This solution is as old as Origen (*Commentary on John* 6.24) who, faced with the textual problem, suggested that the precise site of the healing of "Legion" was Gergesa, the small town in the territory of Gadara, but hardly in the more remote territory of Gerasa. Origen says this is a good example of how biblical writers simply were not concerned to identify certain sites with precision.

Most scholars today would agree with Origen that near Gergesa was the precise site for the healing of "Legion." This view agrees with the general description of the site (Mk. 5:1; Lk. 8:26; cf. *SacBr*, 359–60). In this immediate area, steep hills come down to the shoreline and fit the story of the swine rushing headlong into the sea. No other place on the E side of the sea fits this requirement of the story. The mountainside has caves and hewn tombs where, according to Mark and Luke, the demoniac had taken shelter. The site is identified today with the town of Kursi (spelled variously), just below Wadi es-Samak (see *NEAEHL*, 3:893–96).

II. Gerasa. This town is identified from various sources as a city in Arabia, Decapolis, Gilead, or Perea. Since all of these areas overlap, one may take the references as meaning the same place. Gerasa was a city situated near the Jabbok River about 18 mi. E of the Jordan, about 20 mi. SE of Pella, and 20 mi. N of Philadelphia (OT Rabbah in Ammon). Archaeologists identify it with the modern Jerash. At this distance from the Sea of Galilee, Gerasa could not have been the site of the healing of "Legion." It is doubtful that Jesus ever visited it. This location agrees with the description given by the ancient writers. The geographer Ptolemy says Gerasa was a city in Coelesyria, 35 travel mi. from Pella. Pliny the Elder described it as a city of the Decapolis founded after the Roman conquest of Syria in 65 B.C. Josephus (*War* 1.4.8) mentions it with Pella and Golan as being taken by storm during Alexander Jannaeus's campaign E of the Jordan in about 83 B.C. (see Hasmonean II.C). In his description of the boundaries of Perea (*War* 3.3.3), he mentions Gerasa as one of the cities on the eastern boundary between Perea and Arabia, the other border cities being Philadelphia and Sebonitus. Gerasa is mentioned next by Josephus in connection with the Jewish rebellion against the Romans in A.D. 70.

Apparently Gerasa was rebuilt by the Romans before the revolt began, probably about A.D. 65. Before the war it was a Gentile settlement. In retaliation for the massacre of the Jews at Caesarea, the Jews sent several raiding parties into the Gentile cities of the Decapolis. These forces plundered Gerasa, Philadelphia, Pella, and others (Jos. *War* 2.18.1), and apparently occupied these cities with Jewish patriots. The next allusion to Gerasa concerns its capture during Vespasian's campaign. He dispatched Lucius Annius with a force of cavalry and an army of foot soldiers, who took the city on the first attack, slaughtering a thousand young men, taking their families captive, plundering and burning the city and the surrounding towns (*War* 4.9.1). In the 2nd cent., Gerasa was rebuilt in splendor and remained prosperous for several centuries. It was a leading city of Syria in commerce, culture, and religion. The pagan religions continued among the Gentile population, as is evidenced by the ruins of the temple of Artemis. But Christianity early became important in the city; several churches were built so that by the 5th cent. Gerasa could send a bishop to the Council of Chalcedon.

III. Archaeology. Excavations at the modern Jerash (by the British and American Schools of Oriental Research and Yale University) clearly show that Gerasa was a large and important city already in Jesus'

Colonnaded street in ancient Gerasa. (View to the E.)

time. The excavations uncovered what is to date the best preserved Roman city in Palestine. These ruins date from the 2nd to the 7th centuries and show that the city flourished during this period as a center for religion, culture, and commerce. The forum, with a semicircle of columns still standing, was paved with large cut stones. A main street with columns on both sides leads out of the forum. The modern village of Jerash is situated on the hillside, having been built with stones from the ruins below. Remains of the temple of Artemis, some columns still standing, are on another hillside above the ruins.

The city was large and well planned. Its architecture was of the Corinthian order, quite lavish and imposing, with columns 3–4 ft. in diameter and about 30 ft. high. The ruins also show evidence of a dozen churches that date in the Byzantine period (4th–7th centuries), indicating that this once was a large Christian community. An inscription noted the official establishment of Christianity and discontinuance of pagan worship in the 5th cent.

(See W. A. Thomson, *The Land and the Book* [1882], 333–38, 353, 359; G. A. Smith, *The Historical Geography of the Holy Land*, 25th ed. [1931], 400–407; C. H. Kraeling, ed., *Gerasa: City of the Decapolis* [1938]; C. F. Pfeiffer, *The Biblical World* [1966], 252–54; I. Browning, *Jerash and the Decapolis* [1982]; R. G. Khoun, *Jerash: A Frontier City of the Roman East* [1986]; F. Zayadine, ed., *Jerash Archaeological Project*, 2 vols. [1986–89]; A. Negev in *The Archaeological Encyclopedia of the Holy Land*, 3rd ed. [1990], 193–94; A. Hoffmann and S. Kerner, eds., *Gadara, Gerasa und die Dekapolis* [2002]; D. Kennedy, *Gerasa and the Decapolis* [2007]; *NEAEHL*, 2:470–79.) J. C. DeYoung

Gergasite ger´guh-sit. See Girgashite.

Gergesene ger´guh-seen. See Gerasene.

Gerizim ger´uh-zim (גְּרִזִים H1748). A mountain in central Samaria, near Shechem and about 10 mi. SE of the city of Samaria, especially important as the center of worship for the Samaritans. Rising close to 2,850 ft., today it bears the name Jebel et-Tur. From Mount Gerizim and Mount Ebal (about 3 mi. NE), the sacred sites of Shechem and Jacob's well are visible.

The area is sacred to Jews as well as Samaritans. Here, Abraham and Jacob entered the Promised Land (Gen. 12:6; 33:18). Jacob built an altar, dug a well, and purchased a burial ground at Shechem. The Israelites used it for a burial ground for the bones of Joseph (Josh. 24:32). Both Mount Gerizim and Mount Ebal were the sites used when Joshua gathered all the people of Israel for the ceremony of taking possession of the Promised Land. According to the command of Moses (Deut. 11:29; 27:11–14), Gerizim was to be the mount from which the blessings would be pronounced, while from Ebal would be declared the curse of God upon wickedness. There Joshua read the law of Moses in full to the whole assembly gathered before Gerizim and Ebal, but he built an altar only on Mount Ebal (Josh. 8:30–35).

Joshua called Israel back to Shechem, under the shadow of Gerizim and Ebal, to renew the covenant. There he set up a great stone "under the oak in the sanctuary of the Lord" (Josh. 24:26). This site was sacred to the Israelites in the early days of their occupation of the Promised Land. In the movement toward centralization of worship at Jerusalem under David and Solomon, other worship centers were not looked upon with favor. When the division of the kingdom took place,

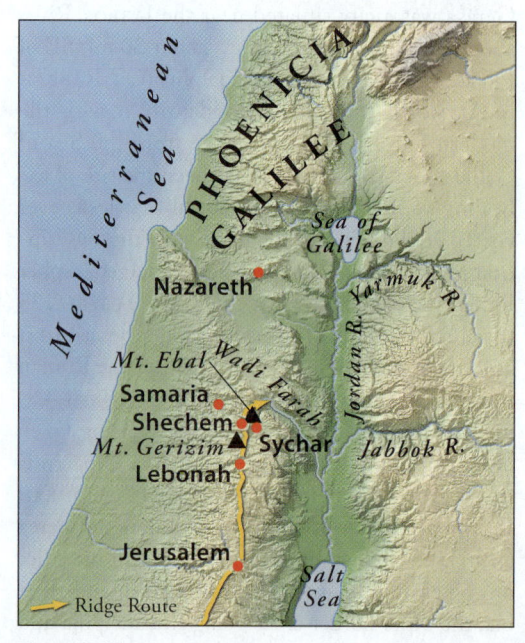

Mount Gerizim.

Mount Gerizim rises above ancient Shechem. (View to the W.)

Jeroboam made Shechem the capital of the northern kingdom (1 Ki. 12:25), discouraged worship at the TEMPLE in Jerusalem, and substituted calf worship at BETHEL and DAN (PLACE). He thereby instigated a new and separate religion, centering on Shechem and Mount Gerizim.

After the king of Assyria resettled northern and central Palestine with pagan peoples, he sent a priest of Israel back to Samaria to teach them the religion of the Jewish remnant (2 Ki. 17:24–34). In this way, the worship of God was preserved, but also perverted. The story of the origin of the Samaritan cult and temple probably has apocryphal elements. On the basis of Neh. 4 and 13:28 and traditions, JOSEPHUS (*Ant.* 11.8.2, 4) wrote that the event leading to it was the marriage of Manasseh, a son of a high priest at Jerusalem, to the daughter of Sanballat, a Gentile official at Samaria. Manasseh was ordered to divorce his pagan wife or leave the priesthood, but Sanballat promised to build a rival temple for him. Some date this event in the time of ALEXANDER THE GREAT, 330 B.C., others a century earlier. The temple was probably destroyed by the HASMONEANS around 110 B.C. (Jos. *Ant.* 13.9.1; *War* 1.11.6).

Although the name Gerizim does not appear in the NT, the most important biblical allusion to it is found in Jn. 4:20–23. The Samaritan woman at the well referred to "this mountain" as the worship center for her people, but Jesus replied: "Believe me, woman, a time is coming when you will worship the Father neither on this mountain nor in Jerusalem. You Samaritans worship what you do not know; we worship what we do know, for salvation is from the Jews. Yet a time is coming and has now come when the true worshipers will worship the Father in spirit and truth, for they are the kind of worshipers the Father seeks." (See *DCG*, 1:644–45; E. G. Kraeling, *Rand McNally Bible Atlas* [1956], 158–59; *ABD*, 2:993; *NEAEHL*, 2:484–92.)

J. C. DeYoung

Geron gihr´on. This name occurs once in the ASV as a rendering of Greek *gerōn*, used with reference to a man sent by ANTIOCHUS Epiphanes "to compel the Jews to forsake the laws of their ancestors" (2 Macc. 6:1). The term, which means "old man" (cf. KJV), is often used in the political sense of "elder, chief," and that is probably its meaning here (cf. NRSV, "an Athenian senator").

Gerrhenians guh-ree´nee-uhnz (Γερρηνοί). The SELEUCID general LYSIAS, in fighting against Judas MACCABEE in 162 B.C., was forced to return to ANTIOCH OF SYRIA because of a deterioration of affairs in the city. Before going N he made peace with the Jews and appointed HEGEMONIDES as "governor from Ptolemais unto the Gerrhenians"

(2 Macc. 13:24 KJV, which however takes the name *Hēgemonidēs* as an adjective, "principal"). Both the text and the exact geographical reference are problematic. Because the context seems to call for a location in the S near the Egyptian frontier, it is commonly taken to be GERAR (so NRSV; cf. *APOT*, 1:151). The Syriac apparently understands this place to be GEZER. A city named Gerrha, which might be the obvious choice on the basis of the Greek spelling, lay inside Egyptian territory, and so is impossible.

G. G. SWAIM

Gershom guhr'shuhm (גֵּרְשֹׁם *H1768*, derivation uncertain; by popular etymology, "an alien there"). **(1)** Firstborn son of MOSES. When ZIPPORAH gave birth to him in Midian, "Moses named him Gershom, saying, 'I have become an alien [*gēr H1731*] in a foreign land'" (Exod. 2:22; cf. 18:3). The only other information given about him is his genealogical data and, probably, the account of his CIRCUMCISION (4:24–26; his name does not actually appear in this passage). According to the book of Judges, a descendant of Gershom named JONATHAN served as priest for the Danites. See DAN (PERSON AND TRIBE). Jonathan made use of idols, however, and his descendants continued this practice until the EXILE (Jdg. 18:3–4). Another descendant of Gershom, SHEBUEL, was an officer in charge of the treasuries during the time of DAVID (1 Chr. 23:15–16; 26:24).

(2) A descendant, and probably clan leader, of PHINEHAS who returned from BABYLON with EZRA (Ezra 8:2).

(3) Variant form of GERSHON in 1 Chronicles.

A. BOWLING

Gershon guhr'shuhn (גֵּרְשׁוֹן *H1767*, possibly from GERSHOM; gentilic גֵּרְשֻׁנִּי *H1769*, "Gershonite"). First son of LEVI, born to him before JACOB and his family went to Egypt (Gen. 46:11). In the Hebrew text of Chronicles, this name almost always appears as Gershom (the only exceptions are 1 Chr. 6:1 [MT 5:27] and 23:6), but the NIV uses the spelling Gershon whenever the reference is to the son of Levi (on the connection between the two names, see *ABD*, 2:994–95). Biblical references to Gershon focus on the Levitical line that descended from him. Discussion of the Gershonites will be organized according to chronological periods.

I. The exodus and the wanderings. In the book of NUMBERS, the Gershonites are divided into two families or clans: LIBNI (apparently called LADAN in 1 Chr. 23:7) and SHIMEI (Num. 3:18, 21). The number of male Gershonites "a month old or more who were counted was 7,500" (3:22); their leader was ELIASAPH son of Lael (3:24). They camped immediately to the W of the TABERNACLE (3:23) and "were responsible for the care of the tabernacle and tent" (3:25) and for carrying the ten linen curtains, the eleven goats' hair curtains, the two skin coverings, the door curtains of the tabernacle, the curtains for the court, the door curtains for the court, the tying cords for all the curtains, and other unspecified equipment (3:25–26; 4:24–26). Two wagons and four oxen were allotted to them for their burdens (7:7).

II. The conquest. The Gershonites were assigned lands within the holdings of Issachar, Asher, and Naphtali in Palestine proper, and in the holdings of the half tribe of Manasseh in Transjordan (Josh. 21:6, 27–33; 1 Chr. 6:62, 71–76). This assignment of land placed the Gershonites in the northernmost extremes on both sides of the Jordan.

III. The monarchy. Although their northern homelands were far from JERUSALEM, biblical evidences show that the Gershonites shared in the central religious life of the nation. Apparently, there were recognized arrangements whereby outlying religious personnel shared in the worship of the central shrine. One hundred and thirty Gershonites helped bring the ARK OF THE COVENANT to Jerusalem (1 Chr. 15:7). A Gershonite, ASAPH son of Berechiah, was the chief of the temple musicians under DAVID (16:4–5). The later prominence of the Asaphite clan of temple musicians probably originates from this office. HEMAN son of Joel was another important Gershonite official (15:17; "son of Joel" may refer to a Gershonite clan). Other offices held by Gershonites are exemplified by three clans (or individuals): Jehieli, Zetham, and Joel, who were "in charge of the treasuries of the temple of the LORD" (26:21–22; cf. 23:8). An individual named Jehiel later appears as a Gershonite office holder (29:8). Despite the unanswered questions which these passages leave, it is clear that the

Gershonites played a significant role in the centralized administration of the nation.

Though the passage should be used cautiously in view of the possibility of textual corruption, 1 Chr. 23:7–10 seems to list ten prominent Gershonite clans who shared in regular temple worship in David's religious bureaucracy: The sons of Ladan (Libni) include the clans of Jehiel, Zetham, and Joel; the sons of Shimei (v. 9; perhaps the same as the Shimei descended from Libni through Jahath; cf. 1 Chr. 6:39–43) include Shelemoth, Haziel, and Haran; and another group called "sons of Shimei" (v. 10) includes Jahath, Zina (Zizah of v. 11), Jeush, and Beriah.

Gershonites maintained their importance in the later monarchy. Several Gershonites participated in HEZEKIAH's cleansing of the temple (2 Chr. 29:12–15). Joah son of Zimmah and Eden son of Joah ("son of Zimmah" and "son of Joah" may be clan designations), are mentioned along with two Asaphites, Zechariah and Mattaniah. Further participation by Gershonites in public religious life is seen in the preaching of Jahaziah, an Asaphite, in the reign of JEHOSHAPHAT (20:14–17) and in JOSIAH's Passover celebration (35:15).

IV. The return from exile. The only Gershonites mentioned during this period are the descendants of Asaph (Ezra 2:41 et al.). A. BOWLING

Gerson guhr´suhn. KJV Apoc. form of GERSHOM (1 Esd. 8:29).

Geruth Kimham gihr´ooth-kim´ham (גֵּרוּת כִּמְהָם H1745 [*Ketib* כמוהם]), possibly "lodging place of KIMHAM"). Also Geruth Chimham. Unidentified place near BETHLEHEM (perhaps named after the son of BARZILLAI, 2 Sam. 19:37–40). After the murder of GEDALIAH, whom NEBUCHADNEZZAR had appointed governor over Judah, Hebrew forces led by JOHANAN son of Kareah fled and stayed in Geruth Kimham on their way to Egypt (Jer. 41:17). C. P. WEBER

Gerzite guhr´zit. See GIRZITE.

Gesem gee´suhm. KJV Apoc. form of GOSHEN (Jdt. 1:9).

Gesham gee´shuhm. See GESHAN.

Geshan gesh´uhn (גֵּישָׁן H1642). KJV Gesham (some later editions). Son of Jahdai, from the tribe of JUDAH, possibly a descendant of CALEB, although the genealogical connection is not stated (1 Chr. 2:47).

Geshem gesh´uhm (גֶּשֶׁם H1774, possibly "[born during] rain season"; variant form גַּשְׁמוּ H1776 [Neh. 6:6, KJV "Gashmu"]). One of NEHEMIAH's opponents in the rebuilding of the walls of Jerusalem (Neh. 2:19; 6:1–2, 6). He was important enough to serve as witness to the Jews' alleged treason. His title, "the Arab," may identify him as the governor of EDOM (*IDB*, 2:386), but scholars have more generally identified him with a N Arabian king referred to as "Gashm son of Shahr" in an inscription from DEDAN in ARABIA and as "Gashm king of Kedar" in an Aramaic inscription from Egypt (see I. Rabinowitz in *JNES* 15 [1956]: 1–9; W. J. Dumbrell in *BASOR* 203 [Oct. 1971]: 33–44). Probably both TOBIAH and Geshem had friendly contacts with the nomads and seminomads who were then infiltrating into Palestine from the S. Furthermore, N Arabian kings profited economically from the trade routes extending from Arabia through Palestine to the Mediterranean coast. A resurgent Jerusalem threatened both of these interests. A. C. BOWLING

Geshur gesh´uhr (גְּשׁוּר H1770, possibly "bridge"; gentilic גְּשׁוּרִי H1771, "Geshurite"). **(1)** A country just E and NE of the Sea of Galilee, corresponding to the southern part of the Golan Heights. This area, along with the land of the Maacathites, was one of the borders of the territory given to JAIR, of the tribe of MANASSEH (Deut. 3:14). The same boundary is mentioned as the limit of the area that the Israelites were able to capture (Josh. 12:5), and its inhabitants are listed as among those whom the Israelites were not able to drive out and who continued to live within Israel (13:11, 13). The Geshurites, along with the Arameans (Syria), took HAVVOTH JAIR (formerly possessed by Jair the Manassite) and other places from the Israelites (1 Chr. 2:23). One of DAVID's wives, MAACAH, was the daughter of TALMAI, king of Geshur (2 Sam. 3:3; 1 Chr. 3:2).

When Absalom (son of David and Maacah) killed his half-brother AMNON, he fled to his grandfather Talmai in Geshur for protection (2 Sam. 13:37–38; cf. 14:23, 32; 15:8).

(2) The term Geshurites apparently can also refer to a people S of the PHILISTINES near SINAI, whose land was not taken originally by the Israelite forces at the time of the conquest (Josh. 13:2). When David was in exile with ACHISH king of GATH, he and his men made raids upon these Geshurites (and other peoples) and led Achish to believe that he was attacking his own people (1 Sam. 27:8).   C. P. WEBER

gesture. Any movement of head, hand, or other part of the body to convey meaning to an observer, as to secure his attention or to guide his action; to emphasize what is being said or is about to be said; or to express strong feeling. A variety of words and phrases convey the different actions of persons in the Bible. People of the ANE were much more given to what Westerners of today would regard as extreme expressions of such emotions as grief, despair, joy, and friendship.

Gestures were used to communicate either with or without speech. Thus, when ZECHARIAH was visited by an angel to inform him that he would have a son, he was unable to speak and had to make signs to express himself (Lk. 1:22). When JOHN THE BAPTIST was born, his relatives made signs to the father to inquire what he should be called (1:62). PETER beckoned to his partners with his hands to help him with the huge load of fish (5:7); and again, after he was released from prison by a heavenly messenger, he used his hand to calm the believers who had gathered for prayer (Acts 12:17). Peter motioned to the beloved disciple to find out who would betray Jesus (Jn. 13:24). PAUL gestured when he began to speak to the Jews in the synagogue at ANTIOCH OF PISIDIA (Acts 13:16), as he did elsewhere (21:40; 26:1). In CAESAREA, Felix motioned to Paul to speak in his defense against the Jewish leaders (24:10).

It may be noted that when the Jews interrupted Paul's speech from the Tower of ANTONIA following his arrest, they showed their indignation by waving their garments and throwing dust into the air (Acts 22:23–24). Stretching out the arm was occasionally used as a signal to attack or go forward, in the assurance that God would work on behalf of his people. MOSES did this at the RED SEA in connection with the parting of the waters, and again at their return upon the Egyptians (Exod. 14:16, 21, 26–27). JOSHUA did the same with a javelin in his hand at the attack on AI (Josh. 8:18–19, 26). The stretching out of the arm often is used figuratively of God to express his mighty acts in Israel's interest (e.g., Isa. 23:11; cf. Acts 4:30). Jesus stretched forth his hand toward his disciples to indicate that they were his true mother and brothers and sisters (Matt. 12:49). XERXES the king gave the traditional gesture of acceptance when he held out the scepter to Queen ESTHER as she approached the throne unbidden at a critical time (Esth. 4:11; 5:2).

Bowing was a common gesture of greeting and reverence. ABRAHAM so greeted his visitors as he was encamped at MAMRE (Gen. 18:2); and so did LOT when they visited him at SODOM (19:1). JACOB bowed himself seven times as he approached ESAU, with whom he hoped for reconciliation (33:2). DAVID fell on his face and bowed three times as he met with JONATHAN to say farewell when he would have to flee to escape from SAUL (1 Sam. 20:41). The two men also kissed each other and wept, another common practice in Bible times, especially when feelings were strong. Esau and Jacob embraced and wept when they met after their long estrangement (Gen. 33:4). JOSEPH kissed his brothers and they wept when his identity was made plain in Egypt (45:15). Such wholesome gestures of love and friendship could be used hypocritically for base purposes, and JOAB did this when he kissed AMASA while concealing the sword with which he murdered him (2 Sam. 20:9). JUDAS ISCARIOT also planted the false kiss of betrayal upon Jesus to deliver him up to his enemies (Matt. 26:49).

Considerable freedom is shown in the variety of postures or gestures in PRAYER and WORSHIP. SOLOMON, EZRA, DANIEL, and STEPHEN all knelt to pray (1 Ki. 8:54; Ezra 9:5; Dan. 6:10; Acts 7:60). Bowing was frequent in worship: ELIEZER, ELIJAH, the BAAL worshipers, and congregations did so (Gen. 24:26; 1 Ki. 18:42; 19:18; Neh. 8:6). People would stand as they prayed, as HANNAH and Solomon did, and, of course, the hypocrites in public (1 Sam. 1:26;

1 Ki. 8:22; Matt. 6:5; Mk. 11:25). Believers would lift up or spread their hands when they prayed (2 Chr. 6:13; Ezra 9:5; Pss. 88:9; 143:6; 1 Tim. 2:8). And we recall the strong gesture of penitence by the TAX COLLECTOR when he struck his breast, not lifting his eyes to heaven (Lk. 18:13).

Hands were joined to pledge fidelity or friendship (2 Ki. 10:15) or were extended in blessing (Lev. 9:22), laid on animals for sacrifice (Lev. 1:4), or clapped to express joy (Ps. 47:1). Weeping expressed either sorrow (Jer. 9:10) or joy (Gen. 46:29). The head might be lifted in pride (Ps. 83:2); or it might be covered in grief, perhaps with putting ashes, earth, or dust on it (Josh. 7:6; 1 Sam. 4:12; 2 Sam. 13:19). Shaking or wagging the head could express contempt (Ps. 64:8). Tearing garments would express grief, consternation, or outrage (Gen. 37:34; Matt. 26:65). Shaking the dust off the feet against a town condemned it for its rejection of God's witness (Matt. 10:14; Acts 13:51). Inclining the ear would indicate a readiness to listen (Isa. 55:3); a "stiff-necked" people would not do so (Jer. 17:23).

The gospel writers take note of various gestures of Jesus during his ministry. He looked with love upon the good but unyielding rich young man (Mk. 10:21). In dealing with a deaf man with impaired speech, Jesus put his fingers in the man's ears, spat and touched the tongue, looked to heaven, sighed, and then gave the healing word (7:33–35). He sighed over the hardness of the human heart (8:12). He looked around with indignation in the synagogue when the leaders opposed his Sabbath healing of an afflicted man (3:5). He picked up little children and laid hands on them to bless them (10:16). In the final hours in GETHSEMANE, Jesus knelt and fell on his face and prayed out of the deep agony of his heart (Matt. 26:39; Lk. 12:41).

N. B. BAKER

Gether gee´thuhr (גֶּתֶר *H1788*, meaning unknown). Son of ARAM and grandson of SHEM, included in the Table of NATIONS (Gen. 10:23). In the parallel list (1 Chr. 1:17), the phrase "the sons of Aram" is missing from the MT, making it appear that Gether was a son of Shem and thus a brother of Aram. It is possible that this passage intends to list the descendants of Shem without distinguishing generations (cf. NRSV), but many scholars believe that the phrase in question dropped out by scribal mistake at an early stage in the textual transmission of the book (cf. NIV).

Gethsemane geth-sem´uh-nee (Γεθσημανί *G1149*, prob. from Heb. גַּת שְׁמָנֵי, "oil press"; see G. Dalman, *Grammatik des jüdisch-palästinischen Aramäisch*, 2nd ed. [1905], 191). A plot of ground where Jesus went to pray before his trial and crucifixion (Matt. 26:36; Mk. 14:32). Gethsemane was a garden or OLIVE grove E of JERUSALEM across the KIDRON Valley (Jn. 18:1), on the MOUNT OF OLIVES (Lk. 22:39). It may have been near an olive press, hence the name (although JEROME thought it meant "oil valley," from Heb. *gay’ H1628*). Both Matthew and Mark give the impression that Gethsemane was a place arrived at only after traversing part of the orchard hillside (Matt. 26:30, 36; Mk. 14:26, 32).

According to Luke and John, Jesus frequently retreated to this hillside and "garden" for rest, prayer, and fellowship with his disciples (Lk. 21:37; Jn. 18:2). He did so on the night of his betrayal. After the Last Supper and the singing of the Passover hymn, he left the upper room (possibly located in S Jerusalem near the Zion Gate), crossed the Kidron Valley, and ascended the Mount of Olives, across the valley from the TEMPLE. Upon entering the area, Jesus spoke to the disciples about their being scattered as sheep, his resurrection and

These ancient olive trees found in the courtyard of the Church of All Nations (possibly the site of Gethsemane) are nearly 1,500 years old.

reunion with them in Galilee, and the temptation and denial of PETER (Mk. 14:26–31). Then he took Peter, James, and John on into Gethsemane and charged them to watch (see JAMES I; JOHN THE APOSTLE). Going a stone's throw farther, he prayed three times for deliverance (14:32–42). His prayer-agony complete, he went out to meet his betrayer. (With regard to the authenticity of Lk. 22:43–44, see BLOODY SWEAT.)

The precise site of Gethsemane is a matter of contention in Christian tradition; different sites are identified by Western, Russian, Armenian, and Greek Orthodox Church authorities (cf. E. G. Kraeling, *Rand McNally Bible Atlas* [1956], 394–404, and map on p. 396). It is generally agreed that Gethsemane was situated on the hillside above the road from Jerusalem to BETHANY. The oldest tradition, dating from Empress Helena's visit to Jerusalem in A.D. 326, fixed the site at the Church of the Tomb of the Virgin, and the place of Jesus' prayer a stone's throw up the hill (Lk. 22:41). This would place Gethsemane about equal distance from St. Stephen's Gate and the Golden Gate. It would have been directly across from the temple. The tradition that eight very ancient olive trees mark the site is probably not well founded, since JOSEPHUS (*War* 6.1.1) records that in A.D. 70 the emperor TITUS cut down all the trees E of the city. (See further J. Wilkinson, *Jerusalem as Jesus Knew It: Archaeology as Evidence* [1978], 125–31, which includes an aerial photograph of the likely site.)

J. C. DEYOUNG

Geuel gyoo'uhl (גְּאוּאֵל H1451, possibly "loftiness of God"). Son of Maki, from the tribe of GAD, and one of the twelve spies sent out by MOSES to reconnoiter the Promised Land (Num. 13:15).

Gezer gee'zuhr (גֶּזֶר H1618, possibly "confined space"). A major city of the N SHEPHELAH, allotted to the tribe of EPHRAIM and assigned to the Levites.

I. Discovery and excavation. The true site of Gezer was first identified by C. Clermont-Ganneau during 1870–73 (see his *Archaeological Researches in Palestine* 2 [1899], 224–75). His investigations led him from Khulda to Tell el-Jezer beside the village of Abu Shusheh, about 17 mi. SE of JOPPA. In 1874, he found some bilingual (Heb.-Gk.) inscriptions on the rocks surrounding the tell that read: ALKIOY tḥm gzr ("the confines of Gezer, [of] Alkios"; see *RB* 8 [1899]: 109–15). Ancient Gezer was situated on the NW edge of the Shephelah. It commands a good view of the plain of ONO (Neh. 6:2), across which passed the main N-S route of the Levant. The lateral trunk road leading into the hill country via BETH HORON led directly to Gezer before meeting the coastal route.

Two major excavations were carried out by R. A. S. Macalister at Gezer in 1902–05 and 1907–09 (see his book, *The Excavations at Gezer* [1912]). In the 1960s, the Hebrew Union College—Biblical and Archaeological School in Jerusalem—began a new series of excavations under the guidance of G. E. Wright, with W. G. Dever as director. The Chalcolithic, Early Bronze I, II, and III, and Middle Bronze II, as well as the Late Bronze, Iron, Persian, Hellenistic, and Roman periods are all found at Gezer. From Macalister's report it seems that the Solomonic age is not represented, but Y. Yadin (in *IEJ* 8 [1958]: 80–86) showed that a true Solomonic gate had been mistaken by Macalister for part of a Hellenistic public building.

II. History. Gezer is first mentioned in THUTMOSE III's list of towns conquered (in his first campaign) in Canaan. The name is written *q-dj-r* (no. 104). Thutmose IV erected a stele in his funerary temple mentioning Khurri (HORITE) prisoners from Gez[er] who were brought to Egypt (*ANET*, 248). A fragmentary CUNEIFORM tablet found at Gezer has an enigmatic allusion to nearby Gittim (GATH or GITTAIM) and has been linked by Albright and others with a campaign by Thutmose IV. Gezer and its princes played important roles in the intrigues among Canaanite cities in the TELL EL-AMARNA age; for example, the ruler of Gezer seems to have been a leader in the attempt by the ʿapiru (HABIRU) to seize the territories of other princes loyal to PHARAOH. He and his successors sought to occupy key towns guarding the approach routes to Jerusalem. Pharaoh MERNEPTAH called himself "the reducer of Gezer"—a boast evidently based on his conquest of the city during a campaign depicted on his victory stele (*ANET*, 378).

The site of ancient Gezer, one of three major cities Solomon fortified along the international trade route leading to Egypt. (View to the NE.)

During the conquest under Joshua, Israel defeated Horam, king of Gezer, when he came forth to support Lachish (Josh. 10:33). The city is mentioned after Beth Horon as being on the border of allotment given to the sons of Joseph (Josh. 16:3). Gezer was given to Ephraim (1 Chr. 7:28), who failed to expel the Canaanites (Josh. 16:10; Jdg. 1:29); later the indigenous population was put to forced labor. The Levitical Kohathites were allotted Gezer as one of their cities in the Ephraimite tribal inheritance (Josh. 21:21; 1 Chr. 6:67 [MT v. 52]).

After David established his capital at Jerusalem (Jebus), the Philistines tried to assert their authority over the hill country by means of the approach routes to Jerusalem, but David chased them as far as Gezer (2 Sam. 5:25; 1 Chr. 14:16). When Solomon came to power, Gezer was taken by the Egyptian Pharaoh and burned with fire (1 Ki. 9:15–17); it was then given to Solomon as dowry for Pharaoh's daughter. Solomon refortified it along with other major chariot cities and strategic towns (e.g., Hazor, Megiddo, Beth Horon). The gates at Gezer were almost identical to those at Hazor and Megiddo; Hazor had a casemate wall in this period like that at Gezer, but Megiddo had a salients-and-recesses wall along with its stone houses in the Solomonic period (contra Yadin).

When Pharaoh Shishak invaded the land in the fifth year of Rehoboam, he launched his drive into the hill country by attacking Gezer (no. 12 on his list); from there he was able to penetrate the uplands and threaten Jerusalem (1 Ki. 14:25–28; 2 Chr. 12:1–12).

Gezer does not appear in the history of the divided monarchy until its conquest by the Assyrian monarch Tiglath-Pileser, either in his campaign against Philistia (734 B.C.) or in his subsequent attack on Israel (733 B.C.). The Assyrian monarch left a relief depicting his siege of the city (*ANEP*, no. 369), and two tablets in Assyrian cuneiform found on the tell itself show that the conqueror established a colony at Gezer. But stamped jar handles and a shekel weight all marked "for the king" reveal that Gezer had returned to Judean control, at least under Josiah and possibly in the reign of Hezekiah.

Other jar handles stamped *Yehud* and *Yerushalem* indicate that Gezer was part of, or had relations with, the postexilic province. According to 1 Esd. 5:31, "sons of Gezer" (KJV, "Gazera"; Gk. *Gazēra*) returned from captivity in Babylon—but the Hebrew parallel texts (Ezra 2:48; Neh. 7:51) have "sons of Gazzam," which is probably correct. A stone slab and a scaraboid with the name of Pharaoh Nepherites (398–393 B.C.) suggest that

Gezer was witness to the conflict between the 29th Egyptian dynasty and the Persian empire.

Prior to the establishment of the HASMONEAN kingdom, Gezer was a Gentile city to which the defeated SELEUCID forces could retreat (1 Macc. 4:15; 7:45; NRSV, "Gazara"). BACCHIDES included it in his chain of strongholds (1 Macc. 9:52; Jos.

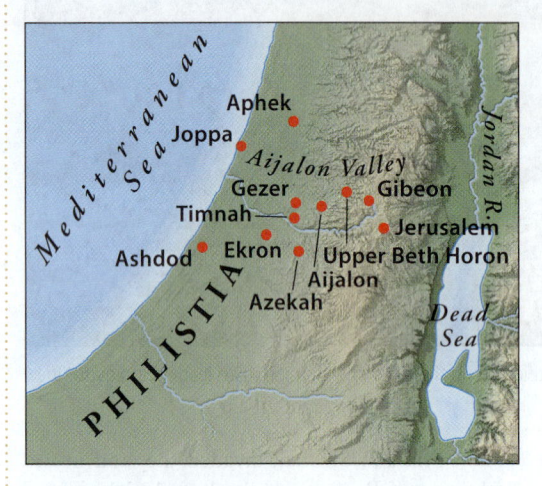

Gezer guards the road to Jerusalem.

Ant. 13.1.3). Later SIMON MACCABEE besieged and took it (1 Macc. 13:43–48 has Gaza, but Jos. *Ant.* 8.6.7 and *War* 1.2.2 correctly read Gezer [*Gazara*]; in 2 Macc. 10:32, "Gazara" may be an error for "Jazer"—cf. 1 Macc. 5:8 and see J. A. Goldstein, *II Maccabees*, AB 41A [1983], 393–94). There he established his son John with a garrison (1 Macc. 13:53; 14:34). Antiochus Sidetes tried to force Simon to surrender Gezer (15:28–35; 16:1–10), but only under the reign of John Hyrcanus did he succeed (Jos. *Ant.* 13.8.3; *War* 1.2.5). After the death of Antiochus, the Roman senate supported Hyrcanus's efforts to retrieve Gezer (Jos. *Ant.* 13.9.2). During the subsequent Roman rule in Judea, Gezer was reduced to a small village. By the Byzantine era it had been completely overshadowed by another town 4.5 mi. SSE, namely, the Emmaus-Nicopolis of EUSEBIUS (*Onomasticon* 66.19—68.2) and the MEDEBA map.

Further archaeological investigation of Tell Gezer will certainly illuminate many aspects of her history and material culture. The famous "high place" discovered by Macalister has now been relocated by the Hebrew Union College expedition; its date is still not certain but appears to belong to the Middle Bronze Age. The Solomonic gate and casemate walls have also been uncovered again. It is hoped that the eastern part of the gate, untouched by Macalister, may provide more accurate stratified evidence of its construction phases. (See further H. Darrell Lance in *BA* 30 [1967]: 34–47; W. G. Dever in ibid., 47–62; J. F. Ross in ibid., 62–72; W. G. Dever et al., *Gezer I, II, IV* [1970–86]; W. G. Dever in *BASOR* 262 [May 1986]: 9–34; J. D. Seger, *Gezer V* [1989]. On the Gezer calendar, cf. W. F. Albright in *BASOR* 92 [Dec. 1943]: 28–30; D. Sivan in *IEJ* 48 [1998]: 101–5.)

A. F. RAINEY

Gezer calendar. See AGRICULTURE V.

Gezrite gez′rit. KJV form of GIRZITE.

Ghor gor. The Arabic term for the ARABAH, the low-lying plain of the JORDAN Valley from the S end of the Sea of Galilee (see GALILEE, SEA OF) to the N end of the DEAD SEA in the S. Its eastern border is formed by the relatively straight cliffs formed when the eastern mountains of TRANSJORDAN fall off to the valley below along the fault line of the Jordan rift. Its W border is much more irregular, being formed by the western mountains of the CISJORDAN range, which protrude into and recede from the valley of Ghor quite brokenly, cut in several places by steep valleys. The largest of these valleys is that of the Jalud River, which comes into the Jordan Valley about 7 mi. below the Sea of Galilee, emptying the plain of JEZREEL to the NW. The Ghor is broad and expansive, as it is at its widest region (about 12 mi., E to W) just N of the Dead Sea. Within this valley, the Jordan River winds and twists its way from the Sea of Galilee to the Dead Sea (see L. H. Grollenberg, *Atlas of the Bible* [1959], 17, pl. 26).

F. W. BUSH

ghost. This English term, which in modern usage refers specifically to the SPIRIT of a dead person that appears in bodily likeness, is very frequently used by the KJV to render Hebrew *rûaḥ* H8120 and Greek *pneuma* G4460, which normally refer to the vital life principle of a person, or to the essence of God, or to the HOLY SPIRIT (however, Lk. 24:37 and 39 uses *pneuma* in the sense of "ghost"; the parallels have *phantasma* G5753, Matt. 14:26; Mk. 6:49). The NRSV also uses "ghost" a few times to render Hebrew *ʾôb* H200 (e.g., Isa. 8:19; NIV, "medium"). See DIVINATION; FAMILIAR SPIRIT.

Ghost, Holy. See HOLY SPIRIT.

Giah gi´uh (גִּיחַ H1632, "spring"). An unidentified site within the territory of the tribe of BENJAMIN, mentioned as being on the route of ABNER's flight from JOAB and ABISHAI (2 Sam. 2:24). It is said to have been E of GIBEON (emended to GEBA by some scholars) and near a hill named AMMAH, probably close to the edge of the wilderness.

F. W. BUSH

giant. This English word (which the NRSV uses in only two passages [2 Sam. 21:16–22; 1 Chr. 20:4–8], and the NIV not at all) may have two meanings. (1) It may refer to a race of beings of superhuman size and strength who appear in the mythology and folklore of most ancient peoples, often at war with the gods. (2) It may also be used to refer to human beings of abnormal and unusual size, usually due to a disease of the pituitary gland, properly referred to as *gigantism*. In modern times medical accounts record individuals over 8 ft. tall, while claims have been made of giants taller than 9 ft.

That "giants" occur in the OT in the latter sense admits of no doubt. GOLIATH of GATH, whom DAVID slew, was "six cubits and a span" in height (1 Sam. 17:4). If the ordinary cubit is meant, this represents a height of c. 9.5 ft. (WEIGHTS AND MEASURES I.A.). Compare also Og king of BASHAN, whose "bed of iron" was 9 cubits long and 4 cubits wide (c. 13 x 6 ft., Deut. 3:11), and the Egyptian whom BENAIAH slew, who was 5 cubits tall (over 7 ft., 1 Chr. 11.23). The account in 2 Sam. 21:15–22 records the exploits of David and several of his men against PHILISTINE giants (although only one is said to be "huge," 2 Sam. 21:20; 1 Chr. 20:6; in Job 16:14, the KJV's "giant" renders Heb. *gibbôr* H1475, "warrior").

The REPHAITES (KJV, "giants") and the Anakites (see ANAK), who were among the original inhabitants of Palestine (cf. Gen. 15:18–21; Num. 13:28, 33), probably concern "giants" in the second sense as well. Although these two terms do not mean "giants" but are rather ethnic names, it is quite certain that they refer to races of people of inordinate size (see esp. Num. 13:32–33; Deut. 9:2). That the Hebrews regarded them as giants in the first sense mentioned above (as is often held)

This Roman marble relief from the 2nd cent. A.D. depicts the struggle of the goddess Athena with the Giants.

seems highly improbable (Num. 13:33 is best understood as an emotional reaction of intimidated men). The only passage that may refer to giants in the first sense is Gen. 6:1–4, where the NEPHILIM (KJV, "giants") are mentioned. Many hold that this text refers to the stories of giants on earth who are descended from union between gods and humans and that it is used by the biblical author as a measure of the effects of human sin (cf. G. von Rad, *Genesis* [1961], 109–12).

F. W. BUSH

giants, valley of the. See REPHAIM, VALLEY OF.

Gibbar gib´ahr (גִּבָּר H1507, "[strong] man"). The ancestor of one of the families who returned with ZERUBBABEL from EXILE (Ezra 2:20). The parallel passage at this point reads GIBEON (Neh. 7:25). Since the returning exiles begin to be listed by their city rather than their ancestor in the immediately following entry (Ezra 2:21; Neh. 7:26), some have argued that Gibbar in Ezra is a textual corruption of the place name Gibeon.

F. W. BUSH

Gibbethon gib´uh-thon (גִּבְּתוֹן H1510, "hill, ridge"). A PHILISTINE city allotted to the Danites (Josh. 19:44) and assigned to the Levites (21:23).

See Dan (person and tribe); priests and Levites. It was while Nadab, son of Jeroboam, was besieging Gibbethon that Baasha murdered him and assumed the crown of Israel for himself (1 Ki. 15:27). Later, the Israelite army was again trying to wrest Gibbethon from the Philistines when word reached them that Zimri had murdered Baasha's son, Elah, and proclaimed himself king. On hearing this, the army proclaimed Omri king, and Zimri committed suicide (16:15–20). The city is identified either with Tell Melat (some 15 mi. SE of Joppa and 3 mi. W of Gezer) or with Ras Abu Ḥumeid (also Ḥamid, c. 3.5 mi. farther NE, but see Gittaim). In either case, Gibbethon was an important fortress on the eastern branch of the Way of the Sea (Via Maris), the route used by Thutmose III in his Syrian campaigns, and by Esarhaddon in his attack on Egypt. It probably had a close relationship with the much larger city of Gezer, which was only about 3 mi. E of Gibbethon. (For a discussion of the cities within the tribal territory of Dan, see B. Mazar in *IEJ* 10 [1960]: 65–77.)　　　　　　　　　　　　G. G. Swaim

Gibea gib'ee-uh (גִּבְעָא *H1495*, "hill" or possibly "highlander"). Son of Sheva and grandson of Caleb, included in the genealogy of Judah (1 Chr. 2:49). Sheva had been born to Caleb through his concubine Maacah (v. 48). Some scholars identify the name Gibea with the town of Gibeah of Judah.

Gibeah gib'ee-uh [גִּבְעָה *H1497* [גִּבְעַת in Josh. 18:28], "hill"; gentilic גִּבְעָתִי *H1503*, "Gibeathite" [only 1 Chr. 12:3]). The name of several locations in Palestine. To form an adequate understanding of the problems of identification connected with this name, the reader should carefully compare the Hebrew spellings of the following names, all of which come from the same root and have approximately the same meaning: Geba (*gebaʿ*), Gibeah (*gibʿâ*), Gibeath (*gibʿat*, construct form of the preceding; cf. Josh. 18:28 and see Gibeath Haaraloth), and Gibeon (*gibʿôn*). Because much of Palestine is hilly country, it is not surprising that a name meaning "hill" was widely used. Unfortunately, the MT exhibits considerable confusion in the use of these names—a confusion not clarified by the Septuagint, which neither follows the MT consistently nor has any other regularly observed practice in its treatment of this name.

Gibeon, properly the chief city of the Hivites who tricked Israel into an alliance to avoid being massacred (Josh. 11:19), can be mistaken for Gibeah of Saul (2 Sam. 21:6) and for Geba (1 Chr. 14:16; cf. 2 Sam. 5:25). Again, Geba and Gibeah should properly refer to different places, but the MT reads Geba in Jdg. 20:10 and 33, where the reference is probably to Gibeah; in v. 31, on the other hand, it reads Gibeah when Geba (according to some, Gibeon) is probably intended. J. Simons (*The Geographical and Topographical Texts of the Old Testament* [1959] §§669–70) finds the usage in 1 Samuel so fluid as to create the impression that the masculine (Geba) and feminine (Gibeah) forms were used interchangeably.

If this assumption is made, one must ask which place the context calls for, rather than relying on the form in the MT to distinguish the localities with any degree of finality. It has been argued that 1 Sam. 13:16 refers to the same place as 14:16, presumably Geba (modern Jebaʿ, relatively close to Micmash), which was more suitable than Gibeah (Tell el-Ful) as the location for the Israelite army in opposition to the Philistine forces in Micmash. It is certain, however, that Saul would keep some of his forces in his capital city (Gibeah, cf. 1 Sam. 13:2), and one can make sense out of the text as it stands. Scholars have not been able to agree on any reconstruction of the exact course of events in this war. Caution is thus necessary. After the readings have been ascertained—and Geba and Gibeon set aside—at least four distinct places named Gibeah remain.

(1) A town in the hill country of the tribe of Judah (Josh. 15:57). It is perhaps the same city identified elsewhere as the home of Micaiah, the mother of King Abijah (2 Chr. 13:2; but see #2 below). Moreover, some believe that Gibea, described as a grandson of Caleb, refers to this town (1 Chr. 2:49). Modern el-Jebaʿ (c. 7.5 mi. WSW of Bethlehem) has been proposed as a possible identification of Judahite Gibeah, but this location is improbable, since the context of Josh. 15:57 suggests the area SE of Hebron.

(2) A town (or hill) in the hill country of the tribe of Ephraim; it was the home of the priest

PHINEHAS, grandson of AARON, and provided the burial place of Phinehas's father, ELEAZAR (Josh. 24:33). Nothing else is known about such a city, unless it was the home of King Abijah's mother (see #1 above). JOSEPHUS (*Ant.* 5.1.29 §119) refers to it as *Gabatha*. Some believe that the word in this passage should be understood as a common noun, "in the hill that belonged to Phinehas." If it does refer to a town, the location cannot be determined.

(3) A hill—known as Gibeath Elohim, "Gibeah [Hill] of God"—in the tribal territory of BENJAMIN where the PHILISTINES had an outpost and where SAUL met a procession of prophets (1 Sam. 10:5, 10). It has been identified with various sites, including Ram Allah, Gibeah of Saul (see #4 below), Gibeon, Geba (it is in fact called Geba in 13:3; see P. M. Arnold in *ABD*, 2:1007–09), and Nabi Samwil (5 mi. WNW of Jerusalem, but see BEEROTH and MIZPAH).

(4) Finally, there is the Gibeah of Benjamin (1 Sam. 13:15), also known as Gibeah of Saul (11:4); it is probably the same as Gibeath (Josh. 18:28 KJV). This Gibeah was first identified with Tell el-Ful (about 3.5 mi. N of Jerusalem) in the 19th cent., a proposal later confirmed by W. F. Albright (*Excavations and Results at Tell el-Fûl (Gibeah of Saul)* [1924]; cf. also his later report in *BASOR* 52 [Dec. 1933]: 6–12). More recently some scholars have argued that it is the same as Geba (Jebaʿ, about 3 mi. farther to the NE; cf. J. M. Miller in *VT* 25 [1975]: 145–66). It is possible that Tell el-Ful was the original site and that SAUL built a fortress there (Gibeah of Saul), but that since the city itself had been destroyed, its name (Geba/Gibeah) was transferred to the neighboring site of Jebaʿ (cf. A. Demsky in *BASOR* 212 [Dec. 1973]: 25–31). By far the most important city by this name in the biblical account, Gibeah of Benjamin first comes into prominence in the book of Judges.

A Levite from the hill country of Ephraim, returning N from Bethlehem, hesitated to spend the night in Jebus (Jerusalem) because it was still controlled by the JEBUSITES. He preferred to press on to Gibeah of Benjamin. When he arrived, no one invited him into his house in spite of the fact that he had his own provisions with him. Finally, a man from Ephraim who lived in Gibeah came along and offered hospitality, but soon the men of the city surrounded his house and demanded that the traveler be surrendered to them for homosexual abuse. To avert this, the Levite sent his concubine out to the mob. After raping her all night, the revelers released her at dawn, but she died. The Levite took her home, dismembered her body, and sent pieces of her throughout the land of Israel, calling for vengeance on the barbarous inhabitants of Gibeah. When the whole tribe of Benjamin defended the culprits, a bloody intertribal war broke out; over 40,000 Israelites and 25,000 Benjamites died. Apparently, the Israelites felt more than vindicated by this "victory," for they then proceeded to murder all the inhabitants of JABESH GILEAD except for 400 young virgins, to obtain wives for the 600 Benjamite survivors of Gibeah (Jdg. 19–21). As this did not provide enough girls for 600 men, they conspired with the Benjamites to abduct women from the annual religious feast at Shiloh.

The obvious parallels with the story of LOT's heavenly messengers in SODOM add to the impression that this city was the very paradigm of evil (cf. Hos. 9:9; 10:9). If it could be shown that the author of this account actually knew the story of Sodom, he should be credited with an unusual subtlety of style, because he nowhere makes the parallel explicit. Nor should it go unnoticed that a later inhabitant of Gibeah, Saul son of Kish, hacked up a pair of oxen and sent the pieces throughout Israel as a call to war to free Jabesh Gilead from a siege conducted by NAHASH the Ammonite (1 Sam. 11:7). Imagine the psychological impact on the Israelite warrior upon the receipt of a piece of gory meat from Gibeah of Benjamin!

At first reading, the story in Judges appears almost as a propaganda piece written to discredit Saul's claims to the throne, but the fact that Saul killed his own oxen in his bid to rescue the inhabitants of Jabesh Gilead, the same city that was massacred to provide wives for the earlier people of Gibeah, goes far to offset any propaganda value that the story might have. In fact, Saul could now be seen as the man from Gibeah who undid an earlier wrong. Later, when Saul became king, Gibeah remained his chief residence (1 Sam. 10:26; 15:34; 23:19). The fortress of the city was destroyed for the second time (the first time having been in the battle to avenge the Levite) either during Saul's lifetime or at the time of his death, possibly during the same battle that cost him his life. It was rebuilt almost immediately on the same plan but fell into disuse shortly after David succeeded in reuniting the country.

When Albright first excavated Tell el-Ful, he thought that the next fortification, a watchtower, was built by ASA (1 Ki. 15:22, reading Gibeah instead of Geba), but when he returned to the site ten years later, the absence of Iron II pottery convinced him that this fortress must date from the late 9th or early 8th cent. The use of almond indicates the loss of the earlier conifers. This tower was destroyed later in the 8th cent., possibly in the Syro-Ephraimite War, or by TIGLATH-PILESER III or SENNACHERIB (cf. Isa. 10:29). It was rebuilt in the 7th cent. and destroyed once more, this time presumably by NEBUCHADNEZZAR in 597 or 586 B.C.

After several centuries, the tower was built again, and this time a village grew up on the eastern slope of the hill which lasted about a century and a half until its destruction in or about the time of the war between PTOLEMY V and ANTIOCHUS III. Still, the site retained its attractiveness, and JOSEPHUS (*War* 5.2.1 §51) wrote of a village there in Roman times that probably came to an end with the destruction of Jerusalem and the dispersion of the Jews in A.D. 70. (This village is of particular interest because a stone manger dating from approximately the time of the birth of Christ was found there, and it is possible that the Savior's first bed was a similar structure.) G. G. SWAIM

Gibeath gib´ee-uhth. See GIBEAH #4.

Gibeath Elohim gib´ee-uhth-el´oh-him. Also Gibeath-elohim. See GIBEAH #3.

Gibeath Haaraloth gib´ee-uhth-hay-air´uh-loth (גִּבְעַת הָעֲרָלוֹת *H1502*, "hill of the foreskins"). Also Gibeath-haaraloth. A hill in the vicinity of JERICHO where CIRCUMCISION was performed on the Israelites who were born after the exodus (Josh. 5:3). Presumably, the place received its name because of this event, but some have thought that even before the arrival of the Israelites it was associated with a pagan circumcision ritual. With regard to the place-name Gibeath (18:28 KJV), some have thought that it refers to Gibeath Haaraloth and others take it with the name that follows (meaning "the hill of KIRIATH JEARIM"), but it is usually understood as referring to GIBEAH of Benjamin.

Gibeathite gib´ee-uh-th*it*. See GIBEAH.

Gibeon gib´ee-uhn (גִּבְעוֹן *H1500*, "hill"; gentilic גִּבְעוֹנִי *H1498*, "Gibeonite"). An important city in the hill country of BENJAMIN, about 6 mi. NW of JERUSALEM (in 1 Chr. 8:29 and 9:25, "the father of Gibeon" is probably an epithet for a major figure in the early history of the city).

I. Biblical record. Gibeon is first mentioned in connection with JOSHUA's assault on the hill coun-

The isolated hill of el-Jib, biblical Gibeon. (View to the NE.)

try. After taking JERICHO and AI, his march would have taken him N of Jerusalem. A delegation from Gibeon came to him, however, under the guise of having taken a long journey (Josh. 9:3–6). Joshua made a peace treaty with them before learning that they had come from the nearby town. Upon discovering the ruse, Joshua did not destroy them but put them in servitude to the Israelites as "woodcutters and water carriers for the house of my God" (9:23). The people involved, who included inhabitants of associated towns (v. 17), were known as HIVITES (11:19, possibly related to the HURRIANS, but see also 2 Sam. 21:2). Their action precipitated the battle of Beth Horon (see BETH HORON, BATTLE OF). ADONIZEDEK, king of Jerusalem, and the other AMORITE kings planned to attack Gibeon; but Joshua, now committed to defend Gibeon by treaty, fought against them. Joshua and his army, after a night march, slaughtered many at Gibeon and chased the remainder over the Beth Horon pass. God sent hailstones and later had the sun stand still at the command of Joshua (Josh. 10:6–14; see DAY, JOSHUA'S LONG). (For the view that the treaty with the Gibeonites followed common practice, cf. F. C. Fensham in *BA* 27 [1964]: 96–100; see also J. Blenkinsopp, *Gibeon and Israel* [1972]; P. J. Kearney in *CBQ* 35 [1973]: 1–19.)

After the division of the land into tribes, Gibeon became a part of Benjamin (Josh. 18:25; 21:17). Centuries later, the old rivalries surfaced because of SAUL's apparent intolerance of non-Israelite peoples in the land. At some point during his reign, he slaughtered many Gibeonites, who subsequently demanded from DAVID revenge on the house of Saul. Since they would not accept money in payment for the blood, David finally yielded up seven of Saul's sons, whom the Gibeonites promptly hung. Only MEPHIBOSHETH was spared (2 Sam. 21:1–9).

The famous contest between the twelve soldiers of ABNER and the twelve of JOAB at the pool of Gibeon had nothing to do with the Gibeonites themselves (2 Sam. 2:12–16). Because all twenty-four of the young men died, the name HELKATH HAZZURIM ("the field of the sword edges") was given to the area by the pool. Since the war by representation was indecisive, Joab chased Abner across the JORDAN but failed to apprehend him (2:17–28).

The last major happening at Gibeon was the religious visit that SOLOMON paid to the city because "that was the most important high place" (1 Ki. 3:4; according to the parallel, 2 Chr. 1:3, the Tent of Meeting was there). While in Gibeon, he had the dream in which God asked him what gift he desired, and the famous king chose wisdom. This place of worship is mentioned twice again (1 Chr. 16:39; 21:29; see HIGH PLACE). The false prophet HANANIAH, whose death JEREMIAH foretold, was from Gibeon (Jer. 28:1–17). After the return from Babylon, MELATIAH the Gibeonite and other men of the city helped NEHEMIAH rebuild walls (Neh. 3:7; cf. 7:25 and see GIBBAR).

II. Archaeological results. From 1956 to 1960, James B. Pritchard directed the expeditions of the University of Pennsylvania Museum to el-Jib, the modern Arabic name of Gibeon (see his book, *Gibeon: Where the Sun Stood Still* [1962]). These expeditions not only thoroughly excavated the most famous feature of both ancient and modern Gibeon, namely, the great pool (2 Sam. 2:13; Jer. 41:12), but they also revealed other interesting aspects of the city. Although el-Jib, because of the similarity of the sound, had been suggested as the site of Gibeon as early as 1838 by Edward Robinson, no certain proof came until the archaeologists

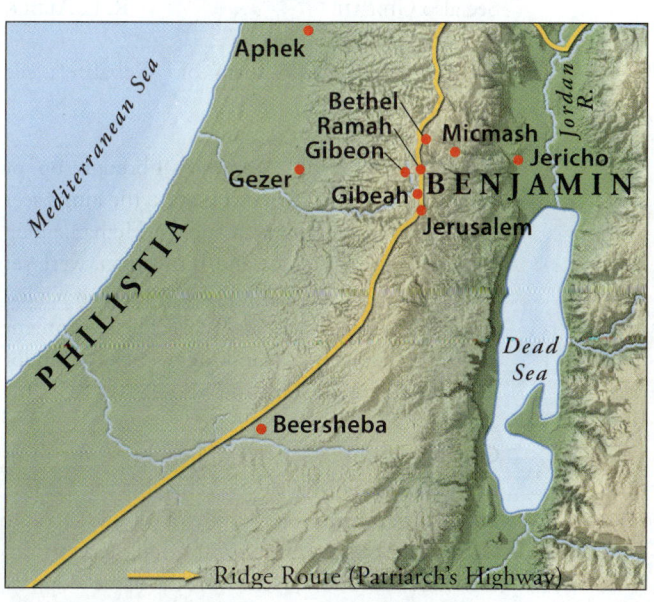

Gibeon lies at a critical internal crossroads in Palestine.

unearthed many jar handles, twenty-four of which bore the name Gibeon. Other handles bore the typical names of Amariah, Azariah, and Hananiah. The jars may have been used in connection with the wine industry of Gibeon. Cut into the solid rock of the hill were some sixty-six cavities, or cellars, in which the wine could be stored at a constant temperature. In the immediate vicinity were the other accouterments of wine making, such as presses and troughs. (During the Roman period, the dead were buried most exquisitely in the necropolis of Gibeon. Several tombs plus a columbarium were excavated, and these produced very fine pottery specimens.)

By far the most spectacular feature was the great pool, 37 ft. in diameter and 82 ft. deep, with a circular staircase of 79 steps cut out of the rock. This pool is one of the best-known archaeological attractions. The pool was never used to hold WATER but was part of a rather complete waterworks that assured the citizens of water even during times of siege. To reach the water required the descent not only of the 79 steps of the circular "pool," but also an additional 93 steps through a tunnel 167 ft. long. At the bottom was the cistern room filled with water from the main spring outside the city wall. This tunnel also was cut from the solid rock, although the crookedness of it indicates that the engineers followed the natural fissures of the rock. See also GIBEAH.   R. L. ALDEN

Giblite gib′lit. KJV form of "Gebalite"; see GEBAL.

Giddalti gi-dal′ti (גִּדַּלְתִּי H1547, "I brought up" or "I magnify [God]"). Son of HEMAN, the king's seer (1 Chr. 25:4). The fourteen sons of Heman, along with the sons of ASAPH and JEDUTHUN, were set apart "for the ministry of prophesying, accompanied by harps, lyres and cymbals" (v. 1). The assignment of duty was done by lot, and the twenty-second lot fell to Giddalti, his sons, and his relatives (25:29).

Giddel gid′uhl (גִּדֵּל H1543, possibly short form of גְּדַלְיָהוּ H1546, "great is Yahweh"; see GEDALIAH). (1) Ancestor of a family of temple servants (NETHINIM) who returned with ZERUBBABEL from the EXILE (Ezra 2:47; Neh. 7:49; the name is apparently omitted in the parallel list, 1 Esd. 5:30).

(2) A servant of SOLOMON whose descendants returned with Zerubbabel from the exile (Ezra 2:56; Neh. 7:58; in 1 Esd. 5:33, the NRSV has "Isdael," but the reading *Geddēl* is preferred by R. Hanhart, *Esdrae liber I*, Septuaginta 8/1 [1974], ad loc.). The "sons of Solomon's servants" (Ezra 2:55 RSV) were descendants of foreigners or of prisoners captured in war who were subjected to forced labor (cf. Josh. 9:23; 1 Ki. 9:21).   F. W. BUSH

Gideon gid′ee-uhn (גִּדְעוֹן H1549, "one who cuts, hewer"). Son of JOASH the Abiezrite, from the tribe of MANASSEH, and the fifth recorded judge of Israel (Jdg. 6–8); also called JERUB-BAAL ("let Baal contend," 6:32 et al.); JERUB-BESHETH in 2 Sam. 11:21.

I. Background. During the period of the Judges there was no predetermined or planned leadership such as exists under a monarchy, where a king is normally succeeded by his son. See JUDGES, PERIOD OF. God raised up individuals to meet special circumstances, and these acted as "judges," ruling Israel. The Israelites were unorganized and the tribes disunited: "In those days Israel had no king; everyone did as he saw fit" (Jdg. 21:25). This left them open to oppression by neighboring tribes. The Israelites repeatedly fell into sin and idolatry, after which God gave them over to their enemies. At the time of Gideon, the oppressors were the Midianites and the Amalekites (see MIDIAN; AMALEK), who periodically plundered the land, destroying what they could not carry away. With their crops destroyed at each planting, the starving Israelites cried to the Lord. God sent a prophet to rebuke them for their disobedience. After seven years of suffering, God delivered the Israelites by the hand of Gideon.

II. Call of Gideon. While Gideon was THRESHING wheat covertly to hide it from the Midianites, the angel of the Lord appeared to him at his home in OPHRA (Jdg. 6:11). When the stranger informed Gideon that he was to deliver Israel, he asked for proof to validate the message. At the angel's request, Gideon prepared food and presented it to the angel, who caused the food to go up in flames, and the angel promptly vanished. It should be noted that the dynamic leadership of Gideon that followed was not the result of public demand, personal desires for leadership, or a high opinion of his own abilities, but only of the knowledge that God had called him and was leading him. For this reason Gideon asked for and received proof of God's call both at this time and later.

That night, following the Lord's instructions, Gideon and his servants pulled down the altar of BAAL, erected an altar to the Lord, and offered a bull, using the wood of the ASHERAH that was by the altar of Baal. When the townspeople learned of this the following morning they wanted to put Gideon to death. But Gideon's father, Joash, refused to deliver him to them, saying that if Baal were a god he could contend for himself and would not need their help. Thus, Gideon was given the name Jerub-Baal, "let Baal contend" (Jdg. 6:32).

III. The battle against Midian. The Midianites and the Amalekites came in from the E, crossed over the Jordan, and set up camp in the Valley of JEZREEL by the hill of MOREH. The Spirit of the Lord came upon Gideon; he gathered the Abiezrites (see ABIEZER) and sent messengers to the rest of the Manassites and also to the tribes of Asher, Zebulun, and Naphtali, asking them to join him in fighting the Midianites. Although Gideon had already acted on faith, he again asked for a sign—an additional miracle to help him in the difficult job ahead and to give faith to others who might have witnessed the event. On one night he left a fleece of wool on the threshing floor, asking for dew on the fleece, but not on the ground. On the following morning he wrung a bowl of water from the fleece although the ground was dry. The next night he asked for the reverse, so he found the fleece dry and the ground wet with dew (Jdg. 6:33–40). Then Gideon and his army of 32,000 men set up camp beside the spring of HAROD on Mount GILBOA.

The Lord made it clear that the coming victory would be his and not the result of superior Israelite might. He thus requested Gideon to send those trembling with fear back home (Jdg. 7:3; cf. Deut. 20:8). The majority, 22,000, returned home, leaving 10,000. But the Lord said there were still too many, so he set up another test based on the method of drinking water. The text as it stands does not seem clear. According to some commentators, the majority got down on their knees, put their faces down to the water, and drank it directly; whereas 300, upright, used their hands to put the water to their mouths. The phrase "lap the water with their tongues like a dog" (Jdg. 7:5) is made somehow equal with "lapped with their hands to their mouths" (7:6), both of these being opposed to those who knelt down. The comparison made between the dog and the 300 men is the standing position. This may have indicated that the 300 were more alert and cautious, as their physical position left them ready for action.

An alternate view (requiring textual emendation) is that the 300 fell prostrate and put their mouths to the water, lapping as a dog laps, whereas the rest were the ones who knelt "with their hands to their mouths" (see Y. Yadin, *The Art of Warfare in Biblical Lands*, 2 vols. [1963], 2:256–60). The virtue of the 300 in this instance would be their willingness to suffer the discomfort of lying in the dirt, if it was the most efficient way of accomplishing a goal. The important part, however, is that only 300 remained. Gideon kept the 300 and sent the rest home.

Having left Gideon with a fighting force of only 300 men, the Lord saw fit to encourage him again. Leading him to the camp of Midian, the Lord caused Gideon to overhear a man relating his dream to a friend. His friend understood the dream to foretell the defeat of Midian at the hand of Gideon

The Spring of Harod at the base of Mount Gilboa, where Gideon chose his 300 men to battle the Midianites.

(Jdg. 7:9–14). This may have been an indication of insecurity among the Midianite forces. In any case, it gave Gideon the confidence to proceed with his plans. That same night Gideon divided his men into three companies and gave them instructions for the attack. They surrounded the camp of Midian with torches hidden inside overturned jars in one hand, and trumpets in the other hand.

At the beginning of the middle watch (about midnight), following the lead of Gideon, they blew the trumpets, smashed the jars, and shouted. The sudden light and noise frightened the Midianites, and the Lord caused them to fight among themselves and to flee while Gideon and his men stood in their places around the camp. The places to which the Midianites fled (Jdg. 7:22) are not positively identified but seem to indicate that they went E, crossing the Jordan, and possibly S into the tribe of Ephraim (cf. S. Tolkowsky in *JPOS* 5 [1925]: 69–74; A. Malamat in *PEQ* no vol. [1953]: 61–65; Yadin, *Art of Warfare*, 2:256–60).

IV. Clearing out of Midianite troops.

God used just 300 men to defeat the Midianites, but the work of destroying the defeated enemy, now spread across the countryside, remained to be done. For this Gideon sent again to Manasseh, Asher, and Naphtali, and also to Ephraim, for assistance to seal off the fords of the Jordan blocking their escape. The Ephraimites caught and killed the two princes of Midian—OREB AND ZEEB—and brought their heads to Gideon (Jdg. 7:23–25).

The men from Ephraim complained that they had not been asked to help with the initial battle. Gideon answered with tact and wisdom that Ephraim had slain the princes of Midian and that he himself had done nothing as great as this. The soft answer turned away their wrath (Jdg. 8:1–3; contrast JEPHTHAH, who in a similar situation later responded to the Ephraimites logically but was unable to prevent conflict, 12:1–6).

Gideon pursued ZEBAH AND ZALMUNNA, the kings of Midian, eastward across the Jordan. On the way he asked for provisions for his 300 men from the towns of SUCCOTH and PENUEL. Both towns refused him, so after threatening them, he proceeded. Gideon caught Zebah and Zalmunna with their army off guard. (Only 15,000 men were left as 120,000 had already fallen.) The surprise attack again routed the Midianites. Zebah and Zalmunna tried to flee but were caught. Returning to Succoth, Gideon took thorns and briers from the wilderness and used them to whip the men of the city. He also broke down the tower of Penuel and killed men there. When he learned that Zebah and Zalmunna had killed his brothers, Gideon killed them also (Jdg. 8:4–21).

V. Aftermath.

From the golden earrings taken in the spoil, Gideon made an EPHOD and took it in his city, Ophra. Although Gideon was so devoted to the Lord that he refused to rule Israel, saying that the Lord should rule over them, the ephod became a "snare to Gideon and his family," affecting all Israel, as it became an object of worship. The land, however, had rest for forty years as a result of his leadership (Jdg. 8:22–28). Gideon had many wives, who bore him seventy sons. He also had a concubine who bore him a son, ABIMELECH. Gideon died "at a good old age," and it was not until after his death that the Israelites again departed from God (8:29–35; subsequently Abimelech slew all but one of his brothers and set himself up as ruler, ch. 9).

VI. Character and influence of Gideon.

The writer of Hebrews includes Gideon as one of the heroes of the faith (Heb. 11:32). He certainly learned to trust God for the impossible. He gave evidence of wisdom in the art of warfare and, also, wisdom along with patience and humility in dealing with the Ephraimites. In contrast, he took revenge against Succoth and Penuel. His error in making and misusing the ephod may be attributed, at least in part, to the ignorance and low moral standards of that time. Israel later remembered her deliverance by Gideon as one of national importance (Ps. 83:11; Isa. 9:4; 10:26). The name of Gideon has become popular in Christian circles and has been used to name groups such as Gideons International, a Bible distributing organization. (See further J. M. Lang, *Gideon and the Judges* [1890]; on the names Gideon and Jerubbaal, cf. J. A. Emerton in *JTS* 27 [1976]: 289–312; for a literary analysis, see E. Assis, *Self-Interest or Communal Interest: An Ideology of Leadership in the Gideon, Abimelech and Jephthah Narratives (Judg 6–12)* [2005]).

C. P. WEBER

Gideoni gid´ee-oh´ni (גִּדְעֹנִי H1551, in form, a gentilic of GIDEON, but meaning uncertain). Father of ABIDAN; the latter was the leader of the tribe of BENJAMIN in the wilderness wanderings (Num. 1:11; 2:22; 7:60, 65; 10:24).

Gidgad gid´gad. See HOR HAGGIDGAD.

Gidom gi´duhm (גִּדְעֹם H1550, possibly "cutting off, clearing"). An unknown location, probably in the E side of the territory of BENJAMIN (Jdg. 20:45). After the rape of the Levite's mistress in GIBEAH, the other tribes of Israel went to battle against the Benjamites, who "fled toward the desert to the rock of Rimmon." Along the flight, the Israelites killed 5,000 Benjamites and pressed after them "as far as Gidom," where 2,000 more died. Some scholars have thought that the word *gidʿōm* should be understood as a verbal form and translate the text, "to their cutting down," that is, until the Benjamites were slaughtered (cf. NEB).

gier eagle jihr. This term (now obsolete) is used by the KJV to render Hebrew *rāḥām* H8164 and *rāḥāmâ* H8168, which are found in lists of unclean birds and refer to some kind of carrion VULTURE (Lev. 11:18; Deut. 14:17; NIV, OSPREY). See also EAGLE.

gift. This English term is used variously in Bible versions to render numerous Hebrew words, especially *minḥâ* H4966 and *mattān* H5508; the most common Greek terms are *dōron* G1565 and *charisma* G5922 (the latter is in the NT restricted to the favors that God grants, both physical and spiritual). In Israel, gifts were presented not only to one's immediate family to mark a betrothal, marriage, birth, or death, but also to superiors in political and religious hierarchy and to the palace and temple. The ultimate gifts are those given to God as tokens of faith and dependence; however, Scripture insists upon the sincerity of the heart. In the early, pastoral societies of the OT, gifts were almost always in kind (Gen. 24:22 et al.), while in the period of the Second Commonwealth and the NT, coinage became the primary basis of both exchange and giving. (See *NIDOTTE*, 2:978–90; 3:205–11; *NIDNTT*, 2:39–44.) See also CONTRIBUTION; CORBAN; SACRIFICE AND OFFERINGS; SPIRITUAL GIFTS.

gift of healing. See SPIRITUAL GIFTS.

gift of tongues. See SPIRITUAL GIFTS; TONGUES, GIFT OF.

Gihon River gi´hon (גִּיחוֹן H1633, "a bursting forth, spring"). One of the four headwaters into which the river flowing from Eden divided (Gen. 2:13; cf. Sir. 24:27). See EDEN, GARDEN OF. Suggested identifications of the Gihon include the Araxes, the NILE, the Shatt el-Hai, the Karun, and even a Babylonian canal. All such identifications seem to overlook the fact that the TIGRIS and EUPHRATES, two of the other headwaters, do not flow out of a common source; hence the account does not literally fit today's geography. Some have suggested that the Gihon River was associated in Hebrew mythical thought with the spring by the same name (see next entry) in JERUSALEM, with ZION regarded as the focal point of the world (cf. *ABD*, 2:1018–19).

G. G. SWAIM

Gihon Spring gi´hon (גִּיחוֹן H1633, "a bursting forth, spring"). The more important of the two springs that supplied WATER to JERUSALEM in OT times (today it is known as ʿAin Sitti Maryam, Arab. ʿEin Umm ed-Deraj). It was Gihon that determined the original site of the city on the hill called OPHEL, just W of the spring. On the assumption that it lay outside the wall of the fortified city, it was long thought that the pre-Israelite inhabitants cut a tunnel down through the rock of Ophel to provide protection for those drawing water when the city was under siege, and that DAVID's men gained access to the city through this tunnel (2 Sam. 5:6–9). The most recent excavations, however, have shown that throughout the biblical period the spring was protected by massive towers (see R. Reich and E. Shukron in *RB* 107 [2000]: 5–17).

The fact that Gihon was chosen as the proper place to anoint SOLOMON as David's successor (1 Ki. 1:33, 38, 45) may have been symbolic; just as David became master of the city at Gihon, so did Solomon. In any event, the selection of this site underscores its ceremonial as well as its strategic importance. It is hardly surprising that an AQUEDUCT was later constructed to make the water more accessible (Isa. 7:3). Some two and a half centuries after Solomon's accession, when SENNACHERIB attacked Judah (2 Chr. 32), HEZEKIAH built a new water system, constructing the famous SILOAM tunnel to provide a safer means of getting Gihon's water into the fortified area (32:30) and refortifying the wall in its vicinity (33:14). In postexilic times, the demand for water outgrew this supply, and the city constructed aqueducts to bring in water from farther away. Pontius PILATE, using temple funds, either built or repaired one of these aqueducts.

(See further K. M. Kenyon, *Jerusalem: Excavating 3000 Years of History* [1967], 15–16, 31, 69–77; Y. Shiloh, *Excavations at the City of David 1978–1982. Interim Report of the First Five Seasons* [1984], 23; P. J. King and L. E. Stager, *Life in Biblical Israel* [2001], 213–15.) G. G. SWAIM

Gilalai gil′uh-li (גִּלֲלַי H1675, meaning uncertain). A priestly musician who participated in the dedication of the rebuilt wall of Jerusalem under EZRA (Neh. 12:36; his name is one of several omitted in the LXX).

Gilboa, Mount gil-boh′uh (גִּלְבֹּעַ H1648, prob. "hill country"). A mountain or range of mountains (today Jebel Fuquʿah), about 8 mi. long and 3–5 mi. wide, lying to the E of the Plain of ESDRAELON, on the border between SAMARIA and GALILEE, some 17 mi. SW of the Sea of Galilee. The highest peak, Sheikh Burqan, is only 1,696 ft. above sea level, but it falls off rather abruptly on the E to the JORDAN, 2,000 ft. below. The western slope inclines more gradually to Esdraelon, 300 ft. above sea level. On these western slopes occurred the last battle and the death of SAUL and his three sons, JONATHAN, ABINADAB, and MALKI-SHUA (1 Sam. 31; 2 Sam. 1; 21:12). The PHILISTINES prepared for war when Israel pressed into the plain and threatened to cut off their access to the Way of the Sea (VIA MARIS, the major trade route from Egypt to Damascus). When they attacked, the Israelite warriors fled, and Saul was seriously wounded. Rather than fall into the hands of his lifelong enemies in this condition, Saul took his own life, one of the few suicides mentioned in the Bible.

The name Gilboa (which has the definite article in Heb. except in 1 Chr. 10:1, 8) occurs in Scripture only in connection with the death of Saul; from before the time of the Israelite conquest, notorious battles were fought in this vicinity. It was at nearby MEGIDDO that THUTMOSE III fought the Canaanites, nearly 850 years before NECO's forces killed JOSIAH on their way to do battle against the Assyrians (2 Ki. 23:29). DEBORAH's battle against SISERA was greatly aided by the Brook KISHON, which takes its rise on Gilboa (Jdg. 5:21). It was not far from here that GIDEON routed the Midianites (6:33).

JEZREEL, summer capital of the house of OMRI (1 Ki. 18:45; 2 Ki. 9:15), was situated on a western spur of Gilboa, about 200 ft. above the plain, commanding both the Way of the Sea and the highway from the Mediterranean to the Jordan. Here JEHU, subverted by ELISHA, murdered both JORAM of Israel and his mother JEZEBEL, and from here he pursued and murdered AHAZIAH of Judah (2 Ki. 9; cf. Hos. 1:4). (See G. A. Smith, *The Historical Geography of the Holy Land*, 25th ed. [1931], 246–50, 259–62.) G. G. SWAIM

Gilead gil′ee-uhd (גִּלְעָד H1680, possibly "rugged country," but see GALEED; gentilic גִּלְעָדִי H1682, "Gileadite"). The name of three persons and of a geographical area.

(1) Son of MAKIR, grandson of MANASSEH, and eponymous ancestor of the Gileadite clan (Num. 26:29, 30; 27:1; 36:1; Josh. 17:1; Jdg. 5:17; 1 Chr. 2:21, 23; 7:14, 17). According to one passage (Num.

View SE from Tel Yisreʾel looking toward Mount Gilboa.

32:40; cf. Josh. 17:1), Moses gave the land of Gilead (see below, #4) to Makir, suggesting that the latter named his son after the name of the land.

(2) The father of Jephthah; because Jephthah was born of a prostitute, Gilead's legitimate sons drove him away (Jdg. 11:1–2).

(3) Son of Michael and descendant of Gad (1 Chr. 5:14; the Gadites lived in Gilead and other areas, v. 16).

(4) A large mountainous region E of the Jordan. Often mentioned in the OT, the name Gilead in its broadest sense can be applied to all of Israelite Transjordan (e.g., Josh. 22:9, where it is contrasted to the land of Canaan, i.e., Cisjordan) or to the entire central section of that area (2 Ki. 10:33). More precisely, Gilead was located in the foothills N of the Plain of Mishor. It was bounded on the W by the Jordan River, extended near the Yarmuk on the N, to the S-N branches of the Jabbok and the Arabian desert to the E, and to the Arnon on the S. Its cities included Jabesh Gilead, Mahanaim, Mizpah, Ramoth Gilead, and Succoth. In NT times, as a part of the kingdom of Herod the Great and his son Herod Antipas, it was known as Perea. The name is still preserved today in several locations (e.g., Jebel Jelʿad, Khirbet Jelʿad, and ʿAin Jelʿad; the Wadi Yabis preserves the name of Jabesh in Gilead; and the name Ramoth is preserved in Tell Ramith, SW of Derʿa).

Rising from the Jordan Valley on the W, 700 ft. below sea level, Gilead reaches heights of more than 3,300 ft. It is a well-watered hill country, thickly wooded (as Absalom found at the cost of his life), and is still well forested with Mediterranean pine and evergreen oak. It is known for its grapes, olives, fruit trees, and pasture lands. It was also proverbial for the "balm of Gilead" (Jer. 8:22; 46:11), an ointment with medicinal value (see balm).

The N part of Gilead was settled as early as the 23rd cent. B.C. It was occupied by the Amorites and Moabites (see Moab) at the time of the Israelite entrance under Moses. Sihon, the king, would not allow the Israelites to pass through his land; this stance resulted in warfare that ended with the land in the possession of the Israelites (Num. 21). The tribes of Reuben, Gad, and the half-tribe of Manasseh did not want to cross over the Jordan with the other tribes, as the Transjordan territory appealed to them.

Moses agreed to give them the land after exacting a promise that they would first help the other tribes subdue the land W of the Jordan, a promise they fulfilled (Josh. 22). The descendants of Makir of the tribe of Manasseh were given Gilead and settled there (Num. 32:39). Moses was allowed to see the land of Gilead as far as Dan (place) from the top of Mount Nebo just before his death (Deut. 34:1). Gilead seems to have been a mixture of Gadite and Josephite elements (Num. 32:39–40; Josh. 13:24–31). Ramoth Gilead was early designated as one of the cities of refuge (Josh. 20:8).

During the period of the early settlement, the tribes E of the Jordan enjoyed a measure of security and did not even come to help their kinsmen W of the Jordan in their struggle with Sisera (Jdg. 5:17). During the time of the judges, the nation of Ammon oppressed the people of Israel in Gilead as part of their attempt to expand their land. The people chose Jephthah, an outcast Gileadite and mighty warrior, as their leader to deliver them. He drove out the Ammonites and secured the land for the Israelites (ch. 11). However, a feud arose between the Ephraimites and the Gileadites because they were not called to participate in the struggle against the Ammonites. The Ephraimites were routed, and when they tried to flee back across the river, they found that the Gileadites had taken possession of all the fords. Anyone who attempted to cross was tested to see if he was an Ephraimite by asking him to say Shibboleth. If he said Sibboleth, they seized him and slew him (ch. 12).

The mountainous region of the Dome of Gilead, N of modern Amman. (View to the NE.)

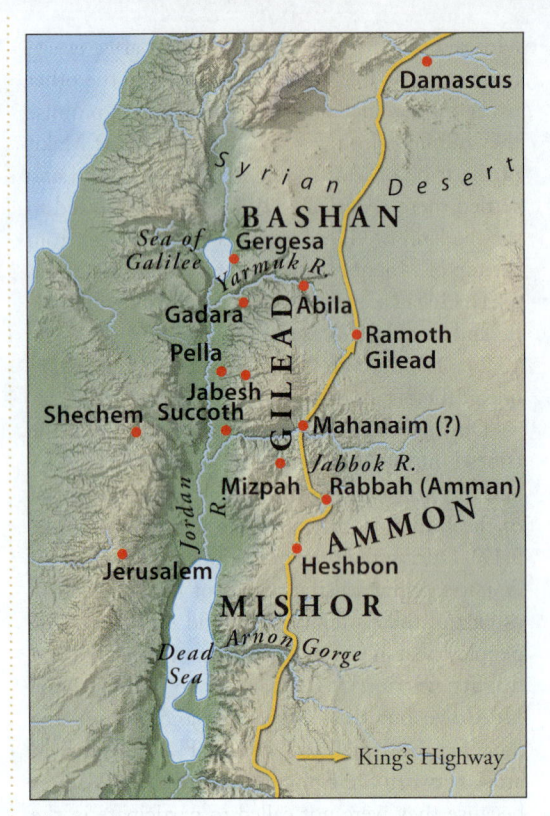

Gilead.

The Ammonites continued to be a threat to the Gileadites in subsequent history. SAUL's first great military victory after becoming king was his rescue of the city of Jabesh Gilead, which was being threatened by NAHASH, king of the Ammonites (1 Sam. 11). After Saul's defeat and death at the hands of the PHILISTINES, ABNER established Saul's son ISH-BOSHETH as king over Gilead (2 Sam. 2:8, 9). It was to Mahanaim in Gilead that DAVID fled when ABSALOM rebelled against him (17:24), and it was in Gilead where the decisive battle was fought that resulted in the death of Absalom and the return of the kingdom to David (ch. 18). Gilead was included in the census made by David (24:6).

ELIJAH was from Gilead (1 Ki. 17:1). During the 9th–8th centuries, DAMASCUS (ARAM or Syria) was a constant threat to the Israelites. AMOS condemned the Arameans for their extreme cruelty, particularly toward Gilead (Amos 1:3–5). He condemned the cruelty of the Ammonites toward innocent women of Gilead in time of war (1:13). Hosea said Gilead was a city of evildoers (Hos.

6:8). Israel and Judah entered into an alliance to wrest Ramoth Gilead from the king of Aram (1 Ki. 22:1–4), resulting in the death of AHAB on the battlefield. JEHU made some kind of protective alliance with SHALMANESER III (c. 837 B.C.), but it did not keep the Aramean HAZAEL from seizing part of Israel, including Gilead (2 Ki. 10:33). As a result of a conspiracy by REZIN of Aram and PEKAH of Israel, TIGLATH-PILESER III invaded the two countries in his campaign of 734–732, utterly destroying the coalition. He occupied parts of Israel, dividing the annexed territory into three provinces, named in the Assyrian lists according to their respective capitals: MEGIDDO (Magiddu), DOR (Du'ru), and Gilead (Gal'aza). He carried part of the population captive to Assyria (2 Ki. 15:29).

In an attempt to restore the empire of David, JOSIAH seized the territory of the former kingdom of Israel that had been Gilead. When Babylon overran the land, no changes were made in the provincial organization established by the Assyrians. EZEKIEL mentions the provinces of Hamath, Damascus, Hauran, and Gilead, already known from the Assyrian period (Ezek. 47–48). JEREMIAH looked to the time of restoration of Gilead to Israel (Jer. 50:19), and OBADIAH foresaw its restoration to Benjamin (Obad. 19). In the postexilic period, TOBIAH was the Persian appointed governor of the territory of Ammon, which had been joined to the province of Gilead.

In 163 B.C., Judas MACCABEE with his younger brother Jonathan campaigned in Gilead (Galaad) with some success, but his power was not sufficient to hold the area permanently, so he took the Israelite population to Judea that wanted to remain members of the Jerusalem religious community (1 Macc. 5:9–54). Gilead in NT times was part of PEREA. (See further M. Noth, *The History of Israel* [1960], 158, 274, 371; Y. Aharoni, *The Land of the Bible: A Historical Geography*, rev. ed. [1979], 38–39 et passim; R. H. Dornemann, *The Archaeology of the Transjordan in the Bronze and Iron Ages* [1983].)

F. B. HUEY, JR.

Gilead, balm of. See BALM.

Gilgal gil´gal (גִּלְגָּל H1652 [with def. article, except Josh. 5:9; 12:23], "circle [of stones]," thus "circuit, territory"). The name of several locations. The most important of these, JOSHUA's encampment near the JORDAN, will be treated last.

(1) A town in the tribal territory of EPHRAIM. The prophets ELIJAH and ELISHAH are said to have gone "from Gilgal" (2 Ki. 2:1) to BETHEL (v. 2) and on to JERICHO (v. 4). On the basis of such limited information, some have identified this Gilgal with the modern town of Jiljulieh, about 7 mi. N of Bethel, but the site cannot be confirmed (cf. Y. Aharoni, *The Land of the Bible: A Historical Geography*, rev. ed. [1979], 280 n. 131). It was possibly the same place where later Elisha threw flour in the pot of death, making the stew harmless (4:38–41). In addition, Mounts EBAL and GERIZIM are elsewhere said to be "near the great trees of Moreh, in the territory of those Canaanites living in the Arabah in the vicinity of Gilgal" (Deut. 11:29–30). This description indicates a place near SHECHEM, and thus likely the same area mentioned in 2 Kings (another possibility is Juleijil, 2.5 mi. SE of Nablus). Because the broader context of Deuteronomy speaks of the Israelites' entering the Promised Land, however, some scholars argue that this Gilgal must be the same as #4 below. The difficulty was handled by a 2nd-cent. sage, Rabbi Eleazar, with the comment (possibly reflecting an ancient tradition) that after crossing the Jordan the Israelites constructed two piles of stones near JERICHO, calling one Mount Gerizim and the other Mount Ebal (*y. Soṭah* 7.21c). The matter is still not satisfactorily resolved.

(2) A region where the Canaanite city of GOIIM (NIV, "Goyim") was located; the name is included in a list of conquered monarchs (Josh. 12:23; the KJV reads, "of the nations of Gilgal"). Because it is mentioned next to DOR (in Naphath Dor) and before TIRZAH, some think the area may have been on the eastern edge of the SHARON Plain (perhaps Jiljulieh, 4 mi. N of APHEK [NT ANTIPATRIS], not to be confused with the Jiljulieh mentioned above, #1). The SEPTUAGINT, however, has GALILEE (rather than Gilgal), a reading followed by the NRSV and other versions. It is even possible that the text should be rendered, "the king of the nations of Galilee" (cf. the expression *gĕlîl haggôyim*, "Galilee of the Gentiles," Isa. 9:1). Some scholars identify Goiim with HAROSHETH HAGGOYIM, which was perhaps in Galilee.

(3) A town or region on the NE boundary of the tribe of JUDAH, facing the Pass of ADUMMIM, "south of the gorge" (Josh. 15:7). Because Adummim is about 6 mi. SW of Jericho, some have identified this Gilgal with #4 below, but the latter was clearly much closer to Jericho. A similar passage (18:17, which describes the SE boundary of BENJAMIN) refers to GELILOTH as facing the Pass of Adummim, and many scholars believe that Geliloth and Gilgal are variant forms of the same name. In any case, the place in question must have been approximately 8 mi. NE of JERUSALEM, but the precise site has not been identified (proposals include Khan el-Aḥmar and ʿAraq ed-Deir).

(4) The Gilgal most frequently mentioned in the Bible is a site "on the eastern border of Jericho" where the Israelites camped soon after entering the Promised Land (Josh. 4:19). There they built a monument of twelve stones (v. 20, but the text does not indicate whether they were arranged in a circle), the rite of CIRCUMCISION was performed (5:8), and the PASSOVER was celebrated (5:10). From this site, the Israelites set out to march around Jericho for seven days. Apparently, Gilgal was their base camp as they made attacks on the hill country, for JOSHUA was found at Gilgal by the Gibeonites after AI was destroyed and after he had built an altar on Mount Ebal (8:30; 9:6). From Gilgal, the Israelites left to defend Gibeon and returned to Gilgal victorious (10:15, 43).

After Joshua had completed most of the conquest (Josh. 18:1), the central sanctuary, including the ARK OF THE COVENANT, was transferred to SHILOH. Gilgal must have continued as a prominent city, however, because it is apparently referred to twice in the book of Judges (Jdg. 2:1; 3:19), and it was later one of three cities on SAMUEL's circuit (1 Sam. 7:16). SAUL was made king in Gilgal (11:14–15), which became a base of military operations (13:4 et al.). Here Saul sought to placate Samuel after he had disobeyed by salvaging some cattle for booty and permitting the enemy king to live (15:7–15). It was in this context that Samuel uttered the famous maxim, "To obey is better than sacrifice" (15:22).

This Gilgal near Jericho is generally accepted as the place against which the prophets HOSEA and AMOS preached, both of whom associate the town closely with Bethel (if BETH AVEN in Hos. 5:15

is a sarcastic alteration of "Bethel"; see also 9:15; 12:11; Amos 4:4; 5:5). On the other hand, because of this association, many scholars think that the Gilgal mentioned by these prophets is a different one, possibly the same as #1 above.

James Muilenburg has done extensive research on the location of Gilgal and has identified it with modern Khirbet el-Mefjir, a little over 1 mi. NE of Jericho (modern Tell es-Sultan; see *BASOR* 140 [Dec. 1955]: 11–27). This site is not without problems (the remains of the sumptuous Ummayyad palace of the caliph Hisham, A.D. 724–732, are there). The strongest alternative site for Gilgal is Khirbet en-Nitleh (3 mi. SE of Jericho), which is covered by many Byzantine ruins. Apart from the Bible, JOSEPHUS is the best and oldest witness. He locates Gilgal fifty stadia from the ford of the Jordan (accepted by nearly all as being at al-Maghtas) and ten stadia from Jericho (*Ant.* 5.6.4). If both Muilenburg and Josephus have the same Jericho and the same ford in mind, then Gilgal can only be Khirbet el-Mefjir, because en-Nitleh is too close to the river. Muilenburg found pottery of the Iron Age in a sounding of Khirbet el-Mefjir, which sets its occupation back at least to 1000 B.C. and dispels any doubts that the site is not sufficiently ancient. (See further F. M. Abel, *Géographie de la Palestine*, 2 vols. [1933–38] 2:337ff.)   R. L. ALDEN

Gilgamesh gil'guh-mesh. A legendary king of the Sumerian city of Uruk (ERECH). Gilgamesh was apparently a historical figure who lived in S MESOPOTAMIA about the end of the 4th or beginning of the 3rd millennium B.C. It was as the great hero and personification of the human condition in the CUNEIFORM literature of later ages that he became famous, figuring in a great many poetic myths from SUMER (e.g., *Gilgamesh and Agga of Kish, Gilgamesh and the Bull of Heaven, Gilgamesh and the Land of the Living*). The portrayal of the character of Gilgamesh includes not only positive heroic virtues, such as strength and loyalty, but also negative, debased aspects, including trickery, tyranny, and the like. This literary tradition passed to the Semites, and he is mentioned frequently in Akkadian literature (see LANGUAGES OF THE ANE II).

The greatest cycle of stories woven around him is the *Epic of Gilgamesh* in twelve tablets (other

One of the cuneiform tablets containing the *Epic of Gilgamesh*, a famous Babylonian narrative describing a great deluge with similarities to the account of the flood in Genesis.

fragmentary versions have survived). The contents are as follows: Gilgamesh has ruled his city of Uruk tyrannically and so the gods prepare a counter protagonist, a wild man, Enkidu; Gilgamesh is warned that Enkidu can be foiled by a prostitute (Tablet I). Enkidu is seduced and becomes like other men; he wrestles with Gilgamesh and the two become fast friends (Tablet II). Enkidu and Gilgamesh go to battle the monster Huwawa (Tablets III–V). ISHTAR attempts to entice Gilgamesh into an affair and has the Bull of Heaven fashioned to punish him when he spurns her; Gilgamesh and Enkidu kill the Bull (Tablet VI). As a punishment for impiety, the gods kill Enkidu by means of a pestilence; Gilgamesh mourns for Enkidu and, grief-stricken, wanders over the earth seeking immortality (Tablets VII–IX). Gilgamesh continues his wanderings and carries on dialogues with various mythological characters about the nature of mortality; he finally comes to the magical land of Utnapishtim, the Sumerian who was destined by the gods to survive the deluge (Tablet X). The account of the flood is told in high-style epic verse by Utnapishtim (Tablet XI), followed by a lament for the mortality of Gilgamesh (Tablet XII).

Although the whole of the poem is of great interest to biblical students, Tablet XI with its detailed description of the flood has been studied for many years. It is a brilliant and gripping tale and is strangely, but not precisely, similar to the account in Genesis. In the 19th cent., some German scholars who stressed cultural parallels saw this cycle and the character of Gilgamesh as a possible anticipation of Christ and the messianic office. This view has been rejected by all but a few authorities. A magnificent relief in the Louvre Museum from the palace of SARGON II at Khorsabad is thought to show a gigantic figure of Gilgamesh strangling a lion.

(See further R. C. Thompson, *The Epic of Gilgamesh: Text, Transliteration, and Notes* [1930]; A. Schott, *Das Gilgamesch-Epos* [1934]; A. Heidel, *The Gilgamesh Epic and Old Testament Parallels* [1946]; P. Garelli, ed., *Gilgameš et sa légende* [1960]; S. N. Kramer, *The Sumerians* [1963], 45–49, 130–31, 134ff., 185–205, 255ff.; J. H. Tigay, *The Evolution of the Gilgamesh Epic* [1982]; A. George, *The Epic of Gilgamesh: The Babylonian Epic Poem and Other Texts in Akkadian and Sumerian* [1999]; id., *The Babylonian Gilgamesh Epic: Introduction, Critical Edition and Cuneiform Texts* [2003].) W. WHITE, JR.

Gilo gi′loh. See GILOH.

Giloh gi′loh (גִּלֹה *H1656*, possibly "rejoicing"; gentilic גִּילֹנִי *H1639*, "Gilonite"). A town in the hill country of southern JUDAH (Josh. 15:51). It was the home of DAVID's counselor, AHITHOPHEL (2 Sam. 15:12; 23:34 [RSV, "of Gilo"]). Some have identified Giloh with modern Khirbet Jala, about 5 mi. NNW of HEBRON, but others prefer an otherwise unknown location farther S, closer to DEBIR.
G. G. SWAIM

Gilonite gi′luh-nit. See GILOH.

gimel gim′uhl (גִּימֶל [not used in the Bible], meaning uncertain). The third letter of the Hebrew ALPHABET (ג), with a numerical value of three. The Hebrew letters are named for their shape, and in the past some have connected *gimel* with the word for "camel" (*gāmāl H1695*); others derive it from a root meaning "throw-stick" (cf. further *HALOT*, 1:168). Its sound corresponds to that of English "hard" *g* (following a vowel, it later became spirantized, probably with a sound similar to that of intervocalic *g* in Spanish).

Gimzo gim′zoh (גִּמְזוֹ *H1693*, perhaps "[place of] sycamore tree"). A town in the SHEPHELAH wrested from King AHAZ by the PHILISTINES (2 Chr. 28:18). The loss of Gimzo and other towns, combined with an Edomite invasion, caused Ahaz to appeal to TIGLATH-PILESER of Assyria for help (28:16). Gimzo is identified with modern Jimzu, some 5 mi. N of GEZER and 15 mi. SSE of JOPPA.

gin. This English term, in its meaning "snare, trap" (now infrequent), is used by the KJV to render the roughly synonymous Hebrew terms *paḥ H7062* (Job 18:9; Isa. 8:14) and *môqēš H4613* (Ps. 140:5; 141:9; Amos 3:5). The latter term may have referred to the lure that draws the victim to the trap (or possibly to the trigger), but its meaning became extended and was applied to the trap itself.
G. G. SWAIM

Ginath gi′nath (גִּינַת *H1640*, possibly "protector" [but the feminine form may reflect a place-name]). The father of TIBNI; the latter contended with OMRI for the throne of Israel after the death of ZIMRI (1 Ki. 16:21–22).

Ginnetho, Ginnethoi gin′uh-thoh, -thoi. See GINNETHON.

Ginnethon gin′uh-thon (גִּנְּתוֹן *H1715* [in Neh. 12:4, גִּנְּתוֹי], perhaps "gardener"). A priest who returned from BABYLON with ZERUBBABEL and JESHUA (Neh. 12:4; KJV, "Ginnetho"; NRSV, "Ginnethoi"). He was among those who affixed their seals to the covenant of NEHEMIAH (10:6). In the days of JOIAKIM, the head of his family was Meshullam (12:16).

girdle. This English term is used frequently by the KJV to render various words that are better translated "belt," "sash," "waistband," etc. See BELT.

Girgashite guhr′guh-shit (גִּרְגָּשִׁי *H1739*). A Canaanite tribe descended from HAM through his son CANAAN (Gen. 10:6) and included in various lists of peoples dispossessed by the Israelites (Gen. 15:21; Deut. 7:1; Josh. 3:10; 24:11; 1 Chr. 1:14; Neh. 9:8; in Jdt. 5:16, "Gergesites"). The personal (and perhaps tribal) name *grgš* appears in 13th-cent.

texts from UGARIT and is probably related (C. H. Gordon, *Ugaritic Textbook* [1965], 381 no. 619). Less likely is the view that the name means "client of [the god] Gesh" (a Sumerian deity of light; see B. Maisler in *ZAW* 1 [1932]: 86–87). The Bible gives no indication of the tribe's locality. Some have suggested a connection with Karkisha, a HITTITE city in ASIA MINOR; others have identified the Girgashites with the Gergesenes (cf. LXX *Gergesaios*; see GERASENE). These and other proposals remain unconfirmed.   H. A. HOFFNER, JR.

girl. This English term is used in Bible versions to render primarily Hebrew *naʿărâ* H5855 and Greek *korasion* G3166. It must be noted that among ancient peoples there was little in the way of a differentiation between the stages of infancy to old age. Such terms as "boy" or "girl" are therefore imprecise, and must be interpreted by the context in which they occur. See CHILD; YOUTH.

Girzite guhr´zit (גִּרְזִי H1747). A Canaanite tribe that, along with those of the Geshurites and Amalekites, was raided by DAVID while he lived in ZIKLAG (1 Sam. 27:8; see GESHUR; AMALEK). Such a tribe is otherwise unknown, and the text is not secure. A Hebrew variant (the *Qere*) is *gizrî*, that is, "Gizrite" or "Gezrite" (cf. KJV, as well as some MSS of the LXX), which would refer to an inhabitant of GEZER. Many scholars have thought, however, that Gezer was too far N for it to be involved in this account. Some have argued that the pair of names Geshurites and Girzites (or Gizrites) is the result either of a careless scribal repetition (dittography) or of a conflation of two different texts (note that the LXX has only one name), and that therefore the original reading was simply "Geshurites." While the solution to this problem remains uncertain, one must allow for the possibility that a people by the name of Girzites did indeed live "in the land extending to Shur and Egypt."

Gishpa gish´puh (גִּשְׁפָּא H1778). KJV, Gispa. A supervisor, along with ZIHA, of the temple servants (NETHINIM) living on the hill of OPHEL (Neh. 11:21). Some have thought that he should be identified with HASUPHA, who is elsewhere mentioned next to Ziha (Ezra 2:43; Neh. 7:46).

Gittah-hepher git´uh-hee´fuhr. KJV alternate form of GATH HEPHER (in Josh. 19:13).

Gittaim git´ay-im (גִּתַּיִם H1786, "[two] winepresses"). A village at the NE edge of the PHILISTINE plain, usually identified with Ras Abu Humeid/Hamid (but see GIBBETHON), about 14 mi. SE of JOPPA and 3.5 mi. NW of GEZER (alternatively, nearby Er-Ramleh, according to Y. Aharoni et al., *The Carta Bible Atlas*, 4th ed. [2002], index; some scholars, however, identify it with GATH Padalla, much farther N and possibly mentioned in 1 Chr. 7:21). Gittaim became a refuge for the indigenous population of BEEROTH (2 Sam. 4:3). It is possible that the people of Beeroth fled at the time that the tribe of BENJAMIN took possession of its allotment or that they, along with the Gibeonites, were attacked by King SAUL (cf. 21:1–2; Beeroth was closely associated with GIBEON, Josh. 9:17). After the return from the EXILE in Babylon, Gittaim was settled by Benjamites (Neh. 11:33).

Gittite git´it. An inhabitant of GATH.

gittith git´ith (גִּתִּית H1787). Often capitalized. A musical term used only in the titles of three psalms (Pss. 8; 81; 84). The meaning of the term is uncertain, but several suggestions have been made. It may refer to a lyre or other musical instrument distinctive to the PHILISTINE city of GATH, or to a type of melody associated with that city. Others believe it is derived directly from the Hebrew word for "winepress" (*gat* H1780), thus referring to a tune sung at the grape harvest or specifically at the Feast of Tabernacles. It has also been suggested that the term should be linked with OBED-EDOM the Gittite, keeper of the ARK OF THE COVENANT (2 Sam. 6:10–11), and that it indicates a melody associated with the religious New Year. See also MUSIC AND MUSICAL INSTRUMENTS VI.C.

Gizonite gi´zoh-nit (גִּזוֹנִי H1604). A descriptive term applied to a certain Hashem, one of DAVID's mighty men (1 Chr. 11:34; the parallel list in 2 Sam. 23:32 says "the sons of Jashen" instead of "Hashem the Gizonite"). The term is gentilic in form and thus appears to refer to an inhabitant of a town named "Gizo" or "Gizon," but such a place is unknown;

by textual emendation, the city of GIMZO has been suggested. The epithet could also be understood as a patronymic, indicating a family name (some Gk. MSS have "Gunite"; see GUNI).

Gizrite giz'rit. See GIRZITE.

glad tidings. See GOSPEL.

Glaphyra (Γλαφύρα). Daughter of Archelaus king of CAPPADOCIA. According to JOSEPHUS, she was given in marriage to Alexander, a son of HEROD the Great (*Ant*. 16.1.2 §11), but her presence caused disturbance in the family (16.7.2 §193). When Alexander was executed by his own father (16.11.7 §394), Glaphyra apparently returned to Cappadocia, remarried, and divorced (Josephus mistakenly calls her a widow, 17.13.4 §350). Some years later she married another son of Herod, Archelaus (ibid.). One of Glaphyra's sons by Alexander eventually became King Tigranes V of Armenia.

glass. A generally transparent or translucent, lustrous, hard, and brittle substance that has passed from a fluid condition, at high temperature, to a solid condition quickly enough to prevent the formation of visible crystals. Glass is formed in nature in three main ways. Rarely a silica glass is formed in small amounts when lightning strikes sand. The concentrated heat fuses the sand. The melt immediately solidifies, forming a fragile tube of silica glass sometimes several feet long. Such tubes are called fulgarites and are generally found in desert environments. Rarely, also, natural glass is formed as the result of localized melting of rock in a large fault zone, the glass generally being black and referred to as pseudotachylite. The most common natural occurrence of glass is as obsidian, a glassy volcanic rock of acidic composition used by early man for making small implements. Early sources of obsidian for countries of the ANE were the Aegean region and Ethiopia. Later obsidian was obtained from Armenia and possibly from Lipari and Pentellera. (See J. R. Partington, *A Textbook of Inorganic Chemistry*, 6th ed. [1950], 760–61.)

Manufactured glass consists primarily of a combination of silicic acid and alkali (sodium or potassium). Probably it originated somewhere in the eastern Mediterranean lands, possibly in Egypt; the Egyptians were already making small glass-covered objects about 4000 B.C. The first glass vessels appear to have been made c. 1500 B.C. In Egypt and in other coastlands, like Syria, soda glass was produced. This glass contains sodium and calcium silicates and is made by fusing white pure sand (silicon dioxide) free from iron compounds, soda-ash (sodium carbonate), and limestone (calcium carbonate) or lime (calcium oxide) in fireclay pots or tanks at 1375°C or above. The soda-ash was obtained from seaweed ash. Bohemian or potash glass contains potassium instead of sodium and was developed in well-wooded countries, particularly Germany, the potassium being derived from charcoal, particularly beech charcoal.

The ingredients of glass are rarely in a pure state, the sand generally containing some iron impurities. The green color they cause, due to ferrous silicate, may be neutralized by adding pyrolusite (manganese dioxide). The resultant glass (Gk. *hyalos* G5613, adj. *hyalinos* G5612) may be clear and transparent and look like still water (Rev. 4:6; 15:2; 21:18, 21). However, if there are numerous minute air bubbles left in the glass, it is translucent and has the appearance of ice. In biblical times, a MIRROR was made of a polished sheet of metal, not of glass.   D. R. BOWES

Glass bottles imitating berries (3rd cent. A.D.).

glass (mirror). See MIRROR.

glass, sea of. See SEA OF GLASS.

glaze. This English term is used by the NIV and other modern versions in Prov. 26:23, where the MT's *kesep sîgîm* (KJV, "silver dross") is often emended to "like glaze," perhaps referring to a shiny metallic oxide of lead that has been used for millennia as a pigment (litharge) and as a glaze on pottery. However, see discussion under DROSS.

glean, gleaning. The verb *to glean* (Heb. *lāqaṭ H4377*) means "to gather the grain left behind by the reapers." The Mosaic law allowed for gleaning by the POOR (Lev. 19:9–10; 23:22), a practice beautifully illustrated in the story of RUTH and BOAZ (Ruth 2:3, 7–8, et al.). The concept is used metaphorically by the prophets (Isa. 17:5–6; Jer. 6:9 [ʿālal *G6618*]; Mic. 7:1 [ʿōlēlôt *H6622*]).

glede. This English term, referring to a bird of prey, is used by the KJV to render Hebrew *rāʾâ H8012* (Deut. 14:13; often emended to *dāʾâ*). Rendered "buzzard" by the NRSV and "red kite" by the NIV, the word no doubt refers to some kind of VULTURE, often identified with the KITE, *Milvus migrans* (see *FFB*, 40–41). See also BIRDS OF PREY; BUZZARD; FALCON; HAWK.

glorification. See EXALTATION OF CHRIST; GLORY; RESURRECTION.

glory. Great honor or praise; used especially of God's majestic splendor.

    I. Terminology
        A. In the OT
        B. In the NT
    II. The glory of God
    III. The glory of God in creation
    IV. The glory of Christ
    V. Eschatological glory

I. Terminology

A. In the OT. Several words have been translated "glory," including Hebrew *hādār H2077* ("splendor, grandeur"), *tĕhillâ H9335* ("renown, praise"), *nēṣaḥ H5905* (cf. esp. 1 Sam. 15:29, where the KJV renders, "the Strength of Israel"), and others. The most frequently used word, however, is *kābôd H3883*, which has a broad range of meaning: "weight, burden, wealth, magnificence, honor." It can be used of human beings to indicate personal influence or substance. JOSEPH, for example, says to his brothers, "Tell my father about all the honor [*kābôd*] accorded me in Egypt" (Gen. 45:13; cf. 31:1). Joseph was a man of wealth and position and was held in high esteem in Egypt, with servants and clothes reflecting that position. Thus he could speak in this way. HAMAN also recounted all "the glory of his riches" (Esth. 5:11; NIV, "his vast wealth"; cf. Ps. 49:16–17; Isa. 16:14; 17:4; 61:6; 66:11).

The magnificent garments of AARON were "for glory and for beauty" (Exod. 28:2 KJV), and the gorgeously apparelled king's daughter is "all glorious" (*kol-kĕbûddâ*, Ps. 45:13). MICHAL, SAUL's daughter, considering that DAVID had behaved in an undignified manner, used the cognate verb (*kābēd H3877*) in the sense of reputation when she sarcastically said to him, "How the king of Israel has distinguished himself today!" (2 Sam. 6:20; cf. Job 29:20; Ps. 4:2; Prov. 21:21; Eccl. 10:1). When used of a kingdom, the word can refer to armies or peoples, as in the phrase, "the king of Assyria and all his glory" (Isa. 8:7 KJV; cf. Ps. 78:61; Isa. 17:3; 21:16). It can also be used with reference to nature (e.g., "the glory of Lebanon," Isa. 60:13; cf. 35:2).

In many instances the word suggests "brightness." After describing the presence of God with the term *nōgah H5586*, "bright light, radiance" (Ezek. 1:4, 28a), EZEKIEL says, "This was the appearance of the likeness of the glory of the LORD" (v. 28b). Consider also Exod. 24:17, where the glory of the God of Israel is said to have "looked like a consuming fire." These various senses—brightness, honor, grandeur—can be combined in applying the word to God to describe his intrinsic worth and majestic splendor. (See further *NIDOTTE*, 2:577–87.)

B. In the NT. The distinctive Greek word for "glory" is *doxa G1518*. This noun (derived from the verb *dokeō G1506*, "to think, seem") means "opinion" or "reputation" in classical literature (cf. the derived English word *dogma*). Such a meaning is occasionally reflected in the NT, as when John says that some of the Jewish leaders preferred the *doxa* (high opinion, fame, praise) of men rather than God's (Jn. 12:43; cf. 5:41–43; 7:18). Almost always, however, the use of the word coincides with the meanings of Hebrew *kābôd*: brightness ("the glory of the Lord shone around them," Lk. 2:9; cf. 2 Cor. 3:9); outward human splendor ("Solomon in all his glory," Matt. 6:29; cf. 1 Cor. 11:15); national splendor ("all the kingdoms of the world and their glory," Matt. 4:8; cf. Rev. 21:24); honor ("you are our glory and joy," 1 Thess. 2:20).

Chiefly, the word refers to the revelation of God in Christ: "the Son is the radiance of God's glory" (Heb. 1:3). The apostle John declares: "We have seen his glory" (Jn. 1:14; cf. v. 18). It was seen in the miracles (2:11) and in the TRANSFIGURATION (2 Pet. 1:16–17). He is "our glorious Lord" (Jas. 2:1). In his incarnate life, the glory of God is seen. The word, as in the SEPTUAGINT, indicates the outshining of the divine glory, but with particular reference to the outshining in Christ. The subjectiveness involved in "opinion" is gone, and in its place is an objective fact—the glory of God in Christ. (See further *NIDNTT*, 2:44–48.)

II. The glory of God. STEPHEN summed up the OT concepts when he referred to "the God of glory" (Acts 7:2). For Israel, God's majesty surpassed all other manifestations of glory. Although the word could refer to armies or wealth, Israel must trust in neither of these, but in the Lord (Isa. 31:1, 3; cf. Pss. 20:7; 62:7). When Israel departed from God, Jeremiah rebuked the people saying, "Has a nation ever changed its gods? / (Yet they are not gods at all.) / But my people have exchanged their Glory / for worthless idols" (Jer. 2:11). Yahweh is Israel's glory. By sinning against him, the Israelites "exchanged their Glory for something disgraceful" (Hos. 4:7). Israel insulted God's glory when it created images of him (Isa. 42:8; 48:11).

This glory belongs to God intrinsically (1 Chr. 29:11). It is not some accidental feature of God's character, but an essential quality in it. His name is majestic (Ps. 8:1; cf. 102:15). The inherent glory of God is obviously in mind in such references as Ps. 29:2, "the glory due his name," or 63:2, "I have seen you in the sanctuary / and beheld your power and your glory" (see also 113:4; 138:5; Isa. 59:19; cf. Pss. 79:9; 96:8). When Isaiah saw the majestic holiness of God, the SERAPHS cried out, "the whole earth is full of his glory" (Isa. 6:3). So majestic is God's glory that to see his face is to die (Exod. 33:20), and it is considered remarkable that any should see his face and live (Gen. 16:13; 32:30; Deut. 4:33; 5:24; Jdg. 6:22–23). Paul writes of "the glory of the immortal God" (Rom. 1:23). A person's glory—wealth, reputation, honor—may be taken away, but that person remains human; God, on the other hand, cannot be God without his glory. For this reason he is jealous about it; his creatures must not infringe upon it. The intention of God is that human beings and all creation should give glory to him. We must not glory in his wisdom, might, or riches, but rather in understanding the Lord (Jer. 9:23–24). He who boasts must "boast in the Lord" (1 Cor. 1:31; cf. 1 Pet. 2:9). This principle is well summed up in the first question of the *Westminster Shorter Catechism*: "Man's chief end is to glorify God." We must not take to ourselves glory that belongs to God.

Much less may we attribute God's glory to false gods. "I will not give my glory to another / or my praise to idols" (Isa. 42:8; cf. 48:11; Rom. 1:23). Having demanded exclusive worship in the first commandment, God prohibits image worship in the second. See TEN COMMANDMENTS. The prohibition arises from an apprehension of God's glory—glory of such a nature that no earthly form can be given to it (Deut. 4:15); it cannot be represented by an idol. John Calvin says, "God's glory is corrupted by an impious falsehood whenever any form is attached to him" (*Institutes of the Christian Religion* 1.11.1; Battles trans., 1:100). Isaiah is forthright on this point. He asks, "To whom, then, will you compare God? / What image will you compare him to?" (Isa. 40:18). He then shows the folly of representing such a glorious person by an idol (cf. 41:7; 44:9–20; 46:5–7). PAUL speaks likewise to the Athenians: "Therefore since we are God's offspring, we should not think that the divine being is like gold or silver or stone—an image made by man's design and skill" (Acts 17:29). God's glory is God himself, and as such he cannot be represented by any human image; nor does he need any such image to glorify him—in fact, in so representing him we dishonor him.

Whereas the glory of God is his essentially and inherently, the major emphasis of Scripture is on its manifestation: the self-revelation of God's being and character. ISAIAH summarizes this point, "Arise, shine, for your light has come, / and the glory of the LORD rises upon you. / See, darkness covers the earth / and thick darkness is over the peoples, / but the LORD rises upon you / and his glory appears over you" (Isa. 60:1–2). When MOSES requested to see God's glory, he was told, "I will cause all my goodness to pass in front of you, and I will proclaim my name, the LORD, in your presence" (Exod. 33:18). Isaiah warns the unfaithful to hide in the dust / from the terror of the LORD, / and from the glory of his majesty" (Isa. 2:10; cf. vv. 19, 21). He had in mind a frightening revelation of God himself. In Num. 14:22, the revelation of his glory is associated with the signs in Egypt. According to A. Richardson, "The glory of God is thus in effect the term used to express what we can comprehend, originally by sight, of the presence of God on the earth."

Specific examples of the appearance of the glory of God may now be considered. When Moses received the law, "the glory of the LORD settled on Mount Sinai," and "the appearance of the glory of the LORD was like a devouring fire on the top of the mountain in the sight of the people of Israel" (Exod. 24:16–17; cf. Deut. 5:24). The glory was also manifest in the cloud that accompanied Israel, and particularly when this cloud was associated with the tabernacle and temple. See PILLAR OF FIRE AND OF CLOUD; SHEKINAH. The tent was to be sanctified by God's glory (Exod. 29:43). When the TABERNACLE was erected, "the cloud covered the Tent of Meeting, and the glory of the LORD filled the tabernacle" (Exod. 40:34; cf. Lev. 9:6, 23). So impressive was the cloud of glory that Moses could not enter the tabernacle. The same phenomena appeared in the TEMPLE (1 Ki. 8:10–11; 2 Chr. 5:13–14; cf. Ezek. 44:4). In 2 Chr. 7:1–2, fire and the glory of the Lord are associated (cf. Exod. 40:38; Num. 9:16; Ezek. 43:2–5; Zech. 2:5).

The cloud of glory also appeared to vindicate and protect God's servants, particularly Moses and Aaron. When the Israelites grumbled at scanty provision, God's glory appeared in a cloud (Exod. 16:7, 10). The same occurred when they were in danger because of the spies' report (Num. 14:10). At KADESH, the people grumbled because of lack of water, and God's glory appeared (20:6). It also appeared for the purpose of settling matters in the dispute with KORAH, DATHAN, and ABIRAM (16:19). In the NT, a bright light arrested Saul of Tarsus on his way to DAMASCUS to persecute the followers of Christ (Acts 9:3; 22:6). The death of Aaron's sons (Lev. 10:2–3) may be considered God's vindication of his glory in the sanctuary (cf. Isa. 2:10, 19, 21). God manifests himself in judgment and brings the pomp, pride, and rebellion of men to nought. In so doing, he protects his servants. Being jealous of his own glory and honor, he is also jealous about the welfare of his people. In this pleasing way, the glory of God appears in the history of his people.

Attention is often drawn to the somewhat physical way in which God's glory is mentioned in the OT. Examples of this are the cloud and fire, already mentioned, and the vision of God granted

During OT times, the manifestation of God's glory sometimes took the form of a cloud.

to Moses (Exod. 33:18—34:6) in the form of a tangible THEOPHANY. The Israelites saw his glory (Deut. 5:24–25). EZEKIEL is particularly notable in this connection; his vision of the glory of God had many physical characteristics. He gives a vivid description of "the appearance of the likeness of the glory of the LORD" (Ezek. 1:28b), which makes this clear. He describes it in many ways, such as a bright shining phenomenon resembling the rainbow (1:28a; cf. 3:12–13; 3:23; 8:4; 9:3; 10:4; 10:18–19; 11:22–23; 43:2). A physical manifestation is also involved in the vision to Isaiah (Isa. 6:1–5; cf. Jer. 17:12).

Too much stress can be laid on this evidence, as though implying that the God of the Hebrews was a physical being. As Ezekiel described the glory of God, he was describing something he saw in a vision (apart from Ezek. 39:21). The vision would have tangible form—it cannot be otherwise—because it is not an abstract idea but a concrete revelation. This does not mean that something physical was present. To the Hebrews, in any case, God was not an absolute abstraction, but one with whom they could have contact, and anthropomorphic terms were inevitable. See ANTHROPOMORPHISM. The Hebrews did not, however, view him as human, or earthly in shape and motion. Taking the Scripture as a whole, such physical conceptions are balanced out by the ethical ideas that attach to God's glory.

In Isa. 6 is a concrete vision, but the reaction of the prophet is not merely one of awe at God's majestic holiness but of humility before his moral attributes. Ezekiel also connects glory with judgment (Ezek. 39:21). It is associated with righteousness in Ps. 97:6, "The heavens proclaim his righteousness, / and all the peoples see his glory" (cf. Isa. 40:4.; 60:1–3). Paul sums up sin as a falling short of God's glory (Rom. 3:23; cf. 1:23; 3:7; 5:2; 2 Cor. 3:18); he also describes the actions of God, the Father of glory, in the realm of wisdom and understanding (Eph. 1:17). It would be a mistake to associate this word primarily with the physical. It endeavors to describe the indescribable God, and human terms are inevitable, but it is not a balanced scriptural view to say that in Ezekiel, or anywhere else, glory is viewed as exclusively physical.

Because the glory of God is so much involved in his self-disclosure, man cannot ignore the revelation in Scripture itself, which is a light shining in a dark place (2 Pet. 1:19–20). Whereas the most glorious revelation is Christ, the extant knowledge of this revelation is in Scripture. The word *glory* thus embraces the whole biblical knowledge of God.

III. The glory of God in creation. The glory of God appears in creation as well as in theophanies. REVELATION itself presupposes the existence of the world to which revelation is made. To receive this revelation the world must be something of worth. An aspect of the glory of God belongs to creation. Several psalms view the whole of nature as praising God (Pss. 8; 148; 150; cf. 29:1–2; 104:31). It all glorifies God: "The heavens declare the glory of God" (19:1). "The voice of the LORD twists the oaks / and strips the forests bare. / And in his temple all cry, 'Glory!'" (29:9). Paul has the same conception in mind in Rom. 1:18–23. Though even God's "eternal power and divine nature" are obvious in the created world, the evils and idolatry of men dishonored his glory. Heavenly and earthly bodies each have their own distinctive glory (1 Cor. 15:40). In nature and in the world's history, God's glory is evident.

At present, many aspects of nature seem against the glory of God. Men concentrate on nature and forget God, or meet one of the maladjustments of nature and curse him. The blight on nature is a consequence of human sin (Gen. 3:17). Ultimately this curse shall be removed and "the earth will be filled with the knowledge of the glory of the LORD, / as the waters cover the sea" (Hab. 2:14; cf. Num. 14:21; Ps. 72:19; Isa. 6:3). Nature, animate and inanimate, human beings included, one day will give due glory to God. Then "the glory of the LORD will be revealed, and all mankind together will see it" (Isa. 40:5; cf. Lk. 3:6).

In reference more particularly to humanity, the word *kābôd* is used in some OT passages to describe a person's self. JACOB thus uses it, "Let not my soul enter their council, let not my glory join their assembly" (Gen. 49:6 lit. trans.; NIV, "Let me not enter…let me not join…"). The SEPTUAGINT here renders the word with Greek *ta hēpata mou* ("my insides," pl. of *hēpar*, "liver"), reading the Hebrew as *kĕbēdî* (from *kābēd* H3879, "liver"). Some suggest that this translation should be followed, in view of the Hebrew tendency to use organs of the body to describe psychological experiences. However, several other poetic passages support the reading *kĕbôdî* (rendered *hē doxa mou* by the LXX; e.g., Job 29:20; Ps. 57:8 [LXX 56:9]; et al.). This usage enshrines a great truth: human beings are made in the IMAGE OF GOD, possessing a glory that distinguishes them from the animals. He is "the image and glory of God" (1 Cor. 11:7).

When God created man, male and female, he declared that his CREATION was very good (Gen. 1:31). Man was intended to glorify God and at first he did this. He truly uplifted God in creation and gave him the glory due to his name (Ps. 96:8; cf. 66:2). This still remains the duty of the creature, however poorly he fulfills it. The case of the healed Samaritan leper illustrates this principle (Lk. 17:18; lit., "Was no one found to return and give glory to God except this foreigner?"). The advice of the PHARISEES, "Give glory to God" (Jn. 9:24), though hypocritically given, is still correct practice. The following considerations make clear that glorifying God covers all of life. Christians are to receive each other "for the glory of God" (Rom. 15:7 NRSV). The speaking and ministry of the Christian are to be "so that God may be glorified in all things through Jesus Christ" (1 Pet. 4:11 NRSV). All of life must be for his glory (1 Cor. 10:31). Our bodies must be kept pure for his glory (6:20; cf. Phil. 1:20). This duty is fulfilled in believers, who "are being transformed into his likeness with ever-increasing glory" (2 Cor. 3:18). On earth they reflect favorably on the honor of God (Eph. 1:6; 1 Pet. 2:9).

Although our whole duty is to glorify God, it is possible for us to become rebels and take to ourselves what really belongs to God. Calvin, having quoted Jer. 9:23–24 and 1 Cor. 1:29, says, "we never truly glory in him until we have utterly put off our own glory … whoever glories in himself, glories against God" (*Inst.* 3.13.2; Battles trans., 1:764). This perfectly sums up what the Lord says about the sin of receiving glory one from another (Jn. 5:41–44). In glorifying God, self-boasting must be excluded (Rom. 3:27; Eph. 2:8–9). The whole trouble since the FALL is the creature's attempt to become as God (Gen. 3:5), and as a result he does not fulfill his true destiny. He ruins his glory when he is a rebel. He is truly glorious only when he looks on God as God and the creature as creature.

IV. The glory of Christ. Whereas ADAM and his posterity failed to glorify God, Christ glorified his Father completely, so that at the end of his earthly life he could say, "I have brought you glory on earth by completing the work you gave me to do" (Jn. 17:4). He did what no person ever did; he glorified God in all he was, said, and did (cf. Heb. 2:6–10).

OT Israel expected the MESSIAH to be glorious. In the wilderness wanderings they possessed a forward look. The tabernacle was to be sanctified by God's glory when erected (Exod. 29:43). This forward look was present in the whole history of Israel; none of the religious achievements was final—more was to follow. The promise of a future glory is especially clear in the prophecy of Isaiah (e.g., Isa. 4:5; 11:10; 24:23; 40:5). Such longings and hopes find fulfillment either in the INCARNATION or the SECOND COMING of the Messiah.

The glory of Christ existed before the incarnation, since he was preexistent (Jn. 17:5; cf. v. 24; 2 Cor. 8:9; Phil. 2:6). This glory must have been personal and entirely divorced from any activity in revelation. But it was also closely related to his incarnate life (Jn. 1:14), which was completely glorifying to God, and which also was full of his own personal glory. He glorified God in making him known (1:18; 17:4, 6). B. F. Westcott, commenting on Jn. 2:11, remarks regarding the fourth gospel, "It represents the whole human life of Christ, under its actual condition of external want and suffering and of external conflict and sorrow, as a continuous and conscious manifestation of divine glory" (*The Gospel according to St. John: The Greek Text with Introduction and Notes* [1908], 100).

Also important to consider is the concept of the SHEKINAH glory (possibly alluded to in the Gk. verb *eskēnōsen*, "dwelt, tabernacled," Jn. 1:14; cf. Rev. 21:3). This term is derived from the Hebrew verb *šākan* H8905, "to dwell," and in the rabbinic writings it is used of God's presence among men, especially as manifested in the tabernacle and the temple. The TARGUMS used this word possibly to avoid any localization of God. Some rabbis spoke of Moses' face being bright because he shared the Shekinah. The idea in the NT can also be associated with the cloud that overshadowed Christ at the transfiguration, when a voice came from the majestic glory (2 Pet. 1:17; cf. Lk. 2:9; Acts 7:2; Rom. 9:4). A similar idea may be conveyed by the comment, "Above the ark were the cherubim of the Glory, overshadowing the atonement cover" (Heb. 9:5).

The glory of Christ, although always present, was also largely veiled in the incarnation. It flashed out in miracles (Jn. 2:11; 11:40) and words of wisdom, but largely "He had not beauty or majesty to attract us to him" (Isa. 53:2). He was just a carpenter to many. Paul maintains that because none of the rulers of this world recognized Christ for what he was, they put him to death (1 Cor. 2:8). He was crucified in weakness (2 Cor. 13:4). The glory was there, but the god of this world so blinded men that they saw his humanity only and not "the light of the knowledge of the glory of God in the face of Christ" (2 Cor. 4:4, 6; cf. Heb. 1:3). The same is still true.

The only instance where Jesus' glory became fully apparent was at the transfiguration (Matt. 17:1–8; Mk. 9:2–10; Lk. 9:28–36; cf. 2 Pet. 1:16–18). The cloud, the symbol of the divine presence, came over the disciples and Jesus, and his exceeding great glory was seen in his countenance and even in his garments. The transfiguration is not recorded in John, for John looks beyond the outward appearance and sees the whole life and death of Christ as a continuous demonstration of the glory of God. The glory of Christ was also seen after his ascension, in the revelation to Stephen (Acts 7:55–56; cf. 6:15), and in the vision that converted Saul of Tarsus (ch. 9; cf. chs. 22; 26). All people are to honor the Son even as they honor the Father (Jn. 5:23). To do this they must see his real glory. The redeemed of the Lord do see it and in heaven they glorify him as they should (Rev. 5:12–13).

It is easier to see the glory of Christ in miracles and in the transfiguration than in the humility of his death; yet this event was his crowning earthly glory. He did not go to it as a helpless victim but as "a victorious being to his crowning." His sufferings were an entrance into his glory (Lk. 24:26). Several other verses refer to the glory of the cross. For instance, "The hour has come for the Son of Man to be glorified" (Jn. 12:23; see also 17:1; Lk. 9:31; Jn. 7:39; 12:16; 13:31–32; 17:4). In Heb. 2:9 he is spoken of as being "crowned with glory and honor because he suffered death," and in Revelation the slain Lamb is viewed as worthy of glory (Rev. 5:12). The gospel, which centers in the CROSS, shows the riches of his glory (Col. 1:27; cf. Eph. 1:18). Paul gloried in the cross (Gal. 6:14). The cross did not enhance his personal glory; it was rather a glorious accomplishment by an already perfectly glorious person.

After his death came the glory of his RESUR-

Artistic motif of Jesus' transfiguration (from the Church of Transfiguration on Mount Tabor).

RECTION and ASCENSION. They are involved in the glory that followed his death (Lk. 24:26). God glorified him by his resurrection and ascension. He was raised from the dead by the glory of God the Father (Rom. 6:4). After being raised, God gave him glory (1 Pet. 1:21). He has been taken up in glory (1 Tim. 3:16) and is now in glory at God's right hand (Acts 7:55–56; cf. Mk. 16:19; Acts 2:33; 3:13; 3:21; 1 Cor. 15:27; Eph. 1:20; Phil. 2:9–11; Heb. 1:3–4). Whereas his whole life was glorious, the resurrection and ascension vindicated all his claims and overshadowed with glory the victory of the cross. This glory was not new, but a resumption of the glory he had before the incarnation (Jn. 17:5, 24).

V. Eschatological glory. Earlier conceptions and hopes are gathered up in the word *glory* when it is used eschatologically. The NT era is the last hour (1 Jn. 2:18) and is in many ways the fulfillment of OT eschatological longings. The glory of the Lord was truly revealed (Isa. 40:5; cf. Ps. 97:6; 102:16; Isa. 24:23; 58:8; 59:19). The NT accepts this truth and applies it to Christ, but it also contains its own eschatological longings. Paul describes longings for the deliverance and glorification of nature (Rom. 8:18–21; cf. 1 Cor. 15; Col. 1:27; 1 Thess. 4:13–18). See ESCHATOLOGY.

The future glory of Christ receives the major emphasis eschatologically. He shall "come in his Father's glory" (Matt. 16:27; Mk. 8:38; Lk. 9:26). He shall come on the clouds with "power and great glory" (Matt. 24:30; Mk. 13:26; Lk. 21:27). He shall sit on his glorious throne (Matt. 19:28; 25:31; cf. Dan. 7:13–14). Even when his teaching regarding the cross upset the disciples, the sons of Zebedee saw his future glory (Mk. 10:37). The glory that always was his will no longer be hidden; it will be revealed (1 Pet. 4:13; cf. Tit. 2:13).

Popularly, heaven is spoken of as glory, and the idea is not absent in Scripture (cf. Ps. 73:24; Jn. 17:24; 2 Pet. 1:17). The future of the Christian may be considered as the restoration of the *doxa* lost at the fall. Adam must have been radiant with God's glory when the divine image was unimpaired (Gen. 1:31). This idea is also reflected in Ps. 8, where man is viewed as crowned with glory and honor. The ideal is, under present conditions, realized only in Christ (Heb. 2). In the latter passage, the comment that "at present we do not see everything subject to [man]" (v. 8) indicates that this also shall be seen in due course. Scripture elsewhere puts the matter more clearly, showing that man shall have the glory restored to him. Christ is the true image of God (2 Cor. 4:4; Col. 1:15) and we are even now "being transformed into his likeness with ever-increasing glory" (2 Cor. 3:18).

Christ is in us as the hope of glory (Col. 1:27). Ultimately, redeemed sinners shall be conformed to this image (Rom. 8:29). We shall be like him (1 Jn. 3:2) and be satisfied with beholding his form (Ps. 17:15). Our bodies shall be like his glorious body (Phil. 3:21; 1 Cor. 15:42–43). Having had the glory restored to us, we will become what we were originally intended to be. The wise shall shine (Dan. 12:3). We will share a glorious inheritance (Eph. 1:18). The riches of God's glory will be shown in us (Rom. 9:23). Christ will be glorified in his saints (2 Thess. 1:10). Crowns shall be given at that day (2 Tim. 4:8; cf. 1 Pet. 5:4). We shall "appear with him in glory" (Col. 3:4). The word that sums up the final state of the believer is *glorification*.

(See further I. Abrahams, *The Glory of God* [1925]; L. H. Brockington in *ExpTim* 57 [1945–46]: 21–25; E. G. Selwyn, *The First Epistle of Peter* [1949], 250–58; A. M. Ramsey, *The Glory of God and the Transfiguration of Christ* [1949]; A. Richardson, *An Introduction to the Theology of the New Testament* [1962], 64–67; B. Ramm, *Them He Glorified: A Systematic Study of the Doctrine of Glorification* [1963]; W. Grudem, *Systematic Theology: An Introduction to Biblical Doctrine* [1994], ch. 42.)

M. R. GORDON

glossolalia glos´uh-lay´lee-uh. See TONGUES, GIFT OF.

gluttony. The term *glutton* can be used to render the participle of the Hebrew verb *zālal* H2361, which means "to be frivolous, profligate" (Deut. 21:21; Prov. 23:20–21). In the NT, it renders Greek *phagos* G5741 (Matt. 11:19; Lk. 7:34) and *gastēr* G1143, lit., "belly" (Tit. 1:12). See SELF-CONTROL.

gnashing the teeth. This expression is used in Hebrew poetic passages to indicate the hatred and scorn of enemies (verb *ḥāraq* H3080, Job 16:9; Pss. 35:16; 37:12; 112:10; Lam. 2:16). The Greek verb *brychō* G1107 is used similarly with reference to the rage of STEPHEN's enemies (Acts 7:54), while the cognate noun *brygmos* G1106 occurs repeatedly in the sayings of Jesus concerning the remorseful gnashing of teeth by those excluded from heaven (Matt. 8:12; 13:42, 50; 22:13; 24:51; 25:30; Lk. 13:28; see HELL). Another verb, *trizō* G5563, describes the epileptic's grating sound (Mk. 9:18).

E. RUSSELL

gnat. This English term, which can refer to various kinds of small, biting, two-winged flies, occurs primarily as a rendering of Hebrew *kēn* H4031 (only pl. *kinnîm*) in connection with the plagues in Egypt (Exod. 8:16–18; Ps. 105:31; some believe the word refers to LICE, while others have suggested mosquitoes, ticks, and maggots). Lands such as EGYPT, with flooding rivers, provide unlimited breeding places for insects like gnats and mosquitoes. Eggs are laid in water, occasionally in damp places, and at certain seasons, when suitable water suddenly becomes available and temperatures are high, breeding is almost explosive. As the adults emerge from the water they go in search of blood, and many kinds are indiscriminate in their hosts. Mosquitoes transmit some of the world's most widespread diseases, including malaria and filariasis.

The details of the OT narrative (Exod. 8:17, "All the dust throughout the land of Egypt became gnats") are clearly figurative to some degree and need not preclude the rendering *gnat*. G. Hort (in *ZAW* 69 [1957]: 84–103) sees the first nine plagues as a logical and connected sequence in which natural phenomena are used by God to fulfill his purpose, the miracle being in the timing, extent, intensity, etc. and above all in their control. The translation *gnat* would perhaps fit this sequence best.

The term is also used once in the NT: "You blind guides! You strain out a gnat [*kōnōps* G3270] but swallow a camel" (Matt. 23:24; from the Gk. word is derived the term *Conopidae*, a family of two-winged flies). The statement alludes to the Jewish orthodox habit of straining wine or drinking it through a piece of cloth to avoid ritual contamination by taking forbidden meat. (See further *FFB*, 35–36.)

G. S. CANSDALE

Gnosticism nos´tuh-siz´uhm. Derived from Greek *gnōsis* G1194, "knowledge," this term is variously applied to certain movements within, or in relation to, early Christianity.

I. Connotations. In the past, the term *Gnosticism* was applied collectively to the majority of those 2nd-cent. movements that called themselves Christian (or borrowed heavily from Christian sources) but were rejected by the mainstream of Christian tradition (represented in such fathers as IRENAEUS, Hippolytus, and EPIPHANIUS). Neither the fathers nor the groups themselves, however, apply the title in this sense. The former use it only of certain groups and designate the whole simply "the heresies," while the latter prefer to use the distinctive names of particular groups. There are, however, certain common features, among them a dominating concern with KNOWLEDGE.

Since these common features (indicated below) appear in some other forms of contemporary Hellenistic religion, and since a concern for knowledge is evident in the NT, there is now a tendency to use the term more widely. Some employ it of any form of dualistic teaching with sharply opposed principles of good and evil that offers knowledge as a key to the struggle, and others apply it to the myth of a supramundane Redeemer found in some forms of Hellenistic religion apparently derived from Eastern, probably Iranian, sources. From different points of view, therefore, the term has been applied to the QUMRAN sect, PAUL, the fourth gospel (see JOHN, GOSPEL OF), and the Alexandrian fathers (see CLEMENT OF ALEXANDRIA; ORIGEN). It seems best for the moment to use the term with reference to the 2nd-cent. Christian and post-Christian movements, without prejudice to the question of their significance for Christian origins. (Many contemporary scholars prefer to use the term *Gnosis* to indicate the general movement, including its 1st-cent. manifestations, while reserving *Gnosticism* for the later, more complex system, characterized especially by the Redeemer myth. Others question the validity of such a distinction.)

II. The common features of Gnosticism. Anyone who reads through the books of Irenaeus or Hippolytus against heresies will be struck by the wide variety of these movements. There are Gnostic systems that make testing intellectual demands, others that depend on mumbo-jumbo and sleight of hand. Some Gnostic leaders are high-minded ascetics, and others are licentious charlatans. Nevertheless, they all offer knowledge—and in a form or degree not to be found outside their own teaching. This concern for knowledge links the higher and the lower forms of Gnosticism. At its lowest, the knowledge offered related simply to power and secrets of the future—the same sort of things as those for which people consulted astrologers and fortune tellers, but put into a religious setting. In its higher forms, it is related to abstract speculation, grappling with problems that had long been obstacles for educated pagans: how came good and evil into the world, and how do they relate to God?

Sometimes, too, it is special knowledge about Jesus that is proffered, on the basis of secret, closely guarded sources. The essential content of the knowledge offered in many of the systems we know of is summarized in a passage preserved in Clement of Alexandria: "who we were, and what we have become, what we were, where we were placed, whither we hasten, from what we are redeemed, what birth is, what rebirth" (*Excerpta ex Theodoto* 78.2). Implied in this description is the thought of the individual SOUL entering the world from the outside and passing from it. And the Gnostic sought the key both to the origins of an evil world and to his salvation from that world.

Knowledge and salvation were keynotes of much 2nd-cent. religion: this is what people wanted from the MYSTERY RELIGIONS and explains their contemporary popularity. The Gnostic teachers sought to provide for these longings in a way that was both Christian and compatible with the basic assumptions about God and the world held by most people of the day. These assumptions might be formed by contemporary philosophy, by mythology, or by astrology; and in different Gnostic systems, these factors appear in differing degrees. What they have in common is a desire to be contemporary.

There was nothing peculiarly Gnostic about the common assumptions: these can be found, for example, in the anti-Christian writer Celsus, whom no one would call a Gnostic. Celsus believed that God is so utterly transcendent that he can have no direct contact with the world; that matter is inherently evil and can have no contact with God; and that human beings, or at least some of them, have within them a spark of the divine which is now incarcerated in the material prison of the body. Man is thus a creature of mixed origin, a mixture of incompatibles (Origen, *Contra Celsum*, passim). It is for such reasons as these that Celsus regards Christianity as self-condemned: the claim that God became man is impossible, since God and matter could not mix. (The old myths talked of the gods appearing in human shape: no one suggested that they *were* human while in it.)

The Gnostics, however, are trying to square Celsus' assumptions with the Christian proclamation. Not surprisingly, both have to give something: the proportions, and thus the degree of closeness to traditional Christianity, vary in the different systems. In some, such as the system of VALENTINUS (who was at one time a serious candidate for the bishopric of Rome), a fairly orthodox Christian confession could be made, though there was little room for it in the system itself. In others, such as apparently the Ophite sect (a serpent-worshipping group), all pretense at continuity with mainstream Christianity was given up, though this did not prevent large-scale borrowings from the Bible and Christian tradition. And, of course, the movements evolved and changed; BASILIDES, for instance, seems to have held a reasonably orthodox view of Christ (Hippolytus, *Refutation* 7.26); but within fifty years, according to Irenaeus, followers of Basilides believed that Jesus was never crucified (*Against Heresies* 1.19.11–12).

Of the movement as a whole, however, we can say the following: (a) It is rationalistic, seeking to answer questions outside the scope of the OT and the apostolic witness, and to do so on wholly non-biblical assumptions. (b) It is mystical, in the sense of pursuing identification with and absorption in the divine (see, e.g., the spectacular Ophite liturgy quoted by Origen, *Contra Celsum* 6.31). (c) It is mythological, employing MYTH to express truth, as an essential supplement to (or in some cases substitute for) the biblical tradition.

Marble carving of the god Mithra slaying a bull (2nd cent. A.D.). Gnosticism had points of contact with the mystery religions such as Mithraism.

III. The Gnostic crux.
The collision of Christian and Greek assumptions directed attention to the origin of evil in the world. For those reared

on Greek assumptions, the question might be formulated as, How does the divinely originated soul become imprisoned in matter, and how can it escape? For teachers believing in the love and goodness of God, these posed particular problems. The general answer is to give a mythological scheme, in which redemption becomes a drama played out among cosmic forces—the "principalities and powers" of the NT, or the astral forces in a good deal of contemporary religion.

IV. The revision of Christian theology.

The central Christian tradition represented in the apostles maintained the peculiar features of the Jewish faith in which it had been born: monotheistic, historical, eschatological, ethical, and exclusive. The Redeemer continued to be styled *Christ*, a direct translation of the Hebrew *Messiah*. The Jewish concern with God's interventions in human history was retained and enlarged: preaching concentrated, indeed, on the historical events of the life and death and resurrection of Jesus. Though the law was abandoned, the idea of a moral commitment directly watched over by God remained. The peculiarly Jewish belief in the resurrection and last judgment was retained, and the Jewish Scriptures continued to be read. And though the idea of a people of God defined by physical descent disappeared, the solidarity of a single "Israel of God," in continuity with the OT Israel, meant the continuing consciousness of a single worshiping community, a "third race" alongside Jew and Gentile. Gnostic reformulation was bound to collide with all these elements.

A. The doctrine of God. GOD is conceived of as remote from all the material creation. The gap between is filled by a hierarchy of intermediary beings, in a descending order of magnitude. These are *aeons*, often linked in pairs or syzygies (usually male and female), and are collectively given the name PLEROMA (fullness). The earliest may be the result of God's creative act; the others emanate from them. There are different myths as to the origin of our world; but all agree that it was a mistake, an accident, the work of an ignorant being, or the mischief of an antigod. One picture of the material universe is that of an abortion self-generated by the inordinate desire of a female aeon (*Sophia*, "wisdom"); and some systems attempt to reconcile this view with such passages as Jn. 1:3 by describing the LOGOS in creation as giving form to the misshapen abortion, which thus combines the principles of good and evil. In other systems, of which the most influential was that of MARCION, creation is the work of a Demiurge, an inferior divinity.

B. The Old Testament. Clearly such a scheme does not reflect the Creator/Vindicator God of the OT. Accordingly, teachers like Cerdo and Marcion frankly abandon the OT and regard themselves as liberating the church from the fetters of the JUDAIZERS. Since one can be truly radical with the OT only by being truly radical with the NT, many of those who wished to keep contact with the apostolic writings were forced to try to accommodate the OT. A long, thoughtful letter from the Valentinian theologian Ptolemy (quoted in Epiphanius, *Panarion* 33) offers a tripartite division of the OT: part is from God, part from Moses acting as law giver, part from the elders. The first part is eternal, if incomplete; the second was temporary and is now abrogated; the third is symbolical and is now transformed.

C. Nature of authority. The Ptolemy already mentioned tells his correspondent, "You will learn the order and the begetting of all these [aeons] if you are deemed worthy of knowing the apostolic tradition which we have received from a succession, together with the confirmation of all our words by the teaching of the Saviour." That is, he is claiming access to a superior source of secret knowledge. Valentinian and other "right wing" Gnostics paid lip service to the same authority as the mainstream church: the Lord and his apostles. They had to show that they possessed reliable knowledge conveyed by the apostles (and thus ultimately from the Lord) which other Christians did not. The Valentinians claimed a tradition from a disciple of Paul called Theudas; the Basilidians from Peter, via one Glaukias, and from Matthias. More exotic groups often chose James the Lord's brother as their source, or Thomas (*Didymus*, "the Twin," being taken to be the Lord's twin) as being very close to the person of the Savior. The now famous Gospel of Thomas (Logion 12) insinuates that Thomas is a source of tradition superior to Matthew and Peter, the apostles associated with the first two Gospels (see THOMAS, GOSPEL OF).

D. Incarnation and atonement. If God's transcendence implies the impossibility of his contact with matter, how could God take a human body, still less suffer in one? There are several Gnostic answers, depending on the degree of closeness to the central Christian tradition. Some reject the idea of INCARNATION altogether: Christ was only an "appearance" of God in human form, he only *seemed* to suffer. Others spoke of the divine Logos resting on the righteous but human Jesus but being withdrawn at the PASSION (the cry of dereliction, Mk. 15:34, was held to be evidence of this). Others again used the traditional language, but emphasized not the historical events of the incarnation, but the relations between the disordered elements of the pleroma, which the incarnation righted. For Basilides the important fact seems to be that Jesus had within himself all the elements of creation; his passion is related to the ordering of its confusion (Hippolytus, *Refutation* 7.27). He is basically interested in the question, Whence comes evil? rather than the question, How is sin forgiven? Likewise Valentinus in the *Gospel of Truth* (discovered at NAG HAMMADI) uses traditional language about the cross without finding a clear place for this very mundane event in his complex drama of redemption among the aeons (see TRUTH, GOSPEL OF).

E. Sin and salvation. Evil is associated with matter, ignorance, formlessness, distortion. Consequently SALVATION means to slough off defilement rather than to receive forgiveness for offenses. Salvation comes as illumination dispelling ignorance, triumphing over the material. The gospel is principally a means whereby people *know* the truth; the cosmic bodies receive the same instruction.

F. Judgment and resurrection. These doctrines were a constant source of difficulty for those who sought immortality in *escape* from the body. RESURRECTION, and the whole eschatological dimension associated with it, is noticeably missing from Gnostic schemes.

G. The church and the Christian life. Some schools divided mankind into three according to the predominant element in their constitutions: (1) the material, who could not be saved; (2) the "psychic," who could receive some purification; (3) and the spiritual, the elite capable of receiving the deep mysteries. Naturally the third class were the Gnostics, the mass of Christians forming the second class. The church becomes the club of the illuminated, not the society of the redeemed. The view that the material is the seat of evil leads, in some systems, to asceticism, celibacy, and vegetarianism; in others, paradoxically, to license, for "liberation" from matter meant its effects were inconsequential.

V. The origins of Gnosticism. Continental scholars have often argued that Gnosticism is of pre-Christian origin, the figure of a cosmic redeemer being taken over from Eastern, specifically Iranian, sources, from which DUALISM also primarily comes. Some would even see the essence of Gentile (indeed, Pauline) Christianity as the superimposition of the Gnostic Redeemer on the historical Jesus. No one has yet shown, however, that the Gnostic Redeemer existed before Christian times, and the Qumran documents have shown that Pauline and Johannine language about knowledge was firmly rooted in Jewish tradition. R. M. Grant has even suggested that Gnosticism itself is of Jewish origin: the fruit of unorthodox speculation working upon an apocalyptic framework that the fall of Jerusalem in A.D. 70 had caused to be reevaluated. Certainly the Nag Hammadi documents suggest the effect of Jewish speculation.

The "Colossian heresy" combined Jewish and ascetic features, philosophical activity, and veneration of astral powers (Col. 2:16–23), and when Paul speaks of the whole *pleroma* dwelling in Christ (1:19), it is tempting to see him taking the word which the Gnostics used of their scheme of intermediary beings, disinfecting it and replacing it, as it were, by Christ. But neither the Colossians nor the Corinthians, nor the groups attacked in the Pastoral Epistles or 1 John, display a Gnostic system of the type reflected in the 2nd-cent. movements. The Corinthians delighted unduly in knowledge (1 Cor. 8:1; 13:8) and wisdom (1:17–31), were unhappy about the thought of resurrection (ch. 15), included both those who questioned whether a Christian could marry (ch. 7) and those whose "liberation" left them indifferent to their bodies' actions (6:12–18). Others possessed "*gnosis* falsely so-called" (1 Tim. 6:20), had mythologies and genealogies (1:4), spiritualized the resurrection (2 Tim. 2:18), played with "Jewish myths" (Tit. 1:14), and knew both severe asceticism (1 Tim. 4:3) and sexual laxity (2 Tim. 3:6). The elder feared those who taught a docetic, "phantom" Christ (1 Jn. 4:1–3). All these show what fertile soil the early church provided for Gnostic teaching; but they show no sign of the systematized Gnosticism of the 2nd cent.

The HERMETIC WRITINGS, some of which are pre-Christian, with their mystical quest for illumination and rebirth, also often remind one of some Gnostic documents; and the mystery religions (with the notorious problems of dating material which they present) afford other parallels. All this simply reflects what was indicated earlier, that Gnosticism was a natural fruit of the 2nd-cent. religious quests in the Hellenistic world, with its Greek assumptions, Eastern religion, and astrological fatalism. These tendencies did not together constitute a system: but, coming into contact with a system or articulated preaching, they could form one. Coming into contact with Christianity, they took the Christian Redeemer and gnosticized him, took the Christian preaching and tore it from its OT roots, took the biblical tradition and sought to make it answer the problems of Greek philosophy, took the Christian convictions about the end and purged away such offensively Jewish features as resurrection and judgment.

Gnosticism was parasitic and took its shape from the system to which it attached itself. Looked at from another point of view, it was cultural, an outcome of the attempt to digest and "indigenize" Christianity. It need not surprise us, therefore, that some of the same tendencies appear in other 2nd-cent. Christians, even among those who brought about the eventual defeat of Christian Gnosticism. It may be hard for us who have been formed in another thought world, and who do not have the same inbred assumptions, to understand either the attractions of the Gnostic systems or the agonies and difficulties of many mainstream Christian theologians. It is the measure of their greatness that, sharing so much with the Gnostics intellectually as they did, by faithfulness to the historic Christ and the biblical tradition they produced an "indigenous" Greek-Gentile Christian thought that retained the primitive preaching and the whole of the Scriptures.

Being a phenomenon arising essentially from a particular historical and cultural situation, Gnosticism was not likely to outlast that situation long. The crisis for Gnosticism probably came with the emergence of the genuinely Iranian, radically dualistic religion of Mani (d. A.D. 277), which was spreading in the Roman empire from the 3rd cent. onward. The MANICHEAN doctrine must have faced many Christian Gnostics with a crucial choice: it could not long be possible to occupy a middle ground between mainstream Christianity and the books of Mani.

VI. The sources. Until the middle of the 20th cent., the Gnostic writers were known almost entirely through the writings of their antagonists. Of these, Irenaeus (*Against Heresies*), Hippolytus (*Refutation of all Heresies*), and Epiphanius (*Panarion*) provide extracts, often sizable, from Gnostic works. The second half of the 20th cent. saw the gradual publication of items from a Gnostic library discovered at NAG HAMMADI in Egypt and containing Coptic translations of works of very diverse character (English trans. in *NHL*). These include many writings further removed from the Christian tradition, some Manichean ones, the *Gospel of Truth* (prob. by Valentinus), and a *Gospel of Thomas* consisting of sayings attributed to the risen Lord (a number of which are gnosticized variants on synoptic sayings). While there is much still to be done in the study of these documents, the conclusion emerging from them is that the early fathers — for all their bias, trenchancy of language, and even exaggerations — present a picture of Gnosticism that is not far from the facts.

(The standard introduction is K. Rudolph, *Gnosis: The Nature and History of Gnosticism* [1984]. Other valuable works include H. E. W. Turner, *The Pattern of Christian Truth* [1954]; R. Bultmann, *Primitive Christianity in its Original Setting* [1956]; R. McL. Wilson, *The Gnostic Problem* [1958]; R. M. Grant, *Gnosticism and Early Christianity*, 2nd ed. [1966]; R. McL. Wilson, *Gnosis and the New*

Testament [1968]; H. Jonas, *The Gnostic Religion: The Message of the Alien God and the Beginnings of Christianity*, 2nd ed. [1970]; W. Schmithals, *The Office of Apostle in the Early Church* [1971], 114–230; B. Layton, *The Rediscovery of Gnosticism*, 2 vols. [1978–81]; E. M. Yamauchi, *Pre-Christian Gnosticism* [1983]; B. Layton, *The Gnostic Scriptures: A New Translation with Annotations and Introductions* [1987]; W. Wink, *Cracking the Gnostic Code: The Powers in Gnosticism* [1993]; A. H. B. Logan, *Gnostic Truth and Christian Heresy: A Study in the History of Gnosticism* [1996]; R. Roukema, *Gnosis and Faith in Early Christianity: An Introduction to Gnosticism* [1999]; K. L. King, *What Is Gnosticism?* [2003]; B. A. Pearson, *Gnosticism and Christianity in Roman and Coptic Egypt* [2004]; C. B. Smith II, *No Longer Jews: The Search for Gnostic Origins* [2004]; A. Mastrocinque, *From Jewish Magic to Gnosticism* [2005]; B. A. Pearson, *Ancient Gnosticism: Traditions and Literature* [2007].) A. F. Walls

goad. A sharp stick used for prodding cattle, particularly during plowing. It could have an iron tip (cf. 1 Sam. 13:21; Heb. *dorbān H1995*) and also could be utilized for cleaning plows, probably with a blade on the other end. Shamgar used an oxgoad as a spear while killing 600 Philistines (Jdg. 3:31; Heb. *bāqār malmād H1330 + H4913*), a detail that possibly reflects the lack of real weapons because of the Philistine iron monopoly. In a metaphorical sense, the words of the wise are compared to goads as they encourage and rebuke (Eccl. 12:11). The only NT use of the term concerns Christ's rebuke to Paul on the Damascus road for kicking against the goads (Acts 26:14; Gk. *kentron G3034*), which refers not to "the prickings of an uneasy conscience over his persecuting activity but [to] the new forces which were now impelling him in the opposite direction to that which he had hitherto pursued" (F. F. Bruce, *The Acts of the Apostles: The Greek Text with Introduction and Commentary*, 3rd ed. [1990], 501, which includes parallels to this proverb in classical literature). H. M. Wolf

Goah goh′uh (גֹּעָה [or גֹּעָת] *H1717*, possibly from גָּעָה *H1716*, "to low, bellow"). KJV Goath. An area in or near Jerusalem that would serve as one of the boundaries prophesied for the rebuilt city (Jer. 31:39; the Heb. text has the locative form *gōʿātâ*). See Gareb (place).

goat. The primary Hebrew word for "goat" (*Capra hircus mambrica*) is *ʿēz H6436*, generally found in nonsacrificial contexts (Gen. 30:32–35 et al.), but also used for sacrificial animals, especially in connection with the sin offering (e.g., Lev. 4:23–24, with *śāʿîr H8538*). Other Hebrew terms include *ʿattûd H6966*, "he-goat" (Gen. 31:10 et al.; fig., "leader," Isa. 14:9), and *gĕdî H1531*, "young goat, kid" (Exod. 21:19 et al.; this word can be used for the young of other animals). In the NT, "goat" is the rendering of Greek *eriphos G2253* (Matt. 25:32 [diminutive *eriphion G2252* in v. 33]; Lk. 15:29) and *tragos G5543* (Heb. 9:12–13; 10:4). In English, male and female goats are properly called he-goat and she-goat, but billy(-goat) and nanny(-goat) are much used.

I. Origin and domestication. Many authorities consider the goat to have been the first domesticated ruminant. The main wild ancestor still survives: the bezoar, or Cretan wild goat (*Capra aegagrus*), which is reddish-brown in summer and gray-brown in winter. Its overall range is from India to Crete, but its numbers have been much reduced; it has disappeared from many areas, and elsewhere is very rare. A few remain in the mountain parts of Crete and an island of the Cyclades. Other wild goats from farther E have contributed to the stock, but the position is complicated. (See F. E. Zeuner, *A History of Domesticated Animals* [1963], ch. 6.) All are hill animals and very sure-

Goats grazing in the wilderness of Judah.

footed; they are browsers as much as grazers. Two factors add to the problem of dating: first, for some time the tame form did not differ markedly from the wild; second, in many cases even experts cannot distinguish some bones of sheep and goats.

The earliest accepted evidence for domestication is from the Neolithic pre-pottery levels of JERICHO, with carbon dating of 6000–7000 B.C. The remains of some horns show damage suggestive of close confinement. Material from N Iran is of similar age, probably indicating an earlier origin from which both areas were supplied. Among the early goats, two types are recognized: those with corkscrew and those with scimitar horns. Gradually the variety increased in size, proportions, color, and hair type; but the wide range of breeds now seen, especially in Europe, is of modern origin. These show a wide range of colors, including black, white, and parti-colored. The only biblical mention of color is the spotted and speckled goats of Gen. 30. Ancient Egyptian art illustrates all these.

II. Uses. The goat was first kept for its milk. The meat of the young was eaten, and it was apparently the standard meal for strangers arriving unexpectedly (cf. Jdg. 6:19). Later, the kid was less highly rated (it is compared unfavorably with a fattened calf, Lk. 15:29–30). Goatskins became the standard material for water bottles in countries of limited rainfall, and the hair was spun and woven into cloth. It seems that the SHEEP was tamed fairly soon after the goat. Sheep began to replace goats in the areas where it could thrive, that is, the less hilly places with better grazing, largely because it yielded much better meat, with ample fat, and WOOL instead of rather coarse hair. The goat was still valued as a milk-producer, but when the domestic cow became available, the goat was more and more confined to the rougher and drier areas. By the time of the PATRIARCHS, sheep and cattle probably greatly outnumbered goats. Milk is mentioned frequently in the OT, but only four passages refer specifically to goats' milk (and three of these deal with the prohibition against seething or boiling a kid in its mother's milk, Exod. 23:19 et al.).

III. Damage to vegetation. Second to humans, and with their help, goats have been the most important land-destroyers in history (see FAUNA). In Mediterranean lands, they climb trees and destroy them by eating twigs and leaves. This is illustrated in ancient art. The goat is hardy and, if allowed to escape, can quickly establish itself and develop a feral race. The damage to vegetation continues, sometimes until the habitat is destroyed; in an island, goats die of starvation.

IV. Place in biblical narrative. Numerous references in both OT and NT show that the goat was important to the Hebrews, though the range of names and total numbers are far below the sheep and cattle. Goats are spoken of in thousands only once (2 Chr. 17:11). In most Western countries, the problem of dividing sheep from goats (Matt. 25:32–33) would never arise, for flocks are unlikely to mix and the two species are not easily confused. This is not so, however, in many lands around Palestine, where they often run together; moreover, native breeds may be alike in size, color, and shape. The usually upturned goat tail may be the only obvious difference.

Apart from one symbolic passage (Dan. 8), the goat seems to have no figurative significance, but some seventy percent of the occurrences refer to animals for SACRIFICE. This would seem to have been its main importance to the Hebrews. In addition, goats' hair was the material woven by Hebrew women to cover the TABERNACLE (Exod. 26:7), and it is still used in tentmaking by the BEDOUIN. The context, which speaks of "finely twisted linen" and colored yarn (v. 1), may imply superior quality cloth, perhaps comparable to cashmere from the Kashmir goat today. It is likely that long-haired races from farther E had become established by this time. In general, little can be inferred from the context about the natural history or habits of the goat. (See further G. S. Cansdale, *Animals and Man* [1952], and *All the Animals of the Bible Lands* [1970]; *FFB*, 36–38; *ABD*, 2:1040–41 and 6:1127–29.)

G. S. CANSDALE

Goath. KJV form of GOAH.

goatskins. See SKIN.

Gob gob (גֹּב H1570, meaning uncertain). An unknown location where DAVID's men battled the

784 GOBLET

Philistines on two occasions (2 Sam. 21:18–19). It was possibly a town close to Gath (mentioned in vv. 20 and 22). The parallel passage, however, has Gezer (1 Chr. 20:4; no place is specified for the second battle, v. 5). On that basis, some scholars read "Gezer" also in Samuel (either the first occurrence only, for which there is some Gk. support, or both), while others think that Gezer and Gob were alternate names for the same place. In addition, many Hebrew mss read Nob, a variant preferred by some on the basis of the personal name Ishbi-Benob (2 Sam. 21:16). Still other scholars identify Gob with Gibbethon (cf. J. Simons, *The Geographical and Topographical Texts of the Old Testament* [1959], 337, §795).

goblet. This English term is used variously in Bible versions to render words and expressions referring to drinking vessels. It occurs only once in

Hittite drinking goblet made of clay and with the image of a horse.

the KJV (Cant. 7:2, for *ʾaggān* H110, "bowl") and in the NRSV (Esth. 1:7, for *kĕli* H3998, "vessel, utensil"). The NIV uses it a few other times as well (e.g., Isa. 51:17, 22, for the expression *qubbaʿat kôs* H7694 + H3926).

God, biblical doctrine of. The Bible says so much about God that we need to think about where to start our discussion. Theologians have sometimes suggested that we focus our thinking around some central divine attribute, like love, infinity, aseity (self-sufficiency), holiness, or power. Others have suggested a focus on God's acts in history, or his Trinitarian persons. There is no single correct approach, unless that approach be simply to recite the Bible from beginning to end. Scripture presents God in many ways, from many perspectives.

One very promising and somewhat neglected approach, however, is to focus on the *Lordship* of the biblical God. The word Lord occurs almost 7,500 times in the NIV, most often referring to God, including many references to Christ as divine. (The term *G/god*, by comparison, appears less than 4,000 times.) But more significant than the frequency of the name is its theological importance. When Moses meets God in the burning bush, God identifies himself by the mysterious phrase, "I am who I am" (Exod. 3:14). This phrase is shortened to "I am" later in the verse. Then in v. 15, God presents his name *Yahweh* (the tetragrammaton *yhwh* H3378, usually represented in English Bible versions with small caps, "the Lord") as "my name forever, the name by which I am to be remembered from generation to generation." Evidently *Yahweh* of v. 15 is somehow related to the "I am" and "I am that I am" in v. 14, either by actual etymology or by mere resemblance to the Hebrew verb *hāyâ* H2118, "to be." See God, names of; I am (who I am).

Yahweh is the name by which God identifies himself to Israel as the head of the covenant relation between himself and them (Exod. 6:2–3, 6; 20:2). He is the Lord; they are his people. Over and over, we are told that God performs his mighty works so that people "will know that I am the Lord" (6:7; 7:5, 17; 8:22; 10:2; 14:4, 18; et al.). The Israelite's fundamental confession was that there was one God, the Lord (Deut. 6:4–5), and the NT Christian's confession is that Jesus Christ is Lord (Rom. 10:9; 1 Cor. 12:3; Phil. 2:11; cf. Jn. 20:28; Acts 2:36). Arguably these confessions represent the fundamental messages of both Testaments and together the central theme of Scripture.

 I. Attributes of Lordship
 II. Acts of the Lord
  A. Miracle
  B. Providence

C. Creation
D. God's decrees
III. Authoritative descriptions of the Lord
A. Names
B. Images
C. Attributes
IV. Conclusion

I. Attributes of Lordship. During the exodus from Egypt, God expounded to Moses the meaning of his name (Exod. 33:19; 34:5–7). These and other passages (like the "I am he" passages in Deut. 32:39; Isa. 41:4; 43:11–13; et al.) that seem intent on expounding God's Lordship present especially the following themes:

(1) The Lord is supremely *powerful*, in sovereign control of the world he has made and of the affairs of human beings. He brings his people out of Egypt by a "mighty hand," with "wonders" and "mighty acts" (Exod. 3:19–20; 4:21; 6:1–5; 20:2). He has mercy on whom he will have mercy (33:19; cf. Deut. 32:39). He reigns over all his works (Pss. 93:1; 97:1; 99:1).

(2) The Lord speaks a word of supreme *authority*. He comes to Moses with a message for Israel, "I AM has sent me to you" (Exod. 3:14), which they may not contradict. Because he is "the LORD your God, who brought you out of Egypt," he has the right to expect obedience: "You shall have no other gods before me" (20:2–3). In Lev. 18:4–5 and in Deut. 6:4–9, too, his Lordship is given as the sufficient reason why Israel must obey his commands. As Lord, he reveals and proclaims, as well as saves (Isa. 43:11–12). Similarly, Jesus' Lordship entails his right to command and to receive obedience (Lk. 6:46; Matt. 7:21–29).

(3) God's Lordship also means his *presence* with his people to bless and judge. The Lord is one who takes a people to be his own, in covenant. The basic meaning of the covenant is God's promise that "I will be your God, and you will be my people" (Lev. 26:12; cf. Gen. 17:7; Exod. 6:7; Jer. 7:23; 11:4; 30:22; Ezek. 36:28; 2 Cor. 6:16; Rev. 21:3–4). So God is *with* them (Exod. 3:12; cf. Gen. 21:22; 26:28; 28:15; 39:3–4; and many other texts). God's presence with Israel is his salvation, deliverance from bondage; but it also takes the visible forms of a cloud and pillar of fire, and of a TABERNACLE pitched among them (Exod. 26), where God dwells. The presence of Yahweh is a presence in blessing, but it can also mean judgment to those who rebel, and that too is part of Lordship (34:6–7). Later, Jesus, IMMANUEL ("God with us," Isa. 7:14; Matt. 1:23), pitches his tabernacle among us (Jn. 1:14), the tent of his own flesh, for in him God dwells with us in human form. In the NT, believers themselves are the temple of God (1 Cor. 3:16–17; 6:19; 2 Cor. 6:16; Eph. 2:21; Rev. 3:12), God's intimate dwelling place.

Power, authority, and presence in blessing and judgment: these do not exhaust the meaning of divine Lordship, but they provide a basic framework for understanding it and therefore for understanding everything the Bible teaches about God. For these attributes of covenant Lordship describe God's relationship not only to Israel and to new covenant Christians, but to the whole world. In Gen. 1, Moses presents CREATION as a parallel to the exodus, in which God by his powerful and authoritative Word (and the presence of his Spirit, 1:2) delivers the world from waters and darkness and makes a place for himself to dwell with ADAM and EVE. So the very regularity of nature is God's covenant with NOAH and with the world (8:20—9:17).

II. Acts of the Lord. Scripture teaches us about God in three ways, roughly corresponding to his power, his authority, and his presence: (1) it teaches us about his mighty acts; (2) it gives us authoritative descriptions of his nature; and (3) it gives us a glimpse into the intimacy of his Trinitarian inwardness. For the third of these, see TRINITY. The remainder of this article will focus on the biblical narrative of God's acts and its authoritative descriptions of him.

God's acts in Scripture include REDEMPTION, REVELATION, PROVIDENCE, CREATION, his eternal planning for creation (theologically called DECREES), and the eternal acts of love and communication among the persons of the Trinity. The last of these, again, will be treated in another article. Revelation will be treated here as an aspect of all God's actions toward his creatures, in the context of AUTHORITY as an attribute of divine Lordship. Redemption is the main story of the Bible, far too long to explore adequately in the present article; but our focus on God's covenant Lordship will bring a redemptive emphasis to our discussion. That leaves us with providence, creation, and the divine decrees to cover at this point. But first we will discuss MIRACLE, a kind of divine act that overlaps the categories of redemption and providence.

A. Miracle. Miracles have sometimes been defined as exceptions to natural law, or as "immediate" acts of God as opposed to acts in which God uses created means. These definitions stress that God is not bound by the structures of the created world, and that is certainly true. But the biblical writers never invoke these criteria to identify events as divine signs and wonders. Indeed, they could not have used these criteria, for like ourselves they did not know exhaustively what natural law is and is not capable of, or how precisely to distinguish an "immediate" act of God from a "mediate" one. Rather, for them, a miracle is an extraordinary event in which God demonstrates his Lordship power, authority, and presence. It is (1) *dynamis G1539*, an event of extraordinary *power* (Matt. 7:22 et al.; cf. Exod. 15:6 et al.); (2) *sēmeion G4956*, an *authoritative* sign that reveals God and often validates a human being as his messenger (Matt. 12:38–39 et al.; cf. Exod. 4:1–5; 7:9–13; 1 Ki. 17:24; Matt. 9:6; Acts 2:22; 14:3; 2 Cor. 12:12; Heb. 2:3); and (3) *teras G5469*, an event that elicits awe and wonder as people find themselves in the *presence* of the living God (Matt. 24:24 et al.; cf. Isa. 6:5; Lk. 5:8). In miracle, God is present in a special way, to redeem or to judge.

B. Providence. As miracle is God's extraordinary working in the world, providence is his more "ordinary" working: his government and preservation of the world from day to day. The difference between miracle and providence is relative rather than absolute, for *extraordinary* and *ordinary* differ in degree. In Ps. 136, the writer gives thanks to the Lord for all his "wonders" (v. 4), mentioning the creation of the world and the miracles accompanying Israel's deliverance from Egypt (vv. 5–15). But also included among the wonders is the truth that God "gives food to every creature" (v. 25). Mentioned at the end of the psalm, it is almost an afterthought, but a telling one: for is God's feeding all creatures any less wonderful or amazing than any of the other wonders? Certainly not.

(1) Providence displays God's *power*, as he directs all nature and history to his intended goal (Rom. 8:18–25, 28–30; Eph. 1:9–11), a creation purified from the curse of SIN. He preserves the world from final judgment until the fullness of his elect people come to repentance and faith (2 Pet. 3:5–9). Providence, then, is the text by which PAUL tells the people of LYSTRA and ATHENS of God's patience with sinners (Acts 14:17; 17:25–28). God is preserving the world because he has redemptive work to do. It is Christ, the redeemer, in whom all things "hold together" (Col. 1:17), for he intends to "reconcile all things to himself" (v. 20).

(2) Providence also displays God's *authority*, for in it we see the work of God's Word. As God's Word created all things (Gen. 1:3; Ps. 33:6), so it directs the course of nature and history (Pss. 147:15–20; 148:5–8). It is this powerful Word that God has given to Israel in Scripture, in laws and decrees (148:19–20; cf. Ps. 19). So providence reveals God's power and his purposes.

(3) And providence is God's *presence* in the world, his "concurrence" in events large and small (Matt. 10:29–30). He rules from on high, but he is also near to us, involved in every little thing that happens.

C. Creation. If God demonstrates his Lordship both in the extraordinary and the ordinary events of nature and history, then certainty he is no less than Lord at the beginning of these events. In creation he makes a world to be his own throne and footstool (Isa. 66:1), his royal palace.

(1) In creation, the Lord expresses incomparable *power*, commanding things to appear that had no existence previously (Gen. 1:3, 6, et al.; Ps. 33:6–9). Scripture never quite says explicitly that God created "out of nothing" (ex nihilo), but that conclusion is inescapable. For Scripture emphasizes many times the universality of creation, that God made absolutely everything in heaven, earth, or sea (Exod. 20:11; Neh. 9:6; Ps. 146:5–6). So everything except God himself is created. There is no uncreated stuff out of which God made the world, and he certainly did not make the universe from his own divine substance, for then the world itself

Within this text, written in the later Jewish script, the Tetragrammaton (YHWH) occurs in paleo-Hebrew letters (first line, second word from right margin).

would be God, as in pantheism. So what did he make the world out of? The only possible answer is "nothing."

(2) We see in creation also the other attributes of Lordship. For he makes all things by his *authoritative Word* (references above; also Jn. 1:1–3; Col. 1:15–16), and by that Word gives names, authoritative interpretations, to his creation (Gen. 1:5, 8, 10), finally declaring them good (vv. 4, 12, etc.). Creation also reveals God's wisdom (Job 38–42; Ps. 104:24; Prov. 3:19; 8:1, 22–36).

(3) And creation also brings God's *presence* to us. For in creation, God enters a relationship with things and people other than himself. He creates "directly," out of nothing, and from the beginning he is present in the world (Gen. 1:2).

So in Scripture creation is a picture of redemption. As God brought the world out of nothing, so in Christ he brought hope from despair, light from darkness, life from death (2 Cor. 4:6). We are his "new creation" (2 Cor. 5:17; cf. Eph. 4:24; Col. 3:10; Gal. 6:15–16). Indeed, in Christ, there will be renewal of the whole heaven and earth (Isa. 65:17–18; 66:22; 2 Pet. 3:10–13; Rev. 21:1–4). See HEAVENS, NEW.

D. God's decrees. The term *decrees* in theology refers to God's eternal purposes for creation. Although Scripture rarely uses *decree* this way (but see Pss. 2:7 and 148:6 in the NIV), it speaks often of God's "plans," "counsel," "purposes," "good pleasure," "will," etc. (Matt. 11:26; Acts 2:23; 4:27–28; Rom. 8:29; 9:11; Eph. 1:5, 9, 11; 3:11; 2 Tim. 1:9; Heb. 6:17; 1 Pet. 1:2). God's acts in history are the result of a wise plan. That plan is eternal (Matt. 25:34; 1 Cor. 2:7; Eph. 1:4; 3:11; 2 Tim. 1:9) and therefore unchangeable (Ps. 33:11; Isa. 14:24; 46:10; Jas. 1:17). God's plan ordains change to occur—it even foreordains temporary defeats of God's purposes—but in itself it does not change. And it is universal (Lam. 3:37–38; Rom. 8:28; 11:33–36; Eph. 1:11). God foreordains human free decisions and attitudes (Gen. 45:5–8; Exod. 12:36; 34:24; Jdg. 7:22; Prov. 16:9; 21:1; Isa. 44:28; Dan. 1:9; Acts 13:38; 16:14), even sinful ones (Deut. 2:30; Ps. 105:24; Isa. 6:9–10; 63:17; Lk. 22:22; Acts 2:23; 4:28; Rom. 9:17; 11:7–8).

If God is Lord in miracles, providence, and at the beginning of world history, then how can he be less than Lord in the *planning* of history? (1) The very fact that God governs the whole world by his plan manifests his incomparable *power*. (2) The wisdom of his plan is the ultimate *authoritative interpretation* of the world. (3) And his sovereign plan creates a *personal bond* between God and his creatures even before the creatures come into existence (Jer. 1:5; Eph. 1:4). So in his decree of ELECTION God chooses those who will receive the blessings of Christ (Jn. 10:27–29; Rom. 8:29–39; Eph. 1:3–11).

III. Authoritative descriptions of the Lord. Under this heading we may distinguish names, images, and attributes.

A. Names. The name *Yahweh*, as we have seen, stresses God's attributes of Lordship and presents God as the head of the covenant with his people. In the NT, as in the SEPTUAGINT, this name is represented with Greek *kyrios* **G3261** (e.g., Matt. 3:3, quoting Isa. 40:3). Another Hebrew word, *ʾādôn* **H123**, "lord, master" (also rendered with Gk. *kyrios*), stresses God's ownership of the creation. With the first person pronominal suffix, the plural form of the word becomes *ʾădōnāy* **H151** (lit., "my lord[s]"), which from antiquity the Jews have substituted for Yahweh, a name considered too sacred to be pronounced. A third name, *ʾĕlōhîm* **H466**, "God," can denote false gods as well as the true God (Pss. 86:8; 95:3; 97:9; et al.; see ELOAH, ELOHIM). As a relatively generic term for deity, it tends to be prominent in contexts where God deals with the creation in general, as in Gen. 1:1—2:4. Like Yahweh, however, it can also be used in contexts of covenantal intimacy, as in the expressions "our/your God" (e.g., Exod. 3:18; Isa. 40:1), and especially "the God of Israel" (Exod. 34:23; Ezra 6:22; Pss. 68:8; 72:18). The corresponding Greek term, *theos G2536*, takes on a more distinct meaning in Paul's writings to designate God the Father in distinction from the Son (1 Cor. 8:6; 2 Cor. 13:14; Eph. 4:4–6). But on the whole the major names of God differ mainly in nuance. Used to designate the one true God over many centuries and many texts, they tend toward interchangeability. For further discussion, including compound names, see GOD, NAMES OF.

B. Images. Images are not sharply distinguished from names and attributes, but they convey the same content in a more pictorial way. *King*, the most frequent image, is almost a name, close to *Lord* in meaning. As King, God rules over the whole earth (see esp. Pss. 93—99), and in a special sense he is the king of Israel (Pss. 5:2; 145:1; Isa. 41:21; cf. 1 Sam. 8:5–7). His kingdom is everlasting (Exod. 15:18; Ps. 93:2), but also historical and temporal. His kingdom is not merely his continuing sovereignty, but also the historical process by which he puts down opposing powers and brings people to recognize his rule. So the original gospel of Jesus is "Repent, for the kingdom of heaven is near" (Matt. 4:17). He is himself the king, who will reign forever and ever (Rev. 11:15; 17:14; 19:16). Similarly, he is *judge* (Gen. 18:25) and *lawgiver* (Exod. 20:2; Lev. 18:1–5; 19:1).

God often describes himself as a shepherd.

Moving from the political to the family sphere, we come to the precious name-image *Father*. God is father to all by virtue of creation (Acts 17:28), but more especially toward his people by virtue of covenant. Like *Lord* and *King*, *Father* is an image of rule. The divine father disciplines his children (Heb. 12:4–11) and demands honor (Mal. 1:6). But he also protects, provides, and guides (Deut. 1:31), showing compassion to his children (Ps. 103:13). The father is the redeemer (Isa. 63:16), reaching out with joy to the returning prodigal (Lk. 15:11–32). The father image becomes more pervasive in the NT, for there we learn to worship in and with the incarnate Son. See FATHERHOOD OF GOD. He is Son by nature, we are sons and daughters by ADOPTION, for his sake (Rom. 8:15). With him we become co-heirs (8:16; Gal. 4:5). So we pray, "Our Father" (Matt. 6:9) and address him by the Aramaic ABBA, "father," as did Jesus (Mk. 14:36; Rom. 8:15; Gal. 4:6). But in his family God is also *husband* (Isa. 54:5; Ezek. 16:6; Eph. 5:25–27). And he is the *kinsman*, the more distant relative who comes to *redeem* us from bondage (Lev. 25:47–53; Exod. 6:6; Job 19:25; Ps. 19:14). God redeems us by the blood of Christ; so Jesus, too, is redeemer (Eph. 1:7).

God is also the *shepherd* of his people (Gen. 49:24; Pss. 77:20; 80:1). SHEPHERD, like some of images already discussed, connotes rule, but also nurture (Ps. 23). God promises to judge the wicked leaders of Israel and will himself become the shepherd (Ezek. 34:11–15). Jesus presents himself as the good shepherd, who lays down his life for the sheep (Jn. 10:11; cf. Lk. 15:1–7).

There are many other personal images of God, such as *potter* (Isa. 64:8; Jer. 18–19; Rom. 9:19–22), *farmer* (Isa. 5; Matt. 13:3–8), *refiner* (Ps. 12:6; Prov. 17:3; Mal. 3:2). Scripture compares him also to animals (e.g., Exod. 19:4; Ps. 17:8; Hos. 5:2). Jesus is both lion of Judah and the lamb who was slain (Rev. 5:5–6). In the inanimate world, *light* is an important image of God, virtually defining him in 1 Jn. 1:5. Light is his GLORY, the brightness of his THEOPHANY. It stands in contrast especially with darkness in the moral sense, human sin. So Jesus is the light of the world (Jn. 8:12), and he appoints his disciples to bear that light (Matt. 5:14–16). *Rock* is also a frequent image of God, indicating strength, protection, unchangeable perfection (Deut. 32:4; Ps. 18:2, 31, 46; 1 Cor. 10:4).

Many have discussed recently the question of divine gender. This is also a question of imagery, because the incorporeal God is not literally male or female. There are feminine images of God in Scripture. God not only fathers Israel, but also gives birth to her (Deut. 32:18; cf. Num. 11:12; Isa. 42:14–15; and the image of divine wisdom in Prov. 7:4; 8:1—9:18). But certainly the predominant imagery for God in Scripture is male, and we should maintain that balance. To think of God primarily in female terms is to compromise the biblical picture of God as father and husband. And, given the biblical principle that men are to be rulers in their homes (Eph. 5:22–23; Col. 3:18; Tit. 2:5; 1 Pet. 3:1, 5–6) and in the church (1 Cor. 14:33–35; 1 Tim. 2:11–15), a predominant use of female imagery creates confusion about God's very rule, his Lordship.

C. Attributes. Attributes are nouns (like *eternity*) or adjectives (like *eternal*) that describe God's nature and character. As such, they indicate his *power* over various aspects of creation, his *authority* as a model for human conduct, and the nature of his interactions with creatures in history, his *presence*. So each attribute presents all three of the aspects of divine Lordship I defined earlier. But some focus on one or another aspect of that Lordship. So I shall discuss them under the general categories of goodness, knowledge, and power, which loosely correspond to the Lordship attributes of presence, authority, and power, respectively.

1. Attributes of Goodness. *Goodness* is a general term of commendation, but most often it refers as a divine attribute to God's benevolence. He is good in blessing his creatures, filling them with good things (Gen. 50:20; Josh. 24:20; Pss. 103:5; 145:9; Acts 14:17). Often the psalmists couple God's goodness with his *mercy* (Heb. *ḥesed* H2876, sometimes translated "lovingkindness," "love," "steadfast love"), his faithfulness to his covenant people (Pss. 100:5; 106:1; 107:1; 109:21; 118:1; 136:1). So God's goodness is a form of his Lordship.

God is good to all his creatures (Ps. 145:9, 13–16; Matt. 5:45; Acts 14:17). How, then, can he permit evil to exist in the world? It may not be possible to provide a thoroughly satisfying answer to this question. The Bible itself presents three responses: (1) Although it is not wrong to ponder this mystery, we may not bring charges against God (Rom. 9:19–21). (2) God brings good from evil (Gen. 50:20; Rom. 8:28), particularly from the worst evil, the crucifixion of the Son of God. (3) In heaven we shall be thoroughly persuaded of God's goodness and justice: all nations will praise him for the revelation of his righteous acts (Rev. 15:3–4). Clearly, though, God is not good to all creatures in the same way, or in the same degree. God's elect experience suffering in this world, glory in the next (Rom. 8:18; 1 Pet. 1:3–9). The wicked often experience the reverse (Lk. 16:19–31; cf. Ps. 73). But nobody can complain that God has not been good to them—he has been far more good, in fact, than any of us deserve.

Love overlaps the concept of goodness but is theologically richer. In general, God's LOVE is his disposition to act for the happiness and welfare of his creatures. It is both affection and action, feelings and deeds. As with goodness, God's love is universal in some respects: he loves his enemies, providing a model for us (Matt. 5:43–48). But there is a special love reserved for God's elect, a love begun in eternity past (Eph. 1:4–5) and defined by the cross of Christ (Jn. 3:16; 15:13–14; Rom. 5:8; Gal. 2:20; Eph. 5:2; 5:25; 1 Jn. 3:16; 4:8–10; Rev. 1:5). That is the love that brings us all the blessings of salvation. Biblical writers marvel at its vastness (1 Jn. 3:1; Eph. 3:17–19). And it is that special love, Jesus' dying for his friends, that serves as the model for Christian love (Matt. 20:25–28; 2 Cor. 5:14–15; Phil. 2:1–11; 1 Pet. 2:21–25).

God's *grace* is benevolent, like his goodness, and it motivates him to save sinners, as does his love. GRACE differs from these other attributes in that the term often emphasizes God's favor to the undeserving, and therefore his sovereignty in choosing those who receive his blessings (Exod. 33:12–19; Rom. 9:15). He chooses Israel despite her disobedience (Deut. 9:4–6) and brings Gentiles into the NT church apart from their obedience to the law (Acts 11:23; 15:10–11; 18:27). So in Paul's writings, God's grace is salvation apart from the works of the law (Rom. 3:21–24; 4:4, 16; 11:6; Gal.

2:21; Eph. 2:8–9). According to 2 Tim. 1:10, God gives us grace in our eternal election, so his grace cannot be based on any of our works. Rather, it gives us power to do good works (2 Cor. 9:8; Eph. 2:8–10).

Scripture also speaks of God's *compassion* or *pity*, his sympathy for the distress of others. These terms represent Greek and Hebrew terms that are strongly emotional. God often shows COMPASSION for his people after they have rebelled and he has judged their sin (Deut. 13:17; 30:3). So his compassion motivates him to grant FORGIVENESS (Ps. 78:38). This is an aspect of God's love and a model for ours (1 Jn. 3:17; cf. Matt. 18:21–35).

God's *righteousness* (the Hebrew and Greek terms can also be rendered "justice") has a more legal, forensic focus than *goodness*. It represents God's standards of conduct, both his own and ours, and therefore the fairness of his judgments (Ps. 9:7–8). But, surprisingly, God's RIGHTEOUSNESS is not only a standard—it is also a means of our salvation. Among God's "righteous deeds" are his deliverance of Israel from Egypt, according to his promises (1 Sam. 12:6–11; Neh. 9:8). God's righteousness is "salvation to Zion" (Isa. 46:12–13; cf. Pss. 40:10; 85:9–10; 98:2–3). And, because Jesus has paid the legal penalty for our sin, God is not only faithful, but also *just* to forgive (1 Jn. 1:9). Thus, as Luther discovered, the "righteousness of God" in Rom. 1:17 is not the terror of God's judgment, but the good news of forgiveness in Christ.

Similarly, God's *holiness*, which at first seems forbidding, is good news to the believer. It is essentially the capacity of God to inspire awe and reverence, the impression of God's whole being upon those who stand in his presence. His HOLINESS is his "separation" from all created reality, his transcendence by virtue of all that makes him divine. But because we are not only creatures, but also sinners, that separation in Scripture takes on a particularly ethical meaning. Upon meeting God, human beings are typically aware of their sins and fearful of judgment (Exod. 20:18–19; Isa. 6:3–5; Lk. 5:8). But, amazingly, God draws his people into his holiness. They become his "holy nation" (Exod. 19:6; 22:31). They are to be "holy because I, the LORD your God, am holy" (Lev. 19:1; 1 Pet. 1:16). Christians are "saints," holy ones (Rom. 1:7; 1 Cor. 1:2), because they belong to Jesus, the holy one. So the psalmist invokes God's holiness as the reason God should deliver him (Ps. 22:1–5). Holiness is not only God's transcendent separation from the world, but also his immanence, drawing near to us and bringing us out of sin into the sphere of his holiness.

God is not only loving, but also *jealous* (Exod. 20:4–6; 34:14), for his love is covenantal, exclusive, even marital. He demands exclusive love from us (Deut. 6:4–5); we may not love other gods (Exod. 20:3). The jealous character of his love, together with his righteousness, leads him to *hate* the wicked (Lev. 20:23; Deut. 25:16; Ps. 5:5; et al.). Indeed, all of us were once "children of wrath" (Eph. 2:3 NRSV) because of our offenses against God. But God's WRATH, in this life, does not preclude forgiveness and salvation. Nor does it exclude God's love in every sense. As God loves his enemies (Matt. 5:43–48) and, indeed, has loved his elect sinners before the beginning of the world (Eph. 1:4–5), we can see that he does sometimes love and hate the same people, in different respects.

2. Attributes of knowledge. We learn of God's knowledge through his *speech*. Only in religions and philosophies influenced by the Bible does the supreme being *speak* to human beings. The Greek gods speak, but they are not supreme; ultimates in Hinduism, Buddhism, and some secular philosophy are supreme in various senses, but they do not speak. So in Scripture God's Word defines him over against the "dumb" idols (Hab. 2:18–20; Pss. 115:5–8; 135:15–18; 1 Cor. 12:2). The biblical God creates the world (Gen. 1:3; Ps. 33:6, 9) and governs the course of nature and history (Ps. 147:15–18) through his powerful word. In the gospel, God's word is God's power of salvation (Rom. 1:16; cf. 1 Thess. 1:5; 2:13; 2 Tim. 1:10). Jesus himself is God's living Word (Jn. 1:1–14; 1 Jn. 1:1–3; Rev. 19:13). The Bible is God's word in written form, "breathed out by God" (2 Tim. 3:16; NIV, "God-breathed"; see INSPIRATION).

God's words are *true*. God is *true* in several senses: (1) He is the authentic God as opposed to the false gods (Jer. 10:9–10). (2) What he says is reliable: his words are truth (Jn. 17:17). He cannot lie (Num. 23:19; Tit. 1:2; Heb. 6:18) or be in error (Heb. 4:12–13). So he is true, though every man is a liar (Rom. 3:4). Scripture thus rebukes the modern theological tendency to decry "mere propositional truth." Propositional truth, verbal correctness, is an attribute of God, and that truth is found in his word. (3) God *does* truth. Truth is an ethical concept in Scripture, a close synonym of *faithfulness* (1 Jn. 1:6; 3:18; 2 Jn. 4). God keeps his promises; he is faithful and true (Deut. 7:5; 32:4; Rev. 3:14; 19:11).

God's *knowledge* is implicit in the truthfulness of his words and in the comprehensiveness of his decree. If he has planned the whole course of nature and history, certainly he knows it. In Scripture, God's KNOWLEDGE sometimes refers to his entering personal covenant relationships rather than merely knowing facts about them (as in Amos 3:2; cf. the concept of foreknowledge in Rom. 8:29; 1 Pet. 1:2; see FOREKNOW). But he also knows all the facts (Ps. 147:5; Jn. 21:17; Heb. 4:12–13; 1 Jn. 3:20).

Some have recently denied that God knows the future exhaustively, because they believe human free decisions cannot be known in advance. But in Scripture knowledge of the future is the test of a true prophet (Deut. 18:21–22) and of the true God in contrast with idols (Isa. 41:21–23; 42:9; 43:9–12; et al.). God and his prophets do know human free decisions in advance, sometimes very specific ones (1 Sam. 10:1–7; 23:11; 1 Ki. 13:1–4; 2 Ki. 8:12), sometimes centuries in advance (Gen. 9:24–27; 15:13–16; 45:5–8; 50:20; 1 Ki. 13:1–4; Dan. 9:20–27). "Open theists" have argued that in some passages God confesses ignorance, as when he visits SODOM and GOMORRAH to "see if what they have done is as bad as the outcry that has reached me" (Gen. 18:21). But this passage, like others (e.g., 3:9; 11:5; 22:12), concerns God's knowledge of the present, not of the future. And such statements do not describe divine ignorance. Rather, here God publicly collects facts as an indictment to justify a coming judgment. He makes his indictment by entering time in theophany. And when he enters time (as with the INCARNATION, Lk. 2:52; see below), he does accumulate knowledge gradually and temporally.

God's *wisdom* is both knowledge and the use of that knowledge in action. All his work in creation and providence reveals his WISDOM (Pss. 104:24; 136:5; Prov. 3:19; Jer. 10:12; 51:15). The NT identifies Jesus as the wisdom of God (1 Cor. 1:30) and finds in him "all the treasures of wisdom and knowledge" (Col. 2:3).

God's *thoughts* are above our thoughts (Isa. 55:8), incomprehensible to us (Rom. 11:33–36). But God has revealed himself so as to give us knowledge that is true, though not exhaustive. We may describe his thought as *logical* in the sense that his faithfulness guarantees the consistency of his word, and his truth excludes falsehood. This is not to say that his thought always coheres with any system of logic developed by human beings.

3. Attributes of power. King JEHOSHAPHAT praised God by saying that "power and might are in your hand, and no one can withstand you" (2 Chr. 20:6). As we have seen, power is one of God's Lordship attributes. Biblical writers frequently observe that God does what he wishes in the world. His plans cannot be thwarted (Job 23:13; 42:2; Pss. 115:3; 135:6; Prov. 21:30; Isa. 14:24–27; 43:13; 55:11; Dan. 4:35). Nothing is too hard for him (Gen. 18:14; Num. 11:23; Jer. 32:17; Zech. 8:6; Mk. 14:36; Lk. 1:37; 18:27). He can do all things (Job 42:2).

Nevertheless, in some senses there are things that God cannot do. He cannot contradict his truth, as we have seen. He cannot lie (Num. 23:19; Tit. 1:2). He cannot (in his transcendent existence) perform actions appropriate only to finite creatures, like celebrating his birthday, taking medicine, buying shoes (though by taking human form he can do all these things). He cannot deny his own nature as God, as by making another god equal to himself. Nor can he change his eternal plan, or fail to keep his promises. But such "inabilities" really underscore the greatness of his power. They are positives, rather than negatives. Similarly, note that God's power often works through weakness (2 Cor. 12:9), a truth exemplified particularly in the cross of Christ. Jesus' death is an apparent defeat of God's purposes; but actually it is the greatest example of his mighty power, which is stronger than man's strength (1 Cor. 1:18, 23–25).

More difficult to explain is the mystery that God does not always get what he desires. He desires for us all to be holy and righteous, but we are not. He

View from Masada to the E across the Dead Sea. Although the Ammonites and Moabites were advancing toward Jerusalem across this landscape, King Jehoshaphat declared before the Lord, "Power and might are in your hand, no one can withstand you" (2 Chr. 20:6).

wills our SANCTIFICATION (1 Thess. 4:3), but our sanctification is never complete in this life. We should note that Scripture speaks of God's *will* (also of his thought, intent, purpose, pleasure, counsel) in two ways: (1) to denote God's eternal decree, which cannot be thwarted and always comes to pass (Gen. 50:20; Pss. 51:18; 115:3; Isa. 46:10; Jer. 49:20; 50:45; Dan. 4:17; Matt. 11:25–26; Acts 2:23; Rom. 9:18–19; Eph. 1:11; Jas. 1:18; Rev. 4:11; cf. also the texts listed at the beginning of this section); and (2) to denote states of affairs God values highly but does not necessarily bring to pass (Pss. 5:4; 103:21; Matt. 7:21; 12:50; Jn. 4:34; 7:17; Rom. 12:2; Eph. 5:17; 1 Thess. 4:3; 5:18; Heb. 13:21; 1 Pet. 4:2). These two senses of God's "will" are sometimes called *decretive* and *preceptive*, respectively. It is in the second sense that God's will is not always done. It is also in that sense that God wills the salvation of all (Ezek. 18:23, 31–32; 33:11; 2 Pet. 3:9).

It may seem odd to think of God's *eternity* under the category of *power*. The theological discussion of ETERNITY centers, rather, on the question of whether God is "within" or "outside" time. But Scripture contains no explicit teaching on that issue. It does, rather, emphasize that for God (in contrast with us) time is no limit. For him, time never passes too slowly or too quickly (Ps. 90:4; 2 Pet. 3:8). He is sovereign over the temporal sequence, so that, for example, Jesus comes precisely at the right time (Gal. 4:4). He sets times and dates by his own authority (Acts 1:7; cf. 17:26; Mk. 13:32). And, as we have seen, he knows past, present, and future with equal vividness. So his relation to time is very different from ours. To us time is a limit, but he rules it. He has *power* over time; he is *Lord* of time. So it is indeed appropriate to consider eternity as a power of God.

Is God "outside" time or "inside" it? The biblical writers do not use these categories. But if God is Lord of time as presented above, the picture of God standing outside time, viewing history all at once, and governing it from outside seems more accurate than the picture of God standing within time, as within a box he cannot get out of. Nevertheless, it is also important to insist that God *enters* time, that he is *present* with his creation at all times, as well as in all places. He is an actor in the drama of history, not only in the incarnation of Jesus, but from the beginning of time.

As an actor in time, God changes in certain ways, as did Jesus in his earthly life (Lk. 2:52). He blesses one day, judges the next. Sometimes he "relents" from announced judgments, in response to human REPENTANCE (Jon. 3:10) or intercessory

PRAYER (Amos 7:1–6). Indeed, God announces such relenting as a settled policy in Jer. 18:5–10. But God does not change in his essential nature and attributes (Heb. 1:10–12; 13:8; Jas. 1:17), in his decretive will (Ps. 33:11), in his faithfulness to keep his covenant promises (Ps. 89:34–37; Isa. 54:10; Mic. 7:19–20; Mal. 3:6; Heb. 6:17–20), or in the truth of his revelation (Rom. 15:4; 2 Tim. 3:16–17).

Similar points can be made about God's relation to *space*. Heaven and earth are his throne and footstool (Isa. 66:1–2); he is greater than they (cf. 1 Ki. 8:27; 2 Chr. 2:6). The theological term (not found in the Bible) for God's transcendence of space is *immensity*, which parallels *eternity* (transcendence of time). But as God is also present in all times, he is present in all spaces as well, omnipresent (Ps. 139:7–10; Acts 17:24–28). So as he is Lord of time, he is Lord of space, beyond its limits, but using it freely for his purposes. His relation to time and space is both transcendent and immanent. See OMNIPRESENCE.

So God is Lord of the material world and of the visible world: thus *incorporeal* and *invisible*. Of course, God can take bodily and visible form as he chooses, in THEOPHANY and INCARNATION. But he is not limited to any physical manifestation. Physical and visible beings are limited to space and time; God transcends these limits. So Scripture speaks of his essential nature as invisible (Rom. 1:20; Col. 1:15; 1 Tim. 1:17; Heb. 11:27).

God's *glory* is, literally, the brightness associated with his theophany (Exod. 16:10) and, more broadly, everything in God that evokes praise (1 Chr. 29:11; Ps. 24:7; Eph. 1:6). Thus when we view the world as God's creation, it reveals his glory (Ps. 19:1), and so do we also as his image and glory (Ps. 8:5; 1 Cor. 11:7). In one sense, we cannot add glory to God. But God himself calls us to "glorify" him, by imaging God to the rest of creation, through obedience. Thus like Jesus we become the "light of the world" (Matt. 4:14–16; Jn. 8:12). So we bring *praise* to him (note that Gk. *doxa G1518* can be translated both "glory" and "praise").

Scripture also relates God's *spirituality* to the glory-theophany (Neh. 9:19–20; Isa. 63:11–14; Hag. 2:5). More generally, God's *Spirit* (= God's "breath") is his presence in the world, performing his work as Lord. He is God's *power* (Jdg. 13:25; 14:6; Mic. 3:8; Lk. 4:14; Rom. 15:19; 1 Cor. 2:4; 1 Thess. 1:5). He speaks with *authority* to and through the prophets (Gen. 41:38; Num. 24:2; 1 Sam. 10:6; Lk. 1:17; 1 Pet. 1:11) and apostles (Matt. 10:20; Lk. 4:14; Jn. 3:34; 14:16–17; 15:26; 16:13; Acts 2:4; 6:10; 1 Cor. 2:4; 7:40; 1 Thess. 1:5; Rev. 2:7; 19:10). And he is God's *presence* (Ps. 139:7; 1 Cor. 3:16; Gal. 4:6), the giver of life (Gen. 2:7; Jn. 3:5–8; 6:63; 1 Cor. 15:45; 2 Cor. 3:6; 1 Pet. 3:18; 4:6), the motivator of godly living (Rom. 8:1–17). But he can also be present in judgment (Isa. 11:1–4; 2 Thess. 2:8; 1 Pet. 4:13–16). Like *Father* and *Word*, *Spirit* is both a divine attribute (Jn. 4:24) and the name of a person of the Trinity.

Because God has all power, he has no needs (Acts 17:24–30) and therefore may be described as *self-sufficient* or *self-contained*, as having the theological attribute of *aseity*. We should not infer, however, that God never suffers. He is, of course, *impassible* in the sense that he can never suffer loss to his being or attributes. But he does experience emotions such as grief (Gen. 6:6; Eph. 4:30), and he expresses that emotion in passionate exhortations (e.g., Ezek. 33:11). He is "distressed" when Israel is distressed (Isa. 63:9). He is the compassionate God, who knows the agonies of his people, not only as the transcendent author of history, but also as the immanent one who is with us here and now. And God the Son, Jesus, really experienced death for us on the cross (Isa. 53:3–4; Rom. 5:6–8; 8:34).

IV. Conclusion. The God of Scripture is *Lord*, powerful, authoritative, and present with his creatures to bless and judge. In all these ways he is supreme, yet always and fully personal. Only the Bible (and other literature influenced by the Bible) presents a God who is both absolute and personal. As mentioned earlier, Hinduism, Buddhism, and many secular philosophies proclaim supreme beings that are absolute in some sense, but impersonal. Polytheistic religions worship beings that are personal, but not absolute. The biblical God is fully absolute, but he also enters personal relationships with us, planning history, speaking to us, loving, judging, redeeming, guiding. If it is reasonable to think that only a personal being can fully account for the rationality of the universe, the human mind, the origin of life, ethical standards, beauty, and the possibility of meaningful existence, then the biblical doctrine of God is also a powerful apologetic for his existence.

(This article summarizes J. M. Frame, *The Doctrine of God* [2002]. See also H. Bavinck, *The Doctrine of God* [1951]; R. T. France, *The Living God* [1970]; J. I. Packer, *Knowing God* [1973]; J. M. Frame, *The Doctrine of the Knowledge of God* [1987]; G. L. Bray, *The Doctrine of God* [1993]; W. Grudem, *Systematic Theology: An Introduction to Biblical Doctrine* [1994], chs. 9–17, which include extensive bibliographical references to classic publications in systematic theology. In addition, note the standard works in OT and NT theology.) J. M. FRAME

God, children (sons, daughters) of. The FATHERHOOD OF GOD and thus the sonship of human beings are valid definitive concepts in biblical terminology. With reference to father and children, the earthly FAMILY bears a true resemblance to the heavenly family. In retrospect, the likeness is evident throughout the Bible, coming into sharp focus in Jesus. The Bible story begins with the natural children of ADAM; continues with the chosen children of ABRAHAM; and concludes with the spiritual children of redemption. All are God's children in one way or another.

   I. Created children
      A. Angelic beings
      B. The whole human race
  II. Chosen children
      A. Israel
      B. Jesus and Israel
 III. Converted children
      A. The unique sonship of Christ
      B. Children of God by faith
      C. Characteristics of God's converted children

I. Created children. In a general sense, all created personal beings are children of God. They are products of his workmanship and bear his image.

A. Angelic beings. Angelic beings are depicted as children of God. See ANGEL. On witnessing the glorious creation of the earth, "all the sons of God shouted for joy" (Job 38:7 KJV). Could it be that God addressed himself to them when he said, "Let us make man in our image, in our likeness" (Gen. 1:26)? Of course the beloved Son "was with God in the beginning. Through him all things were made" (Jn. 1:2–3; cf. Heb. 1:2). But angels did not enjoy an equal sonship relation with Jesus, "For to which of the angels did God ever say, 'You are my Son; today I have become your Father'?" (Heb. 1:5; cf. Ps. 2:7). However, Jesus compared the final state of humans with angels. In the resurrection they would not marry, and "they can no longer die; for they are like the angels. They are God's children, since they are children of the resurrection" (Lk. 20:36).

The debatable passage in Gen. 6:1–4 relates that "the sons of God" married "the daughters of men." According to some scholars, these "sons of God" were angels (for the various views, see SONS OF GOD). It is more likely, however, that the passage refers to natural men who were sons of God by creation. They bore in human form the image of God on one hand, and on the other hand were able to reproduce themselves. In this early age, "When men began to increase in number on the earth," the fact that men of divine image could not only reproduce male offspring but also daughters who were fair and beautiful was a startling revelation. Moreover, that there was sex attraction, resulting in marriage and establishing the chain of reproduction, was exciting enough to report in semimythological terms. Another pertinent factor in this brief report was God's announcement to reduce the human span of life on earth from the former longevity to 120 years. This brief passage may serve well as an

Young bedouin girl. God gives those who believe in him the privilege of being called his children.

appropriate epitaph of the forefathers, the "men of renown" (v. 4) of a bygone age.

In another ancient record, angelic beings are called children of God. "Now there was a day when the sons of God came to present themselves before the LORD, and Satan also came among them" (Job 1:6; 2:1 KJV). Similar ideas are expressed in the Psalms, which speak of the *běnê ʾēlîm*, which means literally, "sons of gods," but is usually translated "mighty ones" or "heavenly beings" (Pss. 29:1; 89:6).

B. The whole human race. All people on earth are children of God by creation. In the process of creation, God endowed human beings with two qualities resembling his—the ability to reproduce his likeness and to rule (Gen. 1:26–28). Just as natural children resemble their parents, men and women resemble God, for he made them in his likeness. Like God, man is rational, emotional, volitional, and spiritual, endowed with freedom of choice. Like a lost child, he is restless for his heavenly Father. Everyone's genealogy may be traced back to God, just as Luke traced Jesus' human lineage through long generations back to "Seth, the son of Adam, the son of God" (Lk. 3:38). Another writer says, "The Son is the radiance of God's glory and the exact representation of his being" (Heb. 1:3). Jesus was God in human form (cf. Dan. 3:25); conversely, then, man resembles God, his Maker and Father, in an amazing way. Even a pagan poet, Aratus of Greece, wrote, "We are his offspring" (Acts 17:28). Likewise, every person on earth can validly claim that he is a child of God by virtue of creation. People of every race, age, and sex are by nature children of God.

II. Chosen children. Since human beings are free moral agents, they may be obedient children of God or rebellious ones (Ezek. 20:21). In the days of NOAH, disobedience was so prevalent that God punished mankind with the flood (cf. Eph. 2:2). People continued to sin and lose their way, so God chose some of his children to help reclaim the others.

A. Israel. God called ABRAHAM to be the progenitor of the Jewish race, chosen to bring salvation to the world (Jn. 4:22). Thus the select race could be called "children of promise" (Gal. 4:28) and "sons of the living God" (Hos. 1:10). Even of these, God said, "the children rebelled against me" (Ezek. 20:21); and he called to them, "Return, O faithless children" (Jer. 3:14 NRSV; cf. 4:22). But the Father's love reformed a REMNANT, who again sang, "O children of Zion, be glad / and rejoice in the LORD your God" (Joel 2:23 NRSV).

B. Jesus and Israel. Jesus fulfilled God's purpose in his chosen children, while confirming God's plan in the race. He said to the SYROPHOENICIAN woman, "First let the children [i.e., the Jews] eat all they want ... for it is not right to take the children's bread and toss it to their dogs [i.e., the Gentiles]" (Mk. 7:27). In this strong metaphor, Jesus was emphasizing the fact that in personal human service he "was sent only to the lost sheep of Israel" (Matt. 15:24). Concerning ZACCHAEUS, he said, "Today salvation has come to this house, because this man, too, is a son of Abraham. For the Son of man came to seek and to save what was lost" (Lk. 19:9–10). The lost that would be saved eventually included the Gentiles, for the Father, in his love, does not want anyone to perish (2 Pet. 3:9). His inclusive love was also portrayed in Jesus' parable of the lost sheep (Lk. 15:3–7). The chosen race (Deut. 14:2) came to full fruition in the chosen Son (Lk. 9:35).

III. Converted children. As the Christian era dawned, a new concept of the children of God was preached. JOHN THE BAPTIST thundered out the explosive truth to the Jews: "And do not think you can say to yourselves, 'We have Abraham as our father.' I tell you that out of these stones God can raise up children for Abraham" (Matt. 3:9). Henceforth, divine sonship would be reckoned on a new basis.

A. The unique sonship of Christ. JESUS CHRIST was the SON OF GOD in a unique way. He was God's "Son, whom he appointed heir of all things, and through whom he made the universe" (Heb. 1:2; cf. Jn. 1:3). He appeared at his baptism with "the glory of the One and Only, who came from the Father" (Jn. 1:14). He called himself "God's Son" (10:36;

cf. 3:16), and God, out of a cloud, called him "my Son, whom I love" (Matt. 17:5). On numerous occasions, Jesus called God "my Father," "my heavenly Father," and similar terms (18:35; 26:39). Moreover, he subordinated his lineage of DAVID to divine lineage (Mk. 12:35–36).

B. Children of God by faith. Through Jesus Christ all the children of Adam as well as those of Abraham are eligible to be eternal children of God. "You are all sons of God through faith in Christ Jesus.... If you belong to Christ, then you are Abraham's seed, and heirs according to the promise" (Gal. 3:26, 29). "In other words, it is not the natural children [*lit.*, children of the flesh] who are God's children, but it is the children of the promise who are regarded as Abraham' offspring" (Rom. 9:8). The criterion for becoming spiritual children of God is faith not flesh. "Flesh gives birth to flesh, but the Spirit gives birth to spirit" (Jn. 3:6), and "those who are led by the Spirit of God are sons of God" (Rom. 8:14). Jesus told some Jews they were not Abraham's children, neither was God their Father, warning them, "You belong to your father the devil" (Jn. 8:44). Through Christ sonship is offered to all who believe. "Yet to all who received him, to those who believed in his name, he gave the right to become children of God" (1:12).

C. Characteristics of God's converted children. Spiritual children resemble God in lives of obedience to him. If you love your enemies, do good, be merciful, and lend to the selfish, "your reward will be great, and you will be sons of the Most High" (Lk. 6:35–36). "How great is the love the Father has lavished on us, that we should be called children of God!" (1 Jn. 3:1). Christians are to live "as children of light" (Eph. 5:8), for they are "all sons of the light" (1 Thess. 5:5). Jesus cherished and taught the fatherhood of God and the sonship of believers. He said, "And do not call anyone on earth 'father,' for you have one Father, and he is in heaven" (Matt. 23:9). He taught his disciples to address God in prayer as "Our Father in heaven" (6:9), and assured them, "Blessed are the peacemakers, for they will be called sons of God" (5:9). See also ADOPTION.   G. B. FUNDERBURK

God, names of. Distinctive of the Hebrew-Christian system is the use of the names for deity as instruments for divine disclosure (see REVELATION). The several names, simple and compound, employed in both the OT and the NT, are not mere human designations or constructs. Rather they are revelatory instruments, appearing at nodal points in the career of the Hebrew people, and reflecting God's self-revelation. Israel's feeling for names reflected the general attitude toward nomenclature that was common to ancient peoples. With them a person's NAME was not a mere designation of familial relationship—not a mere possession—but something distinctly personal. In Semitic culture, names were frequently used to designate a characteristic of the person named. The thought seems to have been that *nomina sunt realia* ("names are the real things"). An example of this type of usage is found in the case of the name of JACOB, meaning "supplanter," whose subject was in actual fact a crafty and self-seeking person. While there is no evidence that in Israelite usage names were held (as in some cultures) to possess magical power, yet they were held in serious regard. This was true concerning personal names; and the same seriousness is apparent in the employment of designations for deity among OT peoples.

I. God's name: general considerations. In some parts of Scripture, God's name is regarded in a strictly singular sense, and the principles surrounding its usage are collectively applied to the several designations of him. Thus we have in the Decalogue, "You shall not misuse the name of the LORD your God, for the LORD will not hold anyone guiltless who misuses his name" (Exod. 20:7 KJV). This prohibition is intended to exclude any fraudulent or flippant use of any of the terms by which God was designated. The third commandment is thus intended as a safeguard placed upon the structure of divine names as a revelatory instrument. The entire pattern of names was to be held in respect as a vital part of the self-disclosure of Deity, so that no aspect of his revealed nature should be regarded frivolously. See TEN COMMANDMENTS.

It should be noted that the way a name is used, rather than its derivation, is most significant in OT usage. While etymology is a highly relevant study in this connection, its conclusions cannot by themselves be accepted as definitive for the understanding of divine names. Nor can the fact that the Hebrews used names for God that were current in the ancient world be held to militate against a special use of names as revelatory in OT times.

Within the divine nomenclature of the OT, there are varying combinations of designations with respect to the "transcendence-immanence" question. These suggest that to the Hebrews, God was understood as being both hidden and present. Again, there is evidence that he was understood in both transcendent and anthropomorphic modes so far as his personal qualities were concerned.

The NT understanding of both the divine names and the divine nature continues and simplifies the OT usage. The names employed to designate the Deity are fewer, and less emphasis is laid upon names themselves as indicative of the nature of God. Whereas in the OT usage nuances and compound verbal structures are employed to convey the qualities of the Deity, in the NT there are characterizations, direct and indirect, that serve to elaborate men's understanding of God's nature.

II. Basic names for God in the OT.

Much of OT criticism has pivoted about the use of two divine names, ʾēl H446 (usually rendered "God") and yhwh H3378 ("the Lord"). These, taken together with the name ʾădōnāy H151 (lit., "my lord[s]"), form what may be considered the basic OT designations for the Deity. These are, as well, simple names, as contrasted with a group of derived and compound names to which attention will be given later.

The name EL (see also ELOAH, ELOHIM) is one of the oldest designations for deity in the ancient world. It forms the basic component for the general term for God in Babylonia and Arabia, as well as with the Israelites. That the conceptions sometimes attached to this term in the world of antiquity were unworthy of the God of the Bible is clear, but this does not diminish the significance of the occurrence of the term in the racial stocks of the ANE. It is a very old term, and many feel that it is reasonable to infer that the term has been retained from a primeval revelation (*Uroffenbarung*).

The name El seems to suggest power and authority. In this connection, John P. Lange says:

An illustration of creation taken from Jenson's Latin Vulgate (1479). The divine name Elohim is closely linked to God's role as Creator.

"Power, greatness, vastness, height, according as they are represented by the *conceptions* of the day, carried to the fullest extent allowed by the knowledge of the day; this is the ideal of *El* and *Elohim*, as seen in the etymological congruity of the epithets joined to those in Genesis" (*A Commentary on the Holy Scriptures* [1865–80], 1:109n.) Its original meaning may have been: (a) to be strong; (b) to have extended sphere of control; or (c) to possess binding force. "It is worth noting that whichever of these meanings we adopt stresses the distance between God and man. In this they are in basic conformity with the basic characteristic of the Semitic concept of God, namely, that what is of primary importance is not the feeling of kinship with the deity, but fear and trembling in the face of his overwhelming majesty. Another point which it is necessary to remark is that they do not identify the Godhead with any natural object, but describe it as the power which stands behind Nature or the overruling will manifested in it" (W. Eichrodt, *Theology of the Old Testament* [1961], 1:179).

The name El as applied to God is general and includes the primary significance of power or ability (Gen. 17:1; 28:3; 35:11; Josh. 3:10; 2 Sam. 22:31–32; Neh. 1:5; 9:32; Isa. 9:6; Ezek. 10:5). Many feel justified in concluding that its employment and wide currency witnesses to a primeval monotheism, from which polytheism represented a lapse. Attention will be given to the frequent use of the plural form *Elohim* in the OT in a later section. For the present, it needs to be said that the name El bears not only the connotation of might, but also the idea of the transcendence of the Deity.

If El was a general term for the divinity in the thought of the peoples of the Bible Lands and ANE, the name *Yahweh* was a specifically Hebrew name for God. (Because it was considered too sacred to be pronounced, the Masoretic mss combine the four consonants YHWH—the tetragrammaton—with the vowels of ʾădōnāy [or of Aram. šēmāʾ, "the name," as some argue] to indicate that in public reading the latter should be substituted. The traditional form *Jehovah* is in effect a hybrid of the two names.) The basic meaning of Yahweh seems to be "he which is" or "he who is truly present." It is difficult to ascertain how widely this name was used during the patriarchal era, though the Bible seems to indicate that it was current in ABRAHAM's day. It was given new emphasis and significance to MOSES (Exod. 3:15–16; 6:3, 6) beyond what was understood by Abraham as he built his altar between BETHEL and AI (Gen. 12:8). Yahweh was revealed as an intensely personal name.

If it be correctly understood that the name was known as early as the birth of ENOSH (Gen. 4:26) and that Abraham had a knowledge of it, then it follows that the revelation to Moses represented a deepening and more personalized usage of the name. It is possible that earlier disclosures of the name had been obscured or even largely lost. The Mosaic use of the term (including the new significance attached to it) set the pattern for subsequent Hebrew thought. With Moses, the name seems to have gained general currency and specific acceptance; but more important, it became intimately associated with the life of Israel as a people. That is, it became the token of a special and crucial self-revelation of God to a special people—a disclosure that tied together the mighty acts involved in the exodus and Israel's self-consciousness as a nation. These acts in turn prepared the way for the intimate involvement of Israel with Yahweh at Sinai. Thus the name Yahweh was tied in inseparably with Israel's national awareness and was inescapably involved in Israel's unique COVENANT relation with the Deity. Vital to this covenant was the fact that Yahweh had taken the initiative and had stepped visibly and unmistakably into Israel's national affairs.

It is significant that the use of this name for God was unique with the Israelites. The other Semitic peoples do not seem to have known it or at least did not use it in reference to the Deity except as contacts with the Hebrew people brought it to their attention. It was the special property of the covenant people. It is significant also that the pronunciation of the name was eventually avoided by the Jews. Scribal usage involved circumlocutions and as well the use of alternate names. This bears witness not only to the significance of the name as a basis for the feeling for nationhood, but also to the respect the people felt for the supernatural source of their history.

It is clear that the name Yahweh was, in the Israelites' consciousness, set over all that which was merely naturalistic. This does not imply necessarily that the Hebrews saw a metaphysical meaning (as for example Aristotle's formula of "essence equals existence") in the "I AM WHO I AM" of Exod. 3:13, but rather, that they understood Yahweh as being existent and active in the here and now. In this connection, Eichrodt suggests that the name "goes much further than the divine names hitherto in use in its emphasis on the concrete nearness and irruptive reality of God, and contrasts vividly for this reason with their generalized statements (earlier names) on the rule and guidance, the exaltedness and eternity of the divine" (*Theology of the Old Testament*, 1:191).

The revelation and the grasp of the name Yahweh by the Israelites clearly marked a landmark in spiritual awareness and in national religious experience. With the exodus the Deity assumed in the mentality of Israel a specifically redemptive role. His "mighty acts" were specifically saving acts, and were so understood. In the deliverance at the Red (or Reed) Sea, Yahweh had shaped the forces of nature to serve the ends of grace and had brought his power to bear upon the nation in a time of historic emergency and crisis.

It is understandable then that the events of the exodus formed the core of Hebrew theology: "I am the LORD [Yahweh] your God, who brought you out of Egypt, out of the land of slavery" (Exod. 20:2). Here is emphasized the specialized quality of God's self-disclosure to the Hebrew people. It goes without saying that objections have been raised to the specificity which is implied here. Such thinkers as Douglas Clyde Macintosh have held that for God to have revealed himself especially and exclusively to the Hebrew people would have been an act unworthy of him, and one ultimately immoral. It is at this point that a sharp antithesis between merely human thought and the biblical insight appears.

The OT insight is that God has taken the initiative in restoring the knowledge-bond that existed between God and fallen humanity, a bond that was fractured at the FALL. And it was through his revelation to Israel of himself under the name of Yahweh that the unfolding of saving history became visible. The unveiling of God's nature by the giving of this name to Israel was of supreme significance to the entire biblical system. See also I AM (WHO I AM).

The third basic name for deity occurring frequently in early Israelite history is *Adonai*. Its root form, *ʾādôn H123* ("lord, master"), does not seem to have been in common use among Semitic peoples generally; in the OT it was used mainly in reference to human beings possessing authority but is also applied to God (cf. Josh. 3:11, "the Lord of all the earth"). Most frequently the plural suffixed form (*Adonai*, lit., "my lord[s]") is employed. In its earliest usage it was evidently a more transcendent term, indicating God's role as one high and above all things. In later usage, it came to indicate a more personal and intimate relation between the Deity and his people. It thus involves not only gradations of relationships but also obligations and duties. The name was frequently used with in combination with Yahweh. In the latter usage, the significance would seem to be that while Yahweh does indeed enter into relationship with his people, he is not to be localized or regarded as the God of any specific place.

III. Combined or secondary names in the OT. In addition to the three names that are frequently regarded to be basic in Hebrew usage, there are several compound or otherwise grammatically qualified forms. Belonging to this group, for lack of other special classification, would be two names that are apparently related to El, namely *ʾĕlôah H468* and the plural form *ʾĕlōhîm H466* (see ELOAH, ELOHIM). The former of these is used chiefly in the book of JOB, being found some forty times there. The name Elohim (often called "the plural of intensity") is used over 2,000 times in the OT to refer to Israel's God. It is frequently used with the definite article, bearing the significance of the one true God. Some have suggested that, by the use of this plural form, the Hebrews went beyond the usual Semitic name El as a fitting designation for their Deity, whom they regarded as being above and beyond all other gods.

Among the compound names for God in the OT, *ʾēl šadday H446 + H8724* represents a clear progression in the self-disclosure of God to the Hebrews of the patriarchal period (Gen. 17:1 et al.; NIV, "God Almighty"; the term *šadday* is used by itself in Num. 24:4 et al.). As EL SHADDAI, the Deity is viewed not only as the creator and sustainer of the universe, but also as the initiator and keeper of covenants. He is thus seen to move clearly in the human sphere, shaping natural forces to spiritual ends. The name seems to have had Babylonian connections. Though some understand it to mean "sustainer" (relating it to the Heb. word for "breast"), it is more likely derived from a root meaning "mountain," indicating strength, stability, and permanence. It has been suggested that the name is basically poetic (it appears most frequently in Job) and that it signifies majestic stability, the reliable refuge. The disclosure of the name is associated closely with the giving of the COVENANT as recorded in Gen. 17. The events associated with this point in Israel's history were intimate and personal ones, centering on the birth of ISAAC, the institution of CIRCUMCISION, and the provisions made for HAGAR and ISHMAEL.

It is significant that this name for the Deity became current in the patriarchal period, in which God's providences toward the Hebrew people were manifested most intimately and also uniquely to the race of Abraham. In this period, the name El Shaddai was an important verbal aid in the pedagogy of the Hebrews. It may be said that in a sense this name formed a bridge in the Hebrew mind between the epoch in which Elohim was the chief designation for the Deity and the period of the reemphasis on the intensely personal and redemptive name, Yahweh.

The name El can also be combined with ʿōlām H6409 (Gen. 21:33; NIV, "the Eternal God"), suggesting the permanence of the Deity, his exaltation above the changes and contingencies of time. He is conceived to be above the flux of natural phenomena. More significant is its combination with ʿelyôn H6610 (Gen. 14:18; Ps. 78:35; NIV, "God Most High"), denoting the highest and therefore supreme Being. See EL ELYON. The term Elyon is also combined with Yahweh and with Elohim, and it frequently occurs by itself. In the use of this name for God, the Israelites gave expression, not in the first instance to the exclusiveness of their God (which was amply expressed elsewhere), but to his supremacy. This name, which occurs in very early Hebrew history, seems to have receded in use until about 1000 B.C., at which time it came again into use, especially in the poetic literature of the OT. Here the OMNIPOTENCE of God is the point of stress (cf. also Aram. ʿillāy H10546, Dan. 3:26 et al.).

Especially common is the combination of the term ṣābāʾ H7372 ("host, army") with Yahweh, with Elohim, and even with both (*yhwh ʾĕlōhê ṣĕbāʾôt*, 2 Sam. 5:10 et al., NIV, "Lord God Almighty"). See LORD OF HOSTS. It is employed to indicate God's role as the One who controls all created agencies and beings. The name is associated with the ARK OF THE COVENANT (e.g., 1 Sam. 4:4; 2 Sam. 6:2) and is employed frequently by the prophets. That it was not merely an appellation equivalent to "Warrior God" is suggested by its large use (nearly 250 times) in the prophetic books. See WARRIOR, DIVINE.

Moreover, the term does not indicate a merely national or racial deity, as witnessed by the prophets' use of it in connection with judgment upon both Israel and the environing nations. Thus the "Lord of hosts" was conceived as being sovereign over *all hosts*, both "things in heaven and things on earth." The name suggests exaltedness, transcendence, and omnipotence. The use of this name implies also a universalistic tendency in Israel's religion during the period of the monarchy. As Eichrodt (*Theology of the Old Testament*, 1:193) points out, it suggests that the early concept of a high God in Israel was sustained. Thus the Hebrews' cultic usage was shaped and conditioned, not by purely national or tribal sentiment, but by a Yahwist faith that possessed universalistic conceptions.

The term ṣûr H7446 ("rock") is used as a name for God several times in the song of Moses (Deut. 32:4 et al.) and also in the Psalms, Isaiah, and elsewhere. The connotation is figurative; the name reflects God's role as a fortress or shield. It occurs in Deuteronomy in a context that suggests both God's greatness and his righteousness. The same combination occurs in Ps. 92:15: "The LORD is upright; / he is my Rock, and there is no wickedness in him." In Deut. 32:15, Moses chides JESHURUN (meaning "Upright One," no doubt an ironical reference to Israel) for forgetting the Rock who as Maker is the source of Israel's security. In v. 31 of the same chapter, Israel's Rock is contrasted with the rock of its enemies; here the reference is to God's strength, as well as to his special relationship to the Israelites, for he confuses their enemies and causes them to triumph in the face of vastly overwhelming numerical odds.

The word qādôš H7705 ("holy") is used as a name of God in several books, especially in Isaiah, where it is employed over thirty times (e.g., Isa. 1:4; 40:25). The term implies separation from all that is unworthy and unrighteous, and carries the connotation also of power, distance from man and the world, and in a certain sense aloofness and inaccessibility. At the same time, God is declared

A rocky escarpment in the Desert of Zin. The strength of God is highlighted when he is called the Rock.

to be "the Holy One of Israel"; thus the motif of transcendence, which might have been the major thrust of the term, is modified by the suggestion of *specialness* with reference to Israel. See HOLINESS.

Two names focus on the greatness of God, *ʾābîr* H51 ("strong") and *gibbôr* H1475 ("hero"). The first is employed in connection with the names of Israel or Jacob (e.g., Isa. 49:26, where it is closely associated with Redeemer); it indicates a Mighty One who strengthens the hands of chosen men (Gen. 49:24) and whose presence is symbolized by the ark of the Lord (Ps. 132:2, 5). The second has a similar significance, and is found in connection with the names El and Yahweh (Isa. 9:6; 42:13; Jer. 32:18).

The name El combines with *rōʾî* H8024 ("seeing, vision") in one passage; the use of the phrase is attributed to HAGAR as she fled into the NEGEV from the ire of SARAH (Gen. 16:13). It also combines with *bĕrît* H1382 ("covenant") on one occasion (Jdg. 9:46; see EL-BERITH). The reference here, however, is to a sanctuary at SHECHEM from whose treasury the citizens of the city gave seventy silver shekels to ABIMELECH to aid him in his struggle for kingship. The actual relation of the sanctuary in the city to the motif of "covenant" is unclear, but some agreements between the sons of Jacob and the Shechemites were probably implied in Jacob's acquisition of land there (Gen. 33:19).

From the foregoing, it seems clear that in OT usage the names describe functions or activities of God, although intrinsic and even metaphysical implications are not wholly absent. More significant still, they represent stages in a progressive self-disclosure of the Deity, a revelation that utilized situations (esp. crucial ones) as vehicles. The entire revelatory process was safeguarded by the third commandment, which prescribed not only a certain economy in the use of divine names, but a scrupulous adherence to norms of truth in connection with their employment.

IV. Names for God in the NT. The employment of names for the Deity in the NT tends to simplify the nomenclature of the OT. The most common name is, of course, *theos* G2536, which occurs more than 1,000 times. Corresponding to El and Elohim, it is expressive of essential deity. In general, its use in the NT takes for granted some familiarity with OT conceptions of the divine Being, whose existence is usually assumed. He is present in depth in all things, yet is independent of the created universe. While no stranger to the world, he is in his essential being transcendent, unmixed with created realities.

The name *kyrios* G3261 ("lord") occurs with great frequency in the NT. It seems to gather together within itself the combined meaning of Adonai and Yahweh. The name is applied to both Father and Son, and at times is the chief signification for Jesus Christ. A close correlate to the name *theos* (Jn. 20:28), it appears as a direct name for Jesus Christ especially in the postresurrection narratives (Lk. 24:34; Jn. 20:18; 21:20).

Thus, in the unfolding of the message of the NT, the richness and variety of OT nomenclature for the Deity was presupposed. This is expressed not only in the wide range of usages of the two terms already mentioned, but also in the carrying over of attributive names from the OT, such as "Most High" and "Almighty" (e.g., Lk. 1:35, 76; Rev. 4:8; 11:17; 21:22).

The most distinctive development in the use of divine names in the NT is the introduction of the name *patēr* G4252, "Father." While the idea of "God as Father" was foreshadowed in the OT, particularly in the relationship existing between Yahweh and Israel, and in the more intimate strains of the devotional literature (Ps. 68:5; 103:13), it remained for our Lord to make the usage concrete and intimate. The term was completely natural to him, and as the divine Son he employed it frequently (Matt. 7:21; 10:32; Lk. 11:13; Jn. 12:49). It is noteworthy that his first recorded words (Lk. 2:49) indicate his awareness of being about his Father's affairs, and that his last discourse on earth centered upon "what my Father has promised" (24:49).

While our Lord claimed that God was Father to him in a unique sense (see Jn. 5:18), yet that relationship was something to be shared (Matt. 7:11; Lk. 11:13). As the Redeemer and Son, he ever called attention to the Father who had sent him into the world. The ease with which he employed the name made it natural for the early Christian community to speak of God as "the Father of our Lord Jesus Christ." It follows that our Lord's language was not philosophical but filial. This name gave dimensions to the understanding of the Deity that neither "God" nor "Lord" could afford.

The thrust of the language of the NT Epistles is that God is the Father of all people in the sense of being the creator and sustainer of all, while at the same time there is an essentially Christian sense in which God is the Father of the regenerate. It is within the context of Christian redemption that the name *Father* comes to its fullest significance.

V. God's nature as revealed by names. It has been noted that God's existence is not argued in detail in Holy Scripture. The names by which he revealed himself in the OT period were, as already pointed out, descriptive largely of the divine activities and functions. It was mentioned further that there was an elaboration of functions (and by implication, of nature also) in the plurality of names.

This truth does not, of course, rule out the possibility that the employment of the varied designations afforded to the Hebrews—and to men and women of the Christian era—a propositional understanding of God's essential nature. The twin qualities of spirituality and personality shine through the OT nomenclature rather clearly. Back of this was the more basic understanding of God's sovereign freedom. He is portrayed as being above any determination outside himself. He existed before the world and is in no way dependent upon the cosmos for his existence.

God is unique in the quality of his freedom. This uniqueness has for its corollary the unitary quality of his being. He thus answers to the Shema (Deut. 6:4): "Hear, O Israel: the LORD our God, the LORD is one." This view, which by the period of the return from the exile had been indelibly impressed upon the mentality of the Hebrews, sums up the Jewish view of God. As sovereignly unique and exclusively unitary, God appears also as sovereign Father. This latter concept developed alongside the regal understanding of Yahweh, and in NT times became a dominant motif. It goes without saying that each of these conceptions is morally and ethically based, this being a corollary of God's holiness.

As almighty, God is shown to act not merely from the fact of irresistible power but also in accordance with that holiness (Lev. 11:44; 1 Sam. 2:2). This quality demands that all that is associated with him shall also be holy: the priests, the ark, the tabernacle, and the people. The purity thus enjoined is not merely a ritual characteristic, although the so-called Holiness Code (Lev. 17–26) has profound ritualistic overtones. But at the same time, the code has strong practical and ethical overtones. In the section dealing with blessings for obedience, God the Lord demands separation from evil as a condition to his making his dwelling with Israel.

The NT usage of designations for God sheds light upon the question of God's LOVE. While in the OT there were racial and national limits to the exercise of divine love, in the NT God's love and benevolence is clearly shown to extend to the whole of mankind. This is the clear implication of the words, "God *is* love" (1 Jn. 4:8). The supreme evidence for this is, of course, shown to be found in the INCARNATION of the Word, and in the sufferings, death, and resurrection of the Incarnate One (4:9, 10).

Something needs to be said, finally, with respect to the relation of God's nature (and esp. as this is revealed through the employment of divine names) to the created world. This question assumes its sharpest form in the issue of transcendence versus immanence. The name El, with its strong overtones of power, clearly suggests God's transcendence. The element of distance applies both to the relation of God to human beings and to the world. The accent falls upon his majesty (Neh. 9:32; Ps. 68:34, 35; Ezek. 10:5) in OT usage and in his role as the Lord of history, Creator of all things, and Ruler of the ages in the NT (1 Tim. 1:17).

In the name Yahweh are combined the two motifs of transcendence and immanence. On the one hand, he was a God of power and ability (Exod. 3:14; 20:2), but at the same time One who was vitally operative in human events. His nearness was, in general, seen in terms of proximity and availability to persons (e.g., Moses and the Israelites). The concept of covenant seems to bring the two motifs into close relationship, for the Mighty Deliverer was also Lawgiver and Provider.

It is significant that the understanding of Deity, particularly as it is revealed progressively through divine names in both Testaments, is singularly free from the twin extremes of deism and pantheism. On the one hand, God is declared and shown to be concerned with the affairs of the created universe and particularly the needs of mankind; on the other, he is intensely personal and thus distinct from all of the empirical universe. It is also noteworthy that the thrust of the scriptural view of Deity avoids the peril of envisioning transcendence in exclusively spatial terms, and as well, that of seeing his immanence in terms of a mixture (or identification) of him with created realities. Rather, God *as spirit* (Jn. 4:24) is essentially and intrinsically independent, and at the same time irreducible to corporeal or material existence.

While many feel that the employment of the plural form *Elohim* leaves the way open to the NT view of a plurality of *Personae* in the One divine Essence, the doctrine of the TRINITY rests primarily upon other grounds than that of the use of names for the Deity. But these names do play an indispensable role in the total movement of history-and-thought by which the eternal God has made himself known to the sons of men. To say the least, these names inform us, not only *that God is*, but also "that he rewards those who earnestly seek him" (Heb. 11:6). (See further W. R. Matthews, *God in Christian Thought and Experience* [1930], 89–110; C. F. H. Henry, *Notes on the Doctrine of God* [1948], 75–91; H. B. Kuhn, "God: His Names and Nature," in *Fundamentals of the Faith*, ed. C. F. H. Henry [1969], 35–55; L. F. Hartman, "God, Names of," in *EncJud* 7:674–79; K. Hemphill, *The Names of God* [2001]; G. H. van Kooten, ed., *The Revelation of the Name YHWH to Moses* [2006].)

H. B. KUHN

God, Son of. See SON OF GOD.

Godhead. A synonym of *godhood* or *divinity*, this English term is used to designate the state, dignity, condition, or quality of a deity, and in Christian theology, of the self-revealed God. The term occurs as early as A.D. 1225, sometimes bearing the more explicit sense of the one divine essence in distinction from personal or hypostatic distinctions within God's nature. Although older encyclopedias used to carry rather extensive essays under this heading, both this term and *godhood* have fallen into increasing disuse and are seldom found in modern Bible versions. B. B. Warfield noted that the disfavor of substantives ending in *-head* "has been followed by a fading consciousness ... of the qualitative sense inherent in the suffix. The words accordingly show a tendency to become simple denotives" (*ISBE* [1929], 2:1268b). Beginning in the 16th cent., the term *Godhead* was used to designate the divine nature of Jesus Christ, as well as the essential nature of the triune God. Some modern writers seem to use the term as a strong synonym for "God."

The word occurs in the KJV as the rendering of two related Greek words: *theion* G2521 (an adjective used substantivally in Acts 17:29) and *theiotēs* G2522 (Rom. 1:20; Col. 2:9). The first word, with the definite article, was in general Greek use for "the divine," which pagan religions saw in almost everything, and PAUL employed it in addressing a heathen audience, but in a context that urges personal faith in the living God. The second word was used by non-Christians with reference to ARTEMIS at EPHESUS, for example, and also later in the context of the imperial cult, and emphasized that quality that gives the divine, as deity, the right to human worship. Paul uses this term in association with the Creator's power upon which all creatures are dependent, and in Colossians he applies it to the incarnate LOGOS, in whom "all the fullness of the Deity lives in bodily form."

The term *Godhead* (or *Godhood*) cannot be applied to the divine essence in distinction from the attributes, since the glory of God is precisely the totality of his attributes, and the attributes constitute his essence. God's being is a living unity, in the sense that each attribute is identical with his essence; the attributes are human distinctions, but they have their basis in the divine nature and are affirmed in view of God's self-revelation. God is the infinite and eternal Spirit, the source, support, and end of all things. He is revealed in Scripture as Lord, Light, and Love—the sovereign creator, preserver, and judge of the universe; the righteous source of moral and religious truth; and the Father of spirits, whose provision of redemption for sinners through the gift of his only Son is the supreme manifestation of love. See also DEITY OF CHRIST; GOD, BIBLICAL DOCTRINE OF.

C. F. H. HENRY

godless. This term, referring to someone who does not acknowledge God, is most often used in the sense "wicked" or "impious." Neither it nor its cognate noun *godlessness* occurs in the KJV (which prefers *ungodly* and *ungodliness*), but the term is sometimes used in modern versions to render such words as Hebrew *ḥānēp* H2868 (e.g., Job 8:13; Isa. 10:6) and Greek *asebēs* G815 (e.g., Heb. 12:16; noun *asebeia* G813, Rom. 1:18 et al.). Note also the term *atheos* G117, which occurs in the NT only once (Eph. 2:12, usually rendered "without God"). See GODLINESS; HOLINESS; RIGHTEOUSNESS.

godliness. In nonbiblical Greek literature, the term *eusebeia* G2354 connotes "reverence toward the gods" and thus is usually rendered "piety, religion." In the NT (aside from Acts 3:12) it occurs only in the PASTORAL EPISTLES (esp. 1 Timothy) and in 2 Peter. The term indicates a devout attitude toward the true God reflected in holy conduct, and it is associated with such concepts as RIGHTEOUSNESS, FAITH, LOVE, KINDNESS, and PERSEVERANCE (e.g., 1 Tim. 6:11; 2 Pet. 1:6–7). Godliness means more than morality and more than mere religious profession. The power and reality of a vital union with God are implied. The corresponding adjective *eusebēs* G2356 occurs three times and is usually translated "devout, godly" (Acts 10:2, 7; 2 Pet. 2:9; cf. the adverb *eusebōs* G2357, 2 Tim. 3:12; Tit. 2:12); note also the noun *eulabeia* G2325, "reverence" (Heb. 5:7; 12:28), and the cognate adjective *eulabēs* G2327, "religious, pious" (Lk. 2:25; Acts 2:5; 8:2; 22:12). In the OT, the term "godly" is sometimes used to render Hebrew *ḥāsîd* H2883, "faithful, devout" (e.g., Ps. 12:1). See also HOLINESS; RIGHTEOUSNESS.

gods. This plural noun usually renders Hebrew *ʾĕlōhîm* H466 (though itself a plural form, it is also applied to the one true God; see ELOAH, ELOHIM and GOD, NAMES OF); in the NT it renders *theoi*, plural of *theos* G2536. Scripture teaches that the original religion of mankind was MONOTHEISM, and that belief in and worship of gods as distinguished from the worship of the true God is to be regarded as a corruption of the earliest faith and religious practice. The apostle PAUL outlined the downward process by which belief in the one true God, known but not worshiped, deteriorated to the most debased forms of IDOLATRY (Rom. 1:18–25).

The first mention of idolatry or polytheism in the Bible occurs in connection with the history of JACOB, whom LABAN accused of having stolen his "gods" (Gen. 31:30), actually the images of household divinities (*tĕrāpîm* H9572, 31:19; see TERAPHIM). From that point on, references to false gods are frequent in the OT. Through the course of Hebrew history and until the end of the Babylonian captivity in the 6th cent. B.C., there was a constant struggle to maintain consistently the purity of monotheism against the constant tendency to lapse into polytheistic belief and worship. There is a typical example of this long continued polemic against false gods in Ps. 115:1–8. By the time of the return from the Babylonian captivity, this tendency of the people of Israel to recognize and honor other gods was effectively and permanently corrected; from then on, to be a Jew was to be a strict monotheist and a hater of idols.

The Hebrew term is possibly applied to heavenly beings in some passages (e.g., Ps. 8:6) and even to human beings (e.g., Exod. 21:6), though the translation of such texts is disputed. Of special interest is Ps. 82:6 (quoted by Jesus in Jn. 10:34), "I said, 'You are "gods"; / you are all sons of the Most High.'" The following verse presents a contrast, "But you will die like mere men; / you will fall like every other ruler." It must be remembered that the context in both Ps. 82 and Jn. 10 is one of strictest monotheism. Jesus' statement that those who were called "gods" were those "to whom the word of God came" (Jn. 10:35) indicates that members of the covenant nation of Israel were meant. The generally accepted interpretation is that in these two passages the reference is to the judges or other rulers of OT times, who are called "gods" not because they were divine, but because they were dignitaries clothed with an authoritative commission from God.

The later JUDAISM, in the context of which the NT revelation was given by God, was the strictest possible monotheism. Among and around the Jews, however, were Gentiles who were polytheists and often idolaters. Hence, the NT emphatically contradicts all claims for divinity of any others than the one true God. At EPHESUS, for example, DEMETRIUS the silversmith objected violently to the preaching of Paul because the latter had said that "man-made gods are no gods at all" (Acts 19:26).

And to the Corinthians the apostle wrote: "there is no God but one. For even if there are so-called gods, whether in heaven or on earth (as indeed there are many 'gods' and many 'lords'), yet for us there is but one God, the Father, from whom all things came and for whom we live; and there is but one Lord, Jesus Christ, through whom all things came and through whom we live" (1 Cor. 8:4–6).

In using the term *gods* for the objects of pagan worship, Scripture does not mean to imply their objective reality, but only their subjective existence in the minds of their worshipers. AMAZIAH king of Judah, after decisively defeating the Edomites, brought back to Jerusalem a collection of Edomite idols, which he then set up and worshiped (2 Chr. 25:14–15), and was rebuked by a prophet of Yahweh for worshiping gods that were manifestly unreal and helpless, since they had not been able to save their own people, the Edomites, from conquest by Judah. Evidently Amaziah, though a worshiper of Yahweh, found it difficult to hold a pure enough monotheism to regard the Edomite gods as mere lifeless images. What is important to note is not merely Amaziah's inconsistency, but the Lord's rebuke to him through the prophet.

In 1 Cor. 10:19–21 Paul sets forth the demonic character of pagan divinities: "the sacrifices of pagans are offered to demons, not to God." While the pagan divinities are nonexistent and mere figments of human imagination (Rom. 1:21–25), still the worship offered to them was claimed and appropriated by DEMONS, who of course are objectively real and aim to oppose the truth of God.

J. G. Vos

goel. This term is a transliteration of the participle of the Hebrew verb *gā'al H1457*, which means "to redeem" or "to act [deliver] as a kinsman." The term is used frequently in the OT with reference to the person who is next of kin and his respective duties. One of those duties was to buy back what his poor brother had sold and could not himself regain (Lev. 25:25–26). He was also the recipient of the restitution that might be due to a next of kin (Num. 5:8). The story of RUTH illustrates the responsibility of the redeemer to purchase land belonging to one deceased who was next of kin, to marry his widow, and to raise up children for the deceased (Ruth 2:20; 4:14). In addition, the *goel* was to avenge any wrong done to a next of kin, particularly murder (Num. 35:12, 19–27). As AVENGER OF BLOOD, he had power to kill the murderer. CITIES OF REFUGE were established throughout Israel for those who accidentally killed another, and in those cities the slayer could not be harmed (Deut. 19:6, 12; Josh. 20:3, 5, 9).

It is quite appropriate then that the term became applied to God in his relationship to sinners. As Redeemer, God may be said to "buy back" what the poor sinner has sold (namely, his life) and cannot regain (see REDEMPTION). God also avenges the wrong done to believing sinners by his judgment against the devil and sin. Furthermore, like a husband, God marries the church, his bride. All of these concepts of God are seen in Scripture. They begin in the OT but are fully developed in the NT.

JACOB spoke of God as "the Angel who has delivered [*haggō'ēl*] me from all harm" (Gen. 48:16). JOB expressed assurance that his *Goel* was alive (Job 19:25). The psalmist called God his Rock and his *Goel* (Ps. 19:14; cf. also 78:35; 103:4). The book of Proverbs calls God the strong *Goel* of the destitute orphan (Prov. 23:11).

It is ISAIAH who most elaborately develops the concept of the divine *Goel*, using the term in reference to God thirteen times. As the Redeemer of Israel, God would rescue helpless Israel (Isa. 41:14), destroy Babylon (43:14), be king of Israel (44:6; 47:4), teach his people to profit and lead them in the way (48:17), be their Savior (49:26; 60:16), be their husband (54:5), show them everlasting love and compassion (54:8), and be their Father (63:16). All of this is conditioned on their turning from transgression (59:20).

Aside from using the Greek word for "next of kin" (*anchisteus*, Ruth 3:9; cognate verb, Lev. 25:26), the SEPTUAGINT renders the Hebrew term with the participial forms of such verbs as *lytroō G3390*, "to redeem" (Lev. 27:13), and *rhyomai G4861*, "to rescue" (Isa. 49:7). These words appear in the NT quite appropriately in reference to God and especially Jesus Christ, who is described as giving "himself for us to redeem us from all wickedness" (Tit. 2:14). PETER tells us that we were redeemed not with gold and silver "but with the precious blood of

Christ" (1 Pet. 1:18–19). Paul refers to Jesus as the one who rescues us "from the dominion of darkness" (Col. 1:13) and "from the coming wrath" (1 Thess. 1:10; note also *exaireō G1975* in Gal. 1:4 and cf. Isa. 60:16 LXX).

From the use of this term it is clear that quite early God's people understood the concept of God as *Goel*. And appropriately, Christ in the flesh became the Redeemer who purchased our lives with his blood and who wrought vengeance on our enemy, Satan. He further made the church his bride. (See R. L. Hubbard, Jr., in *BBR* 1 [1991]: 3–19; *NIDOTTE*, 1:789–94; *NIDNTT*, 3:189–205.)

Gog gog (גּוֹג *H1573*, perhaps related to Akk. *gāgu*, "costly pottery"). **(1)** Son (or descendant) of Shemaiah, from the tribe of REUBEN (1 Chr. 5:4). The names in this list may be included among the herdsmen who settled in the desert E of GILEAD (vv. 8–9).

(2) In an important prophecy, EZEKIEL speaks of "Gog, of the land of Magog, the chief prince of Meshech and Tubal" (Ezek. 38:2; see also vv. 3–23 and 39:1–16). He is viewed as the demonic and sinister leader of ungodly peoples far distant from Israel, whom he leads in a final assault against the people of God. Gog is ignominiously defeated by the intervention of Yahweh upon the mountains of Canaan. The conflict is alluded to in the NT (Rev. 20:7–9).

The origin of the name Gog is uncertain. Many scholars identify him with Gyges, king of Lydia (the Assyrian *Gugu*, c. 660 B.C.), who is said to have expelled the invading CIMMERIANS with Syrian help. See LYDIA (PLACE). Other suggestions include Gaga, mentioned in the TELL EL-AMARNA letters; a Babylonian deity also named Gaga; and Gagi, a ruler of the city of Sabi.

MAGOG (possibly meaning "the land of Gog") was no doubt located in ASIA MINOR and may refer to Lydia (JOSEPHUS says it refers to the SCYTHIANS, *Ant.* 1.6.1). With Gog are associated many peoples: not only MESHECH and TUBAL, of whom he is prince, but also Persia, Cush, Put, Gomer, Sheba, Dedan, and Tarshish—all of whom come from widely separated parts of the earth as a mighty host, like a cloud, to do battle against Israel under the mighty Gog. But God's judgment comes upon the enemies of Israel. Every kind of terror is summoned by Yahweh against Gog, whose defeat is so great that his vast armaments serve as fuel for Israel for seven years, and whose dead are so numerous that it takes all Israel seven months to bury them. Gog appears again in Rev. 20:7–9, where SATAN is depicted after the MILLENNIUM as gathering the godless nations of the whole earth—symbolically represented by Gog and Magog—against the saints and the beloved city, but they are destroyed and cast into the lake of fire.

There are three major divergent interpretations of the story of Gog. Some hold it to present a literal description of a future attack on Israel by certain identifiable nations led by Russia. Others regard it as a symbolic description of some future event—either the final conflict of the nation Israel with unidentified foes, or the final catastrophic struggle between the church and the forces of the world. Still others look upon it as a prophetic parable illustrating not a specific historical event but a great truth—that whenever in history evil forces array themselves to destroy God's people, he comes to the aid of his own. (See P. Fairbairn, *The Interpretation of Prophecy* [1856], 484–93; E. Yamauchi, *Foes from the Northern Frontier: Invading Hordes from the Russian Steppes* [1982]; D. I. Block in *VT* 42 [1992]: 154–72; P. E. Fitzpatrick, *The Disarmament of God: Ezekiel 38–39 in Its Mythic Context* [2004]; *NIDOTTE*, 4:685–87.)   S. BARABAS

Goiim, Goyim goi´im (גּוֹיִם *H1582*, "nations"). **(1)** A territory associated with NE SYRIA and ruled by a king named TIDAL, who joined KEDORLAOMER and other rulers in waging war against the CITIES OF THE PLAIN (Gen. 14:1, 9; NIV and most versions, "Goiim"; TNIV, "Goyim"; KJV, "Tidal king of nations" [cf. LXX, *Thargal basileys ethnōn*]). The common link with Gutium (Kurdistan), which implies an error in the Hebrew consonants, is unlikely. The location of Goiim has depended usually on the proposed identification of Tidal. If Tidal is the HITTITE name Tudhalia (Tudkhaliyas), then the identification of Goiim with a region in Syria would fit the biblical references. It would further support the view that the kings were drawn into a coalition from each of the quarters of the Babylonian empire: Goiim (Hatti) representing the W,

Ellasar (Assyria) the N, Elam the E, and Shinar (Babylonia) the S. Another proposal is that Tidal (reflecting Tudḫula) refers anachronistically to Sennacherib and that therefore Goiim indicates the conglomerate of "nations" that made up the Assyrian empire (see *ABD*, 2:1057). The context, however, gives no reason to understand Goiim as a collective reference to non-Israelite peoples.

(2) A city in "Gilgal" whose king is included in the list of rulers defeated by Joshua (Josh. 12:23; NIV, "Goyim in Gilgal"; NRSV, "Goiim in Galilee" [following LXX]; KJV, "of the nations of Gilgal"). See discussion under Gilgal #2.

D. J. Wiseman

Golan goh´luhn (גּוֹלָן *H1584*, possibly "enclosure"). A city in Bashan assigned to the tribe of Manasseh; chosen by Moses as one of three cities of refuge E of the Jordan, it was allotted to the descendants of Gershon as a Levitical city (Deut. 4:43; Josh. 20:8; 21:27; 1 Chr. 6:71). Josephus describes the district of Gaulanitis in Bashan as a fertile area containing a large population. Golan was the scene of both defeat and victory for Alexander the Great (Jos. *Ant.* 13.13.5). It belonged to the tetrarchy of Philip (see Herod VI).

Eusebius notes that Golan/Gaulan was a large village whose name became attached to the adjoining country. Most probably the territory corresponds to modern Jaulan (Golan Heights), an area bounded by Mount Hermon on the NE, the Jordan and the Sea of Galilee on the W, and the Yarmuk River on the S. The ancient city of Golan is usually identified with modern Saḥm el-Jolan, some 18 mi. E of the Sea of Galilee, on the E bank of the river el-ʾAllan.

H. M. Wolf

gold. A precious metal of bright-yellow color, high density (19.3), and high melting point (1063°C). It is the most ductile and malleable of metals and can be beaten into leaves of less than 0.0001 mm. in thickness. Gold usually occurs in the native state but sometimes as gold tellurides. Native gold is generally alloyed with 10–15% silver, sometimes with copper, and also with iron, platinum, palladium, and rhodium. The more silver present, the whiter the color, while the presence of copper makes the color orange-red. The natural alloy containing 15–45% silver was used for many early coins and is called *electrum*. This word in Greek (*ēlektron*) also means "amber," while in ancient Egypt the term *asem* was used. Like silver and copper, the crystal structure of gold is a face-centered cubic lattice in which each atom has twelve neighboring atoms touching it.

Gold is widely distributed in the earth's crust, but generally only in small amounts, with the average

Prehistoric circles located on the Golan Heights.

proportion in the crust being one part per thousand million. It is found in various igneous rocks, particularly those containing quartz, and their metamorphic derivatives, including the Precambrian Aqaba Granite Complex, which occurs on either side of the Red Sea and from which much of the sedimentary rocks of the Holy Lands were derived. Gold also occurs in many such sedimentary rocks, particularly those resulting from deposition in river channels and along old shore lines. The gold used in ancient times largely or entirely came from alluvial deposits. These occur on the slopes of hills not too far distant from the source of gold-bearing veins or as sands and gravels deposited by rivers in regions with auriferous bedrock, for example, rich gold deposits were known in the valley of the River Pactolus in LYDIA, Asia Minor. In such deposits, the gold is separated from the sand and gravel using a current of water that carries off the particles of lower density, leaving the high-density gold flakes, which sink. The gold is then separated from any remaining material by amalgamation with mercury. The gold-mercury amalgam is then heated to vaporize the mercury leaving a crude bullion (see METALS AND METALLURGY).

Even in predynastic times, the Egyptians made use of gold to embellish stone vessels and to make the handles of flint knives. The washing of gold ores is depicted on Egyptian monuments of the 1st dynasty (2900 B.C.), with gold occurring in Egypt between the NILE and the RED SEA (see MINE, MINING). Gold also occurs in ARABIA (Gen. 2:11; cf. 1 Ki. 10:2) and was imported by SOLOMON from OPHIR (1 Ki. 10:11). While Ophir is often considered to be in Arabia, in Solomon's day it was thought of as an overseas El Dorado (cf. Ps. 45:9; Isa. 13:12), to which joint Hebrew-Phoenician expeditions sailed in the "ships of Tarshish" (Ps. 48:7 et al.). Punt in Somaliland, Zimbabwe in Rhodesia, and Surparaka in India have been suggested as possible locations. Rich gold deposits were also known in ancient times in Lydia, in the lands of the Aegean, and in Persia. Later, deposits were worked in Italy, Sardinia, and Spain, while in the time of the Roman empire the chief source of supply appears to have been Transylvania.

Gold ornaments and utensils have been used since the Bronze Age, with the Sumerians c. 3000 B.C. using gold for domestic and ritual vessels and objects for personal ornament. Corresponding use of gold is recorded for biblical times (e.g., 2 Chr. 9:20; Exod. 25:11; Gen. 41:42, respectively). However the main use of gold has been, and still is, in relation to money and wealth (e.g., Gen. 13:2; Jdg. 8:26; 1 Ki. 10:14). It is taken as the representation of the most valuable of man's material possessions (cf. Ps. 19:10; 1 Pet. 1:7), while visions of things referring to the new Jerusalem speak of pure gold (Rev. 21:18). (See E. S. Dana, *A Textbook of Mineralogy*, 4th ed. [1932], 401–3; J. R. Partington, *A Text-book of Inorganic Chemistry*, 6th ed. [1950], 745–47; *The Zondervan Pictorial Bible Atlas*, ed. E. M. Blaiklock, [1969], 438–43.)   D. R. BOWES

golden calf. See CALF, GOLDEN.

Golden Rule. See ETHICS OF JESUS II.B.

goldsmith. An artisan who makes objects of GOLD. This English term is used a number of times in Bible versions to render the participle of the Hebrew verb *ṣārap* H7671 ("to smelt"), which can also be applied to the SILVERSMITH (as in Jdg. 17:4). The goldsmith's primary work was to hammer gold into shape, or cast it in a mold to form the object desired. These artisans often fashioned both gold and goldplated idols (Isa. 40:19; 41:7; 46:6; Jer. 10:9, 14; 51:17). Gold plating was placed over an idol carved from wood, using nails to hold the gold plate in place. The goldsmiths mentioned in the book of Nehemiah were probably jewelers (Neh. 3:8, 31–32). (Cf. R. J. Forbes, *Studies in Ancient Technology* 8 [1964], ch. 5.) See also CRAFTS; GOLD; OCCUPATIONS.   J. L. KELSO

Golgotha gol'guh-thuh (Γολγοθά G1201, from Aram. גָּלְגָּלְתָּא, "skull" [cf. Heb. גֻּלְגֹּלֶת H1653]). The Aramaic name of the "Place of the Skull," an area near JERUSALEM where Christ was crucified. See CRUCIFIXION. This name appears but three times in the Bible, in parallel passages of the Gospels (Matt. 27:33; Mk. 15:22; Jn. 19:17). Luke, as usual, does not use the Semitic word but only its corresponding Greek term, *kranion* G3191, "skull" (Lk. 23:33; cf. Eng. *cranium*), which the VULGATE in turn translates with Latin *calvaria*, thus KJV, "Calvary."

The author of Hebrews indicates that Jesus suffered "outside the city gate" (Heb. 13:12). Therefore, Golgotha "was near the city" (Jn. 19:20), but not within the city wall in NT times. The Gospels suggest that Golgotha was by a well-traveled road (Matt. 27:39; Mk. 15:21); furthermore, it was visible from some distance (Mk. 15:40; Lk. 23:49). This information has led many to think of it as a hill, but nowhere in the Bible is that so stated.

Although many places around the holy city have been suggested as the site of Calvary, only two are serious contenders for the spot of both the crucifixion and the burial. One primary claim to the site is the Church of the Holy Sepulchre, whose history goes back to the 4th cent. It is within the walls of the old city today, but its supporters maintain that the NT city wall would place it outside the city. Because modern buildings heavily cover all real estate in the area, no excavation is yet possible to determine just where that northern NT wall was. The location of this site can be traced to the 4th-cent. Christian Roman emperor Constantine, during whose reign the historian EUSEBIUS commissioned Bishop Marcarius to find Golgotha and the tomb. The Church of Constantine was then built on the site of Hadrian's Aphrodite temple and named in honor of St. Helena, the emperor's mother. Legend has it that upon excavating for the tomb, a fragment of the true cross was found that effected miracles of healing, and thus certified the site. The tradition that this is the site is very old but it is mostly tradition. Earlier, the pagan emperor Hadrian had deliberately obscured many Christian holy sites with his temples. See SEPULCHRE, CHURCH OF THE HOLY.

The other major contender for the site of Calvary is known today as the Garden Tomb and/or Gordon's Calvary. Suggested by Otto Thenius in 1842, General Charles Gordon declared in 1885 that this was the site of the crucifixion and burial, found some 250 yards NE of the Damascus Gate. Gordon's Calvary is a hill or knoll and is certainly outside the city walls (both modern and NT). The most serious problem with the Holy Sepulchre's location does not affect this choice. A garden and a tomb (in fact, several tombs) are in the immediate vicinity. Those who contest this identification maintain that the hill was part of a ridge that is still visible on the N wall of Jerusalem adjacent to Herod's Gate. Thus it was not a separate hill in NT times. The tombs are at least of Byzantine vintage, but no one can say whether they are older than that. The topographical feature of the hill that makes it look like a skull would not have been present in NT times. In fact, this hill, called by the Jews the "Grotto of Jeremiah," is thought to be a mine site

Modern reconstruction of the uplifted rocky protrusion of Golgotha just outside Jerusalem's Second Wall during the time of the Gospels. (View to the NE.)

developed only in the past two or three centuries. A better explanation of the "place of a skull" would be that either the hill was bare rock, or it served as a cemetery.

Some prefer the latter site because it resembles their concept of JOSEPH of Arimathea's garden (as a result of landscaping by the organization that owns the land). Since the Church of the Holy Sepulchre is a highly decorated building on top of a site, and the scene of much activity, a good imagination is required to see a garden tomb there, but it does have a stronger historical claim. (See further J. Jeremias, *Golgotha* [1926]; G. Dalman, *Sacred Sites and Ways* [1935], 341–81; C. Marston, *The Garden Tomb, Jerusalem* [1941]; L. T. Pearson, *Where Is Calvary?* [1946]; J. Simons, *Jerusalem and the Old Testament* [1952], 282–343; A. Parrot, *Golgotha and the Church of the Holy Sepulchre* [1957]; L. E. Cox Evans in *PEQ* 100 [1968]: 112–36; J. Wilkinson, *Jerusalem as Jesus Knew It: Archaeology as Evidence* [1978], 145–49, 180–94, 198–200.)

R. L. ALDEN

Goliath guh-li´uhth (גָּלְיָת *H1669*, perhaps derived from the Lydian name *Alyattes*; cf. *CAH*, 3rd ed. 2/2 [1975], 513). A warrior from GATH during the reign of SAUL (late 11th cent. B.C.). Representing the PHILISTINES in the Valley of Elah (about 15 mi. W of BETHLEHEM; see ELAH, VALLEY OF), he challenged the Israelites to send an opponent. His challenge went unaccepted until DAVID visited the battleground to bring food to his brothers. David felled the giant with a stone shot from a sling and cut off his head with Goliath's own sword (1 Sam. 17; with regard to the apparent discrepancy between this passage and 2 Sam. 21:19 [cf. 1 Chr. 20:5], see ELHANAN and cf. E. J. Young, *Introduction to the Old Testament*, rev. ed. [1964], 185–86). The height of Goliath was six cubits and a span, over nine feet (1 Sam. 17:4); however, the LXX and the DSS have four cubits and a span, less than seven feet (see J. D. Hays in *JETS* 48 [2005]: 701–14). His coat of mail was 5,000 shekels, about 125 pounds; his spearhead, 600 shekels, about 15 pounds (17:5, 7). His sword was kept at NOB under priestly jurisdiction and later given to David by AHIMELECH, the priest, when David fled from SAUL (21:9; 22:10).

This event illustrates ancient warfare: most of the army was ill-trained and no match for the experienced elite who often engaged in individual combat (cf. the Egyptian story of Sinuhe and Homerian battles; and see R. de Vaux, *The Bible and the Ancient Near East* [1971], ch. 7). Thus, JONATHAN could fight the Philistine garrison single-handedly (1 Sam. 14:6–15). David, Jonathan, and others were not foolhardy; they depended on God and therefore could expect his help. See also ARMY; WAR. C. P. WEBER

Gomer goh´muhr (גֹּמֶר *H1699* [*H1700* in Hos. 1:3], perhaps "completion"). **(1)** First son of JAPHETH and grandson of NOAH; father of Ashkenaz, Riphath, and Togarmah (Gen. 10:2–3; 1 Chr. 1:5–6). Gomer—referring probably to his offspring, the CIMMERIANS (Akk. *Gimirrai*, Gk. *Kimmerioi*)—is mentioned in Ezek. 38:6 as supporting an attack on Israel that will fail because the Lord is defending his people. (Some believe that the "men of Gammad," in Ezek. 27:11, is a copyist's error for Gomer.) The Cimmerians were forced out of S Russia by the SCYTHIANS and crossed over the Caucasus into Asia Minor at the end of the 8th cent. B.C. In the following century, they fought the Assyrians, conquered Urartu (ARMENIA), then subdued PHRYGIA and LYDIA, and fought Greek cities on the W coast. (See *CANE*, 2:1102–04.)

(2) Daughter of Diblaim and wife of HOSEA, the 8th-cent. prophet in Israel during the reign of JEROBOAM II (Hos. 1:3–8). The Lord asked Hosea to take to himself "an adulterous wife" (v. 2; NRSV, "a wife of whoredom"), so he married Gomer and by her had children to whom were given illustrative, or symbolic, names. This marriage pictured the Lord's relationship with his people, who had gone astray into IDOLATRY. Some moralists have questioned the propriety of Hosea marrying a harlot and have proposed the possibility that she was pure at the time of her marriage, but that both the Lord and Hosea knew that she would fall into sin. Hosea is later told to marry "an adulteress" (3:1); some believe that this too is a reference to Gomer after she had left Hosea, being bought again and asked to abstain from harlotry. Whether or not this is Gomer, it illustrates that though God's people sin, he loves them and wants them to return to him, but to refrain from sin. Some argue that these are not actual marriages but simply illustrations. (See N. Snaith, *Mercy and Sacrifice* [1953], 27–38; G. A. F. Knight, *Hosea* [1960], 27–29, 40–65; J. M. Ward, *Hosea* [1966], 3–71.) C. P. WEBER

Gomorrah guh-mor´uh (עֲמֹרָה *H6686*, perhaps "flooded place"; Γόμορρα *G1202*). A city located in the Valley of SIDDIM, probably at the S end of the DEAD SEA. Together with SODOM, it became infamous because of the circumstances of its destruction. Sodom and Gomorrah became bywords for the judgment of God. ISAIAH referred to its sin and its consequent destruction twice in his first chapter, and once later (Isa. 1:9–10; 13:19). JEREMIAH resurrected the horror of its destruction (Jer. 23:14; 49:18; 50:40). Both AMOS and ZEPHANIAH pronounced divine threats in terms of the two famous CITIES OF THE PLAIN (Amos 4:11; Zeph. 2:9). In the NT, Jesus, Paul, Peter, and Jude alluded to these ancient examples of God's retributive wrath (Matt. 10:15; Rom. 9:29; 2 Pet. 2:6; Jude 7).

Gomorrah is first mentioned as the S or E extent of the Canaanite territory (Gen. 10:19).

Some identify Gomorrah with this hill, Tel Numeira, on the SE side of the Dead Sea. (View to the S.)

Abraham's nephew, Lot, chose to live in Sodom. It was then that four eastern kings under the leadership of Kedorlaomer attacked the five cities of the plain (ch. 14). The book of Genesis also records the meeting of Abraham with the angels and their warning to Lot of the imminent destruction of Sodom and Gomorrah (chs. 18–19). Lot escaped and "the Lord rained down burning sulfur on Sodom and Gomorrah" (19:24).

The location of Gomorrah is unknown. Some have argued that it was at the N end of the Dead Sea, but the more widely accepted view is that Gomorrah and the other cities are sunken beneath the shallow waters of the Dead Sea, S of the Lisan peninsula. (See W. F. Albright in *BASOR* 14 [April 1924]: 5–7; id. in AASOR 6 [1924–1925]: 58–62; F. G. Clapp in *AJA* 40 [1936]: 323–44; J. P. Harland in *BA* 5 [1941]: 17–32 and 6 [1943]: 41–54; W. W. Fields, *Sodom and Gomorrah: History and Motif in Biblical Narrative* [1997].)

R. L. Alden

gong. The expression "resounding gong" (NRSV, "noisy gong") is used only once to render Greek *chalkos ēchōn*, "sounding brass," mentioned by Paul to illustrate the futility of the gift of glossolalia if unaccompanied by love (1 Cor. 13:1). See also music, musical instruments III.C; tongues, gift of.

good. This adjective, which occurs hundreds of times in the Bible, is usually the rendering of Hebrew *ṭôb* H3202 (e.g., Gen. 1:2) and Greek *agathos* G19 (e.g., Matt. 7:11) or *kalos* G2819 (e.g., 3:10). The terms have a wide variety of related meanings that often shade off into one another, such as "kind, gracious" (of men, 1 Sam. 25:15; of God, Ps. 86:5); "befitting, appropriate" (2 Sam. 17:7; 1 Cor. 5:6); "highly esteemed" (of a name, Eccl. 7:1); "agreeable, pleasant" (of fruit, Gen. 3:6; of a word, Prov. 15:23); "upright, righteous" (1 Sam. 12:23; Matt. 5:45).

In the Bible, the supreme good is never a matter of speculation, as it was in ancient Greek philosophy; rather, it is directly connected with such concrete concepts as happiness, pleasure, knowledge, etc. God himself is the Good: he is the source of all goodness, and thus there is no good apart from him. "No one is good—except God alone" (Mk. 10:18). It follows that we cannot know the good unless we know God in a right relationship and do his expressed will.

Since goodness is intrinsic to God, all that he does is necessarily good. He declared his own creation good (Gen. 1). The disorder, disruption, evil, and sin that now prevail throughout his world are the result of the rebellion of moral beings originally created good. God's revelation of himself in history was an increasing revelation of his goodness. He made man and woman in his image for fellowship with himself. Even when they flouted him in the FALL, God's loving interest in them continued; he showed his goodness by immediately taking steps to undo the disastrous effects of the fall. His election of Israel as his people, the exodus, the giving of the law, his many deliverances of Israel, the promise and preparation for the coming of the Messiah—all these were evidences of God's goodness; as were the incarnation, the atoning death of his Son, the resurrection, Pentecost.

The Scriptures make clear that history is not haphazard, but that God is working out a plan in history—the consummation of all things in his Son Jesus Christ. In this plan, God's children have an important part (Eph. 1). Some day his goodness will be acknowledged by all of his creation; and he will be all in all. Because of the fall, we are by nature corrupt and capable of doing nothing that is really good (Rom. 7), but because of God's provision in Christ and the Holy Spirit, we can live a life of obedience to and fellowship with our creator. (See *NIDOTTE*, 2:353–57; *NIDNTT*, 2:98–107.) S. BARABAS

goodman. This term is used by the KJV once in the OT to render Hebrew *ʾîš H408*, "man, husband" (Prov. 7:19), and several times in the Gospels, in the phrase "goodman of the house," to render Greek *oikodespotēs G3867*, "master of the house, householder, landowner" (Matt. 20:11 et al.). See HOUSEHOLDER.

goods, community of. See COMMUNITY OF GOODS.

goodwill. See PLEASURE.

gopher wood. This term is used by the KJV to render the Hebrew phrase *ʿăṣê-gōper*, which occurs only once (Gen. 6:14). NOAH was commanded to construct an ark out of this wood, but the meaning of the term is unknown. Scholars have frequently emended it to *kōper*, "pitch," which occurs at the end of the verse (and only there); "wood of pitch" could perhaps be a resinous wood, such as the conifers. Modern versions, however, usually take the term to be a reference to CYPRESS, which was often selected for shipbuilding purposes. See ARK OF NOAH.

H. M. WOLF

gore. This English verb renders Hebrew *nāgaḥ H5590*, which occurs in laws relating to injuries caused by oxen (Exod. 21:28–32). It is also used figuratively with the military connotation of thrusting at the enemy (piel stem, Deut. 33:17; Ps. 44:5; Dan. 8:4; 11:40 [hithpael]; cf. Ezek. 34:21). The false prophet ZEDEKIAH fashioned horns of iron, symbolic of irresistible weapons with which AHAB would gore and thus destroy the Arameans (1 Ki. 22:11 = 2 Chr. 18:10). H. M. WOLF

Gorgias gor´juhs (Γοργίας). A general who, along with two other "able men among the Friends of the king," was selected by LYSIAS (regent over SYRIA under ANTIOCHUS Epiphanes) to destroy the land of Judah (1 Macc. 3:38). He is described as "a man of experience in military service" (2 Macc. 8:9), and was later made governor of IDUMEA (10:14; 12:32).

Guided by Jews who opposed Judas MACCABEE, Gorgias once took "five thousand infantry and one thousand picked cavalry" and left camp by night to attack Judas by surprise (1 Macc. 4:1–2). But Judas learned of it and attacked the weakened Gentile camp. Finding Judas gone, Gorgias's men returned to their own camp, and seeing it in flames, they fled. On another occasion, Gorgias defeated Joseph and Azariah because "they did not listen to Judas and his brothers" nor "belong to the family of those men through whom deliverance was given to Israel" (5:59–62).

Later, when governor of Idumea, Gorgias almost lost his life as one Dositheus, on horseback, seized him and started to drag him away. He was rescued by a Thracian horseman and escaped (2 Macc. 12:32–35). Following this, Gorgias's men were routed (v. 37). (The KJV, with some Greek MSS, reads Gorgias also in v. 36, in place of Esdris.)

C. P. WEBER

Gortyna gor-tiʹnuh (Γόρτυνα). Also Gortyn. A city of south-central CRETE in the plain of Messara, on the River Lethaeus, about 10 mi. from the sea. Next to Knossos, Gortyna was the most powerful city on the island. According to Plato, it was founded by a colony from Gortyn in Arcadia (*Laws* 4). In classical times it and Knossos in league controlled the island, but in later times they were in almost continual warfare (Strabo, *Geogr.* 10). Gortyna allied with Rome in 197 B.C. against Philip V and soon became the most important city of the island. Under the empire it was the capital of the province of Crete and Cyrenaica (see CYRENE).

Much of the ancient city has been excavated by Italian archaeologists, who in 1884 discovered the Gortyn Law Code. It is dated in the middle of the 5th cent. B.C. and deals mainly with laws concerning family rights. Gortyna is listed among the autonomous cities to whom the Romans sent a letter in c. 139 B.C. guaranteeing the rights of the Jews (1 Macc. 15:23). That there were Jews on Crete is clear from statements by JOSEPHUS (*Ant.* 17.12.1; *War* 2.7.1) and PHILO JUDAEUS (*Leg. ad Caium* 36). A. RUPPRECHT

Goshen goh´shuhn (גֹּשֶׁן H1777, possibly "on the mountains" or "mound of earth"). **(1)** A town in the S hill country of the tribe of JUDAH (Josh. 15:51). The precise location is unknown, although some scholars have suggested Tell el-Dhahiriyeh, about 12 mi. SW of HEBRON, or somewhat farther E (cf. J. Simons, *The Geographical and Topographical Texts of the Old Testament* [1959], §§285–87, 497).

(2) An area in S Palestine. The Israelites are said to have subdued the Canaanites "from Kadesh Barnea to Gaza and from the whole region of Goshen to Gibeon" (Josh. 10:41; cf. 11:16). This region was probably between the NEGEV and the hill country, and it may have received its name from the town of Goshen; see #1 above.

(3) A region in EGYPT where JACOB and his family settled (Gen. 45:10 et al.). Goshen is closely linked, and apparently to be identified, with the land and city of RAMESES (Raamses), on the eastern side of the NILE delta (47:11). At the time of the exodus, the Hebrews were still in Goshen (Exod. 8:22; 9:26), and they began their travel from Rameses (Exod. 12:37; Num. 33:3), which city they had helped to build (Exod. 1:11). As the Hebrews also had to work at PITHOM (1:11), Goshen should preferably be within reasonable reach of that city. Furthermore, Goshen lay on a route from Palestine into Egypt, and near the residence of Joseph's pharaoh (cf. data in Gen. 45:10; 46:28, 29; 47:1–6). As JOSEPH (on any reasonable date for the PATRIARCHS) belongs in the Middle Kingdom or HYKSOS periods, his ruler's residence must be one of that general epoch not too far removed from the later Rameses of the 19th dynasty. Finally, Goshen was a good place for keeping cattle (Gen. 46:34; 47:6) and had room for settlers.

Rameses has been located at either Tanis (ZOAN) or near modern Qantir (more likely). As Pithom is indubitably to be located in Wadi Tumilat in the SE delta, Goshen can readily be placed in the territory between Saft el-Henneh in the S (at W end of

The land of Goshen near Tell el-Dabʿa. (View to the N.)

Wadi Tumilat) and Qantir and El-Salhieh in the N and NE. It could hardly be still farther extended up to Tanis. Many scholars specifically identify Rameses with modern Tell el-Dabʿa, just S of Qantir and about 3 mi. NE of Faqus.

This suggested extent would allow Joseph to meet his family in the northern part of Goshen, if they came in by the el-ʿArish route via Qantara toward Qantir; they would perhaps meet Joseph near El-Salhieh. A series of discoveries by Egyptian scholars in the E delta makes it highly probable that a royal residence existed in the 10th and 12th–13th and Hyksos dynasties (including the "Hyksos" town of Avaris) in the same region favored centuries later by RAMSES II for his delta residence of Rameses. Attested by temples and a palace, this residence was the administrative center for the E delta and Palestinian affairs.

The SEPTUAGINT tradition calls Goshen *Gesem Arabias*, this "Arabia" being a later epithet of the 20th Lower Egyptian nome (province), probably extending from Faqus to Saft el-Henneh. It is not quite certain whether the Egyptian inscriptions actually offer an equivalent for Hebrew Goshen. One toponym in Egyptian is written in a way that could be read either *šsmt* or *gsmt*. H. K. Brugsch and E. Naville accepted the reading *gsmt* and equated it with Goshen/Gesem. A. H. Gardiner preferred to maintain the sole reading *šsmt*, keeping it identical with a known place name. Both P. Montet and

Land of Goshen.

J. van Seters have revived the reading *gsmt* and its identification with Goshen. A final verdict is not yet possible, but either way, the topography is not affected.

The role of Goshen as a cattle-raising area fits well into the conditions of the Egyptian delta, with its bull cults (E. Otto, *Beiträge zur Geschichte der Stierkulte in Aegypten* [1938], 6–9, 32–33) and prominent animal-husbandry (H. Kees, *Ägypten* [1933], 10). In the late Hyksos period, the Theban princes even sent their cattle to pasture in the Hyksos-controlled delta (*JEA* 3 [1916]: 103). Under Ramses III, Papyrus Harris I has cattle of the god Amun (see AMON #4) pastured by the Waters of Ra in the very region of biblical Goshen, alongside other districts (A. H. Gardiner, *Ancient Egyptian Onomastica*, 2 vols. [1947], 2:167). (See further E. Naville, *Goshen and the Shrine of Saft el Henneh* [1885]; A. H. Gardiner in *JEA* 5 [1918]: 218–23; E. Naville and A. H. Gardiner in *JEA* 10 [1924]: 28–32, 94–95; J. van Seters, *The Hyksos* [1966], 146, 148, and references.) K. A. KITCHEN

gospel. The Christian message, or good news, of redemption proclaimed by JESUS CHRIST and his apostles. The English term *gospel* (from Old Eng. *gōd*, "good," and *spell*, "tale, talk") renders Greek *euangelion* G2295 (from *eu* G2292, "well," and *angellō* G33, "to announce"). This Greek substantive does not occur in Luke (though he often uses the cognate verb *euangelizō* G2294, middle voice, "to bring good news," e.g., Lk. 1:19); it is used a dozen times in Matthew and Mark (where modern versions usually render it "good news," e.g., Matt. 4:23), a few times in other books (Acts 15:7; 20:24; 1 Pet. 4:17; Rev. 14:6), and most frequently in the Pauline letters (almost sixty times, e.g., Rom. 1:1). The rare noun *euangelia* occurs in two passages in the SEPTUAGINT (2 Sam. 18:20–27; 2 Ki. 7:9; cf. also Jos. *Ant.* 18.6.10 §229). Note also the derivative *euangelistēs* G2296, "proclaimer of good news" (Acts 21:8; Eph. 4:11; 2 Tim. 4:5; see EVANGELIST). For the use of the term *gospel* in the sense of a book that recounts Jesus' life, see GOSPELS.

I. Background. The Hebrew term for "good news" is *bĕśôrâ* H1415, which is not used in the OT with a religious meaning (2 Sam. 4:10; 18:20–27; 2 Ki. 7:9). The cognate verb *bāśar* H1413, however, has the general meaning "to proclaim good news," especially in the sense "bring news of victory," and is sometimes associated with such concepts as RIGHTEOUSNESS and SALVATION (e.g., Ps. 40:9; Isa. 52:7). The participial form is employed in the later chapters of Isaiah to denote the messenger who announces the victory of God, the good news of God's kingly rule (Isa. 41:27; 52:7; cf. 40:9; 61:1). The expectation of such a herald persisted as a hope in rabbinic Judaism.

Among the Greeks, the verb *euangelizesthai* was used often in the context of announcing a victory, and *euangelion* originally meant "reward for good news." The noun (both sing. and pl.) also was used in the Roman imperial cult to signify the "glad messages" of the birth of a future emperor, of his coming of age, and of his accession to the throne. This aspect of the imperial worship is traced generally to Eastern influence, and it is not held that the NT message has been derived from the Roman cult, but we can see that hearers would already associate a religious content with *euangelion* before the advent of Christian preachers.

II. The message of Jesus

A. The kingdom of God. Like JOHN THE BAPTIST, Jesus proclaimed the advent of the KINGDOM OF GOD (Matt. 3:1; 4:17). In summarizing his ministry, the NT writers declare that he traveled the country preaching the good news of the kingdom and healing (e.g., Matt. 4:23; 9:35; Lk. 8:1; 16:16). The term *kingdom* signifies "kingly rule," the almighty, sovereign purpose of God and his royal authority, with its consequences for individual and community alike. According to Mk. 1:14–15, Jesus came preaching the gospel of God, and the substance of his message was that sinners must make the response of REPENTANCE and FAITH in view of the drawing near of God's kingdom.

But this gospel of the kingdom involves more: it bears a close relation to the person of Jesus himself. Jesus was conscious of his messiahship (Lk. 4:16–21) and of his Sonship (Matt. 11:27), and of the fact that the kingdom belongs to his Father (26:29). With his sense of messianic kingship he claims that God's sovereign purposes, revealed in the Scriptures, find historical and visible realization in himself and his ministry (Matt. 13:16–17; Lk. 10:23–24; Jn. 5:39). One may indeed say that Jesus, as the REVELATION of the Father (Jn. 14:9–10), is himself the complete expression of the sovereign rule of God. He is *autobasileia*, the kingdom personified (cf. Matt. 19:29; Mk. 10:29; Lk. 18:29; and see K. L. Schmidt in *TDNT*, 1:589). G. Friedrich has pointed out the importance of Jesus' messianic consciousness in this connection, for if he knew that he was the Son of God who was to die and rise again, then he also realized that he himself was the content of the gospel message (*TDNT*, 2:728).

These considerations indicate that the kingdom Jesus proclaimed was totally unlike that of contemporary expectation. One theme dominates Mk. 8:27—10:45, which represents Jesus teaching his disciples, in emphatic, stereotyped language, that the One whom they have acknowledged as Messiah must suffer and die (8:31; 9:31; 10:33–34).

The climax of that section is 10:45, where Jesus describes his mission in terms reminiscent of the Suffering Servant of Isa. 52:13—53:12. His purpose was to serve and to die as a ransom for many, thus advancing God's kingdom, in obedience to the sovereign will of the Father (Jn. 10:11, 17–18).

B. The invitation to the needy. Because of his identity and his mission, Jesus invites people to himself. Following the statement of Jesus' messianic consciousness, we have the offer of rest to those burdened by the yoke of the law (Matt. 11:28). The good news is proclaimed to the poor and oppressed (Matt. 11:5; Lk. 4:18; cf. Isa. 61:1), and the "I am" sayings of John's gospel are invitations to experience the divine provision for the needy. To respond to the invitation, through repentance and faith (cf. Mk. 1:14), is to experience salvation (Lk. 19:9), to enter the kingdom (18:18, 22, 24), to gain a new and eternal relationship in the family of God (Jn. 3:3–8, 16; cf. Matt. 6:9; Jn. 20:17). This is more than a casual invitation: the parables of Lk. 15 reveal the divine initiative in seeking and saving, and Jesus shows that initiative in action, for his purpose in coming was to make the good news known to all Israel (Lk. 4:43) and to seek and save the lost (19:10), a purpose whose urgency and yearning are well revealed by the lament over Jerusalem (Matt. 23:37).

C. The responsibility of the hearers. Jesus is to be exalted in glory (Mk. 14:62) and is to be the

Greek minuscule MS of the Gospels (A.D. 1271), open to Lk. 6.

final judge (Matt. 7:22–23; 25:31–46). He therefore demands that people should determine their response to him, for to reject his offer means death (Mk. 8:34–38; cf. Matt. 7:13–14), and to ignore is to reject, for neutrality is impossible (Lk. 11:23). Once the step of discipleship has been taken (see DISCIPLE), new responsibilities emerge, for ethical requirements are inherent in the message of Jesus (see ETHICS OF JESUS). The offer of rest provides also a new yoke of OBEDIENCE (Matt. 11:29), for here again Jesus is God's royal authority personified and it is *his* instruction which is to be obeyed (5:22, 28, 32, 34, 39, 44; 7:24–27), since that instruction reveals the will of the Father (Matt. 7:21, 24; Jn. 7:16–17; 14:10). Disciples of Jesus have the responsibility to live, individually and communally, in a manner worthy of their relationship to God, in humility, holiness, compassion, and trust (Matt. 5–7; 18), for their relationship with the Father is one in which he reigns over their life (cf. Matt. 5:3, 9–10, 19–20; 6:33), and their character must consequently reflect that of God himself (5:48). Because of the world in which they live, disciples must bear witness to their Master (5:13–16; Mk. 8:38), and they must fulfill lives of faithful service in view of the final judgment (Matt. 25).

D. The privilege of believers. R. H. Strachan has pointed out that since the kingdom was the Father's kingdom, Jesus taught an identity of purpose and activity between the kingship and the FATHERHOOD OF GOD (*IB*, 7:13). Those who submit to the kingdom are brought to the Father (Jn. 14:6), and they know the experience of divine FORGIVENESS (Matt. 18:23–35; Mk. 2:5–11; Lk. 7:40–48) and PEACE (Jn. 14:27). Believers have the sovereign protection and provision of the heavenly Father (Matt. 6:25–34; 7:7–12; Lk. 12:4–7, 22–32), a loving care that not only removes anxiety throughout life but that also is eternal in its scope (Jn. 10:29). The depth of relationship with the Father into which the message of Jesus brought his followers is reflected in their use of the intimate term ABBA (Mk. 14:36; Rom. 8:15; Gal. 4:6). Jesus speaks not only of his disciples' privileged position as children of the Father, but also of the instruction and guidance they may expect from the HOLY SPIRIT (Lk. 11:13; 12:11–12; Jn. 14–16), who provides the power necessary for living the life of the kingdom (Acts 1:8). Finally Jesus tells of the future blessedness that awaits his followers, when they will share the glorious consummation of his own kingly authority (Lk. 12:32; 22:29–30) and the eternal security of his Father's home (Jn. 14:1–6).

III. The message of the apostles. It will be convenient to consider the apostolic gospel message under the two well-known classifications of missionary preaching (*kērygma* G3060) and Christian teaching (*didachē* G1439), although it must not be supposed that these two aspects of the message were rigidly separated.

A. Missionary preaching. The apostles, too, announce the kingdom of God (Acts 1:3; 8:12; 19:8; 20:25; 28:23, 31). For them also Jesus is the kingdom personified, and the person and work of Christ are frequently the objects of the verb *euangelizesthai* (e.g., Acts 5:42; 8:35; 11:20; 17:18; Gal. 1:16; Eph. 3:8; 1 Pet. 1:11–12). In contrast to the "glad messages" of the imperial cult, there is now proclaimed the one Christian *euangelion* of the kingdom of God, a message of which some might be ashamed (cf. Matt. 11:6; Rom. 1:16; 1 Cor. 1:17, 23), since it is essentially connected with the person and history of Jesus. It is not naturally accepted (2 Cor. 4:3), but needs to be accompanied by the revelatory power of the Holy Spirit (1 Cor. 1:17; cf. 2:4; 1 Pet. 1:12).

In his gospel preaching to pagans (Acts 14:15–17; 17:22–31), PAUL sought to present the Christian message in the way most appropriate to his hearers' circumstances and cultural background. The same is true of the missionary sermons made to Jews and God-fearers in Acts, but it often has been noted that in these addresses one finds the frequent occurrence of certain definite themes. The question of a stereotyped kerygmatic pattern has been much discussed, but space forbids a detailed treatment here. Many scholars support such a pattern in some form (e.g., F. W. Grosheide in *EvQ* 3 [1931]: 62–66; C. H. Dodd in *ExpTim* 43 [1931–32]: 396–400; id., *The Apostolic Preaching and Its Developments* [1936]; M. Dibelius, *From Tradition to Gospel* [1934], 15–30; W. P. Hatch in *JBL* 58 [1939]: 1–13; A. M. Hunter, *The Unity of the New Testament* [1943], 23–25). These writers often differ widely from one another in their analyses, but the work of C. H. Dodd has had great influence upon English-speaking scholars. T. F. Glasson (in *HibJ* 51 [1952–53]: 129–32) has modified Dodd's analysis by listing the essential kerygmatic elements as: (1) the resurrection, (2) the fulfillment of OT prophecy, (3) the death of Christ, (4) the offer of forgiveness, (5) the apostles as witnesses.

Other scholars reject, wholly or partially, a rigid kerygmatic pattern (e.g., F. V. Filson, *Jesus Christ the Risen Lord* [1956], 41–54; C. F. Evans in *JTS* 7 [1956]: 25–41; H. G. Wood in *New Testament Essays: Studies in Memory of T. W. Manson*, ed. A. J. B. Higgins [1959], 306–14; R. H. Mounce, *The Essential Nature of New Testament Preaching* [1960]; J. P. M. Sweet in *ExpTim* 76 [1964–65]: 143–47). Filson analyzes the *kerygma*, but maintains, as do Wood and Mounce, that *kerygma* and *didache* frequently were intermingled in Christian preaching, while Evans, followed by Sweet, prefers to think of many differing *kerygmata* rather than of the *kerygma*. In the present article it is assumed that by his presentation of frequently repeated themes in the Acts sermons, Luke wished his readers to understand that these were the characteristic emphases of apostolic missionary preaching. It also is assumed that the essential *kerygma* consists of the elements most commonly preached, for it appears to be a sound method to follow Glasson's principle of including only the items that are most frequently mentioned, rather than to form a synthesis by utilizing each different particular that may be discovered.

We notice first, however, that a kerygmatic structure has been claimed also for other parts of the NT, particularly for certain "traditional" passages in Paul's epistles. One passage of special importance for Paul's understanding of the *kerygma* is 1 Cor. 15:1–11. In v. 2 Paul says that he will remind his readers in what terms he had preached to them, and in v. 3 he uses the technical vocabulary employed in JUDAISM for transmitting and receiving tradition, which might suggest the existence of an authoritative pattern for Christian preaching. J. Jeremias, among others, maintains that Paul is claiming to have communicated the facts and doctrines that had been given form by his predecessors in the faith (*The Eucharistic Words of Jesus* [1955], 128ff.). Consequently, Paul claims the same preaching as the other apostles (1 Cor. 15:11; cf. Gal. 1:8; 2:1–9). What then is that preaching? It contains a statement of the death of Christ (1 Cor. 15:3–4), an allusive reference to the forgiveness and salvation offered by God ("for our sins," v. 3), an emphasis upon scriptural evidence (vv. 3–4), a stress upon the RESURRECTION OF JESUS CHRIST, corresponding to what is perhaps the most characteristic emphasis of the Acts sermons (vv. 4–8), an insistence upon apostolic witness (vv. 5–8, cf. v. 15).

Looking SW toward Bethlehem. Shepherds were watching their flocks outside Bethlehem when they heard the Good News of Jesus' birth.

There is clearly an inherent logic in this combination of facts and doctrines. The DEATH OF CHRIST, the first article in Paul's summary, was from the beginning a fact of the utmost importance, if not as a soteriological event, certainly as an apparent mystery requiring some explanation and apology. The resurrection, therefore, provided an emphatic vindication of Jesus, an overwhelming proof that he was not a rejected sinner, but the appointed Christ of God. This argument is then complemented by the fact of apostolic witness, which furnishes yet stronger evidence for the validity of the *kerygma*. The further proof, from the Scriptures, would be an essential element of apologetics in a Jewish milieu: with the Jews' strong awareness of God's action in past history, Christian preachers would need to demonstrate that their message was the culmination of the previous revelatory activity of God.

It seems, therefore, both natural and logical that apostolic missionary preaching should consist of a reference to the death of Jesus, three proofs of the validity of the *kerygma,* and a concluding statement of the significance of the events preached: that forgiveness now is offered to those who believe. These five themes correspond to the items in T. F. Glasson's analysis of the *kerygma.* There may be yet another argument contained within 1 Cor. 15:1–11. Before his conclusion Paul tells his readers that he, like the other apostles, has experienced not only the vision of the resurrected Christ, but also the supernatural help of God in his life (vv. 8–10). Such a statement, set in general terms—that human beings can experience supernatural power, and that this power has a connection with Christ—would be another strong argument for the validity of the Christ-centered *kerygma.* It is not surprising to find that such a proof is sometimes used in close conjunction with the elements mentioned above. One may summarize six themes under the following titles: (1) death, (2) resurrection, (3) witness, (4) Scripture, (5) power, (6) forgiveness.

The above emphases form the essence of the missionary message in Acts. They occur as follows: (1) death—2:23, 36; 3:13–15; 4:10–11; 5:30; 10:39; 13:28–29; cf. 26:23; (2) resurrection—2:24–36; 3:15; 4:10–11; 5:30–31; 10:40; 13:30, 33–38; cf. 26:23; (3) witness—2:32; 3:15; 5:32; 10:39–42; 13:31; cf. 26:16–17, 22; (4) Scripture—2:17–21, 25–28, 34–35; 3:18, 21–25; 4:11; 5:30–31; 10:43; 13:16–23, 27, 29, 33–36, 40–41; cf. 26:22; (5) power—2:15–20, 22, 33, 38; 3:12–13, 16, 19–21; 4:9–10; 5:32; 10:38; 13:17–23, 40–41; cf. 26:22; (6) forgiveness—2:21, 38–40; 3:19, 26; 4:12; 5:31; 10:43; 13:38–39; cf. 26:23. An examination of the passages will show that the themes are presented in ways appropriate to the audience. For example, in Acts 2–3 the statements about the death of Jesus effectively contrast the crime of the hearers with the attitude of God; in chs. 10 and 13 more detailed information is given than was necessary in Jerusalem; and in ch. 13 the allusions to OT facts and to God's sovereign power are worked into a typical form of synagogue address.

What, then, is the origin of these particular emphases? The obvious source to whom to look would be Christ himself. Bo Reicke (in *The Root of the Vine: Essays in Biblical Theology,* ed. A. Fridrichsen [1953], 128–60) notes that Jesus sent the disciples on preaching missions, and it would be natural to assume that their preaching then was modelled on his, especially as they were his representatives and considered as an extension or multiplication of his person. Some scholars have argued for an even closer connection between the teaching of Jesus and that of the apostles. B. Gerhardsson, for example, maintains that Jesus taught in rabbinic fashion, with extensive use of memorization, and that the apostles and early church transmitted fixed forms of tradition derived from Christ, in the way that Judaism transmitted the oral Torah (*Memory and Manuscript* [1961], 234, 274–80).

Gerhardsson's thesis has been criticized widely (e.g., by Morton Smith in *JBL* 82 [1963]: 169–76), and it seems improbable in its detailed outworking, but the practice of memorization was so much an accepted feature of ancient education that it does seem possible that the disciples would have learned at least some parts of Jesus' teaching by heart, and it does appear that many items of the apostolic message may be traced back to Jesus. Note the following: Servant of God and Messiah (Mk. 10:45; 14:61–62), the argument from supernatural power (2:9–12; Lk. 11:20), the importance of personal testimony (Matt. 10:27; Mk. 4:19; 10:38), stereotyped references to Jesus' death and resurrection (Mk. 8:31; 9:31; 10:33–34), proof texts from the OT (12:10–11, 35–37). The most common kerygmatic elements occur also in Lk. 24:19–20, 25–27, 44–49. C. F. Evans holds that Luke has simply read back the *kerygma* into his gospel and has presented it in a dramatic form in preparation for the Acts sermons, but it does not seem unreasonable to believe that Luke 24 is an accurate record of events, that the risen Christ answered his disciples' questionings, and that the emphases of his explanation later found expression in their preaching.

Concentration upon particular emphases of the missionary gospel must not blind one to the fact which we have noticed at the beginning of this section: that the one central theme, dominating and unifying all the secondary themes, is Christ himself. The gospel is the gospel of the glory of Christ (2 Cor. 4:4).

B. Christian teaching

1. The privilege of believers. Paul possessed an overwhelming sense of the privileged position granted to him by the grace of God (Eph. 3:8), and not to him only, but to all believers, for the good news of Christ is that the priceless blessing of salvation is a free gift (Rom. 3:24; 6:23), given by the grace of God (Eph. 2:8; cf. Acts 20:24) to all who will accept it by faith (Rom. 3:22, 25). This gospel is God's secret which he has made known to his people (Eph. 6:19; Col. 1:26). It brings salvation (Eph. 1:13; cf. 1 Cor. 15:2), for it is God's own power for saving (Rom. 1:16), revealing the righteousness of God: that gracious, delivering activity by which God rescues the sinner and justifies the ungodly (1:17; 3:26; 4:5).

A stress upon JUSTIFICATION — God's gracious, free acquittal of guilty sinners who trust in Christ — is especially characteristic of Paul's presentation of the gospel message (e.g., Rom. 4:5–7; 8:34). The gospel tells of FORGIVENESS and of RECONCILIATION with God achieved through the cross of Christ (Rom. 5:10–11; 2 Cor. 5:19), for Christ made reconciliation and came proclaiming the good news of PEACE (Eph. 2:16–17; cf. 6:15). Just as the appearance of Christ on earth was "the beginning of the gospel" (Mk. 1:1; cf. Acts 1:1), so in the context of Eph. 2:15–18 the total work of Christ is summarized in the words, "He came and preached peace" (cf. Isa. 52:7; 57:19).

That peace is available for the whole of humanity, for the good news unites Jews and Gentiles and mediates salvation to both alike (Eph. 3:6). All believers have experienced spiritual rebirth from God (1 Pet. 1:3; 1 Jn. 3:9; cf. Jn. 3:3), know the privilege of ADOPTION as God's own sons (Rom. 8:15–23; Gal. 4:5–6; Eph. 1:5), and are set in a new order of existence (2 Cor. 5:17), for there is "a new creation": the believer is "in Christ"; he is united with Christ (Rom. 6:1–11; see UNION WITH CHRIST); he is in "the kingdom of God's beloved Son" (Col. 1:13). In this new life in God's family, the gospel brings the news of the strength that comes from God (Rom. 16:25), for the gift of the Holy Spirit enables believers to live in a way that pleases God (8:1–17, 26–27).

The writer to the Hebrews reminds us that Christians also have constantly the help and care of Christ as the perfect High Priest, who fully understands and sympathizes with the character and circumstances of his people (Heb. 2:14–18; 4:14–16), and 1 Pet. 2:21–25 is an assertion of the understanding Christ has for his afflicted followers (cf. 1 Pet. 5:10). The Christian already is triumphantly secure in the loving care of God, from which nothing can separate him (Rom. 8:28–39), and he is equally secure after death (2 Cor. 5:1–8). Christ is exalted in glory over the whole universe (Eph. 1:20–23; Phil. 2:9; Col. 1:15–17); believers share already in his exaltation (Eph. 1:3; 2:6), and are yet to share in his future majesty in the restored universe (Rom. 8:17–19; 1 Cor. 15:20; Col. 1:5, 27; 2 Tim. 2:12; Heb. 2:10).

2. The responsibility of believers. In apostolic teaching, as in that of Jesus, ethical requirements are inherent in the gospel message. See ETHICS OF PAUL. The new and privileged position that the believer has received by God's grace is intended to lead directly to righteous living (Eph. 2:10). Clear ethical implications are also found elsewhere (e.g., 2 Cor. 5:21; Col. 1:22–23; 2:6–7; Tit. 2:11–14). The Christian message is "the glorious gospel of the blessed God" (1 Tim. 1:11); it is God's address to us, and when God thus speaks, we must listen and yield obedience (2 Cor. 9:13; cf. Rom. 1:5; 16:26). The believer must lead a life that is equally "worthy of God" (1 Thess. 2:12) and "worthy of the gospel of Christ" (Phil. 1:27).

In his ethical teaching Paul often argues explicitly from the well-known facts of the gospel proclamation by which the churches were established. For example, based on such essential facts about Christ are the exhortations to mutual concern (Rom. 15:1–3), to humility and brotherly love (Phil. 2:1–11), to forgiveness (Eph. 4:32), to conjugal love (5:25–30), to holiness and purity (Rom. 6:4; 1 Cor. 6:15–20), and to confidence and hope (1 Cor. 15:20; 1 Thess. 4:13–14). Christians are "called to be saints" (Rom. 1:7); they are united with Christ (6:1–11) and must therefore lead a sanctified life. Their union with Christ involves other responsibilities too. Christ has suffered, and his followers must share that experience (8:17; 1 Pet. 2:21). Christ has brought the gospel, and now Christian believers, who have responded to that good news, must themselves bear it to others (Rom. 10:15; cf. Isa. 52:7; Eph. 6:15; 2 Tim. 4:5).

An identity of purpose has been apparent in the apostolic teaching and that of Jesus. Sometimes actual words of Jesus are employed in ethical instruction (e.g., Acts 20:35), and sometimes one finds striking similarities to the SERMON ON THE MOUNT (e.g., Jas. 1:2, 4–5, 19–22; 2:10, 13; 3:18; 4:4, 10–15; 5:2–6, 10–12). Finally, as in the teaching of Jesus, there is an insistence upon future JUDGMENT: the message of judgment is intrinsic to the gospel (Rom. 2:16), and believers are to live constantly in the light of the judgment seat of Christ (Rom. 14:10; 1 Cor. 3:10–15; 2 Cor. 5:9–10; 1 Pet. 5:4; cf. 2 Pet. 3:11–12). (See further *The Gospel and the Gospels*, ed. P. Stuhlmacher [1991]; *Gospel in Paul: Studies on Corinthians, Galatians and Romans for Richard N. Longenecker*, ed. L. A. Jervis and P. Richardson [1994]; P. T. O'Brien, *Gospel and Mission in the Writings of Paul: An Exegetical and Theological Analysis* [1995].)

IV. Summary. The message of Jesus is ultimately an invitation to men and women to commit themselves wholeheartedly to him, and to experience fully the relationship with the Father which is insured by that discipleship. The message of the apostles is the same, but has now been filled out, from a deepening Christian experience, with the proclamation of all the saving activity of God revealed in the total ministry of Christ, who is the climax of all God's purposes (cf. 2 Cor. 1:20).

D. R. JACKSON

Gospel according to the Hebrews. See HEBREWS, GOSPEL ACCORDING TO THE. Similarly, NAZARENES, GOSPEL OF THE; PHILIP, GOSPEL OF; THOMAS, GOSPEL OF; etc. See also APOCRYPHAL NEW TESTAMENT I.

Gospel harmony. See HARMONY OF THE GOSPELS.

Gospel of Truth. See TRUTH, GOSPEL OF.

Gospels. The first four books of the NT, which relate the life, teachings, death, and resurrection of JESUS CHRIST. Christianity is a historical faith. It is rooted in the INCARNATION and committed to Jesus of Nazareth. Understandably, there is a tremendous interest in the life and teachings of Jesus and in those primary documents that present him.

   I. Use of the term
  II. Oral tradition
 III. Written Gospels
    A. The four Gospels
    B. Relationships
 IV. The fourfold gospel
  V. Historical value

I. Use of the term. Originally, the term GOSPEL had reference to the message of salvation through Christ, and only later was the term used to designate written documents. Its most important antecedent is the OT theme that the SERVANT OF THE LORD, who was to come, would declare good news to the world (Isa. 40:9; 52:7; 61:1). Jesus came preaching the gospel in fulfillment of prophecy (Matt. 11:5; Lk. 4:18). "The time has come.... The kingdom of God is near" (Mk. 1:15). Jesus Christ, the bearer of the good news, was himself the content and substance of the gospel. In Paul's epistles, the gospel is the testimony to Jesus (Rom. 1:3; in the NT, the word is always sing.). An evangelist is one who bears the good tidings (2 Tim. 4:5).

At the beginning of the 2nd cent., the term began to be used for the written account of salvation (*Did.* 15.3–4; *2 Clem.* 8.5). There was, however, only one gospel. The person who declares another gospel is anathema (Gal. 1:8–9). The four works called "the Gospels" are really four records of one gospel. JUSTIN MARTYR was apparently the first Christian to use the word in the plural when he wrote of the "memoirs composed by the apostles called Gospels" (*1 Apol.* 66.3). By that time, the danger of confusion had passed, though the church still spoke, for example, of the "Gospel according to Matthew," not "the Gospel *of* Matthew." God's grace had broken into history, and the news of it was the *good news*. An evangelist was not the writer of a gospel, but a bearer of the message itself. The four Gospels were intended to do that too, and remained anonymous.

These works constitute a new literary phenomenon. They are not biographies as such, for they omit much material normally found in such works; yet they are more like biographies than anything else. They are historical in form; their primary aim is to present the data in such a way that the good news will be very apparent. This accounts for the heavy emphasis in each gospel upon the closing days of Jesus' earthly life and his resurrection. The Gospels are not literary productions; their writers were not literary men. They followed no conventional pattern or form. Each sought to give a portrait of Christ as he saw him from his perspective. (On the debate concerning the genre of the Gospels, see C. H. Talbert, *What Is a Gospel?* [1977]; D. E. Aune, *The New Testament in Its Literary Environment* [1987], 17–76; L. W. Hurtado in *DJG*, 276–82.)

In the days of oral tradition, when eyewitnesses were available to pass on information vital to Jesus' life and ministry, the need for written works was not great. Many regarded the spoken word more highly than the written accounts. With the gradual disappearance of eyewitnesses, by death, the need became acute for written records. Fortunately for the church, such accounts had already been in process of compilation and composition long before the first generation died. The spread of the church throughout the world did as much as anything else to create the demand for written Gospels. Luke composed his two-volume work to meet such a need (Lk. 1:1–4). Written documents were needed for instructing new converts and for teaching the people, as well as for use in public worship. By the end of the 2nd cent., the four Gospels were almost universally accepted, not only as authentic, but as canonical—on a par with the OT Scriptures. Valuable testimony from Papias, Irenaeus, Clement of Alexandria, and Tertullian indicates that the Gospels all originated from the apostolic age. Few ancient documents have such attestation so close to the date of their composition. Their writers had no ambition for literary glory; they desired only to record the message of salvation.

II. Oral tradition. Criticism of the Gospels in modern times has been concentrated on the shadowy area of transmission from event to its recording. Most of the material in the Gospels existed for a time in an oral stage, when it was handed down by word of mouth, before being incorporated into a written document. Jesus was a preacher of the good news. He gave his disciples close instruction privately (Mk. 4:34), and they remembered his words and deeds long after his death.

Form criticism is a method of analysis that seeks to trace this process of transmission. This discipline arose out of some dissatisfaction with the fruits of source criticism, which could not penetrate behind the written materials themselves. Form criticism is, however, inevitably somewhat speculative, because it delves into the few decades after the resurrection, and there is little historical information about the materials handed down during this time. Unfortunately, form criticism became allied to an attitude of historical skepticism in the work of many scholars. Although the investigation of the oral stage is itself quite worthy, this discipline has become almost synonymous with the attempt to discredit the historical integrity of the NT documents.

Form criticism treats the Gospels as primary witnesses not to the life of Jesus but to the beliefs and practices of the primitive church. Although the attempt to find the life-situation of the materials in the Gospels is legitimate, it is quite another matter to assume without proof that the accounts were invented to meet the needs of the church community. Therefore, the reconstruction of units of tradition is highly speculative. One scholar will find a totally different life-situation for a story or saying than another. If form critics would allow for more life-settings with a pre-Easter situation, their

The two small fish that Jesus blessed when feeding the 5,000 may have been sardines from the Sea of Galilee.

whole endeavor would look less suspicious. That the community should first frame its own traditions and then convince itself of their historical integrity is hardly plausible. It is dangerous to start with a hypothetical theory of how the materials were handled, while ignoring the plain testimony in the text to the contrary. The presence of eyewitnesses in the church certainly had a restraining effect on the free creation of historical traditions. The gospel accounts did not grow out of the church's need for them; rather the church grew out of the facts they recorded.

Primitive Christianity was stamped by the impact of the person and work of Jesus. The theory that the community wrote the first life of Jesus in isolation from reliable recollections about him has no foundation and little probability. The church was "colored" by Jesus, not Jesus by the community. Early Christians were interested in stories of Jesus during his historical ministry. The apostles who played a decisive role in the formation of the church were in a position to supply such information. The idea of the free creation and flow of tradition unhindered by historical fact is fanciful and romantic. The presence of the apostles prevented the very situation the form critics assume.

There is no positive evidence that the needs and problems of the early church were read back into the Gospels. Certain of these problems are well known, such as the admission of the Gentiles, tongues, dietary laws, and church government; none of these problems received any significant treatment in the Gospels. On the other hand, there are features in the Gospels that do not reappear in Acts or the Epistles, such as parables, the SON OF MAN title, and the KINGDOM OF GOD. All the data suggests that a clear boundary existed between the history before and after Easter. There is just not enough time available for the developments assumed by the form critics. The "biology of the saga" requires a time lag of centuries for the development of a coherent cycle of myths. There was no time in the 1st cent. for the creation, collection, and collation of community sagas. The gospel story broke into the light of history in a very short time.

Form criticism as a method has been vastly overrated. Jesus gathered disciples around him. These disciples treasured the deposit of his teaching and passed it down in the community that they led after his resurrection. A convincing parallel to what went on in the oral stage of the gospel material would be the rabbinic method of transmission, which was marked by a high degree of accuracy and continuity. The presence of eyewitnesses in the church during the whole period of oral tradition puts a severe limiting factor upon all radical form criticism.

As long as the care employed in transmission is respected, form criticism can aid the understanding of the history of the Gospels in their preliterary stage. The advance in knowledge from this source has not been great. Clearly, the early preachers gave prominence to the PASSION of Jesus and presented the account in connection with the general shape of Jesus' life. As converts were instructed, further stories and sayings of Jesus were added from the memory of the apostles to meet the needs at hand. The catechesis was no doubt largely oral in form, but possibly also accompanied with written accounts. Tradition connects an early tract with the apostle Matthew, and it may have been one of many primitive written sources that assisted the teachers in their work (cf. Lk. 1:1).

III. Written Gospels

A. The four Gospels

1. Matthew. The first gospel breathes the atmosphere of the OT, and makes the transition from the Old to the New a smooth one. At the outset, the writer provides a genealogy linking Jesus to DAVID and ABRAHAM through his legal father JOSEPH (see GENEALOGY OF JESUS CHRIST). His interest in connecting Jesus with messianic prophecies of the OT is apparent throughout. All the significant events in Jesus' life — his birth, birthplace, home, ministry, and death — were in direct fulfillment of OT predictions. Most of the NT manifests the same concern with prophecy, but Matthew demonstrates it to a remarkable degree.

Although he does not state his purpose, as Luke and John do, Matthew endeavors to prove that Jesus is the MESSIAH. To achieve this, the writer gives his gospel a strongly Judaic flavor. Numerous details about contemporary Jewish life and religion are included. Interest in the kingdom of heaven and the messianic king is sustained throughout. Matthew gives great prominence to the teaching ministry of Jesus. Apparently using the Markan narrative as his basis, Matthew inserted five long blocks into it. This feature made Matthew a handy teaching manual in the primitive church. Since Mark is notably short of teaching, the inclusion in Matthew of extensive sermons is a distinct advantage.

In Matthew, narrative and discourse alternate. The pattern of act and word, of *kerygma* and *didache*, is striking. One of the curious features of Matthew is the tension between universalism and particularism. On the one hand, Jesus came exclusively to "the lost sheep of Israel" (Matt. 15:24) and refused to go into the way of the Gentiles (10:5). He would not allow even "the smallest letter" or "the least stroke of the pen" to "disappear from the Law" (5:18). Alongside this narrow particularism, however, is a universalism. The coming of the MAGI, the flight into Egypt, the Great Commission, all point to the universal implications of this gospel. The tension is resolved by observing the progress of saving history. Prior to his death, Jesus exhausted himself in taking the good news to the nation of Israel, who refused it. Near the end of his life, Jesus predicted, "the kingdom of God will be taken away from you and given to a people who will produce its fruit" (21:43). Out of his death and resurrection sprang a "new Israel," a spiritual heir to the promises of God, drawn from every nation under heaven.

Matthew may be regarded as a long edition of Mark. The writer incorporated almost the whole of Mark, abbreviated some of the stories, and added a large amount of non-Markan material. Whereas Mark gave Matthew his framework, Mark did not determine Matthew's purpose. Matthew's emphasis differs from Mark's. The first gospel is an apologetic tract, and the note of fulfillment is prominent. An insistent tradition in the ancient church, going back to PAPIAS, held that the first gospel was originally written in Aramaic or Hebrew (quoted by EUSEBIUS, *Eccl. Hist.* 3.39.15–16; for an analysis of the passage, see R. H. Gundry, *Mark: A Commentary on His Apology for the Cross* [1993], 1026–45). Opinions differ widely over what this may mean. It would seem reasonable, however, to locate the underlying genius of Matthew's gospel and its origins in the earliest Jewish Christian church. See also MATTHEW, GOSPEL OF.

2. Mark. The second gospel is direct and to the point. It is a gospel, not a biography. Mark's readers already knew the story. It has been described as a passion narrative with a preface; the entire movement of the action is toward the cross. The absence of teaching material accents this fact. Mark gives a brief, simple record of our Lord's life and ministry, which fills in some of the details of the apostolic preaching. In accord with apostolic preaching, it begins with John the Baptist and ends with the resurrection (cf. Acts 10:36–43; 13:24–37). The skeleton, or framework, of Jesus' life was given in sermons, but further detailed information was required for use in instructing the people. Obviously, the passion narrative was preserved in definite historical sequence, and it is likely that this was true also of the other material. Mark made no attempt to provide a tight chronology, but it is going too far to suggest he ignored it altogether. In the early church, the Gospel of Mark was overshadowed by Matthew. Mark contained little not found in Matthew, whereas Matthew had much more than Mark. Few wrote commentaries upon it, and eventually the idea circulated that it was a mere abstract of Matthew. Not until the 19th cent. was its identity known as the kernel to the first gospel.

Mark begins and ends abruptly. The approach is blunt and direct. Mark is a gospel of action; movement is more important than discourse. The impression from Mark is a factual, eyewitness account of the life of Jesus. Fascinating details are included in the narration, without any hesitation to get directly to the action. Mark excludes the birth narratives. Jesus' deeds are reported rather than his words. He repeatedly uses the adverb *euthys* G2317, meaning "immediately." Frequently he notes that Jesus taught here and there, but does not pause to tell what he taught. The earliest explanation of this vividness was to find PETER's testimony behind Mark. "Mark became Peter's interpreter and wrote accurately all that he remembered, not, indeed, in order, of things said or done by the Lord" (Euseb. *Eccl. Hist.* 3.39.15). Mark derived his material from the public testimony of Peter the apostle. This would indeed explain the living character of Mark's work.

Many have pointed out the ARAMAIC influences on the second gospel. Mark may well have drawn upon Peter's sermons and lectures, and used them along with other material to construct his gospel. His work has a freshness and confidence of detail that is hard to explain in any other way.

From all indications, Mark was written from ROME for Gentile readers. A comparison of Mk. 15:21 and Rom. 16:13 makes a Roman origin probable, as does the presence of an unusual number of Latinisms in the Greek text. There is also an absence of the Judaic atmosphere so noticeable in Matthew. A comparison reveals that almost every instance of Jewish coloring in Matthew is lacking in the Markan parallel. Mark had Gentile readers in mind in writing his gospel. Where he had to include Palestinian customs, he took pains to explain them (e.g., Mk. 7:3–4), something unnecessary for a Jewish audience. Similarly, the Aramaic expressions that Mark did retain are given a Greek translation (e.g., 14:36).

Mark is "the gospel of Jesus Christ, the Son of God" (Mk. 1:1). The author's central aim was to present the person of the Messiah. Jesus is the SON OF GOD, the glorious SON OF MAN, and the Redeemer. Mark presents a high CHRISTOLOGY throughout. See also MARK, GOSPEL OF.

3. Luke. The third gospel is the longest and the most comprehensive in range and scope. Luke and Acts constitute the largest contribution to the NT of any single writer. Ernst Renan (*Les évangiles et la seconde génération chrétienne* [1877], 283) called the Gospel of Luke the most beautiful book there is. It gives an attractive account that leaves on the reader a deep impression of the personality of Jesus. To have the intention of the writer expressly stated in a prologue (Lk. 1:1–4) is fortunate. Without doubt, the aim of the author was primarily historical accuracy and integrity. His own statement of purpose takes precedence over any speculative theory. He was dominated primarily by a historical concern. The prologue indicates that the writer was well educated, as his excellent prose reveals, and possessed critical historical judgment. He was of the deep conviction that the believer needed to have a solid historical foundation for his faith in Christ, and this he sought to provide.

Although scholars in the past have doubted the trustworthiness of Luke's work, much research has vindicated his integrity in a spectacular way. At numerous points, Luke ties his account to secular history, and his accuracy has repeatedly been proven. He did not, however, write a secular history as such. His aim, in common with all the evangelists, was to

Aerial view looking NE at Wadi Qilt along the road to Jericho, where the parable of the Good Samaritan is set. Only the Gospel of Luke reports this story from Jesus' teaching.

trace the ministry of a unique Person. Like the others, Luke presents history that contains important theological significance. The author presents the beginnings of a movement that in the short space of three decades established itself in the capital of the Roman empire. It began quietly in Judea and extended itself to the center of the world's stage. History itself gave Luke his theme.

As would be expected, Luke's scope is indeed comprehensive; his gospel covers more of Jesus' life than any other. He alone writes about the birth of John the Baptist (Lk. 1:5–25, 57–80), the annunciation to Mary (1:26–38), the adoration of the shepherds (2:1–20), the visit to the temple (2:41–52). He includes an account of Jesus preaching in Nazareth (4:16–30), the miraculous draught of fishes (5:1–11), the woes (6:24–26), the raising of the son of the widow of Nain (7:11–17), the woman saved by Jesus (7:36–50), the women who served Jesus (8:1–3), the Samaritan villages that refused his message (9:51–56), the parable of the Good Samaritan (10:30–37), the incident regarding Mary and Martha (10:38–42), the parable of the friend at midnight (11:5–8), the blessedness of those who obey the Word of God (11:27–28), the parable of the rich fool (12:13–21), the saying about many or few blows (12:47–48), the call to repentance (13:1–9), the healing of another woman (13:10–17), the departure from Galilee (13:31–33), the healing of a man with dropsy (14:1–6), teaching on humility (14:7–14), the parables of the prodigal son (15:11–32) and of the unjust steward (16:1–13), the hypocrisy of the Pharisees (16:14–15), the parable of the rich man and Lazarus (16:19–31), the servant's duty (17:7–10), the healing of ten lepers (17:11–19), a saying about the coming of the kingdom of God (17:20–21), the parables of the unjust judge (18:1–8) and of the Pharisee and the publican (18:9–14), the incident regarding Zacchaeus (19:1–10), the statement about the two swords (22:35–38), Jesus' questioning before Herod (23:6–16), the weeping women (23:27–31), the penitent thief (23:39–43), the burial of Jesus (23:55–56), the conversation on the road to Emmaus (24:13–35), the appearance of the risen Christ at Jerusalem (24:36–49), and the ascension (24:50–53).

Luke's universalism is evident in numerous places. The good news the angels brought was for all people (Lk. 2:14). Simeon foresaw that Christ would be a light for the Gentiles (2:32). John the Baptist was the voice of one crying in the wilderness in fulfillment of Isa. 40:3–5, which includes a line Luke cites, "all mankind will see God's salvation" (Lk. 3:6). Non-Israelites are on a par with the Jews (4:25–27; 9:54; 10:33; 17:16). Luke shows that he is interested in all manner of people. Numerous individuals emerge in his narrative unknown elsewhere—Zechariah, Elizabeth, Zacchaeus, Cleopas. Luke presents several case studies of social outcasts being transformed by the gospel. He mentions thirteen women not found in the other Gospels. Children, also, often appear in his record. This is a gospel of the manhood of Jesus. Everywhere his teaching attracted wide popular interest, and his compassion for the poor and the destitute shone through. The entire ministry of Jesus was an outworking of the saving purpose of God in history. See also LUKE, GOSPEL OF.

4. John. John, as does Luke, gives a clear statement of his purpose (Jn. 20:30–31). John is presenting to the believer and unbeliever alike the historical data upon which saving faith rests. The gospel was intended to be both an evangelistic and a pastoral instrument. John selected a set of signs that he believed would convince his readers of the DEITY OF CHRIST and lead them to place their trust in him. He was concerned that the messianic faith of the church should be filled with the proper content.

There are indications in the gospel that its writer was in a good position to provide this content; the narration gives constant hints of being recorded by an eyewitness. On several occasions, John reveals a detailed knowledge of Jewish life and custom in the period before the fall of Jerusalem. He was aware of the political situation in Palestine. He had an intimate knowledge of the geography of the land. His account abounds with personal allusions and details absent from the synoptic narratives. Undoubtedly, the author intended his readers to take his gospel as real history, not as mere symbol or allegory. The fourth gospel is fully as trustworthy historically as the other three, and at certain points more precise and detailed than they. It is reasonable to assume the historicity of the whole account, since historical errors cannot be demonstrated in the fourth gospel.

The present state of Johannine criticism represents a complete reversal to that of earlier times. John's style is as simple as his thought is profound. He regularly uses common words and paratactic constructions. Although John purposely limited the range of his vocabulary, the effect is dignified and compelling. It abounds with theological theme words that recur again and again (water, light, bread, love, truth).

The first half of the gospel (Jn. 1:1—12:50) presents the revelation of Jesus to the world and is structured around seven signs. The words of Jesus are for the most part occasioned by the miracles in the narrative. The discourses are rather long, often argumentative, and frequently set in the southern ministry of Jesus, in Judea. Jesus' activity around Jerusalem was more directly polemical because the hostility to him was greater there than in Galilee.

Like Matthew, John presents Jesus as the Messiah of OT hope. Jesus approached Israel with a rightful claim to her loyalty. He was disturbed that his own people did not receive him (Jn. 1:11; 5:39, 45–46). The imagery of bread, shepherd, and the Spirit, all root back to OT prophetic passages. John does not quote texts in the way Matthew does, but OT texts continually underline his thought. All the Scriptures point to Jesus. He is the fulfillment of the OT longing. See also JOHN, GOSPEL OF.

B. Relationships

1. The synoptic problem. The first three Gospels are called the Synoptic Gospels because they can be "viewed together"—their similarities noted and their differences examined. A considerable amount of material is common to all three, or to two out of three. Out of Mark's total of 661 verses, some 606 appear, although somewhat abridged, in Matthew, and 380 are found in Luke. Only 31 verses in Mark have no parallel in either Matthew or Luke. In addition, there are some 250 verses common to Matthew and Luke that have no parallel in Mark. Obviously, this synoptic relationship can be viewed in different ways. Many solutions have been proposed, but none has won unanimous agreement.

One of the stable findings of synoptic criticism has been the priority of Mark. It is a striking fact that whereas the order of Mark and Matthew may agree against Luke and the order of Mark and Luke may agree against Matthew, the order of Matthew and Luke never agrees against Mark. In other words, Mark is the stable factor. Most probably, Mark was the source common to the other two, which they generally followed but sometimes altered. This common material is almost entirely narrative.

The non-Markan material common to Matthew and Luke, on the other hand, almost entirely consists of sayings of Jesus. This observation has led to a further hypothesis—the existence of a sayings source, usually referred to as Q. Once the theory of Markan priority is accepted, the existence of Q follows. The 250 verses of common material between Matthew and Luke possess a considerable measure of verbal agreement and occur in much the same order in each gospel. Scholars differ as to the extent of this proposed second source. It might conceivably have contained narrative itself originally. From the data now available, it seems to have been a sayings source only. The need for Q could be bypassed if it is assumed that Luke used Matthew directly; but his alteration of Matthew's careful ordering of the sayings is difficult to explain, unless he had access to information regarding their rightful historical sequence. The purpose of Q can easily be imagined in the early church. As a collection of Jesus' teachings, it would have been a useful manual of church order and teaching.

Some scholars have gone on to detect homogeneity between the material peculiar to Matthew and that peculiar to Luke. Matthew's special material has a Judaistic tone, however; its existence as a source is highly speculative. Luke includes even more special material, which he doubtless collected during his historical research.

2. The synoptics and John. The independence of John from the other three Gospels is significant. There are few incidents in the life of Jesus common to the synoptics and John. Major events and extensive speeches are peculiar to John alone. The presentation of the style of Jesus' ministry is different. There are also certain chronological tensions.

What is the explanation of these differences? John may either be supplementary to, independent of, interpretive of, or a substitute for, the synoptics. If John's readers knew Mark, for example,

John could afford to pass over Mark's account and include stories and sayings not found there. If he wrote independently of Mark, on the other hand, it seems improbable that John could have failed to mention certain historical events, even if he wrote at a very early date before the other Gospels circulated. Some argue that John knew the oral tradition behind the synoptics, but wrote independently of them. The fact that John wrote about Jesus' activities in different locations than those mentioned in the synoptics would explain the lack of parallels. Besides, it is quite possible to harmonize the chronology of John with that of the other three, as Stauffer has shown.

IV. The fourfold gospel. From the first, the four Gospels were considered to be various accounts of one gospel. Soon after the composition of John, the four accounts began to circulate as a fourfold corpus of Scripture. A series of replies to MARCION (who repudiated Matthew, Mark, and John) called the anti-Marcionite prologues prove that the four Gospels were accepted as one collection. About A.D. 170, Justin's disciple Tatian composed a harmony of the Gospels called the DIATESSARON, which became a favorite in the Syriac-speaking church for some years. To Irenaeus, the fourfold gospel was as fundamental as the four corners of the world or the four winds of heaven. Clement of Alexandria, Tertullian, and Origen all agree that these four accounts are the only authentic accounts of the life of Jesus from apostolic times.

V. Historical value. The Christian faith rests upon historical foundations; the four Gospels are primary evidences for its authenticity and validity. An attack on their historical integrity is an attack against the credibility of Christianity itself. Many NT critics still regard the gospel tradition as community fiction handed down by anonymous and miscellaneous individuals. In the light of the evidence, such attempts to discredit the gospel records must be discounted. Historical pessimism is utterly unwarranted. The textual witness for the NT documents is incredibly good, surpassing any comparable instance in Greek or Latin literature. The internal data indicate that all of the Gospels were written inside the 1st cent. and that they contain eyewitness accounts of the highest veracity. The concerted attempt of form critics to undermine their integrity is based upon huge speculation. The Christian faith could scarcely rest upon a more secure basis than what the four Gospels provide.

(See further B. H. Streeter, *The Four Gospels* [1924]; V. Taylor, *The Formation of the Gospel Tradition* [1933]; R. Bultmann, *History of the Synoptic Tradition* [1963]; C. H. Dodd, *Historical Tradition in the Fourth Gospel* [1963]; N. B. Stonehouse, *Origins of the Synoptic Gospels* [1963]; R. G. Gruenler, *New Approaches to Jesus and the Gospels* [1982]; W. Kelber, *The Oral and the Written Gospel* [1983]; C. L. Blomberg, *The Historical Reliability of the Gospels* [1987]; S. D. Moore, *Literary Criticism and the Gospels* [1989]; M. Hengel, *The Four Gospels and the Gospel of Jesus Christ: An Investigation of the Collection and Origin of the Canonical Gospels* [2000]; G. Stanton, *The Gospels and Jesus*, 2nd ed. [2002]; R. A. Burridge, *What are the Gospels? A Comparison with Graeco-Roman Biography*, 2nd ed. [2004]; P. R. Eddy and G. A. Boyd, *The Jesus Legend: A Case for the Historical Reliability of the Synoptic Jesus Tradition* [2007]. Note also the standard introductions to the NT.)

C. H. PINNOCK

gospels, apocryphal. The canonical GOSPELS, which strictly speaking are not biographies, record only a small part of the life and work of JESUS CHRIST. After the apostolic period, a growing biographical interest led to the composition of works intended to fill the gaps, most of them based on imagination or drawing on MYTH and legend. The infancy gospels recount tales of his childhood, or carry the story back to the birth and childhood of Mary. The passion and resurrection, the descent into hell, and the terrors of the underworld are described with additional detail (e.g., *Gospel of Peter, Acts of Pilate, Gospel of Bartholomew*). The Gnostics in particular composed "gospels" containing revelations given in the period between the resurrection and the ascension (see GNOSTICISM). Rarely can one look for the survival of authentic early tradition, and only in the earliest of these documents. (Most of the significant works are reproduced in vol. 1 of *NTAp*.) See APOCRYPHAL NEW TESTAMENT I and separate articles on individual works.

R. McL. WILSON

gossip. Rumor or inappropriate spreading of private information; also, a person who habitually spreads such information. Gossip need not be, but often is, malicious. The English term is used occasionally by modern versions to render several words or expressions (e.g., Heb. *hôlēk rkil H2143 + H8215*, "one who goes about as a slanderer," Prov. 11:13 [KJV, "talebearer"]; Gk. *psithyristas G6031*, "whisperer," Rom. 1:29). See SLANDER.

Gothic Version. See VERSIONS OF THE BIBLE, ANCIENT, V.A.

Gotholiah goth´uh-li´uh (Γοθολιας). KJV Gotholias. Variant form of ATHALIAH (1 Esd. 8:33).

Gothoniel goh-thon´ee-uhl (Γοθονιηλ, prob. from Heb. עָתְנִיאֵל *H6979*; see OTHNIEL). Son of a certain Chabris who was one of the magistrates in BETHULIA (Jdt. 6:15).

gourd. A generic term applied to various trailing or climbing plants (such as the pumpkin and the cucumber). Gourds have very broad leaves; they grow quickly in the E, lengthening themselves by as much as 12–18 in. a day. They wither and die quickly when attacked at their base by insects like wireworms. The term is properly used to render Hebrew *paqquʿōt H7226*, which occurs only once, referring probably to the *Citrullus colocynthis*, a cucumber-like plant with purgative qualities (2 Ki. 4:39). Known in England as the bitter apple, it has a leaf like a squash, and the fruit could easily, therefore, have been mistaken for an edible squash. (Cf. *FFB*, 124–25. Others have thought that the reference is to the squirting cucumber, *Ecballium elatrium*, but it seems unlikely that the student prophet would have gathered such a prickly and spiny fruit for a stew.) It is possible that the *Citrullus colocynthis* is also to be identified with "the vine of Sodom" (Deut. 32:32). See FLORA (under *Cucurbitaceae*). The cognate *pĕqāʿim H7225* refers to ornaments shaped like gourds (1 Ki. 6:18; 7:24). The carving of little gourds alternated with open flowers would have been very attractive. Renaissance painters used plants in their pictures to give a symbolic meaning. Gourds were apparently regarded as symbolic of salvation, and this may be the reason they were used in the temple.

The term *gourd* is also used by the KJV and other versions to render Hebrew *qîqāyôn H7813* (Jon. 4:6–10; NRSV, "bush"; NIV, "vine"). Although some have identified this plant as the pumpkin (*Cucurbita pepo*), most specialists believe it is the castor oil tree (*Ricimum communis*, also known as *Palma Christi*). This plant has huge leaves, which provide excellent shade. It could be used growing over a bower, and grows rapidly. In England, the castor oil plant grows to a height of 4 ft., but in the E it makes a large shade-giving tree. It is certainly a native of Asia. (Cf. *FFB*, 106–7.)

W. E. SHEWELL-COOPER

government. The control and administration of public policy. The Bible begins with God, and all thinking on human government must also begin there. Exclusive stress on human autonomy and self-sufficiency in government leads either to ruthless tyranny or to anarchy. The ideal is an ordered society subject to law, with the consequent possibility of a normal life in the community—something that becomes possible insofar as the biblical conception of the state is, in some measure at least, actually realized.

I. Its source
II. The nature of the state
III. Government in Israel
IV. Government in general
   A. Its divine authority
   B. The duty of obedience
   C. The limits of obedience
   D. The limits of disobedience
   E. Prayer for the government
   F. Participation in government

I. Its source. Human sovereignty as it is exercised in the state has its source in divine sovereignty. See SOVEREIGNTY OF GOD. The starting point is the doctrine of CREATION. God the Creator made all things. All that is owes its beginning to his creative act and to his sustaining power. This inevitably implies God's sovereignty over his creation. Since all is dependent upon him, so everything is subject to him, whether the solar system, the world of nature, or human society.

This creative activity is the work of the TRINITY. God created (and creates) through the agency of his word, and the Spirit of God was (and is) present in life-giving power (Gen. 1; cf. Prov. 8:22–31; Jn. 1:1–4; Col. 1:15–17; Heb. 1:1–3). The Son is not only the One through whom the Father created all things, but also "in him all things hold together" (Col. 1:17). Hence, the sovereignty of God in creation is exercised through Christ. He is not only the Savior of his people but also the Lord of all creation.

This sovereign authority of God over all is expressed in law. Prior to the FALL, God dealt with ADAM in terms of law. The prohibition of the forbidden fruit was the expression in legal terms of the absolute rights of the sovereign God. Adam's disobedience was thus law-breaking, and as such, because the law was the expression of God's will, it was a personal affront to God himself.

SIN, however, not only renders all the world guilty before God, but also has adverse consequences in the sphere of human relationships. God's purpose in creation was that men and women should subject the created order to their control and live in harmony with each other. Sin entered, however, as a divisive influence so that people ceased to contribute to each other's welfare. Instead, they preyed on each other. Hence, it is in the natural course of events that in place of a harmonious society, murder and lust, theft and war appear as symptoms of a humanity that has lost its bearings spiritually.

The law of God, declared to human beings in their fallen condition, is his gracious corrective. This applies both to the law written on the CONSCIENCE of every person and to the revealed law of the OT. Whereas law has a redemptive function in that it shows men and women their sin and so turns them to the Savior, it has also a secondary but nonetheless important function of restraining them from reaping the consequences of their own sinfulness.

God remains the God of GRACE, even in face of Adam's sin and human persistence in willful defiance of their Creator. This grace is seen not only in his redeeming work by which he saves his elect, but also in his gracious dealings with people in general: "He causes his sun to rise on the evil and the good, and sends rain on the righteous and the unrighteous" (Matt. 5:45). If human beings were left to their own devices they would destroy each other. Certainly, social life would be impossible. So God has graciously imposed restraints that ordered social living may be possible.

These restraining influences may be seen in the various sanctions to which people submit themselves—the pressure of conscience, the influence of the family, the customs and standards of the community. The concern in this article is, however, with one particular sphere in which God's gracious restraint is seen; namely, the state, which in Scripture is always viewed as divinely instituted.

II. The nature of the state. The term *state* in this article is employed in its widest sense. There is a wide gulf between the primitive jungle tribe and the highly sophisticated community of a technological society; there is also a deep difference between the totalitarian regime of a fascist or communist dictatorship and the freedom of a democracy. Nonetheless, all of these have certain fundamental characteristics. Each group is a community and not merely a collection of warring individuals. They are not bound together necessarily by national ties, for many different ethnic groups may be knit together under one state; on the other hand, a single ethnic group may be divided into two states.

What constitutes a state, at the rudimentary tribal level and at the most advanced stage, is the common submission of a community to law. Whether it be a tribal chief, a dictator, or a democratically elected parliament, there is an organ of government, and that government exercises authority over those who are subject to its jurisdiction. This authority is expressed by laws that are promulgated (whether the unwritten code of the tribe or the precisely drafted legislation of the modern state). Law is not mere exhortation to the people to conform; it is **enforced**. The government must have the means of compelling its subjects to obey the law and must have the power to impose penalties on those who disobey.

There is no explicit description of the state in Scripture. There is no attempt to define precisely what constitutes the prerogatives of government. All that has been said above is implicit in biblical teaching, whether it is expressed in the narratives of God's dealings with nations, in the record of God's word to kings and those in authority, or in the attitude to the state, either adopted by God's people or prescribed for them by prophets and apostles and by Christ himself.

There are two spheres in which human authority is exercised in Scripture—among the people of God and among men and women in general. In the OT Israel appears as a nation under God in a special sense, but the other nations are also subject to him, and although they may not acknowledge the fact, yet the authority exercised even by pagan kings was entrusted to them by the God of Israel. Similarly in the NT there is the company of the redeemed where the kingly rule of Christ is gladly accepted. There is also the ROMAN EMPIRE in which the believers find themselves under civil control. However, the latter is not a realm where God's sovereign power is absent, for the NT writers echo the prophets of the OT that "the governing authorities … have been established by God" (Rom. 13:1).

The authority of God exercised among his people is an anticipation of the final consummation of the purposes of God when every knee shall bow. That same authority mediated through the agency of human rulers is a standing witness to God's common grace, even to men in a state of rebellion against him. Although some features of government as exercised in Israel are common to any properly ordered state, because of the peculiar position of the chosen people, it is best to consider them separately before looking at the wider aspects of the biblical view of the state.

III. Government in Israel. The ancient nation of Israel was unique in that it was organized as a THEOCRACY. Although the precise form of government varied during the nation's history, the underlying conviction was always there in the OT that the Lord is the true ruler of his people. Whoever exercised rule over the nation, the ultimate authority belonged to God.

The Lordship of God over his people is seen in the way that leaders and kings owed their appointment to him. MOSES was commissioned directly by God to lead the people out of Egypt. It was under his leadership that they ceased to be a collection of tribes and were constituted a nation, the people of the COVENANT. JOSHUA, his successor, owed his position to the same divine commission, and in the stormy days after his death judges were raised up by God to save the Israelites from those who raided them (Jdg. 2:16). See JUDGES, PERIOD OF. In the rise of the monarchy there was the same firm insistence on divine appointment, as SAUL was first selected and then rejected, and as DAVID was summoned to the throne by SAMUEL, God's prophet. The king in Israel was "the LORD's anointed." He was not merely the head of the civil administration or the commander of the army. He was essentially the representative of the kingly rule of God. His government of Israel embodied and illustrated the sovereign authority of the Lord.

Thus in Israel the ideal of creation began to be realized. Because of the sinfulness of those called to govern the nation, this realization was all too often sadly impaired. Nonetheless, a nation was established distinct from the other nations that

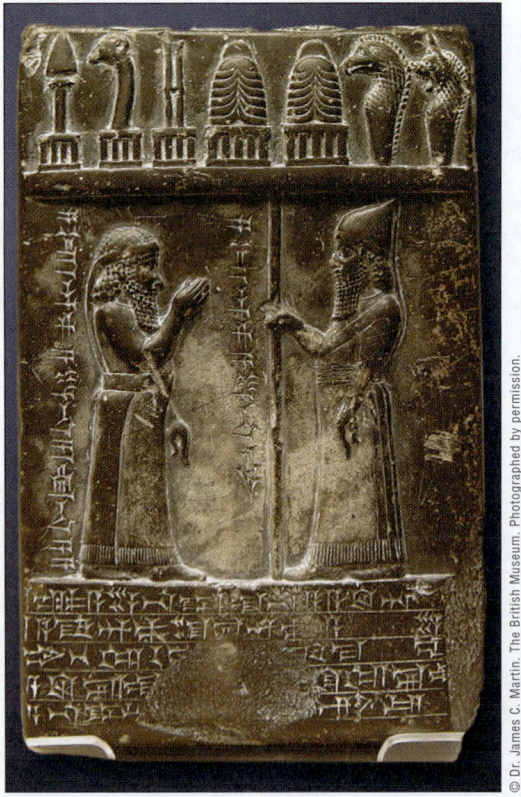

This cuneiform stone tablet from N Babylonia (c. 875–850 B.C.) records a land grant by King Nabu-apla-iddina (on the right) to one of his officials.

surrounded it, and in it God's purposes for his creatures were to some degree manifested. God's original purpose for men and women was that they should live in submission to their Creator, in harmony with their neighbors, and in enjoyment of the bounty of nature. Sin by contrast brought rebellion against God, division among people, and discord into the whole created order. Whereas the original purpose envisaged the communion of human beings with God, the sad consequence of their sin was divine judgment, leading to exclusion from God's presence and to misery.

All this was reflected in ancient Israel. Insofar as the nation submitted to God's law, the original pattern of creation began to be seen. When a godly ruler on the throne led the people in submission to the law, the result was unity in the land between the different tribes. There was peace and security against the disruptive forces from without. "During Solomon's lifetime Judah and Israel, from Dan to Beersheba, lived in safety, each man under his own vine and fig tree" (1 Ki. 4:25). They all enjoyed the fruit of the land, but when they rebelled against God the warnings of Deuteronomy were realized. The nation was divided; they faced plague, pestilence, and famine; they became subject to their enemies, and finally they were banished from the land.

There was also the eschatological element. See ESCHATOLOGY. The glimpses of the glory enjoyed in the land were flickering tokens of the surpassing glory to come at the end of the age, when the Israel of God would be brought into perfect submission to his rule. On the other side, the sin and the consequent judgments were tokens of the solemn outcome of the final DAY OF THE LORD, when the nations that knew not God would be consumed by the fire of his wrath.

There is, of course, the important messianic element in the history of government in Israel. Just as the anointed prophet and priest foreshadowed the Word made flesh, the great High Priest at Calvary, so the king of Israel was a foreshadowing of the messianic king. Thus Jesus began his ministry preaching the gospel of the kingdom. The rule exercised by the kings of Israel failed to declare adequately the sovereignty of the Lord because of the sinfulness of even the best of the kings. In the MESSIAH there is no such imperfection; in him God's rule is perfectly manifested.

Within the CHURCH, Christ's kingship is the dominant truth. The government that is exercised by the spiritual leaders within the redeemed community is really the mediation of the royal government of Christ. To a greater degree than in Israel, the ideal of creation is realized. However, because the church is comprised of people who, although justified, are still sinful, the final realization is yet future, and the Christian still prays, "Thy kingdom come."

This consideration of government in Israel and in the church of Christ has not been a mere parenthesis in the discussion of the biblical view of the state. Apart from its positive value in stressing the ultimate authority of all human government, it needs to be related in a biblical fashion to the wider issues, for it is at this point that historically there has been much confusion. There has been a failure to see the unique character of the theocracy in Israel, with the subsequent misguided attempt to organize nations on a theocratic basis. In a similar way some Christians have viewed the government of God exercised within the church as the blueprint for society, so that the laws of the church become the pattern for the laws of the land.

In the 16th cent., many of the Reformers were clearly dominated by the theocratic ideal. The godly prince of the OT found his fulfillment in the Lutheran, Reformed, or Anglican ruler so that the magistrate had a responsibility to protect the church and to enforce the moral standards that the church declared. In its more ugly manifestation, the magistrate also assumed the further responsibility of defending the "truth" and resisting "error" to the extent of punishing offenders.

This concept of the Christian state fails to do justice to the biblical understanding of the new covenant. It is true that there is in Scripture one covenant of grace. However, within that one covenant there is a period of preparation and a period of fulfillment. When JEREMIAH rejoiced in the prospect of the glories of the new covenant, and when the writer of Hebrews discoursed at length on its implications, they were not using empty words. The OT was a period when God was graciously at work, but it was still a preparatory period. It looked forward to the age of the Messiah, the gospel age, the age of fulfillment. See COVENANT, THE NEW.

The restrictive national character of the old covenant was shattered by the divinely commanded inclusion of the Gentiles. There is no longer a theocratic nation as men and women of every tribe and nation are gathered into the church. The godly prince of the OT finds his fulfillment in the Messiah. To look for a modern counterpart to David or Hezekiah is to miss the concept of the unique kingship of Christ. It may be that the ruler is a true believer, but that does not give him the status that the theocratic concept requires, for in the kingdom of God there is only one king, Christ himself.

For this reason the Anabaptist wing of the Reformation movement (in its more sober and biblical manifestations) insisted on the separate spheres of church and state. The church is the realm of God's special grace where God governs his people by means of those whom he ordains and whom the Spirit endows with gifts for their task. The state is the realm of God's common grace extended to all people. The government, although it is of divine authority, will reflect Christian standards only insofar as the members of that government themselves exercise Christian values.

In other words, a Christian who reaches a position of authority in the state will be motivated by his faith in the same way that a business man is influenced in his decisions by the standards of integrity and righteousness that are his because he is a Christian. This does not mean that the Christian politician can submit a nation including both believers and unbelievers to a pattern of conduct that belongs properly to believers only. The separation of church and state is not a mere slogan. This principle is rooted in the biblical doctrine that there are two realms: secular government and the spiritual household of God. God is at work in both, but each enjoys a relative autonomy—relative, that is, in view of the overriding fact of God's final authority.

IV. Government in general

A. Its divine authority. The more general aspects of human government overlap with some of the elements already discussed concerning Israel and the church. All authority is ultimately from God, and although human beings may either ignore or reject God, he still remains King. People scheme and plot and kill to seize power. Nations go to war and national boundaries change. Dictatorship gives way to democracy or vice versa. But above and beyond all political changes and the ebb and flow of national powers, the Lord God omnipotent reigns.

DANIEL, the prophet, insisted on this derived character of all government when he reminded NEBUCHADNEZZAR that "the Most High is sovereign over the kingdoms of men and gives them to anyone he wishes and sets over them the lowliest of men" (Dan. 4:17; cf. v. 25). This same Nebuchadnezzar was humbled by God, and at another time he was used to carry out God's purposes (Jer. 27:6). The word of the Lord to BELSHAZZAR declared that the fall of his kingdom and the rise of the Medo-Persian empire was by the decree of God (Dan. 5:28). When CYRUS acted to liberate the Jews, it was because the Lord stirred up his spirit (2 Chr. 36:22; cf. Isa. 44:28).

The judgment of God upon nations stresses the same truth that all government is derived from God, and therefore when rulers misuse the responsibility entrusted to them, they are liable to God's judgment. So PHARAOH was overthrown, a great OT illustration of God's supremacy. The PROPHETS declared the same theme, as in the prophetic warnings to the nations by Isaiah, Jeremiah, and Ezekiel. Not only Judah and Israel but pagan nations as well were subject to the moral law, and all alike came under the lash of Amos's passionate invective.

The NT contains the same position. The state for most believers was the Roman empire, paganistic and powerful. But it was established by divine decree. So Christ accepted the authority of CAESAR as the legal authority in civil affairs (Matt. 22:15–22), even though Caesar controlled Palestine by force of arms. PETER counseled the same attitude. Christians were to honor the emperor (1 Pet. 2:17). PAUL, in the emphatic statement already quoted (Rom. 13), insisted that all human authority is derived from God.

Most significant is the fact that divine authority over government is independent of the moral character of the leaders who control the government. NERO was a blackguard, yet the same word

Colossal statue of Amenhotep III, ruler of Egypt during the 18th dynasty (Thebes).

applies—he was to be honored. An institution like the family or the state is devised and established by God, and yet many of those involved may fall far short of the ideal. To destroy the institution, however, is to produce an intolerable chaos. A father may behave like a brute and forfeit any right to respect, but this does not give cause to despise or repudiate the vital necessity of family life and parental authority. No more does the failure of one ruler to administer justly give the right to anarchic overthrow of authority. God in his own way deals with such people. In spite of individual failure, the authority of the office still stands.

B. The duty of obedience. The obvious corollary to the divinely given authority of the state is the obligation to submit to the laws of the land. Obedience to duly constituted civil authority is written into the canons of Christian conduct. To honor the emperor did not mean for Peter simply to pay lip service to the dignity of his office. It meant a readiness to obey the laws that the emperor promulgated, and to submit if need be to the penalties imposed on disobedience. The issue of disobedience for the sake of conscience will be discussed later.

Obedience to the government was practiced by Jesus himself. He lived in the midst of nationalistic resentment of the alien rule of Rome (one of his disciples, Simon the Zealot, was drawn from this background; see ZEALOT). It would have been easy for him to fan the embers of bitterness into a flame of opposition to the Roman occupation, but this he refused to do. The currency bearing Caesar's head was a reminder of the benefits of stable government. The use of that currency was an implicit acknowledgment of the authority of the government that had issued it. Therefore its subjects must obey Caesar in practical ways by paying the tax with the same coinage used to enjoy the privileges of Roman rule. Rome was an alien occupying power, but her government was a fact of the providential ordering of God Almighty. Therefore they must obey, for to refuse to pay the tax would be to rebel against God (see Matt. 22:15–22).

When standing before PILATE, the Lord affirmed the same attitude. The man who tried him was unworthy of his office, and the trial was a travesty of justice. Nonetheless, Pilate was the governor and as such was the representative of the imperial government, and therefore to him Jesus submitted. When Pilate began to bluster, there was a firm word of rebuke—"You would have no power over me if it were not given to you from above" (Jn. 19:11)—but in his general attitude Jesus maintained the same approach as he had earlier in the garden, when he rebuked Peter for using his sword and submitted quietly to arrest.

The apostle Paul followed his master in this as in all other things. His frequent assertion of the essential legality of his actions in the eyes of Roman law is an implicit acknowledgment of the authority of that law. It is a standard to which he saw himself called to conform. When in the final stages of his prolonged imprisonment at Caesarea he made his appeal to Caesar, he was acknowledging the supreme authority of the emperor whose laws he had obeyed and to whose justice he now appealed. When he spoke in explicit terms about the authority of the state and the responsibility involved in citizenship, he expressed a reflection of his own personal attitude. As already noted, he emphasized the divine institution of the state (Rom. 13).

God's purpose in thus ordaining the power of government is a gracious one. It is to restrain evil and punish wrongdoers. Thus the demands of the law for honesty and preservation of life reflect the demands of God. The justice of the law carried out upon evil reflects in some measure the righteous judgments of the Judge of all the earth. This realization lifts the Christian's obedience to a new level. He does not obey merely because it is the best policy and because disobedience to the law if detected will lead to punishment. He obeys "for the sake of conscience." Seeing the hand of God in the demands of the state, hearing the voice of God in the just requirements of the powers that be, and believing himself to be someone not simply subject to the laws of the state but to the authority of God, he yields a willing obedience.

The same applies to the payment of TAX, an echo of Jesus' teaching about Caesar's rights. Since the state is divinely ordained and since obviously it requires money to carry out its divinely appointed function, the citizen must pay taxes to furnish the necessary resources. The Christian, says Paul, will pay taxes for conscience' sake. There will be no manipulation of his tax returns, no defrauding of the tax authorities. The tax demand note is a requirement with heaven's seal upon it, and there must be a scrupulous honesty in complying with it.

The island of CRETE was noted for its turbulence, but Christians even in such an atmosphere were to show a different spirit. Paul wrote to TITUS to remind the Cretans of their responsibility "to be subject to rulers and authorities" (Tit. 3:1). This injunction was linked with the requirement that they should be "ready for any honest work" (RSV). Obedience to the demands of the government means not only an avoidance of what is illegal but also a positive participation in any task that is obviously the responsibility of a loyal citizen.

There is a unanimity in the apostolic teaching. Peter, who once used his sword in GETHSEMANE, had learned his lesson. Whether it is the emperor as the supreme authority, or the various governors who are his representatives, all must be seen by the Christian to be sent by God himself. Government is viewed not simply in its restraining and punitive capacity, but also in its positive role of promoting the public good. The state praises those who do right (1 Pet. 2:14). This public recognition of worth is an implicit acknowledgment of the responsibility of the state to promote moral standards in the community. If the state acts to provide education or welfare for its citizens, the Christian citizen should recognize the positive side of the state's function and should readily pay his taxes to provide the means for accomplishing these programs. This submission is rendered "for the Lord's sake." This involves not only an honest compliance with the state's requirements, but also an ungrudging and ready obedience, since it is not merely a government that makes the demand, but the Lord himself.

C. The limits of obedience. There are, however, limits to the obedience that the state may demand. No one is entitled to qualify his response on the ground of personal inconvenience or of personal dislike of any particular legislation. Once such considerations are substituted for submission, a condition of subjectivism exists that, if unchecked, leads to anarchy. A question of conscience, however, is in a different category. It is one thing when the state imposes repressive measures that may be very hard to accept, or even when the state acts unjustly. In such cases submission is due. It is a very different matter when the demands of the state conflict with the law of God. What is the Christian to do if the government commands him to act in a way that is plainly contrary to Scripture?

Where there is a conflict of loyalties the higher one must take precedence, "We must obey God rather than men!" (Acts 5:29). Although the Lord was quite insistent that one must render to Caesar the things that are Caesar's, he added an important and qualifying requirement, "and to God what is God's" (Lk. 20:25). Caesar had a divinely given authority to which submission was due, but his authority was always subject to a higher authority, God himself. If Caesar then went beyond his prerogatives and required from citizens something that God forbade, then Caesar must be disobeyed.

It must be stressed, however, that disobedience must be limited only to matters of conscience. In every other point the Christian must remain a loyal citizen. It is only at the point where his loyalty to God is in danger of being violated that he must take his stand. This point emerged in Peter's first epistle. He wrote about the likely persecution and suffering that Christians would face. They must be prepared to endure trial for Christ's sake. At the same time he reminded them that it is only in the cause of righteousness that such resistance to the state is permissible. If a Christian suffered the consequences of other unlawful actions he need expect no word of commendation from God (1 Pet. 4:12–13).

D. The limits of disobedience. A further question arises: what form should this legitimate disobedience take? If for the sake of conscience one cannot obey the dictates of the state, how should he show his resistance? Should the disobedience be active or passive? This is no academic issue for it constantly recurs as an existential problem. Is it right, for example, when a dictatorship is repressing the country in general and the church in particular, for a Christian to take part in a conspiracy to overthrow the government? Is it right for Christians to participate in civil disobedience or should a Christian's resistance be that of suffering only?

Any active participation in subversion is apparently ruled out by the basic biblical insistence on the divine authority of government. To take steps to overthrow an existing government is to deny this fact. It suggests that citizens have rejected what is a fact of God's providence, and this the Christian cannot do. He must suffer for conscience' sake and await God's hour of deliverance. It may be that God will use an armed revolt to overthrow a tyranny, for God uses men's schemes and plans even when those who formulate them are not his people and their action may be contrary to his revealed will. However, the Christian cannot himself share in the planning or initiation of such a rebellion. Until the existing regime has manifestly been overthrown, his calling is to submit.

In the matter of civil disobedience, guidance must come from biblical principles rather than from explicitly stated biblical mandates or prohibitions. Neither the OT nor the NT envisaged the type of state as the Western democracies of today, but rather the Bible knew only the authoritarian regime where the subjects' only duty was to obey.

Clearly the situation is different in a democracy where opposition to the government's policies is both allowable and desirable. Indeed, organized political opposition to the government (the political party in power) is the life blood of democracy. No biblical injunction is violated here. The "powers that be" in a democracy are the people themselves acting through their elected representatives. If then by educating public opinion, pressure is brought to bear on the government, or if by the use of the vote the political party in power is defeated, such actions are still consistent with submission to the duly constituted authorities.

Civil disobedience, however, is in a different category. It is one thing to agitate for a particular position, or even to organize demonstrations. These are within the law. But once an activity goes beyond the law, it would appear that at that point such conduct becomes illegitimate for the Christian. There are times when it is difficult to come to a clear decision. There are areas of action that are neither black nor white, but an indefinite gray. At such times the Christian whose attitude to the law is governed by such phrases as "for conscience' sake" or "for the Lord's sake" will give the law the benefit of the doubt.

A situation may also arise when there is a revolt leading to civil war with two competing authorities claiming to be the rightful government. Should the Christian take sides? What is his attitude to be? Again, one must admit that in the confusion that prevails at such a time, it is hard to come to a firm conclusion because of the lack of information, and also because of the misleading propaganda that usually issues from both sides. Christians will stand on their basic position. Since they have accepted the existing government as the one appointed by God, they will continue to treat it as such until it is quite clear that a *de facto* situation has made the *de jure* situation unreal and empty. Recognizing that God has often used rebellion to sweep away a corrupt government, Christians will not cling blindly to the status quo but will be ready to submit with an equal obedience to the new government. One extreme is the readiness to side with any movement that looks likely to topple an unjust government. The other extreme is the conservatism that makes Christians reluctant to accept the inevitability of a change that is already a fact, and to yearn after a day that is gone. The middle course between these extremes is not easy to chart, but unless we constantly relate ourselves to the basic biblical principles, the way will not be merely difficult to chart, but well nigh impossible.

E. Prayer for the government. Paul urged that PRAYER should be offered "for kings and all those in authority" (1 Tim. 2:2). Clearly he was not concerned with the formal prayer that makes a brief and perfunctory mention of the government in the public worship of the church. On the contrary, he embraced the whole range of prayer as he called for "requests, prayers, intercession and thanksgiving" (v. 1). The Christian is to be as fervent in his prayers for the government as he is in what he might be tempted to consider as more spiritual concerns.

It is also important to note that Paul did not add any moral or spiritual qualifications in designating those for whom we are to pray. He knew only too well that a blackguard like Nero might be on the throne as emperor. His own experience verified the corruption that could exist at lower levels of government. His prolonged captivity at CAESAREA had been due largely to the hope of a bribe on the part of the corrupt and immoral FELIX, the governor. But Paul did not qualify his exhortation in any way. If a man is in a position of authority, whatever may be his personal character, he must be prayed for. Even if he is an avowed enemy of the gospel and a bitter persecutor of the church, he is still to be the object of intercessory prayers.

Paul knew from experience the resistance to the gospel on the part of the Roman authorities, who always viewed with suspicion any group that might prove to be a source of disaffection or subversion. The Christians might claim to be unconcerned with political issues, but the fact that they did not conform to the general social pattern marked them out as politically suspect. The likelihood of continuing and intensified persecution was present. To pray for the government was really to pray for the well-being of the church. Paul gave as the aim of this praying, "that we may live peaceful and quiet lives in all godliness and holiness" (1 Tim. 2:2). He was declaring his concern not merely that Christians might enjoy peace, but also that they might be enabled to live as good citizens, respecting the government.

Christians at peace are never Christians at ease. Peaceful conditions in church and state mean opportunities for preaching the gospel. Paul followed this in his own experience. Roman roads were open to travelers because of the protecting might of the Roman legions stationed at strategic points throughout the empire. Those roads provided opportunity for the missionary of Christ who wanted to spread the gospel. Obviously it was a vital matter that these lines of communication be kept open. In modern times civil war and consequent anarchy are closing doors of opportunity. This call to pray for governments in all parts of the world is a continuing aspect of missionary intercession.

Paul also knew from experience the value of CITIZENSHIP as a barrier against injustice. He would not use any external powers to forward the gospel, for "the weapons we fight with are not the weapons of the world" (2 Cor. 10:4). At the same time, when he was subjected to injustice or to the possibility of mob violence or assassination, he was ready to appeal to the authorities. In PHILIPPI he was insistent that the authorities in the town must themselves be subject to Roman justice, which they claimed to administer. In the final resort, as Paul faced the plots of the Jews against his life, he was ready to invoke his right as a citizen to appeal to Caesar. The stable government of Rome was therefore not only a condition of peaceful existence but also was a valuable instrument for restraining unjust attacks on Paul's life. To pray for Paul's evangelistic work, to pray for his protection in carrying out that work, and to pray for the government, were not different areas of intercession, but aspects of the same basic concern.

Paul did not have in view simply the stability of the social order when he urged people to pray for rulers. He was also concerned for them as individuals, who are as much in need of the gospel as any other sinner without God and without hope. He doubtless recognized the possibility of unbelief bordering on incredulity with which many Christians might receive the request that they pray for the emperor's conversion. They might well have doubted whether there was any likelihood of such a remote possibility being realized. Paul reminded them of the width of God's purposes of grace. "God our Savior ... wants all men to be saved and to come to the knowledge of the truth" (1 Tim. 2:3–4). Taken in its immediate context, the words "all men" would seem to refer to all sorts and conditions of men. God's purpose embraces not only the weak things of the world who comprise the bulk of the church, but also rulers. When Paul emphasized God's choice of the humble to confound the mighty (1 Cor. 1:26–29), he did not exclude altogether those from a more exalted social or intellectual position—his phrase was "not many" rather than "not any." Therefore he declared that the gracious purpose of God reaches out to kings, so that prayer for them should petition their conversion.

There may come a time when the government of the day has gone far beyond its rights, and blatant unrighteousness and injustice control a nation. However, the Christian cannot, even then, have recourse to violent means to overthrow such a regime, but he can pray. In the Revelation is described such a conflict between the church and the persecuting state. Therein is a symbolic glimpse of "the souls of those who had been slain because of the word of God and the testimony they had maintained" (Rev. 6:9). They were crying to God for vindication, "How long, Sovereign Lord, holy and true, until you judge the inhabitants of the earth and avenge our blood?" (6:10). This prayer in heaven may well be echoed on earth. The Christian may be prepared to suffer for his testimony, but he is not inactive. God is his vindicator and to God he commits his cause, for in this matter his cause is no more a personal matter since it is the cause of the gospel itself. The psalms provide inspiration for prayer at such a time (Pss. 35:1; 43:1; 119:154) and also provide the ground of hope. The rulers may defy the Lord and his Christ, yet God still reigns. "The One enthroned in heaven laughs; / the Lord scoffs at them" (2:4). The solution may be in the ruler's conversion or in his overthrow, but in either case it is the power of God that will effect it, and believing prayer is faith's laying hold upon this divine power.

F. Participation in government. Is it right for Christians to use their vote? Can the Christian conscientiously enter political life and stand as a candidate for election either at the local or national level? These are questions that are obviously relevant only in a democracy where such possibilities exist. A similar question confronts Christians who live under some form of dictatorship. Is it right for a believer to accept employment that involves carrying out government policy? Does the believer's attitude to the world commit him to a policy of withdrawal from political affairs? As noted above in the matter of obedience to the state, the political context of the biblical writers was different from a democratic situation of today, though very similar to that of many contemporary dictatorships. The Bible does not give definite precept or prohibition, but does provide guiding principles.

An appeal to the situation in Israel seemingly is ruled out because of the unique character of the theocracy. The ruler or king in Israel was involved not only in civil but in spiritual functions as well. However, there is abundant OT illustration of the attitude of godly people toward Gentile and pagan governments. JOSEPH accepted a position of authority in Egypt, DANIEL in Babylon, and MORDECAI in Persia. Their positions are attributed to God's providence. NAAMAN continued to serve the king of Syria, and OBADIAH remained in the service of AHAB, whose apostate northern kingdom approximated the surrounding heathen nations. In the NT there is no hint that the ETHIOPIAN EUNUCH was called upon to renounce the office he held in the court life of his country. The same applies to CORNELIUS, the Roman centurion in Caesarea, Sergius PAULUS, the proconsul in CYPRUS, and the Philippian jailer. When Paul sent greetings to the Philippian church, he associated with him "those of Caesar's household." Although it might be argued that these were only slaves in the palace, it is not probable that Paul would single out palace slaves for special mention. More likely they had an official status that would be of particular interest to a church in Philippi, which was a Roman colony.

Some might accept the legitimacy of employment by government who would question the Christian's entry into political life. In the latter case it is a choice freely taken, and it involves a person not merely in carrying out the policy of the government but also in helping to formulate it. Can a Christian thus be involved? Does the call to come out and be separate not apply here?

One preliminary point needs to be made. There would seem to be no fundamental difference between using one's vote and entering actively into political life. In both cases one is taking an active part. One vote may seem a very insignificant cog in a great machine, but a few hundred such votes can change the whole future of a country. Whether or not to allow a Christian to enter politics is basically the same issue as the question of whether one should vote.

The continuing principle of submission to the powers that be must again be the starting point. Assuming a democratic situation, that authority is vested in the people themselves: those who actually rule the country are there as representatives of the people. The means by which they reach their position of authority is part of the constitution of the social order in which they live. According to the NT the ruler has divine authority, and in a democracy that power is vested in the people. Thus the procedure for electing representatives shares in that divinely given authority. To exercise the vote is thus simply to comply with the standing requirement of Scripture.

As far as active participation in politics is concerned, a Christian should enter only if he or she is strongly motivated by Christian principles of service. A Christian entering a political career encounters special problems. The lust for power, the unfair denigration of opponents, the dubious methods used to finance the party, the underhanded and sometimes dishonest methods employed, deceit for the sake of party advantage—these are some of the features of political life that make it a particularly thorny area for a Christian. Yet, it is in the darkness that the light is needed to shine all the more brightly. Salt is not to be stored but to be used where corruption is likely. The Christian politician thus becomes a moral preservative in an area where corruption is too often an ugly reality. Also, a Christian politician can exert his influence in forming and passing the best possible legislation.

Another live issue is the attitude of the church to the political struggle. Many contend that the church has a political role and should be ready to exercise its powers in a lobby aimed at influencing government policy. The NT reply to this would surely be to stress the respective roles of the church and state. The task of the church, as church, is to preach the gospel, edify the believers, and lead men and women to worship the living God. Individual Christians may enter the political field but they will do so primarily as citizens, not as representatives of a church lobby. However, their convictions will be influenced by the presuppositions of the Christian faith, and they will aim to realize in social life patterns of truth and equity. In this they will be strengthened by their membership in the church and by the fellowship they experience there.

The church as a body aims not primarily at improving the social order; her main objective is the salvation of men and women. The social improvement that may result when many people are saved is desirable, but when the church forsakes her primary task of preaching the gospel to engage in political enterprises, her true mission is lost.

A further consideration is Paul's attitude to the standards in the church and those in the world. Dealing with the problem of discipline at CORINTH, he is quite insistent that high standards be maintained in the church. As for the world outside, he cannot judge them, for they are not subject to Scripture, which provides the criterion of judgment in the life of the church (1 Cor. 5:9–13). The church therefore cannot insist that the state must conform to standards that are only applicable to Christians. The Christian in political life will know the standards, and in his own life he will strive to realize them. Knowing that unregenerate people can be restrained but not regenerated by legislation, and realizing that politics in a democracy is the art of the possible, he must be prepared to work for something less than the ideal lest he make the best the enemy of the good.

Such an active role obviously brings its own problems of conscience. There can come a point when compromise is impossible and when a policy to which one is so committed is a clear violation of the law of God. In such an eventuality the Christian in a dictatorship must do what Daniel did in a similar situation, and face the consequences of disobedience, whereas the Christian in a democratic country has no option but to resign.

(See further J. Calvin, *Institutes of the Christian Religion* 4.20; J. Wesley Bready, *The Evangelical Revival and Social Reform* [1938]; H. F. R.

Catherwood, *The Christian in Industrial Society* [1964]; C. F. H. Henry, *Aspects of Christian Social Ethics* [1964]; id., *Christian Personal Ethics* [1965]; D. Möberg, *Inasmuch* [1965]; L. Verduin, *The Reformers and their Stepchildren* [1966]; A. G. Dickens, *Reformation and Society in 16th Century Europe* [1966]; S. C. Mott, *Biblical Ethics and Social Change* [1982]; E. Bammel and C. F. D. Moule, eds., *Jesus and the Politics of His Day* [1984]; W. E. Pilgrim, *Uneasy Neighbors: Church and State in the New Testament* [1999]; M. Tellbe, *Paul between Synagogue and State: Christians, Jews, and Civic Authorities in 1 Thessalonians, Romans, and Philippians* [2001].)

H. M. CARSON

government, church. See CHURCH GOVERNMENT IN THE APOSTOLIC AGE.

governor. An official appointed to exercise control and administer a province or territory. The English term is used in Bible versions to render a variety of Hebrew terms, especially *peḥâ H7068* (1 Ki. 10:15 et al.), a somewhat vague title that is used, for example, of TATTENAI, the Persian ruler whose satrapy included Palestine, Phoenicia, and Egypt (Ezra 5:3; 6:6), and of ZERUBBABEL and NEHEMIAH as governors of Judah (Ezra 6:7; Neh. 5:14). In the NT, "governor" usually is the rendering of Greek *hēgemōn G2450*, "leader, chief" (e.g., Matt. 10:18).

During the Roman period, the various territories were constituted in different ways, and their governors were of different ranks. The rulers of senatorial PROVINCES, which were kept under control without difficulty, were appointed by the senate and given the title PROCONSUL, their term usually running for one year. Governors of imperial provinces, which were apt to cause trouble for Rome, were appointed by the emperor personally for an indefinite term of office and were called *legates*. The governor of a subdivision of an imperial province was also appointed by the emperor and given the title PREFECT (before the reign of CLAUDIUS, apparently) or PROCURATOR. The NT mentions the following governors who were proconsuls: Sergius PAULUS, governor of CYPRUS (Acts 13:6–7); GALLIO, governor of ACHAIA (18:12); and the unnamed governors of the province of ASIA who lived at EPHESUS (19:38). QUIRINIUS, governor of SYRIA (Lk. 2:2), was a legate. The governors of JUDEA, which was a part of the imperial province of Syria, included PILATE (Matt. 27:2; 28:14), FELIX (Acts 23:26), and FESTUS (Acts 26:32), all of whom were prefects/procurators.

Pontius Pilate and other Roman military governors were stationed at Caesarea Maritima on Israel's Mediterranean coast. The city had amenities such as a stadium, hippodrome, theater, and busy commerce. (View to the N.)

The KJV sometimes uses the word *governor* in ways that are now unusual or obsolete. In the account of the marriage at CANA, "the governor of the feast" and "the ruler of the feast" (Jn. 2:8–9 KJV) are the same person. In Gal. 4:2, "tutors and governors" is better translated "guardians and trustees." And the rendering "withersoever the governor listeth" in Jas. 3:4 refers to the pilot or steersman who takes a ship where he wants.

J. L. KELSO

Goyim. See GOIIM #2.

Gozan goh′zan (גּוֹזָן *H1579*, from Akk. *Guzana*). City and region of the upper valley of the Khabur River (biblical HABOR, a tributary of the EUPHRATES). The capital, modern Tell Halaf, lies on the river where it crosses the border between Syria and Turkey, some 200 mi. E of the NE tip of the Mediterranean Sea. The region was conquered by the Assyrians (2 Ki. 19:12; Isa. 37:12), and later TIGLATH-PILESER III, king of ASSYRIA, transported Israelites from TRANSJORDAN to Gozan (1 Chr. 5:26). It is also one of the areas to which Israelites were deported after SAMARIA fell to Assyria in 722 B.C. (2 Ki. 17:6; 18:11). Gozan was excavated, beginning in 1911, by Baron Max von Oppenheim, who discovered a new culture with excellent pottery (see his book, *Tell Halaf: A New Culture in Oldest Mesopotamia* [1933]; cf. also I. Hijjara, *The Halaf Period in Northern Mesopotamia* [1997].)

C. P. WEBER

Graba grah´buh. KJV Apoc. variant of HAGABAH (1 Esd. 5:29).

grace. In Christian doctrine, this term refers to unmerited divine favor. In summary form, the Christian message is "the gospel of God's grace" (Acts 20:24). The Greek term *charis* G5921 was common in secular usage, but when taken up into the message of Christ it was to become filled out with a new and enriched content. Its usual meaning in classical Greek is "attractiveness" or "charm" (cf. the cognate verb *chairō* G5897, "to rejoice, be glad"), though it can also be translated "favor, kindness, gratitude." The word appears about 170 times in the Greek OT, where it commonly renders a Hebrew word of similar meaning, *ḥēn* H2834 (Gen. 6:8; 19:19; et al.). While the SEPTUAGINT has many expressions to convey the reality of God's saving acts (e.g., *eleos* G1799, "mercy, compassion," rendering *ḥesed* H2876), *charis* is not used in this connection. Moreover, "Not even the higher conception of the Divine *ḥesed* or mercy is able in Judaism to achieve the place occupied by *charis* in Christianity. While the gracious love of God to men had been the real foundation of the prophetic religion of the OT … it has to be noticed that even there the salvation of God was based not upon *charis* but upon the sovereign power and glory of God, upon his 'righteousness,' or 'judgment,' or 'torah'" (W. Manson in *The Doctrine of Grace*, ed. W. T. Whitley [1932], 37).

The process by which the word *charis* came to approximate the NT idea runs somewhat as follows: (1) Its primary reference appears to have been to the state of being charmed or delighted. PLUTARCH, for example, speaks of the "charm" of Homer's poetry and of the talkative person whose unreasonable chatter destroys the *charis* of his deeds (*De garrulitate* 4–5 [504C-D]; LCL ed. of the *Moralia*, 6:403). (2) The word then took on a subjective sense with the thought of "kindly," or "courteous," that is, "a generous disposition"; it is a virtual equivalent for the idea of the willing of good to someone. (3) From this there developed the concrete connotation suggesting a "favor" or "boon"; a favor is the expression of good will, and as such it is to be taken as a token of kindness. (4) As grace implies not only a giver but also a receiver, so it came to denote the gratitude felt by the recipient for the favor bestowed and the thanks by which the gratitude is expressed.

While the NT reflects these various significations, it uses the word in the main with the enriched meaning that comes to it through the work of Christ. Grace is almost a synonym for SALVATION. Always, however, *charis* had the underlying idea of a bestowal of help by an act of one's free generosity. Aristotle could therefore define the term as "helpfulness towards someone in need, not in return for anything [*mē anti pinos*]," nor that the helper may get anything, but for the sake of the person who is helped (*Rhet.* 2.7). Before Bethlehem, the concept of a God of grace who gives himself appears nowhere. PHILO JUDAEUS speaks much of God's "grace," but always in the sense of giving gifts to men. He does confess, "Often when I get rid of a foul suggestion in my mind by a rush of good thoughts, it is God flooding my soul with his grace [*tē heautou chariti*]" (*Leg.* 2.9). Even here, however, although the idea of an undeserved favor is recognized, Philo never rises to the faith that God's presence can enter a human heart. God giving himself in Christ his Son, who finds a dwelling-place in the life of the believer, is "the gospel of the grace of God." (See *NIDOTTE*, 2:203–6; *NIDNTT*, 2:115–24.)

    I. The Synoptic Gospels and grace
   II. The Pauline doctrine of grace
      A. Grace and the Trinity
      B. Grace and justification
      C. Grace and law, works, and nature
   III. Grace in the other NT writings

I. The Synoptic Gospels and grace. The word *charis* is entirely absent from both Matthew and Mark. Luke uses it several times with the sense of "favor" (Lk. 1:30 [cf. also v. 28]; 2:40, 52), but when attributed to Jesus it bears the sense of "credit" or "thanks" (6:32–34; 17:9). The absence of the term in its theological sense from the sayings of Jesus tells against the common view that the early Christians constantly read back into the teaching of Jesus their own faith and sought to justify that faith by crediting its utterance to him. It is also natural that only after Jesus' death and resurrection would the term acquire the rich meaning it has, for example, in the writings of PAUL.

The use of the word in Lk. 4:22 may, however, be taken as a link with the peculiar post-Calvary significance of the concept. The verse reads, "All spoke well of him and were amazed at the gracious words that came from his lips." The Greek phrase *tois logois tēs charitos* (lit. "the words of grace") may indicate more than that the people marveled at Christ's charm as a speaker, or at his winsomeness as an orator. Luke uses the phrase "the word of his grace" (Acts 14:3 NRSV) as equivalent to the gospel (cf. 20:24). Something of this objective sense should possibly be read in the use of *charis* in Lk. 4:22. This proposal is strengthened by an examination of the context, where our Lord reads from Isa. 61:2 and asserts its fulfillment in his coming. The allusion to divine grace is made more obvious still by his omission of any reference to the divine vengeance mentioned in the original passage (cf. 61:2; Lk. 4:22). Jesus was indicating that his presence in the world was to have a result wider and deeper than any nationalistic aid to the people of Israel. While Luke of all the synoptic writers was impressed by the gracious manner of Christ's teaching, he also wished his readers to be aware of the gracious matter of his teaching. The words of our Lord caused marvel because they came as "words of grace, about grace" (A. B. Bruce in *EGT*, 1:490).

Throughout the Gospels in several ways the category of grace was demonstrated in Christ's acts and teaching. He came to fulfill a divine commission. The recurrent phrase "I have come" (Matt. 10:34 et al.) accentuates this task. He had come as the Father's beloved Son to seek and to save that which was lost. That is grace! By his attitude Jesus demonstrated what is meant by grace. He sought out the sinful. This is the new note of the gospel. JUDAISM, though teaching that God was ready to be gracious, was inclined to leave the first step with the sinner. The distinctive thing with Jesus was his taking the deliberate initiative on God's behalf. That is grace!

The whole tendency of Jesus' teaching was in the same direction, indicating that salvation is a matter of God's free generosity. For example, in the sequel to the story of the rich young ruler, the astonished disciples ask, "Who then can be saved?" (Mk. 10:26). Jesus answers that the ultimate right to enter the KINGDOM OF GOD and be saved lies with God. Christ enunciates the gospel of grace in contrast with a message of law and works. A place in his kingdom is not gotten by anything given up for God. It is given by the Father, and the Father's giving is the Father's grace. "What are we to get?" ask the disciples with the parable of the laborers in the vineyard in mind (Matt. 20:1–8). They are reminded of the folly of bargaining with God. The final principle of God's dealing with sinners is a matter of grace.

The parable of the Pharisee and the tax collector shows clearly that "grace is grace" because, though

This church, named Dominus Flevit (The Lord Wept), overlooks Jerusalem and recalls Jesus' love for and gracious plea to the Holy City.

wholly concerned with moral goodness, it does not at all depend upon how moral we are (John Oman, *Grace and Personality* [1917], 189). The symbolism of the Last Supper makes clear Jesus' wish to indicate that the divine purpose of grace was focused in his CROSS. The blood of the cross inaugurated a new covenant and was essential to God as a means and medium of his saving work (see COVENANT, THE NEW). It was no *post factum* explanation of what had happened. From the beginning, the life and work of Christ were read in the category of grace. The story of the cross was not given as an account of how the life of Jesus ended, but as revealing the basis upon which God's grace is assured and secured.

Two broad facts are clear from the record of the Gospels. On the one hand, it is evident that the saving initiative is with God; and, on the other hand, any plea to human merit is ruled out. While Jesus' teaching is not the source of the term *charis*, which describes these two facts, his own person is the source of the "grace" of which the whole NT speaks. It was the apostle Paul who took these twin ideas and included them under the one pregnant term. In this sense, grace is specifically a Pauline concept.

II. The Pauline doctrine of grace. While all the shades of meaning noted earlier are to be found in the NT, not all of them together convey the richness that the term acquired in the theology of Paul. For him, grace was nothing less than the unsought and unbought saving activity of God which made him a debtor forever. The DAMASCUS road encounter with the risen Jesus brought to focus the two basic ideas which unite in the word *charis*—that the saving initiative is with God and that human merit is of no avail. By "grace," then, is meant that salvation is from first to last a gift of God. God's saving relation to humanity has its beginning and ending in his own eternal purpose as the counterfoil of history. He loves because he would love; saves because he would save. God acts in grace; acts without waiting for a sign or a nod from us: this is grace.

The idea of the absoluteness of grace in salvation is specially indicated by the fact that Paul never begins or ends his letters without a reference to grace. In neither case is he adhering to mere convention (Jas. 1:1 is the only instance of the conventional epistolary greeting in a NT letter; cf. also Acts 15:23, 29). By beginning his letters as he does, Paul is suggesting the supremacy of grace as the source from which flow all the blessings of the new order into which God's unmerited favor has brought the redeemed soul. Everything rests on God's free grace in Christ. Coming at the close of his letters, the use of *charis* was a new thing in epistolary literature. In so using it, the apostle was virtually authenticating his position as an apostle to whom the grace of God had come in such abundance.

Paul almost always links grace and PEACE in his greetings, and the two ideas are often associated elsewhere (cf. 2 Cor. 13:11–13; Eph. 6:23–24; 1 Thess. 5:23–28; 2 Thess. 3:16–18; et al.). As the first word of greeting and the last word of farewell, "grace" sums up for the apostle the totality of the blessings that come from God through Christ. "Grace" is the source; "peace," the stream. "*Grace*... denotes the love of God manifested in the form of pardon toward sinful man; and *peace*... the feeling of profound calm or inward quiet which is communicated to the heart by the possession of reconciliation" (F. Godet, *Commentary on the Epistle to the Romans*, rev. ed. [1883], 84).

The apostle concludes his second letter to the Thessalonians with these words: "I, Paul, write this greeting in my own hand, which is the distinguishing mark [*sēmeion G4956*] in all my letters. This is how I write. The grace of our Lord Jesus Christ be with you all" (2 Thess. 3:17–18). There is no reason to suppose (with J. A. Bengel, *Gnomon of the New Testament* [1877], 4:237) that Paul was in the habit of appending the "grace" in a specifically picturesque style of his own, although it may be agreed that if he could have done so he well might, for the word was engraven in multicolors upon his own heart. Paul had a purpose other than personal in adding such a benediction. His letters were, as Dryden has said, "absent-sermons," and the last word for any church as well as the first is *grace*. This must remain the dominant note of the celestial symphony as a Pauline epistle dies away.

A. Grace and the Trinity

1. The grace of Christ. In the salutations the connection of grace with Christ is not as explicit as in the benedictions. The general formula in the latter case is, "The grace of our Lord Jesus [Christ] be with you" (cf. Rom. 16:20; 1 Cor. 16:23; 2 Cor. 13:14; Gal. 6:18; et al.). Paul bases his trinitarian benediction on the order of experience (2 Cor. 13:14). It is the grace of Christ which makes real the love of God—"first the experience of grace of Jesus, and then, through that and only through that, the certainty of the loving Fatherhood of God" (cf. James Moffatt, *Grace in the New Testament* [1931], 151; James S. Stewart, *A Man in Christ: The Vital Elements of St. Paul's Religion* [1935], 140–41).

In 2 Cor. 8:9 Paul sees the grace of Christ displayed in "the poverty" which for our sakes he accepted that we might become "rich." It is by "the grace of Christ" we are called, and to preach any other gospel is anathema (Gal. 1:8). Thus in 2 Thess. 1:12 the grace of God and of the Lord Jesus Christ are associated. Paul then sees grace as founded on the absoluteness of Christ. Only an absolute Christ can meet the sinner's absolute need. Paul never sets before us a relative Christ: a relative Christ might reduce him to our condition, but only by removing him from our need. To be absolute Christ must have originated on God's side, must have that origin and nothing less. Paul preached absolute grace because he proclaimed an absolute Christ. To Paul the self-sacrifice of Christ was one and the same with the grace of God.

2. The grace of God. Paul steadfastly declared that grace is given by God (cf. Rom. 15:15; 1 Cor. 1:3; 3:10; 15:10; et al.), and in no meager fashion either (Rom. 3:24; 5:20; 2 Cor. 4:15; 9:8, 14; 12:9; Eph. 1:7; 2:7; 1 Tim. 1:14). For the apostle, such grace is God's "radiant adequacy." The phrase "the grace of God," says Manson (*The Doctrine of Grace*, ed. Whitley, 43), "signifies the generous love or gift of God by which in Christ salvation is bestowed on man and a new world of blessings opened."

3. Grace and the Holy Spirit. In the epistle to the Hebrews, the Holy Spirit is referred to as "the Spirit of grace" (Heb. 10:29; cf. Zech. 11:10). It is by the Holy Spirit that the love of God manifest in the grace of Christ is made real to believing hearts. Both the individual and the church are the dwelling place of God through the Spirit (cf. 1 Cor. 3:16; 12:11, 13; Eph. 1:12; 2:22; et al.). In this connection note must be taken of the association between "grace" and "power." God's special "favor" and God's diversified "favors" are alike the result of divine grace (cf. Rom. 1:5; 12:3; 15:15; 2 Cor. 8:9; Eph. 4:7; et al.); it is therefore natural to conceive of the relation between them in terms of "power" (1 Cor. 15:10). This association between "grace" and "power" is given special emphasis in 2 Cor. 12:9: "My grace is sufficient for you, for my power is made perfect in weakness" (cf. 2 Tim. 2:11; 1 Pet. 4:10). By referring to grace as the active power of God, grace may be thought of as the presence of the HOLY SPIRIT. For the presence of the Holy Spirit is "power" (cf. Lk. 4:14; 24:49; Acts 1:8; 8:10; 10:38; et al.). Between "grace" as divine "power" and "power" as the presence of the Holy Spirit there is, then, a vital kinship. The experience of being "full of the Holy Spirit" and being "full of grace and power" is hardly to be distinguished (cf. Acts 6:5–8; 1 Cor. 12:4–11; Eph. 4:7–13).

In spite of this association, however, the Holy Spirit is not to be confused with the grace of God, as is done explicitly, for example, by N. P. Williams (*The Grace of God* [1930], 110). This is to confuse association with identification; and in the end is to throw doubt upon the Trinitarian conception of the Godhead, which is authentically biblical. It is therefore rightly said that "the grace of God is the grace of the Father, Son, and Holy Ghost." We may properly refer to it as "the grace of the Lord Jesus Christ" because "the Incarnation of the Son of God is its crowning expression; and it is especially associated with the Holy Ghost in the Christian, because we live under the new dispensation consequent upon the accomplishment of Christ's redemptive work and his appointment of 'another Comforter.' Grace is, nevertheless, the grace of the indivisible Trinity and is not to be equated with any one Person of the Trinity" (O. Hardman, *The Christian Doctrine of Grace* [1937], 34).

B. Grace and justification. Paul begins his exposition of JUSTIFICATION by referring to God's "grace as a gift" (Rom. 3:24 NRSV). To be declared righteous before God by virtue of our acceptance in Christ is altogether of God's spontaneous compassion. The grounds of our justification are variously stated (cf. Rom. 5:9, 18–19; 1 Cor. 6:11). While justification is based upon the objective mediatorial work of Christ for mankind, the channel by which this saving act is made effective in human experience is FAITH. Faith is the instrumental, not the formal, cause: it has the meaning of a living personal trust in a perfect redemption and a present Savior. The summary scheme of salvation is, then, "by grace … through faith" (Eph. 2:8). Grace points back to the ultimate source of God's act of justifying the sinner by his sheer goodwill and mercy. Faith, as our response to God's act in Christ, is a divine work in us—itself a gracious and free gift of God. From first to last the justification of the sinner is a matter of grace: "And if by grace, then it is no longer by works; if it were, grace would no longer be grace" (Rom. 11:6).

Paul sees "the abundance of grace and the free gift of righteousness" (Rom. 5:17 NRSV) as greater and more powerful than the original taint of nature, even when the added stains of actual sinful acts are taken into reckoning, for "where sin increased, grace abounded all the more" (v. 20 NRSV). And grace reigns through righteousness to eternal life through Christ our Lord (v. 21; cf. Tit. 3:5). This teaching does not allow any idea of "cheap grace" (D. Bonhoeffer). Paul will not admit to the perversion of God's free generosity in an antinomian direction (cf. Rom. 6:1–2; Jude 4). He insists rather that the grace of God, which has appeared for the salvation of all, trains us to renounce sinful passions and to await "the blessed hope—the glorious appearing of our great God and Savior, Jesus Christ" (Tit. 2:11–13). Instead of sinning "that grace may abound," the believer is called upon to "grow in grace."

Paul's experience had taught him that God gives and God forgives. He was sure that "all is of grace"—here is the sovereignty of grace. This was the logic of his own sense of being overwhelmed by the mercy of God. The gospel he received and preached taught him that faith was something not confined to his own people after the flesh; and faith was, he knew, the sinner's response by the action of grace to God's initiative. If faith was not limited to Israel neither could grace be. He was assured then that "grace is for all"—here is the sweep of grace.

In no place does Paul state that grace is given to all people. While the word *all* appears in some passages (Rom. 3:22–24; 5:17–18; Tit. 2:11), in each case it is clearly restricted by reference to the immediate context. In the first passage, the word is found in a parenthesis about sinners (Rom. 3:23), and the declaration that people "are justified freely by his grace" (v. 24) points back to "all who believe" (v. 22). In the second passage, the "justification that brings life for all men" (5:18) must be read in connection with the assurance that "those who receive God's abundant provision of grace and of the gift of righteousness reign in life through the one man, Jesus Christ" (v. 17). The NRSV renders Tit. 2:11, "For the grace of God has appeared, bringing salvation to all," which could too easily lead to a universalist conclusion if isolated from the whole drift of the NT. The alternate translation in the note is preferable: "For the grace of God has appeared to all, bringing salvation" (cf. NIV, "For the grace of God that brings salvation has appeared to all men"; TNIV, "For the grace of God has appeared that offers salvation to all people"). In the three passages, then, the most that could be concluded is that salvation is offered to all: in none of them is it declared that all individuals are saved (cf. Jn. 1:16; 3:16; et al.).

C. Grace and law, works, and nature. Paul declares that we are justified by faith (Rom. 3:28) apart from the deeds of the law. Throughout he clearly puts the LAW in antithesis with grace. To follow the law as a way of obtaining salvation is but to increase one's debt (Gal. 5:3) and to fail of the grace of God. But "Christ is the end of the law so that there may be righteousness for every one who believes" (Rom. 10:4). We may say that the law "met its end in Christ," yet it was not just "ended" by him. He is himself its "end" as a means of attaining to a righteousness acceptable to God. The gospel reveals the righteousness of God by faith. At the same time the law is not abolished, but has found its fulfillment in him; here is the "grace of law." Grace, too, cancels out works as a means of attaining salvation (Rom. 11:6). A reward is not reckoned of grace (4:4); thus to receive "grace" is to renounce "works" as a means of justification. The association of faith and works in salvation is impossible, for then "grace would no longer be grace."

It has been contended that nowhere does the NT in general, and Paul in particular, oppose "grace" and "nature." This is argued to justify the medieval maxim, "Naturam non tollit gratia sed perficit" ("Grace does not destroy but perfects nature"). The contention is false. For that is not rightly regarded as grace which is but a *donum superadditum* (an extra gift added to human powers). That is not grace which is a mere auxiliary to our initial efforts. Christ did not come to supplement us at our best, but to redeem us at our worst. Throughout the NT—and especially underscored in Pauline theology—what is reckoned to be of the individual's own origination is assigned to "nature," whereas "grace" is what is given gratis to us. It is the plain teaching of the gospel that we have no natural endowments and no moral deeds that merit favor with God; for if we had, grace would not be grace, and we would have something wherein to glory.

III. Grace in the other NT writings.

Although the term *charis* is less frequent outside the Pauline writings, its occurrences show that the Pauline sense was everywhere the Christian understanding of God's method of dealing with sinners. There is a close kinship of ideas between Paul and the epistle to the Hebrews on the subject of grace. The supreme evidence of "the grace of God" is in Christ's tasting death for everyone (Heb. 2:9). Having a great High Priest, we can come for timely help to "the throne of grace" (4:16). We must beware lest we offend "the Spirit of grace" (10:29) or fail to obtain grace (12:15). Later, the writer contrasts the strengthening of the heart by "grace" with that which comes from "foods" (13:9). It is by this strengthening of grace that the believer is equipped with everything good to do the will of God (13:21). Throughout this epistle, however differently expressed, there is the same idea of grace as throughout the rest of the NT.

The Petrine epistles are no less undergirded by the same sense of indebtedness to God. God is the "God of all grace" (1 Pet. 5:10). It is to the humble that he gives grace (5:5; cf. Jas. 4:6; Prov. 3:34). Standing in the "true grace of God" (1 Pet. 5:12), men and women become "heirs together of the grace of life" (3:7 KJV). This grace is now ours (1:10), and yet there is grace coming to us at the revelation of Jesus Christ (1:13). The sum of the believer's aim must be to "grow in the grace and knowledge of our Lord and Savior Jesus Christ" (2 Pet. 3:18).

James, too, assures grace for the humble; humility is at the same time a fruit of grace and a reason for "more grace" (Jas. 4:6). Christ is the perfect law of liberty so that the liberty into which we are brought is not lawlessness but that which is of God (1:15, 27). To be "rich in faith" (2:5) is to do what God requires. No empty inactive faith saves (2:14–15). The "wisdom that comes from heaven" produces "a harvest of righteousness" (3:17–18). Indeed, in all things we can be but humble receivers of "every good gift and perfect gift" (1:17). Of his own will are we brought into salvation by means of the "implanted word" that is able to save our souls (1:21 NRSV). For James, then, basic to all that we are or do is God's generous acceptance of those who draw near to him (4:8).

Only a few times in the Johannine writings does the term *charis* occur. This scantiness, however, is not especially significant, for John tends to give to LOVE (*agapē G27*) the idea "grace" has for Paul. A difficult use is that of "grace for grace" (Jn. 1:16 KJV). But the intention seems to be to stress the newness and adequacy of God's favor: here is grace on top of grace, and grace following grace—more grace on the foundation of grace and more waves flooding the shore of life from the ocean of grace (cf. NIV, "one blessing after another"; an almost exact equivalent phrase is found in Philo, *Post.* 43, with the meaning of "benefit upon benefit").

This statue represents Jesus forgiving Peter at the Sea of Galilee after the resurrection.

The term, as used in the salutations of the second epistle and of Revelation (2 Jn. 3; Rev. 1:4–5), has a Pauline sense, while nothing could be more apt than that the NT itself should conclude with the renewed benediction, "The grace of the Lord Jesus be with all the saints" (22:21 NRSV). Here the distinctive word of the Christian message finds its climax. In Paul the special emphasis is that grace reaches down to our need: in the Apocalypse, with its special stress on the sovereignty of Christ, there is the assurance that grace reigns from the throne.

The free generosity of God through the self-giving of Christ is throughout what is meant by grace. Christ's self-sacrifice is the supreme demonstration of grace (2 Cor. 8:9; cf. Phil. 2:5–11). He is the incarnate grace of God made available to faith. By grace we are called (Gal. 1:15) and justified (Rom. 3:24) and sanctified (Rom. 6:14). By grace we have an eternal consolation and a good hope (2 Thess. 2:16), and the strength to endure (2 Tim. 2:1). Even liberality is a blessing when conducted in the "grace" of Christ (2 Cor. 8:1, 6, 9, 19; 9:8, 15).

(See further L. S. Chafer, *Grace* [1922]; J. Murray, *The Covenant of Grace* [1954]; J. N. D. Anderson, *Law and Grace* [1954]; C. Ryder Smith, *The Biblical Doctrine of Grace* [1956]; P. S. Watson, *The Concept of Grace* [1959]; G. A. F. Knight, *Law and Grace* [1962]; E. F. Kevan, *The Grace of Law* [1964]; H. D. McDonald, *I and He* [1966], chs. 5–6; R. M. Hals, *Grace and Faith in the Old Testament* [1980]; J. B. Cobb, Jr., *Grace and Responsibility: A Wesleyan Theology for Today* [1995]; T. R. Schreiner and B. A. Ware, eds., *The Grace of God, the Bondage of the Will* [1995]; B. Eastman, *The Significance of Grace in the Letters of Paul* [1999]; R. J. Mouw, *He Shines in All That's Fair: Culture and Common Grace* [2001]; P. F. M. Zahl, *Grace in Practice: A Theology of Everyday Life* [2007]. Note also the standard works on OT and NT theology.) H. D. McDonald

graff. KJV form (now obsolete) of GRAFT.

graft. Grafting (Gk. *enkentrizō* G1596) is the practice of joining a shoot or bud to a growing plant, usually by insertion. A common procedure is to insert a slip of a cultivated tree into a wild plant. In Rom. 11:17–24, however, Paul uses a metaphor that is "contrary to nature" (v. 24), namely, the grafting of a wild olive branch, representing the Gentiles, into the good olive tree, which indicates the place of blessing under the Abrahamic COVENANT. Such a process is unnatural, which is precisely the point (but see C. E. B. Cranfield, *A Critical and Exegetical Commentary on the Epistle to the Romans*, ICC, 2 vols. [1975–79], 2:571–72). Normally, such a graft would be unfruitful. The branches refer figuratively to being in the place of spiritual blessing and fruitfulness. "That unbelieving Jews (branches of the good tree) were broken off that Gentiles might be grafted in, afforded no occasion for glorying on the part of the latter. Jew and Gentile alike must enjoy the divine blessings by faith alone. So Jews who abide not in unbelief shall, as 'the natural branches, be grafted into their own olive tree'" (W. E. Vine, *An Expository Dictionary of New Testament Words* [1940], 1:171). K. L. Barker

grain. This English term, referring to the fruits of cereal grasses in general, occurs very frequently in modern Bible versions as the rendering of various Hebrew and Greek terms. (In all but a few cases, the KJV has CORN, a term that in America refers to maize, which was unknown to the ancient world. In Britain *corn* is the general term for grain, including all the cereal plants, but especially wheat and oats.) The most important agricultural products in ancient Israel were grain, WINE, and OIL—usually mentioned in that order (Deut. 7:13; 11:14; et al.). There are many Hebrew words connected with the raising and processing of grain, such as *gereś* H1762, "crushed [wheat] grain" (Lev. 2:14, 16); *šibbōlet* H8672, "head of grain" (Gen. 41:5–7); *gādîš* H1538, "stacked [sheaves of] grain" (contrasted to *qāmâ* H7850, "standing grain," Exod. 22:6); and others. Note in particular the term *ʾābîb* H26, referring to fresh young ears of barley that could be roasted and that were included in the offering of FIRSTFRUITS (Lev. 2:14). The first month of the religious calendar (corresponding to March-April) was called ABIB because of its agricultural importance.

In PALESTINE all grain was grown during the winter. It was planted soon after the beginning of the rainy season in October (see RAIN). After the rainy season in March and April, the BARLEY began to ripen and the WHEAT followed from a week to a month or more later, depending upon the altitude.

About the first week in June the REAPING began and the whole family, including the children, participated. Reaping was done with a hand SICKLE. The grain was then threshed on a bare, flat circular stretch of ground by having an ox or some other animal drag a THRESHING sledge round and round the floor. The threshed grain was then winnowed by tossing it into the air with a shovel to let the wind blow away the chaff (see WINNOWING). After that the grain was cleaned with a sieve and stored in jars, to be ground into flour with a handmill whenever there was need for BREAD. Normally, the bran was not removed from the meal; when it was, it was called "fine flour." Newly ripened grain was eaten either fresh (Deut. 23:25; Matt. 12:1) or roasted and eaten as grits (Lev. 2:14, 16).

Rye and oats are not mentioned in the Bible, although oats were raised in Palestine. Wheat was the most esteemed grain and was grown wherever the climate made it possible. The best wheat was grown in the fertile valleys of JEZREEL, SAMARIA, and GALILEE, and in the HAURAN in TRANSJORDAN, which in Roman times was one of the great granaries of the empire. The next most common grain of Israel was barley. It was less expensive to grow than wheat because it could be raised on poorer soil, and it also had a shorter growing season. The ordinary food of the poor was barley bread (Jdg. 7:13; Ezek. 4:9; Jn. 6:9); barley was also used to feed horses and cattle (1 Ki. 4:28). SPELT was a hard-grained variety of wheat of poor quality. Grown in Egypt (Exod. 9:32) and in Palestine (Isa. 28:25), it was sometimes mixed with regular wheat to make bread (Ezek. 4:9). MILLET was fed to poultry, but was also eaten by people. EZEKIEL was commanded to use it as an ingredient of the bread he was ordered to prepare (4:9).

Grain stored in jars has been found in a large number of cities excavated by archaeologists. John Garstang, for example, found jars filled with wheat, barley, millet, and oats in the burned debris of JERICHO; and it has been suggested that the full jars are evidence that the city was destroyed after the harvest had been gathered.

In the NT, such Greek terms are used as *sitos* G4992, which can refer to grain generally or to wheat specifically (Lk. 12:18; Acts 27:38), and *stachys* G5092, "head of grain" (Matt. 12:1 et al.; note the stages of the plant, Mk. 4:28). Various aspects of grain farming were used as illustrations by Jesus: the parables of the sower (Matt. 13:3–23; Mk. 4:3–20), the wheat and the weeds (Matt. 13:24–30), the seed growing secretly (Mk. 4:26–29), and the rich man and his barns (Lk. 12:16–21), as well as the metaphor of the grain of

A field of grain ripening in the region of Goshen in Egypt.

wheat buried in the ground to produce fruit (Jn. 12:24). Paul also used the image of the buried grain of wheat as a symbol of the resurrection of the body (1 Cor. 15:37). (Cf. further S. and J. L. Miller, *Encyclopedia of Bible Life* [1944], 1–24; P. J. King and L. E. Stager, *Life in Biblical Israel* [2001], 94–95.) See AGRICULTURE; HARVEST. S. BARABAS

granary. See STORE CITIES; STOREHOUSE.

grape. See VINE, VINEYARD.

grass. This English term is used frequently in Bible versions to render several Hebrew words, especially *ḥāṣîr* H2945 (1 Ki. 18:5 et al.); in the NT, it renders Greek *chortos* G5965 (Matt. 6:30 et al.). Sometimes the reference is to grass for grazing (e.g., Job 6:5; here *dešeʾ* H2013), sometimes to hay (Ps. 37:2), sometimes to plants as a whole (Matt. 6:30). The prophets and psalmists describe human life as grass: "As for man, his days are like grass" (Ps. 103:15). Especially noteworthy are the words of Isaiah: "All men are like grass, / and all their glory is like the flowers of the field. / The grass withers and the flowers fall, / because the breath of the LORD blows on them. / Surely the people are grass. / The grass withers and the flowers fall, / but the word of our God stands forever" (Isa. 40:6–8, partially quoted in 1 Pet. 1:24–25; cf. Jas. 1:11).

grasshopper. See LOCUST.

grating. A grill or network of bars. The word is used to render Hebrew *mikbār H4803*, referring to the bronze lattice-work or mesh that, underneath a projecting ledge, surrounded the lower half of the ALTAR of burnt offering (Exod. 27:4–5; 35:16; 38:4–5, 30; 39:39). Four rings were attached to it. Poles were then passed through the rings, and the altar was carried by them (27:4, 7). Various functions have been attributed to the grating itself, for example, to protect the altar and to support the ledge above it. K. L. BARKER

gratitude. The condition or quality of being grateful; an emotion or sentiment of thankfulness. It implies a warm sense of appreciation for a kindness received, accompanied by a feeling of good will toward the benefactor and a desire to repay the favor. This English term is absent from the KJV and occurs only a few times in modern versions (e.g., Acts 24:3, rendering *eucharistia G2374*; Col. 3:16, rendering *charin G5921*).

The Greek word *eucharistia*, which occurs rarely in the SEPTUAGINT (Esth. 8:13; Wisd. 16:28; Sir. 37:11; 2 Macc. 2:27), is used fifteen times in the NT and is usually translated "thanksgiving" (1 Cor. 14:16 et al.). This term is attested as far back as the 5th cent. B.C. and is found in both PHILO JUDAEUS and JOSEPHUS. It is common in the inscriptions, but there is perhaps only one known example in the papyri, namely, in a letter by the emperor CLAUDIUS where he expresses gratification to a gymnastic club for games performed in his honor. In profane Greek *eucharistia* does not occur in the sense of the *giving* of thanks, and this usage in biblical Greek is confined always to religious contexts.

No motif more adequately recalls the nature of biblical faith than gratitude or thanksgiving. With three insignificant exceptions (Lk. 17:9 [in the expression *echei charin*]; Acts 24:3; Rom. 16:4 [verb *eucharisteō G2373*]) thanks invariably are rendered unto God. It appears only within the context of the COVENANT relationship. Moreover, it is always prompted by a concrete act of the covenant God in human affairs.

In the OT the verb "to give thanks" is *yādâ H3344*, which can also be translated "to praise" and "to confess"; the word for "thanksgiving" is the cognate noun *tôdâ H9343*. Thanksgiving comprises the special note of the Psalter; yet Israel's gratitude to Yahweh rings throughout her history. King DAVID appointed certain Levites "to make petition, to give thanks, and to praise the LORD" (1 Chr. 16:4). This practice was continued by SOLOMON (2 Chr. 5:13; 7:6), by HEZEKIAH (31:2), and by the exiles who returned from Babylon (Neh. 11:17). Ministers were appointed to express thanksgiving publicly (1 Chr. 16:4, 7; 23:30; 2 Chr. 31:2).

Thanksgiving was prominent in Israel's cultic worship. Festival processions en route to ZION filled the air "with shouts of joy and thanksgiving" (Ps. 42:4). Their entrance into the temple was with thanksgiving (95:2; 100:4); the service itself contained melodies of gratitude (147:7). All the tribes ascended to Jerusalem "to give thanks to the name of the LORD" (122:4 NRSV). Israel thanked Yahweh because he ever remained faithful to his covenant with his people (100:4). God's faithfulness was manifested in many ways as he protected the Jewish nation from external foes (7:17). Among the DEAD SEA SCROLLS, the *Hodayot* or Thanksgiving Hymns (1QH) is a document containing over thirty psalms, mostly fragmentary, in which the author renders thanks for acts of God's kindness. Most of these psalms begin with the expression, "I thank you, O Lord," and their style is reminiscent of the Hebrew Psalter.

In the NT thanksgiving to God both for his work (Lk. 17:16) and for his person (2:38) is a major theme. The concept of thanksgiving abounds in PAUL's epistles (Rom. 1:8; 7:25; 2 Cor. 9:15; Col. 1:12; 1 Tim. 1:12). See ETHICS OF PAUL II.D. The NT writers urged their fellow Christians to be grateful (Eph. 5:4; Col. 3:15; Heb. 13:15; Jas. 1:2, 9; 1 Pet. 4:12–14). Among the Gentiles a lack of gratitude was coupled with an absence of the true faith (Rom. 1:21).

Gratitude is pleasing to God (Ps. 92:1) because it is commanded (Ps. 50:14; Phil. 4:6), because

Christ set the example (Matt. 11:25; 26:27; Jn. 6:11; 11:41), and because the heavenly host is engaged in it (Rev. 4:9; 7:11–12; 11:16–17). Gratitude should be offered (1) to God (Ps. 50:14), (2) to Christ (1 Tim. 1:12), (3) through Christ (Rom. 1:8; Col. 3:17; Heb. 13:15), (4) in the name of Christ (Eph. 5:20), (5) in both private (Dan. 6:10) and public worship (Ps. 35:18), (6) at the remembrance of God's holiness (Pss. 30:4; 97:12), (7) before eating (Jn. 6:11; Acts 27:35), (8) upon the completion of great tasks (Neh. 12:31, 40), (9) in everything (1 Thess. 5:18), and (10) at all times (Eph. 1:16; 5:20; 1 Thess. 1:2).

Gratitude can be expressed for (1) the goodness and mercy of God (Pss. 106:1; 107:1; 136:1–3); (2) the gift of Christ (2 Cor. 9:15); (3) Christ's power and reign (Rev. 11:17); (4) deliverance from indwelling sin (Rom. 7:23–25); (5) the nearness of God's presence (Ps. 75:1); (6) our desire to give for God's work (1 Chr. 29:6–14); (7) the supply of our physical needs (Rom. 14:6–7; 1 Tim. 4:3, 4); (8) victory over death and the grave (1 Cor. 15:57); (9) wisdom and might (Dan. 2:23); (10) the triumph of the gospel (2 Cor. 2:14); (11) the reception of God's word (1 Thess. 2:13); (12) the conversion of souls (Rom. 6:17); (13) faith (Rom. 1:8; 2 Thess. 1:3), love (2 Thess. 1:3), and zeal (2 Cor. 8:16) manifested in others; (14) grace bestowed upon others (1 Cor. 1:4; Phil. 1:3–5; Col. 1:3–6); (15) ministers appointed by God (1 Tim. 1:12); (16) all men (1 Tim. 2:1); and (17) everything God permits (2 Cor. 9:11; Eph. 5:20).

Gratitude ought to be accompanied by intercession for others (1 Tim. 2:1; 2 Tim. 1:3; Phlm. 4), by prayer (Neh. 11:17; Phil. 4:6; Col. 4:2), and by praise (Ps. 92:1; Heb. 13:15). Believers are exhorted to be grateful (Ps. 105:1; Col. 3:15). They should (1) resolve to offer praise (Pss. 18:49; 30:12), (2) oveflow with thankfulness (Col. 2:7), (3) magnify the Lord with thanksgiving (Ps. 69:30), (4) enter God's house with praise (100:4), (5) come before God with thanksgiving (95:2), (6) offer thanks habitually (Dan. 6:10), and (7) sacrifice thank offerings to God (Ps. 116:17).

The wicked are averse to thanksgiving (Rom. 1:21); hypocrites mar it with boasting (Lk. 18:11). Biblical examples of true gratitude include (1) the Levites (2 Chr. 5:12), (2) David (1 Chr. 29:13), (3) Jonah (Jon. 2:9), (4) Daniel (Dan. 2:33), (5) Simeon (Lk. 2:28), (6) Anna (Lk. 2:38), and (7) Paul (Acts 28:15). Gratitude lay at the very heart of biblical faith because it formed the only proper response to what God had done for his people. (See J. Calvin, *Institutes of the Christian Religion* 2.8.16; 3.20.28; W. Eichrodt, *Theology of the Old Testament* [1964], 2:271, 299, 372; G. Von Rad, *Old Testament Theology* [1967], 1:224–26; *NIDOTTE*, 2:405–8; *NIDNTT*, 3:816–20.) See also EUCHARIST; PRAISE; PRAYER IV.A; SACRIFICE AND OFFERINGS III.D.3. R. E. PERRY

grave. An excavation or other place used for BURIAL. See TOMB. See also SHEOL.

Hellenistic burial chambers at Tel Marissa, Israel.

gravel. A mix of rock fragments or pebbles. The term is used to render Hebrew *ḥāṣāṣ H2953*, which occurs twice in a figurative sense. In Prov. 20:17 it is used of a liar, showing the consequences of deceitfulness: "he ends up with a mouth full of gravel." In Lam. 3:16 the prophet complains, "He has broken my teeth with gravel; / he has trampled me in the dust." In addition, the KJV uses "gravel" to render the plural of *māʿâ H5054*, a word that occurs only once (Isa. 48:19; NIV, "grains"). K. L. BARKER

graven image. A statue or other reproduction carved from wood, stone, or metal (in contrast to images cast from molten metal). This expression is used frequently by the KJV to render Hebrew *pesel H7181*, which the NIV and other modern versions translate with such equivalents as "image" (e.g., Lev. 26:1), "carved image" (Jdg. 17:3), and "idol" (Exod. 20:4). The form *pāsîl H7178* seems to have the same meaning (Deut. 7:5 et al.). These terms may have served sometimes to distinguish carved images from those that were molten, but not always (cf. Isa. 40:19).

The Israelites were expressly forbidden to make any idolatrous representations of deity, whether carved (Exod. 20:4, 5; Deut. 5:8) or molten (Exod. 32:4; 34:17). The second commandment in the Decalogue prohibits the making of such images in the form of anything seen in the heavens, on the earth, or in the sea. See TEN COMMANDMENTS III. All ancient peoples except the Israelites made images to represent the various gods. The Israelites were commanded by MOSES to destroy all Canaanite forms of idolatry, including graven images (Deut. 7:5; 12:3). In spite of this, throughout their history (Jdg. 17:3, 4; 2 Ki. 21:7; Isa. 42:17), until the return from the Babylonian captivity, they often succumbed to the idolatrous ways of their neighbors.

There has been considerable discussion concerning whether or not all imitative art is forbidden by the second commandment. In deciding this question, it must be kept in mind that certain figures were in fact made by God's own command. Both the TABERNACLE and the TEMPLE contained many objects that required the arts of carving and engraving, such as the two cherubim in the holy of holies (Exod. 25:18, 20), the floral ornamentation of the golden lampstand (25:34), the embroidered hangings of the sanctuary (ch. 26), and the bronze serpent (Num. 21:8–9). In the temple, moreover, there were various figures on the walls, and the molten sea rested on twelve bronze oxen. (See J. Pedersen, *Israel: Its Life and Culture*, 2 vols. [1926–40]; W. Eichrodt, *Theology of the Old Testament* [1961], 1:115–19; *NIDOTTE*, 3:644–46.)

S. BARABAS

gray. This term occurs about a dozen times in the OT, always with reference to gray hair as an indication of old age (it usually renders *śêbâ H8484*, Gen. 43:38; cf. also *śîb H8482*, only in 1 Sam. 12:2; Job 15:10). The term does not occur in the NT. See AGE, OLD; HAIR.

great. This English adjective can be used to render several terms, especially Hebrew *gādôl H1524* (Gen. 1:16 et al.; cf. the noun *gĕdullâ H1525*, "greatness," 1 Chr. 29:11 et al.) and Greek *megas G3489* (Matt. 4:16 et al.). In addition, words that primarily mean "much, many" can sometimes be translated "great" (e.g., *rab H8041*, Gen. 7:11; *polys G4498*, Matt. 2:18 [NRSV, "loud"]). These and other expressions are used in a wide variety of contexts, but the Bible views greatness primarily as an attribute that should be applied to GOD (e.g., Ps. 48:1; Tit. 2:13), his qualities (such as his "great love," Ps. 17:7), and his deeds (Rev. 15:3). (See *NIDOTTE*, 1:827–30; *NIDNTT*, 2:424–27.)

Great Assembly. See SYNAGOGUE, GREAT.

Great Bible. See VERSIONS OF THE BIBLE, ENGLISH.

Great Commission. See COMMISSION, GREAT.

great lizard. This expression is used by the NIV and other versions to render Hebrew *ṣāb H7370*, which occurs only once in a list of unclean animals (Lev. 11:29). It is thought by some to be the *Uromastix spinipes*, a LIZARD characterized by a spiny-scaled tail.

great owl. See OWL.

Great Sea. Biblical designation for the Mediterranean Sea, the body of water W of Palestine, lying between the European and African continents. It was sometimes called simply "the sea" by the Hebrews (*hayyām*, Num. 13:29; Josh. 16:8; Jon. 1:4; cf. Acts 10:6 et al.), but was referred to more often as "the Great Sea" because of its size (*hayyām haggādôl*, e.g., Num. 34:6–7; Josh. 9:1; Ezek. 47:10). Because of its location relative to the land of the Hebrews, it was occasionally called "the western sea" (*hayyām hāʾaḥărôn*, lit., "the sea that is behind," Deut. 11:24; 34:2; Joel 2:20; Zech. 14:8; in distinction from "the eastern sea," *hayyām haqqadmônî*, that is, "the front sea," referring to the DEAD SEA, Ezek. 47:19; Zech. 14:8). Once it is called "the sea of the Philistines" (Exod. 23:31), and once possibly "the sea of Joppa" (Ezra 3:7 KJV; the NIV renders, "by sea … to Joppa").

The Mediterranean is 2,196 mi. in length from Gibraltar to the Lebanon coast, varies in width from c. 600 mi. to 100 mi., and has a maximum depth of c. 2.7 mi. It is the main existing fragment of a great ocean (called Tethys by geologists) that existed at least from the late Carboniferous period to early Tertiary times. Because it is largely an enclosed sea, its saline content is abnormally high. Its divisions include the Aegean, Ionian, Adriatic, Tyrrhenian, and Ligurian seas. Only a narrow strip along the Palestinian coast receives any appreciable amount of rainfall, and the rapid transition to arid desert country is quite pronounced in the E and on the S.

Many great Mediterranean civilizations of ancient times were maritime powers (Egyptians, Phoenicians, Greeks, Romans), but seafaring and sea-trading played almost no part at all in Israel's history and economy. In spite of the long coastline, the sea exerted only a marginal influence on Israel. SOLOMON built a fleet of ships at EZION GEBER on the RED SEA and operated it with the assistance of the PHOENICIANS (1 Ki. 9:26–27; cf. also 22:48), but the Hebrews never did undertake a similar venture on the Mediterranean. This fact may best be explained by the absence of good harbors along the Palestinian coastline. There have been a few harbors of relative importance along the coast, such as ASHKELON, DOR, JOPPA, and ACCO, but a large part of the shoreline, particularly in the S, is backed by a strip of shifting sand, sometimes several miles in width, that blocks the approach to the shore. By contrast, the coastline of SYRIA played an important part in the development of that area, for there are many excellent natural harbors along the Syro-Phoenician coast. Therefore, maritime trade was highly developed there even in the most ancient periods. Byblos (see GEBAL #2) was a noted maritime power in the 3rd and 2nd millennia B.C., and Canaanite TYRE and SIDON played the same role during the early centuries of the 1st millennium B.C.

The cosmic sources of water that were conceived in mythological imagery to be dragons are absent in the Genesis account of CREATION, so little was the influence of the sea on the Hebrews. Though some have argued that the Hebrew term *tĕhôm* H9333 ("the deep," Gen. 1:2) is related etymologically to the Akkadian name TIAMAT (a female creature personifying the primeval ocean), no direct derivation or association can be established. The Hebrews certainly believed that God had absolute power over the seas (Ps. 89:9; Isa. 23:11; Jon. 1:4, 9).

In the early Christian era, the Mediterranean world was ruled by Rome. Her supremacy in the W was established by the defeat of Hannibal of Carthage in the battle of Zama in 202 B.C. In the E, conquest by POMPEY in 63 B.C. made the Mediterranean (as the Romans liked to call it) "Our Sea."

Fishermen on the Mediterranean Sea at the site of Dor.

Under the rule of AUGUSTUS (d. A.D. 14) and his successors, the Mediterranean world experienced for two centuries the *Pax Romana*, a period of peace it had never known before or has enjoyed since.

Some impression of the life and traffic of the Great Sea under the Romans can be obtained from the Acts of the Apostles, and especially the journeys of PAUL. Rome organized imperial trade routes for drawing upon the resources of its provinces around the Mediterranean shores. These and the coastal shipping routes between the ports of Asia Minor and the Levant, as well as those to the islands like CRETE, CYPRUS, and RHODES, provided Paul with easy and relatively fast means of travel on most of his journeys, and some of the habits of the Mediterranean sailor can be learned from Luke's record of those journeys.

Although land-bound, the Mediterranean is certainly large enough to generate fierce storms. In winter, these are caused by the passage of depressions along the sea from W to E, drawing in cold air from the N behind them. In summer, the outblowing winds from the Arabian desert can attain considerable force as they cross the coast of Palestine, and easterly gales therefore occur off-shore to inconvenience shipping. (Cf. W. F. Albright, *Archaeology and the Religion of Israel* [1942], 148–49; J Finegan, *Light from the Ancient Past* [1946], 209–10; Y. Aharoni, *The Land of the Bible: A Historical Geography*, rev. ed. [1979], 9–10, 17; M. Lubetski in *ABD*, 2:1091–92; F. Brandel, *The Mediterranean in the Ancient World* [2001].) See also SEA; SHIPS. F. B. HUEY, JR.; J. H. PATERSON

Great Synagogue, the. See SYNAGOGUE, THE GREAT.

greaves. See ARMOR, ARMS.

Grecia gree′shuh. KJV alternate form of GREECE (only Dan. 8:21; 10:20; 11:2).

Grecian gree′shuhn. A native or inhabitant of GREECE; a speaker of the GREEK LANGUAGE. The KJV uses this term once in the OT (Heb. *běnê hayyěwānîm* [gentilic of *yāwān* H3430, "Greece"], lit., "the sons of the Greeks," Joel 3:6), and three times in the NT (Gk. *Hellēnistēs* G1821, "Hellenist," Acts 6:1; 9:29; 11:20 [NIV, "Grecian Jews" in the first two passages, "Greeks" in the last]).

Greece grees. A geographical area on the S Balkan Peninsula, including the islands and surrounding coasts of the AEGEAN SEA, and inhabited primarily by speakers of the GREEK LANGUAGE.

   I. The name
   II. Geography
   III. Prehistory
   IV. The Mycenaean civilization
   V. The city-states
   VI. Colonization
   VII. The Persian wars
   VIII. The Confederacy of Delos
   IX. The Golden Age
   X. The collapse
   XI. The fourth century
   XII. The empire of Alexander
   XIII. Hellenism

I. The name. Greece (from Lat. *Graecia*, whence *Graeci*, "Greeks") was a geographical term properly applicable to an Indo-European group in the NW corner of the southeastern Mediterranean peninsula of Europe, opposite the "heel" of the Italian peninsula. It is a not infrequent phenomenon of geographical nomenclature that an area and its inhabitants acquire a name on the basis of a smaller region or people group first familiar to those who bestow and perpetuate the name (cf. *Palestine* from the name of the Philistine tribe settled on the SW corner of the land, or *Franks* provided by the French for all Europeans among the people of the Middle E, whose first significant contact with the W was with the armies of the French Crusaders).

The Greeks themselves called their country *Hellas* (cf. Acts 20:2), and the people *Hellenes* (from *Hellēn* G1818), though there seems to be some evidence that this name too was originally applicable to a small tribe in southern Thessaly (Homer, *Iliad* 2.683–84). The name seems to have spread S in the wake of the Dorian invasions, the last wave of tribal migration to infiltrate the peninsula. Although Homer, the earliest Greek writer, used the terms Hellenes and Pan-hellenes, the Greeks generally were named by him in tribal appellations—Achaeans, Argives, Danai; so in the OT, JAVAN and RODANIM may refer respectively to the Ionians (the Greeks of ASIA MINOR) and the inhabitants of RHODES. The name Greece (KJV in Daniel, "Grecia") occurs a number of times in the English Bible (for Heb. *yāwān* H3430, Dan. 8:21; 10:20; 11:2; Zech. 9:13 [NIV also Isa. 66:19; Ezek. 27:19]; in the NT, only Acts 20:2). The term GRECIAN in the KJV is ambiguous, referring sometimes to Greeks proper (Acts 11:20; in such contexts KJV elsewhere employs "Greeks" quite correctly: Jn. 12:20; Acts 14:1; 16:1), and sometimes to Jews domiciled in the Hellenistic cities (Acts 6:1; 9:29; see HELLENISM).

II. Geography. Europe fronts the Mediterranean with three peninsulas, two of them formed by the seaward intrusion of the continent's mountain system. Geographically considered, Greece is the shattered SE end of the mountain core of southern and central Europe. J. B. Bury (*History of Greece* [1913], 1) remarked that ILLYRICUM in the E would have closely resembled Spain in the W if its structure had been cut off N of Thessaly. It would have been a solid mass of land almost touching Asia in the

E, as Spain almost touches Africa in the W. But Greece—the southern and seaward extension of this land and mountain mass—has features of its own to mark it off geographically from Spain's firm square and Italy's spined ridge of land. Greece is a mountainous headland of tumbled terrain, narrow valley plains, ranges, peaks, broken from W to E across its midst by a deep rift, indented by the intruding sea, and scattered around by several groups of islands, notably those of the Ionian Sea (incongruously on the Adriatic shore though Ionia was in W Asia Minor), and of the Aegean (the Sporades and the Cyclades).

The Dodecanese islands and CRETE, though not part of Greece proper, were geographically, ethnologically, and historically associated with the mainland. The geography of the whole area was determined by the submergence in the Mediterranean of a mountain complex that begins with the Alps, sweeps E, N, and S, and finds ultimate emphasis in the Taurus Range of Anatolia and in the strong E-W formations of Crete. In peninsula, upland, and island, as Bury has said, one can trace the ribs of a framework "which a convulsion of nature bent and shivered, for the service, as it turned out, of the human race" (ibid.).

It is a notable fact that Greek history cannot be extricated from its landscape. The rugged peninsula, where the tribes of the Hellenes found precarious lodging place, was no land made for unity. It drove its inhabitants into the arms of the sea. Island, narrow coastal plain, and river valley provided foothold and dwelling. The convulsions of nature that had tumbled the land, and almost divided it in two, had decreed of old that the Greeks should invent the city-state, and thereby democracy and dialectic philosophy, and that history in the dynamic little land should be fragmented, varied, and full of strife.

Nature, sparing of topsoil and tilth land even before the human folly of deforestation, set ancient limitation on the size and growth of communities, and turned men's eyes seaward to open highways of trade and colonization. Like the PHOENICIANS, hemmed between the mountains and the sea, with the incomparable cedar growing on LEBANON behind, and navigable water before, the Greeks became inevitably seafarers, colonists, internationalists. It was the fiat of geography born of geology.

III. Prehistory. Perhaps the beginnings of Greek history proper can be set about the year 800 B.C., the date of the epic poems, when the Aegean world was emerging from a Dark Age of some four centuries. "Prehistory" covers the preceding twenty centuries and those civilizations that have left their rich remains for archaeology to recover—traces of their history, their rise and fall, and their dominant personalities in myth, legend, and tradition.

Stone age cultures have left traces from the Thessalian plain in the N to Crete in the S. The Bronze Age came to the Aegean perhaps by way of ASIA MINOR in the 3rd millennium B.C., and mass migration, probably of the Indo-European peoples who colonized most of Europe, began at this period with wandering groups following the sun, and infiltrating the mainland and the archipelago. (See O. Dickinson, *The Aegean Bronze Age* [1994].)

The first civilization of consequence reached its full flower in the island of Crete, which from its geographical position was in contact with the E end of the Mediterranean and Egypt, as well as exposed to the human pressure of the N and the Aegean. This, the *Minoan* civilization, a name derived from the legendary king Minos, was based on sea power and sea borne trade. It was cultural, artistic, and influential. Spacious, unwalled palaces speak of the wealth, ability, and security of the islanders. In the excellence of the work of architect, painter, and goldsmith, the Minoan culture rivaled Egypt. Two

Christianity reaches Greece.

forms of script have survived. One of them, *Linear B*, has been deciphered, and proves to be a primitive Greek referred to as *Mycenaean*, but it is impossible to say whether this fact does more than indicate the race of a dominant minority, or even a language of trade. If the Cretans were an early wave of Indo-European invasion, perhaps overlaying a neolithic or "Mediterranean" aboriginal stock, that would at least suggest a pattern that history is in the habit of repeating: note, for example, the successive waves of infiltration into Britain—the Belgae, Romans, Germanic tribes, Scandinavians—each divided into numerous ripples. The W coast of America and the S Pacific islands can demonstrate the same periodicity of occupation. The Cretan civilization collapsed about 1400 B.C., somewhat mysteriously, and due perhaps to a complex of natural disaster, social upheaval, and invasion from the N.

IV. The Mycenaean civilization. The infiltrating tribes of the 3rd millennium before Christ took longer to organize on the mainland. In Crete, whether it was first settled or only taken over and ruled by members of this Indo-European folk-wandering, the island itself imposed a certain unity as well as a framework for development that was rapid (as far as such distant evidence can be read) and certainly distinguished.

The first mainland settlements were around CORINTH, in the Argolis, and on the island of Aegina. From these focal points they spread N into the fertile Boeotian plain, where Thebes was later to be dominant, S to Messenia, and W to the Ionian islands, chiefly to Ithaca. This so-called Helladic civilization was not a high or affluent one, except that their pottery was of a fine quality. It is not certain whether these villagers and pastoralists spoke an Indo-European speech. They were not literate.

The first recognizable Greeks came with fire and sword, if the archaeological record of conflagration and ruin is read aright, c. 2000 B.C. They may be called the Achaeans, and it is not certain whether they came through Asia Minor or down the Balkan peninsula. It was the contact of this Middle Helladic civilization with Crete that, from 1600 onward, produced the Mycenaean civilization. It was a fruitful union in which some have sought to see "Minoan imagination yoked to Helladic restraint and order." The phrase might mean more if we had clearer knowledge of the ethnic relationships of the tribes and peoples concerned.

The Mycenaean civilization takes its name from the great fortress of Mycenae in the eastern Peloponnesus, and the period of its greatness is notable for the building of great palaces and mighty fortifications, the development of a strong militaristic feudalism, and vast wealth. The fact that Linear B script is found on the mainland and in Crete may mean that by the 15th cent. Mycenae had actually conquered Crete. Certainly the destruction of the Cretan civilization about 1400, which probably followed the ruin of Crete from natural causes—such as earthquakes—and internal strife, can hardly have been other than the work of Mycenaean invasion. (See W. Taylour, *The Mycenaeans*, rev. ed. [1983].)

About 1200 B.C. occurred an event difficult to assess: the Trojan war, which, as the Roman Horace wrote, found a poet (Homer) who has lived in the imagination of the world. TROY lay on an escarpment with a narrow intervening coastal plain on the Asiatic shore of the Dardanelles. It was an old post of power, as the stratified remains of nine Troys heaped on the site indicate. The story of Helen and the great expedition to recover her need not concern us. The Trojan conflict certainly involved a clash of nations or a vast internecine upheaval, the interpretation depending upon who they were who held the Trojan stronghold. The traditional view is that the subsequent decline of the Mycenaean civilization was due to the blood-letting, the destruction, and the social strain of this great mili-

Mycenaean artifacts from a tomb in Cyprus.

tary adventure. The divided, broken, and weakened culture was ripe for the so-called Dorian invasion.

This was another wave of the folk-migration that had marked the last millennium. The traditional view is that the more primitive Dorians like the Saxons, assaulting a weakened Roman-Britain, came in as a destructive force, and gave Greece and the Aegean a Dark Age of four centuries, across which the Homeric poems look, preserving for another age the folk memories of epic strife in which Mycenaea went down before the Dorians. Rhys Carpenter, however, has suggested another view (*Discontinuity in Greek Civilization* [1966]). His climatological studies, linked with the archaeology of the period, seem to indicate that the Mycenaean civilization died of drought when the rain belts of southern Europe, determined by the meteorological and climatological conditions in the Sahara area, moved N. In consequence, the great centers of Mycenae were slowly depopulated, as a weakened people sought the rainier coasts and westward-facing slopes watered by the Zephyr winds. The Dorians, if this thesis can be maintained, inherited an empty land—and a good land, as the more favorable and moist weather pattern gradually reestablished itself in Greece and the Aegean. The final answer to this question of history awaits further knowledge.

Scholarly views regarding the character of the Dark Age have been altered as a result of some major archaeological discoveries (the product of British excavations during the late 1970s and early 1980s). The city of Lefkandi, on the W coast of the island of Euboea, has revealed a remarkably prosperous culture reaching its height during the 10th and 9th centuries. The evidence suggests that this site may have been the focus of commercial and military collaboration at that time. If so, Greek-speaking tribes in Thessaly and surrounding areas, contrary to what used to be thought, may have been characterized by a significant level of cultural cohesion. (Cf. G. Forrest in *The Oxford History of the Classical World*, ed. J. Boardman et al. [1986], 20–22.)

V. The city-states. From 800 B.C. onward, Greece was reorganizing itself. Civilization, recovering from the trauma of invasion, was building new patterns of life. The city-states emerged as scattered villages syncretized for protection. The villages of Attica, for example, merged their strength under the masters of the Acropolis, and the power of ATHENS began its momentous growth; so, too, Thebes (in Boeotia, NW of Athens) and SPARTA. In the process, monarchy passed to oligarchy. In the process, too, individual "tyrants" arose. In the Greek sense of this word (*tyrannos*), which appears to be merely a Lydian term for "ruler," a tyrant was not necessarily a cruel despot. But since "power corrupts," as Lord Acton put it, "and absolute power corrupts absolutely," there came the coloring that the word inevitably took on.

In this period, the history of Greece is necessarily varied and fragmented. Athens successfully resisted "tyranny" in 630 B.C., and in 594 Solon, a rich member of an emerging industrial class, was given power to institute constitutional reforms on broadly democratic lines. After another crisis of tyranny from 561 to 528, finally in 507 one Cleisthenes introduced a genuinely democratic constitution in which the assembly of citizens had sovereign power. Sparta, meanwhile, where a Dorian group sought over a long period to maintain a kind of "apartheid" over a subject population, organized herself on the basis of the savage code of the half-legendary Lycurgus. It was a rigid, uncultured, military society, whose most lamentable achievement was the destruction of Athens in the great war of 431 to 400, a conflict from which Athens never quite recovered.

The Parthenon in Athens.

All the city-states functioned independently in all the processes and relationships of peace and war. They present a picture of universal history in microcosm. Whereas it may be true that there is properly no history of Greece, but rather the history of the Greek states, it is also true that, despite this ultimately fatal political disunity and dismemberment (with the local jealousy and debilitating petty nationalism that made it impossible for Greece to face Persia, then Macedon, and finally Rome, as a unit of power), there was a consciousness of spiritual oneness. The great sanctuaries of Olympia with its pan-Hellenic games, and Delphi with its oracle, called the "common hearth of Greece," stand for a sense of common origin, common heritage, and common destiny, which, had it found wider political expression, might have changed European history. The world today faces the same vast problem, and Greek history assumes challenging significance.

VI. Colonization. Greek migration to islands and more remote spots along the Mediterranean coastline began with the pressure of the Dorian inroads, or the climatological changes that are alleged to have played their simultaneous part. In discussing the geography of Greece, it was pointed out that the limits imposed by nature on the arable land available enforced emigration. The process continued over several countries. It was, after all, only the maritime extension and projection of the migratory movements that had populated the Mediterranean basin.

From 770 to 550 B.C., with trade vigorous in the inland seas, the process of colonization assumed immense significance for human culture and future European history. Colonies were planted, in the familiar form of city-states, on the coasts of Spain and Southern France, the whole of southern Italy and Sicily, the Black Sea, and the African coast to the Gulf of Syrtis from almost the Nile delta. Greek colonies generally did not penetrate or seek to subdue the hinterland. They remained independent, and some of them—Massilia, Tarentum, Syracuse, for example—became powerful states. ROME, in its early growth, and southern Italy generally, were strongly influenced by the transplanted Greek civilization of what came to be called Magna Graecia, the complex of Greek city-states right around the W and S coasts of Italy from Cumae to Tarentum.

VII. The Persian wars. Ionia was the name given to the Greek settlements on the W end of Asia Minor. In the 7th cent., these city-states, in which Greek art, science, and philosophy had struck their first roots, fell under the control and domination of LYDIA, the inland empire based on SARDIS. In 546 B.C. Lydia fell under the expanding power of PERSIA, which was reaching for the Aegean, as it was also pressing into India and Egypt in one of history's great movements of imperialism. In 499 the Ionian cities rose in revolt against Persia, and Athens, helping the rebels in their hopeless fight, incurred the wrath of DARIUS, the Persian king. He attacked Attica from the sea in 490 but was repulsed at his point of landing, at Marathon, by the Athenians.

Ten years later, XERXES, Darius's successor, dispatched by land and sea a mighty army determined to overwhelm Greece. Halted for a brief time at Thermopylae by the famous Spartan Three Hundred, the great armada rolled into Attica and burned Athens, whose population had withdrawn to the island of Salamis. In the strait of Salamis, in one of the decisive battles of the world's history, the Greek fleets, about half Athenian, shattered the Persian naval arm, upon which the vast expedition depended for communications and supply. Xerxes could do nothing else but withdraw. He left a strong army in Boeotia, and the Greeks, attaining an unusual measure of unity, mustered 110,000 men and broke the remaining remnant of the Persian invasion at Plataea. Salamis and Plataea were decisive. Asia was not to dominate Europe (the Turks were the only comparable foe, twenty centuries later). A remnant of the Persian fleet was broken up at Mycale, also in 479 B.C., and Greece was free to continue her system of government, which found its most significant expression in Athens.

VIII. The Confederacy of Delos. After their victory at Mycale, the confederate Greeks decided to pursue the war against Persia and liberate the Greeks of Asia Minor. A fleet was fitted out and placed under the command of the Spartan Pausanias. The Spartans had from the first shown a strong disinclination to incur responsibilities on behalf of the Asiatic Greeks, or to embark on maritime enterprises. In 476 the allies, disgusted with the arrogance of Pausanias, transferred the command to the Athenians, and Pausanias was recalled to answer to charges of treasonable correspondence with Persia. His successor's orders were disregarded, and Aristeides, the Athenian, was acknowledged as admiral, an arrangement in which the Spartans were forced to acquiesce.

The Peloponnesian squadron returned home, and Athens, now left to take the lead, entered into a compact with the allies. This was the origin of the Confederacy of DELOS. Its object was the expulsion of the Persians from Europe and the security of the Greeks of Asia Minor and the adjoining islands. A definite obligation, either in ships, men, or money, was imposed upon every member, and general conditions were regulated in a common synod, appointed to meet annually in the temple of APOLLO at Delos, where the treasure was placed. Special officers collected the money, ships being sent around the Aegean every spring for this purpose. The first assessment of tribute amounted to 460 talents, payable partly in ships, partly in money.

Such was the confederacy, at first without doubt a just league for resisting the Persians and protecting the Aegean Sea against piracy—a league due to the fear of the Ionians, not to the ambition of Athens. How the transition from leadership to empire took place is not difficult to conjecture, for in any confederacy where there is one member unusually prominent, such a result must follow.

Within ten years the Persians had been driven from Europe and restricted to the inland of W Asia Minor. Then, as the danger from Persia became more remote, the necessity for personal service seemed to many of the allies no longer imperative, and their distaste for its duties led them to commute it for a money payment. The result of this was to put Athens in possession of a steady revenue for a constantly increasing navy, and to inspire her citizens with the idea that they were military overlords with a body of tribute-paying subjects. This change in the relations between Athens and the allies became further intensified when the treasure was removed from Delos to Athens about 455 B.C., and the management of the affairs of the confederacy fell almost exclusively into Athenian hands. Even before this, however, there had been revolts and attempts to secede, all of which had been sternly suppressed by Athens; these became increasingly frequent, as the rule of Athens grew more despotic and her misappropriation of the tribute to her own needs became more open.

Under the administration of Pericles, discontent reached a dangerous height. The tribute now amounted to 600 talents, not an excessive sum considering the number of members. The only outgoings, for many years, had been the support of sixty Athenian triremes (standard warships with oarsmen in groups of three) in the Aegean. There was a surplus of nearly 10,000 talents in the Acropolis, and vast sums had been expended by Pericles on the beautifying of Athens and other purely Attic interests. It was useless for Pericles to urge in answer that, as long as Athens secured the safety of the allies, she was justified in dealing with the surplus revenue as she chose. Clearly, the original object of the confederacy had been lost, and Athens had become—partly from force of circumstances, and later from design—the mistress of the 249 cities whose names stood upon her tribute lists in the time of Pericles; of these Chios, Samos, and Lesbos alone still possessed navies. Thus was the scene set for the clash with Sparta that came inevitably in 431 B.C. and ended the period of Athenian greatness—half a century of astounding creativity, to which a section must be devoted.

IX. The Golden Age. It is the fate of empires to be viewed differently by their immediate beneficiaries and by those who pay, or imagine that they pay, the bill. So it was with Rome and Britain, and with Athens. First gratefully accepted as a leader, Athens became the burdensome imperialist. At the same time, in the eyes of the Athenians, and all who from then till now have been entranced by the spectacle of her achievement in the realms of art, thought, literature, and the mind's creativity, a Golden Age was enjoyed.

The Greeks had emerged from a day of grimmest peril in the wars with Persia. The Athenian response to this challenge was an outburst of spiritual energy scarcely paralleled in history. In a mood of exaltation that believed all things possible to the conquerors of Persia, the people of Attica set to work. They equipped their farmlands with buildings which, three generations later, their Theban enemies found it worthwhile to dismantle and transfer bodily to Boeotia. They rebuilt their shattered city and filled it with monuments, some of which have survived the battering of twenty-three centuries, and stand today a monument to the worth of human effort when willing hands work as one under the inspiration of a grand idea. "In this work," says a modern historian, "Periclean Athens displayed a vitality far superior to that of postwar France. When the French recovered the battered shell of Rheims Cathedral, they performed a pious restoration of each shattered stone and splintered statue. When the Athenians found the Hekatompedon burned down to the foundations, they let the foundations lie, and proceeded, on a new site, to create the Parthenon" (A. J. Toynbee, *The Study of History*, 12 vols. [1934–61], 2:110).

Socially, the characteristics of that age were two. There was first a notable union between culture and democracy (we are not concerned at the moment with the differences between Athenian democracy and ours, nor to assess the part slave labor played in Athenian culture and self-expression). In 5th-cent. Athens, democracy, in a real and significant form, was certainly known. That reality found a voice in literature. The partnership between culture and the Athenian way of life was no artificial product of such patronage as that by which Maecenas rallied the pens of Rome to the service of a new regime. The praise was spontaneous, an undercurrent rather than a stream.

When Aeschylus, for example, wrote his *Prometheus Bound*, he had primarily no political end in view. His theme was the vast problem of suffering and pain. He was hazarding the bold solution of a doctrine of perfectibility applied to God himself. It was the ancient question of the prophet HABAKKUK that the poet had in mind in his tremendous drama of the tormented demigod. And yet the notions of freedom that filled the air and the writer's mind color the whole picture and find involuntary expression in the passing remark, the aside, the ejaculation. For instance: "For tyranny, it seems, is never free / From this distemper—faithlessness to friends. / Wilt thou thus kick against the pricks, aware / That our harsh monarch owes account to none? / … is it plain to you?— / The tyrant of the gods is violent / In all his ways / … But who shall strip his tyrant sceptre from him? / Himself by his own empty-headed counsels. / … Nay, let him reign supreme and work his will / For his brief day—he shall not rule for long."

The same passion for freedom and hatred of all tyranny color the characterization. It marks Hermes as the cunning menial of a royal court; Io as the maiden victim of the unbridled selfishness of kings; Oceanus, so confident and comfortable, as the compromising lover of soft ease, on whose acquiescence all dictatorship is built; and Oceanus's daughters as the unexpected opposition, whose innocence and ignorance, when fired with knowledge, are ready to face death for a name and an ideal.

The first two books of Thucydides' *History* present the same phenomenon. In the reported words of friend and foe, this historian depicts Athens. The climax is the funeral oration (*Hist.* 2.35–46), whose words are carved on a thousand war memorials. It was the first winter of the Peloponnesian War, that conflict a generation long that closed the chapter of Athens' greatness. The bones of those who had died in battle were carried to the Cerameicus beyond the Dipylon Gate. There, as the custom was, an orator spoke in praise of the dead. On this occasion Pericles mounted the platform. Whether Thucydides reported his speech, paraphrased it, or transformed it matters little. Under Pericles' name, its moving sentences stand in the historian's pages as a tribute of love and patriotism difficult to match in literature:

"Athens alone of cities when put to the test excels her reputation. She alone gives her foes no reason to grudge her victory, and her subjects no cause to complain of an unworthy mistress.… we shall need no Homer to sing our praise nor poets, whose verse may delight for the moment but whose fancies will be destroyed by fact.… For such a city these men have nobly fought.… This land in which for generations the same people has ever dwelt, through the merits of our ancestors was handed down to us as a land of liberty.… We live under a political system which does not seek to emulate the institutions of our neighbors.… We are indeed an example to some, but an imitation to none.… We have a deep respect for those in authority and for the laws, especially those which have been ordained for the benefit of the oppressed, and for those unwritten laws which disgrace the breaker of them in the eyes of his fellow men.... We put our trust in the readiness of our stout hearts for the deeds demanded of us.... To sum up, I declare our city to be the education of Hellas."

Illustration might proceed. The early plays of Euripides show the same burning patriotism. Athens in these dramas is ever the refuge for the broken and oppressed. Even a Medea may find asylum there, much more the persecuted children of Heracles and the broken Heracles himself. Athens' very people tread more nobly: "The sons of Erechtheus, the olden, / Whom high gods planted of yore, / In an old land of heaven upholden, / A proud land untrodden of war. / They are hungered and, lo, their desire / With wisdom is fed as with meat; / In their skies is a shining of fire, / And joy in the fall of their feet" (Euripides, *Medea* 824–833 [trans. G. Murray]).

Such ideals sanctified the Athenian struggle with Sparta in its opening years. They could not fail to find a response in the heart of Euripides. The strong awareness of the faults of democracy, and of his own democracy in particular, which was later to inspire satiric portraits of soldiers, and the horror at Athens' own crimes that was to find expression in the *Trojan Women* and ultimately in Euripides' own secession, had not yet gained control. The mood of the *Medea* was unchanged. In that play, the kindly man of Athens, his heart swifter than his head when moral right became a challenge, gave unthinking sanctuary to a criminal. The *Heracleidae*, written in the fourth year of the war, is set in the temple of Zeus at famous Marathon. In these precincts, so redolent of Athenian memories, the children of Herakles (Hercules) sat as suppliant refugees. An Argive herald demanded their surrender. It was simple as that. On such an issue Athens went to war. The play is vibrant with patriotism. Athena moves behind the scenes wrought in the gold and ivory of every democratic excellence. Athens appears as the home of liberty.

Says Iolaus, guardian of the refugees: "God's altar shall prevail, / And the free land whereunto we have come." And the chorus to the arrogant ambassador: "Thou shouldst have shown respect to this free land." And Iolaus again: "If this shall be, if she but ratify / Thine hests, free Athens then no more I know. / Nay, her sons' nature know I, know their mood: / They will die sooner, for in brave men's eyes / The honour that feels shame is more than life." Demophon concluding all argument: "This city which I hold / Is not to Argives subject, she is free ... / King, this advantage have I in your land, / I am free to speak and in my turn to hear. / None, as from other lands, will first expel me. / Ever she chooseth, this our land, / To help the helpless ones in justice' cause. / So hath she borne for friends unnumbered toils" (*Heracleidae*, passim).

Such an attitude is based, sings the chorus in a song that has the simplicity of a Hebrew psalm, on truest piety: "O land / thy path is in justice / O never abandon / thy fear of the Lord. / Who denieth it in thee / close rideth to madness, / when these signs are showing. / For behold God revealeth / clear tokens. He taketh / away evermore the high mind / of the wicked" (*Heracleidae*, 901–9).

These illustrations must suffice to indicate the reality of the partnership between culture and democracy. The quiet grandeur of Sophocles, with its suggestion of a spirit at rest in its environment, and the still perfection of 5th-cent. art displaying life and not reaching painfully for the hidden and the unknown, might illustrate the same theme.

The second characteristic, noted by Pericles in the passage already quoted, was the ability of the age to produce noble leadership and the willingness of the mass to follow. It is not for nothing that the age bore the name of Pericles. With the death of Pericles, says Thucydides, there vanished the outstanding moral example of the time. He had never been led by personal ambition to a pursuit of selfish ends. He was incorruptible. He knew how to restrain the multitude without infringing liberty. He led because he would not flatter, daring, when occasion called, even to provoke. "Thus Athens became a democracy in name, but in fact a monarchy of the foremost citizen," the historian declares.

The achievements of the age were tremendous. Here is the record in brief. Of the world's four supreme tragic artists, three of them appeared in 5th-cent. Athens—Aeschylus, Sophocles, and Euripides. "When the spirit of enquiry meets the spirit of poetry," says Macneile Dixon, "tragedy is born." They met in the vigor of those days. And yet it is difficult to realize that those who watched the half-Shavian drama of Euripides were the sons and daughters of those who saw the first performance of the *Agamemnon* of Aeschylus. In Euripides is realism, the study of such characters as the streets of Athens knew—the self-satisfied husband, the embittered foreign bride, the children of a broken home in time of war, the shell-shocked boy, the epileptic, the ambitious soldier, the cold athlete. The ruler, faced with problems beyond his understanding—the phenomena of religious revival, the moral wreck of war, the woes of the conquered—lives intensely on his stage. In Aeschylus, Shakespeare and Ezekiel are combined. Imagine the fruitful mingling of the tragic power of the dramatist with the spiritual insight and religious fervor of the prophet. Imagine a gift of language that combined the daring and richness of the Englishman's speech with the color of the Hebrew. Such variety made Aeschylus, and such variety of genius marked Athens' tragic stage.

The age produced the finest of the world's historians. In granting this palm to Thucydides—cold, detached, scientific, yet brilliantly imaginative—one should not forget HERODOTUS, the mighty traveler and collector of facts. There is a sense in which the two were spiritual kin. They both ransacked the world for facts. They both sought a law behind phenomena. The validity of Herodotus' generalizations on the Envy of the gods is beside the point. The quest for the principle puts him into the ancestry of Spengler and Toynbee. Herodotus was the first Greek to seek behind events for the forces that determine them. He shared the honor with the prophets of Israel.

The age produced the noblest European mind. Plato was at once the greatest thinker and the greatest writer of Athens and the ancient world. See GREEK RELIGION AND PHILOSOPHY II.B. Plato, like Paul, was as "one born out of due time." He survived the century that gave him birth. Most of his work belongs to the 4th cent., not the 5th; and the 4th cent. was ushered in by a judicial crime, rare in the annals of Athens—the murder of Socrates. The tragedy of 399 B.C. was proof that the glory was departing, and if the mind of Plato, like the mind of Thucydides, lived on and found bitter food for thought in a twilight era, that is Plato's misfortune and the world's. One sees through Plato's personal crisis into the crisis of ancient society. That is why his work is a document of decadence, an utterance of opposition.

If Plato lacked the serenity of a happier past, those who seek for truth in our own anxious day will have the deepest sympathy for his preoccupations, for truth was Plato's quest. It is that passion that made him one with the Athens of calmer years. As he drew to the end of his *Republic*, described by Sir Richard Livingstone in 1947 as "the greatest secular prose work of all time," he wrote significant words: "Is there not another quality which philosophers should possess?" "What quality?" "Truthfulness: they will never intentionally admit falsehood to their minds … and is there anything more akin to wisdom than truth?" "How can there be?" "Can the same nature be a lover of wisdom and a lover of falsehood?" "Never!"

The 5th cent. produced some of mankind's noblest art. Much of the revolt against classical Greek art is the reaction of a dissatisfied and unhappy age against the serenity of a more stable society that believed it knew where perfection lay and expressed itself with confidence. In language, itself an art, Athens produced what is perhaps the most perfect instrument of human expression in the history of speech. Words are the symbols of creative thought. Language reflects the quality of the minds that give it shape and form. If the spirit of Athens at her best was permeated with the passion for truth, one should expect to find that mood translated into the forms of speech—the amazingly subtle verb, the rich facilities of the article, the brilliant invention of the particle that Attic Greek carried to final perfection, enabling the written sentence without stage directions to express irony, deprecate, cock an eyebrow, curl the lip, shrug the shoulders, and represent, in short, to the reading eye the animation of the living voice. These are only three of the many qualities that made Attic speech perhaps the world's most powerful and exact linguistic medium. For vivid conversation and the expression of abstract thought, this is most certainly true. (See GREEK LANGUAGE.)

X. The collapse. This glory withered in a generation. Its monuments remained in stone and written speech. Personalities survived like people "left on earth after a judgment day." Looking back one can see, nevertheless, that the disastrous Twenty-seven Years' War with Sparta was a conflict in which "one unhappy generation of Hellenes dealt their own Hellas a mortal blow, and knew that her blood was on them and their children" (Toynbee, *Study*, 3:292). Those who watched thought of Aeschylus and Herodotus, and murmured three Greek words that were part of the century's contribution to historical thought—*koros, hybris, atē*. With considerable loss of moral content the words may be translated "surfeit," "arrogant behavior," and "disaster." The first suggests the demoralization that comes with prosperity or too complete success, the relaxing of the moral fiber in the favored of fortune; the second implies the consequent loss of mental and moral balance reflected in over-confidence and outrageous action. The third word, also oddly Hebraic in force, contains the notion of the mad blind impulse, by which the spirit, morally ripe for disaster and in the grip of sin unpardonable, is driven into the catastrophic folly of attempting the impossible. However differently the thought of another age may view the relations of cause and effect, the formula covers Athens.

The war with Sparta revealed the ravages of decay. It becomes obvious, as the record proceeds, that "Ichabod" was written, and that Athens was in full career for the sorry days half a century later that felt the lash of Demosthenes' tongue. The marks of decadence are worth studying.

(1) There first appeared the divorce of culture and democracy. The phenomenon may be illustrated by the thought of three penetrating minds. First take Plato, last though he was in time of the three. Plato's last work, the *Laws*, was inspired by a profound hostility to Athenian democracy. It was democracy, in Plato's view, that brought devastation by its crazy militarism upon the very world in which Athenian culture found its air and nourishment.

To turn from the philosopher to the historian and the dramatist is to find in both similar phenomena of opposition. During the summer and winter of 416 B.C. occurred an event of small military importance to which Thucydides sees fit to devote no fewer than twenty-six paragraphs of his fifth book. The Athenians had besieged and captured the little island of Melos, massacred its men, and enslaved its women and children. The island was in no sense a vital strategic base. It was without natural wealth. Why then this bulky place in the historian's narrative? Because Thucydides saw that society was a moral phenomenon, that what men think determines what men do and are, that systems and institutions form, maintain themselves, and fall with the growth, subsistence, and decay of an "ethos."

In the Melos crime, Thucydides saw Athens passing from *hybris* to *atē*. As his manner was, Thucydides proceeded to reveal the moral background of the episode by means of speeches. The debate he reported between the Athenian envoys and the Melian Council had no doubt a solid basis in fact, but its truth is rather psychological than factual. In cold deliberate words, the Athenians explained to the little senate that it suited their convenience that Melos should join the Athenian bloc. They did not suggest that the Melians had in any way wronged them, nor indeed did they lay claim to any shadow of right in such a demand. It was simply Athens' policy that the islands should submit to her. Melos therefore had to make her choice. She was free to submit or be destroyed.

Is it safe, the Melians answered in bitter irony, for Athens thus to flout all morality? Empires after all are mortal and there is world opinion. "We shall risk that," the Athenians answered. The Melians pleaded their neutrality, threatened Spartan intervention, expressed their determination to die rather than be slaves. "A lamentable error of judgment," said the Athenians. The cynical exposition of immoral power politics fills page after page. "They put to death," Thucydides quietly concluded, "all the Melians whom they found of man's estate, and made slaves of the women and the children." So ends book 5. The peace of desolation descended on Melos. Book 6 begins: "And the same winter the Athenians sought to sail with a greater fleet than ever before and conquer Sicily." Sail they did, in a burst of mad ambition, to ghastly and complete disaster.

In the same city, another brilliant mind was brooding over the same dark action. The next spring, when the shipyards of the Piraeus were roaring with preparation for the great Sicilian adventure, Euripides produced his most bitter and tragic play, the *Trojan Women*, which, to quote G. Murray, "set a flame of discord for ever between himself and his people." This somber drama is a masterpiece of black tragedy, a passionate protest against the evils of war difficult to match in all literature. It is a picture of war from the point of view of babes and women set amid the very blood and mud and smoke of shattered Troy. It is the morning after the night of swords. It is conquest seen when the heat of battle is over, and nothing remains but to wait and think. The reader who turns the last page of this terrible drama is not surprised that a few years later Euripides abandoned the city whose glories he had once so movingly extolled, and went away to conclude his life's work, an exile in distant Macedonia.

These three illustrations suffice to mark the reality of the contention that a significant feature of Athens' decline was a revolt of noble minds and a dissolution of the partnership that once existed between culture and the Athenian way of life. Aristophanes might provide similar illustrations. The savage satire of his comedies, and the nostalgic praise of a vanished age that strews them, both reveal an indignant and discontented spirit at war with growing decadence.

(2) Another mark of the age of decline was a collapse of morale. In his third book, Thucydides paused and drew up a balance sheet of war. It is difficult to realize that some of the words are twenty-three centuries old. His austere prophecy that such evils as he saw "will, according to human nature, happen again in much the same way," has proved too unhappily true. He described the sanguinary end of the Corcyraean revolution, and continued:

"Later the whole Hellenic world was convulsed, struggles being made everywhere by the popular chiefs to bring in the Athenians, and by the ruling class to introduce the Spartans. In peace there would have been neither the pretext nor the wish to make such an invitation; but in war with an alliance always at the command of either faction for the hurt of their adversaries and their own advantage, opportunities for bringing in the foreigner were never wanting to the revolutionary parties. The sufferings that revolution entailed were many and terrible, such as have occurred and always will occur so long as human nature remain the same. In

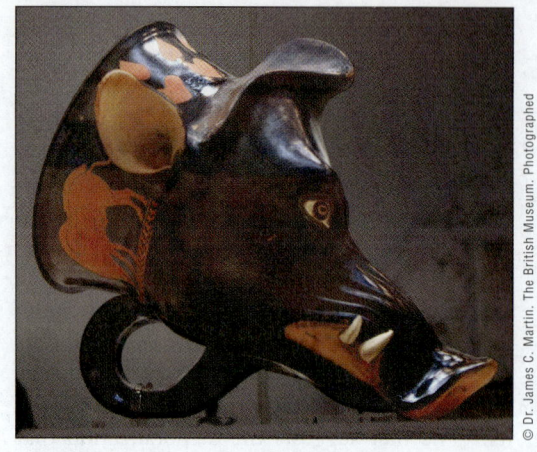

A rhyton or drinking vessel in the form of a boar's head (from Athens, c. 460 B.C.).

peace, states and individuals have better sentiments because they do not find themselves confronted suddenly by imperious necessities; but war takes away the easy supply of daily wants, and proves a rough schoolmaster, that brings most men's characters to the level of their fortunes.... Reckless audacity came to be considered the courage of a loyal ally; prudent hesitation, specious cowardice; moderation was held to be the cloak for unmanliness, ability to see all sides of a question, inaptness to act on any.... Oaths of reconciliation being proffered on either side to meet an immediate difficulty only held good so long as no other weapon was at hand.... The cause of all these evils was lust for power arising from greed and ambition, and from these passions proceeded the violence of parties once engaged in contention.... Meanwhile the moderate part of the citizens perished between the two" (*Hist.* 3:82–83).

(3) The third mark of decadence was the deterioration of leadership. The entry of the "man in the street" upon the stage of Athenian history before the close of the 5th century B.C. is one of the unmistakable symptoms of social decline. Few will advocate an aristocracy of wealth, but an aristocracy of character all healthy people must possess or perish.

The rise of the Athenian common man was no egalitarian process fostered in politics and education. The war, which ruined the landed aristocracy and exalted, as war does, the industrialist, doubtless played a leveling part; but the chief reason was the decay of social discipline and morality already noted. This process was aided by a vast refugee problem and the pauperization that follows invasion. Character deteriorated over wide areas of the populace. Leadership became a quest for power and no longer a patriotic privilege. Party politics and class conflict naturally took shape. The "sailor crowd" of Plato's and Euripides' contempt emerged. This led, meanwhile, to a loss of all view of the common good and supported this leader or that in equal pursuit of selfish advantage. The proletariat so clearly pictured later in Demosthenes' orations—selfish, emotionally unbalanced, venal, narrow-minded, self-assertive, irresponsible, and slothful—appears in clear outline in the documents. It bore the marks of mortal disease.

Athens lost her men of worth and leadership. She lost them in the spirit, she lost them in the flesh. The literal loss of blood in great wars and plagues has played a significant if unmeasured part in the decline of nations. The dilution of the old Roman stock and the vast loss of life from Hannibal to Caesar contributed much toward the modification of the Roman character and its ultimate deterioration. The gaps made at Passchendaele and on the Somme during World War I are still visible in public life, and today suffers from the human loss of yesterday. Athens' heavy casualties in the generation's war with Sparta and in the Great Plague may in the end have determined her failure to rise and triumphantly rebuild her battered greatness. Her talent was simply poured away. A brief return to comparative prosperity brought no resurgence of the spirit and no return to the old level of achievement.

In international politics, Athens' failure to create a commonwealth was another and final decisive factor. The forces that shaped the globe did good and ill when they tumbled the geography of Greece in confusion. The atomization of the Greek people produced the city-state, the medium in which individualism took shape, and this in turn produced philosophy and democracy. The sharp differences of outlook, which environment also determined, proved a barrier to unity. Enlightened Greeks talked of Hellenic unity, but in spite of abortive and halfhearted efforts, unity was never achieved until the sword achieved it—in the hands of the dictator of Macedon, and later of Rome. In the Delian League that Athens built by her naval power after the Persian war, Athens had her opportunity. She failed to grasp it and secure even that measure of loyalty from subject allies that proved Rome's narrow margin of salvation in the war with Hannibal. The modern world on which history has served notice to unite or perish should mark the fact. Athens missed her moment and it never came again.

XI. The fourth century. The story of the great war between Athens and Sparta and their respective allies, whose two long episodes fill the last generation of the remarkable 5th cent., has not been told in detail. Athens struggled back to a measure of life, but the dash and vitality of her great days were gone, and the century was scarcely forty years old when MACEDONIA, considered heretofore the barbarous N, began to rise like a menacing cloud on the horizon.

Philip II of Macedonia was a dynamic dictator of the sort the first half of the 20th cent. knew. His northern kingdom was new, young, and potentially rich. It needed only ruthless leadership, and that Philip could give. It was not exhausted, like the rest of Greece, by war and tension. In natural resources, gold and timber, it was wealthy. Its men were raw, strong, and numerous.

Philip began to press into Thessaly and to menace the southern regions. Athens had many spheres of influence and vital areas of control in his path, and her interests were menaced more than those of any other state. How Philip subverted Athenian strength, deceived, tricked, instigated revolt, softened morale by corrupted politicians and fifth columnists, and finally destroyed opposition in open war, is a story not unfamiliar to the modern world. Its gloom is relieved only by the heroism of the famous orator Demosthenes, who tried in his fine Philippic orations to rouse his weary and decadent people to rise and unite and beat back the menace to their liberty. Demosthenes' light was soon put out. Athens and Thebes were defeated at Chaeronea in 338 B.C., and Macedonia was virtual master of Greece.

To unite Greece, now cowed by Macedonian imperialism, Philip took up the challenge of a great crusade against Persia. In the midst of preparation he was assassinated, but his son, Alexander, a cultured youth educated on the Athenian tradition by Aristotle, took up the legacy of his father.

XII. The empire of Alexander. The project was not as mad as it might seem at first sight, and a curious event had some significance. At the beginning of the 4th cent. B.C., an army of 10,000 Greek mercenaries had been stranded in Persia; the rebel governor for whom they had fought was dead, and his native army dispersed. Their officers were treacherously murdered. The rank and file took up the challenge and cut their way out to the Black Sea, through the Armenian mountains and the snows. An Athenian named Xenophon wrote the stirring story in a book. There is little doubt that the tale had much to do with a decision of the dashing young Alexander, who succeeded his father as king of Macedon in 336 B.C. An empire out of whose heart and depths a little Greek army could boldly march was ripe for conquest.

Alexander was right. He needed a cause to unify Greece, and the old sin of Persia—the invasion of a century and a half before—was as good an excuse as any for aggression. With his well-drilled military machine, which he led magnificently, Alexander marched through the loose-knit Persian empire, and when he died at the age of thirty-two, he was master of a realm that stretched from the Ionian Sea to the Punjab, and from the Caucasus to the Libyan Desert and the borders of Ethiopia. Nor was there anyone to challenge it. Rome, still a city-state, was at grips with the petty problems of security in Italy. See ALEXANDER THE GREAT.

XIII. Hellenism. Thus was HELLENISM born. Alexander, with his strangely international outlook, might have done much with his vast empire. He died, and the great, amorphous mass of conquered territory was divided into four areas of control: metropolitan Greece and three kingdoms. Egypt, which had always been safely defined by the deserts that hemmed the valley of the Nile, fell into the hands of PTOLEMY, one of Alexander's marshals, and the dynasty he founded endured for three centuries, until the suicide, in fact, of CLEOPATRA—last and most amazing of the line—in 30 B.C.

The second successor-kingdom, which had much to do with Palestine, was that of SELEUCUS, another general of Alexander, who eventually asserted his independence from metropolitan Macedon and found himself in control of all the wide northern sweep of lands through which Alexander had marched. Seleucus's boundaries were ill-defined, and wavered with the ebb and flow

Palace ruins of Philip II, father of Alexander the Great, at Vergina.

of strength at ANTIOCH OF SYRIA. At one period, a Greek kingdom was carved out in the eastern marches, which covered modern Afghanistan and NW India. It disappeared in the flux of history, lying as it did beyond the ultimate reach of Rome; but coinage reveals a considerable realm that had its years of power. In the W, the kingdom of PERGAMUM, which its ruler bequeathed to advancing Rome in 133 B.C., was cut from the Seleucid realms. Other kingdoms, too, limited Antioch's westward power from time to time. It was a progressive disintegration of its ill-coherent mass that brought an end to Syrian imperialism, and, gradually restricting the borders of the old successor-empire of Seleucus, left Asia Minor and the Middle E finally a vacuum of power that invited and found Rome's effective intervention. The successful revolt of the Jews under Judas MACCABEE in the 2nd cent. is a recorded illustration of the gradual process by which the Seleucid empire declined.

Thus history brought Roman, Greek, and Jew together, made PAUL of Tarsus with his triple culture possible, and set the scene for modern Europe. Each contribution was essential history. The Roman peace provided the framework for the first activity of the church. It was on a Jewish stage that the events of the Gospels took place. It was Paul, a Jew, who first wrought out the synthesis of the Testaments, but a Jew steeped in Hellenic thought, and writing habitually in the language of the Greeks. Alexander thus brought Greek and Jew together by opening the way for the second great movement of Greek colonization. The culture of the Greeks penetrated as far E as Greek arms had moved, and Hellenism—that subtle blend of language, way of life, and mode of thought—was a stimulus and a catalyst felt far beyond the limits of Greek nationhood.

(The standard work of reference is *CAH*, rev. ed., vols. 2–6 [1973–94]. See also H. D. F. Kitto, *The Greeks* [1951]; N. G. L. Hammond, *A History of Greece to 322 B.C.*, 3rd ed. [1986]; M. Grant and R. Kitzinger, eds., *Civilization of the Ancient Mediterranean: Greece and Rome*, 3 vols. [1988]; S. Hornblower, *The Greek World, 479–323 BC*, rev. ed. [1991]; P. Cartledge, *The Cambridge Illustrated History of Ancient Greece* [1998]; K. H. Kinzl, ed., *A Companion to the Classical Greek World* [2006].)

E. M. BLAIKLOCK

greed. An excessive desire to acquire more than one has (esp. wealth and material possessions), usually leading to inappropriate behavior. This English term occurs primarily as the rendering of Greek *pleonexia G4432* (Lk. 12:15 et al.; KJV, "covetousness"), but the concept is expressed in many different ways.

Scripture regards greed or avarice as IDOLATRY (Eph. 5:5; Col. 3:5), vanity (Ps. 39:6; Eccl. 4:8), and the root of all evils (1 Tim. 6:10). It is something that God abhors (Ps. 10:3), forbids (Exod. 20:17), and even punishes (Job 20:15; Isa. 57:17; Jer. 22:17–19; Mic. 2:2–3). Greed is characteristic of the wicked (Rom. 1:29) and the slothful (Prov. 21:26); it is inconsistent in believers (Eph. 5:3; Heb. 13:5), especially ministers (1 Tim. 3:3). Excessive desire originates in the heart (Mk. 7:22–23), engrosses the heart (Ezek. 33:31; 2 Pet. 2:14), and is never satisfied (Eccl. 5:10; Hab. 2:5).

Greed leads to foolish and harmful lusts (1 Tim. 6:9), departure from the faith (6:10), falsehood (2 Ki. 5:22–25), theft (Josh. 7:21), poverty (Prov. 28:22), misery (1 Tim. 6:10), injustice and oppression (Prov. 28:20; Mic. 2:2), domestic affliction (Prov. 15:27), and murder (1:18–19; Ezek. 22:12). It is commended only by the wicked (Ps. 10:3); believers, on the other hand, hate it (Exod. 18:21; Acts 20:33). Both Isaiah and Habakkuk denounced it (Isa. 5:8; Hab. 2:9); Jesus warned his disciples to beware of it (Lk. 12:15). This sin can cause one to miss heaven (1 Cor. 6:10; Eph. 5:5). It will abound in the last days (2 Tim. 3:2; 2 Pet. 2:1–3), but those who hate it will be rewarded (Prov. 28:16). Believers ought to pray against avarice (Ps. 119:36), put it to death (Col. 3:5), and avoid those guilty of it (1 Cor. 5:11).

Biblical examples include Laban (Gen. 31:41), Balaam (2 Pet. 2:15; cf. Jude 11), Achan (Josh. 7:21), Eli's sons (1 Sam. 2:12–14), Samuel's sons (8:3), King Saul (15:9, 19), Ahab (1 Ki. 21:2–16), Gehazi (2 Ki. 5:20–27), Jewish nobles (Neh. 5:7; Isa. 1:23), Jewish people (Isa. 56:11; Jer. 6:13), Babylon (Jer. 51:1–12), a young man (Matt. 19:22), the Pharisees (Lk. 16:14), Judas (Matt. 26:14–15), Ananias (Acts 5:1–10), and Felix (24:26). (See further J. Calvin, *Institutes of the Christian Religion* 3.7.9; T. Laetsch, *The Minor Prophets* [1956], 151, 161–62; D. M. Lloyd-Jones, *Studies in the Sermon on the Mount*, 2 vols. [1959–60], 2:86–96.)

R. E. PERRY

Greek language. The language of Greece, spoken continuously from very ancient times until the present day. As a member of the Indo-European family, Greek is related to many languages, both eastern (e.g., Persian, Sanskrit) and western (e.g., German, Russian, Latin, and esp. Armenian); but it is very clearly distinctive as well, being the only member of its own branch (contrast, e.g., the Germanic branch, consisting not only of German, but also Dutch, English, the Scandinavian languages, and so on).

Although English too belongs to the Indo-European family, it has in the course of time lost many of the features characterizing this linguistic group. The English verbal conjugation, for example, is limited mainly to marking the third person singular (*I/you/we/they look*, but *He/she looks*) and the past tense (*I looked*). Greek verbs, in contrast, have a large variety of forms to indicate each person, several tenses, and so on (e.g., *blepō*, "I see"; *blepeis*, "you see"; *blepei*, "he/she sees"; *blepomen*, "we see"; *blepete*, "you [pl.] see"; *blepousi*, "they see"; *eblepsa*, "I saw"; *eblepon*, "I was seeing"; *blepsomai*, "I will see"). The only remnant of a noun declension in English is the possessive ending (*Paul's slave*), whereas Greek, in addition to the possessive (one of the functions of the genitive case), can indicate a variety of syntactical relationships through several other endings. Thus the form *doulos* (nominative case) serves primarily to indicate the subject of a sentence, whereas the variation *doulon* (accusative case) serves to indicate the object of a verb (*ho doulos blepei Paulon*, "the slave sees Paul," but *ton doulon blepei Paulos*, "Paul sees the slave"; note that, unlike English, the word order is irrelevant for determining who is the doer or the recipient of an action).

The Greek verb is unique in its use of three voices — not only active and passive but also *middle*, which appears to indicate that the subject is somehow affected by the action (a nuance different from that of a true reflexive). Though there is no true parallel in English, this threefold distinction may be illustrated by contrasting the following sentences: *the mother bathed the child* (active), *the child was bathed by the mother* (passive), and *the child bathed* ("middle" — the child is both the subject of the action and affected by it, but the force of the sentence is not quite the same as *the child bathed herself*). Among other characteristics of Greek, one should keep in mind its extensive use of the adverbial participle. English often uses the participle in this fashion (e.g., *Seeing the officer, John slowed down* = "After/because John saw the officer, he slowed down"), but Greek writers truly exploit this feature, causing much ambiguity that can be resolved only by the context (e.g., Gal. 6:9, *therisomen mē eklyomenoi*, "we shall reap not giving up" [i.e., *if* we do not give up]).

One characteristic of the Greek verb deserving special notice is that it grammaticalizes aspectual distinctions. The term *aspect* refers to the way the action is perceived or presented by the speaker. Probably all languages can express such distinctions through the use of adverbs, periphrasis, etc. In English, *I saw* presents as one whole the action of seeing an event, whereas *I was seeing* could be used of the very same action, but presenting it as a process. Greek can do the same, but it does so grammatically through its verbal conjugations: the *aorist* form *eblepsa* corresponds to "I saw," while the *imperfect eblepon* corresponds to "I was seeing" (though various renderings are possible). Moreover, this distinction is found not only in the past indicative, but also elsewhere, for example, in the imperative, and grammarians are not always agreed regarding the semantic difference involved. In NT interpretation, it is common to exaggerate the significance of the aorist (that it is emphatic, that it indicates a once-for-all event, etc.) over against the so-called progressive forms (supposedly signifying repetition, perseverance, etc.), but their function in the indicative mood is comparable, though not identical, to that of the corresponding English expressions. (Cf. M. Silva in *FCI*, 259–63.)

The rest of this article focuses on the character of NT Greek within the context of the history of the language.

    I. A revolutionary discovery
        A. The language of the Holy Ghost?
        B. The evidence of the papyri
   II. Koine and the evolution of Greek
        A. The Greek dialects
        B. From the beginnings to Alexander
        C. The Koine
        D. From the Atticistic reaction to modern times

III. Deissmann or Turner?
  A. Stylistic diversity
  B. Semitic influence
  C. Is biblical Greek sacred?

I. A revolutionary discovery. At the end of the 19th cent. an aspiring scholar, still in his twenties, looked over someone's shoulder in the library at the University of Marburg. What had caught his attention was the original reproduction of a Greek PAPYRUS that contained the phrase "son of God." The young man, whose name was Adolf Deissmann (1866–1937), would later recall: "I was arrested, fascinated by the *theou huios*, and found myself, as I continued to turn the leaves, everywhere in the world of the New Testament and the world surrounding it" (*Light from the Ancient East: The New Testament Illustrated by Recently Discovered Texts of the Graeco-Roman World* [1928], 346 n. 4). This discovery inspired Deissmann to a lifetime of research. As early as 1895, in the midst of pastoral duties in Herborn, he published his *Bibelstudien*, a book that was to revolutionize scholarly assessment of the NT language and related issues. Indeed, "seldom in the history of scholarship has the work of one man been more influential in rewriting an entire chapter in the book of knowledge" (E. C. Colwell in *IDB*, 2:486). For a proper appreciation of Deissmann's work, however, we must acquaint ourselves with a curious question that had occupied the minds of biblical students for a long time.

A. The Language of the Holy Ghost? The revival of learning at the time of the Renaissance had sent scholars back to the classical languages (for what follows, cf. J. Vergote in *DBSup*, 3:1320–70, esp. cols. 1321–27; J. W. Voelz in *ANRW* 2/25/2 [1984], 893–977). Humanists soon became aware of a phenomenon that had greatly exercised some Christians in the ancient church, namely, the striking differences between the language of their Bible (SEPTUAGINT and NT) and that of other literature. Erasmus, for example, regarded the apostolic style as undisciplined, rough, imperfect, and confused. By the 17th cent. a controversy between *Hebraists* and *purists* was in full swing. The former must have taken their cue from the reformer Théodore Beza, who described Hebraisms as jewels adorning the apostles' writings. On the other hand, the purists, unable to reconcile the presence of "Semitic corruptions" in the NT with the doctrine of INSPIRATION, sought to prove the hopeless thesis that NT Greek was no different from the language of such classical writers as Thucydides and Demosthenes.

The inevitable triumph of the Hebraist camp in the 18th cent. had some unfortunate consequences, such as the tendency to explain grammatical problems by viewing them merely as examples of *anomaly* (abnormality). For some scholars, indeed, NT Greek was characterized mainly by "a total disregard of grammatical propriety and precision" (as stated by G. B. Winer, *A Grammar of the New Testament Diction* [1860], 4). These excesses were gradually corrected, but the conviction that biblical Greek was a peculiar dialect grew stronger. Classical philologists attributed the peculiarity to a supposed Jewish patois in PALESTINE and ALEXANDRIA. However, since the writings of such Jews as the Palestinian JOSEPHUS and the Alexandrian PHILO JUDAEUS did *not* reflect a distinctive dialect, some theologians preferred to explain the character of biblical Greek as one more evidence of divine inspiration. A striking example was Richard Rothe, who argued in 1863 for the appropriateness of the phrase, "a language of the Holy Ghost."

Rothe went on to argue: "For in the Bible it is evident that the Holy Spirit has been at work, molding for himself a distinctively religious mode of expression out of the language of the country which he has chosen as his sphere, and transforming the linguistic elements which he found ready to hand, and even conceptions already existing, into a shape and form appropriate to himself and all his own." These words were quoted with approval by H. Cremer in the preface to his *Biblico-Theological Lexicon of the New Testament* (1883), a work that exerted great influence on NT scholarship and was indeed the precursor to G. Kittel's *Theological Dictionary of the New Testament* (for more details, see M. Silva, *Biblical Words and Their Meaning: An Introduction to Lexical Semantics*, rev. ed. [1994], 22–32).

And the Septuagint scholar Edwin Hatch, without recourse to theological arguments, encouraged a similar attitude by insisting on the need to appreciate the differences between classical and NT Greek: "The difficulty of Biblical Greek really begins when we remember that it was Greek as spoken not merely in a foreign country and under new circumstances, but also by an alien race.... The attitude of [the Jews] towards human life, towards nature, and towards God was so different that though Greek words were used they were the symbols of quite other than Greek ideas.... Biblical Greek is thus a language which stands by itself" (*Essays in Biblical Greek* [1889], 10–11). Hatch's last statement in particular sets forth clearly the real issue: must we sharply isolate the language of the NT in order to understand it?

Not all scholars could see eye to eye with Hatch. T. K. Abbott severely criticized his ideas soon after they were published; he argued, for example, that "expressions characterized as Hebraisms may in not a few instances be paralleled in classical writers, the difference being in their frequency" (*Essays, Chiefly on the Original Texts of the Old and New Testaments* [1891], 66). And H. A. A. Kennedy, who had been inspired to research the vocabulary of biblical Greek precisely because of Hatch's work, found that "the further the inquiry was pushed, the more decidedly was he compelled to doubt" Hatch's conclusions (*Sources of New Testament Greek, or The Influence of the Septuagint on the Vocabulary of the New Testament* [1895], preface). While Hatch had argued that most NT words exhibit LXX influence, Kennedy concluded, "When we consider the exceptional importance of the Greek Bible to the New Testament writers, the astonishing fact is that its influence on their vocabulary is not incomparably greater than it is found to be" (ibid., 165; for a fuller discussion of these issues, cf. Silva, *Biblical Words*, 56–68).

These and other writers (cf. MM, xii-xiii) hinted that, if our knowledge of the popular language were greater, many of the peculiarities of biblical Greek might prove to be nothing but instances of common speech. The most striking anticipation of Deissmann's work was a comment made by J. B. Lightfoot in a classroom lecture in 1863: "... if we could only recover letters that ordinary people wrote to each other without any thought of being literary, we should have the greatest possible help for the understanding of the language of the NT generally" (see J. H. Moulton, *Grammar of New Testament Greek. Vol. 1: Prolegomena*, 3rd ed. [1908], 242).

B. The evidence of the papyri. Even as those words were being spoken, such letters were coming to light in Egypt, where the dry climate had preserved ancient documents written on the fragile pith of the PAPYRUS plant. While some important finds had been made in the first half of the 19th cent., these were but a glimmer of what was to come. "The sites of ancient settlements had always been a legitimate hunting ground for building materials.... In the 1870s, as the cultivated area expanded, the demand for 'fertile earth' or *sebakh* grew enormously.... As ancient sites were stripped, papyri began to appear in masses, just as they had been thrown away in the ancient world on rapidly forming out-door rubbish heaps" (E. G. Turner, *Greek Papyri: An Introduction* [1968], 21). Especially significant were the papyrological discoveries by B. P. Grenfell and A. S. Hunt in Oxyrhynchus.

In addition to copies of literary works, the excavations brought to light day-to-day transactions, private correspondence, and the like, revealing the lives of the common people. Deissmann (*Light*, 7, 9–10) pointed out that in the literary documents the "lower classes are seldom allowed to speak, and where they do come to the front—in the comedies, for instance—they stand before us for the most part in the light thrown upon them from above.... Now, however, thanks to the discovery of their own authentic records, they have suddenly risen again from the rubbish mounds of the ancient cities, little market towns, and villages."

By appealing to various kinds of data, particularly the discovery of many words that had been considered exclusively biblical, Deissmann sought to disprove the uniqueness of the NT language. It was neither a "Holy Ghost language" nor a strange Jewish-Greek dialect, but the common (*koinē*) speech of Hellenistic times. Deissmann's thesis received impressive support when, at the turn of the century, the renowned classical philologist Albert Thumb adopted it in an authoritative study of the Koine (*Die griechische Sprache im Zeitalter des Hellenismus* [1901]). Moreover, the need to apply the new discoveries to grammatical questions inspired

J. H. Moulton in Britain and A. T. Robertson in America to write comprehensive grammars that systematically incorporated the papyrological material. In short, Deissmann won the day, though not without opposition.

But the controversy was revived in the 1960s, primarily because of the work of Nigel Turner, who was given the responsibility of completing Moulton's *Grammar* by writing the volume of syntax. In light of the position taken by the original author in vol. 1 of that work, one is startled to read Turner's judgment that "the strongly Semitic character of Biblical Greek, and therefore its remarkable unity within itself, do seem to me to have contemporary significance at a time when many are finding their way back to the Bible as a living book and perhaps are pondering afresh the old question of a 'Holy Ghost language.' The lapse of half a century was needed to assess the discoveries of Deissmann and Moulton and put them in right perspective. We now have to concede that not only is the subject-matter of the Scriptures unique but so also is the language in which they came to be written or translated" (vol. 3 of Moulton's *Grammar* [1963], 9). This striking reversal demands consideration. Did Turner prove his case? Was Deissmann misguided? What precisely is the significance of the papyri? Before we can attempt to answer these questions, however, we need to make some major digressions.

II. Koine and the evolution of Greek. Definition by negation has always been an indispensable tool of scientific research. We can most clearly and unambiguously describe an object by specifying what it is not. Of course, we can follow this procedure effectively only by grouping objects that are very similar to begin with. We can therefore better understand the character of NT Greek by comparing and contrasting it with other forms of the language. In other words, if we wish to determine whether the language of the NT is "pure" or "semiticized" or "colloquial" or "literary," we must become acquainted with the linguistic variations possible within Greek.

A. The Greek dialects. We can best gain such an acquaintance by surveying the diversity of Greek dialects that characterized the classical period, that is, around the year 400 B.C. (For what follows, cf. esp. L. R. Palmer, *The Greek Language* [1980], ch. 3; note also J. B. Hainsworth, "The Greek Language and the Historical Dialects," in *CAH*, 2nd ed., 3/1 [1982], 850–65; G. Horrocks, *Greek: A History of the Language and Its Speakers* [1997], ch. 1.)

(1) It is appropriate to begin with ATHENS, the intellectual capital of the ancient world. Athens was situated in a region known as Attica, and therefore we use the term Attic Greek to describe the language spoken there. We should keep in mind, however, that because of the cultural predominance of Athens, Attic had become to some extent the standard literary language (at least for prose writing) among the Greeks; the term *classical Greek* therefore normally refers to the Attic dialect. Now someone familiar only with NT Greek would be surprised by various features of Attic, such as (a) a large number of particles that defy translation (these were needed to convey nuances that in English we express by means of sentence intonation; such intonation was not possible in Ancient Greek because voice pitch was a function of the individual word, not the sentence), (b) very free word order, (c) a wide variety of verbal forms relatively uncommon in the NT (e.g., pluperfects and optatives), (d) the use of the dual, which was however mainly confined to poetry, and (e) unusual formations (e.g., *thalatta* for *thalassa*, *leōs* for *laos*).

(2) A second area of importance was *Ionia*. This term refers to the W coast of ASIA MINOR, although the Ionic dialect was spoken in many of the Aegean islands (esp. the Cyclades), in Euboea (the large island north of Attica), and elsewhere. An earlier form of this dialect had been used for the composition of the Homeric poems. It is distinguished from Attic by the following: (a) final -*ē* where we would expect a long -*a* (e.g., *kardiē* for *kardia*), (b) uncontracted vowel combinations (e.g., *ethnea* for *ethnē*), (c) the familiar NT form *thalassa* instead of Attic *thalatta*, and (d) many forms we had not seen before (such as *tōn* for *hō*, *es* for *eis*, *leōs* for *leōs* [NT *laos*], *poleōs* for *poleōs*, etc.).

(3) Next we move to the island of CYPRUS, whose inhabitants spoke a form of Greek very similar to the dialect used in Arcadia (an isolated region in the middle of the Peloponnesus). The inscriptions that have survived from these areas reveal: (a) the

use of long *a* where we would expect *ē* (e.g., *tan* for *tēn*, *phama* for *phēmē*), (b) the sound *w*, represented with a letter called *digamma* (thus *woikias* instead of *oikias*), (c) many peculiar forms (such as *kas* for *kai*, *apy* [with the dative] for *apo* [with the genitive], *peda* for *meta*, *in* for *en*, *pos* for *pros*).

(4) A fourth dialect was common to Boeotia (the area just to the NW of Attica), Thessaly (farther N), and Lesbos (a large island off the coast of Asia Minor, best known as the home of the poetess Sappho). We use the name *Aeolic* to describe this dialect. Although not alike in all respects, the forms of Greek spoken in these areas shared various features, such as (a) most of the items listed in the previous paragraph, (b) some peculiar forms (*emmi* for *eimi*, *ammes* for *hēmeis*, *pempe* for *pente*), (c) the preposition *en* constructed with the accusative case rather than the dative.

(5) A dialect known as *Northwest Greek* was spoken in Phocis and Locris (which were W of Boeotia) and in Elis (on the W coast of the Peloponnesus). Here too we find long *a* for *ē* and the presence of *digamma*, and in addition: (a) the final form *-ti* (e.g., *didōti* instead of *didōsi*), (b) *ka* for *an* and *hoka* for *hote*, (c) first plural suffix *-mes* (cf. the ending of Lat. *amamus*, "we love") instead of *-men*, (d) such forms as *amara* for *hēmera*, and (e) some features found in Aeolic, such as *en* with the accusative and the form *pempe*.

(6) The term *Doric* is used to refer to one final dialect that predominated in the Peloponnesus, including the cities of CORINTH and SPARTA as well as the island of CRETE. This form of Greek shared the features of the previous group, except for the last two sets.

All of this diversity may seem striking, but should not be exaggerated. The topography of the areas populated by Greek speakers encouraged separation (thus the emergence of independent city-states), and this separation accounts for the linguistic variety. These differences, however, were not so great as to prevent communication, and all Greek speakers were conscious of a common heritage reflected in their language. Moreover, the modern linguist is able to see some pattern in the diverse facts listed above. For example, the last two groups are so similar that we can group them together as forms of "West Greek," to be distinguished from all others. It is also clear that the first two groups form one dialect, Ionic-Attic. More controversy surrounds the relation of the two middle groups to the rest of the dialects. Nevertheless, because the shared features probably reflect a common descent, many scholars believe that at an early stage a form that we may call Common Greek split into E and W dialects. The W dialects were subsequently differentiated as Doric and NW, whereas the E dialects developed into three forms, Aeolic, Arcado-Cyprian, and Ionic-Attic (the features shared by NW Gk. and Aeolic are perhaps best explained as the result of subsequent contact between these two groups, but it is possible to argue for a genetic connection between them).

Our knowledge of Greek dialectology was greatly enhanced through the exciting discovery and later decipherment (in the early 1950s) of tablets written in what we now call Mycenaean Greek, a language that shows some affinities with the dialect spoken in Arcadia and Cyprus (cf. Palmer, *Greek Language*, ch. 2). These tablets, which are dated about 1400–1200 B.C., pushed back our knowledge of Greek by several centuries and provided new insights into the history of the language. That history may be reconstructed, with some simplifications, as follows.

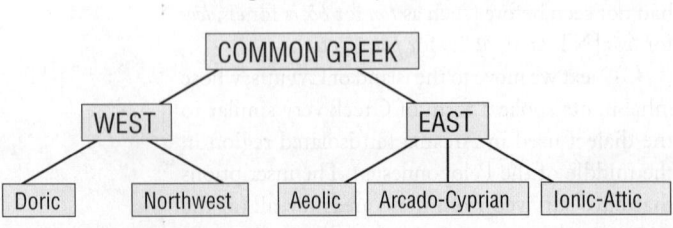

B. From the beginnings to Alexander. Linguistic, archaeological, and historical data allow us to form a tentative picture of the earliest development of Greek. Early in the 3rd millennium B.C., a group of people living perhaps in Central Europe used a form of speech that we may call Proto-Indo-European. In the course of that millennium a series of migrations took place, leading some (the later Celts) to occupy the westernmost areas of Europe, while others went eastward and settled as far as India. No later than 2000 B.C., one such migratory group went S and occupied considerable portions of the Aegean.

```
                    COMMON GREEK
                   /            \
                WEST            EAST
                /  \           /  |  \
            Doric  Northwest  Aeolic  Arcado-Cyprian  Ionic-Attic
```

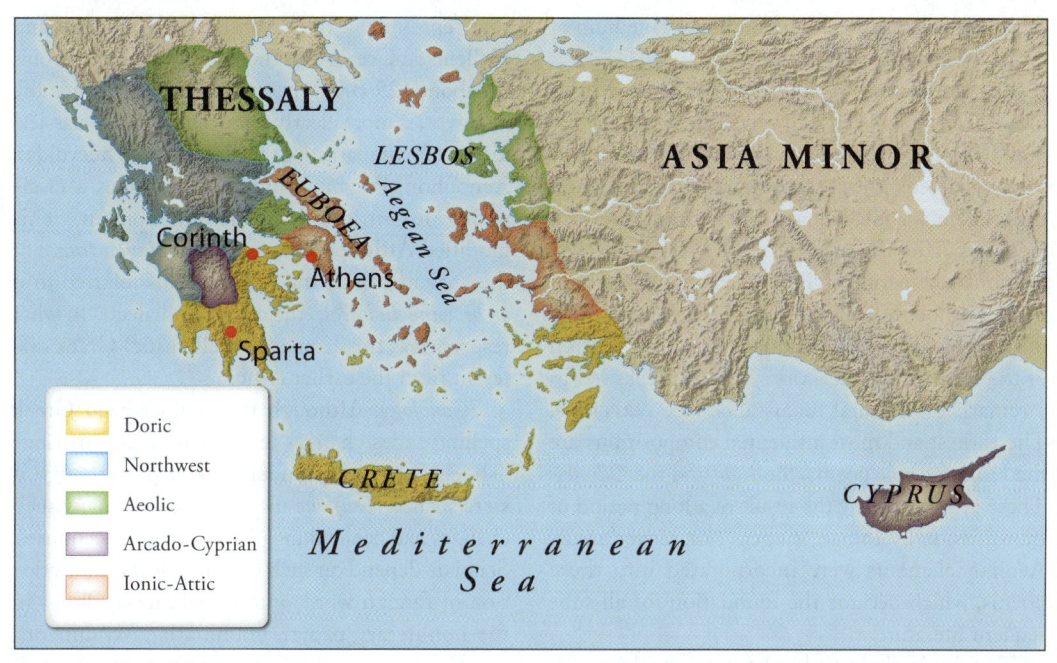

The ancient Greek dialects.

Even at the time of migration, these people probably spoke a distinct form of Indo-European. During the succeeding centuries, naturally, their speech would develop more and more distinctives. (In what follows, an asterisk denotes a prehistoric and therefore hypothesized, unattested sound.) For example, the Proto-Indo-European initial sound *y- changed to z-, as in zygon (cf. Sanskrit yugám, Lat. iugum, Eng. yoke); initial *s- became h, as in the pronoun ho (Sansk. sá); the sound *kʷ changed to either p or t, as in pente (Lat. quinque); the number of cases (eight, as in Sansk.) was reduced to five; and so on. Moreover, this group came in contact with other peoples, both Indo-European (e.g., Macedonians, Thracians, Phrygians) and non-Indo-Europeans. Contacts with the latter are difficult to specify, but traces were left in the Greek language (such as the ending -ssos and vocabulary items like asaminthos, "bathtub," a device apparently not needed before they came to the hot south).

The record suggests that at an early stage there was isolation between those Greeks who occupied the NW areas (Dorians) and those who established the Mycenaean culture in the Peloponnesus (these Mycenaeans eventually destroyed the non-Indo-European Minoan culture of Crete about 1400 B.C.). Toward the end of the 2nd millennium the Dorians, perhaps under pressure from the Illyrians, moved S to the Peloponnesus. This migration, possibly combined with other factors, resulted in the destruction of the Mycenaean culture and introduced a dark period of illiteracy. Some of the Mycenaeans fled to Cyprus while others stayed put in the mountainous central section known as Arcadia. These two groups retained the Mycenaean speech with some changes (thus we can speak of an Arcado-Cyprian dialect), whereas the Dorians, because of their previous isolation, preserved a number of archaic features in their own dialect.

Even before the coming of the Dorians, however, it appears that distinct dialects had surfaced in Thessaly (later to become the Aeolian dialect) and in Attica and Euboea (later to become Ionic-Attic). Perhaps already at this time Ionic and Attic began to develop their peculiar features, such as the shift from long a to $\bar{e}$ and the loss of digamma. After the separation of Attic and Ionic, the former dialect continued to evolve rapidly with a number of innovations, such as vowel contractions. It is worthwhile considering that, among the Greek dialects, it was not the more conservative Dorian but the "progressive" (some might say "corrupted")

Attic that became the dominant literary medium of Greek civilization.

But we are running ahead of our story. Mycenaean Greek had been written down by means of a non-Indo-European syllabary (a script that represents syllables rather than individual sounds), and this system was inadequate for writing the Greek language. After the collapse of the Mycenaean civilization and a period of literary inactivity in written form (although oral literature developed richly during this period), the adoption and adaptation of the Phoenician ALPHABET by the Greeks led to a remarkable cultural renaissance (see WRITING). The earliest and most influential compositions are the Homeric epic poems, the *Iliad* and the *Odyssey*. These are admittedly the result of a long period of transmission by Ionian "singers"; moreover, many Aeolian elements were incorporated into these poems, which became the foundation for all subsequent literature.

The Ionic dialect also became the basis for Hesiod's poems (c. 700 B.C.), whereas Aeolic, particularly Lesbian, played a dominant role in the lyric poetry of the 6th cent. It was in the 5th cent., with the emergence of dramatic literature (esp. Aeschylus), that the Attic dialect took over. Particularly important for the development of Greek prose was the style of the historian Thucydides, who occasionally preferred "pan-Hellenic" forms (e.g., *thalassa*) over those peculiar to Athens (*thalatta*). Although some of the other dialects continued to be used for special genres of literature, by the 4th cent. someone wishing to write anything of importance had to do it in Attic.

C. The Koine. It was this Attic, then, with which ALEXANDER THE GREAT (himself a Macedonian rather than Greek) conquered the cultures of the ancient world. Even before Alexander's time, the Attic dialect had spread to other parts of the Greek world, where "the process of rejuvenescence and fusion [particularly the introduction of Ionic elements] was much more rapid, and it was here that the foundations of the Koine were laid" (A. Thumb in *DAC*, 1:554). This process was however greatly accelerated when Alexander imposed Greek culture on eastern races. The historian Xenophon, who spent many years traveling abroad, wrote in a style that represents a transition between classical and Hellenistic Greek; and the later historian Polybius (d. about 125 B.C.), having spent most of his life in Egypt, is more clearly removed from the classical idiom. (A comparison of the historians Thucydides, Xenophon, Polybius, and Luke provides a fascinating insight into linguistic development.) This modified Attic speech became the *lingua franca* of the ancient world, and grammarians referred to it as *hē koinē dialektos*, "the common dialect." In what respects was this Koine (or Hellenistic) Greek different from the earlier Attic?

Phonology. Although the standardized Greek spelling hides changes in pronunciation (in English, e.g., we now pronounce *through* as though it were spelled *thru*), we may be sure that many such changes had been taking place during the centuries. Scholars depend on such evidence as the transcription of foreign words into Greek, misspellings in the nonliterary papyri, grammarians' comments, etc. For example, the Greek word *rhabdos* ("rod") occurs in the papyri with the spelling *raudos*, which indicates that in the 1st cent. B.C., and probably earlier, the diphthong *au* was being pronounced *av*

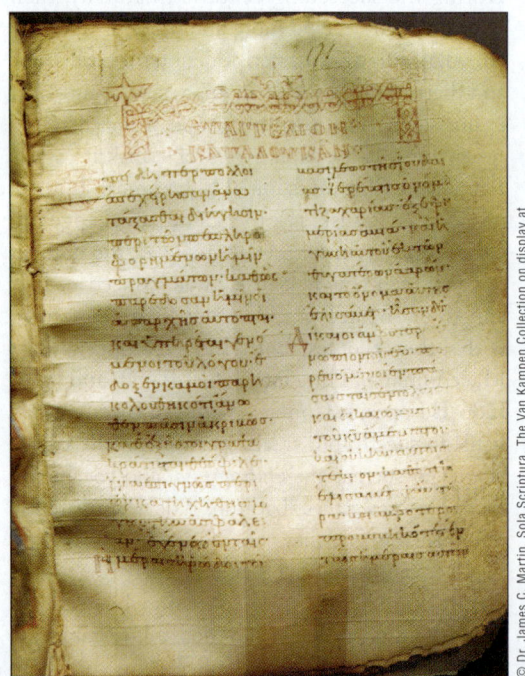

A 9th-cent. Greek minuscule MS of the Gospel according to Luke.

(sometimes *af*), while the consonant *b* (originally a stop or occlusive) had become a fricative, similar to *v*. Both of these features are found in Modern Greek. Similar developments include the pronunciation of *eu* as *ev* (sometimes *ef*), *d* as *th* (as in Eng. *these*), etc.

Another misspelling (common even in the MS tradition of literary works) is the confusion between the omicron, *o*, and the omega, *ō*. In ancient times the distinction between them was simply that *ō* was pronounced about twice as long as *o* (similarly, *ē* twice as long as *e*; the other vowels, *a i y*, could be pronounced either short or long). This distinction, which appears trivial to us, was a very important *phonemic* (i.e., linguistically significant) feature, and it is found in many languages, but as early as the 4th cent. B.C., the system began to weaken, and it had probably disintegrated by NT times. Linked with this change was the shift from pitch accent to stress accent; this development in turn allowed for sentence intonation and made unnecessary the use of many particles. Other changes in vowel and consonant pronunciation took place during Hellenistic times. (These developments are documented, e.g., in several monographs by Sven-Tage Teodorsson, such as *The Phonology of Attic in the Hellenistic Period* [1978]. Although some features of his work have been criticized, the evidence he has collected is of great value.)

Morphology. In most linguistic development, *analogy* (the tendency to regularize, i.e., change unusual forms so that they conform to the familiar) plays a potent role. Thus the unusual Attic declension of *leōs*, "people," was removed by using the pan-Hellenic form *laos*; some *-mi* verbs were increasingly conjugated as omega-verbs (e.g., *deiknymi*, "to show," was treated as though it were *deiknyō*, an already existing alternate form); the so-called second aorist *ēlthon*, "I came," was often modified to the hybrid form *ēlthan* (i.e., using the *a* of the more common first aorist); and so on. Because analogical formations may be regarded as part of a broader tendency to simplify the language, Hellenistic Greek tends to ignore complications like the middle voice and the optative mood. But the Koine also added to the linguistic store by creating thousands of formations and compounds (cf. BDAG, xv-xix).

Syntax. Again simplification seems to be the rule here. The avoidance of complex sentences leads to common word-order patterns (though not a fixed word-order, as in English). Relations that had been expressed merely by the use of case-endings begin to be expressed more and more with prepositions. (It should be noted that growing dependence on prepositions can eventually make case-endings unnecessary; if these case-endings disappear, as in Modern English, a fixed word-order becomes essential.) Moreover, in conformity with conversational style, clauses are coordinated simply with *kai*, "and," as well as other conjunctions, in contrast with the complex subordinated clauses of Attic Greek.

Vocabulary. Many non-Attic words (such as Doric *alektōr* G232, "rooster," for Attic *alektryōn*) became common in the Koine. Contact with foreign languages resulted in numerous loanwords, such as *kaisar* G2790 (Lat. *Caesar*), *angareuō* G30, "to press into service" (from a Persian term used of royal messengers), *sakkos* G4884, "sackcloth" (from Semitic; cf. Heb. *śaq* H8566), etc. Finally, old Attic words acquired new meanings, such as *aretē* G746 "miracle" (formerly "virtue"), *epangelia* G2039, "promise" (formerly "announcement"), etc.

Palmer (*Greek Language*, 176) summarizes and assesses these developments as follows: "Profound linguistic consequences might have been expected from the adoption of what was basically the Attic dialect by users of not merely non-Attic, but non-Greek speech. In fact the changes were remarkably slight. In phonology certain tendencies already observable in the ancient dialects persisted. In the morphology there was simplification and systematization which ironed out a number of Attic idiosyncracies. But the main result of the immense extension of Macedonian power and the use of language for all the purposes and occasions of life in a world empire—government, science, art and literature—was a great enrichment of the lexicon."

D. From the Atticistic reaction to modern times. As one might expect, Greek writers tended to react negatively to many of these linguistic developments and felt compelled to preserve the "pure" language of the great classical authors. Teachers corrected their students if, for example, they used the verb *eucharisteō* G2373, "I thank"; the reason given was that this use could not be attested among the "approved" writers (so Phrynichus, a grammarian who lived in the 2nd cent. A.D.; see Robert Browning, *Medieval and Modern Greek*, 2nd. ed. [1983], 47). And, although some writers (e.g., the historian Polybius, the geographer Strabo, and others) composed respectable works in what we may call a literary Koine, most authors of distinction attempted to reproduce the older Attic dialect. But this dialect was no longer a *living* form, and so their writing is often artificial and stilted; moreover, stylistic infelicities and outright blunders are common. This "Atticistic" movement, however, had tremendous influence and created a division between colloquial spoken Greek and the written form that lingers into our day. As noted previously, early Christians were often troubled by the language of Scripture, for the enemies of Christianity pointed to it as evidence that the new faith was culturally deficient; sensitive to this accusation, church theologians like John Chrysostom were careful to write in atticizing Greek.

Yet the spoken form continued to develop along the lines already outlined. The vowel system was simplified to the extent that *i y ē ei oi* are now all pronounced the same (like *ee* in Eng. *feet*). The aspirates *ph th ch* (which used to be pronounced approximately like the Eng. *p, t,* and *k*) became fricatives (pronounced like English *f, th* [as in *think*], and German *ch*; note that *p t k* have always been pronounced like *p t c* in French or Spanish, that is, without the aspiration characteristic of Eng.). There have been other phonological changes, like the disappearance of initial unaccented vowels (e.g., *mera* for *hēmera* and *ligos* for *oligos*). The morphology has been further simplified by greater regularization, by the disappearance of the dative case, by the restricted use of the participle, and so on. The vocabulary too has been greatly affected: more and more classical words have been dropped, foreign words (esp. Turkish) have been added, and new forms and meanings have resulted from cultural modernization.

During the last two centuries or so many have resisted the introduction of this colloquial Greek (the *dēmotikē*, "demotic," that is, the people's Greek) into the schools and the literature. Most writers, along with newspapers and government publications, have used the *kathareuousa* ("purified"), a peculiar combination of ancient and modern forms. This so-called "language-question," a source of division and political unrest, can be traced directly to the Atticistic movement of the first century. It was not until 1976 that Demotic Greek was recognized as the official language of Greece. What may be called the "standard" form today, as used for example in journalism, is indeed the popular dialect, but with the free use of learned elements. (For a brief and excellent discussion, see the introductory chapter in Peter Mackridge, *The Modern Greek Language: A Descriptive Analysis of Standard Modern Greek* [1985]; for greater detail, R. Beaton, *An Introduction to Modern Greek Literature* [1994], ch. 6.)

III. Deissmann or Turner? We may now return to our central concern: What is biblical Greek? How is it different from other forms of Greek? Is the language itself—and not only the message it communicates—unique? The evidence indicates clearly that NT Greek is *not* peculiar and that therefore Deissmann, Thumb, and Moulton were correct in all essential respects. But what about the objections of Nigel Turner and others?

A. Stylistic diversity. To begin with, one must point out that the term *biblical Greek* encompasses more linguistic diversity than we may realize. While no one will dispute that the language of the SEPTUAGINT and NT books is characterized by some important features not found elsewhere, one can hardly claim that it is all uniform. We cannot, for example, ignore the crucial distinction between translation Greek (LXX) and original Greek. Even within the LXX, one can move from the very literal translation (and the strongly semiticized Greek resulting from it) of parts of Samuel–Kings, to the respectable literary Koine of the Greek Pentateuch, and on to the very free translation, and therefore less semiticized language, of Proverbs (see K. H. Jobes and M. Silva, *Invitation to the Septuagint* [2000], ch. 5).

But let us focus on the NT books. The epistle to the Hebrews has a distinct literary flavor. It begins with a long, carefully worked-out sentence that makes use of assonance (*polymerōs, polytropōs, palai, patrasin, prophētais*—all in the first clause) and many participles. Moreover, the last clause of this sentence (*diaphorōteron par' autous keklēronomēken onoma*, "the name he has inherited is superior to theirs," Heb. 1:4) exhibits his elegant tendency of separating a noun (*onoma*, "name") from its modifier (*diaphorōteron*, "superior"). Without falling into the monotony and woodenness of some forms of atticizing Greek, the author lends his writing a classical ring by the use of particles like *dēpou* and *eaper* (2:16; 3:6), numerous negative adjectives (*amethatētos, akatalytos*), idioms (*hōs epos eipein*, "so to speak," 7:9), and other features.

Although occasional phrases (e.g., "the word of his power" for "his powerful word" in Heb. 1:3) are reminiscent of the LXX style, there is nothing in the *language* of the epistle to the Hebrews (apart from actual LXX quotations) that would have sounded peculiar to a Greek reader. James Moffatt has said of this author: "He has a sense of literary nicety, which enters into his earnest religious argument without rendering it artificial or over-elaborate. He has an art of words, which is more than an unconscious sense of rhythm. He has a style of a trained speaker; it is style, yet style at the command of a devout genius" (*A Critical and Exegetical Commentary on the Epistle to the Hebrews*, ICC [1924], lxiv). Nigel Turner (in his volume on style for the Moulton *Grammar* [1976], 108–12) argues that the author of Hebrews writes "Jewish Greek" and even appeals to Moffatt for support, but the latter (*Commentary*, lxii) speaks of the Semitisms in Hebrews as only "occasional," and adds that "this is a minor point."

In striking contrast to Hebrews, the book of Revelation "seems the work of a man whose knowledge of Greek was imperfect, or at all events to whom Greek was a foreign language" (H. Simcox, *The Writers of the New Testament: Their Style and Characteristics* [1890], 80). For example, Rev. 7:2, translated literally, speaks of an angel who "cried out to the four angels *to whom it was given to them* [*hois edothē autois*] to harm the earth and the sea." Such a repetition of the pronoun is characteristic of Semitic idiom, as is the coordination in v. 14 of a finite verb (*eplynan*, "they washed") with a previous participle (*hoi erchomenoi*, "the ones who come"): "These are the ones who come out of the great tribulation and they washed their robes," where a typical Greek author would have written, "and who washed." Other examples include the use of common Greek words with unusual meanings, such as *thanatos* G2505, "death," in the special sense of "pestilence, plague" (Rev 6:8b; 18:8 [NRSV]; cf. Heb. *māwet* H4638 in Jer. 15:2 [NRSV]). Moreover, the book abounds in what appears to be a series of ungrammatical constructions, although some scholars believe that the author used them consciously for specific reasons. "But from whatever cause or concurrence of causes, it cannot be denied that the Apocalypse of John stands alone among Greek literary writings in its disregard of the ordinary rules of syntax, and the success with which syntax is set aside without loss of perspicuity or even of literary power. The book seems openly and deliberately to defy the grammarian, and yet, even as literature, it is in its own field unsurpassed" (H. B. Swete, *The Apocalypse of St. John* [1908], cxxv).

Between these two extremes (Hebrews and Revelation) lie the rest of the NT writings. Mark, for example, without sharing the anomalies present in the Apocalypse, is written in a simple and inelegant style, with many marks of its Semitic background. Similar to Mark, but smoother in its grammar, is the style of Matthew, while 2 Peter's sentence construction strikes many observers as "cumbersome and occasionally clumsy" (B. M. Metzger in *IB*, 7:56). Studied simplicity, but not harshness, characterize the Gospel of John, whose

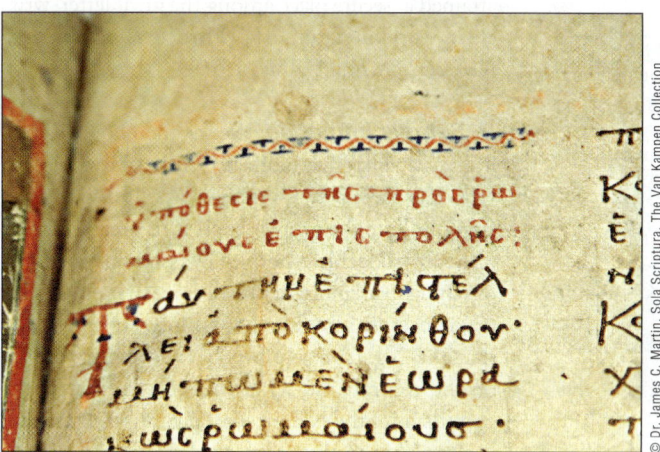

An example of Greek cursive writing from a MS dealing with the Pauline epistles.

"method is not elegant, is not literary; but the result is always worth having" (Simcox, *Writers*, 72). Over against these books stand James and 1 Peter, both of which approach the rhetorical standards of Hebrews. Luke too is capable of writing in the best literary tradition, but one is more greatly impressed by his picturesque style and by a remarkable versatility that allows him to begin with a long and sonorous sentence in the classical style (Lk. 1:1–4), shift suddenly to the language of the LXX for his description of two Jewish births (1:5—2:38), then subsequently and masterfully adjust his style to the circumstances of his narrative.

Almost precisely in the middle of the two extremes stands the language of the Apostle to the Gentiles. On the one hand, PAUL was certainly not motivated by literary pretensions, and therefore his style is clearly to be distinguished from the rhetorical efforts of Hebrews and Luke–Acts. On the other hand, the apostle was a true Greek writer: the grammatical "irregularities he does admit are such as show freedom rather than inexperience in the use of a language" (Simcox, *Writers*, 25). He was unmistakably Jewish (cf. ibid., 27), but at the same time he was "a classic of Hellenism" (Ulrich von Wilamowitz-Moellendorf in *Die griechische und lateinische Literatur und Sprache*, 2nd ed. [1907], 159, who goes on to make the striking statement: "Finally, finally someone speaks Greek again from a fresh, inner life experience"). Because his epistles "express so spontaneously and therefore so eloquently his mind and his message," Paul has attained a "secure place among the great letter-writers in world literature" (F. F. Bruce, *Paul: Apostle of the Heart Set Free* [1977], 15).

B. Semitic influence. We see then how difficult it is to characterize biblical Greek as a whole, for God has used both simple and skillful writers to communicate the gospel. Yet it is not really all that difficult to decide whether Deissmann was right or wrong—assuming that we understand what his real concerns were. He had no interest in denying that the NT language betrays its Semitic origin; on the contrary, he acknowledged freely that the Semitisms of the NT are like "birthmarks," making it clear "that in this great cosmopolitan Book the Greek cosmopolitan language was spoken by men whose home lay in the East" (A. Deissmann, *The Philology of the Greek Bible: Its Present and Future* [1908], 65). Nor did Deissmann ignore "the power of Christianity ... in *transforming* the meaning of the old words" (*Light*, 78). He did argue, however, that these characteristics are not "sufficient reason for scholars to isolate the language of the sacred texts"; whatever Semitisms we find "do not place the Bible outside the scope of Greek philology" (*Philology*, 65). Not only was Deissmann on target, but his main point is really beyond controversy. When we consider the kinds of linguistic features that distinguished the old dialects from each other, it is clear that NT Greek is *not* a dialect separate from the Koine.

Turner has, to be sure, rendered a service in emphasizing the many traits (both stylistic and lexical) that lend to biblical Greek its own distinctiveness. His mistake consisted in supposing that such evidence undermines Deissmannism. For example, Turner showed in one article (*VT* 5 [1955]: 208–13) that biblical Greek, in the use of the adjective *pas* G4246, prefers syntactical patterns different from those common in the papyri, and on that basis argued that the Koine in general was different from the NT language, which may be described as "unique." His own evidence, however, makes it plain that the patterns preferred by biblical Greek are found in the papyri as well, only not so frequently. This was precisely Moulton's point when he stressed that "the ordinary Greek speech or writing of men whose native language was Semitic ... brought into prominence locutions, correct enough as Greek, but which would have remained in comparatively rare use but for the accident of their answering to Hebrew or Aramaic phrases" (*Grammar*, 1:11; cf. also M. Silva, "Bilingualism and the Character of Palestinian Greek," *Bib* 61 [1980]: 198–219; G. H. R. Horsley, *New Testament Documents Illustrating Early Christianity*, vol. 5, *Linguistic Essays* [1989], esp. ch. 1).

The influence of Hebrew and Aramaic on Palestinian Greek is most clearly seen in the vocabulary, which changes more quickly and easily than other aspects of language. The most obvious (though also the most superficial) evidence of foreign influence is the phenomenon of loanwords, as when English "borrows" the Spanish word *sombrero* to describe a particular type of hat for which there is no native English term. Several examples of this tendency are found in the Greek NT, perhaps the best known being ABBA (Aram. for "father"). More interesting is the occurrence of so-called loan translations, that is, attempts to translate an idiom or expression by imitating the word-combination of the foreign language. For example, instead of simply borrowing the word *skyscraper*, Spanish speakers tried to reproduce it with the similar combination *rascacielos*. In the same way, the LXX translators saw the Hebrew idiom *nāśāʾ pānim* ("to lift the face," meaning "to pay regard to a person, to be partial") and rendered it literally as *prosōpon lambanein* (e.g., Lev. 19:15).

Perhaps the most important examples of foreign lexical influence are semantic loans. Rather than borrowing a whole word (a sound combination plus its meaning), speakers who recognize a partial equivalence between a certain native word and the corresponding foreign term may decide, consciously or unconsciously, to borrow "the rest" of the foreign word's meaning—that is, to "extend" the meaning of the native term so that it corresponds more fully to the foreign one. When we say, *I give you my word*, we are using the term *word* in imitation of the French *parole*, with its extended meaning "promise." Some important theological terms in the NT reflect a similar development. The Hebrew term *kābôd* **H3883** ("weight, honor") is difficult to translate when used to describe a brilliant divine manifestation. Because Greek *doxa* **G1518** ("opinion") could be used in the sense of "reputation," the LXX translators chose it to render the Hebrew term, and thus the Greek word took on an extra theological nuance, "glory" (for a more detailed discussion of semantic borrowing, see Silva, *Biblical Words*, ch. 3).

C. Is biblical Greek sacred? Just as we can do full justice to the significance of Semitisms in the NT without accepting the theory of a Jewish-Greek patois, so can we acknowledge the powerful effects of the Christian faith on the Greek language without concluding that biblical Greek is linguistically unique. This question is perhaps more difficult to handle than the previous one. To begin with, students of the classical languages have at times made exaggerated claims about the inherent greatness of Attic Greek; in addition, Christians have often appealed to those claims as somehow strengthening their convictions about divine INSPIRATION.

This tendency is not confined to popular writings. As renown a scholar as C. A. Briggs wrote in the 19th cent. that "the Greek language is the beautiful flower, the elegant jewel, the most finished masterpiece of Indo-Germanic thought." Greek, we are further told, is complex, artistic, beautiful, finished, strong, and vigorous. "Its syntax is organized on the most perfect system.... [the Greek language] wrestles with the mind, it parries and thrusts, it conquers as an armed host." But with the coming of the gospel, "the Greek language had now to perform a work for which it had providentially been preparing, and yet one which it had never yet attempted, namely, to convey the divine revelation to mankind." The result was that this language was "employed by the Spirit of God, and transformed and transfigured, yes, glorified, with a light and sacredness that the classic literature never possessed" (*General Introduction to the Study of Holy Scripture* [1900], 64, 65–67, 70–71; cf. J. Barr's critique in *The Semantics of Biblical Language* [1961], 246ff.).

In response to this approach one must point out, first of all, that modern linguistic science has cast serious doubts on the validity of regarding some languages as inherently better than others. For example, the discovery and analysis of exceedingly complex languages spoken by uncivilized peoples argues against viewing Greek as superior because of its complexity. Every language is adequate with respect to the culture in which it is spoken. By and large, the greatness of Greek resides in its *literature*, not in any inherent qualities of its linguistic structure. Similarly, we must not confuse the worth of Christian doctrines with that of the linguistic medium used to communicate it—though we may certainly appreciate the wisdom of God's providence in choosing a language that enjoyed a rich literary tradition and that had become a universal means of communication.

The fact that Greek is no more sacred than, say, the writing material Paul may have used does not however prevent us from recognizing that the Koine was indeed affected by Christianity. All creative periods in civilization have left their mark on their respective languages. The flowering of learning in 16th-cent. England, for instance, most surely transformed the English language. Again, no one would want to deny that the intellectual power of ancient Athens molded the Attic dialect into a remarkable instrument for analytical expression. We may therefore be sure that Christianity, the most potent spiritual awakening in history, would have had an important effect on linguistic expression. But that fact does *not* make the Greek of the early Christians unique, that is, a language all its own. English-speaking Christians have their own specialized vocabulary and forms of expression—every group with special interests does—but that is no ground for linguistically isolating their speech from "non-Christian English."

From the standpoint of *linguistic structure*, then, biblical Greek is no more and no less than Hellenistic, Koine Greek. While the level of literary sophistication varies from book to book, the NT authors wrote in the simple, colloquial language of the people while avoiding both the near-illiteracy or vulgarity sometimes found in the papyri and, at the other extreme, the artificial and archaizing forms of the Atticists. If we focus on *style*, however, we may indeed speak of biblical Greek as a coherent whole, colored by occasional Semitic idioms and enriched by a vocabulary that gave clear expression to revealed truth.

(Among the works mentioned above, the best introduction is G. Horrocks, *Greek: A History of the Language and Its Speakers* [1997]; an important work that appeared too late to be consulted here is F. Rodríguez Adrados, *A History of the Greek Language: From Its Origins to the Present* [2005]. See also the articles included in *The Language of the New Testament: Classic Essays*, ed. S. E. Porter [1991]. The standard reference works in English for the classical period are H. W. Smyth, *Greek Grammar*, rev. by G. M. Messing [1956]; H. G. Liddell and R. Scott, *A Greek-English Lexicon*, rev. by H. S. Jones et al., 9th ed. [1996]. For the NT and related writings, see F. Blass and A. Debrunner, *A Greek Grammar of the New Testament and Other Early Christian Literature*, trans. R. W. Funk [1961, but note that the German edition has been subsequently revised by F. Rehkopf]; W. Bauer, *A Greek-English Lexicon of the New Testament and Other Early Christian Literature*, 3rd ed. rev. by F. W. Danker [2000]. The older work by A. T. Robertson, *A Grammar of the Greek New Testament in the Light of Historical Research* [1923], contains much useful information, including an extensive introductory section on the character and history of the language. A recent and significant monograph that stresses the continuity of Greek from ancient times to the present is C. C. Caragounis, *The Development of Greek and the New Testament: Morphology, Syntax, Phonology, and Textual Transmission* [2004].) M. SILVA

Greek religion and philosophy

 I. Greek religion
  A. Homeric religion
  B. Primitive religions
  C. Mystery religions
  D. Forms of worship
 II. Greek philosophy
  A. The Pre-Socratics
  B. The age of Plato and Aristotle
  C. The Hellenistic age

I. Greek religion. This account of Greek religion is divided into three parts: the classical religion of the Olympic deities, especially as depicted in the writings of Homer; an earlier religion of fear, some practices of which continued into the classical period; and the mystery religions that later displaced belief in Zeus.

A. Homeric religion. Classical Homeric religion acknowledged ZEUS as its chief god. Zeus was not in any sense the creator of heaven and earth. Neither was he the prime mover, the *ens perfectissimum*, the eternal self-existing being; he was the son of a previous god. Originally there was Chaos, then came Gaea (Earth), who married Uranus (Heaven), and in addition to several monsters this pair produced the Titan gods Kronos, his sister Rhea (whom he married), Tethys, and Oceanus, as well as others.

When Uranus imprisoned his monster offspring, Gaea persuaded Kronos to castrate Uranus, and from his blood the Giants and the fearsome Furies, pursuers of evildoers, came into being. Kronos and Rhea gave birth to Zeus. Fearing that one

Marble bust of Homer. Roman copy after a lost Hellenistic original (blind type) of the 2nd century B.C.

of his sons might unseat him, Kronos wished to devour Zeus as he had devoured some of his other children; but Rhea hid Zeus and saved his life. When of age, Zeus overthrew Kronos and the race of Titans. Zeus thus became the chief deity, the god of the sky; his brother Poseidon became god of the sea, and another brother, HADES, became lord of the underworld.

Zeus, by his sister-wife Hera, was the father of Ares, god of war; but Athena, goddess of wisdom, sprang full grown from her father's forehead. Zeus seduced Leto, his niece, who gave birth to APOLLO and ARTEMIS. He also seduced Dione, the daughter of Tethys and Oceanus, to beget Aphrodite, the goddess of love. Zeus' main occupation, pausing only occasionally to hurl a thunderbolt, seems to have been seducing both goddesses and mortal women. Zeus also set the example, so frequently followed by his worshipers, of unnatural vice with boys.

Other gods are: the crippled smithy Hephaestus, who married Aphrodite (who also became the mother of Aeneas by Anchises of Troy); orgiastic DIONYSUS, the god of drunken revelry; Demeter, goddess of agriculture, sister of Zeus, by whom she had a daughter Persephone, who was abducted by Hades but finally compelled to live in the underworld for only three months a year—an arrangement that produced winter. In addition to these main gods and goddesses were innumerable local spirits of caves, springs, trees, mountains; there were the evil demons, gorgons, and sirens; the lovely nymphs, and the half-man, half-horse centaurs.

The mythology, the stories, the dealings between the gods and men are told chiefly by Homer in his *Iliad* and *Odyssey*. Hesiod and the other sources sometimes give variations on the Homeric accounts. For the present purpose, these will be omitted and attention centered on the Greek concept of the future life.

Little did the concept of the future life encourage morality, as in the conduct of Zeus. All people, good and bad alike, met the same fate in Hades. The only exceptions were a few heroes who were changed into demigods, and a few exceptionally wicked men who had perpetrated special crimes against the gods. For example, Tantalus killed his son Pelops, roasted the body, and served it to Zeus for dinner. For this crime Tantalus had to stand forever in water, which, when he was thirsty and stooped to drink, would recede and disappear; and when he reached up to pick fruit from branches near his head, a wind tantalizingly blew the branches out of reach. Another example is Sisyphus. Zeus had abducted Aegina, daughter of Asopus. Sisyphus told Asopus what had happened and where Zeus had taken his daughter. For this "crime" against Zeus, Sisyphus was condemned to roll a heavy stone up a hill; every time he got it near the top, it rolled down again. All other men descend at death to Hades.

Hades, however, is not a place of punishment. It is simply the abode of the dead, where, as Homer describes, "flit the shades of wornout men." Memory remains, but reason is extinct. No information about those still living trickles down. The dead do not even know whether their friends and family have died. Dismal darkness replaces the sunlight and joy of the upper world. Achilles, himself a king, remarked, after he arrived in Hades, that a menial position on earth was superior to that of a king in the underworld.

The Homeric religion is often pictured as one of happy enthusiasm in the vigorous game of life. The Greeks admired athletes and warriors; they lusted and reveled in drunken feasts; they admired beauty and produced triumphs of sculpture and architecture; and they celebrated their interests in song and story. They could be happy, however, only through deliberate thoughtlessness, for their religion gave them no hope. Death ended it all, and utter dreariness was their uniform fate.

B. Primitive religions. Earlier religions had not been any better. In the Homeric religion there was no fear of the gods. It is true that one had to make proper sacrifices to have a prosperous voyage or to receive some gift; one had to treat them with due respect and attend the public rites—but with ordinary precaution no one was going to get hurt. Contrariwise, the gods of the earlier religion, which lasted perhaps into the 6th cent., were malevolent spirits to be appeased. The practices of this religion continued on through antiquity even though their significance, with certain gruesome details altered, had been forgotten.

The Anthesteria, a three-day spring festival in honor of Dionysus, during which everyone got drunk, preserves elements of a placation of ghosts. One of the sacrifices of this festival is not offered to Dionysus at all; nor, unlike the usual Greek sacrifices, is it eaten by the people. Eating symbolizes either communion or identification with the god. The refusal to eat seems to indicate that the god, ghost, or spirit is being sent away. On the second day of this festival they chewed buckthorn, presumably to get rid of spirits; and a vase painting of the feast shows ghosts emerging from a *pithos*, which was ostensibly a wine jar, but it could have been a casket for the dead.

In the autumn the Eleusinian rites were celebrated. In connection with Hades' rape of Persephone, her mother Demeter in remote antiquity established her temple and worship in Eleusis (a town about 15 mi. W of Athens). These rites became immensely popular, waning only upon the advent of Christianity, but briefly revived by Julian the Apostate. It was a mystery religion, a secret society, forerunner of many similar secret religions of later times; and so well were the secrets guarded, by severe punishment and by devotion to Demeter, that very little is known of the details. A large part of the rites had to do with the purification of women. They washed suckling pigs in the ocean and threw them into a chasm. Sometime later the women dug up the decayed flesh, put it on the altar, and served it as a fertility charm. It is thought by some that in earlier days the women used their own babies instead of baby pigs.

Another evidence of an earlier savage religion is in the worship of Isis, which the Greeks took up at the beginning of the Christian era (see Osiris). Although a late importation into Greece, this Egyptian religion seems to have incorporated a much earlier, purely Greek ritual, in which the initiates stood under a slain bull on a scaffold and were baptized in its blood. After this baptism they ate the bull's flesh. Vase paintings seem to hint its origin in human sacrifice.

C. Mystery religions. Later history brought other forms of religion. With the defeat of the Persians at Salamis—a great victory for the Olympian deities—Homeric religion became more and more a purely civic and patriotic exercise. The gain in patriotism was a loss in religion. Classic worship did not stimulate morality: it had never held out the hope of eternal life, and personal interest and devotion were still further minimized.

At the same time, philosophy and science undermined belief in the myths: it was the clouds and not Zeus that produced rain; the sun was not a god, but a hot stone; and so on. Sophism, though refuted by Plato and Aristotle in the 4th cent., made that century an age of secular individualism. In the 3rd cent., credulity seemed to triumph.

Pure secularism could not satisfy the majority of the people. They were economically prosperous, but this prosperity came through the destruction of the Greek city-states at the hands of Alexander the Great. Rome later absorbed the whole territory. This development eradicated Zeus and patriotism, and left the individual in the hands of capricious Tyche (Luck), now deified. The situation stimulated the need for a more personal religion, and in such a climate mystery religions developed. Some of them may have been continuous with the early rites of fear, but they were so altered as to become

The Pythian oracle at the temple of Apollo was a popular pilgrimage site.

religions of hope. Such mysteries existed as early as 400 B.C.; Orphism and the Eleusinian mysteries existed in some form even earlier; but they began to proliferate in the century before Christ.

In general, these religions were secret societies whose mysteries (secrets) would guarantee a happy future life to their initiates. None of the mysteries included any concept of a RESURRECTION of the body, but in opposition to the idea of Hades they asserted the possibility of a blessed immortality.

Some were more moral than the usual Greek religion. Orphism, with its theory of the transmigration of souls, taught that wrong-doing is punished in this life, but if not, then in the future life. The Pythagoreans were a philosophic school and a religious brotherhood. One of their more moral principles was that of friendship, out of which came the story of Damon and Pythias. They also enforced a set of rules or taboos: members were not to eat beans, for earth spirits came up from below through the hollow stalks to reside in the beans; linen clothing, not woolen, was required; and they would not sit with the left leg crossed over the right. Chiefly, they held that salvation comes by KNOWLEDGE; this principle motivated their serious and principal work in mathematics.

D. Forms of worship. After the apostle PAUL looked around Athens, he remarked that the city was "very religious"; it even had an altar to an unknown god. Strabo agreed with the apostle, for his description of one locality is, "All the region is full of shrines of Artemis, Aphrodite, and the nymphs.... There are also many shrines of Hermes on the roads, and of Poseidon on the sea shore" (*Geogr.* 8.3.12).

There were more than 200 shrines in Athens. Besides the great TEMPLES — triumphs of architecture — many shrines were of modest construction, some without any roofed building, just stone altars in the open, or a post with the head of HERMES on it. There was no central religious authority, and the ritual at any one shrine had no definite connection with the others. One god had many local shrines, and he was worshiped under such different aspects of his nature and with such different traditions that he was hardly the same god from place to place.

The large temples were staffed with priests to care for them, to manage their wealth, and to regulate the dense traffic of state occasions. There were priests for lesser places; but there was no organized priesthood. No particular moral or educational qualifications were required of the priests; rather the qualification was a handsome physique. The office, at least in the larger temples, brought them honor and respect such that they could serve as ambassadors and emissaries in time of war.

The term of office was usually one year; sometimes it was held for life; sometimes, hereditary;

The 5th line of this Greek inscription found at Philippi refers to the new pythia. The related term *pythōn* is used with reference to the Philippian girl who had a spirit of divination (Acts 16:16).

sometimes the priest was selected by lot; sometimes the office was sold to the highest bidder. For many of the lesser shrines there was no priest at all; anyone, especially the father of a family, could offer his sacrifice by himself. Sacrifices were even offered at home: parts of the animal were burned on the hearth and the family ate the rest.

Even in the slaughter houses and butcher shops, such sacrifices were burned before the gods. For this reason, immature Christians refused to eat meat at banquets, suspecting it had been offered to idols (cf. 1 Cor. 8; see FOOD I.K; IDOLATRY). Before the sacrifices were burned, the worshipers examined the pieces, liver, and entrails; if they were firm and of good color, it was a propitious omen. DIVINATION was one of the most frequent features of Greek worship. In addition to the parts of the sacrificed animals, signs of the future were seen in the flight of birds, lightning from Zeus, eclipses, meteors, etc.

That Troy would be captured in the tenth year was indicated by a serpent devouring a sparrow and her eight young (*Iliad* 2.308). The use of natural events as signs declined from 400 B.C. on, and reliance was put on oracles, sacrifice, and astrology. For subsequent developments, see ROMAN RELIGION.

(See further J. Harrison, *Prolegomena to the Study of Greek Religion* [1903]; E. Caird, *The Evolution of Theology in the Greek Philosophers* [1904]; A. Fairbanks, *A Handbook of Greek Religion* [1910]; W. Jaeger, *Paideia* [1939]; M. P. Nilsson, *Greek Popular Religion* [1940]; id., *Greek Piety* [1948]; W. K. C. Guthrie, *The Greeks and Their Gods* [1951]; D. G. Rice and J. E. Stambaugh, *Sources for the Study of Greek Religion* [1979]; W. Burkert, *Greek Religion* [1985; a highly regarded introduction]; P. E. Easterling and J. V. Muir, eds., *Greek Religion and Society* [1985]; M. Grant and R. Kitzinger, eds., *Civilization of the Ancient Mediterranean: Greece and Rome*, 3 vols. [1988], 2:847–1025; T. Grantz, *Early Greek Myths: A Guide to Literary and Artistic Sources* [1998]; P. Cartledge, *The Cambridge Illustrated History of Ancient Greece* [1998], ch. 12.; H.-J. Klauck, *The Religious Context of Early Christianity: A Guide to Graeco-Roman Religions* [2000]; J. D. Mikalson, *Ancient Greek Religion* [2005]; D. Ogden, ed., *A Companion to Greek Religion* [2007].)

II. Greek philosophy. Greek PHILOSOPHY in general had little interest in Greek religion. The philosophic development, a minority movement in any age, is divided into three stages: the Pre-Socratics, whose chief interest was science; Plato and Aristotle, who attacked the problem of epistemology; and the Hellenistic age with its largely ethical emphasis.

A. The Pre-Socratics. Pre-Socratic philosophy began with Thales, a resident of MILETUS in Ionia, who predicted the solar eclipse of 28 May 585 B.C., and so imposed scientific law on hitherto unorganized observations. He and his fellow Milesians, Anaximander and Anaximenes, though they differed on minor details, agreed on the following five universal principles: (1) all things have emerged from a single underlying substance; (2) this substance is eternal: it never came into being and will never cease to be; (3) the substance is inexhaustible, probably infinitely extended in space; (4) our immediate world or cosmos is limited in space and in duration, but other worlds preceded it and will follow upon its dissolution (it is doubtful that the Milesians asserted the existence of many worlds at one time); (5) motion, the processes of nature, the constant change in all things, is spontaneous—the substance is not dead, but alive, and the impetus to change is immanent in it rather than the effect of an extraneous cause.

The assertion of one substance leads to a problem that plagued antiquity and has not been satisfactorily answered to this day. If all things originate from one substance, each thing must or at least can turn into anything else. Observation shows that the bread we eat becomes both hair and fingernails, or, more generally, wheat can become man, dog, and donkey. Water can become fire—the wood of a tree has come from water, and wood burns—and earth can become air. For example, lead comes from uranium, whose properties are far different. How can the existence of qualitative differences be explained, especially if basically everything is the same stuff?

Thales seems to have appealed merely to observation: water becomes steam or air as it changes into fire, and the fire in the lightning turns to rain. This really leaves little basis for Thales' view that water is the cosmic substance and that fire, air, and earth are derivatives. Anaximander made all four derivatives from an unobservable "boundless" substance. It was a stuff in which the qualities of earth, air, fire, and water were so mingled that it had no quality of its own. The process by which the ordinary "elements" with their qualities came from the boundless was a whirling motion, somewhat similar to that of a cream separator.

Anaximenes, the last of the Milesians, identified air as the original substance (because water and earth fall, but air supports itself), and explained the emergence of qualities by condensation and rarefaction. Thus the concept of a natural, mechanical law is the contribution these first philosophers made to civilization.

Heraclitus (c. 525–475 B.C.) lived near Miletus in EPHESUS. His attention was not focused on the generation of qualities, as in later philosophies, but on the fundamental problem of motion itself. If the cosmic substance changes spontaneously, then change is universal: "all things flow" and "no man can step into the same river twice." On the second stepping the river would not be the same because the water would not be the same, and even the bed and banks would have eroded somewhat. Since the river is its bed, banks, and water, therefore nothing remains the same.

This applies to persons too. A man cannot step twice because he is not the same man: "In the same rivers we step and we do not step; we are and we are not." Thus persons and things do not exist; for when we say that something exists, we mean that it does not change, it stands still, it remains what it is and does not become something else. If it is blue and two inches wide, it stays blue and two inches wide. But if everything is in motion, then blue must change, and every quality and dimension is becoming different. Therefore nothing exists.

However, although everything changes, there is one thing that does not change—only it is not a "thing." There is a *law* of change that does not change. Heraclitus called it the LOGOS. The Greek words bear two meanings, so that Heraclitus's sentence can be translated either as "This theory, always true, men do not understand," or as "This Logos, always existing, men do not understand."

If a law be considered a reality, what becomes of the view that the only reality is a single, physical, cosmic stuff? Can *corporeal monism* admit the reality of an incorporeal law? This question Heraclitus in his own day could not understand. He identified the basic substance as fire and at the same time gave it the characteristics of a directing intelligence: "Wisdom is one thing: to understand the mind that governs all things through all"; and "the thunderbolt directs the course of all things"; and "this cosmos, the same for all, none of the gods or men has made, but it always was and is and ever shall be an ever-living fire, kindled in measures and extinguished in measures." Unable to distinguish, Heraclitus confused physical fire with a mechanical law of measurement, and both with a directing mind, which men today would say is neither a law nor a body. Thus problems multiplied and philosophy developed.

The Pythagoreans (alluded to in the section on Greek religion) formed a school in southern Italy about this time and continued all through antiquity. They were mathematicians. Pythagoras himself, a contemporary of Heraclitus, is said to have discovered what we now know as the Pythagorean theorem (the square of the hypotenuse of a right-angled triangle equals the sum of the squares of the other two sides). Without their geometry, astronomy would not have been able to make much headway. Their headway was considerable, for Eratosthenes about 300 B.C. measured the circumference of the earth with an accuracy about just one per cent off modern measurements (he and many others in the ancient world realized that the earth is not flat).

Parmenides (c. 475 B.C.), the chief member of the Eleatic school in Elea, southern Italy, addressed himself directly to the difficulties in Heraclitus and corporeal monism. Parmenides had been preceded by the poet Xenophanes (c. 590–500 B.C.?), who attacked the stupidity and impiety of Greek polytheism. He insisted that there was but one God. Parmenides, not so religious, asserted merely that there is One. He was troubled by a contradiction and therefore an absurdity in previous philosophy. How can a true monist assert a pluralism? How can one thing be another? How can a rational theory be irrational?

Thales had said fire is water, and Heraclitus said water is actually fire, but "pure" logic shows clearly that fire means and can only be fire, nothing else. To say that fire is water is like saying a square is a circle. Not only so, but worse, Parmenides denied that water is water. Undoubtedly the two instances of water have the same meaning, but the word *is* denotes existence. Therefore the sentence means water is an existence. If fire cannot be water because the two words do not have the same meaning, water cannot *exist* because the two words mean different things. It is false that water is water, because it is false that water is. Water does not exist.

What, then, exists? Only that which can be asserted without contradiction or absurdity. Therefore only the existent is existent, or, Being is. Being cannot have originated or come into being. It cannot have come from nonbeing, for nonbeing never has existed for anything to come from it. Nor can Being have come from Being, for Being is Being without any coming. Therefore origination is impossible and Being is eternal, immutable, and changeless. And if Being is changeless, there can be no motion. The earlier philosophies contradicted themselves by asserting both unity and motion, both one body and many differences, both identity and change.

Parmenides could not divest himself of the common notion that reality is corporeal. His one Being therefore was a solid, spherical, homogeneous body. Admittedly men see fire, water, and their differences; they see motion and change, but when they see rabbits jumping out of a hat or a man climbing a rope hanging from nothing, they *know* it is not so. Sensation must submit to reason. Absurdities cannot be true.

The Pluralists, however, could not repudiate sensation. There is a world of many different things; and if corporeal monism is absurd, let us retain motion, reject monism, and assert corporeal pluralism. This can be done in three ways. Empedocles (c. 490–430 B.C.) asserted that there were four elements: earth, air, fire, and water. Their basic qualitative differences are eternal, and the problem of their origination—either from a boundless or from one of them considered as original—is sidestepped. Other differences were somehow to be explained by chemical combinations. The theory of a finite number of qualitatively different elements was much later adopted by 19th-cent. chemistry. Empedocles could not, however, totally ignore the threat of Parmenides. Each element and each atom must be eternal and unchangeable like the Parmenidean Being. If so, motion is no longer spontaneous; matter, no longer alive, is inherently inert, and extraneous moving forces are necessary—two forces, Love and Hate, one to cause mixture and combination, the other to cause dissolution.

Anaxagoras immediately saw that one moving force was sufficient, for every mixing is a separation from previous combinations. Then too, whereas Empedocles was clumsy in clarifying the distinction between inert, corporeal elements and the newly assumed principles of motion, Anaxagoras described his single principle as a mind, totally separate from matter, the wise director of the cosmos. After all, if men's minds direct their bodies, why should not a universal mind direct the Universe? As Socrates complained later on, however, Anaxagoras had difficulty in carrying through this

Bust of Socrates (c. 470–399 B.C.), considered the intellectual father of Hellenistic philosophy. Roman copy after a lost Greek original from the 4th cent. B.C.

part of his theory and never really transcended the mechanistic position.

Empedocles also had made a second mistake that Anaxagoras corrected. It may be good to assume four original qualitative differences, but four are not enough. Since Parmenides had shown that origination is irrational, a philosopher to be a pluralist must assume that every quality is original and eternal. Hence, instead of earth, air, fire, and water, the elements are hair, blood, fingernails, wood, bone, and so on to infinity.

If an infinite number of original qualities seems awkward, and if four are not enough, there is only one other possibility for atomistic pluralism: an infinite number of atoms, of all shapes and sizes, but without any qualities at all. Democritus (c. 460–370 B.C.), a native of Abdera in Thrace, with Leucippus, produced the classic theory of atomism. Each atom is impenetrable and indivisible, the characteristics are purely mechanical or geometrical. Qualities such as hot and cold, wet and dry, do not exist in reality: they are subjective effects of mechanical action in the organs of sensation. For example, if in a compound body the smooth surfaces of the atoms are on the exterior, we receive a sensation of coolness when we touch it; but if the points and sharp edges of the atoms are on the surface, our sensation is one of heat. The atoms themselves are neither cold nor hot, blue nor red, bitter nor sweet, and so on.

Democritus found it unnecessary to posit a moving principle. Each atom moves when and because another atom hits it. There is no point asking what started the first atom on its first motion. There is no first atom and there never was a first motion. However, whereas neither mind nor spontaneity is needed, Democritus, to explain motion, had to invent the concept of empty space. If all space were completely filled with solid atoms, none of them could budge. The Ionians did not need empty space, for their cosmic stuff was alive and nonatomic. Parmenides, too, had virtually equated empty space with nothing, for only body is real. Empedocles and Anaxagoras had not yet seen the implications of pluralism. So the credit for this concept belongs to Democritus, although the later philosophers did not regard it as much of a credit.

The pre-Socratic period, with its scientific interests, may be said to end with the destructive arguments of Zeno, the Eleatic, a disciple of Parmenides. First, the clever story of Achilles and the tortoise proves that motion is impossible. Reduced to its bare, essential mathematics, it argues that for an atom to move to a far point, it must first traverse half the distance; before it can get half way, it must go a quarter way; and before it arrives at the quarter mark, it must arrive at the eighth mark. To start at all, it must exhaust this inexhaustible infinite series; therefore it cannot start. And therefore motion is impossible. Similarly, at any moment of an arrow's alleged flight, it is at rest because its extremities coincide with two points in empty space. But since the flight takes place wholly within a series of moments, the arrow is always at rest and never moves.

Also, sensation is impossible. When an ocean wave "thunders" against the rocks, no atom produces an audible sensation; but the wave is nothing but atoms, therefore it produces no sound. Finally, if there must be space for an atom to exist in, there must be a superspace for space to exist in, and a super-superspace. It would be better never to start such a useless series. Pluralism is refuted.

B. The age of Plato and Aristotle. This new period was introduced by the Sophists. The reaction of these men to the failure of atomism explains why science receded in importance and epistemology became the pressing problem. The early pre-Socratic attempt to give a rational account of the universe failed because Parmenides had shown that corporeal monism is absurd. Zeno had shown that corporeal pluralism is absurd, but if one body cannot furnish an explanation, and if many bodies cannot, and since there must be either one body or many, it follows that the universe cannot be explained at all. Knowledge is impossible. This skeptical conclusion is supported by the Pythagorean theorem. Further study of this early triumph in geometry revealed the existence of irrational numbers, such as the square root of two. If irrationality is embedded in pure mathematics, surely any further knowledge is impossible.

Ordinary Greeks had always acknowledged certain moral truths as well. The murder of parents was wrong—everyone knew that; and so was the neglect of funeral rites, and so on. But the Persian wars had acquainted the Greeks with a foreign code of conduct, the old Greek morality began to break down, and soon no one could know any ethical truth. All knowledge is impossible. If knowledge is impossible, there is no use wasting time on mathematics, astronomy, or ethical principles. A wise man must renounce the life of the intellect and exercise his volition. The problem is to set a goal and achieve it.

The more ordinary Sophists therefore gave lectures in vocational education. They taught navigation or wrestling. The name Sophist, with its evil connotation of making the worse argument appear the better one, got its reputation because most ambitious young men wanted to be instructed in politics. Therefore the Sophists taught the devices of oratory, the knack of swaying audiences and gaining votes. Neither the personal aim nor the political policy is subject to intellectual ethical principles. Simply willing it, or, better, achieving it, makes it right.

There were two outstanding Sophists who, though they may have taught oratory to young politicians, also reflected on the more profound philosophical aspects of their practice. Gorgias, with an Eleatic background, taught that (1) nothing exists; (2) if anything existed, no one could know it; and (3) if anyone could know it, he could not teach it to someone else. Protagoras, with a Heraclitean background, accepted the threefold proposition that (1) all things constantly change; (2) knowledge, since men do not wish to discard the word, is perception; and (3) "man is the measure of all things, of the existence of the things that are and the nonexistence of the things that are not."

The man-measure theory meant that everything is as it appears, no matter to whom. A wind is chilling to a person with a fever; the "same" wind feels exhilarating to someone in good health. It is not the same wind because a wind is an appearance due to the combination of certain external motions and one's sensory organs. The wind is the perception. Since two people cannot have the same sensation, for my toothache is not yours, two people never sense the same thing. Each person lives in a separate world of his own perceptions. Therefore whatever someone thinks is true, that is true for that person, and no one else can judge. This is the theory of relativism, the denial of fixed, eternal truth. This theory was resurrected by William James and John Dewey, pushed to extremes by French existentialism, accepted widely in American education, and taken to further extremes in postmodern thinking. So if Plato can make a pertinent reply, his usefulness cannot be said to have ended in antiquity.

Plato, interested in mathematics, science, and very particularly in ethics and politics, was obliged therefore to defend, first of all, the possibility of knowledge. His preliminary answer to Sophism was that it is self-contradictory. Since Protagoras holds that all beliefs are true, and since many people believe that Protagoras's theory is false, their belief must be true and Protagoras must admit the falsity of his own position. Or, again, if everything is constantly changing and nothing remains fixed, then, as blue does not remain blue and chilling does not remain chilling, neither can seeing remain seeing nor perception perception; from which it follows that if perception is knowledge, it immediately changes into "not-knowledge." The key to the situation and the great absurdity is that in this view everything is relative *except relativism*. There is no fixed truth except the fixed truth that nothing is fixed. Relativism is always asserted absolutely.

Finally, Protagoras had located sensation in the sense organ, so that one eye could sense and know, when the other was closed and could not know. But, replies Plato, this reduces man to a wooden horse of Troy: one soldier sees out of one eye, another does not see out of the opposite ear. Man, however, is not such an aggregate of separate senses. It is the person who senses, not the eye or the ear. The senses unite in one power, the soul or the mind, and it is this power that uses the organs. The eye cannot see a sound and the ear cannot hear a color; but the man perceives both the color and the sound, compares them, and judges that they are different. This is what the horse of Troy could never do.

At this stage of the argument, Plato makes his great, constructive contribution. When corporeal monism met its fate at the hands of Parmenides, the pluralists thought that the fault lay in the monism. When Zeno exploded pluralism, the Sophists gave up hope of rationality. Plato's genius saw another possibility. If neither corporeal monism nor corporeal pluralism can explain the universe, the fault must lie in corporealism. Reality cannot be material. Or, conversely, if knowledge is to be possible, there must be a noncorporeal reality.

In the refutation of Protagoras, Plato had asserted the existence of a soul or mind, necessary to judge disparate sensations. This soul is, of course, incorporeal. Knowledge also requires incorporeal objects for the soul to know. Plato calls these objects Ideas, and his early dialogues explain at length why such objects must exist.

The easiest argument to understand is the one based on the occurrence of common qualities. There is a very small steel cube; here are two ivory dice; here are some blocks that children play with. We call them all cubes. What then is *cube*? If it were one of the physical objects, the others would not be cubes because the others are not that one. If cube were the aggregate of all of them, none of them would be a cube because none is the aggregate. Furthermore, all these cubes could be destroyed, but Cube would remain. Hence Cube cannot be a physical thing; it is an eternal, unchangeable, supersensible object of thought. It is a single, unique Idea, whereas the physical objects are a plurality. So it is with all common qualities. When two or more objects are similar, the similarity is real. It is something that exists: there *is* such a similarity, but these realities are not bodies.

A second argument is that thought and science require such an object. A geometer does not study this one triangle drawn on the blackboard. A physician does not study this one case of measles. The object of geometry is Triangle, and the object of medicine is Health. There are many drawn triangles, of all sizes, equilateral, isosceles, and scalene; but there is only one, definite Idea of triangularity. If a particular triangle drawn on a blackboard were the Idea of triangle and the object of knowledge, then knowledge would disappear when it was erased, for knowledge cannot be knowledge of the nonexistent. To know means to know something. To know nothing means not to know. Hence Ideas exist.

Since Ideas are not sensory objects that can be seen with the eyes, Plato must answer the inescapable question how they can be known. His example is the Idea of equality. When a person sees two peas in a pod or two pebbles on a beach, he carelessly says they are equal. Stopping to think, he knows well enough that they are not exactly equal. It would be better to say they approximate equality. This example shows, first, that the concept of equality cannot be abstracted from experience because equality is never found in experience; and, second, that men actually know equality before they have ever seen two pebbles. They must have known equality before their first experience because at that time they are ready to use the concept in judging that the two pebbles are not equal but approximate equality. Men have to have the concept before they can use it as a norm in judging.

True enough, as youngsters, men may never have consciously thought of equality until the moment they saw the pebbles. At that moment the pebbles remind them of an equality they know without ever having sensed it. Since sensation begins at birth, it follows that before birth men's souls must have existed in the Ideal world where they were in contact with all the Ideas. What is ordinarily called learning is therefore reminiscence. As the lyre of Simmias reminded men of Simmias, although it does not look like him, so the two pebbles, though not strictly equal, remind people of the absolute equality they previously knew but had as youngsters forgotten.

The soul therefore is immortal. It existed before birth and continues to live after death. Because of the soul's immortality and because the Ideas—Ideas of Justice, Temperance, Piety—are immutable, one can reject the relativistic ethics of the Sophists. Knowledge is possible; ethical knowledge can be taught as well as geometry; and both are valid at all times and in all places.

Since intellect and truth have displaced Sophism's unbridled will, the good life is not a life of pleasure, but of knowledge. Pleasures rivet the soul to the body and the body is a tomb (*sōma sēma*, an old Orphic adage of ascetic tendency). The philosopher detaches himself from sensation as much as possible and prepares for pure communion with the Ideas after death. In the *Phaedo*, a relatively early or middle dialogue, Plato is moderately ascetic. In the late dialogue *Philebus*, he recognizes that some pleasures are harmless and even necessary to life. Their admission into the good life, however, is strictly controlled by intellect, knowledge, and truth.

Having thus solved the problem of knowledge and ethics, Plato returned to cosmology. His mathematical physics, his astronomy (in the *Timaeus*), and his invention of the eight-note scale, cannot be reproduced here, nor his adoption of a heliocentric theory later perfected by Aristarchus; but the relation he envisaged between God and the world needs mention. The supreme Being, to which nothing is superior or equal, is the world of Ideas. These Ideas—of Equality, Courage, Man, and so on—are not merely an ordered series of concepts. They are indeed an ordered system, with the Idea of Good in the highest position, on which all other Ideas depend for existence and in whose light alone men can know them. Beyond the status of ordered concepts, the world of Ideas is a living mind. The relatively late dialogue *Sophist* gives the arguments, and the conclusions are further worked out by the Neoplatonists.

Modern students, who have been taught to believe that the world is basically an aggregate of inanimate atoms, must be reminded that in ancient times and even in modern times this has been the minority view. Most philosophers—Hegel and Leibniz, the Stoics and Plato—have held that the universe is a living being. It is all the more natural to conceive of the world of Ideas as a mind. Independently and eternally existing, yet lower in rank than the Ideas, is "God," or the Demiurge, the personal Maker of heaven and earth. The Demiurge is confronted with another independent and eternal being, or rather nonbeing, namely, chaotic space. Since the Demiurge is good and devoid of envy, he wishes to make space good too. To this end he fashions a world-soul and through it produces the visible world here below by using the world of Ideas as a model, or blueprint, and imposing its order on space or matter.

The visible world, therefore, like the world of Ideas, is a living being. Note also that it is not created, as the Hebrew-Christian view has it, but is made out of preexisting stuff. Whereas a particular fashioning may occur at a definite time, the process, as explained below, is without beginning or end. Unfortunately space is inherently recalcitrant. It cannot be made perfect; that is, neither Equality nor Justice, not even Horse and Man, can be perfectly exemplified here below. What is still worse, in a sort of rebellion, the world collapses at intervals and needs to be remade. Thus cosmological history is cyclical as all natural processes are. World follows world, reincarnation follows reincarnation, as day follows night, forever.

Aristotle (384–322 B.C.) was Plato's student but not Plato's disciple. The great difference was carried over into Christian theology, for as Augustine's tendencies, dominant until A.D. 1250, were Platonic, so Thomas Aquinas eventually succeeded in making Aristotelianism the official philosophy of Roman Catholicism. The intricate detail of Aristotle's work is enormous and in many ways admirable. His theory of the syllogism, with perhaps only one alteration in the Middle Ages, was not carried further until A.D. 1850. He wrote several volumes of zoological observations. The eight books on *Physics* define motion with its several species, discuss time, place, and infinity, and propose a theory of a finite universe. The work concludes with the ponderous cosmological proof of the existence of the

Prime Mover, or God, who sits on the circumference of the heavens, blissfully ignorant of the world below.

Aristotle was as greatly opposed to skepticism and sophism as Plato was; but he thought that a world of Ideas beyond the visible world was redundant, that reminiscence of a previous life contradicted the testimony of man's consciousness, and that sensation was a satisfactory basis for higher forms of knowledge. Therefore he asserted that the primary realities are physical individuals, such as Socrates and Mount Olympus. These primary realities are objects of perception, and all learning comes through sensation.

Strictly speaking, people do not see, hear, or touch other people. They see colors, hear sounds, and touch the hard or the soft. These are the special senses and the special sensibles. Some sensations come through two senses: people see and touch magnitude, shape, number, rest, and motion. Beyond the special senses is a *common sense*, common at least to sight and touch, and five common sensibles. By this common sense, persons also compare disparate sensations, for comparison requires the two objects to be presented to a single judge; and as these objects are perceived by sense, the judge must be a sense—not any special sense, but the common sense. Moreover, the perception of the primary realities is "accidental." Higher forms of knowledge, however, transcend sensation and primary realities. There are secondary realities—species or concepts. Socrates is only one of several men seen, and there are other mountains besides Mount Olympus. The common quality in all men or all mountains is the species or concept. It is as unchangeable as a Platonic Idea, but it is not learned in the Platonic manner.

Briefly, the learning process begins in sensation, upon which follow memory images. From these images, the intellect by a process of abstraction detaches the concept, the secondary reality, the definition of the species. This concept or form can be abstracted because it is embedded in the sensory matter, rather than existing independently in an Ideal world. The intellect that does the abstracting is really two intellects. First, there is the passive intellect. As the sense organ requires the stimulation of a sense object before there is any sensation, so there must first be an object of thought before there can be any thinking. Unlike the sense organ, however, which has various corporeal qualities of its own, the mind before it thinks is actually nothing. If it had qualities, these, like colored glasses, would distort the objects of thought, in which case man could never have accurate knowledge. When the mind thinks, it receives the qualities, or better, it receives the object it thinks and thus becomes the object it thinks.

Corresponding to this passive intellect which becomes all things is the active intellect that makes all things. One might suppose that the intellectual objects themselves would stimulate the mind and raise it from possibility to actuality—but no: as color must be actualized by light before it can be sensed, so the active intellect must disengage the concepts or forms from their corporeal matrix and thus actualize them for reception into the passive intellect. Aristotle further says: "it is this [active] intellect which is separable and impassive and unmixed, being in its essential nature an activity.... This intellect has no intermittance in its thought. It is, however, only when separated that it is its true self; and this, its essential nature, is alone immortal and eternal. But we do not remember [the activity of this intellect before our birth] because this [active intellect] is impassive, while the intellect which can be affected is perishable and without this does not think at all" (*De anima* 3.5, 430^{a}17–25).

When Aristotle in another place asserts that the active intellect enters a human being "from without," commentators wonder whether or not the eternal, active intellect is God. In the Middle Ages the Mohammedan philosopher Averroës made this identification and therefore denied individual immortality. Thomas Aquinas had an individual intellect for each person and so tried to support belief in a future life. In any case, Aristotle's theory hardly fits into Christian doctrine, for even on Thomas's interpretation his active intellect is eternal, not merely immortal, and has therefore existed as long as God himself.

Something more must be said about abstraction. So far only the concepts of man and mountain have been actualized. People who lived their life on great plains might never get the concept of mountain; but there are other concepts so basic that without them a person could not think at all. These concepts are called the categories. The word *category*, in Greek as well as in ordinary English, means simply a classification. In philosophy, however, it means the fundamental, inescapable classifications. Whereas Parmenides identified the verb *is* with the meaning of "exist," Aristotle insisted that there are ten different meanings of this verb.

These nine categories are: substance, quantity, quality, relation, and five others that are not discussed at much length. Substance or reality, primary and secondary, has already been mentioned. Quantity, quality, and relation are supposed to be quite distinct, though Aristotle's arguments do not seem conclusive — and if they are not, the system is seriously defective. At any rate, these concepts are the result of further abstraction, and therefore, unlike the Kantian categories, are empirically based.

Beyond this Aristotle must establish the fundamental principles of the various sciences. First of all, the law of contradiction is the law of all being. It is an ontological law and not merely a law of thought; it is a law of thought because it is first a law of being. While this law covers all subjects, each science has in addition its own fundamental laws, without which it could not be kept separate from other sciences. No one of these laws can be so restricted as to cover only a part of a science, nor so general and remote as to combine uncombinable subjects. Geometrical truths, for example, cannot be demonstrated on arithmetical principles. Thus the ideal of a single all-inclusive science is excluded. Today one wonders how Aristotle would explain analytic geometry, not to mention cybernetics, or the contemporary reduction of chemistry to physics. He is honest enough, however, to say, "It is hard to be sure whether one knows or not, for it is hard to be sure whether one's knowledge is based on the principles of each genus or not; and it is precisely this that constitutes knowledge" (*Posterior Analytic* 1.9, 76^{a}26).

After manifold sensations, memory, and wide experience, the intellect abstracts the fundamental laws. This is the process of induction and intuition; and although the processes of opinion and calculation are sometimes mistaken, intuition is foolproof and unfailingly accurate. It is consoling to know that at least part of the time people cannot possibly be mistaken, even if they cannot be sure what part of the time it is.

The most direct contact of Aristotle's philosophy with Christian theology is in his cosmological proof of the existence of God. The argument is extremely intricate; only its general character can be indicated in a brief statement of its five stages. First, motion is eternal: it never began and will never end. Second, since motion presupposes a mover, there must be a single, eternal mover. Third, this eternal cause of motion cannot itself be in motion. Fourth, the unmoved Mover has no magnitude. And fifth, "The mover must of necessity be situated at the center or on the circumference, for these are the principles of a sphere. Now, the things that move most rapidly are those nearest the mover. Since, then, the rotation of the outer sphere is the quickest motion, there is where the mover must be" (*Physics* 8.10, 267^{b}6).

C. The Hellenistic age. After Plato and Aristotle, when Alexander extinguished the independence of the Greek city-states, and with the rise of Roman influence, came the Hellenistic age (see HELLENISM). As the Pre-Socratics had been interested in science, and Plato and Aristotle in epistemology, the Hellenistic age thought it time to emphasize ethics. The schools of the EPICUREANS and the STOICS arose about 300 B.C.

Although ethics presupposes that the epistemological problem has been solved, these schools emphatically rejected the Platonic solution and agreed with Aristotle only on the point that knowledge is based on sensation. They even defended the possibility of knowledge in their own way. Both Epicureanism and Stoicism continued in existence for over five centuries, but they had less and less success in persuading philosophers that they possessed the secret of knowledge. The Epicureans were widely despised, and Stoicism faced difficult criticism. Neither did the school of Aristotle conquer the world; rather it went into eclipse. Plato's Academy turned skeptical. If any philosophy can be said to have surpassed the other at this time, it was skepticism.

A skeptical school was founded by Pyrrho about 300 B.C., continued by Arcesilaus (315–240), who was actually a Platonist, then by the brilliant

Carneades (219–129), by the relatively insignificant Agrippa (who made, however, an excellent summary of the arguments c. A.D. 100), and finally by Sextus Empiricus a century later. The Stoics had asserted the occurrence of a sensory impression so clear and distinct that its veracity could not be doubted. Carneades replied that there is no specific difference discernible among impressions. Dreams and illusions, while they last, are as vivid and convincing as sensations. Furthermore, since people cannot distinguish between twins, it is clear that two different objects can produce the same impression. If knowledge is based on sensation, as the Stoics say, there is no sure knowledge.

Aenesidemus, about the beginning of the Christian era, added that the sense organs of animals differ from those of human beings: dogs receive different odors; birds, different sounds; and flies receive visual impressions different from ours. Why should we assume that our sensations are more accurate pictures of reality than those of the animals? Indeed, animal lovers emphasize the greater acuity of their humble friends. Agrippa reduced the skeptical arguments to five basic points, which emphasize the logical difficulties of nonskeptical philosophies. First, opinions differ on all subjects. Second, to prove the truth of one opinion, philosophers have recourse to a second, and so on ad infinitum. Third, to escape this regress, they go around in a circle. Fourth, they make an assumption, which only begs the question. Finally, all objects are relative to the subject, as Aenesidemus so clearly showed, and hence nothing can be known as it really is by itself.

If knowledge is unattainable, what becomes of ethics and the daily decisions of life? One rule of action adopted by skepticism was, "It makes no difference." One day a skeptic, about to cross a road, jumped back to avoid a four-horse chariot. A friend chided him on his inconsistency: he should not have jumped out of the path of the chariot because it made no difference. "But," replied the skeptic, "that is why I jumped back—it made no difference."

Sextus Empiricus tried to accommodate skepticism to the needs of living. Anticipating pragmatism and John Dewey, he held that the senses were made, not for knowledge, but for use; and when people are hungry they should eat. If someone objects that a statement such as this, relative to the purpose of sensation, purports to be knowledge, Sextus replies that adherence to such principles must be motivated, not by reflection, but by a conscious lack of reflection. Medical theories founded on cosmology are worthless, but empirical medicine can cure disease. Without claiming to know anything, people can formulate practical rules and become proficient—not in science, but in art. Medicine is an art; man did not learn it, he practiced it. Man is a doer, not a knower.

The reaction against skepticism and against Stoicism became prominent and effective with the work of the Neoplatonist Plotinus (A.D. 205–270). Neoplatonism, previously thought to have originated with Plotinus's teacher, Ammonius Aaccus, can be found in the generation that followed Plato. Not only are characteristic Neoplatonic themes found in Speusippus and Xenocrates, the first and second presidents of the Academy after Plato, but Aristotle himself gives, even if mistakenly, a Neoplatonic interpretation of Plato. Nevertheless, it was not until Plotinus wrote six books of nine tractates each, the *Enneades*, that Neoplatonism displaced all the other schools of antiquity.

The weak point in Stoicism, by reason of which the skeptics could so greatly embarrass them, was their empiricism and materialism. Even apart from the skeptics, the Stoics themselves were troubled to give a corporeal explanation to the incorporeal phenomena of meaning or significance, space, and time. Because these difficulties had become acute, the time was propitious for Plotinus to insist that knowledge presupposes spiritual realities.

In one of the first tractates he wrote (*Enn.* 4.7, "On the Immortality of the Soul"), Plotinus rejects the Epicurean atomic soul, the Stoic wax soul, the behavioristic theory of harmony, and the Aristotelian form of the organic body—then puts in their place a pure spiritual being. Briefly, the arguments are that life cannot be explained as an arrangement of inanimate particles, for an arrangement requires a prior arranging mind. Further, if a soul were a material quantity and could be split into inanimate parts, the phenomenon of multiple births could not be explained; each pup of a litter of puppies is a complete dog, he does not have half a soul or part of a soul, but an entire and integral soul. The characteristic of a soul is to remain essentially the same through infinite division, to be entire at every point, to have the derivative part equal to the whole, and this is the characteristic not of body but of incorporeal spirit.

Plotinus analyzes sensation to support the same point. Perception requires the presence of the whole object in the entire unitary soul. If the soul were not unitary but extended, it would be impossible to judge that the perceived color white is different from the perceived taste sweet. Thought even more clearly than perception requires an incorporeal soul. Even the materialistic Stoics admit that human beings can think of empty space and conceptual meaning. No material soul could grasp these immaterial realities.

Seemingly the discussion envisages an individual soul, like that of Socrates. If, however, the essential characteristic of soul is to remain the same and be entire at every point; and if all souls are one in species, as the Platonic argument on common qualities requires; and if, finally, a philosopher is bound to assert the unity of the universe—it follows that all souls must unite in a single world-Soul. Although Plotinus investigates psychology in great detail, he does not use this material to build up an empirical argument to prove the existence of a world-Soul. For this purpose, general Platonic principles are sufficient. He does show how the presupposition of a world-Soul accounts for psychological details, and he thus escapes opposing objections.

One of these objections is that if your soul and my soul are one soul, then I would feel your toothache. Plotinus replies that a single soul in two bodies gives two different combinations, so that unitary Humanity moves when I move but is simultaneously at rest in you. Hence two people will have different impressions, though their soul is one. An analogy is found in a single person when the left hand does not feel the pain the right hand feels. In this case, the soul is entire and complete in each hand, but the impressions are different. So, also, with different persons.

A question arises why the world-Soul, so superior to the human soul, descends and contaminates itself by entering people's bodies and becoming their souls. The answer is that the existence of the world presupposes some principle of duality; the Soul is inherently productive; therefore it descends of necessity and produces human souls and the world that lies even below us. This descent is not all loss, for the Soul's contact with the sensible world heightens its appreciation of the intelligible realm.

Above the Soul is the Divine Mind, or World of Ideas. Were there no such mind, an explanation of human intelligence would be impossible. On occasion people withdraw themselves from the insistent sense impressions and impetuous desires of everyday life and give themselves over to the calm subject of geometry or some deeper philosophical reflection. They may even go beyond reflection and enjoy the beauty of union with the divine. Here human beings are in the realm of Ideas, far above the level of perception.

Stressing the viewpoint of Plato's *Sophist*, Plotinus makes it clear that the Ideas are not just a collection of hypostatized concepts, but are in truth a living mind. At this point, a modern student who has heard of Berkeleyan idealism, or a Christian who makes God's decree dependent on God's activity of thinking, must take care not to misunderstand Plotinus. "Not by its thinking movement does movement arise. Hence it is an error to call the Ideas intellections in the sense that upon an intellectual act in this principle one such Idea or another is made to exist" (*Enn*. 5.9.7). Mind and its objects are not different, the latter inferior to the former: Mind *is* what it thinks.

Philosophy, however, since its purpose is to discover unity, cannot stop with the Mind or World of Ideas, because here duality still remains. There is a multiplicity of Ideas. In knowledge there are subjects and predicates. Unity requires a further ascent above and beyond duality, therefore beyond knowledge, to the ineffable One. Rational argument shows the need of postulating this One; but to be unified with it, man must leave reason behind and experience the One in a mystic vision.

Four times during the six years of Porphyry's study under him, Plotinus enjoyed this communion. This is a state in which ordinary consciousness is suspended. The soul no longer knows whether it has a body, and cannot tell whether it is a person, a living being, or anything real at all. Knowledge is somewhat like seeing sense objects on a cloudy day. In the vision a person sees the Source of the light that made knowledge possible and sees it directly in all its brilliance. This experience is not abnormal: it is the exercise of a faculty that all have but few use; he who has seen, says Plotinus, knows what I mean.

After Plotinus, Neoplatonism continued to the end of antiquity. Only one name, however, needs to be recorded—Proclus (A.D. 410–485). The future was to be in the hands of Christianity. Plotinus himself seems to have known nothing of orthodox Christianity, though he wrote one tractate against GNOSTICISM.

AUGUSTINE was rescued from the MANICHEANS and skepticism by Neoplatonic arguments. Because of this, he gave a Platonic slant to Christian theology, though as he matured in his Christian understanding, he dropped many Neoplatonic details as inconsistent with the Scripture. In the E, an unknown Christian writer appropriated a section of Proclus's writings. Working up two volumes of strong Neoplatonic and mystical cast, he issued them under the name of DIONYSIUS THE AREOPAGITE. This insured their acceptance during the superstitious Middle Ages, seducing even the brilliant Thomas Aquinas, and contributed to the development of pantheism (in John Scotus Erigena) and to a widespread vogue of mysticism. In A.D. 529, the emperor Justinian closed the moribund school, and thus Greek philosophy came to its end.

(See further A. E. Taylor *Plato: The Man and His Work* [1927]; P. Merlan, *From Platonism to Neoplatonism* [1953]; G. H. Clark, *Thales to Dewey* [1957]; W. K. C. Guthrie, *A History of Greek Philosophy* [1962–81]; A. A. Long, *Hellenistic Philosophy* [1974]; A. A. Long, ed., *The Cambridge Companion to Early Greek Philosophy* [1999]; J. A. Arieti, *Philosophy in the Ancient World: An Introduction* [2005]; M. Trapp, *Philosophy in the Roman Empire* [2007]. For Greek texts, translations, and commentary, see G. S. Kirk et al., *The Presocratic Philosophers: A Critical History with a Selection of Texts*, 2nd ed. [1984]; A. A. Long and D. N. Sedley, *The Hellenistic Philosophers*, 2 vols. [1987–89].) G. H. CLARK

Greek versions. See SEPTUAGINT.

green. A COLOR lying between blue and yellow in the visible spectrum; the hue characteristic of foliage. The English term is used to render a variety of words and expressions, such as Hebrew *yereq H3764*, a noun meaning "green [plant], verdure" (Gen. 1:30 et al.), and *raʿănān H8316*, an adjective with the sense "fresh, luxuriant" (Ps. 37:35 et al.). The Greek adjective *chlōros G5952* can be translated "green" (e.g., Mk. 6:39), but this term covers a wide range, including "pale green" or simply "pale" (cf. Rev. 6:8), "greenish-yellow," and even "yellow" (it can be applied to honey, for example). In Lk. 23:31, English idiom requires the translation "when the tree is green" (contrasted to "dry"), but the Greek adjective here, *hygros G5619*, properly means "wet, moist." K. L. BARKER

greet. To salute or welcome upon meeting a person or in a written communication. This English verb is found in the OT mainly as the rendering of the Hebrew expression *šāʾal lĕ-šālôm*, "to inquire about [someone's] welfare" (Exod. 19:7; Jdg. 18:15; 1 Sam. 10:4; et al.), although the verb *bārak H1385*, "to bless," can also be used in this way (e.g., 2 Ki. 4:29). The Hebrew noun *šālôm H8934* ("completeness, welfare, peace") is even today the conventional term for "Hello!" and can be used in a letter with the sense "Greetings!" (cf. Aram. *šĕlām H10720* in Ezra 4:17; it is in fact the standard expression in Semitic languages more generally, e.g., Arab. *salām*).

This usage is reflected in our Lord's instruction to his disciples. "When you enter a house, first say, 'Peace to this house'" (Lk. 10:5), and in Paul's use of *eirēnē G1645* at the beginning of his letters (Rom. 1:7 et al.). In Hellenistic times, the conventional way of beginning a letter was to use the infinitive of the verb *chairō G5897*, "to rejoice" (e.g., Acts 15:23; Jas. 1:1). Paul's unusual formula, "Grace [*charis G5921*] and peace," combines the Hebrew greeting with a Christianized form of the Greek salutation. In addition, the NT often uses the verb *aspazomai G832* ("to welcome kindly, greet," Matt. 5:47 et al.) and the cognate noun *aspasmos G833* ("greeting, salutation," 23:7 et al.). These terms in classical literature can also be used of physical expressions of welcome, such as "embrace" and "kiss." Greetings in the ANE and the Hellenistic age were typically accompanied by such signs of emotion (e.g., Gen. 27:26; Exod. 4:27; 1 Sam. 10:1; Lk. 7:38; Rom. 16:16).

greyhound. The KJV rendering of Hebrew *zarzîr motnayim H2435 + H5516*, an expression of uncertain meaning that occurs only once (Prov. 30:31; both NIV and NRSV translate it as "strutting rooster").

grief. This English term is used variously by Bible translations to render a large number of Hebrew words and expressions (e.g., *kaʿas H4088*, 1 Sam. 1:16 NIV, but NRSV "vexation"; conversely, Ps. 6:7 NRSV, but NIV "sorrow"). It occurs less frequently in the NT, usually as the rendering of Greek *lypē G3383* (e.g., Jn. 16:6; cf. also the cognate verb *lypeō G3382*, Matt. 17:23 et al.). Some have suggested that the biblical writers considered the emotions and attitudes only indirectly, and naturally focused attention on the external circumstances in human experience (cf. R. Bultmann in *TDNT*, 4:313–24). The *cause* of the grief was the true grief. Envisaging a world fallen in all detail and under the judgment of God (Gen. 3:16–17), their perspective went beyond analysis of personal feeling. Grief was related to the groaning in travail of the whole creation, as Paul expressed it (Rom. 8:22), which reflects a prevailing OT sentiment. Grief, however, was not simply punishment or a final state for man; by including the idea of suffering, it was related to the MESSIAH, who was to be the hope of redemption from the guilt indicated by the universal fact of grief (Isa. 53:4; cf. 35:10; 1 Pet. 1:3–7).

Contrary to the prevailing Greek practice of contrasting grief with pleasure, the NT makes grief and grace complementary (Jn. 16:20–21; Heb. 12:11). Paul contrasted a "godly grief" that leads through repentance to salvation with a "worldly grief" that produces death (2 Cor. 7:10 NRSV; NIV, "sorrow"). A spiritual notion of grief that includes various kinds of suffering (2 Cor. 4:8–10; 11:23–28; 12:10) also explains how the Christian is not necessarily hampered by the present course of suffering in life, but may by God's help transcend and transvaluate grief. In some passages (e.g., Jn. 16:20; Rom. 6:6; 2 Cor. 4:8; Gal. 6:14; Phil. 1:29; 3:10; Jas. 1:2; 1 Pet. 2:19), this pattern of grief in complementary relationship with grace can be discerned. See SUFFERING. T. M. GREGORY

griffon. See VULTURE.

grind. A procedure by which GRAIN was reduced to flour through being pulverized between two large stones (e.g., Heb. *ṭāḥan H3221*, Isa. 47:2; Gk. *alēthō G241*, Lk. 17:35). Small hand mills sometimes had holes in the center of the top stone through which the grain was poured (Matt. 24:41). Larger community mills were often powered by animals (Mk. 9:42). See MILL. R. K. HARRISON

grisled. An archaic term used by the KJV to render Hebrew *bārōd H1353*, meaning "spotted, mottled, dappled," and occurring in two passages that describe the appearance of goats and horses respectively (Gen. 31:10–11; Zech. 6:3, 6).

grove. This English term is found occasionally in modern versions with its usual sense of "orchard" (e.g., Deut. 6:11). In the KJV it is used (with one exception, Gen. 21:33) to render Hebrew *ʾăšērâ H895*, the name of a Canaanite goddess, ASHERAH (e.g., 1 Ki. 18:19), though the term occurs more frequently with reference to the wooden cult objects or "sacred poles" (NRSV) by which she was represented (Exod. 34:13 et al.; NIV, "Asherah poles"; the incorrect KJV rendering is based on the LXX, which has *alsos*). It is not always clear which of these two meanings is meant.

guarantee. See DEPOSIT; EARNEST; PLEDGE.

guard. A soldier or group of soldiers assigned to protect an important person or to keep watch over prisoners. In ancient times oriental monarchs had attached to their persons a body of picked men to protect them and carry out their wishes on important confidential matters. POTIPHAR, to whom the Midianites sold JOSEPH, was the captain of PHARAOH's guard, and NEBUZARADAN held the same position in NEBUCHADNEZZAR's BODYGUARD (Gen. 37:36; 41:10, 12; 2 Ki. 25:8; Jer. 52:12; the Heb. term used in these passages is *ṭabbāḥ H3184*, which also means "butcher" or "cook"). The men who formed the royal bodyguard were usually foreigners. DAVID had a corps of 600 foreign mercenaries, made up of KERETHITES and PELETHITES, of whom BENAIAH was the captain (2 Sam. 20:23).

They accompanied DAVID on his flight from ABSALOM (15:18), and formed SOLOMON's escort on the day he was crowned (1 Ki. 1:38, 44).

Members of the Israelite royal guard were known as "runners" (from Heb. *rûṣ H8132*). They appear in the reign of Saul (1 Sam. 22:17). Later, when Absalom and ADONIJAH attempted to seize the throne, they provided themselves with fifty runners as a part of the royal ceremonial (2 Sam. 15:1; 1 Ki. 1:5). In the time of REHOBOAM, the guardroom stood at the entrance to the palace, and it housed the bronze shields that the guards carried when they accompanied the king to the temple (1 Ki. 14:27–28; 2 Chr. 12:10–11). JEHU's guard went with him to SAMARIA to assist in the destruction of the worship of BAAL (2 Ki. 10:25).

HEROD Antipas ordered a member of his guard (*spekoulatōr G5063*) to bring to him the head of JOHN THE BAPTIST on a platter (Mk. 6:27; NIV, "executioner"). PILATE told the Jews to make the tomb of Jesus secure with a guard of soldiers (*koustōdia G3184*)—undoubtedly, the temple police (Matt. 27:65–66). J. L. KELSO

guard, court of the. See COURT (COURTYARD) OF THE GUARD.

Guard, Gate of the. This name (Heb. *šaʿar hammaṭṭārâ*) occurs only once, in the account of the dedication of the rebuilt wall of JERUSALEM (Neh. 12:39; not to be confused with "the gate of the guards" in the temple precincts [*šaʿar hārāṣîm*, 2 Ki. 11:19; see UPPER GATE]). The second group sent by NEHEMIAH to march on the wall went N and then E; after passing over the SHEEP GATE on the NE corner, the procession stopped at the Gate of the Court near the TEMPLE compound. Some have suggested that the Gate of the Court should be identified with the MUSTER GATE (3:31; NIV, "Inspection Gate"); others argue that it should be linked with the COURT (COURTYARD) OF THE GUARD (3:25; Jer. 32:2 et al.). In either case, the precise location of this gate is not known.

guardian. Someone who watches over or protects. This English term is used occasionally in some Bible versions to render various Hebrew and Greek words. Of special interest is the Greek noun *epitropos G2208*, which means basically "a person to whom some task or property has been entrusted." For example, Matt. 20:8 mentions a foreman or manager entrusted with paying laborers, while Lk. 8:3 uses the term with reference to HEROD's steward or household manager (the cognate word *epitropē G2207* is used in Acts 26:12 of PAUL's authorization by the high priests to persecute Christians). A governor with authority from the emperor was also called *epitropos* (it is applied to LYSIAS, who held an important office under ANTIOCHUS, 2 Macc. 11:1; 13:2; 14:2). Paul illustrated the position of Jews under the law by means of a minor in a household who was under the authority of "guardians and trustees" until a certain age (Gal. 4:2; KJV, "tutors and governors"). Under Roman law, the *epitropos* was the legal guardian of a child—potentially if his father was alive, actually if he had died. A trustee (*oikonomos G3874*) was responsible for the child's financial affairs until he was twenty-five. When he came of age, he was free and entered into his inheritance. F. FOULKES

Gudgodah gud-goh′duh (גֻּדְגֹּדָה *H1516*, meaning uncertain). A station in the wilderness wanderings of the Israelites, located between MOSERAH and JOTBATHAH (Deut. 10:7). The name is thought to be a variant of Gidgad. See HOR HAGGIDGAD.

guest. Someone invited to a home or a meal. This English word occurs a few times in the OT, primarily as a rendering of the passive participle of Hebrew *qāraʾ H7924*, "to call" (e.g., the guests of ABSALOM and ADONIJAH at their abortive attempts to usurp the throne, 2 Sam. 15:11; 1 Ki. 1:41, 49). It occurs more frequently in the NT, where it renders especially the participle of *anakeimai G367*, "to recline, dine," or of the compound *synanakeimai G5263*, "to dine with" (e.g., the guests at King HEROD's birthday party, Matt. 14:9; Mk. 6:22, 26; or those mentioned in the parable of the wedding feast, Matt. 22:10–11). Other words and expressions can also be rendered "guest" (e.g., Jdg. 19:23; Job 19:15; Matt. 9:15; Acts 10:23). D. H. MADVIG

guest room. This expression (Gk. *katalyma G2906*) is used of the room in which Jesus and his disciples ate the PASSOVER on the eve of the

896 GUIDEPOSTS

This section of a 1st-cent. home in the village of Tayibeh (Ephraim) may have served as a guest room. (© Dr. James C. Martin)

CRUCIFIXION (Mk. 14:14; Lk. 22:11; the same Gk. word is translated "inn" in Lk. 2:7). It refers to a room that provided facilities for temporary lodging or for banqueting (cf. LXX for the place where SAMUEL and SAUL feasted together, 1 Sam. 9:22, for Heb. *liškâ H4384*, "hall"). The NIV and other versions use "guest room" also to render Greek *xenia G3825*, "lodging," in one passage (Phlm. 22; cf. Acts 28:23). D. H. MADVIG

guideposts. This term is used by some Bible versions to render the Hebrew word *tamrûrîm H9477*, which occurs only once (Jer. 31:21; KJV, "high heaps"). In this passage, the prophet admonishes the returning exiles to prepare for their journey by marking the route to help them find the way back.

guile. This English term, meaning "skillful deceit," occurs eleven times in the KJV, but less frequently in modern translations (not at all in the NIV). Well-known passages where the KJV uses the term include Jesus' statement regarding NATHANAEL, "Behold an Israelite indeed, in whom is no guile!" (Jn. 1:47; NIV, "in whom there is nothing false"), and PETER's affirmation that Christ "did no sin, neither was guile [NIV, deceit] found in his mouth" (1 Pet. 2:22; this passage is a quotation of Isa. 53:9, where the KJV, curiously, uses "deceit"). See DECEIT, DECEPTION; LIE.

guilt. Although this English term in modern usage often refers to a subjective feeling (self-reproach, awareness of having done something wrong), in biblical contexts it indicates the *legal and moral condition* that results from SIN, that is, from a violation of God's law as expressed through the COVENANT. In OT and NT thought there is little or no clear distinction made between sin, guilt, and punishment (cf. Gen. 4:13 where all three ideas may be included). Older versions therefore tend uniformly to employ the word *sin* where modern translations reflect the greater precision of modern English usage. For example, *guilt* occurs only twice in the KJV, but it occurs over 100 times in the NIV and the NRSV as the rendering of a wide variety of Hebrew and Greek terms.

I. OT concept. In general in the OT, the concepts of sin, guilt, and punishment are all implied in the various words used by the biblical authors to denote the violation of God's commandments and its results. Guilt may be incurred, increased, purged, pardoned, remembered, removed, borne, or taken away. (1) The word *ʾāšām H871* usually refers to both moral and ritual transgression (Gen. 26:10; Lev. 4:3 [and frequently in this book]; 1 Chr. 21:3; et al.). (2) David speaks of "the guilt [*ʿāwōn H6411*] of my sin" (Ps. 32:5); this word occurs seventy times in the OT, but not all imply the notion of guilt (cf. Exod. 28:43; Num. 14:18; 1 Sam. 20:8; 2 Sam. 14:32; 19:19; Hos. 12:8). (3) According to the Mosaic law, judges have the responsibility of "acquitting the innocent and condemning the guilty [*rāšāʿ H8401*]" (Deut. 25:1; cf. 1 Ki. 8:32; Job 10:7; Ps. 18:23; Isa. 5:23; 50:9). (Cf. L. Morris in *EvQ* 30 [1958]: 196–210.)

To be guilty of sin is to incur God's wrath both collectively (Exod. 20:5–6; Isa. 65:7; Jer. 14:20) and individually (Deut. 24:16; Ezek. 18:2–4, 14–20). At first, guilt could exist without the individual's awareness of sin, but along with individualization of guilt came the necessity of subjective knowledge (see J. Hempel in *IDB*, 2:155–56). For the psalmists and the prophets, to be guilty of breaking God's laws involves universal shame and repentance (Pss. 38:1–12; 53:2–3; Isa. 1:4–5). A sincere desire to have God remove one's sins or even a willingness to forgive a neighbor's wrongdoing leads to forgiveness and a restoration of purity (Pss. 32:5; 51:1–12; 79:9; Dan. 9:4–19; Sir. 28:2). The idea of sin as a legal *indebtedness* to God, important for an understanding of NT usage, occurs in later JUDAISM; the

Aramaic term *ḥôbāʾ* ("debt") is, in fact, the word commonly used by the rabbis for sin (see *Tg. Onk.* on Num. 14:19; Exod. 34:7; Isa. 53:4, 12).

II. NT concept. The idea of guilt is much less frequent in the NT. Although the word *hamartia G281* usually means "sin," it also occasionally implies guilt, especially the guilt of all people for Jesus' death. In the Synoptic Gospels, especially Matthew, guilt occurs in the context of forgiveness of sin understood as a debt owed to God (Matt. 6:12; 18:21–35; et al.). Guilt as the result of lawlessness (*anomia G490*, equivalent to the Heb. *ʿāwōn*) is also implied in the synoptics in the context of the judgment of God (Matt. 7:23; 13:41).

PAUL deepens the understanding of guilt by universalizing and internalizing the debt to God that results from sin. He speaks about the actual removal of sin by Christ's death as well as the payment of the debt through the justification which God through faith grants the repentant sinner (Rom. 3:24–25; Eph. 1:7; Col. 1:14; et al.). To be "in Christ" (see UNION WITH CHRIST) means to be free from condemnation and guilt (Rom. 8:1–4); it means that the verdict of "guilty" is reversed. Other NT writers reflect the Hebraic understanding (e.g., Jn. 9:41; Jas. 2:10 [*enochos G1944*]; 1 Jn. 3:4). (See further J. G. Simpson in *DCG*, 1:696–98; F. R. Tennant *The Concept of Sin* [1912]; H. R. Mackintosh in *ERE*, 11:538–44; J. Heuschen and B. Vawter in *Encyclopedic Dictionary of the Bible* [1963], 912–18; M. E. Biddle, *Missing the Mark: Sin and Its Consequences in Biblical Theology* [2005].)   L. R. KEYLOCK

guilt offerings. See SACRIFICE AND OFFERINGS.

gull. An aquatic bird of the family *Laridae*, characterized by long wings and webbed feet. The NIV uses this term to render Hebrew *šaḥap H8830*, which occurs twice in parallel lists of unclean birds (Lev. 11:16, Deut. 14:15; NRSV, "sea gull"; KJV, "cuckoo"). G. R. Driver (*PEQ* no vol. [1955]: 5–20) rejected this rendering because it conflicted with his hypothesis that the list consists mainly of BIRDS OF PREY. He suggested "long-eared owl," but it is doubtful whether a bird as rare and local as this owl, which is strictly nocturnal and found in woods, would be separately named and banned.

In contrast, the gulls are numerous, diurnal, and conspicuous.

Ten true gulls and eight other members of the family are recorded in Palestine; five are only rare stragglers, but the others migrate. Those that come from the S often fly up the Gulf of AQABAH to make a landfall at Eilat, before traveling overland. The winter visitors are the commonest, including lesser black-backed and black-headed gulls; their flocks may run into hundreds and they may be seen on the Mediterranean and Red Sea coasts, on the Lake of Galilee, and around the great complexes of fishponds. Only the herring gull nests in Palestine, along with the black, common, and little terns. Most gulls are scavengers and would certainly rank as unclean. It seems much more reasonable to specify them than such uncommon skulkers as the cuckoo and the long-eared owl. (See *FFB*, 71.)

G. S. CANSDALE

gum. A viscous or resinous substance used as incense. It is the product of the *Astragalus tragacantha*, a fair-sized shrub with small pale yellow blossoms. It grows over a wide area in Palestine and the Near E (another possibility is the *Astragalus gummifer*). The gum is gathered by rubbing the plant with a ball of cotton. The English term is used by the NRSV as the rendering of Hebrew *nĕkōʾt H5780*, which occurs only twice (NIV, "spices"). The word is applied to one of the goods carried to Egypt by the Ishmaelite traders who bought JOSEPH (Gen. 37:25); it was also among the "choice fruits" of S Palestine sent by JACOB to Joseph in Egypt (43:11). The term "gum resin" is used by the NIV once (Heb. *nāṭāp H5753*, Exod. 30:34), and also once by the NRSV (Heb. *bĕdōlaḥ H978*, Num. 11:7). (Cf. W. Walker, *All the Plants of the Bible* [1957], 194.) See also FLORA (under *Leguminosae*); SPICE.

D. H. MADVIG

Guni gyoo'ni (גּוּנִי *H1586*, possibly "partridge"; gentilic גּוּנִי *H1587*, "Gunite"). (**1**) Second son of NAPHTALI and grandson of JACOB (Gen. 46:24; 1 Chr. 7:13). His descendants are called Gunites (Num. 26:48; the Lucianic MSS of the LXX at 2 Sam. 23:32 read "Jashen the Gunite" instead of "the sons of Jashen" [cf. also 1 Chr. 12:34], and this variant has been accepted by a few scholars).

(2) A member of the tribe of GAD who settled in GILEAD; he was grandfather of a certain Ahi who is described as head of the clan (1 Chr. 5:15). The connection between these men and the other Gadites mentioned in the context is ambiguous.

D. H. MADVIG

Gur guhr (גּוּר *H1595*, possibly "sojourning"). An incline near IBLEAM (modern Belameh) where AHAZIAH was mortally wounded by JEHU's men as he fled from the threat of assassination after the death of Joram (2 Ki. 9:27). W. F. Albright (in *BASOR* 94 [April 1944]: 21) noted that Gur must be the same as the Canaanite city of Gurra, which is mentioned in a 15th-cent. tablet discovered at TAANACH. A. Zertal (see *ABD*, 2:1090) more specifically identifies Gur with modern Khirbet en-Najjar, on the E side of Wadi Belameh. D. H. MADVIG

Gur Baal guhr-bay´uhl (גּוּר־בָּעַל *H1597*, "sojourn of the lord"). Also Gur-baal. A city in the NEGEV inhabited by ARABIANS (and possibly by PHILISTINES also), whom UZZIAH conquered with the help of God (2 Chr. 26:7; the LXX reads *tēs petras kai epi*, on the basis of which some emend the MT to *ṣûr weʿal*; others emend it to GERAR, following the Tg.). Since the verse mentions also the MEUNITES, Gur Baal was probably in or near the territory of EDOM, SE of the DEAD SEA, but its precise location is unknown. (See J. Simons, *The Geographical and Topographical Texts of the Old Testament* [1959], 371.) D. H. MADVIG

gutter. This English term is used by the NIV in only one passage as the rendering of Hebrew *ḥêq H2668* (lit., "bosom"), which occurs in an architectural context with reference to the channel around the ALTAR (Ezek. 43:13–14, 17; NRSV, "base"). The KJV uses it in two passages: in one of them it renders *rahaṭ H8110*, "trough" (Gen. 30:38, 41); in the other it renders *ṣinnôr H7562*, probably meaning "water shaft," and referring to the tunnel that DAVID recommended to his soldiers as a way of entering Jerusalem to conquer it (2 Sam. 5:8). Dating back to pre-Israelite times, it may be "Warren's Shaft" in the SE hill that leads from the GIHON SPRING to within the city wall (cf. J. Simons, *Jerusalem in the Old Testament* [1952], 168–75, but see JERUSALEM III.B). D. H. MADVIG

gymnasium. In Greece the gymnasium (Gk. *gymnasion*, from *gymnos G1218*, "naked") was originally a place of training for the Olympic games and other athletic contests. By the 4th cent. B.C. it had become as well an educational and cultural center for Greek youths, and was regarded as an essential

The gymnasium of Sardis.

feature of a city. It derived its name from the fact that the competitors exercised naked. The gymnasium consisted of a number of large buildings, which contained not merely places for each kind of exercise—running, boxing, wrestling, discus throwing, etc.—but also baths, a covered portico for practice in bad weather and in wintertime, and outside porticos where philosophers and writers gave public lectures and held disputations. Most of the education of boys and young men was obtained in gymnasiums. In ATHENS there were three great gymnasiums, each consecrated to a particular deity, and each made famous by association with a celebrated philosopher: the Academy, where Plato taught; the Lyceum, where Aristotle held forth; and the Cynosarges, which was the resort of Antisthenes and his followers, the CYNICS.

The Greek institution of the gymnasium never became popular with the Romans, and it was held in horror by orthodox Jews. Nevertheless, a gymnasium was erected in JERUSALEM by hellenizing Jews, under the leadership of the high priest JASON, in the time of ANTIOCHUS Epiphanes, who tried to compel the Jews to give up Judaism (1 Macc. 1:10, 14; 2 Macc. 4:9, 12; 4 Macc. 4: 20). Strict Jews opposed it because it introduced heathen customs and led Jewish youths to exercise naked in public and to be ashamed of the mark of their religion, CIRCUMCISION. It existed until the destruction of Jerusalem by the emperor TITUS. PAUL alluded to the exercises of the gymnasium several times: boxing (1 Cor. 9:26), wrestling (Eph. 6:12), and racing (1 Cor. 9:24; Gal. 5:7; Phil. 3:12–14). See ATHLETE.

S. BARABAS

We want to hear from you. Please send your comments about this
book to us in care of zreview@zondervan.com. Thank you.

ZONDERVAN®

ZONDERVAN.com/
AUTHORTRACKER
follow your favorite authors